The Proceedings of the

2000 Summer Computer Simulation Conference

Edited by
William F. Waite

Vancouver, British Columbia, Canada
July 16–20, 2000
The Coast Plaza Suite Hotel

SCS

ISBN: 1-56555-208-3

Sponsored by the Society for Computer Simulation International

Special Note on 1995 SCSC Proceedings:

The Society for Computer Simulation International has received correspondence claiming that the papers "Collective Learning Systems" by Liviu W. Doroftei and Stephen Lucci and "Collective Learning Automata" by Liviu W. Doroftei and Stephen Lucci which, were published in the Proceedings of the 1995 Summer Computer Simulation Conference, were essentially the class work of Mr. Carsten Oertel and Mr. Gary Takis respectively, carried out for Professor Peter Bock at George Washington University.

Additional copies of the Proceedings are available from:

The Society for Computer Simulation International
P. O. Box 17900
San Diego, CA 92177 U.S.A.

ISBN: 1-56555-208-3

PRINTED IN THE UNITED STATES

PREFACE

Welcome to the 2000 Summer Computer Simulation Conference (SCSC 2000), your portal to the Modeling and Simulation Industry of the 21st Century! The theme for this year's conference is: ***"MAINSTREAM Simulation*** – SCSC 2000 addresses the MAINSTREAM of simulation...in the MAINSTREAM of world-wide business, government, and education."

The simulation industry is changing rapidly in response to economic imperatives and technological opportunity. Fueled by economic pressure, simulation is becoming pervasive in public and private enteprise. Facilitated by emerging standards and infrastructure, the long-awaited simulation intervisibility, interoperability, and re-use among heretofore segmented simulation markets are becoming practical. Simulation application domains that have been insular and specialized are beginning to share concepts, practices, and assets at an accelerating pace.

The SCSC 2000 meeting emphasizes topics of synoptic interest to the entire modeling and simulation community. Papers and panelists from a wide range of application domains were solicited. Consequent participation by diverse simulation communities is expected to heighten awareness at the meeting of the significant similarities that characterize modeling and simulation technology and practice within the industry. By sampling generously across the industry, we expect to discover those topics which are most generally important and which best admit to inter-domain collaboration.

A full program of activities is planned for the SCSC 2000. *Invited Speakers* provide senior executives' views of the evolving simulation landscape. *Paper Sessions* report practitioners' progress in addressing issues of general concern. *Panels* provide cross-domain review of selected issues. *Workshop Sessions* provide a structured, moderated venue for the collegial investigation of topics admitting to subsequent ACTION. And *Exhibits* afford vendors and users of simulation products and services the opportunity to demonstrate their wares and capabilities.

As SCSC 2000 participants, I encourage you to discover *and invent* for yourselves the trends that will dominate the evolution of the 21st Century Simulation Industry!

William F. Waite
General Chair, SCSC 2000

CONTENTS

PAGE AUTHOR(S)

SIMULATION DEVELOPMENT

SIMULATION METHODOLOGIES: LANGUAGES, TOOLS AND TECHNIQUES

CONTENTS

CONTENTS

CONTENTS

Contents

CONTENTS

CONTENTS

Contents

CONTENTS

CONTENTS

CONTENTS

CONTENTS

CONTENTS

SIMULATION DEVELOPMENT

SIMULATION METHODOLOGIES: LANGUAGES, TOOLS AND TECHNIQUES

E.T. of M&S Tools.

Prof. Ir. Maurice S. Elzas
Professor Emeritus, Knowledge Systems,
Applied Computer Science Department,
Wageningen University,
Wageningen, the Netherlands.
E-mail: Elzas@RCL.WAU.NL

Keywords:
Simulation history, Continuous simulation, Discrete simulation, Hybrid simulation, Combined simulation.

Abstract:

The full title of this paper is meant to be "European Tales of Modelling and Simulation Tools". The link with the Extra Terrestrial is relevant because, for many years, Europeans and their ideas in this field most often appeared to come from outer space to our dear colleagues in North America.
Our measurable difference in approach to Modelling and Simulation was largely caused by particular differences in historical and scientific perspective. Also the funding of developments, the nature of the Simulation market and –last but not least- the perceived relative importance of sound theoretical foundations versus methodologies based on practical experience contributed to this gap in appreciation.
The sequel will endeavour to delve into the details of these original differences, highlight successes and failures and will, finally, attempt to give the reasons why, in the past decade, both worlds have become so close knit that any difference remaining is hardly discernible.

1. Introduction:

I clearly remember, when I started travelling to the US and Canada in the early sixties (of last century!) as a person in charge of a sizeable –European- modelling and simulation venture, to have been startled by the fact that many of my American colleagues could hardly believe that there where valuable developments in this field in Europe.
This has again been illustrated in a 1988 SCS publication describing the early days of Simulation [McLeod ea, 1988].

One had to bend over backwards to show that European M&S ideas had any practical value at all.

On the other hand, noticing hundreds of engineers in cubicles in a large hall of a derelict mill in Huntsville, Alabama, all working on a single simulation mission (Apollo) caused relief. It made one feel happy to be able to work in small -highly motivated- groups, as was the case in general in Western Europe.

For many decades, the division was also visible in the nature of the relevant professional societies. SCS being mainly American and AICA, although claiming to be international, mainly European. To become a member of SCS in 1962, as I did, was considered as close to pure folly as one could get.

Travelling was still a bother for most, the dollar outrageously expensive, telephoning unaffordable to us and (snail) mail excessively slow. These practicalities contributed as well in maintaining the communication gap that the initial differences in approach had caused. The advent of the Cold War in the mid-fifties and its associated McCarthyism in the U.S. did not improve matters at all.

Oddly, occasionally, personal friendships developed and these became the main vehicles through which understanding and co-operation gradually –and far too slowly- grew.

The establishment, by the government of the U.S. in the late sixties, of research scouting agencies in a few strategic locations in Europe, finally broke down the remaining barriers through liberal funding of original European work.

It would, however, require the advent of ARPAnet (which now has become Internet), to improve communications so thoroughly as to enable joint work across the ocean at a minimal (and therefore affordable) price.

2. A bit of history:

Although it is probably Archimedes[1] that represents our earliest recollection of a simulation experiment (in a bathtub) with his

[1] Ancient Greek mathematician, physicist, inventor. One of the earliest 'engineers'. Presumed to have lived from about 290 BC to 211 BC. One of his very few remaining publications, the "Method concerning mechanical theorems" is still interesting to this day for us, M&S

"Eureka", the philosophical foundation of our field is clearly attributable to Descartes [France 1596-1650] with his "Discours de la Méthode" [1637]. In this seminal work he establishes the basis for determinism, the principle that allows us, to this day, to compose and decompose systems, models and simulation experiments.

Although calculus and the notion of differential equations had been developed long before, Lord Kelvin [U.K. 1824-1907] was the first person to devise a technique through which the behaviour of functions, governed by this type of equations, could be followed. He solidly established the value of (physical) analogues for computing purposes in this way[2].

O. Reynolds [U.K. 1840-1912] (and his predecessors W. Froude [1810-1872] and S. Stevin [1548-1620] in the Netherlands) intrigued by the relation of small scale experiments to reality invented dimensional analysis, and became in this way the pioneer of validation.

This set the wheels of the connection between experimental and computational physics in motion, theoretically at first through pioneering work by E. Mach [Austria 1838-1916] (yes the one that gave his name to the Mach number). Later on in a more practical vein by work on the simulation of field problems through the use of electrolytes and resistive paper, mainly at the Max Planck foundation in Germany and the Russian Academy of Sciences. The latter Institute continuing this work into the 20th century [Ouchakov]. The early issues of the Journal and Proceedings of AICA clearly illustrate this.

Between the two World Wars, the increasing complexity of aircraft and weaponry provided (in Europe as well as later in the U.S.) a decisive push to build full fledged, almost general purpose, analog computers.

Some were gigantic, like the hydraulic analogue built at the Royal Aircraft Establishment in Farnborough, which filled a huge hangar and was operational until the early sixties.

Also rather small devices were built as the one constructed by Tinbergen [Dutch, one of the founding fathers of econometry]. Confronted, in the mid fifties, with the task to help rebuild the Dutch economy, he undertook to build a full model of the Dutch macro-economy based on water vessels (integrators!) connected to each other with pipes and valves (coefficients). The device worked to satisfaction until the early sixties. I distinctly remember, when visiting him, that he even was satisfied with the leaks in the model, as they reflected –to his opinion- the 'leaky' nature of the actual system that was simulated.

Although this was a period in which mainly special purpose devices were built, a general methodology gradually developed. Analyse problem => make mathematical formulation => attempt to solve analytically => if not possible => construct experimenting device => run (many) experiments => analyse statistically => derive solution. This approach was illustrated 'par excellence' in the –then very popular- movie "the Dambusters", where a British weapon (and its associated bombing system) is seen to be developed for the destruction of dams in the German Ruhr area, where the Nazi's had the bulk of their weapon industry. Of course, the movie the follows up with images of the actual use of the device, thus coming full circle from original idea to utilisation.

A more peaceful application was the fight against disastrous floods, as the one that struck the Netherlands in 1953. A huge, special purpose, analog computer (the DELTAR) was built in the late fifties for this. The machine was used in 'competition' with the digital computers of its time and won easily.

Analog computing was of such an importance in Europe until the early sixties, that even Maurice Wilkes, the world famous digital luminary, started out in this field.

Naturally, aerospace was also an important application for simulation outside America. We even find aircraft factories among the early producers of more general-purpose analog computers like e.g. Short Brothers (Northern Ireland) and Dornier (Western Germany).

As time went by it became clear, also to engineers outside of the simulation community, that good use could be made of this technique in a great many fields. New European manufacturers of general-purpose analog/hybrid computers emerged like e.g. the French Analac, the English Solartron and the German Telefunken.

However, it was only in 1972, with the appearance of "Limits to Growth"[3] on the initiative of the Club of Rome that (digital) Modelling and Simulation really came into the European public domain.

3. Funding, markets and their consequences:

The impact of differences in the funding of applications, tools and techniques between the U.S. and Europe has had a far-reaching influence on how the Modelling and Simulation and its tools evolved on the Old continent.

We, workers in the M&S industry, were often jealous of our American colleagues who seemed to be able to get any new M&S development funded, by the either DoD or NASA.

White elephants notwithstanding, these central sources of funding also provided an additional advantage: guidelines for quality and standardisation.

In Europe, the defence and aerospace establishments played a far more modest role. Moreover our fragmentation in ever so many countries, with different languages, economic systems, cultures; etc. diluted the scarce funds even more.

professionals, because of his discussion of the relative merits of heuristics.

[2] In fact in 1873, he built one of the first simulators ever in order to simulate tidal movement and thus predict the height of tides as dependent on environmental circumstances.

[3] About 2 million copies sold in the Benelux

It was, therefore, clear from day one, that in order to succeed as an M&S community we had to cater for as many different (industrial) applications as possible and provide highly cost-effective solutions.

Referring again to early European publications in the field (AICA Journal and Proceedings) we find application of M&S to the oil and chemical industries, steel making, medicine and operations research at an earlier stage than in America.

Striking as well is the lack in standardisation. Apart from analog computers based on operational amplifiers, quite a number of machines emerged (and where relatively successful) based on esoteric principles like passive circuits or inductive devices.

Moreover, as the majority of the customers did not have any M&S expertise in house, the tool vendors often had to develop the applications to go with the tools they sold. In some cases these would even, be 'fixed' applications. A case that comes to mind is the cattle fodder manufacturer wanting to optimise (nutritional value, price, etc.) the mixture he offers for sale. The M&S vendor develops the (typical OR) application and delivers it as a 'fixed program' analog device to the client. Even when the client got to the stage in which it was far more efficient to simulate and optimise on a digital computer, the only thing that happened was that the original analog program was converted 'as is' to Basic code. Standardisation was a hopeless case under such circumstances!

On the other hand the whole situation had positive aspects as well, awakening the European M&S community at an early stage to the, almost boundless, opportunities of application in almost all areas of industry and science.

As we shall see later, also this advantage had a drawback: the 'easier' programming became, the more individuals and institutions started making their own simulation tools, especially digital simulation languages.

4, The evolution of digital simulation:

Only slightly later than in America, the interest in mimicking analog circuitry on digital computers started in earnest in Europe in the early sixties.

To name a product I know well, having been associated with it since its beginning: the DISAR (Digital Simulation of Analog Reckoning) project was started as a thesis project of one of my students in 1962, stimulated by the vision of Prof. L. Dekker. The product was originally written in ALGOL, converted to FORTRAN in the late sixties, ported to PASCAL in the seventies and its unique 'ripple' integration algorithm has survived to this day.

Of course there were many more experimental developments in this area in the sixties, in Europe just as in the U.S., so much so that in 1967 SCS felt the need to develop a standard containing the minimum requirements for Continuous System Simulation Languages in 1967. [Ziegler, Hoffman 1967] [Rechenberg 1969] [Giloi ea. 1969] [SCI, 1967]

An original European approach, however was to use these languages for assistance in programming and checking out analog computers, which first started at the European Nuclear Research Institute at Ispra (It.). [Green ea. 1961], [Denmead ea. 1967]

However, a major breakthrough was caused in the field of discrete system simulation by the advent of Simula in 1966. Simula was a completely new, strong typed and structured language, originally specifically designed for discrete event M&S, but so powerful that it was later put to use for other (mainly object-oriented) tasks. [Dahl, Nygaard 1966] Interestingly enough this was one of the few, groundbreaking, M&S developments that was initially entirely funded by Norwegian defence money. The 'class' concept that was first used here, has become a standard feature of all O.O. languages these days.

Of course (like mostly the case when a revolutionary product emerges), the language was too terse and too general for some. Specialised languages, based on the Simula concept, emerged e.g. DYMOLA [Elmqvist, 1979] for continuous systems and DEMOS [Birtwistle, 1979] for discrete systems. Both languages have survived to this date, DYMOLA in an expanded form under the name of MODELICA being developed by a whole group of scientists representing a wide field of applications[4].

However, specialisation did not end there, many tools where put into operation, which catered to a specific public or a restricted application field. A remarkable (and rather unique) initiative was the development of WSL'70[5]. The story behind this venture is fascinating enough to be told here. Cees de Wit, a Dutch authority in agricultural production ecology, took a trip to the U.S. in the late sixties. In one of the places where he stayed he chanced to meet Bob Brennan (of NASA, IBM and DSL'90 fame) and was given a thorough 'lecture' on the value of simulation for the development of technical systems. He came back to Wageningen University totally convinced and proceeded, together with this author, to develop a CSSL-definition compatible language that had features especially attuned to the needs of simulation in agriculture. In parallel, he created special –real life- validation facilities in which plants could grow in the same 'odd' circumstances as those to which the simulation models were restrained by their necessarily simplified representation of reality. Doing this he became the first and foremost authority on this subject worldwide.
Two other specialisation initiatives are worth mentioning here:

- *Bond-graph* based simulation languages, of which the best known, and internationally most widely spread, has been TUTSIM a block oriented tool first issued in 1982 for PDP-11 computers and later ported to PC's.
- *Portable* simulation languages emerged focussing on the ease of learning and used for teaching simulation, control, etc. A good example in this category was ISIS [Hay 1978].[Griffin 1978]
- *Comprehensive* simulation languages intended to cater for model description, simulation programming, experiment

[4] see http://www.modelica.org/

[5] Wageningen Simulation Language '70

management and result analysis. Examples of this approach for the area of discrete system simulation are PROSIM [Sierenberg 1979] and SIMPLEX [Schmidt 1988].

5. The 'egghead' approach:

Due to the European cultural heritage, reflected in a specific approach to science and engineering taught at Europe's leading Universities, the general attitude over here has long been one of 'principles first and demands of practice later'.

This resulted in a smaller sensitivity to technology push and the enjoyment of gadgetry in the computing field, which largely governs M&S tools. In fact the attitude has mostly been: before embarking on a new venture, stand back first to see the larger picture.

This explains why, in Europe especially, so much emphasis has always been placed on hardware independent computer programming and M&S tools. Home brews like ALGOL and PASCAL are illustrations in point.

The APACHE venture, which was mentioned in §4, ended in failure (mainly due to the restricted possibilities of analog and digital hardware in the sixties). Nevertheless, the idea of providing programming facilities for simulation that could generate programs for purely digital, hybrid as well as purely analog realisations was still very much alive in the mid seventies. The advances in both hardware areas were such, in the meantime, that the task became feasible.
Notable examples were:

- HARTRAN/HYTROL catering for programming and executing hybrid simulation programs [Giloi 1970]
- ACTRAN compiler for analog/hybrid computation [Rook 1972]
- HL-1 a language for digital, hybrid and analog simulation [Elzas 1973] [Rook 1975], a system, developed through European co-operation, that had the privilege to have 5 customers world-wide (1 in the U.S.)

Another tendency arising from this urge to be hardware independent was to provide a simulation tool or language that could be implemented on top of already existing computer languages and associated compilers (much like CSMP rests on FORTRAN). This in order to be able to ride piggyback on the portability that such languages had already achieved. In the late seventies, the choice of languages was so large, that it became possible to choose the best (lower level) language for the purpose. A case in point was CS-PROLOG, which used the power of the PROLOG inference engine to program and run discrete system simulations. [Futo, Szeredi 1982]

Another, apparently mainly European, worry was the sorry state of numerical methods for handling discontinuities (in otherwise continuous systems) in a simulation experiment. The usual approach had been, until then, to argue the discontinuities away or (manually) adjust integration step sizes until their effect 'disappeared'. Nevertheless, discontinuities are a reality and central feature in many real systems (e.g. phase changes, switching phenomena). Something had to be done. Two people who devoted a sizeable part of their scarce research time to this important issue need to be mentioned here: François Cellier (then at ETH in Zürich) and Dik Kettenis (Wageningen University), working together they broke the deadlock that had been investigated earlier on by Crosbie and Hay at the University of Salford.

Once the discontinuity issue had been tackled, there was no problem –in principle- to realise a long-standing European dream: *one language for all simulation.* Many people started working on this challenge, but only two produced results of scientific value. The first one making the initial (and rather fundamental) step leading to the COSY language definition and interpreter [Cellier 1979]. The second one writing the COSMOS language and compiler extended later to take into account possible execution on parallel digital computers. [Kettenis 1994].

6. Simulation without programs:

This reference to a paper by Luker and Stephenson [Luker, Stephenson 1978] typifies one of the typical developments caused by the fact that, at least in Europe, the late seventies saw ever more 'innocents' use simulation and get bogged down in the process. All these thousands of users represented a tremendous market, as well for the academic community as for the business sector.

As experts we concluded that the user should focus on modelling and simulating his system, and be freed from menial tasks like programming, numerical worries, details of output generation, etc. etc.

Moreover, the early eighties saw the revival of A.I as well through fabled (but often misquoted) successes in Expert Systems as through Reagan's Star Wars initiative. M&S did not have a direct use for the results of these efforts. Nevertheless, our community quickly saw the opportunity that the tools, freshly developed in this other field, offered for enabling possibilities of which we had only dreamt before.

Work started on so-called 'environments' which would offer a simple and interactive interface to the lay user while catering for all M&S tasks from model construction to result interpretation.

This was easier said than done. There are such a multitude of M&S applications that it quickly became clear that the search for one-engine fits all would be futile, at least for the time being.

Moreover, expert users being what they were, soon made clear that they had no need at all for these newfangled 'toys'. Furthermore many of the European lay users where not able to afford themselves costly tools.

The conclusion was that we had –however grudgingly- tot cut up the market again into continuous and discrete, to develop cheaply (and as fast as possible due to the threat of American competition) and be absolutely fool proof.

A number of products reached the market, only one of them addressing the continuous system area: the Conceptual Modeller 100 (better known as CM-100) [Elzas 1988a, 1988b]. About 100 copies of this comprehensive and rather appealing environment were sold. It was used, amongst other applications, for a systems-engineering M&S lab at Wageningen University from 1987 up to 1999 with good success and without crashing once. In the meantime, CM-100 has been superseded by SMART, an environment based on the experience acquired with CM-100, and developed jointly by Wageningen University and Research institutions in its neighbourhood[6].

More success was achieved on the discrete side, where animation and graphics input interface based environments emerged in the early 80's.

Two of them have known sufficient success to be worth mentioning here:

- See Why, a discrete manufacturing facility simulation environment with animated output, constructed by the Systems Research group of the late British Leyland Motors Company. It was originally developed to design the manufacturing, parts management and logistics facilities for the Mini Metro car. Although expensive, the system was successful and sold relatively well in Europe. When British Leyland's business soured, the product was sold to Citroën for its internal use.
- Taylor[7] a product developed by the Dutch F&H Simulators, possessing a graphic input facility, apart from a straightforward Pascal-like programming facility and output in 3D animated form as well as possibilities for statistical analysis. From its origin as a rather coarse and rudimentary environment the software has been developed to professional standards and enjoys a quite solid clientele worldwide.

7. The call for standardisation:

The attitude towards standards has always been quite different in Europe from what is usual in America.

While the U.S. possesses a number of professional society and government sponsored standards institutions the way standards are arrived at and respected is mostly based (certainly in the areas associated with ICT) on the actual situation in the field. Standards are thus mostly 'de facto', whereas in Europe they are mostly 'de jure'. In the former case, the standards are established *after* the market has shown that they are useful and wide spread (e.g. IEEE-bus). In the latter case standards are discussed and decided upon before any product arrives on the market (e.g. the GSM standard).

No wonder that a number of M&S professionals (Europe in this case including Israel and Turkey) took the initiative to try to come to a comprehensive standard for simulation languages in the widest sense. This 'wide sense' meaning in this case that not only languages for the simulation of continuous systems, but also those for the simulation of discrete and/or combined systems had to be covered.

For this purpose T.I. Ören, B.P. Zeigler and this author organised the Sorrento Workshop on International Standardisation of Simulation Languages (SWISSL) in Sorrento, Italy in July 1979.

That the venture was not seen, at that time, as totally superfluous, was illustrated not only by the fact that participants from all over the world made the effort to contribute and participate, but also by the sponsorship of the research branch of the U.S. DoD.

It was a genuinely fascinating workshop. Many relevant issues were covered, from implementation issues to enforcement possibilities and from the role of the existing CSSL standard to the question if all forms of discrete systems could be described by a common formalism. (Tempers flared over this question, but later one of the students of one of the participants worked on a thesis showing possibilities of converting discrete event representations into process oriented ones).

Unfortunately, apart from the fact that some of us became friends for life, nothing came of it then and no progress has been made to this day.

Might this be a point to ponder for this audience or the Society for Computer Simulation?

8. References:

[Birtwistle 1979]	Birtwistle, G.M.: "Discrete Event Modelling on Simula", The Macmillan Press, 1979.
[Cellier 1979]	Cellier, F.E.: "Combined continuous/discrete system simulation by use of digital computers: techniques and tools", ETH dissertation, ADAG Administration & Druck AG, Zurich, 1979.
[Dahl,Nygaard 1966]	Dahl, O-J and Nygaard, K.: "SIMULA – an ALGOL-based Simulation Language", Communications of the ACM, Vol. 9, number 9, pp. 671-678.
[Denmead ea. 1967]	Denmead, J.K. ea.: "Analogue Programming by Digital Computers", Proceedings 5th. International Conference AICA, Lausanne 1967, pp. 279-296.
[Elmqvist 1979]	Elmqvist, H.: "DYMOLA – A Structured Model Language for Large Continuous Systems", Proceedings SCSC 1979, Toronto, 1979.
[Elzas 1973]	Elzas, M.S.: "HL-1 or towards a unique language for all continuous system simulation", Proceedings

[6] More information can be found at http://www.info.wau.nl/SMART/

[7] For more information consult http://www.taylor.com/

7th. AICA conference, Prague, 1973.

[Elzas 1988a] Elzas, M.S.: "Desktop Modelling and Simulation Environments", Simulation environments and symbol and number processing on multi-array processors, Proceedings of the European Simulation Multiconference, Nice, 1988, pp. 389-393.

[Elzas 1988b] Elzas, M.S.: "Expert Simulation Systems in Practice", Proceedings 12th. IMACS World Congress on Scientific Computation, Paris, 1988.

[Futo, Szeredi 1982] Futo, I. and Szeredi, J.: "A discrete simulation ystem based on artificial intelligence methods", Discrete Simulation and Related Fields, ed. A. Javor, North Holland, 1982, pp.135-150.

[Giloi ea. 1969] Giloi, W.K.; Beckert, D,; Liebig, H.C.: "A Flexible Standard Programming System for Hybrid Computation", Proceedings AFIPS SJCC, 1969, pp. 827-841.

[Giloi 1970] Giloi, W.K.: "A standard programming system for hybrid computation and its implementation", Report ESL-R-427, M.I.T. Cambridge/mass., 1970.

[Green ea. 1961] Green, C.; Debroux, A.; delBigio, G.P.;d'Hoop, H.:"Le code APACHE destiné à la programmation d'un problème analogique au moyen d'un calculateur digital", Proceedings 3rd. International AICA Conference, Opatija, 1961.

[Griffin 1978] Griffin, A.W.G.: "Some ISIS Applications", Proceedings 1978 UKSC Conference on computer simulation, pp. 204 – 214.

[Hay 1978] Hay, J.L.: "On the portability of continuous simulation languages", Proceedings 1978 UKSC Conference on computer simulation, pp. 285 – 293

[Kettenis 1994] Kettenis, D.L.: "Issues of parallellization in implementation of the combined simulation language COSMOS", Thesis Delft University of Technology, ISBN 90-9007472-4, 1994.

[Luker,Stephenson 1978] Luker,P.A.; Stephenson, J.:"Simulation without Programs", Proceedings 1978 UKSC Conference on computer simulation, 1978, pp.181 – 191.

[McLeod ea. 1988] McLeod, J. Editor: "Pioneers and Peers", Proceedings of the 1988 Conference, SCS International, 1988.

[Rechenberg 1969] Rechenmberg, P.:"Simulationssysteme für Digitalrechner"; Ph. D. Thesis, TU Berlin, 1969.

[Rook 1972] Rook, P.E.:"Hybrid compilation using ACTRAN", scsc 1972 Proceedings, pp. 298-309.

[Rook 1975] Rook, P.E.:"The HCS-1 Complier at B.A.C.: Experience in Use", AICA Symposium on Simulation langauges for Dynamic Systems, London, 1975.

[Schmidt 1988] Schnidt, B.:"Systems Analysis, Model Construction, Simulation: Methodological Basis of the Simulation System SIMPLEX-II", Simulation environments and symbol and number processing on multi-array processors, Proceedings of the European Simulation Multiconference, Nice, 1988, pp. 39- 51.

[SCI 1967] Simulation Councils Inc.:"The SCI Continuous System Simulation Language (CSSL)", Simulation Vol.9, number 6 (1967), pp.291-303.

[Sierenberg 1979] Sierenberg, R.W.:"Modelling with PROSIM78", Proceedings of the 9th, IMACS World Congress, North Holland 1979, pp.997-1002.

[Ziegler, Hofman 1967] Ziegler, W.; Hofman, P.:"ANAGOL 67, eine blockoorientierte sprache auf ALGOL-basis", Proceedings 5th. International AICA conference, Lausanne, 1967.

Maurice S. Elzas recently retired from his tenured professorship in Knowledge Systems at Wageningen University. He has been active in computers and simulation since the early sixties, both in industry and academia. His work encompassed tool design (hardware and software) as well as methodologies and a wide range of applications. He is still active in research and consulting

AN INTELLIGENT AGENT CONTROLLED METHODOLOGY FOR DETERMINING ADEQUATE MODELS

András JÁVOR[1,2], Gábor SZŰCS[2]
International McLeod Institute of Simulation Sciences
Hungarian Center
[1]Széchenyi István College, H-9026 Győr, Hédervári út 3., Hungary
[2]Budapest University of Technology and Economics, H-1111 Budapest, Sztoczek u. 4., Hungary
E-mail: javor@eik.bme.hu

KEYWORDS

Model analysis, Validation, Discrete simulation, Optimization, Decision support systems

ABSTRACT

A methodology for the reconstruction of models by intelligent agents to describe the real systems adequately is shown. The agents perform their task by changing model structure, parameters and functionalitites characterizing the cause effect interrelations among the objects of the model structure. The main field of application is the area of soft or ill-defined systems. The methodology has been implemented in an AI controlled simulation system and it is illustrated on an example.

INTRODUCTION

In a wide range of fields – where the systems may be investigated by simulation – the difficulty of determining the optimal solution isn't only caused by the high complexity of the models but also by the fact that the model describing the real system adequately is not known. In such cases before investigating the operation and performance of the model by simulation it is a necessary and also difficult problem to determine its architecture.

This is true in many cases as e.g.

(i) micro-, and macroeconomy,
(ii) defense systems dealing with technical, psychological and other aspects,
(iii) financial, marketing problems,
(iv) environmental protection,
etc.

In general these problem fields can be characterized by their highly interdisciplinary nature (Ziegler 1984), and by the presence of certain procedures describing their operation the exact nature and interaction of which is not known sufficiently.

One of these fields is the development of regions (Jávor and Szűcs 1999), where the investments, traffic, environmental pollution, growth of the population, taxation, rate of unemployment, development of the infrastructure, etc. are strongly interrelated. Building of roads connecting an underdeveloped region e.g. may on the one hand promote the investments for allocating industry to the area, but on the other hand may also increase the rate of commuting thereby decreasing the amount of people working in the region. These two factors may thus have oppositely directed effects influencing also the tax income of the area etc.

Another area is the fast merging of informatics and telecommunications with particular emphasis on mobile phone systems, computer networks and applications as m-commerce e.g., where also the interrelation of technical, commercial and human factors have to be considered in the planning phase.

In this contribution a methodology is presented, that is based on the following main disciplines.

- Agents with artificial intelligence capabilities; knowledge bases and inference engines (Jávor 1992) (introduced already earlier as *demons*) monitor the operation of the model, and modify its structure and parameters until an acceptable matching with the real world system to which it is intended to correspond is determined. This search is based on a matching

procedure with historical information collected in advance.
- The models existing already in literature and/or as initial assumptions are used as a starting point and the AI controlled procedure has to provide a better understanding and more correct model for forecasting applications.

This approach may have two important results; beyond the solution of the specific problem, a better and scientifically substantiated insight into the field in general can be achieved that can be used for solving similar problems of the field.

ARCHITECTURE OF AGENTS

The intelligent agents mentioned above have already been applied in various projects, where the models describing the systems investigated were well known and the problem to be solved was to find optimal solutions.

These cases have been concerned with the following fields:
(i) flexible manufacturing (Szűcs and Vigh 1995),
(ii) urban traffic and environment pollution (Jávor 1997).

The scope of the changes performed by the agents in cases, where the aim was to find optimal solutions, has been relatively restricted since the possible structure and parameters of the models could be chosen from a foreseeable set of possibilities.

In case the model describing reality adequately is to be searched, the changes to be undertaken may be chosen from a far wider variety of possibilities.
- As the cause effect relations among the various factors are not known adequately in advance; the structure of the model may be changed during the search considerably.
- Beyond changing parameters of the simulation models (as constants, delay values, capacities) also the functions (linear, quadratic, logarithmic, etc.) may have to be changed.

As a consequence of these aspects the complexity of the intelligent agents has to be increased considerably. The basic structure of an intelligent demon/agent can be seen in Figure 1.

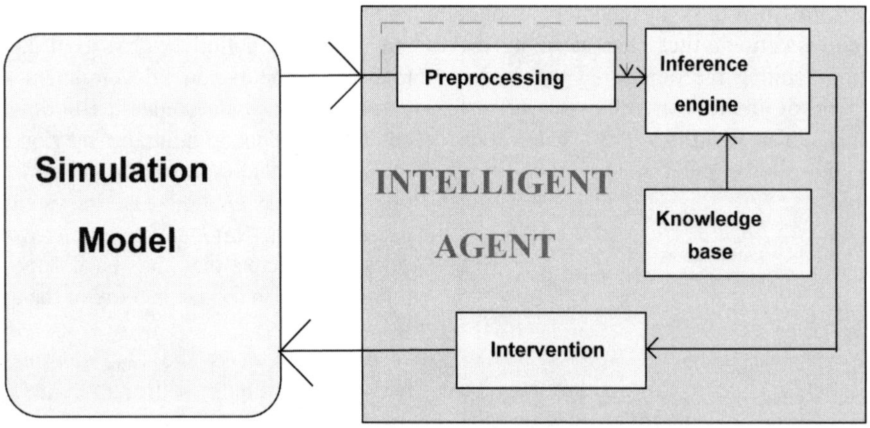

Figure 1 Intelligent agent structure

The advanced version has to contain the following items.

Knowledge base and inference engine subsystem

- A variety of knowledge base shells enabling the insertion of decision rule and frame structured knowledge bases.
- A set of inference engine algorithms as hill climbing, depth first, width first, best first, etc. search strategies.
- Tools to aid the proper execution of the search to avoid possible pitfalls as finding local extreme values instead of the global ones (as e.g. random sampling or rough average sampling).
- Special algorithms for finding saturation points e.g.

- Variable step size control for the search taking into consideration the following aspects:
  (i) multidimensional search,
  (ii) variable step size for the initial search and the final approach to the desired result. Here the speed of the search as well as the convergence of the procedure has to be taken into consideration.
- An advising controlling tool as an aid to determine the most appropriate inference engine and knowledge representation for the task to be solved. This module may apply a learning strategy.

<u>Statistical control subsystem</u>

- In order to make reliable decisions the information collected during the dynamic simulation run by monitoring the simulation model behavior it is necessary to analyze the level of significance and the confidence intervals respectively to determine the required simulation run length for a given evaluation period.
- Preprocessing modules for the data obtained from the simulated model (as e.g. average, standard deviation, correlation functions, etc.).

<u>Intervention subsystem</u>

It has to be stated that the world view i.e. the simulation model structure used has an object oriented nature meaning that it consists of a network of interconnected model element modules. Interventions into the model after having taken the decision by the inference engine using the data collected from the simulation model and retrieved from the knowledge base can be the following.

- Parameters of the model – assigned usually to given model elements – can be changed.
- Functions (mathematical or other as e.g. tables) may be changed as well. Here the possible and feasible set of functions to be chosen from should be given in advance.
- Finally the most complex task to be solved is the change in the model structure. This however is of extreme importance since the determination of cause effect relationships is essentially determined by this.
  Enabling all possibilities for the topology reconstruction with the creation and deletion of arbitrary model elements (contained by the model element library) provides obviously the broadest set of solutions but due to the combinatorically high degree of complexity in practice it would be difficult to realize. It is practical to incorporate a set of practical operations that enable a wide range of feasible changes of the structure.
  Some of the structural change operations that have already been tested are the following:
  - deletion of an arbitrary model element,
  - creation and insertion of an arbitrary model element,
  - connecting or disconnecting the output of an element to the inputs of a set of elements in a step by step way,
  - connecting or disconnecting the outputs of a set of elements to the input of a single element in a step by step way,
  - exhaustive step by step permutation of the elements of a limited model network segment and collecting the information about the corresponding topologies and simulation results.

The architectural principles described above have partly been implemented and tested in the CASSANDRA 3.0 simulation system (Jávor at al. 1994) and further development and corresponding evaluations are in progress.

HIERARCHICAL APPLICATION OF AGENTS

In earlier experiments (Jávor 1997) it has already been shown that the application of more demons/agents for monitoring the simulation model behavior and intervening for model reconstruction can be advantageous since distributed control is more efficient than a single centralized one. In general it can be stated that the hierarchical application of agents, where a "master" supervises his subordinate "slaves" may have advantages in systems of high complexity. Here the "slaves" work in an autonomous way executing the tasks assigned to them and provide rough information to their "master" that collects this from each subordinate agent. After having evaluated the information collected by the supervisor agent it can provide control commands or advises to its subordinates.

AN EXAMPLE ILLUSTRATING THE METHODOLOGY

As a relevant example for trying to determine the effects in an interdisciplinary field has been the problem of the development of regions where the traffic possibilities connecting it to other regions, the unemployment rate, the number of enterprises, financial results and the central redistribution of the finances has been taken into consideration (Jávor and Szűcs 1999). The research work in this field has been continued and the cause effect relation by structural reconstruction of the model performed. The experimental model of a given region using Knowledge Attributed Petri Nets (Jávor 1993) is shown in Figure 2. The *place* elements contain the tokens with the attributes of the states of the significant variables, where the letters indicate the following:

U – Unemployment
T – Traffic
E – Enterprises
W – Working power
P – Population
F – Finances

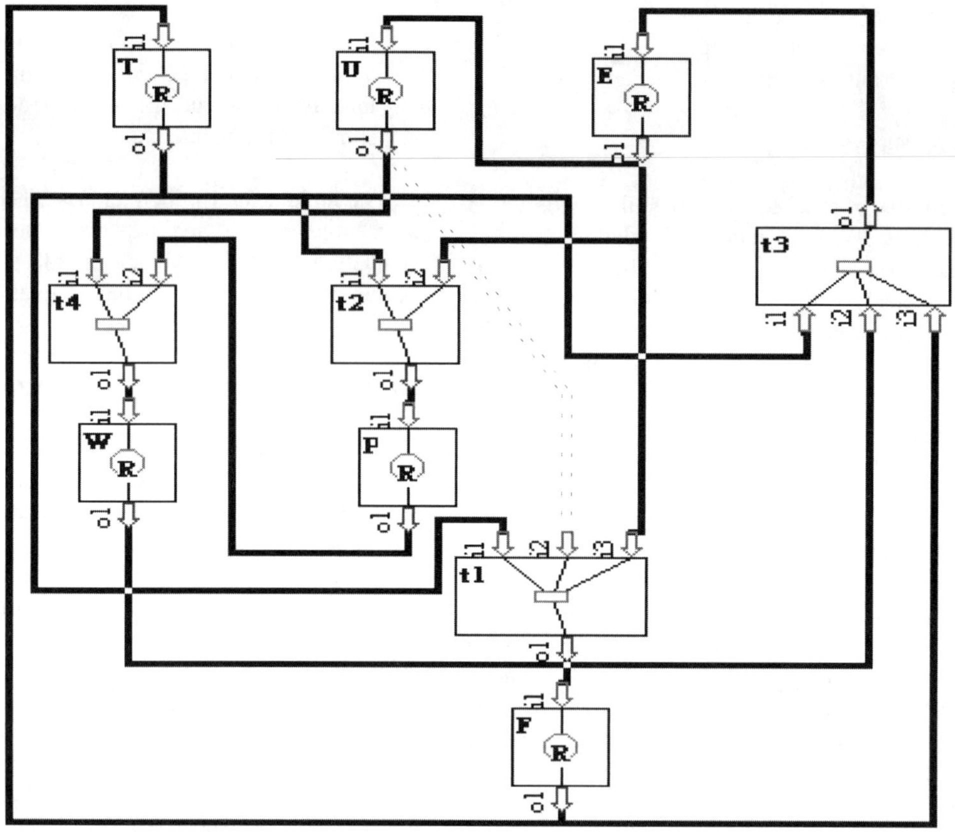

Figure 2 Petri Net model of a region

The refinement of the model has been undertaken in the following ways. The improvement of traffic possibilities among regions may contribute to the increase of working power by the reachability of the region but may also enable working power to leave for other areas by commuting.

The financial results have been considered as a linear function of the number of enterprises, traffic volume, and employment rate. The number of enterprises has been assumed to depend linearly on the available finances, traffic and working power. The change of unemployment rate was a negative linear function of the change of the enterprises. Traffic volume depended on the redistributed finances available (i.e. building of roads). In case of the population the commuting has been considered as a factor and here linear and quadratic functions have been tested. Also the change of the number of enterprises has been considered as an attracting force (which may attract people to the given region (or a neighbouring region having an opposite effect).

RESULTS OF THE AGENT CONTROLLED SIMULATION EXPERIMENT

The experiment has been performed for five regions interrelated via a central financial distributor i.e. the state collecting taxes and distributing money according to given strategies. During the fitting of the model four variables have been considered for each region (number of enterprises, unemployment rate, inter-region traffic, population).

The third possibility i.e. structural reconstruction is indicated in Figure 2, where the dotted line indicates the removal of a connection that means the influence of a factor of the model on an other. In our case it meant that the removal of the direct influence of unemployment on the finances has been omitted from the model which resulted in a better fitting to reality.

In Figure 3 a) b) c) and d) the relative deviations of the simulation results from the 5x4=20 parameters of the actual historical statistical data during the search procedure performed by the intelligent agent can be seen. The notations VFiSj denote the versions of the ith function and the jth structure chosen, where i=1 means linear, while i=2 quadratic function; j=1 indicates that the structural connection is valid, while j=2 that it is omitted (see Figure 2).

In Figure 4 the average of the deviations is shown. In one direction the choice of the functions in the population rate growth is shown. 1 means that the traffic rate influences it in a linear way, while 2 means that the dependence may be quadratic. Consecutively this has been a change of the function. In the other direction the value of the constant used in calculating the financial results has been changed. The results show the average deviations from the historical data.

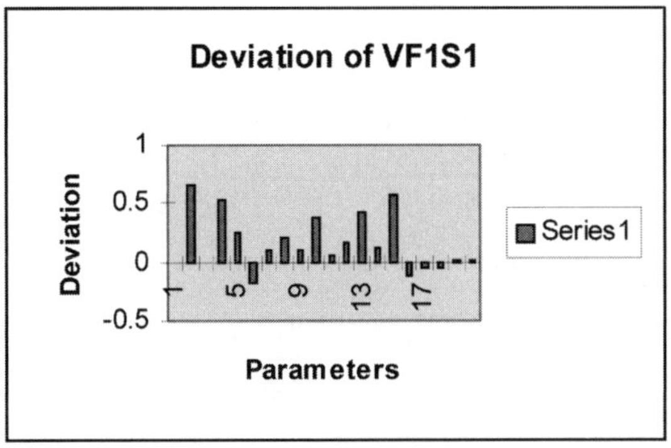

a)

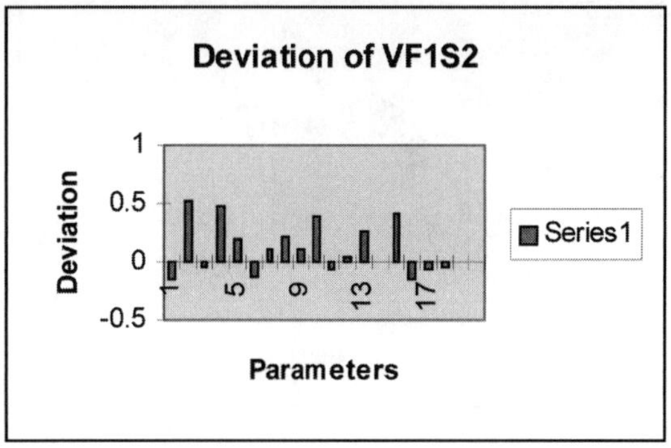

b)

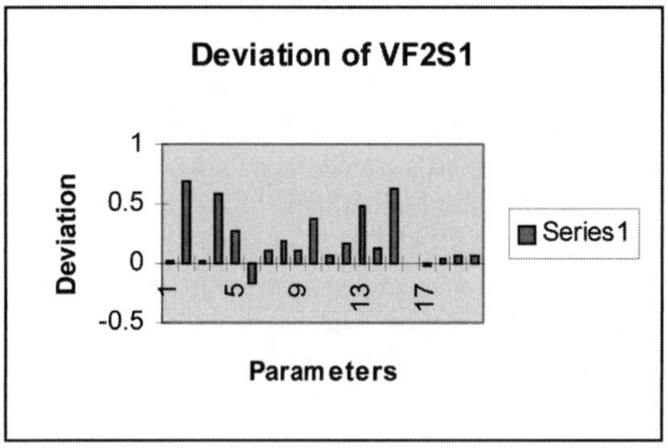

c)

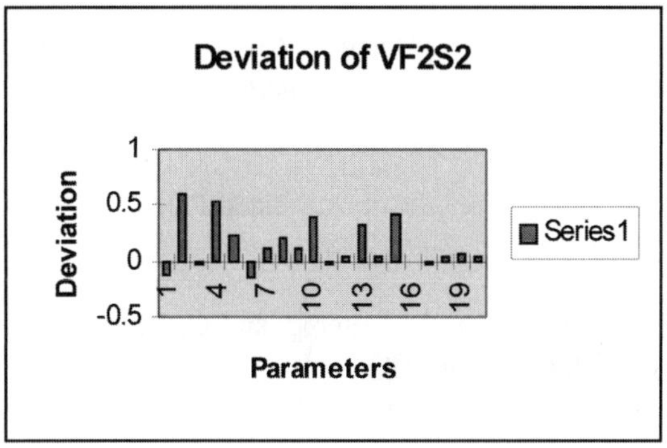

d)

Figure 3 Relative deviations of the simulation results during the search

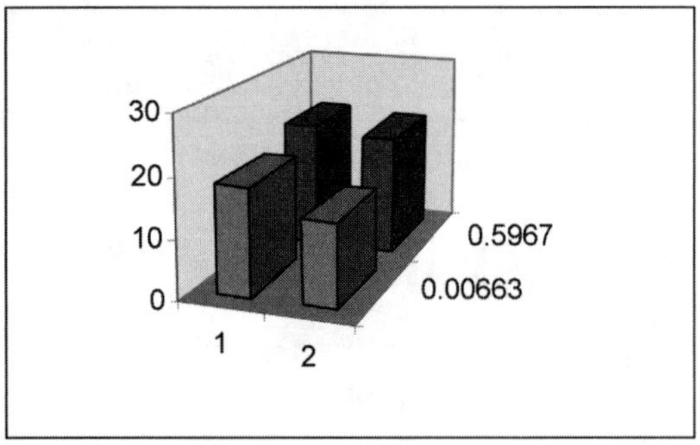

Figure 4 Average deviations

CONCLUSIONS

Summing up it can be stated that the results of the R&D work of applying intelligent agents to determine models representing ill-defined systems more adequately have been promising and the implementation of the advanced version of agents in the CASSANDRA 3.0 simulation system is in progress. Finally it has to be mentioned that the problem described in this paper was – obviously – only an experimental one intended to illustrate the methodology. It is hoped that the approach can be applied in a wide variety of fields including the resolution of human conflicts concerned with peace and/or war as well as the fast growing combined area of informatics and telecommunication networks considering also the human factors, commerce, finances, etc.

REFERENCES

Jávor, A. 1992. "Demon Controlled Simulation." *Mathematics and Computers in Simulation* 34, no. 3-4: 283-296

Jávor, A. 1993. "Knowledge Attributed Petri Nets." *Systems Analysis, Modelling, Simulation* 13, no1/2. 5-12.

Jávor, A.; M. Benkő; A. Leitereg; and G. Moré. 1994. "AI Controlled Simulation of Complex Systems." *Computing & Control Engineering Journal* 5, no. 2: 79-82.

Jávor, A. 1997. "Problem Solving by the CASSANDRA Simulation System Controlled by Combined Mobile and Static AI." In *Proceedings of the Summer Computer Simulation Conference* (Arlington, Virginia, USA, July 13-17),723-728.

Jávor, A. and G. Szűcs. 1999. "AI Controlled Simulation of the Complex Development of Regions". In *Proceedings of the Summer Computer Simulation Conference* (Chicago, Illinois, USA, July 11-15), 385-390.

Szűcs, G. and Á. Vigh. 1995. "Simulation of a Quality Controlled Manufacturing and Assembly System." In *Proceedings of the IMACS Symposium on Systems Analysis and Simulation* (Berlin, Germany, June 26-30), 279-282.

Ziegler, B.P. 1984. *Multifacetted Modelling and Discrete Event Simulation.* Academic Press Inc.

BIOGRAPHIES

András Jávor holds the degrees M.Sc.E.E., Ph.D. and D.Sc. in computer science. He is director of the Hungarian Center of the International McLeod Institute of Simulation Sciences. He is professor at the Budapest University of Technology and Economics and at the Széchenyi István College, where he is also dean of the Faculty of Informatics and Electrical Engineering. He is chairman of the Hungarian Simulation Society and of IMACS/Hungary, secretary of the Board of Directors of EUROSIM and the editorial boards of 5 international scientific journals. His publications exceed 150 items. He was visiting professor 3 times at the Aachen Technical University and invited lecturer several times at various universities in Austria, the Netherlands, Japan and China.

Gábor Szűcs M.Sc.E.E. is a research fellow working with Prof. A. Jávor in the workplaces mentioned above. His publications amount to 12 items.

PONDERING ON A SELF-ORGANIZING ALL-OPTICAL ROUTING SYSTEM

Edward E. E. Frietman, R.C Huntsinger[1] and G.D. Khoe[2]
Pattern Recognition Group, Faculty. of Applied Sciences, Delft University of Technology
Lorentzweg 1, 2628 CJ, Delft, the Netherlands
e-mail: E.E.E.Frietman@tn.tudelft.nl
[1] College of Engineering, Computer Science, and Technology (ECT)
California State University, Chico 95929-0410 USA
e-mail: drralph@ecst.csuchico.edu
[2] Electro Optical Communication Systems, COBRA Institute
Technical University Eindhoven, EH-12, 5600 MB, Eindhoven, the Netherlands
e-mail: G.D.Khoe@tue.nl

KEYWORDS

All-optical routing system, ATM-node, Self-Organizing Neural network algorithms.

ABSTRACT

In the context of nowadays information and communication technologies, the Internet is idealized as a panacea in developing a global information infrastructure. Yet this technology, linking millions of users at academic, industrial, governmental and domestic environments, hasn't come to an accomplishment of the requirements of a large bandwidth and a higher throughput, while data traffic growth has caused significant effects in all parts of the network. So implementations of voice and video applications are yet far from being able to realize. The exploitation of wavelength-division-multiplexing as a technology supporting mechanism completed with the design of a new generation of devices and materials has advanced the arrival of optical communications, ultimately leading to the availability of a packet-switched all-optical network. Such a network not only offers a higher bandwidth than its electronic counterpart, but it also provides for protocol heterogeneity; i.e. the transparency of the transport layer. In exploring such a communication environment, optical packets must be sorted along three dimensions: space, time and wavelength. This paper reflects on some fictitious building stones that arrange an all-optical routing system. Also special attention will be paid on an imaginary alternative that provides for a congestionless routing path when sending data through the network.

1. INTRODUCTION

High traffic handling efficiency and scalability are required to route data packets through a communication network containing large numbers of nodes. To accomplish this mostly a trade-off is made between the complexity of the handling procedure and the availability of an adequate network capacity. In such a case, less communication functionality is required in case of an increasing network capacity. This tendency will ultimately lead to a situation that network node complexity is traded for network transport capacity. In case of relying on a routing algorithm typically an optimization of some performance measure of the network is pursued, like mean packet delay or percentage of successfully delivered packets. See figure 1 for an impression of such a network.

Routing can be performed in a centralised or localised manner. In both cases the path used to route packets between a source destination pair can be static or will be altered depending on network changes and conditions. Adaptive routing algorithms that change the path depending on network conditions may deliver packets with less delay and greater success than static routing algorithms. However, they may not deliver packets in the same order in which they were sent, due to possible changes in the data paths. With centralised routing, a central node that has knowledge of all links in the network and the condition of the links, computes the optimum route for the packet through the network. The central node updates routing tables in the individual nodes of the network so that the packet follows the prescribed route. For localised routing each node makes its own routing decision on where to send the packet, based on information each node has on local links and possibly the whole network. Networks can be broadly classed as either connection-orientated or connectionless networks. In connection-orientated networks the path used for routing of packets is predetermined and fixed prior to sending the packets. Examples of connection-orientated networks are asynchronous transfer mode (ATM) networks and the telephone system. On the other hand in connectionless networks packets are sent without first establishing a routing path. In fact the path packets take to the destination may change from packet to packet. An example of a connectionless network is an IP (Internetwork Protocol) based network.

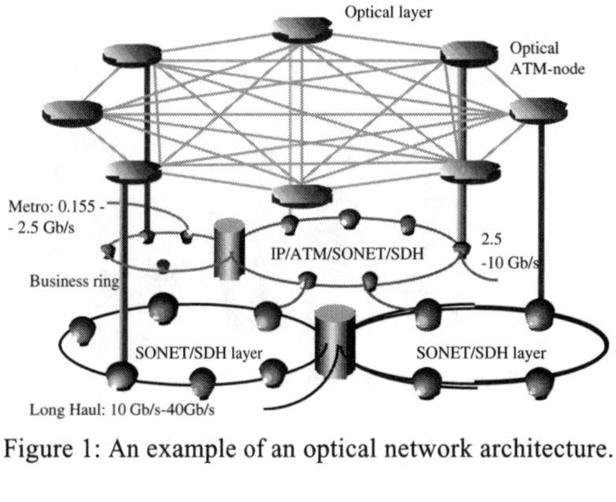

Figure 1: An example of an optical network architecture.

2. DRIVEN BY DEMANDS

There is an increasing demand for high-throughput networks, - supporting end-to-end data rates on the order of several 100 terabits/second (Tb/s) - for voice, video, images, and data communication applications. All-optical networks are a fast emerging technology that promise solutions for bottlenecks introduced by the fact that electronic circuits have limitations towards data rates in excess of 10 Gb/s. Since optical networks offer much higher bandwidths than electronic networks, there can be a change over from the classical time-division multiplexing (TDM) technology, usually performing at transmission speeds up to 10 Gb/s using only one wavelength, towards wavelength-division multiplexing (WDM). While WDM networks have to at most accommodate the speed or data rates of the fastest node, TDM networks have to serve throughputs that are the aggregate of all the data rates of all nodes. WDM, originating from the beginning of the 1990s, exploits a single optical fiber to transport a number of signals simultaneously with each signal operating at a optical routing system, new devices such as optical cross-connects (OXC's) (Alexander 1993), (Johanson 1996) and optical add-drop multiplexers (OADM's) (Kim 1997, Miyakawa 1996) had to be designed.

3. PACKET-SWITCHING NODE

Each node fulfills a crucial function within the network. It distributes the information to predetermined destinations and it incorporates the necessary functionalities of which some of them are processed in the electronic domain, while others resort under an optical processing technique.

3.1 ATM Node Architecture

A representation of a generic structure of an ATM node is depicted in figure 2 (Guillemot 1998). In WDM-based networks, nodes are usually flanked by de/multiplexers, while the actual switching process is carried out at packet level per wavelength and per time slot. Correspondingly, the number of ports is scaled according to the number of connecting fibers times the number of multiplexed wavelengths. Such a configuration leads to a large switching fabric.

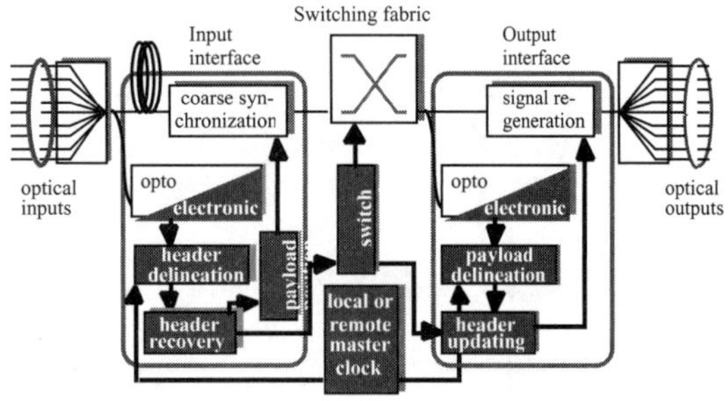

Figure 2: Block diagram of a generic node architecture.

The input interface synchronizes the incoming cell streams relative to a local or remote master clock, this way properly recovering the contents of the header. In most cases electronics isn't involved in recovering the packet payloads. Hence the packet has to be optically synchronized to align the payload time position, which at the same time maintains bit rate transparency.

The output interface ensures physical transmission constraints, such as power levels, wavelength allocations, signal shaping and reinsertion of the modified header.

In the RACE ATMOS (ATM optical switching) project, the switching fabric (also labeled a wavelength routing switch) is not all-optical since it is controlled by electronics. It encodes wavelengths at input level where the packet headers are detected to extract the routing information. It accomplishes contention resolution by buffering the information using optical fiber delay lines with lengths corresponding to a multiple of the packet duration and it selects the packets with the help of a wavelength demultiplexer containing bandpass filters (Masetti 96). To compensate for time jitter endured by the packets within the switching fabric; the necessary payload delineation is implemented after the fibre delay lines at the input interface (Guillemot 1998).

In 1995 a successor was introduced, named KEOPS (Keys to Optical Packet Switching) (Danielsen 1998, Gambini 1998 and Renaud 1997). KEOPS discerns itself from other architectures, including that of the ATMOS platform, in that the optical packet layer is able to handle both bit rates and to some degree also transfer mode transparency. The latter is of importance in both ATM cells and internet protocol (IP) packet switching. In addition to variable bit rates facilities, the switching fabric also allows for broadcasting incoming data packets in the sense that packets from a given input are always converted to the same wavelength.

4. CONGESTION AND ITS IMPACTS

Each link is characterised by its transmission capacity while each node is demarcated by a maximum storing capacity. An increasing delay and a decreasing work-load will result in a declining network throughput. Congestion, in fact, occurs if queue lengths grow disproportionate in a short time, leading to buffer overflow (due to a limited buffer space) and cell loss (due to a low throughput rate). A larger buffer and the implementation of high speed links might offer a solution, but these remedies are rather more reactions on symptoms than less a direct response to the perpetrator.

4.1 Routing Process

Routing, executed in a centralized or localized manner, is a process of determining an optimal trajectory through a network when a message has to be delivered to a more or less predestined destinations. In centralized routing one node is designated to be a network routing manager. It regulates the flow of the messages through the network by updating the routing tables in the individual nodes of the network, this way forcing the packet to follow a prescribed route. In executing its task the necessary routing table will be transmitted to each node simultaneously. This routing algorithm has both advantages and disadvantages. An advantage is that only one node is required to produce a routing table, the others simply use it; resources are saved this way. But the method does not support the necessary conditions when the composition of a network changes. For instance, there is no indication when nodes are overloaded by a large number of messages.

The localized or decentralized manner still uses a formal routing protocol where all nodes make their own routing decisions. Applied in a large geographical area network, the routing table for each node is now developed by its individual network manager. This protocol shows an interesting feature in that it is self-adjusting; it automatically adapts to changes in a network configuration. The routing table, developed by such a network manager, is the result of a static routing protocol. It only changes its configuration if nodes are added or removed. The events are automatically registered.

4.2 Congestion Control

Congestion control, interpreted as a problem of matching the admitted traffic to the available network resources, is of crucial importance for Internet and ATM networks in providing quality of service to competing users in an efficient way. Control can also be classified by the stages that the operation is performed: congestion prevention, congestion avoidance and congestion recovery. Congestion prevention makes the occurrence impossible, while congestion avoidance allows the phenomenon to happen at the costs of efforts to keep the network state always in balance. Recovery is a remedy to remove the congestion state itself and to restrict the damage that has already been done. All these schemes are needed to treat problems inherent to the burstiness of the data traffic, the unpredictability of the resource demands and the required propagation delay versus bandwidth ratio.

4.3 Virtual Deflection Routing

A more or less divergent technique in limiting congestion and preventing cell losses is the method of deflection routing. Cells arriving at an allocated node, that cannot handle that information at that moment, are re-routed to adjacent nodes that can bring about the intended performance bound. So deflection routing prevents congestion by " diffusing" cells around a congested area. Main drawbacks of such a scheme are the chances of a battered delivery of cells and an origination of an unbound transfer delay. One of the alternatives is the exploration of a fully-connect scheme.

4.4 A Fully-Connect Scheme

A *fully-connect* networking topology, seldom used because of its costs, makes the need of switched networks superfluous because of the fact that it is the only connection scheme of which a many-to-many, a many-to-one and a one-to-many structured network can be derived. Figure 3 shows an eight-node organized *version of it.*

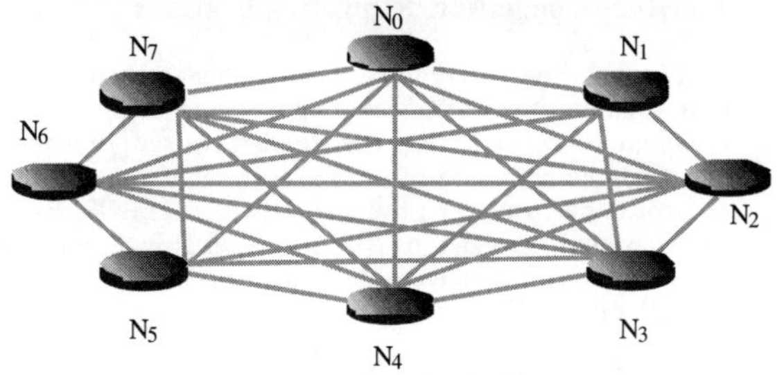

Figure 3: An eight-node organized fully-connect topology.

Let N^{ATM}_i, i = 0, 1, 2, ... M be the ATM nodes in this fully-connect topology. Given an arbitrary interconnection configuration, s_k, k = 0, 1, 2, ... K is denoted the source of a destination d_j, j = 0, 1, 2, ... J where s_k transfers its information to d_j, indicated as $s_k \rightarrow d_j$. An interconnection scheme is defined if and only if all the sets $S(s_k)$ and $D(d_j)$ are characterized. Let $S(s_k)$ and $D(d_j)$ be respectively the set of source nodes of s_k and destination nodes of d_j, that is (Frietman 1995):

$$S(s_k) = \{d_q \mid s_k \rightarrow d_q\},\ q = 0, 1, 2, \ldots J$$

$$D(d_j) = \{s_p \mid d_j \rightarrow s_p\},\ p = 0, 1, 2, \ldots K$$

The *one-to-many*, also called *single broadcast*, interconnection scheme performs a communication protocol that allows information to be transported from any specified source to any arbitrary destination. Assume N_0 has to provides data to N_4 . This can be done through a *direct* transition or in case of a congested N_4, through (M-2) alternate (*double* transition) paths. In the case of a *direct* or *single* transition the source node is $S(d_0) = \{s_0\}$ and equivalently the destination nodes are $D(s_0) = \{d_4\}$ and $D(s_4) = \varnothing$. In the second situation, where a *double* transition is executed, the source node is $S(d_0)=\{s_0\}$, $S(d_1)=\{s_0\}$, $S(d_2)=\{s_0\}$, $S(d_3)=\{s_0\}$, $S(d_5)=\{s_0\}$, $S(d_6)=\{s_0\}$, $S(d_7)=\{s_0\}$, but the destination nodes are now defined as $D(s_0) = \{d_0, d_1, d_2, d_3, d_5, d_6, d_7\}$ and $D(s_0, s_1, s_2, s_3, s_5, s_6, s_7)= \varnothing$. A set with no elements is an empty (or null or void) set and is denoted $\varnothing = \{ \}$.

So for a one-to-many interconnection scheme, there is thus one finite (or none-empty) set of source nodes and one finite set of destination nodes. Practicing these relations imply that there are (M-2) six alternate paths. The direct path is not counted because it is a *direct* transition. See figure 4 for the elaborated situation.

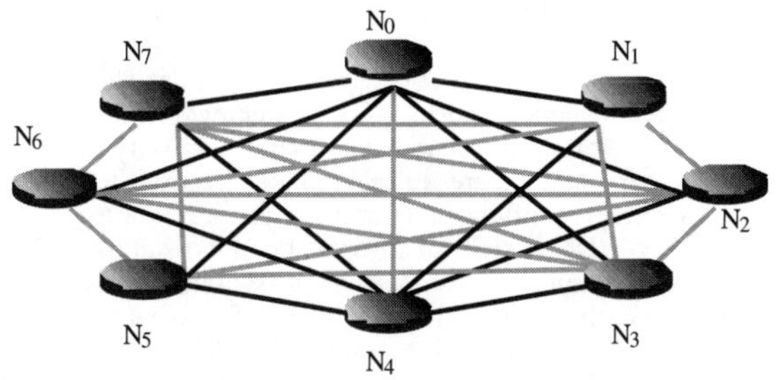

Figure 4: Modes of double transitions or 'hops'.

4.5 Other Congestion Regulating Features

Feedback, necessary to control the phenomenon of congestion, regulates the traffic submitted on ATM connections according to the state of the nodes to be traversed. In making an appropriate choice, questions have to be answered whether control is performed by the length or the growth rate of a queue. Most investigations focus on using growth rate as a parameter, because it indicates in which direction the state of the network moves. If it comes to an execution of the feedback, both an open-loop (with no end-to-end control) as well as a close-loop scheme could satisfy. In the close-loop mode a sending node adjust its cell rate in accordance with the measure of the feedback information retrieved from nodes in the network.

The implementation of the feedback can be done by allocating a combination of bits in the cell-packet to point out the burstiness of the nodes along the flow path, as a function of which the sending node should increase or decrease its rate upon receiving the feedback information.

In contrast to conventional control techniques, neural networks only require a specification of an appropriate learning algorithm, followed by a definition of an interpretation of the signals that flow through the network to ultimately provide a set of application-specific data streams that collectively represent the desired behaviour of the network. The network determines how an input pattern is transformed into an appropriate output pattern by letting the data adaptively modify the weights in its internal structure.

5. BROADCAST ROUTING NETWORK

A network, of which the topology is the basic geometry layout, is expected to span a large geographical area. Where ring, bus and star topologies are mostly found in Local Area and Backbone Networks, star and mesh configurations are commonly exploited in Wide Area Networks. For large geographical areas, only a star and a mesh will satisfy. For a star, each node is connected by an individual point-to-point methodology through a central connection point. Once a cable breaks, only the corresponding node will fail. In a true mesh, which is just a derivative of a *fully-connect* architecture, each node functions as a central connection point while it is connected to every other node by its own point-to-point links.

5.1 A Fictitious All-Optical ATM Node Architecture

All-optical networks put wavelength conversion with optical functionalities (optical cross-connects and add-drop multiplexers) in the place of electronic switching. The usability of the accompanying optical packet switching, offering high speed data rate/format transparency and configurability, is one of the most important features in supporting the various forms (speech, movie etc.) of information transfer in the near future.

In a WDM system an all-optical path is established between two communication nodes, if circuit-switching is performed by wavelength routing. Since Internet traffic is bursty at all time scales, this method will result in a low bandwidth utilization, implying that such paths may not be efficient. Optical packet switching, on the other hand, is suitable for supporting bursty traffic since it allows statistical sharing of the channel bandwidth among packets that belong to different source and destination pairs. Here, the payload (i.e. data) will remain in the optic form, while its header may be processed electronically or preferably optically. To restrict the percentage of the control overhead Lithium Niobate switches (the use of which lies well beyond the facilities offered now) or semiconductor optical amplifiers are very much needed. So the execution of switching, routing and crossconnect tasks at major network hubs, where many fiber trunks each carrying multiple optical channels may terminate, is of crucial importance.

The block diagram, shown in figure 5, indicates the various desired functions. Most of the proposed functionalities are not yet available, so this part of the paper only reflects author's vision for a future generation all-optical ATM node architecture. The functionality of the different blocks will be cursorily discussed.

An all-optical node architecture, being part of a connectionless network, employs a localised routing algorithm where packets are routed by decisions made at each node independently. Each decision reflects a packet address and the state of the links directly connected to the node. In an all-optical option, the issues of contention and overload on outgoing links are especially critical, as currently an optical equivalence of a shift register or a random access memory doesn't exist. As a consequence of this deficiency, data can only be delayed for a limited amount of time by implementing fiber optic delay lines. Consequently the routing algorithm should be sensitive to the state of the node links to avoid excessive packet loss.

While fiber delay lines suffer from insertion losses, multiple reflections in an optical multifaceted cavity unit more efficiently engender time delays in increments of a single transition time. After the light has travelled around in the cavity a predetermined number of times, optically controlled shutters will gate it out of the unit. Self-Electrooptical Effect Devices (SEEDs) can function as an optical shutter (Miller 1985). A second elegant alternative is the coherent transient true-time-delay regeneration method, enabling storage and processing of a large number of broadband delay elements in a single compact crystal, that was introduced by William Randall Babbitt of the Physics Department of Montana State University at Bozeman, Montana.

Synchronization, to efficiently process the data information is obligatory, since each node needs to recognize the header and the end of the packet, and next re-align a modified/replaced header with its payload. So data and clock recovery is a crucial feature. At data rates beyond a few Gbit/s, it becomes increasingly difficult to perform the clock recovery electronically. An ultra fast Optical Phase Locked Loop (OPLL) controlled master clock, that perform at hundreds or even thousands of Tbit/s, is necessary to walk in step with the further processing of the incoming data stream and the settlement of tasks and controls to be executed in the node itself.

The Time-to-Space Converter is meant for the parallellization of the Header and Channel information that is stored in the cell. A solution can be implemented using an Acousto-Optic Deflector (AOD). AOD's, producing a change in first order spot positions in response to a change in the frequency of the input signal, execute a time-to-space (serial-to-parallel) conversion without the use of moving parts. The device, allowing full electronic control of spot positions in one- and two-dimensional directions, can accurately position a laser beam up to a resolution of 2,500 spots. It so to say provides a simple means to deflect an optical beam in a sequential or random access manner. In case the electronic input is a digital word, the spots generated by a vector scan represent the location of the deflected laser beam. The speed of an AOD is determined by the acoustic transit time across the optical aperture. In case the AOD operates in the 1550 nm region, the speed of sound in this material is 5000 m/sec corresponding to a 1.6 ns transit time when traversing 8 µcrons of material.

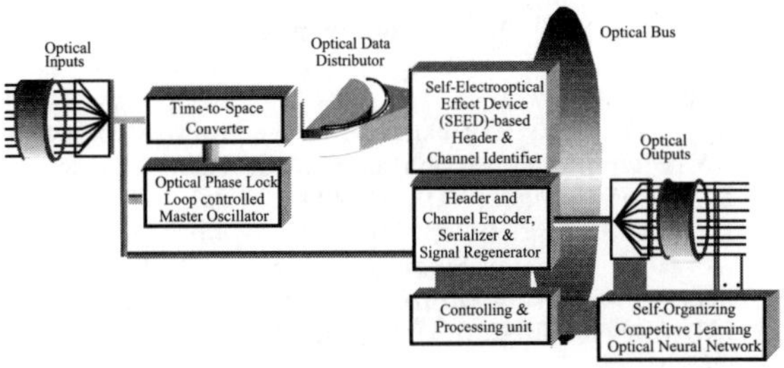

Figure 5: Block diagram of a new generation all-optical ATM node structure.

Moving towards the pico-/femtosecond regime requires the design of an Opto-Optic Deflector (OOD), in which the measure of deflection is determined optically by gradually varying the frequency or the wavelength.

The Header and Channel Identifier, assembled out of optical logic components, decodes the parallelized data (Header and Channel Address) from the Optical Data Distributor. Optical logic (NORs, XORs, XNORs and NANDs) can be realized with SEEDs; a quantum well device consisting of a large number of one nanometer (nm) thick layers alternating between Gallium Arsenic (GaAs) and Aluminium Gallium Arsenic (AlGaAs) (Miller 1985). Such devices, in which in - and outputs are optically controlled, allow parallel processing of the data streams. Performing the process in the optical domain enable multiple devices to be cascaded, so that outputs can directly control inputs of other devices. A symmetric-SEED component stems from two SEED devices that are connected in series, this way creating a flip-flop that can be switched relative to the intensity of the controlling input signals.

The two-dimensional topology of electronic implementations of neural networks limits the number of layers and restricts the measure of globalism of the links, leading to a situation that neural networks has been treated more like algorithms rather than computational architectures. Optical technologies, exploring the third dimension, are ideal for realizing dense networks. Moreover the massive tightly coupled parallelism that occurs in the individual layers of neural networks permits high speeds for any class of computation, next making it attractive for optical computing. Hence optical implementations of neural networks are promising for research in transparent optical packet switching. However, optically organized, but electronically controlled Backpropagation and Hopfield networks have been the only optical neural networks so far demonstrated (Wang 1995 and Giles 1995), genuine realisations of optical versions are sporadic (Psaltis 1989).

The (not yet realized) optical neural network proposed in this paper will exploit an unsupervised self-organizing competitive learning architecture (Kohonen 1982, 1995). Unsupervised learning is an algorithm that collates objects together on the basis of their perceived closeness in an *n*-dimensional hyperspace, where *n* is the number of degrees of freedom of the considered object. The network contains an input layer that represents a vector of the parameters related to the problem under investigation, here the measure of congestion. The neurons in the output layer - also known as the competitive Kohonen layer - are fully connected to the neurons in the input layer, meaning that every neuron in the input layer is linked to every neuron in the Kohonen layer. A neighborhood relation mutually links the neurons. The architecture is shown in figure 6.

The network scheme relies on competitive learning, where neurons compete for the privilege of learning among each other, while the correct answer(s) is (are) not known. This implies that for a certain input vector (values that are fed back from the other nodes in the network), there is only one neuron (out of a cluster of output neurons) that gets activated. To determine which neuron that is, the input vector is compared with the vector that is stored in each of the neurons, the so-called weight-vectors. Only the neuron whose vector most closely resembles the current input vector dominates. So only the "winner" (and in some cases its nearest neighbors) is (are) allowed to learn.

One way to put together a neural network is to use inhibitory connections, where each neuron inhibits every other neuron. A lateral inhibition layer structure demonstrates neurons that inhibit only those that are nearby.

During training a single sample (input) vector $\underline{x}$ is chosen randomly and a process is initialized that searches for similarities between that vector and the weight vectors of the map. The winning neuron $\underline{w}$ is the one whose weight vector has the greatest similarity with the input sample $\underline{x}$, usually defined as the neuron that has a distance $\|\underline{x} - \underline{m}_w\| = \min_i\{\|\underline{x} - \underline{m}_i\|\}$. $\|.\|$ represents the distance measure. The weight vectors which eventually converge to a point of stability, are updated the moment neuron *w* is found.

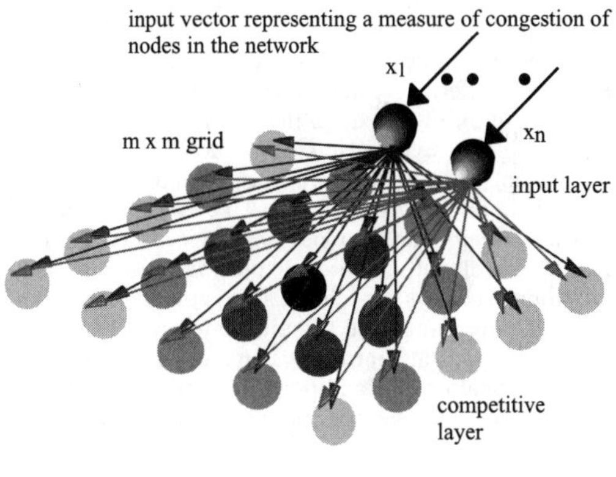

Figure 6: A self-organizing competitive learning architecture. The feature or Kohonen map is located at the bottom.

In the learning process, weight vectors and topological neighbors move closer to the input vector in the input space. A learning rate governs the size of the weight alterations. The update rule for the weight vector of neuron *w* is: $\underline{m}_w(t+1) = \underline{m}_w + K_{wi}(t)[\underline{x}(t) - m_i(t)]$, where *t* denotes the time and $K_{wi}(t)$ the neighborhood kernel around the winner *w* at time *t*. See Figure 6 for the different gradings of gray values centered around the winner. $K_{wi}(t)$, which is usually a non-increasing function of time and of the distance of neuron *i* to the winner *w*, defines the region of influence that the input sample has on the network. The size of the "winner's" neighborhood is generally varied during the training process. In the beginning all the nodes are involved in the learning process, during processing the size of the neighborhood shrinks after each presentation of the complete training set, until it includes only the "winner" itself.

The Header and Channel Encoder, Serializer and Signal Regenerator are respectively allocated to the formation of the new destination, the execution of a parallel-to-serial conversion and the generation of the new data. SEED components can also be used to put together the encoding and parallel-to-serial functionalties. The Controlling & Processing unit takes care of the activities within the node.

The Self-organizing optical neural network section plays a crucial role in the philosophy of the design of a next generation all-optical router. First and foremost it must always process the information, independent from the selected congestion control criteria. This information, reflecting the conditions of the various links that lead to the available (not so congested) destination nodes, determines a "winner" according to which the route will be changed. When using a fully-connect scheme, the congested node will be evaded by forcing the data to undergo a second transition to a nearest node. In case of a network it implies a routing path to another destination.

It is expected that all-optical components can significantly improve on the performance of an optical system. The basic switching domain for optics is obviously space and optical switching fabrics are in fact continuous processing devices that physically route an optical stream of data from one node to another. Probably the biggest advantage is offered by the properties of optical transparency: the routed flows carry information of different calibers based on signal modulation and encoding.

While time is marked as the second domain for traditional electronic switching, performing the same activity in the optical domain is more difficult since photons cannot be stopped easily. So buffering, either realized by delay lines or a multifaceted cavity unit or through the method of coherent transient true-time-delay regeneration, is of crucial importance.

Probably the most important aspects for the near future is to investigate the radius of action of the switching and the multiplexing domain, that stretches from space towards time also including wavelength features. Exploring the parallelism in such evolutions conveys the idea of a growing penetration of optics and photonic integrated circuits into switching, ultimately leading towards all-optical systems of increasing complexity and functionality. The addition of optical neural network techniques is probably the most promising (Frietman 2000).

5. CONCLUSIONS

From a system point of view, the advantages of all-optical ATM networks have to be demonstrated first, because most of present-day research is focused on the design of prototypes with limited functionalities, such as putting to test buffering capabilities and space switching facilities of the core of a switching fabric. It must not be trivialized that advantages of optics, like the transparency of the payload, may not be achievable anymore, if functions of a photonic ATM node are implemented by electronics instead of optics. More efforts should be put into ideas carrying innovative solutions to overcome the ubiquitous problems and to completely change the perspectives in the future. Investigating the features of a self-organizing all-optical routing system could be one of them.

REFERENCES:

Alexander S.B. 1993. " A precompetitive consortium on wide-band all-optical networks." *J. Lightwave Technol.*, VOL. 11, (May): 714-735.

Danielsen S.L., P. Bukhave-Hansen, K.E. Stubkjaer 1998. "Wavelength conversion in Optical Packet Switching." *J. Lightwave Technol.*, VOL. 16, NO. 12 (Dec.): 2095-2109.

Frietman E. E. E. 1995. *Opto -Electronic Processing & Networking: A Design Study: Perspectives of Optical Interconnects in Massively Parallel Processing.* Research Monograph: ISBN 90-900 8690-0, Delft University of Technology Press Office.

Frietman E.E.E., M.T. Hill, G.D. Khoe, 2000. "A Kohonen neural network controlled all-optical router system." In *Special Issue of International Journal of Computer Research* (IJCR), (to be published).

Gambini P. et al. 1998. " Transparent optical packet switching: Network architecture and demonstrators in the KEOPS project." (Invited paper), *IEEE J. Select Areas in Commun.*

Giles C.L., M.W. Goudreau, 1995. "Routing in Optical Multistage Interconnection Networks: A Neural Network Solution," *J. Lightwave Technol.*, VOL. 13, NO. 6 (June): 1111-1115.

Guillemot C. et al. 1998. " Transparent Optical Packet Switching: The European ACTS KEOPS Project Research Approach, *J. Lightwave Technol.*, VOL. 16, No. 12 (Dec.): 2117-2134.

Johanson S. 1996. "Transport network involving a reconfigurable WDM network layer- A European demonstration." *J. Lightwave Technol.*, NO. 14, (June): 1341-1348.

Kohonen T. 1982. "Self-organised formation of topologically correct feature maps. "*Biological Cybernetics* 43: 59-69.

Kohonen T. 1995. *Self-Organising maps*. In Springer Series in Information Sciences, Springer, Heidelberg.

Kim S.Y. et al. 1997." Highly stable optical add-drop multiplexer using polarization beam splitters and fibre Bragg gratings." Techical Dig. OFC'97, paper ThJ3, Dallas, USA, (Febr.)

Masetti F. et al.. 1996. "High speed, high capacity ATM optical switch-es for future telecommunication transport networks." *IEEE J. Select. Areas Commun.*, NO.14 (Jule): 979-998.

Miller D.A.B. 1985. "The quantum well self-electrooptical effect device: Optoelectronic bistability and oscillation, and self-linearized modulation." *IEEE Proc.*, QE-21 (Sept.): 1462-1476.

Miyakawa T. et al. 1996. "An experiment of optical add-drop multiplexer using fibre grating and its limiting factor." Techical Dig. OECC'96, paper 17B3-5, Chiba, Japan, (July).

Psaltis D. et al, 1989. *Optical implementation of Neural Computers. Optical Processing and Computing.* In Optical Processing and Computing. H.H. Arsenault, T. Szopilik and B. Macukow, eds. Academic Press Inc. Harcourt, Boston, 251-277.

Wang C.J., P.N. Weissler. 1995. "The Use of Artificial Neural Networks for Optimal Message Routing." *IEEE Network,:* 16-24.

In Search of Data Distribution Management in Large Scale Distributed Simulations

Azzedine Boukerche and Amber Roy
Parallel Simulations and Distributed Systems
Research Laboratory (PARADISE)
Dept. of Computer Sciences, University of North Texas
Emails: {boukerche, ajr}@cs.unt.edu

Abstract

With the need to do increasingly complex distributed simulations, a considerable amount of effort in the DIS/HLA community is concentrating on the data distribution management (DDM) problem. In large-scale distribution simulations, a large number of entities are simulated, and each entity could be a source of data that might be relevant to only few other entities. Thus, DDM is necessary to provide efficient, scalable mechanisms for distributing state updates and interaction information for distributed simulations. In this paper, we describe DDM in a more general and comprehensive way, and answer basic questions such as "what", "where", "why", and "when" DDM is used. We also provide a good insight of DDM schemes that have been proposed by now and their implementations, and propose a classification of the well known DDM schemes, so that one will be able to unify fundamental concepts pertaining to DDM, and be able to compare them.

1. INTRODUCTION

With the need to do increasingly complex distributed simulations, a considerable amount of effort in the DIS/HLA community is concentrating on the data distribution management (DDM) problem [1, 2, 8, 9, 14, 16]. In large-scale distribution simulations, a large number of entities are simulated and each entity could be a source of data that might be relevant to only few other entities. The aim of DDM is to limit and control the volume of the data exchanged during the simulation, and reduce the processing requirements of simulation hosts by relying events and state information only to those applications which require them, while exploiting the features of the computer network architectures. In this paper, we describe DDM in a more general and comprehensive way, and answer basic questions such as "*what*", "*where*", "*why*", and "*when*" DDM is used. Our main objective is to be able to provide a good insight of DDM schemes that have been proposed by now, so that one will be able to unify fundamental concepts pertaining to DDM, and be able to compare them. It is our belief, that without this holistic vision, relationships among the seemingly disparate aspects of DDM may go unrecognized and chances for optimization, and sources of complications, might be missed.

2. WHAT IS DDM?

In a non-distributed environment, all entities are simulated on one machine. Hence interactions between entities are easy to manipulate using a single heap of events. On the other hand, in a distributed simulation environment, simulated entities might reside on different machines, necessitating data exchange between those host machines. Data Distribution Management (DDM) is basically the mechanism, used by the distributed simulation engine to ensure that the simulated entities have the relevant data they need during the execution of the simulation. The aim of DDM is to reduce the volume of the traffic of data exchanged during the simulation, and the processing requirements of the simulated entities/hosts in the network. In General, DDM can be divided into three phases: (*i*) *express interest* and *availability*; (*ii*) *match*; and (*iii*) *deliver data*. The "express interest" stage involves the declaration of the data requirements given by the application to the infrastructure, which will map them to the current state information in the "match" step, and then will facilitate the transmission of any matching data to the appropriate host and the simulated entity.

2.1 Express Interest and Availability

The initial step in DDM occurs when simulated entities (objects or federates) tell to the infrastructure in which of the distributed world data they are interested in, and which of its own data they wish to make available in the distributed virtual world. In some environments, such as homogeneous systems, interests and availability are usualy expressed on per-entity basis, where each entity notifies the distributed simulation engine (DSE) (i.e., the available infrastructure) of its interest areas. In the HLA world which will be discussed later, interests and availability can be expressed per-entity (object or federate)[1]. The per-federate approach implies that the simulator will collect and combine the interests and availability of each object in the federate, which may be done by the federate's engine. Note that simulated entities (such as objects or federates) can express their interests either statically, i.e., once at system initialization, or dynamically, i.e., multiples times in the course of a simulation

2.1.1 Static

The static method allows the DSE to make optimizations[2], based on the interests and availability. Static interests and availability are usually easier to read by both the human developer and the DSE, since they can be expressed in a

[1] DoD High Level Architecture

[2] which it would not be possible if those interests do not change during the simulation.

configuration file that may be created by a developer and/or generated by the system based upon the initialization parameters. This file can have arbitrary syntax including user comments. It is easy to locate this file, since it does exist as an ASCII text file, which may be desired for logging or debugging purposes. The file can also be parsed and used to create subscriptions and publications. Static subscriptions and publications are simple to manage since after their initial creations they are read-only.

2.1.2 Dynamic

The DSE using the dynamic model must always be ready to (1) read; (2) process the interests and the availability of information; and (3) create the corresponding subscriptions and publications. Hence, it uses complex data structures, which might need to be frequently updated to store these subscriptions and publications. Furthermore, communication and synchronization protocols must be employed to ensure the accuracy of the data. Recall that DDM occurs in the context of a distributed world environment. Therefore, the data structures that keep track of the subscriptions/publications and other information relevant to DDM are also distributed among the hosts and simulated enties. Therefore, it may be necessary to move some of the data among the hosts as the simulator's objects' or federates interests and availability change. DDM is sometimes used to coordinate this type of scenario, which is referred to as a *recursive* use of DDM [18, 19].

For these simulations using dynamic subscriptions and publications, this step may be performed a few times for the same object or federate, whereas it will only be done once for the simulations using the static strategy described earlier. Each time this step is performed, a match is then required.

2.2 Match

Simulated entities express their interests and availability to DSE, which will in turn, creates and/or modify the subscriptions and publications. Next, the subscriptions are compared to the publications in order to determine if there is any intersection region of interests. This process is referred to as a *matching,* since the goal is to find matches between the data being published (i.e., made available), and the objects or federates that are subscribing to (i.e., interested in that data). Matching data must be delivered to the simulated entity, i.e., object or federate that is subscribing to it.

2.3 Deliver and Receive Data

The final phase in DDM involves delivering any published data that matched data subscriptions to the host that is simulating the object (or federates) that made that subscription. While a subscriber may be matched with many publishers, a publisher can be matched with multiple subscribers who are also distributed in the network The delivery of data from the publisher to the subscriber is the main task associated with this step. However, the reception of the data by the subscriber is also part of this phase, which consists of two parts, referred to as *routing data* and *forwarding data.* While the former entails establishing the data transfer pathways between the simulated entities involved in the transfer; the latter involves the actual data transfer. Some researchers do not consider the second part to be truly an element of the DDM. They consider that DDM services are only responsible for the first part, and they only establish connectivity between federates for the data [8]. Other researchers do consider the data transfer to be an integral part of DDM services. In this case, DDM refers to the mechanism used by a PDES[3] engine to automatically marshal the appropriate user-specified data between entities as they move in and out of one another's field of view [13, 14, 16]. In [2], the authors assumed that moving the data among the simulated entities, is an integral part of the entire DDM process, and they considered the delivery and reception of data, including establishing the connectivity and transferring the data, as the final stage of DDM.

2.4 DDM Data Abstraction

In the first phase of DDM, interests and availability are expressed to the DES infrastructure, which will store these information as subscriptions and publications. A *subscription* is basically an abstraction that refers to the set of world data in which a simulated entity (object or federate) is interested in, and a *publication* is an analogous construct that refers to the set of data that the simulated entity is making available to the world. A publication is also knows as an *update.* The entity that expressed an interest or availability, and generated the subscription (or publication) is known as a *subscriber* (or *publisher*). When discussing subscribers and publishers, it is essential to realize that in a virtual environment (VE) using DDM, the data representing the state of the objects in the shared world is distributed among the various hosts simulating them, and the data representing these objects' subscriptions and publications are also distributed. The data representing a subscription does not necessarily reside on the same host as the subscriber. Hence, the infrastructure that supports DDM must use an abstraction whose primary purpose is to manage subscriptions and publications in an efficient and scalable manner. The *Grid* is perhaps the most fundamental abstraction used in such distributed environments. The *Routing Space* is a generalization of this construct. We shall describe each of these constructs in the next subsections.

2.4.1 Grid

A grid is a multidimensional coordinate system whose dimensions represent values in which simulated entities can express their interests or availability. As its name suggests, the grid is partitioned into cells. An example of two dimensions might be longitude and latitude. Those two values might also be represented by one dimension as an ordered LongLat=(longitude,latitude) ordered pair. Dimension values are not necessarily real numbers, they can also be integers or enumeration. They can also represent real-world phenomenon, such as radio frequency, or simulation-specific information, such as object class type or IP addresses. A simulation might have multiple grids, each with different characteristics and employed for different purposes.

For each grid, the following information must be known: (1) the number of dimensions, (2) the *routing variable* which corresponds to each dimension, (3) the mapping of routing variables onto grid coordinates, and (4) the initial cell size for each dimension. While in a fixed-cell grids scheme, the cell

[3] Parallel Discrete Event Simulation

size should be constant throughout the simulation, in a variable-cell grids one, the cell size may change, and thereby they provide a finer (or broader) resolution as opposed to the fixed cell approach.

Hierarchical grids[4] consists of multiple levels of grids, each with a different cell size, and a fine resolution resides at the lower grid levels. Hierarchical grids are usually represented using quadtrees and/or octtrees[5].

2.4.2 Routing Space

A *routing space* is basically a grid without cells, i.e., a multidimensional space without partitions. It has the following characteristics: multiple dimensions, routing variable, and mapping of routing variable to routing space coordinates. However, the initial cell size is not applicable [18]. Note that just like there may be several grids in a simulation, there may be multiple routing spaces as well.

2.4.3 Region

Regions are subsets of a particular grid or a routing space, and they can have up to the same number of dimensions. A region may have fewer dimensions than the grid or routing space if no interests were expressed in at least one of the dimensions. At least one pair of values (called *extents)* that specifies the maximum and minimum values of the regions is assigned to each dimension. along that dimension. Regions are defined by their extents.

3. WHEN CAN DDM BE USED?

DDM has now become a common, if not a mandatory function of an infrastructure supporting large scale distributed simulations. Recently, there has been growing interest in simulation interoperability, and hence the advent of the DoD[6] High Level Architecture (HLA). DDM is being used by several simulation systems that are HLA-compliant, as well as other heterogeneous environments. However, not all distributed simulations are equally able to take advantage of the optimization provide by DDM. Recall that DDM can only be used in systems when the data representing the virtual world is distributed according to the shared world environment, as opposed to the replicated world.

3.1 Replicated World

Simulations that use protocols for inter-hosts communication, such as SIMNET and DIS-compliant systems, do not have any middleware that can store or coordinate the state of the virtual world. The protocol-based method of implementing a heterogeneous environment implies the use of a replicated virtual world. Each simulation must keep track of the state of the world, meaning that it may be replicated on many of the hosts that are part of the environment. Clearly this is inefficient in terms of host memory usage as well as network traffic, since every update to the virtual world must be transmitted to all hosts.

DDM is not applicable in a replicated world environment,

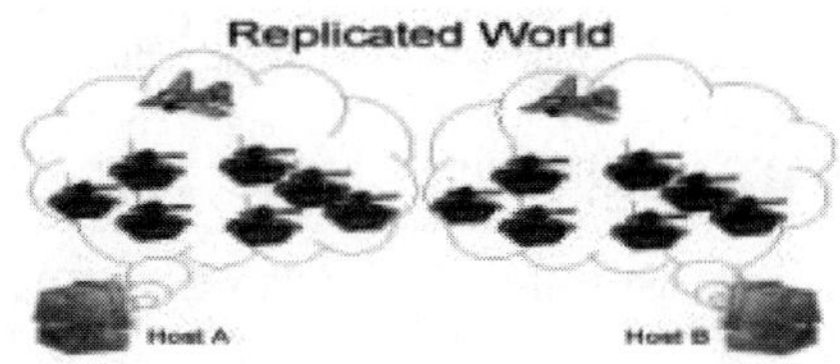

since by definition all hosts need all data associated with the state of the world. Thus, the paradigm of replicated worlds

disallows doing any data filtering. Most DIS-compliant simulations fit into the replicated world model. However, it would be more accurate to categorize them as *stateless* systems, i.e., they have no notion of a shared virtual world. DIS uses IP/UDP broadcasts to send to every host every state change that occurs within the virtual world. The simulators must then construct their own world based upon the messages they have received. In addition, DDM cannot be used when there is no middleware layer to mediate between the simulations and the network, which is true for DIS-compliant systems. Some DIS-compliant systems have been modified, and so no longer use the DIS broadcast protocol. Instead a middleware has been added to perform some of the DDM services. The DoD is encouraging all DIS simulations to be HLA-compliant, and thus to use the shared world paradigm in order to benefit from the DDM services.

3.2 Shared World

The observation that all hosts do not need all data lead to the conclusion that the replicated world paradigm is generally not very efficient. Fortunately, heterogeneous environments that use an efficient infrastructure can avoid it , because the infrastructure can serve to store the data associated with the state of the world among the hosts, and thereby simulating a shared memory architecture using the a shared world paradigm. One of the main features of the infrastructure is to ensure that each host gets, in a timely manner, the data that it needs.

This feature shall help to reduce the use of memory and the processing power, by reducing the total amount of data that needs to be received, evaluated, and stored. However, these gains can be easily negated by the additional network load of the synchronization messages transmitted, the processing time incurred by the infrastructure while performing the necessary computations, and the potential bottleneck while requiring the data that will be managed by the infrastructure. These overheads are the result of the additional coordination and organization required by having the data distributed among the various hosts, and ensuring that the hosts shall receive only that the data they are interested in.

DDM mechanisms seek to meet the data requirements of hosts while minimizing its associated overhead. Inefficient DDM

---

[4] , a cross between the fixed and variable cell-grids

[5] because they have proven to speed up the search process.

[6] Department of Defense

schemes can have a devastating effect on the performance and the scalability of any distributed simulations. Thus, DDM is necessary and it is a critical part of any infrastructure that shares the data relevant to the state of the virtual world.

4. WHY USE DDM?

Distributed simulations systems make use of DDM in order to reduce the amount of data received by individual simulations in large-scale distributed simulations. Specifically, DDM aims to limit the data exchanged among the distributed hosts by only sending data to those hosts that are running a simulation that requires that particular data.

The fundamental observation leading to this strategy is that practically all of the real-world objects being simulated will be interested in only a fraction of the objects contained in the entire simulation. For example, a plane is primarily interested only in those ground vehicles, such as tanks, that are close to it. It is probably not concerned with the position of any other tanks, some of which might be thousands of miles away. Without DDM schemes, the host simulating the plane can not elect to only receive information about certain objects, namely the ones that are within the plane's radar range. It will get an update message anytime any other vehicle (or simulated entities), changes its position. The cost of these irrelevant data transmission can be very high. Sending data to a host that is not interested in, puts an un-necessary burden on the sending and especially the receiving host, besides flooding the network.

DDM is used because it performs the desirable task of reducing extraneous data transfer. If limiting the amount of information sent and received is so advantageous, why then is unneeded information sent in the first place? The obvious answer is that the sender did not know it was unneeded by the eventual receiver. To understand why this might happen, one needs to be familiar with the methods used to store the data associated with the virtual world in a distributed simulation.

5. WHERE IS DDM APPLICABLE?

In this section, we shall describe where DDM fits in terms of other modeling and simulation concepts. Before we proceed further, we will review, first, terms associated with the High Level Architecture (HLA).

5.1 High Level Architecture (HLA)

HLA represents a common framework within which compliant simulation components can be interconnected to build federations of cooperating simulations. The HLA is comprised of three elements defined in three documents:

(1) An Interface Specification which describes the way compliant simulations interact during operation (with one another and with the runtime infrastructure)
(2) An Object Model Template Specification which specifies the form in which simulation elements are described.
(3) A set of HLA Rules which establish guidelines and define relationships among federating compliant simulations.

The HLA also promotes interoperability and reuse among compliant simulations within an HLA federation and across functional M&S communities. The purpose of the DoD HLA is to allow diverse simulators, called federates, distributed among several hosts, and thereby creating a Virtual Environment (VE) in which all federates can participate. The HLA can be linked to a header file that specifies the functions that need to be called to perform certain tasks. The RTI[7] provides a set of services that allow HLA compliant federates to interact with one another in the execution of a federation. All federation communications go through the RTI. It is important to understand that the HLA is NOT the RTI. Continuing with our analogy, the RTI can be seen as the source code that carries out the functions declared in the header file. RTI is a separate process from the federates, but one that all federates can and must access in order to interact. The *federation* is primarily a conceptual grouping of federates that does not usually have a "life of its own" in terms of an executable piece of software separate from that of the federates. However, a federation does contain information that is not part of the individual federates. This data can be seen as supplementary documents that are not directly used by the federates or the RTI but are intended for human readers. It can also take the form of configuration file, definition type file, and other text that is read and used by the software that implements the federation, namely the federates and the infrastructure.

5.2 Run Time Infrastructure (RTI)

RTI is a software that allow federates to interact with each others. Parts of the infrastructure may be distributed to various hosts, but although it may be running on the same machine as a federate, it is both conceptually and concretely separate from and independent of the federate. A federation could theoretically be run using one RTI, and then be executed again using another RTI. The federates would probably need to be re-linked so that the HLA calls would invoke the other RTI, but they should not need to be recompiled.

2.4.1 DIS

In addition to using an infrastructure, there is another way to implement a heterogeneous environment: using the communication DIS[8] protocol allowing diverse simulation systems to interact with each other's. The Protocol Data Units (PDUs) which are to be exchanged among the simulated entities (or hosts) specify this protocol. We differentiate between an infrastructure and protocol because DIS is a set of rules and conventions, and not an executable software like the RTI. As such, the influence of DIS is confined to the data-link layer of the distributed simulation system. There is no DIS

[7] Run Time Infrastructure

[8] Distributed Interactive Simulation

protocol component that mediates between distributed VE[9] applications and the physical network, whereas the RTI software acts as a "middleware" layer [7]. Thus, in order for two applications on different hosts in a DIS-compliant distributed VE to interact, they must exchange PDU that are sent and received directly over the network. Here, we are referring to simulations that are strictly DIS-compliant and not those that use the DIS PDUs but have added additional software. This software may be complex and needs to be known by the distributed applications, giving its characteristics similar to that of an infrastructure and not necessarily a pure-DIS compliant system.

6. DDM PHASES

In this section, we shall describe the implementation details of the three phases of DDM described earlier.

6.1 Express Interest and Availability

Objects (or federates) usually express their interests or their availability to an infrastructure, such as the RTI, in terms of regions. For instance, an entity carrying a sensor that can only detect signals in a certain frequency range would only be interested in a subset of all possible frequency values, and it would then specify the upper and lower limits of its detection capability as the start and end of the extent[10]. The figure below shows the steps that are generally taken in performing the "express interest and availability" phase of DDM. The objects or federates express their regions of interest or availability to the infrastructure, which then locates the host of the grid or the routing space where this information will be published or subscribed[11].

(1) If routing spaces are used, the regions may basically be stored "as is." Conceptually this means that the routing space

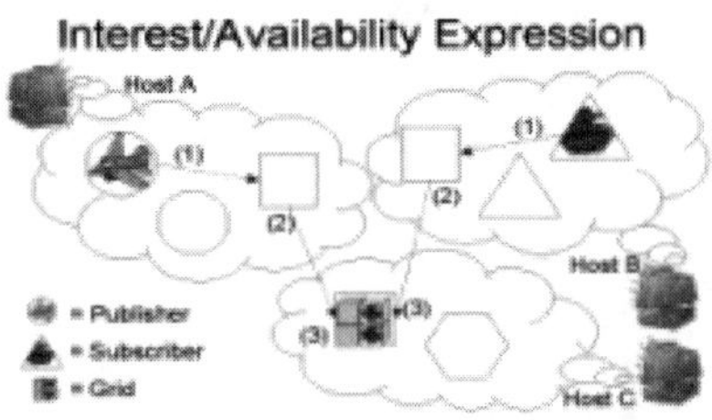

is populated with various regions representing subscriptions and publications.

(2) If the grid method is used, the regions are mapped onto grids. Some regions terminate between cell boundaries, thus the subscription (publication) may be bigger than the interest

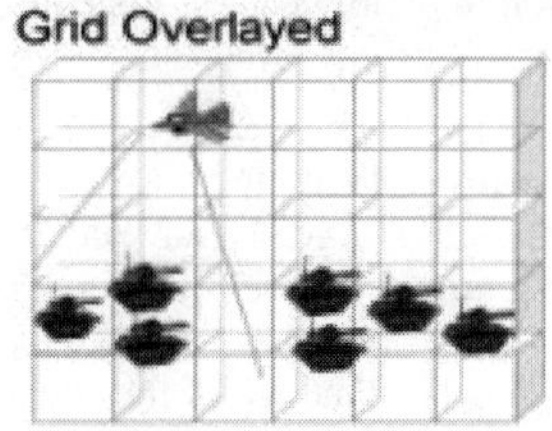

or availability of a region that it represents. In this case, only the object or federate knows the real interest or availability region, since the RTI infrastructure has stored the expanded subscription or publication, and it is in the process of converting from the region into the grid. Hence, additional filtering might be needed. The basic implementation of the subscriptions and publications is based upon the use of two lists (subscriber and publisher lists) assigned to each cell.

6.2 Match

Matching should be done as quickly and accurately as possible. However, these goals are very hard to achieve.

(1) If the Routing Space is used, the matching between subscription and publication regions entails performing calculations to determine the intersection between them, which we refer to as the intersection region.

(2) If only grids are used, then the Grid-based matching scheme might result in a superfluous match because the interest and availability regions may have been expanded slightly in the mapping to the grid to reach the closest cell boundary. However, when using the grid data structure to store the publications and subscriptions, matching is rather straightforward and very fast. A match occurs in any cell that has at least one subscriber and at least one publisher. If this condition is met, then there is a publisher making data available and a subscriber that is interested in that same data.

6.3 Delivery and Receipt of Data

In this section, we will investigate the basic data transfer schemes that have been developed.

6.3.1 Point-to-point and Multicast schemes

Most distributed simulation systems use either point-to-point (unicast) or multicast protocols to transfer and send data among the hosts. Multicasting allows an entity to send information to one IP address representing one group or channel that multiple other hosts (or entities) may join to

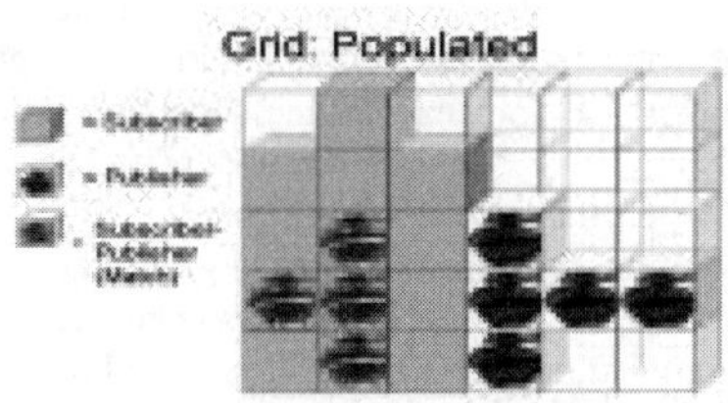

receive the data. If there are objects (or federates) on multiple hosts that are interested in the same data, as if often the case, the host of the object (or the federate), making that data available, benefits from using the multicast approach. The one-to-many nature of multicast allows the sender to transmit

[9] Virtual Environment

[10] The extent of the frequency dimension of the regions could be the single pair, e.g., (100, 500) MHz, or multiple pairs such as (100, 300) MHz) AND (600, 900) MHz.

[11] Recall that once this has happened, I refer to them no longer as interests and availabilities but subscriptions and publications.

the information to multiple hosts, instead of forming one-to-one connections[12] with each one.

6.3.3 Multi-level Transfer

Point-to-point and multicast can both be used in a single simulation using a multi-level transfer scheme. One protocol may be used to send data across a Wide-Area-Network (WAN), whereas the final leg of the trip across a Local-Area-Network (LAN) is done using another protocol. For example, data may be transmitted using TCP/IP over a WAN to a designated host that acts like a router and multicasts the data to the hosts on its LAN. Multi-level transfer can be well integrated with the hierarchical grids where different grid levels are distributed at various hosts. A grid of a lower resolution can be used during the initial matching. Next, the matching data can be sent to a grid of higher resolution that resides on a different host. This scheme provides the same accuracy as the high-resolution grid alone, but that fine-grained matching is only done after an initial match has been successfully conducted, thereby reducing the load on the hosts that maintain both grids. However, the need for data transfer between the hosts might introduce additional network latency. Another common approach is to distribute the grid levels of increasing resolution at the "decreasing" levels of the network so that more and more accurate matching occurs, e.g.,, e.g., WAN to LAN network.

7. HOW IS DATA TRANSFER INITIATED?

The following two figures show how the transfer occurs. It is important to understand that there are two types of communication happening. The first type convies to the DDM-specific information between the infrastructure's parts running on different hosts and between the local architecture that is used and the application. The second part corresponds to the transfer of the actual domain-specific data, which is sometimes referred to as *data forwarding*.

The rest of this paper will focus upon the data forwarding stratgies. When a match is detected on the host representing the publications and subscriptions, this host must convey, either by point-to-point or multicast communication, the "relevant information" to the "appropriate host." Then, the same host takes the "appropriate action" and facilitates the publisher's sending of the data to the subscriber.

7.1 Sender-based Transfer

If a sender-based transfer is used, the "appropriate host" corresponds to the host of the object that is publishing the data (Host B, see figure below). The "relevant information" sent will be a list of the subscribers, and the "appropriate action" will consist of transmitting the subscriber information to the publisher so that it can send its data to the subscriber using point-to-point or multicast schemes. Thus, all subscribers must join the publisher's multicast group if each objetc has not done so already, and the publishers agents can do the join. If a message must be sent to the subscribing host or to the hosts to do the join, this is quite similar to the receiver-based transfer paradigm. For this reason, sender-based transfer is more commonly used with point-to-point communication.

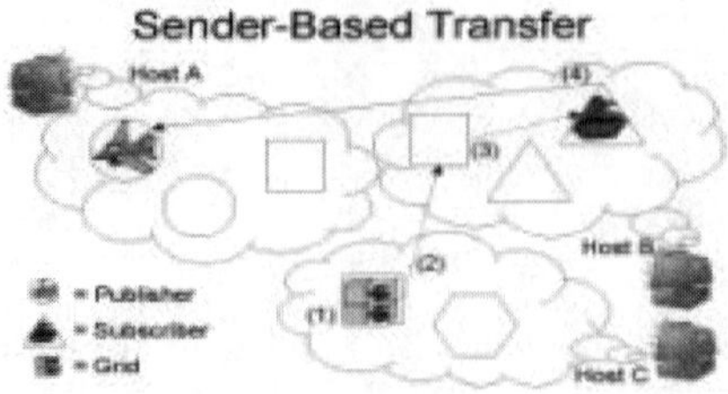

7.1.1 Distribution List

For a grid-based approach using sender-based transfer, the most common data structure used to keep track of the subscribers is the *distribution list*, i.e., this list records the subscribers to which a simulated entity must send data. Recall that for each grid cell, there are two lists: asubscriber and publisher lists. The distribution list is created/updated by combining every subscriber list from the cells matching the entity's publication. Since several subscribers could be on the same host, an optimization is to prune the distribution lists so that a particular data item is sent only once to any host [14]. If a dynamic interest and availability expression is permitted, the distribution lists may be updated quite frequently. In practice, however, the update can be better viewed as creating a new distribution list that should replace the old one. This is very useful for time-managed simulations since the infrastructure that supports the distributed simulation has a record of the state of the publisher-subscriber matching corresponding to the different logical simulation times [16]. Thus, the old lists mus be kept for future references.

7.2 Receiver-based Transfer

If a receiver-based transfer is used, the host of the subscriber (Host A, see Figure below) must be notified when there is a match, given the information regarding the publishers that match the subscription, and must instruct the subscriber to take action that will facilitate the data transfer from the publisher to the subscriber. If a multicast is used, the subscriber host will join the group(s) on which the publisher is transmitting the data. With the point-to-point transfer scheme,

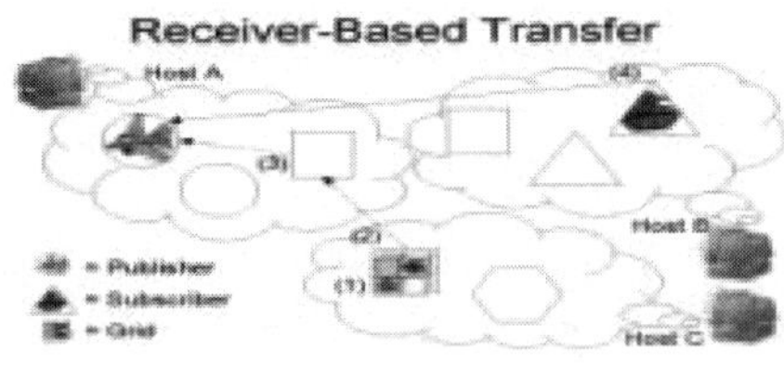

the subscriber's host must cause the publisher's host to transmit that data, which could theoretically be done using the agents. In practice, receiver-based transfer usually uses multicast and sender-based usually uses point-to-point transfer. Though, there may be some elements of both startegies in any scheme. For example, in receiver-based multicast, the sender might be notified at some point to stop transmitting on a particular group because it has no subscribers, and may later be told to resume transmitting on that group. In this case, the sender will periodically take actions in order to control the transfer, even though the algorithm is considered as a receiver-based.

[12] Such TCP/IP

8. HOW ARE MULTICAST GROUPS ASSIGNED

In systems multicast based transfer, how the hosts are assigned to multicast groups is a critical part of DDM, in particular the "deliver and receive data" phase. Group assignment is the process of directing objects or federates to send to or receive data from a particular multicast address, which is referred to as a multicast group or channel. Static assignment is easier to implement, however, allowing the multicast groups to be configured dynamically will provide more flexibility than the static one. Assignment may be cell-based, publisher-based, or intersection-based.

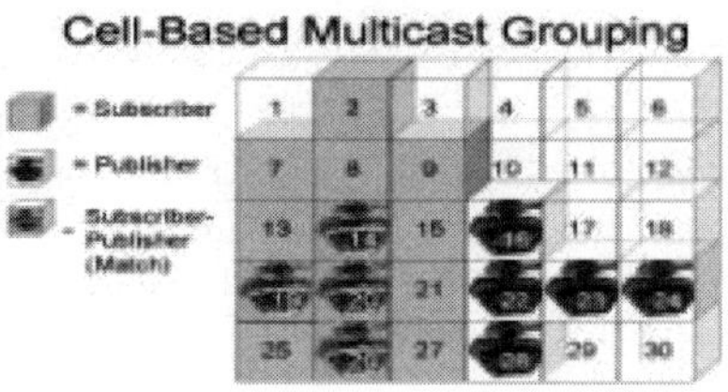

8.1 Cell-Based

In a cell-based multicast group assignment, each cell is associated with a multicast address. Publishers always transmit on that channel. Any subscribers merely join the group to receive the data, meaning that the matching is done implicitly. A drawback with this approach is that the publisher might be transmitting on a channel to which no one is listening,

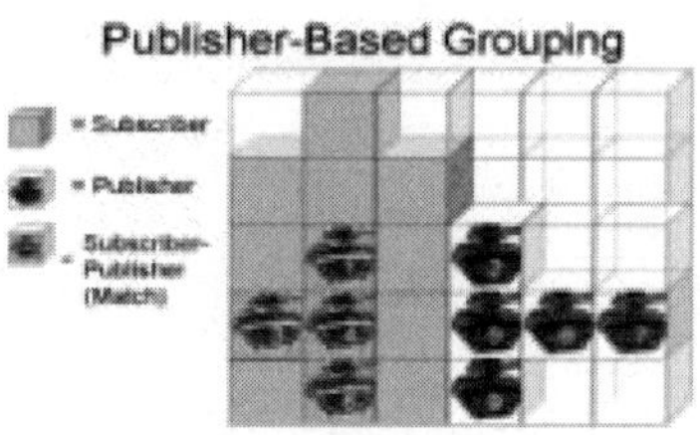

thereby burdening the network with data that no one will read.

8.2 Publisher-based

Cell-based assignment can only occur with grids, but both grids and routing spaces can use the publisher-based approach, where cells containing or regions representing publishers are assigned to a group to which they are to send data, and matching subscribers are instructed to listening on that channel and receiving it. If availability expression is dynamic, publisher-based assignment must be dynamic since the cells or regions involved may be deleted or added in the course of the simulation. An advantage of the publisher-based assignment is that less multicast groups are required, since only those cells or those regions associated with the publishers are assigned. Since there are a finite number of multicast group addresses, it is beneficial to be frugal in using this limited resource [19] A complication of this method is that the subscribers must be told which group to join, depending on the results of the matching operation. Note that in the cell-based method, the subscribers and publishers did not need to know about each other. The problem of a publisher sending data on a channel that no subscribers have joined[13] is still present. However, this problem is solved using the intersection-based method.

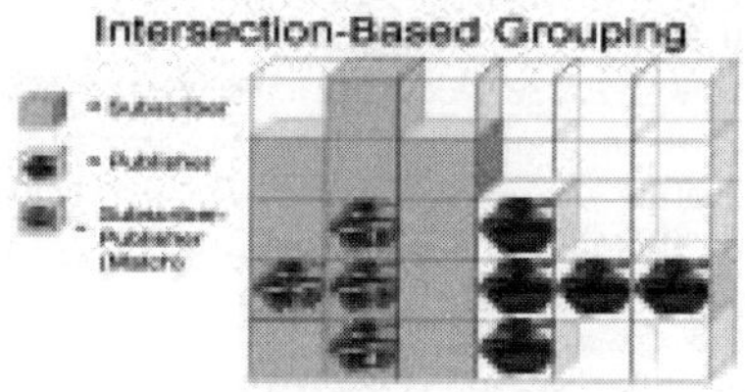

8.2 Intersection-based

Intersection-based assignment designates groups only to cells in which a match is detected or to the intersection regions. The publisher is instructed to transmit on that group, and the subscribers are directed to join that group and receive the data. These assignments are more dynamic than the previous two methods, since a change in either a subscription or a publication can effect the matching cells or intersection regions. This approach is also more accurate than the previous schemes, in the sense that publishers will only send data on the channels in which at least one subscriber has joined.

8.4 Clustering

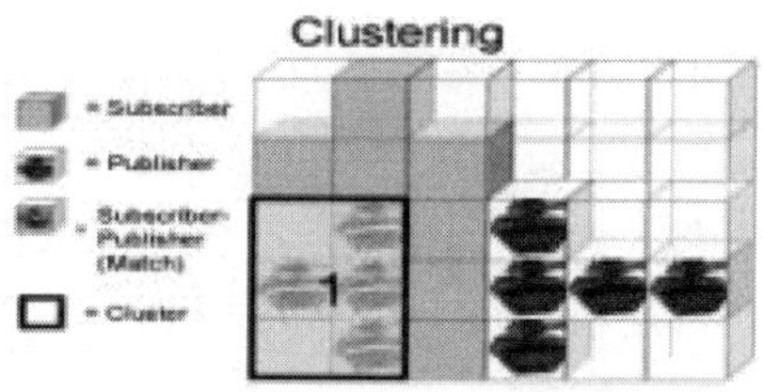

Clustering is a technique that, when used with any of the three algorithms described above, combines cells or regions, normally associated with different multicast groups and assigning them to one cluster, which in turn is assigned to a group. Clustering can also be used with other grouping algorithms [2]. The use of agents to perform the clustering has also been proposed [3]. In all cases, the goal of clustering is to reduce the number of multicast groups, using dynamic clustering based schemes

8.5 Virtual Multicast Router

Another approach to reduce the muticat groups is to decouple the multicast abstraction from the hardware limits of the network, which is the purpose of a Virtual Multicast Router mechanism. A Virtual Multicast Router (VMR) is a computer that is responsible for directing multicasted packets to other VMR and/or broadcasting the received packets to all hosts on its portion of the network. To perform a "virtual multicast" a host simply sends the packets to its VMR, which will then routes them appropriately. This method has the advantage of being compatible with practically any network, whereas traditional multicast is not supported in some networks. The interested may wish to consult [4] for more details.

---

[13] Similar problem arise with the cell-based scheme

9. CONCLUSION

In this paper, we have described DDM problem in a more general and comprehensive way. We have provided a good insight of DDM services that have been proposed by now, as well as their implementations. We also proposed a simple classification of the well known DDM schemes, so that one will be able to unify fundamental concepts pertaining to DDM, and be able to compare them.

REFERENCES

[1] A. Boukerche and A. Roy, "Dynamic Grid-Based Multicasting Group Assignment in DDM", UNT TR, 2000

[2] Ali Berrached. "Alternative Approaches to Multicast Group Allocation in HLA Data Distribution Management." SIW 1998. No. 98S-SIW-184

[3] J. O. Calvin and D. J. VanHook, "Agents: An Architectural Construct to Support Distributed Simulation," Proc. of the 11th Workshop on Standards for the Interoperability of Distributed Simulation, September 1994.

[4] Jiung-Yao Huang. "Virtual Multicast Router Over Internet." TR- Tamkang Univ. Tamsui, Taipei Hsien, Taiwan.

[5] C. R. Karr, D. Reece, R. Franceschini. Synthetic Solders. IEEE Spectrum ,March 1997 (pp. 39-45)

[6] M. R. Macedonia, and M. J. Zyda, "A Taxonomy for Networked Virtual Environments." IEEE Multimedia Vol. 4, No. 1, 1997.

[7] M. R. Macedonia, "Exploiting Reality with Multicast Groups: A Network Architecture for Large-scale Virtual Environments." Proc. of SIW 1994. No. 94-11-163

[8] K. L. Morse and J. S. Steinman, "Data Distribution Management in the HLA: Multidimensional Regions and Physically Correct Filtering," Proc. SIW Spring 1997.

[9] K. L. Morse. "Interest Management in Large-Scale Distributed Simulation." UCI Technical Report #96-27.

[10] S. J. Rak, "HLA/RTI Data Distribution Management in the Synthetic Theater of War." Proc. SIW , 97F-119.

[11] Company website: http://209.102.89.195/rtime_web/netscape/rt_about_simnet.html

[12] Roger D. Smith. "Disaggregation in Support of Intelligence Training", 19th Inter-Service/Industry Training, Simulation, and Education Conf. (I/ITSEC) Proc Dec, 1997.

[13] J. S. Steinman, "Logically Correct Data Distribution Management in SPEEDES."

[14] Jeffrey S. Steinman "Parallel Proximity Detection and the Distribution List Algorithm." 1994 Parallel And Distributed Simulation Workshop Pages 3-11.

[15] Stricom Company Web site: www.stricom.army.mil/PRODUCTS/MODSAF

[16] Ivan Tacic and Richard. M. Fujimoto, "Synchronized Data Distribution Management in Distributed Simulations." Spring SIW Proc. 1997, No. 97S-SIW-045,

[17] Tele-Learning Web Site. "Collaborative Virtual Environments Examples." http://www.ipswich1.demon.co.uk/celia/assign2/telecveeexamples.html

[18] Daniel J.Van Hook, "Data Distribution Management in RTI 1.3." Proc. SIW No. 98S-SIW-206.

[19] Daniel J. Van Hook, Steven J. Rak, and James O. Calvin, "Approaches to Relevance Filtering," Proceedings of the 11th SIW , September 1994.

Design and Implementation of High Performance and High Fidelity Wargame Simulation System

Atsuo Ozaki†, Masakazu Furuichi†, Katsumi Takahashi†, and Hitoshi Matsukawa‡

† *Mitsubishi Electric Corporation Information Technology R&D Center*
5-1-1 Ofuna, Kamakura, JAPAN
e-mail: {ozaki, furuichi, kats}@isl.melco.co.jp

‡ *Mitsubishi Electric Corporation Kamakura Works*
325, Kamimachiya, Kamakura, JAPAN
e-mail: Hitoshi.Matsukawa@kama.melco.co.jp

KEYWORDS

Parallel and distributed simulation, HLA, Wargame, Model design, Interactive simulation

ABSTRACT

Simulation based education and training, especially wargame simulations are being widely used in the field of defense modeling and simulation communities. In order to efficiently train students and trainees, the wargame simulations must have both high performance and high fidelity. In this paper, we discuss design and implementation issues for a prototype of parallel and distributed wargame simulation system. This wargame simulation system is based on High Level Architecture (HLA) and employs some optimization to achieve a high performance and high fidelity simulation system.

1 INTRODUCTION

We have been developing a high performance large scale moving object simulation for a distributed system. As part of this study, we have developed a middle-ware for parallel and distributed simulation environment (MARINE) and a MARINE based wargame simulation for the workstation cluster system (WGSS)[1][2][3]. In the MARINE, High Level Architecture (HLA) has been employed to achieve a flexible and scalable simulation system.

In the wargame simulation, players on the blue team and the red team compete in tactics and strategy using information gained through the simulation. There are several problems in the wargame simulation:

- when the simulation time step is increased, a collision between moving objects does not take place and nearby objects cannot be detected;
- when a large number of objects must be simulated, we require not only parallel processing, but also optimization so as to reduce the computational cost.

WGSS has employed several techniques for guaranteeing the simulation fidelity at a user defined level, and for reducing the computational cost in the detection. These techniques are aimed at solving the above mentioned problems.

In this paper, we outline the wargame simulation and MARINE, and discuss the design and implementation of MARINE based WGSS. We also discuss the effectiveness of our optimization method in the detection process.

2 WARGAME SIMULATION

Wargame simulation, a commander level training or educational simulation for tactics and strategy, has been used in the command post exercise (CPX). In general, the players and several operators who support the players spend a few days or hours in the simulation. A player controls a corps as commander of the blue team or red team utilizing information acquired through the simulation. The players' actions, decisions, analyses and so on, are the criteria for evaluating the players, rather than victory or defeat in the simulation. A mechanism for recording the sequence of events and for recalling and replaying the simulation are required for this evaluation, which is made by the judges. Wargame simulation is based on a cycle of movement ⇒ detection ⇒ battle ⇒ estimation of damage of the battle ⇒ refueling", and the simulation progresses by repeating this cycle. The followings are the two major problems in wargame simulation.

Go through accident (GTA): Each object's so-called "PlatForm(PF)" moves $\Delta t \times v$ at every simulation time step Δt, where Δt is the simulation time unit for simulating one cycle and v is the speed for the individual PF. For instance, if Δt is large, an aircraft and a cruise missile (CM) might be going through each other, though they must actually collide (see Figure 1). The frequency of this accident can be reduced by making Δt smaller.

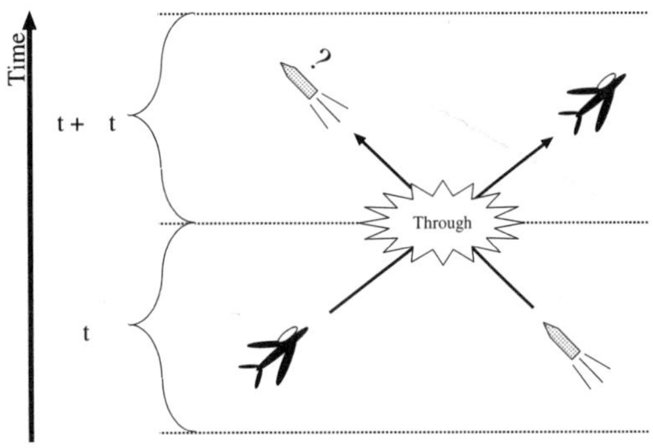

Figure 1: Go through accident

Computational cost problem in detection process (CCP): The computational cost in the detection process is the order of N^2 where N is the number of PFs in the blue team as well as the red team. This computational cost is significant when a large number of objects must be simulated for the training, all of which must perform in real time.

JTLS[4] represents a wargame simulation, assigning a small Δt to every PF to avoid GTA. A sub-field of the simulation space, called "Hex", is defined in JTLS, and the battle between PFs is started when the PF crosses the Hex. Hex also has been applied in the detection process. For example, a PF detects only the PFs on the same Hex. In these JTLS methods:

- the execution of simulation is inefficient, since every PF, even a low speed PF, must be simulated by a small Δt;
- the simulation results are affected by the statically defined Hex.

3 MARINE: Middleware for Parallel and Distributed Simulation Environment

MARINE is used as a middle-ware on the distributed systems for ease in constructing the application program and for reducing programming cost. By using MARINE, the application programmer can construct the application program without concern over the communication between the workstations. MARINE consists mainly of the following library and components.

Class Library: MARINE provides a class library (MCL) for the application programmer. The programmer can create any PF just by defining the behavior of the PF on the MCL provided object class.

Simulation Engine: The MARINE Simulation Engine (MSE) is a core component of MARINE. It consists of the event queue, prioritized by simulation time, and the scheduler (see Figure 2). The scheduler picks up an event out of the event queue and simulates the event in simulation time order.

Distributed Object Management Table: The MARINE Distributed Object Management Table (MDOMT) manages not only the local object, the so-called "native object", but also the "foreign object," simulated on the other workstations (see Figure 2). MDOMT uses a declaration management and an object management of HLA. The communication between MDOMTs is based on HLA Communication. The attributes of the objects are reflected in every MDOMT, when the objects in any workstation are updated. Therefore, the object can refer to any foreign object only by referring to the local MDOMT. The interaction between the objects on the different workstations also can be executed, as if the objects were on the same workstation, but only by sending an event to the target foreign object of the local MDOMT. The information on distance between the objects can be also reflected in MDOMT.

The number of MSE with MDOMT can be increased depending on the size of the problem.

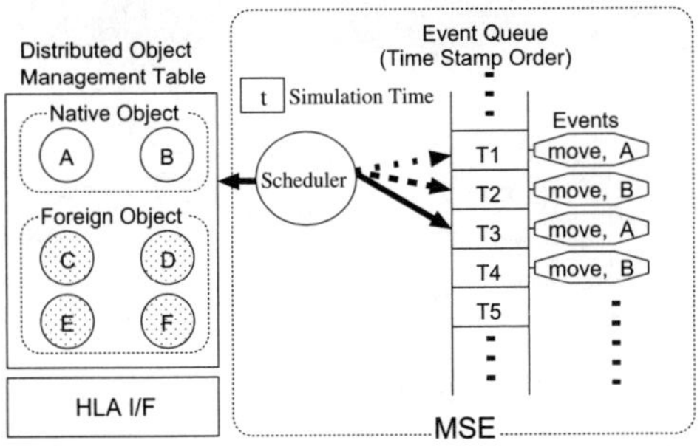

Figure 2: MARINE Components

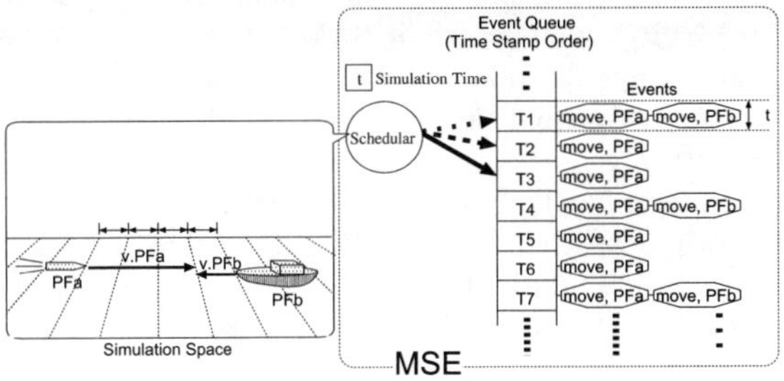

Figure 3: Example of the method for achieving a more efficient simulation fidelity by exploiting MSE.

4 WARGAME SIMULATION SYSTEM based on MARINE

In this section, we explain the methods for more efficiently achieving a simulation fidelity and for reducing the computational cost of the detection process. These methods integrate GTA and CCP by taking simulation space as free space (no sub-fields). We also explain the system structure, each federate of the federation and the animation tools.

4.1 MASF: Method for more efficiently achieving a simulation fidelity

GTA is an inevitable problem when the simulation is based on a discrete event simulation. One of the methods to reduce the frequency of GTA is to make Δt smaller, such as with the JTLS method. But this method is inefficient since the movement of a battleship during Δt is much different from the movement of an aircraft over the same time interval. We have proposed a method for more efficiently achieving a simulation fidelity (MASF) by exploiting a property of MSE. In the MASF, every PF has its own Δt which depends on its current speed. MASF guarantees that a GTA has not happened when the PFs are close to each other within σ. This distance, σ, is defined as a "simulation fidelity." The "simulation fidelity" can be defined by the user. For instance σ could be defined as a nautical mile.

Each PF updates its Δt_{PF}, a time interval to the next simulation, using its current speed (see Equation (1)). Therefore, in general Δt_{PF} is larger when the PF is at low speed, and Δt_{PF} is smaller when the PF is at high speed. The scheduler of MSE advances the simulation time by a constant simulation time unit δt, which satisfies Equation (2), and simulates the event by taking it out of the event queue. The next Δt_{PF} is calculated by Equation (1) when the PF has been simulated, and the event for simulating the PF is rescheduled in t+Δt_{PF} of the event queue.

$$\Delta t_{PF} = \sigma / speed\ of\ PF \tag{1}$$

$$\delta t \ \leq \ ^{\forall}\Delta t_{PF} \tag{2}$$

Figure 3 shows an example of MASF when a high speed PF (PFa) and a low speed PF (PFb) are in the simulation space. PFa is the PF which has the higher speed v.PFa out of two PFs. Therefore δt is set to the value shown in Equation (3), which is derived from Equations (1) and (2), and PFa is scheduled at every δt (see Figure 3). The event "move, PFx" in Figure 3 shows the event for simulating one cycle of PFx.

$$\delta t \ = \Delta t_{PFa} \tag{3}$$

Note that Δt_{PFb} is set to the value shown in Equation (4) by using Equations (1) and (3), since the speed of PFb, v.PFb, is $\frac{1}{3}\times$ v.PFa. Therefore PFb is scheduled at every $3 \times \delta t$ (see Figure 3).

$$\Delta t_{PFb} = 3 \times \delta t \tag{4}$$

When the distance between PFs is within σ, this situation can be detected without fail by using MASF. Therefore, GTA can be avoided by making some judgment when the PFs are within σ.

Almost no wargame simulations handle a SAM (Surface-to-Air Missile) as a PF but rather they take it as an event. In these simulations, a problem may occur when a low speed PF, e.g. a battleship, launches a SAM toward the CM. The amount of time for detecting CM and launching SAM is limited or zero because a low speed PF has been simulated at a low frequency. To avoid this situation MASF has employed a critical condition mode (CCM) in which the PF in a state of battle is simulated as $\Delta t_{PF} = \delta t$. The PF, which is in a state of battle, means that the PF is attacking by itself or the PF is being attacked by any PF. The attacking PF is PFa and the PF being attacked is PFb in the case of Figure 4. In this case, PFb falls into CCM when the PFc launches CM (PFa) to PFb. When PFa and PFb enter a state of battle, an HLA interaction message for CMM is sent from PFa to PFb. As soon as the PFb receives this message, PFb starts the simulation in CMM by letting $\Delta t_{PFb} = \delta t$. When the battle has been completed, PFb re-starts the simulation based on Equation (1).

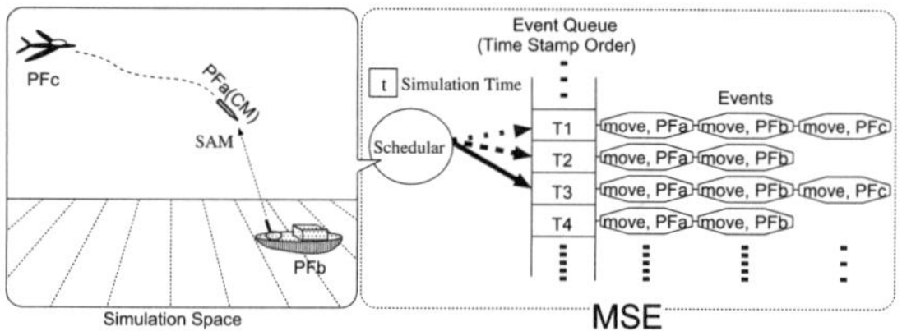

Figure 4: Critical Condition

By employing MASF, GTA is avoided and an efficient execution is achieved. Employing CMM in MASF can also retain the fidelity of the simulation.

4.2 MRCC: Method for reducing a computational cost in detection process

In the detection process, to detect or not to detect is decided by the distance between PFs. Therefore, every distance between the PFs must be calculated by using the position, e.g. latitude, longitude and altitude, of each PF. However, the distance value does not need to be calculated exactly when the distance between PFs is beyond the range of detection (RofD). Using this feature of the detection process, we propose a method for reducing the computational cost (MRCC), in which the distance is calculated at every δt only for pairs of PFs that have a possiblility of being detected, i.e. within RofD.

Specifically, P_{ij} in Equation (5) for every pair of PFs (PF_i,PF_j) is calculated at every δt (see Figure 5). Here, PF_i and PF_j belong to different teams.

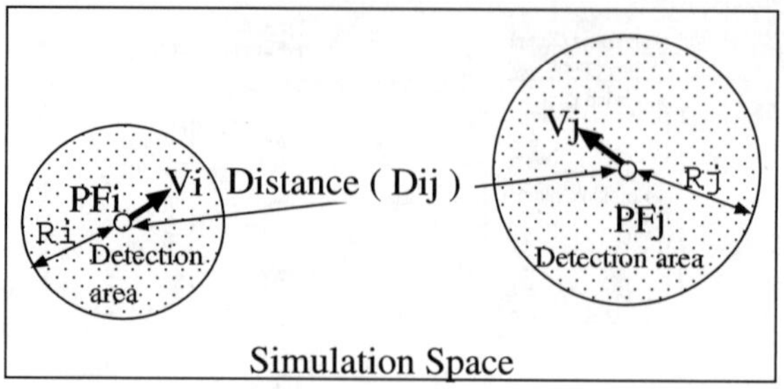

Figure 5: The distance between PFs

$$P_{ij} = \frac{|V_i| + |V_j|}{D_{ij}^{(s)} - max(R_i, R_j)} \times (t - s) \qquad (5)$$

- t: current simulation time
- $D_{ij}^{(s)}$: the distance between PF_i and PF_j at simulation time s.
- s: the simulation time at $D_{ij}^{(s)}$ was calculated
- $|V_i|$, $|V_j|$: the maximum speed of PF_i and PF_j.
- $max(R_i, R_j)$: the bigger radius of the detection area between PF_i and PF_j.

When the calculation of P_{ij} for every pair has been completed, the distance between the PFs at the current simulation time t, ($D_{ij}^{(t)}$), is calculated for the pairs which satisfy Equation (6). The pair of (PF_i, PF_j) has the possibility of being within the RofD when the condition specified by Equation (6) has been satisfied (derived from Equation (5)). The pairs satisfying Equation (7) also have their distances calculated since it is necessary to calculate the distance between the pair, which is already within the RofD.

$$P_{ij} \geq 1 \qquad (6)$$

$$D_{ij}^{(s)} - max(R_i, R_j) \leq 0 \qquad (7)$$

MRCC mentioned above has been introduced in WGSS to reduce the computational cost of the detection process by calculating only the pairs which are within the RofD. This method is inferior to the JTLS method-employing Hex, but the detection result is not affected by a sub-field as Hex.

4.3 Federation Structure

Figure 6 shows an example of the system structure as well as the federation structure of WGSS. The federation is composed of **ConsoleFed**, **MoFed**, **DisFed** and **GW-Fed**[2]. **ConsoleFed** that mediates between players actions and the simulation system. **MoFed** simulates a cycle of "movement ⇒ detection ⇒ battle ⇒ estimation of damage of the battle ⇒ refueling". **DisFed** manages every pair of PFs and calculates the distance between the PFs for these pairs. Finally **GW-Fed** collects the simulation results and sends these results to the animation system. In this Figure 6, MoFed1 simulates the PFs of Red Team and MoFed2 simulates that of Blue Team. The circled PFs in MDOMT of each MoFed are the native objects and other (PFs) in MDOMT are the foreign objects (see Figure 6). eRTI[5] has been employed as the RTI of WGSS, because the performance of the logical time synchronized federation is higher than those of other RTIs. In this system, double Ethernets for simulation data and for animation tools have been used to avoid degrading of the network performance.

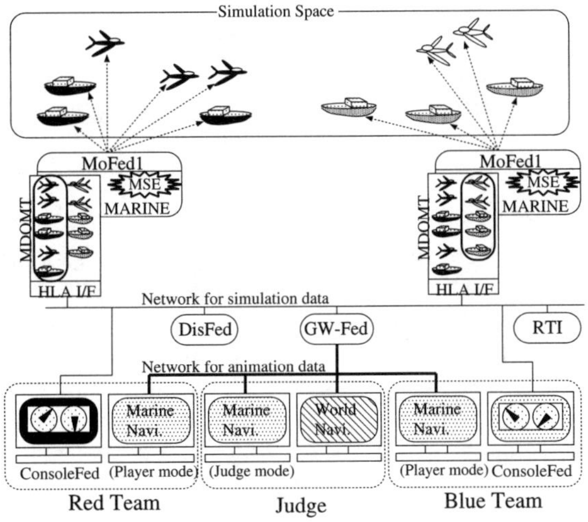

Figure 6: Example of the federation and system structure of MARINE based WGSS.

4.4 Federates and Animation Tools

Figure 7 shows one cycle in each federate on three workstations. In this section, the federates and animation tools are outlined.

ConsoleFed (Console-panel Fed): ConsoleFed has a GUI to mediate a player's interaction with MoFed. The player can control the PFs of MoFed through this GUI. This is achieved by sending an HLA interaction message from ConsoleFed to MoFed. The detection results from MoFed are subscribed in Con-

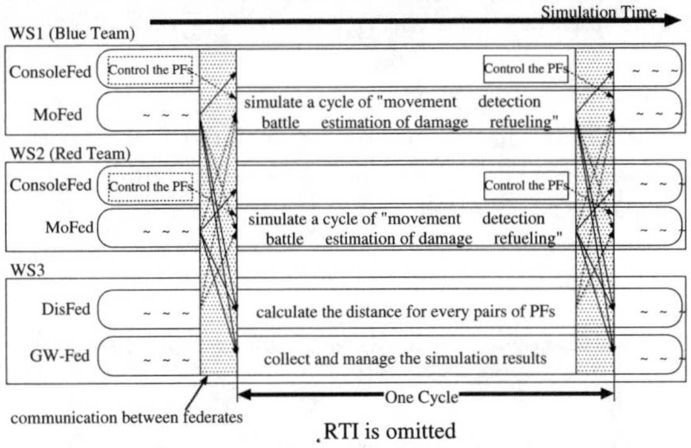

Figure 7: The process of one cycle in each federate of WGSS

soleFed, displayed on GUI, and are used by players in the state of battle.

MoFed (Moving-object Fed): MoFed manages a squadron and simulates PFs of this squadron by the interactions from ConsoleFed or SafFed. SafFed is similar to ConsoleFed without players. It is basically a user defined scenario file. The distance values between PFs for every pair are subscribed from DisFed and used in the detection process in MoFed. The number of MoFeds can be increased depending on the required number of squadrons.

DisFed (Distance Fed): The position of all of the PFs are subscribed in DisFed and used for calculating the distance between PFs at every simulation time based on Equations of section 4.2. These calculated distance values are published to MoFed.

GW-Fed (GateWay Fed): GW-Fed subscribes the attributes of the PFs and the detection results. These data are customized by a request from animation tools and sent to these tools.

Animation Tools: We developed a 2-dimensional animation tool called "Marine Navigator" and a 3-dimensional animation tool called "World Navigator". In the wargame simulation, the player must view the war situation from his team's point of view. Therefore Marine Navigator employs three different modes of view, "Blue team mode", "Red team mode" and "Judge mode", with the ability to switch to any other mode at any time. In the judge mode, all information for PFs can be displayed. In the other two modes, the blue or red team mode, PFs for the player's team and detected PFs for the other team are displayed. Figure 8 shows the blue team mode in GUI of Marine Navigator, in which the information for any PF by the blue team can be displayed, but the information for detected PF with the red team is limited. Figure 6 shows an example screen shot of World Navigator, which is used by the judges.

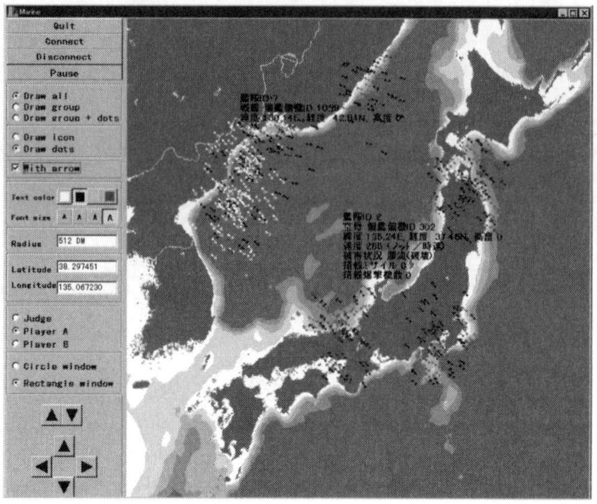

Figure 8: GUI of Marine Navigator in players mode.

Figure 9: Example screen shot of World Navigator

5 DISCUSSION

In this section, the characteristics of MRCC and an optimization to MRCC are discussed.

Equation (8) shows the calculation cost of MRCC.

$$M \times N \times T_P \quad + \quad \sigma \times M \times N \times T_D \qquad (8)$$

- M: the number of PFs of blue team.
- N: the number of PFs of red team.
- T_P: the execution time to calculate P_{ij} (see Equation (5)).
- T_D: the execution time to calculate D_{ij}
- ρ ($0 \leq \rho \leq 1$): the proportion of the number of pairs, which calculate D_{ij} ,to the total number of pairs.

Equation (9) shows the calculation cost when there is no optimization.

$$M \times N \times T_D \qquad (9)$$

Equation (10) must be satisfied if MRCC is greater than for the situation where there is no optimization (derived from Equations (8) and (9)).

$$\rho < 1 - \frac{T_P}{T_D} \qquad (10)$$

Therefore, MRCC should be applied when the application model has satisfied Equation (10). The values of T_P and T_D shown in Equation (11) have been acquired from a preliminarily experiment.

$$\left.\begin{array}{l} T_P = 1[\mu sec] \\ T_D = 8[\mu sec] \end{array}\right\} \qquad (11)$$

$$\rho < 0.875 \qquad (12)$$

By substituting the values of Equation (11) into Equation (10), we arrive at Equation (12). Therefore, MRCC is greater than for the situation of no optimization when the percentage of the pairs of PFs in RofD is less than 87.5%. This means that 93.5% of PFs are in the RofD of each team when M=N. Therefore, MRCC brings about an improvement in almost all models. Figure 10 shows E=$(\frac{Tno\_optimization}{Tmrcc} - 1) \times$ 100(%), a ratio of improvement on the no optimization situation. Here, $Tmrcc$ is an execution time when MRCC is applied, and $Tno\_optimization$ is an execution time for the no optimization situation. The result shows that E=166.7% can be obtained when 50% of PFs are in RofD, and E=640.1% can be obtained when 10% of PFs are in RofD for each team.

Next, three ways of optimizing MRCC are discussed. First, the pairs either approaching each other or not can be reflected in P_{ij}, which enhances the

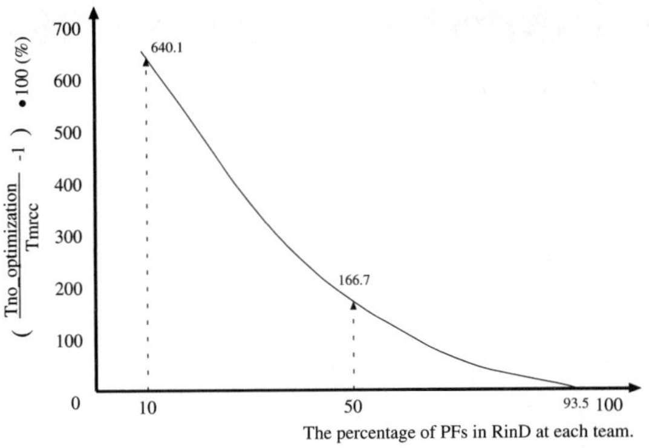

Figure 10: The ratio of improvement for MRCC

accuracy of RofD. In this optimization, T_P becomes larger but ρ can be held to a small value. The second is using a relation of PFs derived from Equation (6) when t_{PF} is being calculated. The next time to simulate PF_i can be set to the simulation time satisfying Equation (13), if there is no event initiated by PF_i during this time interval. By this optimization, Δt_{PF} can be increased when the PF would not be in RofD.

$$P_{i \exists j} \geq 1 \qquad (13)$$

Third is to calculate the distance only for high priority pairs, i.e. only for the pairs with the larger values of P_{ij}, by introducing a λ (> 1) (see Equation (14)).

$$P_{ij} \geq \lambda \qquad (14)$$

In this optimization, the player can increase the priority of interesting PF when this PF is first detected, since the first PF detected has the highest priority. If the detection for a pair must be executed and the distance of this pair is not calculated at the current simulation time, then the most recent distance value of this pair is used.

6 CONCLUSIONS

This paper has outlined the design and implementation of MARINE and MARINE based WGSS. In the WGSS, MASF and MRCC have been applied, in which GTA can be avoided by MASF. These methods have the advantage of enhancing not only performance but also simulation fidelity, since the simulation is not affected by a sub-field set beforehand. The conditions for influencing MRCC have also been derived and the optimization of MRCC has been discussed to achieve further reduction in the computational cost.

Our future work will be in the performance evaluation of WGSS and verification of MASF and MRCC. The parallelization of DisFed and its evaluation are also planned.

References

[1] M. Furuichi, A. Ozaki, K. Takahashi, H. Matsukawa, "Design and Implementation of Parallel and Distributed Interactive Wargame Simulation Environment and its Evaluation - An Overview -," In Proc. of 17th Japan Simulation Technology Conference, pp.113–116, 1998.

[2] A. Ozaki, M. Furuichi, K. Takahashi, H. Matsukawa, "Design and Implementation of Parallel and Distributed Interactive Wargame Simulation Environment and its Evaluation," In Proc. of 17th Japan Simulation Technology Conference, pp.117–120, 1998.

[3] A. Ozaki, M. Furuichi, K. Takahashi, H. Matsukawa, "Extended Wargame Simulation System based on High Level Architecture," In Proc. of 18th Japan Simulation Technology Conference, pp.259–262, 1999.

[4] Jeff Nielsen, "Challenges in Developing the JTLS-GCCS-NATO Federation", 98FallSIW, pp.973–982, 1998.

[5] M. Furuichi, M. Mizuno, H. Miyata, "Performance Evaluation Model of HLA-RTI and Evaluation Result of eRTI," Proc. of the '97 Fall Simulation Interoperability Workshop, vol. II, pp.1099–1109, 1997.

EFFECT OF AUTOMATIC LOAD BALANCING IN CONSERVATIVE DISTRIBUTED SIMULATION

Jouni Ikonen and Jari Porras
Lappeenranta University of Technology
P.O. Box 20, FIN-53851
Lappeenranta, Finland
{ Jouni.Ikonen, Jari.Porras}@lut.fi

KEYWORDS

Load balancing, load distribution, distributed simulation, cellular network simulation, conservative simulation

ABSTRACT

In this paper load balancing for conservative distributed simulation is discussed. Simulation uses a GSM cellular network as example application. Tests have been run on a network of workstations, connected by Ethernet. The time which simulation Agents in workstations have to wait for other Agents has been used as load indicator. This way a single load indicator can represent both the internal load caused by simulation and load caused by other processes in the workstations. The load indicator has been tested with simulation experiments. Some results from load balancing experiments are also discussed.

INTRODUCTION

Simulation has become an important tool in many areas of industry. In economics it is used to model the effects of stock market fluctuations (Hutchinson 1998), in meteorology it is used for acquiring more accurate weather forecasts (Eerola and Järvenoja 1999) and in communication networks it is used for tuning different parameters (Perrone and Nicol 1998; Pham, Brunst and Fdida 1998; Zeng, Bagrodia and Gerla 1998) to mention a few applications. What is common for all these applications is that increased computing power has enabled more accurate models. Without additional computation power the more accurate models would have required more computation time and there is not always enough time to obtain a more accurate model. A popular example is a weather forecast (Kumar et al. 1994) as it is not feasible to predict weather for the next day if the calculation of the prediction takes 24 hours or more.

The demand for faster simulation requires methods for harnessing the power of multiple processors. This can be achieved by distributed simulation with a network of workstations. A common alternative is to use super computers. In this work the use of distributed simulation in a network of workstations (NOW) is considered and some problems are tackled.

A distributed simulation environment, Diw*orse*, is presented. Diw*orse* can be used to simulate problems in a network of workstations. The problem has to be divided into parts and the connections have to be established between these parts. The operation of Diw*orse* and GSM simulation experiments are studied. Diw*orse* is based on an optimized version of the Chandy-Misra Null message protocol (Chandy and Misra 1979; Porras et al. 1997) and the load balancing and synchronization problems associated with it are also considered. Performance tests are carried out using Diw*orse*. In earlier work the effect of different computing and networking hardware, communication protocol options, etc. has been studied (Ikonen 1999). The results from earlier work indicate that the parameters of the communication protocol must be considered carefully. It is shown that partitioning of the problem to the workstations must be done with expertise of the application, otherwise the gain from parallel execution can be lost. The need for run time load balancing is also shown. Load balancing is needed to keep the simulation running smoothly on the network of workstations, when there are other load sources than the simulation. In this paper suitable load indicators, usage of load indicators and automatic load balancing is discussed.

DISTRIBUTED WORKSTATION SIMULATION ENVIRONMENT – DIW*ORSE*

Diw*orse* is based on the Manager-Agent concept. An example of the distributed simulation environment, Diworse, is shown in Figure 1. The environment is composed of workstations, simulation software and an interconnection network. The core of the environment is the simulation software. An Agent process is run in each workstation participating in a simulation. The simulation Agent is composed of the Scheduler, logical processes (referred to as LPs later), queues and the communication interface. The Scheduler serves as the communication element of the simulation. A single Scheduler is needed in each workstation participating in the simulation. The Scheduler sends and receives messages and transmits them to appropriate logical processes according to the sender and receiver information included in the messages. The Scheduler controls the execution of logical processes using the round robin method, i.e. logical processes are executed sequentially inside a workstation. Logical processes are the main elements in distributed simulation. They represent both the simulation application and the distribution. A Manager process is used also in Diworse. Its purpose is to control the simulation, collect results and handle error situations. It does not participate in the actual simulation.

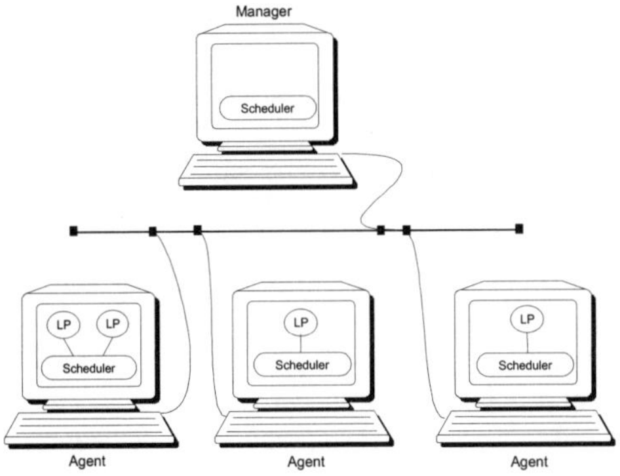

Figure 1. The distributed workstation simulation environment; *Diw*orse.

The Scheduler handles communication in each Agent. The structure of a simulation Agent is illustrated in Figure 2. Normally there is only one simulation process in a workstation. This is to avoid context switches, so that the processes do not have to force each other to be stored temporarily into disk in the case of lack of available memory. The size of the process is application specific and combining all simulation processes in a workstation makes the total size of processes in a workstation smaller as the static libraries are included only once, queues can be shared, etc.

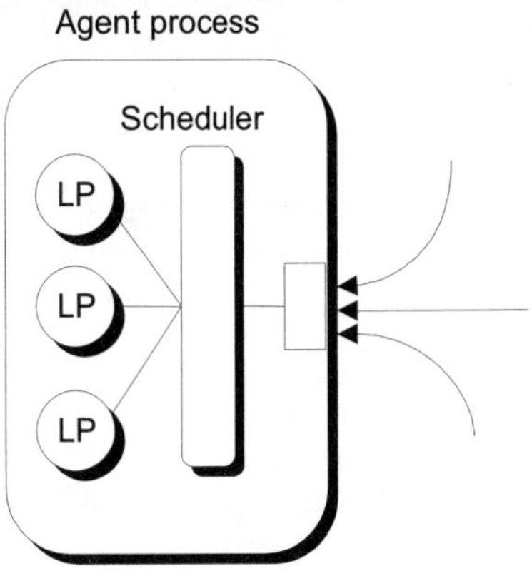

Figure 2. The structure of a simulation Agent.

Simulation in Diw*orse* requires the user to model the simulation problem. In practice this means deciding how to divide the problem into logical parts (LPs). The user has to keep in mind that the division of the problem will affect the amount of information exchanged between LPs. Information that go through an interconnection network should be minimized. The user has to define the logical communication channels between LPs. Only LPs which have a defined channel between them can communicate directly with each other.

SIMULATION PROBLEM

A GSM network simulation is used as an example application. It was chosen because of its requirement for computing power and the demand from industry to reduce the simulation time. The GSM system is composed of mobile equipment, a base station subsystem and a network subsystem. Each base transceiver station (later referred to as transmission tower or base station) has a set of frequencies that it can use. These frequencies are divided into time slots. A call normally reserves one time slot from a frequency. This way multiple users can concurrently use the same frequency. If the radio interface of the system is simulated, the interest of the simulator could be the radio interference on a radio channel caused by other users, devices, etc. Other points of interest could be to create a signal quality estimate for an area or estimate the need of call capacity. The users can move around with their cellular phones, and a handover must be performed between cells if a user moves from a cell to another during a call. If the cell, into which the user is moving, does not have capacity to handle the call, the call must be terminated. Calls terminated by the network are very irritating for the user and must be minimized to keep customers happy.

There are many ways in which LPs can be defined, and as mobiles (MS) on the area of a single BSS are always connected to only one BSS it is not a very far-fetched idea that BSS and MS logical processes could be combined. The combined MS and BSS would free the user from deciding how to distribute these two tasks that communicate a lot with each other. It would also be possible to take a totally different approach for the simulation of GSM mobile networks, e.g. the LP could simulate a frequency used by base stations. How much the LPs would communicate with each other should be considered when selecting LPs and when distributing LPs over a network. Often LPs are chosen so that they present logical parts of a real life problem, like cellular phones, users and base stations.

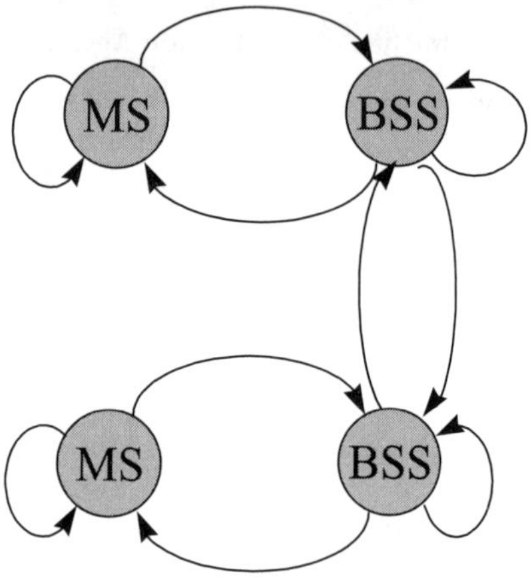

Figure 3. Logical processes for the area of two mobile cells.

DISTRIBUTED LOAD BALANCING REALIZATION

Partitioning of the simulation problem between workstations is an important task. With a good partitioning, the workstations can carry out their tasks as independently as possible. This means that there are fewer message transmissions between workstations, which minimizes the delay caused by the network. Running the simulation in a single workstation minimizes the network usage, but it will hardly speed up the simulation. A better approach is to divide the problem evenly into all workstations according to the relative speeds of the workstations. This can be realized by analyzing relative speeds of the workstations and distributing the problem to the workstations according to the analysis. The volume of messages exchanged between logical processes are not necessary known beforehand. An attempt to do automatic static load distribution has been to use Metis software (Karypis and Vipin 1995) for graph partitioning.

A 5-fold increase in simulation time, with bad partitioning, is shown in simulation experiments (Ikonen and Porras 1999). The results show that good simulation time requires expertise with the application. The load balancing approach could be used to free the user from this. A simulation could be started with a random LP distribution and load balancing could be used to relocate the LPs. A good distribution requires an analysis of communication between LPs and information about the location of LPs.

Load balancing can be realized with multiple methods. A centralized approach can be used, where a centralized entity knows the state of whole system. The central entity can monitor load and issue load balancing orders as needed. In distributed load balancing decisions are made by distributed entities. Distributed approach makes things more complicated and negotiation must be done, between entities, who can move some work and where.

It is not usually known what the load situation of a workstation is after a simulation has been started. Therefore static division of the problem to the workstations might not be very effective. A better approach is to do an initial division and later improve it. Load balancing of the work can be done in a centralized or a distributed manner. In centralized method a Manager process studies the load situation in participating hosts and decides if there are resources available. Even if suitable workstations are available there must be decision logic to select the task to move. The selection is not a trivial problem, as all tasks do not communicate with each other and the communication volume between tasks varies. An optimal setup is reached when the simulation in the workstations is progressing evenly and communication between them is minimized. In practice this means that workstations have been given work according their capabilities.

EXPERIMENTS

Efficient load balancing requires suitable load indicators. The suitable measurements must be determined. One commonly available indicator is the load in the workstation. In a Unix workstation the load is a function of the length of the processor queue. This kind of load indicator has been used e.g. in (Boukerche and Das 1997). However, queue length is an unsuitable load indicator for Di*worse* as there is only one simulation Agent in each workstation. Change of Unix load indicates that there are more jobs in a workstation, but it does not represent internal load caused by the simulation. The simulation Agents should have work according their capabilities. If one of the Agents has to use more time to complete its tasks, other Agents have to wait and this would slow down the whole simulation. The load indicator should represent both the internal load of the simulation Agent and the load in the workstation. A suitable indicator seems to be the time the Agent must wait for messages from other Agents. If the Agent has little to do and the processor has no other tasks, it will complete its tasks quickly and send created messages to other Agents. If the workstation is slow, has other processes or a lot of simulation tasks, it takes longer to process simulation tasks and sending of created messages to the other Agents is delayed. By measuring, how long the Agent must wait for messages reveals its relative performance compared to the other Agents. If an Agent has waited for a long time for messages it is relatively fast and a potential target for additional simulation load. If an Agent has waited only a short time for messages from other Agents, it is slow and simulation could be improved by transferring some work away from that Agent.

RESULTS

The GSM simulation was run with nine workstations. Workstations and Ethernet were reserved exclusively for the simulation experiments. Simulations were run with GSM call loads varying from 100 to 800 calls/h / cell. The average call time was 1 minute. Initially simulation was divided into logical parts and these parts were distributed into the workstations. For initial runs the user analyzed the distribution and distributed three MS + BSS –pairs for each workstation. Analysis of the time, which simulation Agents in the workstation waited for each other are shown in Figure 4. The time, which is used, does not change notably as the simulation load is increased. However, there is a notable difference in the times, which different Agents have to wait for each other. This indicates that the distribution of the LPs could possibly be improved. Agents 1, 5 and 8 (Figure 4) a wait long time for messages. Long wait time implies that they could do more work. Agents 3, 6 and 9 do no wait for a long time. Moving some work from Agents 3, 6 and 9 to Agents 1, 5 and 8 could equalize imbalance between Agents.

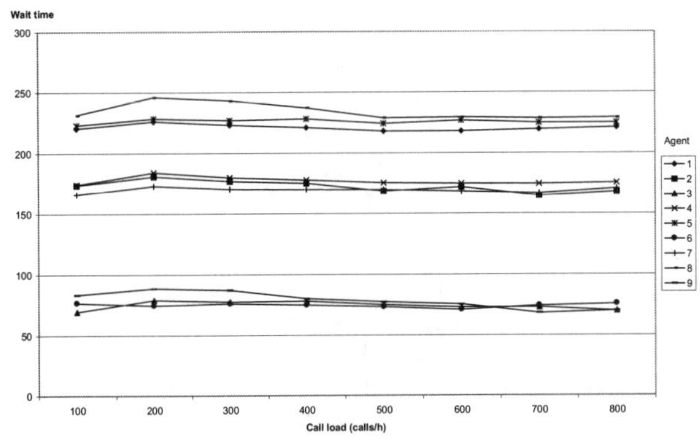

Figure 4 Time which simulation Agents in different workstations have to wait for messages, when there is 3 BSS+MS pairs in each workstation.

The user equalizes the load by moving a BSS+MS –pair from each of 3 the most loaded Agents to 3 least loaded Agents. Results from this experiment are presented in Figure 5. Time which simulation Agents spend waiting is reduced notably. Now also the used simulation load affects the wait time.

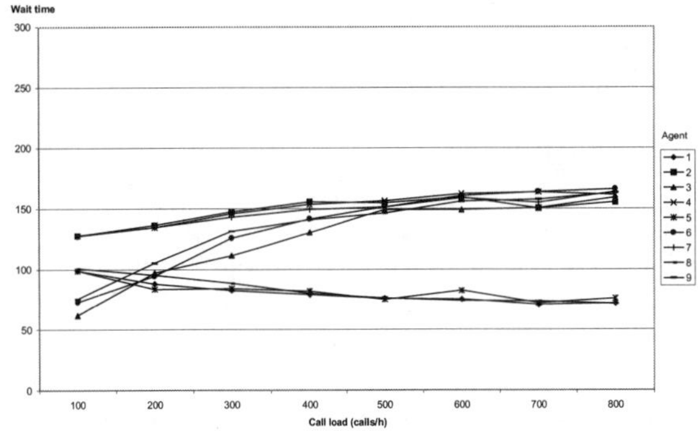

Figure 5 Time which simulation Agents in different workstations have to wait for messages, when load distribution is improved according to measurements.

Figure 6 presents the total time used for simulation. With less calls/h there is a notable difference between the execution times, but the difference diminishes as load increases. The difference between execution times is 1 to 15 percent. The figure presents also the case where external load is present. External load in a workstation participating into simulation clearly slows down the simulation. By allowing the simulation to adapt to changed load situation this difference can be compensated partially.

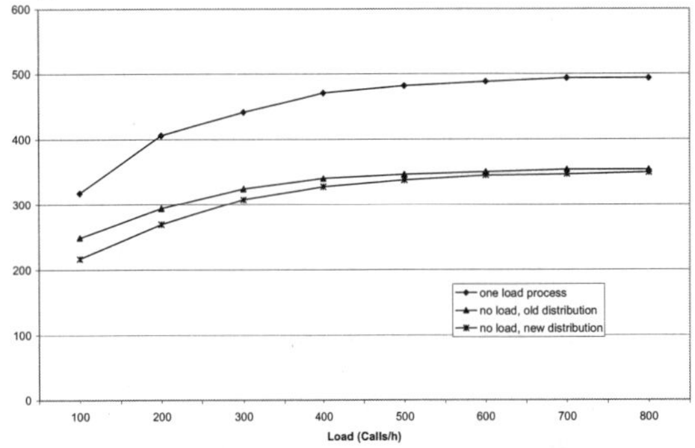

Figure 6 Execution time used for simulation with 2 different LP distributions and under influence of external load.

Simulation tests with automatic load balancing were able to balance the work between workstations. However in initial tests the time used for getting the system into a balanced state took so long that the simulation run should be much longer than 10 minutes. However this result is reasonable as initially the load balancing system was designed for long simulation runs (over 1 day).

Transfer of a single LP from a workstation to anther takes about half of a second, including required queues locking, snapshot and transfer. The time used for the transfer operation is reasonable if the simulation time is expected to be long and transfers are infrequent. How frequently transfers are executed must be constrained with suitable thresholds.

CONCLUSIONS

Usage of office workstations for distributed simulation is not feasible if the changes of use during the simulation are not considered. Applying dynamic load balancing to the simulation can compensate these load changes. Suitable load measurements are however needed and the usage of time how long simulation Agents in the workstations wait for each other is proposed as a suitable measurement. Suitable thresholds are also needed to avoid all gains in execution speed to be used only to transfer LPs. Rational LP transfer decisions require information, how LPs are connected to each other. This information must be used when selecting an LP for transfer to try to avoid increase in network traffic.

REFERENCES

Boukerche A and Das S. K. 1997. "Dynamic Load Balancing Strategies for Conservative Parallel Simulations." In *Proceedings of the 1997 workshop on Parallel and distributed simulation.* (Austria , June 10 - 13), 20 – 28.

Chandy K and Misra J. 1979. "Distributed Simulation: A Case Study in Design and Verification of Distributed Programs", *IEEE Transactions on Software Engineering*, 440-452.

Eerola K. and Järvenoja S. 1999. "The Use of Supercomputers in Operational Weather Prediction." *CSC report on scientific computing 1997-1998*. 175-180. http://www.csc.fi/english/publications/cr97-98/.

Hutchinson M. O. 1998. "The use of fuzzy logic in business decision-making"; *Derivatives Quarterly*, New York; Summer 1998, Vol. 4, Iss. 4, 53-67.

Ikonen J. 1999 "*Limitations of software, network and hardware in distributed simulation*", licentiate thesis, Lappeenranta University of Technology. http://www.lut.fi/~jikonen/

Ikonen J. and Porras J. 1999. "Load Balancing in Conservative Simulation." In *Proceedings of the 11th European Simulation Symposium and Exhibition in Industry*, (Erlangen-Nuremberg, Oct. 26-28).

Karypis G. and Vipin Kumar V. 1995. "*MeTis: Unstrctured Graph Partitioning and Sparse Matrix Ordering System.*" Version 2.0. http://www-users.cs.umn.edu/~karypis/metis/

Kumar V., Grama A., Gupta A. and Karypis G. 1994. "*Introduction to Parallel Computing, Design and Analysis of Algorithms.*" The Benjamin/Cummings Publishing Company, Inc., Redwood City, California.

Perrone L. and Nicol D. 1998. "Rapid Simulation of Wireless Systems." In *Proceedings of the 1998 workshop on Parallel and distributed simulation*, 170-177.

Pham C., Brunst H. and Fdida S. 1998. "Conservative Simulation of Load-Balanced Routing in a Large ATM Network Model", In *Proceedings of the 1998 workshop on Parallel and distributed simulation*, 142-143.

Porras J., Hara V., Harju J. and Ikonen J. 1997. "Improving the Performance of the Chandy-Misra Parallel Simulation Algorithm in a Distributed Workstation Environment." In *Proceedings of the 1997 Summer Computer Simulation Conference* (Arlington, NJ, July 13-17). 657-662.

Zeng X., Bagrodia R. and Gerla M.: 1998. "GloMoSim: A Library for Parallel Simulation of Large-scale Wireless Networks", In *Proceedings of the 1998 workshop on Parallel and distributed simulation*, 154-161.

BIOGRAPHY

Jouni Ikonen received Master of Science degree from Michigan Technological University in 1994, Master of Science degree in 1995 and Licentiate of Technology in 1999 from Lappeenranta University of Technology. He is currently working as research engineer at Lappeenranta University of Technology. His interests include distributed simulation, wireless networks and data communications. His doctoral studies have been supported by Nokia Foundation, Sonera Foundation, Cultural Foundation of Finland, Foundation of Technology and Lappeenranta University of Technology Foundation.

Jari Porras received Master of Science degree from Michigan Technological University in 1993, Master of Science in 1993, Licentiate in Technology degree in 1996 and Doctor of Technology degree from Lappeenranta University of Technology in 1998. Currently he is working as a professor at the Lappeenranta University of Technology. His main research interests are the use of clustered workstations for distributed computing, parallel algorithms and cellular networks.

From the Scull to the Face: Advances in Inverse 3D-Simulation

Dietmar P.F. Möller[1,2], Björn Kesper[1], Stefan Bergstedt[1]
[1]University of Hamburg, Department Computer Science, Chair Computer Engineering
Vogt-Kölln-Str. 30, D-22527 Hamburg, Germnay
McLeod Institute of Simulation Sciences, German Center
[2]College of Engineering, Computer Science and Technology, California State University, Chico
Chico, California 95929-0003
Erhard Godehardt[3], Jens-Albrecht Koch[4]
[3]University of Düsseldorf, Clinic of Thoracic and Cardiiovascular Surgery
Moorenstr. 5, D-40225 Düsseldorf, Germany
[4]University of Düsseldorf, Department of Diagnostic Radiology
Moorenstr. 5, D-40225 Düsseldorf, Germany

Keywords:

Inverse Simulation, analysis, identification, synthesis, state space notation, scull, face, 3D-simulation

Abstract:

The paper describes modeling which determines systems inputs from given systems response data at the systems outputs. Inverse simulation in this way can be introduced as allowing determination of time history of outputs needed to achieve specified time history for selected sets of inputs., which is of importance in the medical application domain of organ reconstruction.

1. Introduction

Inverse problems apppear in mathematical physics and mathematical analysis, as well as in geophysics, acoustics, electrodynamics, tomography, medicine, archaeology and ecology. One example is the surface reconstruction of the human heart, where the model is used for procedures of minimal cardiac procedures to bridge the time until transplantation for patients with dilatative cardiomyopathy [1]. Another challenging topic in the field of inverse modeling and simulation is the estimation and reconstruction of missing information. There are many examples from forensic medicine – and archaeology as well. Consider the problem that we have to reconstruct the face of a human according to a skull (and to some other, additional information like gender, age, constitution, race and so on). In this case, the reconstruction is quite often based on artistic methods (the method "Gerassimov", see [2], [3]) or on the superposition of parts of different photographs over the skull (sometimes combined with computer-based methods of blending and morphing). Until now, there are no originally "3D-methods" in use.

1.1 Inverse modeling at the very first

Inverse modeling is based on the systems theory methodology which contains topics like analysis, identification and synthesis [4]:

- analysis: given U representing system future, X as system present situation, and S as the model predicting the future of Y. Assuming that the system model is an accurate representation of the real system under test, analysis techniques allow the prediction of system behavior.
- identification: given time histories of system input U and system output Y, usually obtained from experimentation on the real system, result in a model S and state variables X, which are consistent with the sets of U and Y.
- synthesis: given input U and some desired outputs Y, we find model S such that U acting on S will produce system outputs Y.

Moreover modeling dynamical systems and testing the transient behavior we use the state space notations of controllability and observability:

- controllability: given system described by the controlled vector-field $dx/dt=f(x, u)$ is said to be controllable if $\forall a,b$, $\exists u$ and $T>0$ such that the solution to $dx/dt=f(x, u)$ and $x(0)=a$ yields $x(T)=b$. Clearly, the finite-dimensional linear system $dx/dt=Ax + Bu$ is controllable if and only if the matrix $[B\ AB\ A^2B\ \ldots\ A^{\dim(x)-1}B]$ has full row rank.
- observability: given linear time-invariant system is described being observable if and only if there exists a set of differential equations satisfied by the behavior of the system of the following form that puts observability into evidence: $v_1=R'(d/dt)v_2$.

1.2 Introduction into inverse modeling

Dynamic system investigations normally consider a system defined by

$$z' = f(z, u);\ z(0)$$
$$y = g(z)$$

with z(0) as initial condition, z as the system state vector, u as the control vector and y as the output vector. Conventional solution finding of that type of dynamic processes is done simulating y(t) for a given u(t) and a given set of x(0). Inverse simulation involves calculation of the control input of time history u(t) which is required in order producing a given output time history y(t) given by:

$$y' = dy/dz\ z' = dg/dz\ f(z, u)$$

In simple cases, as shown in [6], where the equation above is invertible with respect to the variable u it is possible creating an equation of the form

$$u = h(z, \dashrightarrow)$$

Substituting this equation into the very first equation of z′ results in

$$z' = f\{z, h(z, \dashrightarrow)\} = F(z, \dashrightarrow).$$

The last two equations provide a complete statement of the inverse model with ⇢ given and the vector y to be determined.

Due to the previous assumptions from systems theory as well as from state space approach, inverse modeling can be stated as synthesis in the context of systems theory and/or as obserbability approach from the state space notation point of view.

Due to that situation we are really able to handle the very complex processes in medicine on the basis of inverse modeling, using real inverse 3D simulation, as shown in this paper for organs and surfaces.

1.3 3D Simulation

Today, 3D simulation is used in many applied fields. We are interested in the application to medicine, when inner organ have to be outlined. Some details are discussed in the chapter on the segmentation of inner organs (see also [1]).

1.4 Reconstruction

Mathematically geometric (medical) subjects can be interpreted as embedded contour within an image plane

$$(x, y) \in \Re^2$$

of a reconstruction framework concept. The contour itself can be assumed as

$$\exists(s) = (x(s), y(s))^T$$

where x and y are the coordinate functions and s ∈ [0,1] the parametric domain. The shape of a contour subject to an image I (x,y) can be described [5] by the functional

$$\Im(\exists) = E(\exists) + \Gamma(\exists)$$

The functional given above can be interpreted as representation of the energy of the medical contour. Hence the final shape of this medical contour corresponds to a minimum of energy. Due to that the first term of the functional given above can be introduced as internal deformation energy

$$\Xi(\exists) = {}_0\int^1 \Lambda_1(s)\ |\ \delta\exists/\delta s\,|^2 + \Lambda(s)\ |\delta\exists^2/\delta s^2|^2\ \delta s.$$

This equation describes the deformation of a stretchy, and flexible medical contour, with $\Lambda_1(s)$ as tension of the medical contour and Λ_2 (s) as rigidity.

In accordance with the calculus of variations, the medical contour ∃ (s) , which minimizes the energy ℑ (∃) must satisfy the Euler-Lagrange equation [5]

$$-\,\delta/\delta s\,(w_{1*}\,\delta\exists/\delta s) + \delta^2/\delta s^2\,(w_{2*}\,\delta^2\exists/\delta s^2) + \nabla P(\exists(s,t))=0$$

The vector partial differential equation, introduced above, describe the balance of internal and external forces when the medical contour rests at equilibrium. Therefore the first two represent the internal stretching and bending forces respectively, while the third term represents the external forces that couple the contour to the image data.

1.5 Suggested steps for the very first

The suggested steps for inverse 3D-simulation are as follows:

1. Identify essential objects.
2. Identify attributes used describing above objects.
3. Build class hierarchy based on common attribute groupings.
4. Classify each object and prepare object class structure table.
5. Repeat steps 1–4 for interactions. Identify interactions and associated parameters, build hierarchy, classify interactions and prepare the interaction class table.
6. Prepare initial attribute and parameter tables.
7. While constructing data types, lexicons, and routing space tables, iterate with earlier tables, especially the attribute and parameter tables.
8. Verify the potential attributes or parameters have not been overlooked and/or modify existing ones as necessary.

2. From Scull to Face

2.1 Segmentation of Inner Organs

CT and MR measurements result in very good representations of inner sections of the human body. Nevertheless the segmentation of separate organs, and the representation of real 3D reconstructions based on soft shapes from the measurements, is up to now, a task, which had not been solved in a sufficient manner.

The different segmentation methods are based on the assumption, that the grey values of the measured dot space can be interpreted as the border between organs. Conventional methods are based on dot pursuit algorithms which have the important disadvantages of:

- The resulting models are primarily voxel based, and due to that fact limited for carry on the signalprocessing procedure.
- If gray values are within gaps, they will be considered within the 3D model, but an actual polish fit is necessary.
- Vague data of in vivo as well as in vitro measurements of organs, like heart, liver, lung, etc. result in a significant deterioration, and hence the extracted 3D model will be inaccurate.

Treating the disadvantage of the methods discussed above, we developed, for the area shape reconstruction of the human heart, a specific morphing algorithm, the so called Multi Level B-Spline approximation for 3D modeling.

The data, obtained from the respective CT and MR measurements are being weighted in accordance to the gray values which, thereafter, being treated as a projection onto a free space allocation area, the Non Uniform Rational B-Spline, the so called NURBS.

Due to the mathematical representation within the projection reference point in the direction of the vector of the projection, the given space domain will be deformed in a successive manner one after the other. By that, the influence on the dot projection will be more severe weighted and thereby global more effective onto the respective free space allocation area. In a sequence of steps, the influence of weighting factors will be more and more reduced, hence the deformation will be effect only local areas of the representations in between.

Changing the order of the polynoms of the original space description function, and the number of iteration steps, used, allows a problem dependent approximation of the dot space dependent information description.

Using appropriate weighting factors, and simultaneous distortion of the models through all the dots, single and remote dots will be smoothed automatically, whereby also from the CT and MR pictures 3D models can be extracted. Moreover, as an initialization, a rough approximation of the human organs can be extracted, and hence, the clinical expert knowledge will influence the process of reconstruction. Due to that intrinsic power of the methodology, used, after a few iteration cycles, an exact description of the heart is possible.

Based on constraints of the most important dots, single sub domains of the outcome space domain can be manipulated. Based on the knowledge of the position of single organ compartments, e.g. the left and right ventricles of the heart, the target oriented deformation of the basis space domain is possible (in [1], we have shown an application of our method to the segmentation of the human heart, see Fig. 1).

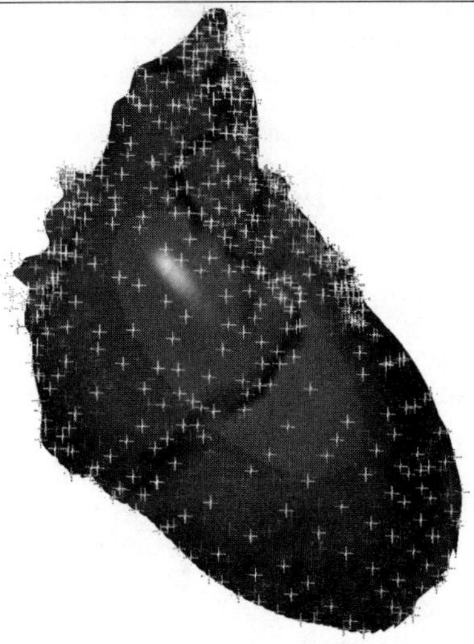

Fig. 1: Reconstructed human heart

The methodology developed, fits as well in the situation of less data, as well as in the situation of huge data sets. In case of missing data sets as well as vague data sets, the methodology, developed, is able to process the data sets in an automatic manner, due to the fact, that locations with ill defined data sets, need no more deformability, after a couple of iteration steps.

Modeling with NURBS free space domains allow simple and easy correction of the model by the physician, as user. Simply pulling the generated space domain, and justification of the dependencies within the influence domain, the model can be much more completed or much more detailed compartments of the heart can be modeled in a manual manner.

For a better understanding, the generated model can be used with the embedded virtual reality visualization environment. Multimedia aspects like figures, animation, etc. are also easy as well as powerful to use.

2.2 Segmentation and Reconstruction

In forensic medicine as well as in archaeology, there is need for reconstruction methods. Especially, to a given skull the face has to be estimated and reconstructed. Many of us know the vivid reconstructions of Australopitecus afarensis or Homo neandertalensis from the Museum of Natural Sciences in New York which are based on Gerassimov's method. This method is that of a sculptor who uses his knowledge about the different thickness of muscles and tissues on the bones (based on additional knowledge like the gender, age, constitution or race of the person whose shape has to be reconstruction by estimating the missing information using some basic information and rules.

We are starting a computer-based method for the reconstruction of faces on skulls. The skulls and faces of a representative sample of people is to be scanned. The scans will be taken using MR methods since these procedures have no side effects to healthy persons. To these scans (which are voxels), our method for the segmentation of inner organs is applied to get NURBS representations of the individual skulls and faces. These models are stored together with additional information about the gender, age, constitution or race of each person in the sample.

For a skull, to which a face has to be estimated or reconstructed, the following process will be started:

1. The skull is scanned.
2. To the voxel information, the segmentation procedure, based on NURBS, is applied.
3. The "nearest neighbor" from the data base is found (see Fig. 2).

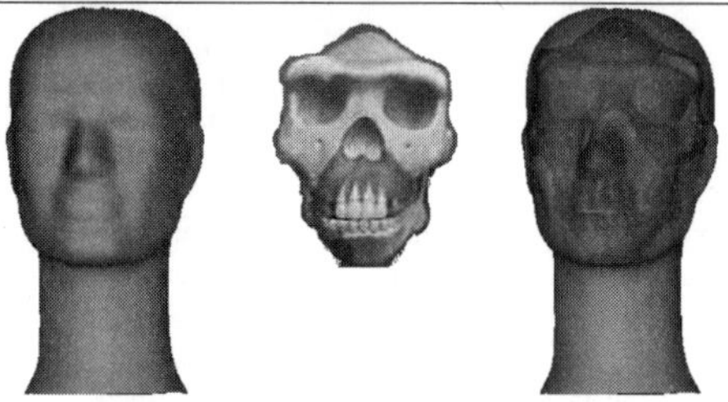

Fig. 2: Finding the nearest neighbour

4. This nearest-neighbor skull from the data base is morphed onto the new skull. The parameters of the morphing algorithm are stored (see. Fig. 3).

IMPLEMENTATION OF JAVA 3D API FOR MULTI-AGENT SYSTEM OF VIRTUAL ELECTRICAL-ENGINEERING LABORATORY

A. Dewi, J.L. Coulomb, and R. Pacaut
Laboratoire d'Electrotechnique de Grenoble, *INPG/UJF CNRS UMR 5529*
ENSIEG BP 46, 38402 Saint Martin d'Hères, France
e-mail : Alita.Dewi@leg.ensieg.inpg.fr, Jean-Louis.Coulomb@leg.ensieg.inpg.fr, Roland.Pacaut@leg.ensieg.inpg.fr

Electrical-engineering laboratory, facet, scene graph-programming model, virtual reality environment.

ABSTRACT

Virtual reality (VR) environments are now being widely created in engineering technology in order to model and simulate a system that is composed of autonomous components with many interactions. Agent oriented has been acknowledged as the competent approach for defining the components. A VR environment of the electrical-engineering laboratory modelled as a multi-agent system is developed in relation to the issues surrounding the utilization of numerical simulation system that is more and more complex. An object oriented API that was designed for writing three-dimensional graphics applications is implemented for realizing this VR environment. It is shown that the Java 3D's scene graph-based programming model could support the decomposition structure of multi-agent model.

INTRODUCTION

To understand the concepts in engineering technology, it is necessary to do actual experience or hand-on practice. But, this activity is often expensive and logistically complex or dangerous. Numerical simulation software has been developed as a solution. The engineers can create a computerized simulation model for simulating the actual experience. Complexity of the concepts that has to be represented makes the utilization of the numerical simulation software (system) more and more complex. It is overlong and not easily comprehensible.

Experiment in laboratory has been considered as natural studying method for understanding the phenomena or the concepts of technology and science. The method would be adapted in the utilization of numerical simulation system by developing environment that makes the engineers as if doing an experiment when they are exploring the system. This study deals with development of virtual electrical-engineering laboratory (VEEL) in which the electromagnetism, mechanical and thermal characteristics of electrical device are studied (A. Dewi 2000).

The laboratory with the activities inside is a system that cannot be defined as a whole but as a set of autonomous components with many interactions. This system needs specific tools that have to be versatile, sizeable and to enforce interactive and co-operative work. The VR technology seems to be very powerful in this context. Here, the meaning of VR is not as a graphic animation in 3D world and not also as a tool for interactive simulation. But, it is as a tool for interactive prototyping (Chevaillier 1999). The engineers will be able to move in the VEEL, to interact with the VEEL's components (electrical device, electrical source, and measuring apparatus) and also to substantially change the characteristics of the components whenever or however he wants.

The concept of AMF model has been used for developing the architecture model of VEEL system. This concept provides a fine composition of facet in each agent and the parallel communication concept of the PAC model (J.Coutaz 1990). Within multi-agent model, an interactive application is decomposed into a treelike structure (hierarchy) of autonomous and co-operative components.

Java 3D is an object-oriented API. With Java 3D API, applications construct individual graphics element as separate object and connect them together into a treelike structure called a scene graph (Henry 1997). Thanks to the scene graph-programming model Java 3D API could support realization of the multi-agent model, with a structure of program that follows or meets the multi-agent's structure.

In this paper, the technique of implementing Java 3D API in order to define an multi-agent-oriented system will be presented. First, it is described the multi-agent model of the VEEL system. The discussion then proceeds to the behaviors of agents composing the VEEL system and the interactions between these agents. Finally, it is discussed the structure of classes representing the agents and the agent's facets.

AMF MODEL

While concerning to the three objectives of architecture model in general, AMF model has been developed in order to solve the two problems found in implementing the multi-agent model (F. Tarpin 1999). For the first problem, AMF proposes a more fine decomposition of interactive agent.

According to this model, there is no limitation for number of facet in each agent and there is no compulsory facet.

In relation to the second problem, function of Control facet is described by two components: communication port and administrator of control. The communication port defines the service proposed and utilized by the facet. The administrator of control that is elementary entity of Control facet manages connection between communication ports.

Like as PAC model, interactive agents of an application are hierarchically organized based on the composition rule where root agent of the interactive application is ancestor of the other interactive agents (child agents). In this context, the each child agent could be direct component or be indirect component for the root agent.

JAVA 3D PROGRAMMING PARADIGM

Java's scene graph-based programming model provides a simple and flexible mechanism for representing and rendering scenes. A scene graph consists of Java 3D objects, called nodes, arranged in a tree structure. The individual connection between Java 3D nodes always represents a directed relationship: parent to child. The scene graph organizes and controls the rendering of its constituent nodes (objects).

The nodes of Java 3D could be classified into two categories: Group nodes and Leaf nodes. Group node serves to group together one or more child nodes and to define a spatial group that contains all geometry defined by its descendants. While, Leaf node specifies the graphics state attributes (parameters) through its constituent appearance objects and geometry objects. The graphics state of Leaf node is defined by the nodes in a direct path between the scene graph's root and the Leaf node. The Leaf node has no child, and only one parent.

The most common node that changes the graphics state is TransformGroup node. The TransformGroup, which is one of Group nodes, can change the position, orientation and scale of the objects below it.

VEEL

Definition

VEEL is a computerized model representing an electrical-engineering laboratory and the activities happen inside. The specifications of this model are the concept of electrical-engineering laboratory and the application objective of VEEL that is could be used as interface for exploring a numerical simulation system. The VEEL is developed as virtual reality environment where its components could behave like the real ones, and it allows the user to directly interact with the components.

Electrical device, which is the examined object in the laboratory, has been modelled by decomposing its components. Each model of the components defines geometry, material and characteristics parameters of the electrical device. Furthermore, the characteristic parameters describing behavior or function of the electrical device in whole are attached to the electrical device model containing all its component models.

Architecture Model of VEEL

Architecture model of VEEL has been created by implementing the AMF model. Fig. 1 presents the hierarchy of interactive agents of VEEL.

The root agent of VEEL (*VELaboratory*) is composed of two child agents: *Cupboard* and *Experiment*. *VELaboratory*'s presentation component (Presentation facet) visualizes the experiment room in which there is the virtual experiment table.

The *Cupboard* agent organizes the process of developing experiment circuit. Presentation component of this agent presents the room containing virtual drawers of electrical devices, of experiment objectives and of electrical device' condition. In the experiment room, the *Experiment* agent manages the creation of the virtual experiment circuit on the virtual experiment table. This agent decomposes into *Device* agent that contains agents of electrical-device category, and *Montage* agent that contains agents of experiment objective category.

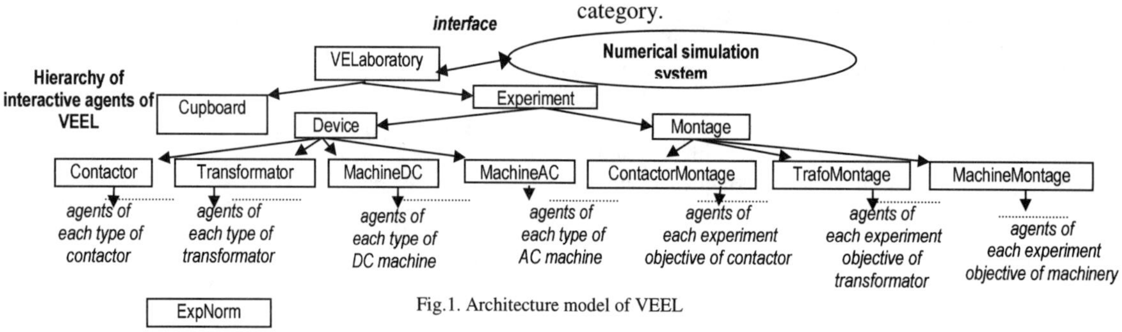

Fig.1. Architecture model of VEEL

The each agent of electrical-device category is composed of agents representing electrical device included in the category. In the same way, each agent of experiment objective category is composed of agents of experiment objective.

Presentation facet of each electrical device agent defines geometry and physical behavior parameters. The value of these parameters is specified by its Abstraction facet. For each experiment objective agent, the component of presentation visualizes virtual electrical device, virtual measuring apparatus, and information for the user. And then, the component of abstraction specifies experiment procedure (protocol) and calculation of electrical device characteristics that will be visualized on the virtual measuring apparatus or be animated by the Presentation facet of related electrical device agent.

Communication between *Cupboard* agent and *Experiment* agent or children of *Experiment* agent is managed by Control facet of *VELaboratory* agent. In Abstraction facet of *VELaboratory* agent, it is defined the interfaces of numerical simulation system that will be used for calculating magnetic field of the examined electrical device.

ExpNorm agent that represents experiment standard provides, for certain experiment objective, the information about electrical device conditions, constraints, input parameters, and experiment procedure. This agent is independent, so that it could become child of any agent that needs the information.

Interaction Model of VEEL

Fig. 2 depicts the experiment process within VEEL that is used for describing the interaction model of VEEL. Process of human-machine interaction happens after the user has determined the problem that will be examined

Developing the experiment circuit is done in cupboard room. The user interacts with virtual drawers and menu of electrical device, of experiment objective, and of electrical device condition. In the last of each choosing, the system will show related virtual object in the experiment room. This process could not be done if the user uses the existing file.

After developing the experiment circuit, the following process is conducting the experiment. This process start with defining the input parameters through the menu dialog that is shown by the system each time the user clicks on the virtual electrical device. The virtual experiment circuit is set on by turning on the virtual electrical source and connecting it to the virtual electrical device. For this action, the system shows the menu for determining which numerical method (numerical simulation system) that will be used for calculating magnetic field.

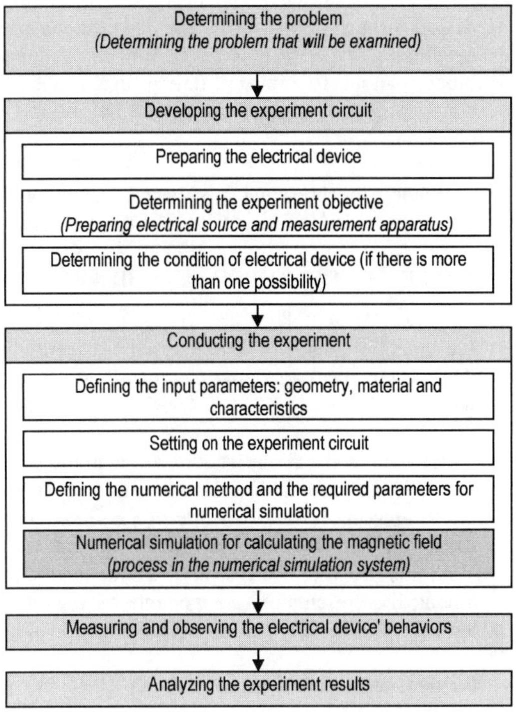

Fig.2. Experiment process within VEEL

When calculation process in the numerical simulation system has finished, *VELaboratory* agent will send the magnetic field to the experiment objective agent that has been chosen. This magnetic field, later, is used for calculating the mechanical and thermal characteristics of the electrical device. The system will visualize the characteristics on the virtual measuring apparatus and animate the physical behavior of electrical device through the virtual electrical device. The user could also see the value of additional characteristics or characteristics that is not directly related to the experiment objective by choosing it on the list menu.

Analyzing the experiment result is for creating description according to the theory. In this case, the user could use the information that is provided by the *ExpNorm* agent.

The user could also study the influence or the function of each component that composes the electrical device by removing the not studied components. Later, the removed components could be shown again. For this process, the user clicks on pop menu, and then the system will respond this action by showing or by hiding the related component.

Changing the experiment objective or the electrical device means doing again the experiment process from developing experiment circuit. While, changing value of input parameters means doing again the process of conducting the experiment circuit before measuring and observing.

Saving the present experiment or opening the existing experiment is specified in the *VELaboratory* agent.

IMPLEMENTATION OF JAVA 3D API

Java 3D API has been implemented for creating the Presentation facets of the interactive agents. While, the Abstraction facets and the Control facets have been built with Java API.

Thanks to the scene graph-programming model of Java 3D API, the presentation (human interface) of VEEL could be decomposed into a structure of presentation components that is agree with the structure of the interactive agents. With this structure, we ease to distribute interaction elements among the presentation components by regarding to which agent that will react upon the each interaction element.

Scene Graph of Presentation Facet

Fig. 3, Fig. 4 and Fig. 5 present scene graphs of all VEEL's presentation components from the root agent to the last child agent (for example *ContRelaiE* agent). The scene graph of child agent is attached to the scene graph of its parent agent by the function of *addSceneContent()*. Presentation component of Cupboard agent will be independently displayed of *VELaboratory*'s presentation component, so that it is not part of VeelRoot.

The composition of scene graph should meet the interaction mechanism of interaction model. For example, SwitchGroup node in the scene graph of *Cupboard*'s presentation component (see Fig. 6) is used for supporting the mechanism of closing or opening each drawer. And then, BranchGroup node with detach capability is implemented in order to display presentation component of certain agent that is active.

As in Fig. 4, for example, scene graph of electrical device could represent the structural decomposition of the electrical device and meet the requirement to study influence of each component. Each Leaf node represents each electrical device' component. As mentioned above, the characteristic parameter describing function of the electrical device in whole is attached to Group node (*tgConte*) that groups all its components.

Structure of Classes

AMF Model provides the concept of modeling and also the code of realization. This code contains Java classes of AMF objects: Agent, Port, Facette, Administrateur, et. VEEL objects (interactive agents their components are linked with the AMF objects through a relation of association (see Fig. 7).

```
public static FacetteUnive facet;

public PresCupboard(String name) {

        viewPosition = new Vector3d(3.0, -7.5, 14.0);
        lightDirection = new Vector3f(0.0f, -20.0f, -30.0f);
        GraphicsConfiguration gConfig =
        SimpleUniverse.getPreferredConfiguration();
        canvas = new Canvas3D(gConfig);

        facette = new FacetteUnive(name, canvas, viewPosition,
        lightDirection);
        .....................
}
```

Fig.7. Implementation of AMF objects

FacetteUnive class has been developed as the heritage of AMF's Facette class. Object of this class will be associated with Presentation facet (VEEL object) that should have virtual universe for displaying geometry and physical behavior of agent containing the Presentation facet.

The AMF objects are called as AMF motor, because they manage the communication between two facets in one interactive agent or in another interactive agent. While, the VEEL objects that could be considered as duplicate of AMF objects are responsible for generating and treating data.

The Administrateur and Port are usually not duplicated because they only do the connection between Presentation facets and between agents.

The classes of VEEL objects are independent. Like as relation between AMF objects and VEEL objects, object of parent agent and object of child agent is linked with the relation of association. Fig. 8 and Fig. 9 present the structure of class for agent and for agent that is composed of some child agents.

Library of VEEL is composed of packages for each interactive agent. Package of each agent contains classes defining components of the agent.

```
public static Agent agent;
public static PresCupboard pres;
public static AbsCupboard abs;

public Cupboard(String name){

        agent = new Agent(name);
        pres = new PresCupboard("cup_presentation");
        agent.ajoute(pres.facette);

        abs = new AbsCupboard("cup_abstraction");
        agent.ajoute(abs.facette);
        ................
}
```

Fig.8. Structure of class for a VEEL's agent

```
public static AgentCompose agentCompose;
public PresVELab pres = new PresVELab("presentation");

public VELaboratory(){

        agentCompose = new AgentCompose("veelagent");
        agentCompose.ajoute(pres.facette);

        Cupboard agentC = new Cupboard("agent_cupboard");
        agentCompose.ajoute(agentC.agent);

        Experiment agentE = new Experiment("agent_experiment");
        AgentCompose.ajoute(AgentE.agent);

        ......................
}
```

Fig.9. Structure of class for a VEEL's parent agent.

CONCLUSION

The VEEL system is realized by creating classes that represent agents and facets. A class of agent is made up of abstraction facet object, presentation objects and administrator objects relate to control facet. As an interactive object, agent is capable of initiating events and of reacting to the events. The Java 3D's behavior and interpolator nodes could support these characteristics.

The scene graph-programming model has helped to develop structural classes of the VEEL's presentation components (VEEL's Presentation facets) that is agree with the structure of VEEL's interactive agents. Furthermore, it has also made easier to realize the electrical devices model developed by implementing the structural decomposition method.

Decomposition of multi-agent model allows accelerating the action of application to the user. This is important for application requiring direct manipulation.

REFERENCES

A. Dewi, J.L. Coulomb and R. Pacaut. 2000. "Virtual Laboratory for Analyzing Electrical Device' Characteristics." submitted for publication, *IEEE -CECF' 2000*, Milwaukee - USA.

Henry Sowizral; Kevin Rushforth; and Michael Deering.1997. *The Java 3D API Specification.*Addison-Wesley.

J. Coutaz; L. Nigay; and D. Salber. 1990. *Software Architecture Modelling for Interactive Systems, The Encyclopedia of Human Computer Interaction.* Wiley.

Pierre Chevaillier; Fabrice Harrouet; Patrick Reignier; and Jacques Tisseau. 1999. "Virtual Reality and Multi Agent System for Manufacturing System Interactive Prototyping." *International Scientific WorkShop on VIRTUAL REALITY AND PROTOTYPING,* Laval - France.

F. Tarpin Bernard and B.T. David. 1999."AMF: un Modèle d'Architecture Multi Agent Multi Facettes." *Techniques et Sciences Informatiques*

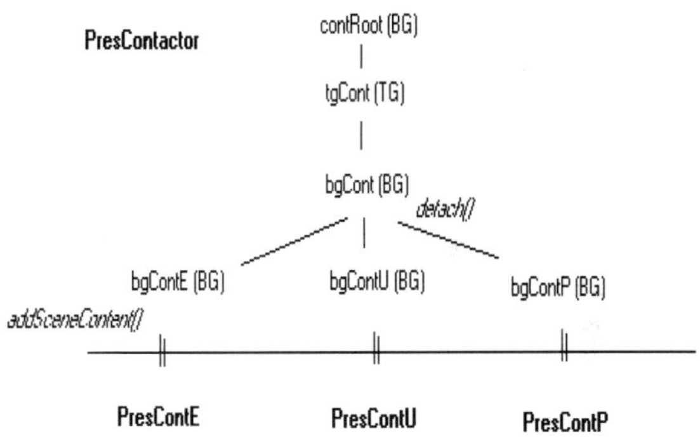

Fig.3. Scene graph of *Contactor*'s Presentation facet

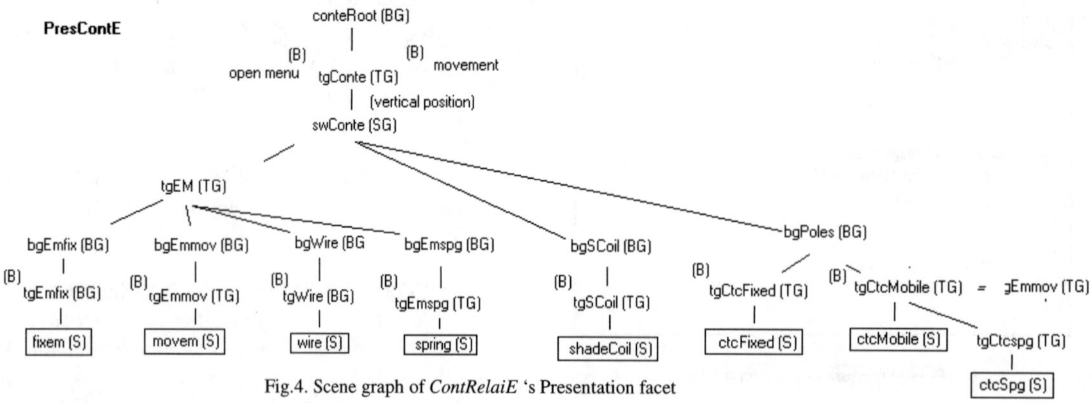

Fig.4. Scene graph of *ContRelaiE* 's Presentation facet

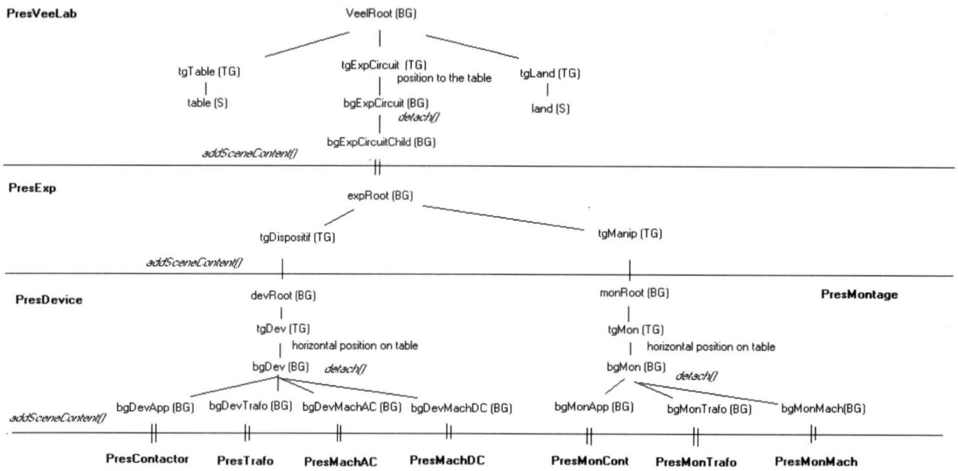

Fig.5. Scene graph of VEEL's presentation components

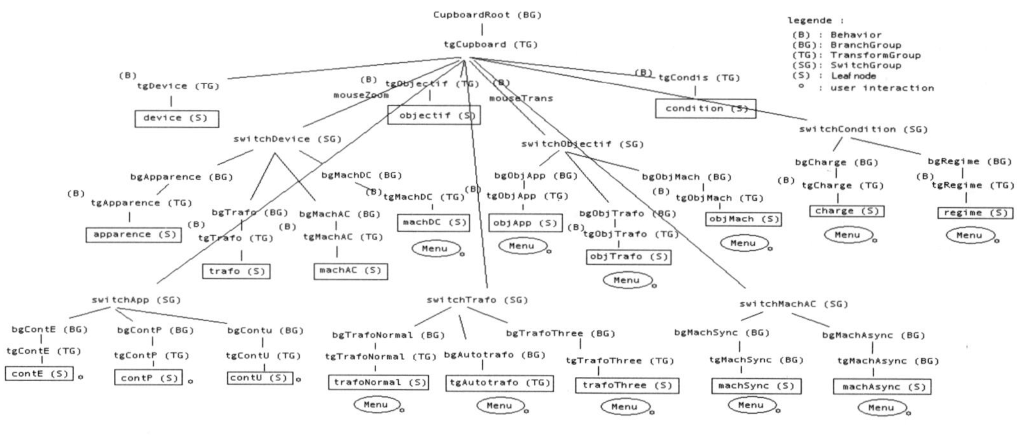

Fig.6. Scene graph of *Cupboard*'s Presentation facet

Digital System Prototyping Using Altera's Design Laboratory Package

Hamid Vakilzadian
Department of Electrical Engineering
University of Nebraska-Lincoln
Lincoln, NE 68588-0511
E-mail: hvakilzadian@unl.edu

Abstract

Field Programmable Gate Arrays provide an important platform for verification of the functionality of a digital system and for constructing a working model fast. This is especially important in both research and teaching where designs can be easily modified, reprogrammed, and implemented rapidly. This also helps in building student confidence to take on more challenging and complex design projects and to reinforce the concepts taught in the classroom. Altera Corporation funds proposals from academic institutions for Design Laboratory Packages. These are used for design and implementation of many complex projects. This paper describes Altera tools used for design entry, simulation, verification, and prototyping at various abstraction levels. It also includes the description of a small instructional processor that was partially simulated part of the digital system design course.

1.0 Introduction

Filed programmable gate arrays provide a convenient medium for verification of functionality and rapid prototyping of digital systems. The use of high-level description languages in this environment permit parts of existing designs to be reused by revising the description and simulating it to check that it behaves the way it was meant. Since rapid prototyping depends heavily on a set of hardware and software technologies, the construction of a system proceeds quickly. This allows the validity of a concept to be tested more easily, rapidly, and economically. Also, through this process, a number of alternatives may be examined, choosing the one that best fits the design constraints. However, the price paid for this speedy implementation is, in some cases, sacrificing some performance parameters such as speed, power, or area.

Even though the tools used for complex programmable-logic-device (CPLD) implementation support various design specifications including schematic capture, rapid prototyping will not be effective unless the design specification is captured through hardware description languages (HDLs). Computer-aided design (CAD) tools, then take these descriptions and map them into more detailed representations, such as interconnected gates, suitable for implementation.

Altera's Design Laboratory Package is used in the Department of Electrical Engineering, University of Nebraska-Lincoln as both research and teaching tool to implement design projects using hardware description language methodology. The educational objective is to allow the systematic incorporation of the technologies developed by RASSP (Rapid Prototyping of Application Specific Signal Processors) program into digital-system course sequence to expedite the student learning and their familiarity with new design techniques and the state-of-the-art tools.

The remainder of this paper is organized as follows. Section 2 presents a brief description of the RASSP program. Section 3 provides an explanation of Altera's development board and CAD tool. This is followed by design entry methods and simulation in Section 4. Delays in programmable logic devices and timing analysis are discussed in Section 5. To provide the expert users with a tool to change the critical timing, Section 6 describes briefly the Altera's floor-plan editor. Section 7 gives a description of small processor followed by some concluding remarks in Section 8.

2.0 What is RASSP?

To improve the way complex digital systems are designed and manufactured, the Department of Defense (DoD) in cooperation with Tri-Services initiated a major effort to produce a technology to reduce the time from design concept to fielded prototype by at least a factor of four. The motivation for this initiative was the need for inexpensive embedded signal processors for use in a wide range of electronic systems that requires coordination and improvements in *processor architecture, design methodology, and electronic design infrastructure.*

To improve the *processor architecture*, the RASSP program focuses on the scaleable and modular architectures for programmable embedded hardware and software. These include scaleable interconnects, smart interfaces, and reliable real-time software that are reusable and simple to upgrade and maintain.

To improve the *design methodology* the RASSP program emphasizes development techniques that have been widely used and have demonstrated their value. Concurrent engineering, top-down and spiral design, and simulation-based design methods, such as, virtual prototyping and executable specifications are the main focus points.

To improve the *design infrastructure*, the focus of RASSP is on system-level design tools for development and integration of better architectural tradeoff and selection tools that can play a valuable role in a top-down and codesign-oriented design processes.

3.0 Altera Design Laboratory Package

Altera University Program has funded the Department of Electrical Engineering, University of Nebraska-Lincoln with fifteen Design Laboratory Packages for student design experience. Each package can support many small-to medium-scale designs on a single chip and includes MAX+PLUS II Student Edition development software, UP 1 Development Board, EPM7128S and EPF10K20 CPLDs on the UP 1 board, and a cable (ByteBlaster) for downloading designs from the development platforms.

3.1 MAX+PLUS II and UP1 Development Board

The MAX package supports schematic capture and text-base hardware description language design, including Altera Hardware Description Language, AHDL [1], VHDL [2], and VERILOG [3]. It provides support for programming, compilation, and verification of a design for the EPM7128S and EPF10K20 devices. Some of the features of this software include the on-line help, an integrated design environment, and an intuitive graphical user interface.

The UP 1 board includes MAX 712S and FLEX 10K20 devices. These chips have over 2,500 and 20,000 gates respectively. Although most of the class projects can be performed using either chip, the higher density FLEX is used in many projects because the pushbuttons and light emitting diode (LED) can be utilized directly without additional jumper wires. Both chips are programmable using the byte-blaster cable.

The EPM7128S chip includes 128 macrocells, each with a programmable-AND/fixed-OR array and a reconfigurable register with independently programmable clock, clock enable, clear, and preset functions. The AND/OR network of the macrocell is used to implement Boolean expressions in sum-of-product form. Parallel expanders of this chip allow extra product terms to be borrowed from adjacent macrocells for logic functions needing more than five product terms.

FLEX EPF10K20 chip is based on reconfigurable Static Random Access Memory (SRAM). Since the configuration stored in SARM is lost whenever power is removed, a small external Programmable Read Only Memory (PROM) is usually used to load programming information automatically when the device is powered up. The EPF10K20 chip has 1,152 logic elements and 6 embedded array blocks. Each logic element (LE) consists of a 4-input look-up table (LUT), a programmable flip-flop, and dedicated signal paths for carry and cascade functions. Figure 1 shows schematic of a single logic element.

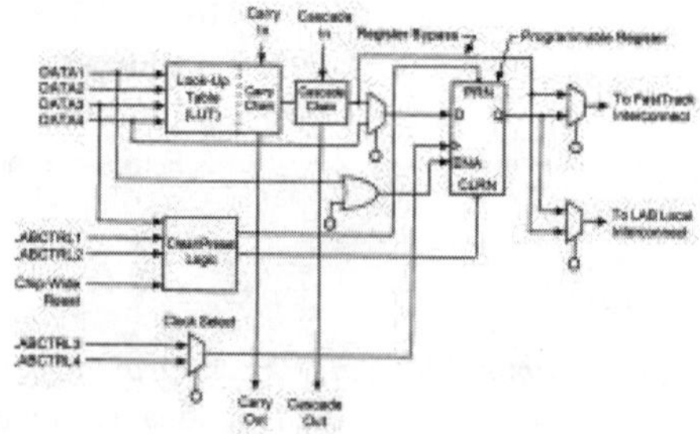

Figure 1. Schematic of FLEX 10K Logic Element

Each embedded array block of EPF10K20 provides 2,048 bits of memory, which can be used to create RAM, ROM, or first-in first-out (FIFO) functions. The embedded array blocks can also be used to implement logic functions, such as multipliers, microcontrollers, state machines, and digital signal processing (DSP) functions.

4.0 Design Entry and Simulation

A design may be entered using either *graphic editor* or the *text editor*. The *text editor* supports entering designs in VHDL, VERILOG, or AHDL languages. No matter which editor is used for design entry, the menu driven windows, templates, and symbol libraries make the task of entry very simple. An XOR gate developed using the graphic editor is shown in Figure 2. In the figure, inputs PB1 and PB2 are assigned to push buttons at pin numbers 28 and 29 and output is tied to the LED at pin number 14.

MAXPLUS2 supports design descriptions at various abstractions such as behavioral, data follow, and structural.

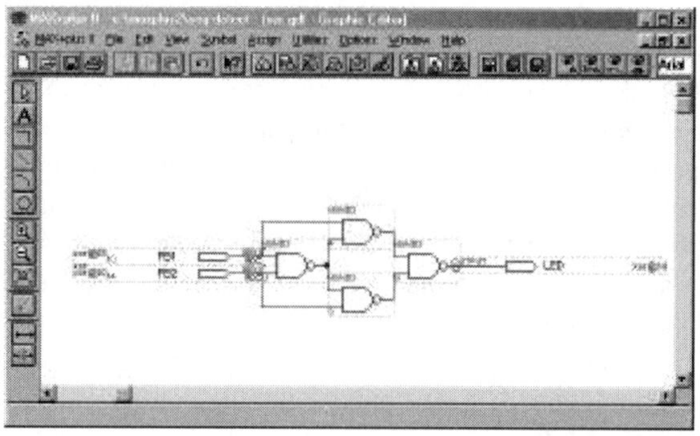

Figure 2. Schematic Diagram of an XOR Gate

Before downloading a design (in text or schematic form), the description must be assigned into either FLEX or

MAX chip. The compiler and simulator use this info to setup the internal connections and reconfigure the internal registers. It is also used for routing the design into the correct CPLD. Figure 3 shows the compilation results of the XOR gate shown in Figure 2. This window is common for all design entry forms. The compiler generates various files for timing and netlist extraction as well as files for generating report and synthesizing logic.

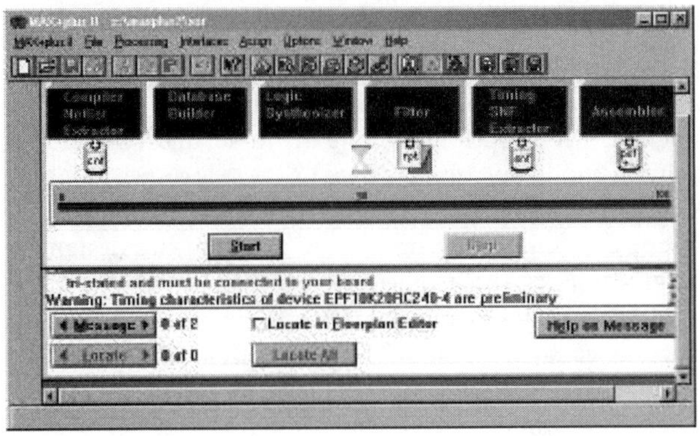

Figure 3. Compilation of the XOR gate

. To simulate the model, stimuli for the inputs must be provided. The stimuli can be in trace form or as text in a vector file (*.vec). Depending on the form of stimuli (trace or vector), the output generated by MAXPLUS II will be in trace form (Figure 5) or table form (*.tbl).

MAXPLUS II supports many VHDL and VERILOG constructs and attributes for simulation, however, to comply with hardware and synthesis constraints, a subset of the language constructs are supported.

Figures 4 and 5 show the trace setup for simulation of the XOR gate. The inputs and outputs for setup are extracted from the timing file (*.snf).

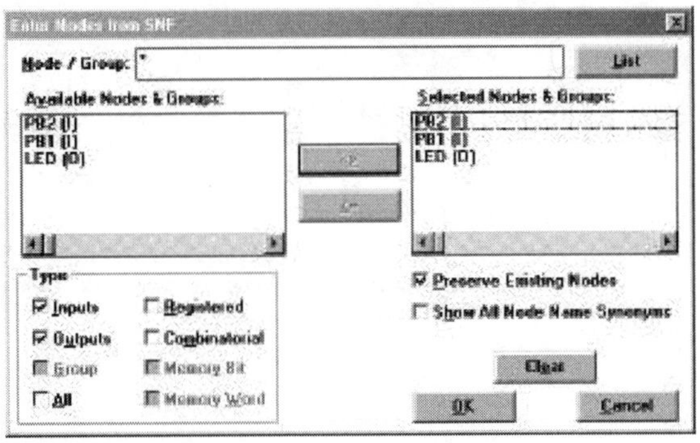

Figure 4. Input/output setup for the XOR gate

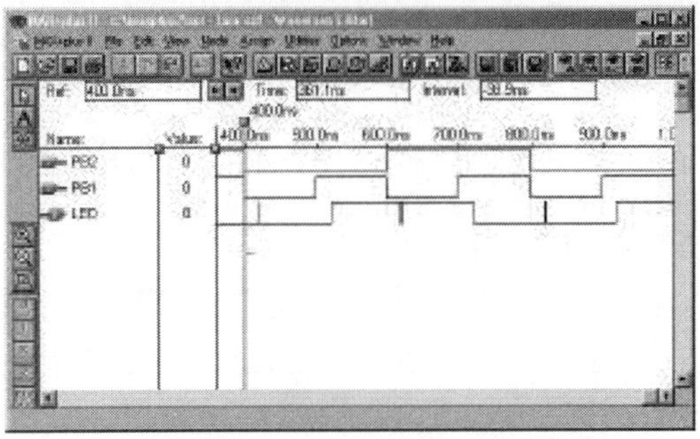

Figure 5. The XOR-gate timing simulation

5.0 Timing Analysis

Altera's FPGA timing is affected by:

- Input and output buffer delays
- Routing interconnect delays
- The internal logic delay of the circuit

Figure 6 shows a matrix of input to output delay times for the XOR-gate. This delay is the same delay time seen in the simulator. They include the input-to-output buffer delays and the interconnect delays inside the FPGA. The XOR-gate logic delay is very small compared to the rest of the device delays. These values vary with different Altera CAD tools and different chip speed grades. Other timing analysis options include setup time, hold time, and clock rate for sequential circuits.

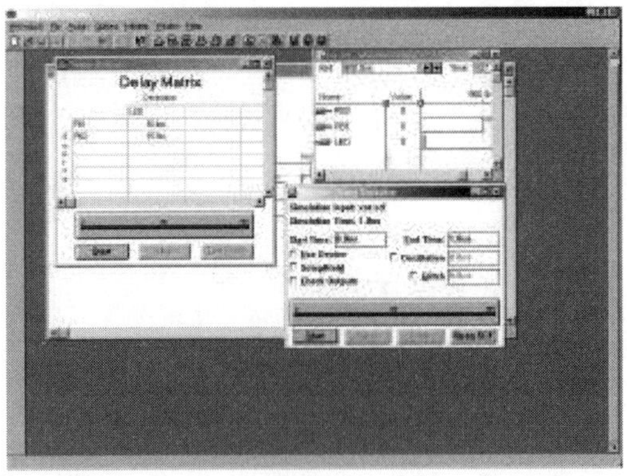

Figure 6. Input-to-output timing delays for XOR gate

6.0 The Floorplan Editor

The floorplan editor is used by experts to help them manually place and move portions of logic circuits to different logic cells inside the CPLD. This is done in an attempt to achieve faster timing or better utilization of the CPLD. This feature is used in very large designs that contain subsections of hardware that include critical high-speed timing. For non-expert users, the automatic placement-and-routing tool is recommended. Figure 7 shows the compiler's automatic physical placement of the logic design inside the CPLD.

There is a lot of empty space in the floor plan since the XOR gate uses a very small area of the chip. Pins and logic cells used in the design are *color-coded*. If we move the design to other areas in the chip, it will make small changes to the circuit timing because of the change in the interconnection delays inside the chip.

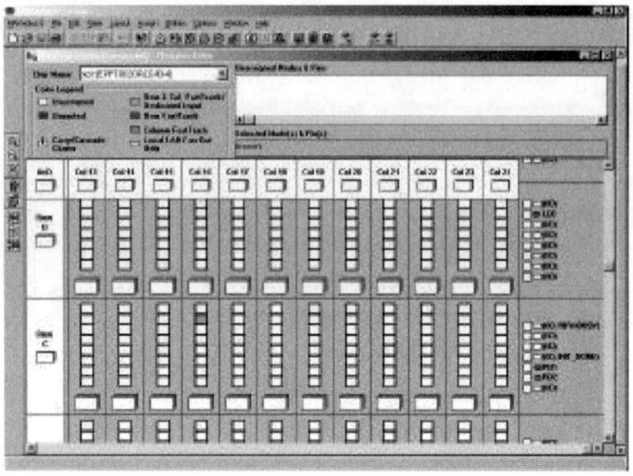

Figure 7. The XOR gate floor plan with automatic placement

7.0 A Small Instructional Processor

This example shows the behavioral-level modeling and simulation of a small single address processor with a

Mnemonic	Operation	Opcode
LDA	AC <= AC + contents of memory location	00
STA	contents of memory location <= AC	01
JMP	PC <= jump address	02
ADA	AC <= AC + contents of memory address	03
BNE	PC <= branch address if AC<>0	04

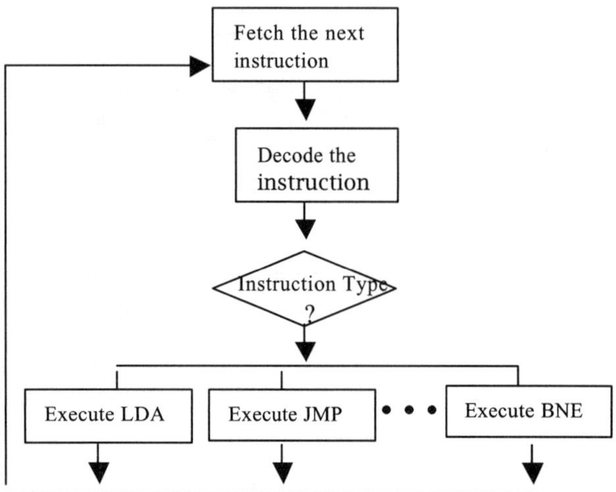

Figure 8. A flowchart of execution cycle

limited instruction set, developed part of the class project as described in [4]. Even though the processor has capacity for 256 different instructions, modeling and simulation of only five are shown. These instructions are load accumulator (LDA), store accumulator (STA), jump (JMP), add to accumulator (ADA), and branch if the content of the accumulator is not equal to zero (BNE). The instructions, operation code and operation is performed by each are shown in the following table. In the table AC is accumulator and PC is the program counter

The VHDL description also based on [4] is provided on the next page. In the description, lpm_ram_dq is the main system memory, which is initialized with the user program. A simple user program to set the size of the memory and to sum three values (X+Y+Z) is shown in Figure 9. The VHDL design fits nicely into the FLEX chip. The description follows the standard register transfer design for the processors. That is, the fetch cycle reads the instruction into the instruction_register (IR) while incrementing the program_counter (PC). The instruction in IR is then decoded and executed based on the operation code.

The timing diagram for reset, clock, state, program_counter, instruction_register, register_A (accumulator), memory_address_register, memory_data_register_out, and memory_write are shown in Figure 10. As seen from this figure, at 700ns, accumulator is loaded with AAAA and at 1300 nsec with FFFF.

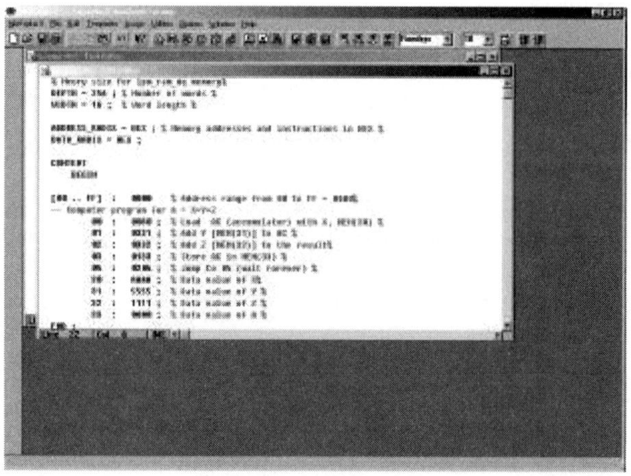

Figure 9. The instruction file to be loaded into memory

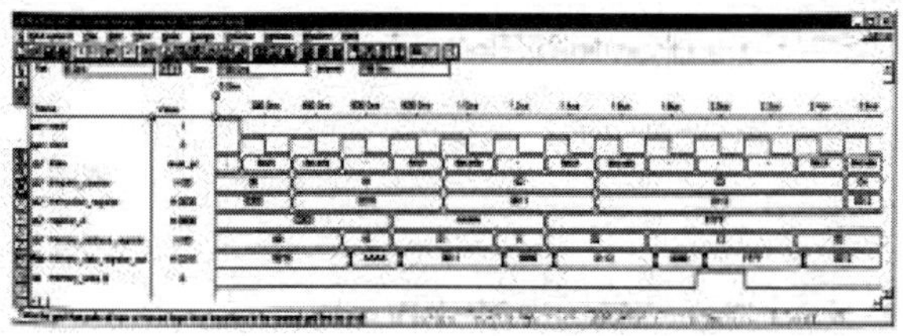

Figure 10. Simulation results of SIP

8.0 Conclusions

CPLDs provide a convenient medium to design, simulate, verify the functionality of a design, and to implement a prototype model fast. Their value in research for investigating better and compact designs and implementing complex signal processing algorithms is enormous. Using this technology new and innovative alternatives to replace the traditional design techniques are now investigated.

Altera's design laboratory package has helped our student to take more challenging and real-world design projects part of their design courses. The integrated design environment of MAXPLUS II permits the students to gain working knowledge of designs in a variety of formats ranging from schematic-capture to high-level description languages (VERILOG, VHDL, and AHDL). Since learning hardware description languages and their support tools are time consuming, MAXPLUS II provides this basic learning platform. This platform is followed later by Mentor Graphics tools for more complex system modeling and simulation.

7. 0 References

[1]Altera University Program Design Laboratory Package, Altera Corporation

[2] "IEEE Standard VHDL Language Reference Manual", IEEE Std 1076-1987, The Institute of Electrical and Electronic Engineers, Inc., 1988.

[3] Donald E. Thomas and Philip Moorby, *The Verilog Hardware Description Language*, Kluwer Academic Publishers, 1991.

[4] James o. Hamblen and D. Michael Furman, *Rapid Prototyping of Digital* Systems, Kluwer Academic Pub. 2000.


```
Library IEEE;
USE IEEE.STD_LOGIC_1164.ALL ;
USE IEEE.STD_LOGIC_ARITH.ALL ;
USE IEEE.STD_LOGIC_UNSIGNED.ALL;
LIBRARY lpm;
USE lpm.lpm_components.ALL;
ENTITY SIP IS
       PORT ( clock, reset_PC : IN STD_LOGIC;
              program_counter_out : OUT STD_LOGIC_VECTOR (7 DOWNTO 0)   ;
              register_AC_out     : OUT STD_LOGIC_VECTOR (15 DOWNTO 0) ;
              memory_data_register_out : OUT STD_LOGIC_VECTOR (15 DOWNTO 0));
END SIP;
ARCHITECTURE behavior OF SIP IS
    TYPE STATE_TYPE IS (reset, fetch, decode, execute_add, execute_load,
              execute_store, execute_wait1, execute_wait2, execute_jump, execute_branch);
       SIGNAL state: STATE_TYPE;
       SIGNAL instruction_register, memory_data_register: STD_LOGIC_VECTOR (15 DOWNTO 0);
       SIGNAL register_AC   : STD_LOGIC_VECTOR (15 DOWNTO 0);
       SIGNAL program_counter      : STD_LOGIC_VECTOR (7 DOWNTO 0) ;
       SIGNAL memory_address_register : STD_LOGIC_VECTOR (7 DOWNTO 0) ;
       SIGNAL memory_write : STD_LOGIC ;
       BEGIN
              memory: lpm_ram_dq
              GENERIC MAP (LPM_WIDTH => 16,
              LPM_WIDTHAD => 8,
              LPM_FILE=> "program.mif",
              LPM_INDATA =>"REGISTERED",
              LPM_OUTDATA =>"UNREGISTERED",
              lpm_address_control => "UNREGISTERED")
              PORT MAP (data => Register_AC,
                        Address => memory_address_register,
                        we => memory_write,
                        inclock => clock,
                        q => memory_data_register);

              program_counter_out <= program_counter ;
              register_AC_out <= register_AC;
              memory_data_register_out <= memory_data_register ;
              PROCESS (CLOCK, RESET)
                     BEGIN
```

```
                IF RESET ='1' THEN
                        state <= reset_pc ;
                ELSIF clock'EVENT AND clock ='1' THEN
        CASE state IS
        WHEN reset_pc =>
                program_counter <= "00000000";
                memory_address_register <= "00000000";
                register_AC <="0000000000000000";
                memory_write <= '0' ;
                state  <= fetch ;
        WHEN fetch =>
                instruction_register <= memory_data_register ;
                program_counter <= program_counter + 1;
                memory_write <= '0' ;
                state <= decode ;
        WHEN decode =>
                memory_address_register <= instruction_register (7 DOWNTO 0) ;
                CASE instruction_register (15 DOWNTO 8) IS
                        WHEN "00000000" => state <= execute_load ;
                        WHEN "00000001" => state <= execute_store ;
                        WHEN "00000010" => state <= execute_jump ;
                        WHEN "00000011" => state <= execute_add ;
                        WHEN "00000100" => state <= execute_branch ;
                        WHEN OTHERS     => state <= fetch ;
                END CASE ;
        WHEN execute_load =>
                register_ac <= memory_data_register ;
                memory_address_register <= program_counter ;
                state <= fetch ;
        WHEN execute_store =>
                memory_write <= '1' ;
                state <= execute_wait1 ;
        WHEN execute_jump =>
                memory_address_register <= instruction_register (7 DOWNTO 0) ;
                program_counter <= instruction_register (7 DOWNTO 0) ;
                state <= fetch ;
        WHEN execute_add =>
                register_ac <= register_ac + memory_data_register ;
                memory_address_register <= program_counter ;
                state <= fetch ;
        When execute_wait1 =>
                memory_write <='0' ;
                state <= execute_wait2 ;
        WHEN execute_wait2 =>
                memory_address_register <= program_counter ;
                state <= fetch ;
        WHEN execute_branch =>
                If Z_flag = '0' THEN
                        Memory_address_register <= instruction_register (7 DOWNTO 0);
                        Program_counter <= instruction_Register (7 DOWNTO 0) ;
                END IF ;
                State <= fetch ;
        WHEN OTHERS =>
                memory_address_register <= program_counter ;
                state <= fetch ;
        END CASE ;
    END IF ;
  END PROCESS;
END behavior ;
```

MMTS MODELLING METHODOLOGY EXTENSIONS

John M. Creagh
Department of Mathematics and Computing
Cork Institute of Technology
Rossa Ave, Cork
Ireland
Email : jcreagh@cit.ie

Keywords : Discrete-Event Simulation, Traffic Simulation, Modelling Methodology, MMTS, SIM-ENG.

ABSTRACT
MMTS is a discrete-event modelling methodology, which is suitable for traffic simulation. Extensions to this methodology are proposed in this paper. The transport entity is a special purpose entity responsible for handling the departure of events from normal entities. The functionality of the transport entity is enhanced. MMTS generates the specification of a simulation model. A MMTS model contains sufficient information so that the model may be presented directly to simulation software for simulation. Extension to the MMTS model specification is proposed, whereby additional information may be included for result processing. Therefore, the MMTS model specification may include information for controlling the results generated by the simulation software.

1. INTRODUCTION

Computer simulation may be considered closely linked to the field of software engineering in both design and implementation (Schruben 1983, Law and Kelton 1991; Fiskwick 1992). Many software engineering design techniques such as object oriented design (Hill 1996), and modular, reusable component design such as HLA (Yu et al. 1998), are now incorporated into computer simulation.

This paper proposes extensions to the discrete-event modelling methodology MMTS (Creagh 1998). MMTS uses a top-down approach for the design phase of a model. The design phase is subdivided into three sections : conceptual model, entity model and entity refinement model. The MMTS modelling methodology is suitable for traffic simulation, since the flow of events (or traffic flow) is clearly specified in the entity model. MMTS models contain sufficient detail whereby they may be input directly to a simulation program. SIM-ENG (Creagh 1999) is an example of a simulation engine, which accepts MMTS models for simulation.

Conceptual Model
: The conceptual model presents the highest level view of the simulation model. The major components of the simulation model are identified in the conceptual model, including the flow of events.

Entity Model
: The entity model consists of a refinement of the conceptual model. Event flow is clearly identified. The components identified in the conceptual model are used to specify the entities and their types. An entity is defined as a component, which is effected by the flow of control of events during the simulation. Three types of entity are defined. The *Arrival Entity* acts as a source of arriving events into the system. The *Normal Entity* receives events, processes events according to the event received, and finally the event departs. The *Transport Entity* is a special purpose entity, which is responsible for handling the departure of events from entities and transporting them to other entities.

Entity Refinement Model
: The entity refinement model provides a detailed specification of each entity of the entity model. Various parameters/fields are specified for each entity including queuing requirements, probability distribution algorithms and departure of event policies.

Extensions to the transport entity are proposed. The entity model provides a clear view of the flow of events in the model. Clouding of this view is avoided by restricting the entity model to three types of entity. Additional types of transport entity are now proposed, whereby the details of the entity are specified in the entity refinement model.

MMTS specifies a modelling methodology for the generation of a simulation model. MMTS is not concerned with the implementation details of the simulator. This paper proposes optional specifications to the entity refinement model for controlling the result processing of the simulation.

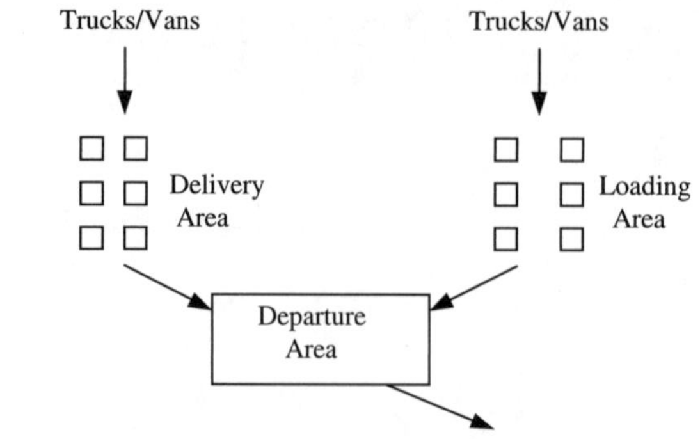

Figure 1 (a) Conceptual Model

2. MMTS MODEL DESIGN OVERVIEW

An overview of MMTS modelling is presented using a "simplified wholesale warehouse" example. This example is further referenced in section 4 below, to help illustrate some of the result processing options added to MMTS.

The conceptual model presented in figure 1 (a), illustrates the arrival and departure of trucks and vans to a warehouse. Trucks/vans may enter the delivery area or the loading area. Goods are unloaded at the delivery area. Six unloading bays exist, whereby queuing is required if more that six vehicles wish to unload. Goods are loaded at the loading area. Six loading bays exist, whereby queuing is required if more than six vehicles wish to load. All vehicles must depart at the departure area for security reasons. The components of the conceptual model are trucks/vans, the delivery area, the loading area and the departure area. Refining the conceptual model leads to the entity model as illustrated in figure 1 (b). The arrival entities A0 and A1 represent the arrival of trucks/vans to the system. Event flow is clearly illustrated in an entity model. The normal entity N2 represents the delivery area with six servers (i.e. six unloading bays). The normal entity N3 represents the loading area with six servers. Finally, the departure area is represented by the normal entity N4. The entity refinement model is presented in figure 1 (c). This model contains sufficient information so that the model may be presented to a simulation program for execution. Each entity is specified in isolation. The fields for each entity include queuing information, service information and departure information.

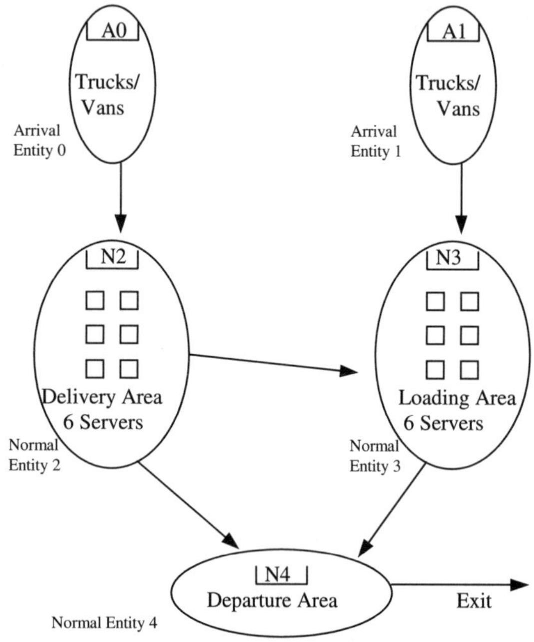

Figure 1 (b) Entity Model

3. TRANSPORT ENTITY EXTENSIONS

The transport entity is a special purpose entity responsible for the transportation of events from entity to entity. The transport entity does not have a queue, and does not effect the system clock. It receives events, and then transports them immediately to their destination. Figure 2 illustrates the transport entity.

A0 Entity 0
Type : Arrival Entity

Arrival Algorithm Type: Poisson parameters : mean = 12 per hour.
Departure To : Entity 2

A1 Entity 1
Type : Arrival Entity

Arrival Algorithm Type: Poisson parameters : mean = 10 per hour.
Departure To : Entity 3

N2 Entity 2
Type : Normal Entity

Service Algorithm Type: Exponential parameters : mean = each bay services 3 vehicles per hour.
Queue Type: FIFO parameter : unified queue.
Departure To : Depart Entity 3 probability 0.14 Depart Entity 4 probability 0.86
Number of Servers : 6

N3 Entity 3
Type : Normal Entity

Service Algorithm Type: Exponential parameters : mean = each bay services 3 vehicles per hour.
Queue Type: FIFO parameter : unified queue.
Departure To : Entity 4
Number of Servers : 6

N4 Entity 4
Type : Normal Entity

Service Algorithm Type: Exponential parameters : mean = service 28 vehicles per hour.
Queue Type: FIFO parameter : unified queue.
Departure To : Exit System
Number of Servers : 1

Figure 1 (c) Entity Refinement Model

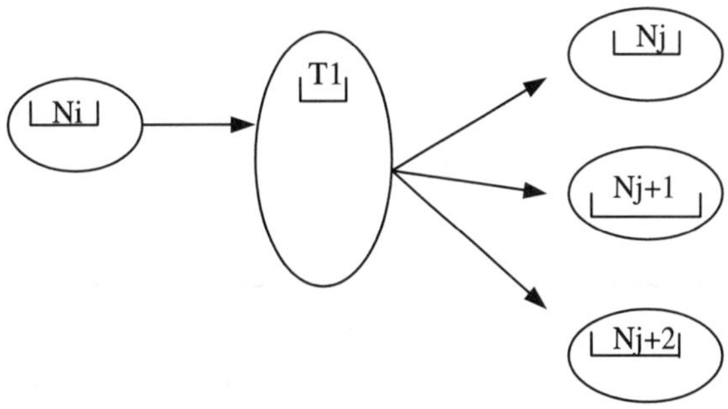

Figure 2 (a) Class A : Single input to transport entity with multiple outputs.

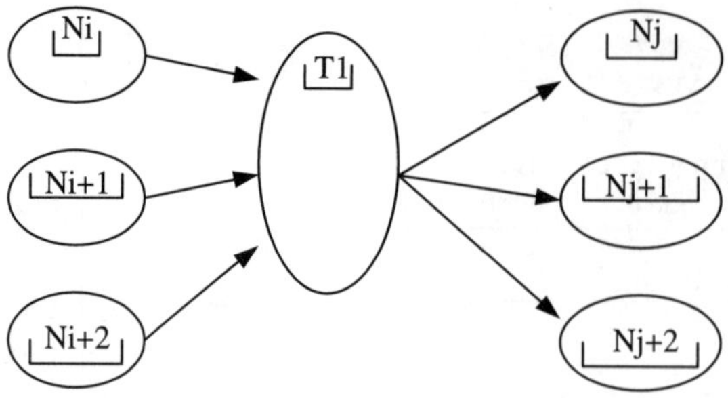

Figure 2 (b) Class A or Class B : Multiple inputs to transport entity with multiple outputs.

The purpose of the transport entity is receive an event, decide the destination, and finally to deliver the event to the destination. This paper proposes to enhance this decision making by providing a series of options. The transport entity is divided into two classes. The class A transport entity is not concerned with the source of the arriving event. If a single input transport entity, then the transport entity must be class A. If a multiple input transport entity, then for class A, the source of an event does not affect the output destination. The class B transport entity has its output destination decision dependent on the source of the input.

Tables 1 and 2 list the transport entity types. Two fields are added to the transport entity in the entity refinement specification. The class field specifies class A or class B. The second field specifies the type of transport entity and its associated parameters.

4. RESULT PROCESSING

Quite often, a simulation model is developed for a specific problem. A typical example is for the evaluation of a particular traffic problem. A simulation model is developed to determine the performance under a variety of operating scenarios. In these situations, the output requirements of the simulator are known at the model development stage. Therefore, this paper proposes to extend the entity refinement model. Additional information is needed to specify result processing requirements.

Name	Parameters	Description
Round Robin	None.	Using a Round Robin scheme, deliver the first event the first departure entity, the second event to the second departure entity etc., in a circular manner.
First Entity Free Server.	None.	Check each departure entity. The first departure entity with a free server receives the event.
First Entity Free Server (with Round Robin).	None.	Using a Round Robin scheme, deliver to the next entity, which has a free server.
Shortest Queue.	None.	Check all departure entities. Deliver the event to the entity found with the shortest queue.
Probability.	Probability value for each departure.	The event is delivered to the departure entity based on some probability.

Table 1 Class A transport entity types

Name	Parameters	Description
One to one.	None.	There exists the same number of inputs and outputs. A one to one correspondence exists, whereby events that arrive at the first input depart to the first output, events that arrive at the second input depart to the second output etc.
One to one, except if full.	None.	A one to one correspondence between input and output exists. However, when the output entity does not have a free server, then the other output entities are checked to find a free server.
Group Management.	Group specification parameters.	The inputs are specified as groups. The outputs are specified as groups. An event that arrives from an input group is directed to a specific output group.

Table 2 Class B transport entity types

The wholesale warehouse example of figure 1 above is used to assist in illustrating the result processing options. The first option is the specification of multiple simulation runs (Creagh 1999). This is made possible, (a) by allowing range values within the fields, of the entity refinement model. For example, suppose that the delivery area is to be tested for 5..14 unloading bays (i.e. Number of Servers of entity N2 of figure 1 (c) is specified as 5..14). Also, the loading area is tested for 5..14 loading bays. Therefore, 10 x 10 = 100 simulation runs are specified. If 20 replications of each simulation are specified, then 10 x 10 x 20 = 2000 simulation runs are required. The MMTS modelling methodology is not concerned with implementation issues. However, by allowing options to specify multiple simulation runs, this may give the specific implementation sufficient information to subdivide the execution of the simulation. SIM-ENG (Creagh 1999) is an example, whereby the multiple simulation runs are distributed over a network of PCs/workstations, thus providing load sharing.

The second option is that of recording/tracing. Additional fields are added to the entity refinement model, which allow the specification of the recording of data as a simulation execution proceeds. For example, record the clock time(s) when the queue increases past four entries for a particular entity. Another example, record the clock time(s) when less than five servers are busy at a particular entity.

The third option is the specification of result processing of information to assist in output analysis. Such specification is appended to the entity refinement model in a result specification section. Examples include, co-ordinate the output of different simulation runs into graphs or tables of data.

5. CONCLUSION

This paper presents extensions to the MMTS discrete-event simulation modelling methodology. MMTS is suitable for traffic simulation. The expansion of the functionality of the transport entity is proposed. The different types of transport entities are specified at the entity refinement model, thus avoiding adding additional complexity to the entity model. The transport entity is a special purpose entity responsible for the transportation of events from entity to entity. The additional transport entity types allow this transportation functionality to be enhanced. The second extension of MMTS is the addition of result processing specification to the entity refinement model. A MMTS model contains sufficient detail so that it may be presented to simulation software, however, MMTS is not concerned with the implementation details of the simulation software. The MMTS model specification may include additional information to direct the simulation software result processing. This optional feature may be useful for many simulations, whereby the result processing decisions may be known at the model design phase. One such benefit is the specification of multiple parameters in an entity, implying that multiple simulation runs are required. This may be quite common in performance evaluation scenarios. By specifying multiple simulation runs, the simulation implementation software may distribute the simulation runs. The simulation engine SIM-ENG is one such example, whereby simulation load is distributed over a network of PCs/workstations if multiple simulation runs are specified.

REFERENCES

Creagh, J.M. 1998. "MMTS : A Modelling Methodology for Traffic Simulation". *Proceedings of the SCS 1998 Summer Computer Simulation Conference, Reno, Nevada*, (July) : 393-403.

Creagh, J.M. 1999. "SIM-ENG : A Traffic Simulation Engine". *Proceedings of the IEEE/SCS 1999 Annual Simulation Symposium, ASTC'99, San Diego, CA*, (April) : 4-10.

Fishwick, P.A. 1992. "An Integrated Approach to System Modeling Using a Synthesis of Artificial Intelligence, Software Engineering and Simulation Methodologies." *TOMACS.* Vol 2. No. 4 (Oct) : 307-330.

Hill, D.R.C. 1996. *Object-Oriented Analysis and Simulation.* Addison-Wesley Publishers Ltd.

Law, A.M. and Kelton, W.D. 1991. *Simulation Modeling & Analysis.* 2nd Edition. McGraw-Hill,

Yu, L.C., Steinman, J.S. and Blank, G.E. 1998. "Adapting Your Simulation for HLA." *SIMULATION.* Vol 71:6, 410-420.

Schruben, L. 1983. "Simulation Modeling with Event Graphs." *Communications of the ACM.* Vol 26. No. 11 (Nov) : 957-963.

A SIMULATION METHODOLOGY DESCRIPTION OF CONTAINER PLACEMENT USING A UNIQUE SYSTEM TO CONTROL THE LOGISTICS

Mhamed Itmi [1,2]

Ralph Huntsinger [2]

Patrick Jarjoui [1]

Jean-Pierre Pécuchet [1]

(1) INSA de Rouen BP 08
PSI Laboratory
76131 Mt-St-Aignan, France
xxx@insa-rouen.fr

(2) California State University, Chico
Computer Science Department
Chico, California 95929-0410, USA
xxx@ecst.csuchico.edu

KEYWORDS

Logistics, object oriented design, software components, software reengineering.

ABSTRACT

This paper deals with discrete systems simulation in the domain of logistics. The aim of our work was to develop a simulator regarding a container terminal. A prototype has been designed and implemented. To improve the system and add new functionality, we proceed to the reengineering of the model. After remembering the original features of the prototype, we describe our approach using components for Reverse Engineering and we give highlights on some extensions currently studied.

I - INTRODUCTION

The part of the container sea-borne trade is steadily expanding, especially as far as we are concerned with "handle with care" or high added value products (manufactured products, perishable goods...). This kind of traffic has significantly increased, and is mainly concentrated in the great industrial areas: North America, Europe, and Asia. To respond to the increasing trade and to decrease the working costs, it is necessary to improve the use of existing areas by introducing new storage techniques and new working methods. The considerable cost of infrastructure requires a simulation based evaluation before considering any change in one of the three main parameters that are:

-the geometric configuration of the site and the placement of containers,

- working methods and resource control,

- equipment investment.

We were interested in container terminal simulation. The intent is to obtain a model that offers the ability to define the resource allocation policies at various levels. In order to define the work organization, the system takes into account the team view of managing various kinds of resources.

We developed a container terminal simulator prototype for the validation of specifications in that way. The system uses the paradigms of Object-Oriented Design to represent entities and Process Oriented Simulation relating to object dynamics. This prototype is called SGTC (a System for Container Terminal Management).

II - MAIN CARACTERISTICS OF THE MODEL

This system has two particularities (Serin et al. 1995):

One corresponds to the resource management through the objects labeled 'resource providers' and 'multi-resource-controllers'. The resource allocation is managed by a resource-provider. This object manages only one type of resource. To reflect the decision hierarchy in the organization structure, we can define several control levels for each resource: it consists of many resource providers that are able to manage it. Resource providers can share the same type of resources and are consulted according to a priority fixed by the user. Very often we need to gather different kinds (classes) of resources like machines, transports, etc. to coordinate the functioning of the system. However, the strategies for allocation may be different. So, a set of heterogeneous resources cannot be combined in the same resource provider. To solve this problem we created the 'multi-resource-controllers'.

The second particularity of SGTC is the type of simulation, which is a simulation by processes and complementary processes. These concern the work allocation policies:

- the process-oriented server-customer relationship including tasks and services,
- the process-oriented simulation diagrams.

The behavior of each entity is described through the process approach, which is widely considered the most natural one. The interactions between entities are obtained through a customer/server model. For modularity, the process of a customer is described in terms of sub-processes.

The prototype SGTC is actually under a general validation process after it has been validated a first time by a particular port handling contractor. The model will be improved by some changes and some extensions to become more adapted to different kinds of terminals. We also want to add new functionality to the system. We take into account these steps in common with the maintenance step to work out the design of the model in a Reverse Engineering process. To improve the software, and particularly its maintenance, we will benefit from the software component approach.

III - THE REVERSE ENGINEERING PROCESS

1- Software engineering

Software engineering is the activity of the design and implementation of products and the procedures to improve production of software and its follow-up. The need for such methods grew up over the past few years as information systems became more and more complex. A lot of tools and methods exist to help project managers and developers in their tasks. Life-cycles describe steps needed in software engineering like specifications, implementations, and test phases. Reverse Engineering is the activity of analyzing components of a system and their interactions with the aim to describe it at a higher level of abstraction. Re-engineering means examination, understanding, and alteration of program code, in order to enhance performance, maintainability and functionality.

We represent the component levels in layers from the bottom level to the top level (system components, communications, database access, user interface, business components). The levels in the middle are common task components. Components of the same level are represented in a horizontal manner. Our work in (Itmi and Tricaud 1999) helps us to work out the software engineering steps. The new architecture of SGTC is based on a layer model using components in each layer. The main layers are presented in figure 1. We can distinguish from the bottom: the lower, medium, high and business layers. These layers are made of components. In fact, the components are logical packages in the sense of UML (Unified Modeling Language (Rumbaugh et al. 1997)).

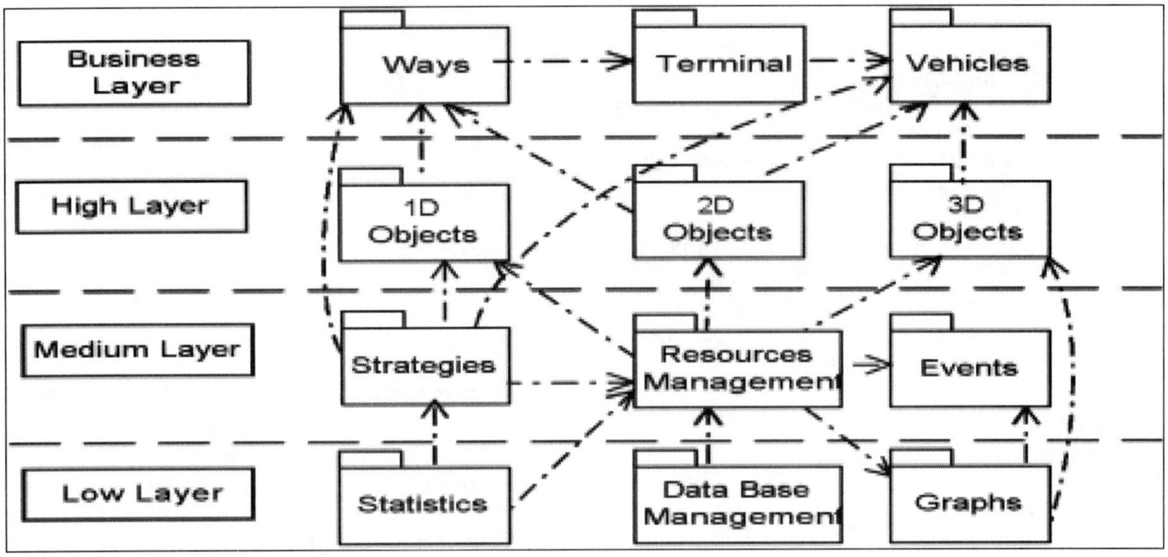

Figure 1 : Components in layers

2- The Layers and their components

For analysis and design, the UML recommends the use of a dynamic view of a logical and a physical model to perform object oriented analysis and design. The overall model contains several model elements and the relationships between them. A notation provides graphical icons to represent each kind of model element and relationship.

Logical packages serve to partition the logical model of a system. They are clusters of highly related classes that are cohesive and loosely coupled to other clusters. We use them to group classes, interfaces and other packages. In our reverse engineering process, the system components are logical packages.

We recall the meaning of different kinds of links that may appear:

- A dependency relationship is a dotted line with an arrowhead at one end. Roughly, it shows that the client class depends on the supplier class to provide certain services. It is also used between logical packages.
- An association relationship is an oblique or orthogonal line. It usually represents a semantic connection between two classes.
- The meta relationship shows the connection between a class and its metaclass. It is an arrowhead pointing toward the metaclass.

In the following, we will only give a description of some packages and some classes with their links. Our objective is more to give highlights about the reverse engineering process than to present the system details.

First, let us describe roughly the main layers with their components (packages):

- The package "Probabilities" concerns all the packages dealing with basic probability and stochastic calculus.
- The package "Graphs" concerns various approaches to graphs including optimization calculus.
- The package "Resources" concerns the resource management.
- The package " 2D-Objects" concerns the management of objects with 2-dimensions.
- The package "Ways" concerns the ways things are specified.

Each package has its own object hierarchy. We avoid multiple inheritance to permit a model implementation with no constraint on the choice of a programming language. Let us describe now several components.

In figure 2 we give the description of the "Ways" package.

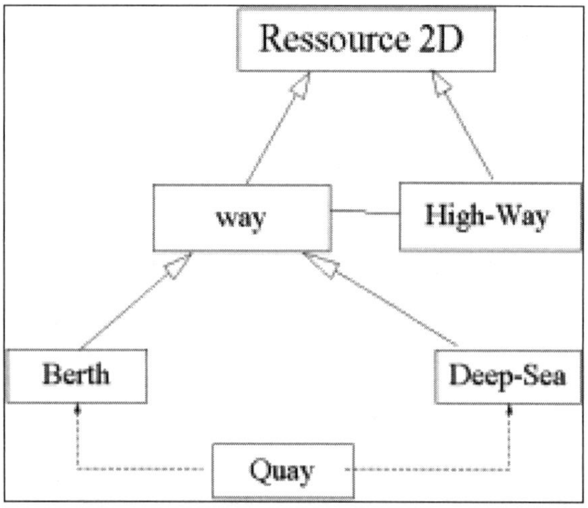

Figure 2 :The package "Ways".

The package "Resources-Management" is described in figure 3.

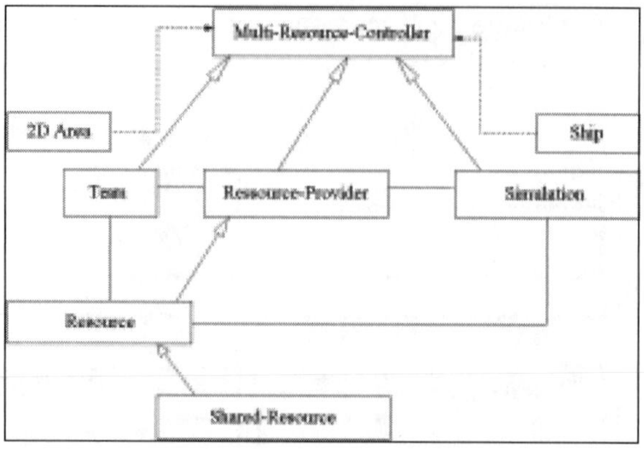

Figure 3 : The package "Resources management".

3- Other extensions and further work

To improve the system, other components are currently studied. They concern:
- Strategies: one example appears in figure 4. These strategies concern the displacement of vehicles, manipulation of containers, calculus methods, etc...
- Explanation: such a component will help the user to better understand the dynamics of the system (Itmi et al. 2000).

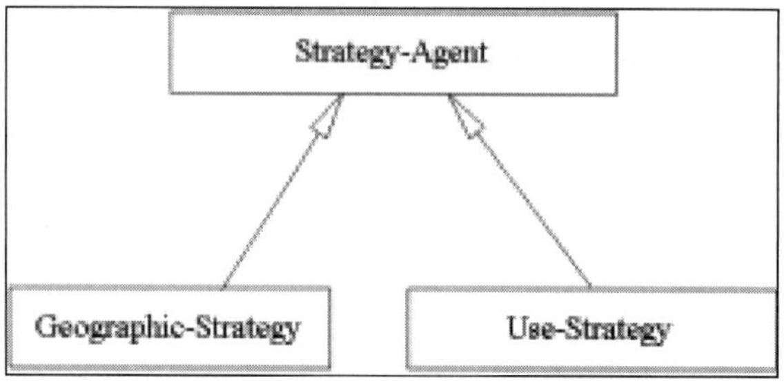

Figure 4 : The package "Strategies".

These components will also deal with an intelligent user-interface, which is also work in progress.

IV - CONCLUSION

Our objective is to obtain a new version of a simulation software based on components for reasons of maintenance and development of new functionality. We found that the method we presented for the reverse engineering based on layers and packages is satisfactory. It permits one to reach the objectives by manipulation of components. The use of market libraries of components will also be useful in the implementation phase.

This work is supported by the French Ministry of Equipment and the Region of Haute-Normandie. Several papers on type this research have been published in International Conferences and were a part of two Ph.D. thesis. This paper concerns a part of an actual third thesis and is published here for the first time.

REFERENCES

Itmi M., Morel D., Pecuchet J.-P. and Serin F., Villefranche L. 1995. "Eco-Problem-Solving For Container Stacking." In *Proceedings of the 1995 Systems, Man and Cybernetics Conference* (Vancouver, Br. Columbia, Oct. 22-25). IEEE, pp. 3810-3815.

Itmi M., Pecuchet J. P. and Coic A. 1997. "Machine learning in system simulation. An application to a port container terminal." In *Proceedings of the 1997 Summer Computer Simulation Conference* (Arligton, Virginia, Jul. 13-17). SCS, pp. 715-719.

Itmi M., Huntsinger R. C. and Pecuchet J. P. 2000 "A method for an embedded explanation subsystem for simulation systems: a proposal for an intelligent simulation environment." In *Proceedings of the 2000 Summer Computer Simulation Conference* (Vancouver, Br. Columbia, Jul. 15-20). SCS, to appear.

Itmi M., Tricaud S. : "Incremental Software Reverse Engineering Activity and Object Oriented Methodology." In *Proceedings of the 1999 Summer Computer Simulation Conference* (Chicago, Illinois, Jul. 11-15). SCS. pp. 33-36.

Rumbaugh, J., Jacobson, I. and Booch, G. "Unified Modeling Language Reference" Manual, ISBN: 0-201-30998-X, Addison Wesley, est. Publication Dec. 1997

Serin F., Villefranche L., Itmi M. and Pecuchet J.-P. 1995 "Resource Control Model for Simulation." In Proceedings of the International Conference on Industrial Engineering and Production Management (Marrakech, Morocco, Apr. 4-7). IEPM'95-FUCAM, 364-370.

REAL-TIME TRAFFIC GENERATION FOR A DRIVING SIMULATOR USING MATLAB

Harold Klee
School of Electrical Engineering and Computing Science
University of Central Florida
Orlando, FL 32816
email:klee@mail.ucf.edu

KEYWORDS: Real-time Simulation, Simulators, Transportation

ABSTRACT

A multi-year project was initiated to introduce autonomous vehicles in the UCF Driving Simulator for real-time interaction with the simulator vehicle. This paper describes the progress during the first year.

A traffic network consisting of several one and two-way roads, an outer loop and intersections with traffic control devices was created. It is completely defined in terms of a set of nodes and links.

Using a Windows PC, MATLAB was used to calculate positions and headings of simulated vehicles with respect to the link/node coordinate system of the network. The link/node vehicle coordinates are transformed in the PC to x,y and heading coordinates for communication to the simulation control program running in the host computer.

MATLAB was chosen because of its powerful data analysis, visualization and programming environment, extensive library of mathematical functions and its capability to produce easily customizable GUI's.

Initial traffic densities on the links are set by the user as are the arrival patterns of new vehicles entering the network at the source nodes. An onscreen map of the network displaying the simulated traffic movement, with zoom and scroll is useful for off-line software development purposes. The traffic generation frame rate is a function of the number of cars and other factors which affect the computational load on the PC.

Traffic generation output is interpolated to synchronize with the basic simulator frame rate which is dictated by the vehicle dynamics model.

INTRODUCTION

The UCF Driving Simulator has evolved since the mid 1990's into a midrange simulator with the potential to conduct research in transportation, human factors and real-time simulation. In 1995, a joint UCF research team began a project to enhance the capabilities of the simulator to incorporate modern hardware and software technology. A Silicon Graphics Onyx Reality Engine with two 200 MHz MIPS processors, two raster managers and 192 MB of memory was acquired and installed as the central host computer for the system. It was upgraded in 1999 with two additional 200 MHz MIPS processors and two more raster managers. The system runs a real-time version of the Unix operating system and is sufficiently powerful to control system I/O, integrate a sophisticated vehicle dynamics model, perform data logging operations, and run a 3-channel color video display with 960 x 680 fixed resolution on each channel. Three video projectors were acquired, and a wrap around curved screen providing a 160-degree field of view was installed. The UCF Driving Simulator is shown in Figure 1.

A preliminary validation study comparing the driving behavior (primarily forward speed) of subjects along a section of road in the simulator and the real world counterpart in an instrumented vehicle was conducted in 1998 (Klee 1998). A view from the simulator is shown in Figure 2.

Certain types of roadway improvement projects related to road geometry, sight distances, sign placement, traffic calming, etc. could be tested in the simulator. However, the absence of vehicular traffic in the visual data base precludes its use as a training device or as a testbed for studies involving traffic operations where traffic interaction is essential.

A multi-phase research study was initiated in 1999 to create external traffic movements viewable by the driver in the simulator and also develop a limited scenario generation capability. In the initial phase, there was no attempt to introduce autonomous vehicles, i.e. vehicles whose movements reflect an awareness of each other's presence as well as that of the simulator vehicle. Instead, the primary focus was assuring that all vehicles remain properly registered with respect to the centerlines of each road.

TRAFFIC GENERATION

A traffic network consisting of several one and two-way roads, an outer loop and intersections with traffic control devices was created and shown in Figure 3. Unlike the visual database used in the validation study, this roadway network is purely fictitious and was created as a prototype for evaluation of the traffic generation routines.

A previous real-time traffic simulation study (Balfour and Andrews 1998) utilized a link/node type of description for a network of roads. The nodes are placed along the network at locations which define the permissible traffic patterns. The nodes are connected by links which allow the vehicles to be properly registered on the roads. A link/node description of a roadway network is not unique, however regardless of its definition, it is a starting point for the process of artificially generating vehicles for insertion in the network.

A database of link properties was created to describe the entire network topography, i.e. node types at either end (source, sink or intermediate), neighboring links, transition probabilities for moving from link to link, and relevant geometrical data. A cell array L with 140 rows, one for each link (see Figure 3), stores the complete set of link properties, some of which are entered directly by the user and others which are calculated internally.

L{i, 1}:	Link Identifier ('L1', ... , 'L140')
L{i, 2}:	Link Type ('ST', 'RT', 'LT', 'UT')
L{i, 3}:	Link Start Node ('N1', ... , 'N209')
L{i, 4}:	Link Start Node Type ('SRC', 'INT')
L{i, 5}:	Link Start Node Road ('R1', ... , 'R8')
L{i, 6}:	Link End Node ('N1', ... , 'N209')
L{i, 7}:	Link End Node Type ('INT', 'SNK')
L{i, 8}:	Link End Node Road ('R1', ... , 'R8')
L{i, 9}:	Link Upstream Links ('L1', ... , 'L140')
L{i, 10}:	Link Downstream Links ('L1', ... , 'L140')
L{i, 11}:	Link Transition Probabilities ([0], [P1, P2], [P1, P2, P3])
L{i, 12}:	Link Length (ft), calculated from link node data for 'ST' links or (h, k, r, θ) for 'RT', 'LT', and 'UT' links
L{i, 13}:	Link Speed Limit (mph)
L{i, 14}:	Link Start Node x,y coordinates
L{i, 15}:	Link End Node x,y coordinates
L{i, 16}:	Heading (rad) with respect to positive x axis for 'ST' links or (h, k, r, θ) for 'RT', 'LT', and 'UT' links

Running on a Windows PC platform, MATLAB (ver 5.3 Math Works) was used to calculate positions and headings of simulated vehicles with respect to the link/node coordinate system of the network. MATLAB was chosen because of its powerful data analysis and visualization, extensive built-in library of mathematical functions, programming environment, and its capability to produce easily customizable GUI's.

Uniquely identified vehicles are initially placed on each of the 140 links according to a default or user's initial density specification. Link/node vehicle coordinates, consisting of the link number, distance along the link from the upstream node, and heading are transformed in the MATLAB PC to x,y and heading values in the coordinate system of the 3D modeling software used to create the visual database. This transformation guarantees the vehicles will be properly registered with respect to the centerlines of the roads. These coordinates are communicated over a network to the simulation control program running in the host computer, a Silicon Graphics ONYX computer. New link/node vehicle coordinates are established each frame, i.e. a complete pass through the traffic generation loop.

New vehicles entering the network are introduced at source nodes 'N100', 'N101', ... ,'N109' (see Figure 3) in a stochastic fashion based on default or user defined average arrival rates. Current vehicles are removed when and if they arrive at sink nodes 'N200', 'N201', ..., 'N209'. On the PC side, an onscreen map of the network displaying several different views of the simulated traffic movement, frame by frame, is useful for off-line software development purposes. The view selection menu allows the user to track a specific vehicle, view selected links, view the entire network, or track the simulator vehicle. An individual frame snap shot showing traffic at one of the intersections is shown in Figure 4. The network map is not rendered when the simulator is running in order to minimize the traffic generation cycle time on the MATLAB PC.

The vehicle dynamics model executes on the host at the basic simulator frame rate of 30 Hz. Currently, the simulator's positional coordinates from the vehicle dynamics model is not processed by the MATLAB traffic generation software. Consequently, the externally generated traffic does not respond to the presence of the simulator vehicle.

Instead, for each frame of traffic generation, previously recorded simulator vehicle profile data (t,x,y,heading) is read from an external file to account for the location of the simulator vehicle. This is done to test the MATLAB algorithm for locating the nearest link to the simulator vehicle, a requirement for future integration of the real simulator vehicle and intelligent traffic generation. There is no intelligence in the simulated traffic as the vehicles are either randomly advanced along the links each frame or deterministically placed for purposes of creating specific scenarios.

The traffic generation frame rate is a function of the number of cars and other factors which affect the computational load on the PC. Initial results of timing the traffic generation loop subject to various loads indicate a sustainable frame rate in the neighborhood of 1 Hz. Interpolation is used to produce vehicle traffic coordinates synchronized with the basic simulator frame rate to assure smooth trajectories of the rendered vehicles. A single frame lag is the penalty associated with using interpolated values based on "old" traffic coordinates to determine the current positions of the simulated vehicles. A snapshot of traffic viewed from inside the simulator is shown in Figure 5. Video clips of the PC traffic generation output and the view of traffic from the simulator are available for downloading at the CATSS (Center for Advanced Transportation Simulation Systems) website (http://www.ucf.edu/catss).

Despite the absence of intelligent traffic, as a result of the first year's research, specific scenarios can be programmed to evaluate driver's responses to various types of stimuli. A recently initiated study is investigating the situational awareness of elderly drivers and their ability to perform routine driving tasks. Subjects were asked to travel along a prescribed path in the network shown in Figure 3 with scripted external traffic movements viewable in both directions. Driving characteristics such as ability to maintain longitudinal and lateral control, traffic sign recognition, behavior at signalized intersections, obeying speed limits, car-following tendencies, gap acceptance at intersections are the primary components to be monitored and evaluated. The traffic generation routine for this scenario was developed along with the required data logging routines. Other possible scenarios involve programmed vehicle movements where one or more vehicle trajectories pose a threat to the simulator driver.

FUTURE RESEARCH

The next phase of the research will address the issues of intelligent movement of traffic and recognition of the simulator vehicle. The primary objective during the first year was creating a framework for describing a traffic network and producing vehicles in a visual scene which are properly registered with respect to the roads in a real-time simulation environment. In the future, with intelligent traffic populating the visual database, alternative designs for moving traffic safely and expeditiously can be evaluated in a simulated environment. The actual (or proposed) roads and surrounding features displayed in the simulator will be generated from existing CADD files and digital photography.

REFERENCES

Balfour, R.; Andrews, B. 1998. "3-Dimensional Roadway Traffic Simulation and Modeling for Design, Public Education and Conflict Resolution: A New York Case Study." Report by The National Aviation and Transportation Center, Long Island, New York.

Klee, H.; C. Bauer; E. Radwan; and H. Al-Deek. 1999. "Preliminary Validation of Driving Simulator Based on Forward Speed." Transportation Research Record Committee on Simulation and Measurement of Vehicle and Operator Performance, Nov. 1999.

Figure 1 The UCF Driving Simulator

Figure 2 View From Inside The UCF Driving Simulator During Validation Study

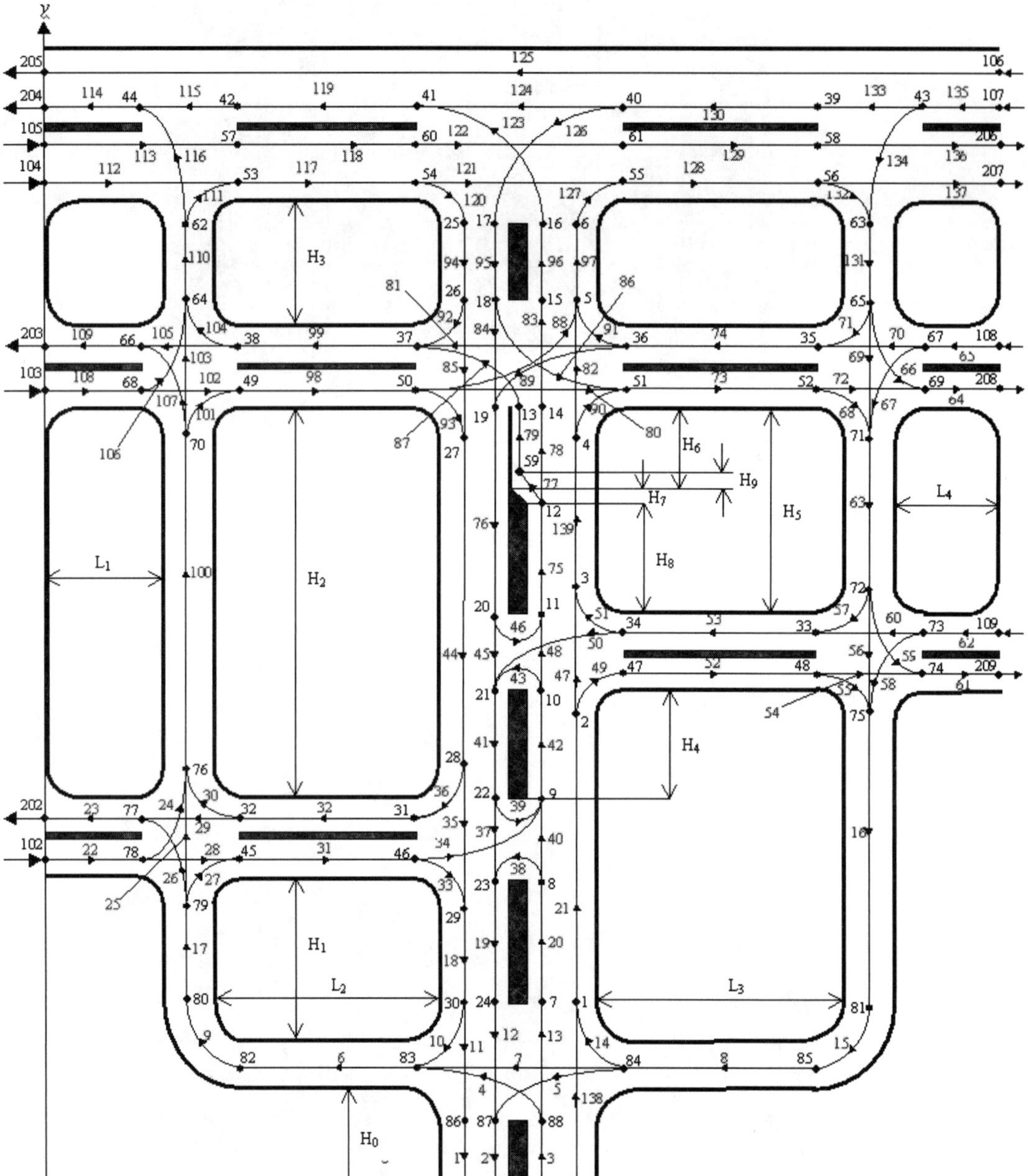

Figure 3 Roadway Network for Traffic Generation

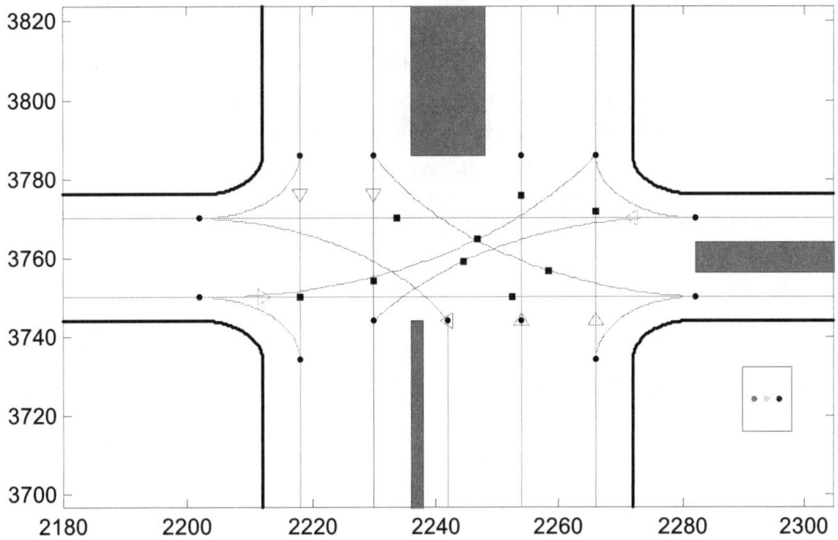

frar

Figure 4 Snapshot of Roadway Network Intersection from PC Traffic Generation

Figure 5 View from Simulator of External Traffic

THE NEED FOR DEBUGGING TOOLS FOR DECLARATIVE EQUATION BASED SIMULATION LANGUAGES.

Peter Bunus, Peter Fritzson
PELAB, Programming Environment Laboratory
Department of Computer and Information Science,
Linköping University, S-581 83, Linköping, Sweden
{petbu,petfr}@ida.liu.se

KEYWORDS

Modelica language, Debugging framework, Declarative equation based modeling language.

ABSTRACT

The primary focus of this paper is the subject of understanding the underlying mechanism of debugging equation based languages. Such an understanding will help the simulation practitioner to build models confidently and use debugging techniques more thoroughly.

In this paper, we first give an introduction to declarative equation based programming languages and the consequences equation based programming has for debugging. At the same time we examine the particular debugging problems posed by Modelica, a declarative equation based modeling language. A brief overview of the Modelica language is also given.

We also present our view of the issues and solutions based on a proposed framework for debugging declarative equation based languages. We believe that there is a clear need for debugging tools that would eliminate most of the problems presented in the paper and allow the designer to concentrate on the modeling aspects.

INTRODUCTION AND MOTIVATION

Simulation models are increasingly being used in problem solving and in decision making since engineers need to analyze increasing complex and heterogeneous physical systems. In order to support mathematical modeling and simulation a number of object-oriented and/or acausal modeling languages have emerged ASCEND (Piela et al. 1991), Dymola (Elmqvist 1978), gPROMS, NMF (Sahlin et al. 1996), ObjectMath (Fritzson et al. 1995), Omola (Andersson 1994), SIDOPS+ (Breunese an Broenik 1994), Smile (Kloas et al. 1995), U.L.M-Allan (Jeandel et at. 1996) and VHDL-AMS (IEEE 1997).

The advantage of such a modeling language is that the user can concentrate on the logic of the problem rather than on a detailed algorithmic implementation of the simulation model.

A significant part of the simulation design effort is spent on detecting deviations from the specifications and subsequently localizing the source of such error. Several studies have been conducted to see how much time goes into debugging. According to (Parasoft 1997) the debugging phase of software development takes 60-70% of the overall development time and debugging is responsible for 80% of all software projects overruns. Based on these facts we should attach substantial importance to the debugging phase during all the phases of the software development. That would require the development of new programming environments tools as well as new and improved debugging techniques. We believe that debugging will be an essential step in the modeling and simulation process with a declarative equation based language, as well as for other languages.

Currently, few or no tools are available to assist developers debugging declarative equation based modeling languages. Since these languages usually are based on object-orientation and acausal physical modeling, traditional approaches to debugging are inadequate and inappropriate to solve the error location problem. To begin to address this need we propose a methodology for implementing an efficient debugging framework for high level declarative equation based languages and to adapt traditional debugging techniques and algorithms to such languages.

The concept of declarative programming is inspired by mathematics where it is common to state or declare what holds, rather than giving a detailed stepwise algorithm on how to achieve the desired goal as is required when using procedural languages. Unlike procedural languages such as FORTRAN, C, Pascal, formulas and relationships can be entered in any order. In declarative programming, computational structures of data elements, functions, and equations can be specified e.g. by giving formulas in predicate logic (Broy 1991).

To begin to address the need for debugging we propose a methodology and a framework for efficient debugging of high level declarative equation based languages. Our first target language for the implementation of the framework will be the Modelica modeling language.

The debugging framework should also address issues about model checking, simulation model verification, and validation. Our aim is to provide a complete environment which will assist the programmer at each stage of the simulation process. We strongly believe that in the case of equation based languages static debugging, run time debugging and various methods for model checking and validation methods complement each other. None of these should be overlooked when designing an environment for the modeling and simulation process.

The main focus of the debugging framework should be the interaction between models and as well as the independent validation of each developed model. This will be beneficial for the modeler by providing guidance at each stage of the simulation model building process. This will be a powerful tool for assessing the correctness and the credibility of simulation models.

As far as we know there is no good general purpose debugger available for declarative equation based languages. Also, there is no efficient debugging framework for the Modelica simulation language. In order to achieve a reasonable degree of correctness for simulation, the debugger should detect bugs in the early stages of the modeling process.

In the following section, the Modelica equation based simulation language is briefly introduced. In the next section the current problems from the debugging point of view are presented and possible debugging solutions to the currently encountered problems are briefly given. Lastly a summary is provided and future work and concluding remarks are given.

THE MODELICA MODELING LANGUAGE

Before describing the difficulties of debugging a declarative equation based language, we will acquaint the reader with Modelica, a declarative equation based modeling language.

Modelica is a new language for hierarchical object-oriented physical modeling which is developed through an international effort (Fritzson and Engelson 1998; Elmqvist et al. 1999). The language unifies and generalizes previous object-oriented modeling languages. Modelica is intended to become a *de facto* standard. The language has been designed to allow tools to generate efficient simulation code automatically with the main objective to facilitate exchange of models, model libraries and simulation specifications. It allows defining simulation models modularly and hierarchically and combining various formalisms expressible in the more general Modelica formalism. The multidomain capability of Modelica gives the user the possibility to combine electrical, mechanical, hydraulic, thermodynamic etc, model components within the same application model. Compared to other equation based languages available today, Modelica offers four important advantages from the simulation practitioners point of view:

- Acausal modeling based on ordinary differential equations (ODE) and differential algebraic equations (DAE). There is also ongoing research to include partial differential equations (PDE) in the language syntax and semantics.
- Multi-domain modeling capability which gives the user the possibility to combine electrical, mechanical, thermodynamic, hydraulic etc., model components within the same application model.
- A general type system that unifies object-orientation, multiple inheritance, and generics templates within a single class construct. This facilitates reuse of components and evolution of models.
- A strong software component model, with constructs for creating and connecting components. Thus the language is ideally suited as an architectural description language for complex physical systems, and to some extent for software systems.

The reader of the paper is referred to (Modelica Assoc. 1999a) and (Modelica Assoc. 1999b) for a complete description of the language and its functionality. Shorter overviews are available in (Elmqvist et al. 1999) and (Fritzson and Engelson 1998).

Modelica Acausal Modeling.

At the lowest level of the language equations are used to describe the relations between the quantities of a model. As was mentioned before, one of the distinctive features of Modelica is the acausal programming model. The equations should be stated in a neutral form without consideration of order of evaluation of elements in the model. Modelica computation semantics does not depend on the order in which equations are written. However, this property complicates the debugging process.

For instance the equation `a = b + c;` can be used as three different assignment statements :

`a := b + c;` or `b := a -c;` or `c := a - b;`

depending on the context where the equation and the corresponding variables `a`, `b`, and `c` are instantiated.

The acausality makes Modelica library classes more reusable than traditional classes containing assignment statements where the input-output causality is fixed, since Modelica classes adapt to the data flow context in which they are used. The data flow context is defined by telling which variables are needed as *outputs* and which are external *inputs* to the simulated system. From the simulation practice point of view this generalization enables both simpler models and more efficient simulation. The declarative form allow a one-to-one correspondence between physical components and their software representation.

Modelica Classes

Modelica programs are built from classes, like in other object oriented languages. The main difference compared with traditional object-oriented languages is that instead of functions (methods) equations are used to specify the behavior. A class declaration contains a list of variable declarations and a list of equations preceded by the keyword `equation` An example of a low pass filter in Modelica from (Modelica Assoc. 1999a) is shown below.

```
class LowPassFilter
    parameter Real T=1;
    Real u, y (start=1);
equation
    T*der(y) + y = u;
end LowPassFilter;
```

The model class can be used to create two instances of the filter with different time constants and "connecting" them together as follows.

```
class FilterInSeries
    LowPassFilter F1(T=2), F2(T=3);
equation
    F1.u = sin(time);
    F2.u = F1.y;
end FilterInSeries;
```

Modelica Subtyping

The notion of subtyping in Modelica is influenced by the theory of objects (Abadi and Cardelli 1996) The notion of inheritance is separated from the notion of subtyping. According to the definition, a class *A* is a subtype of a class *B* if class *A* contains all public variables declared in the class *B*, and types of these variables are subtypes of the types of corresponding variables in *B*. For instance, the class `TempResistor` is a subtype of `Resistor`.

```
class Resistor
     extends TwoPin;
     parameter Real R;
 equation
     v = R * i;
end Resistor;

class TempResistor
     extends TwoPin;
     parameter Real R, RT, Tref;
     Real T;
equation
     v = I * (R+RT * (T - Tref));
end TempResistor;
```

Subtyping is used for example in class instantiation, redeclarations and function calls. If variable a is of type *A*, and *A* is a subtype of *B*, then a can be initialized by a variable of type *B*.

Note that `TempResistor` does not inherit the `Resistor` class. There are different equations for the evaluation of `v`. If equations are inherited from `Resistor` then the set of equations will become inconsistent in `TempResistor`, since Modelica currently does not support named equations and replacement of equations. For example, the specialized equation below from `TempResistor`:

```
v=i*(R+RT*(T-Tref))
```

and the general equation from class Resistor

```
v=R*i
```

are inconsistent.

Modelica Connections and Connectors

Equations in Modelica can also be specified by using the `connect` statement. The statement `connect(v1, v2)` expresses coupling between variables. These variables are called connectors and belong to the connected objects. Connections specifies interaction between components. A connector should contain all quantities needed to describe the interaction. This gives a flexible way of specifying topology of physical systems described in an object-oriented way using Modelica.

For example, Pin is a connector class that can be used to specify the external interfaces for electrical components that have pins. Each Pin is characterized by two variables, voltage and current. A connector class is defined as follows:

```
connector Pin
     Voltage v;
     flow Current i;
end Pin;
```

Connection statements are used to connect instances of connection classes. A connection statement `connect(Pin1,Pin2)`, with Pin1 and Pin2 of connector class Pin, connects the two pins so that they form one node. This implies two equations, namely:

```
Pin1.v = Pin2.v; Pin1.i + Pin2.i = 0
```

Implementation of the Modelica Simulation Environment

The simulation of a Modelica model involves some preparatory stages. The diagram in Figure 1 shows how a typical simulation works.

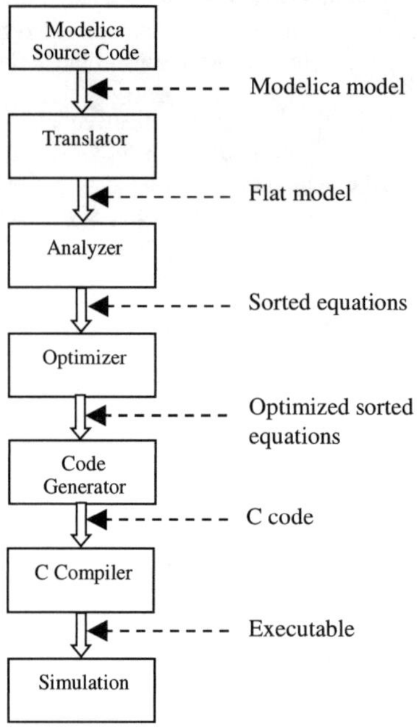

Figure 1Translation stages leading to a simulation of a Modelica model

One should note that the simulation models are expressed in declarative form and not in procedural form. The declarative form cannot be used directly for simulation. Thus, it is necessary to manipulate it in a way in which the procedural form is further generated. Classes, instances and equations are translated into a flat set of equations, constants and variables.

After flattening, all the equations are topologically sorted according to the data dependencies. Simplification algorithms remove most equations. If two syntactically equivalent equations appear, only one copy of the equations is kept.

Then independent equations are converted to assignment statements. If a strongly connected set of equations appears, this set is transformed by a symbolic solver which performs a number of algebraic transformations to simplify the dependencies between the variables. It can also solve a system of differential equations if it has a symbolic solution. Finally, C code is generated, and linked with a numeric differential and algebraic equation solver.

The initial values can be taken from the model definition. If necessary, the user specifies the parameter values. Numeric solvers for differential equations (such as LSODE, part of ODEPACK) give the user the possibility to view about the values of specific variables at a specific moment in time. As the result functions of time can be computed for a time interval $[t_0, t_1]$ and displayed as a graph or saved in a file. This data presentation is the final result of a dynamic system simulation.

In most cases (but not always) the performance of generated simulation code (including the solver) is similar to hand-written C code. Often Modelica is more efficient than straightforwardly written C/C++ code, because additional opportunities for symbolic optimization are used.

A Modelica simulation terminates when the simulation clock exceeds the specified simulation horizon (the time period over which the model is to be simulated).

From the debugging point of view after equation flattening the hierarchy of models is not preserved and any concept of data and equation dependency may be lost or at least obscured. Some of the error messages generated after this phase by the Modelica simulation environment are meaningless for the user.

For example the following Modelica `model`:

```
model A
    Real x,y;
equation
    x = 2 * y;
end A;

model B
    A a;
    Real x[10];
equation
    x[5] = a.y;
end B;
```

is translated to following equations:

```
B.a.x = 2 * B.a.y
B.x[5] = B.a.y
```

The structure is mostly lost, but the variable names in the output give an hint about their origin.

The translator translates from Modelica source code to an internal representation of the resulting set of equations in order to adapt the equations to the optimizer and to the code generator. It should be noted that the flat Modelica representation is not at all adapted for debugging purposes. For the proposed debugging framework another internal representation should be created.

One future goal will be to create a usable and efficient translator which should be able to transform the Modelica code into a more flexible internal form supporting debugging related information. One possible approach would be to use a compiler generation system, e.g. RML, to produce a Modelica translator from natural semantics specifications with added debugging information and functionality (Kågedal and Fritzson 1998).

Currently there are two design and simulation environments for Modelica: the Dymola tool with Modelica Language Support developed by Dynasim and Mathmodelica developed by MathCore. The MathModelica is an extension of the Modelica modeling language with the main goal to work within the Mathematica environment (Fritzson et al. 1998). The environment use extensively the principles of literate programming (Knuth 1984) and integrates most activities needed in simulation design: modeling, symbolic processing, transformation and formula manipulation, input and output data visualization. A first debugger implementation should target first the MathModelica environment because of the easy access to the intermediate form of the code and most operations that require information about model structuring are implemented in a nice and secure way. Since MatModelica works with the Mathematica environment the possibility of building an incremental debugger for this environment must to be considered

ARISING DIFFICULTIES WHEN DEBUGGING EQUATION BASED LANGUAGES

In this section, we first discuss declarative equation based programming languages and the consequences equation based programming has for debugging. At the same time we examine the particular debugging problems posed by the Modelica modeling language. Equation based declarative programming presents new challenges in the design of programming environments.

Actually, there exist two independent parts in most equation based languages.

- The algorithmic part which may be debugged using traditional debugging techniques. This part is similar to a conventional programming language.
- The equation part for which traditional debugging facilities are useless

Based on this structure of the language we should note that it is impossible to test or debug using only one debugging technique for the whole source code. The proposed debugging framework should contain different approaches to different parts of the source code in order to correctly locate the error.

At the first stage an automatic static analysis is performed on the source code in order to check for declaration errors. This is already done by the Modelica compiler. Next, each algorithmic section of the source code should be debugged using traditional debugging techniques. The algorithmic debugging may have to be performed simultaneously with the equation validation debugging.

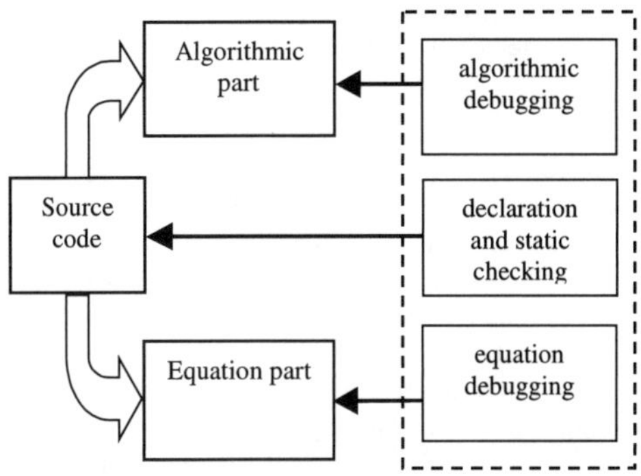

Figure 2. Source code decomposition and debugging frameworks subsystems.

Traditional Debugging Techniques.

The application of algorithmic debugging techniques (Shapiro 1982) and generalized algorithmic debugging techniques (Fritzson et al 1992) to the evaluation of structural procedural languages is an approach which has found increased applicability over the past years. In order to use these approaches successfully on the algorithmic part of an equation based language we must pay close attention to methodological issues, both in order to ensure the generality of this approach to this part of the language and to ensure a communication with other debugging techniques used for the equation part of the language. To ensure the above mentioned communication between different debugging techniques for different parts of the language, presents a major challenge in our research.

Traditional approaches to debugging are inadequate and inappropriate to solve the error location problem in equation based languages. The fundamental problem is that conventional debuggers and debugging techniques are based on observation of execution events as they occur.

Even nontraditional declarative debugging techniques such as the above mentioned algorithmic debugging method, are inadequate for equation-based languages. In order to see this, consider invoking an algorithmic program debugger (Shapiro 1982) on a functional/logic program after noticing an external symptom of a bug. The debugger executes the program and builds a trace execution tree at the function level while saving some useful trace information such as function names and input/output parameter values. In other words, the algorithmic debugging method is dependent on the use of functions and function calls in the language. In the case of declarative equation based languages, there is no clear execution tree and the inputs and outputs are not clearly stated inside the model. Therefore using an algorithmic debugging technique is useless.

One of the most commonly generated error messages by the Modelica compiler is the "missing equation", which means that the overall model is unsolvable due to a wrong stated or missing equation in one of the submodels. The "missing equation" is detected very late in the compilation phase, after the equation flattening. In that case it is impossible to confirm a fault location because of the lack of detail and formal specifications at this level. A typical generated error message is shown below:

```
DAE with 12 unknown scalars and 11 scalar
equations.
Error: Model is singular:
The number of non-trivial (scalar) equations is 9.
The number of (scalar) variables is 10
Translation aborted
Error: 1 error was found.
```

The error message is a very general one, and it is very hard to derive the exact location of the "missing equation" in the submodel in order to eliminate the fault. The failure symptoms and a correct equation oriented dependency analysis should be used by the debugger to confirm the location of the fault. One solution will be to build an equation data flow dependency graph.

In conclusion we can take a look on why errors are hard to find in a declarative equation based language:

- There is a cause-effect gap between the time or space when an error occurs and the time when the error becomes apparent to the programmer.
- The acausality of the language eliminates the use of program traces as a debugging guide.
- The transformation process from the declarative form to the procedural form looses or obscures a lot of model structure information which might be useful for debugging purposes.
- Even in a highly structured system which uses extensively hierarchical and modular simulation models surprise and unreliability occur because the human mind is not able to fully comprehend the many conditions that can arise mainly because of the interactions of the components.
- Debugging is in some sense harder to perform on a declarative equation based language because much run-time debugging must be replaced by compile-time static checking.

Connection checking and debugging.

At the connection checking level we need a set of rules and or functions which can look for inconsistencies. In the Modelica modeling language a set of connection rules has been identified in the specific libraries in which there are very strict rules. Therefore it is possible to specify domain knowledge within the reusable model components. For example, in the mechanical library there are constraints on connecting objects together.

Fault recognition techniques help the programmer formulate hypotheses about fault location and identity. The problem of this approach is the incompleteness of any knowledge base of faults (Viravan 1994).

A knowledge base of common fault patterns should be incorporated into the debugger framework. This approach to a particular library with the generated compiler error message will form a cooperative problem solving environment, where the debugger library oriented expertise to error pattern matching and the knowledge base incorporated in the debugger work together to find the fault.

A common approach to this problem is to use a fault localization tool such as a program slicing tool and a fault recognition tool used as a pattern matching tool (Viravan 1994).

A further goal related to this part is to investigate how a test data set and other domain knowledge can enhance the debugging .

Assertion Derivation.

One of the Modelica language built-in debugging features is the use of the assertion statement which provides an automatic assertion at simulation time. The intent is to execute a model and to report the failed assertion to the user if the expression evaluates to false. The means of reporting a failing assertion are dependent on the simulation environment and are sometimes dependent on the particular behavior of an application model.

In the current Modelica implementation no assertion derivation techniques is implemented so the user does not have the possibility to backtrack through the history of derivations in order to correctly locate the bug. When an assertion is evaluated to false the current evaluation of the model is stopped and an error message is generated. This can save the modeler from examining large traces of simulated code. It is a quality of implementation issue to generate a good error message if the assertion fails.

The proposed debugging framework should provide a mechanism for automatic assertion derivation in order to correctly locate a bug.

SUMMARY AND CONCLUSIONS

The declarative approach of the Modelica language is very useful in model building for simulation applications. To simulate declarative models further model manipulations are necessary in order to generate the low level executable procedural form.

This paper presents our view on the issues and some solution proposals regarding the proposed debugging framework for declarative equation based languages. From the literature and from the actual implementation of some declarative equation based languages we can notice that not a single system can deal with the whole debugging problem. Further research should deal with the problem of how different debugging technologies can interact with each other for the overall validation and debugging of simulation models expressed in equation based declarative languages.

Though the methodology approach shows some promising results, there is much work to be done. Currently, an extension of the Modelica internal representation in order to support a debugging framework is underway.

The presented work is planned to be extended in several ways. We plan to build a prototype implementation of our debugging framework first for the Modelica modeling language and then gradually extending our approach to other equation based languages. Writing a complete debugging environment for a declarative equation based language requires a set of techniques which are qualitatively and quantitatively different from other techniques used to debug traditional languages.

We intend to include more user interaction in the debugging process because the automatic fault correction may be constrained by the specific domain knowledge incorporated in the language domain libraries. By using an advanced debugging framework, simulation practitioners should be in a position to build models faster and use debugging tools during the model development process, and be more confident than the models they build reflect system complexities precisely as intended.

There is no lack of problems in debugging declarative equation based languages and the growing use of these languages in simulation practice make the need for a debugging framework obvious and urgent.

REFERENCES

Abadi, M. and L. Cardelli. 1996. "A Theory of Objects." Springer Verlag, ISBN 0-387-94775-2.

Allan, B.A.; V. Rico-Ramirez; M. Thomas; and K. Tyner. 1996. "ASCEND IV - A Portable Mathematical Modeling Environment." ICES Technical Report. Carnegie-Melon University. (Oct).

Andersson, M. H. I. 1994. "Object-Oriented Modeling and Simulation of Hybrid Systems." PhD thesis ISBN LUTFD2 / TFRT--1043—SE. Department of Automatic Control, Lund Institute of Technology, Lund, Sweden.

Breunese, A.P. and J.F. Broenik. 1994. "Modeling mechatronic systems using the SIDOPS language." In *Proceedings of ICBGM'97, 3rd International Conference on Bond Graph Modeling and Simulation, Simulation Series,* (Vol.29, No.1). The Society for Computer Simulation International., 301-306.

Broy, M. 1991. "Declarative specification and declarative programming." In *Proceedings of the Sixth International Workshop on Software Specification and Design.*, 2 –11.

Elmqvist, H. 1978. "A Structured Model Language for Large Continuous Systems." PhD thesis TFRT-1015, Department of Automatic Control, Lund Institute of Technology, Lund, Sweden. 1978.

Elmqvist, H.; S. E. Mattsson and M. Otter. 1999. "Modelica - A Language for Physical System Modeling, Visualization and Interaction." In Proceedings of the 1999 IEEE Symposium on Computer-Aided Control System Design (Hawaii, Aug. 22-27).

Fritzson P.; N. Shahmehri; M. Kamkar; and T. Gyimothy. 1992 "Generalized Algorithmic Debugging and Testing." *ACM Letters on Programming Languages and Systems 1*, NO.4 (Dec): 303-322.

Fritzson, P.; L. Viklund.; D. Fritzson; J. Herber. 1995 "High-Level Mathematical Modelling and Programming". *IEEE Software 12* NO. 4 (Jul.): 77-87.

Fritzson P.; V. Engelson; J. Gunnarsson. 1998. "An Integrated Modelica Environment For Modeling, Documentation and Simulation." In *Proceedings of the 1998 Summer Computer Simulation Conference* (Reno, Nevada, USA, July 19-22).

Fritzson P and V. Engelson. 1998. "Modelica, A Unified Object-Oriented Language for System Modeling and Simulation." In *Proceedings of ECOOP'98 (the 12th European Conference on Object-Oriented Programming)*(Brussels, Belgium, Jul. 20-24).

IEEE. 1997. "Standard VHDL Analog and Mixed-Signal Extensions." Technical Report IEEE 1076.1. IEEE.

Jeandel, A.; F. Boudaud; P. Ravi ER; and A. Buhsing. 1996. "U.L.M: Un Langage de Modélisation, a modelling language." In *Proceedings of the CESA'96 IMACS Multiconference.* (Lille, France).

Kågedal, D. and P Fritzson. 1998. "Generating a Modelica Compiler from Natural Semantics Specifications". *In Proceedings of Summer Computer Simulation Conference* (Reno, Nevada, USA, Jul. 19-22).

Kloas, M.; V. Friesen; and M. Simons. 1995. "Smile — A simulation environment for energy systems." In *Proceedings of the 5th International IMACS-Symposium on Systems Analysis and Simulation* Vol. 18–19 of Systems Analysis Modeling Simulation, Gordon and Breach Publishers., 503-506.

Knuth, D.E. 1984. "Literate Programming" *The Computer Journal,* NO27(2) (May): 97-111.

Modelica Association 1999. *Modelica – A Unified Object-Oriented Language for Physical Systems Modeling - Tutorial and Design Rationale Version 1.2*(Dec).

Modelica Association 1999. *Modelica – A Unified Object-Oriented Language for Physical Systems Modeling – Language Specification Version 1.3.* (Dec).

Parasoft. 1997. "It's a Bug-free World After All." Technical Paper PS-9710-DV3.

Piela, P.; T. Epperly; K. Westerberg; and A. Westerberg. 1991. "ASCEND: An object-oriented computer environment for modeling and analysis: the modeling language." Computers and Chemical Engineering 15, NO.1 :53–72.

Sahlin, P.; A. Bring; and E.F. Sowell. 1996. "The NeutralModel Format for Building Simulation, Version 3.02." Technical Report. Department of Building Sciences, The Royal Institute of Technology, Stockholm, Sweden.

Shapiro Ehud Y. 1982. *Algorithmic Program Debugging.* MIT Press (May).

Viravan, C. 1994. "Enhancing Debugging Technology". Ph.D. dissertation, Purdue University.

A METHOD FOR AN EMBEDDED EXPLANATION SUBSYSTEM FOR SIMULATION SYSTEMS: A PROPOSAL FOR AN INTELLIGENT SIMULATION ENVIRONMENT.

Mhamed Itmi [1,2] Ralph Huntsinger [2] Jean-Pierre Pécuchet [1]

(1) INSA de Rouen BP 08
PSI Laboratory
76131 Mt-St-Aignan, France
xxx@insa-rouen.fr

(2) California State University, Chico
Computer Science Department
Chico, California 95929-0410, USA
xxx@ecst.csuchico.edu

KEYWORDS

Explanation, reasoning, simulation, knowledge systems.

ABSTRACT

In this article, we show that an explanatory component in a simulator will help the user to better understand the dynamics of its system. As explanation is a set of themes related to knowledge systems, we discuss it in order to place it within the framework of simulation. An approach to its integration in simulation is presented.

I - INTRODUCTION

The ease and the comfort of use and the efficiency of computerized decision-making systems are increased when these are equipped with means of explanation and dialogue with the user. These means make it possible to mitigate the insufficiencies of communication and give justification of the choices which were made to generate the obtained results. The simulation systems could profit largely from these extensions. They could communicate information on the state of the simulated system and the dynamics that led it there, thus exceeding a simple trace of execution. The interactivity and graphic animation would be also enriched.

The design of an explanatory system makes it possible to improve the comprehension of a calculated situation. With the addition of a dialogue module, interactivity is favored at the same time, reinforcing the acceptance of the system by the users. These points of view find their origins in Artificial Intelligence (AI) where the same problems have been posed. The fields of dialogue and explanation in Knowledge Based Systems (KBS) were a great success.

In this paper we are interested in explanation in a simulation system. It gives the user the possibility of asking the system explanations as if he/she was dealing with a human expert. That would enable him/her to be ensured of the competence of the system and thus to accept or dispute its results. After having pointed out the links with AI, we will propose an architecture for such a system. We will not be interested here in the search considerations concerned with the dialogue and natural language.

II - THE EXPLANATION IN KBS AND SIMULATION SYSTEMS

1- The usual explanation in simulation systems

One wishes to answer questions of the type: why, why not, how or what? Criticisms were formulated on the explanatory inefficiency of simulation systems. One can summarize them in three points (Belattar 1997; Laraba 1999):

- Case of graphic animation: the observation of the dynamic behavior of the system allows, at least, to increase the confidence of the users in the proposed solution. It also presents the disadvantages due to the requirements in memory and calculations, moreover it does not take into account the state changes in the system according to the simulator's choices.
- The trace constitutes an accurately reflecting explanation of the dynamics of the simulated system. However, it is a heavy and rudimentary tool to answer the questions of the user. During experimentation in simulation, choices are made by the simulator and never appear in the results.
- Interactivity: it is noted that when it is possible, it does not make it possible to answer questions explaining the choices of the simulator such as "how?" or "Why?"

2- The explanation in the KBS

The explanation improves the ease of communication of a KBS with the user. The system produces information justifying the reasoning followed to arrive to a given result. One can for example read in (Greboval 1994) points of view on the modeling of the explanatory reasoning within the framework of the Expert System. In (Swartout and Moore 1993), the ability to be explained makes the system more transparent and thus facilitates its acceptance by the user. According to (Swartout and Moore 1993), it is a process of construction of a coherent history linking the concepts and results of the system to what the user understands and accepts. The explanation is a complex task requiring reasoning and proper knowledge. In (Paris & al. 1988; Wick and Thompson 1989) one distinguishes the line of reasoning from the line of explanation. The first is comparable with the trace of execution, i.e. the recording of the steps of inference carried out by the system from the input data to the conclusion. The second consists of steps of inference suggested to the user in order to convince him/her that the solution obtained by the system is correct. These two lines must arrive from two distinct processes: one is used for the resolution of problems and the other to produce explanations. The systems that present the trace of the execution as an explanation confuse these two lines. We believe that these approaches for explanation in the KBS are useful in simulation systems.

III - TOWARDS THE DEVELOPMENT OF THE EXPLANATION IN SIMULATORS

1- General point of view

One can approach the explanation in two different ways:
- The first is based on the trace of the execution (explanation by introspection). In this case, the system must extract the necessary information for explanation.
- The second manner seeks to rebuild the explanation (explanation by concocting). Even if it uses the trace results, it requires an independent reasoning of the trace. It is a new problem resolution.

An explanatory module is necessary for the development of this explanation. It will have to consider various types of explanations: to make a synthesis of the followed reasoning, to provide " rebuilt " explanations, etc...

2- Modeling of the explanatory reasoning

Explanatory information that will be presented to the user must have an internal representation. This internal representation should be based on one of the three approaches of the modeling of the explanatory reasoning:
- Ascending approaches or explanation driven: They leave the trace of the resolution of a problem to transform it, adapt it or enrich it. The transformation of the object to be explained is made possible thanks to the relational representations used.
- Downward approaches or directed by the goals explanation: One wishes to present an explanatory speech to the user. Its plan is conceived in a downward way by the decomposition of the goals of speech in sub-goals until obtaining the primitives of speech. The sub-goals are generally associated with the intentions of the speech.

- Hybrid approaches: They combine the preceding approaches in order to cure their weaknesses: these are insufficiency of explanatory strategies of the trace and not taking into account the explanation currently in construction.

3- Basic knowledge for the explanation process

In (Paris & al. 1988) two kinds of principal knowledge are highlighted:

- Linguistic knowledge: this is necessary for the task of explanation. They relate to the language and explain its use.
- Knowledge of the field: it is those which are necessary to the problem resolution and explanation. They are not necessarily used in the phase of problem resolution.

One can also add to this knowledge those which relate to the model of the user and to the knowledge of strategy or control. These last are required to be able to explain the reasoning which has been used.

IV - APPROACH FOR AN EXPLANATORY MODULE IN SIMULATION

We can proceed in two manners:

a- By the addition of explanatory components to an existing system of simulation.

b- By the realization of a simulation system integrating the environment of explanation.

In (Belattar 1997), each component of the first case is an expert system using one or more knowledge bases. From our point of view, this way raises difficulties primarily related to the ignorance of the system control. Indeed, even if we can have a trace, the system operates like a black box. It will not allow the explanatory component to approach the knowledge of strategy. For example, in a situation of routing of a given resource, the trace will provide the rough history of the routing. The knowledge of " Why? " in this routing will not be answered. It is the case with the Petri net of the figure 1 below. The resource "token" will be consumed after the firing of one from the three transitions X, Y or Z. One or more tokens will be produced in the places at the output of these transitions. One could preserve the trace of it. For the explanation, it would be necessary to have the strategy adopted for the resolution of the conflict. We considered here the Petri net as a formal model used in the internal representation of the system. Even if it would be the effective tool for simulation, the problem would remain posed. Indeed, it is well-known that the Petri net graph of representation of a real situation becomes complex. Seeing the run of the tokens one will not be able to answer questions such as " Why transition Z was selected? " or " Why not choose transition X? "

In the b) case above, there are systems based primarily on techniques of AI. In (Sharma 94) the system suggested adopts this approach. An approach of integration as that of (Zeigler 96) which makes it possible to define an expert system as a component of the simulation model. The problem of control must be taken into account to work out the explanation.

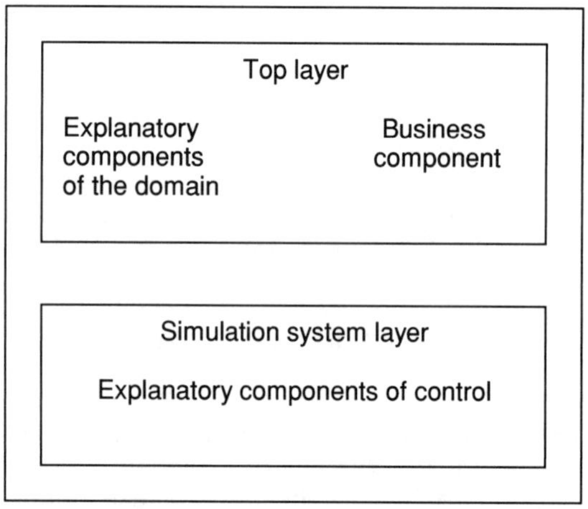

Figure 1 : Cas d'un conflit

A model of explanatory knowledge was presented in (Laraba 1999). It was inspired by the KADS method (Knowledge Acquisition Design Structuring, see (Wielingra et al. 1992)). This model includes three layers of explanatory conceptual models:

- The first models constructive knowledge (explanatory strategies, explanatory principles and knowledge of control).
- The second models contextualized knowledge (trace of the reasoning, knowledge of the field) and generators (linguistic knowledge and contained basic explanation).
- The third models contextual knowledge (the trace of the explanatory reasoning and history of the dialogue) and of co-operation (to determine the role of the system and the user in the development of the explanation).

We propose in figure 2 below, a diagram simplified for the architecture of an explanatory system of simulation. It is presented in two layers according to the point of view of the software components. The first corresponds to the components relating to the business. Second is in fact the concatenation of other layers (system components, communication...). We have named it the simulation system layer.

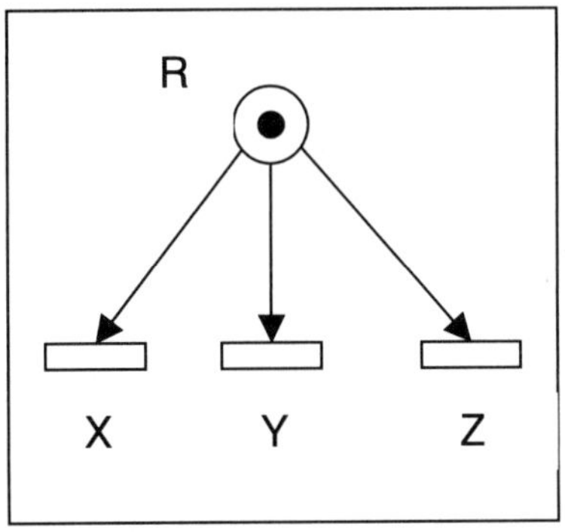

Figure 2: A simplified architecture for an explanatory simulator

We saw that to work out the explanation, we need " raw material ". We focus on the "matter" coming from control and the "matter" coming from the field. The higher layer corresponds to the business level. We will put the knowledge from the field there. It will vary according to the field of application of the simulation system. The simulation system layer will be specialized in the knowledge of control. It comes from the management of queues, strategies of resolution... The conceptual models suggested today are often based on multi-agent systems: specific knowledge will be necessary to explain, for example, the results due to a co-operation of agents... It may also be interesting to explain a concept badly understood by the user.

IV - CONCLUSION

In this paper we show the need to have an explanatory module for simulation. This module makes the simulation system be an explanatory knowledge based system. Then, it will be possible to justify the choices operating during the calculations. An outline of architecture for the explanatory system is proposed. Its refinement in terms of software components is under development.

REFERENCES

Belattar, B., 1997. "Apports de l'Explication en Simulation" In *Proceedings of the 1st MOSIM conference* (Rouen, France, June 1997). Editions HERMES, 527-537.

Laraba, E.H., 1999. "SIMEX : Une Architecture de Tâches pour un Simulateur Explicatif" In *Proceedings of the 2nd MOSIM conference* (Annecy, France, October 1999). SCS Publications, 231-235.

Paris, C.L., Wick M.R., Thompson W.B., 1988. "The Line of Reasoning Versus The Line of Explanation." In *Proceedings of the AAAI Workshop on Explanation*, (St-Paul, USA, 1988), 4-7.

Swartout, W.R. & Moore, J. 1993. "Design for explainable Expert Systems." *In IEEE Expert*, vol. 6, no. 3, 1991

Wick M.R. & Thompson W.B. 1989. "Reconstructive Explanation: Explanation as Complex Problem Solving." In *Proceedings of IJCAI*, (Detroit, USA, 1989). 135-140.

Greboval M.H. 1994. "La Production d'Explications, Vue Comme une Tâche de

Conception: Contribution au Projet Aide" Phd thesis. Université de Technologie de Compiegne. France. 1994.

G. Sharma, R.G.S. Asthana, S. Goel, 1994. "A knowledge based simulation approach for train operation and planning" In *Simulation* Vol. 62, N°6, Juin 1994. SCS Publications, 381-391.

B.J. Wielinga, A. Th. Shreiber, J.A. Breuker, 1992. "KADS: a modeling approach to knowledge engineering". In *Knowledge Acquisition*, Vol. 4, no 1, 1992.

Bernard P. Zeigler, Tae H. Cho, Jerzy W. Rozenblit, 1996. "A knowledge based simulation Environment for Hierarchical Flexible Manufacturing" *IEEE Transactions on Systems, Man, And Cybernetics, Part A: Systems and Humans*, Vol. 26, N°1, Janvier 1996. 81-90.

AN INTEGRATED SPREADSHEET APPROACH TO SIMULATION INTERFACES

James F. Leathrum, Jr., Roland R. Mielke, and Taylor Frith
Virginia Modeling, Analysis and Simulation Center
Old Dominion University

ABSTRACT

If the base simulation code is removed from a simulation, the remaining effort is data oriented. Generally the effort can be characterized by a user interface, input analysis, output analysis, and database access. Simulation languages (such as MODSIM, SIMAN, Csim) and simulation tools (such as Arena and Promodel) are classically focused on managing entities, time, and possibly animation. Past experiences in simulation development show that an inordinate amount of time and effort is spent on user interface and data management development. A common environment that is language and tool independent is presented to reduce the development effort and create an environment in which simulation users are comfortable. This paper presents the needs requirements for an interfacing effort. It then develops a platform-independent, software architecture to support these needs. Two case studies of the use of the new environment are presented based on a port simulation (PORTSIM) and a traffic analysis simulation (for Busch Gardens – Williamsburg).

INTRODUCTION

If the base simulation code is removed from a simulation, the remaining effort is data oriented. Generally the effort can be characterized by a user interface, input analysis, output analysis, and database access. Simulation languages and simulation tools are classically focused on managing entities, time, and possibly animation. Past experiences in simulation development show that an inordinate amount of time and effort is spent on user interface and data management. A common environment that is language and tool independent is presented to reduce development effort and create an environment in which users are comfortable.

This paper presents the needs requirements for an interfacing effort. It then develops a platform- independent software architecture to support these needs. An implementation of the architecture is described using Excel. Finally, two case studies of the use of the new environment are presented.

PROBLEM DEFINITION

The primary issue addressed in this paper is data management. The flow of information required for a simulation is depicted in Figure 1. Data management is loosely defined to include the following components:

- User Interface – The User Interface allows the user to generate or interact with the data used to drive the simulation. It also allows the user to define the simulation process and view results.
- Internal Data Management – The storage of data and generation of appropriate data to the simulation engine is an important simulation issue.
- Input Analysis – Input analysis provides a mechanism to analyze the input data prior to simulation. This may include the determination of appropriate distributions describing the data or visualization of the data.
- Database Access – Databases provide a convenient mechanism for management of common or shared data. As such, it is common in simulation to have a database component.
- Output Analysis – Data generated by a simulation is frequently in a very raw form. Output Analysis allows this data to be distilled to an understandable form, extracting pertinent information, and preparing it for display back to the user or for passing to an external agent.

These concepts are common across simulations and problems associated with them are solved repeatedly. Each simulation language or tool has its own support environment, often not meeting the needs of the user. Within an organization, it is also desirable to have a consistent interface environment, even if the simulation engines are different

The proposed software architecture attempts to establish a development environment where the construction of the user interface and data management structure is easy, professional, and reusable. It is disconcerting to hear simulation stories about 50,000 lines of simulation code and 50,000 lines of user interface/data management code. The problem is that these efforts frequently require rewriting

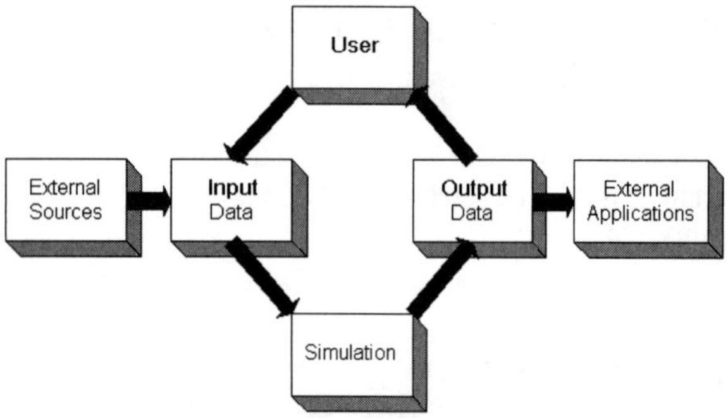

Figure 1. Simulation Process Flow.

standard capabilities prevalent in existing applications that can be reused in the simulation context.

SELECTION OF A DEVELOPMENT ENVIRONMENT

It is proposed here to simply use software tools for what they do well and not continuously reinvent the wheel. Data management is a well-solved problem in spreadsheet and database application tools. Database tools do not generally provide a high level of data analysis like spreadsheet tools. For this reason, a spreadsheet is chosen as the primary development platform for the new environments.

The spreadsheet tool must support the following characteristics: database access (such as ODBC), user interface development, external programming access, and data analysis capabilities. The environment selected for this work is Microsoft Office, primarily to support customer needs and to work in their predefined office environments. Excel provides all of the necessary features, especially through the use of Visual Basic for Applications (VBA) and Forms. However, the architecture is designed for implementation in similar environments such as Star Office. An added benefit to the selection for one customer is the ability to modify the spreadsheet themselves for a customized interface without having to recompile the simulation itself.

SOFTWARE ARCHITECTURE

A spreadsheet based, software architecture is presented for simulation management. Given the system requirements discussed previously, the primary goal of the architecture is easy internal and external management. Internal management refers to the data management (referencing, storage, etc.) internal to the spreadsheet structure. External management refers to the management of information at the file level. Frequently these goals contradict each other.

To minimize file size, common management structures (interface, utilities, etc.) are segmented from the scenario based data. The first incarnation of the spreadsheet based concept kept everything within a single workbook. For a relatively simple interface and data, the Busch Gardens simulation described later required 3 Mbytes per scenario. Since there may be numerous scenarios for a single simulation application, this was unacceptable, prompting the development of a new architecture.

The new architecture is shown in Figure 2. The input user interface is the primary control point. It is where a scenario is defined, the data is input to the simulation tool, and the output user interface is activated. It also manages the flow of data. Each component in the architecture is described in more detail.

Input User Interface

The primary focus of the Input User Interface is to handle input data required for a scenario. However, the Input User Interface also controls the simulation process, routing data to the appropriate repository and activating the simulation process. Where necessary, input data analysis may be required. Data may be historical and require

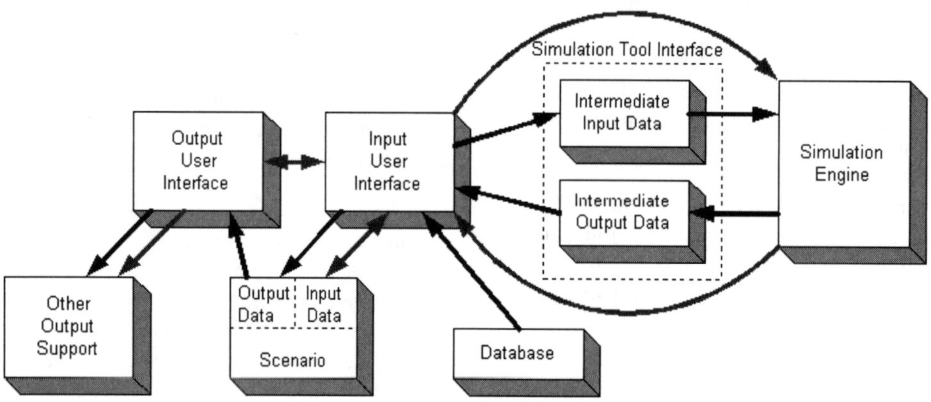

Figure 2. Software Architecture.

conversion to appropriate distributions, or users may require the ability to construct complex distributions. The Input User Interface may also be required to manage multiple simulation runs in order to generate statistically meaningful output if the simulation engine does not handle it directly.

Current development focuses on a Web page based look and feel, a request made by MTMCTEA for the PORTSIM project discussed later. The intent is to put the user in a comfortable environment where he can navigate around the data. Buttons are used for navigation, text for data input and review, and graphs to provide an alternative view of the data or distributions.

Scenario Spreadsheet

The scenario spreadsheet maintains all data specific to a scenario. A separate file is maintained for each scenario, thus reducing the total size of files and simplifying the transfer of information. To keep all information in one file, both input and output data are maintained, though organized internally on separate sheets.

Input data is defined as specific to scenario resulting in a single run or set of runs. It is user defined or the result of default values (pre-populated on scenario creation). The output data is the direct results of the simulation as provided by the simulation tool.

A final management issue for version control is that a scenario is only valid for a specific database version and must be locked to the database. Therefore, the database version must be kept in the spreadsheet and verified by the Input User Interface. An example illustrating this concept from the port simulation described later is that a scenario defines a set of ships to be used. The ship characteristics are kept in the database and referenced by the simulation engine. If an older database is used which does not have all ships of the current version, the scenario will be unable to execute as is.

Database

The database maintains information common across scenarios. It tends to be slowly changing and ideally is not modifiable by the Input User Interface for version control reasons. The importance of data integrity in the database is crucial and cannot be emphasized enough.

Simulation Engine

The simulation engine is the actual simulation. It executes the simulation run, or multiple runs, generating appropriate data. It is also responsible for any run-time animation, a strength of many simulation tools and languages, and not supported in spreadsheets, nor should it be.

Simulation Engine Interface

The Simulation Engine Interface is an intermediate interface to pass data from the Input User Interface to the Simulation Engine and vice versa. Ideally the exchange can be done using existing structures such as Visual Basic for Applications (VBA), but may have to take the form of in intermediate data form such as a flat text file. The cases when an intermediate data form is required are:

- the Simulation Engine does not support a direct interface to the spreadsheet (VBA, etc.), and
- the Simulation Engine was developed prior to the inclusion of the new interface structure.

The second point is key in that it is easy to integrate existing simulations to the software architecture using this mechanism. The PORTSIM project as described later is a prime example

Output User Interface

The Output User Interface provides visualization of output data for after action analysis. Modern spreadsheets have powerful visualization capabilities in the form of charts and reports. Graphs can be in the form of line plots, histograms, scatter charts, etc. General reports are enhanced by the ability to sort and hide data. Finally, multiple run analysis is available by use of statistical measures such as confidence intervals.

Other Output Support

Other support may supply capabilities not available in spreadsheets. For example, if after action animation is required then a time log will be required which can be generated to an alternate tool to perform the animation. The need for after action animation arises if the run time speed of the simulation is not conducive to animation or if the animation is the result of analysis from multiple runs.

CASE STUDIES

Two case studies are presented to illustrate the use of the software architecture and spreadsheet environment to support simulation development. They are developed in different simulation environments to support varying levels of effort. The PORTSIM project is a seaport simulation while the Busch Gardens project is a traffic flow analysis.

PORTSIM Project

Model Description. The Port Simulation (PORTSIM) system is a discrete-event simulation that facilitates the

Figure 3. PORTSIM Main Screen.

analysis of movements of military unit equipment through worldwide seaports and allows for detailed infrastructure analysis. The seaports under consideration tend to be commercial operations where complete access to all port facilities is not feasible. PORTSIM was designed by modeling the general processes in a port and then allowing the specification of process times and available resources to define a specific port's characteristics. A complete description of the process logic for PORTSIM can be found in (Nevins *et al.* 1998a). Other PORTSIM work appears in (Nevins *et al.* 1998b, Leathrum *et al.* 1997, Leathrum and Frith 2000, Leathrum *et al.* 2000).

PORTSIM assists planners in comparing and selecting ports and it determines port throughput capability and utilization of critical resources. PORTSIM is designed to answer the following questions:

- How long does it take to move equipment and supplies through the seaport (closure)?
- What and where are the potential bottlenecks and limiting resources to movement through the seaport?
- Why are operations not completed by the required time?
- What are the implications if certain seaport resources are constrained or available?

What is the port throughput capability given explicit assumptions on assets, resources, and scenarios?

PORTSIM process modeling addresses two modes of operation. The first mode focuses on embarkation processes and encompasses the major activities of reception, staging, and ship loading. Reception activities include all processes needed to accept cargo items at the entry points to the port and transport those items to the staging areas. The entry points to the port are the gates for highway entry and interchange yards for railway entry. Staging activities encompass all processes necessary to part cargo items in appropriate locations before ship arrival as well as to inspect individual items. Finally, ship loading activities include all processes needed to call forward the cargo items to the berths when whips arrive and to load them onto the ships by means of the appropriate loading method.

The second mode of operation in PORTSIM focuses on debarkation processes and encompasses the major activities of ship unloading, staging, and clearance. Ship unloading activities include all processes needed to offload the vessels that arrive at the berths and transport the cargo to the staging areas. Debarkation staging activities are similar to embarkation staging activities and encompass the parking and inspection of cargo items at the port. Finally, clearance activities allow the cargo items to be moved from the port onto the highway or railway infrastructure. This activity involves the loading of commercial highway assets such as flatbed trucks and chassis as well as the loading of railway assets such as trains made up of flatcars and boxcars.

Simulation Management Development. PORTSIM was originally developed with a radically different user interface/data management structure. (Nevins *et al.* 1998b) The design was driven by the use of SimGraphics (CACI 2000b) which is directly supported by the development language, MODSIM (CACI 2000a), to build the user interface. This interface was deemed inadequate, requiring a redesign. Argonne National Laboratories put in a relatively major effort to develop a Java interface while the Virginia Modeling, Analysis and Simulation Center (VMASC) has put in a minimal effort to develop the structure presented here. The introductory screen is shown in Figure 3.

The first step in developing the system was to organize the data. An analyst wants data organized according to his current operational concern. For example, when considering flatbeds, all characteristics and processing times associated with flatbeds are maintained on a single sheet in the spreadsheet. However, when looking at the port, an analyst may want to look at the gates where one item will be the flatbed processing time. The spreadsheet structure makes it trivial to cross reference this item on multiple sheets.

The database maintains port and ship information. Figure 4 demonstrates the interface to the database for constructing a ship list. The user has easy access to all ship characteristics to make his choices. The actual ship list is scenario dependent, thus is maintained in the scenario spreadsheet, not the database.

The definition of process time parameters in the simulation is actually complicated. The process times are actually complex processes themselves, allowing for multimodal distributions, ordered distributions, and blocking distributions (Leathrum et al. 2000, Frank 1999). The

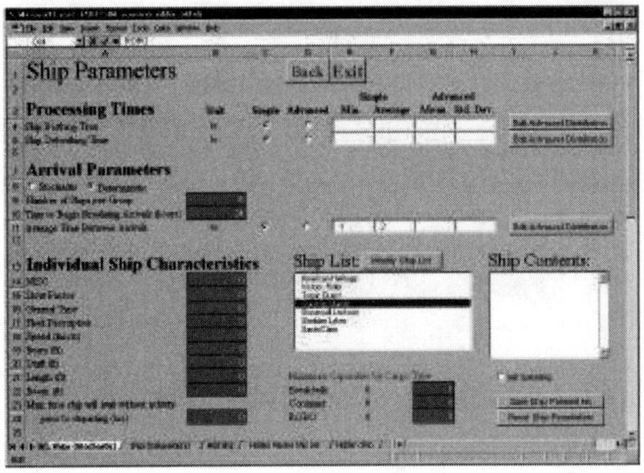

Figure 4. PORTSIM Ship Parameter Selection.

interface to support this has been developed in Excel, but is beyond the scope of this paper.

The original PORTSIM interface involved the construction of a text file to maintain all scenario specific information, obviously an ill suited structure for easy maintenance. The program also generated an output text file for interpretation by application specific software to generate reports (in postscript) and graphs. To avoid a major effort in rewriting the interface between the data and the MODSIM simulation, the scenario text file and output text file have been maintained as the Simulation Engine Interface. When the simulation code is executed, Excel generates the scenario file in the appropriate format, runs the simulation, waits for the simulation to finish, reads the data from the output text file, and saves it in the scenario spreadsheet in an appropriate format.

The output capabilities involve creating reports that can be searched, sorted, and output to Word, and the ability to generate graphs to visualize the data. A level of analysis is done using Excel's capabilities to produce information like confidence intervals. This gives the user information about the likelihood that the simulation will reach a given point within the allotted time.

Busch Gardens

Model Description. Guests arriving at the Busch Gardens - Williamsburg Theme Park regularly obstruct traffic flow on major arteries leading from nearby expressways to the park. The state of Virginia is constructing a new interstate highway interchange, called the Grove Interchange, which will funnel traffic directly from Interstate 64 into the theme park beginning in spring 2000. However, this interchange requires the construction of a new park toll plaza facility and access roads for entering the park, and totally reverses the traffic flow to the existing parking lot system. Simulation presents the opportunity to study the affects of the new system for planning purposes prior to completion of construction. The enterprise simulation described in this paper will be used in the near term to assess and validate system design and proposed new parking strategies. Longer term, the simulation tool will be used to assist in planning operating strategies for park expansion and to rehearse appropriate responses to unusual events such as special entertainment events and in-park vehicle breakdowns. (Mielke 2000)

The immediate concern of the Busch Gardens management staff is to assess if the new parking infrastructure and the proposed parking strategy will perform as expected. It is imperative that arriving park traffic not back up at the toll plaza to the extent that traffic flow on Interstate 64 or US Route 60 is impeded, even for days when customer demand is very high. It also is important that park guests are able to park in a reasonable period of time without experiencing long traffic delays in the approach to the toll plaza or on the service roads leading to the parking lots. Additionally, there is initial concern that the ten-lane toll plaza may not be adequate to accommodate the anticipated traffic flow. Longer term, the management staff desires a decision support tool to assist in planning operating strategies for future park expansion and to rehearse appropriate responses to unusual events such as special entertainment events and in-park vehicle breakdowns. The tool also should support "what if" planning concerning the level and allocation of staffing required to achieve adequate customer service levels.

Simulation Management Development. The Busch Gardens project was VMASC's first endeavor to produce an Excel interface to a simulation. It does not utilize the full software architecture previously described, but demonstrates some other capabilities. The main screen of the simulation is shown in Figure 5. The simulation itself was developed in Arena (Systems Modeling), taking advantage of the flexible development environment and automated animation.

Busch Gardens makes traffic planning decisions based on Virginia Department of Transportation (VDOT) data and internal data, both in crude forms. It was obvious that a user interface in Arena to handle this crude data would likely be cumbersome. Thus the use of Excel was born. Arena also easily supports 2-D animation during run-time. Excel does not support animation, so this component of Arena is maintained.

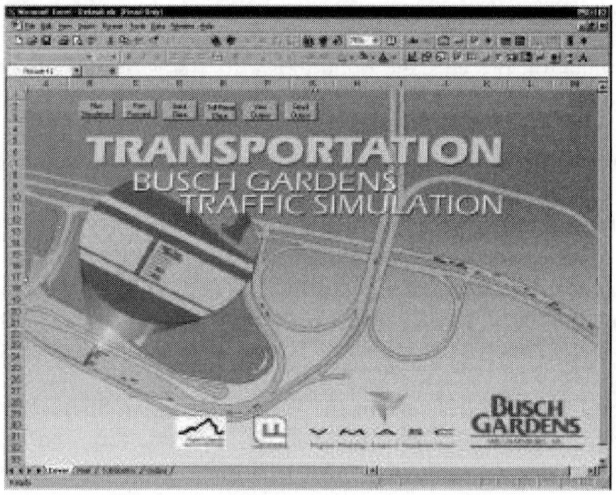

Figure 5. Busch Gardens Main Screen.

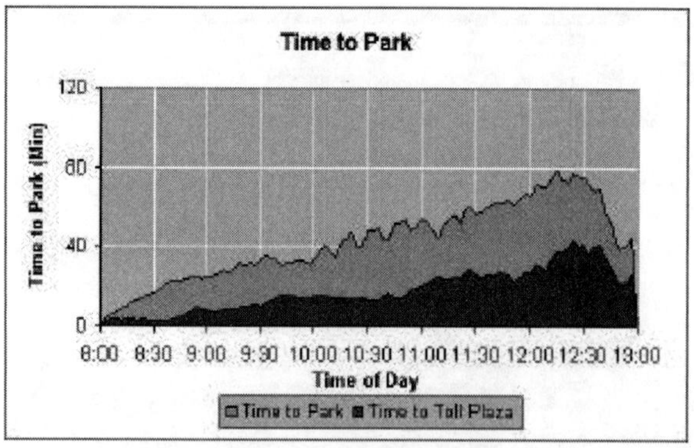

Figure 6. Busch Gardens Output Analysis.

The key difference between the Busch Gardens structure and PORTSIM is the Simulation Engine Interface. Because Arena supports VBA, it was prudent to have arena extract data directly from the Excel spreadsheet. The format of the data used by the simulation is not conducive to the user interface, so internal to Excel, the data is transformed on hidden sheets in preparation for simulation. It was possible on the output side to directly write data into Excel, but due to time constraints, a text file was used to interface Arena's output with Excel.

The Busch Gardens project also demonstrates the benefits of the software architecture. All input data, user interface, output data, and VBA code is maintained in all scenario spreadsheets. The result is very large scenario spreadsheets, on the order of 3 Mbytes per spreadsheet. PORTSIM, on the other hand, requires less than 300 Kbytes per scenario spreadsheet with much more data and more elaborate interfaces.

CONCLUSIONS

The spreadsheet interfaces created for both the PORTSIM project and the Busch Gardens project proved simple to build and provided capabilities to the customers satisfaction. The customers were very comfortable in a spreadsheet environment, and felt like they were not learning a new tool to interface with the simulation (this perception may not have been real, it may have just been a comfort level). The resulting interface has been easy to maintain, and the customer has even been able to modify it themselves to provide feedback (providing a certain level of ability in Excel). The interface has also been proposed to potential future customers of VMASC and the concept has been well received. Thus VMASC is looking to this approach to reduce development time while providing a professional quality interface.

REFERENCES

Nevins, M., C. Macal and J. Joines. 1998. "A Discrete-Event Simulation Model for Seaport Operations." *Simulation* 70, no. 4 (Apr.): 213~223.

Nevins, M., C. Macal, R. Love, and M. Bragen. 1998. "Simulation, Animation and Visualization of Seaport Operations." *Simulation* 71, no. 2 (Aug.): 96~106.

Leathrum, J., R. Mielke, M. Meyer and J. Joines, C. Macal and M. Nevins. 1997. "Strategies for Integrating Commercial and Military Port Simulations," *Proceedings of the 1997 ASEM National Conference*, (Virginia Beach, VA, Oct.), 37~42.

Leathrum, J. and T. Frith. 2000. "A Reconfigurable Object Model for Port Operations," to appear in *Proceedings of the Summer Computer Simulation Conference, SCSC 2000*, (Vancouver, BC, July).

Leathrum, J., T. Frith and P. Frank. 2000. "Simulation Structures for a Reconfigurable Port Model to Support Military Cargo Operations," submitted to *The International Workshop on Harbour, Maritime & Multimodal Logistics Modelling and Simulation*, (Oct.).

CACI, Co. 1999. *MODSIM III, Object-Oriented Simulation, Reference Manual.*

CACI, Co. 1999. *SIMGRAPHICS !! User's Manual.*

Systems Modeling. *Arena Standard.* http://www.sm.com/sim/arena/default.htm

Frank, P. 1999. *A Generic Object-Oriented Random Variate Model for Discrete Event Simulations: Separating the Data Model from the Process Model.* Master's Thesis, Old Dominion University, (December).

Mielke, R., J. Leathrum, M. Rohatgi, K. Kunam, S. Yelamanchi, B. Bacon-Williams, P. Ake, G. Clayton and W. Lugo. 2000. "Busch Gardens Traffic Management Simulation." *Proceedings of the Advanced Simulation Technology Conference - BIS 2000.* (Washington, DC, Apr.): 145~150.

DEVS-BASED MULTI-FORMALISM MODELING AND SIMULATION IN MODELICA.

Peter Bunus, Peter Fritzson
PELAB, Programming Environment Laboratory
Department of Computer and Information Science,
Linköping University, S-581 83, Linköping, Sweden
{petbu,petfr}@ida.liu.se

KEYWORDS

Modelica language, DEVS formalism, Object-oriented simulation, Modeling tools.

ABSTRACT

In a comprehensive modeling and simulation environment, it is desirable to integrate models specified in different modeling formalisms and to extend modeling language constructs to support multi-domain and multi-formalism modeling. This paper discusses a DEVS (Discrete Event System Specification) model library specified in Modelica.

In this paper we present an object oriented implementation of Discrete Event System Specification (DEVS)-based models in Modelica and show how such a discrete formalism can be integrated in the Modelica simulation environment. The developed Modelica reusable library enables the modeler to specify models directly in the DEVS formalism using a graphical editor for connection diagrams. DEVS-based models, atomic, as well as coupled, are defined by Modelica class definitions which specify the model interface, set of states and component systems by data definitions and behavior and couplings by special Modelica class constructs.

A short overview of the DEVS formalism and of the Modelica language constructs and the discrete event simulation capabilities of the language are also given in the paper.

INTRODUCTION

Modelica is a new language for hierarchical object-oriented physical system modeling which is developed through an international effort (Fritzson and Engelson 1998; Elmqvist et al. 1999). The language unifies and generalizes previous object-oriented modeling languages. Modelica is intended to become a *de facto* standard. The language has been designed to allow tools to generate efficient simulation code automatically with the main objective to facilitate exchange of models, model libraries and simulation specifications. It allows defining simulation models modularly and hierarchically and combining various formalisms expressible in the more general Modelica formalism. The multidomain capability of Modelica gives the user the possibility to combine electrical, mechanical, hydraulic, thermodynamic etc. model components within the same application model.

The Modelica capabilities to incorporate multiple modeling formalisms inside the Modelica formalism was demonstrated by using statecharts as a visual formalism for the specification and modeling of complete reactive systems (Ferreira, and Oliveira 1999), bond graphs (Broenink 1997) for modeling the dynamics of physical systems, and Petri nets (Mosterman et al. 1998) as a visual formalisms to model discrete event behavior.

However, many issues of standard discrete event packages have not yet been considered in the Modelica language design such as: queue handling, statistical information gathering, discrete distributed simulation protocols, etc. However, our findings suggest that Modelica has the proper features for expressing discrete-event formalisms that exploit the advantages of the object-oriented paradigm.

Since DEVS offers an expressive framework for modeling, design, analysis and simulation of hybrid systems, the Modelica language simulation capabilities are extended by using the new developed library. The DEVS library implementation in Modelica is intended to serve as a powerful simulator in the Dymola and MathModelica modeling and simulation environments. The use of these environments and the employment of the DEVS formalism allow us to develop cost-effective and safe simulators through using a formal specification paradigm. Also this library implementation serves as a test on the Modelica language versatility for supporting different simulation model formalisms and not just multidomain simulation. The non-causal modeling capability of the language, based on ordinary differential equations (ODE) and differential algebraic equations (DAE) for continuous time is extended by using discrete event modeling in the same application domain.

In this paper, we first give a very brief introduction to DEVS and the consequences discrete modeling formalisms have for modeling language design. At the same time we examine the particular discrete language constructs of Modelica. A brief overview of the Modelica language is also given with an emphasis on the modular and hierarchical modeling facilities of the language. The language features for handling discrete variables and how the variables are changing during simulation will be described. We will also present some basics of the Modelica DEVS library realizations of the modeling concepts and its use is shown through some simulation examples. We conclude with an outlook concerning further development based on the implemented library.

A BRIEF LOOK AT THE DEVS FORMALISM

The Discrete Event System Specification formalisms (DEVS) is one of the basic formalisms for discrete event modeling and also provides a basis for specifying discrete event models in a hierarchical, modular way (Zeigler 1984). DEVS embodies the concepts of system theory and modeling. The hierarchical model development offers advantages such as fast model development, model reuse, and easy model validation and verification. DEVS, a system theory based formalism, provides a formal representation of discrete event systems analogous to the role as differential equations serve for continous systems.

Atomic DEVS models describe the functionality of basic system entities from which larger models are built. Based on (Zeigler 1984) an atomic model with static structure is defined by a 7-tuple:

$M = \langle X, Y, S, \delta_{\text{int}}, \delta_{ext}, \lambda, ta \rangle$ where

- X,Y are the set of input and output values.
- S is a set of sequential states.
- $\delta_{\text{int}} : S \to S$ is the internal state transition function.
- $\delta_{ext} : Q \times X \to S$ is the external state transition function where Q is the total state set defined by $Q = \{(s,e) \mid s \in S, 0 \le e \le ta(s)\}$, e is the time elapsed since the last transition.
- $\lambda : S \to Y$ is the output function
- $ta : S \to \Re^{+}_{0,\infty}$ is the time advance function, defines the time span from one event to next internal event

The interpretation of these elements can be summarized as follows: At any time the system is in some state *s*. If no input value X is received at the input port of the model the system will stay in state s for time $ta(s)$. When the resting time ta expires the output function λ determines the output $\lambda(s)$, and changes to state $\delta_{\text{int}}(s)$. If an external event occurs $x \in X$ before the expiration time $ta(s)$, the external transition function δ_{ext} will specify the next state of the model $s' = \delta_{ext}(s, e, x)$.

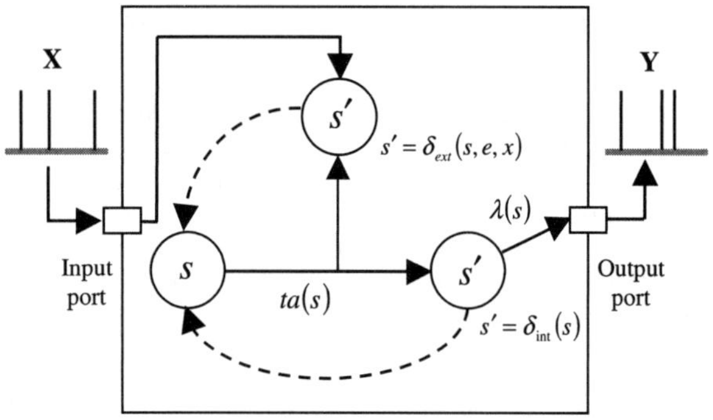

Figure 1. Atomic DEVS behavior and specification.

Several atomic DEVS models can be connected together to form a coupled model. The communication between objects is performed through the coupling mechanism as part of the simulation process.

A coupled DEVS model specification with ports includes the external interface (input, output ports and the values that the messages are carrying) and the coupling requirements which are formally defined as :

$$CM = \langle X, Y, D, \{M_d \mid d \in D\}, EIC, EOC, IC, SELECT \rangle$$

where:

- *X*, *Y* are the set of input and output values.
- *D* is the set of the component names.
  for each $d \in D$ $M_d = \langle X_d, Y_d, S, \delta_{ext}, \delta_{\text{int}}, \lambda, ta \rangle$ is a DEVS.
- *EIC* is the external input coupling (connects external inputs to internal component inputs)
- *EOC* is the external output coupling (connects component outputs to external outputs)
- *IC* is the internal coupling (connects component outputs to component inputs)
- *SELECT* is the tie-breaking function with the main goal to arbitrate between components in case of equal next time event times

Detailed descriptions of the definition of the atomic and coupled DEVS can be found in (Zeigler 1984).

The state behavior of the formalism is event-like. DEVS distinguishes two types of events:

- Internal events – are time scheduled and handled by the internal transition function.
- External events – are handled by the external transition function and occur upon the arrival of an input at one of the input ports.

THE MODELICA MODELING LANGUAGE

Modelica is a new language for hierarchical object-oriented physical modeling which is developed through an international effort effort (Fritzson and Engelson 1998; Elmqvist et al. 1999).

Compared to other modeling languages available today, Modelica offers four important advantages from the simulation practitioner point of view:

- acausal modeling based on ordinary differential equations (ODE) and differential algebraic equations (DAE). There is also, ongoing research to include partial differential equations (PDE) in the language syntax and semantics.
- Multi-domain modeling capability which provides the user with the capability to combine electrical mechanical, thermodynamic, hydraulic etc. model components within the same application model.
- A general type system that unifies object-orientation, multiple inheritance, and templates within a single class construct. This facilitates reuse of components and evolution of models.
- A strong software component model, with constructs for creating and connecting components. Thus the language is ideally suited as an architectural description language for complex physical systems, and to some extent for software systems.

Modelica can be used for mixed continuous and discrete models. The Modelica hybrid features allow modeling of discontinuities, changes in structure, and discrete events in a very reliable way (Mattson et al. 1999). The continuous simulation capabilities of the language is not the subject of this paper. For the discrete part of the language, the synchronous data flow principle with the single assignment rule is employed (Otter et al. 1999).

The reader of the paper is referred to (Modelica Association 1999a) and (Modelica Association 1999b) for a complete description of the language and its functionality. Shorter overviews are available in (Fritzson and Engelson 1998; Elmqvist et al. 1999). Some of the language constructs which emphasize the Modelica language discrete features and the modular and hierarchical modeling facilities of the language will be described in the rest of this section.

Discrete Constructs

In Modelica, there are two different statements to handle discrete changes: the `when` statement which allows modeling of phenomena that occur at a specific time instant, like a change of state variable values, and the `if-then-else` conditional expressions which allow modeling of phenomena with different expressions in different operating regions.

`When` clauses have been introduced in Modelica to express instantaneous equations, i.e. equations that are valid only at certain points, e.g. at discontinuities, when specific conditions become true. The condition of the `when` clause should be a `discrete Boolean` scalar or vector expression and its general form and syntax is shown below.

```
when condition then
   equations
end when;
```

It is also possible to use a vector of conditions instead of only one condition and in such a case the equations are active whenever any of the conditions becomes true.

```
when {condition1, condition2, ...} then
   equations
end when;
```

Modelica Classes

Modelica models are built from classes, like in other object oriented languages. The main difference compared with traditional object-oriented languages is that instead of functions (methods) equations are used to specify the behavior. A class declaration contains a list of variable declarations and a list of equations preceded by the keyword `equation`. An example of a low pass filter in Modelica taken from (Modelica Association 1999b) is shown below.

```
class LowPassFilter
   parameter Real T=1;
   Real u, y (start=1);
equation
   T*der(y) + y = u;
end LowPassFilter;
```

The keyword `parameter` specifies that the quantity is constant during a simulation run, but can change values between runs. This is a very convenient way for the user to modify the behavior of the developed model between simulation runs.

The `LowPassFilter` class can be used to create two instances of the filter with different time constants and "connecting" them together as follows.

```
class FilterInSeries
   LowPassFilter F1(T=2), F2(T=3);
equation
   F1.u = sin(time);
   F2.u = F1.y;
end FilterInSeries
```

While we would like objects to communicate with each other, the communication is performed through the coupling mechanism as part of the simulation process. Modelica defines a special class type called `connector` which is used to declare the structure of connection points and may not contain equations. A connector must contain all quantities needed to describe the model interaction. For example, Pin is a connector class that can be used to specify the external interfaces for electrical components that have pins. Each Pin is characterized by two variables, `v` for voltage and `i` for current. A connector Pin class is defined as follows:

```
connector Pin
   Voltage v;
   flow Current i;
end
```

A common property of many electrical components is that they have two pins. This means that it is useful to define a "blueprint" model class, e.g. called `TwoPin`, that captures this common property. This is a partial class since it does not contain enough equations to completely specify its physical behavior, and is therefore prefixed by the keyword `partial`. Partial classes are usually known as abstract classes in other object oriented languages.

```
partial class TwoPin
   Pin      p, n;
   Voltage  v;
   Current  i;
equation
   v = p.v - n.v;
   p.i + n.i = 0;
   i = p.i;
end TwoPin;
```

The `TwoPin` class has two pins, `p` and `n`, a quantity `v`, that defines the voltage drop across the component and a quantity `i`, that defines the current into pin `p`, through the component, and out from pin `n`.

Equations in Modelica can also be specified by using the `connect` statement. The statement `connect(v1, v2)` expresses coupling between variables. These variables are called connectors and belong to the connected objects. Connections specifies interaction between components. A connector should contain all quantities needed to describe the interaction. This gives a flexible way of specifying topology of physical systems described in an object-oriented way using Modelica.

Connection statements are used to connect instances of connection classes. A connection statement `connect(Pin1, Pin2)`, with `Pin1` and `Pin2` of connector class `Pin`, connects two pins so that they form one node. This implies two equations, namely:

```
Pin1.v = Pin2.v
Pin1.i + Pin2.i = 0
```

DEVS LIBRARY IN MODELICA

Our developed DEVS library was implemented and tested in the MathModelica and Dymola modeling and simulation environments.

The MathModelica modeling environment contains an extension of the Modelica modeling language with the main goal to work within the Mathematica environment (Fritzson et al. 1998). The environment use extensively the principles of literate programming (Knuth 1984) and integrates most activities needed in simulation design: modeling, symbolic processing, transformation and formula manipulation, input and output data visualization.

The Dymola (Elmqvist et al. 1996) and MathModelica simulation environments are built to optimally support the realization of reusable model libraries.

Using the Dymola or MathModelica simulations environments together with the implemented DEVS library removes the need for programming by providing the means for graphical model building with little or no knowledge of the Modelica language syntax. The goal of these environments GUI is to allow the simulation modeler to form a clear mental image of the model's structure and function. Furthermore the MathModelica environment also support literate programming, thus providing a clear and intuitive way of presenting the simulation model.

The Dymola and MathModelica compilers map the modular hierarchical structure into a flattened computer program. This approach is not well suited to simulate systems with complex structure changes (Pawletta and Pawletta 1995) and also is not suitable to debug the simulation model (Bunus and Fritzson 2000), because structure information is lost in the transformation process. One of our future approaches will adapt the simulation environment to the abstract simulation concept (Zeigler 1984) which transform the modular system specifications in computing models in a one to one manner providing in that way an extensive debugging support for the developed library.

DEVS-based models, atomic as well as coupled, are defined by Modelica class definitions which implement the model interface and a set of states. Due to the hierarchical property of the implemented library, users can quickly expand their new developed models.

When developing models and model libraries for a new application domain it is good to start by defining a set of connector classes. A common set of connector classes used in all components in the library supports compatibility of the component models. A DEVS atomic model input or output port connector is defined as follows:

```
connector cconnect
// connector for DEVS input and output ports
   discrete Boolean outp;
end cconnect;
```

The discrete Boolean variable will carry the discrete signal between the models. In order to illustrate the usage of the connector port we can build a wrapper class for the build-in Modelica `sample` operator.

```
model SampleTriggerSignal
// generates sample trigger signals
   cconnect outsignal;
   parameter Real startTime = 0;
   parameter Real period = 1;
equation
   outsignal.outp = sample(startTime,period);
end SampleTriggerSignal;
```

A common property of the most atomic DEVS models is that they have two ports (one input port and one output port) and two state variables (`sigma` and `phase`). At this stage of the modeling phase it is useful to define an "interface" model class that capture the common properties of the two ports atomic DEVS models. Further decompositions are also possible but in order to keep the explanations simple the following interface model is taken into account:

```
partial model DEVSTwoPorts
  cconnect input;     //input port
  cconnect output;    //output port
  discrete Boolean phase(start=true);
       //the model always start in active mode
  Real sigma;
  Real e(start = 0); //elapsed time
equation
  //no equations at the moment
end DEVSTwoPorts;
```

Next we will present a number of DEVS models and discuss their implementation and behavior in order to illustrate the Modelica language discrete modeling capabilities. Our next example implementation will be an atomic DEVS model of a Generator which outputs a sequence of job identifiers with a specific period. The generator has two basic state variables: `phase` and `sigma` and extends the previously presented model `DEVSTwoPorts`. We have also added an input port "stop" to the generator, which when simulated, stops the generator from producing any more outputs as is shown in Figure. 2.

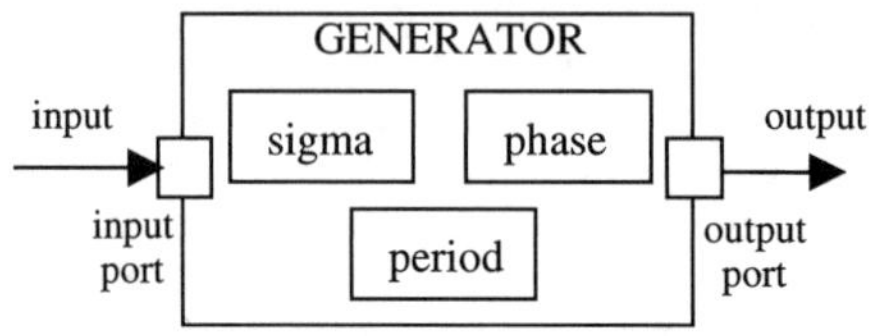

Figure 2. Structure of the DEVS generator.

```
model DEVSStopGenerator
   extends DEVSTwoPorts;

   //the period of the generated output signal
   parameter Real period = 1;
   Boolean internalEvent
   Boolean externalEvent;

   discrete Real prevt;
   Boolean stopActivated(start=false);
equation
   //stop signal received as input
   externalEvent = input.outp;
   internalEvent = sample(0,period);
   when externalEvent then
             stopActivated = true;
   end when;
```

```
   when internalEvent then
            prevt = time;
   end when;
   e = if internalEvent or stopActivated
          then 0 else time - prevt;
   sigma = period - e;

  //internal and external event actions
   when{externalEvent, internalEvent} then
       phase = if edge(externalEvent)
          then phaseExtTransition(pre(phase))
         else phaseIntTransition(pre(phase));
   end when;
   output.outp =
     outputFuncDEVSStop(phase,internalEvent);
end DEVSStopGenerator;
```

In Zeigler's implementation (Zeigler 1990) every DEVS model comunicates with its world through a set of input and output ports. Therefore we defined the set of input and output ports for our mode by using the following port declarations `cconnect input` and `cconnect output`. The DEVSGenerator model use the following utility functions which are applied to the state of the model:

```
function phaseExtTransition
   input Boolean phase;
   output Boolean outphase;
algorithm
   outphase:= false;
end phaseExtTransition;

function phaseIntTransition
   input Boolean phase;
   output Boolean outphase;
algorithm
   outphase:= if phase then true else false;
end phaseIntTransition;

function outputFuncDEVSStop
   input Boolean phase;
   input Boolean internalEvent;
   output Boolean signalOut;
algorithm
   signalOut := if phase and internalEvent
                 then true else false;
end outputFuncDEVSStop;
```

Since `DEVSStopGenerator` is itself a DEVS model it can be tested in a stand-alone fashion or it can be connected to other models. A stop signal generator can be connected to the input port of our generator which generates a stop signal at a given time specified by the `stopTime` parameter value. For testing purposes the following model can be developed:

```
model testDEVSStopGenerator
   //model for testing the DEVSStopGenerator
   DEVSStopGenerator
       stopGenerator(period=1);
   GenerateStopSignal
       stopSignal(stopTime= 6.2);
equation
   connect(stopSignal.outsignal,
                     stopGenerator.inputSet);
end testDEVSStopGenerator;
```

A connection diagram of the simulated models is given in Figure 3 and a plot of simulation results using Dymola is given in Figure 4.

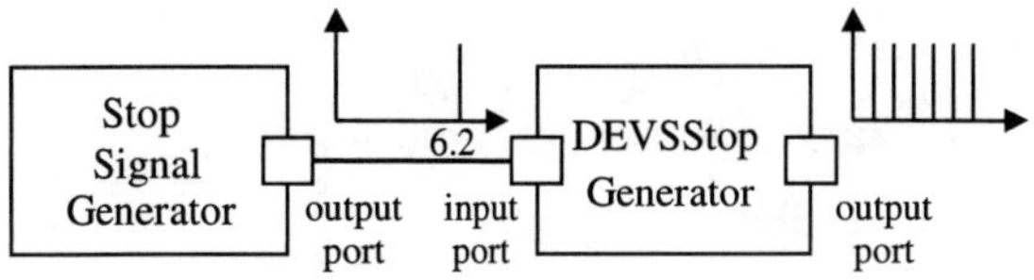

Figure 3. Connection diagram of the DEVSStopGenerator

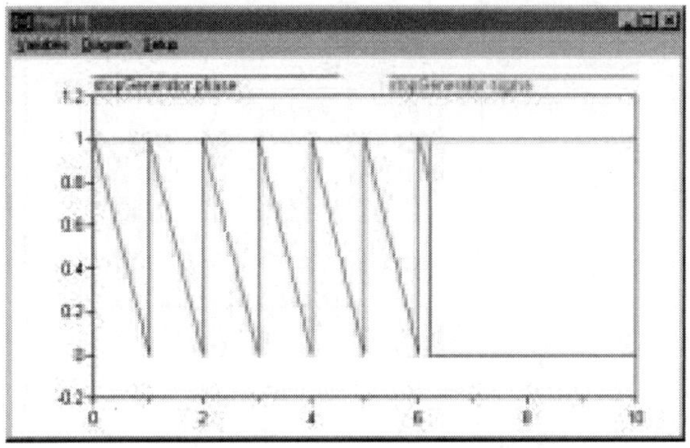

Figure 4. Plot of simulation results using Dymola

The following example shows in part the Modelica realization of a simple DEVS coupled component by placing three simplistic processors in series to form a pipeline (Figure 5.). Generator outputs are considered to be jobs and the processors take some time to process them. Inside the atomic representation of processor model only the time it takes to complete a job is represented, not the detailed manner in which the processing is done. When a processor receives a job, it stores the job and goes into mode "busy". Since the processor has no buffering capabilities, if it is already busy, it ignores incoming jobs. When the processor has finished processing it outputs the job and returns to "passive".

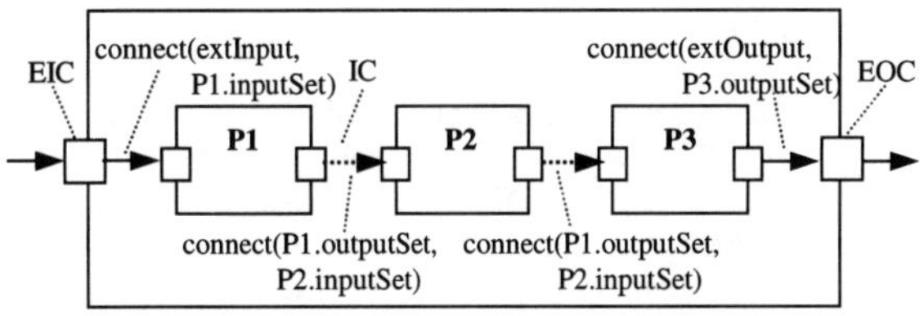

Figure 5. DEVS pipeline coupled model

An implementation of the coupled pipeline DEVS model in Modelica can be described as follows:

```
model DEVSCoupledPipeLine
   cconnect extInput;
   cconnect extOutput;
   DEVSProcessor
         P1(pTime=1),P2(pTime=1),P3(pTime=1);
equation
   connect(extInput,P1.inputSet);
   connect(P1.outputSet, P2.inputSet);
   connect(P2.outputSet, P3.inputSet);
   connect(extOutput,P3.outputSet);
end DEVSCoupledPipeLine;
```

The coupled DEVS pipeline model can be tested by the following model and the trajectories of the simulated model are given in Figure 6.

```
model testCoupled
   DEVSCoupledPipeLine pipeLine;
   DEVSGenerator generator(period=4);
equation
   connect(generator.outputSet,
                          pipeLine.extInput);
end testCoupled;
```

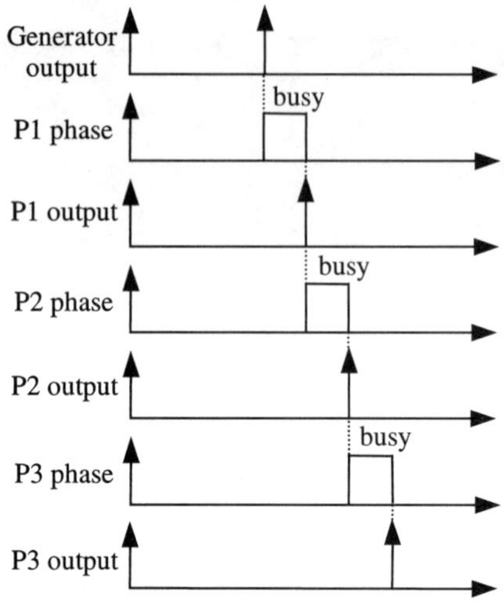

Figure 6. Trajectories for DEVSCoupledPipeLine model

SUMMARY AND FUTURE WORK

We have presented an extensible and reusable DEVS library specification in Modelica. The implemented library exploits concepts from object oriented design and analysis, as well as the DEVS formalism, to support the development of modular and reusable simulation models. The developed library can also be used in the graphical environments of MathModelica and Dymola with drag and drop features, allowing the composition of DEVS models.

Our future work will concentrate on the extension of the developed DEVS library to support multi-formalism combined discrete/continuous (DEVS&DESS) modeling and simulation. The hybrid system modeling and simulation capability of the Modelica language was demonstrated by a series of practical implementations (Mattsson et al. 1999). The equation based approach of the Modelica language has the advantage that a discrete formalism can be easily combined with a formalism based on continuous differential algebraic equations and therefore the implemented DEVS library can be easily extended to the DEVS&DESS formalism. We will also investigate the possibility of building import/export facilities from and to other simulation environments improving in that way the connectivity of the simulation environment.

The goal of this paper was to analyze the Modelica language capabilities in implementing a DEVS library and to test the modeling performance of the Dymola and MathModelica simulation environments in that context.

REFERENCES

Bunus, P.; P. Fritzson. 2000. "The Need for Debugging Tools for Declarative Equation Based Simulation Languages". In *Proceedings of the 2000 Summer Computer Simulation Conference* (Vancouver, B.C. Canada, Jul. 16-20).

Broenink, J.F. 1997. "Bond-graph modeling in Modelica." In *Proceedings of the ESS'97 European Simulation Symposium* (Passau, Germany, Oct. 19-22.).

Elmqvist, H.; S. E. Mattsson and M. Otter. 1999. "Modelica - A Language for Physical System Modeling, Visualization and Interaction." In Proceedings of the 1999 IEEE Symposium on Computer-Aided Control System Design (Hawaii, Aug. 22-27).

Elmqvist, H.; D. Bruck; M. Otter. 1996. *Dymola – User's Manual.* Dynasim AB, Research Park Ideon, Lund.

Ferreira, J.A. and J. P. Estima de Oliveira. 1999. "Modeling Hybrid Systems Using Statecharts and Modelica." In *Proceedings of the 7th IEEE International Conference on Emerging Technologies and Factory Automation* (Barcelona, Spain, Oct. 18-21).

Fritzson P. and V Engelson. 1998. "Modelica - A Unified Object-Oriented Language for System Modeling and Simulation." In *Proceedings of the 12th European Conference on Object-Oriented Programming* (ECOOP'98 , Brussels, Belgium, Jul. 20-24).

Fritzson P.; V. Engelson; J. Gunnarsson. 1998. "An Integrated Modelica Environment For Modeling, Documentation and Simulation." In *Proceedings of the 1998 Summer Computer Simulation Conference* (Reno, Nevada, USA, July 19-22).

Knuth, D.E. 1984. "Literate Programming" *The Computer Journal,* NO27(2) (May): 97-111.

Mattsson, S.E.; M Otter; and H Elmqvist. 1999. "Modelica Hybrid Modeling and Efficient Simulation" In *Proceedings of the 38th IEEE Conference on Decision and Control, CDC'99* (Phoenix, Arizona, USA, Dec 7-10).

Modelica Association 1999. *Modelica – A Unified Object-Oriented Language for Physical Systems Modeling - Tutorial and Design Rationale Version 1.2*(Dec).

Modelica Association 1999. *Modelica – A Unified Object-Oriented Language for Physical Systems Modeling – Language Specification Version 1.3.* (Dec).

Mosterman, P.; M. Otter; and H. Elmqvist. 1998. "Modeling Petri Nets as Local Constraint Equations for Hybrid Systems Using Modelica" In *Proceedings of the 1998 Summer Computer Simulation Conference -98* (Reno, Nevada, USA, July 19-22.).

Otter, M.; H. Elmqvist; S.E. Mattsson. 1999. "Hybrid Modeling in Modelica based on the Synchronous Data Flow Principle" In *Proceedings of the 1999 IEEE Symposium on Computer-Aided Control System Design, CACSD'99* (Hawaii, August 22-27).

Pawletta, T. and Pawletta, S. 1995. "*Simulation of modular hierarchical systems with discrete structure changes.*" In *Proceedings of the 40th Anniversary Conference KoREMA* (Part 1, Zagreb, pages 356 – 359).

Zeigler B.P. 1990. *Object Oriented Simulation with Hierarchical, Modular Models.* Academic Press London.

Zeigler B.P. 1984. *Multifaceted Modeling and Discrete Event Simulation.* Academic Press, London.

Zeigler B.P. 1976. *Theory of Modeling and Simulation.* John Wiley, New York.

APPLICATION OF THE CELL-DEVS PARADIGM USING N-CD++

Javier Ameghino Gabriel Wainer.

Departamento de Computación. Facultad de Ciencias Exactas y Naturales
Universidad de Buenos Aires.
Planta Baja. Pabellón I. (1428) Buenos Aires. ARGENTINA
gabrielw@dc.uba.ar
http://www.dc.uba.ar/people/proyinv/celldevs

ABSTRACT

Cell-DEVS is an extension of the DEVS formalism that allows the definition of cellular models. We have developed a tool implementing these theoretical concepts, making easy the definition of complex cell spaces with explicit timing delays. Here, we show the use of the paradigm through different application examples. Complex applications can be implemented in a simple fashion, and they can be executed effectively.

Keywords: Modeling methodology: DEVS models, cellular automata, Cell-DEVS models; Simulation tools.

INTRODUCTION

The DEVS formalism, defined in (Zeigler 1976, Zeigler 1984, Zeigler *et al.* 2000) is a modular and hierarchical approach for discrete-event simulation. A DEVS model can be described as composed of several submodels, which, once tested, can be reused.

We have interested in describing real systems that can be represented as cell spaces. Cellular Automata (Wolfram 1986) is a well-known formalism to describe these systems. They are defined as an infinite n-dimensional lattice of cells whose values are updated according to a local rule. This is done simultaneous and synchronously, using the present cell state and those of a finite set of nearby cells (called its **neighborhood**).

Cellular automata usually require large amounts of compute time. The use of a discrete time base also constrains the model precision. Timed Cell-DEVS solves these problems by using the DEVS paradigm to define a cell space where each cell is defined as an atomic model (Wainer and Giambiasi, 2000). The goal is to build discrete-event cell spaces, improving their definition by making the timing specification more expressive. Cell-DEVS atomic models can be specified as:

$$TDC = < X, Y, I, S, N, delay, d, \delta_{INT}, \delta_{EXT}, \tau, \lambda, D >$$

In this case, **X** is the set of external input events, **Y** is the set of external output events, and **I** is the model's modular interface. **S** is the set of sequential states for the cell, and **N** is the set of input events. **Delay** defines the kind of delay for the cell, and **d** its duration. Finally, there are several functions: δ_{INT} for internal transitions, δ_{EXT} for external transitions, τ for local computations, λ for outputs and **D** for the state's duration function.

Each cell uses a set of N inputs to compute the future state. They are received through the model interface, and are used to activate the local function. A delay can be associated with each cell, allowing deferring the transmission of the execution results. A **transport** delay allows us to model a variable commuting time for each cell with anticipatory semantics (every scheduled event is executed). Using **inertial** delays, the semantics is preemptive: some scheduled events are not executed due to a small interval between two input events. Therefore, the outputs of a cell are not transmitted instantaneously, but after the consumption of the delay. The model advances through the activation of the internal, external, output and state's duration functions, as in other DEVS models.

Once each cell is defined, they can form a coupled model:

$$GCC = < Xlist, Ylist, I, X, Y, n, \{t1,..,tn\}, N, C, B, Z >$$

Here, **Xlist** is an input coupling list, **Ylist** is an output coupling list and **I** represents the model interface. **X** is the set of external input events and **Y** the external output events. The **n** value defines the dimension of the cell space, **{t1,...,tn}** is the number of cells in each dimension and **N** is the neighborhood set. **C** is the cell space, **B** is the set of border cells, and **Z** a translation function.

This specification defines a coupled model composed of an array of atomic cells. Each of them is connected to its

This work was partially supported by ANPCYT Project 11-04460, UBACYT Project JW10, and COMPAQ Latin America Corporation.

neighborhood. As the cell space is finite, the borders should be provided with a different behavior than the rest of the space. Otherwise, the space is wrapped, meaning that cells in a border are connected with those in the opposite one. Finally, the Z function defines internal and external couplings.

Using these formal specifications, a simulation tool was developed. The following sections will be devoted to show how the tool can be used to develop cellular models.

A SIMULATION TOOL BASED ON CELL--DEVS

N–CD++ (Rodríguez and Wainer, 1999) is a tool built following the formal specifications of Cell-DEVS. The tool includes a specification language that allows describing the behavior of each cell. A cell space is defined including its size, influencees, neighborhood and borders. Using these parameters, a complete Cell-DEVS is built using the formal specifications.

The behavior of a cell is defined using rules with the form:

VALUE DELAY { CONDITION }

Each rule indicates that if the *CONDITION* is satisfied, the state of the cell will change to the designated *VALUE*, and it will be *DELAY*ed the specified time. If the condition is not valid, the next rule is evaluated (according to the order in that they were defined), repeating this process until a rule is satisfied.

The specification shown in Figure 1 shows the rules for the "Life" Game (Gardner, 1970). They indicate that if a cell will remain active when the number of active neighbors is 3 or 4 (using a transport delay of 10 ms). If the cell is inactive and the neighborhood has 3 active cells, the cell activates. Otherwise case, the cell is inactive.

```
Rule: 1 10 { (0,0) = 1 and ( truecount = 3 or
             truecount = 4 ) }
Rule: 1 10 { (0,0) = 0 and truecount = 3 }
Rule: 0 10 { t }
```

Figure 1. Definition for the Life game.

The language permits to manipulate n-dimensional references. Likewise, a neighborhood can be composed of non-adjacent cells, and the neighborhood's dimension can be similar or inferior to the model's dimension.

The most common operators are included: boolean (*AND*, *OR*, *NOT*, *XOR*, *IMP* and *EQV*), comparison (=, !=, <, >, <= and >=), and arithmetic (+, -, * and /). In addition, different types of functions are available: trigonometric, roots, power, rounding and truncation, module, logarithm, absolute value, minimum, maximum, G.C.D. and L.C.M. Other existing functions allow to check if a number is integer, even, odd or prime.

Some functions allow to query the cell state of the neighborhood: *truecount, falsecount*, *undefcount* and *statecount*(*n*).

Some common constants are defined: *pi*, *e*, certain constants used in the domains of the physics and the chemistry (gravitational constant, acceleration, light speed, Planck's constant).

The *Time* function returns the global simulated time. Functions *RadToDeg* and *DegToRad* are used for the conversion of angles expressed in radians to degrees and viceversa. There are functions for the conversion of polar and rectangular coordinates and temperatures in Celsius, Fahrenheit or Kelvin degrees.

Other functions allow to obtain values depending on the evaluation of a certain condition. *IFU*(*c*, *t*, *f*, *u*) evaluates the *c* condition, and if it is *True*, it returns the *t* value. If it is *False*, it return *f*, and *u* if it is *undefined*. On the other hand, the function *IF*(*c*, *t*, *f*) returns *t* if *c* evaluates to *True*, and *f* otherwise.

Finally, several functions are used to generate pseudorandom numbers using different probability distributions. We have included Uniform, Chi Square, Beta, Exponential, Φ, Gamma, Gaussian, Binomial and Poisson distributions. The introduction of random conditions presents new problems. For example, in the rule:

10 100 { random >= 0.4 }

the condition is evaluated to *True* in the 60 % of the cases, and to *False* in the rest. Therefore, the model could return all the rules evaluated to *False*, even when the model is well specified. The tool automatically identifies these cases, and assigns the *Undefined* value to the cell, informing this situation and continuing with the simulation.

Space *zones*, defined by a cell range, can be associated with a set of rules different than the rest of the cell space.

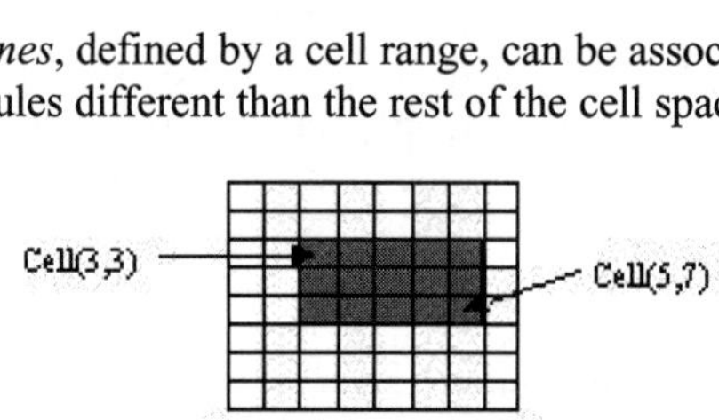

Figure 2. A Zone defined by the range {(3,3)..(5,7)}

Cellular models can be integrated to a standard DEVS hierarchy. Therefore, input/output ports can be defined for the cell space. The *portInFunction* directive is used to query the value of a message arrived in an input port. On the other hand, output ports are activated using the *send* function.

APPLICATION EXAMPLES

This section is devoted to describe how to implement different Cell-DEVS models using N-CD++.

We first show an example of excitable media, a phenomenon appearing in several real systems. For instance, the nervous tissue of the heart muscle is an excitable medium where a wave travels through the heart in every heartbeat. Magnetic fields, forest fires, etc. also can be represented as modifications of these models.

Three states can be recognized. For instance, in a heart tissue these states represent a cell that is resting, excited or recovering. In a forest fire, the states could represent a cell without fire, burning or burnt. Any of these models are defined as:

```
[ExMedia]
type : cell            dim : (9,9)
delay : transport      border : wrapped
neighbors : (-1,-1) (-1,0) (-1,1) (0,-1)
neighbors : (0,1) (1,-1) (1,0) (1,1) (0,0)
localtransition : Ex-rules

[Ex-rules]
rule : 0 100 {(0,0)=0 and statecount(2)=0 }
rule : 2 100 {(0,0)=0 and statecount(2)>0 }
rule : 1 100 { (0,0) = 2 }
rule : 0 100 { (0,0) = 1 }
rule : { (0,0) } 100 { t }
```

Figure 3. Definition of an excitable media model.

We first define the Cell-DEVS coupled model and its parameters: size, neighborhood shape, kind of delay and borders. The *Ex-rules* section represents the local computing function for the model. Here, the first rule defines that when the cell and its neighbors are not excited (value *0*), the cell must keep resting. The second rule means that if the cell is resting and there are excited neighbors (value *2*), the cell is excited. Third and fourth rules mean that the cells remain in a specific state. In every other case (*t* means "True"), the cell keeps its present state.

Figure 4 shows the results obtained when this model executes. It shows the evolution of this excitable media model using different neighborhoods. Figure 4a uses all the adjacent neighbors, as defined in Figure 3 (Moore neighborhood). Figure 4b uses four adjacent cells (N-S-E-W), and Figure 4c shows a hexagonal lattice on a square grid.

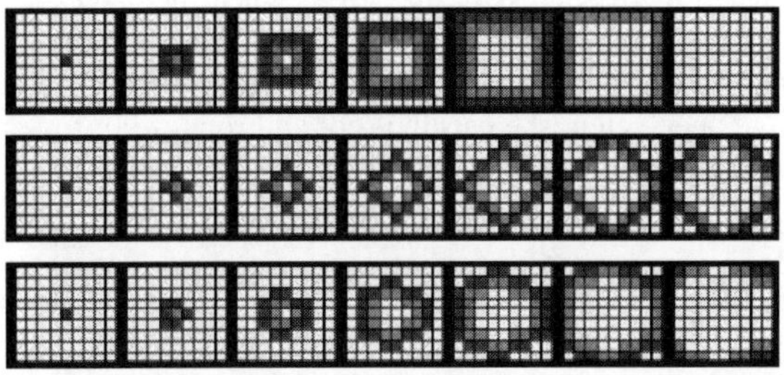

Figure 4. Results of ExMedia with different Neighborhoods: (a) Moore; (b) Von Neumann; (c) hexagonal grid.

The following example represents a surface tension model.

```
[Tension]
type : cell            dim : (40,40)
delay : transport      border : wrapped
neighbors : (-1,-1) (-1,0) (-1,1) (0,-1)
neighbors : (1,-1) (1,0) (1,1) (0,0) (0,1)
localtransition : Ten-rules

[Ten-rules]
rule : 0 100 { statecount(0) >= 5 }
rule : 1 100 { t }
```

Figure 5. Surface tension model specification

We see the definition of the Cell-DEVS coupled model parameters: a grid of 40x40, Moore neighborhood, transports delays and wrapped borders. We have two states: the presence (value *1*) or absence (value *0*) of particles. This model can be represented as a "majority vote" system. In each step, the new state depends of most neighbors. It remains in the cell if at least 5 of the 9 are occupied; otherwise it becomes empty. The following figure shows how particles concentrate where there is bigger tension. The resulting behavior of the surface is a high level representation of the majority vote rules defined earlier.

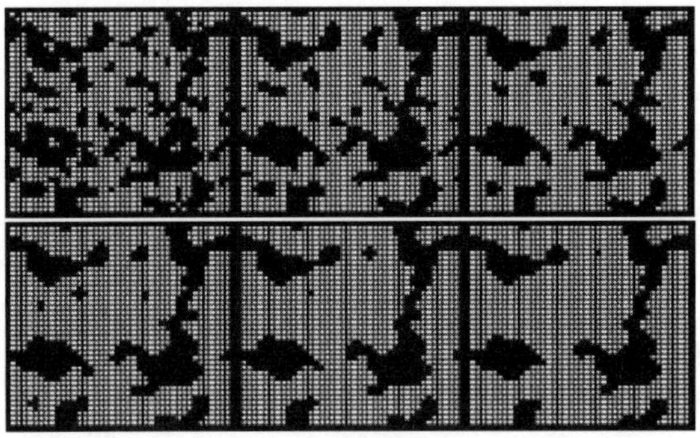

Figure 6. Execution results of the Surface Tension model.

The next example is an ecological model of ants moving in the ground. The ants eat grass in two steps: first, they eat the leaves and then the root. Hence, we have three grass states: *1* when there is grass in the cell, *2* when the leaves have been eaten, and *3* or *4* for empty cells. When an ant find grass, she eat it and rotates 90° to the right. When the leaves have been eaten, she eats the root and rotates 90° to the left. If there is no grass, she continues moving ahead.

```
[vants]
type : cell                  dim : (10,10,2)
delay : transport            border : wrapped
neighbors: (-2,0,0)  (-1,-1,0)  (-1,0,0)
neighbors: (-1,1,0)  (0,2,0)  (0,0,1)
neighbors: (0,-2,0)  (0,-1,0)  (0,0,0)  (0,1,0)
neighbors: (1,-1,0)  (1,0,0)  (1,1,0)  (2,0,0)

localtransition : calculus
[calculus]
...
rule:{if((0,0,0)=45,31,(trunc((0,0,0)/10)*10)+
1) } 100 { cellpos(2)=0 and (0,0,1)=2 and
((0,0,0)=25 or (0,0,0)=35 or (0,0,0)=45) and
(fractional((-1,0,0)/10)*10)!=7 and
((fractional((-1,1,0)/10)*10)=8 or
(fractional((-2,0,0)/10)*10)=7 or
(fractional((-1,-1,0)/10)*10)=6) }
...
rule : { (trunc(((0,0,0)/10))*10) + 1 } 100
{cellpos(2)=0 and (0,0,1)=4 and ((1,0,0)=25 or
(1,0,0)=35 or (1,0,0)=45)}
...
rule : { (0,0,0) + 1 } 100 {cellpos(2)=1 and
(0,0,0)<7}
rule : 1 100 {cellpos(2)=1 and (0,0,0)>=7}

rule : { (0,0,0) } 100 { t }
```

Figure 7. Specification of the ant's model

We use four states to represent the present direction, combined with the grass state. For instance, a value *13* means that there is grass (*1*) and the ant is going north (*1*: S; *2*: E; *3*: N; *4*: W). This model needs extra information to control the movement of the ants to avoid collisions. Then, we define auxiliary ant directions to analyze the possibility of collision (5: S; 6: E; 7: N; 8: W).

We have two surfaces, the first representing the grass and the ants, and the second used as collision flags. When a cell in the second surface have the value *1* we must analyze only rules that determine whether there are collisions or not. When the value of the cell is *2* we must analyze only rules to compute the next position of the ants. This is shown in the first rule in Figure 7. The following rule is used to move the ant once we know that we can move it. The *cellpos* function allows us to know which surface we are using, providing two different behaviors.

The following figure shows the execution of the model using the tool. The dark cells contain grass, and an ant moving in the lower rows is eating them. The ant behaves using the rules recently explained. We also can see the growth of the grass, represented as a change of state for the lighter cells, where a long delay is used.

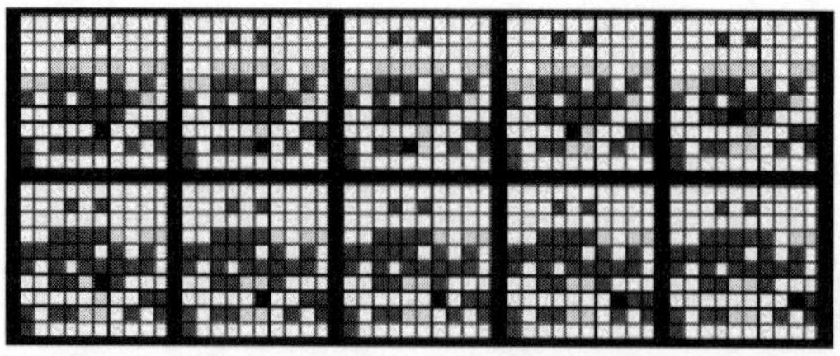

Figure 8. Execution results of an ant foraging model.

Our last example shows the simulation results for a watershed model. This model, previously introduced in (Moon *et al.* 1996), represents a hydrology system built as a cell space. The watershed is represented as small cells organized in several layers (air, surface water, soil, ground water, and bedrock). The rainfall input is partially retained by vegetation, and the rest infiltrates.

```
[Watershed]
type : cell             dim : (30,30,2)
delay : transport       border : nowrapped
neighbors : (-1,0,0)  (0,-1,0)  (0,0,0)  (0,1,0)
neighbors : (1,0,0)  (-1,0,1)  (0,-1,1)  (0,0,1)
neighbors : (1,0,1)  (0,1,1)
localtransition : Hydrology

[Hydrology]

rule : {0.0022 + (0,0,0) - if ((-1,0,0)!=?) and
((0,0,1)+(0,0,0) > ((-1,0,1) + (-1,0,0)),
((0,0,0)+(0,0,1)-(-1,0,0)-(-1,0,1))/1000)*
(0,0,0))/1000),0)-
if((1,0,0)!=?) and ((0,0,1)+(0,0,0))> ((1,0,1) +
(1,0,0)),((0,0,0) + (0,0,1) - (1,0,0) -
(1,0,1))/1000)*(0,0,0))/1000),0) - if((((0,-1,0)
!= ?) and
((0,0,1)+(0,0,0)) > ((0,-1,1)+(0,-1,0)) ,((0,0,0)
+ (0,0,1)-(0,-1,0)-(0,-1,1))/1000)
*(0,0,0))/1000),0) -
if((0,1,0) != ?) and ((0,0,1) + (0,0,0)) >
((0,1,1) + (0,1,0)),(((0,0,0) + (0,0,1) - (0,1,0)
- (0,1,1))/1000) * (0,0,0))/1000),0) + if((-
1,0,0) != ?) and ((-1,0,1) + (-1,0,0)) > ((0,0,1)
+ (0,0,0)),((-1,0,0) + (-1,0,1) - (0,0,0)-
(0,0,1))*(-1,0,0))/1000),0) + if((1,0,0) != ?)
and ((1,0,1) + (1,0,0)) > ((0,0,1) +
(0,0,0)),((1,0,0) + (1,0,1) - (0,0,0) - (0,0,1))
* (1,0,0))/1000),0) + if((0,-1,0) != ?) and ((0,-
1,1) + (0,-1,0)) >((0,0,1) + (0,0,0)), ((0,-1,0)
+ (0,-1,1) - (0,0,0) - (0,0,1)) * (0,-
1,0))/1000),0) + if((0,1,0) != ?) and (((0,1,1) +
(0,1,0)) > (0,0,1) + (0,0,0)),((0,1,0) + (0,1,1)
- (0,0,0) - (0,0,1)) * (0,1,0))/1000),0) } 1000 {
cellpos(2)=0 }
rule : { (0,0,0) } 1000 { t }
```

Figure 9. Watershed model specification

Figure 9 shows the implementation of the model using the tool. The rules represent the accumulation of water. It takes the present water of the cell, and the rain fell up to the present moment is added. Then, we consider how much water must be passed to the neighbors, and how much water is received from the inverse neighborhood. Several layers are represented as planes in a three dimensional model.

We can see the execution results of this model in the Appendix. In the first figure we show an initial state, representing the slope of the terrain before raining. Each cell occupies 1m x 1m. The second figure shows the execution results after intense rain (0.0022 mm/s) after 10 minutes of simulated time. We can see that the rain is accumulated in the lower levels of the terrain, and a river is formed.

CONCLUSION

The tool N-CD++ can be used for modeling and simulation of n–dimensional Cell–DEVS. This approach improves the development, checking and maintaining phases, facilitating the testing and reuse of their components. Input/output port definitions allow defining multiple interconnection between Cell-DEVS or DEVS models. We also can develop multidimensional models, making the tool a general framework to define and simulate complex generic models.

The tool was built using a standard version of C++, which allowed is to provide different versions running in several platforms without additional cost. At present, N–CD++ has been successfully tested in Windows 95/NT, Linux, AIX, IRIX, HP-UX and Solaris. A simulation server has been built, and soon it will be available to do simulations using a Web-based approach.

The tool and the examples are the public domain and they can be obtained in:
"http://www.dc.uba.ar/people/proyinv/celldevs".

REFERENCES

Gardner, M., 1970. "The Fantastic Combinations of John Conway's New Solitaire Game 'Life' ". *Scientific American, 23* (4), pp. 120-123.

Moon, Y.; Zeigler, B.; Ball, G.; Guertin, D., 1996. "DEVS representation of spatially distributed systems: validity, complexity reduction". *IEEE Transactions on Systems, Man and Cybernetics*. pp. 288-296.

Rodríguez, D.; Wainer, G., 1999. "New Extensions to the CD++ tool". In *Proceedings of SCS Summer Multiconference on Computer Simulation*. 1-7.

Wainer, G.; Giambiasi, N., 2000. "Timed Cell-DEVS: modelling and simulation of cell spaces". In *Discrete Event Modeling & Simulation: Enabling Future Technologies*, to be published by Springer-Verlag.

Wolfram, S. , 1986. *Theory and applications of cellular automata*. Vol.1, Advances Series on Complex Systems. World Scientific, Singapore.

Zeigler, B., 1976. *Theory of modeling and simulation*. Wiley.

Zeigler, B., 1984. *Multifaceted Modelling and discrete event simulation*. Academic Press.

Zeigler, B.; Praehofer, H.; Kim, T., 2000. *Theory of Modeling and Simulation: Integrating Discrete Event and Continuous Complex Dynamic Systems*. Academic Press.

BIOGRAPHIES

Gabriel A. Wainer received the Licentiate degree (M.Sc., 1993) and Ph.D. degree (1998, with honours) of the Universidad de Buenos Aires, Argentina, and DIAM/IUSPIM, Université d'Aix-Marseille III, France. He is Assistant Professor at the Computer Sciences Dept. of the Universidad de Buenos Aires, Argentina. He has been working in the same department since 1988. He published more than 40 articles in the field of operating systems, real-time systems and Discrete-Event simulation. He has been head of several research projects related with computer modelling and simulation. He is author of a book on real-time systems and co-author of a book on Operating Systems.

Javier Ameghino is a Licentiate (M. Sc.) student at the Computer Sciences Department of the Universidad de Buenos Aires, Argentina. He worked in several private companies in Buenos Aires. At present he works at COMPAQ Latin America Corporation (Buenos Aires).

APPENDIX – Execution results of the Watershed model.

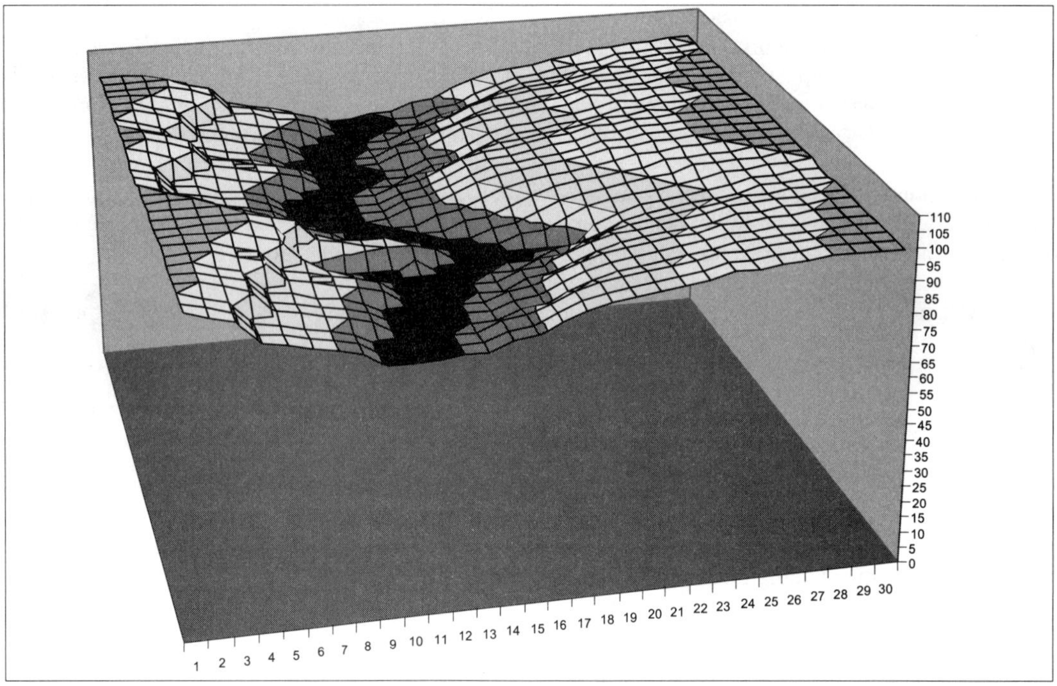

Figure 10. Initial height values for a watershed.

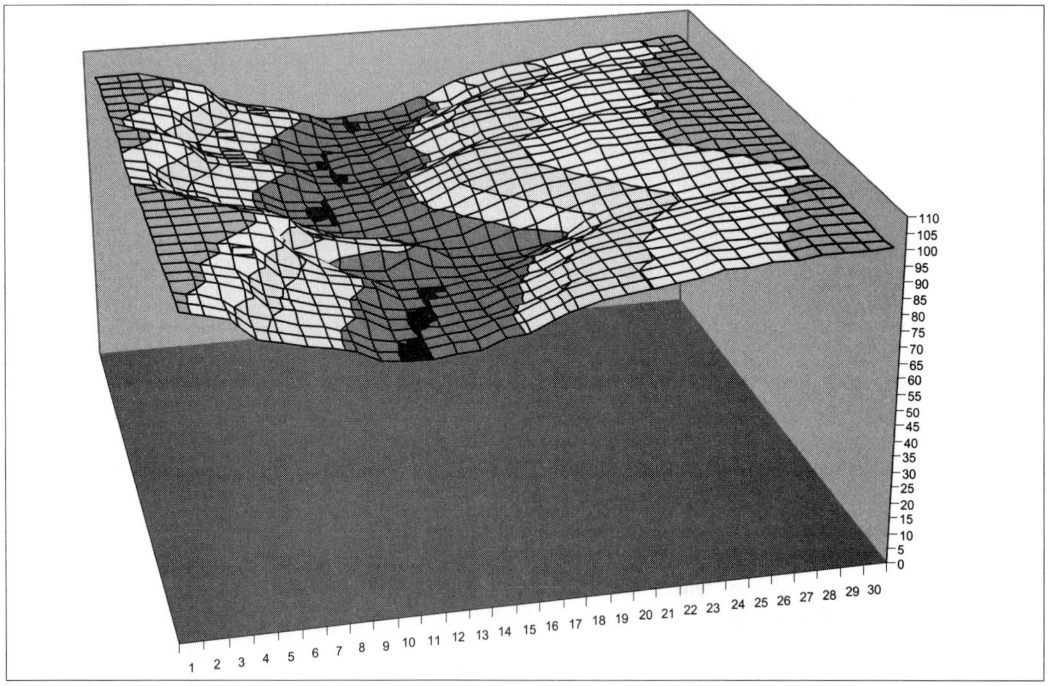

Figure 11. Height values after rain.

ASL/NSL: A MULTI-LEVEL COMPUTATIONAL MODEL FOR DISTRIBUTED NEURAL SIMULATION*

Alfredo Weitzenfeld
Departmento Académico de Computación
Instituto Tecnológico Autónomo de México
Río Hondo #1, San Angel Tizapán, CP 01000
México DF, MEXICO
alfredo@lamport.rhon.itam.mx

Sebastián Gutiérrez
Department of Information and Computer Science
University of California, Irvine
Irvine, CA 92697-3425, USA
seguti@ics.uci.edu

Keywords: Neurosciences, Distributed processors, Continuous, Differential equation solvers, Hierarchical

ABSTRACT

As neural systems become large and complex, sophisticated tools are needed to support effective model development and efficient simulation processing. Initially, during model development, rich graphical interfaces linked to powerful programming languages and component libraries are the primary requirement. Later, during model simulation, processing efficiency is the primary concern. Workstations and personal computers are quite effective during model development, while parallel and distributed computation become necessary during simulation processing. We give first an overview of modeling and simulation in NSL/ASL together with an example. We then discuss current and future work with the system in the development and simulation of modular neural systems executed in a single computer or distributed computer network.

INTRODUCTION

In this paper we present an overview of the ASL/NSL computational model for the simulation of neural systems. This work is motivated by the quest to simulate animal-like behavior as faithfully as possible based on existing ethological, physiological and anatomical neural data. At the higher level these models are described in terms of *schema* (Arbib 1992) modules corresponding to behavior agents (ethology) simulated with ASL (*Abstract Schema Language*) (Weitzenfeld 1993). At the lower level, neural networks are described in terms of neural modules (physiology and anatomy) simulated with the Neural Simulation Language NSL (Weitzenfeld and Arbib 1994). Many models have been developed and simulated with ASL/NSL (see Weitzenfeld *et al.* 2000a for examples of models involving perception, visuomotor coordination, motor control as well as technological neural applications).

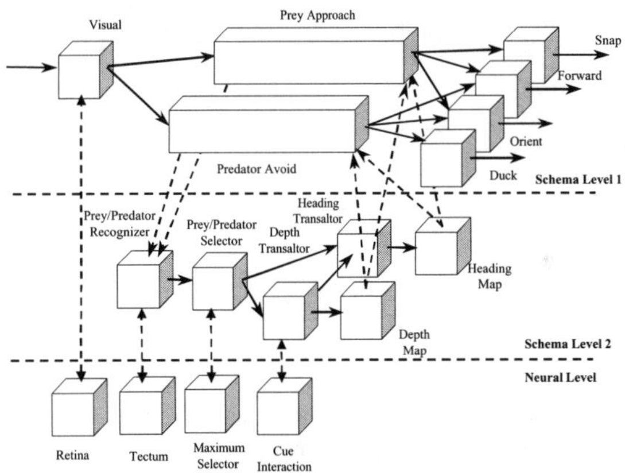

Figure 1. Schema hierarchy for the toad's prey acquisition and predator avoidance models. The top two levels correspond to schema levels (1 and 2) and the lower level corresponds to neural modules.

For example, in Figure 1 we show a simplified diagram of the toad's prey acquisitions and prey avoidance model (Cobas and Arbib 1992), (schema level 1) involving *perceptual* and *motor* schemas. The external visual input is processed to generate

* We thank the NSF-CONACyT collaboration grant (#IRI-9522999 in the US and #546500-5-C018-A in Mexico), the CONACyT REDII grant in Mexico, as well as the "Asociación Mexicana de Cultura, A.C.".

appropriate motor actions: forward, orient, snap and duck. Schemas at this level are decomposed and delegated to the next level down (schema level 2) where schemas perform more specific tasks. Prey approach and predator avoid schemas delegate their tasks to a *schema assemblage* composed of a prey/predator recognizer, a prey/predator selector, depth and heading translators and maps. Next level down, different neural modules: *Retina*, *Tectum*, *Maximum Selector* and *Cue Interaction*, if available, implement the actual neural network processing.

SCHEMAS AND NEURAL NETWORKS

To better understand the underlying computational model, ASL/NSL defines a tree-like schema or module hierarchy as shown in Figure 2.

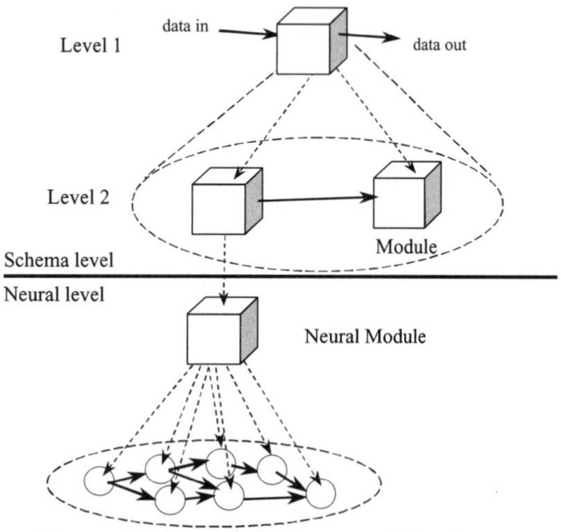

Figure 2. The ASL/NSL computational model is based on hierarchical interconnected modules. A schema module at a higher level (level 1) is decomposed (dashed lines) into additional interconnected (solid arrow) schema submodules (level 2). At the lowest level, neural modules are implemented by neural networks (circular objects).

Starting by the root module (known as the model), modules are further decomposed into additional *submodules*, having no limit on how many levels this may reach. At the same abstraction level, modules are interconnected (solid arrows), while at different levels modules have their task delegated (dashed arrows). Networks of submodules – *module assemblages* – are seen in their entirety in terms of a single higher-level module and may be implemented independently from each other in both top-down and bottom-up fashion, an important benefit of modular design. At the higher abstraction levels, the detailed module implementation is left unspecified, only specifying the module's interface and what is to be achieved. At the lowest level, schemas are implemented by neural modules.

As a computational unit, every module incorporates its own local structure and control mechanisms. Every module defines an external interface made of a set of unidirectional input and output *ports* supporting data passing between modules together with a set of public methods that can be externally invoked from other modules. Communication between modules is in the form of asynchronous message passing for both data and methods. Internally, communication is hierarchically managed through anonymous data port reading and writing. Externally, communication is managed through dynamic port *connections* (solid arrows) - links between output ports in one module to input ports in another module - and *relabelings* (dashed arrows) - module ports at one level in the hierarchy are linked to similar input or output ports at a different level. The hierarchical port management approach enables the development of neural architectures where modules may be designed and implemented independently and without prior knowledge of the complete model or their final execution environment, encouraging component reusability and permitting module execution in a distributed fashion (Weitzenfeld *et al.* 2000b).

For example, consider the *depth perception* problem where a three dimensional scene is presented to the two eyes. The depth perception model developed by House (1989) uses two systems to build a depth map, one driven by *disparity* cues - difference in retina projection - while the other is driven by *accommodation* cues - receiving information about focal length. The corresponding simplified ASL/NSL model consists of a *Stereo s* root module and three interconnected submodules: *Retina r*, *Depth m* (accommodation) and *s* (disparity), as shown in Figure 3.

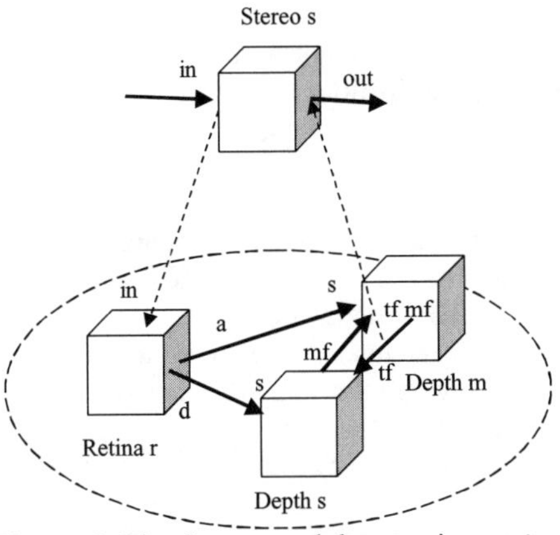

Figure 3. The *Stereo* module contains an *in* input port and an *out* output port. It is further decomposed into a *Retina* module containing an input port *in* and two output ports, *d* and *a*, for disparity and accommodation, respectively. The *Depth* module consists of an input port *s*, receiving data from the *Retina*, a second input port *tf*, receiving input from the other *Depth* module, and an output port *mf*.

NEURAL SIMULATION

Neural networks define the lowest level in the computational model. In general, neural simulation varies depending on whether it relates to artificial o biological systems. Artificial neural networks often require two-stage simulation process, (1) an initial training phase and (2) a subsequent processing or running phase. On the other hand, biological neural networks usually require a single running phase, in which behavior and learning may be intertwined. Initially, during the model development, the simulation process involves interactively specifying aspects of the model, such as network input and parameters values, as well as simulation control and visualization. As the model becomes more stable, efficiency becomes the primary concern of the simulation process and concurrency play an important role, not only as a way to increase processing performance but also to model neurons more faithfully (Weitzenfeld and Arbib 1991). Yet, large and complex models may require hours or even days of processing time and distributed computing may play a key role in speeding up computation.

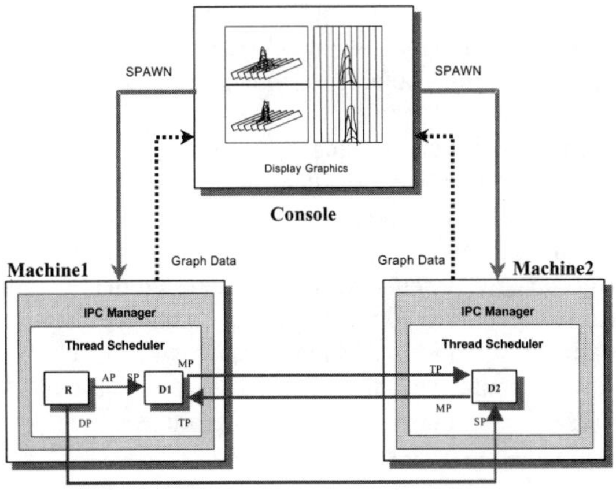

Figure 4. The distributed architecture of ASL/NSL is conceptualized as a set of autonomous (processing) nodes. Each node may contain one or more schema modules that communicate via asynchronous message passing. The nodes do not share a common address space and they are connected by unidirectional communication links along which messages are transmitted. A communication link is not necessarily a direct link, It can be any network path connecting these schemas

Sequential and Distributed Processing

ASL/NSL provides an architecture to support both sequential and distributed (as well as parallel) simulations. In the sequential simulation, neural dynamics are executed one equation at the time where the output from one neuron is immediately fed as input to the next one. In NSL the same procedure is applied to modules, where each module would get executed in a predetermined order sending newly generated output port values immediately to their corresponding interconnected input ports. This approach simplifies simulation results in that the order of computation depends directly from the order of computation. To further simulate brain-like concurrent behavior while doing sequential processing, NSL interleaves module execution while buffering output from one module to the next one, making processing order unimportant. In the distributed simulation, all simulation control as well as graphical display take place in the *console* in one of the machines responsible for distributing processing among local and/or remote machines (see

Figure 4). The actual distribution is specified by the user or automatically generated by the system depending on the available machines in the network.

Since neural models are processing and communication intensive, a distributed simulation requires monitoring and resource management capabilities in order to improve overall simulation performance. Particularly, we are interested in (1) identify processing bottlenecks, such as unnecessary serializations between schemas or excessive model fragmentation, (2) accomplish a cost-effective use of the resources in the system and (3) optimize communication performance.

Reflective meta-level architectures add introspective capabilities to computational systems by providing dynamic adaptability to internal and external processing constraints (Smith 1982). Here, the computation activities are separated into base and meta level activities, representing the application execution and the structures used to control its execution respectively. This separation of concerns allow us to monitor and reason about aspects of communication and resource management without affecting the normal behavior of the underlying application execution. In fact, meta-level facilities allows to provide more adequate control of modular neural networks (Smieja and Muhlenbein 1992), as well as improve the computational efficiency of the network (Boers and Kuiper 1993) in a semantically clean manner.

Meta-Level Architecture

In order to represent the resource and communication activities going on behind the scenes without interfere with the on-going computation (called also perturbation), the meta-level architecture is design as follows: (1) Each schema module has a meta-schema, which represents the meta-level capabilities of the base-level schema module, (2) The communication between the schema and its meta-schema is synchronous, in order to guarantee the integrity and semantics of the neural simulation that could be violated by some interleaving execution between the meta and base level, (3) Each meta-schema is composed by a computational and communication model, (4) The computational model gathers resource information of the schema it represents, (5) The communication model monitors the incoming/outgoing communication of its schema to identify possibly communication bottlenecks and evaluate different distribution strategies of the neural model through postmortem visualization of the communication primitives.

The computational model gathers the information by accessing the internal structures of the kernel in a modular way. Thus, it may be visualized as an plug-in component tailored to an specific architecture, which traces the following information for a particular schema module: (1) The node workload, (2) The statistic information of the node, such as number of processes, memory and virtual memory available and (3) performance statistics of the schema module such as real cpu time (cpu-ticks), amount of memory allocated, number of threads, priority assigned and total size of the schema. On the other side, the communication model uses a client-server logging event model for communication primitives, in order to minimize the degree of perturbation, while measure: (1) Ports communication throughput, (2) Message queue size, (3) Number of messages remaining in the queue and (4) Message properties, such as size of the message, type of the message, who is the sender, who is the receiver.

The client-server logging event model works similar to PGPVM (Brad Topol *et al.* 1994), but without synchronization barriers. That is, there is a centralized server which communicates with the underlying network in order to satisfy communication service requirements while providing distributed buffered trace in PICL (*Portable Instrumented Communication Library*) format (Geist *et al.* 1991) as follows (see Figure 5):

1. The message send request is intercepted by the meta-schema
2. The message properties are registered and a log event for the transmission is generated and saved in a local buffer
3. The transmission request is sent to the communication server (eSvr), which in turn sent it to the underlying network
4. The underlying network sent the message and return and acknowledge to eSvr
5. eSvr return the control to the meta-schema, which resume the base level application

6. At the end of the simulation, each meta-schema sent the collected information to eSvr
7. eSvr consolidate the information and save it in the trace database
8. A post processing of the information is required in order to create a trace file, which will be the input of the postmortem visualization program ParaGraph (Heath and Etheridge 1991)

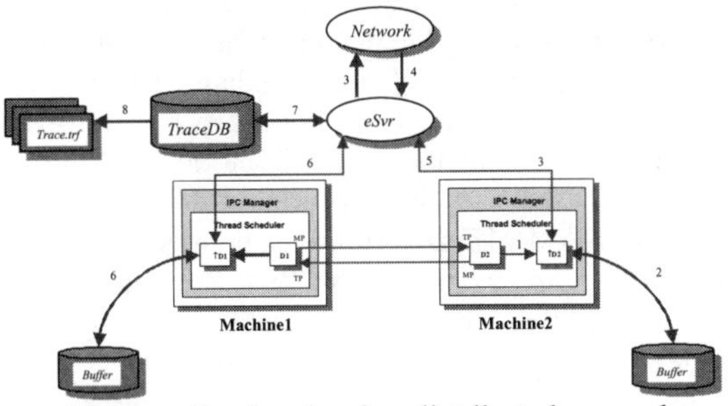

Figure 5. A simple distributed neural model composed of two schema modules **D1** and **D2**, in which communication is restricted to their port interconnections

SIMULATION RESULTS

In this section we present the results of the depth perception distributed simulation, realized with the parameters shown in Table 1.

System endTime	*System delta*	*Differential delta*	*Differential integration*
2.0	0.05	0.05	Euler

Table 1. Simulation and approximation method parameters.

Model	*CPU (MHz)*	*Disk (GB)*	*RAM (MB)*	*Operating System*
Ultra-1	200	1	32	Solaris 2.6
Ultra-10	333	1	128	Solaris 2.6
Sparc-5	170	0.5	32	Solaris 2.6

Table 2. Hardware and operating system parameters.

The underlying network infrastructure is a shared Ethernet 10 baseT and the hardware specifications shown in Table 2.

One of the most interesting parts of the simulation was the frequency and volume of communication. As we can see in Figure 6, the communication between *Depth1* and *NslConsole* (ranked node 0) or *Retina* (node 1) is frequency intensive, while communication between *Depth1* and *Depth2* (node 3) is volume intensive

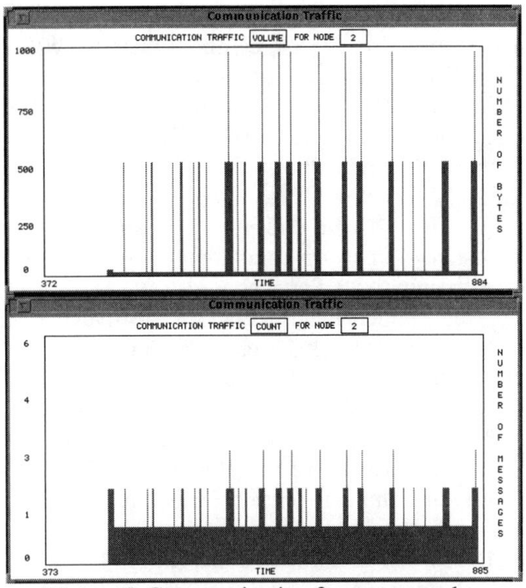

Figure 6. Communication frequency and volume of *Depth1*

The *lamport* diagram of space-time, mainly knowledge as the happens before relation, shown in Figure 7 displays the order of the events during the simulation

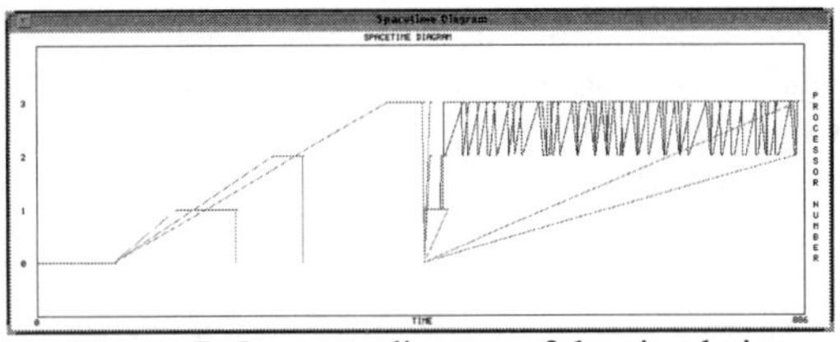

Figure 7. *Lamport* diagram of the simulation with node 0 as the Nsl Console, node 1 as *Retina* and nodes 2 and 3 as *Depth1* and *Depth2* respectively.

REFERENCES

Arbib, M.A., 1992, "Schema Theory", *Encyclopedia of Artificial Intelligence*, 2nd Edition, Editor Stuart Shapiro, 2:1427-1443, Wiley.
Boers, E.J., Kuiper, H., 1993, "Biological Metaphors and the Design of Modular Artificial Neural

Networks", Master Thesis, Dept. of Computer Science and Experimental and Theoretical Psychology, Leiden University, Netherlands.
Cobas, A., and Arbib, M.A., 1992, "Prey-catching and Predator-avoidance in Frog and Toad: Defining the Schemas", *J. Theor. Biol* 157, 271-304.
Geist, G., Heath, M., Peyton, B., and Woley, P, 1991, "A User's Guide to PICL", Technical Report ORNL/TM-11616, Oak Ridge National Lab.
Heath, M., and Etheridge, J., 1991, "Visualizing the Performance of Parallel Programs", *IEEE Software*, 8(5):29-39.
House, D., 1989, "Depth perception in frogs and toads: A study of in neural computing", *Lecture notes in Biomathematics*, 80, Springer-Verlag.
Smieja, F.J., Muhlenbein, H., 1992, "Reflective Modular Neural Network Systems", Technical Report, German National Research Center for Computer Science, May.
Smith B, 1982, "Reflection and Semantics in a Procedural Languages", Technical Report 272, Laboratory of Computer Science, Massachusetts Institute of Technology.
Topol, B., Sunderam, V., and Alund, A., 1994, *PGPVM Performance Visualization Support for PVM*, Technical Report CSTR-940801, Emory University.
Weitzenfeld, A., 1993, "ASL: Hierarchy, Composition, Heterogeneity, and Multi-Granularity in Concurrent Object-Oriented Programming", *Proceedings of the Workshop on Neural Architectures and Distributed AI: From Schema Assemblages to Neural Networks*, USC, October 19-20.
Weitzenfeld A & Arbib M, 1991, "Concurrent Object Oriented Framework for the Simulation of Neural Networks", *Proceedings of ECOOP/OOPSLA'90 Workshop on Object-Based Concurrent Programming, OOPS Messenger*, 2(2):120-124.
Weitzenfeld, A., Arbib, M.A., 1994, "NSL, Neural Simulation Language", *Neural Networks Simulation Environments*, Editor J. Skrzypek, Kluwer.
Weitzenfeld, A., Arbib, M., Alexander, A., 2000a, *NSL - Neural Simulation Language: System and Applications*, MIT Press (to be published).
Weitzenfeld, A., Peguero, O., Gutierrez, S., 2000b, "NSL/ASL: Distributed Simulation of Modular Neural Networks", *Proc of MICAI 2000*, Acapulco, Mexico.

BIOGRAPHY

Alfredo Weitzenfeld is currently an Assistant Professor at the Computer Engineering Department at the Autonomous Technological Institute of Mexico (ITAM). He received his BS in Electrical Engineering from Israel Institute of Technology (TECHNION). He has an MS in Computer Engineering and a PhD in Computer Science both from the University of Southern California, where he was a Research Assistant Professor. In Mexico he is the co-founder of CANNES Laboratory for Brain Simulation and a member of the Mexican National Research System (SNI) as well as a member of the Doctoral Advising Committee at the National Autonomous University of Mexico (UNAM). He is currently supported by Mexico´s funding agency CONACyT. Previously he has received grants from NSF-CONACyT collaboration projects with a number of US academic institutions. His main research interests include simulation systems, software engineering, artificial intelligence, neural networks and robotics.

Sebastian Gutiérrez is currently pursuing a Ph.D. from the University of California, Irvine. He received his BS in Computer Engineering from the Autonomous Technological Institute of Mexico (ITAM). He worked as Research Assistant at CANNES Laboratory for Brain Simulation. His main research interests include semantic foundation for composition of communication services in open distributed systems, neural networks and clustering for scientific computing.

COMPUTING A CANONICAL BOND GRAPH FROM A COMPONENT-CONNECTION REPRESENTATION

Bruno Robisson and Jean-Gabriel Ganascia
Laboratoire d'Informatique de Paris 6
Université Pierre et Marie Curie
4, place Jussieu 75005 PARIS
e-mail: {bruno.robisson, jean-gabriel.ganascia}@lip6.fr

KEYWORDS

BOND GRAPHS - FUNCTIONAL REPRESENTATION - SCIENTIFIC DISCOVERY

ABSTRACT

This paper proposes away to create a tool to discover new power electronic circuits. The first step of the proposed approach is to generate electrical circuits without redundancy. For that, a representation of electrical networks is constructed such that one single representation corresponds to several structurally distinct circuits all of which are equivalent, i.e. "function in the same way". First, the classical component-connection representation is used to define the equivalence between circuits. Then, this equivalence is expressed mathematically using the notion of 2-isomorphism, which is closely related to a particular decomposition of graphs called the Tutte decomposition. We have developed an algorithm to transform a circuit into a bond graph based on this decomposition. Contrary to existing algorithms, the algorithm developed here computes a canonical bond graph from a circuit. Finally, we show that this representation is fully adapted to the generating process.

INTRODUCTION

Scientific discovery is a subfield of artificial intelligence which aims to create tools to discover "novel, interesting, plausible and intelligible knowledge about the objects of study" (Valdés-Pérez, 1999). Some programs, in particle physics, mathematics, chemistry, linguistics or molecular biology, already perform this task successfully. But, to our knowledge, nothing has yet been done in power electronics. This field is in constant evolution because many components with new characteristics are produced. As the functioning of power electronic circuits is complex and as the set of possible circuits is large, an exhaustive search for devices corresponding to a given specification is intractable by hand. That's why we propose to create a system which performs this task automatically.

The approach is divided into two main stages. In the first one, which has been implemented, all the electrical circuits of a given size are generated, after which the uninteresting ones are discarded by applying constraints based on simplification rules and on basic functioning criteria. In the second stage, qualitative analysis tools will be designed to search in this created data base for those devices which satisfy given specifications.

This approach is viable only if this data base is complete and as small as possible. The problem of generating process is to find a representation of electrical networks such that the same representation is associated with several distinct but equivalent circuits, i.e. those that function in the same way. Thus, the representatives of a set of equivalent circuits are generated instead of the representatives of a physical circuit. The elaboration of such a representation is presented in this paper.

Section 1 gives the class of circuits that are taken into account and a brief overview of their component-connection representation. This classical representation is unfortunately not adapted to the problem but is very useful, first to define the equivalence between circuits and next to express it mathematically. In the second section, a more suitable one called bond graph representation is described and the algorithm which associates a single bond graph with a circuit is presented. Finally, by analyzing properties of such bond graphs we show that this representation and this *ad hoc* algorithm fully solve the problem.

1 COMPONENT-CONNECTION REPRESENTATION

1.1 Hypothesis and Description

Physical electrical networks are modeled by network elements, connected to each other with "ideal" wires. Their functioning is described using the classical Kirchhoff model, i.e. the sum of the currents at each connection and the sum of the voltages along each circuit are zero. In what follows, networks are composed entirely of dipoles, selected from among ideal current sources (noted S_f), voltage sources (S_e), switches (S_w), resistors (R), inductances (L) or capacitors (C). These dipoles are assumed not to be physically oriented, which means that capacitors are not polarized, sources are reversible and switches are bidirectional and ideal. Given this hypothesis, a component-connection representation of a physical network is an edge-labeled graph. Each dipole of the network corresponds to an edge of this graph and, as wires are "ideal", each connection between components corresponds to a vertex. The graph which expresses the interconnection between components of a circuit is called a *topology*. It is obtained by deleting the labels of the edges of its component-connection representation.

Since there is a bijection between circuits and their component-connection representation, it cannot be used to solve the problem but it will be used to express it formally. Henceforth, a circuit and its component-connection representation will be not distinguished.

1.2 Definition of the Equivalence between Electrical Circuits

Foster was the first to attempt to enumerate topologies in (Foster, 1932). To avoid redundancy, he proposed a raw definition of the electrical equivalence between them. After this preliminary work, Whitney improved the definition in (Whitney, 1933) and we have extended it to electrical circuits. Thus, two circuits are said to be *equivalent* if there is a bijection between the edges of their component-connection representation such that corresponding edges are associated with the same dipole, and such that the same current will flow through those corresponding dipoles.

Example The two circuits in Figure 1 have equivalent equational systems obtained by applying Kirchhoff's voltage and current laws and Ohm's law. So, the same current will flow through corresponding dipoles, which means that these two circuits are equivalent.

Whitney studied the properties of Kirchhoff's laws to express mathematically the equivalence between topologies.

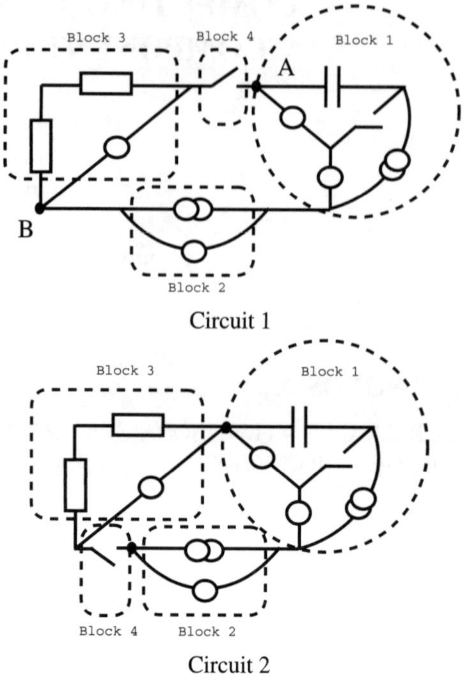

Figure 1: Equivalent electrical circuits.

1.3 Mathematical Formulation

Equations corresponding to Kirchhoff's current and voltage laws are written respectively from an independent set of cuts and an independent set of circuits (Chen, 1971). Consequently, graphs having the same set of cuts and the same set of circuits have interesting electrical properties. Whitney studied these graphs and to do so he defined 2-isomorphism. This notion and the notion of m-connexity are presented briefly here; Berge describes this graph theory terminology more precisely in (Berge, 1973).

Let G be a connected graph. An n-separation of G is a pair (H,K) of edge-disjoint subgraphs of G satisfying the following three conditions: $H \cup K = G$, H and K have exactly n common vertices and H and K have at least n edges. A graph is said to be m-connected if it has no n-separations for any $n < m$.

Let G be a 2-connected graph and (H,K) a 2-separation of G. H and K have, by definition, two vertices d and c in common. A switch operation on G at (H,K) is defined by interchanging d and c in K. Thus, a 2-connected graph G is said to be 2-isomorphic to another 2-connected graph G' if G' is obtained from G by a sequence of such switches.

From the result of Whitney on the equivalence between topologies, we obtain the fact that two circuits are equivalent if they are 2-isomorphic. For example, circuit 1 in Figure 1 has a 2-separation with vertices A and B as hinges. By interchanging A and B in this circuit, we obtain circuit 2. So, they are 2-isomorphic and thus equivalent.

This result formalizes and generalizes a well-known property of electrical circuits, which is that the permutation of the order of elements or blocks of elements in series does not modify the equational system obtained by applying Kirchhoff's voltage and current laws and Ohm's law. However, this physical property is not expressed by the component-connection representation; we have therefore preferred to use bond graph representation which, based on physical primitives, seems to be more adapted to our problem.

2 BOND GRAPH REPRESENTATION

2.1 Description

Bond graphs are vertex labeled graphs used to represent physical systems and especially electrical networks (Perelson, 1976). In this formalism, dipoles are connected to each other with edges called bonds and with *serial* or *parallel* vertices called junctions. These junctions are symbolized respectively with "1" or "0". In bond graphs associated with structures containing only dipoles, the degree of vertices corresponding to dipoles is one. These vertices are called *external*.

Example Figure 2 shows a network and its associated bond graph. It has two junctions and five external vertices. The parallel connection between the capacitor and the current source is symbolized by a parallel junction, and the serial connection between this set of two dipoles, the resistor, the switch and the voltage source is symbolized by a serial junction.

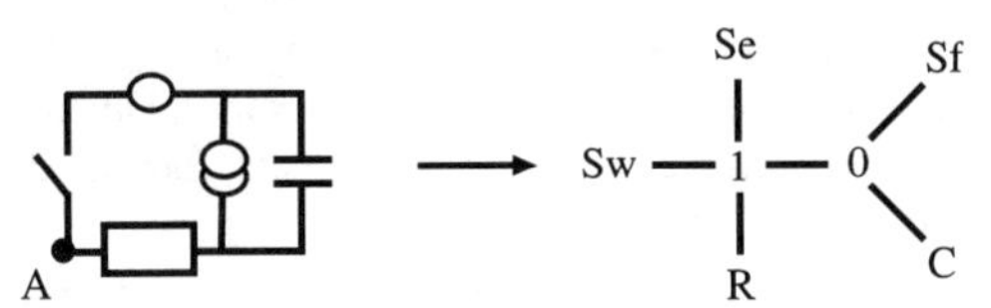

Figure 2: A network and its associated bond graph.

In this representation, the order of elements in series does not appear. For example, if the switch and the resistor are permuted in the network in Figure 2, the component-connection representation is modified but not the bond graph. This shows that a bond graph may represent equivalent but structurally distinct electrical networks.

However, algorithms proposed in (Karnopp and Rosenberg, 1975) and in (Birkett and Roe, 1988) for transforming a network systematically into a bond graph provide several bond graphs for a single circuit. In fact, the associated bond graph is related respectively to a particular ground or to a particular planar representation. For example, by choosing point A as the ground in the circuit in Figure 2, we obtain the bond graph shown in Figure 3. However, the resistor does not appear explicitly in series with the voltage source and the switch.

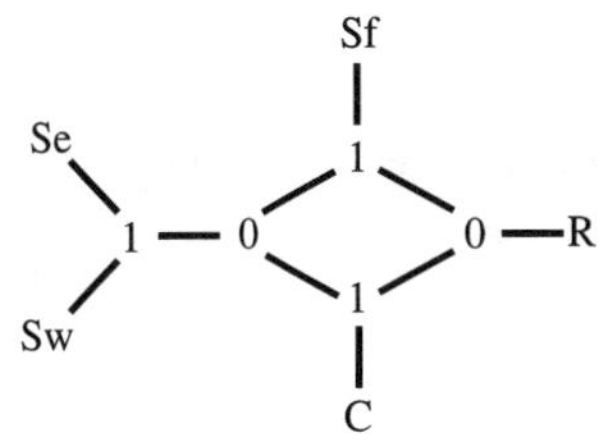

Figure 3: Another possible bond graph for the circuit shown in Figure 2.

With such algorithms, it's impossible to obtain a single representation of a set of equivalent circuits, so we propose another algorithm which allows this. From now on, we suppose that networks are 2-connected; if they were not, they could be decomposed into independently functioning sub-networks.

2.2 From a Network to a Single Bond Graph

The problem is to identify the circuit topology in terms of serial or parallel connections. An "inspection method" was suggested in (Karnopp and Rosenberg, 1975) to perform this task; this paper proposes an algorithm to formalize the method. First, the initial graph is decomposed into blocks of elements. The Tutte decomposition, described in (Tutte, 1984), has been chosen because it is closely related to 2-isomorphism. Next, each element of this decomposition is transformed into a bond graph compound and finally, these compounds are connected to each other to obtain the canonical bond graph.

Tutte Decomposition A Tutte decomposition decomposes a 2-connected graph G into its set of "3-blocks" called $D(G)$. These blocks, which are not exactly subgraphs of G, are either a 3-connected graph, a polygon (i.e. a cycle with at least 3 edges) or a bond (ie. a connected loopless graph on two vertices but with at least 3 edges). Tutte proved that a tree $T(G)$ can be built with elements of $D(G)$ so that each vertex of $T(G)$ is a single element of $D(G)$ and so that each edge of $T(G)$ corresponds to a 2-separation of G. Thus, two graphs with the same Tutte decomposition are 2-isomorphic.

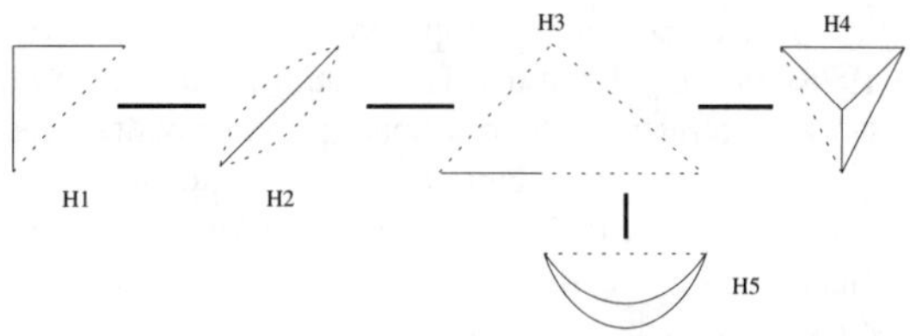

Figure 4: The Tutte decomposition of the circuit shown in Figure 1.

Figure 4 shows the tree associated with the Tutte decomposition of circuit 1 in Figure 1 (dipoles are not included for clarity). This graph is decomposed into one 3-connected graph, two polygons and two bonds. The eight dotted edges are called virtual edges. By merging and deleting the virtual edges of adjacent elements of $D(G)$ in $T(G)$, the graph G is rebuilt.

An algorithm for computing recursively the set of "3-blocks" is proposed in (Hopcroft and Tarjan, 1973). The polygons are composed of elements or blocks of elements which are in series and the bonds are composed of elements which are in parallel. These two types of graphs will naturally correspond to serial and parallel junctions respectively in the bond graph formalism.

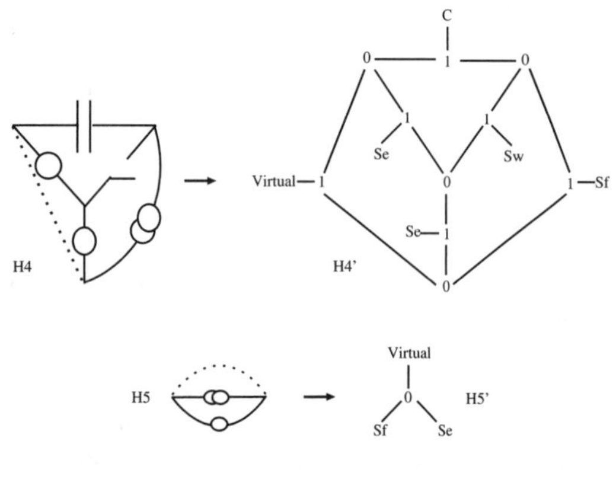

Figure 5: Two examples of graph transformation.

Graph Transformation To obtain the bond graph associated with a graph G, each element $H \in D(G)$ is first associated with a bond graph compound H'. The transformation depends on the type of H as follows:

If H is a 3-connected graph, each vertex of H is associated with a parallel vertex of H' and each edge of H is inserted between parallel vertices of H' using a serial vertex.

If H is a polygon, H' is a serial junction linked with vertices having the same labels as edges of H.

Similarly, if H is a bond, H' is a parallel junction linked with vertices having the same labels as edges of H.

Figure 5 shows a 3-connected graph, a bond and their associated bond graph compounds.

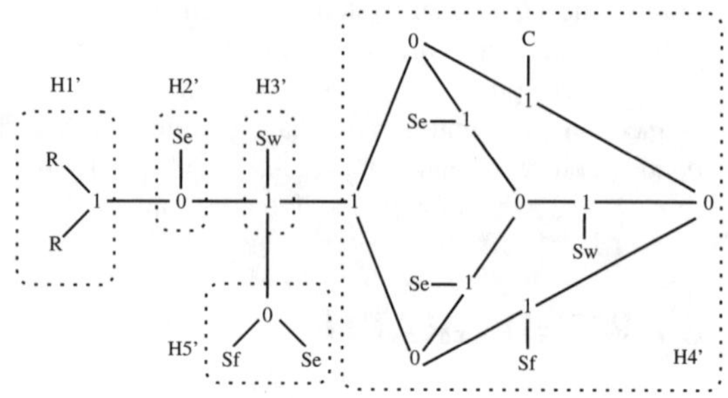

Figure 6: The bond graph associated with circuits in Figure 1.

Connection of Bond Graph Compounds Finally, these compounds are connected if their antecedents are adjacent in the tree $T(G)$. For that, the vertices corresponding to virtual edges are merged and suppressed. Next, the two edges which were associated with these two vertices are merged. Each of these edges corresponds to a 2-separation in the initial graph. The bond graph in Figure 6 is obtained from circuits 1 or 2 in Figure 1.

2.3 Properties

As explained above, each edge inserted between bond graph compounds corresponds to a 2-separation in the initial graph. Consequently, the switch operations at those 2-separations transform the initial graph into a 2-isomorphic one but do not modify the associated bond graph. Therefore two 2-connected circuits are 2-isomorphic if their bond graphs are isomorphic.

With this property, a mathematical reformulation of the definition given in 1.3 is possible. In fact, we can now assert that two 2-connected circuits are equivalent if their associated bond graphs are isomorphic. For example, circuits 1 and 2 in Figure 1 are equivalent because they are both associated with the bond graph in Figure 6.

In addition, Tutte proved that the decomposition presented in 2.2 is unique, which means that for any given circuit there is one and only one bond graph. Thus, this bond graph is the representation of several distinct circuits all of which are equivalent.

CONCLUSION

By formalizing the inspection method proposed by Karnopp, the algorithm proposed in this paper associates a canonical bond graph with an electrical circuit. This bond graph is a representation of a set of circuits that function in the same way. This property is useful to generate a data base of electrical circuits. In addition, bond graphs can be used to test easily the constraints applied for the discarding of uninteresting devices. In fact, many of these constraints can be expressed in terms of serial or parallel compositions of dipoles and, as these compositions are fully expressed using the bond graph formalism and the proposed algorithm, the constraints are easily computed.

Therefore, the algorithm must be generalized to networks with oriented n-port elements and the properties of bond graphs thus obtained need to be studied. In particular, causality propagation algorithms may have to be slightly modified.

References

Berge, C. (1973). *Graphs and algorithms*. North Holland.

Birkett, S. and Roe, P. (1988). The mathematical foundations of bond graphs. *Journal of the Franklin Institute*, 326:329–350.

Chen, W. (1971). *Applied Graph Theory*. North Holland, Amsterdam.

Foster, M. (1932). Geometrical circuits of electrical networks. *Transaction of the American Institute of Electrical Engineers*, 51:309–317.

Hopcroft, J. and Tarjan, R. (1973). Dividing a graph into tri-connected components. *SIAM Journal of Computing*, 2:135–158.

Karnopp, D. and Rosenberg, R. (1975). *System Dynamics - A Unified Approach*. Wiley, New York.

Perelson, A. (1976). Bond graphs and linear graphs. *Journal of the Franklin Institute*, 302:159–185.

Tutte, W. (1984). *Graph Theory*. Addison-Wesley.

Valdés-Pérez, R. (1999). Principles of human-computer collaboration for knowledge discovery in science. *Artificial Intelligence*, 107:335–346.

Whitney, H. (1933). 2-isomorphic graphs. *American Journal of Mathematics*, 55:245–254.

MULTI STAGE MONTE CARLO OPTIMIZATION IN VISUAL BASIC

William Conley
Business Administration
University of Wisconsin at Green Bay
Green Bay, Wisconsin 54311-7001
E-mail: conleyw@uwgb.edu

Philip J. May
Schneider Logistics
Green Bay, Wisconsin 54303
E-mail: philmay@execpc.com

KEYWORDS

Mathematical programming, Visual BASIC, Monte Carlo

ABSTRACT

Simulation has long been an attractive solution approach for generating probabilities in complex systems. These types of simulations will certainly continue and be advanced in our new century. However computers are now so fast and accessible that simulation techniques such as multi stage Monte Carlo optimization (MSMCO) are increasingly viable for solving general multivariate optimization problems; where the goal is not a set of probabilities but an optimal solution.

Three examples will be presented here and Visual BASIC with MSMCO will be used because it is currently a popular programming language and its popularity is likely to last for a long time.

INTRODUCTION

Multi stage Monte Carlo optimization (MSMCO) is a general purpose simulation technique that can be used to solve or approximate the solution to difficult multivariate optimization problems that occur in business, industry and engineering. Although it can be used on linear problems, it will be featured here on several nonlinear multivariate optimization problems to show its power and versatility.

The idea behind MSMCO is that each optimization problem has a sampling distribution of feasible solutions. Therefore, all that is necessary to solve it, is to create a simulation that crosses that sampling distribution to its maximum or minimum solution. The best approach is to have a stage one simulation that randomly looks at thousands of feasible solutions and finds and stores the best one (largest for maximizing and smallest for minimizing). Then centered about this best answer so far, a stage two simulation based search is done in a smaller region and its best answer is found and stored. Then a stage three simulation is done in a further reduced region centered about this new best answer so far.

This process continues for as many stages as are needed to obtain the desired level of accuracy needed for the answer. Any computer language with loops, if statements, arrays and the capacity for using random numbers can be used to create the multi stage Monte Carlo optimization programs. Visual BASIC is the language used here, because it is featured on many computers and used by so many people. Three applications will be presented including; a chemical blending system to be optimized, a system of nonlinear equations transformed into an optimization problem and a nonlinear multivariate product mix problem subject to various constraints. The product mix problem will feature a company making six products with a limit on total productive capacity and separately developed demand curves for each of the six products. The idea being that as the price of a product is lowered, more units are sold but at less revenue per unit. Therefore the company seeks to determine how much of each of the products to make to stay within its productive capacity limits and still reach its revenue goal. The downward sloping demand equations plus the total capacity requirements make this a challenging problem to solve theoretically. However a five second run of a Visual BASIC MSMCO simulation will solve the problem.

One MSMCO Visual BASIC program will be included and explained. It will also be mentioned how it can be modified for other applications, including the ones presented here, plus ones that other practitioners might encounter in applications work.

EXAMPLE ONE

Five input chemicals are run through a refinery yielding six output compounds. The chemicals react nonlinearly and their yield equations for the six outputs are given on the left hand sides of the system

$x_4x_1 + x_3x_5 = 840{,}303$ ounces of compound one
$x_5x_2 + x_2x_3 = 620{,}511$ ounces of compound two
$x_1x_5 + x_4x_4 = 988{,}695$ ounces of compound three
$x_1x_3 + x_1x_5 = 961{,}137$ ounces of compound four
$x_2x_4 + x_5x_2 = 711{,}165$ ounces of compound five
$x_3x_2 + x_3x_4 = 520{,}044$ owners of compound six

where the right hand sides represent the current demand for the six output compounds subject to $O \leq x_i \leq 1000$ tons for i = 1, 2,...5 for the input chemicals.

The refinery solves this current system (to meet its sales requirements—the right hand side values) by minimizing the sum of the absolute values of the differences between the left and right hand side of each equation with the following multi stage Monte Carlo optimization program in Visual BASIC.

The ten stage simulation printout follows the program yielding an answer of x_1 = 807 tons, x_2 = 521 tons, x_3 = 453 tons, x_4 = 627 tons and x_5 = 738 tons of the input chemicals one through five that should produce the desired amounts of the output compounds.

```
Sub Sheet1()
ActiveSheet.Range("B3.H13").ClearContents

Dim a (1 to 5) As Variant
Dim b (1 to 5) As Variant
Dim l (1 to 5) As Variant
Dim n (1 to 5) As Variant
Dim u (1 to 5) As Variant
Dim x (1 to 5) As Variant
Dim p As Long
Dim m As Long
Dim j As Variant
Dim i As Variant
Dim f As Variant
Dim k As Variant
Dim q As Variant
Dim r As Variant
Dim s As Variant
Dim t As Variant
Dim v As Variant
Dim w As Variant
Dim z As Variant
Dim Start, Finish, TotalTime As Integer

Randomize (1)
Let f = 2
Let m = 9999999
For q = 1 To 5
  Let b (q) = 0
  Let a (q) = 500
  Let n (q) = 1000
Next q
Start = Timer
For j = 1To 10
  For i = 1To 7500
    For k = 1 To 5
      If a (k) – n (k) / f ^ j < b (k) Then l (k) = b (k)_
      Else l (k) = a (k) – n (k) / f ^ j
      If a (k) + n (k) / f ^ j > n (k) _
        Then u (k) = n (k) – l (k)
        Else u (k) = a (k) + n (k) / f ^ j – l (k)
      x (k) = Int (l (k) + Rnd ( ) * u (k))
      Next k
  r = x (4) * x (1) + x (3) * x (5) – 840303
  s = x (5) * x (2) + x (2) * x (3) – 620511
  t = x (1) * x (5) + x (4) * x (4) – 988695
  v = x (1) * x (3) + x (1) * x (5) – 961137
  w = x (2) * x (4) + x (5) * x (2) – 711165
  z = x (3) * x (2) + x (3) * x (4) – 520044
  If r < 0 Then r = -1 * r
  If s < 0 Then s = -1 * s
  If t < 0 Then t = -1 *t
  If v < 0 Then v = -1 * v
  If w < 0 Then w = -1 * w
  If z < 0 Then z = -1 * z
  p = r + s + t + v + w + z
  If p < m Then a (1) = x (1): a (2) = x(2): _
    a (3) = x (3): a (4) = x (4): a (5) = x (5):_
    m = p
  Next i

Finish = Timer
Total Time = Finish – Start

Active Sheet.Range ("b2").Activate
ActiveCell.Offset ( (j), 0).Value = a (1)
ActiveCell.Offset ( (j), 1).Value = a (2)
ActiveCell.Offset ( (j), 2).Value = a (3)
ActiveCell.Offset ( (j), 3).Value = a (4)
ActiveCell.Offset ( (j), 4).Value = a (5)
ActiveCell.Offset ( (j), 5).Value = m
Next j
ActiveCell.Offset (11, 6).Value = TotalTime & "seconds"

End Sub
```

The Printout of the Ten Stage Simulation

x_1	x_2	x_3	x_4	x_5	Total Error
842	521	517	689	649	261105
740	478	466	616	856	84971
833	543	447	615	708	49512
846	539	446	632	688	22035
836	535	449	629	704	17156
824	530	448	629	720	8162
811	523	453	627	734	4342
808	521	453	627	737	1669
807	521	453	627	738	0
807	521	453	627	738	0

8 seconds

The program works as follows:
After the various arrays and variables are declared Randomize (1) starts the random number generator for drawing the sample feasible solutions. The b, a, and n arrays set the search region to be $O \leq x_i \leq 1000$ for i = 1, 2....5. The For j loop sets up a ten stage simulation drawing 7500 sample feasible solutions (the For i loop) at each stage. The k loop draws five "random" numbers for the five x values for each function evaluation. The k loop also controls the repositioning and narrowing of the search as it crosses the feasible solution space to the solution. The transformed function follows the k loop.

EXAMPLE TWO

Solve the nonlinear system

$$x_1x_3 + x_2 = 6277$$
$$x_2x_4 + x_5 = 1283$$
$$x_1x_5 + x_4 = 5762$$
$$x_2x_3 + x_1 = 2147$$
$$x_4x_5 + x_3 = 2801$$

by minimizing

$$f(x_1, x_2, x_3, x_4, x_5) = \left|x_1x_3 + x_2 - 6277\right| + \left|x_2x_4 + x_5 - 1283\right| + \left|x_1x_5 + x_4 - 5762\right| + \left|x_2x_3 + x_1 - 2147\right| + \left|x_4x_5 + x_3 - 2801\right|$$

to zero using MSMCO with Visual BASIC.

The previous example's program can be used once it is adjusted for this new function. A three second run of seven stages (sampling 7500 feasible solutions at each stage) yielded a printout of

x_1	x_2	x_3	x_4	x_5	Error Term
86	35	70	44	66	1149
90	27	68	43	62	617
86	29	71	41	67	229
88	29	71	44	65	190
88	29	71	43	65	95
88	29	71	42	65	0
88	29	71	42	65	0

Therefore $x_1 = 88$, $x_2 = 29$, $x_3 = 71$, $x_4 = 42$ and $x_5 = 65$ is the solution.

EXAMPLE THREE

A company is making six products and has a total hourly production goal, a production cost goal, an inventory cost goal, a unit set up time goal, a machining time goal, a packaging time goal and a revenue goal given in the following equations

$x_1 + x_2 + x_3 + x_4 + x_5 + x_6 = 1{,}000$ total hourly production goal
$2x_1 + 7x_2 + 15x_3 + 6x_4 + x_5 + 3x_6 = 7{,}551$ production cost goal
$3x_1 + 4x_2 + 6x_3 + 5x_4 + 7x_5 + 8x_6 = 4{,}729$ inventory cost goal
$2x_1 + 3x_2 + x_3 + 3x_4 + 2x_5 + x_6 = 1{,}999$ set up cost goal
$2x_1 + 7x_2 + 3x_3 + 5x_4 + 2x_5 + 4x_6 = 4{,}127$ unit set up time goal
$3x_1^{.89} + 4x_2^{.78} + 5x_3^{.91} + 3x_4^{.93} + 2x_5^{.75} + 6x_6^{.94} = 2{,}081$ machining time goal
$4x_1^{.97} + 6x_2^{.68} + 3x_3^{.88} + 4x_4^{.92} + 10x_5^{.72} + 3x_6^{.91} = 1{,}984$ packaging time goal
$34x_1^{.87} + 46.x_2^{.93} + 28x_3^{.90} + 29x_4^{.92} + 45x_5^{.79} + 20x_6^{.94} = 21{,}130$ revenue goal

Again modifying our example one Visual BASIC program for minimizing this six variable function (call it $g(x_1, x_2, x_3, x_4, x_5, x_6)$) that is the sum of the absolute values of the differences between the left and right hand side of each equation yields the solution of

$x_1 = 255$, $x_2 = 315$, $x_3 = 290$, $x_4 = 42$, $x_5 = 30$ and $x_6 = 68$.

So given their current requirements and limitations (right hand sides of the equations) they should make 255, 315, 290, 42, 30 and 68 units of products one through six respectively.

CONCLUSION

Every chemical plant, every factory production setting or any business or enterprise can be viewed as one big optimization problem ready to be simulated in Visual BASIC with MSMCO or one of the other so called "genetic algorithms." This could lead to more sophisticated and accurate business planning and forecasting, with the knowledge that at least an approximate solution to a difficult nonlinear optimization problem is possible with simulation and Visual BASIC. Frequently this "approximation" turns out to be the true optimal. When it is not the true optimal it is at a minimum the best course of action out of millions of alternatives.

BIOGRAPHIES

William Conley is professor of Business Administration and Statistics at the University of Wisconsin at Green Bay. He is a member of Phi Beta Kappa and a senior member in the Society for Computer Simulation. He is a fellow in the Institution of Electronic and Telecommunication Engineers of India and was inducted into the Albion College Athletic Hall of Fame. Hobbies include golf, tennis, jogging and listening to music.

Philip J. May works for Schneider Logistics on various finance and transportation problems. He is a 1999 summa cum laude graduate of the University of Wisconsin at Green Bay, where he received the University Leadership Award and was elected to Who's Who of American Colleges and Universities. He is an expert in Visual BASIC and a considerable user of internet applications. Hobbies include skiing, golf and reading.

STATISTICAL OPTIMIZATION AND THE MINIMAX TRANSFORMATION

William Conley
Business Administration
University of Wisconsin at Green Bay
Green Bay, Wisconsin 54311-7001
E-mail: conleyw@uwgb.edu

KEYWORDS

Education, Optimization, Monte Carlo, Sampling

ABSTRACT

Computers have become so quick and powerful that large scale simulation techniques such as multi stage Monte Carlo optimization can be used to solve difficult multivariate optimization problems and systems of equations when combined with the minimax transformation.

The minimax transformation attempts to minimize the maximum equation error at each stage of the simulation when used in conjunction with multi stage Monte Carlo optimization.

Presented here will be four minimax examples. First a minimax forecasting problem will be presented as an alternative to the least squares approach. Then three nonlinear systems of varying size and difficulty will be presented followed by a discussion of the strengths and limitations of the minimax and multi stage simulation approach.

INTRODUCTION

A statistical optimization technique called multi stage Monte Carlo optimization (MSMCO) can be used to solve systems of equations, by minimizing the errors between the left and right hand sides of each equation in the system.

Typically a system such as

$$f(x_1, x_2, \ldots x_n) = c_1$$
$$g(x_1, x_2, \ldots x_n) = c_2$$
$$\vdots$$
$$r(x_1, x_2, \ldots x_n) = c_k$$

would be transformed to minimize

$$a(x_1, x_2, \ldots x_n) = |f-c_1| + |g-c_2| + \ldots |r-c_k|$$

and solved using MSMCO, which would make repeated random searches in an ever reducing search region centered about the best answer so far as the simulation proceeds. This approach is designed to drive the simulation as far as possible across the feasible solution space of $a(x_1, x_2, \ldots x_n)$ to the minimum (or a near approximation).

One difficulty with this approach is that with larger systems (more than five equations) one, two or three of the error terms could be dominated by the other fast dropping error terms. This would lead to say, for example, four of six equations being solved (in a six equation system).

This can be overcome by using the minimax transformation that minimizes the maximum error of the equations at each stage of the simulation. Referring to the previous example we would define

$$E_1 = |f-c_1|$$
$$E_2 = |g-c_2|$$
$$\vdots$$
$$E_k = |r-c_k|$$

and then minimize

$$b(x_1, x_2, \ldots x_n) = \text{Maximum}(E_1, E_2, \ldots E_k)$$

as the MSMCO simulation proceeds. This eliminates the problem of leaving any error terms behind. So when the maximum error term is driven to zero, the complete system is solved.

However even this approach can run into problems on particularly difficult large systems. The minimax simulation runs the risk of getting pinned down in a local optimal and never getting out. There are several ways around that difficulty too. Some type of averaging of several MSMCO simulations along with minimax attached to the sum of the absolute values approach can work. Also minimizing the median error term in conjunction with the minimax transformation can lead to improved results.

These extra simulations and transformations exist at a price, namely usually longer run times for the simulation. However our era of powerful pc's and mainframes is making computer time cheaper and shorter for most tasks. TRW has announced in January 2000 that its new computer chip will do 69,000,000,000 operations a second. It is an exciting time to be in the computer simulation field.

A MINIMAX FORECAST EXAMPLE

Find the forecasted equation of the form $y = B_1x_1 + B_2x_2 + B_3(x_1\ x_2)^{.5}$ that minimizes the maximum absolute error on the following data set using multi stage Monte Carlo optimization (MSMCO).

x_1	x_2	y
20	50	37,037
10	10	10,260
10	80	43,427
16	75	46,335
40	12	21,220
75	25	41,927
50	50	51,300
95	20	42,587
70	45	55,509

The MSMCO simulation seeks to minimize $f\ (x_1,x_2,x_3)$ = maximum of $(E_1,E_2,E_3,E_4,E_5,E_6,E_7,E_8,E_9)$ where

$$E_1 = \left| B_1 20 + B_2 50 + B_3 SQR\ (20.50) - 37037.0 \right|$$

$$E_2 = \left| B_1 10 + B_2 10 + B_3 SQR\ (10.10) - 10260.0 \right|$$

$$E_3 = \left| B_1 10 + B_2 80 + B_3 SQR\ (10.80) - 43427.0 \right|$$

.
.
.
.

$$E_9 = \left| B_1 70 + B_2 45 + B_3 SQR\ (70.45) - 55509.0 \right|$$

and SQR means take the square root. The BASIC language simulation program for this problem is

```
1   REM MINIMAX FORECAST
2   REM WITH MULTI STAGE
5   DIM A(3),B(3),L(3),N(3),U(3),X(3)
6   DIM E(9),ER(9),P(9)
7   F=2
8   RANDOMIZE
9   M=1.0E21
10  FOR I2=1 TO 3
12  X(I2)=0
14  A(I2)=500
15  N(I2)=1000
16  NEXT I2
18  FOR J=1 TO 18
19  Q=F**J
20  FOR I=1 TO 20000
21  FOR K=1 TO 3
30  IF A(K) - N (K) / Q < X(K) THEN 50
40  GO TO 60
50  L(K) = X(K)
55  GO TO 65
60  L(K) = A(K) – N(K) / Q
65  IF A(K) + N(K) / Q > N(K) THEN 80
70  GO TO 90
80  U(K) = N(K) – L(K)
85  GO TO 100
90  U(K) = A(K) + N(K) / Q – L(K)
100 B(K) = (L(K) + RND*U(K) )
101 NEXT K
103 P(1) = B(1)*20+B(2)*50+B(3)*(20*50)**.5
104 E(1) = ABS (P(1) – 37037.0)
105 P(2) = B(1)*10 + B(2)*10+B(3)*10
106 E(2) = ABS (P(2) – 10260.0)
107 P(3) = B(1)*10 + B(2)*80 + B(3)*(10*80)**.5
108 E(3) = ABS (P(3) – 43427.0)
109 P(4) = B(1)*16+B(2)*75+B(3)*(16*75)**.5
110 E(4) = ABS (P(4) – 46335.0)
111 P(5) = B(1)*40+B(2)*12+B(3)*(40*12)**.5
112 E(5)  = ABS (P(5) – 21220.0)
114 P(6) = B(1)*75+B(2)*25+B(3)*(75*25)**.5
115 E(6) = ABS (P(6) – 41927.0)
116 P(7) = B(1)*50+B(2)*50+B(3)*(50*50)**.5
117 E(7) = ABS(P(7) – 51300.0)
118 P(8) = B(1)*95+B(2)*20+B(3)*(95*20)**.5
119 E(8) = ABS (P(8) – 42587.0)
120 P(9) = B(1)*70+B(2)*45+B(3)*(70*45)**.5
121 E(9) = ABS (P(9) – 55509.0)
130 MM=0
131 FOR I5=1 to 9
132 IF E (I5) < MM  THEN 137
133 MM=E(I5)
137 NEXT I5
140 IF MM < M THEN 160
150 GO TO 190
160 M=MM
161 A(1) = B(1)
162 A(2) = B(2)
163 A(3) = B(3)
165 FOR I7 =1 TO 9
166 ER (I7) = E(I7)
168 NEXT I7
190 NEXT I
195 PRINT A(1), A(2), A(3), M
200 NEXT J
201 END
```

The eighteen (lines 18-200) stage simulation draws (line 20) 20,000 sets of B_1, B_2 and B_3 at each stage always minimizing the maximum E_i error in an ever narrowing and repositioning search for the optimal. The K loop lines 21-101 controls the reading in all of sample feasible solutions and it also controls the ever narrowing focus search for the optimal. The printout of the best answer at each of the eighteen stages is

B_1	B_2	B_3	Maximum Error
118.471	326.72	573.022	389.367
105.248	318.858	602.041	162.426
100.229	312.539	615.202	99.3477
100.229	312.539	615.202	99.3477
101.785	314.788	610.549	56.125
102.562	314.51	609.195	14.2656
103.097	314.875	608.045	8.79688
103.169	315.162	607.532	7.25781
102.949	314.988	608.103	1.98828
103.021	314.996	607.967	1.35547
102.969	314.99	608.052	.753906
102.968	314.976	608.064	.628906
102.99	314.999	608.012	.451172
102.996	315.008	607.994	.416016
102.995	315.005	607.997	.404297
102.995	315.005	607.997	.404297
102.997	315.009	607.992	.402344
102.998	315.011	607.988	.398438

Therefore $y = 102.998x_1+315.011x_2+607.988(x_1x_2)^{.5}$ with maximum E_i error of .398438 is a good equation fit for the data.

A NONLINEAR SYSTEM EXAMPLE

Use MSMCO and the minimax transformation with a five stage simulation drawing 20,000 feasible solutions at each stage in the region $O \leq x_i \leq 11$ for $i = 1, 2, \ldots 8$ to find an all whole number solution to the system

$$x_1^5 + x_4^2 x_8 = 33{,}173 \quad (1)$$

$$x_5^5 + x_1^2 x_7 = 8{,}416 \quad (2)$$

$$x_7^5 + x_3^2 x_6 = 101{,}089 \quad (3)$$

$$x_6^5 + x_1^2 x_8 = 59{,}369 \quad (4)$$

$$x_2^5 + x_4^2 x_6 = 17{,}536 \quad (5)$$

$$x_8^5 + x_3^2 x_7 = 4{,}335 \quad (6)$$

$$x_3^5 + x_2^2 x_6 = 161{,}492 \quad (7)$$

$$x_8^5 + x_5^2 x_8 = 3{,}305 \quad (8)$$

$$x_4^5 + x_2^2 x_5 = 59{,}343 \quad (9)$$

The solution of $x_1 = 8$, $x_2 = 7$, $x_3 = 11$, $x_4 = 9$, $x_5 = 6$, $x_6 = 9$, $x_7 = 10$ and $x_8 = 5$ is produced in just seconds. The previous program can be used for this example once it is modified for eight variables, and integer solutions in the desired range with the new function inserted.

A THIRD EXAMPLE

Use MSMCO and the minimax transformation with a seven stage simulation drawing 10,000 feasible solutions at each stage in the region $O \leq x_i \leq 100$ for $i = 1, 2, \ldots 7$ to find an all whole number solution to the system

$$x_1^2 x_3 + x_2x_4 = 184{,}617 \quad (1)$$

$$x_4^2 x_7 + x_3x_5 = 177{,}944 \quad (2)$$

$$x_2^2 x_4 + x_4x_6 = 188{,}235 \quad (3)$$

$$x_7^2 x_7 + x_1x_3 = 514{,}088 \quad (4)$$

$$x_3^2 x_3 + x_2x_5 = 17{,}037 \quad (5)$$

$$x_5^2 x_4 + x_1x_6 = 125{,}379 \quad (6)$$

$$x_4^2 x_2 + x_2x_4 = 142{,}128 \quad (7)$$

$$x_5^2 x_5 + x_1x_7 = 139{,}611 \quad (8)$$

$$x_7^2 x_1 + x_2x_5 = 560{,}013 \quad (9)$$

$$x_6^2 x_6 + x_3x_7 = 48{,}576 \quad (10)$$

The solution of $x_1 = 87$, $x_2 = 63$, $x_3 = 24$, $x_4 = 47$, $x_5 = 51$, $x_6 = 36$ and $x_7 = 80$ is produced quickly. Again the previous program can be used once it is modified for seven variables and ten equations and the new transformed minimax function and bounds.

A FOURTH EXAMPLE

Use MSMCO and the minimax transformation with an eight stage simulation drawing 15,000 feasible solutions at each stage in the region $O \leq x_i \leq 12$ for $i = 1, 2, \ldots 10$ to find an all whole number solution to the system

$$x_1^6 + x_2x_4 + x_8 = 262{,}283$$

$$x_2^6 + x_4x_5 + x_{10} = 2{,}986{,}083$$

$$x_3^6 + x_9x_{10} + x_2 = 262{,}266$$

$$x_4^6 + x_1x_2 + x_3 = 1{,}771{,}665$$

$$x_5^6 + x_7x_8 + x_9 = 262{,}231$$

$$x_6^6 + x_3x_5 + x_7 = 1{,}000{,}075$$

$$x_7^6 + x_6x_8 + x_9 = 1{,}771{,}641$$

$$x_8^6 + x_1x_2 + x_8 = 117{,}752$$

$$x_9^6 + x_8x_4 + x_2 = 1{,}000{,}089$$

$$x_{10}^6 + x_1x_5 + x_8 = 1{,}771{,}632$$

The solution of

$x_1 = 8$, $x_2 = 12$, $x_3 = 8$, $x_4 = 11$, $x_5 = 8$, $x_6 = 10$, $x_7 = 11$, $x_8 = 7$, $x_9 = 10$ and $x_{10} = 11$

is similarly produced in seconds.

CONCLUSION

What would happen if MSMCO and minimax were tried on a system with one thousand variables and equations. The easy answer is to say that it would not solve the system (assuming the system had a solution) because even if the optimal solution region were located that "random sampling" would have to hit all 1,000 numbers exactly (and that's unlikely) to get the exact solution.

However real valued arithmetic can be used and those answers then rounded to the nearest whole number for a try at the optimal when one requires an all whole number solution.

Also outer loops can be put around the multi stage simulation to repeatedly average (coordinatewise) thirty or forty or one hundred MSMCO solution attempts. This usually greatly improves the prospect for an optimal or useful approximate solution.

The powerful and inexpensive computers of the twenty-first century could make simulation the dominant solution approach in engineering and business mathematics.

BIOGRAPHY

Dr. William Conley is a member of the Business Administration and Mathematics faculty at the University of Wisconsin at Green Bay. He is a member of Phi Beta Kappa and the author of over 150 publications. He was inducted into the Albion College Athletic Hall of Fame and is a senior member of the Society for Computer Simulation. He is also a fellow in the Institution of Electronics and Telecommunications Engineers. He has a Ph.D. in mathematics from the University of Windsor.

SNOOPY A NEW CALENDAR QUEUE STRUCTURE

Kah Leong, Tan
Li-Jin, Ian Thng
Chi Chung, Ko

Department of Electrical Engineering
10 Kent Ridge Crescent
National University of Singapore
Singapore 119260

Keywords: Optimization, Calendar Queue, SNOOPy CQ, Future Event List

ABSTRACT

Discrete event simulations need a priority queue to schedule events according to their timestamp. Up to 40% of the time may be spent on the management of the pending event set. Thus the choice of a efficient data structure is vital to the performance of discrete event simulations. A conventional Calendar Queue (CQ) and Dynamic Calendar Queue (DCQ) are two data structures that promises O(1) time complexity regardless of the size of the pending event set. CQ however performs poorly over skewed event distributions or changes in the event distribution. DCQ improves on the CQ by adding a mechanism to detect the two scenarios above and redistribute events when necessary. Both of these data structures determine their operating parameter (bucket width) by sampling of events. Sampling sometimes fails to provide a good estimate for an optimum bucket width to use. This paper proposes a novel approach to determine the optimum operating parameter of a calendar queue based on its performance statistics and guarantees O(1) performance. Henceforth, we named our calendar queue adopting this mechanism, Statistically eNhanced with Optimum Operating Parameter Calendar Queue (SNOOPy CQ). Our experiment results showed that SNOOPy CQ offers a consistent O(1) performance and, in certain scenarios, executes up to 100 times faster than DCQ and CQ.

1 INTRODUCTION

Discrete event simulations are widely used in many research areas to model complex system's behavior. In discrete event simulation a system is modeled as a number of logical processes that interact among themselves by generating event messages with an execution timestamp associated with each of the messages. The pending event set (PES) is a set of all generated event messages that have not been service yet. A PES can be represented by a priority queue with messages with the smallest timestamp having the highest priority and vice versa. The choice of a data structure to represent the PES can affect the performance of a simulation greatly. If the number of events in the PES is huge as in the case for a fine-grain simulation, it has been shown that up to 40% of the simulation execution time maybe spent on the management of the PES alone [Comfort, 1984].

A Calendar Queue is a data structure that offers O(1) time complexity regardless of the number of events in the PES. To achieve this the Calendar Queue, which consists of an array of linked lists, tries to maintain a small number of events over each list. However Calendar Queue performs poorly when event distributions are highly skewed or when event distributions changes.

A Dynamic Calendar Queue (DCQ) [Oh and Ahn, 1999], has been proposed to solve the above-mentioned problem by adding a mechanism for detecting uneven distribution of events over its array of linked lists. Whenever this is detected, DCQ re-computes a new operating parameter for the calendar queue and redistributes events over a newly created array of linked lists.

Both the DCQ and CQ compute their operating parameter based on sampling a number of events in the PES. Sometimes the choices of samples are not sufficiently reflective of the optimum bucket width to use for the PES. When this occurs, performance of the DCQ and CQ degrade significantly and the newly resized calendar will not be able to maintain their O(1) processing complexity.

This paper proposes a novel approach in estimating an optimum operating parameter for a calendar queue. This approach is based on the past performance matrices of the calendar queue which can be obtained statistically. This approach provides an O(1) processing complexity for the calendar queue under all standard benchmarking distributions. It is also not susceptible to estimation error associated with the sampling method used in DCQ and CQ.

This paper is organized as follows. In section 2 we present in detail how a conventional CQ and DCQ operates, and their associated shortcomings. In section 3 we describe the statistical data-bucket width relationship used by the SNOOPy CQ algorithm. Utilizing this relationship, section 4 describes the SNOOPy CQ mechanism in pseudocode. In section 5, the performance graphs of SNOOpy CQ, DCQ and CQ under different situations are presented, compared and analyzed. Finally section 6 summarizes the content of this paper.

2 CQ AND DCQ

A quick understanding on the working of the calendar queue can be obtained by following the illustrated example below.

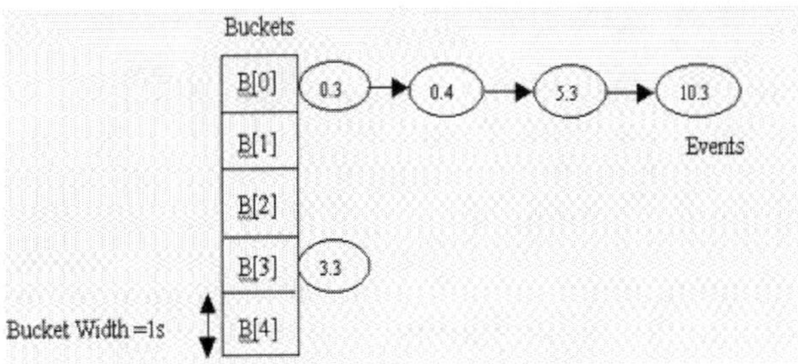

Figure 1: A Conventional Calendar Queue

A calendar can be represented by an array of buckets as shown in the figure above. Each bucket contains a linked list of events. Each bucket represents a single day of the calendar year. For the example above a year consists of five days. The length of a day is in turn represented by the bucket width and for this case it is 1 s. A year for the above calendar is thus 5 s. Events are sorted according to the day and year they fall into. Looking at the calendar above it can be seen that the events' timestamps can be mapped to the calendar year and day according to the Table 1

Table 1: Event Timestamp Mapping

Event timestamp		Calendar Year	Calendar Day
0.3		0	1
0.4		0	1
5.3		1	1
10.3		2	1
3.3		0	4

It can be seen that any events falling on the same calendar day regardless of their calendar year is inserted into the same bucket and sorted in increasing time order. All day one events are stored into bucket 0 or B[0], and all day N events are stored into bucket N-1 or B[N-1]. Let's assume we would like to insert a new event with timestamp 4.3 s. Mapping this timestamp to that of the calendar shows that it falls on day 5 and year 0 (4.3 modulo 5). Thus this new event will be inserted into B[4].

For dequeuing of events the calendar queue always keep track of the current calendar year and day it is in. It will dequeue the earliest events that falls on the current calendar year and calendar day. If no such event is found it will proceed on to search the next bucket. When all the buckets have been cycled through the current calendar year will be incremented by 1 and current calendar day will be reset back to day 1(B[0]).

The number of buckets of a calendar is of the power of two. Buckets are doubled or halved everytime the number of events exceeds twice that or decreased below half the current number of buckets. During this resize operation a new value of operating parameter (bucket width) will be calculated. The new bucket width to used will be estimated from sampling the average inter-event time gap from the first few hundreds events. With this new bucket width a new calendar will be created and all the events in the old calendar will be recopied over.

The resize heuristic described above for the calendar queue suffers from the following problems:

1) Since resizing is done only when the number of events doubled or halved that of the current number of buckets, calendar queue would not be able to adapt itself if there is a drastic change in event distribution but not on the number of events.
2) Sampling the first few hundreds of events for estimation of an appropriate bucket width to use may not give an accurate estimate for the optimum bucket width especially when event distribution is highly skewed.

Dynamic Calendar Queue (DCQ), tries to improved on the conventional calendar queue by adding the following mechanism. DCQ keeps track of the Average Enqueue Cost (AEC) and the Average Dequeue Cost (ADC). AEC is defined as the average number of events that need to be skipped through before an insertion can be made on a linked list. ADC is defined as the average number of buckets that need to be searched through before the event with the earliest timestamp can be found.

DCQ computes AEC and ADC after every N enqueue or dequeue operations, where N is the number of buckets in the calendar. If the AEC or ADC computed exceeds a preset threshold indicating a change in event distribution, DCQ forces a resize operation. A new bucket width will be computed based on sampling of events around the most populated bucket. Although DCQ can detects and forces a resize operation when an uneven distribution of events in its buckets is detected, DCQ still suffers from the following problems:

1) The DCQ heuristic suffers from inherent instability and may perform better than conventional CQ in same situation but performs worse in others.
2) Calculation for of an optimum bucket width to use just by sampling events around the most populated bucket does not guarantee a good estimate everytime. It can give a better estimate then the estimation method used by conventional CQ in some situation but not all. This leads to the instability problem described in (1).
3) When both AEC and ADC does not exceed the threshold no further optimization of bucket width will be done although possible.

SNOOPy CQ uses a novel approach in estimating an optimum bucket width to use without resorting to sampling of events. It also incorporates an algorithm that does further optimization of bucket width from time to time to achieve optimum performance. The statistics behind obtaining an optimum bucket width for a calendar queue will be described in the next section.

3 STATISTICS BEHIND SNOOPY CQ

Performance of a priority queue can often be measured by the average number of searches performed for a set of enqueue and dequeue operations (a hold operation). Thus to optimize a calendar queue we will need to minimize ADC+AEC. Let's define the average searches done for a hold operation as Average Total Cost (ATC). Assume that the current ATC, ADC and AEC for a calendar queue is *Oldcost*, C_D and C_E respectively. And assume that currently $C_D > C_E$. Let the current bucket width of the calendar queue be *Oldbucketwidth*. Thus we have,

$$Oldcost = C_D + C_E \qquad (1)$$

Our objective is to find a new bucket width, *Newbucketwidth*, that minimizes expression (1). Let the optimum resize factor be k such that

$$Newbucketwidth = k \times Oldbucketwidth \qquad (2)$$

And this factor k minimizes expression (1) above. Since $C_D > C_E$, the calendar queue at the moment makes more searches through empty buckets before dequeuing an event than searches through the linked list for enqueueing an event. Thus to rectify this situation k must be bigger than 1. In other words we must increase the bucket size to decrease the number of empty buckets and effectively decreasing C_D. Let's assume that when we increase the bucket width by a factor of k, C_D will decrease by a similar factor k. AEC will also be affected by this resizing. If we increase the calendar bucket width by a factor k, more events will reside in each bucket, thus increasing AEC. Let's assume C_E will be increased by a factor k, when bucket width is increased by a similar factor. Table 2 shows the effect on the calendar variables before and after the resize operation.

Table 2: Variable Values for Calendar Queue

Variables	Before resize	After resize
Bucket Width	*Oldbucketwidth*	*k×Oldbucketwidth*
ADC	C_D	C_D /k
AEC	C_E	$k \times C_E$
ATC	$C_D + C_E$	$C_D /k + k \times C_E$

From the table above we propose the new ATC, *Newcost*, as a function of resize factor k as

$$Newcost = C_D /k + k \times C_E \qquad (3)$$

By differentiating (3) with respect to k, and equating it to zero, we find that the optimum k that minimizes the ATC is given in the equation below

$$k = (C_D / C_E)^{0.5} \qquad (4)$$

Substituting (4) into (2), we obtain the expression below that gives an estimate of an optimum bucket width to use that minimizes the ATC.

$$Newbucketwidth = (C_D / C_E)^{0.5} \times Oldbucketwidth \qquad (5)$$

For the case $C_E > C_D$, using similar arguments, expression (6) below can be derived for the optimum new bucket width.

$$Newbucketwidth = (C_D / C_E)^{0.5} \times Oldbucketwidth \qquad (6)$$

Thus, the same equation can be used in order to obtain an estimate for an optimum bucket width to use for both situations. Substituting this value of k into Table 2 we obtained the following values for the calendar variables in Table 3.

Table 3: Variable Values for Calendar Queue

Variables	Before resize	After resize
Bucket Width	*Oldbucket-width*	$(C_D/C_E)^{0.5} \times Oldbucketwidth$
ADC	C_D	$(C_D \times C_E)^{0.5}$
AEC	C_E	$(C_D \times C_E)^{0.5}$
ATC	$C_D + C_E$	$2 \times (C_D \times C_E)^{0.5}$

From Table 3 it can be observed that for optimum operation the value of ADC and AEC are the same.
As for the ATC, since,

$$(C_D^{\ 0.5} + C_E^{\ 0.5})^{2.} \geq 0$$
$$C_D + C_E + 2 \times (C_D \times C_E)^{0.5} \geq 0$$
$$2 \times (C_D \times C_E)^{0.5} \leq C_D + C_E \qquad (8)$$

Equation (8) shows that the ATC after resizing will always be smaller or equal to that ATC before resizing. Thus this resize algorithm is stable and will eventually converge to the true optimum bucket width that minimizes ATC after a few resize operations even if estimates for ADC and AEC are not so accurate.

4 SNOOPY CQ

SNOOPy CQ is very similar to that of DCQ except for the algorithm used for estimation of bucket width. SNOOPy CQ computes a new bucket width to be used based solely on the current bucket width and the performance statistics ADC and AEC. Initially when queue size is small and performance statistic is not available SNOOPy CQ relies on the DCQ algorithm to compute bucket width. Only when the queue size exceeds a certain threshold does SNOOPy CQ takes over the task of computing bucket width from DCQ.

It has been shown in section 3, that optimum performance occurs when ADC is same as AEC. To achieve this, SNOOPy CQ initiates performance fine-tuning even when ADC or AEC differs significantly from each other. SNOOPy CQ will initiate a bucket resize operation whenever the ratio of a 10 samples moving average of ADC/AEC differs by more than a factor of two (MADC> 2 × MAEC or MADC < 0.5 × MAEC). The moving averages, MAEC and MADC, is the average for the 10 most recent values of AEC or ADC respectively. This algorithm ensures that both ADC and AEC will have approximately the same value for optimum operation.

The pseudo-code for SNOOPy CQ for an enqueue operation is given in Figure 4 and for the resize operation in Figure 5. A description of all the variables used is given in Table 4 below.

Table 4: Description of Variables

Variable	Description
CalQSize	Keeps track the number of enqueued events
CalTop-Threshold	The threshold for upward resizing
EnqCnt	Keeps track of the number of events skipped before a successful insertion into a linked list
SumEnqCnt	Accumulated EnqCnt since the last resize operation
EnqSearch	The number of enqueue operations done since the last resize operation
DeqCnt	Keeps track of the number of buckets skipped before a successful removal of the most imminent event
SumDeqCnt	Accumulated DeqCnt since the last resize operation
DeqSearch	The number of dequeue operations done since the last resize operation
AEC	SumEnqCnt/EnqSearch
ADC	SumDeqCnt/DeqSearch
MAEC	Average value for 10 most recent AECs
MADC	Average value for 10 most recent ADCs

```
enqueue( ) {
(1)enqueue new event to the appropriate bucket;
(2)  set  EnqCnt  to  the  number  of  events  to
visit;
(3) calQSize++;
(4) if (calQSize > calTopThreshold) {
(5)   calResize(2 * calNBuckets);
(6)   SumEnqCnt = 0;
(7)   EnqSearch = 0;
(8) }else {
(9)     SumEnqueueCnt += EnqCnt;
(10)   EnqSearch++;
(11)   if (EnqSearch > calNBuckets) {
(12)       if((SumEnqCnt/EnqSearch>2)
           ||(MAEC/MADC>2)| |(MAEC/MADC<0.5)){
(13)              AEC=MAEC;ADC=MADC;
(14)         calResize(calNBuckets);}
(15)       else{
(16)       Collect Moving Average of AEC;
(17)          EnqSearch = 0;
(18)          SumEnqCnt = 0; } } } }
```

Figure 2: Enqueue() Pseudo Code of SNOOPy CQ

Line (3) to (8) shows the static resize algorithm of a conventional CQ that resizes only when calQSize exceeds twice that of the current number of buckets. The dynamic resize algorithm of SNOOPy CQ is given by line (9) to (18). SNOOPy CQ dynamic resize algorithm is very similar to that of DCQ except on line (12) and (16). On line (12), SNOOPy CQ adds additional condition for resize whenever the ratio of 10 Samples Moving Average for AEC and ADC differs by more than a factor of 2. On line (16), moving average data of AEC is collected and this is absent in the DCQ algorithm. The effect of line (12) and (16) is to further fine tune the bucket width for optimum performance during steady state by ensuring that AEC and ADC does not differ much from one another.

The pseudo code for the calendar resize operation calResize( ) is given in Figure 3 below.

```
calResize(N){
(1)if( EnqSearch>64 && DeqSearch>64 )
(2)     bucketwidth = (ADC/AEC)^0.5bucketwidth;
(3)else
(4)   calculate bucketwidth using DCQ algo;
(5)reset MAEC and MADC collected;
(6) redistribute events using the new bucket-
width calculated;
   }
```

Figure 3: Enqueue() Pseudo Code of SNOOPy CQ

From figure 3, it can be seen that when the number of statistical samples are big enough to get an accurate estimate for AEC and ADC then only SNOOPy CQ bucket width estimation algorithm is triggered. If there is not sufficient amount of data to compute a good estimate of AEC or ADC the standard DCQ bucket width estimate algorithm will be used. Line (5) resets the MAEC and MADC obtained since a resize operation changes the *bucketwidth*. MAEC and MADC measure the moving average of AEC and ADC for at constant *bucketwidth*.

5 EXPERIMENTS AND RESULTS

The classical Hold and Up/Down model are used to benchmark the performance for a conventional calendar queue (SCQ), DCQ and SNOOPy CQ. The priority increment distributions used are the Rect, Triag, Camel(x,y) and Change(A,B,x) distributions as were used by Oh and Ahn [1999] and Rönngren et al.[1993]. Camel(x,y) represents a 2 hump distribution will x% of its mass concentrated in the two humps and the duration of the two humps is y% of the total interval. Change(A,B,x) interleaves two priority distribution A and B together. Initially x priority increments are drawn from A followed by another x priority increments drawn from B and so on. The shapes of the priority increment distributions used are shown in Figure 4.

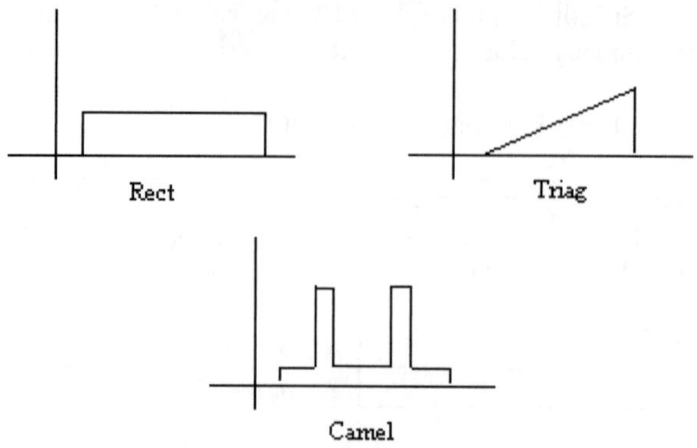

Figure 4: Benchmarking Distributions

The Classical Hold and Up/Down model represent two extreme cases and are frequently used to show the performance bounds of PES implementations [Vaucher and Duval, 1975]. The number of hold operations performed is 100 × the queue size. Loop overhead time is eliminated using another dummy loop as was described by Rönngren and Ayani[1997]. Figure 5 shows the Hold results under Triag and Camel(98,01) distribution for SCQ, DCQ and SNOOPy CQ.

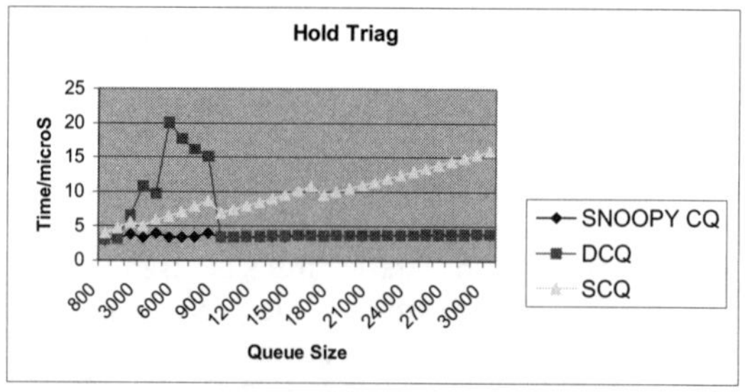

(a)

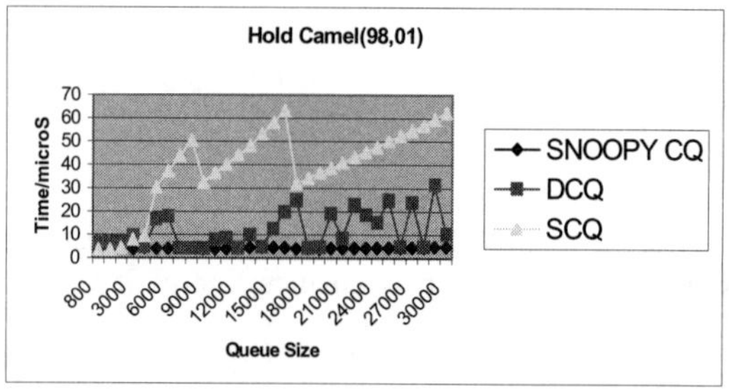

(b)

Figure 5: Average time per Hold operation under Hold Model

It can be observed that out of the three queue implementations SNOOPy CQ seems to be least affected by the type of distribution used with average hold time between 3 to 5 µs for all priority increment distributions. DCQ performance is erratic for Triag and Camel(98,01) distributions. Average hold time varies from 3 to 30 µs. SCQ performance is the worst among the three queue implementations with average hold time varying from 3 to 65µs for the two distribution tested. Both DCQ and SCQ suffer from the same problem in estimating the optimum bucket width to use just from sampling of events. For DCQ sampling of events around the most populated bucket seems to give a good estimate for some situation but not all. Thus, the inconsistent performance as shown in graph (a) and (b).

Two other distributions used for the Hold benchmark are the Change (camel9801(9-10), Triag(0-0.0001), 2000) and Change (Triag(9-10), Rect(0-0.0001), 2000). Camel9801(9-10) represents the camel(98,01) in the range of 9 to 10. Triag(0-0.0001) distribution represents the Triag distribution in the range of 0 to 0.0001 Triag(9-10) represents the Triag distribution in the range of 9 to 10, and finally the Rect(0-0.0001) represents a Rect distribution in the range of 0 to 0.0001. The results of the Hold benchmark are shown in Figure 6.

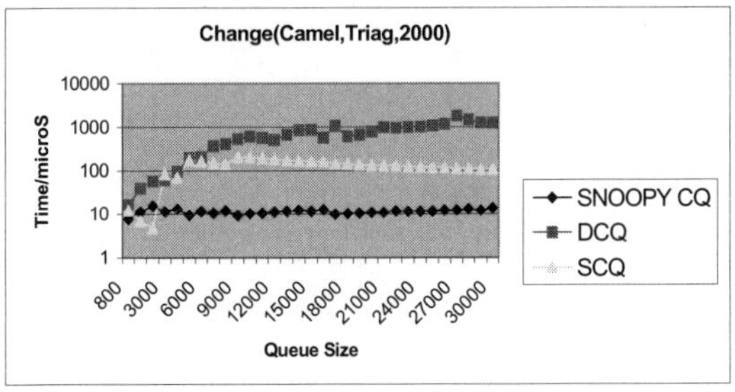

(a)

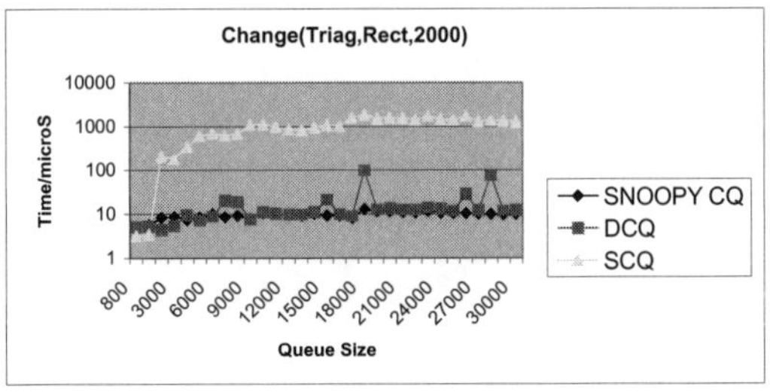

(b)

Figure 6: Average time per Hold operation under Change(A,B,x)

From these two graphs it can be seen that SNOOPy CQ adapts to changes in distribution easily with average hold time in the range of 10µs for (a) and (b). The resize hueristics for SCQ and DCQ fails miserably for (a), with average hold time of 100µs and up to 1000µs. In (b), the DCQ heuristic could adapt itself for certain queue sizes but not all. Average hold time ranges from 10µs to 100µs. SCQ on the other hand fails to adapt at all due to its static resize algorithm. Average hold time deteriorates to 1000µs for large queue sizes. Again from these two graphs, it is evident that estimating an optimum bucket width to use just by sampling of events does not offer consistent performance under all situations unlike the SNOOPy CQ resize heuristic.

For the Up/Down model a total of 10 cycle of filling up the Calendar up to the required queue size followed by complete emptying of the calendar was done. The average time per Hold operation is then computed and plotted against different queue sizes. The plots for SCQ, DCQ and SNOOPy CQ under Triag and Camel(98,01) distribution are given in Figure 7.

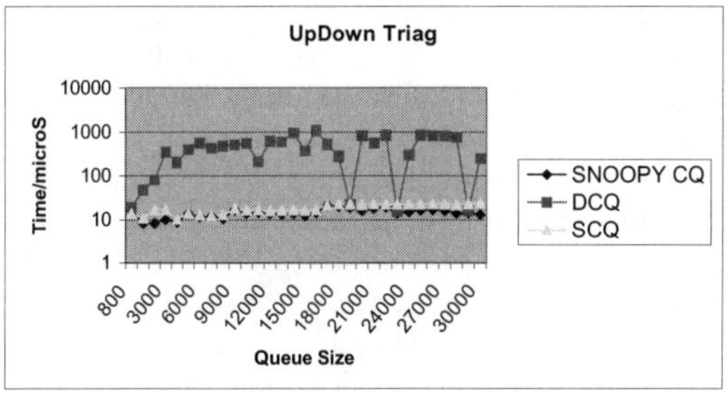

(a)

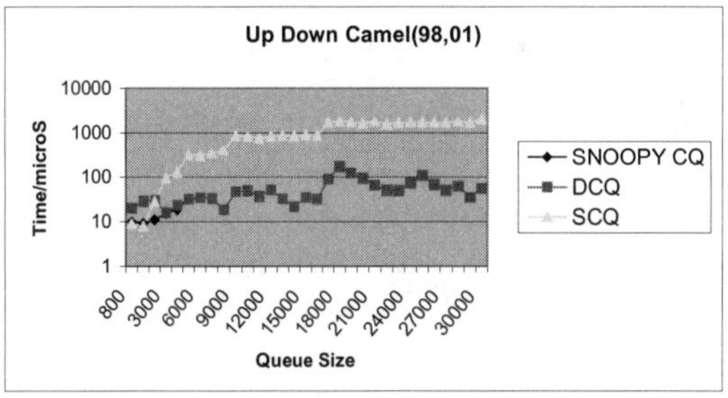

(b)

Figure 7: Average time per Hold operation under Up/Down Model

Graph(a) shows that the DCQ resize heuristic is sensitive towards the Triag distribution. The heuristic tends to estimate a bucket width that is too small just by sampling events around the most populated bucket.

Graph (b) shows that SCQ resize heuristic is sensitive towards Camel(98,01) distribution although resize operations happen often enough. This is due to the fact that SCQ determines the bucket width inaccurately by just sampling the first few events.

Graphs in Figure 7 also illustrate that the SNOOPy CQ heuristic has the ability to estimate an optimum bucket width to be used under both the Triag and Camel(90,01) distributions tested.

6 CONCLUSION

Choosing the correct data structure to use to implement a PES for a simulator is important to speed up simulations when simulations generate huge number of events. Calendar Queue and Dynamic Calendar Queue are two data structure that are often used to implement the PES. Both of these data structures perform well under some situation but badly in others. The resize heuristic of CQ and DCQ could not guarantee a good estimate of an optimum bucket width to use under all situations. This paper proposes a novel approach in estimating the optimum bucket width to use based on performance statistics of the calendar. The data structure employing this approach is called Statistically eNhanced with Optimum Operating Parameter Calendar Queue (SNOOPy CQ). The statistical aspect behind SNOOPy CQ has been explained and implementation of it in pseudo-code was outlined. Experimental results from the Hold and Up/Down model shows that SNOOPy CQ consistently offers O(1) processing complexity under a wide selection of different distributions, unlike SCQ and DCQ. In the worst-case scenario SCQ and DCQ are 100 times slower than SNOOPy CQ, while in the best-case scenario their performance is of similar order with SNOOPy CQ.

REFERENCES

Comfort, J.C., 1984. The simulation of a master-slave event set processor. *Simulation 42, 3 (March), 117-124.*

Oh, S., and Ahn, J.. 1999. Dynamic Calendar Queue. In *Proceeding of the 32nd Annual Simulation Symposium.*

Rönngren, R., Riboe, J., and Ayani, R. 1993. Lazy Queue: New approach to implementing the pending event set. *Int. J. Computer Simulation 3, 303-332.*

Rönngren, R., and Ayani, R. 1997. Parallel and Sequential priority Queue Algorithms. *ACM Trans. On Modeling and Computer Simulation 2, 157-209.*

Vaucher, J. G., and Duval, P. 1975. A comparison of simulation event lists. *Commun. ACM 18, 4(June), 223-230.*

AUTHOR BIOGRAPHIES

TAN KAH LEONG is a Research Scholar in the Department of Electrical and Computer Engineering, National University of Singapore (NUS). He received his B.Eng from NUS. His research interests include O-O simulation and neural networks. He can be contacted at `<engp9186@nus.edu.sg>`.

DR THNG LI- JIN, IAN is a lecturer in the Department of Electrical and Computer Engineering, National University of Singapore. His research interests include O-O simulation, signal processing and communications. He can be contacted at `<eletlj@nus.edu.sg>`.

A/P KO CHI CHUNG is the Deputy Head of Research and a lecturer in the Department of Electrical Engineering, National University of Singapore. His research interests include signal processing and communications. He can be contacted at `<elekocc@nus.edu.sg>. His home-page is located at http://www.ee.nus.edu.sg/ee/view1.asp?user=elekocc`

ITERATION TIME INTERVAL VERSUS EVENT DRIVEN EVALUATION OF A STOCHASTIC CONTINUOUS MODEL

Martin Albertyn
Gennan Systems (Pty) Ltd
Armscor Building, 370 Nossob Street, Erasmuskloof, Pretoria
PO Box 7063, 0001 Pretoria, South Africa
e-mail: martina@armscor.co.za

KEYWORDS

Simulation model, Stochastic model, Continuous model, Iteration time interval, Event driven model.

ABSTRACT

The key objective is to compare two methods which can be utilized to model a stochastic continuous system. A system from the "real world" is used as the basis for the simulation modelling techniques that are presented. The conceptualization phase indicates that the basic model has to incorporate both stochastic and deterministic elements. The basic model is used as the prototype for the development of the two subsequent models that represent the different methods. The first model utilizes an iteration time interval evaluation method while the second model utilizes an event driven evaluation method. The length of the iteration time interval of the first model and adequate sample sizes for both models are investigated. The methods are authenticated by the verification and validation of the models. The methods are compared and the results are discussed. Conclusions are presented and strengths and weaknesses of the methods are considered and discussed.

INTRODUCTION

The system which is used as the basis for the simulation modelling techniques illustrated in this paper, is a continuous process plant. The plant produces chemical products from coal. A simplified schematic representation of the plant is shown in figure 1: "Continuous process plant". The plant is representative of a real continuous process plant (and also of any stochastic continuous system with complex interrelationships). Changes to the original data are incorporated to protect client confidentiality.

The original need for a simulation model of the plant arose because the plant management identified the necessity of a decision support tool at a strategic level. In a plant of this size and complexity it is extremely difficult to predict what the effect of proposed changes is going to be on the operation of the plant. The complex interrelationships that define the operation of the plant, as well as random events such as failures of equipment can be dealt with in a simulation model. The main objectives of the model are to identify problem areas ("bottlenecks") in the system and to study the effect of projected scenarios on the system. Projected scenarios may include added capacity at bottlenecks, changes in the support philosophy, etc.

The objective of this paper is to compare two methods which can be utilized to evaluate the basic simulation model that represents this plant. The basic simulation model is used as the prototype for the development of the two subsequent models that represent the different methods. The first model utilizes an iteration time interval evaluation method while the second model utilizes an event driven evaluation method.

BASIC MODEL DEFINITION AND CONCEPTUALIZATION

For the purpose of this paper, the basic simulation model is not addressed in detail. Only a brief overview of the most important concepts is presented. Albertyn (Albertyn 1995) provides a detailed explanation of the development of the basic simulation model.

To demarcate the model it is necessary to define the system being considered. The composition and process logic of the plant can be derived from figure 1. For the purpose of the model, the total plant is considered to consist of 20 smaller plants and 147 modules. A module can be seen as a group of equipment that has a specific function. Some plants consist of groups of different types of modules. Parallel lines of modules in a plant are referred to as "trains". The plant has a complex switching capability. This implies that if one of the modules of a train goes down, the whole train is not necessarily rendered inoperative.

FIGURE 1: CONTINUOUS PROCESS PLANT

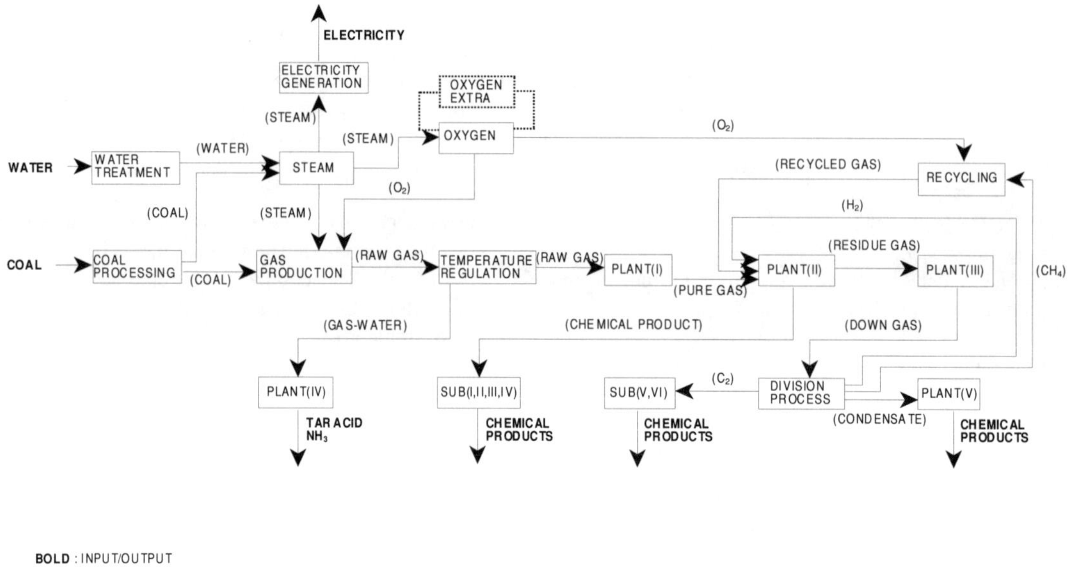

The following key characteristics of the plant can be identified:

a) It is a "continuous flow" plant.
b) Some elements of the plant have a stochastic nature.
c) The plant possesses complex interrelationships.

In the "real world" the "time between failures" and the "time to repair" are stochastic events. This is in contrast to services which start at predetermined times by the decommissioning of the module for a predetermined time interval. The service schedules and service durations are strictly chronological events and thus can be handled in a deterministic manner. The complex interrelationships are manifested in both the composition and the operation of the plant. The plant has feedback-loops and does not have a simple serial or parallel configuration. The switched on or off logic of the different modules also presents complex interrelationships from an operational point of view. The continuous nature of the plant implies that all 147 modules are in a way intrinsically interlinked. A breakdown in production (caused by service or failure) at one point, does have an immediate effect on upstream and downstream operations.

The throughput of the total plant depends on the capacities and the availabilities of the different modules. The availability of a module depends on the service schedule and the occurrence of failures. To model throughput at any given time, the status of each individual module must be known. The model also needs to identify the module group that represents the momentary "bottleneck" in the system at that specific moment in time. This point is the momentary "driver" that will determine the maximum possible throughput. From this point the switched on or off logic, for upstream and downstream module groups, can be determined. The philosophy of maximum possible throughput will lead to all the modules in the identified "bottleneck" module group being switched on. In contrast to this, the upstream and downstream module groups could have some modules that are not switched on. Due to the complex interrelationship characteristic of the plant, the identification of the momentary "bottleneck" and the determination of the associated switched on or off logic, require complex deterministic calculations. With the module status known and the momentary "bottleneck" identified, the switched on or off logic can be determined and the throughput can be calculated.

If all of the previously mentioned procedures are included in a model and evaluated at predetermined time intervals, the results should approximate the operation of the real plant.

EVALUATION METHOD CONCEPTUALIZATION

In the previous section it is indicated that the basic simulation model should be evaluated at predetermined time intervals. Two possible ways to handle the model evaluation are to utilize an iteration time interval evaluation method or an event driven evaluation method. The first method evaluates the model at predetermined iteration time intervals while the second method evaluates the model every time an event takes place.

The basic principles of the iteration time interval evaluation method can be found in classical mathematics. In classical mathematics the behaviour of a continuous system is usually modelled with the help of differential equations. Analytical solutions can, however, only be found for rather simplistic systems. As soon as more complex differential equations are encountered, numerical methods seem to be the only viable solution. One such method involves the discretisation (division into discrete elements) of the continuous behaviour of a system into behaviour at specific intervals in time. The behaviour of the system is evaluated at the start of every time interval and is assumed to remain constant for the duration of the time interval. The total behaviour of the system is then found by the summation of the behaviour at the different points in time.

If the time interval between evaluations is chosen in accordance to the dynamic response characteristics of the system, the results obtained can be a very close approximation of the real process. Systems with quick or fast dynamic response characteristics, will necessitate the use of a very short time interval between evaluations to capture the behaviour of the system. This is especially true for simulations that are used to study the performance of aircraft and missile systems. It stands to reason that a continuous process plant can also be modelled in this way. It is common practice to use a constant time interval, referred to as an iteration (repetition) time interval, between evaluations.

The event driven evaluation method works on the principle that the behaviour of the system can only change if an event takes place and assumes that the behaviour is constant between events. Thus, the behaviour of the system will remain constant until an event takes place that necessitates the re-evaluation of the system to determine the new behaviour. The total behaviour of the system is then found by the summation of the behaviour between the different points in time that events took place.

Six distinct different events that warrant scrutiny can be identified:

a) The beginning and end of the simulation run.
b) The decommissioning and re-commissioning of modules for scheduled services.
c) The failure of modules and the re-commissioning after repair.

The basic difference between the two methods is that the iteration time interval method evaluates the model with a time interval that is of constant length, while the event driven method evaluates the model with a time interval that is of variable length, depending on the events that take place.

MODEL CONSTRUCTION

ARENA models are used to compare the two evaluation methods. (ARENA is a simulation software package from Systems Modeling Corporation.) Statistical distributions (Pegden *et al.* 1990) are used to model the stochastic elements. The first model (Model(I)) utilizes an iteration time interval evaluation method and the second model (Model(II)) utilizes an event driven evaluation method. (Both models were developed from a basic simulation model that contained all the necessary modelling elements, except the evaluation method.)

A novel feature of the ARENA models are that they are generic in terms of modules, module groups and plants, thus facilitating easy implementation of changes and further developments. The model constructs that model the services and failures are also to a large extent generic but not so the constructs that model the process logic (because of the complex interrelationship characteristic of the plant). Survey results (Simulation Fax Survey Results 1993) indicates the growing importance of "user-friendliness" of software. Seen in this perspective, the inputs to the models are handled with the help of input files.

INVESTIGATION OF THE ITERATION TIME INTERVAL LENGTH

In a previous section it is indicated that if the time interval between evaluations is chosen in accordance with the dynamic response characteristics of the system, the results obtained can be a very close approximation of the real process.

Investigation of the processes involved in the continuous process plant suggests that an iteration time interval of one hour should be appropriate for Model(I). (There are some services that decommission modules for a period of one hour.) The validity of this assumption is tested by starting with a very short iteration time interval and increasing it until the answers start to deviate from the perceived correct one. In this instance, the perceived correct answer will be the one generated with the shortest iteration time interval.

Table 1: "Effect of iteration time interval" shows the results generated by variation of the iteration time interval from 0,125 to 24 hours in Model(I).

TABLE 1
EFFECT OF ITERATION TIME INTERVAL

ITI (hour)	Gaspr (mn^3/h)	n	Dev(I) (%)	Dev(II) (%)	RT (min)
0,125	1344494	7	0,000	0,190	225,1
0,25	1344206	12	-0,021	0,169	110,5
0,5	1344021	8	-0,035	0,155	55,5
1	1344569	10	0,006	0,196	27,7
2	1343966	6	-0,039	0,151	14,1
4	1342309	8	-0,163	0,028	7,2
6	1339571	13	-0,366	-0,176	4,9
12	1334160	13	-0,769	-0,580	2,6
24	1322744	8	-1,618	-1,430	1,4

Where:
ITI : Iteration time interval (hour)
Gaspr : Mean Gas production (mn^3/h - normalised cubic meter per hour)
n : Minimum sufficient sample size
Dev(I) : Deviation from 0,125 hour iteration time interval value (%)
Dev(II) : Deviation from "real world" value (%)
RT : Runtime for 20 replications (minute)

Kelton (Kelton *et al.* 1998) defines replications as identical, independent simulation runs. *"Each run starts and stops the same way and uses the same input-parameter settings (that's the "identical" part), but uses separate input random numbers (that's the "independent" part) to generate* (the stochastic events like) *the inter-arrival and service times."*

Twenty replications of a simulated time period of 18 months were completed for every iteration time interval. From these, the mean and the standard deviation from the mean is calculated. (The output from Gas production is used as the variable of comparison.) Using the standard deviation, the corresponding minimum sufficient sample size (with an allowance for a 0,5 % deviation from the "real world" mean value and a 99 % confidence interval) is calculated - see next section for a detailed explanation. The number of replications completed in all instances should be more than, or equal to, the minimum sufficient sample sizes calculated for the answers to be taken as representative of the simulated scenario. A scrutiny of column three of table 1 indicates that this constraint is adhered to.

The results in table 1 are graphically depicted in figure 2: "Effect of iteration time interval".

FIGURE 2: EFFECT OF ITERATION TIME INTERVAL

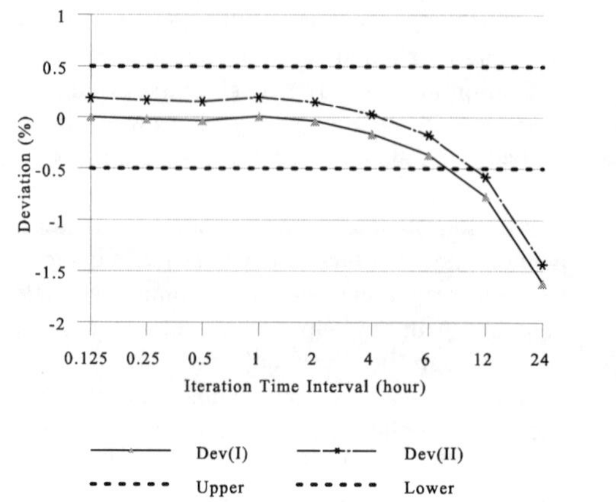

Where:
Upper : Upper (0,5 %) deviation boundary
Lower : Lower (-0,5 %) deviation boundary

A scrutiny of table 1 and figure 2 indicates that the deviation from the perceived correct answer (the 0,125 hour iteration time interval value) increases with an increase in iteration time interval. If a deviation of 0,5 % is taken as an acceptable deviation, all iteration time intervals up to and including six hours seem acceptable. The original assumption of using a one hour iteration time interval thus seems to be validated by this exercise. (Table 1 and figure 2 also indicate the deviation from the "real world" mean value of Gas production and again if a deviation of 0,5 % is taken as an acceptable deviation, all iteration time intervals up to and including six hours seem acceptable.)

The downward trend in deviation is caused by a fall in the output of Gas production if the iteration time interval is increased. This happens because the system always strives towards maximum throughput and would have resumed maximum throughput as soon as possible after the return of a module from service or failure. This return is delayed if the iteration time interval is long. The system is thus modelled as operating at a lower throughput than that which is actually possible for the remainder of the iteration time interval.

DETERMINATION OF ADEQUATE SAMPLE SIZE

The results from a stochastic model may show slight variation between different replications because of the randomness of the chance events such as breakage. This implies that, during the simulation run of a scenario, more than one replication has to be completed in order to find answers that are "stabilized" and representative of the simulated scenario. The minimum sample size that is needed to get a mean value that is representative of the simulated scenario can be calculated with the help of an equation from Crow (Crow *et al.* 1960).

Column three of table 1 shows the minimum sufficient sample sizes needed for Model(I) for iteration time intervals ranging from 0,125 to 24 hours. The minimum sufficient sample size needed for Model(II) is 11 replications.

Twenty replications of a simulated time period of 18 months were completed for every instance. From these, the mean and the standard deviation from the mean is calculated. (The output from Gas production is used as the variable of comparison.) Using the standard deviation, the corresponding minimum sufficient sample size is calculated. The sample size is calculated with an allowance for a 0,5 % deviation from the "real world" mean and a 99 % confidence interval. That corresponds to a maximum error of the estimate of 0,5 % from the "real wold" mean or a bandwidth of the answers from the 20 replications of no more than 1 % of the "real world" mean value. The number of replications completed in all instances should be more than, or equal to, the minimum sufficient sample sizes calculated for the answers to be taken as representative of the simulated scenario. A scrutiny of column three of table 1 for Model(I) and the required value of 11 replications for Model(II), indicates that this constraint is adhered to.

MODEL VERIFICATION AND VALIDATION

The verification involved the checking of the operation of the logic in terms of the chemical processes involved and the working of the other model constructs in terms of the services and breakages. The number of services and breakages generated were counted and evaluated against their "real world" values.

The models are validated by determining the deviation of model results from the "real world" values in a known scenario. Twenty replications of a simulated time period of 18 months were completed for both models. The deviation from the "real world" mean value (of Gas production) of the simulation results for Model(I) are shown in column five of table 1. The simulation results deviates only 0,147 % from the "real world" mean value for Model(II).

If a deviation of 0,5 % from the "real world" mean value is taken as an acceptable deviation, all iteration time intervals up to and including six hours render acceptable results for Model(I) and the results of Model(II) are also acceptable. It can therefore be accepted with a high level of confidence, that both models are valid representations of the real continuous process plant.

MODEL COMPARISON

The two models can be compared in terms of accuracy, ease of use, simplicity of construction, runtimes etc.. From this comparison the strengths and weaknesses of the models can be identified.

In terms of **accuracy** there is no significant distinction between the two models, provided that iteration time intervals of less than six hours are used in Model(I).

There is no difference between the **ease of use** of the two models, both use exactly the same input files and are manipulated in exactly the same way.

As far as **simplicity of construction** is concerned, Model(I) is more straightforward than Model(II). Model(II) requires additional logic to identify when the next event will take place and consequently requires more model constructs. This leads to a slightly bigger model size for Model(II), compared with Model(I).

The **simulation runtimes** for Model(I) for iteration time intervals ranging from 0,125 to 24 hours are indicated in column six of table 1. The simulation runtime for Model(II) is 13,3 minutes and it is comparable to the simulation runtime of 14,1 minutes for Model(I) (with an iteration time interval of two hours).

Strengths of Model(I)

a) Accurate and easy to use.
b) Simpler model construction and smaller model size.
c) Modeller can achieve short runtimes by increasing the iteration time interval up to the acceptable limit.

Weakness of Model(I)

a) Modeller cannot accept the results as being representative of the simulated scenario without first going through the somewhat cumbersome exercise of determining a bandwidth of iteration time intervals that would render valid results.

Strengths of Model(II)

a) Accurate and easy to use.
b) No need to determine a bandwidth for iteration time intervals that would render valid results.

Weaknesses of Model(II)

a) More and complex model constructs needed to identify the

next event (leading to a bigger model size).

b) Simulation runtime is a given, depending on the computational speed of the computer.

CONCLUSIONS

It can be accepted with a high level of confidence (proved through verification and validation) that both models are valid representations of the real continuous process plant. The two methods demonstrated in this paper to model a stochastic continuous system can thus be accepted as authentic and valid methods of modelling. Any one of the models can be implemented with confidence in any further projected scenario analysis and "what if" studies.

There is no clear, distinct "better" option when these two methods are compared. Both models are accurate (provided that the correct iteration time interval is used in Model(I)) and both are easy to use. Model(I) has the advantage of easier construction compared to Model(II) because the latter has to identify when the next event will take place (leading to additional constructs and more complexity). On the other hand, Model(II) is inherently always correct because the effect of every change is incorporated the moment that it takes place.

The simulation runtime is fixed for every specific simulated scenario with Model(II) and depends on the computational speed of the computer. Thus, the modeller has no other option than to increase the computational speed of the computer if shorter runtimes are required. If the equivalent scenario is modelled with Model(I) however, the modeller does have some leeway in terms of simulation runtimes. The modeller can increase the iteration time interval (within the bandwidth boundaries identified) and in such a way maybe achieve a more favourable simulation runtime. For example, the previous results indicate that a simulation run of Model(I) (with an iteration time interval of two hours) and the same simulation run of Model(II) will have comparable simulation runtimes of about 14 minutes. If shorter runtimes are required the modeller have the option available of increasing the iteration time interval of Model(I) to six hours and still obtain valid results - with a simulation runtime of only about five minutes.

This may be especially important when the modeller is using an automated optimizing software tool such as OptQuest. (OptQuest is an automated simulation software package from Systems Modeling Corporation that can be used in conjunction with ARENA to optimize simulation models.) These automated optimizers tend to evaluate a lot of different scenarios (especially in bigger models with many variables) to try to identify an optimum solution. In such an instance shorter simulation runtimes are of paramount importance, otherwise total simulation runtime for the optimizing process can easily get out of hand.

It should be noted that the results presented in this paper do not necessarily reflect the behaviour of systems that seem similar, but in fact have different response characteristics. Prospective modellers are cautioned against blindly accepting these results as indicative of how other systems will behave. It should be stressed that simulation modelling results can only be accepted with a high degree of confidence after the verification and validation of that specific model.

REFERENCES

Albertyn, M. 1995. *Modelling of a Stochastic Continuous System.* Unpublished Masters Thesis, Department of Industrial and Systems Engineering, University of Pretoria, Pretoria, 1-73.

Crow, E.L.; F.A. Davis; and M.W. Maxfield. 1960. *Statistics Manual.* Dover Publications Inc., New York, 48.

Kelton, W.D.; R.P. Sadowski; and D.A. Sadowski. 1998. *Simulation with Arena.* WCB McGraw-Hill, Boston, Massachusetts, 36.

Pegden, C.D.; R.E. Shannon; and R.P. Sadowski. 1990. *Introduction to Simulation Using SIMAN.* McGraw-Hill Inc., New York, 46-51.

Simulation Fax Survey Results. 1993. *Industrial Engineering*, May 1993, vol.25, no.5, 10.

* * * * *

A Scalable Deadlock Avoidance Algorithm for Flexible Manufacturing Systems with Mixed Choices in Part Routing

Robert P. Judd
School of Electrical Engineering
and Computer Science
Ohio University
Athens, OH 45701

Wenle Zhang
School of Electrical Engineering
and Computer Science
Ohio University
Athens, OH 45701

Robert Lipset
Department of Industrial and
Manufacturing Systems Engineering
Ohio University
Athens, OH 45701

Keywords: Manufacturing, Deadlock, FMS

ABSTRACT

A new deadlock avoidance algorithm for flexible manufacturing systems that contain both multiple capacity resources and mixed choice in part routing is presented. The method determines whether moving a part to its next step is safe, unsafe, or undetermined. This classification is linear in complexity. Part movements that are classified as undetermined are further analyzed using another procedure, which attempts to empty the system virtually to determine whether the move is safe or not. It is polynomial in complexity. By adjusting a simple tuning parameter, the size of the set of possible undetermined classifications returned can be made arbitrarily small at the cost of increasing the order of the algorithm. An example showing the application of the method is provided.

1. INTRODUCTION

In the past decade, considerable research has been performed on the topic of developing deadlock control policies for flexible manufacturing systems. Some of the significant works have adopted Petri net models as a formalism to describe the manufacturing system. (Banaszak and Krogh 1990) proposed a *deadlock avoidance algorithm* (DAA) that developed a restriction policy to guarantee that no circular wait situations will occur. (Viswanadham *et al.* 1990) developed a deadlock avoidance algorithm that used a look-ahead policy. Structural properties of PNs such as siphons are used in (Barkaoui and Abdallah 1995; Ezpeleta *et al.* 1995) to determine potential deadlock situations.

Another formalism is to describe the manufacturing system using graphs. In this approach the vertices represent resources and the edges represent product part flows between resources. (Cho *et al.* 1995) developed the concept of bounded circuits with empty and non-empty shared resources to detect deadlock. (Fanti *et al.* 1996) developed a simple graph-theoretic method for deadlock detection and recovery in systems with multiple capacity resources. (Judd and Faiz 1995) derived a set of static linear inequalities that, when satisfied, avoid deadlock. (Lipset *et al.* 1997) expanded upon (Judd and Faiz 1995), and quantified both necessary and sufficient conditions for deadlock to occur in a manufacturing system. (Judd *et al. 1*999) developed a polynomial complexity deadlock avoidance algorithm by classifying part movements.

The major contribution of this paper is to extend our previous method presented in (Judd and Faiz 1999) to allow flexible manufacturing systems with both mixed (single & multiple) capacity resources and choices in part routing (MCRC). Two types of choices will be considered. One is called free choice; the other, conditional choice. The simple stack structure used in (Judd *et al.* 1999) is no longer adequate to handle the complexity involved in MCRC systems. Instead, a new recursive algorithm, called *dynamo*, is developed. Previously, part movements have been divided into two major categories, i.e. *live* moves and *dead* moves. A *dead* move will cause a non-deadlocked system to enter a deadlocked state, and a *live* move will not cause a non-deadlocked system to enter a deadlocked state. With conditional choices, we will have another major category called *conditional dead* (abbreviated as *deadc*) moves. If a move causes a non-deadlocked system to enter a deadlocked state along some, but not all, conditional choice branches, then the move is a *conditional dead* move.

The algorithm categorizes a large class of moves as live in linear time. These moves will be termed *safe* moves. Furthermore, the same algorithm identifies a class of dead or deadc moves, which will be termed *unsafe* or *unsafec*, respectively. Moves that cannot be determined to be either safe, unsafe, or unsafec will be classified as *undetermined.*

The proposed approach does not stop at that point. By surrounding the classification scheme with another simple algorithm, called *empty_system*, many of the undetermined moves can be declared either safe or unsafe in polynomial time. Basically, the improved algorithm will create a virtual system and make the proposed undetermined move. It then tries to empty the system using only safe moves. If it can, then the proposed move must be live. Notice that for this approach, not all the safe moves need to be found at any given state of the virtual system. As long as one safe move is found, the state can be advanced. Section 2 discusses the MCRC model, Section 3 analyzes the classifications, Section 4 presents the algorithms and Section 5 gives an example using the proposed algorithm.

2. MCRC SYSTEM MODEL

A MCRC system consists of a set R of resources such as machines, robots, AGVs, etc. and a set P of product types. Each resource has capacity cap(r)≥1. At any point in time, the system contains a set Q of parts. Each part q belongs to a product type $p \in P$ and each product type p possesses a process plan that describes the resource sequence required to produce it. Each required resource is called a process step. Each part q has a current step n. $\mathbf{s} = \{n, n \text{ is } q\text{'s current step}, \forall q \in Q\}$ is a vector representing the system state. With choices, process plans need not be fixed and sequential, but are finite. By *choice* in part routing, we mean that the part's next step can be chosen from a set of resources. By *free choice*, we mean that the system controller has the right to dispatch the part to any one of these resources. By *conditional choice*, the part's next step must be selected according to some external condition. An example condition is routing based on inspection result.

2.1 Process Plan Representation

Our method to represent a process plan with choices in part routing is to "straighten" the plan. Steps with no choices are listed resource by resource sequentially, and steps that have choices are listed branch by branch sequentially. Each branch further consists of sequences of resources and other branches in an iterative manner. In this way, each process plan can still be represented as a sequence of resources. However, this is not complete. Our method associates each process plan with two additional data structures. One is *choices*, a vector that counts the number of choices for each step. The other is *branches*, a matrix that identifies the next step for every current step; each step corresponds to a column of the matrix. With choices, a process plan can have more than one terminal step. In our method, all terminal steps are given the same next step number, which is the length of the actual plan plus one. Three functions are defined for this method. Function choices(q, n) returns the number of choices at step n of the plan of part q. Function choice_type(q, n) returns the type of the choice as one of none, free or conditional. Function next(q, n, b) returns the next step of part q after step n on branch b. See the example in Section 5.

2.2 The Wait Relation Graph

A MCRC system can be described by a digraph, called a *wait relation graph* (WRG), which consists of a set of nodes to represent resources of the system and a set of arcs to represent individual process steps for all product types.

A *path* in a wait relation graph G is a set of nodes that are connected to one another within the graph. A *closed path* starts and ends on the same node. A *simple circuit* is a closed path with no repeated nodes, except for the common starting and ending node. A *semi-closed* path is a path that is not closed but contains a closed path. The portion of a semi-closed path that is not on the closed part of the path is called a *tail*.

When a part q in a resource must follow a particular arc a to its next resource, then arc a is said to be *committed*, and we also say that part q commits arc a. With choices added, a part in a resource can follow any one of a set of arcs either chosen by the system controller (free choice) or the external condition (conditional choice).

3. ANALYSIS OF POTENTIAL MOVES

In this section, we first discuss the structural and dynamic properties of a WRG. We then present the classifications of part moves.

3.1 Structural Properties

The function len(p) returns the number of steps in process plan p. Function res(p, n) provides the resource required in the nth step of process plan p. Functions cap(r), len(p), res(p,n), choices(p,n), choice_type(p,n) and next(p,n,b) are all independent of the system state. They are therefore structural properties of the system graph G.

The following functions also depend only upon the structure of the graph G and can be stored as simple lookup tables that are accessed by the proposed algorithms. Therefore, the evaluation of these functions will not be considered in determining the computational complexity of the proposed algorithms. Function converge(r) returns true if more than one arc enters resource r. Any product type p in step n of its process plan is associated with a unique arc a in G. Function closed(p, n) (or, circuit(p, n)) returns the set of all of the closed paths (simple circuits) in G that a part of product type p in step n of its process plan belong to; that is, the set of closed paths (simple circuits) that contain a. If the part at step n has free choice, then functions converge and closed must be checked for each choice.

3.2 Dynamic Properties

Function step(q,s) returns the current process step of part q, step(q,s)=0 indicates that the part is ready to enter the system. class(q) returns the part type of part q. Function free(r,s) returns the number of free units left in resource r. Function empty(r, s) returns true if resource r is empty of parts and false if it contains parts. part(r,s) returns the set of all the parts currently held in resource r. These functions are dependent on the system state s.

3.3 Dynamic Path (Subgraph) Construction

A dynamic subgraph is formed by concatenating the resources in the plan of the candidate part until a different part is encountered. The subgraph is continued by appending (chasing) the resources of the new part's process pl an. When a multiple capacity resource is seen, the dynamic subgraph will be split into several branch paths. If free(r, s) > 0 for the resource, then a special path corresponding to the part entering the resource is constructed. The part is called the *ghost part* with respect to this resource because the resource does not actually contain the part. Paths are also constructed for all the parts contained in the resource.

The dynamic subgraph for a multiple capacity system will look like a cyclic tree. As shown in Figure 3.1, there are three possible types of paths that can exist in such a dynamic subgraph:

i) an open path,
ii) a closed path that includes the original part q, and
iii) a semi-closed path in which the original part q is on the tail.

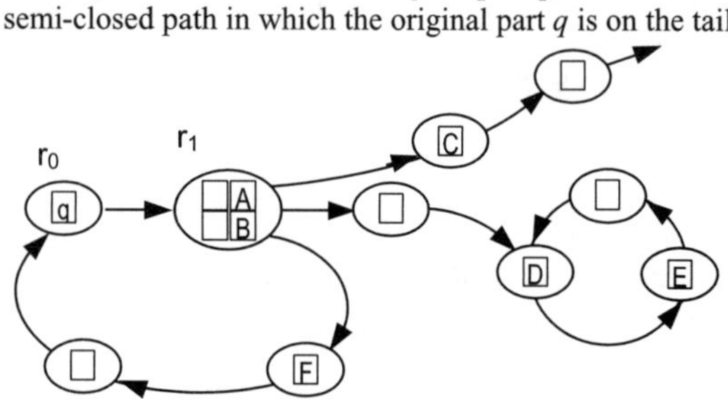

Figure 3.1. Three types of paths at a multiple capacity resource

For systems with choices, at a step with choice, the dynamic subgraph will be split into several branch paths. Each branch path can also assume one of the three types shown in Figure 3.1.

Paths on the dynamic subgraph are terminated when either the terminal resource of the plan for the current part is reached or when a part is encountered for the second time.

Dynamic subgraphs are simple to find (linear complexity) and analyze. We will use dynamic subgraphs in our analysis instead of the wait relation graph G that represents the entire system. This will improve computational complexity; however, some interactions among the structural paths may be overlooked.

A *canonical semi-closed path* (CSC) is a semi-closed path with a part on the tail that enters the closed portion of the CSC, and a part on the closed portion that leaves the CSC through its key resource. The *key resource* is the resource that connects the tail and the closed portion of the CSC. The part on the tail that enters the key resource first is called the *initiating part*, and the first part to leave the closed portion through the key resource is called the *pivot part*. All CSCs must have at least one free unit in the key resource. An example is shown in Figure 3.2.

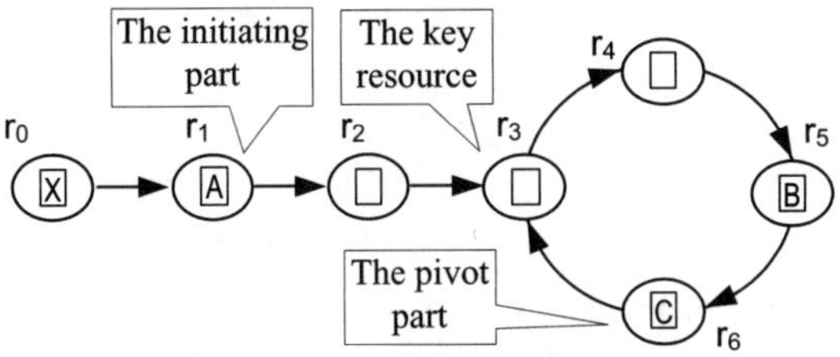

Figure 3.2. A canonical semi-closed path example

A CSC is *simple* if the dynamic path starting with the initiating part results in only one simple circuit for the closed path. That is, the initiating part and all parts in the key resource have the same dynamic path. It is *complex*, otherwise. Complex CSCs can be divided into five major types: *multiple* CSCs, *parallel* CSCs, *multi-level* CSCs, *serial* CSCs and *iterative* CSCs.

A CSC is *multiple* if the closed portion of the CSC has resources with multiple out-going arcs (they can be seen as *generalized choices*, either because of parts with free choices or multiple capacity resources with multiple parts going different directions), which produces multiple closed paths that correspond to each combination of arcs. The closed portion of the CSC is the union of all these closed paths. Figure 3.3 is an example.

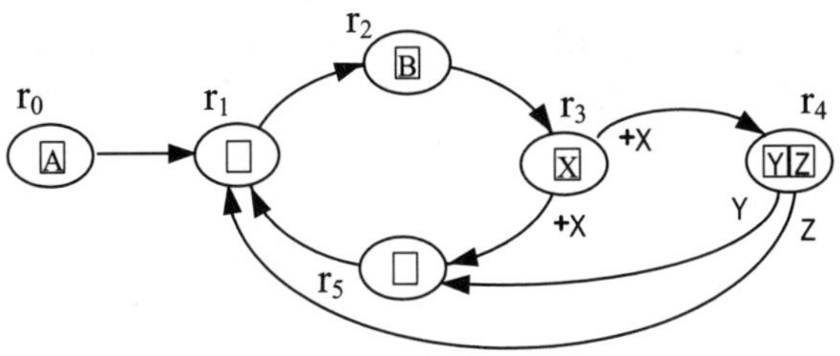

Figure 3.3. A multiple CSC example

A *parallel* CSC is a special case of multiple CSC where only the key resource can have multiple out-going arcs. Figure 3.4 is an example.

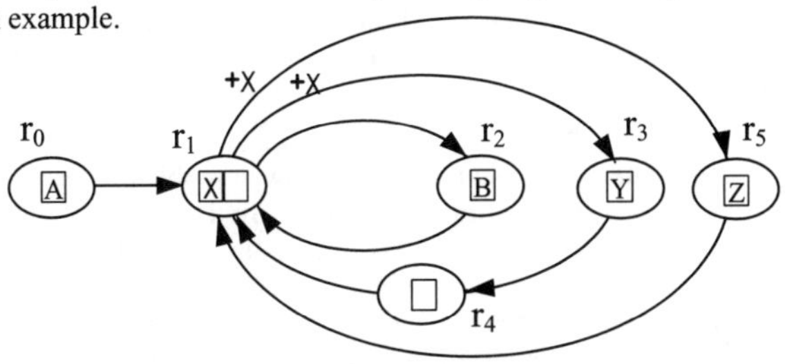

Figure 3.4. A parallel CSC example

A *multi-level* CSC is a CSC where two or more CSCs, c_i, $i = 1{\sim}k$ $(k \geq 2)$, are joined together at their key resource, and the pivot part of one CSC c_i becomes the initiating part of the next CSC c_{i+1}. An example is given in Figure 3.5.

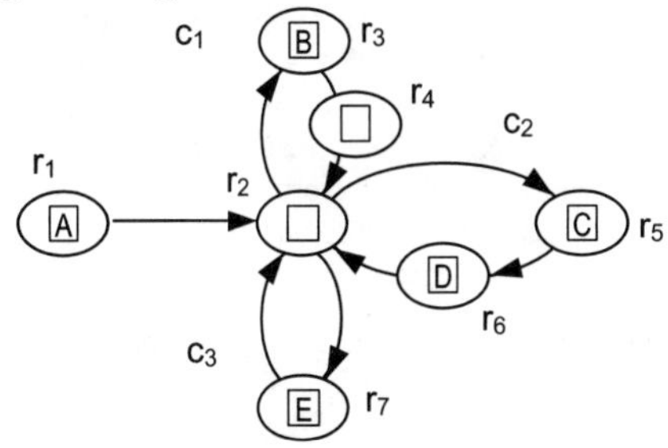

Figure 3.5. A multi-level CSC example

Definition 3.1: Suppose that the choices (either from a part with free choices or a non-empty multiple capacity resource) in the closed portion of a multiple/parallel CSC are fixed; then a simple CSC is formed. This simple CSC is called a *component* CSC of the multiple/parallel CSC, and the multiple/parallel CSC can be reconstructed as the union of all its component CSCs.

In Figure 3.3, the multiple CSC has 3 component CSCs: $r_0r_1r_2r_3r_5r_1$, $r_0r_1r_2r_3\,r_4r_5r_1$ and $r_0r_1r_2r_3r_4r_1$.

A CSC may be formed by combining other CSCs. A *serial* CSC is formed by taking individual CSCs and joining them end-to-end, as illustrated in Figure 3.6. The closed portions are joined together at their key resources, where each key resource is distinct. The tail for each closed portion includes the original tail along with the portion of each closed path that connects the original tail with the key resource.

An *iterative* CSC has its key resources connected together by a closed path, as shown in Figure 3.7. More complicated CSCs can be formed by combining the various types of CSCs.

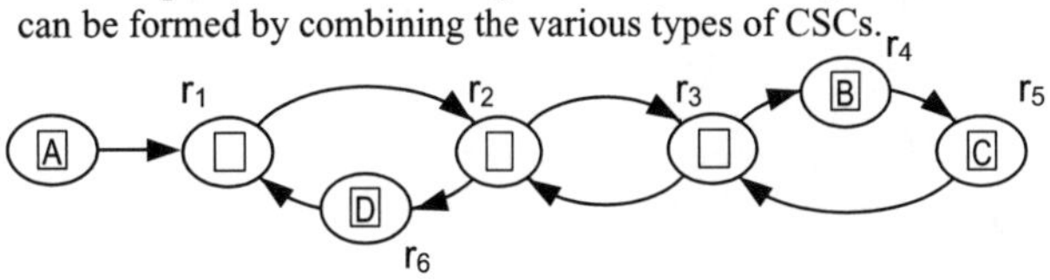

Figure 3.6. A serial CSC example

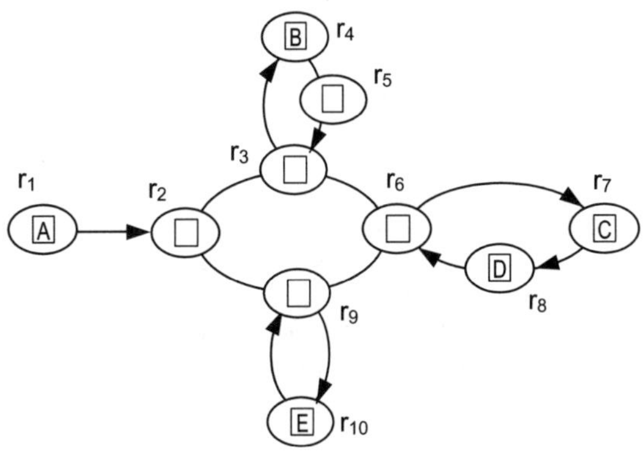

Figure 3.7. An iterative CSC example

3.4 Classifications of Part Moves

When the manufacturing system is in any particular state *s*, a part is capable of being moved or can enter the system if the next resource in its process plan has at least one free unit. Such a part is termed *enabled*. *s'* denotes the state of the system after such a move. Enabled parts must be analyzed to determine whether the move (state change) will result in deadlock. The following subsections list conditions by which the proposed move can be classified as safe, unsafe or undetermined. It can be shown that this classification can be performed with linear complexity.

In this section, we summarize the eight classes presented in (Judd *et al.* 1999). Class 5 is modified, and two new classes will be added in Section 3.5

Class 1 (safe) refers to a part at its terminal step. *Class 2* (safe) is a part whose next resource is non-converging. *Class 3* (safe) is a part that does not move onto any new circuits.

Classes 4 through 8 are based on the construction of a dynamic subgraph. *Class 4* (safe) is for a part on a free exit.

Class 5. Let S_{CSC} be the set of all states for a CSC such that the pivot part has not yet entered the key resource. Then moving the initiating part on the CSC into its key resource is a class 5 move if it deadlocks the closed portion of the CSC for all $s \in S_{CSC}$. Since, by definition, the pivot part must leave the system through the key resource, a class 5 move is a dead move and will be classified as unsafe.

Lemma 3.2. Propagating the initiating part on a simple CSC into the key resource is a class 5 move, if,

i) the key resource has only one free unit; and
ii) all the resources (except for the key resource) on the closed portion are filled and their parts all commit to arcs on the closed portion.

Proof. Once the initiating part is moved into the key resource, no part is enabled on the closed portion of the CSC, so the pivot part can no longer leave the CSC. The CSC is in primary deadlock. ■

Lemma 3.3. Propagating the initiating part on either a multiple or parallel CSC into the key resource is a class 5 move, if,

i) the key resource has only one free unit; and
ii) if propagating the initiating part is a class 5 move for all the component CSCs.

Proof. This is a direct result of Lemma 3.2. ■

Lemma 3.4. Propagating the initiating part on a multi-level CSC into the key resource is a class 5 move, if,

i) the key resource has only one free unit;
ii) propagating the initiating part is a class 5 move for c_1; and
iii) propagating the pivot part on c_i is a class 5 move for c_{i+1}, $i = 1 \sim k\text{-}1$.

Proof. Clearly none of the pivot parts for c_i, $i = 1 \sim k\text{-}1$, can be moved, otherwise c_{i+1} will be placed into deadlock. Also, moving the original initiating part will place c_1 into deadlock. ■

For the purpose of classifying part moves, a CSC can be *reduced* by replacing the closed portion of the CSC with only the key resource and adjusting the key resource such that its capacity is increased to hold all the pivot parts of the CSC. Also, if any component CSC has a free resource, then the key resource is adjusted to have a free unit.

An example is given in Figure 3.8. Suppose we are analyzing a CSC whose closed portion $c = c_1 \cup c_2$. c_1 could be a serial or iterative CSC. There must exist a CSC that includes c_2 and a tail that extends into c_1, we call this CSC2. Then CSC2 can be reduced to the key resource only.

CSC2 can be simple, multiple, parallel or multi-level. Notice, if the key resource is a multiple capacity resource with a part in it, the part will be replaced by the pivot part(s).

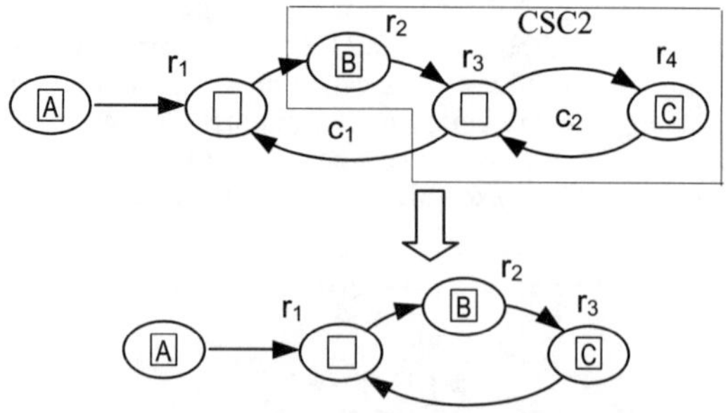

Figure 3.8. CSC reduction

More complicated class 5 moves can be analyzed through the process of CSC reduction. This reduction will be performed logically by the algorithm introduced later. The system graph will not be physically reduced.

Class 6 (undetermined_0) denotes a part that moves on a closed path, but is neither a class 2 nor a class 3. *Class 7* (undetermined_1) is a part on an open path but is not a class 4 move. *Class 8* (undetermined_1) refers to a part that is on the tail of a semi-closed path.

3.5 Conditional Choices

As described later, in Section 4.2, the above classification is also used by *empty_system* to empty the virtual system. As long as a part *q* is not classified as unsafe, *empty_system* should be invoked to try to clear the system and determine the final class for part *q*.

Once in the virtual system, if a part *q* has choices, then *q* will be classified along each choice. For free choices, the best class (if we order from best to worst as safe, undetermined and unsafe) among all choices can be chosen since the system controller can determine which choice to select. On the other hand, for conditional choices, the worst class should be chosen since no external condition is available in the virtual system. If the worst class is not unsafe, then along which choice should *empty_system* advance part *q*? Unfortunately, there is not enough information for *empty_system* since the external condition is not available. A naive method for *empty_system* is to try to clear the system based on trials made on every conditional choice. That is, try to advance the part on each individual choice branch and try to clear the system, until all choices have been tried. Only if the system can be cleared on every choice, should *empty_system* declare safe, otherwise unsafe. The problem with this method is the complexity is no longer polynomial.

Our method to avoid this computational problem is based on the observation that we might be able to find a way to combine trials made on every choice. The idea is to *split* the part to the next resource step on every choice if the part has conditional choices. Therefore, after the split, there will be multiple instances of the same part existing in the virtual system. Only one of the split parts is real; all others are fictitious.

To represent this type of move, instead of creating, say, three different parts, we assign the three next step numbers to the part. That is, with conditional choice and the part splitting concept, the *state of a part* should be redefined to reflect the splitting. Now the part state is a set of steps instead of a single step value. For example, suppose a part X is at step 5 and has three choices. The next steps are 6, 8, and 11, respectively. Then part X has a set of steps with only one element – step 5. After splitting, it has a set of steps with three elements – 6, 8, and 11 to represent that part X now has 3 splits. The first split is at step 6, the second is at step 8 and the third is at step 11.

Function *step* is also redefined to return the set of steps of a part. After splitting, step(X) = {6, 8, 11}. If the set of steps of a part has more than 1 element (step), then the part has been split. Each step in the set is called a *split* of the part.

Naturally, we will also have an opposite operation, that is, to *merge* a set of part splits. If after splitting, every split part's next step is the same, then these splits can be merged at the next step.

Definition 3.5: A part q at a conditional/free choice step is *enabled* if its next step (n_1) resource on every/any choice either is free or already has a split n_1 of part q.

Two new classes will be added based on conditional choices. One is safe and numbered class 2b. The class number 2b is used because the move does not involve any closed path examination. The other is conditional unsafe and numbered class 5b.

Class 2b. Advancing a split part whose next step is n_1 to a resource that contains a split n_1 of the same part will cause the two splits to merge and is therefore safe.

Class 5b. Given a CSC whose closed portion has conditional choices. Then moving the initiating part on the CSC into its key resource is a class 5b move, if some component CSCs are class 5 moves and some are not because of conditional choices. A class 5b move is a deadc move and will be classified as unsafec.

If a component CSC1 with conditional choices has a free resource on its closed portion, and another component CSC2 with conditional choices is filled, then moving the initiating part is a dead move if CSC2 is chosen. Moving the initiating part is not a dead move if CSC1 is chosen. Then by definition, a class 5b move is a deadc move.

Example 3.6. Examples of both class 5 and class 5b are illustrated in Figure 3.9. Part q is unsafec. This is because the component CSC1 = $r_0r_1r_2r_3r_2r_1$ is a class 5 move and CSC2 = $r_0r_1r_2r_3r_4r_1$ is not a class 5 move.

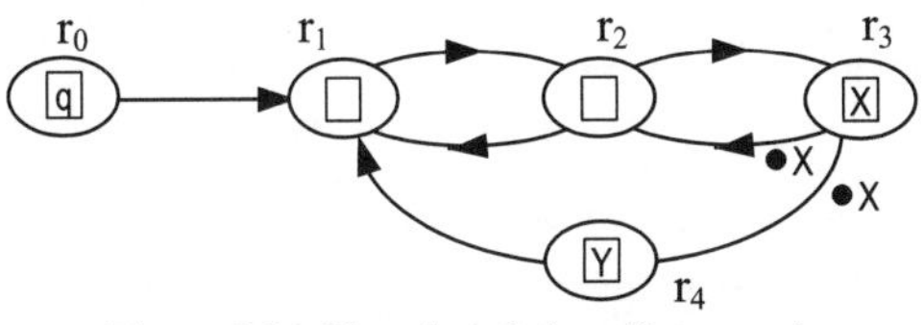

Figure 3.9. Class 5 and class 5b examples

Class 5b is different from class 5 in that class 5 is certain to be a dead move, while class 5b may not be dead if the conditional choice part involved selects certain alternatives.

Class 5b is different from the undetermined classes in that an undetermined class means that there is not enough information, while class 5b means that if the candidate move is made, there is some probability to deadlock the system. Therefore, since we know it is dangerous to make the move, and to assure deadlock-free system operation, the move should not be allowed.

3.6 Enabled Paths and Ratcheting

Because of the splitting, *empty_system* may enter a state where it cannot find a safe or undetermined move. Normally, *empty_system* would declare unsafe. However, we can take advantage of the fact that only one of the splits corresponds to a real part and all others are fictitious. The idea is to try to find an *enabled path* instead of an individual part. Then the parts on an enabled path can be cycled—this is called *ratcheting*. After ratcheting, some parts might be able to exit the system or advance safely, thus helping to empty the system. This is not guaranteed. The system may still be unable to advance after ratcheting.

There are two types of enabled paths. The first type has part splits in series, and is called a *serial enabled path*. An example is given in Figure 3.10. X_1 and X_2 are two splits of part X. Starting with split X_1 of X, then Z is seen, then another split X_2 of X is seen, then Y is seen and then X_1 is seen again. So we have an enabled path $X_1 \rightarrow Z \rightarrow X_2 \rightarrow Y \rightarrow X_1$. The ratcheting shifts parts on the path in turn.

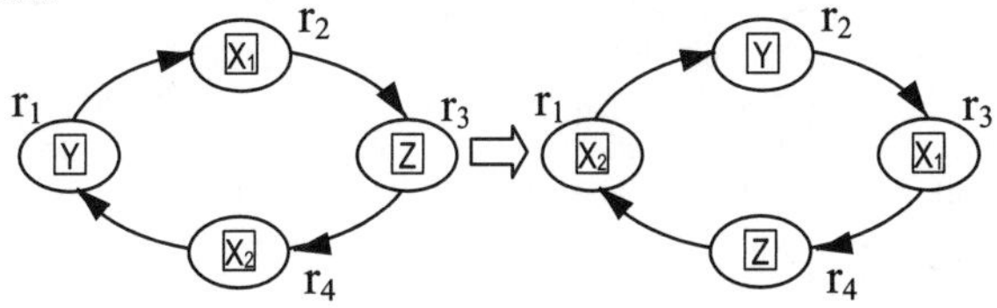

Figure 3.10. Serial enabled path and ratcheting

The reason we can perform the ratcheting is that, in reality, only one of X_1 and X_2 is real, meaning either r_2 or r_4 is free. If r_2 is free, then Y can be moved to r_2, X_2 can be moved to r_1 and Z can be moved to r_4. If r_4 is free, then Z can be moved to r_4, X_1 can be moved to r_3, and Y can be moved to r_2.

The second type of an enabled path has two splits of a part in parallel on free choices on the path, and they can be merged. This type of an enabled path is called a *parallel enabled path*. This path has a *diverging point* and that point must be at a free choice step. An example is given in Figure 3.11. Y_1 and Y_2 are two splits of part Y and part X has a free choice of r_2 or r_3. Starting with part X, we have two free choice branches with splits Y_1 and Y_2 on those branches, and the two splits can merge at the next step. So we have an enabled path $Z \rightarrow V \rightarrow X \rightarrow Y_1 \rightarrow Z$ plus $X \rightarrow U \rightarrow Y_2 \rightarrow Z$. The ratcheting shifts parts on the path in turn with two exceptions:

i) X will be split to both r_2 and r_3;

ii) Y_1 and Y_2 will merge to r_5.

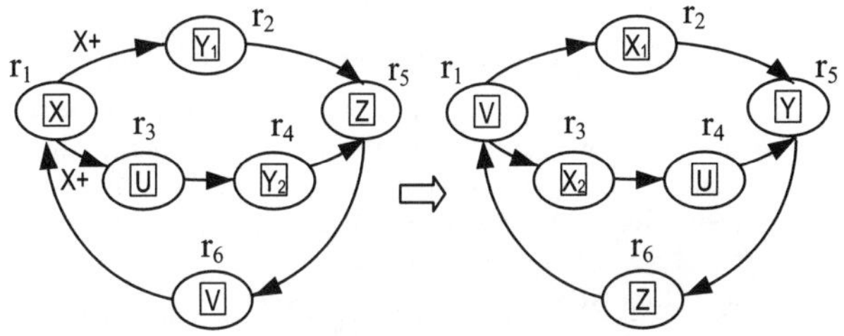

Figure 3.11. Parallel enabled path and ratcheting

The reason we can do this is that, in reality, only one of Y_1 and Y_2 exists, meaning either r_2 or r_4 is free. If r_2 is free, then X can be moved to r_2, V can be moved to r_1 and Z can be moved to r_6. If r_4 is free, then U can be moved to r_4, X can be moved to r_3, V can be moved to r_1 and Z can be moved to r_6.

4. DEADLOCK DETECTION ALGORITHM

To determine whether advancing a candidate part q results in a live state, we have developed three major algorithms: *dynamo*, *empty_system* and *live*, which constitute our deadlock avoidance policy for the MCRC system model. Algorithm listings and detailed theoretical results can be found in (Zhang 00).

4.1 Algorithm *dynamo*

Algorithm *dynamo* determines the type of move for a candidate part q (on each of its choices, if any) according to the classes presented in section 3. The algorithm first checks whether the move is one of the first four classes of safe moves. If none of those classes applies, then the algorithm starts the construction of the dynamic subgraph which is stored in an AND-OR tree C. The tree has three types of nodes: terminal nodes, AND nodes, for conditional choice parts and OR nodes for free choice parts or non-empty multiple capacity resources. As the construction of the subgraph progresses, the algorithm tracks the free resources it encounters in set R and the parts it sees in set Q. When a path in the dynamic subgraph meets one of the stopping criteria specified in section 3.3, the algorithm examines the type of the stopping criterion, the set Q, and the set R to determine the proper classification. If the candidate part has choice, then the best-suited class of move will be decided after classification on every choice has been made.

In addition, the algorithm has another condition that stops the recursion (and guarantees linear complexity) that is not one of the aforementioned stopping criteria. We refer to this as a *stop-check-and-go* mechanism.

4.1.1 Dynamic Path Status

Each of these conditions is associated with a status value. Status values are sorted in ascending order. Table 4.1 gives the status values and associated stopping conditions. *dynamo* examines all possible paths in a dynamic subgraph and keeps track of the one with the best-suited status. It then makes conclusions on whether the proposed move is live or not based on this optimal path within the dynamic subgraph. Also defined are two other statuses, UNSAFE and UNSAFEC. UNSAFE is used to conclude a dead move and UNSAFEC is used to conclude a conditional dead move.

Table 4.1. Status values and order

Value	Name	Stopping criterion
1	EXIT	A part at its terminal step / on a free exit.
2	PST	A part seen the second time.
3	RST	A free resource seen the second time.

1) *PST*. A PST status is defined when a part is seen for the second time. PST means that a part is found on either a closed dynamic path or on a semi-closed path. An exception is when the PST is seen after an UNSAFE on an open path. In that case, undetermined (PST) is still the value desired.

2) *RST*. An RST status is defined when a free resource is encountered for the second time, indicating a (component) CSC is found. The resource is the key resource, also called the *RST resource*. The part leading the path to the RST resource for the first time is the initiating part of the CSC. The part leading the path to the RST resource for the second time is the pivot part, also called the *RST part*. A flag is used to determine if the space in the RST resource is needed to avoid deadlock. An RST with a false space flag means that the RST resource is seen for the second time without seeing any other free resource after the first time it is seen. Essentially, this means moving the initiating part into the key resource is a class 5 move for this component CSC.

3) *EXIT*. This status is the best status. EXIT status means either the candidate part or another part can exit. Even though EXIT as a status is better than RST, the algorithm gives higher priority to detect RST over EXIT unless the proposed part is at its terminal step. The reason is to make sure that the dynamic path has enough space to accommodate the proposed part, so that the part that is found to exit actually can exit. A part at a free choice step is given an EXIT status as long as EXIT is found on one of the choices. On the other hand, a part at a conditional choice step receives an EXIT status only if EXIT is found on every choice.

At a non-empty multiple capacity resource or a choice step, the algorithm will find the best-suited status by choosing the lowest status value from parts in multiple capacity resources or choices of free choice steps, and by choosing the highest status value from choices of conditional choice steps.

4.1.2 The Stop-Check-and-Go

The stop-check-and-go mechanism is performed when status RST is detected. This mechanism implements the CSC reduction. Using this technique, the algorithm eventually reduces the CSC to a single resource with the pivot part(s) in it.

The stop. If the path encounters a resource for the second time that has at least one free unit (RST), then: i) the path stops; ii) the last part that would have entered the RST resource (*RST part*) and its process step are recorded in tree C, and; iii) we return to the point when the RST was visited for the first time.

The check. As the algorithm returns to the RST resource, any resources with free capacity will be flagged.

The go. When the algorithm returns to the RST resource, the flag indicates whether space on the CSC can be used. If the flag is true, all the RST parts in C will be chased further to determine which one will produce the optimal path.

It is easy to show that *dynamo* directly uses the definitions given in section 3 to classify all moves, and that these classifications can be done with complexity that is linear in system size L, measured by the sum of lengths of all process plans.

4.2 Algorithm *empty_system*

Given a set of parts Q in state $\mathbf{s}$, *empty_system* attempts to find a set of moves that will remove all parts from the virtual system using only safe moves. It invokes algorithm *dynamo* on every enabled part. *Empty_system* will execute all the safe moves first. Parts returned with status EXIT from *dynamo* will be taken out of the virtual system immediately. Parts returned with status MERGE or SAFE0 will be merged or advanced. One of the parts returned with status SAFE1 will be advanced, and the set of enabled parts will be re-evaluated. If only undetermined_0 moves exist, then it will arbitrarily pick one and proceed. In the case that only SAFE1 or undetermined_0 moves exist, preference will be given to parts not at a conditional choice step. And in the cases that no further enabled parts exist, or all parts returned with status UNSAFE or UNSAFEC, the algorithm will try to find an enabled path and perform the ratcheting. If no enabled path can be found, then it will return FALSE. The algorithm continues this cycle until it empties all parts from the system; it then returns TRUE. It returns FALSE if the system cannot be emptied. It can be shown that this algorithm is polynomial in complexity.

4.3 Algorithm *live*

Among the three algorithms, *live* is the algorithm to be called first to determine whether a proposed move is live. It further invokes *dynamo* to perform the classification. Its complexity is linear in L unless *dynamo* returns undetermined (status EXIT and PST), in which case it will invoke *empty_system* and the complexity is therefore $O(L^3)$. *Live* begins by classifying the proposed part move. A virtual move is made if the proposed move is found to be undetermined. *Live* then attempts to find a way to empty the virtual system to determine whether the original proposed move is indeed live. It is impossible for this algorithm to mistakenly return true for a dead move, since the move is either classified as safe immediately or a sequence of moves that empties the system is found.

In a few cases, it will be possible for *live* to return false for a live move. This will happen if, while emptying the virtual system, a state is reached where no enabled parts are safe moves, multiple undetermined_0 moves are detected, and the undetermined_0 move that is chosen results in deadlock of the virtual system, whereas selecting a different undetermined_0 move would not have. Although examples can be constructed that have this behavior, these types of systems are not typical of actual manufacturing systems.

5. EXAMPLE

Example 5.1. Let the manufacturing system in Figure 5.1 be composed of seven resources r_1, r_2, r_3, r_4, r_5, r_6, and r_7. r_4 has capacity 2. All other resources are of unit capacity. Suppose the system manufactures three types of products, p_1, p_2 and p_3, specified by the following process plans: $p_1=r_1r_2r_3r_4$, $p_2=r_4r_3r_2r_1$, p_3 is given in Table 5.1. Assume parts X belongs to p_1, Z belongs to p_2, Y, U, V and W belong to p_3.

Table 5.1. Process plan for p_3

step No.	1	2	3	4	5	6	7
resource list	r_4	r_5	r_6	r_7	r_3	r_2	r_1
choice type	c	f	-	c	-	-	-
choices	2	2	1	2	1	1	1
branches	2 3	5 6	4	6 7	6	7	8

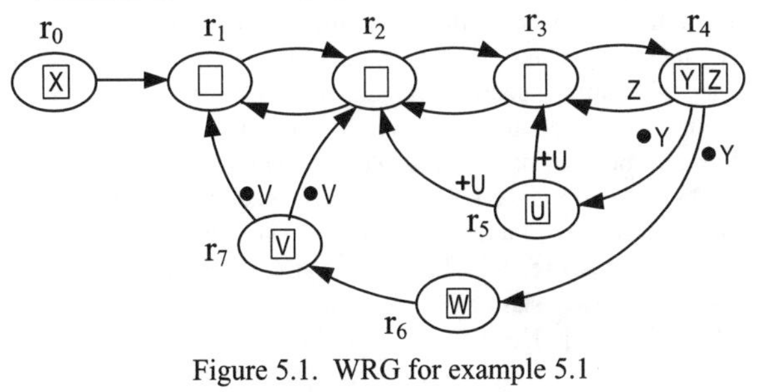

Figure 5.1. WRG for example 5.1

Suppose we want to know whether introducing X to r_1 is live. We first call *live*. *Live* calls *dynamo* to classify part X and *dynamo* will classify X as undetermined (U can exit). *Live* then will virtually move part X to resource r_1 and invokes *empty_system* to try to clear the system. Parts X, Z, and U are enabled. *dynamo* classifies both Z and U as UNSAFE and X as undetermined_0. So X is advanced to r_2. Now, parts X, U, and Z are still enabled. Again, *dynamo* classifies both Z and U as UNSAFE and X as undetermined_0. X is advanced to r_3. U and V are now on a free exit, and are removed. Then W is on a free exit, and it will be removed. In this fashion, the system is cleared of all parts.

Because *empty_system* finds a sequence of moves to empty the system, *live* declares that part X is a live move.

6. DISCUSSION

A minor modification to the *empty_system* algorithm would make a classification returned from *live* both necessary and sufficient conditions for determining deadlock. The change would involve trying all undetermined_0 moves if no safe moves existed, instead of selecting one arbitrary move of this type. If that change is made, however, *live* can no longer be guaranteed to terminate in polynomial time. A counter could be used in *empty_system* to limit the number of searches of undetermined_0 moves. This counter would then be a tuning parameter to trade off the algorithm's complexity versus the degree of completeness to which the algorithm can determine all live moves.

REFERENCES

Banaszak, Z. and B. Krogh. 1990. "Deadlock Avoidance in Flexible Manufacturing Systems with Concurrently Competing Process Flows." *IEEE Trans. Robotics & Auto.* 6, no. 6: 724-733.

Barkaoui, K., and I. B. Abdallah. 1995. "Deadlock Avoidance in FMS Based on Structural Theory of Petri Nets," *IEEE Symp. Emerging Tech. & Factory Automation*, 499-510.

Cho, H., T.K. Kumaran, and R. Wysk. 1995. "Graph-Theoretic Deadlock Detection and Resolution for Flexible Manufacturing Systems," *IEEE Trans. Robotics & Auto.* 11, no. 3: 550-527.

Ezpeleta, J., J. M. Colom, and J. Martinez. 1995. "A Petri Net Based Deadlock Prevention Policy for Flexible Manufacturing Systems," *IEEE Trans. Robotics & Auto.* 11, no. 2: 173-184.

Fanti, M., G. Maione and B. Turchiano. 1996. "Deadlock detection and recovery in flexible production systems with multiple capacity resources," *Industrial Applications in Power Systems, Computer Science and Telecommunications Proc. of the Mediterranean Electrotechnical Conference*, 237-241.

Judd, R. P. and T. Faiz. 1995. "Deadlock Detection and Avoidance for a Class of Manufacturing Systems." *Proceedings of the 1995 American Control Conference*, 3637-3641.

Judd, R., W. Zhang, P. Deering, and R. Lipset. 1999. "A Digraph-Based Deadlock Avoidance Policy For Automated Manufacturing Systems with Multiple Capacity Resources", *Proceedings of the 1999 Summer Computer Simulation Conference*, 143-148.

Lipset, R., P. Deering, and R. P. Judd. 1997. "Necessary and Sufficient Conditions for Deadlock in Manufacturing Systems," *Proceedings of the 1997 American Control Conference*, 1022-1026.

Viswanadham, N., Y. Narahari, and T. Johnson. 1990. "Deadlock Prevention and Deadlock Avoidance in Flexible Manufacturing Systems Using Petri Net Models," *IEEE Trans. on Robotics and Auto*.6, no. 6: 713-723.

Zhang, W. 2000. "Scalable Deadlock Avoidance Algorithms for Flexible Manufacturing Systems", Ph.D. Dissertation, Russ College of Engineering and Technology, Ohio University.

A SIMULATION TECHNIQUE FOR CODESIGN OF HARDWARE/SOFTWARE

Jianming CAI †, I. E. Ritchie ‡, and David W. Lloyd Ψ

† Department of Computing, Information Systems, and Mathematics, London Guildhall University, 100 Minories, London EC3N 1JY, U.K. Email: jcai@lgu.ac.uk

‡ Computing Research Centre, School of Computing and Management Sciences, Sheffield Hallam University, Pond Street, Sheffield, U.K. Email: i.ritchie@shu.ac.uk

Ψ Department of Computer Science, University of Manchester, Oxford Road, Manchester, U.K. Email: lloydd@ cs.man.ac.uk

ABSTRACT

A novel co-simulation technique plus its system target architecture and supporting software libraries and packages, is dealt with in this paper. The technique has been developed especially for performance analysis in the realm of codesign of hardware/software. The main contribution of it lies in the capacity for the system target architecture to be exploited against the system performance. The content of the paper begins with a brief review on both emulation and simulation techniques that are widely utilized in the codesign research. The co-simulation and virtual prototyping methods are highlighted. The proposed co-simulation technique and its virtual prototyping model are described and the layered bus protocol and the supporting VHDL packages and libraries are introduced. Furthermore, a case study is undertaken. The design and implementation of RDS (Radio data System) co-simulation program are presented and simulation results are examined in detail. Finally, conclusions and further research directions are drawn.

KEYWORDS

Real-time, Performance Evaluation, Co-simulation, Codesign, VHDL, Object-based Specification

1. INTRODUCTION

Improving system performance is an essential issue in the codesign of hardware/software. It is of paramount importance in codesign of hard real-time embedded system. The system performance can be analyzed in implementation, emulation, or simulation. The implementation approach has been rejected in this project because of huge cost and inflexibility. The emulation technique is carried out on its physical prototype platform, whereas simulation is executed in software simulators. In the codesign discipline, this type of simulation is often referred to as *co-simulation* since it deals with heterogeneous system with both hardware and software components in it. In addition, the term *performance analysis* involves both *performance estimation* and *evaluation* for codesign process. The work in this paper relates to performance evaluation. We therefore use the term *performance evaluation* in the context, instead of *performance analysis*.

A great deal of effort has been traditionally spent on emulation techniques to evaluate the performance of codesign system. One of the good reasons is that a codesign system can be emulated by its prototype target architecture. It is composed of microprocessors, ASICs (*Application Specific Integrated Circuits*) and buses. Hardware and software components generally communicate via a global memory as the rendezvous. Despite the fact that it could predict accurate system performance, the emulation approach is expensive and inflexible especially in terms of exploitation of system target architecture. It can in fact only proceed when prototyping hardware components are all available.

In contrast to emulation, the software simulation has the following range of advantages: low cost, flexibility, and short design turnaround time. Because of these advantages, there has been a growing interest in co-simulation techniques [1, 2]. The co-simulation can be either software-based (C/C++) or hardware-based (VHDL/other HDLs) but neither of them suits the task alone. The software-based offers good support for functional verification for those individual components but behaves awkwardly when dealing with the performance evaluation for hardware components and communications between heterogeneous components. On the other hand, the hardware-based favours the performance evaluation for individual hardware components but provides no mechanism to support the evaluation of software counterparts plus communications. Another drawback of the hardware-based co-simulation lies in its simulation efficiency (simulation performance itself). As the density of hardware circuit increases, driven by advancing technologies, traditional event-driven hardware simulators become increasingly incapable of responding to a huge number of events, which would have to take hours or even days to complete the simulation. To achieve high-performance solutions, EDA vendors started to switch the interest to a new technique, *cycle simulation*, which does not take account the detailed circuit timing but computes the steady state response of the circuit at each cycle boundary [3]. Nevertheless, the simulation at the behavior level (i.e. high level) is not ideal for this problem because of dramatically decreasing number of event at this level.

Co-simulation tools which emerged during late 90's, such as the *Seamless CVE™* from the Mentor Graphics [4], only support primitive system target architectures. They are confined in the single bus system, which can easily fall into the communication bottleneck problem inherited in this type of target architecture [5].

2. THE CO-SIMULATION PROJECT

The co-simulation project is an indispensable part of the research into the object-based codesign approach, collaborated in three institutions in the UK. In the object-based approach, the overall system is specified by using an object-based graphical notation (PARSE process graphs) and PARSE BSL descriptions [6, 7] that have been since extended to incorporate hardware specific functionality. From PARSE specifications, the processes are converted to VHDL and C programs for hardware/software implementations and the communication channels are synthesized in components invoked from a VHDL library. This project is intended to tackle the problem of predicting system performance through co-simulations in VHDL programs.

In general, the performance of a codesign system is associated with both the performances of individual component and the communication cost. While other codesign researchers study the communication cost in mathematical models [8, 9, and 10], this research has focused on the experimental perspective rather than statistical models. We prefer this path because of the following observations. Most codesign systems are hard real-time embedded system with strict timing requirements. Co-simulation techniques could provide a reliable and accurate prediction in respect of system timing. Besides, compared with statistical analysis that is proven to be effective to design general distributed network system incorporating communications through relay mechanism and via uncertain transmitting routes, the target architecture for codesign system is static and so is the communication route. This feature indicates the communication in codesign system is relatively "well-behaved" and thus able to be simulated, built on its physical architecture model.

The objectives of the project can be justified for the following reasons. First, modern embedded systems are no longer bounded by the single bus target architecture. The virtual prototyping plus co-simulation technique can readily provide a solution to the effectiveness, flexibility, and cost for performance evaluation. Second, since hardware/software components in a codesign system are generally clocked independently (asynchronously) and the number of components may change in line with both the system cost and performance, the layered asynchronous multi-bus target architecture is well suited to this reality.

In this project, the design of a generic layered bus protocol and the VHDL packages and libraries have been achieved. Apart from inter-process communications based on the layered buses, the VHDL co-simulation program is inserted in timing annotations for individual hardware/software components. The performance evaluation with the technique can be accurate to system clock cycles.

This project has employed a hardware-based co-simulation approach, i.e. the co-simulation supported by VHDL simulation environment. This route has been pursued because of the following merits. First, VHDL language furnishes hardware design. Its simulator provides the performance evaluation for hardware components. Secondly, thanks to the VHDL synthesis tool, most of the VHDL design can be automatically synthesized towards hardware circuitry. It speeds the time to market and improves the design quality of hardware component. Following this path, however, requires software components and the communication between hardware and software to be adroitly dealt within a unified co-simulation program. The chief difficulty has resulted from different nature between hardware and software design, in which a hardware designer has to handle circuitry timing by using special timing statements provided in VHDL whereas the timing in software is handled by operating system. Utilizing this feature properly, however, we can fully manipulate the system timing with respect to hardware, software, and the communication.

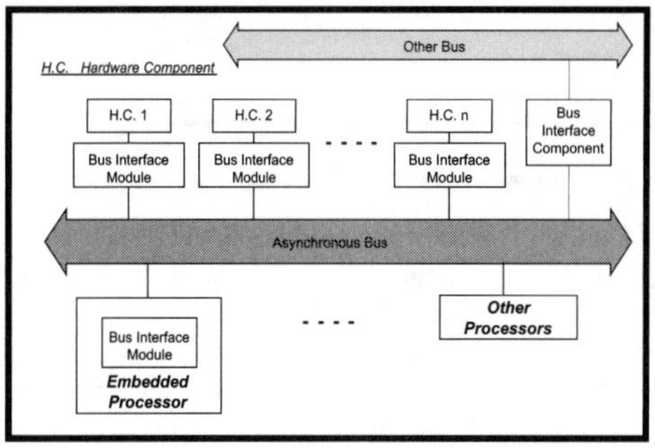

Figure 1. Generic System Target Architecture

Figure 1 illustrates our virtual prototyping model for the target architecture aforementioned, based on which the backbone system buses undertake the bulk of communication tasks. The number of system buses and the designation of bus throughput can now be exploited against the system performance. A component is connected to a selected system bus according to certain criteria so as to satisfy the system performance and/or hardware costs. Notice that, despite other communication mechanisms such as direct hard-wired connections or interrupts although supported in this model, they are not the focus of this project at present. In order to relieve the user of the burden of understanding complex bus handshaking protocol, VHDL packages and libraries have been developed, which can be directly called from user's VHDL simulation program. The asynchronous bus itself consists internally of four parallel sub-buses. They are *Data Transfer Bus* (DTB), *DTB Arbitration Bus*, *Control Bus* (CB), and *Address Bus* (AB) respectively. Apart from normal control lines typically in other bus protocols [11], two extra control lines are required to clarify the following positions:

- the DTB transfer occurs on same/different bus (line *sd* in Figure 2)
- the DTB transfer is blocked/non-blocked (line *sa* in Figure 2)

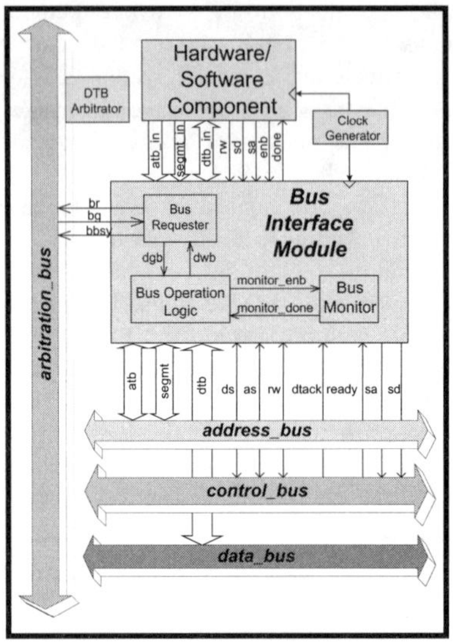

Figure 2. Bus Interface Module

Figure 2 enlarges the *bus interface module* (BIM). It is a regular system component, inserted between individual component and the system bus. It is composed of three sub-components: *Bus Requester*, *Bus Operation Logic*, and *Bus Monitor* that communicate with each other in internal signals. While the bus requester is connected to the arbitration bus to apply for control of the DTB, the bus operation logic and the bus monitor are all connected to the DTB, CB, and AB to complete handshaking and data transfer. The bus monitor is crucial in this protocol to avoid the deadlock resulted from the blocked DTB transfer (*Synchronous Channel* in PARSE).

In the PARSE object-based codesign approach, while a codesign application is synthesized with its low-lever system architecture, the system components are readily mapped to its target structure and the object-based properties are conceptually maintained. In particular the simulation programmer can implement system communication paths directly, using components provided in a VHDL library and following guidelines established in the codesign approach. This programming style looks rather like assembling of components previously developed, which promotes the component reuse. It ultimately helps create robust simulation programs.

Two types of communication channel in the specification are currently synthesizable that are *synchronous* (rendezvous) and *asynchronous* (buffered) channels. Due to its characteristic nature, the synthesis of synchronous channels is stressed as follows.

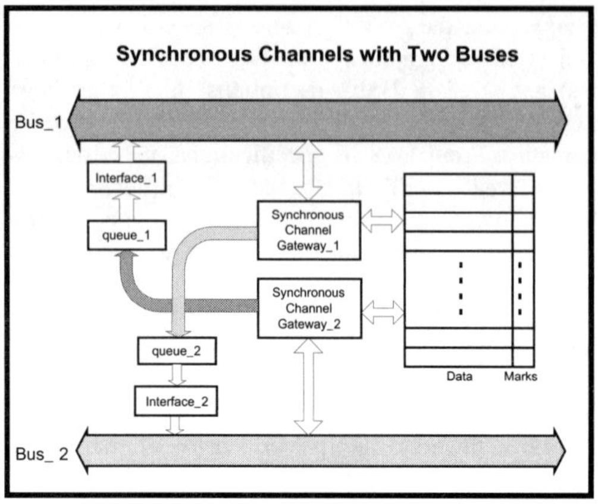

Figure 3. Bus Interface Component

The key to implementing synchronous channels is a global memory for the rendezvous for both sender and receiver. Each synchronous channel is assigned to a number. Both sender and receiver place the number on the ATB when they communicate. Apparently, all synchronous channels communicating on the same system bus can be organized in a standard component plus a chunk of memory. In addition, each channel has a one-bit mark as an indication of either a sender or a receiver waiting for the message from other side. By manipulating the mark, a sender or a receiver is able to release the system bus and trigger the monitor once they have to wait at the rendezvous, which prevents the potential system deadlock.

A complex situation rises where the sender and receiver are allocated on different system buses. This forces the communication to go through different system buses. A special component is thus designed to tackle this problem. Its internal structure has been shown in Figure 3. The *bus interface component* (BIC) connects different system buses, providing a common gateway across system buses. All synchronous channels across system buses can be pegged into this component with a piece of global memory. In Figure 3, the *Synchronous Channel Gateway_1*, *queue_2*, and *interface_2* form a synchronous communication path from the components on Bus_1 to the components on Bus_2. The *Synchronous Channel Gateway_2*, *queue_1*, and *interface_1* instead amalgamate into the opposite path. This symmetrical structure enables us only to discuss the path from Bus_1 to Bus_2.

In addition to data transfer handshaking with its counterpart on Bus_1, the Gateway_1 takes care of message storage and retrieval and bookkeeping. After a component on Bus_1 gains control of the DTB1, it contacts the Gateway_1 and the channel identity is added to the ATB1. It is understandable that both Gateway_1 and Gateway_2 concurrently access the global memory and the protection against the data inconsistency has to be imposed upon. Same problem exists between queue_1/queue_2 and Gateway_2/Gateway_1. The mutual exclusion must be imposed where appropriate. The receiver on BUS_2 waiting for the message coming or the sender on BUS_2 waiting for the receiver ready needs to be waken up as soon as the condition is satisfied. Because of unpredictable difference of speed between two system buses, the discharge messages from Gateway_1 have to be put in the queue_2 and let the Interface_2 apply for DTB2 acquisition and inform their counterparts.

Similar principles are applied to synthesizing asynchronous channels. The primary difference is that each asynchronous channel needs a separate chunk of memory as a buffer for the channel. The interlock or mutual exclusion also plays a key role.

The ARM embedded processor [12] has been adopted in the target architecture to embody the software component. This was chosen on account of its low power consumption and the support derived from its *Software Development Toolkit* (STD) In principle, any other embedded processor could have been chosen. For simplicity, we also suppose that each software component in the specification is assigned to an individual processor. Thus, the Co-BSL specification for a software component will be converted to a C program (the ANSI C in the case of STD). The ARM STD is a C cross-development tool-set. It represents a fully integrated development environment, based on Windows 95/NT 4.0. A thorough description of the environment can be found in [13]. The following three features can be evaluated by the STD: code and data size, overall execution time, and the time spent in specific parts of an application. The performance evaluation discussed here is related to overall execution time and the time spent in specific parts of an application. Although the code and data sizes are highly beneficial to codesign, they will not be discussed in this paper. The overall execution time and the time spent in specific parts of an application can be obtained by running debugger within the STD. As a C program executes, the STD counts the total number of clock ticks taken, and report this figure to user either through the debugger's $clock variable, or indirectly through a C library function such as clock (). Because of debugger's symbolic feature, any program section can be assessed against clock ticks, and the time delay in this particular section can be acquired.

On the other end of the spectrum, the efficiency of a synthesized hardware design, including its time delay, circuit area, or power consumption etc., can be predicted by hardware synthesis tools. The hardware performance has been exclusively researched into at the high-level synthesis (HLS) arena since early 80's and a number of synthesis algorithms and tools have been developed [14]. A major benefit is that most hardware components can now be automatically synthesized and the VHDL synthesis tool can be fully exploited. The evaluation of hardware performance is therefore a relatively less demanding job in this project.

The VHDL co-simulation program, on the whole, includes both timing delays for hardware and software components plus the time delays for communications over system bus(es). The time delays for hardware and software components are resulted from hardware synthesis and symbolic debugging in the STD, whereas the communication delay directly accumulates during the VHDL simulation. They are all counted in the number of clock cycle. The entire time delay from a VHDL simulation session represents the performance of a codesign system. The performance evaluated in the co-simulation could be accurate to system clock cycles. Since the simulation is at the behavioral level, it avoids problems of efficiency and generally runs to completion within minutes.

A special VHDL library that supports up to two asynchronous system buses is currently available although more bus layers will be added at a late stage. The system synthesis process is thus no more then an assembly of individual components.

3. THE CASE STUDY

The feasibility of the proposed technique has been tested in the case study, namely *Codesign of Radio Data System* (RDS). The RDS [15, 16] is a typical hard real-time embedded system. It was initially intended to assist the car receivers in proper tuning. Owing to ever-growing demand on radio data information and technology advances, its potential use has been well beyond its original goal. It can be foreseen that researches into low power, low cost, and multi-application RDS equipment will draw a great deal of attention from both academic and commercial societies.

In this case study, however, we assume that the RDS receiver's function has been expanded to listen concurrently to two different RDS transmitters and the data received are all simplified as integers. This assumption is justified because the modern RDS system is reasonably expected to encompass variety of new applications and the simplified data type enables us to concentrate on demonstration of above-mentioned co-simulation technique.

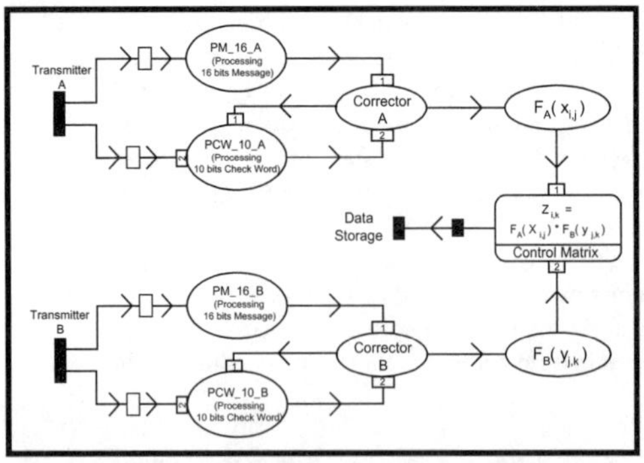

Figure 4. Low-level Process Graph for RDS

The RDS receiver has been specified in the enhanced PARSE process graph and refined as in Figure 4. Inter-process communications are specified as synchronous/asynchronous channels. In the hardware/ software partitioning phase, processes are dispatched to either hardware or software components in accordance with system criteria. Communication channels are synthesized, supported in components stored in the VHDL library. The simulation stimuli are assumed as two sets of integers. They are transmitted via *Transmitter A* and *B*. Integers in group A are the elements of Matrix A and integers in group B are the ones in Matrix B. After transformed in the F_A and F_B, Matrix A is then multiplied by Matrix B in the control process *Control Matrix*. The results from the multiplication are preserved in the external entity *data storage* through an asynchronous channel.

The simulation was carried out on the ModelSim VHDL simulation platform. Simulation results indicate that the performance of RDS can be duly improved when the target architecture with two system buses is introduced and the allocation of individual component is carefully planed.

Among simulation outcomes, two typical groups have been selected for comparison, which are displayed in Table1 and Table2 respectively. In the first column of the tables, in addition to the process names in the process graph, there are four extra components summoned from the VHDL library for synthesizing communication paths. The BUS1_SYN_BUF is a component for synchronous channels on bus_1, whilst BUS2_SYN_BUF is its counterpart on bus_2. The BUS_1_2_SYN_BUF is a component for cross bus synchronous channels and the ASYN_BUF is the one for the asynchronous channel in the specification graph. The clock cycles assigned to individual components are listed in the second column and the time delays are shown in the third column. The last column indicates whether a particular component is allocated on bus_1 or bus_2. The last row of each table discloses the time stamp on final datum received from the process *Control Matrix*. It is evident that once the second bus introduced the system performance is accordingly improved, notwithstanding original individual parameters remain same.

Table 1

PROCESS NAME	CLOCK	TIME DELAY	BUS
PM_16_A	500 NS	500 NS	1
PCW_10_A	500 NS	500 NS	1
Corrector A	500 NS	1000 NS	1
F(A)	500 NS	300 NS	1
PM_16_B	500 NS	500 NS	1
PCW_10_B	500 NS	500 NS	1
Corrector B	500 NS	1000 NS	1
F(B)	500 NS	300 NS	1
Control Matrix	500 NS	1000 NS	1
Storage	500 NS	100 NS	1
BUS1_SYN_BUF	500 NS	500 NS	1
BUS2_SYN_BUF	N/A	N/A	N/A
BUS_1_2_SYN_BUF	N/A	N/A	N/A
ASYN_BUF	500 NS	500 NS	1
LAST_ELEMENT_RECEIVED	N/A	***2287100 NS***	N/A

Table 2

PROCESS NAME	CLOCK	TIME DELAY	BUS
PM_16_A	500 NS	500 NS	1
PCW_10_A	500 NS	500 NS	1
Corrector A	500 NS	1000 NS	1
F(A)	500 NS	300 NS	1
PM_16_B	500 NS	500 NS	2
PCW_10_B	500 NS	500 NS	2
Corrector B	500 NS	1000 NS	2
F(B)	500 NS	300 NS	2
Control Matrix	500 NS	1000 NS	1
Storage	500 NS	100 NS	1
BUS1_SYN_BUF	500 NS	500 NS	1
BUS2_SYN_BUF	500 NS	500 NS	2
BUS_1_2_SYN_BUF	500 NS	500 NS	1 & 2
ASYN_BUF	500 NS	500 NS	1
LAST_ELEMENT_RECEIVED	N/A	***2231600 NS***	N/A

4. CONCLUSIONS AND FUTURE WORK

The conventional performance evaluation for codesign system excessively relies on the emulation technique, which is expensive particularly when the system target architecture is exploited for the improvement of system performance. The co-simulation technique proposed in this paper provides one of solutions to this problem. In addition, this research advocates object-based system synthesis method that helps transfer high-level co-specification to its low-level implementation and retain object-based properties. The co-simulation program produced in this technique is therefore more reliable and easy to maintain from the viewpoint of Software Engineering.

The case study demonstrates the practicality of the proposed co-simulation technique.

The future work has been directed towards improving simulation accuracy, analyzing impacts on system performance under different component allocation schemes, and the possibility of automation of generation of the co-simulation program.

REFERENCES

1. Antoniazzi, A. Balboni, W. Fornaciari and D. Sciuto, "Co-synthesis and Co-simulation of Control-Dominated Embedded Systems", *Design Automation for Embedded Systems*, Kluwer Academic Publisher, 1996
2. Claudio Passerone, Luuciano Lavagno, Massimiliano Chiodo and Alberto Sangiovanni-Vincentelli, "Fast Hardware/Software Co-simulation for Virtual Prototyping and Trade-off Analysis", *Proceedings 34th DAC*, Anaheim, CA, USA, 1997
3. Murali Bharathala, "VHDL Times", viewlogic Systems, Inc. *http://www.vhdl.org/vhdl_intl/vtimes*, 1998
4. Russ Klein and Ross Nelson, Seamless CVE™ Hardware/Software Co-Verification Technology, *http://www.mentorg.com/codesign*, 1997
5. M. Edwards, "Software Acceleration Using Coprocessor: is it worth the effort?", *Proceedings of the Fifth International Workshop on Hardware/Software Codesign*, IEEE Computer Society Press, 1997
6. Jianming Cai, D W Lloyd and I E Jelly, "Modeling Mobile Communication Systems in the Integrated PARSE and VHDL Environment", The Proceedings of The 9th International Conference on Wireless Communications, 9-11 July 1997, Calgary, Alberta, Canada
7. Jianming Cai, D W Lloyd and I E Jelly, "Modeling and Simulating Radio Data Systems", The Proceedings of The 1st International Symposium on Communication Systems and Digital Signal Processing, 6-8 April 1998, Sheffield, UK
8. Ken Hines and Gaetano Borriello, "Dynamic Communication Models in Embedded Systems Co-Simulation", *Proceedings of 34th Design Automation Conference*, Anaheim, CA, USA, 1997
9. J-Y. Brunel, E.A. de Kock, W.M. Kruijtzer, H.J.H.N. Kenter, W.J.M. Smiths, "Communication Refinement in Video Systems On Chip", *Proceedings of Seventh International Workshop on Hardware/Software Codesign*, Rome, Italy, 1999 , pp. 142 146
10. Peter Voigt Knudsen and Jan Madsen, Communication Estimation for Hardware/Software Codesign, *Proceedings of the Sixth International Workshop on Hardware/Software Codesign*, IEEE Computer Society Press, 1998, pp. 55-59
11. Joseph Di Giacomo, Digital bus handbook, McGraw-Hill, 1990
12. S.B. Furber, ARM System Architecture, Addison-Wesley, 1996
13. Advanced RISC Machines Ltd. (ARM), ARM Software Development Toolkit, User Guide & Reference Guide, 1997
14. Paul Camposano and Wayne Wolf (Eds.), High-Level VLSI Synthesis, Kluwer Academic Publishers, 1991
15. Peter L Mothersole and Norman W White, Broadcast Data System, Teletext and RDS, Butterworths & Co. (Publishers) Ltd., 1990
16. RDS Forum-News, WWW address: http:// www.org.uk/rdsupgrade.html, 14th, Jan. 1998

THE OPTIMIZATION OF THE SINTERING OPERATION BY THE COMPUTER SIMULATION

Juzo Shibata
Division of Human Information Science
Kanazawa Institute of Technology
7-1 Ohgigaoka,Nonoichi,Ishikawa 921-8501,Japan
e-mail : shibata@neptune.kanazawa-it.ac.jp

KEYWORDS
mathematical simulation,computer model, numerical calculation,pertial differential equations,optimization

ABSTRACT
This research is related to the mathematical simulation for the sintering plant of the iron ore. The coke combustion reaction and the decomposition reactions of limestone have been taken into account. The process performance of the sintering machine is affected by various factors, such as blend ratio of coke, water content of raw material, blend ratio of limestone, melting properties of raw material the decomposition reactions of limestone and the atmosphere conditions in ignition furnace. Because the high temperature gas from the ignition furnace flows downward through the packed layer of raw material, the heat exchange occurs between solids and gases. Here assumed there is the analogy between heat transfer and mass transfer. This model including respective equations is consisted of simultaneous nonlinear partial differential type of twenty equations having many operation parameters. Using the initial operating conditions, this mathematical model, which includes empirical formulas of the pressure drop in each zone, can predict the change in the suction air volume with the movement of moisture, temperature distribution with the oxygen concentration and the progress of sintering operation can be quantitatively evaluated.This critical concentration can be estimated and showed the changes of the temperature distribution of the bed layer with operating time.

Introduction

This research describes the mathematical models for elucidating the sintering phenomena and analyzing quantitatively the inner situations of the ermal decomposition of limestone ,the melting process of iron ore and the solidification process of molten ore are included as the elemental equations. In addition, the vaporization of moisture and the recondensation of vapor were included in this mathematical model. Therefore, the model can obtain more actual results than previous papers. The volume of air passed through the sinter bed markedly affects the rate of heat transfer and that of coke combustion in the sinter bed. The behavior of wind is important in clarifying the characteristics of the sintering process. Thus, the attention is focussed on the characteristics of the wind volume and the pressure drop in the sinter bed. The changes in the pressure of each zone in the sinter bed were investigated experimentally by use of a sintering test pot and were analyzed theoretically. The relationship between the pressure drop in the sinter bed and that in each reaction zone is investigated, and the factors that govern the wind volume required are revealed. The humidity concentration in the flow gas causes to decrease the partial pressure of oxygen concentration. The amount of moistere condensation largely depends on the difference between the wet bulb temperature of flow gas passing through the sinter bed and the temperature of the raw sinter mix. The moisture condensation zone forms at a high rate and reaches the bottom of the sinter bed in a short time. The gas flow resistance of the moisture condensation zone is larger than that of the initial raw sinter bed, so these phenomena affect each other.

MATHEMATICAL MODEL

The simulation model is constructed from eighteen non-linear partial differencial equations.

The most fundamental phenomena in this process is the heat exchange between gas flow and solid. Here it can be discribed as the following equations from the enthalpy balance viewed from gas.

$$\partial (V \cdot Cg \cdot T) / \partial x + b \cdot h \cdot (T - t) = \partial (\varepsilon \cdot V \cdot Cg \cdot T) / \partial y \qquad (1)$$

The heat transfer coefficient;b between gas and solid around a simple particle can be expressed empirically as following equation;

$$h \cdot D / s = 2.0 + 0.6 \cdot (n \cdot d \cdot w \cdot \rho_g \cdot u)^{1/2} \cdot (Cg \cdot u / s)^{1/3} \qquad (2)$$

From the enthalpy balance on the solid side,

$$b \cdot h \cdot (T - t) + Rc^* \cdot Hc + Re^* \cdot He = (1-\varepsilon) \cdot \partial (c \cdot t) / \partial y = (1-\varepsilon) \cdot \rho_c \cdot \partial H / \partial y \qquad (3)$$

According the bed temperature changes the melting and solidification process of the Iron ore happen.

These phenomena can be presented as follows:
The enthalpy change in melting and solidification process,

$$\partial H / \partial y = -(\partial H / \partial t) \cdot (\partial t / \partial y) \qquad (4)$$

Here,

$(\partial H / \partial t)$ shows the change of the latent heat of solids, and it is assumed to be constant during melting,

$$\partial H / \partial t = Const = f \qquad (5)$$

The sum of $\partial H / \partial t$ should be equal to H_{m0},

Then,

$$\int (\partial H / \partial t)\, dt = f \cdot (t_2 - t_1) = H_{m0} \quad (6)$$

So,Finally, the equation is given by:

$$f = H_{m0} / (t_2 - t_1) \quad (7)$$

This is relating to the melting function of raw material.

The coke combustion in sinter bed is the most important reaction. The main reaction of coke is the formation equation of the carbonic dioxide gas

$$C + O_2 \rightarrow Cco_2 \quad (8)$$

here main reaction is considered.

The reaction coefficient of carbon combustion ;

K_r can be expressed ,

$$Kr = 3.92 \times 10^9 \cdot \sqrt{t} \cdot \exp(-44000 / q \cdot t) \quad (9)$$

where q is gas constant,

Co_2 is oxygen concentration.

The overall reaction coefficient;

K c* could be expressed with mass tranfer coefficient,

$$Kc^* = 1 / K_f + 1 / Kr \quad (10)$$

The mass tranfer coefficient;

K_f of oxygen gas is derived from the following equation.

Here assumed there is the analogy between the heat transfer and the mass transfer ,

$$K_f \cdot D / Dg = 2.0 + 0.6 \cdot (n \cdot d \cdot w \cdot \rho_g \cdot u)^{1/2} \cdot (u / \rho_g \cdot Dg)^{1/3} \quad (11)$$

Reaction rate per coke particle.

$$r_c^* = 4 \pi r^2 \cdot Kc^* \cdot Co_2 \quad (12)$$

Material balance for coke particle

$$-\partial r / \partial y = 4 \pi r_e^2 (\rho_c / Mc) \cdot r_c^* \quad (13)$$

The decomposition rate of lime stone,

$$re^* = 4 \pi r_e^2 \cdot ke \cdot (Cco_2^* - Cco_2) \quad (14)$$

Material balance for and limestone particle

$$-\partial r_e / \partial y = 4 \pi r_e^2 \cdot (\rho_c / Mc) \cdot re^* \quad (15)$$

From carbon dioxide balance in the flow gas the next is discribed as following:

Balance for oxygen and carbon dioxide in gas

$$-\partial (V \cdot Cco_2 / \rho) / \partial x + Rc^* + Re^* = \partial (\varepsilon \cdot Cco_2) / \partial y \quad (16)$$

Material balance on oxygen gas can be discribed as

$$-\partial (V \cdot Co_2 / \rho) / \partial x - Rc^* = \partial (\varepsilon \cdot Co_2) / \partial y \quad (17)$$

Equation of the continuity viewed on the fluid side,

$$-\partial V / \partial x + Mc \cdot Rc^* / \rho_c + Me \cdot Re^* / \rho_e = \partial (\varepsilon \cdot \rho) / \partial y \quad (18)$$

In the case of developing the fundamental equations relevant to the drying process, the first stage of the drying process and the second stage of the falling rate period. Moisture condensation and drying process can be expressed from the material balance on the fluid. In wet zone,there are additional vapor condensation,then the ratio of the water in the solid raises gradually.

Therefore,the condensation of moisture can be suppressed by reducing the humidity of the gas or raising the temperature of the raw sinter mix.

Material balance for moisture. viewed from gas and solid:

$$-\partial (V \cdot W) / \partial x = R_w^* \quad (19)$$

From the material balance of the water content in the raw materials,

$$(1 - \varepsilon) \rho_s \cdot \partial w / \partial y = R_w^* \quad (20)$$

Moisture Condensation and Drying Region Enthalpy balance, viewed from gas and solid in the wet zone,

$$\partial (V \cdot Cg \cdot T) / \partial x + b \cdot h \cdot (T - t) = R_w^* \cdot H_w + (1 - \varepsilon) \cdot \partial (c \cdot t) / \partial y \quad (21)$$

It is assumed that the drying process is ruled by heat transfer from hot gas flow in the layer.

Velocity equations for constantiate drying and decreasing-rate drying processes:

Drying process in the constant rate period,

$$R_w^* = b \cdot h \cdot (T - t) / H_w \quad (22)$$

For the falling rate period is expressed,

$$R_w^* = \{ b \cdot h \cdot (T - t) / H_w \} \cdot (w - w_e) / (w_c - w_e) \quad (23)$$

Through this drying process,the water in the upper solids move into the gas bulk flow as the vaper.

The moisture condensation zone forms at a high rate and reaches the bottom of the layer in a short time. Then this vapor from the flow gas attach to the down of layer and are cooled by the lower part of solid, then the vapor condences again on the solid surface.

Moisture condensation rate can be expressed as following,

Velocity equation for moisture condensation process:

$$R_w^* = V \cdot (\partial Ws / \partial T) \cdot (\partial T / \partial x) \quad (24)$$

$$\partial Ws / \partial T = k_w \cdot \exp(0.057 \cdot T) \quad (25)$$

Here Ws is the saturation humidity curve of suction gas.

Another important factor is the sintering wind volume. The gas flow resistance of the moisture condensation zone is larger than that of the initial raw packed bed.

The pressure changes; P of each zone are estimated by the following equation,

$$dPg / dx = k_{1,i} \cdot \mu \cdot V + k_{2,i} \cdot \rho_g \cdot V^2 \quad (26)$$

Here $k_{1,i}$, $k_{2,i}$ are pressure drop coefficients for each phenomena.

NUMERICAL CALUCULATION

Caluculation Method of this model, the numerical solutions can be obtained by computer-based numerical computations. It was found from the computations that there existed a maximum step size of the difference as required for obtaining stable solutions and that the solutions could be illustrated on the two characteristic curves regarding the time and distance variables. In general,partial diffrential equations are classified in three type,the first is the hyperbolic type second is the parabolic type and the third is the ellipitic type. This mathematical model belongs to the second order hyperbolic type. This type partial differencial equation has two characteristic curve On these curve,these equations of this model can be treated as the ordinary differential equations. So it becomes more easier to be solved. The numerical solutions are obtained on the integral curve. It was found from the computations that there existed a maximum step size of the difference as required for obtaining stable solutions and that the solutions could be expressed on the two characteristic curves regarding the time and the distance variables.

On the basis of this model having many operation parameters,the numerical solutions can be obtained by computer based step by step calculation. Then the virtual operation can be achieved ,it was carried about eleven million steps for one operating case. Using the initial operating conditions only,this mathematical model which includes empirirical formulas of the pressure drop in each zone can predict the change in the suction air volume with the movement of moisture and the progress of sintering after ignition. As a result,it can be clarified that the temperature distribution in non steady state. Using this model, the changes of the temperature distribution with the oxygen concentration were theoretically investigated. The critical concentration can be estimated as the changes of the temperature distribution of the bed layer with operating time. It is considered that the sintering reaction will not take place under this value. Thus,with the other operating conditions kept unchanged, the value is considered the lower limit of critical oxygen concentration. It can be also obsereved that there the same hesitation to rise solid temperature. It caused the coke reaction rate were not enough, the maximum temperature of solid can not be developed. While the concentration is raised over critical value,the temperature distribution expands along the distance from the bed surface. This describes the mathematical model for elucidating the sintering phenomena and analyzing quantitatively the inner situation of the sinter bed. Here caluculated three typical cases for moisture content in the through gass of the sintering bed. The maximum temperature of solid tends to increase as the distance from the bed surface. If the temperature distribution are gradually decrease, a intermediate case, here the sinter reaction almost stopping, but recovered finally. The case that the concentration in gas flow were calculated also. The numerical analysis showed that the suction air volume remains actually constant within a certain range even if the other operating conditions are varied. By using this model, the changes in the temperature, wind volume and wind pressure throughout the sinter bed including the reaction zone were theoretically investigated. Given the initial operating conditions, the mathematical model, which includes empirical formulas describing the pressure drop in each zone, can predict the change in suction air volume with the movement of moisture and the progress of sintering after ignition. The effects of these factors on the reaction rates and the temperature distributions of the sinter bed can be quantitatively evaluated by the mathematical model.

CONCLUSION

The effects of operating factors on the reaction rates and the temperature distributions of the sinter bed can be quantitatively evaluated by the simulation model. On the basis of the findings obtained by use of the model, there are some limitting condition to develop heat pattern in the bed. Here,it is clearly decided the critical humidity concentration in the suction gas. The effects of these factors on the reaction rates, the temperature distribution of the sinter bed and critical conditions for the flue gas recirculation can be quantatively evaluated. It is seemed that high vapor existance decreases the coke combustion reaction.

As a result, the waste gas recirculating method will increase the amount of moisture condensation in the sinter bed and decrease the maximum temperature in the bed. Then it should be paid enough compensation for the high temperature gas. By this virtual simulation technics developed here, the optimum condition can be dicided cleared for every cases. The results of these analysis have been utilized in developing the new technics for the sintering process as well as improving the machine.

NOMENCLATURE

Cco_2 : carbon dioxide concentration
Cg : specific heat of gas
Co_2 : oxygen concentration
c : specific heat of solid
H :melting variable
Mc : molecular weight of carbon
Me : molecular weight of limestone
r : radius of coke particle
r_c :radius of limestone particle
Rc*:coke reaction rate for bed
Re*:limestone reaction rate for bed
R_w*:moisture moving rate
T :gas temperature
t :solid temperature
V :suction gas volume
w_c :critical moisture content,
W :moisture content of gas
Ws :saturated moisture content
w_e :equilibrium moisture content
w :moisture content of solid
x:distance from bed surface
h:heat transfer coefficient
b:specific surface area
r_c*:coke reaction rate for particle
r_e*:limestone reaction rate for particle
Hc:heat of coke reaction
He:heat of lime stone reaction
H_w :latent heat of vaporization
ε :voidage of bed
y:time since ignition
ρ_c ;density of coke
ρ:density of gas
ρ_s ;density of bed

REFERENCES

1. J.Shibata,Y.Hosotani,N.Konno,T.Sato,H.Suzuki , I.S.I.J.International,Vol.35, No.11,1995 ,p.1340
2. Y.Hosotani,N.Konno,J.Shibata,T.Sato ,Testu to Hagane,Vol.81,No.1,1995,P.34
3. J.Shibata,Proceeding of the 6th International Conference on Mathematical Modelling, Vol.11,1988,p.956

ANALYZING THE SENSITIVITY OF SIMULATION PARAMETERS

James F. Leathrum, Jr. and Lars Karlberg
Virginia Modeling, Analysis and Simulation Center
Old Dominion University

ABSTRACT

Simulations which are heavily data driven can be difficult to analyze. As the number of parameters grows, the ability to understand their effect on simulation results becomes increasingly difficult. Looking to improve a process by modifying the parameters requires a lot of insight from the user, thus requiring a domain expert. This paper presents an experimental process for comparing the affects of various parameters in a simulation. The process has been implemented as an analysis tool in Excel to set up and run experiments using the simulation and then analyze the result by ranking the affect of various parameters on the chosen measure of effectiveness. The process and tool are demonstrated on a port simulation (PORTSIM) that analyzes the ability to move military cargo through a port in a time of crisis. The results provide some insight into the PORTSIM model and identify areas where cost can be saved and where throughput can be increased.

INTRODUCTION

Simulations tend to be data dependent, however the majority of effort is placed on the model and simulation development, and little effort is placed on the data. When effort is placed on the data, the emphasis is on analyzing input data and output data. However, a primary purpose of simulations is to determine the necessary resources to complete a process within certain constraints. Generally, this involves a domain expert intuitively adjusting the parameters in a simulation until an acceptable result is obtained. This paper presents a process to assist the analyst in performing studies to determine how to better perform the process with available resources by constructing experiments on interesting parameters to identify those parameters most like to improve the process.

It is fairly straightforward to perform an experiment on a single simulation parameter. One simply defines a range of values over which the parameter is to be varied and the increment over that range. A smaller increment gives more detail but takes longer to gather the data. An appropriate measure of effectiveness is also chosen as the measure to evaluate the affect of the parameter. Example measures of effectiveness include throughput, capacity, and time to completion.

The difficulty arises when trying to compare different parameters. Parameters are very different in nature. Consider a simulation where the measure of effectiveness is the time to completion. Parameters such as number of available resources generally improve the time to completion as the value increases. However, increasing processing time parameters actually degrades the performance.

This paper proposes a method for normalizing the results of various types of parameters to allow direct comparison. An automated process of running experiments to gather the data necessary to compare parameters is presented. Finally, a visualization of the data is presented that allows an immediate determination of the relative affect of different parameters. The final analysis of the parameters is separated into two measures:

- *Available freedom:* defines how much slack exists in a parameter allowing the analyst to reduce requirements without affecting the measure of effectiveness.
- *Performance:* defines how directly increasing requirements on a parameter benefits the performance of the measure of effectiveness.

The final analysis actually allows an analyst to rate the importance of different parameters relative to a base scenario based on the above two measures. In this manner, the analyst can identify parameters where his effort should focus to improve system performance.

EXPERIMENTAL METHOD

The experimental method involves the running of experiments, the gathering of data, and the analysis of results. The experiments are conducted by varying the parameters in a simulation relative to a base scenario selected by the user. The currently proposed method involves the varying of one parameter at a time to determine the simulation's sensitivity to that parameter about the base scenario. Future work considers a multi-parameter sensitivity analysis, but the current work only varies one parameter at a time and then compares the sensitivity of different parameters in an attempt to identify those parameters that present the largest room for improvement. The analysis of the parameters can be described in seven steps described in this section.

Measure of Effectiveness

The analyst has to define a measure of effectiveness by which simulation results are judged. That measure that is most important to the process results should be selected. The current work only allows a single measure of effectiveness, though it is acknowledged that there are various competing goals in complex simulations. Currently, analysis of multiple measures of effectiveness requires separate analyses. Examples of measures of effectiveness are throughput, capacity, time to completion and cost.

The desired affect on the measure must also be determined. When using throughput as the measure of effectiveness, an increase is generally desirable. However, when using the time to completion as the measure, a reduction in time is generally desirable.

Base Scenario

Experiments are performed to determine the sensitivity of the parameters about a fixed base scenario, not across the ranges of all scenarios. The assumption is that the analyst has a scenario on which improvement is desired. This scenario becomes the base scenario that defines the initial values of all parameters. Then a single parameter will be varied at a time, keeping all other parameters fixed to the values defined by the base scenario.

Parameter Characterization

Not all parameters affect the result in the same manner. An increase in one parameter might be a benefit and an increase in another parameter might be a penalty. The parameters must be manipulated so that these two conditions can be compared. An important assumption made in this work is that the affect of all parameters is either an increasing or decreasing function. Comparing parameters whose results contain either minima or maxima requires further analysis.

The first step is to characterize the parameters into like groups. Several general groups have been defined, though individual simulations may require different groupings:

- *Resources:* resources refer to entities required for processing, such as a forklift to move an item.
- *Capacities:* similar to resources, capacities involve the amount of something available such a storage capacity.
- *Process times:* these times are how long different activities require, such as moving from one location to another.
- *Interarrival times:* defines the rate at which entities arrive in the simulation. Interarrival times are generally data driven, but occasionally they are a programmable value for the system to prevent queue overloads.

Note that generally the first two groups result in an increase in performance as the amount increases, while the latter two result in a decrease in performance as the amount increases.

Experiment Definition

Once the parameters and measure of effectiveness for a base scenario are characterized, experiments can be defined. This involves identifying those parameters of interest, and the range over which those parameters are to be considered. A separate scenario is defined for each different parameter value for all parameters.

Simulation

The complete set of scenarios defined above are then simulated to generate data on the measure of effectiveness. One goal of this work was to automate both the generation of the scenarios and the execution of the scenarios as these tend to be lengthy manual processes.

Data Collection

The results of the simulation runs need to have the appropriate data extracted in preparation for analysis. This also should be an automated process as manually analyzing each result is time consuming.

Data Analysis

The first step of data analysis is to massage the results so that different parameters can be directly compared. The convention is chosen that the measure of effectiveness should be plotted as an increasing function, thus an increase in value represents a benefit. This may be contrary to how the measure of effectiveness is generally analyzed, but consistency in analysis over all measures of effectiveness and all parameters was selected as the mode of operation.

Figure 1 demonstrates how parameters are plotted. The parameters are changed as a percentage from the value in the base scenario. Thus each different parameter plotted on the graph has it's value for the base scenario defined as 0% on the X-axis. Changes in parameters which expect a penalty in the measure of effectiveness correspond with negative percentages on the X-axis. Changes in parameters which expect an improvement in the measure of effectiveness correspond with positive percentages on the X-axis.

The percent change in the measure of effectiveness is plotted on the Y-axis. An improvement in the measure of effectiveness corresponds with a positive percentage and a penalty corresponds with a negative percentage. All parameters will have a 0% change in measure of

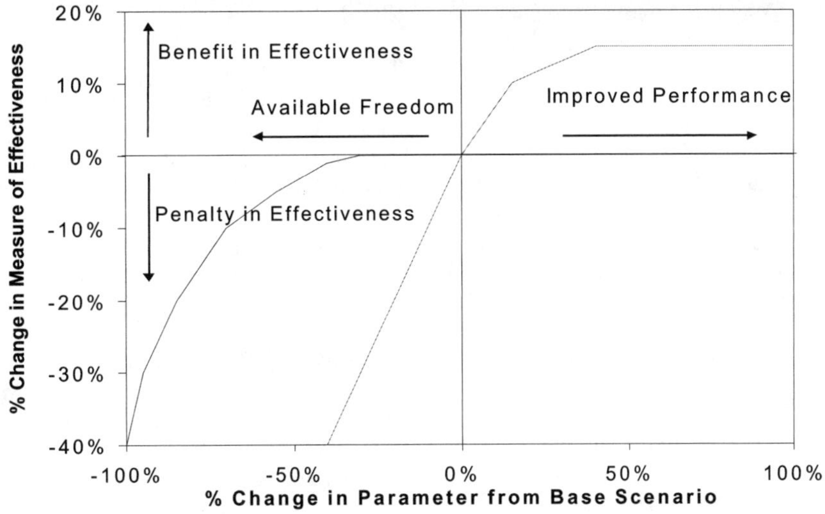

Figure 0. Graphical Representation of the Comparison of Parameters.

effectiveness for a 0% change in parameter so all curves will pass through the origin.

Consider the case where the measure of effectiveness is the time to completion. A reduction in value corresponds with an improvement, therefore, a value less than the base scenario is plotted as a positive percentage. A value greater than the base scenario is plotted as a negative percentage. When a parameter corresponding with a number of resources is increased, an improvement is expected, thus the percent change is positive, and decreases are mapped as negative percentages. When a processing time parameter is increased, a penalty in the measure of effectiveness is anticipated, resulting in the percent change being plotted as negative percentage, and a decrease being plotted as a positive percentage. Thus the signs of the percent changes are inverted where appropriate to align the measure of effectiveness.

When a positive slope is detected at the origin, the associated parameter has a potential to improve the performance. Therefore, the desire is to increase the percent change in parameter from the base scenario. When comparing two parameters, emphasis should be placed on adjusting the parameter with the largest slope as it has a more direct affect on the performance.

If a zero slope is detected at the origin, then increasing or decreasing the percentage has no change in performance. In fact, the potential to move the percent change in the negative direction corresponds with slack in the system. The parameter can be moved in the negative direction until a positive slope is detected. An example is that if an abundance of a resource is available so that there are idle resources throughout the simulation run, the plot will identify how many resources could be left out, potentially reducing operational costs.

IMPLEMENTATION OF AN AUTOMATED METHOD IN EXCEL

In order to release the analyst from time consuming processes during the analysis, an interface in Excel has been built to construct and analyze the experiments. Excel was chosen due to its data analysis capabilities and the ability to easily create user interfaces and programmable capabilities. The benefits of a spreadsheet-based interface to simulations is presented in (Leathrum, et. al., 2000).

The interface makes the creation of test scenarios faster. The user can create all the scenarios for one parameter in seconds. The interface is built so that parameters are varied with respect to a base scenario, thus creating a set of test scenarios. Test scenarios are created in whatever format the simulation accepts as input. The running of the scenarios is then automated. On completion, data is automatically collected and organized in charts that easily allows the analyst to visualize the change in effect for that parameter. The results of multiple experiments can then be presented together to allow a direct comparison.

CASE STUDY: PORTSIM

The method to test the operating parameters is implemented as a proof of concept in the port simulation PORTSIM. PORTSIM is a simulation that analyzes the flow of military equipment through commercial seaports (Nevins *et al.* 1998, Nevins *et al.* 1995, and Leathrum and

Frith 2000). The process described here will eventually be integrated into the final PORTSIM interface (Leathrum *et al.* 2000).

PORTSIM background

PORTSIM is a tool used for planning operations, where the military is given a portion of a port. Planners can, by using this software, compare and select ports and determine available throughput, time to completion, and utilization of critical resources.

PORTSIM is designed to answer the following questions:

- How long does it take to move equipment and supplies through the seaport (closure)?
- What and where are the potential bottlenecks and limited resources to movement through the seaport?
- Why are operations not completed by the required time?
- What are the implications if certain seaport resources are constrained or available?
- What are the port throughput capability given explicit assumptions on assets, resources and scenarios?

PORTSIM runs in two modes. The first mode uses embarkation processes, which include reception, staging and ship loading. Reception processes are the acceptance of cargo at the gate or railway interchange yard. It also includes cargo transfer to the staging areas. Staging includes the processes that are required for parking and inspecting cargo before ship loading. The ship loading calls forward cargo to the berths when ships arrive and loads the cargo onto the ships.

The second mode of operation is debarkation. This includes ship-unloading activities, debarkation staging activities and clearance activities. The debarkation processes are similar to embarkation processes but they are proceeded in reverse order. This paper focuses on the port of embarkation processes as an example.

PORTSIM handles all cargo items, ships and port infrastructure as individual objects. A typical scenario can include over 10,000 pieces of equipment. The types of cargo PORTSIM handles are vehicles, containers and palletized cargo. The transportation that is used to and from the port is: highway (flatbeds, chassis, vans), rail (flatcars, boxcars), and ships (RORO, containers, breakbulk, and FSS). The availability and priority of port resources can be determined, to make the scenario as realistic as possible.

Simulation study

The port of embarkation processes are under consideration in this simulation study. It involves moving 9164 pieces of cargo (containers and vehicles) through the Port of Savannah. The cargo arrives on 1224 transports (commercial highway and rail) and leaves on 10 ships. An initial set of resources is defined and the simulation is run as a base scenario. The goal then is to improve the simulation performance and reduce the number of resources allocated where available.

Measure of Effectiveness. There are numerous potential measures of effectiveness in PORTSIM such as throughput and the average time cargo spends in the port. A crucial measure in any scenario is the time to closure, or how long it takes all cargo to clear the port. This is the measure applied in this work.

Categorization of Parameters. The categories determined in PORTSIM are resources (container handlers, chassis, drivers, inspectors, etc.), capacities (staging area capacity, etc.), process times (loading times, inspection times, etc.), and the arrival profiles (time between arrival of cargo carrying transports – rail and highway).

Experiment Definition. For this study, five parameters are considered. The resources number of berths, number of inspectors, and number of drivers are considered. The processing times load time for a vehicle on a ship (RORO), vehicle gate processing time, and flatbed gate processing time are considered. Each is varied by increasing and decreasing its value from the base scenario value.

Date Analysis. The data analysis is divided into two parts: resources and process times, and then they will be combined for a final analysis.

Figure 2 shows the results for the resources that were considered. Note that the number of berths has a direct affect on the time to closure. Increasing the number of berths improves performance (reduces the time to closure) and decreasing the number degrades performance. Also note that there is an upper limit to the number of useful berths, after which point, adding more berths does not improve performance.

Alternatively, changing the number of drivers and number of inspectors has no affect around the base scenario. In fact, a large degree of slack has been identified in both. The number of inspectors in the base scenario can be reduced by as much as 75% without affecting performance and the number of drivers can be reduced by as much as 83%. Obviously this presents the potential for great savings in cost. Caution should be taken when

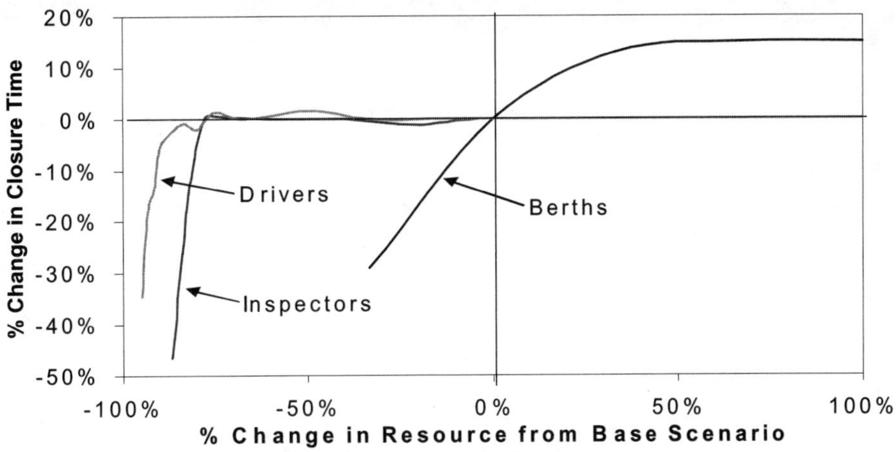

Figure 2. Resource Parameter Analysis.

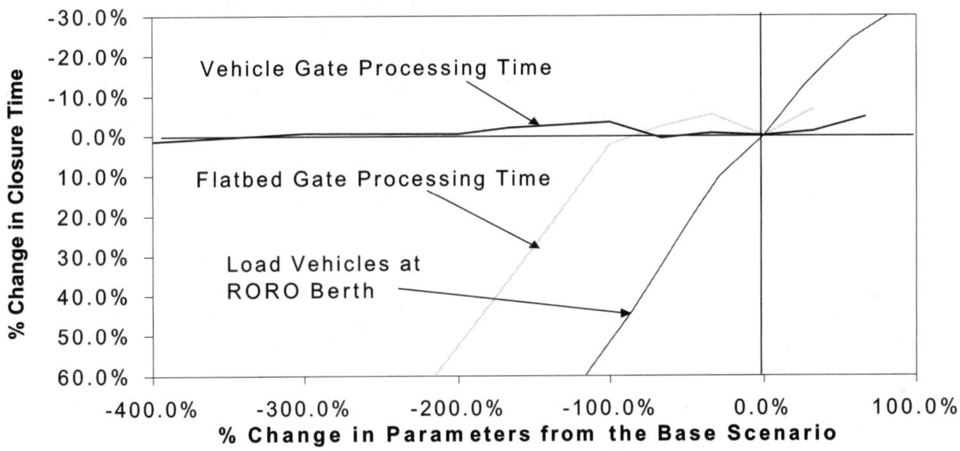

Figure 3. Processing Time Parameter Analysis.

reducing both. While the study shows the affect of reducing them individually, until the system can handle adjusting multiple parameters simultaneously, a new study should be run with both parameters reduced to ensure they are not codependent.

Figure 3 demonstrates the result of the processing times. Around the base scenario, changing the gate processing times has no affect. This is due to the fact that cargo ends up waiting in a staging area to be loaded on a ship. Thus the processes of getting cargo into staging are not critical. In fact, should other processing be required at the gate, the gate processing times can be increased to a certain degree (corresponding to moving in the negative direction on the X-axis) without degrading performance.

Ship loading times do have a direct impact on performance. The time to load vehicles on a ship using the roll-on, roll-off (RORO) process where vehicles are driven onto the ship using a ramp has significant impact. Finding a way to reduce that time provides direct impact on performance. It should be noted that changing this parameter in real life may be impossible, but it does identify that should the opportunity arise, it is a worthwhile effort to reduce this time.

Figure 4 is the composite of Figures 2 and 3, allowing the analyst to directly compare the impact of spending time to adjust different parameters. It just so happens that the RORO loading time and the number of berths have very similar impact. Increasing the number of ships that can berth by increasing the number of berths by a given percentage is virtually identical to decreasing the loading time by the same percentage (up to the limit of useful berthing space).

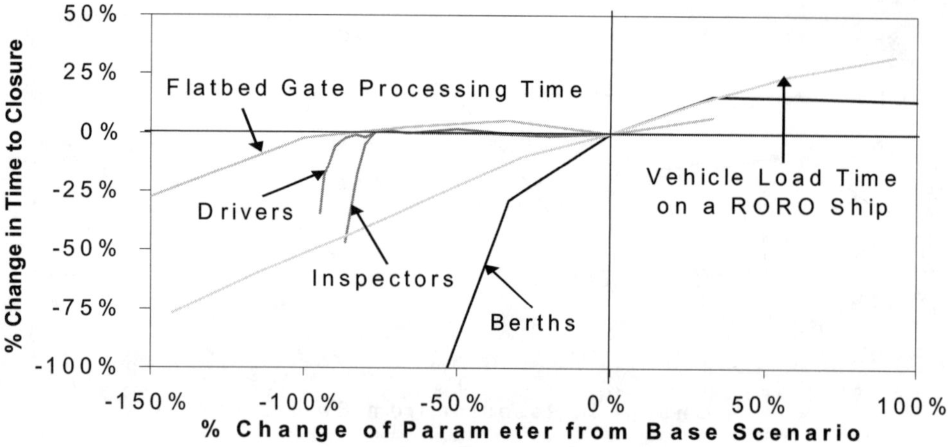

Figure 4. Complete Parameter Analysis.

FUTURE WORK

It was noted earlier that this work only adjusts one parameter at a time. But parameters may be dependent, so that while slack may be identified for two parameters, that does not mean that both may be reduced without affecting performance. Either can be reduced individually by the amount indicated, or both may be reduced to a lesser degree if dependence exists. This is not a major effort to add to the current work, though it would reduce the ability to visualize the affect of many parameters at once.

Some work has also been initiated in comparing parameters that are unequal in characteristics. A prime example is the berths. In the study done here, the characteristics of all berths were made the same. However, in real life, not all berths are the same, thus not all ships can dock at all berths. This means that adding one berth to the simulation may not have the same impact as adding a different berth. In this case, effort is being made to rank the individual berths as to their importance to the simulation.

CONCLUSIONS

The work presented in this paper has been applied to the PORTSIM project. It is not in use by the analysts to at the current date, but has been applied to the validation and verification process for the model. The experimental process and resulting visualization demonstrated several mistakes in the simulation that were not apparent from single run tests. One example is that when studying the affect of the staging area capacity, the capacity could be dropped to about 400 sq. ft. with no degradation in performance. This resulted in identifying an implementation error in the staging area processes. So long as one piece fit in the staging area, the simulation continued unimpeded due to the presence of an infinite queue at the entrance to staging. When repaired, the experiments were run again demonstrating correct behavior. This has led analysts to believe that the experimental process will provide them necessary insight to the processes to simplify the process of identifying bottlenecks and waste in the simulation.

REFERENCES

Nevins, M., C. Macal and J. Joines. 1998. "A Discrete-Event Simulation Model for Seaport Operations." *Simulation* 70, no. 4 (Apr.): 213~223.

Nevins, M., C. Macal and J. Joines. 1995. "PORTSIM: An Object-Oriented Port Simulation." *Proceedings of the 1995 Summer Computer Simulation Conference*, 160~165.

Leathrum, J. and T. Frith. 2000. "A Reconfigurable Object Model for Port Operations," to appear in *Proceedings of the Summer Computer Simulation Conference, SCSC 2000*, (Vancouver, BC, July).

Leathrum, J., R. Mielke and T. Frith. 2000, "An Integrated Spreadsheet Approach to Simulation Interfaces." to appear in *Proceedings of the Summer Computer Simulation Conference, SCSC 2000*, (Vancouver, BC, July).

AN APPROACH FOR DYNAMIC SYSTEM MODEL VALIDATION AND SIMULATION

Gregory L. Mealy and Arwen M. Warlock
Litton/TASC
55 Walkers Brook Drive
Reading, MA 01867
glmealy@tasc.com;amwarlock@tasc.com

KEYWORDS: Aerospace, Estimation, Parameter Identification, Model Evaluation, Validation

ABSTRACT

The Airframe Coefficient Estimation System (ACES) implements a parameter estimation–based model validation approach applicable to nonlinear dynamical system models. Model parameter estimates are determined as corrections to an *a priori* model by processing measured system response in an extended Kalman filter (EKF). Details on mapping general dynamic systems described via state-space or input-output (transfer function) models into the ACES EKF formulation are included. The use and functionality of ACES, accessible through a Microsoft Windows® style GUI, is described. A concrete example of the approach – missile aerodynamic parameter estimation – is formulated and results (using simulated data) demonstrating the technique and its effectiveness are given. Finally, current applications of the technique are described.

INTRODUCTION

Modern dynamical systems are increasingly complex and difficult to analyze. This has led to the development of increasingly sophisticated simulations to explore various facets of system behavior. However, the usefulness of these simulations is limited by their validity. Specifically, are the models, which form the core of the simulation, adequate to represent the process being simulated? This paper describes one approach to validating and/or improving these dynamic models by making use of measured data from the process being simulated. The method employs an extended Kalman filter parameter estimator to determine corrections to a model by comparing predicted behavior with actual system response.

TASC, under Air Force Operational Test and Evaluation Center (AFOTEC) sponsorship, developed a tool – the Airframe Coefficient Estimation System (ACES) – to assist designers or analysts in developing accurate mathematical models using a full complement of parameter estimation, data manipulation, simulation prediction and analysis functions. Motivation for the development of this tool came from a problem consistently encountered during the design of high-performance tactical missiles: predicting the aerodynamic forces and moments the missile will experience. An accurate mathematical model of the airframe's aerodynamic behavior is needed for autopilot and guidance law design and for predicting missile performance.

Since ACES incorporates a fully stochastic model of the subsystem being estimated, it functions as an integrated estimation and prediction tool. Initially, the ACES system uses data gathered during flight tests to estimate corrections to *a priori* models of the major missile airframe components: autopilot, actuator and aerodynamics. In particular, this processing yields estimates of the variability in the parameters in addition to their baseline value. Thus, not only is the mean (nominal) value determined, but also its expected range. Using these data in the 6-DOF missile simulation component of ACES, yields Monte Carlo performance predictions of the missile flyout for trade studies to identify missile dynamic performance sensitivities or for comparison with measured flight test data.

PARAMETER ESTIMATION APPROACH

Extended Kalman Filter (EKF)

The ACES parameter estimation approach assumes that the dynamical system of interest can be written in the form

$$\dot{\underline{x}}_s(t) = \underline{f}_s(\underline{x}_s(t), \underline{u}(t), \underline{a}_0, t) + \underline{w}(t) \qquad (1)$$

where:

$\underline{x}_s$ is the vector of system states

t is time

$\underline{f}_s$ is a nonlinear differentiable function

$\underline{u}(t)$ is a vector of control inputs

$\underline{a}_0$ is the nominal set of model parameters

$\underline{w}$ is a zero mean gaussian noise having spectral density matrix, Q(t),

while the true system takes the form

$$\dot{\underline{x}}_s(t) = \underline{f}_s(\underline{x}_s(t), \underline{u}(t), \underline{a}, t) + \underline{w}(t) \qquad (2)$$

where $\underline{a} = \underline{a}_0 + \Delta\underline{a}$. The EKF estimates the system state and parameter perturbations by augmenting the system state with the correction states, viz., $\underline{x} = [\underline{x}_s \quad \Delta\underline{a}]^T$, where $\underline{x}_s$ contains the dynamic system states and $\Delta\underline{a}$ is the vector of parameters to be estimated. The first-order differental equation for the composite state vector, $\underline{x}$, is given by

$$\dot{\underline{x}} = \underline{f} + \underline{\tilde{w}} = \begin{bmatrix} \underline{f}_s(\underline{x}_s, \underline{u}, \underline{a}, t) \\ \underline{\tau}^{-1} \end{bmatrix} + \begin{bmatrix} \underline{w}(t) \\ \underline{w}_a(t) \end{bmatrix} \quad (3)$$

where the original dynamical equations are explicitly shown to be a function of the true model parameter set, $\underline{a}$. The estimated parameters are assumed to be modeled as first-order Markov processes (with time constants $\underline{\tau}$) to allow the possibility of time variation.

The correction terms are estimated using information contained in observations of the actual system behavior taken at discrete points in time. Generally, these measurements are a nonlinear function of the state in the form

$$\underline{z}(t_k) = \underline{h}_k(\underline{x}(t_k), t_k) + \underline{v}(t_k) \quad (4)$$

where

$\underline{z}$ is the vector of measured quantities

$\underline{h}_k$ is the nonlinear, differentiable observation function

$\underline{v}_k = \underline{v}(t_k)$ is a vector of Gaussian measurement errors with zero mean and covariance, R_k.

Equations 3 and 4 comprise a system to which the EKF algorithm is applied to estimate corrections to the model parameters. Since the EKF is a linearized estimator, the nonlinear dynamic and observation functions must be linearized about the current best estimate of the state, $\hat{\underline{x}}(t)$.

The EKF algorithm (Gelb *et al.* 1974) operates in a prediction-correction fashion. The prediction (or state propagation) between observations is obtained by solving the nonlinear system equations:

$$\dot{\hat{\underline{x}}}(t) = \underline{f}(\hat{\underline{x}}(t), \underline{u}(t), t) \quad (5)$$

for $t_{k-1} \le t < t_k$ with $\hat{\underline{x}}(t_{k-1}) = \hat{\underline{x}}(t_{k-1}^{+})$. When new data are received at each time t_k, the estimate is updated (corrected) via

$$\hat{\underline{x}}(t_k^{+}) = \hat{\underline{x}}(t_k^{-}) + K_k\{\underline{z}(t_k) - \underline{h}_k(\hat{\underline{x}}(t_k^{-}), t_k)\}. \quad (6)$$

Here, $\hat{\underline{x}}(t_k^{-})$ is the optimum estimate prior to the incorporation of the measurement $\underline{z}(t_k)$, and $\hat{\underline{x}}(t_k^{+})$ is the optimum estimate immediately after processing $\underline{z}(t_k)$. The matrix K_k is the Kalman gain matrix. To calculate this matrix, first define the error covariance matrix, P(t), as

$$P(t) = E\{\tilde{\underline{x}}(t)\, \tilde{\underline{x}}(t)^T\} \quad (7)$$

where $\tilde{\underline{x}}(t) = \hat{\underline{x}}(t) - \underline{x}(t)$. The propagation equation defining changes in the error covariance matrix is

$$\dot{P} = FP + PF^T + Q \quad (8)$$

where $F = F(\hat{\underline{x}}(t), \underline{u}(t), t) = \left.\frac{\partial \underline{f}}{\partial \underline{x}}\right|_{\underline{x}(t)=\hat{\underline{x}}(t)}$. The Kalman gain matrix is computed using

$$K_k = P_- H_k^T \left[H_k P_- H_k^T + R_k\right]^{-1} \quad (9)$$

where $P_- = P(t_k^-)$ is $P(t)$ just before the measurement at time t_k and $H_k = H_k(\hat{\underline{x}}(t_k^-), t_k^-) = \left.\frac{\partial \underline{h}_k}{\partial \underline{x}}\right|_{\underline{x}(t)=\hat{\underline{x}}(t)}$.

Analogous to the state vector update, the covariance update equation,

$$P_+ = \left[I - K_k H_k^T\right] P_- \left[I - K_k H_k^T\right] + K_k R_k K_k^T \quad (10)$$

defines the error covariance just after applying the measurement at time t_k. Equation 8 is used to calculate the estimation error covariance between measurements; Eqs. 9 and 10 are used to calculate the Kalman gain matrix for use in Eq. 6 and to update the estimation error covariance matrix at a measurement, respectively. Note that the linearization in the EKF is associated with the covariance (and hence, gain) calculation. The form of Eq. 10 is chosen to aid in maintaining the symmetry of the covariance matrix.

Transfer Function to State Space Mapping

Frequently, system models are defined in terms of transfer function block diagrams. These models can be readily incorporated into the state space formulation used in ACES. Given a general transfer function of the form

$$T(s) = \frac{Z(s)}{U(s)} = \frac{a_{n-1}s^{n-1} + \cdots + a_1 s + a_0}{s^n + b_{n-1}s^{n-1} + \cdots + b_1 s + b_0}, \quad (12)$$

it is possible to construct an arbitrary number of equivalent state space representations of the form $\dot{\underline{x}} = F\underline{x} + L\underline{u} + \underline{w}$ and $\underline{z} = H\underline{x} + \underline{v}$ which is the linear equivalent of Eqs. 1 and 4. The unique form chosen for use in ACES is the observable canonical form and has a well defined set of state variables that result in a specific form for the system dynamics matrix. For a model derived solely from a transfer function, the representation is linear and Eqs. 8, 9 and 10 are exact.

For the transfer function in Eq. 12, the observable canonical form state space representation (Chen 1970) is: $\underline{x} = [x_1,\ x_2,\ \ldots,\ x_n]^T$ where each element of the state vector is defined by the recursion

$$\dot{x}_i = -\, b_{i-1} x_n + x_{i-1} + a_{i-1} u,\ i = 2, \ldots, n, \quad (13)$$

$$\dot{x}_1 = -\, b_0 x_n + a_0 u. \quad (14)$$

To provide a concrete example, consider the simple first–order lag model

$$T(s) = \frac{a_0}{s + b_0}. \quad (15)$$

Within the transfer function of Eq. 15 there are two parameters that may be in error: the gain, a_0, and the inverse time constant, b_0. The ACES parameter estimation formulation assumes that each parameter may be expressed as a model value plus an additive error that is small relative to the true value (*i.e.,* the model is close to the true value). For example, let a_0^T denote the true value of the transfer function gain and a_0^M the modeled value. Then $a_0^T = a_0^M + \Delta a_0$ where Δa_0 is the error in the modeled value of a_0. A similar expression holds for b_0.

The ACES formulation is straightforward. First, the system state vector is augmented with the parameters to be estimated, viz.,

$$\underline{x} = [x_a \quad \Delta a_0 \quad \Delta b_0]^T. \tag{16}$$

Then, the differential equations are written as

$$\underline{\dot{x}} = \underline{f}(\underline{x}, u) = \begin{bmatrix} -(b_0^M + \Delta b_0)x_s + (a_0^M + \Delta a_0)u \\ -\Delta a_0 / \tau_a \\ -\Delta b_0 / \tau_b \end{bmatrix} \tag{17}$$

The relevant linearized dynamics, and measurement matrices for the augmented state vector are:

$$F = \begin{bmatrix} -(b_0^M + \Delta b_0) & u & -x \\ 0 & -1/\tau_a & 0 \\ 0 & 0 & -1/\tau_b \end{bmatrix}\Bigg|_{\underline{\hat{x}}, \underline{u}} \tag{18}$$

and $H_k = [1 \quad 0 \quad 0]$. (19)

The time constants (τ_a and τ_b) are included to allow a possible time–variation in the parameter estimates. Setting $1/\tau=0$ forces the parameter to be constant.

Compound System Example

Real world systems are generally more complicated than a single transfer function. For illustrative purposes consider the block diagram in Figure 1. This example illustrates how cascaded transfer functions with an included (differentiable) nonlinear element, and a switching nonlinearity are modeled. This system has three inputs, u_1, u_2, and u_3, and one output, O. The five internal states, x_1, x_2, x_3, x_4, and x_5 are outputs of individual transfer functions that comprise the system. The input to the transfer function for x_4 is either x_1 or $x_2+c_3u_2$ switching based on the relative sizes of x_3 and O. The variable x_4 is fed through a nonlinear function, g, and so the input to the transfer function for x_5 is $g(x_4)$. A state space representation, $\underline{\dot{x}} = \underline{f}(\underline{x}, \underline{u}, t)$, of the example shown in Figure 1 is given by a system of five differential equations, namely,

$$\dot{x}_1 = -c_2 x_1 + c_1 u_1 \tag{20}$$

$$\dot{x}_2 = -c_5 x_2 + c_4 u_2 \tag{21}$$

$$\dot{x}_3 = -c_7 x_3 + c_6 u_3 \tag{22}$$

$$\dot{x}_4 = -c_9 x_4 + c_8 \begin{bmatrix} H(x_3 - c_{12}x_5)x_1 \\ +(1 - H(x_3 - c_{12}x_5))(x_2 + c_3 u_2) \end{bmatrix} \tag{23}$$

$$\dot{x}_5 = -c_{11} x_5 + c_{10}\, g(x_4) \tag{24}$$

where the function, H, is the Heaviside, or unit step function. Assume that measurements can be made of the output and one internal state, x_4, thus $\underline{z} = \underline{h}(\underline{x}) = (x_4, \quad c_{12}x_5)^T$. In this example there are twelve parameters, the c_i, which may be in error. The ACES parameter estimation formulation assumes that each parameter can be written as a baseline model value plus a small perturbation. For example, $c_1 = c_1^M + \Delta c_1$, where c_1^M denotes the baseline value and Δc_1 the small perturbation.

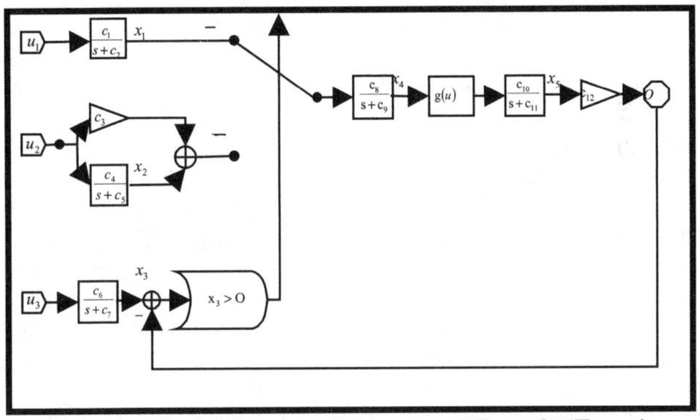

Figure 1 Block Diagram of Compound Transfer Function Model with Nonlinearities

THE AIRFRAME COEFFICIENT ESTIMATION SYSTEM (ACES)

The ACES system is built around a Microsoft Windows® style Graphical User Interface (GUI) that provides the user with full control over the setup and execution of the parameter estimation or simulation options. Starting ACES brings up the main window with eight menu bar items. Figure 2 shows a corner of the main window with the Configure menu item selected. The "Processing" option must be selected and defined before continuing with the remainder of the program setup.

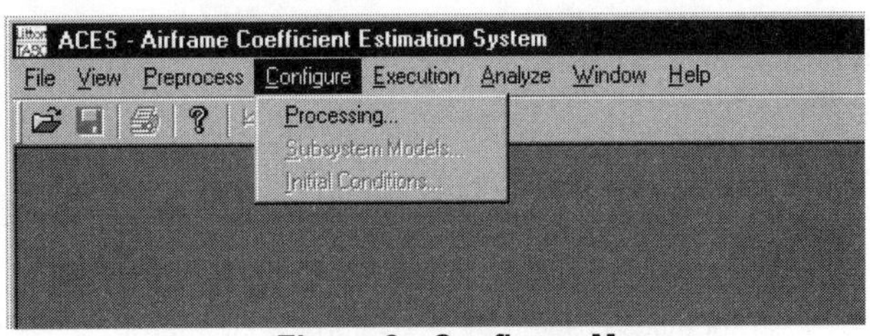

Figure 2 Configure Menu

Selecting "Processing" brings up the dialog box shown in Figure 3. Here, the type of processing (parameter estimation, simulation, etc.) is specified as are the type of missile subsystem and the relevant input and output file names. This, and other dialog boxes used to select models, model correction coefficients and initial conditions, are context sensitive and are matched to the type of processing selected by the user.

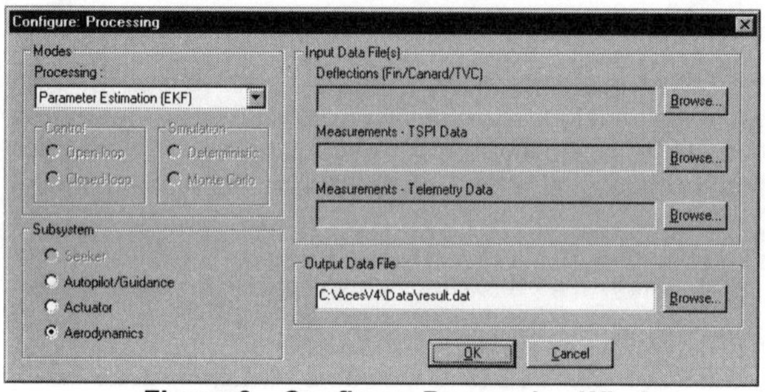

Figure 3 Configure Processing Window

Construction of objects during program execution is defined by the user through the GUI. By selecting the desired system configuration and operating mode, and then starting simulation execution (from the Execution menu in the main window), the user causes the main ACES program to construct the appropriate Simulation Engine (SimEngine). Once constructed, each SimEngine then constructs the simulation entity class that implements specific processing e.g., *aceExtKalmanFilter* for parameter estimation and all other classes necessary for execution of the selected process. These classes fall into three basic groups: Dynamics, Model Specific classes and Data Management.

- Model dynamics specific classes which encapsulate the properties (data and functions) of the formal model of the missile and its subsystems. These classes are composed of general parent classes and derived child classes specific to each particular model type (*e.g.,* aerodynamics, autopilot and actuator). The model dynamics parent classes are: *aceModelDynamicsVec* ($\underline{f}$ in Eq. 2), *aceModelDynamicsMat* (F in Eq. 8), *aceModelMeasurementVec* ($\underline{h}$ in Eq. 6) and *aceModelMeasurementMat* (H in Eq. 9)
- The class *aceModelInterface* encapsulates all of the missile specific code (*e.g.,* calls to external functions that calculate the aerodynamic forces and moments). This interface class is used by the missile aerodynamic data classes which perform several tasks in an aerodynamic specific but airframe independent manner. In the actuator and autopilot implementations the dynamics classes use *aceModelInterface* directly.
- Data management within ACES is provided by a set of Data Manager classes: *aceFlightDataManager* for measured flight data, the simulation/estimation output data manager (*aceOutputDataManager*), and a manager (*acePlotDataManager*) for plotting data contained in the binary output files created by *aceOutputDataManager* .

There are two main elements to the EKF calculations – propagate and update. Within the advanceToTime method of class *aceExtKalmanFilter*, a test is made to determine if a measurement is available at the current time. If it is, the update method (shown in Figure 4) is invoked to implement the Kalman update equations (Eqns. 6 and 10). Prior to, and following, the update calculation, the writeData method of class *aceOutputDataManager* is invoked to store the filter data. Methods associated with classes *aceModelMeasurementVec* and *aceModelMeasurementMat* are invoked to compute measurement–related quantities used in the update calculation.

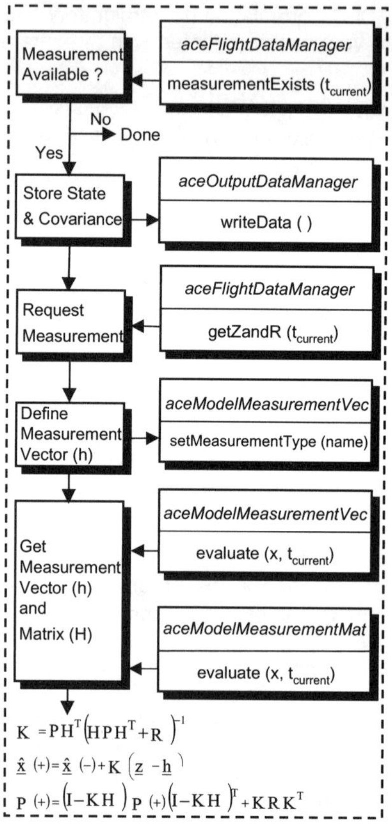

Figure 4 Update Method

Following the update, or if no update is performed, the propagate method is executed which advances the filter state estimate and covariance matrix to the next time by solving Eqns. 5 and 8. This method uses the mathematical utilities *IntegrateVec* and *IntegrateMat* in class *aceIntegrate* and the dynamics model classes *aceModelDynamicsVec* and *aceModelDynamicsMat*.

ACES also provides analysis capabilities including: statistical analysis of the Monte Carlo data and graphical display of the estimation or simulation results. Through the Graphical User Interface (GUI), the analyst can plot the simulation data or parameter estimates as a function of time or another parameter.

AERODYNAMICS EXAMPLE

To illustrate the use and performance of ACES, consider the six degree of freedom (6-DOF) missile aerodynamics example defined below.

Formulation

The state vector for the missile 6-DOF dynamics is

$$\underline{x}_s = \left[\underline{v}^B \quad \underline{r}^I \quad \underline{\omega} \quad \underline{\upsilon}\right]^T \tag{25}$$

where

$\underline{v}^B$ is the body velocity 3 vector

$\underline{r}^I$ is the inertial position 3 vector

$\underline{\omega}$ is the body rate 3 vector

$\underline{\upsilon}$ is the body orientation 3 vector.

The inputs to the system are a set of control deflections

$$\underline{u} = [\delta p \quad \delta q \quad \delta r]^T \tag{26}$$

where δp, δq, and δr are the effective roll, pitch and yaw commands, respectively. The 6-DOF equations of motion are given by

$$\dot{\underline{x}}_s = \underline{f}_s(\underline{x}_s) + \underline{f}_{aeromodel}(\underline{x}_s, \underline{u}) + \underline{f}_{\delta aero}(\underline{x}_s, \underline{u}) \tag{27}$$

where $\underline{f}_s$, $\underline{f}_{aeromodel}$, and $\underline{f}_{\delta aero}$ are the underlying system dynamics, baseline model, and parameter correction terms, respectively. The dynamic function, $\underline{f}$, is broken into three pieces here because the baseline aerodynamic model, which describes the forces and moments acting on the missile, takes the form of data tables derived from wind tunnel testing. The functional dependence is not written explicitly, rather forces and moments are evaluated using a table look-up. The functional form for corrections to the model are derived from a Taylor series expansion in the independent variables in the data tables. For example, the parameter correction terms for the z-component of the acceleration are $QA_{ref}C_N/m$, where Q is the dynamic pressure, A_{ref} is the aerodynamic reference area, m is the mass and C_N is the normal force perturbation term which takes the form

$$C_N = C_{N0} + C_{N\alpha}\alpha + C_{N\delta q}\delta q + C_{N\alpha\delta q}\alpha\delta q + \ldots \tag{28}$$

where α is the angle-of-attack. One or more of the set of possible parameter corrections, e.g., C_{N0}, $C_{N\alpha}$, $C_{N\delta q}$, can be selected by the user and are then added to the state vector.

Results

The ACES implementation of the aerodynamic model was verified through a set of sample calculations using simulated truth data. Pseudo flight test results were generated using synthetic measurement data created by introducing a perturbation into the baseline model in a previously validated simulation code. These data were used as inputs and measurements to the ACES parameter estimation process. The *a priori* model for the missile aerodynamics used in ACES was the original (unperturbed) aerodynamic model. Two different tests are described here.

In the first case, a constant perturbation was added to the normal force coefficient. ACES was run with two levels of uncertainty in the velocity measurements, *i.e.*, with measurement error covariances of 0.01 (m/sec)^2 (higher confidence) and 1 (m/sec)^2 (lower confidence). Figure 5 shows that ACES has no trouble estimating the constant perturbation, and that it converges to the solution faster when the velocity measurement uncertainty is smaller. The rate of convergence is determined not only by the quality of the measurement data, but also by the filter allocation, among the estimated states, of the weighted difference between the predicted measurements and the observations. Direct measurement of model states yields a faster estimate, while states related to the measurements through more complicated dynamics require a longer interval. The initial transient in the state estimate shown in the figure is a common result as the filter adjusts the covariances to be consistent with the model dynamics and observations.

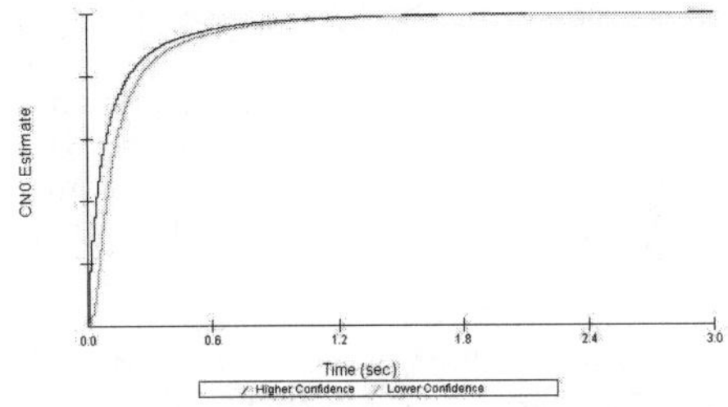

Figure 5 C_{N0} Estimate

For the second case, an angle-of-attack dependent perturbation of 6α was introduced into the normal force coefficient. The prototypical ACES three-step process for parameter estimation was then followed. First, the unmodeled forces and moments needed to match the measured data were estimated. Unmodeled forces or moments are terms representing the total force (or moment) difference between the value derived from the aerodynamic model and the actual value consistent with the measurements. These are time-varying and are compared by the analyst to the functional forms that the estimates can take. For example, two of the curves in Figure 6 are the unmodeled z-axis aero-force estimate from the uncorrected model and the angle-of-attack, α. The shapes are similar, leading the analyst to further investigate if there is an alpha dependence to the necessary correction. The estimate of the unmodeled z-axis aero-force in the figure provides a good example of the initial estimation transient.

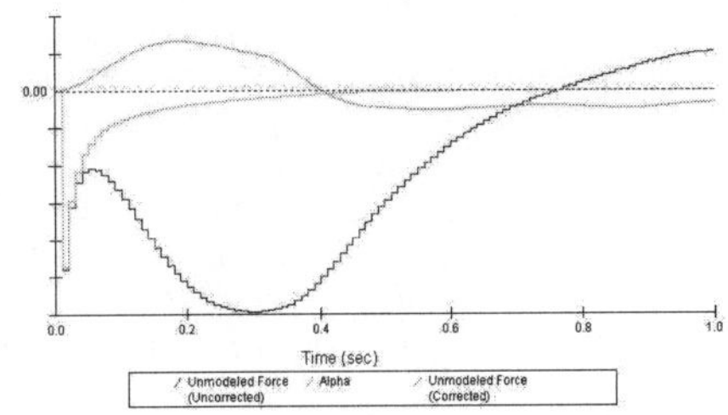

Figure 6 $C_{N\alpha}$ Estimate

Alternately, the analyst could chose one (or more) of the correction terms and run ACES to compute the value of the correction. If the selected term is not an actual contributor to the error, the filter will provide an estimate for the coefficient near zero. Due to the linearized nature of the solution, convergence is much more rapid when reasonable prior estimates of the coefficients are used, thus motivating the approach utilizing unmodeled forces and moments.

The next step is to make an estimate of the candidate correction coefficient, in this case $C_{N\alpha}$. Since the maximum value of α is approximately six times the maximum normal force*, the value of $C_{N\alpha}$ is expected to be approximately 6. Refining the estimate entails using the current estimate as an initial value for the correction term and re-running ACES to re-estimate the selected parameter until the changes are sufficiently small.

The third step in the process is to include the estimated correction in the baseline model and re-estimate the unmodeled forces. The third curve in Figure 6 is the unmodeled force estimate when the alpha dependent correction is added to the baseline normal force coefficient. The unmodeled force in the corrected case converges to zero, indicating that the corrected model matches the observed missile behavior.

The efficacy of the ACES parameter estimation process is demonstrated by comparing the aerodynamic coefficients and state variables from the corrected model to the synthetic data from the perturbed reference simulation run. Figure 7 shows the comparison of the normal force from the baseline and corrected models as well as the truth data. The truth and corrected curves are indistinguishable.

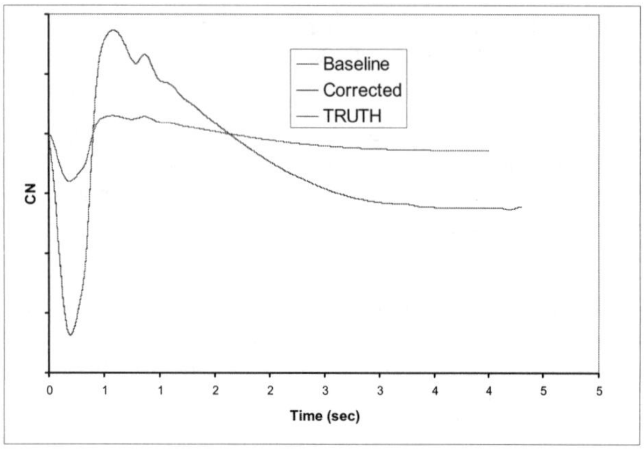

Figure 7 C_N Baseline-Corrected Model Comparison

Figure 8 depicts a similar comparison for the z-component of velocity. Again the truth and corrected model curves are indistinguishable. These plots illustrate the impact of aerodynamic coefficient differences on missile state. While the closed-loop environment provides a reduction in the effect of a coefficient difference (200-300% change in C_N yields a much smaller ~20% change in V_z), there remains a measurable change in missile performance. As shown in these figures, ACES processing can reduce the aerodynamic coefficient model errors to a level for which performance prediction error is negligible.

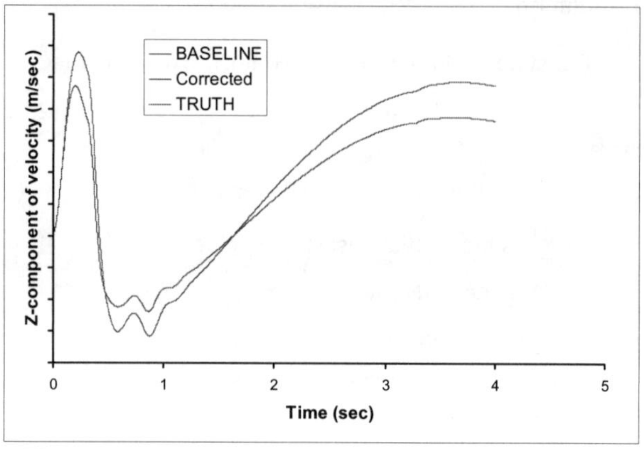

Figure 8 V_z Baseline-Corrected Model Comparison

SUMMARY AND FUTURE WORK

The approach described in this paper uses an EKF algorithm and real world observations to estimate correction terms to established dynamical system models. The approach has broad application to systems describable by differential equations, although the ACES system applies this approach specifically to missile autopilot, actuator and aerodynamics models. Autopilot and actuator models typically consist of a series of transfer functions, pure gains, and nonlinear elements including switches. Aerodynamics models typically follow Newton's laws of motion with forces and moments calculated by a look-up in a table derived from wind tunnel test data. As shown in this paper, models of either nature are readily handled with the ACES system. The full capabilities of ACES are only briefly outlined in this paper.

AFOTEC's goal is to employ the ACES technology to improve the fidelity of existing missile models. Currently, TASC is preparing to process flight test data to bring the current missile models into better agreement with real-world observations. Results from this processing will be presented in a future paper.

REFERENCES

Chen, C.T.; 1970. *Introduction to Linear System Theory.* Holt, Rinehart and Winston, Inc. New York.

Gelb, A.; J.F. Kasper Jr.; R.A. Nash; C.F. Price; A.A. Sutherland, Jr. 1974. *Applied Optimal Estimation.* The M.I.T. Press, Cambridge, MA.

* The graph shows the z-axis force which is opposite in sign from the normal force.

SINGLE-PASS SIMULATION FOR OUT-OF-ORDER MECHANISMS OF SUPERSCALAR PROCESSORS

R-Ming Shiu and Chung-Ping Chung
Department of Computer Science and Information Engineering,
National Chiao Tung University, Hsinchu, Taiwan 30050, R.O.C.
Computer & Communications Research Laboratories
Industrial Technology Research Institute, Chutung, Taiwan 310, R.O.C.
e-mail: rmshiu@csie.nctu.edu.tw

KEYWORDS Computer performance, microcomputers, combined simulation.

ABSTRACT

Trace-driven simulation is popular in evaluating the performance of superscalar processors. As the trace lengths grow, single-pass trace simulation techniques need be developed to evaluate many sets of design configurations in one simulation run. However, these techniques are traditionally only suited to storage systems obeying the inclusion property. This paper proposes single-pass simulation techniques for superscalar processors. The major difficulty in the task is that the pipeline and the out-of-order mechanisms do not show the inclusion property. To overcome this difficulty, we place the incoming instructions in a unified instruction progression queue, and enumerate the possible pipeline states with a pipeline state vector. The speedup of this single-pass simulation over the conventional simulation for superscalar processors is 2.32 in terms of simulation time when 10 sets of configurations are simulated.

1. INTRODUCTION

Contemporary microprocessor designs achieve higher performance through advanced out-of-order mechanisms. For good decision making, trace-driven simulation is often used to evaluate the large number of design configurations (Johnson 1991). It can give very accurate and detailed performance data than the analytical modeling, and is more efficient than the software-based emulation (Holliday 1992). The time required by a trace-driven simulation is in proportion to both the length of the simulated trace, and the number of alternative configurations evaluated. The trace lengths of generally accepted benchmark suites have grown indefinitely nowadays. For example, the computer simulation time of some of the SPEC95 benchmarks may be several days for only one design configuration (Case 1995). Several techniques, such as *trace sampling* (Laha 1988, Chame 1993) and *trace reduction* (Wang 1991), have been developed to reduce the trace length without sacrificing accuracy. Another approach, called the single-pass simulation, has been proposed to evaluate many sets of design alternatives in one simulation pass for systems with certain particular properties.

The single-pass simulation techniques for storage systems have been extensively studied. Mattson *et al* (1970,1971) explored the single-pass simulation technique, known as the *stack simulation*, to evaluate memories of various sizes. They declared that when the data stored in the memory possess the *inclusion property*, then all the stored data can be presented using a stack, and the performance can be evaluated in a single trace pass. This technique has been applied to designs of different storage hierarchies. Gecsei extended this technique to simulate multiple-level memory hierarchies (Gecsei 1974). Silberman extended it to simulate delayed-staging storages (Silberman 1983). Thompson and Smith extended it to simulate both write-back caches and sector caches (Tompson 1989). Hill and Smith extended it to simulate caches of various associativities, and called their work the *all-associativity simulation* (Hill 1989). Wang and Baer extended the all-associativity simulation to include write-back cache simulation (Wang 1991). Sugumar and Abraham used a binomial forest to represent the stack, and thus sped up the all-associativity simulation (Sugumar 1995). And Wu and his colleagues extended the all-associativity simulation to include MP cache simulation (Wu 1995, 1993).

However, uses of these techniques are limited to storage systems obeying the inclusion property. In this research, we intend to develop a single-pass simulation applicable to superscalar processor designs. The major difficulty in the task is that the pipeline and the out-of-order mechanisms do not show the inclusion property. To overcome this difficulty, we place the instructions presently in the pipeline into a unified *instruction progression queue*, and enumerate the possible pipeline states with a *pipeline state vector*. Though this queue has no inclusion property, several operations such as trace read, queue insertion/deletion, and dependency check can be maintained globally.

The remainder of this paper is organized as follows. Section 2 creates a simulation model and presents the conventional simulation algorithm for superscalar processors. We develop the single-pass simulation in Section 3. Section 4 shows the experimental results. Finally, in Section 5, we conclude this research.

2. SIMULATION MODEL

A general simulation model contains following four components is built: the *instruction trace*, the *processor model*, the *instruction progression queue*, and the *conventional simulation algorithm for superscalar processors*.

2.1 Instruction Trace

Each entry of the input trace to the simulation model represents an instruction encountered in the program execution trace. We define an *instruction trace* as follows:

* This paper presents partial result of a research project financed by both NSC of R.O.C. under no. NSC 87-2622-E-009-009 and the industry.

Definition 1. Instruction trace— An *instruction trace* $IX = [(xeu_1, xr1_1, xr2_1, xbt_1), (xeu_2, xr1_2, xr2_2, xbt_2), \ldots, (xeu_T, xr1_T, xr2_T, xbt_T)]$ is the input trace to the simulator, where $(xeu_t, xr1_t, xr2_t, xbt_t)$ is the *t*th instruction, whose execution unit is xeu_t, source registers are $xr1_t$ and $xr2_t$, and output register is $xr1_t$. If any register is not used, the corresponding value of $xr1_t$ or $xr2_t$ is 0. If the instruction is a taken branch, xbt_t is *true*; otherwise xbt_t is *false*. □

2.2 Processor Model

The block diagram and pipeline stages of the processor model are shown in Fig. 1(a). Instructions are orderly fetched from the instruction cache, decoded, and dispatched into a centralize reservation station (RS). A branch target buffer (BTB) may be added aside the fetcher for branch prediction. Instructions in RS with ready operands and available execution units are issued out-of-order from RS to execution units while the in-order state is kept in a reorder buffer (ROB). A memory order buffer (MOB) may be added aside the load/store unit (LSU) to keep the order of loads and stores. Results of instructions are written out-of-orderly to ROB via the result buses, and are written back to the register file (retired) orderly from ROB.

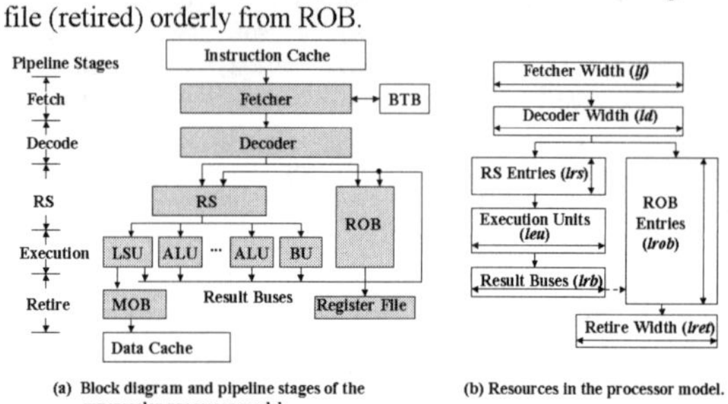

(a) Block diagram and pipeline stages of the superscalar processor model. (b) Resources in the processor model.

Fig. 1 Block diagram of the processor model and resources in the model.

In this processor model, the caches of different configurations can be evaluated in a single pass with traditional stack simulation. Furthermore, the BTB of different configurations can be evaluated in a single pass with a modified stack simulation though the prediction states in them have no inclusion property. This difficulty can be overcomed by enumerating the prediction states with a *prediction state vector*, thus we can properly update prediction state with a finite state automata.

In this research, we focus on the single-pass simulation of the pipeline and the out-of-order mechanisms. For simplicity without losing generality, we assume that all the execution units are the same and their latency is one cycle. Thus, the processor model can be simplified to become the resource limitations as shown in Fig. 1(b). We elaborate the resource limitations of all configurations evaluated with a *resource limitation list* defined below:

Definition 2. Resource limitation list — The *resource limitation list* of configuration *c* is:

$RL(c) = (lf(c), ld(c), lrs(c), leu(c), lrb(c), lrob(c), lret(c))$,

where $1 \leq c \leq C$, C is the number of configurations evaluated, $lf(c)$ is the fetch width, $ld(c)$ is the decode width, $lrs(c)$ is the number of entries of RS, $leu(c)$ is the number of execution units, $lrb(c)$ is the number of result buses, $lrob(c)$ is the number of entries of ROB, and $lret(c)$ is the retire width. □

Each configuration evaluated can be represented by a resource limitation list. In our experiment, for illustrative purposes, we focus our attention on canonical *c*-issue superscalar processors, i.e., $RL(c) = (c, c, 2c, c, c, 4c, c)$, where $lrs(c)$ is $2c$ for ample decoupling, and $lrob(c)$ is $4c$ for ample storage of instructions in RS, Execution, and Retire stages.

During simulation, we keep tracking the usage of these resources with a *resource use list* defined below:

Definition 3. Resource use list — The *resource use list* of configuration *c* is:

$RU(c) = (uf(c), ud(c), urs(c), ueu(c), urb(c), urob(c), uret(c))$

Each element in *RU* tracks the usage of corresponding resources in *RL*. □

2.3 Instruction Progression Queue

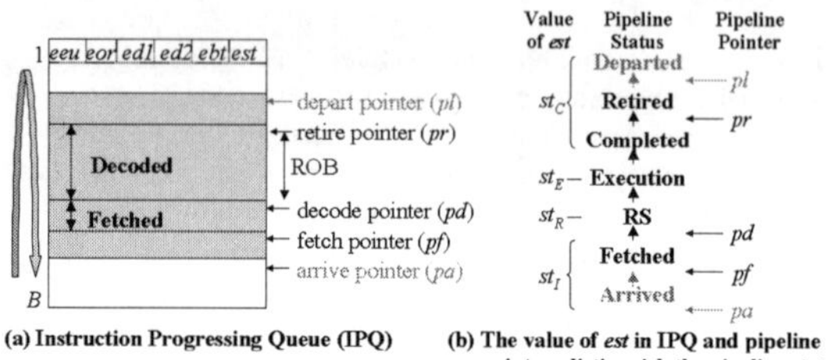

(a) Instruction Progressing Queue (IPQ) (b) The value of *est* in IPQ and pipeline pointers distinguish the pipeline status

Fig. 2. The instruction progression queue and the pipeline status.

During simulation, an *instruction progression queue* (IPQ) is used to keep track of the pipeline status and the dependence status of the instruction operands. The IPQ is a circular queue as shown in Fig. 2(a) which is defined in Definition 4. The pipeline status is indicated by the *pipeline pointers* to be defined in Definition 5 and the value of *est* field in IPQ, as shown in Fig. 2(b). The shadowed pipeline status and pointers in Fig. 2 are only used in single-pass simulation algorithm in Section 4.

Definition 4. Instruction progression queue — The *instruction progression queue* (IPQ) of size *Q* is a circular queue:

$IPQ(c) = [q(1, c), q(2, c), \ldots, q(Q, c)]$,

where $1 \leq c \leq C$, and $e(i, c) = (qeu(i, c), qor(i, c), qd1(i, c), qd2(i, c), qbt(i, c), qst(i, c))$ is the *i*th entry in IPQ of configuration *c*, whose execution unit is $qeu(i, c)$, output register is $qor(i, c)$. The instruction depends on the instructions whose IPQ positions are $qd1(i, c)$ and $qd2(i, c)$. If no corresponding instruction is depended on, the value of $qd1(i, c)$ and $qd2(i, c)$ is 0. If the instruction is a taken branch, $qbt(i, c)$ is *true*; otherwise $qbt(i, c)$ is *false*. The field $qst(i, c)$ tracks the pipeline state of the instruction. An active instruction must be in one of the following states: in-order (including arrived and fetched), in RS, in execution unit, and completed (including completed, retired, and departed). $qst(q, c)$ is st_I, st_R, st_E, and st_C, respectively. □

The IPQ at any point of time must be large enough to store all instructions present in the processor model at any point of time, i.e., $Q > \max(lf(c) + ld(c) + lrob(c))$, where $1 \leq c \leq C$.

Definition 5. Pipeline list — The *pipeline list* of configuration *c* is:

$$P(c) = (pf(c), pd(c), pr(c)),$$

where $1 \leq c \leq C$, $pf(c)$ is the fetch pointer, $pd(c)$ is the decode pointer, and $pr(c)$ is the retire pointer. The *q*th entry in IPQ(*c*) is fetched if $pf(c) < q \leq pd(c)$, is decoded and dispatched if $pd(c) < q \le pr(c)$, and is retired if $pr(c) < q \le pf(c)$. All the comparisons are circular. □

2.4 Dependency Check

In this out-of-order mechanism, instructions in RS can be issued if their depended on instructions are completed. In the simulation, the depended on instructions are identified and stored in *ed1*, *ed2* upon an instruction entering IPQ. The dependency are checked by a *register unit* defined as follows:

Definition 6. Register unit — The *register unit* is:

$$RES = [res(1), res(2), \ldots res(R)],$$

where R is the register unit size of the processor and $res(r)$ points to the IPQ entry of the most recent instruction that writes to the rth register. If no instruction in IPQ writes to the rth register, $res(r) = 0$. □

An *Arrive_RES* procedure is called to identify the dependent on instructions when an instruction is entering IPQ. And a *Depart_RES* procedure is called when an instruction is leaving IPQ. Thus an instruction in RS can check if its operands are ready by a *Check_Ready* function.

```
Procedure Arrive_RES (p, qor, qd1, qd2);
Input p: integer; (the recently entered IPQ position)
Output qor, qd1, qd2: integer; (qor, qd1 and qd2 of the recently entered IPQ position)
begin
qor := xr1_t;                                      //Store output register
if xr1_t = 0 then qd1 := 0 else qd1 := res(xr1_t);  //Check Dep.of r1
if xr2_t = 0 then qd2 := 0 else qd2 := res(xr2_t);  //Check Dep.of r2
if xr1_t ≠ 0 then qes(xr1_t) := p;                 //Update register unit
end
```

```
Procedure Depart_RES (p, qor);
Input p (the leaving IPQ position), qor(qor of p): integer;
begin
if qor ≠ 0 and res(r1) = p then res(r1) := 0;      //Update Reg.
end
```

```
function Check_Ready (qd1, qd2, c: integer): boolean;
begin
 Check_Ready := (qd1=0 or qst(ed1,c)=st_C) and
                (qd2=0 or qst(qd2,c)=st_C));
end
```

2.5 Conventional Simulation Algorithm

The *conventional simulation algorithm for superscalar processors*, shown in Fig. 3, is used as the basis to develop our single-pass algorithm for superscalar processors. The input to the algorithm is the instruction trace. The most significant performance metric of processors is the *execution cycle count*. The output from the algorithm is the *execution cycle count vector* $N = [n(1), n(2), \ldots, n(C)]$, where $1 \le c \le C$ and $n(c)$ is the execution cycle count of configure c.

We first develop the procedures and functions used in the algorithm. We use a *Circular_Inc* function to circularly increment the pipeline pointers:

```
function Circular_Inc (p: integer): integer;
begin
 if p = Q then Circular_Inc := 1; else Circular_Inc := p + 1;
end
```

A *Retire* procedure is used to simulate the retire stage of the processor. The procedure repeatedly increments the retire pointer as long as there is available retire width and all previous instructions are completed.

```
Procedure Retire (c);
Input c: integer; (specifies a configuration)
begin
uret(c) := 0;                                        //Reset retire width
while uret(c)<lret(c) and pr(c)<pi(c) and qst(pr(c),c)=st_C do//Retire rules
  uret(c) := uret(c) + 1;                            //Consume retire width
  urob(c) := urob(c) - 1;                            //Release ROB entry
  Depart_RES (pr(c), qor(pr(c), c));                 //Departing RES
  pr(c) := Circular_Inc (pr(c));                     //Increment retire pointer
end
```

An *Execute* procedure is used to simulate the execution stage of the processor. The procedure scans IPQ beginning from the retire pointer to the dispatch pointer. Once an instruction in execution unit is found, it completes the instruction if there is an available result bus.

```
Procedure Execute (c);
Input c: integer; (specifies a configuration)
begin
urb(c) := 0;                                         //Reset used result bus number
pt(c) := pr(c);                                      //Assign template pointer
while urb(c) < lrb(c) and pt(c) < pi(c) do           //Complete rules
  if qst(pt(c)) = st_E then                          //If instruction in execution unit
    urb(c) := urb(c) + 1;                            //Consume result bus
    ueu(c) := ueu(c) - 1;                            //Release execution unit
    qst(pt(c), c) := st_C;                           //Change to complete state
  pt(c) := Circular_Inc (pt(c));                     //Increment template pointer
end
```

An *RS* procedure is used to simulate the RS stage of the processor. The procedure scans IPQ beginning from the retire pointer to the dispatch point. Once an instruction in RS is found, it issues the instruction to execution unit if there is an available execution units.

```
Procedure RS (c);
Input c: integer; (specifies a configuration)
begin
pt(c) := pr(c);                                      //Assign template pointer
while uex(c) < lex(c) and pt(c) < pi(c) do           //Execute rules
  if qst(pt(c)) = st_R and                           //If instruction in RS and ready
    Check_ready (qd1(pt(c), c), qd2(pt(c), c), c) then
    ueu(c) := ueu(c) + 1;                            //Consume execution unit
    urs(c) := urs(c) - 1;                            //Release RS entry
    qst(pt(c)) := st_E;                              //Change to execution state
  pt(c) := Circular_Inc (pt(c));                     //Increment template pointer
end
```

A *Decode* procedure is used to simulate the decode stage of the processor. The procedure repeatedly increments the decode pointer when there are available decode width and ROB entries.

```
Procedure Decode (c);
Input c: integer; (specifies a configuration)
begin
ud(c) := 0;                                          //Reset decode width
while ud(c)<ld(c) and pd(c)<pf(c) and urob(c)<lrob(c)do //Decode rules
  ud(c) := ud(c) + 1;                                //Consume decode width
  urob(c) := urob(c) + 1;                            //Consume ROB entry
  pd(c) := Circular_Inc (pd(c));                     //Increment decode pointer
end
```

A *Fetch* procedure shown is used to simulate the Fetch stage of the processor. The procedure repeatedly fetches new instructions into IPB and increments the fetch pointer when there is available fetch width and no taken branch has been encountered.

Procedure Fetch (*c*);
Input *c*: **integer**; (specifies a configuration)
begin

```
1.uf(c) := 0; bt :=false;                                    //Reset fetch width
2.while uf(c) ≠ lf(c) and t ≤ T and not bt do                //Fetch rules
3. uf(c) := uf(c) + 1;                                       //Consume fetch width
4. qeu(pf(c), c):= xeu_t; qbt(pf(c),c):= xbt_t;              //Place new Instr.
5. qst(pf(c), c) := st_1; bt := xbt_t;                       //Get new instruction
6. Arrive_RES(pf(c),qor(pf(c),c),qd1(pf(c),c),qd2(pf(c),c));
7. pf(c) := Circular_Inc (pf(c));                            //Increment fetch pointer
8. t := t + 1;                                               //Next instruction
```

end

The conventional simulation algorithm shown in Fig. 3 simulates the behaviors of processors with configurations from 1 to *C*. For each configuration, it initializes the pointers, resource usages, and the register unit, and then repeatedly calls the Retire, Execute, RS, Decode, and Fetch procedures sequentially to simulate the pipeline activities in every cycle.

Algorithm Conventional_Superscalar (*IX*, *RL*, *N*) ;
Input: *IX* (instruction trace), *RL* (resource limitation list);
Output: *N* (execution cycle count vector);
begin

```
1. for c := 1 to C do                                        //For all configurations
2. n(c) := 0;                                                //Reset cycle count
3. P(c) := (1, 1, 1, 1);                                     //Reset pointers
4. urs(c) := 0; ueu(c) := 0; urob(c) := 0;                   //Reset resource usages
5. for r := 1 to R do res(r) := 0;                           //Reset register unit
6. t := 1;   //For all instructions
7. while t ≤ T do                                            //While still have instructions
8. Retire (c);  Execute (c);  RS (c);                        //Retire, Execute, and RS
9. Decode (c);  Fetch (c);                                   //Decode, and Fetch
10.n(c) := n(c) + 1;                                         //Increment cycle count
```

end

Fig. 3. The conventional simulation algorithm for superscalar processors.

The time complexity of the conventional simulation algorithm is $O(C \times T \times Q)$. However, this algorithm scans the trace and checks dependencies for every configuration evaluated.

3. SINGLE–PASS SIMULATION

In this section, a single-pass simulation is developed First, the pipeline status problem is pointed out. Then the *pipeline state vector* is used to solve this problem. Finally, the *Arrive* and *Depart* procedures is designed to complete the single-pass simulation algorithm.

3.1 Pipeline Status Problem

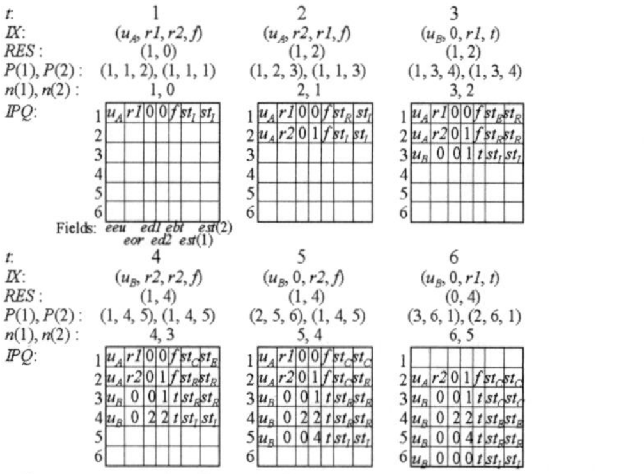

Fig. 4. An example of the pipeline status problem.

To apply the single-pass simulation to evaluate the processors, instructions executed with different configurations must be put into a unified IPQ. However, the pipeline statuses of processors with different configurations are not the same. Consider the example shown in Fig. 4. Assume two configurations of canonical 1- and 2-issue superscalar processors with two registers are evaluated. The IPQs are shown by concatenating the pipeline states of the two configurations in sequence. The entries are updated according to the conventional simulation algorithm, and the two state fields, pipeline pointers, and execution cycles are modified individually. In this example, if the instructions is a branch, *xeu* and *eeu* are u_B, otherwise they are u_A. During progression of the six instructions, the pipeline status distinguished by the state fields and the pipeline pointers of different configurations are not the same. We call such difference the pipeline status problem.

3.2 Pipeline State Vector

To solve the pipeline status problem, we concatenat the states of all configurations evaluated to become a *pipeline state vector* as follows.

Definition 7. Pipeline state vector—A *pipeline state vector* at IPQ position *q* is:

$$qstv(q) = [qst(q, 1), qst(q, 2), \ldots, qst(q, C)],$$

where the *c*th state of the vector is the state in IPQ of *c*. □

We modify the IPQ to become the concatenation of pipeline state vectors which also contains some other fields. Since these fields are all configuration independent, we can remove the index of the configuration from the representations of the entries. We call the modified IPQ the *IPQ with pipeline state vector* and define them as follows:

Definition 8. IPQ with pipeline state vector— The *IPQ with pipeline state vector* (IPQ′) of size *Q* is a circular queue:

$$IPQ' = [q'(1), q'(2), \ldots, q'(Q)],$$

where $q'(i) = (qeu'(i), qor'(i), qd1'(i), qd2'(i), qbt'(i), qstv(i))$ is the *q*th entry in IPQ′, whose execution unit is $qeu'(i)$, output register is $qor'(i)$. This instruction depends on the instructions whose IPQ position are $qd1'(i)$ and $qd2'(i)$. If no corresponding instruction is dependend on, the value of $qd1'(i)$ or $qd2'(i)$ is 0. If the instruction is a taken branch, $qbt'(i)$ is *true*; otherwise $qbt'(q)$ is *false*. The field $qstv(q)$ records the pipeline state vector of the instruction. □

Fig. 5 shows how the IPQ is transferred into the IPQ′. In Fig. 5(a), the IPQs of configurations from 1 to *C* are listed. The pipeline state vector *qstv* enumerates the states of various configurations as shown in Fig. 5(b).

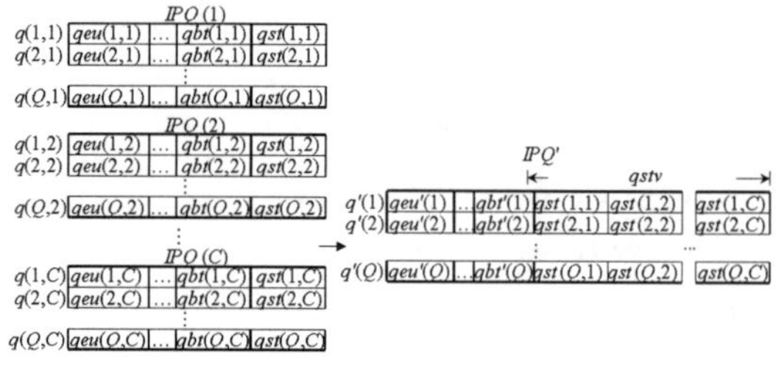

(a) IBQ of different configurations. (b) IBQ with state vectors.

Fig. 5. Turning IPQ into IPQ′.

3.3 Single-Pass Simulation for Superscalar Processors

We propose a single-pass simulation on IPQ′ to evaluate the processors of various configurations. Since instructions arrive at and depart from the processor globally in this algorithm, the original Retire procedure is divided into *Depart* and *Retire_S* procedures, and the original Fetch procedure is divided into *Arrive* and *Retire_S* procedures. In these procedures, arrive pointer *pa* and depart pointer *pl* are used to point at the IPQ′ positions of arriving and departing instructions, respectively; *test width ut(c)* is used to preview the fetch width; and *ready vector* $RDY = [rdy(1), rdy(2), \ldots, rdy(C)]$, where $1 \le c \le C$ and $rdy(c)$ is used to track if the arrived instructions are enough to do the pipeline action of next cycle in *c*.

A *Depart* procedure is used to depart the instructions that retired in all configurations to depart IPQ′. The procedure repeatedly increments the depart pointer when all previous instructions have been departed.

```
Procedure Depart;
begin
df := true;                                  //Set depart flag
while df do                                  //Continually departing
  c := 1; //For all configurations
  while df and c ≤ C do;                     // Test if stop departing
    if pr(c) = pl then df := false;          //Check to stop departing
  if df = true then                          //If departing is not stopped
    Depart_RES(pl, qor′(pl));                //Depart RES
    pl := Circular_Inc(pl);                  //Increment depart pointer
end
```

A *Retire_S* procedure is similar to the Retire procedure except that it does not call the Depart_RES procedure.

```
Procedure Retire_S (c);
Input c: integer; (specifies a configuration)
begin
uret(c) := 0;                                //Reset retire width
while uret(c)≠lret(c) and pr(c)≠pi(c)and qst(pr(c),c)=stC do//Retire rules
  uret(c) := uret(c) + 1;                    //Consume retire width
  urob(c) := urob(c) - 1;                    //Release ROB entry
  pr(c) := Circular_Inc (pr(c));             //Increment pointer
end
```

An *Arrive* procedure is used to place a new instruction into IPQ′. The procedure places a new instruction, increments the arrive pointer, and checks if any configuration is ready for the pipeline action in next cycle.

```
Procedure Arrive;
begin
if pa + 1 ≠ pl and not (pa = Q and pl = 1) then         //Arrive rules
  qeu′(pa) := xeut; qbt′(pa) := xbtt;                    //Place instruction
  for c := 1 to C do qst(pa, c) := stI;                  //Set to in-order state
  Arrive_RES (pa, qor′(pa), qd1′(pa), qd2′(pa));         //Check dependence
  pa := Circular_Inc (pa);                               //Increment arrive pointer
  t := t + 1;                                            //Next instruction
  for c := 1 to C do                                     //For all configurations
    if rdy(c) = false then                               //If not ready for next cycle
      if ut(c) + 1 = lf(c) or xbtt then rdy(c) := true;  //Check ready rules
      else ut(c) := ut(c) + 1;                           //Consume test width
end
```

A *Fetch_S* procedure is similar to the Fetch procedure except that it does not place new instructions into IPQ′.

```
Procedure Fetch_S (c);
Input c: integer; (specifies a configuration)
begin
uf(c) := 0; bt := false;                     //Reset retire width
while uf(c) ≠ lf(c) and not bt do            //Check fetch rules
  if qbt′(pf(C)) = true then bt := true;     //Check taken branch
  uf(c) := uf(c) + 1;                        //Consume decode width
  pf(c) := Circular_Inc (pf(c));             //Increment fetch pointer
  rdy(c) := false; ut(c) := 0;               //Reset ready state and test width
end
```

The *single-pass simulation algorithm for superscalar processors*, shown in Fig. 6, simulates the behavior of processors with configurations from 1 to *C* in a single pass. It repeatedly calls the Depart and Arrive procedures and checks the ready vector. If any configuration is ready, it calls the Retire_S, Execute, RS, Decode, and Fetch_S procedures sequentially to simulate the pipeline action in one cycle.

```
Algorithm Single_Pass_Superscalar (IX, RL, N);
Input: IX (instruction trace), RL (resource limitation list);
Output: N (execution cycle count vector);
begin
for c := 1 to C do                                      //For all configurations
  n(c) := 0;                                            //Reset cycle count
  P(c) := (1, 1, 1, 1);                                 //Reset pointers
  urs(c) := 0; ueu(c) := 0; urob(c) := 0;               //Reset resources
  ut(c) := 0; rdy(c) := false;                          //Reset ready state and test width
for r := 1 to R do res(r) := 0;                         //Reset register unit
pa := 1; pl := 1;                                       //Reset arrive and depart pointers
t := 1;                                                 //For all instructions
while t ≤ T do                                          //While still have instructions
  Depart;                                               //Depart from IPQ′
  Arrive;                                               //Arrive at IPQ′
  for c := 1 to C do                                    //For all configurations
    if rdy(c) = true then                               //If ready for next cycle
      Retire_S (c); Execute (c); RS (c);                //Retire, Execute, and RS
      Decode (c); Fetch_S (c);                          //Decode, and Fetch
      n(c) := n(c) + 1;                                 //Increment cycle count
end
```

Fig. 6. The single-pass algorithm for superscalar processors.

The time complexity of this single-pass simulation algorithm is $O(C \times T \times Q)$. However, this algorithm scans the trace and checks the dependencies only once, and evaluates the processors of all configurations interested.

4. EXPERIMENTS

To show the speedup of the single-pass simulation algorithm for superscalar processors to the conventional simulation algorithm, we build a trace-driven simulator. In this section, we first examine this simulator. Then the advantages of our approach are demonstrated by comparing the simulation time of the different algorithms.

4.1 The Simulator

We build a trace-driven simulator to measure the execution times of both the conventional algorithm and the single-pass simulation algorithm on a lightly loaded SUN Ultra-1 workstation. The source codes of SPECint95 benchmark suite (Case 1995) are compiled with GCC compiler. The executable benchmarks along with the input files are executed on Linux OS in x86 compatible PCs. The traces are retrieved by the system call "ptrace()" and are read into our simulator to evaluate the performance of the simulation models we proposed in Section 2.

4.2 Simulation Time

In Fig. 7, we show the simulation times of the eight benchmarks using:

(a) the conventional algorithm for canonical c-issue superscalar processors defined in Section 3.2, where $c = 1 \sim 10$, denoted tc_c;

(b) the single-pass simulation algorithm for canonical c-issue superscalar processors, where $c = 1 \sim 10$, denoted ts_{10}; and

(c) the trace read time, denoted tt.

On average, for canonical c-issue superscalar processors, the simulation time of the single-pass simulation algorithm for $c = 1 \sim 10$ is 3.06 times that of the conventional algorithm for $c = 10$ ($ts_{10}/tc_{10} = 3.06$). However, with this increase in simulation time, the stack simulation algorithm can simulate the behaviors of 10 various configurations, as opposed to only 1. On average, the speedup of the single-pass simulation algorithm over the conventional algorithm is 2.32 ($\left(\sum_{c=1}^{10} tc_c\right)/ts_{10} = 2.32$). The speedup will be higher if the ratio of tt is much higher, or if the number of configurations to be evaluated is increased. And even if tt is set to zero for all cases, the average speedup is still 1.70 ($\left(\sum_{c=1}^{10}(tc_c - tt)\right)/(ts_{10} - tt) = 1.70$).

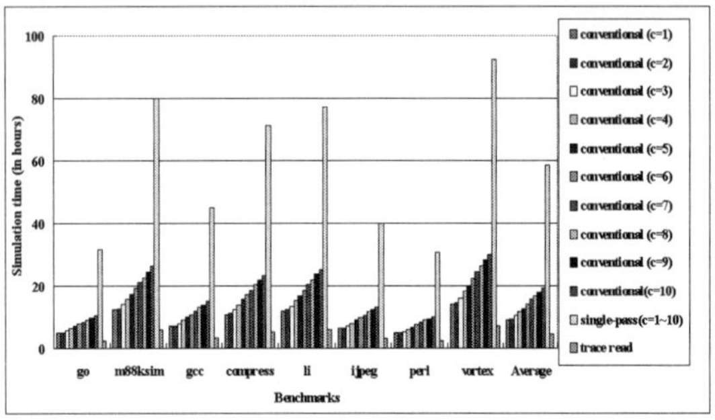

Fig. 7. Simulation time of the simulation algorithms and the trace read time.

5. Conclusions

In this paper, we show our work of developing a single-pass simulation algorithm to measure the performance of superscalar processors of various configurations. Traditionally, single-pass stack simulation worked only on caches and storages have the inclusion property. The major difficulty in this work is that the pipeline status of processors with different configurations are not the same nor have inclusion property, thus instructions of different configurations can not be put into a unified IPQ. To overcome this difficulty, we have proposed to use pipeline state vector to enumerate the possible pipeline states of an IPQ entry for different configurations. And a speedup of 2.32 has been observed in our previous simulation study, based on typical system parameters in current technologies.

For simplicity, we have concentrated only on the pipeline and out-of-order mechanism. By integrating the traditional stack simulation of caches, BTBs, and other storages, however, our simulator can easily become a platform of a complete single-pass simulation for whole superscalar processors. Furthermore, by extending the resource limitation list and with simple modification, our methods can be extended to evaluate more sophisticated mechanisms and policies of superscalar processors.

As the complexity of processors and the trace lengths of the benchmark programs grow, single-pass simulation technique for superscalar processors, favored by the fact that it reads the trace and checks the dependencies only once, is certainly a more desirable design aid. Furthermore, similar to superscalar processors, many hardware devices involve pipeline, cache, BTB, storages, and out-of-order mechanism. Our methods can be facilitated to develop a single-pass simulation for these devices.

References

Mike Johnson, *Superscalar Microprocessor Design,* Prentice Hall, 1991.

Holliday, M. A. and C. S. Ellis, "Accuracy of Memory Reference Traces of Parallel Computations in Trace-Driven Simulation," *IEEE Tran. Parallel and Distributed Systems*, vol. 3, no. 1, Jan. 1992, pp. 97-109.

Case, B., "SPEC95 Retires SPEC92," *MicroProcessor Report*, Aug. 1995, pp. 11-14.

Laha, S., J. H. Patel, and R. K. Iyer, "Accurate Low-Cost Methods for Performance Evaluation of Cache Memory Systems," *IEEE Trans. Computers*, vol. 37, no. 11, Nov. 1988, pp. 1325-1335.

Chame, J. and M. Dubois, "Cache Inclusion and Processor Sampling in Multiprocessor Simulations," *Proceedings of 1993 ACM SIGMETRICS*, May 1993, pp. 36-47.

Wang, W. H. and J. L. Baer, "Efficient Trace-Driven Simulation Methods for Cache Performance Analysis," *ACM Tran. Computer System*, vol. 9, no. 3, Aug. 1991, pp 222-241.

Mattson, R. L., J. Gecsei, D. R. Slutz, and I. L. Traiger, "Evaluation techniques for storage hierarchies," *IBM Systems Journal*, vol. 9, no. 2, Feb. 1970, pp. 78-117.

Mattson, R. L., "Evaluation of Multilevel Memories," *IEEE Trans. Magnetics*, vol. Mag-7, no. 4, Dec. 1971, pp. 814-819.

Gecsei, J., "Determining Hit Ratios for Multilevel Hierarchies," *IBM Systems Journal*, vol. 18, no. 4, Jul. 1974, pp. 316-327.

Silberman, G. M., "Stack Processing Techniques in Delayed-Staging Storage Hierarchies," *Communications of the ACM*, vol. 26, Nov. 11, 1983, pp. 999-1007.

Tompson, J. G. and A. J. Smith, "Efficient (Stack) Algorithms for Write-Back and Sector Memories," *ACM Tran. Computer Systems*, vol. 7 No. 1, Feb. 1989, pp. 78-115

Hill, M. D. and A. J. Smith, "Evaluating Associativity in CPU Caches," *IEEE Tran. Computers*, vol. 38, no. 12, Dec. 1989, pp. 1612-1630.

Sugumar, R. A. and S. G. Abraham, "Set-Associative Cache Simulation Using Generalized Binomial Trees," *ACM Tran. Computer Systems*, vol. 13, no. 1, Feb. 1995, pp. 32-56.

Wu, Y. W. and R. Muntz, "Stack Evaluation of Arbitrary Set-Associative Multiprocessor Caches," *IEEE Tran. Parallel and Distributed Systems*, vol. 6, no. 9, Sep. 1995, pp. 930-942.

Wu, C. E., Y. Hsu, and Yew-Huey Liu, "Efficient Stack Simulation for Shared Memory Set-Associative Multiprocessor Caches," *Proceedings of 1993 International Conference on Parallel Processing*, 1993, pp. I-163-170.

INITIAL TRANSIENT PERIOD DETECTION FOR STEADY-STATE QUANTILE ESTIMATION

Jong-Suk R. Lee, Don McNickle[†] and Krzysztof Pawlikowski
Department of Computer Science and [†]Department of Management
University of Canterbury
Christchurch, New Zealand
E-mail: {ruth, krys}@cosc.canterbury.ac.nz

KEYWORDS

Steady-State Simulation, Quantile Estimation, Initial Transient Period Detection

ABSTRACT

Performance of stochastic dynamic systems such as computer and telecommunication networks is often assessed by quantiles of, for example, system's response times or experienced delays. Thus, estimation of quantiles during stochastic simulation of computer and telecommunication networks is an important issue. However, unlike estimation of mean values, estimation of quantiles requires that simulation output data (observations) have to be stored for processing in several steps. Thus, QE (quantile estimation) requires large amounts of computer storage as well as longer computation time than for example, estimation of mean values. Several approaches for estimating quantiles in the method of RCs (regenerative cycles) and other methods have been proposed to reduce these problems. For sequential steady-state QE using the methods, like batch means and spectral analysis, one must first eliminate the effect of the initial transient period. However, heuristic rules or statistical tests specifically for detecting the initial transient period when estimating the steady-state quantiles have not been developed yet. In this paper, we study properties of statistical tests for detecting the initial transient period (originally developed for estimating mean values), when applied to estimating steady-state quantiles in a sequential simulation. We have also investigated statistical tests in terms of appropriateness for implementing them in a fully automated simulation package.

1 INTRODUCTION

Simulators are often more concerned with the extreme performance of simulated systems characterised by quantiles, than with its average behaviour, when simulating a dynamic stochastic system, such as a computer or a telecommunication network. Quantiles are convenient measures of entire ranges of values of simulation output data, and are particularly useful for planning necessary capacities for various resources, comparing the overall performance of alternative designs or establishing minimum standards of performance. Therefore, from a practical point of view, the problem of reliable estimators of quantiles during stochastic simulation is quite important.

The pth quantile of a random variable X equals Q_p if

$$Pr[X \leq Q_p] = p.$$

Let $x_1 \leq x_2 \leq \ldots \leq x_n$, $x_i \geq 0$, be the ordered sequence of n observations of a random variable X, collected during the simulation. The usual point estimator of the pth quantile is given by

$$\hat{Q}_p(n) = x_{\lfloor n*p+1 \rfloor}, \quad 0 < p < 1 \tag{1}$$

where $\lfloor z \rfloor$ denotes the integral part of z.

The problem with using this formula is that, especially in the case of correlated sequences of observations, the length of sample sequence required for achieving an adequate statistical error of the pth quantile $\hat{Q}_p(n)$ can be very large and impossible to predict in advance. Direct application of Equation (1) in quantile estimation (QE) requires large amounts of computer storage for storing the entire sequence of observations since sorting through the entire sequence of output data is required whenever a new observation is recorded (Heidelberger and Lewis 1984; Jain and Chlamtac 1985).

Clearly, repeating storing and sorting of the entire sequence for a QE is impractical in the long runs required for estimating steady-state parameters. Several approaches for avoiding these storing and sorting difficulties when estimating quantiles and their statistical error in the method of RCs and other methods have been proposed for non-sequential procedures in Heidelberger and Lewis 1984; Iglehart 1976; Jain and Chlamtac 1985; Seila 1982.

Another problem commonly encountered in simulating systems, especially using method other than RCs, is that the performance measures observed during the initial transient period of a simulation run are not typical of the system's true behaviour. It normally takes some time for the effect of the starting conditions to become insignificant and for the simulation model to reach steady-state. If the problem is to obtain performance measures for the model under steady-state conditions, then the analyst must eliminate the initialisation bias of observations collected during an initial transient period of a simulation run.

To do this, ideally, observations should be collected only after the system has reached steady-state. A problem with this approach is that how one can recognise that steady-state has been achieved. A number of ways to estimate the length of the initial transient period of steady-state simulations have been proposed in (Cash et al. 1992; Goldsman et al. 1994; Schruben 1982; Schruben et al. 1983). Basic problems related with the existence of initial transient periods can be found, for example, in Pawlikowski 1990; Randhawa and Baxter 1992; Wilson and Pritsker 1978. The length of the initial transient period has traditionally been determined using different heuristic rules.

More precise measures of the length of the initial transient could be obtained by using various statistical tests invented to test the stationarity of data sequences. These tests operate in a hypothesis testing framework, formally testing the null hypothesis that *there is no initialisation bias in the output mean* against the alternate hypothesis that initialisation bias in the output exists.

Our motivation is to find a robust initial transient period detector especially for steady-state QE which could be used in practical applications of sequential steady-state simulation and could also be implemented in a fully automated simulation package like Akaroa-2 (Ewing et al. 1999). In Section 2, we have summarised two statistical tests for detecting initialisation bias. In Section 3, we discuss the automatic detection of the initial transient period for steady-state QE. We also present the numerical results of two sequential detection methods of initial transient period, especially applying them in a fully automated simulation package Akaroa-2 (Ewing et al. 1999) in Section 4. Finally, our findings are summarised in Section 5.

2 STATISTICAL TESTS

In this section, we summarise two statistical tests for detecting the initial transient period in steady-state mean estimation.

2.1 Schruben Test

Stationarity tests based on variance estimation methods using standardised time series were first proposed by Schruben (Schruben 1982) using the maximum estimator of the variance, and improved on by Schruben et al. (Schruben et al. 1983) especially using a weighted area estimator.

Rejection or acceptance of the hypothesis that the given subsequence of observations is stationary, or equivalently, that the initial transient period is not included in the observations, depends on the statistic calculated from the considered sequence. Despite the sophisticated theory hidden behind these tests they are quite simple numerically, and can be applied to a wide class of simulated processes.

A practical problem when implementing one of these tests is that they require a priori knowledge of the steady-state variance σ^2 of the simulated process which is not normally available when the test is applied because the system is still in its initial transient period. These tests solve this problem by estimating the steady-state variance over the latter portion of the collected data. This is done on the assumption that this latter portion of data is more representative of the steady-state behaviour of the system, thus giving a better estimate of the steady-state variance. The effectiveness of this test is strongly dependent on how accurate the variance estimator is.

2.2 Goldsman, Schruben and Swain Test

The Goldsman, Schruben and Swain (GSS) test which is a natural generalisations of previously proposed tests in (Schruben 1982) and (Schruben et al. 1983), was proposed and tested in (Goldsman et al. 1994). In this test, observations $x_1, x_2, \cdots, x_n$ are divided into b batches of length m (assume $n = bm$). Variance estimators based on the first b' batches are compared to the corresponding estimators from the remaining $b - b'$ batches. If these estimators are deemed to be significantly different, then we say that an initial transient is present, and would likely bias point estimators of the steady-state mean.

The empirical results of the GSS test using different variance estimators of the batch means, standardised time series, and linear combinations of these estimators give a good agreement with the more extensive studies in Cash et al. 1992; Schruben 1982; Schruben et al. 1983. Furthermore, they stated that using the maximum estimator, and the combination of batch means and maximum estimator are the most powerful tests for detecting the presence of initial transient bias. For the GSS test, the compromise choice of $b \approx 8$ with the large enough batch size m and $b'/b \approx 0.75$ were recommended in Cash et al. 1992.

3 AUTOMATIC DETECTION OF INITIAL TRANSIENT PERIOD FOR STEADY-STATE QE

A common way of dealing with such an initialisation bias is to take a large (possibly wasteful) number of observations in an attempt to overwhelm the initialisation effects. Another method is simply to delete (truncate) a portion of the output from the beginning of the simulation run. This presumably allows the simulation to warm up before data are retained for analysis. The simulation experimenter would then hope that the biasing observations had been eliminated or their effects ameliorated. Of course, if the output is truncated too early, then significant bias might still be present. If it is truncated too late, then good observations are lost.

Most of the proposed heuristic rules and statistical tests for detecting the initial transient period are developed for the case of estimating the steady-state mean of the system. Specific heuristic rules or statistical tests of detecting the initial transient period especially for estimating steady-state quantiles have not been developed yet.

Two methods for automatic detection of the length of the initial transient period have been proposed: one proposed by Pawlikowski (Pawlikowski 1990) based on Schruben's test (Schruben 1982) with the method of spectral analysis used for the variance estimator (Heidelberger and Welch 1981), and another one proposed by Jackway and deSilva (Jackway and deSilva 1992) based on the same Schruben's test (Schruben 1982) with an autoregressive method used for the variance estimator. The former initial transient period detection method is implemented in a simulation package Akaroa-2 (Ewing et al. 1999). For estimating the steady-state mean, the initial transient period is well automatically and sequentially detected in Akaroa-2.

A sequential procedure for estimating steady-state quantiles based on the method of spectral analysis for the variance of the quantile estimates has been proposed in (Raatikainen 1990). The procedure has not been fully automated since the length of the initial transient period for the steady-state QE has to be decided beforehand. Another method for estimating steady-state quantiles in sequential simulation has been proposed in (Lee et al. 1999). Unlike the method proposed by Raatikainen (Raatikainen 1990), this approach uses a fully automated detection procedure for the initial transient period. Therefore, we have an immediate question if the currently available detection methods of the initial transient period proposed for estimating the steady-state mean are directly applicable for detecting the initial transient period especially when estimating the steady-state quantiles.

To check whether the initial transient period detection method implemented in Akaroa-2 is suitable for sequential QE or not, we can validate the initial transient period detection method of Akaroa-2 in a simple way. One suggestion for the validation is that just after the initial transient period the value of (say) the 0.9 quantile of the waiting time in the queue for an $M/M/1/\infty$ queueing system with the traffic intensity $\rho = 0.8$ should be very close to its theoretical steady-state 0.9 quantile, which can be calculated by

$$\max\left(0, \frac{E[w]}{\rho}\ln[10 * \rho]\right), \tag{2}$$

where $E[w]$ is the steady-state mean waiting time in the queue for the $M/M/1/\infty$ queueing system. If not, some of the results on quantiles may be suspect since it means that the initial transient period detection method in Akaroa-2 applied when estimating steady-state quantiles does not work properly, i.e., initialisation bias still exists even after deleting all observations collected in the initial transient period.

4 NUMERICAL RESULTS

First, to see the suitability of the initial transient period detection method implemented in Akaroa-2 when estimating the steady-state quantiles, we did the above simple suggestion. The results are depicted in Figure 1. The empirical values have been obtained from 100,000 independent waiting times of the first recorded customer over 100,000 independent simulation runs for the $M/M/1/\infty$ queueing system, after passing the initial transient period which has been suggested by the initial transient period detection method originally implemented in Akaroa-2.

The empirical 90th quantile and the empirical mean waiting time in the queue for the first recorded cus-

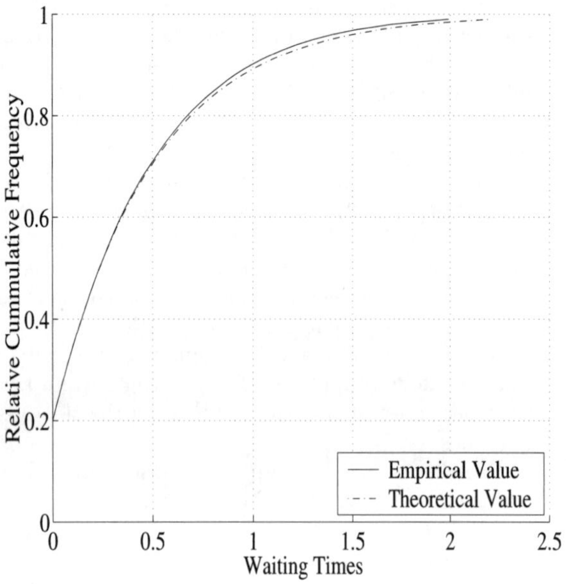

Figure 1: Comparisons of theoretical and empirical values when using Schruben's test for detecting an initial transient period ($M/M/1/\infty$ at traffic intensity $\rho = 0.8$)

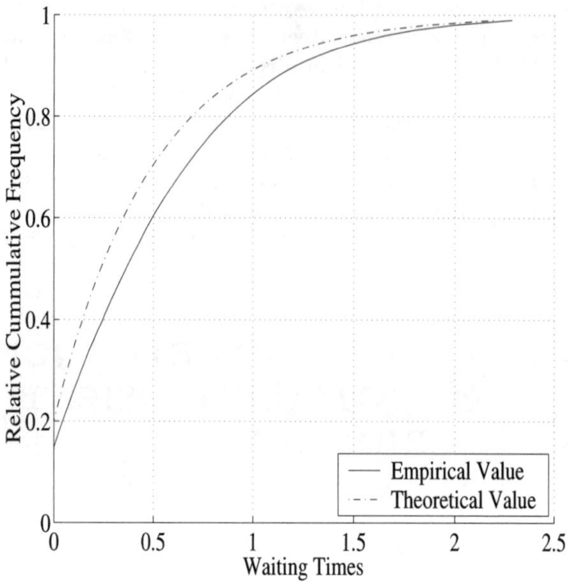

Figure 2: Comparisons of theoretical and empirical values when using the GSS test for detecting an initial transient period ($M/M/1/\infty$ at traffic intensity $\rho = 0.8$)

tomer after passing the initial transient period were calculated from 100,000 independent waiting times recorded after passing the initial transient period from each of 100,000 simulation runs, and compared with the theoretical steady-state values, which can be calculated by using Equation (2), of the mean waiting time in the queue for the $M/M/1/\infty$ queueing system.

The simple experiment is showing that the 90th quantile of the $M/M/1/\infty$ queueing system when estimating the mean waiting time in the queue is indistinguishable from its steady-state quantile - they are extremely close; see Figure 1. In such a situation we have the first evidence that the length of initial transients for quantiles and means should be close. This experiment is very modest, but at least gives some justification for using the initial transient period detection method, originally developed and applied for detecting the initial transient period in the case of estimating the steady-state means, implemented in Akaroa-2 especially when estimating quantiles. Therefore, an initial transient period detector developed for applying when estimating the steady-state means does seem to work adequately for quantiles as well.

Secondly, to find the better statistical test for detecting an initial transient period for steady-state quantiles, we have also investigated the performance of the GSS test based on the maximum estimator of the standardised time series which was reported as giving the best performance in (Cash et al. 1992; Goldsman et al. 1994). The GSS test is also implemented in the simulation package Akaroa-2 (Ewing et al. 1999). The empirical and the theoretical results of the GSS test and Schruben's test are depicted in Figure 2.

When comparing Figure 1 and Figure 2, the GSS test, based on the maximum estimator of the standardised time series, clearly shows much worse performance than Schruben's test, based on the method of spectral analysis, since the empirical values are much far from the theoretical values.

Another comparison of Schruben's test and the GSS test is presented in Table 1. These empirical statistics are obtained from 100,000 independent simulation replications (the same data of Figure 1 and Figure 2) for $M/M/1/\infty$ queueing system at traffic intensity $\rho = 0.8$ with the required relative statistical error of 10% or less, at the 0.95 confidence level.

The mean waiting times in steady-state when applying Schruben's test and the GSS test; (see the second column of the third and the fourth rows of Table 1,) are calculated by averaging 100,000 independent waiting times collected just after the initial transient period from 100,000 independent simulation replications. The

Table 1: Statistics obtained after applying Schruben's test and the GSS test for detecting the initial transient period

	Waiting Time	Total Observations	Transient Observations	Relative Length of Transient
Theory	0.4	47,443	326	0.69%
Schruben's Test	0.384	42,104	455	1.08%
GSS Test	0.507	41,434	390	0.94%

numbers of total observations and transient observations in the third and the fourth column of the third and the fourth rows of Table 1 are obtained by averaging the final total observations and the final transient observations recorded from 100,000 independent sequential steady-state simulation executed in Akaroa-2 with Schruben's test and the GSS test for detecting the initial transient period, respectively. The last column of the third and the fourth rows of Table 1 is the proportion of transient observations (the fourth column) over total observations (the third column).

The theoretical convergence of the mean waiting time in the $M/M/1/\infty$ queueing system at traffic intensity ρ = 0.8 to steady-state can be depicted in Figure 3 (McNickle 1991). (Note, we have assumed 6 initial customers at time zero since it gives interesting non monotone convergence to steady-state.) If we make the assumption that we are in steady-state when the mean waiting time is very close (within 0.0001 and 0.0005) of the steady-state value, then we can achieve steady-state within 0.0001 and 0.0005 after 432 and 326 customers, respectively.The theoretical mean waiting time and the theoretically required total and transient observations, with the required relative statistical error of 10% or less at the 0.95 confidence level, in the $M/M/1/\infty$ queueing system at traffic intensity $\rho = 0.8$ are also presented along with the empirically obtained results in Table 1.

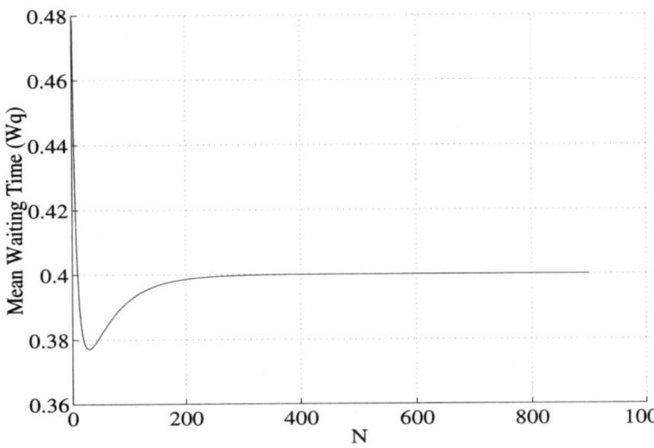

Figure 3: Theoretical convergence of waiting time in $M/M/1/\infty$ queueing system at load 0.8 (Initial customer number at time zero = 6)

As we can see from Table 1, the mean waiting time obtained from Schruben's test is much closer to the theoretical value than the mean waiting time obtained from the GSS test. This suggests that Schruben's test for detecting the initial transient period may be better than the GSS test since the mean waiting time calculated from 100,000 first customers recorded after passing the initial transient period should be very close to the theoretical value. To eliminate or reduce the effect of the initial transient period for estimating steady-state parameters, in general, deleting a little bit longer length of the initial transient period detected using Schruben's test seems desirable.

5 CONCLUSIONS

In this paper, we have studied properties of statistical tests of detecting the initial transient period, especially in terms of the propriety of the current state of the art in the initial transient period detection methods when applying them for estimating steady-state quantiles in a sequential steady-state simulation. The experiment is done in a very modest way, but at least gives some justification for using Schruben's test for detecting the initial transient period implemented in Akaroa-2 when estimating quantiles. Therefore, an initial transient period detector originally developed and applied for estimating steady-state means does seem to work adequately for estimating steady-state quantiles as well. Schruben's test for detecting the initial transient period seems better than the GSS test since Schruben's test suggests a longer end point of the initial transient period.

REFERENCES

Cash, C. R.; D. G. Dippold; J. M. Long; and W. P. Pollard. 1992. "Evaluation of Tests for Initial-Condition Bias." *Proceedings of the 1992 Winter Simulation Conference*, 577-585.

Ewing, G.; K. Pawlikowski; and D. McNickle. 1999. "Akaroa-2: Exploiting Network Computing by Distributed Stochastic Simulation." *13th European Simulation Multiconference* (Warsaw, Poland), 175-181.

Goldsman, D.; L. W. Schruben; and J. J. Swain. 1994. "Tests for Transient Means in Simulated Time Series." *Naval research Logistics Quarter*, 41, 171-187.

Heidelberger, P. and P. A. W. Lewis. 1984. "Quantile Estimation in Dependent Sequences." *Operations Research*, 32, no. 1: 185-209.

Heidelberger, P. and P. D. Welch. 1981. "A Spectral Method for Confidence Interval Generation and Run Length Control in Simulations." *Communications of the ACM* 25: 233-245.

Iglehart, D. L. 1976. "Simulating Stable Stochastic Systems, VI: Quantile Estimation." *Journal of the Association for Computing Machinery*, 23, no. 2: 347-360.

Jackway, P. T. and B. M. deSilva. 1992. "A Methodology for Initialization Bias Reduction in Computer Simulation Output." *Asia-Pacific Journal of Operational Research*, 9, 87-100.

Jain, R. and I. Chlamtac. 1985. "The P^2 Algorithm for Dynamic Calculation of Quantiles and Histograms Without Storing Observations." *Communications of the ACM*, 28, no. 10: 1076-1085.

Lee, J. R.; D. C. McNickle; and K. Pawlikowski. 1999. "Quantile Estimation in Sequential Steady-State Simulation." *13th European Simulation Multiconference* (Warsaw, Poland), 168-174.

McNickle, D. C. 1991. "Estimating the Average Delay of the First N Customers in an $M/Erlang/1$ Queue." *Asia-Pacific Journal of Operational Research*, 8, No. 1: 44-53.

Pawlikowski, K. 1990. "Steady-State Simulation of Queueing Processes: A Survey of Problems and Solutions." *ACM Computing Surveys*, no. 2: 123-170.

Raatikainen, K. E. E. 1990. "Sequential Procedure for Simultaneous Estimation of Several Percentiles." *Transactions of The Society for Computer Simulation*, 7, no. 1: 21-44.

Randhawa, S. U. and L. K. Baxter. 1992. "A Study in the Application of Schriber's Truncation Rule to Simulation Output." *Transactions of The Society for Computer Simulation*, 9, no. 3: 175-192.

Schruben, L. W. 1982. "Detecting Initialization Bias in Simulation Output." *Operations Research*, 30, no. 3: 569-590.

Schruben, L. W.; H. Singh; and L. Tierney. 1983. "Optimal Tests for Initialization Bias in Simulation Output." *Operations Research*, 31, 1167-1178.

Seila, A. F. 1982. "A Batching Approach to Quantile Estimation in Regenerative Simulations." *Management Science*, 28, no. 5: 573-581.

Wilson, J. R. and A. A. B. Pritsker. 1978. "A Survey of Research on the Simulation Startup Problem." *Simulation*, 31, 55-58.

AUTHORS' BIOGRAPHIES

JONG-SUK RUTH LEE is currently a PhD student in computer science from the University of Canterbury, Christchurch, New Zealand and a student member of IEEE. Her research interests are sequential quantitative stochastic simulation and distributed simulation of telecommunication networks.

DON MCNICKLE is a Senior Lecturer in Management Science on the Department of Management, University of Canterbury, New Zealand. His research interests include queueing theory and statistical aspects of simulation. He received a PhD in Mathematics from the University of Auckland, New Zealand. Member of ORSA.

KRZYSZTOF PAWLIKOWSKI is an Associate Professor (Reader) in Computer Science at University of Canterbury, Christchurch, New Zealand. He received his PhD degree in Computer Engineering from the Technical University of Gdansk, Poland. The author of over 80 research papers and four books. His research interests include stochastic simulation, distributed processing, ATM, optical and wireless telecommunication networks, and teletraffic modelling. Senior member of IEEE.

SOME PROBLEMS IN SEQUENTIAL SIMULATION WITH SELF-SIMILAR PROCESSES

Hae-Duck J. Jeong, Don McNickle[†] and Krzysztof Pawlikowski

Department of Computer Science and [†]Department of Management
University of Canterbury
Christchurch, New Zealand
E-mail: {joshua, krys}@cosc.canterbury.ac.nz

KEYWORDS

Self-Similar Processes, Sequential Simulation, Teletraffic Generators.

ABSTRACT

It is generally accepted that self-similar processes may provide better models for teletraffic in modern telecommunication networks than Poisson processes. If stochastic self-similarity of teletraffic is not taken into account, it can lead to inaccurate conclusions about performance of networks. Thus, an important requirement for conducting simulation studies of networks is the ability to generate long synthetic self-similar sequences of incremental processes, to transform them into inter-event time intervals, and to do this accurately and quickly. A case study is discussed to show how many observations and how much time are needed in steady-state simulation of queueing models with self-similar input processes. This is compared with simulation run lengths of the same queueing models fed by Poisson processes.

1 INTRODUCTION

The search for accurate mathematical models of data streams in modern telecommunication networks has attracted a considerable amount of interest in the last few years. The reason is that several recent teletraffic studies of local and wide area networks, including the world wide web, have shown that commonly used teletraffic models, based on Poisson or related processes, are not able to capture the self-similar (or fractal) nature of teletraffic (Leland et al. 1994; Likhanov et al. 1995; Paxson and Floyd 1995; Ryu 1996), especially when they are engaged in such sophisticated services as variable-bit-rate (VBR) video transmission (Garrett and Willinger 1994; Krunz and Makowski 1998; Rose 1997). The properties of teletraffic in such scenarios are very different from both the properties of conventional models of telephone traffic and the traditional models of data traffic generated by computers.

The use of traditional models of teletraffic can result in overly optimistic estimates of performance of telecommunication networks, insufficient allocation of communication and data processing resources, and difficulties in ensuring the quality of service expected by network users (Beran 1992; Neidhardt and Wang 1998; Paxson and Floyd 1995). On the other hand, if the strongly correlated character of teletraffic is explicitly taken into account, this can also lead to more efficient traffic control mechanisms.

Several methods for generating pseudo-random self-similar sequences have been proposed. They include methods based on fractional Gaussian noise (Mandelbrot 1971), fractional ARIMA processes (Hosking 1984), the $M/G/\infty$ queue model (Krunz and Makowski 1998; Leland et al. 1994), autoregressive processes (Cario and Nelson 1998; Granger 1980), spatial renewal processes (Taralp et al. 1998), etc. Some of them generate asymptotically self-similar sequences and require large amounts of CPU time. For example, Hosking's method (Hosking 1984), based on the F-ARIMA$(0, d, 0)$ process, needs many hours to produce a self-similar sequence with 131,072 (2^{17}) numbers on a Sun SPARCstation 4 (Leland et al. 1994). It requires $O(n^2)$ computations to generate n numbers. Even though exact methods of generation of self-similar sequences exist (for example: (Mandelbrot 1971)), they are only fast enough for short sequences. They are usually inappropriate for generating long sequences because they require multiple passes along generated sequences. To overcome this, approximate methods for generation of self-similar sequences in simulation studies of telecommunication networks have also been proposed (Lau et al. 1995; Paxson 1997).

An important requirement for conducting simulation studies of telecommunication networks is the ability to generate long synthetic self-similar sequences of incremental processes, long enough to ensure arbitrary statistical precision of the final simulation results. Very little is known on appropriateness of selection of specific inter-arrival processes and production of inter-event time intervals for arrival counts generated by an FGN process still remains an open research issue (Jeong et al. 1999b; Leroux and Hassan 1999; Paxson 1997).

Three methods for generation of self-similar sequences were considered in (Jeong et al. 1999). In this paper we study an additional method, based on *Fractional Gaussian Noise* and *Daubechies Wavelets* (*FGN-DW*) which has promising properties, and consider the transformation of count processes into inter-arrival processes. This generator was proposed in (Jeong et al. 1999a). Then, the inter-arrival processes are used in steady-state simulation of queueing models with self-similar input processes.

A summary of the basic properties of self-similar processes is given in the next section. Generation and transformations of the *FGN-DW* count processes are described in Section 3. In Section 4, a case study is discussed to show how many observations and how much time are needed in steady-state simulation of queueing models with self-similar input processes (called $SSM/M/1/\infty$). This is compared with simulation run lengths of the same queueing models fed by short-range dependence (SRD) processes such as $M/M/1/\infty$ queueing system. The influence of the Hurst parameter on simulation run-length is also analysed, before the final conclusions are formulated.

2 SELF-SIMILAR PROCESSES AND THEIR PROPERTIES

Basic definitions of self-similar processes are as follows: A continuous-time stochastic process $\{X_t\}$ is strongly *self-similar* with a self-similarity parameter H $(0 < H < 1)$, known as the Hurst parameter, if for any positive stretching factor c, the rescaled process with time scale $ct, c^{-H}X_{ct}$, is equal in distribution to the original process $\{X_t\}$ (Beran 1994). This means that, for any sequence of time points $t_1, t_2, \ldots, t_n$, and for all $c > 0$, $\{c^{-H}X_{ct_1}, c^{-H}X_{ct_2}, \ldots, c^{-H}X_{ct_n}\}$ has the same distribution as $\{X_{t_1}, X_{t_2}, \ldots, X_{t_n}\}$.

In discrete-time case, let $\{X_k\} = \{X_k : k = 0, 1, 2, \ldots\}$ be a (discrete-time) stationary process with mean μ, variance σ^2, and autocorrelation function (ACF) $\{\rho_k\}$, for $k = 0, 1, 2, \ldots$, and let $\{X_k^{(m)}\}_{k=1}^{\infty} = \{X_1^{(m)}, X_2^{(m)}, \ldots\}$, $m = 1, 2, 3, \ldots$, be a sequence of batch means, i.e., $X_k^{(m)} = (X_{km-m+1} + \ldots + X_{km})/m, k \geq 1$.

The process $\{X_k\}$ with $\rho_k \to k^{-\beta}$, as $k \to \infty, 0 < \beta < 1$, is called *exactly self-similar* with $H = 1 - (\beta/2)$, if $\rho_k^{(m)} = \rho_k$, for any $m = 1, 2, 3, \ldots$. In other words, the process $\{X_k\}$ and the averaged processes $\{X_k^{(m)}\}$, $m \geq 1$, have identical correlation structure. The process $\{X_k\}$ is *asymptotically self-similar* with $H = 1 - (\beta/2)$, if $\rho_k^{(m)} \to \rho_k$, as $m \to \infty$.

The most frequently studied models of self-similar traffic belong either to the class of fractional autoregressive integrated moving-average (F-ARIMA) processes or to the class of fractional Gaussian noise processes; see (Hosking 1984; Leland et al. 1994; Paxson 1997). F-ARIMA(p, d, q) processes were introduced by Hosking (Hosking 1984) who showed that they are asymptotically self-similar with Hurst parameter $H = d + \frac{1}{2}$, as long as $0 < d < \frac{1}{2}$. On the other hand, the incremental process $\{Y_k\} = \{X_k - X_{k-1}\}, k \geq 0$, is called the *fractional Gaussian noise* (FGN) process, if $\{X_k\}$ represents a fractional Brownian motion (FBM) random process. This process is a (discrete-time) stationary Gaussian process with mean μ, variance σ^2 and $\{\rho_k\} = \{\frac{1}{2}(|k+1|^{2H} - 2|k|^{2H} + |k-1|^{2H})\}, \quad k > 0$. A FBM process is characterised by three properties (Mandelbrot and Wallis 1969): (i) it is a continuous zero-mean Gaussian process $\{X_t\} = \{X_s : s \geq 0$ and $\quad 0 < H < 1\}$ with ACF given by $\{\rho_{s,t}\} = \{\frac{1}{2}(s^{2H} + t^{2H} - |s-t|^{2H})\}$, where s is time lag and t is time; (ii) its increments $\{X_t - X_{t-1}\}$ form a stationary random process; (iii) it is self-similar with Hurst parameter H, that is, for all $c > 0$, $\{X_{ct}\} = \{c^H X_t\}$, in the sense that, if time is changed by the ratio c, then $\{X_t\}$ is changed by c^H.

Main properties of self-similar processes include:

- *Slowly decaying variance.* The variance of the sample mean decreases more slowly than the reciprocal of the sample size, that is, $Var[\{X_k^{(m)}\}] \to c_1 m^{-\beta_1}$ as $m \to \infty$, where c_1 is a constant and $0 < \beta_1 < 1$.

- *Long-range dependence.* A process $\{X_k\}$ is called a stationary process with *long-range dependence (LRD)* if its ACF $\{\rho_k\}$ is non-summable, that is, $\sum_{k=0}^{\infty} \rho_k = \infty$. The speed of decay of autocorrelations is more hyperbolic than exponential.

- *Hurst effect.* Self-similarity manifests itself by a straight line of slope β_2 on a log-log plot of the R/S statistic. For a given set of numbers $\{X_1, X_2, \ldots, X_n\}$ with sample mean $\hat{\mu} = E\{X_i\}$

and sample variance $S^2(n) = E\{(X_i - \hat{\mu})^2\}$, Hurst parameter H is presented by the *rescaled adjusted range* $\frac{R(n)}{S(n)}$ (or *R/S statistic*) where $R(n) = \max\{\sum_{i=1}^{k}(X_i - \hat{\mu}), 1 \leq k \leq n\} - \min\{\sum_{i=1}^{k}(X_i - \hat{\mu}), 1 \leq k \leq n\}$ and S is estimated by $S(n) = \sqrt{E\{(X_i - \hat{\mu})^2\}}$. Hurst found empirically that for many time series observed in nature, the expected value of $\frac{R(n)}{S(n)}$ asymptotically satisfies the power-law relation: $E[\frac{R(n)}{S(n)}] \rightarrow c_2 n^H$, as $n \rightarrow \infty$, with $0.5 < H < 1$, where c_2 is a finite positive constant. The Hurst parameter H is typically about 0.73, observations X_k from SRD processes are known to satisfy $E[\frac{R(n)}{S(n)}] \rightarrow c_3 n^{0.5}$ as $n \rightarrow \infty$, with c_3 a finite positive constant. This discrepancy of the H values obtained by LRD and SRD processes, i.e., $H = 0.73$ and $H = 0.5$, respectively, is generally referred to as the *Hurst effect*; see for example (Beran 1994; Cox 1984; Leland et al. 1994).

- *1/f-noise.* The spectral density $f(\lambda; H)$ obeys a power law near the origin, i.e., $f(\lambda; H) \rightarrow c_4\lambda^{1-2H}$, as $\lambda \rightarrow 0$, where c_4 is a finite positive constant and $0.5 < H < 1$.

3 TELETRAFFIC GENERATION AND SIMULATION

We claim that the *FGN-DW* transformation is sufficiently fast for generation of synthetic self-similar sequences, to be used as simulation input data (Jeong et al. 1999a). Let us briefly introduce the *FGN-DW* method itself.

3.1 Generation of Self-Similar Teletraffic Using FGN-DW

The general strategy behind our method is the same as in (Paxson 1997). The algorithm consists of the following steps (for more detailed discussions, see (Jeong et al. 1999a)):

Step.1 Calculate a sequence of values $\{f_1, f_2, \cdots, f_n\}$ using $f(\lambda; H) = c_f|\lambda|^{1-2H} + O(|\lambda|^{min(3-2H,2)})$ where $c_f = \sigma^2(2\pi)^{-1}sin(\pi H)\Gamma(2H + 1)$ and $O(\cdot)$ represents the residual error, $f_i = \hat{f}(\frac{\pi i}{n})$, corresponding to the spectral density of an FGN process for frequencies from $\frac{\pi}{n}$ to π.

Step.2 Adjust $\{f_i\}$ by multiplying them by realisations of an independent exponential random variable with mean equal 1.

Step.3 Generate a sequence $\{x_1, x_2, \cdots, x_n\}$ of complex numbers such that $|x_i| = \sqrt{\hat{f}_i}$ and the phase of x_i is uniformly distributed between 0 and 2π. The random phase technique, taken from (Schiff 1992), preserves the distribution of spectral density of $\{\hat{f}_i\}$, but ensures that different sequences generated using the method will be independent. It also makes the marginal distribution of the final sequence normal. The phase randomisation makes the different frequency components independent (Paxson 1997).

Step.4 Calculate two synthetic coefficients of orthonormal Daubechies wavelets which are used in the inverse discrete wavelet transform (IDWT) (Nartallo et al. 1996). Then, generate the approximately self-similar FGN sequence in time domain by using the IDWT from $\{x_i\}$. We use the Daubechies wavelets (Daubechies 1992) because it produces more accurate coefficients of wavelets than Haar wavelets (Wickerhauser 1994).

Using the above steps, the proposed *FGN-DW* method gives a fast generator of well approximated self-similar sequences of numbers representing FGN processes which can be interpreted as differential arrival rates.

3.2 Transformation of Self-Similar Count Processes into Inter-Arrival Processes

Simulation studies of telecommunication networks require generation of arbitrarily long sequences of inter-arrival times of transmitted data packets. Therefore, a mechanism is needed to transform self-similar processes representing the arrival counts, or differential arrival rates (see the above subsection.), into suitable sequences of inter-arrival times of packets, while preserving appropriate characteristics (Jeong et al. 1999b). In this paper, we use a count process generated by *FGN-DW* to obtain exponential inter-arrival distribution.

Let $F_Y(y)$ be a marginal cumulative density function (CDF) corresponding to a process $\{Y_k\}$. Then the process $\{Y_k\}$ with the desirable marginal CDF $F_Y(y)$ is produced from the process $\{X_k\}$ by using the following transformation. Given a self-similar sequence of the *FGN-DW* process $\{X_k\}$, we can transform the marginal distribution by mapping each number as $\{Y_k\} = F_Y^{-1}(F_N(X_k)),\ k = 1, 2, \ldots$.

In order to estimate the CDF, we use that from Cody 1969. Rational approximations for the complementary error functions erfc (x), with maximal relative errors ranging down to between 6 x 10^{-19} and 3 x 10^{-20} were proposed by (Cody 1969).

The CDF of the exponential distribution is $F_X(x) = 1 - e^{-\lambda x}$. To generate exponential variates, the inverse transformation is defined as: $\{Y_k\} = -(1/\lambda) * \log(F_N(X_k))$.

4 NUMERICAL RESULTS

We look at how many observations and how much time are needed in sequential steady-state simulation of a queueing system with self-similar input processes. An $M/M/1/\infty$ and $SSM/M/1/\infty$ queueing systems have been simulated in the method based on spectral analysis when one simulation engine is used in AKAROA-2 (Ewing et al. 1999), a fully automated tool of sequential simulation designed for stopping simulation with a pre-specified statistical precision of the final results.

Figure 1 shows the number of theoretically required observations, and the mean number of empirical observations need for stopping simulation with the required statistical precision, for different values of traffic intensity ρ, when analysing steady-state mean response time in an $M/M/1/\infty$ queueing system. Each mean experimental run length of simulation is an average over 30 replications. Confidence intervals of relative half-widths of 10% or less, at 0.95 confidence level, are also shown in Figure 1. While for $\rho \leq 0.6$ the mean number of empirical observations is slightly higher than the number of theoretically required observations, for $0.6 < \rho \leq 0.9$ the mean number of empirical observations is lower than the number of observations required theoretically. Both numbers quickly grow as $\rho \to 1$. The range of the reported mean numbers of empirical observations needed is between 1787 and 128211.

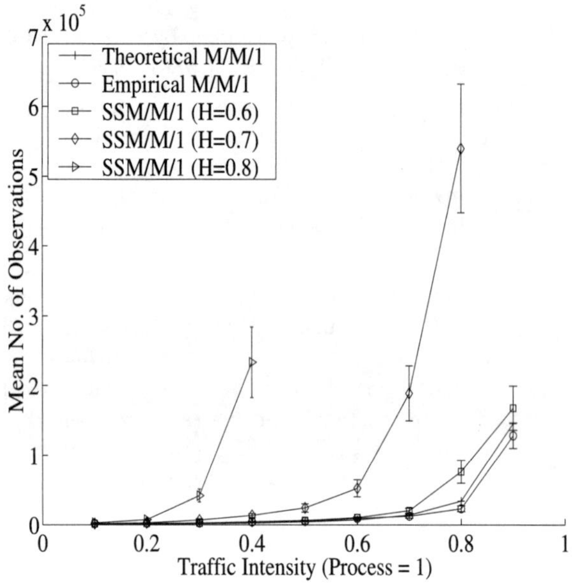

Figure 1: Mean numbers of observations needed in sequential analysis of steady-state mean response time: in an $M/M/1/\infty$ and $SSM/M/1/\infty$ queueing system with relative precision $\leq$ 10%, 95% CI when one simulation engine is used.

The results in Figure 1 show that, analysis of an $SSM/M/1/\infty$ queueing system with self-similar input processes requires many more observations than an $M/M/1/\infty$ queueing system. The mean number of observations, or simulation run length, significantly increases with H of the input stream. For $\rho = 0.4$ and each H = 0.6, 0.7 and 0.8, the mean number of empirical observations for the $SSM/M/1/\infty$ queueing system is 4484 (13.4%), 13540 (242.4%) and 233023 (5791.9%), respectively, while for $\rho = 0.4$, the $M/M/1/\infty$ queueing system needs 3955 observations (($\cdot$ %) are the relative increases of the run-length against the $M/M/1/\infty$ queueing system). For $\rho = 0.8$ and each H = 0.6 and 0.7, the mean number of empirical observations for the $SSM/M/1/\infty$ queueing system is 76373 (228.4%) and 539781 (2221.2%), respectively, while for $\rho = 0.8$, the $M/M/1/\infty$ queueing system only needs 23524 observations.

Figure 2 shows the mean response time needed in the sequential analysis of a steady-state simulation in an $SSM/M/1/\infty$ and an $M/M/1/\infty$ queueing system with a relative statistical error $\leq$ 10%, 95% CI. Even though $\rho = 0.4$, for $H = 0.6, 0.7$ and 0.8, the mean response time of the $SSM/M/1/\infty$ is 0.174 (4.8%), 0.206 (24.1%), and 0.3291 (98.3%) seconds, respectively, but the mean response time of the $M/M/1/\infty$ queueing system is 0.166 seconds. For $\rho = 0.8$ and $H = 0.6$ and 0.7, the mean response times of the $SSM/M/1/\infty$ queueing system are 0.6722 (35.5%) and 2.086 (320.6%) seconds, respectively, while for $\rho = 0.8$, the mean response time of the $M/M/1/\infty$ queueing system is only 0.496 seconds.

Therefore, the mean response time of the $SSM/M/1/\infty$ queueing system in Figure 2 rapidly increases as H increases, while the mean response time of the $M/M/1/\infty$ queueing system slowly increases.

Thus, the results tell us that performance of queueing systems under Poisson processes and self-similar processes are very different. If self-similar processes are taken into account in simulation studies of telecommunication networks, they will give more realistic results than Poisson processes. We may also face difficulty in sequential steady-state simulation of a queueing system when the H value is especially very high, since methods of long bulk generation with self-similar processes require a large amount of time.

5 CONCLUSIONS

We have examined the main issue of stochastic simulation of telecommunication networks with self-similar teletraffic. We looked at how many observations and how much time are needed in sequential steady-state simulation of a queueing system with self-similar input processes. As we have shown, assuming self-similar inter-arrival processes, one needs many more observations to obtain the final simulation results with a required precision than when assuming Poisson inter-arrival processes. To secure a predefined statistical precision of simulation final results, one would need to generate arbitrary long sequences of inter-arrival times, and this would need to be done sequentially. At this stage, an algorithm for sequential generation of self-similar sequences has not been proposed.

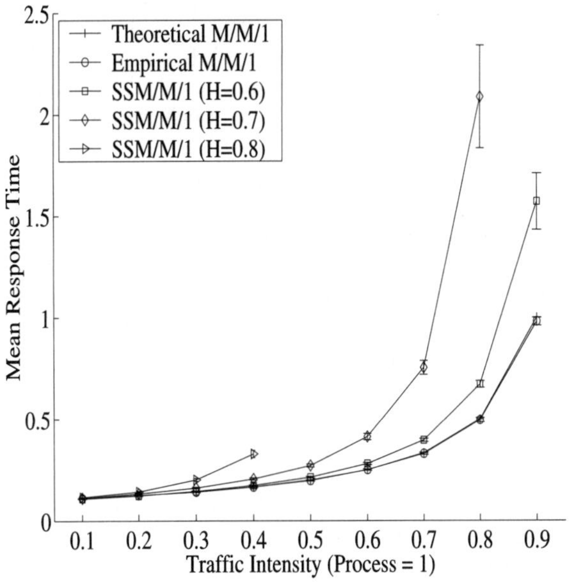

Figure 2: Mean response time needed in sequential analysis of steady-state mean response time: in an $M/M/1/\infty$ and $SSM/M/1/\infty$ queueing system with relative precision $\leq 10\%$, 95% CI when one simulation engine is used.

ACKNOWLEDGEMENTS

The authors wish to acknowledgement the financial support of Telecom New Zealand (Research Grant 4500286492).

REFERENCES

Beran, J. 1992. "Statistical Methods for Data with Long Range Dependence." *Statistical Science*, 7, no.4: 404-427.

Beran, J. 1994. *Statistics for Long-Memory Processes.* Chapman and Hall, New York.

Cario, M.C. and B.L. Nelson. 1998. "Numerical Methods for Fitting and Simulating Autoregressive-to-Anything Processes." *INFORMS Journal on Computing*, 10, no.1: 72-81.

Cody, W.J. 1969. "Rational Chebyshev Approximations for the Error Function." *Mathematics of Computation*, 23, no. 107: 631-637.

Cox, D.R. 1984. "Long-Range Dependence: a Review." *In Statistics: An Appraisal.* Iowa State Statistical Library, The Iowa State University Press, 55-74.

Daubechies, I. 1992. *Ten Lectures on Wavelets.* CBMS-NSF Regional Conference Series in Applied Mathematics, SIAM Press, Philadelphia, Pennsylvania, 61.

Ewing, G.; K. Pawlikowski; and D. McNickle. 1999. "AKAROA-2: Exploiting Network Computing by Distributing Stochastic Simulation." In *Proceedings of 13th European Simulation Multiconference, ESM'99* (Warsaw, Poland), 1: 175-181.

Garrett, M.W. and W. Willinger. 1994. "Analysis, Modeling and Generation of Self-Similar VBR Video Traffic." In *Computer Communication Review, Proceedings of ACM SIGCOMM'94* (London, UK, Aug.), 24, no. 4: 269-280.

Granger, C.W.J. 1980. "Long Memory Relationships and the Aggregation of Dynamic Models." *Journal of Econometrics*, 14: 227-238.

Hosking, J.R.M. 1984. "Modeling Persistence in Hydrological Time Series Using Fractional Differencing." *Water Resources Research*, 20, no. 12 (Dec.): 1898-1908.

Jeong, H.-D.J.; D. McNickle; and K. Pawlikowski. 1999. "A Comparative Study of Three Self-Similar Teletraffic Generators." In *Proceedings of 13th European Simulation Multiconference, ESM'99* (Warsaw, Poland), 1: 356-362.

Jeong, H.-D.J.; D. McNickle; and K. Pawlikowski. 1999a. "Fast Self-Similar Teletraffic Generation Based on FGN and Wavelets." In *Proceedings of the IEEE International Conference on Networks, ICON'99* (Brisbane, Australia), 75-82.

Jeong, H.-D.J.; D. McNickle; and K. Pawlikowski. 1999b. "Generation of Self-Similar Time Series for Simulation Studies of Telecommunication Networks." In *Proceedings of the First Western Pacific and Third Australia-Japan Workshop on Stochastic Models in Engineering, Technology and Management* (Christchurch, New Zealand), 221-230.

Krunz, M. and A. Makowski. 1998. "A Source Model for VBR Video Traffic Based on $M/G/\infty$ Input Processes." In *Proceedings of IEEE INFOCOM'98* (San Francisco, CA, USA, Mar.), 1441-1448.

Lau, W-C.; A. Erramilli; J.L. Wang; and W. Willinger. 1995. "Self-Similar Traffic Generation: the Random Midpoint Displacement Algorithm and Its Properties." In *Proceedings of IEEE ICC'95* (Seattle, WA), 466-472.

Leland, W.E.; M.S. Taqqu; W. Willinger; and D.V. Wilson. 1994. "On the Self-Similar Nature of Ethernet Traffic (Extended Version)." *IEEE/ACM Transactions on Networking*, 2, no. 1: 1-15.

Likhanov, N.; B. Tsybakov; and N.D. Georganas. 1995. "Analysis of an ATM Buffer with Self-Similar ("Fractal") Input Traffic." In *Proceedings of IEEE INFOCOM'95, 985-992.*

Leroux, H. and M. Hassan. 1999. "Generating Packet Inter-Arrival Times for FGN Arrival Processes." In *The 3rd New Zealand ATM and Broadband Workshop* (Hamilton, New Zealand), 1-10.

Mandelbrot, B.B. 1971. "A Fast Fractional Gaussian Noise Generator." *Water Resources Research*, 7: 543-553.

Mandelbrot, B.B. and J.R. Wallis. 1969. "Computer Experiments with Fractional Gaussian Noises." *Water Resources Research*, 5, no. 1: 228-267.

Nartallo, C.M.; N.G. Prelcic; S.J.G. Galan; and C.S. Cabanelas. 1996. "Wavelet Toolbox for Matlab." Available through http: //www.tsc.uvigo.es/ ~wavelets/uvi_wave.html.

Neidhardt, A.L. and J.L. Wang. 1998. "The Concept of Relevant Time Scales and Its Application to Queueing Analysis of Self-Similar Traffic (or Is Hurst Naughty or Nice?)." In *Proceedings ACM SIGMETRICS'98* (Madison, Wisconsin, USA, Jun.), 222-232.

Paxson, V. 1997. "Fast, Approximate Synthesis of Fractional Gaussian Noise for Generating Self-Similar Network Traffic." *ACM SIGCOMM, Computer Communication Review*, 27, no. 5: 5-18.

Paxson, V. and S. Floyd. 1995. "Wide-Area Traffic: the Failure of Poisson Modeling." *IEEE/ACM Transactions on Networking*, 3, no. 3 (Jun.): 226-244.

Rose, O. 1997. *Traffic Modeling of Variable Bit Rate MPEG Video and Its Impacts on ATM Networks.* PhD thesis, Bayerische Julius-Maximilians-Universität Würzburg.

Ryu, B.K. 1996. *Fractal Network Traffic: from Understanding to Implications.* PhD thesis, Graduate School of Arts and Science, Columbia University.

Schiff, S. J. 1992. "Resolving Time-Series Structure with a Controlled Wavelet Transform." *Optical Engineering*, 31, no. 11: 2492-2495.

Taralp, T.; M. Devetsikiotis; and I. Lambadaris . 1998. "Efficient Fractional Gaussian Noise Generation Using the Spatial Renewal Process." In *Proceedings IEEE International Communications Conference (ICC'98)* (Atlanta, GA, USA, Jun.), S41.3.1-S41.3.5.

Wickerhauser, M.V. 1994. *Adapted Wavelet Analysis from Theory to Software.* A K Peters, Ltd., Wellesley, Massachusetts.

BIOGRAPHY

Hae-Duck Joshua Jeong is currently a PhD student in Computer Science from the University of Canterbury, Christchurch, New Zealand and a student member of IEEE. His research interests are teletraffic modelling in telecommunication networks, stochastic simulation and multimedia.

Don McNickle is a Senior Lecturer in Management Science on the Department of Management, University of Canterbury, New Zealand. His research interests include queueing theory and statistical aspects of simulation. He received a PhD in Mathematics from the University of Auckland, New Zealand. Member of ORSA.

Krzysztof Pawlikowski is an Associate Professor (Reader) in Computer Science at University of Canterbury, Christchurch, New Zealand. He received his PhD degree in Computer Engineering from the Technical University of Gdansk, Poland. The author of over 90 research papers and four books. His research interests include stochastic simulation, distributed processing, ATM, optical and wireless telecommunication networks, and teletraffic modelling. Senior member of IEEE.

SIMULATION OF MOLECULAR PROCESSES USING PETRI NETS: Comparison of Mitosis and Meiosis

Isaac Barjis[1], **Isan Barjis**[2], **Joseph Barjis**[3]

[1,2] *Department of Computer Science, International Center of Information, the Netherlands.*
http://is.twi.tudelft.nl/~barjis/ici.html

[3] *Department of Information Systems & Software Engineering, Delft University of Technology, The Netherlands.*
e-mail: J.Barjis@is.twi.tudelft.nl; http://is.twi.tudelft.nl/~barjis

Keywords: *Mitosis and Meiosis, Molecular processes, Petri net, Discrete simulation*

ABSTRACT

This paper discuses application of Petri nets in biological process. The results reflecting in this paper are part of the ongoing research towards analyzing, modeling and simulating biological and molecular processes using Petri nets. This paper, in particular, shows how mitosis and meiosis and their molecular processes can be modeled and analyzed using Petri nets. Also it shows how the Petri net technique could be used to compare the two biological processes (mitosis and meiosis). In order to construct a Petri net model of mitosis and meiosis and then to use the model in order to compare these two processes, one should know the molecular events and reactions that occur in both processes. So firstly the paper will describe molecular events and reactions that occur through out the process of mitosis and meiosis, and then based on that information a Petri net model is constructed. This model captures all involved molecular events and reactions that occur in the process of mitosis and meiosis.

1. INTRODUCTION

In this paper efforts of authors from two different fields, one from computer science another from biomedical science are put together to study molecular (biological) processes from computing point of view. In its turn it is another one step towards bringing computer science and molecular biology closer and call it bioinformatics.

Bioinformatics is the study of the inherent structure of biological information and biological systems. It brings together the avalanche of systematic biological data (e.g. genomes) with the analytic theory and practical tools of mathematics and computer science. Bioinformatics integrates courses and research in biology (molecular biology) with computer modeling and information sciences (Barjis and Barjis, 1999; Baxevanis and Ouellette, 1998).

This paper includes both biological and analytical approaches towards the comparison of Mitosis and Meiosis.

From the computer science we apply the Petri net modeling technique to model the Mitosis and Meiosis processes. Petri nets are a tool for the study of systems. Petri net theory allows a system to be modeled by a Petri net, a mathematical representation of the system. Analysis of the Petri net can then, reveal important information about the structure and dynamic behavior of the modeled system. This information can then be used to evaluate the modeled system and suggest improvements or changes or simply understand the nature of the system under study (Peterson, 1981). The Petri nets are formalism and a graphical language for the design, specification, simulation and verification of systems (Peterson, 1981; Jensen, 1997). The Petri net structure consists of places and transitions. Corresponding to these, a Petri net graph has two types of nodes. A circle represents a place (states); a rectangle represents a transition (events, activities, actions, operations).

The content of this paper is divided into two sections. In the section two Petri net models of the Mitosis and Meiosis processes and their joint model are introduced. Each Petri net model is provided with thorough description of all reactions and molecular events that occur during the Mitosis and Meiosis processes. Conclusions that are derived from the results of this paper are represented in the conclusion part of this paper. Finally, suggestions for future works are given at the end of this paper.

2. PETRI NET MODELS OF THE MITOSIS AND MEIOSIS

In this section we apply Petri net theory to study and compare the differences in Mitosis and Meiosis. In particular, in the following two subsections, Petri net models will be developed for both Mitosis and Meiosis, and the differences between them will be pointed out in the text and will be shown in the joint Petri net model of the Mitosis and Meiosis. This modeling methodology will be helpful in visualizing, and simulating the process of Mitosis and Meiosis. However, before developing a Petri net model, one should know the molecular events that occur in both, Mitosis and Meiosis. For more complete description look at (Karp, 1996).

2.1. The Mitosis process

Mitosis is the complex process that apportions the new chromosomes equally between daughter cells i.e. it is the way in which most cells divide, so that the chromosomes within the nucleus of the original cell are exactly duplicated into two daughter cells, so we could say that Mitosis is a stage or a process in cellular replication or growth. In both unicellular and multicellular eukaryotes, cellular replication is a cyclical process of growth, mitosis and cytokinesis (cell division/ division of cytoplasmic material). In most cases, the two process are linked with mitosis rapidly followed by cell division. The cycle of growth, mitosis and cell division is called cell cycle, where cell cycle in proliferating somatic cell, consist of two phases: the mitotic phase (called M phase) and the inter phase. Interphase consist of 3 stages: gap 1 (called G1)- which is presynthesis stage and the cell prepares for DNA and Chromosome replication, Synthesis stage (S stage) – where the replication take place, gap 2 (G2)- which is postsynthesis stage and the cell prepares for cell division or the mitosis phase. That is, the precise replication of chromosomes take place in inter phase and then mitosis occurs, resulting in the distribution of a complete chromosome set to each of the progen nuclei. The inter phase can be named as replication process as it is shown in Petri net model of figure 2.1, but we would not concentrate into details of inter phase as the aim is to compare mitosis and meiosis rather then to describe the cell cycle.

The process of mitotic divisions consists of definite sequence of operations, as it will be described later. The mitotic divisions process consist of distinguishable stages, and these are prophase, metaphase, anaphase and telophase. In each of these stages definite molecular events, and sequence of operations occur which will be described in same details and will be shown in detailed Petri net model. However a compact Petri net model is developed in this paper and represented in figure 2.1.

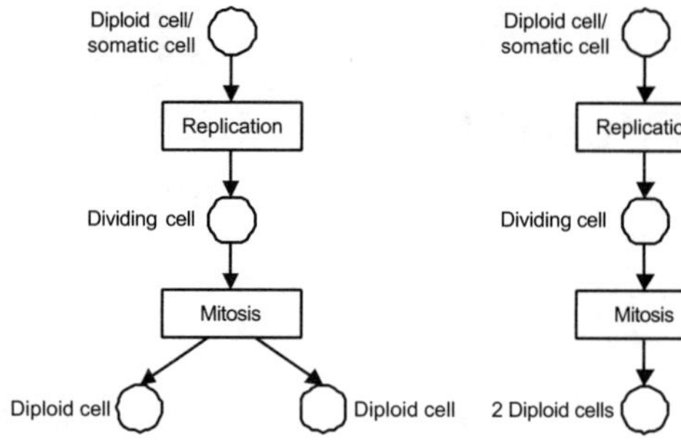

a) b)

Figure 2.1. The Petri net model of the Mitosis process.

The Petri net model of figure 2.1 illustrates that a diploid cell (a cell which has two allels (copies) of each gene) produces two haploid cells after each cycle of mitotic divisions.

This process can be represented by Petri net in two ways. The first way, when two diploid cells are represented as two separate places (see figure 2.1a), the second way, when both diploid cells are represented by one place (see figure 2.1b).

2.2. The Meiosis process

Meiosis is special type of cell division that gives rise to gametes (sperm and egg cells), and it occurs only within the ovaries and testes. In this form of cell division haploid cells (a cell which has only one allele of each gene) are produced from diploid cells. So a pre-mitotic cell is diploid cell, which has two allele of each gene, where each allele is descended from different parents (mother and father), so they are homologus (i.e. their gene are similar but are usually not identical).

Unlike mitosis, meiosis is not responsible for cell proliferation, but it is responsible for sexual reproduction. It occurs in all sexually reproducing eukaryotes, through one round of chromosome replication and two rounds of nuclear division, and produces 4 haploid cell/gamete cells from each diploid cell.

In the first meiotic division the chromosome number is reduced from diploid to haploid, and this process consist of four cytologically distinguishable stages, which are prophase I, metaphase I, anaphase I, and telophase I. The second meiotic division is very similar to a mitotic division, that have been described earlier. This division phase consist of prophase II, metaphase II, anaphase II, and telophase II. This process is modeled by Petri net and depicted in figure 2.2.

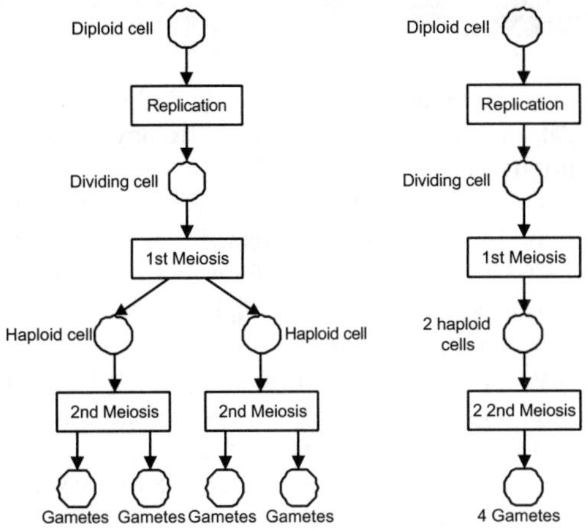

a) b)

Figure 2.2. The Petri net model of the Meiosis process.

The Petri net model of figure 2.2 clearly illustrate that 2 haploid cells are produced in the first meiotic division process, and the second meiotic division process gives rise to 4 gametes (sperm or egg cells).

As in the case with mitosis, this process can be also represented by Petri net in two ways. The first way, when four gametes are represented as four separate places (see figure 2.2a), the second way, when all gametes are represented by one place (see figure 2.2b).

One of the advantageous features of the Petri nets is that Petri nets allow to describe a complex processes in a convenient compact and integrated manner. Especially high level Petri nets (HLPN) such as predicate transition Petri nets and colored Petri nets allow to use one place (or transition) for several parallel or serial states (or activities) distinct by colors or other dates (Jensen, 1997).

2.3. A Petri net model of Mitosis & Meiosis

Since, HLPNs are out of the scope of this paper lets look how a sample place transition Petri net, used in this paper, can model two various processes (mitosis and meiosis) into one joint model. The resulting joint model of mitosis and meiosis is represented in figure 2.3 below.

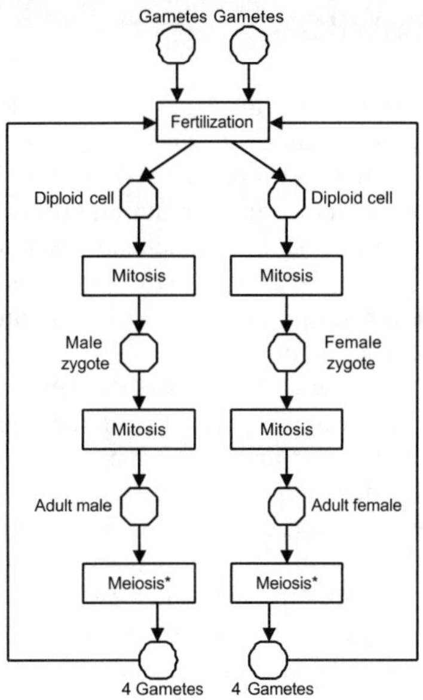

Figure 2.3. The Petri net model of the Mitosis and Meiosis processes (*meiosis occur in sex organs only).

Summarizing the results and purpose of this paper the following outcomes can be drawn.

From the description of the mitosis and meiosis processes the following conclusions can be made. Firstly, the mitosis and meiosis processes are dynamic processes, which change their states after each operation. Secondly, there some random, conditional, and optional processes take place in these processes. In respect to the described peculiarities, inherent to the mitosis and meiosis processes, we consider that Petri nets can more adequately model and formalize most of the molecular processes.

In developing a Petri net model of the molecular processes, we find out operations (in terms of Petri net referred to as events or activities), which take place in these processes, and states, which are reached after each of these operations. In other words we trace the sequence of operations from the beginning to the end.

Having a detailed model of any molecular process in the form of Petri net model, it is easy to analyze and simulate it using common techniques for analyzing and simulating the behavior of Petri nets or other discrete event simulation tools. But it should be noted that there is also an alternative way towards simulation and analysis - programming.

For this alternative way, there should be a procedure how to describe the graphical elements of the designed Petri net models in terms of programming language. Once, all the elements are described e.g. in modular form, a complete program compiled from these modules can be executed (run) in a computer. However, we leave this question for the future research.

3. CONCLUSION

The main purpose of this paper is to develop modeling methodology for the modeling and comparison of mitosis and meiosis using Petri nets. This methodology helps formalization, modeling and simulation of the mitosis and meiosis. Therefore the first conclusion is that dynamic processes of molecular and biological systems in general, the mitosis and meiosis in particular can be modeled as a discrete dynamic system.

Two areas can benefit from such a methodology that has been presented in this paper: to stimulate research and to assist teaching. For the teaching purposes, this model would help educational institutions in teaching the process of meiosis and mitosis. It would help students to see this process visually, and understand it better. It would help to follow the molecular events and reactions that occur through out the process of meiosis and mitosis. The model will help to visualize and see the differences between the two processes by the movement of tokens of the Petri nets from state to state, and explain how molecular events, reactions and operations together provide these process to occur. It would help to visualize the actual biological process and see how the substrates and precursors bind or disassociate in order to complete the process of meiosis and mitosis. This paper can be also useful for the training program offering molecular biology with modeling and information sciences integrated into the individual courses, to train students in the use of computational techniques in the study of molecular and biological processes (systems).

For the research purposes, one can use this methodology for the mitosis and meiosis modeling and simulation. Finally, it seems that the results of this paper are one of the first efforts to apply discrete systems modeling technique such as Petri net to molecular-biology processes. In its turn it is another one step towards bringing computer science and molecular biology closer and call it bioinformatics.

4. FUTURE RESEARCH

As a future research it is planed to investigate an appropriate tool for analyzing and simulating the developed models, and study how Colored Petri nets (Jensen, 1997) can be applied for more complex biological (molecular) processes. Colored Petri nets have a considerable advantage when dealing with complex processes. It is also planned to develop hierarchical Petri net models of various biological processes.

REFERENCE

Alberts, B., Bray, D., Lewis, J., Raff, M., Roberts, K., and Watson,J.D., 1994. Molecular Biology of the Cell, (3rd edition). Garland.

Barjis, J.; Barjis, I. Formalization of the Protein Production by means of Petri Nets. In the proceedings of the IEEE International Conference on Information, Intelligence and Systems (Symposia) November 1-3, 1999, Washington, DC, pp. 4-9.

Baxevanis, A. D. and Ouellette, B.F.F., 1998. Bioinformatics - A Practical Guide to the Analysis of Gene and Proteins, John Wiley.

Hawkins, J.D., 1997. Gene Structure and Expression. Cambridge University Press.

Jensen, Kurt, 1997. Colored Petri nets. Basic Concepts, Analysis Methods and Practical Use, Volume I. Springer-Verslag.

Karp, G. 1996. Cell and Molecular Biology. Wiley

Peterson, James L., 1981. Petri net theory and the modeling of systems. Prentice-Hall, Inc., Englewood Cliffs, NJ.

Stryer,L., 1995. Biochemistry, (4th edition). Freeman, USA.

ABOUT AUTHORS:

Isaac Barjis /Ph.D. student/ Diploma (degree) in medicine from Russia, B.Sc. in Biomedical Sciences and Nutrition from London, UK). He worked or works in Russia, UK and the Netherlands. From 1998 he started work with the International Center of Information, headquartered in the Netherlands, as a scientific manager and had many achievements, and been awarded by the Center for his achievements.

Isan Barjis /Ph.D. student/. He works in the Netherlands. From 1998 he started work with the International Center of Information, headquartered in the Netherlands, as a scientific researcher.

Joseph Barjis /Ph.D., Associate Academician of the International Informatization Academy, Chairman of the International Center of Information, headquartered in the Netherlands/ MSc. in Computer Science in 1991; Ph.D. in Computer Science in 1996; Ph.D. in Information Systems in 1999. He worked or works in: Russia, United Kingdom and the Netherlands. Currently he works as a senior researcher in the department of Information Systems & Software Engineering at Delft University of Technology.

PARTIAL FUZZYFICATION OF HYBRID TIME-DISCRETE COMPARTMENT MODEL OF PARACETAMOL

Aleš Belič, Rihard Karba, *Iztok Grabnar, *Aleš Mrhar
Faculty of Electrical Engineering
Tržaška 25
*Faculty of Pharmacy
Aškerčeva 7
University of Ljubljana, 1000 Ljubljana, Slovenia
ales.belic@fe.uni-lj.si

Keywords: Dynamic models, Compartmental models, Pharmacokinetics, Optimization, Fuzzy models.

ABSTRACT

Modelling of biological systems is often problematic. The lack of measurements and theoretical knowledge of the processes is the main problem. Limitations of theoretical knowledge have significant influence on model structure whereas the lack of measurements affects model parameter estimation procedures. The combination of both limitations can result in unreliable models. However, a lot of knowledge exists in form of various "recipes" that are also called expert knowledge, which are very awkward to implement in conventional modelling. Paracetamol is an antipiretic and analgesic drug, available as tablets, syrup and suppositories. The modelling aim was to characterize differences in bioavailability of two suppositories, fast and slow drug-releasing. Differences are supposed to occur because of different pathways of absorption in rectum for the two formulations. Each mechanism was known, however, they were not investigated systematically. The measurements were carried out on four healthy volunteers. Plasma levels of paracetamol were measured, at the same time urine was collected and analysed for paracetamol and its metabolites. Compartment modelling was chosen because of its transparent structural relation to the real system. The model parameters were estimated with Genetic algorithm.

Partial fuzzyfication allowed successful combination of expert knowledge and measurements. Furthermore, the particular knowledge of processes involved in rectal absorption of paracetamol was systematically included in the model and the reasons for different bioavailability of the two formulations were elucidated.

INTRODUCTION

Many simulation problems arise from hybrid discrete-continuous models. Special integration methods with ability to detect discrete changes of values in the model are needed for reliable simulation runs. On the other hand, discrete changes are not very likely to occur in biological systems. Therefore it is sensible to avoid time discrete simplifications in the model if it does not add unnecessary complexity to the model, concerning the modelling objective.

Paracetamol is an antipiretic and analgesic drug, available as tablets, syrup and suppositories. The modelling aim was to characterize differences in bioavailabilities of two suppositories, fast and slow drug-releasing (Chicco et al. 1999). Differences are supposed to occur because of different pathways of absorption in rectum of both formulations, however, the relation cannot be modelled with linear model. The measurements were carried out on four healthy volunteers. Plasma levels of paracetamol were measured. At the same time urine was collected and analysed for paracetamol and its metabolites. Compartment model (Godfrey 1983; Wagner 1993) was chosen because of a transparent structural relation to the real system. Absorption mechanism from rectum was treated as sub-model. Model parameters were estimated by simultaneously fitting the adaptive model responses to the three measured time courses. Genetic algorithms were used as optimization routine because of number of parameters to be set (Belič et al. 2000). Sub-model with time-discrete changes of absorption rate was chosen, to get as simple and as transparent as possible sub-model. However, to achieve acceptable fit to the measured data absorption rate had to be changed at least three times during a simulation of one dose kinetics. Moreover, time courses of discrete changes of absorption showed no resemblance between the subjects for the same suppository formulation and no pattern between different suppository formulations in the same subject. Since the model was not uniquely identifiable, parameter estimation procedure was repeated several times, but no pattern could be found among the results. Therefore, absorption sub-model was designed as fuzzy sub-model. Since it was clear from the literature that absorption in rectum is time-variable process, the observation interval was divided between four fuzzy sets named pre-absorption phase, transition from pre to main absorption phase, main absorption phase, and terminal absorption phase. Gaussian membership functions were chosen because they provide smoother time course and because they can be explained as probability densities of responding parameter values. Singletons were used as output functions, representing absorption rate in the responding absorption phase. Parameters of fuzzy sub-model were estimated together with the rest of model parameters.

GENETIC ALGORITHMS (GA)

Basic idea of GA is to search for optimal solution by applying natural laws of genetics and evolution. Different GAs have been proposed and tested in the literature, each being optimal for a given problem. However, there was no universal solution for all optimization problems and very likely never will be. In the frame of this work two GAs have been tested (Belič et al. 2000); simple GA (Goldberg 1989; Gen and Cheng 1997) and parallel GA (Levine 1994). It has been known (Levine 1994) that larger populations of problem solutions are not always better in problem space exploration. It is suspected that best genetic material e.g. parameter set, prevails too slowly over less successful subjects than in smaller populations. Therefore, the convergence of algorithm is much slower and results are usually away from optimum. On the other hand, parallel algorithm divides the whole population into smaller subpopulations. That enables faster convergence of the solution in subpopulations. At the same time algorithm explores the problem space better, since each subpopulation usually distributes over different part of problem space. Migrations of subjects between subpopulations take place at regular intervals. This model is much closer to natural evolution of species and also works considerably better in problem space exploration.

Important stage in each modelling cycle (Matko et al. 1992; Cellier 1991) is model parameter estimation. If the model structure is derived from physiological characteristics it is usually non-identifiable and unique solution of the problem does not exist. However, sometimes it is sufficient to find an acceptable solution in the set of solutions. That requires a method that is not very exact but can explore large parameter spaces in relatively short time. GAs represent a successful compromise between stochastic and deterministic search algorithms. By balancing stochastic and deterministic component of the algorithm, convergence speed can be set to achieve the desired effect. When searching in large parameter spaces and when exact solution is not very important, stochastic component must prevail over deterministic one. That is just what the modelling in Pharmacokinetics and Pharmacodynamics (PK-PD) requires.

MODELLING

Compartment models were used because of transparent structural relation to the system. As the absorption mechanism showed time-varying character, it was modelled with time-varying rate constants. Absorption rate constants were described with step functions, therefore, the model remained piece-wise linear. With this model acceptable fit to the measurements was achieved, however, the model provided no additional information from systemic point of view. Therefore, absorption was modelled with fuzzy sets.

Discrete Time-Varying Compartment model

Modelling began with linear compartment model based on physiological background of the drug (Figure 1). However,

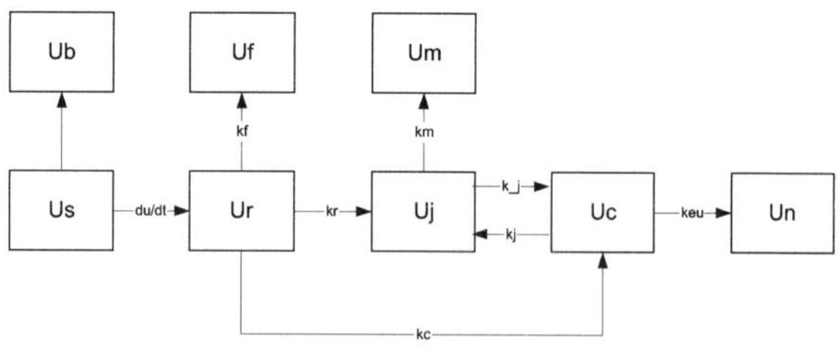

Figure 1: Linear compartment model of paracetamol pharmacokinetics. Labels have the following meaning: Ub - cumulative compartment of suppository, Us - suppository compartment, Uf - faeces compartment, Ur - rectal compartment, Uj - liver compartment, Um - metabolites compartment, Uc - central compartment, Un - unchanged paracetamol compartment, kf - transfer speed to faeces compartment, kr - transfer speed from rectal to liver compartment, kc - transfer speed from rectal to central compartment, km - speed of metabolism in liver compartment, k_j, kj transfer speed from liver to central compartment and vice versa, keu - elimination from central compartment.

it was not possible to explain the data with this model satisfactorily. Therefore certain changes had to be made to the model structure (Figure 2). Absorption mechanism from rectum was treated as sub-model. Sub-model with time-discrete changes of absorption rate was chosen, to get as simple and as transparent as possible sub-model. To achieve acceptable fit to

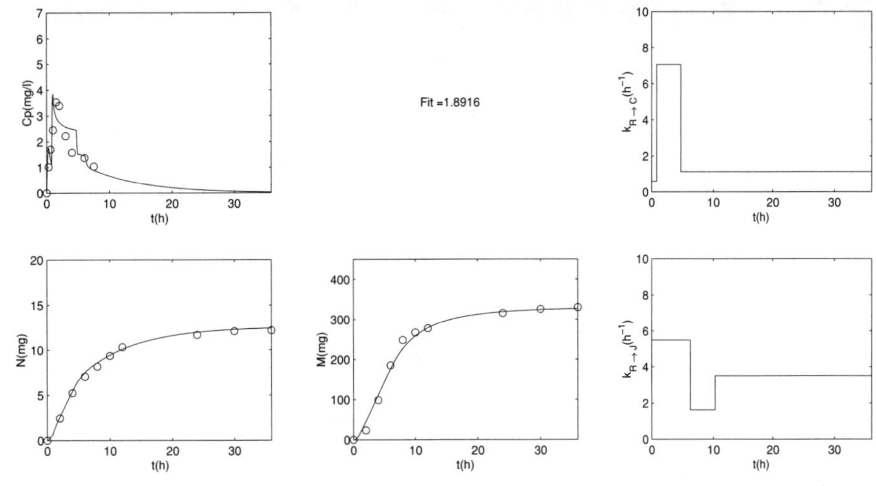

Figure 3: Response of the discrete time-varying model in comparison to measured data for fast formulation. Plasma concentrations - upper left-hand corner, unchanged paracetamol in urine - lower left-hand corner, metabolites in urine - middle, time course of transfer speed from rectal to central compartment - upper right-hand corner, time course of transfer speed from rectal to liver compartment - lower right-hand corner, Fit - the value of fit function.

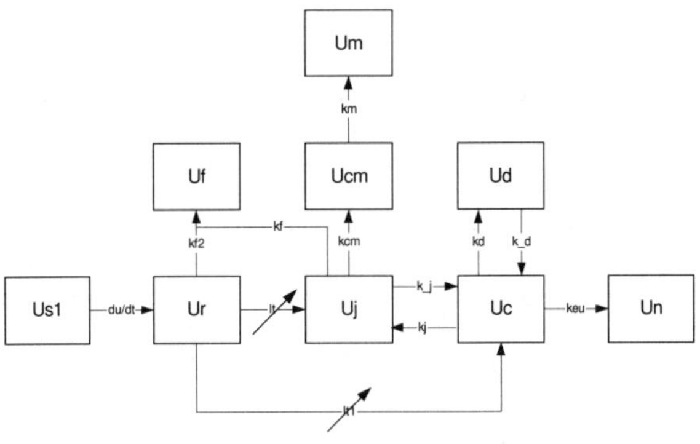

Figure 2: Time-varying compartment model of paracetamol pharmacokinetics. Additional labels have the following meaning: Ucm - central compartment for metabolites, Ud - periferal compartment, kf - transfer speed from liver to faeces compartment, It - time-varying transfer speed from rectal to liver compartment, It1 - time-varying transfer speed from rectal to central compartment, km - speed of metabolites elimination, kd, k_d - transfer speed from central to periferal compartment and vice versa.

the measured data absorption rate had to be changed at least three times during a simulation of one dose kinetics (Figure 3). However, time courses of discrete changes of absorption showed no pattern between the subjects for the same suppository formulation and no pattern between different suppository formulations in the same subject. Since the model was not uniquely identifiable, parameter estimation procedure was repeated several times, and again no pattern could be found among these results.

Partial Fuzzyfication of the Model

Absorption sub-model was redesigned to fuzzy sub-model. Since it was clear from the literature that absorption in rectum is time-variable process, the observation interval was divided on four fuzzy sets named pre-absorption phase, transition from pre to main absorption phase, main absorption phase, and terminal absorption phase. Gaussian membership functions were chosen because they provide smoother time course and because they can be explained as probability densities of responding parameter values (Figure 4). Singletons were used as output functions, representing absorption rate in the responding absorption phase. Parameters of fuzzy sub-model were estimated together with the rest of model parameters. Smoother time course of model responses was, however, not the main contribution of the fuzzy sub-model (Figure 5). Pattern in time course of the absorption could now be seen. The pattern was even more obvious when observing positions of membership functions and their responding output functions (Figures 6 and 7).

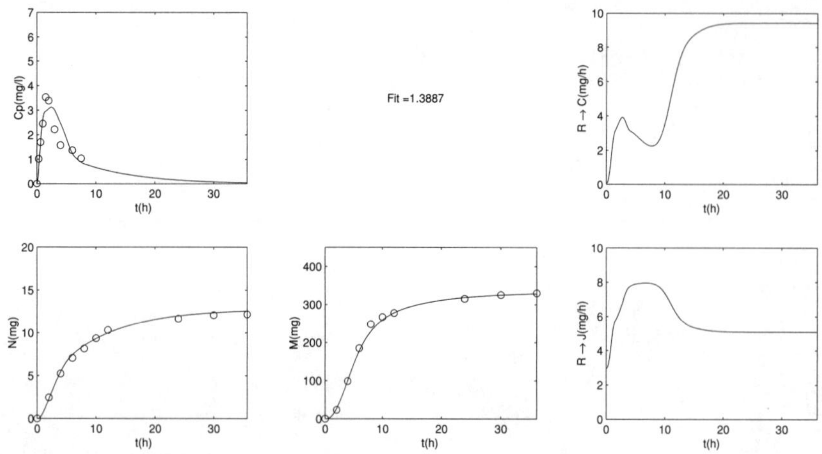

Figure 5: Response of the fuzzy time-varying compartment model in comparison to measured data for fast formulation. Plasma concentrations - upper left-hand corner, unchanged paracetamol in urine - lower left-hand corner, metabolites in urine - middle, time course of transfer speed from rectal to central compartment - upper right-hand corner, time course of transfer speed from rectal to liver compartment - lower right-hand corner, Fit - the value of fit function.

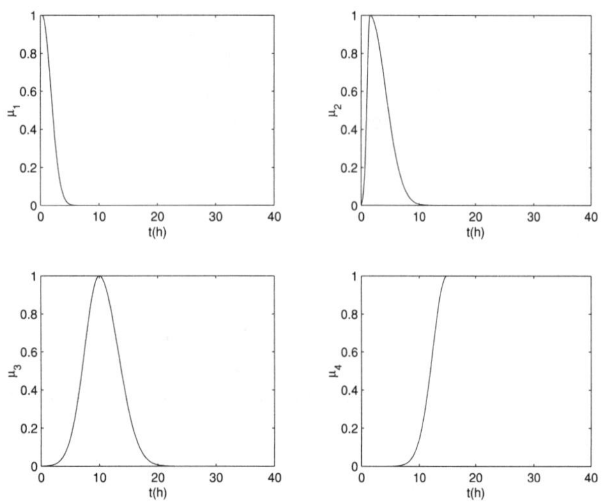

Figure 4: Membership functions for absorption fuzzy sub-model.

SUMMARY

Let us summarize as follows:

- The processes involved in paracetamol absorption are known, however, their combined effect on the absorption was not yet investigated.
- Partially fuzzyfied model was developed to systemically elucidate the processes involved in paracetamol rectal absorption.
- Membership functions of absorption sub-model correspond with phases of absorption found in the literature (Chicco et al. 1999).
- Output functions describe the importance of absorption phases.
- The model can systemically explain the reasons for different bioavailability of the two formulations.
- Expert knowledge and measured data were successfully combined.
- Genetic algorithms represent successful tool for estimation of model parameters for non-identifiable models.
- Larger portion of drug is available to the organism from slow formulation than from fast formulation, because the absorption directly to central compartment is faster, which reduces first-pass effect in the liver and herewith the loss of active substance.

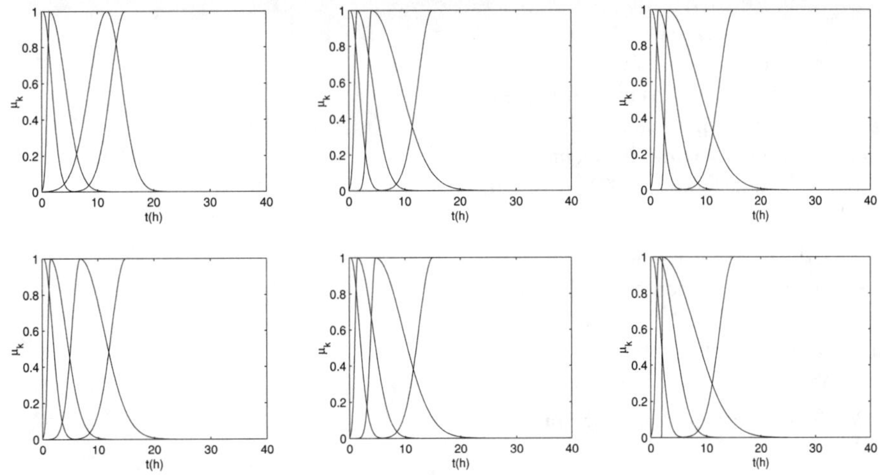

Figure 6: Membership functions for three sets of "optimal" model parameters for subject G, above - fast formulation, below - slow formulation.

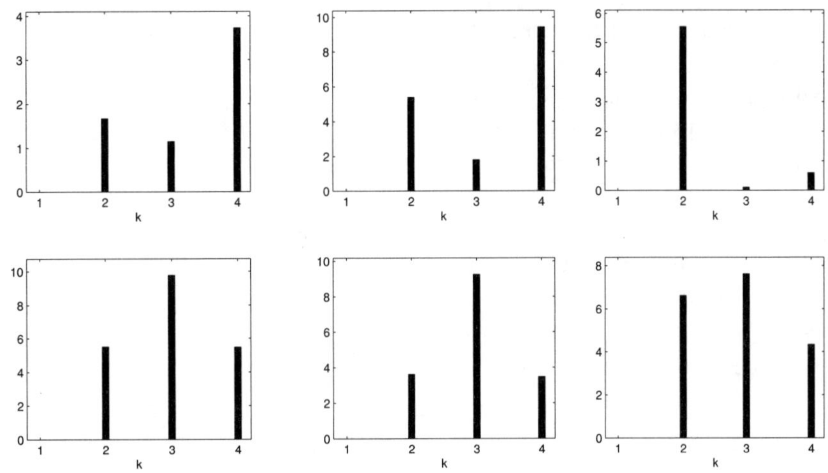

Figure 7: Output functions for three sets of "optimal" model parameters for subject G, above - fast formulation, below - slow formulation.

REFERENCES

Belič, A.; R. Karba; I. Grabnar; A. Mrhar; and D. Andrejič. 2000. "The role of Genetic Algorithms in Pharmacokinetic - Pharmacodynamic Modelling and Evaluation. " In *3rd Mathmod Proceedings*, Volume 2, (Vienna University of Technology, February 2-4, 2000), Argesim, Vienna, Austria, 587–590.

Belič, A.; R. Karba; I. Grabnar; A. Mrhar; and B. Potočnik. 2000. "Expert Knowledge Inclusion in Pharmacokinetical Models. " In *3rd Mathmod Proceedings*, Volume 2, (Vienna University of Technology, February 2-4, 2000), Argesim, Vienna, Austria, 583–586.

Cellier, F. E. 1991. *Continuous System Modelling* Springer-Verlag, New York.

Chicco, D.; I. Grabnar; A. Škerjanec; D. Vojnovic; V. Maurich; N. Realdon; E. Ragazzi; A. Belič; R. Karba; and A. Mrhar. 1999. "Correlation of in vitro and in vivo paracetamol availability from layered excipient suppositories. " *International Journal of Pharmaceutics* NO. 189(2): 147–160.

Gen, M. and R. Cheng. 1997. *Genetic Algorithms & Engineering Design* John Wiley & sons, inc., New York.

Godfrey, K. 1983. *Compartmental Models and Their Application* Academic Press, London.

Goldberg, D. E. 1989. *Genetic Algorithms in Search, Optimization, and Machine Learning* Addison Wesley Publishing Company, New York.

Levine, D. 1994. "A Parallel Genetic Algorithm for the set Partitioning Problem. " Doktorska disertacija ANL 94/23, Argonne National Laboratory, Argonne, IL, USA.

Matko, D.; R. Karba; and B. Zupančič. 1992. *Simulation and Modelling of Continuous Systems: A Case Study Approach* Prentice Hall, New York.

Wagner, J. G. 1993. *Pharmacokinetics for the Pharmaceutical Scientist* Technomic Publishing inc., Lancaster.

AN EVALUATION FRAMEWORK TO SUPPORT ACCURACY ANALYSIS OF COMPUTER ASSISTED SURGERY SYSTEMS

Warren J. Viant
Dept. of Computer Science
University of Hull
Hull, HU6 7RX, UK
e-mail: w.j.viant@dcs.hull.ac.uk

Keywords: Computer-assisted surgery, Model analysis, Validation, and Statistical analysis.

ABSTRACT

This paper describes the development of a novel evaluation framework for the characterisation of the accuracy within a complex real-time system. The framework diagrammatically describes the registration process and simulates the error propagation chain based on the principle that errors can be described through the use of a normal distribution model.

BACKGROUND

The development of prototype Computer-Assisted Surgery (CAS) systems is increasing. A direct consequence is a requirement for an objective method to quantitatively assess CAS performance for implant placement during development and before the commencement of clinical trials (Viant et al. 1999). Lea (Lea et al. 1995) introduced a diagrammatic notation, the Lea diagram, for describing registration strategies. The notation uses a graph-theoretic framework to visually describe the registration connectivity between system components. Two main elements exist within the notation: the node, representing either physical or abstract objects; and links, representing actions. Lea states that although this diagrammatic technique provides a good representation of the registration problem it does not provide any indication of the system accuracy.

AN EVALUATION FRAMEWORK

The evaluation framework takes the main components of the Lea diagram, namely the node and the link, and expands and augments them with a normal distribution error model supported by a set of computer simulations. Templates have been developed enabling rapid decomposition of a registration problem into a framework compatible form. The templates are linked with a set of generic and application specific error models. Figure 1 illustrates an evaluation framework of a Passive Arm, a typical CAS subsystem. The Passive Arm includes three components represented by nodes on the diagram: IRED, an array of infrared diodes; Cannula socket, a tube for the support of a surgical cannula; and a Spider, a local co-ordinate system. Two measurement devices are also represented: Co-ordinate Measurement Machine (CMM); and Optical Position Localiser (OPL). The purpose of the CMM is to calibrate the Passive Arm. The purpose of the OPL is to provide real-time tracking of the IRED array on the Passive Arm and hence the position of the surgical cannula.

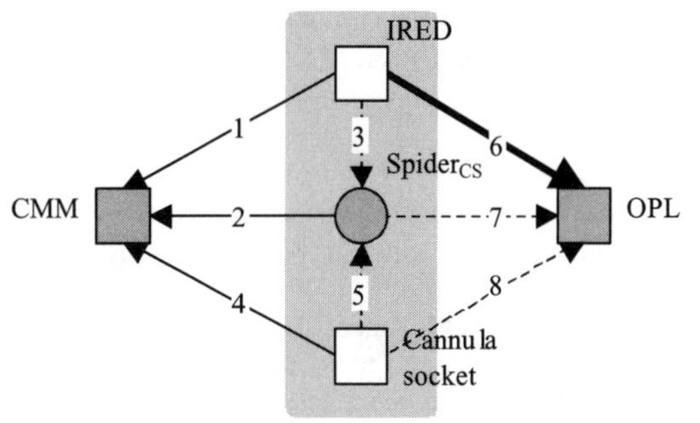

Figure 1. An evaluation framework of a Passive Arm

Label	Feature accuracy	Co-ordinate System accuracy	Operation / Description
1	N(0.000, 0.017^2)	N(0.000, 0.000^2)	*Measure* IRED
2	N(0.000, 0.012^2)	N(0.000, 0.006^2)	*Measure* Spider$_{CS}$
3	N(0.001, 0.017^2)	N(0.001, 0.002^2)	*Transform* to Spider$_{CS}$
4	N(0.000, 0.015^2)	N(0.000, 0.000^2)	*Measure* Cannula socket
5	N(0.007, 0.016^2)	N(0.007, 0.003^2)	*Transform* to Spider$_{CS}$
6	N(0.000, 0.416^2)	N(0.000, 0.000^2)	*Measure* IRED
7	N(0.030, 0.296^2)	N(0.296, 0.164^2)	*Register* Spider$_{CS}$ to OPL$_{CS}$
8	N(0.168, 0.085^2)	N(4.945, 0.083^2)	*Transform* to OPL$_{CS}$

Table 1. Description of the links in an evaluation framework of a Passive Arm

Table 1 contains the related normal distribution modelling information and other link properties, associated with Figure 1. Labels on the links within the diagram provide a one to one mapping with rows in the table. Feature and co-ordinate system accuracy figures are generated by the underlying computer simulation and summarised as mean and standard deviation values. The final registration error is available in row 8 of Table 1.

Nodes

The Lea diagram introduced the concept of a node to represent key features within the registration strategy. Nodes that exist on the same physical superstructure are represented in the original Lea diagram as a *motion group,* presented as a rounded box. Nodes within a motion group are constrained to maintain a constant spatial relationship with all other nodes in the group. The evaluation framework extends the node concept to include:

Abstract node (circle): Abstract concept or non-physical features e.g. the surgical plan.

Co-ordinate system node (shaded circle): A refinement of the abstract node, an arbitrary location in space defined by a co-ordinate frame. This node has one set of normal distribution error models per attached measurement link. Each error model is relative to the node at the other end of the associated measurement link e.g. $Spider_{CS}$.

Physical node (square): Physical feature involved in the registration strategy e.g. IREDs.

Measurement node (shaded square): A refinement of the physical node and represents the class of physical objects that are capable of measurement e.g. CMM or OPL. This node contains an implicit co-ordinate system.

The rationale behind the node extension is threefold. A distinction at the node level aids in the normal distribution modelling, by both simplifying the concepts and increasing clarity. The node extension is a prerequisite of the error model templates, the building blocks of the normal distribution model. Diagrammatic clarity is improved with the distinction between physical and abstract objects.

Links

The original Lea diagram introduced links to connect nodes. Lea states "Links represent the act of measurement which establishes a known spatial relationship between the objects represented by the two nodes" (Lea et al. 1995). The link does not represent the actual spatial relationship, as two objects may be spatially related even though a link has not established the fact.

To capture the dynamic aspects of registration Lea introduced the concept of an *event* and the *induced link.* When objects move relative to one another, measurements (links) that were previously valid become invalid. An event is used to tag all the links that simultaneously become invalid. Events are presented as numeric values on the links (in the augmented diagram they have been moved to the table). For clarity, links that never become invalid, i.e. links between nodes in the same motion group, are not tagged. The induced link represents a spatial relationship between two nodes that is derived from an indirect connection of links via a common third node. The induced link can only be derived if the indirect connection of links to the third node is tagged with the same event or all three nodes belong to the same motion group. The induced link is considered persistence and is presented as a dotted line.

The temporal aspects of links can also be represented in the original Lea diagram with the *transient* or *sustained link.* The transient link represents a discrete measurement operation between two nodes, presented as a thin solid line e.g. link between the CMM and cannula socket node. The sustained link represents a continuous measurement operation between two nodes, presented as a thick solid line e.g. link between the OPL and the IRED nodes.

It is within the link structures that the distinction between the original and augmented Lea diagrams becomes evident. The augmented Lea diagram makes a stronger distinction between types of link than the original. The types of link are associated to a specific normal distribution simulation. The following list of link types is not exclusive but is extendible, dependant on the nature of the registration strategy being evaluated. Currently the link types include: measurement, transformation, registration and reconstruction. The original Lea diagram presented the link as a straight line, of varying widths and styles, joining two nodes. This representation is maintained along with representation of transient, sustained and induced links. Links in the augmented Lea diagram are mapped to rows in an associated table by numeric labels. The event tags are also moved to the table. These decisions were taken so as maintain the clarity of the original diagram.

Links in the augmented Lea diagram are directional, with an arrow indicating the sense. Traversal of the link in the direction of the arrow is a forward traversal and against the arrow is an inverse traversal.

Problem representation

The basic registration problem illustrated in Figure 1 contains: a measurement node, the CMM; a physical node, the IRED array; and a co-ordinate system node, the Spider local co-ordinate system. The local co-ordinate system on the Spider is based around a set of physical features, which in this case can be measured by the CMM. Both the IRED array and the Spider co-ordinate system belong to the same motion group, represented by the rounded box, and hence have a fixed spatial relationship. Table 1 contains the accuracy with which the CMM can measure the two nodes attached to links 1 and 2, along with an event tag and temporal key. The simulator, using the accuracy measurement from link 2 as input data, calculates the error propagation to the co-ordinate system. A co-ordinate system has one set of normal distribution error models per measurement link connected to the node. Each error model is relative to the node at the other end of the associated measurement link.

The normal distribution error model provides accuracy information for each link within the augmented Lea diagram. This information enables an understanding the error propagation and resultant accuracy of a CAS system. Once the Lea diagram is completed, the normal distribution error models are added to the table in a two-stage process. A normal distribution error model is created for each measurement link within the diagram. The values for the statistical model are derived from manufacture's equipment specifications, through experimentation or through simulation. If measurement links exist between co-ordinate system nodes and measurement nodes, then the error propagation model for the co-ordinate system is also generated. In Table 1 the normal distribution models are added for the measurement by the CMM of the IRED array and the Spider co-ordinate system features. The error propagation model for the Spider co-ordinate system is also generated. An iterative error propagation cycle ensures that all remaining induced links are modelled. The sequence of this iteration follows the order of the event tags in the Lea diagram.

To capture the essential functionality of a system, careful thought has to be given to how the individual error models are constructed and how they interact. The implementation of the error model calculation is therefore specific to a particular application. For example, decisions have to be taken as to which, if any, features are to be considered reference features with zero error. This depth of knowledge is only available on an application-by-application basis. There are however many similarities in the implementation of the error models. These similarities are explored later in this paper, where a number of error model templates are developed. The aim of the templates is to provide both a basis for error model development and to provide examples of the logic behind the development of the error models.

Connectivity

Lea made some observations concerning the connectivity of nodes in the original diagram.

Basic connectivity: Registration requires that there exist a simultaneous connected sub graph containing the plan, the involved anatomy and the tool.

Control connectivity: Control requires that the robot (or other active positioning device) must also be a part of the simultaneous connected sub graph

Sustained connectivity: Continuous registration despite tool motion and patient motion requires that the simultaneous connected sub graph consist entirely of sustained and induced links.

A fourth observation concerning the connectivity can now be added.

Error model connectivity: Error propagation requires that there exists a connected sub graph for the purpose of fulfilling basic, control and sustained connectivity such that all links contain an error propagation model.

If the fourth observation holds then the augmented Lea diagram as part of the evaluation framework is capable of generating an error model for any CAS system.

Graph reduction

Lea states that "Nodes connected by untagged sustained or induced links may be collapsed into one node". This condition for graph reduction still holds with the inclusion of the error model. Graph reduction is to be encouraged for large simulations, provided that the reduced components are expanded in an additional diagram elsewhere.

PATTERNS WITHIN THE FRAMEWORK

The template approach is based on the premise that an evaluation framework for a CAS system contains a number of recurring patterns within the node and link structure. Identification of these patterns permits a logical decomposition of the problem into a number of sub-problems. Each sub-problem can be mapped directly onto an existing error model template. This process both decreases the time required to develop a framework and reduces the possibility of introducing errors during model creation. The use of templates during framework development is analogous to using an existing class hierarchy within a software development process. The templates detailed in this paper are sufficient to describe the general registration problem and more specific x-ray registration problems. If a sub-problem does not map directly to an existing template, then a new specialised template can be created e.g. x-ray source reconstruction.

Template preliminaries

In Figure 2, node A is connected to node B via a link directed towards B. This link establishes the spatial relationship between nodes A and B. Mathematically this relationship is defined as:

$$B = RA + t$$

Where R is a 3x3 rotation matrix and t a translation vector defining the transformation between the co-ordinate system local to A and the co-ordinate system inherent to B.

A convention in the augmented Lea diagram is that all links are directed towards a co-ordinate system, either explicit or implicit. In Figure 2 the link is directed towards the measurement node B, as this node type contains and implicit co-ordinate system. When a link exists between two co-ordinate system nodes, the direction of the link is unconstrained. This convention ensures that the direct connection of nodes that are not co-ordinate systems is prohibited and consistency is maintained across evaluation frameworks. The co-ordinate system nodes and the measurement nodes are fully interchangeable in all of the model templates, as are the abstract and physical nodes.

Generic templates have been developed for error propagation, transformation, registration and co-ordinate system transformation. Application specific templates have been developed for x-ray projection, x-ray source reconstruction and x-ray target reconstruction application.

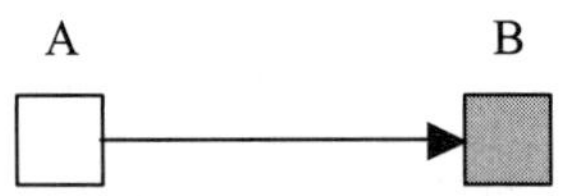

Figure 2. A link between a physical node A and a measurement node B.

Transformation template

The error transformation template represents the process by which the positional accuracy of a node can be transformed to an alternative co-ordinate system. The prerequisites are the positional accuracy of the node in the existing co-ordinate system and the transformation error between the existing and alternative co-ordinate systems. In Figure 3, A is the feature whose positional accuracy is to be transformed from co-ordinate system B to co-ordinate system C. Two variants of the error transformation template are required to fully describe the transformation process. The difference between type 1 and type 2 is the direction of the transformation link between nodes B and C.

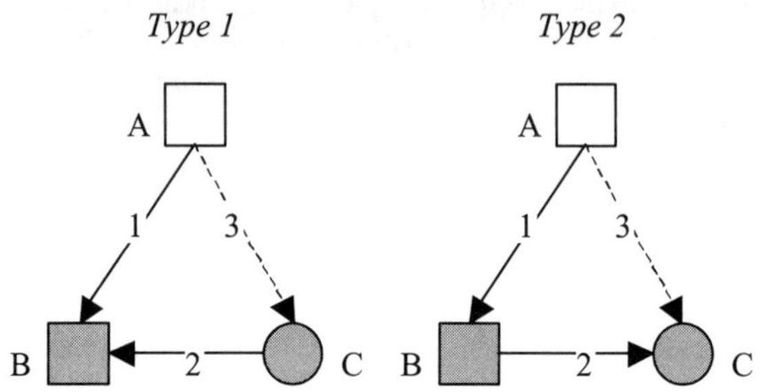

Figure 3. Transformation template

SIMLULATION STATES

The error templates provide the flow of control for the evaluation framework simulation. The templates are derived from a direct mapping of the nodes and links, following system decomposition. The static and dynamic behaviour of the simulation is determined by a set of states associated with each link and node. Many of these states will be initially undefined. Upon successful completion of the simulation all states should be fully defined.

Link States

The state of the each link comprises three independent components.

Positional accuracy of the feature. The positional error with which a feature's position can be determined is represented with a 3D normal distribution model.

Transformation error incurred when traversing the link. The transformation modelling method detailed later in the paper is adopted for the representation of the transformation error when traversing a link. In summary, three 3D normal distribution models are used to model the effect of rotation about the three orthogonal axes located at the centre of gravity of the feature. Translation is modelled independently to rotation. The models are duplicated to enable inverse traversal of the link. Representation of the transformation error as a rotation about an arbitrary axis is also included. This model, redundant in terms of the simulation is used to reduce the complexity of the transformation models summarised above to provide a simplified form for output in a summary table

Transformation represented by the link. Accurate simulation of a system is dependent on defining the working volume of all components. For example, it is not possible to precisely model the accuracy during x-ray registration, if the working volume of the components is unknown. The normal distribution model is also employed in a secondary role as a random generator of transformations constrained by the working volume. A 4D normal distribution model represents an arbitrary axis and angle of rotation. A 3D normal distribution model represents the translation. The use of the normal distribution model for transformation generation provides an elegant solution to the problem of feature position determination. Each feature is ensured a randomly distributed placement across their defined working volumes.

Node States

The node states comprise only the geometric configuration of the represented features. For example, the node state associated with the IRED node in Figure 1, is defined as a set of 3D co-ordinates that describe the configuration of the IREDs within the IRED array. The co-ordinates are relative to a local co-ordinate system.

Simulation States

The simulation state comprises the number of iterations and the datum distance used to evaluate the co-ordinate system errors following a successful simulation.

TRANSFORMATION ERROR SIMULATION

The transformation template represents the process by which the positional accuracy of a feature A can be transformed from one co-ordinate system B to a second co-ordinate system C, given the positional accuracy of the feature in the first co-ordinate system and the error propagation between the two co-ordinate systems. The process is represented on the augmented Lea diagram as a transformation link between the feature and the second co-ordinate system.

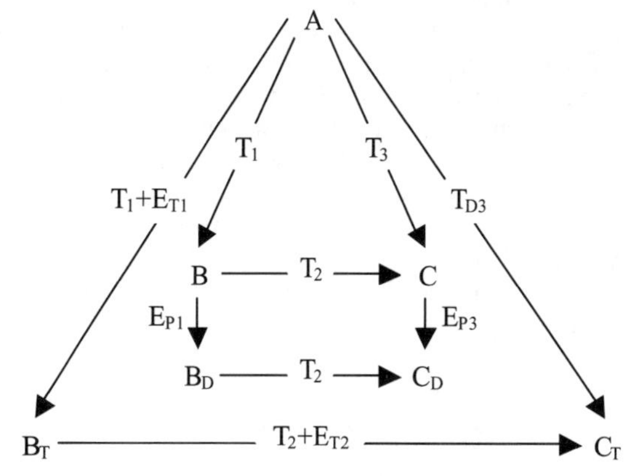

Figure 4 Simulation of transformation type 1 error

The simulation of the type 1 transformation error is illustrated in Figure 4. Type 2 transformation errors differ only in the transformation process between co-ordinate systems B and C.

A, perfect geometry of the feature A.
T_1, transformation that maps feature A's local co-ordinate system onto co-ordinate system B
E_{T1}, induced error from traversal of link between A's local co-ordinate system and co-ordinate system B.
E_{P1}, accuracy with which the position of the feature A is known relative to co-ordinate system B.
B, geometry of A, transformed error free by T_1 to co-ordinate system B.
B_D, geometry of B, when perturbed by positional accuracy E_{P1}.
B_T, geometry of A, transformed by T_1 with traversal error E_{T1} to co-ordinate system B.
T_2, transformation that maps co-ordinate system B onto co-ordinate system C
E_{T2}, induced error from traversal of link between co-ordinate systems B and C.
C, geometry of B, transformed error free by T_2 to co-ordinate system C.
C_D, geometry of B_D transformed error free by T_2 to co-ordinate system C.
C_T, geometry of B_T, transformed by T_2 with traversal error E_{T2} to co-ordinate system C.
E_{P3}, accuracy with which the position of the feature A is known relative to co-ordinate system C, obtained through comparison of C and C_D.
T_3, transformation that maps A to C, obtained through registration.
T_{D3}, transformation that maps feature A to C_T, obtained through registration.
E_{T3}, induced error from traversal of link between A's local co-ordinate system and co-ordinate system C, obtained through comparison of T_3 and T_{D3}.

An example of transform error between two co-ordinate systems can be found on link 3 of Figure 1 and Table 1. In this example the error model for the IRED array is to be transformed from the CMM co-ordinate system to the Spider's co-ordinate system. The creation of this transformation link (link 3) is possible because an alternative route exists between the IRED node and the Spider co-ordinate system node via the CMM node. Comparison of this link geometry with the framework patterns reveals that link 3 can be simulated with a type-1 transformation template. The modelled accuracy with which the IRED array can be measured by the CMM, and the error propagation for the Spider co-ordinate system can be found in the Table 1.

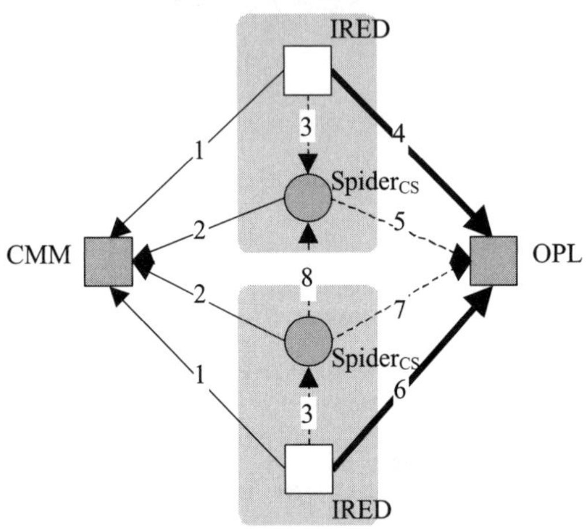

Figure 5. An augmented LEA diagram of a Passive Arm calibration experiment

VALIDATION OF THE FRAMEWORK

The validation strategy for the framework is based on the premise that the process of registration is sufficiently complex as to require a large number of samples in order to achieve consistency. Therefore validation of the framework is achieved by comparison of the results from simple repeatable experiments with those from corresponding evaluation frameworks. One such validation experiment is the repeated positioning and measurement of a Passive Arm using both an OPL and a CMM. The associated framework is illustrated in Figure 5. Figure 6 shows the actual data, where N=30, overlaid onto the simulated data, where N=10,000. In this validation experiment a correlation between the actual and simulated data can be observed. Similar results have been achieved with other validation experiments.

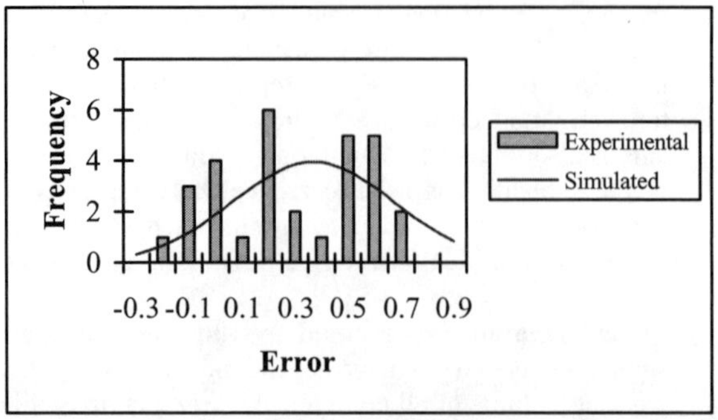

Figure 6. Experimental data overlaid onto the simulated d ata for framework validation.

However the reliability of the current validation approach has to be questioned given the original premise that a large sample size is required for consistent results. More conclusive validation experiments are being developed to overcome this shortfall. The practical limitations of performing physical experiments with large sample sizes, where N=10,000, is the primary issue being addressed.

DISCUSSION

The extension of the Lea diagram into an evaluation framework linked with computer simulated error propagation modelling provides a valuable tool for the development of CAS systems. In particular this novel approach enables testing of virtual CAS components within a simulated CAS environment. The framework not only enables the final accuracy of the proposed system to be determined prior to component assembly, but also the propagation of errors throughout the system. Error propagation analysis permits the primary error sources to be identified and targeted for future development, if a more accurate CAS solution is required.

The framework is also applicable for confidence testing of a completed CAS system. The ability of the framework to exhaustively test the accuracy of the registration components of a system makes it ideally suited to this role.

REFERENCES

Lea JT, Santos-Munne JJ, Peshkin MA, MMVR3, San Diego, Jan 1995. *Diagramming Registration Connectivity and Structure,*

Viant WJ, Phillips R, Mohsen A, Sherman KP, Hafez M, Chawda M, Bielby MS, Zhu Y, Griffiths JG, CARS '99, Paris, June 23-26 1999. *Computer Assisted Positioning of Cannulated Hip Screw,*

M&S Standards Track

Simulation Standards Activities at SISO

Presented at Summer Computer Simulation Conference
July 17, 2000
Vancouver, BC

Simulation Interoperability Standards Organization

Who is SISO?

- Who are our customers, and what do they want?
- How do standards help?
- What is SISO's role?
- What products should/is SISO developing?

Simulation Interoperability Standards Organization

Who are our customers?

- Organizations that need to condition (train), or educate a constituency through rehearsal, repetitive conditioning, behavioral modification...
- Organizations that need to discover or predict the outcome of a situation through an experimental process

Simulation Interoperability Standards Organization

What Do Those Customers Want?

Training and Education Customers

- To assemble a system from as many existing components as possible, which meets or exceeds training requirements, for a minimum investment

Research Customers

- To assemble a system from as many existing components as possible, which answers the research questions with the required degree of confidence, for a minimum investment

Simulation Interoperability Standards Organization

How Do Standards Help?

Interoperability Standards

- Enable simulation "parts" to be plugged together for rapid assembly of systems. Enable reuse of "parts" developed for one system in another application.

Accreditation Standards and Practices

- Provide confidence to the user that the assembled system is providing meaningful, valid results to the degree specified in the accreditation.

Simulation Interoperability Standards Organization

What is SISO's Role?

Be the Open Community Forum To:

- Identify areas where standards can enable interoperability and reuse
- Feed back industry needs to sponsors
- Develop, review, accredit, and archive standards
- Get community buy-in, grass-roots support for standards
- Educate and evangelize industry as to what's available
- Be the "nexus" for related and complementary products

Simulation Interoperability Standards Organization

"Diffusion of Innovations" by E. Rogers

Figure 1-1. Diffusion Is the Process by Which (1) an Innovation (2) Is Communicated Through Certain Channels (3) Over Time (4) Among the Members of a Social System.

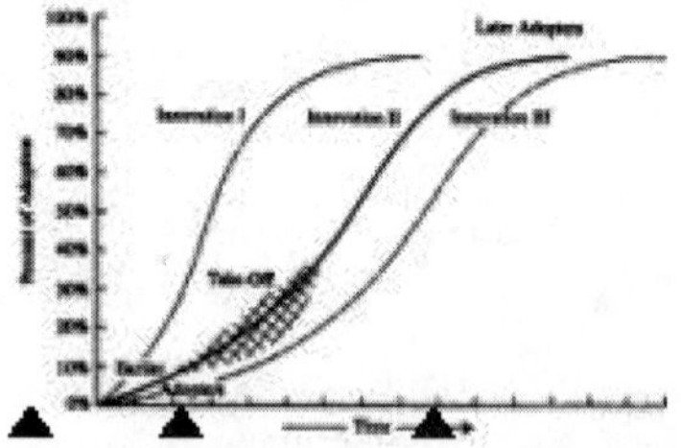

A Vision Virtually Reality Reality

SISO Simulation Interoperability Standards Organization

What Products Should SISO be Developing?

- Network Interoperability Standards
- Content Interchange Standards
- Accreditation Standards and Practices

SISO Simulation Interoperability Standards Organization

Network Interoperability Standards

HLA Regimes Each Needing Reference FOM Standards

High Order Wargaming	Small Unit Training & Combat Dev.	Platform Training & Combat Dev. (RPR FOM)	Platform T&E	CAD/CAM/CAE High Fidelity Engineering Models

Data Exchange

SISO Simulation Interoperability Standards Organization

Content Interchange Standards

- SEDRIS (Environmental Representation)
- Standard interchange format for physics models
- Standard interchange format for behavioral models
- Standard interchange format for simulation data (logger file format, AAR analysis format, statistical results...)
- Standard interchange format for scenario data

SISO Simulation Interoperability Standards Organization

Accreditation Standards

Rating system for validity of a simulation for a particular use:

- Categorization example:

  SISO Level 4 - Simulation of an aggregated unit. Individual entities are not modeled. Statistical model driven by Monte Carlo technique. Not to be used for physics prediction. Experimental accuracy not considered valid below 85% repeatability.

- Practices Example:

  When combining SISO Level 3 and SISO Level 4 simulations, the results must be considered SISO Level 4 validity.

SISO Simulation Interoperability Standards Organization

What Products is SISO Currently Developing?

- DIS - IEEE 1278 series, Network Protocol and Data Standard
- High Level Architecture (HLA) - IEEE 1516 series, Application Programmer's Interface (API) and Data Standards.
- Realtime Platform Reference Federation Object Model (RPR FOM) - SISO Native Standard for Platform Simulation Interoperability within HLA.
- Synthetic Environment Data Representation and Interchange Standard (SEDRIS) - Proposed ISO Standard for terrain and environment data.

SISO Simulation Interoperability Standards Organization

User Community Forums

- Analysis Forum
- Research, Development, and Engineering Forum
- Test and Evaluation Forum
- Small Team Training Forum
- Staff-Level Training Forum

SISO Simulation Interoperability Standards Organization

Specialty Area Forums

- Infrastructure Track
  - Run-Time Infrastructure and Communications Forum
  - Live Interaction Form (joint)
- Federation Development Track
  - Federation Development Process Forum
  - Exercise Management Forum
  - Verification, Validation, and Accreditation Forum
  - Testing Forum
- Environment Track
  - Simulated Natural Environment Forum
  - Sensor Modeling Forum (joint)
- C4ISR (Command,Control,Communications, Computing, Intelligence, Surveillance, and Reconnaissance)Track
  - C4I Forum
  - IO/ISR Forum
  - Sensor Modeling Forum (joint)
  - Live Interaction Form (joint)
- Applications Track
  - Vehicle/Weapon System Modeling Forum
  - Human Decision-Making and Behavior Representation Forum
  - Federation Implementers' Forum
  - Logistics Forum

SISO Simulation Interoperability Standards Organization

Virtual Forums

- Topics of continuing interest
  - Not a one-shot "special session"
  - Expected to continue over several Workshops
- Of interest to multiple communities
  - No single "home" within current Forum structure
- Involve sessions in two or more Forums
  - Typically start with a Monday evening kickoff session
- Led by a Virtual PRP
  - Typically including a CC member and selected PRP members from the participating Forums

SISO Simulation Interoperability Standards Organization

How to Get Involved:

- Subscribe to Forum reflectors via the SISO Web page:

  http://www.sisostds.org "Reflectors"
- Come to the Simulation Interoperability Workshops
- Run for one of the SISO Committees.

SISO Simulation Interoperability Standards Organization

Scheduled Dates for Next SIWs

- September 17 - 22, 2000
- March 25 - 30, 2001
- September 9 - 14, 2001

10th Conference on
Computer Generated Forces & Behavior Representation
Holiday Inn, Orlando May, 2001

1st European SIW
University of Winchester (UK) June 25-27, 2001

SISO Simulation Interoperability Standards Organization

Framework for Standards

Jack Sheehan, DMSO Data Engineer

Defense Modeling & Simulation Office
jsheehan@dmso.mil, 703-998-0660 x448

University of Texas at Austin
sheehan@arlut.utexas.edu, 215-361-2026

Thoughts on Knowledge Management

No direct correlation between IT investments and business performance or knowledge management. "A dollar spent on the same system may give a competitive adv antage to one company but only expensive paperweights to another." *Erik Brynjolfsson*

Analysis of IT investments by technology economist Paul Strassmann concludes that there is **no relationship whatsoever between computer expenditures and company performance**.

John Seely Brown, director of Xerox Park Research Center underscores that U.S. industry has invested **more than $1 trillion in technology** (over 20 yr period), but has realized **little improvement in the efficiency or effectiveness of its knowledge workers**.

Brown attributes this failure to an **organization's ignorance of ways in which knowledge workers communicate and operate through the social processes of collaborating, sharing knowledge, and building on each others' ideas**.

(excerpted from MORS mini-symposium at NPS in February 2000)

Framework for Standards

- → **Changes in the Nature of the Problem:**
  - ⇨ Information-Intensive Warfare
  - ⇨ Measures of Mission Success
  - ⇨ Customer Perspectives
- **Require Changes in the Nature of Solutions**
  - ⇨ An Analogy from Circuit Theory
  - ⇨ Applied to Modeling and Simulation
- **Framework for Data Provisioning**
  - ⇨ Create Information Sharing Partnerships Identify Key Information Classes
  - ⇨ Designate Authoritative Sources
  - ⇨ Develop Common Semantics and Syntax
  - ⇨ Implement Exchange-Centric Standards

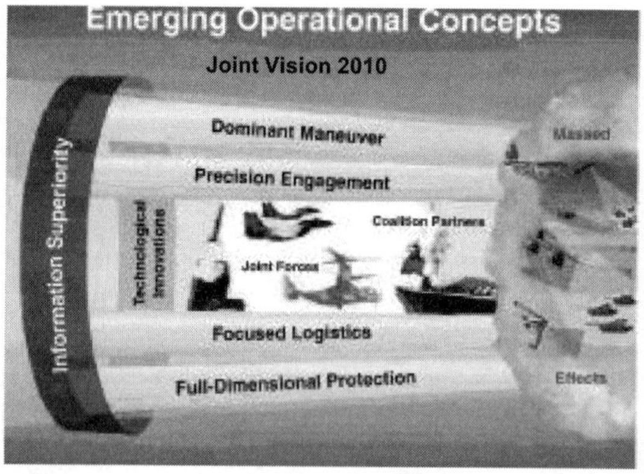

Information-Intensive Warfare, Digitization of the Battle blurs distinctions between simulations and operations

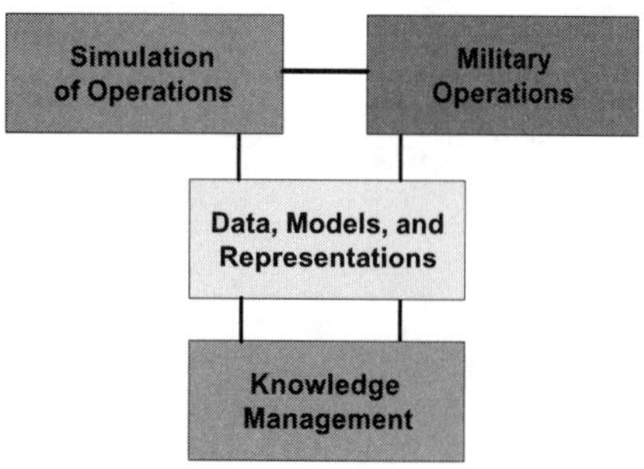

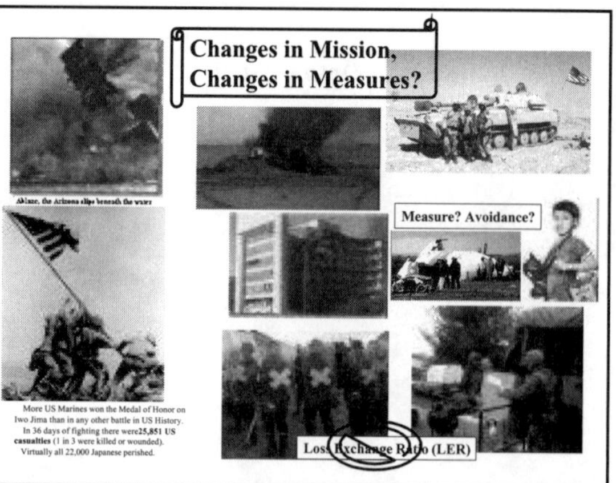

Perspectives

- The Warfighter cares about <u>Credibilty</u>.
- The Developer cares about <u>Completeness</u>.
- The Program Manager cares about <u>Cost</u>.

Achieving all three requires that Knowledge Management focus on <u>Content Composability</u>

Framework for Standards

- Changes in the Nature of the Problem:
  - ⇨ Information-Intensive Warfare
  - ⇨ Measures of Mission Success
  - ⇨ Customer Perspectives
- → Require Changes in the Nature of Solutions
  - ⇨ An Analogy from Circuit Theory
  - ⇨ Applied to Modeling and Simulation
- Framework for Data Provisioning
  - ⇨ Create Information Sharing Partnerships Identify Key Information Classes
  - ⇨ Designate Authoritative Sources
  - ⇨ Develop Common Semantics and Syntax
  - ⇨ Implement Exchange-Centric Standards

Analogy from Circuit Theory

Open-Loop, Forward Gain

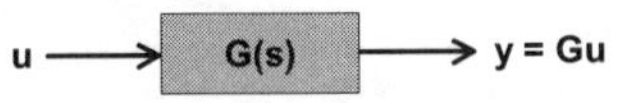

Closed-Loop, Feedback Control

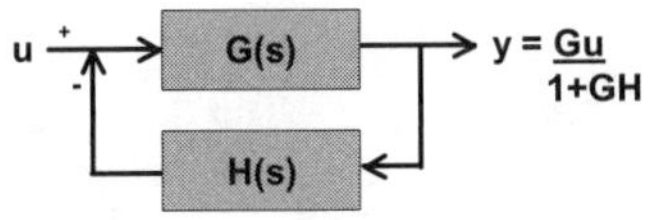

As Is: Open Loop, Forward Gain

<u>Technology Pushes Content:</u>

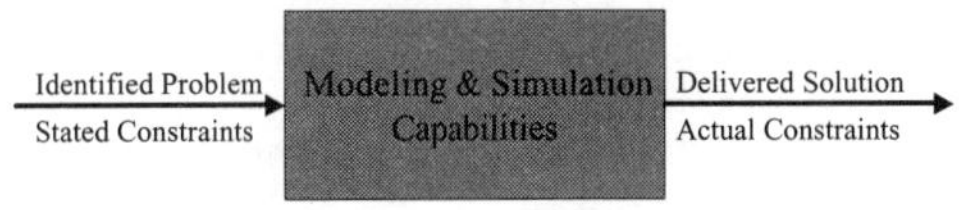

To Be: Closed Loop, Feedback Control

<u>Content Pulls Technology:</u>

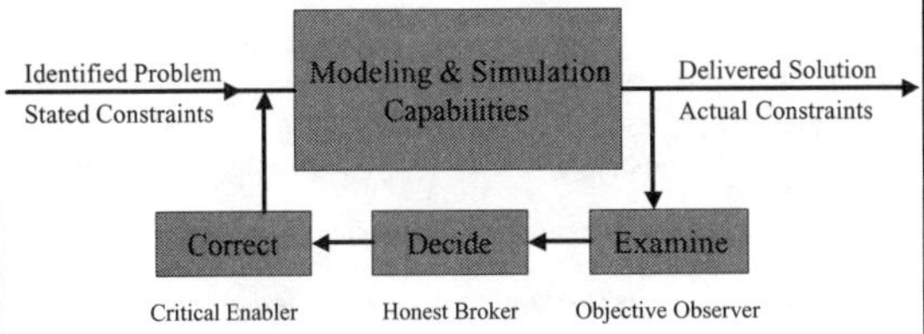

→ **Knowledge Management is the Key**

Data Engineering Process

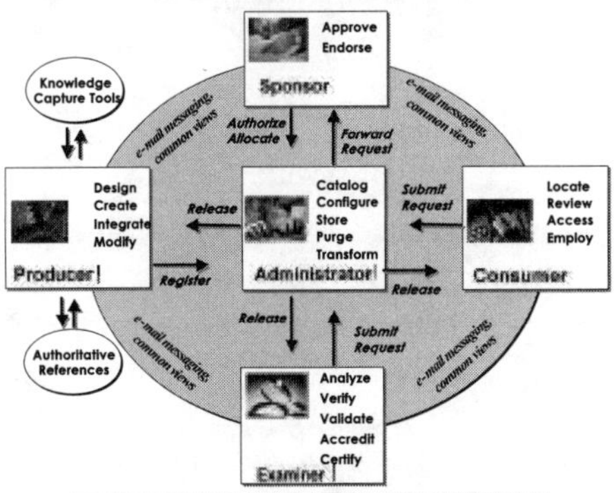

Implemented in the CMMS Model Library

Framework for Standards

- Changes in the Nature of the Problem:
  - ⇨ Information-Intensive Warfare
  - ⇨ Measures of Mission Success
  - ⇨ Customer Perspectives
- Require Changes in the Nature of Solutions
  - ⇨ An Analogy from Circuit Theory
  - ⇨ Applied to Modeling and Simulation
- → Framework for Data Provisioning
  - ⇨ Create Information Sharing Partnerships Identify
  - ⇨ Identify Key Information Classes
  - ⇨ Designate Authoritative Sources
  - ⇨ Develop Common Semantics and Syntax
  - ⇨ Implement Exchange-Centric Standards

Key Concepts

- It's Content that Counts
  - ⇨ Enforcing and administering access control drives everything else
- Formal Collaborations
  - ⇨ Partners: shared funding, shared decision making
  - ⇨ Associates: shared products
  - ⇨ Observers: shared discussion
- Focus on Content Exchange
  - ⇨ Common semantics for logical structure and meaning
  - ⇨ Neutral formats for data exchange
- Use before Re-use
  - ⇨ "Fill it and they will come... "
  - ⇨ "Add value for the original requirement and they will stay... "
  - ⇨ "Focus on the food label, not the diet"
  - ⇨ "Do the hardest one early, the easy ones will follow"

Framework for Standards

- Changes in the Nature of the Problem:
  - ⇨ Information-Intensive Warfare
  - ⇨ Measures of Mission Success
  - ⇨ Customer Perspectives
- Require Changes in the Nature of Solutions
  - ⇨ An Analogy from Circuit Theory
  - ⇨ Applied to Modeling and Simulation
- Framework for Data Provisioning
  - ⇨ Create Information Sharing Partnerships Identify
  - → ⇨ Identify Key Information Classes
  - ⇨ Designate Authoritative Sources
  - ⇨ Develop Common Semantics and Syntax
  - ⇨ Implement Exchange-Centric Standards

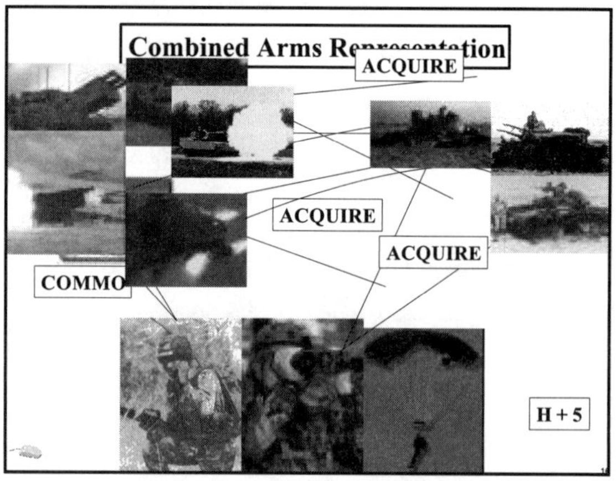

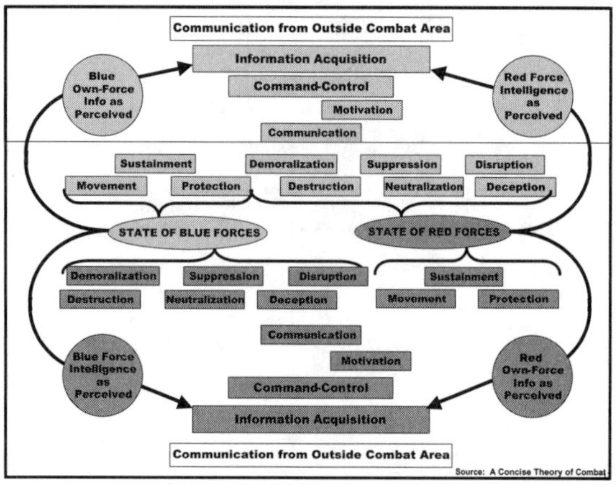

Key Information Classes Summary (1/2):

- The Warfighter's Perspective (missions, operations, tasks) is th e Central Organizing Principle. The Systems, Platform, Equipment Perspective plays as supporting role defined by the Warfighter's Perspective.
- Key Information Classes include are subdivided into:
  - ⇨ Entities, Processes, and Environment.
- Entity-focused information classes include:
  - ⇨ Force Structure (order of battle: unit, electronic, logistics load-out, etc)
  - ⇨ System C&P (to move, sense, communicate, engage, replenish)
  - ⇨ Targets and Facilities (both static and mobile)
  - ⇨ Weapons Effects (damage, attrition, suppression, etc.)

Key Information Classes Summary (2/2):

- Process-focused information classes include:
  - ⇨ Doctrine and Tactics
  - ⇨ C4ISR, Logistics
  - ⇨ Human and Organizational Behavior
- Environment-focused information classes include:
  - ⇨ Integrated Natural Environment (Terrain, Ocean, Air & Space)
  - ⇨ Civil and Political Environment

Framework for Standards

- Changes in the Nature of the Problem:
  - ⇨ Information-Intensive Warfare
  - ⇨ Measures of Mission Success
  - ⇨ Customer Perspectives
- Require Changes in the Nature of Solutions
  - ⇨ An Analogy from Circuit Theory
  - ⇨ Applied to Modeling and Simulation
- Framework for Data Provisioning
  - ⇨ Create Information Sharing Partnerships Identify
  - ⇨ Identify Key Information Classes
  - → ⇨ Designate Authoritative Sources
  - ⇨ Develop Common Semantics and Syntax
  - ⇨ Implement Exchange-Centric Standards

Data Engineering Strategy

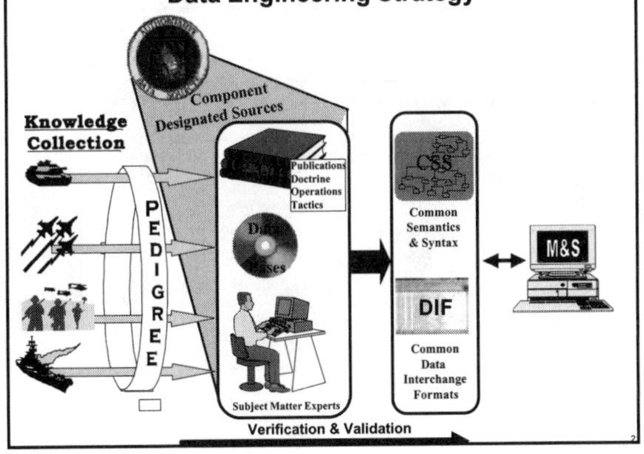

Identifying Source Data with ADS

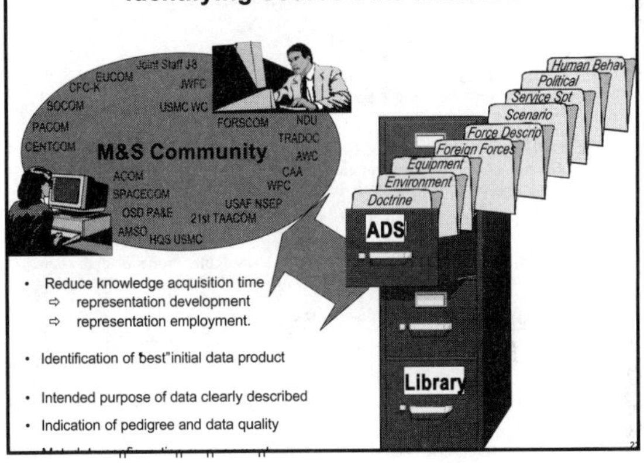

Authoritative Data Sources Summary (1/2):

- A simulation is <u>only</u> as good as the data which drives it.
- If you need help figuring out where to begin, MSIAC is a good place to start.
  - ⇨ Navigate to the DMSO home page – link to MSIAC home page.
- If you have a solid notion of what you need, but dont know where to find it, the ADS Working Group is a good way to get pointed to the best starter data:
  - ⇨ Navigate to the DMSO home page – link to the appropriate ADS-WG member: AMSO, AF/XOCP, M&S Environmental EA's, etc.
  - ⇨ Or navigate directly to the appropriate Service/Component ADS Library.

Authoritative Data Sources Summary (2/2):

- If you are of an established data provisioning community:
  - ⇨ Joint Data System for QDP,
  - ⇨ Virtual Data Center for BMDO,
  - ⇨ Joint Integrated Data Preparation Center for JFCOM
  - ⇨ Human and Organizational Behavior

Work through your designated representative on the above groups.

- If you still need help, contact one of the ADS Working Group co-chairs:
  - ⇨ Mike Hopkins, DMSO (mhopkins@dmso.mil) or
  - ⇨ Lt Col Katherine Rowe, AF/XOCP (roweka@af.pentagon.mil)

Framework for Standards

- Changes in the Nature of the Problem:
  - ⇨ Information-Intensive Warfare
  - ⇨ Measures of Mission Success
  - ⇨ Customer Perspectives
- Require Changes in the Nature of Solutions
  - ⇨ An Analogy from Circuit Theory
  - ⇨ Applied to Modeling and Simulation
- Framework for Data Provisioning
  - ⇨ Create Information Sharing Partnerships Identify
  - ⇨ Identify Key Information Classes
  - ⇨ Designate Authoritative Sources
  - → ⇨ Develop Common Semantics and Syntax
  - ⇨ Implement Exchange-Centric Standards

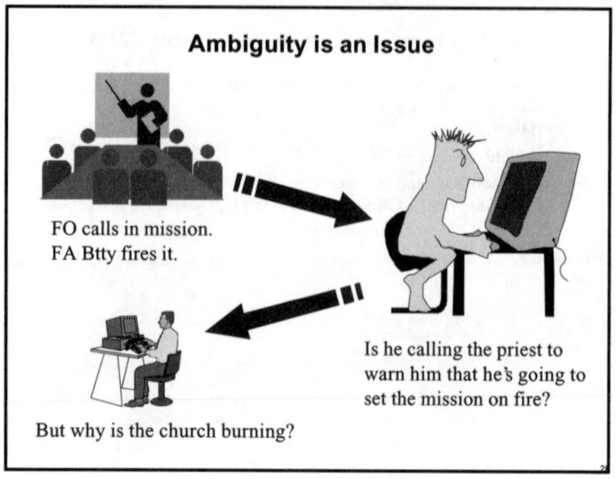

Common Semantics and Syntax

SYNTAX:
the symbols and structures which may be used in a representation and the ways that those symbols may be arranged with the allowed structures.

SEMANTICS:
the content or meaning embodied in the symbols and symbol arrangements defined in the syntax.

COMMON SEMANTICS and SYNTAX:
the implementation-independent logical representation of structure and content (meaning) of a particular model or data element within the specified scope and context of a recognized standard.

CSS is composed of:	Examples:
⇨ Lexicona	⇨ Entity, Task, Class names
⇨ Templates	⇨ JSIMS FDP, C4ISR-AF
⇨ Style Guides	⇨ UML guide for CMMS

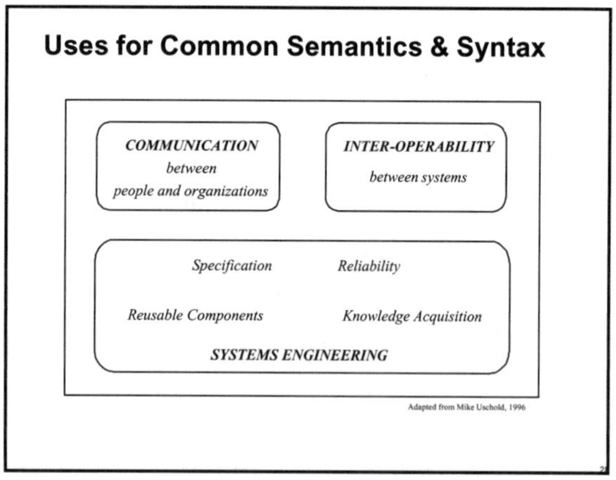

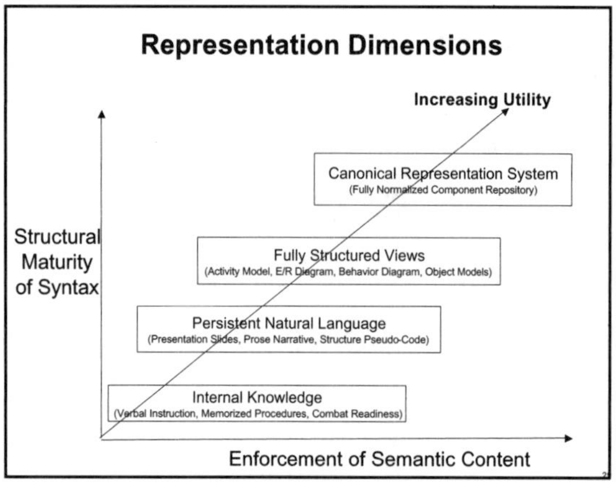

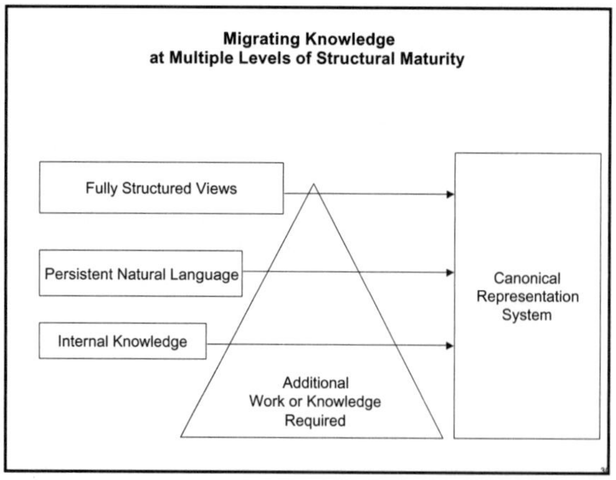

Framework for Standards

- Changes in the Nature of the Problem:
  - ⇨ Information-Intensive Warfare
  - ⇨ Measures of Mission Success
  - ⇨ Customer Perspectives
- Require Changes in the Nature of Solutions
  - ⇨ An Analogy from Circuit Theory
  - ⇨ Applied to Modeling and Simulation
- Framework for Data Provisioning
  - ⇨ Create Information Sharing Partnerships Identify
  - ⇨ Identify Key Information Classes
  - ⇨ Designate Authoritative Sources
  - ⇨ Develop Common Semantics and Syntax
  - ⟶ ⇨ Implement Exchange-Centric Standards

Data Interchange Format

FORMAT:
the set of symbols and structures which define the physical implementation of data (BNF, SQL, bits & bytes) conforming to a specified semantics and syntax.

DATA INTERCHANGE FORMAT:
an intermediate format required to convert data from a set of input formats which share a common semantics and syntax to a set of output formats without loss or distortion of content.

DATA INTERCHANGE MECHANISM:
a set of tools, utilities, or application programming interfaces which perform the conversion into and/or out of a data interchange format

DIF composed of:	Examples:
⇨a CS&S	⇨HLA-OMT, SEDRIS Representation
⇨a physical format	⇨HLA-OMT-DIF, SEDRIS Transmittal, UOB-DIF, CMMS-DIF

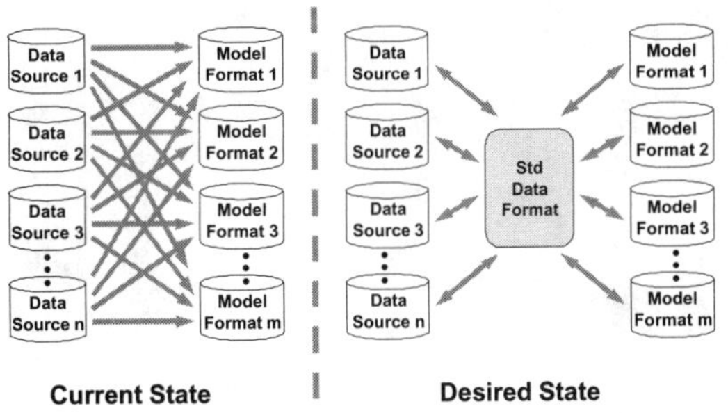

Data Standards Summary:

- Enforce the Standard <u>between</u> major applications; encourage PMs to make pragmatic choices about where and when to embrace the Standard <u>inside</u> the application.
- If you need help with Data Standards, contact the:
  - ⇨ Appropriate Service Standards Category Coordinator (Army in the lead, Navy and AF making excellent strides) via their respective M&S management offices.
  - ⇨ The M&S Executive Agents for Intell and Environment (Terrain, Ocean, Air & Space) via DMSO.
  - ⇨ The M&S Functional Data Administrator (Bob Senko, DMSO, rsenko@dmso.mil)

Unit Order of Battle (UOB) Data Access Tool (DAT)

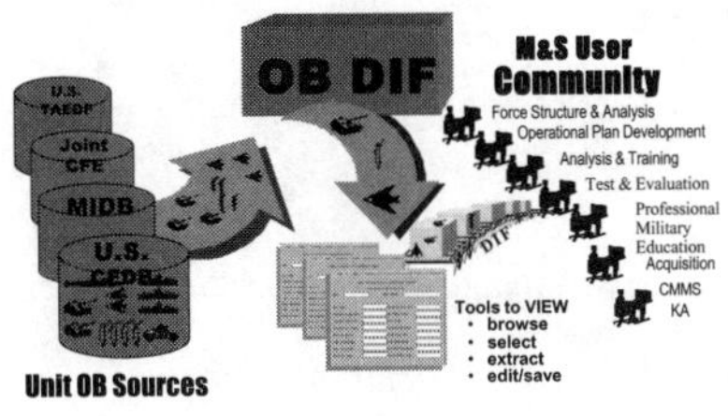

Access Tool to Task Organize & Produce TOs in Standard Format

CMMS Toolset Architecture

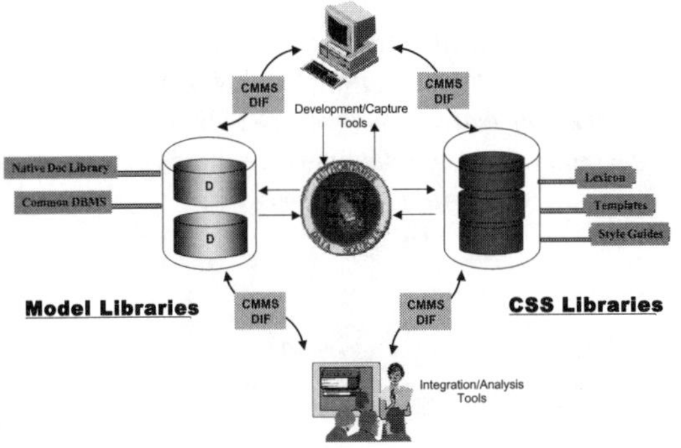

"SBA is SMART for the Army"

17 July 2000

SMART: A Little Historical Perspective...

1997...New MILDEP briefed on OSD Simulation Based Acquisition (SBA) Initiative

"SBA...this is not about small business...give me a new name; one that captures the idea of collaboration among the 3 communities"

LTG Paul J. Kern, Military Deputy to the Assistant Secretary of the Army (Acquisition, Logistics and Technology)

SMART: A Little Historical Perspective...

SIMULATION & MODELING ACQUISITION REQUIREMENTS TRAINING — SMART

SMART is a process in which we capitalize on Modeling and Simulation (M&S) technology to address the issue of system development and life-cycle costs through the combined efforts of the requirements, training and acquisition communities.

SMART: A Little Historical Perspective...

2000...Observations by the Army Acquisition Executive and the former President of Disney Imagineering Creative Technology...

"The Army has made significant progress in the last 3 years with SMART...first there was the 'get out of my office I don't want to hear about this' phase... "

Hon. Paul J. Hoeper

Mr. Bran Ferren

"...Then the long period of silence with no opinion and comment..."

"...and now we are moving into the 'if I don't get on board quickly, I am going to be left behind' phase."

SMART Vision

"Be a world leader in Modeling and Simulation to continuously improve Army effectiveness through a disciplined collaborative environment in partnership with industry, government, and academia."

Larry R. Ellis, Lieutenant General, GS, Deputy Chief of Staff for Operations and Plans

Paul J. Kern, Lieutenant General, GS, Military Deputy to the Assistant Secretary of the Army (Acquisition, Logistics and Technology)

Walter W. Hollis, Deputy Under Secretary of the Army (Operations Research)

What Will SMART Achieve?

- Reduced Total Ownership Cost (TOC), Time to Initial Operating Capability (IOC), and Logistics Tail
- Increased Supportability, Maintainability, and Military Worth
- More Effective, Cost Efficient Training at Individual, Crew, and System Level

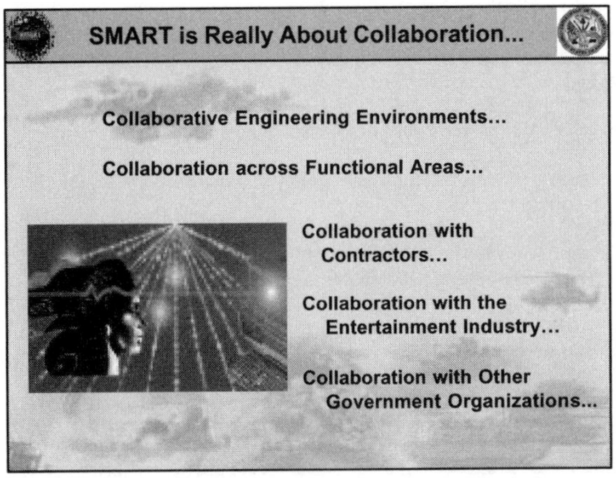
SMART is Really About Collaboration...
Collaborative Engineering Environments...
Collaboration across Functional Areas...
Collaboration with Contractors...
Collaboration with the Entertainment Industry...
Collaboration with Other Government Organizations...

SMART Collaborative Engineering Environments...
Integrated Digital Environments
•Distributed Product Description
•Data Protection/Security
•Data Access
•Causal Networking

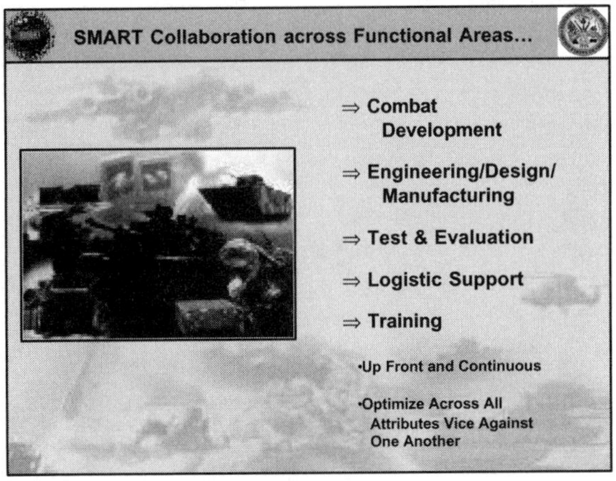
SMART Collaboration across Functional Areas...
⇒ Combat Development
⇒ Engineering/Design/ Manufacturing
⇒ Test & Evaluation
⇒ Logistic Support
⇒ Training
•Up Front and Continuous
•Optimize Across All Attributes Vice Against One Another

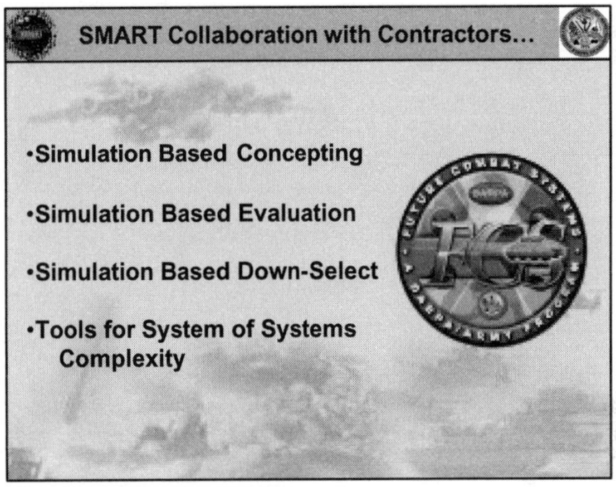
SMART Collaboration with Contractors...
•Simulation Based Concepting
•Simulation Based Evaluation
•Simulation Based Down-Select
•Tools for System of Systems Complexity
FUTURE COMBAT SYSTEMS
FCS
A DARPA/ARMY PROGRAM

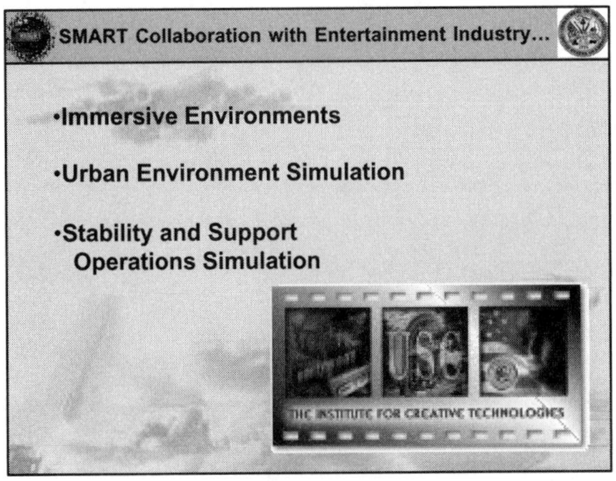
SMART Collaboration with Entertainment Industry...
•Immersive Environments
•Urban Environment Simulation
•Stability and Support Operations Simulation
USC
THE INSTITUTE FOR CREATIVE TECHNOLOGIES

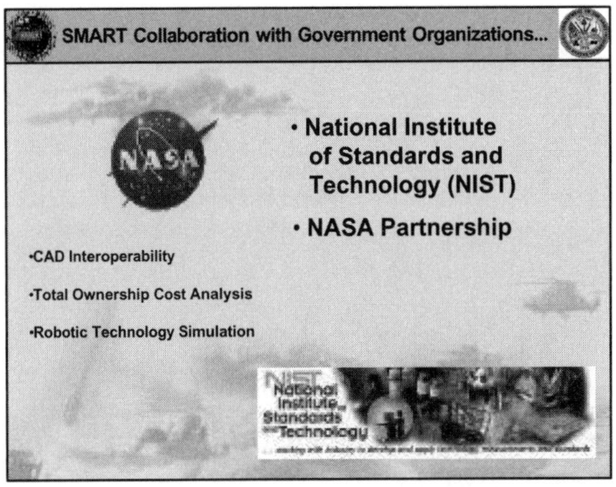
SMART Collaboration with Government Organizations...
NASA
• National Institute of Standards and Technology (NIST)
• NASA Partnership
•CAD Interoperability
•Total Ownership Cost Analysis
•Robotic Technology Simulation
NIST National Institute of Standards and Technology

SMART Points to Ponder

...A Note on Standards:

"In fact standards free companies to innovate much more rapidly, and profitably than do proprietary approaches. When standards define architectures, interfaces, and basic communications, companies can innovate 'on top of the standard'. We can focus on high-value capabilities without having to rewrite the architecture or interface"

Lew Platt, Chairman, CEO & President, Hewlett-Packard

A SMART Way Ahead

⇒ **SMART is about breaking stovepipes**

⇒**SMART is about the Army doing business in the digital Information Age**

⇒**SMART is about reducing total ownership costs and fielding more effective systems quicker**

⇒**SMART is about integrating the Requirements Generation, Acquisition and Training communities**

Army is committed...SMART is how we will build the Objective Force

Conceptual Modeling

Furman Haddix, Ph.D.
Applied Research Laboratories
University of Texas at Austin
Sponsored by DMSO

Introduction

- Why is conceptual modeling important?
- Why should I care?
  - What does it mean for M&S Development?
  - What does it mean for Software Development?

Conceptual Modeling

- Conceptual Modeling Concepts
- Conceptual Models
- Using Standards for Conceptual Models
- Summary and Conclusions

conceptual modeling

- Used in many sciences (andpseudosciences) with different connotations:
  - Nursing
    - The holistic conceptual model for the structure and the development of the Nursing Science is empirical and stems clearly from the observation and maybe from my premonition that a new century delimits certain understandings.
  - Physics
    - Conceptual Model of Super Universe and Relativity Hypothesis
  - Psychology
    - Everyday spatial metaphors form a non-technical conceptual model that helps us understand the self, relationships, virtues, science and spiritual beliefs.
  - Education
    - Conceptual Model: The conceptual framework for the School of Education forms the basis for course content, stated student outcomes, instruction, and assessment.

Conceptual Modeling

- Conceptual Model is a generic term (refer to conceptual modeling)
- We're better served by modifying an overloaded term unless its meaning is clear from the context.
  - (Simulation) Conceptual Model
  - (Federation) Conceptual Model
  - (Mission Space) Conceptual Model

What is a Model?

- A purposeful approximation or abstraction of an entity, a behavior, or a model of an entity or behavior.
  - A model is inherently inaccurate, else it would be the entity or behavior, not a model of the entity or behavior.
  - The value is in the fidelity of the entity or behavior with respect to the primary purpose of the model.
    - Too much fidelity→
      - Drives model development costs too high because of unneeded detail
      - Communicates inefficiently (model usage costs too high) because user must separate wheat from chaff
    - Too little fidelity→
      - Drives implementation costs too high, because of chaos and redundant repetition in developer/SME communication channels

Some Conceptual Model Thoughts

- Conceptual Model
  - A representation which serves to facilitate the understanding of a real world context, situation, object, or abstractions of the above.
- Conceptual Model in Software Development
  - Used to satisfy multiple definitions, including:
    - A representation of the problem space suitable as a basis for solution space development
    - A representation of the solution space providing a bridge between the problem space and the implementationaka a conceptual design
- Simulation Conceptual Model
  - An abstract or generic view of the modeling and simulation problem space generalized from instances of related requirements, experience, science, and doctrine, and providing a suitable basis for solution space development (design and implementation).

Large-scale Modeling and Simulation Development (LS M&S D)

- Large-scale Modeling and Simulation is not the only significant application of conceptual modeling
- Significant characteristics of largescale modeling and simulation development include:
  - Clear divisions of responsibility
    - SME Knowledge Producers
    - SME Knowledge Validators
    - (Conceptual and/or Object) Modelers
    - System Designers
    - System Implementers
    - System Testers
    - Simulation Accreditors
  - Scope of project requires multiple of all resources

Starting with the Real World

- There is a problem which motivates funding a (LS M&S D) solution
- Define the Problem (Scope of problem space)
- Describe the User Functionality that could solve the problem (User Space)
- Develop the Domain-based Derived Requirements (Mission Space)
- Identify the algorithms, science, etc., to approximate the Mission Space (Synthetic Representation)
- Combine all of the above into a Simulation Conceptual Model

Supporting Conceptual Models (Specification)

- Document requirements gathering, definition, description, and (front-end) analysis.
- Examples include
  - Conceptual Models of the User Space (CMUS)
  - Conceptual Models of the Mission Space (CMMS)
  - Conceptual Models of Synthetic Representations (CMSR)
- E.g., conceptual models of the mission space constitute representational requirements for simulations.
  - CMMS, if of appropriate scope, fidelity, etc., provide a simulation dependent, but implementation independent benchmark for a simulation.

Primary Conceptual Models (Analytical)

- Implementation independent; backend description and analysis; simulation dependent issues become more significant.
- Potential for component reuse is less because in the primary conceptual model user requirements are explicitly included, as opposed to some supporting conceptual models, e.g., CMMS, where only their effect on scope, fidelity, etc., is recognized.
- Requirements analysis
- Easily contaminated with Conceptual Design (High level Design Issues)
- Examples include
  - Simulation Conceptual Model (SCM)
  - Federation Conceptual Model (FCM)

What is a Simulation Conceptual Model?

- A Simulation Conceptual Model is implementation independent, but simulation dependent.
  - Independent of implementation concerns, e.g., programming language, but issues addressed and level of detail with which they are addressed depend upon simulation objectives.
  - Represents important aspects of a simulation.
  - An important purpose -- communication of concepts regarding the thing being modeled.
  - Address issue or related set of issues in a meaningful manner; but still abstract, a pale imitation of reality.
  - It is not the design or the implementation, but ideally, it addresses all the concepts and constraints relevant to the design and/or implementation → A design or implementation which "fits" the simulation conceptual model will be satisfactory with regard to simulation requirements

A Dependency Model of a Typical SDP

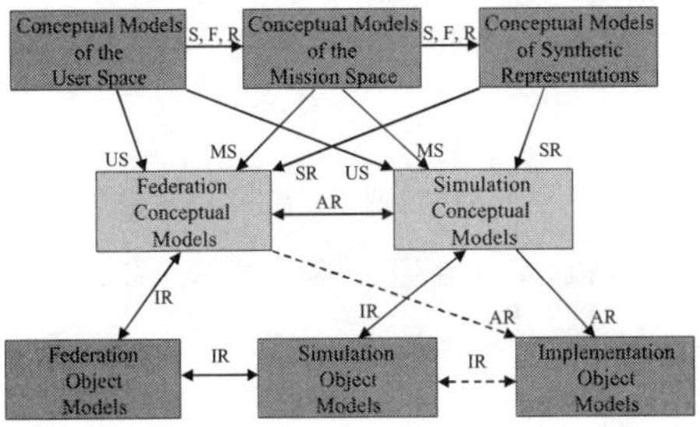

S - Scope
F - Fidelity
R - Resolution

US - User Space
MS - Mission Space
SR - Synthetic Representation

AR - Analytic Requirements
IR - Interface Requirements

A Federation-Centric Model of SDP

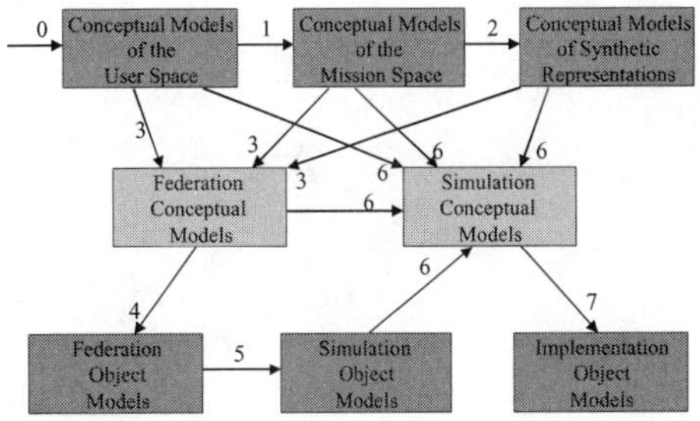

A Simulation-Centric Model of SDP

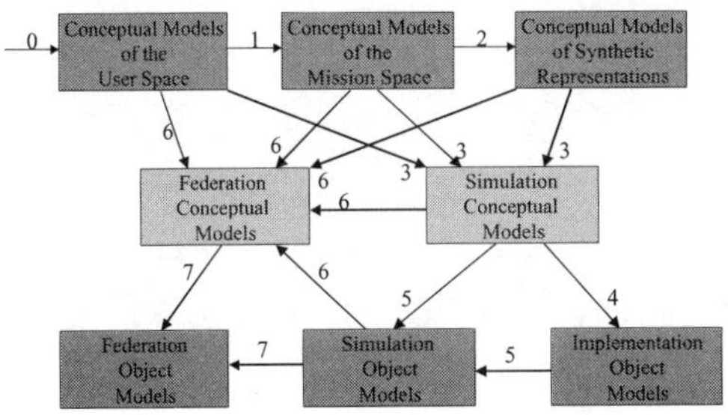

A Dual-Purpose Model of SDP

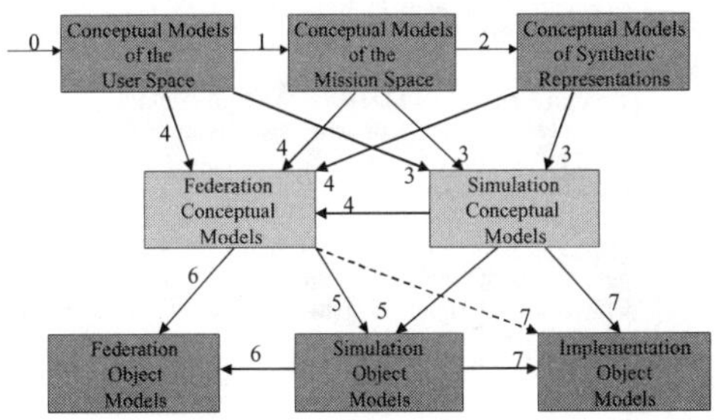

Why Standards for Conceptual Models?

- Military executes extremely complex processes.
  - Process execution depends upon human factors, terrain, weather, wide variety of equipment concerns
  - Worst constraint on military processes– execution of most has opposing forces attempting to execute their processes.
- Developing affordable specifications demands reuse
- Reuse is possible
  - I worked on the Fire Support Automated Test System in early 90's.
  - We designed a development process focused on small grained reuse
  - Today additional missions are still being added to this system
  - Small grained reuse has caused development costs (per mission) to decline each year. Costs today are less than 50% of what they were ten years ago.
- This same reuse can occur within other programs and across programs; however, standards are necessary to achieve this.

What Issues Should Be Addressed by Standards for Conceptual Models?

- Spectrum → None, Internal, External
- Focused Knowledge Acquisition and Engineering
- Small-grained Reuse Potential
- Common Semantics and Syntax
- Examination Descriptions

Focused Knowledge Acquisition and Engineering

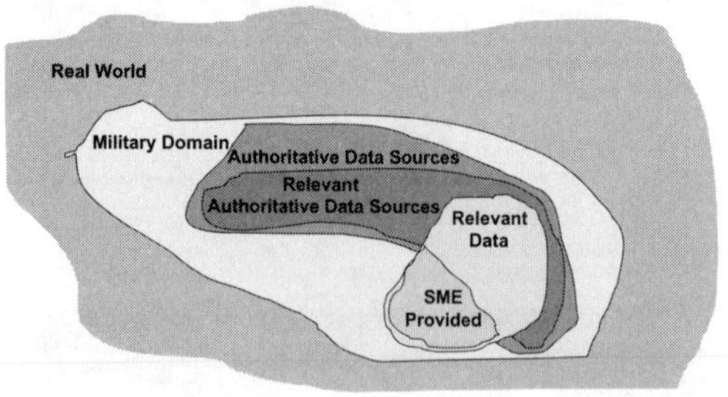

What is a Conceptual Design?

- Micro-level
  - Conceptual design of a program
    - Pseudocode
    - Flowchart
    - …
    - Enough detail to be verifiable against requirements
    - High-level enough to have one-to-many translation to code
- Macro-level
  - Conceptual design of a simulation or system
    - System Design
    - Segment Design
    - Initial Software Design
    - Detail Software Design
    - Above predicated on assumption that design documentation is a tool of essential solution space analysis

What's the Difference between a Conceptual Model and a Conceptual Design?

- Domain
  - Conceptual Model → Problem Space
  - Conceptual Design → Solution Space
- Inheritance
  - Used in Conceptual Modeling to avoid redundant documentation (reuse of detail descriptions)
  - Used in Conceptual Design to provide re-use of base class functionality
- Purpose
  - Conception Model →Provides clear, concise, explicit description of system functionality
  - Conceptual Design → Provide basis for implementation which is characterized by robust, efficient execution
- Constructs
  - May be very similar→ Facilitates Common Semantics
  - May be very different→ See Domain, Inheritance, and Purpose above

Conceptualization of Conceptual Model and Conceptual Design

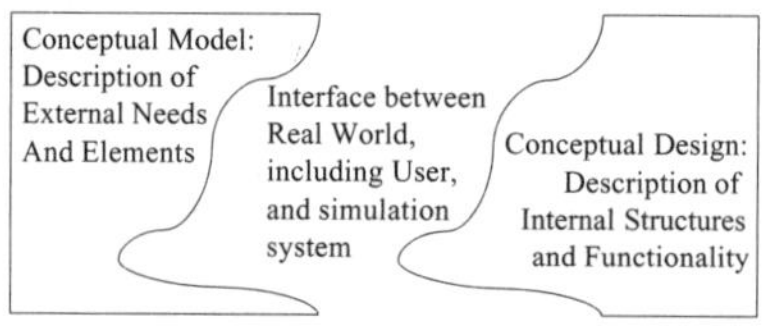

- The simulation is the hand which fits the conceptual design's glove. The real world is the hand which fits the conceptual model's glove. Ideally, the two gloves have a tight fit.

Conceptual Model and Conceptual Design: Summary

- Conceptual Model
  - What:
    - Description of functionality to be provided and how that functionality interacts with the operational environment
- Conceptual Design
  - How:
    - Description of system implementation and how implementation constructs interoperate to produce desired (required) functionality

Disciplined Development Approach Requires Common Focused Context

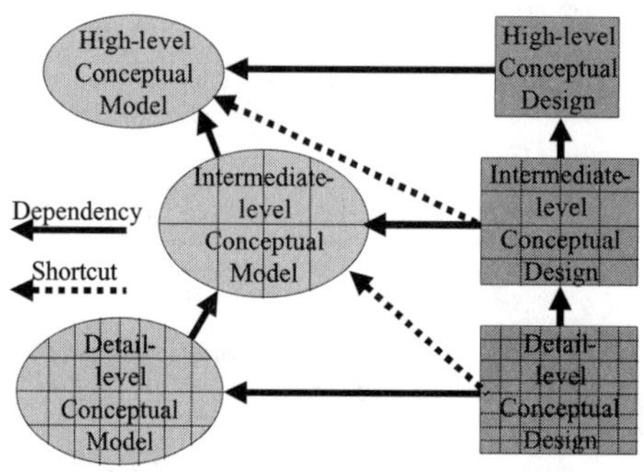

Common Semantics and Syntax

- Joint Force Order is given: "Secure the Building!"
  - Navy turns the lights out and coffee pot off and goes home
  - Army checks the building for inhabitants and lays down a defensive perimeter
  - Marine Corps begins by preparing to assault the building
  - Air Force goes to landlord's attorney's office negotiating a lease on the building

Simulation Examination

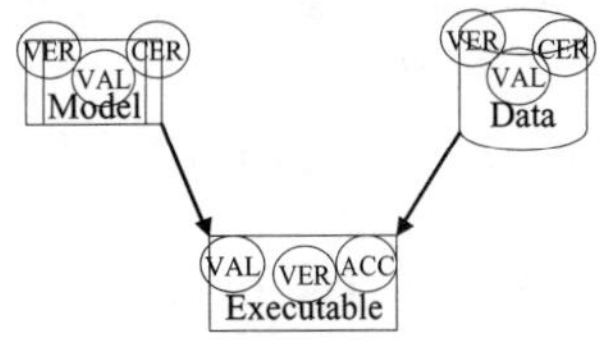

- Can I reuse verification?
  - Is specification the same or similar?
- Can I reuse validation?
  - Is need the same or similar?
- Can I reuse certification or accreditation?
  - Were validation and verification reusable?

Similar Problem with Using Term "Object"

- Problem with using "conceptual model" is like that of object in object-oriented programming (OOP).
  - Everyone knows what an object is!
    - It is a thing!
  - Proper use of the term object, if it is not the most generic use, requires a modifier or context.
    - When we start using subject and verb in the same context, or when we use the modifiers "direct" and "indirect", we are using object in the sentence structure sense.
    - Once we use object-oriented, many of us leap to the conclusion, we are dealing with an object-oriented design (OOD) or OOP context
      - An object is an instance of a class with characteristic attributes and behaviors
- Use of object in domain knowledge development (problem space) is not the same as in OOP/OOD (object-oriented design) development environment (solution space)

Of Conceptual Models, Conceptual Designs, and Object Models

- The great gulf between artifacts
  - Conceptual Models are composed of Testable Requirements
  - Conceptual Designs are composed of development artifacts which taken together should satisfy Testable Requirements
  - Conceptual Models are about "What"; Conceptual Designs are about "How"
- What are Federation and Simulation Object Models?
  - These are interface specifications–part of the Conceptual Design
    - The FOM imposes constraints on components of the Federation
    - The SOM represents constraints imposed on one Federate

When is an Interface a Requirement and When Not?

Answer: An internal interface is usually not a requirement, but a design constraint. An external interface is usually both a requirement and a design constraint.

- An Unfortunate Fact:
  - The definition of external and internal depends upon one's current point of view
    - An internal interface for a simulation may be an external interface for a system segment
    - An internal interface for a segment may be an external interface for a software module
    - An internal interface for a software module may be an external interface for a program or for an object

What is an Object Model?

- Object Models are implementation dependent
  - An object model is an artifact of a specific implementation methodology
  - An object model is a representation of a simulation element after implementation dependent decisions have been made
    - For example, implementation formats have been determined versus required formats.
    - A required format is one due to an environmental requirement -- If a communications device is simulated, its message formats may also have to be simulated.
    - An implementation format may be an abstraction of the real world format if reproduction is not a requirement.

Object Models (Developmental)

- Federation Object Model (FOM)
- Simulation Object Model (SOM)
- Implementation Object Model (IOM)
  - FOM and SOM could be considered parts of the IOM
    - FOM and SOM concerned with only external interfaces
    - IOM concerned with both external and internal interfaces

HLA Object Model Purpose

- Provide a commonly understood mechanism for specifying the exchange of data and general coordination among members of a federation
- Provide a common, standardized mechanism for describing the capabilities of potential federation members.
- May be a Federation Object Model (FOM) or a Simulation Object Model (SOM)

Implementation Object Model

- The model of the implementation
  - Just as the CMMS is an abstraction one step removed from the real world; the IOM is an abstraction one step removed from the synthetic world implemented by the simulation.

How Conceptual Models Facilitate Simulation Development

 → 
- Real World → CMUS

→ 
- Real World → CMMS

→ 
- Scientific Representations of Real World → CMSR

→ Synthetic World of Simulation Developed
- using SCM, FOM, IOM, …

How Standards Facilitate Conceptual Model Development

- Module A Simulation

- Module B Simulation

- Module C Simulation

→ Well-formed Conceptual Models → Integratable Software

Conclusions

- Start with Focused Context
- Use commonly understood terms
- Plan for standards and small-grained reuse and interoperability
  - Intra-program (big savings)
  - Inter-program (made practical by 2 programs following common standards)
- Standard Descriptions of VV&A and VV&C
- Greatly reduce costs of development by improving potential for interoperability and reuse
- Improve DoD Effectiveness

Data Standards Approaches and Solutions

Roy Scrudder
Applied Research Laboratories
The University of Texas at Austin
scrudder@arlut.utexas.edu

2000 SUMMER COMPUTER SIMULATION CONFERENCE
M&S STANDARDS TRACK

The Need for Standards

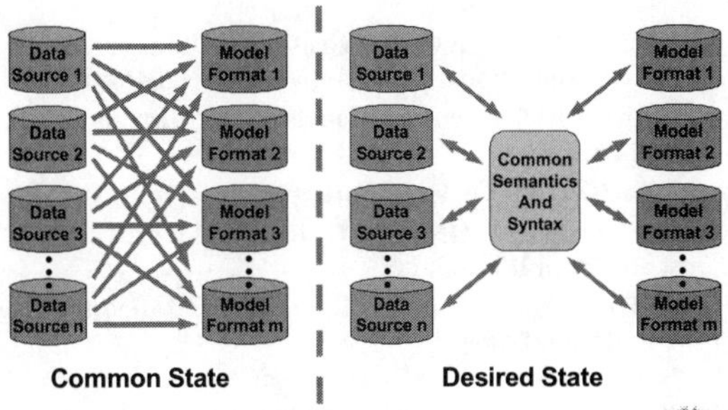

2000 SUMMER COMPUTER SIMULATION CONFERENCE
M&S STANDARDS TRACK

Approaches to Developing Standards

Effectiveness

- Commercial dominance by a major high-volume player (e.g. Intel, Microsoft)
- Making if free but good (the Web)
- Government funding of a really useful thing (TCP/IP)
- Standards committees (slow)
- Edict (rarely works with technology)

Source: James Oyler, President and CEO, Evans and Sutherland, at DMSO Industry Days 2000

2000 SUMMER COMPUTER SIMULATION CONFERENCE
M&S STANDARDS TRACK

Approaches to Developing Data Standards

- Top Down
  - Consensus formed among a group of key stakeholders
  - DISA "Tiger Teams" including terrain, meteorological and oceanographic
- Single, dominant system
  - GCCS and the C2 Core Data Model
- Bottom Up
  - Formal modeling and integration of requirements from multiple legacy systems
  - Electromagnetic and threat data standards

2000 SUMMER COMPUTER SIMULATION CONFERENCE
M&S STANDARDS TRACK

US DoD Data Standardization

- Based on a single, extremely large relational (IDEF1X) DoD Data Model with dozens of views
- Initially a process (IDEF0) model was to accompany the data model, but has not been kept up-to-date
- Standardizes individual data elements
- Limited registration to legacy systems
- Changes and additions approved by Functional Data Administrators
- Majority of growth occurred in 1995 timeframe

2000 SUMMER COMPUTER SIMULATION CONFERENCE
M&S STANDARDS TRACK

M&S Data Requirements

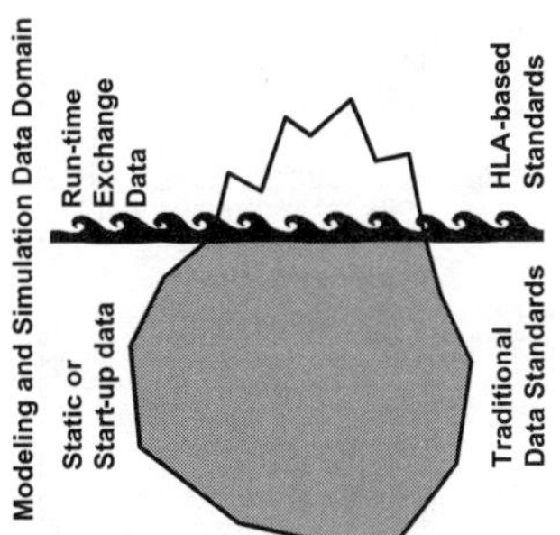

- The majority of data standardization is concerned with static or start-up data
- M&S must also be concerned about run-time exchange of data
- Static and dynamic data elements are often related

2000 SUMMER COMPUTER SIMULATION CONFERENCE
M&S STANDARDS TRACK

M&S Community Success Stories

- SEDRIS – Synthetic Environment Data Representation and Interchange Specification
- CMMS – Conceptual Models of the Mission Space
- UOB – Unit Order of Battle
- HLA OML & OMDD – Object Model Library and Data Dictionary
- JDBE – Joint Database Element for Modeling and Simulation
  - Universal Threat System for Simulators
  - Electromagnetic Environment Data Standards

Common Threads of Success

Standard	Data Model	Data Element Definitions	Physical Format	Devel. Approach
SEDRIS	Modified Rumbaugh	Data Dict. and Coding Stds.	Binary	Top-down
CMMS	IDEF1X	CMMS DRIS	XML	Top-down
UOB	IDEF1X	DoD Data Elements DIF Document	CSV & Fixed width XML	Bottom-up
HLA OML & OMDD	Tables IDEF1X	Object Model Template	Tagged Files / XML	Top-down
UTSS & EM Env.	IDEF1X	DoD Data Elements	None	Bottom-up

Lessons Learned

- Data elements are not enough
  - Data model is necessary to put the data elements in context
  - Process model defines the data elements
  - Data models (or portions thereof) are more easily reused than data elements
- Data elements must be rigidly defined
  - Textual definition
  - Domains
  - Format (including precision and accuracy)

Emergence of XML-Based Standards

- A meta-language for defining and structuring data interchanges
- Similar in appearance to HTML, but the tags are defined by the users
- XML documents are defined by
  - Document Type Definition (DTD)
  - XML Schema
- Rapidly becoming the standard for business-to-business (B2B) data interchange

Data Standards Development Approach

Activity	Products
Define scope of data standardization effort	Operational architecture definition Process model
Identify stakeholders	Office of primary responsibility (steward) & legacy systems
Capture data requirements - Reverse engineer legacy systems - Forward engineer new requirements	Data models Data dictionaries
Integrate data requirements - Normalize legacy requirements - Integrate data models	Data model & data dictionary Mappings to legacy systems and new requirements
Establish Data Interchange Format	Select representation format Define DIF structure

DMSO

Mike Hunsucker,
ASNE MSEA
for V. Dobey, MSEA(Ocean)

What is the INE?

Sun Tzu * Stated --

Know the enemy, know yourself; Your victory will never be endangered.

Know the ground, know the weather [Know the Environment]; Your victory will then be total.

* Chinese Military Strategist, approx. 300 B.C.

INE Overall Concept

The Challenge

Create a physically consistent, crossdomain authoritative "ground truth" of the natural environment that meets user requirements

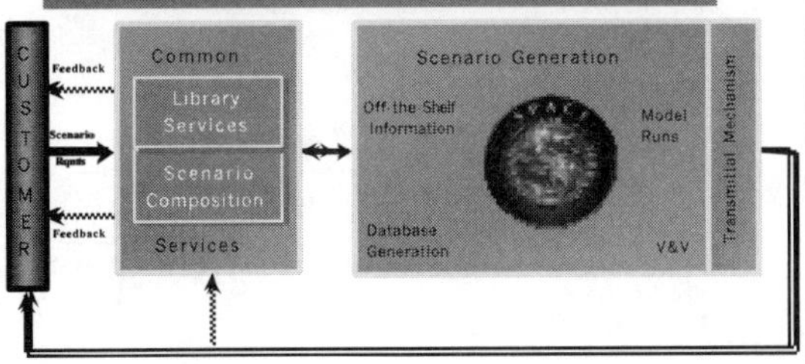

Integrated Natural Environment Program Concept

- **Incorporate the INE Strategy developed by the MSEAs**
- **Unify the DMSO projects under single management and with common purpose**
- **Focus environmental technologies for M&S on the integration and evaluation phase**
- **Build on existing capabilities to conduct experimentation, prototyping and demonstration**

Integrated Natural Environment Program Projects

- **Requirements/Common Data Model (Reqs/CDM)**
- **Master Environmental Library (MEL)**
- **Environmental Scenario Generator (ESG)**
- **Synthetic Environment Data Representation and Interchange Specification (SEDRIS)**
- **Environmental Books on the Shelf (EBS)**
- **INE End-to-End Prototype (INE^{3}P)**

Integrated Natural Environment Program Projects

- **Requirements/Common Data Model (OARCDM)**
  - **Improve understanding of M&S users requirements for environmental data**
  - **Coordinate requirements with environmental data producers**
  - **Expand the data model initiated by JSIMS/WARSIM on the Terrain Common Data Model development to include**
    - **Air & Space**
    - **Ocean**

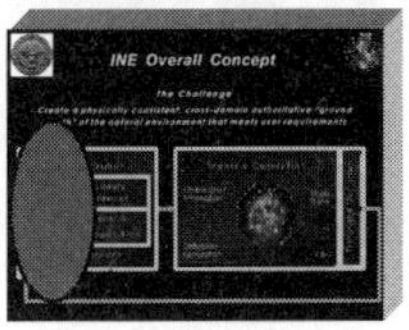

Integrated Natural Environment Program Projects

- **Master Environmental Library (MEL)**
  - Improve DOD environmental data users' ability to discover, access, subscribe and get delivery of authoritative environmental information through:
    - Providing Life Cycle Support to existing sites
    - Standing up new resource sites, improve access to restricted data
    - Enhancing the software tools to submit queries, process data requests and testing

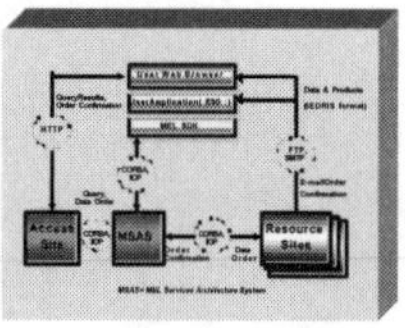

Integrated Natural Environment Program Projects

- **Environmental Scenario Generator (ESG)**
  - Continue the evolution of the former Weather Scenario Generator into a more general use ESG that will handle ocean and terrain information as well as the atmospheric data it currently handles
  - Improve the scenario generation template to address additional space weather requirements
  - Extend data mining capabilities to access atmospheric and space archives and implement related techniques applicable to other domains (ocean and terrain)
  - Develop the INE Process Controller to orchestrate the production of data sets for a fully integrated environment
  - Demonstrate the Just in Time (JiT) atmospheric and space data set production capability at an operational producer facility

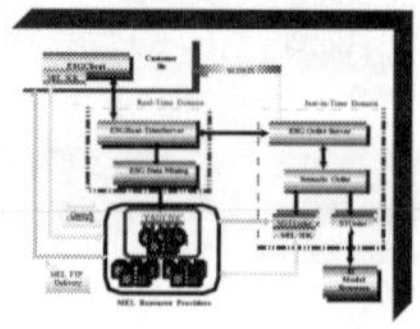

Integrated Natural Environment Program Projects

- **Synthetic Environment Data Representation and Interchange Specification (SEDRIS)**
  - Field SEDRIS interchange components to include training support
  - Develop formal documentation for the specification and initiate formal standardization process
  - Continue tools verification and support interchange experiments for data in all domains
  - Develop partnerships for use of SEDRIS maturing products in C3I and GIS domains
  - Develop transition plan

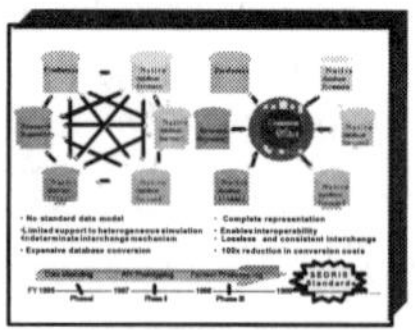

Integrated Natural Environment Program Projects

- **Environmental Books on the Shelf (EBS)**
  - Develop and demonstrate terrain database development technology:
    - low- and medium-to-high resolution terrain databases
  - Promulgate worldwide low-resolution terrain databases that are
    - MEL-accessible & SEDRIS available
      - "Cleaned and deconflicted" archives (3)
        - Feature data, elevation data, and 3Dmodels/texture data
      - Integrated archive based on integrated Triangulated Irregular Network (iTIN)
      - Standard feature data model (STRICOM TCDM)
      - SEDRIS "unambiguous representation" technology

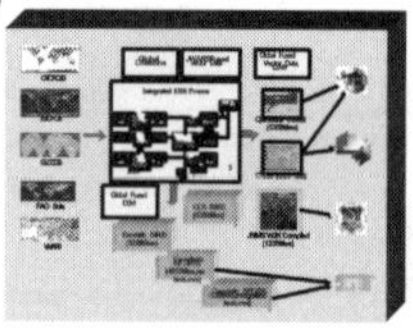

Integrated Natural Environment Program Projects

- **INE End-to-end Prototype**
  - Perform a case study paper walk-through to validate the INE Strategy and Concept
    - Provide complete technical documentation and lessons learned
  - Conduct a live test end-to-end demonstration of the INE Strategy emphasizing the atmospheric domain
    - examples of inter domain interactions between the atmosphere and the ocean and between the atmosphere and terrain using existing capabilities will also be explored
  - The results of the end-to-end demo will be in SEDRIS Transmittal Format

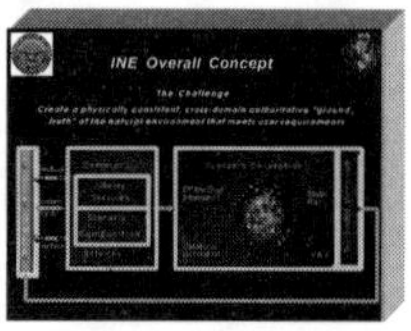

Prototyping use of the Environment in Realtime Simulation (The Environment Federation)

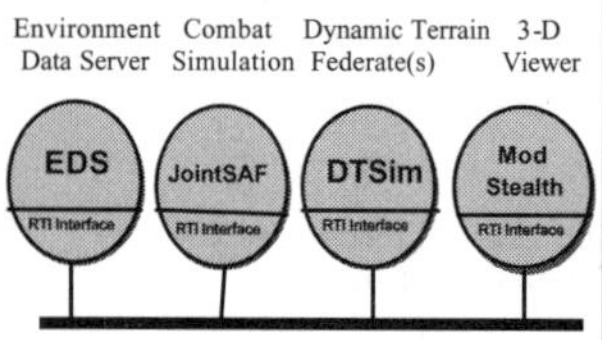

EDS	Dynamically changing weather
JointSAF	Simulated forces
DTSim	Terrain Changes
ModStealth	Renders 3-D visualization

Cross area project: HLA & Environment

- Reuse of SEDRIS Data Coding Standard at runtime (FOM Contents)
- Reuse of STOW Federates
  - Upgraded to current HLA standard
  - Use of Agile FOM Interfaces
  - FOM design for reuse

Standards in the INE

- **Architecture standards:**
  - Joint Technical Architecture Standards, with the goal of Defense Information Infrastructure/Common Operating Environment (DII/COE) compliance
- **Data Transfer Format standards:**
  - Vector Product Format (NIMA)
  - Standard simulator database Interchange Format (SIF)
  - Basic Imagery Interchange Format (BIIF)
  - GRIB and BUFR (WMO)
  - National Imagery Transmission Format Standard (NITFS)
  - SEDRIS Transmittal Format

Standards in the INE (cont.)

- **Metadata standards:**
  - ISO/TC211 (standard for geospatial data), part 15 (metadata)
  - Federal Geographic Data Committee
  - Geographic Information Locator Service, and
  - U.S. Imagery and Geospatial Standard (USIGS) metadata formats,
  - with the goal of ensuring consistency with emerging Joint METOC Conceptual Data Model (JMCDM), SEDRIS, and HLA metadata standards
- **Data Consistency standards:**
  - Defense Data Dictionary System (DDDS) standard data elements, including JMCDM and USIGS data model components
  - Global Change Master Directory
  - Uniform Joint Task List (UJTL)
  - SEDRIS data representation standards

Standards in the INE (cont.)

- **Information Processing Standards:**
  - ANSI Z39.50 information search
  - SEDRIS spatial reference
  - FIPS 173 spatial data transfer standard
- **Model/Algorithm and Database Standards:**
  - DoD METOC data producer standard operational models
  - Navy Oceanographic & Atmospheric Master Library (OAML) models and databases
  - NOAA atmospheric and oceanographic climatological databases
  - NOAA National Center for Atmospheric Research databases
  - Other U.S. Government-owned standard climatology databases

A VIRTUAL STANDARDS ORGANIZATION

Tammie L. McClellan and Elizabeth A. Griffin
Institute for Simulation and Training
3280 Progress Drive
Orlando, FL 32826
Email: tmcclell@ist.ucf.edu and agriffin@ist.ucf.edu

KEYWORDS: Database Management Systems, Virtual Organization, Standards, Internet

ABSTRACT:
Imagine an organization that exists only in a virtual environment. It has no corporate headquarters or home office. There are no time clocks to punch or conference rooms waiting for meetings to begin. It does have thousands of volunteer members though voting on management positions, collaborating on the development of thousands of pages of highly technical modeling and simulation standards covering industry, academia, and governments both domestic and foreign! It conducts dozens of meetings each day involving hundreds of people in multiple countries, all at work on producing the standards needed to make M&S work, whether for a complex military force-on-force simulation or for the latest tourist attraction simulator at the local theme park. In fact, this "virtual organization" even pulls together three conference per year where managers and engineers come together and put finishing touches on their products and share ideas through the social forum afforded by their gathering. While many talk of a "paperless office", this organization, the Simulation Interoperability Standards Organization (SISO), has actually achieved it. This paper will describe the "virtual organization" and the tools, applications, and mechanisms that allow the organization to be productive.

The Simulation Interoperability Standards Organization (SISO) originated over ten years ago with a small conference held April 26-27, 1989, called, "Interactive Networked Simulation for Training". This conference grew into the DIS Workshops, later evolving into the Simulation Interoperability Standards Organization (SISO).

SISO focuses on facilitating simulation interoperability and component reuse across the DoD, other government, and non-government applications and seeks to serve the broad Modeling and Simulation (M&S) community by:

- Providing a forum for the interchange of new ideas, concepts, and technology through the Simulation Interoperability Workshops (SIW) and the Conference on Computer Generated Forces and Behavioral Representation (CGF-BR).
- Educating M&S practitioners and sponsors regarding implementation through tutorials held at the Workshops and through the quarterly publication of an on-line technical magazine titled "Simulation Technology".
- Supporting the development of standards, practices, and guides for use in various applications.

Each of these components serves as an integral part of the development of M&S Standards. The Workshops and Conferences provide a wide based forum for identifying needs and candidates for standardization. The Tutorials, offered by SISO at the SIWs, provide a way to educate the M&S community on the basics of M&S as well as the new developments in M&S Standards, tools and methods. The Simulation Technology on-line magazine provides a way to update the community on progress being made in technology and standards development. Last but not least, the standards development component of SISO serves to gain consensus amongst the M&S community in order to develop the best methods and practices for interoperable simulation.

So how does SISO do all this?

Based on the description above of the broad and diverse efforts SISO is trying to accomplish, one would think that there is a large office building somewhere filled with a staff to support all these efforts. This assumption though is far from the truth. SISO is a legally constituted non-profit organization with NO home office, NO dedicated staff, NO paperwork, and NO telephones! It exists only in a virtual environment. How does this organization operate then? It has thousands of volunteers and the use of the Internet.

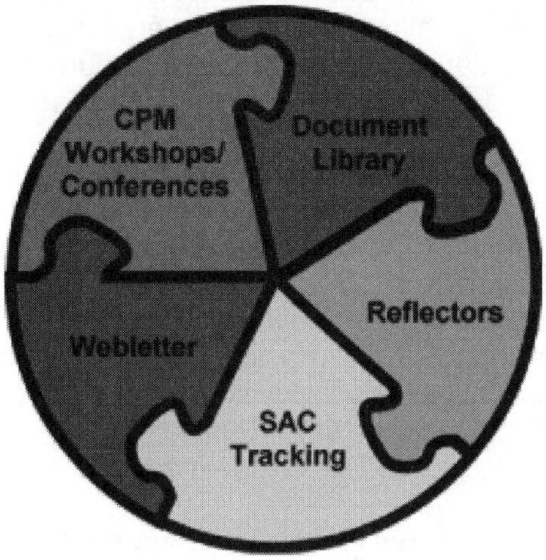

Figure 1

Many organizations talk of a "paperless office", but the Simulation Interoperability Standards Organization has actually achieved it. In fact for SISO, there has never been any other approach. Even in the early days of DIS, volunteers worldwide realized that working strictly in the physical world was slow, expensive, and very time consuming. Spurred by the need to reduce costs while increasing product/standards production, SISO quickly built all its key operations in the virtual world of the World Wide Web.

Members communicate continuously via email (Reflectors) while working on many individual products simultaneously (SAC Tracking). Documents are made available to members and the public instantaneously via the SISO electronic Document Library. When it comes to planning the workshops (which include peer review of professional papers leading to selection for presentation), SISO again returns to an electronic format with use of the Conference Papers Management system. Even the SISO magazine, "Simulation Technology", is created and published via the web. All of these activities occur without paper while involving volunteers across the U.S. and the World!

The following sections will explain the tools, applications and mechanisms that allow this organization to be productive. They will demonstrate how Information Technology (IT) has been used in the standards development process and how a standards organization, such as SISO, has successfully used IT to conduct its operations. Although the applications were customized and tailored to suite the specific needs of SISO, each could be used by other organizations with minor adjustments.

SISO's World Wide Web Site

As eluded to, the World Wide Web is the "home base" for this "virtual organization". It is the SISO web site (http://www.sisostds.org) that serves as the hub and primary means for this organization to conduct business and communicate with its members (Figure 1). This is no ordinary web site however. It is comprised of various web-based, relational database applications that track and manage the efforts of the organization. Most of the site is dynamically created before it is ever presented to the end user. This delivery method ensures that the public and members of SISO receive the most accurate and current information available.

To assist SISO in creating its "virtual organization", the Institute for Simulation and Training (IST) created the SISO web site and its database-driven, web-based applications this paper discusses. Each application is designed to function with a backend Microsoft Access database (with the ability to upgrade to SQL server

URL - http://www.sisostds.org/

Figure 2

when necessary) and was created with a middleware product called ColdFusion by Allaire, Inc. The applications were optimized to work with the most commonly used browsers (MS Internet Explorer and Netscape) and use JavaScript for authentication and validation of data. No JAVA, ActiveX or other languages that are commonly blocked by firewalls (due to security) are used.

Conference Papers Management (CPM) Twice a year SISO holds the Simulation Interoperability Workshop and once a year the Conference on Computer Generated Forces and Behavioral Representation. Both efforts provide a wide based forum for the interchange of new ideas, concepts and technology, and for identifying needs. The events include tutorials, papers on state-of-the-art experiences identification and discussion of interoperability issues, and presentation of proposed solutions. As these solutions are prototyped and demonstrated, they become candidates for possible standards within relevant simulation communities.

Organizing and conducting these events is no simple feat, and it is further complicated by the fact that the “staff” of the organization is spread around the world. All professional papers submitted to the workshop and/or conference, must also undergo peer review prior to selection for presentation, thus increasing the coordination effort required.

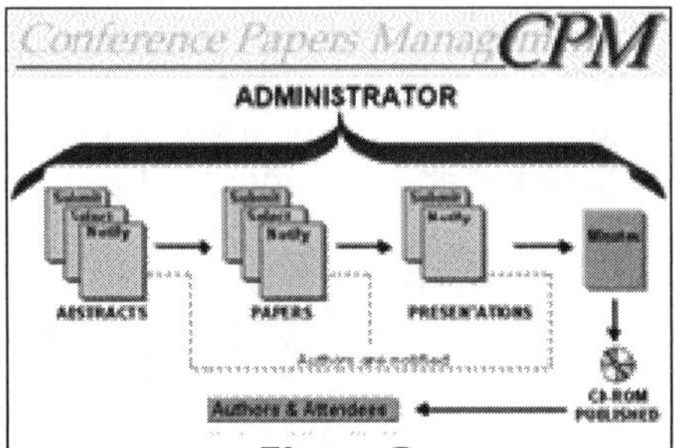

Figure 3

To aid in this process of preparing and publishing papers and proceedings, the Conference Papers Management (CPM) system was developed. It is an entirely web-based relational database used to assist the Workshop/Conference Coordinator in managing the events leading up to the Workshop/Conference (Figure 3). Specifically, the CPM supports:

- Abstract entry, peer review (to include dissemination to reviewers around the world), and automated invitation for paper submission,
- Paper upload, virus scan and format conversion, peer review and prioritization, and automated invitation for presentation,
- Presentation upload, virus scan and format conversion
- Submission of meeting minutes from the Workshop forums
- Final production of the workshop/conference proceedings via CD-ROM

Because the CPM tracks every submission from beginning to end, automatically handling the dissemination of the abstracts and papers for peer review, the withdrawal or denial of a paper, etc., SISO has saved considerable time, effort, and resources compared with previously used manual methods.

Webletter Virtually every organization has tried publishing a company/organization newsletter and SISO is no different. The effort in doing so though can be very time consuming, labor intensive, and costly. To reduce the cost and effort of publishing, IST created a web-based newsletter application called the Webletter. SISO uses this application for the quarterly publication of its magazine titled "Simulation Technology" (Figure 4). This on-line magazine

Figure 4

provides a way to update the M&S community on progress being made in the technology and standards development. It has become a very successful outreach effort for SISO.

What makes the Webletter so useful is that the entire process of article collection, issue creation (to include layout and design), and publication is all done via the web. Through the use of web forms, SISO members can easily submit their articles for use in upcoming issues. The Webletter editor is then automatically notified via email of any new submissions and he/she can then review, edit, and select the articles to be used in the creation of the next publication.

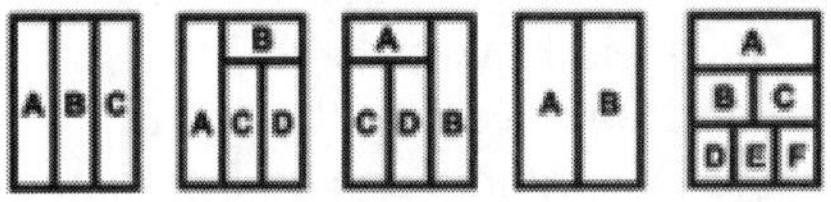

Figure 5

Creating a new issue is easy. The editor first selects from anyone of 5 template designs (Figure 5). From there, a wizard like process leads the editor through the selection of articles and placement within the chosen template. Once all the articles have been selected for the given issue, publication occurs immediately upon decision of the editor with the press of a button. The current issue is then placed online with the previous issue automatically moving into the archive of back issues. All issues (current and past) can also be searched.

Standards Activity Committee (SAC) Tracking System To support the collection of ideas and the development of a standard (Figure 6), the SAC Tracking system was created. It is used by SISO sponsored Product Development Groups (PDGs) as a collaborative tool for document creation and review.

Using the web interface created, SISO members submit their idea for a new "standard" or "product". This "idea" (and the descriptive information that explains it) is stored in a backend database and an email is sent to an administrator to review the idea's validity. From there, with the press of a button by the administrator, the idea is posted to the web site for review. Other members interested in pursuing the development of the idea can then volunteer to be either editors or reviewers. This "volunteering" also occurs via the web interface provided and all submissions are stored in the database. A lead editor is then selected to move the document forward.

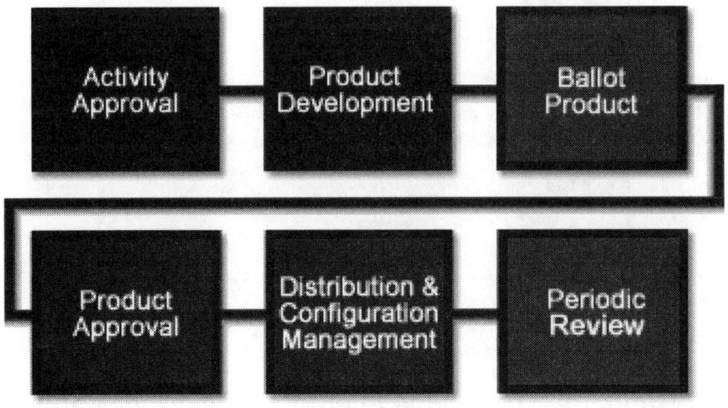

Figure 6

Upon development of the first draft, the document is posted to the web site for review (Figure 7). This process involves parsing the document into sections and importing them into the database. Each section is stored as a separate record in the database to facilitate the tracking of individual comments. At the editor's discretion, the document review phase can be set to private (requiring a password) or public. Reviewers then submit their comments, section by section, via the web interface provided. Using the administrative area created, the editor then reviews the comments submitted and determines the best resolution for each. The resolution assigned for each comment is then emailed automatically back to the original submitter. This review process can occur for every draft of the document.

Figure 7

At some point, the document will reach what the editor and other volunteers believe to be its final version and they will call for a vote. Just as the review phase occurred, the voting also happens through the web interface created. The public is notified (via the Reflectors) and requested to vote on the document. Voting and tallying of the results are all also performed by the application and provided to the editor. Based on the vote, the editor can call for an update of the document or request the document be moved forward and voted upon by the Standards Activity Committee (SAC). If approved by the SAC, the document is stored in the SISO Document Library for dissemination.

Document Library Given the numerous documents and products created by SISO, there was a strong need to store these files in a common location for dissemination to SISO members. The Document Library provides for just that. Documents of any format can be electronically stored within the server for quick access by authorized users.

Visitors who upload their documents are required to include descriptive information, which later makes it possible for other visitors to search for the document (Figure 8). All documents are automatically scanned for viruses, sent through an approval chain for review, and converted to other formats if necessary. The entire process is automated (except for some file conversions and human approval decisions) thus significantly reducing overhead and maintenance costs.

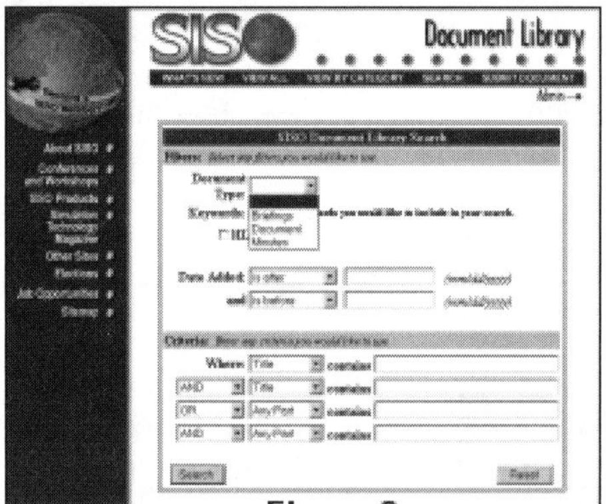

Figure 8

The administrative area is quite robust and contains many features that contribute greatly to the application's overall presentation and interface. The administrative area is accessible only to assigned administrators and available functions are based upon permissions granted by the Main Administrator. Just as any public library would operate and organize its materials, the Document Library provides numerous ways of categorizing its contents and managing it. Directories and folders can be created for storing documents of a particular subject area together and keywords and other filters can be tagged to each document for quick and easy retrieval. To reduce administration of the library, "sub-librarians" can be created through the administrative console and placed in charge of specific sections (directories and folders) of the library. Additional functions available are briefly outlined below:

- Add New Documents
- Edit/Accept/Delete/Order Existing Documents
- View ALL Documents
- Search ALL Documents
- Assign and Set Permissions for Sub-Administrators
- Edit/Delete Sub-Administrators
- Assign/Delete/Expire PIN Codes for Users
- Create New Directories (folders) with or without password protection
- Edit/Delete Existing Categories/Sub-Categories
- Add/Edit/Delete Keywords
- Submit and Retrieve Files by Email
- Access to Documents can be Restricted by password and/or domain (IP) address

Reflectors Reflectors, also known as electronic conferences or mailing lists, are used by SISO to facilitate communication amongst its member population through email.

The primary tool used is the List Processor, an Internet mail server that allows individuals to join and leave the various discussion groups at their discretion. Whenever someone wishes to communicate with the group, they address a single message to the server where it is copied and sent to every current member of the list. Beyond the traditional service of a list processor though, a unique interface (Figure 9) was built to "reflect" all email traffic to the web site where it is indexed for searching. The ability to fully search the archive of email traffic is valuable to new members joining SISO, and current members who want to stay abreast of other areas within SISO. To ease the process of subscribing and unsubscribing from a list, a web front end was also created to interface with most of the standard list server processes.

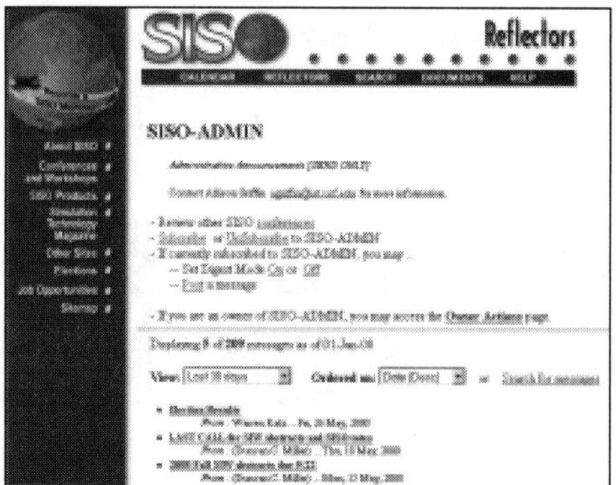

Figure 9

Summary

Without the use of the Internet, the efficiency and effectiveness by which SISO operates would not be possible. The members of SISO though not only manage to communicate, they manage to be productive. On top of this they are productive in a paperless world. They have learned through trial and error how to best utilize the tools they have to work with. They have discovered new tools that make their jobs easier and they have developed their own applications where there were none. SISO is a model to follow and its methods and processes should be considered by other organizations for potential adoption.

References

Journal
Goldiez, Brian. 1999. "Origins and Early Days of the Workshop." Simulation Technology, Volume 2, Issue 1 (September 10)

Special Publication
Simulation Interoperability Standards Organization. 1999. "SISO-ADM-002-1999 SISO P&P Revision 2.0." SISO Document Library, http://www.sisostds.org/doclib/doclib.cfm?SISO_RID_1001384.

Special Publication
Simulation Interoperability Standards Organization. 1997. "Vision-A Global Modeling and Simulation Community." SISO Document Library, http://www.sisostds.org/doclib/doclib.cfm?SISO_RID_1000022.

Web Site
Institute for Simulation and Training (IST)
http://www.ist.ucf.edu

Institute for Simulation and Training (IST)
Information Technology Department
http://www.sc.ist.ucf.edu

Web Site
Simulation Interoperability Standards Organization (SISO)
http://www.sisostds.org

Web Site
Simulation Technology Magazine
http://www.simulationtechnology.org

Biographies

Tammie L. McClellan is an Associate in Simulation and Deputy Program Manager for Information Technology at the Institute for Simulation and Training, University of Central Florida. She is responsible for the logical and physical design, development, integration, testing, quality assurance, configuration management, installation, and operations management and technical support of the information, data, and databases of the Information Technology group's clients. She also manages the accounting for all IT contract accounts and reporting to sponsors. Ms. McClellan has a BS in Accounting from the University of Central Florida in 1994 and over 7 years of experience in the Information Technology field. Her experience in the information field, specifically the World Wide Web and database connectivity, make her a pioneer in the field.

Elizabeth A. Griffin is an Associate in Simulation at the Institute for Simulation and Training, University of Central Florida. She has been working in the field of simulation for 4 years and is currently the project lead on the Support to the Simulation Interoperability Standards Organization. In the past, Allison participated in the HLABDS-D Proto-federation project. She also has over ten years experience in the field of nuclear power generation and the manufacture of nuclear fuel rods. Ms. Griffin has a B.S. in Mechanical Engineering from the University of Alabama at Birmingham in 1983 and a M.S. in Simulation Systems from the University of Central Florida in 1996.

Policies and Procedures as They Pertain to Standards

James Hunt
Ballistic Missile Defense Organization
National Missile Defense Joint Program Office
1725 Jefferson Davis Highway, Suite 502
Arlington, Virginia 22202
703-604-3232 Fax:703-604-3121
e-mail: James.Hunt@bmdo.osd.mil

Todd Repass
Axiom Corporation
307K W Maple Street, Suite K
Vienna, Virginia 22183-8613
703-558-8711 Fax:703-860-9507
e-mail: toddrepass@aol.com

KEYWORDS: Modeling, Simulation, National Missile Defense, Policy, Standards, Baseline, Verification, Validation, Accreditation, Reference Federation Object Model

ABSTRACT:

The National Missile Defense (NMD) Program officially transitioned from a technology program to an acquisition program on April 1, 1997 with the establishment of the NMD Joint Program Office (NMD JPO). The established objective of the NMD Program was to be prepared for a Deployment Readiness Review (DRR) by June 2000 with possible deployment as early as the year 2005. The NMD Program is dependent on a robust, yet flexible, Modeling and Simulation (M&S) Program to supplement and complement the flight test and ground test programs to demonstrate deployment readiness. This briefing addresses the critical role that M&S standards play in the policy, procedures, and execution of the NMD M&S Program. Specific lessons learned associated with M&S baseline management; Verification, Validation, and Accreditation (VV&A); and Reference Federation Object Model (FOM) are discussed.

BRIEFING

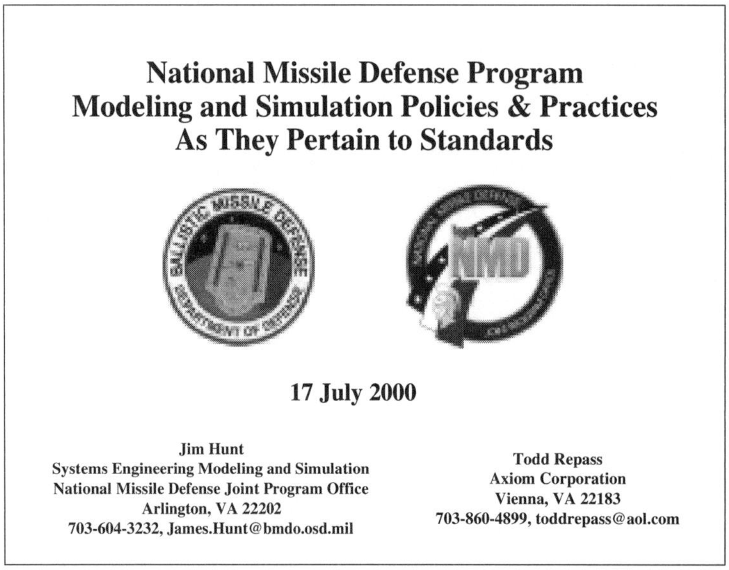

• We are very pleased to have the opportunity to be a part of Summer Computer Simulation Conference 2000 and to discuss our modeling and simulation (M&S) experiences within the National Missile Defense (NMD) Program. Our discussion today centers on the NMD M&S policies and practices as they pertain to the use and application of standards.

• The NMD Program M&S strategy has been developed and executed under the guidance of the NMD System Engineer, Mr. Dennis Mays, and the NMD Deputy for Integration, Mr. Keith Englander. Currently, Mr. Jim Hunt is the NMD lead for the execution of the M&S Program.

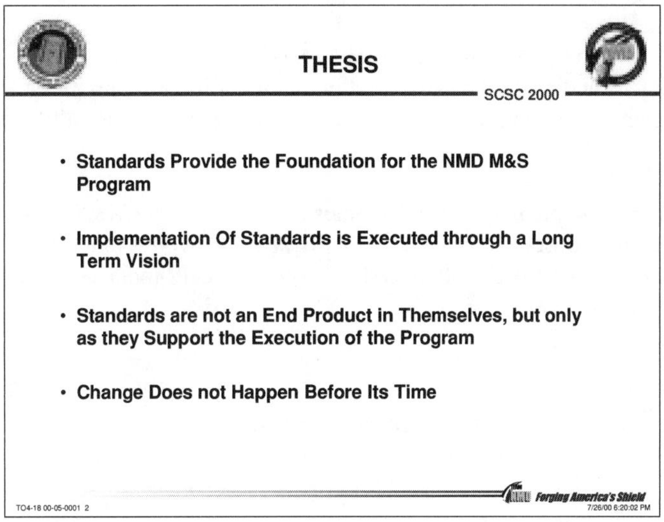

• Our thesis for this discussion is that standards have served as the foundation for the definition and execution of the NMD M&S Program. As the M&S Program has evolved, a small number of very basic concepts have been at the center of the vision on which the M&S is based.

• The implementation of standards and their resulting effects are realized through the execution of a long-term vision. While the implementation of a standard may have a short effect, the pay-off is in the long term.

• We constantly have to remind ourselves that a standard, a procedure, a format, is not an end into itself, but only as it supports the execution of the NMD Program.

•As we have evolved the NMD M&S Program, we have, on numerous occasions, been tempted to decree the establishment of a standard procedure, a process, a definition, a format and, almost without exception, we have rediscovered that "nothing happens before its time." That is, when dealing with such a diverse community as National Missile Defense, the implementation of a standard requires socialization across the entire program, and at an appropriate time, it will be accepted or rejected.

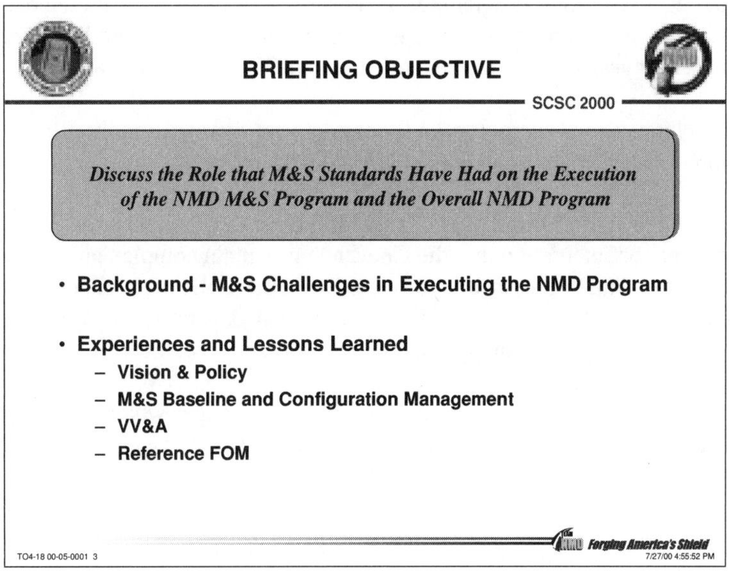

•The objective of our briefing today is to discuss the role that standards have had on the development and execution of the NMD M&S Program and the subsequent impact on the NMD Program.

•We will first review the evolution of the NMD Program from a set of distinct program offices, each with missions and objectives, budgets, staffs, contracts, and products; to a single integrated joint program office and a single lead system integrator contractor. This program evolution provided numerous challenges to the definition of an NMD system level M&S Strategy.

•We wish to focus our attention to the implementation of policies that make up the M&S Vision; then, discuss the importance of establishing and maintaining the M&S Baseline; look into the critical contributions that VV&A has provided and close with some ongoing work in the definition of an NMD Reference Federation Object Model (Reference FOM) to support the establishment of an NMD M&S architecture.

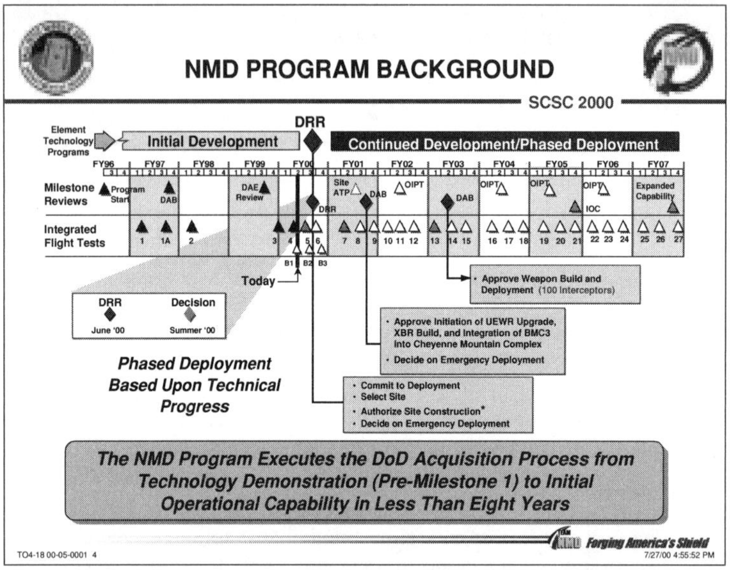

•The NMD Program grew from a number of Element Programs, each of which had its own mission, acquisition plan, schedule, and products. Additionally, each of the Element Program Offices brought their unique M&S approach and their models and simulations. On April 1, 1997, the NMD Joint Program Office (JPO) was established with the overall responsibility of executing the NMD Program. This responsibility included the integration of the Element Program Offices into the JPO and specifically, integrating the M&S programs and strategies into an overall NMD M&S strategy.

•In May 1998, the Lead System Integration Contractor (LSI) contract was awarded and the Boeing Team became part of the NMD Program bring their unique M&S strategy and their set of models and simulations.

•The Program has two major Defense Acquisition Decisions (DABs). One in the summer of FY-01, which focuses on the decision to build radar systems and the integration into the Cheyenne mountain complex and the second, is the FY-03 decision to build and deploy the interceptors. The Deployment Readiness Decision (DRR) to be made this summer is not designated as a DAB Review but carries a similar high-level review. Initial Operational Capability (IOC) for the NMD System is in FY-05. The NMD Program is executing in eight years what a normal DoD program executes in 15 to 20 years

•The NMD M&S program has had to be flexible enough to adapt to these changes while providing the structure and procedures to maintain pace with the NMD Program. The underlying standards that we will discuss have provided that structure and flexibility.

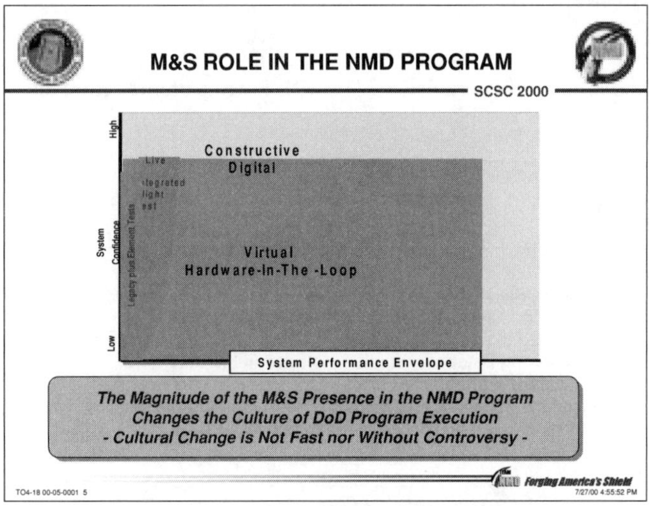

•The NMD Program is a simulation intensive program. The current program includes a total of 21 flight tests prior to IOC. The virtual hardware-in-the-loop test tools or simulators are also being relied on very heavily to provide data supporting the design and deployment decisions. However, the preponderance of the data supporting the NMD Program will be the product of constructive simulations. As the NMD Program development and integration strategy evolves, one of the major objectives of the test program, both flight-testing and ground testing, is the production of data to support the anchoring of constructive simulations.

•The heavy dependence of the NMD Program on simulations to achieve the acquisition schedule has required changes in the normal or accepted methods of acquisition and those changes do not occur fast or without controversy.

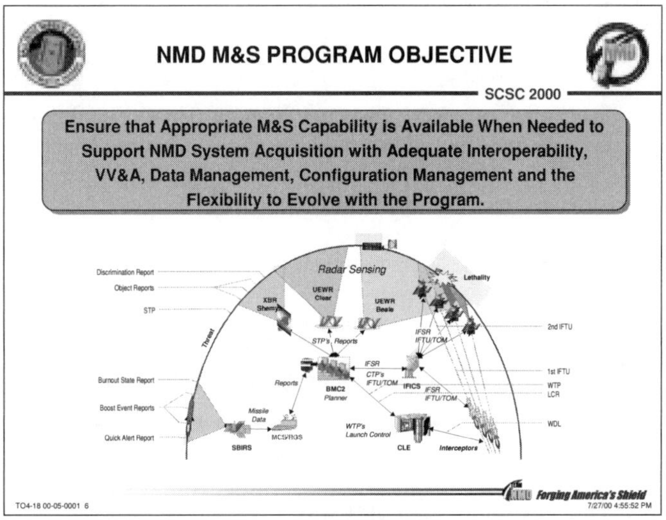

•In 1997 when the NMD M&S Program objective was established, the two key components were to provide the required capability at the time when the NMD Program needed it and to provide the necessary flexibility to support a very dynamic acquisition schedule.

A major advantage provided by the NMD Program in establishing the M&S objective is that the mission space associated with NMD is bounded; the NMD System architecture including interfaces to external systems is bounded; the organization is defined; and the technology areas are focused. Therefore, the required M&S Program is also bounded.

•An additional advantage present in establishing an M&S objective was that we only had to solve the problems with the NMD Program. We were free to copy anyone's good ideas, processes and procedures, standards, and documents.

•Additionally, it was recognized that the policy and standards were necessary to support this objective and that an organization to implement the concepts needed to be established.

•The M&S Program was documented in the Modeling and Simulation Support Plan (MSSP) that was signed by the NMD System Engineer in May of 1999 and is currently in revision. The MSSP was patterned from the Army's requirement for a Simulation Support Plan.

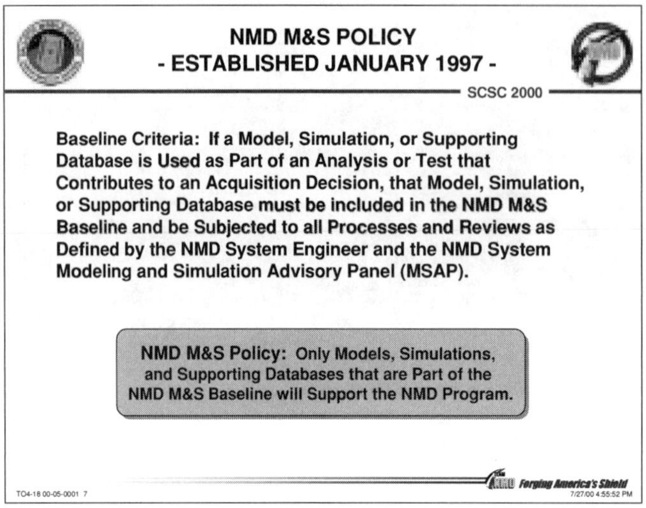

•The initial policy established in 1997 within the NMD M&S Program was that only models and simulations that are part of the NMD M&S baseline would be used to support the program. This policy has established the M&S baseline as the standard for the M&S Program.

• We have had to adapt this policy to the unique needs of the NMD program and have divided the baseline into two parts: Performance and Threat Signatures and Environments. This separation was necessary in that the technology supporting the two types of modeling are so different that we found that different types of expertise were necessary.

•The Performance Baseline was also divided into two parts: Core and Support. The Core baseline makes up the performance simulations that provide data supporting acquisition decisions while the support baseline simulations are used in engineering analyses. Core simulations must have V&V programs in place to support accreditation, implement a configuration management process, and become HLA compliant.

•The Core Baseline has functioned as the center of the M&S program.

•The Modeling and Simulation Advisory Panel (MSAP) was established to coordinate the execution of the M&S Program.

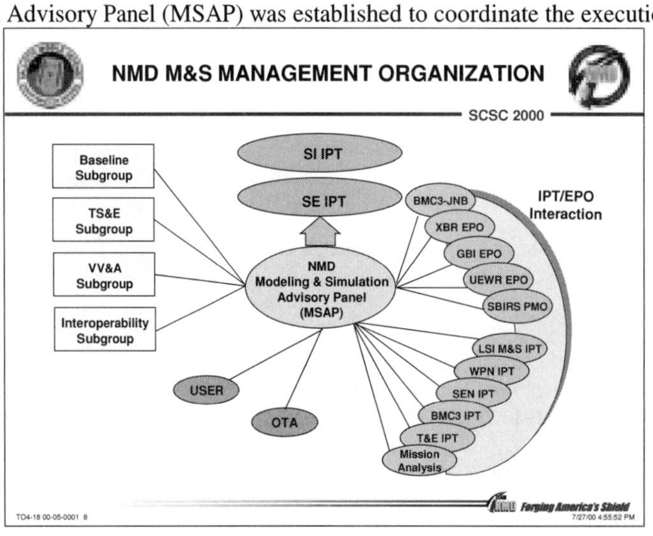

The MSAP is co-chaired by NMD JPO M&S Lead and a representative of the LSI M&S organization. The initial functions of the MSAP were the communications and coordination of the M&S Program that is now evolving more toward a real advisory body. It is chartered by the NMD PEO and has met on a quarterly basis. It includes representatives of all NMD M&S organizations.

Currently, four subgroups are active within the MSAP.

– The Baseline Subgroup is responsible for reviewing and recommending additions and deletions to the Performance Baseline. It is also responsible for tracking the Version descriptions and configuration management of the Baseline entries.

–The Threat Signatures and Environments (TS&E) Subgroup is responsible for reviewing and recommending additions and deletions to the TS&E Baseline; reviewing and recommending accreditation for TS&E models imbedded in performance simulations; and review and certification of the threat representations.

–The VV&A Subgroup is responsible for the overall establishment and coordination of the NMD VV&A process and procedure. The Subgroup is responsible for recommending accreditation for each NMD acquisition event requiring accreditation.

–The Interoperability Subgroup is responsible for the interoperability and reuse of the NMD M&S. This includes the coordination of a Program-wide HLA strategy and has recently introduced the concept of a Reference Federation Object Model (Reference FOM). The Interoperability Subgroup is viewed as the Object Broker for future NMD FOMs and SOMs (Simulation Object Models).

The MSAP reports directly to the System Engineering Integrated Product Team (SE IPT).

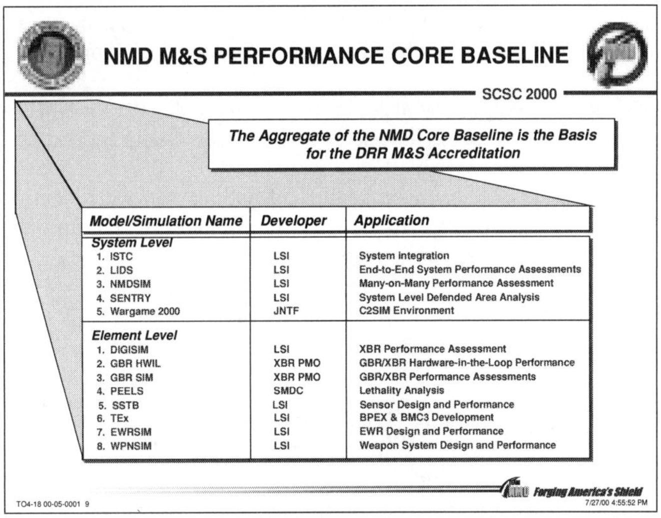

Model/Simulation Name	Developer	Application
System Level		
1. ISTC	LSI	System integration
2. LIDS	LSI	End-to-End System Performance Assessments
3. NMDSIM	LSI	Many-on-Many Performance Assessment
4. SENTRY	LSI	System Level Defended Area Analysis
5. Wargame 2000	JNTF	C2SIM Environment
Element Level		
1. DIGISIM	LSI	XBR Performance Assessment
2. GBR HWIL	XBR PMO	GBR/XBR Hardware-in-the-Loop Performance
3. GBR SIM	XBR PMO	GBR/XBR Performance Assessments
4. PEELS	SMDC	Lethality Analysis
5. SSTB	LSI	Sensor Design and Performance
6. TEx	LSI	BPEX & BMC3 Development
7. EWRSIM	LSI	EWR Design and Performance
8. WPNSIM	LSI	Weapon System Design and Performance

This is the Performance Baseline that has been accredited to support the DRR decision that is ongoing. The VV&A Subgroup decided that the accreditation of the entire baseline was desirable for DRR rather that accrediting each individual entry. This approach has worked very well in the fast paced NMD Program where analysis and accreditation are being worked in parallel. In a small number of cases, caveats to a simulation have been identified resulting in the use of alternative analysis methods.

•NMDSIM and SENTRY were added to the Baseline during the January MSAP meeting as a mitigation for the late availability of LIDS. Both simulations have been accredited for support for DRR.

•This baseline will be updated to support the upcoming System Critical Design Review (SCDR) and the 01 DAB.

•The concept of the M&S Baseline has worked well to provide the basis for DRR M&S accreditation in accordance with DoD and BMDO policies. It has also provided the discipline and structure to support the accreditation decision.

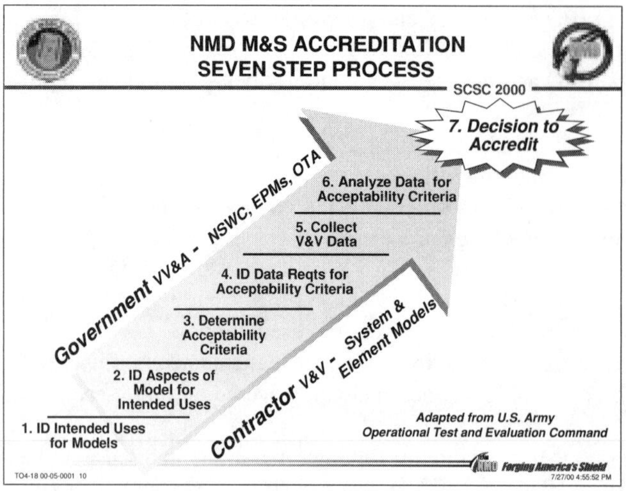

•VV&A has played a major role in the evolution of the NMD strategy and has had an overall positive effect on the NMD Program execution. It has functioned very similar to the discipline associated with a preliminary or system design review. The reality that the review will take place; that it will be very detailed; that it requires well documented results all contribute to the positive effect of the product.

• The NMD program has adopted the seven-step accreditation process used by the Army Operational Test and Evaluation Command. It has provided the structure and the flexibility necessary for the NMD Program.

•The ISTC (Integrated System Test Capability) in Huntsville, AL was the trailblazer for NMD VV&A activities supporting early Integrated Ground Tests (IGTs). The first baseline accreditation effort was in support of DRR.

•During the DRR Accreditation process, 11 Major caveats and 165 Minor caveats were identified. Further analysis of the DRR data showed that the 11 major caveats were not violated which enabled removing them from the major category. The Minor caveats are candidates for upgrade of the appropriate simulations.

•The VV&A process has provided visibility across the entire M&S effort.

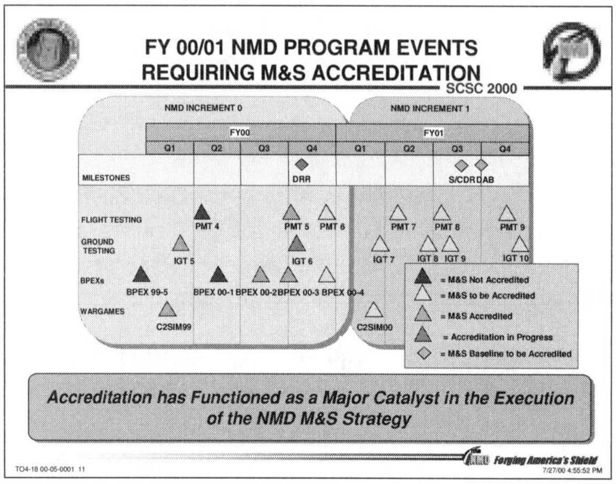

•As mentioned earlier, ISTC was the trailblazer for VV&A activities with in the NMD Program followed by the Command and Control Simulations (C2SIMs) based on the WARGAME 2000 simulation and the BMC3 simulation TEx.

•Additional accreditation events are the 01 and 03 DABs, which will require the accreditation of the total Performance Baseline. Pre-mission Testing and Battle Planning Exercises have also been identified as accreditation events as data from these activities are candidates for being included in acquisition decisions.

•Within the NMD Program, accreditation has functioned as a major catalyst in the overall execution of the NMD M&S Program.

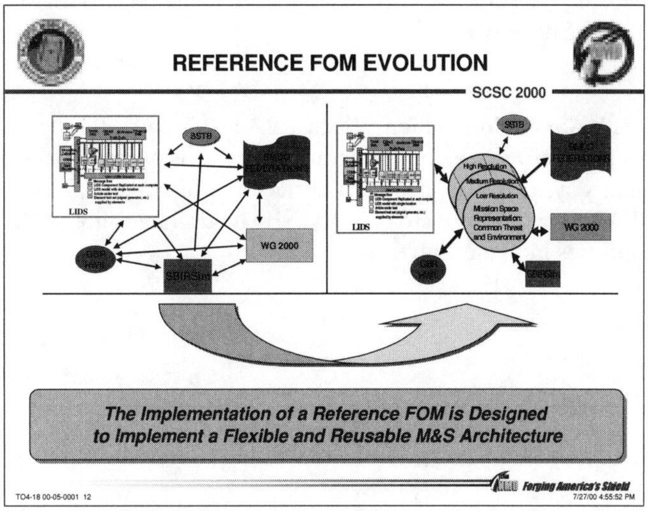

•At the June MSAP meeting, the Interoperability Subgroup introduced the concept of an NMD Reverence Federation Object Model (FOM). This Reference FOM is not viewed as an executable federation but as a top-level reference or standard to support the definition and description of federations within the NMD Program.

•Currently, the M&S architecture is made up of standalone element and system simulations. We believe that the Reference FOM will be the basis for the evolution of an NMD M&S Architecture that supports interoperability and reuse.

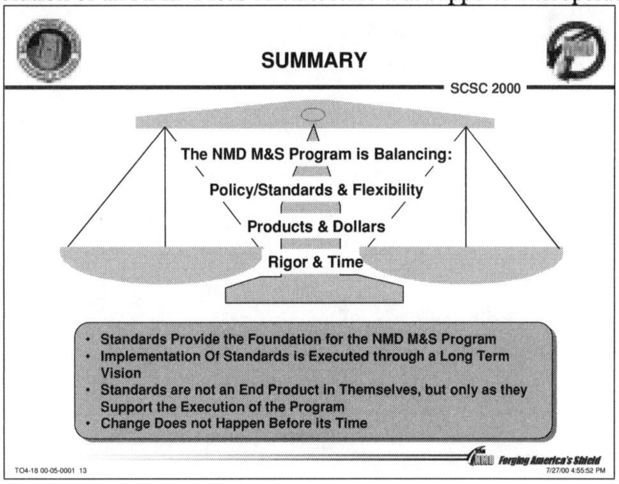

•In summary, The NMD M&S Program has been an effort in balancing policy and standards with flexibility; products with dollars; and rigor with time; all under the constraint of limited dollars, a very aggressive schedule, while knowing that the NMD Program will change as it evolves toward deployment.

•In conclusion, we would like to emphasize:
- –Standards have and are providing the foundation for the NMD M&S Program,
- –The presence of a long-term vision is necessary for implementation of the standards,
- –Standards must be applied in a manner that supports the execution of the program, and
- –We must continue working the vision as change takes time.

AUTHOR BIOGRAPHIES

James Hunt is the National Missile Defense Program Systems Engineering Lead for Modeling and Simulation, System Verification, and Software Development. He has a BSEE from VA Tech and an MPA from Troy State. He has extensive experience in DoD system acquisition and is a certified Acquisition Professional in Program Management, and in Systems Planning, Research & Development, and Engineering.

Todd Repass is a Senior Manager with Axiom Corporation, Vienna, VA and is currently supporting the Modeling and Simulation Program for the National Missile Defense Joint Program Office. His professional experience has been in research, development, and acquisition of military systems with the Naval Surface Warfare Center, Dahlgren, VA, the Space and Naval Warfare Systems Command (SPAWAR), and with private industry. He holds a Bachelor of Arts in Physics from Berea College and Master of Science in Statistics from the University of Iowa.

AMS
Army Model and Simulation Office

Modeling and Simulation Standards Development

Mr. Bruce Donlin
Army Model and Simulation Office

Into the 21st Century

Bottom Line: What will Standards do?

SMART "Goals"	M&S Standards
• Substantially Reduce the Time, Resources, and Risk Associated with the Acquisition Process;	• Reduce Time / Cost Avoidance - Reuse of algorithms, heuristics, and techniques
• Increase the Quality, Military Worth and Supportability of Fielded Systems, While Reducing their Operating and Sustaining Total Ownership Costs;	• Reduce Risk - Improved credibility / easier Validation, Verification, and Accreditation
• Enable Integrated Product and Process Development (IPPD) Across the Full Acquisition Lifecycle.	• Supports IPPD - Creates opportunities for the Army's analytic, training, and acquisition communities to leverage their model and simulation development efforts

Into the 21st Century

What is a Standard?

Definition

(from the Army's M&S Master Plan):

- Broad context to include procedures, practices, processes, techniques, data, and algorithms.
- Source of relevant standards will vary with each standards category.

Need not connote a restrictive environment... can have built in flexibility for use

Into the 21st Century

The Army's Standards Categories

M&S Areas
- Computer Generated Forces
- Deployment
- Logistics
- Mobilization
- Cost Representation

M&S Support
- Architecture
- C4I Integration
- Data
- VV&A
- Object Management
- Visualization

M&S Funct Elements
- Acquire
- Attrition
- Dynamic Environment
- Cmd Decision Modeling
- Communications Systems
- Move
- Terrain

Into the 21st Century

Standards Development Process

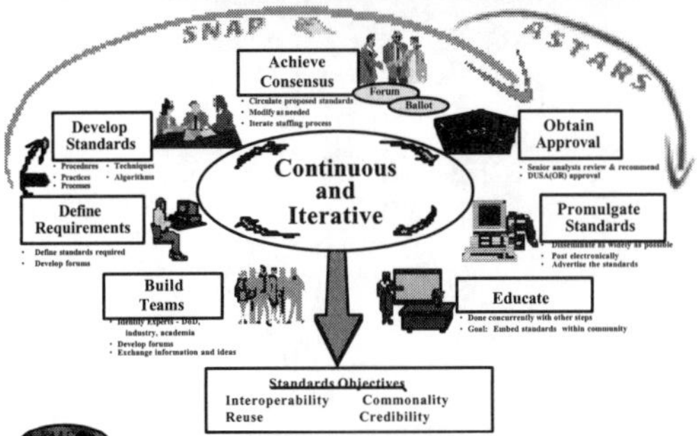

Into the 21st Century

High Payoff Areas

- ✦ Expeditious and accurate generation of terrain data
- ✦ Integration of real world C4I systems and simulations
- ✦ Standardized threat representation and development of threat data repository
- ✦ Standard methods and common requirements for data/scenario generation
- ✦ Representation of human behaviors, to include command decision modeling
- ✦ Modeling to facilitate analysis of (joint) mobilization issues
- ✦ Information Operations
- ✦ Integration of logistics within simulations
- ✦ Acquisition life cycle cost modeling
- ✦ Use of M&S to complement live testing
- ✦ Physics of failure

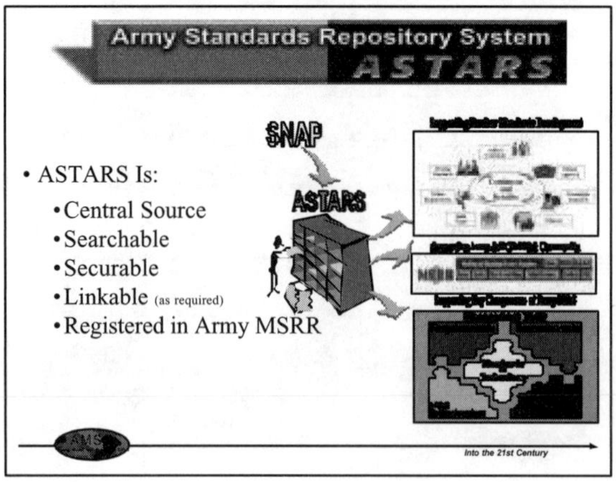

Army Standards Repository System
ASTARS
SNAP
ASTARS
• ASTARS Is:
•Central Source
•Searchable
•Securable
•Linkable (as required)
•Registered in Army MSRR
Into the 21st Century

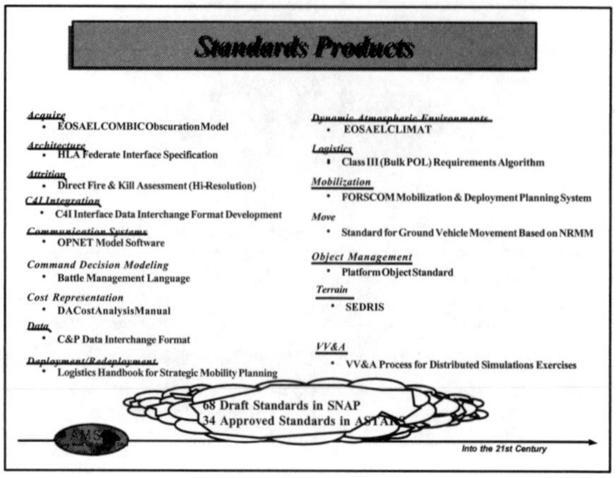

Standards Products
Acquire
• EOSAEL COMBIC Obscuration Model
Architecture
• HLA Federate Interface Specification
Attrition
• Direct Fire & Kill Assessment (Hi-Resolution)
C4I Integration
• C4I Interface Data Interchange Format Development
Communication Systems
• OPNET Model Software
Command Decision Modeling
• Battle Management Language
Cost Representation
• DA Cost Analysis Manual
Data
• C&P Data Interchange Format
Deployment/Redeployment
• Logistics Handbook for Strategic Mobility Planning
Dynamic Atmospheric Environments
• EOSAEL CLIMAT
Logistics
• Class III (Bulk POL) Requirements Algorithm
Mobilization
• FORSCOM Mobilization & Deployment Planning System
Move
• Standard for Ground Vehicle Movement Based on NRMM
Object Management
• Platform Object Standard
Terrain
• SEDRIS
VV&A
• VV&A Process for Distributed Simulations Exercises
68 Draft Standards in SNAP
34 Approved Standards in ASTARS
Into the 21st Century

The Naval Training Meta-FOM

Jeff Bergenthal
Lockheed Martin Information Systems

Doug Clark
Analysis & Technology, Inc.

Agenda

- Background
- Why A Meta-FOM
- NTMF Goals
- The Envisioned Solution
- Making it Happen
- Developing the FOM
- Next Steps in the FOM Development
- Acknowledgements

Some Motivation JV 2010* and 2020

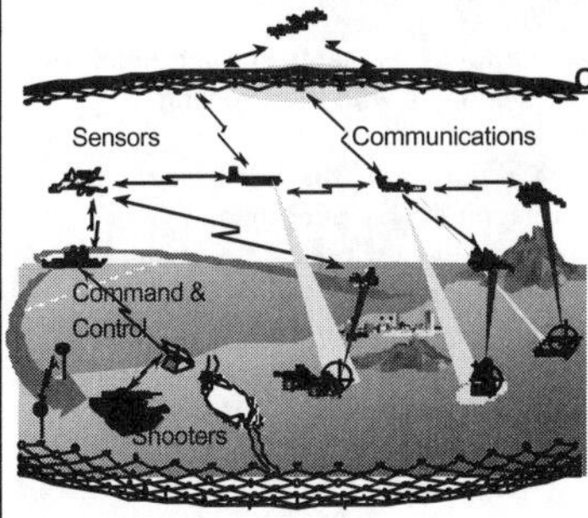

Emerging Operational Concepts

- Dominant Maneuver
- Precision Engagement
- Focused Logistics
- Full-Dimensional Protection

*Adapted from J6 Brief

Background

- Network Centric Warfare requires interaction and cooperation across a broad range of Naval systems:
  - Requires interoperability among simulation & training (S&T) systems in a *meaningful* way.
- Battlespaces represented in Naval S&T systems differ in both content & resolution.
- Ad hoc Government/Industry working group meetings have met to:
  - Explore the value of interoperability
  - Determine a methodology for achieving meaningful interoperability

Why a Naval Training Meta-FOM

- Provides a venue for standardizing the representation of the mission space
- Necessary to eliminate duplication of effort for recreating mission space elements (synthetic natural environment and battle space entities) build once and reuse often acquisition philosophy including cost savings
- Leads to higher interoperability through the creation of a standard lexicon, semantics, data dictionary, taxonomy,...
- Eliminates multiple interfaces to federations and federates (point to point solutions)
- Provides training commands a framework of understanding for their synthetic training capabilities allowing them to create federations to support training needs and objectives.

Do We Want This?

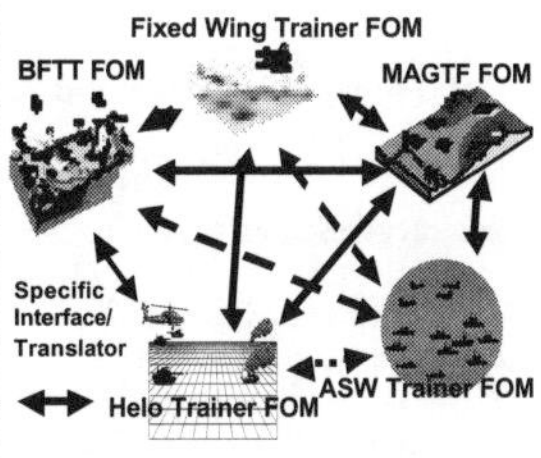

Multiple Naval Training FOMs with Multiple Interfaces

Or Do We Want This?

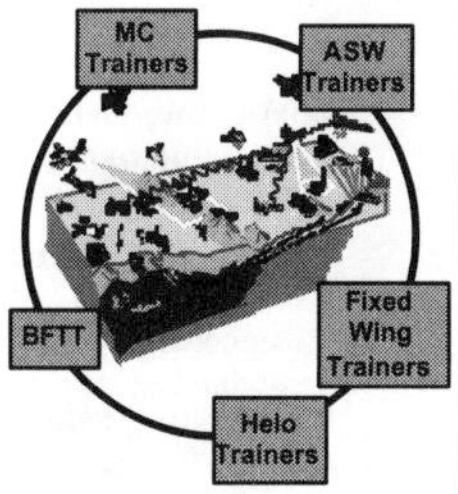

One Naval Training Meta-FOM

NTMF Goals

- Address three needs within Naval simulation & training systems:
  - The need for the force to be able to train as they will fight.
  - The need for a common synthetic battlespace that can be established as a "standard."
  - The need for the simulation & training systems to evolve as the force, weapons systems, and threat evolves.

Train As the Force Will Fight

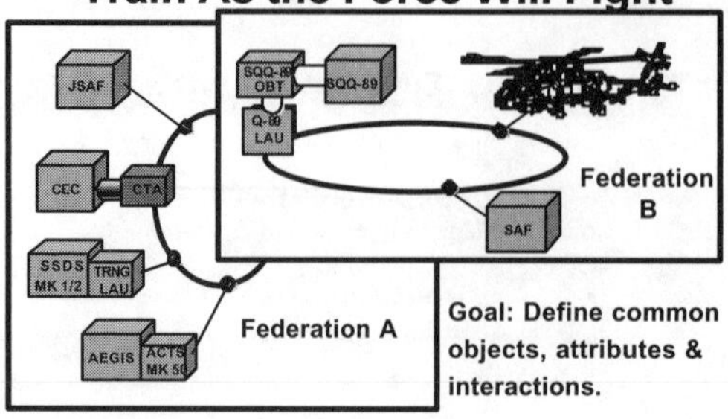

Goal: Define common objects, attributes & interactions.

Common Synthetic Mission Space

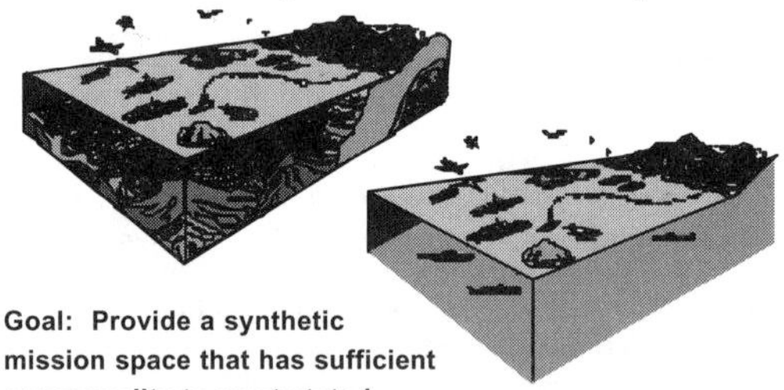

Goal: Provide a synthetic mission space that has sufficient commonality to meet stated training objectives.

Evolving Mission Space

- The NTMF provides a rapidly available starting point for training systems to keep pace with the evolving mission space.
- Naval mission space is not static, the force, weapons systems and the threat all evolve over time.
- In particular the NTMF allows for the S&T systems to evolve with the mission space:
  - Inclusion of data & models allows for evolution of second order factors (e.g., is the SNE representation robust enough to model a new sensor in a sufficiently realistic manner?)

Envisioned Solution

- Naval Training Meta-FOM (NTMF) focused on Tier 1 and Tier 2 training systems
- Meta-FOM will encompass:
  - A reference FOM from which individual Naval training federations can be drawn.
  - "Standards" for data and models to be used by the federates to obtain consistency and fair fight within a Naval training federation (i.e., meaningful interoperability)
  - Best practice guidance for developing a particular FOM from the "standard" FOM.

Envisioned Solution

- A "standard" Meta-FOM will evolve over time to cover additional federates and federations
  - FOM agility will be essential
- Data and models are a formalization of "federation agreements"
  - Convergence over time
- Data and models available for reuse:
  - New simulation & training systems
  - Pre-planned program improvements of legacy systems

Making it Happen- The NTMF Process

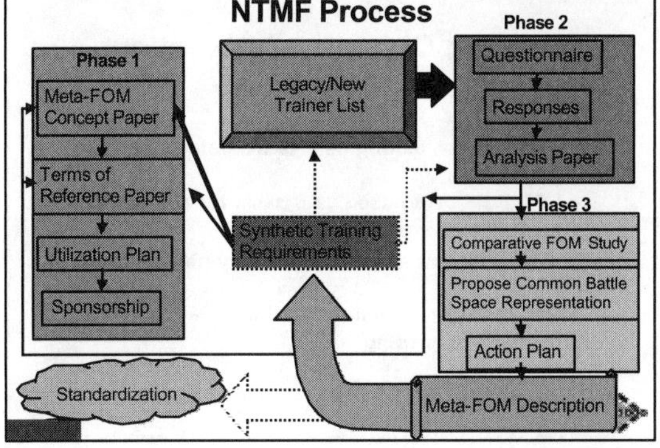

Determining Requirements

- 20 legacy systems identified as candidates and POC identified
- Detailed questionnaire developed:
  - Basic system information
  - Interoperability aspects
  - Synthetic mission space description
- Questionnaire submitted to system POCs

Questionnaire Examples

1 General Description of the Model/Simulation's Purpose
   Indicate the Functional Usage of the Model/Simulation
2 What other simulation systems do you have a requirement to interoperate with?
   Which time models does the simulation support?
3 What sensors does the simulation support?
   What portion of the acoustic spectrum does the simulation use in its model?

Analysis of Responses

- 14 responses received covering surface, subsurface, air, and ground domains
- All systems run in real time (1:1)
- General level of detail is at the entity/contact level
- Support a wide range of missions, platforms & weapons
- Wide variety of sensors and spectral ranges
- SNE must encompass atmospheric, oceanographic and terrain data & effects

Use Cases

- Two use cases are being developed for federations of near term systems of interest:
  - Subset of the total number of systems
  - Provide broad coverage over the synthetic battlespace:
    - Missions-Combined ASW and Strike
    - Synthetic Natural Environment
    - Sensors
    - Platforms
- Basis for scenarios to be used in federation testing

Use Case Matrix

	Combined ASW	Shore-based re-supply	Strike	CSAR	Operational maneuver from the sea	Air defense	Theater missile defense	Joint operations	Surface warfare
Training device /program									
GASS	Y	N	N	N	N	N	N	Y	Y
BFTT	Y	N	Y	N	Y	Y	Y	Y	Y
VA-Class OBT	Y	N	Y	N	N	N	N	N	Y
JT CTS	N	N	Y	N	N	Y	N	Y	N
SMMTT	Y .25	N	Y	N	N	N	Y (ISR)	?	Y
COSTD	Y	N	Y	N	N	N	Y	N	Y
H60 TU/S/R	Y	Y	N	Y	Y	N	N	Y	Y
MAGTF	N	N	N	Y	Y	N	N	Y	N
SETI	Y	N	N	N	N	N	N	N	Y
BFTT/JCTCS	Y	N	Y	N	Y	Y	Y	Y	Y
F-14	N	N	Y	Y	N	Y	N	Y	N
Totals	8	1	7	3	4	4	4	7	8
PRI	3B		1			4			3a

The NTMF is using an Abbreviated Federation Development and Execution Process (FEDEP)

- Activities focused on FEDEP Steps 2 - 4
  - Reuse
- Requirements based on training scope and objectives
  - Multiple federations
  - Training data
- Concurrent activity addressing Step 1 products:
  - Terms of Reference
  - Concept Paper

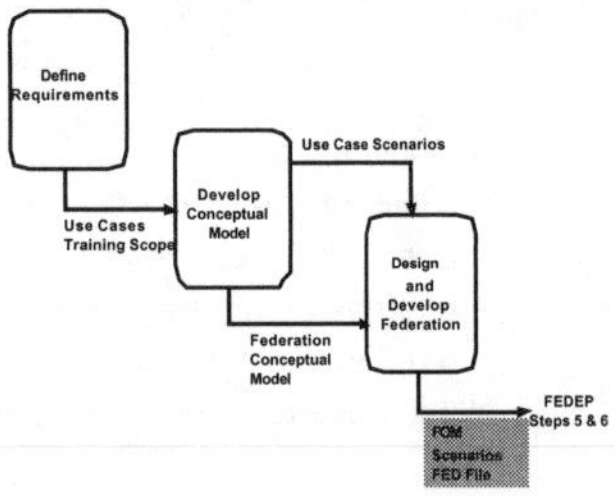

Defining Objects & Interactions

- Initial efforts are focused on defining commonalties and differences among near term systems of interest:
  - RPR FOM being used as a basis for comparison
  - Identify and explain additions
- Resolve differences when there is conflict or overlap
  - Use cases provide input to this
- Define what's missing

Where we are Today

- NTMF Charter and Terms of Reference published
- FOM Questionnaire
- Members of the Working Group include:
  - Navy Laboratories
  - Chief Of Naval Operations Organizations
  - Navy Systems Commands
  - Marine Corp
  - Academia
  - Trainer developers and Implementers
- Point(s) of Contact
  - Doug Clark, Development Lead- 703-418-8667
  - Peter Kassal, Chair-703-602-1782/643

Next Steps in the NTMF Development

- Beta version of NTMF in late CY01
- Follow FEDEP Steps 5&6 during CY01,CY02 for near term systems of interest
- Test objectives of federation testing:
  - Verify specific aspects of interoperability for each federation
  - Begin to identify and quantify the effects of inconsistencies

Why a "standard"?

- A "standard" provides a rapidly available starting point for the NTMF to keep pace with the evolving mission space.
- A "standard" will provide a synthetic natural environment that has been accepted by the training community.
- A "standard" that includes a mission space representation, including common models and data as well as syntax and semantics will promote meaningful reuse and interoperability.
- A "standard" will reduce acquisition and pre planned product improvement costs.

Summary

- Need for interoperability and a "standard" synthetic mission space has been recognized across the training community.
- Ad hoc group formed to address the need
  - Cooperative effort of Government and Industry personnel including program managers, developers, users and modelers.
- NTMF concept supported by the Navy Modeling and Simulation office N6M.
- Plan of action and milestones have been developed and are being implemented.

Acknowledgements

- Mike O'Neal, PMS430 Program Manager (Major Acquisition Program Manager)
- Peter Kassal, PMS430 Technical Director and Chair NTMF Working Group

BACKUP

Why a Naval Training Meta-FOM

- Provides a venue for standardizing the representation of the mission space
- Necessary to eliminate duplication of effort for recreating mission space elements (synthetic natural environment and battle space entities) Build once and reuse often acquisition philosophy
- Leads to higher interoperability through the creation of a standard lexicon, semantics, data dictionary, taxonomy,...
- Eliminates multiple interfaces to federations and federates (point to point solutions)
- provides a framework of understanding for training commands of their synthetic training system capabilities to allow them to create training federations to supports training needs and objectives

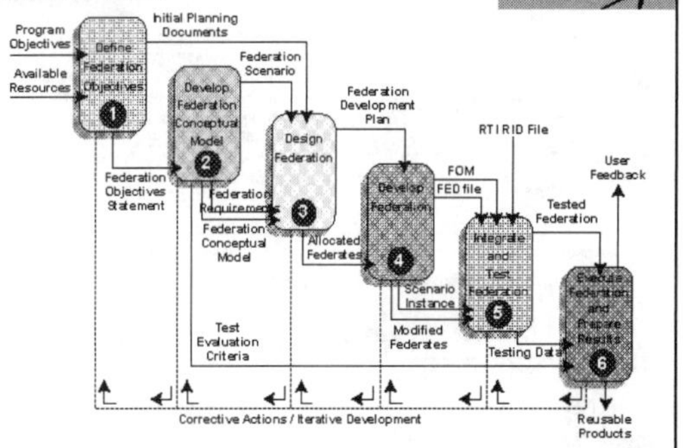

Can They All Train Together?

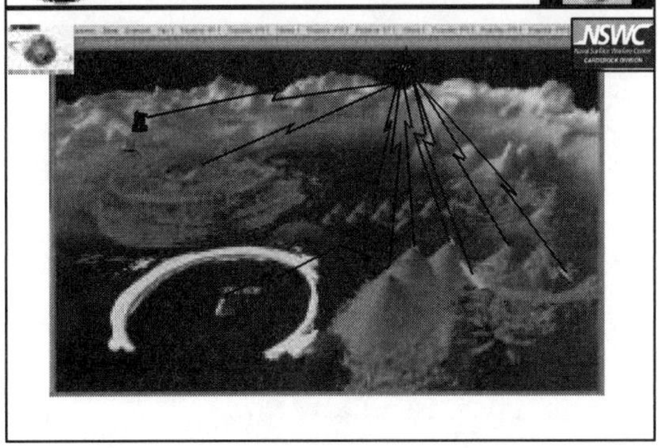

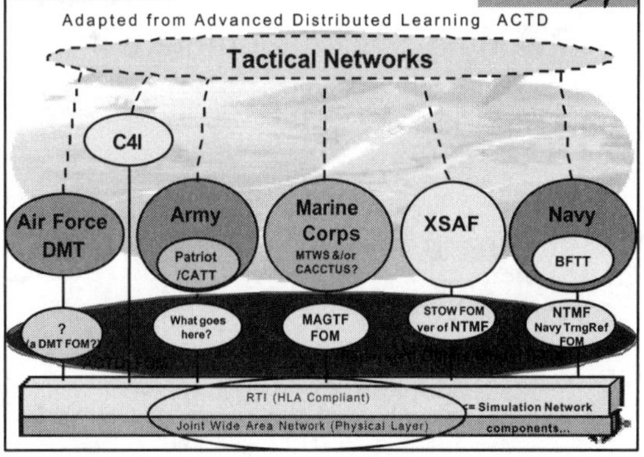

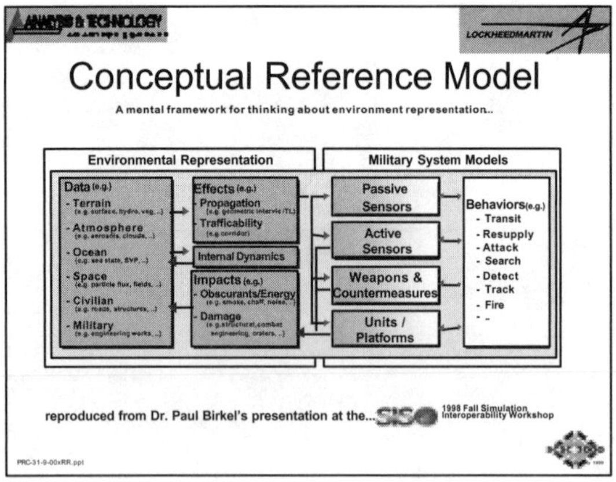

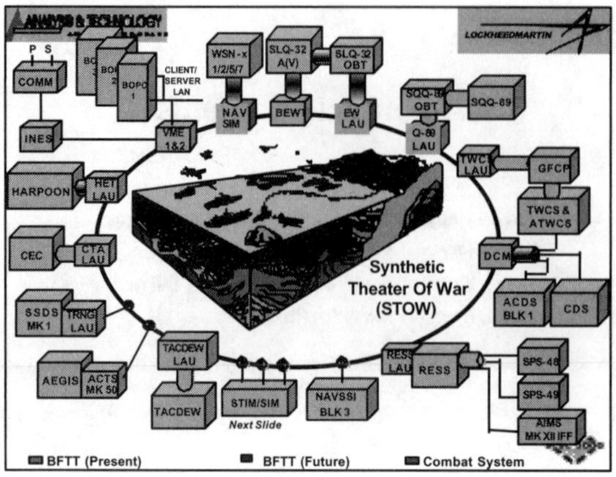

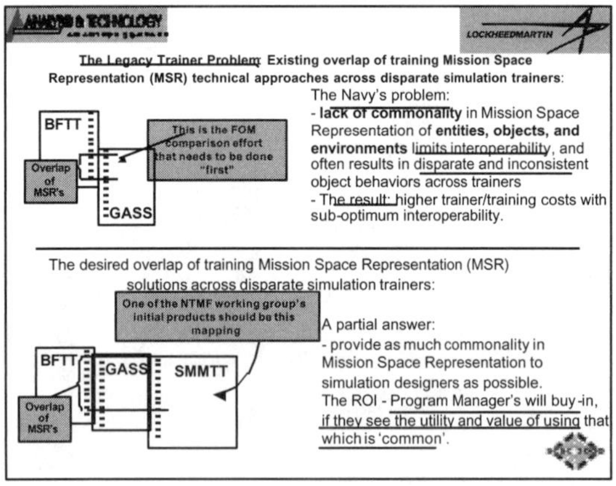

Today's Situation	Way Ahead
• Inability to train as a Team	• BFTT, JTCTS, NTMF
• Limited ability for Fleet units and school houses to connect training systems	• MMTT, SMMTT
• Unable to provide realistic coordinated training	• BFTT, MMTT, SMMTT, JTCTS
• Different manufacturers / vintages / environment & target databases	• HLA, Retire, NTMF, SCDL ATAS
• Unrealistic representation of physics based models	• NTMF, MARVEDS

Training Systems of Interest

- Focus on Naval Tier 1 and Tier 2 systems
- Near term systems of interest:
  - BFTT
  - GASS
  - SMMTT
  - SH-60B/R Upgrade
  - JTCTS
  - MAGTF, Marine System

Attaining an Authoritative Environment:

SEDRIS in the Real World

Mike Hunsucker
ASNE MSEA
for V. Dobey, MSEA(Ocean)

What is SEDRIS?

Synthetic Environment Data Representation and Interchange Specification

Tackling the Requirements Problem

Very large number of users with both common & unique requirement

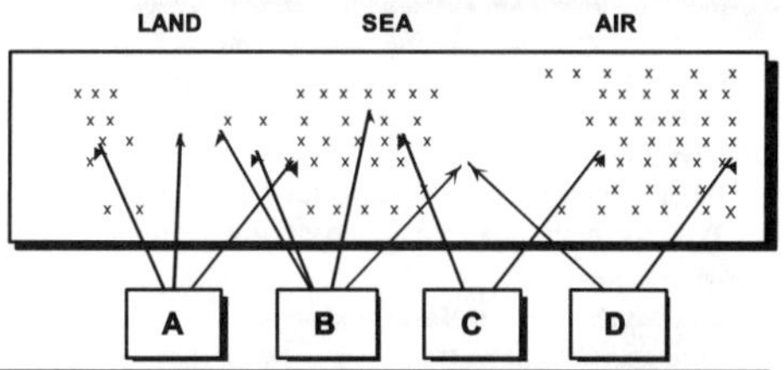

Agencies or companies that produce environmental databases

***The Key:** Small number of environmental database builders (in contrast to environmental data user)*

SEDRIS Program

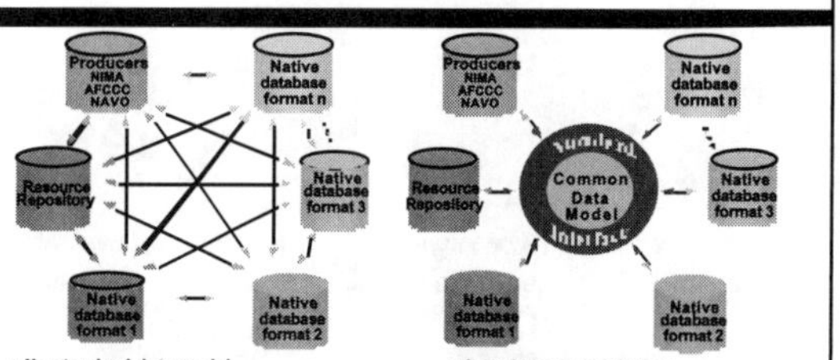

- No standard data model
- Limited support to heterogeneous simulation
- Indeterminantinterchange mechanism
- Expensive database conversion

- Complete representation
- Enables interoperability
- Lossless and consistent interchange
- 100x reduction in conversion costs

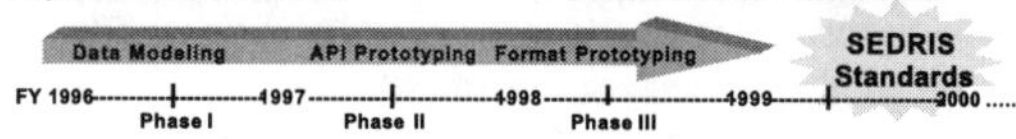

SEDRIS Objectives

- Articulate and capture the complete set of data elements and associated relationships needed to fully represent environmental data:
  - *Data Representation Model (DRM)*
  - *Environmental Data Coding Specification (EDCS)*
  - *Spatial Reference Model (SRM)*
- Provide a standard interchange mechanism to pre distribute environmental data and promote database reuse among heterogeneous applications
- Support the full range of applications across all environmental domains (terrain, ocean, atmosphere, and space)

Describe Environmental Data

- The grammar, syntax, and structural semantics provided by the DRM
- The comprehensive, accurate, and efficient coordinate reference frames provided by the SRM
- And the classification and attribution schemes provided by the EDCS

These three powerful components allow data providers to express and describe their data objects, and the internal relationships, clearly and unambiguously.

Exchange Environmental Data

- **The access mechanisms provided by the Read and Write APIs, which are coupled to and reflect the data representation model**
- **And the mediabased format**

These two practical components (coupled with the previous three) allow data providers and consumers to develop applications that can access, manipulate, and interchange all types of environmental data efficiently through a common interface, while promoting sharing and reuse.

Technology Components of SEDRIS

- ***Data Representation Model (DRM):*** **Provides syntax and structural semantics for representing environmental data and databases**
- ***Spatial Reference Model (SRM):*** **Unified and robust description of the coordinate systems, along with an accurate, efficient, and fast software implementation**
- ***Environmental Data Coding Specification (EDCS):*** **Provides "thing" level semantics (classify/attribute scheme)**
- ***Software Interface Specification*** **(Read and Write Application Programmer Interfaces (APIs))**
  - **Allows ease of access**
  - **Lowers the barrier-to-entry in software development**
- ***SEDRIS Transmittal Format (STF):*** **Platform independent storage and transmission of data**

Spatial Reference...

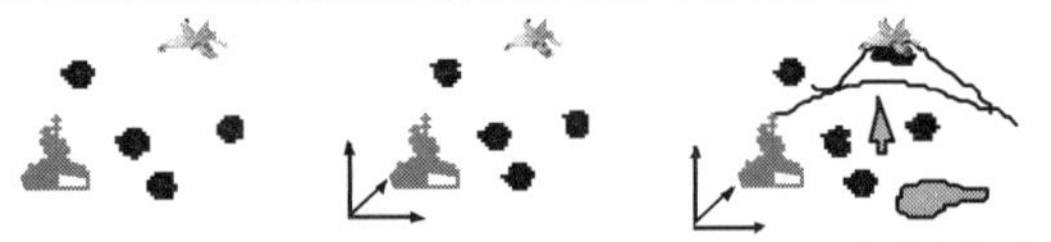

Systems

The void ...

Systems, *where?*

Start with locating your systems; sometimes that's about all you could afford in legacy simulations.

Systems, *and what else?*

Define the context within which systems engage; and that context can advantage, or disadvantage, ...

Defining and using a consistent spatial reference framework is critical for M&S interoperability

- **System models (men, material, ...)**
- **Environmental data, models, phenomena**

Spatial Reference Model Requirements

- ***Completeness:***
  - **Include coordinate systems in common usage**
  - **Tie those systems together into a common framework**
  - **Educate the system developer** (e.g., What's a horizontal datum? A vertical datum?)
- ***Accuracy:***
  - **Generally higher than required for C4ISR systems**
  - **Typically better than 1 cm up past geosynchronous orbit**
- ***Performance:***
  - **Computation speed: Never fast enough!**
  - **Support environmental data sets dominated by location data**
  - **Reduce costs for simulation using heterogeneous coordinate systems (spatial reference frames)**

SEDRIS Spatial Reference Frames

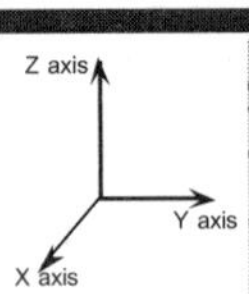

Arbitrary ORM	Local Space Rectangular	LSR2	2D	
		LSR	3D	
Earth-Centered, Earth-Fixed	Geocentric	GC	3D	
Earth-Surface, Global	Geodetic	GD2	2D	
		GD	3D	
Earth-Surface, Local (Topocentric)	Local Tangent Plane	LTP2	2D	
		LTP	3D	
	GCS	GCS	3D	
Earth-Surface, Projection-Based	Mercator	M	2D	
		AM	3D	
	Oblique Mercator	OM	2D	*Spherical ERM Only*
		AOM	3D	
	Transverse Mercator	TM	2D	
		ATM	3D	
	Universal Transverse Mercator (60)	UTM	2D	
		AUTM	3D	
	Lambert Conformal Conic	LCC	2D	
		ALCC	3D	
	Polar Stereographic	PS	2D	
		APS	3D	
	Universal Polar Stereographic (2)	UPS	2D	
		AUPS	3D	
	Equidistant Cylindrical	EC	2D	*Spherical ERM Only*
		AEC	3D	
Earth-Centered, Rotating (Inertial & Quasi-Inertial)	Geomagnetic	GM	3D	
	Geocentric Equatorial Inertial	GEI	3D	
	Geocentric Solar Ecliptic	GSE	3D	
	Geocentric Solar Magnetospheric	GSM	3D	
	Solar Magnetic	SM	3D	

SEDRIS at Runtime

- **Unambiguous representation of environmental data**
  - ***Data Representation Model:*** **Complex data elements in object-based model**
  - ***Data Coding Standard:*** **Well-specified data element definitions / semantics**
  - ***Spatial Reference Model:*** **Completeness, accuracy, performance**

  Experimental Application (at runtime)
- **Efficient interchange of environmental data (pre-simulation runtime)**
  - ***Interface Specification:*** **Platform and language independent APIs, with reference implementation**
  - ***Transmittal Format:*** **Assures architecture neutral data exchange, when required**
  - **Tools and applications: Inspect, evaluate, verify, transform, ...**

  Replaced by RTI (at runtime)

Transmittal Format Requirements

- ***Platform Independence:***
  - Both software and files
  - Adapts to platform's word order
- ***Fully Support the SEDRIS Data Representation Model:***
  - Full expressive power of the DRM
  - Data driven via DRM support functions
  - Completely lossless with respect to objects instantiated by the data provider
- ***Space Efficient Media Storage:*** Minimal overhead with respect to the size of the SEDRIS objects stored
- ***Run-time Efficiency:***
  - Efficient with respect to both memory and processing time
  - Heavier emphasis on extraction performance than on insertion
- ***Insulate Developers from Implementation Details:*** Format and software can evolve independently from applications
- ***Leverage Existing Format Standards where it makes sense:*** Images and Data Tables

Attaining an Authoritative Environment

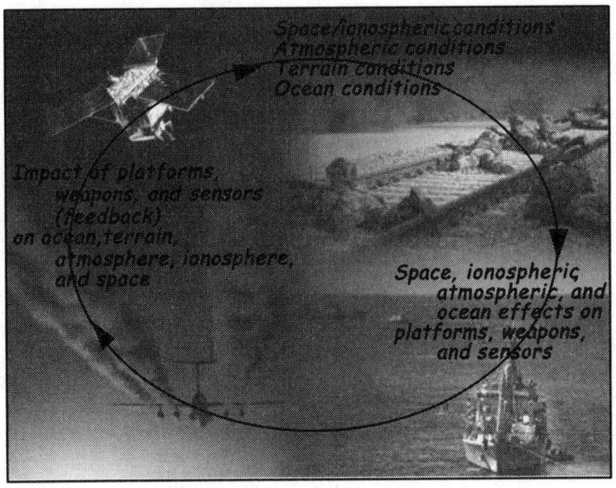

Characteristics of METOC Data

- Sampled values representing a continuous phenomenon
  - Gridded data, linear profiles, regional observations
  - Uniformly spaced time samples
- Complete representation usually requires assembling data from multiple sources and multiple files
  - 3-D, multi-quantity grids often disassembled into 2D, one-quantity files
  - Observations, analysis, forecasts, scientific models
- Each source may use a different format
  - Ad-hoc based on sensor, numeric application, textual report, ...
  - International standards: World Meteorological Organization (WMO)

METOC Data Sets

- Atmospheric Forecast Data
- Atmospheric Observations
- Ocean Forecast Data
- Ocean Observations
- Climatology
- Bathymetry
- Marginal Ice Zone
- Space Wx Observations

Meteorology, Oceanography & Space Data

We need technologies to:

- Provide stronger and more explicit structuring of complex data formats, especially for data integration
- Eliminate consumer dependency on data format
- Provide more than one way to represent data

Space Data Sets

- IonosphericScintillation
- Electron Density Profile
- Solar Energetic Particles
- Solar Electromagnetic Emissions
- MagnetosphericPlasma
- Geomagnetic Fields
- Solar Wind
- AuroralEmissions
- Interplanetary Magnetic Fields
- AuroralPrecipitating Particles
- Cosmic Rays
- Auroral Electrojet
- Total Electron Count (Vertical)
- Neutral Density
- Trapped Energetic Particles

...Environmental Effects and Impacts

DARPA, LockheedMartinDatabases

Spatial Reference Frames

Spatial Reference Frames (SRF) serve to locate coordinates in a multidimensional space (generally either two or three-dimensional). They are specified in two parts:

- A geometric description (model) of a reference object embedded in (and serving to orient) that frame referred to as an *Object Reference Model (ORM)*
  - An Earth Reference Model (ERM) is a special case of an ORM
- A *Coordinate System (CS)* specifying how a tuple of values uniquely determine a location with respect to the origin of that frame. By extension, that tuple also specifies a location with respect to the reference object.

SRF = ORM + CS

SEDRIS Program

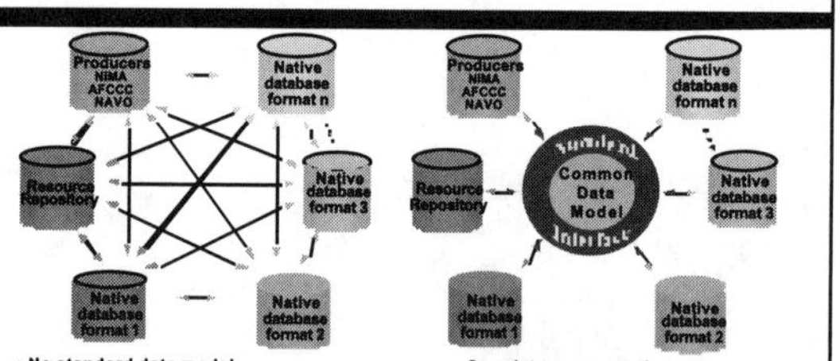

- No standard data model
- Limited support to heterogeneous simulation
- Indeterminant interchange mechanism
- Expensive database conversion

- Complete representation
- Enables interoperability
- Lossless and consistent interchange
- 100x reduction in conversion costs

Summary

SEDRIS is:

- An integrated collection of tightly coupled technologies that allow complete and unambiguous representation of environmental data
- An infrastructure technology that can be used in many applications
- An open development process and has benefited greatly from the significant contributions of practitioners from all environmental domains
- In use and rigorously tested, and its foundational concepts have not changed in more than two years

To get More Information...

- Visit the SEDRIS web site *www.sedris.org*
- Request SEDRIS Development Team Resources:
  - Proceedings from the SEDRIS Technology Conferences (STCs), February 11-12 and September 28-30, 1999
  - Next STC: August 22-24, 2000 - Snowbird, Utah
  - Various video tapes, tutorials and presentations
- Attend Commercial Courses

A realistic environment obtained and reused through SEDRIS

Navy C4ISR Communication Modeling Standard

Albert K. Legaspi, Ph.D

Navy Modeling and Simulation Management Office
OPNAV N6M Technical Support Group
SPAWARSYSCOM PD-13 TSG
4301 Pacific Highway
San Diego CA 92110-5115
legaspi@spawar.navy.mil

Carl Ivancic

Network Communications Consulting
6325 Oakridge Road
San Diego, CA 92120
(619) 286-4723
ncconsulting@home.com

Keywords: C4ISR, NETWARS, Communication Effects, FOM

ABSTRACT: The Navy Modeling and Simulation Management Office (NAVMSMO) N6M is responsible for the centralized management of Navy Modeling and Simulation (M&S) activities, coordination of M&S efforts across functional areas, and development of policies and procedures for Navy M&S standardization. The Navy also participates in M&S efforts throughout the DoD and the Joint Services to ensure that Naval interests are addressed, and most importantly, to provide technical feedback to the standards process and procedures of the Navy. One area of active participation is in a Joint Chiefs of Staff (JCS) J6 initiative called Network Warfare Simulation (NETWARS). The objectives of NETWARS are to provide a common M&S framework for communications burden analysis for a Joint Task Force (JTF), and a robust analysis capability to assist in communication planning that includes assessments of the impacts of leading edge technologies on JTF communications. The NETWARS Standards Group was formed to develop a modeling standard to enhance the re-usability and interoperability of models throughout the Joint Services. The Navy has led the development of an approach that involves a classification of network applications, devices and protocols into Network Element Classes. Focusing on J6's communication analysis requirements, the Navy derived a set of Measures of Effectiveness/Performance (MOE/MOP), which were used in the derivation of essential attributes for each specific network element class. The work presented in this paper is the basis for the NETWARS Reference Federation Object Model (FOM). This reference FOM serves a dual purpose: (a) It provides a necessary and sufficient set of attributes for a communication modeling environment to participate in a NETWARS simulation run. (b) It provides information on the types of data that may be available for other simulations that participate in a federation.

1. Introduction

The Navy Modeling and Simulation Management Office (NAVMSMO) OPNAV N6M is responsible for the establishment of guidelines, policy and procedures for Modeling, Simulation, and Analysis in order to provide for Navy-wide requirements in this area. As part of a major on-going effort in enhancing reuse, NAVMSMO has established a Navy Modeling and Simulation Information System (NMSIS) to provide a central repository for Modeling and Simulation (M&S) guidelines, policy, instructions, and information on various models that are being used or developed. It is envisioned that potential model designers will access the information from NMSIS to facilitate development of their models. Recognizing that there are many modeling environments in use or under development, NAVMSMO considers it essential that model capabilities be made known and easily available to the general M&S community.

In order to facilitate the re-use of models Navy-wide, NAVMSMO invests in the development of standards for communication system models. Additionally, NAVMSMO engages in the study and documentation of the Command, Control, Communications, Computers, Intelligence, Surveillance, and Reconnaissance (C^4ISR) modeling environment through capture of capabilities of classification. The intent of this task is to further enhance the Navy's thrust toward reusability and interoperability of communications networks modeling and analysis efforts.

Domain	Composition	Example
Network	Nodes connected by communication links	End System, Router
Node	Process objects and lower-level nodes	Router
Process	Finite State Transition Diagram	TCP Connection Process
Proto-C	Open language for protocols and algorithms	Priority Queueing Algorithm

Figure 1. OPNET Modeling Hierarchy

The purpose of this paper is to present the network simulation standards development performed for the NAVMSMO. The objective of the standards documentation is to promote model reusability and interoperability and assist in the development of High Level Architecture (HLA) Simulation and Federation Object Models (FOMs) through standardization of attributes. This report documents the set of list classes and attributes of the Reference FOM. The approach is intended to minimize the impact to model development and to leverage definitions from existing commercial and Department of Defense (DoD) models, Information Exchange Requirements (IERs), and established standards.

The results of this effort can be used to facilitate the development of a core, reusable, communications M&S capability such as the NETwork WARfare Simulation (NETWARS) program. The standards are primarily intended as a starting point for engineers and developers who are embarking on the development of new models. The standards provide a framework for model development as well as a reference for key attributes that are required for proper model functionality. While legacy models can be modified to conform to the standards, the intent is to guide and assist M&S developers in building new models of communications devices (i.e. routers, switches, etc.). The utilization of the standard element classes and attributes is intended to apply to most communication modeling environments.

2. Communication Modeling Approach

This section presents the standard network modeling approach and the hierarchy of communications network models.

2.1 Modeling Environment

The OPtimized Network Engineering Tools (OPNET) Modeler/Radio tool by MIL-3 provides the current modeling environment in NETWARS. While the Reference FOM is applicable to most modeling environments, the OPNET modeling environment provides a good example of the hierarchy, modularity, and parameterization of models upon which the network modeling approach is based. OPNET provides a hierarchical modeling environment as shown in Figure 1. At the *process model* level, a finite state transition diagram is used to represent the behavior of an algorithm or protocol. The process model may have embedded code based on Proto-C language constructs. At the middle level, the *node model*, discrete functions such as buffering, transmitting, receiving, and processing data packets are performed by separate objects, some of which may rely on an underlying lower level process model. These objects can be connected together to form a higher-level node model. At the highest level, node objects based on underlying node models are deployed and connected by links to form the *network model*. The network model defines the specific communications system that is simulated.

2.2 Model Development

Network model development utilizes the OPNET modular network modeling environment as illustrated in Figure 2. The hierarchical and modular approach is used to model systems at the highest network/subnetwork levels down to the lowest process levels by assembling the components with the appropriate parameters. Thus, model development is characterized by parameterized and modular models in order to maximize model reuse and potential study options.

As shown in Figure 2, typical network models can be composed of subnetwork modules that are interconnected by channel media models. The subnetwork models are composed of clients/servers, links, and routers/gateways. The communications between clients and servers are characterized by the use of reliable protocols such as the Transmission Control Protocol (TCP) and unreliable protocols such as the User Datagram Protocol (UDP). The clients and servers can also utilize protocols such as Ethernet for basic network connectivity. Links are defined by type (e.g., point-to-point or bus) and configuration

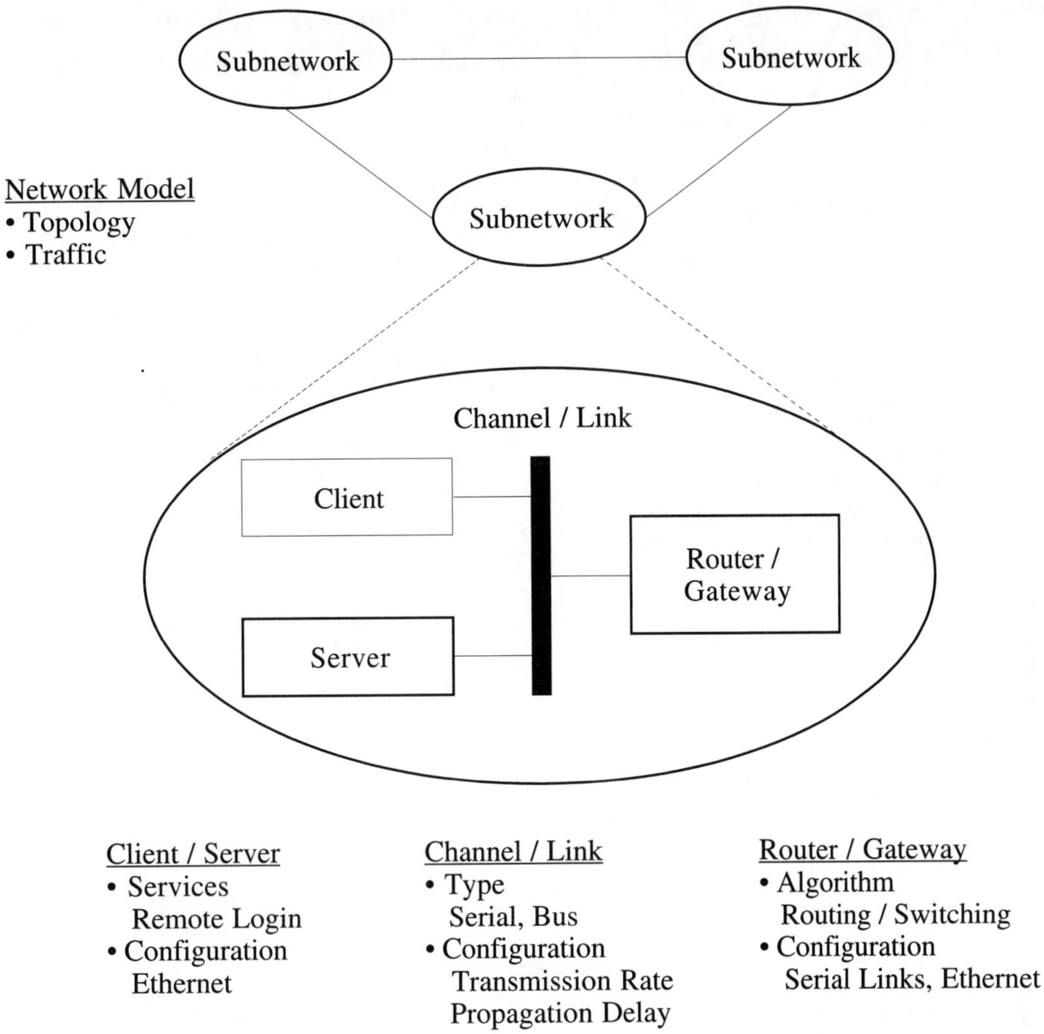

Figure 2. Network Modeling Environment

parameters (e.g., transmission rate and propagation delay). Gateways are characterized by switching/routing algorithms and port connectivity configurations (e.g., serial links and Ethernet).

The development approach involves an incremental build of capabilities that are verified at intermediate levels to ensure confidence in the results obtained from subsequently more complex models and simulations. The hierarchical and modular model development plan involves the construction of individually validated models from the process level to the network level which then become the foundation of the final system model and simulation.

2.3 Model Validation

Model validation criteria ensure the proper operation of process, node, and network models. Model validation criteria consist of both functional and performance characteristics. Functional validation is achieved by tracing traffic flows through predetermined scenarios to verify proper network model operation. Network model performance validation is achieved by monitoring statistical probes of associated network elements. In general, deterministic traffic scenarios are run in order to facilitate comparisons of predicted versus simulated results. A validated model is used as an operational and performance baseline in subsequent analyses. The validated models developed in a task can be added to a reusable model library.

2.4 Model Standards Development

The model standards development complements the modular framework of the network modeling environment which provides the ability to create network models from parameterized combinations of lower level models. The development of model standards is expected to evolve and grow with increased participation and support from the M&S community. At a minimum, model standards should provide increasingly valuable guidelines to diverse modelers to assist them in the development of reusable communications models.

3. Standard Model Components

This section describes the components of the model standards and their definitions. As illustrated in Figure 2, the modular framework of the network modeling environment provides the ability to create network models from parameterized combinations of lower level models.

3.1 Model Classes

Communications elements are grouped into model classes. The model classes are presented in Section 4.

3.1.1 Minimum Attributes

Each model class has an associated minimum set of attributes that describes the functionality and performance of the communications device. The minimum attributes for each model class are presented in Section 4. Depending upon the desired level of model fidelity, the value of each attribute may or may not be defined. For some high fidelity models, it may be necessary to include more attributes. This document attempts to present a minimum set of attributes that are common to all high fidelity models in that functional class.

3.1.2 Attribute Types

The six different types of attributes are as follows:

- **String** – Text string value
- **Real** – Double precision floating point number
- **Integer** – Long integer number
- **Boolean** – True/False, 1/0, Enabled/Disabled, On/Off
- **Enumerated** – Datatype that can be assigned only a finite set of values
- **Complex** – Datatype that consists of a group of multiple attribute types in a single structure

3.1.3 Attribute Classifications

For model development purposes, attributes are also classified as mandatory/optional and static/dynamic.

3.1.3.1 Mandatory and Optional Attributes

An attribute is designated as *mandatory* if it is required to adequately model a device at all levels of fidelity. If it is possible to model the device functionality at some level of fidelity without the attribute, then the attribute is designated as *optional* or *not mandatory*. The illustration in Figure 3 provides a visual representation of the concept of mandatory attributes with respect to the levels of modeling fidelity. As shown in Figure 3, models of the lowest level of fidelity are composed entirely of *mandatory* attributes, and models of higher fidelity are composed of *mandatory* and *optional* attributes. Examples of *mandatory* attributes are *interface_name* and *interface_speed* for device interfaces. The *interface_name* attribute is required to identify an interface and the *interface_speed* attribute is an essential parameter of the device functionality. Examples of *optional* attributes are *interface_state* and *interface_failure* for device interfaces. These attributes are used to define the current availability state and the state change characteristics of an interface. While high fidelity models might likely include these attributes, they are not necessary to model the basic device functionality in all simulation cases.

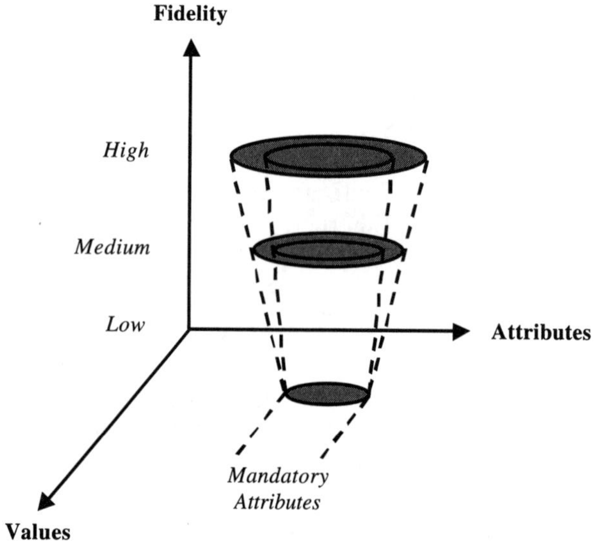

Figure 3. Mandatory Modeling Attributes

3.1.3.2 Static and Dynamic Attributes

An attribute is designated as *static* if its value must remain constant during the course of a simulation. An attribute is designated as *dynamic* if its value must be capable of changing during the course of a simulation. The static/dynamic aspect of an attribute is also designated as *dynamic* if the dynamic or static capability of the attribute is not essential for all cases and can be left to the discretion of the developer. An example of a *static* attribute is *object_name*, which defines the name of the communications device. An example of a *dynamic* attribute is *orbit_latitude* for a satellite model that has time-varying orbit position parameters. The device *object_state* attribute is designated as *dynamic* under the static/dynamic classification, because the capability for an object state change is determined by the designer/developer based on system analysis requirements.

4. Model Classes and Minimum Attribute List

This section presents an overview of the network element class models and their respective minimum set of attributes. Attributes are also classified as *mandatory/optional* and *static/dynamic*. Further descriptions and details of attributes can be found in [3] where each attribute has an associated definition, type, units, and default value. Actual device examples for some model classes are also provided. The device examples include data for their respective attribute values. The complete set of network element classes and examples can be found in [3].

The network element classes are shown in Table 1.

4.1 Common Attributes

To organize attributes and to enhance manageability, some attribute groups are referenced within classes. These groups are for organizational purposes. The attributes in Table 2 correspond to those attributes that are common to communications device models.

The *mode_name* attribute refers to the name of the mode of operation of the device model. The *inheritance* attribute consists of a list of attributes (e.g., *position*, and *object_state*) with values that are inherited from other objects. The *object_state* attribute indicates whether the device is enabled or disabled. The *object_failure* attribute indicates the state change (failure/repair) characteristics of the device. Definitions of all attributes can be found in [3].

4.1.1 Interface Attributes

Interfaces refer to the parts of devices that connect to communication links. The group of attributes in Table 3 includes attributes that are common to communications device interfaces. The *device_id* and *link_id* attributes support the ability to define link connectivity and resulting network topologies.

4.1.2 Message Attributes

Messages represent the information that passes through the communication system or network. Messages are represented by complex datatype parameters in object interactions such as message arrivals, generation, routing, and transmission. Table 4 lists the minimum set of attributes contained in message structures.

The *msg_data_field* attribute provides support for data encapsulation capabilities.

4.2 Radio

Table 5 lists the minimum set of attributes for communications device models with radio functionality.

The value of the *radio_bandwidth* attribute is related to the values of the rate and modulation attributes.

4.2.1 AN/WSC-3(V) Radio

Source: AN/WSC-3(V) Operation and Maintenance Instructions [1]; Jane's Military Communications 1996-97 [2]

Table 6 provides an example instantiation of the radio network element class.

Table 1. Network Element Class Descriptions

Class	Description
Antenna	Antenna models.
ATM Communication Layers	ATM communications device models with attributes drawn from ATM protocol layer functionality.
Communications Link	Serial, bus, and radio communications link models.
Encryption Device	Communications device models with Key Generator (KG) encryption device functionality.
End System	Communications device models with workstation (client/server) functionality.
OSI Communication Layers	Unique and hybrid/composite models, which support communications devices that do not fit in any one class. Model attributes are drawn from the applicable Reference Model of OSI layer functionality.
Networking Equipment	Communications devices with network (gateway, router, bridge, switch, hub) functionality.
Radio	Communications devices with radio functionality.
Satellite	Communications device models with satellite functionality.

Table 2. Common Attributes

Attribute	Type	M/O[1]	S/D[2]
object_name	String	M	S
object_version	String	M	S
mode_name	String	M	S
icon_name	String	M	D
inheritance	Complex	O	S
position_x position_y position_z	Real	M	D
velocity_x velocity_y velocity_z	Real	O	D
object_state	Boolean	O	D
object_failure	Complex	O	D

1. Mandatory (M) or optional (O) attribute.
2. Static (S) or dynamic (D) attribute value.

Table 3. Interface Attributes

Attribute	Type	M/O	S/D
interface_name	String	M	S
interface_type	Enumerated	M	S
interface_speed	Real	M	D
interface_medium	Enumerated	M	S
interface_data	Complex	M	S
interface_protocols	Enumerated	M	S
interface_address	String	M	D
interface_state	Boolean	O	D
interface_failure	Complex	O	D
device_id	String	M	S
link_id	String	M	D

Table 4. Message Attributes

Attribute	Definition	Type	M/O
msg_source	Source	String	M
msg _destination	Destination	String	M
msg _priority	Priority	Real	O
msg _date	Message creation time	Real	O
msg _death	Perishability time / Time-to-live	Real	O
msg _protocol	Protocol	Enumerated	O
msg _id	Identification number	Integer	M
msg _seq_no	Sequence number	Integer	O
msg _overhead	Overhead size	Real	O
msg _error_code	Forward Error Correction (FEC) / Code	Complex	O
msg _size	Size	Real	M
msg _data_field	User-defined data	Complex	O

Table 5. Radio Attributes

Attribute	Type	M/O	S/D
Common attributes			
Interfaces	Complex	M	D
tx_rate	Real	M	D
tx_power	Real	O	D
tx_modulation	Complex	O	D
tx_frequency	Real	O	D
radio_bandwidth	*Real*	*O*	*D*

Table 6. AN/WSC-3(V) Radio Attributes

Attribute	Type	Units / Range
Common attributes		
Interfaces	Complex	
tx_rate	Real	FSK - 75 bps; PSK - 75, 300, 1200, 2400, 4800, 9600 bps
tx_power	Real	30 W AM, 100 W FM and data mode
tx_modulation	Complex	AM; FM; FSK - 75 bps; PSK - 75, 300, 1200, 2400, 4800, 9600 bps; External Modem
tx_frequency	Real	225-399.975 MHz
radio_bandwidth	*Real*	*7000 channels in 25 kHz steps*

4.3 Antenna

Table 7 lists the minimum set of attributes for antenna models. To provide maximum flexibility and to address custom antenna designs, antenna patterns are defined through the use of the *antenna_gain* attribute.

Table 7. Antenna Attributes

Attribute	Type	M/O	S/D
Common attributes			
Interfaces	Complex	M	D
antenna_gain	Complex	M	D
antenna_orientation	Complex	O	D

4.3.1 Shakespeare Model 4243 VHF Broadband Antenna

Source:

http://www.shakespeare-ce.com/military/4243.htm

Table 8 provides an example instantiation of the antenna class.

Table 8. Shakespeare Model 4243 VHF Broadband Antenna Attributes

Attribute	Type	Units / Range
Common attributes		
Interfaces	Complex	1 50 OHM Coax
Antenna_gain	Complex	See Figure 4.
Antenna_orientation	Complex	Phi:90 Theta:0

The antenna gain pattern for the Shakespeare Model 4243 at 85 Megahertz (MHz) is shown in Figure 4. Antenna orientation parameters ϕ and θ are utilized to indicate the antenna orientation. They are illustrated in Figure 5.

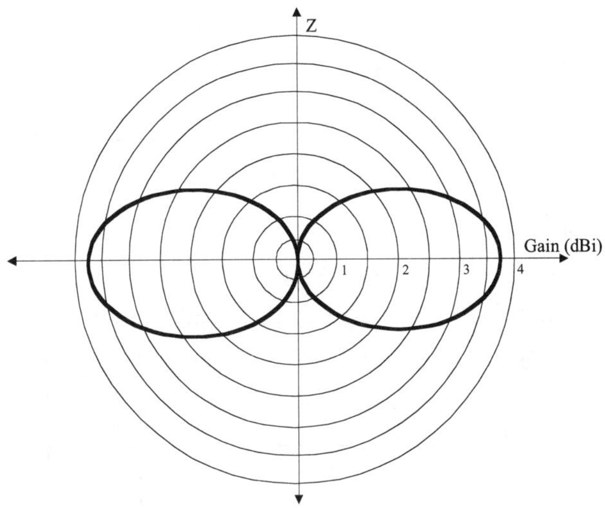

Figure 4. Shakespeare Model 4243 Gain Pattern at 85 MHz

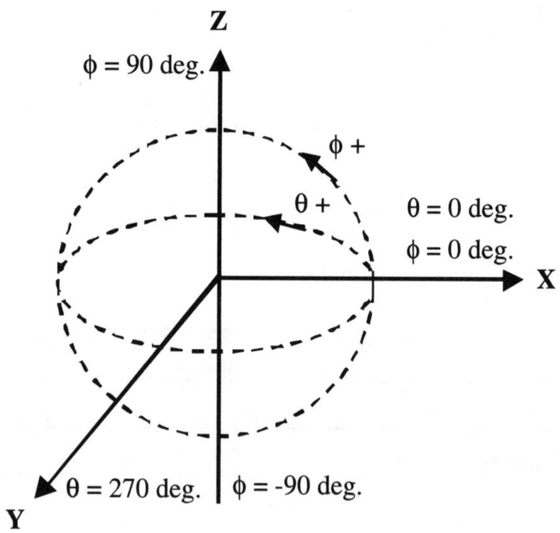

Figure 5. Antenna Orientation Parameters

4.4 Communications Link

The following table lists the minimum set of attributes for serial, bus, and radio communications link models. Communications link models provide the means for environmental effects on data/message transmissions. The environmental effects are parameterized through the use of the *error_allocation* attribute.

Table 9. Communications Link Attributes

Attribute	Type	M/O	S/D
object_name	String	M	S
icon_name	String	M	D
position_x position_y position_z	Real	M	D
link_type	Enumerated	M	S
link_medium	Enumerated	O	S
transmission _rate	Real	M	D
propagation_ delay	Real	M	D
error_ allocation	Complex	O	D
interface_ids	String	M	D
link_state	Boolean	O	D
link_failure	Complex	O	D

5. HLA Reference FOM Representation of Model Classes

The work presented in the previous section formed the basis for the HLA Reference FOM. This work is presented in detail in [3]. The tabular format, syntax and terminology that were used follow that of the HLA Object Model Template (OMT). The HLA Object Model Development Tool (OMDT) was used to create the Reference FOM representation of the model classes.

The current Reference FOM contains definitions of the initial set of network element classes, the respective minimum attributes, and message handling interactions. Datatype definitions include representative enumerated and complex types along with cardinality specifications. Other attributes and parameters were set as the OMDT default values.

6. Unified Modeling Language Representation of Model Classes

A Unified Modeling Language (UML) representation of the model classes is shown in Figure 6. An example UML diagram with definitions of UML terms is shown in Figure 7.

7. Summary and Conclusions

The JCS has a requirement for a simulation environment to support JTF communications burden analyses. Rigor in the modeling environment is required to accurately identify areas of the network for improvement. Confidence in the results is required to provide the warfighter with a higher degree of trust in the communication plans. Modeling flexibility and robustness are required to provide planners with the capability to experiment with a variety of scenarios in order to optimize plans for deployment. In order to fulfill these requirements, a variety of reusable, interoperable, validated models must be available. This work supports the validation process by providing developers with a minimum set of attributes that are essential for models. In addition, this standard provides a common modeling framework to enhance reusability and interoperability of communication models, and to support potential federations of C4ISR simulations.

8. Acknowledgments

The authors would like to acknowledge the sponsorship and support of this effort by the NAVMSMO N6M. The authors would also like to acknowledge the assistance of Mr. Chris Alspaugh of Network Communications Consulting in the development and testing of the Reference FOM. In addition, the authors would like to thank Dr. Michael Hieb of AB Technologies and Mr. Alspaugh for their assistance in reviewing this paper.

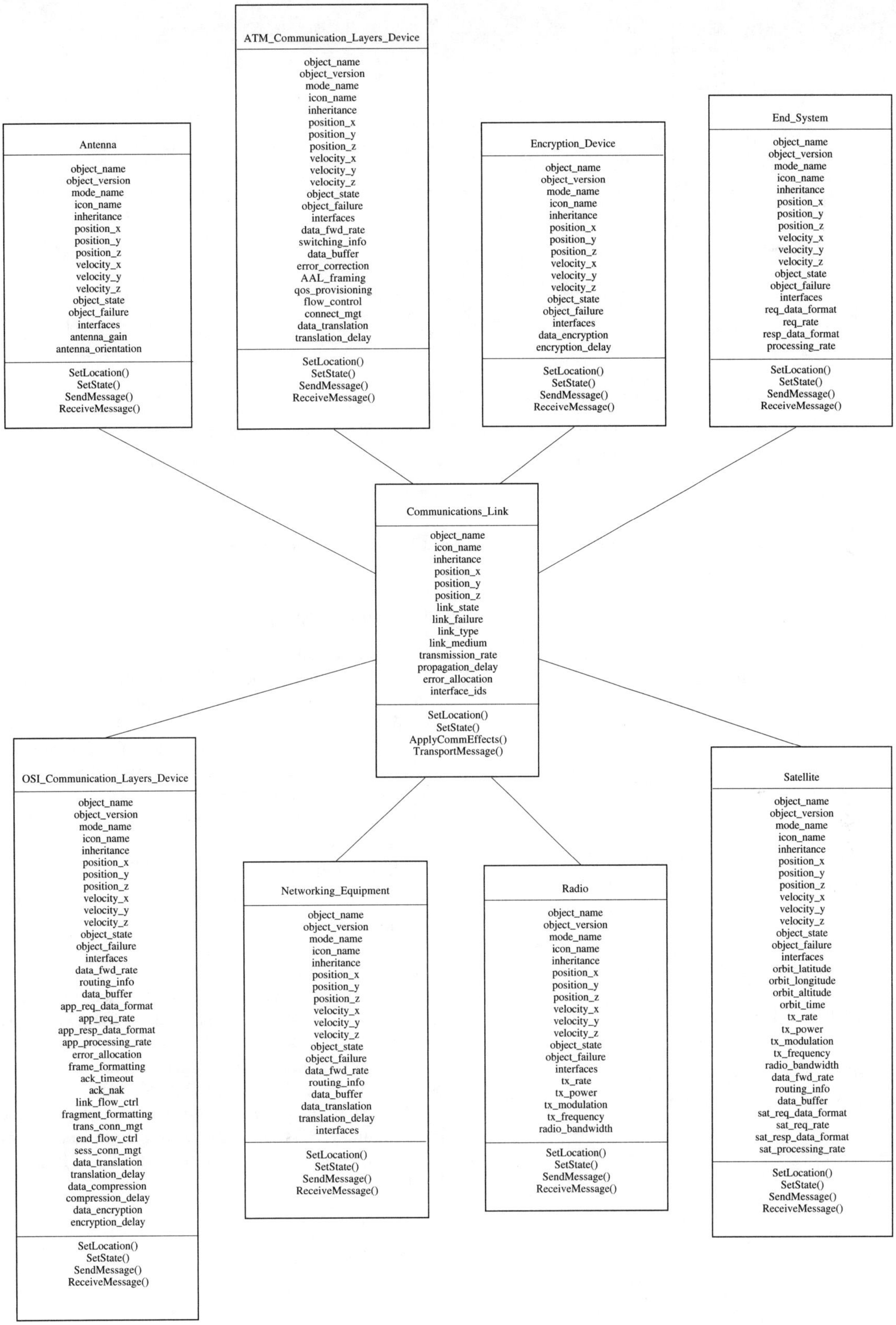

Figure 6. UML Representation of Model Classes

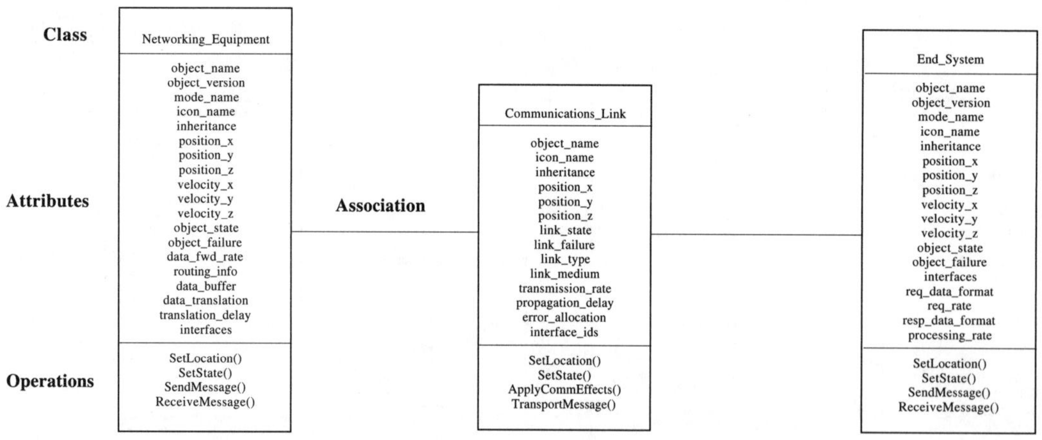

Class - Description of a set of objects that share the same attributes.

Attribute - Named property of a class that decribes a range of values that instances of the property may hold.

Operation - Implementation of a service that can be requested from any object of the class to affect behavior.

Association - Structural relationship that describes a set of connections among objects.

Figure 7. UML Example and Definitions

9. References

[1] *AN/WSC-3(V) Operation and Maintenance Instructions*, E-Systems, 31 May 1987.

[2] *Jane's Military Communications 1996-97*, Jane's Information Group, Inc., 1996.

[3] *C4ISR Communication Modeling Standards*, Navy Modeling and Simulation Management Office, December 1999.

[4] *High Level Architecture (HLA) Object Model Template Version 1.3 Draft*, Defense Modeling & Simulation Office, http://www.dmso.mil/, 5 February 1998.

[5] W. Sudnikovich, J. Roberts, J. Lacetera, *Implementation of a Prototype C4I FOM*, Spring 1999 Simulation Interoperability Workshop, Paper Number 99S-SIW-061.

[6] *The Unified Modeling Language User Guide*, G. Booch, J. Rumbaugh, I. Jacobson, Addison-Wesley, 1999.

10. Author Biographies

Albert K. Legaspi is the Deputy Director of the Technical Support Group (TSG) for the Naval Modeling and Simulation Office OPNAV N6M and is attached with SPAWAR Systems Command PD-13. He is currently the Navy technical representative to the Joint Chiefs of Staff NETWARS project. Dr. Legaspi holds a B.S. in Electrical Engineering and Mathematics, M.S. and Ph.D in Electrical Engineering, all from UCSD and UCLA. Dr. Legaspi was the chairperson of IEEE Communication Society for San Diego Charter in 1995.

Carl Ivancic is the Chief Technical Officer and Senior Systems Engineering Consultant for Network Communications Consulting. He has over fourteen years experience in communication systems engineering, modeling and simulation, network engineering research, requirements development, program management, system integration, and test support. Mr. Ivancic has previously held senior engineering and program management positions with TRW, Trident Data Systems, and SAIC. Mr. Ivancic holds a B.S., Magna Cum Laude, and a M.E. in Computer & Systems Engineering from Rensselaer Polytechnic Institute. He is a member of Tau Beta Pi and Eta Kappa Nu.

An Update of the HLA Standardization Efforts

Presented to:
SCSC 2000
M&S Standards Track
18 July 2000

Mike Lightner
The AEgis Technologies Group, Inc
Orlando, FL
MLightner@AEgisTG.com
(407) 380-5001

9/8/00

Outline

- Why HLA?
- How Did HLA Come to Be?
- What is the HLA?
- How is the HLA Being Standardized?
- What's the Status of the IEEE Process?
- What Changes will the IEEE Version Bring?

9/8/00 2

Why HLA? Must Respond to Change:

Continuing Squeeze on Resources
- Shrinking, dispersed force structure
- Competition for O&M funds limits field exercises
- Need to carefully examine every investment

More Demanding Operational Requirements
- New, more complex missions
- Vastly expanding mission space
- Increased complexity of systems and plans
- Increasing demand for joint operations
- No traditional way to address

Much More Technical Capability at Less Cost
- Communications and Computers
- Advanced software technology
- Displays/human-machine interfaces
- Data storage and management

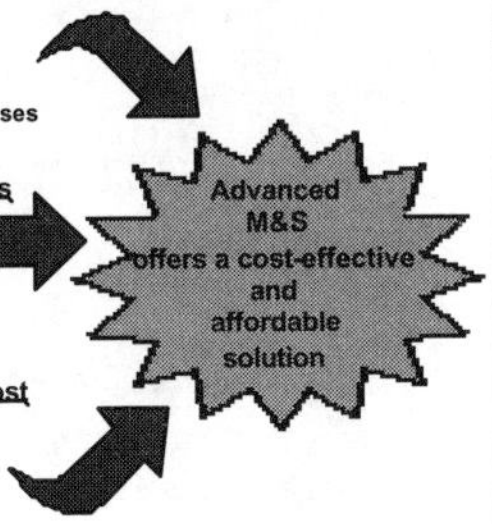

9/8/00 3

Why HLA? Some Basic Truths:

- No single, monolithic simulation can satisfy all needs. Must have, and effectively use, multiple M&S assets.
- All uses of simulations and useful ways of combining them cannot be anticipated in advance. Need a composable approach to constructing federations of simulations using well-defined interfaces.
- Must be able to accommodate future technological capabilities and a variety of operating configurations. Need to insure specific simulation functionality is separated from the underlying runtime infrastructure.
- M&S is NOT free! Must manage & use our M&S smartly.

9/8/00 4

Why HLA? Critical Part of Solution:

- Need an infrastructure which was applicable to broad range of functional areas and M&S assets and which could evolve with new technology innovations.

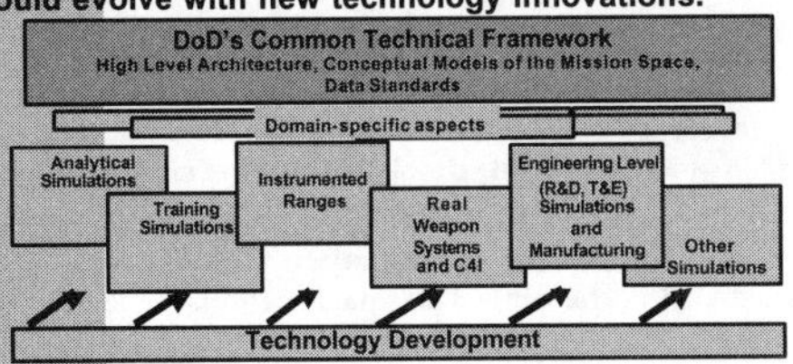

9/8/00 5

How Did HLA Come to Be?

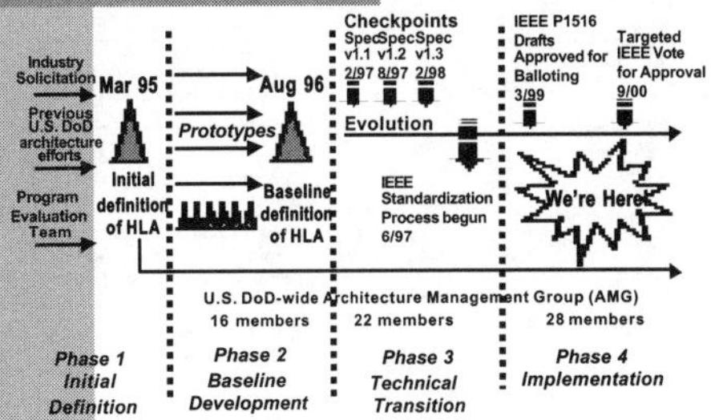

9/8/00 6

What is the HLA? Its Components:

- The High Level Architecture is comprised of three elements:
  - An Interface Specification which describes the way compliant simulations interact during operation
  - An Object Model Template (OMT) Specification which specifies the form in which simulation elements are described
  - A set of HLA Rules for Federates and Federations which define relationships among federating compliant simulations

9/8/00 7

What is the HLA? A Functional View:

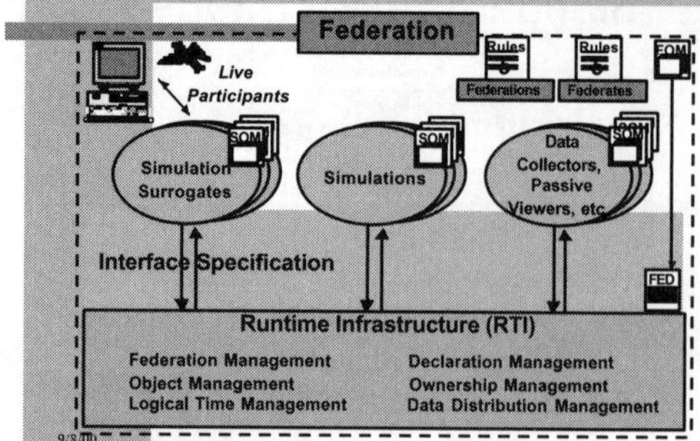

9/8/00 8

HLA Standardization Initiatives

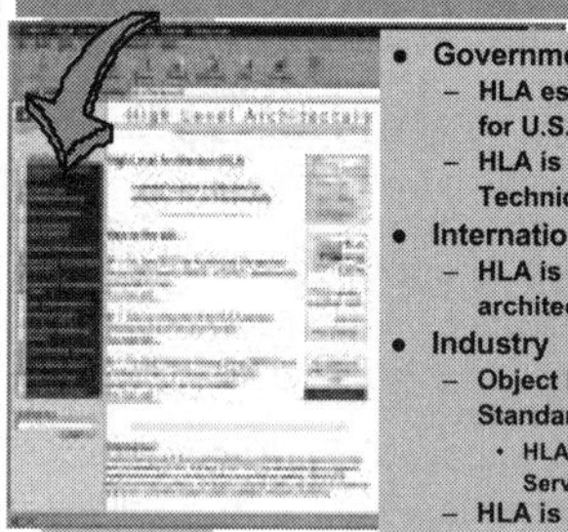

- Government
  - HLA established as technical architecture for U.S. DoD Simulations
  - HLA is a part of the U.S. DoD Joint Technical Architecture (JTA)
- International
  - HLA is named as NATO standard architecture in NATO M&S Master Plan
- Industry
  - Object Management Group (OMG) Standardization
    - HLA Interface Specification and RTI Services were approved as OMG standards
  - HLA is a draft IEEE standard, IEEE P1516
    - Anticipated IEEE approval in Sep 00

9/8/00

HLA IEEE 1516 Series

A Review of the IEEE Process

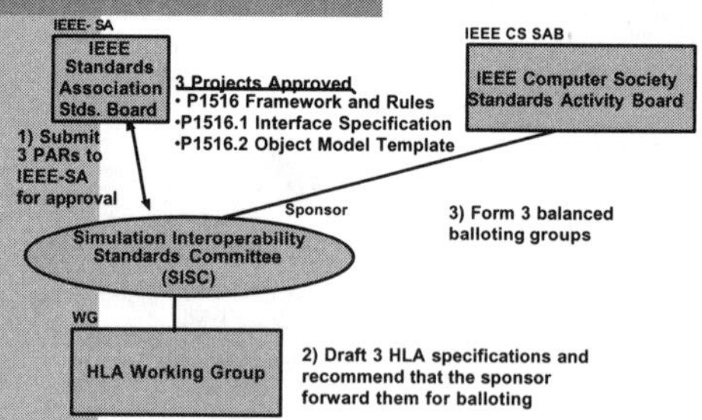

9/8/00 10

HLA IEEE 1516 Series

A Review of the IEEE Process

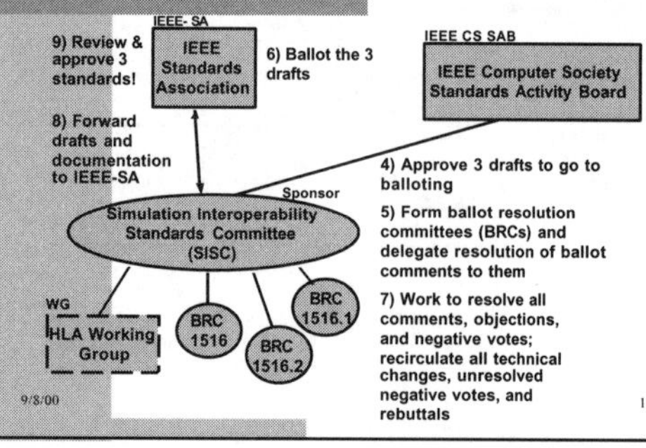

9/8/00 11

HLA IEEE 1516 Series

Summary of Editorial Changes

- Formatting/Consistency Corrections/Improvements
- Typographical Corrections / Wording Clarifications
- All Definitions/Acronyms used in all of the P1516 Series Specifications.
- Addition of IEEE Prescribed Up Front Matter like Abstract, Copyright, Disclaimers, Participants etc.
- OO Concepts vs HLA OMT discussion (which was already in the OMT specification) modified and included in the other two specifications.

9/8/00 12

HLA IEEE 1516 Series
Summary of Technical Changes

- Creation of a Rationale Annexes.
- Addition/modification of Technical Definitions.
- Inclusion/modification of appropriate terminology and/or wording in the descriptive text to insure proper interpretation and consistency of the specifications.
- Some new Support and Federation Management services.
- DDM services significantly enhanced and improved.
- Slight changes to MOM , Time & Ownership Management.

9/8/00 13

HLA IEEE 1516 Series
Summary of Technical Changes

- All I/F Specification service areas improved.
- New I/F service description <-> API mapping clause.
- Improvements and enhancements made to the APIs.
- Significant Enhancements to OMT
  - New Tables and Annexes added
  - Existing Tables and Annexes modified
  - Some existing tables replaced
- Improvements made to OMT datatypes.
- DIFs now based on XML.

9/8/00 14

Need More HLA Insights?

- DMSO HLA Homepage provides full service access to the broad HLA user community. For direct access to the HLA Home Page set your bookmarks to

  http://hla.dmso.mil

- HLA Training and Education is available. See HLA Home Page for details. Also there are HLA Tutorials here at the SCSC on Thursday.

9/8/00 15

IEEE 1516 Process Details
The HLA Working Group

The Working Group formed, chose our tools and started our work.

The first thing the Working Group did was to ponder the task that was handed us.

9/8/00 16

IEEE 1516 Process Details
Summary of WG Activity

HLA Working Group

3 full comment and review cycles

Drafts posted online; comments were accepted from anyone

Responded to all 706 comments received

- Mtg 1: March 1998, Orlando, FL
- Draft 1: April 20, 1998, 213 comments
- F&W: 37, I/F Spec: 98, OMT: 78

- Mtg 2: June 1998, Austin, TX
- Draft 2: July 27, 1998, 255 comments
- F&W: 18, I/F Spec: 165, OMT: 72

- Mtg 3: Sept. 1998 Alexandria, VA
- Draft 3: Nov. 16, 1998, 238 comments
- F&W: 13, I/F Spec: 138, OMT: 87

- Mtg 4: Jan. 1999, San Diego, CA
- Approval to forward three final drafts to SISC for balloting

- Final Draft: March 9, 1999

9/8/00 17

IEEE 1516 Process Details
The Ballot Resolution Committees

With the SISC vote to forward the drafts for balloting we toasted ourselves...

... and handed our work off to the IEEE BRCs.

9/8/00 18

IEEE 1516 Process Details

Forming the Ballot Groups

Thus, the BRCs formed. However, having now had some experience, decided we needed some different tools.

Ballot Groups were also formed.

9/8/00 19

IEEE 1516 Process Details

IEEE 1516 HLA Framework & Rules

1st Ballot Results

Ballot group size	87		
Affirmative votes	56		
Negative votes	22		
Abstention votes	0		
Votes	78	90%	Returned
		0%	Abstention
Affirmative votes	56		
Negative votes	22		
Votes	78	72%	Affirmative

9/8/00 20

IEEE 1516 Process Details

IEEE 1516.1 HLA Interface Specification

1st Ballot Results

Ballot group size	80		
Affirmative votes	34		
Negative votes	35		
Abstention votes	5		
Votes	74	93%	Returned
		6%	Abstention
Affirmative votes	34		
Negative votes	35		
Votes	69	49%	Affirmative

9/8/00 21

IEEE 1516 Process Details

IEEE 1516 HLA Object Model Template

1st Ballot Results

Ballot Group Size: 85
Affirmative Votes: 40
Negative Votes: 36
Abstention Votes: 1

Votes 77 — 90% Returned, 1% Abstention

Affirmative Votes: 40
Negative Votes: 36

Votes 76 — 53% Affirmative

9/8/00 22

IEEE 1516 Process Details

The Goal: Consensus

The BRCs worked with the balloters to do all we could to understand their concerns and reach consensus.

9/8/00 23

IEEE 1516 Process Details

IEEE 1516 Ballot Resolutions

Count of Ballot Item Type	Ballot Item Type			
D	Content	Editorial	Objection	Grand Total
Accept	25	62	23	110
Accept w/BRC changes	46	15	28	89
Reject	7	0	16	23
Balloter was non-responsive in discussion of reject	1	0	0	1
Withdrawn by balloter	0	0	1	1
Grand Total	79	77	68	224

9/8/00 24

IEEE 1516 Process Details

IEEE 1516.1 Ballot Resolutions

BRC Response	Ballot Item Type: Content	Editorial	Objection	Grand Total
Accept	69	76	95	240
Accept w/BRC changes	36	18	70	124
Balloter was non-responsive in providing additional information	0	0	9	9
Reject	3	5	8	16
Balloter was non-responsive in discussion of reject	2	0	5	7
Withdrawn by balloter	21	3	28	52
Grand Total	131	102	215	448

9/8/00 25

IEEE 1516 Process Details

IEEE 1516.2 Ballot Resolutions

BRC Response	Ballot Item Type: Content	Editorial	Objection	Total
Accept	56	70	48	174
Accept w/BRC changes	25	5	14	44
Reject	18	16	2	36
Withdrawn	0	0	12	12
Grand Total	99	91	74	264

9/8/00 26

IEEE 1516 Process Details

The Result: Consensus

We experienced different reactions from the balloters...

...but in the end we were able to work most of the issues and come to consensus or understanding.

9/8/00 27

IEEE 1516 Process Details

The Future

We've now passed the recirculation ballots. So we're racing for the finish line of IEEE approval where we fully intend to have one heck of a celebration.

9/8/00 28

And When We're Done Its Off We Go To The...

MIKE REED BOB

BRC Editors' Retirement Home

9/8/00 29

Simulation System Architectures

Object Oriented HLA Interface Design For Military Simulations

S. B. Hall, S. M. Venkatesan, D. B. Wood - Lockheed Martin Space Systems
H. S. Sarjoughian, B. P. Zeigler - University of Arizona

Abstract:
We describe here a general purpose object-oriented HLA Interface developed at Lockheed Martin Space Systems' Advanced Simulation Center. The intent of this effort is to save the modeler the highly elaborate task of incorporating HLA-specific code into a simulation, by wrapping all the complex details of HLA connectivity into one interface package. This HLA Interface does not duplicate any functionality in HLA, and in fact is arguably a necessary complement to it. Even though this work was an offshoot of our other efforts to refine the DEVSHLA simulation engine, it is disjoint from DEVSHLA, and is powerful enough to work with any simulation engine, as illustrated by our applications.

1. Motivation:

Since the advent of the High Level Architecture, the focus of the military simulation community's efforts has been to (1) understand HLA compliance and the issues of and emerging standards in simulation inter-operability (2) train their simulation engineers in the details of HLA in a variety of ways (3) identify and involve HLA products and vendors to accelerate compliance efforts, and (4) resurrect trusted and top-notch, but non-object-oriented legacy systems with new HLA wrappers. The experience seems to be positive in general, while forcing the simulation engineers through the HLA learning curve, away from developing traditional simulation components.

We have worked on a variety of legacy validated systems as well as new projects that need interoperability, and have seen the need for a core HLA design philosophy to guide the development teams and identification of common and shared efforts in this area. The philosophy underlying our specific effort was that we can and must facilitate the development of robust, powerful, interoperable, and extensible enterprise simulation software that goes beyond HLA compliance. Such a distributed simulation middleware must provide a clean conceptual and architectural separation of the Engineering Simulation from the component that supports distributed computing (in this case, the HLA Interface). The overall distributed computing should be so transparent that a federate should be able to encapsulate the communication with another federate as across a "hole in the wall". In fact, this view encapsulation is not new and is already supported in software systems such as the CORBA IDL (Interface Definition Language). In order to make such a clean separation in any general event-driven distributed setting, we are forced to rely on the full power of object-oriented methodology. In such a setting, the event driver (for instance our HLA Interface combined with the RTI) needs to operate without knowing the full class or logic details of the constantly evolving engineering simulation. Our specific interface development effort was started in C++ and can be readily translated into Java.

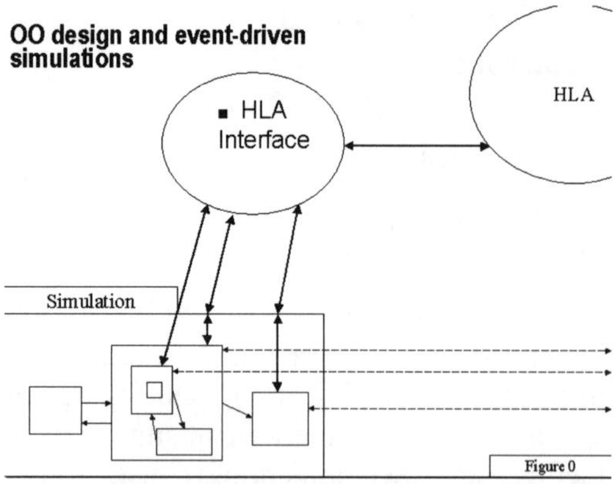

2. Design Objective:

Our primary objective was to develop a general purpose HLA Interface Module that is disjoint architecturally from any engineering simulation. The HLA Interface Module needs to be plug-and-play; allowing non-simulation engineers to continue to build their models and simulations as they traditionally do. Then with just basic OO knowledge, they would make these simulations HLA compliant by plugging in the HLA Interface Module.

A few words may be needed to indicate whether a single simulation protocol is necessary or not (see comments with yellow highlight under the "The Advantages" heading). Our overarching general objective was to quickly ramp up knowledge of distributed simulation design methodology (with emphasis on HLA), and finally to illustrate how easy distributed design can be if carefully approached. Our immediate purpose was of course to enable rapid prototyping of powerful HLA compliant simulations.

3. How is the HLA Interface different from HLA?

In order to understand the need for a HLA Interface, we need to point out that the Interface does not replace any functionality of HLA/RTI, and is purely complementary to it. In fact its only purpose is to encapsulate all the HLA functionality for the engineering simulation designer so that he/she can develop code that is almost completely independent of HLA/RTI, and with some simple compiles and links creates a full fledged HLA federate. In fact, this is what we believe most people in our industry want to see made available, if not developing it themselves. In short, what our HLA Interface does do is

(1) fully automate the declaration of HLA classes (including all the class handles and flags) and fully automate the registering of all HLA objects (including all the object handles and flags)
(2) fully automate all the callbacks from HLA, and the calls to HLA
(3) provide an environment in which the simulation engineer can develop a HLA federate, say without using the word "RTI" in code (this so that the same federate code can in the future be used to couple to a middleware other than HLA).

4. HLA Interface and DEVSHLA:

Our design started with trying to separate the HLA component from the Devs component in the DEVSHLA engine developed at University of Arizona. This Devs component is a software rendition of the theoretically rich Devs formalism, which in short captures complex discrete event systems by a grammar that describes hierarchically interconnected temporal automata. As mentioned before, the idea was to architecturally separate the Devs engine from the HLA component (they were already conceptually separate). In doing so, we started realizing the need for a full fledged HLA interface that is of value to the entire HLA community, in that it can couple with an arbitrary simulation engine while shielding the engine from the HLA connectivity. As it turns out, the HLA Interface has already coupled effortlessly with the Devs engine, making Lockheed Martin's JOINT MEASURE simulation framework more flexible, powerful, and efficient.

5. HLA Interface Design Details:

To achieve our objective, several classes were developed to augment those in the standard DMSO HLA implementation. The main classes are now briefly introduced (we are not providing the class diagrams in order to avoid unnecessary details)

1. HLA_Federate: responsible for (a) overall federation and time management, (b) for "parsing" the .fed file, and (c) for initiating declaration management

2. HLA_ObjectClass: responsible for (a) overall declaration management for ObjectClasses, (b) overall object management through a Dynamic Model Registry, which includes model setup and delete (local), discovery and remove (remote) (c) Callback management (receive), Update (send), (d) model find routines, send and receive flag management, and (e) ownership services . The User has to provide a function named cloneDiscoveredObject, which tells the inteface what sort of "proxy" or "endomorph" the user wants created in response to discovery of a remote object.

3. HLA_InteractionClass: responsible for (a) overall declaration management for Interaction Classes, (b) maintenance of models that wish to receive interactions (callbacks), (c) definition of receiveInteraction and sendInteraction, (d) find routines, and flag management.

4. HLA_FederateAmbassador

5. baseAttribute and baseParameter classes (to enable dynamic binding), hlaAttribute and hlaParameter classes (that maintain the handles and general flags). The user has to derive attribute and parameter classes from the base classes that are simulation specific, and which are added to attribute and parameter lists maintained in the simulation models (these user defined attribute and parameter classes hold arbitrary class objects that are transported across the network by the RTI). The general design of this class hierarchy is shown in Figure 1, and this enables the automated maintenance of HLA related aspects in mirrored hlaAttributes and hlaParameters, and the automatic transport of objects across the network

6. quantizer classes which can be attached to user defined attribute and parameter classes for update purposes

7. data structures (Element, Set, etc)

In our two classes HLA_InteractionClass and HLA_ObjectClass, we maintain in a class-static container all the Interaction and Object Classes published by or subscribed to by this federate. Roughly speaking, this container's contents correspond to the object classes and interaction classes specified in the fed file. The advantage of this design is that a fed file parser can automatically build this container. Callbacks to the components from the appropriate HLA_InteractionClass or HLA_ObjectClass are through virtual functions defined in the component, and calls from the component to the HLA Interface cause the Interface to exercise the rtiAmbassodor appropriately, while hiding all the details from the component.

Each HLA_ObjectClass object in turn has a component list where we maintain pointers to all the component that need to register an object of this class, and this list is populated by a very simple registerObjectClass call from the component. This registry is used to do a callback on the component when the federateAmbassador is exercised by the RTI. To do this, we require a couple of obvious things from the component:

(1) First, the component itself (which can be as complex as needed) should derive from a common root class such as Object or Entity, so that the HLA Interface does not need to know any of the specific simulation component classes;

(2) Second, the attribute list (maintained in the simulation component), and a mirrored attribute list (maintained along with all the handles, but without the

values in the HLA_ObjectClass object) need to be derived from a common root class in order that the incoming attribute reflections can virtually update the simulation component's attribute, without the HLA Interface knowing any attribute classes specific to the simulation (See Figure 1).

The HLA specification does not support data transparency across operating systems or platforms. Thus sending class objects over the network must be at least partially addressed, and we did that by adding functions to reconstruct remote objects from the reflected values. However we did not address network and platform related issues in this reconstruction.

Each HLA_InteractionClass object has a similar structure, except that, since interaction classes do not involve registered objects, we maintain a container list of components that would use this interaction class. Again, we require derivation from a common root class as explained above for the components as well as the parameters.

6. The Benefits:

We believe the benefits of this approach are:

1) The simulation designer is free to define complex objects of his/her choice, and the HLA interface remains unchanged. In other words, the HLA Interface can be coupled with any simulation (or engine) The approach is general and independent of simulation engine in that we can have optimistic, time-warp, or some mixture of simulation protocols.
2) If necessary, the core of the simulation can have minimum object orientation (i.e. legacy systems) with simple object wrappers for registry purposes.
3) The simulation designer can define local endomorphic images of named remote objects (without registering them) so that these images can be automatically updated by the RTI.
4) Attributes and parameters can be associated with user defined quantizer classes which will define how these must change before updating must occur.
5) The interface provides flexibility to handle ownership and other issues.
6) With application of parallel/distributed high performance computing, it may be possible to reduce the execution of complex simulations from weeks/ months to hours/days.
7) HLA expertise can be locally developed for enterprise wide use, and for a faster push towards compliance.
8) The approach adds very little code weight, and is essentially platform independent.

7. Integration Experience:

We integrated our HLA Interface with

1. Joint Measure Simulation Platform (DEVS based): JOINT MEASURE is our simulation development platform that has been used for developing various high fidelity discrete event simulations. Our test case was a DARPA funded project to study trade-off between network traffic and signature fidelity requirements in a tank-helicopter discrete event simulation. The tank federate's signature in arbitrary terrain (with line of sight and cloud factor taken into account) determines the signature as received by the helicopter federate sensors. This signature is associated with quantizer objects which determine when the signature packet will be transmitted. The simulation runs indicated that using HLA produced the expected trade-off. Similar techniques can be used to develop any Joint Measure based HLA Compliant high fidelity discrete event simulations.

2. Pursuer Evader (DEVS based)

3. HelloWorld and FoodFight (DMSO examples)

8. Conclusions:

An Interface design should attempt to be (a) powerful, extensible, and scalable, (b) practical, and easy to understand, (c) motivate beginners, yet be very useful to experts, (d) develop once, use many times, instead of the other way around.

We have tried hard to keep these in mind in our own HLA Interface design.
We are yet to add features like the fedfile parser, DDM, etc. We are planning to build a GUI to partition a simulation into HLA federates.

9. References:

Hall, S. B., B. P. Zeigler, et al. (1999). Joint Measure: Distributed Simulation Issues In a Mission Effectiveness Analytic Simulator. SIW, Orlando, FL.

Zeigler, B. P., G. Ball, et al. (1998). The DEVS/HLA Distributed Simulation Environment and Its Support for Predictive Filtering. ECE Dept., UA, Tucson, AZ, DARPA Contract N6133997K-0007.

Zeigler, B. P., S. Hall, et al. (1999). "Exploiting HLA and DEVS to Promote Interoperability and Reuse in Lockheed's Corporate Environment." Simulation J. 74(4): 288-295.

10. The HelloWorld Example Outline:

```
Country::Country( char* name, double pop, int remoteFlag)
                    : Entity(name)
  { // define attributeList and parameterList
  myFederate->addObject(this); }
void Country::evolve( double grantTime )
 { //change country's attributes and set sendFlags }
void Country::objectUpdate ()        //callbacks
  { //attributeValues automatically modified by HLA_Interface
   // use modified attribute values and reset receiveFlags }
Entity * cloneDiscoveredObject(char * theTag)
  { Country * remoteCountry = new Country( theTag, 0.0, 1 );
    //pop is 0.0, remote = 1
   return remoteCountry; }
int main(int argc, char *argv[])     {…………………...
   myFederate =  new HLA_Federate( name, fedExecName, fedFile, ...);
   myCountry = new Country(……., 0 ); //remote = 0
   myMessage = new commObject(….);
   myFederate->addInteraction(myMessage);
   //register initial objects: dynamically created or discovered objects
   // will be handled inside event loop
   myFederate->setUp();
   int counter = 0;
   while ( counter++ < numberOfTicks-1 ) { …..
     { myFederate->requestTimeAdvance( requestTime );
       myCountry->evolve(grantTime);
       myFederate->updateAttributeValues(myCountry,……….);
       myFederate->sendInteraction(myCountry);  ……}
  delete myFederate;
  return 0; }
```

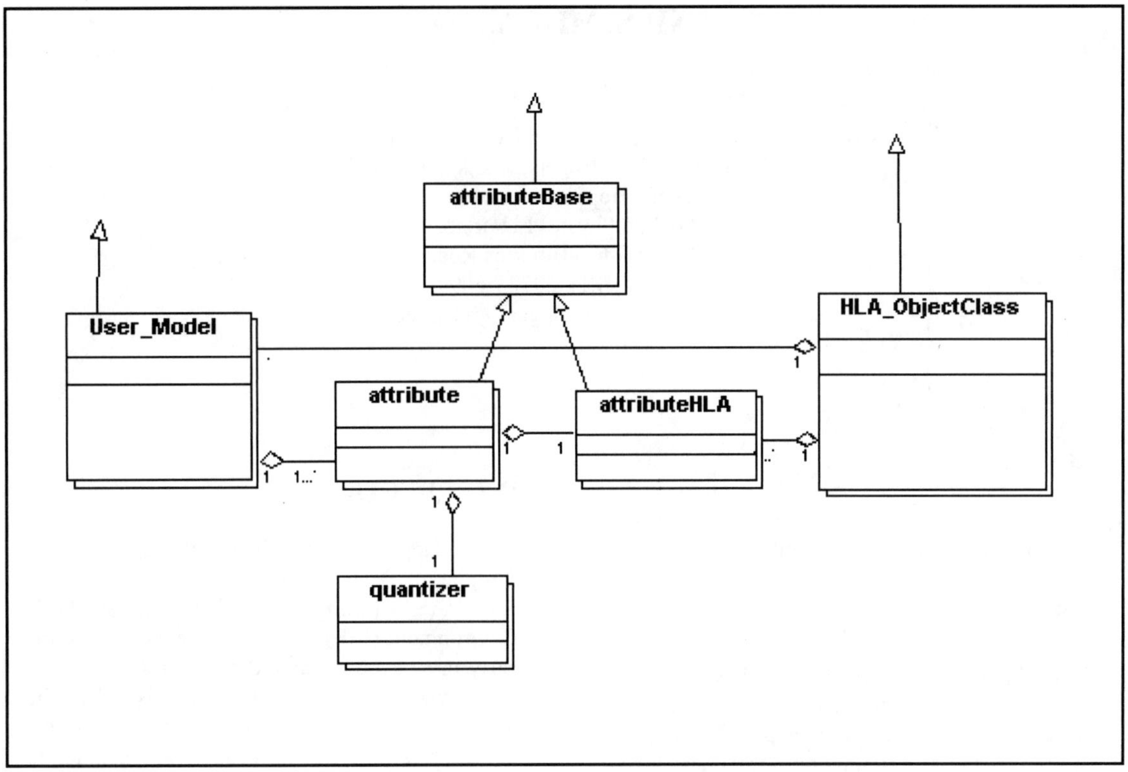
attributeBase
User_Model
HLA_ObjectClass
attribute
attributeHLA
quantizer
1
1
1
1
1
1
1
1

Figure 1.

AN INTEGRATED ARCHITECTURE FOR SPACECRAFT DESIGN AND SIMULATION

Andrew Goldfinger, David Silberberg, Lien Doung', John Gersh, Martin Gomez,
John Hunt, Gabe Rogers, Frank Weiskopf
Johns Hopkins University
Applied Physics Laboratory
11100 Johns Hopkins Road
Laurel, MD 20723-6099
e-mail: andy.goldfinger@jhuapl.edu

KEYWORDS

Aerospace, Distributed Processors, Standards, Design, Knowledge Sustainment.

ABSTRACT

Traditionally, spacecraft design has been a slow and laborious process. The translation of the designer's concept into a practical design, and the testing and simulation of this design has occurred in a piecemeal fashion. Our goal is to replace this cumbersome procedure with a coherent, user friendly, rapid approach.

The vision is the following. The designer has an idea. A user interface is provided to enable the designer to express his idea rapidly. This description becomes the core of an abstract model based on standard component interactions. The design team then refines the model in incremental steps, each step leading the design to become more detailed and practical. As this is done, simulations are melded into the design so the abstract model becomes a working model of the spacecraft.

The Johns Hopkins University Applied Physics Laboratory (JHU/APL) has been working on the development of this vision. A three-tiered knowledge-based architecture has been arrived at. This architecture is being demonstrated through construction of a simulation of a spacecraft attitude control system.

INTRODUCTION

The Department of Defense, through its Simulation Based Acquisition (SBA) initiative, and NASA through the Intelligent Synthesis Environment (ISE) program are encouraging the early use of modeling and simulation (M&S) as tools in spacecraft design. This has led to the following vision. A designer has an idea. A user interface is provided to enable the designer to express his idea rapidly. This description becomes the core of an abstract model based on standard component interactions. The design team then refines the model in incremental steps, each step leading the design to become more detailed and practical. As this is done, simulations are melded into the design so the abstract model becomes a working model of the spacecraft.

As part of this process, the designer considers the possible use of a component such as a reaction wheel manufactured by a commercial company. He visits the vendor's web site and finds a simulation of the wheel. He either downloads this simulation and melds it into his growing model, or executes the simulation in place as part of a distributed architecture. He is able to select either of these choices since the developers of the reaction wheel simulation have adhered to a set of standards that have become adopted internationally by the spacecraft design community.

The Johns Hopkins University Applied Physics Laboratory (JHU/APL) has been working on the development of this vision. A three-tiered knowledge-based representation architecture has been arrived at. These tiers are defined as follows:

(1) Design: the abstract representation of the designer's ideas and concepts.

(2) Knowledge: an integrated abstract repository to describe the design of a spacecraft in terms of its components and interactions and a representation of the practical knowledge necessary to translate the abstract design into a working simulation. This knowledge is itself subdivided into three layers:

(a) Standards: a set of standards representing spacecraft component objects and their behaviors and interactions

(b) Component Simulation Descriptions : a representation of the repertoire of the models and simulations that can be used to emulate behavior of the spacecraft component objects and can be combined in a plug-and-play fashion

(c) Subsystem Designs: representations of the decomposition of the subsystems into components and their interactions.

(3) Simulation: the practical, executable simulation/model of the spacecraft, which can be run through a distributed architecture.

DESIGN TIER

The Design Tier will be linked to a facile user interface that will allow a designer to rapidly express his design concepts. The principal idea is that a designer should be able to concentrate on design – not software. A design language with a high degree of expressive directness will be employed to facilitate rapid translation of the designer's ideas into a distributed spacecraft simulation that is captured by design tools and product model formats such as STEP (IOS 1994).

Also present in this layer will be component descriptions, standard spacecraft classes and methods. At present we are investigating which technologies will be used to represent this information. The components may be created ab initio or use may be made of a modeling tool such as Rational Rose.

KNOWLEDGE TIER

Once captured by the design layer, the goal will be to translate these ideas into an executable model of the spacecraft, which will occur in the simulation tier. To enable this to occur, use will be made of an intermediate tier, the knowledge tier. This tier will itself be divided into three layers,

Topmost is the standards layer. This layer contains abstract knowledge about the standard classes, their methods and their parameters (classes may contain both methods and parameters since we will not enforce a rigid object oriented discipline). It also describes the relationships between the classes, such as inheritance hierarchies. Examples of objects in this layer are the standard class MassiveObject (any spacecraft component with mass) and PoweredObject (any component drawing power). Typical methods would be getMass() (get the mass of a massive object) and getPower() (get the power of a powered object). Alternatively, parameters such as Mass or Power could be published to obviate the overhead of method calls.

Also present in this layer will be standards for classes representing components, such as attitude sensors or actuators, along with their associated methods and parameters.

The middle layer consists of component simulation descriptions. These present a menu of tools that can be used by the design to create the executable model. For example, a component such as a reaction wheel (an attitude actuator) will be represented by a standard class, which inherits from the MassiveObject and PoweredObject classes. A desciption of the simulation modeling this component will be present in the middle layer. This description will either be written ab initio or downloaded from the web site of a vendor providing the component.

As the designer expresses his ideas, the various component simulations will be melded together into a workable model using the information present in this layer.

The various components described in the standards and component description layers are traditionally combined into well defined subsystems, such as the attitude control subsystem. Knowledge of such combinations, and the component interactions within them, is contained in the lowermost layer, the subsystem design layer.

SIMULATION TIER

Third is the simulation tier. This level is more concrete than the preceding two tiers. It contains practical knowledge of the simulations being used to build the model: their locations, file formats, and so on. It is within this tier that the executable federated simulation is constructed and executed. It is also within this tier that the results of the simulation are captured and stored, to be made available to the knowledge sustainment activity described below.

ARCHITECTURE

To produce a working distributed simulation, software will be used to extract information from the three tiered knowledge base and translate this information into an executable simulation. To make this process concrete, and to demonstrate it, we must choose a distributed simulation architecture.

We have chosen the High Level Architecture (HLA) (DOD 1996) as the distributed simulation architecture we will use.

HLA is defined by a set of rules captured in well defined formats such as the object model template (OMT), the Federation Object Model (FOM), and the component Simulation Object Models (SOM). Once the objects and interactions of the various components are defined, the Run Time Infrastructure (RTI) is used to provide interfacing services, such as federation, declaration, object, ownership, time and data distribution management.

SOM's are produced from information in the top two layers of the knowledge base tier. The FOM is generated from information about the object interactions contained in the design tier.

If a designer wishes to download a simulation of a star camera (an attitude sensor) from a vendor's web site, he can be assured that the software author has adhered to industry wide standards embodied in the standard FOM's and SOM's. Therefore, this simulation can be inserted into his growing federated model in a plug and play fashion.

KNOWLEDGE SUSTAINMENT

A significant amount is learned during the design, analysis and testing phases of spacecraft development. A perennial problem is the storage and retrieval of this information so that it becomes readily available to other workers on the same or subsequent missions. The process of facilitating this is called knowledge sustainment.

At present, much progress is being made in the theory of knowledge based approaches to design (Coyne 1990, Brazier 1998). This progress has been translated into practical use through the CommonKADS methodology (Schreiber 1993), which is becoming a de facto standard in Europe. It is this technology we intend to use in developing our knowledge sustainment component.

Let us consider a design that is in a partial state of completion. The knowledge accumulated in the knowledge base contains, in addition to the standards, components and designs that were described previously, such additional information as requirements, cost models, and so on. In addition, as the growing model is executed, additional information such as execution results and performance data are accumulated. The knowledge base also contains retrieval information that defines the procedures that can be used to select, interpret and display data within the database. Thus, the simulation results database might contain results from a simulation exectution. A CommonKADS tool would use the retrieval information to extract results from the simulation results database and make these results available to the designer via text or a display.

STANDARDS

Early work on realization of our vision has concentrated on the development of the standards for interoperable distributed simulation of spacecraft.

The goal is to develop standards that allow rapid development of mixed fidelity distributed simulations of spacecraft. It should be possible to include both new and heritage models in a plug and play fashion. To achieve this end, we have begun by studying a number of previously designed spacecraft to determine which design features they have in common, and which are sui generis. Since it will be necessary for the standards to become industry wide if our vision is to be realized, we will be seeking the collaboration of other academic, government and commercial spacecraft designers in the process. At present, we are working with The Jet Propulsion Laboratory and The Goddard Space Flight Center.

The three spacecraft we have analyzed are TIMED, a scientific earth orbiting spacecraft that is in the design phase; MSX, a large and very complex near earth spacecraft containing a variety of imaging sensors; and NEAR, a deep space mission that is currently in orbit around an asteroid. We found that it is necessary to decompose a generic spacecraft along both functional and physical boundaries. Functionally, we chose to maintain the classical subsystems: attitude determination and control, command and data handling, instruments/payload, mechanical and structural, navigation, power, propulsion, telecommunications, and thermal control. These subsystems are in turn decomposed into components. Thus, for example, the attitude system contains both actuators, such as reaction wheels, and sensors, such as star cameras. Physically, we found it necessary to capture properties common to hardware components such as the distribution of mass and the generation of heat, and common to software components such as data flow. We also found that we had to define standards for environmental "truth" models (that must be provided by the overall M&S system designer) such as attitude dynamics and vibrational behaviors.

We have observed, in the decomposition process, that components bear two types of relationships to one another. Systems or subsystems and their components bear a "has-a" relationship. Thus, an attitude systsem "has-a" reaction wheel and a power subsystem "has-a" battery. In addition, various components bear an "is-a" relationship to general classes: a reaction wheel "is-a" MassiveObject and a battery "is-a" HeatProducingObject. The "has-a" relationships define subsystem composition while the "is-a" relationships determine the hierarchy of class inheritances. Through the "is-a" relationship, spacecraft components inherit methods and parameters. For example, the reaction wheel object inherits the getMass() method from the MassiveObject class, and the power parameter from the PoweredObject class.

In addition to the standard methods and parameters inherited by the component objects, there may be unique methods and parameters. For example, the reaction wheel object, in addition to the above mentioned getMass() method must also have its own set of methods including setTorqueCommandVoltage(), getWheelSpeed(), getWheelMomentum(), and getWheelTorque().

In creating standards, we have come to the realization that there are two types of information that are required to proceed through the design process to create a working model of the system: *specification information* and a *simulation interface definition* (see Figure 1). The *specification information*, parameters such as mass, peak power, input voltage, operating temperature limits, etc., is generally used at the design stage as an engineer is selecting appropriate components to use in his design. For example, in an attitude control system design, the designer will need to select reaction wheels from among those that are available. To narrow the list, he will look at peak torque, peak angular momentum, and mass to see that the wheel can meet the performance requirements while satisfying any mass limitations imposed upon him at the system level. Using the specification information, it becomes easy to quickly narrow the list of candidate hardware prior to proceeding to the simulation phase where more detailed performance trade-offs are evaluated. Furthermore, once an engineer has added a reaction wheel to his design, the rest of the specification information for that component is available to the other subsystems. For example, the power engineer can take a look at the peak power and operating voltage of the wheel to see if it fits within his planned implementation.

The second part of a component standard is the *simulation interface*. The goal of standardizing the simulation interface is to create plug-and-play capability among spacecraft component models. To be able to use any reaction wheel model in an attitude control system simulation the engineer needs to know that the interface to the component model is the same for all other models. Consequently, items such as wheel speed and instantaneous angular momentum would be expected as part of a reaction wheel model. Furthermore, for an item like a reaction wheel, we would require that it provide not only its true instantaneous speed (and hence angular momentum) which would be needed for an attitude dynamics "truth" model, but also a reported speed that represents a modeled tachometer output to the control system.

The two-part standards for each spacecraft component include a predefined set of specification data for the component (for example a reaction wheel must specify its peak torque and angular momentum) and a description of the simulation interface. Component attributes that are part of the specification data (for example peak power) may or may not also be part of the simulation interface; similarly, attributes of the simulation interface may or may not also be represented in the specification data. Using the power as an example, peak power is a static value that would not need to be passed among components in a distributed simulation, however instantaneous power may be a simulation attribute for the component but would have no meaning as specification data.

To simplify and potentially reduce the amount of data that is passed around a distributed simulation, we allow flexibility in the selection of the data attributes that are required as part of the simulation side of the standard. Any component model must provide only its very basic information that makes that component what it is. For example, the reaction wheel simulation must accept a command torque to the wheel and is expected to output its current angular momentum, rate of change of momentum, and tachometer estimate of the its speed; it is not, however, required to provide instantaneous current usage to the power system (though it may). In essence, we allow each component model to attach a shopping list of its supported standard interfaces. Any individual component model must support only the minimum set of attributes and interactions which qualify it to be classified as a reaction wheel, star tracker, battery, etc. If a vendor implements a model that includes characteristics above and beyond the minimal set required, those additional characteristics must conform to base classes of objects which have been defined, for example MassiveObject, PoweredObject, and ThermalObject. Finally, as with the specification data, the standards include the flexibility to allow custom attributes for a component to be added while still ensuring conformance to the standard.

PROGRESS

To date, we have completed the following:

(1) decomposed a generic spacecraft into functional and physical subsystems and components
(2) developed an initial list of components and their interactions
(3) developed an initial list of inheritance classes
(4) designed the knowledge-based architecture
(5) designed the knowledge base
(6) selected HLA as the test-bed distributed simulation platform and selected a platform for implementation.

We are currently developing, as a test and demonstration case, a simulation of the Thermosphere, Ionosphere, Mesosphere Energetics and Dynamics (TIMED) satellite's attitude control system. This system includes a number of flight computers, actuators and sensors. In addition, there is a truth model for attitude dynamics.

The design of a demonstration simulation is simple in principle, but complicated in execution. A minimal set of federates which can demonstrate our concept is the following:

a) A model of a reaction wheel (i.e. an actuator capable of exerting a torque on a spacecraft)
b) A model of an inertial reference unit (i.e. a sensor capable of measuring the angular rate of a spacecraft)
c) A simple controller, which commands the reaction wheel to generate the torque required to force the angular rate to zero.
d) A rotational dynamic truth model, which outputs the angular rates as a function of time given the spacecraft's moments of inertia and the torque on it.

To free a spacecraft designer from the need to be very familiar with HLA and C++ programming, considerable use will be made of autocoding. Building on the knowledge base portion of this project, a tool has been generated that can autocode the essential underpinnings of HLA when given a Simulation Object Model (SOM) file – an HLA construct that defines a simulation's input and output interfaces. While the autocoded file thus generated will have no "physics", it will allow a spacecraft designer to easily insert the code that implements the desired behavior.

Once the basic architecture has been demonstrated, it will be made available to other collaborators in the spacecraft design industry. Only through interorganizational cooperation can industry wide standards be arrived at.

REFERENCES

Brazier F.M.T.; van Langen P.H.G.; Treur J. April 1998. *Strategic Knowledge in Design: a Compositional Approach.* Knowledge Acquisition Workshop 98. Banff, Canada,

Coyne R.D.; Rosenman M.A.; Radford A.D.; Balachandran M.; Gero J.S. 1990. *Knowledge-Based Design Systems*: Addison-Wesley Publishing Company

DOD (Department of Defense) 15 August 1996 *High Level Architecture Object Model Template Version 1.0*, http://hla.dmso.mil/

IOS (International Organization for Standardization). 1994. *Industrial Automation Systems and Integration – Product Data Representation and Exchange (STEP) – Part I: Overview and Fundamental Principals.* ISO 10300-1:1994. http://www.iso.ch/infoe/catinfo.html

Schreiber A.; Wielinga B.J.; Breuker J.A. editors. 1993. *KADS: A Principled Approach to Knowledge-Based System Development.* Volume 11 of Knowledge-Based Systems Book Series: Academic Press, London.

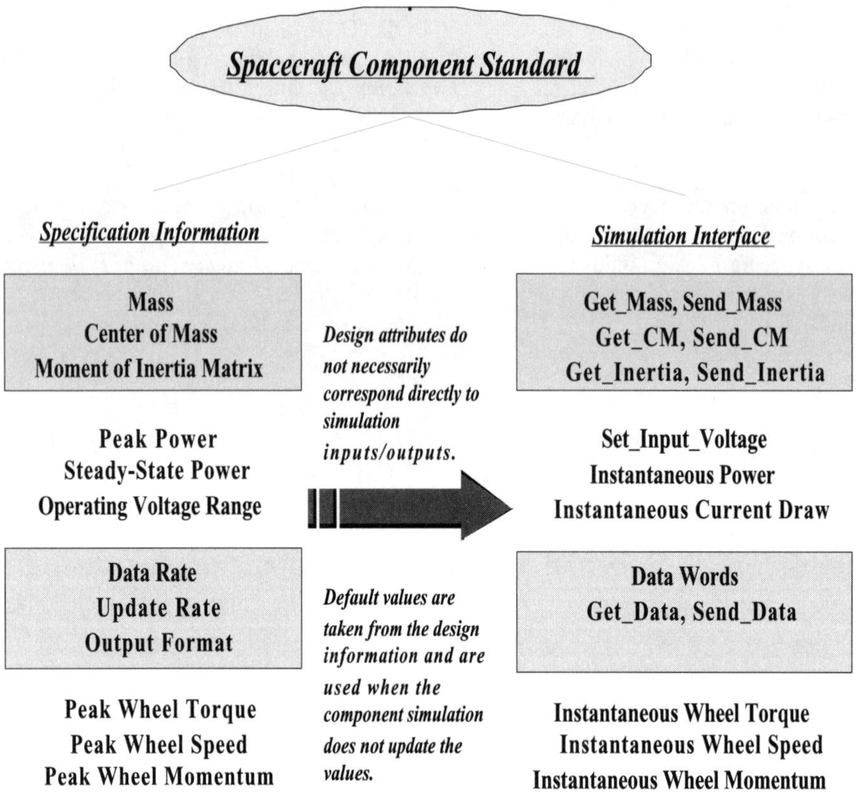

Figure 1: The Two Part Standard

HLA-FEDERATE REPRODUCTION PROCEDURES IN PUBLIC TRANSPORTATION FEDERATIONS

Thomas Schulze
Steffen Straßburger
Otto-von-Guericke University of Magdeburg
School of Computer Science
PSF 4120
39102 Magdeburg, Germany
e-mail:{tom, strassbu}@isg.cs.uni-magdeburg.de

Ulrich Klein
Fraunhofer Institute for
Factory Operation and Automation IFF
Factory Ecology Department
Sandtorstrasse 22
39106 Magdeburg, Germany
e-mail: Uklein@iff.fhg.de

KEYWORDS

Transportation, Discrete simulation, Distributed simulation

ABSTRACT

This paper summarizes our conceptual and prototypical work related to the dynamic composition of heterogeneous distributed simulations using the High Level Architecture for Modeling and Simulation (HLA). Previous studies of the authors and within the HLA community have shown that federates other than of simulation type are feasible. The reproduction of federates during runtime (so-called "cloning") has been identified as basic dynamic pattern, allowing the creation or exchange of federates of the same or different type. The paper provides an overview of different cloning strategies within or external to a given federation and applies them to the public transportation domain. Finally, the potential of cloning strategies on the component (HLA: federate) level is described.

1 MOTIVATION

With the advent of the High Level Architecture it became feasible for the first time to build simulations and simulation based information systems (federations) in a distributed manner using heterogeneous simulations and other software or hardware components (the federates). In view of the HLA support for interoperability and reusability, federates can be (re-)combined to form simulations / information systems. As long as software adheres to the HLA specifications (e.g., strictly using the object model templates and the HLA RTI interface), it can act as a federate. Previous studies by the authors and the HLA community have shown that federates can also consist of online information systems, databases, etc. Different federates with identical object models can be used to offer the same objects in a real operational system or in training mode (e.g., one time using an online GPS-based fleet management system and a simulation in training mode). This flexibility is a major breakthrough in simulation based system design but in most cases has been limited to the pre-run-time. Once a set of federates is used for starting a federation execution, it remains the same (late entering federates are allowed, though).

The cloning approach presented in this paper tries to extend the flexibility of system composition to run-time. Federates can be created as copies of existing federates, and while the status and the external representation (in HLA the object model) remains the same, a different internal implementation can be used. This approach is not limited to one time management, rather it includes the parallel management of different time axes in order to allow e.g. ad-hoc forecast functionality. In this way a method for simulation model initialization is also derived, preventing the overhead incurred by starting at an empty-and-idle status.

2 CLONING TECHNOLOGIES IN SIMULATION ENVIRONMENTS

2.1 Related Work

The term "Cloning" in relation with distributed simulation was first introduced in literature in 1997 by (Hybinette and Fujimoto 1997, 1998). In their approach logical processes (LPs) of a parallel simulation are cloned, i.e., copies of logical processes of a parallel simulation are created during the execution of the simulation. The copies (clones) of the original logical processes would initially have the same state as the original processes, but possibly behave differently at a later point in time because of some user interaction. The intention of this is to conduct multiple what-if-analysis at the same time, e.g., by having multiple clones each evaluating the consequences of different strategies at the same time.

The main motivation for the approach taken by Hybinette/Fujimoto is to have as few as possible copies of logical processes running at the same time due to performance and resource issues. This is done by association of several "virtual" LPs to one "physical" LP until a virtual LP behaves differently and needs to be created physically.

Kindler (Kindler 1999) and Novack (Novack 2000) developed together the nested-simulation or reflective-simulation approach. The goal of this approach is to start a new simulation inside an existing simulation. The internal simulation delivers information that will be used by the original simulation. It is necessary to copy the state of parts or the whole original simulation model for starting the internal simulation. This approach has been developed for monolithical simulation models only.

2.2 Cloning in HLA-Federations

Since the idea of cloning simulations for the reasons of conducting multiple what-if-analysis and providing as-fast-as-possible forecasts could also be very useful and valuable in the context of HLA federations, concepts and prototypical solutions for developing a similar technique for HLA federations have been investigated. Different cloning technologies for HLA federations have been developed at the University of Magdeburg. The following techniques are suggested:

Internal Cloning: Internal cloning refers to the process of making a copy of one or more HLA federates and have them join the same federation as the original federates (Figure 1). The federates must take appropriate steps for distinguishing between messages (i.e., updates, interactions, and the like) between original federates and cloned federates. Possible solutions would incorporate special attribute and parameter tags for each update or interaction which is issued. The simpler case would be to clone federates which have only a passive behavior. How this approach could be used is described below in the discussion of the streetcar federation prototype, which serves as the demonstration federation for the cloning techniques described here.

External Cloning: External cloning refers to the process of making a copy of one or more HLA federates and have them join a different federation than the original one (Figure 2). The major advantage of an external cloning procedure is that it allows the cloned federates to apply a different time management scheme, e.g., they could switch from a real-time simulation to an as-fast-as-possible forecast. This is also an approach providing more flexibility compared to the original cloning technique from Hybinette and Fujimoto, where all LPs were executed in one simulation requiring all simulations to run on the same time axis.

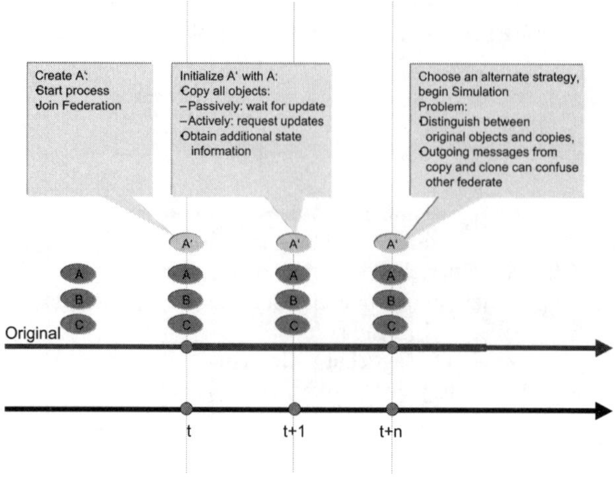

Figure 1:Suggested Procedure for Internal Cloning

External cloning also eliminates the need to distinguish between message traffic between original and cloned federates, which is an important issue in the case of internal cloning.

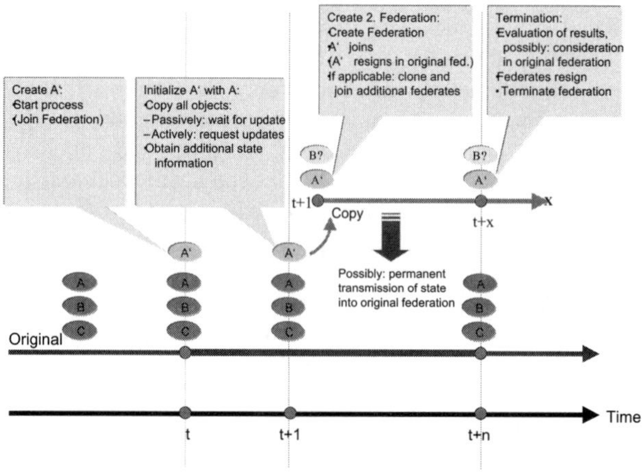

Figure 2: Suggested Procedure for External Cloning

Exchange of Federates at Runtime: Since exchanging federates with the same simulation object model (SOM) at runtime of a federation is a process which is (up to a certain extend) related to the issue of cloning of federates it will also be discussed here. The suggested procedure for exchanging federates at runtime includes the following steps (Figure 3):

- Create a copy (clone) or start a replacement federate
- Join this federate to the federation
- Acquire objects from original federate
- Resign the original federate

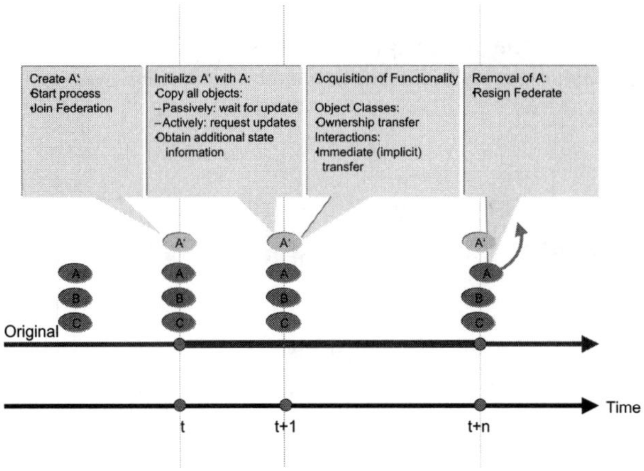

Figure 3: Suggested Procedure for Exchanging Federates at Runtime

2.3 Implementation Issues

In the cloning approach by Hybinette/Fujimoto the communication infrastructure (the Georgia Tech Time Warp Operating System, GTW) had to be enhanced for realizing the cloning. For the cloning of HLA federates, this cannot easily be done. Therefore different alternatives have been investigated.

A major prerequisite for the cloning of HLA federates is a technique for saving and restoring the state of a running simulation model. In the ideal case a simulation system would offer a built-in function for doing this itself. Examples for such simulators are GPSS/H and Simplex. GPSS/H offers the checkpoint function which saves a memory footprint to the hard disk and thus allows a later restoration of the model state. Simplex allows the user to schedule breaks for a certain simulation run. When reaching a break, the entire model state is also written to hard disk and can be resumed later.

Most commercial simulation systems do not offer a functionality for saving and restoring the state of a running simulation model. Therefore alternative means for copying the state of a simulation model have been investigated. The simulation system which served as the reference system for these investigations was SLX. The most important reason for this choice was the availability of a reliable HLA interface for this tool (Straßburger *et al.* 1998) and the possibility to easily be able to implement modifications or enhancements, in case they should deem necessary.

The difficulty when implementing the cloning or replication process for a simulation model is to cover all relevant model elements. Besides replicating the obvious items, e.g., object instances registered with a federation, other items need to be included, too. This relates for instance to certain simulator internals, like the state of random number generators, state of statistics already collected, etc.

Another question relates to the fact of how the state information from the original HLA federate to the replicated federates is transmitted. One could use external means, e.g., files, pipes, or a network connection. On the other hand one could also use means provided by HLA and its RTI itself. This is the path we chose for our prototypical implementation. The approach used here has some similarities to the object transfer approaches discussed in (Myjak *et al.* 1999a) and (Myjak *et al.* 1999b).

In our approach the original federate starts the cloned federate upon the occurrence of a certain event, e.g., by receiving an certain interaction, or command via the HLA Management Object Model (MOM). The clone is based on the same SLX source code like the original federate. After startup the clone detects the fact that it is indeed a clone and undergoes a special initialization phase. In this phase the clone requests updates for all object instances the original federate has registered in the federation. Also, additional information regarding the internal status of the original federate is transmitted. The clone is thus enabled to build up an almost identical copy of the internal state of the original federate. Some limitations apply regarding statistics and other details. More information can be obtained from (Albrecht 2000).

After the state of the original federate is replicated in the clone, the clone can enter its normal execution cycle. The further process depends on the aims for the cloning process. In an internal cloning procedure, the clone would co-exist with the original federate. This is most trivial in the case that the clone is passive and does not send messages (updates/interactions) to other clones. If this is not the case, further efforts need to be taken to distinguish between messages from the clone and the original.

An alternative aim could be to perform a forecast simulation. In this case, the clone could resign from the original federation and create/join a new one (possible in conjunction with other clones).

The third alternative would be a replacement of the original federate. In this case the clone would additionally request the transfer of ownership of object instances from the original federate. Then the original would resign and the clone would take over the responsibility for modeling the acquired object instances.

3 CLONING IN PUBLIC TRANSPORT FEDERATIONS

The HLA-related cloning is a new technology enabling a broad range of new and flexible applications. We are convinced that cloning technology will promote the use of simulation in traditional and new application areas. On a more general level application-oriented simulation models can be divided into three categories: design of systems, management of systems, and staff training applications. This paper presents three cloning technology examples from the second and third general application areas described above. The examples are focusing on public transport federations. Public transport has been selected because most people have related background and their own experiences. Furthermore, public transportation prototypes already have served as demonstrations for other advanced HLA-based work, such as online-/realtime-federates.

3.1 Support for operative management - forecast

An increasing number of simulation models is used in the operative management of public transportation systems. These models help for example managers to evaluate the system capacity for new transportation tasks, for breakdown- or accident-related changes in the number of available vehicles and for changes in the availability of staff. They give support to the management of systems for analysis of throughput and detection of bottlenecks. The management wants to evaluate operating decisions in relation to the performance of the system. In general the aim of models of this category is to support the operative management. The management wants to gain experiences from the future. We call these dedicated models Management Simulation Models (MSM).

MSM require greater level of detail than models for transportation system design. For example, complex control mechanisms and strategies may have to be implemented. On the other side, the MSM must be initialized with the state of the real system. For this task two possibilities exist: The simulation can start from a null-and-idle-status and run until it reaches the current state of the real system (e.g., using a trace file), or the model can be initialized directly with the state of the real system.

We prefer the last possibility using the external cloning procedure. The basic idea is to use one current-state-federation as a mirror of the current real system state. A real-time simulation model (federate) exists inside this federation and this federate will be updated permanently by online-data. The time advancement in the simulation federate will be paced by the real-time. This way it can be ensured that the simulation model maps the current system state. When the management wants to get decision support, the simulation federate will be cloned and it will be placed in a new federation.

The new federation has to contain the cloned federate and optionally other federates for human-interactions and visualization. This simulation federate operates as fast as possible and has to return a forecast considering the new conditions. The advantage of this solution is that the simulation model is indeed initialized by the current state of the real system.

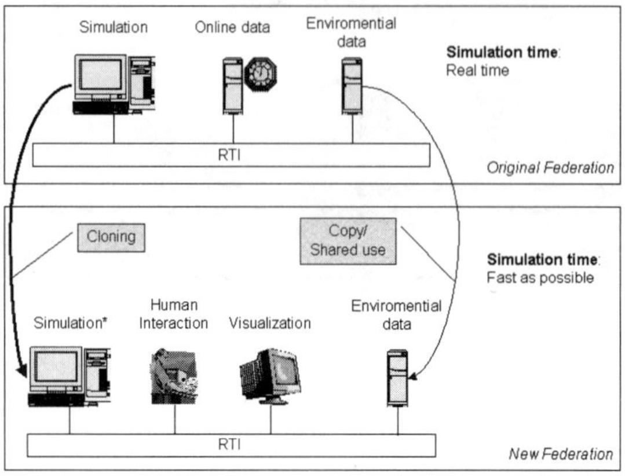

Figure 4: Suggested Procedure for External Cloning

3.2 Support for operative management – different strategies

Operative management is often confronted with the issue of choosing between different decision alternatives. Simulations can help to support the process of choosing the best suited decision. This can either be done by providing as-fast-as-possible forecasts, as discussed in the previous section, or by evaluating many different alternatives at the same time.

For the latter approach we suggest the internal cloning procedure: Several copies (clones) of a simulation model are created within the same federation. Each clone evaluates a different strategy. One implication of running within the same federation is that usually the same time management needs to be applied. This is also the approach which was chosen by Hybinette and Fujimoto.

In case of real-time proportional federations, this approach is therefore best suited for situations, where no immediate decision at a fixed time needs to be performed. In situations where an immediate decision is necessary, many as-fast-as-possible forecasts (faster than real-time) for all different strategies are needed.

Running multiple simulation copies within the same federation has the advantage that each copy can use any other information provided from other federates. This is especially important in the case of on-line transportation simulations using some sort of real-life data source. In this case each simulation copy can use this on-line data and perform its strategy evaluation based on this data.

The evaluation of different strategies based on this approach can be useful for strategic planning of traffic schedules, e.g., by comparing how different routing alternatives would influence the throughput of the system. The optimization of riding times, avoidance of traffic delays, and the minimization of necessary transportation devices can be additional target dimensions.

3.3 Support for staff training

Training is one of the most important application areas of simulation technology in the military and civil domain. This is due to the rareness of the events to be trained, costs or danger incurred by real training or the non-existence of the appliances or systems to be used or trained.

The training of staff can be executed in a pure training environment or in combined training and real life environments.

In the fist case the trainee operates in a traditional closed pure training environment. The trainee is integrated as an human player in the federation. He has to react on actions that will be delivered by a data supplier federate. The federation is completed by any other passive information and visualization federates. A training session can start with a data supplier federate focused on simple tasks. The trainee can thus be limbered up. After the warm-up period this supplier federate will be exchanged by an other. This new federate can deliver the real data online from the underlying transportation system. The trainee does not perceive that he has to respond to the real conditions. The trainer observes the reactions of the trainee and he/she can exchange the data supplier federate again. The exchange of federates during runtime will be applied.

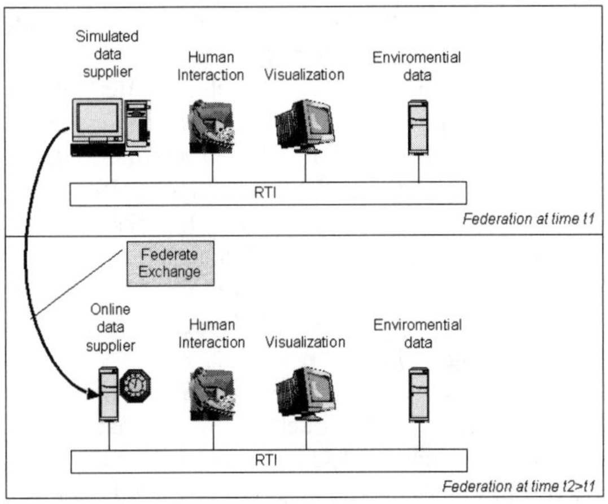

Figure 5: Suggested Procedure for Federate Exchange

In the second case the trainee acts in an open or integrated training environment. He is integrated in the real control and command structure but his reactions will not influence the real process. The control and command federation consists of the active human dispatcher federate, the online data supplier federate and other necessary federates for visualization and data bases. When the trainee will be integrated the dispatcher federate will be cloned and this federate will be the trainee-federate in the federation. The trainee does not work in an artificial training environment. He is integrated in the real system, using it in an "personal" training mode. The internal cloning will be used for this application.

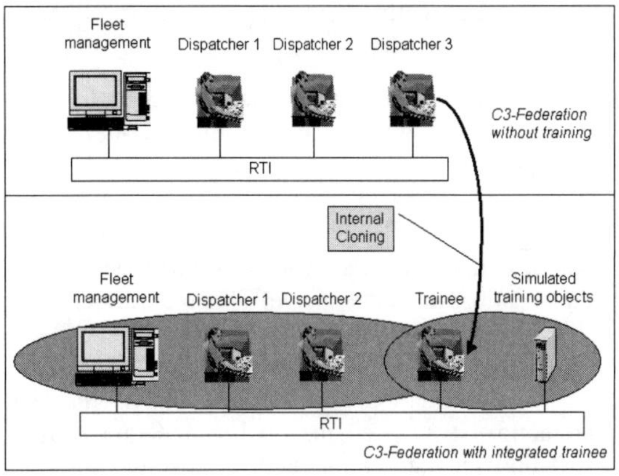

Figure 6: Suggested Procedure for Internal Cloning

4 PROTOTYPE

The prototype for test and demonstration of the cloning approaches has been a federation modeling the streetcar system of the city of Magdeburg (Schulze *et al:* 1999).

4.1 Internal Cloning

In this target scenario the simulation federate of the federation is cloned. The clone joins the original federation and requests information about all registered objects from the original federate, i.e., all streetcars currently moving through the city. After receiving updates for all objects the clone starts simulating the streetcar traffic based on the current schedule or any other chosen routing strategy. In opposite to the original federate the online positions for the vehicles will no be regarded. The cloned federate simulates the public traffic system without the real perturbations. Since the clone has a passive behavior, i.e., it does not send updates to other federates except the visualization component, no special mechanisms for distinguishing between original and cloned objects need to be introduced. The visualization federate can show both object types and thus visualize the different routing strategies chosen for the streetcars.

4.2 External Cloning

In this target scenario the simulation federate is cloned, too. It also requests information about all registered objects from the original federate. After that it resigns from the original federation. The clone is then used to perform an as-fast-as-possible forecast of the streetcar traffic. This enables the user to obtain an impression how a certain situation will develop and if bottlenecks will be likely to occur. For this forecast the cloned federate needs to advance simulation time faster than real-time. Therefore it can

- run independently from other federates without joining a new federation
- join a new federation and cooperate with other (cloned) federates, e.g., the visualization component.

4.3 Exchange of federates at runtime

In this scenario the on-line data source of our federation is exchanged by an off-line data source. This replacement is a straight-forward process: The off-line federate is started. It retrieves all necessary state-information from the on-line, e.g., the current simulation time, time stamp of the last update/interaction sent. Then the on-line federate resigns and the off-line federate starts sending position updates. This procedure is useful for operator training. By switching from a real system to a simulated scenario (without the need for the operator to know if the scenario is real) reactions to certain situations can be tested and trained.

5 CONCLUSION

The paper derived the cloning process on the component (HLA: federate) level as basic pattern of dynamic system composition applications, e.g., dynamic system reconfiguration, ad-hoc forecast analysis, and training applications.

The distinction between external description (in HLA the object models) and internal implementation details allows the creation or exchange of federates with the same external description and the same or different internal "nature" (e.g., simulation, online process, database or human-in-the-loop). This approach also covers the use of different time axis in order to allow, e.g., as-fast-as-possible forecasts during a real-time main application.

The public transportation domain has been chosen as application area for the prototypical work of the authors. Future steps include real-life prototypical applications of the different cloning strategies and the development of cloning and dynamic system management tools. The potential of cloning and other dynamic patterns is considered enormous, requiring considerable research and tool support.

ACKNOWLEDGEMENTS

This work has been supported by the Magdeburger Verkehrsbetriebe GmbH (MVB) by provision of their public transportation schedule and online positioning system. The geographic baseline data used in the visualization federate of the public transportation prototype has been provided by the Landesamt für Datenverarbeitung und Vermessung, Saxony-Anhalt, Germany.

REFERENCES

Albrecht, G. 2000. *Konzeption und Implementierung von Cloning-Techniken in HLA Federations*. Master's Th esis. Institute for Simulation and Graphics. Otto-von-Guericke University Magdeburg. July 2000 (In Progress).

Hybinette, M., and R. Fujimoto, 1997. Cloning: A Novel Method for Interactive Parallel Simulation. In *Proceedings of the 1997 Winter Simulation Conference*, pp. 444-451. ed. S. Andradóttir, K.J. Healy, D.H. Withers, and B.L. Nelson.

Hybinette, M., and R. Fujimoto, 1998. Dynamic Virtual Logical Processes. *Workshop on Parallel and Distri buted Simulation (PADS'98),* May 1998.

Kindler, E., 1999. Nested simulation of container yards. In *Proceedings of the Simulatiuo n und Visualisierung 99 Magdeburg*, ed. O. Deussen, P. Lorenz und V. Hinz, 247-259. SCS-Europe BVB, Ghent, Belgium 1999.

Novack, P., 2000. Reflective simulation with Simula and Java. In *Proceedings of the Simulatiuon und Visualisierung 2000 Magdeburg*, ed. T. Schulze, P. Lorenz und V. Hinz, 183-196. SCS-Europe BVB, Ghent, Belgium 2000.

Myjak M., S. Sharp, T. Lake, K. Briggs, 1999a. Object Transfer In HLA. In: *Proceedings of the Simulation Interoperability Workshop*, Spring 1999.

Myjak M., S. Sharp, W. Shu, J. Riehl, D. Berkley, P. Nguyen, S. Camplin, M. Roche, 1999b. *Implementing Object Transfer In the HLA*. . In: *Proceedings of the Simulation Interoperability Workshop*, Spring 1999.

Straßburger, S., T. Schulze, U. Klein, J.O. Henriksen. 1998. Internet-based Simulation using off-the-shelf Simulation Tools and HLA. *In Proceedings of the 1998 Winter Simulation Conference*, eds. Medeiros, D.J. and E. Watson, Washington D.C.

Schulze, T., S. Straßburger, U. Klein, 1999. On-Line Data Processing in Simulation Models: New Approaches and Possibilities Through HLA. In *Proceedings of the 1999 Winter Simulation Conference*, pp. 1602-1609. December 5-8, 1999. Phoenix.

Using *Joint MEASURE* to Study Tradeoffs Between Network Traffic Reduction and Fidelity of HLA Compliant Pursuer/Evader Simulations

S. B. Hall, S.M. Venkatesan, D.B. Wood - Lockheed Martin Space Systems
H.S. Sarjoughian, B.P. Zeigler - University of Arizona

We describe some results of a DARPA funded study[1] that investigated HLA network traffic reduction versus simulation fidelity tradeoffs that arise from predictive contract methodology. In particular, we report on several approaches to the use of endomorphic models and their associated parameter update quantization schemes. The study required the development of an HLA compliant Test Bed consisting of two Joint MEASURE[2] federates; one running a platform with various sensors and the other running a platform with a dynamically changing signature.

Joint MEASURE is a mission effectiveness simulator that has been used to assess the vulnerability and lethality of a variety of DoD air, land and sea platforms as well as numerous proposed systems of systems. It can run as a fully standalone simulation with an elaborate GUI (scenario creation, simulation display, statistical analysis), GRASS[3], XRT[4], and STK[5] support, and a powerful emulation of radar systems, ballistic, cruise, guided, and many other advanced missile systems, satellites, data communication, line-of-sight, and weather functionality. It also has a tightly integrated HLA functionality as part of its core simulation engine DEVS/HLA[6], an HLA-compliant implementation of the DEVS formalism.

The Test Bed developed for the DARPA study supports the evaluation of alternative distribution strategies in the context of a realistic, analytically oriented, DoD relevant scenario. The set of scenarios supported by the Test Bed all involve at least one Pursuer and one Evader. Analyses of such scenarios play a critical role in, for example, attempts to find effective solution to the fleeing TEL[7] problem.

The Pursuer in these scenarios is typically configured with a variety of sensors including infrared and/or radar and possibly one or more weapon systems. The Pursuer's objective is typically to seek and destroy the Evader. The Evader is configured with a full complement of signature models and is typically attempting to evade and escape the Pursuer.

The signatures of the Evader are of two basic types: emitted and reflected. Emitted signatures are available to passive sensors (e.g., infrared). Reflected signatures are available to active sensors (e.g., radar). Many factors contribute to the dynamic nature of the Evader's signature including the azimuth, elevation, frequency and polarization of the emission as well as the platform's mission timeline, altitude, 'speed', and configuration. The Evader's movement relative to the Pursuer varies in 6 dimensions over time and the environment influences the propagation differentially in both time and space due to dynamic weather and terrain affects.

Unfortunately, the dynamic quality of these signatures threatens to undermine much of the possible performance gain realized by distributing the simulation because of flood of messages that must be transmitted over network. The Test Bed was created to address these and similar issues.

This paper reviews the use of endomorphic models[8] to reduce message traffic and the role of quantizers in maintaining the state of endomorphs. Simulation performance measurements are presented for alternative architectures along with their impact on the accuracy of the study results.

1. Goals of the DEVS/HLA Validation Test Bed.

The design and development of the DEVS/HLA Joint MEASURE validation test bed was driven by the desire to satisfy the following four objectives:

- Establish the practicality of using the DEVS/HLA approach in an industrial strength application.
- Demonstrate that remote models can be efficiently accessed for analytically demanding purposes through the use of endomorphs.
- Explore the impact of alternative distribution strategies on performance and fidelity.
- Quantify the resulting performance and fidelity improvements and/or tradeoffs.

[1] DARPA Advanced Simulation Technology Thrust (ASTT) Contract #N6133997K-0007
[2] Lockheed Martin's Mission Effectiveness Analysis Simulator for Utility, Research and Evaluation
[3] FSF's GIS: Geographical Resource Analysis Support System
[4] A set of dynamic Motif-based chart and graphs that support data visualization
[5] A satellite availability and coverage tool with strong visualization support.
[6] Developed by Bernard Zeigler at the University of Arizona.
[7] Transportable Erector Launcher
[8] A local 'replica' of a remote model that is interacted with directly but whose state is maintained by the remote parent.

Joint MEASURE, an industrial strength constructive simulation in regular use within Lockheed Martin, was chosen to serve as the foundation of the test-bed. An overview of Joint MEASURE and its architecture is provided in the section that follows.

2. Joint MEASURE Validation Test Bed Architecture

2.1 Joint MEASURE Overview

The Joint MEASURE (Mission Effectiveness Analysis Simulator for Utility, Research and Evaluation) project began in 1994 to provide simulation based analytical support for the assessment of the utility of new and proposed sensors, weapons and C^3 (communication, command and control) systems. Joint MEASURE has the following notable features:

- Mission effectiveness analysis oriented.
- High performance Monte-Carlo DEVS (discrete event based) modular architecture.
- Integrates a full GIS (for environmental modeling) and statistical toolkits (for results analysis).
- Incorporates analyst friendly GUI supporting: scenario definition, system specification and runtime 2-3D dynamic data displays.

Figure 1 below presents a top-level architecture of Joint MEASURE. Analysts and application developers are involved in developing additional reusable model (in orange) while infrastructure developer maintain and enhance the blue and white central core of Joint MEASURE.

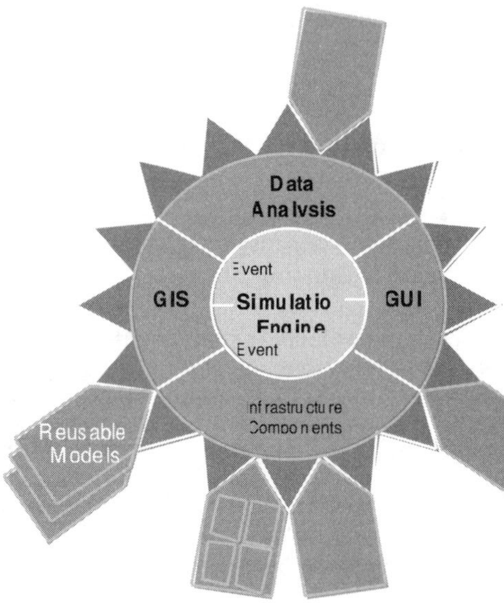

Figure 1. MEASURE's ComponentArchitecture

Figure 2 presents two screenshots of the many graphical user interfaces available to analysts during the process of the specification of new systems and the way they are to be used as well as the post-run tools available to support the results analysis process.

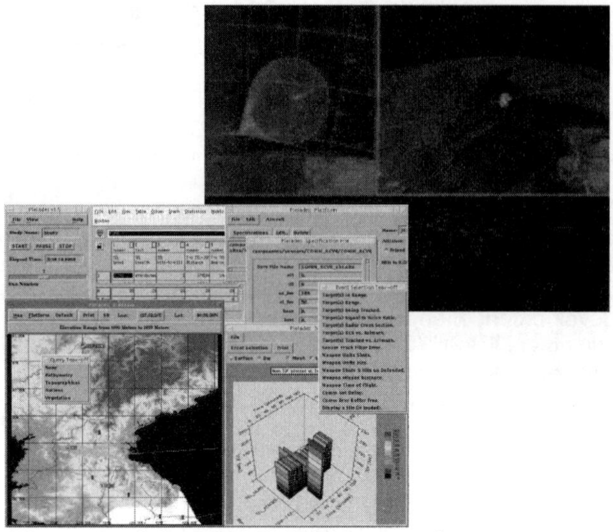

Figure 2. Joint MEASURE Screenshots

2.2 Typical Joint MEASURE Applications

Joint MEASURE has a broad range of applicability to system and system-of-systems mission effectiveness analysis. A review of a few of the projects that have utilized Joint MEASURE can however help communicate the applicability of the tool. The following subsections briefly characterize four recent applications.

2.2.1 High Energy Lasers (HEL) and Space Based Lasers (SBL)

Lasers have recently emerged as conceivably practical weapons. Joint MEASURE has been used on several recent efforts to assess the most practical and effective design of these new weapons including an SBL study where it was used to:

- Automatically import government supplied scenarios that define the nature and behavior of the hostile forces to be engaged by the system(s) under design (e.g. TM93).
- Analyzes alternative constellations of lasers and mirrors
- Analyze alternative SBL designs (freq., power, jitter, optics)
- Analyze alternative battle-managers (weapon and sensor resource scheduling).

2.2.2 Joint Composite Tracking Network (JCTN)

The JCTN project is focused on the utility and feasibility of widely distributing sensor measurement data to be fused together with other measurements for improved tracking and discrimination. Joint MEASURE was used to assess the feasibility and consequent utility of JCTN as a function of the following factors:

- Alternative communication distribution systems (including space based relays) and message filtering algorithms.
- Alternative sensor fusion (tracking) algorithms, including message time delay, from heterogeneous sensors.

2.2.3 Space Operations Vehicle (SOV) / Common Aero Vehicle (CAV) / Space Maneuvering Vehicle (SMV)

The SOV is a next generation reusable launch vehicle that can be rapidly 'turned-around' and relaunched. It can piggyback multiple maneuverable and reentry-able payloads. Joint MEASURE was used to assess the impact of the following:

- Alternative turn-around conops and SOV performance capability's impact on launch frequency.
- Alternative launch frequencies and payload performances on mission measures of effectiveness (MOE) s.

2.2.4 Arsenal Ship / Deepwater / DD21

The Navy is currently designing its next generation of ships and the Coast Guard is looking to modernize its fleet. Many features including ship speed, stealth, sensors, weapons and C3I influence the mission effectiveness of alternative candidates (e.g., its lethality and vulnerability). Joint MEASURE has been used to assess the following factors:

- The impact of alternative signature versus speed tradeoffs on survivability.
- The impact of improved off-board sensors and communications on mission success.
- The impact of alternative battle-group conops on lethality and vulnerability.

2.3 The Non-Distributed Joint MEASURE Architecture

Joint MEASURE is fundamentally architected around the concept that interactions between platforms are overwhelmingly emissions (electromagnetic, acoustic, pressure-wave) based. Emissions are subject to propagation delays, loss of signal strength and the addition of environmental noise and that they may carry structure and/or meaning. The reliable (and high-performance) modeling of these emissions based interactions is at the heart of the Joint MEASURE. The architecture defines the following three kinds of domain models. Figure 3 depicts these fundamental models and their interfaces.

2.3.1 Platform(s) - Top Level Modeling Components

Platform models represent physically locatable entities or vehicles. They have the following features:

- Encapsulate subsystems models, e.g.: Hull (with global state), Sensors (both transmitters and receivers), Weapons, Communications (both receivers and transmitters), C^2 (command and control).
- Interact (indirectly) with other platforms via 'emissions'.

2.3.2 Spatial Event Generator (Logger) - Infrastructure Component

The Logger is responsible for processing the route plans of the various platforms along with their various sensor and communication capabilities and predicts when interactions are, under ideal circumstances, possible. The Logger informs platforms when they are 'within range' of other platforms. Platforms are responsible for updating the Logger when their route or sensor capabilities change. The Logger, in short, has the following features:

- Calculates when emission based events could occur.
- Publish and subscribe oriented.
- Handles detection, firing and collision events.
- Accesses the Geographical Information System (GIS) to access environmental limitations (e.g. terrain blockage).

2.3.3 Propagator - Infrastructure Component

The Propagator represents the environment through with emissions travel. It makes extensive use of the GIS system to access how the spatial and temporal context of the simulation impacts the emissions being propagated. It salient features include:

- Determines signal and noise strength and latencies.
- Interfaces to a GIS system (GRASS) for environment models including: terrain elevation, vegetation coverage, soil type, historical 4D weather data, ocean wave models and smoke dispersion models amongst others.

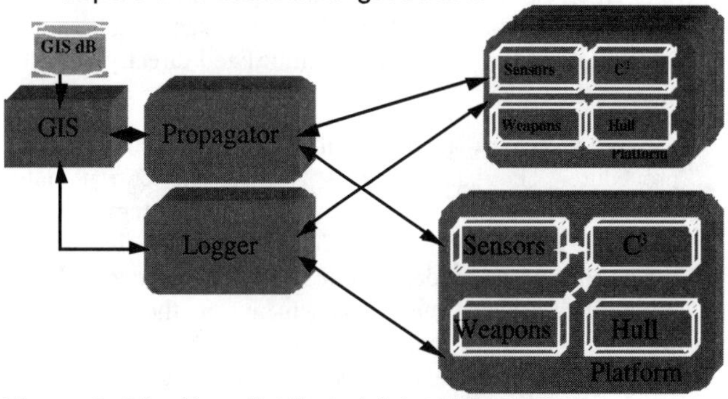

Figure 3. The Non-distributed Joint MEASURE Architecture

convinced that cloning technology will promote the use of simulation in traditional and new application areas. On a more general level application-oriented simulation models can be divided into three categories: design of systems, management of systems, and staff training applications. This paper presents three cloning technology examples from the second and third general application areas described above. The examples are focusing on public transport federations. Public transport has been selected because most people have related background and their own experiences. Furthermore, public transportation prototypes already have served as demonstrations for other advanced HLA-based work, such as online-/realtime-federates.

3.1 Support for operative management - forecast

An increasing number of simulation models is used in the operative management of public transportation systems. These models help for example managers to evaluate the system capacity for new transportation tasks, for breakdown- or accident-related changes in the number of available vehicles and for changes in the availability of staff. They give support to the management of systems for analysis of throughput and detection of bottlenecks. The management wants to evaluate operating decisions in relation to the performance of the system. In general the aim of models of this category is to support the operative management. The management wants to gain experiences from the future. We call these dedicated models Management Simulation Models (MSM).

MSM require greater level of detail than models for transportation system design. For example, complex control mechanisms and strategies may have to be implemented. On the other side, the MSM must be initialized with the state of the real system. For this task two possibilities exist: The simulation can start from a null-and-idle-status and run until it reaches the current state of the real system (e.g., using a trace file), or the model can be initialized directly with the state of the real system.

We prefer the last possibility using the external cloning procedure. The basic idea is to use one current-state-federation as a mirror of the current real system state. A real-time simulation model (federate) exists inside this federation and this federate will be updated permanently by online-data. The time advancement in the simulation federate will be paced by the real-time. This way it can be ensured that the simulation model maps the current system state. When the management wants to get decision support, the simulation federate will be cloned and it will be placed in a new federation.

The new federation has to contain the cloned federate and optionally other federates for human-interactions and visualization. This simulation federate operates as fast as possible and has to return a forecast considering the new conditions. The advantage of this solution is that the simulation model is indeed initialized by the current state of the real system.

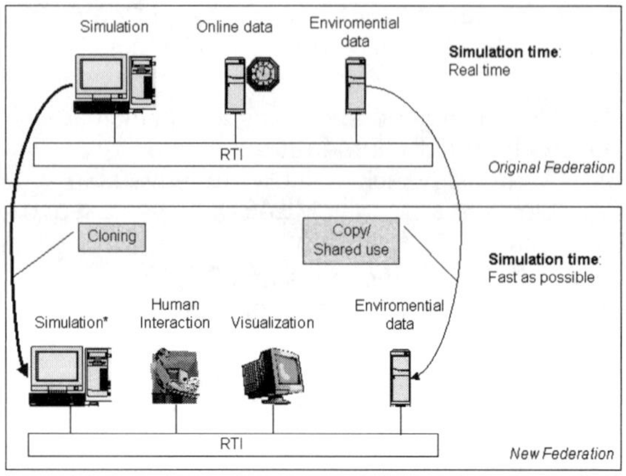

Figure 4: Suggested Procedure for External Cloning

3.2 Support for operative management – different strategies

Operative management is often confronted with the issue of choosing between different decision alternatives. Simulations can help to support the process of choosing the best suited decision. This can either be done by providing as-fast-as-possible forecasts, as discussed in the previous section, or by evaluating many different alternatives at the same time.

For the latter approach we suggest the internal cloning procedure: Several copies (clones) of a simulation model are created within the same federation. Each clone evaluates a different strategy. One implication of running within the same federation is that usually the same time management needs to be applied. This is also the approach which was chosen by Hybinette and Fujimoto.

In case of real-time proportional federations, this approach is therefore best suited for situations, where no immediate decision at a fixed time needs to be performed. In situations where an immediate decision is necessary, many as-fast-as-possible forecasts (faster than real-time) for all different strategies are needed.

Running multiple simulation copies within the same federation has the advantage that each copy can use any other information provided from other federates. This is especially important in the case of on-line transportation simulations using some sort of real-life data source. In this case each simulation copy can use this on-line data and perform its strategy evaluation based on this data.

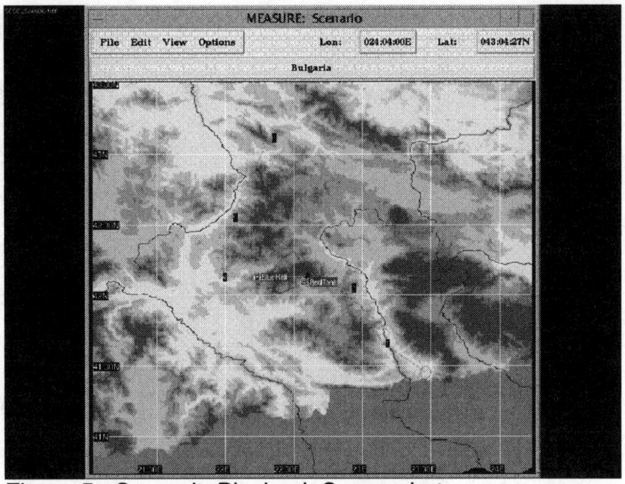

Figure 5. Scenario Playback Screenshot

3.2 Distribution Rules and Guidelines

The architecture rules and guidelines that follow define the class of distribution architecture that the data in this paper studies:

3.2.1 Distribution Approach Rules and Guidelines

1. Models are distributed to processors on the basis of red/blue affiliation.
2. All models are responsible for maintaining remote endomorph(s) (updates).
3. All detection/tracking is performed locally against endomorphs
4. Other interactions (e.g. detonations) are transmitted over the network. (interactions)

3.2.2 Endomorph Update Rules and Guidelines

1. Models maintain their own (possible dynamic) signature databases.
2. Models monitor (with local logger support) position of possible detectors.
3. Models update selected signature cell values in response to:
   A. Dynamic changes in their own signature cell values.
   B. Motion derived changes in detector bearing and eleation.
4. Updates are quantized in order to control the update frequency.

3.2.3 Test Bed Support Guidelines

1. Quantization parameters can be easily manipulated.
2. Number of processors over which the simulation is distributed can be readily increased.
3. Endomorphs can be eliminated altogether.

4. Sample Results

This section summarizes the results obtained by varying the quantizer level in the architecture described above and executing the two scenario variants also described above. The message traffic reductions reported here reflect the reductions due to the tank model's quantized updating of its endomorph. The reduction in simulation fidelity is assessed via a variety of measure including time in track and track error (a measure of how accurately the tracker is performing).

4.1 Scenario 1 Results

Scenario 1 produced fewer detections than Scenario 2. The data are however comparable in most important respects. Figure 6 displays both the dramatic drop in message traffic as a function of increasing quantizer level and the relatively strong track error correlation coefficient obtained by correlating the highest fidelity data with the quantized data. The correlation remains strong until the 1dB level and only drops off significantly after the 5dB level.

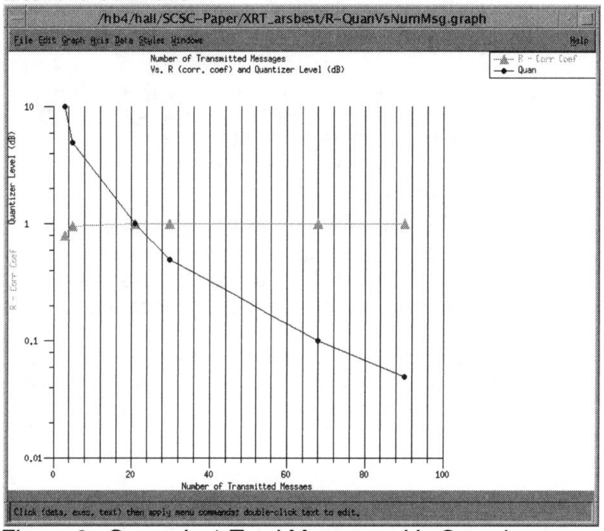

Figure 6. Scenario 1 Total Messages Vs Quantizer Level

Figure 7 displays the track error correlation vs. the quantizer level directly revealing the drop off that begins at 1 dB.

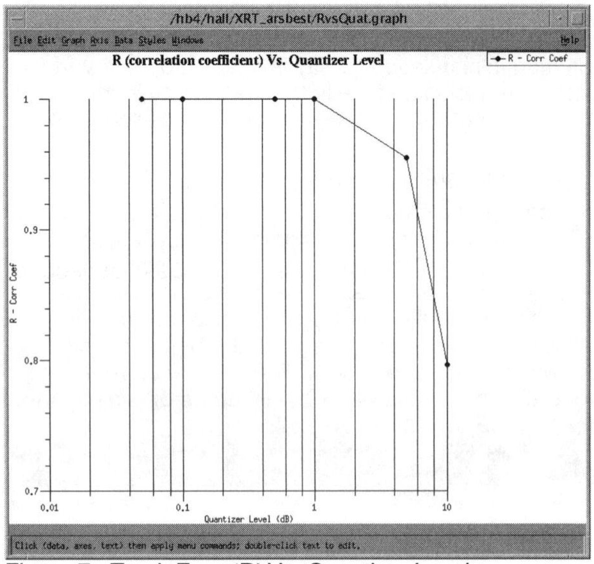

Figure 7. Track Error 'R' Vs. Quantizer Level

4.2 Scenario 2 Results

Scenario 2, while exhibiting more subtle behaviors, reveals similar quantizer trends as does scenario 1. Figure 8 once again shows the dramatic decrease in HLA message update traffic as a result of increasing quantizer level.

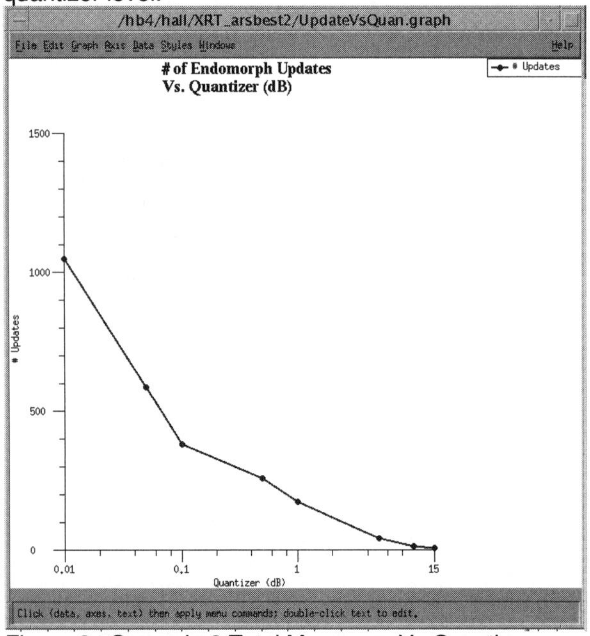

Figure 8. Scenario 2 Total Messages Vs Quantizer Level

Figure 9 is a sample of the data generated for use by the analyst. It displays one frame of a movie constructed from the various quantizer levels. It reveals what the radar receiver is seeing in the quantized run in comparison to the 'actual' signature.

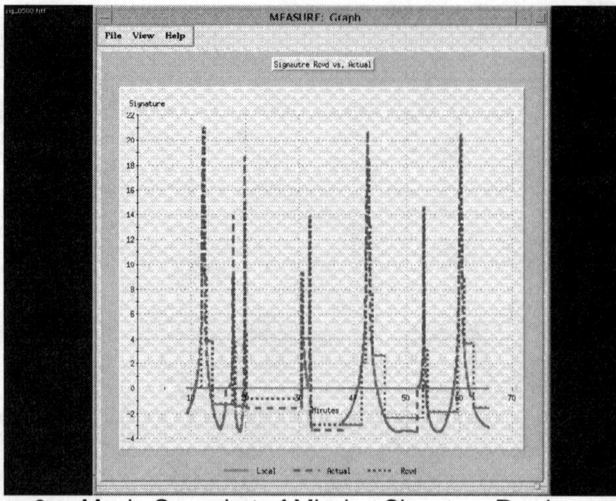

Figure 9. . Movie Snapshot of Mission Signature Rcvd vs. Quantizer Level

Figure 10 is another sample of data generated for the analyst. This movie sequence is generated from the various quantizer levels. This sequence reveals the Monte-Carlo probability that the tank was being tracked by the radar at various times in the scenario for the various levels of the quantizer.

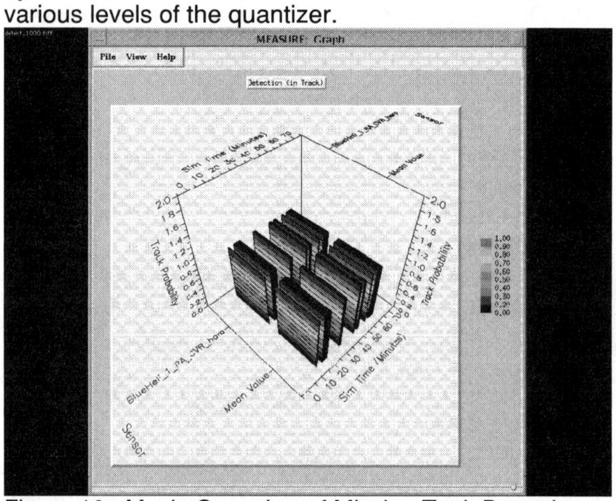

Figure 10. Movie Snapshot of Mission Tank Detection vs. Quantizer Level

Figure 11 is a single frame (quantizer level) from a third movie sequence similar to Figure 10 but reveals the track error as a function of mission time for each of the levels of the quantizer.

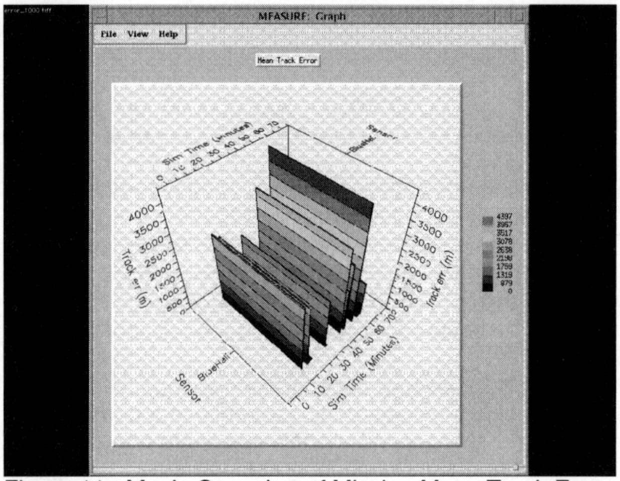

Figure 11. Movie Snapshot of Mission Mean Track Error Vs Quantizer Level

Figure 12 reveals again the strong track error correlation that remains above .99 until the quantizer exceeds the 1dB level.

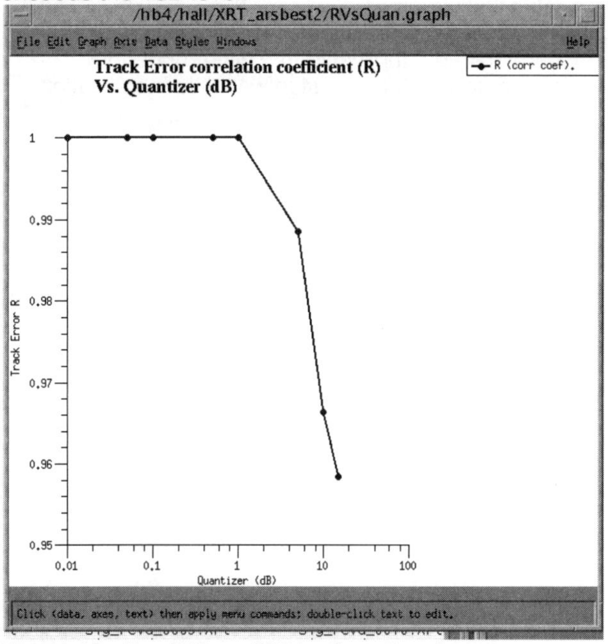

Figure 12. Track Error 'R' Vs. Quantizer Level

5. Discussion of Alternative High Performance Distributed Architectures

A number of subtle differences can be identified in the approach used to distribute a simulation of this class. The best approach would seem to be a function of the details of the models and their fidelity. Some of the options are listed below. Each of these architectures can be investigated within the current test-bed but further research is necessary to quantify their affect and to reliably predict the best approach for a given simulation.

5.1 Option 1:

- Complete Signature is initial transmitted.
- Orientation is quantized and transmitted.

This option requires the model to download the entire signature structure to the endomorph and then update the endomorph in response to quantized changes in its absolute orientation. Benefits include that the model does not need to know the relative location of the sensor. Disadvantages include: high update rates for rapidly maneuvering and rough terrain traversing vehicles; the lack of synchronization with the sensor receiver's relative bearing and the inapplicability of the approach to models which dynamically generate signatures or interpolate them from established sets of values.

5.2 Option 2:

- All Routes and route changes are broadcast.
- Signatures are quantized and updated independent of accesses.

This option requires the model to update the endomorph's signature only when the relative bearing of the sensor exceeds the quantizer value. Benefits include the possibility of specifying the quantizer in terms of the resolution of the RCS structure and thereby producing perfect fidelity. Disadvantages include the unnecessarily high update rates for rapidly maneuvering vehicles especially in the context of relative low scan rates and the added complexity of the need to maintain the relative position of the sensor and predict when the quantizer threshold will be exceeded (predictive quantization[11]).

5.3 Option 3:

- All transmissions are broadcast.
- Signatures are quantized and updated only when accessed.

This option requires that the transmitter simultaneously send all emissions across the network and to the endomorph. The model updates a single signature value in the endomorph only on the occasion that the endomorph is being 'scanned' and the current value has diverged from the 'actual' value by more than the quantizer threshold. Benefits include the synchronization of updates with actual 'scans'. Disadvantages include the need

[11] Zeigler, B.P., et al. (1998). The DEVS/HLA Distributed Simulation Environment and Its Support for Predictive Filtering, ECE, Technical Report, The University of Arizona, Tucson, Arizona.

to transmit all sensor transmitter emission and the implementation complexity that results from the lack of a zero-time advance in HLA.

5.4 Option 4: (hybrid)

- Routes and emission rates are broadcast.
- Signatures are quantized and updated as by local determination

This option requires that the model maintain (and predict) both when the sensor's relative position will change beyond the resolution of the signature structure and/or the quantizer threshold and when the endomorph will next be scanned. Its responsibility is to update the endomorph only when the endomorph is about to be scanned and the current value diverges from the actual value by the quantizer threshold or more. Benefits include the elimination of the need to send all sensor transmitter emissions in exchange for an emission rate. Disadvantages include implementation complexity, model processing demands and the lack of applicability to models with episodic scan patterns.

5.5 Broadcast restricted to models conservatively capable of interaction.

All of the above strategies benefit from the use of the Spatial Event Predictor (Logger) which controls the distribution of messages to only those models that are conservatively capable of interaction.

6. Summary

The following summary observations are offered:

- The Joint MEASURE high performance HLA distribution architecture test bed has proven to be an easy to use, flexible and effective means of evaluating a variety of performance enhancing alternative architectures.
- The quantizer approach offers the promise of substantial reduction in HLA message traffic along with the consequent run-time performance improvement while maintaining a predictable level of fidelity.
- The best approach for maintaining fidelity while reducing message traffic depends on a number of factors that are apparently specific to the details of the simulation. Addition research is necessary to simplify the identification of the best approach for a specific simulation.
- The combination of the quantizer approach with the Spatial Event Predictor developed in the original Joint MEASURE is a particular powerful combination.
- The approach developed here is sufficiently generic to be applicable to a wide range of distributed HLA application with little modification.

Contact: steve.hall@lmco.com 408-742-2903

THE JOINT WARFARE SYSTEM (JWARS) ARCHITECTURE
A CLIENT-SERVER, DATABASE CENTRIC SIMULATION SYSTEM IN SMALLTALK

Ronald D. Painter
CACI, Inc.
1600 Wilson Blvd.
Suite 1300
Arlington, VA 22209
e-mail: rpainter@hq.caci.com

KEYWORDS
Discrete Simulation, Stochastic, Military, Simulation Architecture, Smalltalk

ABSTRACT

JWARS is a stochastic discrete event simulation that must run much faster than real time. It must simulate campaign level of warfare with a balanced representation of multi-sided combat. The JWARS system includes the warfight and the inter- and intra-theater mobility, all at unprecedented resolution across the breadth of a campaign simulation. The JWARS architecture was specifically designed to allow the JWARS Program to meet demanding system requirements. There are requirements for ease of use for both input and output along with strict configuration management of the data. This led to a database centric solution for data storage with a sophisticated Human Computer Interface system. This data centric approach required detailed attention to the mapping of Smalltalk objects to RDBMS structures. The requirement for fast, Monte Carlo simulation runs separated the HCI system from the Simulation System allowing each repetition of a given scenario to be ran on separate machine(s)/processor(s). The JWARS system also includes a JWARS administrative control system (JACS) which handles the Simulation System runs and allows users to connect to running simulations and visualize results as they occur. This paper describes the components of the JWARS architecture, with particular emphasis on how a Visual Age Smalltalk's development environment was used to support major design changes efficiently.

BACKGROUND

The Joint Warfare System (JWARS) is being developed as a closed-form analytic model of joint military operations. Its purpose is to support joint military analysis, primarily focusing at the theater, strategic and operational levels of war. JWARS will address joint warfare as specified in the JWARS Operational Requirements Document (ORD).

Predecessor models to JWARS were developed by the various services to address their particular issues. These models were developed in the 70s and 80s using the then state-of-art computers (mainframes) and programming languages (FORTRAN and SIMSCRIPT II.5®). While these programs have been ported to modern computers, their architectures do not allow them to be easily expanded to meet current requirements for the JWARS program.

JWARS design decisions are based on stated system requirements from the JWARS Operational Requirements Document, prime contractors' Statements of Work, analyst interviews, and implicit requirements derived from predecessor models. These design requirements lead to numerous derived requirements that are allocated to the various components of the architecture.

Below is an overview of the JWARS system-level requirements the system must support:

- Simulate joint military operations in a balanced manner.
- Allow the proper representation of Command, Control, Comminations, Computers, Intelligence, Surveillance and Recognizance (C4ISR) systems through perception-based models.
- Handle stochastic phenomena
- Require no human intervention during the simulation.
- Allow analysts to build studies and scenarios within the tool through a modern Graphical User Interface (GUI).
- Manage studies and excursions on studies.
- Reduce significantly the time required to prepare a study.
- Improve the usefulness of the resulting data from the simulation over current simulations.
- Require much faster than real-time execution runs.

- Allow the user to have traceability of results.
- Allow verification and validation of the simulation.
- Employ modern object-oriented design practices in the building of the JWARS system that allows the users to change the model to meet future requirements.

To support this complex set of system requirements, the JWARS is being constructed with several design features that address specific system architecture issues:

- Technical Reference Model (TRM) compliant architecture that permits maximum use of Commercial Off-The-Shelf (COTS) / Government Off-The-Shelf (GOTS) software to be incorporated in the system in a plug replaceable manner.
- Client-Server architecture that allows the off-loading of services type tasks to other processors/ computers when using the JWARS system.
- Kernel based architecture that uncouples the JWARS executable code from the GUI interfaces and development environment. This allows the JWARS system to be fully testable at all stages of development.

TECHICAL DISCUSSION

Two fundamental decisions concerning the JWARS architecture were driven by the need to execute multiple stochastic replications of a single "scenario" at much faster than real time run speed. These design decisions form the foundation of the JWARS architecture and are reflected in the selection of almost all other design approaches taken throughout the system.

First, the simulation engine was separated from the HCI interface. The de-coupling of the simulation run from the Human Computer Interface (HCI) has several advantages and one significant disadvantage. The major advantages of de-coupling are:

- Multiple simulation runs/repetitions can be run in parallel distributed across machines and networks.
- The HCI user can select the simulation run/repetition to be observed switching that selection at will and disconnecting at anytime
- The HCI user can analyze previous runs or set up future runs while a simulation is running
- The simulation objects cannot be tied to graphical interactions that can cost CPU time even when not being used.
- The simulation must be run against data sets that are archived in the Oracle database repository and all output must be saved to the repository.

The primary disadvantage is that the user needs interactive access to the running simulation execution when preparing data sets. However, the simulation data required to support set up is not directly accessible to the HCI.

The second underlying design decision was to make the simulation system of JWARS a monolithic component instead a distributed sub-system. While system designers can argue that a single run can be completed quicker when distributed over multiple computer resources, JWARS could not ignore the fact that multiple replications will always run more rapidly over multiple computer resources when the individual simulation runs are not being distributed internally. The replication requirement also brought into play the ability to perform simulation runs in "batch" mode since the end-users often do not want to commit massive computer resources during normal working hours and/or may not actually get access to the needed resources during those hours.

Figure 1 shows the JWARS architecture resulting from the separation of the Human Computer Interface (HCI) from the Simulation System. The JWARS Administrative Control System (JACS) was required to allow batch mode operation of the simulation runs. It also looks at the available resources and distributes the simulation runs both across the resources and over time.

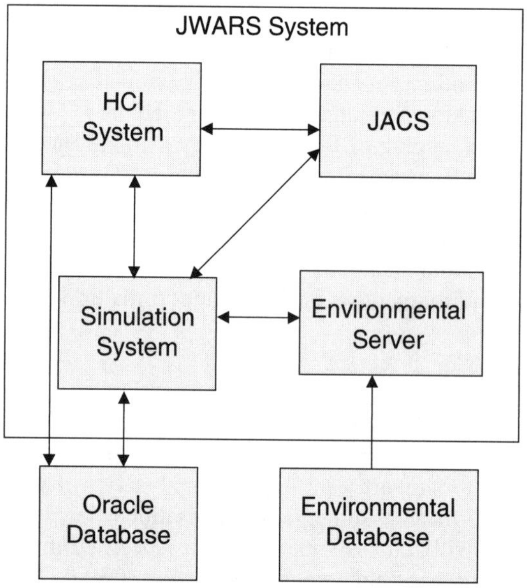

Figure 1: JWARS System Architecture

Dividing the JWARS architecture into multiple subsystems provides distinct advantages but requires difficult design tradeoffs. The architectural design, the advantages and the design tradeoffs for each of the JWARS subsystems will be described.

The HCI System

The HCI System provides the user interface into the simulation. Figure 2 shows the Technical Reference Model (TRM) view of the HCI system. The user can work in any one of three environments: developer, entity modeler or analyst. The developer environment provides the development of new objects and includes extensions to the

Smalltalk VisualAge environment such as automatic code generation. In addition, the developer's environment includes a GUI interface that allows the in-field developer to extend a Battle Space Entity (BSE) with limited new behavior. The BSE architecture is discussed in greater detail in the Simulation System discussion.

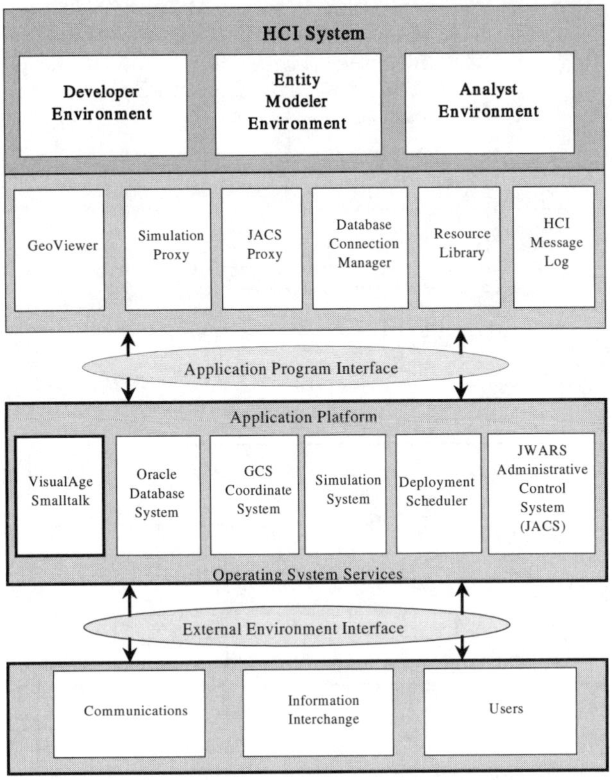

Figure 2: HCI System Architectural View

The entity modeler environment also allows the user to create BSEs from the implemented Smalltalk objects by attaching platform, sensor, communication, logistics and C2 objects and creating the instance data for these objects. Scenario development is also part of the entity modeler environment. The analyst environment is the richest environment. An analyst can create studies, manage studies, run the simulation along with excursions and analyze the results. The HCI System is developed as a series of workflow steps. These are developed from requirements derived from the JWARS ORD, work flow/screen flow, and analyst interviews.

The workflows are:

1. User Signs On to JWARS
2. Analyst Associates EEAs => MOE => Study
3. Analyst Modifies a Scenario
4. Analyst Creates a Scenario
5. Analyst Sets up and Runs the Simulation
6. Analyst Generates MOE/MOP Reports

To mitigate the issues associated with de-coupling the HCI from the simulation system, JWARS provides information exchange between the two sub-systems via a publish-subscribe mechanism. The data to be exchanged has to be defined explicitly and any data change requires modification to both systems. The publish-subscribe mechanization has the publishing system always publishing the data but the data is sent between the systems only when subscriber systems are present. The computational time involved in construction of the publication "packet" for HCI consumption even when an HCI system is not present is significant; therefore, the JWARS design required checking for the presence of subscribers before construction of these subscription packets. Also, the data publication from the simulation to the HCI is asynchronous with the simulation; therefore, the data being received by the HCI at any given time can be considerably behind the current state of the simulation. This demands that any interaction of the HCI with the simulation occur only when the simulation has been paused. To reduce this latency, the simulation system looks to see if an HCI system is connected and synchronizes with it on a periodic basis to keep the HCI in relative time synch with the simulation.

The JWARS Administrative Control System (JACS)

The JWARS Administrative Control System (JACS) allows the JWARS analyst to start multiple batch runs distributed across the network and monitor individual simulation executions in the distributed environment. Each run of the simulation must be associated with a single user running a single scenario. The JACS system allows multiple users to be running multiple simulations on the same hardware at the same time. The JACS allows users to connect the HCI system to any running simulation and monitor the results. Each computer designated to run JWARS simulations has a "mini" JACS running at all times with parameters that specify the computer's performance. A central JACS communicates with the "mini" JACS systems and maintains connections to all HCI systems. When the user submits a run, it schedules the run that will usually include a number of repetitions with different random seeds based on the availability of computer resources. The user can also schedule runs to be run at a later time. The central JACS keeps track of each running simulation through reporting from the "mini" JACS systems. Figure 3 shows the TRM architectural view of the JACS.

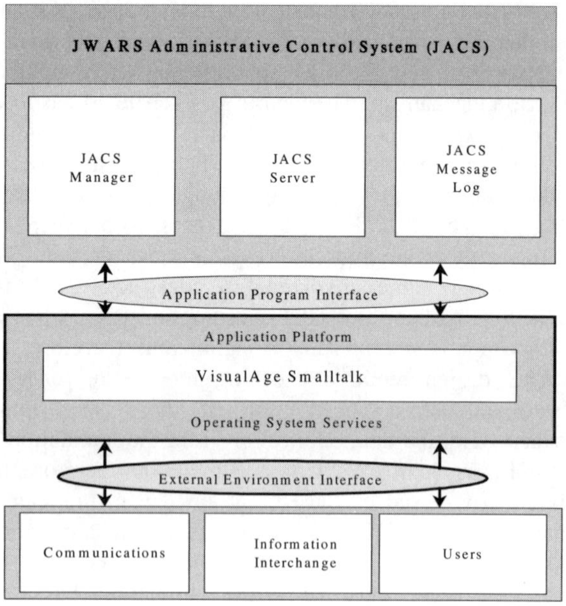

Figure 3: JACS Architectural View

The Simulation System

The Simulation System is the heart of the JWARS system. Figure 4 shows the TRM architectural view of this system. The JACS starts the simulation system whenever a repetition of a simulation is to be performed. The JACS passes the simulation a data packet that gives the simulation the information needed to retrieve the proper data sets from the Oracle database. The simulation retrieves the initialization data from the database, initializes and runs the repetition collecting and storing outputs (instruments) to the database. When connected to an HCI System, it produces log information and map data as directed by the HCI.

The Simulation System is divided into the problem and simulation domains. The military systems functionality is incorporated in the Battle Space Entities (BSE) of the problem domain. BSEs generally represent aggregates of real world systems. For example, brigades, flight groups, ships and command headquarters are JWARS BSEs. The BSE is comprised of the physical equipment and behaviors to use the equipment and make decisions. The simulation domain provides the services needed by the BSEs to interact with each other and the environment. It also provides the discrete event engine to run the simulation and the data collection mechanisms to save results from the simulation. The simulation domain holds the "truth" model on where all entities are and their state. The BSEs hold perception of the battlespace. This perception is derived from data via sensors and communications with other BSEs. The algorithms that allow interactions between BSEs and the environment can be changed without having to rework the BSEs. This feature has been critical for improving runtime performance of the simulation. The fidelity of sensor interaction algorithms has been revised a number of times without having to change the BSE sensors.

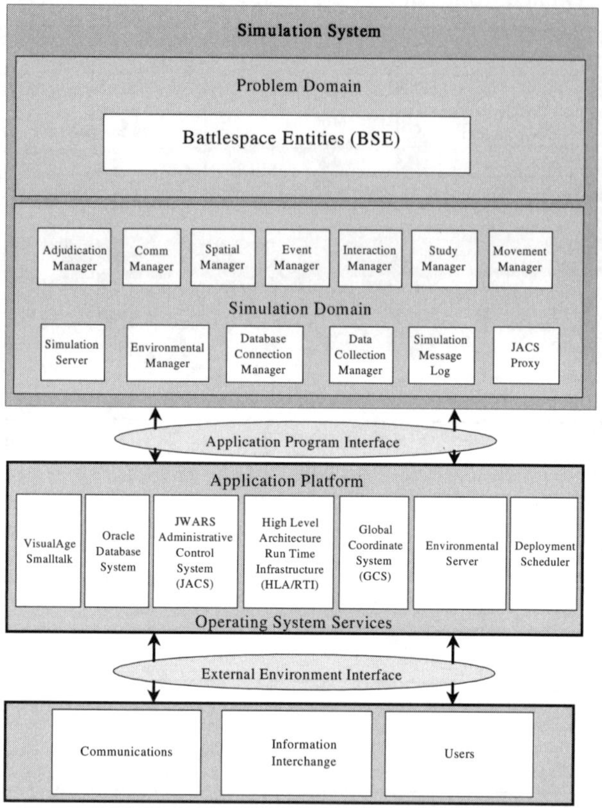

Figure 4: The JWARS Simulation System

The Battle Space Entity is the only object type that can interact with other objects or the environment. Having only one object type in the warfare environment greatly simplifies the interface between the problem and simulation domains. The BSE is designed to allow it have maximum flexibility in what it can represent.

Figure 5 shows the basic structure for the BSE. The BSE is essentially a holder object. The BSE has a set of standard component objects and can own, control or hold any number of other BSEs. Each component can have a class hierarchy of derivatives. At the BSE level only the C2 presently has hierarchical components. The C2 in addition to having hierarchical derivatives can have "plug-ins" added to add functionality to the particular C2. Figure 5 shows a few of the current plug-ins available. The Platform object interacts with the MovementManager allowing the BSE to move in the environment. The CommManager interacts with the Communications Architecture to pass messages between BSEs. The ResourceManager supplies information about the BSE to the simulation domain and interacts with the

DeploymentScheduler for the delivery of needed resources. The BSE can have as many sensors as desired.

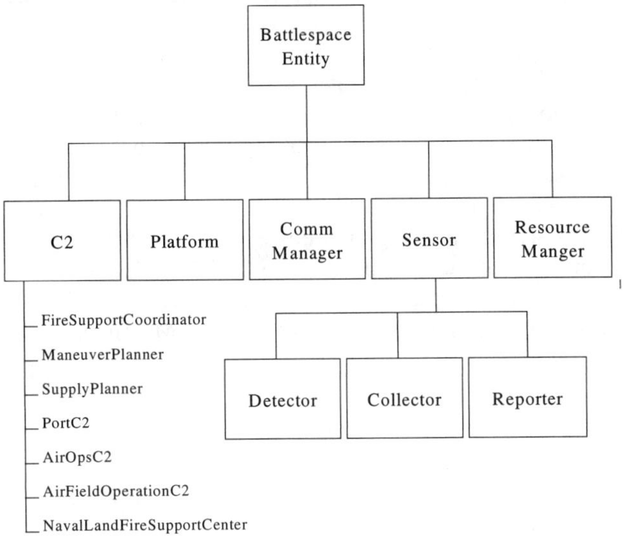

Figure 5: The BattlespaceEntity Structure

Each Sensor is a holder for a Detector, Collector and Reporter that have hierarchical derivations. The Detector interacts with the InteractionManager to "detect" potential targets. The Collector determines which targets are seen and may identify and classify the targets depending on the type of sensor. The Reporter creates reports which are given to the C2 for processing. The user builds sensors by selecting a detector, collector and reporter from the appropriate class hierarchies and configures them with data.

Using associations instead of inheritance in composing the BSE allows the BSE to represent a wide variety of physical objects. For example, an airfield, which holds squadrons of aircraft, supplies, etc. and a bridge can be constructed from the BSE structure.

The Environmental Server

A single Environmental Server provides environmental data for all Simulation systems. A terrain data set in compact terrain database (CTDB) format is required for the "playbox" of the joint warfare. The detail for the data set is user defined. The more detailed the data set, the slower the performance of the server. Three dimensional weather and general environmental conditions based on real world collected data are loaded and integrated with the CTDB.

The Simulation System uses the Environmental Manager to retrieve the required data from the environmental server. Table 1 shows the data currently available to the JWARS simulation through the environmental server. The data is time variant usually changing every 4 to 6 hours. The Environmental Server can supply raw data (e.g., temperature) or processed data such as line-of-sight.

1) IlluminationManager (Time Based)
   a) Day / Night Determination
   a) Julian Date
   a) Light Level / UJTL Light Level Descriptor
   a) Time of next Sunrise / Sunset
1) AtmosphereManager (Coordinate Based)
   a) Air Temperature / UJTL Air Temperature Descriptor
   a) Barometric Pressure / UJTL Barometric Pressure Descriptor
   a) Cloud Ceiling
   a) Humidity / UJTL Humidity Descriptor
   a) Icing Intensity / UJTL Icing Intensity Descriptor
   a) Low Cloud Amount
   a) Low Cloud Base
   a) Low Cloud Type
   a) Precipitation Rate / UJTL Precipitation Descriptor
   a) Total Precipitation / UJTL Total Precipitation Descriptor
   a) Precipitation Type / UJTL Precipitation Type Descriptor
   a) Visibility / UJTL Visibility Descriptor
   a) Weather Band
   a) Wind Vector
1) OceanManager
   a) Ocean Depth / UJTL Ocean Depth Descriptor
   a) Sea State / UJTL Sea State Descriptor
   a) Sonic Layer Depth
   a) Water Temperature / Water Temperature Descriptor
1) TerrainManager
   a) Geometric Line-of-Sight
   a) Probabilistic Line-of-Sight
   a) UJTL Harbor Depth Descriptor
   a) UJTL Land Locked Water Depth Descriptor
   a) UJTL Ocean Depth Descriptor
   a) UJTL Soil Type Descriptor
   a) Terrain Elevation / UJTL Terrain Elevation Descriptor
   a) UJTL Vegetation Descriptor
   a) Water Depth

Table 1: Environmental data available from the Environmental Server

JWARS Data Model

JWARS is a data driven model requiring hundreds of megabytes of input data for a single run and writing hundreds of thousands of output records (instruments). The requirement that the user must be able to associate the input data used to create the output data sets and trace changes to the input data from a baseline data set demands the use of a configuration management scheme. A database approach was selected over a file based configuration management system for a number of reasons. These include:

1. The source data sets for JWARS are hosted in database systems

2. Databases are virtually system independent unlike file systems
3. Databases are optimized for storage and retrieval of large amounts of data
4. Databases have built in mechanisms for offline archiving of data

Using a database solution, the versioning of input and output data is done internally to the JWARS system by converting objects to byte streams before data storage. In effect JWARS uses a standard RDBMS as an object store. The building of the JWARS data model proved to be an iterative process since performance is the driving factor. Considerable rework of designs was required in the JWARS system interfaces to the Smalltalk and Smalltalk Oracle interface methods themselves. Most database interfaces are designed for transactional processing where the user interacts with a small number of data records over and over again from an enormous data archive. Simulation models require a large amount of data infrequently and virtually never retrieve the same record twice. Much of the normal caching of data proved to get in the way of simulation performance both in terms of memory footprint and speed of execution.

In saving and retrieving of objects from the database, the size of the object complex being saved and the complexity of object associations greatly effect performance. Also, the HCI System often wanted the data in a much simpler representation than the simulation needed for execution. As a consequence, a single input data object was developed. The data object is hierarchically organized along warfare functionality areas and has over 300 separately stored components. The components are organized with respect to GUI requirements. The simulation upon reading a component has methods to convert the data into objects that have full warfighting functionality.

The object based data model has allowed the developers to easily reorganize data including adding and deleting data structures without having to touch the Oracle database tables. The objects, which are stored as a LONG RAW oracle type, are not editable or viewable outside the JWARS system. The output instruments are handled in the same manner as input data and are tagged with the run information that allows complete traceability from input to output.

SUMMARY

The JWARS system architecture has been designed to meet a complex set of domain representation, end user interface, and performance requirements. By selectively distributing the system components, this architecture allows for multiple modes of operation and efficient use of computer resources in the analytical environment.

BIOGRAPHY

Dr. Ronald Painter is the Chief Scientist for Modeling and Simulation at CACI, Inc. and has been the technical lead for the JWARS project since its inception in 1997. He has been the architect and lead developer of a number of simulations including the Ships Combat System Simulation (SCSS) for evaluating shipboard antimissile defense systems, the System Level Air-To-Air Simulation (SLAATS) for the AMRAAM DSARC analyses, SimMaster, a modeling environment, in which nine major simulations have been built and SARSIM, a Coast Guard search and rescue simulation. He has a Ph.D. in Theoretical Solid State Physics from Michigan State University.

AN OVERVIEW OF THE JOINT MODELING AND SIMULATION SYSTEM (JMASS)

Vernon K. Handley and **Peter M. Shea**
Dynetics, Inc.
P.O. Box 5500
Huntsville, AL 35814-5500
vernon.handley@dynetics.com and pete.shea@dynetics.com
Capt. Mark Morano
Joint Modeling and Simulation System (JMASS) Program Office
ASC/SMJ Building 28
2145 Monahan Way
WPAFB, OH 45433-7017
mark.morano@wpafb.af.mil

KEYWORDS

JMASS, HLA, Modeling and Simulation, SBA, C++

ABSTRACT

The Joint Modeling and Simulation System (JMASS) is a simulation support environment that includes a collection of well-defined, well-documented interface standards to which models can be built. JMASS provides software tools that help users build representations of real-world systems, configure those models, assemble them into simulations, execute those simulations, and process the results. As a tri-service product with nearly 300 registered users, JMASS partners include the U.S. Army, Navy, Air Force, Department of Defense (DoD), Defense Intelligence Agency (DIA), and industry. With object-oriented technology applied throughout, a single set of source code executes in the Windows NT, Sun Solaris, and SGI IRIX computing environments. JMASS currently serves the acquisition, test and evaluation, and scientific and technical intelligence communities with a standard engagement and engineering-level simulation framework. It provides a critical element in the technical portion of the overall simulation based acquisition (SBA) strategy. JMASS will comply with the High Level Architecture (HLA), which provides a common technical framework to ensure interoperability of different simulation components. This paper provides an overview of the concept, operation, and utility of JMASS.

1.0 JMASS BACKGROUND

In the early days, there was little formalized modeling and simulation, but Operations Research developed during World War II began to fill in the gap with pure mathematical models. As general-purpose computers came into more widespread use in the 1960s, large many-on-many engagement models were used to describe event interactions among various friendly and enemy entities, such as aircraft and surface-to-air missile (SAM) sites. The 1970s brought a proliferation of standalone, more detailed engineering and engagement models with differing assumptions and limitations and with results that often differed widely. We saw the development of SAM simulations such as the Enhanced SAM Simulation (ESAMS). Modeling of enemy command and control led to SUPPRESSOR. The 1980s brought model hierarchies to provide a set of tools for logically consistent results where an output of one could be an input to another. Because the cost of model development was significant, reusability became a hot topic. Integrated modeling systems with object-based technologies were proposed as a technological solution to reduce development and ownership costs. In the 1990s, JMASS was an early joint development in this area followed by the Joint Simulation System (JSIMS) and the Joint Warfare Simulation (JWARS).

JMASS was originally designed to support the high-fidelity engagement level analyses required for weapon system development and acquisition. Since the early 1990s, JMASS has progressed from a UNIX-only solution to a compact and efficient system requiring less than 100 Mbytes of disk space. Initial operational capability (IOC) is scheduled for early 2001 with full operational capability (FOC) scheduled for 2004. When completed, JMASS will be a complete simulation system consisting of a defined set of standards and specifications, an efficient simulation engine, tools to assist the analyst user and model developer, and an infrastructure of validated threat models. A single set of source code, including the graphical user interface (GUI), executes in the Windows NT, Sun Solaris, and SGI IRIX computing environments. In the coming year, JMASS will become compliant with HLA, which will allow JMASS to interoperate with other simulations. JMASS currently provides an infrastructure for training and customer support. A Model Developer Reference and a comprehensive User's Manual are provided with the JMASS software. Context-sensitive on-line help will be available in future releases. Training and customer support are available from the JMASS Program Office (JPO). Details are available at www.jmass.wpafb.af.mil.

2.0 JMASS UTILITY

Four levels of analysis are presented in ***Figure 1***. Force structure studies based on multi-day, many-on-many scenarios fall into the Campaign category. Mission analyses include system trade-off studies based on tailored scenarios and fewer, more detailed systems. The Engagement and Engineering categories include studies of system and subsystem performance based on the interactions among a few highly detailed objects. Results, not models, can be aggregated and passed up the pyramid. JMASS works at the engineering and engagement level, but in the near future, the greatest utility of JMASS will be in support of analyses at the tactical/engagement level.

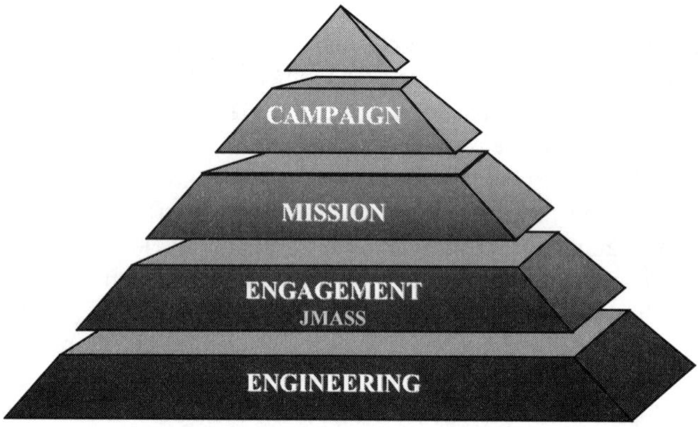

Figure 1. Levels of Analysis

JMASS currently serves the acquisition, test and evaluation, and scientific and technical intelligence communities with a standard engagement and engineering-level simulation framework. It provides a critical element in the technical portion of overall SBA strategy. By placing weapon systems in a virtual environment, JMASS provides a framework for analyzing the design and performance of weapon systems considered for procurement. In this manner, JMASS complements other DoD modeling and simulation programs such JSIMS and JWARS. JMASS is not a part of JSIMS and JWARS, but rather generates data that can be validated for use in either JSIMS or JWARS.

3.0 JMASS DESCRIPTION

As depicted in ***Figure 2***, JMASS is composed of four distinct parts: legacy model functional implementation, red threat models, blue digital system models, and the architecture. The JMASS architecture and models are discussed in this section.

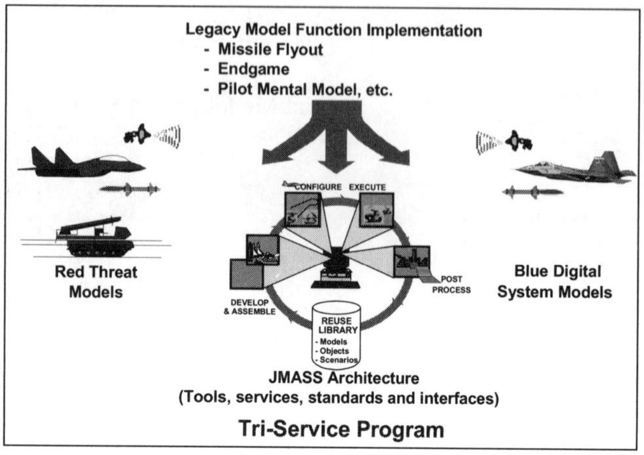

Figure 2. The Four Parts of JMASS

JMASS models typically correspond to real-world physical objects such as aircraft, radar, missiles, electronic countermeasure (ECM) systems, or missile seekers. JMASS defines and provides a standardized set of file formats and application program interfaces (APIs) that allow these models to be developed such that interoperability is achieved. The primary file format specification captures model design information, and a sophisticated code generator transforms the design information into a code framework to ensure that all architecture capabilities are accessible to the model developer. Model developers are required only to fill in behavior code for their models and understand and use the service APIs to ensure interoperability with other models. To facilitate model reuse, JMASS takes an open-systems approach and uses common object-oriented language that includes GUIs and applications based on commercial standards such as Microsoft Windows, POSIX, ANSI C++, and OpenGL. The JMASS open architecture allows customization and extensibility. The standard tool suite is accessible through native drag-and-drop file managers for both Windows NT and UNIX platforms. The provided GUI tools are implemented in Tcl/Tk allowing them to run on Windows NT, Sun Solaris, and SGI IRIX. Site-specific tools may be added to the architecture to customize and extend design and analysis capabilities.

3.1 JMASS Architecture

JMASS provides standard service modules for scheduling, spatial services, data recording, message logging, as well as physical environments for the atmosphere and terrain. User-supplied physical environment and atmosphere models may be substituted if desired. A discrete event-based scheduler is the default, but real-time, frame-based, or HLA time-management approaches could be employed. A hierarchical six-degrees-of-freedom spatial manager with two derivatives is provided to maintain and extrapolate states of spatial entities within the simulation. The standard data recorder can provide simulation output in binary, MATLAB, and/or ASCII format. The message logger displays color-coded messages during the simulation run and stores these messages to a file. Architecture services will be plug-and-play in the IOC JMASS.

Designed to help engineers develop simulations quickly and easily, JMASS provides tools that permit model developers to concentrate on algorithms instead of software. The standard tool suite is accessible through native drag-and-drop file managers for both Windows NT and UNIX platforms. ***Figure 3*** shows some of these tools. The Builder tool provides automated code generation, dependency generation, compilation, and linking. It isolates the user from compiler and file system details but still offers detailed control through makefiles. The Configuration GUI provides for initializing simulation attributes and selecting data for recording. The Execution tool displays color-coded messages while running the simulation. It also provides for profiling and debugging the simulation. Command line execution is also supported.

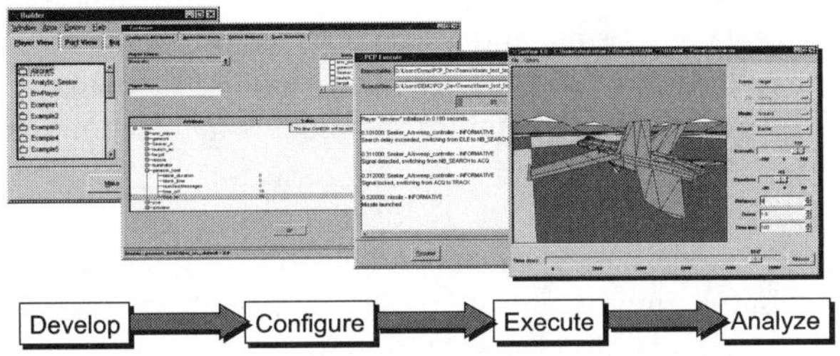

Figure 3. JMASS Modes of Operation and GUI Tools

The Automated Model Conversion Tool (AMCTool) will be incorporated into future releases of JMASS. It is a visual programming tool used to support model development by providing an automated approach for converting Simulink models to JMASS components.

JMASS provides a study manager called the Flexible Automated Study Tool (*FAST*) designed to support engineering analysis studies that use JMASS. *FAST* distributes multiple runs over a local area network for parametric and statistical analyses. It also collects data and provides tools for data reduction and analysis. *FAST* allows analysts to run experiments by varying one or more simulation inputs, distribute these experimental runs across multiple computers, and then graphically analyze the results.

JMASS includes an analyst-quality visualization tool called *SimView* that is used to visualize the spatial behavior of players simulated in JMASS. Support for *SimView* in JMASS is provided by the *SpatialInfoPlayer*. The developer does not have to do any additional programming within the models to support visualization. *SimView* is designed to support analysts' needs by providing visualization of players in three space.

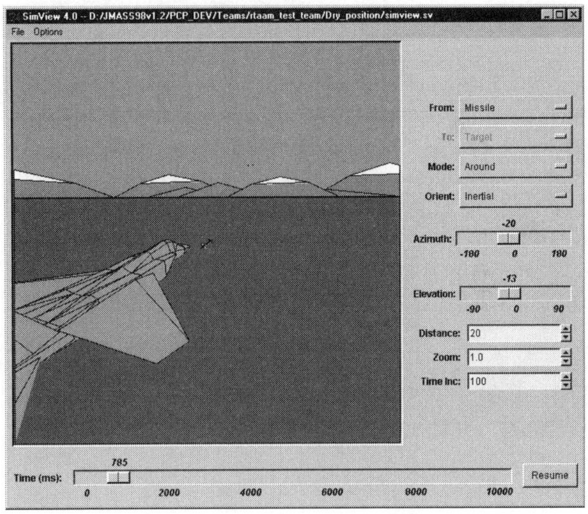

Figure 4. SimView Analyst Quality Visualization Tool

To use *SimView*, the user must first execute the simulation scenario. Executing a scenario that contains the *SpatialInfoPlayer* generates a .sv file with all the data *SimView* needs to replay the scenario visually. A window similar to that shown in ***Figure 4*** will be displayed when initiated. A number of controls on the *SimView* playback window allow the user to adjust playback rate and provide a variety of viewing angle and zoom options that can all be changed during playback.

JMASS also includes a cross-platform, post-processing plotting tool called *JPlot*. *JPlot* reads JMASS Binary Journal Data (BJD) files created during execution of a simulation scenario and displays the data in a spreadsheet, from which the user may select columns/rows of data for plotting. *JPlot* provides a wide variety of options, which permit axes scaling and styling, polar

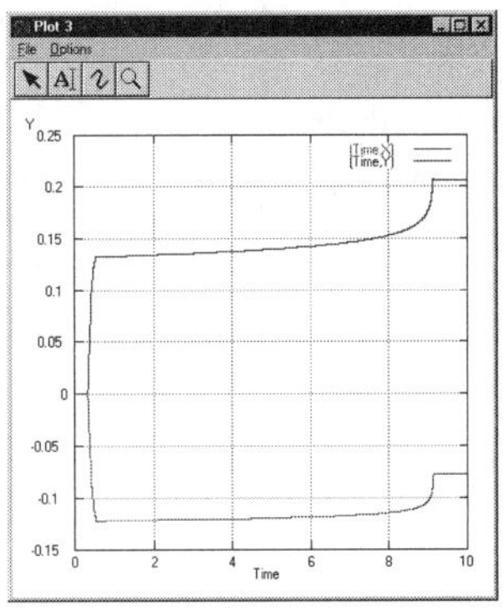

plots, linear-linear, log-linear, and log-log plots, and the overlaying of plots of the same type. Additional options permit 3-D plotting, grids/no grids, color coding, and annotations. A typical plot is shown.

JMASS is an open architecture with a well-defined API that makes it relatively easy to interface commercial products. This has been demonstrated with Simthetica from Computer Explorations, Inc. A sample output snapshot is shown in ***Figure 5***.

Figure 5. Simthetica Display

The JMASS tool *BJD_to_Text* converts JMASS binary journal data (BJD) files into ASCII text files for use with other tools such as Microsoft Excel or MATLAB. JMASS also provides the capability to record data in MATLAB binary format. These data can be loaded directly into the MATLAB workspace for data analysis and plotting, and for presentation-quality visualization.

The JMASS analyst tools are being extended by a number of users. These customized tools and GUIs are tailored for particular analyses. One example is the Tcl/Tk-based JMASS Analyst Capability Kit (JACK) being used by the Air Force Operational Test and Evaluation Center (AFOTEC). This tool will be available for future releases of JMASS. Another example of tool extensibility is the Java-based analysis tool, JTEAM, which has been developed by the Air Force Information Warfare Center (AFIWC) for internal use. The JTEAM analyst "dashboard" is shown in ***Figure 6***.

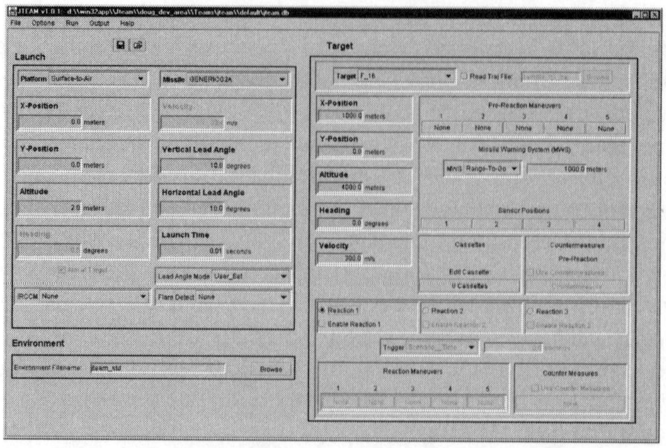

Figure 6. JTEAM Analyst Dashboard GUI

3.2 JMASS Models

JMASS provides architectural services through a well-defined API. JMASS models are referred to as players and typically correspond to real-world physical objects such as aircraft, radar, missiles, ECM systems, missile seekers, etc. JMASS supports multiple levels of detail. The level of detail of a JMASS model can be developed or selected to match the scenario to be executed. JMASS permits the model detail to be varied across the simulation and across the model itself. The APIs are robust enough to handle both high and low levels of detail permitting both high and low detail models to be used in the same simulation. Similarly, within a model, the level of detail can be focused in those areas that are stressed by the application or use. The detail in the models strongly affects the speed of the JMASS simulation. The architecture (simulation engine) has low overhead so that run time is determined/ driven by the number and detail of the models included in the simulation.

JMASS models may be subdivided into digital system models (DSMs), environmental models, and ancillary models. DSMs are typically divided into friendly (blue) and threat (red). Threat DSMs are developed and validated by the appropriate Intelligence Centers. They will plug and play in JMASS without requiring that new code be written, which would necessitate revalidation of the threat DSMs. HLA will provide a means for these validated threat DSMs to interoperate with other available JMASS or non-JMASS simulations.

Environmental models in JMASS model the environment for the particular sensor domains of interest in the simulation. JMASS currently has a radio frequency (RF) domain environmental model designed primarily to handle the radar-directed weapon systems and sensors. Additional environments for the infrared (IR) and undersea domains are required for FOC.

Additional ancillary models, the *SpatialInfoPlayer* and the *SpatialObserver* player, are available to provide additional functionality and support information to the simulation. These models and the additional functionality they offer will be described later.

The primary tool for modeling ECM systems in JMASS is the Generic ECM (GenECM) toolkit. GenECM is a flexible, generic, general-purpose ECM signal generator that provides the capability to exercise the various threat SAM and air-to-air missile models with realistic electronic combat (EC) environments for checkout, evaluation, and test of EC techniques, as well as for evaluation of the effectiveness of threat counter-countermeasures. GenECM provides a foundation of object-oriented EC components to populate a JMASS component library for use by EC hardware developers. The GenECM model has a modern object-based structure and design that permit it to be rapidly reconfigured to reflect the specific hardware structure of a particular EC system. GenECM is designed to facilitate focused fidelity, permitting the various components of the ECM suite model to operate at different levels of detail. GenECM was also designed to fully utilize the advanced features of the JMASS signal packet interface. GenECM supports all three of the typical ECM response types: repeater, transponder, and noise.

Threat models are developed, validated, owned, and maintained by the appropriate threat Scientific and Technical Intelligence (S&TI) Centers. Currently, three different levels of detail are being developed to support different kinds of analysis. These levels of detail are referred to as sub-analytic, analytic, and EC-capable. All three are object-based in the sense that the software design is organized in the same manner as the hardware being modeled, at least down to some level of decomposition. For each hardware object, there is a corresponding software object, and signals flowing between the hardware objects correspond to the data flowing between software objects in the simulation. The sub-analytic and analytic models are faster running, but in no way are they EC predictive in their behavior. They may have EC responses "hard-wired" into their behavior code but they have to be told what technique is attacking them and they must have a prescripted behavioral response available for that technique. They do not simply respond to the signal environment presented to them by the environment player.

The EC-capable models have the ability to exhibit truly predictive ECM behavior for a broad class of EC modulations. Ideally, these models will be based on detailed hardware design and measurement data. Signals that could represent multiple overlapping signals from the target, the ECM, and/or the environment are combined into a single composite signal and presented to these models through the antenna component, and they respond accordingly. Advanced modeling techniques allow non-linearities to be accurately simulated with baseband processing of the signals, not at the RF or intermediate frequency (IF) of the system being modeled. This has a tremendous effect on the overall computational cost and efficiency of the model.

JMASS comes with a simple aircraft player that can be used as an RF target or a missile-launch platform. It currently has a configurable constant radar cross section (RCS) value and the ability to perform prescripted maneuvers in both the pitch and yaw planes. It is not intended to be a full aerodynamic aircraft model, but rather a moving platform that can act as a target aircraft or launch aircraft for air engagement scenarios.

Two players are delivered with JMASS that do not represent any physical entity but are useful in supporting analysis. These are the *SpatialObserver*, which computes the point of closest approach (PCA) between two players, and the *SpatialInfoPlayer*, which produces the *SimView* output file.

The *SpatialObserver* monitors the relative spatial states between pairs of spatial components and ultimately calculates the PCA. Multiple pairs may be monitored by a single instance of the *SpatialObserver* class. The *SpatialObserver* dynamically schedules the next observation between the pairs of spatial entities. This allows resolution to be increased as the entities approach each other.

The *SpatialInfoPlayer* extracts the data needed for *SimView* with respect to a specified reference spatial object. The recorded data are written to an output file with the extension .sv. This file can be used by *SimView* to display the objects in three space. Objects to be recorded must have observations configured for them. The rate at which the states will be recorded is set by the *SpatialInfoPlayer* update interval.

The JMASS Modular Object-Oriented Simulation Environment (*JMOOSE*) is the most widely used RF environment player for JMASS. It provides signal representation and modulation processes approximating the phenomena experienced in short-wave RF operation in the range of 100 MHz to 100 GHz. The JMASS event time-management concept is designed for pulsed systems such as radars, RF seekers, RF countermeasure equipment, and identification friend or foe (IFF) systems. However, careful design will allow simulation of continuous wave (CW) systems as well. *JMOOSE* interfaces with JMASS are simple and reliable and are mandatory for systems that will interact with the RF environment, including any vehicle with an RF cross section detectable by RF electronic sensors.

An electro-optical (EO)/IR environment model is being designed and prototyped.

4.0 JMASS INTEROPERABILTY THROUGH HLA

JMASS is designed to handle high-fidelity, tightly coupled simulations of interactions between ECM and the intended victim. For these applications, the latency associated with HLA and simulations distributed across a network is highly undesirable. HLA is designed to enable interoperability between various simulations across a network. HLA provides a much looser coupling than does JMASS. JMASS provides a tight framework for plug-and-play operation of tightly coupled models interacting through shared memory on a single- or multi-processor computer.

JMASS will comply with HLA, which provides a common technical framework to ensure interoperability of different simulation components. Since HLA is a general-purpose architecture designed for simulation reuse and interoperability, it will be the standard through which JMASS simulations will communicate with other simulations. This will allow for high-fidelity, tightly coupled models interoperating within JMASS to interoperate with other simulations through HLA. This will provide a portal to HLA for legacy models that are ported to JMASS or provide for interaction with actual hardware. For instance, JMASS could simulate a high-fidelity missile shooting at a target that is actually a man-in-the-loop aircraft simulator, with the two interacting via HLA.

JMASS will only implement unconstrained, unregulating time management. JMASS will support the use of any of the HLA time-management schemes through its ability to plug new schedulers into the JMASS architecture.

5.0 FUTURE JMASS

Future releases of JMASS will provide real-time capability, parallel simulation processing, simplified model integration capability, improved installation efficiency, and improved GUIs. Model design tools and 2-D contour and 3-D topology map visualization will be added. Legacy model conversion processes along with undersea and EO/IR/ultraviolet (UV) environment improve-ments will be incorporated. Improved customer support via website and beta site testing will be available soon.

6.0 SUMMARY

For the past 10 years, JMASS has had a significant impact on the definition and concept of modeling systems. JMASS has evolved as an object-based technology for reusable, interoperable models. It provides a simulation architecture and tool set for model development compliant with architectural standards. Deeply rooted in the acquisition and test and evaluation community, JMASS best supports engagement-level analyses. JMASS is key to twenty-first century engagement modeling.

ACKNOWLEDGEMENTS

Information for this paper was gleaned from many sources, including material presented at the April 2000 JMASS Customer Conference in Dayton, OH. Special thanks are extended to **Ms. Cindy Porubcansky**, JMASS Program Office (ASC/SMJ) Program Manager, for her guidance and support, and to **Mr. Bill McQuay**, Technical Advisor for the Collaborative Simulation Technology and Applications Branch, Information Directorate, Air Force Research Laboratory, Wright Research Site, for his material on the history of modeling and simulation and JMASS.

AUTHOR BIOGRAPHIES

Vernon Handley is a Principal Engineer at Dynetics, Inc., Huntsville AL. He holds a BSEE from the Georgia Institute of Technology and an MSEE from the University of Alabama in Huntsville. As a model developer and systems analyst, he has been involved with JMASS for over ten years. He currently leads JMASS training and outreach activities.

Pete Shea is the Chief Engineer for Dynetics' JMASS development activities. He holds a BSEE from Clemson University and an MSEE from North Carolina State University. He has been active in JMASS model, tool, and architecture development since the early 90s.

Capt. Mark Morano is Director of the Support Team at the JPO. In this capacity he oversees JMASS training and outreach activities.

ASDA - AN AUTOMATIC DISTRIBUTED SIMULATION ENVIRONMENT

Sarita Mazzini Bruschi, Regina H. C. Santana and Marcos José Santana
Instituto de Ciências Matemáticas e de Computação (ICMC)
Universidade de São Paulo (USP)
Caixa Postal 668 – São Carlos – SP – Brazil
{sarita, rcs, mjs}@icmc.sc.usp.br

KEYWORDS Automatic simulation environment, distributed simulation, SRIP and MRIP techniques

ABSTRACT

This paper presents ASDA, an automatic distributed simulation environment. Automatic environments are normally built aiming at either making easier the generation of a product or helping inexperienced users to develop a product, that could be difficult without such kind of environments. In this work, the product is related to distributed simulation programs and aims at reaching both objectives presented above by allowing the utilisation of previously developed sequential simulation programs (*MRIP* technique) and the development of new distributed or sequential simulation programs (*SRIP* and/or *MRIP* techniques).

INTRODUCTION

Simulation has been adopted in many different application areas mainly due to its flexibility and low cost. However, sequential discrete-event simulation presents some disadvantages (specially the simulation time) when it is necessary to simulate complex models or even more detailed models. Additionally, the simulation program has to be executed several times in order to guarantee that the input data randomness will not influence the simulation results.

Some solutions using several processors have been proposed aiming at decreasing the simulation time (Heidelberger 1988; Fujimoto 1990), comprising distributed simulations: SRIP (Single Replication in Parallel) and MRIP (Multiple Replications in Parallel).

Distributed simulation offers several advantages over the traditional sequential simulation: besides the speedup, the simulation can be adapted to the hardware structure available (for instance, if few processors are available, several processes may be simulated in a unique processor). However, the main factor to reach good performance is the requirement for the user to have expertise on distributed simulations together with good knowledge about the application. This is related to the possibility of maximizing the parallel-program load-balancing and minimizing the required communication. Thus, to reach good performance in a distributed simulation the user needs (Bruschi *et al.* 1999):

- to know deeply the system to be simulated and its model in order to exploit all the inherent parallelism;
- to analyze the best way to split the model with the aim at maximizing the load-balancing and minimizing the communication;
- depending on the model, to know which synchronisation protocol gives the best performance;
- to know the architectural features of the used platform, making possible to evaluate the compromise between load-balancing and communication, i.e., to define when it is worth to spoil the load-balancing in favor of minimizing the communication and vice-versa.

All these factors can bound the usage of distributed simulation, once they require advanced knowledge on parallel/distributed computing and on simulation from the user.

This paper presents a general overview of the design of a novell distributed simulation environment called ASDA. This environment removes the bound imposed by the need of knowledge on parallel/distributed computing and simulation, helping the users to develop simulation programs. The users will be able to choose between traditional sequential simulation programs and distributed simulation programs.

DISTRIBUTED SIMULATION

Distributed simulation has been developed targeting at decreasing the time of a sequential simulation. Thus, two solutions have been proposed: SRIP (Single Replication in Parallel) and MRIP (Multiple Replications in Parallel). These solutions basically differ in the way the system is modelled, as discussed ahead.

Single Replication in Parallel (SRIP)

The *SRIP* (Single Replication In Parallel) technique is based on the decomposition of the simulation model into logical processes, running on different processors and communicating to each other by means of message passing protocols. However, a critical SRIP problem is the warranty of synchronism for the several processes composing the simulation program. Several protocols have been developed and grouped into two wide categories: conservative and optimistic protocols (Fujimoto, 1990). Another kind of solution that has been researched comprises the asynchronous approach, where no synchronisation protocol is used (Pham & Fdida 1995).

The main feature of the conservative protocols is the execution of an event only when it is safe, i.e., when there is no possibility of a causality error occurrence. While this cannot be guaranteed, the process stays blocked, making possible to have both loss of performance and deadlocks (Fujimoto, 1990). The many conservative mechanisms available differ in the way the deadlock is handled. Some of them prevent the deadlock occurrence and other ones recover the system from deadlocks. The CMB protocol (Bryant 1977; Chandy & Misra 1979) prevents deadlock by means of the adoption of null messages.

The optimistic protocols do not avoid the causality errors, allowing all events to be processed. A detection and recover mechanism is adopted to recovery the simulation from possible errors, leading to a consistent state. This protocol has the advantage of exploiting all the implicit parallelism where the conservative protocols could not proceed (Fujimoto 1990). The Time Warp mechanism is the most known optimistic protocol and it is based on the Virtual Time paradigm (Jefferson 1985).

Both classes of protocols have their own set of advantages and disadvantages. The choice between them is not an easy task and it is dependent on the application features and on the computer architecture considered.

Multiple Replications in Parallel (MRIP)

In *MRIP* (Multiple Replications In Parallel) (Ewing *et al.* 1999) independent instances of the same sequential simulation program are replicated in parallel, running based on different random seeds. Each replication sends its partial results at the end of the run to a global analyser, where the final results are evaluated. When the accuracy defined by the user is reached the simulation stops.

In contrast to SRIP, MRIP can be easly applicable to any system, independently of the inherent system parallelism. However, there are some situations where the MRIP technique is inappropriate (Glynn & Heidelberger 1992):

- A single replication can not be executed on a unique processor;
- The output is almost deterministic.

Although this method seems very simple, some care has to be taken regarding to the number of processors (number of replications), the length of each replication and the length of the deletion period to generate a valid confidence interval (Glynn & Heidelberger 1992).

ASDA

The ASDA (***Ambiente** de **Simulação** **Distribuída** **Automático*** – in portuguese) environment evolve as an evolution of an automatic sequential simulation environment developed at the Distributed Systems and Concurrent Programming Group – ICMC – USP called ASiA: ***Ambiente** de **Simulação** **Automático*** in portuguese (Santana et al. 1996; Santana et al. 1996a). The ASiA is a supporting tool for distributed computing system performance evaluation, that allows the user to simulate a model without a deep knowledge about simulation. The environment automatically generates the simulation program based on a graphic specification, given by the user. The ASiA aims at taking the user away from the task of translating the model into a simulation program.

Thus, ASDA also aims at taking the user away from the task of translating the model into a simulation program and it goes further: the simulation program generated in this case is a distributed simulation program. Furthermore, the user is taken away from the details of communication and synchronisation and the distributed simulation features.

The ASDA purpose is to make available to the users an automatic environment where distributed simulation can be developed in an easy and fast way. Users that deal with this environment can have different levels of knowledge, including both extremes: users with advanced simulation knowledge and users that have only superficial knowledge in both simulation and parallel computing.

Thus, ASDA also offers the necessary flexibility to help different user profiles, meeting to the following requirements:

- It allows the complete generation of a distributed simulation program by an inexperienced user;
- It offers flexibility to more experienced users as they are allowed to modify the generated programs;
- It allows the utilisation of previously developed sequential simulation programs.

ASDA is basically composed of 6 modules: User Interface, Graphic Specification, Code Generator, Software Interface, Replication and Scheduling Modules as can be seen in figure 1 (modular structure diagram).

In order to keep the flexibility eligible by the experienced users and still offering the facilities required by the inexperienced ones, ASDA has a friendly User Interface Module. From this interface, the user can choose among specifying a new simulation model; using a developed simulation program or defining the scheduling variables (policy, hardware, etc.).

If the user choice is to define a new simulation model, it is necessary to specify the model by means of the Graphic Interface Module. When the graphic specification is ready, the program code is generated by the Code Generator Module and the replications are started (if necessary) by the Replication Module.

If the user chooses to use a previously developed simulation program, the Software Interface Module is activated and the program is sent to the Replication Module. All generated process are taken to the scheduling module and that is responsible for starting and controlling their execution.

User Interface Module

This module is responsible for the interaction between the ASDA environment and the user. A tutor system helps the user giving information about system modelling and performance evaluation (platform versus system to be simulated versus protocol). Based on this information the user chooses if a new simulation program will be generated (SRIP, MRIP or SRIP + MRIP approaches) or a previously developed simulation program will be used (MRIP approach). The configuration of variables for the scheduling module are also handled in this module.

Graphic Interface Module

The Graphic Interface Module is responsible for allowing the user to use the facilities available to model the system. Three system modelling approaches are widely used: Queuing Nets, Petri Nets and Statecharts. Whereas Petri Nets and Statecharts are able to represent parallelism, Queue Nets are able to represent the most important feature in computing systems: the queues. Petri Nets and Statecharts can not straightly represent this feature; on the other hand Queuing Nets can not represent system parallelism.

A novell modelling approach is under developing at the Distributed System and Concurrent Programming Group – ICMC – USP with the objective of joining the most important features found in each of the traditional approaches. The new specification will be used in ASDA, being introduced in this module, allowing the user to specify a large variety of systems.

Code Generator Module

This module is responsible for generating the simulation program based on the information given by the user (by means of the model), the user's knowledge and the tutor system. In this module the user must choose among the SRIP (stand-alone execution), MRIP (a sequential simulation program replicated) or SRIP + MRIP techniques.

After having the model fully specified, the simulation program code is automatically generated, which will depend on the simulation technique adopted. With SRIP, the code uses one of the synchronisation protocols (optimistic, conservative or neither), taking into consideration the model and the architecture of the system where the simulation will be executed. With MRIP, a sequential simulation program is generated. The user can either define which is the technique appropriate to its application or ask for help from the tutor system.

In this module, a database with simulation libraries/languages allows the user to choose the target language used and for each library/language considered there is a pattern file with the program sequence to be generated (a template).

The MRIP code generation is simpler than the SRIP one because it is actually a sequential simulation program. In the SRIP technique it has to be considered the model division into logical processes and also the synchronisation protocol.

Software Interface Module

This module is made active when the option to use a developed sequential simulation program is selected. The inclusion of this module in the environment was motivated by the large number of existing sequential simulation programs. Using the idea of replication (MRIP), it is possible to use these programs and decrease the simulation time required to obtain the results within the required accuracy.

The main idea of the interface module software is to have interfaces to functional-extensions of programming languages, such as SMPL or ParSMPL, and simulation programs languages, such as GPSS and SLAM. The interfaces provide a way to modify the program in order to construct a new program, following the MRIP technique. The new program is then sent to the Replication Module.

Replication Module

The Replication Module starts the replications and controls the execution, making all the calculation to decide when the simulation must stop. Two basic components make part of this module: the MRIP master and the MRIP slave.

The main function of MRIP master is to activate the MRIP slaves, receive and process the information sent by the slaves. The MRIP slave starts the replication (the sequential simulation program), collects the data and sends them to the MRIP master.

Scheduling Module

The main purpose of the schedule is to distribute the services (process, tasks, threads, etc.) to the process resources (processors, memory, disk, etc.) available. This task can be done in many different ways, depending on the scheduling policies. The scheduling performance will depend on (Souza *et al.*, 1999):

- The objective of the platform used;
- The available hardware;
- Multitask environments;
- Different application classes;
- Different workloads.

The Scheduling Module will join two research areas at the Distributed System and Concurrent Programming Group – ICMC - USP: parallel computing and performance evaluation. A novell process scheduling environment called AMIGO (Dyn**AM**ical Flex**I**ble Schedulin**G** Envir**O**nment) has been developed (Souza *et al.,* 1999) and will be also included in the ASDA.

The AMIGO purpose is to eliminate the gap between theory and practise in the process scheduling area, introducing flexibility to the scheduling algorithms and making transparent to the users the factors involved in the choice of a scheduling policy. AMIGO makes available a set of scheduling policies in an easy and organised way and in a unique environment.

CONCLUSIONS AND FINAL REMARKS

Many factors must be taken into consideration to develop a distributed simulation such as the model to be simulated, the available hardware and the technique used for synchronisation.

ASDA was proposed aiming at helping both expert and inexperienced users in the task of developing a distributed simulation.

ASDA is composed of 6 integrated modules that allows the users to define a new distributed simulation program or to use a previously built sequential simulation program. The techniques adopted by the environment are: SRIP and MRIP.

A tutor system helps the user to choose the option that will give the best performance depending on the available hardware, the model to be simulated and the technique.

This new distributed simulation environment has potential to clarify the development and use of distributed simulation, offering an easy and straight automatic approach.

ACKNOWLEDGEMENTS

The authors would like to thanks the financial support given to the Distributed System and Concurrent Programming Group – ICMC – USP by the Brazilian Foundations FAPESP, CAPES and CNPq.

REFERENCES

Bruschi, S.M.; R. Spolon; R.H.C. Santana; M.J. Santana. 1999. “Simulation as a Tool for Computer Architecture Teaching.” In *Proceedings of the 1999 Sumemr Computer Simualtion Conference* (Chicago, Illinois, Jul): 81-86.

Bryant, R.E. 1977. “Simulation of Packet Communications Architecture Computer. Massachusetts Institute of Technology.” Technical Report 188, Massachusets Institute of Technology, LCS.

Chandy K.M. and J. Misra. 1979. “Distributed Simulation: A Case Study in Design and Verification of Distributed Programs.” *IEEE Transactions on Software Engineering*, V.SE-5, NO.5: 440-452.

Ewing G.C.; K. Pawlikowski; D. Mcnickle, 1999. “Akaroa-2: Exploiting Network Computing by Distributing Stochastic Simulation”. In: *Proceedings of the 1999 European Simulation Multiconference ESM-99*, (Warsaw, Poland, Jun). 175-181.

Fujimoto, R.M. 1990. "Parallel Discrete Event Simulation." *Communications of the ACM 33*, NO. 10 (Oct.): 31-53.

Glynn P.W. and P. Heidelberger. 1992. “Analysis of initial Transient Deletion for parallel Steady-State Simulations.” *SIAM J. Sci. Stat. Comput*, V.13, NO.4: 904-922.

Heidelberger, P. 1988. “Discrete Event Simulation and Parallel Processing: Statistical Properties.” *SIAM J. Stat. Comput*, V.9, NO.6: 1114-1132.

Jefferson, D.R. 1985. “Virtual Time”. *ACM Transactions on Programming Languages and Systems*, V.7, NO.3: 404-425.

Pham, C.D.; S. Fdida 1995. “Relaxation of Synchronization Constraints in Parallel Simulation of ATM Network”. In *Proceeding of the Anglo-French Workshop on Formal Methods, Modelling and Simulation for System Engineering Dassault Electronique* (St-Quentin en Yvelines, France, Feb).

Santana, M.J.; R.H.C. Santana; R. Spolon; R. Spolon. 1996. "Automatic Generation of Discret-System Simulation Programs" In *Proceedings of the 1996 Summer Computer Simulation Conference* (Portland, Jul.). 133~138.

Santana, M.J.; R.H.C. Santana; R. Spolon; R. Spolon. 1996. "A Graphical User-Interface for an Automatic Simulation System." In *Proceedings of the 1996 Summer Computer Simulation Conference* (Portland, Jul). 139~143.

Souza P.S.; M.J. Santana; R.H.C. Santana,1999. AMIGO – A Dynamical Flexible Scheduling Environment. In *5th International Conference on Information Systems Analysis and Synthesis – ISAS’99.* (Orlando).

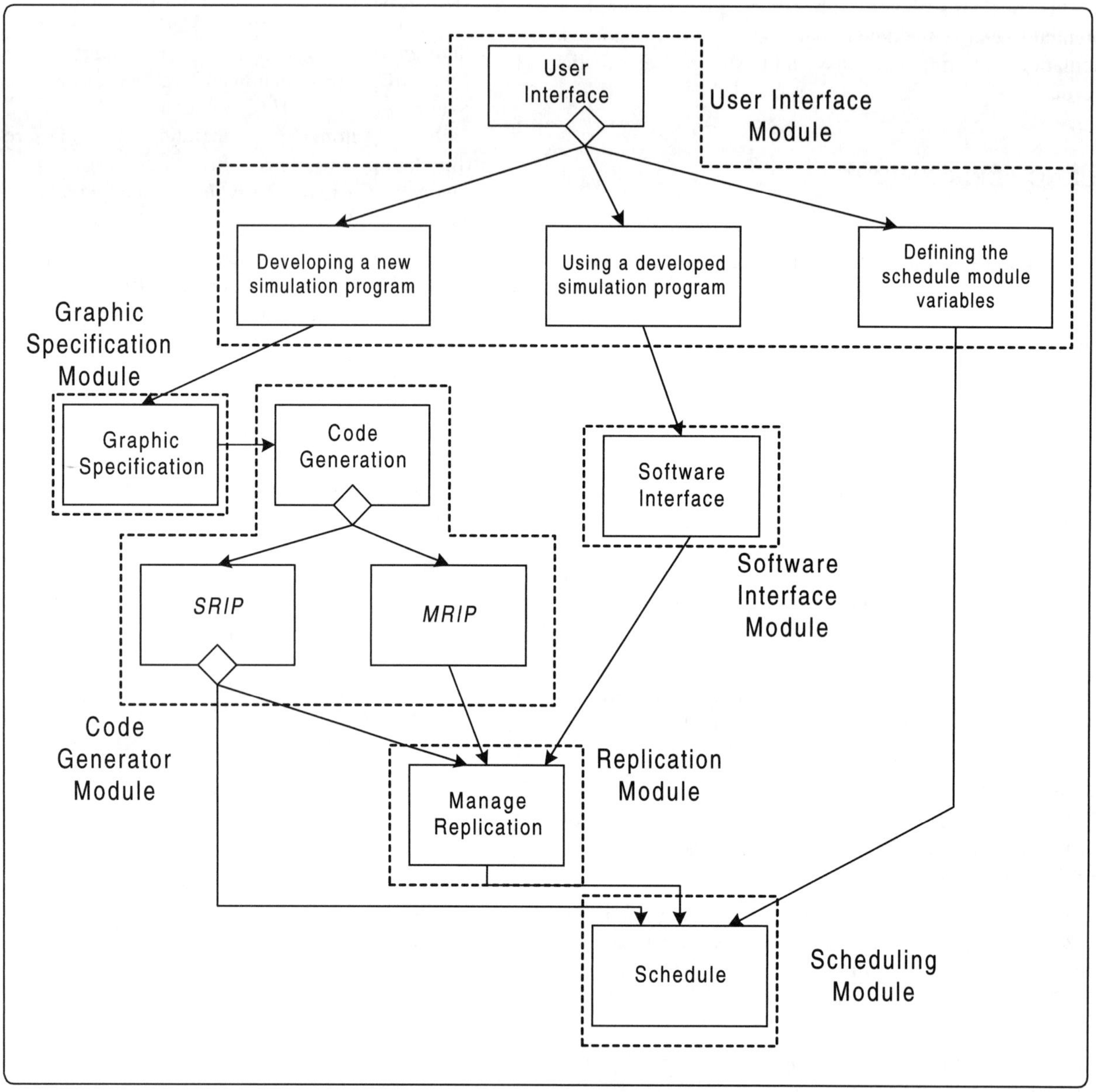

Figure 1. The ASDA modular structure.

MODELING WEB SERVERS USING JAVA AND SILK

Emmett Burke
Symbi Systems, Inc.
816 SW Normandy Terr.
Seattle, WA 98166 USA
emmett@symbi.com

Richard A. Kilgore
ThreadTec, Inc.
P. O. Box 7
St. Louis, MO 63006 USA
kilgore@threadtec.com

KEYWORDS

Computer performance, Distributed processors, Web Servers, Java, Silk

ABSTRACT

The performance of web servers is an issue of some common concern in the Internet community. The issues of client session generation, embedded files, protocols, the web server process model, file serving, and scheduling of processes onto Symmetric Multi-Processor (SMP) systems need to be addressed together. We show how to model these issues for web servers using classes within the Java-based, object oriented Silk simulation environment. The classes described focus on the detailed description, analysis and improvement of the web server process model using the popular Apache web server software. The extension of the classes to other types of distributed systems is indicated.

1 INTRODUCTION

As more and more business and personal communication becomes transported by the internet, the performance of the hardware and software systems supporting web-based communication will become critically important issues. Internet performance is dependent on a large number of factors, each of which limits the capability of the overall system. Detailed understanding and improvement of each of these separate components and their interaction is crucial to the improvement of the entire system.

Three areas have been proposed for improving the ability of a web site to handle increased workloads (Hu 1997). The first group of methods focuses on the replication or mirroring of the Web site information to multiple machines that are either clustered or distributed (Katz 1994). The second group of methods revolves around a similar capacity increase through offloading volume through caching (Luotonen 1994; Cao 1997; Chankhunthod 1996). Only the third group of methods addresses the capacity issue through increasing the productivity of the web server itself. It is common practice to engineer a manufacturing facility to optimally allocate a fixed set of resources to better meet service level targets. The same principles apply in web server software, where the interaction of this software with the computer architecture supporting its execution can be tuned to get the greatest efficiency possible.

Web server software allows you to serve content over the Internet using the Hyper Text Markup Language (HTML). The web server accepts requests from browsers like Netscape and Internet Explorer and then returns the appropriate HTML documents. A number of server-side technologies can be used to increase the power of the server beyond its ability to deliver standard HTML pages; these include CGI scripts, server-side includes, SSL security, and Active Server Pages (ASPs). Although a large number of web server software packages have been developed, the freeware Apache server software is the web-wide market leader.

As of June 1999, the Apache server software supported about 60% of all servers running Unix, Windows 95/98, and Windows NT and Linux which represented nearly 4 million installations (Internet.com Corp, 2000). The most recent release is version 1.3.2 (http://www.apache.org/dist/). The origin of the Apache server (the name comes from the description: "a patch-y server") was in an informal group of users required by circumstance to patch, maintain, upgrade and port the public domain HTTP daemon developed by Rob McCool at the National Center for Supercomputing Applications at the University of Illinois, Urbana-Champaign. When the development of that httpd stalled after his leaving the NCSA in mid-1994, the webmasters who had developed their own extensions and bug fixes that were in need of a common foundation for development, support and distribution (Apache Group, 2000).

To continue to improve the productivity of the internet infrastructure, it would seem important to develop high fidelity, flexible and robust tools for quantitatively characterizing the behavior of web server software like Apache. Yet few published results have addressed the role of simulation modeling in exposing the inefficiencies and exploring solutions for general-purpose and domain-specific applications. Those few that have explored the issue have found circumstances where 60% improvement in throughput could be achieved through performance improvement techniques in the Apache server (Hu 1997) and through the use of other server software and HTTP approaches (Hu, J. 1998). There is clearly a need for more research into the benefits of alternative approaches to the software and hardware mix needed by businesses to meet their server demands.

As proven in other applications, dynamic, complex systems may require dynamic, complex solutions that can only be spawned through system understanding and experimentation. Often, that system understanding for network architectures can only be economically obtained through simulation rather than through expensive prototypes. Discrete event simulation has been frequently applied to the larger internet infrastructure optimization issues and special purpose simulators have been built for these studies (ns-2, University of California-Berkeley, 2000). The purpose of the research described in this paper is to apply a general-purpose, object-oriented, simulation environment to the problem of modeling the interaction of server, web server software and web clients. Specifically, we desire to

- model the core web server performance issues of http protocol, file access, replication, caching and multi-processor scheduling
- model the consequences of routing, front-end processing (firewalls) and network congestion latency on web server performance
- model domain-specific client demand patterns and client-side service levels
- model server-side application processing, such as database engine performance on either the web server machine or a linked machine
- model with a library of extendible, robust, readable and reusable classes for web server architecture simulation

In Section 2 we summarize the web server behavior and client behavior studied at the domain level. Section 3 describes the process oriented, object-oriented, Java-based Silk software and explain the role of message objects and push-pull orientation in modeling web server systems. Section 4 describes the specific application model using the Silk design classes. Section 5 describes future work and extension of the classes to other types of distributed systems

2 WEB SERVER AND CLIENT PROCESSES

In this section, we give a brief overview of our understanding of the working of the Apache web server on a machine with a Unix-based TCP/IP implementation.

In the HTTP protocol, for each URL fetched, a browser establishes a new TCP connection to the appropriate server, sends a request on this connection and then reads the server's response. HTTP 1.1 supports persistent connections, but most browsers and servers today do not use HTTP 1.1. To display a typical Web page, a browser may need to initiate several HTTP transactions to fetch the various components (HTML text, images) of the page.

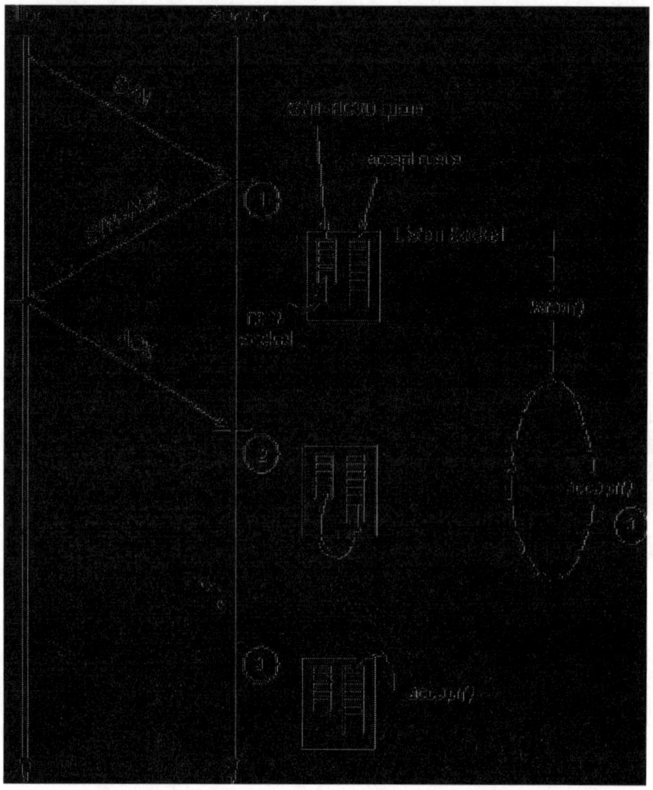

Figure 1: HTTP Connection Establishment Timeline

Figure 1 shows the sequence of events in the connection establishment phase of an HTTP transaction. When starting, the parent Apache process is created which *listens* for connection requests on a socket bound to a well-known port--typically port 80. When a connection establishment request (TCP SYN packet) from a client is received on this socket (Figure 1, position 1), the server TCP responds with a SYN-ACK TCP packet, creates a socket for the new, incomplete connection, and places it in the listening socket's SYN-RCVD queue. Later, when the client responds with an ACK packet to the server's SYN-ACK packet (position 2), the server TCP removes the socket created above from the SYN-RCVD queue and places it in the listen socket's queue of connections awaiting acceptance (accept queue). Each time the Apache server process executes the *accept()* system call (position 3), the first socket in the accept queue of the listen socket is removed and returned. After accepting a connection, the Apache server--either directly or indirectly by passing this connection to a helper process, reads the HTTP request from the client, sends back an appropriate response, and closes the connection.

There are a number of well-known potential inefficiencies in this architecture. The first comes from the TCP "slow start algorithm" which is intended to avoid an investment of bandwidth in an unreliable connection in a network by ensuring that each TCP sender doesn't overwhelm the network (Sun, 2000). The algorithm mandates that the first transmission be a single packet. If the recipient acknowledges the first packet successfully (i.e. the communication doesn't time out and the recipient believes that the packet has arrived without error), the sender sends two more packets. Successful transmission results in the sender sending yet more packets in parallel, until the capability of the underlying network is reached and one or more packets are not acknowledged successfully. Essentially the sender uses ACKs as a "clock" to regulate and gradually increase the rate packets are injected into the network until it reaches equilibrium.

The TCP specification describes another technique known as "delayed ACK", which concerns the receive side. The technique calls for an acknowledgment of a data packet to be delayed for a short period of time - the delayed-ACK interval. Different TCP implementations use different delay intervals. The TCP specification (RFC1122) mandates that the delayed-ACK interval must be less than 0.5 second. Delayed ACK serves to give the application an opportunity to send an immediate response, in which case the ACK can be piggybacked with the packet carrying the response. This technique is very useful, both in saving the network bandwidth and in reducing the protocol-processing overhead, and is widely adopted by TCP implementations. The TCP standard also recommends that an ACK not to be delayed for more than two data packets. This is to keep the slow start algorithm on the sender side flowing, which counts on the ACK packets coming back from the receive side in order to strobe more data packets into the network.

Another well-known problem exists with many traditional implementations of TCP/IP that limits the throughput of a Web server. Many web server systems have small default and maximum values for limits on the maximum backlog on a listen socket. This backlog is an upper bound on the sum of the lengths of the SYN-RCVD and accept queues. Since this threshold can be reached when the accept queue and/or the SYN-RCVD queue fills, a low value can limit throughput by refusing connection requests needlessly. As discussed above, the SYN-RCVD queue can grow because of long round-trip delays between server and clients, and high request rates. If the limit is too low, an incoming connection may be dropped even though the Web server may have sufficient resources to process the request. Even in the case of a long accept queue, it is usually preferable to accept a connection, unless the queue already contains enough work to keep the server busy for at least the client TCP's initial retransmission interval.

Clearly there are a number of queuing, timing and scheduling issues related to the execution of the web server processes and the interaction of the web server processes with the TCP process, disk and memory. To model these issues, researchers have relied on a number of simplifying approaches regarding the nature of the processes and their interaction with single or multiple processors. The detailed interaction of the web server software and disk directory and other logging operations have also been overlooked. Only through detailed simulation of all of the significant events of these processes can you properly quantify the relationships and performance for a given set of client demands.

Prior models have also been simplifying assumptions regarding the distribution of client demands placed on these web server processes. The SPECweb99 (SPECweb99, 1999) benchmark is typical of techniques for modeling Web workloads that define "typical" distributions for client demand. These simplistic approaches may not result in realistic demand patterns that mimic actual client interactions. The primary assumption in workload generation involves the creation of independently generated requests for files of sizes consistent with an anticipated workload. What this scheme fail to properly model is the nature of the embedded file requests that accompany the initial client web page request. As some of these files may be required for page navigation, the client session may be waiting until all of these files have been received and the "think-time" starting point should not begin until the complete page has been received.

3 SILK SIMULATION CLASSES

An important result of this work was the achievement of a true implementation of object-oriented simulation design for web client and web server modeling and execution using Java and the Silk classes (ThreadTec, 1996). The Silk classes are a Java Application Programming Interface for general-purpose, discrete-event, process-oriented, object-oriented simulation.

This section describes the uniqueness of the Silk entity-thread approach for creating simulation classes

The power, flexibility and scalability of Silk derive directly from Java and the seamless way in which the simulation-related extensions that constitute Silk have been integrated into the language. Achieving such a high level of integration would not be possible were it not for a unique combination of features in the Java language. Java presents a simple, yet powerful framework that greatly facilitates the implementation of object-oriented design methodology and its capabilities for creating flexible, modular, and reusable programs. Silk has implemented simulation using Java's built-in support for multi-threaded execution, which is essential to representing in a natural way the inherently concurrent flow of entities in process simulation models.

Silk is a wholly object-oriented modeling formalism in which system objects and their software implementation are patterned after real-world objects. The system objects are entities that have *data* (attributes, characteristics, properties, etc.) that represent the *state* of the objects and a *process* method that describes the *behavior* of the object. In an object-oriented simulation approach, the association between the state of an object and it's process is made explicit via *encapsulation* whereby both are defined in an integral, self-contained unit called a *class*. Each *instance* possesses its own unique copy of the state-related data defined by the class but shares the common *process*. *Inheritance* is a mechanism by which new classes can be defined as extensions of existing ones. The derived class has all the characteristics and behaviors of the parent class (which may itself be derived from others) plus some added functionality in the form of new process behavior. In this application, parent classes of server processes and messages (packets) have created templates for both the data and process methods of subclasses. (The user-defined Process class in this example should not confused with the common Silk process method which all Silk entities inherit.) The object view of the foundation Apache web server software model in our research is shown in Figure 2 below.

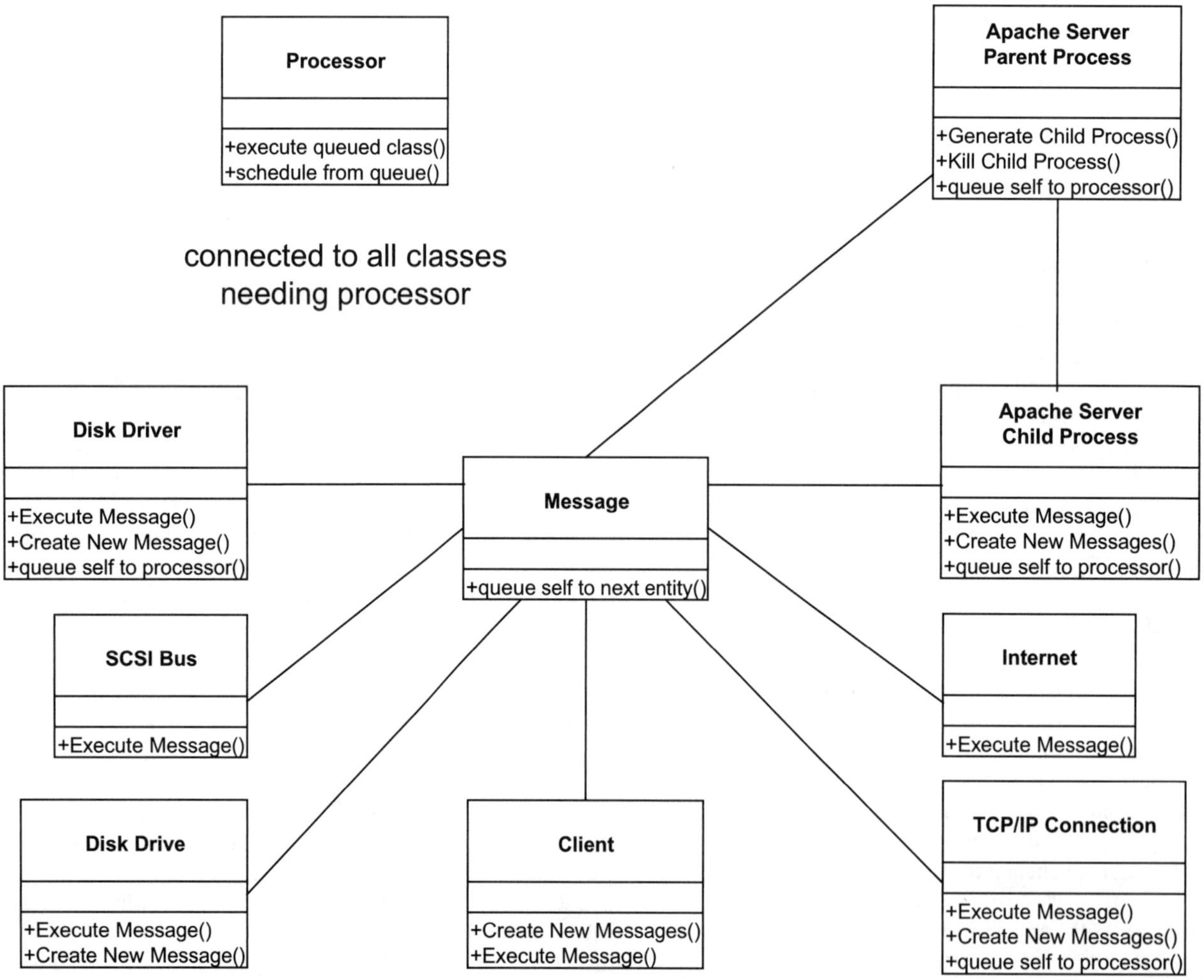

Figure 2: Object view of Apache web server simulation

The distinguishing feature of our implementation of the objects in Silk is the combination of message push and process pull. Most commercial simulation software is restricted to a push-type assembly-line world-view. The focus in this approach is on transient entities whose aim is to complete a series of process steps, each of which may require a set of passive, unintelligent, capacity-limited resources. For simplistic models, this approach is often sufficient. However, in multitasking, distributed architectures, there is almost always a need to model active, intelligent resources who from a modeling standpoint are more naturally seen to control decision making within the system rather than the transient entities being acted upon. For this situation, a pull-oriented description of activity from the process point-of-view yields a more natural and efficient model of the system dynamics. This eliminates the need for the traditional simulation design that must handle this interaction through the creation of executive entities whose purpose is to manage the interplay between the transient entities and static resources. In the model described below, there is a one to one correspondence between system objects and simulated objects with no need for executive objects controlling the system.

Support for multithreaded execution is an essential aspect to the implementation of the Silk web server modeling classes. Thread-based entity representation and the natural process-oriented modeling capability are made possible only in Java. Instances of classes that extend *Entity* run as separate threads of execution that are alternately suspended and resumed to coordinate the time-ordered sequencing of entity movements in the model. A thread is suspended when the corresponding entity encounters an predetermined wait at a *delay( )* method or a status delay, the most general of which is modeled by the *while(condition( ))* construct. Also, a Silk entity-thread can reside simultaneously in any number of queues. This is a particularly useful feature for modeling certain types of dynamic behavior or for decomposing a wait time or queue length into constituent parts. This is ideal for research into the latency components of web server packet entities.

4 SILK CLASSES FOR SERVER SIMULATION

Figure 3 shows the inheritance structure used for the Silk classes created for the basic Apache Web server simulation library. The Message class forms the parent for both TCP packets and other generic data packets involved in inter-process communication. A convenient Timer class is available to all processes or messages to model time-out behavior. The Process class interacts with the Processor class to create independent lightweight processes that wait for message arrivals or scheduled execution times. Servers are defined as a collection of Processors, Disks, Pagcs and Files. New Server configurations can be created by changing the data and process method behavior of these classes without modifying the other classes. Likewise a parent Client class is configured to support the creation of a number of independently behaving client types according to the nature of clients each server is designed to service. This modularity of class design is central to the achievement of the reusability goal to allow convenient systems data and behavior changes.

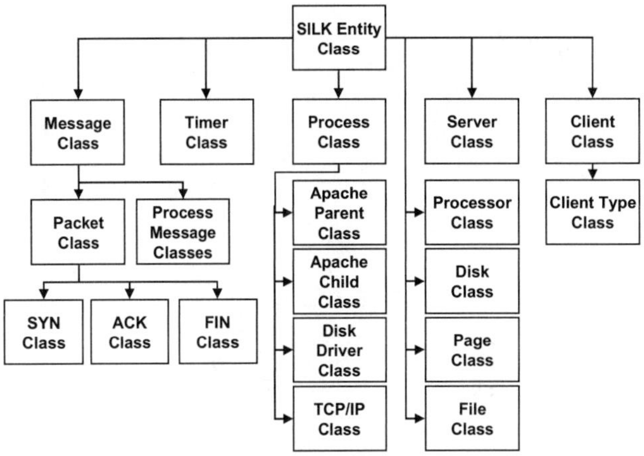

Figure 3: Silk web server class inheritance

To insure proper correspondence between the system object view and our Silk simulation object representation, we continued the use of Unified Modeling Language (UML, 2000) tools by preparing an Event Trace. The partial Event Trace shown in Figure 4 describes the sequence of interactions between the Silk simulation classes and the corresponding system objects. This diagram is the primary mechanism for the server system architect and simulation engineer to document their shared understanding of the interactions and verify the execution of the simulation event trace.

5 RESULTS AND FUTURE WORK

The simulation class code and results from the execution of the Silk web server classes are available at http://www.threadtec.com/models/Silk012_0WebServer/. Among the many extensions of our research is the issue of modeling the interaction of web-server software and database access that is fundamental to the evolution of e-commerce applications. The multiple application, multiple processor and multiple server designs promoted in this domain require enormous investments in hardware and software. The use of web-server level simulation early in the architecture design process may be crucial to avoiding solutions that mask inefficiency with hardware solutions that only add to the network congestion. Likewise, Silk classes similar to those used in this web-server research are being employed in analysis of distributed systems architecture for commercial

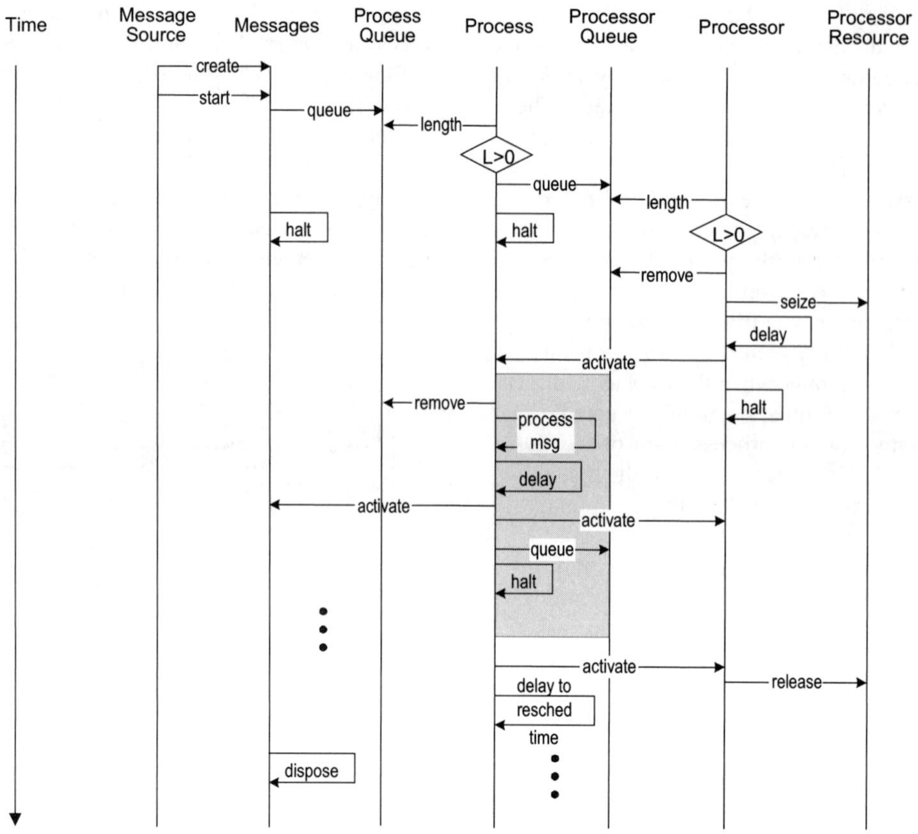

Figure 4: Silk web server Event Trace for server processes

and defense applications. These models have been validated against concurrent prototype-based architecture development activities. Our experience has been that the Silk simulations are an ideal complement to other architecture design and analysis tools and offer insight into system inefficiencies and paths for improvement.

REFERENCES

Apache Group, Apache FAQ, http://www.apache.org/ABOUT_APACHE.html, 2000.

Banga, G. and P. Druschel, "Measuring the Capacity of a Web Server", *USENIX Symposium on Internet Technologies and Systems (SINTS)*, 1997.

Cao, P. and S. Irani, "Cost-aware WWW proxy caching algorithms," *USENIX Symposium on Internet Technologies and Systems*, 1997.

Chankhunthod, A., P. B. Danzig, C. Neerdaels, M. F. Schwartz and K. J. Worrell, "A hierarchical internet object cache," in *Proceedings of the 1996 USENIX Technical Conference*, 1996.

Crovella, Mark E., Robert Frangioso and Mor Harchol-Balter, "Connection Scheduling in Web Servers", *USENIX Symposium on Internet Technologies and Systems*, 1999.

Hu, James, Sumedh Mungee and Douglas C. Schmidt, Principles for Developing and Measuring High-performance Web Servers over ATM, *Proceedings of INFOCOM '98,* 1998.

Hu, Yiming; Ashwini Nanda and Qing Yang, "Measurement, Analysis and Performance Improvement of the Apache Web Server". In *Proceedings of the 18th IEEE IPCCC'99*, 1999.

Improving Restart of Idle TCP Connections, Vikram Visweswaraiah and John Heidemann , Technical Report 97-661, University of Southern California, November 1997.

Katz, E. D.; M. Butler, and R. McGrath, "A scalable web server: The NCSA prototype," *in WWW'94 Conference Proceedings*, 1994.

Luotonen, A. and K. Altis, "World Wide Web proxies," in *WWW'94 Conference Proceedings*, 1994.

ns-2, Network Simulator, 2000. http://www-mash.cs.berkeley.edu/ns/

SPECweb99, 1999 Standard Performance Evaluation Corporation, 1999.http://www.specbench.org/osg/web99/

Sun Microsystems, http://www.sun.com/sun-on-net/performance/tcp.slowstart.html, 2000.

ThreadTec, Inc. *Silk®, A Java-Based Process Simulation Language,* http://www.threadtec.com/papers/paper2/paper2.html., 1997

UML (Unified Modeling Language), Rational Software, 2000. http://www.rational.com/uml/index.jtmpl

Web Server Comparisons, 2000. http://webcompare.internet.com/cgi-bin/quickcompare.pl

AN ABSTRACT SIMULATION MODEL FOR MIXED LANGUAGE HARDWARE SIMULATION

André S. Windisch
Department of Computer Science
Technical University of Chemnitz
09111 Chemnitz, Germany
e-mail: andre.windisch@informatik.tu-chemnitz.de

Electrical Engineering, Verification, Combined, Mixed-Language, Simulation, Hierarchical Model

ABSTRACT

This paper presents an abstract simulation model for mixed-language hardware simulation. Based upon this model the simulation semantics of both hardware simulation languages and mixed-language hardware simulation systems can be formally defined thus unifying these heretofore distinct domains. The formalization of simulation semantics is founded on a fixed set of abstract semantic primitives; a hierarchical simulation architecture, different simulation data classes, simulation processes and intra-process communication, three different simulation time domains, and an adaptive scheduling algorithm. Supported time domains include the untimed, the discrete-time, and the discrete-event domain with time being modeled as a tuple consisting of a continuous time value and a n-dimensional delta vector. The scheduling algorithm performs a delta-cycle accurate adaptive scheduling of subsystems based on their time domain. The concepts presented in this paper were verified by an implementation prototype of a mixed-language hardware simulation system.

1 INTRODUCTION

The increasing size of integrated circuits is giving rise to the creation of complete hardware systems on a single chip. Such a System-On-Chip (SoC) is usually composed of a set of interacting components, called cores, which denote domain-specific subsystems (e.g. mechatronic or fluid subsystems). This changing nature of the integrated circuits has led to a paradigm shift in hardware design which is accompanied by the creation of new hardware description languages (HDL) for SoC design. These new languages extend the semantics of older HDL towards system level design by incorporating new concepts for abstract data types, abstract communication, different simulation scheduling mechanisms, and protocol based design.

The current consensus in the hardware design community is that there will never be a single, domain-independent HDL. Instead, future SoC designs will consist of various interacting cores each implemented in a different, domain-specific HDL. This requires that multiple HDL must conform to some common semantic principles in order to achieve meaningful simulation results for SoC designs. Furthermore, it demands the formalization of HDL specific simulation semantics which is usually informally defined by the HDL reference manuals. Ideally, formalization of simulation semantics of the various HDLs should be based on a single formal model that could then also be used for defining simulation semantics of mixed-language hardware simulation systems.

2 RELATED WORK

Numerous projects on the formalization of simulation semantics have been carried out in the past decade. Adopting a classification scheme for mixed-language design presented in (Jerraya and Ernst 1999), these projects follow two main streams for formalization which can be characterized as either *language based* or *computation-model based* approaches.

The first category, language based approaches, comprises projects focusing on the formal description of simulation semantics for both single *languages and mixed-language systems*. A formalization of the VHDL (IEEE 1993) simulation cycle based on Abstract State Machines (Gurevich 1994) was carried out by (Börger *et al.* 1994) and extended by (Sasaki *et al.* 1997) for the mixed-signal language VHDL-AMS. An axiomatic description of the hardware description language Verilog (IEEE 1996) is presented in (Fiskio-Lasseter 1998). Similar formalizations exist for most hardware description languages but are too numerous to be quoted. A classification of mixed-language systems is given by (Jerraya 1998) defining two abstract architectures, called *compositional and co-simulation approach*, for mixed-language simulation. In the compositional approach simulation is based on a common intermediate representation into which all source languages are translated. In the co-simulation approach language specific simulators are composed to form a mixed-language simulation system. Based on this approach (Sasaki 1999) formalizes Verilog-VHDL simulation interoperability by defining both the language specific simulation cycles and the resulting mixed-language simulation cycle using Abstract State Machines.

The second category, computation-model based approaches, focuses on the formalization of both computational models and frameworks incorporating different models of computation. One of the initial frameworks for simulation of heterogeneous systems is Ptolemy (Buck *et al.* 1994) which allows integration of any model of computation into a predefined hierarchical architecture. A denotational framework for comparing models of computation which is based on the notion of signals is given in (Lee and Sangiovanni-Vincentelli 1996). An open simulation platform for the distribution of cores, called Open Model Interface (OMI), is presented in (Obilisetty 1999). This model combines discrete-time and discrete-event simulation.

3 THE ABSTRACT SIMULATION MODEL

This paper introduces an abstract simulation model for mixed-language hardware simulation, called Hardware Simulation Model (HSM). This model incorporates concepts for the formalization of simulation data, simulation architectures, simulation processes and intra-process communication, simulation timing, and scheduling. As opposed to the Ptolemy project which defines a "non-dogmatic" simulation kernel, HSM provides a single predefined scheduling algorithm that adapts itself to a fixed set of supported simulation timing domains. Thus, HSM provides a semantic framework for the formal definition of simulation semantics based on a fixed set of semantic primitives. Based on this model the simulation semantics of both current HDLs and mixed-language simulation systems can be formally defined thus unifying these heretofore distinct domains.

3.1 Simulation Architecture

HSM provides an abstract simulation architecture that allows the hierarchical creation of simulation systems from simulation subsystems. Formally, this simulation architecture of a hardware simulation system S at hierarchy level n is defined as the four tuple

$$S_n = \langle SMU_n, SKU_n, SCU_n, SDU_n \rangle \qquad n \in \mathbb{N}$$

containing a simulation model unit (SMU), a simulation kernel unit (SKU), a simulation communication unit (SCU), and a simulation data unit (SDU). Thereby the *simulation model unit* at level n denotes the model under simulation and comprises either a non-empty set of simulation model processes (SMP), realizing model specific behavior, or a non-empty set of level (n–1) simulation subsystems. Thus, either

$$SMU_n = \{ SMP_{n,i} \mid i \in \mathbb{N}; i > 0 \} \qquad \text{for any n or}$$

$$SMU_n = \{ S_{(n-1),i} \mid i \in \mathbb{N}; i > 0 \} \qquad \text{for any n>0.}$$

The execution of a simulation model unit in the context of a simulation system is controlled by the associated *simulation kernel unit* that contains a non-empty set of simulation kernel processes (SKP);

$$SKU_n = \{ SKP_{n,j} \mid j \in \mathbb{N}; j > 0 \}$$

For reasons of uniformity the set of simulation processes $\{ SP_k \mid k \in \mathbb{N}; k > 0\}$ is defined which comprises all SKP and SMP of a single, possibly hierarchical, simulation system S.

Communication between SMU and SKU of a simulation system is performed through a *simulation communication unit* (SCU) that is defined by

$$SCU_n = \{ SCI_{n,j,i} \in SKU_n \times SMU_n \}$$

as the non-empty set of simulation communication interfaces (SCI) where $SCI_{n,j,i}$ connects $SKP_{n,j}$ with either $SMP_{n,i}$ or $S_{(n-1),i}$. Thus, for a given level n the communication interfaces define a partial ordering on the simulation processes of S_n.

Exchange of simulation data between either $S_{(n-1),i}$ or $SMP_{n,i}$ of S_n is governed by a shared data structure, called *simulation data unit* (SDU). This is a set containing a single future event list (FEL) and a number of simulation data items (SDI)

$$SDU_n = \{ SDI_{n,l} \cup FEL \mid l \in \mathbb{N}; l > 0 \}$$

with each item denoting an interface object used for communication between the simulation subsystems or the SMPs at the same level. Each write operation on a timed SDI also adds an event to the totally ordered (with respect to the time domain $\mathbb{T}$) list of events of the FEL. A SDU_n can also be accessed by any SKP_n residing in the same simulation system. Thereby, a SKP can update any SDI denoting interface objects to a higher level simulation system. Furthermore, a SKP can read the next time stamp with respect to its own local virtual time (LVT) from the internal FEL. For this purpose a SDU provides the function nextTime: $\mathbb{T} \rightarrow \mathbb{T}$ which returns the time stamp of the next event or the predefined maximum time value t_{max} if no further events exist.

The abstract simulation architecture defined above can also be represented graphically as shown in Figure 1 below. In this figure dashed rectangles denote sets which group entities whereas solid rectangles are used to represent entities. Furthermore, simulation data exchange between the simulation processes via SDU is indicated by bi-directional dashed arrows.

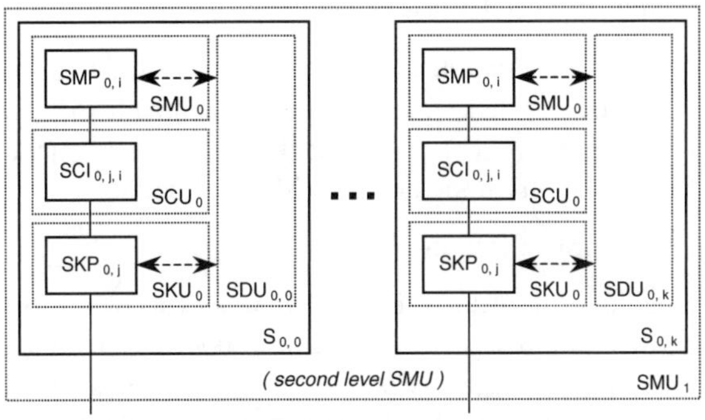

Figure 1 The abstract simulation architecture

The reason for introducing a hierarchical architecture is two-fold: First, it allows a simple handling of large scale simulation systems and, second, it supports an efficient partitioning of the overall model across the simulation system. Thereby, the hierarchical architecture can be optimized to have an equivalent amount of data flow on each level of the hierarchy. Moreover, since a simulation subsystem can be controlled by more than SKP, HSM provides the possibility to create n-dimensional simulation hypercubes for the efficient simulation of heavily loaded network or transputer models.

3.2 Simulation Data

HSM introduces four abstract classes of simulation data items (SDI) that are distinguished by their time and space properties. The time property defines whether or not a data item class has a notion of simulation time. Additionally, the space property specifies whether a data item class supports buffering of multiple values or just a single value.

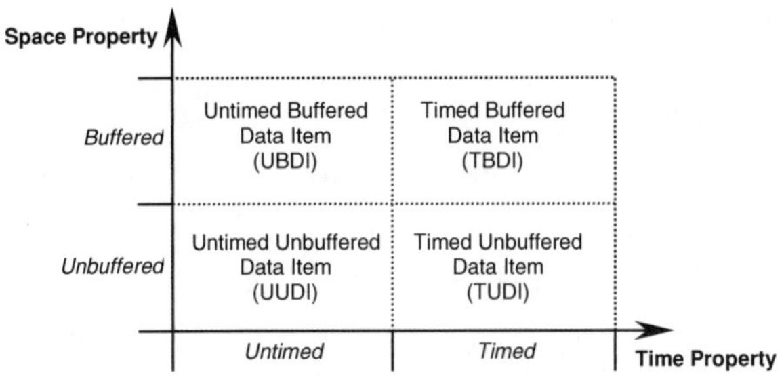

Figure 2 Classification of simulation data items

This classification scheme for data items can be graphically represented as shown in Figure 2. Moreover, the above defined data classes can be formalized using tuple notation. Given the identifiers $\mathbb{C}$, $\mathbb{D}$ and $\mathbb{T}$ denoting the domains of Characters, abstract Data and Time, respectively, the above data classes are defined by

$$\text{UUDI} = \langle \text{name, value} \rangle$$
$$\text{TUDI} = \langle \text{name}, \{ (\text{time}, \text{value})_i \} \rangle$$
$$\text{UBDI} = \langle \text{name}, \{ \text{value}_i \} \rangle$$
$$\text{TBDI} = \langle \text{name}, \{ (\text{time}, \{ \text{value}_j \})_i, \text{delay} \rangle$$

with $name \in \mathbb{C}^m$, $value \in \mathbb{D}$, $time, delay \in \mathbb{T}$ and $i, j \in \mathbb{N}$. Clearly, the definitions above closely resemble, in the order of appearance, the semantics of variables, signals, streams and channels as known from various hardware description and programming languages. However, the introduced formalization proved necessary since the semantics of these objects varies from language to language.

For the manipulation of data items HSM defines the two operations *read()* and *write()* that are polymorph with respect to the different data classes :

- *UUDI and UBDI.* The operation write: $\mathbb{D} \rightarrow$ VOID either assigns a new value to a UUDI object or appends a new value to the totally ordered set of values of a UBDI object. Ordering of this value set is such that it realizes FIFO behavior. The operation read: VOID $\rightarrow \mathbb{D}$ either reads and returns the value of a UUDI object (non-destructive read) or removes and returns the first value from the value set of a UBDI object (destructive read). In case of an empty set the value $\perp$ is returned which is part of all data domains $\mathbb{D}$.
- *TUDI and TBDI.* Operation write: $\mathbb{T} \times \mathbb{D} \rightarrow$ VOID either adds a new (time, value) pair to the totally ordered set of time-value pairs of a TUDI object or appends a new value to the totally ordered set of values associated with the corresponding time of a TBDI object. As before, ordering of this value set is such that it exhibits FIFO behavior. The operation read: $\mathbb{T} \rightarrow \mathbb{D}$ either reads and returns the value of a TUDI object (non-destructive read) or removes and returns the first value from the value set of a TBDI object (destructive read) for the specified time. In case of an empty value set the value $\perp$ is returned.

In addition to these operations HSM defines a method *event*: $\mathbb{T} \rightarrow$ BOOLEAN for all timed data classes which returns true if the value of a TUDI or TBDI has changed at the specified simulation time. Otherwise this method returns false.

As previously mentioned, all level n data items SDI_n of a simulation system S_n are gathered in its corresponding simulation data unit SDU_n. In the presented abstract simulation model each SDU is modeled by a separate *tuple space* which is a collection containing a set of data item tuples and exactly one FEL tuple. A tuple space denotes a shared data structure that provides controlled access for parallel processes via the predefined operations out(T), in(T), and read(T). The operation out(T) allows processes to output tuple T into the tuple space. On the contrary, tuples can be read from tuple space by any process by calling either in(T) or read(T) which are a destructive and non-destructive read operation, respectively. For a more detailed discussion of tuple spaces the interested reader is referred to (Gelernter 1985; Carriero and Gelernter 1986).

The advantages of using tuple spaces are that they model data on an abstract level, provide concurrent access to the data, and hide the actual physical implementation which may be distributed. Moreover, based on the predefined tuple space operations the aforementioned read() and write() operations on SDI can be implemented. For instance, the write() operation on UUDI can be defined as an atomic operation that first removes the corresponding SDI tuple by calling in(T), then changes its value, and finally puts the tuple back into the tuple space using out(T). This definition of atomic operations is based upon law-governed tuple spaces as introduced by (Minsky and Leichter 1994).

3.3 Processes and Communication

As previously stated, HSM employs simulation control interfaces (SCI) for the communication between simulation processes. Thereby, each $SCI_{n,i,j}$ connects exactly one $SKP_{n,i}$ with either exactly one $S_{(n-1),j}$ or exactly one $SMP_{n,j}$. Internally, a SCI is structured as a 4-tuple containing four directed links

$$SCI = \langle \text{activate, complete, cancel, domain} \rangle$$

Each of these links is strongly typed, i.e. it can only carry one type of message. Within the abstract simulation model all links are assumed to be secure, i.e. no messages sent on those links can be lost.

- The link *activate* is used by SKP_n to start simulation of the connected $S_{(n-1)}$ or SMP_n. The activation message contains as parameters the LVT of the sending SKP and all changed input SDIs $\in SDU_n$ of the controlled subsystem.
- The link *complete* is used by $S_{(n-1)}$ or SMP_n to signal successful completion of a simulation step to its connected SKP_n. The message contains as parameters the future LVT calculated by the controlled subsystem and all changed output SDIs $\in SDU_{(n-1)}$ of the controlled subsystem.
- The link *cancel* is used to indicate failed activation of a $S_{(n-1)}$ or a SMP_n. Activation of the first fails in case neither an internally nor an externally generated event triggers a new simulation cycle. Activation of a SMP fails when evaluation of its associated activation rule returns false (please see below).
- The link *domain* allows simulation kernel processes to retrieve the simulation timing domain $m \in M$ of the connected $S_{(n-1)}$ or SMP_n. The set of supported simulation timing domains M is defined by

  $$M = \{ \text{ut, dt, de} \}$$

  consisting of the elements *untimed* (ut), *discrete-time* (dt), and *discrete-event* (de). Among the elements of M a precedence is defined, such that ut $\angle$ dt $\angle$ de, which is used to determine the simulation timing domain of subsystem compositions. Thereby, the simulation timing domain of the composed system is determined by the highest timing domain of one of its simulation subsystems. Thus, composing untimed and discrete-time systems yields a discrete-time system whereas a composition of discrete-time systems with discrete-event systems results in a discrete-event system. This composition schema is based on the implicit assumption that the timing of all discrete-time systems is defined in multiples of a common clock rate. This requirement holds for all synchronous hardware designs but can not be met for asynchronous designs. Thus, the latter must be modeled using discrete-event timing.

After discussion of the inter-process communication protocol inherent to HSM the remaining part of this subsection focuses on the formal definition of the simulation processes. A level n simulation model process $SMP_{n,j}$ with index j is defined as the 5-tuple

$$SMP_{n,j} = \langle f, C, a, t, m \rangle$$

where

- *f* ... is the non-strict function to be executed.
- *C* ... represents the communication interface. Thus, $C \subseteq SCU_n$ is the set comprising all simulation control interfaces that are connected to this simulation model process. Formally,

  $$C = \{ SCI_{n,x,j} \in SCU_n \mid \forall x \in \mathbb{N} \}$$

- *a* ... is the associated association rule. This is an expression in first order predicate logic which may contain predicates checking for events on timed SDI, comparison of values of SDI and checks for specific simulation times. During simulation of a simulation model process its activation rule can be changed dynamically which allows to change sensitivity of the process to a different set of SDI for a specific simulation time.

- *t* ... is the local virtual time (LVT) associated with this process instance and $t \in \mathbb{T}$. The LVT can only be changed in response to an activation message received on one of the activation links. If a SMP is connected to more than one SCI then this process is only activated upon a receive of activation messages on all SCIs. In that case LVT is set to the minimum of all received activation times.
- *m* ... represents the simulation timing domain associated with this process instance. The type of model determines the scheduling policy applied by the connected SKP.

Similarly to a simulation model process a level n simulation kernel process $SKP_{n,i}$ with index i is defined as the 5-tuple

$$SKP_{n,i} = \langle f, C, D, t, m \rangle$$

where

- *f* ... represents the scheduling function of this simulation kernel process (see subsection 3.5).
- *C* ... denotes the communication interface of this process instance. This interface can be divided into a lower communication interface (LCI) and an upper communication interface (UCI), where

  $LCI = \{ SCI_{n,i,x} \in SCU_n \mid \forall x \in \mathbb{N} \}$ and
  $UCI = \{ SCI_{n+1,y,i} \in SCU_{n+1} \mid \forall y \in \mathbb{N} \}$
- *D* ... specifies the data mapping scheme applied by this kernel. This scheme consists of an input (IDI) and an output data interface (ODI) defining the mapping of input and output parameters between the containing simulation systems and a higher level simulation system.
- *t* ... is the LVT of this SKP.
- *m* ... represents the simulation timing domain associated with this process instance. This timing model is calculated according to the timing composition schema introduced earlier on.

3.4 Timing

Various hardware description languages contain two-dimensional time models where the first dimension specifies the *simulation time* and the second dimension a *delta time* $\in \mathbb{N}$. Delta time does not represent any real simulation time. It is used to describe zero-delay feedback loops between model processes in a discrete-event simulation by providing an ordering mechanism for events with identical simulation time. This ordering is based on the explicit enumeration of zero-delay events such that delta time of a generated event is equal to the current simulation delta-time incremented by one. Thus, delta time ensures determinism of simulation by defining a strict causal ordering on events.

In HSM this time model is adapted to the inherent hierarchical structure and generalized to a *n-dimensional delta time* model for level n simulation systems S_n. Thereby, the nth delta dimension defines the ordering for zero-delay events at level n. These events can be generated within the corresponding SMU_n by the contained $S_{(n-1)}$ or SMP_n and are therefore stored in the FEL of the associated SDU_n. Thus, control of level n events and management of level n delta cycles for any S_n must be performed by the corresponding SKU_n as shown in Figure 3 below. However, SMPs are always controlled by a level 0 delta in order to ensure a correct delta cycle accurate scheduling of all SMPs.

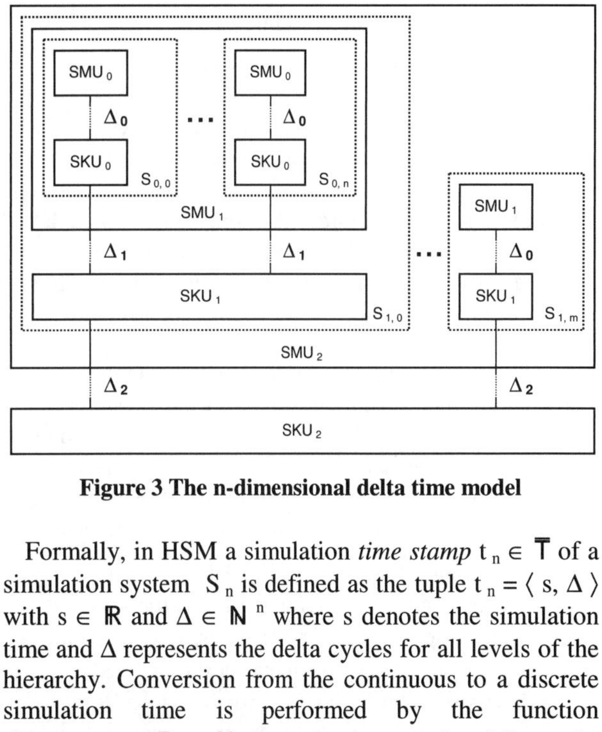

Figure 3 The n-dimensional delta time model

Formally, in HSM a simulation *time stamp* $t_n \in \mathbb{T}$ of a simulation system S_n is defined as the tuple $t_n = \langle s, \Delta \rangle$ with $s \in \mathbb{R}$ and $\Delta \in \mathbb{N}^n$ where s denotes the simulation time and Δ represents the delta cycles for all levels of the hierarchy. Conversion from the continuous to a discrete simulation time is performed by the function *discrete_time*: $\mathbb{R} \rightarrow \mathbb{N}$ whose implementation follows the definition given in (IEEE 1999). As stated there, the continuous time values 1.0 and 0.0 correspond to the discrete time values 1 sec and 0 sec, respectively. As the time resolution for discrete time within the HSM we define 1 fs since smaller resolutions are not supported by any of the current hardware descriptions languages.

On the set $\mathbb{T} \times \mathbb{T}$ we define the relations ">", "<" that are necessary for the comparison of simulation time stamps. Clearly, these relations only define a partial ordering on time stamps since the inherent hierarchical architecture only imposes a partial ordering on the simulation processes. Hence, only the time stamps of related simulation processes can be compared. Thus, for any given simulation system S_n and the two time stamps $t = \langle s, \Delta \rangle$ and $t' = \langle s', \Delta' \rangle$

$$t < t' \text{ iff } s < s' \text{ or } s = s' \text{ and } \exists i \in \mathbb{N}, i \leq n; \Delta_i < \Delta'_i$$

$$t > t' \text{ iff } s > s' \text{ or } s = s' \text{ and } \exists i \in \mathbb{N}, i \leq n; \Delta_i > \Delta'_i$$

In the same way we can define the equivalence relation "=" $\subseteq \mathbb{T} \times \mathbb{T}$. Again, due to the partial ordering of the simulation processes within a simulation system S_n only time stamps of related simulation processes can be compared for a specific level n. Given the above definitions for t and t' the relation "=" is formalized by

$$t = t' \text{ iff } s = s' \text{ and } \forall i \in \mathbb{N}, i \leq n; \Delta_i = \Delta'_i$$

In the above three definitions comparison of delta cycles is possible because of the HSM inherent delta-cycle accurate scheduling algorithm which maintains global delta states on each level of hierarchy.

3.5 Scheduling

Scheduling in the HSM is carried out by a non-empty set of inter-connected simulation kernel processes that are distributed across different levels of the hierarchical simulation architecture. As previously stated, each simulation kernel process contains the predefined HSM scheduling function *f* which implements an *adaptive scheduling* algorithm. The term adaptive scheduling refers to the ability of this function to perform context specific scheduling depending on the simulation timing model of the scheduled simulation subsystems and on possible control by a set of higher level simulation kernel processes. The structure of a level n SKP and its associated scheduling algorithm are shown in Listing 1 below using an object-oriented pseudo-code notation.

A simulation kernel process SKP_n is parametric on its associated simulation data unit SDU_n, the set of its upper communication interfaces UCI $\subseteq SCU_{n+1}$, and the set of its lower communication interfaces LCI $\subseteq SCU_n$. Upon SKP initialization [lines 4 to 6] the LCI is divided into the three distinct subsets lci_ut, lci_dt, and lci_de which schedule associated untimed, discrete-time, and discrete-event simulation sub-systems, respectively. This scheduling is performed by domain specific schedulers, one for each LCI subset, which are instantiated by the scheduling function [lines 16 to 18] prior to the first scheduling cycle.

```
1   class SKP_n( SDU_n sdu, SCI_n+1[] uci, SCI_n[] lci) ≡
2   {
3
4     SCI_n[] lci_ut = getSubSystems( lci, ut);
5     SCI_n[] lci_dt = getSubSystems( lci, dt);
6     SCI_n[] lci_de = getSubSystems( lci, de);
7
8     SCI_n+1 × SCI_n  idi = getInputDataMapping();
9     SCI_n × SCI_n+1  odi = getOuputDataMapping();
10
11    Domain          m   = getComposedDomain();
12    Time            t   = getInitialTime();;
13
14    void f() ≡
15    {
16      UT_Scheduler s_ut = new UT_Scheduler( lci_ut);
17      DT_Scheduler s_dt = new DT_Scheduler( lci_dt);
18      DE_Scheduler s_de = new DE_Scheduler( lci_de);
19
20      TIME[ uci.size()]  uci_time = getUCITime();
21      TIME[ 4]           lci_time;
22
23      while true
24      {
25        if uci ≠ NIL then
26        {
27          ∀ i ≤ uci.size(),
28            uci_time[ i]= uci[ i].activate.time(),
29            sdu.set( idi, uci[ i].activate.data());
30        }
31
32        if MIN( uci_time) > t or sdu.changed() then
33        {
34          t = MIN( uci_time);
35
36          lci_time[ 0] = s_ut.schedule( t);
37          lci_time[ 1] = s_de.schedule( t);
38          lci_time[ 2] = s_dt.schedule( t);
39          lci_time[ 3] = s_ut.schedule( t);
40
41          uci_time = MIN(lci_time,sdu.nextTime( t));
42
43          if uci ≠ NIL then
44          {
45            ∀ i ≤ uci.size(),
46              uci[ i].complete.time( uci_time,
47                sdu.get( odi, uci[ i]));
48          }
49        }
50        else
51        {
52          if uci ≠ NIL then
53          {
54            ∀ i ≤ uci.size(),
55              uci[ i].cancel.time( t);
56          }
57          else
58          {
59            exit();
60          }
61        }
62
63      }
64
65    }
```

Listing 1 The HSM adaptive scheduling algorithm

The scheduling cycle itself can follow two different policies: *controlled and free scheduling*. The latter is selected when a SKP does not have an upper communication interface, i.e. it resides in SKU_n of a simulation system S_n. In that case the next simulation time step is determined by events occurring inside or at the interfaces of the controlled simulation subsystems S_{n-1}. The simulation terminates if no new events are generated [line 59]. As opposed to that, *controlled scheduling* is applied when a non-empty set of upper communication interfaces is present. In that case scheduling is synchronized by activation messages on all

UCI which can be received in any order [lines 25 to 30]. These messages carry as parameters the new simulation time stamp determined by the higher level SKP and an possibly empty array of changed higher level SDI. Since the simulation time stamps contained in the different activation messages may not be identical the future LVT is calculated as the minimum of the received values [line 32]. Again the simulation subsystems are only scheduled [lines 36 to 39] if the future LVT is greater than the current LVT or in the case that events on higher level SDI occurred. Termination or skipping of the scheduling cycle are reported to higher level SKP by sending completion [lines 43 to 48] or cancel messages [lines 52 to 56], respectively. The first message type takes as parameter the calculated future LVT and an array of changed SDI which are mapped to higher level SDI as defined by the output data interface ODI. The latter message carries only the LVT thus requesting a re-scheduling for this simulation time from the higher level SKP.

The actual scheduling of simulation subsystems is performed by the three domain specific scheduler instances [lines 36 to 39] in sequential order starting with the untimed subsystems, followed by discrete-event, discrete-time, and again untimed subsystems. Thereby, discrete-time subsystems are only scheduled if the current scheduling cycle is not a delta cycle. This requirement ensures that associated input SDI that are driven by discrete-event subsystems are stable. Scheduling of untimed subsystems is performed in a cycle until all controlled subsystems are stable. Thus, scheduling of dynamic data-flow networks is possible. Since untimed subsystems can be both driven from and drive timed SDI scheduling of these subsystems has to be performed twice before and after the scheduling of timed subsystems.

Clearly, the presented delta-cycle accurate adaptive scheduling algorithm emulates a *conservative parallel discrete event simulation (PDES)* (Fujimoto 1990; Lin and Fishwick 1995). In HSM the hierarchical architecture and the scheduling function f ensure that the causal relation among time consecutive events will be maintained at all times during simulation. Thus, the local causality constraint is satisfied since every simulation process executes events in non-decreasing time stamp order and refuses processing of events with time stamps less than the its LVT. Furthermore, both the input waiting rule and the output waiting rule are met; a simulation process only executes after it has received an activation message on each UCI link and a SKP nether sends activation messages on a LCI with time stamps larger than its LVT. Moreover, deadlock between simulation processes is avoided by the n-dimensional delta-time model where the delta delay serves as the look-ahead. At the current stage HSM does not contain mechanisms for an application of optimistic PDES scheduling techniques although this simulation model could be integrated. However, it was omitted on purpose since only very few of the current HDL simulators contain implementations of rollback mechanisms.

4 APPLICATION OF THE MODEL

The abstract simulation model presented in the previous section was verified by a prototype implementation of a mixed-language hardware simulation system. Currently, this simulation system allows co-simulation of models implemented in either VHDL or SystemC by coupling the language specific simulators to a possibly hierarchical set of backplanes. In this simulation architecture each simulator and backplane instance is run in a separate physical process.

In this simulation system a backplane incorporates both a single SDU and a SKU containing exactly one SKP. All simulation control interfaces, such as UCI and LCI, are implemented as socket interfaces carrying typed messages with each message type representing a single link (e.g. activate, complete, ...). The messages are encoded using a byte-oriented encoding scheme that ensures a consistent representation of messages on different physical platforms.

Both VHDL and SystemC simulators have identical architectures each consisting of an application specific static set of SMP, a single SKP controlling all SMP via separate SCI, and a single SDU. Furthermore, both languages support discrete-event simulation and provide slightly differing delta-delay mechanisms for modeling of zero-delay feedback loops. Moreover, inherent to both languages is the concept of a *resolution function* which defines data-flow behavior for multiple SDI sources (each associated with a different SMP) driving a single SDI sink. In HSM resolution can be modeled as a static data-flow network based on untimed SMP. However, the concept of data-flow must be altered to support triggering of SMP execution on partially defined input vectors; this can be achieved by appropriate activation rules.

5 CONCLUSION

This paper presented a newly developed abstract simulation model for mixed-language hardware simulation. Based upon this model the simulation semantics of both language specific simulation systems and composed systems for mixed-language simulation can be formally defined. Formalization is based on the notion of an abstract simulation that incorporates definitions of hierarchical simulation architecture, simulation data, simulation control interface, simulation time, and domain-specific adaptive scheduling. The model was verified by a prototype of a mixed-language simulation system for the languages VHDL and SystemC.

Future work will focus on the refinement of both the described mixed-language hardware simulation system and the model. The latter will be extended by a continuous simulation timing model and in addition will be further formalized using process algebraic notation.

ACKNOWLEDGEMENTS

This work was funded by Infineon Technologies Munich, CPD DAT ADM. For their ongoing support I would like to thank the responsible managers Dr. Mrva and Dr. Ecker. Furthermore, I am indebted to Thomas Schneider (Darmstadt University of Technology), Alan Southall (Siemens, Corporate R&D), Jochen Mades (Infineon Technologies, Corporate R&D), and Stefan Schulz (University of Arizona) for valuable comments and contributions to this work.

REFERENCES

Börger, E.; U. Glässer; and W. Müller. 1994. "The Semantics of Behavioral VHDL'93 Descriptions." In *Proceedings of the European Design Automation Conference EURO-DAC* (Grenoble, Sept. 19-23). IEEE CS Press, 500-505.

Buck, J.; S. Ha; E. A. Lee; and D.G. Messerschmidt. 1994. "Ptolemy: a Framework for Simulating and Prototyping Heterogeneous Systems." *International Journal of Computer Simulation* (April).

Carriero N. and D. H. Gelernter. 1986. "The S/Net's Linda kernel." *ACM Transactions on Computer Systems*, 4(2), May.

Fiskio-Lasseter, J. 1998. "A Formal Description of Behavioral Verilog Based on Axiomatic Semantics." Technical Report TR-98-04. Department of Computer and Information Science, University of Oregon (Aug.).

Fujimoto, R. M. 1990. "Parallel Discrete Event Simulation." *Communications of the ACM*, Vol. 33, No. 10 (Oct.), 31-53.

Gelernter, D. H. 1985. "Generative communication in Linda." *ACM Transactions on Programming Languages and Systems*, 7(1), January.

Gurevich, Y. 1993. "Evolving Algebras 1993: Lipari Guide." In *Specification and Validation Methods*, E. Börger, editor. Oxford University Press, 9-36.

Institute of Electrical and Electronics Engineers (IEEE), Inc. 1993. *VHDL Language Reference Manual.* IEEE Standard 1076-1993. IEEE Press, Los Alamitos, CA.

Institute of Electrical and Electronics Engineers (IEEE), Inc. 1996. *Standard Hardware Description Language Based on the Verilog Hardware Description Language.* IEEE Standard 1364-1995. IEEE Press, Los Alamitos, CA.

Institute of Electrical and Electronics Engineers (IEEE), Inc. 1999. *IEEE Standard VHDL Analog and Mixed-Signal Extensions.* IEEE Standard 1076.1-1999. IEEE Press, Los Alamitos, CA.

Jerraya, A. 1998. "Multilanguage Specification for System Design". In *System-level Synthesis* (NATO ASI), A. Jerraya and J. Mermet, eds. Kluwer Academic Publishers.

Jerraya, A. and R. Ernst. 1999. "Multi-language System Design." In *Proceedings of the Conference on Design, Automation and Test in Europe* (Munich, Germany, March 9-12). IEEE CS Press, 696-699.

Lee, E.A. and A. Sangiovanni-Vincentelli. 1996. "Comparing Models of Computation." In *Proceedings of the Conference of Computer Aided Design ICCAD* (San Jose, CA, Nov. 10-14).

Lin, Y. and P. A. Fishwick. 1995. "Asynchronous Parallel Discrete Event Simulation." Technical Report TR-95-005. Department of Computer and Information Science, University of Florida.

Minsky, N. H. and J. Leichter. 1994. "Law-Governed Linda Communication Model." Technical Report LCSR-TR-221. Department of Computer Science, Rutgers University, March.

Obilisetty, S. 1999. "Open Model Interface (OMI): A Silent Revolution." Tutorial No. 5 at *International HDL Conference and Exhibition HDLCon.*

Sasaki, H.; K. Mizushima; and T. Saski. 1997. "Semantic Validation of VHDL-AMS by an Abstract State Machine." *In Proceedings of the BMAS'97* (Arlington, VA, October 20-21). 61-68.

Sasaki, H. 1999. "A Formal Semantics for Verilog-VHDL Simulation Interoperability by Abstract State Machine." In *Proceedings of the Conference on Design, Automation and Test in Europe* (Munich, Germany, March 9-12). IEEE CS Press, 353-357.

VIRTUAL PROVING GROUND INTEGRATION

Darrell Bench
U.S. Army Test and Evaluation Command (ATEC)
Developmental Test Command (DTC)
Aberdeen, Maryland 21005-5055
benchd@dtc.army.mil

K.L. Hall
Virtual Proving Ground Integration
Amtec Corporation
Huntsville, Alabama 35816-3429
klhall@amtec-corp.com

S166

KEYWORDS: Testing, Evaluation, Simulation, Integration, Collaboration.

ABSTRACT

Recent trends in the Department of Defense (DOD) have been "downsizing" and "doing more with less". Materiel systems are becoming more complex and more costly; however, the mandate is to minimize development and sustainment (life cycle) cost. To deal with this dilemma, everyone involved in the acquisition process, whether technology developer, Program Executive Officer (PEO), Program Manager (PM), Product Manager, tester or evaluator, has been directed to use modeling and simulation (M&S) to reduce acquisition cycle time and cost.

DOD's Simulation Based Acquisition (SBA) envisions all participants in the process being linked through a common, computer-based, collaborative environment. A family of models of the systems being developed, and of the environments in which the system is intended to operate will be created to more efficiently develop and analyze alternatives. Testing will be expanded to include immersing system models into complex synthetic battlefield-representative environments including the communications between elements of a system of systems. Virtual Proving Ground (VPG) is the U.S. Army Test and Evaluation Command (ATEC), Developmental Test Command's (DTC's) implementation of SBA and SMART initiatives.

INTRODUCTION

The SBA and the Army's Simulation and Modeling for Acquisition, Requirements and Training (SMART) concepts dramatically change the roles of testers and evaluators. They are being asked to predict performance of systems based on a balanced test program using models and simulations with reduced amounts of live testing. Testers are working with the "evaluator" to validate models and simulations. The testers are using simulations to optimize the planning, conduct, and reporting of "live" tests. These models and simulations are also used to generate performance data beyond the test envelope.

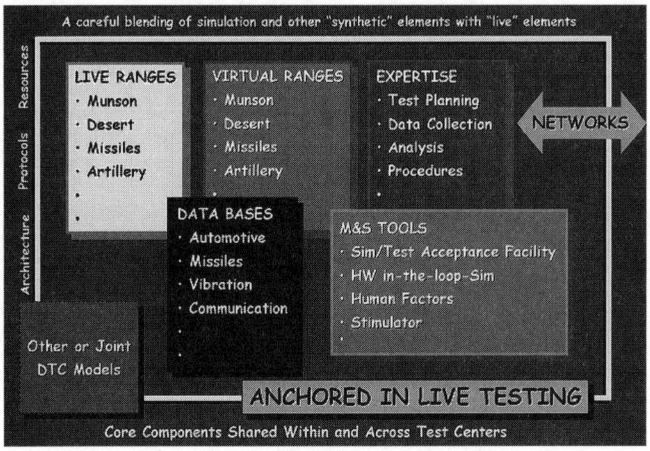

Figure 1 – Virtual Proving Ground Concept

VPG is a supplement to the T&E mission previously performed by the DTC Test Centers. Test Centers (TCs) will continue to test as they have in the past; however, VPG will permit the TCs to provide more and better test results with reduced testing as compared to the past. The result will be more responsive customer support, at reduced cost, with fewer test units. VPG will consist of conventional M&S/T&E facilities with supporting tools as shown in Figure 1.

These supporting tools include virtual environments, databases from previous simulations and tests, common simulation objects (for reuse in M&S); common architectures (for sharing data, between users/facilities), common protocols (so shared data can be understood), common interfaces (to support distributed simulation), and units under test (hardware/software). VPG will be used to develop the right mix of simulation and live testing to ensure effective and efficient support for materiel systems over the entire life cycle.

Why VPG?

DoD and Army direction is toward an Acquisition Process in which DoD and Industry are enabled by robust, collaborative use of simulation technology across all acquisition phases and programs.

VPG is DTC's response to this direction.

VPG Consists Of:

- Conventional & HWIL test facilities
- Models and Simulations
- Virtual Environments
- Databases
- Data elements from previous simulations and tests
- Common objects (for reuse in models and simulations)
- Common architectures (for sharing data between users/facilities)
- Common protocols (so shared data can be efficiently utilized and understood)
- Common interfaces (so tools and models can be "plug-and-play")
- Hardware/software (units under test)

Why VPG Integration?

- To encourage sharing of knowledge and resources among DTC Test Centers, the T&E community, and the larger modeling and simulation community
- To facilitate multi-test center operations where feasible
- To enable DTC to provide more efficient and effective developmental test support to the Army
- To develop common VPG tools for use across DTC and the DoD community.

Who Will Benefit?

Both the test community and the customer.

Benefits for the tester:

- Perform the test mission with fewer test items (more cost effective)
- Increased understanding of simulation technology and the insight it provides for understanding units under test and analyzing test results
- Supports "safety" and "environmental" assessments with minimum risk to personnel and property
- Minimizes "false starts" (supports pre-test rehearsal)
- Facilitates the "prediction" of test results
- More confidence in test data (verified by simulation)
- Quick look analysis to validate successful data collection from a test event

Benefits for the customer:

- Fewer test items required to evaluate system performance
- Increased understanding of test item performance across the full range of expected operational conditions
- Reduces overall acquisition cost
- Reduces test time (schedule)
- Test results utilized to validate models and simulations
- Powerful tool for data analysis and trouble shooting
- Improved data requirements generation
- Improved test support across total life cycle of materiel system (cradle to grave)

VPG FOCUS

VPG responds to three high-level needs within the Developmental Test and Simulation communities. These overarching needs drive all major goals and objectives. The needs are:

Warfighter

The need to support emerging warfighting concepts as defined by DOD.

New Weapon Systems

The need for improved infrastructure capabilities to support the testing of current and advanced weapon systems over their full performance envelope.

SMART/SBA/STEP

The need to support Acquisition Reform, including increased use of Modeling and Simulation (M&S) along with the **S**imulation and **M**odeling for **A**cquisition, **R**equirements and **T**raining **(SMART)**, Simulation **B**ased **A**cquisition (**SBA**) and **S**imulation, **T**est and **E**valuate **P**rocess (**STEP**) initiatives of the U.S. Army and the Office of the Secretary of Defense (OSD).

TEST CAPABILITIES DESCRIPTION

The focus of the VPG is on DTC Test Centers, Facilities, Simulations, and the Plan to expand their capabilities while simultaneously reducing their support costs. To address these challenges, the test capabilities deployed by the VPG will include:

- Cost-Effective Interoperability between simulation capabilities and Range test resources, across all phases of the acquisition process, and between DTC test center resources and system under test resources and,
- To Provide Cost-Effective Development and Maintenance of Simulation Systems for support or Testing and Training and the SBA process.

VPG will provide the design, development, and operational validation of these two integrated test capabilities. Together, these capabilities foster interoperability, reuse, and efficiency between cooperating DTC Test Centers or Ranges, Facilities, and Simulations. Interoperability is defined as the ability to allow the resources of one facility to interface with one or more other facilities as seamlessly as if they were an integral part of their organic systems. Reuse is the ability to use the same products at multiple facilities. Effective reuse is an optimization of commonality and flexibility that recognizes the unique requirements of individual facilities within a common core environment or domain. Reuse enables significant savings in long-term development and maintenance costs and is an effective and efficient path to sharing and interoperability. Interoperability presupposes underlying communication capability and operational coordination appropriate to the type of resources involved. The synergism among capabilities will permit effective testing of new and enhanced weapons systems and has the potential to vastly improve the scope and fidelity of army wide combined testing and training. The VPG will work within the Army to transition the VPG products to organic support and to promulgate the capabilities throughout the DoD Modeling and Simulation community.

VPG provides Virtual Ranges and Test Capabilities to customers for their use early in system design and development, and across the total life cycle (cradle-to-grave).

All acquisition programs that use DTC test Ranges, Facilities, and Simulations will benefit from these new capabilities. All programs and users will benefit, however, not every potential user may need all aspects of these capabilities or require them simultaneously. An incremental development approach will be used both to reduce risk and to introduce the most cost-effective functions as early as possible.

PROVIDE COST-EFFECTIVE INTEROPERABILITY

VPG products will provide interoperability so that disparate resources can be integrated to support the objectives of a specific test mission or exercise. The complete span of interoperability solutions will allow more efficient testing of new, more advanced and interoperable weapons. Moreover, VPG products will enable exchange of information with tactical systems and directly support emerging warfare initiatives.

VPG will provide cost-effective interoperability:

- ***Between Range Test Resources*** Interoperability between range test resources will allow sharing data and control information among Range instrumentation and other Ranges (DTC Test Centers) test resource categories (e.g., a range with a hardware-in-the-loop laboratory or a range with a simulation). This capability will allow expansion of the test environment (land, air, space area) as well as adding participants (either live, virtual, or constructive) to increase mission realism or access to specialized range test resources to avoid duplication of instrumentation investments. In addition, interoperability between test resources will enable specialized, transportable instrumentation to be capable of being cost-effectively deployed to many ranges, i.e., instrumentation reusability among ranges.

- ***Across All Phases of the Acquisition Process*** Interoperability across phases of the acquisition process will allow DTC Ranges to support SMART, SBA, and STEP. These concepts are designed to reduce costs and increase the reliability of weapon systems by applying successful commercial practices. Cost of testing is reduced because investments in simulations in earlier acquisition phases can be leveraged, rather than duplicated, in later stages. Reliability is increased because of the iterative approach inherent to SMART, SBA, and STEP, where results from field tests are incorporated back into models, in a "model-test-model" paradigm. Overall cost of acquisition is reduced because system evaluators can merge information from multiple acquisition phases, maximizing insight to system performance. In addition evaluators can use simulations to complement and replicate testing wherever possible for critical and one of a kind prototypes.

- ***Between DTC Test Center Resources and System Under Test Resources*** Interoperability between test center resources and system under test (SUT) C4ISR resources will allow DTC test ranges to better test integrated weapon systems and new warfighting doctrine. With a battle management perspective, test engineers will be able to extract pertinent tactical information to better understand performance of not only a system under test but also a suite of systems under test (or a System of Systems). Furthermore, test engineers will employ test resources as surrogates of tactical systems (e.g., a range radar, serving as a tactical radar, cueing a system under test), enabling cost-effective "system of systems" testing to conduct sensor-to-shooter timeline assessments.

Large-scale live tests and exercises are constrained by environmental concerns, geographical limitations, safety regulations, and treaty restrictions. For example, deployment of test equipment, participants, and support resources for a major operational test exercise typically has a severe environmental impact. Use of models and simulations can innocuously expand the size of a small live event and provide the necessary insight without the large quantities of resources required to support large exercises. Cost-effective interoperability will provide the necessary infrastructure so complex test missions can be conducted, saving time, cost, and risk to acquisition program managers. A complex test mission involves either integrating capabilities from different test resource categories or linking multiple, geographically dispersed resources together or both, to support the test requirements of an acquisition program.

COST-EFFECTIVE SUPPORT TO T&E AND SBA PROCESS

Cost Effective Development and Maintenance will take advantage of commercially proven practices which rely on a common, but flexible architecture across multiple systems sharing many similar characteristics. The architecture will be used as a baseline for software building blocks that can be assembled into multiple instrumentation systems, while still allowing for unique single system needs. High percentages of each system will be built from these basic building blocks, avoiding the need to develop and maintain millions of additional lines of software across DTC Test Centers. Standards for hardware will promote easy interfacing to multiple systems and effective acquisition strategies for commonly used equipment. Integrated processes for development of simulation systems will allow multiple developers, both government and commercial, to offer different solutions to common requirements with confidence that their offerings will be applicable to a large market of systems adhering to the architecture and standards.

Anticipated Operational Support Concepts Three key Operational Support Concepts describe how the Cost-Effective Interoperability and the Cost-Effective Development and Maintenance capabilities will be employed. These three Operational Support Concepts are:

- Virtual Testing
- A Cooperative Methodology for Supporting DTC Test Centers and Resources
- Continuous Insight Throughout the Acquisition Process

The Virtual Test concept represents the primary user's (i.e., range user's) perspective of utilizing VPG products, to support cost-effective development strategies. The Cooperative Methodology for Supporting DTC Test Centers and Resources forms the basis for building the systems which can assemble DTC Virtual Ranges appropriate for supporting customer needs. Continuous Insight specifically addresses program support and implementing SMART, SBA, and STEP.

TECHNICAL APPROACH

DTC test centers are jointly developing the VPG. Even though their test commodities are diverse, there is considerable commonality or potential for commonality in test processes and procedures. Each test center contributes unique experience, knowledge and capabilities for testing in specific commodity areas to VPG development. DTC will leverage this expertise by designating specific test centers to be the lead, with other test centers providing support, for developing a particular capability horizontally across the command. Spiral development techniques will be used to continually improve VPG capabilities for the next ten or more years.

The overall approach is based upon a Systems Engineering (mixed with common sense) approach to the development of the underlying Technical Architecture to support the Virtual Proving Ground. The overarching philosophy used throughout this approach is one of balancing a rigorous Systems Engineering approach to system development with a build-prototype-fix-evolve process.

Thus VPG integration is being carefully planned using the DoD Joint Technical Architecture as a model foundation. Operational requirements are collected, converted to system requirements, and to technical requirements. From the system and technical requirements a definition of the VPG blueprint is developed followed by an inventory of current VPG capabilities and resources. Capabilities/resources remaining to be developed to reach the Objective VPG are derived by removing capabilities and resources covered by current inventory from the blueprint. The VPG Roadmap shown in Figure 2 provides the plan and process to reach the Objective VPG.

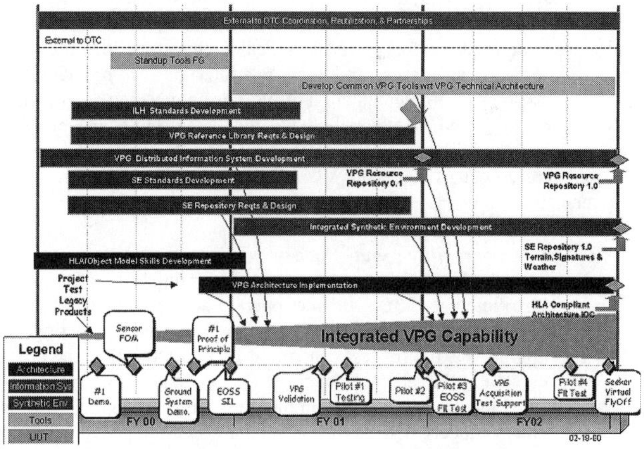

Figure 2 – Virtual Proving Ground Roadmap

The set of operational requirements from the test centers is the motivation and justification for implementation of the capability defined as the VPG end-state. Developing the VPG system requirements for all the test centers into a functional needs inventory enables analysis and discovery of common function opportunities for reuse, areas of commonality, joint development, and generation of cost estimates. The set of technical requirements based upon standards is the basis for compatibility and interoperability within and across the test centers. Generation of a total detailed needs set from the system and technical requirements enables identification of VPG requirements satisfied by the inventoried current capability. The VPG remaining "needs list" results when the items satisfied by the inventory list are removed from the total detailed needs list. The remaining needs list allows prioritization, funding allocation, and assignment of responsibility to test centers.

Objective Integrated VPG

By 2007, DTC will have developed an integrated VPG test capability. The test capability will consist of shared common-use simulations, models, databases, objects, synthetic environments, and architectures connected with standard interfaces and protocols. The VPG will be horizontally integrated across test centers sharing capabilities through common processes, assets, and methodologies. VPG will not only support Developmental Testing (DT) but also Operational Testing (OT), Training and future materiel systems upgrades. The horizontal integration across test centers is facilitated by the efforts of the VPG functional working groups.

An essential element of the Objective VPG is represented by the mature VPG Core Capability which is to evolve in response to the test center needs.

VPG Core Capability

The core capability can be grouped into five functional areas and their related components as follows:

1. Architecture,
2. Integrated Information Systems (Databases/Data Standards),
3. Synthetic Environments,
4. Tools, and
5. Unit Under Test Interface.

Architecture According to the IEEE definition, "Architecture is the structures or components, their relationships, and the principles and guidelines governing their design and evolution over time." The definition for a Technical Architecture used by the Army is "A minimal set of rules governing the arrangement, interaction, and interdependence of the parts or elements whose purpose is to ensure that a conformant system satisfies a specified set of requirements. The technical architecture identifies the services, interfaces, standards, and their relationships. It provides the technical guidelines for implementation of systems upon which engineering specifications are based, common building blocks are built, and product lines are developed." Based on these definitions, and the previous work of the Architecture Focus Group, the VPG Architecture is broken into three components:

- ***Interoperability and Reuse*** VPG components will be developed conforming to accepted standards to allow distributed resources to inter-operate across, and within, test centers. A foundation will be implemented consisting of upgraded skills for test center and DTC personnel in the areas of High Level Architecture (HLA) and Object Model development and use. From this foundation of upgraded skills object models will be developed for VPG components within and across the DTC test centers. These object models will be provided for re-use to the DTC community for local/wide area distributed applications. Protocol/Standards translator services will be utilized where proven to add value in achieving interoperability.

- ***Simulation Environment*** An environment to support the seamless development, execution, and analysis of VPG operations will be developed. This will include a basic set of VPG run-time services for distributed applications. Interfaces will be provided to key implementation tools.

- ***Connectivity Standards*** Network connectivity standards are being adopted between Test Centers to support real-time and non-real-time VPG operations. Connectivity between test centers will be based upon the ISO 7 Layer Model.

Multi-level Security The future Test Center local and distributed VPG based tasks are likely to require multi-level security on computer and network elements as well as the integrated test environment. The implementation pace will be strongly influenced by the multi-level technology available from commercial and government sources. Development of a small group of multi-level solutions may be necessary specifically for VPG.

Integrated Information Systems (Data Standards / Databases) Standard data elements are being defined including nomenclatures, item names, and data types. Data interchange formats for files and data are being established. They will also develop a repository of M&S resources linked to DA and DoD repositories.

Common Synthetic Environments A Synthetic Environment (SE) is a representation of natural and man-made environmental influences on a system under test. A representation can be any combination of (virtual) simulations or (physical) stimulators. A system under test can be any combination of models, hardware, humans, etc. The acceptable representation level of detail required is dependent upon the specific test objectives and "testspace". The SE includes the (input) data description of the environment to be represented. DTC expects to evolve into an increasingly important activity in the simulation-based acquisition community by becoming the source of synthetic environment models for use in simulations, validated with "ground truth" data. The VPG Synthetic Environment will Include both natural and tactical environments, integrate from engineering level subsystem models to aggregate system of systems simulations, provide robust synthetic environment for all commodity areas, and allow total immersion of a system-under-test into the synthetic environment. VPG will maximum use of existing and emerging synthetic environment resources. The objective of the Synthetic Environment Focus Group (SEFG) is to identify and develop a core set of synthetic environments requirements in eight primary areas that are applicable across DT:

SE Control Most of the test centers have SE control requirements for a variety of environments. These requirements may or may not be applicable for use by all test centers, thus the goal is to identify those characteristics that might be common across all or multiple test centers. SE control includes, but is not limited to, specifics such as:

- Standards for SE interface and data representation
- Operational protocols (for linking heterogeneous simulations / live hardware for time synchronization, prioritization, etc. as required for test setup, control, and after action review)
- Heterogeneous model integration

Digital Terrain All of the test centers have digital terrain requirements for a variety of environments. These requirements may or may not be applicable for use by all test centers, thus the goal is to identify those characteristics that might be common across all or multiple test centers. Digital terrain includes, but is not limited to, specifics such as:

- Cultural details: Buildings, power lines, detailed like data
- Thematic data: soils, roads, hydrology, geology, buildings, bridges
- Terrain elevation changes: Digital elevation maps, material class maps, material properties, vegetation height maps, cultural features, 3D
- Vegetation: Foliage, complex conductivity
- Detailed test site characterization

- Temperatures: Cloud interactions, soil types at given times of day, year, or month
- Solar radiation
- The ability to deform geometry of terrain (soil / tire interaction)

Weather / Meteorology All test centers have weather / meteorology requirements for a variety of environments. These requirements may or may not be applicable for use by all test centers, thus the goal is to identify those characteristics that might be common across all or multiple test centers. Weather includes, but is not limited to, specifics such as:

- Ability to get in the model and pull some data out, to run real data during a test and pull it out, for transport and diffusion
- High resolution wind profiler
- Historic climatic data at specific locations
- Meteorological database: Clouds, weather conditions (rain, sun, sleet), wind
- Effects on EO, IR, acoustics, MMW images and transmission, on obscurants and countermeasures
- Flight dynamics modeling, EO, MMW propagation, atmospheric effects, icing
- Transport/Diffusion of chem/bio (clouds)

Propagation All of the test centers have propagation requirements for a variety of environments. These requirements may or may not be applicable for use by all test centers, thus the goal is to identify those characteristics that might be common across all or multiple test centers. Propagation includes, but is not limited to, specifics such as:

- Electro-magnetic ranging from millimeter wave up to infrared
- Co-site interference (with antennas or emitters radiating so close together that they couple into one another)
- Electro-optic including visible and IR
- Acoustic

Signatures All of the test centers have signature requirements for a variety of environments. The goal is to identify those characteristics that might be common across all or multiple test centers. Signatures includes, but is not limited to, specifics such as:

- Battlespace interference, EM/message
- Missile flight IR/EO targets, EMP, E3, laser, nuclear, MMW
- IR/UV (backgrounds - urban and battlefield, vegetation, chem/bio agents)
- Real chem/bio signatures
- Low frequency SAR, hyperspectral
- Photographic imagery
- Acoustics, targets, humans, cultural, countermeasures, terrain
- Real-time scene generation and projection

Platform Dynamics / Induced Disturbances All test centers have platform dynamics requirements for a variety of environments. The goal is to identify those characteristics that might be common across all or multiple test centers. Platform Dynamics / Induced Distrubances includes, but is not limited to:

- Vibration and shock
- Flight dynamics models
- Nuclear blast effects
- Storage effects

Battlespace Environment Most of the test centers have battlespace environment requirements. These requirements may or may not be applicable for use by all test centers, thus the goal is to identify those characteristics that might be common across all or multiple test centers. Battlespace environments includes, but is not limited to, specifics such as:

- Capturing analytical level data/models into battlefield simulations
- Live/Virtual integration
- Dynamic C4I scenario generation
- IEW dynamic modeling

Stimulators Most of the test centers have stimulator requirements for a variety of environments. These requirements may or may not be applicable for use by all test centers, thus the goal is to identify those characteristics that might be common across all or multiple test centers. Stimulators includes, but is not limited to, specifics such as:

- Ability to provide a bi-directional link from the virtual to the live world
- Ability to 'project' the synthetic environment into the live hardware

VPG Tools The VPG Tools functional area component is concerned with the development of modeling and simulation tools to assist in the three phases of testing within the VPG: Test Planning and Setup, Test Execution, and Test Analysis and Reporting.

Test Planning and Support Tools to assist the VPG tester in pre-test functions include:

- Test planning and optimization,
- Scenario development,
- Test rehearsal,
- Route planning,
- Instrumentation laydown,
- Test data requirements and tracability,
- Tools to support Cost as an Independent Variable, and
- Verification, validation, and accreditation support tools.

Test Execution Tools to assist the VPG tester in test execution functions include:

- Test conduct,
- Distributed test control,
- Data collection and reduction,
- Safety analysis and prediction, and
- Test visualization tool.

Post-Test Analysis and Reporting Tools to assist the VPG tester in post-test analysis and reporting include:

- Automated report generators,
- Simulation based analysis tools, and
- Test playback 'After Action Review' tools.

Unit Under Test Interface The interfacing of the Unit Under Test will apply the Interface Control Document approach to assure integration of the VPG components and the UUT. DTC must acquire not only the models but also the hardware, software, and expertise required to integrate the models within the VPG and operate them during tests conducted in VPG.

Unit Under Test Hardware/Software Hardware and software along with combinations of the two will be combined with the models of subsystems and processes not available or found advantageous to model to provide system level test environments. Varying mixes of models, hardware, and software will allow collaborative test environment to be available from early concept to retirement of a system and will provide the means for all involved with the system to work together locally or from remote sites.

All Digital UUT Models The unit under test models are detailed digital simulations of the real systems under test constructed or modified in such a manner as to be interoperable with the other VPG functional components. These models are usually developed by a non-DTC entity (prime contractor, Research, Development and Engineering Center (RDEC), Army Research Laboratory (ARL), etc.).

Examples of planned UUT components are:

- Computer aided design solid models,
- Mechanical analysis tools,
- Electromagnetic analysis tools,
- Thermal analysis tools,
- Mobility models,
- Antenna models,
- Survivability/Lethality models,
- Reliability, availability, and maintainability models,
- Human factors engineering models,
- Environmental effects models/databases, and
- Aging effects models/databases.

VPG INTEGRATION STRATEGY

The strategy for achieving an integrated VPG as represented in Figure 3 is based on a spiral development process which balances between the Focus Group lead technology integration efforts and the customer requirements. VPG Integration will be implemented in incremental builds of an

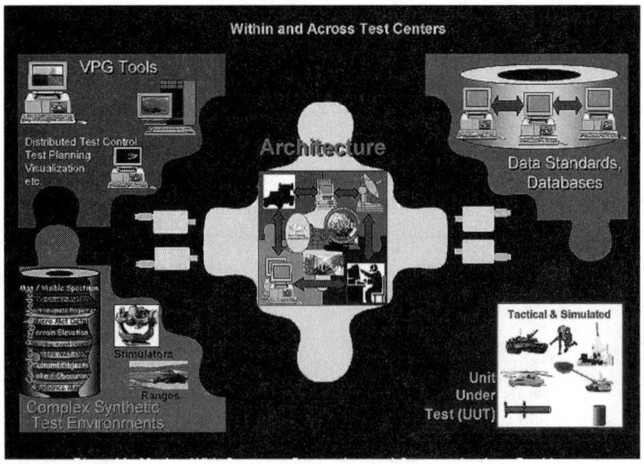

Figure 3 – Overall Integrated Virtual Proving Ground

Integrated VPG: accomplished through the execution of pilot projects which will be conducted in support of Commodity Product Managers to develop, improve and validate the VPG tools, synthetic environments, and architecture. Lessons learned will be promulgated throughout the VPG community and utilized to improve processes for future projects. To facilitate this process, the individual Focus Groups (Synthetic Environments, Architecture, Data Bases, and Tools) and DTC Test Centers will develop their own related Roadmaps coordinated with each other to implement the Master VPG Roadmap.

VPG Integration Planned To Be A Series Of Builds

A series of integration events will occur between FY00 and FY07 to accomplish the Integrated VPG Initial Operational Capability. These events will consist of VPG core component development, integration element development, pilot project application and execution.

Pilot Projects

Pilot projects will be conducted in support of Commodity Product Managers to develop, improve and validate the VPG tools, synthetic environments, and architecture. Lessons learned will be promulgated throughout the VPG community and utilized to improve processes for future projects. To facilitate this process, the individual Focus Groups (Synthetic Environments, Architecture, and Data Bases) and DTC Test Centers will integrate pilot project activities within their roadmaps.

SUMMARY

Several factors have converged to make implementation of a new modeling and simulation based approach to test and evaluation an urgent activity. These factors are summarized by strong emphasis upon each new or improved product being developed with reduced funds, a shorter development time, improved performance, increased reliability, and supported with a significantly reduced government staff. Modeling and simulation (M&S) has proven to provide excellent results when testing is planned to allow adequate verification, validation, and accreditation (VV&A). Proper implementation of VPG will apply the strong leverage of M&S to the total development process. This in turn will allow the product development/improvement process to meet the goals of future product being developed/improved with reduced funds, a shorter development time, improved performance, increased reliability, and supported with a significantly reduced government staff.

The key to developing a comprehensive simulation based test capability in a cost effective manner, is the development of an Integrated VPG. The goal is to develop a common set of tools, synthetic environments and databases (connected through a common set of architectures), for use by all TCs to support a distributed mix of "real" and "simulated" materiel system components for supporting testing and evaluation. VPG is being developed through an incremental engineering approach, using developmental and pilot projects, to develop, improve and validate VPG tools, synthetic environments, and architecture. VPG will make DTC tools and synthetic ranges/ facilities available to the entire acquisition community (including private industry).

VPG Integration is well underway with promising results. The Keys to this success (and continued success) are:

- Centralized VPG vision across the Command
- Focused "top-down" management
- Empowered Program Manager and strong support team
- Involvement of management and workforce at each test center
- Requirements driven (vs. solution pull) development process
- Communication with and partnership with customer base
- Understanding and meeting customer needs
- Every player is a "winner" (win-win situation)

VPG is a winning strategy that will help DTC implement innovative, effective, and efficient test processes, procedures, and capabilities to support integrated M&S/T&E across the total life-cycle of Army materiel systems.

Implementation and Evaluation of a Distributed Interactive Simulation Architecture for Group Interaction and Coordination: A Case Study in Interference Detection and Resolution in Naval Radar Units *

K. SRINIVASAN, S. RAMASWAMY

Software Automation and Intelligence Laboratory, Department of Computer Science and Center for Manufacturing Research

Tennessee Technological University, Cookeville TN 38505. Phone: (931)-372-3448 Email: srini@acm.org / srini@ieee.org

Abstract: In last year's conference, a two-level architecture for the implementation of a distributed simulation environment for interference detection and frequency assignment in naval radar units [1]. In this paper, we present the current implementation and results obtained and the performance analysis of each of the three algorithms namely locally autonomous, master-slave and negotiation based algorithms for interference resolution. The locally autonomous algorithm is designed to be useful in totally chaotic conditions, while the master-slave algorithm is designed to be useful in deterministic situations. The negotiation-based approach is designed as a suitable alternative for situations that fall in between these extremes.

I. Introduction

At last year's conference, we presented a paper describing a two-level architecture for the implementation of a distributed simulation environment for interference detection and frequency assignment in naval radar units [1]. The Java-based distributed interactive simulation was designed as a two level architecture incorporating *i)* multiple radars on each ship controlled through a lower-level intra-ship interference control module and, *ii)* multiple ships in a group coordinated through a higher-level interference control module. This is shown in Figure 1. Each ship's interference detection and control mechanism would be composed of these two separate levels, called a control agent, dynamically coordinating with one another in eliminating interference problems. In addition, the control agent is a multi-threaded architecture that incorporates the maintenance of a distributed data base system that contains periodically updated radar information. In that paper, we presented a two-level distributed interactive simulation architecture for the interference resolution.

As stated in [1], the approach had the following advantages to enhance the simulation environment: *i) Intra and Inter Ship Interference:* Interference resolution is *one* of the issues addressed by a control agent that has a two-level architecture, a lower level and a higher level. The lower level resolves the interference problem if the source of interference is within the ship. If the source of interference is not from within the ship, then the lower level passes the responsibility to the higher level. The higher level of the control agent detects the source *(outside)* of interference. If the source is a radar of another ship within the group, it may resolve the interference problem in one of the following modes, viz. Master-Slave, Locally Autonomous, or the Negotiation based mode. *ii) Two-level Architecture:* A two level approach helps in balancing the local goals and the system goals and developing appropriate data structures and encapsulation techniques for addressing such concerns appropriately. Here the local goal of each control agent is to provide interference free operating frequencies to radar units on the ship and the system goal is to provide interference free operating frequencies for all radar units on all the ships within the group. *iii) Group Coordination Strategies:* Using the proposed architecture, it is easy to implement and study algorithms for group coordination. Different coordination and group management (arbitration, election of a group representative, determining group membership eligibility, rescinding / retaining group memberships, etc.) algorithms may be selectively implemented and comparatively evaluated. *iv) Localized Databases*: The two-level structure also incorporates a separate database associated with every control agent. By creating a separate thread of control for coordinating -i.e. report and maintain - database related information to legal group members, the simulation now provides for any individual control agent to assume control whenever it is decided that a group coordinator is no longer available. *v) Generic Test-bed*: The two-level implementation provides a generic test-bed for studying performance issues such as the available reaction time w.r.t. the speed of detection of an interference and its subsequent resolution, estimation of the percentage of false alarms and the consequences of subsequent actions, etc.

Each agent (ship) in the simulation is composed of one or more radars. Hence, interference for a given radar may be due to either of the following three reasons: *i)* another radar in the same ship, *ii)* radar of another ship in the same group, or *iii)* an external interference. AS in [1], in this paper the first two cases are referred to as intra-radar interference and inter-radar interference. The interference problem is resolved by either

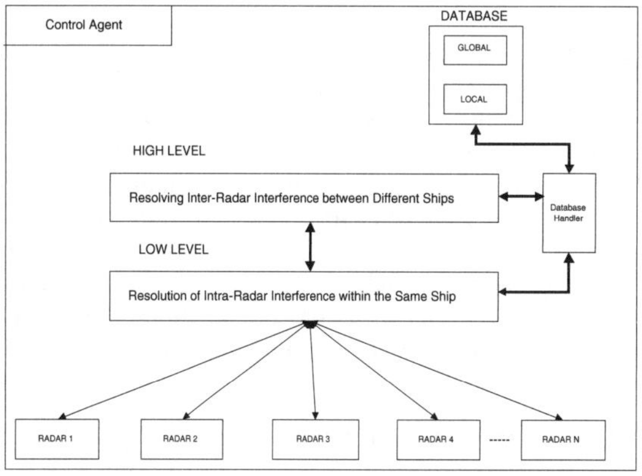

Figure 1. Two-level Control Agent Architecture

* This research is currently being conducted at the Software Automation and Intelligence Laboratory (SAIL) in the Department of Computer Science at Tennessee Technological University and is supported, in part, by grants from the National Science Foundation (#DMI 9896235) and the Center for Manufacturing Research at Tennessee Technological University.

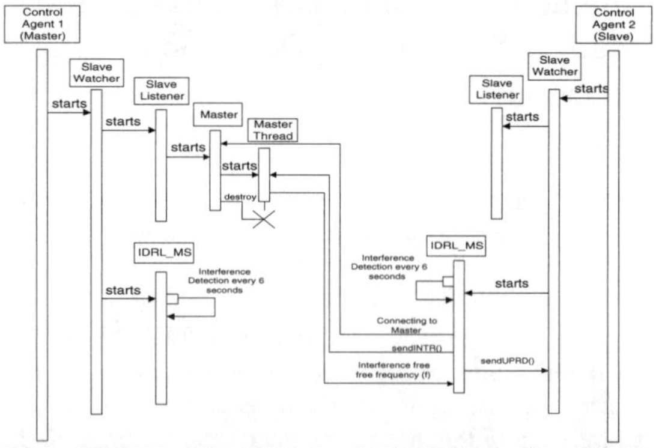

Figure 2. Interaction diagram in the Master-Slave Mode

changing the radar's frequency, bandwidth or position. The desirable alternative is for the interference resolution process to change a radar's frequency.

In this paper, the performance of each approach for interference resolution, viz. Master-Slave, Locally Autonomous, or the Negotiation, is determined by the time taken by each approach to detect, resolve the interference and update the database.

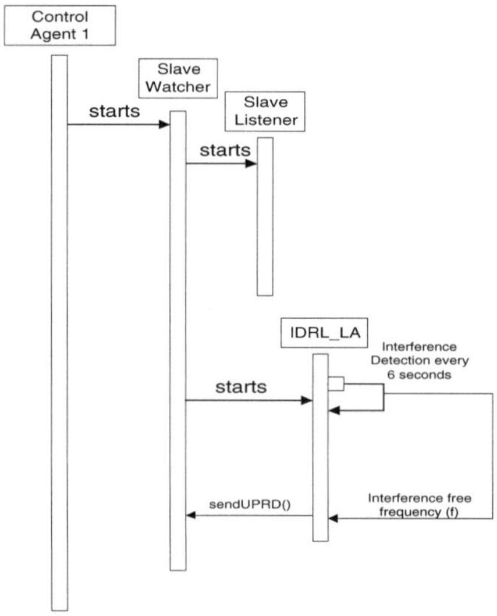

Figure 3. Interaction diagram in the Locally Autonomous Mode

The rest of this paper is organized as follows. The paper is organized as follows: Section II explains as to how each of the three algorithm viz. locally autonomous, master-slave and negotiation-based algorithms are implemented in the two-level software agent. Then each of the algorithms is evaluated based on the time taken by each algorithm to detect and resolve interference under different set of test conditions. Performance evaluation of each of the algorithm is discussed in Section III. Section IV concludes the paper.

II. The Control Agent Architecture

The control agent (ship) can be configured to operate in either of the following modes viz. Locally Autonomous, Master-Slave (Centralized) or Negotiation based modes. The following sections explain elaborately how each of the approaches mentioned above is used to detect and resolve interference using class interaction diagrams.

II. A. Master-Slave Approach

When the control agent is started in the master-slave mode the first ship that starts up becomes the master. The interaction diagram as to how interference is resolved in the master-slave mode is shown in Figure 2. The object initiating the interaction is placed at the left and increasingly more subordinate objects are placed to the right. The events that occur as time progresses are shown in increasing order of time from top to bottom along Y-axis. All the ships that join the group are slaves and the first one remains as their master until and unless it gets destroyed or leaves the group. In that case the ship that joined the group second becomes the new master control agent. This process goes on. The IDRL_MS class takes care of the detection and resolution of the interference problem. This class has two parts *i)* detection and *ii)* resolution. The detection fragment of the thread is active in all the control agents but the resolution fragment of it is active only in the current master. Hence whenever a ship detects an inter-radar interference it contacts the master and informs the master about the source causing the interference. The master randomly generates a new interference free frequency for this ship and sends it. Once the ship updates its radar and ship information in the database it acknowledges to the master. The detection algorithm checks for interference every six seconds. Thus resolution occurs every six seconds if there is interference.

II. B. Locally Autonomous Mode

In the locally autonomous mode each ship is its own master. Whenever it detects an external interference, it switches to a new interference free frequency and updates the database. The main difference between the master-slave and locally autonomous mode is that both fragments of the IDRL_LA class are active in locally autonomous mode. The interaction diagram as to how interference is resolved in the locally autonomous mode is shown in Figure 3. Then it broadcasts the new copy of the database to all the ships in the group. As in the case of the master-slave mode, the detection algorithm checks for interference every six seconds. Thus resolution occurs every six seconds if there is interference.

II. C. Negotiation Mode

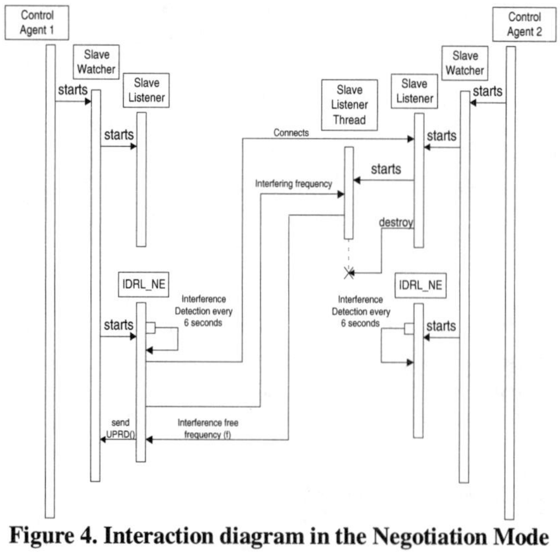

Figure 4. Interaction diagram in the Negotiation Mode

Negotiation is a process in which parties that a have conflict talk to each other in order to resolve the conflict and arrive at a solution that is mutually beneficial. Whenever there is interference between two ships the one that detects the interference first starts negotiating with the ship that is causing the interference. The interfering ship assigns a new interference free frequency to the ship that detected the interference. The ship that detected the interference then switches to this new frequency and updates the radar information in the database and broadcasts the new copy of the

Case IA: All Radar Units with 0.4 MHz Bandwith									
Locally Autonomous Mode									
	Number of Ships in the Group								
Radar/Ship	2	3	4	5	6	7	8	9	10
1	223	236	239	247	268	1234	2698	4556	8067
2	231	238	245	255	271	1943	3756	6706	9143
3	234	240	247	262	1244	2903	4223	7022	9532
4	236	243	248	268	1327	3055	4620	7537	9836
5	236	245	253	270	1521	3114	5210	8240	10057
Master-Slave Mode									
	Number of Ships in the Group								
Radar/Ship	2	3	4	5	6	7	8	9	10
1	342	411	420	423	534	745	921	1138	1169
2	421	421	426	440	576	850	950	1146	1254
3	422	453	470	518	645	778	953	1190	1287
4	427	464	555	579	712	939	1022	1220	1325
5	432	561	565	622	768	989	1085	1240	1381
Negotiation Mode									
	Number of Ships in the Group								
Radar/Ship	2	3	4	5	6	7	8	9	10
1	381	381	390	391	395	398	406	418	421
2	383	385	391	393	398	408	413	427	445
3	386	388	392	413	421	424	430	446	453
4	388	390	400	414	432	438	447	456	464
5	390	391	401	408	425	440	456	461	467

Table 1. All Radar Units with 0.4 MHz Bandwidth

database to all the ships in the group. If two ships detect that they are interfering with each other at the same time, then both of them assign a new interference free frequency to each other. As mentioned in the other modes, the detection algorithm checks for interference every six seconds. Thus resolution occurs every six seconds if there is interference. The interaction diagram of how negotiation occurs between two ships having interference is shown in Figure 4.

Case IC: All Radar Units with 1.2 MHz Bandwidth									
Locally Autonomous Mode									
	Number of Ships in the Group								
Radar/Ship	2	3	4	5	6	7	8	9	10
1	202	213	232	245	279	2508	6063	8106	10075
2	203	215	234	246	290	3352	6797	8402	11468
3	207	218	239	249	1419	4223	7242	8954	12313
4	216	218	244	255	1646	4922	7367	9476	14176
5	221	242	259	279	1819	5384	7962	10030	16021
Master-Slave Mode									
	Number of Ships in the Group								
Radar/Ship	2	3	4	5	6	7	8	9	10
1	346	425	496	513	800	1250	2652	3166	5177
2	403	433	511	547	923	1325	2836	3422	5251
3	417	461	532	556	973	1440	2912	3735	5486
4	418	508	541	591	1028	1976	2998	4091	5544
5	426	511	557	652	1101	2541	3120	4322	5628
Negotiation Mode									
	Number of Ships in the Group								
Radar/Ship	2	3	4	5	6	7	8	9	10
1	382	383	392	396	402	404	416	421	423
2	385	385	390	402	405	407	425	435	454
3	388	389	399	412	413	418	430	448	458
4	389	395	401	417	427	435	443	457	466
5	393	395	399	421	427	440	449	455	469

Table 3. All Radar Units with 1.2 MHz Bandwidth

Initially the control agent starts the SlaveWatcher class, which in turn starts the SlaveListener and the IDRL_NE classes. The SlaveListener class runs in an infinite loop ready to accept client connections. The IDRL_NE class has the interference detection and resolution algorithms in it. This thread again runs in an infinite loop and checks for interference every six seconds. Let us consider the case when control agent 1 detects that it is having interference from control agent 2. It connects to the SlaveListener of control agent 2 and starts negotiation. The SlaveListener starts a new thread SlaveListenerThread in order to negotiate with control agent 1. This way it can accept any number of client connections for negotiation at the same time. Then control agent 1 informs control agent 2 that one of its radar units is interfering and passes the interfering frequency to it. The SlaveListener thread

Case IB: All Radar Units with 0.6 MHz Bandwith									
Locally Autonomous Mode									
	Number of Ships in the Group								
Radar/Ship	2	3	4	5	6	7	8	9	10
1	201	221	230	241	261	2056	5554	7272	10034
2	200	221	233	254	266	3404	5929	7528	11339
3	196	223	237	255	704	4154	6216	8112	12250
4	201	226	238	256	1325	4529	6660	8780	13193
5	218	228	241	259	1418	5233	6948	9776	14356
Master-Slave Mode									
	Number of Ships in the Group								
Radar/Ship	2	3	4	5	6	7	8	9	10
1	347	425	496	513	578	781	907	1118	1278
2	401	433	509	553	608	821	944	1141	1337
3	414	466	531	555	673	867	974	1187	1378
4	414	501	540	595	707	903	1055	1261	1391
5	425	510	556	653	764	922	1092	1278	1421
Negotiation Mode									
	Number of Ships in the Group								
Radar/Ship	2	3	4	5	6	7	8	9	10
1	384	384	391	392	395	398	411	421	421
2	387	385	391	392	397	416	413	437	463
3	389	385	400	403	410	420	436	454	465
4	390	388	401	421	426	433	451	455	466
5	390	390	402	422	433	436	451	460	469

Table 2. All Radar Units with 0.6 MHz Bandwidth

then randomly generates a new interference free frequency and sends it to control agent 1. Control agent 1 switches it's radar to this new frequency, updates the database and propagates the new copy of the database to all the ships in the group.

III. Performance Evaluation

In order to evaluate the performance of each of the three approaches viz. locally autonomous, master-slave and negotiation based approaches, based on the time taken by each of the approaches to detect, resolve the interference and update the database, a test code is plugged individually into each of these modules. The test module that is used is the same for all three modes. It writes the ship name and time into the report file whenever interference is detected and resolved by any of the ships in the group.

Interference is created between ships by manual entry between two or more ships having more than one radar unit on each of them. Whenever interference is detected by any of the ships in the group, the time at which the interference was detected is written into a report file using a file output stream by the test module that is plugged into the code. Similarly the time at which interference is resolved and the database is updated is also logged into the report file.

The following assumptions are experimental assumptions that are made while evaluating the performance of each of the

Case II: Homogeneous Distribution, All radars on same ship have same bandwidth									
0.4 MHz -2 Ships, 0.6 MHz- 2 Ships, 1.2 MHz - 2 Ships, 2.4 MHz - 2 Ships, 5 MHz - 2 Ships									
Locally Autonomous Mode									
	Number of Ships in the Group								
Radar/Ship	2	3	4	5	6	7	8	9	10
1	223	236	239	247	268	1234	2698	4556	8067
2	231	238	245	255	271	1943	3756	6706	9143
3	234	240	247	262	1244	2903	4223	7022	9532
4	236	243	248	268	1327	3055	4620	7537	9836
5	236	245	253	270	1521	3114	5210	8240	10057
Master-Slave Mode									
	Number of Ships in the Group								
Radar/Ship	2	3	4	5	6	7	8	9	10
1	342	411	420	423	534	745	921	1138	1169
2	421	421	426	440	576	850	950	1146	1254
3	422	453	470	518	645	778	953	1190	1287
4	427	464	555	579	712	939	1022	1220	1325
5	432	561	565	622	768	989	1085	1240	1381
Negotiation Mode									
	Number of Ships in the Group								
Radar/Ship	2	3	4	5	6	7	8	9	10
1	381	381	390	391	395	398	406	418	421
2	383	385	391	393	398	408	413	427	445
3	386	388	392	413	421	424	430	446	453
4	388	390	400	414	432	438	447	456	464
5	390	391	401	408	425	440	456	461	467

Table 4. Radar Units within the ship with Same Bandwidth

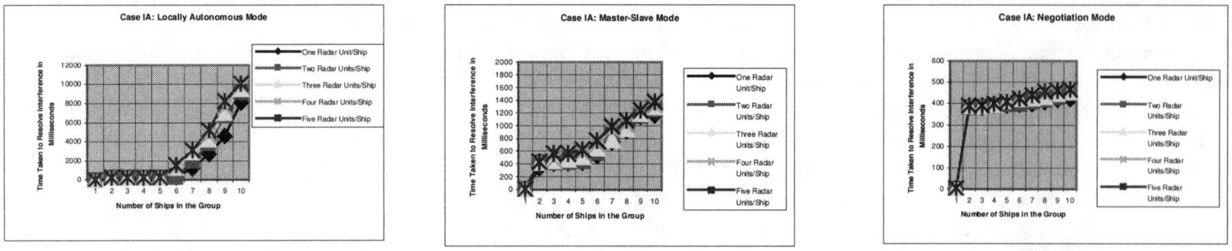

Locally Autonomous | Master-Slave | Negotiation

Figure 5. Performance Plots for Case IA

above-mentioned approaches:

- All radar units in all the ships in the group have the same receiver threshold power of –70 dB.
- All radar units in every ship in the group have the same peak transmitting power and threshold.
- In all the test cases the moderate ducting factor is used while calculating the propagation factor

III. A. *Case I*

This case involves three sub-cases: Case IA - where all radar units have 0.4 MHz bandwidths, Case IB - where all radar units have 0.6 MHz bandwidhs, and Case IC - where all radar units have 1.2 MHz bandwidths. Table 1 provides the observed performance data for Case IA, while Figure 5 plots the performance data. Similarly, Table 2 and Table 3 provide the observed performance data for Cases IB and IC, while Figure 6 plots their respective performance data. The frequency range is 1300 MHz to 1400 MHz for cases IA and IB while the frequency range for case IC is 1300 MHz to 1450 MHz. In each of the above three cases all radar units in every ship have the same bandwidth. This way the performance of the three algorithms can be evaluated with the bandwidth remaining invariant.

Interference is created between ships and the time taken to resolve interference is calculated in the above three cases using each of the three algorithms viz. locally autonomous, master-slave and negotiation-based algorithms.

It can be evidently noticed from the tables and plots

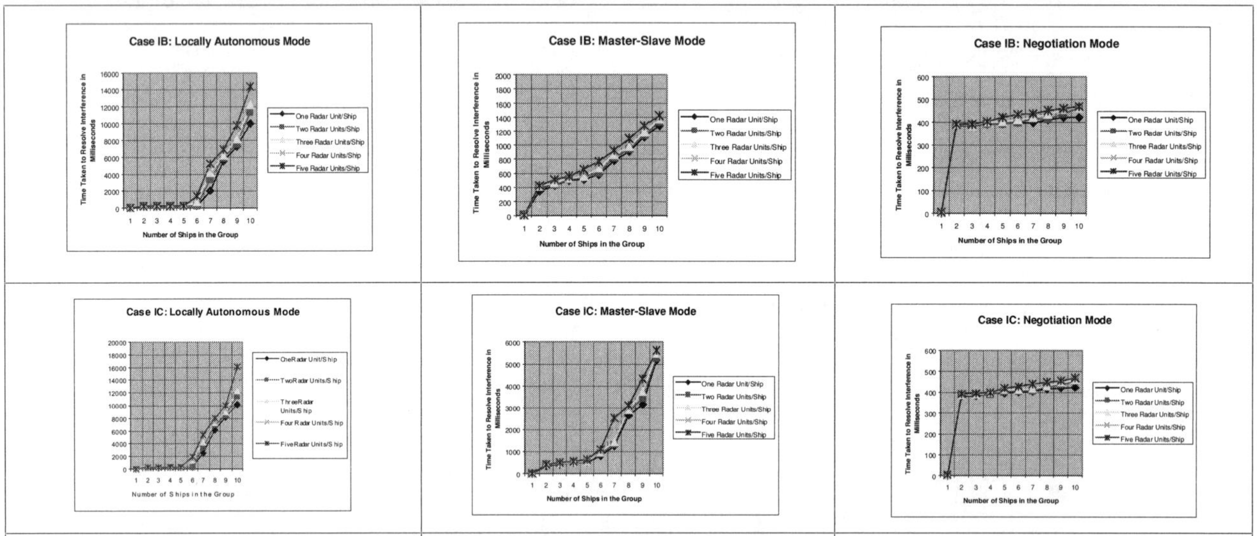

Locally Autonomous	Master-Slave	Negotiation

Figure 6. Performance Plots for Case IB and IC

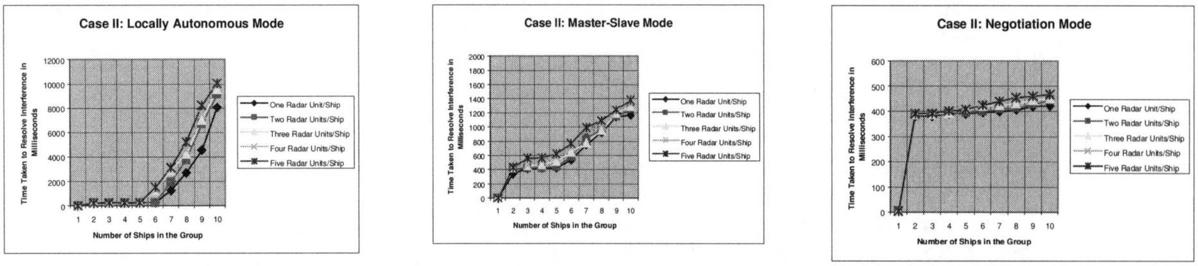

Locally Autonomous | Master-Slave | Negotiation

Figure 7. Performance Plots for Case II - Heterogeneous Ships, Homogeneous Radar Units

that the negotiation based approach for detecting and resolving interference is much more efficient compared to the master-slave and locally autonomous based approaches for Case I.

III. B. Case II

Case III: Heterogeneous Distribution, All Radar Units on same Ship have Different Bandwidths									
0.4 MHz, 0.6 MHz, 1.2 MHz, 2.4 MHz, 5 MHz - Radar Units in Each Ship									
Locally Autonomous Mode									
	Number of Ships in the Group								
Radar/Ship	**2**	**3**	**4**	**5**	**6**	**7**	**8**	**9**	**10**
1	213	215	225	245	265	2418	6555	8098	10067
2	215	217	239	252	560	3444	7142	8378	11241
3	216	218	248	258	1418	4334	7581	8776	12148
4	217	224	256	262	1749	5665	7717	9005	15078
5	221	238	260	278	1964	6282	7937	9882	16090
Master-Slave Mode									
	Number of Ships in the Group								
Radar/Ship	**2**	**3**	**4**	**5**	**6**	**7**	**8**	**9**	**10**
1	355	416	482	516	991	1204	2155	3166	5177
2	395	430	502	552	1004	1295	2394	3422	5276
3	415	452	523	560	1043	1395	2588	3735	5533
4	417	497	529	590	1106	1866	2764	4091	5615
5	425	514	545	642	1164	2393	2916	4322	5735
Negotiation Mode									
	Number of Ships in the Group								
Radar/Ship	**2**	**3**	**4**	**5**	**6**	**7**	**8**	**9**	**10**
1	383	384	394	403	410	418	431	443	446
2	382	386	402	407	413	420	429	453	455
3	394	398	403	418	418	427	441	458	458
4	396	399	404	423	432	446	442	465	471
5	397	400	408	429	434	446	449	467	475

Table 5. Radar Units within the ship with same bandwidth

In this case, all radar units in every ship have the same peak power and threshold. In order to study the effectiveness of the three chosen algorithms in a heterogeneous environment, radar units with different bandwidths are used for each ship. That is, while all radar units within the ship have the same bandwidth, radar units in other ships have other bandwidths. For example, all units on Ship1 may have a bandwidth of 0.4 MHz, while all units on another ship, Ship2, may have a bandwidth of 1.2 MHz.

The bandwidths of radar units in the ten ships is as follows: 0.4 MHz –two ships, 0.6 MHz-two ships, 1.2 MHz – two ships and 5 MHz-two ships. The chosen frequency range for this case was 1300 MHz to 1530 MHz. As in case I, interference is created between radar units in different ships and the time taken to detect and resolve interference is calculated using each of the three algorithms.

III. C. Case III

In this case, each ship has radar units with different bandwidths. The bandwidth of the five radar units in each of the ten ships is as follows: 0.4, 0.6, 1.2, 2.4, 5 MHz respectively. The frequency range for this case is 1300 MHz to 1450 MHz. In order the study the effectiveness of the three algorithms in a heterogeneous environment, radar units with different bandwidths are used in used in a single ship. Thus each ship has five radar units of the same kind with five different bandwidths. Interference is created between ships and the time taken to resolve interference is determined using each of the three algorithms and plots are made with the results obtained.

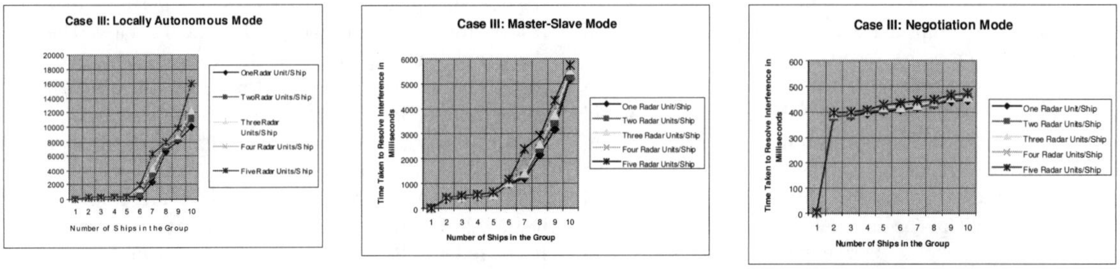

Locally Autonomous Master-Slave Negotiation

Figure 8. Performance Plots for Case III - Homogeneous Ships, Heterogeneous Radar Units

Cases I-III are used in order to obtain the performance and effectiveness of the algorithms. Here by performance we mean the time taken by the algorithm to detect, resolve and update the database when there is interference between radar units.

Case IVA: Overloading, All Radar Units with 2.4 MHz Bandwidth									
Locally Autonomous Mode									
	Number of Ships in the Group								
Radar/Ship	**2**	**3**	**4**	**5**	**6**	**7**	**8**	**9**	**10**
1	221	223	344	712	2110	8191	16233		
2	217	225	379	1065	3230	8756	17425		
3	198	216	423	1163	4745	9178			
4	195	245	512	244	6771	10163			
5	230	234	620	1450	7189	12578			
Master-Slave Mode									
	Number of Ships in the Group								
Radar/Ship	**2**	**3**	**4**	**5**	**6**	**7**	**8**	**9**	**10**
1	350	445	481	640	843	1517	2320		
2	355	411	537	656	975	1628	2651		
3	367	424	528	750	1056	1777			
4	344	450	585	789	1178	1845			
5	410	466	633	810	1221	1978			
Negotiation Mode									
	Number of Ships in the Group								
Radar/Ship	**2**	**3**	**4**	**5**	**6**	**7**	**8**	**9**	**10**
1	390	396	409	438	460	466	521		
2	395	428	415	429	456	477	525		
3	411	430	427	440	445	421			
4	420	445	454	442	478	456			
5	433	405	441	460	465	478			

Table 6. Case IV a: Overloading Available Frequency Range with 2.4 MHz Radar bandwidths

From cases I, II, III it can be observed that the time taken by the negotiation based approach is extremely better compared to the master-slave and locally autonomous based approaches. An important point to note here is that the scale used for the time taken to resolve interference on y-axis is different for the three algorithms in the different cases.

Case IVB: Overloading, All Radar Units with 5 MHz Bandwidth									
Locally Autonomous Mode									
	Number of Ships in the Group								
Radar/Ship	**2**	**3**	**4**	**5**	**6**	**7**	**8**	**9**	**10**
1	198	228	306	814	2265	9033	15442		
2	205	231	377	978	3451	10171	17621		
3	221	219	445	985	4783	11045			
4	206	265	437	1032	5972	12855			
5	242	290	625	1170	6911	14033			
Master-Slave Mode									
	Number of Ships in the Group								
Radar/Ship	**2**	**3**	**4**	**5**	**6**	**7**	**8**	**9**	**10**
1	341	435	441	696	948	1649	2519		
2	395	445	499	716	1004	1781	2802		
3	412	476	513	781	1035	1987			
4	398	481	568	865	1102	2114			
5	423	486	665	914	1195	2270			
Negotiation Mode									
	Number of Ships in the Group								
Radar/Ship	**2**	**3**	**4**	**5**	**6**	**7**	**8**	**9**	**10**
1	380	408	428	432	466	433	512		
2	386	424	436	447	441	464	578		
3	412	437	445	451	480	445			
4	434	451	468	479	457	477			
5	441	459	461	467	468	485			

Table 7. Case IV b: Overloading Available Frequency Range with 2.4 MHz Radar bandwidths

III. D. Case IV

This case has two sub-cases: Case IVA and Case IVB. This case is used to overload the algorithms by narrowing the

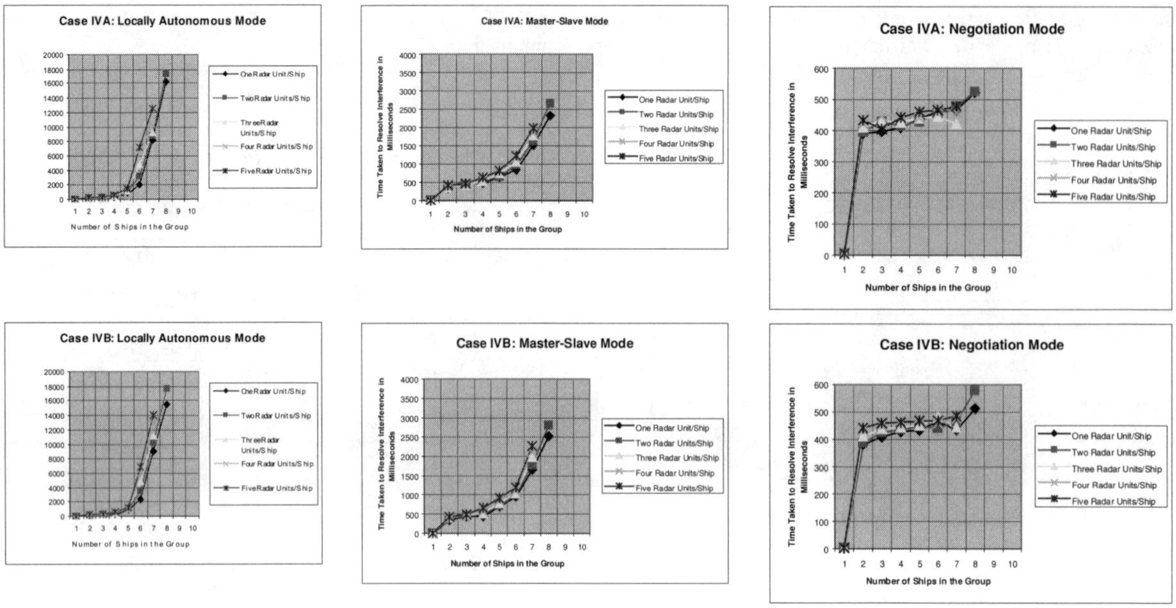

Locally-Autonomous Master-Slave Negotiation

Figure 9. Case IV - Tolerance Analysis

frequency range and introducing more radar units than possible into the system and study whether each of the algorithms provide the theoretically optimal solution. In Case IVA, all radar units in all the ships have the same peak power and threshold. All radar units are set to 2.4 MHz bandwidths. In theory, radar units operating on a 2.4 MHz bandwidth need a minimum frequency separation of 5 MHz in order to avoid interference. Therefore the frequency range is set to 1300 to 1500 MHz and all five radar units in the ten ships are set at the above mentioned radar parameters. Thus the algorithms must be able to fit forty out of the fifty radar units at their desired interference-free frequencies. Our objective is to study and find out how many radar units each of the algorithm can provide with interference free frequencies. This measure gives the tolerance of each of the algorithm.

Similarly, in Case IVB, all radar units have 5 MHz bandwidths. The minimum frequency separation required between radar units order to avoid interference is 10 MHz. Therefore the frequency range is set to 1300 MHz to 1700 MHz and all five radar units in the ten ships are set at the above mentioned radar parameters. Again, theoretically each of the algorithms must be able to fit forty of the fifty radar units at their desired frequencies. The measure of how many radar units each of the algorithm is able to provide interference free frequencies provide the tolerance of the algorithm.

It was found that all three approaches used for interference detection and resolution viz. locally autonomous, master-slave and negotiation based approaches fit 37 out of the 40 radar units that could theoretically fit in the given frequency range. The algorithms are thus found to be 92.5% efficient in finding interference free frequencies for their radar units.

III. E. Conclusions

The three different algorithms for radar interference detection and resolution viz. locally autonomous, master-slave and negotiation based algorithms were implemented in the two-level software agent program. Under different sets of tests, the negotiation based algorithm proved to performing better compared to master-slave and locally autonomous modes with regards to the time taken by each algorithm to detect and resolve the interference and update the database. Then finally a stress analysis was done on the three interference resolution algorithms by narrowing the frequency range and introducing more radar units than possible into the system and the point each of the algorithm fails was determined. In cases IVA and IVB, all the three algorithms fit 37 out of the 40 radar units into the frequency range. All the three algorithms were found to be 92.5% efficient in finding interference free frequencies for its radar units within a specified frequency range.

IV. Acknowledgements

The authors wish to thank Prof. P. K. Rajan, Dr. Jeff Frolik and Prof. Roger L. Haggard of the Electrical and Computer Engineering Department at Tennessee Technological University for their helpful and insightful suggestions for conducting the performance evaluation experiments.

V. References

1 K. Srinivasan, J. Cherry, T. Scalf, N. D. Cannon, S. Ramaswamy, "A Two-level Distributed Interactive Simulation Architecture for Radar Frequency Assignment" *1999 Summer Computer Simulation Conference*, July 1999.

THE TESTING OF DISTRIBUTED REAL-TIME SYSTEM

Hu HuaPing, Xiao XiaoQiang & Jin ShiYao
School of Computer Science
National University of Defense Technology
Changsha, Hunan, P. R. China, 410073
E-mail: hphu@nudt.edu.cn

KEY WORDS

Distributed systems, Real-time, Test bed, System test, Reliability.

ABSTRACT

Test (test bed) is the key to guarantee the quality and reliability of computer systems. In this paper, we firstly introduce a high reliability, hard real-time distributed system and its test bed's main functions. The general description and implementation details of the test bed are presented, the difficulties and key points to realize the test bed are shown. Finally, the testing results are presented.

This test bed has been successfully applied in testing an Information Processing System (IPS), and it has good effect on improving the development quality, system reliability and system stability. Testing results show that our IPS is greatly met users' requirement and the test bed can test IPS efficiently.

1. INTRODUCTION

With the computer application domain widening, more and more departments, especially those critical ones, rely highly on computer systems. In fields like finance, aviation, aerospace, defense and industry control, computer systems' breaking down means invaluable loss of lives and properties. The high reliability of computer system is required in these fields (Hu Huaping et al. 1998).

Test is the key to ensure the computer system (especial the software) quality and reliability. With the difficulty and complexity of testing increasing, testing can be divided into four levels: unit testing, integration testing, validity testing and system testing (Zheng Renjie 1992).

This paper focuses on system testing. System testing consists of recovery testing, completeness testing, intensity testing, performance testing and so on (Qi Zhichang et al. 1997).

In practice, more than one kinds of testing are used to meet the testing requirements. There are three basic testing methods, which are black-box testing, white-box testing and gray-box testing (Michael R. Lyu, 1996). Black-box testing is also called function testing, which concentrates on program or software's external characters. White-box testing is also called structure testing, which centers on their internal implementation. The gray-box testing is the combination of the previous two methods. The test bed introduced in this paper is a system testing tool of a high reliability, hard real-time distributed system. Black-box testing is mainly adopted.

This paper is organized as follows: First, the tested system and its main functions are introduced briefly in section2. Then, the test bed general description and its implementation details are shown in section 3. Section 4 presented the keys and difficulties in realizing the test bed. At last, the testing results are presented and the results show that our IPS is greatly met users' requirement and the test bed can test IPS efficiently.

2. THE TESTED SYSTEM AND MAIN FUNCTIONS OF TEST BED

The tested system is a high reliable and hard real-time (the service time is measured in *ms*) distributed system.

It can be divided into two symmetric parts, with each part composed of front-end processor, service processor, back-end processor and online backup processor; the whole system works in dual-mode. The system is tightly coupled by special interconnection network to meet hard real-time communication, which is measured in *ms*. To perform soft real-time communication, the system peripheries are connected to the HUBs via two pairs of Fast Ethernet (100MB/s). In addition, the system also includes offline backup processor (OBP), network administration processor, monitor processor, control processor and gateway processor. (Hu Huaping et al. 2000)

In this system, the users are divided into three kinds. The 3rd kind users have the highest priority, the 1st kind users have the lowest priority, and the priority of 2nd kind users is in the between. Besides, there are 3 types of service requests. It is very important to develop one test bed to improve the system quality, shorten both the system and the large system debugging cycle, and ensure the system reliability. On the other hand, because there are nearly ten different branches involved in developing this system, and the major application software is coded by themselves, it is impossible to perform completeness testing. The test bed main functions are listed below (Hu Huaping et al. 1999):

a) Model the interface and function of the Send/Receive System (SRS).

b) Based on the technical requirements, the following performance indices of 1st kind service request are tested:

- System throughput
- Mean Response Time (MRT) for each type service requests
- How system throughput is affected by the rate of different type service requests.

c) Enable the system debugging before it is incorporated with other related systems.

d) Provide a system test bed, in case of the large system test or system failure.

3. SYSTEM OUTLINE

3.1 Hardware/Software Environment

The related software is installed in the OBP, which can be used as a Develop Processor (DP). In case of testing, or system failure, the DP can be connected to IPS via High level Data Link Controller (HDLC), or Network Interface Card (NIC) to perform the role of SRS. The test bed can generate the input data to IPS and collect the corresponding results from HDLC. The testing environment is shown in Fig.1.

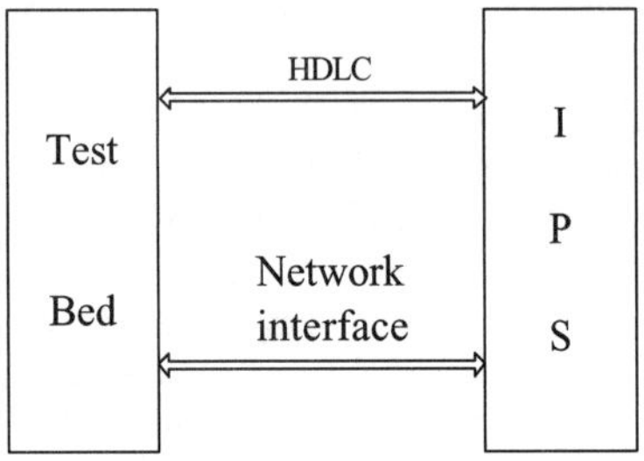

Fig.1 Hardware and interface evironment of test bed

The supporting software environments are:

- Real-time UNIX Operating System and its corresponding developing environment;
- C/C++ developing tool;
- Graphical interface development tools-OSF/Motif;
- Network software

3.2 General Description

The test bed can run either in manual mode or in automatic mode.

In manual testing mode, only one single user service request is concerned, the aim is to test system correctness. While in the automatic testing mode, a large quantities of users are concerned, the system overall performance is measured. The test bed workflow is shown in Fig. 2.

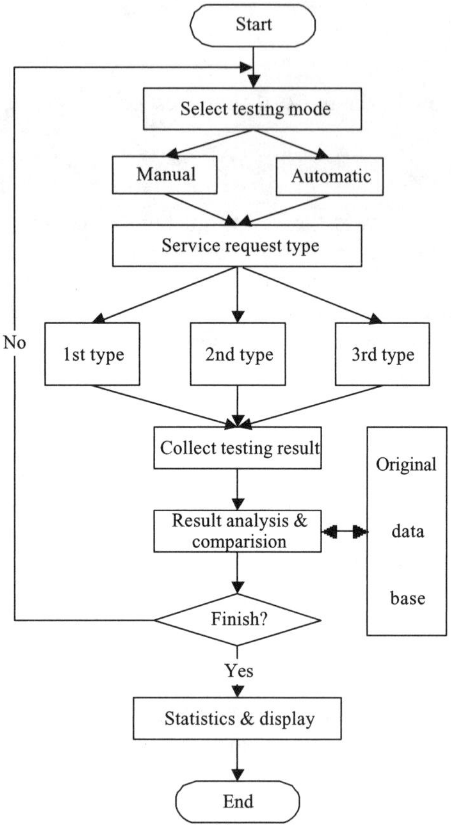

Fig. 2 The workflow of test bed

Manual Testing Mode. The user information, such as location, service request type, user type, user identification (ID), whether to add random error, are all inputted via interface. Then, the manual testing mode is activated, and the simulation data is generated and sent to IPS via HDLC. When output information (the computed results or the forwarded information) is generated and sent to test bed via HDLC, the Result Collection Monitor Module (RCMM) will be activated and hence gets the data. The useful data, such as user location, computed results or forwarded information, are extracted and sent to the Result Collection and Statistic Module (RCSM). The incoming messages will be handled differently according to their service request types. Based on the service request type and user ID, standard results can be retrieved from the built original database, and comparison and analysis will be made. At last, the testing results (such as response time, user location, precision, success or fail flag) will be displayed.

Automatic Testing Mode. After the testing parameters (such as the test time, the rates of different service request types, and the rates of different kinds of users, the distribution of arrival time interval) are set, according to the distribution and rates, the corresponding simulation data are created and sent to the IPS continuously. The test bed will fetch the data produced by the IPS, and do certain statistics and analysis. The automatic testing won't stop until the end of test time comes. Automatic testing mode mainly tests system performance to see whether they satisfy the developing requirement. The detail indices are listed in the following:

a) MRT of each service request type

For the 1st type service request:

- The MRT of 1st kind users is no greater than 10 seconds.
- The MRT of 2nd kind users is no greater than 6 seconds.
- The MRT of 3rd kind users is no greater than 4 seconds.

For the other type service requests, the MRT should be no greater than 10 seconds.

b) System throughput

We mainly concern how the system throughput is affected by the rates among different request types and different kinds of users. When system throughput reaches maximum, the rates among different request types and different kinds of users can be calculated.

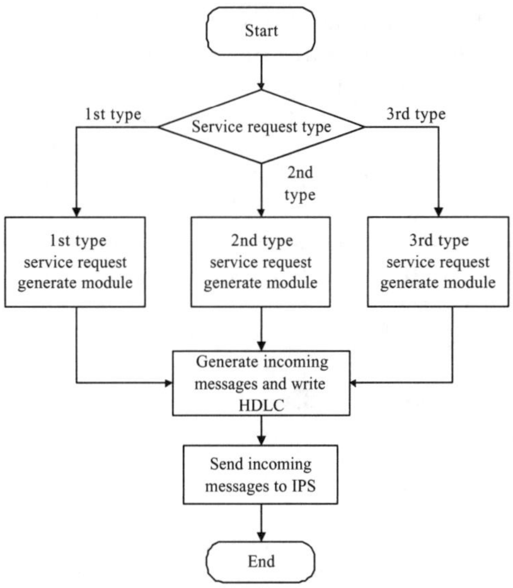

Fig. 3 Input event processing Module

3.3 Input Event Handling Module (IEHM)

IEHM is used to simulate the function of the SRS. Given raw data and some calculated results, it can produce incoming messages in the required format and timely send them to the IPS. Its flow chart is shown in Fig. 3.

3.4 Result Collection and Monitor Module

The output messages produced by the IPS are received by RCMM, and according to their format, extracted them, then sent the results into the Common Data Region (CDR). Its flow chart is shown in Fig. 4.

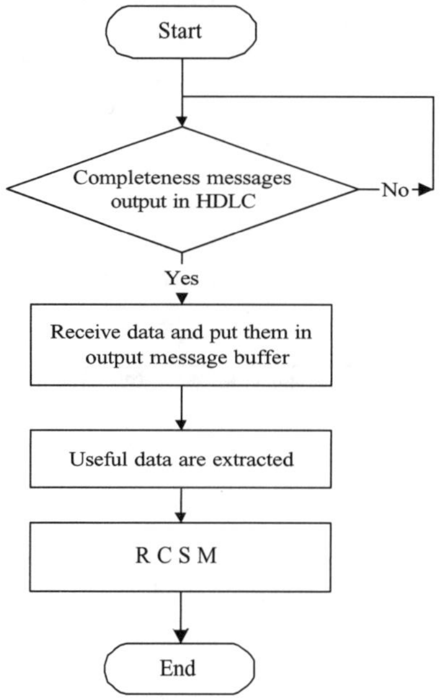

Fig. 4 The flow chart of RCCM

3.5 Result Collection and statistic Module

RCSM reads data from the CDR (which is filled by RCMM) and places them into a list. According to their service request types, different result handling modules will be called. As mentioned, standard results will be retrieved from the original database according to the service request type and user ID. After compared and analyzed, the final results will be acquired and placed into an array. After doing the related performance analysis and statistics, old data will be of no use and can be overwritten by new ones. The system performance index is shown in graph.

4. DIFICULTIES AND KEY POINTS

4.1 Multi-threads Programming

Multi-threads can run parallel in the same program. HDLC can only be preempted by one process.

In order to test the system real-time, the read and write to HDLC must run in parallel. If the read and write operation to HDLC is programmed in two processes, the two processes can also run in parallel. However, because the switch between two processes is quite often, and the initialization and termination of HDLC must be undergone at each switch, the real-time of system can not be satisfied.

In our implementation, multi-thread programming is adopted, the read operation to HDLC and write operation to HDLC are parallel threads in the same process, each thread writes or reads HDLC timely. The shared and excluded of HDLC is realized by the lock mechanism of two threads, the flow chart of multi-thread is shown in Fig. 5.

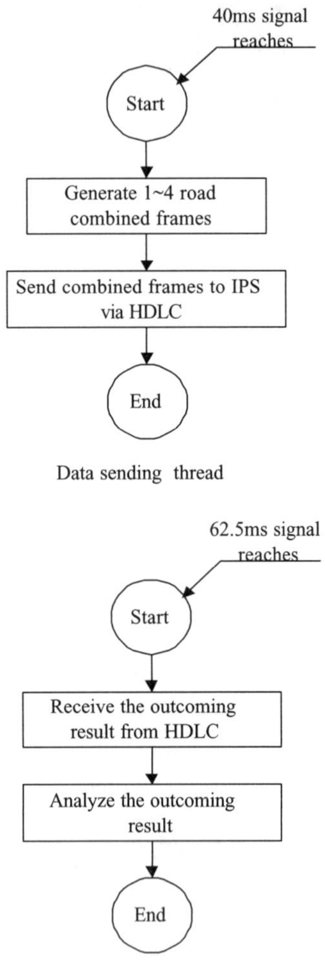

Fig. 5 The flow chart of multi-thread

4.2 Construction of the test cases

As mentioned, the test of the IPS is based on the test cases, and thus the generation of test cases is of critical importance.

Unfortunately, it is impossible to try all kinds of cases. The 1st type service requests will have no less than 10 thousands kinds of different cases. If all types of service requests are considered, the workload involved in the completeness testing is terrible. So how to construct the test cases quickly and effectively is the key to implement the test bed.

After negotiation with the clients and a detailed analysis of the incoming message structure, the combined random selecting with fixed original data sources is used to construct test cases. So to the 1st type service request, 8×250 typical test cases are used, 8 ×250 test cases and 12×250 cases are chosen separately for the 2nd type and 3rd type service request. The selected test cases can basically ensure the creditability of the performance indices. In addition, clients can also use the manual testing mode to try those "unreasonable" cases to test system correctness and system fault-tolerant function.

4.3 Real-time Test of Distributed Real-time Systems

Many difficulties, such as network real-time, task schedule, will arise when real-time characteristics are introduced into distributed systems. So another key to develop such kind of system is how to test system real-time. Both automatic testing mode and manual testing mode are used to overcome this difficulty. Thus, not only the overall system performance and real-time, but also a single user service request, can be tested.

4.4 Test of Software/Hardware Combined System

The IPS is a complex system involving various kinds of devices. As mentioned previously, in order to realize the hard real time communication, The hard real time part is interconnected via the internal interconnection networks, and the system peripheries are connected by two pairs of 100MB/s fast Ethernet to satisfy the need of soft real time communication. The involved software includes system software (UNIX OS), software on the shelf (Oracle, network administration software, firewall, etc) and much self-developed software. It is rather difficult to make the whole system run and ensure all the processors perform their functions correctly. Besides the interfaces and function testing, recovery testing, intensity testing, function testing are also integrated.

5 TEST RESULTS

5.1 MRT of third Kind Users (1st Type Service Request)

For the 1st type service request, the input rate of 3rd kind users is 150requst/S, after IPS runs ten minutes, the RCMM is stimulated, and the statistics results are listed in table 1. The statistics results show: The MRT of IPS is met the request of users which isn't greater than 4 seconds.

Table 1. MRT of 3rd kind users

Number of Service request (10 thousand)	MRT(Units: ms)
1	2760
2	2620
3	2940
4	2620
5	2560
Average	2700

5.2 System Throughput

In order to test IPS throughput, the input rate of test bed is changed from 100 request/s to 300 request/s, the testing results are listed in table 2. The testing results show: IPS system throughput is 200 request/s, which is greater than users required.

Table 2. Test result of system throughput

Rate of test bed input	**Rate of IPS output (Average)**
100 request/s	100 request/s
150 request/s	149 request/s
200 request/s	199 request/s
250 request/s	200 request/s
300 request/s	200 request/s

6. CONCLUSIONS

Our test bed has improved the reliability and quality of IPS, shortened the IPS and the whole system debugging cycle. Although the testing results show that our IPS is greatly met users required and the test bed can test IPS efficiently, there are still many things need improving and perfecting, such as the flexible of input interface, the correctness of input data, the display of statistics result and so on.

REFERENCE

Hu Huaping et al.1998. "The Study and Realization of High Reliability Distributed Real-time System", *Chinese Computer Research and Development*, Vol.35, No.9 (Sept.): 841~845.

Hu Huaping et al. 2000. "The Study and Realization of Distributed Real-time System Test Bed", *Chinese Measurement & Control Technology*, Vol.19, No.2 (Feb.), 55~58.

Hu Huaping et al. 1999. "The Switch technology Study of High Reliability, Hard Real-time Distributed System", *The Journal of National University of Defense Technology*, Vol.21, No.12 (Dec.), 80~83.

Michael R. Lyu. 1996. "Handbook of Software Reliability Engineering", McGraw-Hill Companies, 356~377.

Qi Zhichang et al. 1997. "Software Engineering", *Chinese High Education Publishing Company*, Beijing, 236-258.

Zheng Renjie. 1992. "Computer Test Technology", Qinghua University Publishing Company, Beijing, 47~55.

BIOGRAPHY

Dr. Hu HuaPing was born in 1967. He received the M.S. degree and. Ph.D. degree in Systems Engineering from National University of Defense Technology (NUDT), Changsha, P. R. China, in 1991 and 1995 respectively. He has been a Post-doctor in Computer Science and Technology at the same university. Now he is Assistant Research Fellow of Department of Computer, NUDT. He has published more than 50 papers in professional journals and conference publications. His research interests include performance evaluation of computer systems, Modeling and simulation of complicated system, fault tolerant system study.

Dr. Xiao XiaoQiang was born in 1972. He received the M.S. and the Ph.D. degree in computer science in 1996 and 2000 respectively. Now he is working in the National Laboratory for Parallel and Distributed Processing (PDL). He has published more than 20 papers and his current research focuses on high performance architecture and performance evaluation.

Prof. Jin ShiYao was born in 1937. He is a famous professor in PDL. He is also the tutor of Ph.D. students. His interests include computer architecture, performance analysis and high performance computer.

PERFORMANCE IMPROVEMENT OF EXTENDED AIR DEFENSE TESTBED (EADTB) VIA SYNCHRONOUS PARALLEL ENVIRONMENT FOR EMULATION AND DISCRETE EVENT SIMULATION (SPEEDES)

Ray Smith
TRW Space and Missile Systems
213 Wynn Dr.
Huntsville, AL 35805
ray.smith@trw.com

Archie Morris
Kottmann Inc.
513 Sparkman Dr.
Huntsville, AL 35816
archie.morris@kottmann.com

Keywords: Military, Parallel Simulation, Optimistic Scheduling, Discrete Event

ABSTRACT

The is a highly flexible constructive military simulation with a modeling scope that ranges from land and sea to air and space based entities. It allows the detailed analysis of one-on-one interactions as well as the more general analysis of larger engagement to force-on-force level scenarios. The EADTB is an event-stepped simulation and can be run in real-time or non-real-time modes. The modeling paradigm is an object-based architecture where each entity in a scenario is comprised of building blocks. The model algorithms are general-purpose and completely configured by input data. Fidelity and performance of simulated entities is user-selectable, and the experiment logic used by each simulated entity is driven by "rulesets." Because of this capability to construct and run high fidelity objects, there is a significant runtime performance challenge. The focus of this paper is on the approach we are investigating for overcoming this runtime challenge.

The algorithms for the various models have been streamlined and honed to a significant degree to improve speed. Running as a single-threaded, sequential simulation, little further improvement can be realized without reducing the level of detail and flexibility of the models. Some form of parallelization is necessary. A number of constraints make the task to parallelize more challenging. With more than two million lines of Ada code, it is desirable to preserve the architecture and code as much as possible. Strict repeatability and causality have been maintained thus far and must not be compromised, even though some relaxation would make speedup easier. Based on review of the technologies available, we have determined that some form of optimistic scheduling is the most promising solution given these constraints.

Fortunately, the architecture of EADTB lends itself to parallelization, and we have been able to successfully integrate with the SPEEDES engine as the scheduling mechanism. Preliminary work with a pseudo-EADTB prototype, has allowed us to overcome the Ada-to-C++ language barrier and to produce some promising timing results. The SPEEDES developer has provided selected special-purpose interfaces that have allowed us access to required SPEEDES facilities. Currently we are in the process of integrating SPEEDES with significant portions of the actual EADTB models.

Through this effort we are attempting to surface and find solutions to all the problem areas that have to be addressed in a full-scale integration. While we anticipate significant technical challenges to accomplishing a successful full integration, we continue to find solutions to the problems we're encountering. The goal continues to appear feasible that we can achieve order-of-magnitude speedup while running within the memory space available, and without significant breakage of the already-developed models. The end result will be a system in which the models operate without the knowledge that they are running in parallel or occasionally are being rolled back. They simply schedule and execute events. Performance improvement for larger and more complex scenarios should be achieved in a scalable manner simply by adding more processors.

The details of our successful, groundbreaking prototype work have been previously reported (Smith, Andress, and Parsons 1999). This paper extends the report to our recent experience with SPEEDES integration into the actual EADTB models. It discusses some of the more innovative approaches to achieving parallelism, and provides additional insight on the approach to retrofitting an existing simulation to SPEEDES. Many of these findings have application to new developments and are being incorporated into the SPEEDES baseline.

Introduction

The modeling approach used by EADTB is to provide all the building blocks through a carefully constructed interface, so that experimenters can fairly rapidly put together scenarios. Specific System Representations (SSRs) are first assembled from component parts (Sensors, Comms, Platform, Thinkers) each of which has been assembled from lower level parts. For example an F-15 SSR can be constructed, then selected for deployment as a Scenario Element (ScenEl) on a gameboard complete with environmental features. A master set of SSRs is provided from which users can select and modify as needed, or users can construct their own SSRs from scratch. EADTB provides a toolkit of algorithms that the user configures to represent these systems. The C3 behavior of the systems is specified via user-written "rulesets" which are supported by symbols (which can be thought of as "sub-programs") that perform standard calculations, issue commands, or retrieve data. A taxonomy of over 1200 symbols is available for this purpose. Users need not be programmers, and aside from ruleset translation, no software building is required for generating or altering scenarios. EADTB is primarily focused on the mission/engagement level of modeling vs. the engineering or campaign levels. A more detailed description of the simulation and its uses is provided in another conference paper (Hunter and Elliott 2000).

As previously reported (Smith, Andress, and Parsons 1999), in the initial phase of this investigation, we constructed a small pseudo-EADTB prototype to mimic the some of the most important characteristics of EADTB. A mechanism for the Ada to C++ interface was worked out so that the SPEEDES developer provided c-callable interfaces to the required SPEEDES methods. The integrated SPEEDES/EADTB model allowed us to test for feasibility of the approach, in terms of whether we could precisely preserve model behavior when running in parallel, whether there was sufficient memory to support rollback, and whether we could significantly reduce run-times. These questions were all answered affirmatively based especially on a 1000 ScenEl scenario. The integration approach was to define each ScenEl as a SPEEDES simulation object (rather than going to lower level components within a ScenEL because of the extensive interaction between components). A single SPEEDES event type was defined for EADTB and the details of the event were encapsulated for handling within the existing EADTB structure. The level of impact to the existing EADTB model code was determined not to be prohibitive, and the speed-up for one 1000 ScenEl scenario was a factor of almost twelve using 32 processors. Factors affecting speed-up including event granularity, the level of object interaction, and the availability of data distribution management to reduce rollbacks were discussed in the previous paper (Smith, Andress, and Parsons 1999).

The second phase of our performance improvement effort is to do a partial integration of SPEEDES with our actual EADTB models. The objective of this phase is to surface all significant issues related to integration, to devise mechanisms for dealing with these issues, to provide a design approach for full integration with EADTB, and to provide estimates of the projected speed-up as well as the level of effort to complete full integration. In order to avoid having to deal with all 2.3 million lines of code, we have carefully constructed a set of scenarios, which execute a limited number of EADTB event types. Thus only that portion of code that executes these events needs to be examined and instrumented for rollback support.

EVENT SCHEDULING AND EXECUTION

The first order of business was to replace the EADTB event scheduler with the SPEEDES scheduler. This turned out to be surprisingly straightforward because of the modular, generic nature in which EADTB schedules and executes events, and the limited information about an event needed by SPEEDES. Once we had worked out the mapping of the EADTB event priority scheme to the SPEEDES scheme, and had encapsulated the event data for passing to SPEEDES, we were able to complete the scheduler switchover and verify identical behavior in the sequential mode of execution.

PERSISTENT DATA HANDLING

The next and more challenging step was to provide state saving calls for all persistent data involved with the execution of events. Some data is transient – created and destroyed during the execution of an event and is of no concern to rollback. Other data "persists" between events and whenever a piece of this persistent data is modified, its old value must be state-saved prior to modification. State saving consists of simply calling a SPEEDES method and passing the address and length of the data, which is about to be modified. SPEEDES archives a copy of this data, and if a rollback occurs, automatically re-stores the state of persistent data to the rolled-back time. Thus whenever a rollback occurs, EADTB is basically oblivious to the fact, and simply executes events supplied by the SPEEDES scheduler. The key is finding modifications to all persistent data, and inserting state saving calls to SPEEDES. Ideally in a new development effort using SPEEDES, the programmer would simply select a specially-built rollbackable type (rb_float, rb_integer, rb_boolean, etc.) for persistent data elements. These rollbackable types have their assignment operators overloaded so that state saving occurs automatically whenever the values are modified. Because of language safety issues, Ada does not directly provide assignment operator overloading. We did investigate the use of the Ada95 "controlled type", which provides a somewhat similar capability. However, we found that the level of control was not the same, and although this mechanism could be made to work, it is not run-time efficient for this purpose. Additionally the effort to switch over all our persistent data to these new types would have been fairly extensive. Even in the C++ environment, developers must be wary of the cost of rollbackable types, and not over use them. For example if a persistent data object happens to be modified multiple times during the execution of an event, it really only needs to be state saved once. Most persistent data resides within structures such as records and containers (lists, queues, stacks, trees, maps, etc.). Studies have shown that if more than about 20% of a data structure is modified, it is more efficient to state save the entire structure ("block copy state save"), than to piecemeal state save individual components ("incremental state save"). Some of the persistent data structures are non-contiguous in memory (e.g. may have embedded pointers to data). In some cases it is necessary to "flatten" the structure in order to state save. Hopefully there will be only a few instances where we have to resort to this mechanism.

For a retrofit situation, the big challenge is to locate all the persistent data. In the Ada world, it turns out that persistent data is defined as all "package" level data objects. While this knowledge helps tremendously in identifying persistent objects, there is still a challenge. In order to help with this search, we developed a tool, which works in conjunction with the GNAT Ada debugger to provide a directed run-time trace of event logic. We then used this dynamic call tree to focus our examination of code for persistent data assignments. This still leaves a fairly significant manual task. A pitfall in this process is that care must be taken to avoid state saving data on the run-time stack. Usually persistent data will not be on the stack, except that occasionally, due to the use of call-by-value, an argument may be copied onto the stack during execution inside a called function or procedure. In Ada we must force the persistent parameter to be passed by reference. One mechanism to do this is to insert pragma interface FORTRAN directives for these procedures.

The remaining issue with respect to persistent data is to make dynamic memory allocation/deallocation rollbackable for persistent objects. In Ada this means we must use "storage pools" so that we can intercept "new" and "free" processing for persistent objects, and in turn invoke SPEEDES functions. Thus we must locate and change the data types of all pointers to persistent data within EADTB.

While the primitive rollbackable types were not very useful to us, we did find that rollbackable versions of "containers" are needed. When persistent objects are stored within containers, these structures must be rollbackable by having state saving calls inserted at the appropriate points. We are currently in the process of constructing these containers. Within EADTB, this is a challenging task because of the extensive use of nested, generic containers (e.g. a collection of lists of dynamic arrays). Having access to the SPEEDES rollbackable containers would be useful, except that the semantics of the containers are not always compatible with the EADTB container semantics.

SCENARIOS

Our initial scenario is composed of two aircraft, which are each commanded to fly to specific points, then to begin flying racetracks. The portion of EADTB code involved with executing these events is very limited so that we could fairly quickly get EADTB running on multiple processors in parallel. In order to force rollbacks, we artificially added periodic queries by each aircraft to get the other's current position via its SPEEDES object proxy. Once we got this scenario running correctly in parallel, we replicated the aircraft to look at loading and performance. A second scenario involved adding a sensor, which performs periodic scans and detects each aircraft as it goes in and out of coverage. This added some limited sensor and thinker processing to the logic. Figure 1 shows a screen capture of this executing scenario. With state saving calls inserted, this scenario seems to be functioning, but currently when we add more sensors we get failures, which we think are due to not having found and saved all persistent data. A third scenario involves adding a command center ScenEl to which the sensors report tracks. This increases the amount of Sensor and Thinker logic involved, and introduces COMM message processing into the mix.

each of the receivers. This eliminates having to copy and pass the message contents which can be large when the message involves track or plot data. Once all receiving ScenEls have gotten the message, the sending Thinker then frees the memory associated with the message, as triggered by a feedback mechanism. In order to keep message passing efficient, especially since now messages must be rollbackable, the SPEEDES developer has provided a shared memory management mechanism. Since a message is read-only after it is created, it can be put into shared memory, and receiving objects on multiple processors may access it freely. The new SPEEDES mechanism allowed us to create these messages in shared memory, pass pointers to receiving ScenEls, and use the advancement of global virtual time, as the trigger to free the memory. The related issue with COMM modeling is the bookkeeping associated with message routing, delays, losses, and delivery time slots. The original

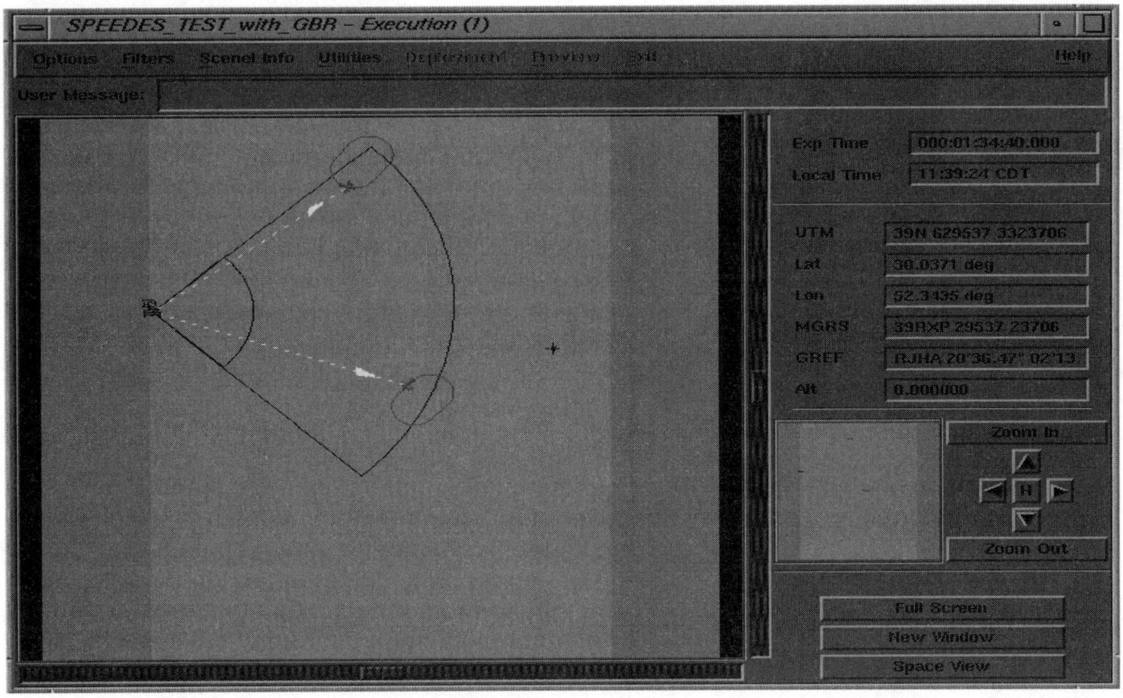

Figure 1 Test Scenario with Sensor and Two Aircraft

COMMUNICATIONS MODEL

The issue of COMM modeling is significant in parallelizing EADTB because of the interaction between communicating ScenEls. Our design in sequential EADTB is to pass a pointer to the message contents to

design handled this bookkeeping in a central store in which receipt of a message by each ScenEl caused message state data to be modified. We are in the process of changing the COMM model, to eliminate this feedback mechanism and to employ another new SPEEDES capability that uses a shared memory mechanism to ensure that message receipts are not duplicated.

EVENT CANCELLATION

Some processes in EADTB involve cancellation or retraction of previously scheduled, but unexecuted events. For example, whenever a new path command is received from a ruleset for an aircraft, the model first cancels the pending update_move event, then schedules a new update_move consistent with the new command. Also in some event processing we need to query the event queue to see what is pending. The SPEEDES developer has provided an interface that allows a ScenEl to access and cancel any event that it has scheduled (even if it is scheduled for another ScenEl), but does not allow access to any event it did not schedule (even if the event was scheduled for it by another ScenEl). This is adequate for most purposes, but in the case where a ScenEl is destroyed, we must modify EADTB to mark it as dead and simply stop executing events for it rather than deleting the events.

the scenario display is comprised of Recorded Data Items (RCDs). In parallel mode, these RCDs will be generated from multiple nodes at varying simulation times. SPEEDES provides an ExoStream functionality, which is used to rollbackably merge and sort the RCDs and release each record upon passage of global virtual time (called "commit"). By the same token other EADTB outputs must use ExoStreams (trace and error logs). The mechanisms for output have been implemented so that the process in Figure 2 can be accomplished. Some minor work remains to debug the process to drive scenario display via socket access, but the SPEEDES mechanism functions perfectly.

FORKING

The processing sequence for EADTB is to initialize, load, configure, and then execute. In the load phase,

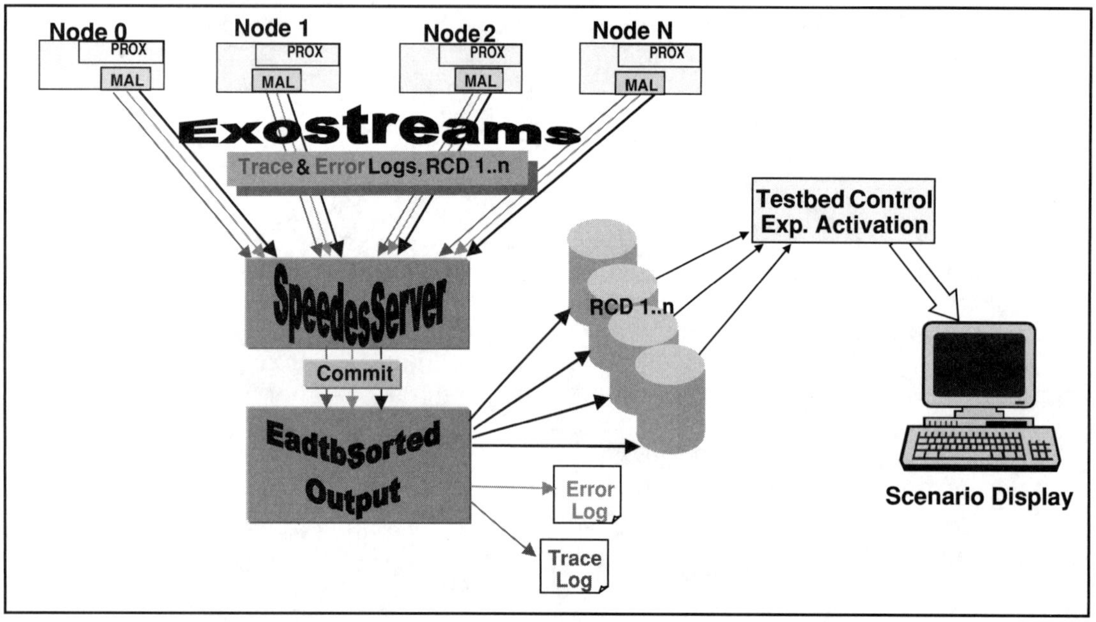

ROLLBACKABLE I/O AND SCENARIO DISPLAY

In an optimistic parallel execution process, external interfaces require special handling. In EADTB all input data is basically loaded at the outset of an execution and the external input interface can be terminated thereafter. Thus because loading takes place while EADTB is a single process, there is no issue relative to parallel processing. However, for model output, there is an issue. In EADTB output for analysis and to drive

all the component SSR level (or static) data is retrieved from the oracle database, and all the ScenEl level deployment data (dynamic or instance data) is retrieved. During the configure process, pointers from the dynamic data are generated to the shared static data, some initial RCDs are generated, and initial events are scheduled. Because of the need to access data across ScenEls during configure, our design is to wait until after configure to invoke SPEEDES execute which forks EADTB to all the specified nodes and assigns ScenEls to nodes. Thus to enable waiting until after configure to fork, we must queue up the initial events to be scheduled via SPEEDES until after configure. The initial event to be processed by each node, then extracts the appropriate events for its ScenEls and issues the SPEEDES schedules. Likewise the initial RCDs must be queued for sending after the fork. These processes have been implemented, however some work remains to be done to allow merging of the error and trace log versions prior to and after the fork.

EVENT DESTINATIONS

In SPEEDES all events must be scheduled for some simulation object and then executed on behalf of that object (called the "current" object). In EADTB some events have a null destination ScenEl. These include weather and 24-hour clock changes, events executed in general by the COMMs model, and events which must be executed even if the destination ScenEl dies prematurely such as some of the Pk draw modeling. In order to meet the SPEEDES requirement, we have adjusted the destination ScenEl in some cases to be the source ScenEl. We have also introduced an artificial ScenEl "0" for use as the destination in some cases. We may need to introduce an artificial ScenEl on each node, and take care to prevent these artificial ScenEls from becoming bottlenecks due to being required to handle too many events.

STATUS AND PLANS

The process of identifying problematic areas and of devising workable solutions is continuing. We do not need to actually fully implement all solutions during this phase but rather make certain that the solutions are sufficient. SPEEDES development continues and new capabilities and efficiency mechanisms are being introduced. Some of the enhancements we will need include Data Distribution Management (DDM) so that unnecessary object interaction can be reduced. For example whenever objects move which are outside a sensor's field of view, the sensor should not be impacted, especially if the sensor is operating at a different simulation time and updating the position of such an object would trigger an unnecessary rollback of the sensor. Something like a "smart" proxy needs to be implemented so that subscribers who have not queried the proxy for the object since the last proxy update, need not be rolled back. Use of a position error tolerance would allow the old proxy state vector to continue to be used for extrapolation as long as possible. A memory mechanism could be used to eliminate multiply extrapolating ScenEl states for the same time.

Before a decision to commit the program to full integration with SPEEDES, more sample integration must be done. Finding and state saving persistent data continues to be a time-consuming task. We are investigating some other tools to help with this including consideration of having Ada Core Technology, the GNAT Compiler support organization, build some special tools. The issue of Thinker context data for rule sets and the various weapon and engageability data maps and structures need to be further investigated for state saving. General ruleset processing needs further study.

We continue to monitor the development of the SPEEDES HLA capability to support interoperability. We also anticipate taking advantage of the access to other simulation objects which is provided when operating with another simulation which is using SPEEDES.

References

Hunter, R. and Elliott, S., "Advanced C3 Simulation and Analysis Using EADTB," Society for Computer Simulation International, Proceedings of the 2000 Summer Computer Simulation Conference, July, 2000.

Smith, R., Andress, R., and Parsons M., "Scalable Speed_Up of Existing Military Simulations Without Re-Implementation", *TRW Systems and Information Technology Review Journal*, Vol 7, No. 1, Spring/Summer 1999.

Simulation System Life-Cycle Evolution

PANDA: AN APPROACH TO SIMULATION SOFTWARE ENGINEERING, DEVELOPMENT, AND INTEGRATION

Jeffrey Wallace
Consultant
jeffrey.w.wallace@att.net

Captain Joseph Celano, USN
Space and Naval Warfare Systems Command
(SPAWAR) PMW 131
celanoj@spawar.navy.mil

Dr. Larry Peterson
SPAWAR Systems Center San Diego
Code D44202

KEYWORDS

Software development, software architecture, model representation, simulation paradigms, distributed simulation, simulation interoperability.

ABSTRACT

Various forms of simulation have been a mainstay technology for scientific and engineering disciples for many decades. From physics, to civil engineering, to operations research, the need to study, design, or predict the behavior of a complex system can often be satisfied through the application of simulation techniques. Over the past half-century a large body of knowledge and many software tools have been developed to aid in the design and analysis of simulations. Methodologies and software packages for domain specific needs as well as more general solutions have been developed. Typically these approaches rely on the application of a single software technology, such as imperative programming, and result in a software system whose sole function is as a digital simulation. This approach has been effective for simulation of isolated systems and loosely coupled federations of systems.

The **Pa**rallel Simulatio**n** **D**evelopment **A**rchitecture (PANDA) initiative emerged as an outgrowth of the shared experiences of several Department of Defense (DoD) R&D efforts into simulation software engineering environments and the practical application of these efforts in the execution of the U.S. Navy's Joint Simulation System (JSIMS) Maritime program. The PANDA initiative seeks to enable diverse simulation development approaches to be unified in a rigorous manner into the mainstream of modern software engineering, development, and integration theories and tools. This paper outlines the theory and reasoning behind PANDA, provides an overview of an instantiation of this architecture,

INTRODUCTION

Over the last two decades efforts at developing large-scale simulations spanning many levels of system resolution have been attempted. The combat models developed by operations researchers in support of defense department decision-makers are an example. These efforts to develop simulations of large parts of reality, from switching circuits to human decision-making, have made use of most of what is known about software technologies and techniques. These efforts require the application of a number of technologies. For example, declarative programming is typically used to model human decision-making, while static portions of models are written in imperative languages for efficiency. However, most expert systems are designed as stand alone packages and only provide loosely coupled interfaces to imperative languages. This is true of other software technologies and has hampered their general use to address modeling and simulation in a consistent and integrated manner.

Recent DARPA and DoD initiatives have goals far beyond the use of these large simulations as single-user tools. They have embarked on ambitious efforts at providing distributed simulations using virtual reality for training, virtual prototyping of hardware, and for analytical uses. This community is unlikely to meet these goals without a significant improvement in the underlying development environment and infrastructure for simulation software and it's relationship to business enterprise information systems.

The **Pa**rallel Simulatio**n** **D**evelopment **A**rchitecture (PANDA) initiative, as a solution to many of the problems identified above, has four basic elements:

- An evolving abstract simulation CASE tool architecture that permits common software framework and pattern generation while allowing for a variety of subject-matter domain specific higher level modeling representations.

- An approach to the integration of simulation software CASE tools with the larger CASE tool industry.
- An approach to the integration of enterprise information systems with simulation systems.
- An evolving government and industry collaboration to consider the business aspects of PANDA and to continue the evolution and execution of the technical approach.

This contributes in a significant way to the further definition of the theory, concept, and implementation of distributed product descriptions (DPDs) and the required infrastructure to support various components of collaborative environments (CEs). In addition, PANDA supports long-term systems engineering of Simulation-based Acquisition (SBA).

The PANDA initiative also has had a significant and immediate return on existing investments by:

- Providing key simulation development infrastructure components which the Joint Simulation System (JSIMS), the Joint Modeling and Simulation System (JMASS), the Joint National Test Facility's Wargame 2000 (WG2K), and the Extended Air Defense Testbed (EADTB) programs utilize to reduce development cost and risk significantly.
- Stimulating government and industry co-investment in R&D for SBA infrastructure and life-cycle product support based on market share and business case considerations, as is happening in the JMASS community due to the adoption of the key tenets in the PANDA approach.
- Stimulating the implementation of open standards in open forums for common software frameworks with a significant application in SBA infrastructure and DoD market share, such as the Parallel Discrete Event Simulation (PDES) User's Group, which provides a forum for industry, academia, and government to guide the development of simulation infrastructure technology for use in JSIMS, JMASS, WG2K, and EADTB.

A successful CE, whether software production is involved or not, must support a wide variety of operational architectures, as Figure 1 illustrates. To permit the support and rapid deployment of this diversity of system structures, we require middleware, and middleware development capabilities, with the following features:

- *Data Integration* - this permits direct access to original record, and allows the data to be derived from multiple sources, or the parties that own the data.
- *Application or Model Integration* - enabling and automating reuse and encapsulation allows the exploitation of existing algorithmic knowledge while permitting the sharing of transient information.
- *Ability to Add Value Non-Intrusively* - The reasoned and automated approach allows the transformation, aggregation, and the filtration of data, while allowing the addition of incremental custom services. Making a simulation High Level Architecture (HLA) compliant, for instance, is more often than not quite intrusive, and up until recently very expensive.
- *Enterprise-Capable* – A sound development environment must allow ubiquitous access to all enterprise partners and provide robustness, reliability, and real-time performance.

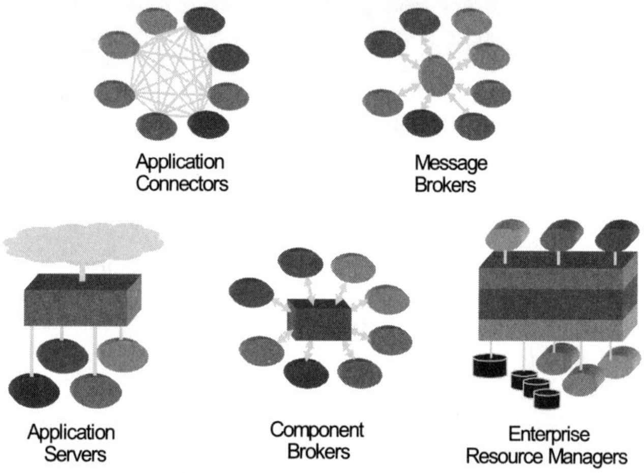

Figure 1. Sample of operational architectures to be supported by PANDA.

Thus, PANDA seeks to provide the development environment support, along with underlying execution frameworks, required to support simulations deployed in these various operational architectures.

To show how many of these problems have been solved, we first discuss the relevant simulation software engineering issues that need to be addressed. We next discuss the requirements placed on simulation execution frameworks, highlighting the need to understand model and simulation integration mechanics. We then address the types of simulation CASE tool interoperability required. Finally, we present the results from the initial use-case of the PANDA approach, the JSIMS Maritime program. In particular, we present the software development productivity metrics resulting from the application of the PANDA approach to simulation development by the JSIMS Maritime program.

Simulation Software Engineering Issues

In this section we outline the challenges facing the simulation development and user communities that PANDA seeks to address. As software development in most other domains outside of the scientific and technical communities becomes increasingly sophisticated and productive, we must address why simulation development is so difficult and has not, in general, derived the same productivity improvements as other domains like enterprise resource systems development and use.

Simulation Software Reuse

In most sectors of the software development industry, cost and time-to-market are reduced through the reuse of existing software in new applications. Techniques and capabilities to wrapper or otherwise abstract interfaces to existing software modules abound, but these techniques are difficult to achieve in the simulation community. This is due to the differing ways in which simulation time is represented and real-world concepts are mapped and represented in software.

Thus, to achieve real reuse of simulation software, an approach to mapping various simulation time mechanisms and real-world representation techniques are required to create reusable simulation software and integrate existing simulation components. In certain simulation domains we have developed an approach in PANDA to solve this key aspect of the reuse problem, called the Unified API [McGraw 2000]. This is being used in both the JSIMS and JMASS programs to reuse existing simulation code written to a certain API, while new code is added to these programs using a different simulation API.

Standardized model interfaces

The idea of standardized model interfaces is a difficult concept for the modeling and simulation (M&S) community, since different domains within the simulation community require different models. However, there is an increasing recognition that significant similarity and commonality exists among simulation applications and that there are a significant number of cases where a common model interface can be defined for multiple applications.

In a variety of large M&S programs we see model API standardization to enable multiple developing agents within the scope of a single effort. The largest of these, JSIMS, must coordinate the input of over ten developing agents. As another example, JMASS must be used by industry to contribute to the design and engineering of military hardware. As such, with no standardization, coordinating these various elements into a coherent, valid simulation would be practically impossible. Current instantiations of PANDA, such as that in the JSIMS Maritime program, allow the rigorous representation of a variety of standard model interfaces.

Simulation interoperability

As resources become increasingly scarce, a need exists to reuse different models across multiple simulation domains. A different approach to interoperability, different from standardized model APIs, addressing deeper issues such as different execution frameworks and simulation control paradigms must be addressed. The High Level Architecture (HLA) standard developed by the Defense Modeling and Simulation Office (DMSO) defines a common basis for simulation interoperability at the level of granularity of a simulation. While this approach is addressed in PANDA via code generation and HLA APIs used to develop low-level simulation components and models, there are other ways to combine existing models and simulation components into a single HLA federate, or HLA compliant simulation.

In addition, software architectures that already provide for application interoperability, such as the Defense Information Infrastructure Common Operating Environment (DII COE) [DISA 1999a], desire to have simulations as part of their application suite. DII COE developers, such as those building software for the Global Command and Control System [DISA 1999b] need an interoperability approach that overcomes the limitations confronting simulation software reuse. This problem is addressed in PANDA by observing the software engineering principles common to all successful application architectures such as the DII COE. This is accomplished by carefully building up the underlying simulation execution frameworks in PANDA by factoring the different simulation execution framework component subsystems into rigorous layers with well defined and generalized interfaces relating and separating them [Steinman 1998, McGraw 2000].

Development Process and Model Composition

In a compositional development environment [Deutsch 1989, Meyer 1989], such as the existing instantiations of the PANDA approach, software creation may be viewed as a constructive activity wherein a system exhibiting a desired functionality is composed from a set of existing components, in this case mathematical models and simulation components representing some phenomenology or thing in the real world. When building simulation systems from components in PANDA, development can be characterized by a number of processes, including:

- *Conceptualization:* A model of the application domain is formulated which partitions the desired functionality of the system into components (analysis and design).

- *Accumulation:* Existing components are evaluated and those satisfying various aspects of the requirements for each component are identified.
- *Evaluation:* The best existing component (or set of components) is selected for each component of the conceptual design.
- *Adaptation:* The selected components are adapted to the specific requirements of the conceptual components.
- *Composition:* The adapted components are composed to meet the desired characteristics of the system under construction.
- *Expansion:* The new component is evaluated and added to the repository of reusable components.
- *Implementation:* The alternative to compositional reuse; if a suitable candidate cannot be found, and then it must be implemented from scratch.

In this compositional model of software development, the Accumulation, Evaluation, and Adaptation activities can be conceptually grouped into the process of software reuse.

Feedback occurs between the Conceptualization and Reuse processes when the conceptualization is influenced by the availability of components. This influence can be either in the form of re-partitioning within the parameters of the original design, or of relaxing design constraints. If no candidate artifacts that satisfy the requirements are found, the designer may revise the conceptualization under a different design strategy to increase the opportunity for reuse, or may elect to implement the needed component [Prieto-Diaz 1987].

Feedback occurs between the Reuse and Composition processes when interface requirements dictate certain adaptations that may not be feasible with a particular artifact. Within the Reuse process, failure to adapt a selected component signals the need to consider the "next-best" candidate; when all candidates are exhausted, then a re-evaluation and relaxing of design requirements must occur.

Whenever the conceptual design must be altered, the tradeoffs between changing the design and implementing a new software component exhibiting the right characteristics must be considered. Whenever a new component is created, either by adaptation of an existing component or by implementation, the new component becomes a candidate for inclusion in the reuse repository.

At this time, these processes are best implemented manually in PANDA in the guise of the Software Engineering Institute's (SEI) Capability Maturity Model (CMM) key process areas. Increasingly vendors are supplying development environment support with SEI CMM certifiable process models embedded, such as those in the Rational ClearCase-ClearQuest tool suite for performing configuration management and change request management.

Additionally, automated support to implement the above listed processes has been present in the R&D community for some time [Whitehurst 1995]. This level of sophistication in simulation software development environments has not been incorporated in the current generation of simulation CASE tool suites, and is in general absent from the current generation of CASE tools. However, the problem of incorporation of metadata about source code uses and associated operators, or "intelligence" into design environments and repositories is quite similar to the problems faced by the CAD community in intelligent design and collaboration environments. Given the success and progress this community has made for nearly a decade, we expect this capability in the near future in software development and user environments.

Figure 2 illustrates the basic categories of software development tool and use required to minimally implement PANDA.

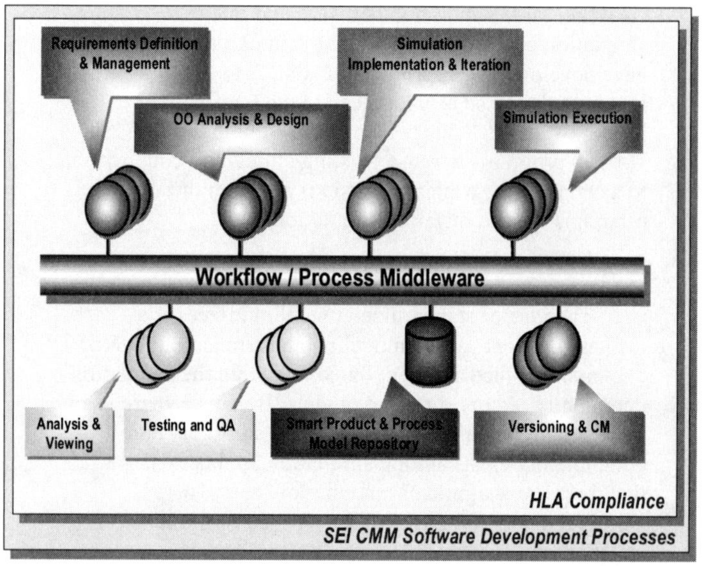

Figure 2. Basic simulation CASE tool suite component categories for PANDA.

We now address the mechanics of implementing these processes in simulation development and use environments. In particular, we show the need for software module integration abstractions and implementation techniques in the simulation domain that are analogous to those found in the business and small computing domains. The problem, however, is that the implementation strategies for integration in the business and small computing software domains does not scale to very large problem sizes with near-real-time performance, and in general do not have the requisite robustness and fault-tolerance features.

MODEL AND SIMULATION INTEGRATION BY SOFTWARE ENGINEERING INTERFACES

To mold existing models and simulations into a virtual single executable simulation system that optimizes the efficiency of execution is not always possible, unlike the Microsoft COM and DCOM architectures, and the Common Object Request Broker Architecture (CORBA) for general purpose computing. This problem has recently been solved for a significant spectrum of simulation problem types, most notably those with a logical time structure which may or may not be synchronized with some hardware clock system, and in general require no more than best-effort or firm real-time execution guarantees.

Indeed, one of the major problems in developing general purpose simulation execution frameworks which provide rich sets of representation and interaction mechanisms and can be run faster-than-real-time, are the difficulties involved in providing functions that allow the synchronization of logical time with some hardware clock. The computational overhead to provide fine-grained, hard-real-time synchronization guarantees is quite large and is hard to implement for complex problems.

In the course of implementing a unifying simulation execution framework for PANDA and its predecessor programs in the Navy and Army, many simulation execution frameworks have been used over the past decade [CACI 1991, Whitehurst 1991, 1995, and 1998]. As a result of an Office of Naval Research effort that concluded in 1996, the SPEEDES simulation framework was chosen as the most promising simulation execution framework with which to leverage ongoing DoD investments to more quickly achieve the desired integration capabilities [Steinman 1998 and 1999].

Viewed in this light, SPEEDES is being used as an execution efficient, scalable, and robust time-dependent model and simulation domain analog to COM, DCOM, and CORBA, that provides features such as: location transparency (distributed computing); a set of supported APIs for module integration allowing for abstraction; and encapsulation mechanisms which support legacy code reuse, to mention a few of the most important features for this discussion.

Figure 3 illustrates the basic concept behind this approach. Given $\boldsymbol{n}$ time-dependent models $\mathbf{M}_1, ..., \mathbf{M}_n$, which may have been independently executed as simulation in their own right, we isolate the software mechanism used to manipulate time in each model. We then map this mechanism into the SPEEDES Unified API, which contains the spectrum of modeling APIs and their subsequent timing approaches, from continuous to discrete-event. This mapping, or *API translation*, is implemented in a *compatibility library*, and allows the infrastructure model software to be linked to the SPEEDES libraries for runtime execution as a virtual single, composite simulation.

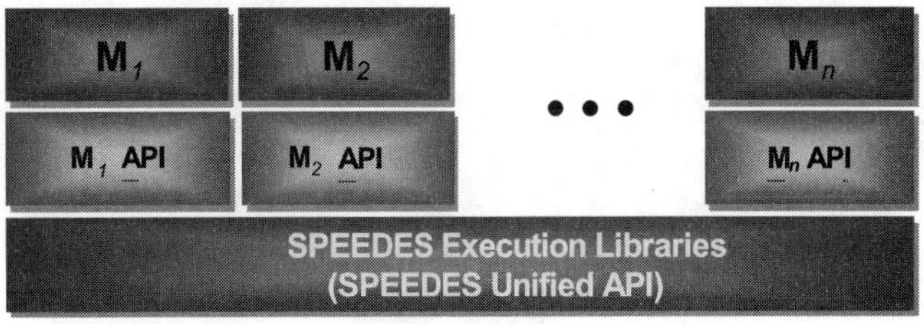

Figure 3. PANDA model integration strategy implemented using SPEEDES.

This approach to API translation was first demonstrated by the authors in the context of the JMASS program in an advanced technology demonstration, and is now being implemented in JMASS as a risk-reduction effort. In addition, this approach to system integration and software interoperability methodology that is being successfully utilized on the JSIMS program in support of an HLA-based simulation system architecture.

In the next section we discuss how this methodology extends to simulation CASE tool interoperability.

SIMULATION CASE TOOL INTEROPERABILITY

In order to rapidly produce realistic, predictive real world system representations in models and simulation for use in the wide variety of operational architectures illustrated above, with the desired characteristics, the problem of using many CASE tools to represent domain specific problem formulations in historically and psychologically founded symbol systems must be addressed. As will be demonstrated in our presentation of the software productivity metrics on the JSIMS Maritime program, the impact of natural and convenient symbol system representations from which software source code is generated is of prime importance in terms of the cost and time-to-market to get a simulation or its results into the user or operational community.

To address these issues, consider the situation where a variety of subject matter experts must collaborate to produce a single simulation system with many conceptually different domains. There is typically a symbol system that subject matter experts in a given domain of phenomenology choose or prefer to express their various models. In order to allow a cost-effective, timely solution to their problem, given that enough market critical mass exists, simulation CASE tool vendors will create a tool which supports a given symbol system. The problem arises, as we have indicated in the preceding discussion, in the fact that most tool vendors build their own internal mechanisms for the time-coordination and interaction coordination of the time-evolving simulation. As we have indicated in the section above, a solution to the problem illustrated in Figure 4 below needs to be constructed.

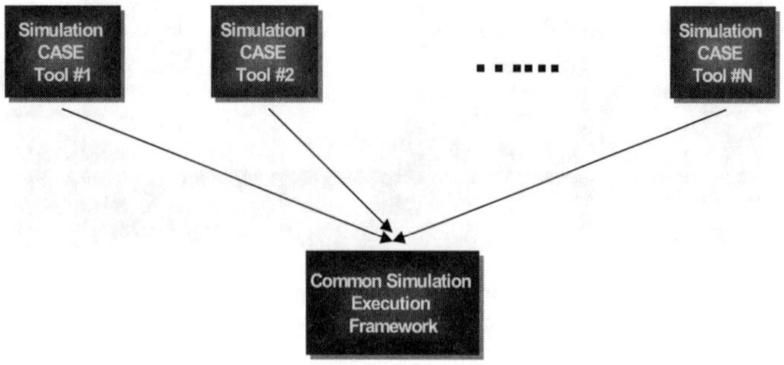

Figure 4. Many-to-one mapping of Simulation CASE Tools to a single Simulation Execution Framework.

In our programs, this has been done with the SPEEDES simulation execution framework with the following simulation CASE tools: the HPCMO's IMPORT v2.0 simulation development tool, Project Technology, Inc.'s (PTI) Bridgepoint has been used for all of the software development on the JSIMS Maritime program, and OriginalSim, Inc.'s OSim for a SPAWAR sponsored PANDA Industry Day.

Figure 5 illustrates the converse of the previous circumstance, that of having a common simulation CASE tool which generates multiple simulation execution frameworks.

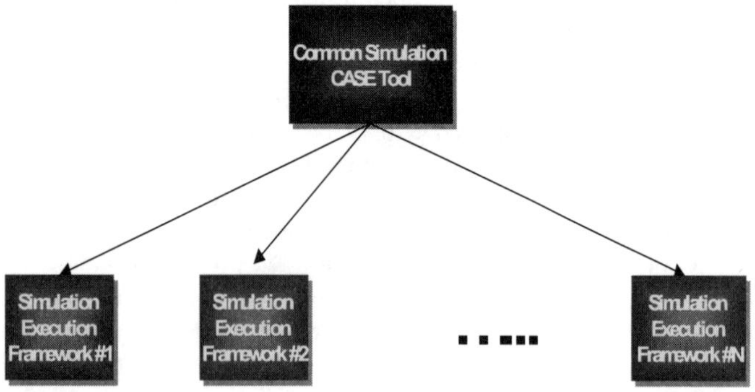

Figure 5. One-to-many mapping of a single Simulation CASE Tool to multiple simulation execution frameworks.

The usefulness of this capability has been demonstrated with both the IMPORT tools [Whitehurst 1995 and 1998] and Bridgepoint.

Consider Figure 6, which more explicitly illustrates the use of Bridgepoint in the software development process.

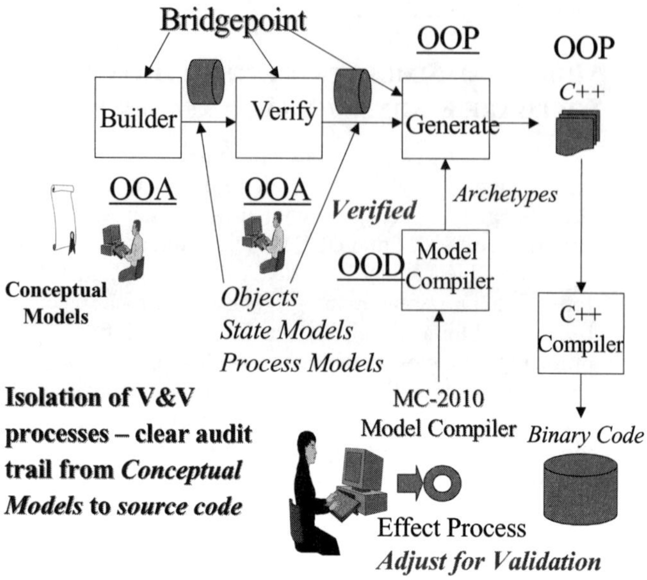

Figure 6. Use of the Bridgepoint tool suite in the software development process.

The Bridgepoint tool suite has the ability to generate multiple execution frameworks by virtue of using multiple ***Archetype Libraries*** with a given ***Model Compiler***. In addition, different model compilers are available from PTI for a variety of domain specific uses, from hard-real-time execution frameworks, to the MC 2010 model compiler used by the JSIMS Maritime program to generate the SPEEDES simulation framework.

In the next section we present the software development metrics recorded by the JSIMS Maritime using the PANDA approach, with the Bridgepoint tool suite as the centerpiece of the development environment shown in figure 2 above.

PANDA USE CASE: JSIMS MARITIME

The JSIMS Maritime program planned on using state-of-the-art software development approaches during the formative part of the program when formal cost estimates were being developed concurrently with a technical approach that would maximize the Navy's return on their scarce resources for meeting the fleet user's needs for JSIMS.

As a result of the authors' experiences on a successful line of R&D on simulation software engineering, combining the Army's Integrated Simulation Language Environment (ISLE) project, and the Navy's High Performance Computing Object Technology Transfer

(HOTT), the experience was gained to understand how to apply the use of tool suites like Bridgepoint and SEI CMM software development process guidelines to develop a highly efficient simulation software development process for JSIMS Maritime. Additionally, the stated goal on the JSIMS Maritime program was to attempt to achieve the software development productivity levels predicted by the Revised Constructive Cost Model (REVIC) for software cost estimation.

The REVIC model predicted that given near-optimal conditions, a rate of 900 source lines of code (SLOC), fully tested, debugged, documented, could be developed per person-month of labor. The ability of the JSIMS Maritime program to actually achieve this goal was deemed highly unlikely, given that the industry average for nominal software development activities is approximately 197 source-lines-of-code per person-month. We note that this implies factoring in all direct and indirect labor costs in computing this metric. Figure 7 illustrates the JSIMS Maritime software development metrics achieved during Build 2 with direct costs only.

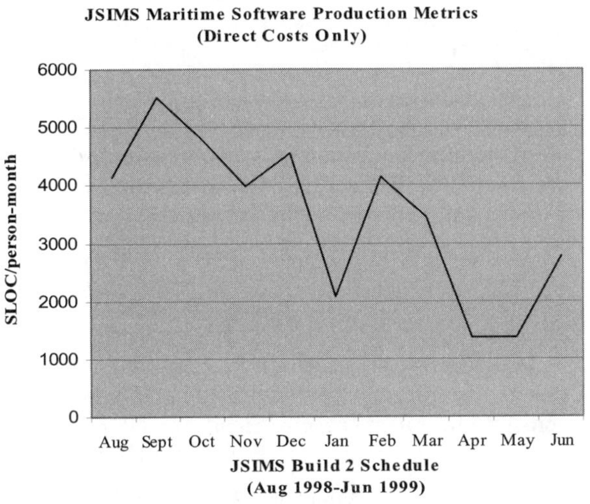

Figure 7. JSIMS Maritime SLOC metrics for JSIMS Build 2, direct costs only.

The drop-offs in productivity were due to instability in various JSIMS program execution elements, upon which JSIMS Maritime production was dependent. Even accounting for such irregularities, a high level of productivity was attained.

In Figure 8 we show the metrics, except the indirect labor costs are factored into the productivity metric figures. Note that the average productivity for JSIMS Maritime over the ten months spent developing software for Build 2 was approximately 640 SLOC/person-month, which compares quite favorably with the industry average of approximately 200 SLOC/person-month. We note that the level of 900 SLOC/person-month predicted by REVIC was in fact achieved during periods when programmatic conditions were stable.

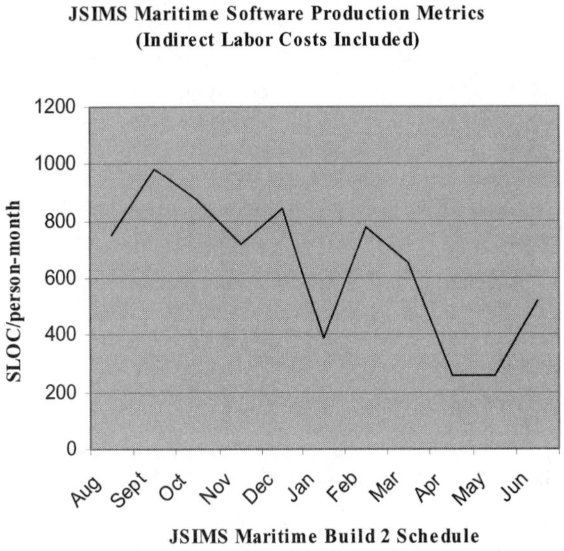

Figure 8. JSIMS Maritime SLOC metrics for JSIMS Build 2, all cost effects shown.

Finally, Figure 9 shows the growth of the JSIMS Maritime source code base over the during the development phase of JSIMS Build 2.

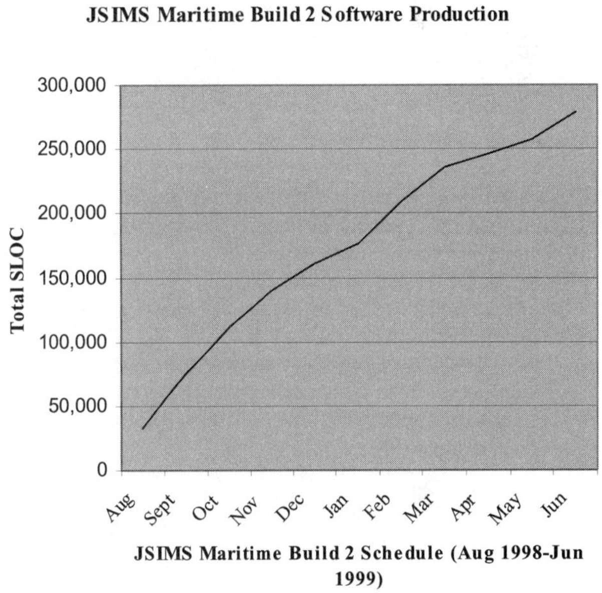

Figure 9. JSIMS Maritime software production during JSIMS Build 2.

Worth noting is that during the ten months of development on JSIMS Maritime, over 250,000 source lines of code were produced with 7 people providing the direct labor, an extremely high sustained productivity rate.

CONCLUSIONS

Our experiences on the JSIMS Maritime program indicate that more effort should be expended in proliferating the PANDA approach to simulation software engineering, development, and integration, due to the large impact this has made on the cost, schedule, and performance aspects of large-scale simulation development.

In addition, we feel the following areas deserve attention to further augment the advances we have documented in this paper. This would involve the following areas:

- A systemic specification tool that aids in the conceptualization process by managing catalogs of inter-object associations and frameworks.
- A systemic reuse agent based upon case-based reasoning which attempts to retrieve artifacts based upon their participation in inter-object associations and frameworks that exhibit similar roles and relationships.
- While evaluation and adaptation at the object class level is probably best left to the human developer, systemic evaluation based upon analogical measures can be performed by the reuse agent. This can lead to an automated identification of candidate entities based on the observation that they assume similar roles.
- Given that a particular entity or architecture is chosen based upon the recommendations of an automated reuse agent utilizing case-based reasoning, domain specific terminology can be translated from one domain to another based upon the analogical mapping (adaptation process).
- The identification of analogical architectures, such as those found in the process of translating simulation APIs, provides a framework or basis of composition that could be either directly re-useable, or form the basis for creation of a specialization (accumulation and evaluation).

REFERENCES

[CACI 89] CACI Products Company. 1989. *ModSim: A Language for Object-Oriented Simulation, Reference Manual, Release 1.0*, Contract DABT60-86-C-1382, Deliverable A-009, CACI Products Company, 1989.

[Deutsch 1989] Deutsch, Peter L. *Design reuse and frameworks in the smalltalk-80 systems*. In Ted J. Biggerstaff and Alan J. Perlis, editors, Software Reusability, volume 2, chapter 3, pages 57-72. ACM Press, New York, NY, 1989.

[Meyer 1989] Meyer, Bertrand. *Reusability: The case for object-oriented design*. In Ted J. Biggerstaff and Alan J. Perlis, editors, Software Reusability, volume 2, chapter 1, pages 1-34. ACM Press, New York, NY, 1989.

[McGraw 2000] McGraw R., *et al*, "Integration of SPEEDES into the JMASS Architecture," To appear in *The Proceedings of the 2000 Summer Computer Simulation Conference*, Society for Computer International, July 2000.

[Prieto-Diaz 1987] Prieto-Diaz, R. and P. Freeman. *Classifying software for reusability*. IEEE Software, 4(1):6-16, January 1987.

[Steinman 1998] Steinman, Jeffrey, "Scalable Distributed Military Simulations using the SPEEDES Object-Oriented Simulation Framework," *Object-Oriented Simulation 1998*, Wallace, J. and J. Steinman Eds., Society for Computer Simulation International, 1998.

[Steinman 1999] Steinman, Jeffrey, "A Tutorial on the SPEEDES Simulation Framework," At the 1999 Fall Simulation Interoperability Workshop.

[Whitehurst 91] Whitehurst R. A. 1991. "Simulation Using an Interpretive, Object-Oriented, Rule-based Approach," In *Object-Oriented Simulation 1991*, Ege R. Ed., Simulation Councils, Inc., January 1991.

[Whitehurst 95] Whitehurst R. A. and V. P. Morrison. 1995. "IMPORT: A Language for Simulation of Complex Systems," In *Object-Oriented Simulation 1995*, Roberts C., T. Beaumariage, C. Herring, J. Wallace Eds., Simulation Councils, Inc., January 1995.

[Whitehurst 1998] Whitehurst R. A. and J. Brutacao. 1998. "Parallel Execution of Process-based Simulation Models," In *Object-Oriented Simulation 1998*, Wallace J. *et al* Eds., Society for Computer Simulation International, January 1998.

INTEGRATION OF SPEEDES INTO THE JMASS ARCHITECTURE

Robert M. McGraw[1], Richard A. MacDonald[1], Jeffrey S. Steinman[1], Jeffrey W. Wallace[2], R. Douglas Buchy[3]
[1]RAM Laboratories, Inc. Solana Beach, CA
[2]Consultant to SPAWAR PD 13, PMW 131, San Diego, CA
[3]Deputy Program Manager, JMASS Program Office, Dayton, OH

Keywords: Distributed Simulation, High Performance Computing, Simulation-based Acquisition, High Level Architecture, Time management

ABSTRACT

The DOD simulation community is striving to develop and utilize simulations frameworks that reduce cost and promote scalability, portability, and interoperability across a wide variety of disciplines. In order to support an interdisciplinary approach, simulation frameworks must provide simulation services such as advanced time-management, data time tagging, repeatable time/event synchronization, communication via shared memory architectures, and dynamically including or excluding models during simulation. One method of supplying these simulation services would be to integrate simulation architectures with an existing framework that supports high performance computing (HPC) applications.

An approach is presented for integrating the SPEEDES (Synchronous Parallel Environment for Emulation and Discrete Event Simulation) Modeling Framework (SMF) within the JMASS architecture. This basic approach involves integrating the SPEEDES simulation engine within JMASS using the SPEEDES Distributed Simulation Management Services (DSMS) and the SPEEDES Modeling Framework (SMF) as a foundation to develop an interface library to the JMASS Application Program Interface (API). By using SPEEDES, HPC services required to support complex simulations will be inherently provided. Additionally, features such as code generation, model interoperability, and support for multi-modeling, will also be provided. The resultant integrated framework will allow the execution of JMASS simulations on a wide variety of parallel and distributed high performance computers (which includes MPPs), and computing environments, thus extending the portability and scalability of the current JMASS system.

INTRODUCTION

Today's military is increasingly reliant on the use simulation to reduce cost. However, these simulations themselves are often costly in terms of not only development time but also simulation time. In order to address these cost issues, the DOD has turned to architectures and frameworks that reduce cost by promoting, scalability, portability, and interoperability. The Joint Modeling And Simulation System (JMASS) is a tri-service simulation environment that addresses these issues. JMASS utilizes an object-based technology for developing an interoperable common model set by specifying a collection of well-defined, well-documented interface standards to which a JMASS model should be built. The resultant simulation system supports engineering and engagement-level simulations with non-real time interaction among models of varying levels of detail. This includes support for the development of detailed digital models of red, blue and gray systems for use in electronic warfare analysis.

In the future, goals for JMASS will be to expanded to support other Tri-Service domains[1]. For example, the Navy's requirements for a simulation system that supports simulation-based acquisition encompasses a variety of simulation domains. For instance, different naval organizations (NAVAIR, NAVSEA, SPAWAR) utilize a wide range of commercial tools and application-specific simulations over diverse computational areas. NAVAIR programs require simulation-based acquisition that supports the design of airframes and power plants, the design of weapons systems and countermeasures, and the C4ISR integration. NAVSEA programs require simulation-based acquisition that supports the design of hulls, topside, weapons systems and countermeasures, as well as the integration of C4ISR systems. The Space and Naval Warfare (SPAWAR) Systems Command requires simulation-based acquisition support for the design of C4ISR hardware design and integration and testing (Teknowledge Corporation, 2000).

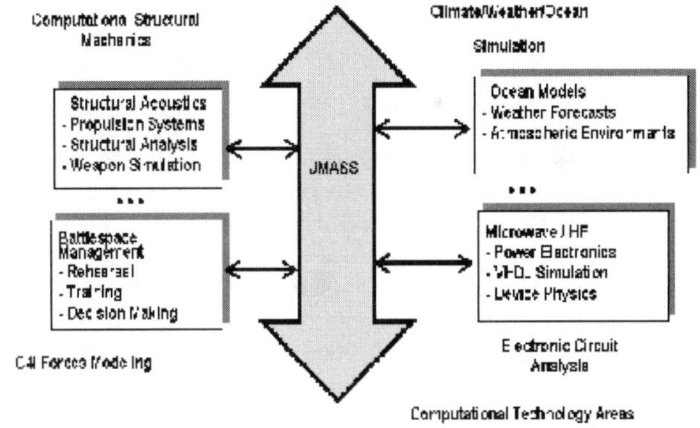

Figure 1: Interdisciplinary Approach to JMASS

In order to satisfy the design and acquisition requirements of each of these Navy programs, a simulation infrastructure must support a wide variety of simulation paradigms. Navy design and integration programs require simulations to support disciplines such as computational fluid dynamics, computational structural mechanics, computational electromagnetics, computational thermodynamics, electronic circuit design, environment modeling, terrain modeling, climate, weather, and ocean simulation, C4I forces modeling, civilian and military infrastructure modeling, and analytic attribute evolution modeling. To fully support these

[1] http://www.jmass.wpafb.af.mil

requirements, JMASS must support simulations for each of these areas as shown in Figure 2.

Simulations and environments that are employed in each of these diverse computational areas often have very different developmental front-ends, execution frameworks, and back-end analysis capabilities, as shown in Figure 3. Full simulation for such multi-interdisciplinary Navy programs requires the co-simulation and interoperability of these execution frameworks. In order to provide this capability, JMASS must implement the features required by various Navy application-specific and commercial simulation tools. These features may include provisions for discrete or continuous simulation, support for modeling of ordinary and partial differential equations, support for model synchronization, and support for simulation involving models consisting of multiple degrees of freedom and resolution.

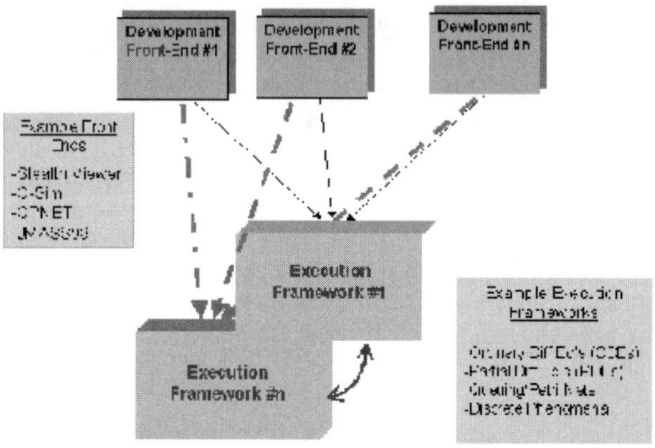

Figure 2: Multiple Execution Frameworks

In addition to developing application-specific simulations, the Navy employs a wide variety of simulation tools. The commercial simulation tools have included a wide variety of simulation features. These features include continuous simulation, discrete simulation, Monte Carlo simulation, differential equation-based simulations, partial differential equation-based simulations, queuing-based models, and Petri Net models. Other simulation modes that are supported include real-time simulation, faster-than-real-time simulation, man-in-the-loop simulation, and hardware-in-the-loop simulation.

To these simulations and environments, JMASS must extend its current set of modeling services to provide support for high performance computing applications. These services include support for advanced time-management algorithms to permit real-time and faster-than-real-time simulation, data time tagging, repeatable time/event synchronization, dynamically starting, stopping, pausing and aborting executions, saving and reloading model states, and dynamically including or excluding models during simulation. One method of supplying these simulation services would be to integrate the JMASS architecture with an existing framework that supports high performance computing (HPC) applications. SPEEDES is such a framework.

SPEEDES

SPEEDES is a high performance computing (HPC) simulation framework that supports parallel and distributed simulation for computationally intense problems. SPEEDES maintains HPC features such as advanced time management and support for shared memory communications structures.

In the early 1990's, several Department of Defense (DoD) simulation infrastructure projects began to explore how to provide interoperability between multiple simulations executing on different computing platforms (Kanarick 1991, Loral 1992, Peckham 1999, Weatherly 1993). One of those projects, SPEEDES, was started in 1990 by NASA under DOD contracts by the Jet Propulsion Laboratory for the Ballistic Missile Defense Organization (Steinman 1998). SPEEDES' primary goal was to provide interoperability between objects distributed across large numbers of processors using a common simulation engine. One of the key features of SPEEDES is its ability to preserve causally correct event processing in a repeatable manner without sacrificing parallel performance or imposing constraints regarding how simulated objects may interact. The SPEEDES work resulted in more than thirty publications and four government patents[2].

In the mid-1990s, the DOD officially acknowledged the importance of providing interoperability between its simulations. The Defense Modeling Simulation Office (DMSO) began to explore the idea of defining a High-Level Architecture (HLA) that would provide the necessary means to achieve interoperability between disparate simulations (Dahmann, Kuhl, et al 1998, Dahmann and Lutz 1998, Steinman 1997, Yu 1998)[3]. Likewise, starting in 1996, the SPEEDES development effort has closely mirrored that of HLA.

Currently, several mainstream DoD projects are looking at SPEEDES to combine interoperability and high-performance by using a common simulation engine. SPEEDES applications can combine to form larger, more capable simulations. SPEEDES is currently being extended to provide interoperability with:

- HLA federations through a gateway that can "talk to" any RTI meeting the HLA standard
- External HLA federates operating in a computer network environment
- HLA federates represented as SPEEDES nodes that execute on high-performance computers

All of the above combinations are interoperable with each other.

The development of SPEEDES is currently under configuration management with the PDES User's Group acting as the Configuration Management Board. Members of the Configuration Management Board are members of the SPEEDES user community: Joint Simulation System (JSIMS), Wargame 2000 through the Joint National Test Facility (JNTF), Space and Naval Warfare (SPAWAR) Systems Command, the Extended Air Defense Test Bed (EADTB), and the Joint Modeling and Simulation System (JMASS).

---

[2] http://www.speedes.com

[3] http://hla.dmso.mil

SPEEDES ARCHITECTURE

A layered software architecture strategy provides a bottom-up approach to software development that allows higher-levels of functionality and abstraction to be built upon lower-levels. SPEEDES has evolved using software-layering principles and the spiral process model. Figure 3 shows the various layers of the SPEEDES architecture. The layered approach isolates critical functionality, while extending capability through higher-level abstractions. Several of these areas are described below.

Internal Communications Layer

The foundation for portable distributed simulation in SPEEDES is supported through internal communications libraries. The SPEEDES Communications Library (Van Iwaarden 1999) achieves interoperability between different operating systems, networks, and inter-process communication mechanisms through a common interface that we have been able to implement and optimize across all the major types of parallel and distributed computing environments. Such environments include shared memory multiprocessor machines, networks of computers, and/or large scale message-passing supercomputers.

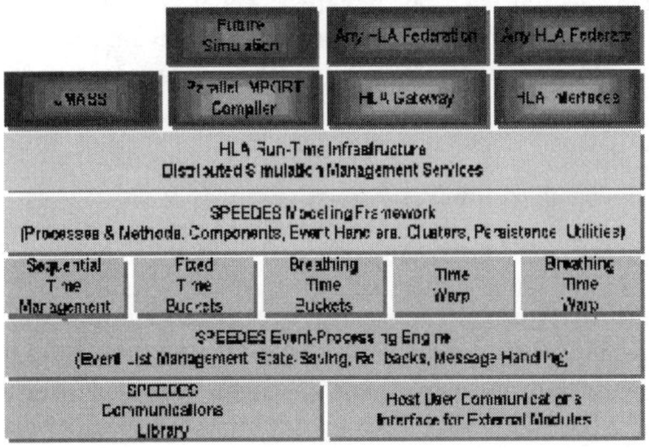

Figure 3: The SPEEDES Architecture.

External Communications Layer

SPEEDES provides a second communications infrastructure that facilitates message passing with external modules. SPEEDES decouples its internal message-passing infrastructure from its external message passing system in order to optimize the implementation of each separately. Internal communication is accomplished by sending messages through shared memory, local high-speed networks (or both); external communications are transmitted through distributed network environments. Separating external and internal communication systems enables external modules to join and leave SPEEDES simulations without disrupting internal synchronization mechanisms.

Event Management Layer

SPEEDES provides an optimistic, rollback-based, event-management layer that can be used to support multiple time management schemes (Fujimoto 1990, Steinman 1994). Disabling the rollback mechanism at run time permits conservative time management algorithms to synchronize event processing. Currently, lookahead-based conservative time management is available.

Lazy cancellation is also provided by SPEEDES. Lazy cancellation is implemented in a manual mode where users can write virtual methods that determine whether events are permitted to roll forward following a rollback. In the future, SPEEDES will automate lazy cancellation through a built-in touch-depend system that tracks the dependencies between events and state variables. A rolled back event can later be rolled forward if the straggler that induced the rollback does not touch any of the state variables that the event depends on. All rollbackable operations in SPEEDES are rollforwardable (Steinman 1993, West 1988, West 1996) and thereby support lazy cancellation.

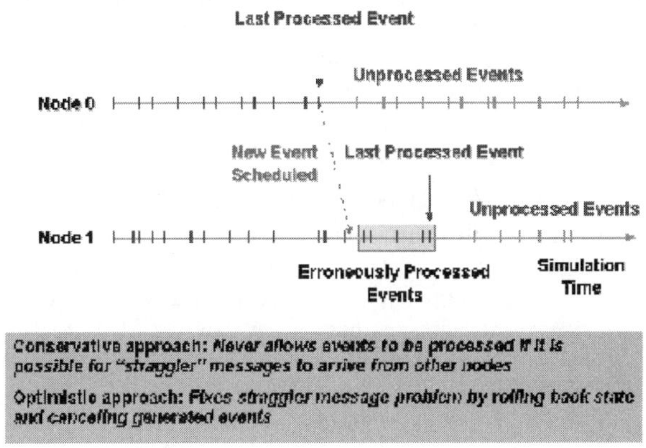

Figure 4: Distributed time management.

Persistence, the ability to save the state of a simulation to a disk, is also supported by SPEEDES (Van Iwaarden 1999). Whenever a SPEEDES simulation dynamically creates a rollbackable object, SPEEDES records its address and block size in a default persistent database that it manages directly in high-speed memory. Similarly, whenever the simulation sets a rollbackable pointer, SPEEDES records the linkage between memory blocks in the database.

By transparently providing persistence in the rollback mechanism, SPEEDES simulations can automatically participate in checkpoint/restarts. During a checkpoint, SPEEDES packs all objects on each node into a compressed buffer and then writes the buffer to disk. Each node writes to its own file. SPEEDES can later read these files during a restart to reconstruct the entire simulation from the point where the checkpoint was originally made. This capability provides further fault tolerance for SPEEDES applications.

Time Management Layer

Guaranteeing logically correct time management in a distributed computing environment involves many challenges. Each simulated object must process its events in ascending time order to maintain repeatability and causality. The challenge is to allow any object to schedule events for any other object at any logical time in the present or future.

SPEEDES utilizes lookahead to provide some processing concurrency by limiting how tightly in time objects can interact. Without lookahead, conservative time management algorithms can only permit the object with the smallest time tag to process its next event. This is because all other objects must wait just in case their actual next event is scheduled by the current event. This fact prohibits concurrent event processing, thereby serializing the simulation.

The most capable solution to the time management problem is to allow objects to process their events optimistically, but then roll them back when receiving *straggler* events (an event whose time tag is in the past). Rollbacks restore state variables and retract events generated during the rolled-back simulated time interval. When a simulation engine schedules events for different nodes, it sends event-scheduling messages. Rollbacks must therefore retract those sent messages by further sending *antimessages*. When another simulation node receives an antimessage, it may have already processed the retracted event. The most popular optimistic algorithm of this type is called Time Warp (Jefferson 1985).

SPEEDES uses Breathing Time Warp (BTW) to implement optimistic time management (Steinman 1995, Steinman 1998). This algorithm provides the flow control necessary to ensure stable simulation execution. BTW achieves such flow control by releasing event messages only when they are likely to be valid. Events that have a high probability of being rolled back hold onto their messages initially. This strategy significantly reduces both antimessage traffic and rollbacks.

The SPEEDES Modeling Framework Layer

The SPEEDES modeling framework uses four fundamental abstractions as building blocks for the rest of the framework. These abstractions, shown in Figure 5 using an extended Unified Modeling Language (UML), are (1) object managers, (2) simulation objects, (3) events, and (4) messages (Steinman 1998).

One *object manager* instance for each kind of simulation object resides on each node. Object Managers group different kinds of simulation objects together into subsets in a distributed manner. An object manager decomposes its simulation objects to SPEEDES nodes and remembers their locations when responding to requests for simulation object handles.

Simulation objects represent the simulated entities. Their state variables must be comprised of rollbackable data types. All event management responsibilities for individual entities reside in the base class simulation object where SPEEDES maintains pending unprocessed events as well as uncommitted processed events. A SPEEDES scheduler, residing on each node, continually determines which simulation object processes its next event. Processed events are committed when their time tags are less than the time tag of the earliest unprocessed event in the simulation (Fujimoto 1990, Jefferson 1985, Steinman 1995).

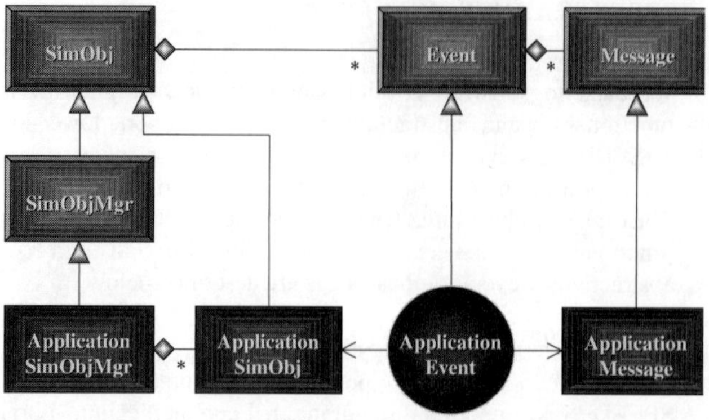

Figure 5: UML diagram of the fundamental classes in the SPEEDES Modeling Framework.

Time-tagged *events* are C++ objects that are managed by simulation objects. Unprocessed events with future time tags are stored in a pending event queue. Processed events with time tags in the past are stored in an uncommitted event queue until SPEEDES commits them. When processing an event, SPEEDES stores state variable changes in the event object. This allows SPEEDES to roll back uncommitted events when necessary. An event may associate with only one simulation object at a time because (1) simulation objects may be on different nodes, (2) simulation objects may be at different logical times, and (3) rollback dependencies are coordinated by simulation objects.

Components & Event Handlers

Building on these fundamental abstractions, SPEEDES provides a higher-level component-based set of modeling tools to promote expressive and clear semantics, reusability, and maintainability. *Components* encapsulate an abstraction, such as a piece of equipment, that can be dynamically added or removed from a simulation object. Examples include sensors, trackers, weapon systems, communications, command & control, position, cargo, etc. Components usually contain one or more application-level models that are controlled by processes and event handlers. Models do not require inheritance. By keeping model associations one-way (i.e., models are only used by other objects within the component), SPEEDES preserves maximum reusability.

Events as Methods & Processes

SPEEDES provides another way to schedule and process events. Users can define methods in their simulation objects to be invoked as events. Applications can schedule these event methods using a type-checked event-scheduling interface provided by SPEEDES. The macro, DEFINE_EVENT_METHOD, generates this specialized event-scheduling function in addition to an event object and a message. This macro relieves users from the necessity of writing event objects and messages.

SPEEDES also provides support for process model constructs (Whitehurst 1998) inside event methods with a few simple macros. Processes are event methods that can pass simulated time without exiting. The WAIT statement is the simplest process model construct. Processes can wait specified time periods and then "wake up," continuing where they left off.

TECHNICAL APPROACH

In order to provide the simulation services of the SPEEDES Simulation Framework to JMASS, a straightforward development approach will be followed. The goal of this approach is to provide JMASS with a plug-and-play capability using SPEEDES. In order to provide this capability, a JMASS Compatibility Library will be developed. This JMASS Compatibility Library interfaces the Unified API.

SPEEDES Unified API

The SPEEDES Unified API provides a unified interface for applications to interact with the SPEEDES Simulation Framework (SSF). This unified API provides macro-ized APIs for generating interfaces for Events, Processes, and Event Handlers for the applications that interact with SPEEDES. The Unified API is used to generate C++ code to provide these interfaces. The Unified API provides an implementation for the four major approaches to general time-evolving system representations in the SSF. These approaches include methods for representing events as objects, events as methods, processes as objects, and processes as methods. Additionally, the SPEEDES Unified API provides a "Plug-in" mechanism that allows simulation objects for a given application to be plugged into the SSF.

JMASS API

The JMASS API defines the interface for all applications that wish to interact JMASS-compliant simulations. Specifically, for simulation framework applications (i.e. the simulation infrastructures) the key subset of APIs includes the JMASS *Player* class APIs and the JMASS *Port* class APIs. These APIs interact with the time-evolving elements of JMASS simulations. The time evolving components in JMASS are derived from the JMASS *Player* class APIs. The interactions of time-evolving components in JMASS are derived via the JMASS *Port* class APIs (Esmond 1999).

JMASS Compatibility Library Development

The JMASS Compatibility Library provides the interface between the SPEEDES Unified API and the JMASS API. This library allows JMASS applications to interact via the SPEEDES Simulation Framework. The basic idea behind the development of the JMASS Compatibility Library is to take each API that represents a time-evolving component or component interface, and develop a mapping from that API to the SPEEDES Unified API. This entails taking the virtual JMASS functions, represented by these APIs, and defining that function using the SPEEDES Unified API. Figure 6 illustrates a simple example for developing the JMASS Compatibility Library representation for the JMASS *Update()*API using *DEFINE_EVENT* of the SPEEDES Unified API.

EXAMPLE

The example details the *Update* API as represented in JMASS by the virtual function *Update()*. This particular example was taken from the set of JMASS Training Examples, Example 6 (JMASS 1999). The *Update()* virtual function performs an update in JMASS using the JMASS Player APIs *update*, *schedule_update*, and *update_time*. Of these APIs, the Update() API, is used to evolve
time.

```
void Example6::Update ()
{
  PCP::Trace pcpTrace(this, "Example6::Update",
                              pcpTraceCmd,
  pcpNumTraceCmds);
  PCP::Trace *w = &pcpTrace;w=w;
  //= USER MODIFIED CODE #Update_CODE_BODY#

  controller->control_it(control_msg);
  schedule_update(update_time + update_interval);
  return;

  //= USER MODIFIED CODE #Update_CODE_BODY#
}
```

Figure 6: JMASS Update API

```
#include "SpExecute.H"
#include "SpBuiltInMacros.H"
#include "player.H"

DEFINE_EVENT_METHOD_0_ARG(UpdateEvent,
                10,
                player,
                Update);

void PlugInJmass()
{
   PLUG_IN_EVENT(UpdateEvent);
}
```

Figure 7: JMASS Compatibility Library Implementation

The JMASS Compatibility Library implementation for the JMASS *Update()* API is shown in Figure 7. In order to implement this function using the SPEEDES Unified API, both the *SpExecute.H* and *SpBuiltInMacros.H* SPEEDES header files are required. Additionally, the JMASS header file *player.H* is required to implement the *Update()* function for this library component.

The SPEEDES Unified API implementation of *Update()* is performed using the *DEFINE_EVENT_METHOD* API. The zero-argument version of this API is selected because the *Update()* virtual function has no arguments. The event definition is *UpdateEvent* based on SPEEDES naming conventions. The *player* entry refers to the JMASS simulation object that is being implemented. The *Update* entry refers to the virtual function being implemented. Finally, in order to plug in elements into SPEEDES, the *PlugInJMass()* function is defined. For this example, only the event, *UpdateEvent* needs to be plugged into SPEEDES. This plug-in is implemented using the SPEEDES Unified API *PLUG_IN_EVENT*.

SUMMARY

An approach has been presented for integrating SPEEDES within the JMASS architecture. The proposed approach provides a low-risk, yet straightforward, method for providing JMASS a simulation framework that supports HPC applications. By utilizing advanced time management and shared memory communications structures already present in the SPEEDES Simulation Framework, simulation services such as real-time simulation, faster-than-real-time simulation, data time tagging, checkpoint restart, dynamic simulation control, and persistence can be afforded to all users of JMASS. Additionally, the use of SPEEDES will provide JMASS Users with a parallel and distributed simulation capability that supports multi-modeling and CASE tool applications. By implementing this approach, SPEEDES-JMASS can better address the simulation demands of both the DOD and commercial simulation communities.

ACKNOWLEDGEMENTS

The author wishes to thank the JMASS Program Office and SPAWAR PD-13 for their support in this effort.

REFERENCES

Dahmann J., Kuhl F., Weatherly R. 1998, "Standards for Simulation: As Simple As Possible, But Not Simpler – The High Level Architecture For Simulation." Simulation, Vol. 71, No. 6, Dec. 1998, Pages 378-387.

Dahmann J., Lutz R. 1998, "Persistent Federations." 1998 Spring Simulation Interoperability Workshop, No. 98S-SIW-059.

Esmond, Marvin. 1999. Joint Operations Requirements Document for Joint Modeling and Simulation System.

Fujimoto R. 1990, "Parallel Discrete Event Simulation." Communications of the ACM, Vol. 33, No. 10, Pages 30-53.

Jefferson D. 1985, "Virtual Time." ACM Transactions on Programming Languages and Systems, Vol. 7, No. 3, pages 404-425.

JMASS Training 1999. JMASS Program Office Presented by Dynetics.

Kanarick C. 1991, "A Technical Overview and History of the SIMNET Project." In Proceedings of the 1991 Advances in Parallel And Distributed Simulation Conference, Pages 104-111.

Loral Systems Company 1992, "Strawman Distributed Interactive Simulation Architecture Description Document." Prepared for Program manager – Training Devices Naval Training Systems Center, Orlando, FL, ADST/WDL/TR-92003010, Vols. 1 and 2.

Peckham M. 1999, "High Level Architecture Gateway for Wargame 2000." In Proceedings of the 1999 Fall Simulation Interoperability Workshop. Paper 99F-SIW-140.

Steinman J. 1993, "Incremental State Saving in SPEEDES Using C++." In Proceedings of the 1993 Winter Simulation Conference, Pages 687-696.

Steinman J., Wieland F. 1994, "Parallel Proximity Detection and the Distribution List Algorithm." In Proceedings of the 1994 Parallel And Distributed Simulation Conference (PADS'94), Pages 3-11.

Steinman J., et. al. 1995, "Global Virtual Time and Distributed Synchronization." In Proceedings of the 1995 Parallel And Distributed Simulation Conference, Pages 139-148.

Steinman J. 1997, "The NSS HLA-Integration Framework." 1997 Spring Simulation Interoperability Workshop, No. 97S-SIW-071.

Steinman J. 1998, "Scalable Distributed Military Simulations Using the SPEEDES Object-Oriented Simulation Framework." In Proceedings of the Object Oriented Simulation Conference (OOS'98), Pages 3-23.

Teknowledge Corporation, Navy Requirements for JMASS To-Be Technical Reference Architecture, January 2000.

Van Iwaarden R., et. al. 1999, "A Combined Shared Memory – TCP/IP Implementation of the SPEEDES Communications Library." In Proceedings of the 1999 Fall Simulation Interoperability Workshop. Paper 99F-SIW-095.

Van Iwaarden R., et. al. 1999, "Persistence Memory Management for Checkpoint and Restart of SPEEDES." In Proceedings of the 1999 Fall Simulation Interoperability Workshop. Paper 99F-SIW-109.

Weatherly R., Wilson A., Griffin S. 1993, "ALSP – Theory, Experience, and Future Directions." In Proceedings of the 1993 Winter Simulation Conf4erence, Pages 1068-1072.

West D. 1988, "Optimizing Time Warp: Lazy Rollback and Lazy Re-evaluation." Master's Thesis, University of Calgary, January 1988.

West D., Panesar K., 1996, "Automatic Incremental State Saving." In Proceedings of the 1996 Parallel And Distributed Simulation Conference (PADS'96), Pages 78-85.

Whitehurst A., Brutocao, J. 1998, "Parallel Execution of Process-Based Simulation Models." In Proceedings of the Object Oriented Simulation Conference (OOS'98), Pages 115-120.

Yu L., Steinman J., Blank G., 1998, "Adapting Your Simulation For HLA." Simulation, Vol. 71, No. 6, Dec. 1998, Pages 410-420.

USING FOM AGILITY IN COTS PRODUCTS TO CUSTOMIZE HLA TOOLS FOR THE JMASS PROGRAM

By Warren Katz
MÄK Technologies, Inc.
185 Alewife Brook Parkway
Cambridge, MA 02138
617-876-8085 x113
wkatz@mak.com

KEYWORDS:

FOM, COTS, HLA, Software Engineering, Tools

ABSTRACT:

The JMASS Program required a long-term technical solution for 3D visualization and Data Logging of battlefield simulation data. Though they had developed some custom prototype applications for this need, for the long-term they wanted to investigate leveraging an existing suite of commercial products and customize them to be interoperable with the JMASS environment. MÄK Technologies was awarded the contract to modify its suite of COTS products for 3D visualization, data collection, and data playback within the JMASS environment. The 3D-visualization tool is based on MÄK's commercial Stealth, and Data Logging is based on MÄK's commercial Data Logger. The mechanism by which this customization was achieved was FOM Agility, an architectural aspect of the VR-Link networking toolkit, which underlies all of MÄK's products. FOM Agility enables custom HLA FOMs to be easily integrated into any VR-Link based application, making that application interoperable within the custom HLA federation. This paper describes how FOM Agility works, and how MÄK's commercial products were quickly customized with a new HLA-compliant JMASS FOM to make them interoperable with the JMASS environment.

INTRODUCTION:

JMASS is a simulation framework that enables users to define models, combine models into simulations, execute the simulations, and perform post-processing analysis. To support this framework, tools were needed that support 3D visualization, data recording, and data playback of the JMASS scenario. These tools needed to be HLA-compliant and operate within the JMASS environment. These tools were to be used by a wide-spectrum of JMASS users with varying level of computer experience, making it imperative that the tools were robust and easy-to-use, with intuitive user interfaces.

MÄK proposed modifying versions of the VR-Link, Stealth, and Data Logger COTS tools to support scenario 3D visualization, data recording, and data playback. The modified tools had to meet the requirements of JMASS-compliance, HLA-compliance, robustness, ease-of-use, and flexibility. The advantages to incorporating COTS products into the JMASS environment were decisive to the program:

- **Reduction in Lifecycle Cost:** By utilizing a COTS product, JMASS is able to not only leverage years of existing software development, but also have access to dedicated support staff, professional documentation, and continual upgrades, enabling the program to stay current with new and evolving standards. By amortizing these costs over a large customer base, a COTS company is able to provide these services for a minimal maintenance fee. To implement a custom solution, the JMASS program would have had to pay a contractor for non-recurring engineering, operation and maintenance costs, as well as any future modifications, including support for different FOMs and future HLA specifications.
- **Reduction in Schedule:** By utilizing a COTS product, JMASS was able to leverage a substantial amount of existing HLA software, thereby reducing the development time. In the future, JMASS will be able to quickly adapt to changing standards by updating to new versions of HLA COTS tools. This insulates JMASS users from worrying about changes in the HLA specification, such as the change from RTI 1.0.3 to RTI 1.3, and the planned change to IEEE 1516.

- **Reduction in Risk:** By utilizing a COTS product, JMASS leveraged a robust, proven solution that already supports hundreds of customers and thousands of simulators. In addition to a strong technical solution, JMASS has access to an expert support staff ensuring successful integration of current and future software versions.

The MÄK Stealth is available for Windows 95/98, Windows NT, and SGI Workstations. The Stealth is OpenFlight compatible. It has a comprehensive Graphical User Interface (GUI) that enables users to fly through the virtual world using a choice of interfaces and to attach to simulated entities in one of eleven view modes. The MÄK Data Logger is available on both Unix and WINTEL platforms. It has a comprehensive GUI that enables users to quickly record and playback HLA data. Both of these tools are based of MÄK's commercial networking toolkit, VR-Link.

TECHNICAL APPROACH

Dynetics acted as consultants throughout the duration of the program. They are the company responsible for implementation of JMASS 98.

Internally, JMASS players communicate using JMASS ports. Externally, JMASS is able act as an HLA federate, transmitting object and interaction data through an RTI. In order to minimize the cost and risk of integrating COTS tools within JMASS, MÄK took advantage of the new JMASS HLA prototype, based on JMASS 98 1.0, developed by SAIC (standard JMASS releases will not be HLA or DIS compliant until JMASS 5.0).

To work within JMASS, there needs to be a mapping between the JMASS FOM/SOM and the internal data structure used by MÄK's COTS products. Since all the products are based on VR-Link, this mapper only needed to be developed once and could be used by all of MÄK's COTS products. By isolating the JMASS modifications to a single piece of code, JMASS users are able to incorporate new releases of MÄK's COTS products directly from the CD with no additional modifications.

JMASS flexibility made it impossible for a tool to know beforehand what objects and interactions were going to be used in the scenario. Through MÄK's FOM-Mapping approach, MÄK COTS products are able to dynamically load-in, during runtime, the mapping between the specific JMASS FOM and the COTS internal data structures. This technology enables MÄK's COTS products to support different JMASS scenarios without any modifications.

DETAILED APPROACH

Figure 1 illustrates how MÄK's COTS tools were incorporated into the JMASS environment MÄK enhanced VR-Link by incorporating a JMASS FOM-Mapper Tool. The Tool was used to create a mapping of the objects and interactions defined in the JMASS FED-file to the internal data structures used by the MÄK Stealth, Data Logger. The Stealth was modified to incorporate a JMASS Model Mapper which enable users to map JMASS players to user-defined 3D models. The MÄK Stealth and Data Logger communicate with JMASS through HLA using VR-Link. Users can view the exercise during execution and record data for AAR. Using the VR-Link development libraries, users can extend the JMASS FOM Mapper to incorporate new simulation concepts.

JMASS FOM Mapper:

The JMASS FOM Mapper Tool is illustrated in Figure 2. The JMASS FOM Mapper Tool obtains the attributes and interactions used in the exercise from the FED File. Through a GUI, JMASS users can map the attributes and interactions to their VR-Link counterparts. For example, in Figure 2, the FOM attribute *position* is mapped to the VR-Link function, *setLocation*. Once all the mappings are complete, the JMASS FOM Mapper Tool automatically creates a JMASS FOM Mapper Software Stub. JMASS users will complete the JMASS FOM Mapper filling in the software stub with the specific mapping required between the JMASS defined data and by the VR-Link data.

For example, based on the mapping in Figure 2, code similar to the following would be generated to map between the position attribute and VR-Link:

```
DecodePosition(void * value, DtEntityStateRespository *esr)
{
    DtVector vec;
    // User places conversion between FOM representation (value) and VR-Link's internal representation (vec)
    // Example conversion may include coordinate conversion or unit conversions
    setLocation (vec);
}
```

Once completed, the JMASS users compile the software stub into a JMASS FOM Mapper. Through the VR-Link development libraries, users have access to any of the VR-Link functions to assist in the creation of the JMASS FOM Mapper. This includes coordinate conversion routines, time utilities, and attribute and interaction callbacks and accessor/mutator functions. The resulting FOM Mapper is dynamically loaded into the Stealth and Data Logger during execution to support 3D visualization and data recording and playback of the HLA data.

While it was not technically feasible to completely automate the FOM-Mapping process, there are ways in which MÄK assisted the JMASS user throughout the process, such as:

- **Implementation of a sample FOM Mapper:** To support the final demonstration, MÄK and Dynetics created a JMASS FOM Mapper. Dynetics was involved in this task to lend expertise in the types of attributes and interactions typical of a JMASS exercise and to provide valuable feedback on the ease-of-use and robustness of the tool.
- **Explanation of FOM creation process:** MÄK provided an extensive, easy-to-follow description outlining how the sample FOM Mapper was created. In addition, MÄK provided a detailed description of the VR-Link internal data structures and provided example mappings of typical JMASS attributes and interactions.

GUI-based Model Mapper

MÄK modified the Stealth to incorporate a graphical Model-Mapper to enable JMASS users to specify their own 3D representation (via OpenFlight .flt files) for JMASS players. The Model-Mapper exports a Stealth configuration file that is read during start-up. Without the GUI-based Model Mapper, JMASS users would need to edit the Stealth configuration file by hand. This Model Mapper is a JAVA-based application will be included as a standard feature in all future Stealth releases.

Display Modifications

In order for the JMASS user to know how simulated time is progressing, MÄK modified the Stealth to display the passage of time. In the Stealth, a clock display was added to the Heads Up Display. To visualize terrain as well as dynamic players, each visualization system requires a terrain data set. The Stealth requires MultiGen OpenFlight-format databases, which can be constructed from JMASS DTED terrain data sets via COTS tools such as either MultiGen or TerraVista.

CONCLUSION

One of the advantages of the HLA is the ability to develop custom FOMs for unique federations. This enables the unique data transmission requirements of families of simulations to make use of the generic underlying infrastructure of the RTI. The disadvantage of this architecture is that interoperability with standard tools becomes difficult. As FOMs change, COTS tools must have the ability to be easily adapted to the new data communications requirements. FOM Agility through the use of FOM Mappers, provides such a mechanism. In this way, MÄK's entire line of COTS HLA products was quickly converted for use in the JMASS environment, saving the program the prohibitive expense of recreating custom versions of these general purpose tools.

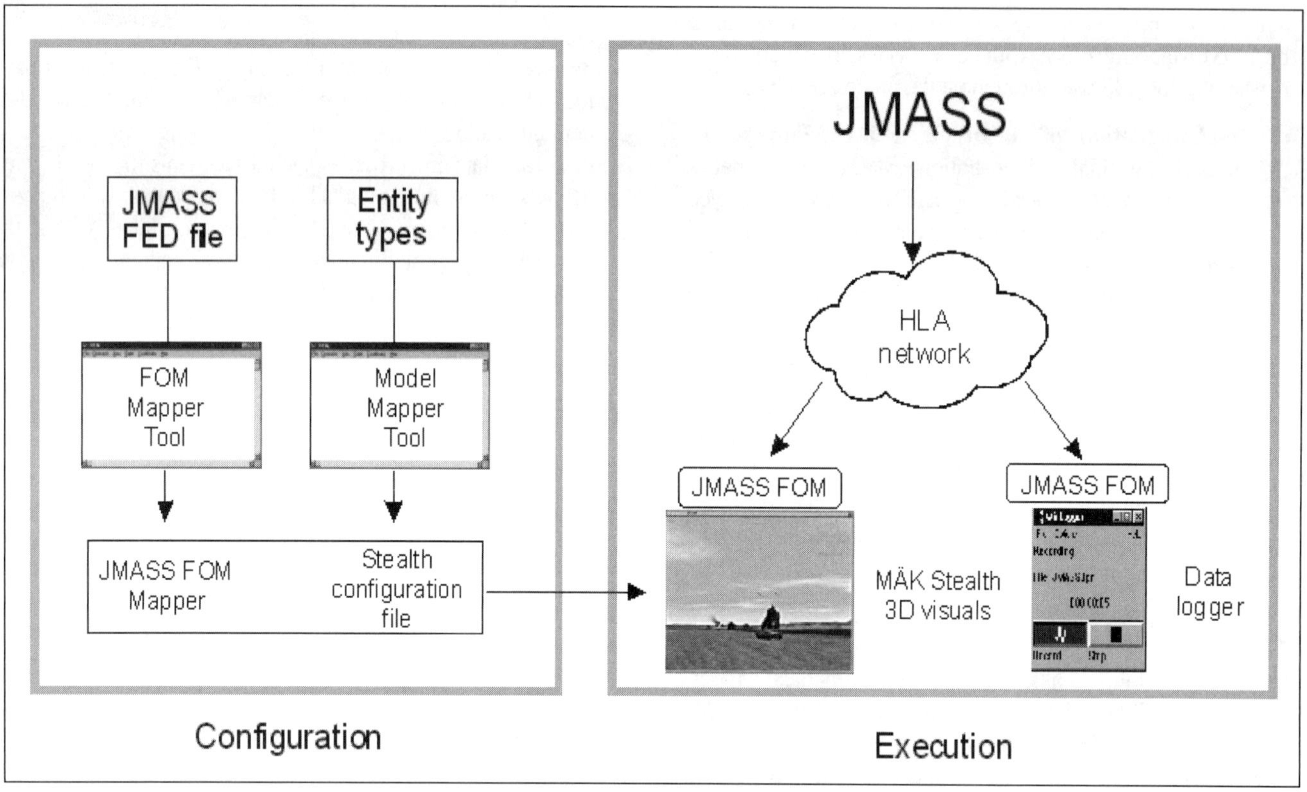

Figure 1.0. Incorporation of MÄK's VR-Link, Stealth, and Data Logger to support JMASS 3D visualization and data logging.

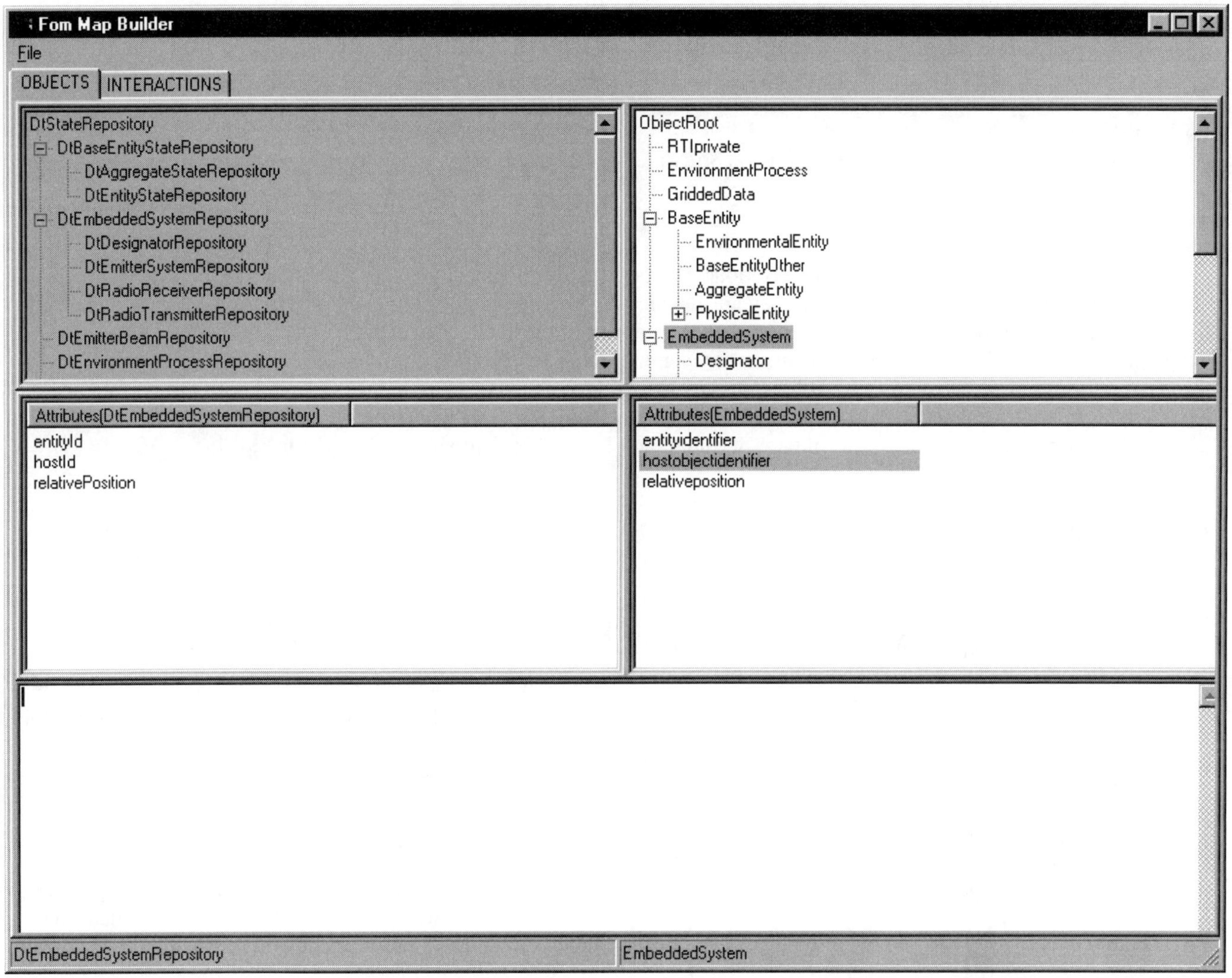

Figure 2. Illustration of the JMASS FOM Mapper Tool

OSIM – INTEGRATING SIMULATION ACROSS THE E-ENGINEERING CHAIN

Carl Byers and Roanne Levitt
OriginalSim Inc.
5524 St. Patrick Suite 302
Montreal, QC Canada H4E 1A8
Email: cbyers@originalsim.com and rlevitt@originalsim.com

KEY WORDS
Collaboration, Engineering, Model and Simulation Software Management, SBA

ABSTRACT
Geographically distributed engineering organizations who perform development together with their suppliers and partners are able to produce products more effectively if they are connected with systems that facilitate collaboration, access specialized domain expertise, reinforce process, and support the management of the intellectual capital created through the product development process. The systems these teams create can be even more effectively developed if simulation is used throughout the organization at every step of the product life cycle to assess designs, reduce risk, and optimize performance. These organizations should conduct their product development using Simulation-enabled e-Engineering Chains – the fourth pillar of the e-Enterprise and the core facilitator of Simulation Based Acquisition.

E-ENGINEERING CHAINS

What are they?

e-Engineering Chains are web-based collaborative environments that connect the engineering organization of an enterprise together with related stakeholders both within that core enterprise and within the extended virtual enterprise consisting of suppliers, partners and customers.

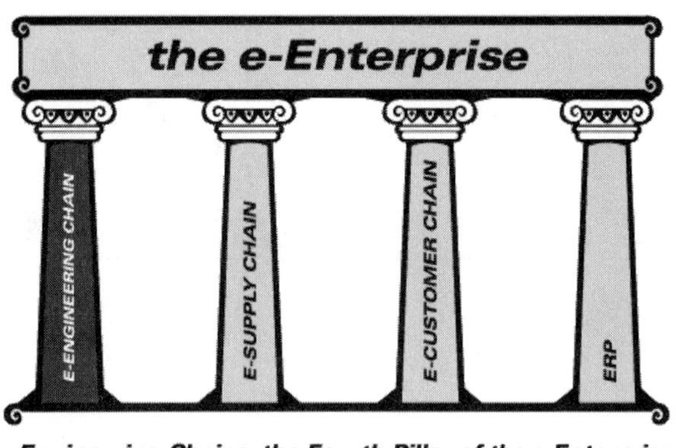

e-Engineering Chains: the Fourth Pillar of the e-Enterprise

Figure 1

e-Engineering Chains do for the engineering and product development organization what supply chains do for the manufacturing organization, customer relationship management systems do for the marketing and sales organization, and enterprise resource planning (ERP) systems do for the financial and administrative organization. As such, e-Engineering Chains for the fourth pillar of enterprise integration, and are a fundamental element of an enterprise strategy for improved performance, efficiency, synchronization and profitability.

At their most fundamental level, e-Engineering Chains are process-enabled engineering information portals containing a version-controlled repository of engineering and product data, accessible via a web browser with the appropriate tools and applications, from anywhere in the world.

How are they used?

e-Engineering Chains are all about integrating people with each other and with their tools, applications and data, and facilitating their improved performance and innovation with process-based enablers.

The manner in which an e-Engineering Chain is integrated varies with each organization – the tools used are different, the systems produced are different, the corporate processes are different. However, the common element is the need to facilitate design innovation and improved system cost/performance through the application of the creative talents and knowledge of a diverse group of geographically distributed subject matter experts.

The e-Engineering Chain is not just about development; it also involves all the other organizational elements involved with the system or product life cycle:

- Salespeople working with customers to define new requirements should work closely with the engineering organization to address engineering issues and performance or historical cost data;
- During bid development and early system analysis, the distributed subject matter experts within the enterprise with knowledge in mechanical, software, electronics, control systems and other design elements of the product must be tapped to perform initial design trade-offs and to optimize cost versus performance;
- During detailed design and development, those experts must work even more closely with the virtual engineering network including suppliers and partners to conduct more rigorous development, analysis and simulation to further optimize performance and reduce cost;
- If a system is to move into manufacturing, design for manufacturability should be considered early in the design and development process to ensure that an optimized production environment can be achieved; as a result, manufacturing engineers must be an integral part of the e-Engineering Chain; and,
- After a system is fielded, the maintenance and service organization should be integrated within the e-Engineering Chain to be able to access the engineering and simulation data to perform troubleshooting and preventative maintenance and provide failure information to the engineering database.

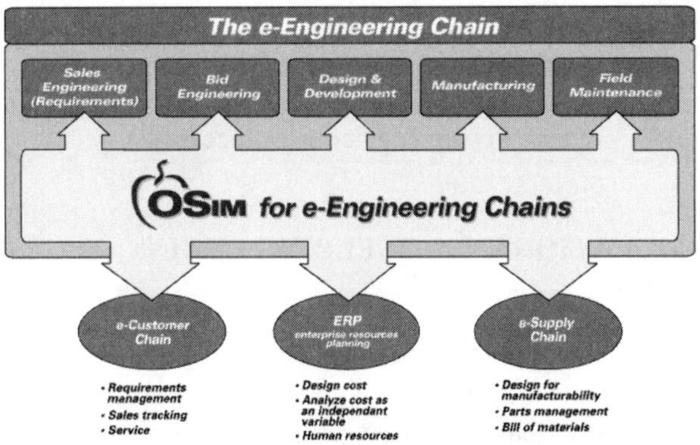

Figure 2

With an integrated e-Engineering Chain, all participants involved across the enterprise in the life cycle of a product, can be connected together and have access to the current and historical information related to the product requirements, product design, and test and maintenance data.

e-Engineering Chains should also be integrated with the other three pillars of enterprise information integration:

- The Customer Relationship Management system supports the management of customer contacts, tailored proposals, preliminary design specifications, and marketing communication strategies;
- The ERP system provides labor rates, production costs, human resource planning and requires project performance and cost data; and,
- The e-Supply Chain system requires the manufacturing bill of materials, supplier costing, and parts ordering information generated by the engineering activity.

Why should they be used?

e-Engineering Chains provide value to the enterprise. They integrate product data and manage intellectual capital with version controlled, web-accessible repositories; they integrate and synchronize people with improved communication and collaborative knowledge sharing; and, they manage chaos with processes for re-use, best practices, and standardization.

The result is less wasted time looking for the right version of the right thing, less wasted time trying to coordinate with people, faster access to pieces of the solution that can be reused from previous projects, and access to the right experts at the right time. In turn, this leads to better, cost-optimized designs, faster development, and development cost savings.

E-ENGINEERING CHAINS AND SBA

Simulation Based Acquisition (SBA) is a broadly defined initiative to improve the acquisition process for complex systems such as aircraft, ships, and vehicles and to substantially reduce the development and per unit cost as well as the development time for those systems. Objectives of 50% reduction in life cycle cost and time to deployment are frequently cited.

In order to achieve these objectives, the SBA initiatives target three key areas:

- Education of the acquisition community to adopt collaborative processes and invest in up front risk reduction activities;

- Cultural changes to embrace collaboration and information sharing instead of stove-piping and information hoarding; and,
- Collaborative technologies to facilitate the sharing of information and faster decision processes involving companies, their customers, and suppliers/partners.

SBA is to acquisition what the four pillars of enterprise integration are to the enterprise – a means to build better systems, faster, and cheaper. The e-Engineering Chain, as the fourth pillar of the e-enterprise, is essential to success in achieving these SBA objectives: the web-based collaborative environment with version controlled repositories connects people, manages information, and fosters an environment of knowledge sharing supported by process.

INTEGRATING SIMULATION ACROSS THE E-ENGINEERING CHAIN

Simulation is a key word in the phrase "Simulation Based Acquisition". Within the SBA context simulation is intended to be a tool and function that occurs at every step of the product life cycle to reduce risk, optimize cost, verify performance, and troubleshoot failure. As such, simulation should be used across every functional element of the e-Engineering Chain and the results obtained should be used to continuously improve product development activities.

Some examples:

- Salespeople and end-user customers defining new requirements should use simulation to assess and demonstrate prototype concepts, confirm and refine requirements, and visualize what they will be buying;
- During bid development and early system analysis, the distributed subject matter experts in different engineering domains should use simulation as part of their analysis to perform initial design trade-offs and to analyze cost as an independent variable to optimize cost versus performance;
- During detailed design and development, simulation should be used at the component, sub-system, and system level to more rigorously assess designs before they are committed and whenever an element of the design changes;
- The manufacturing environment should be simulated to verify design for manufacturability as well as to assess production alternatives, manufacturing bottlenecks, and perform supply chain inventory analysis, and;
- The maintenance and service organization should be able to access the simulation environments to conduct failure analysis and predictive troubleshooting.

Simulation is a tool similar to others, such as CAD/CAM, CASE, or EDA, used in the design and development of complex systems. However, the impact of simulation is significantly higher because of the value it can provide when used continuously throughout every phase of the product life cycle, by every participant across the e-Engineering Chain.

Simulation e-Engineering Chains (an aside)

An integral subset of the complete e-Engineering Chain is the Simulation e-Engineering Chain. For dedicated simulation applications, or the evolution of complex simulations and models throughout the product life cycle, the Simulation e-Engineering Chain is an environment to:

- Connect together the domain experts, programmers, model developers and others involved in building, assessing, testing and analyzing the results of complex simulation models;
- Manage, version control, and access and re-use simulation models;
- Remotely run simulation models and direct results to other interested parties;
- Integrate the myriad of tools and applications used to build, run, and deploy simulation models such as Matlab, Simulink, Matrix-X, OSim S/M, ADAMS and many others; and,
- Facilitate standardized model development with processes such as the HLA Federation Development and Execution Process (FEDEP) and other software engineering processes.

SIMULATION E-ENGINEERING CHAINS – A CASE STUDY

OSim for e-Engineering Chains

OriginalSim has produced OSim a web-based product for e-Engineering Chains. OSim incorporates a web server, SQL database, version management, session management, security management, and integration to leading engineering products and enterprise applications such as Rational Rose, Matlab, OSim S/M, MS Office, MS Project, and Revic. Additional capabilities and applications will be integrated based on product plans and customer requirements.

OSim allows any participant in the e-Engineering Chain to access project-related artifacts and knowledge stored in the version-controlled repository, from any location via a web browser. The user can communicate with other team members or create new artifacts and view or modify existing artifacts using the tools that should be used within the enterprise, and upload the artifact to be version controlled and available for the rest of the team according to the next steps of the enterprise engineering process.

OSim S/M for Simulation Model Development

OriginalSim also produces OSim S/M (formerly OSim Framework), an integrated development environment that facilitates the development of complex physics based simulation applications compliant with the High Level Architecture (HLA) standards using a visual model development GUI and automatic code generation.

Simulation e-Engineering Chains linking Boeing and USAF NAIC

The Boeing Company is under contract to support the US Air Force National Air Intelligence Center (NAIC) in, among other tasks, the development and management of simulation models.

In a recently initiated pilot project to improve software engineering processes for development and deployment of simulation and models at the NAIC, Boeing purchased several licenses of both OSim and OSim S/M for installation at their offices in Dayton, Ohio and at the NAIC.

The initial pilot project will involve the integration of three products: Rational Rose, Simulink from The MathWorks, and OSim S/M, in a visual development environment from model conception, through implementation and HLA compliant application generation. Each individual involved in each phase of the simulation model development activity will be connected through the OSim e-Engineering Chain environment to facilitate collaboration and the artifacts produced by each application or team member will be managed and version controlled by the OSim repository.

Initial installation has been completed in Q2 2000 and the first phase of the pilot project will be completed before September 2000.

Preliminary results of this pilot project will be discussed at the SCSC presentation in July.

SUMMARY

e-Engineering Chains represent a collaboration technology that will vastly improve the product development processes within enterprises developing complex systems using geographically dispersed development teams, partners and suppliers. They allow access by every team member to the right information, at the right time, with the right tools, regardless of their physical location, avoiding costly duplication, wasted downtime, and miscommunication.

Simulation is a critical tool to be used throughout the complete e-Engineering Chain across every phase of the product life cycle to reduce risk, improve product designs and reduce time to market and life cycle cost.

Combined, Simulation-enabled e-Engineering Chain solutions such as OSim represent the greatest potential for success in the difficult battle to bring better products to market faster and cheaper, as envisioned by SBA.

AUTHOR BIOGRAPHIES:

Carl Byers is the President and CEO of OriginalSim, the developer of the world's first e-Engineering Chain solution and the world's first HLA simulation integrated development environment. Mr. Byers holds an MBA from York University, Toronto and a B.Sc. in Engineering Physics from Queen's University at Kingston.

Roanne Levitt is Director of Product Development for OriginalSim where she leads the team developing, deploying, and supporting the OSim product suite. Ms Levitt has over ten years of product development experience in organizations including Microsoft and Philips and holds a B.Sc. in Mathematics and Computer Science from McGill University in Montreal.

INTEGRATING SIMULATION WITHIN THE PRODUCT-ENGINEERING LIFE CYCLE

Jean-Marc Naud
Virtual Prototypes Inc.
4700 de la Savane, suite 300
Montreal, QC, Canada
naud@VirtualPrototypes.ca

KEYWORDS

Product-Engineering, Simulation Life Cycle, HLA, Development Tools, Data Management

ABSTRACT

Simulation is a key technology to help optimize the product-engineering task. Simulation can be used at all stages of the product-engineering life cycle. The mechanisms necessary to allow simulation work to be integrated with product engineering work are: coordination with the engineering activities, common management of the engineering and simulation data and the availability of a simulation infrastructure. Advanced software technologies supporting reusable components, flexible object models and collaborative access to data are necessary. The SEQUOIA project is currently under way and consists of an investigation of these technologies and of the development of associated tools.

INTRODUCTION

This paper discusses the use of simulation during the full life cycle of the engineering of a product. Simulation is a technology that has many applications: training, analysis, stimulation, testing, etc. Some of these applications can be combined to support new product development. The integration of simulation within the product-engineering life cycle is becoming more and more important as new products are getting more and more complex. Product developers are faced with significant challenges as they have to manage requirements, evolve their product through prototyping, get feedback from potential users, iteratively test the evolving system, manage the product engineering information, etc. To do this, they must successfully use all the technologies that are available to them. One of these key technologies is simulation. Already the use of simulation during the design phase, Simulation Based Design (SBD) has received a significant share of interest. In this paper, we look at how the use of simulation can extend to the full product engineering life cycle leading to what we can call: "Simulation Based Product Engineering" or "Virtual Product Engineering". This is a parallel concept to the Simulation Based Acquisition (SBA) strategy put forth by the U.S. DoD (Albergo and Thomen 2000). SBPE is more targeted toward product developers while SBA is viewed from the acquisition side but they share most of the same ideas.

The first section of the paper provides a summary of the standard product-engineering life cycle. It is followed by a discussion of the aspects of the product life cycle that can benefit from simulation. The requirements for the simulation systems are then put into the context of the current state of simulation systems development.

The following three sections provide elements of solutions necessary to reach the full benefits from integrating simulation within the product-engineering life cycle. These are the coordination of engineering activities, the management of engineering data elements and the provision of a simulation infrastructure.

Finally, we discuss tools and technologies that are being experimented with to help put in place the infrastructure necessary to support the integration of simulation within the product-engineering life cycle.

THE PRODUCT-ENGINEERING LIFE CYCLE

While there are various approaches to the product engineering process, especially in terms of the sequence of events, there are key activities that are agreed upon. While the number of activities used to decompose the product engineering cycle as well as the terminology varies, most of the time they will fall under the following categories:

- setting the product vision;

- defining the requirements
- analyzing and designing the system;
- implementing the system;
- testing the system;
- deployment (code, documentation, training);
- support and maintenance;

These activities are normally supported by a project management structure, a systems engineering approach and a configuration management system. The sequence of activities can be linear or it can include prototyping and/or evolutionary cycles.

The product engineering cycles are getting shorter as the competitive pressure to be first to market is growing. System integrators for large systems are facing shorter development schedules as deployment time for systems and manufacturing schedules are being cut. The challenges faced by product engineering teams are:

- to insure that the final systems meets the requirements of the users;
- to coordinate work activities and find the optimal sequence of development;
- to identify reusable elements in order to increase productivity;
- to integrate teams from various business units and various companies;
- to integrate various technologies and platforms;
- to manage the engineering artifacts produced during the engineering life cycle;

Faced with those challenges, product engineers have been looking to simulation as a means to help them increase the likelihood of successfully developing the right product in the most productive manner.

SIMULATION IN THE ENGINEERING LIFE CYCLE

Traditionally the use of simulation has been for system integration testing and for training. However the simulation systems for those two aspects were not developed in synergy.

There is a push to use more simulation and introduce it earlier in the design process to save production time and rework costs later on. Simulation use is increasing as it demonstrates its usefulness in enabling more robust designs earlier in the development process using a virtual environment. There are significant cost savings in solving problems or bad design issues early on before starting the actual manufacturing of a product or the deployment of a new system. At the same time, the simulation must be capable of rapidly providing answers.

But simulation can be used for more than just the design work. It can be used at each phase of the product-engineering life cycle:

- to help set the vision;
- to better identify requirements;
- to help in analyzing and designing the system by enabling early evaluations, potentially with users in the loop;
- to provide mechanisms to support unit testing during the implementation phase, by replacing elements not yet developed;
- to provide the virtual environment necessary to test the integrated product;
- to enable the deployment of a training systems;
- to help management evaluate progress;
- to help validate that user requirements were met;
- during support and maintenance to help identify and fix problems;

As can be seen from this list of applications for simulation during the product-engineering life cycle, not only does it serve many purposes but it should also be used by many different engineering teams working either on different parts of the product or on different aspects of the life cycle.

One of the main challenges of the systems engineers is to allow those various engineering teams to work in a coordinated fashion and to increase the information flow between teams and between phases in the life cycle. By using a proper information management system and by using simulation to make this information dynamic rather than static, the product engineering team will be able to communicate information and exchange reusable components in a way not possible without those tools. Simulation is an enabler of successful collaboration between engineering teams.

SIMULATION SYSTEMS DEVELOPMENT

Developing simulation systems for complex products that are part of a complex environment is itself a complex task. The standard approach has been to assign the development of the various simulation systems needed to support a product engineering effort to different teams that share little coordination. As an example, the team in charge of developing the training system for a new product would develop a simulation system independently of the team developing simulation components to help do unit testing.

However, while the simulation systems goals in this example are different, there is still a significant amount of synergy that can be established between the two teams. The solution to enable this synergy is to create a new way of building simulation systems. This new way of doing things should:

- allow systems to be built from reusable components;
- provide underlying frameworks that are applicable to various simulation domains;
- enable the dissemination of information about the state of simulation component development across the various teams;
- provide a configuration management system for the simulation components that are developed;

With the proper mindset and the proper tools, it should be possible to significantly streamline and optimize how simulation systems are built and used within the product-engineering life cycle. The key is to focus on the core simulation needs, to establish an infrastructure to support reusable components and to put in place an engineering data management system that allows work activities to be coordinated and that enables seamless communication.

Coordinating Activities

During the product engineering processes, everything is put in place to coordinate the activities of the product development teams. What is also needed is the creation of a simulation team with which the product activities are also coordinated. It is important to provide a central focus for simulation needs. Because, just as the product will evolve over time, so will the simulation components, i.e., the simulation has a life cycle that needs to be coordinated with the product life cycle. The evolution of the simulation system should parallel the product evolution; new product requirements should find their way as requirements of the simulation systems.

It is important to synchronize the product-engineering schedule with the simulation system schedule to insure that simulation components are ready when required by the product engineers.

The key to achieve a proper coordination of the activities with respect to simulation is to:

- put simulation as a key element of the systems engineering process;
- assign responsibility for the simulation aspect of the product engineering life cycle;
- break-up the design of the simulation system in reusable components that provide functional aspects of the simulation;
- coordinate the development of those components with the product schedule;

Managing Engineering Data

The product engineering team needs to use an engineering data management system to store the artifacts produced during the engineering effort. This data management system has to provide mechanisms to quickly retrieve information and data as well as provide mechanisms to identify relationships between those.

Once such a system is in place, it is important that artifacts produced for simulation be stored within that system, as they are an inherent part of the engineering process. The simulation components need to be classified and organized according to their functionality, purpose, usage, limitations, etc. Idem for relationships, i.e., simulation components should be linked to product requirements, product functions, design elements, testing scripts, training needs, etc.

As an example, it might be important to know that a given simulation components has been built to emulate a given piece of hardware, based on a given design documents, to meet a stated requirement. Such information has to be maintained and properly manage by a system that allows it to be rapidly retrieved and which provides a proper configuration management system.

In addition, simulation can provide a new dimension to such a system. With simulation, not only can the data be retrieved and viewed statically, but now it can also be animated. As an example, if a requirement specifies that a given device will display a warning when some conditions will apply in the environment it operates in, a system engineer should be able to launch a simulation application that validates this requirement directly from the engineering data management system. This is possible because the data management system will know of all the elements necessary to launch a simulation system built for a given purpose. This is the concept of Smart Product Models (Eirich 2000).

Providing a Simulation Infrastructure

In order to launch simulation systems that use the components stored in the repository, these components have to be designed based on a common set of standards and they have to be built for a common execution platform. In other words, there needs to be a defined simulation system infrastructure in order to support the concept of reusable simulation components.

One element of this simulation infrastructure is the run-time execution framework that allows distributed simulation components to interoperate. The US DoD has developed a standard, the High Level Architecture (HLA), that includes an element called the Run Time Infrastructure (RTI). The RTI provides this execution framework. With the mechanisms provided by HLA and the RTI, it is now possible to develop distributed simulation components that can interact via a common execution platform. This is a necessary element of the solution for implementing the simulation based product engineering system. However, additional frameworks and technologies are needed to complement what is provided by HLA. It is necessary to have frameworks for the modeling of the time, of the environment and of the systems, for the management of events and the linkage of components, as well as tools for creating and managing the simulation components that are built by a project engineering team.

USING SOFTWARE TOOLS

To enable the vision described above, it is necessary to elaborate the right technologies and to develop tools that implement them.

These technologies should be based on modern software techniques that allow rapid application development through component assembly and the use of flexible object models.

The tools should support the HLA concepts and augment them to enable their users to create and manage software components that are built for multiple use. They have to allow controlled access to these components and provide mechanisms to link them to the engineering data management system. The tools should also provide the foundation frameworks that are necessary to insure that simulation components can be linked together.

SEQUOIA PROJECT

Faced with the above requirements for simulation software development tools, we have started a project, named SEQUOIA, to investigate these technologies and to develop software tools that would enable the integration of simulation within the product engineering process.

The SEQUOIA project was initiated to investigate the development of sophisticated integrated environments that that would facilitate the development of complex systems through the use of reusable components and of dynamic object models. Techniques such as visual development and template-driven code generation are also being used to increase the productivity of simulation component developers. The SEQUOIA concept is also based on a collection of frameworks for common simulation needs. In particular, the simulation executive supports mixed-mode time management (time-step and event driven).

For the distribution aspect, SEQUOIA relies on the HLA RTI. It provides a front-end development tool to HLA by allowing users to benefit from a distributed system framework that significantly simplifies the task of developing HLA-compliant systems.

System Overview

A diagram providing an overview of SEQUOIA's functionality appears in Figure 1. SEQUOIA provides an Integrated Visual Development Environment (IVDE) called SimDesigner that allows the visualization and editing of complex software application through various visual editors. Each editor contributes to creating the Simulation System Model (SSM). The SSM is made up of a System Object Model (SOM), of logical components that are hierarchically organized, of presentation elements, of sub-system and application information. The hierarchical organization is a result of the composability of SEQUOIA through its component mechanism. The goal of the SEQUOIA architecture is to enable an easy access to each individual component in a complex application and to understand its relationship with the other elements without having to go through realms of code. Some additional information about this system can be found in a previous paper (Naud 1999).

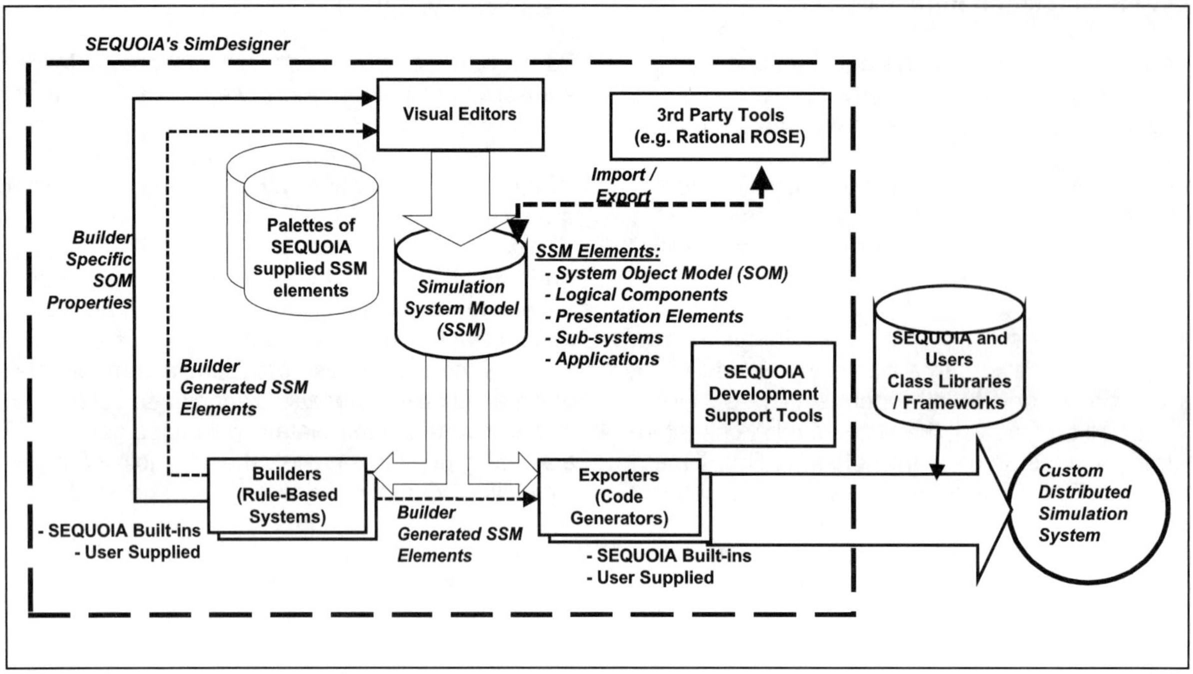

Figure 1 – System Functional Overview

SEQUOIA includes builders that can automatically deduce some of the SSM elements by analyzing, through a rule-based system, the System Object Model, and data exporters that generate code (of other data files) from the data elements in the SSM in order to create a custom distributed simulation system.

Part of SEQUOIA is an HLA Integrator module that includes the System Object Model Editor and the code generators for the objects and the data distribution. It allows users to generate the wrapper code necessary to pass on and receive the attribute values. A mechanism to import the System Object Model generated using other tools (Rational ROSE, DMSO's OMDT) is being developed to facilitate the process. There is also a set of middleware software that simplifies the most common tasks done with the HLA-RTI. Those are the Distributed System Infrastructure (DSI) and the Dynamic Object System (DOS). Those systems have been described in a previous paper (Naud 2000).

Central to SEQUOIA is the SSM repository that provides the mechanism to store and manage simulation components. Our goal is to link this repository within an Engineering Data Management (EDM) with which we would implement the key relationships between the product engineering data and the simulation components.

Project Status

The SEQUOIA project is well under way and many important concepts have been implemented and validated. The code generators for HLA integration are functional and a first evaluation by potential users has shown significant productivity increase for the development of HLA-compliant systems.

Work on the component system is on going and preliminary results are very encouraging. It has been significantly easy to reuse components in context not initially anticipated.

We have been investigating methods to provide collaborative access to the SSM repository and are looking into integration with existing tools.

CONCLUSION

In this paper, we presented a vision of product development where simulation is fully integrated to the engineering task.

We believe that many benefits will come out of such an approach, in particular in the area of simulation component reuse across functional areas (testing, evaluation, analysis, training, etc.).

We also believe that HLA is an important part of the technology needed to make this vision happen. We stated that tools that support those concepts are needed to insure an efficient implementation within a product engineering organization.

An overview of the SEQUOIA project that aims at developing tools that enable the vision put forth was then given.

It is our belief that the advanced software concepts used in SEQUOIA, such as dynamic objects, hierarchical components, integrated visual development, and code generation, will significantly impact the simulation application software development process. We feel that it will aid in reducing the cost, time and risk associated to such projects. And it will help integrate simulation within the product-engineering life cycle enabling the products to be developed more effectively.

ABOUT THE AUTHOR:

Mr. Jean-Marc Naud is Director of Technology at Virtual Prototypes Inc. He holds a bachelor degree in Engineering Physics and a M.Sc. in Project Management. He has more than 14 years of experience in the fields of military simulation, synthetic environments and simulation systems architecture. Mr. Naud's research interests are object-oriented modeling applied to simulation, meta-models, dynamic object systems, distributed simulation systems and more recently visual development and componentware.

REFERENCES

Albergo, E.J. and D. Thomen. 2000, "Simulation Based Acquisition, The Way Ahead", In Proceedings of the 2000 Spring Simulation Interoperability Workshop, Orlando, Florida.

Eirich, P. 2000, "Systems Architecture for a Low Cost Collaborative Environment for SBA Decision-Making", In Proceedings of the 2000 Spring Simulation Interoperability Workshop, Orlando, Florida.

Naud, J-M. 1999, "Simulation Models as Components in an HLA World", In Proceedings of the 1999 Spring Simulation Interoperability Workshop, Orlando, Florida.

Naud, J-M.; M. Pourzandi and Y. Lagacé. 2000, "An HLA-Based Distributed System Infrastructure", In Proceedings of the International Training and Education Conference (ITEC 2000), The Hague, The Netherlands.

A SIGNAL REPRESENTATION FRAMEWORK FOR THE HETEROGENEOUS SIMULATION OF OPTICAL COMPONENTS, SYSTEMS AND NETWORKS

Olaf Lenzmann, Igor Koltchanov
Virtual Photonics Ingenieurgesellschaft mbH
Carnotstrasse 6, 10587 Berlin, Germany

Arthur Lowery, Rod Vance
Virtual Photonics Pty. Ltd.
187 Grattan Street, 3053 Carlton, Victoria, Australia

e-mail: o.lenzmann@virtualphotonics.com

KEYWORDS

Signal Representation, Photonics Simulation, Approximation Techniques

ABSTRACT

To handle the inherent technical complexities in the design of optical components, systems and networks, sophisticated design tools are required. Due to the wide range of scales involved – from wavelength-sized resonators in lasers and filters, to interactions in global networks – such tools need to provide highly advanced simulation technology. To address this need, we have developed the *Photonic Transmission Design Suite* (PTDS). It contains the *Optical Network Simulation Layer* at its core, which implements a novel simulation framework with a dynamic, object-oriented signal representation that can be tailored to the needs of a variety of modeling tasks.

We discuss the challenges encountered in the development of the simulation framework and the principal signal representations that it provides. These representations enable us to describe signals on different levels of detail; the framework provides the freedom to mix these representations within one simulation as appropriate with very few restrictions.

This paper highlights the fundamental design concepts of the signal representation framework, which guarantee flexibility and openness for future extensions. The approach that we pursue to represent signals is object-oriented and highly dynamic, allowing to change the structure of signal representations even at run-time: *signals* are constructed in a modular fashion by aggregating *signal properties*, which model different aspects of a signal, and which can mutually interact. *Physical signal properties* are used to capture physical aspects of a signal, such as its sampled waveform or a statistical description of it, whereas *logical signal properties* represent ancillary information on a signal, like the modulation kind employed (e.g., amplitude or frequency modulation, RZ or NRZ coding), the coded bit sequence, etc. By introducing signal properties that themselves aggregate signals, the containment concept can be applied recursively. Using PTDS, we show an application of the different signal representations.

INTRODUCTION

Technical advances in recent years – especially the advent of optical amplification and wavelength division multiplexing (WDM) – have brought about new challenges in the design and evaluation of optical components, systems and networks. Systems performance is limited by complex non-linear phenomena, making numerical simulation a necessity (Hamster and Lam 1998). We have developed the Photonic Transmission Design Suite (Breuer et al. 2000) that provides a framework in which designs are composed from pre-defined, parameterizable building blocks. It allows to perform a range of analyses, based on simulating the propagation of time-dependent signals through the design. The simulator adheres to a *dataflow model of computation* (Lee and Sangiovanni-Vincentelli, 1998), where building blocks behave as *actors* that consume, process and produce *tokens*, which represent (excerpts of) a physical signal.

Due to the extremely high bandwidth of optical signals, sophisticated modeling and simulation techniques are required to achieve accurate results with reasonable computational effort. Different design objectives require different modeling approaches, as for instance the characteristics of an optical amplifier can be modeled on different levels of detail, ranging from a simple gain factor to the solution of complex rate equations. These different detail levels do not only apply to models of, for instance, optical components, but also to the way signals are represented. Because of the analogue, non-linear nature of optical systems, the influence of a single component can have significant impact on the characteristics of an entire system. Therefore, heterogeneous simulations are of great importance to allow modeling of crucial parts of a design in great detail, while modeling the bulk of the design in a simplified manner to achieve a reasonable trade-off between simulation performance and accuracy. Again, this trade-off applies both to models and signal representations: some signals are of direct interest, while for others only their *effect* is important (consider a modulated transmission channel and a pump signal for an optical amplifier).

Efficient Modeling of Wideband Systems

The introduction of *dense wavelength division multiplexing* (DWDM) in optical communications has been the major driver for the development of memory- and time-efficient simulation concepts. Today's commercial DWDM systems provide bit rates of 10 GB/s per channel, carried on up to 160 channels spaced 100 GHz apart; this implies a total optical bandwidth of DWDM signals on the order of a couple of THz. Due to the non-linearities inherent in optical system, these signals need to be modeled in their entirety, i.e., a strictly frequency selective consideration is not feasible. The traditional numerical representation of such signals employs bandpass sampling at the Nyquist-Rate, which leads to prohibitive computation time requirements, since simulations need to cover time spans of at least a few thousand bits in order to generate meaningful results: simple calculation shows that gigabytes of sampled data need to be processed when following this approach. While block-wise processing of data – models exchange arrays of sample data instead of individual sample values – allows much more efficient computation by reducing overhead, it gives rise to new modeling problems and implies huge memory requirements.

A number of efforts have been successful in mitigating these problems by introducing approximate signal representations: transmission channels under direct consideration are modeled as sampled signals, whereas other channels are approximated by statistical descriptions of signal and noise contributions (e.g., Rasmussen 1999). This enables the development of more efficient, albeit less accurate models. The approaches taken by the groups differ mainly in the flexibility of the signal representation employed: to our knowledge, all concepts introduce a fixed representation by defining the signal contributions as hard-coded structures with certain properties, aggregated in arrays. While this guarantees maximum performance, it does not lend itself very well to extensions, but imposes strict constraints on the modeling approaches used.

The development of our simulation framework has initially been driven by the same concept of signal approximations. However, our realization of this concept goes far beyond other approaches, as it bases on an extensible, object-oriented design. We believe that the flexibility thus gained outweighs the associated performance penalty by far.

Supporting Heterogeneous Modeling Techniques

The key challenge for a design framework is to provide the flexibility to employ the modeling technique that is appropriate for a given problem. This does not only require the capability to support different global modes of computation. Instead, the ability to mix and interoperate different modeling techniques, and thus different signal representations within the simulation of one design is needed. Designs can be modeled on different levels of detail: more detailed approaches usually require more sophisticated models, execute slower, consume more memory, but yield more accurate results. However, only very detailed models allows for (almost) all physical effects.

Modeling approaches can be classified according to two broad categories: *Numerical approaches*, which usually exchange and operate on signals in the form of sampled signal data. These approaches base on techniques as digital filtering and methods to numerically solve differential equations. Numerical approaches can be further sub-classified according to whether they operate on arrays of sample data or on individual samples at a time; the former concept allows more efficient simulation, but has restrictions as it cannot model feedback loops with delays shorter than the time span covered by one array of samples. Especially to model lasers, approaches based on individual sample processing are required (Lowery et al. 1996). The second general class of approaches operates on a statistical representation of signals, where a signal is described by its power, noise level, and other parameters. Such statistical models are often very simple, i.e., of low level of detail. On the other hand, highly sophisticated semi-analytical solutions are known for some problem sets (Richter and Grigoryan 1999), enabling simulations that allow for all significant physical effects but are orders of magnitude more efficient than traditional numerical approaches. In this case, models operate for instance on power, average timing and amplitude jitter values of signals.

In complex designs, different kinds of approaches need to coexist to model the system adequately and efficiently. Moreover, allowing a designer to freely choose the level of modeling detail enables him to refine the simulation results at the cost of increased computation time. This ability supports the different requirements in different phases of the design process. The challenge for the implementation of building blocks within a design tool is to comprise models of different detail levels in order to model components according to the required level of detail, but also to handle any input signal configuration properly. The main challenges for a design framework are:

- To enable models to use signal representations that suit the problem at hand.
- To provide mechanisms that allow uniform handling of different signal representations.
- To offer supporting functionality for signal processing that can handle any possible combination of signal configurations.

SIGNAL REPRESENTATIONS

In this section, we introduce some basic concepts of signal representation, before we describe the principal representations provided by our simulation framework.

Signal Windows

In the scope of the simulation framework, a signal is defined by one or more *signal windows*, each of which is a computational object that describes the signal over a certain period of time, using some kind of signal representation. For instance, the first window might cover the first millisecond of a signal, the second window the second millisecond, and so forth. Any signal window is tagged with its start time t_0 and duration T. Similarly, each window covers a finite bandwidth and holds according values that define the center frequency f_C and the bandwidth Δf of the spectral range that it covers. In the case of sampled representation, the product $T*\Delta f$ defines the number of samples per window. This number must obviously be an integer, but for efficiency reasons we restrict it to be a power of two, thus allowing the use of fast Fourier transforms on an entire block of samples.

Common Time Window

A frequent operation during simulation is the addition of two signals. To yield proper results, the argument signal windows need to be aligned in time and frequency before addition can take place. In the case of sampled signal representations, this addition can be performed efficiently in the frequency domain, given that all signals involved adhere to the same spacing of sample points in the frequency domain. We achieve this by introducing a *common time window* T_C that globally defines the maximum time duration of a signal window, and thus the minimum spacing of values in the frequency domain. Shorter windows may be defined with the restriction that T_C/T is a power of two.

Block-wise vs. Individual Sample Representation

We define a signal representation to be *block-wise*, if the product of bandwidth and duration of a signal window is greater than one. If on the other hand, this product is exactly one, each signal window degenerates to a single sample, which we denote as *individual sample representation*.

Boundary Conditions

In the case of block-wise representation, the assumption of *periodic boundary conditions* can be made, meaning that a signal is fully described by a single window that is periodically repeated in time. This requires that all simulation models generate signals that are periodic within the signal window duration; models of signal sources, for example, need to quantize their emission frequencies to a multiple of the frequency grid spacing $1/T_C$, which can be a severe limitation. For many computations, however, this assumption is beneficial, as it allows the use of circular convolution and thus complies with the implicit assumptions of the Fourier transform.

In the standard case of *aperiodic boundary conditions*, a signal is described by a sequence of signal windows adjacent in time. In principle, this allows models to generate arbitrary frequencies. However, this would make the frequency alignment of signal windows computationally very demanding, as it would require re-sampling and quasi-ideal filtering of signals in the time domain. Therefore, allowing arbitrary signal frequencies seems only feasible if the frequency range of signal windows is globally fixed. This in turn does not comply with the usual application of block-wise representations to model wideband signals, which require a frequency selective representation of individual channels of interest. Hence, we have restricted models to generate frequencies quantized to the grid spacing mentioned above in the aperiodic case too, allowing us to perform signal addition efficiently in the frequency domain without generating aliasing artifacts.

With individual sample representation, aperiodic boundary conditions are obviously implied, leading to certain restrictions when mixing this representation and models assuming a periodic block-wise operation. Further, the use of this representation is restricted to signals occupying the same frequency range in order to avoid on-the-fly re-sampling, as discussed above.

Principal Signal Representations

There is a set of principal representations that we use to approximate signals within PTDS. These are:

- *Individual Samples*, where each signal window represents a single time-domain sample of a signal.
- *Sampled Bands*, which represent a signal block-wise by an array of samples that can be given either in time or frequency domain.
- *Parameterized Signals* that represent a signal block-wise by a set of statistical quantities including its average power and state of polarization. We assume parameterized signals to be mutually uncorrelated, meaning that the addition of any two such signals adds the respective powers. This assumption leads to wrong results if the two signals are correlated, in which case their fields would need to be added, allowing for the relative phase. This limitation is inherent to a statistical description.
- *Noise Bins*, which are represent white, Gaussian noise, and which carry information on the spectral power density of the noise and its state of polarization, much like a parameterized signal.
- *Compound Signals*, which model signals through containment of sets of sampled bands, parameterized signals and noise bins. Thus, compound signals provide an extremely flexible means to represent signals by modeling them using an adequate combination of the above signal representations.
- *Logical signal*s, which are defined to aggregate logical signal properties, as opposed to the previously introduced signal types, which exclusively aggregate physical properties by default. A logical signal is used to comprise information on one *channel of transmission*, like the channel's signal source, the bit sequence modulated onto it, modulation type and pulse shape used, etc. Since a physical signal waveform can carry a number of multiplexed channels of transmission, sampled bands and parameterized signals can be associated with logical signals in a one-to-many relationship. This relation is constructed indirectly via unique signal labels (handled by according properties) and not via containment, as a channel of transmission may be present in more than one physical signal. The mechanisms to maintain and track these relations are tedious in detail and go beyond the scope of this paper.

Figure 1 depicts the principal signal representations.

CONCEPT AND DESIGN

To gain maximum flexibility, we have designed our signal representation framework in an object-oriented way, using C++ as implementation language. OO concepts like polymorphism and late binding – virtual methods in C++ – as well as OO patterns like *delegation*, *composite* and *listener* (Gamma at al. 1995), enable us to provide the programmer of models with a signal-, not an operation-centric API, which hides most of the complexity associated with proper handling of different signal configurations. The following description neglects a number of implementation details for the sake of clarity.

Base Classes

A fundamental design decision is to separate the class hierarchy into a part addressing individual sample representation and a part addressing block-wise signal representations, both sharing a common base class. This is motivated by the goal to provide a flexible and dynamic block-wise representation, which implies a prohibitive overhead when each object carries just one sample value. A common base class helps to keep method signatures simple, by accepting both types of data as arguments.

Base class `SignalWindow` contains parameters defining the signal window's time and frequency position. Note that the time and frequency values are not represented by floating point numbers, but by dedicated data types that apply quantization to prevent round-off errors: frequency values are quantized to a grid defined by $1/T_C$, time values to a grid defined by $1/\Delta f$; hence, the quantization grid for time values is depending on the duration of the signal window.

Derived from `SignalWindow` is class `Sample`, which provides individual sample representation, holding an according sample value. Note that for instances of this class the product of its inherited members T and Δf yields one.

Defining Signals by Aggregation

In order to provide a highly dynamic and extensible signal representation framework, we pursue a concept where the structure of data representing a signal is defined at run-time rather than at compile-time. We achieve this by defining class `Signal` as a container, which holds objects that constitute the properties of the signal, according to the *composite* pattern. This approach makes it possible to change signal descriptions at run-time by adding or removing properties, in contrast to a conventional concept, where signals are defined statically using inheritance at best.

Signal Properties

A number of classes are derived from `SignalProperty`, implementing different aspects of a signal. They are classified into *physical properties*, which describe the physical signal waveform, either by a sampled or by a statistical representation, and *logical properties*, which convey ancillary information on a signal, like a signature of its source, the modulation type and pulse shape used, etc.

Interaction of Signal Properties

Since signal properties are not mutually independent, a mechanism is required to enable information exchange between properties held in the same container object. This is achieved by applying a modification of the *listener* pattern, where signal properties know their container and can notify it of changes by sending a message, which itself is a first-class object. The container can react to the message and usually relays it to all properties it contains, which in turn can react as required. Thus, manipulations on any property can be propagated through the entire composite.

Some properties provide different views of the same data, and need therefore to interact closely: a property representing the power of a signal needs for instance to cooperate with a property holding the sampled waveform to provide a consistent behavior. When a client changes the sampled waveform, the power property needs to be notified and must re-compute its value from the sample data. To avoid unnecessary updates, signal properties generally implement a lazy mechanism, which tracks changes but performs actual updates only as required.

Automation of Signal Properties

Any property implementation needs to overload some inherited methods, which allow the framework to provide generic processing of signals and signal properties without knowledge of the actual semantics of the derived classes. For instance, each property class must implement the member `operator+=()` to provide objects with the capability to add another property instance of the same type to itself, allowing for the time and frequency offset as defined by the respective container signal objects if required. This allows a generic implementation of the `operator+=()` of class `Signal`, where all properties of the argument signal are added to matching properties of the target signal, and unmatched properties are simply copied to the target. To allow for types of properties that cannot define a meaningful addition operation, a property instance is free to reject the addition operation in which case itself and the argument property are discarded from the target signal. The benefit of this approach is that the introduction of new properties does not affect the implementation of class `Signal` at all, but still can provide new functionality.

Physical Signal Properties

The most important physical signal property classes that are currently implemented in our framework are:

- Class `SampleArray`, which holds an array of sample data and provides functionality to transform these data between time and frequency domain.
- Class `Power` that represents the average power of a signal, and which cooperates with class `SampleArray`, if an instance of this property is present in the same signal. If not, the signal is described statistically and the power property itself provides the normative reference for the power of the signal.
- Class `Polarization` that represents the state of polarization of an optical signal by a *Stokes vector*, and which also cooperates with class `SampleArray`, if an instance of this property is present. If not, the signal is described statistically and the polarization property itself provides the normative reference for the state of polarization of the signal.
- Class `SignalStatistics`, which captures statistical properties of a signal, as its timing and amplitude jitter. This property is used mutually exclusively with `SampleArray` – this constraint is enforced at run-time – because the sampled waveform cannot be adjusted to changes in these statistical quantities in a well-defined way.

Logical Signal Properties

A great number of logical properties have been implemented so far. Some of them are:

- Class `Modulation`, capturing the scheme and the associated parameters of the modulation that is applied to a signal. Derived classes represent concrete modulation schemes, such as amplitude shift keying.
- Class `PulseShape` that captures the shape of the original pulse launched into a system. Derived classes represent Gaussian pulses, solitons, etc.
- Class `BitSequence` that stores the original bit or symbol sequence modulated onto a signal.
- Class `SignalLabel`, which holds an arbitrary string that is used as symbolic name of a signal.

Basic Signal Classes

Some *basic signal classes* are derived from `Signal` in order to introduce type safety for the principal signal representations. These derived classes rely entirely on the functionality provided by their base class to model signals by aggregating properties. In addition, they add code to guarantee the existence of certain properties, depending on the derived type. Moreover, the basic signal classes introduce *alias* member variables that point to known properties of the signal to allow an efficient access of these properties – the base class implementation only is able to iterate over the whole set of properties.

Compound Signals

To implement the compounded signal representation, *compound properties* are introduced, each of which contains a set of one type of basic signal objects, all of which cover the same time span but different, disjunct frequency positions. Inserting a basic signal object that spectrally overlaps one of the objects already in the set is automatically handled by the compound property, merging the overlapping sections into the existing objects. In the case of sampled signals, the restriction to array lengths equal to two to the power of N can result in automatic up-sampling and thus to recursive merges of spectrally adjacent signals.

From the point of view of the compounded signal, these compound properties are ordinary properties that transparently support the addition operation, which merges two such signal sets into one; this is a complex operation as it requires to merge signal objects overlapping in frequency. Further, compound properties provide transparent propagation of messages, rendering them "invisible" in the message flow between their container object and the signal objects they contain.

Class `CompoundSignal` is derived from `Signal` and guarantees to contain one instance of compound properties holding sampled bands, parameterized signals and noise bins, respectively.

PERFORMANCE

This section discusses the performance bottlenecks of the concept.

Individual Sample Representation

The individual sample representation suffers from the problem that class `Sample` is derived from class `SignalWindow`, since the inherited member variables are partly redundant, and especially since these values could in most cases be handled more efficiently by global settings. However, experience has shown that the additional memory consumption is not critical since simulations usually do not produce too many sample objects simultaneously. Instead, objects are processed sequentially, and memory can be re-used.

Signal Creation

The software design of the block-wise signal representations that we have presented incurs run-time overhead as it models all signal properties by first class objects, which in addition communicate mutually through message passing. Hence, the instantiation of a signal object requires the creation of a number of contained signal property objects. Further, each time a property is added to a container, an according message is sent to all properties already present in the container; this is required to allow the properties to "get to know" each other, as some property types cooperate. Generally, neither of these issues has proven to be a bottleneck. One special case, however, can cause severe performance problems: recall, that compound signals use signal properties that in turn aggregate other basic signal objects. While for sets of sampled bands and parameterized signals, the number of contained objects is usually on the order of a few tens to hundreds, the collection of noise bins can easily reach the size of thousands. The original procedure for adding an element to a container requires sending messages to all previously contained elements, leading to a complexity that scales exponentially. To overcome this problem, we have simply modified the according compound properties such that messages announcing the addition of an element are not sent, but the completion of an addition phase is signaled by a message and container elements can then scan the set if required. Currently, such scanning is not required, but it would imply a complexity scaling with N^2.

Signal	Time
Noise bin	65 μsec
Sampled band (array length 2048 samples, no array initialization)	270 μsec
Compound signal with one sampled band	410 μsec
Compound signal with 8 sampled bands and 160 parameterized signals	78 msec
Compound signal with 10,000 noise bins	1536 msec

Table 1: Time for life-cycle operations on different signal types.

Table 1 lists the combined con- and destruction times of various signal types, using an Intel 350 MHz Pentium II PC running Linux for the benchmark. Compared with the computing time for standard simulation algorithms, which are on the order of a few milliseconds to several days, the overhead imposed by object life-cycle operations can in most cases be neglected. Only in rare situations, where a very large number of noise bin objects are used and the simulation algorithms are trivial, the overhead is significant.

Adding Signals

Another potential bottleneck is the addition of signals. Again, the critical issue is related to handling sets of noise bins, while all other aspects cause no problems in terms of performance. Two sets of noise bins are added such, that the resulting set does not contain any two spectrally overlapping noise bins. This obviously requires that overlapping bins are appropriately added; to preserve the spectral noise density, in the case of two partially overlapping noise bins N_1 and N_2, the result is a set of bins N_1', N_2', and N_3, as depicted in figure 6. Performing this operation on two unordered set of noise bins, containing N and M bins respectively, requires to check for matches between any combinations of bins, implying a N*M complexity. However, we store signal objects spectrally ordered in the sets, such that matching overlapping signals can be done with at most N+M operations.

APPLICATIONS

This section describes two "real-life" applications of the signal representation framework that we have presented.

Efficient Representation of Wideband Signals

Optical amplifiers, mostly Erbium Doped Fiber Amplifiers (EFDA), are a crucial element of modern optical communication systems. One of their important characteristics is the noise that they add to the amplified signal. This noise is extremely broadband in nature, covering some 10 THz. Although the actually amplified signal covers only a small fraction of that bandwidth, it is important to capture the entire amplifier noise in order to model saturation effects of cascaded EDFAs. Further, optical amplifiers need to be *pumped* to achieve amplification. Therefore, the design and evaluation of EDFAs requires the application of all principal signal representations. Figure 7 depicts the PTDS simulation setup, modeling the optical amplification of a four channel WDM signal using an EDFA. Figure 8 shows the resulting output in the form of an optical spectrum of the signal. A wide spectral region of about 18 THz is covered by noise bins, with the four transmission channels modeled by individual sampled bands, and the pump source represented by a parameterized signal. Figure 9 gives an impression of the internal composition of the resulting signal object, showing a screenshot of an interactive signal browser. For historical reasons, some of the class names found in the figure differ from those presented here. The simulation takes a few seconds to run; using the traditional method by sampling the entire spectrum would increase computation time by orders of magnitude and would require gigabytes of memory.

Using Logical Signals

The prominent use of logical signals within a simulation is to enable receiver models to regenerate the initial signal that they ideally should have received and to derive performance measures from comparison with the actually received signal. Typical applications comprise designs in which the transmission of a signal is simulated, with the receiver side estimating the bit error rate (BER). Using logical channels allows the receiver to access the modulated bit sequence for BER estimation as well as to perform synchronization.

CONCLUSIONS

We have developed a signal representation framework based on an object-oriented, extensible design concept. We have discussed the principal signal representations and their application, have mentioned the bottlenecks encountered, and have discussed counter-measures taken to overcome them. The signal representation framework is successfully used as the basis of a commercial design product, proving the practicability of the concept.

REFERENCES

Hamster, H. and J. Lam. 1998. "PDA: Challenges for an emerging industry" *Lightwave*, August 1998, Penwell Publishing

Breuer, D.; et al. 2000. "Photonic Design Automation: The Photonic Transmission Design Suite" *DesignCon 2000 Conference Proceedings*, W325

Lee, E.A. and Sangiovanni-Vincentelli, A. 1998. "A framework for comparing models of computation" *IEEE Transactions on computer-aided design of integrated circuits and systems*, Vol. 17, No. 12, Dec. 1998

Rasmussen, C.J. 1999. *Transmission Analysis in WDM Networks*. Ph.D. Thesis, Technical University of Denmark

Lowery, A.J.; P.C.R. Gurney; X-H. Wang; L. V. T. Nguyen; Y-C. Chan; and M. Premaratne. 1996. "Time-domain simulation of photonic devices, circuits and systems" *Technical digest of Physics and Simulation of Optoelectronic Devices IV*, (San Jose, CA, Jan. 29 – Feb. 2), vol. 2693, pp.624-635

Richter, A. and V. S. Grigoryan. 1999. "Efficient approach to estimate collision-induced timing jitter in dispersion-managed WDM RZ systems" *Proceedings of OFC'99* (San Diego, CA, Feb. 23–26), WM33, pp. 292-294

Gamma, E.; Helm, R.; Johnson, R.; and Vlissides, J. 1995. *Design patterns: Elements of reusable object-oriented software*. Addison-Wesley

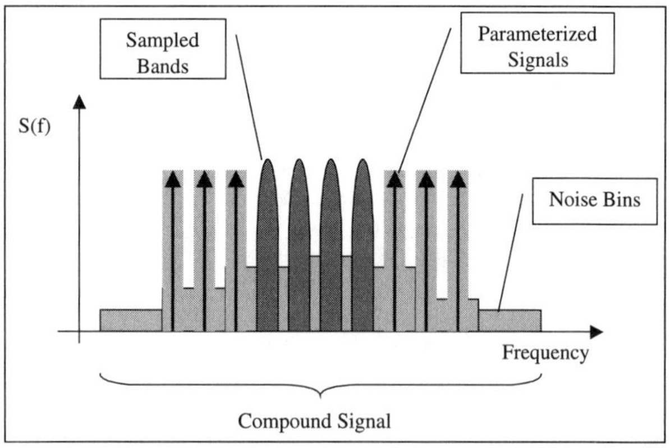

Figure 1: Spectral view of principal signal representations.

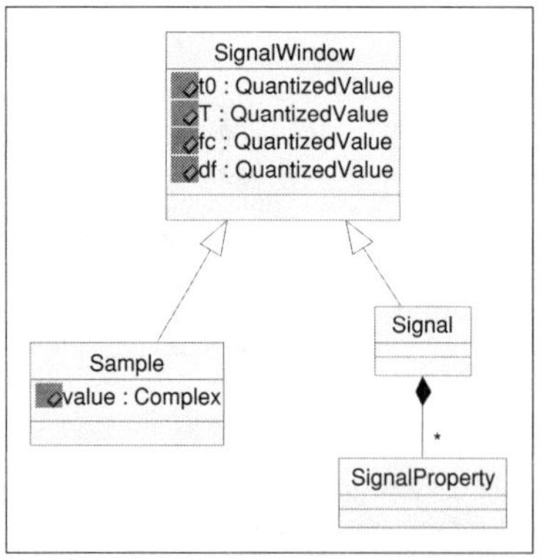

e 2: UML class diagram of signal representation base class

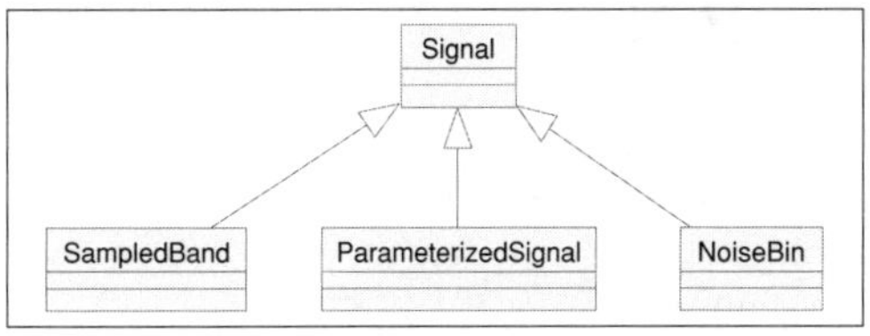

Figure 1: UML class diagram of basic signal representation classes.

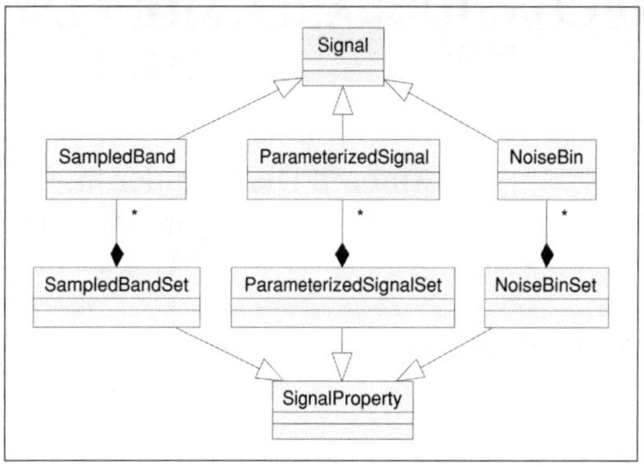

Figure 2: UML class diagram for compound signal properties.

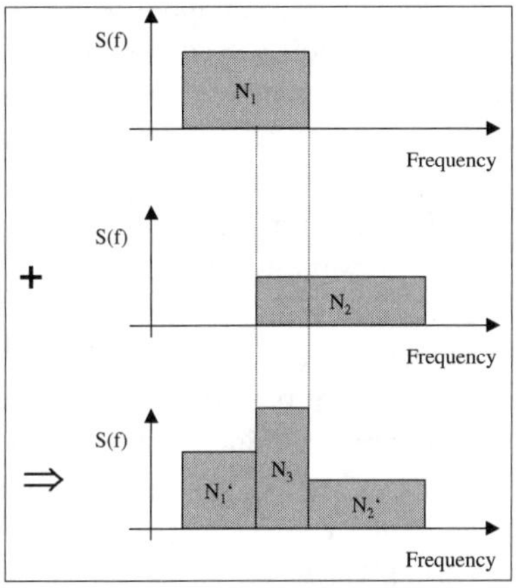

Figure 3: Noise bin adaptation during addition to preserve spectral noise density information.

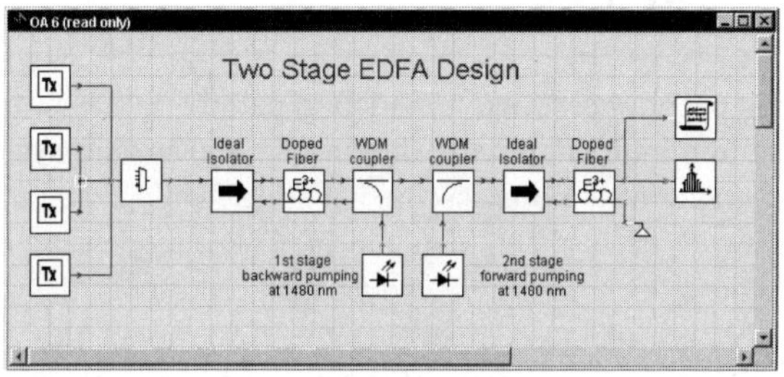

Figure 4: Setup of for simulation of an optical amplifier design (EDFA).

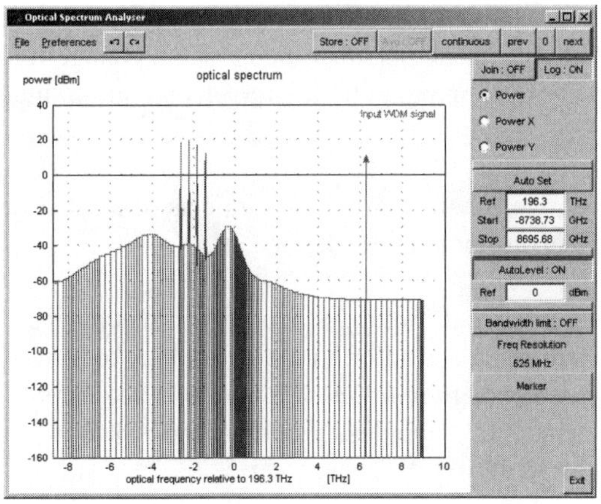

Figure 5: Optical spectrum of EDFA output signal.

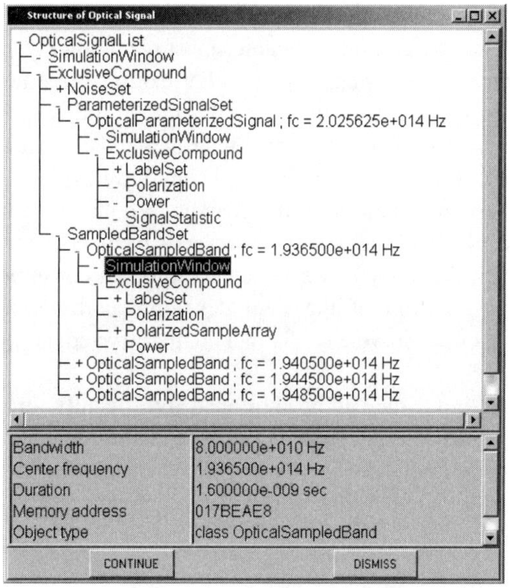

Figure 6: Structure or simulation output signal.

RECONFIGURABLE MODELS: A MODELING PARADIGM TO SUPPORT SIMULATION-BASED DESIGN

Antonio Diaz-Calderon, Christiaan J. J. Paredis[1], Pradeep K. Khosla
Department of Electrical and Computer Engineering
Institute for Complex Engineered Systems
Carnegie Mellon University
Pittsburgh, PA 15213, USA
E-mail: paredis@cmu.edu

KEYWORDS

reconfigurable model, object-oriented modeling, model space, component libraries, VHDL-AMS.

ABSTRACT

In this paper, we define a modeling paradigm that provides simulation support for the design of mechatronic systems. The paradigm supports associating more than one simulation model with each system component. These models are organized in a *reconfigurable model* that represents the entire model space of the component. The elements of this space are models that vary from abstract (conceptual) to concrete (fully determined), thereby supporting the evolutionary nature of the design process. They allow the designer to work with high-level concepts that can be specialized at later stages in the design process.

INTRODUCTION

Because of the intense competition in the current global economy, successful companies must react quickly to changing trends in the market place. For example, the need for a new product can be triggered by the introduction of new technologies, changes in customer demands, or fluctuations in the cost of basic materials and commodities. To capitalize on these imbalances in the market, a company must conceive, design, and manufacture new products quickly and inexpensively. Because the design process consumes a significant portion of the total development time, a shorter design cycle provides a distinct competitive advantage.

The design cycle can be shortened significantly through virtual prototyping. A virtual prototype enables the designers to test whether the design specifications are met by performing simulations rather than physical experiments; a physical prototype is only needed for final testing. Not only does virtual prototyping make design verification faster and less expensive, it provides the designer with immediate feedback on design decisions. This in turn promises a more comprehensive exploration of design alternatives and a better performing final design. To fully exploit the advantages of virtual prototyping, however, simulation models have to be accurate and easy to create.

Creating high-fidelity simulation models is a complex activity that can be quite time-consuming. To take full advantage of virtual prototyping, it is necessary to develop a modeling paradigm that supports model reuse, that is integrated with the design environment, and that provides a simple and intuitive interface which requires a minimum of analysis expertise. This paper introduces such a paradigm: *composable and reconfigurable modeling*, which is based on model composition from system components.

Reconfigurable models allow the designer to model systems in a hierarchical fashion. Initially, a system can be described by high-level components and the interactions between them. The models of the high-level components can then be refined iteratively without having to modify the system-level model description. As a result, the system model can be incrementally adapted as more detailed design features become known. This is in contrast to most currently available modeling environments in which a small change in the system description may require a large change in the model structure.

In this paper, we consider simulation models of mechatronic systems. Mechatronics can be defined as

> "A technological field that combines mechanics with electronics and information technology to form both *functional interaction* and *spatial integration* in components, modules, products and systems." (Breunese 1996)

1. Corresponding author.

To provide simulation support to the mechatronic design approach, we need modeling tools that capture system behavior across energy domains. In recent years, a number of modeling languages have emerged that capture mathematical models of mechatronic systems. These languages are based on object-oriented principles, and include Dymola (Dynasim AB 1999, Elmqvist *et al.* 1993), OMOLA (Anderson 1994), NMF (Sahlin 1996), and—more recently—Modelica (Elmqvist 1998) and VHDL-AMS (IEEE 1999).

Although these modeling languages are object oriented in nature, they do not permit the model *structure* to be easily modified. Instead, only mechanisms for parameter reconfiguration are provided. Given the evolutionary nature of the design process, it would be desirable to accommodate reconfiguration of the model structure also.

In de Vries' work with polymorphic models (the MAX system), he suggests an approach to achieve structure configuration (de Vries *et al.* 1995). His polymorphic models are similar to our concept of reconfigurable models; however, they present the following limitations:

- An instance of a model is considered an implementation. This forces a new type to be defined for each new set of parameter values for an implementation.
- Models are represented by bond graphs, which limits their applicability to lumped parameter systems.

To overcome such limitations, we propose a system representation based on two concepts: *interface* and *implementation*. In this model representation, systems are described from a systems engineering point of view where subsystems interact with their environment through energy exchange. The interface of a system describes the interaction through a set of ports. The implementation, on the other hand, describes a system's internal behavior. The interface and implementation together define a complete model of a system. A direct consequence of this new representation is that it is possible to assign different implementations to the same system interface, thereby achieving reconfigurability of models. We call system models that are based on this modeling paradigm *reconfigurable models.*

Because reconfigurable models are an extension of port-based models, we will first describe the port-based modeling paradigm.

PORT-BASED MULTI-DOMAIN MODELING OF MECHATRONIC SYSTEMS

To provide better support for simulation-based design of mechatronic systems, we have developed a modeling and design paradigm based on composition. A wide variety of products, ranging from consumer electronics to cars, contain mostly off-the-shelve components and components reused from previous design generations; for instance, in cars, the portion of completely new components is often less than twenty percent. As a result, the design of such systems consists primarily of the configuration or assembly of existing components.

The modeling of such systems can also be viewed as composition. We can obtain a system level simulation model, by combining the component models with the models that define the interactions between the components. Assuming the models for individual components already exist in a component library, and that the physics of the interactions between the components have been modeled in a library of interaction models, a system level simulation model can be generated through the composition of existing component and interaction models. To support modeling through composition, we have developed a port-based modeling paradigm.

A port-based modeling paradigm

In our modeling paradigm, subsystems interact with each other through ports (Diaz-Calderon *et al.* 1998, 1999). As noted above, ports represent localized points on the boundary of the system where energy exchange between the system and the environment takes place. At a port, energy flows in and out of the system. Consequently, there is a port for each interaction point, and each port will belong to an energy domain. For example, consider an electric transformer with four terminals. Each terminal represents a port through which electrical energy flows in and out of the transformer. In this example, the ports belong to the electrical energy domain; this captures the flow of power in terms of the voltages and currents on the two sides of the transformer.

The energy flow through a port is represented by means of two variables: an *across* variable and a *through* variable. Across variables represent values measured between a global reference point and the port. For instance, the across variable at one of the ports in the transformer represents the voltage between the physical terminal and ground. Through variables represent values measured through the element; e.g., the current in the transformer example.

Connections between ports represent the interactions between different components. A connection between two ports represents the energy exchange between two subsystems and imposes algebraic constraints on the port variables involved in the connection. In general, these

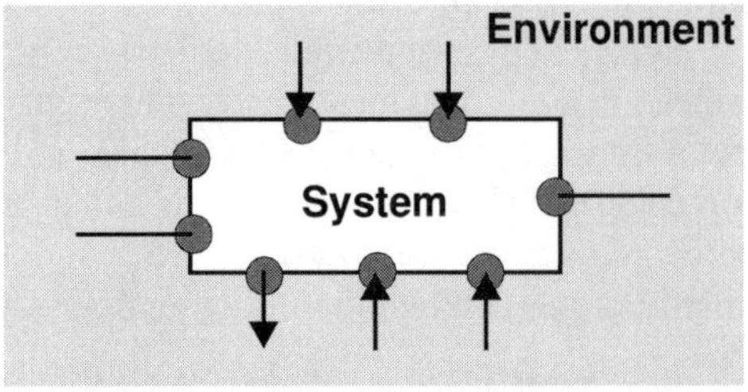

Figure 1: Model of an engineering system. Energy ports are represented by non-directed lines while signal ports are represented by arrows.

constraints take two forms: one form enforces the equality of the across variables, and the second enforces the sum of the through variables to be zero.

Physical interactions that represent energy exchange have no predefined direction. Therefore, we capture a physical interaction with undirected connections representing non-causal interactions. This approach to modeling reflects the physical interactions more accurately and relieves the modeler of specifying the input/output relations, as would be required in a modeling environment such as Simulink.

Besides ports and connections that model energy flow, we also consider signals and signal ports. No energy flows through the signal ports, and the interaction between signal ports is causal. That is, signal ports have a predefined input-output direction that constrains the signal flow between components. Signal and signal ports capture a system based on a block diagram description similar to Simulink.

The system's ports are collectively grouped into an interface, which defines the interaction points of the system with the environment. In this way, we can describe systems as self-contained entities, whose interactions with the environment can be described independently of the internal behavior of the system, as illustrated in Figure 1.

The port-based modeling paradigm can describe component interactions in any energy domain as long as the interaction is not distributed but lumped. Consider for example a flexible beam. A finite element model may describe the behavior of the beam. However, presuming that the interaction points of the beam are localized at the two ends, we can describe its interaction with the environment with two ports located at the two ends. Thus, our modeling paradigm is limited to interactions that are localized at a finite number of points on the boundary of the system.

As illustrated in Figure 2, the port-based modeling paradigm also supports a hierarchical model structure. The hierarchy

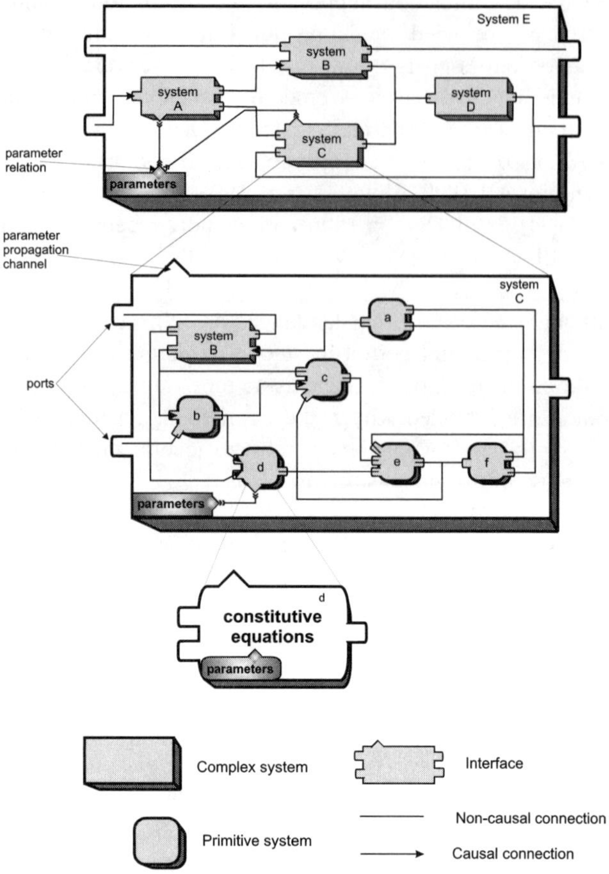

Figure 2: Hierarchical model structure

can have any number of levels; however, in order to transform it into an adequate simulation model, the hierarchy must be terminated with *primitive* systems, or systems that cannot be divided into smaller subsystems. *Compound* systems on the other hand are composed by connecting primitive models or compound models at a lower level in the hierarchy.

Equation-based modeling

The behavior of a primitive system can be specified using either of two formalisms, depending on whether the system is energy-based or not. Both formalisms represent the behavior of the system with a set of *constitutive equations.* The difference between the two types of systems lies in how the constitutive equations are specified and how the system's topology is described.

In the first formalism, the behavior of non-energy-based systems is described using a procedural approach. In this case, a signal quantity represents the quantity that is available to the environment through the interface of the system. Constitutive equations of this kind are described as assignments (causal equations) that compute the value of a signal quantity based on the inputs to the subsystem.

In the second formalism, the behavior of energy-based systems can be represented using a graph-based model (Diaz-Calderon *et al.* 1999). Each edge in the graph has two associated quantities, called *branch quantities*: *across quantity* and *through quantity*. These quantities are analytic functions of time (i.e., they are piece wise continuous with a finite number of discontinuities). Across quantities, represent effort such as voltage, temperature, or pressure that are the result of a measurement taken across two energy ports of the system. Through quantities represent flow such as current, heat flow rate, or fluid flow rate that are the result of a measurement taken in series with the component. To illustrate this, consider an example of an electrical network. Here, the vertices of the graph represent equipotential nodes in the circuit, and edges represent branches of the circuit through which current flows. The measurement taken across two nodes defines the across branch quantity, while the measurement taken in series with the component defines the through quantity.

The constitutive equations are expressed by relating the across and through quantities of one or several branches—for example, a resistor has a single branch, and its constitutive equation (Ohm's law) relates the voltage across (the across quantity) and the current through (the through quantity) the resistor.

Constitutive equations define the behavior of a subsystem without specifying a particular causal direction. The causal direction emerges only when the equations are combined with constitutive equations of other subsystems, and the quantities that are external to the subsystem are specified. A quantity is external to the subsystem if its value is computed using a constitutive equation that is not part of the constitutive equations of the subsystem. For example, when the constitutive equation of a resistor is combined into a larger system of equations, either the voltage or the current will be defined externally; Ohm's law is causally oriented to reflect this: $v := iR$ or $i := v/R$. In the first case, the voltage v is computed from the current i, which is computed using an external equation. Similarly, in the second case, the current i is computed from the voltage v.

The equations appearing in the model can be of several kinds: *ordinary differential equations*, *algebraic equations*, or *differential-algebraic equations*. Ordinary differential equations (ODE) can represent the variation of quantities as a function of a single variable, such as time. Therefore, ODEs are used to represent lumped parameter models. Algebraic equations do not contain partial or total derivatives. When a model includes both ODE and algebraic equations, the resultant system of equations is called a differential-algebraic system of equations (DAE). In this type of system, algebraic equations represent constraints among the state variables defined by the set of ODEs.

Constitutive equations of both types (i.e., non-causal and causal) may include a combination of branch quantities and signal quantities. We call these types of models *hybrid models* since they describe the interaction of energy-based systems with non-energy-based systems. An example of this type of behavioral description would be an electromechanical system controlled by a digital controller.

If the system is compound, its behavior is described according to the structural arrangement of subsystems, which in turn may be compound or primitive. This unambiguously defines the topological constraints among components. Consequently, a compound system can be reduced through a sequence of algebraic transformations into a primitive model that exhibits the same behavior.

Meta knowledge

Whether using a compound or primitive model to describe a system's behavior, constitutive equations do not provide sufficient information to reason about the properties of the system since they are based on implicit assumptions and approximations. In other words, the context in which a model of a system can be applied is not explicit. If such knowledge were explicit, one could not only reason about the applicability of the model to a given problem, but also decide when models having similar properties can be interchanged.

One kind of meta knowledge that we consider is the *operating region* of the model. The operating region defines the space of admissible values for the quantities of the model, which provide meaningful results. Outside this space, the model may provide erroneous results that invalidate its application. To ensure that a model is used within its operating region, we explicitly express its bounds through the *operating conditions* of the model. Operating conditions are conditional expressions on the quantities of the model and explicitly define the sub-domain for each quantity for which the equations stated in the model are valid.

When it is necessary to define multiple operating regions, for example to capture a large portion of the system's operating region, operating conditions are disjointed. Each element of the disjunction represents a valid operating region that has an

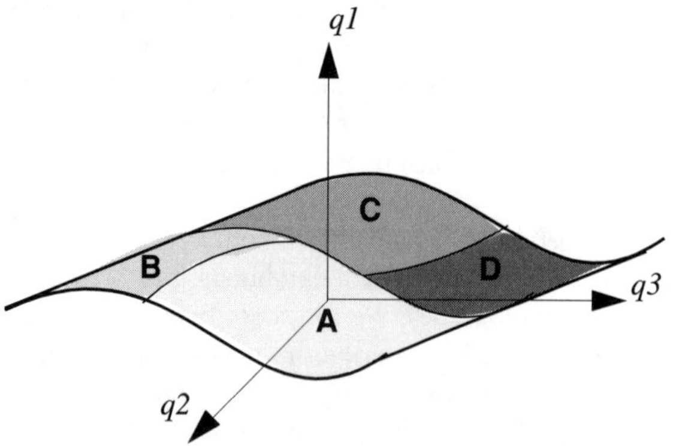


```
model process
quantities
  q1, q2, q3
equations
  if OC1(q1, q2, q3)
    RA(q1, q2, q3)=0
  elif OC2(q1, q2, q3)
    RB(q1, q2, q3) = 0
  elif OC3(q1, q2, q3)
    RC(q1, q2, q3) = 0
  elif OC4(q1, q2, q3)
    RD(q1, q2, q3) = 0
end process
```

Figure 3: Segmentation of the domain based on different operating regions

associated set of constitutive equations. In other words, operating conditions allow us to segment the domain of the quantities involved in the constitutive equations. Consequently, we can obtain a model that is applicable within a larger operating region of the system. For example, consider the operating region of the system shown in Figure 3. The domains of the three quantities define the solution space of the system. The operating conditions given as a function of the three quantities (represented by the functions OC_i) segment the space into four regions *(A, B, C,* and *D),* each of which has an associated set of equations (represented by the function R_j) that describe valid behavior under these conditions.

Current support for port-based modeling

Using object-oriented modeling principles, it is possible to describe a port-based model that is composable and hierarchical (Elmqvist 1998, Sahlin 1996, Anderson 1994, IEEE 1999). However, in an object-oriented modeling paradigm, there is not necessarily a clear separation between the interface of the model and the implementation of its behavior. Often both concepts are merged together into a single modeling entity. In this modeling approach, only parametric reconfiguration is allowed. However, to evaluate the design at different levels of detail, changes in structure should also be supported. This is achieved with reconfigurable models.

RECONFIGURABLE COMPONENT MODELS

In a reconfigurable model, the interface of the model and the implementation of its behavior are considered to be two separate concepts. By considering these two concepts independently, it is possible to associate different implementations with a single interface, achieving a structural modification of models, and consequently, creating a *reconfigurable model* (Figure 4). In addition to the traditional changes in parameter values, a reconfigurable model provides a mechanism to describe changes in the model structure by using the principles of *composition* and *instantiation.*

The composition principle denotes the mechanism by which the formal behavior of the component is described in terms of interfaces of subcomponents and their interactions. Since composition unambiguously represents topological constraints among components, a composed model given by the pair $\langle\Phi|\phi_c\rangle$ can be reduced to a primitive model $\langle\Phi|\phi_p\rangle$ which exhibits equivalent behavior, where $\langle\Phi|\phi\rangle$ represents the binding of implementation ϕ to interface Φ.

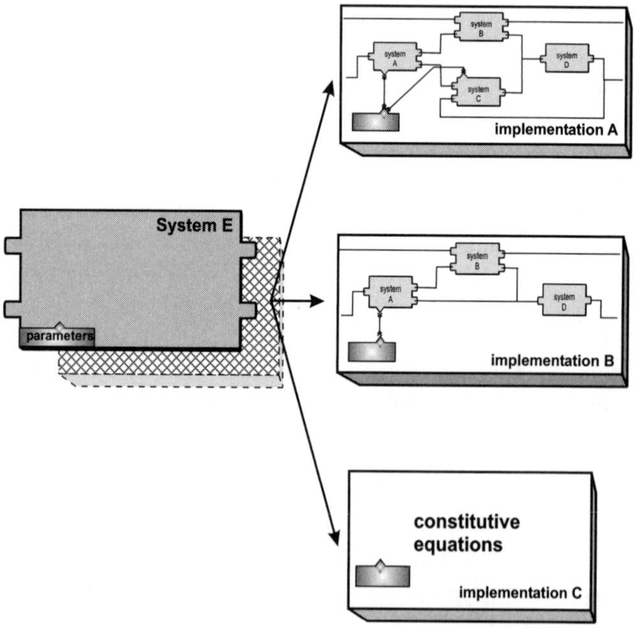

Figure 4: A reconfigurable system model.

As a result of the principle of instantiation, compound implementations are abstract. They are a composition of abstract interfaces, that still need to be bound to implementations to specify the behavior completely. Consequently, instantiating a compound component (i.e., a component with a compound implementation) requires the recursive instantiation of each interface in the component.

Reconfigurable models are hierarchical in nature. Based on the composition principle, we define self-contained implementations of a system in terms of the composition of subsystem interfaces; i.e., a compound implementation. However, a hierarchical system defined by reconfigurable models is not fixed. Rather, it changes as implementations are bound to the interfaces (model instantiation) that describe the compound implementation. Specifically, binding different implementations to an interface results in a different structural arrangement and thus a different hierarchical structure.

The second principle—the principle of instantiation—describes the mechanism by which the interface of a model is bound to its implementation. An implementation that meets the requirements of an interface, can generally be bound to it. However, the semantics of the resulting model must be consistent with the context in which the model is used. For example, consider the case of a resistor and a capacitor whose interfaces both include the same set of interaction points (two electrical terminals). In such a case, an implementation that satisfies the interface for the resistor will also satisfy that of the capacitor. However, the semantics of the resulting model will differ; hence they cannot be interchanged. In summary, we will allow bindings that produce models having the same semantic meaning.

There are two kinds of implementations that can be bound to an interface and maintain a consistent semantic interpretation of the model. These are implementations with different representations of equivalent behavior, and implementations with different behavior. Accordingly, if τ and κ are two implementations that satisfy interface Φ, then,

$$SEMANTICS(\langle\Phi|\tau\rangle) = SEMANTICS(\langle\Phi|\kappa\rangle) \quad (1)$$

The instantiation principle also provides the basis for defining a family of systems (i.e., the model space of a component). An interface that can be bound to different implementations by the instantiation principle defines a family of systems. All members of the family will show the same interaction characteristics but with different formal behavior. This method of describing membership of an element in a set is referred to as a *type* in the theory of computational objects and can be phrased as follows (Abadi and Cardelli 1996):

> "The type of an object provides the semantic information that completely characterizes the object but not its behavior."

An interface defines a type, each member of which is a subsystem having a unique formal behavior. Based on this observation, it is possible to organize system models into a type hierarchy. This type hierarchy is derived from a type system that provides the notions of subtype and supertype (Abadi and Cardelli 1996).

Let the symbol <: represent a reflexive and transitive subtype relation between interfaces I and I', then:

Definition *Subtyping.* I' <: I if I' has the same ports and parameters as I and possibly more, and the following conditions pertain:

1. The types of the ports are subtypes of types of corresponding ports in I.
2. The types of the parameters are subtypes of the corresponding parameters in I.
3. The semantics of the parameters are equivalent to the semantics of the corresponding parameters in I.

Based on the definition of subtype (and its complement, supertype), two operations can be defined on the type hierarchy, namely, *specialization* and *generalization*. Specialization involves finding an interface for the same family of components that includes more detail, while generalization involves finding an interface that is less specific. These operations are carried out by traversing the hierarchy in either a downward direction (specialization) or an upward direction (generalization).

Definition *Specialization.* Let x and y be two interfaces. Interface y is a specialization of interface x, denoted $y \xrightarrow{S} x$, if and only if the type of y is a subtype of the type of x, and for any system S that contains x, y can be substituted for x while maintaining the same semantics. This can be stated formally as:

$$\begin{aligned} y \xrightarrow{S} x \Leftrightarrow\ & TypeOf(y) <: TypeOf(x) \wedge \\ & (\forall S|_x,\ S\langle x \ll y\rangle \rightarrow \\ & SEMANTICS(S|_y) = SEMANTICS(S|_x)) \end{aligned} \quad (2)$$

where the operator $S\langle x \ll y\rangle$ should be interpreted as "x is substituted by y in S" and $S|_x$ should be read "the system S

evaluated with interface *x*". Similarly, it is possible to derive the property of generalization based on the supertype relation.

Parameter handling

In addition to the ports, it is also important to include the parameters in the interface. Model parameters describe fundamental characteristics of the system. For example, inertia and torque constants specify the invariant properties of a system that represents an electric motor; they are constant quantities that do not change value throughout the entire simulation.

In defining parameters of lower level subsystems, two kinds of parameters can be identified: *formal* and *actual* parameters. A formal parameter is defined locally in the interface of the subsystem, and it is used by a bound implementation. An actual parameter contains the value of an argument that is related to a formal parameter in a call to the model, and it is defined by the environment. The value of the argument is the value of an expression defined in terms of the formal parameters in the current scope. Parameter composition ensures that the parameters of the system are propagated to all the subsystems that were incorporated into the compound implementation.

The principles of instantiation and composition together with parameter propagation provide the infrastructure required to define reconfigurable models.

SUMMARY

In this paper, we have described a modeling paradigm based on reconfigurable component models that supports the design of mechatronic systems. In this paradigm, mathematical models consist of two elements: interface and implementation. The interface defines the mechanism by which the model interacts with its environment, while the implementation describes the behavior of the component. Model reconfiguration is achieved when the model of a component is defined by binding an implementation to an interface.

ACKNOWLEDGMENTS

This research was funded in part by DARPA under contract ONR # N00014-96-1-0854, by the National Institute of Standards and Technology, by the NSF under grant # CISE/IIS/KDI 9873005, by the Pennsylvania Infrastructure Technology Alliance, and by the Institute for Complex Engineered Systems at Carnegie Mellon University.

REFERENCES

M. Abadi and L. Cardelli, *A theory of objects*. Monographs in Computer Science, Springer-Verlag, New York, 1996.

M. Anderson. "Object-oriented modeling and simulation of hybrid systems," Ph.D. Thesis, Department of Automatic Control, Lund Institute of Technology, Lund, Sweden, 1994.

A. P. J. Breunese. "Automated support in mechatronic systems modeling," Ph.D. Thesis, Department of Electrical Engineering, University of Twente, Enschede, The Netherlands, 1996.

A. Diaz-Calderon, C. J. J. Paredis, and P. K. Khosla, "A modular composable software architecture for the simulation of mechatronic systems," presented at ASME Design Engineering Technical Conference, 18th Computers in Engineering Conference, Atlanta, GA, September 1998.

A. Diaz-Calderon, C. J. J. Paredis, and P. K. Khosla, "A composable simulation environment for mechatronic systems," presented at SCS 1999 European Simulation Symposium, Erlangen, Germany, October 1999.

Dynasim AB, "Dymola." Lund, Sweden, 1999.

H. Elmqvist, F. E. Cellier, and M. Otter, "Object-oriented modeling of hybrid systems," presented at European Simulation Symposium, Delft, The Netherlands, October 1993.

H. Elmqvist, S. E. Mattsson, and M. Otter, "Modelica: The new object-oriented modeling language," presented at The 12th European Simulation Multiconference, Manchester, UK, June 16-19 1998.

IEEE, 1076.1 Working Group, "Analog and mixed-signal extensions for VHDL," IEEE, 1999.

P. C. Piela, T. G. Epperly, K. M. Westerberg, and A. W. Westerberg, "ASCEND: An object oriented computer environment for modeling and analysis. 1- The modeling language," *Comput. Chem Engng*, vol. 15, no. 1, pp. 53-72, 1991.

P. Sahlin. "Modeling and simulation methods for modular continuous systems in buildings," Ph.D. Thesis, Department of Building Sciences, Division of Building Services, Royal Institute of Technology, Stockholm, Sweden, 1996.

T. J. A. de Vries and A. P. J. Breunese, "Structuring product models to facilitate design manipulations," presented at International Conference on Engineering Design, Praha, August 22-24 1995.

Modeling the Web: Linking Discrete and Continuous

Narsingh Deo
School of Computer Science
University of Central Florida
Orlando, FL 32816
USA
deo@cs.ucf.edu

Bruce Litow
School of Information Technology
James Cook University
Townsville, QLD. 4811
Australia
bruce@cs.jcu.edu.au

Pankaj Gupta
School of Computer Science
University of Central Florida
Orlando, FL 32816
USA
pgupta@cs.ucf.edu

KEYWORDS: webgraph, WWW model, search engine.

ABSTRACT

The World Wide Web can be modeled as a directed graph in which a node represents a web page and an edge represents a hyperlink. Currently the number of nodes in this gigantic webdigraph is estimated to be approaching a billion, and is growing without any centralized control. Recent studies suggest that despite its chaotic appearance, the web is a highly structured digraph, in a statistical sense. This paper explores some of the salient features of the webdigraph—both discrete and continuous. Knowledge of these properties can be used to attain efficiency and comprehensiveness in WWW navigation. These properties may be determined with a combination of experimental and analytic tools.

1. WWW AS SPAGHETTI

The World Wide Web (WWW) can be viewed in two very divergent ways. From an internal standpoint it is a TCP-compliant application, HTTP with related software, *e.g.*, support for Java and a set of associated programming and data communications problems and solutions. We are interested in the other equally-important way of viewing WWW, which is external and extensional. From this standpoint, WWW is a vast and continuously growing repository of information: textual as well as audio and video. The sheer mass of material and the apparently chaotic nature of WWW can make locating, acquiring and organizing information for a specific purpose both time consuming and difficult. This runs exactly opposite to the promise of WWW, namely that all information can be made readily available to the world's population all of the time. The first challenge to overcome in attaining this laudable goal would be to find methods for efficiently and comprehensively navigating WWW. Efficiency has to be defined in WWW-intrinsic terms. That is, one wants to minimize the number of links that must be followed to reach a desired piece of information from a designated starting point. Comprehensiveness means that most relevant information is actually obtained during the navigation. At present neither efficiency nor comprehensiveness can be reliably achieved.

Much of the effort in devising search methods for navigating WWW is based on knowledge engineering. This is a promising approach provided one knows how deep (how many links overall) the search should continue and how comprehensively relevant sections of WWW have been identified. Knowledge engineering is most appropriate when the field of search has been significantly narrowed to the point where with some certainty most of the relevant information resides in visited pages. At this point, knowledge-engineering techniques can be used to amplify relevance and filter less relevant material away so that the user can then apply interface techniques, *e.g.*, visualization to examine the results. There is need of a set of methods that can exploit structural properties of WWW to accelerate the search process so that it actually reaches the threshold where knowledge engineering can be profitably applied. A summary of WWW data collection and characterizations of aspects of WWW appears in (Pitkow 1997). However, a WWW model does not 'emerge' from these data, as the elements of any model must be formulated mathematically.

Recent work suggests that despite its chaotic appearance, WWW is highly structured, but in a statistical sense. Models have been proposed which reproduce certain experimentally determined features of WWW and these features could be exploited to attain efficiency and comprehensiveness in WWW navigation. Section 2 discusses some preliminary considerations about WWW that play a crucial role in assessing WWW models. Section 3, includes some observation on present search engines. Section 4 is a survey of some of the most important contributions to the identification of structure in WWW. Section 5 contains the concluding remarks.

2. HOW SHOULD WWW BE MODELED?

WWW is Not the Internet

Any discussion of WWW in the extensional sense must begin by disengaging it from the Internet. The Internet is a constellation of data communications technologies, which are not relevant to the present discussion of the WWW structure. To highlight this statement, let us ask a simple question: "What is the correspondence between the distance (minimum number of hyperlinks) from one WWW page to another and the minimum number of IP router hops required to realize the traversal?" The answer is generally that there is no correspondence. It may be a three-hyperlink jump, but nine routers might have to be involved in the best of circumstances on the Internet. Internet topology and traffic are defined by data communications lines and resource allocation issues in entities like routers or operating systems. There are valuable studies of the Internet and the impact certain kinds of WWW activities have on it as a resource issue (Claffy 1999; Crovella and Bestavros 1995). However, WWW and the Internet do not directly influence each other. The smallest useful component of WWW is a page, which we take to be a single HTML file. A page can be resolved into smaller elements such as cross-linked subdocuments (HTML files) and multimedia objects, *e.g.*, digital images. This level of detail is not necessary for an analysis of WWW structure. Since WWW is the sum total of all of the authoring decisions made by individual designers of a page, the WWW links reflect semantically motivated, intentional acts by human beings. The topology of WWW in not influenced by data communications or systems considerations. Recent studies about WWW structure show that it resembles collective behavior reminiscent of complex physical systems and thermodynamics. Thus, despite the impossibility of direct modeling at the microscopic level, WWW structure can be modeled.

More on Building Blocks: WWW as a Digraph

It is reasonable to model WWW as a directed graph where each node represents a page and each edge a hyperlink. The graph-theoretic terms used in this paper can be found in any standard graph-theory book such as (Deo 1974). In Section 4, we will see that some progress has been made in identifying the kinds of subgraphs that can be regarded as intermediate-scale objects. These objects are of the highest importance in defining web structure and in developing new approaches to efficient and comprehensive navigation.

To draw one more distinction between Internet and WWW structures, the word 'site' has various meanings when applied to WWW. From the Internet standpoint, a site is a principal IP address. It derives its importance from being identifiable as a reachable target on the Internet. From the WWW standpoint, its usage is hard to pin down. As an interesting exercise in both WWW search and the framing of the definition here are some URL's, that have conflicting definitions of the term WWW site (FOLDOC; Netlingo; Webopedia). Whatever appropriate definition eventuates, it will not coincide with IP site.

3. SEARCH ENGINES

The WWW has more than one billion pages and is growing rapidly. A search engine is useful to locate information in this vast space. According to URL Beaucoup.com, currently there are more than 2,500 search engines (16,240 according to URL SearchPower.com), but searching on WWW is still far from perfect. Most of the search engines can be broadly classified into two categories—text-based and directory-based. There are other type of search engines like meta-search engines, *e.g.*, dogpile.com, metacrawler.com, mamma.com, etc. The meta-search engines send search query to several search engines and show all the results simultaneously.

Search engines consist of three major components: spider, index, and search engine program. The spider or crawler starts with an initial set of URL's called seed URL's, retrieves the webpages of the seed URL's and follows the links to other sites from those pages (Cho and Garcia-Molina 1999). Keywords found on a webpage are added to index or catalog of the search engine. The search engine program finds the relevant pages, from the millions of pages recorded in its index, that match a query and returns them to the user after ranking them in order of relevance.

Ranking the pages returned by search engine according to relevance is extremely important, especially for queries returning huge number of pages. This is done by ranking-function heuristics, which are based on the frequency of occurrence of keyword, and sometimes on the position of keyword in the page. However, such strategies may not deliver correct information. For example, some sites may have a keyword repeated many times to attract web traffic or gain favorable ranking.

One of the factors in the effectiveness of a text-based search engine is the number of webpages indexed in its database. As of April 11, 2000, *Inktomi* has the largest database with 500 million pages indexed, *Fast* has indexed 340 million pages. *Altavista* has 350 million pages indexed as of May 1, 2000. Thus, 50% of WWW is yet to be indexed. The keyword searches performed by the current search engines typically turn up huge volumes irrelevant responses. Vast inconsistency in number of hits for two similar queries on a search engine is another serious problem. For example, a query for "Oscar award" on *Altavista* search engine resulted in 1,480 hits while "award Oscar" yielded 1,208,710 hits (Deo *et al.* 2000; Greenlaw and Hepp 1998).

4. MODELS OF RANDOM GRAPH

Erdös-Rényi Model

The earliest model of random graph was proposed by Erdös and Rényi (Erdös and Rényi 1960) in which we start with n isolated nodes, and each of the $\frac{n(n-1)}{2}$ pair of nodes is connected with a uniform probability p. This model does not does not take into account the increasing number of nodes in the network nor does a uniform probability p of edge formation between all pairs of nodes reflect the real-life WWW.

The Small-World Network I

Much of the research into WWW structure has been inspired by the small-world model of random networks. Milgram (Milgram 1967) appears to be the first to articulate the basic properties of small-world networks. It is a well-founded folklore that each individual is indirectly linked through a short chain of acquaintances to practically anyone else in the world. The small-world effect has been identified in disparate contexts including epidemiology, power networks, networks of movie actors, and WWW. Watts and Strogatz (Watts and Strogatz 1998; Watts 1999) suggested a probabilistic graph-evolution as the process underlying small-world networks. Evolution starts with a ring lattice with each node connected to its d nearest neighbors. Then the existing $\frac{n.d}{2}$ edges are randomly reassigned to distant nodes with some probability ρ in a round robin fashion. The rewired-edges connect nodes that are actually apart from each other by a distance more than L_{random}, where L_{random} is the number of edges in the shortest path, averaged over all pairs of nodes. The chief feature of this model, which can be viewed as yielding random chordal rings if we start with a ring lattice, is that a region of values for ρ produces evolution unlike the Erdös-Rényi type random graph evolution. On entering this region from below, the expected diameter of a small-world network decreases dramatically, while the expected clustering is only slowly varying throughout the region. Clustering is a measure of the extent to which the neighbors of a node form a complete graph, and it provides the basis for redefining site in purely WWW structural terms. This behavior and the values of clusters in this region are unlike those in Erdös-Rényi random-graph evolution. When $\rho = 0$, we keep the original regular graph, and when $\rho = 1$, we get an Erdös-Rényi type random graph.

Small-World Network II

Analysis of the small-world model has gone well beyond the description provided by Watts and Strogatz. Important examples of both results and analytical tools appear in papers by Moore, Newman and Watts (Moore and Newman 2000a; Moore and Newman 2000b; Newman *et al.* 1999). Like the Watts-Strogatz model, the Moore-Newman-Watts model is based on undirected graphs.

The mathematical model presented in (Newman *et al.* 1999) establishes a connection between the discrete small-world network and a continuous version. It is a mean-field model, meaning that the variables are all taken to be expected values. The notion of a cluster, which is the key concept for WWW, is a random variable in this model. For a given distance l (number of edges) and random node v, the expected number of nodes within distance l of v is determined. These nodes break up into clusters and their number is a random variable. Using the continuous model, good estimates for these variables are obtained, and corresponding estimates for the discrete model can be obtained (with a suitable confidence measure) that reflect granularity. (Newman *et al.* 1999) prove that these parameters are scale-free, *i.e.*, independent of the size (number of nodes) of the network. This is only true for 'large' networks, however. The notion of 'large' network can be made precise in terms of the corespondence between their continuous and discrete models.

Moore and Newman (Moore and Newman 2000a) have couched their analyses in epidemiological terms. In their small-world model, additional edges are added randomly giving an expected number of $\phi . d . n$ new edges. Here ϕ, d and n denote the new edge probability, number of neighbors in the original ring-lattice, and the number of nodes, respectively. Moore and Newman consider the following situation in a small-world network. Some fraction f of nodes is populated by individuals who will contract a disease if exposed to it. We need to determine $P(j)$, the probability that a randomly chosen node i belongs to a connected cluster of j nodes. A cluster has an epidemiological significance. If any node i contains an infected individual, $P(j)$ is the probability that j people will be consequently infected because there are very short paths from the original infected individual to all others in the cluster. This epidemiological notion has an obvious WWW interpretation provided one can sensibly define the cluster concept to reflect semantic relevance.

The method in (Moore and Newman 2000b) permits the calculation of a threshold value of f at which the expected size j of infectious outbreak diverges. This represents an epidemic. They also derive an asymptotic expression for $P(j)$ in the neighborhood of this threshold value of f.

Small-World Algorithmics

Kleinberg points out that although WWW may have small-world characteristics, it is another matter to exploit them efficiently. Given that a graph has small expected-diameter, how does one compute a shortest or near-shortest path from one node to another? A model for one approach to this question is given in (Kleinberg 1999b). This model has a two-dimensional grid with directed edges. The long-range contact of a node in this model is more and more clustered in its vicinity by increasing a parameter r, where r is a structural parameter that defines the degree distribution. The probability of an edge between nodes u and v is proportional to $[L(u, v)]^{-r}$ where $L(u, v)$ is the distance between nodes u and v. Using this as an extension of the

Watts-Strogatz model, Kleinberg devised a decentralized algorithm that finds a near-shortest path in expected time, which is polylogarithmic in the size of the graph. The algorithm considers the problem of passing a message from node u to another node v. It assumes that every node knows the location of the target node in the network. In addition, every node knows the location and long-range contact of all nodes that have met the message. Kleinberg proved that at $r = 2$, the decentralized algorithm takes best advantage of the geographic structure of network and produces chains having length proportional to $\log n$, where n is the number of nodes in grid. As r increases, the long-range contacts of a node become less useful in moving the message through a longer distance. In each step, a node i chooses a contact that is as close to the target node v as possible. Their model can be extended to q-dimensional network and the decentralized algorithm gives the best polylogarithmic-length path for $r = q$.

In connection with Kleinberg's extension of the small-world model, there is another model for random graphs obeying a scale-free power law for degree. This power-law random-graph model $P(\alpha, \beta)$ has n nodes each with degree d (Aielo *et al.* 2000). The degree distribution depends on α and β where α is the logarithm of number of nodes with degree 1 and β is the log-log rate of decrease of number of nodes of given degree. Here, n and d satisfy the relationship $\log n = \alpha - \beta \log d$. The model is closer to the one in conventional random-graph theory and is based on a distribution over all graphs satisfying certain parametric constraints. We believe that simpler, birth/death process models which are closer to physics in spirit may be more suitable for robust application to WWW structure studies.

The Clever Project Model

This model takes into account the creation of new pages in WWW graph as well as the removal of the existing ones. Most newly created pages will have links to existing pages of interest to the user. A "locally dense" subgraph is created around a topic of common interest by linking the scattered pages. This model has four characteristic discrete stochastic-processes—creation processes C_v and C_e for node and edge creation, respectively; and deletion processes D_v and D_e for node and edge deletion, respectively. A node is created independently at each time step with probability $\lambda_c(t)$, and similarly a node is deleted with probability $\lambda_d(t)$. All edges incident on a node are deleted, once the node is deleted. These probabilities $\lambda_c(t)$ and $\lambda_d(t)$ are determined to reflect the growth rate of WWW, the half-life of pages, etc. In edge-creation process, at each step σ edges are added from a node v to nodes chosen independently and uniformly at random with a probability ψ. In addition, σ edges are copied from a randomly-chosen node u to node v with probability $1 - \psi$. This means, we create edges from node v to node w, if (u, w) is an edge. In edge-deletion process, a randomly-chosen node is deleted at each step with a probability δ. The Clever Project group claims that (Kleinberg *et al.* 1999c) this model captures the aggregate process of page creation in WWW.

The Barabasi-Albert Model

The small-world models cannot be applied directly to WWW because the numbers of links and pages in WWW themselves are variables. These models do not accomodate about a birth/death process in which new pages are created, how new links are formed (possibly through editing old pages) and how both links and pages can be deleted. Two new models have been proposed recently to explain some of the empirical findings concerning overall WWW structure, taking on board the reality of the birth/death process.

Barabasi and Albert (Barabasi and Albert 1999) have described a mean-field theory that reproduces one of the most significant empirical findings about WWW, namely, the probability that a page or node i has degree d_i is $\frac{A}{(d_i)^c}$, where A is proportional to the square of average degree of the network, and c is a constant. The two key assumptions upon which their model is based are:

1. At each successive time step, a new node with a random, but bounded number of outgoing edges is added to the network.
2. The probability that a link from the new node goes to an existing node i is $\frac{d_i}{\sum_j dj}$, where the denominator sum runs over all existing nodes. The coefficient A in the power law depends on the expected outdegree. The Barabasi-Albert model does not account for the reconnection of existing nodes. Addition of new edges takes place only when new nodes are added in the system. However, in real-life WWW the new links are added continuously between old nodes.

Two other models are also investigated analytically by Barabasi and Albert with neither yielding a scale-free power law for node indegree.

The Huberman-Adamic Model

A different model that accounts for another scale-free empirical finding about WWW has been proposed by Huberman and Adamic (Adamic 1999; Huberman and Adamic 1999). They derive a model that exhibits an inverse, scale-free power law for the probability that a site s has N_s pages. In their analysis, a site is an undefined term, but the data they use appears to require that a site be defined as a principal IP address. It remains only a partially defined term in their model and in their data collection.

The basis of Huberman-Adamic model is an equation governing the number of pages (a random variable) at a site as a function of time. This model uses an explicit time step. The equation has the form

$$N_s(t+1) = N_s(t) + g(t+1).N_s(t)$$

Here, $N_s(t)$ is the number of pages at site s at time step t and $g(t)$ is a universal growth rate, which is independent of a site. This growth rate is further specified by the law $g(t) = g_0 + \xi(t)$, where g_0 is the basic, constant rate and $\xi(t)$ is essentially a Brownian motion variable. This gives a Wiener-process exponential law for the expected value of $N_s(t)$, which involves time t explicitly. The authors make an argument that a reasonable measure for the probability of $N_s(t)$ pages at site s is given by a weighted integral which eliminates dependence on t and yields a scale-free inverse power-law $\frac{c}{N_s^\gamma}$, where c is constant and exponent γ is in the range $[1, \infty]$. The manipulation that yields this scale-free law is not entirely clear-cut.

In a short note, Huberman and Adamic (Adamic and Huberman 2000) criticize the Barabasi-Albert model based on its prediction that older pages have larger indegree than newer pages. Empirical data appears to show no correlation between age of a page in WWW and its indegree. The two models make different assumptions about the creation of new links and the appearance of new pages.

Another Empirical Study

In one of the most extensive study until now, (Broder *et al.* 2000) analyzed link structure of 203 million pages and 1.5 billion links. Three different sets of experiments were conducted in two *Altavista* web crawls. The first experiment verified the power-law distribution of indegree (incoming links) of a webpage as reported by (Barabasi and Albert 1999; Kumar *et al.* 1999). The outdegree (outgoing links) distribution was also found to exhibit the power law, except in the initial segment.

The second set of experiments explored the connected components of the undirected web graph obtained by ignoring the edge directions, and found that about 91% of the nodes are connected together. In addition, the nodes with high indegree do not affect connectivity of the webgraph. The strongly connected component (SCC) in the directed webgraph accounts for only 28% (56 Million) of total number of webpages in the experiment. The sizes of connected component in undirected webgraph and SCC in directed webgraph follow the power-law distribution.

The third experiment ran Breadth-First Search (BFS) twice from randomly-chosen starting nodes: in forward and backward directions. These searches reveal that for some starting nodes, only the forward or backward BFS traversal covered 100 Million nodes and for some starting nodes, both forward and backward traversal covered 100 Million nodes. The starting nodes in latter case lie in the SCC. The nodes in connected component found in undirected webgraph (91% of entire sample) form four distinct regions. There is a set of newly formed nodes called IN having outgoing links and another set of introvert nodes called OUT having incoming links (like corporate and e-commerce sites). There exists a directed path from any node in IN to SCC and a directed path from SCC to every node in OUT. Another set of nodes called TENDRILS do not have any directed path from and to SCC but there exists a directed path from nodes in IN to TENDRILS and from TENDRILS to nodes in OUT. Each of IN, OUT and TENDRILS region occupies about 21% of total number of nodes. The study shows that only 24% of the time there exist a directed path between any two randomly-chosen nodes, and if it exists, the average distance between them is about 16.

The WWW Communities

As we have pointed out, above the level of a page in WWW there are many choices for levels of aggregation of pages. WWW site has conventionally meant not an IP address, but rather a collection of pages defined by design. Usually this amounts to a topical significance; *e.g.*, pages pointed to from some anchor page, often referred to as a home page. In some cases, a site is coherent with respect to some semantical interpretation, *i.e.*, the pages are all about different aspects of one 'thing' but more often the home page is just the hub of the collection.

Another notion of WWW site can be defined through link counting. Here, we consider some notion of locality, *e.g.*, some subnet IP address range and then measure the ratio of the links among all pages inside the range to all the links going outside the range. The threshold of this ratio for assigning pages to a single collection is arbitrary. A more precise formulation can be obtained by computing SCC's. However, in some situations pages related to a main topic might not point outside of themselves, so that the SCC condition could be too stringent to capture many collections of pages that should be identified as sites. Two papers (Gibson *et al.* 1998a; Gibson *et al.* 1998b) have identified two kinds of pages that together make possible a computational concept of a WWW community of pages. This notion may be quite close to that of a cluster in the Newman-Moore-Watts small-world model. One kind of pages represent authorities on a focused topic while the other kind represent hubs which conduct a search to authorities.

The ingenious aspect of this WWW community theory is that a simple, iterative algorithm is presented which identifies authorities and hubs. The algorithm makes use of the adjacency matrix of a subgraph of WWW. However, the community is computed as a function of WWW topology alone. For a broad-topic search, the algorithm starts with a root set *S* of pages returned by a text-based search engine (Gibson *et al.* 1998a). The set *S* forms a small induced subgraph focused on the query topic and it is expanded to cover all the pages that point to or are pointed by any page in set *S*. Each page, *x*, has non-negative authority weight $a(x)$ and non-negative hub weight $h(x)$. In a single iteration, $a(x)$ is replaced by the sum of $h(x_i)$'s of all the pages *i* pointing to *x* and $h(x)$ is replaced by the sum of the $a(x_j)$'s of all the pages *j* pointed by *x*. The iterative process converges to return authority and hub for the query. Thus, the algorithm uses the link structure of subgraph of root set *S*.

The evolution of link structure of web is influenced by the browsing patterns of people. Knowledge of Web communities can be exploited to enhance browsing and searching (Gibson *et al.* 1998b). Tools using information about WWW link topology can help users adopt "link-based" browsing methodologies and enable navigation approaches that effectively use the global structural information.

5. CONCLUSION

The World Wide Web is an extremely interesting and new type of random digraph. At present, it is only dimly understood. In this paper, we have pointed out some of the features that may characterize the webdigraph. A great deal more remains to be discovered.

6. ACKNOWLEDGMENTS

This work was partially supported by a contract from Honeywell.

7. REFERENCES

Adamic, L. 1999. "The Small World Web." Technical Report. Xerox PARC, Palo Alto, CA.

Adamic, L. and B. Huberman. 2000. "Technical Comment to 'Emergence of Scaling in Random Networks'." *Science 287*, (Mar.): 2115.

Aielo, W.; F. Chung; and L. Lu. 2000. "A Random Graph Model for Massive Graphs." In *Proceedings of 32nd ACM Symposium on Theory of Computing* (Portland, Oregon, May 21-23). ACM SIGACT, 1-9.

Barabasi, B.; R. Albert; and H. Jeoung. 1999. "Mean-field Theory for Scale-free Random Networks." *Physica A*, No. 272: 173-187.

Broder, A.; R. Kumar; F. Maghoul; P. Raghavan; S. Rajagopalan; R. Stata; A. Tomkins; and J. Wiener. 2000. "Graph Structure in the Web: Experiments and Models." In *Proceedings of the 9th International World Wide Web Conference* (Amsterdam, Netherlands, May 15-19).

Cho, J. and H. Garcia-Molina. 1999. "The Evolution of the Web and Implications for an incremental Crawler." Technical Report SIDL-WP-1999-0129. Stanford Digital Library Technologies Project, Stanford University, Stanford, CA. (Dec.)

Claffy, K. C. 1999. "Internet Measurement and Data Analysis: Topology, Workload Performance and Routing Statistics." Technical Report. Cooperative Association for Internet Data Analysis, La Jolla, CA.

Crovella, M. and A. Bestavros. 1995. "Explaining World Wide Web Traffic Self Similarity." Technical Report TR-1995-015. Department of Computer Science, Boston University, Boston, MA. (Aug.)

Deo, N. 1974. *Graph Theory with Applications to Engineering and Computer Science*. Prentice-Hall, Englewood Cliffs, N.J.

Deo, N.; B. Litow; and P. Gupta. 2000. "Modeling the Web: Linking Discrete and Continuous." Technical Report CS-TR-00-003. School of Computer Science, University of Central Florida, Orlando, FL. (May).

Erdös, P. and A. Rényi. 1960. "On the Evolution of Random Graphs." *Publications of the Mathematical Institute of the Hungarian Academy of Sciences 5*: 17-61.

FOLDOC: Online Dictionary of Computing, URL:http://wombat.doc.ic.ac.uk/foldoc.cgi?query=site&action = search.

Gibson, D.; J. Kleinberg; and P. Raghavan. 1998. "Inferring Web Communities from Link Topology." In *Proceedings of the 9th ACM Conference on Hypertext and Hypermedia* (Pittsburg, PA, June 20-24). ACM SIGWEB, 225-234.

Gibson, D.; J. Kleinberg; and P. Raghavan. 1998. "Structural Analysis of the World Wide Web." *Position paper at the WWW Consortium Web Characterization Workshop* (Cambridge, MA, Nov. 5).

Greenlaw, R. and E. Hepp. 1998. *In-line/On-line: Fundamentals of the Internet and the World Wide Web*. McGraw-Hill, Ave. of the Americas, N.Y., 177-181.

Huberman, B. and L. Adamic. 1999. "Evolutionary Dynamics of the World Wide Web." Technical Report. Xerox PARC, Palo Alto, CA.

Kleinberg, J. 1999. "Authoritative Sources in a Hyperlinked Environment." *Journal of ACM 46*, No. 5 (Sept.): 604-632.

Kleinberg, J. 1999. "The Small-World Phenomenon: an Algorithmic Perspective." Technical Report 99-1776. Department of Computer Science, Cornell University, Ithaca, N.Y. (Oct.).

Kleinberg, J.; Kumar R.; Raghavan P.; Rajagopalan S; and A. Tomkins. 1999. "The Web as a Graph: Measurements, Models and Methods." *Lecture Notes in Computer Science 1627*, (July): 1-17.

Kumar, R.; P. Raghavan; S. Rajagopalan; and A. Tomkins. 1999. "Trawling the Web for Emerging Cyber-Communities." In *Proceedings of 8th World Wide Web Conference* (Toronto, Canada, May 11-14).

Milgram, S. 1967. "The Small World Problem." *Psychology Today 2*: 60-67.

Moore, C. and M.E.J. Newman. 2000. "Epidemics and percolation in small world networks." Working Paper 00-01-002 , Santa Fe Institute, Santa Fe, N.M. (Jan.).

Moore, C. and M.E.J. Newman. 2000. "Exact Solution of Site and Bond Percolation on Small-World Networks." Working Paper 00-01-007. Santa Fe Institute, Santa Fe, N.M. (Jan.).

NetLingo.com: Internet Language Dictionary.
URL: http://www.netlingo.com/lookup.cfm?term=site.

Newman, M.E.J.; C. Moore; and D. Watts. 1999. "Mean-Field Solution of the Small-World Network Model." Working Paper 99-09-066. Santa Fe Institute, Santa FE, N.M. (Sept.).

Pitkow, J. 1997. "Summary of WWW Characterizations." Technical Report. Xerox PARC, Palo Alto, CA.

Watts, D. and S. Strogatz. 1998. "Collective Dynamics of 'Small-World' Networks." *Nature 393*, (June): 440-442.

Watts, D. 1999. *Small Worlds: The Dynamics of Networks between Order and Randomness*. Princeton University Press, Princeton, N.J.

Webopedia: Online Computer Dictionary for Internet Terms.
URL: http://webopedia.internet.com/TERM/w/web site.html.

BUILDING A NETWORK SIMULATOR USING DISTRIBUTED OBJECT TECHNOLOGY

Dimitrios Vergados, John Soldatos, Evangelos Vayias, Nikolas Protopsaltis and Nikolaos Mitrou.

Telecommunications Laboratory
Department of Electrical Engineering & Computer Science
National Technical University of Athens
Heroon Polyechniou 9, Zographou Athens
GR 157 73, Greece
Tel: +30 1 772 2558
Fax: +30 1 772 2534
Email: {nproto;vergados}@telecom.ntua.gr

KEYWORDS
ATM, CAC, Call level, Routing, Resource Management.

ABSTRACT

ATM will become the main backbone component of the network infrastructure. The important feature of ATM is the support for different traffic characteristics and QOS requirements. This paper presents the architecture of an ATM Simulator that operates at the call level, exposes the power of such a tool in evaluating different control architectures for ATM networks and presents the status of a prototype implementation. It also describes the overall architecture of the simulator, illustrates the innovative features and elaborates on the potential benefits behind building and using such a tool, also identifying possible advantages against other candidate solutions. The implementation of the simulator provides a toolkit allowing the assessment, testing and comparative evaluation of CAC algorithms and caters for smooth incorporation of other essential parts of the architecture, such as components for advanced Resource Management and Routing strategies.

1. INTRODUCTION

ATM has been proposed as a target technology for overcoming the difficulties in existing transfer modes, allowing the creation of the B-ISDN [14],[19]. One of the major objectives of ATM is "The provision of a wide range of services to a broad variety of users utilizing a limited set of connection types and multi-purpose user-network interfaces". Consequently, much effort has been put on standardisation efforts, and standards have been established to facilitate its deployment and several vendors have already proceeded with implementations, either proprietary or based on the proposed standards, e.g. [1]. There are still several open issues; ongoing research activities aim at providing solutions to persisting thorny points (see [11] for an overview). Among the issues, that feature this research dimension, is the evaluation of control strategies that addresses vital ATM functions Algorithmic schemes for CAC [5],[25], Routing [6],[23], [29], and Network Resource Management [10], [16], [21], [24], are characteristic examples of such strategies. There is also a necessity for an environment (a "testbed"), that would be appropriate for organising and carrying out experiments ("trials") on ATM algorithms [2],[3],[18]. There are several efforts for developing simulation tools for ATM networks, targeting the needs of several research projects, i.e. the NIST [7], developed by the National Institute of Standards and Technologythe ICM [4] and the YATS [9] simulators, developed in the scope of the European projects ACM and EXPERT respectively.

This paper presents the architecture of an ATM Simulator that operates at the call level, exposes the value of such a tool in evaluating different control architectures for ATM networks, and identifies additional benefits that result from the proposed architecture [20],[27]. The overall architecture of the simulator illustrates the innovative features and elaborates on the potential benefits behind building and using such a tool, also identifying possible advantages against other candidate solutions. Apart from describing the architecture of the simulator, in the paper the progress of the implementation process is reported, underlining the simulation capabilities that have already been implemented.

The paper is structured as follows: after this introductory section, section 2 illustrates the innovative features of the simulator, identifying possible advantages against other developed tools. Section 3 describes the overall architecture of the simulator. and in the following section discusses the implementation status of this novel tool. Finally section 5 concludes the paper.

2. RELATED WORK

There are several efforts for developing simulation tools for ATM networks. A brief description of the already developed simulators is provided trying to compare the different characteristics and functionalities.

First, the PlanNet simulator [Alta Group, Inc., http://www.sysnet.com/plannet.html] is a commercial network simulator, which provides simulation capabilities for capacity planning and topology testing. A GUI has been developed for simulation control and the description of the Topology. The topology modules include LAN Segment modules, WAN Modules, Interconnect Modules and traffic generators. The PlanNet provides also tools for analyzing the performance of the simulated network.

The NEST Simulator [Dept of Computer Science, Columbia University, ftp://ftp.cs.columbia.edu/nest] consists of a simulation server and client monitors. This simulation server manages the context switching and the appropriate scheduling of the execution of a process. The simulated events need to be synchronized with the global simulation clock. The manipulation of external or internal real – time events needs to be synchronized as well. The development language is C. The description language uses a GUI language for the description of the network topology and C for the description of the communication protocol. The GUI provides two graphical monitoring tools and the Network Topologies consists of Node and Link modules.

The REAL [Dept. of Computer Science, Berkley University, http://minie.cs.adfa.oz.au/REAL] is a simulator for studying the dynamic behavior of flow and congestion schemes in packet switch data networks. It provides the NEST simulator with node and link configurations. The REAL Node entities are sources, gateways and sinks. The simulation report includes node ID, type, queuing delays, cell drops and round trip time. The development language is C and the description language is a script language named NetLanguage 4.0 to provide NEST configurations. The simulator report includes node ID, type, queuing delays, cell drops and round trip time.

The Opnet Simulation Model [MIL3 Inc., http://www.mil3.com] [26] one of the most important tools, is expanded in three layers which are used to describe the data and control flow and the topology. It is developed in C or C++ programming language, uses a multi – windowing graphical user interface which runs under X Windows for several platforms. The description language is a C enhanced with communication and simulation specific routines and is used to specify the process behavior FSA. It also supports Interrupt processing and scheduling, Process management, Packet manipulation, routing algorithms and others. It uses three basic node entities, animation capabilities for visualizing simulation events and provides tracing tools that allow the user to view pre-defined and user-defined tracing statistics. There are also standard and user specified probes to collect data and statistics. There is an Analysis Tool which evaluates the results of a simulation and can present the statistics graphically as well.

The Maryland Routing Simulator (MaRS) [Department of Computer Science and Institute for Advanced Computer Studies, University of Maryland http://ftp.digital.com/pub/net/simulators] is designed to provide a platform for the evaluation and comparison of network routing algorithms. It is a discrete event simulator implemented in C. It considers the target system as a physical network a routing algorithm and a workload. A node, a link, a routing, a link-cost are some of the components and a performance monitor component is used to evaluate and compare the routing algorithms. MaRS provides a mechanism to record event occurrences and user specified messages to a file.

Apart from the general network simulators we have the NIST and VINCE which are ATM Network Simulators. NIST [National Institute of Standards and Technology, http://www.niuf.nist.gov] [7] is an event driven simulator, which can be used as an ATM Network planning tool or ATM protocol performance analysis. It also provides tools for topology creation and results analysis. A configuration default considers of four classes of components, which are the switches, the physical links, the terminal equipment and the ATM Applications. The development language for NIST is C and X Windows are used as a programming platform for the user. NIST uses C for the communication protocol as well. The network modules provided by NIST are ATM switches, B – TE components, ATM applications and Link Components. It provides tools for displaying information about a parameter in graph form.

The VINCE [Naval Research Laboratory, http://sun1000e.pku.edu.cn/on_line/ATM/atm_faq_html/FAQ/ATM_FAQ/F/F1.htm] is a software package for the development of protocols in ATM Networks. It is publicly available and provides a set of general abstractions that can be used in place of switch networking code and vendor – supplied host for ATM networking. Its goal is to provide ease in introducing experimental signaling and routing to running ATM networks. It is implemented as a module system based around a single core, which maintains a set of structures relevant to ATM protocol work. The development language is C. The node description is provided by the following entities: A Terminal, a port and a switch. The link description is provided by the following network entities: Call, Connection, Path and Virtual Switch.

Several simulation tools have also been developed in the scope of research projects, such as the ICM[4] and the YATS [9] simulators, developed in the scope of the European projects ACM and EXPERT respectively. However, such tools target specific needs of these research activities rather than being general-purpose ATM simulation applications. A more general ATM simulator is QUARTS-II [8] targeted mainly at simulating routing algorithms in the P-NNI reference model.

The design of our simulator together with the graphical user interface enable the development of complex and highly customisable network settings without resorting to some sort of "scripting" language. In particular, the provision of a graphical user interface unburdens the simulator operator from the chores of defining the experiment configuration by writing plain text files and obtaining the desired results through similar file processing procedures. Another important feature of the design is the use of inter-object communication for the execution of the simulation logic, i.e. invocation of methods exported by each object instead of message passing. Combined with distributed object programming architectures such as CORBA or Java RMI, this design allows to promptly transform the tool to a distributed simulator, by spreading the computational objects across several machines. Distributing the components of a simulator in several machines is very efficient in cases of complex configurations, where the overall computational load would be too high to be handled by a single machine.

3. OVERALL SIMULATOR'S ARCHITECTURE

The design of our ATM Simulator is based on state of the art concepts and technologies [12]. These schemes guarantee a flexible and efficient architecture, as well as key features such as object orientation, flexibility, scalability, user friendliness, speed and robustness. Figure 1 depicts roughly the main components of the architecture of the simulator. The design of our simulator together with the graphical user interface enable to define complex and highly customisable network settings without resorting to some sort of "scripting" language. The main components of the simulation tool include:

(a) the *Core Simulation Environment*, which performs the simulation by applying given algorithmic schemes to the desired simulation configuration. This is the heart of the simulation environment. Its major role is to initialise a specific experiment according to traffic parameters and algorithmic schemes for Resource Management [32], Routing and CAC [31], [33]. Specifically, the design focuses on the central element of an ATM network, which is the ATM switch. The object that emulates an ATM switch is the most sophisticated one, as it plays the major role with respect to the main objectives of the simulation tool. Thus the objects' design attempts to take into account every task performed by a real ATM switch with respect to the desired functionality of the call-level Simulator. This is accomplished through the use of objects that are designed to act as specific network components. The simulation environment contains a number of "top-level" object and a "second-level" object which appropriately "customized" can be incorporated in a switch "top-level" object. The top-level" objects represent functions and algorithmic tasks, and the "second level" ones perform tasks such as Call Admission Control, Route Selection, Call Generation.
The communication between the various objects of the core simulation environment is achieved through inter-object communication (realized either in a centralized or in a distributed manner), which relies on the ability of a "top-level" object to access methods and attributes of a peer object. This communication enables complex protocols and specifications to be implemented in this simulated environment. A "second-level" object appropriately "customised" (sub-classed in Object-Oriented Programming terms) can be incorporated in a switch "top-level" object, thus determining the behaviour of the switch with regard to one of the above functions. This renders the simulator tool highly modular and facilitates changes in the algorithms used for several control functions [18]. Furthermore, the objects of the core simulation environment export interfaces to the other components of the simulator. Specifically, they interface with the main module to provide information needed for tasks requiring a global view of the environment, they accept information from the main module so as to update their local contexts (e.g., their Route Information Base).

(b) the *Main Module*, which creates the core simulation

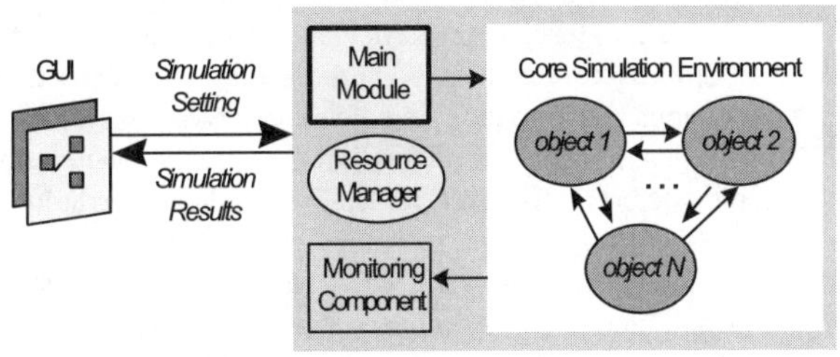

Figure 1 - Overall architecture of the simulator

environment according to given input parameters, maintains a global view of the simulated network and parameters during the evolution of a specific trial. In particular, an operator uses the graphical front end to produce the simulation scenario (i.e. physical/logical configuration & call generation parameters). This information is conveyed through the network, to the main module, which undertakes to build a core simulation environment that conforms to the provided parameter. In addition, it initialises the simulation on the operator's demand. Therefore, this module has the potential for performing tasks that require a universal picture of the simulated network, or accumulated central intelligence. This justifies the communication of this module with two other components of the simulator, namely the *Resource Manager* and the *Monitoring Component*.

(c) the *Resource Management* component, which is responsible for applying network resource management strategies to the simulated network, achieving high utilization and performance. The goal of the *Resource Manager* is to provide logical configurations based on the Virtual Path (VP) concept in order to facilitate and speed up admission control and routing. To this end, the Resource Manager communicates with the Main Module, so as to obtain any necessary information for the simulation components and their state. Although, the Resource Manager could well be integrated into the Main Module, this modular approach allows flexible replacement of this component, with other that use different algorithms. Therefore, the Resource Manager is actually an object that is dynamically loaded according to the operator's choice. In this way, this simulation environment allows evaluation of several resource management strategies and assessment of their efficiency.

(d) the Monitoring Component, which collects statistics relevant to a simulation section. These figures mainly involve measurements at the call level (e.g., allocated bandwidths, effective bandwidths, number of active calls, number of rejected calls, total number of calls, call blocking ratio) and are conveyed from the object of the simulation core to this component. In the sequel, this information is forwarded to the *Graphical Front End*, which displays them graphically.

(e) the *Graphical Front End*, which acts as a user console and viewer, by accepting user interaction and displaying simulation results. In particular, an operator uses the graphical front end to define the setting of a simulation session, to produce the simulation scenario (i.e. physical/logical configuration & call generation parameters). Moreover, it displays results in a graphical fashion, during the run-time. After the end of the simulation session, the user can access cumulative results and view collective statistics and diagrams that show the evolution of several parameters in time. Thus, the users of the simulator can be classified into two main categories:
   - users that simply monitor a simulation session,
   - users (operators) that define a simulation scenario and initialise the simulation procedure.

4. SIMULATORS FEATURES – CURRENT IMPLEMENTATION STATUS

The implementation of the simulator has already started based on the general guidelines described above.

Specifically, three major distributed software entities (each one encapsulating various objects) can be distinguished:

- a *terminal* entity, which provides the means for formulating the parameters of the various Call Request(s) to the ATM network and selecting the CAC scheme to be evaluated.
- a *Virtual Switch* entity, which holds information about the current status of an individual ATM switching node in terms of its configuration and resources
- a *CAC & Routing* entity, that applies and evaluates the selected CAC schemes (after performing some simplistic static routing of the calls)

In the sequel, we elaborate on each of these entities and underline their pertinence to the original design. Figure2 provides an overview of the interactions between the various component types.

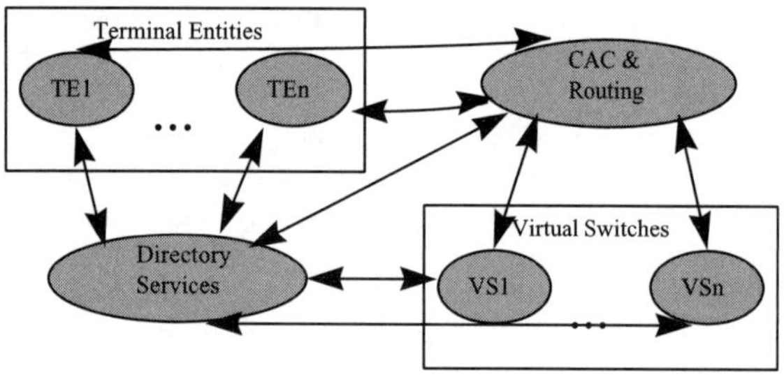

Figure 2 - Interactions between the distributed entities of the Simulation Tool

The Terminal Entity is a piece of software emulating the function and role of a user's ATM terminal requesting connectivity through the ATM network, according to the needs of a QoS aware application. Thus, the terminal entity provides a Graphical Interface allowing the operator of the simulation to specify:

- The Source and Destination ATM Networking Nodes
- A *QoS-level* indication in terms of delay and loss that the data units of this stream may tolerate.
- A *Traffic Profile*, describing the type of traffic it generates This is defined by the values of a set of parameters, which constitute the *Traffic Descriptor* of the stream. The operator of the terminal entity is allowed to select among various traffic models. Currently, Exponential ON/OFF traffic sources, as well as Markov Modulated Rate Processes are supported.
- A CAC algorithm to be used for admission control of this specific call request

In the scope of our simulation environment it is also essential to have QOS indications being specified by the operator (human user or hared coded in the application), since they constitute scrucial parameters of the CAC evaluation process. In a realistic terminal an application call request will rarely specify ON/OFF or MMRP traffic profiles, since these do not constitute apt traffic models for most of the applications. Moreover, in most cases the application can not describe its traffic in such a formalistic and precise way. However, these models are essential towards testing and evaluating various CAC strategies, as well as towards validating theoretical results. In the scope of our simulation environment it is also essential to have QOS indications being specified by the operator, since they constitute crucial parameters of the CAC evaluation process. After specifying these parameters a unique call reference number is assigned to the call request, which is in the sequel conveyed to the CAC & Routing entity for further processing, according to the logical configuration of the simulation environment, and the selected CAC scheme.

The Virtual Switch Entity constitutes a virtual representation of an ATM switching node[34]. It consists of a set of objects that capture all the essential information of the ATM switch that may be needed by the simulation environment. In particular, this entity comprises a (super) object that contains information for the node as a whole, such as identification information (e.g. name, address). Moreover, this super-object encapsulates data structures holding Port objects. The Port objects capture information items relating to the node's ports, such as the port line rate (linkBW), the port name, the post status. In addition, each port object contains a pointer to a data structure of VPL (Virtual Path Link) objects that hold properties of Virtual Paths that either originate or terminate at the specified port. Information items included within VPL objects are the VPI and the bandwidth allocated on this Virtual Path. Note also that VP Cross-Connections are represented through Pointers to other VPL objects. The Virtual Switch entity interacts with the CAC & Routing Agent for the purpose of providing information related to simulation configuration. Once CAC is performed on a node (hop), the corresponding Virtual Switch object has to be updated so as to represent the actual state of the simulated network.

The CAC & Routing Entity is the most crucial component of the simulator for CAC evaluation and testing.

It performs all the calculations that are necessary for coming up with the CAC decision. Then it compares the various schemes but keeping track of accepted and rejected calls, as well as of the resulted network utilisation. As already outlined, the terminal and virtual switch entities provide the logical configuration of the simulated network and the characteristics of the call to be handled. The simulation setting is completed through a number of Routing Tables (one for each virtual switch) which are given to this entity for the purpose of routing the various call requests. Each Routing table contains enumerated routes for all possible source destination pairs. Each one of the 'labeled' routes is also characterised from the QoS metric that supports.

Once the CAC & Routing Entity receives a Call Request from a Terminal Entity, it creates a new thread which carries out the CAC & Routing process for the request. Thus, the multithreaded nature of the system guarantees efficient simultaneous processing of several calls. Concurrent processing of calls is important when two calls or more calls (of the same QoS) are simultaneously destined in the same output port of a switching node. The concurrency problem is sorted out by blocking the processing of other calls once some other call of the queue is processed at the same output port.

The CAC & Routing process for each individual call is the following:

1. A route is initially selected for the call (by a Routing component), according to the source destination pair of the request. The routing table of the source node is examined and a route fulfilling the target QoS criterion is selected from the list of routes of the specified source destination pair. The routing in the rest of the switches is based on the 'label' of the selected route. The structure of the routing table held in every node for the purpose of routing based on the label of the selected route is depicted in Figure3.
2. The CAC function is performed in each one of the virtual switches of the selected route. The CAC process fails if just one of the switches rejects the call. In such a case, an alternate route is selected, and the hop by hop process is repeated. The CAC decision succeeds for a call, when the request has been accepted from every node within a route.

Whenever there are more than one possible route for a specified source destination pair, the above-mentioned routing strategy chooses a route at random. Although this source routing strategy is rather simplistic, it is sufficient for comparing various CAC schemes. The CAC function, is a method of the CAC object. Different CAC objects correspond to different CAC schemes. Each of these schemes takes into account the information supplied by the terminal entities and the virtual switches. Moreover, all the CAC objects present three interfaces:

- a constructor that takes as parameters the Call Request and references to objects holding the logical configuration of the simulated network
- the CAC function which returns a *boolean* result
- a method that takes as input a vector of resources (e.g. bandwidth) associated with the CAC scheme and returns an updated version of this vector as a result of the accepting a call request

As a result, any number of different CAC schemes can be provided to the Simulator provided which implements these three generic interfaces. All CAC schemes are made available to the simulator operator.

With respect to the architecture of the simulator the CAC object [31] and the Routing Component [32] along with the logical configuration information form the core simulation environment. Thus, there are no provisions for evaluating resource management strategies such as bandwidth reallocation mechanisms, or even buffer management techniques. These features along with the Graphical Front End that will enable viewing of the simulation results through the WWW are under development.

```
NodeID

Number of SD (Source Destination) Pairs
SourceID DestinationID  (First SD Pair)
Number of Routes  (First SD Pair)
  (InPort, OutPort, InVPI, OutVPI, NextHopID) QoSClassID (Route #1)
  (InPort, OutPort, InVPI, OutVPI, NextHopID) QoSClassID (Route #2)
 ---------------------------------------------------------
  (InPort, OutPort, InVPI, OutVPI, NextHopID) QoSClassID(Route #n)


SourceID DestinationID  (Second SD Pair)
Number of Routes  (Second SD Pair)
  (InPort, OutPort, InVPI, OutVPI, NextHopID) QoSClassID (Route #1)
  (InPort, OutPort, InVPI, OutVPI, NextHopID) QoSClassID (Route #2)
 ---------------------------------------------------------
  (InPort, OutPort, InVPI, OutVPI, NextHopID) QoSClassID (Route #n)
 ---------------------------------------------------------
 ---------------------------------------------------------
 ---------------------------------------------------------

SourceID DestinationID  (n-th SD Pair)
Number of Routes  (n-th SD Pair)
  (InPort, OutPort, InVPI, OutVPI, NextHopID) QoSClassID (Route #1)
  (InPort, OutPort, InVPI, OutVPI, NextHopID) QoSClassID (Route #2)
 ---------------------------------------------------------
  (InPort, OutPort, InVPI, OutVPI, NextHopID) QoSClassID (Route #n)
```

Figure 3 – Format of the Routing Table maintained at each ATM node

5. CONCLUSIONS

This contribution proposes an architecture, for a tool capable of simulating trials and providing call- level metrics. The paper discusses an implementation framework based on state of the art object-oriented technologies.Apart from illustrating the architecture of this novel tool, the paper discusses an implementation framework based on state of the art object-oriented technologies. The current implementation of the simulator provides a toolkit allowing the assessment, testing and comparative evaluation of CAC algorithms. It also caters for smooth incorporation of other essential parts of the architecture, such as components for advanced Resource Management and Routing strategies. Therefore, this contribution delves into implementation details, since the development of this simulation tool is an on-going process.

Specifically, the current capabilities of the simulator allow evaluation of different CAC schemes. This initial capability of the simulator exposes a major benefit of the modular, object oriented design of the tool: Different schemes can be evaluated provided that the user implements an object (*CAC object*) that exports appropriate interfaces to the rest of the simulator. In addition, the design of our simulator together with the graphical user interface enable to define complex and highly customisable network settings without resorting to some sort of "scripting" language. Several research initiatives aim at enabling researchers and engineers to understand the traffic characteristics and their impact on control mechanisms through measurement, simulation and analytical studies. Under these circumstances, simulation tools have a role to play.

7. REFERENCES

[1] ITU-T Rec I.150, B-ISDN Asynchronous Transfer Mode Functional Characteristics, Helsinki March 1-12, 1993

[2] Meurisse W. et al., EXPERT Deliverable AC094/EXPERT/P3.2+WP4.2/DS/R/P/04/B2, "Initial Specification of BandwidthManagenent, March 1996

[3] T'Joens Y. et al., REFORM Deliverable A208/BELL/WP1/DS/P/002/B1, "REFORM Systems Requirements and Analysis", December 1996

[4] ICM Deliverable 3 R2059/VTT/TEL/ DS/R/004/b1

[5] Hui J., "Resource Allocation for Broadband Networks", IEEE Trans. On Communications, Vol. 6, No.9, Dec 1988, pp. 1598-1608

[6] Bertsekas D. and Gallager R., Data Networks, Englewood Cliffs, NJ: Prentice Hall, 1992

[7] Golmie et al., The NIST ATM/HFC Network Simulator, Operation and Programming Guide, Ver. 3.0, March 1998

[8] Sivabalan M. and Mouftah H.T., QUARTS-II: A Routing Simulator for ATM Networks, IEEE Communications Mag., May 1998

[9] Baumann M., YATS – Yet Another Tiny Simulator, User's Manual, Ver. 3.0

[10] Friesen V., Harms J. and Wong J., "Resource Management with Virtual Paths in ATM Networks", IEEE Network, October 1996

[11] Mitrou N.M., "Traffic Control in ATM: a review, an engineer's critical view and a novel approach", to appear in Computer Networks and ISDN Systems, 1999

[12] Ash G.R. and Schwartz S.D., "Traffic Control Architectures for Integrated Broadband Networks", Int. Journal of Digital and Analog Communication Systems, Vol. 3, No. 2, April-June 1990

[13] Cooper R.B., "Introduction to Queueing Theory", London: Collier-Macmmilan Ltd., 1972.

[14] Minzer S.E., "Broadband ISDN and Asynchronous Transfer Mode (ATM)", IEEE Communications Magazine, Vol. 27, No. 9, September 1989

[15] Schwartz M.I., "Telecommunications Networks: Protocols, Modeling and Analysis", Addison-Wesley, 1987

[16] Ohta K., and Sato K., "Dynamic Bandwidth Control of the Virtual Paths in an Asynchronous Transfer Mode Network", IEEE Trans. On Commun. Vol. 40, July 1992, pp 1239-1247

[17] ATM Forum, ATM Traffic Management Specification, Version 4.0, February 1996

[18] EXPERT Deliverable AC094/EXPERT/WP51/D/R/I/011/B1, "Report on Source Traffic Modelling & Network Models", F.Aglan, et al.

[19] Chen T. and Liu S., "ATM Switching Systems", Artech House Inc., Norwood, MA 02062

[20] Object Management Group, *"The Common Object Request Broker: Architecture and Specification"*, 2.0 ed., July 1995.

[21] Sato K. and Sato K-Y., "Virtual Paths and Link Capacity Design for ATM Networks", IEEE J. on Selected Areas in Communications, Vol. 9, Jan. 1991, pp. 104-111

[22] ATM Forum, Private Network-Network Interface Specification Version 1.0, March, 1996

[23] EXPERT Deliverable AC094/EXPERT/WP3.2/D/R/P/08/B1, "Interim Report on Bandwidth amd Routing Trials", Marias G. et al., Dec. 1996

[24] Burgin J., and Dorman D., "Broadband ISDN Resource Management: The Role of Virtual Paths", IEEE Communications Mag., Sept. 1991, pp. 44-48

[25] Saito H. and Shiomoto K., "Dynamic Call Admission Control in ATM Networks", IEEE JSAC, Vol. 9, Sept. 1991, pp. 982-989

[26] OPNET Modelling Manual (Release 3.0), Modelling vol.1

[27] Bhatt, S., et al. "Parallel Simulation Techniques for Large-Scale Networks", IEEE Comm. Magazine, vol. 36, no. 8, August 1998, pp. 42-47

[28] Redlich Jens-Peter, Masaaki Suzuki, and Stephen Weistein "Distributed Object Technology for Networking", *IEEE Commun. Magazine*, Oct. 1998

[29] Schwartz M. and Stern T., "Routing Techniques used in computer communication networks", IEEE Trans. on Communications, Vol. 28, 1980

[30] S. J. Golestani, "Congestion - free communication in broadband packet networks," IEEE Trans. Comm., vol. 39, 1991, pp. 1802–1812.

[31] Perros H. and Elsayed K., Call Admission Control Schemes, IEEE Comm. Mag, Nov 1998, p. 82.

[32] Gelenbe E., Mang X. and Onvural R., Bandwidth Allocation and Call Admission Control in High-Speed Networks, IEEE Com. Mag, May 1997, p. 122

[33] Knightly E. and Shroff N., Admission Control for Statistical QoS: Theory and Practice, IEEE Network, March/April 1999, p. 20

[34] G. Kormentzas, J.Soldatos, E.Vayias, K.Kontovassilis, N.Mitrou, "An ATM Switch-Independent MIB for Portable Deployment of Traffic Control Algorithms", in Proc. COMCON '99 Conference, Athens, Greece, June 2nd, 1999

Naval Aviation Training Systems Interoperability Maturation Model

Daniel J Paterson
Naval Air Warfare Center Training Systems Division
<patersondj@navair.navy.mil>

CAPT Rory Fisher
PMA205
<FisherRH@navair.navy.mil>

Keywords
Distributed Synthetic Environment, Maturity Model, High Level Architecture, Federation Interoperability

ABSTRACT: *The Naval Aviation Training Systems TEAM has developed a draft High Level Architecture (HLA) Interoperability Maturation Model for the measurement of HLA Compliant Federations. This Model proposes five Levels of Maturity for Naval Federations addressing a scaled set of training requirements. For example a Level 1 Federation achieves basic HLA compliance, (Usually using a Gateway approach) where a Level 5 Federation achieves Federation wide Mission Rehearsal Training and essentially a 'fair-fight' between simulations. A key consideration in building these networked simulations is how to ensure that all of the participating Federates in a networked virtual environment synchronize their shared states and environment. Special recognition goes to the Naval Air Systems Command (NAVAIR) HLA Integrated Product Team (IPT) for the development of this Model.*

1. DEPARTMENT OF DEFENSE

In 1991, the Department of Defense established the Executive Council on Modeling and Simulation. The purpose of this council is to establish overall policy for the development and use of modeling and simulation within the Department. The Executive Council promulgated its vision for modeling and simulation in March 1992. The vision states that modeling and simulation will provide readily available, operationally valid environments for use by Department of Defense components. From an operational perspective, modeling and simulation will allow the components to train jointly, develop doctrine and tactics, formulate operational plans, and assess war-fighting situations. On the technical side, modeling and simulation will support technology assessment, system upgrade, prototype and full-scale development, and force structuring. The vision expects that common use of modeling and simulation environments will allow greater cooperation between the acquisition and operations communities. Further, the vision requires that modeling and simulation requirements will be constructed from affordable, reusable components interoperating through an open-systems architecture.

2. DEFENSE MODELING AND SIMULATION OFFICE (DMSO) AND HLA

2.1. ARCHITECTURE MANAGEMENT GROUP (AMG)

The Defense Modeling and Simulation Office (DMSO) is leading an effort to further HLA development through the DoD-wide Architecture Management Group (AMG).

The HLA Baseline Definition was completed by DMSO on 21 August 1996 as a DoD initiative. It was subsequently approved by the Under Secretary of Defense for Acquisition and Technology [USD(A&T), 1996] as the standard technical architecture for all DoD simulations on 10 September 1996.

DoD policy established two cut-off dates. Starting in October 1998, no funds (no-pay date) would be provided to develop or modify simulations that are not High Level Architecture compliant. In October 2000, (no-play date) all simulations that are not compliant with the High Level Architecture are to be retired. DMSO has established HLA compliance categories to track simulations that will become HLA compliant and simulations that are exempt from compliance.

2.2. SIMULATION INTEROPERABILITY STANDARDS ORGANIZATION (SISO)

In 1996, a new organization, SISO was established to develop standards for simulation interoperability. It is aimed at simulation developers, simulation users, and analysts from a broad range of government, industry, and academic communities. The new organization is an outgrowth of the Distributed Interactive Simulation (DIS) Workshops sponsored by the U. S. Army Simulation, Training and Instrumentation Command (STRICOM).

SISO operates as a non-profit standards and educational corporation. DIS Workshops have changed to Simulation Interoperability Workshops (SIW). SISO provides an open forum that promotes the simulation interoperability through the exchange of ideas, examination of technologies, and development of consensus standards.

The SISO High Level Architecture Standards Development Group [1516], [1516.1], [1516.2] is sponsoring a Draft IEEE specification for HLA. The Draft IEEE specifications are currently being balloted by the Simulation Interoperability Standards Committee of the IEEE, with the latest ballots due 26 June, 2000.

2.3. SOME USEFUL HLA DEFINITIONS

HLA Compliance – When a Federate has completed the DMSO HLA Interface Compliance testing (4 Steps). Compliance testing only ensures that the Federate meets the HLA Interface Specification. Compliance testing does not mean a Federate is interoperable with another federate, just that it meets the HLA interface specification.

Federation Object Model - One FOM per federation. FOMs document all shared information (e.g., objects, interactions), and inter-federate issues (e.g., data encoding schemes).

Simulation Object Model - One SOM per federate. SOMs document salient characteristics of a single federate. SOMs presents objects and interactions that can be used externally. SOMs are a subset of the FOM.

Object Model Template –The Object Model Template is used to foster interoperability and reuse of simulations and simulation components via the specification of a common representation framework. This includes object classes, interaction classes and parameters of a HLA Simulation Object Model (SOM) which when combined with other federation members SOMs creates the Federation Object Model (FOM).

Methods Of Constructing HLA Interfaces – The following 3 approaches are used to adopt simulations to operate with HLA: (Figure 2)

Gateway Approach – The Gateway approach 'bridges' between an existing federate interface and HLA, usually with no changes to the existing federates code. Examples include the STRICOM DIS/HLA Gateway, and NAWCTSD's (NAWCTSD Gateway) Simulation Middleware Object Classes (SMOC) code in "Gateway Mode".

Middleware Approach – "Middleware" software is added to federate to support HLA interfaces, usually in the form of a new software module. An example is the NAWCTSD SMOC running in "Middleware" mode.

Native Approach - Basic federate code is (re)designed to incorporate HLA calling functions and data callbacks. Only completely redesigned or new federates can provide a "Native" approach.

2.4. WHY HAVE A MATURITY MODEL

One major reason to have a capability maturity model is because HLA means many different things to many different users. A conceptual maturity model can convey much more meaning than a plain statement, "this system is HLA compliant." As NAVAIR federations develop and Federates become "HLA COMPLIANT" a conceptual maturity model is needed to measure what "HLA compliance" means to the user community. By developing the NAVAIR Interoperability Maturation Model the users can measure the training capability of the Federation, not the technical dialog of interoperability centered around interchanging FOMs and SOMs.

Developing NAVAIR Federations, Federates, Federation Object Models (FOMs) and Simulation Object Models (SOMs) can be downright expensive and must be tied to a hard user driven training requirements or a "Return on Investment" (ROI) training strategy. The key to Federation interoperability is the shared synthetic environments that allow users, defined here as "NAVAIR Pilots and Crew Members", to interact (with synthetic objects) in a natural manner. The formulation of NAVAIR Federations using the Interoperability Maturation Model helps to established a tie to real training requirements against the Levels of Interoperability Maturity. At the lowest level the Interoperability Model allows for NAVAIR federations to exist, which meet the DoD HLA Mandate for HLA Compliance using some very basic Gateway

Implementations. At the highest level the Interoperability Model measures the Federation Mission Rehearsal scenario capability and introduction of distributed training as part of the users core training "Curriculum". The Model is mdesigned such that a Level 5 Federation must also meet all the requirement of a Level 4 Federation, which must also meet all the requirements of a Level 3 Federation.

3. NAVAL AVIATION TRAINING SYSTEMS, INTEROPERABILITY MATURATION MODEL

The challenge that NAVAIR federates face is the need to provide a distributed training Environment that provides support for NAVAIR Federations plus support for larger DoD Federations. The development of a NAVAIR federation has direct training implications on current NAVAIR training pipelines and curriculum. To guide Federation development and measure the Training Effectiveness and ROI of the NAVAIR Federations the following draft NAVAL Aviation Training Systems Interoperability Maturation Model (Figure 1) was formulated.

Figure 1

As currently shown in Figure 1, the NAVAL Aviation Training Systems Interoperability Maturation Model ties Training Requirements to Levels of Interoperability between NAVAIR Federations. This approach of mapping Training Requirements to actual Federation Training Capabilities provides a ROI training strategy. The ROI training increases as NAVAIR Federations increase the Model level in which they train their users. The Model is designed as a "Road Map" for Federations to develop along. As Federations migrate from Levels 1 to 5 they increase their interoperability and allow users to interact with other users in a natural manner.

3.1. INTEROPERABILITY MODEL LEVEL 1

Level one is defined by the following requirements. 1) Federate investigated Federation/Federate Interoperability requirements 2) SOMs and FOMs developed for existing DIS capable systems 3) Gateway implementations complete for current DIS Capable systems and 4) HLA Certification complete for Gateway Systems.

Level 1 covers the case of DIS compliant systems using a DIS-to-HLA Gateway (Figure 2). Gateways act as "Bridges" between the DIS network and the HLA Federation performing a translation role. Gateways are attractive for initial federation construction due to their low risk of implementation and extremely low costs. Gateways also are a very productive first step into a HLA Federation and usually are implemented with no changes to any existing lines of code. There are drawbacks with this approach notably the limitation of the Gateway tied to an existing interface (DIS for example), which may not grow or scale to meet changing Federation needs.

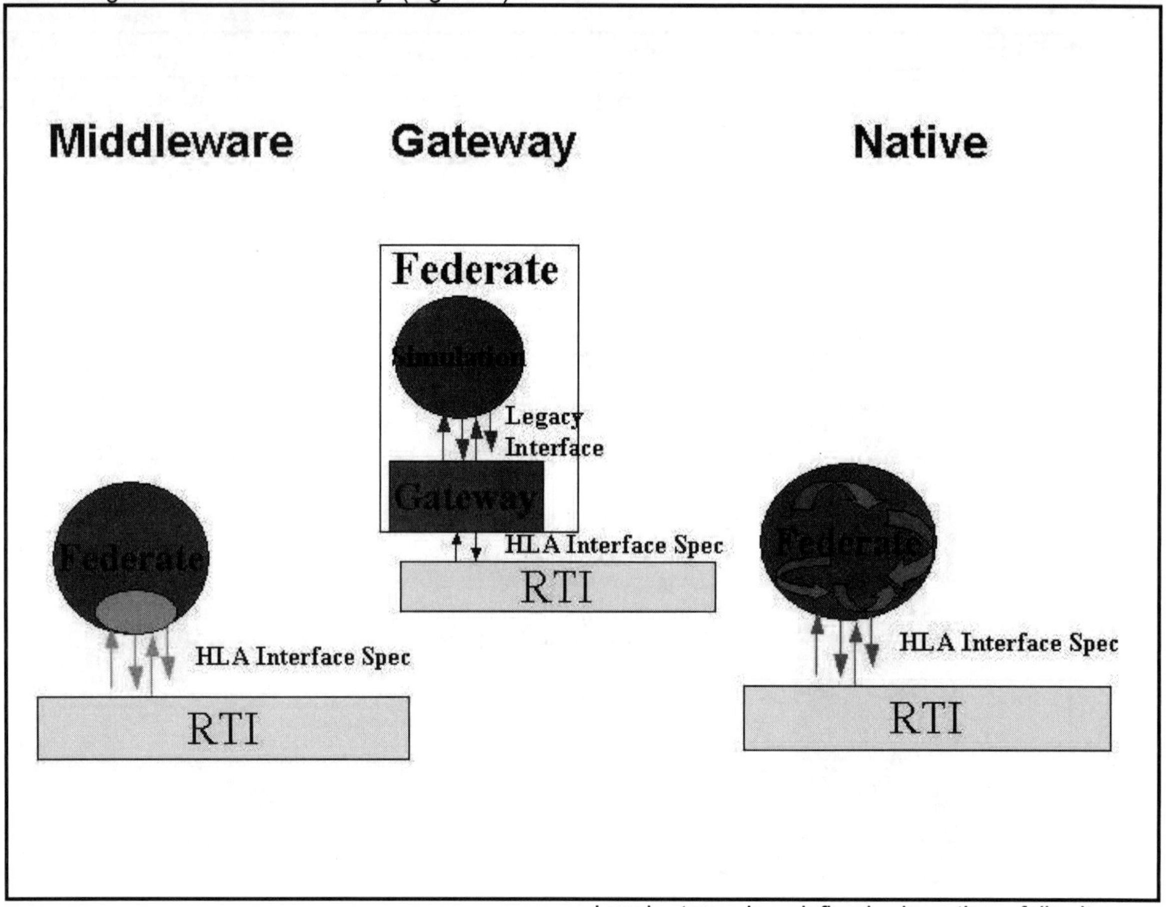

Figure 2

Completing Level 1 does provide an initial training value for the least cost with a good ROI.

3.2. INTEROPERABILITY MODEL LEVEL 2

Level two is defined by the following requirements. 1) Identify additional systems for networking 2) Interoperability issues investigated between federates 3) SOMs and FOMs developed/mapped, a broader Federation established and 4) demonstration of connectivity completed.

Completing Level 2 provides the first demonstration of connectivity among federates and provides the users their first look at what Interoperability between multiple simulations (broader Federation) brings to their training environment.

Completing Level 2 does provide the simulation with a demonstration of training value for a modest cost with a good ROI.

3.3. Interoperability Model Level 3

Level three is defined by the following requirements. 1) Common Models identification 2) Common Data identification and 3) Performance Measurement requirements.

Completing Level 3 means the Federation has a solution for the common data, model, and Performance Measurements collection problem. This means the user will see a common environment and will not become frustrated by simulation "glitches".

3.4. Interoperability Model Level 4

Level four (Figure 6) is defined by the following requirements. 1) Native/Middleware and Gateway Implementations 2) Interoperability criteria evaluated with necessary upgrades 3) Limited Federation training opportunities and 4) Incorporation of Exercise Control and full Performance Management tools.

Completing Level 4 means the Federation has added the "Tools" required for distributed training including Exercise Control and Performance Management. This means the user will be able to perform in limited Federation training opportunities.

3.5. Interoperability Model Level 5

Level five is defined by the following requirements. 1) Distributed Training as part of core "Curriculum" 2) Established infrastructure (communications, maintenance, logistics, CM) 3) Scenarios on demand and 4) In-Situ data and Mission Rehearsal level scenario capability.

Clearly, completing Level 5 means the Federation has established itself as ready for daily Mission Rehearsal Training and can provide the user with realistic 'fair-fight' training scenarios. This means the user will be able to perform in unlimited Federation training opportunities.

4. Conclusion

The development of the NAVAL Aviation Training Systems Interoperability Maturation Model is a step toward providing user requirements in the form of levels of interoperability to the formation of NAVAL Aviation Federations. By following the model process from bottom to top the user gets increased training opportunities and higher levels of system performance as the Federates climb up the levels in the model.

A simple example of this process is to look at the difference between a Level 1 and Level 5 Federation. The Level 1 Federation is using DIS-to-HLA gateways, obtaining immediate HLA compliance and allowing users to just see each other in their visual/radar/Electronic Warfare systems. This Level may be initially attractive until the user discovers that a 'fair-fight' scenario is not probable with mismatches in databases and models. When all the steps are completed for a Level 5 Federation, the databases and models are all in a single environment allowing the user to see the environment naturally. This leads to a 'fair-fight' scenario and Mission Rehearsal capabilities, which do not exist today.

The end result of completing the task of Networking Naval Aviation trainers will be a paradigm shift in how the users train. No longer will trainers be stand-alone devices with limited interoperability. The networked Naval Aviation Trainer will provide exciting new capabilities with the user involved in multi-service training and fleet wide training on a daily basis. Finally the user (using existing simulators) will be come involved in, and help along, the development of new tactics and weapon systems.

5. REFERENCES

[USD(A&T), 1996] USD(A&T) Memorandum, "DoD High Level Architecture (HLA) for Simulations," September 10, 1996, URL: **http://www.dmso.mil/docslib/mspolicy/usdat.html**

[1516] SISO High Level Architecture Standards Development Group, "*Draft Standard for Modeling and Simulation (M&S) High Level Architecture (HLA) - Framework and Rules*," Draft specification, currently being balloted by the Simulation Interoperability Standards Committee of the IEEE. April 1999.

[1516.1] SISO High Level Architecture Standards Development Group, *"Draft Standard for Modeling and Simulation (M&S) High Level Architecture (HLA) - Federate Interface Specification,"* Draft specification, currently being balloted by the Simulation Interoperability Standards Committee of the IEEE. April 1999.

[1516.2] SISO High Level Architecture Standards Development Group, *"Draft Standard for Modeling and Simulation (M&S) High Level Architecture (HLA) - Object Model Template (OMT) Specification".* This is a Draft specification, currently being balloted by the Simulation Interoperability Standards Committee of the IEEE. April 1999

6. Bibliography

DANIEL J. PATERSON is an electronics engineer with the Naval Air Warfare Center, Training Systems Division, Simulation & Models Division, Modeling & Simulation Development Branch in Orlando Florida. He is currently the technical leader of the NAWCTSD Interoperability Laboratory, with research papers on HLA Gateways and Data Distribution Management.

In 1992 he received his MSEE degree from the University of Central Florida. In 1976 he received his BA in Mathematics from Jacksonville University, Jacksonville Florida.

In 1977 he received his Naval Flight Officer Wings from the US Navy. He spent 8 years flying in Naval Patrol Aircraft, before transferring to the US Naval Reserves where he spent another 12 years flying as a Reserve Officer for the US Navy.

Captain Rory H. Fisher is the current Aviation Training Systems Program Manager (PMA-205) responsible for the acquisition and life cycle support of all training systems (aircrew devices, maintenance training suites, and courseware) supporting Navy and Marine Corps Aviation.

His education includes a B.S. in Aerospace Engineering from the U. S. Naval Academy (1973), an M.S. in ASW Systems Technology from the Naval Postgraduate School, graduating with highest distinction from the Naval War College, and completion of the Program Manager's course at the Defense Systems Management College.

Captain Fisher served as a patrol plane commander, mission commander, and instructor pilot in all variants of the P-3 and was the Commanding Officer of Patrol Squadron Forty Eight based at Moffet Field. His acquisition tours included Executive Officer of Air Test and Evaluation Squadron One (VX-1); Assistant Program Manager (Systems and Engineering)/P-3 Class Desk; Military Director of Research and Engineering for the Naval Air Warfare Center, Aircraft Division; Director of Program Management for Aircraft Division; and Assistant Deputy Commander for Operations and Support (Air-1.0B) for the Naval Air Systems Command (NAVAIR) prior to his assumption of command of PMA-205.

NAVAIR HLA Integrated Product Team Members: Captain Rory H. Fisher, CDR Mike Holmes, Mike Hennessy, Gary Fraas, Cathy Matthews, Claudia Slaton, and Daniel Paterson.

RELATIONSHIP BETWEEN VV&A AND BEST PRACTICES IN SOFTWARE ENGINEERING

Captain Joseph Celano
Space and Naval Warfare Systems Command (PMW 131)
4301 Pacific Highway (Bldg C-60), San Diego, CA 92110
Phone: 858-537-0120
Email: celanoj@spawar.navy.mil

Marcia A. Stutzman
Logicon Information Systems and Services
Logicon, Inc., A Northrop Grumman Company
55 John Clarke Road, Middletown, RI 02842
Phone: 301-317-9698, Email: mstutzman@logicon.com

Candace L. Conwell
Space and Naval Warfare Systems Command (PMW 131E)
4301 Pacific Highway (Bldg C-60), San Diego, CA 92110
Phone: 858-537-0184
Email: clc@spawar.navy.mil

KEYWORDS: Modeling, Simulation, Verification, Validation, Accreditation, Software Engineering, CMM

ABSTRACT

Innovations in computer and visualization technologies have rendered modeling and simulation (M&S) an increasingly viable and attractive means to reduce project costs and to "extend the envelope" for analysis, tests and training applications otherwise limited by low availability of resources or high risk to personnel or assets. M&S has become central to both defense and commercial programs as a way to mitigate risk and reduce time to market. Architects, educators, media and medical communities are rapidly embracing M&S. M&S affects many aspects of our professional and personal lives and we, as users and as providers of M&S, are acutely aware that M&S should be examined for credibility prior to use. Unfortunately, it is difficult to inspect many M&S systems for suitability for a specific user's intent simply because the sponsor did not ensure that good software engineering practices were followed. M&S is increasingly software-intensive and thus suffers many of the ills that plague software development efforts both commercially and within the Department of Defense (DoD). Tools and processes do exist and program sponsors are in the unique position of being able to ensure that these resources are employed to protect the investment in M&S and to protect those who will be affected by the use of M&S, whether it be for Battle Group training or weapons systems acquisition decisions. This paper describes the relationship between good software acquisition practices and model verification and validation (V&V). The combination of the Software Engineering Institute's (SEI) Capability Maturity Models (CMMs) (CMM and Capability Maturity Model are trademarks registered by Carnegie Mellon University) with a verification, validation, and accreditation (VV&A) process will ensure that the upfront expenditures for improving our M&S development and maintenance will provide positive return on investment and will mitigate risks that the M&S will be inappropriately applied.

BACKGROUND

Until relatively recently, M&S within DoD had been conducted in isolated pockets and often by a close-knit group of Subject Matter Experts (SMEs) and modelers. The SMEs were often "warriors-turned-modelers." Some of these "isolated pockets" are still functioning today, providing reliable and credible M&S to the user. In the early 1990's, political and economic events created an environment of declining resources which prompted a demand for 'reusable' M&S as well as the dawn of large-scale, multi-purpose, multi-resolution warfare M&S. Meanwhile, tremendous improvements in processing and graphical capabilities have made M&S more affordable. These affordable, graphical capabilities have also whetted the appetite for more detail or for what is often called "physics-level" modeling. Additionally, the development and early implementations of the High Level Architecture (HLA) Run Time Interface (RTI) opened new avenues for federation across simulations. Thus, the requirements for M&S continue to outpace even the rapid advances in technology.

The growth of simulation requirements within DoD has been mirrored by a tremendous surge of M&S application in industry and commerce. The automobile industry continues to be a major user of M&S. Aerospace corporations are using M&S to gain the competitive edge. Architects are using simulation to convince city planners to approve designs for ballparks and buildings. Construction teams and architects use M&S to design and plan building projects. Attorneys use M&S to present their cases to juries. Weather predictions are based on high performance modeling. Medical schools are investigating the use of simulation for education, training and even certification for selected procedures. Local and state governments across the country are employing M&S to analyze transportation, environment and police issues. School systems plan bus routes using M&S. The use of M&S is becoming increasingly significant in many aspects of our personal and professional lives and has already affected our checkbooks because costs (and presumably, any benefits) are distributed across consumers and citizens.

Those of us who are in the business of M&S are eager to harness technology, including high performance computing, to meet our customers' simulation needs. We are also in the best position to know that misuse of M&S can lead to decisions that can have adverse consequences. Within DoD, acquisition professionals and Test and Evaluation (T&E) managers are using the DoD-mandated VV&A process to ensure that M&S are evaluated for specific uses. Other Federal agencies without mandatory processes for VV&A are likely to be encouraged by internal legal counsel to implement V&V practices where necessary to reduce risks involved in use of M&S.

SOFTWARE MANAGEMENT CRISIS JEOPARDIZES M&S BENEFITS

V&V is chartered by the using organization to ensure that the M&S is suitable and that limitations and assumptions are well understood. Except for trivial uses that do not merit the expenditure, V&V of an M&S will involve an inspection of M&S documentation. Examples of non-trivial uses of M&S in the military include mission rehearsal and T&E, and surgical training in medical schools. These M&S should be subjected to considerable scrutiny for obvious safety and liability reasons. Unfortunately, in too many cases management of M&S programs has neglected to implement processes that provide traceability through documentation. Without documentation, there will be no way (short of reengineering the code) to ensure that all the user's requirements are implemented, coded correctly and tested. It is not likely that SMEs will want to read code to determine if the M&S has adequately represented a "real heart" in sufficient detail to analyze a new drug's affect on nerve synapse activity. To do so would be cost prohibitive.

The lack of documentation is one symptom of a software crisis that has been examined and solved on paper for the last decade. The processes that produce quality systems are defined and available, but seldom implemented. Even when program managers understand the benefits of software engineering versus coding, they are frequently heard to complain that their sponsors will not pay the upfront costs to implement these procedures. In many cases within DoD and elsewhere, the sponsor will look for "product" and will go to the laboratory or contractor that will fulfill the functionality requirements regardless of the quality. This tendency to want "code" now rather than insisting on well-designed and documented functionality is analogous to the tendency of stockholders to prefer dividends to investment. In the long run, everyone is short-changed, because without investment, quality deteriorates and products will fail to win customer loyalty.

The fact that software systems development in the United States often fails to deliver usable products to the customer has been documented in the CHAOS report (Standish 1995) and in even more recent research. In 1987, the Defense Science Board, chaired by Fred Brooks, conducted a study to evaluate the causes of software problems that result in frequent schedule slips, poor performance and unhappy customers. Norm Brown, the founder of the Software Program Manager Network, describes the situation well:

> *"The DoD, despite its deep dependence on software for virtually all its systems, has been slow to address the thorny problem of poor software-project management, ever pursuing instead the latest software "silver bullet" quick, painless solutions to complex problems. The DoD is not alone in this quest, which also is common in the commercial software industry. Of course, there are no silver bullets, and chasing them only postpones real improvement.*
>
> *Assessment of many large-scale software projects suggests that the largest single cause of poor software management is poor understanding of essential management practices and techniques of what works and what does not. This lack of understanding is echoed in what I call the senior management problem: corporate or government executives responsible for software often do not understand the critical aspects of large-scale software development. Management's lack of understanding leads to unwillingness to support the needed infrastructure (such as training and tools) and process improvements. It also results in failure to effectively support the entire software team, contractual and other actions that erode the team's credibility and processes, and unrealistic commitments of time and money (Brown 1996)."*

The lack of commitment to quality software engineering jeopardizes the benefits we seek from M&S, when M&S systems are coded rather than engineered, we essentially throw money down the drain. More money chases that bad money when we find user organizations responding to the DoD VV&A mandate with V&V plans that are paperwork drills rather than carefully tailored risk-reducing evaluations of the M&S' ability to support the use. A common complaint from M&S developers supporting VV&A efforts is that they do not have the documentation to support V&V and, therefore, V&V is "too costly." Actually, documentation is needed within a M&S program to maintain common understanding of system requirements and to ensure that system functionality is understood by the test developers and by the users. Configuration control involves the management of user manuals, analyst guides, system specifications and model description documents or Conceptual Model (Sargent 1999). The cost of documentation is a cost of providing a supportable product. Nowhere in the world of hardware-based products (such as automobiles or houses or computers) would a customer choose to buy products that are not well documented and configuration-managed. When your taillight needs replacing, you fully expect the auto dealer to know which part to order and that it will snap on nicely. When you buy an espresso machine, you look for the directions when you open the package. When you purchase a $3,000 computer, you expect documentation. When a customer uses a million-dollar model, he should be able to read a descriptive document that describes the model capabilities, assumptions and limitations. He should know that if he finds problems, he can submit them to a configuration control process and that they will be documented, prioritized, fixed (eventually), and that a Version Description Document will describe version capabilities and outstanding trouble reports. He should know that a Test Plan and test procedures have been tailored to requirements and that the Test Plan is documented so that releases and changes are tested. The sponsor should be able to read test reports and to examine outstanding enhancement requests and trouble reports. M&S, like other software, can be managed.

The processes for good software engineering are defined, but until they are used for M&S, credibility will be difficult to establish because V&V will be perceived as "too costly". V&V will be "blamed" for costs that, except for validation, represent costs that will be incurred for any software that will be usable and useful to the end user. Even validation costs are critical in order to provide the users with meaningful documentation. Thus, documentation is a prerequisite for successful use by the end user. The inspection of system documentation for V&V is just one of the reasons systems need to be documented. The costs of documentation are not allocable to V&V but do make V&V possible. This is a chicken-and-egg problem for some legacy systems. Prospective users of an M&S are expected to fund the costs of VV&A for their use. If there is no documentation for their M&S of choice, then the bill for V&V is going to be inordinately high and the prospective user is likely to seek another M&S system that will cost less to V&V for the specific use. The undocumented M&S cannot be V&V'd and will lose customers.

The legacy problem may not be solved unless a long-term sponsor is motivated to invest in upgrading the processes and products that underlie the M&S. For "new construction" M&S, the use of commercial best practices will mitigate program risks while also ensuring that prospective users will find it much easier to evaluate the M&S capabilities to support their needs.

SOFTWARE ENGINEERING AND V&V SOLUTIONS

There are a number of software process improvement paradigms that can be used to improve the quality of M&S. The V&V process complements general software engineering best practices by adding emphasis on V&V of a user's specific criteria. V&V are included in most software engineering methodologies but the validation of M&S, particularly those used in critical areas such as defense, medicine, and transportation, will require more emphasis on validation that the implemented abstraction of the "real world" is appropriate for the given use. One de facto standard for software engineering processes is presented below, followed by a discussion of V&V.

CMM as a Best Practice for Software Engineering and Acquisition

Both Government and industry recognize the need to improve software acquisition and software development processes. To advance the practice of software engineering in DoD, the Office of the Under Secretary of Defense for Acquisition, Technology, and Logistics (OUSD(AT&L)) sponsors the SEI operated by Carnegie Mellon University. The SEI was established in December 1984 as a federally Funded Research and Development Center (SEI 2000).

In 1999, the Honorable Jacques S. Gansler, USD(AT&L), made it policy that all software (including M&S) providers for ACAT I programs would have to prove compliance with the CMM for Software (SW-CMM) at Level 3 as a technical consideration for contract award (Gansler 1999). In March 2000, the Naval Air Systems Command (NAVAIR), expanded the scope applying the SW-CMM Level 3 requirement to all ACAT programs (I, II, III, and IV) within NAVAIR and the Naval Aviation Program Executive Offices (NAVAIR 2000). Level 3 compliance must be evaluated using an approved Software Capability Evaluation (SCE) method.

SEI Capability Maturity Models

The SEI CMMs were developed to help organizations improve their software engineering management practices.

- The SW-CMM is a de facto standard used to judge the maturity of an organization's software processes and to identify what is required to mature of those processes. Organizations use the SW-CMM to assess their ability to develop and maintain software and as a guide to improve their software processes.
- The Software Acquisition CMM (SA-CMM) is a model for improving an organization's software acquisition processes.

The CMMs provide the frameworks to achieve that needed improvement. By institutionalizing better processes for M&S acquisition and development, organizations can incorporate requirements for VV&A at the beginning of the acquisition cycle, manage those requirements throughout the design and development, mitigate risks, and build confidence in a functionally superior, more credible M&S product.

Software Capability Evaluation

The CMM establishes a frame of reference for performing a SCE (pronounced 'ski'). A SCE evaluates the management maturity level of an organization's software process. A SCE can identify risks associated with a project or contract for acquiring and building high-quality, dependable software on schedule and within budget. The findings from a SCE may be used to define, and potentially reduce, the risks in awarding a contract. Evaluations are also performed on existing contracts to monitor an organization's process performance and improvement.

The SA-CMM and the SW-CMM are synergistic. They are used together to address the acquisition and development of high quality products. Both of these CMMs identify key process areas (KPAs) with associated goals for several levels of maturity. CMM levels of maturity are achieved sequentially.

Maturity Level 1 (Initial) of both CMM models is characterized as ad hoc and chaotic, with few processes defined and success depending on individual effort. Maturity Levels 2 (Repeatable) and 3 (Defined) are described in Table 1. Maturity Levels 4 (Quantitative) and 5 (Optimizing) further refine the process focus.

The CMMs describe KPAs with related activities and processes that are necessary to achieve the goals considered important to evaluate an organization's capability. We introduce the selected KPAs below.

Table 1. Maturity Levels 2 and 3

Level	SA-CMM	SW-CMM
2 Repeat-able	1. Basic software acquisition project management processes established to: • plan all aspects of the acquisition • manage software requirements • track project and contractor performance • manage the project cost/ schedule baselines • evaluate the products and services, and • successfully transition software support activity. 2. Project team reacting to circumstances 3. Process discipline in place to repeat earlier successes	1. Basic project management processes are established to track cost, schedule, and functionality 2. The necessary process discipline is in place to repeat earlier successes on projects with similar applications.
3 Defined	1. Documented standard software acquisition process 2. All projects use tailored version for acquiring software 3. Proactive Project & contract management 4. Risk management is integrated into all aspects of the project 5. Training provided	1. Organization-wide documented standard software process for management and engineering activities 2. All projects use a documented and approved version of the organization process for developing and maintaining software 3. Training provided

Role of the Acquirer of M&S Software

The SA-CMM (Cooper et al. 1999) describes the acquirer's role in the software acquisition process and addresses the functions that support software acquisition. The SA-CMM provides a structured framework to guide and assess organizations in maturing their acquisition capabilities both in the acquiring and maintenance phases of the M&S life cycle.

Although the SA-CMM currently is not mentioned in DoD policy, organizations cannot continue to afford having immature acquisition capabilities. An SW-CMM Level 3 development effort coupled with an SA-CMM Level 1 acquiring effort can often lead to a SW-CMM Level 1 delivery capability. While the Level 3 developer is often criticized for an inferior product, the reality is that an immature acquiring process can force poor practices upon the developing organization (Jarzombek 1999).

SA-CMM Level 2 Repeatable. The process capability of a Level 2 acquisition organization is stable for planning and tracking the software acquisition because documented procedures provide project level repeatability. The Requirements Development and Management KPA is of prime importance to Level 2 M&S acquisition. This KPA calls for the establishment of "common and unambiguous definition of requirements" for use by the M&S manager, sponsor, developer, tester, and user.

Requirements development and management begins with the translation of operational or user requirements into specifications and ends with the transfer of responsibility for the support of the software products. Direct participation from the M&S user is needed to ensure that system-level requirements are well understood. The process ensures that software requirements are baselined and that all subsequent requirements changes are controlled. Requirements management includes establishing and maintaining agreement among people involved in the acquisition with the objective of specifying requirements that are unambiguous, traceable, verifiable, documented, and controlled.

SA-CMM Level 3 Defined. The process capability of Level 3 acquisition organizations can be summarized as being controlled, since performance, cost, schedule, and requirements are under control and software quality is tracked.

At this level, the acquisition organization's standard software acquisition process is established, including the processes for software contract management and internal project management. Management and engineering activities are integrated. Risks are identified and managed throughout the acquisition. The Risk Management KPA has the most direct impact on containing the costs of M&S V&V.

Risk management is the process associated with identifying risks, evaluating their impact and probability, developing strategies to mitigate the effect, tracking each risk, and implementing the defined mitigation strategy when required. A Level 3 acquisition organization has a defined process for identifying and quantifying risks associated with software acquisition. The risks can be tracked in a controlled manner, so that mitigating action can be taken at the appropriate time.

CMM Application to M&S Acquisition

SA-CMM Level 2 maturity for *Requirements Development and Management* is essential during development or evaluation of an M&S Conceptual Model. Once established, this capability facilitates the on-going Requirements Traceability. If requirements must change during or post software development, the traceability to the baseline and rationale for the change needs to be captured to ensure consistency across the product and to support the credibility and accreditation decisions.

Acquisition Risk Management, an SA-CMM Level 3 capability, is also applicable throughout the acquisition process. Risk management capabilities are particularly critical during the final stages of M&S acquisition, when the credibility and accreditation decisions are made. As the organization matures, the capability to quantify risks and to track probability of occurrence improves. Accreditation decisions, which assess the value of the M&S to the decision-makers, are particularly amenable to the types of statistical analyses that characterize advanced risk mitigation techniques. The use of the SA-CMM and the requirement that the software supplier be evaluated at SW-CMM Level 3 are initial steps in risk management.

Disciplined requirements management is essential to a successful M&S effort. Any organization acquiring M&S should be operating at Level 3 to ensure the ultimate delivery of a well-built, quality software product that meets all specifications, and is produced on schedule and within budget.

Role of the Software Developer

The SW-CMM (Paulk et al. 1993) describes the software developer's role and addresses software engineering functions. The SW-CMM provides a framework for assessing the maturity of an organization's software development capabilities. The software developer can use the SW-CMM to determine current process maturity and as guidance in selecting process improvement strategies. An acquisition organization can use the SW-CMM as an auditing tool to judge the maturity of its software providers.

SW-CMM Level 2 Repeatable. At the Repeatable Level, policies for managing a software project and procedures to implement those policies are established. The software process capability of Level 2 organizations is characterized as disciplined because planning and tracking are stable and earlier successes are repeatable.

The KPAs at Level 2 focus on establishing basic project management controls. Two KPAs with direct impact on M&S projects are *Requirements Management* and *Software Configuration Management.*

- *Requirements Management* - Establishes a common understanding between the customer and the M&S project team of the customer's requirement.

The SW-CMM *Requirements Management* KPA is a direct parallel of the SA-CMM *Requirements Development and Management* KPA. The acquirer establishes the basic requirements, including non-technical requirements such as milestones and schedule. These requirements are the basis for the contract between the acquirer and the provider. The software provider uses them as the basis for establishing cost and schedule, planning, performing, and tracking the M&S project activities. In order to maintain control of their activities, developers must review initial requirements, baseline their allocation to software, and review / adjust all planning documents if requirements change. Requirements bound the M&S project; remaining cognizant at a management level of all changes to requirements helps contain requirements-creep and the escalating costs and schedule delays it causes.

- *Software Configuration Management*-Establishes and maintains the integrity of the M&S product throughout the product's software life cycle.

Configuration management involves identifying the exact version of all software that would be needed to replicate the M&S product at specified points in time, controlling changes to that software, and maintaining traceability of those changes. The software under configuration management must include any software delivered to the customer and commercial software, such as compilers, that might change the performance of the delivered software. Many tools are available to support change control and traceability. Proof of configuration management is a requirement for accreditation of the use of a M&S in DoD.

SW-CMM Level 3 Defined. In a Level 3 organization, standard organization-wide software processes are in place, along with a training program to develop identified management and technical skills. Each project may tailor the organization's standard software processes to create a coherent, defined software process that meets the needs of the particular project. The commonality of the standard software process promotes better upper management insight into a project and allows projects to share data and "lessons learned" more easily.

The KPAs at Level 3 address both project and organizational issues, as the organization establishes an infrastructure that institutionalizes effective software engineering and management processes. Two Level 3 KPAs especially pertinent to M&S are *Software Product Engineering* and *Peer Reviews.*

- *Software Product Engineering* - Consistently performs a well-defined engineering process that integrates all the software engineering activities to produce correct, consistent M&S products effectively and efficiently.

Product engineering is the application of the project's software process to the technical activities of the project. The Requirements Management processes, developed primarily as a tracking mechanism in Level 2, are expanded to include active analysis and rationale development. Software architecture and code design becomes controlled, rather than ad hoc, efforts. Testing is to requirements, rather than to software design. A consistent, well-defined development process reduces risk and builds the customer's confidence in the M&S product.

- *Peer Reviews* - Remove defects from the M&S products early and efficiently.

Peer reviews involve a methodical examination of software and related documentation by other programmers to identify defects and possibilities for improvement. Peer reviews have proven highly effective in detecting errors prior to test; with some programs showing as much as an 80 percent reduction in coding errors. Delivering M&S products that function correctly will gain the user's confidence

CMM Application to M&S Development

The SA-CMM and SW-CMM are synergistic and should be used in parallel since they address the same requirements, proceed on the same schedule, and pursue the same objectives.

SW-CMM is applicable during the coding and functional testing phase and supports continuous Requirements Traceability and Risk Mitigation tasks.

The Level 2 emphasis on project management and tracking is evident in the early stages of software requirements analysis. A solid contract is based on mutual understanding of the requirements. Software integrity is supported with early establishment of configuration management.

At Level 3, the focus of SW-CMM is wider. The product engineering and peer review concepts institutionalize traceability of all technical requirements from M&S product development inception through testing.

VERIFICATION, VALIDATION, AND ACCREDITATION

Because the need for credible, cost-effective, and efficient M&S is so great, the DoD directed each of the Services to develop a VV&A process in January 1994. This process is intended to provide the end user with information needed to determine whether and how the results of a model or simulation can be applied to decisions that ultimately affect the warfighter. DoD Directive 5000.59 *DoD Modeling and Simulation Management* directed the Department of the Navy (DON) to establish VV&A policies and procedures for all M&S applications and also established the Defense Modeling and Simulation Office, or DMSO, as it is most commonly known today. In April 1996, DoD Instruction 5000.61 DoD *Modeling and Simulation Verification, Validation, and Accreditation,* which assigned responsibilities and prescribed procedures for the VV&A of DoD M&S, was promulgated. DMSO followed up with the publication of the *DoD Verification, Validation, and Accreditation Recommended Practices Guide (RPG)* in November 1996 and the online Year 2000 Edition (Build One) in May 2000. The RPG is written for use by M&S developers and users. The target audience includes decision-makers and program mangers that need a quick overview of VV&A and information on the accreditation process, as well as the technical staff that performs the V&V.

V&V is ideally independent of the M&S management, reporting to the user chain of command. VV&A is not a duplication of the developer's Software Quality Assurance (SQA). SQA is the M&S manager's check that the developer is meeting developmental software specifications and standards. VV&A is the process that ascertains for a prospective user whether the selected M&S will be suitable for the intended use. Thus VV&A is designed to assure the user and to mitigate the risk that the user will make decisions based on invalid or malfunctioning M&S.

A single M&S system can be employed by any number of users, each of who may employ the system for somewhat different purposes and over a different range of input data. Still, it is very probable that a good number of any user's requirements would be among the original system requirements. If CMM Level 3 processes have been followed for development and maintenance of a given M&S, then the original requirements will have already been verified. So wherever there is a nice one-to-one match between the requirements of the new user or customer and previously implemented requirements, verification will have already been completed for those functions. Previously tested and inspected system requirements are unlikely to be risk areas. Documentation, logic- and code- "walkthroughs" will have been performed on those requirements. Validation will involve SME review of the conceptual model and M&S results to determine whether the key algorithms support the user's desired fidelity.

Department of the Navy VV&A Process

The DON established the Department of the Navy Modeling and Simulation Management Office (DONMSMO) in April 1994 with the publication of SECNAV Instruction 5200.*38 Department of the Navy Modeling and Simulation Program.* The DONMSMO was charged with developing a common VV&A process for use by both Navy and Marine Corps activities. In April 1999, the DON Verification, Validation, and Accreditation policy was established with the issuance of SECNAV Instruction 5200.40 *Verification, Validation, and Accreditation of Models and Simulations*, which describes a VV&A process that is both flexible and tailorable.

VV&A Roles and Responsibilities. The key players in the performance of Navy VV&A are the M&S Proponent and the Accreditation Authority. SECNAVINST 5200.40 describes the roles they play and the responsibilities they have in acquisition and development of M&S. The Navy VV&A Handbook, a companion to the instruction, is currently being staffed for approval as a Navy M&S VV&A Standard. The handbook amplifies information in the SECNAV Instruction and provides practical guidance for those responsible for implementing VV&A.

Accreditation of M&S Used in Navy T&E. 5200.40 also designates the Commander Operational Test and Evaluation Force (COMOPTEVFOR) as the Accreditation Authority for M&S used to support operational test and evaluation (OT&E) activities. As the Operational Test Agency for the Navy, COMOPTEVFOR accredits all M&S used to supplement the OT&E of weapons systems, as well as any M&S used in combined developmental test/operational test events. Early and continuous involvement between the M&S Proponent and COMOPTEVFOR is needed to ensure that both have a common understanding of the M&S requirements.

While COMOPTEVFOR is the accreditation authority for M&S used to support Navy OT&E decisions, COMOPTEVFOR does not perform the V&V. As the accreditor, COMOPTEVFOR's role is limited to identification of test requirements and acceptability criteria. Programs with systems under test should begin coordination with COMOPTEVFOR early, plan V&V tasks to meet the projected requirements, and be prepared to describe how the selected M&S will be used in the test. Furthermore,

Program Managers need to set aside resources and schedule time to adequately perform the necessary V&V activities when targeting an accreditation for OT&E. Funding for accreditation is the responsibility of the M&S Proponent.

CONCLUSION

M&S systems are often software-intensive. Industry standard best practices are available to program sponsors for development of robust and useful systems that can be V&V'd without extraordinary efforts.

The key to V&V for M&S is an underlying software engineering process that maintains and documents traceability.

Program sponsors who develop M&S can and should employ CMM processes (or equivalents) for acquisition and development of M&S.

Program sponsors who use M&S to reduce risk in their programs will benefit from using M&S that have been developed in accordance with CMM processes because the M&S will be more robust, supportable, useful and significantly less difficult to verify and validate for their specific uses.

REFERENCES

Brown, Norman. 1998. Software Program Management Network (http://spmn.com/isms_article.html).

Carnegie Mellon University Software Engineering Institute. 2000. http://www.sei.cmu.edu/

Cooper, J. M. Fisher, and S. W. Sherer. 1999. *Software Acquisition Capability Maturity Model (SA-CMM) Version 1.02.* Technical Report CMU/SEI-99-TR-002, ESC-TR-99-002. http://www.sei.cmu.edu/

Defense Modeling and Simulation Office. 2000. *VV&A Recommended Practices Guide Year 2000 Edition Build 1.* May. http://www.msiac.dmso.mil/vva

Department of Defense. 1996. *Department of Defense Verification, Validation and Accreditation (VV&A) Recommended Practices Guide*, Defense Modeling and Simulation Office, Alexandria, VA, Nov. http://www.dmso.mil/

Department of Defense Directive. 1999. Department of Defense Directive 5000.59 *DoD Modeling and Simulation (M&S) Management, Change 1.* May. http://www.dmso.mil/

Department of Defense Instruction. 1996. *Department of Defense Instruction 5000.61 DoD Modeling and Simulation (M&S) Verification, Validation, and Accreditation (VV&A).* Apr. http://www.dmso.mil

Department of the Navy. 1994. Secretary of the Navy Instruction 5200.*38 Department of the Navy Modeling and Simulation Program.* Apr. http://navmsmo.hq.navy.mil/

Department of the Navy. 1999. Secretary of the Navy Instruction 5200.40 Verification, Validation, and Accreditation (VV&A) of Models and Simulations. Apr. http://navmsmo.hq.navy.mil/

Gansler, J. S. 1999. *Software Evaluations for ACAT I Programs.* The Under Secretary of Defense for Acquisition, Technology and Logistics (USD(AT&L)) policy memorandum. Oct.

Jarzombek, J. 1999. Integrating Acquisition with Software and Systems Engineering: Providing More Structured Guidance to Better Satisfy the Needs of Users. *The Journal of Defense Software Engineering*, Volume 12 Number 8. Aug.

Kresa, K. 2000. *1999 Annual Report Defense. Aerospace. Cyberspace.* Northrop Grumman Corporation, Los Angeles, CA.

Naval Air Systems Command. 2000. *Interim Policy on Software Evaluations for Naval Aviation Programs.* AIR-1.1/SEI00/89. Policy memorandum. Mar.

Paulk, M.C., B. Curtis, M. B. Chrissism, and C.V Weber. 1993. *Capability Maturity Model ® for Software, Version 1.1.* Technical Report CMU/SEI-93-TR-024, ESC-TR-93-177. http://www.sei.cmu.edu/

Sargent, R.G. 1999. Validation and verification of simulation models. In Proceedings of the 1999 Winter Simulation Conference. ed. P.A. Farrington, H.B. Nembhard, D.T. Sturrock, and G.W. Evans, 39-48. IEEE, Piscataway, NJ.

The Standish Group International, Inc. 1995. *CHAOS.* West Yarmouth, MA. http://standishgroup.com/visitor/chaos.htm

AUTHOR BIOGRAPHIES

CAPTAIN JOSEPH CELANO is the Director of the Synthetic Battlespace and Analysis Program Office at Space and Naval Warfare Systems Command. He manages several major M&S acquisition programs including Joint Simulation Systems (JSIMS) -Maritime, Naval Simulation System (NSS) and Navy Joint Modeling and Simulation System (JMASS). Additionally, CAPT Celano leads the integration of the SPEEDES distributed high performance computing simulation engine within both JSIMS and JMASS.

CANDACE L. CONWELL is a Computer Scientist at the Space and Naval Warfare Systems Command. She is a graduate of the Naval Postgraduate School. Ms. Conwell has 23 years of C4ISR and M&S experience, including the design, development, testing of simulation systems, scenarios and associated databases. While a member of the DONMSMO Technical Support Group, she led the DON VV&A Program spearheading publication of the VV&A instruction, coordination of the VV&A Handbook, and ongoing development of an online VV&A Turbo Tool that automates the production of VV&A related documents.

MARCIA A. STUTZMAN is a Senior Principal Analyst at Logicon Information Systems and Services, an SW-CMM Level 3 software developer (Kresa 2000). She currently supports the Navy M&S VV&A Program and previously supported the Navy Test and Evaluation M&S Management Office. Ms. Stutzman also provided program management and technical support to the Office of the Secretary of Defense Threat Systems Office's Threat Simulator Validation Program. While in the U. S. Army, she served as an Intelligence Research Analysts with duty at the National Security Agency. Ms. Stutzman earned her Bachelor's of General Studies Degree from Indiana University at South Bend.

PERFORMANCE EVALUATION OF COMMUNICATION SYSTEMS USING FORMAL DESCRIPTION TECHNIQUES

Luc Hohwiller and Serge Wendling
Laboratoire MAGE
Université de Haute-Alsace
4, rue des frères Lumière
F-68093 MULHOUSE Cedex (France)
e-mail : luc.hohwiller@khe.siemens.de, s.wendling@univ-mulhouse.fr

KEYWORDS

Formal Description Techniques, performance evaluation, Estelle, time in Estelle, simulation, modeling formalism.

ABSTRACT

Computer simulations provide support for performance evaluation of communication systems where analytical methods can no longer be used, due to growing complexity of real systems. Computer simulations involve computer models which describe the systems in a modeling language and use a simulation environment for model execution. The formal language Estelle has been designed for the description of distributed, communicating, concurrent information processing systems with particular application in communication protocols and services of Open Systems Interconnection (OSI) architectures. Estelle provides a well accepted and powerful formalism based on communicating automaton. Our contribution is to demonstrate that Estelle can also be used as a modeling and simulation language for performance evaluation purposes of communication systems.

INTRODUCTION

Communication systems have taken a central place in our daily modern life. It has become of highest importance to make sure that communication systems are suitable for their dedicated applications, and that they meet the required performance and reliability. Performance evaluation has therefore become a central point in system design and validation. Computer simulation may be a solution for modern and future communication systems, since their performance evaluation has become analytically intractable due to their growing complexity.

Our interests emphasize the modeling formalisms and simulation languages for performance evaluation of communication systems based on OSI protocols. The formal languages Lotos, SDL and Estelle have been designed for the specification of computer based communication protocols (Kenneth 1993). Formal description techniques are considered as specification, validation and verification techniques for complex systems. Estelle belongs to those techniques in the area of distributed, concurrent and safety-critical communication systems. Estelle provides powerful expression capabilities for modeling logical behavior of such systems and formal languages advantages. We try to extend the application area of Estelle language to the performance evaluation of communication systems in order to take benefit of its rich expression capabilities and its formal basis.

In this paper, we first review the performance modeling and simulation issue. After having analyzed Estelle language for performance evaluation, we present a method to use Estelle as a modeling and simulation language for performance evaluation purpose. The approach is demonstrated and validated on the performance evaluation of fieldbus networks.

1. PERFORMANCE MODELING AND SIMULATION

Whenever new systems are to be designed or existing systems have to be tailored, performance evaluation can help to predict the impact of any changes on the system performance. Performance evaluation aims at forecasting system behavior in a quantitative way for decision support, system optimization, validation or verification by evaluating alternative system concepts and designs.

The purpose of performance simulation is to estimate what the measurement would be if the simulated system were to be measured directly. Simulation enables to play "what if" games with various system parameters or system architectures and use it as both a design and an analysis tool. Simulation has therefore become a fundamental solution for system performance analysis and forecasting.

Nevertheless, simulation can be a pitfall, if some basic rules are not considered, development steps are skipped or bypassed. Thus, it is advised to follow rigorously the well established simulation life cycle and its steps (Banks 1998; Maillot and Wendling 1996). To be able to get the required performance information about a system by simulation, the system and its performance aspects must be modeled in order to be measured during simulation run. Consequently, the conceptual modeling formalism and the simulation language used for performance evaluation must support the specification and the measurement of quantitative performance aspects of the system to be evaluated. The selection of a modeling language and a simulation environment are therefore essential since they provide the tools and expression capabilities to model and evaluate system performances.

2. PERFORMANCE EVALUATION IN ESTELLE

After a brief introduction to Estelle and its application areas, we analyze the language for being a suitable modeling and simulation language for performance evaluation purpose.

2.1. Introduction to Estelle

The Formal Description Technique (FDT) Estelle (Extended State Transition Language) is a formal language for the specification of distributed, concurrent communication systems based on OSI communication model. Estelle has been developed by the ISO and was standardized in 1989 (Estelle 1989). The language is based on communicating non-deterministic extended finite state machines (EFSM). EFSM are widely used in communication systems design and have a wide range of modeling capabilities. A system description in Estelle consists in a hierarchical interconnection of modules whose behavior are described by state machines. The state machines communicate by exchanging messages through bi-directional channels with FIFO queues. Estelle uses ISO 1982 standard Pascal to describe the state machines as well as the data processing. The language was developed with protocol engineering in mind, and accordingly, it is mainly used in this area.

Estelle specifications may serve as a basis for validation, functional simulation and animation, code generation, prototyping, testing, conformance testing.

2.2. Performance evaluation requirements

This section discusses the expression capabilities necessary for a modeling and simulation language to be suitable for performance evaluation of communication systems. For performance evaluation, system performance has to be modeled in order to be measured during simulation run. Time expression and management play a central role in performance evaluation. For evaluating system performances, the modeling language must permit to specify quantitative time consumption on the one hand, and to measure time delays on the other hand. A global system time that controls time progress is mandatory as well. To perform performance measurements, a mechanism to access the global time must be provided in order to compute elapsed time between two events during model execution. A performance data storage support must also be provided by the modeling and simulation language to record performance data.

2.3. Time expression in Estelle

Time expression and computation is a general weakness of many modeling languages because performance aspects have been less important in the past. Time aspects in modeling languages make their specification and execution semantic more complex. Time expression is also particular in Estelle, because it is not the intention of a specification language to provide language constructs to express quantitative system aspects. Estelle aims at describing the logical behavior of systems leaving performance aspects to the implementation step.

The only Estelle statement dealing with time is the delay clause. It is aimed at the specification of time constraints like timeouts of communication protocols.

Estelle (intentionally) has therefore a rudimentary notion of time. The only assumptions about time flow are the following two:

- time progresses as the computation does,
- the progression time is uniform with respect to "delay" clauses values of transitions involved.

The Estelle definition of time and expression capabilities are insufficient for performance evaluation.

2.4. Time enhancement proposals

Estelle does not cover non-functional system expression aspects such as time delay or execution time. It provides a lot of features for describing logical behavior of communication systems, but misses a way to express time performance and has no execution time model. Language extensions and tool specific solutions to express time performance in Estelle have been proposed for language enhancement but have never been normalized (Estelle 1989). They have been reviewed in (Fischer 1998) and may be classified in two groups :

- specification oriented enhancements,
- and performance evaluation oriented extensions.

The specification oriented enhancements aim at the specification of system time constraints (real-time) whereas performance evaluation oriented extensions aim at forecasting execution times of specification implementations. Performance evaluation oriented Estelle extensions come towards the system performance evaluation requirements. Unfortunately, the proposed solutions are tool and vendor specific (Hendaz and Budkowski 1995) and available performance measurement features are restricted. This initiated the motivation to define a modeling and simulation method in standard Estelle for time performance evaluation purpose, independently of any tool.

3. MODELING TIME IN ESTELLE

Time consumption in communication systems may belong to one of the three categories: processing time, waiting time (queuing, timeout) or transmission time.

To model those time consumptions in Estelle, we use Estelle timer modules (Fig. 1.). They include two states (*wait_for_start* and *wait_for_timeout)* and implement a spontaneous delayed transition (Fig. 2.).

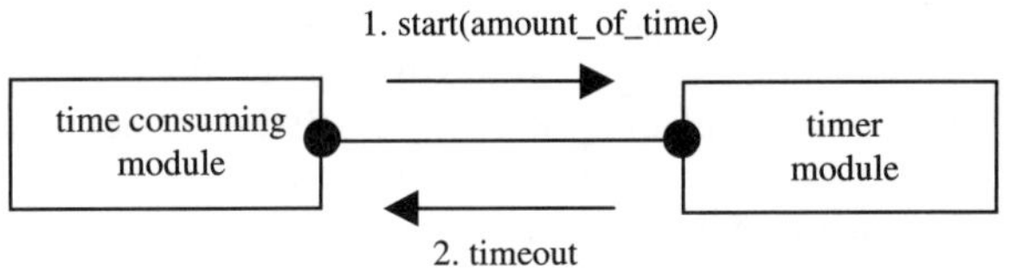

Fig. 1. Time consumption with a timer module

The concept we developed is to express time flow by using timeouts. Timer modules are used to generate a *timeout* interaction after a specified amount of time has elapsed. If an Estelle module needs to consume time, it is connected to a separate Estelle timer module. Each time the Estelle module needs to consume time, it sends a *start* interaction to the timer module (Fig. 3.) and waits for receiving the associated *timeout* interaction (Fig. 4.).

The *start* interaction sent to the timer module includes the amount of time (number of time units) to consume (Fig. 5). At reception of a *start* interaction, the timer module runs from the *wait_for_start* state into the *wait_for_timeout* state, starting the time countdown from the delayed transition. When the specified amount of time has elapsed, the timer returns in its initial *wait_for_start* state and sends a *timeout* interaction back to the time consuming module. The time countdown may be aborted by sending a *cancel* interaction to the timer module.

All the timer modules in the system must run in parallel and in a asynchronous way to ensure uniform time

```
body TimerBody for TimerModule;
var amount_of_time : integer ;

state WAIT_FOR_START,WAIT_FOR_TIMEOUT;

initialize to WAIT_FOR_START
  begin
  end;

trans
{ fired when timer is started }
  from WAIT_FOR_START to WAIT_FOR_TIMEOUT
    when TIMER_IP.start(amount_of_time)
      begin
      end ;

{ waits for amount of time }
  from WAIT_FOR_TIMEOUT to WAIT_FOR_START
    delay(amount_of_time)
       begin
          output TIMER_IP.timeout;
       end ;

{ countdown canceled }
  from WAIT_FOR_TIMEOUT to WAIT_FOR_START
    when TIMER_IP.cancel
       begin
       end ;
end;
```

Fig. 2. Estelle body for the timer module

```
TRANS
   FROM        state_1
   TO          wait_for_time_out
   WHEN        module_ip.interaction
   PROVIDED    conditions
   PRORITY     priority_level
   BEGIN
     OUTPUT    timer_ip.start(amount_of_time)
   END
```

Fig. 3. Transition for starting time consumption

```
TRANS
   FROM      wait_for_time_out
   TO        state_2
   WHEN      timer_ip.timeout
   BEGIN
     actions_1
     ...
     actions_n
     OUTPUT  module_ip_1.interaction_1
     ...
     OUTPUT  module_ip_n.interaction_n
   END
```

Fig. 4. Transition for receiving timeout

```
channel timer_to_module
(module_role, timer_role);

by module_role :
   start(amount_of_time: integer);
   cancel;
by timer_role :
   timeout;
```

Fig.5. Channel declaration for timer module.

```
module timer_module systemprocess;
   ip module_ip: timer_to_module
   (timer_role) individual queue;
end;
```

Fig. 6. Header declaration for the timer module.

progress in the system model. This can be guaranteed when all Estelle modules are subsystems which requires to set the *system* Estelle attribute to all of them, including the timer modules (Fig. 6.).
The introduction of time in Estelle requires the definition of a time model for the simulation execution. The time model required for performance modeling specifies that :

- research for transitions to be fired,
- firing of transitions,
- transition code execution,
- sending interactions,

do not consume any time during model execution. This Estelle simulation execution model has been implemented in the XEC Estelle-toolset (Thees and Gotzhein 1998).

4. TIME PERFORMANCE MEASUREMENT IN ESTELLE

The evaluation of system time performance is mainly based on measuring the time elapsed between two events in system execution. The measurement of time delays in model execution requires access to the simulation time.
We introduced a global timer for managing time progress in Estelle during simulation execution. A Pascal Estelle primitive function returning the current time advance in time units, called *now*, has been defined and implemented in the XEC Estelle toolset. This enables to read the current simulation time advance at any time during simulation execution by calling the *now* function in any transition code. To measure time performances, two different approaches may be used in Estelle : on-line or off-line performance measurement.
Off-line approach consists in recording all performance information of the system during simulation execution. When simulation is finished, the system performance is evaluated by computing the data collected during simulation run. The collected output data are system tracing information reporting the system execution events with time stamp. Time delays are calculated by analysis and tracing the simulation output records.
On-line approach consists in measuring and recording the time delays during simulation execution, using virtual measurement instrumentations, part of the simulation models.
For recording simulation data, we use file manipulation functions implemented in Estelle inline C code.

5. FIELDBUS PERFORMANCE EVALUATION USING ESTELLE

We validate our approach of using Estelle for performance evaluation on PROFIBUS-DP (PROFIBUS 1994) fieldbus networks. Fieldbus networks provide a communication facility for distributed real-time process control applications supported by isolated field devices such as controllers, actuators and sensors. From the design stage of a fieldbus plant on, it is necessary to ensure that the real-time constraints of the control applications will be met by the fieldbus network. Fieldbus network simulation has therefore become mandatory for performance forecasting and system parameter tuning. We show on a PROFIBUS-DP network simulation how PROFIBUS-DP devices are modeled in Estelle and how network reaction times can be measured during simulation.

5.1. Fieldbus device modeling

Fieldbus network devices are based on OSI communication models. Each field device is composed of two interconnected parts: a network communication protocol (OSI layer 2) and a process control application (OSI layer 7). The Estelle device model structure maps the fieldbus device structure (Fig. 7.).
The asynchronously execution of control application and network communication is assured by using Estelle subsystems for each module.

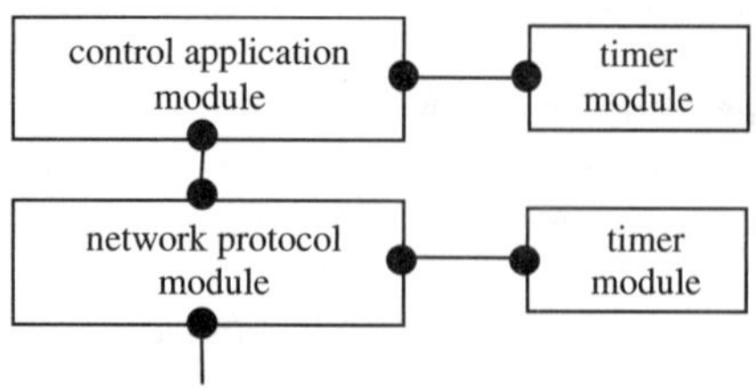

Fig. 7. Architecture of an Estelle fieldbus device model

5.2. Network performance measurements

Network performance measurements aim at testing alternative network configurations and evaluating reaction times for decision support and validation.
We have chosen the on-line performance evaluation approach. A measurement protocol has been designed and implemented into the Estelle modules of the fieldbus applications. An extra Estelle module is used as virtual delay measurement device (Fig. 8.).

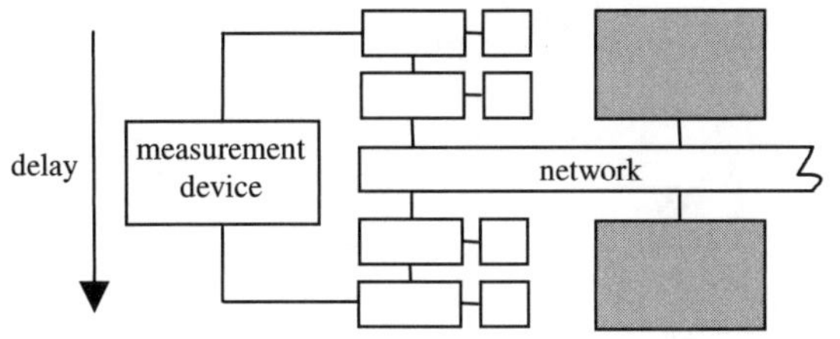

Fig. 8. Estelle configuration for delay measurement

Reaction time measurements consist in following steps:

1. start delay measurement,
2. send an output data to the process,
3. stop measurement when output data has arrived to the process.

Due to asynchronous execution of application and protocol in field devices, reaction times are random variables varying between a minimum and a maximum delay of time. A great number of measurements are therefore required to get relevant reaction times.

5.3. Modeling and simulation environment

A PROFIBUS-DP network simulation starts with the design of a network configuration using available Estelle component models. The Estelle code of the system configuration is then compiled and linked with the instantiated Estelle component models (library) in order to build an executable file (Fig. 9.). When the simulation is started, model parameter values are read from a specified file for initialization. Performance data are recorded in an output file during simulation execution. Performance analysis is carried out off-line (Fig. 10.)
XEC efficient object code generation provides a high-speed execution that enables to reach real PROFIBUS-DP network execution speed up to 1.5 Mbaud bus transmission rate.

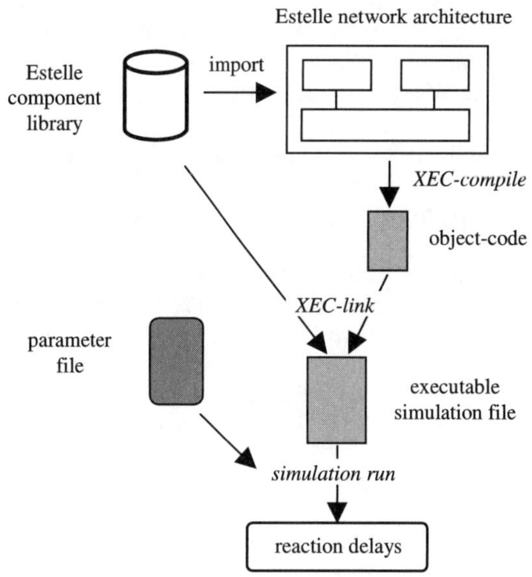

Fig. 9. Simulation process overview with XEC

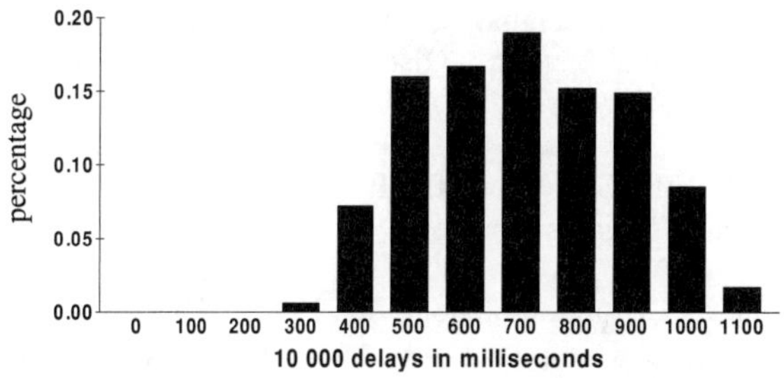

Fig. 10. Repartition of measured network reaction times

CONCLUSION

We have analyzed the formal specification language Estelle for performance evaluation purpose of communication systems. Estelle is a powerful modeling formalism but doesn't support performance evaluation. Nevertheless, we have successfully defined, implemented and validated a performance evaluation method using timer modules. An Estelle time model for simulation execution has been defined and implemented in an experimental Estelle toolset. The approach has been illustrated on the evaluation of reaction times of fieldbus networks for decision support.
Using Estelle as modeling and simulation language enables to take advantage of a formal network protocol description for modeling the network components. Automatic simulation code generation from Estelle conceptual models avoids model verification task.

REFERENCES

Banks, J. 1998. *Handbook of Simulation: Principles, Methodology, Advances, Applications, and Practice.* John Wiley & Sons, ISBN 0-471-13403-1.

Estelle 1989 – *A Formal Description Technique based on an Extended State Transition Model*, ISO/IEC 9074, International Organization for Standardization.

Fischer, S. 1998. "Real Time and Estelle: A Comparison of Approaches" In *Proceeding of the 1rst International Workshop on the Formal Description Technique Estelle.*

Hendaz, M. and Budkowski, S. 1995. "An enhanced Estelle Simulator for Performance Evaluation" In *Actes du Colloque Francophone sur l'Ingénierie des Protocoles CFIP'95*, ISBN 2-86601-468-5.

Kenneth J. Turner. 1993. *Using Formal Description Techniques An Introduction to Estelle, LOTOS and SDL*, John Wiley & Sons, ISBN 0-471-93455-0.

Maillot, Y. and Wendling, S. 1996. "VHDL as a Modeling Language within a General Simulation Environment for Discrete Event Systems." In *Proceedings SCSC'96*, 127-132.

PROFIBUS 1994. DIN E 19245 Part 3, PROFIBUS Nutzer Organisation.

Thees, J. and Gotzhein, R. 1998. "The eXperimental Estelle Compiler - Automatic Generation of Implementations from Formal Specifications" In *Proceedings of The 2nd Workshop on Formal Methods in Software Practice (FMSP'98).*

M&S for Life Cycle Management at Sandia National Laboratories*:
From Engineering Simulations to Enterprise Modeling

Patrick Chavez[1], Paul Nielan[2], Russell Skocypec[1], and Paul Yarrington[1]
[1]Sandia National Laboratories, Albuquerque, NM 87185
[2]Sandia National Laboratories, Livermore, CA 94551

KEY WORDS

computer systems, computer software, numerical methods, continuous simulation, validation

INTRODUCTION

Sandia National Laboratories has responsibility for designing all non-nuclear components for the U.S. nuclear weapons program, as well as performing a wide variety of energy research and development projects. More generically, Sandia works on assignments that broadly respond to military and economic national security threats. In conjunction with this work, Sandia encourages and seeks partnerships with appropriate U.S. industry and U.S. government groups to collaborate on emerging technologies that support our mission. The breadth and depth of Sandia's scientific endeavors span every discipline required to fulfill our national defense mission and have consistently contributed to the US's technological and economic well being. This broad focus has led to revolutionary advances in multiple science and technology areas including for example, advanced manufacturing, materials and processes, modeling and simulation, computational and information sciences, nanotechnology, electronics, pulsed power, and engineering sciences.

In the area of modeling and simulation (M&S), Sandia is engaged in an unprecedented effort to revolutionize engineering and manufacturing. This effort intends to reduce the reliance on traditional physical build and test methodologies through increased use of digital modeling and simulation approaches. Sandia is developing and applying advanced M&S technology as part of the Department of Energy's (DOE's) Accelerated Strategic Computing Initiative (ASCI), including a major effort to move high performance computing (HPC) far beyond its current level of performance. Although driven by national security needs, many of the capabilities developed are helping solve complex industrial problems of a scope never before feasible. For example, visualization of oil and gas reservoirs, modeling the entire life cycle of manufactured products such as tires, or simulating an airliner crash are just a few samples of the cooperative work Sandia performs for non-defense projects. This paper presents some of the goals, efforts, capabilities, and accomplishments of the M&S efforts at Sandia National Laboratories ranging from engineering simulations to enterprise modeling.

* Sandia is a multi-program laboratory operated by Sandia Corporation, a Lockheed Martin Company, for the United States Department of Energy under Contract DE-AC04-94AL85000.

MODELING & SIMULATION

U.S. national policy, budgetary and time constraints on non-nuclear testing, and loss of production capability call for a new means of verifying the safety, reliability, and performance of the U.S. nuclear stockpile. While new weapon production has ceased, the ability to design nuclear weapons, analyze their performance, predict their safety and reliability, and certify their functionality as they age is essential for conscientious management of the enduring stockpile. Recent dramatic advances in computer technology make virtual testing and prototyping viable alternatives to some traditional physical test-based methods. The possibility of managing the entire life cycle of complex devices and systems lies in simulation-based performance models of the components, subsystems, and systems and in the models of materials synthesis, manufacturing processes, aging, and disposition.

Sandia has identified five segments of a system's life cycle in which the development and use of M&S can provide dramatic increases in effectiveness and decreased costs. The first segment is Simulation-Driven Concept Exploration, in which simulation technologies such as intelligent software agents, generative analysis, variable/reversible aggregation and disaggregation, collective/cooperative behavior, genetic optimization and uncertainty quantification are used to explore massive trade spaces. The second segment is Simulation-Based Design, Test, Evaluation and Manufacture. Technologies including massively parallel and commodity-based high performance computing, the "right" level of coupled physics models, multi-model federates, manufacturing M&S, and virtual/synthetic environments for visualizing massive datasets will enable high-confidence simulation-based design, acquisition, test and evaluation.

The third segment is Personnel Protection Simulation and Analysis, in which physics-based M&S is integrated into vulnerability assessment tools. These tools address issues such as explosive and chemical/biological threats, genetic algorithms for bio-event early warning/epidemiological prediction, probabilistic risk assessment, and virtual reality to visualize threats and enhance training so that personnel protection can transition from "vulnerability assessment" to "situation awareness." The fourth segment is Predictive

M&S for Sustainment Logistics. Here, technologies such as design for reliability, system reliability, electronics reliability, predictive failure/physics of failure, prognostic algorithms for diagnostic sensors, spares optimization/supply chain management, and large-scale optimization techniques are used to transition from "reactive" to "predictive" maintenance, sustainment and logistics. The fifth segment is Simulating Comprehensive Information Connectivity, in which low-power cryptography, high-speed secure network system phenomenology models, ad-hoc wireless network technology, distributed computing, and intelligent software agents for information assurance are used to enable rapidly changing reconfigurable communication networks for effective knowledge management.

Another critical M&S capability that spans these life cycle segments is the simulation of human behavior in complex adaptive systems including individual and group behavior through techniques such as layered learning, neural networks, genetic algorithms, genetic programming, expert systems and autonomous adaptive systems. Humans are a vital element in virtually all complex systems of interest.

Preliminary versions of virtual testing and prototyping exist today. However, to meet the needs of the future, simulation applications must achieve higher-resolution, three-dimensional, full-physics, and full-system capabilities. This level of simulation requires HPC far beyond the current level of performance. DOE's ASCI program is creating the leading-edge computational modeling and simulation capabilities to meet this need. The ASCI initiative is being accomplished through a collaboration of Lawrence Livermore National Laboratory, Los Alamos National Laboratory and Sandia National Laboratories. ASCI activities within the initiative are organized to support multiple strategies including...

- high-end computing platforms,
- advanced applications, and
- robust problem solving environments.

HPC PLATFORMS

The objective of the HPC platform strategy is to stimulate the U.S. computer manufacturing industry to create high-end computers with speeds and memory capacities thousands of times greater than currently available. It is estimated that computer-based engineering life cycle applications will require a several orders-of-magnitude increase in computing performance above the best computers currently available. Access to these high-end supercomputing capabilities will give scientists and engineers the ability to develop and use high-performance, "full-system", "full-physics" predictive codes and to consider classes of problems that are now intractable with current computing power. In order to support full-physics, full system simulation, 100's of TeraOPS and beyond are required. The HPC platform effort is bridging the gap between Giga- and Tera-scale computing through the following approaches (Figure 1).

- Accelerate high-performance computing.
- Maintain affordability by accelerating existing technology trends.
- Demonstrate scaleable balanced 100-TeraOPS computing platforms.
- Develop software to take full advantage of hardware capabilities.

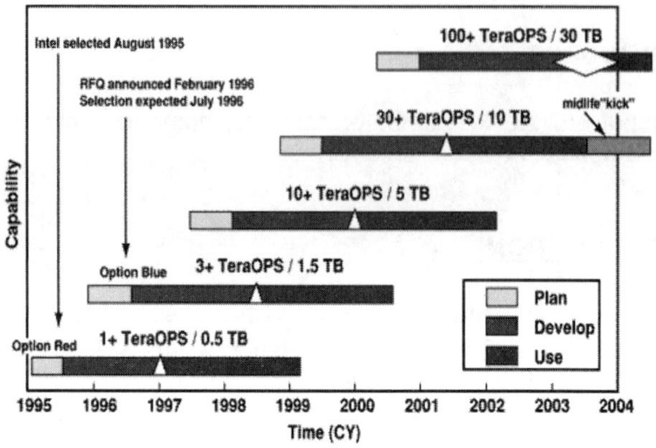

Fig. 1: HPC Platform Goals

The requirement for predictive simulations leading to a platform performance objective of 100's of TeraOPS requires a broad balance in platform capabilities, advanced application development, and an integrated problem-solving environment. This imposes requirements for appropriate memory, memory bandwidth and latency, disk capacity, parallel I/O bandwidth, and external networking. Partnerships to develop alternative methods for achieving the end goal of 100's of TeraOPS are being pursued. For example, single computer company partnerships have already provided a major increase in computing resources as evidenced by Sandia's TeraOPS computer (Figure 2). This computer recently achieved a record speed of 2.8 TeraOPS and is heavily used for a variety of defense and science applications.

Fig. 2: Sandia's TeraOPS Computer

An alternative HPC platform strategy is to aggregate "commercial-off-the-shelf" (COTS) technology in scaleable architectures to develop high-performance computers at affordable costs. Already under development at Sandia is the CPlant™ computing cluster that ranks in the world's top 100 computing platforms and was used to break the world record for large database sorting.

ADVANCED APPLICATIONS

There are two broad science and technology (S&T) areas related to advanced application development: 1) engineering S&T and 2) computer and information S&T. Engineering S&T at Sandia is focused on the revolution in engineering and manufacturing with the imperative of creating a model- and simulation-based life cycle engineering environment. Life cycle engineering, at Sandia, is considered to be a comprehensive and validated modeling and simulation capability that enables "cradle-to-grave" stewardship of the products for which Sandia is responsible. This concept is intended to change the way Sandia's products are engineered, allowing us to move from traditional physical build and test-based processes to computation-driven processes supported by high performance computing. Basic research to improve the fundamental understanding of, for example, the physics of multiphase flows, complex flows through porous media, fluid/structural interactions, and complex geomechanics is underway. This is in conjunction with developing, deploying, validating, and verifying the corresponding modeling and simulation capabilities.

Computer and information S&T are also vital to the development of advanced M&S simulations. Important areas in this field include the development of new mathematical methods, algorithms, and software tools including for example, efficient parallel matrix solvers and massively parallel computer operating systems. Other developmental efforts in the computational and information sciences area range from discovery of new methods for finite element meshing and load balancing to the creation of immersive visualization environments. Such work at Sandia has won many national and international awards and has led to numerous major patents and commercial licenses.

Additionally, in regards to advanced applications, Sandia is aggressively pursuing the verification and validation of models and simulations. Verification is the process of ensuring that the problem is solved accurately while validation is the process of ensuring that the right problem is solved. Because it is necessary to place increased reliance on computer simulations when making engineering judgments, the uncertainties associated with these calculations must be well understood and, over time, reduced. These uncertainties arise from many sources, errors in coding, inadequate approximations, physical processes not represented in the code, and user errors. The goal of both verification and validation is to reduce the total uncertainty associated with modeling and simulation calculations. Reducing any individual uncertainty to zero at the expense of leaving others large clearly fails to minimize the overall uncertainty; therefore a balanced effort is underway that addresses all sources of uncertainty.

Representative of the many advanced applications developed at Sandia is the CTH computer code. CTH is a multi-material, large deformation, strong shock wave, solid mechanics code that supports multi-phase, elastic-viscoplastic, porous and explosive materials. A recent interesting scientific application of the CTH code was the numerical simulations of the impact of the comet Shoemaker-Levy 9 on Jupiter (Figure 3). With many organizations attempting to simulate this unique event, Sandia's simulations were the only ones to follow comet debris from the time of impact through the time when debris was ejected from the fireball. In the weeks preceding the impacts, Sandia published several papers predicting that the explosion would be directed outward along the fragment's path of entry, that an incandescent fireball would rise into view within a minute of impact, and that a plume of debris would rise into sunlight. Because of these predictions, Sandia was credited with alerting the astronomical community to look for these phenomena. The accuracy of the predictions provided qualitative verification and validation for modeling events involving very large energy releases of approximately one million megatons.

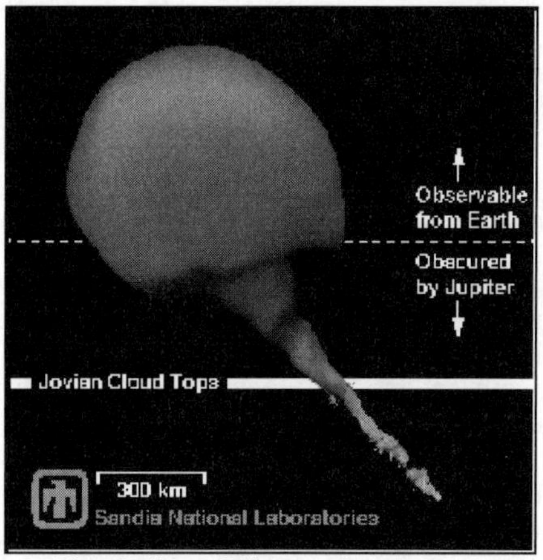

Fig. 3: Simulation of Shoemaker-Levy 9 Impact

The Cooperative Research and Development Agreement (CRADA) between Goodyear and Sandia also provides many illustrative examples of Sandia's M&S capabilities. Sandia has developed many computer-based analysis tools for predicting the thermal and mechanical responses of structures. These tools are being extended and customized in the Sandia-Goodyear partnership for the purpose of simulating and predicting tire manufacturing elements such as the shaping and curing processes, and tire performance characteristics such as rolling resistance and hydroplaning (Figure 4). By doing this, the new computational tools can reduce the number of prototypes that must be built and tested, which will ultimately get new tires to market sooner.

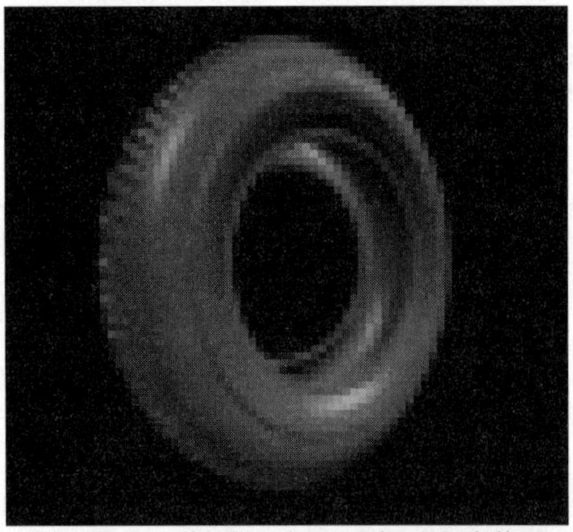
Fig. 4: Sandia-Goodyear Tire Modeling

Under another complimentary Sandia-Goodyear CRADA, researchers are using a variety of analytical techniques, including neutron scattering, to study the structure and properties of various materials used in tire fabrication. They are gaining an understanding of the aging and reliability of elastomers and developing methods for predicting material lifetimes. They are also developing advanced materials with improved properties. A third Sandia-Goodyear project is seeking ways to predict tire vibration for ride quality and noise applications. All of these efforts have a direct relation to Sandia's primary defense mission, through the underlying engineering analysis codes used in the studies.

PROBLEM SOLVING ENVIRONMENTS

The fundamental goal of the ASCI Problem-Solving Environment (PSE) program is to provide to application developers and users accelerated access to HPC including advanced applications. Strategies employed within the PSE effort to achieve this fundamental goal include...

- products based on industry standards,
- end-to-end solutions that directly enable applications developers and users, and
- a focus on building a balanced HPC PSE.

In addition, PSE solutions have to be scalable to provide balanced computing systems for application users up to the TeraOPS scale.

To accomplish these goals PSE is...

- supporting the rapid development of predictive simulation codes that are adapted for the efficient use of massively parallel computers, and
- ensuring that the power of the application/platform combination can be readily applied by Sandia scientists and engineers.

In regards to these, Sandia is developing engineering application code development frameworks and is embarking on a journey to provide customized, web-accessible simulation-based tools directly to the desktop computer.

SIERRA

Historically at Sandia, small software development teams have developed and maintained engineering codes for their particular application. The increasing demands upon software applications to keep up with improvements in algorithms and hardware place a tremendous strain on the teams. In particular, three emerging technologies that are each difficult to "back fit" into an existing engineering software architecture include adaptivity, multi-physics, and parallel algorithms. Each technology is difficult in itself to implement in an existing code. Taken together, the task is overwhelming.

At Sandia, we are also increasingly finding that our code developers are spending less time on the development of improved physics capabilities, and more time struggling with computer science issues related to establishing and maintaining software facilities associated with advanced hardware technologies. Examples of such software facilities are parallel communication including parallel input/output (IO). Because of each team's responsibility for its own code's development, this attention to computer-science issues has resulted in duplication of effort.

As in most organizations, legacy codes at Sandia represent a tremendous investment. Although individually valuable, the coupling of these codes to represent more complex phenomenon has primarily been limited due to computer science related issues. Where coupling of two or more codes has occurred, the time to perform a complete computer analysis with the coupled codes is often excessive. Typically, the codes must be executed in sequence, with a special translator program executed in between each set of coupled codes to translate the results of the one code into the input format expected by the other code. Because of the demands on laboratory computers, the processing sequence to perform a coupled-code analysis could extend over a period of several weeks since each subsequent task in the sequence may occupy a much later position in the queue.

In response to the above, SIERRA's main goal is to provide an environment for parallel, adaptive, coupled-code development. To achieve this goal, an object-oriented architecture of software services that are common to engineering codes and a set of software tools to manage the code development process are being developed. SIERRA's software architecture is based upon the observation that Sandia's analysis codes share a common computer science basis that logically should be implemented once and used by all of our codes (Figure 5). The capabilities of parallel communication, parallel IO, and the transfer of solution fields from one code to another for the purpose of coupling are being built into SIERRA so that they can be used by all

Sandia codes. Once a code is built within the SIERRA framework, it can either be run in stand-alone mode or be coupled. Because such codes "speak the same language," coupling will be inherently more flexible than was ever historically possible. For example, several Sandia components employ a manufacturing process known as resistance welding. To accurately model the residual stresses induced by this process requires the coupled solution of electrical, thermal, and mechanical fields. Other important applications of coupling range from weapon surety in fuel fires to tire manufacturing processes.

Fig. 5: SIERRA Architecture

SIERRA represents a software architecture where the framework has been broken into a set of building blocks upon which the engineering simulation codes are built. The codes have been factored into those parts that deal with the more abstract computer science portions, mainly associated with data movement and data management, and into those that deal with the engineering algorithmic implementation. This allows engineering codes built upon SIERRA to have more immediate access to the functionality developed by the computer science researchers. A goal is to leverage Sandia's computer science algorithmic research and development across many engineering applications. Application development with SIERRA also promotes software reusability. Objects created by SIERRA or application developers are available for reuse by others. Thus one can leverage critical application components, which increases productivity and encourages consistency.

SIERRA offers the following services to the engineering application developer (Figure 6).

- *Multi-mechanics infrastructure* which provides the capability to rapidly couple single physics applications into a multi-physics package.
- *Adaptivity infrastructure* that allows for increasing and decreasing spatial resolution based upon specific engineering criteria.
- *Surface mechanics infrastructure* that provides an abstraction of a surface and a set of interfaces for performing mechanics operations on the surfaces
- *Scalable linear equation solvers* for solution of sparse systems of equations on distributed and shared memory parallel architectures.
- *Parallel IO* that is independent of the file format and provides the ability to write results or restart files in parallel to one or more neutral file formats.
- *Dynamic load balancing* that provides for moving mesh objects and their associated data from one processor to another.
- *Parallel services* that separate the engineering from the parallel implementation.
- *Data services* that provide data structures and functionality to separate the data bookkeeping from the engineering.

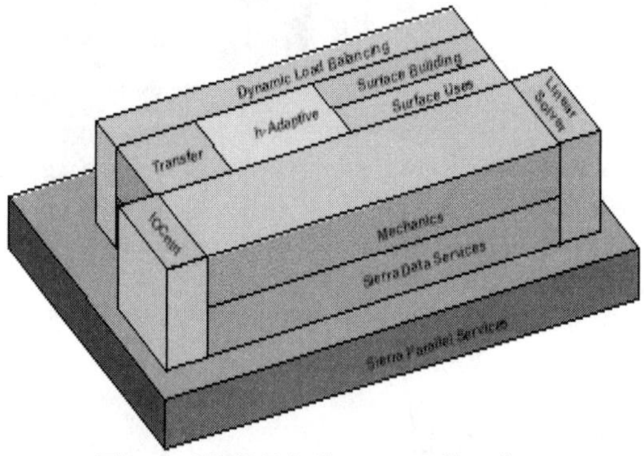

Fig. 6: SIERRA Common Services

WEB-ACCESSIBLE SIMULATION-BASED TOOLS

Historically, computer modeling and simulation has required substantial levels of software and hardware subject matter expertise. This conflicts with the desire for ubiquitous M&S to maximize the benefits that these technologies offer. The challenge is then to provide easy-to-use, useful, integrated, and validated modeling and simulation capabilities that are accessible by the broader science and engineering community throughout the product life cycle. More specifically, computer-based modeling and simulation tools are needed that are accessible via the desktop computer and allow the design engineer, for example, throughout the product life cycle to quickly, conveniently, safely, securely, and reliably explore a design space. Moreover, the tools must transparently incorporate an integrated set of capabilities (e.g., modeling, meshing, analysis, and visualization) that execute on diverse and distributed computing hardware from workstations to TeraOPS computers.

At Sandia, customized, web-accessible modeling and simulation tools are being developed that bring advanced applications and HPC to the desktop computer (Figure 7). This effort will be expanded considerably in the coming years with the goal of disseminating previously restricted modeling and simulation capabilities to the broader Sandia design and engineering community. Easy and convenient access to modeling and simulation tools will promote earlier and more extensive use of simulation capabilities throughout the entire product life cycle. Additionally this access should also decrease the demand for expensive physical prototypes and testing, as well as reducing the longer times needed to develop the physical models and tests which remain necessary. The tools also leverage the valuable and limited human resources that provide design, modeling, and simulation expertise.

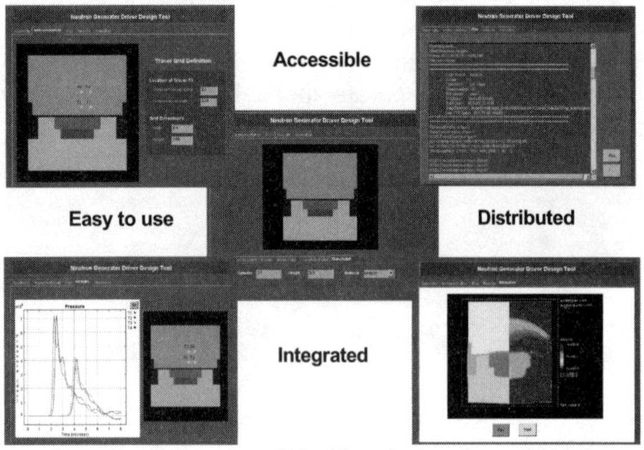

Fig. 7: Web-accessible Simulation-based Tool

ENTERPRISE MODELING

Beyond physics-based engineering simulations, Sandia is involved in an enterprise modeling and simulation effort. Enterprise modeling and simulation attempts to capture all of the pertinent attributes of a business or institutional entity and express these attributes in a simulation environment. These attributes include the physical, financial, personnel, management, and safety processes and information flows that are part of the enterprise being studied. When an enterprise model (EM) is constructed and used properly, it corresponds to the real business enterprise.

The primary objective for enterprise modeling and simulation is to provide a better idea of how an enterprise will respond to various cost and funding scenarios, policy changes, surveillance findings, technology changes, and regulatory changes. The EM is expected to be able to process all aspects of the factors that will bear on performance of the enterprise. Some examples of the types of situations that the EM will have to deal with include…

- changes in the number of sites in the enterprise and their responsibilities,
- response to failures,
- changes in production processes,
- capital investments,
- changes in the specific regulations, and
- changes in overall funding.

In response to this need, the CoMPASS (A Confederation of Models to Perform Assessments in Stockpile Stewardship) project is being cooperatively developed across the DOE (Figure 8). CoMPASS unifies a set of distributed, classified enterprise models across the DOE. These models describe products and processes, from interactive simulations of manufacturing operations representing the flow of produced entities (both parts and information) between plants in the DOE, to the detailed record of assembly and reliability fault tree equations of individual systems. A major goal of CoMPASS is to enable better decisions regarding production, stewardship, and dismantlement plans, options, and investments.

Fig. 8: DOE Enterprise Modeling

SUMMARY

Sandia National Laboratories is pursuing a broad M&S program ranging from cooperative development of HPC platforms, to advanced applications development including enterprise modeling, to making widely available the HPC environment at the desktop. The overarching goal of this effort is nothing short of revolutionizing the engineering and manufacturing life cycle process by shifting from nearly exclusive reliance on traditional physical build and test-based processes to substantially greater reliance on digital model and simulation-based processes. Capabilities ranging from the world's fastest computers to a variety of advanced engineering analysis codes and tools, to modern code development architectures have already been developed and are in use. These capabilities will serve as a basis for the next phase of the revolution. Sandia actively encourages and engages in mutually beneficial M&S partnerships with U.S. industry and U.S. government groups.

DISTRIBUTED SIMULATION AND MODELING FOR VIRTUAL ENTERPRISES

Alptekin Erkollar
Institute for Business Informatics and Application Systems
University of Klagenfurt
Klagenfurt, A-9020, Austria
e-mail: alp@ifit.uni-klu.ac.at

Keywords

Supply Chain Management, Distributed planing, Enterprise Resource Planing, Simulation, Virtual Enterprises

Abstract

This paper deals with the question of distributed Planing, Enterprise Resource Planing, simulation for improving planning of relationship within a virtual enterprise, e.g. Business to Business and Business to consumer. A strategy is presented which starts from network analysis as is used by today's Planing Systems, transforms a local planning network into a simulation model, uses that model for simulation experiments in order to find a global plan and a feasible enterprise resource planning (ERP).

INTRODUCTION

The success of enterprises and enterprise networks (virtual enterprises) makes specific demands on the deliveries of planning and modeling. Today's planing systems are not fully prepared for these demands because of the relatively fixed nature of their planning data structures (local planning nets) that hardly may be integrated into an overall planning structure. Moreover, these systems rely upon deterministic input parameters and fixed work sequences, which does not correspond to the situation in virtual enterprise environments. On the other hand supply chain management offers a large potential for the enterprises to reduce cost and improve customer service performance. Simulations of this relations between different activities (or Enterprises) can help in these objectives by implementing of new policies. Supply chain involves modeling of multiple enterprises across the chain and get quite complex. With the support of simulation can be found of bottleneck or planing mistakes. Supply chain management make planing and managing of the process possible for the manufacturing, transport, distribution and information flow between supplier, enterprises and customer. Any activity in this chains can be locally improvement. However, the improvements made locally have not always contributed to global improvements in the supply chain performance. In this case simulation can be use for the finding an optimally combination. The need of simulation supply chain processes to allow decision makers to explore various options and scenarios. One of the major issues in the creation of supply chain simulation models is the level of detail that each of the links in the chain should be modeled at. In any simulation study, the level of detail modeled depends on the purpose of the effort. With the focus on supply chain performance, the level of detail for the manufacturing tasks varies among different efforts (e.g. constant capacity, deterministic parameters, fixed throughput). Within this paper will be presented an approach that extends Enterprise Resource Planning (ERP) and resource availability based planning (as is provided for by traditional PPC and planing systems) by simulation support: Planning networks are converted and integrated into an overall simulation model, this model then is used for simulation experiments in order to find an acceptable solution, which is finally returned to the global planing systems concerned. This NETSIM (Network Simulation) concept, fits into the dynamic scenario of virtual enterprises as well as it provides substantial enhancements to traditional planning (Deterministic or stochastic basis). The paper is organized in 6 sections. The state-of-the-art in PPC-Systems and their integration with other business information systems will be presented after the introduction. Then, the NETSIM concept is introduced together with a discussion of its advantages for virtual enterprises. The next section gives an outline of the NETSIM Prototype. The paper ends with a summary.

TODAY'S PPC SYSTEMS, SUPPLY CHAIN AND SIMULATION

Actual PPC systems mainly use network analysis as a planning mechanism. I.e. they work with monolithic nets that do neither allow for alternative work flows nor for the dynamic integration of varying subnets (reflecting the production structure of components within a heterogeneous enterprise network). The primary objective of supply chain management is to achieve the right balance of customer responsiveness and low inventory levels with an aggressive cycle time. For this purpose must be planed very low cycle times and synchronization between production, inventory and transportation. Producing enterprises, therefore, actually face among others the following problems (Fandel 1994, Hitomi 1996, Ruis-Torres 1998, Taj 1998):

- There is no common process model nor integrated or integrating means for computerized modeling, simulation and optimization.
- There are neither means for automated re-design and re-structuring of models based on optimization results nor for the iterative improvement of process dynamics.
- While many of the existing simulation software can be used as a platform for building supply chain models, there is not any tool available commercially that provides pre built features for this purpose.

For the solutions of this problems comprehensive process modeling concepts are needed as well as a coupling of powerful tools for simulation and optimization. Complete product models, descriptions and related data can be exchanged using existing standards like PDDI (Product Definition Data Interface), PDES (Product Data Exchange using STEP), STEP (Standard for the Exchange of Product Model Data), EDIFACT (Electronic Data Interchange for Administration, Commerce and Transport), HLA (High Level Architecture).

Another deficiency comes from the fact that conventional PPC systems model temporal data like transportation times, processing times, machine preparation times, down times etc. by input values that enter the calculation as fixed entities. In reality, however, these data are subjected to variations (Erkollar and Mayr 1997). Network analysis tries to cope with that restriction by calculating the values each from an optimistic value, a pessimistic value and from the expectation. For reasons of simplicity, however, often only average values are considered. Thus, what actually happens in reality is that deviations are considered only insufficiently so that bottlenecks and delays are not always transparent to the planner.

NETSIM CONCEPT AND SUPPLY CHAIN MANAGEMENT

The basic idea of NETSIM (NETwork SIMulation) Concept (Erkollar 1998) is to provide a stochastic interpretation of deterministic networks (as managed by PPC-Systems) using probability distributions for input values and control variables. Thus, using NETSIM, a (virtual) manufacturer will be able to consider deviations that might occur during production when searching for an optimal schedule. To do so efficiently, the extraction of the PPC's network and its transformation into a simulation model is supported by NETSIM interconnection and interface modules (see figure 1). This should be possible for arbitrary pairs of PPC-Systems and Simulation tools, the NETSIM prototype, however, is restricted to the coupling of SAP R/3 and Arena. The supply chain model used in NETSIM very basic elements. All activities will be defined on the basis of Manufacturing activities, Transportation, Business Processes and Orders.

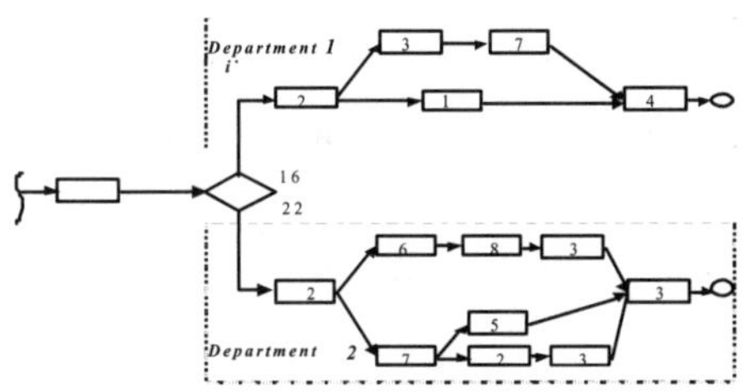

Figure 1: Integrating of different Graph with the support of decision node (in a global Graph)

The simulation results are either forwarded to an optimization tool or directly fed back into the PPC system. To sum up, the NETSIM approach consists of

- extracting the Process (Activity) network of each member of the (virtual) enterprise consortium,
- replacing the constant parameters of these networks by suitable distributions,
- extending the networks by alternative process sequences and the corresponding decision points,
- integrating the simulation models into a comprehensive one, it will be called manufacturing net, which thus represents the structure and processes of the whole (virtual) enterprise (Erkollar 1998).

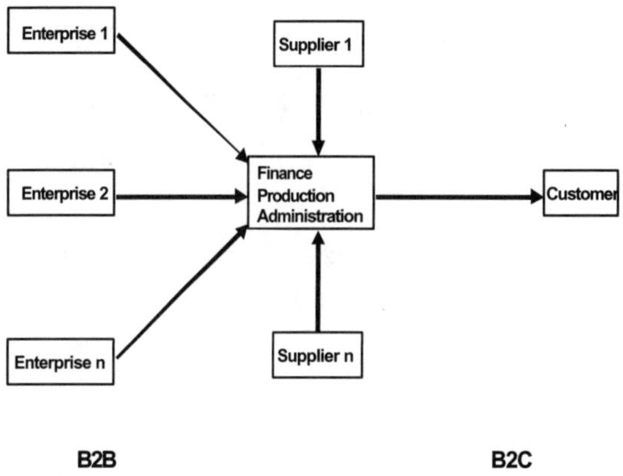

Figure 2: A typical Virtual Enterprise structure

It is not intended to reach a complete automation of production planning. The planner rather will be supported in finding the most appropriate schedule out of a number of validated alternatives. Thereby, he can observe and consider influences that activities may have on others, and resulting alterations of the critical activities. Moreover, for ERP he may take into account additional input values like availability of tools, materials, workers, machines etc. (see figures 2 and 3).

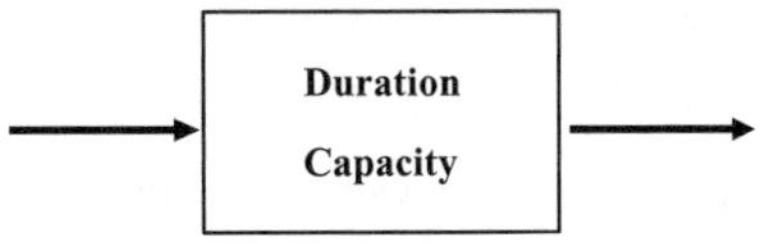

Figure 3: Task definition in conventional networks

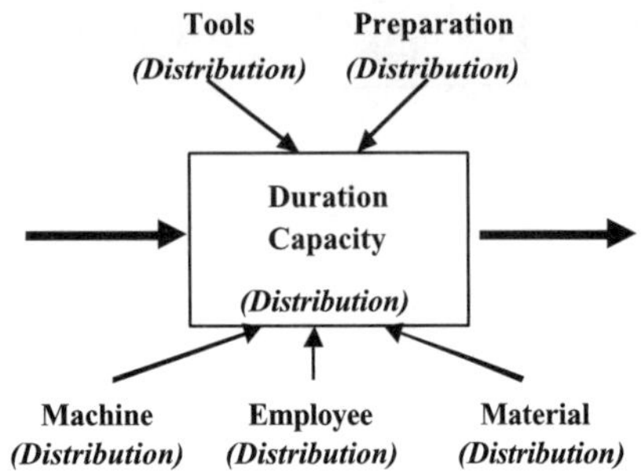

Figure 4: Extended specification of work units (Task) in NETSIM

As a side effect, using the simulation model (Blazewicz 1996), the entire production process may be visualized. This can support the user to find out bottlenecks, that emerge during the production process (Vollman 1997), and to better consider due dates. Finally, the simulation model also might be used for analyzing and improving the factory layout.

PROTOTYPE

The manufacturing represents an abstract simulation model, since it includes all data that are necessary for simulation (Erkollar and Mayr 1999). It may easily converted into a concrete ARENA simulation model. For handling the different components of such a model was developed an ARENA template (snapshot see figure 5). Using this template the model parameters may be analyzed, modified, resp. provided with initial values and/or boundaries.

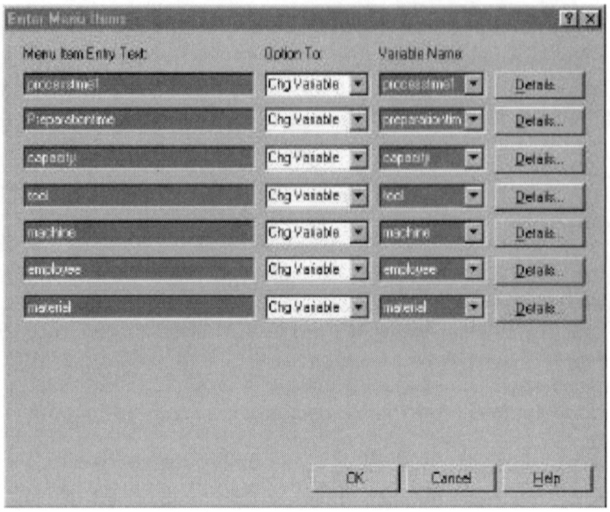

Figure 5: NETSIM screenshot showing work unit variables

Another template (in this case a SAP R/3 connection) serves for selecting one or more product(s) or product groups (i.e. different networks) that are to be analyzed together. To so, data have to be extracted from several SAP R/3 database tables. Clearly, in practice a planner (user) would find it convenient to be able to manipulate NETSIM parameters not only before but also concurrently to a running simulation experiment in order to see and evaluate immediately the consequences of his considerations (see Figure 6).

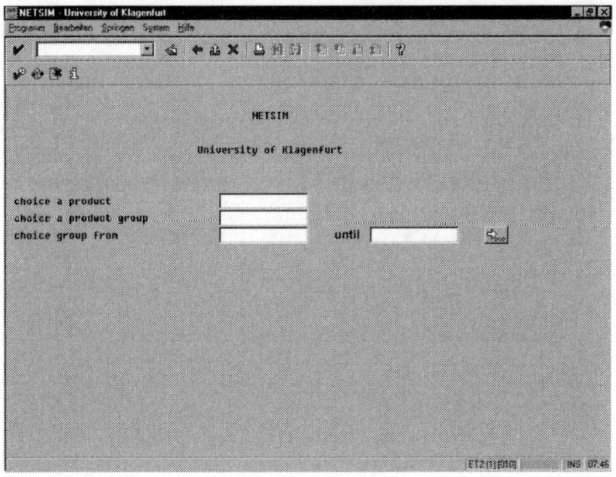

Figure 6: NETSIM template for PPC Ssystem

SELECTION OF OPTIMIZED PLANS

After an alternative-oriented working plan is completed by the cooperating functional units, a particular subnet has to be identified out of it as an optimized working plan. This is done by an iterative procedure which consists of three steps: First, starting with the latest due date, a (deterministic) backward scheduling is carried out. As a result, subnets which do not conform to restrictions like the earliest starting time can be eliminated from the total network. The goal of the second step is to find a preferred working plan with respect to the restrictions by taking into account costs as well as time consumption and due dates. If such a plan can be found, it is validated by a stochastic simulation (third step). Otherwise, the optimization procedure as described below can be started. If the simulation shows that the plan cannot be performed, the iteration of the procedure continues with choosing another preferred subnet in step two.

If no one of the studied working plans is feasible, a simulation-based parameter optimization can be carried out. The simulation input can be differentiated between model data (working plan network, resources), decision data and parameter (time- and quantity information) together with their boundaries and degree of freedom. For the optimization time information (target times) can be assumed to be constant while the other parameters (just quantities – see above figure 7– so what else?) of the model can be varied. The stochastic simulation then reveals the distributions of the target parameters with their upper and lower bounds, serving as starting point for parameter variation. Which procedure is used for this depends on the user respectively on the model conditions. The most important result here is the consideration of availability of production resources in the analysis.

This procedure allows to take the interactions between the tasks into account and secure changes in critical tasks. Furthermore it is possible to visualize the manufacturing process via the model and the simulation for detecting bottlenecks which might appear during the manufacturing process. Here, it is also possible to examine the outputs of actions which can be taken against the bottlenecks.

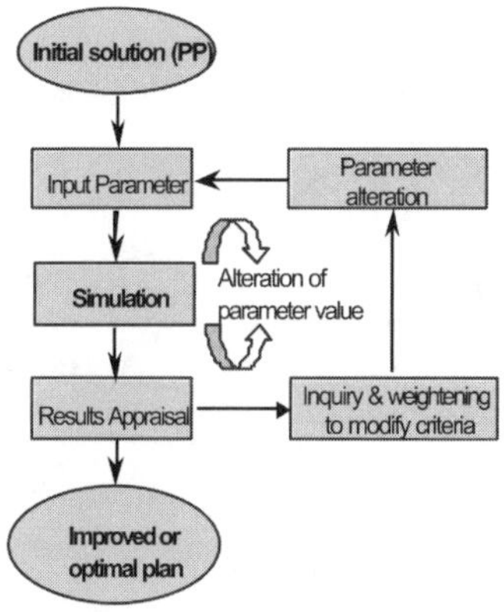

Figure 7: the “optimization loop”

For that purpose the NETSIM prototype has been extended to a version allowing for on-line parameter manipulation (NETSIM-Active).

USABILITY AND UNDERSTANDABILITY

The simulation model is an abstraction of the real world. It should enable communication between simulation expert, decision maker and employee. Wrong abstraction in this context could cause inaccurate or wrong results. It must be considered that the information capability of the model is not dependent on the model precision (see (Erkollar and Mayr 1998)). From a specific level of detail, further refinement complicates the interpretation of the model behavior and so lowers the acceptance and the benefit of the simulation (Figure 10). Especially the different representation views abstraktion/generalisation from NETSIM alleviated the understanding of the constructed models.

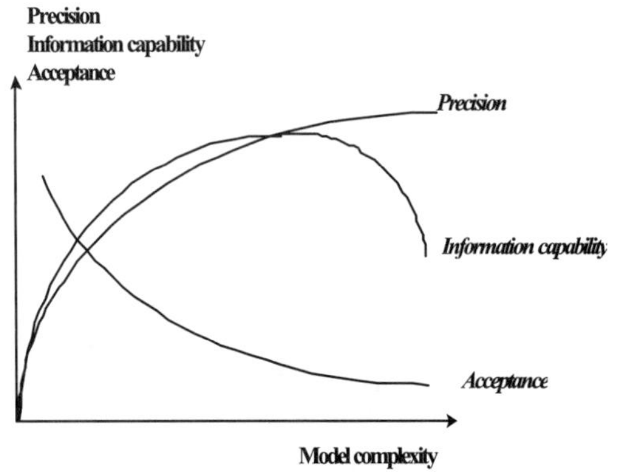

Figure 10: Evaluation criteria for the model quality, [Er98].

CONCLUSION

The integration of PPC systems, simulation and optimization tools allows for substantial enhancements of the planning process and more realistic planning results within a producing enterprise. This extends to the integrated planning in virtual factories of the future, which need for their success even more correct and reliable results. The member companies of virtual cooperatives may use different PPC systems. Consequently, a platform has to be implemented which allows for the integration of arbitrary PPC Systems. Therefore, a reference model is needed for an unified description of the different systems' interfaces. A subsequent work will be driven into this direction as well as into the integration of existing optimization tools. Another task to will be the analysis and research concerning automatic means for a kind of integrating simulation models that goes beyond the above described coupling, similarly to the integration of database schemata. A tool will be implemented for the description of manufacturing flow. Actual results on integrating dynamic models (e.g. state charts) may be used as a starting point for that purpose.

REFERENCES

Blazewicz J.; Ecker K.H.; Pesch E.; Schmidt G.; Eglarz J. (1996): *Scheduling computer and manufacturing processes*, Springer Verlag Berlin-Heidelberg.

Erkollar, A.; Mayr, H. C. (1998): The Netsim Concept and its application. In (A. Bargiela, E. Kerckhoffs ed.) Proc. ESS 98: Simulation technology:Science and Art, pp. 543-545.

Erkollar, A.: The NETSIM Modeling Concept. (1998) In (M. Engeli, V. Hrdliczka ed.) Proc. ASIM'98, Zurich, pp. 323-330.

Erkollar, A.; Mayr, H.C. (1999): Planning in Virtual Enterprises Using the NETSIM Approach: an application report, In Proc. PICMET 99, Technology and Innovation Management, Portland, Oregon-USA)

Fandel, G.; Francois, P.; Gubitz, K.M. (1994): PPS-Systeme. Springer Verlag,

Hitomi, K. (1996): Manufacturing Systems Engineering. Taylor&Francis.

Ruiz-Torres, A.J.; Nakatani, K. (1998): Application of real-time Simulation to Assign due Dates on Logistic-Manufacturing Networks. Proc. WSC'98, Washington, December.

Taj, Sh.; Cochran, D.; Duda, J.W.; Linck, J. (1998): Simulation and Production Planning for Manufacturing Cells. Proc. WSC'98, Washington, December.

Vollmann, Th.E. (1997): Manufacturing Planning and Control Systems. McGraw-Hill.

Simulation Based Acquisition
Where are the Savings?

Prepared For:

2000 Summer Computer Simulation Conference
Simulation System Live-Cycle Evolution Task

Prepared By:

William Grigson
John Chapman
Simulation Division
IIT Research Institute
12443 Research Parkway, Suite 302
Orlando, FL 32826

May 15, 2000

Simulation Based Acquisition
Where are the Savings?

Shrinking procurement dollars and aging weapons systems necessitate the adoption of an approach to reduce cost and schedule of acquisition efforts. Simulation Based Acquisition (SBA) has been widely touted as the approach providing the solution. The purpose of this paper is to promote a definition of SBA and establish a strategy for implementing SBA. Unlike the recently released SBA Roadmap, the approach in this paper is program and product centric as opposed to "M&S" centric. SBA, in concept, is quite simple and is compliant with Acquisition Reform.

In spite of the simplicity of the SBA concept, OSD, the Services and industry have been wrestling with the implementation of Simulation Based Acquisition for at least the past 2 years, having achieved minimal progress (as measured by the limited adoption of SBA within the Acquisition community). Has this lack of progress been due to the deficiency in ownership of the SBA effort by personnel tasked to define it? Or has this lack of progress been due to an inappropriate understanding of SBA? Perhaps the conclusion is that there is no defined SBA methodology clearly depicting cost and/or schedule savings.

SBA Definition

In simple terms, SBA is defined as "basing acquisition decisions on simulation results." **(Figure 1)** How does one know when requirements are finished? With SBA, requirements are complete when modeling or simulation results indicate that the stated requirements achieve mission success and are capable of being implemented in accordance with a feasible cost and schedule. How does one know when a design is compliant? With SBA, a design is compliant when a comprehensive model has been developed which can be demonstrated through simulation to meet functional and performance requirements and can be built within the desired cost and schedule. (In SBA, when cost is addressed, it should be addressed in the context of Total Cost of Ownership.)

What is SBA?...

Basing { Acquisition } Decisions on Simulation Results

PLUS...SBA Includes Life Cycle Product Support...

Basing { Requirements, Acquisition, Logistics, Cost, Training Systems } Decisions on Simulation Results

Figure 1 Definition of SBA

Is this all there is to Simulation Based Acquisition? The answer is basically yes. Decisions to continue to the next milestone or event in the acquisition process must be substantiated with modeling or simulation results. Does this mean literally everything must be simulated – all functions, or all systems or all subsystems? No. It is impractical to assume all requirements features or all design details either could or should be modeled. Would adoption of SBA require that the only rationale for requirements, design, or acquisition decisions come entirely from simulation results? No. However, adoption of SBA would require that simulation results provide a basis for the majority of acquisition decisions. It would be appropriate to establish policy delineating this requirement. Should such policy require that the acquisition decisions always be in agreement with simulation results? No. However, deviating from simulation results to pursue a course either in conflict with simulation results or unsubstantiated with simulation results should require justification. Program/Product managers (PM's) are responsible for managing technical risk, schedule risk, and cost risk. They manage these risks by, 1) making educated decisions, 2) performing trade studies, 3) developing prototypes and also 4) by building and executing simulations. There are appropriate times and occasions for each approach to managing risk. The benefit to simulation is that once built, many excursions or versions of a prototype can be evaluated with minimal increase in cost for each version. A simulation, or software prototype, can be significantly more cost effective than a hardware prototype due to the ability to be modified at a significantly lower cost.

Conversely, PM's should never blindly follow simulation results. It is incumbent upon a PM to understand the utility of a simulation and the relative fidelity of the models involved. There is a process in which a PM develops an understanding of the models involved in a simulation and the relative realism of those models in providing information on an acquisition effort. This process culminates in the PM's decision to use the model and is known as the accreditation process. A PM should only accredit models for specific purposes and then only subsequent to verification and validation of the model. SBA becomes, for all practical purposes, the utilization of accredited, evaluated simulation results as a primary basis for sound acquisition life cycle decisions.

The commercial sector has made claims of significant savings through the use of modeling and simulation in a variety of product programs. One example is the Dodge Intrepid, depicted in **Figure 2** below. The fundamental question is whether DoD acquisition processes can benefit from similar based initiatives.

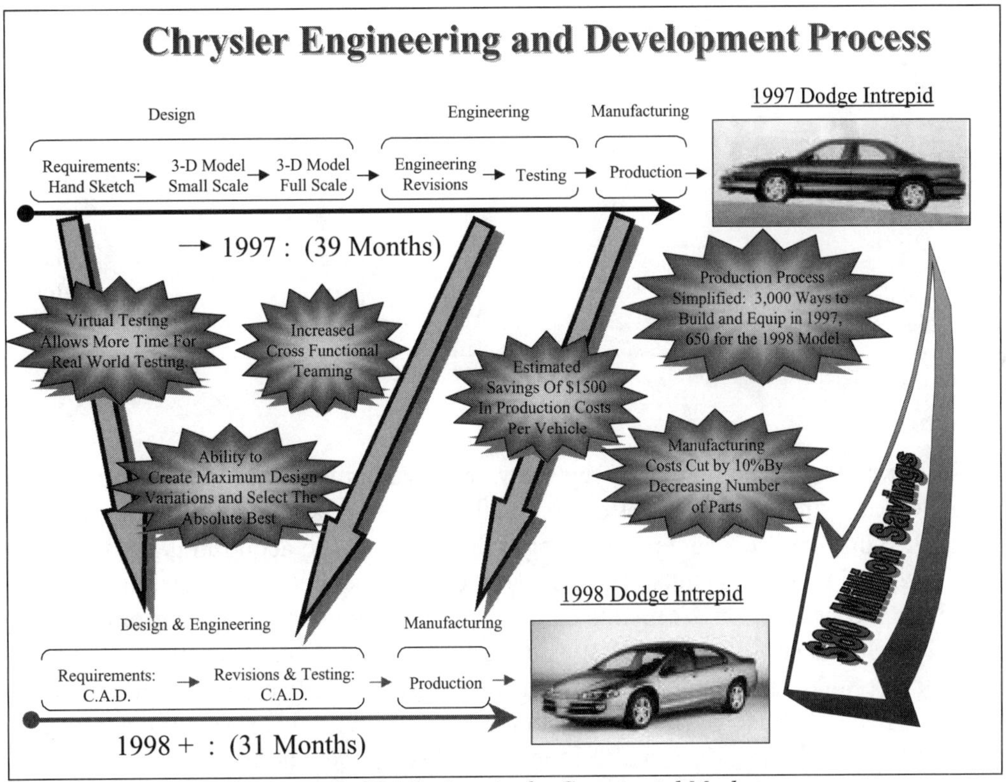

Figure 2 SBA Savings in the Commercial Market

SBA Analogy

Is there a recognizable process that can help us relate to SBA? Yes. Migration from the traditional acquisition process to the SBA model is very similar to the evolution from traditional software development to the current prototyping approach in use in today's software development efforts.

The DoD software development methodology has evolved in recent years from a serial process, e.g., requirements, design, code, and test to an evolutionary prototyping process involving the user, developer, and tester, etc. in an integrated team **(Figure 3)**.

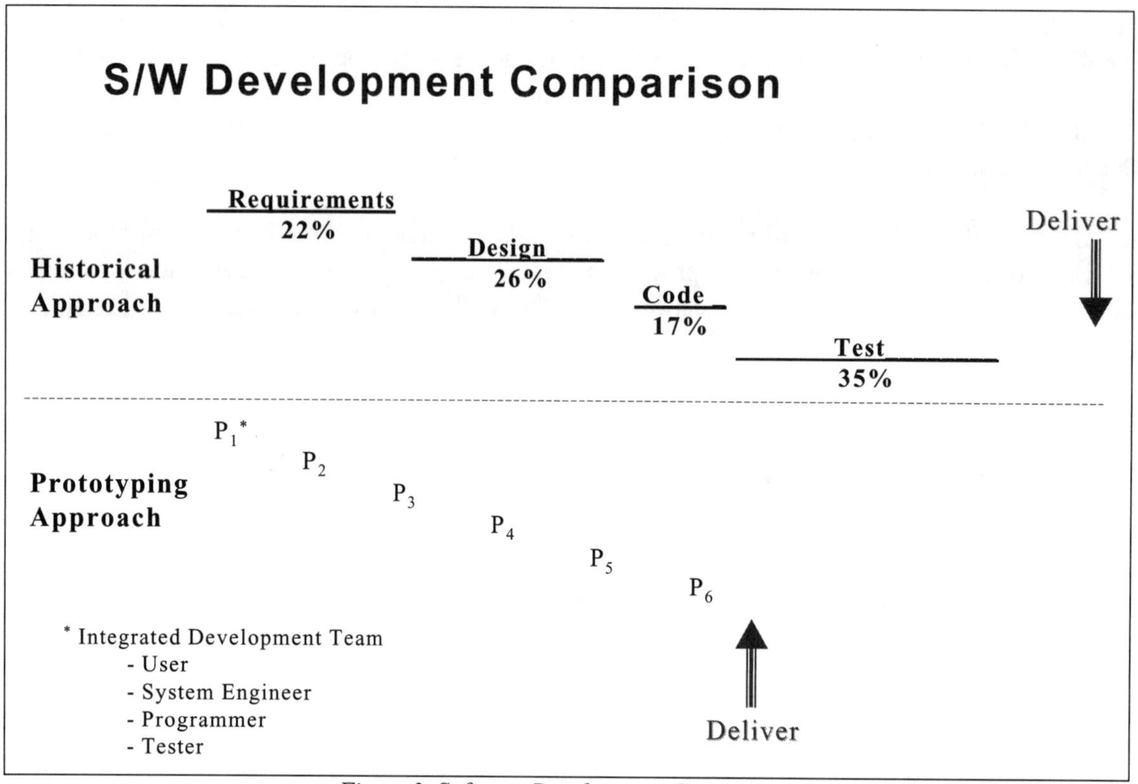

Figure 3 Software Development Comparison

The SBA paradigm is analogous to the software development approach of prototyping. After all, models and simulations are, or can be, software instantiations of the desired system being acquired. Similar to software prototyping – the system to be acquired is modeled and simulations executed to reveal results. Each version of the model/simulation is, in fact, a prototype of the end product. SBA results can be used to demonstrate 1) requirements compliance, 2) design compliance, 3) logistics compliance, and 4) cost compliance **(Figure 4)**. Once simulation results are evaluated, the models and/or simulations are modified in hopes of obtaining better results or discovering new limitations. Note with this strategy the conventional acquisition activities and milestones are no longer serial segmented activities, and the previously produced formal documentation is no longer necessary. In other words, PM's do not use a set of documents (end products of specific phases) as the basis for readiness to progress to the next phase. In fact, the bulk of interim products should be soft copy models and databases, which are at some point in the development process, captured and placed under configuration control.

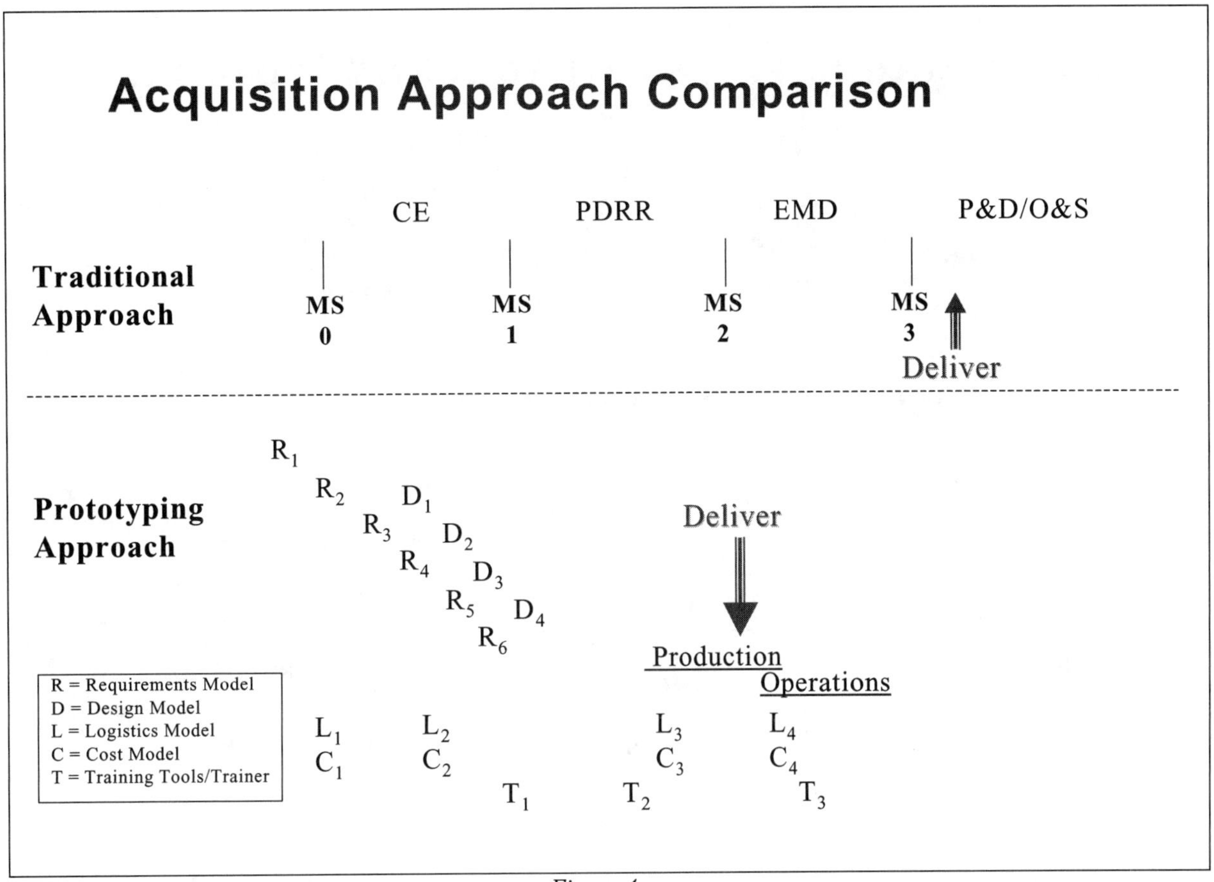

Figure 4

The Savings

The SBA approach encourages design efforts to begin prior to completion of requirements definition. It also results in a shorter development effort. SBA has some additional benefits such as the evolution of training devices prior to the actual product. What changes with SBA is the serial process of requirements, design, build, test, production, and O&M is now traded for an overlapping iterative process. The mounds of paper required in the serial process (documented agreed to requirements etc.) are not required in the SBA process. **Figure 5** provides the answer as to where savings are found. The savings come from the elimination of the tasks and work effort associated with a conventional acquisition effort. The basis for transition to the next phase is a validated, verified, accredited simulation under configuration control as opposed to a mound of paper products, which took months or years to build, and which typically have multiple interpretations.

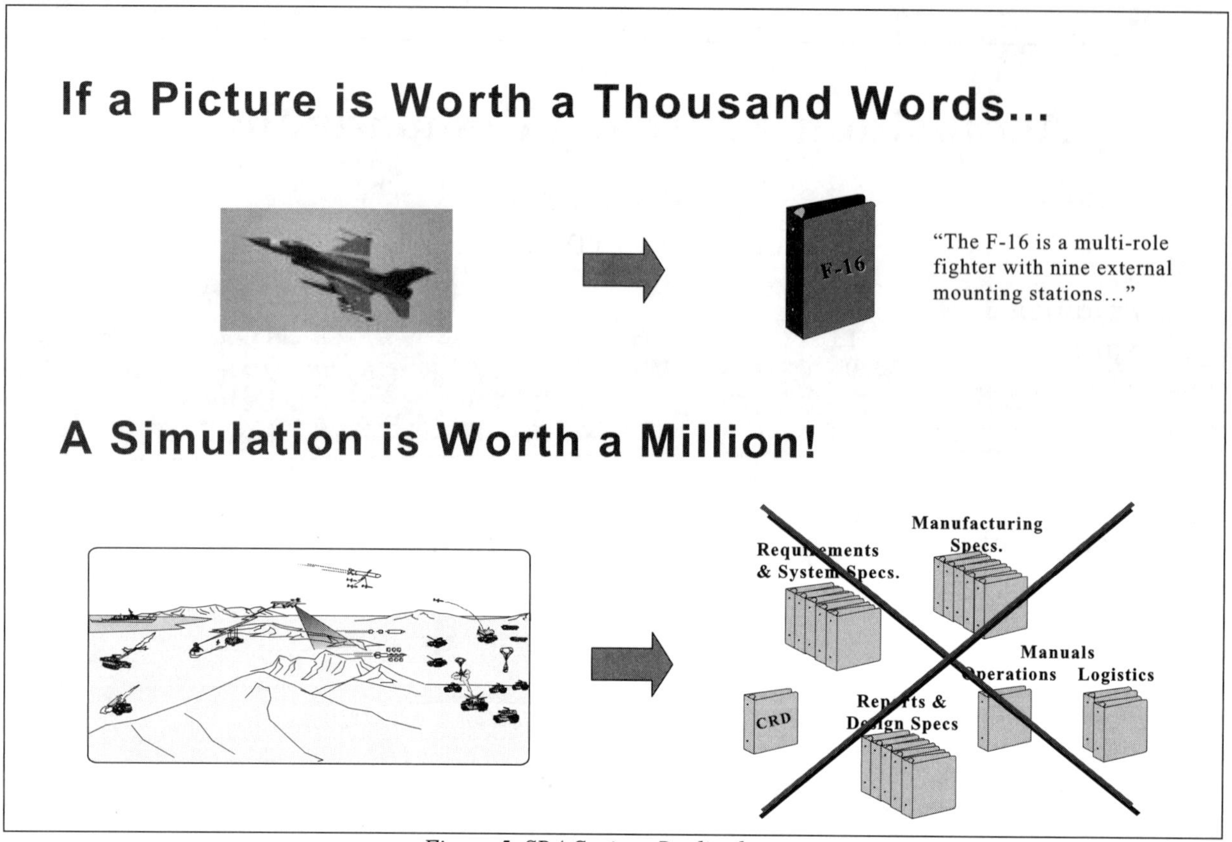

Figure 5 SBA Savings Realized

As was stated above, the requirements and design processes overlap. The SBA process requires an IPT team composed of the functional engineering disciplines. The role of the engineer may change with SBA. For example, the test engineer's role in SBA is not to always conduct tests, but to perform model verification, i.e. the test engineer verifies that the model performs in accordance with requirements. The test engineer also performs model validation ensuring model behavior that emulates real world behavior. Real world behavior may or may not be captured via live test. Decisions are made by the PM to build physical prototypes and conduct live tests in accordance with the program's risk mitigation plan. Both the types of things simulated, and the level of detail of items simulated are, established by the PM – as dictated by cost trades and risk avoidance criteria.

SBA Benefits and Recommended Approach

SBA not only offers a cost-effective approach for acquisition efforts; it is also integral to the process of achieving another major DoD objective – Joint Interoperability. What is SBA's tie to interoperability? What implementing mechanism exists to ensure SBA can be employed to address Joint Interoperability?

The decision in 1996 that all models and simulations would become HLA compliant by 1999 or at that point become unfunded, provides the mechanism to utilize SBA to ensure Joint Interoperability, and additionally provides a process for evaluation of systems under acquisition. HLA compliance mandates that Federations be established with specific run time infrastructures (RTIs). However, there are few ground rules for the establishment of HLA Federations. This raises the question of who decides in which Federations an object model should participate? In other words, who establishes the Federations? Who establishes the ground rules for the Federation? Specifically, who determines which Federation(s) should be used to evaluate virtual prototypes, e.g., who establishes the Federation(s) which will be used to validate or authenticate, or accredit the DD 21, Crusader, AAAV, and F-22 virtual prototypes? Who establishes the Federation(s) to be used as the evaluative environments for Requirements assessment, sensitivity analysis, and design assessment? The current process for Federation establishment is via voluntary participation. Is it appropriate to make billion dollar acquisition decisions on simulation results generated from voluntarily (uncontrolled) developed HLA Federations? The answer to these questions will be addressed in a subsequent paper.

DMSO, with the support of several service organizations, is facilitating the development of various federations. These Federations may or may not address issues of the acquisition community, but they are certainly providing an experience base for future efforts. In the mean time it is appropriate to begin a transition from the traditional acquisition approach to the future SBA approach. **Figure 6** depicts this transition process where as an interim step we begin to identify and replace those work efforts for which simulation is not just a substitution for the traditional task but an improvement over that task – more definitive results with less time and cost.

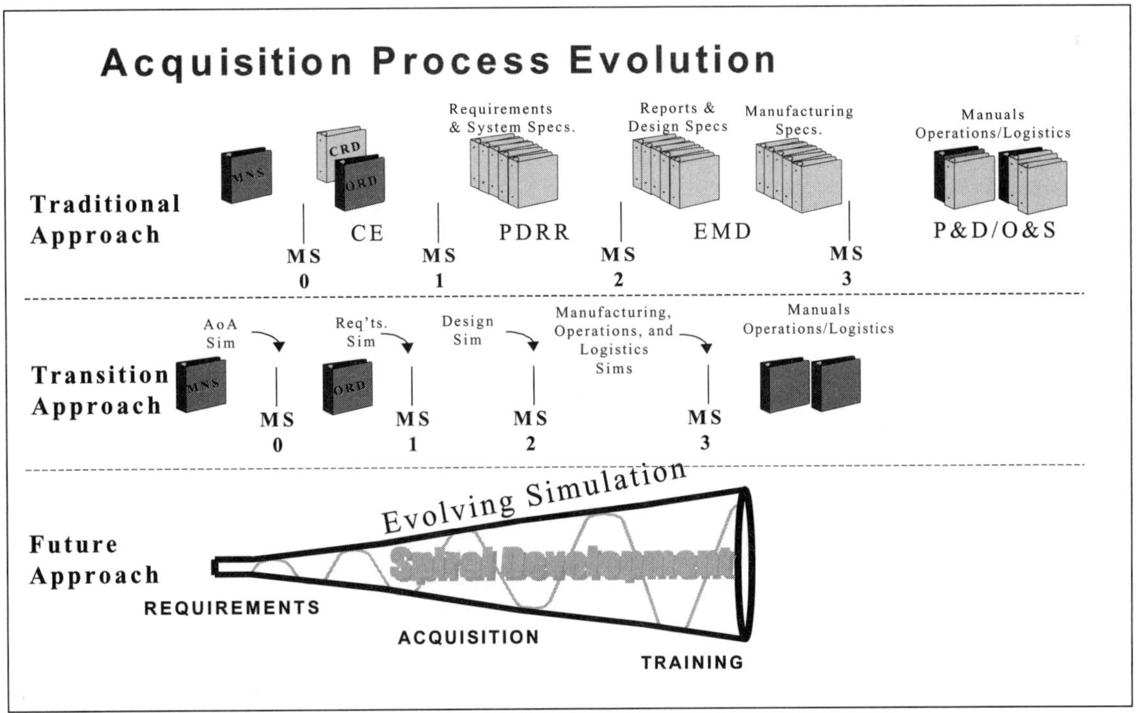

Figure 6 Acquisition Process Evolution

Controlling and Understanding Simulation Significance

AN INTEGRATED APPROACH TO EVALUATING SIMULATION CREDIBILITY

Paul R. Muessig, Ph.D.
Naval Air Warfare Center, Weapons Division (Code 418000D)
1 Administration Circle
China Lake, CA 93555
muessigpr@navair.navy.mil

Dennis R. Laack and John J. Wrobleski
Computer Sciences Corporation
711 Daily Drive
Camarillo, CA 93110
drlaack@csc.com, jwrobles@csc.com

KEY WORDS

Model credibility, model evaluation, verification, validation, accreditation

ABSTRACT

Discussions about simulation credibility tend to focus on the issue of "validation", i.e., how well simulation predictions match real world observations. While validation is certainly a most direct and intuitively accessible measure of simulation credibility, the validation process has numerous well-known limitations. Validation is by no means the only measure of simulation credibility, however. This paper identifies and categorizes a spectrum of information that can be used to evaluate simulation credibility more robustly than reliance on validation results alone. It also describes a method by which the nature, scope and depth of information necessary to establish simulation credibility for a particular application can be determined from an analysis of the risks associated with that application.

INTRODUCTION

What makes a simulation “credible”, and what activities contribute to a determination of simulation “credibility”? The modeling and simulation (M&S) community has tended to focus on “validation” activities (i.e., comparisons of simulation outputs with various types of “real world” data) as the primary hallmark of simulation credibility. This emphasis is hardly surprising; it is difficult to imagine a more direct and intuitively appealing measure of simulation credibility. Moreover, the validation process is amenable to scientific rigor; when performed without prejudice in accordance with the scientific method it yields an objective measure of confidence in simulation predictions.

The validation process is not without its drawbacks, however. For example, validation tests tend to be limited in scope relative to the range of predictive capabilities of most simulations, a fact that limits the range over which simulations can be declared "valid". Validation data also tend to be difficult and costly to obtain under conditions that match the predictive constraints of the simulation being evaluated. This means that "real world" data will always contain factors not accounted for by the simulation. Disentangling what is a simulation artifact from what is a data artifact can be a troublesome and speculative process that reduces the value of validation results as a measure of simulation credibility. Finally, some simulations simply cannot be validated in the commonly accepted sense of the term. (Campaign level military simulations come to mind.)

Are there any other measures of simulation credibility? What are those measures, and what kind of confidence do they contribute to simulation outputs? This paper explores one approach to answering these questions, and provides guidance on how to integrate these measures into a robust evaluation of simulation credibility for specific applications.

WHAT MAKES A SIMULATION "CREDIBLE"?

The authors have been involved with all facets of simulation credibility assessment for over ten years. Based on this experience, we have repeatedly seen five key factors that contribute to the evaluation of simulation credibility:

Capability

Simulations are abstractions of reality; they do not simulate all aspects of the "real world", nor do they need to. In order to be considered credible for use in a particular application, a simulation need only represent those aspects of the "real world" that are important to the intended use. These "capability requirements" are derived from an analysis of the application in which the simulation will be used. These requirements must then be compared to actual simulation capabilities to determine whether or not the simulation has all the features necessary to produce credible outputs for the intended use.

Analysis of the intended use of the simulation should lead to a complete description of simulation capability requirements, including:[1]

- A clear description of the intended use of the simulation;
- A listing of the physical entities that must be simulated, the functions they must perform within the simulation, and the degree of fidelity to which these functions must be simulated;
- A description of the environment in which the physical entities will interact, and the rules under which different entities will interact with each other and with the environment.

Descriptions of simulation capability should follow a similar outline:

- A clear description of the purpose for which the simulation was developed;
- A listing of the physical entities included in the simulation, the functions they perform within the simulation, and the degree of fidelity to which these functions are simulated;
- A description of the environment in which the physical entities interact within the simulation, and the rules under which different entities interact with each other and with the environment.
- A summary of assumptions and limitations in simulation design and implementation that impact the scope of potential applications in which the simulation can be credibly used.

Once we know the intended use of a simulation and the capability requirements that flow from it, we are in a position either to specify requirements for simulation development and design or to assess the capabilities of existing simulations against these requirements. The credibility of a simulation is a function of its ability to meet the most important elements of required capability as determined by the intended use. While intuitively obvious in principle, we have observed in practice that both simulation capability requirements and descriptive information about simulations are rarely documented in terms that allow for easy comparison and evaluation.

Software Accuracy

By software accuracy we mean the degree of error-freeness of the simulation software. One must be able to demonstrate on the basis of software test results not only that the software passed all the planned qualification tests, but that the nature scope and depth of those tests was matched to the complexity of the simulation and the risks associated with simulation use. The more complex a simulation is, the more difficult it is to specify and execute a robust software testing program that will unambiguously demonstrate the degree of software accuracy achieved. A poorly scoped software test program with ambiguous or undocumented acceptance criteria can easily result in a relatively meaningless formal "qualification" of the software. In addition, the higher the risks associated with use of the software, the more important it is that the testing be robust enough to demonstrate such accuracy.[2]

Another factor of equal importance to software test results is the quality of the resources applied to software testing. The more complex a simulation is, the more important it is to apply seasoned resources to the planning, management and execution of the test program. It is not enough to rely on "best commercial practices"; one must establish that these practices are actually being applied by qualified personnel. Such an assessment normally requires an evaluation of the software development process used, the quality and appropriateness of the resources applied, and the nature, scope and depth of the artifacts produced.

[1] Readers will recognize elements of sound conceptual model development practice in this description.

[2] One need only refer to the recent disasters with the Ariane rocket system and the Mars lander program to see the impact of even minor software errors on high-risk applications of software.

These factors related to the quality of software test results are frequently overlooked in assessments of simulation credibility, the common practice being instead to treat the results of software testing as a brute fact to be accepted at face value. But software accuracy is a function not only of V&V results; it is a function of how much confidence the simulation user can have in those results.

It is interesting to note that software accuracy will have an important effect on validation efforts as well. If comparisons between test data and simulation predictions do not yield acceptable results, where might the problem lie? The test data could be corrupted or inaccurate; the simulation may not account for some essential feature of the real world; or there may be an error in the software. The more one can demonstrate software accuracy, the easier it becomes to trace unacceptable validation results to data problems or inadequacies in simulation functionality.

Data Accuracy

By data accuracy we mean two things: (1) the appropriateness and error-freeness of all simulation data, and (2) the accuracy of any data transformations performed to convert data from one form to another.

We have found it convenient to divide simulation data into two categories: embedded data and run-time data. Embedded data are those that are typically "hard wired" into simulation software and do not often change. They consist of fixed parameters that characterize a specific physical system or system behavior, as well as physical constants. Examples of the former would be the specific operating frequency and power output of a radar; examples of the latter would be the speed of light and Boltzmann's constant. Run-time data are variable sets of data fed to in to the simulation at run time. They typically consist of data that affect scenario conditions within the simulation. Examples are terrain databases, environmental databases, aerodynamic tables, etc. We make this distinction between types of simulation data because we have found that the rigor with which data accuracy is pursued in simulation development depends in large part on which of these two categories the data fall in.

Embedded data accuracy is normally addressed during software development and testing. We have found, however, that specific documentation of data sources, histories and accuracy assessments tend to be neglected in typical software development documentation. Instead, heavy reliance on the (mostly anecdotal) "corporate memory" of the development effort substitutes for documented evidence of data accuracy. If the development effort is small and the development environment is stable[3] this may pose little risk to the credibility of simulation outputs. For complex simulations developed in more "dynamic" development environments, however, informal and subjective assessments of embedded data accuracy detract from confidence in simulation credibility and make it harder to diagnose errors in simulation output.

We have also observed that the assessment of run-time data accuracy tends to be handled rather passively: as long as the data are obtained from a recognized source, the assumption is made that the data are both appropriate and accurate, often without further inspection. For example, terrain databases obtained from the National Environmental Mapping Agency (NEMA) are automatically assumed to be appropriate, accurate and usable "as-is". Reliance on the credibility of "authoritative data sources" as a guarantee of data accuracy can easily obscure the need for more detailed inspection and assessment of run-time data, especially for high-risk simulation applications.

As noted above, data accuracy is also a function of the accuracy of data transformations within the simulation. It is clear that unit conversions, coordinate transformations, and data pre- or post-processing algorithms all need to be tested to ensure that good data going in do not become corrupted before being acted upon by simulation algorithms. The nature of these activities tends to be informal, however, and their scope and depth need to be assessed against the risk associated with the intended use of the simulation.

While simulation developers and users will agree with all or most of this in principle, we have found in practice that the degree of rigor with which data accuracy is assessed and documented needs to be evaluated in light of simulation complexity and the risks associated with the intended use of the simulation.

Results Accuracy

By results accuracy we mean the degree of correlation between simulation predictions and real world observations. This is where the term "validation" applies, but there are different types of validation, each of

[3] By "stable" we mean either a low turnover rate in the personnel applied to the development effort OR a well documented development audit trail OR both.

which carries implicit assumptions about how the "real world" is defined:

- Validation Against Other Simulations. Comparison of simulation outputs with the outputs of other "accepted" simulations is called "benchmarking". The value of the comparison depends on how credible the "accepted" simulation is. One must be able to document the basis upon which the "accepted" simulation is considered credible in order for the comparison to have any meaning. As with run-time data accuracy, we have observed a tendency to passive acceptance of benchmark simulation suitability.

- Validation Against Expert Opinion. Here, simulation design and outputs resulting from well-defined input conditions are reviewed and evaluated by Subject Matter Experts (SMEs). This process is usually called "face validation". The value of face validation as a contributor to simulation credibility depends upon the nature, scope and depth of SME experience relative to the type of simulation being evaluated. It also depends on the scope and depth of information presented to the SMEs. One must document not only the results of face validation, but also whether or not the right people with the right experience evaluated the right data for the right (i.e., the intended) application.

- Validation Against Test Data. This is what most people think of when the term "validation" is used. It is certainly the most direct and scientifically rigorous means of ascertaining simulation credibility. In addition to the drawbacks mentioned in the Introduction, however, the value of this method of assessing simulation credibility depends on the credibility of the data used to compare with simulation outputs. The validation process should include an explicit assessment of the validity of the validation data. This assessment should include an evaluation of the test instrumentation used, its inherent measurement accuracy, its calibration history, and any other characteristics that might impact the validity of the validation data set. It should also include a description of any data reduction, smoothing or filtering algorithms applied to the data, why these were chosen, and what impact they had on the validity of their representation of the "real world".

Regardless of the type of validation used, the value of the results is proportional to the quality and accuracy of the real world standard against which the simulation is compared. In nearly all cases, actual data from tests or real world observations is considered better than SME judgements, which are, in turn, considered better than benchmarking against another model that represents the real world.

Usability

Our definition of simulation usability is not framed in terms of "ease of simulation use", but rather in terms of "reduced probability of simulation misuse". This operational definition stems from the twin observations that simulations are credible only within a well-defined usage context, and only when they are properly used within that context. Any simulation attribute that reduces the probability of simulation misuse enhances its credibility within a given context.

By usability, then, we refer to that collection of simulation user support features that facilitate credible use of the simulation and reduce the probability that it will be employed inappropriately. Examples of such features are: training in proper simulation use and interpretation of outputs; accurate and comprehensive simulation documentation (User's Manuals, Analyst Manuals, Programmer's Manuals, etc.); on-call technical support for simulation users; simulation user groups that meet on a regular basis; the existence and implementation of a sound configuration management process for the simulation, both during and after development; the availability of trained simulation operators and analysts who can run the simulation and interpret its outputs correctly; and any other support feature that can help simulation users ensure credible use of the simulation.

Of these, configuration management is worthy of special mention as an indicator of simulation usability. Configuration management is the “glue” that ties the version of the simulation being used to all of the V&V results and to simulation documentation. Without a well-structured and effective configuration management program, the simulation user cannot be sure that any of the information used to demonstrate capability, accuracy, or usability really applies to the version of the simulation that is being used. Under these conditions, evaluating simulation credibility will be problematic.

Note that simulation usability is a necessary, but not sufficient, condition for simulation credibility. No simulation user support feature, no matter how well designed to minimize the probability of simulation misuse, will militate against improper use of the simulation. In all cases, the aphorism that "a fool with a tool is still a fool" applies.

HOW MUCH INFORMATION IS ENOUGH?

To determine how much information is enough to establish simulation credibility for a particular application one must know how much credibility the application requires. The level of simulation credibility required is, in turn, dependent on the level of risk associated with how the simulation will be used. The greater the potential adverse consequences of using inappropriate or erroneous simulation outputs, the greater will be the amount of simulation credibility required and the greater will be the amount of information necessary to demonstrate simulation credibility.

Consider the case of two potential applications of an air combat training simulation: training pilots to fly low (i.e., as a standard flight training tool) and training pilots to execute a critical mission to bomb a specific target (i.e., as a mission rehearsal tool). Assume that validation results demonstrate that the simulated radar depiction of a power plant was visually acceptable, but that the geographic location of the power plant was off by 1000 meters.

What is the impact of this result to each of the applications? In the case of the flight training application, the physical location of the power plant is immaterial, and the risk of "negative training" is low. The goal, after all, is to learn to fly low and not hit things, wherever they are. In the case of using the simulation as a mission rehearsal tool, however, the physical location of the power plant relative to surrounding features is critical. In the actual mission the pilot would be expecting the target to be in one location but it would actually be somewhere else, with potentially disastrous consequences for pilot safety and mission success.

Clearly these two cases involve very different levels of risk. Use of the simulation for mission rehearsal requires a greater level of demonstrated simulation credibility than using the simulation for low-level flight training. This means that more information will need to be collected and evaluated to establish simulation credibility for the mission rehearsal application.

Risk is a concept easily understood but difficult to quantify in objective terms. Even so, several texts and documents have attempted to introduce some degree of uniformity in quantifying risk.[4] One very common approach is to consider risk as the product of two components: the impact (or consequences) of an event and the probability or frequency of the event's occurrence. In most cases the factors in this "equation" cannot be quantified absolutely, but can be subjectively evaluated using principles similar to those described in MIL-STD-882C, "System Safety Program Requirements". The general process for determining the overall level of risk first requires quantification of the impact severity and probability for each separately identified risk factor.[5] Using these two elements an overall level of risk is assigned. This process is repeated for each particular risk factor, and the highest level of risk associated with the application is selected as the level that drives the credibility requirement. The criteria used in each step of the process are all subjective, but they are explicitly stated, subject to expert review and consensus, and can be tailored to the specifics of individual problems. The details of the process for determining simulation credibility requirements have been described by Muessig et al.[6]

Once the risks that could accrue from erroneous simulation outputs have been evaluated the amount and type of information needed to make an adequate assessment of simulation credibility can be determined. This is done using a Simulation Credibility Assessment Guide that has been developed by the authors.

SIMULATION CREDIBILITY ASSESSMENT GUIDE

The guide is divided into six major sections (see Tables I through VI). The first section addresses the determination of simulation credibility requirements; the following sections address the various aspects of simulation credibility discussed above. The first column of Tables I through VI identifies the major questions associated with each of the credibility components. The next column of each table identifies the type(s) of information used to answer each of the questions. In many cases, there are several types of information that apply to a single question. The third column identifies specific sources for each information

---

4 See, for example, Steele, Lowell W. 1989. *Managing Technology, The Strategic View*. McGraw-Hill, pg 118.

5 A risk factor is a specific type of outcome or result. For example, one risk factor might be injury or death of personnel; another might be damage to equipment; a third might be damage to a particular part of the environment.

6 Muessig, P. R., Laack, D. R. and Wrobleski, J. J. "Optimizing the Selection of VV&A Activities A Risk/Benefit Approach." In *Proceedings of the 1997 Summer Computer Simulation Conference*. Arlington VA. pp 855-860.

type. These three columns basically define the information space that establishes simulation credibility.

The three columns on the far right side of each table provide guidance as to which information source or sources are needed to mitigate particular levels of risk. Note that greater levels of application risk require more detailed information to establish simulation credibility. Note also that the assignment of specific information requirements to specific levels of risk is subjective, and should be tailored to meet the requirements of individual applications. The assignments listed here are reasonable based on the authors' experience. In some cases, the table provides some flexibility to allow the user to select from two or three alternative information sources to establish the required level of credibility.

In practice, the process outlined above, and the credibility assessment tables that result, would work as follows. To make a robust assessment of simulation credibility one needs to know how much credibility the intended use of the simulation requires in the capability, accuracy and usability dimensions, and what information about a simulation's capability, accuracy, and usability characteristics will establish this level of credibility. The risk analysis approach described above would be used to determine how much and what type of information would be required to establish the required level of simulation credibility. These information requirements would then be compared with available information about the simulation, and a list of credibility shortfalls would be compiled. Each element of this list would then be evaluated for its impact on application risk. Unmet requirements for simulation credibility that have acceptable (i.e., low risk) work-arounds would be removed from the list. Unmet requirements for simulation credibility that have no acceptable work-arounds would generate a requirement for more detailed information in the appropriate category.

It should be noted that the Tables provided are only examples of the output of the process described above. Simulation users must tailor the guidance provided here to the particular circumstances of their specific applications. The guidance provided here establishes a clear set of criteria for developing a simulation credibility assessment plan. It also provides a clear basis for explaining the logic that underlies such a plan, thereby permitting an independent assessment of its validity.

SUMMARY

The benefit of categorizing the key elements of simulation credibility as we have is that it provides a convenient way to associate standard V&V activities with the types of credibility they provide. Our categories of simulation credibility also serve to point out areas where standard V&V activities fall short of fully addressing all aspects of simulation credibility, and they suggest other types of information that might be equally important. The result is a more robust set of metrics by which simulation credibility can be evaluated. The risk techniques outlined here then allow simulation users to determine how much and what specific types of information are needed to establish sufficient credibility for their intended application. This information can form a convenient basis both for V&V and simulation credibility assessment planning.

ABOUT THE AUTHORS

Paul R. Muessig

Dr. Muessig is currently Director of the Joint Accreditation Support Activity (JASA) at the Naval Air Warfare Center, Weapons Division, China Lake, CA. JASA's goal is to support weapons system acquisition and testing programs with credible integration of M&S into program objectives. Dr. Muessig has extensive experience in VV&A methodology development, planning and execution in support of numerous M&S applications in acquisition and testing. He has also worked as a defense analyst at the Center for Naval Analyses in Washington, D.C., contributing to survivability analyses for advanced technology aircraft, and leading model validation efforts for the Advanced Low Altitude Radar Model (ALARM). Dr. Muessig holds a B.S. in Chemistry from St. Joseph's University and a doctorate in Physical Chemistry from Brown University.

Dennis R. Laack and John J. Wrobleski

Messrs. Laack and Wrobleski are retired combat Naval Aviators with extensive experience in directing and managing research, development, acquisition, and testing of naval aircraft, weapons and related systems. For the five years they have provided management and technical assistance to the Joint Accreditation Support Activity (JASA), including original contributions in the areas of accreditation requirements determination, M&S acceptance criteria development, and V&V requirements derivation. Mr. Laack holds a B.E.E. from Marquette University, an M.S. in Systems Acquisition Management, and both an M.S. and an Ae.E. in Aeronautical Engineering from the Naval Postgraduate School. Mr. Wrobleski holds a Bachelor of Aerospace Engineering and Mechanics from the University of Minnesota, and both an M.S. and Ae.E. in Aeronautical Engineering from the Naval Postgraduate School. Both are employed by Computer Sciences Corporation in Camarillo, California.

Table I: M&S Credibility Requirements Matrix

M&S Credibility Requirements Issue	Items Required	Item Description	Typical Sources	Needed When Risk is...		
				Low	Moderate	High
What do you need the simulation to do?	Application Description and M&S Requirements	The Application Description defines the overall problem to be solved, the outputs needed from the simulation, and how these outputs will be used in the solution. Specifically describes what the model will be used for and how it will be used in the context of the problem. M&S Requirements must include functional, fidelity and operating requirements. Also specifies required input data sets (e.g., embedded system parameters and constants, look-up tables, runtime inputs, etc.) and input data quality (accuracy) requirements.	Application Description must be developed for each specific application based on what the simulation will be used for. If the simulation is being developed for the specific application, the Application Description and some of the M&S Requirements can sometimes be derived (or inferred) from top level S/W Design documentation. Some programs actually develop an "intended use statement" that identifies some of the items mentioned, but it is rarely comprehensive enough by itself to meet the requirements of this information element. Some of the M&S Requirements are unique to each application and must be generated by the analysts who will be using the M&S either via documented study requirements or interviews.	Verbal Description is Sufficient	Req'd	Req'd
How much confidence do you need in simulation outputs?	Risk Analysis Results	Identifies type of risks arising from potential errors in simulation outputs, assesses the probability of the risk actually occurring, and determines the impact of the risk. Result is an assessment of the level of risk associated with the application, which sets the scope and depth of V&V (and related) activities required to mitigate this level of risk.	Must be developed for each specific application. It is essential to obtain consensus on risk elements, impacts, probabilities and levels among technical, operational, and management personnel. These people must be intimately familiar with the decisions to be made based on simulation outputs, as well as the system(s) being simulated and their use. The risk analysis should be based on the Application Description.	Informal	Formal with Documented Results	Formal with Documented Results

Table II: M&S Capability Requirements Matrix

M&S Capability Issue	Items Required	Item Description	Typical Sources	Needed When Risk is...		
				Low	Moderate	High
Does the simulation do what you need it to do?	Functional Breakdown and Description of Model	Describes what the model actually does. Must describe: M&S functions and relationships between functions; the level of fidelity at which each function is modeled; function level I/O and I/O relationships between functions; the hardware, software, and training needed to operate the model properly and interpret the outputs correctly.	User Documentation (Users' Manual, Programmers' Manual, Analysts' Manual)	Any One	Req'd	Req'd
			Software Design Documentation, possibly including Data Flow Diagrams		Any One	Either One
			Conceptual Model documentation			
	List of Limitations due to Assumptions and Errors	Describes model assumptions and known errors, and assesses their impact on model use. The resulting limitations should be correlated with each of the functions in the Functional Breakdown, but may also be useful at the overall simulation level. List should ID any and all assumptions and/or errors of each M&S function (or of the model as a whole) that are implicit or explicit in the model's design and/or coding, as well as the implications of these limitations on appropriate or acceptable uses of the simulation.	Software Design Documentation, User Documentation are the most typical sources for inherent assumptions and limitations arising from the algorithms used. Configuration Management Databases are useful sources for known errors. Some assumptions and limitations may also be found in Verification or Validation Reports but may not be explicitly stated as an assumption, limitation, or error.	Desirable		Req'd

Table III: M&S Usability Requirements Matrix

M&S Usability Issue	Items Required	Item Description	Typical Sources	Needed When Risk is...		
				Low	Moderate	High
Do you have confidence that the simulation is being run properly?	Demonstration of the Computer Hardware and operating system suitability	Test results that show that the hardware and operating systems used to host the model or simulation (if different than that used to develop the M&S) will allow it to run correctly and produce consistent results across platforms.	Information on M&S portability across platforms is usually found in the user documentation associated with the simulation. If this information is not documented, test results will be needed to demonstrate portability.	Req'd	Req'd	Req'd
	Operator Qualifications	Information to demonstrate that the operators running the simulation have the expertise and knowledge to properly set up the simulation, execute it, and operate all associated tools and utilities. Typical information includes experience with the specific model being used, formal training on the model, and experience with the hardware, software, and interface devices being used.	This information is usually gathered from biographies or interviews with the operators.	Req'd	Req'd	Req'd
Can you convince others of your interpretation of simulation outputs?	Analyst Qualifications	Information to demonstrate that the analysts using the simulation have the expertise and knowledge to properly generate the input data and interpret the outputs. Typical information includes experience with the specific model being used, formal training on the model, experience in performing similar analyses and experience or training in M&S based analysis techniques.	This information is usually gathered from biographies or interviews with the analysts. It may also be found in prior accreditation assessment reports.	Req'd	Req'd	Req'd
	Demonstration of Pre- and Post- processor acceptability	Information that shows that any auxiliary tools and utilities used to format or load input data, or to convert, record, and visualize model outputs are suitable for the intended purpose(s). The type of information usually presented includes descriptive documentation of the tools and utilities being used for those purposes.	User documentation associated with the simulation may list tools and utilities that are compatible with it. If this information is lacking, user documentation for the tools and utilities may contain information that will aid the determination of tool compatibility with the simulation.			Req'd

Table IV: M&S Software Accuracy Requirements Matrix

M&S S/W Accuracy Issue	Items Required	Item Description	Typical Sources	Needed When Risk Is...		
				Low	Moderate	High
How much confidence do you have in the accuracy of the software?	S/W Development Process Description	The "process description" should include a description of the development paradigm and how it is being implemented (including the use of CASE tools); a logical process for defining, tracing, and testing requirements throughout development; Configuration Management during the development process, and adequate provision for documentation of all of these activities.	Look for a S/W Development Plan (SDP) or a Configuration Management Plan that outlines the development process used. If the development is underway, these plans should describe the process currently being used.	Either One	Req'd	Req'd
	S/W Development Resources Description	The resource description should include a description of the H/W environment and the S/W engineering tools that will be/were used; the qualifications of the personnel who will/did code the S/W and perform CM functions, and who will be/was responsible for production of key documentation and testing. A history of similar simulation development experience should also be included.	Check the SDP or other management plans that might contain such information. If this information isn't in existing documentation, discussion with the software developers and managers will be necessary to obtain as much of this information as possible, even if anecdotal. Evidence of simulation development qualifications may be available in SEI Capability Maturity Model evaluation reports.		Any Two	Req'd
	S/W Development Artifacts	"Artifacts" refers to the evidence (usually documentary in nature) that S/W development is actually being implemented in accordance with the guidelines and specifications called out in the SDP (or its equivalent). Documentary artifacts must also be in compliance with known (or acceptable) standards and practices for format, content, currency and applicability to the current version of the S/W.	Look for standard documentation that reflects the current state of the S/W and that conforms to known standards for information content. The most important examples are Configuration Management Histories and Logs.			Any Two
			Model Documentation (User Manual, Programmers' Manual, etc.)			
			S/W Design documentation (particularly a documented set of requirements and a conceptual model)			
	S/W Development V&V Results	V&V results include all evidence that the code has been developed according to the design and is free of critical errors. The types of results will include reports from design reviews, code walk-throughs, regression testing on model changes, S/W testing, and supplemental V&V efforts of previous M&S users.	Requirements Trace Reports	Either One	Either One	Either One
			Reports of Design Reviews, Peer Reviews, and/or Logical Reviews			
			Code Walk-Through reports	Any One	Any Two	Any Three
			S/W Problem Change Request Logs			
			Module S/W Test Reports			
			Subsystem S/W Test Reports			
			System S/W Test Reports			
	S/W Management Process Description	The "process description" should include a description of the post development management of the software. This should include processes for documenting, implementing, tracking and testing M&S changes resulting from either requirements changes or software errors. Processes should also exist for keeping all software documentation current with the software.	Check the S/W Management Plan, Configuration Management Plan, V&V Plan, etc. to determine if they address M&S life cycle activities. If these documents only address development activities, look for other documentation that describes the life-cycle management activities.	Any Two	Required	Required
	S/W Management Resources Description	The resource description should summarize the nature and extent of resources currently being applied to simulation management and support. The information should indicate whether sufficient funding and experienced personnel are being applied to ongoing documentation support, configuration management support, regression testing, user group support, training, technical support, etc.	Check any management plans that might contain such information. If this information is not in existing documentation, discussion with the model managers and/or software developers will be necessary to obtain as much of this information as possible, even if anecdotal.		Desired	Required
	S/W Management Artifacts	"Artifacts" refers to the evidence (usually documentary in nature) that S/W maintenance is actually being conducted in accordance with the guidelines and specifications called out in the SMP (or its equivalent).	Configuration Management Database status reports, system Change Requests (SCRs) and/or System Trouble Reports (STRs)		Any One	Any Two
			Up-to-date Model Documentation (User Manual, Programmers' Manual, etc.)			
			CCB and User Group meeting minutes			
			Updated S/W Design documentation			
	Post-Development S/W V&V Results		S/W Problem Change Request (SPCR) Logs that correlate V&V results with specific versions of the S/W		Either one Coupled with S/W Mgmt Items above	Either one Coupled with S/W Mgmt Items above
			Alpha- or Beta- test reports for both new requirements testing and regression testing			
			Specific verification reports for the M&S version being used	Note 1	Note 1	Note 1
			History of successful usage in similar applications	Note 2		
	Note 1:	If the scope and depth of the specific verification results equates to the scope and depth of development V&V required for a particular level of risk (Item 4D), this element can be substituted for all the above items dealing with the quality of the software (all				
	Note 2:	This item alone can be used as evidence of sufficient quality for low risk applications (it can replace all items above for Issue 4)				

M&S Data Accuracy Issues	Items Required	Item Description	Typical Sources	Needed When Risk Is...		
				Low	Moderate	High
How much confidence do you have in the quality and suitability of input data obtained from outside sources?	Data Quality Profile	A body of metadata that describes the database, its source, specifications, intended usage, history, and how it was collected. Metadata elements should exist at the database, data element, and data value levels.	Metadata elements should be available from the data producer or may exist in the same archives that contain the database itself. A list of essential metadata elements considered necessary for different risk levels is contained in Sheet 2 of this Excel Workbook.	Either one. Depth of Information indicated in Data Accuracy Sheet 2	Either one. Depth of Information indicated in Data Accuracy Sheet 2	Either one. Depth of Information indicated in Data Accuracy Sheet 2
	Independent Assessment of Data Quality	An independent assessment is prepared by the data user when the Data Quality Profile is inadequate, incomplete, or does not exist. This assessment addresses the key metadata elements listed in the Data Quality Profile.	Information that indicates the quality of test data can generally be found in documents such as test plans, laboratory procedures, calibration records, test reports, etc. Information that indicates the quality of data collected through surveys or monitoring operations can generally be found in data collection plans, reports, and raw notes.			
	Data Manipulation Verification	This item refers to the verification of any data manipulation done by the user. "Data manipulation" includes operations such as: editing, subset selection, merging, aggregation, transformation, estimation, interpolation, etc. Verification includes any activities that are done to ensure that the data manipulation steps are correct and do not introduce unknown errors.	Verification of data manipulation procedures may be documented in M&S verification reports (when done in conjunction with M&S development). Other data manipulation should be reviewed and verified as part of the M&S accreditation process and documented in the accreditation report. This documentation should describe the verification techniques that were used.	Req'd at cursory level	Req'd	Req'd
How much confidence do you have in the quality and suitability of self-generated input data ?	Description of Data Quality Assurance Process for self-generated data	An assessment by the data user of the process, equipment, tools, instrumentation, etc. used in generating the data. This assessment should generate information similar to that included in the critical metadata elements of the Data Quality Profile.	Information that indicates the quality of test data can generally be found in documents such as test plans, laboratory procedures, calibration records, test reports, etc. Information that indicates the quality of data collected through surveys or monitoring operations can generally be found in data collection plans, reports, and raw notes.	Req'd. Depth of Information indicated in sheet 2	Req'd. Depth of Information indicated in sheet 2	Req'd. Depth of Information indicated in sheet 2
	Description of Data Quality Assurance Resources for self-generated data	This item refers to the verification of any data manipulation done by the user. "Data manipulation" includes operations such as: editing, subset selection, merging, aggregation, transformation, estimation, interpolation, etc. Verification includes any activities that are done to ensure that the data manipulation steps are correct and do not introduce unknown errors.	Verification of data manipulation procedures may be documented in M&S verification reports (when done in conjunction with M&S development). Other data manipulation should be reviewed and verified as part of the M&S accreditation process and documented in the accreditation report. This documentation should describe the verification techniques that were used.	Req'd at cursory level	Req'd	Req'd

Table VI: M&S Output Accuracy Requirements Matrix

M&S Output Accuracy Issues	Items Required	Item Description	Typical Sources	Needed When Risk Is...		
				Low	Moderate	High
How much confidence do you have in the simulation outputs?	Benchmarking Results	Documents the results of comparisons between simulation (or simulation component) outputs and those of a "standard" or widely accepted simulation. Benchmark simulations are generally of greater fidelity than the simulation (or component) under review and are characterized by some "stamp of approval" from a recognized authority. Benchmark results should include the name and source of the standard simulation; why it is (or should be) considered a "reference" simulation, which parameters between simulations (or components) were compared (and why), what the results of the comparison were, and what these results imply about the credibility of the outputs from the simulation under review.	Benchmarking results are usually documented in either a validation report, a briefing that describes the results of the comparison, or an Accreditation Support Package for certain models. These reports would generally be prepared by previous users. They might also be available through the model manager or individual Service M&S databases. If these results are for a previous model version, they must be accompanied by model management activities that are appropriate to your application risk (as outlined in items 4E, 4F, and 4G).			
	Face Validation Results	Describes the results of subject matter expert opinions about simulation realism and accuracy. This should be based on a structured review of simulation (or component) outputs, sensitivities, and/or design. When face validation is a review of the simulation design, the documentation should state whether the representations are realistic and whether any assumptions that underly the design are acceptable from the perspective of the intended use. Documentation should describe which aspects of the simulation were reviewed (and why), who participated in the review, why one should trust their opinions (e.g., biographical information), what the results of the review were, and what these results imply about the credibility of the simulation.	Face validation results are typically documented in a Face Validation report (or an Accreditation Support Package for certain models) or a previous Accreditation Assessment Report (if the face validation was done as part of an accreditation assessment). If the review was a validation of the design, the results may be reported in a design review report (either a formal report or an annotated briefing). These reports would generally be prepared by previous users. They might also be available through the model manager or individual Service M&S databases. If these results are for a previous model version, they must be accompanied by model management activities that are appropriate to your application risk (as outlined in items 4E, 4F, and 4G).	Any One		Either both of these
	"Results" Validation Documentation	Describes the results of comparisons between simulation (or component) outputs and data collected from tests or operation of the real system(s) or process(es) being simulated. The documentation should include a description of the source data used in the comparison, how where and how it was obtained, and why it should be considered representative of the real world. Issues relating to data quality (e.g. instrumentation accuracy, calibration, test scenario realism, etc.) should be addressed in the validation report. The correlation between model outputs and real world data should be stated in quantitative terms rather than merely stating that the correlation was "good". Any anomalies and their impact on model usage should be explained.	"Results" validation is typically documented in a Validation Report (or an Accreditation Support Package for certain models). In some cases, results validation might be documented with an annotated briefing. These reports would generally be prepared by the simulation developer or previous users. They might also be available through the model manager or individual Service M&S databases. If these results are for a previous model version, they must be accompanied by model management activities that are appropriate to your application risk (as outlined in items 4E, 4F, and 4G).		Either One	Or this item is required

SOFTWARE ENGINEERING AND SIMULATION CREDIBILITY

Ronald L. Ketcham and Paul R. Muessig
Naval Air Warfare Center, Weapons Division (Code 418000D)
1 Administration Circle
China Lake, CA 93555-6100
Ketchamrl@navair.navy.mil, muessigpr@navair.navy.mil

KEY WORDS

Software Engineering, Software Quality Assurance, Configuration Management, Requirements Management

ABSTRACT

Most people think of "validation" as the hallmark of simulation credibility. But some simulations, by their very nature (e.g., mission level models, highly complex physics-based simulations, etc.) are notoriously difficult to validate. There are also situations in which the process of validation, even if feasible, cannot keep pace with the dynamic nature of simulation evolution, or where the cost of validation data is prohibitively high. Are there any other "hallmarks" of simulation credibility that can help us in cases like these? This paper demonstrates that significant insights into simulation credibility can be obtained via detailed examination of the software engineering processes and practices by which the simulation was developed and is maintained. The nature and value of good software engineering processes is often unknown, or under-appreciated, by the end-users of simulation results and therefore is often overlooked as a barometer of simulation credibility.

INTRODUCTION

To explore this topic we will use DoD mission-level models as a starting point. These models have unique characteristics when compared to other model categories on the DoD M&S model pyramid[1] which make them exemplars of simulations that have rapidly changing requirements and that are difficult to validate. Of all the model categories included, mission-level models have the widest range of applications, a fact that has resulted in these simulations having large and diverse user bases. The DoD has three mission-level models in wide use today: Suppressor, JIMM (Joint Interim Mission Model, formerly known as SWEG), and EADSIM. These models are used in a wide variety of applications by the acquisition and analysis communities. They are used to evaluate the potential effectiveness of new systems and platforms, different tactical employments, and even various command and control approaches. Recently, these models have also seen growth in the user base among the testing and training communities. This great diversity of users and applications means that these mission-level models are constantly called upon to meet new requirements at an ever-increasing rate. Suppressor and JIMM typically have over 100 new requirements specified over a two-year period. The dynamic nature of these models has emphasized the value of good model management and software development processes.

The second characteristic mentioned above is the difficulty of validating these models. First, they can never be validated in their entirety because the data will never exist. Individual functions within the simulation may be validated, but validation of their integration would require data from actual large-scale combat situations. Such data are very difficult to come by, and are rarely collected in actual combat given the obvious press of higher priorities. Also, there are human factors incorporated in mission-level models that pose serious validation problems. For example, we cannot measure human reaction times in the fog of war on a test range; the environment is simply too artificial. Moreover, the value of any structured validation data that might be collected is diminished in a test situation due to human safety considerations. This limits us to validation of mission model functional components. For example, we can get data to validate sensor detection ranges or examine missile kinematics. Finally, validation efforts have a limited shelf life for mission-level models. As these highly dynamic models change over time, validation results become obsolete. Due to these limitations, it was not surprising to us

[1] See, for example, the Air Force Standard Analysis Toolkit web site: http://www.oas.kirtland.af.mil/restrict/toolkit/index.html

to find in a recent review that both Suppressor and JIMM lack any current validation results in support of their credibility, despite their wide employment.[2]

Are there any other indicators of simulation credibility that can be employed when little, or no, validation data exist, or when the requirements generation environment is very dynamic? We propose that an evaluation of the software engineering processes employed to develop and maintain the simulation can provide insight into the credibility of the simulation. We will use the SEI Capability Maturity Model to examine this issue.

CAPABILITY MATURITY MODEL

In the early 1990's, the Software Engineering Institute (SEI) at Carnegie-Mellon University developed the Capability Maturity Model (CMM). The primary purpose of the tool was to provide the Department of Defense (DoD) assistance in assessing the ability of software development organizations to deliver quality software products within cost and schedule constraints. The CMM is intended to provide the software development customer a means to evaluate the maturity of candidate software developers and their ability to perform as specified (Paulk *et al.* 1995). The CMM provides a framework for identifying the maturity of the organization from level 1 (the most immature) to level 5 (the most mature). The Level 1 organization has no documented software development processes and executes a software development project primarily by writing code and putting out fires. The level 5 organization has well defined and documented processes addressing key software development activities, as well as a trained and disciplined development team that implements those processes. The level 5 organization even has established processes for identifying and fixing weaknesses within its development processes. Table 1 depicts the five levels of maturity for a software development organization. Each level, except Level 1, has unique Key Process Areas (KPAs) which characterize the activity focus for that level. To move from one level to another, a software development organization must demonstrate competence in all of the KPAs both at and below its level of maturity.

While the more mature software development organization may well develop quality software on time and within budget, but will it also develop a more credible simulation? Figure 1 provides some data that support this hypothesis.[3] It shows that defects per KSLOC (thousand lines of source code) decreases monotonically as CMM maturity level increases. A Level 1 organization averages 9 defects per KSLOC, while a Level 5 organization averages only 0.1 defects per KSLOC. The data also show that it takes a Level 5 organization about 1/4th the time as a Level 1 organization to produce software that has only 1/9th the number of errors in it. Put another way, a Level 1 organization spends four times as much time producing nine times as many errors as a Level 1 organization. This difference can be expected to have a profound impact on simulation credibility. The chart also shows that over 3/4ths of the software organizations surveyed were at or below CMM Level 2.

Level	CHARACTERISTICS	Key Process Areas
5 Optimizing	Continuous process capability improvement	Process change management Technology change management Defect Prevention
4 Managed	Quantitative measurement of process and qualitative management of product	Software Quality Management Quantitative Process Management
3 Defined	Software Processes Defined and Institutionalized	Peer Reviews Inter-group Coordination Software Product Engineer Integrated Software Management Training Program Organization Process Definition Organization Process Focus
2 Repeatable	Management Controls in place; stable planning and product baselines	Software Configuration Management Software Quality Assurance Requirements Management Software Project Tracking and Oversight Software Project Planning Software Subcontract Management
1 Initial	Ad-hoc, Putting out Fires	None

Table I: Capability Maturity Model Levels and KPAs

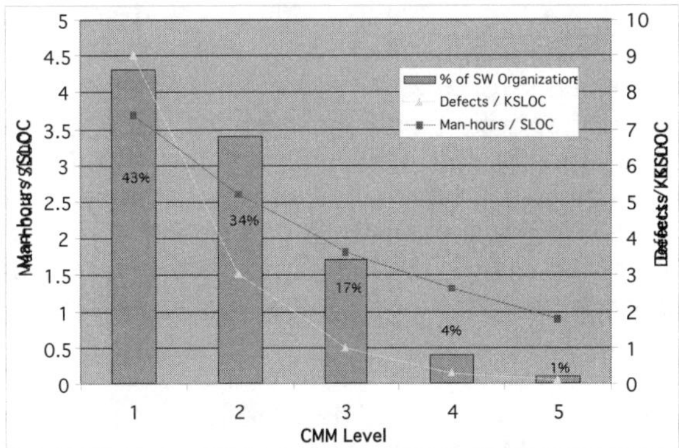

Figure 1: Software Coding Error Rates and Man-Hours per SLOC as a function of CMM Level

[2] See, for example, Accreditation Support Package, Level I for JIMM and Suppressor, available on the JASA web site (http:\\www.nawcwpns.navy.mil\~jasa).

[3] Briefing by RAdm. Joseph Dyer to the NAVAIR Senior Steering Group, 30 August 1999, "Software Implementation Team Status Report".

There are many ways that the software engineering processes used in the development and maintenance of a simulation can contribute to (or detract from) simulation credibility. One way is reflected in the ability of the processes used to capture and document the expertise of recognized Subject Matter Experts (SMEs) in each area of required simulation functionality, and to translate this expertise into documented simulation requirements. The process must be robust enough to accurately translate those requirements into simulation design, implement the design in software, and verify its correct implementation. Simulation credibility is directly related to the degree to which these tasks have been accomplished accurately. The CMM captures this sequence in the Key Process Areas of Requirements Management, Peer Reviews, Configuration Management, and Software Quality Assurance. The following section will detail these KPAs, the potential contribution each can make to simulation credibility, and the methods that can be used to assess if these factors are being adequately incorporated into simulation development and maintenance.

Requirements Management

Requirements definition is one of the most critical aspects of software development, and is a good indicator of the potential for success of the development effort in terms of schedule, cost, and software quality. On the surface this may appear to be a simple exercise, but it is difficult to implement correctly and comprehensively. The primary obstacle is that users (who must define and "own" the simulation requirements) and developers (who must implement these requirements in software) often have two different worldviews and speak in two different languages. For example, the user of a mission-level model views the simulation in terms of specific platforms, systems, tactics, and engagements; the developer of the simulation sees objects, data structures, algorithms and events. In many cases both participants are ignorant of the other's area of expertise or the necessary contribution that the other makes to simulation credibility.

According to the CMM, the purpose of Requirements Management (RM) is to establish and maintain a common understanding of simulation requirements between the developer and the end-user of the simulation under development. Well-documented requirements serve the same function as the Rosetta stone, enabling user requirements to be translated into terms understood by the developer, and enabling the developer's design to be translated into terms understood by the user.

Requirement definition is an inherently tedious and laborious task to the typical SME. A proper requirements document defines simulation requirements in sufficient detail to enable accurate implementation and verification of the simulation design. The less the developer understands the system or phenomenon being simulated, and the level of fidelity at which it must be simulated, the more a good requirements document becomes essential. In many cases the user does not understand or appreciate the need for this level of definition, and may not be inclined to assemble the requisite SME expertise to assist with requirements definition. Even if the right SMEs are assembled, they may lack an understanding of the developer's need for detail, as much as the developer often lacks experience in the simulated subject matter.

Requirements must originate from appropriate SMEs selected or approved by the user. Simulation credibility is only as good as the SMEs who define the requirements. While it is sometimes delegated to the developer to draft the initial simulation requirements, the user must not abdicate responsibility for (or ownership of) them. The user must fight to identify and overcome any communication barriers between SMEs and the developer, ignore the tedium, roll up his sleeves and ensure that the job gets done correctly. The developer can and should assist in this process of free and open communication and collaboration. He must ensure that the user's SMEs have supplied sufficient detail for the design phase of development.

At some point in the requirements definition process the "real world" gets abstracted. Planes and ships become "platforms"; radars, infrared detectors, and human eyes become "sensors". The best abstractions lead to more elegant and maintainable code. However, the essence of the subject matter must not be lost in the process of abstraction. The SME can ensure this does not happen by being an active participant in the requirements definition process. SMEs should participate in this process throughout the design phase of simulation development. Once simulation requirements are documented, the developer should produce design documents detailing how requirements are to be implemented in software.

Real world abstraction also takes place at this point. For example, Integrated Air Defense Systems become "acyclic graph data structures". Design documents should be drafted in a manner that the user can fully understand and comprehensively review. It must be insured that critical elements of the requirements are not lost in the design phase.

Requirements documentation should not only define the specific requirements, but should also specify the verification methods and success criteria to be used for each requirement. All requirements should be specified in such a manner as to be testable. If they cannot be tested, then how will their correct implementation be verified? The SME should assume ownership of the test description and specification for successful implementation of the design into software.

One of the best ways to mitigate risk in the requirements phase is to develop requirements incrementally. This has sometimes been referred to as "rapid prototyping". This is an especially useful approach to the development of complex simulations such as mission-level models. Requirements can be broken down into separate model builds, and drafted in separate development cycles. This allows SMEs to refine and add to requirements as each build, or prototype, is delivered, and as experience with (and insight into) the simulation is gained. The breakdown of requirements also facilitates using multiple panels of SMEs, recognizing that experts may only have expertise in particular subsets of the entire scope of the simulation. The key pitfall with the approach described above is requirements creep after requirements have been frozen. Once requirements have been frozen, new requirements should wait until the next development cycle.

Below are some of questions that can help a user to assess how well simulation requirements are being managed. As described above, the credibility of the resultant simulation is, in part, determined by the adequacy of the answers to these questions. They all give some indication as to whether the expertise of the recognized SMEs was adequately captured and correctly implemented in the simulation:

- Did appropriate and qualified SMEs generate simulation requirements? What is the breadth and depth of the collective experience of the SME panel? Do they have relevant community recognition or acceptance?

- Does the developer have simulation experience in the SME's area of expertise? (This helps facilitate a common understanding of simulation requirements between developers and SMEs.)

- To what extent did the SMEs participate in the generation of simulation requirements? Did they generate the requirements document, or was the task delegated to the developers? Did they review and comment on design documents?

- Are the simulation requirements well documented, comprehensive, and in sufficient detail for the developer to translate them into simulation design and code?

- Are the requirements testable? If so, are the tests well defined, and are success criteria documented with each requirement?

- Were requirements developed incrementally? How have the builds been divided? Has this process been used to refine requirements as the SME gains experience with the simulation? Has the requirement definition process been tailored to enhance the participation of focused SMEs?

- Were requirements frozen during design, implementation and testing? If not, how was the traceability of requirements maintained during development?

<u>Peer Review</u>

The Peer Review KPA also plays a significant role in ensuring simulation credibility. The goal of peer reviews is to prevent and remove defects in the simulation as early and as efficiently as possible. Peer reviews involve a methodical examination of software work products by the producers' peers to identify errors and other potential problems. For our purposes, we choose to include SMEs in the definition of peers, along with other software developers. The work products to be reviewed include requirements documents, design documents, test reports, and even the source code. When peer reviews are minimal, or nonexistent, the user runs substantial risk of the end-product not meeting requirements, or even worse, containing undetected errors.

As stated earlier, simulation credibility is enhanced when SMEs play a review role throughout the development cycle. By reviewing design documentation, SMEs can verify that the implementation methods chosen by the developer are true to their defined requirements. This same logic applies to other software development artifacts, such as test reports.

Even non-SMEs can play a significant role in enhancing simulation credibility through peer reviews. Other programmers can detect common implementation errors during detailed code walkthroughs, such as incorrectly indexedloops or common mathematical equation errors. While some of these may be detected during testing, this is not always the case. Peer reviews of this nature can also help developers enforce coding standards and improve implementation techniques to enhance the long-term maintainability of the simulation software. This may be critical to enhancing credibility in simulations that continue to grow and evolve rapidly over time.

The following are some key questions to ask regarding peer reviews that are aimed at improving simulation credibility:

- Does the development process call for planned periodic peer reviews? If so, what types of reviews are conducted? How often?
- What software work products are reviewed? Are review criteria and goals explicitly articulated?
- Are SMEs encouraged to participate in the peer review process? Are review materials, such as design documents written with their areas of expertise in mind?
- Do SMEs utilize opportunities for peer review? Are they effectively integrated into the review process?
- How are reviewers concerns captured and addressed, and what products result from reviews? Are these products structured to assist in the assessment of simulation credibility?

Software Configuration Management

The next KPA considered is Software Configuration Management (SCM). The general purpose of SCM is to establish and maintain the integrity of the software products throughout the simulation's life cycle. Within this general definition there are many specific functions handled by SCM. Since their stated purpose is to maintain the integrity of the simulation, all of these functions when executed properly enhance the credibility of the simulation. Therefore, the existence of a rigorous and robust SCM process is a positive indicator of simulation credibility.

The scope of SCM activities is too broad to cover here in its entirety. Therefore, three aspects of the SCM process have been selected for further discussion.

Requirements Tracking. Requirements for simulations such as mission-level models change constantly. A key function of the SCM process is requirements tracking (as opposed to Requirements Management, discussed above). Once requirements are documented, either initially in a requirements document or later through Requirements Change Forms of some type, they are entered into the SCM system. Here their status is tracked through implementation, testing, and closure. Requirements tracking enhances simulation credibility by increasing the probability that simulation requirements specified by SMEs will get implemented in software in a controlled and disciplined manner. Users will better understand the capabilities of each new release of the simulation to meeting their needs.

Configuration Control Board (CCB). The CCB, in one form or another, is usually the managing authority over the simulation development process. The CCB should be populated with the stakeholders of the simulation, i.e., with those who have a vested interest in the future of the simulation. The CCB has many roles and responsibilities. In practice, these roles and responsibilities are sometimes divided up among multiple governing boards. For example, a Configuration Review Board (CRB) may be established to rank change requests (new requirements) by technical merit and need. This ranking is then sent to the CCB to be finalized based on programmatic (budget and cost) concerns. In whatever form this body takes, the CCB is a key forum to capture the interests of simulation users and their SMEs. A well run CCB with active participation by the SMEs will help to ensure that simulation development is managed in such a way to enhance credibility.

SCM Database. The SCM database contains all proposed requirements and known errors in the simulation, along with the status of each. At any given time, this database will give potential users insight into the limitations and errors contained within the simulation. This allows the user to assess the impact of these limitations to a specific application.

The following are some key questions to ask regarding SCM that are aimed at improving simulation credibility:

- Is there a documented SCM process? Are the nature, scope and depth of activities robust enough to capture and control problems with software, documentation and databases?
- Are simulation requirements well tracked and controlled?
- Are known errors documented in the SCM database?
- What is the Change Request or Trouble Report submittal process? Is this process open and easily accessed by all users and SMEs?
- Are users and SMEs able to review the SCM database at all times?
- Is there an active CCB (or its equivalent)? Does its membership include users and SMEs? Do SMEs participate actively in the CCB?
- How well does the CCB function? Is it an active body providing the developer with good insight into user requirements, or does it function as a "rubber stamp" for the model manager?

Software Quality Assurance

The final KPA to be examined is Software Quality Assurance (SQA). The role of SQA is to ensure that all-relevant software development standards and processes are applied correctly. If this function is treated as a matter of faith, simulation managers and users may remain blind to many problems that exist within the software development effort. The following are some of the significant functions of SQA that have an impact on simulation credibility (Humphrey 1989):

- SQA ensures that a requirements traceability matrix, or similar device is used to show that simulation capabilities cover the requirements specified by SMEs.
- SQA ensures that an implementation traceability matrix, or similar device is used to show that SME-specified requirements are implemented in the design.
- SQA reviews documentation to ensure that all documents satisfy established standards and are kept current.
- SQA reviews all development artifacts to ensure they are being adequately maintained.
- SQA periodically reviews SCM to ensure it is maintaining proper baseline control as well as full change records for requirements, design, code, test, and documentation.
- SQA reviews all test reports to ensure all testing is performed as appropriate and that the simulation satisfies established acceptance criteria.
- SQA monitors all peer reviews to ensure they are conducted as planned, that the results are documented, and that all follow-up items are executed.

SQA is recognized as a specific discipline that is best served by a trained and dedicated staff. Simulation credibility is directly related to how well SQA verifies proper execution of all processes, specifically those that ensure the expertise of the SMEs are fully realized within the simulation.

SUMMARY

This paper has described the connection between good software development processes and enhancing simulation credibility. We have demonstrated this relationship using a subset of the CMM framework. However, the contribution of the CMM to simulation credibility is not limited to these four KPAs. Other KPAs, such as Software Quality Management (from CMM Level 4) and Defect Prevention (from CMM Level 5) may be of use in this regard.

Also, while the CMM appears to be a good approach to categorize and evaluate software development processes, it is not the only framework that may have merit as an indicator of simulation credibility. For example, Object Oriented Design and Analysis (OOD&A) can enhance the maintainability and extensibility of a proposed simulation. In a simulation that will undergo a rapid and continuous evolvement of requirements, OOD&A may significantly promote credibility if applied well.

We have demonstrated that there exists a causal link between simulation credibility and the quality of software engineering processes and resources applied. These insights can be applied by all parties involved in simulation development - the developer, the end-user, and the simulation evaluator - to enhance simulation credibility.

Although this paper has focused on mission-level models, it should be clear that all simulations could benefit from the relationship between good software development processes and simulation credibility as demonstrated here. All simulations will have enhanced credibility by being developed and maintained with software engineering practices that promote the implementation of the expertise of qualified SMEs, while at the same time preventing, identifying, and removing defects.

REFERENCES

Humphrey, W.S.. 1989. *Managing the Software Process*. Addison-Wesley Publishing Company, Inc., Reading, Massachusetts.

Paulk, M.C., Weber, C.V., Curtis, B., Chrissis, M.B., *et al*. 1995. The Capability Maturity Model: Guidelines for Improving the Software Process. Addison-Wesley Publishing Company, Inc., Reading, Massachusetts.

ABOUT THE AUTHORS

Ronald L. Ketcham

Mr. Ketcham is currently an Accreditation Support Analyst with the Joint Accreditation Support Activity (JASA) at the Naval Air Warfare Center, Weapons Division, China Lake, CA. He is currently the Lead Accreditation Agent for the Joint Strike Fighter (JSF) Program. Mr. Ketcham has extensive experience in software engineering and VV&A. He gained much experience in the CMM as Project Manager of the Analyst's Work-Bench (AWB) in the early 1990's. Mr. Ketcham holds an A.B. in Economics from Transylvania University (in Lexington, Ky.) and an M.S. in Economics and Industrial Engineering from Iowa State University. He is currently working on an M.S. in Computer Science with California State University at Chico.

Paul R. Muessig

Dr. Muessig is currently Director of the Joint Accreditation Support Activity (JASA) at the Naval Air Warfare Center, Weapons Division, China Lake, CA. JASA's goal is to support weapons system acquisition and testing programs with credible integration of M&S into program objectives. Dr. Muessig has extensive experience in risk-based VV&A methodology development, planning and execution in support of numerous M&S applications in acquisition and testing. He has also worked as a defense analyst at the Center for Naval Analyses in Washington, D.C., contributing to survivability analyses for advanced technology aircraft, and leading model validation efforts for the Advanced Low Altitude Radar Model (ALARM). Dr. Muessig holds a B.S. in Chemistry from St. Joseph's University in Philadelphia, and a doctorate in Physical Chemistry from Brown University in Providence, Rhode Island.

Qualification: An Incremental Approach to Modeling and Simulation Verification, Validation, and Accreditation

LCDR Chris Miller, PMS 451
Michael Lee, PMS 452
Joe Uzdzinski, SPA
John Shelby, SPA
Phil Lyle, SPA
Ellis Sutter, Lockheed-Martin

Introduction

The effective use of Modeling and Simulation (M&S) in systems acquisition is predicated on how accurately the M&S represents the functionality of the systems they represent. Even more importantly, the efficacy of M&S is also a function of the confidence the users have in the utility of the M&S. Since confidence is critical to the credible use of M&S, structured M&S Verification, Validation, and Accreditation (**VV&A**) processes have evolved as a way of enhancing user confidence in M&S and of documenting that confidence. However, these activities are typically used only for high-visibility efforts of great importance. M&S ***Qualification*** provides a means to establish documented levels of confidence appropriate to the associated M&S task.

The acquisition program manager who requires M&S to develop his system is challenged to ensure the fidelity and accuracy of the M&S he requires while containing the cost and time it takes to develop and accredit the M&S. He is also challenged to manage M&S development, verification, validation, and accreditation while his attention is properly focused on accomplishing his system acquisition. This article outlines a process, M&S Qualification, that augments traditional M&S VV&A through developing streamlined M&S assessment processes for establishing and documenting confidence in M&S. The goals of this M&S Qualification process are to provide credibility and traceability in the use of M&S in support of program applications. Potential by-products of this process are to reduce accreditation costs, reduce the time required to execute the overall accreditation process (when accreditation is necessary), and control the imposition of additional requirements tangential to the purposes of the acquisition program that impact schedule or cost.

M&S Qualification is a structured means to establish varying levels of confidence in M&S applications. As a supplement to classical Verification, Validation, and Accreditation, Qualification is a technical assessment of the suitability of a particular model or simulation for a particular application. Qualification posits and documents user confidence in particular M&S and serves to "bin" M&S for future consideration as well as to document acceptance for current purposes. Furthermore, it is often the case that qualification-like efforts are routinely used in acquisition, so that implementation amounts to little more than documenting ongoing efforts with a structured framework.

This article will address methodologies of achieving and documenting confidence in M&S and will present the use of the Qualification concept through a case study of its use in the Navy's Theater Ballistic Missile Defense (**TBMD**) program.

Modeling and Simulation Verification, Validation and Accreditation Overview

Confidence is established and documented by the M&S application sponsor through a *Verification, Validation and Accreditation* process. The Department of Defense defines Accreditation as "the official certification that a model, simulation or federation of models and simulations is acceptable for use for a specific purpose."[1] The steps in the VV&A process to achieve that official certification are discussed below [2].

M&S Requirement

The VV&A process actually begins when the initial requirement for M&S is identified. The intended use for the M&S is stipulated (e.g., design development, performance prediction, test and evaluation) and the fidelity and accuracy required of the M&S for that specified use are specified. (Note the primacy of the *intended use* in this step of the process.) These specified fidelity and accuracy requirements are the foundation of the acceptability criteria the M&S will have to ultimately satisfy and from these acceptability criteria a body of detailed metrics is elaborated. The metrics are key to an objective determination that the M&S does, in fact, meet the acceptability criteria that satisfy the requirements.

An approach to obtaining the required M&S is then chosen. The approach could be to use legacy M&S, modify legacy M&S, or develop new M&S. The approach taken is hopefully the approach with the best promise of yielding M&S that achieves all acceptability criteria. However, determining the optimal M&S approach, if not mandated by higher authority, may require a combination of traditional and new methods. For that reason, iterative processes known as *Verification and Validation* (V&V) are applied to the M&S approaches selected to better establish the level of confidence that is a precursor to accreditation. An Accreditation Plan that outlines the acceptability criteria, metrics, M&S approach and generally defines the application of V&V methodologies for the M&S requiring accreditation is developed by the M&S application sponsor to guide these activities.

Verification and Validation

The developer of the M&S considered for accreditation (also known as the M&S Proponent or MSP) implements a V&V Plan approved by the M&S application sponsor. This V&V plan augments the Accreditation Plan by describing the selected methodologies[3] of verification and validation that will be utilized for the M&S under consideration and detailing the data collection and analysis processes that will ensure the M&S satisfies the metrics derived from the specified acceptability criteria. Verification processes are analysis techniques designed to establish the degree to which a specific M&S accommodates the design criteria of the developer or, in other words, how well the developer met his design specifications. Validation processes are analysis techniques that determine the degree to which the M&S satisfies the fidelity and accuracy stipulated for it, or in other words, how well the M&S accommodates the M&S application sponsor's functional specifications. This distinction between verification and validation is important because early in the life of a complex system acquisition. M&S may be vital to design development and performance prediction activities, yet empirical data to validate the M&S will not be available when the M&S will need to be used. In that case, verification can at least give the program manager confidence that the M&S in use is at least well wrought and conforms to the conceptual models that led to the design.

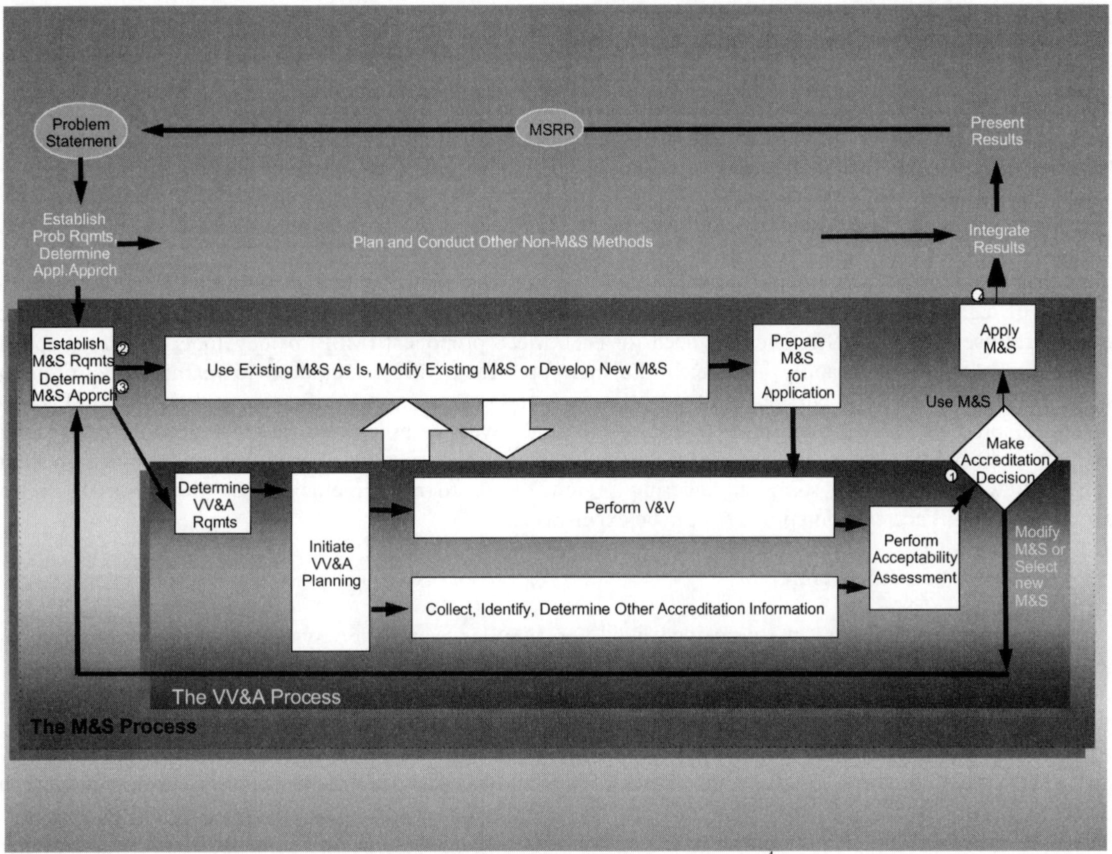

Verification, Validation, and Accreditation[4]

Accreditation Decision

The MSP executes the V&V plan. The conceptual model (statement of assumptions, logic, algorithms and limitations) is examined, followed in order by V&V of the design, implementation, and application of the M&S. The further along this sequence the V&V can progress, a function of the external data available for the analyses, obviously the greater the degree of confidence that can be reposed in the M&S. After data collection, the MSP performs an acceptability assessment and recommends accreditation to the M&S application sponsor based on how well the M&S satisfied the acceptability criteria.

The M&S application sponsor makes the decision to accredit. He can decide to accredit the M&S for use as is, use as is with limitations, or use after modification. He can decide to require more V&V, in effect deferring the accreditation decision, or he can demur on accreditation of the M&S entirely. Clearly, these last two decisions entail both financial and time implications that may impact program schedule. The figure above depicts the VV&A process endorsed by the Department of Defense.

Preconditions for Accreditation

There are some preconditions on M&S implicit in the VV&A process discussed above. These preconditions primarily concern the design discipline practiced by the M&S developer. The developer must employ software specification definition and coding practices that facilitate requirements traceability, error detection and correction, and modification to accommodate the volatility inherent in complex systems. The developer must exercise rigorous Configuration Management, documented in a viable Configuration Management Plan that is the product of corporate climate and not just a contract deliverable. These preconditions are sufficiently critical to serve as selection criteria to be used by the M&S application sponsor when he considers his M&S tool set and developers.

Accreditation Challenges

Now, after discussing the Accreditation Process whereby one can either repose confidence in the fidelity and accuracy of particular M&S, or at least accept accountability for its efficacy, it is time for a look into the hard face of reality. The face of reality is: Accreditation costs money, Accreditation takes time, and Accreditation expertly exposes the biases and organizational jealousies replete in any complex system acquisition process.

Accreditation Costs Money

It is not unusual for a complex system acquisition program to begin concept definition activities supported by a body of legacy M&S, often consisting of competing simulations, augmented by additional M&S as needed. The potential use of this M&S implies the need for each M&S proponent (MSP) or developer to define, specify, code, document, verify and apply his M&S. Furthermore, each MSP is required to maintain Configuration Management on his M&S, encouraged to develop and execute a meaningful Verification and Validation Plan, and expected to complete an Accreditation Plan as needed. The layers of programmatic oversight to monitor and/or participate in the MSP's efforts, consisting of technical working groups, integrated product teams, simulation control panels, review panels, and systems engineering review, needs to be implemented by the program as well. Resourcing the M&S accreditation processes can be expensive.

Accreditation Takes Time

The process that turns the perceived need for M&S in a complex system acquisition program into functional, useful, and accredited M&S is designed to reinforce the aim of achieving sufficient fidelity or accuracy in the M&S for the intended use. This fidelity or accuracy is in fact a necessary proviso for any accredited M&S, justifying a multi-layer process of requirements review, redefinition, confirmation and calibration.

M&S is subject to both computer software development practices as well as the systems engineering practices that turn requirements into system design. The actual complex system acquisition program may be in fact a development and procurement of hardware or hardware with embedded "tactical" software only, yet to properly manage the M&S desired, the program management will have to tackle software development processes in ways somewhat alien to the real focus of the program.

Between the Program Manager and the MSP in the process to acquire and accredit M&S will be a Systems Engineer, a Systems Engineering Team (with an M&S engineer as a member), an M&S Integrated Product Team, an Accreditation Review Panel, a Simulation Control Panel, a M&S Working Group, a Configuration Advisory Board, and one or more Technical Working Groups or Technical Advisory Groups. If the MSP is a contractor, some, or all of these layers are apt to be duplicated, or even augmented, in the contractor's internal organization. The execution of the review and management by these various groups may be especially time-consuming.

Accreditation Can Produce Organizational Challenges

Within the Program Executive Office, Theater Surface Combatants, (PEO TSC), the Navy Area TBMD Program, PMS 451, and the Navy Theater Wide TBMD Program, PMS 452 (mission programs), are supported by several product programs, including the AEGIS Program Office, PMS 400B, and the STANDARD Missile Program Office, PMS 422. See page 11 for a further description of the organizational structure. Each of these product programs has its own accreditation management structure and teams. In PMS 400B, there is a separate system-level Accreditation Review Panel (ARP); and in PMS 422, a missile-level Simulation Accreditation Review Panel (SARP). Each of these management review teams is involved in overseeing the VV&A efforts of their respective program M&S. In addition, many of these same models and simulations are also being accredited for mission-level milestones and critical decisions. The coordination of these various VV&A efforts has been especially challenging.

The Program Manager's M&S Challenge

The program manager is challenged to ensure the fidelity and accuracy of the M&S the program requires while containing the cost and time it takes to develop and accredit the M&S. He is also challenged to control the management of M&S development and Accreditation while he is focused on the development and acquisition of his respective system. Appendix A provides an overview of the VV&A process, as applied in the Navy TBMD Programs. The section that follows outlines a process, M&S Qualification, that augments the traditional M&S Accreditation process by introducing a streamlined, incremental process for establishing and documenting confidence in M&S. The goals of M&S Qualification is to enable a continuous process of building and quantifying confidence in the M&S throughout the development and application of M&S as it is used to support the program as well as to facilitate accreditation as needed.

Modeling and Simulation Qualification

M&S Qualification is a structured means to establish varying levels of confidence in M&S applications. As a supplement to Accreditation, it posits and documents user confidence in particular M&S. Qualification serves to "bin" M&S for future consideration as well as for to document acceptance for current purposes. Five acceptance levels used to specify successively greater levels of confidence or acceptance afforded specific M&S are summarized in the table and discussion below.

Level	Name	Description
0	Undetermined	No requisite visibility within program No documentation required
1	Subject Matter Expert Advocacy	SME recommendation Model description required
2	Registration	Comparison of model results to baseline results Implementation Plan and documented results required
3	Verification	Comprehensive model evaluation relative to its specification Implementation Plan and documented results required
4	Validation	Comparison of model results to empirical data Implementation Plan and documented results required

M&S Acceptance Levels (Qualification)[5]

Acceptance Level 0 (Undetermined)

Acceptance Level 0 M&S are not formally recognized. Assignment of Acceptance Level 0 to M&S is little more than a statement that the M&S exists. This level of M&S does not require or receive external scrutiny.

Acceptance Level 1 (SME Advocacy)

Acceptance Level 1 identifies M&S championed by a Subject Matter Expert (SME) for use in a particular application. M&S characterized with this level of acceptance may be useful for initial requirements definition activities or evaluation of particular technical issues as they arise in the program. With the degree of accountability that SMEs already possess for the accomplishment of many of these activities, their advocacy for M&S to support their efforts is often sufficient to establish the level of confidence appropriate for this use of M&S.

Acceptance Level 2 (Registration)

Acceptance Level 2 identifies M&S that have undergone comparison with similar function M&S, or a Registration process. M&S at this level may be useful for trade studies or system assessments. Registration is a process, depicted in the figure below, of comparing, or benchmarking the output of two or more M&S to ensure consistent results from consistent assumptions and inputs. The M&S proponents (MSPs) of the M&S undergoing this analysis reconcile any differences and re-run cases, iterating this process as often as needed, until either acceptable results are achieved or additional effort is not warranted. A registration process has often been part of M&S development since most M&S developers compare the products of M&S under development with existing M&S products. When legacy M&S begins to entail supportability and maintainability difficulties because of changed coding standards, obsolete host hardware, or evolving capabilities in the system under simulation that can't be accommodated, new M&S designed to overcome these shortfalls will enter the M&S constellation through an initial Registration with the M&S to be replaced.

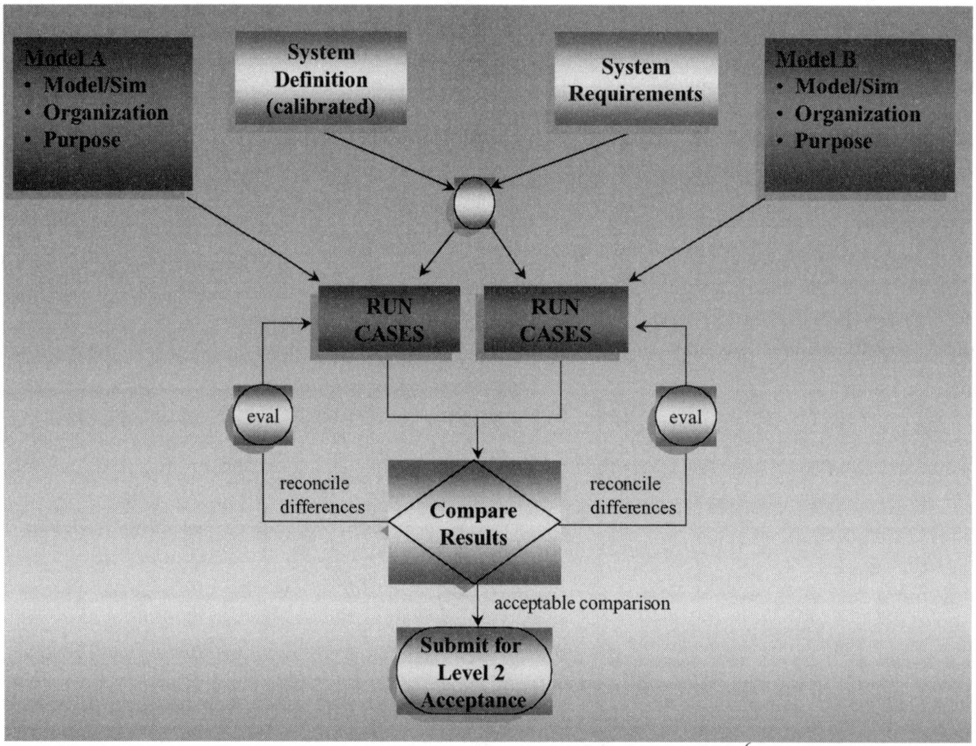

Registration Process Execution (Acceptance Level 2)[6]

Acceptance Level 3 (Verification)

Acceptance Level 3 M&S have undergone verification, i.e., the M&S have been demonstrated to accurately represent the developer's conceptual description and specifications. This is demonstrated through methods such as documentation review, SME's review, registration as described above, functional decomposition, design walk through, code walk through, or sensitivity analysis.

Acceptance Level 4 (Validation)

Acceptance Level 4 M&S have successfully completed a rigorous validation process and have been demonstrated to accurately represent the real world from the perspective of the intended uses of the M&S. Validation methods may include comparison with actual system test results, review of existing validation documentation, SMEs' review, registration with other validated M&S, or functional decomposition (relative to test data).

Comparison of Qualification and Accreditation Processes

As illustrated in Figure below, there is an obvious relationship between Acceptance Levels 1-4 and the stages of the traditional VV&A process. Each Acceptance Level implies the prior application of one or more V&V methods. SME advocacy provides a basis for peer review, registration is a direct comparison of M&S results, and the verification and validation levels have obvious correlation to the process of accrediting M&S. Because of this similarity, prior Qualification process documentation may be acceptable to accreditation review panels as one or more of the components of the V&V materials required for accreditation.

Note from the figure below that the Qualification process Acceptance Levels, as they map to the Accreditation process, are not necessarily progressively ordered. For instance, a particular M&S with Acceptance Level 1 confidence can be verified and accredited if deemed necessary without achieving intermediate assignment of Acceptance Levels 2 through 4. This is what is meant by binning M&S. M&S is binned in an Acceptance level for internal programmatic uses. When the anticipated use of the M&S warrants formal Accreditation, previous qualification efforts may facilitate the choice of any additional the specific V&V methodologies to accomplish its accreditation.

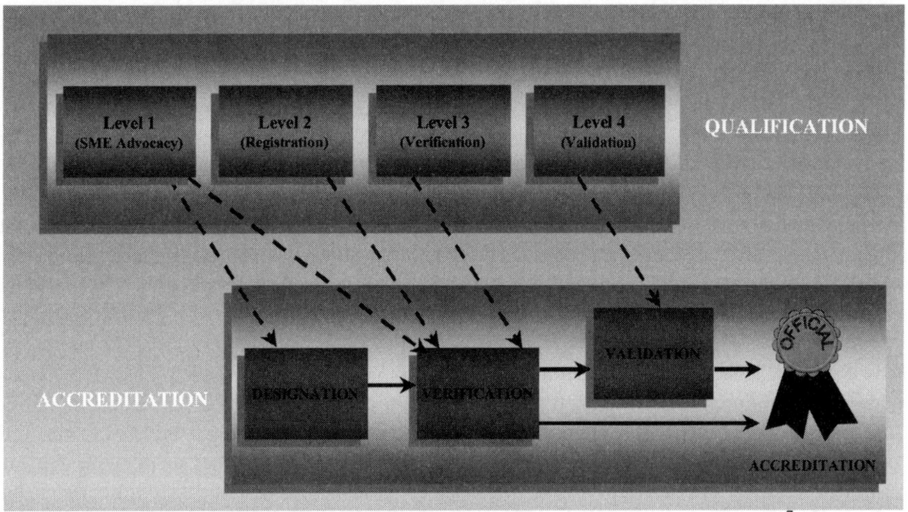

Simplified Relationship of M&S Qualification to M&S Accreditation[7]

The following section discusses how this Qualification Process has been successfully utilized in the Navy's TBMD Program to delineate confidence level in M&S and to contain the costs associated with achieving that confidence.

Navy TBMD M&S Management

Navy TBMD has implemented management processes designed to coordinate and facilitate M&S development and use across the mission and product programs. One key element to the management of M&S in Navy TBMD are the Modeling and Simulation Working Groups (MSWGs) established by the Navy Area and NTW TBMD Programs to facilitate the management of all M&S activities. These MSWGs are government – industry teams and include representation from the Navy Area and NTW Mission Program Offices, the AEGIS and STANDARD Missile Product Program Offices, key supporting laboratories (NAVSEA, Dahlgren Division, the

Johns Hopkins University Applied Physics Laboratory (JHU/APL) and the Massachusetts Institute of Technology Lincoln Laboratory (MIT/LL), prime contractors (Lockheed Martin and Raytheon) and key M&S support contractors. Expertise resident in the MSWGs is instrumental in the preparation of Navy TBMD M&S guidance documentation which includes M&S Management Plans, M&S Accreditation Plans, M&S Milestone Reports, M&S Data Handbooks, M&S Catalogs, and M&S Configuration Management Plans. The MSWGs provide technical review in the selection, development, and application of M&S supporting Navy TBMD Program Systems Engineering and Test and Evaluation efforts.

Navy TBMD Program M&S management processes are also designed to accomplish the important function of establishing confidence in the ability of M&S to predict or simulate system and threat characteristics. In the case of M&S used to support critical performance predictions or post-test analysis, Accreditation, or the traditional VV&A processes, determine and document that confidence. However, as previously discussed, with the expense and length of the traditional accreditation process, a need for a more flexible means for determining and documenting confidence in M&S internal to the TBMD Program has manifested itself. Navy TBMD has developed, and is applying the M&S Qualification processes briefly outlined above to supplement traditional VV&A. The M&S Qualification process facilitates the use of M&S within the Navy TBMD Program by formally qualifying M&S to levels of confidence suitable to early phases of development and by binning M&S to streamline future V&V efforts when greater confidence is needed. The Navy TBMD Program relies on accredited M&S to support critical reviews and milestone decisions, while M&S Qualification processes generally suffice to document internal TBMD Program M&S acceptance.

Navy TBMD M&S Accreditation Management

The Mission Program Managers are the Accreditation Authorities for M&S utilized in the development of their system processes up until Operational Testing - by direction, the Commander, Operational Test and Evaluation Forces (COMOPTEVFOR) is the Accreditation Authority for independent Operational Testing for U.S. Navy programs.[8] As the Accreditation Authority, the Mission Program Manager appoints an Accreditation Review Panel (ARP), coordinating membership with the Product Programs when Product Program developed legacy M&S is involved, and designates the M&S for accreditation by notifying the ARP in writing of the appropriate MSP for the model requiring accreditation. The ARP either confirms that the V&V methods previously utilized to support the accreditation of legacy M&S are sufficient or identifies additional V&V methods required for accreditation from those detailed in the Mission Program Accreditation Plan. The ARP also nominates a Simulation Control Panel (SCP) to assist them in the technical review of the V&V efforts. The MSP performs the V&V as required and reports the results via the SCP to the ARP. The ARP recommends (if appropriate) accreditation to the Mission Program Manager. For Operational Testing, COMOPTEVFOR determines the actual V&V methodologies to be used and the review panel composition.

In cases where a Mission Program formally accredits M&S developed through the offices of a Product Program, the accreditation documentation cites the Product Program accreditation documentation and delineates any differences in the application of the model for Mission Program purposes. (These differences from Product Program applications could be in scenarios, representation of tactics, forces, opposing forces or doctrine for example.) The Mission Program accreditation documentation also includes an assessment of any limitations the Product Program developed M&S may have relative to the Mission Program application. The following figure depicts the process to formally accredit M&S in Navy TBMD.

Note that the key players in the accreditation process are the Program Manager (or COMOPTEVFOR for Operational Testing) as the Accreditation Authority, an expert panel, or ARP, established by him, a SCP of experts who assist the ARP, and the MSP. The ARP and SCP are formal boards, with appointing letters, tasking instructions, funding documents, memoranda of understanding and agreement, and the other paraphernalia associated with establishing formal boards comprised of membership from many different organizations. It should also be stated that the act of Accreditation is not considered delegable. Accreditation is in effect a formal statement to higher authority of TBMD Program capabilities, fundamental assumptions, and design trade off decisions. Considering that all of this is subject to scrutiny and second guessing by some who are not proponents of the TBMD Program, only the Program Manager should be, and is, empowered to authenticate such a formal statement.

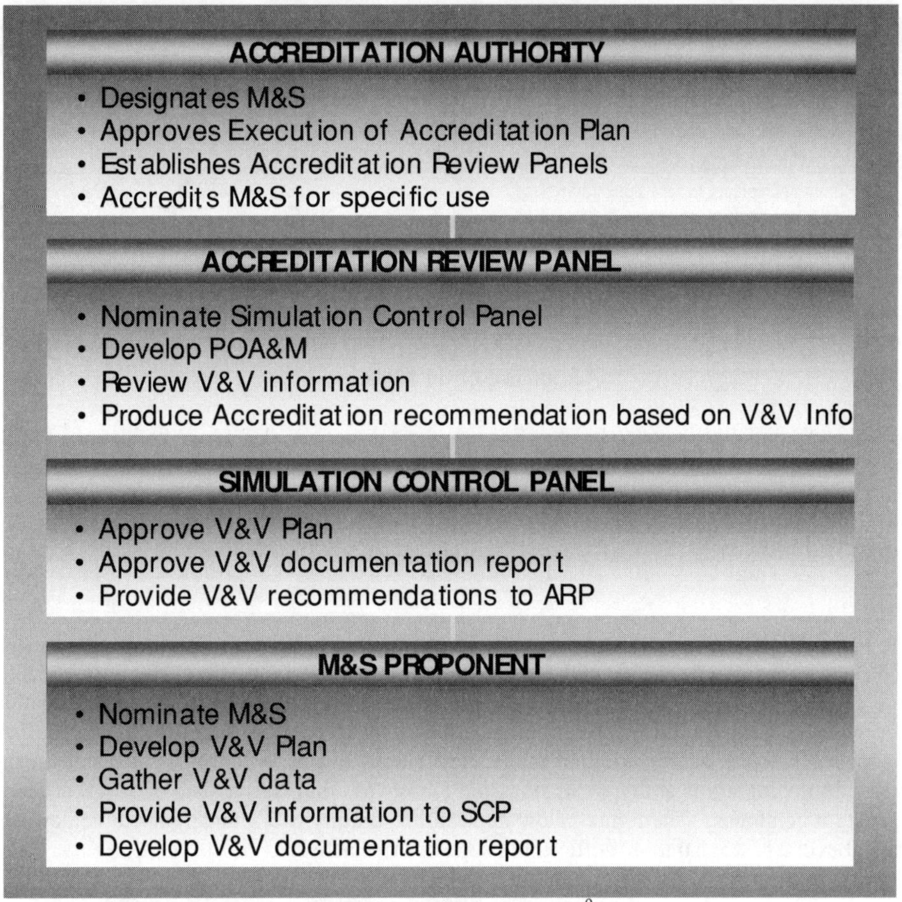

M&S Accreditation Process[9]

Navy TBMD M&S Qualification Management

The Navy TBMD M&S Qualification process is very similar to the Accreditation process, with the Systems Engineer taking the place of the Program Manager as the authority who assigns acceptance levels. The MSWGs stand in for the ARPs and existing Integrated Process Teams or Technical Oversight Groups (TOGs) replace the specific purpose SCPs. The process is advanced by the fact that the MSWGs and TOGs are typically existing and recognized groups composed of individuals with a significant history of working together. The MSWGs and TOGs very often include the concerned MSPs. Not all of these groups are engaged in reviewing and awarding each acceptance level - the higher acceptance levels warranting increasing more oversight than lower levels. The actual processes used to assign and document specific Acceptance levels to M&S are described below.

Assignment of Acceptance level 1 is essentially a "bottoms-up" process, most often initiated by SMEs. Acceptance level 1 M&S is most apropos for the earliest stages of development when M&S is used to facilitate general operational assessments of system capabilities and to assist in the definition of system level requirements through trade studies. This process ensures that working level Navy TBMD Program representatives monitor the SMEs to an extent sufficient to establish confidence in their contributions to TBMD system level requirements descriptions. Again, this level of confidence in M&S is adequate in the early stages of the Navy TBMD Program life cycle. The flowdown of requirements to more detailed specification as the life cycle continues provides ample opportunity to refine this broad brush picture and hence to increase the confidence level in the used M&S to coincide with the degree of systems requirement definition required. The following figure depicts the role of the MSWG and the Mission Program Systems Engineer in the Qualification Process that results in Level 1 acceptance.

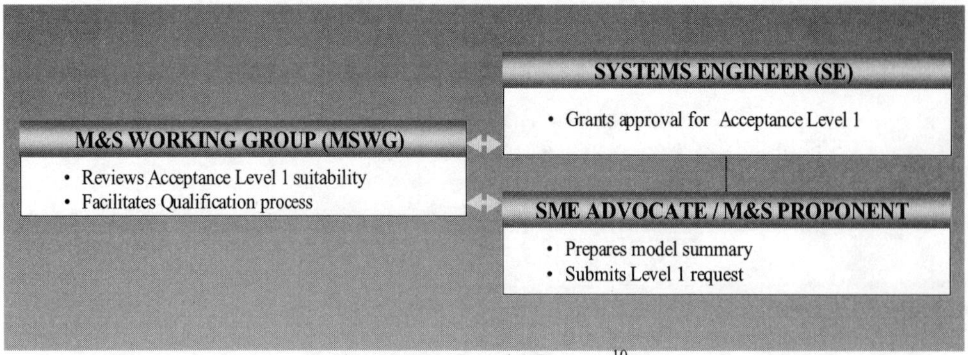

Acceptance Level 1 Process[10]

Establishing an initial acceptance level in this less formal manner also serves to identify M&S, and equally importantly, MSPs with future utility to the Program. More versions of M&S (versions proposed by competing contractors and/or supporting acquisition program organizations) can be surveyed at this point, and M&S results compared with little enabling commitment on the part of senior program management. In effect this positions the Navy TBMD Program to attain a minimal level of confidence in M&S as they evolve in their application to the program.

As the Navy TBMD Program progresses to the stage when more detailed trade studies are conducted, cost trade off analyses are considered, and formal System Requirements Reviews and System Concept Reviews are scheduled, more confidence in the M&S supporting the program is necessary. The Level 2 Qualification process, or, as described previously, Registration or direct comparison of M&S results, is key to further defining the Navy TBMD M&S tool set. Again, senior program management does not have too much invested in the use of any particular M&S and the program is at this point amassing a body of comparative data on M&S efficacy that will be useful as the program continues. The figure below depicts the scrutiny M&S undergoes to achieve the acceptance level (Acceptance Level 2 or Registration) sufficient to support these activities.

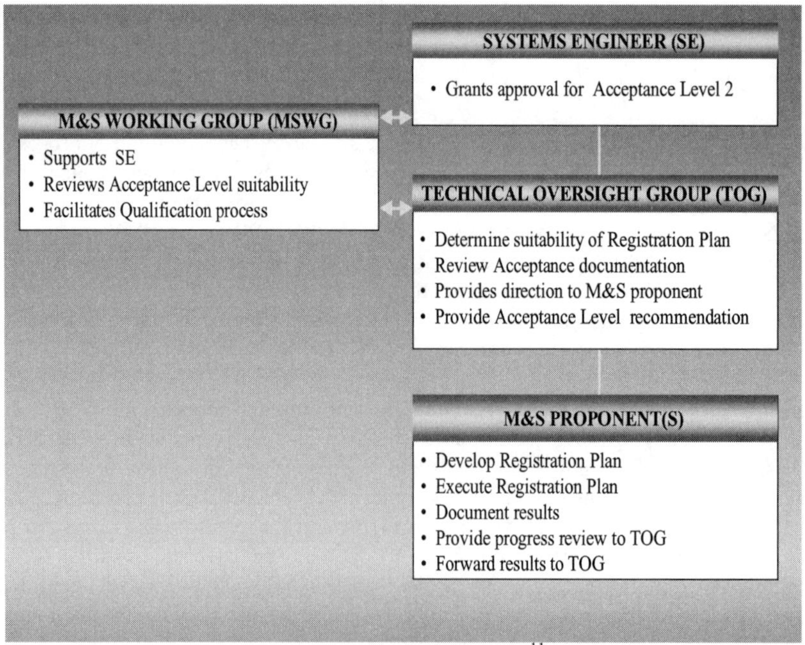

Acceptance Level 2 Process[11]

Assignment of Acceptance Level 2 is also a bottom-up process. However the increasing criticality or influence of the M&S at this level of confidence warrants more scrutiny or formality. It is important that all MSPs be afforded the opportunity to present their M&S fairly and that the expertise residing in the MSWG and TOG be utilized to the fullest in the evaluation or judgement of the M&S undergoing registration.

Registration is of particular importance to the Navy TBMD Program. Legacy M&S with proven performance and utility that enjoys high confidence in traditional Anti-Air Warfare analysis may not necessarily be suited to accommodate the degree of extrapolation necessary to make it useful for Navy TBMD roles. However, new M&S that may have good potential for the desired enhanced performance is more apt to achieve requisite acceptance if it can first be demonstrated to achieve results similar to the legacy M&S when functioning in the domain of the legacy M&S.

Further along in the life cycle of Navy TBMD, M&S will have more impact since M&S results will be supporting design decisions and will be used to justify the expenditure of funds. Clearly, the Navy TBMD Program desires the highest achievable confidence in M&S supporting critical experiments performance predictions, critical reviews such as Systems Functional Review, Preliminary Design Reviews and Critical Design Reviews, and Developmental Testing pre-test predictions. Yet at the stage of the life cycle when these activities occur, little empirically derived data that can confirm M&S performance is available. M&S used in these roles will initially be subjected to rigorous verification methodologies resulting in Acceptance Level 3 (Verification) and later compared or validated with real world test data as it becomes available resulting in Acceptance Level 4 (Validation). This iterative process is supported by the management oversight constructs in the figure below.

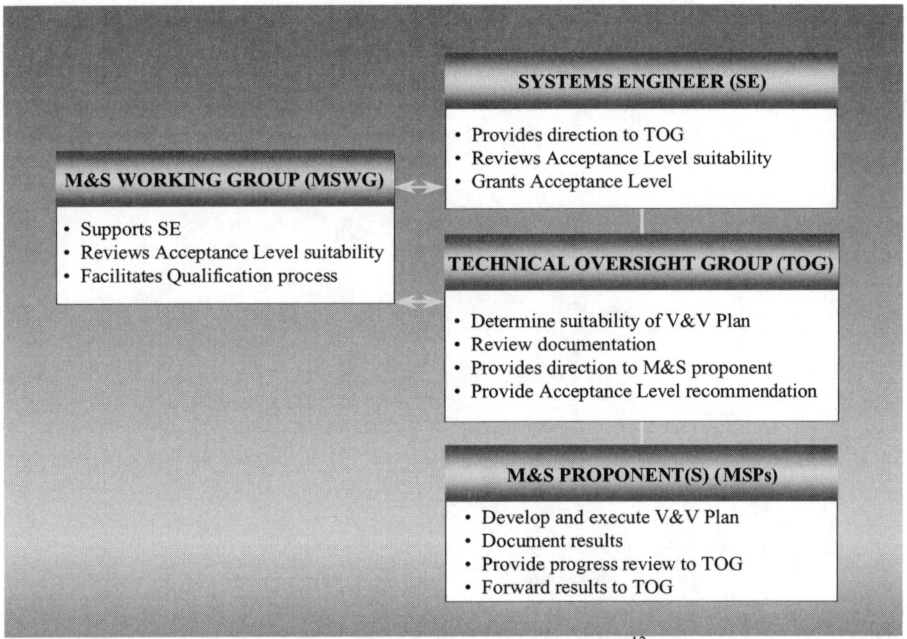

Acceptance Levels 3 and 4 Processes[12]

The processes that result in assignment of Acceptance Levels 3 and 4 are identical. Acceptance Level 3 can be either a technically driven bottom-up process or a directed top-down requirement. Frequent use and increasing confidence in particular M&S may warrant Acceptance Level 3 assignment as de facto recognition of the soundness of ongoing engineering practices by the M&S developer. Likewise, a Navy TBMD Mission Program Manager may direct the Verification of particular M&S for a specific purpose at a critical juncture of his Program. Acceptance Level 4 is always a top down requirement and represents programmatic commitment to use specific M&S for very key purposes. From the perspective of the Navy TBMD Program, Validation, or Acceptance Level 4 is the desired condition for M&S supporting performance prediction, design reviews, and pre-test analysis roles, but since that is not possible, Verification will have to suffice until Validation can be accomplished.

At this stage in the life of the Navy TBMD Program, Qualification is directly supplementing traditional VV&A processes. With the iterative nature of the Qualification process at Acceptance Level 3, M&S will achieve

Acceptance Level 4 by the time it is needed to support Operational Testing pre- and post- test analysis and the decision to enter production. Furthermore, a history of use, a record of V&V, and most importantly, a TBMD community- wide confidence in the M&S will exist by this stage of the Program which should greatly facilitate formal Accreditation by the Mission Program Manager.

Case Study: Application of Qualification to the Navy Theater Wide TBMD Program

This case study discusses the role played by M&S in the Navy's TBMD Program and illustrate the Program's experiences with traditional VV&A practices which resulted in the evolution of the Qualification Process described above. The case study concludes with a discussion of the benefits the Navy's TBMD Program has realized through utilization of the Qualification Process.

The Navy Theater Ballistic Missile Defense Program

The mission of the Navy's TBMD Program is to develop the sea borne capability to successfully intercept and destroy tactical ballistic missile threats that will be encountered in the world's littorals by either United States forces or the forces of our Allies. To accomplish this mission, the Program Executive Office Theater Surface Combatants (PEO TSC) has implemented two mission programs, the Navy Area TBMD (Area) Program and the Navy Theater Wide (NTW) Program to develop near and longer term (with more capabilities) systems. In developing the systems, the PEO has drawn upon the success the AEGIS and STANDARD Missile programs have achieved in developing the capability to intercept and destroy aircraft and cruise missile threats to afloat forces. The prior existence of these (and other) programs, coupled with the multi-mission capability requirement for the ships that will deploy with TBMD systems, has driven a PEO organizational structure that tiers TBMD mission programs over the programs developing specific products such as radars, computers, missiles, and communications systems utilized to accomplish the TBMD mission. The figure below depicts this Mission Program and Product Program structure of the PEO.

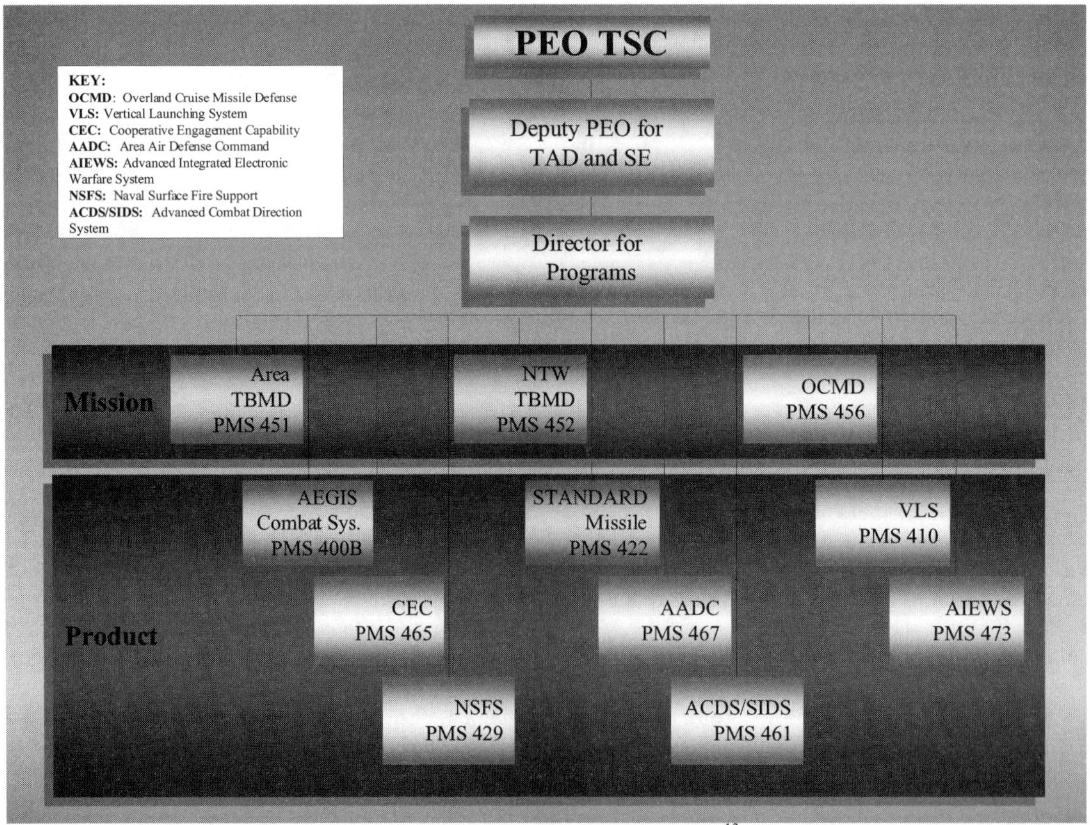

Navy TBMD Organizational Structure[13]

As shown in the picture, the Navy TBMD is managed by the mission programs, Area TBMD (PMS 451) and Navy Theater Wide TBMD (PMS 452); and are supported by the product programs, AEGIS (PMS 400B) and STANDARD Missile (PMS 422). The Navy TBMD Programs are also part of an extended family of programs that includes the Theater High Altitude Area Defense (THAAD), PATRIOT, Medium Extended Air Defense System (MEADS), and Airborne Laser (ABL) Programs. This family of programs is managed by the Ballistic Missile Defense Organization (BMDO).

M&S in Navy TBMD

The Navy TBMD Area and NTW Programs rely on a broad range of M&S to support activities throughout their entire acquisition life cycle. In both programs, M&S assists in design and development processes. In addition, M&S is being used in the Area TBMD Program in engineering level performance predictions and in supporting test planning and execution. Analysis activities in the NTW Program have been focussed on operational capability assessments and trade studies. Both programs will rely on M&S for some degree of system performance verification, and both programs will participate in Family of Systems M&S, wargaming and similar processes.

M&S replicates the environments in which the eventual hardware and software systems, ranging from ship based constructs to missiles, will have to operate. M&S provides the best intelligence community estimated threats the systems will have to counter. M&S provides the means to "flow down" requirements in the development of subsystem and component specifications during systems engineering processes. M&S also provides surrogate stimuli to replicate the functions of yet to be built components for system level analysis.

A large number of the models and simulations utilized in Navy TBMD is legacy M&S derived from prior Product Program development efforts. For instance, there are two versions of M&S simulating STANDARD Missile flight, three simulations for AEGIS SPY-1 radar operation, and a number of Footprint M&S. While the Navy TBMD Program has endeavored control these M&S by designating M&S tool sets as a means of reducing duplication, there is not as yet enough confidence in one model for each purpose to entirely accomplish this goal. The figure on the following page illustrates the current state of Navy TBMD M&S.

It should be stated here that this figure, as complex and inclusive as it seems to be, does not include all the M&S utilized in Navy TBMD Programs. Note that there are two SM 6-DOF (STANDARD Missile 6 Degrees of Freedom) models. Also FIRMTRACK, SEATRAP and SPECTRM are all radar models with some degree of overlap.

Use of Qualification in the Navy Theater Wide TBMD Program

An example of Level 2 qualification, Registration, occurred recently when the Navy Theater Wide program conducted a comparison of the results of five models that have been developed by different support agencies to access predicted system performance against a range of threat theater ballistic missiles. Each of the models was run against a common set of threats, each threat with exactly the same radar and infrared signatures, and the results compared.

The model outputs chosen for comparison included the times from interceptor missile launch to various key events, such as first launch opportunity, and other predictions concerning range, distance and velocities. A sample of the model outputs are shown in the table on page 15 below.

An example of Level 3 qualification, Registration, occurred recently when the Navy Theater Wide program conducted a comparison of the results of five models that have been developed by different support agencies to access predicted system performance against a range of threat theater ballistic missiles. Each of the models was run against a common set of threats, each threat with exactly the same radar and infrared signatures, and the results compared.

The model outputs chosen for comparison included the times from interceptor missile launch to various key events, such as first launch opportunity, and other predictions concerning range, distance and velocities.

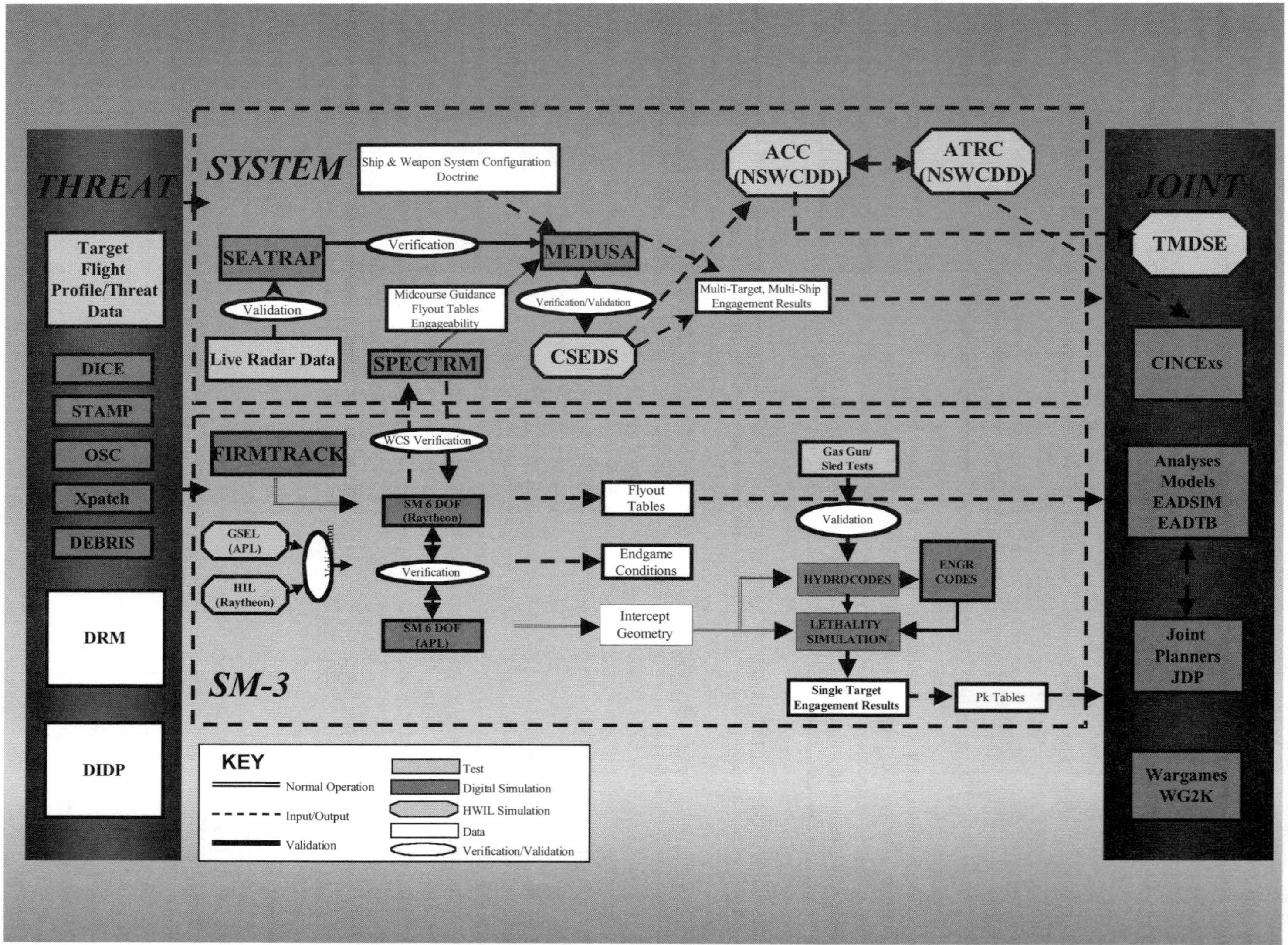

Navy Theater Ballistic Missile Defense Modeling and Simulation[14]

A sample of the model outputs are shown in the table below. Two cases were actually examined, from four different ship positions.

This side by side comparison of model results allowed each model developer to examine how their model's predictions compared with the other models used in the analytic community and resulted in several of the models being modified. This methodology allowed for statistical analysis of the results and a quantitative assessment of the overall agreement (or disagreement) between the models.

Event	unit	Model A	Model B	Model C	Model D	Model E
Time Event #1	(s)	9.45	8.0	10.0	9.0	10.0
Time Event #2	(s)	10.45	11.6	11.7	10.9	11.6
Time Event #3	(s)	13.4	13.0	13.0	12.9	12.1
Time Event #4	(s)	13.6	13.8	13.7	14.0	13.9
Time Event #5	(s)	26.35	24.0	25.2	26.8	26.56
Metric						
Range #1	(km)	5.6	6.12	6.5	5.7	7.1
Distance #1	(m)	195.3	149.67	167.0	114.0	105.7
Velocity #1	(km/s)	1.29	1.39	1.07	1.39	1.38

Example Results of NTW Model Registration (CASE 1, Position 1)

It is important to note that none of these models have yet been required to undergo a rigorous VV&A process because the NTW acquisition program is still in the early stages. However, by subjecting these models to the Registration process the program system engineers have a method to ascertain what degree of confidence to place in the results of each model and to understand where and why some model results differ from each other.

Benefits of Qualification

The M&S Qualification Process, as used by Navy TBMD to supplement the M&S Accreditation Process, has resulted in a number of benefits to the Program. In terms of management, the use of existing boards, MSWGs, TOGs and IPTs, translates to cost avoidances in that formal tasking, funding and administrative capital in the form of appointment letters, etc., do not have to be expended. Furthermore, with the Program Manager not personally involved until the last critical phases of the process that establishes formal confidence in particular M&S, the systems engineering level of the program can consider more M&S in the early stages of the program. This in effect provides a technical assessment of the M&S through the assignment of recognized confidence levels for further consideration as the Program progresses. The Qualification Process affords opportunities for lower organizational levels in the Mission and Product Programs to resolve disagreements without invoking program management levels.

Summary/Conclusions

This article has presented a process that augments the traditional Verification, Validation, and Accreditation processes in assigning confidence in M&S used in the acquisition of complex systems. The process outlined, termed the Qualification Process, can be applied to any acquisition process involving the use of M&S. By no means should Qualification be considered as replacing Accreditation; the firm statement of confidence in particular M&S for specific purposes by the Program Manager at key events or milestones in his program is fundamental in terms of sound program management and accountability. Qualification offers a way to ensure confidence in the use of all M&S as it develops in conjunction with the program.

Footnotes

1. Department of Defense Instruction 5000.61 "Department of Defense Modeling and Simulation Verification, Validation, and Accreditation" dated 29 April 1996.

2. The VV&A process described here is taken from the "Department of Defense Verification, Validation and Accreditation Recommended Practices Guide" dated November 1996, Chapter 5.

3. ibid. Chapter 4.

4. ibid. Page 5-3.

5. Navy Theater Wide Modeling and Simulation Plan, dated 20 August, 1999, paragraph 7.2.

6. ibid.

7. ibid. Paragraph 7.2.2.

8. SECNAVINST 5200.40 "Verification, Validation, and Accreditation of Models and Simulations" dated 19 April, 1999, paragraph 5.d.

9. Navy Theater Wide Modeling and Simulation Plan, dated 20 August, 1999, paragraph 7.1.

10. ibid. Paragraph 7.2.2.

11. ibid. Paragraph 7.2.3.

12. ibid. Paragraph 7.2.4.

13. ibid. Paragraph 5.

14. ibid. Paragraph 8.2.1. This figure actually depicts NTW Program M&S interrelationships. The Area Program differs in that it utilizes fuzing M&S that are not required to simulate the NTW kinetic warhead. Area also does not require the STAMP simulation since it doesn't operate in the regime postulated by that M&S.

LCDR Chris Miller served as the Machinery Repair Officer in the destroyer tender USS YOSEMITE (AD19) in the US Atlantic Fleet and as the Combat Systems and Communications Officer in the amphibious assault ship USS ESSEX (LHD 2). He graduated from the United States Naval Academy with a BS in Mechanical Engineering in 1986 and the Naval Postgraduate School with an MS in Electrical Engineering in 1991. His graduate work was focused on the modeling of submarine navigation systems. He also worked in DIS in the development of the Navy's shipboard Battle Force Tactical Trainer (BFTT) system. He is currently the Modeling and Simulation (M&S) Manager in the Navy Area Theater Ballistic Missile Defense (TBMD) Program Office.

Michael Lee is the M&S Manager in the Navy Theater TBMD Program Office. Joe Uzdzinski is the M&S Program Manager at Systems Planning and Analysis (SPA), Inc. Also at SPA, Inc., John Shelby is the chief technical editor of the Navy Area TBMD Accreditation and Performance Verification Plans and Phil Lyle is the Navy Area TBMD Program Manager. Ellis Sutter is the Navy Theater Wide TBMD Program M&S Manager at Lockheed Martin, SE&I.

VERIFICATION & VALIDATION OF THE JOINT WARFARE SYSTEM (JWARS) CONCEPTUAL MODEL

Michael L. Metz
Innovative Management Concepts, Inc.
45625 Willow Pond Plaza
Sterling, Virginia 20164
e-mail: mmetz@imcva.com

KEYWORDS: Military, Validation, Verification, JWARS, Conceptual Model

ABSTRACT: Verification & Validation of the US Department of Defense's Joint Warfare System (JWARS) simulation's Conceptual Model is being completed. This paper, written from the V&V Agent's perspective, describes the elements of the JWARS Conceptual Model as they were assembled together by the V&V Agent, the V&V activities associated with them, and the results to date. Additionally, this paper compares the JWARS Conceptual Model elements with those recommended by Dr. Dale Pace in his research described in his Simulation Conceptual Model Development paper that was presented at the Spring SISO-SIW meeting in Orlando, FL, in March 2000.

INTRODUCTION

The Joint Warfare System (JWARS) simulation is being developed by the US Department of Defense's (DoD's) Office of the Secretary of Defense (OSD) for use in theater level warfare analysis. In May 1995 the Deputy Secretary of Defense approved the Joint Analytic Model Improvement Program (JAMIP) and directed OSD's Program Analysis & Evaluation Directorate, in cooperation with the Joint Staff (the support staff of the US Joint Chiefs of Staff), to develop a state-of-the-art, closed-form simulation of joint, campaign-level warfare that: represents uniquely joint functions and processes, and component warfare operations; is based on joint doctrine; is capable of representing future warfare; and, supports analysis.

The future users of JWARS include the Joint Staff, the US military Services, the US regional and functional combatant commands, OSD, Joint Task Forces, other DoD organizations, and industry. The planned JWARS applications include: force assessment; force planning and execution (both deliberate planning and crisis action planning); system effectiveness and trade off analysis; and, concept and doctrine development and assessment.

JWARS development began in April 1997 and the Verification & Validation (V&V) effort began in September 1997. One of the primary tasks of the V&V Agent , as detailed in the JWARS V&V Plan (JWARS Office 1998), is to validate the JWARS Conceptual Model (CM). JWARS development is now in process and Release 1.1 was made in January 2000. Release 1.1 is the first in a series of releases that will culminate in a final Release 1 that will be used for user testing and will be designated as the Limited Initial Operating Capability (IOC) for study execution. JWARS requirements are contained in the JWARS Operational Requirements Document (Joint Staff, J-8 1998). This paper addresses the Conceptual Model validation conducted to date for JWARS Release 1.1.

CREATING A VIRTUAL JWARS CONCEPTUAL MODEL

JWARS development does not include a formal CM product, requiring the V&V Agent to create a virtual CM from the available development artifacts. The Defense Modeling and Simulation Office's (DMSO's) description of a CM (DMSO 1996) includes everything in the simulation development process that occurs between the user requirements gathering phase and the design phase. For JWARS this included the

Joint Application Design (JAD) Packages, the Conceptual Model of the Mission Space (CMMS) document, and the algorithm descriptions

Elements of the JWARS Virtual Conceptual Model. Throughout the development of the JWARS V&V process the representatives of the Defense Modeling and Simulation Office (DMSO) on the JWARS V&V Oversight Group consistently identified CM Validation as one of the required tasks. Although the JWARS software development process did not include an artifact or deliverable identified as the JWARS CM the V&V Agent realized that there was an identifiable concept for going from the JWARS requirements as identified in the ORD to the design. From this concept the V&V Agent created a virtual JWARS CM made up of the following artifacts: Joint Analysis Design Packages; the JWARS Conceptual Model of the Mission Space (CMMS); and JWARS Algorithm descriptions.

The JADs were the derived requirements packages for each JWARS thread (or process) that bounded and specified a particular development work package. The JADs were developed concurrently with the JWARS CMMS and provided a great deal of detail about the processes and the entities, actions, tasks, and interactions of the warfare functionality included in them.

The JWARS CMMS evolved from a largely text description of JWARS entities, actions, tasks, and interactions into an enterprise view (provided by the JWARS Enterprise Model) of a United States led coalition and Joint Task Force. By examining various views of the JWARS CMMS an analyst and coder could see how the different organizations worked together and how functional control, orders, communications, and resources were identified, requested, and allocated. The JWARS CMMS also provided the best view of the problem domain architecture.

The JWARS Algorithm Descriptions provided identification of each algorithm used in JWARS as well as some of the conditions, limitations, and assumptions related to them. Although not as well documented as the V&V Agent would have liked, the algorithm descriptions formed a key part of the virtual CM.

Initially scenario validation was not part of the V&V Agent's CM validation. However, during the third year of the V&V effort the V&V Agent proposed to add this task to the JWARS V&V processes. This recommendation is under consideration by the JWARS Office.

VALIDATING THE VIRTUAL JWARS CONCEPTUAL MODEL

This paper describes the Verification and/or Validation of each of these artifacts, along with problems and recommendations for changes in the development and V&V processes. The final part of this section will describe the results of each of these V&V activities and the status of the JWARS CM.

JAD Verification and Validation. JAD V&V was the first V&V process conducted by the V&V Agent. Initially the JAD Packages were not well standardized and the validation process was not formal enough for the V&V Agent to complete the JAD V&V. After the V&V Agent's recommendations for format and content standardization and a more formal subject matter expert (SME) review were implemented by the JWARS Office JAD V&V was improved. The verification process included a review of the format to insure the correct items were included and the validation process included SME review (during sessions at the JWARS Office and via emailed responses to the V&V Agent by those who could not attend) to insure that the information was correct. Many comments were received from the SME community for each JAD and each was adjudicated with the JWARS Office to make sure the proper changes were made to the JADs to correct or refine them.

Conceptual Model of the Mission Space (CMMS) Validation. Initial validation of the text-based JWARS CMMS was unsuccessful due to insufficient SME review of the product. Partially due to this and the adoption of a new Unified Modeling Language (UML) based development process, the JWARS Enterprise Model was adopted as the JWARS CMMS. The V&V Agent was more successful in obtaining comments about the new CMMS and validation was completed after adjudicating the refinements and corrections from the SME community.

Algorithm Validation. Initial algorithm validation was not completely successful. The V&V Agent provided all the information obtained from the JWARS Office to the Validation Authority (the JWARS User Subgroup members) but they were unable to complete the validation due to a lack of information about the algorithms and their inability to place the algorithms in context of the simulation. For the second attempt at algorithm validation the V&V Agent provided a more complete validation package (including limitations, conditions, data input, data output, and algorithm source) that were developed during a lengthy analysis of the JWARS Algorithms with the JWARS developers. This algorithm validation process is ongoing at this time.

COMPARING THE VIRTUAL JWARS CONCEPTUAL MODEL TO DR. PACE'S CONCEPTUAL MODEL CONSTRUCT

This section of the paper compares Dr. Dale Pace's recommendation (Pace 2000) for elements of a CM with what was available for JWARS and describes how the lack of certain elements adversely affected the JWARS V&V process. Dr. Pace includes the elements shown in Figure 1 in his proposed CM and the JWARS CM elements are shown along with their validation status. Key differences include the lack of a simulation domain and system domain validation for JWARS. Due to cost constraints in the JWARS V&V process and the ORD's focus on the problem domain it was decided that the JWARS V&V effort should be concentrated on the problem domain. Also, the current JWARS V&V effort does not include data V&V as that role is assigned to OSD's Joint Data System (JDS). In the Interactions the JWARS CM does not include design artifact validation as that is a verification process in the JWARS V&V effort.

Figures 2a and 2b show another view of Dr. Pace's proposed CM and the elements of the JWARS CM that maps to that view. Dr. Pace begins with requirements for a simulation and the simulation context elements that support the requirements process and constrain the simulation. The JWARS CM includes most of these elements in the JAD products, the Conceptual Model of the Mission Space product, the algorithm descriptions, and the problem domain architecture. In Figure 2b (Pace's CM Specifications) the same JWARS CM elements are shown (plus data) in the specification role for a CM.

Pace also lists the required documentation for a CM (Figure 3) and the corresponding JWARS documentation, or lack of it, is shown along with their validation status. The key difference is the lack of a single JWARS CM document that identifies the CM elements. Also, the JWARS system and simulation domain artifacts and documents were not validated for reasons discussed above and the Simulation Development Plan, as represented by the JWARS Software Development Process, was not validated.

Although a virtual CM, the JWARS CM meets most of Dr. Pace's critical requirements for a CM and most of these elements have been or are in the process of being validated. The V&V Agent believes that a more robust and documented CM would have benefited JWARS development and the subsequent V&V effort. With the exception of requiring more time and resources, the lack of a formal and robust CM has not severely hampered JWARS development or the V&V of the development.

HOW A ROBUST CONCEPTUAL MODEL AIDS THE V&V PROCESS

We support DMSO's effort to develop, standardize, and support Conceptual Modeling standards for simulation development within DoD. The JWARS V&V effort would have been aided by the presence of a robust and documented CM in at least two important ways, including reducing the time and effort required to gather and validate the virtual JWARS CM and providing everyone involved in the JWARS effort a clearer picture of how the developers were going to go from a formal requirements set to the simulation design. We believe that CM standardization will both improve the simulation development process and the V&V of completed simulations. If adopted (and combined with appropriate verification, validation, and accreditation activities) these CM standards will reduce simulation development risk and provide a higher probability of user accreditation and use of the completed simulation.

REFERENCES

CONFERENCE PROCEEDINGS:

Pace, D.K. 2000. "Development and Documentation of a Simulation Conceptual Model." In Proceedings of the 2000 Spring Simulation Interoperability Workshop Papers, April 2000.

SPECIAL PUBLICATION:

Defense Modeling and Simulation Office, 1996. Department of Defense Verification, Validation, and Accreditation Recommended Practices Guide.

JWARS Office, 1998. Joint Warfare System (JWARS) Verification and Validation Plan, Version 3.0.

Joint Staff J-8, 1998. Joint Warfare System (JWARS) Operational Requirements Document (ORD), 27 August 1998.

TABLES & ILLUSTRATIONS

Comparing Pace's Proposed Conceptual Model to the JWARS Virtual Conceptual Model

Pace's CM	JWARS CM	Validated?
Assumptions	Included with Algorithms	Yes
Algorithms	Algorithm Documentation	Yes
Relationships/Architecture	Architecture View Simulation Domain Problem Domain System Domain	 No Yes No
Data	Meta Data Requirements	No (Joint Data System)
Entities	JADs CMMS	Yes Yes
Actions	JADs CMMS	Yes Yes
Tasks	JADs CMMS	Yes Yes
Processes	JADs CMMS	Yes Yes
Interactions	JADs CMMS Design Artifacts	Yes Yes No (Verified)

Figure 1

CM Components Compared

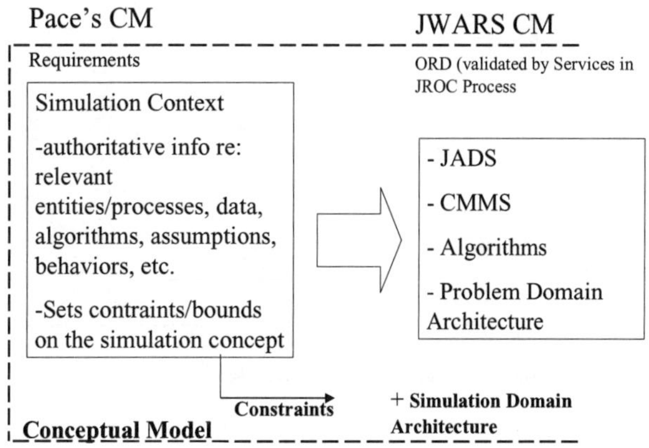

Figure 2a

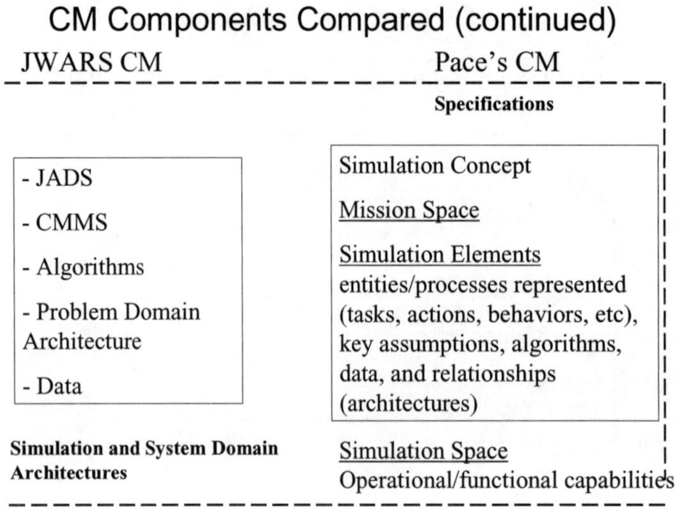

Figure 2b

Documentation: Comparing Pace's Proposed Conceptual Model to the JWARS Virtual Conceptual Model

Pace's CM Documentation [1]	JWARS CM Documentation	Validated?
CM Portion Identification	None	NA
Principal Simulation Developer POCs	Available	NA
Requirements & Purpose	ORD	Yes (by Services)
Overview	ORD, JWARS Overview Briefing, iterated)	Yes No
General Assumptions	Embedded in architecture documents In algorithm descriptions (limited)	No Yes
Identification of Possible: States Tasks, Actions, Behaviors, Relationships, Interactions Events Parameters & factors for entities/processes	 None JADs, CMMS Scenarios JADs, CMMS, Scenarios	 No Yes Yes (proposed) Yes
Identification of algorithms	Algorithm Descriptions	Yes
Simulation Development Plans	JWARS SDP	No
Summary & Synopsis	None	NA

[1] Functionally equivalent to IEEE/EIA 12207 Standards for Information Technology Life Cycle Processes

Figure 3

BIOGRAPHY

Michael Metz, Technical Director of the Joint Warfare System (JWARS) Verification and Validation Program at Innovative Management Concepts, Inc., is a specialist in the design, development, verification, validation, and accreditation of simulations. He has been involved in the development of the RAND Strategy Assessment System, the Joint Resource Allocation Model, the Naval War College Air Model, JWARS, and TASCFORM. He is a member of the Defense Modeling and Simulation Office's Verification, Validation and Accreditation (VV&A) Technical Working Group and its VV&A Technical Support Team.

Simulation Conceptual Model Issues[1]:
Development Methods (Part 1),
Interaction With Simulation Requirements (Part 2), and
Impact on Simulation Development Costs and V&V Costs (Part 3)

Dale K. Pace
The Johns Hopkins University Applied Physics Laboratory
11100 Johns Hopkins Road
Laurel, Maryland 20723-6099
(240) 228-5650; (240) 228-5910 (FAX)
dale.pace@jhuapl.edu

Keywords: conceptual model, validation, fidelity, simulation, requirements, costs, economics

ABSTRACT A simulation conceptual model is a simulation developer's way of transforming modeling requirements into a detailed design framework, from which the software, hardware, networks, and systems/equipment that will make up the simulation can be built. Part 1 of this paper discusses fundamental issues in simulation conceptual model development with guidelines for conceptual model decomposition, for abstraction in describing simulation elements, and for documenting the conceptual model. Development of an explicit conceptual model that is complete, consistent, clear, and correct will cause most deficiencies in simulation requirements to become evident, as discussed in part 2 of the paper. Detection and correction of such requirements deficiencies early is important for affordable, successful simulation development since the majority of software faults are attributed to requirements deficiencies. A high quality conceptual model can improve the quality of simulation requirements, thereby reducing simulation development costs, which is addressed in part 3 of the paper. A quality conceptual model provides a solid basis for judgment about simulation capabilities for conditions not specifically tested, and can contribute substantially to confidence in simulation results – this enhances simulation value.

Introduction

A simulation conceptual model is a simulation developer's way of translating modeling requirements (i. e., what is to be represented by the simulation) into a detailed design framework (i. e., how it is to be done), from which the software, hardware, networks, and systems/equipment that will make up the simulation can be built. A conceptual model describes a simulation developer's concept about the simulation and its pieces by assumptions, algorithms, characteristics, relationships, and data. Taken together, these describe how the simulation developer understands what is to be represented by the simulation (entities, actions, tasks, processes, interactions, etc.) and how that representation will satisfy simulation requirements.

This paper has three sections. Part 1 addresses development methods for simulation conceptual models. Part 2 discusses interactions between conceptual model development and simulation requirements. Part 3 is concerned with the impact of the simulation conceptual model on both simulation development cost and costs for simulation verification and validation (V&V). This introduction also examines paradigms for simulation development and their relation to the simulation conceptual model. This important topic needs to be understood before discussing the three parts of this paper. The introduction also presents a simulation conceptual model construct that is assumed by the rest of the paper.

Paradigms for Simulation Development. A standard development paradigm exists for High Level Architecture (HLA) distributed simulations, the federation development (FEDEP) model -- currently a six step process (version 1.4 is described at http://hla.dmso.mil/federation/fedep/fed/) shown in Figure 1. HLA uses "federation" for the collection of simulations ("federates") in a distributed simulation.

Various paradigms exist for development of a unitary (i.e., non-distributed) simulation, a federate in HLA parlance. Some are linear (such as the waterfall paradigm) and some are iterative (such spiral development and rapid prototyping

[1] The work reported in this paper was performed under sponsorship of the Defense Modeling and Simulation Office (DMSO), with oversight by Ms. Simone Youngblood, the DMSO Director for Verification, Validation, and Accreditation (VV&A). The views are those of the author and should not be construed to represent views of DMSO or of any other organization or agency, public or private.

paradigms). Figure 2 identifies key elements of all development paradigms. In iterative paradigms one passes through these elements more than once before they become final. I use "development" for modification of an existing (legacy) simulation as well as for a new simulation.

Comparison of Figures 1 and 2 reveals important differences in the way that development processes are described; but the differences are semantic, not functional.. In Figure 2, the problem statement expresses purpose, objective, or goal. If a simulation is selected as the tool to address the problem, then simulation requirements are used to capture the idea of the problem statement. The simulation conceptual model then is the developer's translation of those requirements into specifications, from which the simulation is built – specifications contain adequate detail to support design and implementation decisions. "Requirements" normally lack such detail. This is the connotation for a simulation conceptual model which is used later in this paper. By contrast, the federation conceptual model precedes federation requirements in the FEDEP process shown in Figure 1 (more detailed description of the FEDEP process makes it clear that development of the federation scenario, the federation conceptual model, and federation requirements are interwoven, parallel, and iterative). The FEDEP uses "federation objectives" in a manner more like "requirements" for unitary simulation developments. The FEDEP uses "federation requirements" more like "specifications" in most unitary simulation developments. Unless these terminology differences are understood, it is easy for confusion to result when the relationship of a simulation conceptual model to requirements and the relationship of a federation conceptual model to federation requirements are discussed.

As Figure 2 shows, there is consciousness of reality when the problem statement is formed (the dotted line between them) and reality sets boundary conditions upon representational aspects of the simulation (the simulation context). Many confuse fidelity (an absolute intrinsic characteristic) and validity (a relative characteristics that depends upon intended application). This is why the conceptual model combined with reality data is the validity referent (since it incorporates intended application) and reality (without reference to intended application) is the fidelity referent. Figure 2 also indicates how reusable components may be derived from the simulation as well as results from its use.

Simulation Conceptual Model Construct.

The current version of the DoD *Glossary of Modeling and Simulation Terms* [1] does not define "simulation conceptual model." It follows the approach of the Distributed Interactive Simulation (DIS) community by defining "conceptual model" as the agreement between the simulation developer and user about what the simulation will do. The connotation for simulation conceptual model used in this paper is that found in the current (revised) version of the DoD *Recommended Practices Guide for Verification, Validation, and Accreditation (VV&A)* [2]. A simulation conceptual model is "a simulation developer's way of translating modeling requirements (i. e., what is to be represented by the simulation) into a detailed design framework (i. e., how it is to be done), from which the software, hardware, networks (in the case of distributed simulation), and systems/equipment that will make up the simulation can be built." A conceptual model is the collection of information that describes a simulation developer's concept about the simulation and its pieces. That information consists of assumptions, algorithms, characteristics, relationships, and data, which describe how the simulation developer understands what is to be represented by the simulation (entities, actions, tasks, processes, interactions, etc.) and how that representation will satisfy simulation requirements. The more perspicuous and precise the conceptual model, the more likely the simulation development will satisfy requirements and demonstrate that requirements are satisfied (i.e., validation).

A simulation conceptual model *should be* a primary mechanism for clear and comprehensive communication among simulation developer design and implementation personnel (systems analysts, system engineers, software designers, code developers, testers, etc.), simulation users, subject matter experts (SMEs) involved in simulation reviews, and evaluation personnel, such as those involved in verification, validation, and accreditation (VV&A). A simulation's conceptual model addresses the simulation context, simulation elements, and the simulation concept. Each of these is discussed briefly below. The relationships among these are illustrated by Figure 3.

The *simulation context* provides "authoritative" information about the domain which the simulation is to address. In simulations with realistic representation of physical processes, the laws of physics and principles of engineering are part of the simulation context. For many military-related simulations, the simulation context includes standard organizational structures and general doctrine, strategy, and tactics. Documentation of the simulation context may merely be a collection of pointers and references to sources that define behaviors and processes for things that will be represented within the simulation. Special care, especially for distributed simulations, must be used when algorithms are taken from more than one source to ensure that sources do not employ contradictory assumptions or factors (such as different models for the shape of the Earth, differences in characterizing the environment, etc.). The simulation context establishes boundaries on how the simulation developer can properly build the simulation.

The *simulation concept* describes the simulation developer's concept for the entire simulation application (all the federates and other pieces in a distributed simulation, i.e., everything that comprises the simulation) and explains how the simulation developer expects to build a simulation that can fully satisfy user-defined requirements. The *simulation context* establishes constraints and boundary conditions for the *simulation concept.* If the simulation is concerned with realistic representation of missile flight, then laws of physics and principles of aerodynamics are part of the *simulation context*, making the *simulation concept* accommodate conservation of momentum, etc. Unrealistic, cartoon representation of missile flight would not necessarily be so constrained. The *simulation concept* includes *simulation elements*, i.e., the things represented in the simulation. The *simulation concept* is the total of all *simulation elements* and specifies how they interact with one another. This is essentially the *mission space* part of the *simulation concept.* The *simulation space* part of the *simulation concept* includes *all additional information needed* to explain how the simulation will satisfy its objectives. Such *additional information* often addresses control capabilities intended for the simulation, such as pause and restart capabilities, data collection and display capabilities, and how data and simulation control factors can be entered into the simulation (by keyboard, by voice, by gesture or touch, or by feedback from other parts of the simulation). *Simulation space* characteristics can range from identification of specific kinds of computing systems (hardware and operating systems that the simulation must run upon) and timing constraints so that real systems can be part of the simulation (such as hardware in the loop unitary simulations or involvement of live forces in distributed simulations) to the kinds of simulation control capabilities described above. Some simulation space considerations are closely related to implementation issues for the simulation, such as selection of a parallel computing architecture with its implications for the algorithms used.

A *simulation element* is the information describing concepts for an entity, a composite or collection of entities, or process which is represented within a simulation. It includes assumptions, algorithms, characteristics, relationships (interactions with other things in the simulation), data, etc. that identify and describe that item's possible states, tasks, events, behavior and performance, parameters and attributes, etc. A simulation element can address a complete system (such as a radar), a subsystem (such as a radar antenna), an element within a subsystem (such as a circuit within a radar transmitter), or even a fundamental item (such as an atom). It can also address composites of systems (such as a ship with its collection of sensors, weapons, etc.). A person, part of a person (such as a hand), or a group of people can be addressed by a simulation element—as can a process such as environmental effects on sensor performance. A simulation element can also be used for an individual parameter (such as power of a radar).

Quality of a simulation conceptual model is measured by completeness, consistency, coherence, and correctness.

Completeness: the simulation conceptual model identifies *all* representational entities and processes of the problem domain ("mission space"), and *all* control and operating characteristics of the simulation ("simulation space") needed to ensure that simulation specifications fully satisfy requirements.

Consistency: representational entities and processes within the conceptual model are addressed from compatible perspectives in regard to such features as coordinate systems and units, levels of aggregation/deaggregation/precision/accuracy/etc., and descriptive paradigms.

Coherence: the conceptual model is organized so that all elements of both mission space and simulation space have function (i.e., there are not extraneous items) and potential (i.e., there are no parts of the conceptual model which are impossible to activate).

Correctness: the simulation conceptual model is appropriate for the intended application and has potential to perform in such a way as to fully satisfy simulation requirements.

Part 1: Conceptual Model Development Methods

There are four basic steps in simulation conceptual model development: 1) collect authoritative information about the simulation context, 2) identify entities and processes to be represented in the simulation (decomposition), 3) develop simulation elements (abstraction), and 4) define interactions and relations among simulation elements. These steps are iterated until the conceptual model is completed. Widely accepted approaches do not yet exist for how to perform these steps. This part of the paper presents ideas about collecting authoritative information about the simulation context; then makes suggestions about simulation decomposition. Next the paper addresses representational abstraction, with particular attention to formal methods and knowledge engineering techniques that pertain to simulation conceptual models and to the importance of developing the simulation conceptual model within the framework of simulation theory. This section concludes with discussion of conceptual model documentation.

1.1 Authoritative Information about the Simulation Context. The first step in conceptual model development is to collect authoritative information about the intended application domain (the simulation context). Development of the simulation concept and collection of authoritative information for the simulation context is likely to occur iteratively as entities and processes to be represented in the simulation become more clearly defined. Authoritative descriptions of military activities such as contained in Conceptual Models of the Mission Space (CMMSs) in the Defense Modeling and Simulation Office (DMSO)'s repository [3] can be used in the simulation context when appropriate for a simulation's intended application, as can the laws of physics and similar principles.

It is unlikely that the documented simulation context, should one exist, will address everything needed to fully describe the domain that a simulation is to address. CMMS endeavors emphasize a disciplined procedure by which the simulation developer is systematically informed about the real world and a set of information standards that simulation SMEs employ to communicate with and obtain feedback from military operations SMEs. Common semantics and syntax, a common format database management system (DBMS), and data interchange formats (DIF) are keys to removing potential ambiguity between ideas of the warfighting SMEs and simulation development SMEs. A CMMS toolset provides these keys, but information beyond that likely to be obtained in the first level abstraction (i.e., the CMMS itself) may be required. SMEs may be "called upon to fill in details needed by [simulation] developers" that are "not provided in doctrinal and/or authoritative sources." [4]

Caution is required here also. It has also long been known that inserting a knowledge engineer (or other agent to transform information) in the role of an intermediary between the expert and the knowledge-based system (or simulation developer) may create as many problems as it solves [5]. Many approaches have been developed to address this potential problem. For example, Sharp developed a process to ensure that the expert and the knowledge engineer or program developer have the same understanding of the information being acquired and transferred to a knowledge-based system or to some other form of expression [6].

The more complete and clearly stated a simulation context is, the easier it will be to understand how one simulation entity (or simulation in a federation) may differ from another in its assumptions about the domain which is addressed. This becomes very important when questions of compatibility among simulations (federates) considered for a distributed simulation implementation (federation) are addressed as well as in assessment of coherence and compatibility of simulation parts.

1.2 Simulation Decomposition. The second step in conceptual model development is to identify entities and processes that must be represented for the simulation to accomplish its objectives. This enumeration process is fundamental in conceptual model development. Here basic decisions are made about the level of detail and aggregation that is appropriate to support simulation requirements. These decisions determine whether a system (such as a radar) will be represented as a single entity, as a composite of subsystem entities (such as an antenna or receiver), or as a composite of composites of ever smaller entities (to whatever level of detail is needed for the purpose of the simulation). Decisions are made about the level of representation of human decisions and actions. For example, in the movement of a platform (tank, aircraft, ship, etc.), are decisions and responses of all personnel involved (the crew) represented implicitly as a single aspect of the movement control process? Or does each individual involved get represented explicitly (as in a tank simulator with a position for every member of the crew)?

Booch, Rumbaugh, and Jacobson [7] identify four basic principles of modeling: 1) The choice of what models to create has a profound influence on how a problem is attacked and how a solution is shaped, 2) Every model may be expressed at different levels of precision, 3) The best models are connected to reality, and 4) No single model is sufficient. These principles show modeling to be an art which has not yet matured to a scientific method.

Conceptual model decomposition determines the simulation elements in the conceptual model. This establishes the scope of representation in the simulation and the discernible levels of the simulation. A six-item rationale can guide determination of what simulation elements should be in the conceptual model. These six items form a checklist for conceptual model decomposition. Using this rationale will help a conceptual model to be complete and coherent.

1) *There should be a specific simulation element for every item (parameter, attribute, entity, process, etc.) specified for representation by simulation requirements.* This re-emphasizes the importance of appropriate requirements for the simulation. Since a primary function of the conceptual model is to facilitate transformation of requirements into specifications, there must be complete tracking of items in the requirements

to the conceptual model. This establishes the minimum level of detail in simulation decomposition.

2) *There should be a specific simulation element for every item (parameter, attribute, entity, task, state, etc.) of potential assessment interest related to the purpose of the simulation.* This emphasizes understanding potential uses of the simulation clearly so all measures of performance (MOPs), measures of effectiveness (MOEs), and measures of merit (MOMs) that might be associated with the simulation are fully accommodated by the conceptual model. This has important implications for simulation space aspects of the simulation (especially data collection and display capabilities) as well as for representational aspects of mission space.

3) *As far as possible, there should be "real world" counterparts (objects, parameters for which data exist or could exist, etc.) for every simulation element.* The potential impact of data and metadata structures on simulation elements and on the overall simulation conceptual model should not be underestimated. Credibility for simulations with realistic representations is always enhanced when there is easy correspondence between its elements and the real world so that direct comparisons can be made more readily.

4) *Wherever possible, the simulation elements should correspond to standard and widely accepted decomposition paradigms to facilitate acceptance of the conceptual model and effective interaction (including reuse of algorithms and other simulation components) with other simulation endeavors.* Clarity and credibility of a simulation conceptual model are enhanced when such standard paradigms are employed.

5) *Simulation elements required for computational considerations* (such as an approximation used as a surrogate for a more desirable parameter which is not computationally viable) *that fail to meet any of the previously stated rationale should be used only when absolutely essential.* Computationally intensive problems may require approximations or less rigorous mathematical expressions. Such should be used only when necessary, and a clear statement of the reason for use should be included as part of the conceptual model.

6) *There should not be extraneous simulation elements.* Elements not directly related to simulation requirements, not implied directly by potential assessment issues, and without a specific counterpart in the real world or in standard decomposition paradigms should not be included in the simulation conceptual model. Every extraneous simulation element is an unnecessary source of potential simulation problems. Eliminating extraneous items from a simulation conceptual model removes unnecessary potential sources of errors, and follows the principle of parsimony encapsulated in Ockham's Razor.

General guidance about construction of an HLA federation is available [8]; however, rationale for how to decompose a HLA federation (or other distributed simulation) into federates (component simulations) is embryonic. Pollack and Baker [9] developed HLA-specific software metrics for use in determining the appropriate level of decomposition in a specific HLA application. These metrics provided a quantitative measure for achieving a balanced federation in the effort to optimize the sometimes competing goals of utility and efficiency. Applying these metrics to a specific legacy simulation and a baseline federation object model (FOM) identified the need for further decomposition to effectively support the intended application. As others perform similar assessments, it is likely that a set of metrics having general utility will emerge and become accepted by the community. Until these metrics are developed, it will be necessary for those designing a distributed simulation to consider the availability of compatible simulation components as well as computational and bandwidth factors in determining how to best decompose the distributed simulation (HLA federation) for the intended application.

1.3 Representational Abstraction of Simulation Elements. The third step in conceptual model development is development of simulation elements. Identification of simulation elements in conceptual model decomposition determines the scope of subject representation and the discernible levels possible in the mission space. How the characteristics of the simulation elements are abstracted determines the accuracy and precision of the representation. Because no single model is sufficient, the unified modeling language (UML) that Booch et al. [10] developed has nine kinds of diagrams (class, object, use case, sequence, collaboration, state chart, activity, component, and deployment) to fully express the five most useful views (use case, design, process, implementation, and deployment) that comprise the architecture of a software-intensive system. Similarly, representational abstraction for simulation elements needs a multifaceted descriptive approach.

Simulation fidelity is a complex function of the scope and discernible levels of the simulation as well as accuracy, precision, and other parameter quality characteristics. Substantial attention has been paid to describing simulation fidelity, with progress being made toward standardizing connotations for fidelity-related terms and awareness of issues associated with simulation fidelity [11]. Widely-accepted principles for determining required levels of fidelity and abstraction approaches that will produce them have not yet evolved.

Knowledge engineering abstraction principles can be helpful in developing a simulation conceptual model. Knowledge engineering typically is broken into three phases (knowledge acquisition, knowledge elicitation, and knowledge representation) and usually identifies three knowledge structures: declarative knowledge (why things work the way they do), procedural knowledge (how to perform a task), and strategic knowledge (the basis for problem solving). Typically different acquisition, elicitation, and representation techniques are used for each kind of knowledge. Unfortunately, these approaches do not yet allow abstraction to be performed as a scientific method; it remains an art [12]. Casual review of recent articles in such publications as Elsevier's *Journal of Data and Knowledge Engineering* [13] reveal that contemporary researchers often develop a "new" descriptive language or formalism for the problem at hand because their techniques do not yet have broad, general application capabilities.

Failure to fully account for uncertainties and errors that may exist in data and information used as the basis for models, algorithms, entity characteristics and behaviors, processes, and other aspects of a simulation is a common problem in simulation verification and validation [14]. This issue is closely associated with the subject of simulation fidelity and an important consideration in representational abstraction.

As a simulation conceptual model is developed, it should be evaluated by completeness, consistency, coherence, and correctness criteria. It is important to record model assessments and note why the model is changed in response to the evaluation, and how criteria for a quality conceptual model are met more fully. Otherwise, rationale for some changes (and their benefits) may be lost as time passes, and lessons learned from the conceptual model development will not be so readily available for use in subsequent developments.

1.4 Relationships. The fourth step in conceptual model development addresses relationships among simulation elements to ensure that 1) constraints and boundary conditions imposed by the simulation context are accommodated, and 2) simulation space issues (such as control capabilities that allow the simulation to be stopped, backed up in time, restarted, etc. or that identify data to be collected during the simulation) are addressed.

1.5 Simulation Theory. Conceptual model development should always be done within the context of simulation theory, such as Application Domain Modeling [15] or Discrete Event System Specification (DEVS) [16] methodology, to ensure that conceptual model development has coherence and can be related directly to simulation development. Sarjoughian and Zeigler developed a collaborative method for employing DEVS constructs in HLA federation development [17]. YEROOS, an acronym derived from "**Y**et another project on **E**valuation and **R**esearch on **O**bject-**O**riented **S**trategies," is a collaborative venture of researchers from Belgium, Switzerland, Argentina, and Senegal housed at the QANT Research Unit of the University of Louvain in Louvain-La-Neuve, Belgium, investigating and publishing theoretical foundations for conceptual modeling. It provides another approach [18].

1.6 Documentation of the Simulation Conceptual Model. Lack of distinct documentation of the simulation conceptual model has been a major problem in simulation developments in the past. Many simulation contracts fail to require distinct documentation of the simulation conceptual model. Lack of adequate documentation of the simulation conceptual model makes it much more difficult and costly to validate simulations and reduces their potential reuse. This is true for parts of the simulation as well as for the simulation as a whole. It has been recommended that simulation conceptual model documentation employ the scientific paper approach, even if also employing the design accommodation approach [19]. The nine items below are suggested for documenting a portion of the conceptual model (such as a simulation element) or of the entire simulation conceptual model:

1) Conceptual model portion identification;
2) Principal simulation developer point(s) of contact (POCs) for the conceptual model (or part of it);
3) Requirements and purpose;
4) Overview;
5) General assumptions;
6) Identification of possible states, tasks, actions, and behaviors, relationships and interactions, events, and parameters and factors for entities and processes being described;
7) Identification of algorithms;
8) Simulation development plans; and
9) Summary and synopsis.

Discussion of these items may be found at the DMSO website for the *VV&A RPG* and elsewhere [20]. This list is functionally equivalent to the 10 items in the generic content guidelines from IEEE/EIA Industry Implementation of International Standard ISO/IEC12207 *Standard for Information Technology Software Life Cycle Processes* for describing a planned or actual function, design, performance or process: date of issue and status, scope, issuing organization, references, context, notation for description, body, summary, glossary, and change history [21]. As more simulation developers use this standard approach to documentation for the simulation conceptual model (and its parts), reliable comparison of simulations (and simulation parts) will become easier and more affordable.

Part 2: Interaction With Simulation Requirements

Simulation requirements and conceptual model development are a classic "chicken-egg" pair. They each stimulate and derive from the other. Conceptual model development may begin prior to completion of simulation requirements. Conceptual model development may reveal problems with simulation requirements, especially if there has not been a rigorous validation of simulation requirements or if the best of contemporary requirements engineering practices have not been employed comprehensively. As the conceptual model is developed to fully satisfy simulation requirements, inconsistencies and lack of balance among the requirements (some very lax and others very stringent) may become apparent. Development of the conceptual model may reveal serious holes in the requirements: areas where the simulation developer is not told what the simulation should be able to do. A good simulation development program will insist upon the best contemporary requirements engineering practices, will encourage early rigorous validation of simulation requirements, and will ensure that requirement deficiencies uncovered during conceptual model development are corrected.

Development of an explicit complete, consistent, clear, and correct conceptual model will cause most simulation requirement deficiencies to become evident. Such deficiencies are inconsistencies and contradictions, holes, inclusion of extraneous demands, lack of balance, and lack of clarity. These are not a critique about what the simulation is to do. Detection and correction of requirements deficiencies early is important for affordable, successful simulation development since the majority of software faults are attributed to requirements deficiencies. It can cost up to 100 times as much to correct a fault later as it would have cost to correct it early.

Finalization of requirements and conceptual model development often occur iteratively; each process stimulates the other. "Finalization of requirements" means verification and validation of requirements so that they are complete, consistent, and clear. This should not be confused with "requirements creep," the expansion of requirements for additional functionality that normally occurs over the life of a simulation project. In software projects, a requirements creep of 20% a year of project duration is common and is planned for by wise program managers. Requirements creep is due in part to increased understanding about the problem, a result of information growth [22]. "Finalization of requirements" has to occur iteratively as "requirements creep" adds additional requirements. Since the simulation conceptual model is responsive to simulation requirements, the conceptual model must also evolve with changes in simulation requirements. This is one reason that effective configuration management is needed for both requirements and the simulation conceptual model, at least to the extent of tracking unique identification for the evolving versions of requirements and conceptual models with clear indications of which is related to the other.

Simulation consumers, those who use simulation results, usually develop simulation requirements. They seldom are expert in the formal methods that would allow requirements to be stated with mathematical precision. Simulation specifications and the requirements from which they are derived through the simulation conceptual model are typically stated in natural language (even when a CASE tool is used to facilitate tracing requirements to implementation). This "informal" approach to requirements limits simulation potential to be proven correct because of the "ambiguity, context sensitivity, and vagueness inherent in natural language in specification" [23]. And worse, the best practices of contemporary requirements engineering often are not applied in developing requirements for the simulation, causing benefits that result from the application of those best practices to be missed.

It may be impossible to fully express requirements for a simulation, the conceptual model embodying those requirements, and the specifications derived therefrom in precise, mathematically formal terms because the simulation subject is too complex, those expressing this information have limited fluency in mathematical languages, or their mastery of the formal descriptive format is incomplete. When mathematically precise formal methods cannot be used fully, even partial use can provide benefit, allowing simulation parts to have provable correctness. This is true for each simulation element, its associated requirements, and specifications as well as for the overall simulation conceptual model, requirements, and specifications.

A long term goal of the simulation community should be increased competence with set theory, propositional logic, predicate logic, etc. which are the foundation for formal development environments such as those employed with languages like the Vienna Development Method (VDM) from IBM laboratories in Vienna or Z developed at Oxford University. Increased familiarity with these topics within the simulation community would encourage use of more formal and precise methods for simulation requirements and specifications, as well as for the conceptual model which connects them and for the simulation elements contained within the conceptual model. The more that such formal approaches can be used, the greater the utility of various "automatic" verification tools so that the scarce resource of knowledgeable, competent personnel can be focused more on validation issues to ensure that the simulation not only works properly but that it is really working as intended, motivating NASA's emphasis upon the value and utility of formal methods [24]. Movement toward greater use of more formal constructs in requirements and specifications is a general trend as software engineering matures [25]. Such is essential to allow more use of automation in verification and validation of software and simulation, especially during design and early stages of development [26].

Improvement in simulation requirements has major benefits. Half of software errors are attributed to requirement deficiencies and errors. Cost to correct an error caught early may be only a few percent of what it would cost to correct that same error later in the development cycle [27]. This contribution to improved requirements makes formal conceptual model development very valuable. Formal conceptual model development is likely to produce a description of the simulation that allows more reliable estimation of required simulation development resources.

Part 3: Impact on Simulation Development Cost and V&V Cost

The 1999 Simulation Validation (SIMVAL) Workshop noted that simulation development cost is a function of requirements stability and complexity, simulation size and complexity, availability of reference data, availability of usable commercial and government off-the-shelf (COTS/GOTS) elements, maturity of the development process and stability of the enterprise culture, security requirements, and the acceptability level of credibility and risk that the simulation will not achieve its objectives [28]. Verification and validation (V&V) costs are also impacted by these factors plus the availability of simulation documentation and V&V personnel expertise. Some of these factors are obviously impacted by the quality of the simulation conceptual model. A good conceptual model helps to clarify (and thereby stabilize) simulation requirements. A good conceptual model will make it easier to determine if available COTS/GOTS elements will be useful for the simulation. However, other factors, such as security requirements and the availability of reference data, are not so obvious impacted by the way the simulation conceptual model is developed.

Simulation development cost estimation is difficult, especially from a total life cycle perspective. No widely accepted paradigm exists for describing simulation development costs or the portion of costs that is appropriately allocated to verification and validation (V&V) activities. Often significant aspects of simulation cost (such as data collection and algorithm development required for adequate representation of some aspect of the subject addressed by the simulation) are handled outside simulation development. Likewise, initial development cost for a distributed simulation may be reduced by a decision to use live forces (actual systems) in the federation so that adequate representation of such entities and processes do not have to be developed, but later it may be necessary to expend additional resources to develop such representation because the live forces anticipated for use in the distributed simulation (HLA federation) are not available as originally expected. These complexities make this section difficult.

This paper focuses on parts of the cost story about which it can provide insights. The April 2000 issue of *CrossTalk: The Journal of Defense Software Engineering* identifies ten cost estimation web sites (http://www.stsc.hill.af.mil). These resources provide insight about current state of the art in estimating software development costs.

Quality and stability of requirements is a major factor in the cost of developing a simulation. Unclear, incomplete, and inconsistent requirements can cause substantial re-work in simulation development and can lead to a product that may not fulfill its objectives. Half of software errors are attributed to requirement deficiencies and errors. Cost to correct an error caught early may be only a few percent of what it would cost to correct that same error later in the development cycle [29]. A high quality conceptual model can improve both the quality and stability of simulation requirements, thereby reducing simulation development costs by preventing errors from requirements deficiency and by enabling earlier detection of faults. In addition, this will enhance credibility in the completed simulation. A quality conceptual model provides a solid basis for judgment about simulation capabilities for conditions not specifically tested, and can contribute substantially to confidence in simulation results – which enhances the value of the simulation.

The cost of a simulation that does not satisfy requirements can be very high. The simulation may never be used – with all the development effort lost. The simulation may produce results that lead to catastrophe, especially if the simulation provides information used by decision makers and system control mechanisms. A quality conceptual model clarifies where the simulation produces reliable information, and where its results may not be accurate, increasing the likelihood that the simulation will fully satisfy requirements.

V&V cost are also complex. Various cost estimation methods have been developed to estimate costs for software

IV&V (which is mainly related to simulation verification), for V&V of distributed simulation exercises (which does not account for V&V of the individual simulations), and for simulation verification [30]-[33]. Typically these costs are 5-20% of simulation development cost. The sticky wicket in V&V costs is validation costs because the dominant factor is not the size and complexity of the simulation, but the level of credibility (assurance of correctness) required by the simulation's intended application. For simulations which must function correctly at all times, such as simulations involved in safety critical applications, validation requirements can cause V&V costs to be more than half of simulation development costs [34]. A quality conceptual model has great potential to reduce validation costs by making simulation capability clear for conditions other than those specifically tested. A quality conceptual model, documented as suggested, will reduce the effort required by SMEs to assess simulation capabilities. Without adequate documentation of the conceptual model, SMEs involved in simulation validation have to expend resources to essentially re-engineering a conceptual model for the simulation so that they can evaluate the simulation. Not only does a good conceptual model reduce simulation development costs by preventing errors caused by requirement deficiencies, it also reduces V&V costs since V&V resources do not have to be spent addresses the errors that were prevented.

At present, there is inadequate information to allow even a rule of thumb estimation for the potential cost benefit of improvements in conceptual model development, but it is the author's opinion (supported by the material presented above) that the savings from developing a quality conceptual model for a simulation are far greater than the additional cost of doing it the right way instead of the usual haphazard and incomplete way.

Conclusion

Developing a quality conceptual model for a simulation is important. It will help to clarify and stabilize simulation requirements. It will help to reduce simulation development cost and the cost of V&V for the simulation. It will enhance the simulation's credibility. This article has provided suggestions about how to decompose the simulation, about representational abstraction for simulation elements, and about conceptual model documentation. These ideas are important for simulation sponsors and users as well as for simulation developers and V&V personnel. Improvement in development and documentation of simulation conceptual models is essential to support current visions for simulation reuse and to increase capabilities of affordable simulations.

This paper has been somewhat frustrating because it does not provide as specific guidance as one would like. The reason for this is simple. Much of what the paper concerns, how to develop a simulation conceptual model and how to estimate simulation development cost and the cost for simulation V&V, is more art than science. Prescription of rules for these processes would be inappropriate because rules with general applicability do not yet exist. Therefore, the paper has been limited to more basic principles for guidance, and tries to illuminate enough of the issues involved to provide insight about how to do these things.

References

[1] DoD *Glossary of Modeling and Simulation Terms*, available from the Defense Modeling and Simulation Office (DMSO) website: http://www.dmso.mil.

[2] Department of Defense (DoD) *Recommended Practices Guide for Verification, Validation, and Accreditation (VV&A)*, available from the Defense Modeling and Simulation Office (DMSO) website: http://www.dmso.mil.

[3] Jack Sheehan, Terry Prosser, Harry Conley, George Stone, Kevin Yentz, and Janet Morrow, "Conceptual Models of the Mission Space (CMMS): Basic Concepts, Advanced Techniques, and Pragmatic Examples," *98 Spring Simulation Interoperability Workshop Papers,* March 1998, Vol. 2, pp. 744-751.

[4] Thomas H. Johnson, "Mission Space Model Development, Reuse and the Conceptual Models of the Mission Space Toolset" *98 Spring Simulation Interoperability Workshop Papers,* March 1998, Vol. 2, pp. 893-900.

[5] B. R. Gaines, "An Overview of Knowledge Acquisition and Transfer," *International Journal of Man-Machine Studies*, Vol. 26, No. 4 (April 1987), pp. 453-472.

[6] John K. Sharp, "Validating an Object-Oriented Model," *Journal of Conceptual Modeling*, Issue No. 6, December 1998 [http://www.inconcept.com/JCM].

[7] Grady Booch, James Rumbaugh, and Ivar Jacobson, *The Unified Modeling Language User Guide*, Addison-Wesley, 1999.

[8] Current versions of HLA Federation Development and Execution Process (FEDEP) Model, HLA Interface Specification, and Run-Time Infrastructure-Next Generation (RTI-NG). Available from http://www.dmso.mil .

[9] Anne F. Pollack and John P.Baker, "Federation Decomposition: HLA Metrics," *99 Fall Simulation Interoperability Workshop Papers,* September 1999.

[10] Grady Booch, James Rumbaugh, and Ivar Jacobson, *The Unified Modeling Language User Guide*, Addison-Wesley, 1999.

[11] Gross, David C (redactor), "Report from the Fidelity Implementation Study Group", 99S-SIW-167, *1999 Fall Simulation Interoperability Workshop Papers*, March 1999.

[12] http://church.cse.ogi.edu/~walton/know_eng.html.

[13] http://www.elsevier.com/inca/publications/store/5/0/5/6/0/8/.

[14] Patrick J. Roache, *Verification and Validation in Computational Science and Engineering*, Albuquerque, NM: Hermosa Publishers, 1998.

[15] G. N. Hone and M. R. Moulding, "Developments in Application Domain Modelling for the Verification and Validation of Synthetic Environments: Training Process and System Definition." *Proceedings of the Spring 1999 Simulation Interoperability Workshop*, March 15-19,1999, Orlando, FL.

[16] B. P. Zeigler, T.G. Kim, and H. Praehofer, *Theory of Modeling and Simulation,* 2nd ed., 1999, New York, NY: Academic Press.

[17] Hessam S. Sarjoughian and Bernard P. Zeigler, "The Role of Collaborative DEVS Modeler in Federation Development," *99 Fall Simulation Interoperability Workshop Papers,* September 1999.

[18] http://yeroos.qant.ucl.ac.be/yeroos.html.

[19] Dale K. Pace, "Development and Documentation of a Simulation Conceptual Model," *99 Fall Simulation Interoperability Workshop Papers,* September 1999.

[20] http://www.dmso.mil.

[21] James W. Moore, "An Integrated Collection of Software Engineering Standards," *IEEE Software*, November/December 1999, pp. 51-57.

[22] Mike Nelson, James Clark, and Martha Ann Spurlock, "Curing the Software Requirements and Cost Estimating Blues: The Fix is Easier Than You Might Think," *Program Manager*, Vol. XXVIII, No. 6, Defense Systems Management College (DSMC) 153, November-December 1999, pp. 54-60.

[23] Nimal Nissanke, *Formal Specification: Techniques and Applications*, Springer-Verlag, 1999.

[24] http://eis.jpl.nasa.gov/quality/Formal_Methods/index.html.

[25] Software Engineering Institute "Introduction," Vol. 2, No. 1, March 1999, *SEI Interactive: Software Requirements Engineering* [http://www.sei.cmu.edu/products/sei.interactive].

[26] http://archive.comlab.ox.ac.uk/formal-methods.html.

[27] Mike Nelson, James Clark, and Martha Ann Spurlock, "Curing the Software Requirements and Cost Estimating Blues: The Fix is Easier Than You Might Think," *Program Manager*, Vol. XXVIII, No. 6, Defense Systems Management College (DSMC) 153, November-December 1999, pp. 54-60.

[28] Glasow, Priscilla and Dale Pace, "SIMVAL 99 Final Report," Military Operations Research Society (MORS), March 26, 1999.

[29] Mike Nelson, James Clark, and Martha Ann Spurlock, "Curing the Software Requirements and Cost Estimating Blues: The Fix is Easier Than You Might Think," *Program Manager*, Vol. XXVIII, No. 6, Defense Systems Management College (DSMC) 153, November-December 1999, pp. 54-60.

[30] Lewis, R.O. 1992. Independent Verification and Validation: A Life Cycle Engineering Process for Quality Software. John Wiley & Sons, New York.

[31] Dale K. Pace, "An Aspect of VV&A Costs," *PHALANX*, Vol 30, No. 1, March 1997, pp.12-15.

[32] Department of Defense (DoD) *Recommended Practices Guide for Verification, Validation, and Accreditation (VV&A)*, available from the Defense Modeling and Simulation Office (DMSO) website: http://www.dmso.mil.

[33] Jordan, W., Charen, D., Cotten, C., and Lewis, R. 1995. Planning, Optimizing, and Costing Verification, Validation, and Accreditation (VV&A) for Distributed Interactive Simulations (DIS). Proceedings of the 1995

Summer Computer Simulation Conference, Ottawa, Canada, July 24-26. Society for Computer Simulation, pp. 597-602.

[34] J. P.Bowen and V.Stavridou, 1994. "Safety-Critical Systems and Formal Methods," Chapter 1 in *Toward Verified Systems*, J. Bowen, Elseview Science B. V., New York, pp. 3-33.

About the Author

Dale K. Pace, a member of the Principal Professional Staff of The Johns Hopkins University Applied Physics Laboratory, is a specialist in operations research, modeling and simulation, analysis, and wargaming. He was a SIMVAL 99 co-chair and is a member of the DMSO VV&A Technical Working Group and its VV&A Technical Support Team. He was the initial lead for the validation part of the IV&V team for Wargame 2000 and he is *Simulation's* Associate Editor for Validation. He served as SCSC '91 Program Chair and General Chair for SCSC '95. He has been the principal contributor to the simulation conceptual model section of the 2000 version of DoD's *Recommended Practices Guide (RPG) for VV&A.*

****

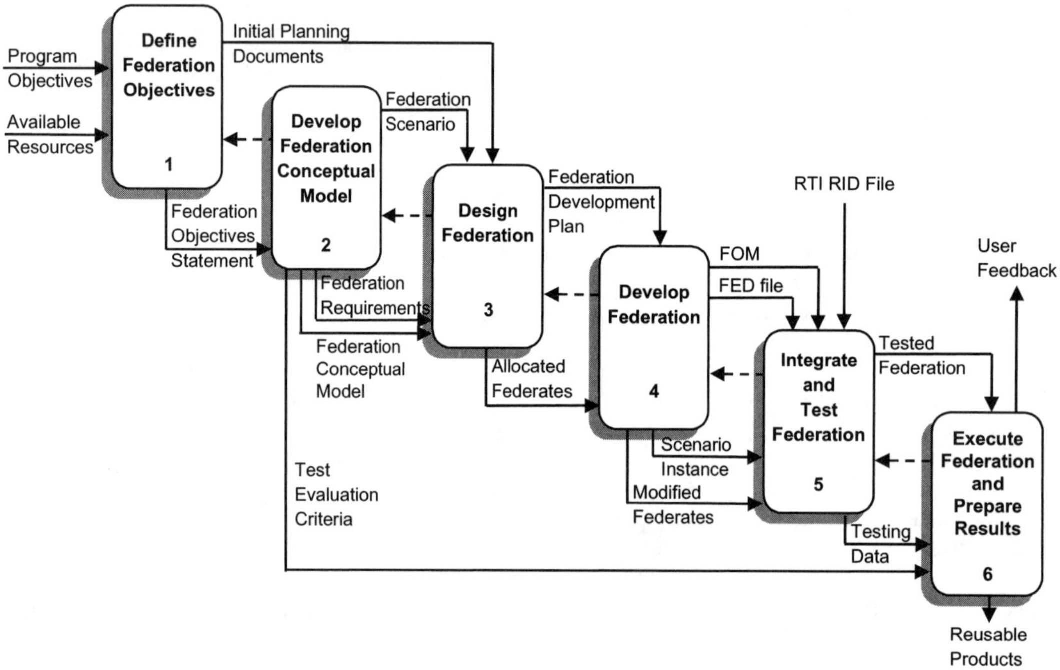

Figure 1. Six-Step FEDEP Process (Version 1.4)

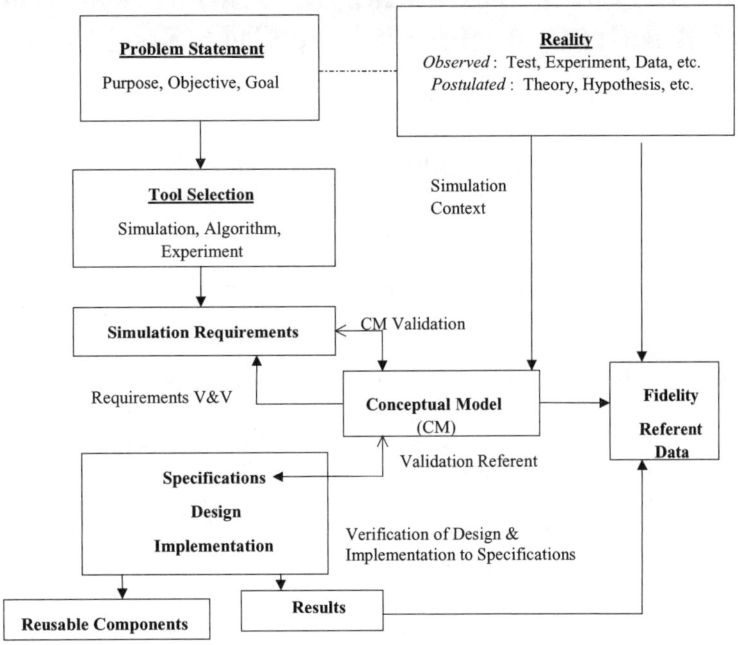

Figure 2. Simulation Development Elements

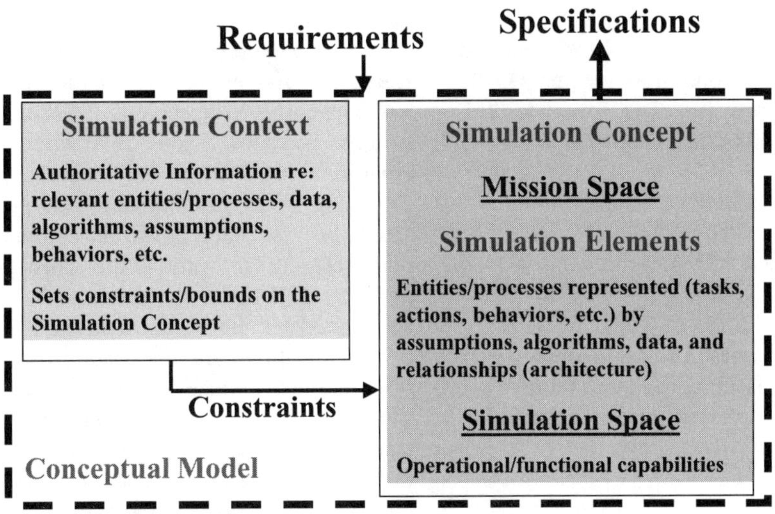

Figure 3. Conceptual Model Components

Knowledge Acquisition for Simulation Requirements: Resolving Ambiguity the CMMS-DD Way

Ronald Smits
Bruce A. Harris
Dynamics Research Corporation
60 Frontage Road
Andover, MA 01810
978-475-9090 ext.1498
bharris@drc.com, rsmits@drc.com

KEYWORDS: Conceptual Modeling, CMMS, Data Dictionary,

ABSTRACT: With the proliferation of taxonomies in the Modeling and Simulation (M&S) community and associated linguistic challenges, a cohesive approach is needed to taxonomy integration. This paper will present a case study, with lessons learned, on the continued developments in taxonomies for the Defense Modeling and Simulation Office's (DMSO) Conceptual Model of the Mission Space (CMMS) toolset. It serves as a review of the state-of-the-art in development of taxonomies and ontologies that support M&S activities broadly sponsored by DMSO. The paper's broad focus is on an evaluation of organizational schemas that appear to offer advantages to DMSO efforts in bridging the linguistic and conceptual differences between M&S activities and warfighters. The development of doctrinally correct, logically consistent, and linguistically unambiguous taxonomies requires the judicious adherence to an established plan, complete with V&V. The paper describes efforts that focused on:

(a) Evaluating existing CMMS-DD taxonomy sufficiency and applicability.
(b) Research and development of M&S-approved taxonomies.
(c) V&V for M&S approved taxonomy (ies).
(d) Mapping existing taxonomies to M&S taxonomies.
(e) Filling CMMS-DD consistent with M&S taxonomy needs and appropriate mapping to exterior taxonomies.

INTRODUCTION

If one examines the doctrinal and other sources produced by and for military Service components, vast differences in jargon can be observed. There is no lack of linguistic ambiguity among Services, between the military language and the English language, and between military language and M&S language. Each domain, be it military, civilian, M&S, or logistics, etc., seems to promulgate a private language, loosely derived from English, that intends to capture concepts, processes, and procedures that are supposedly unique to that domain. The effort to structure data and institutionalize data standards extends beyond the definitional aspects of terms. As important as the semantics are, the structure of semantics in a recognized syntax deserves equal attention. That syntax is often referred to as the taxonomy of a data source or data product.

The M&S community faces difficult challenges in creating realistic and authoritative representations of what we commonly refer to as the real world of the military mission space. While assessing the utility of taxonomies for M&S, the transition from the real-world warfighter jargon, presented in doctrinal and operations data products, to the synthetic representation of that action or task should be facilitated. As the transition is made from these operational data products through the internal processes of other user communities, preservation of original intent is a concern. Linguistic and conceptual challenges must be confronted and overcome to specify a realistic representation of the actions, entities, and interactions in the synthetic environment. A "common" resource serves the purpose of providing access to domain data products for users not normally associated with that domain, or cross-domain purposes, by informing the cross-domain user of the producer's intent. By necessity, a common resource accommodates the needs of users of different domains. By organizing the data (or data-products) into a common resource, the producer of the common resource attempts to categorize the existing products into an ontology or taxonomy. While assisting in the population of the common resources, the organizational structure of the resource also guides intended users in their search for information or data.

Much research has been conducted on taxonomy and ontology development in general. Not all this research directly relates to military operations. Discussions and debates on methods to structure military domain knowledge, often conducted to assist outsider understanding of the warfighter's domain, can quickly become acrimonious and parochial. The study and use of taxonomies, ontologies, taxons (as a taxonomic group in a formal nomenclature), or a combination thereof, can create an almost toxic atmosphere in which bias and prejudices run rampant. However, many of the findings and conclusions regarding their feasibility for capturing and categorizing knowledge are relevant regardless of domain. This paper presents a synthesis of some leading studies in their respective fields in a later section and presents a CMMS-DD data model derived from a compilation of taxonomy and ontology (tax-on). For now, a general discourse regarding differences and similarities between taxonomy and ontology is provided.

TAXONOMIES AND ONTOLOGIES

Taxonomies are widely researched and employed in scientific literature, biology probably foremost, while other areas of academia embrace ontology to facilitate enterprise modeling. A primary distinction between taxonomy and ontology appears to be the conceptualization of the organizing classes or hierarchy. A taxonomy typically resembles a tree structure of progressively more detailed classes. Within each branch a commonality, explicitly defined, exists, but instance data is placed at the lowest possible sub-class, consistent with the defining characteristics of the branches and sub-classes. A taxonomy is a hierarchy of concepts. In addition to the basic *isA* relation, *partOf* relation may also be used from time to time in a taxonomy.

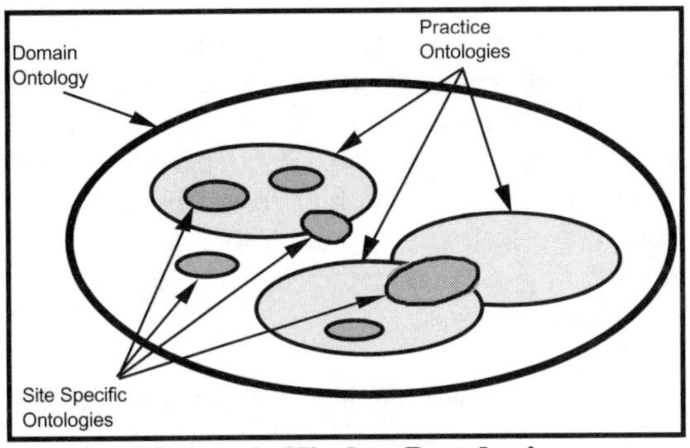

Figure 1. Kinds ofOntologies

In examining an ontology, the relationships between the classes and concepts that define the organizational structure appear of more importance. Initially, the term "ontology" was used in philosophy as a "theory of existence." Following Thomas Gruber [1][2][3], the Artificial Intelligence (AI) community adapted ontology as "an explicit representation of conceptualization." Ontology is an explicit and precise description of concepts and relations that exists in a particular domain such as a given organization, a study field, or an application area. Mike Uschold [4][5][6] developed an "Enterprise Ontology" to model business enterprises, along with a guide for building the ontology. Benjamin Perakath [7] and his team expanded on that work and constructed the IDEF5 method to capture ontology. In their research they describe and define the central concepts of ontology at three levels of generality: domain ontologies, practice ontologies, and site-specific ontologies (Figure 1). The following section more closely examines the leading theories and practices in ontological development.

Ontologies

In this section, four papers are reviewed from the body of knowledge examined on ontological development and its role in knowledge acquisition and sharing.

Gruber's Approach. Thomas Gruber developed the idea at Stanford University's Knowledge Systems Laboratory to use formal ontologies as a way of specifying content-specific agreements for the sharing and reuse of knowledge among software entities. Intelligent agents, capable of querying and answering queries, are employed to share information between knowledge-based systems. Agents that operate in a distributed AI environment, communicate across systems using statements in a formal knowledge representation. Gruber asserted this form of knowledge sharing involved conventions at three levels: representation language format, agent communication, and shared knowledge content specifications.

Case studies illustrated the capability of an extensible representational vocabulary to minimize or eliminate bias, specifically encoding bias. The case studies also illustrated the capability and scalability of the necessary commitment to the ontology. Where a strong theory basis exists, axioms can be developed relatively easily for most concepts, resulting in real implementation constraints for the agents. Where such a strong theoretical underpinning does not exist, such as in the bibliographic exchange of information, the ontological commitment did not require constraints that would unduly impose on the world being modeled.

Uschold's Enterprise Ontology Concept. In an extension of Gruber's work and the Knowledge Interchange Format (KIF), Mike Uschold set out to develop an enterprise model. The overall goal of enterprise modeling is to take an enterprise-wide view of an organization that can then be used as a basis for making decisions. He defined "ontology" as the shared understanding of some domain of interest that may then be used as a unifying framework to solve problems. As ontology embodies some "world view," it is often conceived as a set of concepts (e.g. entities, attributes, processes), their definitions and their inter-relationships. Such a conceptualization can be implicit or explicit. Ontology most frequently refers to an explicit conceptualization.

An ontology can have different forms, ranging from highly informal (such as loosely expressed in natural language) to rigorously formal (with meticulously defined terms with formal semantics, theorems and proofs of such properties as soundness and completeness). Uschold identified thee main categories of uses for ontologies, communications, interoperability, and systems engineering (Figure 2).

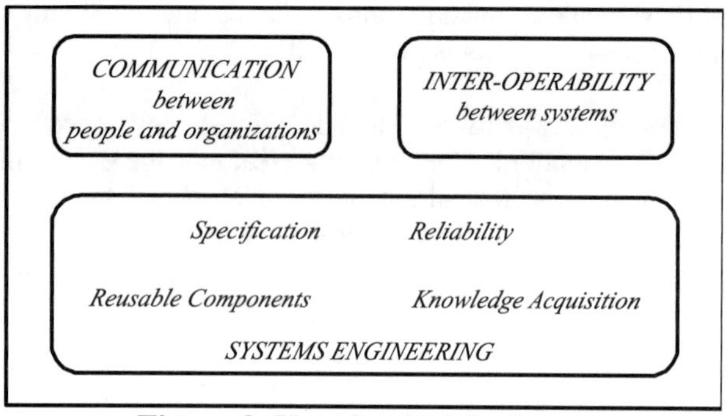

Figure 2. Uses for Ontologies

In building an ontology, a number of questions are addressed, such as purpose and scope, capture, coding, integration of existing ontologies, and evaluation.

In further efforts, Uschold and others developed the Enterprise Ontology, an implementation experiment of the theoretical approach advocated by them. The Enterprise Ontology provided a comprehensive description, with a collection of terms and definitions, relevant to business enterprises. The study formalized the natural language definitions of the informal (prototype) ontology into a formal "Ontolingua," the formal ontology language. Ontolingua is a formal language based on the KIF [8]. During the formalization process, the team characterized several issues that might also be confronted by others when converting an informal ontology into a formal one. These issues included:

(a) Deciding when a term did not need to be explicitly defined.
(b) Representing terms from different perspectives.
(c) Determining when and how to introduce new terms to fill gaps, to amplify informal ontology, or to formalize logical connections where such relationships were not obvious from informal ontology.

IDEF5 Approach. Benjamin Perakath and his team developed an Integrated Definition (IDEF) method to capture ontology descriptions. The reviewed report provides a comprehensive description of the IDEF 5 Ontology Description Capture Method. The report is designed for multiple audiences, to include knowledge engineers and application domain experts interested in developing, documenting, storing, and sharing domain knowledge, and system analysts and designers interested in managing knowledge effectively for both design and analysis purposes.

One of the primary benefits associated with ontology is the standardization of terminology. Coordinating large projects across functional areas or domains and the diversity of concepts and jargon necessitate a standardization of relevant vocabulary. Such standardization also provides strong motivation for use and reusability of the ontology. Large, revisable ontology databases containing structured, domain-specific information allow access to meet current needs. The IDEF5 method fulfills this need by providing a mechanism to acquire, store, and maintain scaleable and re-useable ontologies.

The IDEF5 ontology development process consists of five activities:

(a) Organizing and Scoping: This activity involves establishing the purpose, viewpoint, and context for the ontology development project and assigning roles to the team members.
(b) Data Collection: This activity involves acquiring the raw data needed for ontology development.
(c) Data Analysis: This activity involves analyzing the data to facilitate ontology extraction.
(d) Initial Ontology Development: This activity involves developing a preliminary ontology from the acquired data.
(e) Ontology Refinement and Validation: This activity involves refining and validating the ontology to complete the development process.

IDEF5 employs two languages: the schematic language (Figure 3) and the elaboration language. The schematic language is perhaps closest to IDEF1 and IDEF1X; it provides a relatively easy to use graphical language that has been tailored to express the most common forms of ontological information.

The elaboration language contains all definitions and characterizing axioms, in a structured text language with the full expressive power of first-order logic and set theory. This language can express a broad range of conditions, or relations, or facts needed to express a given kind of thing, property, relation, or process found in a domain. The syntax of the language uses a prefix notation and parentheses to delimit expressions. The alphabet for the language consists of the standard alphanumeric and punctuation characters.

The *core* of the IDEF5 Elaboration Language, which enables the expression of axioms, is based on the KIF.

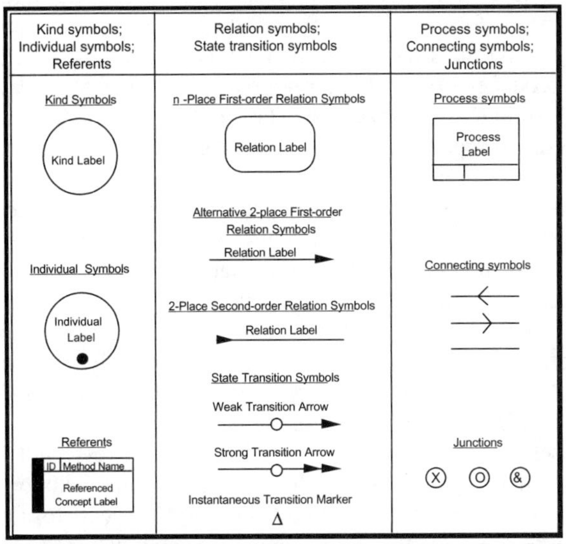

Figure 3. IDEF5 Schematic Language Symbols

Slattery's Study. After first reviewing some of the approaches to global ontology, Norma Slattery [9] argues that several challenges remain with the global ontology approach. She suggests the result of ontology engineering is the integration of systems at the *data* level, that is, below the database application level. Recognizing that a syntactic interface is necessary but not sufficient for semantic interoperability, Slattery asserts that the data level of integration is where owners and users of the knowledge base will realize true interoperability. To test that argument, she selected the military domain as an example. Figure 4 shows Slattery's ontological view of the military domain, where she saw the greater challenge to Jointness as the "military cultural mindset, rather than the semantic differences." Her study of joint integration by means of ontological tools focused on the areas of commonality, the common "business" units.

The study examined the achievability of the Joint Services Ontology. Arguably, the central database of the Joint Services Ontology is important, because it is through this that the "data in the plethora of military and associated databases can start to be effectively mined to yield the information needed to support advanced uses of information technology by military leaders and warfighters." Slattery selected the IDEF5 methodology, since it appeared most mature and most general for ontology engineering purposes.

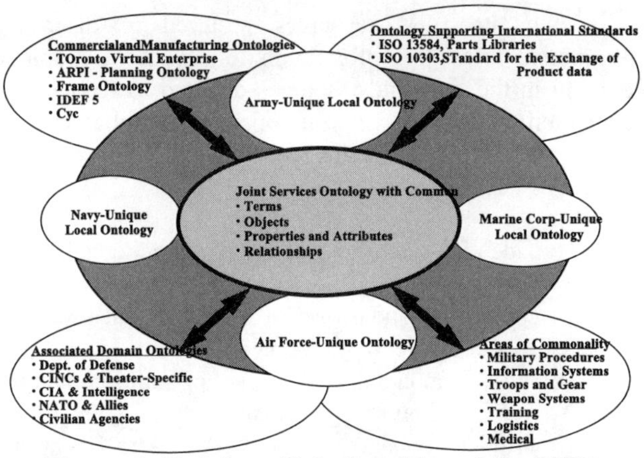

Figure 4. Ontology Relationships of the Military "Universe" and Tangential Domains

Both the Schematic Language and the Elaboration Language were envisioned to be used in the development of the Joint Services Ontology. Slattery's study was only carried out at an aggregate level, but illustrated the enhanced communication within the military domain between decision-makers and analytical activities, if the ontology would serve as a common database of domain objects and its standard definition. A consequence of enhanced communication would be increased reuse and data sharing.

Taxonomies

In this section, several noteworthy projects are reviewed to illustrate the methodology and techniques commonly used during the development of taxonomies. They serve to define characteristics common to organizing schemas applicable to military organizations, activities, or simulations. First, an overview of the assumptions and constructs underlying the Authoritative Data Sources project is presented. Next, a study by Michael Fineberg, who developed a taxonomy for the modeling of human behavior that has broad applicability to military operations, is reviewed. Finally, efforts by Michael Collins and his team to develop a taxonomy for battle management systems used in military simulations is examined.

ADS. As part of the overall strategy for standardization of "data," DMSO sponsored the development of the Authoritative Data Sources Project. The ADS identifies government and commercial data producers and repositories in the United States and around the world. It sets out to capture a standard set of metadata - data about data - that describes and provides a pedigree to the sources. As such, ADS supports structured data mining. The ADS was developed to assist the knowledge acquisition process by identifying the best sources for starter-information and to reduce the time and resources required to discovery authoritative reference information to support a dramatic reduction in the time and resources devoted to Knowledge Acquisition while improving interoperability and assuring a high degree of fidelity with the real world.

The ADS is designed:

(a) To identify government and commercial data producers.

(b) To capture a standard set of metadata that describes and provides a pedigree to the sources.

(c) To have components affix a level of authoritativeness to each source based on recognized standards.

(d) To provide tools to support M&S users in rapidly identifying sources appropriate to their needs.

In analyzing "authoritative sources" the focus was on guiding the user to data sources on either the classified Secret Internet Protocol Router Network (SIPRNET) or the unclassified sources on the Internet. A dynamic effort, the ADS has at this point catalogued over 1061 sources. Of these, the Services and DoD Agencies have designated 458 as Authoritative, Approved or Other. The number of additional candidates that have been identified for cataloging and subsequent inclusion in the database stands at 862 and that number grows daily. The ADS Library catalogs these data sources using a formal taxonomy with 13 top-level categories and 373 subcategories.

Fineberg's Approach. Michael Fineberg [10] conducted a study to determine a systematic approach to the modeling of human behavior in synthetic forces (SF). This study was in direct support of the DoD Modeling and Simulation Master Plan's Objective 4, Human Behavior Representation. Fineberg reports on the Behavioral Taxonomy Project (BTP), the overall purpose of which was increased interoperability and reuse of models and data.

The BTP developed a new behavioral taxonomy that provided some important elements:

(a) A common conceptual view of human behavior: The development of a conceptual model of human behavior (CMHB) allowed model developers to better understand fundamental relationships between human behavior and its antecedent conditions.

(b) A syntax for the language of human behavior: The development of a comprehensive and flexible integrating structure for the organization of human behavior into classes.

(c) The semantics or meanings for human behavior terms: A series of action verbs, populating the taxonomy, and their respective meaning for use across research, development, and user communities.

In developing the taxonomy, the report examined the relevant literature on human behavior classification and taxonomies from the past 35 years. This review highlighted the need for a description of the structure and model underlying the structure of the taxonomy. Both the user and the producer of the taxonomy greatly benefit from creating an explicit categorization. The reviewed literature was roughly divided into taxonomies for individual operators and taxonomies for groups and teams, since the development of taxonomies and the approach used is dependent on the goals of the developer. Although different approaches to taxonomy development were reviewed, three key issues were involved: the why, what, and how of class definition. Classes need objective and concise definitions, where the classes are exhaustive and mutually exclusive, with utility and validity, and clearly established relationships between tasks (for behavior models) and classes. None of the behavioral taxonomies reviewed had used such techniques. Fineberg observed that taxonomies are developed for the purpose they are intended to serve, without much regard to wide applicability, without the strict application of the "exclusivity" principle (orthogonality). As such, most taxonomies are not easily transferable to other systems and lack a conceptual model. The lack of a conceptual model is apparent since most taxonomies are developed heuristically. Developing one unified, multi-purpose behavioral taxonomy was the goal of Fineberg's project.

The report developed a model to understand human combatant behavior under stress (Figure 5). The model follows a "stimulus-decision-response" paradigm within a set of antecedents that shape the "decision-response" conditions. The CMHB suggests generic battle stress conditions and the combat tasks for particular scenarios interact in creating an environmental demand for individual combatants or crews.

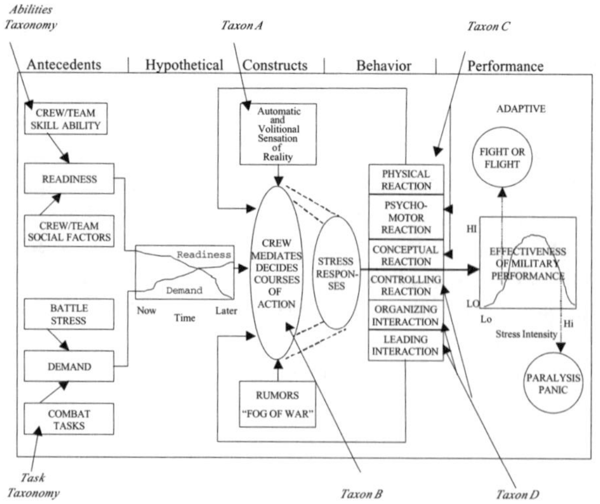

Figure 5. Conceptual Model of Human Behavior

The proposed taxonomy, based on a model of information processing, developed operational definitions for all of the terms listed, specifying the meaning of the behavior and a process for measurement of the behavior. The four taxons are (A) Sensation, (B) Mediation, (C) Reaction, and (D) Interaction.

AN ORGANIZING STRUCTURE FOR CMMS-DD

The construction of mission space models, the individual components of the CMMS, requires a multi-step process. Knowledge about the domain needs to be acquired, but not all knowledge is relevant. The analyst needs to develop a focused context before gathering domain information within that context. Next, the information needs to be formalized to enable software engineers to use their favorite modeling tools to construct a mission space model.

The exchange of domain knowledge is vitally important to the modeling and simulation process. In the past, knowledge gathered to support simulation efforts was often incomplete, not well documented, ambiguous, and not reusable. The costs associated with the KA are substantial and the need to construct authoritative and accurate simulation systems within constrained resources has increased. The CMMS Toolset Architecture as part of the DMSO Data Engineering strategy intends to mitigate risks associated with the development of military simulations.

The CMMS-DD, or the CSS, assists the SME or analyst in turning gathered domain information into formalized data that can be used and understood by software engineers. Its applicability extends beyond that scope, however. By providing authoritative explanations of term-definition combinations, the CMMS-DD can serve many users not traditionally considered part of the M&S domain. The CMMS-DD structure should accommodate the needs of these different users to fulfill its potential. The next section of this paper examines some structures for capturing domain information.

Data Organization and Enterprise Modeling

The CMMS-DD was primarily constructed by mining relevant term-definition combinations from Joint and Service publications. The gathering of these authoritative combinations into a single resource provides interested parties with easy access to this data. It is the organization of the data into a meaningful structure, however, that creates the "value-added" to the resource, as shown in the review of the literature earlier.

CMMS-DD exists in a relationship to other tools developed to support the building of conceptual models. The use of unambiguous term-definition combinations in the context of the appropriate domain would greatly facilitate the reuse of the produced models, while reducing development risk and cost. The need to bridge

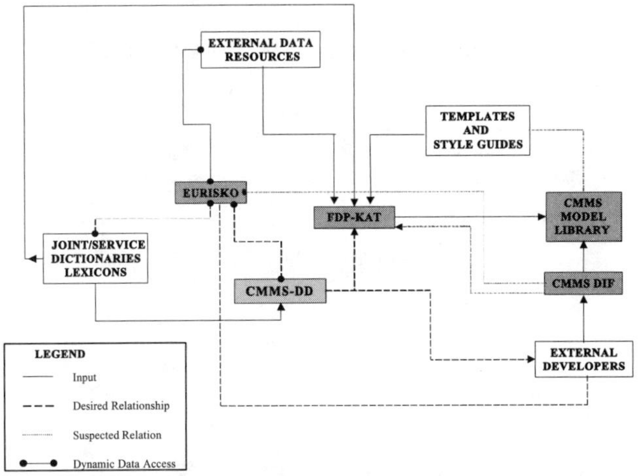

Figure 6. DMSO-Sponsored KA Tool Interactions

the linguistic gap between the warfighter (often the SME) and the simulation developer (a SME in his or her own right) is paramount to the success of the CMMS-DD. This can be accomplished by removing linguistic ambiguity present within the different military domains and between the military domain and the simulation developer's domain. Understanding the function (purpose) the CMMS-DD fulfills within this constellation of tools is important. Data exchanges between the tools occur and the CMMS-DD intends to bridge an "information gap" between different domains. Figure 6 illustrates the interactions among some of the tools and tool users in the development of a conceptual model.

CMMS-DD Structure

John Zachman [11][12] introduced an architecture for enterprise modeling that represents a mix between a taxonomy and ontology. He examined how information could bridge the gap between the strategy (expectations) and implementation(s) for an enterprise. This bridge was the enterprise architecture. The challenge faced by information systems was to capture those components that create an enterprise environment that was conducive to change.

Zachman found by studying aircraft manufacturing and building construction that the method to accurately represent a "product" largely depended on one's perspective. He discovered a set of representations was necessary to accommodate these different viewpoints. Additionally, he identified intersecting representations for the characteristics of the "product" itself, such as the production process, the material used, who built it, etc. The Zachman framework (Figure 7) resulted from the realization that these product characteristics can be completely represented in six columns. The "user" viewpoints can be represented within each column as a distinct row for the enterprise architecture.

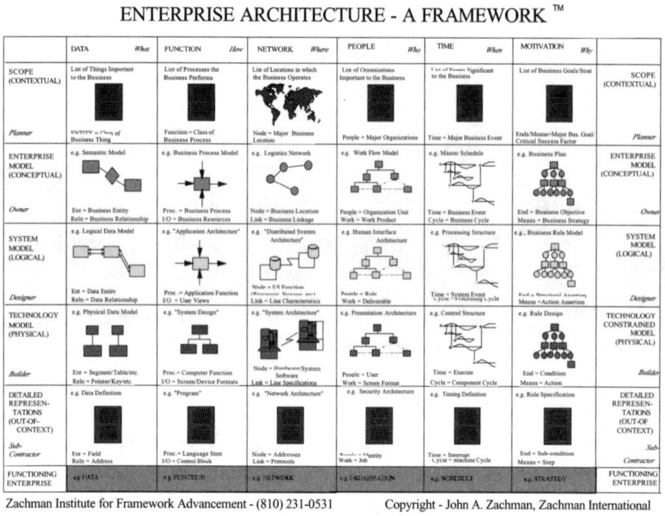

Figure 7.Zachman's Framework

The columns in the framework represent the "what, how, where, who, when, and why" of the enterprise. These columns capture succinctly all aspects related to a "product" for any particular point of view *within* the enterprise. The material description is captured in the "What" column, with a focus on entities and relationships. This column describes what makes up organizational information, the data. Data, however, needs to be related to other data, so this column also describes the relationships that should be maintained among the data. The functional description is contained by the "How" column and describes the input-process-output model of the enterprise. Its focus is the functions and arguments, or describes "how" the data ("what") is used. Next, the location is represented in "Where" column, describing the flow of information and work within the enterprise. The connections between the different locations should be identified in this column as well. "Who" describes the allocation of work to people and organizations involved.

Finally, "When" is used to communicate event-to-event relationships that establish performance criteria and quantitative levels of enterprise resources, while the "Why" column's focus is on ends and means. It describes the motivation of the enterprise, the objectives (ends) and its strategies or methods (means).

For the CMMS-DD, term-definition combinations need to be assigned attributes that uniquely identify their location in a data model. Expanding Zachman's framework to include a third dimension enables the access to data from all required viewpoints. The data (term-definition combination) can be stored at only one instance in the model and therefore is uniquely identified by its use. Figure 8 provides a graphical representation of the three-dimensional data model. The CMMS-DD data model uses the column format (focus or abstraction perspective) from Zachman's Framework, modifies the participant perspectives, and adds the domain perspective. Each of these three perspectives is briefly discussed below.

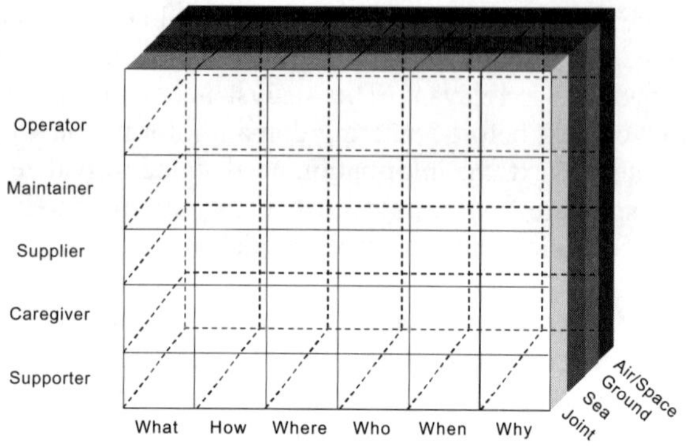

Figure 8. CMMS-DD Data Model

Domain Perspective. In defining the domain perspective, two choices present themselves. First, one could use the Services as the attribute that places data in the respective slice. The Army may define a term differently from the Air Force and thus, given a similar Participant and Focus, the data could be differentiated based on Service. For a term that is defined or described differently (even just slightly) within a Service, as is often the case, given the same Participant and Focus, the analyst filling the data model would be required to choose among these combinations. This would lead to "second-guessing" the needs of the Service and the SME. By removing the Service orientation from the Domain perspective, a choice by the CMMS-DD analyst represents the preferred term-definition combination for the CMMS Toolset, without restricting the Services to define the term differently. The CMMS-DD analyst can thus avoid a parochial view and instead concentrate on capturing all relevant domain concepts. The categories chosen for the domain perspective are related to the operational (or physical) environment.

Participant Perspective. The Participant perspective in Zachman's Framework often represents successive viewpoints. They reflect the need to develop, manage, maintain, and use the information system in the enterprise. The business of the military can arguably be described as the protection and enforcement of national security interests through the use of military force. This leads to five categories of participants. The first group identified includes those who operate the equipment that delivers military force, the operators. Next are those who maintain the equipment, the maintainers. Someone has to supply the equipment and its consumables, the suppliers. All these participants require care to stay healthy and ready for duty. Caregivers are in the business of providing health and welfare to the force. Finally, all these folks need to be paid, transferred, fed, housed, and directed. Supporters provide these needed functions.

Focus/Abstraction Perspective. The Focus or Abstraction perspective of the CMMS-DD can be mapped to doctrinal references of what needs to be done by whom, how, when, where, and why. The SMEs involved with KA would like to access the data in relation to the terminology for which they develop products. Such categories include equipment, tasks, missions, task performers, organizations, information items, locations, etc.

While the Zachman generic column terms are relevant in Service doctrine, a simple "translation" of those terms to an easily understood and bound term is more problematic. If the "what" is equipment, it leaves operations to migrate to the "how" or "why" column. The question that could be asked about the placement of terms in the "how" or "why" column must link to another attribute of the term-definition combination: the part-of-speech (POS) attribute.

The "what" column could very well differentiate between nouns (equipment) and processes (operations), if the generic column name is maintained. To store a task in the three-dimensional model, the analyst would assign the verb property in the POS attribute and place the term-definition combination in the "how" column.

CMMS-DDTaxon

The CMMS-DD data model stores four attributes for each selected term-definition combination. Each entry in the CMMS-DD will be identified with the focus or abstraction of the term-definition combination, its applicable (physical) domain environment, its participants' perspective, and the part-of-speech that the entry refers to. Figure 9 lists the possible values for the four attributes.

FOCUS/ABSTRACTION	PARTICIPANT	DOMAIN	P-O-S
What	Operator	Joint	Noun
How	Maintainer	Ground	Verb
Where	Supplier	Sea	Process
Who	Caregiver	Air/Space	
When	Supporter		
Why			

Figure 9. CMMS-DD Attribute Values

VERIFICATION AND VALIDATION

When discussing verification and validation, several issues take center stage. Not only the scope of the V&V effort should be determined, but also the semantics of V&V. What needs to be "verified" and/or "validated?" What is involved in V&V of a data dictionary? Ultimately, it is the customer who determines the program's needs for traceability and accuracy for the resource. Programmatically, V&V add costs early to the development process, but should save resources later.

For the purpose of the CMMS-DD, the need to establish clear and concise business rules to populate the resource was established in earlier work [13]. This stated need was taken one step further in the current effort, by clearly establishing the requirements and constraints for the organizational structure of the resource. For the life cycle of the CMMS-DD, it is envisioned that at a minimum, "verification" will take place by the customer at each major milestone. The verification of the CMMS-DD taxon as a meaningful representation for the military domain and a useful methodology to structure domain knowledge would greatly enhance the resource's potential for use and re-use.

Next, business rules approved by the customer need to restrict the population of the CMMS-DD to provide the degree of authoritativeness and accuracy required. These business rules need to address the constraints and mining criteria, in addition to the explicit declaration of the attributes and meta-data required for the data entered into the resource. Automated tools can greatly assist in the systematic population of the resource by enforcing the strict application of the approved business rules. To that end, a data entry tool will be used to ensure all involved analysts can mine and process data consistently.

Ultimately, the goal of the CMMS-DD is unambiguous and authoritative semantic descriptions of data elements required to communicate knowledge about the military domain. Business rules, tools, source selection criteria, mining criteria, categorizations, and semantically unambiguous descriptions all serve to advance the ability to communicate concepts clearly between and across domains. Therefore, the CMMS-DD should be able to withstand the same scrutiny as the simulations it intends to enhance.

SUMMARY

Constructing mission space models requires the collaborative efforts of many individuals and organizations. Communicating requirements, specifications, desires, and intents clearly among and across all involved parties has been a major obstacle. The CMMS-DD intends to bridge that linguistic gap by capturing domain knowledge and concepts in an authoritative and unambiguous fashion.

Data resources can be structured using taxonomies and ontologies, each with advantages and disadvantages that are well documented in the literature. For the CMMS-DD, a combination of the two is proposed, resulting in a three-dimensional data model that can uniquely capture military domain knowledge from a variety of perspectives. The data model includes vantage points for participants, focus, domain, and part-of-speech. Together with a robust suite of support tools (verified business rules, categorization schema, capture tools, taxonomy mapping) the CMMS-DD can provide confidence and traceability to the data (term-description combinations) entered. The resource should withstand a level of scrutiny that is equal to the integrity required from military simulations. The verification and validation of the resource can and should be enabled and simplified by the very tools that support its development.

REFERENCES

[1] Gruber, Thomas R., "Ontolingua: A Mechanism to Support Portable Ontologies," Stanford University, Knowledge Systems Laboratory, *Technical Report KSL-91-66*, March 1992 Revision.

[2] Gruber, Thomas R., "A Translation Approach to Portable Ontology Specifications," *Knowledge Acquisition,* 5(2): pp.199-220. http://ksl-web.stanford.edu/knowledge-sharing/papers/ontolingua-intro.rtf

[3] Gruber Thomas R., "Toward Principles for the Design of Ontologies Used for Knowledge Sharing," Originally presented at International Workshop on Formal Ontology March 1993. 23 August 1993 http://ksl-web.stanford.edu/knowledge-sharing/papers/onto-design.ps

[4] Uschold Mike, *et al*, "The Enterprise Ontology," *The Knowledge Engineering Review*, Vol. 13, Special Issue on "Putting Ontologies to Use" (eds. Uschold, M. and Tate, A.), Cambridge University Press. ftp://ftp.aiai.ed.ac.uk/pub/documents/1998/98-ker-ent-ontology.ps

[5] Uschold Mike, *et al*, "Ontologies: Principles, Methods and Applications," *Knowledge Engineering Review*, Volume 11, Number 2, June 1996, Cambridge University Press, February 1996. http://www.aiai.ed.ac.uk/project/enterprise/enterprise/ontology.html

[6] Uschold Mike, "Building Ontologies: Towards a Unified Methodology," Expert Systems '96, 16th Annual Conference of the British Computer Society Specialist Group on Expert Systems.

[7] Perakath, Benjamin C., *et al*, "Ontology Capture Method (IDEF5)," Armstrong Laboratory AL/HR-TP-1994-002, Air Force Materiel Command, 21 September 1994. http://www.idef.com/downloads/rtf/idef5.rtf

[8] Genesereth, M. R., *et al*, "Knowledge Interchange Format Version 3.0 - Reference Manual," Report Logic-92-1, Logic Group, Stanford University, CA. 1992 http://logic.stanford.edu/kif/Hypertext/kif-manual.html

[9] Slattery, Norma J., "A Study of Ontology and Its Uses in Information Technology Systems," Proceedings of the 1997 Software Engineering & Economics Conference, 1997. http://www.mitre.org/support/papers/swee/papers/slattery/21_slattery.doc

[10] Fineberg, Michael L, "A Comprehensive Taxonomy of Human Behaviors for Synthetic Forces," Institute for Defense Analyses, Alexandria VA 22311-1772, November 1995.

[11] Zachman, John A. "A Framework for Information Systems Architecture," *IBM Systems Journal*, vol. 26, no. 3, 1987. IBM Publication G321-5298.

[12] Zachman, John A. and J.F. Sowa, "Extending and Formalizing the Framework for Information Systems Architecture," *IBM Systems Journal*, vol. 31, no. 3, 1992. IBM Publication G321-5488.

[13] Harris, Bruce A., *et al*, Final Report Conceptual Models of the Mission Space Data Dictionary, Defense Modeling and Simulation Office, Alexandria, VA 22311, 31 December 1998.

AUTHOR BIOGRAPHIES

BRUCE HARRIS is the program manager for the CMMS Data Dictionary project for the Dynamics Research Corporation. In addition to his 30 years experience in military force planning and analysis as an Army officer, he has an extensive background in conceptual modeling and requirements analysis. One of his earlier projects involved the Universal Joint Task List and the definition of performance measures for joint tasks and operations.

RON SMITS is a systems analyst for Dynamics Research Corporation. He is the DMSO CMMS DE liaison to the NASM program and brings 16 years experience flying operational fighter aircraft to the simulation world. He has been involved with the CMMS Data Dictionary and NASM conceptual models since joining DRC in 1998.

A MENTAL MODEL FOR SIMULATION STATISTICAL ANALYSIS

Yu-Hui Tao
Dept. of Information Management
I-Shou University
Kaohsiung, Taiwan
ytao@isu.edu.tw

Shin-Ming Guo
Dept. of Industrial Management
I-Shou University
Kaohsiung, Taiwan
smguo@isu.edu.tw

KEYWORDS: mental model, pilot run, simulation statistical analysis

ABSTRACT

Many practitioners who have basic simulation training can not comfortably perform simulation statistical analysis. This paper proposes a conceptual model that contains two cognitive principles, two analysis indicators, and an expert heuristic, which help a practitioner form an appropriate mental model for facilitating their simulation statistical analyses. Instead of a fixed and exact heuristic, the proposed model works as a high-level generalized template for guiding the simulation statistical analysis.

INTRODUCTION

A typical simulation analysis project includes problem definition, simulation modeling, simulation programming, simulation statistical analysis, and recommendation (Law and Kelton 1991). To many simulation practitioners, after going through a disastrous simulation modeling and programming, the tedious and profound statistical analysis make them uncomfortable. To our observations, it is because that not only statistics itself is a difficult skill to learn, but also simulation statistical analysis is often squeezed to the minimum in either the classroom teaching or in the field practice due to time constraint. As a result, it usually takes much longer for simulation practitioners to facilitate the knowledge and experience of simulation statistical analysis.

While there are many simulation references, it is difficult to find the practical process to perform simulation statistical analysis in either the literature or textbooks. Statistical Expert System for Simulation Analysis (SESSA) (Mellichamp and Park 1989) provides a collection of statistical procedures such that its user can choose a statistical procedure from the corresponding class of simulation tasks. Warwick Expert Simulation (WES) (Taylor and Hurrion 1988) provides a computer-assisted approach for executing a simulation analysis. Both SESSA and WES ignored the resource constraint emphasized in a framework for computer-assisted simulation analysis (Tao and Nelson 1997). Simulation analysis is a difficult skill (Sharnon 1985) for novice to acquire its knowledge and experience in order to become proficiency. Therefore, it is particularly important for the beginners to learn both the knowledge and experience about simulation analysis from the beginning.

As a result, this paper addresses these issues by presenting an empirical mental model of simulation statistical analysis for comparison problems. The purpose of this mental model is to provide a conceptual template for inexperienced simulation practitioners, who then can customize it to their own simulation mental model. We present the mental model and its components in Section 2, illustrate this model with an excerpt of an expert problem-solving process in Section 3, justify this model according to its quality, and conclude this paper in Section 5.

SIMULATION STATISTICAL MENTAL MODEL

Simulation modeling, programming, and statistical analysis are interrelated in practice and usually from a complex process. In order to focus this work on the statistical aspect of the simulation analysis, simulation modeling and programming were excluded from the proposed mental model.

Data Sources

The primary data sources upon which the proposed mental was based are the result of a formal knowledge acquisition process from a simulation expert and the log files recorded by the three simulation experts while solving the same simulation problem:

1. Four problem-solving protocols and structured interviews from our primary expert (Tao 1995). There are four experimental cases (M/M/1, (s, S) inventory, 3-station tandem system and classic machine repair system, see (Tao 1989) for detailed system descriptions) performed by an expert. The problem-solving processes were videotaped, transcribed, analyzed with various interviews from the same simulation expert throughout the knowledge acquisition stage.

2. Airline reservation system analyzed by three Goldsman, Schmeiser and Nelson (Goldsman 1991). Three simulation experts solved an airline reservation system with different approaches (interactive analysis, ranking and selection and multiple comparison procedures) and analysis environments, but reached the same conclusion at the end. The log files recorded the detailed problem-solving processes and the article summarized the analysis processes that matched many of what we observed and concluded in the other source.

The Mental Model

A comparison problem has two main sub-problems, initial-bias detection and core comparison, due to the different characteristic of commonly known steady-state and terminating simulation (Tao and Nelson 1997). As a result, our model has two cognitive principles, two analysis indicators, and an expert heuristic that works for both the initial-bias detection and core-comparison sub-problems (See Figure 1). The cognitive principles serve as the mental guide for making decisions during the analysis, while the analysis indicators provide up-to-date measurements for planning the design and predicting the required experimental time. Both the cognitive principles and the analysis indicators contribute significantly to the heuristic in managing the time constraint for simulation statistical analysis. These components form the minimum requirements for representing the simplified version of expert's simulation statistical problem-solving process.

Cognitive principles:
1. The best possible answer within available resources.
2. Sequential experimentation.

Design Indicators.
1. Data generation speed.
2. Error Levels.

Expert Heuristic for initial-bias or core comparison:
1. Select a system instance if there are multiple system instances.
2. Start a small run.
3. Calculate data generation speed and error-level statistics.
4. Perform initial-bias detection or core comparison with statistical procedures, including any assumptions checking.
5. Redesign the experiment with updated information.
6. Decide to proceed or modify the design based on the time constraint.
7. Start the pilot run and repeat steps 3 to 7 until the initial-bias period or core-comparison is determine.

Figure 1. Simulation Mental Model

Cognitive Principles

The cognitive principles are the pre-requisite that needs to be planted in the practitioner's mind before starting a simulation analysis. These two cognitive principles are generalized enough to work with all types and stages of simulation statistical analyses:

1. **The best possible answer within available resources.** "The goal of SEDA (Simulation Experiment Design and Analysis) problem solving, in practice, is to produce a simulation result within a desired error level under the real time constraint (Tao and Nelson 1997)." In the same article, resource is identified as one of the eleven constructs in simulation analysis and the critical factor affecting the process of simulation analysis. In practice the available resources limited what can be accomplished, and thus the resources should be monitored and not sacrifice the answer with some unreachable analysis process.

   For example, in M/M/1 comparison problem, our expert found out that he had taken too much to just make sure that the initial-bias period of a system instance would pass Schruben's test while he already felt comfortable with the visual-plot examination. He decided to stop the investigation in order to proceed the core comparison for an answer of the best possible system instance. In fact, he not only stopped the initial-bias detection of current system instance, but also applied the initial-bias period to other four system instances because the one he investigated was the most congested system and all the system instances were similar. If he was not concerned about the time constraint and stopped the investigation on initial-bias task, he might not even get any comparison result.

2. **Sequential experimentation.** The sequential experimentation is to perform simulation analysis one small step at a time initially, then repeat the analysis and gradually expand it toward better results. When the resources become a problem, the sequential experimentation has a better opportunity to offer an answer within a certain error level.

   For example, when Schemiser (Goldsman 1991) found out that it might take seven days to generate the appropriate data based on his initial analysis, he decided to spend more time in understanding the situations first. He ran an overnight run to generate more data and realized that there was a mistake in the original estimate of the design. He felt relieved because he did not waste seven days to find it out. Moreover, this overnight experiment suggested that the total experimentation was looking shorter than the worst-case projections. Therefore, each time he generated a little more data, he gained more insights about the system instances and thus derived better designs.

   This sequential experimentation can help to incrementally build the results instead of starting from scratch in every experimental design during the problem-solving process. Accordingly, sequential experimentation provides a feasible means to reach the goal for a best possible answer within available resources.

Analysis Indicators

The analysis indicators are the tools compared to the cognitive principles as the mindset for efficiently assisting the simulation analysis. The following two analysis indicators are updated whenever a new data set is generated so that the practitioners are well informed for planning the experiment and making decisions:

1. **Data generation speed.** In order to be aware of the resource constraint, it is important to monitor the data-generation time. The data generation speed may be seconds per replications in both steady-state and terminating simulation. However, the number of observations in a replication needs to be notified in steady-state simulation. For example, both Schmeiser and Goldsman (1991) used seconds per replication in the airline reservation system that is a terminating simulation problem. Also, our expert obtained the average seconds per 2500-obsercations replication in the standard M/M/1 that is a steady-state simulation problem. The principle is that the unit needs to be able to predict the data generation time for a new design. It is this simple indicator that helps a simulation practitioner to calculate the time required for generating the data in a new experimental design for managing the time constraint.

2. **Error Levels.** In simulation analysis, the error levels are usually represented by some statistics, such as the standard deviations, standard errors, confidence intervals, or results of hypothesis tests. Occasionally, there may be visual inspecting procedures or methods, such as histogram for normality assumption and means plot for initial-bias recognition, where the error levels are represented as the inspectors' self-confidence. The error levels should be recalculated for every new data set for the accuracy of estimates. For example, Schmeiser (1991) used a rule of thumb called *significant digit* in his analysis: "Stated in significant digits, $Y_1 = 11.1 \times 10^4$, $Y_2 = 10.3 \times 10^4$, $Y_3 = 9.4 \times 10^4$, $Y_4 = 0.8 \times 10^4$. System 4 appears to be an order of magnitude from being competitive." The significant digit is determined by zeroing the integer digits of the point estimate affected by standard error. In the above case, the numbers 11.1, 10.3, 9.4 and 0.8 were results of the significant-digit rule.

   These two analysis indicators were used repeatedly in all the cases we studied at various points of the problem-solving processes. They are the critical tools that simulation experts identified and utilized to efficiently tackle the simulation problems.

The Expert's Heuristic.

The proposed heuristic is a simple procedure derived from the protocol data and confirmed in interviews. The heuristic itself is only a shell for organizing the simulation statistical analysis. It is the practitioners who need to fill in the details such as illustrated below.

Step 1. Select a system instance if there are multiple system instances

Most of the multiple-system comparison cases we studied started with one system instance. It is reasonable for the experts to focus on one system for understanding the problem and environment first. With the knowledge acquired from the first system instance, the experts can repeat or expand to other system instances their analyses.

The question becomes what system instance to pick? Some of the decisions were due to the client's needs or preferences. In the (s, S) inventory case, our expert picked system instance 3 because the client preferred it. Some of the decisions might be from the practitioner's knowledge or experience. For example, in the 3-station tandem queue system, our expert started with system instance 1 since the arrival-rate over service-rate ratio was the highest and thus might be the most congested system instance. Inexperience practitioners who can not decide what to do can pick any system instance to start with. Our expert did this in the classic machine repair system.

Starting with a right choice can sometimes make the analysis more efficiently. For example, Out expert picked the most congested system instance in the 3-station tandem queue system to start with and later applied the initial-bias period to other systems. The intuitive reason was that the initial-bias period of the most congested system should be the longest.

Step 2. Start a small run

The first run is to quickly generate some data in order to obtain information before planning a design. To most practitioners, the difficulty is on what is a small run? Since the initial goal is to collect information for step 3, particularly the data generation speed, the target is to generate enough data for estimating the data generation speed. For example, our expert ran 1 replication of size 1000 for the classical machine repair case and ran three replications of 8-hour simulation time in the 3-station tandem queue case.

On the other hand, generating the data should not take too long, say over 5 minutes, since otherwise it losses its purpose. For example, in the (s, S) inventory case, the initial data generation speed was "instantaneous". Even though our expert did not do anything further, we think that it would be a good option for the inexperienced practitioners to increase the number of replications and obtain a meaningful rough estimate, such as seconds per 10 replications. Also, in our interviews, the expert suggested to stop the run and reduce the data size if it passed your patient as a 'short' run.

Step 3. Calculate data generation speed and error levels such as means and standard deviations

This step is important in the sense that it provides measurable tools to step 5 for designing a new experiment, and to step 6 for judging the resource concern. See Section 2.2.2 for the details.

Step 4. Perform initial-bias detection or core comparison with statistical procedures, including any assumptions checking

The purpose is to force the practitioners to review the impacts from the new data set, and help them accumulate experiences to meet the time constraint. We do not suggest any particular statistical procedures or methods in our heuristic, and it should be the practitioners' choices and preferences. As a reference, our expert started with visual procedures in all his analysis but verified his judgments with test procedures as much as possible from all his fours problem-solving cases. For example, in the two steady-state cases, our expert used the time plot and cumulated-mean plot in determining the initial-bias trend, but verified the results by Schruben's test procedure.

Assumption checking is a necessary step in confirming the validity of the statistical procedure for initial-bias detection or core comparison. For example, our expert checked the normality and equal variance of the MCB (Multiple Comparison with the Best) procedure in the airline reservation problem.

Step 5. Redesign the experiment with updated information

The concept of sequential experimentation is to repeat the analysis cycle and at each cycle a new design is presented based on the new information collected since the last design. An experiment is stopped either because of the results meet the pre-specified error levels or the simulation runs out of time. Based on the error levels, the design can be drawn up to allowable levels. For example, Schmeiser indicated "The standard error estimate of 21000 minutes has only b-1 = 4 degrees of freedom, ... We are interested only in detecting differences between the best system and inferior system when the difference are in fact at least 3000 minutes. So the standard errors will need to drop to at most 1500 minutes, or 1/14 the current value. Therefore, the number of replications needs to be about 14^2 times longer: 5000 replications. "

Step 6. Decide to proceed or modify the design based on the time constraint

To inexperience simulation practitioners, determine what to do with the proposed design is a difficult task since it takes experience to judge. As a result, this heuristic provides a control point so that the practitioners can take the simple analysis indicators in Step 3 as tools for adjusting a design based on resource constraints. For the same example as in Step 5, Schmeiser continued the analysis as the following: "This means the worst-case projected experiment time is 5000 replication times half a minute per replication times four systems: Seven days." This is a typical expert's way to consider new design and estimate the time it takes.

With the knowledge above, Schmeiser then could consider what to do with this new design: "Rather than begin a seven-day experiment so soon after starting the comparison, and since it is time to go home for the day, we first run an overnight experiment." This demonstrates a cautious concern in spending a lot of time in a design that based only on very few data. If the new design would have only taken one day to run, the course of action might have been completely different.

Step 7. Execute the pilot run and repeat steps 3 to 7 until the initial-bias detection or core comparison is accomplished

Once the new design is decided, this step executes the experiment and brings the cycle back to step 3.

Although the heuristic has a minor variation in steps 4 and 6 for compensating initial-bias detection and core-comparison sub-problems, it is generalized enough for accommodating different types of simulation analyses, such as different analyses demonstrated by Goldsman, Nelson and Schmeiser in the airline reservation system. The heuristic provides a directional for simulation analysis that can be enhanced with tactics not discussed in this article. Examples of simulation analysis tactics are how to choose a system among competitive system in step 1 and how to choose the initial design for execution speed and error levels in step 2 (Tao 1998).

To simulation practitioners, this heuristic may not seem to be too different from what are normally known. However, our model focuses on the mental preparation of the cognitive principles before the analysis, and utilizes the analysis indicators to judge the designs and required resources in the heuristic. The following section presents a sample case solved by our primary expert, which demonstrated the sequences could be adjusted to the experiences or the problem-solving needs.

AN EXAMPLE

This simulation mental model is illustrated by our expert's problem-solving protocol script of a classical machine repair system for demonstrating the initial-bias process. We have rearranged the cases to roughly match our heuristic for illustration purpose.

A classical machine-repairing problem includes 14 identical machines and 10 machine operators (see Figure 2.) The mean machine failure time is 1 time unit. There are three different system instances with the number of repairmen and mean repairing time as (2, 0.16667), (3, 0.25) and (4, 0.3334), respectively. The goal is to find the shortest expected waiting time for machine repairing in the long run. The following steps are excerpts adapted from the verbal protocol transcript where only system instance 1 being analyzed for determining its initial-bias period.

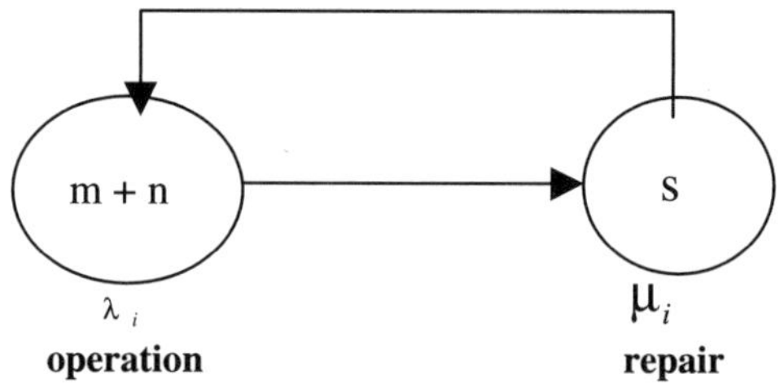

Figure 2. A Classical Machine-Repair System

Step 1. "Run system 1 for the speed."

Step 2. "Let's look at the input data file. I will run 1 replication of 1000 observations."

Step 3. "It took about 4 seconds to run 1 replication of size 1000."

Step 4. "Go into S (a statistical software) and reading the output raw data. I just want to see a time plot about the data here is not obvious initial bias in the means. We start the system with no machine failures. But it does not look like an increasing trend. Instead it comes back to zero very often. My initial guess is that I am not worry about the initial-bias condition. But do I fool myself? Let me perform the initial bias test first...All test results say zeros. That means no significant bias is detected. Let's look at the different direction. Hum, interesting. The combined test rejects this time."

Step 5. "I could use multiple replications to check it. I am going to run 5 replications of size 50."

Step 6. "Run system 1 again."

The above steps corresponded to the first cycle of our heuristic in detecting the initial-bias period. We omitted a lot of details and only presented the parts related to our heuristic so that the example would look reasonably clear to the users. The expert did not calculate the error levels since at this cycle he only concerned about the data generation speed.

Step 4. "I want to get the average across the replications. Plot the mean plot. It is a little low in the first. Maybe a little departure in the middle. To throw the first 100 observations is safe, I think. Let's do the initial-bias test. Combined test rejected. The first half of the sample mean is still a little greater than the second half. The correlation is .267. We think throwing the first 100 should be safe, though there are mild positive correlation."

In both step 4's, the expert started with visual-plot examination and then a test procedure. The expert did not continue the initial-bias detection even though the test result still failed. However, he was confident with the trend of mean plot and he concluded that deleting the first 100 observations should accomplish the goal for initial-bias detection. Notice that the expert did not check the data generation speed since it still ran fast.

JUSTIFICATIONS

The usability for this mental model is to provide a simple, easy to use, resource-concerned and experienced-oriented guidance to inexperienced simulation practitioners:

1. **Simple:** The model contains only five elements: two cognitive principles, two analysis indicators and a simple generalized heuristic. The model is a simplification of the abstracted experts' problem-solving approach.

2. **Easy to use**: The heuristic may seem to be common except that two analysis indicators need to be tracked and two cognitive principles need to be monitored in new experimental designs. With the example illustrated in Section 3, we believe that inexperienced simulation practitioners should be able to apply the proposed mental model in their own analysis.

3. **Resource-concerned**: The practical purpose for having a mental model is primary due to the potential resource constraint that is one of the most critical components in simulation analysis (Tao and Nelson 1997). In the model, the resource constraints were converted into the time constraint. Because of the two analysis indicators this model has predicting power in managing the resource concern in the sequential experiment.

4. **Experiences-oriented**: There are very few literature about the general description of simulation-analysis process empirically or theoretically (e.g., Goldsman 1991;,Mellichamp and Park 1989; Ramachandran et al. 1988;Taylor and Hurrion 1988) Even though the components of the model may not be easily seen in the literature, they are commonly practiced by the experienced simulation practitioners. The motivation of the knowledge acquisition was to explore and to confirm the unwritten experts' processes that were long missing in the literature.

CONCLUSION

This paper presented a conceptual mental model for simulation statistical analysis. Not only we argued that this model has good characteristics, but also we applied this mental model into an web-based computer-based training system for simulation statistical analysis [11] with good initial test results. The ultimate goal of this article is to promote practical models of simulation processes in the literature so that the practitioners can learn both the knowledge and experience from the beginning.

ACKNOWLEDGEMENTS

This paper is partially sponsored by National Science Council of R.O.C.: NSC 87-2218-E-214-013.

REFERENCES

Goldsman, D., Nelson, B.L. and Schmeiser, B. 1991. Methods for selecting the best system, In B. L. Nelson, W.D. Kelton, and G.M. Clark, editors, *Proceedings of 1991 Winter Simulation Conference*, 177-186, Phoenix, Arizona.

Law, A.M. and Kelton, W.D. 1991. *Simulation Modeling & Analysis. Mc*Graw-Hill.

Mellichamp, J.M. and Park, Y.H. 1989. A statistical expert system for simulation analysis, *Simulation*, 52(4), 134-139.

Ramachandran, V., Kimbler, D.L., and Naadimuthu, G. 1988. Expert post-processor for simulation output analysis. *Computers Industry and Engineering*, 15(14), 98-103.

Shannon, R.E. 1985. Intelligent simulation environments. In P.A. Luker and H.H. Adelsberger, editors, *proceedings of Intelligent Simulation Environments*, San Diago, Calif., 150-156.

Tao, Y. 1989. A simulation testbed for simulation procedures, Master Thesis, Department of Industrial and Systems Engineering, The Ohio-State University, Columbus, Ohio.

Tao, Y. 1995. A framework for computer-assisted simulation experiment design and analysis, Ph.D. Dissertation, Department of Industrial, Welding and Systems Engineering, The Ohio-State University, Columbus, Ohio.

Tao, Y. and Nelson, B.L. 1997. Computer-assisted simulation analysis, *IIE Transactions*, 29(3), 221-231.

Tao, Y. 1998. Simulation analysis tactics, working paper, I-Shou University, Kaohsiung, Taiwan.

Taylor, R. and Hurrion, R.D. 1988. An expert advisor for simulation experimental design and analysis. In *AI and Simulation*, Henson, T. (ed.), Society for Computer Simulation, 238-244.

Web-based computer-based training system for simulation statistical analysis. http://www.im.isu.edu.tw/project/simulation/index.htm.

DYNAMIC MODEL-BASED MANAGEMENT OF EXPORT SUPPLY CHAINS

Dr. Doug Seeley, Emerging Networks, Inc.
1073 Newport Ave., Victoria, British Columbia V8S 5E2
e-mail: daseeley@pinc.com
Bob Bridges, Riccardo Macri, and Tony Griffith,
InterDynamics Pty. Ltd., Level 24
Santos House, 91 King William St
Adelaide S.A., Australia 5000
email: bob@interdynamics.com

KEYWORDS: Decision support, Planning system, Interactive simulation platform, Simulation-embedded optimization, Supply chains.

ABSTRACT

The synchronized and integrated response of commodity supply chains to the changing demands of an international marketplace is crucial to retaining a global edge. Various decision support applications require coordination amongst a number of stakeholders to support this goal. When a causal and dynamic model (simulation) is used as the means of decision support, applications can be termed, *dynamic model-based.* This paper describes the successful application of a model-based approach to the export of grain in Western Australia and the export of coal along the east coast of Australia. The integration capabilities of highly visual, discrete simulation were used to develop a *common reference model* with a suite of applications. These reference models then enabled the planning, scheduling and allocation of resources in associated industrial regions. Because of the degree of *dynamic congruence*, we were able to provide robust and effective planning tools which operators could handle easily, especially by embedding simulation evaluations of the dynamic model into associated algorithms. Successfully combining the model-based approach with the dynamic congruence of a common reference model, and by utilizing this model in application algorithms, can be termed "model-based management". It may well augur an expansion of the application of simulation.

INTRODUCTION

The synchronized and integrated response of commodity supply chains, to the changing demands of an international marketplace is crucial for its effectiveness. It enables industrial regions to sustain global competitiveness. Demand forecasting, harvesting (clearance strategies), bulk handling, and cargo assembly are important and often complex challenges to meeting this requirement, especially when lead times are long. Harmonizing schedules between stakeholders, while integrating the planning of chain capacity and throughput, can make the supply chain's response very effective. However, establishing the required collaboration between the stakeholders make up such export chains, especially in a context in which they have been frequently competitive with each other, can take significant effort. Part of the effort is in a necessary change in thinking from optimizing independent parts, to working with the interdependence of the parts in order to optimizing the whole system.

An opportunity exists to use the integration capabilities of highly visual, discrete simulation to develop reference models for the group of stakeholders in a supply chain. These reference models then enable the planning, scheduling and allocation of resources in these industries into a *Coordinated Planning System* (CPS). Traditionally, most simulation projects have been undertaken in order to provide decision-support for engineering design, "what-if" investigations and the evaluation of business development alternatives. For about five years, we have been using dynamic, discrete simulation models of appropriate granularity, in order to provide on-going management tools in scheduling and planning. This makes it possible to provide decision support based upon dynamic modeling, rather than upon the often rudimentary models implicit in most information systems and enterprise resource planning (ERP) tools. In effect, our approach can be termed "Dynamic Model-based Management" (DMBM).

EXAMPLES

Our work in supply chains has been focused upon what is termed "bulk commodity export chains." The diagram below is a general schematic of how these export chains work in our experience with grain, coal, sugar, nickel (import) and other minerals. See Figure 1. The export process consists of a clearance (harvest) of the commodity from mines, farms, refineries or process plants in response to arriving ships, given current stockpile conditions at the source, intermediate receival points, or at the port. Commodities such as coal (Bridges *et al.* 1998) are transported to the port by rail or other transportation. If stockpiles are not ready, production has to be generated and loaded by the transport as quickly as possible to avoid delaying ships. Such delays can generate significant *demurrage costs* to mines on behalf of the shippers. Foreknowledge of arriving ships gives mines lead time to ensure that stock will be ready for the ship. Effective use of the rail network requires regular and predictable levels of movements. Effective use of the port and its stockpile yard depends on good foreknowledge and preparation for incoming ships for all mines. Hence, all stakeholders have a strong requirement to forecast incoming ships accurately (the ordered list of ships by ETA is called a *shipping stem*). Common access to an accurate-as-possible shipping stem is perhaps the most powerful lever in starting a coordination dialogue between stakeholders.

The export of grain is another example of an export commodity chain with significant economic impact. The grain system, since it is a seasonal harvest, also requires effective forecasting of production yields distributed over time. Stockpiling can also be distributed in different areas such as individual farms and bulk receival points. As with coal, there are also distinctions of grade and type of product for which the bulk hander is responsible. The railway transports the grain to storage at the ports. Different ships will have requirements for different grain products, and these are assembled at the port for loading on the ship. The shipping stem is especially important here, as it also contains the ship's product requirements. These requirements are taken by the bulk handlers in order to anticipate future cargo assembly, and may often require refinements to the clearance strategy in order to ensure that the anticipated product requirements will be met at the port with minimal delay. These arrangements in turn, will affect the scheduling of rail and truck transport. Hence, the opportunities for effective coordination and synergy in these commodity export chains is amply evident.

CHAOS AND THE DYNAMICS OF BUSINESS SYSTEMS

It has become fashionable as a management practice to refer to some of the principles emerging from the study of complex adaptive systems, as *order emerging from chaos*. The bottom-up and self-organizing capabilities of such systems do enable intelligent solutions to emerge on their own. But chaos is being used by some as a kind of euphemism for random variation, with the mistaken impression that some averages will effectively account for the variation. However, such ideas along with various "*keep it simple*" decision-making attitudes, are masking the generation of chaos in system behaviour by the imposition of inappropriate order on top of variation, dynamics and interdependency. In fact, what can occur in business systems is not the emergence of order from chaos, but rather *order-induced chaos*.

The well-known *bullwhip effect* in retail supply chains is a good example of order-induced chaos. Amongst other factors, the batching of periodic orders and an over-reliance upon historical data, create delays, distortions and feedback effects which can create a very unstable situation.

But what is less understood, is the chaos induced by taking simplistic approaches to the dynamics of demand and supply, capacity and work practices, as well as multi-threaded production streams. Simplification is often induced by the priority given to financial reporting which is utilized for decision making without accounting for the dynamics of demand and capacity over time. Averaging, aggregating and other means of keeping things simple, as they are reported up the hierarchy towards board level, also contribute to this phenomenon.

Routine averaging and assumptions of uniformity of time-dependent variations can lead to the mis-application of capacity in management practice by producing wasteful congestion. This can be exacerbated by poor recovery times which can lead to excess work-in-process buffering. In some situations, congestion can lead to system breakdown when it impacts the capacity of other interdependent work stations. Some perceive that such chaos requires frequent management "fire fighting", when it should signal the requirement for a better design of workflow interdependency, and overall capacity management.

Another way in which dynamics and interdependency are often ignored is when unit costs, unit profit and marginal evaluations do not account for the interactions between the multiple threads of production in systems producing multiple goods and services which share production resources. Such metrics can distort the perceived advantages of changes in process improvement and product mix offerings. Costing systems, even activity-based systems, fail to effectively plan for marginal advantages in multi-threaded environments, and are not equipped to estimate the true impact of internal *synergy*.

Goldratt in his "drum-buffer-rope" (Goldratt and Fox 1986) approach to scheduling in the manufacturing sector has ably shown how chaos is induced by hyper-efficiency. The attitude that every resource should be running at full capacity is simply erroneous in production systems with interdependent processing and different capacities. This attitude of requiring all work-stations to work at full utilization while ignoring their interdependence, can be seriously counter-productive.

INTERDEPENDENCE, DYNAMICS AND MEASUREMENT

The usual focus of a stakeholder in a supply chain is upon maximizing one's self-benefit by acquiring inputs at a minimal cost, and then supplying the chain downstream with the lowest internal costs for transportation or processing. However these cost containment strategies do not consider interactions downstream, and the internal decision-making mechanisms and attitudes preclude acting in a manner which would optimize the performance of the overall chain. This kind of sub-optimization is sometimes acknowledged within organizations as *sub-optimization* or as narrow "silo thinking". By not tuning operations to the throughput performance of the chain, the competitiveness of the supply chain suffers in the marketplace to the benefit of none of the stakeholders.

Corporate cultures rarely encourage the "big picture" thinking required to produce the synergy and effective coordination to make supply chains effective. A large part this difficulty are the entrenched mechanisms and fixed attitudes about what constitutes good decision-making. What underlies sub-optimization and silo-thinking is the mistaken belief that by optimizing the behaviour of the parts independently, that the whole picture will be optimized. This simply ignores the existing interdependencies and leaves no room for actual synergy between stakeholders to occur.

Hence, a key component of our implementation strategy is demonstrating the impacts and opportunities associated with acknowledging interdependency through visualization. This is accomplished by animating dynamic models of the entire supply chain in a manner which makes these interdependencies clear in a highly graphic manner. Moreover, this approach also highlights the impacts of non-uniform demand dynamics and the role of managing capacity to meet their surges and gaps. Seeing these opportunities emerge from the visualizations can be highly motivating to the stakeholders.

At first however, each party needed to be convinced of the efficacy of model-based planning and scheduling within their own domain. These management activities were then blended carefully with the dynamic modeling capabilities of simulation and the operational realities on the ground. Proceeding in this manner, we were able to provide robust and effective planning tools which operators could handle.

Another crucial component of the implementation strategy was the use of *holistic performance indicators*. Such indicators have direct impact upon the overall throughput performance; e.g. goods shipped per time unit, overall cycle times, timely market satisfaction, return sales, etc. These are necessary in order to avoid the sub-optimization limitations of narrowly conceived performance indicators, and to have the stakeholders moving together in a direction which benefits the entire export supply chain.

There is another class of performance measures which greatly enhance overall performance which could be termed *flow indicators* between stakeholders, or between management units within an organization. When the flow of goods and services to the operation downstream is regular, predictable and in relatively level quantities which match demand in a timely manner, the downstream unit can best optimize their own operation.

With the harmony of such interdependent linkages, overall performance can be optimized. However, it also requires advance warning of surges and gaps in external demand. When this is possible, a coordinated response across the supply chain can adjust capacity settings to meet the demand appropriately.

DYNAMIC CONGRUENCE AND MODEL-BASED DECISION MAKING

Conventional decision-making in organizations typically focuses upon budgets and average measurements that are highly aggregated over time, and aggregated over production threads, utilizations, efficiencies and theoretical capacities. This loss in granularity of decision data can have serious consequences on profitability when the details of resource allocations, service quality, scheduling and planning are based upon coarse and simplified data. Even mathematical optimizations, although based upon clever formulations and algorithms, are undermined by the coarseness of unit cost, unit profit, and uniform production rates. They are undermined even further when the dynamic nature of demand is ignored and when uniform resourcing approximates quite non-linear circumstances. Rarely do they embed assumptions of how the organization actually works via the interdependent (causal) relationships in productive processes.

Behind almost everyone of these sources is an implicit model of how the organization functions in its dynamic environment, usually a model which hardly acknowledges any dynamics whatsoever. This approach is like feeding a Formula One driver data which describes the performance of the auto during the previous race, or averaged over the past five races, and expecting it to assist the driver's current situation in the middle of today's race. These traditional sources do not provide a very effective self-image for the dynamic organization. Such images are static, often dated, may not blend with other IS images, and may be out of synchronization with each other.

Moreover, information systems (IS), even ERP, often have implicit assumptions which assume static, uniform and non-causal relationships. The emphasis of such systems has been data-oriented, and on support for financial reporting. Neither emphasis focuses on the process threads which constitute the productive capacity of the organization, nor on their real-time management. Although ERP systems are transaction-based, and hence support some measure of financial integration, they rarely model the causal relationships in the organization, making difficult to produce live management applications in their context. Addressing these inadequacies is where the use of dynamic models which embed accurate causal relationships can offer a lot to effective decision-making and live management.

By incorporating the latest demand, supply and production data, especially when it approaches real-time, a dynamic and causal model can effectively reflect the live operational context of the organization on an on-going basis. When stochastic elements are set aside but dynamic profiles retained, runs of the dynamic model can now evaluate various alternatives in a rapid manner on a PC. When stochastic analysis is necessary repetitions can easily be carried out against different sampling seeds. When choices are limited to those which are practical to implement, the number of alternatives which need to be examined to obtain a very good solution, to a decision are similarly contained.

A dynamic model can embed the necessary causal relationships in the organization. This is a practical and effective approach which basically shows *how* the organization works, contrasts with "black box" mathematical optimization.

This is particularly true when practical schedules and plans require generation. Every mathematical optimization embeds an implicitly model of how the organization works in the domain being optimized. These rarely embed any of time-dependent behaviours, process interdependence, congestion in non-linear response to near capacity situations, or true multi-threaded costing. In contrast, a dynamic, causal model can handle such requirements, even though evaluation will take longer. Delivering these capabilities means that such models deliver a *dynamic congruence* to the behaviour of the actual organization. A comparison to the models embedded in IS systems (e.g. relational databases) or in conventional optimization and operations research (OR) follows:

MANAGEMENT FEATURE	IS and OR Embedded Models	Animated, Dynamic & Causal Models
Financial Data	good, although often focused on unit data (problematic)	real-time financials are possible
Operational Data	IS is poor (data-centric), but OR can focus very well on special tasks.	As good as the granularity of the model (complexity grows non-linearly with detail).
Time-dependent Data	IS is poor (largely static relationships), OR can approximate with piece-wise linear components	Excellent
Causal Relationships	IS is poor (focused on dataflows), OR can handle some limited cases	Good. Excellent if productive flows modeled directly.
Concurrency	Difficult because of coordination & competition.	Excellent if modelling platform is multi-threaded.
Visualization	Can be built on top of software.	Some platforms animate in a direct fashion.
Scheduling	Good with OR, but schedules may not be robust	Robust schedules can be routinely achieved.
Optimization	Excellent with OR but may be sensitive or not robust.	Can be very robust when embedded in algorithm, but evaluation may be slower.
Integration	ERP (IS) can financially integrate, but less equipped for operational management	A Common Reference Image (CRI) can be used throughout the organization.
Practicality	Depends on IS design; resistance to OR as a "black box" can occur.	Easier to frame operation interactions in familiar terms.

A dynamic model of the entire productive capacity of an organization, and which embeds causal relationships at an appropriate granularity, can serve as a reference model for the entire organization. In animated form, it becomes a Common Reference Image or CRI. When decision-making is made with management tools which utilize a CRI, a very effective method for the integration of decision-making across the organization becomes attainable. It can be termed "dynamic model-based".

MODEL-BASED PLANNING SYSTEMS

Using causal, dynamic models with perhaps both discrete and continuous components to base on-going decision-making upon throughout the organization, leads naturally to what can be termed *model-based planning systems*. Production schedules, supply schedules, resource allocations, capacity management and planning over various time horizons all become attainable with the common reference of the dynamic model at their core. With the computational power readily available on desktops, the algorithms for these management activities can utilize a dynamic model to generate their schedules. An evaluation (run) of the dynamic model can be embedded into the required algorithms.

For optimization purposes, this embedding of a simulation in an algorithm to evaluate the "*objective function*" as it were, would appear on the surface to be computationally very demanding when compared to the evaluation of a polynomial which represents benefit or cost. There are three factors however, which have made this a practical approach in our work: These are:

- Many embedded constraints in causal dynamics,
- Building robustness and user-comprehensibility into the algorithm, and
- Building "importance" into the algorithm.

The first is that the dynamic model, by accurately representing the causal relationships in the actual system, has effectively embedded the constraints which a mathematical optimization would undertake and many that it would not. Each kind of constraint increases the complexity of such optimization. Hence a dynamic model is able to include additional constraints which are too complex to work with normal optimization. The result is that the search space of potential solutions is drastically reduced in comparison to conventional optimization.

The second factor is that instead of focusing on an exact optimization, we focus instead upon an excellent, but robust and practical result in our planning algorithms. Practical means that possible plans are i) constructed in a manner which is comprehensible to the managers involved, ii) particular, but easy-to-implement timing and sizing constraints are embedded in the algorithm, and iii) alternatives are chosen with steps which correspond to the way that the manager could consider making changes. This latter point means that when operational contingencies require changes to the schedule or plan being used, that such changes are relatively small adjustments to a robust solution (i.e. it is not very sensitive) and make sense to the user, and do not require an entirely new formulation and solution as would happen in mathematical optimization.

The third factor is that relative importance can be easily factored into the planning algorithm when the plan is constructed in a progressive manner, similar to the way in which many manual planners do. Importance can embed such considerations as i) heavy utilization, ii) contractual significance of a service or production run, and iii) balancing the allocation of resource capacity between baseload requirements and on-demand requirements. By progressively populating a plan/schedule which is under construction, with the more important of the remaining required productions or services, robustness is built in. But the evaluation of the dynamic model yields another benefit; a reduction in the space of choices for placing the next progressive step. When each step embeds heuristics such as maintaining an overall flow balance, these robust algorithms can be very effective, while also producing results which are comprehensible to the implementers.

When causal threads are used to model the way an organization works, the resulting model lends itself easily to decision-making which can be framed in a whole-of-business view, while still respecting the dynamic realities at operational levels. Causal threads follow the interdependencies in process sequence of all of the intentions that the organization is pursuing. Its Common Reference Image serves as a mediating intelligence for the organization to truly deliver on integrated decision-making. When the underlying software platform embeds this multi-threaded and causal perspective (Seeley *et al.* 1995, Warren *et al.* 1998), such as Planimate™ (formerly SimView), the construction of animated management tools for this purpose is relatively straight forward.

Practical planning and scheduling does not take the monolithic approach whereby a schedule is set in stone at some point in time and left to the next planning period. Rather circumstances in the organization and in the demand stem often change, creating the requirement of an easily modified plan which results in adapted plans that perform well. This requires that the planning system (dynamic model plus planning applications) have access to live sources of data about changing demand and resource availability. It is also important that system users be able to interactively change settings and revise scheduling, for example capacity settings and revised work practices.

In the Diagram 2 is a somewhat generic example of applying model-based management to planning by using a common reference model for a suite of planning applications (see next section). Live (almost real-time) input triggers updates to shared information in the reference model. Schedules and plans are derived for application on a regular basis and when changing conditions require it. Various stakeholders in the system can view appropriate aspects of the suite of applications via an Application Pages Server (APS) on the Internet. This technology of basing decisions upon a dynamic and causal model then, becomes in effect, *Dynamic Model-based Management* (DMBM).

COORDINATED PLANNING SYSTEMS FOR BULK COMMODITY EXPORT

This model-based management approach has been applied to the export of grain in Western Australia and the export of coal along the east coast of Australia in what can be termed Coordinated Planning Systems (Seeley and Bridges 1999). The export of grain in Western Australia (WA) involves several stakeholders; the AWB (Australian Wheat Board, who market grain on behalf of farmers), CBH (cooperative bulk handlers who gather grain at receival points and also manage the port facilities), the Grain Pool of WA (other than wheat), and the rail carrier Westrail (who also provide truck transportation as it is required). The application required the eventual formation of a WA Grain liason group which commissioned an integrated dynamic model for decision-making about the grain export chain, accessed by all of the stakeholders. This became an "industry platform" providing a common reference image from which various management tools were derived including:

- *the Grain Viewer* -- provides participants with access to latest forecasts of the port inventory.
- *Cargo Assembly Planner* -- provides a priority list of cargo needed at port.
- *Clearance Planner* -- investigates of options for clearing grain from rail sections and receival points.
- *Rail Capacity Planner* -- investigates of throughput capacity of the rail system
- *ETA Management Tool* -- improves the predictability (estimated times of arrival, ETAs) of the shipping program
- *AWB Shipping Tool* -- investigates the relationship between the marketing, shipping, and clearance programs.

The planning system was built over a period of 30 months from original conception to the first export chain coordinations under the leadership of the transport carrier, WestRail. See Figure 2. During this period a number of applications were built for the various stakeholders independently.

Shortly after the system was commissioned, a large market opportunity caused by the failure of Canadian wheat export, was very profitably addressed by the planning system. A considerable effort was required to interface various corporate cultures in order to make coordination possible. Once confidence in the overall approach (buy-in) was attained, the liason committee approved the development of the Coordinated Planning System.

A somewhat more centralized approach has been applied in Queensland for several years now to assist the export of coal, carried to port by Queensland Rail (QR). In these export commodity chains, coordination was required between the various mines in regional basins served by QR, and the port facilities which loaded the ships. There is also some indirect coordination with shipping agents and the buyers supplying the ships. Although each mine has some stockpile capacity, it is usually the port which has significant stockpiling resources available. Although annual contracts provide mines with some idea of likely on-going demand, ships often approach the port with little anticipation, requiring the mines to load the ship quickly and avoid demurrage charges. The railway used to be required in an "on-demand" manner to the mines, until they started acting proactively to make train services more regular. This resulted in liason committees between the stakeholders forming, and the gradual increase in the level of coordination to everyone's benefit. There are several such coal platforms for coal, some centered on the rail carrier and others at various stages of integration into independent industry planning platforms.

COORDINATING SUPPLY CHAINS WITH MODEL-BASED MANAGEMENT

We have had success with the following implementation process. Initially a prototype of the common reference model is shown to the stakeholders in order to promote an industry-wide approach, this is often occurred after work individually with one of the stakeholders. More work with individual stakeholders is often required for them to buy into the process, and have confidence that the dynamic models assist them and enable them to pursue their own objectives. As this is happening, coordinating relationships between parties is cultivated.

In order to make this firm and practical, the establishment of contractual arrangements in support of a mutual self-interest for the parties involved was crucial. These are typically in the form of incentives for timely product movements and finding a balance between baseload and on-demand requirements. Agreements on some information sharing in the common reference image was required in order to ensure that sensitive corporate data was not compromised while coordinating operational data was exchanged. These arrangements enabled the parties involved to take coordinating initiatives with each other which then cultivated a spirit of collaboration.

Currently these model-based planning systems are migrating from a system of access to a private bulletin board, to an Internet server producing private ASP pages for browsers. As this is happening, a natural role is evolving for the provider of the industry planning system to be the steward of the export chain's "big picture" and services. An advantage in these developments has been the availability of a simulation platform which enables end-user software tools to be rapidly prototyped and developed, such as the authors' own simulation platform, Planimate™. Its built-in capabilities for direct animation and for handling the concurrency of multi-threaded models has been particularly effective.

A NEW ROLE FOR SIMULATION: DYNAMIC MODEL-BASED MANAGEMENT

Our industrial experience has convinced ourselves and our clients that dynamic model-based management is an effective way to develop planning and scheduling systems, especially ones which span the stakeholders of supply chains. The combination of animated visualizations, adaptability to changing circumstances, incorporation into planning and scheduling algorithms, and accessibility via Web browsers augurs an expanding and successful future for this approach.

An important feature is the dynamic congruence offered by causal models which accurately represent the multi-threaded logic and interdependencies of how organizations and supply chains actually work. Object-oriented software is easy to maintain and work with because the software structures mirror the actual information structures in the application system. In a similar manner, dynamic causal systems mirror the actual organization congruently and make applications developed in this manner easy to maintain, to extend capabilities and to inter-operate with other software. This makes the overall planning system robust. This appears to be an innovative way to extend the conventional use of simulation into an ever broadening range of applications.

REFERENCES

Bridges, R.D., Buckley, N., Goodall, J., Seeley, D.A.; 1999, "Joint Industry Planning Platforms for Coal Export Supply Chains", *Proceedings of Coal 98*, University of Wollongong, N.S.W., Australia.

Goldratt, E.M., Fox, R.E.; 1986, *The Race*, North River Press, Croton-on-Hudson, N.Y.

Seeley, D. A., Bridges, R.D.; 1999, *Supply Chain Dynamics* (Course Notes, Institute of Transportation Studies, University of Sydney), at site: www.interdynamics.com

Seeley, D.A., Warren, J.R., Marcel Jobing, M., Johannes van Dijk, J., Macri, R.; 1995, "Smoothing the Productive Flows of Business with SimView", in *Proceedings of the Summer Simulation Conference*, Ottawa, pg. 373.

Warren, J.R., Jobing M., van Dijk, J., Seeley, D.A., Macri, R.; 1998, "The SimView Graphical Simulator for Participatory Decision Support", in *Information Systems Innovation and Diffusion*, Idea Group Pub., Hershey, PA.

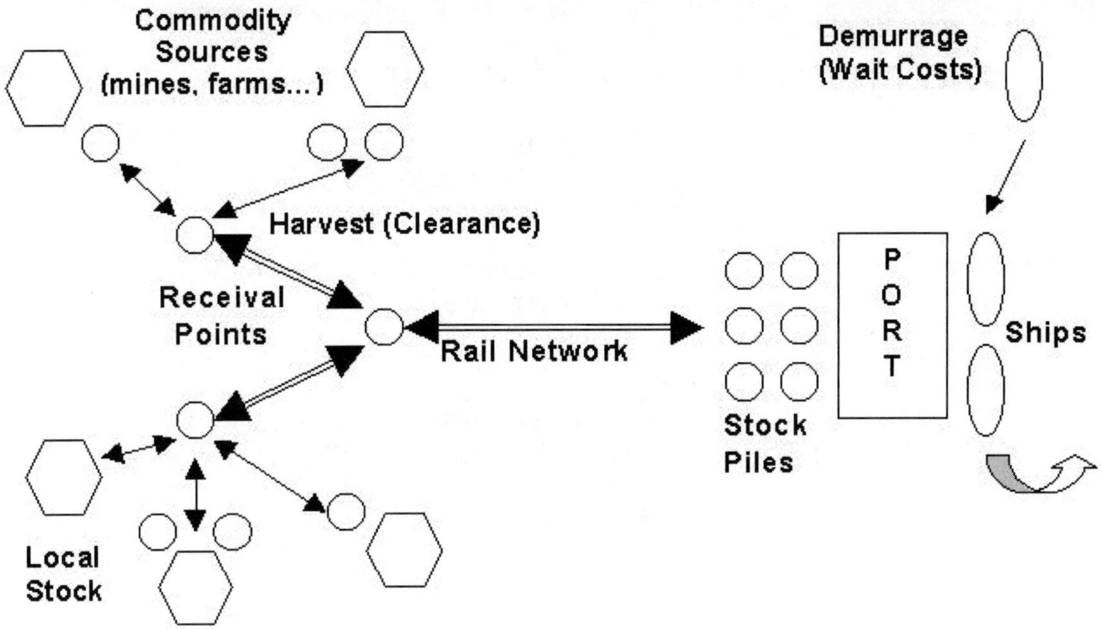

Figure 1: Schematic of a Bulk Commodity, Export Chain

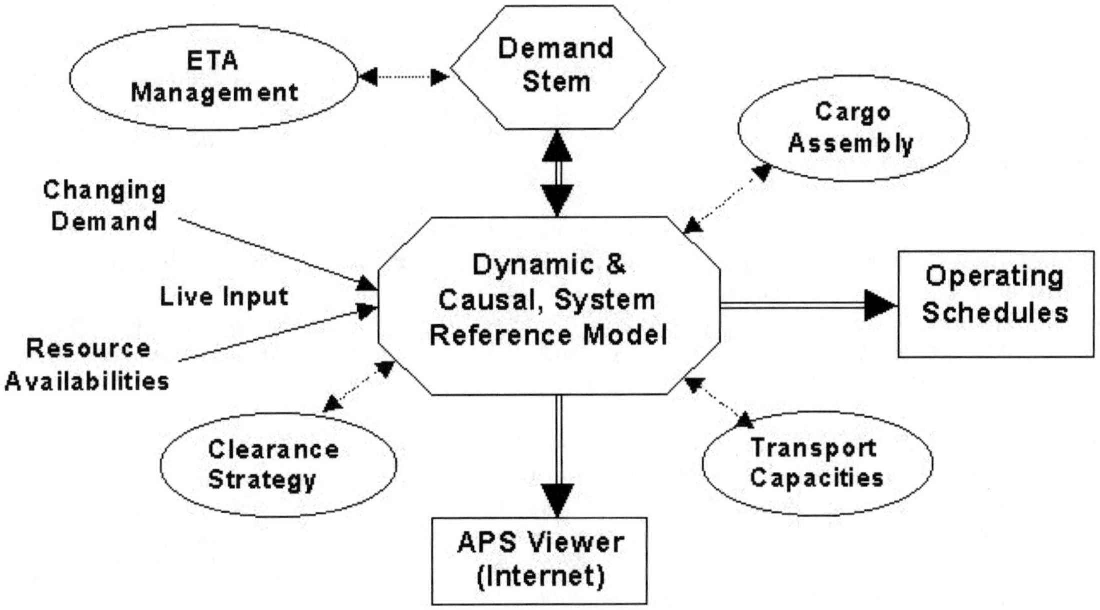

Figure 2. Dynamic Model-Based Management

ACCREDITATION: WHAT IT IS AND WHAT IT ISN'T

BETH VANN
and DR. KEN KAWANO
AEgis Technologies Group, Inc.
6703 Odyssey Drive, Suite 200
Huntsville, Alabama 35806
bvann@aegisrc.com

JOHN PATE
System Test and Evaluation Directorate,
National Missile Defense Joint Program Office
System Test and Evaluation Directorate (JNT), ISTC Program
PO Box 1500 (Attn: BMDO/JNTS)
Huntsville, Alabama 35807
jpate@hiwaay.net

KEYWORDS:
accreditation, certification, National Missile Defense, integrated ground test, hardware-in-the-loop, software-in-the-loop, test and evaluation, verification, validation

ABSTRACT:
The Ballistic Missile Defense Organization (BMDO) Directive 5002 states that accreditation is certification by competent authority that a T&E resource produces realistic, unbiased, credible measurement of specific performance or suitability parameters when operated within a specific domain of scenario and environmental conditions for the examination of a specific test issue.

It is essential in discussing accreditation, that the object being accredited is uniquely identified. It is also critical that the criteria which must be satisfied for accreditation, be clearly and unambiguously articulated. The formulation of the accreditation criteria must also be traceable to the specific domain of scenario and environmental conditions for the examination of a specific test issue. A clear distinction must also be made between the credible and unbiased reporting of the performance vis a vis an evaluation of the quality (goodness/badness) of the performance of a given Element Representation.

Using the National Missile Defense (NMD) Integrated System Test Capability (ISTC) as an instance, this paper describes 1) the development of the accreditation criteria, 2) the identification of caveats and limitations on the use of data collected, 3) the implications of accreditation; and discusses how and why the accreditation process does not assess the performance of the NMD Element Representations. Accreditation, does declare that the data collected during an Integrated Ground Test (IGT) is unbiased and realistic, and that the data collected can subsequently be analyzed to assess the performance of the Element Representations, subject to identified caveats and limitations on the usage of the data obtained.

1.0 INTRODUCTION

Using the National Missile Defense (NMD) Integrated System Test Capability (ISTC) as an instance, this paper describes how the ISTC Accreditation effort is compliant with existing policy guidance, and reflects the strategy for Government Accreditation of ISTC for Developmental Test and Evaluation (DT&E) made by the NMD Joint Program Office (JPO).

1.1 Purpose

To elucidate and provoke discussion on the meaning of "Accreditation" in the context of Models and Simulations and the role it plays in test resources, test beds, and Hardware-In-The Loop (HWIL) / Software-In-The-Loop (SWIL) test facilities.

1.2 Overview

This paper describes the 1) development of the accreditation criteria, 2) the identification of caveats and limitations on the use of data collected, and 3) the implications of accreditation based upon experience in the DT&E accreditation decision made by the NMD JPO for ISTC's use in Integrated Ground Tests (IGTs).

2.0 BACKGROUND

2.1 What is the NMD?

2.1.1 NMD Management

The NMD JPO of the Ballistic Missile Defense Office (BMDO) is managing the Program. The Lead System Integrator (LSI) has the responsibility of managing the development and integration of the NMD Elements to deliver the NMD System. In addition, the LSI is responsible for the execution of the DT&E and System Verification programs. In support of these programs, the LSI will use simulation for Analysis, Design Verification, Integration, and Test & Evaluation (T&E).

2.1.2 NMD Description

The NMD is the integration of weapon, sensor, battle management, command, control and communications systems designed to provide protection against limited ballistic missile attacks targeted at the United States, including Alaska and Hawaii. The National Ballistic Missile Defense (BMD) mission provides surveillance, warning, cueing, engagement, interception and negation of threat objects prior to impact on US targets. This capability is achieved through integration of the NMD system with the Integrated Tactical Warning and Attack Assessment (ITW/AA) network to execute the BMD mission.

The NMD system is composed of space-based and ground-based sensors, ground-based interceptors, and an associated Battle Management/Command, Control and Communications (BMC3) capability. The NMD mission functions include detection, discrimination, and tracking; logistics and readiness; and collateral and theater support operations.

The NMD deployment is an evolutionary process based on an initial capability, known as Capability 1. The NMD system architecture employs the following elements:

- Ground-Based Interceptor (GBI)
- Ground-Based Radar-Prototype (GBR-P) (Prototypical of the objective X-Band Radar (XBR))
- Battle Management/Command, Control and Communications (BMC3) including In-Flight Interceptor Communications System (IFICS)
- Upgraded Early Warning Radar (UEWR)
- Defense Support Program (DSP)
- Space-Based Infrared System (SBIRS)

The Deployment Readiness Program incrementally develops interceptor, sensor and BMC3 technology. As the technology matures, the system capability correspondingly improves.

2.1.3 NMD Acquisition Approach

The NMD System is a Simulation Based Acquisition (SBA). Simulation is required since it is impractical to perform real world tests to answer many of the performance questions concerning a possible NMD System. Alternative architectures and Elements can be evaluated using accredited simulations anchored to actual test data. Since the simulations will be extrapolations of the models of the objective system, verification and validation (V&V) of the simulation and models provides the confidence needed to accept the simulation results.

2.2 What is the ISTC?

2.2.1 ISTC Description

The ISTC is a NMD system-level, HWIL/SWIL test tool. It is a computer-based system for testing actual NMD element data and signal processors and software in an integrated configuration through the use of simulated environments. The ISTC provides the capability to evaluate the performance of the prototype NMD system, determines the interoperability of the incremental software builds used in the NMD system, and determines the operational suitability of the human interfaces in the NMD system.

To achieve its purpose, the ISTC:

- Provides for the physical incorporation of the actual mission and communications processors of the NMD system,
- Utilizes the actual software that is installed in the mission and communications processors,
- Operates in real-time,
- Drives the NMD system processors with realistic scenarios,
- Subjects the system assets to realistic threat and environment effects in demanding scenarios, and
- Collects data to support post-test system-level performance analysis.

The ISTC has the capability to integrate all of the major components of the NMD system. The test configuration is a representation of individual elements operating in concert, as part of an overall architecture, and its objective is to provide an accurate exercise of the NMD system under realistic stresses that would be encountered in an operational environment. The ISTC is also the only cost-effective means to assess the effects of hostile environments including nuclear effects on the real-time responses of the integrated NMD system's computers.

2.2.2 ISTC Architecture

Individual elements of the NMD system are represented in the ISTC on stand-alone computer stations known as nodes. Each node incorporates actual NMD element mission and communications processors that execute actual element software. The individual element nodes are interconnected by a NMD system communication network driven by real-time system interfaces, and threat and environment input data. The nodes are also connected by separate ISTC networks that control the test equipment. The ISTC supplies the autonomous nodes with simulated threat and environments, natural and man-made, that are consistent for each NMD element in the test scenario.

The ISTC architecture is composed of a Test & Control (T&C) Segment, Global Environment (GE) Segment, System Performance Monitor (SPM) Segment, Element Segments consisting of one or more Element nodes, and an External Interface (I/F) Driver Segment. These segments and nodes are tied together via a Tactical Communications Network and Test Networks.

The following NMD elements are currently represented within ISTC - the NMD BMC3, GBR-P, UEWR, Weapon System, and DSP/SBIRS. These Element Representations are on a development path to the objective system.

2.3 ISTC Accreditation History

An integrated government – contractor Accreditation team was instrumental in the development of a capstone accreditation strategy and supporting assessment processes and recommendations that led to the formal accreditation of the ISTC for three major NMD T&E milestones: IGT Three, Four and Five. These processes and the tests they supported are on the critical path of the simulation based acquisition process supporting the acquisition and initial deployment decision for a National Missile Defense System.

3.0 THE ACCREDITATION PROCESS

Having asserted that accreditation has been accomplished, it would be beneficial to examine what is accreditation and how accreditation was accomplished in the context of ISTC for use in IGTs.

3.1 What is Accreditation?

The Ballistic Missile Defense Organization (BMDO) Directive 5002 states that "accreditation is certification by competent authority that a T&E resource produces realistic, unbiased, credible measurement of specific performance or suitability parameters when operated within a specific domain of scenario and environmental conditions for the examination of a specific test issue."

The crux of the process called "accreditation" is to insure that the given simulation "produces realistic, unbiased, credible measurements of specific performance or suitability parameters" and in those instances where such is not the case, to specifically identify the limitations on the use of data and analysis produced by the given simulation. Activities and analysis must be undertaken to define the degree to which the data produced by the specified test resource represents a true measure of the individual and collective performance of the various components of the system as a whole. Accreditation is not an assessment of the quality of the performance of the simulation nor is it a measure of the goodness/badness of the individual integrated components. Accreditation, properly executed, provides a basis whereby one can establish the level of confidence (believability) in the results of a simulation --- both in terms of the data collected (measurements) and conclusions reached as a result of the analysis (performance) of the data. Accreditation by its very nature, defines the bounds on the appropriate use of the data and conclusions from a given simulation.

It must be recognized that M&S are abstractions and may not duplicate actual observed phenomena but provide an approximation of observed behavior. Therefore, accreditation procedures are the formal process by which the application sponsor gains confidence in the M&S for its intended purpose. Any use of the results of an M&S is often considered de facto accreditation and the M&S application sponsor will be held responsible for the results of an M&S that has not been formally accredited. However, the preferred method of accreditation involves an a priori determination that the M&S is appropriately qualified before use.

3.2 Development of the Accreditation Process

It is essential in discussing accreditation, that the object being accredited be uniquely identified. It is also critical that the criteria which must be satisfied for accreditation, be clearly and unambiguously articulated. The formulation of the accreditation criteria must also be traceable to the specific domain of scenario and environmental conditions for the examination of a specific test issue. A clear distinction must also be made between the credible and unbiased reporting of the performance of the test resource vis a vis an evaluation of the performance of the system, subsystem or element under test.

To accomplish the ISTC accreditation, the team broke new ground in establishing a detailed accreditation planning and execution process to develop meaningful criteria consistent with applicable directives and sound engineering judgement. The team formalized the process in the publication of an overarching Capstone Accreditation Plan upon which subsequent Detailed Accreditation Plans for each specific integrated ground test were derived. These accreditation documents, and the incorporated processes, set a high standard and serve as a basis for future NMD ISTC and test resource accreditation planning.

Efforts included:

- Identification of the Accreditation Authority. (Normally the sponsor of the simulation)
- Clarifying the specific domain of scenario and environmental conditions. (This was specified in the Detailed Test Plan associated with the simulation under consideration.)
- Clarifying the specific test issue(s). (These were derived from the stated Test Objectives and Test Requirements cited in the Detailed Test Plan and Technical Interface Control Document.)
- Identifying and tracking the given test resources (Basic resources --- Element Representation, Framework, Common Test Environments, etc --- were specified in the Detailed Test Plan.)

It is critical to note that each IGT is a continual work in progress. Thus, it is essential that changes in scenario and environmental conditions, specific test issues and test resources (changes in Builds, Versions, Revisions, etc.) be constantly monitored. Tracking these changes is mandatory to insure that appropriate V&V activities, accreditation criteria, data collection efforts and acceptability assessments are addressing the most current configuration of the test resource to be used in a given test.

3.3 Acceptability Criteria

Any accreditation process adopted for use must answer the question; "Will this M&S meet my objectives?" The M&S application sponsor appoints an accreditation agent to establish a set of acceptability criteria by which to determine the suitability of the M&S for the intended use. These acceptability criteria are unique to each problem and give key insights to potential solutions. Acceptability criteria therefore become a set of standards that a particular M&S must meet to be accredited for a given use. In all cases, the accreditation agent must identify and articulate the acceptability criteria. Failure of an M&S to achieve a particular acceptability criterion does not automatically result in disqualification. Such an occurrence may result in an evaluation of the criticality of the criterion to overall success and may merely serve to restrict the range of applicability of the M&S at hand.

How are appropriate accreditation criteria developed?

This is, itself a stand-alone topic for discussion. At the top level, however, development of acceptability criteria is an analytical process of identifying and articulating questions (criteria) which must be answered to insure that the resultant data collected during simulation execution is not biased. An integral part of this criteria development process is to insure that any special considerations of the Accreditation Authority are incorporated into the formulation of the accreditation criteria. Formulation of the accreditation process must also take into account data collection requirements and limitations on the collectability of the requisite data.

The resultant criteria are formalized and documented in a Detailed Accreditation Plan specific to a given Test Resource for use in a Specific Test. For the NMD DT&E program this Detailed Accreditation Plan was formally approved by the Accreditation Authority and represented a de facto declaration of the requirements which had to be met for the given test resource to be accredited.

Once we accept that accreditation is the assessment of a test resource to provide data which when analyzed, allows us to assess the performance of the system, subsystem or element under test, we can begin the accreditation process.

3.4 Needs-Driven V&V

ISTC is being developed as a test resource to meet NMD system developmental and operational test and evaluation requirements. The specific V&V activities identified for execution and formal documentation in the ISTC V&V Plan have been selected with the goal of satisfying the fundamental data needed for accreditation decisions.

The ISTC V&V activities definition is driven by data requirements that support BMDO and other government agency accreditation decisions. The accreditation data requirements influence the identification and selection of V&V data products during the ISTC V&V activity definition/design process. The ISTC V&V accreditation data products are subsequently flowed down to entities to be evaluated (units-under-test), then to pertinent V&V activities (with associated procedures and evaluation criteria), and finally to the agents or staff resources necessary to execute the activities. Identification of the accreditation data requirements, V&V data products, associated units-under-test, applicable V&V activities and V&V agents comprise the ISTC V&V Plan. The ISTC V&V Plan optimizes the potential for accreditation by ensuring the ISTC V&V activities planned for execution are responsive to the information needs of the Accreditation Authority.

3.5 Identification of Caveats and Limitations

An inherent assumption is that a given Element Representation is on the development path to the objective system. If the Element Representation was the objective system, the observed performance of the Representation would be identical to that of the objective system. If the Element Representation possesses only a subset of the capabilities of the objective system, then by definition, the observed performance would only be a subset of the performance of the objective system.

The key feature of the ISTC Accreditation Team's efforts was the development and implementation of a process, which identified the caveats and limitations associated with the disparate participating NMD Element Representations used in each IGT. This was accomplished prior to the execution of runs for record for each IGT that provided data used to assess the degree of successful integration and the relative status of the participating NMD Elements.

Caveats provided warnings on the analysis and use of the test data produced. Limitations identified capabilities or performance shortfalls for the incorporated NMD Element Representations. These caveats and limitations were keyed to the objectives and requirements of a given test and were incorporated into the final acceptability assessment and accreditation recommendation provided to the Accreditation Authority for the ISTC-based, developmental test and evaluation activity; i.e. integrated ground test.

4.0 IMPLEMENTATION OF THE ACCREDITATION PROCESS

To implement the accreditation process, the Accreditation Team designed, developed and executed a stepwise process which provided for the documentation of the many and varied steps in the integration of previously disparate systems into a coherent whole. A concerted effort maximized the successful incorporation of previous verification and validation efforts and defined new requirements and procedures that were subsequently implemented.

A key feature of the process was to develop a method of assessing and documenting that the ISTC Test Framework did not bias the performance of the Element Representations integrated within it. A significant aspect of this process was to maintain a clear distinction between processes and procedures which provided assurances that the test resource was not biasing performance versus assessing the performance of the incorporated components i.e., a defacto performance assessment of the NMD System.

The ISTC Accreditation Team tries to insure that when a Representation is integrated into the ISTC and tested, the information reported by ISTC accurately represents the performance of the Element Representation. Inherent in this is the need to insure that the performance of the Element Representation accurately represents the real-world entity.

At the fundamental level, the objective of the ISTC Accreditation Process is to establish that the performance of each of the integrated Element Representations, singularly as well as in concert with other integrated Element Representations is accurately reported. This is the key to accreditation. It is imperative that we distinguish between reporting vis a vis evaluating performance.

Conceptually this sequentially entails 1) establishing the stand-alone performance of a given Representation; 2) establishing the performance of the Representation as the only participant incorporated into the ISTC Framework; 3) establishing the performance of the Element Representation when incorporated as one of several participants in the ISTC Framework; and 4) establishing the performance of the Element Representation when operated in the context of an integrated system operating in the defined scenario (s) environment.

4.1 Establishing the Performance of a Given Representation

For each integrated ground test, the LSI Element Integrated Product Team (IPT)/Element PM is responsible for the V&V and certification of their Element Representation in ISTC prior to its use. The ISTC PM is responsible for certifying the Framework, the Common Test Environment and the Global Environments used in the ground test.

The developer/sponsor of the given Representation establishes the performance envelope of the Representation. The Representation Sponsor must conduct and document the requisite verification, validation and testing of their respective Representation. Inherent in this process is the identification and documentation of what the given Element

Representation functionality is for the prototype HWIL/SWIL or digital model. A critical feature of this process is configuration management of the Element Representations throughout the process. This is especially critical in that an inherent feature of the ISTC is the continual development of new Builds; Versions; Revisions, and upgrades, etc., which are incorporated when technically feasible, to insure that the best available Representations are used in a given test. Accurate configuration management insures an accurate tracking of "upgrades" necessary to insure that accreditation activities accomplished to date are still valid and/or are re-executed as required.

Execution of the forgoing places an upper limit on the expected performance of the given Representation and establishes a performance baseline for the given Representations. The test community will not accredit the ISTC for use without formal PM/LSI certification that their Element Representation is a faithful representation and is ready for use given the specified caveats and limitations.

4.2 Establishing the Element to Framework Performance of a Representation

This is completed by individually incorporating a given Representation into the Test Framework and using various test drivers to represent the remainder of the Representations to be used in the test (simulation suite). Testing at this point is designed to examine the performance of the Representation as well as the Framework when they are coupled with each other. Two fundamental questions need to be answered: When coupled, 1) does the Framework affect the performance of the incorporated Element Representation; 2) does the incorporated Representation affect the performance of the Framework? If yes, one must then identify and assess the degree and direction of the impact. In both instances, it is essential to identify the nature (degree and direction) of the impact. Is it enhancing or degrading? Is it constant or intermittent? Is it an across-the-board effect or limited to certain sections of the test spectrum? Can the problem be fixed (negated), and will it be? The results of these findings and actions must all be documented and all changes maintained under strict configuration management.

4.3 Establishing the Element to Element Performance of the Representation

In an ideal world, the next series of events would entail the stepwise incorporation of various combinations of Element Representations into the Framework, and determining how each of the combinations operate in concert. As a practical matter, however, resource constraints generally necessitate the incorporation of all Representations, the test environments and the Framework into an integrated entity. This integrated entity then is used to examine the effects of interactions between the various Representations, test environments and Framework. Testing at this point is focused on identifying and documenting the effects of the interactions among the incorporated Representations insofar as they do or do not affect the performance of each individual Representation. This also represents a "find and fix" period. In any case however, configuration management must be maintained so that the test configuration can be unambiguously identified.

4.4 Establishing the Integrated System Performance of the Representation

To assist in the analysis, the foregoing processes are performed incrementally, using several "standard" scenarios. This facilitates the identification, isolation and resolution of problem areas. To establish that the integrated system functions in the defined scenario environments, a series of trials are conducted using the various scenarios identified in the Detailed Test Plan (DTP). Ideally, several runs are made for each test scenario identified in the DTP. The purpose of these tests is to insure that the integrated test resource operates in the regime of scenarios specified. At the completion of these integrated tests, the integrated configuration is "locked down" and brought under formal configuration control.

To this point, all efforts have been focused on identifying the various components of the test resource, the degree of accuracy with which data is transferred between components, the identification of shortfalls (both intrinsic and extrinsic) of a Representation, and the degree to which data is accurately reported (recorded). This coupled with the Accreditation Caveats and Limitations delineate the degree to which the ISTC test resource can be used to produce data to meet the DT&E Requirements. This analysis identifies the degree to which the Representations accurately generate, transmit, receive and process data in an integrated environment and is documented in an "Acceptability Assessment and Accreditation Recommendation Report" which is provided to the Accreditation Authority for decision.

After formal accreditation, a "Runs for Record" campaign is executed to generate and collect NMD System and Element performance data which is subsequently analyzed to assess the performance of the integrated system.

5.0 OBSERVATIONS AND CONCLUSIONS

Several observations are supported by The AEgis Technologies Group's experience in Accreditation Planning for ISTC and other similarly complex tools.

5.1 Conclusions

As evidenced by our experiences in the accreditation of the ISTC for use in IGTs, a common, reoccurring misperception is that Accreditation is synonymous with an evaluation of the goodness of a given Representation participating in the Ground Test. We have tried to demonstrate here, as well as when we were working on the accreditation of the ISTC, such is not the case.

As a process, accreditation provides a means for identifying the degree to which data exchanged among participants is consistent with what a given Representation produces and what a receiving Representation expects. It attempts to identify (and quantify, if possible) the instances in which data is enhanced or degraded (in terms of quality, quantity and timeliness) when transmitted between participants. It formally uses a caveats and limitations process as an open forum to identify shortfalls in the simulation and delimits the expectations on the information that can be gleaned from the execution of the simulation. An unexpected benefit of the process is the examination of the historical listing of caveats and limitations which supports assessments of the Element's development and maturation. The accreditation process also identifies the outer limits of the degree to which the test requirements and objectives can be expected to be met. The process also identifies the limits to which data obtained from the simulation can be used.

As a statement, accreditation is a formal declaration by the Accreditation Authority (DT&E Sponsor) that the test resource is suitable for the specified purpose. It formally recognizes the limitations of the Representations being used in the test and the impact such limitations will have on meeting the stated requirements and objectives of the test. It also identifies the limitation on the value and use of data obtained from the test.

The ISTC Accreditation process does not measure or assess the goodness/badness of the objective NMD system, the incorporated Element Representations or the objective system components. That measurement can only be obtained by an analysis of the data resulting from the execution of the integrated test configuration. Accreditation is a process whereby the sponsor of a test which utilizes ISTC can assess the degree to which it meets the purpose and requirements that form the basis of the test. Alternatively stated, the function of the accreditation process is to establish that in the integrated configuration of the test resource, the individual Element Representations and the Framework do not adversely (or beneficially) affect the results in an unintended fashion and where unavoidable, to quantify the nature of such effects.

5.2 Observations

A key feature of the ISTC accreditation process is the early identification of the caveats and limitations associated with the various Representations to be used in the simulation. An initial request for written input with follow-on, face-to-face forums was found to be very advantageous in identifying and establishing the impacts of various caveats and limitations on participating Elements. This mechanism was also a very valuable means of identifying the impacts that various caveats and limitations would have on the degree to which the test objectives and requirements can be met.

Maintaining timely cognizance of the configurations of the various Representations being used in the integrated configuration is also essential. As noted, the ISTC is a HWIL/SWIL simulation. New Software Builds, Versions, Revisions, are constantly being developed and incorporated when technically feasible. It is essential that these "upgrades" are accurately tracked to insure that accreditation activities accomplished to date are still valid and/or re-executed as required.

6.0 REFERENCES

[1] National Missile Defense Joint Program Office, "*Capstone Accreditation Plan for Developmental Tests/Integrated Ground Tests*", 11 January 1999, Report No. EJ-ISTC99-RP006_rB.

[2] National Missile Defense Joint Program Office, "*Detailed Accreditation Plan for Integrated Ground Test-5*", 5 Oct 1999, Report No. EJ-ISTC99-RP033.

[3] National Missile Defense Joint Program Office; *"ISTC Acceptability Assessment and Accreditation Recommendation Report for Integrated Ground Test-5*", 11 October 1999, Report No. EJ-ISTC99-RP034.

[4] National Missile Defense Lead System Integrator, "*Integrated Ground Test-5 Detailed Test Plan***",** 21 September 1999, Report No. D743-10163 Draft.

[5] Department of the Army, Pamphlet 5-11, "Verification, Validation and Accreditation of Army Models and Simulations", 30 September 1999.

[6] National Missile Defense Lead System Integrator, "Verification and Validation Plan", 15 October 1999, Report No. EJ-LSII99-RP001.

ACKNOWLEDGMENTS

This work was supported by the Integrated System Test Capability Product Office, System Test and Evaluation Directorate of the National Missile Defense Joint Program Office.

AUTHOR'S BIOGRAPHIES

BETH VANN is a Systems Engineer with AEgis Technologies Group in Huntsville, Alabama. She supports the Accreditation of the ISTC and previously served as the VV&A Lead Engineer for the Common Test Environment areas of the ISTC. Miss Vann was awarded a BS degree in Computer Science from the University of Alabama-Huntsville (UAH).

DR. KEN KAWANO is a Senior Systems Engineer with AEgis Technologies Group in Huntsville, Alabama. He received a BS in Chemistry from the Massachusetts Institute of Technology, Cambridge, Massachusetts and a PhD in Organic Chemistry from the University of Wisconsin, Madison, Wisconsin.

JOHN PATE is an Aerospace Engineer with the US Army Aviation and Missile Command (USA AMCOM) assigned to the System Test and Evaluation Division, US Army National Missile Defense Joint Program Office (NMD JPO) in Huntsville, Alabama. He serves as the government's Verification, Validation and Accreditation Lead for NMD test resources, including the real-time, NMD element simulations within the NMD Integrated System Test Capability. Mr. Pate has a BS in Aerospace Engineering from the Auburn University.

FOCUSING ON CREDIBILITY AND CONFIDENCE - U.S. NAVY MODELING AND SIMULATION VERIFICATION, VALIDATION, AND ACCREDITATION

Brian J. Hall
Operational Test and Evaluation Force (Code 01B3)
7970 Diven Street, Norfolk, VA 23505-1461
Phone: 757-444-5546, ext.-3288
Email: hallb@cotf.navy.mil

Candace L. Conwell
Space and Naval Warfare Systems Command (PD-13 TSG)
4301 Pacific Highway (Bldg C-60), San Diego, CA 92110
Phone: 858-537-0184
Email: clc@spawar.navy.mil

Marcia A. Stutzman
Logicon Information Systems and Services
55 John Clarke Road, Middletown, RI 02842
Phone: 301-317-9698
Email: mstutzman@logicon.com

KEYWORDS: Modeling, Simulation, Verification, Validation, Accreditation

ABSTRACT

Department of Defense (DoD) has directed the Service Components to use modeling and simulation (M&S) to reduce time, resources, and risks of acquisition, to increase the quality of systems acquired, and to improve system performance. In the post Cold War era of declining defense budgets, reduced manning and rapidly evolving technology and threats, M&S can provide tailored test environments that extend test envelopes to augment live testing. Effective and cost-efficient testing of critical systems will involve tailored verification, validation and accreditation (VV&A) processes driven by the Accreditation Authority's definition of acceptable M&S use in testing. This paper examines the M&S accreditation process the United States Navy's independent operational tester, Commander Operational Test and Evaluation Force (COMOPTEVFOR) employs to ultimately ensure a high level of confidence in the M&S used to supplement operational test and evaluation (OT&E).

INTRODUCTION

Normally a "senior official" in the M&S user's organization or chain of command makes the accreditation decision for use of an M&S. One important exception is the use of M&S for operational testing. COMOPTEVFOR makes the accreditation decision for all M&S used in OT&E. COMOPTEVFOR represents the fleet and the taxpayer in assessing whether an M&S is suitable for use in OT&E. Program Managers anticipating OT&E and intending to use M&S should coordinate as early as possible with COMOPTEVFOR. A common understanding between COMOPTEVFOR and the Program Manager of the planned employment is necessary to support VV&A. This paper maps COMOPTEVFOR's accreditation process and practices with the Department of the Navy (DON) VV&A Process.

POLICY

Modeling and simulation is defined as the use of models, including emulators, prototypes, simulators, and stimulators, either statically or over time, to develop data as a basis for making managerial or technical decisions. Digital M&S is a specialized subset of software and can be described as a detailed, complete, and unambiguous set of requirements implemented as a computer application that models or simulates a threat weapon, combat or support system's intended function or functions. Verification, validation, and accreditation refer to the processes used to ensure the application of M&S results are appropriate for a specific purpose. Properly performed and documented verification and validation (V&V) are necessary and essential to the accreditation decision process. Accreditation is a decision that demonstrates the Accreditation Authority has a high level of confidence that a particular M&S is representative of the weapons system, has demonstrated the required fidelity, and is credible to use for a particular application.

Department of Defense

Because the need for credible, cost-effective, and efficient M&S is so great, the DoD directed each of the Services to develop a VV&A process in January 1994. This process is intended to provide the end user with information needed to determine whether and how the results of a model or simulation can be applied to decisions that ultimately affect the warfighter. DoD Directive 5000.59 *DoD Modeling and Simulation (M&S) Management* directed that the Department of the Navy establish VV&A policies and procedures for all M&S applications and also established the Defense Modeling and Simulation Office, or DMSO, as it is most commonly known today.

In April 1996, DoD Instruction 5000.61 DoD *Modeling and Simulation (M&S) Verification, Validation, and Accreditation (VV&A)*, which assigned responsibilities and prescribed procedures for the VV&A of DoD M&S, was promulgated. DMSO followed with the publication of the *DoD Verification, Validation, and Accreditation Recommended Practices Guide (RPG)* in November 1996. The online version, *Verification, Validation, and Accreditation Recommended Practices Guide (RPG) Year 2000 Edition Build 1* was released in May 2000.

The web-based RPG provides a quick overview of VV&A. The RPG addresses five roles involved in the VV&A process: M&S User, M&S Developer, M&S Program Manager, V&V Agent, and Accreditation Agent. The roles played by the M&S User and M&S Program Manager are similar to, but not entirely the same as, the Accreditation Authority and M&S Proponent that are described in the Navy instruction and this paper.

Department of the Navy

The DON established the Department of the Navy Modeling and Simulation Management Office (DONMSMO) in April 1994 with the publication of SECNAV Instruction 5200.*38 Department of the Navy Modeling and Simulation Program.* The DONMSMO was charged with developing a common VV&A process for use by both Navy and Marine Corps activities. In April 1999, the DON Verification, Validation and Accreditation Program was established with the issuance of SECNAV Instruction 5200.40 *Verification, Validation, and Accreditation of Models and Simulations*.

KEY PLAYERS

SECNAVINST 5200.40 identifies the key players in the performance of VV&A as the M&S Proponent and the Accreditation Authority. Figure 1 shows how those players fit into the overall acquisition structure when the M&S is used to supplement OT&E. The Navy M&S VV&A Handbook is currently being staffed for approval as a Navy M&S VV&A Standard. The handbook amplifies the information in the SECNAV instruction and provides practical guidance for those persons in the Navy and Marine Corps who are responsible for implementing VV&A.

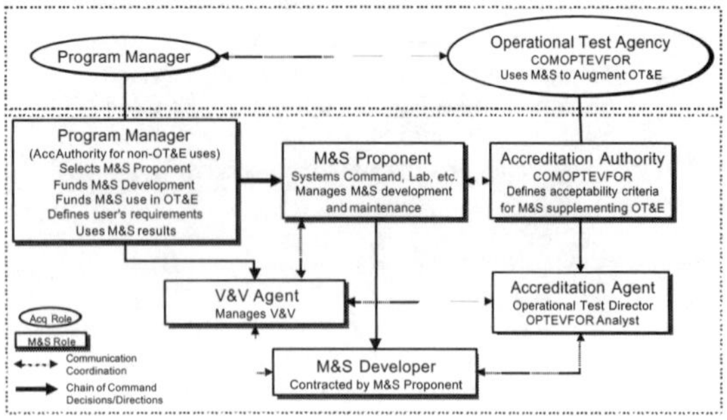

Figure 1. VV&A Players When M&S Augments OT&E

Accreditation Authority. The Accreditation Authority is the individual with the responsibility and/or authority to decide whether an M&S is credible for an intended use. In most cases, the Accreditation Authority is a senior official designated within the organization that uses the results or products from a specific M&S application. The Accreditation Authority determines how much V&V it will take to establish confidence that the M&S is suitable for the user's intended use. The Accreditation Authority represents the M&S user.

M&S Proponent. The M&S Proponent is responsible for defining M&S and V&V requirements, developing the accreditation and V&V plans, implementing the plans, documenting the results, and submitting all documents to the DONMSMO. Additionally, the M&S Proponent ensures that all other related M&S processes, such as configuration management, are established and functioning. The M&S Proponent acquires the M&S application by contracting with the M&S Developer for development of a new M&S or modification of a legacy M&S. The M&S Developer may be a DoD laboratory, a Federally Funded Research and Development Center, or a commercial contractor.

Accreditation Agent. The Accreditation Authority may designate an Accreditation Agent to plan, manage and/or conduct the accreditation assessment for the M&S. Accreditation Agents are intimately familiar with the intended use of the M&S and possess the expertise to make informed judgments. Accreditation Agents work closely with the M&S Proponent and the Verification and Validation Agent(s) to assemble the Accreditation Package and to develop a recommendation for the Accreditation Authority. The Accreditation Agent's organization may be internal to or independent of the Accreditation Authority's organization.

V&V Agent. The V&V Agent is the organization designated by the M&S Proponent to coordinate, manage and/or conduct the V&V for an M&S application.

Commander Operational Test and Evaluation Force. COMOPTEVFOR is the independent Operational Test Agency reporting directly to the Chief of Naval Operations (CNO) on the effectiveness and suitability of major weapons systems. SECNAVINST 5200.40 designates COMOPTEVFOR as the Accreditation Authority for M&S used to support operational test activities in the Navy. COMOPTEVFOR accredits all M&S used to supplement the OT&E of weapons systems, as well as any M&S used in combined developmental test (DT) / operational test (OT) events. Early and continuous involvement between the M&S Proponent and COMOPTEVFOR is needed to ensure that all parties involved have a common understanding of the M&S requirements.

DON VV&A PROCESS

While COMOPTEVFOR is the accreditation authority for M&S used to support Navy OT&E decisions, COMOPTEVFOR does not perform the V&V. As the accreditor, COMOPTEVFOR's role is to identify test requirements and acceptability criteria. Programs with systems under test should begin coordination with COMOPTEVFOR early, plan V&V tasks to meet the projected requirements, and be able to describe how the M&S will be used in the test. Furthermore, Program Managers need to set aside resources and schedule time to adequately perform and document the necessary V&V activities when targeting an M&S for accreditation for OT&E. Funding for accreditation is the responsibility of the Program Manager for the system under test.

Figure 2 provides a graphic overview of the DON VV&A process for M&S. Enclosure 1 to SECNAVINST 5200.40 describes the process in detail and should be reviewed for specific information. The DON VV&A process is flexible and tailorable. In order to maintain a balance between M&S requirements and real-world resource constraints, the VV&A process is tailored for each application to fit four sets of considerations including the intended use, the Accreditation Authority's requirements, resource constraints, and the type(s) of M&S involved, whether new development, modified, or legacy. As Figure 2 indicates, the Accreditation Authority is involved from the beginning of the M&S design and development in defining the M&S acceptability requirements, through documenting plans for and reports of VV&A activities.

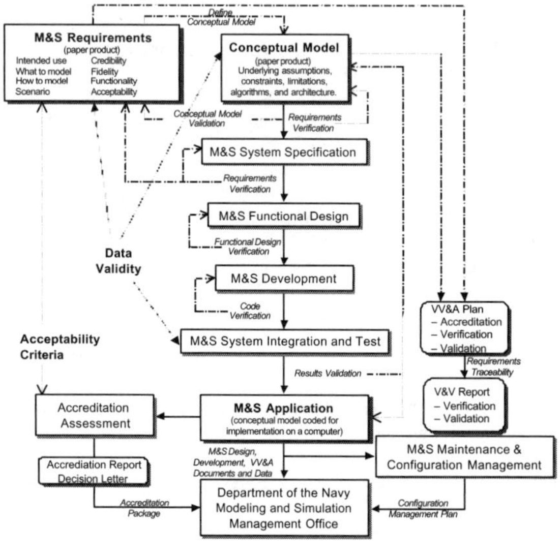

Figure 2. DON VV&A Process

COMOPTEVFOR ACCREDITATION

COMOPTEVFOR Instruction 5000.1 *Use of Modeling and Simulation (M&S) In Operational Testing* was published in September 1995. The COMOPTEVFOR policy memorandum (Ser 00T/312) *Accreditation of Modeling and in Support of Operational Test and Evaluation* issued April 1998 and Policy and Information Notice 99-01 *COMOPTEVFOR Modeling and Simulation Accreditation Documentation* distributed in May 1999 have been updated and incorporated in 5000.1. COMOPTEVFOR's vision is to be at the forefront of intelligent incorporation of M&S into operational testing.

The COMOPTEVFOR Accreditation Process compliments the DON VV&A Process, is concurrent with the M&S Development Process, and satisfies the requirements of SECNAVINST 5200.40. Figure 3 depicts the COMOPTEVFOR Accreditation Process. The process begins by COMOPTEVFOR communicating with the Program Manager to determine the sufficiency of assets and resources for test. A determination will be made at this time if there is a need to use M&S in a program.

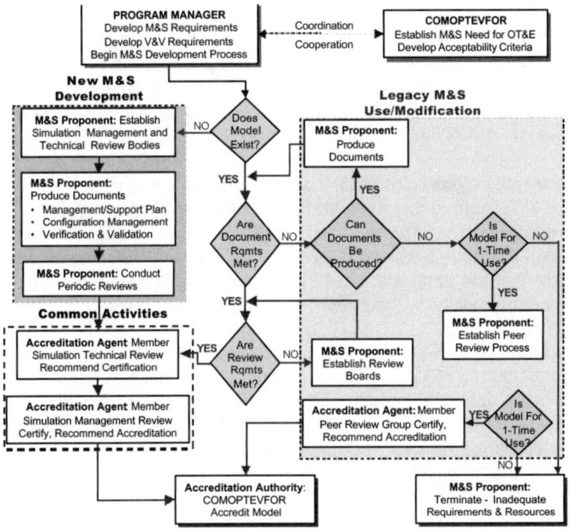

Figure 3. COMOPTEVFOR Accreditation Process Synopsis

The Operational Tester is involved from the start of the M&S development in defining the M&S requirements from which the conceptual model is based and from which the V&V is planned. The Operational Tester is also involved in the review of the Conceptual Model. The Conceptual Model describes the developer's interpretation of the M&S requirements. The conceptual model includes text, diagrams and equations to describe underlying assumptions, constraints, limitations, algorithms, and, where necessary, architecture. This review helps to determine whether the M&S can support the acceptability requirements. The M&S may need modification to meet those requirements.

COMOPTEVFOR works closely in an integrated environment with the M&S Proponent, V&V Agent(s), the contracted M&S Developer, and various subject matter experts to define the acceptability criteria, or requirements, for validation and accreditation of the M&S.

M&S Resource Requirements

Early involvement, proper identification of M&S requirements and close coordination with the M&S Proponent are essential to the development of a functional model or simulation. M&S development resources must be identified as early as possible to enable the Program Manager to budget appropriately. Resources reflect the financial and material requirements for accreditation as well as the Operational Tester technical expertise required to augment the Simulation Management and Technical Review boards formed as part of the M&S development process. As Accreditation Agent, the Operational Test Director serves on the Simulation Management board while the Analyst is a member of the Simulation Technical Review board. M&S observation and review are conducted at both the managerial level and the technical level on a regular basis. Model development progress is evaluated at each phase of operational testing.

Types of M&S Accredited

COMOPTEVFORINST 5000.1 applies to all M&S used to supplement operational testing to include pure mathematical simulations and computer/hardware-in-the-loop hybrid simulations. COMOPTEVFOR's memorandum of 29 April 1998 described ten specific cases for which M&S accreditation would be required:

1. All new M&S
2. Enhancements and modifications of existing M&S
3. Hardware-in-the-loop hybrid simulations
4. Land-based test facilities
5. Threat target simulators and stimulators in support of OT&E
6. Legacy M&S
7. Human-in-the-loop hybrid simulations
8. Existing land-based test facilities
9. Existing threat target simulators and stimulators, along with those under development and those postulated for future use in support of OT&E
10. All M&S in support of OT&E, whether embedded in weapons systems, implemented as stand-alone systems, or integrated with other M&S systems for distributed simulation

COMOPTEVFOR makes the distinction between (a) M&S used in the OT&E of weapons systems, and (b) software intensive systems under test, or M&S, which are components of embedded training and testing tools. In the former case, the principal decision-maker for accreditation is COMOPTEVFOR. In the latter case, the weapon system or platform sponsor decides whether the M&S is adequate to perform a specified task. However, COMOPTEVFOR may evaluate the performance of the M&S as satisfactory (or unsatisfactory) just as in any other aspect of the system(s) under OT&E.

All M&S considered as potential candidates for use to supplement OT&E are considered by default as "non-accredited". This status is changed after the M&S has undergone the V&V process and designated as "accredited" for use in supplementing OT&E in a specific test event. If later modifications alter the operational representation of an accredited M&S without sufficient V&V to document the changes, then COMOPTEVFOR may choose to non-accredit a previously accredited model for that particular test event. Additionally, re-accreditation of M&S are required if modifications to a weapons system under test are major and significant. The Program Office should contact the Operational Test Director to decide on the best course of action.

Acceptability Criteria

Operational Testers must clearly define required model functionality early in the development cycle. Acceptability criteria is established by the responsible OPTEVFOR functional warfare division and briefed to COMOPTEVFOR as an integral component of the Test and Evaluation Master Plan (TEMP) approval process. Testers coordinate with M&S personnel to determine what is feasible, cost effective, and credible. It is imperative that the specific acceptability criteria be determined. Measurable criteria are the most useful. Some criteria may be evaluated on a pass/fail basis. Often the evaluation is a subjective assessment by a subject matter expert (SME) and in these cases, the SME's name and professional credentials should be annotated within the V&V Report.

Upfront involvement enables the Program Manager to accurately estimate the potential benefits of the M&S to reduce program cost, improve product quality, and project completion time.

Testers input should include the anticipated range of data over which the model may be accredited for use, limitations that would render the model unacceptable for use, and conditions that would preclude model accreditation. The acceptability criteria are updated on a cycle corresponding to requirements updates (i.e., Operational Requirements Document (ORD) or TEMP revisions, major milestones) or as needed on a case-by-case basis. Acceptability criteria are traceable to critical operational issues (COIs) resolution.

Rolling Airframe Missile Block 1 Example

The Joint Accreditation Support Activity (JASA), located at the Naval Air Warfare Center Weapons Division (NAWCWD), China Lake, California, developed the Simulation Support Plan for the NAWCWD 6 Degree-of-Freedom (6DOF) Simulation of the Rolling Airframe Missile (RAM) Block 1. For this M&S application, COMOPTEVFOR defined high-level requirements in the following areas: overall, ship systems, launcher, missile, lethality, target, environment, scenario, output, support, and accreditation. To demonstrate that the high level requirements are met, the VV&A efforts focuses on individual detailed requirements. Examples of JASA derived requirements follow:

- **Intended Use:** Use M&S to mitigate OPTEVFOR's assumed risk in making decisions based on a statistically insignificant test population. Specifically, M&S should be used in the resolution of the following COI and system performance requirements identified in the ORD and the TEMP.

- **COI Missile Effectiveness -** Will the RAM Block 1 missile, when properly supported by sensor systems, yield acceptable probabilities of kill (P_K) throughout missile engagement envelopes against the current and projected threats under all natural environmental conditions and in clear and electronic attack (EA) environments?

- **Detailed M&S Requirement:** M&S shall predict the performance of the RAM Block 1 system for those engagements and conditions that were observed during DT/OT from immediately after successful launch throughout the missile flight.

- **Acceptability Criteria:** For engagements and conditions observed during DT/OT and for which adequate test data is available, predictions of RAM performance from immediately after successful launch throughout the missile flight shall match recorded flight test results to a degree that is acceptable to the RAM Simulation Working Group SMEs.

- **Assessment Method:** Overlays comparing simulation results from post flight analyses with measured flight test results from DT/OT shots will be presented to the RAM Simulation Working Group at the certification review.

The RAM 6DOF simulation is currently under review for accreditation by COMOPTEVFOR.

Developmental and operational testing of the RAM Weapon System were conducted from August 1998 through August 1999. This included firing Block 1 missiles during simulated attacks by anti-ship cruise missiles and threat-representative surrogates against the unmanned, remotely controlled Self Defense Test Ship. RAM models and supporting models are being validated with Fiscal Year 99 test results. Simulations will be run with these models to examine predicted performance under conditions of parameter excursion, in preparation for Follow-on Operational Test and Evaluation (FOT&E) of the RAM Block 1. (Office of the Secretary of Defense, Director, Operational Test and Evaluation FY99 Annual Report).

INTEGRATING ACCREDITATION WITH ACQUISITION

DoD Regulation 5000.2R (Change 4) *Mandatory Procedures for Major Defense Acquisition Programs (MDAPs) and Major Automated Information System (MAIS) Acquisition Programs*, dated 11 May 1999, directs that M&S shall be applied throughout a system's life-cycle in support of acquisition activities such as requirements definition, program management, design and engineering, efficient test planning, and results prediction; and to supplement actual test and evaluation, manufacturing, and logistics support.

Additionally, Program Managers must integrate the use of M&S within program planning activities; plan for the life-cycle application, support, and reuse of models and simulations; and integrate M&S across the functional disciplines.

An essential element of the Program Manager's acquisition strategy is the M&S approach, which should include planning for accreditation. The M&S approach iterates through the acquisition process to become increasingly more definitive. VV&A are applied to ensure that the application of M&S results is appropriate for supporting a system acquisition decision.

Figure 4 depicts a generic accreditation schedule for the accreditation of M&S used to augment operational testing integrated over three acquisition phases in accordance with SECNAVINST 5200.40. The acquisition phases depicted include Phase I Product Development and Risk Reduction, Phase II Engineering and Manufacturing Development, and Phase III Production.

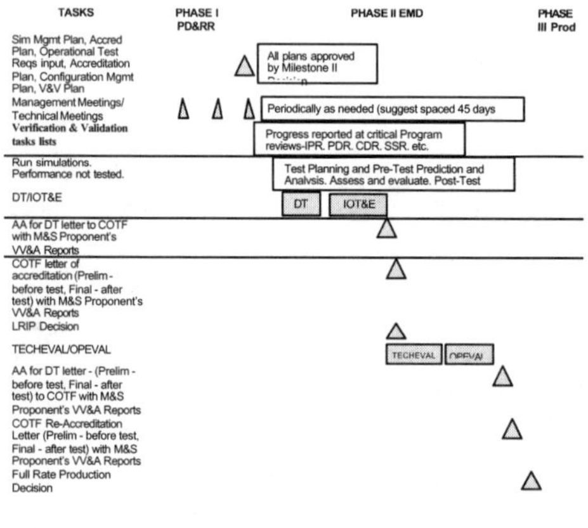

Figure 4. Generic Integrated Accreditation Schedule

The Assistant Chief of Staff of the responsible COMOPTEVFOR warfare division may sign a contingent letter regarding accreditation with a final list of V&V tasks needed to qualify for accreditation (after final test). COMOPTEVFOR signs the accreditation decision letter.

M&S ACCREDITATION EXAMPLES

Following is a partial listing of accreditations that COMOPTEVFOR performed in the past year. COMOPTEVFOR accredited the following M&S for supplementing Operational Evaluation (OPEVAL) or FOT&E. The accreditation letters and supporting reports in these cases were signed by COMOPTEVFOR.

- F/A-18E/F Manned Air Combat Simulator 3 (MACS 3) and F/A-18C/D MACS 2 Simulator (FA/-18 E/F Super Hornet Program OPEVAL)
- TOMAHAWK Land Attack Missile (TLAM) Mission Validation System (MVS) / Register Level Simulation (RLS) Version 4.1 to support the TOMAHAWK Theater Mission Planning Center (TMPC) Version 3.1 (Advanced TOMAHAWK Weapons Control System (ATWCS) Program FOT&E)
- TOMAHAWK Land Attack Missile (TLAM) Shipboard Environment and Missile Simulation (SEMS) Version 2.0 to support Advanced TOMAHAWK Weapons Control System (ATWCS) Launch Control Group – Replacement (LCG-R) (ATWCS use in TOMAHAWK Missile Program FOT&E)
- Computation of Vulnerable Area and Repair Times (COVART) Version 4.1 (MV-22 Osprey Program OPEVAL)
- Air Combat Environment Test and Evaluation Facility (ACETEF) MV-22 Full Mission Simulation (FMS) (MV-22 Osprey OPEVAL)

COMOPTEVFOR also completed accreditations for M&S used to supplement Operational Assessment (OA) test events. The Assistant Chief of Staff of the responsible COMOPTEVFOR warfare division signs the OA accreditation letter. A partial listing follows:

- Simulation II/Scenario Structured Torpedo Operational Requirements Model (SIM-II/SSTORM) (Virginia (SSN 774) Class Attack Submarine Program)
- Surface Combat Systems Center (SCSC), Wallops Island, Virginia and the Multi-Function Land Based Test Site (LBTS), Port Hueneme Division, Dam Neck, Virginia, to support Cooperative Engagement Capability (CEC) AN/USG-3 Equipped E-2C Aircraft (CEC E-2C Program)

Accreditations currently under review by COMOPTEVFOR are the following:

- NAWCWD RAM Block 1 Six Degree-of-Freedom (6DOF) Simulation (RAM Block 1 Program FOT&E)
- Naval Surface Warfare Center, Crane Division, Seeker Test Van and Airborne Turret Infrared Measurement System Pod to support MUJ-52/B (BOL-IR) Infrared Countermeasure (OA)

Examples of M&S being considered for use in OT&E are:

- Total Mine Simulation System (TMSS)
- Suite of M&S proposed to support RAM Block 1 Program FOT&E:
  - Front End Simulation (ship sensors and fire control) of Ship Self Defense System
  - NAWCWD Combined Simulation
  - Joint Service Endgame Model (JSEM)
  - Associated target models
  - Background imagery

Some current and future programs not already mentioned above, which rely heavily upon the use of M&S and will require accreditation for use in OT&E, are the following:

- AIM-9X Sidewinder Air-To-Air Missile
- Integrated Surface Ship ASW Combat System (AN/SQQ-89)
- Joint Standoff Weapon (JSOW)
- LPD 17 Amphibious Transport Dock Ship
- MK 48 ADCAP Torpedo Upgrades
- Navy Area Theater Ballistic Missile Defense (TBMD)
- Navy Theater Wide (NTW) TBMD
- Ship Self Defense System
- Twenty First Century Destroyer (DD 21 Land Attack Destroyer Class)
- Land Attack Standard Missile
- Tactical TOMAHAWK Weapon Control System (TTWCS)

In the recent past, COMOPTEVFOR non-accredited some M&S for use in OT&E to support a specific test phase. Non-accreditation decisions are unfortunate because they can potentially impact acquisition milestones and add significant risk to the program. Successful weapons program test matrices should include adequate resources to resolve critical technical parameters (CTPs) and COIs without relying solely on M&S in case the M&S is non-accredited. It appears that some M&S advocates tend to be overly confident without weighing the consequences of non-accreditation decisions. Therefore, in order to minimize program risk, in addition to adequate V&V, test resources are required in sufficient quantities so that CTPs and COIs can be resolved if the M&S is unable to be used due to a non-accreditation decision. Also, previously accredited M&S must be re-accredited for each future OT phase.

In all cases, the accreditation decision letters and supporting reports are forwarded to DONMSMO for inclusion in the Navy Modeling and Simulation Catalog.

CONSEQUENCES: AUDIT

There are also consequences for not expending the time and funds necessary to conduct V&V. Verification and validation are necessary to produce the body of evidence required by the Accreditation Authority to assess and make a decision about M&S credibility. One possible consequence is that COMOPTEVFOR will not accredit an M&S to be used to augment test planning, test conduct or analyses and, therefore, additional and expensive live assets will be needed to meet milestone decisions. Another example of a type of consequence follows.

The Office of the Inspector General (IG) for DoD conducted an audit to evaluate DoD models used in generating quantitative munitions requirements. Specifically, the IG evaluated Service-level models and assumptions used in generating quantitative requirements.

The Marine Corps use two different methods to determine its munitions quantities - computer modeling applications and SME estimates. Service-level models are used to generate quantitative requirements by identifying the quantities and types of munitions needed to defeat specified threats. SECNAV Instruction 5200.40 M&S requires VV&A for M&S used significantly in supporting the development of the Department of the Navy Program Objectives Memorandum (POM).

Department of Defense Audit Report No. 99-051 *Marine Corps Quantitative Munitions Requirements Process* (December 1998) found that the Marine Corps did not independently verify, validate, and accredit or identify that the requirements generation models it used had been verified, validated and accredited. As a result, the Marine Corps potentially miscalculated its munitions requirements, and did not meet the Commanders in Chief operational objectives. The Marine Corps concurred with the recommendations in the report and is in the process of ensuring the models are verified, validated, and accredited as required.

SUMMARY

"Those who can't wait for accredited models and simulations, will go forward without success."

RADM Kathleen K. Paige, ASN(RDA) Chief Engineer
DMSO Industry Days, 25 May 2000

Accreditation of Navy M&S is not just a suggestion it is a policy that is necessary to ensure the credibility of all M&S used to make Navy decisions regarding national defense, systems procurement, systems safety, budgets, and the safety of our men and women in uniform.

Change is difficult, but change must occur for Navy M&S to be proven credible. No longer can Navy validate M&S without documentation of its capabilities, limitations, and constraints. No longer can Navy use M&S that are not accredited for the specific use.

The Department of the Navy promulgated M&S VV&A procedures and processes through SECNAVINST 5200.40. COMOPTEVFOR has embraced the instruction and tailored its VV&A process for OT&E.

Tailoring the VV&A process is key. No two M&S are alike, therefore, the process to V&V any M&S should be unique. Identify, schedule and execute the V&V tasks required to meet the acceptability criteria. Work with the Accreditation Authority to define precise requirements.

The advantages of effective and credible M&S are numerous. Inadequate attention to the VV&A process can lead to non-accreditation for use of M&S in OT&E.

Program Managers anticipating the use of M&S to supplement OT&E should begin coordinating with COMOPTEVFOR as soon as the need is identified.

The Department of the Navy VV&A Process should evolve to include adequate attention be paid to M&S acquisition and development in order to integrate VV&A requirements definition, traceability, and management throughout those processes. The V&V costs, which are now considered additional, would then be included as part of the normal process of development. Accreditation for a specific use would be the only service a potential M&S user would fund.

REFERENCES

Coyle. Philip E. 1999. *Director, Operational Test and Evaluation Fiscal Year 98 Annual Report*. Feb. http://www.dote.osd.mil/reports/FY98/98tocmain.html

Defense Modeling and Simulation Office. 2000. *VV&A Recommended Practices Guide Year 2000 Edition Build 1.* May http://www.msiac.dmso.mil/vva

Department of Defense Directive. 1999. Department of Defense Directive 5000.59 *DoD Modeling and Simulation (M&S) Management, Change 1.* May. http://www.dmso.mil/

Department of Defense Instruction. 1996. *Department of Defense Instruction 5000.61 DoD Modeling and Simulation (M&S) Verification, Validation, and Accreditation (VV&A).* Apr. http://www.dmso.mil/

Department of Defense Regulation. 1999. Department of Defense Regulation 5000.2R (Change 4) *Mandatory Procedures for Major Defense Acquisition Programs (MDAPs) and Major Automated Information System (MAIS) Acquisition Programs.* May.

Department of the Navy. 1994. Secretary of the Navy Instruction 5200.*38 Department of the Navy Modeling and Simulation Program.* Apr. http://navmsmo.hq.navy.mil/

Department of the Navy. 1995. Commander Operational Test and Evaluation Force Instruction 5000.1 *Use of Modeling and Simulation (M&S) In Operational Testing.* Sep. http://www.cotf.navy.mil/otd/

Department of the Navy. 1998. Commander Operational Test and Evaluation Force policy memorandum (Ser 00T/312) *Accreditation of Modeling and in Support of Operational Test and Evaluation.* Apr. http://www.cotf.navy.mil/otd/

Department of the Navy. 1999. Commander Operational Test and Evaluation Force Policy and Information Notice 99-01 *COMOPTEVFOR Modeling and Simulation Accreditation Documentation.* May. http://www.cotf.navy.mil/otd/

Department of the Navy. 1999. Secretary of the Navy Instruction 5200.40 Verification, Validation, and Accreditation (VV&A) of Models and Simulations. Apr. http://navmsmo.hq.navy.mil/

Kilikauskas, Michelle. 2000. *Accreditation Simulation Support Plan NAWCWD 6 Degree-of-Freedom (6DOF) Simulation of the Rolling Airframe Missile (RAM) Block 1.* Joint Accreditation Support Activity. Jan. http://www.nawcwpns.navy.mil/~jasa/

National Partnership for Reinventing (NPR) Government. 1999. Hammer Award Highlights. http://www.npr.gov/library/awards/hammer/hamrhlgt.html

Office of the Inspector General Department of Defense. 1998. Marine Corps Quantitative Munitions Requirements Process. Audit Report No. 99-051. Dec. http://www.dodig.osd.mil/audit/reports/index.html

Coyle. Philip E. 2000. *Director, Operational Test and Evaluation Fiscal Year 99 Annual Report*. Feb. http://www.dote.osd.mil/reports/FY99/index.html

AUTHOR BIOGRAPHIES

BRIAN J. HALL is the Modeling and Simulation Manager for the Commander Operational Test and Evaluation Force, United States Navy, in Norfolk, Virginia. He received his Master's and Bachelor's of Science Degrees in Mechanical Engineering from Virginia Tech. Mr. Hall serves as consultant and advisor to the command warfare department analysts and operational test directors in the planning and conduct of operational tests employing models and simulations. As principal advisor to the command staff on the selection, accreditation, and application of models and simulations, he provides expertise on the verification, validation and accreditation of models and supports the planning and execution of cost-effective verification, validation and accreditation programs.

CANDACE L. CONWELL is a Computer Scientist at the Space and Naval Warfare Systems Command. She is a graduate of the Naval Postgraduate School. Ms. Conwell has 23 years of C4ISR and M&S experience, including the design, development, testing of simulation systems, scenarios and associated databases. While a member of the DONMSMO Technical Support Group, she led the DON VV&A Program spearheading publication of the VV&A instruction, authoring of the VV&A Handbook, and ongoing development of an online VV&A Turbo Tool that automates the production of VV&A related documents.

MARCIA A. STUTZMAN is a Principal Analyst at Logicon, Inc. where she supports the Navy Modeling and Simulation (M&S) Verification, Validation and Accreditation Program. Previously, she provided program management support to the Director, Navy Test and Evaluation Modeling and Simulation Management Office. Her experience in M&S includes the Missile and Space Intelligence Center's design, development, verification and validation of the integrated SA-5 Simulation System, as well as the reengineering of the SA-10 Simulation System code to produce Model Requirements and Development Manuals. Additionally, she provided program management and technical support to the DoD Threat Systems Office Validation Program for threat simulators, the CROSSBOW Committee, and the Joint Modeling and Simulation System Program. Ms. Stutzman served as an Intelligence Research Analyst and Russian linguist in the U. S. Army with duty at the National Security Agency. She earned her Bachelor's of General Studies Degree from Indiana University at South Bend.

SIMULATION APPLICATIONS

SIMULATION-BASED SYSTEM ENGINEERING

AN INTEGRATED SYSTEMS ENGINEERING PROCESS FOR PERFORMING LIFE CYCLE COST TRADE-OFFS

William R. Ealy and Gregory W. Barnett
Lockheed Martin Advanced Technology Laboratories
1 Federal Street, A&E Building
Camden, NJ 08102
wealy@atl.lmco.com

KEYWORDS

System Engineering, Signal Processing, Signal Processors, Computer Aided Analysis, Performance Analysis

ABSTRACT

Technology improvements are leading to complex systems that allow warfighters to perform more effectively. Innovative computer aided engineering (CAE) tools and methods are needed for designers to develop and optimize these sophisticated systems. This paper focuses on the development of integrated system engineering concepts and tools that can form the basis for developing future systems. The paper describes the system engineering processes and tools developed and demonstrated under the DARPA Rapid Prototyping of Application Specific Processors (RASSP) program to meet emerging CAE and Cost as an Independent Variable (CAIV) requirements. The RASSP processes and tools were assembled to demonstrate the ability to provide design teams with the capability of assessing life cycle costs of electronic systems at the start of the program and throughout the design process.

INTRODUCTION

Technological advances are leading to highly complicated system concepts. These systems are becoming so sophisticated that our ability to design them cost-effectively is difficult using current design practices. New design processes and CAE tools are required to design systems that warfighters need to maintain a tactical advantage. As one of the two prime contractors for the DARPA RASSP program, Lockheed Martin Advanced Technology Laboratories (ATL) developed and demonstrated a number of new processes and tools for meeting these design challenges. The RASSP program goal was to reduce the development and manufacturing time and life cycle costs of signal processors by a factor of four. ATL identified and investigated the following areas as major factors for achieving the required process improvements and life cycle cost savings.

- Hardware/software co-design process and virtual prototyping concepts and tools to ensure first pass design success.
- Commercial of the shelf (COTS) model year architecture (MYA) concepts to enable low cost technology upgrades.
- An integrated system engineering processes and tools for performing life-cycle cost trade-offs throughout in the design and support phases of the program.

Under the RASSP program, ATL investigated, developed and demonstrated processes and tools for each of these critical design areas. As part of RASSP, ATL also developed a life cycle cost modeling process. The processes, tools and cost modeling techniques developed are described below.

HARDWARE/SOFTWARE CO-DESIGN PROCESS

ATL's RASSP design process, shown in Figure 1, was based on an integrated codesign methodology in contrast to the standard practice of separating hardware and software development activities after the design requirements and specification definitions. Our hardware/software codesign process is partitioned as a function of design abstraction level (i.e., system definition, architecture definition, and detailed design). At each level the hardware and software requirements and design issues are addressed jointly. Combined hardware/software design solutions are investigated and evaluated. Virtual prototypes evaluate and verify the evolving hardware/software designs throughout the process. Outputs from the system design and virtual prototyping efforts make design and cost benefit decisions. These

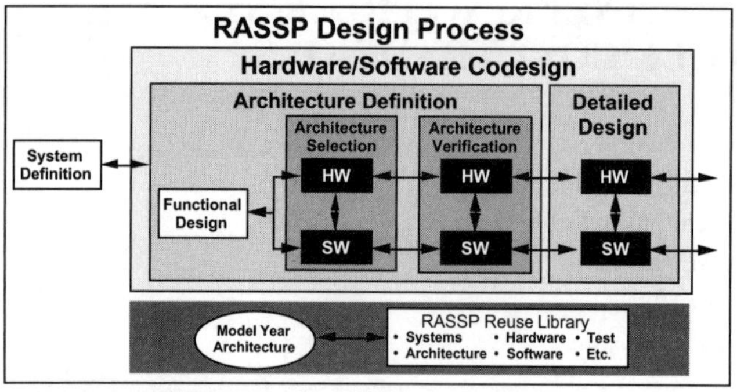

Figure 1. RASSP Integrated Design Process

codesign and virtual prototyping processes allow developers to identify and resolve hardware/software integration issues throughout the entire development effort, instead of waiting until the final system integration and test phase when problems can have significant cost and schedule impacts.

The process relies on early architecture design trade offs using full functional and behavioral virtual prototypes of candidate COTS designs. These independent hardware/software models are mapped and evaluated for a wide range of candidate designs. Designs can be modeled, integrated and validated using detailed hardware/software functional and behavioral virtual prototypes prior to final hardware implementation. During final integration and test, virtual prototypes can rapidly uncover and resolve integration problems. Finally, the resulting virtual prototypes provide a low cost process for verifying functional extensions and hardware upgrades prior to implementation.

Our hardware/software codesign process uses a top-down virtual prototyping process for early architecture design trade-offs and verification, and autocoding techniques for final hardware/software implementation. RASSP design processes focused on extensive use of COTS DSP devices and components. Figure 2 shows the virtual/rapid prototyping design environment resulting from ATL's RASSP development efforts.

The RASSP design process uses graphical algorithm development, virtual prototyping and autocoding tools to simplify development and implementation using COTS multiprocessor components. As part of RASSP, ATL is a pioneered in the development of a data flow based software development process. We integrate and demonstrate graphical algorithm development, virtual prototyping and software autocoding tools. These tools let designers capture and simulate signal processing applications using hierarchical data flow graphs. Once the algorithms are verified, designers partition and map the graph functions onto multi-

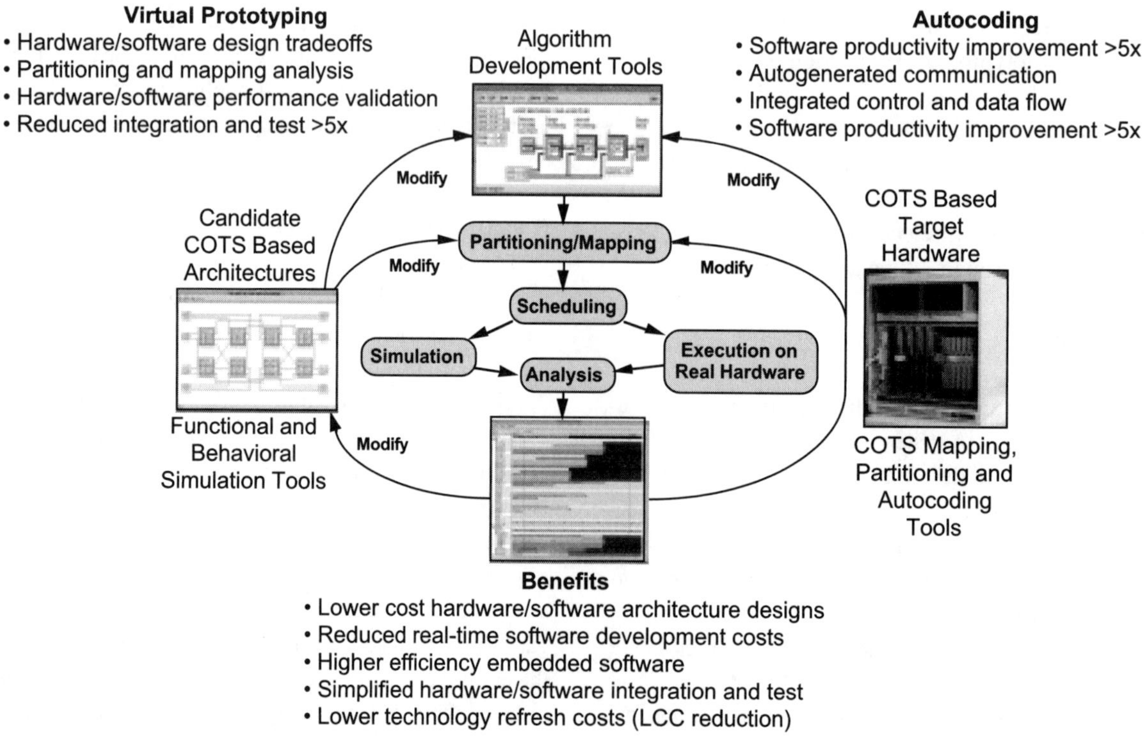

Figure 2. Virtual Prototyping/Rapid Prototyping Design and Development Environment

processor DSP boards and generate the real-time code for the individual processors. During final integration and test, data flow graph and hardware mapping changes are accomplished in one to two hours, significantly reducing the final integration, test time and cost.

INTEGRATED SYSTEM TOOL DESCRIPTION

Systems engineering decisions early in a project significantly impact schedule and cost. Decisions are typically based on the impact to the current phase of a project, rather than the project's overall life cycle. Decisions made during the conceptual system design phase typically determine the total costs incurred over the entire life cycle. To help integrated product development teams (IPDTs) make these trade-offs, the concurrent engineering environment shown in Figure 1 was developed. This integrated system engineering design environment, shown in Figure 3, consisted of Ascent Logic's RDD-100, Price Systems' parametric cost estimation models and Management Sciences' (MSI) RAM-ILS toolset. Design information passed among these tools provides design, cost, reliability, availability, and maintainability support for the IPDT.

This environment provides the IPDT with information to make decisions early, when changes are easy and inexpensive. It allows engineers to make decisions based on current and life cycle impacts of the change, which is essential to reducing total program costs. The capabilities for each of the individual tools are briefly described in following paragraphs.

RDD-100

The RDD-100 tool is the central tool of the integrated toolset. RDD-100 provides requirements analysis, functional analysis, and physical decomposition capabilities. It provides the IPDT with three different views of the system: a requirements view, a functional view, and a physical view. The requirements can be related to the functions and the functions can be allocated to the physical architecture. The interrelation of these three views enables users to automatically generate the lower specification documents from the RDD-100 database. The physical view enables analysis of cost, reliability and maintainability.

Cost Estimation Tools

The toolset uses the PRICE Systems' parametric cost estimation tools for life cycle cost analysis. These tools are modified to allow access to the PRICE models through parameters contained within the RDD-100 requirements database and provide development and life cycle costing information back to the RDD-100 database. The PRICE Systems' tools include a set of four parametric cost estimation models that are summarized in Table 1.

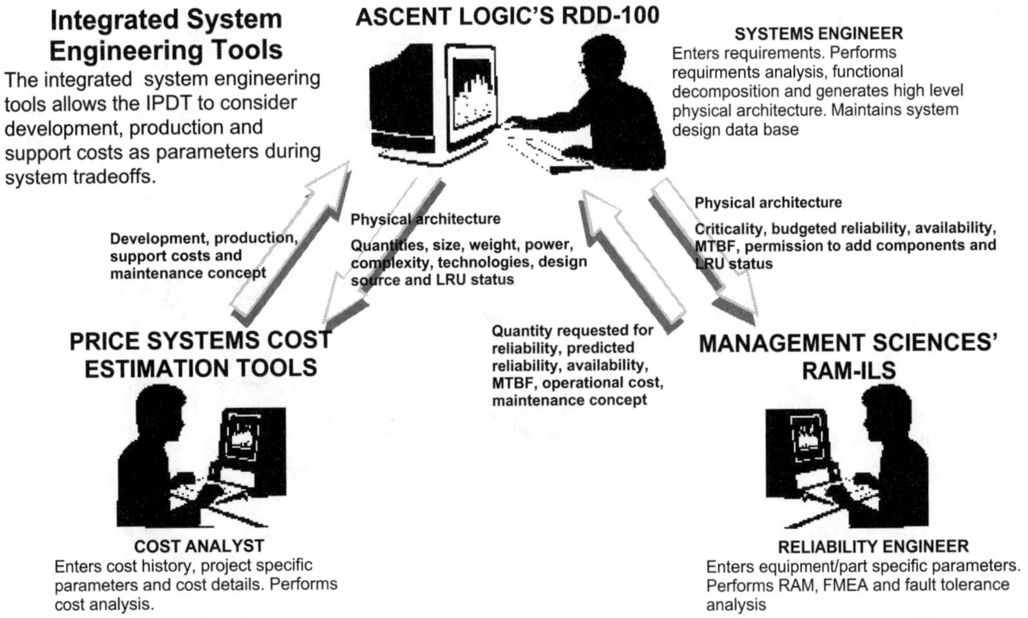

Figure 3. Concurrent Engineering Environment

Table 1. Price System's Individual Cost Estimation Models

PRICE H: This model specifically addresses the costs associated with development and production of hardware. This tool can use outputs of the PRICE M tool.
PRICE HL: This model uses data generated by PRICE H and calculates the hardware life-cycle costs, including sparing for a deployment environment.
PRICE M: This model specifically addresses electronic-module-level hardware development and production costs. It allows engineers to specify individual ASIC and FPGA components to get a detailed cost estimate at the lowest levels.
Software: This model estimates both development costs and life-cycle support costs for software.

RAM-ILS Tools

MSI's RAM-ILS tools calculated reliability, maintainability, and availability of a system. This toolset performed mean time between failure (MTBF) and availability calculations. If a system doesn't meet the MTBF requirements, the tools perform cost driven trade-offs and recommend where redundancy can be added to meet the system requirements.

The integrated system engineering environment uses RDD-100 to capture and analyze the requirements, to define the functional behavior of the system and to allocate the requirements and functions to the subsystems. PRICE cost estimating tools estimate the development, production and support costs for the system. The RAM-ILS tools perform reliability and maintainability analyses.

The integrated system tools provide an integrated system engineering environment where trade-offs considering a product's complete life cycle can be performed. Engineers obtain complete life cycle costs using the system tools without becoming an expert cost analyst. Cost performance trade-offs use the integrated tools to optimize the system design over multiple disciplines. The integrated system engineering tools analyze cost impacts during requirements and specification definition phase and throughout the detailed design effort.

RASSP COST MODEL

Using RASSP concepts and tools, ATL developed a life cycle cost modeling process to identify development opportunities to reduce development, manufacture and support cost of complex signal processors, and predict the life cycle cost savings resulting from RASSP methodology, COTS MYA concepts, and infrastructure technology improvements. This cost modeling process is depicted in Figure 4. The process used the following steps:

1) Definition of the signal processing requirements and a life cycle program plan
2) Establishment of hardware and software processor configurations each life cycle phase that leverages projected COTS MYA processing technology improvements
3) Capture hardware and software components and system life cycle support requirements using the Price cost models for each phase of the system's life cycle
4) Computation and compilation of the development, production and support costs for all of the life cycle phases

To illustrate the process, we developed an example of its uses. The example used a "hypothetical" air to air/air to ground airborne radar system, with a multiphase, 25 year development and deployment life cycle. The system was initially designed to meet air-to-air surveillance requirements; later it was extended to provide air-to-ground SAR imaging mode. The phases of the life cycle are shown in Figure 5 and include normal Demonstration/Validation (DEM/VAL) and Engineering and Manufacturing Development (EMD) phases. Following EMD, system production lasted four years and resulted in a total of fifty systems. A Preplanned

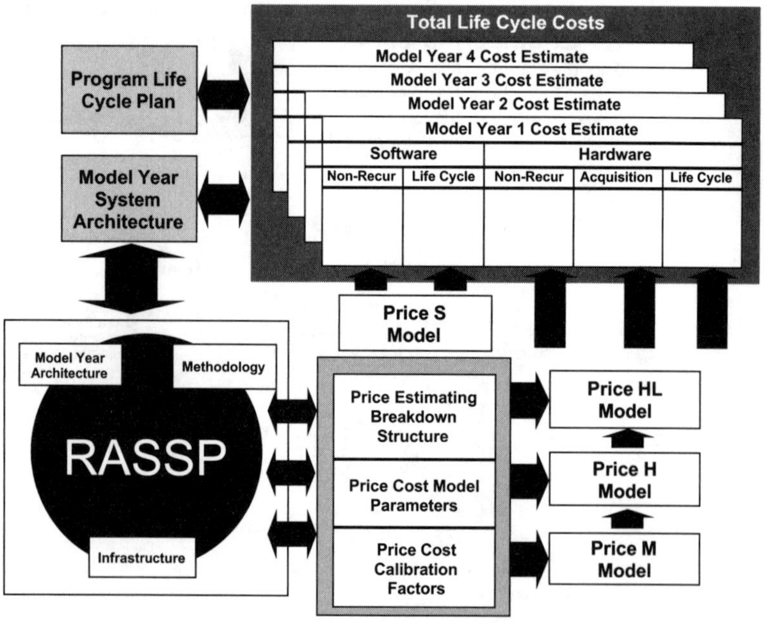

Figure 4. ATL's RASSP Cost Modeling Process

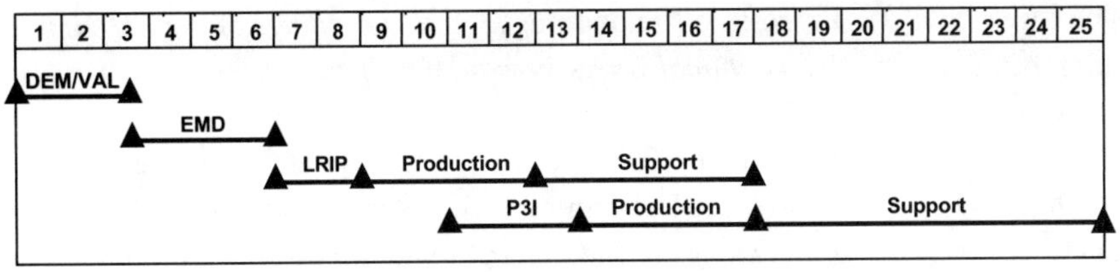

Figure 5. Airborne Radar Life Cycle Phases

Product Improvement activity for the SAR imaging mode started in the eleventh year and was produced and deployed over a seven year period. The fifty systems were continuously supported over the 25 year program.

Life cycle cost estimates were developed using both standard practice and RASSP processes and COTS MYA technology. The standard practice system design is based on a custom ASICs to minimize production hardware. Two RASSP based cost estimates were developed. One uses a COTS design for all phases of the system's life cycle. The second applies RASSP's hardware/software codesign concepts to a portion of the COTS design and custom DSP design to reduce hardware production costs. The RASSP process model, based on a COTS MYA design approach, leverages commercial processor technology improvements during the system's life cycle. By the P3I phase, COTS technology improvements allowed the entire system to be migrated back to an all COTS approach for the final system configuration.

Table 2 summarizes the life cycle costs for the standard practice and both RASSP design approaches. The total costs and improvement factors for each approach are broken down by development phase and engineering, manufacturing and deployment/ support costs. The overall improvement factor for the RASSP COTS based approach is 3.8x. This factor increased to 4.6x when the custom DSP design is used in the production and support phases of the program. A key factor in achieving these improvements is the ability to leverage COTS processor technology advances through the system's life cycle. Leveraging COTS signal processing technology improvements minimizes the amount of hardware manufactured and supported. More than 90% of the life cycle costs are associated with manufacturing and support costs. By enabling low cost, COTS MYA upgrades or custom designs, RASSP's integrated system engineering technology provides the path to significant life cycle cost savings.

The results also show the RASSP processes and tools significantly impact engineering development costs. The COTS based approach development costs were reduced by a factor of 6.2x. This factor dropped to 3.6x for the custom DSP approach, because of non-recurring engineering costs for custom process design. Still the RASSP engineering costs were less than 30% of standard practice costs.

This example demonstrates ATL's RASSP cost modeling process and illustrates how RASSP processes, COTS MYA concepts and infrastructure developments to reduce a signal processor's life cycle cost. Using this example, a life

Table 2. Summary of RASSP Airborne Radar Life Cycle Cost Model Example

RASSP Life Cycle Costs and Improvement Factors					
	ASIC Based	COTS DSP Based Design		DSPs/ASIC Based Design	
	Pre RASSP Cost ($M)	Post RASSP Cost ($M)	Improvement Factor	Post RASSP Cost ($M)	Improvement Factor
	Breakdown by Development, Production, and Support				
Development	$123.4	$47.5	2.6x	$52.3	2.4x
Production	$330.4	$114.3	2.9x	$95.9	3.4x
Support	$831.3	$174.8	4.8x	$128.6	6.5x
Total LCC	$1,285.1	$336.7	3.8x	$276.8	4.6x
	Breakdown by Engineering, Manufacturing and Support				
Engineering	$51.9	$8.4	6.2x	$14.5	3.6x
Manufacturing	$401.9	$153.5	2.6x	$133.7	3.0x
Support	$831.3	$174.8	4.8x	$128.6	6.5x
Total LCC	$1,285.1	$336.7	3.8x	$276.8	4.6x

cycle cost improvement of between 3.8x and 4.6x was achieved by applying RASSP technology developments to leverage COTS processor improvements. The keys to achieving these life cycle cost reductions were:

1) Tailoring the signal processors life cycle development, production and support plans to leverage COTS technology improvements.
2) Using COTS or existing designs (design reuse) during the DEM/VAL and EMD phases to minimize non-recurring engineering and manufacturing costs.
3) Leveraging RASSP enabled cycle time, cost and risk reductions to accomplish cost savings during pre-production and product improvement system upgrades.

SUMMARY

Under the DARPA RASSP Program, ATL explored, investigated, developed and demonstrated a wide range of advanced design processes and concepts for reducing the cost of signal processor development and manufacture. Three of the key development efforts were:

1) The development of an integrated hardware/software design process and virtual prototyping environment to support simulation based designs of complex signal processor.
2) The development of an integrated system engineering environment to allow CAIV trade-offs throughout the entire development process.
3) The establishment of COTS MYA concepts and design reuse to reduce the total development, acquisition and support costs for complex military systems.

Using the RASSP cost modeling process, we demonstrated the impact of these three technologies on the life cycle cost for future signal processing systems. By applying RASSP concepts and techniques we project as much as 4.6X reduction in life cycle costs. The results also demonstrate that using hardware/software codesign, virtual prototyping, integrated system engineering tools and COTS MYA can significantly lower development, manufacturing and support costs.

REFERENCES

Schaming, W. 1997. "Hardware/Software Co-Design in the Rapid Prototyping of Application-Specific Signal Processors Methodology." In *Proceedings of the VHDL International Users Forum.* (Oct.)

Barnett, G. 1998. "An Integrated Systems Engineering Toolset for Performing Life Cycle Cost Tradeoffs." In *Proceedings of the Acquisition and Logistics Initiative MTS Conference.* (Nov.)

Lockheed Martin Advanced Technology Laboratories. 1996. "RASSP Cost Model Report Version 1.0." RASSP Contract Report (May).

RASSP Program Web Site, www.atl.external.lmco.com/projects/rassp.

BIOGRAPHIES

Mr. Ealy has over thirty-four years in developing advanced sensor and signal processing systems. After 19 years with the US Army's Night Vision and Electro-Optics Laboratory, where he was responsible for a wide variety of advanced development projects, he joined Lockheed Martin's Advanced Technology Laboratories. Since then he has been responsible for managing a broad range of signal processing research and development efforts. Recently he was a key participant in ATL's RASSP development program, leading the RASSP Cost Modeling Process effort discussed in this paper, as well as the SAIP Prototype Signal Processor benchmark demonstration effort. Mr. Ealy received his undergraduate degree in Mathematics and Physics from Indiana University of Pennsylvania and holds a Master Degree in Computer Aided Design and Engineering from University of Michigan.

Mr. Barnett is a Principal Member of the Engineering Staff at Lockheed Martin's Advanced Technology Laboratories in Camden, NJ. He has led the development effort for an integrated system engineering toolset, developed radar system concepts, and has refined and implemented algorithms on embedded signal processors. He was a radar systems engineer at Lockheed Martin's Ocean and Radar Sensor Systems in Syracuse, NY prior to his current position.

Research on Supporting Environment Technology for Virtual Prototyping

Xudong Chai*

Yuan Mao**

Bo Hu Li**

Guangleng Xiong*

*Tsinghua University National CIMS Central, Beijing 100081

**Beijing University of Aeronautics and Astronautics, Beijing 100083

<bohuli@moon.bjnet.edu.cn>

Key Words: Virtual Prototyping, architecture, supporting environment

ABSTRACT

In this paper, based on research on connotation, architecture and its key technologies for Virtual Prototyping, a Virtual Prototyping supporting environment for complex system composed with some subsystems including mechanical subsystem, electronical subsystem, software subsystem and control/ kinetics simulation subsystem is introduced. The supporting environment apply integrated framework technology and provides a standard-based computing environment to support integration of different technologies and enable its user to develop and execute distributed collaborative engineering and virtual prototyping session. Furthermore, the integration approaches of two typical simulation languages (i.e., continuous system simulation language ICSL and continuous/discrete event simulation language IHSL) with control/ kinetics simulation integrated framework are also introduced.

1 INTRODUCTION

Since the late 1980s, Competition among manufacturing enterprises has become more and more intense. The core of the race is competition of product innovation based on new technology. Under the impact of the continuous development strategy, various manufacturing enterprises must solve the problem of T(Time to market), Q(Quality), C(Cost), S(Service) and E(Environment) to increase their competitive strength. On the other hand, the world is being changed to a knowledge economy era, modern information technology is growing quickly and being applied more and more widely. All these facilitate the development and revolution of traditional manufacturing industry. Among these, virtual prototyping technology, which is the key enabling technology of new advanced manufacturing model——agile manufacturing, is the focus of the study in many countries.

2 VIRTUAL PROTOTYPING

2.1 Concept

Virtual Prototyping technology is a new product development approach, it is intended to provide an all-digital front-end for product development based on computer model of product. A virtual prototype is a simulatable digital one which combining simulation models of various engineering disciplines, it resembles the physical product as closely as possible in terms of visual, auditory, haptic, functional and behavioural characteristics. Virtual Prototyping technology supports concurrent engineering methodology, it involves kinematics and kinetics modeling theories and implementation techniques of multi-body system, it is a synthetic technology based on virtual reality, advanced modeling and simulation techniques, information management techniques and user interface techniques.

Virtual prototyping technology is the expansion of CAx (e.g., CAD, CAM, CAE, etc.)/ DFx(e.g., DFA, DFM, etc)techniques. Virtual prototyping technology further integrates information technology, advanced manufacturing technology and advanced simulation technology, and applies these technologies in the whole life circle and the whole system of complex system. Virtual prototyping technology introduces comprehensive management capability, stresses to analyze the complex system from the view of the system level, and supports "top down" design pattern of complex system. It improves the limitation of CAx/DFx techniques, which mainly focus on the information modeling and integration of product themselves and pay more attention to analysis in product component level. The core of Virtual Prototyping is integration technology for engineering design technology, M&S technology and VR/Visualization technology (see figure 1.).

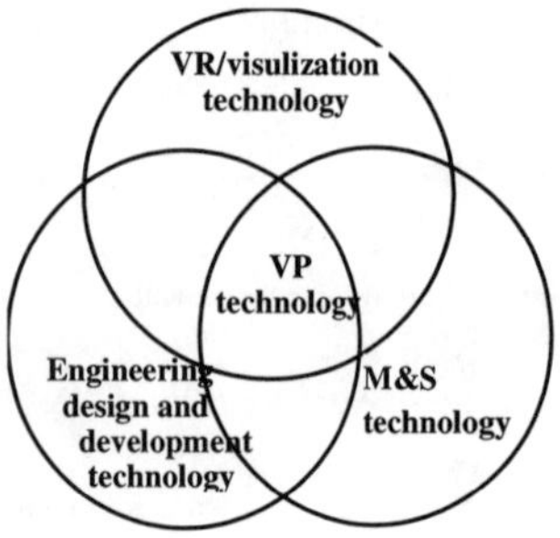

Figure 1 VP integration technology

Virtual prototyping means the process of using these virtual prototypes instead of, or in combination with, physical prototypes for innovation, test and evaluation of product designs to compress development cycles, decrease product cost and improve the accuracy of development to meet the needs of the customer and the market.

2.2 Virtual Prototyping Architecture

A complex system is often composed of multiple subsystems, such as electronic, machinery, software and control. The virtual prototyping architecture is illustrated in figure 2.

This architecture consists of system level, electronic subsystem, mechanical subsystem, control subsystem, software subsystem, virtual prototyping engine, VR/visualization environment and environment model database, product model database, etc.. Each of subsystem is composed of design/development and appearance/function/behavior M&S of product subsystem respectively. System level is responsible for design/development and appearance/function/behavior modeling and simulation for virtual product on system layer, such as the kinematics/kinetics M&S, prototype behavioral M&S in special environment, etc.. Virtual prototype engine simulates the prototype by appearance/function/behavior and feeds the simulation data into VR/visualization environment. After VR rendering, the prototype is shown by appearance/function and various behavior in virtual environment.

3 VIRTUAL PROTOTYPING SUPPORTING ENVIRONMENT

3.1 Feature

In order to support the development of virtual prototype, the supporting environment should have the following features:

(1) Provide different kinds of modeling and supporting tools, resource and supporting system expediently and reliably to facilitate the concurrent working and effective use of M&S technology.

(2) Support reuse and interoperability of data, model, simulation application and other supporting system (e.g., network, tools, etc.) among various functional disciplines, government and industrial department.

(3) Provide advanced, multi-domain supported M&S environment.

(4) Support VR/Visualization .

(5) Support concurrent engineering methodology.

(6) Adopt popular (GOTS/COTS：Government/Commercial Off-The-Shelf) product and standards that is available and widely used currently to minimize new tools and infrastructure development.

7) Be open, scaleable, and flexible, permitting various implementation approaches.

3.2 Supporting environment

Virtual Prototyping supporting environment supports the development of complex product, it consists of system and domain frameworks (including electronic, mechanic, software and control/kinetics simulation sub-systems). A layered architecture is shown in figure 3, including system information platform, system framework layer, domain framework (sub-system framework) layer, application system framework layer and multi-disciplinary collaborative work layer.

(1) System information platform

The system information platform provides soft-bus to achieve the plug-and-play based on "system soft-bus" under distributed and heterogeneous environment, supports integration of different technologies and enables its user to develop and execute distributed collaborative engineering and virtual prototyping session.

The standard computing environment is a supporting environment based on distributed object computing, and it supports most of the technical standards (e.g., CORBA, Java RMI, RTI, HTTP, etc.) under current distributed environment. Various management tools and services in system framework layer can be achieved under this environment.

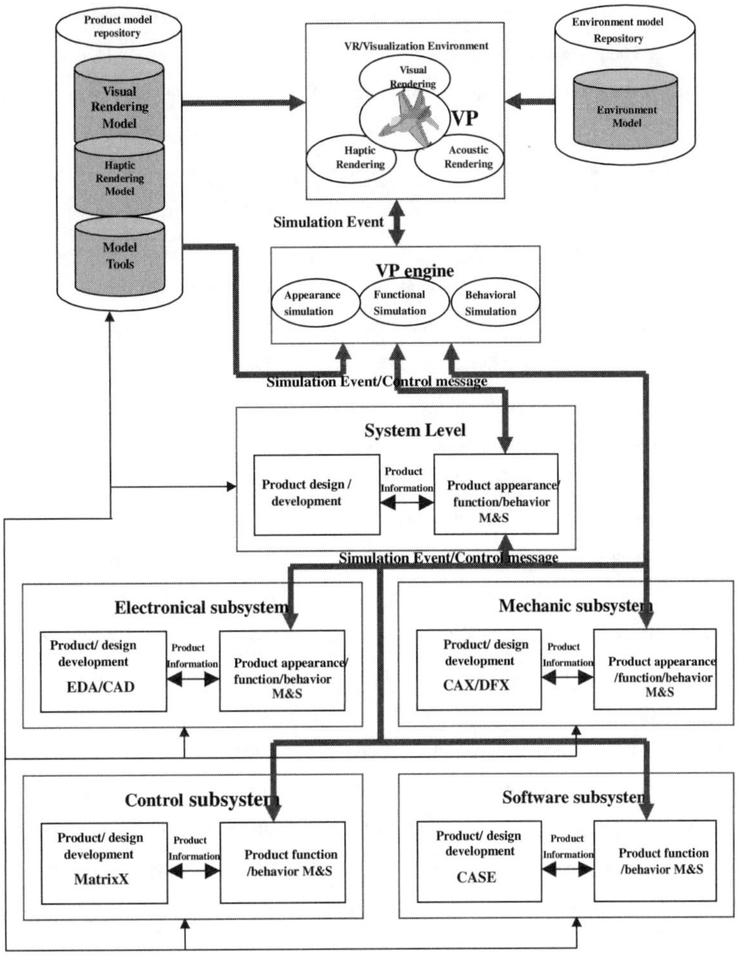

Figure 2. Virtual Prototyping Architecture

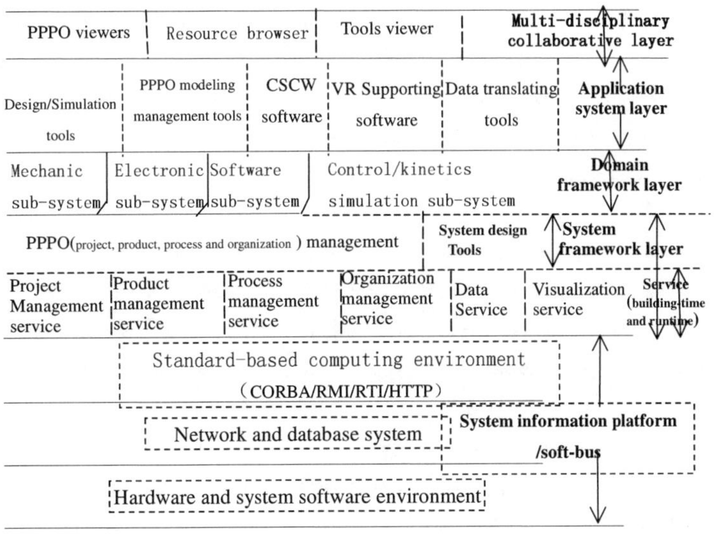

Figure 3. VP Supporting Environment

2) System framework layer

It provides system design tools and services for application system, achieves inter-domain information and process integration in the enterprise. System design tools include project, product, process and organization management. These design tools are achieved by various building-time and runtime services (e.g., project management services, product management services, process management services, organization management services, data management services, visualization services, etc.).

(1) Project management services support various activities, including project data management, project estimation, project budget, project plan, project requirement, project working-time accounting, project progress, project supervision and project invoice, etc.

(2) Product management services describe product structure , design analysis information and related documents, set product structure-tree model, achieve product configuration and version management, electric repository management, data object management, product cell data management, product data management (e.g., extraction and submission) , etc. At the same time, these services provide the support for process and organization viewers, support data share and consistency across different domains, achieve product information integration.

(3) Process management services support the whole process of product development. By setting visualized work-flow model, process management services support enterprise process reengineering , and control the concurrent implementation of the process.

(4) Organization management services serve description of people's organization structure in product development activities and definition and management of product development team, person, workgroup, project staff, roles and access privilege. By setting people organization pattern and providing flexible method, these services provide effective management for person to support team collaborative work.

(5) Data management services manage object model, simulation, standard, strategy, database, distributed product data model(DPDM), document, tools, federation resource and environment in the enterprise.

(6) Visualization service provides friendly human-computer interaction pattern.

3) Domain framework layer

It includes four sub-domain frameworks, i.e., electronic, mechanic, software and control/kinetics simulation sub-domain frameworks. Each domain framework supports its own product integration, PPPO modeling and management, tools encapsulation and integration respectively. It supports integration and concurrency of product development, and achieves global information and procedure integration among different departments and different platforms based on system framework layer.

In which, control/kinetics simulation domain framework supports product modeling and simulation, integration and interoperability of simulation tools/software, kinetics simulation of mechanic product, system level simulation of complex product and distributed interactive simulation. Furthermore, it supports the management of simulation activity and result, provides synthetic simulation environment. The framework supports integration and interoperability of different domain framework by system soft-bus, and supports different domain frameworks and systems to acquire new product by distributed product database. The framework supports concurrent engineering(CE) by providing product data management, process management, organization management and collaborative workbench.

4) Application system

It consists of mechanic domain application software(e.g., Ax/DFx, PDM, etc.) , electronic domain application software(e.g., EDA software, microwave CAD/CAT software, etc.) , software domain CASE tools, and M&S domain tools. At present, most of design and manufacturing application system have their own integration environment (called domain framework), e.g., MENTOR EDA's Falcon framework in electronic design domain, SDRC's Metaphase in mechanic design, etc.. System framework integrates these application software and sub-domain frameworks as legacy systems. Corresponding tools include: desktop, project management tools, work-flow management, collaborative tools, simulation tools, federation development tools, lexical analysis/translator、design tools, analysis tools, etc..

5) Multi-disciplinary collaborative layer

It provides work viewers , including project, process, organization, product model, and product data viewers of different layers or different disciplinary domains, related interoperability tools , and WEB browser connected to distributed product model database or other sub-domains. It supports different disciplinary IPTs (Integrated Product Team) to achieve collaborative work on the same virtual object.

4 HLA/RTI -BASED TOOLS INTEGRATION

ICSL is a user-friendly continuous system simulation language. It can undertake modeling and simulation for dynamic system and control system and provide well external interface to support external function and subroutine written in FORTRAN. IHSL is a continuous/discrete event simulation language. It does not only provide modeling and simulation function for general discrete event simulation language, but also for continuous system expressed in differential equation format and continuous/discrete event hybrid system. ICSL and IHSL have been integrated in control/kinetics simulation subsystem.

In order to support interoperability for models developed by different simulation tools and accomplish integration for different tools by HLA/RTI, it is necessity to build a HLA interface into these tools. It also means to develop a tool-specific HLA interface to enable the simulation tools to use RTI services through the HLA Application Programming Interface(API). It is shown in figure 4.

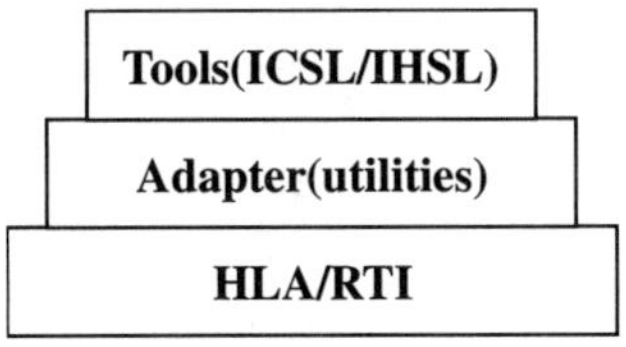

Figure 4. HLA/RTI-based Tools Integration

There are many existing methods to enable simulation tools to access the HLA API(RTI). The modular wrapper method is used to enhance flexibility and interoperability and simplify integration. The different adapters have been built to encapsulate all critical RTI services. The original simulation, the wrapper, and the local RTI constitute the federate.

The HLA interface for ICSL uses external programming interface of ICSL, because ICSL is an open and extensible architecture offering external FORTRAN interface. The ICSL can call arbitrary utilities in the adapter. The adapter is implemented as a function library and provides access to the HLA API. This method allows the ICSL model to have to explicitly use HLA functionality in themselves. The utilities that the model can call should correspond to the methods defined in the HLA Interface Specification.

For IHSL, the source code of the runtime system of IHSL has been extended with HLA functionality. The model description of a IHSL model does not include any HLA specifics. The only way to connect a IHSL model to other federates is by providing a special adapter which specifies the mapping of IHSL variables to HLA data structure according to the SOM and performs the tasks automatically, such as initialization routines, synchronization with other federates, sending/receiving messages, data types conversion between tool-specific and FOM. This solution is to allow IHSL simulation system to handle all RTI services internally, which is transparent to model developer.

5 FURTHER WORK

Our work shows that Supporting Environment based on integrated framework technology supported by standard-based computational environment provides an effective approach for developing complex virtual product. Especially, HLA-RTI based control/kinetics simulation sub-system provides an integrated platform for different simulation tools to facilitate interoperability and reuse and construct virtual prototype. Furthermore, we will keep on integrating more simulation tools including electronic, mechanic and control system simulation tools to support functional and behavioral simulation for complex product. Other ongoing efforts are to integrate some design tools and practise this VP Supporting Environment in some complex aerospace product development.

REFERENCES

Li, Bo Hu, Quan, Chun Lai, Zhu Wen Hai ,Xiao,TianYuan and Han, Xiang Li, "*Concurrent Engineering and Virtual Manufacturing*", Chinese Economic Press, 1999 (in Chinese)

Robin Frost , “Simulation Based Acquisition An Ongoing Look”, 98F-SIW-229.doc

Li,B.H.,Tong,J.,Song,X.,Chai,X.D.,Li,X.Y., “*Concurrent Distributed Interactive Simulation Engineering and Its Support Environment*”, The Proceedings of the Summer Computer Simulation Conference, 1998,eds. Mohammad S.Obaidat,

Franco Davoli, Danny Demarinis, pp.225-230

Schulze, T., StraRBurger, S., and Klein, U., "*Migration of HLA into Civil Domains: Solutions and Prototypes for Transportation Applications*", SIMULATION 73:5, 296-303.

Yu Lois C., Steinman, Jeffrey S., and Blank, Gary E., " Adapting You Simulation for HLA", SIMULATION 71:6, 410-420.

ARCHITECTURE CONCEPTS FOR SIMULATION-BASED ACQUISITION OF COMPLEX SYSTEMS

Dr. Bipin Chadha and John Welsh
Lockheed Martin Advanced Technology Laboratories
1 Federal Street, A&E Building
Camden, NJ 08102
bchadha, jwelsh@atl.lmco.com

KEYWORDS

Architecture, Federation, Enterprise, Complex Systems, Simulation-Based Acquisition

ABSTRACT

The ability to make good design decisions early is a significant driver for simulation-based acquisition to effectively lower life-cycle cost and cycle time. Building virtual prototypes, enabling one to analyze the impact of decisions, achieves effective simulation-based acquisition processes. Virtual prototypes need to support a comprehensive set of analyses that will be performed on the product; hence, all aspects of product data and behavior need to be represented. Building virtual prototypes of complex systems being designed by a multi-organizational team requires new architectural concepts and redesigned processes. Implementation of these new architectures is complex and leveraging commercial technologies is necessary to achieve feasible solutions. One must also carefully consider the state of the current commercial technologies and frameworks as well as the organizational and cultural aspects of organizations that use these systems. This paper describes key architectural principles that one must address for a cost-effective implementation. The paper then discusses key architectural concepts and trade-offs that are necessary to support virtual prototypes of complex systems.

INTRODUCTION

Lockheed Martin, government, and industry partners, and supply chain members are developing and manufacturing large, complex systems. Using simulation-based acquisition and design strategies to develop cost-effective virtual prototypes of these systems presents enormous challenges. One will use virtual prototypes, intended to support a product's entire life-cycle, for multiple purposes, including system engineering during conceptual design and for warfighters during training. Therefore, virtual prototypes must capture all information related to a product's definition and must provide mechanisms to incorporate all aspects of a product's behavior. Product complexity forces organizations to share the design and manufacturing of these products; therefore, the virtual prototype must be shared. Detailed knowledge of a subsystem typically resides with the supplying organization, so it is critical that the supplier organization creates and manages the virtual prototype of that subsystem. Management of the virtual prototype's complexity is important to ensure that developments focus on areas of sufficient benefit; otherwise, the implementation cost of the virtual prototype could be unbounded. Well-designed architectures are key to managing complexity. The following key goals will ensure a cost-effective virtual prototype:

- Create a multi-domain product model that is open, extensible, integrated, and synchronized.
- Integrate equations and/or behaviors with the relevant product data, thereby enabling evaluation of functional performance and optimization of life-cycle costs.
- Create executable representations of the system with multi-level fidelity to support multi-level analysis.
- Execute simulations for analysis and demonstration.

MYTH OF COMMONALITY IN ARCHITECTURE

The trend in information technologies is toward common systems, tools, and processes. While this is a trend away from disjointed systems, it is unrealistic to assume there will ever be a single process or system that satisfies every need in a multi-business organization. Figure 1

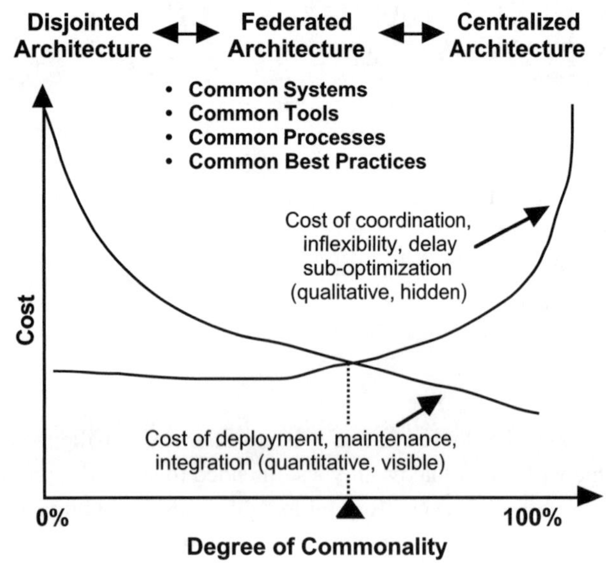

Figure 1. *Federated Architecture Provides an Optimal Solution*

shows diminishing returns as the degree of commonality increases beyond a limit. Figure 2 shows that hidden or ignored qualitative factors increase costs, while easily quantifiable and visible metrics decrease costs. In this example, maintenance, deployment, and integration represent quantifiable costs, while coordination and changes and implementation delays represent qualitative factors that cause significant cost penalties in overall solutions. Most approaches ignore qualitative factors that become important as commonality approaches 100 percent. Existing architectures only account for technical aspects and ignore cultural and organizational aspects. The critical issue is not commonalities in architecture but understanding the trade-offs to determine the right amount of commonality for a given domain in a given context. The same can be said for any given standard. Standards should be evaluated in context to determine whether they are applicable, mature, and cost effective for the problem at hand. Applying a standard just because it is a standard is likely to produce less than desirable results.

Better virtual-prototyping architectures are needed to address this dichotomy among business needs and capabilities available with commercial off-the-shelf (COTS) solutions. A federated approach (Chadha 1997) provides the flexibility to deal with these current trend factors. Federation implies that one has established a degree of interoperability among business systems. Interoperability enables a shared-information area and provides a set of operations that can be initiated in a controlled fashion by one system operating on information in the shared/private area of another system. Members can join a federation to share information and functionality on a program and they can leave when the effort is finished. Federation provides a low-risk alternative to existing technology investment strategies, and it enables organizations to bring new tech-

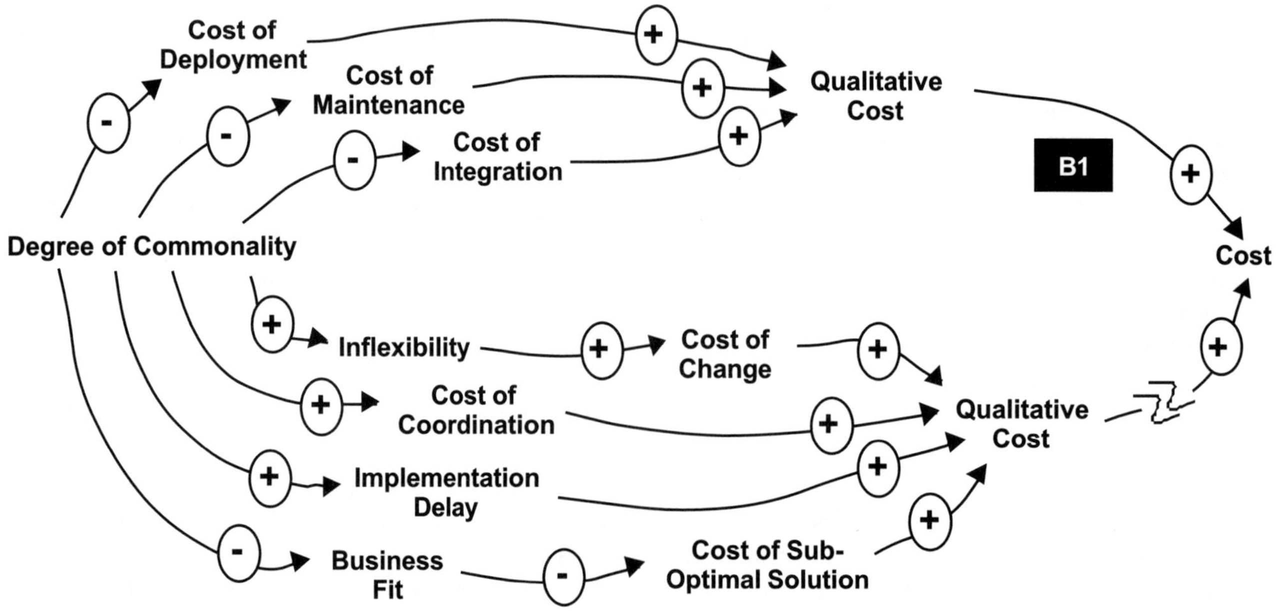

Figure 2. *Architecture Trade-Off Model*

nologies in a modular fashion instead of requiring a total upgrade of the internal business-system architecture ("*big bang*" approach). A federated architecture enables programs to implement a total-systems view and it also provides the ability to optimize supply chains at a global level.

GUIDING PRINCIPLES

Several principles guide the development of the architecture. These principles are useful in information technology and other domains, such as lean manufacturing (Womack, Jones, and Ross 1990) and systems thinking (Senge *et al.* 1999):

- Leverage COTS tools and technologies to the maximum extent possible.
- Focus on federated approaches instead of homogeneous information-system approaches.
- Provide information (and resources) only when needed.
- Provide only needed information (no more, no less).
- Do not carry information defects to the next step.
- Put in place a process that discourages the generation of defects.
- Information should be owned by the entity that is most suited to keep it current/accurate.
- Information must be accessible by those who have or may have a need.
- Account for soft/qualitative factors.

The focus is on *guiding principles* as opposed to hard-design constraints. This allows one to realize benefits in most cases and to avoid penalties associated with exceptional cases.

ARCHITECTURE FOR SIMULATION-BASED ACQUISITION

The principle objective of the virtual-prototyping architecture is to reduce the complexity of the system being designed to implement the virtual prototype. The architecture must also help achieve modularity and reuse of components that make up that architecture. Above all, the architecture must be able to evolve over time as the operating environment changes. This includes changes in requirements, expectations, organizational structures, business processes, and technologies. One must apply the principles of Cost as an Independent Variable (CAIV) analysis for systems design to the architecture for the virtual prototype.

Architecture Concepts

Rapidly evolving software, network, and associated technologies require innovative concepts to leverage their benefits in the architectural approach. This section provides an overview of some of these concepts or architectural patterns, which represent foundational technologies for virtual prototyping architectures.

Internet Architecture. The virtual-prototype architecture will need to be highly scalable and evolvable. The Internet provides an architecture that is highly distributed and scalable. It derives these properties via simple mechanisms, such as decentralized control, small set of ubiquitous standards, and hyperlinking information across independent web servers. It continues to evolve in a bottom-up fashion as content and new technologies are being added. Nodes on networks can be clients and/or servers, and each can perform the role that is necessary for operation. The ability of enterprise agents to hyperlink to each other across the network and to travel across clients and servers will provide essentially unlimited scalability for the architecture.

Common Object Request Broker Architecture. The Object Request Broker (ORB) is a basic architectural construct that sits between clients and makes requests. The ORB mechanisms can support all interactions among various architectural components.

One can statically define interfaces in an interface definition language (object management group IDL), which defines the types of objects according to operations that may be performed on them and the parameters to those operations. The IDL is language independent and bindings to several programming languages, such as C++ and Java, are available. Note that ORBs do not provide complete data-management functions or object-domain functionality. They facilitate the communication without necessarily understanding what is being communicated. They also interoperate via the Internet Inter-ORB Protocol (IIOP), which specifies a standardized interoperability protocol for the Internet.

Federated Architecture. A federation implies a loosely-coupled system distributed across the Internet or Intranet, where participants join or leave the federation without breaking it and where they function on their own when not a part of it (Figure 3).

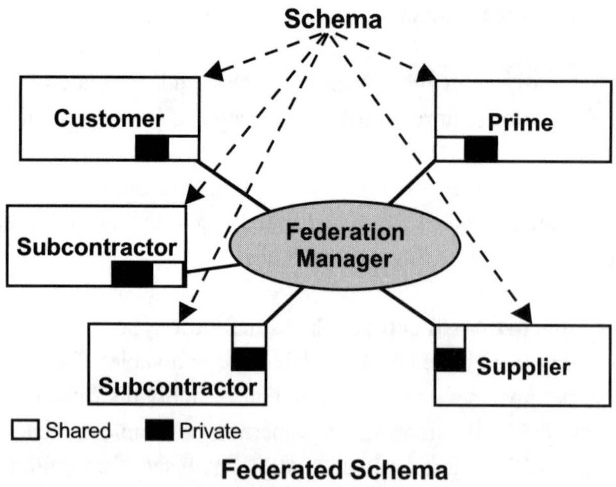

Figure 3. *Federated Architecture Concept*

The federation provides a low-risk alternative to existing technology-investment strategies, enabling organizations to bring new technologies in a modular fashion as opposed to the *big bang* approach, which requires replacement of most or all of the information systems for a technology upgrade. Mechanisms, such as smart-proxy objects, achieve federation.

Smart Proxy Objects. An innovative concept is the "proxy" object, which provides a surrogate or placeholder for another object to control access to it (Figure 4) (Gamma *et al.* 1994). A proxy object resides in the local environment and represents an object residing in a remote environment. The proxy handles requests made to it and forwards them to the real object for further processing, which returns the results back to the proxy object. The proxy then forwards the results to the requester. Therefore, clients only work with the proxy object in the local environment. They are insulated from the details and how-to of dealing with objects in remote environments. These proxies are not the same as those in the ORBs; however, they will use proxy objects and services provided by the ORBs for their operation. Proxy objects provide tremendous flexibility in implementation approaches, enabling variable degrees of information replication and flexible behavior via tailorable business rules. Proxies can be implemented to various levels of complexity, starting from simple uniform resource locators to complex, tightly-coupled proxy objects.

Component-Based Architecture. A key concept that enables realistic and affordable development of the architecture is the ability to build in modular, reusable components. A component is a reusable software program that can be easily added to or combined with other software programs, enabling construction of sophisticated programs in a modular fashion. One can divide the architecture into components via well-defined interfaces. Interfaces allow small components to be grouped to create complex systems that would otherwise be impractical to build. Concepts of interfaces allow objects to be typed across many dimensions. Objects can adhere to many different interfaces without the burden of multiple inheritance. This also allows one to build information models from the bottom-up and not use the monolithic, top-down information model. The impact of component-based architectures is a significant gain in productivity. The use of this design strategy is rapidly gaining acceptance by the information-technology community. Both COM+ and Java use component-based architectures.

Systemic Behavior. Systemic approaches (Senge *et al.* 1999) differentiate between systemic behavior and compo-

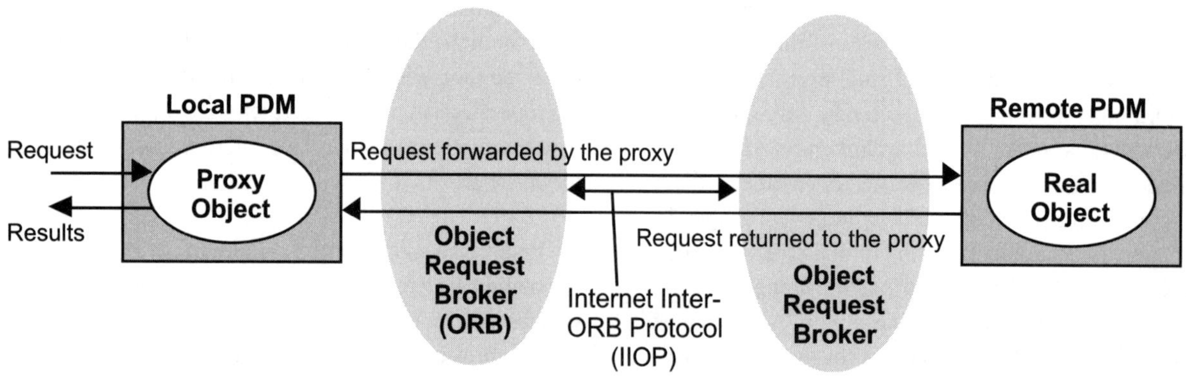

Figure 4. *Proxy Object Concept*

nent behavior. Systemic behavior is the behavior of a system that emerges due to interactions among components. This behavior is not a result of a collection of behaviors of the components. Complex dynamic systems exhibit a wide variety of systemic behaviors that can only be understood by analysis at the systemic level. The following characteristics of component interactions determine the systemic behavior:

- Everything is connected to everything.
- System exhibits properties and behaviors different from the parts.
- There are no independent variables.
- System structure drives system behavior (especially the feedback loops).
- Many effects are indirect and delayed.
- Many dependencies are non-linear.
- Behavior is dynamic.

Systemic issues also result in unpredictable behavior in complex systems leading to "system accidents" (Perrow 1984). Causes can be traced to tight coupling and complex interactions between components of the system. The virtual prototypes of complex systems therefore need to represent these interactions and couplings to be effective in predicting and avoiding some of these complex behavioral modes.

The systemic behavior is modeled via causal loop diagrams (Senge *et al.* 1994) as shown in Figure 5. Causal loops embed the properties of causes and effects, feedback loops, delays, and non-linearity among components of a system. Understanding the causal links enables the architects to decompose a system such that the complex interdependencies reside within a subsystem while few interdependencies remain between subsystems (Alexander 1964).

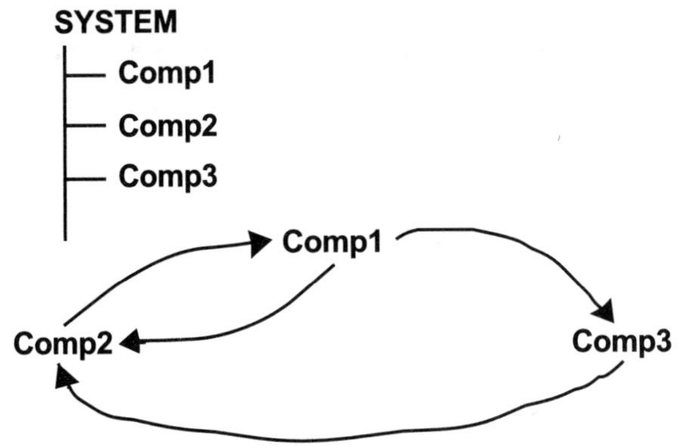

Figure 5. *System Representation via Hierarchy and Causal Loops*

Many systems engineering approaches either ignore these effects or model them simply as static interfaces.

Existing simulation approaches are attempting to address these issues by integrating various analysis tools. While that is helpful, it assumes that the interactions are simple and linear and that there are no cross dependencies. System-level models and systemic approaches are needed to address complex system behavior and cross-domain integration issues. Therefore, the simulation-based-acquisition architecture must incorporate systemic behavior. It is only then that the optimization at the system level becomes meaningful.

IMPLEMENTATION ISSUES

In addition to typical cultural and organizational issues that one must address in architecture strategies (Chadha 1997), a key implementation issue is the use of a top-down versus a bottom-up approach. We recommend a hybrid of the two based on the following observations:

- Bottom-up is relevant when there is little understanding of the problem.
- Top-down can completely address the problem (no items are missed).
- Bottom-up enables the problem to be addressed in small chunks.
- Top-down works in relatively stable environments; bottom-up is suitable for rapidly changing environments. The basic issue is whether one can completely solve the problem before the problem changes.
- Top-down is more efficient when there is a low probability of going astray and the emergent behavior due to component interaction is predictable and well understood. This implies that all the systemic interactions and causalities among components are known and accounted for (Perrow 1984).
- Bottom-up is more forgiving of mistakes and dead-end design paths. This is because mistakes are made on a smaller scale and are caught earlier and it is possible to change the system by rearranging components.
- Top-down is about "knowing it all" at the start; whereas, bottom-up is about "learning it" along the way.
- Top-down has slower design/implementation cycles; whereas, bottom-up has faster design/implementation cycles.
- Apply top-down at the conceptual level but apply bottom-up for details.

A hybrid of both approaches fits most real-world situations. Most projects start top-down before shifting to bottom-up at implementation, where the focus is on reuse of available, existing, or previously developed components. Strategies can also shift emphasis among top-down and bottom-up at multiple points in the development process. New or innovative developments are typically bottom-up (Kelly 1998). Strategies typically shift to top-down as processes mature, experience increases, and the problem is better understood.

SUMMARY

Virtual prototyping is critical to the cost-effective design of complex systems. New architectural concepts are emerging to support virtual prototyping of complex systems across company boundaries. When implementing virtual-prototyping architectures, realize there are limits to benefits achieved through commonality across distributed implementations and that soft/qualitative factors play an important role in architectural trade-offs. This paper outlined key architectural principles and concepts that improved the practicality of large-scale virtual-prototyping efforts. Many COTS tools and technologies are emerging to support implementation of these concepts. Effectively leveraging these tools and technologies will manage the scope of the effort while maintaining cost and schedule constraints. Bottom-up and top-down design approaches have advantages but a hybrid approach is best for most implementations.

REFERENCES

Alexander, C. 1964. "Notes on the Synthesis of Form," *Harvard University Press*.

Chadha, B. 1997. "A Federated PIM for Supply Chains," DH Brown Symposium.

Gamma, E., et al. 1994. *Design Patterns: Elements of Reusable Object-Oriented Software*, Addison-Wesley.

Kelly, K. 1998. *New Rules for the New Economy*, Viking.

Perrow, C. 1984. *Normal Accidents*, Basic Books.

Senge, P.M., et al. 1994. *The Fifth Discipline Fieldbook*, Currency Doubleday.

Womack, J.P., Jones, D.T., Roos, D. 1990. "The Machine that Changed the World," *MIT Press*.

"The Common Object Request Broker: Architecture and Specification," Revision 2.0, OMG, July 1995, Updated July 1996.

BIOGRAPHIES

Dr. Chadha is the principal investigator on enterprise engineering, supply-chain integration, and process-improvement initiatives at Lockheed Martin Advanced Technology Laboratories. He leads the Smart Product Model architecture team for Lockheed Martin's DD 21 program. He is a member of the ASME Engineering Information Management Committee and Supply Chain Council, and he chairs Lockheed Martin's Product Data Management Interfaces Working Group. He received his Ph.D. in Mechanical Engineering from Georgia Institute of Technology.

Mr. Welsh manages the enterprise-technology organization, leading collaborative-engineering projects for ship systems, mission-level analyses, and logistics-supply-chain improvement at Lockheed Martin Advanced Technology Laboratories. He has over 20 years technical and managerial experience on enterprise software, systems engineering, and electrical engineering. He has a Bachelors degree in electrical engineering from Villanova University and a Masters degree in systems engineering from the University of Pennsylvania.

Military Systems Simulation

WEAPONS DESIGN ANALYSIS USING 1-METER TERRAIN RESOLUTION BATTLEFIELD SIMULATORS

Wolfgang Baer, Bard Mansager, William G. Kemple
Naval Postgraduate School,
Monterey CA
baer@cs.nps.navy.mil
bkmansag@nps.navy.mil
kemple@nps.navy.mil

Major James Illingworth
TRADOC Analysis Center - Monterey
Monterey, CA
illingwj@trac.nps.navy.mil

KEYWORDS

High Resolution Terrain, Real-time Simulation, Line-of-Sight, Weapon Design

ABSTRACT

Simulation of battlefield systems in operational scenarios require the calculation of concealment, cover, and detectability to properly evaluate their performance and effectiveness on the battlefield. In the past so called "high resolution" simulations such as Janus and the Combined Arms and Support Task Force Evaluation Model (CASTFOREM) typically performed such calculations using geometric line-of-sight (GLOS) on 25-meter terrain resolution and model micro-terrain effects statistically. Results provided by such simulations do not account for the individual soldier's ability to take advantage of local cover and concealment in an individual engagement while carrying out tactical missions.

New 1-meter terrain analysis tools developed by personnel at the Naval Postgraduate School(NPS), the U.S. Army Training and Doctrine Command (TRADOC), and independent contractors have allowed substantial improvement in our ability to simulate individual engagements and assess the effects of micro terrain features on tactical mission success. This paper introduces the architecture and fast ray-tracing algorithms capable of calculating realistic 1-meter terrain perspective views in real-time on PC based platforms. We then describe how this algorithm is extended to perform view-based line-of-sight calculations (VLOS) and replace the old GLOS approach. This new technique calculates a small perspective view for each simulation player pair of interest. The perspective view is then analyzed. Partial player visibility, sensor location, major obscurant, and background contrast information are now all available and can be used to perform deterministically modeled detections and engagement effectiveness calculations.

We conclude the paper with case studies conducted to analyze the effectiveness of various system designs utilizing the 1-meter terrain tools now available. We describe the ability to select routes, modify tactics, and analyze engagement opportunities when accounting for high-resolution terrain features. Sample analysis results are presented to show the effects of design alternatives on mission performance.

INTRODUCTION

The objective of this paper is to describe the use of a high-resolution terrain simulation to conduct analysis of tactical operations and battlefield system characteristics. In specific we review a study conducted to determine the impact of a mast-mounted sight on a scout vehicle with respect to target acquisition opportunities and susceptibility to detection.

Research efforts supported by TRAC-Monterey and NPS faculty have developed a micro terrain visualization engine and line-of-sight generator known as PVNT. This system shows promise in providing simulated analysis of new battlefield systems in tactically realistic scenarios in order to assess the value of design features to tactical wartime operations. Using this tool, we conducted several tactical scenario experiments consisting of defining enemy defending positions and vehicle paths using a 1:50,000 scale topographic map as a decision aid. These routes are compared with routes selected after using the PVNT simulation knowledge of micro-terrain as a decision aid. Results indicate positions typically changed by 200 to 400 meters while line-of-sight times for scenarios change by 20% to 30% when micro terrain features are added to the scenario generation decision process. This reflects the more accurate use of cover and concealment by defending troops as well as better selection of view-points from which scout vehicles could survey the terrain.

Positions and routes selected interactively with PVNT were automatically densified to 1-second troop movement files using the mobility capabilities of a modified Janus model. Such troop movement scenarios were then used to calculate line-of-sight results at each second between all opposing force entities. For simulations lasting on the order of two hours of real-time resulted in over 14,000 position updates and 720,000 LOS calculations. These were statistically analyzed to quantify the effect of system design features and their use in realistic terrain.

Key to the success of these simulations was the ability to calculate LOS in a simulation environment that allowed effects such as the partial concealment of vehicles and soldiers by the micro-terrain features including trees, bushes and rocks.

PVNT High Resolution Simulation Background

The US Army test facility at Fort Hunter-Liggett, CA (FHL) had a high fidelity battlefield replication system known as Pegasus. This system provides the capability to generate a 1-meter terrain database and a one centimeter target view database for use in weapon substitution, command and control applications, and after action test review. The system has been relocated for operation at other sites such as Fort Hood, TX. Terrain databases have been generated for use in operations at locations such as Yuma, AZ. Perspective view and line-of-sight capabilities represented by the Fort Hunter-Liggett legacy systems have been migrated to low cost PC NT computers by students and researchers at NPS and is now being maintained by Nascent Systems Inc. The code is called PVNT.

Several years ago investigation of porting costs, performance, and platform cost analysis had shown that both the cost and maintenance of future systems would greatly benefit from the utilization of low cost PC hardware and standard software. A combination of NPS students and research efforts has now successfully ported the perspective view generation and line-of site software to a PC NT platform. The availability of high speed low cost PC based workstations at substantially lower prices than those currently employed to host the software has greatly enhanced the cost effectiveness of 1-meter and higher resolution terrain databases.

PVNT is now operating on symmetric multi-processor platforms under NT, and Windows. The code is demonstrable, reasonably stable, and a specialized version has been perfected to the point at which it is an operational component of the Rotary Pilots Associate test being conducted by US Army Test and Experimentation Center (TEXCOM) TEXCOM at Yuma during the Summer of 1999. Sample copies of executables along with sample1-meter terrain data are available on CDROM from Dr. Baer at NPS. The general code however is undocumented, without operations manuals, and shows instabilities, especially when run on arbitrary PC platforms encountered at average distribution sites.

PVNT PROGRAM DESCRIPTION

The PVNT program primary function is to generate video realistic perspective views in real time from 1-meter terrain databases. In order to achieve sufficient coverage for large areas, the 1-meter terrain database [Baer93] using a 32 bit integer to describe each one meter post in a 2.5D Voxel format. Elevation is stored in the top 11 bits and represents the top of the visible feature. This is referred to as "bottom of the sky" elevation. A 10x10 sq. Km area requires 400 megabytes (MB) of data. This is still beyond the capacity of most machines. Typically 64 MB of memory are reserved for terrain, however, a 512 MB memory model has been used on large memory machines. Hence a hierarchical range dependent data structure is used to dynamically load 1, 4, 16, and 64 meter data pixels surrounding the instantaneous view-point. As the view-point moves, this data is updated. Several options exist in the program for loading alternative data volumes, rates, and patterns each one suitable for different applications. These option include:

- Cone Load – loads 1-meter data along a view cone instead of a cylindrically symmetric area
- Update Rate Control – limits the amount of data loaded per view calculation
- LOS High Resolution Update - Places 1-meter data around viewer, targets, and major ground obscurants between the target pairings.

Though memory in modern machines is continuing to drop in cost, the data volume is a primary technical obstacle. The 2.5D Voxel format requires one tenth the storage capacity of vector formats because no polygon outline is required. In order to achieve the same storage capacity using polygons requires increasing the size of a single polygon to cover several elevation postings to reduce the polygonal database size. We have found that the compaction by combining adjacent meter posts with identical element can reduce the data volume by 40% to 60%, however beyond that data loss or statistical substitution of textures is required.

The speed of the PVNT is based upon a unique all integer inverse ray trace algorithm [Baer91]. Rays are projected from the viewer's eye point by incrementing the ray tip length by one meter and testing if the ground has been hit. When hit, the terrain elements, coordinates, and view distances are stored in an array the same pixel dimension as the perspective view. If the ground has not been hit the ray is incremented once more. For a 1024x1024 view, which can scan to 20 Km, the inner loop would execute approximately 20 Billion times per picture. To allow real-time operation on PC machines several tricks are employed. These include:

- All integer ray increment in the inner loop;
- Process in vertical columns;
- Elevation calculations in shifted integers to match the terrain data format; and
- Adjust the ray increment to match the terrain resolution

With these optimizations a 1024x1024 view executes at approximately 2 frames per second (fps) on a 400 Megahertz (Mhz) Pentium machine and can process an equivalent 50 million polygons per second. This number is subject to interpretation since polygons are not used, (90 degree field of view from a 100 meter helicopter over a one meter polygon density is assumed). It should also be noted that the inverse ray trace algorithm automatically performs the painter's algorithm for hidden surface removal and avoids a Z-buffer. A Z-buffer is only used for target template insertion described below.

Besides extremely fast image processing speeds, the PVNT implementation also provides a capability to perform real time surface rendering. Stripping the elevation pixels from the terrain element and running the remainder through a rendering look-up table accomplishes this task. The look-up table is segmented for target to viewer angle. The rendering look-up table is 4 MB and can be calculated off line. This allows material surface property maps to be translated to radiometric emission values on the fly. Hence, shadowing, time of day, view angle, and some weather effects can be handled in real time.

The availability of a fast perspective view generation engine on a generic PC platform is the key to route planning and improved line-of-sight algorithms discussed below.

PVNT Route Planning

Route planning and defensive position selection proceeds as follows. The subject matter expert selects an approximate set of way-points and enters these on a PVNT map view. Once entered, he sequentially visits each point and uses the perspective view capability to examine the terrain as it looks from the position. The route is then adjusted to account for local obscurants, elevation variations, and mission objectives.

Figure 1 shows a screen capture of a map with route points(dashed line) and a perspective view seen by the operator. Note that a view cone is outlined as a white triangle while tree sides seen on the map are colored red and seen as dark spots in the perspective view.

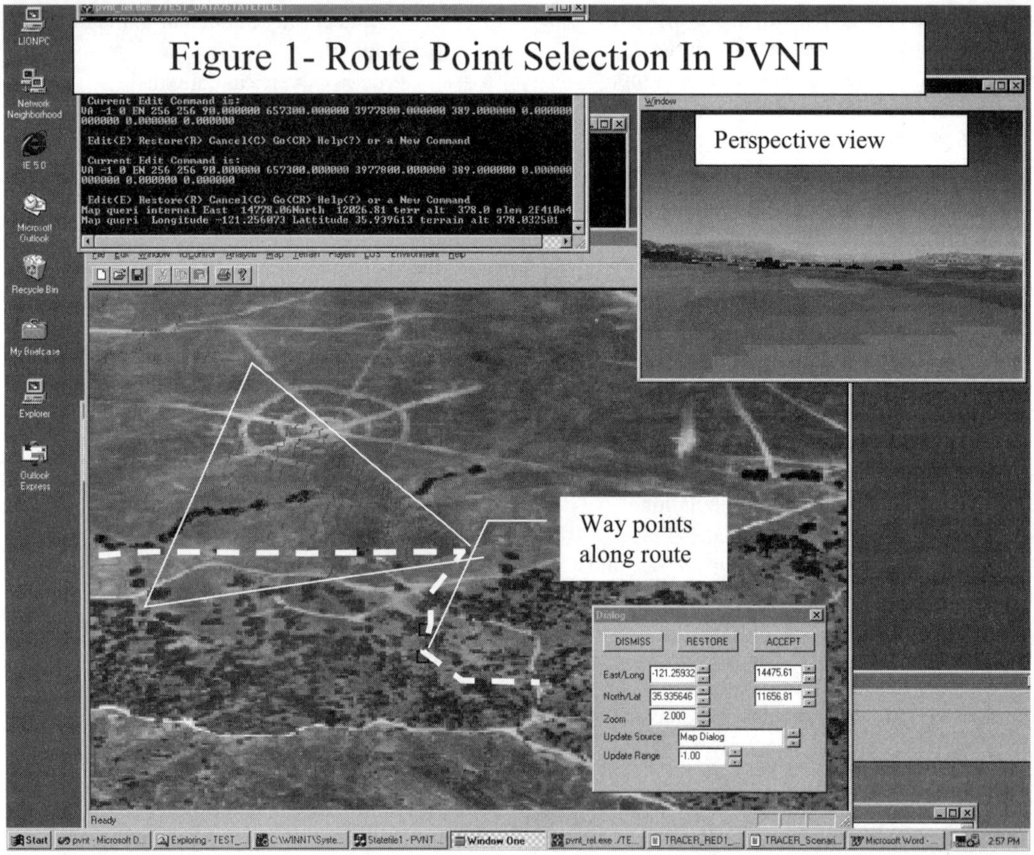

Figure 1- Route Point Selection In PVNT

PVNT LOS Algorithm

The line-of-sight calculation is performed as follows:

- Enter parameters defining a target template aspect as seen from the viewer;
- Enter view and target position;
- PVNT generates a perspective view from the viewer to the target;
- PVNT inserts the target template into the perspective view using a Z-buffer algorithm; and
- PVNT processes the view with the target and performs a pixel count of the target in view.

Figure 2 below shows the perspective view with a template of a vehicle. Note that the target, colored red in the white circle, is partially obscured by the bushes and only the left side of the body is shown along with the mast and the sensor pod on top of it.

The ability to generate full perspective views rapidly allows PVNT to perform such more sophisticated LOS calculations then those using a direct geometric line paring approach. Advantages of this method are:

- Partial visibility handled;
- Viewer can be hidden and only the sensor exposed; and
- Foreground background contrast available for detection calculations

In our study the primary output of this calculation was the fractional visibility of a target and its slant range. If a target had a fractional visibility of 50%, half of the possible pixels were exposed to the viewer.

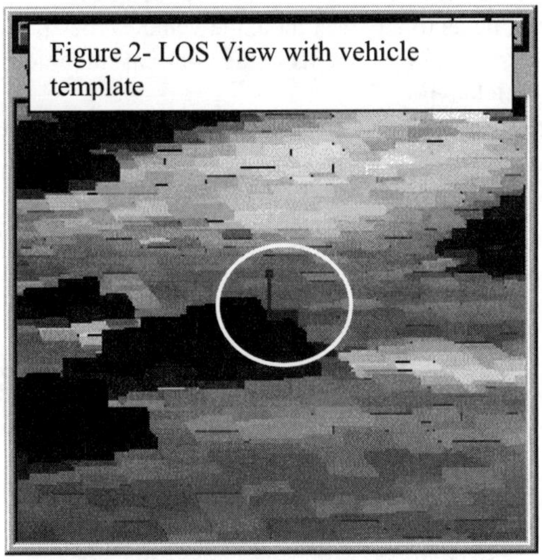

Figure 2- LOS View with vehicle template

SCOUT VEHICLE CASE STUDY

The objective of the study was to determine the impact of a mast-mounted sensor on a battlefield system with respect to target acquisition opportunities and susceptibility to detection. The measures of performance are, given a tactical scout mission, which vehicle type has more inter-visibility to the enemy while remaining less exposed to those enemy targets. The tactical scout mission required each vehicle to move through a suspected enemy position. LOS result comparisons between the vehicle-target pairings regarding the presented area of the target were done. This included both presented area of the enemy targets and presented area of the friendly vehicles while moving through the terrain.

Several methodologies are available for analysis. The generation of weapons effectiveness potential (KEM96) generates terrain maps from stationary players. Routes can be drawn on these maps and compared for effectiveness. This novel method shows great promise in that a single map can provide significant insight into the effectiveness of a weapon over a large geographic region. More traditionally, this simulation generates a large number of LOS data, which is then analyzed. We employed this methodology to generate and analyze different vehicle scenarios in high-resolution terrain. Details of the methodology are described in the next section.

Methodology

Step 1 : A subject matter expert using high resolution terrain knowledge from PVNT interactively chooses defensive positions which maximized visibility and minimized exposure.
Step 2 : A second subject matter expert selects route way points for two scout vehicles also using PVNT. This includes travel points and stop points at which sensing takes place. The routes are chosen without knowledge of the opposing player positions.

Figure 3 shows a diagram of the player positions and two planned routes. Vertical boxes indicate stop points. Vehicle 1 selected a 18.2 km. route defined by 310 points and 7 halt points. Vehicle 2 selected a 17.2 km route defined by 283 points and 6 halt points.

Fig.3 Zone Recon Vignette

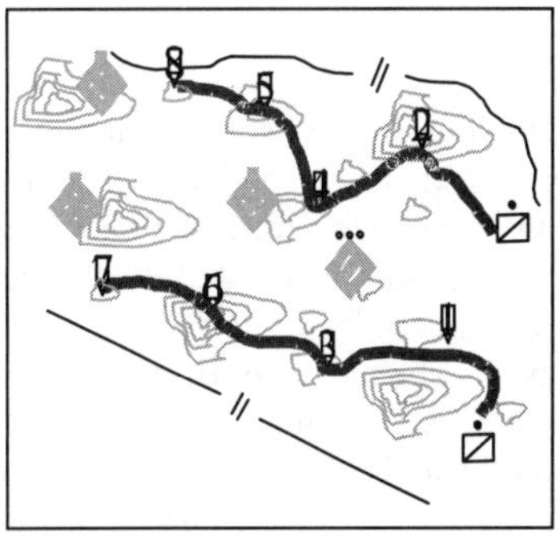

Step 3: The player positions and route way points are formatted by a Data Analysis Tool (DAT) and sent to Janus. Janus densifies the route using its mobility model by inserting time stamps and

PVNT LOS generation commands. A 56 MB file containing over 7000 route waypoints for each vehicle is created. This is for a mission lasting two hours and five minutes in real time.

Step 4: The scenario command file was sent to PVNT, which performed over 749,000 PVNT commands to include position updates and LOS calculations using a 64x64 pixel view template. Run time was 5.5 hours and 778,000 lines of ASCII output were generated. Each output line indicated the red and blue player pair for which LOS was calculated as well as the range, target size, and fractional visibility of the target.

Step 5: The Data Analysis Tool converted The PVNT output file with the LOS results into a Microsoft ACCESS database. Using Structured Query Language (SQL) statements on the database, performance measures were evaluated and graphs were generated through automation.

Study Results

Two vignettes were defined and run through the methodology described in the last section. The first, called the Infiltration vignette, involved two blue vehicles on routes attempting to minimize exposure. The second, called Zone Reconnaissance, included two vehicles attempting to maximize their knowledge of enemy force locations. Two different vehicle types were given the same mission. Yet, through the use of the Subject Matter Expert, each vehicle was employed using it's capabilities. On the whole, the difference between the vehicle with the mast and the vehicle without the mast visibility during travel was insignificant. This was expected since both vehicles were of similar size and moving along similar routes at the same speed.

At stop points (see figures 4a and b) however in the zone recon vignette, the mast mounted vehicles had a total of 67 Inter-visibility (IV) segments (both Blue 1 and Blue 2) versus the 52 IV achieved by the non-mast mounted vehicle type. The most significant differences occurred at Observation Point 2 (OP2) (Blue 1), OP5 (Blue 1), and OP4 (Blue 2). The mast mounted vehicle type had inter-visibility to enemy targets at OP2 and 5 (Blue 1) while the non-mast mounted vehicle types had no IV segments. At OP4 (Blue 2), Vehicle Type 1 had LOS to 6 more targets than Vehicle Type 2. Figures 4a, and 4b show a comparison of Vehicle Type 1 versus Vehicle Type 2 at the stop points.

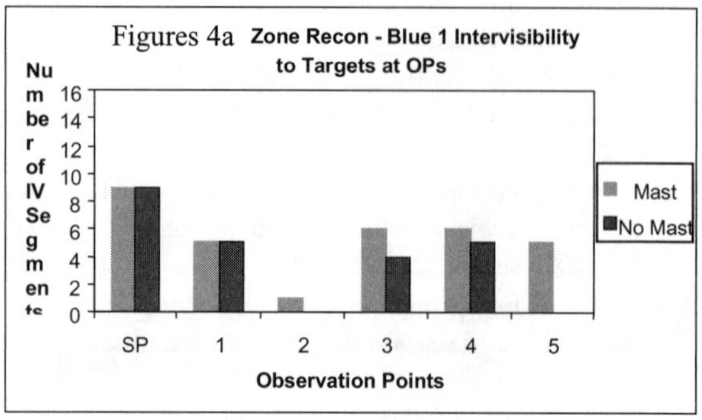

In the infiltration vignette, there was no significant difference in the number of enemy IV segments to the vehicles at the observation points. Enemy targets had a total of 92 IV segments to the mast mounted vehicle type versus 96 IV segments to the non-mast mounted vehicle type.

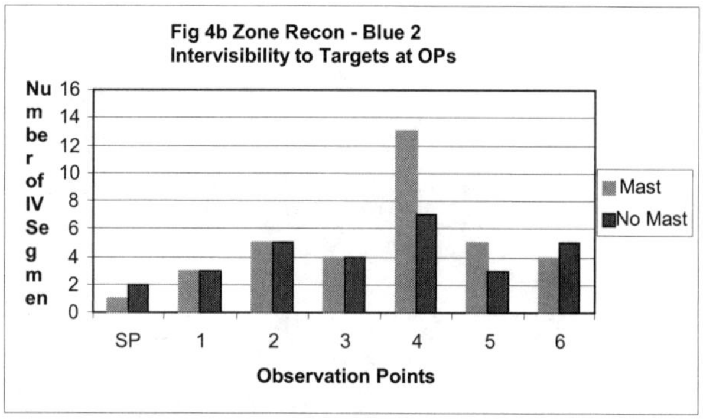

From the results of the study, it is unclear whether one vehicle provides a distinct advantage over the other. In both vignettes, the mast mounted vehicle type shows improvement over the non-mast mounted vehicle with respect to the percent of enemy targets to which it achieves line-of-sight (LOS) and the total number of IV segments at the OPs. In both vignettes, the mast mounted vehicle types has more IV segments at greater ranges than the non-mast mounted vehicles. For this paper, however, the methodology is much more significant than the individual results. A few comments are therefore in order.

In high-resolution terrain using partial target inter-visibility calculations, the LOS is not reciprocal. Some red players could see the blue player when the reverse was not true. This is contrary to our experience with geometric line-of-sight results. We examined several such differences and found for example, a stationary player could be hidden behind a bush, but able to see over the top. Such phenomena make the LOS calculations more realistic although accuracy checks developed with older technologies are not always applicable.

In addition to LOS calculation results, the high- resolution simulator proved to be an effective tool for operational route planning. PVNT visualization allowed the Armor SME to "see" the terrain. The panoramic view from the perspective of the scout observer greatly enhanced route planning and line-of-sight clearance. PVNT "playback" of routes allowed a basic ability to review the tactical movement of the scout

CONCLUSION

The use of high-resolution terrain simulators has been shown to be a significant aid in analyzing tactical importance of weapon design features, which depend on concealment, cover, and camouflage. In addition to LOS calculations, the impact of mission planning utilizing knowledge of micro terrain features has been demonstrated. Future work will concentrate on the improvement of a user-friendly interface, automation of data paths to other simulators and the expansion of 1-meter databases to cover more areas of the world.

REFERENCES

[Baer91] " Implementation of a Perspective View Generator", Transputing '91, P. Welch et. al., Vol. 2 pp. 643-656, ISOPRESS Amsterdam, 1991

[Baer93] "An Approach for Real-Time Terrain Database Creation from Aerial Imagery", by W. Baer and J. R. Akin, *SPIE Proceedings Vol. 1943-17 OE/Aerospace and Remote Sensing Conference*, 12-16 April 1993.

[Baer95]"Global Terrain Database Design for Realistic Imaging Sensor Simulation", W. Baer and C. Reed, *Proceedings 13'th DIS Workshop on Standards for Interoperability of Distributed Simulations*, Vol I, p. 19 ,Sep 18-22 1995

[Kem96] " Computer Visualization of Battlefield Tenets", Kemple, W.G. and Larson, H. J. , Mathematical Computer Modeling, Vol. 23, No. ½ (1996): pp. 25-37

BIOGRAPHY

WOLFGANG BAER is a Research Assistant Professor of Computer Science at the Naval Postgraduate School specializing in data capture, high-speed algorithms, and parallel computers for real-time battlefield application.

MAJOR JAMES ILLINGWORTH is an Operations Research Analyst at the TRAC-Monterey office. His interests are in terrain generation, relational databases, and simulation modeling. He specializes in integrating relational databases into simulations, statistical analysis of data, and virtual modeling of military weapon systems.

BARD MANSAGER is a Senior Lecturer of Mathematics at the Naval Postgraduate School specializing in combat modeling, systems engineering and antitank missile analysis.

WILLIAM G KEMPLE is the Associate Director of the Institute for Joint Warfare Analysis. His research concentrates on combat weapons effectiveness models and display methodologies.

THE DEPARTMENT OF DEFENSE AIR AND SPACE NATURAL ENVIRONMENT MODELING AND SIMULATION EXECUTIVE AGENT: SUPPORTING A FRAMEWORK TO ENSURE AUTHORITATIVE REPRESENTATION OF ENVIRONMENTAL DATA FOR SIMULATIONS

Mike S. Hunsucker, Ronald D. Haynes, Darrell L. Lucas,
Frederick N. Turcotte, Thomas N. Walker

Dynamics Research Corporation
Office of the Air and Space Natural Environment
Modeling and Simulation Executive Agent
151 Patton Avenue, Room 156
Asheville, NC 28801
mike.hunsucker@afccc.af.mil

KEYWORDS Model Credibility, Deterministic, Environmental Science, Aerospace, Man-machine Interfaces

ABSRACT

The Under Secretary of Defense for Acquisition, Technology, and Logistics (USD(AT&L)) created the Air and Space Natural Environment (ASNE) Modeling and Simulation Executive Agent (MSEA), along with the Ocean and Terrain Executive Agents. The MSEAs' task is to help bridge the gap between the providers of natural environmental data and the Department of Defense (DoD) modeling and simulation (M&S) community. The Air Force Director of Weather is designated the Air and Space Natural Environment Executive Agent. As environmental subject matter experts, the ASNE MSEA mission is to ensure the consistent representation of the natural environment in DoD modeling and simulation. The ASNE MSEA office is developing an air and space environmental infrastructure to support DoD M&S programs.

The DoD Modeling and Simulation Master Plan, DoD 5000.59-P, states, "Models of military operations depend on interaction with representations of the natural environment including permanent and semi-permanent manmade features. This requires authoritative three-dimensional representations of the terrain, oceans, atmosphere, and space. These representations are complex in design and require significant funds and time to build. Therefore, the complexity should be commensurate with the simulation's functional requirement for detail given the scope of what is being modeled. Additionally, environmental representations must be seamless [consistent/realistic] in terrain, ocean, atmosphere, and space boundary regions to present fully integrated data for M&S use."

USD(AT&L) chartered the DoD Modeling and Simulation Executive Agents to work with the Defense Modeling and Simulation Office (DMSO) to build the infrastructure so the authoritative representations cited above could be available to the emerging Joint simulations in a cost-effective and timely manner. A "one size fits all" solution will not work. An infrastructure capable of responding to simulation users and developers in a just-in-time manner with the "authoritative representation" of the integrated natural environmental data appropriate to their needs is ESSENTIAL.

This paper emphasizes the office's Joint role that ensures an authoritative representation of the natural environment is available to Joint simulation programs like the Joint Simulation System (JSIMS), the Joint Warfare System (JWARS), and the Joint Modeling and Simulation System (JMASS). Historically, there was very little weather play in simulations because it was too expensive or too hard to retrofit legacy M&S systems with a weather-play capability. This is about to change; the new DoD M&S programs like JSIMS (training), JWARS (analysis), and JMASS (acquisition) will be interactive with the air, space, oceans, and terrain (physical and manmade structures) natural environment and take into account the effects of the natural environment on simulation objects.

BACKGROUND

The Military Services have been involved in modeling and simulation activities for many years. Before 1990, the field of M&S was marked by fragmentation and limited coordination of activities across the Services and across functions. Many activities were Service-specific with limited interoperability and re-use. In the decade of the 90s, DoD acted to consolidate modeling and simulation efforts. While taking control of the overall direction of modeling and simulation, DoD, nonetheless, designated the Services and certain Agencies as Executive Agents in managing the development and maintenance of M&S applications in their areas of expertise, including the arenas of Intelligence and the Natural Environment. DoD recognized that representation of the natural environment and the processes by which the natural environment affects systems were not well integrated into the Service's simulations. Simulations typically were conducted without incorporating the effects of the natural environment or included the natural environment only in limited ways. Simulations assumed clear skies, dry terrain, and low surf conditions. Incorporating weather into simulations was viewed as too hard to do, too costly, or too time consuming. Those parts of the natural environment that were incorporated tended to be high-cost, one-of-a-kind data bases embedded within the software code of a simulation and not re-usable. However, DoD recognized that simulations do not have real credibility without incorporating the effects of the natural environment. Consequently, the USD(AT&L) placed special emphasis on the natural environment and established Executive Agents responsible for coordinating all aspects of DoD modeling and simulation related to representations of the natural environment domains. The Navy is responsible for the Ocean domain, the National Imagery and Mapping Agency (NIMA) is responsible for the Terrain domain, and the Air Force is responsible for the Air and Space domains.

Military training and operations traditionally dominate military activities. Operations remain important as evidenced by the roles of DoD in Kuwait, Somalia, Bosnia, and Kosovo, to name a few. In the early 1990s, however, M&S began to emerge as a very important part of DoD's ability to do its job. There are a number of reasons for this new emphasis and focus. First, as manpower and materiel declined, there were fewer forces that were more widely dispersed. Money for training was diverted to pay for operations and DoD needed to make better investment decisions. Second, the tempo of operations (OpsTempo) for military forces increased significantly during this decade. The flavor and complexity of the missions changed, also. DoD needed to cover more territory with more sophisticated systems and plans. With fewer forces and more operations involving allies, there was a need for more joint and combined training. There was no historical way to deal with these new issues. Third, technology was improving rapidly and its cost was decreasing, especially in communications and computers. New software tools and user interfaces came on-line and there were improvements in the ability to store and handle large volumes of data. DoD recognized that advanced modeling and simulation was a way to make better decisions in the face of declining resources, to train for and determine courses of military action, and to do it at lower cost. The importance of incorporating the effects of the natural environment to the credibility of simulations was a part of this recognition.

ENVIRONMENTAL EFFECTS

While consistent representations of the natural environment within each domain are important, cross-domain consistency is equally important. The atmosphere and ocean should evolve in a dynamically and physically consistent way during the course of a simulation, although changes in the ocean are generally at a slower pace than the atmosphere. Terrain features evolve very slowly, except when modified by the actions of simulation participants. If berms are built or buildings destroyed, these should be reflected with changes in the terrain. Properly integrating these domains is crucial--when the wind blows hard, surf conditions in the ocean should be high. When it rains, the terrain should get wet. If an object on the terrain is generating smoke or dust, atmospheric visibility should be reduced. However, it's important to note here that representing the environment is only part of the problem. Realistically capturing the effects of the environment on the warfare domain objects is what is important to the simulations. It isn't the natural environment itself that's important in a simulation. It's the outcomes of interactions between warfare domain objects and the natural environment that are important. It is on the basis of outcomes that analysis is performed, that courses-of-actions are determined, and that systems are evaluated.

The Executive Agents adopted this common objective to achieve the mission. This objective provides a physically consistent, dynamic environment within and across domains. This concept is essential to ensure that simulation outcomes affected by the natural environment will be realistic. Clear skies will give way to rain and decreasing ceilings; dry terrain will become wet and muddy; rain will add to the acoustic background noise in the ocean; and sea state will be affected by wind. While these changes in the environment may be nice to know, they are really incidental to the effects they cause on warfare domain objects in a simulation. Warfare domain objects (aircraft, satellites, tanks, ships, etc.) will interact with the rain and reduced ceilings to find targets are obscured. Tanks and trucks will find their speed is reduced; they even may be immobilized. Submarines' acoustic sensors will be adversely affected by increased ambient noise. Amphibious assault vehicles may not be able to operate in heavy surf. Space weather effects like ionospheric scintillation should effect communications systems.

SPECTRUM OF SUPPORT

Modeling and simulation is applied across a range of applications. Simulation-based acquisition processes are helping determine how best to spend declining defense appropriations to acquire new generations of defense systems. Here, these new systems are being designed, built, tested, and operationally evaluated almost entirely using modeling and simulation. M&S is used in a broad range of operations and training scenarios from the individual soldier or pilot to a Joint Task Force battlestaff. Modeling and simulation allows planners to assess Joint warfighting situations, conduct operational planning and mission rehearsal, determine weapons and force mixes, and test the effectiveness of various courses-of-action. With the advent of the Joint Warfare System, M&S will play a pivotal role in determining defense budget requirements for the 21st Century. In all these application areas, the natural environment plays a part. For M&S to be credible, the effects of the natural environment must be considered.

Since the modeling and simulation community operates across a wide spectrum of resolution, the depiction of the natural environment must be available in a range of resolutions. At the narrow end of the spectrum, a limited number of natural environmental parameters or data sets are required to meet limited M&S objectives involving system, sub-system, and component simulations for acquisition and test and evaluation decisions. Such simulations may entirely involve software objects in a simulated natural environment with no human-in-the-loop and operate far faster than real time.

In the middle of the spectrum, larger numbers of natural environmental parameters or data sets are needed to support planning and engagement or mission rehearsal simulations. At the engagement or mission rehearsal level, people train or rehearse missions using the natural environment through virtual simulations that usually run in real time. That is, people operate simulated equipment to experience operating in an adverse environment or practice a mission to exploit it. Visualization of the natural environment plays a major role in these human-in-the-loop simulations. The trainees can affect the outcomes of the simulation and learn. Mission rehearsals provide warfighters with advance knowledge and preparation to improve their ability to exploit expected environmental conditions and destroy a target. Their actions affect the outcome of the simulation.

Finally at the broad scope, large numbers of natural environmental parameters or data sets are needed to support campaign-level planning. Battlestaffs are trained or commanders are determining courses-of-action. Constructive simulations like these involve simulated people in simulated equipment. People make decisions to initiate the action in the simulation, but the outcomes of the simulation are determined statistically and reported to the decision-makers. There usually is no visualization in these simulations that may be executed at hundreds up a thousand times faster than real time.

AUTHORITATIVE REPRESENTATION

Across this range of simulation interests, the resolution in space and time of the required environmental parameters depends on the purpose of the simulation and the environmental data of interest. This is called <u>authoritative representation</u>, a very important concept to understand. The DoD Modeling and Simulation Master Plan describes the need for authoritative representations of the natural environment. The real M&S requirement, then, is providing such an environmental representation. The authoritative representation of the natural environment is THE ONE in which finer resolution adds no new information to the end product. That is, if a user of that representation further interpolated or extrapolated the data, the additional data points still would produce valid results. This is an extremely important point. Since it's costly to produce environmental scenarios, there's no need to produce one with more resolution than is necessary. If a single scenario can be produced that meets the needs of each warfare domain object (whether it's a sensor, a system, a platform, or an aggregated object like a tank battalion), then that is the only resolution that needs to be provided. The simulation then can aggregate, interpolate, or extrapolate the data to meet its own needs and each level will be valid.

WHAT'S DIFFERENT ABOUT M&S

So far we've talked about the terrain, oceans, atmosphere, and space domains and the importance of realistic, physically consistent representations of these domains for M&S. Additionally, we explained what authoritative representation means regarding the resolution of environmental data sets. A few points need to be discussed about "what's different about M&S" from operational support. These differences are important to understand.

In modeling and simulation, the actual requirement is about the ability to meet a requirement. A requirement is defined as a task performed under conditions to meet standards. For example, the task could be to "take that hill." The simulation could plan to practice that task under "hot and dusty" or "wet and windy" or any other combination of conditions. The simulation then could require the hill be taken under certain standards, like with the forces on hand or given a time constraint to see what forces would be required to take the hill in a certain amount of time under those conditions. So for modeling and simulation, it's not about predicting whether it will be "hot and dusty," it's about finding "hot and dusty" conditions and representing those conditions and providing them to the simulation.

M&S is not about the ability to accurately forecast an event three or four days in advance. It's about providing the simulated natural environment that consists of both ground truth and forecasts. This simulated natural environment must be provided as an authoritative representation appropriate for a simulation during the simulation run time such that users can evaluate the effects of those conditions on their forces. It's also important to note that using both forecasts and ground truth is about inferring or determining effects. It's not about weather for weather's sake; simulation users care about the effects of that weather not the weather itself.

Currently in both the real world and in M&S, forecasts are used so that a decision-maker can infer possible effects ahead of time and factor these into the decision-making process. In the real world, real forces "go out" and interact with the natural environment and real effects (results) occur.

In M&S, models of forces, sensors, and systems "go out" during simulation run time and interact with a simulated natural environment, the authoritative representation of the natural environment, to determine outcomes. M&S requires these interactions be accurately modeled so outcomes (effects) can be determined. In the real world, Mother Nature provides the ground truth natural environment, but in simulations, someone produces the authoritative representation of the natural environment. This ability to provide the authoritative representation of the natural environment is important to M&S and the MSEAs.

OUR EMPHASIS

The air and space natural environment provider must produce in an authoritative (physically consistent) manner those elements and parameters necessary to provide the intelligent air and/or space objects with the attributes needed to determine environmental effects on the objects. We advocate those development efforts that have the greatest payoff or can accelerate support to the M&S community. In particular, we sponsor projects to improve the ability to determine cloud amounts (both from above and below) and types, icing, turbulence, visibility, and surface wind gusts. In the space environment, we advocate on-going development efforts to improve the specification of important space weather parameters that impact satellite-based communication, navigation, and surveillance systems.

The MSEAs for the natural environment are focusing their efforts in five major areas.

The first area is providing support to certain major modeling and simulation programs, including the emerging Joint M&S programs that were designed at the outset to incorporate the effects of the natural environment. These new systems will replace legacy simulation systems that do not or minimally incorporate the natural environment. These programs are

- the Joint Warfare System, or JWARS, a premier analytic simulation being developed by DoD;
- the Joint Simulation System, or JSIMS, a constructive training simulation to be used by all of DoD; and
- the Joint Modeling and Simulation System, or JMASS, to support Simulation Based Acquisition and Test and Evaluation.

The Executive Agents act as an extended staff to provide subject matter expertise for the Joint simulation community. The Executive Agent for Air and Space established Liaison Offices at the JWARS, JSIMS, and JMASS Program Offices, as well as at DMSO, to serve as extended staff members. Additionally, personnel from the MSEAs provide input and guidance as members of various tiger teams and working groups and as applied research program managers.

These programs were among the first to state requirements for incorporating environmental data and effects in the simulations. The MSEAs focused early efforts on capturing the comprehensive environmental support requirements for these programs that bounded the problem and helped capture the majority of the requirements for the entire M&S community. The MSEAs are working to improve the infrastructure needed to meet the entire range of environmental support requirements for modeling and simulation.

Second, the Executive Agents collaborate on a DMSO-sponsored project known as the Synthetic Environment Data Representation and Interchange Specification, or SEDRIS. SEDRIS will establish a common standard for transfer of environmental data among the various participants in a simulation. This project assures the simulation user community that a single data transfer standard for environmental information is needed.

The third focus area is as advisors to the simulation user community in verifying and validating natural environmental data. We assist in verifying that the natural environmental information acquired for use in a simulation was "done right." We assist in validating that the data acquired for use in simulations is the right information needed by that simulation. In these ways, the Executive Agents aid in accrediting that a simulation is appropriate for its intended use.

Fourth, the Executive Agents collaborate on another DMSO-sponsored project known as the Master Environmental Library or MEL. This project addresses access to a variety of environmental resources. The MEL specifically is designed to be a one-stop environmental shop, or library, containing information about natural environmental data sets and eventually algorithms and weather effects tools useful to the modeling and simulation community. It will contain information about natural environmental data sets and how to order them. This will simplify the simulation users' problems in locating and retrieving natural environmental data suitable for simulations.

The fifth focus area is to develop the capability for a user to specify a need for an environmental data set and have it produced "to order" and on a "just-in-time" basis. The Executive Agents are collaborating on developing this capability called the Environmental Scenario Generator or ESG. The ESG provides the M&S customer like an exercise coordinator with the ability to generate a customized environmental scenario data base containing the parameters and conditions required to impact the simulation. These data bases will maintain realistic inter- and intra-domain consistency. ESG delivers the scenario data bases in a standard format like SEDRIS. ESG is a significant development in the environmental support capability for M&S programs. This capability uses a "fuzzy logic" search engine and allows users to find "matches" in historical archives for the atmospheric, space, and ocean environmental data describing the conditions desired. When matches are found, ESG extracts the available coarse resolution data, places it on an appropriate grid, and derives additional needed parameters. When the existing data are not sufficient or missing, ESG initiates a model run (atmospheric or oceanic) to produce (recreate) the historical event (the scenario) at the resolution necessary to support the needs of the users.

PROJECTS

The Air and Space Executive Agent initiated a number of applied research projects to develop new technology and address the capability shortfalls.

ACMES and ESG

The Advanced Climate Modeling and Environmental Simulations project, or ACMES, at the Air Force Combat Climatology Center (AFCCC) provides a new capability to generate high-resolution climatology data for regions of the world that have little or no data from which to derive such information (Doggett 2000). It also dovetails perfectly into the M&S support infrastructure to meet the need to provide a "just-in-time" capability to produce high-resolution atmospheric data to meet simulation requirements.

The ESG, previously described, enables users to "discover" data that meet their needs, or when they do not exist, request that they be produced in a timely manner. ACMES is just one of the atmospheric capabilities mentioned in the ESG project to produce needed data sets when no actual historical data sets contain the parameters or resolution required for a particular simulation. Triggered by ESG that provides desired dates, regions, time periods, etc., ACMES produces (recreates) the historical event (scenario) at the resolution necessary to support the needs of the users.

To ensure the capabilities being developed are appropriate to the needs of the simulation communities, outreach programs to major developing simulations such as JWARS, JMASS, and JSIMS were started in 1998. ESG provides the infrastructure allowing the M&S community to obtain authoritative environmental scenario data that meets their needs in a timely, cost-effective manner. Interoperability among simulations and re-use will be enhanced through use of standard data and standard interchange mechanisms.

Warfighter Weather Effects (WxFX)

WxFX is an Air Force Weather project that leverages the ACMES project and the Army Research Laboratory's work on the Integrated Weather Effects Decision Aids, or IWEDA (Hummel, et al. 2000). It will provide the capability to produce weather effects information for both M&S and operational customers using high resolution historical weather data. WxFX, like IWEDA, automates the translation of raw weather data into weather intelligence (effects). WxFX is currently in development and will be transitioned to initial operational status at AFCCC when funding permits. The ultimate goal of this project is to develop physics-based weather effects decision aids. This work is expected to have big payoffs for operations as well as the emerging Joint simulations.

Cloud Scene Simulation Model Statistics (CSSM Stats)

The Air Force Research Laboratory's Cloud Scene Simulation Model (CSSM) was developed to take coarse scale cloud and moisture data from weather models and render it in finer resolution for use in deterministic simulations. In fiscal years 1997/98, ASNE MSEA supported development of radiometrically correct renditions of cloud scenes. In fiscal year 1999, the CSSM Statistics project, or CSSM Stats, leveraged the work completed in the CSSM effort to develop statistics on clouds that can be used by major simulation systems (Mozer, et al. 2000). Since these simulations operate at aggregated levels (above the platform level) and at many times faster than real time speeds to determine effects on performance, stochastic versus deterministic methods are needed to determine line-of-sight ranges when clouds are present. Instead of rendering a detailed cloud scene, then calculating if a given sensor can "see" a target, probabilities can be used if they are accurate and available. Using the developed capabilities of CSSM, sensitivity tests were conducted with sensors of various wavelengths using varying cloud amounts, bases, tops, and types. Probability distributions were developed that can be used during simulation run time. These probabilities are improvements to the heuristic pilot "rules of thumb" that state, for example, that when there are more than a certain percentage of clouds below the aircraft, the probability of achieving a cloud-free line-of-sight to a particular location of interest is marginal. CSSM Stats quantifies "marginal" as a distribution that is sampled during run time.

Space Weather

The ASNE MSEA initiated space environmental projects, also. One of the most promising projects deals with ionospheric scintillation. IonScint is one of the space effects parameters most needed by the emerging Joint modeling programs as well as legacy systems being brought forward for High Level Architecture (HLA) compatibility. Scintillation is one of the ten most important space parameters identified in earlier studies on M&S requirements due to its effect on satellite communications and navigation signals. This work also will benefit warning and forecast capabilities that do not currently exist or are too rudimentary to be effective.

The ionospheric scintillation project is designed to provide satellite communications (SATCOM) effects with high spatial and temporal resolution. JSIMS, in particular, will train battlestaffs in decision-making processes; they must learn to plan for realistic SATCOM outages during exercise play. The environmental scenario must depict these variations realistically. The project will deliver an algorithm that provides the data needed as a training aid for daily planning and operations decisions. The result is used by battlestaffs to determine SATCOM effects and in making decisions on the employment of space assets.

CONCLUSION

The ASNE MSEA, along with the Ocean and Terrain MSEAs, has a number of projects underway to ensure that natural environment data providers have the capabilities to support simulation programs. We anticipate that both the government and private sectors increasingly will be using M&S as a basis for analyzing courses-of-action, equipment acquisition, as well as training and mission rehearsal. The end result for M&S is that there soon will be every reason to incorporate the natural environment into simulations if that fact is important to realistic results. The needed data will be available in a timely manner and will be the "right data" for the intended uses. The ordering process will be customizable by individual users and the price should be affordable. That should please the warfighters and acquisition agencies of developing simulations like JWARS, JSIMS, and JMASS. To take advantage of these capabilities, simulation developers should be preparing to accept and use the environmental data. They no longer need to be concerned with producing it, worrying about its availability, or worse yet, paying exorbitant fees to get it. The requisite data sets literally will be at their finger tips.

REFERENCES

Department of Defense, Under Secretary of Defense for Acquisition, Technology, and Logistics. *Modeling and Simulation (M&S) Master Plan, DoD 50059-P*, October 1995.

Doggett, M. K., 2000. "Advanced Climate Modeling and Environmental Simulations (ACMES): Bringing DoD Climatological Support into the 21st Century." *Preprints, 16th International Conference, Interactive Information and Processing Systems (IIPS) for Meteorology, Oceanography and Hydrology*, Long Beach, CA, American Meteorological Society, January 9-14, 2000, 42-44.

J. R. Hummel, T. B. Baines, M. S. Hunsucker, and J. D. Liechty, 2000, "The Incorporation of High Resolution Climatological Data to Support the Development of Environmental Tactical Decision Aids for the Warfighter." *Preprints, 2000 Summer Computer Simulation Conference*, Vancouver, British Columbia, Canada, The Society for Computer Simulation International, July 16-20, 2000.

Mozer, J. B.; G. P. Seely, S. C. Gordon, D. J. Smalley, 2000, "Cloud Impacts for Aggregate Military Simulations Using CSSM Statistics." *Preprints, 16th International Conference, Interactive Information and Processing Systems (IIPS) for Meteorology, Oceanography and Hydrology*, Long Beach, CA, American Meteorological Society, January 9-14, 2000, 50-53

System of Systems Integration (SoSI) - A "SMART" Way of Acquiring Army C4I2WS Systems

By

Richard S. Pei
US Army Communications-Electronics Command
Fort Monmouth, NJ, USA

Introduction

The tactical battlefield has changed significantly due to the increased range, precision and lethality of weapon systems. This extended battle space coupled with increasing sophistication in military technology creates a new operating environment for maneuver forces on the future battlefield. On the "information centric" battlefield of the future, all sensor and weapon systems/platforms will be linked together in a seamless network – a "system of systems" environment – using an information grid operating in near real time. The information battle space where weapon systems will operate will become increasingly complex and intricate.

The complex "system of systems" battlefield, combined with the turbulence of defense drawdown – both on the operational AND Research and Development (R&D) communities – underscores the need for the Army's acquisition community to establish a new robust, diversified, and agile capability/process for effective collaborative research, development, and engineering.

Simulation Based Acquisition (SBA) is a relatively new Department of Defense (DoD) initiative, aimed at reinventing the systems acquisition process through the robust, collaborative use of information and simulation technologies. The Army's implementation of the SBA construct is titled Simulation and Modeling for Acquisition, Requirements, and Training – SMART. The Army leadership believes that the acquisition process is continuous – from the warfighter identifying a material deficiency through system disposal. Modeling and simulation should not be optimized only for acquisition but throughout the Army's acquisition, requirements, and training communities – a 'systems' approach.

The overall mission of CECOM is first to conduct total life cycle management of Command and Control, Communications, Computers, Intelligence and Electronic Warfare and Sensors (C4IEWS) Battlefield and Power Projection Systems. Its second function is to establish the architectural framework and systems engineering to ensure integrated solutions throughout the battlespace and its sustaining base. It is the responsibility of the CECOM Research, Development and Engineering Center (CERDEC) to support its parent organization, CECOM in executing its overall mission, primarily by 1) Develop a comprehensive architecture for the Army to encompass sustaining base to tactical echelons, 2) Ensure vertical integration with and across system domains, 3) Develop & engineer robust C4IEWS capabilities for the soldier, 4) Ensure horizontal integration across all architecture efforts, tech base, hardware and software, and 5) Promote and support system of systems integration.

In order to allow the CERDEC to execute its functional responsibilities of systems optimization, architecture development and developing integrated solutions, there is recognition that we need to focus on the problems/issues associated with integration of C4I2WS systems from a System of Systems level. This is to mean that besides the integration of the components and sub-systems within a weapon system, such as an Unmanned Aerial Vehicle (UAV), we also must also analyze its missions and functions in conjunction with all the other battlefield platforms, both ground and airborne, such that the overall military capabilities of the fighting force including the UAV can be optimized. As such, a new process and RD&E environment to facilitate this System of Systems Integration (SOSI) is required. The details of the SOSI environment will be the focus of our discussions that follows.

System of System Integration (SoSI)

In order to pursue development, integration, interoperability, and overall optimization of new C4I2WS systems to perform in the complex Information Centric Battlefield of the future, the CERDEC, under the leadership of its Director, Dr. Louis

Marquet, initiated the "System of Systems Integration (SoSI)" program to enable it to more effectively and efficiently support its customers in accomplishing their missions under the SMART acquisition paradigm.

Our goal of SOSI is to integrate our core competencies and teaming with our partners and customers to expedite and improve the RD&E process. Our objectives are: 1) Collaborate closely with Battle Labs and TRADOC Schools to ensure R&D models, simulations, and prototypes support the requirements process, 2) Develop, provide, and integrate R&D models, simulations, and prototypes as part of technology generation, insertion and transition, in support of PM systems, and 3) Collaborate closely with training system developers and testing system developers to ensure R&D models, simulations, and prototypes transition and integrate into their efforts.

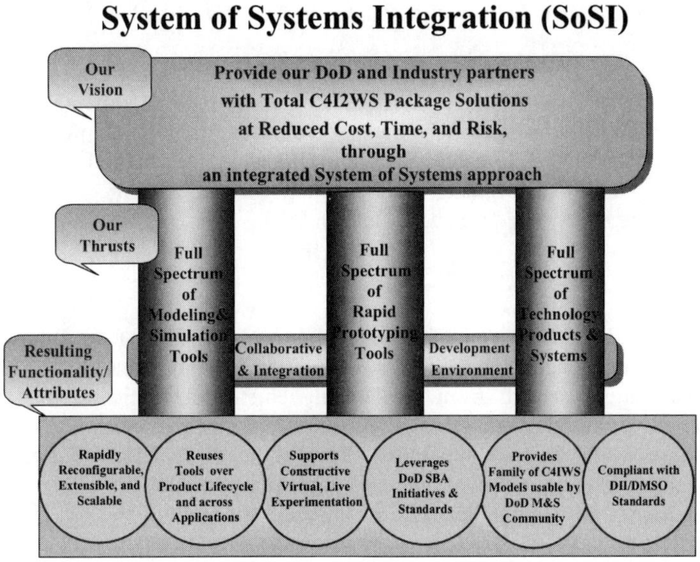

Figure 1. CERDEC SOSI Vision, Thrusts, and Attributes

Portrayed conceptually at Figure 1 is our SoSI vision. Our overall vision is as stated: To Provide CECOM and Its Customer Base with a System of Systems Integration Capability to Rapidly Prototype, Evaluate, Field and Support Optimized, Integrated, Affordable and Supportable Total Package C4I2WS Solutions at Reduced Cost, Time and Risk.

Our vision is supported by three primary thrusts or "pillars":

1) A full spectrum of M&S tools
2) A full spectrum of rapid prototyping tools,
3) A full spectrum of C4I2WS technology products & systems, and
4) A collaborative development and integration environment to facilitate the Integrated Product Process Development (IPPD) process in the planning and execution of SOSI thrusts.

These pillars lay on a foundation of desired functionality and attributes, which take advantage of evolving initiatives within DoD.

In order to save dollars and be compatible with other DoD initiatives, we want to leverage the emerging DoD and Dept. of the Army initiatives, and be complaint with their emerging standards as well as those of the Defense Information Infrastructure (DII) and Defense Modeling and Simulation Office (DMSO), to include the M&S standardization and architectural development (e.g. HLA, MSRR, etc.).

We design the SOSI environment so that it is rapidly, reconfigurable and scalable. In this way it can be rapidly be redirected and shared to support a wide range of programs and mission application areas.

We want the M&S representations of our whole C4I2WS product line, and want the capability to support constructive, virtual, live experimentation or hybrids of each, in conjunction with other collaborators.

Once we develop these modeling tools, we want to assure their reuse over the various life cycle phases of a product as well as share them horizontally across product/mission areas.

Finally, we would hope that once we develop and validate a family of authoritative C4I2WS models , they would be deposited in online M&S repositories, so that they may be made available to the DoD and allied M&S community at large.

The task of implementing the SoSI vision above falls on the SoSI Integrated Product Team (IPT) which has been chartered since January 1999. The work of the SoSI IPT has been focused on developing interoperable C4I2WS models/simulators, establishing a collaborative environment for all stakeholders, as well as improving the infrastructure and simulation facilities required to conduct collaborative distributed research, development and engineering (RDA) of C4ISR systems. The goal is to implement a capability to rapidly prototype, evaluate, field and support optimized, integrated, affordable and supportable total package C4I2WS solutions for the Army at reduced cost, time and risk.

SoSI Sensor-Shooter Experiment Federation

Under SoSI, CERDEC has successfully integrated its core modeling and simulation (M&S) laboratories into a distributed, scaleable, plug and play collaborative engineering and experimentation federation that can readily duplicate and simulate complete sensor-to-shooter operational threads, from the platform/vehicle level all the way up to Joint Task Forces level, to support PEO/PMs, Battle Labs, Warfighters, and other Army/Joint/Coalition activities in executing their mission/functions/tasks of the SMART acquisition process. Figure 2 below depicts the federates of the SoSI Sensor-Shooter Experiment Federation and the diverse set of virtual, live, and constructive models/simulators and C4ISR systems available for plug-n-play within the federation depending on the experimental requirements.

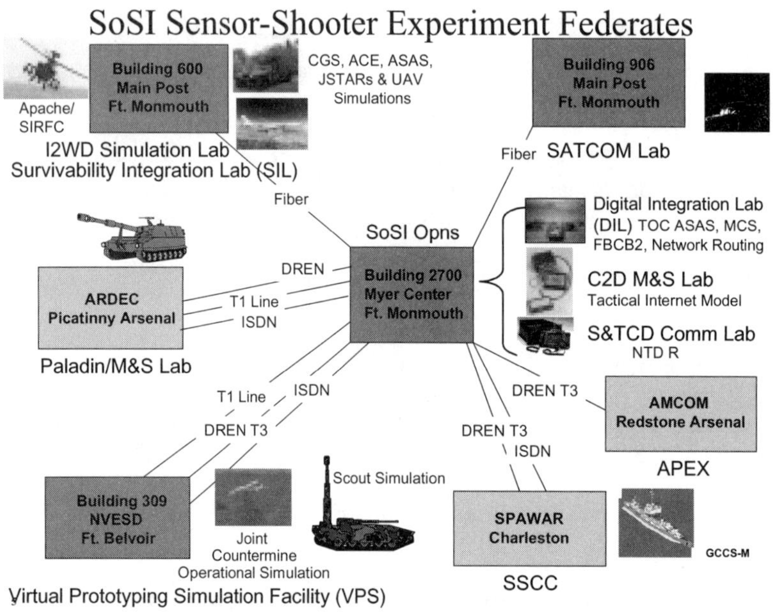

Figure 2. SoSI Sensor-Shooter Experiment Federates

To demonstrate the capabilities of the SoSI Engineering/Experimentation Environment in supporting SMART/SBA activities described above, the SoSI IPT, in collaboration with the Armaments RD&E Center, Picatinny Arsenal and Missile RD&E Center, and the Navy SPAWAR Charleston, S.C., has designed and conducted a series of distributed virtual/live sensor to shooter simulation experiments. A realistic operational vignette was specifically developed to exercise interactions between simulated systems such as the JSTARS Radar, Unmanned Aerial Vehicle, Tactical Internet, SINCGARS Radio, Apache Longbow Radar and Suite of Integrated RF Countermeasures Sensor, Precision Kill & Attack Missile System and the PALADIN Fire Support System, and real/live systems to include the Common Ground Station, All Source Analysis System, Maneuver Control System, Force XXI Battle Command Brigade and Below, and the Global Command and Control System – Army/Maritime. (See Figure 3)

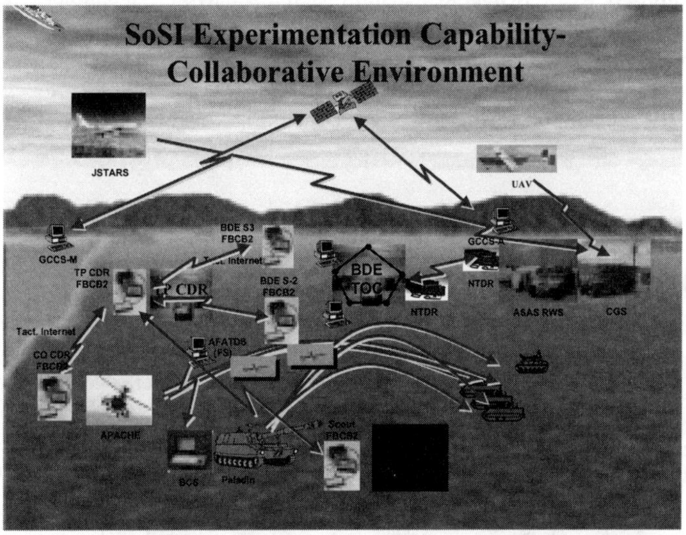

Figure 3. SoSI Experimentation Capability Collaborative Environment

The SoSI Demonstration marked the first time within CECOM that a comprehensive simulation experiment involving all four of the RDEC Directorate's simulation labs was conducted over the distributed network connections provided by the RDEC's Digital Integration Lab. The SoSI experiments demonstrated the robust capability of the SoSI Federation to support system concept developments, simulation based design tradeoff studies, etc. This SoSI capability will benefit and help the Army community to:

1. Integrate multiple programs and systems acquisition projects to achieve substantial reduction in risk and total ownership cost as well as increase in quality and military capability for the warfighter

2. Assemble resources that can be shared in a distributed manner to facilitate research, development, test, and evaluation (RDT&E) (i.e., developmental T&E) that brings about superior C4I2WS systems with advanced technologies to battlefield readiness many years faster than is presently achievable with current acquisition practices

3. Support technical orientation to the operational community for early requirements definition, tradeoff determinations, and warfighting concept generation

4. Facilitate the determination of the technical feasibility of new technology or system and permits tradeoffs in simulation rather than expensive "metal bending"

5. Help prepare new technologies or systems for insertion into the operational assessment environment early through virtual representation

6. Support iterative refinement of new system or product improvement, and

7. Provide a robust collaborative environment for Joint Services and industry for C4I2WS research and development initiatives.

This SoSI sensor to shooter experimentation capability has been successfully demonstrated to executives and senior leadership from OSD, DA, AMC, and TRADOC, including LTG Paul Kern, Military Deputy to the Army Acquisition Executive, Dr. Walter Hollis, Deputy Under Secretary of the Army, and Dr.Vitalij Garber, Director of Interoperability, OSD. As a result these demonstrations, the SoSI project was named one of the pilot SBA pilot efforts within DoD.

AMC RDEC Federation

A important objective of the SoSI program is to extend its capabilities to other Army stakeholders. As such, the CERDEC has teamed with other Army Materiel Command (AMC) Major Subordinate Commands, namely the Aviation & Missile Command (AMCOM), the Tank, Automotive & Armaments Command (TACOM), Soldier, Biological & Chemical Command (SBCCOM), and Simulation, Training & Instrumentation Command (STRICOM), to start the process of establishing an AMC RDEC Federation. The AMC RDEC Federation is conceptually shown at Figure 4 below.

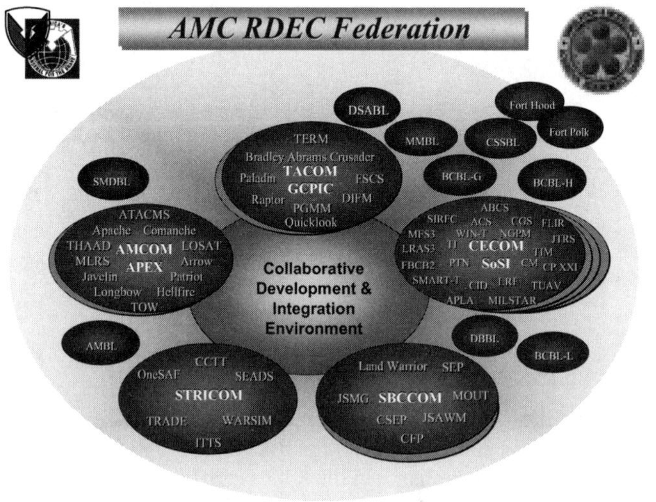

Figure 4. AMC RDEC Federation

The core of this federation consist of a joint collaborative development, integration and engineering environment such that the aggregated modeling, simulation, technical and engineering capabilities of AMC can be brought to bear to support the application of SMART principles to the acquisition of key Army systems such as the Future Combat System. The concept of the AMC RDEC Federation was successfully demonstrated by the AMC Team, which included CECOM, AMCOM, TACOM and STRICOM, at the Army's SMART Conference 2000 hosted by the Office of Assistant Secretary of Army for Acquisition, Logistics and Technology (ASA(ALT)), Los Angeles, 25-28 January 2000. This demonstration showed for the first time live, virtual, and constructive simulators/models from the four AMC commands integrated into a large-scale force-on-force and Military Operations Urban Terrain (MOUT) simulation on the floor of the conference. The demonstrated was so well received that plans are being formulated to include it as part of the October 2000 AUSA Symposium at Washington D.C. and the AMC Technology Demonstration to members of the Congress/Senate on Capital Hill planned for February 2001.

Conclusion

In summary, the CECOM RD&E Center recognize that M&S and virtual prototyping tools are critical for developing and optimizing sensor systems, and integrating them into a network centric information grid. We understand that SBA and SMART implementation is a necessary step if we are to develop products quicker , cheaper, and faster with lower programmatic/cost risk). However, we also realize that further tailoring will have to be done in order to address CECOM's unique needs for system of Systems Integration.

Because of the complexity of the problem sets and the large number of partners, and stakeholders involved in the development of a C4I, Information Warfare, and Sensor, we will have to pay more attention than others to the development of a distributed collaborative environment which will support the systems acquisition process

The CERDEC has chartered an Integrated Product Team to develop a detailed SoSI implementation plan and have already built a baseline SoSI Experiment Federation for support of SBA/SMART programs. Although we are not where we want to be just yet, we will be fully utilizing our current SoSI capabilities to support the immediately needs of our customers. We also are aggressively improving our SoSI facilities, capabilities and processes towards building the capabilities to allow us to better serve our customers in the RD&E of C4I2WS technology and systems to fulfill Army's future requirements as they are being formulated under initiatives such as the Brigade Combat Team/Objective Force.

ADVANCED COMMAND, CONTROL AND COMMUNICATIONS (C3) SIMULATION & ANALYSIS USING EXTENDED AIR DEFENSE TESTBED (EADTB)

Robert W. Hunter, TRW Inc.
Steve D. Elliot, Decisive Analytics Corporation
213 Wynn Drive
Huntsville, Alabama 35905
bob.hunter@trw.com

KEYWORDS
Command, Control & Communications Analyses
Extended Air Defense TestBed
Joint Data Network
Military

ABSTRACT

This paper presents a brief overview of the EADTB simulation and discusses one example of its usage focusing upon C3 analyses. The major characteristics of EADTB are described, along with the unique features that make it well suited for simulation and analysis of C3 systems. Some discussion is also given of how scenario elements interact within the simulation.

A brief description is given of how EADTB has and is being used to study C3 issues related to the Joint Data Network (JDN). These studies have already identified several areas where MilStd-6016 needs to be enhanced, clarified or corrected. MilStd-6016 is the Tactical Digital Information Link (TADIL) J message standard that governs the JDN. This has highlighted the importance of the need for the Simulation Based Acquisition process and use of EADTB to verify and test decision making processes to assure that they will be both robust and flexible. Robust: so that minor errors, inconsistencies and omissions in the data don't cause catastrophic C3 failure. Flexible: so that as the battlefield situation unfolds, a C3 process reacts to it and can overcome prior decisions that may have been erroneous.

INTRODUCTION

Real world military C3 processes must rely on information that is very often inaccurate, imperfect, and incomplete. Furthermore, the available data upon which decisions are based may vary among the different sites making decisions, and this can give rise to conflicting decisions. In addition, these C3 processes must rely on communication networks for the transmission and reception of information that they need in order to fight effectively. Limited bandwidth and high loads for these networks can introduce finite and significant delays for the flow of information among battlefield entities. This accumulation of information errors, discrepancies and staleness has been described as significantly contributing to the "fog of war".

To make meaningful simulation assessments of C3 processes, this "fog of war" must be modeled accurately because it is a key attribute of the joint service warfighter environment. This means that the data being used to support decisions at each site must be explicitly modeled as well as the characteristics of the networks used for distribution of decisions that are made and data that is sent. Once these data and their distribution are modeled, the decision logic that operates on these data must also be accurately represented.

EXTENDED AIR DEFENSE TESTBED

The EADTB is a simulation system ideally suited for studying the performance and issues associated with C3 systems. It is a large, variable fidelity simulation system for warfare analysis, and has some unique features that make it particularly suitable for C3 analyses, as will be described later in this paper.

The EADTB has been developed by an integrated TRW/Raytheon (formerly Hughes Aircraft Company) team for the Testbed Product Office of the U.S. Army Space and Missile Defense Command, and the Ballistic Missile Defense Organization. Raytheon has overall program management responsibility, while TRW is responsible for software development. Development began in September 1989 and continues today with one or two major software releases each year (the current version is 4.4.2). These releases add new features and capabilities requested by the Government and the system's users.

As an event-stepped, constructive simulation that can be run in real-time or non-real-time, in either an interactive or a batch mode of operation, the EADTB is a complete simulation system for experiment preparation, execution, display, analysis, reporting, and exchange. The model algorithms are general-purpose and configured by input data. The performance of simulated entities is data-driven, and the experiment logic used by each simulated entity is driven by "rulesets." Furthermore, the EADTB provides a highly flexible modeling environment. This allows users to choose the level of detail/fidelity for the characteristics of each simulated entity. These characteristics include physical attributes, plus decision making, sensory, and communication capabilities. In addition, entities may be aggregated at whatever level is appropriate for the study being conducted. This allows the analysis of detailed one-on-one/single engagement scenarios, as well as larger force-on-force/theater/global conflicts. The modeling scope of the EADTB ranges from land and sea, to air- and space-based entities.

The EADTB Modeling Paradigm

EADTB's modeling paradigm is an object-based architecture where each entity in a scenario is comprised of building blocks. There are four types of building blocks that may be used to describe an entity:

- *Platform* — describing physical attributes and capabilities;
- *Thinker* — describing decision making capability and logic;
- *Sensor* — defining sense capabilities (optional);
- *Communication* — defining communication capabilities (optional).

Each entity is associated with only one *platform* (although a platform may support other entities), however, it may have multiple *thinker*, *sensor*, or *communication* components, depending on the level of detail required. All of the building block components of an entity are affected by the simulated environment, including weather factors, that they are in. Figure 1 is a pictorial representation of a simulated Theater High Altitude Area Defense (THAAD) Tactical Operations Center (TOC) with a THAAD radar that is detecting a Tactical Ballistic Missile (TBM). The THAAD TOC in this example, is a platform that has a single thinker component, two communication components, and no sensor components. One of the communication components is used to communicate with external non-THAAD entities, while the other is used to talk to the THAAD radar. The THAAD radar is a platform that has one thinker, one communication, and one sensor component. The TBM is a relatively simple entity that has only a platform and a single thinker component.

- The complete set of logical rules that the entity will use to act and react;
- User-defined and written using a simplified programming language that is interpreted at runtime;
- Able to utilize up to 1,258 predefined callable procedures/subroutines to perform a wide variety of functions;
- Written and modified at the user's discretion without requiring any source code changes to the EADTB.

Thus, the EADTB ruleset is a very flexible way to represent Battle Management, Command, Control & Communications (BMC3) logic within the simulation.

For a C3 entity being modeled, the ruleset is where all of the stimulus/response logic for messages are implemented. The ruleset also contains the controlling logic and interfaces to the platform, sensor, and communications components. This includes the representation of tracking filters, threat evaluation, engagement logic, cueing, resource management, guidance and control, etc. The ruleset specifies the exact processing to be done when a certain message is received, which data items in the message to utilize, how these items are to be interpreted, and what they are to be used for. The ruleset also defines the sequence of events that can cause a certain message to be sent out. This definition includes the events that trigger the sending of the message, and gives values to the data items in the message, identifies who the message is to be sent to, and when it should be sent. This provides a way to implement the detailed transmit-and-receive rules for messages as defined in various MilStds and the C3 system-specific requirements as defined in their individual requirements documents. The ruleset for a thinker is user-defined, so the user can modify the ruleset whenever needed to add additional message processing logic or investigate

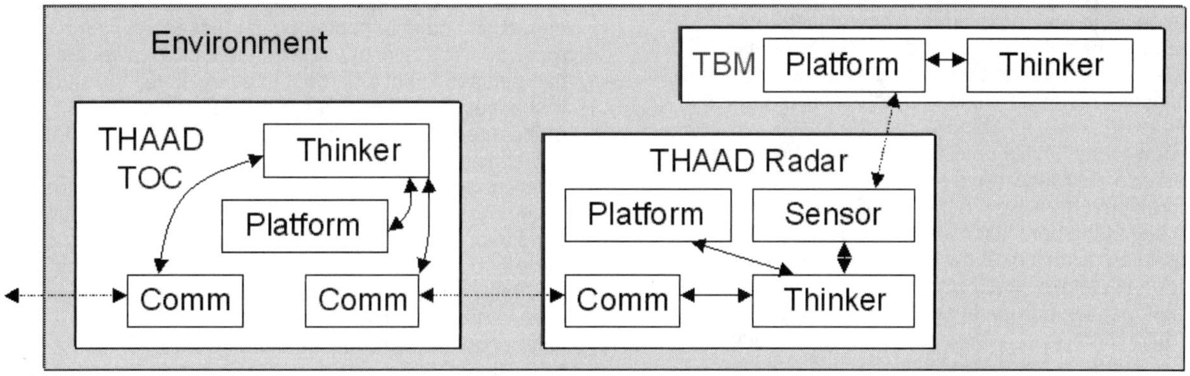

Figure 1. Example of EADTB Object-Based Modeling Architecture

EADTB Rulesets

One of the unique characteristics of EADTB is that the actions and reactions of every entity in a scenario are determined by the "ruleset" of the thinker for that entity. A ruleset is:

alternative transmit/receive rules. This is a particularly important characteristic for modeling the usage of a communication network by a variety of battlefield systems that may be connected to it. It allows the interoperability of these systems to be simulated, evaluated, and studied for possible improvement areas. The EADTB ruleset construct provides a powerful way to simulate the usage of the communication networks by different weapon systems, and the effects of the networks on weapon system actions and performance.

Modeling Imperfect Perception

Real-world BMC3 processes must rely on information that is inaccurate, imperfect, and incomplete. The data upon which decisions are based may vary among the different sites where decisions are made. There is also a finite delivery time for the flow of information among battlefield entities. Real-world entities must rely on communication networks for the transmission and reception of information that they need in order to fight effectively. Thus, the attributes of the problem being studied must be preserved in the simulation being used to support the analysis. In other words, the data being used to support decisions must be explicitly modeled, as well as the distribution of the data, and the distribution of the decisions made. The EADTB software and data architecture are fully support these modeling objectives.

A second unique characteristic of the EADTB is that the thinker for each entity in a scenario, has its own set of perception data that is separate and distinct from the perception data held by every other thinker. This perception data is based only on what has been perceived using sensors or received in a message. An entity does not have access to truth data about other entities in the scenario. This means that the actions and decisions made by an entity are based solely on its locally held perception data and the rules embodied in its ruleset. This allows direct modeling of the data being used to support decisions by each entity. For example, if an EADTB thinker is depending on receiving a message to obtain a key piece of data, and the message is not received, then the data is not known and the ruleset decision is either wrong or not made at all. If the message arrives late, the ruleset decision may have already been made with stale/erroneous data, or the decision may be delayed. If an EADTB thinker is depending on a simulated sensor to report incoming hostile objects, and the sensor does not resolve closely-spaced objects, then the thinker will not know how many hostile objects are approaching. This same sensor will also have associated with it certain measurement errors, so the thinker will not know exactly where any of the detected objects are located. These effects, in combination, show that the separate perception data for each thinker well represents the imperfect, aged data that real weapon systems must rely upon in order to carry out their mission. This partitioning of truth data from perceived data allows a simulation of the "fog of war" that exists during real conflicts, and even during training exercises.

This feature of separate perception data for each thinker is augmented by the EADTB's explicit representation of the communications networks being studied. Real-world network topology, complete with relays, gateways, line-of-sight restrictions, range restrictions, susceptibility to jamming, message error rates, and so forth, can all be modeled. In addition, the network resources assigned to each network participant, and the performance of the radio equipment are included in the model.

In summary, it can be seen that the EADTB's capabilities provide an accurate representation of real-world C3 systems, both from a communications standpoint, and from the standpoint of how they impact the effectiveness of the battlefield systems in carrying out their missions. Furthermore, it allows the interoperability of these C3 systems to be simulated, evaluated, and studied for possible improvement areas. The success of this modeling approach is due to the following factors:

- Representation of all key aspects of the problem;
- The ruleset construct provides a powerful way to simulate the usage of the communication networks by different C3 systems, and the effects of these C3 systems on weapon system actions and performance;
- Separate perception data for each thinker to model the imperfect, aged data that real weapon systems must rely upon, in order to carry out their mission;
- Partitioning of truth data from perceived data allows a simulation of the "fog of war";
- Explicit representation of the data upon which decisions are based, as well as the communication systems that are used for distribution of such data and decisions.

Interactions of Scenario Elements

Figure 2 provides an overview of how different scenario elements interact within the EADTB, and how these interactions are used to build the perception data for a thinker. In this example, scenario element "A" has one or more thinker components where each has its own set of perception data. This perception data contains information about itself, perceptions of other scenario elements, and data contained in messages that it has received. The ruleset contains the logical rules that the thinker uses to act and react to every simulated situation that arises, and uses a set of pre-defined callable procedures, (called "symbols" within the EADTB), to carry out its actions/reactions. There are currently 1258 different symbols that a ruleset may access to perform a wide range of functions, and the release of each new version of the EADTB provides additional symbols to perform new functions that have been requested by simulation users. The thinker's ruleset uses symbols to access data from the scenario element's platform component, e.g. current location, heading, or fuel remaining. Other symbols are used to give instructions to the platform component to carry out a specific command, e.g. move to another location, or launch a missile.

In a similar way, the ruleset uses symbols to receive data from, or issue commands to, the sensor and communication components that are part of the scenario element. Sensor data includes track file reports, plot file reports, sensor resource information, status data, and so forth. Sensor commands include search commands, track

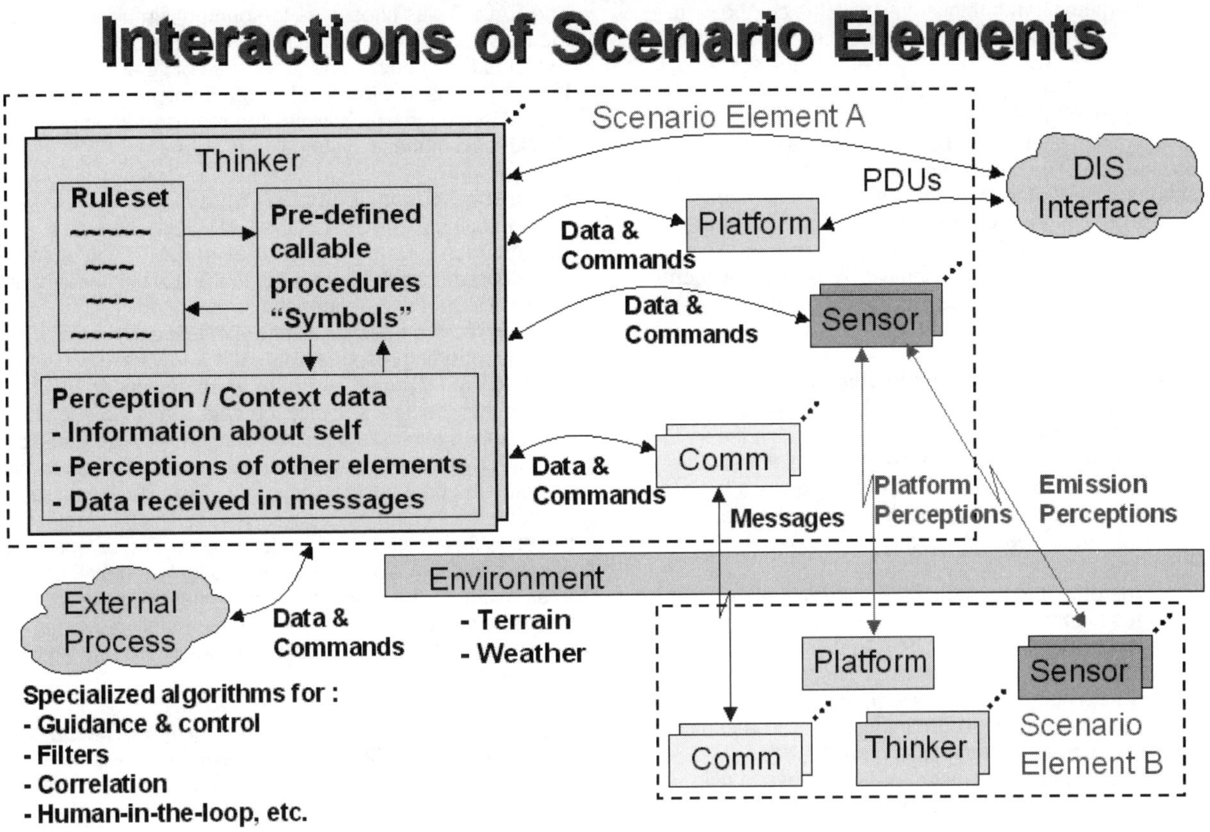

Figure 2. Interactions of Scenario Elements to Produce Perception Data for a Thinker

commands, detection confirmation commands, aiming commands, etc. Communications data includes the contents of messages, status of message queues, status of the communication component, and so forth. Communications commands include commands to send messages and manage the message queues. This process of interaction with the platform, sensor, and communication components, allows a thinker to build its knowledge base of perception data that is used for all of its decisions.

This example also shows a second scenario element, "B", that is perceived by "A". The sensor of A may sense the emissions of a sensor of B, and vice-versa. The sensor of A may detect the platform of B, because of the signature characteristics of the platform. In addition, a communication component of A may send and receive messages from a communication component on B. These interactions are all influenced by the terrain and weather environment that exists between the scenario elements. When these components interact, new data becomes available for the controlling thinker to access, thus increasing its perception knowledge base.

A scenario element in the EADTB also has two additional interfaces that it may use for interactions. The first is an interface with a Distributed Interactive Simulation (DIS) network. The DIS interface may interact directly with any thinker or platform component using DIS Protocol Data Units (PDUs). The PDUs allow simulated entities within the EADTB to perceive the state and actions of simulated entities on the DIS network and vice-versa, while also allowing both sets of entities to transmit messages, issue fire commands and issue detonation commands. The second additional interface is between a thinker and a computer process that is external to the EADTB processes. This external process interface provides the capability for a thinker to substitute or augment the predefined ruleset symbols with user provided algorithms. Examples of these algorithms include:

- A specialized guidance and control function for a guided missile;
- A specific correlation algorithm for a radar system tracker;
- A unique track filter for a tactical operations center;
- An operator console allowing ruleset decisions to be made by a human-in-the-loop.

The interfaces that a thinker has with the components that comprise its own scenario element, the interactions of these components with other components in the scenario, the ability to send and receive PDUs over the DIS interface, and the interface with an external process, all combine to allow a thinker to build its unique set of perception data. The careful modeling of these interactions and interfaces to ensure that a thinker does not have access to truth data about other scenario entities is a cornerstone of the EADTB modeling paradigm. This ensures that a thinker's perception data is based solely on perceptions and not other data that it should not have access to.

Data Available for C3 System Analysis

During scenario execution or playback, the EADTB provides utilities that allow the analyst to visualize the flow of messages on a simulated network. In addition to these message transmission visualization tools, there is a large volume of recorded data that the EADTB can provide for detailed post-run analysis of message traffic.

From the data that is available, it is possible to extract an enormous amount of information about how, when, and why a message traveled from point A to point B within the simulation. This allows a thorough analysis to be performed of the communications architecture itself, as well as the BMC2 behind the communications. These data can be sorted, filtered, merged, summarized, and tabulated in an endless number of possible ways to gain insight into the issues of interest for the analyst. Whether the focus of the analysis is broad or narrow, the data is available to support it. The context for some example analyses could be:

- The entire communications network
- A certain entity on the network
- The messages associated with a specific function
- The messages in a certain time window
- The messages associated with a certain threat
- A single message

The EADTB provides several standard and commercial off-the shelf (COTS) tools to assist in the data reduction effort, and the user may write his/her own analysis scripts/tools to meet specific data analysis requirements.

JOINT DATA NETWORK (JDN)

The JDN is the primary communications network that will be used by the elements of a Theater Missile Defense (TMD) architecture to exchange surveillance, engagement, and status data during a war. Like all communications networks, the JDN has a limited bandwidth and care must be taken to limit and control the data flow in order not to overload the network and introduce message delays which would degrade the quality of the data content. For the last three years, the TMD System Engineering and Integration (SE&I) Contractor has been tasked with analyzing the JDN in order to verify that the network will support the planned TMD architecture when fielded over the next ten years. The EADTB was chosen as the primary simulation tool for the detailed analysis of the JDN in the full TMD Family of Systems (FoS) environment because of its ability to model these systems at a low level of detail and because of its ruleset language which allows the representation of the full BMC3 logic of these systems.

Reporting Responsibility (R2) Study

Modeling of the JDN in the EADTB began with a Ballistic Missile Defense Organization (BMDO) sponsored study of reporting responsibility on the JDN in January of 1998. MilStd-6016 defines the content and transmit/receive rules for all of the messages on the JDN, and the reporting responsibility (also known as "R squared", or R2) rules. R2 rules were developed to assure that the best surveillance data is available to all units, and to minimize the surveillance message traffic on the JDN by restricting reports on any specific target to the unit with the best track quality (TQ). This TQ is calculated for each track using a simple equation, which combines the effects of position and velocity error. The objective of this first BMDO EADTB study was to look at how these R2 rules might work in a theater environment composed of various elements of the TMD FoS by modeling them in detail in EADTB using the MilStd-6016 as the reference.

The JDN (also referred to as TADIL-J) is a communications system that is used for both Theater Ballistic Missiles (TBMs) and air-breathing threat data. The EADTB JDN R2 Study was limited to the study of TBMs only. The JDN is used in general to link battalions within the same service, and to link the various service elements together. Surveillance data is reported periodically on the JDN using three types of messages: TBM Track Reports, Launch And Impact Point Reports, and the TBM Drop Track messages. The TBM Track Report is used primarily for sensor cueing and situational awareness, while the Launch And Impact Point Report is generally used to determine whether defended assets are threatened. The TBM Drop Track message is used to terminate reporting on targets that have been killed or that have impacted the ground. The EADTB configuration used for the JDN R2 Study modeled these messages and others at a detail level not attempted previously in a digital simulation that represents all of the major FoS elements.

A complex set of EADTB ruleset code and data called the "JDN Thinker" was developed by the Joint National Test Facility (JNTF) to model all of the JDN rules and message processing defined in MilStd 6016. This thinker was installed on a number of service-developed representations of defense elements in EADTB. This provided a theater architecture where each element had a common representation of the JDN processing rules provided by MilStd-6016. Scenarios were created in the EADTB with combinations of defense elements linked into a JDN network that considered both physical modeling of the RF connectivity of the elements, and the constraints of bandwidth. Most of the fields in the messages were modeled in detail and the timing and processing of messages were consistent with all R2 and transmit/receive rules in the MilStd.

The analysis for the JDN R2 Study was intended specifically to wring out the defense system representations, the JDN Thinker, and the communications model in the basic EADTB framework. This was done by concentrating on two of the most important system elements (PATRIOT and AEGIS lower tier), and deploying them in various scenarios made up of two or more batteries of PATRIOT only, AEGIS only, and a joint deployment. Different deployment geometries and minor changes to attenuate radar signals were used to provide various circumstances where R2 would shift from one element to another because of changes in Track Quality. Various sized threats were run against the different deployments to stimulate different message sequences and timing. For each scenario, extensive post processing was used to extract the detailed timing and sequence data for all of the JDN messages being exchanged by the elements. In this way, the JDN Thinker was eventually tested extensively enough to assure us that it represented all of the rules from MilStd-6016. From that point, it was possible to evaluate the performance of the JDN R2 rules in a simulated theater environment and determine where corrections and clarifications to the rules were required.

The EADTB JDN R2 Study took place over a period of six months and was a collaborative effort amongst the TMD SE&I, the Systems Analysis Contract (SAC), the service developers of the defense elements, the JNTF, the Testbed Product Office (TPO), and the EADTB development contract. The results and conclusions were briefed to various BMDO department heads in the summer of 1998. The analysis performed on the JDN Study resulted in the submission of fifteen separate Interface Change Proposals (ICPs) to the organizational working group that controls the MilStd-6016 document to clarify and correct the wording. These ICPs were intended to clarify the drop track and lost track rules, establish rules on setting time and state in TBM track messages, clarify the data update request rules, correct the rules for fields in engagement status messages, and clarify various terms and definitions.

Other C3 Studies

Following the successful completion of the EADTB JDN R2 Study, two other major studies using EADTB have been taken on by the TMD SE&I. The first was in early 1999 and was an analysis supporting the development and release of a Systems Requirements Document (SRD), and the second (which is still on-going) is an EADTB study to support the development of a JDN System Performance Specification (SPS). The SRD Study resulted in a dramatic improvement in the performance fidelity of the various defense system models, and set the stage for various other BMDO-sponsored studies. The SPS Study was kicked off in Sept/99 and required several enhancements to the EADTB framework in order to perform the study. These enhancements included the ability to use real correlation algorithms in the rulesets using an external process (coded in C++) and the addition of Time Slot Reallocation (TSR) to the communications model. The SPS Study requires that the EADTB model the JDN in enough detail to evaluate the effect of timing and synchronization errors, sensor registration, data registration, and correlation performance on the overall effectiveness of the network. Some preliminary results should be available from this study be the end of summer 2000.

CONCLUSIONS

The EADTB has been described, along with its object-based modeling paradigm and the way that entities interact within the simulation. It has been shown that the EADTB is ideally suited for studying the performance and issues associated with C3 systems because of its explicit modeling of the perception data for each simulated entity, and the separation of this perceived data from the truth data. This explicit representation of the data upon which decisions are based, as well as the communication systems that are used for distribution of such data and decisions, allow the "fog of war" to be accurately modeled. The EADTB is also well-suited for studies of C3 systems because the rulesets for each entity in a scenario allow a thorough and detailed representation of the message processing logic, transmit rules, and receive rules for each message that is modeled.

There is an extensive amount of data available from the EADTB to support the analytical process, both during and after scenario execution. This data can provide valuable insights into the performance and function of the C3 systems being studied, and can be manipulated in a variety of ways to produce whatever view of the data is required.

An overview was provided of the JDN and the interest of the BMDO in studying it. In particular, the JDN Reporting Responsibility study was described, along with a synopsis of the major findings that came from it. These findings would not have been possible without the detailed simulation capabilities of the EADTB. Finally some ongoing BMDO sponsored efforts to analyze JDN issues were outlined. These studies demonstrate the utility of the EADTB to support detailed analyses of JDN related issues.

In summary, it was shown that the capabilities of the EADTB allow an accurate representation of real-world C3 systems, both from a communications standpoint, and from the standpoint of how they impact the effectiveness of other battlefield systems in carrying out their missions. Furthermore, it allows the interoperability of these systems to be simulated, evaluated, and studied for possible improvement areas.

A COMPREHENSIVE SIMULATION PLATFORM FOR INTRUSION DETECTION IN DISTRIBUTED SYSTEMS

K. Mantha, R. Chinchani & S. Upadhyaya
Department of Computer Science & Engineering
State University of New York at Buffalo
Buffalo, New York 14260
shambhu@cse.buffalo.edu

K. Kwiat
Air Force Research Laboratory
525 Brooks Road
Rome, New York 13441
kwiatk@rl.af.mil

KEYWORDS

Computer security, distributed systems, intrusion detection, simulation

ABSTRACT

This paper[1] describes the simulation of an attack recognition system in a distributed environment. The underlying technique of attack recognition is based on assertion checking. An auxiliary process called watchdog queries the users for a scope-file, from which an assertable plan called Sprint plan is generated. The sprint plan consists of carefully derived assertions, which forms the basis for attack monitoring. Two environments are simulated for the purpose of testing and evaluation of the intrusion detection system. First, a general academic environment with limited security restrictions is simulated. Second, a virtual banking environment with stringent security requirements is simulated. Different attack scenarios are simulated for the purpose of testing the recognition system.

1 INTRODUCTION

As today's commercial applications are becoming more and more distributed, they also become vulnerable to attacks across the network. This difficulty raises the need for concurrent intrusion/anomaly detection. Though a variety of techniques exist, the detection latency of these systems remains high, since most of them rely on audit trail analysis as the base-line approach. Unfortunately intrusion detection schemes based on audit trail analysis do not offer much in terms of damage containment, as they are passive, after-the-fact solutions [1].

[1]The work was supported, in part, by the 1999 Summer Research Extension Program, AFOSR Contract F49629-93-C-0063

This paper describes the simulation of an on-line attack recognition system in a distributed environment. The underlying technique is described in detail in a previous paper [2]. In this scheme, prior to starting a session on a computer an auxiliary process called a watchdog first queries the users for a scope-file and then generates a table called Sprint plan. The sprint plan is composed of carefully derived assertions that can be used as a basis for concurrent monitoring of user commands. The plan is general enough to allow a normal user to perform his task without much interference from the watchdog and is specific enough to detect intrusions both external and internal. The focus of current paper is the simulation of two environments for the purpose of testing and evaluating this intrusion detection system. First, a general academic environment with limited security restrictions is simulated. Second, a virtual banking environment with stringent security requirements is simulated. Different attack scenarios, both internal abuse and external attacks are simulated and tested.

Some background and related work are given in Section 2. An overview of the concurrent intrusion detection system is given in Section 3. Section 4 describes the implementation of the watchdog monitor. The simulation of the test environments is described in Section 5. Experiments and results are given in Section 6. The paper concludes with a brief discussion.

2 BACKGROUND

Intrusion detection is a critical phase of information survivability. A model for intrusion detection was first given by Denning [3], which uses audit trail analysis as a basis of detection. The existing intrusion detections systems (IDS) are frequently classified into misuse and anomaly detection models [4]. The anomaly detection approach is based on the idea that an attack on a system will be different from the normal activity and an intruder will exhibit a pattern of behavior different from the normal user [5]. In the misuse detection approach, the IDS watches for indications of specific, precisely representable activities of system abuse. The IDS includes a collection of known intrusion signatures, which are encapsulations of identifying characteristics of specific intrusion techniques. If a new attack comes in, the system is most likely to fail to detect it. USTAT is a Unix based real-time intrusion detection tool developed by Ilgun et al. [6]. It uses state transition analysis where penetration is identified as a sequence of state changes from a known initial state to a final compromised state. Several real-time network-monitoring tools have been developed over the past years. NADIR [7] is a Network Anomaly Detector and Intrusion Report tool. DIDS [8] is Distributed Intrusion Detection System, which looks and correlates multiple machine connections to the initial login. The project called EMERALD (Event Monitoring Enabling Response to Anomalous Live Disturbances) [9] aims at developing a distributed monitoring scheme, which uses a combination of signature engine and profiler engine within the monitor. The research team at Purdue is developing an adaptive network monitoring technique using autonomous agents [10].

3 OVERVIEW of CIDS

Our concurrent intrusion detection system (CIDS) uses verifiable assertions similar to the notion of control flow checking in fault tolerance [11], [12]. In this scheme, the user starts a session on a computer in a standard way by logging in. The system's watchdog then queries the user for a session-scope. This is the summary of the intended system usage in that particular session. Once the scope-file is submitted, the user is allowed to continue with his session. Before the user starts his session the watchdog does the monitoring of the user. This involves the translation of the scope-file into a sprint (Signature Powered Reasonable Instruction Table) plan. This gives a mechanism for monitoring the user behavior. When the user is in session, the watchdog monitors the user commands and checks if the command is the one he originally intended to execute. Any significant deviation from the plan is an indication of potential intrusion. Figure 1 shows the basic block diagram of the CIDS.

To implement this scheme in a distributed computing environment, a watchdog process is set up for each user on a given node. However, the process remains dormant until a user starts a session on a node. These watchdogs are essentially instances of the same process, monitoring the various sessions. They remain restricted to local nodes, but once operational interact with a master watchdog which is responsible for the coordinated distributed system monitoring. Figure 2 shows the overall architecture for the network of computers consisting N nodes and a file server.

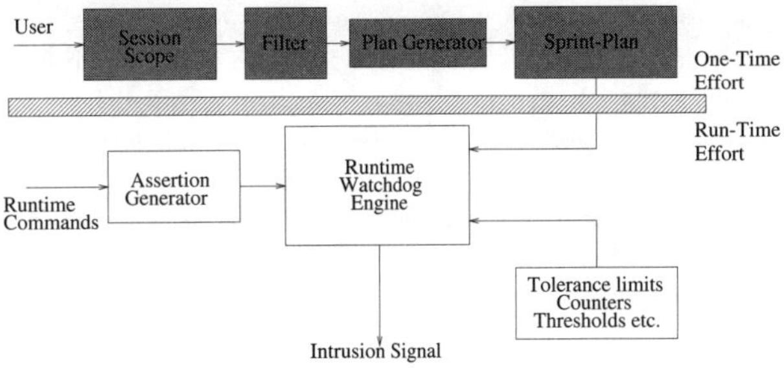

Figure 1. Flow Diagram of CIDS

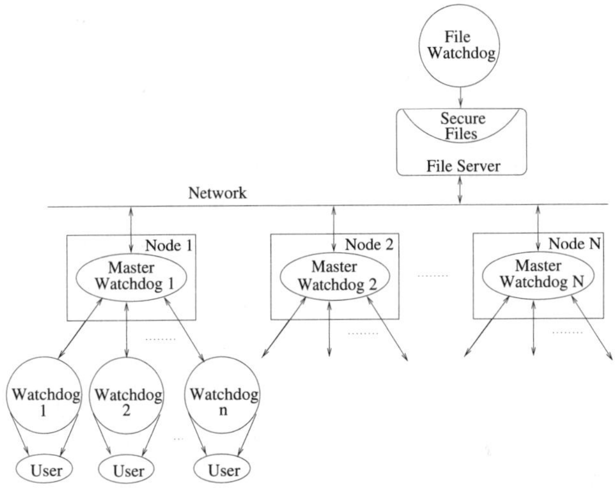

Figure 2. Architecture of Distributed CIDS

Each local area network has a separate watchdog called a file watchdog. The function of the file watchdog is to monitor access to secure files on the file server as shown in the figure.

4 IMPLEMENTATION OF CIDS

The session-scope can be fed into the system in a variety of ways. We use a graphical user interface (GUI) to simplify the process of the user input. With the help of the GUI a few simple checks are done while logging into the system. Figure 3 shows the flowchart of the steps taken by the watchdog when the user logs in. If the login is valid, the watchdog queries the user about the application the user is going to work in that particular session. Based on the application a preselected list of inputs containing the system resources available for the user is provided in a GUI, where the user can select the scope of the session. The watchdog queries the user about his multiple login intent. If the user wishes to open multiple sessions, a list of all the hosts a user can connect to in the network is generated. The scope file thus obtained is given to a converter, which is built into the watchdog. The converter converts the scope-file into a sprint plan consisting of verifiable assertions. A verifiable assertion is a quadruple of the form: *(Subject, Action, Object, Period)* where *subject* is a user (along with additional identifiers such as terminal ID, IP address etc.), *action* is an operation performed by the subject such as login, logout, read, execute and *object* is a receptor of actions such as files, programs, messages, records, terminals, printers etc. A temporal characteristic called *period* signifies the time interval for the usage of a given user command. A formatter formats this spring plan into a format that can be used for comparison.

It is possible that a user's scope exceeds the preselected system resources input list and so the watchdog provides the user with a text area, where the user can type his intent. This text is sent to an intelligent and learning software agent to convert it into the sprint plan. The architecture of this agent is shown in Figure 4.

The watchdog sends the user-defined text to the software agent using the watchdog/agent interface. This is then passed on to a parser, which parses the text looking for known keywords. These are then sent to the execution module. The job of the execution module is to schedule the inputs coming from individual watchdogs as there is one software agent per master watchdog even though there is one watchdog per user, to reduce the overhead on the system. The execution module then looks into the agent database to generate the appropriate mapping for the keywords. If it is not available in the database then it tries to do its job by communicating with other agents on the network doing similar work. The communication between the agents is achieved using KQML (Knowledge Query and Manipulation Language), a protocol that extends these agents to share their knowledge and work towards cooperative problem solving. This is achieved using the agent/agent interface. Once the mapping is done, it is formatted into the sprint plan.

Once the one-time monitoring effort is complete i.e., the sprint plan is generated, the user is allowed to proceed with his normal operation. Every user activity on the system is converted to an atomic operation by the watchdog's preprocessor. The output of the preprocessor is similar to the sprint plan, and is used by the watchdog for comparison with the actual sprint plan. Site-specific details, if any, are also given to the comparator. Any violation is reported to the master watchdog. The architecture of the monitor/comparator unit is shown in

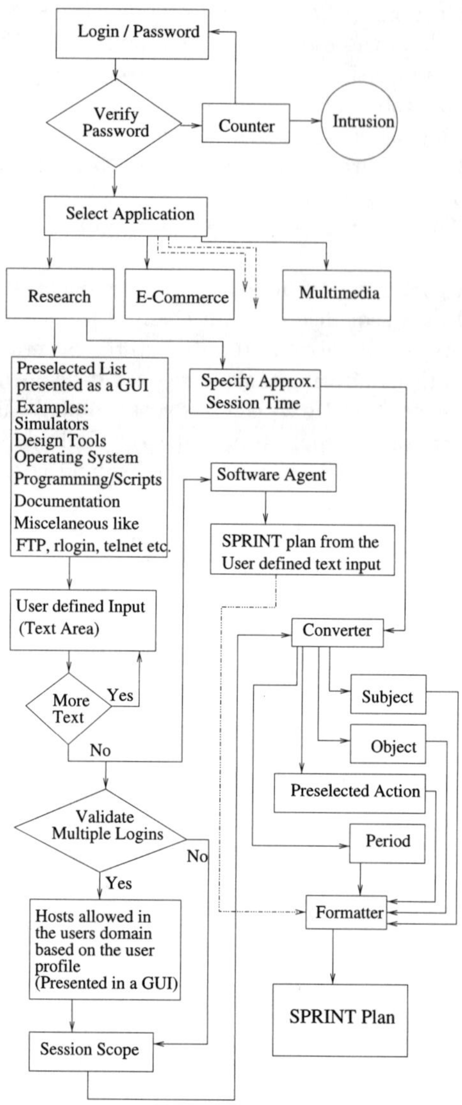

Figure 3. Flowchart of Sprint Plan Generation

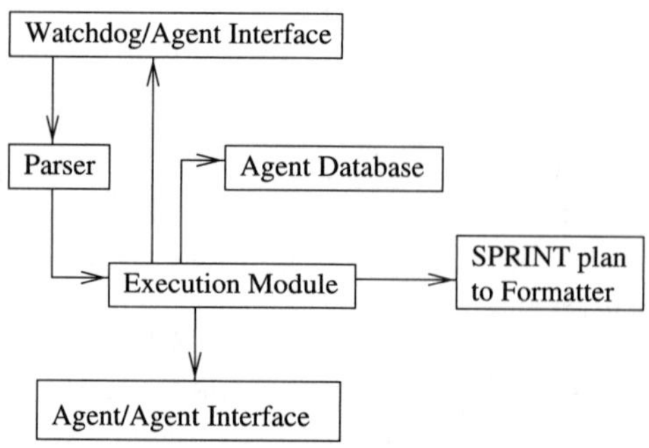

Figure 4. Software Agent Architecture

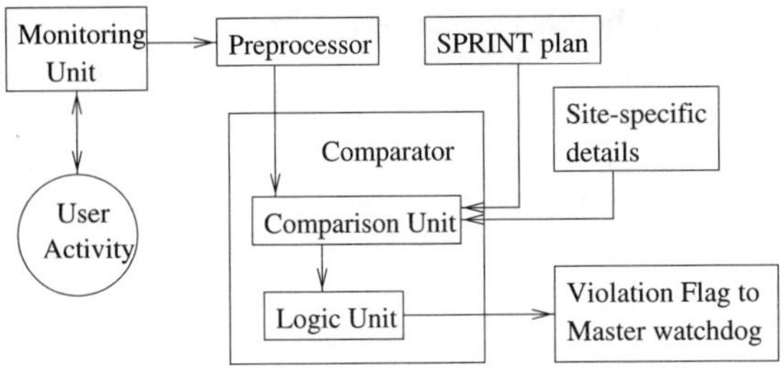

Figure 5. Monitor/Comparator Unit

Figure 5.

The comparator consists of a comparison unit and a logic unit. The comparison unit does all the comparisons and if there is a mismatch then it is passed to the logical unit, which determines the violation flag level, by which the counters are to be raised. For instance, if the user selects a Unix system and types "*I want to work on my research paper*", then the software agent resolves the text into a set of atomic operations. In this case, these atomic operations can be treated as commands that are typed at the Unix prompt. If the agent knows that this particular user uses LaTeX software, the output from the agent will be *latex#bibtex#slitex#ispell#text-editor*. This is based on the fact that the user will use a text-editor to type in the contents of the paper, and later will invoke the LaTeX software by typing the command latex at the Unix prompt. If he uses latex then he probably will use bibtex and so on. The # here is just a separator between different commands.

5 TEST ENVIRONMENTS

We chose two distinctive test environments for simulation. The first one is a student/faculty user environment in a university setting with limited security constraints. The second one is a virtual banking environment with stringent security requirements.

5.1 Simulating a University Environment

The basic architecture is client-server based. Such a setup allows us to derive some test cases from the published descriptions of well known attacks and in developing site-specific test cases based on the security policy. It also helps us to consider both sequential and concurrent intrusions. In a sequential intrusion, a single person issues a single sequence of commands from a single terminal or a workstation window. In concurrent intrusion, one or more intruders issue sequences of commands from several terminals, computers or windows. The command sequences work cooperatively to carry out an attack. For example an intruder can open multiple windows on a workstation and connect to a target computer from each window and try to distribute the suspicious behavior among them. The platform allows us to simulate basic sessions such as telnet, ftp etc. Synchronization can be achieved which lets us specify a fixed execution order of events.

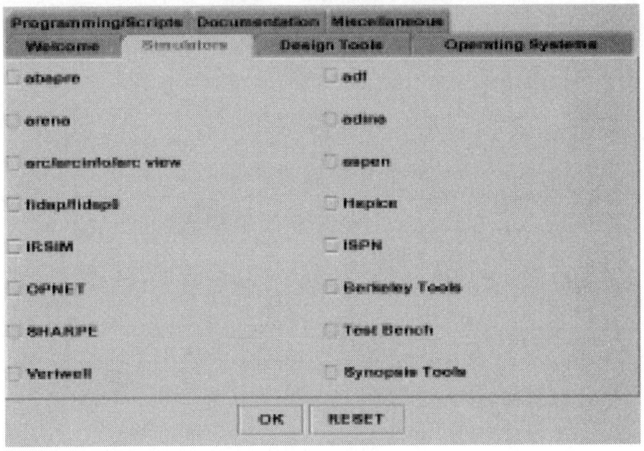

Figure 6. Choice of Simulators on a System

When the student/faculty user logs in with a userid/password submission, password verification is done first. If the user is authenticated to login he will be provided with a series of GUI windows to specify the scope of the session. The user selects the application he is going to work on. If, say, the user selects Research as the application, the user is provided with a preselected input list containing various categories such as simulators, design tools, operating systems, programming languages, scripts, documentation and miscellaneous items such as ftp, rlogin etc. Figure 6 shows the screen image of the GUI illustrating the simulator choices.

The user just needs to check the tasks he intends to perform. Once this is done the watchdog queries the user if he intends to perform any other activities that are not present in the predetermined list. The user is also queried if he intends to open multiple sessions.

The various components of the sprint plan (not shown) are combined together by a formatter to obtain the final sprint plan. Figure 7 shows a run-time monitoring setup for a 1-user, 2-hosts system on a single server.

The sprint plan generated for the user is stored at a secure location on the server. As soon as the user logs in to a host, the watchdog checks to see if there is a sprint plan already existing for the user, if there is none, it generates a new one. If a sprint plan already exists, the user is allowed to proceed with his normal activity. The watchdog continuously monitors the user and compares

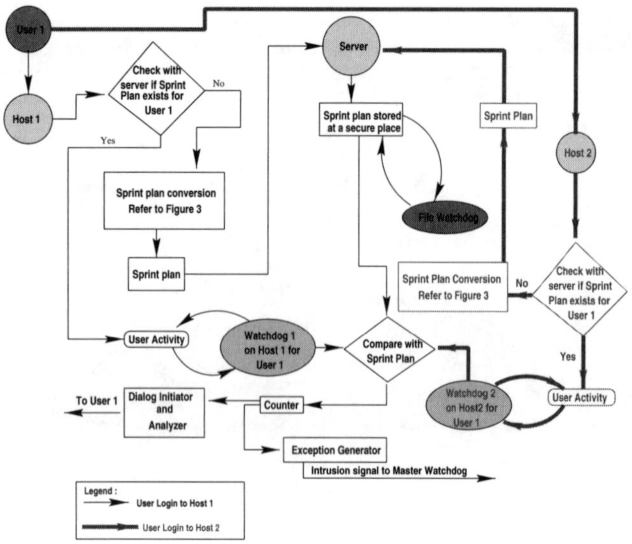

Figure 7. Run-time Monitoring Setup

it with the sprint plan.

5.2 Virtual Banking Test Environment

The second test platform is a virtual banking environment with stringent security requirements. The main focus here is on the employees in the bank who are the users of the banking software. Misuse intrusions can be tested in detail here. The employees in a bank might have access to sensitive data and there is always a possibility of misusing privileges. The environment supports multiple banks with multiple accounts, with multiple access to all the accounts. The virtual banking system can be accessed by a wide variety of employees starting from the president of the bank to the teller in a bank. A session-scope is provided by the employees who login to the system with an authenticated userid and password with the help of a GUI. Once the user submits his scope file, the watchdog converts it into a sprint plan. Once this conversion is complete, the user gets the access to the bank system.

The employees can work in different areas of the banking system such as bank operations, business banking, credit/lending division, e-commerce, investment banking, monitoring etc. If the user is working in the bank operations division then some of the features provided to the employee are creating new accounts, opening existing accounts etc. It also supports a variety of accounts such as checking, savings, loan, mortgage, etc. The system allows the user to do things such as profitability analysis, generate reports etc. The system contains two databases, which the user can access. A transfer tool is provided for transferring balances for one account to another and from one database to another.

The watchdog continuously monitors the user activity in the system. The file watchdog is built into the systems database, which monitors the database accesses and communicates with the master watchdog to report any illegal transactions or access violations. The system is written in Java [13] and uses SQL queries to query the database. The database is custom made and is also implemented in Java. JDBC has been used for the connectivity between the bank system and the bank database. All the GUI components are light-weight, built using JFC Swing [14].

6 EXPERIMENTAL RESULTS

We report the results of our simulation on the university environment only. The metrics used are detection coverage and performance.

There is usually no simple procedure to identify appropriate test cases for an intrusion detection system. A variety of intrusion scenarios are considered based on some common practices of system usage. These scenarios are grouped into four categories, viz., one-user without multiple logins, one-user with multiple logins, multiple users without multiple logins and multiple users with multiple logins. Two set of experiments are performed in each of these categories, first with the worst case, where a user selects all the entities provided in the session-scope GUI by the watchdog and the second where a user selects only a few entities. The tests are performed by treating the logins as four different cases, with up to two users at a given time. The first case is where both logins are legitimate. In the second case, the first login is from a legitimate user and the second login is from an intruder. In the third case, the first login is from the intruder and the second login is from the user and finally the fourth case where both logins are from intruders.

Some of the selections of the intrusive activity simulated are transferring the /etc/passwd file from one host to another, password-cracking by comparing the entries in the /etc/passwd file to entries in another file, using a dictionary file for the same, exploiting the vulnerabilities such as rdist. The system is able to detect all the intrusive activities and terminate the connection for the logins of intrusive users except in the worst case scenarios of one-user with multiple logins and multiple users with multiple logins, where a small number of intrusive activities was not detected. The system has also generated a few false positives, flagging an intrusion when normal user activity is taking place. This happens when the user selects only a few entities from the session-scope.

Since Java is used for implementation, moderate impact on system performance is expected. When new connections are made or more users login, the system load increases. However, this increase is only marginal because there is no need to maintain any large data structures for each user or connection. The main server on which CIDS is running is a Sun Ultra Enterprise 450 Model 4400 and the clients are Sun Ultra 5's running Solaris 2.7.

A normal user in a university environment is assumed to have about six to eight processes running on the system at a given time. There is one watchdog dedicated for each user which makes it one more process per user on the system. This watchdog process does not use many run-time resources and hence may not become an overhead to the system.

In order to quantify the overhead of the CIDS, we eliminated all unrelated activities in the test environment, started the CIDS and allowed the users to login. We analyzed the average load per minute (no. of jobs in the run queue on Unix) and the storage overhead in kB against the number of users on the system. At this particular stage of implementation without much optimization, the operation is very stable for about 15 users. The load on the system tends to increase as the number of monitored users increases beyond 15. The storage overhead (325 kB for a single user) increases at a constant rate with the number of users. When the session-scope is large, the watchdog maps it to a huge sprint plan. The storage used by the CIDS in our study corresponds to the worst case scenario where a user selects all the entities from the session-scope provided by the watchdog in a GUI.

7 CONCLUSION

The concurrent intrusion detection prototype described in this paper is in its preliminary stage and the experiments reported are very basic. Our simulation shows that on-line intrusion detection using assertion checking is feasible, that is, low performance overhead and good detection coverage. This approach is an alternative to conventional audit trail analysis based intrusion detection schemes.

More detailed experiments with complex intrusion scenarios are planned. This requires further enhancements to the sprint plan generation and consideration of structural and temporal sequence checking. Similar experiments will also be conducted on the virtual banking application.

References

[1] J. Feldman, J. Giordano, and J. Palmer, "Information survivability at Rome laboratory," *1997 IEEE Information Survivability Workshop*, 1997.

[2] S. Upadhyaya and K. Kwiat, "A distributed concurrent intrusion detection scheme based on assertions," *SCS Int. Symp. on Perf. Eval. of Comput.and Telecom. Systems*, pp. 369–376, July 1999.

[3] D. Denning, "An intrusion-detection model," *IEEE Transactions on Software Engineering*, vol. SE-13, pp. 222–232, February 1987.

[4] S. Kumar and E. Spafford, "A pattern matching model for misuse intrusion detection," *Proceedings of the 17th National Computer Security Conf.*, pp. 11–21, October 1994.

[5] H. Javitz and A. Valdes, "The sri ides statistical anamoly detector," *Proc., IEEE Symp. on Research in Security and Privacy*, pp. 316–371, May 1991.

[6] K. Ilgun, R. Kemmerer, and P. Porras, "State transition analysis: A rule-based intrusion detection approach," *IEEE Trans. on Software Eng.*, vol. 21, pp. 181–199, March 1995.

[7] J. Hochberg, K. Jackson, C. Stallings, J. McClary, D. DuBois, and J. Ford, "NADIR: An automated system for detecting network intrusions and misuse," *Computers & Security*, vol. 12, pp. 253–248, May 1993.

[8] S. Snapp, S. Smaha, T. Grance, and D. Teal, "The DIDS Distributed intrusion detection system prototype," *USENIX, 1992 Technical Conference*, pp. 227–233, June 1992.

[9] P. Porras and P. Neumann, "EMERALD: Event monitoring enabling responses to anomalous live disturbances," *National Information Systems Security Conf.*, pp. 353–365, Oct. 1997.

[10] J. Balasubramaniyan, J. Omar, G. Fernandez, E. Spafford, and D. Zamboni, "An architecture for intrusion detection using autonomous agents," *Department of Computer Sciences, Purdue University, Coast TR 98-05*, 1998.

[11] M. Namjoo, "Techniques for concurrent testing of VLSI processor operation," *Proc. International Test Conference*, pp. 461–468, November 1982.

[12] S. Upadhyaya and B. Ramamurthy, "Concurrent process monitoring with no reference signatures," *IEEE Transactions on Computers*, vol. 43, pp. 475–480, Apr. 1994.

[13] P. Deitel and H. Deitel, *Java How to Program.* Prentice Hall, 1999.

[14] S. Pantham, *Pure JFC Swing.* SAMS, 1999.

Using Market Mechanisms to Simulate the Balancing of Supply and Demand for Fault-Tolerant Network Resources

Kevin Kwiat, Ph.D.
Air Force Research Laboratory
AFRL/IFGA
525 Brooks Rd.
Rome, NY 13441-4505
e-mail: kwiatk@rl.af.mil

Keywords: Market-Based Control, Replication, Economic Models, Fault Tolerance

Abstract

Economics, being the study of resource allocation problems, is sought to provide the answer to managing large-scale information systems. Market demand for resources will drive up the value of those resources given that they are in limited supply. Information, however, is an easily duplicated quantity in computers, but once the information is multiplied it must be judiciously placed within the network for it to be accessible. While indicating that limited network resources curtail repeated duplication of information, the value for information is not constant and changes with time. Increasing demand for some quantity of information strongly indicates that its value to the system is becoming more critical. Lack of demand indicates that there may be an oversupply. An approach to using market mechanism to address supply and demand fluctuations in the information domain is simulated in the context replicating critical information and reducing less relevant information in the dynamic allocation of network resources. This approach examines a market-based technique for generating replicas, maintaining consistency between generated between them, and using them to provide fault tolerance.

1 Introduction

In engineering, economics has always been a factor. Especially when resources are redundantly applied for the purpose of fault tolerance does the ensuing cost become more acute. Replicating a resource is a design consideration that takes into account the dependability gain from the expenditure made to allocate the necessary resources. Allocating computational resources for non-fault-tolerant applications have adopted economic models [1]. The use of such models has been largely based on mimicing a free-market economy. The phenomena they exhibit was described as early as 1776. It was then that Adam Smith in his *Wealth of Nations* recognized an individual pursuing his own self-interests inadvertently advances the public interest as if being led by "an invisible hand to promote an end which was no part of his intention."[2] Considerable motivation to using a market-based approach was provided in the middle of the 21st Century by John von Neumann (of computer fame) and Nobel Prize-winning economists Kenneth Arrow and Gerard Debreu. In a revolutionary proof they showed that under certain limited conditions there will always exist at least one set of prices that will *exactly* balance the supplies and demands of potentially millions of goods that may be sourced from many different regions, and produced and sold at different times [2]. The proof, however, is merely an existence one, and does not specify how the balance is achieved. Economic models have since been applied in the attempt to control a computer system's resources in a nearly optimal way. An early application [3] of a market-mechanism to managing information systems required users to bid for computer time as opposed to rigid allocation schemes that often left time allotments unexpended and the computer idle. With a competitive market-based approach even the most impoverished users had access to the machine when no one else wanted it. With the emergence of distributed systems, market-based mechanisms were applied to load-balancing of programs to increase the efficiency of multiple resources. Technology has now evolved to the point where it is realistic to support a simulated economy that is not merely confined to a small set of cooperating computer programs but scaled to a global information system. Given the immense size of the global network there are special problems associated with merely modeling it [4]. Therefore the need for an "invisible hand" to provide an autonomous way to allocate and deallocate the resources.

2 Supply and Demand as Replication Drivers

Determining the amount of redundancy to assign to a task is based on the tasks criticality; however, computational tasks generate information and the criticality of the information produced, in turn, determines the importance of the task. The value of the information is ultimately determined by the user, but how the user will use the information is paramount. The user may initiate some action based on the information, or use it to create new information Therefore, given the extent of networking there are vast possibilities to share information. Information from one source may be combined with that from another. Composing information yields additional information that may be of higher value than either of the individual sources can provide. Yet, the composition may be valueless if it lacked one of its components - regardless of how little *data* that component provides. The value of some information may not be known at the time the information was created, because it may be targeted to undergo some combination and that will elevate its value. This has important implications for replication: the degree of criticality of information sources cannot be statically defined. Thus considerable oscillations will occur primarily to adjustments in supply and demand [5].

3 Market Analogies

The potentially large geographic area that the distributed information system can span has made it analogous to the electric power grid[6]. The corresponding *information grid* formed of distributed systems has similar attributes: infrastructure for large-scale pooling of resources, dependable service requirements, consistency of service, and pervasiveness. The parallels between the two grids are also in the complexity of control. Now that the technical challenges of efficient generation of power and high-voltage transmission have been overcome, the technical challenge is managing and monitoring this system [6]. The information grid covers the concerted use of high-performance networking, computing, and advanced software resources. By creating markets and letting prices allocate the resources, the information management issue can be solved through an ongoing and on-line simulation of an economy that exhibits the same phenomena as a real one: it admits arbitrary scale, heterogeneity of resources, decentralized asynchronous operation, and tolerance of localized failures. These derived benefits are compelling and recent advances in computing and communications enable the serious contemplation of building computational markets to control critical information networks and the application services layered on top of them.

The recent deregulation of power markets serves as an analogy for the potential of market-based models for the information grid. It was reported in *The Wall Street Journal* that economists contend that opening electricity markets to competition will greatly reduce power outages [7]. Former monopolies now facing competition from independent power producers that can sell electricity through the power grid can no longer restrict the market's ability to use prices for controlling resource consumption. While possibly eliminating electric shortages in the power grid, an economic model for the corresponding information grid could also use prices to largely eliminate computational shortages. Without a mechanism such as prices to mediate allocation, the seemingly abundant resources of the information grid would become mostly inaccessible.

A more recent report in *The Wall Street Journal* shows a reversal from what was predicted earlier: because of deregulation the United States national power generation/delivery capability is now much less robust than it was ten years ago. A critical national commodity such as electricity went from a state where the infrastructure was relatively robust and dependable (although not the least expensive) to being much more fragile. This has been attributed to lack of a guaranteed profitable market in certain geographical areas. Resulting in the free market not providing the redundancy required for robustness in this vital commodity and newly established regional grid operators assuming responsibility for much larger areas than those formerly overseen by the former individual local utilities [8].

4 Fault Tolerance Models for Distributed Information Systems

This author attributes the previous anomaly in the electric grid to lack of a model that would accurately predict the result of deregulation. This inaccuracy resulted from lack of knowledge of the power network's organization. Therefore, adopting supply/demand models for computer networks and analogizing these networks with those of the electric grid, requires chosing network structures that are tractable to ensure that they can support the requirements for consistency and fault tolerance.

On such approach uses the local-area network (LAN) approach to computational distribution. Here services are aggregated into processors connected to a LAN. In this environment, replicated services are made consistent through broadcasting of data update commands. Tolerance of failed processors on the LAN is through majority voting. Lack of a single centralized voter in the LAN is due to the commensurate complexity of each processor. The voting itself is therefore distributed also among the processors hosting the replicated service. The current convention for distributed voting is to employ the two-phase commit protocol [9] where the participants first share their votes and then the majority result is committed to the user by one of the processors chosen to be the coordinator of the majority vote. Typically, the probability of coordinator failure during the committal phase is negligible; but when viewing processor failures as a direct result of cyber-attack, the two-phase commit protocol has been shown to be deficient [10]. This led to the use of an *interface module* in what is essentially a reversal of the two-phase commit protocol: there is a committal to the module first and then the processors vote. The interface module buffers the "pre-committal" and allows for any dissenting processor to decide if a new majority should be asserted to the module. This scheme has been shown to offer an increase in security and performance without loss in fault-coverage [11]. Simulation results show that the interface-module approach is adaptive to changes in replication levels within the LAN.

The supply/demand model would build upon the use of the interface module to allow it to adjust replication levels in response to localized changes in the perceived levels of criticality of the services within the LAN. The decision to adjust supply levels will most likely reside in the interface module that will also serve as the LAN's gateway to the wider information grid. The decision to adjust supply levels of a service will be relative to those that exist within the LAN ; however, a supply of services may be global in nature and thus span several LANs.

Distributed voting and decision making is applicable to global changes in supply and demand. The computational cost for voting in a wide area network (WAN) has been shown to be greater than using the interface module approach [12]. Absorbing such a cost is justifiable given that no single source within the wide area network can have global knowledge of the information grid and not present a single point of failure. The issue of what agent holds the financial stake in resources distributed within a WAN is open, and suggests that tracking these resources will accrue additional cost.

Although the market models for resource management within the information grid have been studied and show promise, the accompanying issue of resource replication control requires further investigation into the infrastructure that will manage the fault tolerance mechanisms. Referring to the restructuring of the power grid, William Sweet in the June 2000 issue of *IEEE Spectrum* stated: [13]:

> Whether the talk is of generation and transmission capacity, distribution lines or control equipment, service personnel of simulation engineers, it is the same story: too few resources to easily satisfy demands made on systems designed for radically different requirements.

5 Solutions and Challenges

Elements to overcome the problem of automatic response to supply and demand are being found in the distributed fault tolerance schemes being developed for local- and wide-area networks. The analogy of the electric power grid strongly indicates that structural issues are important for employing market-mechanisms for managing the resources of the information grid. The monitoring of services and the decision processes to adjust service supplies must also be distributed and fault-tolerant.

6 Conclusion

An analogy has been drawn between the electric power grid and the information grid. The real-world power grid serves to simulate the evolving information grid. The free-market economic model applied to the former has had some potentially drastic effects on the dependability of the system, yet supply and demand are intuitively clear drivers for managing resource replication in the information grid. Simulation of highly fault-tolerant schemes that deal with replication within a LAN indicate that they are compatible with market approaches. While schemes to address supply and demand issues across a wide-area network are being explored, the approach adopted for the LAN restrict supply and demand adjustments only to those services that are local. This will yield only local optimizations. In order to achieve optimizations on a more global scale, there needs to be a way to maintain consistency in updating the distributed data and voting on computations across a wide-area. Identically distributing tasks and employing wide-area network voting is possible, but, cost withstanding, the parallel of the information grid to the power grid implies that breaking up control does not enhance dependability. Instead, voter interaction requires knowledge of assured network operation so that voters can be depended upon to communicate accurately the status of the resources they represent.

References

[1] Donald Ferguson, Christos Nikolaou, Jakka Sairamesh, and Yechiam Yemini, "Economic Models for Allocating Resources in Computer Systems," *Market-Based Control: A Paradigm for Distributed Allocation,* Scott H. Clearwater Editor, World Scientific, 1996.

[2] Paul A. Samuelson and William D. Nordhaus, *Economics,* Sixteenth Edition, McGraw-Hill, 1998.

[3] I. E. Sutherland, "A Futures Market in Computer Time," *Communications of the ACM,* **11**, 1968.

[4] J. Cowie, D. M. Nicol, and A.T. Ogielski, "Modeling the Global Internet," *Computing in Science & Engineering,* Vol. 1, No. 1, 1999.

[5] Ken Steiglitz, Michael Honig, and Leonard Cohen, "A Computational Market Model Based on Individual Action," *Market-Based Control: A Paradigm for Distributed Allocation,* Scott H. Clearwater Editor, World Scientific, 1996.

[6] Larry Smarr, "Reasons for Computational Grids," *The Grid: Blueprint for a New Computing Infrastructure,* Ian Foster and Carl Kesselman editors, Morgan Kaufmann Publishers, 1999.

[7] Michael Peevey, "Lights Out for Regulated Utility Monopolies," *Wall Street Journal* July 19, 1998.

[8] Rebecca Smith, "New Rules, Demands Put Dangerous Strain on Electricity Supply," *Wall Street Journal,* May 11, 2000.

[9] Jim Gray and Andreas Reuter, *Transaction Processing: Concepts and Techniques,* Morgan Caufmann Publishers, 1993.

[10] Benjamin Hardekopf and Kevin Kwiat, "Exploiting the Overlap of Security and Fault Tolerance", *Proceeding of the Academia/Industry Working Conference on Research Challenges,* IEEE Computer Society and ACM, April 2000.

[11] Kevin Kwiat and Benjamin Hardekopf, "Performance Analysis of an Enhanced-Security Distributed Voting Algorithm," *Proceedings of the Symposium on Performance Evaluation of Computer and Telecommunication Systems,* SCS Press, July 2000.

[12] Benjamin Hardekopf and Kevin Kwiat "Secure Distributed Voting in a Wide-Area Network Using Untrusted Voters," submitted to *Symposium for Reliable Distributed Systems,* October 2000.

[13] William Sweet, "Restructuring the Thin-Stretched Grid," *IEEE Spectrum,* **37**, No. 6, June 2000.

TARDEC'S Embedded Simulation System for Ground Vehicles

Sharon Chase, Kevin Hope and Rob Kaplowitz
U.S. Army Tank-automotive and Armaments Command
AMSTA-TR-R MS264
Warren MI, 48397-5000

KEYWORDS: Embedded Simulation, Personal Computers, Mission Rehearsal, Battlefield Visualization

ABSTRACT

Embedded Simulation is the concept of embedding the capability in the vehicle to allow a 'virtual world' to be displayed to the crew and to have virtual interaction with vehicle subsystems in support of the following missions: Training, Mission Rehearsal, Battlefield Visualization, Command Coordination and Test & Evaluation. Embedded Simulation can potentially be applied to every ground weapon system in the Army. This range of systems includes legacy systems that may have no on-board computer or software to other legacy or emerging systems that have highly advanced and sophisticated embedded systems architecture. The U.S. Army's Tank Automotive Research Development and Engineering Center (TARDEC) VETRONICS Simulation Facility (VSF) team, is developing an Embedded Simulation System (ESS) to incorporate into ground combat vehicles.

Some of the concerns of developing an ESS to support multiple ground vehicle platforms, are cost and flexibility of the system. In order to alleviate some of these concerns, the TARDEC VSF team is developing an architecture for a low cost B-Kit capable of integrating with multiple vehicle architectures. The B-Kit will be composed of off-the-shelf PC compatible hardware packaged into a ruggedized box.

The Embedded Simulation System (ESS) B-Kit will first be integrated and tested as part of the VETRONICS Technology Testbed (VTT) System Integration Lab (SIL). In October 2000, the ESS will also be part of the VTT vehicle when it is field tested at Camp Grayling, MI. In August 2001 at Ft. Hood, the ESS will be used in the VTT at the Inter-Vehicle Embedded Simulation Technology (INVEST) Science and Technology Objective (STO)'s demonstration.

This paper will describe the hardware and software that comprise the B-Kit architecture. The lessons learned from developing the B-Kit architecture will be included in the paper. In addition, the results of any testing that have occurred will be included in the paper.

INTRODUCTION

Embedded Simulation (ES) is one of the technologies that will support the Army After Next. ES will provide the soldier with a chance to rehearse a mission in the real vehicle, and enhanced training locally and in remote locations.

The Simulation, Training and Instrumentation Command (STRICOM) and the Tank-Automotive Research, Development & Engineering Center (TARDEC) are working jointly to develop a common hardware and software architecture that will enable successful integration of ES into ground combat vehicles. STRICOM efforts are being worked under the Inter-Vehicle Embedded Simulation Technology (INVEST) Science Technology Objective (STO) and TARDEC's efforts are being worked as part of the Vehicle Electronics (VETRONICS) Technology Testbed (VTT) under the Inter-Vehicle Electronics Suite (INVEST) STO.

During the development of an Embedded Simulation System (ESS) for ground combat vehicles, the engineers realized that there are three possible architecture choices. The first architecture choice is called a stand-alone Embedded Simulation System. A completely separate subsystem with its own processing, image generator and software that is connected via the data bus, video-bus and power-bus would be used to support ES in the ground combat vehicle. The second architecture choice is called the Integrated Embedded Simulation System. To support the additional requirements of Embedded Simulation, the Integrated approach uses the current vehicle subsystems and upgrades the vehicle's own computer and software architecture. The third architecture choice is called the Hybird Embedded Simulation System. The Hybird approach is a combination of a stand-alone subsystem and an Integrated architecture.

The TARDEC VETRONICS Simulation Facility (VSF) team, is developing an ESS which will use the stand-alone ES Architecture as the first step to Embed Simulation into the vehicle. This architecture is the least expensive and provides the least interface with the vehicle. On the other hand, this architecture will not provide some of the features of the fully integrated ESS and it will take up more space in the vehicle.

In Horizontal Technology Integration (HTI) terms, the item that is common across platforms is known as the "B-Kit". Where as, any items unique to a given vehicle that are required to integrate the HTI item into the vehicle is known as the "A-Kit". Since the goal is to incorporate the TARDEC VSF Embedded Simulation System into multiple ground vehicle platforms, it is referred to as the B-Kit.

The purpose of this paper is to describe the hardware and software that comprise the B-Kit architecture. A brief description of the Vetronics Technology Testbed (VTT) is provided. Any lessons learned from developing the B-Kit architecture are included through out the paper. In addition, the results of testing the B-Kit hardware are included in the paper.

Vetronics Technology Testbed (VTT)

As mentioned earlier, the B-Kit effort is a part of the larger VTT development effort under the INVES STO. The VTT vehicle is a modified Bradley A0 hull, representing a future scout/cavalry vehicle. The VTT is not equipped with actual target acquisition sensors, laser ranging capability, or weapons, the B-Kit will provide a simulation of these elements.

Several key technologies will be included in the VTT to demonstrate their ability to function in a combat vehicle environment while contributing to crew workload reduction. These technologies include: speech recognition, 3D audio, indirect vision driving, advanced user control handles and embedded simulation.

B-Kit Hardware

Two main factors were considered when deciding what type of hardware to use for the B-Kit. The first factor was cost. The B-Kit hardware needed to be inexpensive and easily obtained. The second factor was physical size of the B-Kit. To make the B-Kit more practical, it should take up as little room in the vehicle as possible. The Personal Computer (PC) platform has had major advancements in the areas of cost and in the reduction of the physical size of the hardware components. For these reasons, it was chosen to build the B-Kit with PC components.

To reduce the size of the B-Kit even further, it was decided to design and build our own ruggedized computer boxes. This would eliminate some of the wasted space that would be present in a common PC case. A prototype of our ruggedized computer boxes was built in April of 2000.

The prototype was comprised of an ATX motherboard, a PIII 450 Mhz CPU, 256 Megs of RAM, a Fast Ethernet network card, an AT power supply, a 9 GB hard drive, and a Quantaum3D Raven 3D/2D video accelerator card. These components were mounted in a 16" x 10" x 6" Hoffman metal box.

The total B-Kit will consist of eight of these ruggedized computer boxes networked together to run the Embedded Simulation Software. The B-Kit will be responsible for providing eight visual outputs. Each computer box is only capable of providing a single visual output, therefore eight computer boxes are required to make up the B-Kit. Each box should contain mostly the same components as the others. The only differences would be in the processor speed and the amount of RAM in each computer. We are currently conducting performance tests to determine what processor speed and amount of RAM will be needed for each computer.

B-Kit Shake Test

It was uncertain as to whether or not the design of our ruggedized boxes would hold up under the normal operation of a vehicle. There were two main concerns. The first one was that the video card and the network card would not stay seated in the slots of the motherboard due to the vibration caused by the vehicle. The second concern was that the hard drive would fail due to the vibration caused by the vehicle. Before building anymore ruggedized computer boxes, it was decided to put the first prototype box through a shake and shock test that would simulate 6000 miles of driving. General Dynamics Land Systems in Sterling Heights Michigan conducted the test.

Instead of testing just a single box, it was decided to test all eight boxes mounted the same way that they would be mounted in the vehicle. The eight boxes were lined up in stacks of two (See Figure 1). Each stack had about a four-inch gap between it and another stack. The four boxes on the bottom of the stacks were bolted to a base plate. The four top boxes were attached with Velcro to the bottom boxes. A wooden plank was place on top of the four stacks and strapped down to the base plate. Seven of the eight boxes were empty and the other one was the prototype box. The base plate was mounted on shock mounts, which were mounted to the base of the shaker table.

The initial setup included three accelerometers to record the forces on the B-Kit. A single-axis accelerometer was attached to the base of one of the shock mounts. This accelerometer was used as a reference because it recorded the exact forces exerted by the shaker table. A second single-axis accelerometer was attached to the outside of the box that contained the computer. The shaker table could only move in one axis, so the first two accelerometers were attached so that they recorded the forces in the same direction in which the shaker table was moving. The third accelerometer used was tri-axial and it was attached to the top (the side of the hard drive commonly referred to as the top when it is in a standard mounting) of the hard drive.

The proposed sequence of testing the B-Kit was as follows. The B-Kit was to be vibrated for three fifty-minute periods in the X-axis. Each fifty-minute period would use a different profile of pulses that the B-Kit would be subjected to. Next the B-Kit was to be subjected to shock pulses in the X-axis, both positive and negative shock. Then the B-Kit would have to be rotated 90 degrees on the shaker table to be tested in the Y-axis. Three fifty-minute profiles were to be run for testing in the Y-axis. These profiles would be different than the profiles used in the X-axis testing. Then the B-Kit was to be subjected to shock pulses in the Y-axis. The head of the shaker table would then have to be rotated 90 degrees to test the B-Kit in the Z-axis. Five twenty-four-minute profiles were to be run to test in the Z-axis. Then the B-Kit was to be subjected to shock pulses in the Z-axis. The prototype box would be up and running during the test to signal if and when a failure occurred.

The prototype box made it through the first fifty-minute profile in the X-axis without any problems. During the second fifty-minute profile in the X-axis, the power supply failed. One of the screws of the power supply that held the circuit board in place had worked its way loose and shorted out the circuit board. We did not have another power supply that would fit inside the metal box, so a different style power supply was mounted on top of the B-Kit and used to power the computer so testing could resume.

During the third X-axis profile and the first stage of the X-axis shock test, the hard drive accelerometer showed signs of the hard drive banging against something. The main cause of this turned out to be the high temperature in the box. When the original power supply failed, the fan was disconnected and couldn't be easily reconnected to the new power supply. The high temperature caused the rubber mounts of the hard drive to soften and become more flexible, which allowed the hard drive to move more freely and bang against the lid of the box. The fan was reconnected to the new power supply to reduce the heat in the box and some foam was added to help dampen any collision between the hard drive and the lid before the test was continued.

After vibration testing, shock testing was conducted in the X-axis. The test specification stated that the B-Kit would have to survive three thirty-g pulses in the positive direction and three thirty-g pulses in the negative direction. The magnitude of the pulses was stepped up from 7 to 15 to 22 to 27 to the 30-g level. So the B-Kit actually had to survive a pulse at each of these levels before taking three pulses at the 30-g level. This process was done in the negative X direction also. The B-Kit survived all 6 30-g pulses in the X-axis.

The B-Kit made it through three fifty-minute profiles of vibrating in the Y-axis without any complications or failures. There were complications and eventually a failure during the shock testing in the Y-axis. The B-Kit survived all of the pulses in the positive Y direction. The first 30-g shock in the negative Y direction caused the B-Kit computer to lockup. It was rebooted and it came back up without any problems. The second 30-g shock in the negative Y direction caused the B-Kit computer to reboot itself. It came up without any problems. The third 30-g shock damaged one of the sectors on the hard drive, which prevented it from rebooting successfully.

It was decided to quickly develop a new fixture with a different hard drive-mounting scheme and shake it as opposed to shaking and shocking the dead hard drive in the Z-axis. The new fixture had springs attached to the hard drive in addition to the rubber mounts. The new fixture was strapped down on top of the B-Kit assembly and then shaken for fifty minutes using the third X-axis profile. The setup was then ran through the shock tests in the Y-axis. The new hard drive was also video taped to help identify any abnormal movements. The data from these last tests was not available yet, so no assessment has been made to determine if the better mounting scheme worked.

Overall, a great deal was gained from conducting the shake and shock tests. We realized the importance of securing all possible nuts and bolts with glue or some other means. This goes for both the parts we assemble in-house and those assemblies purchased from outside vendors, i.e. power supply. We also now feel confident that our design is stable enough to survive the vibrations of an operating vehicle. Possible benefits could arise from further investigating possible ways to lessen the impact seen by the hard drive from shock pulses.

B-KIT SOFTWARE

The B-Kit Software consists of many software modules operating in close coordination with one another, as well as synchronization with the VTT. The Department of Defense is migrating away from military proprietary hardware and software standards and towards open systems. The Linux operating system running on generic single or multiple processor IBM compatible personal computers was a logical environment. This will enable us to easily upgrade existing systems, as faster processors and image generators (video cards) become available. A sample B-Kit software architecture diagram can be found in Figure 2.

To support the VTT's various missions, the B-Kit will operate in various states, and within each state multiple modes. Depending upon the state and mode, each B-Kit module may operate differently. To explain how each module operates in the various states and modes is outside the scope of this paper.

We must have a method for testing and evaluating the VTT on the battlefield. Due to cost, it is impractical for us to use the VTT alongside friendly forces and against an enemy "red" force. We must turn to simulation where we can fight our actual VTT alongside virtual friendly forces and against virtual enemy forces. There are multiple B-Kit modules which when operating together will accomplish this goal.

To facilitate host-to-host communications, we have developed a Process Interface Unit (PIU). The PIU enables the developer of each B-Kit module to send and receive data messages without having to worry about who is receiving the data that developer wants to send, and sending the data that the developer wants to receive. With minor modifications, the PIU will share data across any number of hosts. The PIU has been developed over several years on past ground vehicle simulation programs and we anticipate continuing to reuse it on future programs. The PIU operates asynchronously and in near-real time.

As the VTT's A-kit and B-Kit use separate message formats, we developed an A-Kit interface module. The A-Kit interface's sole responsibility is to transfer data between the A-Kit and B-Kit, while performing all required data massaging.

Modular Semi-Automated Forces, or ModSAF, is a Department of Defense developed high-resolution force-on-force exchange model. It has the capability to simulate accurately the performance of both friendly and enemy weapons systems and tactics. ModSAF uses a very detailed graphical display that allows the user to see the progress of the battle as it's evolving. No single ModSAF scenario, or simulated battle, will allow us to fully evaluate the VTT. We will use multiple ModSAF scenarios in the VTT evaluation and the B-Kit must facilitate the loading and running of multiple scenarios. Although we are using ModSAF in its standard release, we've had to develop B-Kit modules that allow us to send and receive data to and from ModSAF.

The Simulation Control Manager was developed to perform the tasks done by a simulation operator (i.e. Start/Stop Simulation). The Simulation Control Manager will receive a selected scenario from the user. The scenario will vary based on the state of the VTT. The Simulation Control Manager will then launch the remainder of the B-Kit modules including the Computer Generated Forces Interface (CGFI) module. It is the CGFI's role to actually launch ModSAF with the appropriate scenario. The CGFI module was developed to facilitate communication between ModSaf and the B-Kit (i.e. Starts ModSaf, tells ModSaf what scenario to load).

As ModSAF is off-the-shelf software, it hasn't been modified to understand the native B-Kit data messages. To provide entity information between ModSAF and the B-Kit a separate B-Kit module has been developed. It is the job of the Network Interface Unit (NIU) to perform this communication. Using either the Defensive Department's Distributed Interactive Simulation (DIS) or High Level Architecture (HLA) protocols, the NIU will monitor the B-Kit's PIU message traffic and translate and transmit the relevant data via DIS/HLA to ModSAF. Likewise, the NIU will also monitor ModSAF's DIS/HLA message traffic and translate and transmit the relevant data to the B-Kit via the PIU.

When fully implemented, the B-Kit will display multiple three dimensional battlefield views to the VTT operators. Within the B-Kit, X-IG from Carmel Applied Technologies, Inc. is an Open GL based three dimensional graphics engine we're using to render and display all our graphical requirements (Website for Carmel Applied Tech. http://www.catinet.com/products/xig/FAQ/index.htm). For the VTT, we are developing high-resolution terrain databases, corresponding to each site where the VTT will be tested and evaluated. X-IG will load and render the appropriate database, as needed. In the B-Kit, there will be a total of seven views. There are five camera views, which are fixed to the relative position of the VTT vehicle and two simulated sensor views, which can move independent of the vehicle. X-IG can operate across multiple workstations and uses its own scheme for host-to-host communications. The B-Kit module developed to act as the interface between the B-Kit and X-IG, is World. The World module also keeps track of the other entities.

During VTT operation of all the scenarios, there must be a way to monitor, evaluate, and log soldier performance. The After-Action-Review (AAR) module logs the soldier's operations to disk for data collection, statistical analysis, and the ability to playback three-dimensional battlefield imagery at a later time.

The Battlefield Visualization (BV) capability allows the operator to move independent of the vehicle in all three dimensions to observe the battlefield conditions around the VTT. The BV capability is an operational enhancement available to the VTT operator. It is typically used prior to engagement of enemy forces.

To complete B-Kit functionality, there are other software modules that perform various data manipulation and computations and communicate solely through the PIU. The Sight/Weapons module controls the VTT's two independent simulated sensor views and the VTT's simulated 25mm cannon. The Command and Control (C2) module passes messages in the standard military digital message format, between the A-Kit and the B-Kit. Types of messages involved will depend upon the particular ModSAF scenario being run. Mobility will track or compute position and orientation of the VTT vehicle. Vulnerability allows the VTT vehicle to be killed during scenario execution. For training purpose, Vulnerability can be enabled or disabled as needed.

CURRENT STATUS

The development of a common ESS architecture by TARDEC and STRICOM has been divided into several phases. The first phase was the demonstration of a prototype B-Kit at the December 1998 I/ITSEC conference.

In January 99, the second phase of the B-Kit architecture was started. The objective of phase 2 is to focus on ruggedization and miniaturization of the B-Kit architecture.

FUTURE PLANS

For phase 2, the ESS B-Kit hardware and software that is being developed will first be tested as part of the VETRONICS Technology Testbed (VTT) System Integration Lab. Phase 2 will conclude in October 2000, with the B-Kit being field tested as part of the VTT vehicle. This field test will be conducted at Camp Grayling, MI.

For phase 3, the B-Kit will again be used in the VTT and will be demonstrated at Ft. Hood during the Inter-Vehicle Embedded Simulation Technology (INVEST) Science and Technology Objective (STO's) demonstration. The INVEST STO demonstration will occur in the summer of 2001. It is being planned for 2004, that the B-Kit will be demonstrated in the Crewman's Associate Testbed STO.

REFERENCES

[1] Paul Bounker, John Brabbs, Curt Adams; " Low Cost Embedded Simulation System for Ground Vehicles" 1999 Interservice/Industry Training, Simulation and Education Conference (I/ITSEC 99) Proceedings, Nov 29, 1999.

AUTHOR'S BIOGRAPHIES

Sharon Chase is a Computer Engineer at TARDEC's VETRONICS Simulation Facility (VSF). Her research interests include distributed simulation and software engineering. She has a Bachelor of Science in Computer Science and Engineering from Milwaukee School of Engineering in Milwaukee, Wisconsin. She also has a Master of Science in Software Engineering from Monmouth College in West Long Branch, New Jersey.

Kevin M. Hope is a Computer Engineer at TARDEC's VETRONICS Simulation Facility (VSF). His research interests include Linux operating system, distributed simulation and computer generated forces. He has a B.S.E degree in Computer Engineering from Kettering University (formally GMI) in Flint, Michigan.

Rob Kaplowitz is a Simulation Engineer at TARDEC's VETRONICS Simulation Facility (VSF). He holds a Bachelor of Science degree in Industrial Engineering from the University of Massachusetts at Amherst.

Figure 1: Setup for B-Kit Shake Test

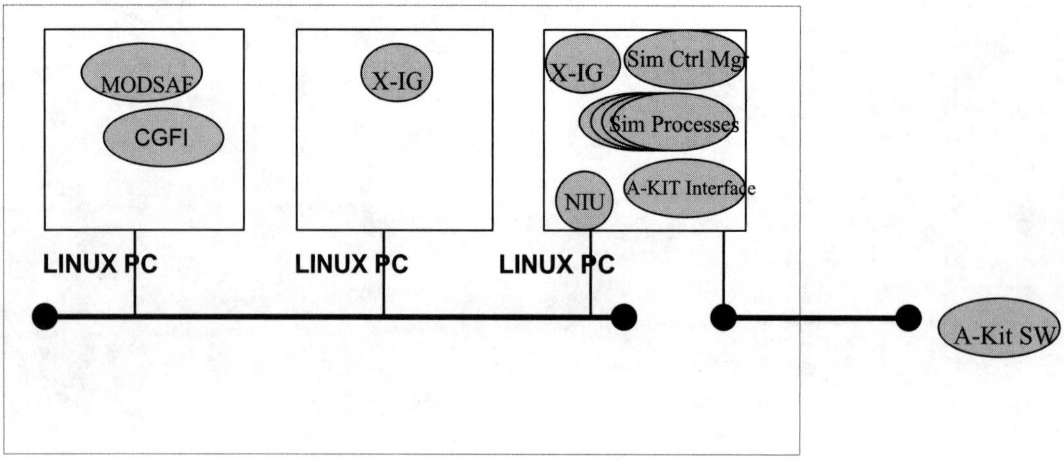

Figure 2: B-Kit Software Architecture

A RECONFIGURABLE OBJECT MODEL FOR PORT OPERATIONS

James F. Leathrum, Jr. and Taylor Frith
Virginia Modeling, Analysis and Simulation Center
Old Dominion University

ABSTRACT

A model is presented to simulate the flow of military cargo through a commercial seaport. The model needs to reflect actual port configurations rather than generalize the port. This means that the sequence of operations may vary from port to port. The model is developed to capture the processes and the reconfigurable nature of the system. The purpose of the model is to provide a common language for domain experts and simulation experts to discuss the infrastructure and processes associated with a port operation. The model does not directly model the software (that is another level of modeling), though it is developed in an object-oriented fashion to help bridge the gap between the domain experts' view and the software model. Within the object structure, flowcharts are used to describe processes as that is the common language for the domain experts. The model requirements are presented in this paper along with a basic presentation of the model and how it addresses the requirements.

INTRODUCTION

A model is presented for port simulations. A rigorous model is developed prior to implementation and then come to agreement by both domain experts and developers. This improves the dialogue between the domain experts and developers by providing a common template from which to discuss both process issues and implementation issues. The most important requirement of the model is that it must be understandable to the domain experts assisting in defining the processes while still addressing implementation requirements.

The result of the work is a model that allows one to dynamically step through the processes utilizing web pages with hyperlinks to allow one to step between the processes. The model describes the processes for a new implementation of PORTSIM, a port simulation analyzing the ability to move military cargo through a commercial seaport in a time of crisis. The resulting object-oriented model is described in the paper. The port is partitioned into *port areas* which have dedicated processes associated with them (examples include berths, staging areas, and gates). The underlying communication mechanism is presented which allows the flow of cargo and resources between the port areas to be easily defined. The resulting structure can be driven by a user interface or by GIS data.

PORTSIM

The Port Simulation (PORTSIM) system is a discrete-event simulation that facilitates the analysis of movements of military unit equipment through worldwide seaports and allows for detailed infrastructure analysis. The seaports under consideration tend to be commercial operations where complete access to all port facilities is not feasible. PORTSIM was designed by modeling the general processes in a port and then allowing the specification of process times and available resources to define a specific port's characteristics. A complete description of the process logic for PORTSIM can be found in (Nevins *et al.* 1998a). Other PORTSIM work appears in (Nevins *et al.* 1998b, Nevins, *et al.* 1995, Leathrum *et al.* 2000).

PORTSIM assists planners in comparing and selecting ports and it determines port throughput capability and utilization of critical resources. PORTSIM is designed to answer the following questions:

- How long does it take to move equipment and supplies through the seaport (closure)?
- What and where are the potential bottlenecks and limiting resources to movement through the seaport?
- Why are operations not completed by the required time?
- What are the implications if certain seaport resources are constrained or available?
- What is the port throughput capability given explicit assumptions on assets, resources, and scenarios?

PORTSIM process modeling addresses two modes of operation. The first mode focuses on embarkation processes and encompasses the major activities of reception, staging, and ship loading. Reception activities include all processes needed to accept cargo items at the entry points to the port and transport those items to the staging areas. The entry points to the port are the gates for highway entry and interchange yards for railway entry. Staging activities encompass all processes necessary to part cargo items in appropriate locations before ship arrival as well as to inspect individual items. Finally, ship loading activities include all processes needed to call forward the cargo items to the berths when whips arrive and to load them onto the ships by means of the appropriate loading method.

The second mode of operation in PORTSIM focuses on debarkation processes and encompasses the major activities of ship unloading, staging, and clearance. Ship unloading activities include all processes needed to offload the vessels that arrive at the berths and transport the cargo to the staging areas. Debarkation staging activities are similar to embarkation staging activities and encompass the parking and inspection of cargo items at the port. Finally, clearance activities allow the cargo items to be moved from the port onto the highway or railway infrastructure. This activity involves the loading of commercial highway assets such as flatbed trucks and chassis as well as the loading of railway assets such as trains made up of flatcars and boxcars. The port of debarkation processes are the focus of this paper.

MODEL REQUIREMENTS

The model has the following requirements:

1. *Understandability*. The model is the primary language for conveying of ideas between the domain experts and the simulation experts. This posed a difficulty in that the desired modeling language for the simulation experts was UML (Rational 1999) as it closely models the object-oriented nature of the simulation. However, the domain experts were not familiar with the constructs in UML and preferred flowcharts. The result is the use of UML in Visio, but modified to have a flowchart structure for the definition of process flow within an object operation.
2. *Address concurrency*. One of the difficulties with flowcharts is that it is difficult to demonstrate concurrent activities. However, concurrency is a major component of a port simulation as each cargo item in the port is effectively undergoing concurrent processes. This has an effect when competing for resources. Therefore, the handling of resources properly is crucial.
3. *Address potential deadlock situations*. Deadlock can easily arise when concurrent processes are competing for resources. An attempt is made to identify potential deadlock situations and address them in the model prior to implementation.
4. *Reconfigurable*. Individual seaports can be widely varying in the configuration of port areas such as berths, staging area, and gates. The processes within each port area is consistent, but the order that the port areas are encountered in a military operation may vary. Thus the objects defining the port areas must be reconfigurable in the order that cargo objects encounter them.
5. *Scalable*. The final implementation is on a Windows NT platform and will require the ability to run scenarios involving divisions containing upwards of 100,000 pieces of cargo. While scalability will not be inherent in the model, modeling decisions will be made to keep memory and processor requirements at a minimum for each cargo item.
6. *Maintainability*. The model must be easily maintained as it undergoes a period of major revision during the design cycle. The model is captured by the simulation experts and reviewed by the domain experts. Each operation in the model underwent numerous modifications, both in process definition and in general structure. Therefore, it was crucial that the model be easily updated.

MODEL DESCRIPTION

The first step taken in developing the model was to identify a general macro level flow of cargo through a port, identifying all pertinent resource needs. Figure 1 presents a general flow of cargo arriving via ship and leaving either by highway or rail. As mentioned in the model requirements, the order of the port areas is reconfigurable, but this is the general flow of cargo. This diagram assists in identifying the major components for design in the model. In particular, the ovals identify *port areas*, or areas where processes occur, the rectangles identify *resources*, and the arrows between port areas identify *transit requirements* to move cargo and resources between port areas. Each of these is discussed in more detail along with the model conventions and the port structure.

Model Conventions

The model has been developed in Visio. Processes are defined using flowcharts. Objects are defined graphically with objects being rounded rectangles and object operations begin ovals. The model is very interactive. HTML pages are generated from the Visio drawings. When viewing an object, clicking on an object within that object (a rounded rectangle) takes the user to the image for the selected object. Clicking on an object operation (an oval) takes the user to the flowchart for that operation. When viewing a flowchart, if another operation is referenced, clicking on that reference takes the user to the flowchart for that operation. A button also exists on flowcharts to allow the user to go to the object for which that operation is defined.

Port Structure

The port is defined as an object containing sets of port areas (berths, anchorage, staging, loading, gates, interchange yards and rail spurs). It also contains resource pools holding resources that are centralized in the port. The last piece of the port object is a transit object that defines a network of the port areas handling the routing of cargo and resources through the port, thus supporting a reconfigurable port.

Port Areas

Port areas define the points in a port where processes occur. The port areas are:

- *Anchorage*. Anchorage is where ships wait for a berth to become available and for a pilot and the necessary tugs to become available.
- *Berths*. Berths handle the docking of ships and unloading of cargo.

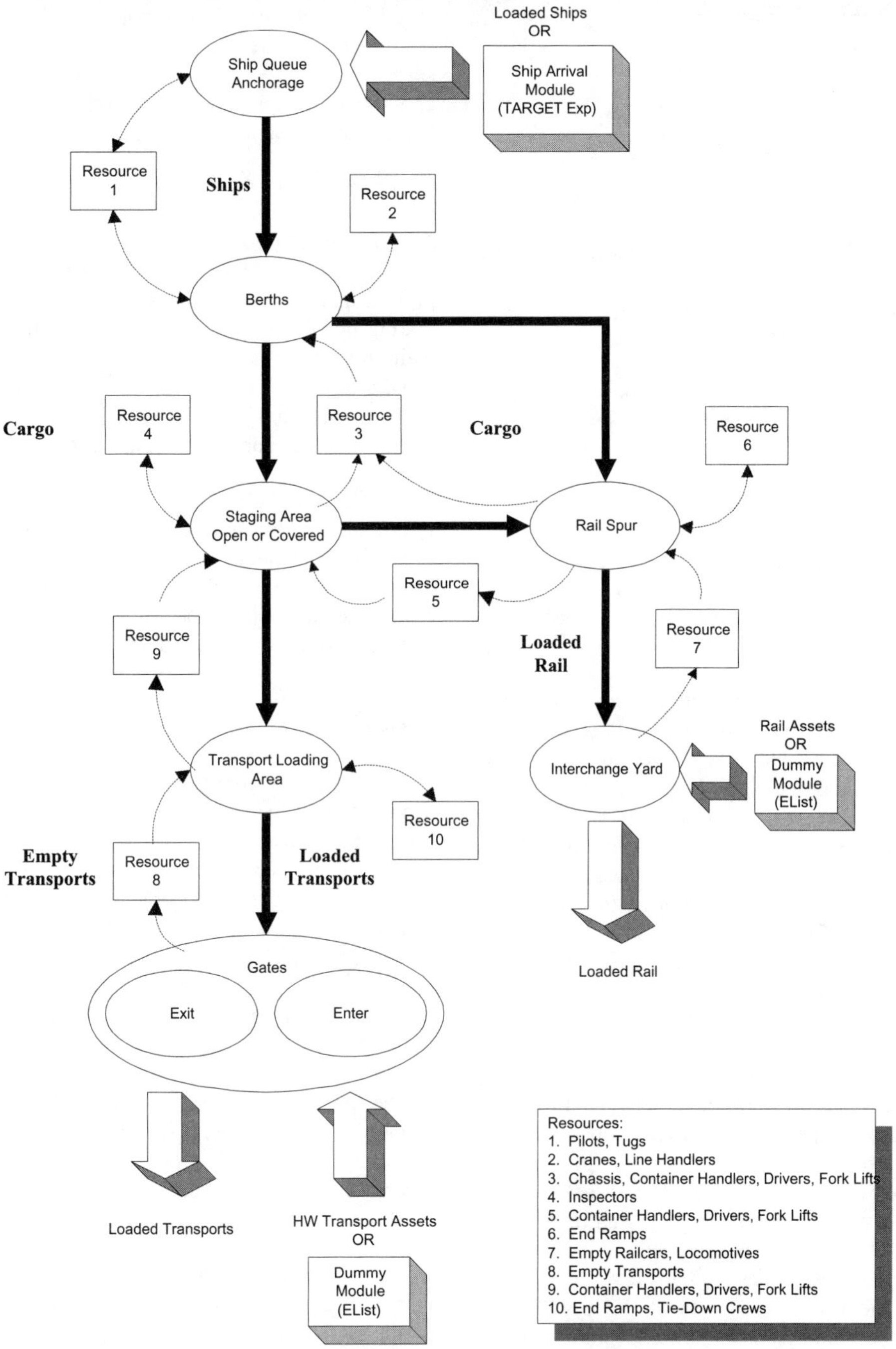

Figure 1. PORTSIM Macro Flow.

- *Staging*. Staging areas are where cargo is stored until resources become available which can move the cargo out of the port. While in staging, vehicles are also inspected.
- *Loading*. Loading areas are where cargo is loaded onto highway transports.
- *Rail spurs*. Rail spurs are the same as loading areas, except that cargo is loaded on rail cars.
- *Interchange yards*. These are holding areas for rail cars where appropriate rail cars are routed to a rail spur to create a train.
- *Gates*. All highway transports must pass through a gate both to get into the port and to leave the port. After waiting in a queue, the transports then are also delayed at the gate.

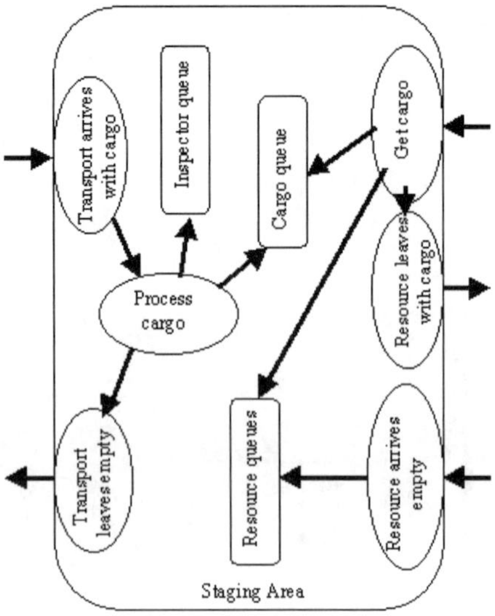

Figure 2. Staging Area Object.

The general structure of all port area objects are constructed the same.

Each port area has a common set of operations defining the arrival and departure of cargo and resources. A cargo arrival operation handles the arrival of a resource carrying cargo. The resource could be a ship, truck, train, forklift, container handler, etc. Cargo departs the port area on a resource through a common cargo departure operation. Empty resources arrive and leave a port area in similar operations. The empty resource operations allow resources to return to another port area to get more cargo. An example port area structure for the staging area is shown in Figure 2.

Internal to each port area, there are operations defining the processes unique to that port area and resource pools holding the resources necessary for the processes. In Figure 2, the Process Cargo operation involves inspection and parking of cargo. The process is described in a flowchart as shown in Figure 3. The model is interactive in that the user may click on the oval for Process Cargo in Figure 2 which results in moving to Figure 3. The Get Cargo operation is a call forward method where a transport calls forward cargo to be loaded when the transport arrives at the port. The resource pools in the staging area handle inspectors, drivers, and container handlers (for transporting cargo for loading). There is also a cargo queue holding cargo that is available for loading.

It is noted that port areas have limited capacities. However, multiple cargo can be concurrently transiting to a port area, each requiring space. If one fills the port area, then the other would be forced to wait outside the port area, but this would result in an infinite queue. To address this, port areas have a request space capability. Prior to having cargo begin the transit to a port area, space is requested in the port area. The granting of space not only indicates that space is available, but that space has been reserved for the cargo even though it has not arrived. Then when the cargo leaves the port area, it releases its space.

Resource Pools

Resource pools are described briefly here. Resource pools hold objects for resources. Operations on the resource pools support putting one or more resources in a pool and getting one or more resources from a pool. The operations wait for sufficient resources to be available prior to satisfying the request. Requests are satisfied in a first come, first serve fashion. The processes to support resource pools are beyond the scope of this paper.

The correct use of resources in the processes is important to address deadlock. Deadlock is addressed by reviewing the sequence that resources are requested to ensure that two objects cannot get partial resource requirements and then be forced to wait on each other to release resources. The model presents a forum to study this relationship.

Transit Object

The transit object is the basis for the reconfigurable capabilities of the model. Port areas do not directly access each other. Instead, when a resource is to move between port areas, with or without cargo, the source port area passes the resource to the transit object. The resource carries with it a final destination for the resource. Given the final destination, the transit object determines the next port area the resource must pass through en route to the destination. It also determines the random variate object defining the transit time for the resource to get to the next port area and delays the resource for the appropriate time before passing it to the port area object. The random variate object is actually a complex model handling multimodal distributions, ordered processes, and blocking processes (Frank 2000). The transit object structure is shown in Figure 4.

The transit object is programmable by defining for pairs of primary sources and primary destinations (comprised of berths, staging areas, and off the port) a route for each resource type (different resources may take different routes to get from one place to another. A route is defined as a sequence of port areas transited to get to the destination. For each pair of port areas, a random variate object is also programmed defining the transit time.

Port Area Connections

The model also gives examples of how two port areas are connected for all successive port areas in Figure 1. This

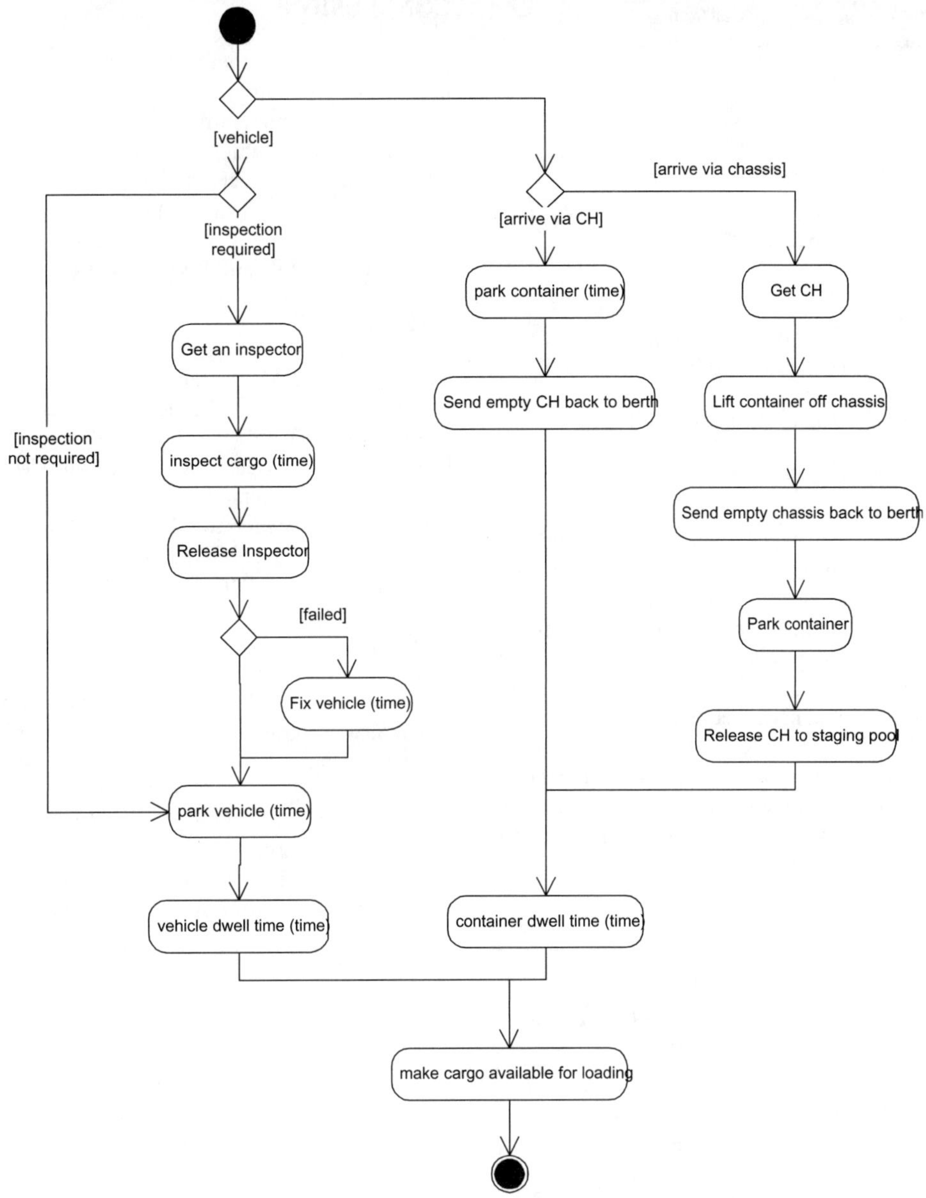

Figure 3. Flowchart for Process Cargo in the Staging Area Object.

is to help the domain expert understand the structure. An example connection is shown in Figure 5 for the transition for a berth area to a staging area. In the connection diagram, each port area is shown, though not necessarily in its entirety. In Figure 5, the whole staging area object as seen in Figure 2 is not shown. Only that portion associated with the connection to the berth is shown. Once cargo is placed in the cargo queue, it is disconnected from the berth processes as it now is waiting to be call forwarded to a loading area or rail spur.

An interesting side point is that the port area connections proved to be a key tool for conversing with the domain experts. By taking the figure and animating it in PowerPoint, the domain expert is easily able to follow the flow of the model. The PowerPoint presentation is provided on the web with the same hyperlink capabilities as the Visio document to allow the user to get to the object diagrams and flowcharts.

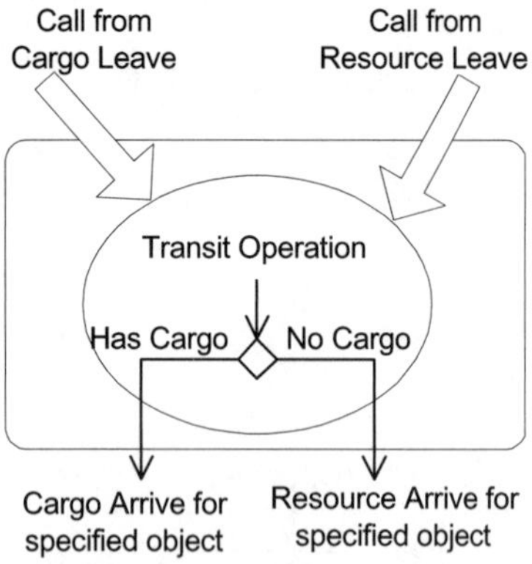

Figure 4. Transit Object Resource Routing.

IMPLEMENTATION ISSUES

While the focus of this paper is on the model and not the simulation, the relationship between the model and the implementation should be briefly mentioned. The model shown in this paper is a model of the processes, not a software model. This is the primary reason that UML was not appropriate as a modeling language. However, several of the constructs used in the model require some significant software modeling. An example is the resource pool. Rather than change to a new modeling language, the same constructs were used to model the software in these cases as needed. The structures proved sufficient to address both the system model and the software model.

CONCLUSIONS

The primary benefit of the model development shown here has been the improved communication with the domain expert. To accomplish this, a simple diagram structure was necessary and an interactive capability was necessary to allow for both a macro and micro view of the processes. The animation of the port area connections proved a real benefit in providing an annotated macro-level walk through the processes while still giving access to the flowcharts.

REFERENCES

Nevins, M., C. Macal and J. Joines. 1998. "A Discrete-Event Simulation Model for Seaport Operations." *Simulation* 70, no. 4 (Apr.): 213~223.

Nevins, M., C. Macal, R. Love, and M. Bragen. 1998. "Simulation, Animation and Visualization of Seaport Operations." *Simulation* 71, no. 2 (Aug.): 96~106.

Nevins, M., C. Macal and J. Joines. 1995. "PORTSIM: An Object-Oriented Port Simulation." *Proceedings of the 1995 Summer Computer Simulation Conference*, 160~165.

Leathrum, J., T. Frith and P. Frank. 2000. "Simulation Structures for a Reconfigurable Port Model to Support Military Cargo Operations," submitted to *The International Workshop on Harbour, Maritime & Multimodal Logistics Modelling and Simulation*, (Oct.).

Frank, P. 1999. A Generic Object-Oriented Random Variate Model for Discrete Event Simulations: Separating the Data Model from the Process Model. Master's Thesis, Old Dominion University, (December).

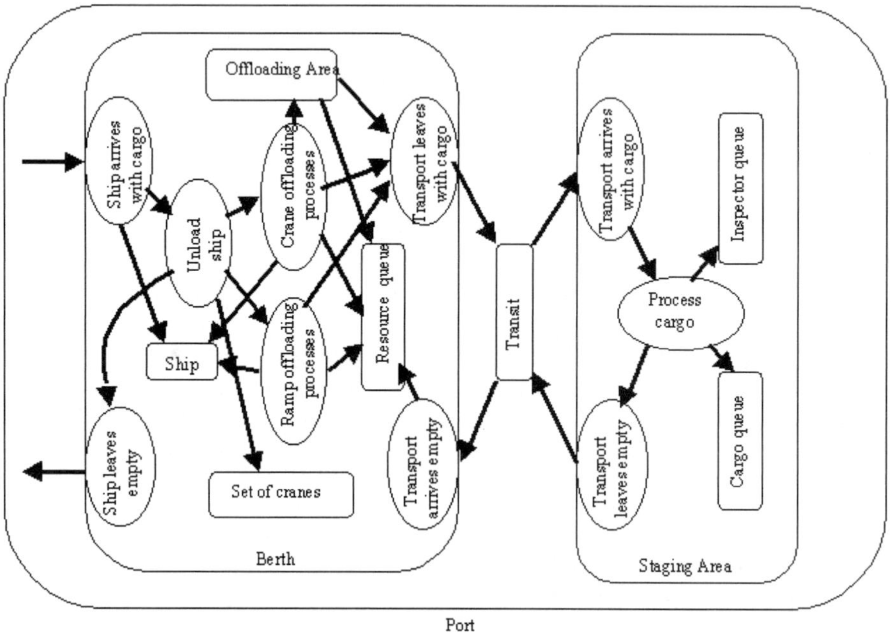

Figure 5. Relationship between a Berth Area and a Staging Area.

TBMD IN JWARS: HOW MUCH DETAIL IS APPROPRIATE?

Barry L. Mitchell and Jacqueline K. Telford
The Johns Hopkins University
Applied Physics Laboratory
11100 Johns Hopkins Road
Laurel, Maryland 20723-6099
e-mail: barry_mitchell@jhuapl.edu

KEYWORDS

JWARS, Campaign Modeling, Model Fidelity, Monte Carlo Simulation

This paper describes a study the authors conducted to determine the appropriate granularity for Probability of Kill (Pk) tables representing Theater Ballistic Missile intercept outcomes in the Joint Warfare System (JWARS). The authors use an empirical approach to demonstrate how and why highly detailed Pk tables in JWARS could, if too few Monte Carlo trials are conducted, cause confusion and lead to bad analysis conclusions from JWARS. The authors then apply principles of statistical test sample sizing to form a theoretical basis for determining the appropriate level of detail for Pk tables in force-on-force or campaign models like JWARS.

INTRODUCTION

Determining the appropriate detail in military models is a perplexing problem facing many analysts and model builders today. Too often models are built without sufficient thought of how analysts will use them and are loaded with excess detail that tax runtime and diminish analytical insight.

We recently conducted a study to determine the appropriate granularity for Probability of Kill (Pk) tables representing Theater Ballistic Missile Defense (TBMD) intercept outcomes in the Joint Warfare System (JWARS). JWARS is a state-of-the-art campaign model that is currently being developed under sponsorship of the Office of the Secretary of Defense.

JWARS uses the Monte Carlo technique to handle stochastic input parameters. This approach is generally superior to deterministic methods because the simulation output represents a distribution of possible warfare outcomes and because problems in treating single or small numbers of battlefields units, inherent in deterministic approaches, are overcome by the Monte Carlo technique. However, long JWARS runtimes could jeopardize the ability of analysts to run a sufficient number of Monte Carlo trials for analysis to be meaningful. The projected runtime to simulate a 100-day warfare campaign in JWARS is 2½ hours.

We used an empirical approach to demonstrate how highly detailed Pk tables in JWARS could, if too few Monte Carlo trials are conducted, cause confusion and lead to bad analysis conclusions from JWARS. We then applied principles of statistical test sample sizing, from test and evaluation theory, to form a theoretical basis for determining the appropriate detail for Pk tables in force-on-force or campaign models like JWARS. Using this theory, we computed the number of Monte Carlo sample sizes needed to distinguish between two adjacent Pk cells and then inverted the process to determine the appropriate Pk table granularity, given the number of Monte Carlo trials that can be afforded by the JWARS user.

The findings of this study serve as a cautionary note to those who demand more detail in military simulations than warranted and demonstrate test sample sizing as a novel and potentially useful method to estimate simulation significance in Monte Carlo simulations.

EMPIRICAL DEMONSTRATION

In this section we use an empirical approach to demonstrate how highly detailed Pk tables could lead to misleading analysis if an insufficient number of Monte Carlo trials are executed.

A candidate method for representing TBMD in JWARS is illustrated in Figure 1. The performance of defensive weapon systems such as PATRIOT or THAAD in negating incoming TBMs is modeled via Pk grids spread over the extent of the weapon system footprints. The Pk associated with each cell represents the probability of kill against TBMs attacking assets located in that cell, and may be a function of TBM type, range, trajectory loft, etc.

Highly detailed footprints with lots of grid-cells lead to less granularity in the simulation results, assuming a sufficient number of Monte Carlo trials can be executed to reveal differences in performance between two adjacent cells.

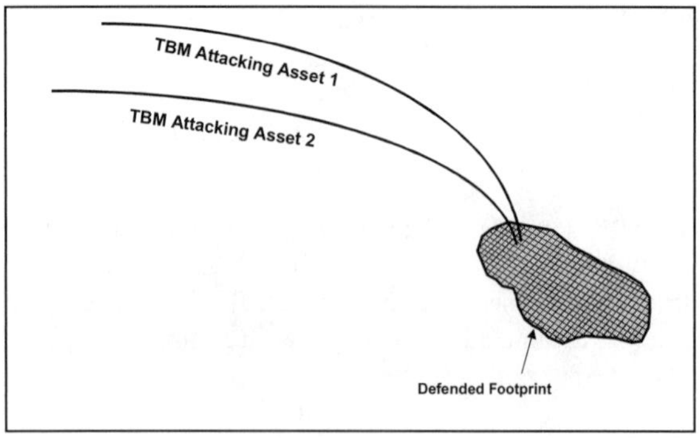

Figure 1. Two TBMs Attacking Assets In Adjacent Pk Cells.

We coded a short FORTRAN simulation, as illustrated by the flowchart in Figure 2, to demonstrate how many Monte Carlo trials are necessary to reveal differences in Pk values between two adjacent Pk cells. Engagement outcomes are determined by drawing random variates from a uniform distribution [0.0 to 1.0] and then evaluating the success or failure of particular engagements by comparing the random draws to Pk values.

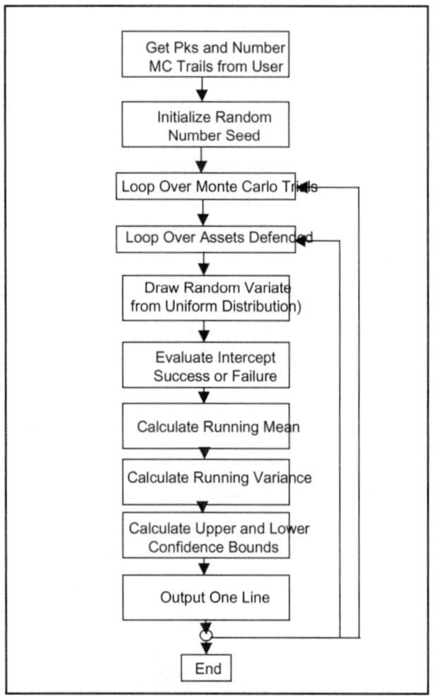

Figure 2. Flowchart for the Empirical Demonstration.

The simulation assumes the two assets are each attacked one time during the war and repeats the process for N-Monte Carlo trials. The cumulative Probability of Kill (Pk) and 2-sigma confidence bounds for the Pk are calculated as the simulation progresses through the N-Monte Carlo trials. We assert that differing Pk values in adjacent cells cannot be distinguished in the output of the simulation if the 2-sigma confidence bounds overlap.

We ran the simulation for two cases: 1) with the adjacent cells having Pk values of 0.7 and 0.8; and 2) with the adjacent cells having Pk values of 0.7 and 0.9. We ran 500 Monte Carlo trials and used three different random seeds for both cases. 500 Monte Carlo trials in JWARS would roughly require 50 days to execute on a single processor, assuming a 2½-hour runtime per 100-day campaign.

Example results from the empirical demonstration are shown in Figures 3a and 3b.

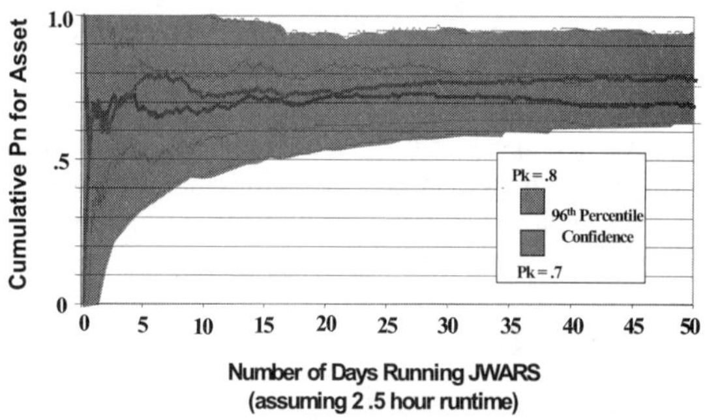

Figure 3a. Example Result With Adjacent Cells Having Pk Values of 0.7 and 0.8.

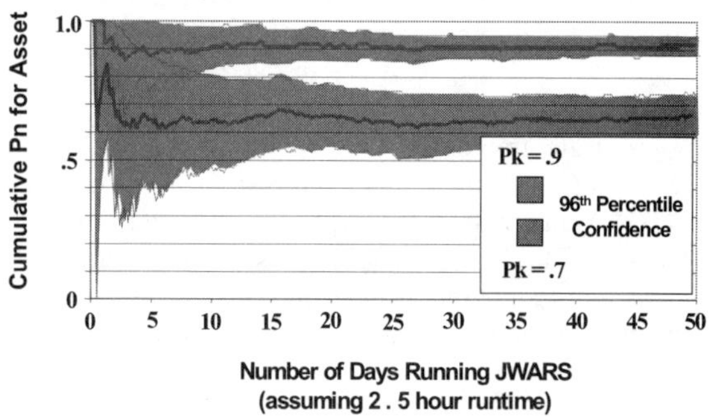

Figure 3b. Example Result With Adjacent Cells Having Pk Values of 0.7 and 0.9.

In none of our runs for the first case were we able to distinguish between Pk values of 0.7 and 0.8 for adjacent cells with 2-sigma confidence, even after 500 Monte Carlo trials. For the second case, where adjacent cells had Pk values of 0.7 and 0.9, we were able to distinguish the Pk values with 2-sigma confidence for all cases. But the earliest this happened was after 77 Monte Carlo trials (or eight days of running JWARS on a single processor), as shown in Figure 3b.

The ability to distinguish differences in Pk values between adjacent Pk cells or from one run to the next is necessary for good analysis. The following example illustrates this point.

Let us suppose that a JWARS analyst makes two sets of Monte Carlo runs, one with a weapon system having a Pk = 0.7, and the other with a weapon system having a Pk = 0.8. If the analyst does not execute enough Monte Carlo trials then he will not be able to distinguish the impact on the warfare outcome resulting from differences between the two weapon systems. In fact, the results can be extremely misleading. It is quite possible, lacking a sufficient number of Monte Carlo trials, that the lesser weapon system could out-perform the more capable weapon system, leading to counterintuitive and misleading results. We observed this in our simulation runs.

In our empirical demonstration we assumed the two assets are attacked only one time during the war. Multiple attacks on the same cells during a war would lessen the required number of Monte Carlo trials needed to differentiate Pk values. This effect is not linear because the confidence bounds change with the square root of the number of trials. So, for example, attacking each asset 10 times during the war instead of one time would not reduce the required number of Monte Carlo trials by a factor of 10.

More importantly, the TBMD Pk values are just one of hundreds, perhaps thousands, of stochastic input parameters in JWARS. The ability to distinguish the impact of changing Pk values will be more difficult, i.e., will require many more Monte Carlo trials than indicated in our analysis, when other random variables are simultaneously impacting the warfare outcome.

THEORETICAL BASIS FOR DETERMINING APPROPRIATE DETAIL

In this section we apply statistical sample sizing, from test and evaluation theory, to form a theoretical basis for determining how many Monte Carlo trials are necessary to distinguish differences between two adjacent Pk cells, or between the same Pk cell for two analysis cases. We accomplish this by recognizing that a series of random Pk draws in a simulation is a binomial distribution, bin (N, p), where N is the number of Monte Carlo trials and p is the constant Pk value. The 90 percent exact binomial confidence bounds for N-Monte Carlo trials use the inverse beta function and are computed as:

lower bound = 1 – betainv(0.95, N(1-p)+1, Np)
upper bound = 1 – betainv(0.05, N(1-p), Np+1)

Figure 4 illustrates 90 percent confidence bounds as a function of Monte Carlo trials for binomial distributions having Pk values of 0.7, 0.8, and 0.9. As shown in the figure, approximately 175 Monte Carlo trials (i.e., 18 days of continuous JWARS execution on a single processor) are needed to distinguish between adjacent Pk cells, or from one analysis run to the next, for Pk values of 0.8 and 0.9 with 90 percent confidence. 260 Monte Carlo trials (i.e., 26 days of continuous JWARS execution on a single processor) are needed to distinguish between Pk values of 0.7 and 0.8.

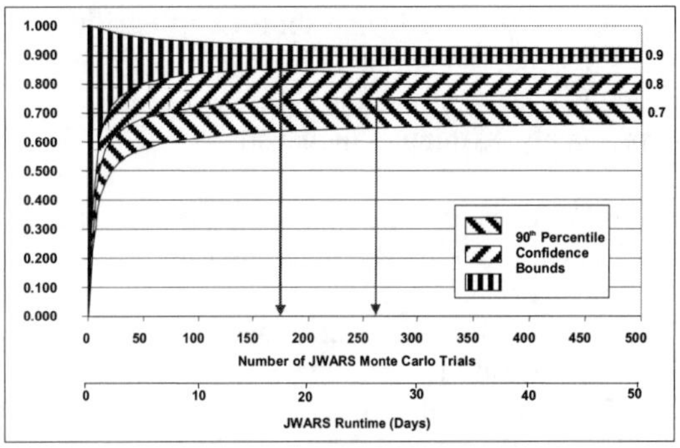

Figure 4. 90 Percent Confidence Bounds for Pk Values of 0.7, 0.8, and .9.

Using a similar approach, we extended the results of Figure 4 to calculate the theoretical criteria for Pk granularity in JWARS. These results are shown in Figure 5 for percent changes about Pk values of 0.7, 0.8, and 0.9.

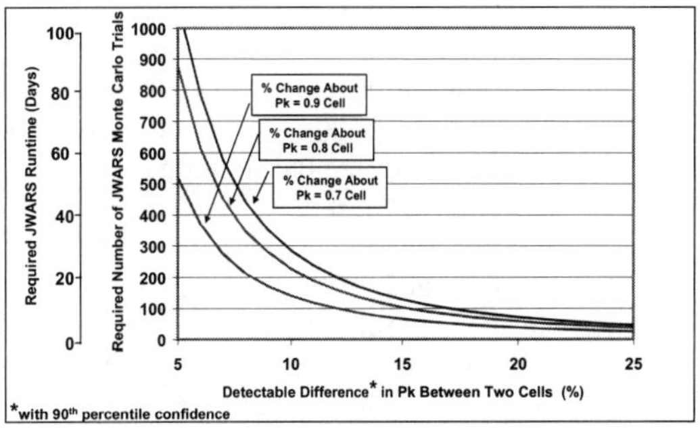

Figure 5. Theoretical Criteria for Pk Granularity.

The results in Figure 5 imply that fine-grained Pk cells will provide no useful purpose in JWARS if users cannot afford at least several hundred Monte Carlo trials. It is unlikely that JWARS users will be able to detect Pk differences between adjacent cells of less than 20 percent unless the footprint cells are made large, quite possibly one uniform cell over the entire footprint for each weapon system. Smaller differences in Pk can be detected if the Pk cells are large because many TBMs will impact into the same region, leading to a much larger statistical sample size per warfare execution.

The Monte Carlo sample size problem applies as well to Pk tables modeled as a function of altitude and downrange in force-on-force models, but these models generally have shorter runtimes than JWARS, so achieving a sufficient number of Monte Carlo trials is typically easier in these models. In a previous study we achieved many thousands of Monte Carlo trials using the Extended Air Defense Simulation (EADSIM) using massive multiprocessor computers located the Joint National Test Facility (JNTF) in Colorado Springs, Colorado. The runtime for each EADSIM Monte Carlo trial was approximately 30 minutes in that study.

The results shown in Figure 5 will impact the types of analysis that can be accomplished using JWARS. It likely will not, however, restrict analysts from answering the primary question concerning ballistic missile defense at the campaign-level, which is "What is the impact of TBMD on the warfare outcome?"

It is possible that analysts may be able to run JWARS in parallel on multiple processors to achieve a large number of Monte Carlo trials in a much shorter time than shown in this paper. But, as discussed in the last section, Pk is just one of many random parameters in JWARS, and assessing the impact of different Pk values will be more difficult than indicated in this paper when other random variables are simultaneously impacting the warfare outcome.

A major drawback to the Monte Carlo method is that analysts generally must execute many more runs than absolutely necessary to insure the solution has converged. In other words, it is difficult to tell whether the solution has converged until long after the solution is converged. We have speculated that the test sample sizing method for determining the required number of Monte Carlo trials, as applied in this study, may be extensible to multivariate problems. Our study considered only binomial distributions for one parameter, TBMD intercept Pk. We speculate the method could have application to problems having M-stochastic parameters, each having its own, unique distribution.

SUMMARY

We have demonstrated that fine-grained Pk cells will provide no useful function in JWARS if users cannot afford enough Monte Carlo trials to distinguish between Pk cells, either in footprints grids or Pk tables based on downrange and altitude. It is unlikely that analysts using JWARS will be able to detect differences between footprint cells of less than 20 percent unless the Pk cells are very large, or possibly constant over the entire footprint. Massive multi-processing of JWARS to obtain sufficient numbers of Monte Carlo trials is another possible solution. We have also shown how counterintuitive and misleading analysis can occur if highly detailed Pk tables are used without executing enough Monte Carlo trials for the differences between Pk values to be distinct.

AUTHOR BIORGRAPHIES

Barry Mitchell is a member of the principal professional staff at the Johns Hopkins University Applied Physics Laboratory (APL). He holds a B.S. in Aerospace Engineering from the University of Cincinnati and a M.S. in Applied Physics from the Johns Hopkins University. Since joining APL in 1986, Mr. Mitchell has been involved in test & evaluation and modeling & simulation projects related to the Trident Missile and ballistic missile defense programs. He previously worked for the McDonnell Douglas Corporation in Houston, Texas.

Jacqueline K. Telford is a statistician and member of the principal professional staff at the Johns Hopkins University Applied Physics Laboratory (APL). She holds a B.S. in mathematics from Miami University in 1973 and M.S. and Ph.D. in statistics from North Carolina State University in 1975 and 1979, respectively. Since joining APL in 1983, she has been involved in reliability analysis and testing, test sizing, and planning for Trident missile programs. She previously worked for the U.S. Nuclear Regulatory Commission in Bethesda, Maryland.

SCRIPTED ARCHITECTURE: AN ALTERNATIVE WAY TO BUILD DEFENSIVE MISSILE SYSTEM SIMULATIONS

Ray Sells
DESE Research Inc.
315 Wynn Dr., Suite 2
Huntsville, AL 35805
(256) 837-8004; e-mail: rsells@dese.com

KEY WORDS
scripting, architecture, flight simulation

ABSTRACT
Significant challenges still exist in constructing and maintaining large missile defense simulations. The complexity of the models and their size makes these simulations difficult to construct and maintain. Current approaches to addressing these challenges focus on the idea of "frameworks" where various models are bound together in a common simulation environment.

This paper describes an alternative to the "framework" approach that, besides reducing the time and effort build simulations, offers an alternative software development process with many advantages. A scripted architecture approach to building simulations is described that leverages the power of newer scripting languages. These typeless data languages are used to bind together existing models with little or no changes. After describing the many advantages to this approach, a simple example is presented illustrating the mechanization and benefits of the scripting approach.

1. INTRODUCTION

Simulations for defensive missile systems are becoming increasingly difficult to build as they become more realistic. These simulations typically include all the elements of a defensive weapon system including the weapon, sensor, and command and control elements. The approach to building these large and complex simulations has typically been to define a common "framework" or architecture and then to force-fit the models for the constituent elements into this framework. The overall goal of the framework is to provide a "plug-and-play" feature for incorporation of its constituent models. However, the models can only be plugged into the framework if their interfaces and functionality meet the constraints imposed by the framework.

Figure 1 is an abstract representation of building large simulations with a framework. In this approach, models are built to a common architecture specification and made to conform and fit into a framework where interfaces (both code and functionality) are well defined. The framework itself provides all the normal simulation infrastructure functionality such as input/output, numerical integration, event triggering and sequencing, and supporting libraries. Typically, the framework is homogeneous, meaning it is built in a single language such as C++ or Ada and models must have interfaces into the particular language's data structures to fit into the framework.

Figure 1. Conventional Simulation Architecture

The ability of frameworks to provide a "plug-and-play" feature for the models is a very powerful concept but this goal is frequently not fully realized. Disadvantages of the framework approach include existing models usually require extensive changes to fit into framework (as shown by the morphing of model shapes in Figure 1), a change in framework necessitates that model code be rewritten, and models are not interchangeable between different frameworks.

2. SCRIPTED ARCHITECTURE DESCRIPTION

The explosion of activity in the area of scripting languages suggests a completely different methodology for simulation development as an alternative to frameworks. The seminal paper on scripting is given by the creator of one of the most prominent scripting languages (Ousterhout 1998). In addition to being an excellent introduction to scripting languages, the paper emphasizes the use of scripting as a whole new technique of software development.

In a phrase, scripting languages can be described as *batch command languages on steroids*. Scripting languages are interpretive in nature (as opposed to compiled) and let the programmer interact with the operating system using a high-level set of commands to control the execution of separate programs. The scripting language provides the capability to control exchange of information between the executing programs as well as performing a wide range of computations within the scripting language itself.

The key feature of scripting languages that enables linking of models into a single cohesive application is that they are *typeless*. All data is stored in one format (commonly strings or objects that can be universally operated on) and hence the programmer need not be concerned with data types such as *float* or *int*. Thus data can be easily exchanged and processed since the programmer need not be concerned with data types and compatibility issues.

The typeless feature of scripting languages suggests a whole new approach to constructing large simulations composed of individual models. Instead of making a centralized framework and force-fitting the models to conform to the framework, scripting languages can be used to make the "framework" conform to the models. This approach is abstractly represented in Figure 2. The idea is to use existing models and simulations "as-is" and to bind them together using the typeless feature of scripting languages. "Glue" routines are easily written in the scripting language itself to ensure all interfaces are compatible between the linked models and tools. The resulting simulation appears to the user to be a single application even though the larger simulation is composed of many models and constituent simulations.

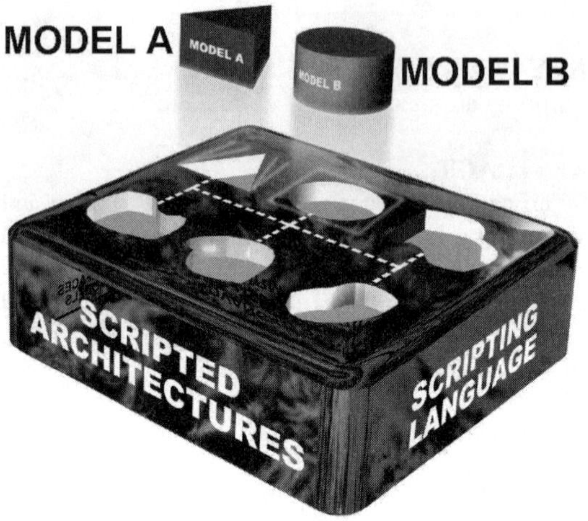

Figure 2. Simulation Architecture Using Scripting Languages

Figure 3 is a common structure for a simulation built using a scripted architecture. Disparate, standalone applications (models/tools) are linked together using an executive written in a scripting language. The executive takes care of executing the proper application at the correct time, handling and passing data between applications, and intermediate and auxiliary calculations. A graphical-user-interface (GUI), also written in the scripting language, is the means that the user interacts with the executive and hence the underlying applications. This structure is general and can accommodate a large variety of simulations. For example, in a missile defense battlefield simulation, separate models for the sensors (radar), weapon elements (interceptors), and mission planning and control elements could easily be bound together into an integrated battlefield simulation. The wargame scenario would be specified by the user via the GUI and the executive would then handle the instructions and execution of the underlying models.

Figure 3. Template for Scripted Architecture Simulation

Several scripting languages are available that offer the simulation developer a wide variety of options and features to choose from. Three scripting languages stand out in particular in terms of maturity and the size of the user community: Perl, Tcl, and Python. Perl is characterized by its compact syntax so that complex commands can be programmed with a minimum of code. It has enjoyed particular acceptance in the web applications community due to its strengths in text processing. Tcl (Tool command language) was originally written by Dr. John Ousterhout who has pioneered scripting in general. The most widely used graphics and GUI library used with most scripting languages, Tk, was originally written for Tcl. Python is distinguished by its object-oriented capabilities which were built into the language kernel itself and not as an add-on library.

Regardless of the individual strengths and weakness of each language, they all have several features in common which are potentially attractive to the simulation developer. All manipulate data typelessly freeing the programmer from the low-level tasks of ensuring data type compatibility. All are cross-platform and have mature stable versions for Unix, Windows, and Macintosh platforms. The scripting languages are all open-source and in the public domain. They are actively supported by the original developer as well as a community of users that contribute upgrades and bug fixes. Extensive and high quality documentation from the world-wide web and independent publishers is available. Several public domain libraries, including libraries for graphics and GUI-building, are available for each scripting language. These libraries and tools are all characterized by being very easy to use allowing even novice programmers to quickly build and prototype GUIs and graphical displays. The most popular graphics library, Tk, is compatible with all three of the scripting languages mentioned.

3. SCRIPTED ARCHITECTURE ADVANTAGES

The advantages of using a scripting language for simulation development are technical as well as organizational. Implicit in using a scripting language for development is the implementation of a modularized software development strategy.

Perhaps the chief advantage of a scripted simulation architecture is that it reduces the degree of coordination, communication, and cooperation between members of the development team. This is the whole idea behind software modularization in the first place - to allow the individual development teams to build their parts independently while spending a minimum of time on coordination. The larger the project, the larger the percentage of time spent on coordinating, managing, and communicating versus developing and integrating the models themselves. The high degree of modularization inherent in the scripting approach greatly reduces the requirement and resources required for coordination and integration.

Because the constituent models are used as-is, the originating organization retains complete control over its model or tool. In most cases only executable code need be provided with a description of input/output files. From an organizational and political viewpoint, no requirements are put on developers regarding tools and methodologies that they must use to develop their software. There are no requirements for formatting of interfaces since it is immaterial to the integrator using a scripting language how the data is formatted or typed. Incompatibilities between data types and formats are easily handled due to the typeless nature of the scripting language.

Implicit decomposition and partitioning of development responsibilities results when using a scripted architecture approach. Lines of responsibility are automatically drawn and maintained between the constituent model developers and the integrator.

Traceability of models to their standalone versions is maintained since the standalone versions of the models are what are actually executed in the integrated simulation. This increases the ability to debug as well as to modify and update code in the models. Updates to models are easily incorporated into the integrated simulation as long as the interfaces don't change. Scripted code in the executive can easily be adapted if the interfaces do change.

Finally the interpretive nature and easy-to-use graphics libraries of the scripting languages provide a quick way to prototype and develop GUI's. The quick and easy GUI toolboxes provided as a part of the standard distributions of the scripting languages allow even novice programmers to build GUIs. This encourages a spiral development methodology since the simulation designers can now actually build the GUIs.

4. EXAMPLE SCRIPTED ARCHITECTURE IMPLEMENTATION

To illustrate these concepts, this section briefly describes a simple application that was built using a scripted architecture approach. Separately developed pieces are integrated together into an apparently single cohesive application using the Tcl scripting language. This process of merging these models with a scripting language is used to compare the scripted architecture approach for building simulations over the traditional framework approach.

The example begins with a task to construct a missile fly-out model for missile defense analyses. The application should include a graphical time-history display of trajectory parameters as well as displaying the trajectory itself on a global graphics display. The resulting application should provide a GUI for the user to control execution and specify parameters.

A standalone interceptor missile trajectory model written in C (Sells 1997) and a Java world graphics display were already available for use in the task. A normal approach to this task would be to attempt to find reusable code fragments in existing codes and models and then integrate them into a common framework in C++ or Ada. A platform-specific GUI and graphics library would then be used to construct the display. Due to the quick-turnaround nature of the task, time and resources were not available to rewrite and adapt these models into a framework-type architecture. This was an excellent opportunity to implement and evaluate an alternative scripted architecture approach.

The existing C missile fly-out model is strictly a console-based application with no GUI or graphics. The fly-out model generates trajectories in terms of range and altitude based on user-input missile characteristics. Output is a time-history of trajectory parameters printed to a console display as shown in Figure 4. The standalone Java tool plots trajectories on world map grid as shown in Figure 5. Each of these tools was developed independently for separate tasks and execute as standalone tools.

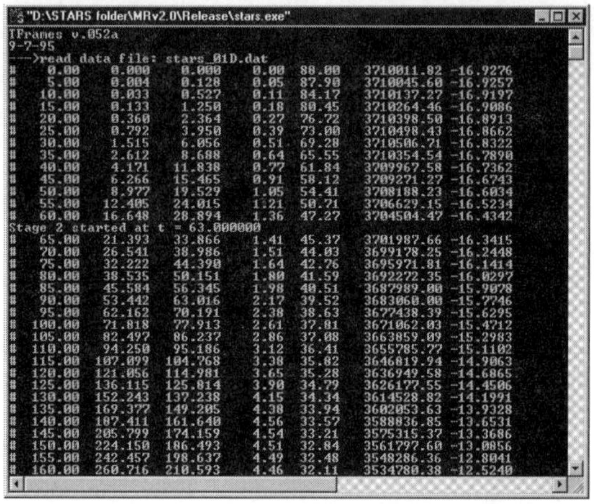

Figure 4. Simple Console Output for Interceptor Missile Trajectory Model

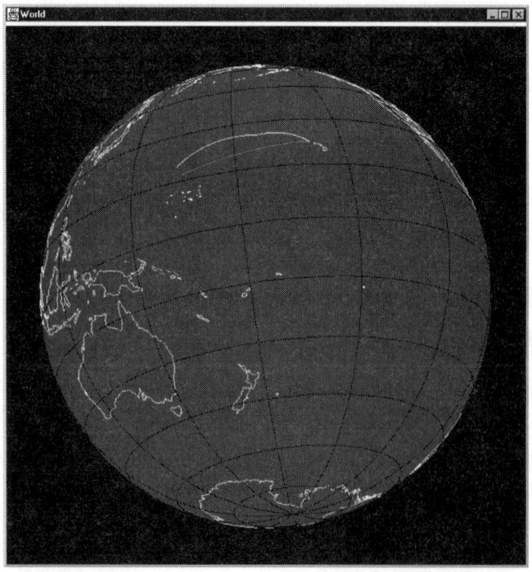

Figure 5. Graphic Display of Trajectory from Java Tool

Tcl was used to integrate the missile flight model written in C and the visualization tool written in Java. The resulting application is shown in Figure 6. Tcl code was used to build the GUI and an executive to control execution of the fly-out and world plotting tool at user request. The executive intercepts normal printed output and plots it on three strip-charts simultaneously as the fly-out model executes. The executive also provides the capability to plot the captured trajectory data on the world graphics display from a button in the GUI.

The utilization of Tcl to integrate these standalone tools into an apparently single application illustrates several key concepts of scripting. The existing applications were used "as-is" with no changes. In fact executable code was used for each of the tools with not one single line or character of source code changed. In comparison with the high-level languages normally used in frameworks, remarkably few lines of code were needed to construct the scripted executive and the display in Figure 6. All execution of the two tools is controlled from one common interface through an attractive GUI with all the widgets users are accustomed to (buttons, slider bars, etc.). Data between the underlying programs is transparently handled by the scripting language. Printed output is intercepted, processed, and displayed graphically by the executive.

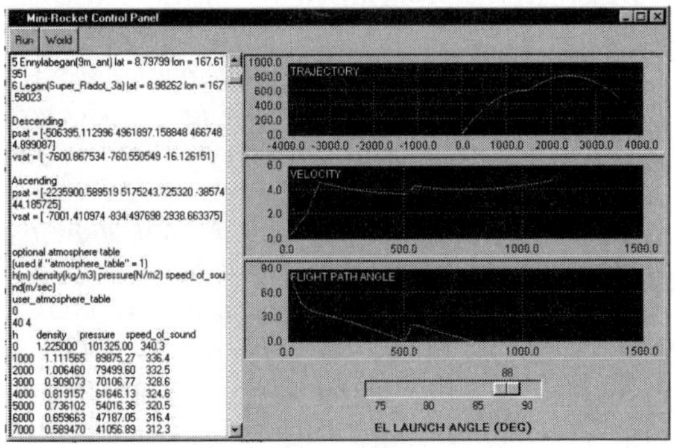

Figure 6. GUI Display for Integrated Interceptor Missile Fly-Out Model and Java Graphics Tool

An enhancement to the scripted trajectory application would be adding missile planning elements to formulate trajectory instructions prior to launch. A separate standalone program to formulate mission planning data using iteration of fly-outs from the interceptor missile model can easily be integrated into the existing scripted application. This illustrates that while this example is simple and uses only two models, the scripted architecture is flexible and can be expanded ad infinitum to build models of varying degrees of complexity.

5. SUMMARY

Scripting is an efficient way to bind together disparate models and tools into a single cohesive application with a GUI. It also suggests an alternative software development process where modularization and partitioning are automatically enforced. Results shown in this paper using real models suggest that scripting is an attractive alternative for building large-scale simulations, including simulations beyond the domain of missile defense simulations.

REFERENCES

Ousterhout, J. K. 1998. "Scripting: Higher Level Programming for the 21st Century." IEEE Computer Magazine, March 1998.

Sells, H.R. 1996. "An Object-Oriented Approach to Simulating Multiple-Staged Missiles," In *Proceedings of Society for Computer Simulation Southeastern Simulation Conference*, (Huntsvillle, AL).

Mr. Sells is Director of Advanced Technology at DESE Research, Inc. where he is principally involved in analysis and simulation of strategic and theater missile defense interceptor systems. He received the BS and MS degrees in Mechanical Engineering from Tennessee Technological University and has completed extensive work in control systems at the University of Alabama in Huntsville. He has published work in the diverse areas of thermal analysis, shock isolation, autopilot design, missile guidance, systems analysis, simulation architecture, and object-oriented simulation design.

Interoperability Policy Roadmap

Paul W. Sutton
Interoperability Manager
Advanced Concepts and Technology (PD 13 TSG)
Space and Naval Warfare Systems Command (SPAWAR)
4301 Pacific Highway
San Diego, CA 92110-3127
(619) 553-9632
psutton@spawar.navy.mil

Keywords:
C4I System, DII COE, HLA, Interoperability, JTA, Model

ABSTRACT: The labyrinth of interoperability policy can present many obstacles to unwary, unsuspecting C4I (Command, Control, Communications, Computers, Intelligence) or M&S (Modeling and Simulation) program managers, system developers, and users. This paper provides a roadmap to help weary managers, developers, and users find their way through this complex, confusing, and often frustrating maze of policies.

1. INTRODUCTION

The purpose of this paper is to provide a roadmap of interoperability policy for C4I and M&S system developers and users. First, however, it is necessary to define the concept *interoperability*. Interoperability has been previously defined as:

"The ability of the systems, units, or forces to provide services to and accept services from other systems, units, or forces, and to use the services so exchanged to enable them to operate effectively together. The conditions achieved among communications-electronics systems or items of communications-electronics equipment when information or services can be exchanged directly and satisfactorily between them and/or their users." (Chairman of the Joint Chiefs of Staff [CJCS] 1995)

"The ability of a model or simulation to provide services to and accept services from other models and simulations, and to use the services so exchanged to enable them to operate effectively together." (Department of Defense Directive [DoDD] 5000.59 1994)

One can infer then, that there are at least two different perspectives of interoperability, the systems perspective and the simulation perspective. Put another way:

"Truth is that which serves the interests of a people. Two groups of people locked in combat cannot be expected to have the same truth."
-- Albert B. Cleage, Jr.

Is interoperability a problem? One of the first and most poignant examples is taken from Operation *Urgent Fury,* the battle of Grenada, in 1983:

"MG Trobaugh, Commanding General of the 82nd Airborne Division, was a very frustrated commander throughout the effort, not only at communications, but at the entire C2 structure. At one period MG Trobaugh landed on the island and tried to effect coordination with Admiral Metcalf, anchored less than ten miles away. Problems ensued due to radio, COMSEC, and frequency incompatibility that did not allow the land-based commander to talk to the overall command headquarters, something that proper J6 planning and coordination should have prevented. MG Trobaugh could see the ship anchored only a few miles away but could only talk intermittently via a satellite link." (Fasulo 1996)

O.K., interoperability was a problem, but is it still a problem? Some very recent disturbing findings (Odell, et. al. 1999) indicate that while some progress has been made, very serious C4I interoperability problems remain unsolved:

"First, future naval coalitions involving the U.S. will be stratified into groups of nations, based on C4I interoperability, with gaps between groups. Not all nations will be able to take on all missions.

We found that interoperability is likely to be poor for the Joint Planning Network, in part because of the allied navies' shortage of SATCOM bandwidth relative to the U.S. Navy and the proliferation of both U.S. and allied systems. Interoperability of sensor-to-shooter networks is also expected to be poor, because of the U.S. near-exclusive hold on most systems of this type.

The Navy, however, does not have a coherent game plan to promote combined C4I interoperability or to specify how different initiatives should be prioritized. Nor does it have any developed doctrine and procedures on using advanced information technology specifically for working with allies"

So interoperability is a problem, but what does policy have to do with it? Why is interoperability policy important? Interoperability policy defines the *what, who, why,* and *where* of interoperability programs. It defines what actions will be taken, who is responsible for them, why they must be taken, and where they're to be performed. Interoperability plans and procedures add the *how* and *when,* in that they define processes for performing the actions and provide schedules for their completion. This recent statement illustrates the increased importance attached to interoperability by DoD:

"Interoperability will be a key determinant in the acquisition of new weapons and a greater set of interests will be brought into the decision making process. There will also be a single focal point to coordinate all interoperability activities.

With the start of the new fiscal year on 1 October, the DoD acquisition officials will begin considering interoperability as a "key performance parameter" in the development of individual weapon systems and military equipment. For the first time equipment will be fielded in part to achieve commonality with the equipment of other US military services or allied capabilities.

'Weapons will be judged by their ability to 'plug and fight',' said Vitali Garber, the DoD's director of interoperability - a position recently created by DoD acquisition chief Jacques Gansler as a central authority for interoperability." (Bender 1999)

Similarly, M&S project funds can be withheld, or permission to play with other simulations denied, because a simulation is not HLA (High Level Architecture)-compliant – things that are required by DoD (Department of Defense) interoperability policy (Undersecretary of Defense [Acquisition & Technology] 1996).

2. THE POLICY CONUNDRUM

Now that we've established that interoperability is a problem, that it's important, and that interoperability policy is important, we can turn our attention to the next question, *"Is interoperability policy a problem?"* At least one high official within DoD issued a recent statement that supports the view that it <u>is</u> a problem:

"The 'architecture and management [of the Defense Information Infrastructure] have failed to provide the security, interoperability and economy originally envisioned,' Arthur Money, DOD's chief information officer, told a joint hearing of the Procurement and Research and Development Subcommittees of the House Armed Services Committee." (Verton 1999)

The labyrinth of interoperability policy can present many obstacles to unwary, unsuspecting C4I (Command, Control, Communications, Computers, Intelligence) or M&S (Modeling and Simulation) program managers, system developers, and users. The purpose of this paper is provide a roadmap to help weary managers, developers, and users find their way through this complex, confusing, and often frustrating maze of policies. It is hoped that this paper will help the reader to better understand interoperability policy by condensing, comparing, contrasting, and presenting the basic elements of interoperability policy in a form that helps bring order, meaning and understanding out of chaos.

3. METHOD

Two basic approaches were taken to analyzing interoperability policy, automated information retrieval & text analysis methods, and manual, semi-automated techniques such as the construction of information matrices with spreadsheets.

3.1 Automated Text Analysis & Information Retrieval – SMART

The technique developed by Dr. Gerard Salton for automated information retrieval and text analysis is called the vector-space model (Salton, et. al. 1975), which is similar to an n-space dot product of a vector representing a query and a vector representing a document. The elements of each vector are words, word stems, and word pairs found in the documents. The result of the n-space dot product is a scalar value between zero and one, with zero being a document pair having no common terms and one being a document pair having all (100 percent) common terms. A 1.0 scalar value is always achieved when a document is compared to itself.

Automated interoperability policy document information retrieval and text analysis was performed with a freely available and extremely mature software tool called System for the Mechanical Analysis and Retrieval of Text (SMART), which implements the vector-space model (Salton 1983).

3.2 Manual Analysis

First, a "Top-10 List" of interoperability policy documents was drawn up from those policy documents that had high relevance scores computed by SMART with a list of interoperability policy concept terms, which itself was made by eliminating very rare (low frequency) and very common (high frequency) interoperability policy concept terms. Some judgment was also used to decide just what or wasn't a policy document – a policy document had to belong to one of three categories, policy directives, standards mandates, and implementing memoranda.

Second, interoperability policy statements and element were manually extracted from each of the documents in the "Top-10 List" by common text outlining and summarization techniques.

Third, an Interoperability Policy Roadmap was constructed by manually examining each policy document to determine its precedence and dependence upon related policy documents. Directives at higher levels of the organization typically spawn related, implementing directives at lower levels; with more process details being added at successively lower levels.

Fourth, an Interoperability Policy Element Document Presence Matrix was constructed to relate all interoperability policy elements to each interoperability policy document in the "Top-10 List."

Last, a C4I and M&S Systems Interoperability Policy Elements Comparison Matrix was constructed by sorting and placing interoperability policy elements side-by-side for both the C4I and M&S domains. This matrix made it possible to visually identify the completeness and consistency of interoperability policy in both the C4I and M&S domains.

4. ANALYSIS RESULTS

The analysis of interoperability policies in both the C4I and M&S domains is discussed here. Two kinds of analysis results are presented and discussed, Automated Text Analysis & Information Retrieval, and manual analysis.

4.1 Automated Text Analysis & Information Retrieval Results

Analysis results for Document-to-Document Relevance, Document-to-Interoperability Policy Concept Term List Relevance, Policy Concept Term List Discriminatory Value, and the Document Interoperability Policy Concept Term Presence Matrix are discussed in the following sections.

4.1.1 Document-to-Document Relevance. In Figure 4.1.1 we can see that the following C4I interoperability policy documents are strongly related to one another (document-to-document relevance between 0.6 and 0.8), with the bolded policy directives being strongly related to more than one other directive (Science Applications International Corporation [SAIC] 1999):

Top-10 Interoperability Policy Documents

		1 CJCSI 6212.01A, C4I Interoperability	2 DoDI 4630.8, C3I Interoperability Procedures	3 DoDR 5000.2-R, MDAP & MAIS Procedures	4 DoDI 5000.61, M&S VV&A	5 DoDD 4630.5, C3I Interoperability	6 JTA Version 2.0	7 DoDD 5000.59, M&S Management	8 SECNAVINST 5200.38, DON M&S Program	9 USD(A&T) Memo, HLA	10 USD(A&T) Memo JTA Ver. 2.0
1	CJCSI 6212.01A, C4I Interoperability										
2	DoDI 4630.8, C3I Interoperability Procedures	0.7									
3	DoDR 5000.2-R, MDAP & MAIS Procedures	0.5	0.5								
4	DoDI 5000.61, M&S VV&A	0.3	0.5	0.3							
5	DoDD 4630.5, C3I Interoperability	0.7	0.8	0.4	0.4						
6	JTA Version 2.0	0.5	0.4	0.3	0.3	0.2					
7	DoDD 5000.59, M&S Management	0.3	0.6	0.4	0.8	0.5	0.3				
8	SECNAVINST 5200.38, DON M&S Program	0.2	0.2	0.2	0.4	0.2	0.3	0.4			
9	USD(A&T) Memo, HLA	0.2	0.3	0.2	0.4	0.3	0.3	0.5	0.4		
10	USD(A&T) Memo JTA Ver. 2.0	0.2	0.3	0.2	0.2	0.2	0.3	0.3	0.2	0.2	

Figure 4.1.1 Document-to-Document Relevance

- ***DoDD 4630.5, C3I Interoperability***
- *DoDI 4630.8, C3I Interoperability Procedures*
- ***CJCSI 6212.01A, C4I Interoperability***

In the M&S domain, however, we see that the top-level M&S interoperability policy directive, ***DoDD 5000.59***, *M&S Management*, is strongly related to the following policy directives from both domains:

- *DoDI 5000.61, M&S VV&A*

♦ *DoDI 4630.8, C3I Interoperability Procedures*

Interestingly, the directive *DoDI 4630.8, C3I Interoperability Procedures* is strongly related to policy directives in both domains. It seems to act as a kind of link between the two domains.

It is also interesting to note that the top Navy M&S interoperability directive, *SECNAVINST 5200.38, DON M&S Program*, isn't strongly related to any other policy document.

4.1.2 Document-to-Interoperability Policy Concept Term List Relevance. Table 4.1.2 lists the SMART-computed relevance scores for the "Top-10" interoperability policy documents in descending order (SAIC 1999). In this case, each document was compared to a specific list of interoperability policy concept terms rather than the more general list of interoperability terms that were used to compute document-to-document relevance.

Interoperability Policy Document	Policy Concept Term Relevance Score
CJCSI 6212.01A, Compatibility, Interoperability, and Integration of C4I Systems, 30 June 1995	0.3040
DoDI 4630.8, Procedures for Compatibility, Interoperability, and Integration of C3I Systems, 18 November 1992	0.2988
DoD Regulation 5000.2-R, Mandatory Procedures for Major Defense Acquisition Programs (MDAPs) and Major Automated Information Systems (MAIS)	0.2689
DoDI 5000.61, DoD Modeling and Simulation Verification, Validation, and Accreditation (VV&A), 29 April 1996	0.2496
DoDD 4630.5, Compatibility, Interoperability, and Integration of C3I Systems, 12 November 1992	0.2389
JTA Version 2.0, Sect. 1	0.2325
DoDD 5000.59, DoD Modeling and Simulation (M&S) Management, 4 January 1994	0.2305
SECNAVINST 5200.38, Department of the Navy Modeling and Simulation Program, 10 October 1994	0.1784
USD(A&T) Memo 10 September 1996, DoD High Level Architecture (HLA) for Simulations	0.1684
USD(A&T) Memo 30 Nov 1998, DoD Joint Technical Architecture (JTA) Version 2.0	0.1493

Table 4.1.2 Document-to-Interoperability Policy Concept Term List Relevance – The "Top-10" List

4.2 Manual Analysis Results

Analysis results are summarized in the following sections: (1) policy document precedence and dependence; (2) C4I and M&S Systems Interoperability Policy Elements Comparison; (3) policy completeness; (4) policy consistency; and (5) policy effectiveness and efficiency.

4.2.1 Interoperability Policy Roadmap – Policy Document Precedence and Dependence.

Reviewed interoperability policy documents receive their authority and mandate from higher management and command authority levels or echelons. This hierarchy of authority is diagrammed for Navy M&S Program Managers in Figure 4.2.1-1, which depicts the interoperability policy document precedence and dependence relationships existing within the list of interoperability documents having the highest relevance to interoperability policy concept terms. Figure 4.2.1-2 provides a similar roadmap for Navy C4I system program managers; it deletes references to M&S interoperability policy documents. It also adds some specific Navy C4I interoperability policy references that are uniquely C4I, but were not analyzed or included in the original interoperability policy document database.

4.2.2 C4I and M&S Systems Interoperability Policy Element Mapping. The author independently extracted interoperability policy elements from each interoperability policy document in the "Top-10 List" (see Table 4.1.2). These policy elements are primarily concerned with prescribed policy actions or the "what" of interoperability policy; they include very few references to the "who, why, or where." The policy elements extracted by the author are also not the same as those extracted by the interoperability study authors (SAIC 1999), but they are based upon them. Finally, interoperability policy elements are condensed to an abbreviated form of short phrases or statements that can be easily displayed and sorted in a matrix.

4.2.2.1 C4I Systems Interoperability Policy Element Mapping. C4I systems interoperability policy elements are mapped to interoperability documents in the "Top-10 List," as shown in Figure 4.2.2.1. Related C4I systems interoperability policy elements are grouped together and alternately shaded in gray or white to distinguish one conceptual group from another.

Figure 4.2.2.1 also shows that with one exception, all the C4I systems interoperability policy elements are confined to six C4I systems policy documents (6212.01A, C4I Interoperability; DoDI 4630.8, C3I Interoperability Procedures; DoDR 5000.2-R, MDAP & MAIS Procedures; DoDD 4630.5, *C3I Interoperability; JTA Version 2.0; USD(A&T) Memo JTA Ver. 2.0*). Virtually none of them come from M&S policy

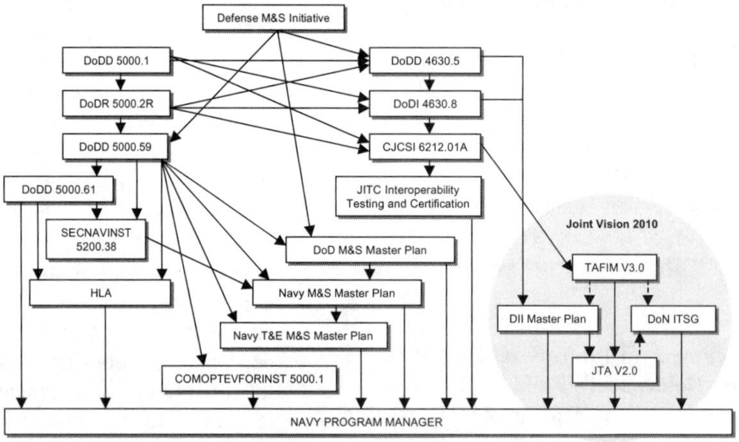

Figure 4.2.1-1 M&S Interoperability Policy

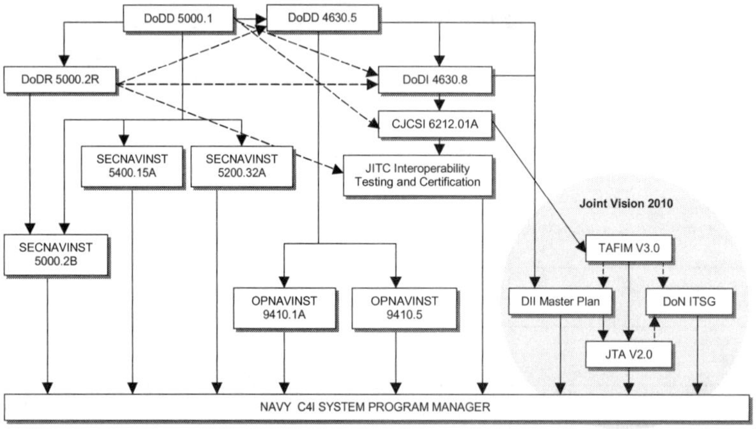

Figure 4.2.1-2 C4I Interoperability Policy

documents. This is what was expected since C4I policy documents deal with issues that are common to both C4I and M&S, while M&S policy documents are largely confined to M&S issues.

4.2.2.2 M&S Systems Interoperability Policy Element Mapping. M&S systems interoperability policy elements are mapped to interoperability documents in the "Top-10 List," as shown in Figure 4.2.2.2. Related M&S systems interoperability policy elements are also grouped together and alternately shaded in gray or white to distinguish one conceptual group from another.

A closer inspection of Figure 4.2.2.2 also reveals that M&S interoperability policy elements are largely confined to four M&S policy documents (*DoDI 5000.61, M&S VV&A; DoDD 5000.59, M&S Management; SECAVINST 5200.38, DON M&S Program; and USD(A&T) HLA Memo*). Virtually none of them come from the four C4I policy documents. This time, however, more than half of the M&S interoperability policy elements come from JTA-related interoperability policy documents (Defense Information Systems Agency [DISA] 1997) rather than M&S interoperability policy documents – this was not expected.

4.2.3 Comparison of C4I and M&S Interoperability Policy. Once both C4I and M&S interoperability policy elements have been mapped to their respective policy documents it is then relatively simple to compare C4I interoperability policy elements with M&S interoperability policy elements for completeness and consistency. Table 4.2.3 provides a side-by-side comparison of both C4I and M&S interoperability policy elements that have been sorted, collated, and

Interoperability Policy C4I Systems	Top 10 Interoperability Policy Documents 1	2	3	5	4	10	6	7	8	9
C4I systems all for Joint use	X	X		X						
C4I systems approved interface standards list		X								
C4I systems information exchange requirements		X								
C4I systems interoperability requirements list		X								
C4I systems standardized information flow procedures and formats		X								
C4I systems, interfacing systems mandatory guidance in TAFIM			X							
Certification of C4I system operation within Joint interface		X								
Certification of C4I systems compatibility		X		X						
Certification of interoperability requirements by CJCS procedures	X	X		X						
Certification of systems integration		X		X						
Combined tests verify interoperability in combined operations		X								
Compatibility development, coordination, review procedures by CJCS				X						
Compatibility requirements conform to interoperability policy				X						
Compatibility requirements tested, validated, meet standards		X		X						
Compatibility satisfactorily addressed throughout life cycle			X	X						
Compatible w/ existing, planned Joint, allied, combined C4I systems, ops		X	X	X						
Compatible with other C4I systems	X	X								
Consistent with U.S. standards and STANAGs		X								
Consistent (new systems w/ interoperating systems) standards application		X								
Data interchange standards ensure that application formats share data					X					
DII COE shall be used by C4I systems & M&S systems					X					
Doctrine compatible with interoperability requirements		X								
Doctrine concepts & operational procedures approved by CJCS				X						
Doctrine concepts & operational procedures for Joint and combined ops				X						
Follow-on Test and Evaluation (FOT&E) to assess interoperability			X							
Human-computer interface mandated standards in Appendix B					X					
Incompatibility, integration, interoperability problems reported		X								
Information modeling and information mandated standards in Appendix B					X					
Information processing mandated standards in Appendix B					X					
Information systems security mandated standards in Appendix B					X					
Information transfer mandated standards in Appendix B					X					
Infrastructure access anywhere, anytime, any mission	X	X		X						
Integratable, integrated	X	X								
Integrated with Joint, combined C4I systems, operations		X		X						
Integration development, coordination, review procedures by CJCS				X						
Integration requirements tested, validated, meet standards		X		X						
Integration satisfactorily addressed throughout life cycle			X							
Interface standards validated and approved		X								
Internet (closed network model) standards prescribed for C4I systems & M&S					X					
Interoperability complies DoDD 4630.5, DoDI 4630.8, and CJCSI 6212.01A			X							
Interoperability development, coordination, review procedures by CJCS				X						
Interoperability requirements assessed during MNS, ORD validation		X								
Interoperability major consideration each milestone decision point			X							
Interoperability major decision for MDAP/MAIS start			X							
Interoperability reqmts consistent with C4I system architectures		X								
Interoperability reqmts consistent with C4I system integration reqmts		X								
Interoperability reqmts consistent with C4I system interface standards		X								
Interoperability reqmts consistent with C4I system procedures		X								
Interoperability requirements conform to interoperability policy										
Interoperability requirements documented	X	X								
Interoperability requirements identified during C4I reqmts validation		X		X						
Interoperability requirements meet standards		X								
Interoperability requirements tested	X	X								
Interoperability requirements validated		X		X						
Interoperability satisfactorily addressed throughout life cycle			X							
Interoperability waivers not permanent	X									
Interoperable horizontally & vertically	X									
Interoperable with allied C4I systems, operations		X	X							
Interoperable with combined/multinational C4I systems, operations		X		X						
Interoperable with existing C4I systems requiring data exchange	X	X								
Interoperable with Joint/multiservice C4I systems, operations	X	X		X						
Interoperable with planned C4I systems requiring data exchange	X	X								
Joint C4I Interoperability Requirements Database with MNSs, ORDs		X								
Joint tests verify interoperability in Joint operations		X								
JTA (Joint Technical Architecture) Version 2.0 implemented						X				
JTA mandated by DoD						X				
JTA mandates standards for emerging, existing, planned capabilities						X				
JTA req'd for all capabilities that produce, use, or exchange electronic info						X				
JTA req'd for all systems that give the warfighter an operational capability						X				
Mapping, charting, geodesy data standards, space support interoperability		X								
MNS and ORD complies with interoperability policy		X								
Open systems architecture standards and protocols established					X			X		
Operational procedures compatible with interoperability requirements		X								
ORD includes C4I system communications, protocols, standards			X							
ORD includes C4I system integration into C4I architecture			X							
ORD includes C4I system Joint use considerations			X							
ORD includes C4I system procedural & technical interfaces			X							
OT&E plans include compatibility, interoperability test objectives		X								
Recertified when required by hardware or software modifications	X									
Seamless, transparent, open systems infrastructure, development	X		X		X					
Standard data elements shall be exchanged by C4I systems and M&S					X					
Systems design and integration uses the technical architecture					X					
TEMPS include compatibility, interoperability test objectives		X								
Test & Evaluation (T&E) in all acquisition phases to verify interoperability		X								

Figure 4.2.2.1 C4I Systems Interoperability Policy Element Map

Interoperability Policy	1	2	3	5	6	10	4	7	8	9
Top-10 Interoperability Policy Documents	CJCSI 6212.01A, C4I Interoperability	DoDI 4630.8, C3I Interoperability Procedures	DoDR 5000.2-R, MDAP & MAIS Procedures	DoDD 4630.5, C3I Interoperability	JTA Version 2.0	USD(A&T) Memo JTA Ver. 2.0	DoDI 5000.61, M&S VV&A	DoDD 5000.59, M&S Management	SECNAVINST 5200.38, DON M&S Program	USD(A&T) Memo, HLA
M&S (Modeling & Simulation) Systems										
Accreditation documentation maintained & accessible							X			
Accreditation procedures by CJCS for Joint federations, M&S							X			
Accreditation responsibility of M&S application sponsor							X			
Common databases developed								X		
Common tools developed								X		
Data interchange standards ensure that application formats share data					X			X		
Data interchange(exchange) standards & protocols established								X		
Data verified, validated, and certified							X			
DII COE shall be used by C4I systems & M&S systems					X					
Federation accredidation of Joint M&S and Joint federations							X			
Federation appearance, behavior, completeness are acceptable							X			
Federation data exchange is accurate and comparable across elements							X			
Federation elements can exchange data							X			
Federation Execution Details Data Interchange Format - FED DIF					X					
Federation performance, fidelity, interoperability are acceptable							X			
Federaton response times commensurate with use across elements							X			
HLA (High Level Architecture) mandated for all M&S					X					X
HLA managed by EXCIMS AMG										X
HLA supercedes DIS and ALSP										X
Human-computer interface mandated standards in Appendix B					X					
Information modeling and information mandated standards in Appendix B					X					
Information processing mandated standards in Appendix B					X					
Information systems security mandated standards in Appendix B					X					
Information transfer mandated standards in Appendix B					X					
Internet 5-layer network model standards prescribed for C4I systems & M&S					X					
Internet standards and protocols established, followed								X	X	
Interoperability standards and protocols developed, implemented, followed								X	X	
Interoperable with combined/multinational C4I systems, operations									X	
Interoperable with Joint/multiservice C4I systems, operations									X	
JTA (Joint Technical Architecture) Version 2.0 implemented						X				
JTA maintained by DISA						X				
JTA mandated standards for emerging, existing, planned capabilities						X				
JTA req'd for all capabilities that produce, use, or exchange electronic info						X				
JTA req'd for all systems that give the warfighter an operational capability						X				
M&S No pay date, 10/1/99, all M&S that are not HLA-compliant										X
M&S No play date, 10/1/01, all M&S that are not HLA-compliant										X
Object Model Data Dictionary					X					
Object Model Template Data Interchange Format - OMT DIF					X					
Open systems architecture standards and protocols established					X			X		
Seamless, transparent, open systems infrastructure, development	X		X		X					
Standard data elements shall be exchanged by C4I systems and M&S					X					
Standard Simulator Data Base Interchange Format - SIF					X					
Synthetic Environment Data Representation Interchange Spec - SEDRIS					X					
Systems design and integration rules for technical architecture					X					

Figure 4.2.2.2 M&S Systems Interoperability Policy Element Map

C4I Systems	M&S (Modeling & Simulation) Systems
	Accreditation documentation maintained & accessible
	Accreditation procedures by CJCS for Joint federations, M&S
	Accreditation responsibility of M&S application sponsor
C4I systems: all for Joint use	
C4I systems: approved interface standards list	
C4I systems: information exchange requirements	
C4I systems: interoperability requirements list	
C4I systems: standardized information flow procedures and formats	
C4I systems, interfacing systems: mandatory guidance in TAFIM	
Certification of C4I system operation within Joint interface	
Certification of C4I systems compatibility	
Certification of interoperability requirements by CJCS procedures	
Certification of systems integration	
Combined tests verify interoperability in combined operations	
	Common databases developed
	Common tools developed
Compatibility development, coordination, review procedures by CJCS	
Compatibility requirements conform to interoperability policy	
Compatibility requirements tested, validated, meet standards	
Compatibility satisfactorily addressed throughout life cycle	
Compatible w/ existing, planned, Joint, allied, combined C4I systems, ops	
Compatible with other C4I systems	
Compliant with U.S. standards and STANAGs	
Consistent (new systems w/ interoperating systems) standards application	
Data interchange standards ensure that application formats share data	Data interchange standards ensure that application formats share data
	Data interchange (exchange) standards & protocols established
	Data verified, validated, and certified
DII COE shall be used by C4I systems & M&S systems	DII COE shall be used by C4I systems & M&S systems
Doctrine compatible with interoperability requirements	
Doctrine concepts & operational procedures approved by CJCS	
Doctrine concepts & operational procedures for Joint and combined ops	
	Federation accreditation of Joint M&S and Joint federations
	Federation appearance, behavior, completeness are acceptable
	Federation data exchange is accurate and comparable across elements
	Federation elements can exchange data
	Federation Execution Details Data Interchange Format - FED DIF
	Federation performance, fidelity, interoperability are acceptable
	Federation response times commensurate with use across elements
Follow-on Test and Evaluation (FOT&E) to assess interoperability	
	HLA (High Level Architecture) mandated for all M&S
	HLA managed by DMSO
	HLA supersedes DIS and ALSP
Human-computer interface mandated standards in Appendix B	Human-computer interface mandated standards in Appendix B
Incompatibility, integration, interoperability problems reported	
Information modeling and information mandated standards in Appendix B	Information modeling and information mandated standards in Appendix B
Information processing mandated standards in Appendix B	Information processing mandated standards in Appendix B
Information systems security mandated standards in Appendix B	Information systems security mandated standards in Appendix B
Information transfer mandated standards in Appendix B	Information transfer mandated standards in Appendix B
Infrastructure access anywhere, anytime, any mission	
Integratable, integrated	
Integrated with Joint, combined C4I systems, operations	
Integration development, coordination, review procedures by CJCS	
Integration requirements tested, validated, meet standards	
Integration satisfactorily addressed throughout life cycle	
Interface standards validated and approved	
Internet 5-layer network model standards prescribed for C4I systems & M&S	Internet 5-layer network model standards prescribed for C4I systems & M&S
	Internet standards and protocols established, followed
Interoperability complies DoDD 4630.5, DoDI 4630.8, and CJCS 6212.01A	
Interoperability development, coordination, review procedures by CJCS	
Interoperability maintainability assessed during MNS, ORD validation	
Interoperability major consideration each milestone decision point	
Interoperability major decision for MDA/PM/AIS start	
Interoperability reqmts consistent with C4I system architectures	
Interoperability reqmts consistent with C4I system integration reqmts	
Interoperability reqmts consistent with C4I system interface standards	
Interoperability reqmts consistent with C4I system procedures	
Interoperability requirements conform to interoperability policy	
Interoperability requirements documented	
Interoperability requirements identified during C4I reqmts validation	
Interoperability requirements meet standards	
Interoperability requirements tested	
Interoperability requirements validated	
Interoperability satisfactorily addressed throughout life cycle	
	Interoperability standards and protocols developed, implemented, followed
Interoperability waivers not permanent	
Interoperable horizontally & vertically	
Interoperable with allied C4I systems, operations	
Interoperable with combined/multinational C4I systems, operations	Interoperable with combined/multinational C4I systems, operations
Interoperable with existing C4I systems requiring data exchange	
Interoperable with Joint/multiservice C4I systems, operations	Interoperable with Joint/multiservice C4I systems, operations
Interoperable with planned C4I systems requiring data exchange	
Joint C4I Interoperability Requirements Database with MNSs, ORDs	
Joint tests verify interoperability in Joint operations	
JTA (Joint Technical Architecture) Version 2.0 implemented	JTA (Joint Technical Architecture) Version 2.0 implemented
JTA maintained by DISA	JTA maintained by DISA
JTA mandated standards for emerging, existing, planned capabilities	JTA mandated standards for emerging, existing, planned capabilities
JTA req'd for all capabilities that produce, use, or exchange electronic info	JTA req'd for all capabilities that produce, use, or exchange electronic info
JTA req'd for all systems that give the warfighter an operational capability	JTA req'd for all systems that give the warfighter an operational capability
	M&S No pay date, 10/1/00, all M&S that are not HLA-compliant
	M&S No play date, 10/1/01, all M&S that are not HLA-compliant
Mapping, charting, geodesy data standards, space support interoperability	
MNS and ORD complies with interoperability policy	
	Object Model Data Dictionary
	Object Model Template Data Interchange Format - OMT DIF
Open systems architecture standards and protocols established	Open systems architecture standards and protocols established
Operational procedures compatible with interoperability requirements	
ORD includes C4I system communications, protocols, standards	
ORD includes C4I system integration into C4I architecture	
ORD includes C4I system Joint use considerations	
ORD includes C4I system procedural & technical interfaces	
OT&E plans include compatibility, interoperability test objectives	
Recertified when required by hardware or software modifications	
Seamless, transparent, open systems infrastructure, development	Seamless, transparent, open systems infrastructure, development
Standard data elements shall be exchanged by C4I systems and M&S	Standard data elements shall be exchanged by C4I systems and M&S
	Standard Simulator Data Base Interchange Format - SIF
	Synthetic Environment Data Representation Interchange Spec - SEDRIS
Systems design and integration rules for technical architecture	Systems design and integration rules for technical architecture
TEMPS include compatibility, interoperability test objectives	
Test & Evaluation (T&E) in all acquisition phases to verify interoperability	

Table 4.2.3 Comparison of Existing C4I and M&S Interoperability Policy

shaded to clearly show: (1) which C4I interoperability policy elements have no counterpart elements in M&S interoperability policy documents; (2) which M&S interoperability policy elements have no counterpart elements in C4I interoperability policy documents; and (3) which interoperability policy elements are common to both C4I and M&S interoperability policy.

4.2.3.1 Completeness. Completeness of interoperability policy will be analyzed and discussed in the context of Table 4.2.3 and other policy analysis work performed in the interoperability policy study (SAIC 1999). Table 4.2.3 suggests four categories of interoperability policy completeness that should be discussed, interoperability policy elements that are: (1) in C4I, but not in M&S; (2) in M&S, but not in C4I; (3) in both C4I and M&S; and (4) not in C4I or M&S.

4.2.3.1.1 Interoperability Policy Elements in C4I, not in M&S. The following types of interoperability policy elements are found in C4I interoperability policy documents, but not in M&S policy documents (bolded policy elements can be made common to both domains):

- **Certification and re-certification**
- **Compatibility**
- **Doctrine**
- **Integration**
- **Interface standards**
- **Interoperability problem reporting**
- **Interoperability requirements**
- **Interoperability testing, OT&E, T&E**
- **Mapping, charting, geodesy data standards and specifications**
- **Mission Need Statement (MNS) and Operational Requirements Document (ORD)**
- **Interoperability waivers**

4.2.3.1.2 Interoperability Policy Elements in M&S, not in C4I. The following types of interoperability policy elements are found in M&S interoperability policy documents, but not in C4I policy documents (bolded policy elements can be made common to both domains):

- **Accreditation**
- **Common databases and tools**
- **Data interchange standards and protocols establishment**
- **Data VV&C**
- Federations
- High Level Architecture
- **Internet standard and protocol establishment**
- No-pay / no-play deadlines for architecture conformance
- **Object Model Data Dictionary (OMDD)**
- **Object Model Template Data Interchange Format (OMTDIF)**
- **Risk management (SECNAVINST 5200.38 only)**
- Standard Simulator Data Base Interchange Format (SIF)
- Synthetic Environment Data Representation Interchange Format (SEDRIS)

4.2.3.1.3 Interoperability Policy Elements in both C4I and M&S. Table 4.2.3 also show which types of interoperability policy elements are found in both C4I and M&S interoperability policy documents by shading those policy elements that are common to both domains. These common (bolded) elements are summarized below:

- **Data interchange standards for applications sharing**
- **Defense Information Infrastructure Common Operating Environment (DII COE)**
- **Human-computer interface standards**
- **Information modeling, processing, systems security, and transfer standards**
- **Internet 5-layer network model**
- **Internet standards and protocols**
- **Interoperable with Joint and combined C4I systems and operations**
- **Joint Technical Architecture (JTA)**
- **Open systems architecture standards and protocols**
- **Seamless, transparent open systems infrastructure**
- **Standard data elements exchanged by C4I systems and M&S applications**
- **System design and integration rules for technical architecture**

Interoperability policy elements that are common to both the C4I and M&S domains should not present any special problems to program managers or system users. Instead, they tend to raise questions as to *why more interoperability policy elements that are unique to either the C4I or M&S domain are not common to both of them.*

4.2.3.1.4 Interoperability Policy Elements not in C4I or M&S. What may by more important to any thorough analysis of interoperability policy elements is not revealed by Table 4.2.3 – that is the types of interoperability policy elements that are missing entirely from interoperability policy directives in both domains. Some that are brought to mind by Figure 2.1 include technology integration, formal interoperability theory and modeling, and interoperability performance measurement and standards.

Technology Integration. Nothing can more quickly render interoperability policy elements obsolete than major new advances in information technology. In software development for example, "componentware" or software through components" promises significant breakthroughs in interoperability, but none of the interoperability policy directives mention it. Similarly, today's interoperability policy elements do no reflect recent improvements in data transfer rates and latency made possible by recent advances in data communications technology. Some examples include: (1) the use of lasers for intra-satellite data transfer rates of 1 GBPS; (2) cooled lasers that produce faster, single-wavelength optical signals on existing fiber-optic cables at speeds up to 10 trillion BPS; and (3) routers that use only mirrors to direct network traffic sixteen times faster than electrical switches do. When interoperability policy, such as the JTA, mandating the use of older, outdated information technology standards which don't reflect current technology advances, it can result in the program manager and "C4I warrior" being saddled with information systems and an infrastructure that provide worse performance than would otherwise be made possible by updated standards.

Simulation Based Acquisition (SBA). The omission of Simulation Based Acquisition (SBA) from interoperability policy documents is equally distressing considering its special emphasis in recent acquisition reform measures. This topic is discussed extensively in the Navy Modeling and Simulation Master Plan, but is not specifically mentioned in any of the interoperability policy documents that were analyzed.

Formal Interoperability Theory & Modeling. A formal, unified theory of interoperability performance and related, explanatory models are needed to underpin interoperability policy making in both the C4I and M&S domains. Without this formal basis, common performance measures and metrics cannot be used to measure and compare interoperability performance in either domain; and the effects of changes in interoperability policy can never be known or understood.

Interoperability Performance Measurement & Standards. Interoperability performance must be made measurable by adopting metrics which are common to both domains, and which validate a formal, testable theory of interoperability. Only then will it be possible to write interoperability performance standards that can be used by policy makers to specify what levels of interoperability performance are actually achievable. Current interoperability policies are conspicuously mute on the subject of what level of interoperability performance can or should be achieved. Without quantified performance goals and common measures, it is impossible to set realistic goals or know whether they've been accomplished.

4.2.3.2 Consistency.

"The only completely consistent people are the dead." -- Aldous Huxley

One view of consistency is concerned with faithful and accurate interpretation and implementation of policy at successively lower organizational levels. A lower-level organization must issue specific policies that faithfully and accurately implement the broader policy statements of a higher command authority.

Reviewed policy documents receive their authority and mandate from higher management and command authorities, as shown in the document hierarchies depicted in Figures 4.2.1-1 and 4.2.1-2.

Another view of consistency deals with the technical attributes and details used to describe policy elements in each domain. These inconsistencies are described in greater detail below in Section 5.2.

4.2.4 Interoperability Policy Effectiveness and Efficiency. The effectiveness and efficiency of interoperability policy cannot be determined because no validated theory or models of interoperability performance currently exist that explain how interoperability works and what causes interoperability performance to vary. There are, therefore, no associated standard measures or metrics of interoperability performance that can be used to gage whether changes in interoperability policy cause any perceptible changes in interoperability performance.

There are some measures and metrics of interoperability in the C4I domain, but they are largely confined to message formats and tactical data link standards and specifications. They do not provide a single, quantified, validated measure of interoperability performance that can be used in either domain.

5. CONCLUSIONS

The following conclusions may be drawn from the above results.

5.1 Interoperability Policy Completeness

Interoperability policies are generally incomplete because C4I interoperability policy does not include policy elements in the M&S domain that should be common to both the C4I and M&S domains. Conversely, M&S interoperability policy does not include policy elements in the C4I domain that should also be common to both domains. Finally, both the C4I and M&S domains have excluded critical policy elements that should also be common to both, but are conspicuously absent:

- Technology integration
- Formal interoperability theory and modeling
- Interoperability performance measurement and standards

5.2 Interoperability Policy Consistency

Interoperability policy documents were found to be generally consistent with one another from one organizational level to the next, with the following exceptions.

5.2.1 Policy Focus. C4I system and M&S policy documents are markedly different when it comes to their focus on interoperability. Interoperability is a major focus of C4I policy documents as evidenced by their higher correlation with interoperability policy concept terms in the interoperability policy document database (SAIC 1999). Interoperability is not a major focus of M&S policy documents as evidenced by their lower correlation with interoperability policy concept terms in the interoperability policy document database (SAIC 1999).

5.2.2 Requirements. C4I interoperability policy ensures that C4I system interoperability requirements: (1) are identified and assessed during system requirements (MNS, ORD) validation; (2) are documented; (3) meet standards; (4) are tested; (5) are validated; (6) are addressed throughout the system's life cycle; (7) are a major consideration for MDAP/MAIS start and each milestone decision; (8) are consistent with C4I system architecture, integration requirements, interface standards, and procedures; and (9) conform to interoperability policy. M&S policy does not provide explicit guidance on interoperability requirements. The only reference to interoperability requirements in M&S policy documents is in the *DoD M&S Master Plan* (DoD 1995). This oversight could result in the failure of simulation/C4I system interfaces to provide successful interoperation of simulations and C4I systems.

5.2.3 Standards. C4I interoperability policy provides message format standards, tactical datalink standards, tactical database standards, and internet standards. M&S policy provides architecture standards and internet standards. Navy M&S policy (Department of the Navy Instruction [SECNAVINST] 5200.38 1994) is inconsistent in its reference to the DIS (Distributed Interactive Simulation) standard and technology, instead of HLA (High Level Architecture). Neither domain provides an interoperability performance standard. Interoperability performance standards are needed by policy makers to specify what levels of interoperability performance are actually achievable. Without quantified performance goals and common measures, it is impossible to set realistic goals or know whether they've been accomplished.

5.2.4 Interfaces. Interfaces are explicitly addressed in reviewed C4I interoperability policy documents, which require approved, validated interface standards (SAIC 1999). Interfaces are not explicitly addressed in M&S policy documents. It is impossible to assess the effectiveness or efficiency of simulation/C4I system interfaces without such interface standards.

5.2.5 Validated Theory. A formal, unified theory of interoperability performance and related, explanatory models are needed to underpin interoperability policy making in both the C4I and M&S domains (Sutton 1999). A formal theory of interoperability and related explanatory models are not now available in either the C4I or M&S domains. It is impossible to write a meaningful interoperability performance standard without a sound theoretical basis.

5.2.6 Performance Metrics & Measurement. Quantified interoperability performance measures and metrics are not available in either the C4I or M&S domains (Sutton 1999). It is, therefore, impossible to measure and compare interoperability performance in either domain; and the effects of changes to interoperability policy can never be known or understood.

5.2.7 Testing. C4I interoperability policy requires: (1) Test and Evaluation (T&E) in all acquisition phases to verify interoperability; (2) Test and Evaluation Master Plans (TEMPs) and Operational Test and

Evaluation (OT&E) plans which include compatibility and interoperability test objectives; (3) interoperability requirements tests that verify interoperability in Joint and combined operations; and (4) DISA maintenance of a database of C4I system interoperability requirements and test results. M&S policy does not include comparable, explicit interoperability test requirements for the interoperability of models and simulations. It is, therefore, impossible to assess the effectiveness or efficiency of simulation/C4I system interfaces without similar, comprehensive testing policy elements.

5.2.8 Accreditation and Certification. DISA has certification authority (CJCS 1995) for reporting the interoperability of C4ISR systems (SAIC 1999). There is no certification authority for the interoperability of simulation/C4I system interfaces. Certification of interoperability of C4I systems is explicitly addressed by C4I interoperability policy, but the interoperability of M&S systems is not explicitly addressed by DoD, Joint, or Navy policy. component level of policy document. M&S HLA compliance is addressed by M&S policy, but it does not guarantee interoperability of one simulation with another, or with a C4I system through a simulation/C4I system interface.

5.2.9 Processes and Procedures. C4I interoperability policy defines detailed, explicit processes and procedures for achieving C4I system interoperability, but M&S policy does not. Both the C4I and M&S communities have clearly defined organizational mandates for carrying out policy, but processes and procedures are clearer and more precise in the C4I domain than they are in the M&S domain.

5.2.10 Risk Management. Simulation interfaces with live (real C4I systems) simulations or virtual simulations could result in situations where: (1) a real pilot is presented with both real and synthetic targets, but can't differentiate one from the other; (2) a real air raid occurs while a ship's C4I system is receiving synthetic targets during an exercise; and (3) a real missile launch occurs while a ballistic missile defense system is being exercised with synthetic missiles. C4I or M&S interoperability policy does not completely define or emphasize specific requirements for risk mitigation in such situations.

6. RECOMMENDATIONS

The following recommendations are made to improve both C4I system and M&S interoperability policy completeness, consistency, effectiveness, and efficiency.

6.1 Interoperability Policy Alignment

Interoperability policy elements in the C4I and M&S domains should be aligned with one another to improve policy completeness and consistency.

6.1.1 Interoperability Completeness. It is recommended that interoperability policy elements in the C4I domain that are not also in the M&S domain (see Table 4.2.3) be added to the M&S domain as discussed above. Similarly, it is recommended that interoperability policy elements in the M&S domain that are not also in the C4I domain be added to the C4I domain.

6.1.2 Interoperability Consistency. It is recommended that interoperability policies be amended to make interoperability policy elements in the C4I and M&S domains consistent with one another as prescribed in Section 5.2 above

6.2 Interoperability Policy Effectiveness and Efficiency

It is recommended that interoperability performance metrics be defined that can be used to measure interoperability in both the C4I and M&S domains. It is also recommended that these metrics be based upon a validated, tested theory of interoperability and associated explanatory models.

It is also recommended that the business process for achieving interoperability be formally modeled to provide a baseline for process improvement in both domains. It is further recommended that the effectiveness and efficiency of this process be measured and tracked by monitoring changes in interoperability performances that result from process improvements or policy changes in both domains.

6.3 Interoperability Program Establishment

It is strongly recommended that Joint, DoD, and DoD component policy makers in both domains adopt a common, coordinated interoperability program similar to the one depicted by Figure 6.3. Such a program will provide a validated, tested theory of interoperability and associated, explanatory models, which in turn will provide a rational basis for interoperability performance metrics and measurement. Metrics and measurement will then make it possible to write a meaningful interoperability performance standard that can then be used as a guide to establish, quantitative interoperability performance standards, which in turn can be used to rewrite interoperability policy to include realistic interoperability goals that are actually achievable.

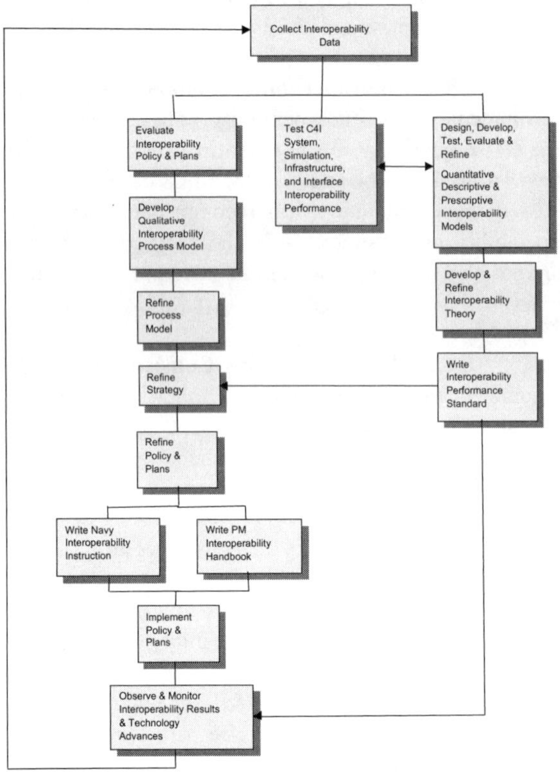

Figure 6.3 Interoperability Program Architecture

7. ACKNOWLEDGEMENTS

The author wishes to acknowledge the contributions of Dr. Vitali Garber, DoD Director of Interoperability, CAPT Steve Chapman, Director of NAVMSMO, Mr. Jim Weatherly, TSG Director, and Mr. Dave Merritt, PD 13 Program Director. The interoperability program and this work would not be possible without their keen insights and special efforts.

8. REFERENCES

Bender, B. 1999 "DoD Expands Pursuit Of Interoperability," *Jane's Defence Weekly* (29 September).

Chairman of the Joint Chiefs of Staff (CJCS) Instruction 6212.01A. 1995. *Compatibility, Interoperability, and Integration of Command, Control, Communications, Computers, and Intelligence Systems.* CJCS, Washington, D.C. (30 June).

Defense Information Systems Agency (DISA). 1997. *JointTechnical Architecture (JTA), Version 2.0 (1st draft).* Washington, D.C. (31 October).

Department of Defense (DoD). 1995. *Modeling and Simulation (M&S) Master Plan.* DoD 5000.59-P. Defense Modeling and Simulation Office (DMSO), Alexandria, VA (October).

Department of Defense Directive (DoDD) 5000.59. 1994. *DoD Modeling and Simulation (M&S) Management.* Deputy Secretary of Defense, Washington, D.C. (4 January).

Department of the Navy Instruction. 1994. *Department of the Navy Modeling and Simulation Program.* SECNAVINST 5200.38. Secretary of the Navy (SECNAV), Washington, D.C. (10 October).

Fasulo, LTC R.K. 1996. *Joint Communications Interoperability.* U.S. Army War College, Carlisle Barracks, PA (29 March).

Odell, R.R.; P. Morley; K. Gause; and F. Ruiz-Ramon. 1999. *Toward a U.S. Navy Strategy for C4I Interoperability with Allies.* Center for Naval Analyses, Alexandria, VA (April).

Salton, G. and M.J. McGill. 1983. *Introduction to Modern Information Retrieval.* McGraw Hill, New York.

Salton, G.; A. Wong; and C.S. Yang. 1975. "A Vector Space Model for Automatic Indexing", *Communications of the ACM,* 18, No. 11 (Nov), 613-620.

Science Applications International Corporation (SAIC). 1999. Technical Report, *Modeling and Simulation Interoperability Study: DoD, Joint, and Navy Policies.* SAIC, San Diego (1 October).

Sutton, P. 1999. "Interoperability: A New Paradigm." in *Computational Intelligence for Modeling, Control & Automation: Neural Networks & Advanced Control Strategies.* M. Mohammadian, Ed. IOS Press, Amsterdam, 351-361.

Under Secretary of Defense (Acquisition & Technology) [USD(A&T)]. 1996. Memorandum, DoD High Level Architecture (HLA) for Simulations. USD(A&T), Washington, D.C. (10 September).

Verton, D. 1999. "DOD revamping massive information architecture." *Federal Computer Week.* 25 (February).

AUTHOR BIOGRAPHY

Paul Sutton is the Navy Interoperability Manager in the Technical Support Group (TSG) of SPAWAR PD 13, which provides direct support to the Navy Modeling & Simulation Management Office (NAVMSMO), OPNAV N6M. He holds a Bachelor of Science degree in General Engineering from the U.S. Naval Academy, and a Master of Science degree in Management from San Diego State University. He has more than thirty years experience in distributed, interactive modeling and simulation, advanced networking engineering, systems engineering, software engineering, and project management. He has previously taught both undergraduate and graduate courses at U.S. International University, San Diego State University, the University of San Diego, and the University of La Verne.

USING XML TO SHARE OFFLINE SIMULATION DATA

Lee W. Lacy
Dynamics Research Corporation
3505 Lake Lynda Drive, Suite 100
Orlando, Florida 32817
407-380-1200 x104
e-mail: LLacy@DRC.com

MAJ Theodore D. Dugone
US Army TRAC-Monterey
P.O. Box 8692
Monterey, California 93943
831-656-4057
dugonet@ trac.nps.navy.mil

KEYWORDS: Military, XML, Data Interchange Format

ABSTRACT:

Simulations are becoming increasingly interoperable. Standards such as the Distributed Interactive Simulation (DIS) protocols and the High Level Architecture (HLA) have enabled heterogeneous simulations to execute within the same simulated environment. However, development of offline simulation support applications continues to be "stovepiped".

New initiatives are being pursued to support the sharing of offline simulation data and information. The purpose of these efforts is to enable simulation systems to share reusable information. The ability to reuse simulation data and information results in reduced simulation development and exercise preparation costs.

Data standards support the sharing of information by creating "common languages" for legacy and new systems' offline data interfaces. The eXtensible Markup Language (XML) is being used to define these standards for many simulation-related applications including HLA Data Interchange Formats (DIFs). XML is also being employed in e-business data interchange applications. The use of XML for sharing simulation data demonstrates techniques for leveraging new Internet-related standards in the simulation community.

Recent research conducted for the U.S. Army's Training and Doctrine Command (TRADOC) has focused on sharing simulation scenario data and Computer Generated Forces behavior descriptions using XML-based standards. This research can be expanded to support a variety of offline simulation data interchange requirements.

This paper provides recommendations on using XML to develop data sharing standards to support sharing offline simulation data and provides examples from the TRADOC research. These recommendations include specification of data requirements, development of supporting logical data models, and the evolution of the data models into XML Document Type Descriptions (DTDs).

INTRODUCTION

Major advances have occurred in linking heterogeneous simulations. Standards such as the Distributed Interactive Simulation (DIS) protocols and the High Level Architecture have enabled distributed simulations to communicate during execution. However, offline simulation support applications continue to proliferate proprietary and "ad hoc" file formats that discourage the sharing of information.

BACKGROUND

The problem of sharing data among offline simulation support applications can be addressed using the eXtensible Markup Language (XML). Certain types of data benefit more than others from XML Data Interchange Format (DIF).

Problem Definition

Simulation support applications have been developed in a "stovepiped" manner. Reusing offline data, such as simulation scenarios, currently requires point-to-point interfaces between scenario generation systems. Standard DIFs enable various applications to develop import and export interfaces to a common data standard, thereby reducing the number of interfaces required from $O(n^2-n)$ to $O(2n)$.

The development of DIFs results in reuse capabilities of both data and code. Reuse results in cost savings benefits.

A large investment has been made by the DoD to define open standards in support of interoperability. Some of these efforts support DoD data standards in sharing in general (e.g. DISA's DII COE initiative).

XML to the Rescue

The extensible Markup Language (XML) is a metalanguage that can be used for data interchange. (Goldfarb, 1998). XML can also facilitate data repositories such as the U.S. Army's Functional Description of the Battlespace (Stone, 1998) (Garingo, 1999).

XML can be used to support almost any type of data, through the use of HTML-like tags. However, the most appropriate use of XML is to markup ASCII type data that's shareable.

XML interchange files are used for defining DIFs for vertical domains such as pharmaceutical prescriptions, the human genome sequence, and HLA simulation data (Lacy, 1999b).

Offline simulation data spans a continuum from information of interest to a broad community to proprietary information of interest to only one organization. This continuum equates to the spectrum of simulation implementation independent to simulation implementation specific.

Offline Simulation Domain Definition

A variety of types of data support offline simulation support applications. These range from highly reusable information to local data that is of little interest to other applications. The most reusable information is the simulation independent information (e.g., scenario data). The least reusable information is information such as local hardware or network configuration data that is of interest only to a particular installation of a simulation for a particular exercise.

XML DIF DEVELOPMENT PROCESS

Specific processes have been developed for creating and publishing DIFs (Gravitz, 1999). Our recommended process for DIF development is similar to traditional software or simulation development models of specifying requirements, designing, coding, testing, and distributing. Our process involves:

- Defining the data requirements to scope the interchange file's contents,
- Developing a flexible logical data model (preferably in a formal language such as IDEF1X) (Bruce, 1992),
- Evolving the data model into a commented XML Document Type Description (DTD) file (Megginson, 1998),
- Demonstrating and testing the XML DTD with sample data, and
- Documenting and evolving the standard in a collaborative environment.

This process has been successfully followed on two U.S. Army projects that have been performed to standardize the interchange of simulation scenario data and Computer Generated Forces (CGF) behavior specifications.

EXAMPLES OF SIMULATION SHARING INITIATIVES

Examples of XML data standards developed for offline simulation data include recent work by the U.S. Army's Training and Doctrine Command (TRADOC) Analysis Center (TRAC) in Monterey, California. These efforts were focused on developing XML data interchange formats for simulation scenarios and CGF behaviors.

XML Scenarios Data Interchange Format

Simulation systems would operate more effectively if they shared scenario data. Scenario data could be shared between scenario generation systems prior to initialization. Additionally, scenario developers could reuse scenario contents from other simulation systems if they were able to access the other systems' scenario data. The task of developing scenario-related tools would be simplified if scenario data was available in a standardized format.

Recommendations have been made in the past for interchanging scenario data using standard data interchange formats. XML has been specifically recommended for use in scenario interchange (Hunt, 1999).

The High Level Architecture (HLA) Dynamic Scenario Builder (DSB) initiative focused on improving the timeliness, quality, and cost-effectiveness of developing scenarios (and associated tools) for HLA simulations by standardizing the interchange of scenario data. (Lacy, 1999a)

The standard development process consisted of reviewing legacy simulation scenario data, defining an HLA scenario logical data model, developing an XML DIF for exchanging scenario data, and specifying common requirements for compliant systems. (Lacy, 1999c)

Major elements of the simulation scenario data model include:

- Metadata,
- Organization,
- Simulation Object,
- Information Item,
- Environmental Area, and
- Event.

Additional entities define relationships between these entities. A set of property classes entities have been used to associate data-driven values with entities.

CGF Behavior Specifications

Computer Generated Forces (CGF) systems are increasingly data driven. New Army CGF systems such as Warfighter's Simulation 2000 and OneSAF require behavior specifications that are read by the simulation software (Karr, 1999). Developers of CGF systems invest significant resources into developing CGF behaviors and authoritative conceptual models of domain expertise to support behavior development.

The process of describing accurate representations of CGF is very complex (Pew, 1998). The process for developing a CGF Behavior Specification DIF involved reviewing the results of prior tasks to identify requirements, categorizing the required information into categories, designing a set of logical data sub-models, and developing an XML DTD to represent the model.

It became apparent that the logical data model could not only support implementation-independent representations of behaviors. The model had to support legacy systems that have chosen to represent knowledge using a particular language or method. The initial model supports a variety of representation methods. However, additional knowledge representation sub-model entities will be required to support new representation techniques such as neural networks, case based reasoning, and active networks.

The concepts used to represent higher-level behaviors such as planning are very difficult to represent in a data model.

The logical data model was separated into the following major sub-models, in increasing level of complexity:

- Metadata,
- Knowledge Representation Constructs,
- Declarative,
- Procedural, and
- Strategic.

The definition of these sub-models is based on commonly identified Knowledge Representations categories (Pace, 2000).

EMERGING INITIATIVES

A variety of U.S. military efforts are being conducted that relate to offline simulation application data standards. These include the Future Combat Systems (FCS) Integrated Data Environment (IDE), and the DARPA Agent Markup Language (DAML).

FCS Equipment Characteristics

The FCS program is evaluating industry proposals for meeting FCS requirements. The FCS effort employs principles of Simulation Based Acquisition (SBA) and strategies based on the Simulation and Modeling for Acquisition, Requirements, and Training (SMART) initiative. (AMSAA, 2000)

A Simulation Support Plan (SSP) is being developed to document the Modeling and Simulation (M&S) strategy for the FCS program. The SSP will identify the set of M&S tools that will be used to develop and assess FCS concepts.

The FCS IDE is a network-based environment being developed to support collaboration within the government and with industry. The IDE will serve as a repository for M&S data. This data will be provided to the IDE by Authoritative Data Sources (ADS) and contractors proposing concepts. The data will be utilized by various M&S applications to compare and contrast proposed concepts.

XML data standards are being developed to support the submission of the concept description data. These standards are primarily focused on supporting the equipment characteristics data required for analysis.

DARPA DAML

The Defense Advanced Research Projects Agency (DARPA) is developing a language called the DARPA Agent Markup Language (DAML). DAML will be based primarily on the Resource Description Format (RDF). RDF is a metadata standard that can be expressed using XML. DAML markup is intended to be understandable to DAML-enabled user agents and programs. (Rapoza, 2000)

DAML represents the next generation of data interchange because it adds semantics to the interchange process, rather than relying on syntax-only specifications of XML data standards.

SUMMARY

XML is a useful metalanguage for standardizing the representation of offline simulation data. These standards should be developed by defining data requirements, designing logical data models, and coding XML DTDs. This process has been followed in the HLA DSB and CGF behavior specification projects.

REFERENCES

AMSAA (2000), Future Combat Systems Combined Analysis Plan, February 2000.

Bruce, T. A. (1992), *Designing Quality Databases with IDEF1X Information Models.*

Garingo, G. (1999), "XML to Facilitate Interoperability Between Repositories". *Proceedings of the Spring '99 Simulation Interoperability Workshop*, Paper 99S-SIW-175. March, 1999.

Goldfarb, C. F., Prescod, P. (1998), *XML Handbook.* Prentice Hall.

Gravitz, P. (1999). "Common Activities in Data Interchange Format (DIF) Development. *Proceedings of the Spring '99 Simulation Interoperability Workshop*, Paper 99S-SIW-177. March, 1999.

Hunt, Ken. 1998. "A New Paradigm for Developing and Maintaining Scenarios for Distributed Simulation. Proceedings of the Spring '99 Simulation Interoperability Workshop, Paper 99S-SIW-179. March, 1999.

Karr, C., Holbrook, R. (1999) "Modeling Command and Control in WARSIM 2000". *Proceedings of the 8th Computer Generated Forces and Behavioral Representation Conference*, May 11-13, 1999. Orlando, Florida.

Lacy, L.; Stone, G. III; D, T. D. (1999a) "Sharing HLA Scenario Data". *Proceedings of the Fall '99 Simulation Interoperability Workshop*, Paper 99F-SIW-190. September 1999.

Lacy, L., Stone, G.; Dugone, T. (1999b) "XML Data Interchange Format Standards for HLA-Related Data Interoperability". *Proceedings of the Southeastern Simulation Conference '99*

Lacy, L., Dugone, T. , (1999c), "High Level Architecture (HLA) Dynamic Scenario Builder (DSB)", Final Technical Report TRAC-Monterey.

Megginson, D. (1998). *Structuring XML Documents*. Prentice Hall. 1998.

Miller, G. J. (1999). "An XML Representation of HLA Object Models. *Proceedings of the Spring '99 Simulation Interoperability Workshop*, Paper 99S-SIW-089. March, 1999.

OneSAF, 1999). OneSAF Operational Requirements Document (ORD), Version 1.1, August 16, 1999.

Pace, D. (2000) "Simulation Conceptual Model Development". *Proceedings of the Simulation Interoperability Workshop*, Spring 2000.

Pew, R., Mayor, A. (Eds.) (1998). *Modeling Human and Organizational Behavior: Application to Military Simulations*. Washington D.C.: National Academy Press.

Rapoza, J. (2000) "DAML Could Take Search to a New Level", PC eek Online, Volume 17, Number 6, February 7, 2000. on-line: http://www.zdnet.com/pcweek/stories/news/0,4153,2432538,00.html

Stone, G., Pettitt, B. (1998) "Future Battlespace Implications to Computer-Generated Forces", *Proceedings of the 7th Computer Generated Forces – Behavior Representation Conference.*

ACKNOLWEDGEMENT

The scenario and CGF work described in this paper was supported by contracts from TRAC-Monterey with STRICOM and TRADOC funding. The FCS equipment characteristics work described in this paper was supported by Booz-Allen and Hamilton as part of their DARPA/Army FCS Integrated Date Environment project.

AUTHOR BIOGRAPHIES

LEE LACY is the Director of Orlando Operations for Dynamics Research Corporation. Lee has worked on training and simulation projects including embedded training research, CCTT, WARSIM 2000, and JSIMS. He is currently researching simulation data interchange for the Army's TRADOC Research and Analysis Center. Lee serves on the Board of Directors for the National Center for Simulation.

MAJ THEODORE D. DUGONE is an Army officer with over ten years of commissioned service. He graduated with a B.S. in biology from Pittsburg State University in 1988 and was commissioned in the Field Artillery. He completed an M.S. in Operations Research from the Colorado School of Mines in 1998. He is currently an operations research analyst at the U.S. Army Training and Doctrine Command (TRADOC) Analysis Center (TRAC) in Monterey, California.

ROLE OF HARDWARE-IN-THE-LOOP (HWIL) SIMULATION IN THE PRODUCTION PROCESS OF AN AIR DEFENSE MISSILE SYSTEM

David M. Curry, Craig A. Combs and Miranda Oden
U. S. Army Aviation and Missile Command
Attn: AMSAM-DSA-SH-TM (Miranda Oden)
Redstone Arsenal, Alabama 35898
e-mail: oden-mh@redstone.army.mil

KEYWORDS

Hardware-in-the-loop (HWIL), cost as an independent variable (CAIV), production, production test equipment, statistical process control (SPC), test parameters

ABSTRACT

For over twenty-five years, hardware-in-the-loop (HWIL) simulation has played a vital role in the development and acquisition process of the Stinger missile system. This paper describes the role of a detailed HWIL simulation in the production process of this air defense missile system, and its historical significance in the evolution of the Stinger missile. The HWIL simulation is an important tool used by the missile producer to evaluate the effects of changes in production parameters on system performance. This paper discusses the interaction of the HWIL simulation with all phases of missile production including such items as correlating the simulation to factory test equipment, tolerance studies, parts interchangeability, engineering change proposals, and other areas throughout the life cycle of the missile system. A brief description of the Stinger missile will be included.

INTRODUCTION

Stinger is a small surface to air missile originally designed to be launched from a soldier's shoulder. Due to its size and accuracy, it has since been integrated onto a variety of ground and air vehicles. Since its inception twenty-five years ago, the missile has undergone numerous performance enhancing upgrades. Throughout this life cycle, simulation has played an increasingly important role. Originally, the simulation was developed to support missile design and testing. Since that time, the complexity and accuracy of the simulation has increased to the point where it is now used in virtually every phase of the system's life cycle beginning with cost trade analyses, transitioning through development and production and finally supporting fielded hardware with failure analysis.

There are a variety of methodologies used in modeling small surface to air missiles. These range from a semi-physical model to a detailed all digital model. For Stinger programs, we chose to utilize a HWIL simulation. This simulation provides a detailed assessment of Stinger missile from development to fielding. Analysis of flight and simulation data has demonstrated that the validated Stinger HWIL simulation is a powerful tool for requirement definition, missile design, test flight analysis, missile performance assessment and hardware fielding.

2.0 MISSILE DESCRIPTION

seeker and a proportional navigation system that operates independently after initial aiming and launching by the operator. The weapon system is a ready-to-fire unit consisting of a missile round (guided missile in a launch tube), a separable gripstock, a battery coolant unit (BCU) and an Identification Friend or Foe (IFF) system. This system is compatible will all platforms capable of firing a STINGER missile and is effective against all types of fixed wing aircraft, helicopters, unmanned aerial vehicles, and cruise missiles. The ready-to-fire weapon weighs 35.0 lbs. and is 60 inches in length. There are currently four generations of the STINGER missile: 1) Basic STINGER, 2) STINGER Post, 3) STINGER-RMP and 4) STINGER-RMP Block I. The Stinger evolution chart is shown in Figure 1.

SYSTEM	CHARACTERISTICS	DESCRIPTION
BASIC	• Passive IR Homing (Fire and Forget) • Proportional Navigation • U.S./NATO Compatible IFF • Blast Warhead • Manportable • No Field Maintenance	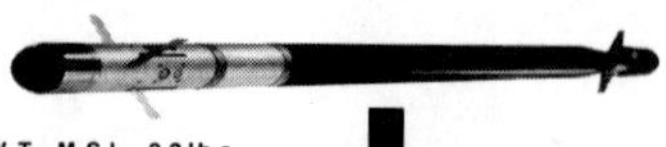 WT. MSL. 23lbs DIAM: 2.75 in LENGTH: 60 in
POST	ADDS: • Passive IR/UV Guidance • Rosette Pattern Image Scanning Techniques	 WT. MSL. 23lbs DIAM: 2.75 in LENGTH: 60 in
RMP	ADDS: • Reprogrammatic and Additional Processing Capability	 WT. MSL. 23lbs DIAM: 2.75 in LENGTH: 60 in
RMP BLOCK I	ADDS: • Software Upgrades • Roll Frequency Sensor	 WT. MSL. 23lbs DIAM: 2.75 in LENGTH: 60 in

Figure 1. Stinger Evolution

3.0 SIMULATION DESCRIPTION

The Stinger-RMP simulations are one-to-one base (real-time), six degree of freedom (6DOF) hybrid (analog/digital) HWIL simulations of the missile system. A block diagram of the simulation is shown in Figure 2. The target/countermeasure/background scene generator and optical scan/IR/UV detector block is a special purpose digital computer based system for generating complex representations of the IR and UV target signatures as functions of time and spatial positions. Target, background, and countermeasure signals are summed to form the detector output signals. Target aspect angle and intensity variation with aspect angle and range are simulated to represent target maneuver and range closure.

The Signal Processing Unit (SPU) incorporated into the simulation is the guidance section electronics fabricated on circuit card assemblies rather than actual missile hybrid micro electronic assemblies to provide access to the microprocessor and memory through a software development station. The wing servo model, also implemented on the analog computer, is a detailed model of the operation of the motor driven wing actuator. Analog implementations are used for these models because of the high frequencies, which must be simulated.

The remaining elements of the simulation, the airframe and geometry models are implemented in the digital domain to obtain the accuracy needed for terminal intercept calculations.

The Stinger Simulation Working Group formally validated the HWIL simulation in November 1996. The Army Test and Evaluation Command (ATEC) subsequently accredited the simulation.

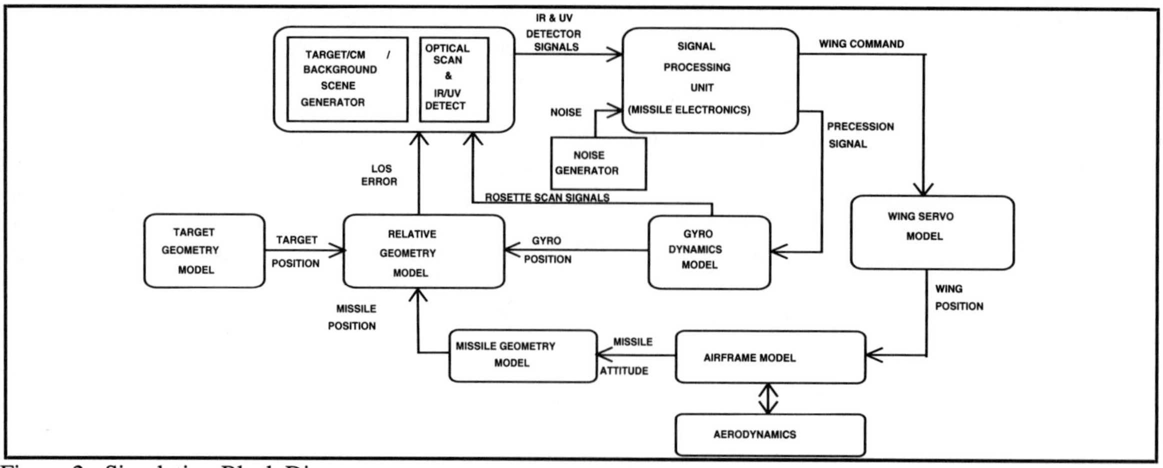

Figure 2. Simulation Block Diagram

4.0 SIMULATION CORRELATION WITH PRODUCTION

Development of the original Basic Stinger simulation employed the model-test-model philosophy. The simulation was used to support missile design. In turn, the initial product design was used concurrently to support simulation development. The simulation was validated by performing flight tests and comparing the predicted simulation results to the actual flight test results. At the completion of missile development, the simulation was fully validated and accredited by the analysis and missile user community. The validated simulation was then used to assess missile performance across a wide array of target engagement conditions, evaluate system modifications and to perform cost trade-off and tolerance studies.

At the completion of the Basic Stinger development, the HWIL simulation was an established tool for supporting design and assessing performance. The relative significant missile modifications required for Stinger Post also necessitated dramatic changes to the simulation. These changes were focused in the target models, signal processing unit and countermeasure generation system. For the most part, the airframe was unchanged. This enabled the use of the Basic Stinger digital airframe model to assess aerodynamic shifts due to changes in optical dome shapes. Following these early airframe excursions, the various components of the Stinger Post simulations were combined and the model-test-model philosophy was repeated. Employing the same model-test-model philosophy, flight test results were again utilized to validate modifications made to the simulation.

A major use of the simulation was to conduct formal and informal Performance Assessments (PA). The PA provides a basis for characterizing the capability of the Stinger-Post weapon system in a broad range of environments to ensure that performance requirements were met or exceeded. The simulation runs for the PA included variations of specific weapon system parameters over an expected manufacturing tolerance. Upon completion of the PA, single point sensitivity studies were conducted to determine the effects of environmental variability on the missile/target intercept point for a given engagement as a function of variations in target size and intensity. These studies led to better test-to-test repeatability, direct verification of the parameters that should be controlled during the manufacturing process and a closer relationship of test parameters with performance parameters. Also, by utilizing the results of the simulation, product reliability was increased through the elimination of potential tolerance issues. The simulation continued to evolve with missile improvements. The validated Stinger Post simulation was used as a baseline for development of the Stinger RMP simulation. The simulation, when correlated with production and testing, provided a cost-effective tool for evaluating development and production modifications. The simulation was used to evaluate system modifications and to perform cost trade-off and tolerance studies. Due to changing components throughout the Stinger life cycle, simulation allowed hardware and software design issues to be addressed and resolved before introduction into missile hardware. Not only did this save time, but also allowed more cost-effective design improvements to be developed and tested. Along with design, the simulation was used to conduct production tolerance studies. Once developed, production parameters were fed back into the HWIL simulation. After the simulation replicated product performance, the simulation parameters were correlated with production parameters to determine where critical production parameters could be relaxed while not degrading overall missile performance. Also, the simulation enabled evaluation of hardware changes to prior missile configurations. The ultimate benefit of these studies was a reduction in the cost of the missile.

During the Stinger RMP program, the simulation was also utilized to evaluate hardware tolerance test parameters. The goal of these studies was to determine the outcome on missile performance by varying key parameter tolerance modifications. As an example, a study was conducted to determine the effect on Stinger-RMP weapon system PH due to tolerance changes to twenty-two Guidance Assembly/Guidance Section production test parameters. Since the production test parameters were not identical to directly controllable missile parameters, a set of controllable missile parameters whose variations would correspond to the test parameter changes was developed. The test parameters were correlated to combinations of nineteen missile parameters. These parameters were simultaneously varied in a normal distribution over the corresponding missile tolerance ranges within a three-sigma deviation span. A subset of the RMP Performance Assessment (PA) engagements was used, comprising six target groups, which included fixed-wing, maneuvering and non-maneuvering targets, both benign and with countermeasures (CM), and rotary wing targets in both benign and CM environments. The results of the study showed that the overall system PH and PK at the requested tolerance were equivalent to the current tolerances. Therefore, no clear pattern of system degradation was apparent for a single tolerance limit.

Functional modeling of parameter variations helped to establish sublevel performance requirements, and subsequently, test station requirements. The methodology and detail used to develop the simulation enabled it to reproduce production test parameters at a subcomponent level. By performing these tests on the simulation, stack up tolerances could be evaluated quickly and easily. This enabled tolerance levels to be properly set to maximize performance while minimizing cost. Missile development, simulation and test equipment (TE) continue to be correlated together and grow by feeding off one another. All begin as piece part items and are matured to complete operational systems. Development and test parameters from design and early test are fed into the simulation to replicate performance. The simulation is then used to modify/enhance development of the missile system and TE. Parameters from the initial development and testing of the system are used to begin initial development of the simulation. Several development and test parameters are used to ensure the simulation matures to replicate true system performance.

Utilization of the aforementioned test parameters allowed development of a validated simulation, which can in turn be used to assist in the future development and growth of the missile system and test equipment. The factory TE can be reproduced using the simulation to determine impacts of changing parameters. Also, the TE and simulation can be used in tandem to evaluate system modifications to ensure actual test results correlate with simulation results. The correlation between these entities allows confidence in changing system parameters without degrading system performance. This correlation provides for simultaneous growth and maturation of the missile system, test equipment and simulation.

Another step linking test and simulation is the comparison of parameters measured in guidance section testing (GST) and missile system testing (MST). The results of missile checkout tests performed on the guidance assembly are important sources of data for developing and maturing the simulation. Certain major GST and MST parameters are measured each time the simulation is checked out on the computer to ensure accuracy. The mean values of the parameters obtained will be compared with guidance section and missile system level parameters to ensure the specified tolerances are met.

The simulation evolved in the early stages of development of Basic Stinger in which requirements were established followed by a model-test-model approach depicted in Figure 3. To a point, Stinger Block I simulations were used to perform up front cost analysis and performance trade-offs. This established the initial system requirements. The simulation was then used to define sublevel requirements in a way that maximized production efficiency. This evolutionary use of the simulation is depicted in Figure 4.

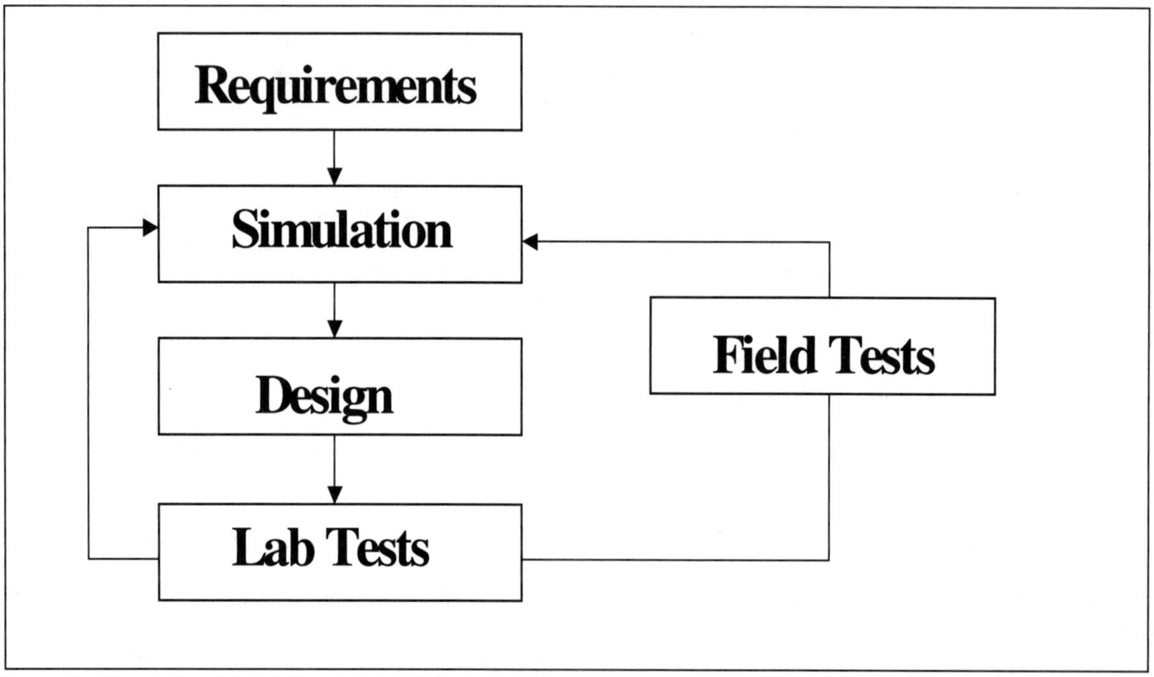

Figure 3. Simulation Model-Test-Model Philosophy During Basic Stinger Development

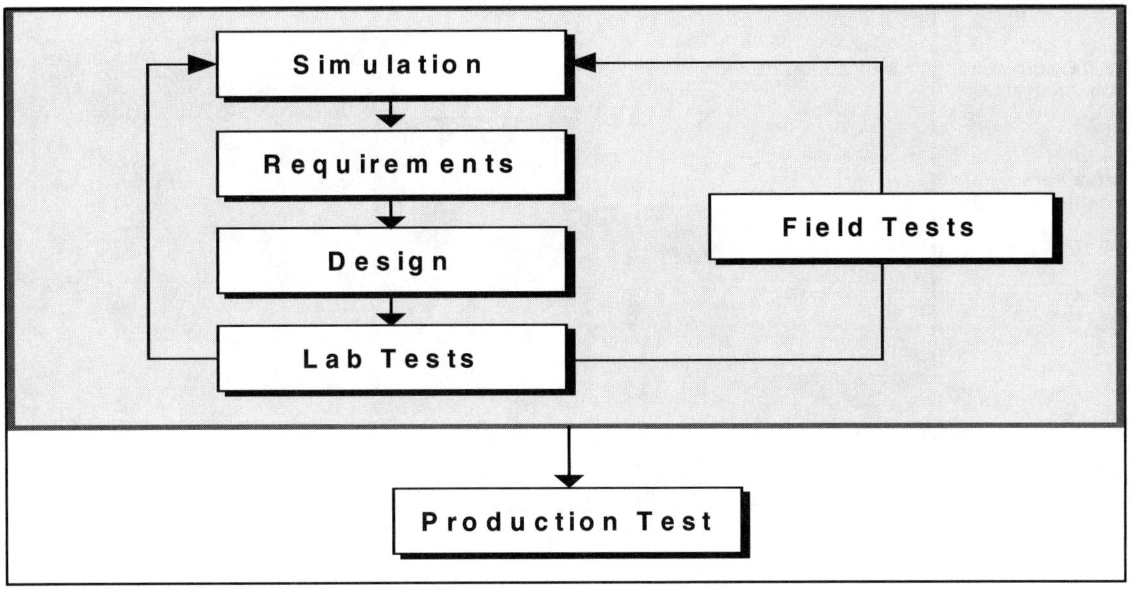

Figure 4. Simulation Model-Test-Model Philosophy During Stinger Block I Development

The Stinger Block I improvement used the simulation from the earliest concept stages. The simulation was used in Cost As an Independent Variable (CAIV) analyses to determine the best trade-offs between cost and performance. These types of studies were only possible because the simulation was mature and complete enough for results to be trusted in the decision process early in the program. Figure 5 depicts the increasing role of the simulation in the Stinger Life Cycle.

The validated Stinger RMP simulation was refined to improve accuracy for development of the Block I Missile. Requiring only minor modifications, the simulation was used to assess proposed missile changes and their impact on system performance. Cost as an independent variable (CAIV) analysis was conducted at the onset to determine which parameters were deemed most important before actually upgrading the missile system. Still employing the model-test-model philosophy, a validated simulation is developed. This simulation is then utilized to support production efforts, perform failure analysis, and to support field hardware.

Ultimately, a gross simulation model is developed and used to perform cost as an independent analysis (CAIV) analysis and to evaluate system level requirements at the onset of a new program. This leads to component requirements and test, which allows for refinement of the model and clarification of systems requirements. Ultimately, a product evolves, is fabricated and is tested. Detailed data from this test can then be used to verify/validate the simulation and subsequently correct and refine the product.

As the simulation grows and evolves with the development of the missile system, many of the components in the breadboard electronics of the signal processing unit are modified and upgraded. In some cases, an entire hybrid microelectronic assembly (HMA) may be redesigned. Because the HWIL simulation utilizes a SPU with circuit card assemblies (CCA) that are identical, from a component standpoint, with the missile HMA's, changes and upgrades can be quickly effected.

This feature makes it straightforward to use the simulation to evaluate the effects of electronic component interchangeability. An example of this was a study conducted during the Block I development program to evaluate missile performance with various "mix and match" HMA's from several phases of missile production. This study was quickly accomplished because the CCA's utilized in the study had already been verified as part of the simulation validation process.

The simulation can also be utilized to evaluate system performance with other new components such as the rocket motor. This type of study requires a formal revalidation of the simulation via detailed post flight analysis before a formal performance can be conducted.

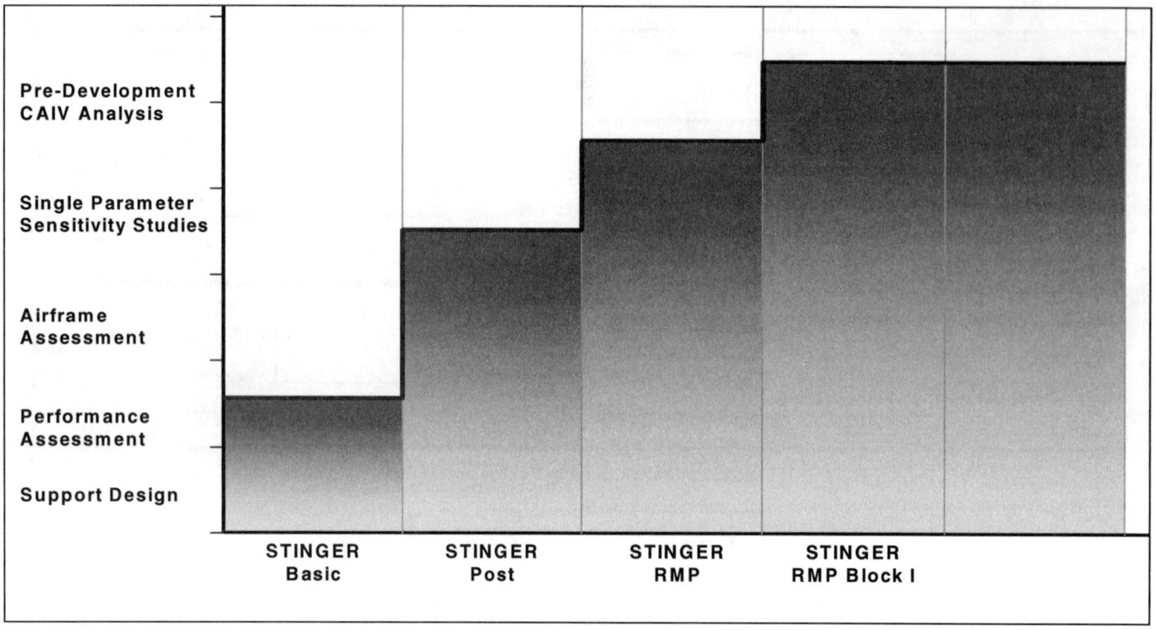

Figure 5. The Increasing Role of HWIL Simulation in the Stinger Life Cycle

At times the simulation is used for other special studies not defined in the above paragraphs. Examples of these are performance against non-specification countermeasures and targets, system performance in alternate applications, evaluation of design modifications, flight failure analyses to determine root cause of in-flight failure not attributable to hardware failure and flight software evaluation studies to verify/confirm performance predictions. These studies are usually performed by special request when additional data is needed to meet specified requirements. The HWIL simulation is an important tool used by the missile producer to evaluate the effects of changes in production parameters on system performance.

5.0 CONCLUSIONS

The HWIL simulation is a powerful tool used throughout all phases of the system's life. Due to the limited resources with respect to time and money, problems can no longer be tested away. Simulation allows for cost analysis and requirements definition to be performed from the onset, leading to a smoother transition into development, production and fielding. Intangibly, use of simulation has enabled the user to utilize the system in an optimum, cost-effective manner.

As the Stinger missile was upgraded, common components of the simulation from previous generations were used to assist in early developmental analysis. Over time, the building block approach to improving the simulation with each subsequent missile improvement created a model that was more complex, accurate and useful. Ultimately, a simulation evolved which is capable of supporting every phase of the product life cycle from predevelopment CAIV through fielded hardware failure diagnosis.

6.0 AUTHORS

Craig Combs is Chief Engineer of the Short Range Air Defense (SHORAD) Project Office at the U.S. Army Aviation and Missile Command. He has over fifteen years experience in management of the development, validation and usage of hardware-in-the-loop simulation.

David Curry is Project Support Engineer in Systems Simulation and Development Directorate for simulation of Stinger missile systems. He has over thirty years experience in planning, developing, validation and usage of hardware-in-the-loop simulation.

Miranda Oden is a Project Support Engineer of the System Analysis and Development Branch of the SHORAD Project Office. She has four years experience with the Stinger programs and simulations.

Modeling and Simulation in Human Factors Engineering

HUMAN OPERATOR MODELS IN CONSTRUCTIVE SIMULATIONS: A REVIEW

David G. Hoagland and S. Narayanan
Department of Biomedical, Industrial, & Human Factors Engineering
Wright State University, Dayton, OH 45435
Dayton, Ohio

Keywords: modeling and simulation, human operator behavior, performance, military, architecture, distributed interfaces, HLA.

ABSTRACT

While it has long been recognized that problems do exist in simulating realistic human behavior during simulated exercises, little has been done to objectively analyze how the requirements of commonly used military simulations drive the development of ongoing human modeling projects. A review and assessment of some of the current state-of-the-art of both constructive simulations and human modeling is needed if we wish to "bridge the gap" between the decision maker's needs of simulation and the developers of human modeling products. It is the identification of this domain space, general attributes and promising solutions which underlie the motivations behind this paper.

OBJECTIVES

The objective of this paper is to review and assess the state-of-the-art in military constructive simulations with a focus on their current implementation of human performance and/or behavioral representation. In addition, this paper attempts to highlight some of the problems associated with the development of human performance models in relation to their integration with constructive mission/engagement level models used with commonly accepted interface technologies and practices.

The Defense Modeling and Simulation Office (DMSO) recognized the shortcomings in representing human behavior and requested that the National Research Council (NRC) establish a panel on Modeling Human Behavior and Command Decision-Making. The panel was charged to review the current state-of-the-art in developing and implementing human behavior representations (HBRs), and evaluate their potential for military simulation application with an emphasis on the challenging areas of cognitive, team, and organizational behavior (Pew & Mavor, 1998). The scope included computational modeling of human behavior and decision making in the military at individual, unit, and command levels. The panel's tasks were to: (1) review and assess HBRs in current military simulations, (2) assess state-of-the-art of HBRs in the research community, and (3) recommend a research and development agenda to the DMSO.

NRC STUDY

The study approach was to review constructive models and simulations used across all three services, of which 11 were identified and studied from the Army, 4 from the Navy, 3 from the Air Force, and 6 jointly across all the three Services. The models and simulations were evaluated along three axes: Types (live, virtual, constructive); Uses (training, analysis, and acquisition); and Levels (individual combatant, unit level, command and control level). In addition, the panel focussed on a few key HBR components that were felt to greatly affect the following military decision-making activities:

1. Assessing current state of the battle (battlefield visualization, situation assessment, and tactical picture generation).
2. Planning (scheduling and resource allocation, wargaming and problem solving).
3. Developing a course of action (executing a course of action, executing planned activities, monitoring plan deviations, replanning, rescheduling and reallocating resources).

In the panel's assessment, almost all human performance and behavioral representations rely exclusively on either virtual-based human-in-the-Loop (HITL) decisions, or on rule-based or decision table approaches. Perception and situation awareness are often assumed to be perfect, and focused solely on visual stimuli. Communications in the models are focused on verbal message passing and ignore non-verbal communications. In addition, low-level planning is only beginning to be addressed (e.g., route planning). And surprisingly, there were no representations or accounting of physiological factors (injury, heat, stress, fatigue), psychological factors (motivation, fear,), nor organizational factors (chain of command, teaming).

In general, there appears to be a great degree of reliance on HITL simulation when high level decisions must be made by even small teams. There is a high reliance on "scripting" and close following of initial battle plans, along with practically no existing or primitive representation of a commander's "mental model" of current/future situations. Other limitations include: inflexible rule-based or decision table approaches used to model doctrinally-correct tactical decision-making; no models for plan generation or course of action analysis; no mechanisms for "learning" from past engagements; and no explicit accounting for organizational impact on situation assessment or decision making. Finally, there is no mechanism for evaluating future developments in information-centered aspects of warfare including data visualization, decision aids, information warfare, etc.

THE DOD MODELING AND SIMULATION MASTER PLAN (MSMP)

The Department of Defense's Modeling and Simulation Master Plan (MSMP) presents many objectives to further the re-use and interoperability of simulations and models employed for defense purposes. The human behavior representation (HBR) objective and associated issues will be discussed in greater detail. The MSMP states that the Services are to develop authoritative representations of individual human behavior, groups and organizations. Representations of humans and their behavior include human capabilities and limitations; individual and group performance; effects of organizational configuration and environment on performance; command, control and communications; and doctrine and tactics.

Sub-Objective 1: Develop Authoritative Representations Of Individual Human Behavior.

This research must tackle the problem of extending existing constructive models of combat operations to include individual combatants. It must also work towards the development of generic models of individual human capabilities, limitations, and performance (including physiological and psychological). At the same time, human-based architectures and tools must provide the capability to rapidly construct models of individual human behavior for specific applications on demand.

Sub-Objective 2: Develop Authoritative Representations Of The Behavior Of Groups And Organizations.

As one can imagine, extending the capabilities of models of individual humans into an organizational behavioral domain becomes much more complex. Yet, the need in DoD constructive simulation is no less a requirement. At this level of aggregation in the DoD's Modeling and Simulation Master Plan, the objectives for unit and organizational behavior mirror those for single operators of weapon systems. To begin with, team models are needed which extend existing simulations of combat operations to cover friendly, threat, and neutral forces over all levels and functional areas. Secondly, research must address the development of generic representations of the behavior of groups and organizations, or model a wide variety of potential adversaries and non-combatants (e.g., insurgents, terrorists, etc.). This also includes social, political, or economic behaviors that may be required to adequately portray non-traditional forms of warfare. And like Sub-Objective 1, architectures and/or tools must provide the capability to rapidly construct models of group and organizational behavior for different applications.

HUMAN MODELS AND ARCHITECTURES

Many human models and architectures exist, therefore, discussion will center on those human-based modeling components which, through different degrees of application, have been used in military exercises. This view was taken as a way to view models of human components at a modular level, i.e. cognition, perception, etc, which, even though may have been developed as a means to prove research theories without a provision to allow them to interface (pass data) with other models and/or simulations, remain invaluable sources of human behavior representation (HBR) data.

General Discussion of Models of Human Behavior

Common to most human models are sub-models of behavior (sensing, perception, cognition, and so on) arranged in a serial or parallel arrangement. To understand the underlying theories of human models interacting with a complex environment, Pew and Mavor (1998) illustrate a generic model based on Broadbent's modified stage model (1957). Within this model, the human interacts with the battlefield through a series of sub-activities requiring certain amounts of "internal" resources to input incoming data, process actions, and outputting data for the next step. The elements that comprise this model are discussed below.

Sensing and Perception models transform representations of external stimulus energy into internal representations that can be operated on by cognitive processes.

Memory consist of short term working memory (holds information temporarily for cognitive processing) and long-term memory (holds large amounts of information for long periods).

Cognition encompasses a wide range of processing functions:

Learning models represent the process of altering knowledge, factual or procedural.

Decision making models the process of generating and selecting alternatives.

Situation Awareness (SA) refers to the modeled individual combatant's state of knowledge about the environment; SA is the process of achieving this knowledge.

Multitasking models the process of managing multiple, concurrent tasks.

Planning which refers to reviewing and outlining the steps necessary to achieve a selected objective.

Motor behavior models the physical actions selected by cognition. Planning, decision making, and other "invisible" cognitive activities could be considered to ultimately manifest themselves in observable behaviors which affect the human's interaction and performance with the battle field.

Review of Human Models/Architectures

The following is a partial list of human modeling architectures that represent a wide cross-section of theory, application, and maturity levels (Pew & Mavor, 1998). Some of the items studied were either models, architectures or a combination of both in which isolated or brand new models could be developed, run, and archived.

* ACT-R: Adaptive Control of Thought (Anderson, 1993)
* COGNET: COGnition as a NEtwork of Tasks (Zachary et al., 1996)
* EPIC: Executive-Process Interactive Control (Meyer & Kieras, 1997)
* MIDAS: Man-machine Integrated Design and Analysis System (Laughery & Corker, 1997)
* OMAR: Operator Model Architecture (Deutsch & Adams, 1995)
* Soar: Symbolic Operator Architecture (Polk & Rosenbloom, 1994)

Key attributes of human behavior were organized using the Broadbent model and analyzed in detail by the NRC panel. They include: Attention and Multi-Tasking, Memory and Learning, Situation Awareness, Decision Making, Planning, and Behavior Moderators. A summary of the findings, conclusions and recommendations are listed below for each of these HBR components.

- **Attention and Multi-Tasking.** The panel discovered two main thrusts for models in attention and multi-tasking: psychological models (resource theory, strategic workload management, task management, and connectionist models), and classical engineering models (queuing theory, optimal control theory). They concluded that relevant models in this component were not well-developed and that some of the computational models are somewhat ad hoc. They recommended that Attention and Multi-Tasking sub-models be developed and incorporated into HBRs to reflect limited-resource processing and workload-induced performance decrements.

- **Memory and Learning.** Memory models in Soar, ACT-R, and EPIC were considered more advanced, however, on average human models generally did not seem to adequately represent this important human component. This was found to be an area that needed much improved representation for both short term and long term memory if HBRs where to incorporate some form of learning in a dynamic constructive simulation environment.

- **Situation Awareness (SA).** The panel found that some of the simulations had explicit SA representations and also had incorporated some learning and "behavior moderators". The SA technologies which permitted these advances are production rule systems, case-based reasoning, and Bayesian belief networks. The primary problem with this HBR component is that most of these models and architectures need validation studies and independent tests to prove out the representation of tactical as well as strategic awareness of the battle space.

- **Decision Making.** The panel found two basic decision making approaches: one that focuses on belief formation (e.g., SA-driven action selection), and another that focuses on decision analysis (e.g., complex game theoretic analysis). Utility theory is the basis for advanced decision making models which incorporates variability via probabilistic choice models and represent individual differences via shaped utility functions. In addition, judgmental errors are assumed and the models also incorporate adaptability via exemplar learning. The conclusions were that further work in decision making is needed by developing decision making models in a stepped fashion by building on utility theory, and also by incorporating learning and memory to support planning.

- **Planning**. Quite a bit of contrast was found between doctrine and actual practice because, while military planning is doctrinally well-specified, real-world situations caused actual behaviors to deviate significantly. It was recommended that planning models in HBRs should start with doctrinal planning processes as a base and then evolve into non-doctrinal behaviors.

- **Behavior Moderators**. Two types of moderators were considered: 'external' moderators (physiological stressors, physical workload, fatigue, and cognitive workload), and 'internal' moderators (intelligence and cognitive 'style', experience, training, expertise, personality, emotions, attitudes, cultural values). It was felt that efforts to succinctly and accurately model these areas were just beginning, and remain critical to military HBRs.

MILITARY CONSTRUCTIVE SIMULATIONS.

Simulations commonly used today are quite numerous, as well as specialized, across the DoD Services (Navy, Air Force, Army). This paper's review will be limited to a recently developed mission-level architecture called JIMM or (Joint Interim Mission Model), with a focus on HBR.

Review of the Joint Interim Mission Model (JIMM)

JIMM represents the next cycle of modeling and simulation upgrades for users of military constructive simulations. The primary impetus behind the creation of JIMM was to bring together the key strengths of SWEG's electronic warfare simulation and man-in-the-loop simulation with Suppressor's air-to-air modeling environment and operator tactics.

The JIMM environment is a data driven, event-stepped general purpose conflict simulation system. This simulation can be used as a reactive scenario generator to analyze mission level conflicts either standalone or in unison with other external simulations, simulators, and/or stimulators. It provides an operationally realistic environment in which to support decision making at upper command and control levels and below to subordinate organizations within a chain of command. JIMM command and control processing provides a medium level of fidelity, and if additional fidelity is required, JIMM's architecture allows for external assets (usually distributed) to provide a link to manned simulators, hardware stimulators, and computer simulations.

JIMM's basic building block for modeling entities is a *cognition-action* object pairs (c/a) which may be joined with other elements as appropriate as shown in Figure 1. Each player (whether a human, vehicle, or group of vehicles) is defined by attributes and capabilities (sensor antenna pattern, fuel usage, etc.), susceptibilities (signatures, P_k (Probability of Kill) tables, etc.), and tactics (rules of engagement, formations, etc.). Within this layer, each player is maintained as a set of memories: knowledge of its relationships to other players, its situation (both real and perceptual), its mission, its plans (orders, etc.). The Action Object deals with physical phenomena: move, shoot, communicate, sense, jam, etc., while the Cognition Object deals with perceptual phenomena: notice, digest, react, review, plan and adapt.

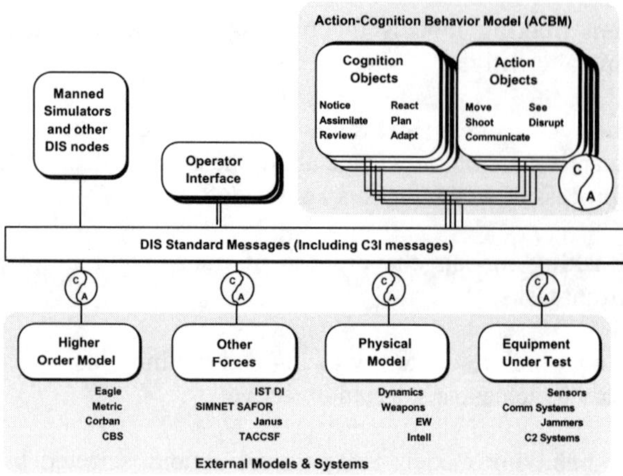

Figure 1. The JIMM environment.

Action Objects.

Action Objects must be discussed in the context of *players* and *functions*. A player represents, to some degree of fidelity, things that exist in the real world and are a mapping of those things to structures that make the simulation of a conflict possible. A player can represent a single entity (an aircraft) or a collection of entities (a flight of four F-15s) with JIMM describing players as objects, along with the relationship between those players. The level of detail used to explicitly represent a player is up to the user and is typically dependent upon analysis factors required in the simulation.

Six basic functions to represent the processes involved in a conflict can be specified by a JIMM user as listed below (with examples in parentheses):

- **Sense** (hardware based functions, i.e. infrared seeker, acquisition radar)
- **Talk** (mobile radio, microwave relay)
- **Shoot** (missile, bomb)
- **Disrupt** (electronic jammer, flare)
- **Move** (aircraft, submarine)
- **Think** (pilot, staff section, computer)

Other significant features in JIMM include:

- **Signature** (radar cross section, presented area)
- **Tactics** (command orders, standard operating procedures)

During run-time, JIMM schedules functions and tasks as specified by the user during his/her set-up of JIMM's databases for an example simulation scenario. It is important to note that the sensing function drives JIMM's simulation. Physical aspects of system sensing are separated from aspects of the human's mental processing.

Cognition Objects (Thinking).

The user can specify Cognition Objects which deal with perceptual phenomena: notice, digest, react, review, ponder and adapt. In addition, the user specifies time delays for each thinking activity and can specify the 'capability' to evaluate and rank the accuracy of intelligence data by a perceived data item. The Cognition Object deals with perceptions of the battlefield, while the Action Object deals with the physics of the battlefield. This is accomplished using the following activities arranged in a configuration somewhat like the Broadbent Modified Stage Model wherein external stimuli is noticed, compared to data stored in memory, and then reacted upon to move towards a desired end state

- **Planning** - measures progress towards goals and assesses the need for changed strategy.
- **Reviewing** - evaluates the quality and quantity of information. It may throw away perceptions, draw conclusions, request action.
- **Adapting** - alters the way the entity evaluates and reacts to situations.
- **Reacting** - manages the entity's and subordinate's physical resources.
- **Noticing** - filters information to short term memory based on entity activity.
- **Digesting** - moves information to medium term memory.
- **Do Next** - allocates time to the other six objects.

SUMMARY AND FUTURE STUDY

This study provides an initial assessment of today's military simulation domain in an effort to understand current representations of human behavior. The domain space for integrating models and architectures of humans into military simulations can be described through examination of these three components as shown in Figure 2 below. With this framework in mind, we can also show how the acquisition, research and training and wargaming functions fit within this domain space. Future study should be accomplished to better quantify the spectrums of this problem domain, their orthoganality and intrinsic attributes.

The horizontal axis pertains to the nature of simulation environments in which models of human behavior will operate. At one end of this spectrum, military simulations contain high fidelity models supported by well-defined levels of engineering data and detail. Research and development applications abound in this part of the domain whereupon researchers create and validate theories of human cognition and other behavioral factors using a single human as the basis for their work. At the other end of the spectrum, are low- fidelity simulations, optimized to the aggregation of hundreds (perhaps thousands) of entities and intelligent agents.

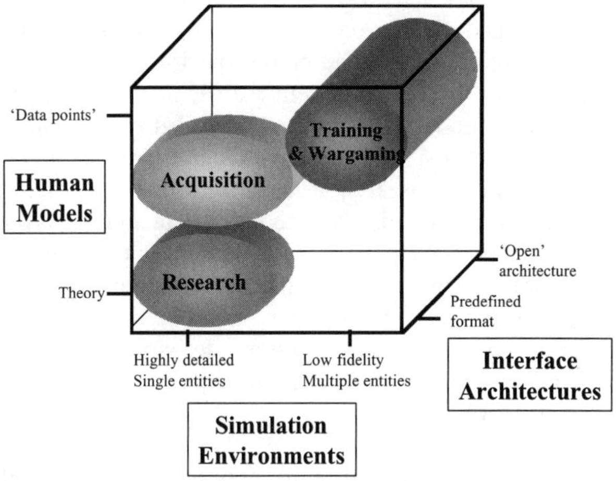

Figure 2. Integration of Modeling Architectures for Military Simulations.

The vertical axis covers the human models themselves. At one end of the axis are the detailed models of visual, motor, or cognitive functions (to name a few) primarily based on localized studies and interpretations (theories) of observed behavior and processed measurement data. In the other extreme are simple values, or 'data points' (i.e. eye movement time = 0.5 seconds), or perhaps simple equations with static variables of human information processing (like time to react or probability of error). As a part of this domain space, the acquisition community uses the quickest and cheapest solutions to derive requirements for weapon systems, usually at the expense of realistic representation of human behavior. Acquisition program schedules are typically too short for the development and incorporation of valid models based on proven research theory. Both research and acquisition applications use established protocols and formats to conduct their work – usually for the same reasons that acquisition has failed to effectively employ research theories, namely, due to cost, time, and the work associated with trying some thing new.

Finally, the depth axis covers the distributed interface architectures (protocols and software) which continue to glue together the M&S community. From legacy systems to new software solutions, these distributed architectures range from predefined data content (PDU) to aid in interoperability on one hand, to the new HLA approach of providing software and data management services which are common and 'open' across multiple simulations on the other. Training and wargaming applications are a major part of this domain space.

One of the challenges facing modelers of human behavior is compatibility *within the larger context* of constructive simulations. Human models in military simulations today tend to be tightly coupled to scenario generations and simulation systems. In these systems, a cognition model may depend on the specific context of the simulation system, and is therefore difficult to extract. So while human modeling is typically derived from a single approach or theory, or at most a mixture of a few approaches, future research needs to pursue 'standardizing' the objects and underlying data (both content and format) in order to support widely-accepted constructive simulation architectures. Another major hurdle is bringing together technical specialists who have valuable insights into different aspects of human cognition, decision making and other factors listed in this paper to help define this sorely needed standard.

In summary, there currently appears to be no single methodology for addressing the many needs and requirements of M&S users who depend on simulation results for making critical decisions regarding military weapon systems. Instead, what has happened is that autonomous organizations have increasingly relied upon themselves to research, develop, exercise, and even market individual models and simulations. While a few models have gained a larger number of accepted users over others, the problems of increasing the realism of human representation in the military have been compounded. Until the plethora of DoD policies migrate themselves into standard business practice across all the Services will the human modeling community have the opportunity to insert itself in readily compatible fashion. The optimal approach for accomplishing this insertion is an area ripe for future study.

REFERENCES

Anderson, J.R. (1993). *Rules of the Mind.* Hillsdale, NJ: Lawrence Erlbaum.

Broadbent, D.E. (1957). A mechanical model for human attention and immediate memory." *Psychological Review*, 64, 205-215.

Deutsch, S.E., & Adams, M. (1995). The operator-model architecture and its psychological framework. In *Proceedings of the Sixth IFAC Symposium on Man-Machine Systems*. Cambridge, MA.

Jones, R. (1999). SWEG/JIMM C[2] Processing and Application for Decision Support at the JFACC Level and Below. TRW Inc. Systems & Information Technology Group. Information & Technical Services Strategic Business Unit. Albuquerque, NM. 27-28 April 1999.

Laughery, K.R., & Corker, K.M. (1997). Computer modeling and simulation of human/system performance. In *Handbook of Human Factors*, II Edition, G. Salvendy, ed., New York, NY: John Wiley & Sons.

Meyer, D.E., & Kieras. (1997). A computational theory of executive cognitive processes and multiple task performance. Part I. Basic Mechanisms. *Psychological Review*. 104: 749-791.

Pew, R., & Mavor, A. (1998). *Modeling Human and Organizational Behavior*. National Academy Press: Washington D.C.

Polk, T.A., & Rosenbloom, P.S. (1994). Task-independent constraints on a unified theory of cognition. In *Handbook of Neuropsychology*, 9, F. Boller & J. Grafman, eds., Amsterdam, Netherlands: Elsevier.

Zachary, W., Le Mentec, J.-C., & Ryder, J. (1996). Interface agents in complex systems. In *Human Interaction with Complex Systems*. C.N. Ntuen & E.H. Park, eds., Kluwer Academic Publishers.

BIOGRAPHIES

DAVID G. HOAGLAND received his Bachelor's of Aeronautical Engineering degree from Ohio State in 1985, where upon he joined the US Air Force as a civilian engineer at Wright-Patterson AFB. As a crew systems engineer working in the Aeronautical Systems Division, he was involved in the design, development, testing and acquisition of major weapon systems. He currently serves as Program Manager for Combat Automation Requirements Testbed (CART) Program with the Air Force Research Laboratory and is also a student at Wright State University obtaining a Master's degree in Human Factors Engineering.

S. NARAYANAN received his doctoral degree in industrial and systems engineering from Georgia Tech in 1994. He is an associate professor of industrial and human factors engineering at Wright State University. His research focuses on a model-based approach to design interactive systems to aid humans in cognitively complex tasks such as planning, control, decision making, information seeking, and troubleshooting.

DOMAIN-RELEVANT PERFORMANCE ANALYSIS IN HUMAN-IN-THE-LOOP DISCRETE-EVENT SIMULATIONS

Ling Rothrock
Department of Biomedical, Industrial, and Human Factors Engineering
Wright State University
Dayton, Ohio 45450
e-mail: lrothroc@cs.wright.edu

KEYWORDS

Man-in-the-loop simulation, performance analysis, discrete simulation, statistical analysis, software engineering

ABSTRACT

This paper presents a method of performance measurement and analysis in human-in-the-loop discrete-event simulations based on the concept of time windows. Operators in modern control systems, or computer simulations of those systems, are confronted with an array of complex, real-time decision tasks. Often, the human operator assumes the role of a supervisory controller and oversees a mostly automated task execution process. In extreme circumstances, operators may only manage by exception – where human intervention is treated as an anomalous event. Hence, human-computer communications play a critical role in the effectiveness of the system as a whole. The construction of measures and design of analysis criteria to evaluate performance in these systems should, therefore, inform the investigator of shortcomings in the communications process.

The performance measures and analysis method presented in this paper are based on human-computer communications in the simulation domain. In fact, operator actions are situated in the context of task demands of the domain. Moreover, the organization of the situated action becomes an emergent property of continuous interactions between the operator and the computer. An adaptation of signal detection theory to the proposed method to measure latency as well as accuracy is explained. The use of the blackboard architecture to determine task demands and interpret operator actions will also be presented. The measures were implemented in a US Navy command and control task, and an analysis of the results will be discussed.

Typically, performance measures represent either a tally of human responses to fixed external stimuli or the extent to which operator activities meet expectations. The method presented in this paper does neither, but rather measures the ability of an operator to communicate, via actions, with the controlled computer in a complex decision environment.

INTRODUCTION

Human activities in complex and dynamic decision environments present measurement and performance quantification challenges to researchers who seek to better understand human-machine interactions. These environments are characterized by uncertainty, simultaneous events, time pressures, and shifting goals. Traditional laboratory studies using classical decision theory concepts are insufficient to account for human activities in dynamic tasks (Beach and Lipshitz, 1993). On the other hand, the unconstrained nature of real-world domains makes it difficult to quantify and measure human performance in operational settings (Doherty, 1993).

Human-in-the-loop simulations provide a means for the researcher to bridge the gap between a Spartan laboratory setting and a largely unconstrained real-world setting (Brehmer, Leplat, and Rasmussen, 1991). In fact, Howie and Vicente (1998) have shown that operator performance in a complex and dynamic simulation can be mapped to different path diagrams that represent distances to a goal state. Also, Hogg et al. (1995) demonstrated that operator performance in a control room simulation could be evaluated in terms of signal detection theory (SDT). Moreover, multiple researchers have utilized time, in the form of temporal constraints, to evaluate human performance (Moray et al., 1991; Laudeman and Palmer, 1995; Raby and Wickens, 1994).

This paper introduces a performance measurement framework for human-in-the-loop simulations, called time windows, that incorporates a temporally constrained SDT measure, as well as a blackboard architecture that opportunistically evaluates windows of opportunity for human activities. The expanded signal detection theory framework will be discussed first. The use of a blackboard model to generate time windows will then be covered. The simulation architecture that incorporates the blackboard model and the time window framework will be discussed next. Following this, some results from an experiment using a human-in-the-loop simulation will be used to highlight the utility of time windows. Finally, some conclusions from the research will be drawn.

TEMPORALLY CONSTRAINED SDT

Signal detection theory conceptualizes a detection task (i.e. a task to detect the presence of a particular signal) as one in which the operator must decide whether the sensory stimulation present at any moment reflects the presence of a signal or irrelevant noise. Figure 1 illustrates the different possible outcomes of human performance in an SDT analysis. The two correct outcomes in the SDT analysis are Hit (correctly detecting a signal) and Correct Rejection (correctly perceiving noise).

Response	**State of the world:** Signal	Noise
Detected	Hit	False Alarm
Not Detected	Miss	Correct Rejection

Figure 1. Signal Detection Theory Outcomes

While a SDT analysis can account for numerous human activities (see Wickens 1992 for a survey), it was not designed to measure human performance in a dynamic context. That is, in situations where required responses are dictated by shifting task demands and conflicting goals, SDT fails to capture the temporal aspect of decision making.

<table>
<tr><th rowspan="2">Response</th><th></th><th colspan="3">State of the world: Task Demand</th><th>No Task Demand</th></tr>
<tr><th></th><th>Early</th><th>On-time</th><th>Late</th><th></th></tr>
<tr><td rowspan="2">Action</td><td>Correct</td><td></td><td></td><td></td><td rowspan="2">False Alarm</td></tr>
<tr><td>Incorrect</td><td></td><td></td><td></td></tr>
<tr><td>No Action</td><td colspan="4">Miss</td><td>Correct Rejection</td></tr>
</table>

Figure 2. Time Window Outcomes

Consider, however, the claim made by Kirlik, Walker, Fisk, and Nagel (1996) that success in dynamic decision making for skilled performers is due to heuristic strategies based on perception and pattern recognition of relevant information in the environment. If one accepts this claim, then one can extend the concept of a signal to some piece of perceptual information or pattern. Moreover, the response to the perceptual information can be thought of as heuristic actions to meet a certain operator objective. The revised SDT shown in Figure 2, therefore, contains outcomes that reflect the relationship between the presence of a task demand (i.e. relevant perceptual information), and operator heuristic actions associated with the demand. Therefore, accurate performance is characterized by an action that is not only correct, but that must also be taken within time constraints dictated by the task demand.

While the time windows framework may be capable of characterizing performance accuracy in dynamic tasks, the problem of time window generation and monitoring remains. To address the problem, one must consider how a component of a simulation can opportunistically (i.e. at the most opportune time) determine task demands based on perceptual information available to the operator. The most suitable tool for solving the problem was determined to be the blackboard model.

BLACKBOARD MODEL

The blackboard model (Nii 1986) of problem solving is a structured case of opportunistic problem solving. It has been used as an effective tool in computer problem solving applications (Vranes et al. 1992), as well as operator aiding in a supervisory control context (Rubin et al. 1998). In an opportunistic reasoning model, pieces of knowledge are applied in a forward or backward chaining fashion at the most opportune time. A blackboard model consists of three major components: the knowledge sources that contain domain knowledge required to solve the problem; the blackboard data structure, which is a global database in which partial and full solutions are kept; and the blackboard control, which is an opportunistic simulation object that guides problem solving by choosing and activating appropriate knowledge sources.

Knowledge Sources

In the context of time windows, the knowledge sources for the blackboard model are those objects that can act on the simulation environment. Moreover, these objects contribute information to the blackboard that are relevant to the frequency and timeliness of operator activities.

For instance, consider a human-in-the-loop simulation where the human operator assumes the role of an air traffic controller monitoring aircraft entering and leaving U.S. airspace. In this instance, each aircraft object is considered as a knowledge source because it provides information that enables the operator to act. More importantly, when the operator is guided by a perceptual or pattern recognition mode of operation, the information provided by the object prescribes how the operator should act.

Blackboard Data Structure

The blackboard holds time window information in the form of computational and solution-state data produced by the knowledge sources. Moreover, it facilitates manipulations at multiple levels of hierarchy.

Returning to the air traffic controller example, the blackboard accommodates all data regarding each aircraft object. For instance, one time window associated with an aircraft object that has just moved into U.S. airspace requires that aircraft identification be made. At a lower level of analysis, another time window associated with the same object specifies that its identification friend/foe signature, which narrows the possible identities of the object, must be ascertained. Thus, the window at the lower level of abstraction supports the identification window at a higher level of analysis.

Blackboard Control

The control of the blackboard occurs through a simulation object that monitors changes on the blackboard and decides what action to take next. The control is based on opportunistic reasoning, and applies knowledge sources in a forward chaining manner from time window creation to time window completion.

Recall that, in the air traffic controller example, a time window was associated with an aircraft object entering U.S. airspace. The blackboard control object created the time window based on two factors: proximity of the aircraft object to the United States, and the knowledge that if an aircraft object entered the U.S., it must be identified by air traffic control authorities. Also, as an operator acts upon an aircraft object to identify it, each action is updated on the blackboard so that the control object can build linkages to indicate that the existing time window has been satisfied. Moreover, if the aircraft object leaves U.S. airspace, its location data alerts the control object so that it can complete the time window.

SIMULATION ARCHITECTURE

As a point of departure, the general simulation architecture first developed at the Georgia Institute of Technology will be used (Chu et al. 1991). The integration of the blackboard model within the simulation framework is depicted in Figure 3.

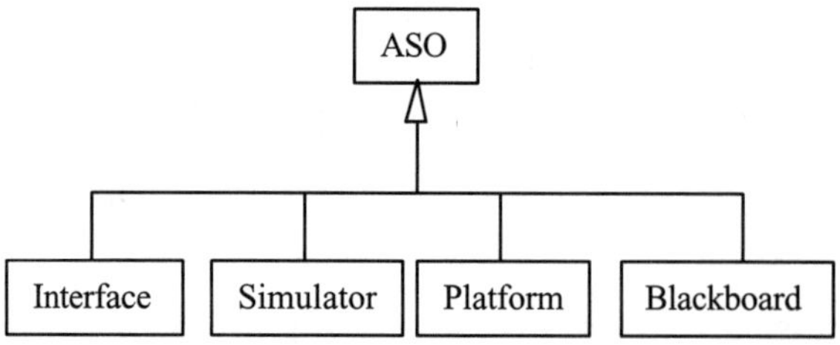

Figure 3. Class Diagram of Simulation

The active simulation object (ASO) is used as a base class so that events may be scheduled by methods contained in the four subclasses. The Interface class contains display parameters as well as methods for rendering the graphical user interface. The simulator class contains methods to control an experimental simulation. The platform class represents platforms (e.g. planes, trains, or automobiles) that exist in the simulation environment, and contains methods that allow those objects to act upon the environment. The blackboard class contains parameters to define the blackboard as well as methods to create, modify and complete time windows.

An illustration of the time window concept within an object-oriented simulation framework is shown in the form of a sequence diagram in Figure 4. A sequence diagram is a model that describes how groups of objects collaborate in some behavior (Fowler and Scott 2000). Each box above the diagram represents an object. Each vertical line represents the object's life during the interaction. Chronological events flow from left to right.

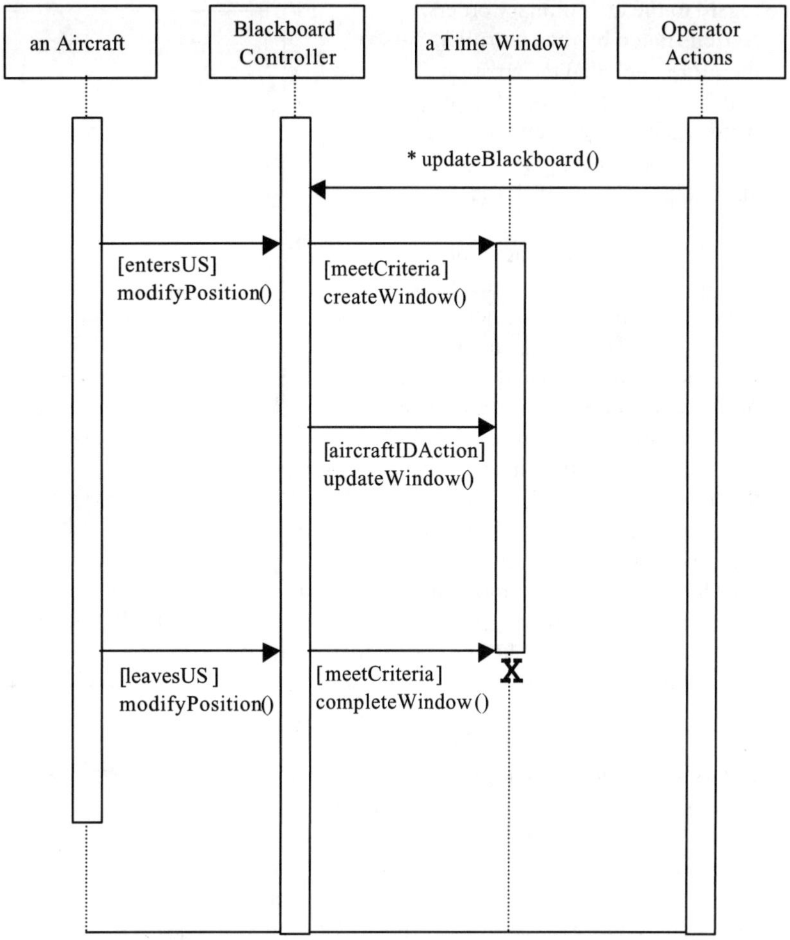

Figure 4. Time Window Sequence Diagram

Thus, Figure 4 illustrates the simulation activities that lead to the creation, update and completion of a time window. As the aircraft enters U.S. airspace, its position is modified on the blackboard. Once the blackboard controller determines that the aircraft is entering and must be identified, it creates a time window associated with the aircraft. All the while, operator actions are being posted to the blackboard and are continuously monitored by the controller. When, and if, an operator action satisfies the task demand of the time window (i.e. aircraft ID action), the time window information is updated to indicate that it has been satisfied. When the aircraft leaves U.S. airspace, the blackboard controller notes that criteria for window completion have been met, and destroys the time window object.

EMPIRICAL RESULTS

The human performance evaluation concepts discussed in this paper were implemented in a series of experiments in a simulation of a military command and control environment (for details, see Hodge et al. 1995). Subjects in the experiment assumed the role of an air defense officer for a naval warship, and were given several tasks to perform. They were told to follow nine military orders (or rules of engagement) in the performance of their tasks. Rules 1-5 were dependant on the proximity of hostile aircraft (i.e. fighter jets and helicopters) in the simulated environment to his/her position. Rules 6-7 regulated the control of his/her air resources (i.e. friendly fighter jets). Rules 8-9 specified that all unknown aircraft must be correctly identified.

The simulation was structured so that the blackboard controller monitored operator activities, and states of objects in the environment, with regard to the nine military orders. Actions taken by the controller, therefore, included the creation, update, and completion of time windows in association with an order as well as an object (e.g. a hostile aircraft in violation of an order).

The experiment involved the training and testing of 72 male undergraduates from a major university. Six training conditions were used that varied in the form of post-scenario feedback and on-line decision aiding. The training conditions were implemented during the training phase of the experiment, and were removed during the testing phase. The objective of the experiment was to determine the degree of transfer of performance improvement from an augmented environment (in which the operator was trained) to an impoverished environment (in which the operator was tested).

An area of interest for the present discussion is the relevancy of the time window measures to actual performance. To evaluate this, the results of one test scenario were examined to determine significant factors that contribute toward good or poor performance. Factor analysis was used to determine groupings of relevant variables that were based on the time window construct. All statistical calculations and graphical presentations were done using STATISTICA (StatSoft 1999). The variables examined were:
(R1ERR-R9ERR) Number of errors committed in executing Rules 1-9 tasks;
(EARLY) Number of errors committed in executing tasks early;
(ONTIME) Number of errors committed while executing the task on time;
(LATE) Number of errors committed while executing tasks late;
(FA) Number of errors committed due to inactivity (False Alarms);
(MISS) Number of errors committed due to lack of task demand (Misses);
(TOTERR) Total number of errors committed;
(MTACT) Mean reaction time after time window created for all rules;
(R1MT-R9MT) Mean reaction time after time window created for Rules 1-9.

The scree curve, shown in Figure 5, indicates the amount of variance accounted for by each extracted factor. It is evident that the first two

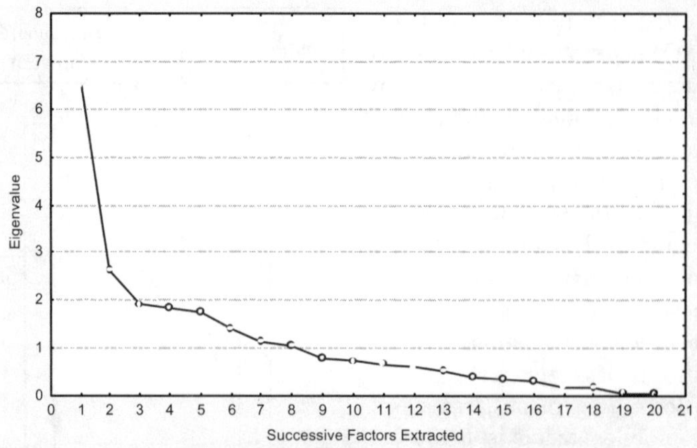

Figure 5. Scree Plot for Successive Factors Extracted

factor account for the majority of variance in the data. Further investigation of the factor loadings (Table 1) indicates that several variables are highly loaded (highlighted and italicized values) on the first factor. The data thus suggests that these variables are highly correlated with one another and represent a common underlying variable.

Table 1. Factor Loadings for Each Variable
Factor Loadings (Unrotated)
Extraction: Principal components
(Marked loadings are > .700000)

	Factor 1	Factor 2
R1ERR	0.47473	0.005897
R2ERR	0.596595	0.177064
R3ERR	0.397408	0.641766
R4ERR	0.504267	0.629091
R5ERR	0.533064	0.135893
R6ERR	0.193651	-0.23048
R7ERR	0.128955	-0.2354
R8ERR	***0.777529***	-0.0616
R9ERR	***0.838927***	-0.00973
EARLY	0.135972	-0.11019
ONTIME	-0.03609	0.14514
LATE	0.608829	0.161879
MISS	0.687744	-0.11765
FA	0.359625	0.702544
TOTERR	***0.953719***	0.222183
MTACT	***0.75915***	-0.48702
R1MT	0.355906	0.275087
R2MT	0.144494	-0.15424
R3MT	-0.19848	-0.04234
R4MT	-0.26438	-0.1525
R5MT	0.250999	-0.41994
R8MT	***0.743501***	-0.51731
R9MT	***0.719211***	-0.48481
Expl.Var	6.508721	2.626776
Prp.Totl	0.282988	0.114208

DISCUSSION AND CONCLUSIONS

The variables highlighted on Table 1 presents an interesting finding. They show that identification tasks (R8 & R9) are highly correlated with the total number of errors as well as the mean reaction time after window creation (i.e. latency). Thus, the results suggest that correct identification of unknown aircraft objects is key to good performance.

In conclusion, this paper presented a method to represent a temporally constrained signal detection theory for dynamic task performance measurement, as well as a blackboard model-based mechanism to implement the time window framework. Through use of factor analysis, it was shown that the time window construct can be used to determine task latency as well as accuracy.

REFERENCES

Beach, L. R. and R. Lipshitz. 1993. "Why Classical Decision Theory is an Inappropriate Standard for Evaluating and Aiding Most Human Decision Making." In *Decision Making in Action: Models and Methods.* G. A. Klein, J. Orasanu, R. Calderwood and C. Zsambok, eds. Ablex Publishing Corp., Norwood, NJ. 21-35.

Brehmer, B.; J. Leplat and J. Rasmussen. 1991. "Use of Simulation in the Study of Complex Decision Making." In *Distributed Decision Making: Cognitive Models for Cooperative Work*. J. Rasmussen, B. Brehmer and J. Leplat, eds. John Wiley & Sons Ltd., New York.

Chu, R. W.; P. M. Jones and C. M. Mitchell. 1991. "The Georgia Tech Payload Operations Control Center Simulation: Design and Implementation in C++." In *Proceedings of the Object-Oriented Simulation Track of the 1991 Society for Computer Simulation Multiconference*, (Anaheim, CA).

Hodge, K. A.; L. Rothrock; A. C. Kirlik; N. Walker; A. D. Fisk; D. A. Phipps and P. E. Gay. 1995. "Training for Tactical Decision Making Under Stress: Towards Automatization of Component Skills." Human Attention Performance Laboratory Technical Report-9501. Georgia Institute of Technology, School of Psychology.

Hogg, D.; K. Folleso; F. Strand-Volden and B. Torralba. 1995. "Development of a Situation Awareness Measure to Evaluate Advanced Alarm Systems in Nuclear Power Plant Control Rooms." *Ergonomics* 38, NO. 11: 2394-2413.

Doherty, M. E. 1993. "A Laboratory Scientist's View of Naturalistic Decision Making." In *Decision Making in Action: Models and Methods.* G. A. Klein, J. Orasanu, R. Calderwood and C. Zsambok, eds. Ablex Publishing Corp., Norwood, NJ. 362-388.

Fowler, M. and S. Kendall. 2000. *UML Distilled: A Brief Guide to the Standard Object Modeling Language*. Addison-Wesley, Reading, MA.

Howie, D. E. and K. J. Vicente. 1998. "Measures of Operator Performance in Complex, Dynamic Microworlds: Advancing the State of the Art." *Ergonomics* 41, NO. 4: 485-500.

Kirlik, A.; N. Walker; A. D. Fisk and K. Nagel. 1996. "Supporting Perception in the Service of Dynamic Decision Making." *Human Factors* 38, NO. 2: 288-299.

Laudeman, I. V. and E. A. Palmer. 1995. "The Quantitative Measurement of Observed Workload in the Analysis of Aircrew Performance." *The International Journal of Aviation Psychology* 5, NO. 2: 187-197.

Moray, N.; M. I. Dessouky; B. A. Kijowski and R. Adapathya. 1991. "Strategic Behavior, Workload, and Performance in Task Scheduling." *Human Factors* 33, NO. 6: 607-629.

Nii, P. 1986. "Blackboard Systems." Technical Report KSL 86-18. Knowledge Systems Laboratory, Stanford, CA.

Rubin, K. S.; P. M. Jones and C. M. Mitchell. 1988. "OFMspert: Inference of Operator Intentions in Supervisory Control Using a Blackboard Architecture." *SMC* 18, NO. 4: 618-637.

StatSoft, Inc. 1999. STATISTICA for Windows [Computer program manual]. StatSoft, Inc., Tulsa, OK.

Vranes, S.; M. Lucin; M. Stanojevic; V. Stevanovic and P. Subasic. 1991. "Blackboard Metaphor in Tactical Decision Making." *European Journal of Operational Research* 61: 86-97.

Wickens, C. D. 1992. *Engineering Psychology and Human Performance*. HarperCollins Inc., New York.

ACKNOWLEDGMENTS

The author would like to acknowledge the support of Dr. Alex Kirlik of the Georgia Institute of Technology while conducting this research.

SOCIO-TECHNICAL MODEL OF COMPLEXITY, AMBIGUITY AND EMERGENCE IN TEAM SITUATION AWARENESS

Tetsuo Sawaragi, Kiyoaki Murasawa

Dept. of Precision Engineering, Graduate School of Engineering, Kyoto University
Yoshida Honmachi, Sakyo, Kyoto 606-8501, Japan.
Email: sawaragi@prec.kyoto-u.ac.jp

Keywords: Team situation awareness, garbage can model, naturalistic decision-making, real-time multitasking.

ABSTRACT

In this paper, we present a socio-technical model for simulating organizational behaviors and performance of the team situation awareness. For this purpose, we introduce Cohen's "Garbage Can Model" that was originally introduced in a field of organization theory for explaining anarchy of organizational behaviors. We extend the original Garbage Can Model for finding out the bottlenecks in which the coordination and synchronization among the team members and artifact systems are broken and team situation awareness is lost under the time-varying loads of tasks. This is applied to the analysis of the high-tech aircraft accident that occurred in Columbia in 1995, which is a well-known accident caused by the dis-coordination between the human and the automated aircraft.

INTRODUCTION

As a framework of human-system interactions, an international civilian aviation organization (ICAO) has provided with a SHELL model, where SHELL represents; Software, Hardware, Environment, and Liveware. Wherein, liveware represents a human actor and/or a decision-maker such as an operator in the plants and a pilot in aviation, who has the interacting relationships between each of the above components including another liveware. This latter liveware represents human personnel who are in contact with the former human. This framework is extended by the addition of another component of management ("m") that is called an *m*-SHELL model. The mechanism invoking most of critical human errors is a result of malfunctions occurring at interactions among these five components. Usually, a trivial malfunction at some interface of a pair of the above components occurs, that is often left unconscious and is propagated to other parts of interactions silently leading to a catastrophe. J. Reason is naming this phenomenon as a "Swiss Cheese Model" putting an emphasis on that catastrophe is caused by an accidentally linked chain of trivial pitfalls. Current high-tech work environments where a human crew has to collaborate with each other being mediated by highly advanced automations or task-offload aiding tools is apt to have potential sources of invoking human errors due to the complexity of the interactions of the six components of the *m*-SHELL model. This would be more serious for an emergency situation under a severe time pressure. It is no longer sufficient that operators perform without significant errors, but it is necessary to design a total system so that they perform correctly within absolute time criteria. For this purpose, training and education of the human crew are not sufficient, rather some systematic approach to designing artifacts taking into account of interactions among human, artifacts and environment.

In this paper, we present a simulation test bed by which human dynamic interactions within the team members and with the externally provided task workloads are generated. For this purpose, we introduce Cohen's "Garbage Can Model" that was originally introduced in a field of organization theory for explaining anarchy of organizational behaviors. We extend the original Garbage Can Model for finding out the bottlenecks in which the coordination and synchronization among the team members and artifact systems are broken and team situation awareness is lost under the time-varying loads of tasks.

The simulation is applied to the analysis of the high-tech aircraft accident that occurred in Columbia in 1995, which is a well-known accident caused by the dis-coordination between the human and the automated aircraft. We present how our model can replay the emergence of the complex behaviors formed by three parties (i.e., air traffic controllers and two pilots taking different roles of pilot flying and pilot non-flying). By changing the parameters of commanding organizational structures, of participants' resources and of external workloads, we generate how the team behaviors are expected to change. Then, we derive general conclusions on what and where the bottlenecks of coordination were as a source of that accident. Through such a case study, we show how our modeling method can be used in the analysis of accidents as an alternative to the conventional causality-based error-investigation approach.

TEAM SITUATION AWARENESS

In a field of human factors research, *situation awareness* (SA) has been investigated for a long time (Endsley, 1995). Endsley defined SA as consisting of the three different levels: Perception of elements in current situation, comprehension of current situation, and projection of future status. SA is not only a snapshot of how a human grasp his/her immediate presence at some moment, but should be modeled as much more dynamic, chained activities. SA is a phenomenon occurring at the front end where two different time scales meet with each other; one with the time stream of occurrence of external demands and the other with the human internal cognitive cycle based on his personal experience and knowledge (Sawaragi, T. and Katai, O., 1998).

An idea of situation awareness of individual decision-makers is extended towards a group or team SA (Salas, E., et al., 1995). Team SA represents far more complexity than does simply combining the situation awareness of individual team. Team SA involves unique activities, such as coordination and information sharing, and performance in many complex systems depends on the coordinated activities of a team of individuals. Teamwork consists of behaviors that are related to team member interactions and are necessary to establish coordination among individual team members to achieve team goals. Each individual member possesses a unique level of situation awareness but that team SA could not be calculated simply as the sum of the situation awareness achieved by each member. In order to model such a complex, dynamic process of team situation awareness, we introduce ideas from management and social organization theories.

GARBAGE CAN MODEL FOR TEAM SA

The complexity of team SA originates from the following issues. A stream of coming demands is not processed one by one by the team in the order of their arrival (i.e., not first-in-first-out); some ongoing issues may be suspended and some other issues thrown into the organization later than the previous one might be prioritized to be processed and completed. In some other cases, due to the conflicts among the available resources within the team, priorities among the demands in process may be changed. Here, we would like to stress that simultaneous, chained activities for different demands may interact with each other, not independently. This interaction is both dependent upon the external factors such as the ways of arrivals of the demands and upon the internal factors such as the availability of *resources*, communication channels and authority relationships. In the latter case, it may be also possible that some pending problems may be resolved not by some members' intentional efforts but by some other factors (i.e., problems themselves may disappear). That is, a team behavior is not the single sum of individual decision-makers or problem solvers, but is rather an "open" and "ambiguous" process, and the management for such a complexity will be a critical issue especially under a time-bounded situation (i.e., an emergency).

For the purpose of simulation, here we introduce a *garbage can model* (*GCM*) (Cohen, M.D., et al., 1972), which was originally introduced in a field of organization theory for explaining anarchy of organizational behaviors. We attempt to discuss the interaction dynamics of an artifact agent as well as of a human with the external task demands from a management perspective using this GCM (Fig.1).

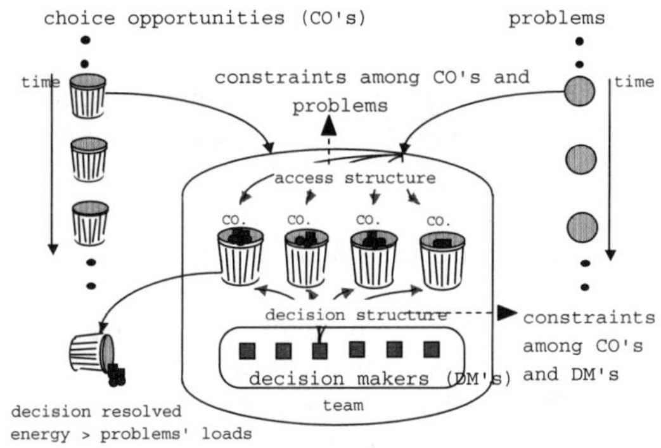

Fig.1 Cohen et al.'s Garbage Can Model

The principal components of the GCM is as follows:

- **problems**: The concern of people inside and outside the team.
- **choice opportunities**: Occasions when a team is expected to produce behavior that can be called a decision.
- **participants**: The human resources of the team contributing to decision-making.

Participants as well as problems are thrown into choice opportunities modeled as garbage cans, and when the total amount of energy thrown into the garbage can exceeds the energy that is required to solve the problems thrown into that garbage can, that choice opportunity turns out to be resolved. That is, the problems belonging to that garbage can are regarded as resolved, and then they disappear. The constraints on which problems and which participants are allowed to be thrown into which choice opportunities can be varied (i.e., an *access structure* and a *decision structure*, respectively). Under these constraints, problems as well as participants are allowed to be allocated into one of the choice opportunities, but even after they are thrown into to a particular choice opportunity, they are allowed to move to another choice opportunity anytime whenever some criteria is satisfied. That is, problems may disappear from that choice opportunity and participants may come and go. In this way, the garbage can model can simulate a descriptive organizational behavior of problem solving. Herein, there defined four types of problem solving as follows:

- **Decision by resolution**: Problems are resolved by the invention of necessary energies.
- **Decision by oversight**: Problems are resolved before they are recognized as "problems".
- **Decision by flight**: Unresolved problems turn out to be resolved as a byproduct of other problems' status. Flight triggered by a single problem's disappearance (flight 2) and enabled by all problems' disappearance (flight 1).

GCM can simulate an organizational behavior consisting not only of conventional logical relations prescribed by access and decision structures but also of other relations such as a one of *temporal synchrony* that is of the importance when we discuss human-factor issues.

In this work, we attempt to simulate team SA using this garbage can model taking the correspondence between the GCM entities and the SA components as follows. The problems of GCM correspond to the demands provided externally to the team, and we regard individual team members as a participant of GCM. Each of choice opportunities of GCM corresponds to an individual chain of decision-making activities that the team is faced with.

Fig.2 shows how the behavior of a single garbage can (i.e., a choice opportunity) proceeds during 50 time units as a stream of demands comes in. Wherein, to simulate movements of problems and participants to other choice opportunities, we model this fluid participation and problems as a random process. During this period, if one of the four resolution types occurs, the garbage (i.e., problems) within that can are renewed and another cycle resumes from an empty can. In the upper of the figure, we show when and what types of resolution occur. We investigate how the organizational behavior evolves as the demands from the external environment changes. Fig.2(b) shows a summary of this experiment. One trial continues for 250 time steps, and the figures show the average of the ten trials. The load coefficient (*LC*) determines the effective loads incurred to the organization, and we can vary the amount of demands by changing this coefficients; a larger coefficient represents a heavier demands. Frequency of the choice opportunities represents how many times the choice opportunities are renewed during the 250 time steps. An inverse number of this frequency represents an averaged duration needed to one choice opportunity to be completed. Right three columns in the figure show the proportions of the types of resolution change as the coming demands vary.

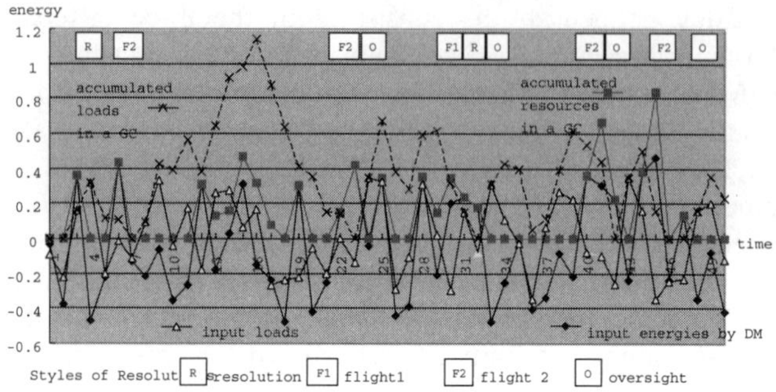

(a)

increase ↑ loads ↓ decrease

Load Coef.	freq. of COs.(per 250 times)	oversight(%)	flight(%)	resolution(%)
LC=1.0	38.1	0.318	0.40720822	0.2753
LC=0.8	72.4	0.348	0.33594479	0.3158
LC=0.6	76	0.362	0.28900629	0.3492
LC=0.4	101.1	0.351	0.24071779	0.4085
LC=0.2	114.3	0.358	0.18122443	0.4611

(b)

Fig.2 An output of a single garbage can model.

As mentioned before, a team is usually faced with multiple choice opportunities, each of which is simultaneously ongoing. Thus, the interactions among multiple choice opportunities do occur in many ways. Moreover, how the problems and the participants move among the multiple choice opportunities does depend upon the current states of the multiple choice opportunities (i.e., status of amounts and kinds of the garbage). Complex behavior emerging out of interactions among those factors can be simulated by usage of the multiple garbage cans model. We have simulated a variety of organizational behaviors using multiple garbage can model and discovers a number of typical emerging patterns of a team that cannot process the workloads appropriately and leads to the disorder. Some of them are summarized as follows:

1. Entrance of too difficult problems to be resolved (i.e., causes existing in the external, not in a team).
2. A team's tendency to examine possibilities too long before acting.
3. A team's persistence on a single issue or activity in failing to be interrupt-driven enough.
4. A team's tendency to jump from issue to issue without satisfactory resolution of any (i.e., too interrupt-driven)

in failing to synthesize or converge multiple views of the situation.

The behaviors caused by the above except the first one are all related more or less to the *interaction* issues within the team or organization. In such cases, it is difficult to uniquely identify a particular cause (i.e., a single person or demand) as a source of errors. This is because many types of relations are *emerging* and *lost* during the dynamic interactions. The most typical relation is the one formed by a time-temporal synchrony on what kinds of task demands are coming simultaneously and conflict status of the other members. We expect our proposing simulation system will function well for finding out such an interaction issue causing the emergence and/or loss of relations.

APPLICATION TO HIGH-TECH AIRCRAFT ACCIDENT

The simulation is applied to the analysis of the high-tech aircraft accident that occurred in Columbia in 1995. This is a well-known accident as the first fatal accident to a B757 in 13 years of exemplary service and as the one caused by the dis-coordination between the human crew, air traffic controller, and the automated aircraft. Probable causes are identified in the final accident report of 1996 (Ladkin, P.B., 1996), but this was actually caused by the unexpected dis-coordination that emerged out of the interactions among the human crews and the automated devices.

The following is a summary of the accident quoted from (Gerdsmeier *et al.*, 1997):

> *The accident aircraft, an American Airlines Boeing 757-223, hit mountainous terrain while attempting to perform a GPWS escape maneuver, about 10 miles east of where it was supported to on the instrument arrival path to Cali Runway 19. Approaching from the north, the crew had been expecting to use Runway 1, the same asphalt but the reciprocal direction, which would require flying past the airport and turning back, the usual procedure. They were offered, and accepted, a 'straight-in' arrival and approach to Rwy 19, giving them less time and therefore requiring an expedited descent. The crew were not familiar with the ROZO One arrival they were given, became confused over the clearance, and spent time trying to program the FMC to fly the clearance they thought they had been given. A confusion over two navigation beacons in the area with the same identifier and frequency led to the aircraft turning left away from the arrival path, a departure not noticed by the crew for 90 seconds. When they noticed, they chose to fly 'inbound heading', that is, parallel to their cleared path. However, they had not arrested the descent and were in mountainous terrain. Continued descent took them into a mountain, and the GPWS sounded. The escape maneuver was executed imprecisely, with the speedbrakes left out, as the aircraft flew to impact.*

We develop how our model can replay the emergence of the erroneous behaviors in this accident formed by the air traffic controller on the ground (ATC), two pilots (i.e., pilot flying (PF) and pilot non flying (NPF)) in the air. Sources of the simulation are gathered from the communication voice records that were officially presented in the report. The critical part of the accident is that the crew in the air could not reply promptly to ATC's clearance requests, which was caused by failing in inputting right way points to FMS when the flight plan was changed.

According to the final accident report of 1996 (Ladkin, P.B., 1996), the probable causes are listed as follows:

- The flight crew's failure to adequately plan and execute the approach to runway 19 at SKCL and their inadequate use of automation.
- Failure of the flightcrew to discontinue the approach into Cali, despite numerous cues alerting them of the inadvisability of continuing the approach.
- The lack of situation awareness of the flightcrew regarding vertical navigation, proximity to terrain, and the relative location of critical radio aids.
- Failure of the flightcrew to revert to basic radio navigation at the time when the FMS-assisted navigation became confusing and demanded an excessive workload in a critical phase of the flight.

In addition to the above, the following contributing factors are identified:

- The flightcrew's ongoing efforts to expedite their approach and landing in order to avoid potential delays.
- The flightcrew's execution of the GPWS escape maneuver while the speedbrakes remained deployed.
- FMS logic that dropped all intermediate fixes from the displays in the event of execution of a direct routing.
- FMS-generated navigational information that used a different naming convention from that published in navigational charts.

Gerdsmeier *et al.* has analyzed the Cali accident by usage of *WB-graph* (*Why-Because graph*) in terms of causality interconnecting accident-related states and events (Gerdsmeier *et al.*, 1997). They picked up 59 states and events. We specified the actors (i.e., components of *m*-SHELL) that are responsible for the individual issues. Tracing the paths leading to the catastrophe by referring to how the actors interact. The source nodes of that model may indeed represent reasons for the accident which have no further reasons lying behind them. Or they can be regarded as *contingencies*, that is, events or states which need not have occurred, but whose conjunction was sufficient to ensure that the accident happened. As Gerdsmeier *et al.* have insisted, the most important is the fatal combination of circumstances as a result of interactions, rather than the individual source nodes. These are actual causes of the accident, and they may be missed in the conventional investigation using methods of a causal analysis only from a viewpoint of *external* observers and/or experts. A more careful method for evaluating such interaction-related components of the accident, then, would be needed that can simulate the interacting processes from a viewpoint of actors, rather than observers, enabling to detect such significant events for which we can formulate an avoidance response.

In case of the Cali accident, clearly the most significant event to be distinguished is the crew's action in taking the ATC's offer to land on Rwy 19 approach, which largely constrained and altered their subsequent actions and decisions. That is, this decision led directly to the crew's *high workload* that brought about many aspects of undesirable environment; their loss of situational awareness, communication confusion, and lack of attention to indicators of their situation, etc. We have to note that this workload should not be measured by the amount of the physical efforts to perform it with, but must be in *cognitive overload*. This cognitive overload brought about by a particular decision is related to the amount of radically-disjointness property among the subsequent scenarios, and we have to develop some logically and computationally sufficient means of assessing this. In the following, we attempt to use the aforementioned GCM for this purpose.

As an extension of the original GCM, we newly introduced constraints among the choice opportunities as a *task hierarchy*, that is a *means-end* relation among the choices making up the group work. Moreover, we defined constraints among individual participants and choice opportunities as well as constraints among problems and choice opportunities. As for decision types, we newly define the following two types specific to such a hierarchical task structure.

- **Decision by resolution:** a choice is made at an opportunity after all subordinate choices are made in decision by resolution in the original meaning of GCM.
- **Decision by flight:** a choice is made at an opportunity in spite of some subordinate choices not yet made.

For our implementing purpose, we give up modeling all the scenarios observed in the Cali accident, and we concentrate upon a series of dis-coordinated events and states initiated by crew's accepting the ATC's offer to use Rwy 19 approach to Cali airport. At that time the major confusion of the crew (PF and PNF) was brought about as a result of communication problems with the ATC. These problems concern with CRW's identifying the way points (i.e., beacons) and with exchanging clearances, that is amalgamated by CRW's troubles in manipulating their FMC displays to know the current horizontal position of the aircraft. Therefore, we concentrate only upon this duration and simplify the problem by picking up the following four choice opportunities for the following investigation using GCM. These four opportunities correspond to:

- CRW's confirmation of the approach (i.e., the ROZO 1 arrival).
- ATC's giving clearances for the approach.
- ATC's confirmation of the current position of the aircraft relative to Tulua VOR.
- CRW's report of the positions of the aircraft relative to Tulua VOR to ATC.

The configuration of the airport and Tulua VOR and Rozo NDB as well as Romeo NDB, that CRW wrongly input the destination in FMC instead of the intended 'Rozo', is illustrated in Fig.3. Further, we consider only two decision-makers of ATC and CRW, and PF and PNF are not discriminated but are treated as one actor of CRW. Constraints on the decision structure and the access structures are straightforwardly determined according to the regulation for the landing procedures. Problems correspond to such individual items and procedures to be checked and done during the before-landing period by ATC and CRW. Quantified parameters of energies assigned to each problem are defined experientially according to their workloads, while the energies of the participants are regarded as cognitive resources of the crew.

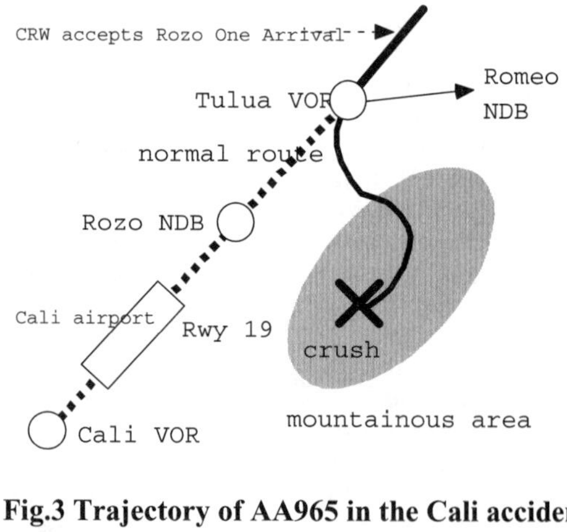

Fig.3 Trajectory of AA965 in the Cali accident

We changed some of the parameters of the original model in three different ways and investigated into how the emergent behavior of the crew would be. The parameters that are varied in the experiments are:

- Constraints among choice opportunities and the participants as well as the problems that reflect the different operational procedures prescribing individual crew members' decision making responsibilities.
- Energy resources of the participants that reflect how much of the individual crew's cognitive resources and skill levels are available.
- Required energies of the individual problems to change the workload to the team.

SIMULATION RESULTS

Experiment 1: Variation of Operational Procedures Prescriptions

We assume two candidates of operating procedures as follows by changing the constraints on the decision-makers for the two problems of "to identify the current horizontal position of the aircraft" and "to decide the aircraft's heading" in two ways. One candidate referred to as case 1 is that the former is accessed only by CRW, while the latter is accessed only by ATC. The other candidate referred to as case 2 is that both decision-makers are accessible to these problems.

Fig.4 shows how the GCM's outputs vary in these two cases. The left and right graphs correspond to case 1 and case 2, respectively. Fig.4(a) shows how the status of the four choice opportunities varies along the time. Vertical items represent the four opportunities, each of which starts to exist when plots appear in the respective horizontal lines. Shifts among the opportunities show the decision-makers move among the choice opportunities. Even though the decision-makers move, choice opportunities do not always terminate with decision by resolution, but may be terminate with decision by flight. The decision by resolutionis denoted by unfilled marking, while the decision by flight is denoted by usual filled marking.

For instance, in the left of Fig.4(a) choice opportunity #1 terminates in decision by resolution, while choice opportunity #2 terminates in decision by flight since its lower choice (i.e., #1) is not made yet when #2 terminates at time 2. On the contrary, choice opportunity #1 as well as #3 and #4 terminate in decision by resolution. Fig.4(b) shows the status of the problems in each of the choice opportunities shown in the vertical items. Although there exist eight problems in total, we show only status for the six problems. At first all the problems become active at time 1, remain in the particular garbage cans (i.e., choice opportunities) for a particular time period, then finally they disappear when the choice opportunities in which the problems are thrown into are made in some way. Problems may move among different garbage cans, which is observed only in case 2 (i.e., Fig.4(b)(right)). Fig.4(c) shows how the ERC indices for the four choice opportunities change along time. The ERC, energy required to choice, represents energies more needed to decision. When the ERC descends below the zero horizontal axis, that choice is regarded as made. As shown in Fig.4(c)(left), choice opportunity #2 is made at first, being followed by #1, #4 and #3, which is consistent with the terminating times shown in Fig.4(a)(left).

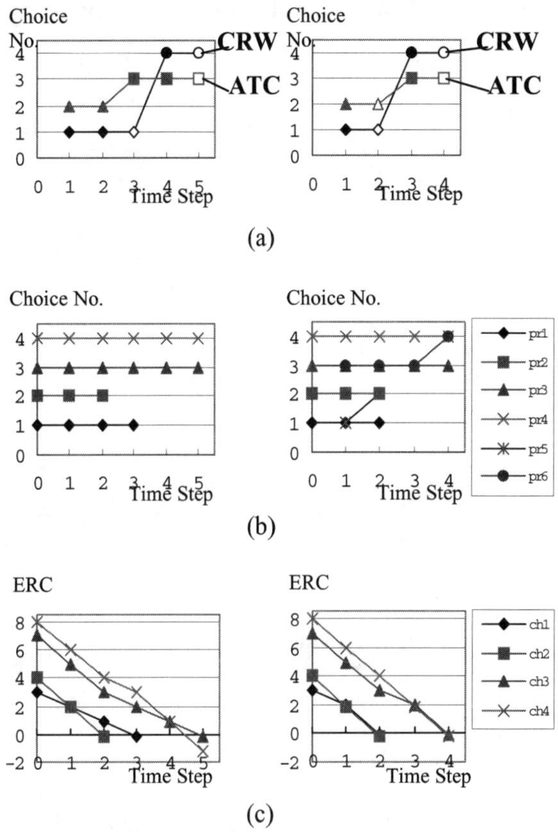

Fig.4 Variations of constraints

From these results, we can compare case 1 and 2 as follows. Under a procedure of case 1 prescribing the fixed accessibility for ATC and CRW, the time needed for all the choice opportunities to be resolved is longer than under case 2 prescribing the more flexible accessibility. Moreover, in the former, decision by flight is observed, while in the latter all the decisions are by resolution. Activities in choice opportunities in #1 and #2 as well as activities in #3 and #4 are performed *concurrently* (Fig.4(a)(right)), which resulted in the prompt resolution by the team. The integral of positive ERC values in Fig.4(c) are related to how much cognitive workloads of the two participants are active during the team problem solving session, and the result presents that case 2 is lower than case 1.

Experiment 2: Variation of Cognitive Skills

Next we simulate how the organizational behaviors may change when the skill levels of the two participants are varied. We reflect this by changing the parameters of the energy that each decision-maker can throw into the garbage can at one time. We set in two ways; in case 3 energy available to CRW is set less than energy available to ATC, and in case 4 vise versa. This means that CRW takes double times to process the same task as compared with ATC in case 3. The total amount of the energy is set to the same in both cases.

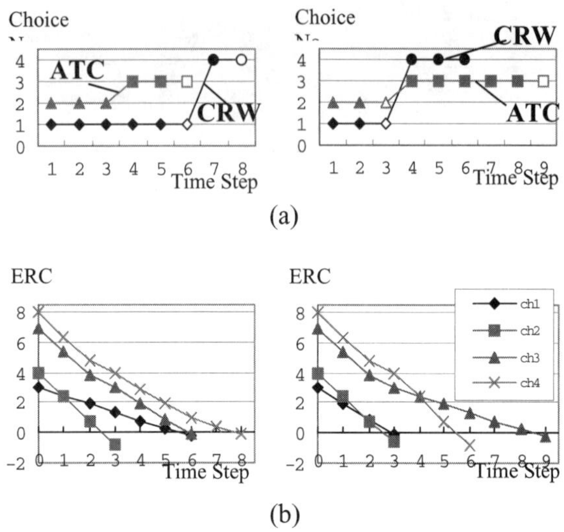

Fig.5 Variations of skill levels

Fig.5(a) presents how the status of the four choice opportunities evolves along time in each setting. It is observed that decisions by flight are observed in choice opportunity #2 in case 3 and in #4 in case 4. Fig.5(b) shows the evolutions of the ERC indices, which show that experienced cognitive workloads in total are different according to which partner is less skilled, although the total sum of the skill levels of the team members remain constant. Actually such imbalance among the training and experience levels of the participants were one of the major probable causes of the Cali accident.

Experiment 3: Variation of Difficulty of Problem

Finally, we change the parameters of the ERP, energy required to the problem, of a particular problem in continuous ways, simulating how the teamwork evolves when the difficulty of a particular problem is changed. We changed the ERP of the problem of CRW's identifying the current horizontal position of the aircraft in ten different ways. Fig.6(a)-(j) show the results concerning with the activities in each of the four choice opportunities. We can notice that the organizational behaviors evolve monotonously while the ERP varies between 1.0 and 4.0 (i.e., Fig.6(a) to (d)), where the decision by flight is observed in choice opportunity #2. In the followings with ERP=5.0 to 7.0, one more decision by flight is observed in #3 as well. Then, with ERP=8.0 (i.e., Fig.6(h)), a drastic change is observed, where choice opportunity #1 is abandoned on the way to decision and CRW's energies are thrown into #4 from #1. Even in this case, decision made in #4 is by flight and the total time needed for all the opportunities turn out to be resolved drastically increases. This behavior simulate a situation in which all the participants are in severe confusion and they fail in concentrating upon the pressing issues but their attentions are sparsely distributed among a number of choice opportunities. That is, this is a team's tendency to jump from issue to issue without satisfactory resolution of any, which is exactly what happened in the Cali accident.

The followings are the summary of the experiments and findings we obtained from the simulation.

- A change of the constraints among choice opportunities and the decision-makers sometimes alters the emerging problem solving types drastically.
- Even a slight change of skill levels of a particular member may drastically change the ways and the amount of the communication among the team members. Especially, the emergent behaviors are very sensitive to the symmetric properties among the team members' abilities.
- Robustness of the team against externally coming and/or internally occurring workloads could be discussed in terms of the team designs and the bottlenecks appearing against those changes of workloads are predicted.

We believe our modeling method can be used in the analysis of accidents as an alternative to the conventional causality-based error-investigation approach.

CONCLUSIONS

In this paper, we presented a simulation testbed in which team SA is modeled and a variety of behaviors emerging out of interactions among the external factors and the internal factors. We showed that the timing as well as the workload of the task demands can affect much upon the team behaviors.

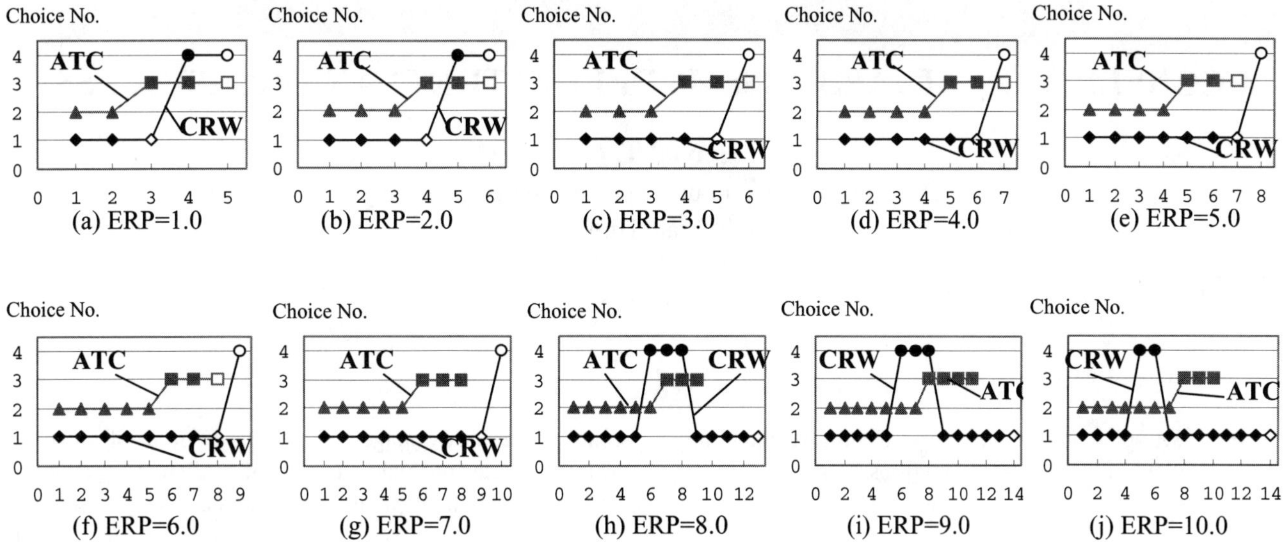

Fig.6 Variations of difficulties of a problem

When we consider about the appropriate interface design for a human, we have to deal with the above complexity. Conventional designs have concentrated upon only the local optimization issues such as how to display the information, how to build correct warning systems, etc.. For seeking for the human-centered design of the artifacts, we have to shift our attention into more global optimization and/or management issues taking such interaction dynamics into account.

ACKNOWLEDGMENTS

We thank Capt. Akira Ishibashi, who was a senior captain at All Nippon Airways Corp. and is now at Waseda University and Japan Institute of Human Factors, for his providing us an opportunity to know about the Cali accident and useful suggestions from his proficient pilot's perspectives.

REFERENCES

Cohen, M.D., March, J.G. and Olsen, J.P. (1972). A Garbage Can Model of Organizational Choice, *Administrative Science Quarterly*, **17**-1.

Endsley, M.R. (1995). Toward a Theory of Situation Awareness in Dynamic Systems, *Human Factors*, **37**-1, pp.32-64.

Flach, J.M. (1996). Abstraction, Coordination, and Situational Awareness: Implication for Use-Centered Design, in Ntuen, C.A. and Park, E.H. (eds.), *Human Interaction with Complex Systems: Conceptual Principles and Design Practice*, Kluwer Academic Publishers, Boston, MA.

Gerdsmeier, T., Ladkin, P, Loer, K. (1997). *Analysing the Cali Accident with a WB-Graph*, University of Bielefeld, Research Report RVS-RR-97-01.

Hutchins, E. (1994). Where is the Intelligence in a System of Socially Distributed Cognition? *Advances in Japanese cognitive science*, Vol.7, pp.67-80.

Klein, G.A. *et al.* (1993). *Decision Making in Action: Models and Methods*, Ablex Pub. Corp., Norwood, NJ.

Ladkin, P.B. (1996). *AA965 Cali Accident Report*, University of Bielefeld.

Lave, J. (1988). *Cognition in Practice*, Cabbridge Univ. Press.

Suchman, L.(1994). The Structuring of Everyday Activity, *Advances in Japanese cognitive science*, Vol.7, pp.41-57.

Sarter , N.B. and Woods, D.D.(1991). Situation Awareness: A Critical But Ill-Defined Phenomenon, *The Int. Journal of Aviation Psychology*, **1**-1, pp.45-57.

Sawaragi, T. and Katai, O.(1998). Modeling Recognition-Primed Decision Making under Time Pressure and Multiple Situational Contexts, *Preprints of the 7th IFAC/IFIP/IFORS/IEA Symposium on Analysis, Design and Evaluation of Man-Machine Systems*, pp.269-274.

Sawaragi, T. and Katai, O. (1999). Bio-Informatic Activity Modeling for Human-Artifacts Symbiosis under Resource Boundedness, *Artificial Life and Robotics*, **3**, pp.45-53.

Woods, D.D.: Towards Theoretical Base for Representation Design in the Computer Medium: Ecological Perception and Aiding Human Cognition, in Flach, J. et al. (Eds.), *Global Perspectives on the Ecology of Human-Machine Systems*, Vol.1, Lawrence Erlbaum Assoc.

A CONFLICT OF METAPHORS: MODELING THE PLANNING PROCESS

Michael T. Cox
Department of Computer Science and Engineering
Wright State University
Dayton, OH 45435-0001
mcox@cs.wright.edu

Keywords: artificial intelligence, mixed-initiative planning, state-space planning, goal transformations.

ABSTRACT

Many mixed-initiative planning systems attempt to integrate humans and AI planning systems so that a synthesis results in higher quality plans. In the AI community, however, the dominant model of planning (and virtually all problem-solving) treats cognition as a search processes. Candidate planning actions are represented as operators consisting of preconditions, post conditions, and variable bindings. Such operators can change the state of the world through their effects. Planning is therefore search from an initial state to the goal state by means of operator and variable binding choices. The alternative we propose is to cast planning as a goal manipulation problem whereby the user can establish and "steer" goals through a visual interactive simulation of the planning domain. Users need not know details of the underlying technology, especially the specific representations and search algorithms used. They are instead presented with a visual representation of the world and the capacity to create goals, to associate goals with resources, and to shift goals along various dimensions, thereby adjusting the behavior of the simulation. In our system called GTrans, an underlying planner takes these user-defined parameters and generates plans and feedback so that the user can further adjust his intention toward better solutions. The result is a metaphor more suited to known human approaches, especially at the operational level of planning.

INTRODUCTION

Significantly the first two selections (Georgeff 1990; Hendler, Tate and Drummond 1990) of the influential *Readings in Planning* compilation unambiguously define the planning process as a search task. This assumption is so ingrained that few question the arrangement. However especially in the mixed-initiative planning and dialogue communities (Burstein 1994; Cox, 1999; Ferguson, Myers, and Smith 1998; Haller, McRoy, and Kobsa 1999) where the human user is an active participant in the planning process, some researchers are starting to formulate alternative metaphors that avoid some of the disadvantages of the search point of view. For example, Ferguson and Allen (1998; Allen, Ferguson and Schubert 1996) treat planning fundamentally as an interactive conversation between the human and the machine. In this paper we propose another alternative to search. That is from the standpoint of a human user, planning can be viewed as a goal manipulation process.

The classical search metaphor is either a search through a space of possible plans or a search through a space of possible world states (or *both*. See Kambhampati and Srivastava 1996). The prototypical metaphor is that of state-space search as first embodied in STRIPS (Fikes and Nilsson 1971). Given an initial state, I, and a goal state, G, the task is to search for a sequence of steps that transform I into state S such that S contains G. State-space planners, such as the PRODIGY planning and learning architecture (Carbonell *et al.* 1992; Veloso *et al.* 1995), perform linear or nonlinear search through a space of action sequences where actions are represented as operators. An operator can be applied when its preconditions are met and its variables bound thereby changing the state through its effects. However, humans (especially those that are unfamiliar with AI planning theory) often have difficulty understanding planning in these terms. Pre- and post-conditions and variable bindings are not the types of choices natural to all users. We offer an alternative that represents a mixed-initiative approach to planning.

Instead of search, the metaphor our interface supports is *planning as goal manipulation process*. The user's task is to define the goals or objectives of a system, to assign resources to the goals, and to assign relative importance between goals over time. That is, goals are not some static state provided by the user to the system as input. Instead goals are dynamically changing states that the user steers through the planning process. Classes of transformations exist that the user applies to change the goals from one state to another.

The following section critically examines search as a metaphor used in planning. The subsequent section overviews the research we have performed in mixed-initiative planning that supports the metaphor of planning as a goal manipulation process. This research is divided into changes to the underlying planner and the changes to the interface with which the user interacts with the planner. We conclude with a brief discussion.

THE PROBLEMS OF SEARCH

Search has been a dominant model for planning for a number of reasons. Importantly the model is formal enough to construct proofs and informal enough to implement and obtain empirical results. Computationally search captures important aspects of planning with a simple uniform mechanism and with a domain-independent representation. From any state of the world, new states can be generated by considering what happens if an action occurs. An action makes changes that are reflected in new states becoming true that previously were not and in other states becoming false that previously were true. For example if one block (e.g., BlockA) is placed on another (e.g., BlockB) by the action stack, then the world is different. BlockA is now on BlockB, and BlockB, which was formerly "clear" of other blocks, is no longer clear.

More formally the stack operator is shown in Figure 1. The operator has two variables, <ob> and <underob>, representing the top and bottom objects respectively. These variables are bound to particular tokens in the blocksworld such as BlockA and BlockB. The preconditions for the operator to be applied are that the bottom object be clear and the top be held (by a virtual robot arm). The effects of performing this action is that the top object is no longer being held and the bottom object is no longer clear (the delete-list) and that the top object is now clear, the arm is empty, and the top object is on the lower one (the add-list).

stack

<ob>: type OBJECT
<underob>: type OBJECT

Pre: (clear <underob>)
(holding <ob>)

Del: (holding <ob>)
(clear <underob>)

Add: (clear <ob>)
(arm-empty)
(on <ob> <underob>)

Figure 1. Stack Operator (Representation adapted from Veloso *et al.*, 1995)

A set of such operators along with an object type hierarchy define a domain suitable for search. A set of goals along with a collection of objects and their relationships define a search problem.

Naive users (i.e., ones not familiar with the technology, rather than the domain) often have problems with this arrangement. For example users understand forward search from the initial state better than backchaining from the goals.[1] This backwards search finds an operator that can achieve a goal, and then searches for operators that can achieve unmet preconditions.

Furthermore, associated planning choices such as variable binding assignments are also user-unfriendly. For example if the stack operator from Figure 1 is chosen for some reason to achieve the condition that BlockA is clear given the state of the block being held by the robot, then the variable <ob> is determined (i.e., it is bound to the object BlockA). However, the variable <underob> is not determined and must be bound to some other object for the operator to be instantiated and applied. Random choices could be any object of type OBJECT in the current problem. A user would have to realize that a relevant candidate object to use in the binding should be an object different from BlockA, that already is on the table, and is clear. Many objects may exists that suit these constraints, but the constraints may not be obvious from the operator definition. Given N objects in the problem, the user selects candidates from the listing. However, if N objects of type OBJECT exist and the goal state has two arguments of this type, then the user must select from N^2 choices (each object could be identical). In general, for a predicate of with Q arguments, each type of which has amount(arg-i) instances, the number of choices is $\prod_{1 \le i \le Q} \text{amount(arg-i)}$.

The PRODIGY system was modified to allow the user to make any decision that the system itself could (Cox and Veloso 1997b), but in terms of variable binding choices, the user is often presented with such a large number of choices that they will not fit on a single screen and must be scrolled through.

Recent alternatives to classical STRIPS-like planning now exist. Making user understandability worse (although making planning more tractable), Blum and Furst (1997) have created a new algorithm (Graphplan) for the planning process. Their method represents possible plans as a plan-graph structure. The plan-graph is created by forward search, and,

1. This informal observation originates from the authors experience with teaching planning in AI classes to computer science students rather than from a formal empirical study.

the shortest plan is extracted from the graph by backward search. Kambhampati, Parker, and Lambrecht (1997) have made progress at making Graphplan more goal-directed, but this does not help in terms of user understandability. Although this algorithm is faster and more tractable in large domains, the representation is less accessible to the user.

The most extreme example of a recent advances in AI planning techniques is by Kautz and Selman (1996). Their algorithm, called walksat, represents plans as CNF boolean expressions and the planning problem as a boolean satisfaction task. The change of representation and algorithm is more efficient, but, it is hardly a model of planning that one would wish to present to a naive (or even expert) user.

Finally, a number of researchers are recognizing additional deficiencies with traditional planning systems developed in the AI community. Chien *et al.* (1996) make the claim that because of tractability problems with large real-world planning problem, full automation is not realistic. Consequently plans must be understandable and easy to modify by users. They further argue that the pragmatics of planning environments require support tools to support the life-cycle of plans. Thus planning aids such as those that support knowledge acquisition and plan verification are required. Finally, they (as well as Pollack and Horty 1999) argue that there is more to planning than just plan generation. Plan management consists of replanning in the face of exogenous change, considering other agent's goals, and managing constraints such as time, plan quality, and flexibility.

Departing from classical planning metaphors, the next sections will discuss an alternative to the classical approach. We examine the modeling of planning as a goal manipulation task and show how this metaphor is realized in a mixed-initiative system called GTrans.

MIXED-INITIATIVE PLANNING

Our research has mainly concentrated on two avenues with which to include the user as an active participant in mixed-initiative systems. First one can change the algorithms, representations, and parameters of the planner with which the user interacts. Second one can change the interface through which the user interacts with the planner. We examine both in turn.

Changing the Planner

In earlier research, we modified a standard planning system to enable more reasonable goals. As a result this effort has allowed us to broadly address choices of goal representation within a mixed-initiative planning system. A state-space planner takes as input a set of ground literals states that compose the top-level goals of the user. A ground literal is a predicate whose arguments are instances in the problem. However, when specifying a goal, users tend to make three departures from this framework (Cox and Veloso 1997a).

- Users specify goals as actions rather than states
- Users mix abstract and grounded goals
- Users include subgoals along with top-level goals

Using an expanded goal vocabulary, we modified the PRODIGY state-space planner to handle these three cases. We then experimented with various ways the user and planning system can interact. One way was embodied by the JADE system (Veloso, Mulvehill, and Cox 1997; Mulvehill and Cox 1999). It integrates a version of PRODIGY called Prodigy/CBMIP with a plan construction tool called ForMAT2. Prodigy/CBMIP sends the ForMAT2 user suggested actions rather than mandatory actions. The user can reject, accept, or ignore each suggestion. Conversely the user provides to the planner constraint information that makes planning more efficient. The most relevant details are available in Cox and Veloso (1997a).

Changing the Interface

To directly support the goal manipulation metaphor, we recently implemented a preliminary interface through which the user manipulates both the goals and the problem. In such an approach, the interface hides many of the planning algorithms and representations from the user and instead emphasizes the goal manipulation process.

The interface, called GTrans, presents a direct manipulation interface to the user that consists of a graphical map with drag and drop capability for objects superimposed upon the map surface. GTrans helps the user create a problem file that is internally represented as described in the previous section. That is, a planning problem consists of a set of objects, a set of relations between these objects, and a set of goals to achieve.

At initialization time an exchange of information occurs between GTrans and PRODIGY. An extension to PRODIGY allows the system to read and analyze the current domain file. The systems then sends to GTrans information about object types and about goal choices. To assemble a list of object types from which the user may choose to include in a given problem, PRODIGY outputs a set of lowest-level object types from the semantic hierarchy.

Figure 2 shows a user selecting another F15 object to add to the current planning problem.[2] A small icon is placed on the map with the pointing device to represent an object of the selected type. Looking ahead and closely at Figure 3, the reader can detect two infantry and three F15 icons near the lower left part of the map.

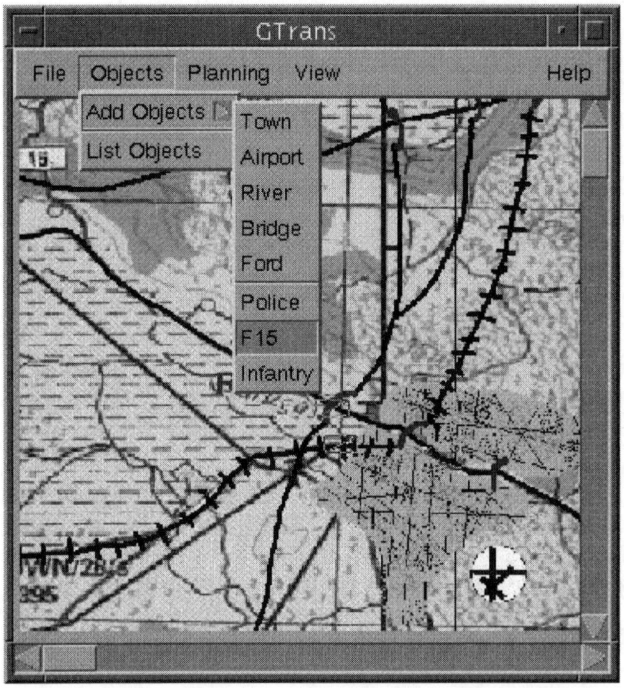

Figure 2. Adding objects to the problem with GTrans

To support goal classification information PRODIGY reads each operator from its domain file and sends to GTrans a list of all primary effects from each operator. The effects are represented as (predicate arg1-type arg2-type ... argN-type). GTrans then can associate objects defined on the map with goals relevant to each.

For example the **damage** operator has the following state specification within its add-list as its sole effect.

(is-damaged <air-force> <crossing>)

In the current domain file, two types of crossings exist (fords and bridges) and one type of air-force unit exists (F15). Therefore the potential goals associated with this effect is as follows.

(is-damaged <F15> <ford>)
(is-damaged <F15> <bridge>)

2.GTrans can save and reload scenario configurations, including object map-coordinates, so, the problem is not represented simply as a standard PRODIGY problem file by GTrans.

Goals can be created in two ways. The user can drag a mobile object[3] from its location on the map to another object. If a goal relationship exists between these two types of objects, the system will present a pop-up menu with any relevant goal states that can be created. Depending the objects of each type, GTrans will create cascaded pop-up menus appropriately. For example if a particular F15 unit is moved over a ford the former goal choice is appropriate, whereas the latter is true when moving it over a bridge.

Alternatively a user can press Control-LeftMouse upon an object on the map. If goals are associated with the object's type, the system will provide a cascaded choice of goals with possible resources to be assigned to the goals. Figure 3 illustrates this method.

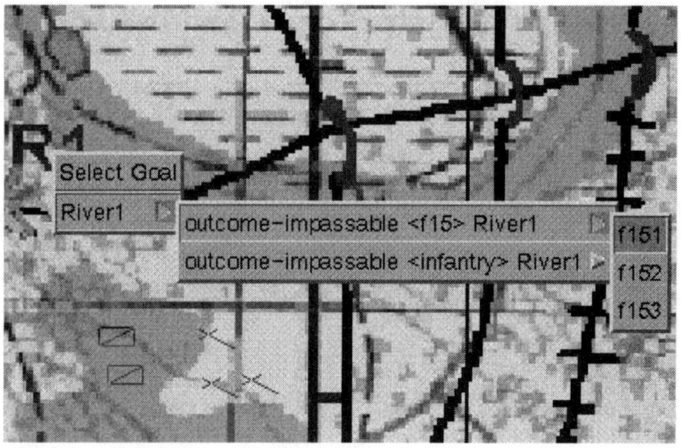

Figure 3. Creating a goal in GTrans

The user has selected the river designated at the symbol R1 with the left mouse button while holding down the control key. This pops up a menu displaying the types of goals relevant to a river. In this case the goal of achieving the state of the river being impassable is relevant. The user can choose either air units or infantry resources to associate with the goal. Here the user is selecting from among three available F15 air units.

GTrans is not simply a problem creation tool, however. With respect to goal manipulation, GTrans provides a unique facility to transform or *steer* the goals in response to PRODIGY responses. When the user receives feedback from the underlying planner (either a successful plan that may not be acceptable by the user, a failure to generate any plan, or an apparent problem due to PRODIGY taking too long), the user can asynchronously modify the goals and send them

3.Prompted during the initial use of a domain by GTrans, the user must differentiate mobile from immobile object classes.

back to the planner for another round of planing. The user does this by selecting a *goal transformation* that moves the goal within a space of possible goals (Cox and Veloso 1998).

Figure 4 shows a series of dialogue boxes that allow the user to change the goal of having the river be impassable (perhaps not enough resources exists to carry this out). By right-clicking on a current goal (represented as a "G" icon on the map), the user is presented with the Current Goals window. The user selects the goal to change, clicks on a "Transformation" button to get a list of potential transformations, and then from the Goal Transformations window, selects the "Transform" button to produce a goal that is "close" to the original goal. Because the erosion transformation moves the goal predicate itself down a level of abstraction, the goal changes to achieving the state of reduced transportation capability rather than the state of impassability. Cox *et al.* (in press) report further details on this feature.

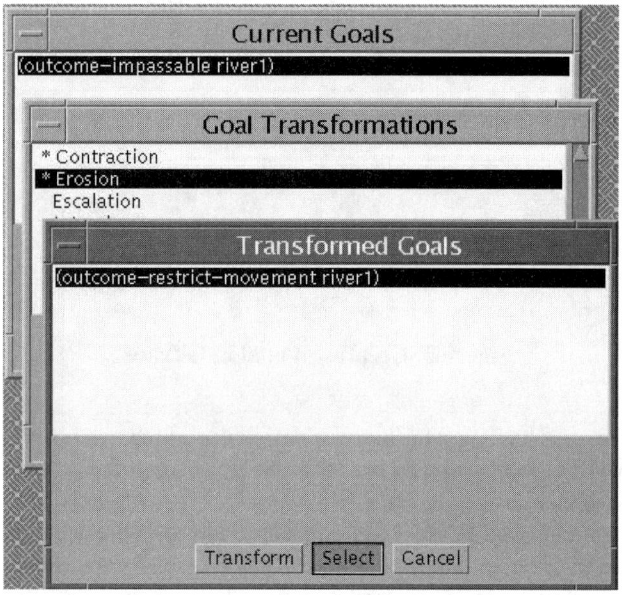

Figure 4. Performing an *erosion* goal transformation in GTrans (taken from Cox *et al.* in press)

CONCLUSION

Although the arguments presented here may appear reasonable, we have not yet obtained empirical results to rigorously support the benefits of our alternative model of planning. Despite this condition indirect evidence does exist. Das, Kar, and Parilla (1996) have psychological data from human subjects to support their theory that human planning can be classified into three distinct types. At the lowest level is *operations planning* that chooses actions to carry out immediate goals. As plan generation this level is most similar to the model of planning as search, although they do not claim that search processes implements the cognitive mechanism underneath. At the highest level is *activity planning*. This is a general orientation for broad life themes such as planning for retirement. Between the two is a kind of planning they call *action planning*. This level is more abstract than operations planning and includes plan management and environment monitoring. This theory is consistent with our view of planning as a process that manages goals, assigns resources to goals, and adjusts goal priorities over time. Our work is also very consistent with the operational level of military planning (Kent and Simons 1994; Thaler and Shlapak 1995).

This paper has contrasted two models of planning as a conflict of metaphors, but, the models are not mutually exclusive. Search is still an important AI technique that can be used in mixed-initiative systems as illustrated in this paper. However, we argue that search is not an appropriate metaphor to present to the user. This is still a hypothesis. Evaluation of this claim is necessary to state it with a significant degree of confidence.

ACKNOWLEDGEMENTS

This paper is supported by the Dayton Area Graduate Studies Institute under grant #HE-WSU-99-09 and by AFOSR under grant number F49620-99-1-0244. The author thanks Golam Rasul and Chaitresh Srinivas for their work on the implementation of the GTrans system.

REFERENCES

Allen, J. F., Ferguson, G., and Schubert, L. K. (1996). Planning in Complex Worlds via Mixed-Initiative Interaction (pp. 53-60). *Advanced Planning Technology: Technological Achievements of the ARPA/Rome Laboratory Planning Initiative*, AAAI Press.

Blum, A. and Furst, M. (1997). *Artificial Intelligence, 90* (1&2): 279-298.

Burstein, M. (Ed.). (1994). *ARPA/Rome Laboratory Knowledge-based Planning and Scheduling Initiative Workshop Proceedings*. San Francisco: Morgan Kaufmann.

Carbonell, J. G., Blythe, J., Etzioni, O., Gil, Y., Joseph, R., Kahn, D., Knoblock, C., Minton, S., Perez, A., Reilly, S., Veloso, M. M., and Wang, X. (1992). *Prodigy4.0: The Manual and Tutorial*. Technical Report, CMU-CS-92-150. Computer Science Department., Carnegie Mellon University.

Chien, S., Hill, Jr., R., Wang, X., Estlin, T., Fayyad, K, and Mortenson, H. (1996). Why real-world planning is difficult: A tale of two applications (pp. 287-298). In M. Ghallab and

A. Milani (Eds.) *New Direction in AI Planning*. Amsterdam: IOS Press.

Cox, M. T. (Ed.) (1999). *Proceedings of the AAAI-99 Workshop on Mixed-Initiative Intelligence*. Menlo Park, CA: AAAI Press.

Cox, M. T., Kerkez, B., Srinivas, C, Edwin, G., and Archer, W. (in press). Toward agent-based mixed-initiative interfaces. In *Proceedings of the 2000 International Conference on Artificial Intelligence*. CSREA Press.

Cox, M. T., and Veloso, M. M. (1997a). Controlling for unexpected goals when planning in a mixed-initiative setting. In E. Costa and A. Cardoso (Eds.), *Progress in Artificial Intelligence: Eighth Portuguese Conference on Artificial Intelligence* (pp. 309-318). Berlin: Springer.

Cox, M. T., and Veloso, M. M. (1997b). Supporting combined human and machine planning: An interface for planning by analogical reasoning. In D. B. Leake and E. Plaza (Eds.), *Case-Based Reasoning Research and Development: Second International Conference on Case-Based Reasoning* (pp. 531-540). Berlin: Springer-Verlag.

Cox, M. T., and Veloso, M. M. (1998). Goal Transformations in Continuous Planning. In M. desJardins (Ed.), *Proceedings of the 1998 AAAI Fall Symposium on Distributed Continual Planning* (pp 23-30). Menlo Park, CA: AAAI Press / The MIT Press.

Das, J. P., Kar, B. C., and Parilla, R. K. (1996). *Cognitive planning: The psychological basis of intelligent behavior.* London: Sage Publications.

Ferguson, G., and Allen, J. F. (1998). TRIPS: An Integrated Intelligent Problem-Solving Assistant (pp. 26-30). In *Proceedings of the Fifteenth National Conference on Artificial Intelligence*. Menlo Park, CA: AAAI Press.

Ferguson, Myers, and Smith, S. (Eds). (1998). *Proceedings of the Interactive and Collaborative Planning Workshop.* Held in Conjunction with the Fourth International Conference on Artificial Intelligence Planning Systems. CMU, Pittsburgh, PA.

Fikes, R. E., and Nilsson, N. J. (1971). Strips: A new approach to the application of theorem proving to problem solving. *Artificial Intelligence*, *2*: 189-208.

Georgeff, M. (1990). Planning (pp 5-25). In J. Allen, J. Hendler, and A. Tate (Eds.), *Readings in planning*. San Francisco: Morgan Kaufmann.

Haller, S., McRoy, S., and Kobsa, A. (Eds.). (1998). *Computational Models of Mixed-Initiative Interaction*. New York: Kluwer.

Hendler, J., Tate, A., and Drummond, M. (1990) A Review of AI Planning Techniques (pp. 26-49). In J. Allen, J. Hendler, and A. Tate (Eds.), *Readings in planning*. San Francisco: Morgan Kaufmann.

Kambhampati, S., Parker, E., and Lambrecht, E. (1997). Understanding and extending Graphplan (pp. 260- 272). In *Recent advances in AI planning: Proceedings of the Fourth European Conference on Planning, ECP97*. Berlin: Springer.

Kambhampati, S., and Srivastava, B. (1996). Universal classical planner: An algorithm for unifying state-space and plan-space planning (pp. 61-75). In M. Ghallab and A. Milani (Eds.) *New Directions in AI Planning*. Amsterdam: IOS Press

Kautz, H., and Selman, B. (1996). Pushing the envelope: Planning, propositional logic, and stochastic search (pp. 1194-1201). In *Proc. of the Thirteenth National Conference on Artificial Intelligence*. Menlo Park, CA: AAAI Press.

Kent, G. A., and Simons, W. E. (1994). Objective-based planning (pp. 59-71). In P. K. Davis (Ed.), *New challenges for defense planning: Rethinking how much is enough*. Santa Monica, CA: RAND.

Mulvehill, A., and Cox, M. (1999). Using Mixed Initiative to Support Force Deployment and Execution. In M. T. Cox (Ed.), *Proceedings of the 1999 AAAI-99 Workshop on Mixed-Initiative Intelligence* (pp. 119-123). Menlo Park, CA: AAAI Press.

Pollack, M. E., and Horty, J. F. (1999, winter). There's more to life that making plans (pp. 71-83). *AI Magazine*.

Thaler, D. E., and Shlapak, D. A. (1995). *Perspectives on theater air campaign planning*. Santa Monica, CA: RAND.

Veloso, M. M., Carbonell, J. G., Perez, A., Borrajo, D., Fink, E., and Blythe, J. (1995) Integrating planning and learning: The PRODIGY architecture. *Journal of Theoretical and Experimental Artificial Intelligence. 7(1)*: 81-120.

Veloso, M. M., Mulvehill, A. M., and Cox, M. T. (1997). Rationale-supported mixed-initiative case-based planning. In *Proceedings of the Fourteenth National Conference on Artificial Intelligence and Ninth Innovative Applications of Artificial Intelligence Conference* (pp. 1072-1077). Menlo Park, CA: AAAI Press.

EVALUATION OF HUMAN PERFORMANCE IN A SIMULATED UCAV CONTROL STATION

Jesse R. Lucas, MS
Jennie J. Gallimore, Ph.D.
Wright State University
Department of Biomedical, Industrial, and Human Factors Engineering
207 Russ Engineering Center
Dayton, OH, 45435

KEYWORDS

UCAV, automation, command and control, interactive simulation, symbology

ABSTRACT

The Suppression of Enemy Air Defenses (SEAD) mission is a dangerous military aviation attack against enemy surface to air missiles (SAMs). The military is thus pushing to eliminate the airborne pilot with ground controlled Uninhabited Combat Aerial Vehicles (UCAVs). This raises many questions concerning the human machine interaction with the command and control ground system.

A simulated command station was designed and implemented using Java on a windows-based operating system with point and click manipulation capabilities. The simulation system allows users to keep track of UCAV parameters such as fuel and airspeed, define new waypoints, and track, identify and destroy enemy targets. A number of performance parameters can be measured, including correct target identifications, targets not identified, targets not destroyed, non-targets destroyed, UCAVs returned on time, average time of range incident, and number and average number of times UCAVs were in target range and did not take action.

This paper describes the simulation system and reports results of a study conducted to investigate human performance using the simulated UCAV mission while varying the number of UCAVs being supervised (1, 2 or 4), symbology (Mil Std 2525 vs pictorial symbols), and level of system automation (low or high). Results indicated that number of UCAVs supervised and level of automation affected performance. In general, when the number of UCAVs supervised is constant, a high level of automation is often non-degrading to many performance measures and can enhance performance. However, due to a reliance on automation in high stress missions (controlling 4 and sometimes 2 UCAVs) many non-targets are destroyed by consenting controllers.

BACKGROUND

The objective of SEAD is to destroy, neutralize, or temporarily degrade enemy air defenses in a specific area by physical attack or electrical warfare. Suppression of enemy air defenses (SEAD) prevents systems from radiating, either through physical damage or by intimidation. The mission requires detection, location, identification, and destruction of important elements of enemy air defenses. Identification and attack on the enemy targets have to be quick and without error. This is an obviously dangerous mission, and taking the human out of the aircraft would reduce the risk to human life. Thus, the concept of implementing UCAVs in the SEAD mission was developed. Some of the advantages that a UCAV has over a conventional *in*habited combat aerial vehicles are operational persistence, potentially lower life-cycle cost, no hazard to crew, and more maneuverability (NWV 1995).

The military has been using controlled uninhabited aerial vehicles (UAVs) for reconnaissance missions for many years now (Clark 1999). The utility of the UAV has developed and diversified over the years. UAVs have been and continue to be successfully used in some of the following ways: decoys, scouts, reconnaissance platforms, surveillance platforms, highly maneuverable bombs, and transports (Christner 1991). Today the UAV is hoped to take on the responsibility of an uninhabited *combat* aerial vehicle (UCAV) (Clark 1999; DARPA 2000; Fulghum 1996; Fulghum 1997; Jones and Barnhart, 1998). Incorporating these uninhabited vehicles into military missions has been fruitful, though a real challenge for command and control station designers.

To make the problem even more complex, controllers will not only have to be aware of one UCAV within enemy territory, literature indicates that perhaps a single controller will control anywhere from 1 to 8 aircraft (NWV 1995; Barnes and Matz 1998). Current UAV reconnaissance systems are monitored by two controllers (Field Manual 34-25-2 1995; Barnes and Matz 1998). In order for a single controller to handle multiple UCAVs in a combat setting, many features will have to be automated for the controller.

SYMBOLOGY

It will not be easy for a single controller to stay aware of the entire mission status, especially when having to recognize, identify, and perhaps destroy individual targets - depending on the target's capabilities. In order for the controller to stay aware of the entire mission status, individual targets must be easily recognized and the capabilities clearly represented.

The MIL-STD-2525 (1999) is designed to eliminate conflicts within various sets of symbology via a single standard. The typical 2525 symbol (i.e., the icon part) represents a generic type of target, such as long rang missile launcher platform. To know more about the capabilities of the long rang missile launcher (e.g., heat seeking, radar navigated, radar seeking, etc.) accompanying label(s) must be read and interpreted. Also it is easy to confuse similar icons without reading the textual label that distinguishes them as illustrated in Figure 1-A. In a SEAD mission there is not much time for reading the fine print, and the more time taken to interpret a symbol representing a threat, the greater chance there is of loosing situation awareness.

An alternative symbology set is suggested that incorporates information about the item within the symbol itself, thus eliminating the need for cluttering, time consuming fine print. Human's find it easier (faster) to retrieve information about something when it is stored in a physical representation format (Ware 2000). A colored silhouette of the item would represent all relevant information about the item that is necessary to complete a dynamic, time sensitive mission without error. During flight training pilots are trained to determine the affordances (capabilities) of an enemy aircraft by the shape of that aircraft's silhouette (personal communication with Patzek, M. on 25 June, 1999. AFRL/HECI, Michael.Patzek@he.wpafb.af.mil). They can determine how to engage a particular aircraft just by observing the outline of that aircraft.

Though the 2525 symbology does an excellent job of distinguishing between items, an alternative symbology would more readily communicate the affordances of the item. For instance, the UCAV controller would know immediately by the shape of the symbol that s/he was looking at a radar seeking, long range missile launcher, threat. The controller then knows that s/he can turn off her/his active sensors to avoid attack on the UCAV. An alternative symbolology, as seen in Figure 1-B, can be thought of as an information icon, rather than a data center of facts that must be integrated for interpretation, analogous to the 2525 symbolology.

Controllers are highly trained with a set of symbology. Just prior to a given mission, controllers review the specific targets that are likely to be seen in the area (personal communication with Patzek, M. on 25 June, 1999. AFRL/HECI, Michael.Patzek@he.wpafb.af.mil). Ambiguities between target types can be addressed at this time and can be resolved by simply editing symbols before mission start time.

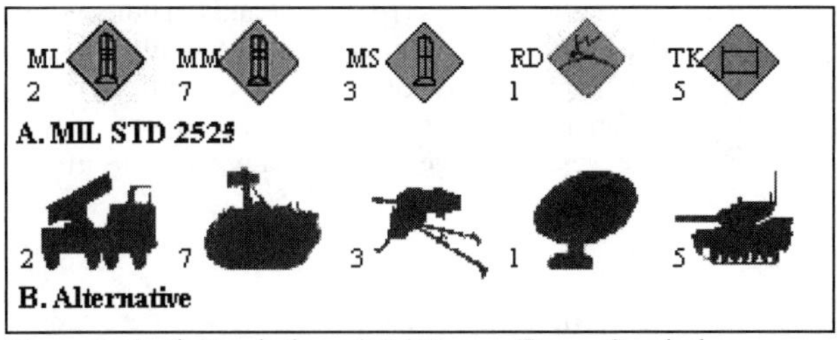

Figure 1. Both Symbology Sets' Enemy Target Symbols

AUTOMATION

With the onset of automated decision aids, interfaces are moving from being directly manipulated to indirectly managed. Function allocation trends increasingly place tasks under the responsibility of highly automated systems (Weber, Reinhardt, and Miller 2000). In general a system has one goal or several goals in which many components, both automated and human, work together to best reach the goal or goals. In the past controllers have directly controlled the system by reading gauges and turning knobs. Today's controllers work with the system to retrieve relevant information, plan situational strategies, and perform control actions (Coury and Semmel 1996). Monitoring for failures and odd situations the automation is incapable of handling are important jobs of the human controller (Endsley 1996).

It has become the controller's job to obtain appropriate information in which s/he is to plan responses to encountered situations (Coury and Semmel 1996). One can conclude that a primary goal for an intelligent user interface is to enhance situation awareness by acting as the intermediary between a controller and the processing systems that provide situational information (Moiser and Skitka 1996; Coury and Semmel 1996). The human controller and the automated portion of the human-computer system must be capable of communicating information, strategies, and commands to each other. Since the controller uses the interface to interact with the problem, the system must be able to effectively communicate information about the state of the system to the controller (Coury and Semmel 1996; Moiser and Skitka 1996).

The communicative capabilities of automated decision aids range across many levels and depend on the environment and the situation at hand. Mosier and Skitka (1996) describe 6 capability levels of automated decision aids.

- Display or highlight raw data that needs to be attended to.
- Provide system monitoring and alert signals.
- Display trends and the results of diagnosis with confidence information.
- Display potential predicted consequences for a particular course of action.
- Provide wrong decision protection.
- Provide action directive.

Many times automated systems don't make it obvious what their limitations are. Controllers may view automated aids as having superior skills and the most efficient way of getting decisions made and tasks done – especially if the workload for the controller is high (Mosier and Skitka 1996). Reducing workload is another major function of automation. Endsley found that monitors of an automated system performed better than did manual controllers in a flight task (Endsley 1996). Endsley suggests that, as monitors, subjects may have been able to distribute their excess attention to other displays and tasks.

Turning a human controller from a performer into an observer can, in and itself, negatively affect situation awareness, even if the controller is able to function as an effective monitor, and this can lead to significant problems in taking over during automation failure (Endsley 1996). This is due to the loss in situation awareness. However, automation used to lower workload may not necessarily imply an increase in situation awareness (Endsley 1996). The implication for the design of intelligent user interfaces is that situation awareness and action planning (the work) must be closely coupled (Moiser and Skitka 1996). By implementing Mosier and Skitka's 6 capability levels of automated decision aids properly, given each specified task or situation within the control environment such that situation awareness is accurate and complete, controllers can act to bring their systems into conformance with their goals (Endsley 1996).

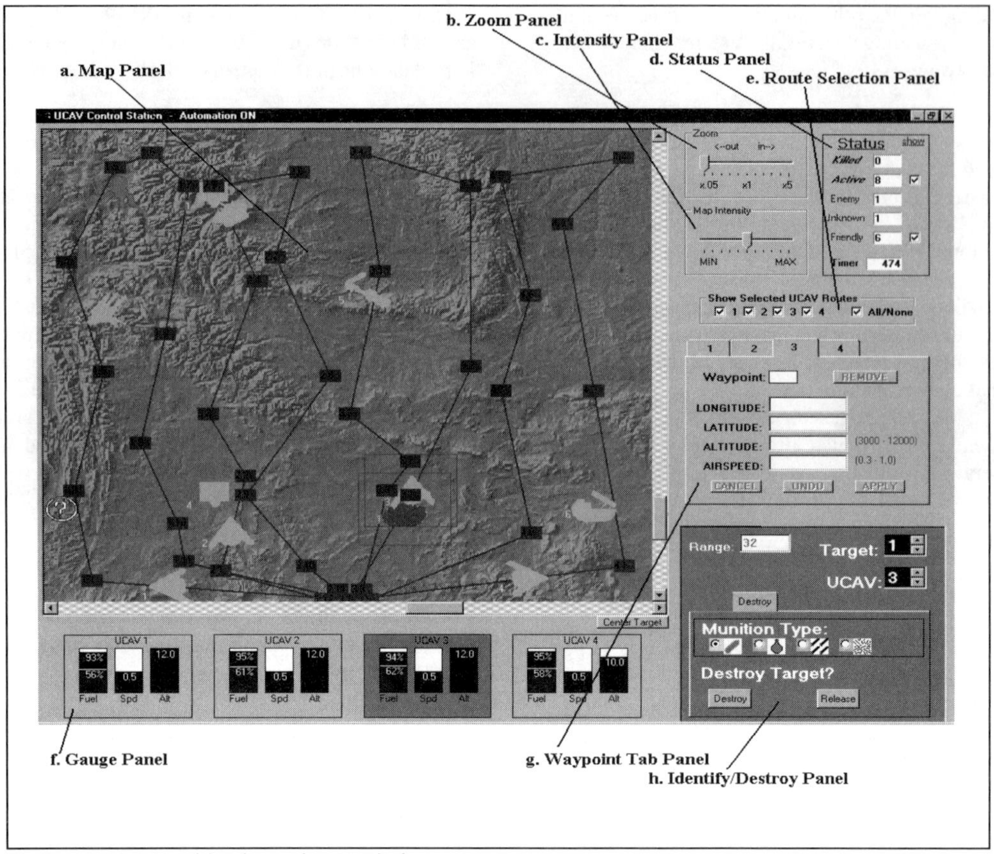

Figure 2. Interface with Alternative Symbology

INTERFACE and SIMULATION

The interface design goal was to provide the UCAV controller with an optimal interactive interface for the SEAD mission. The interface and simulation software was created using JAVA on a Windows PC platform. The interface was displayed on a 21 inch monitor, with input via mouse and keyboard.

The SEAD mission is flown by simulated UCAVs within an enemy territory populated by several known, unknown, and hidden targets. The simulation/interface can handle up to 4 UCAVs that travel along individual predetermined flightpaths, as illustrated in Figure 2. The flightpaths were made up of waypoints connected by lines. Waypoints are destinations on the map display. Each UCAV moves from one waypoint to the next along the lines connecting the waypoints. Waypoints can be moved, added, or deleted. Waypoints can be used to set a UCAV's airspeed and altitude as well as heading. Airspeeds, altitudes, and flightpaths are all preprogrammed before a mission begins, but can be changed at any time during the mission.

As the UCAVs fly along their individual routes the controller monitors and controls the UCAVs in order to identify unknown targets, destroy enemy targets, and return the UCAVs to base safely. As the UCAVs fly along their route, targets are detected via satellites, friendly ground radar, the UCAVs themselves, or other sources. Thus enemy and unknown targets were randomly appearing at seemingly random locations on the map as the UCAV control station database is updated by all these sources. A controller can adjust UCAV routes as targets appear on the map panel. They then identify unknown targets using sensors onboard each UCAV and destroy enemy targets using ammunitions onboard each UCAV.

Onboard each UCAV there are two sensors used for viewing targets remotely. One is an Infrared (IR) sensor and the other is an Electro Optical (EO) sensor. Each can be used for looking at different types of unknown targets. UCAVs must be within the range of 5000 feet (about 1 mile) from an unknown target to view the target with either sensor. Range is measured in hundreds of feet; thus 5000 feet is displayed as a range of 50.

Each UCAV has an unlimited supply of 4 different types of ammunitions. The 4 different types include: , , , and . Symbols, rather than names were used to avoid subject biases, reversal errors, and alleviate memory burdens. Each are used for destroying different types of targets. UCAVs must be within the range of 50 (5000 feet, about 1 mile) from an enemy target to destroy the target with any ammunitions.

Any type of target, other than friendly, may put a radar lock on a UCAV any time it is in range (50). This means that the target can track the exact UCAV location, and thus is able to harm the UCAV quickly. No UCAVs are actually damaged or destroyed. It was felt that destroying UCAVs or changing the nature of the UCAVs performance would confound any analyses. The price of avoiding these confounds was a lack of absolute realism. These features can be added to the simulation.

At any time a UCAV could lose altitude or airspeed and fall below the proper range. It is the controller's job to monitor and adjust each UCAV's airspeed and altitude to be sure it stays within the proper range.

The interface can be used by the controller to handle all aspects of mission operation. Figure 2 is a snapshot of the controller's interface used to control and command the UCAVs in the simulated SEAD mission. Control panels are layered, status panels are shown side by side, and the UCAVs, targets, and the flight paths are all realistically represented within a single map screen.

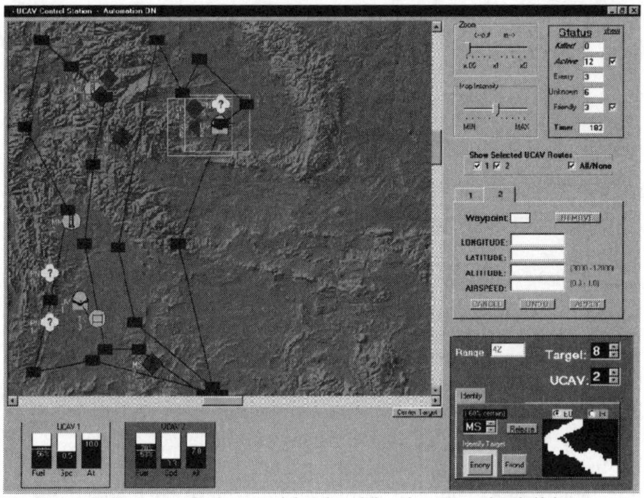

Figure 3. 2525 Symbology with Identification Panel Visible

Many features are automated in the interface/system. For example, UCAVs automatically follow the indicated flight paths and sensors are automatically rotated and focused when viewing specific targets. The interface supports many levels of automation capabilities and communication of those capabilities. Using Mosier's and Skitka's categories for levels of automation the automated features are categorized below:

- **Display or highlight raw data that needs to be attended to:** Remaining mission time is shown continuously through the SEAD mission. Controllers translate this data into the amount of time to move from one waypoint to another and the amount of time to spend on each target (depending on its priority). Also targets are automatically queued when they are within range of a UCAV.
- **Provide system monitoring and alert signals:** UCAV and target are outlined in red when a target has a UCAV in radar lock. Altitude and airspeed are monitored and highlighted red when out of safe flying boundaries.
- **Display trends and the results of diagnosis with confidence information:** Automatic identification of targets is accompanied by an accuracy percentage (i.e., probability of being correct).
- **Display potential predicted consequences for a particular course or action:** The fuel gauge not only displays the amount of fuel left at a particular instant, but also displays the estimated amount of fuel left at the estimated time of that UCAV's return to the base. This allows the controller to see the consequences of extending the flight path or increasing speed along a segment of the path.
- **Provide wrong decision protection:** As new targets appear, waypoints are automatically added to the flight paths, but controllers are still able to adjust those waypoints to better approach the target or fit mission limitations (e.g., time).
- **Provide action directive:** When targets are automatically queued unknown targets are queued such that the identification panel appears (see Figure 3), and already identified targets are cued such that the ammunition selection (i.e., destroy panel) panel appears (see Figure 2), thus giving direction to the type of action that needs to be accomplished for the particular target. In addition, the proper ammunition or sensor is automatically selected (100% accurate), and targets are automatically identified (75% accurate).

EXPERIMENT

An experiment was conducted to examine the effects of three independent variables on controller performance: Number of UCAVs (1, 2, or 4), Level of Automation (high or low), and Symbology (MIL STD 2525 or alternative). The following dependent measures were analyzed during a simulated 8 minute SEAD mission: Portion of Targets Correctly Identified, Portion of Enemy targets not Destroyed, and Average Time of Non-Radar Range Incidents.

It was hypothesized that when automation was set to high, the controller would reach, identify, destroy more enemy targets, and remain in range of enemy radar for less time than when using low automation. It was also hypothesized that as the number of UCAVs being controlled increased from 1 to 4, UCAVs would be in range of targets more often, time in range would increase, and the percentage of targets identified and destroyed would decrease. The type of symbology set was expected to have no effect on controller performance indicating that an alternative symbology that allows for affordances and direct perception performs equally well as a set that relies on abstract icons and textual messages.

METHOD

Sixteen undergraduates from Wright State University were trained for one hour on the objectives of the SEAD mission and how to use the control interface. During training participants learned to use the interface and identify one of the two sets of symbols.

The participant was informed that it was important that the mission area (i.e., area covered by the original UCAV routes) was monitored for targets within mission time. All threatening targets needed to be identified and/or destroyed to allow safe access for the bombers that were to theoretically come after each SEAD mission.

Automation was considered at two levels: high and low. The high automation mode contained the items described previously plus these extra automated features that were not present in the low automation mode: automatic target queuing in order of preference, automatic (i.e., suggested) identification (75% accurate), automatic ammunition type selection, and automatic flight path generation for new targets off current path.

RESULTS AND DISCUSSION

An ANOVA was conducted for each of the 3 dependent variables. Results for each are briefly discussed.

Portion of Targets Correctly Identified

The portion of targets correctly identified is the ratio of targets correctly identified divided by the total number of targets to be identified. Figure 4 illustrates the significant interaction between Level of Automation and Number of UCAVs $\underline{F}(2, 28) = 5.56$, $\underline{p} = 0.0093$. When participants were controlling 4 UCAVs under low automation the portion of targets correctly identified (**X** = 0.775) was significantly different from all other conditions except when controlling 4 UCAVs with high automation. When controlling 4 UCAVs with high automation performance is not significantly different than when controlling 1 or 2 UCAVs under either automation level.

The results indicate that when controlling 1 or 2 UCAVs the level of automation did not affect performance. Adding 2 more UCAVs and providing high automation resulted in similar performance, thus workload was reduced because of automation.

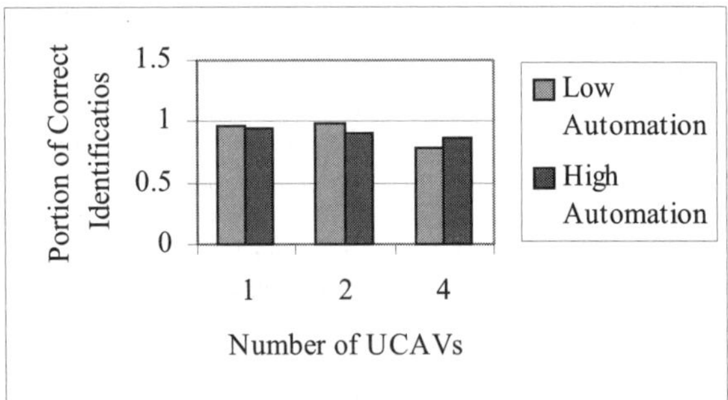

Figure 4. Portion of Targets Correctly Identified.

Portion of Enemy Targets not Destroyed

The portion of enemy targets not destroyed is the ratio of the number of enemy targets actually destroyed in a mission divided by the number of enemy targets to be destroyed in a mission. Figure 5 illustrates the significant interaction between Level of Automation and Number of UCAVs $\underline{F}(2, 28) = 3.70$, $\underline{p} = 0.0377$. There was a significantly higher portion of targets not destroyed when controlling 4 UCAVs with low level of automation compared to all other conditions. Without the higher level of automation, the workload for 4 UCAVs affects the controller's ability to destroy a higher percentage of enemy targets.

The results indicated a significant main effect for Automation $\underline{F}(1, 14) = 8.19$, ($\underline{p} = 0.0126$). A significantly greater portion of targets were left undestroyed with the Low level of Automation (**X** = 0.020) than with the High level of Automation (**X** = 0.001). The results indicated a significant main effect for Number of UCAVs $\underline{F}(2, 28) = 4.05$, ($\underline{p} = 0.0284$). A significantly greater proportion of targets were left undestroyed when 4 UCAVs are controlled (**X** = 0.020) than when 1 UCAV is controlled (**X** = 0.000).

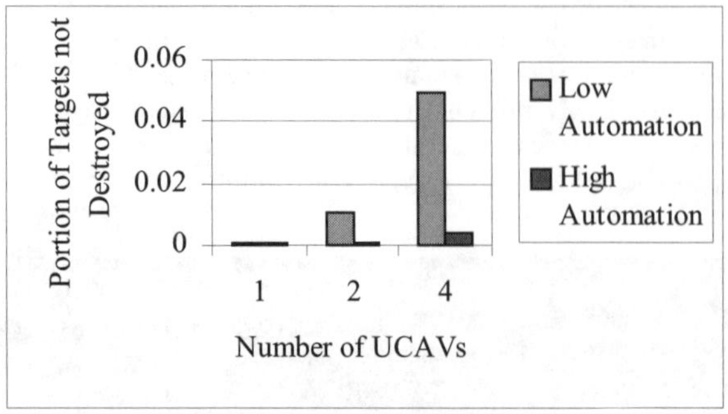

Figure 5. Portion of Targets not Destroyed

Average Time of Non-Radar Range Incidents

A non-radar range incident is when a UCAV enters into target range of a target that does not put the UCAV into radar lock. The average time of non-radar range incident is the total time UCAVs were in non-radar range divided by the number of times they were in non-radar range. Figure 6 illustrates the significant interaction between Level of Automation and Number of UCAVs $\underline{F}(2, 28) = 10.17$, ($\underline{p} = 0.0005$). For all conditions of Number of UCAVs, adding automation improved performance. The average time of non-radar range incident is significantly greatest when 4 UCAVs are being controlled and the automation level is low (**X** = 6.488). The difference in performance between high and low automation when there are 4 UCAVs is larger than the differences when controlling one or two UCAVs. When high automation is activated performance is similar across the levels of UCAV, until performance when controlling 1 UCAV being significantly different than performance with either 2 or 4 UCAVs. Providing high Automation with 4 UCAVs brings performance down to that found when users are controlling 1 or 2 UCAVs with low automation. In general when automation is low, performance deteriorates as the number of UCAVs increase. But when automation is high, performance remains similar.

A significant main effect for Automation was found $\underline{F}(1, 14) = 60.86$, ($\underline{p} = 0.0001$). With the Low level of Automation the average time of a non-radar range incident was significantly higher (**X** = 1.963) than with the High level of Automation (**X** = 1.154). This is likely due to the fact that it takes participants more mouse clicks to destroy a target or identify a target when Automation is at the Low level. A significant main effect for Number of UCAVs was indicated by the results $\underline{F}(2, 28) = 34.42$, ($\underline{p} = 0.0001$). With 4 UCAVs to control, the average time of non-radar range incident was greater (**X** = 4.631) than when 1 (**X** = 2.592) or 2 (**X** = 2.979) UCAVs were controlled.

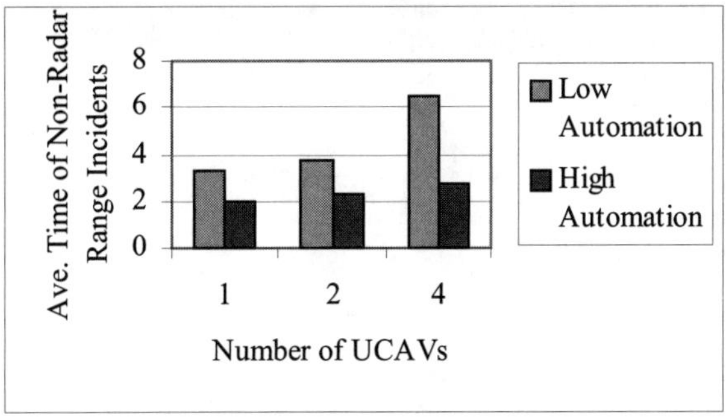

Figure 6. Average Times of the Non-Radar Range Incidents

CONCLUSIONS

The simulation/interface creates an environment that contains tasks much like those that a real UCAV controller would have to perform to accomplish a SEAD mission in an actual combat setting. The simulation/interface system was designed to allow for an analysis of uncertainties about UCAV interface design, including: the number of UCAVs a single controller can manage, how proper automation of features effect performance, and the type of symbology that should be used in such a dynamic mission. The simulation provided an environment in which controller performance could be measured so that the user-interface design can be evaluated and analyzed. The data from the experiment could also be used to populate a computer-based simulation in the future.

The trend in all the dependent measures indicate that a controller's performance significantly drops when s/he controls 4 UCAVs at a low level of automation. Given adequate amount of automated features, properly communicating with the controller the capabilities and limitations of the system, a single controller was able to control 4 UCAVs with performance not significantly different than when controlling 2 or even 1 UCAV. In fact it may be considered better, because with 4 UCAVs a greater number of targets are being addressed than with 1 or 2 UCAVs to control.

As hypothesized, there were no significant differences in performance related to Symbology indicating that the alternative symbology is just as good as the 2525 symbology. The advantage that the new symbology has is that it does not require a descriptive label. From observing the participants interacting with the system during the experimental trials, it was obvious that when using the 2525 symbology, the controllers relied heavily on the descriptive labels accompanying the symbols. This was perhaps due to the fact that, with the 2525 symbology, short, medium, and long range missiles are only distinguished by either counting the number of lines within the center of the symbol (see Figure 1) or reading the accompanying label.

ACKNOWLEDGEMENTS

This research was sponsored by AFSOR, contract # F49620-97-1-0231.

REFERENCES

Barnes, M.J. and M.F. Matz. 1998. “Crew Simulations for Unmanned Aerial Vehicle (UAV) Applications: Sustained Effects, Shift Factors, Interface Issues, and Crew Size.” *Proceedings of the Human Factors Ergonomics Society 42nd Annual Meeting*: 143-147.

Christner, J.H. 1991. “Pioneer Unmanned Air Vehicle Accomplishments During Operation Dessert Storm.” SPIE Vol. 1538 Airborne Reconnaissance XV. Hunt Valley, Maryland: 201-207.

Clark, R.M. 1999. Uninhabited Combat Aerial Vehicles: Airpower By The People, For The People, But Not With The People, Thesis [Online]. www.au.af.mil/au/database/research/ay1999/saas/clark_rm.htm Thesis, School of Advanced airpower studies, Air University, Maxwell Air Force Base, Alabama (June).

Coury, B. and R. Semmel. 1996. “Supervisory Control and the Design of Intelligent User Interfaces.” In *Automation and Human Performance: Theory and Application* ’96, Lawrence Erlbaum Associates, Inc. Mahwah, N.J., 221-242.

Endsley, M. R. 1996. Automation and Situation Awareness. In *Automation and Human Performance: Theory and Application ’96* Lawrence Erlbaum Associates, Inc. Mahwah, N.J., 163-181.

Fulghum, D. A. 1996. “F-16As May Fly Again As Unmanned Combat Vehicles” *Aviation Week and Space Technology* 4 (Nov.): 28-29.

Fulghum, D. A. 1997. New Control Systems Sparks UAV Success. Aviation Week and Space Technology 19 (May): 40-41.

Jones, C.A. and M.S. Barnhart. 1998. “Crew Simulations for Unmanned Aerial Vehicle (UAV) Applications: Sustained Effects, Shift Factors, Interface Issues, and Crew Size” Proceedings of the Human Factors and Ergonomics Society 42nd Annual Meeting: 143-147.

Mosier, K.L. and L.J. Skitka. 1996. “Human Decision Makers and Automated Decision Aids: Made for Each Other?” *Automation and Human Performance: Theory and Application* ’96, Lawrence Erlbaum Associates, Inc. Mahwah, N.J., 201-220.

Ware, C. 2000. *Information Visualization: Perception for Design.* Morgan Kaufmann Publishers, San Francisco, CA.

Weber, J.; A. Reinhardt; and R. Miller. 2000. “Tight Labor? Tech to the Rescue.” *Business Week, n3673,* 20 (Mar.): 36-37.

Defense Advanced Research Projects Agency (DARPA) 2000. Unmanned Combat Air Vehicle (UCAV) [Online]. www.darpa.mil/tto/programs/ucav.html, 2 (June).

Field Manual 34-25-2. 1995. Unmanned Aerial Vehicles (UAVs) [Online]. http://www.fas.org/irp/doddir/army/fm34-25-2/index.html, Department of the Army, Washington, DC. (June)

New World Vistas: Air and Space Power for the 21st century (NWV) 1995. Information Applications volume [Online]. http://ecs.rams.com/afosr/afr/sab/edu/menu/any/sabmnia.htm, 15 (Dec.).

Common Warfighting Symbology 1999. Military Standard 2525B [Online]. http://www-symbology.itsi.disa.mil/symbol/mil-std.htm. 29 (Jan.).

Transportation, Marine and Automotive Applications

Applications of PSPICE CAN Calculator to Analyze Effects of Emissions from Automotive Data Busses

Andrew Rusek, School of Engineering and Computer Science, Oakland University, Rochester, MI 48309, phone: 248 370-2181, fax: 248 370-4633, e-mail: rusek@oakland.edu.
Dan Stevens, Core Networking, DaimlerChrysler, phone: 248 576-7021, e-mail: ds94@dcx.com
Kurt Olzmann, Core Networking, DaimlerChrysler, phone: 248 576-9001, e-mail: kao@dcx.com
Frederick Miesterfeld, Senior Technical Specialist, DaimlerChrysler, 800 Chrysler Drive, Auburn Hills, MI, 48326
Phone: 248 576-3504, fax 248-576 7021, e-mail: fom@dcx.com
Henry Catherino, US Army Tank Automotive Command TACOM, Warren, MI

ABSTRACT - The PSPICE program is applied as a graphic calculator to compute frequency components of the waves transmitted through automotive data busses with twisted pair transmission lines. The components are obtained directly from a mathematical expression instead of retrieving them through the time-domain analysis and subsequent FFT processing. In many cases, the calculations yield larger number of signal harmonic components than the number calculated through the PSPICE PROBE FFT processor. In particular, an example is shown where the calculator displays 500 spectral components while the PSPICE PROBE shows about 50 components. As a result, the PSPICE PROBE cannot be used to cover the full range of frequencies of interest. The CAN (Controller Area Network) calculator was applied as a useful educational tool to enhance computing capability of PSPICE simulations involving spectral analysis of the waves transmitted in data busses. It was also very convenient in technical evaluations of tolerances of the data bus drivers.

INDEX TERMS – Automotive data bus, spectral analysis, PSPICE, CAN.

I. INTRODUCTION

The concept of dominant effects, introduced in [6] by Clayton Paul, has been very useful in analyzing emissions from automotive data busses. In single wire busses the source of radiated emissions is a signal itself directly transmitted through the wire. In a twisted pair, or other symmetric transmission lines, the source of radiation is an uncompensated part of the signal caused mainly by asymmetry of the driving pulses, especially within the frequencies covering AM and FM radio bands.

The paper presents a PSPICE [5] based calculator that is applied to compute harmonic components of typical, trapezoidal signals with additional filtering. The spectrum is subjected to filtering passing through filters introduced in terms of a transfer function. The calculations of conducted and radiated emission levels presented in the paper are based on the Controller Area Network (CAN) standards for twisted pair drivers. The radiated emission spectrum is computed taking into consideration lower frequency part of an antenna transfer function determined based on CISPR 25 measurement setup [1]. The magnitudes of the signal spectral representation are displayed together with references chosen arbitrarily from [3] and [1]. It should be noted that the PSPICE based calculator can be a very useful tool serving to evaluate effects of variation of signal and filter parameters on the EMC performance, but its best application is in conjunction with regular time-domain PSPICE simulation. The calculator becomes a very convenient enhancement and extension of the time-domain analysis applied to evaluate the EMC performance of automotive data busses with CAN drivers, especially when very large number of harmonics is of deep concern, which is the case observed in many EMC applications. The paper describes the structure of the calculator and the results of selected simulations. Major simulated results are practically verified in a circuit with two generators and a summing network.

It is important to observe that the calculator method can be applied whenever an analytical math expression can be derived for source waves. Initially, the waves are assumed to be trapezoidal. Then the spectra are computed and further processed by filters whose characteristics are introduced in terms of transfer functions. Great flexibility of PSPICE algorithms, including variable step of iterations and automatic supply adjustments, makes the PSPICE easier to use than the MATLAB.

II. THE STRUCTURE OF THE CAN CALCULATOR

The CAN calculator has been prepared to speed up and simplify the processes of analysis of EMC parameters of

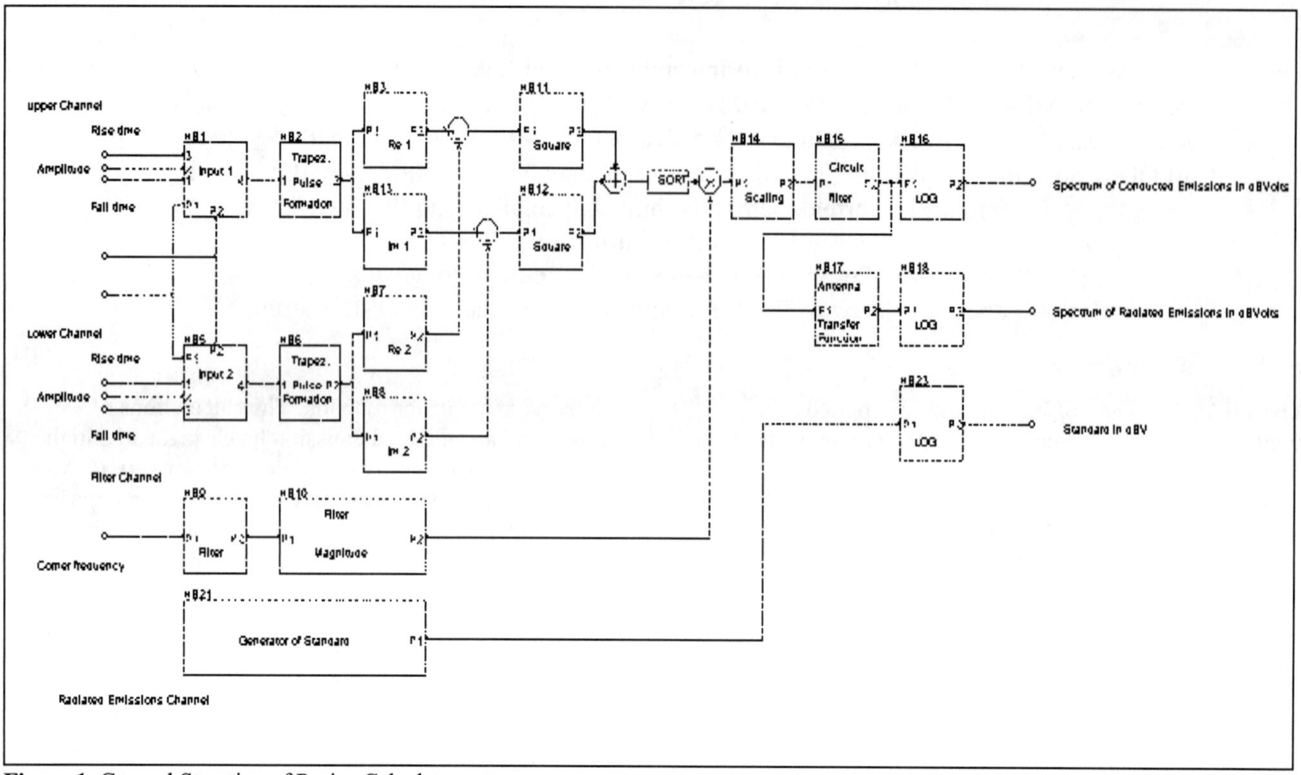

Figure 1. General Struction of Pspice Calculator

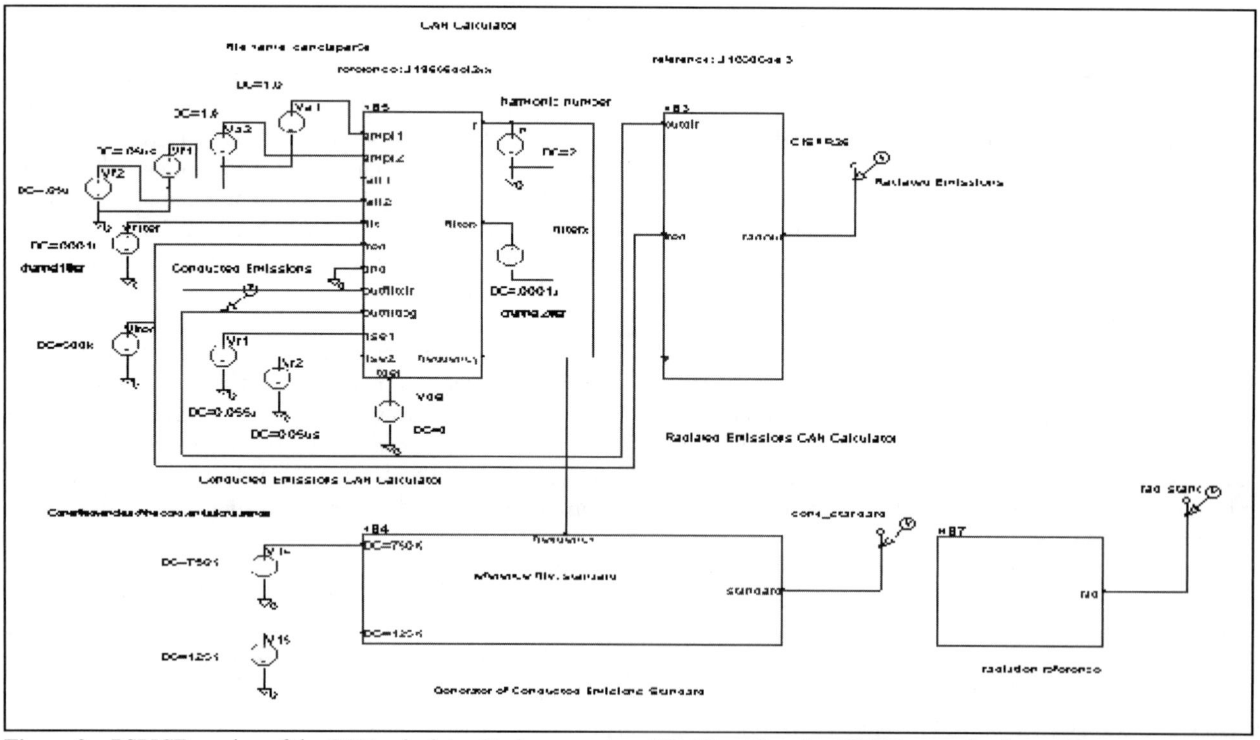

Figure 2. PSPICE version of the CAN calculator. Basic parameters: TR, TF = 50ns, f = 500KHz, amplitudes = 1V are nominal values for both channels.

automotive data busses [6]. The calculator structure resembles an analog computer, which is composed of generic system blocks, like multipliers, integrators, and other mathematical blocks, mixed with classical PSPICE circuit components. A general block diagram of the calculator is shown in Figure 1. In the upper channel, the spectral components of one pulse are calculated, the spectral image of the other pulse is computed in the lower channel. The final results are presented in terms of spectrum magnitude versus frequency. One channel can be disabled to determine behavior of a single wire driver. The spectrum is scaled according to the characteristic of the filter, which is included in the presented version of the calculator. Additional scaling and unit adjustment is done in other blocks, like Scaling and LOG blocks. Figure 2 illustrates the PSPICE block implementation Inside the blocks are the basic functions represented by the equations serving to compute Fourier spectra, filter transfer function, antenna transfer function, and equations for references. All functions are composed of PSPICE blocks, like multipliers, summers, and dividers, trigonometric and logarithmic operators, etc. The results of calculations are displayed in dBV for RMS magnitude values of the spectral components. The frequency units are plotted in volts, so that 1KV corresponds to 1KHz. Any other magnitude units can be introduced by changing built-in scaling factors.

A set of equations applied to find the spectra is as follows:

$$C_n = -j\frac{A\alpha}{2\pi n}e^{-0.5j\omega_o(T+T_R)}$$

$$\text{where } \alpha = \frac{\sin\beta}{\beta}e^{-0.5\ \omega_o T_j} - \frac{\sin\gamma}{\gamma}e^{-0.5\ \omega_o T_j} \qquad (1)$$

and $\beta = 0.5n\omega_o T_R$, $\gamma = 0.5n\omega_o T_F$

If a delay between the pulses is introduced, then Fourier coefficient for the delayed channel are expressed as follows:

$$c_{nd} = c_n\, e^{-j\, n\, \omega_0\, T_D} \qquad (2)$$

Additionally, the meaning of the other terms is as follows:

c_n - Fourier coefficients for trapezoidal waves of upper channel,
c_{nd} – Fourier coefficients for lower channel,
A – Pulse amplitude,

T_0 – Period ($T0 = \frac{1}{f_0}$),

T_R – Rise time (1 and 2 for upper and lower channel respectively),
T_F – Fall time (1 and 2 for upper and lower channel respectively),
T_D – Delay time between the pulses,
n – Integers ($-\infty$, ……, -1, 0, +1, ……, $+\infty$).

Equation (1) and (2) are used in the calculator to determine magnitude of the two-sided spectrum. The calculator finally plots magnitudes of the single-sided spectrum.

III. EXAMPLES OF SIMULATIONS AND TESTS

The examples shown here include a group of selected cases to demonstrate basic features of the calculator, and to show how small deviations from pulse symmetry can cause excessive emissions. For the clarity of graphical presentation, parametric sweeps of parameters yielding families of multiple curves are avoided.

Before applying the calculator to compute spectral components of the trapezoidal waves, filtered or unfiltered, it is important to evaluate basic wave parameters and their limits from the point of view of timing of an applied network. The parameters of the pulses chosen for simulations, whose results are presented in the paper, are based on practical measurements of typical CAN transceivers, like Phillip's PCA82C250. The bit rates, corresponding to 250 KHz and 500 KHz repetition frequencies, are chosen to demonstrate possible EMC problems where excessive conducted emissions may cause undesired interference into AM radio reception. In practice, small variations of the bit rate result in frequency modulation, which is translated by AM receiver filters into an AM signal recognized by the receiver. Obviously, the receiver should be tuned close to the frequency of bit repetition or close to its harmonics. Table 1 lists basic parameters of the waves and the filters used in presented simulations. Major effects demonstrated here include changes of emissions due to small deviations of pulse amplitudes, pulse delay misalignment, rise and fall time differences, channel filter misalignments, and changes of the of the bit rate. Figure 3 shows introductory results of simulations when filter and pulse parameters are symmetric.

The calculated levels represent numerical background noise (noise floor) for conducted and radiated emissions, which are well below the reference levels (standards). The other interesting feature of the calculator that is tested is the capability of the calculator to display a large number of harmonic components. Figure 4 shows the results of computations resulting in 500 frequency components (max. number in this case is 750), reaching 250 MHz and

Table 1

Q-ty	Fig	TR1	TR2	TF1	TF2	TD	A1	A2	f	Tfilt1	Tfilt2	Comments
Units		ns	ns	ns	ns	ns	V	V	KHz	ns	ns	----------
No												
1	3	100	100	100	100	0	1.00	1.00	500	0	0	Noise floor
2	6	100	100	100	100	0	1.02	1.00	500	0	0	Amplitude mismatch
3	7	100	100	100	100	0	1.05	1.00	500	0	0	Amplitude mismatch
4	8	100	100	100	100	2	1.00	1.00	500	0	0	Delay test
5	9	100	100	100	100	5	1.00	1.00	500	0	0	Delay test
6		105	100	100	100	0	1.00	1.00	500	0	0	Rise time mismatch
7		105	100	105	100	0	1.00	1.00	500	0	0	Rise and fall time mismatch
8	10	100	100	100	100	0	1.00	1.00	500	50	52.5	Filter mismatch
9		100	100	100	100	0	1.05	1.00	500	50	50	Filtering
10		100	100	100	100	0	1.05	1.00	500	200	200	Strong filtering
11		100	100	100	100	0	1.05	1.00	250	50	50	Low bit rate and filtering

Table 2. Description of the results.

No.	Figures	Conditions	Comments, conducted emission	Comments, radiated emissions
1.	3	Noise floor, no filtering Full symmetry	-60dBV reference, -120dBV floor level	-140dBV reference, -180dBV floor level
2 and 3	6 and 7	20mV, 50 mV amplitude mismatch, no filtering	4 -6 freq. Components above the standard, MW AM freq. range	2-3 freq. Components above the standard
4 and 5	8 and 9	2ns, 5ns delay mismatch no filtering, amplitude, rise, fall time symmetry	7-9 components move close to standard, MW AM freq. Range, HF spectrum part moves closer to the standard	2-3 components above the standard
6 and 7		Rise time, rise and fall time together, no filtering, amplitude, delay symmetry	as above	as above
8	10	Asymmetry in filtering, 50ns and 52,5ns time constants, symmetry of other parameters	3 components above the standard , HF parts more attenuated	2 components above the standard, HF parts more attenuated
9, 10		50ns and 200ns filter time constants, 50mV amplitude difference, symmetry of other parameters	50ns - 5 components above the standard, HF parts reduced 200ns – 3 components above the standard, HF parts reduced	3 components above the standard, HF parts reduced 2 components above the standard, HF parts reduced
9 and 11		250KHz and 500KHz, 50ns filtering, 50mV amplitude difference, symmetry of other parameters	250KHz – 7 components above the standard (up to 1.75MHz) 500KHz – 5 components above the standard (up to 2.5MHz)	4 components above the standard 2 components above the standard

representing the spectrum of an arbitrary CAN signal, while its FFT spectrum obtained from the PSPICE probe does not reach such a high number (Fig. 5), but the PSPICE time-domain simulation is always helpful to establish desirable shapes of pulses, which can satisfy communication requirements of the CAN, like timing [2].

As shown in all simulations without filtering, the standard levels are exceeded within the medium AM RF bands. Although the first order filter, whose time constant can be controlled, reduces the levels of emissions at higher frequencies, the filter time constant misalignment can introduce very high emission levels. The most critical changes of the spectrum are observed when amplitudes of the pulses are mismatched, which is shown in Figures 6 and 7. Table 2 summarizes the most interesting features of the simulated results.

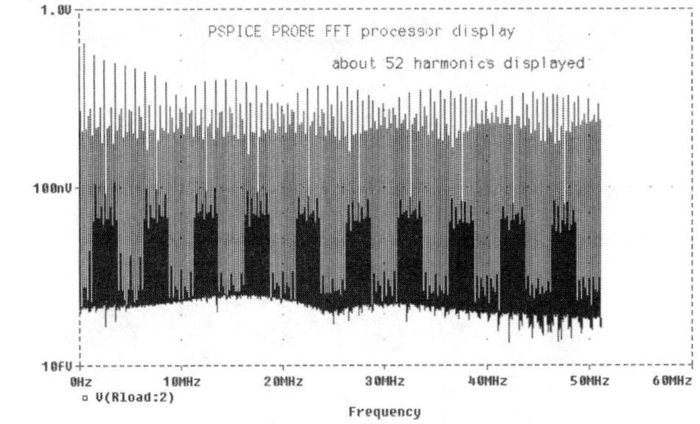

Figure 5. Conducted emissions using Pspice Probe.

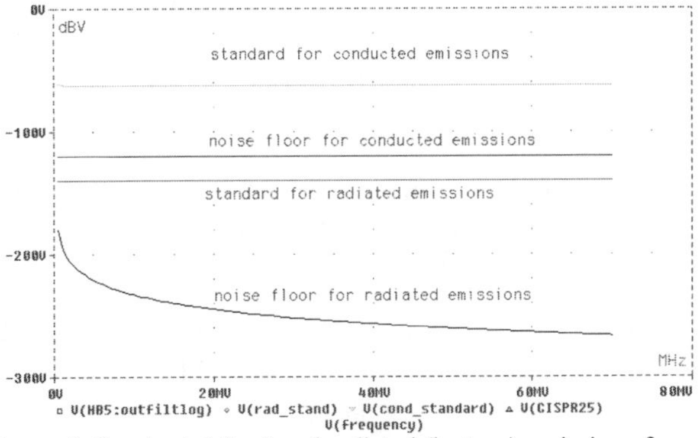

Figure 3. Conducted (top) and radiated (bottom) emissions for symmetric pulse. This represents the noise floor of the Pspice Calculator.

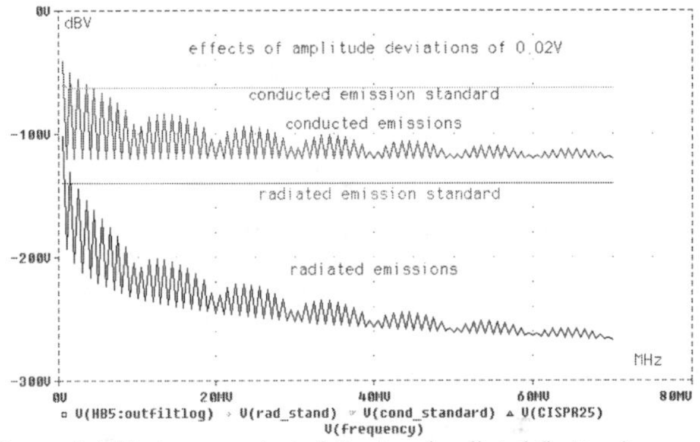

Figure 6. Effects on conducted (top) and radiated (bottom) emissions an amplitude mismatch of $20mV$.

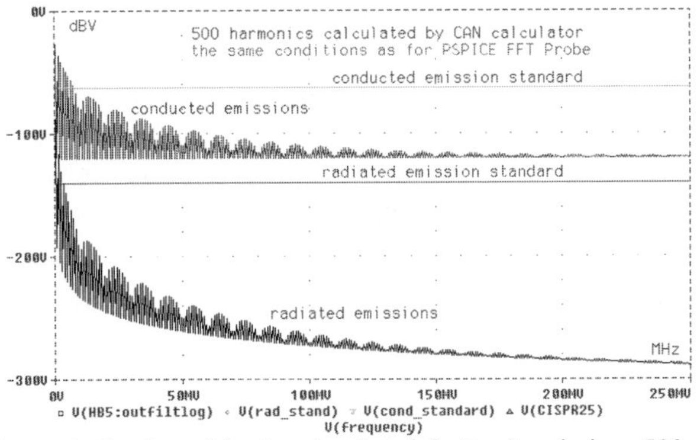

Figure 4. Conducted (top) and radiated (bottom) emissions 500 harmonics using Pspice Calculator.

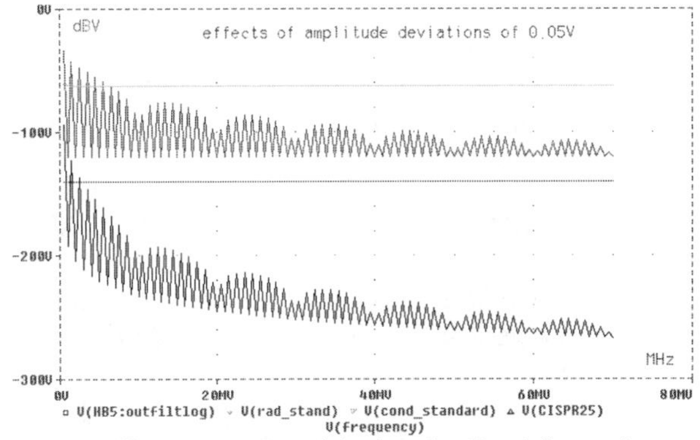

Figure 7. Effects on conducted (top) and radiated (bottom) emissions an amplitude mismatch of $50mV$.

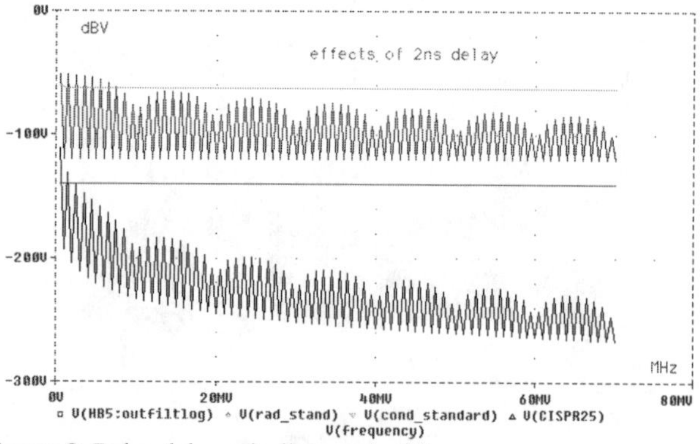

Figure 8. Pulse delay misalignment of *2ns*.

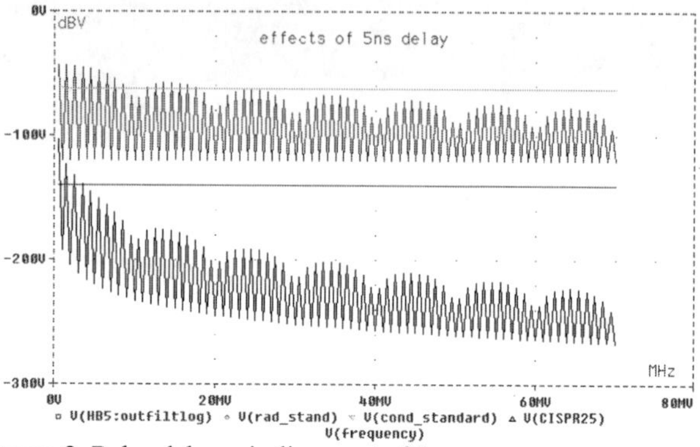

Figure 9. Pulse delay misalignment of *5ns*.

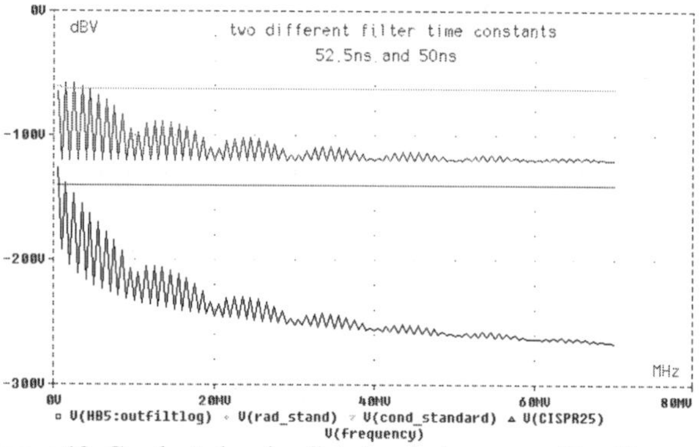

Figure 10. Conducted and radiated emissions caused by filter time constant misalignment.

IV. SUMMARY

The PSPICE based calculator, developed to enhance its classical time-domain simulations and the SPICE PROBE processing power, was used to find spectra of the pulses controlling the automotive communication busses. The calculator computes a large number of harmonics for typical symmetric or asymmetric waves applied to carry information in automotive data busses. The spectrum of the waves is displayed in a form suitable to compare with various standards and to observe effects of pulse and filter parameter tolerances on the bus EMC performance, especially critical within the AM radio frequencies.

The PSPICE program was chosen as a tool that provided many generic mathematical blocks in addition to the time-domain analysis used for preliminary evaluation of the pulses. The examples of simulations, included in the text, showed that even small deviations from symmetry could introduce excessive levels of emissions in AM and FM bands.

REFERENCES

[1] CISPR 25, Reference No. CISPR 25, 1995, 1995-11.

[2] Dietmayer, K., K. Overberg, 1997 "CAN Bit Timing Requirements," SEA Paper 970295, (Feb. 24-27): 1-8

[3] Eisele, H., H. W. Lutjens, 1995 "EMC Measures for Class C Communication Systems Using Unshielded Cable," SAE Paper 950298, (Feb., 27)-(Mar. 2): 131-139.

[4] Macfarlane, I. P. 1999 "A Probe for the Measurement of Electrical Unbalance of Networks and Devices," IEEE Trans. Electromagnet. Compat., vol. 41, (Feb): 3-14

[5] MicroSim EDA Software, 1996.

[6] Paul, C. R. 1992 "The Concept of Dominant Effect in EMC," IEEE Trans. Electromagnet. Compat., vol. EMC-34 (Apr.), 363-367.

[7] Rusek, A., D. Stevens, F. Miesterfeld, 1999 "Development of Tests and Modeling of EMC Effects in Automotive Data Busses," Proc. 2-nd Int. Conf. Inf., Comm.& Sign. Proc., Singapore, (Dec.)

DYNAMIC SIMULATION OF DKM MODELS OF ROBOTIZED SHOVEL FOR SURFACE MINING

R.M.M. Changirwa, S. Frimpong, Szymanski, C.Meng
Centre for Advanced Mine Design Research
School of Mining and Petroleum Engineering
University of Alberta, Edmonton, Canada
e-mail: rchangirwa@civil.ualberta.ca

KEYWORDS

Excavation, automation, mining intelligence, robotization, modeling.

ABSTRACT

Large-scale surface mining operations are increasingly demanding large-capacity shovels for achieving production targets under the varying field constraints. These shovels are equipped with sophisticated on-board instrumentation technology, which requires knowledgeable operators to understand and use them in a typical mining environment. Automation and robotization of mining shovels have received attention in academia and industry for increased productivity and efficiency. Research effort in these areas has been underway for several years but no promising results have been achieved for developing suitable technology for industry. A shovel linkage system consists of four major parts, including the mobile crawler base, the articulated boom, the stick and the dipper. This linkage system is used to perform the complex function of material digging, removal, swinging, loading, dumping and maneuvering in the mining environment. Thorough understanding and abstraction of the kinematics and dynamics of an operating shovel form the basis of any automation and robotization technology. The main objective of this study is to advance knowledge and frontiers in mining shovel automation and robotization for higher productivity and efficiencies in surface mining operations.

In this study, the authors use the merged dipper-kiosk-manipulated $(DKM)^2$ theory and concepts to model the kinematics and dynamics of the operating shovel. The dipper and stick are multi-faceted system with additive kinematics and dynamics to the mechanics of the entire system. Mathematical models of the dipper are developed and used in the $(DKM)^2$ model to study the influence of the dipper system on the directional trajectories and stability of the operating shovel. Homogeneous transformation functions are developed to study the contact force and torque of the dipper in its varying cutting planes. These functions are used to develop a production model of the operating shovel in a given periodic paradigm. The stochastic processes underlying the production function are modeled and simulated over an extended production period. The results of the simulation experiment show that the predicted dipper profiles for excavation and loading are parabolic, collinear and vertical depending on the planes of motions. The dipper profiles for hoisting, swinging and dumping are elliptical and sinusoidal depending on the planes of motion. Simulation experiments are currently underway to calibrate the automation and robotic models and to generate comparative results between these models and conventional operator-controlled productivity models. This research provides significant results to create knowledge and understanding in shovel automation and robotization for surface mining operations. It also expands research frontiers in this important surface mine production engineering.

INTRODUCTION

In an effort to achieve productivity and safety goals necessary to enhance their competitive position in the coming millenium, the mining industry is shifting gear towards automation and robotization of equipment and operations. A shovel (see Figure 1) and its operations form a composite process, excavation and loading present complex problems to be introduced in the same. The principal task of a shovel is to dig and move surface and subsurface material from its original location to a loading location by lowering the dipper, digging, pushing, and/or pulling soil, then lifting, swinging, and emptying the dipper in a hopper or truck. In execution of this task a human operator controls the motion of the shovel manually by using the visual feedback provided through personal eyes. The entire dig-and-load process entails equipment motion constraint, often quite tightly, by the workspace geometry.

This complexity is attributed to stochastic character of material which, in theoretical considerations [Vaha and

Skibniewski, 1993] is usually substituted by deterministic, simplified models. In addition, the typical excavator, with three links and three actuators, gives three degrees of freedom versus two components of equivalent force acting on the bucket/dipper tip.

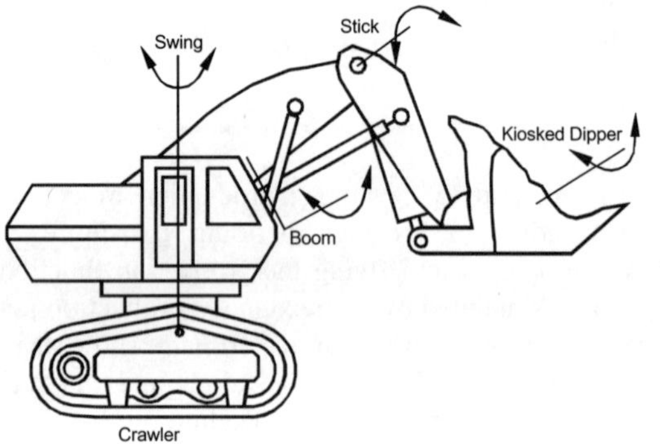

Figure 1: Shovel Schematic System.

The third reason is that the reaction between bucket/dipper and ore, in some of its positions, may be applied to its back instead to its tip. Automation and robotic motion and path control are essential to improve the productivity and the effective use of expensive construction machines [Bernold, 1993; Cannon, 1999; Sundareswaran and Arditi, 1988]. Researchers [Lipsett and Carroll, 1998] have recently undertaken research into automating hydraulic shovel excavation and loading. To use and control mining equipment pragmatically in this environment, their operations, the kinematics and dynamics must be well understood. As a step in this direction, the development of $(DKM)^2$ model will provide an insight into the automation and robotization of shovel digging and loading operations in unstructured in environment. $(DKM)^2$ is desired to perform two different kinds of tasks: digging in the terrain and loading work in the same. This can also be applied other excavators.

$(DKM)^2$ MODEL

A kiosked dipper shovel linkage system (see Figure 1) consists of four major parts: the mobile crawler mounted base, boom, stick and dipper. The last three are co-planar and rotate around the crawler base acting as a swing joint. In addition, each of these parts has components allowing the creation of a co-ordinate and simulation model system that is suitable for the analysis to be done. The dipper and boom are a multifarious system with kinematics and dynamics that are additive to the mechanics of the entire shovel system. The shovel mechanism can be modelled as a kinematic chain as shown in Figure 2.

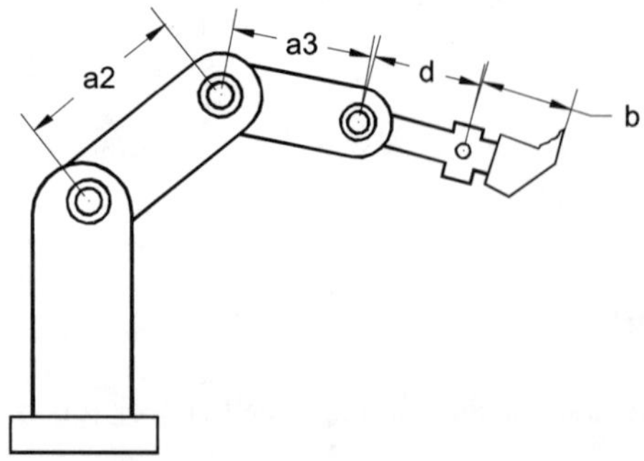

Figure 2: ShovelKinematic Chain.

During digging, the crawler base (swing joint) is clutched firm as the other links move in a plane. Modelling the shovel is apparent employing mathematical models that are commonly utilized for robotic manipulators. Researchers [Denavit, 1955; Singh, 1995] have derived and used the composite transform that relates the joint displacements to positions and orientation of the end-effector (dipper). An entire system for the automatic or semiautomatic operation of an excavator is described in [Seward et. al. 1988]. This research presents kinematic relations between three joint angles and the position of the bucket in a fixed coordinate system and also discusses the use of a position and sensor (force and vision) feedback qualitatively. Similarly, other systems for an excavator designed for automation and robotization are presented in [[Bernold, 1993; Cannon and Singh, 1999] by testing and characterizing the system components. Although the forces between the soil and a tool (bucket) during the digging operations are studied in [Bernold, 1991] and [Bullock et. al., 1990], the kinematic relations of the bucket pose, the joint variables, and the lengths of the actuators are not described in either work.

An attempt to describe the kinematics of an excavator is presented in [Vaha et. al., 1991] by defining the coordinate frames by an ad hoc approach. The forward and backward kinematic relations between the pose of the bucket and the angles of the joint shafts for an excavator are described. However, the coordinate frames are not assigned systematically. Moreover, no relations between the joint shaft angles and the positions (lengths) of the cylinder rods in the hydraulic actuators are given. Thus, the kinematic relations presented in [Vaha et. al., 1991] do not completely describe the configuration of the machine.

Of the models reported, Koivo's [Koivo 1994 establishes a complete set of kinematic equations for excavators by following the Denavit-Hartenberg (DH) guidelines [Koivo

1989], which are well known in robotization. While Koivo and Vaha [Vaha et. al., 1991] models have kinematics and systematic in common, Koivo's asignment of coordinate system is different where DH guidelines are employed. The homogeneous transformation matrices relating any two adjacent coordinate frames in the system are given. The forward and backward kinematic equations covering the pose of the bucket, the angular positions of the joint shafts, and the lengths of the hydraulic actuators are presented. Mathematical models of the dipper mechanism are developed and used in the global shovel model to study the influence of dipper system characteristics on the directional trajectories and stability of the shovel during digging and loading. Following Denavit-Hartenberg convention [Denavit, 1955; Koivo, 1989], the parameters for a shovel are presented in Table 1.

Table 1 DH Shovel Parameters

Link	a_n	d_n	α_n	θ_n
1	a_1	d_1	90	θ_1
2	a_2	0	0	θ_2
3	a_3	0	0	θ_3
4	a_4	0	0	θ_4

The remaining parameter values in Table 1 are determined similarly by following DH guidelines. The homogenous transformation matrix in equation 1 is in the general form as follows:

$$A_{n-1}^{n} = \begin{bmatrix} -\cos\alpha_n \sin\theta_n & \cos\theta_n & \sin\alpha_n \sin\theta_n & a_n \cos\theta_n \\ \cos\alpha_n \cos\theta_n & \sin\theta_n & -\sin\alpha_n \cos\theta_n & a_n \sin\theta_n \\ \sin\alpha_n & 0 & \cos\alpha_n & d_n \\ 0 & 0 & 0 & 1 \end{bmatrix} \quad (1)$$

The substitution of the parameter values of Table 1 for n=1,2,3,4 into equation 1 gives the homogenous transformation matrices as:

$$A_0^1 = \begin{bmatrix} 0 & c_1 & s_1 & a_1c_1 \\ 0 & s_1 & -c_1 & a_1s_1 \\ 1 & 0 & 0 & 0 \\ 0 & 0 & 0 & 1 \end{bmatrix} \quad (2)$$

$$A_1^2 = \begin{bmatrix} -s_2 & c_2 & 0 & a_2c_2 \\ c_2 & s_2 & 0 & a_2s_2 \\ 0 & 0 & 1 & 0 \\ 0 & 0 & 0 & 1 \end{bmatrix} \quad (3)$$

$$A_2^3 = \begin{bmatrix} -s_3 & c_3 & 0 & a_3c_3 \\ c_3 & s_3 & 0 & a_3s_3 \\ 0 & 0 & 1 & 0 \\ 0 & 0 & 0 & 1 \end{bmatrix} \quad (4)$$

$$A_3^4 = \begin{bmatrix} -s_4 & c_4 & 0 & a_4c_4 \\ c_4 & s_4 & 0 & a_4s_4 \\ 0 & 0 & 1 & 0 \\ 0 & 0 & 0 & 1 \end{bmatrix} \quad (5)$$

where $c_n = \cos\theta_n$; and $s_n = \sin\theta_n$. Matrix A_{n-1}^{n} relates the representations of a point in the two adjacent frames as indicated by (1).

In order to study the contact force F_c and torque T_c, a coordinate system is set up at the dipper tip as shown in Figure 3. The force R represents the component of contact force F_c in the Y_{n+1} direction (see Figure 4). The contact force with respect to the coordinate frame (X_n, Y_n, Z_n) can be derived using the transformation matrix in equation 1:

$$F_c = A_{n-1}^{n} \begin{pmatrix} \mu R \\ R \\ 0 \end{pmatrix} \quad (6)$$

Substituting equation 1 into equation 6 and rearranging:

$$F_c = \begin{bmatrix} -s_n \cos\alpha_n & c_n & s_n \sin\alpha_n & a_nc_n \\ c_n \cos\alpha_n & s_n & -c_n \sin\alpha_n & a_ns_n \\ \sin\alpha_n & 0 & \cos\alpha_n & d_n \\ 0 & 0 & 0 & 1 \end{bmatrix} \begin{pmatrix} \mu R \\ R \\ 0 \end{pmatrix} \quad (7)$$

whereas the contact torque Tc, which depends on the force distribution function $f(Z_{n+1})$ along the Z_{n+1} axis [Zhou and Skibniewski, 1994], when the dipper is maintained on the line contact, can be obtained as follows:

$$T_c = \left[\int_{-z/2}^{z/2} Z_{n+1} f(Z_{n+1}) dZ_{n+1}\right] A_{n-1}^{n} \begin{bmatrix} \dfrac{\mu}{\sqrt{\mu^2+1}} \\ Z_{n+1} \times \dfrac{1}{\sqrt{\mu^2+1}} \\ 0 \end{bmatrix} \quad (8)$$

COMPUTATION AND SIMULATION

In order to facilitate modelling and simulation, some of the DKM equations were modified. In equation 8 distribution function, f (Z_{n+1}) was assumed to take a function of the form:

$$f(Z_{n+1}) = \sin KZ + 1$$

In tandem, FORTRAN codes were developed for the modelled and simulated parameters. The input data used in the current research work is shown in Table 2.

Table 2: Input Data for DKM Model

Material specific gravity	1.6
Value of μ	0.1-0.8
Value of K	129-300 Nm^{-1}
Material width	8 m
Material depth	10 m

EXPERIMENTAL FACILITIES

As an important part of this research study, a laboratory for shovel system is being set up to undertake appropriate experimental studies associated with $(DKM)^2$ robotization technology. The goal of the facilities is two-fold. First, to validate the $(DKM)^2$ and allied robotization models. This will provide insight into shovel's dynamics and kinematics. Second, to use the results in designing and improving the operation of the $(DKM)^2$ robotization technology for mining industry. For the automatic and robotization operation of a shovel, dipper digs material and swings to load a truck or hopper.

Major equipment in this laboratory will include an industrial robot outfitted with a shovel kiosked dipper and force/torque sensor to serving as a shovel boom and a self-inclining testbed for various fine and coarse sands, a hopper to serve as a truck, pneumatic return line, data acquisition and optical systems. The proposed facilities layout is shown in Appendix (Figure 5).

RESULTS AND DISCUSSION

The conceptual motion of the dipper involves digging, filling the dipper, lifting dipper, swinging to reach the hopper vertically upwards and lowering to empty dipper into the hopper. The predicted trajectories involve x-z, x-y and y-z planes. A family of predicted dipper profiles for dig-and-load cycles is shown in Figure 6. Curve AB represents parabolic behavior of dipper as it digs in x-z plain. Curve BC shows vertical collinear profiles as the dipper is lifted up. Curve CD shows parabolic loci of the dipper as it swings to reach a hopper. Curve DE shows vertical profiles as dipper lowers to empty material. Dig-swing-dump profiles, simulated for 60 seconds, are illustrated in Figure 7. The results show elliptical profiles while digging and approximately sinusoidal for swinging the dipper to dump. In Figure 8, the generated torque profiles during horizontal motion of the dipper in the excavated bed are illustrated. Unique aspect is that these profiles exhibit sinusoidal spectra.

CONCLUSIONS

The paper has presented a $(DKM)^2$ robotization model for a mining shovel digging and loading operations in unstructured in environment. Least intricate models for capturing shovel controllability and stability presented provided an insight into automation and robotization of shovel digging and loading. Theoretical predictions of dig-and-load motion by dipper in 3D setting indicate parabolic and collinear families of profiles.

FUTURE WORK

Our intention is to conduct comprehensive modeling for automation and robotization of a mining shovel. The project is in the process of procuring an industrial robot manipulator so that we can modify for shovel digging and loading laboratory testing. A computer program development for control of the robotized shovel is progress. We anticipate field-testing will be carried out in a surface mine.

NOTATION

a_n	link parameter on the model
F_c	contact force
R	component of the contact force in the Y axis
T_c	contact torque
ϕ	angle between the dipper and the Y axis
θ	angle of rotation of the links
μ	coefficient of friction for the excavated bed
α	DH angle of rotation about Z-axis
λ	friction angle

REFERENCES

Bernold, L.E., Experimental studies on mechanics of lunar excavation, Journal of Aerospace Engineering, ASCE, 4(1), 9-22, 1991.

Bernold, L.E., Motion and path control for robotic excavation, Journal of Aerospace Engineering, ASCE, 6(1), 1993.

Bullock, M.D., Apte, M.S., and Oppenheim, I.J., Force and Geometry constraints in robot excavation, Proc. Space '90, Engineering Construction and Operations in Space II, ASCE, 960-969, 1990.

Cannon, H. and Singh, S., Models for automated earthmoving, in Proc. Of the 5th International Symposium on Experimental Robotics, 1999.

Denavit, J. and Hartenberg, R.S., A kinematic notation for lower mechanism based on matrices, ASME J. Applied Mechanics 22:215-221, 1955.

Koivo, A.J., Fundamentals for control of robotic manipulators, J. Wiley and Sons, Inc., New York, NY, 42-49.

Lipsett, M.G., and Carroll, M.S., Modelling and Monitoring the Performance of Mining Shovels, Syncrude R&D Technical Seminar, November 4, 1998.

Seward, D.W., Bradley, D.A., and Bracewell, R.H., The development of research models for automatic excavation, Proc. 5th int. Symp. On Robotics in constr., International Association for Automation and Robotics in Construction, 703-708, 1988.

Singh, S., Synthesis of tactical plans for robotic excavation, PhD thesis, Carnegie Mellon University, Pittsburg, PA, USA, 1995.

Sundareswaran, S. and Arditi, D., Current state of automation and robotics in construction, Proc. 5th int. Symp. On Robotics in constr., International Association for Automation and Robotics in Construction, 175-184, 1988.

Vaha, P.K., and Skibniewski, M.J., Cognitive force control of excavators, ASCE Journal of Aerospace Engineering, 6 (2), April 1993.

Vaha, P.K., Skibniewski, M.J., and Koivo, A.J., Kinematics and trajectory planning for excavation, ASCE Construction Congress, ASCE, 100-111, 1991.

Zhou, Y. and Skibniewski, M.J., Construction robot force control in cleaning operations, Journal of Aerospace Engineering, ASCE, 7(1), 33-49, 1994.

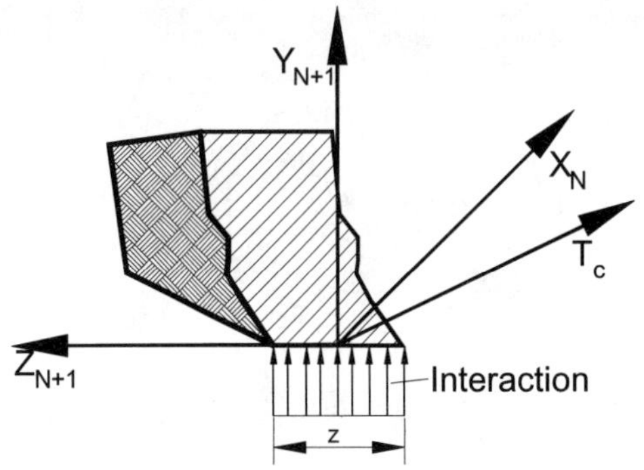

Figure 3 Dipper Tip Forces Set-up.

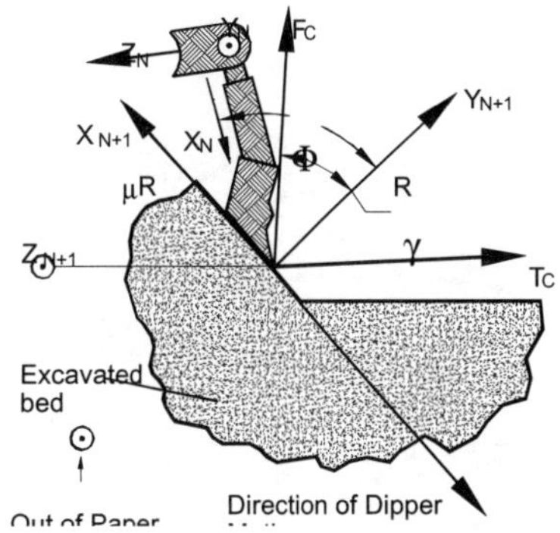

Figure 4 Dipper/material interaction.

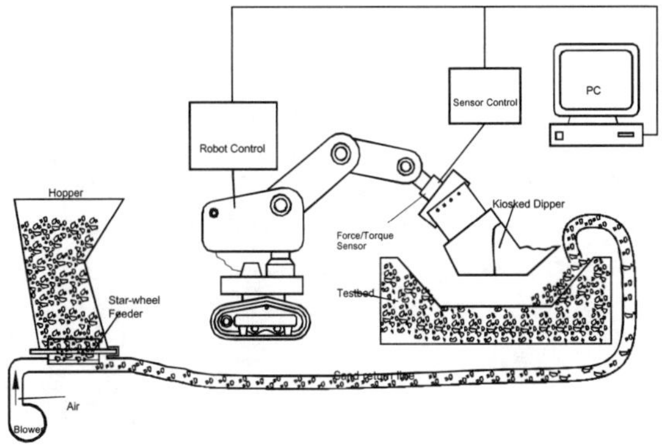

Figure 5 Proposed Robotized Shovel test System

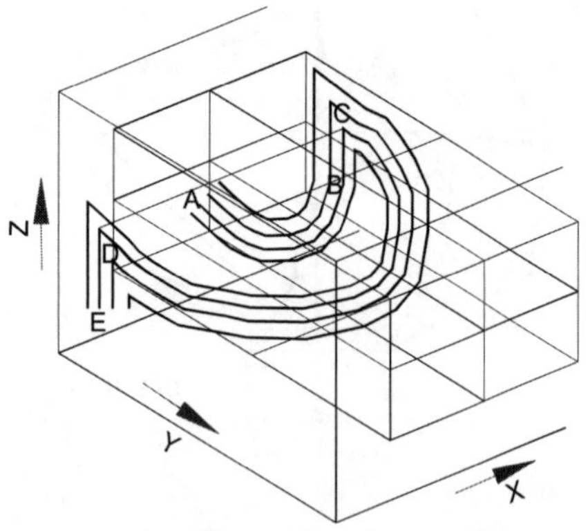

Figure 6 Predicted Dipper Profiles.

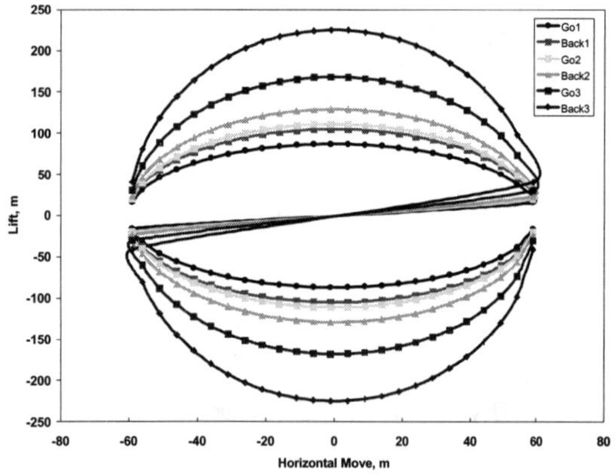

Figure 7 Simulated Dig-Swing-Dump

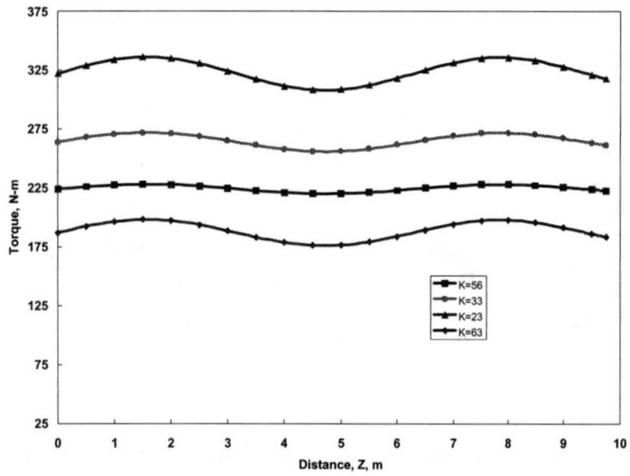

Figure 8 Torque Profiles.

ELIST8: A SIMULATION SYSTEM FOR TRANSPORTATION LOGISTICS PLANNING SUPPORT

Mary D. Braun, Gordon R. Lurie, Kathy L. Simunich,
Charles N. Van Groningen, Hanna J. Vander Zee, and Mary Ann Widing
Decision and Information Sciences Division
Argonne National Laboratory
9700 South Cass Avenue
Argonne IL 60439
e-mail: duffy@dis.anl.gov

KEYWORDS

Discrete simulation, military, transportation, Java

ABSTRACT

Planning for the transportation of large amounts of equipment, troops, and supplies is a complex problem. Many options, including modes of transportation, vehicles, facilities, routes, and timing, must be considered. The amount of data involved in generating and analyzing a course of action (e.g., detailed information about military units, logistical infrastructures, and vehicles) is enormous. Software tools are critical in analyzing these plans.

ELIST (Enhanced Logistics Intra-theater Support Tool) is a simulation-based decision support system that assists military planners in determining the logistical feasibility of an intra-theater course of action. The scenario data used by the ELIST simulation includes the units to be moved, their required movements and activities, an infrastructure database, a vehicle database, and a set of simulation parameters and constraints. Analysts can use the simulation to evaluate the overall success of a plan (determined by required delivery dates), as well as to view detailed information on such things as over- and under-utilized resources, infrastructure bottlenecks, and individual trips. The simulation can be run for as many days as desired or stopped at any time. The state of all queues and resources, and the location and activities of all entities, can be examined using many options for reports and graphs.

The current version of ELIST (v.8) employs a discrete event simulation developed in Java. Java fulfills a primary requirement for multi-platform execution. In addition, the object-oriented framework has greatly facilitated entity and process development within the simulation. This paper describes the problem domain and the modeling approach taken, and presents the representations used for entities, events, facility resources, network links, and other objects. The benefits and problems involved with developing and executing the simulation in Java are discussed.

INTRODUCTION

ELIST (version 7) has been successfully used in the military logistics community for a number of years to assist in planning analyses and training exercises (Macal *et al.* 1995). Ongoing use of ELIST7 has led to requests for more detail, more capabilities, more flexibility, and more speed. ELIST7 runs at a fairly aggregate level, in which individual transports are not explicitly modeled; instead transportation capabilities are represented in short-ton-miles/day. ELIST7 is primarily a C language tool and uses formatted files for input.

ELIST8 was conceived to model the transportation of military cargo at the individual vehicle level, requiring a much more detailed simulation than in ELIST7. This version was to more easily integrate with other models and tools in the fort-to-foxhole logistical arena. It uses the Oracle DBMS for data persistence (rather than flat files) and to facilitate data sharing with other models. In addition, the new system was required to run on multiple platforms, specifically Windows machines and Sun workstations. Because the desired changes, to the simulation in particular, were so significant, modifying the existing ELIST7 would not have been efficacious. ELIST8 is a completely new system.

We decided to develop the new version in Java for a few reasons. First, Java easily provides the platform independence we required. Second, Java provides native support for a number of required and potentially useful capabilities. The JDBC (Java Database Connectivity toolkit) supports multiple DBMSs. Graphical user interface, networking and internet, and multi-threading capabilities are all available. In addition, we wanted the advantages of an object-oriented programming language. Finally, the team was experienced with other object-oriented languages and was eager to try out Java. We did have two concerns. First, we were concerned that the immaturity of the language and changes in the ongoing development of Java itself might impact our effort. Second, the execution speed of this semi-interpreted language might hamper acceptance of the system. We did assume that execution speed would be a universal issue and would lead to faster virtual machines in time. Our findings on these issues are discussed later.

MODEL

The model underlying the ELIST simulation is based on many discussions with military logisticians. The simulation is based on their requirements, experiences, and observations. ELIST models the intra-theater movements of personnel, equipment, and supplies by limited transportation assets over a constrained transportation infrastructure. The purpose of the system is to aid the planners in evaluating the potential success of a theater leg of a transportation plan, analyzing vehicle and facility requirements for a given plan, and identifying possible bottlenecks in infrastructure or process. Because users often require trade-offs between speed and accuracy, the model has been designed so that different degrees of detail may be applied to different portions of the scenario data. The experienced analyst thus has choices for focusing on specific aspects of the plan when time is limited. These detail/aggregation choices will be discussed in the following subsections.

Six modes of transportation are modeled in ELIST: road, including line haul operations, rail, water, air (fixed-wing), helicopter, and pipeline. (At this time air and pipeline are not yet implemented in ELIST8.) ELIST can model either the home theater or a foreign theater.

The main inputs to the model are:

- Unit data (the entities to be moved),
- Vehicle data,
- Transportation infrastructure data for the theater, and
- A set of model parameters.

Unit Data

The military units and their required activities originate from the Time Phased Force Deployment Data (TPFDD.) This format is used by the joint forces to represent deployment plans. Additional data were needed for ELIST as well as for other models, so the Expanded TPFDD (ETPFDD) was developed. The ETPFDD contains an operational hierarchy, as well as a compositional hierarchy, of unit data. Each unit may be composed of other units as well as quantities of commodities. ELIST is primarily concerned with the commodities, which are the entities to be moved through the simulation.

Commodities can be represented at multiple levels of aggregation. In Figure 1, for example, the unit ULN 3AG9C is composed of amounts of the following commodities: Personnel, Aircraft Tonnage, Oversized Tonnage, and Outsized Tonnage. At level 2, only aggregate weight is known (the numbers shown are measurement tons and short tons.) The Oversized Tonnage is also shown at the more detailed levels 3 and 4. At level 4, individual vehicles or containers are represented along with their weights, lengths, widths, heights, and areas.

The analyst can specify the level of detail to be modeled either by individual units or for the entire scenario. Aggregate unit components start out as single entities, but as they are transported through the simulation, they can be split into multiple smaller entities. Often the components are split so they can fit on transports. Discrete entities, on the other hand, must fit dimensionally onto their transports and cannot be divided.

The set of commodities used in a scenario is dynamic. Each commodity is classified in one of five commodity categories: PAX (personnel), POL (liquid fuel), RORO (Roll On Roll Off equipment), Breakbulk, and Container. The commodity categories are used throughout the model to determine how the cargo can be loaded on and off transport vehicles, how it should be stored, and various other activities. The actual commodity is used to determine possible modes of transportation and to select vehicle types.

In addition to unit compositions, initial unit locations and all subsequent movement requirements are included in the ETPFDD. The simulation is driven by the scenario units and their movement requirements. A movement requirement includes a destination node and a required delivery time. A mode of transportation may also be specified. Possible requirements have been expanded from those in the original

Figure 1. Sample Compositional Unit Hierarchy

Level	Unit	ID	Commodity								
ULN	3AG9C										
	3AG9C	PAX P951	Personnel	10							
2	3AG9C	BLK D1632	Aircraft T	11.0	5.00						
2	3AG9C	OVR D1633	Oversized	766.0	307.30						
3	3AG9C	A2D D279	Oversized	766.0	307.30						
4	3AG9C	A2D D595	Oversized	2	11.0	2.80	166	83	55	96	TRAILER CARGO
4	3AG9C	A2D D602	Oversized	2	29.5	8.30	265	95	81	175	TRUCK CARGO 2-
4	3AG9C	A2D D609	Oversized	2	4.0	0.50	109	62	44	46	TRAILER CARGO
4	3AG9C	A2D D616	Oversized	3	6.3	1.20	132	64	53	58	TRUCK UTILITY
4	3AG9C	A2D D623	Oversized	17	38.7	16.50	249	111	97	191	ARMORED RECON
2	3AG9C	OUT D1634	Outsized T	52.0	24.70						

TPFDD to include any number of intermediate or follow-on destinations, staging and other types of delays, marry up and assembly with other entities, and transitions into vehicles that in turn can be used as transportation assets.

A large set of units may be involved in activities all over the world, so ELIST allows the analyst to select the country or countries of interest. ELIST is an intra-theater model, and does not focus on strategic (overseas) deployment. Only those activities in the theater of interest will be modeled. If no other information is available, all units will start out as available and ready to move at their first location in the scenario. Alternately, another (external) model can be used to generate strategic arrivals of loaded ships and aircraft into the theater.

Vehicle Data

ELIST has data on every vehicle type that might be used. The model uses information such as payload, cargo area dimensions, curb weight, average speed, and average on-load and off-load times.

ELIST uses a vehicle grouping called an *asset* in order to specify preferences of how to move specific commodities. An asset is a set of vehicle types that will be used in the same ways in the plan. Examples are a set of similar heavy trucks or a set of tanker railcars. Commodity-asset rules list (in order of preference for each commodity) the assets that may be used to transport that commodity. Conditions based on lateness and distance may be included in these rules.

A specific collection of vehicles is defined for a scenario. There are multiple ways that the analyst may choose to represent vehicles in the simulation. First, a vehicle can be modeled as *fully tracked* or as a *capability asset*. A fully tracked vehicle is a discrete entity that makes loaded and empty trips and that always has a current location in the network. A capability asset, on the other hand, is a vehicle (or set of vehicles) considered to be generally available. Such a vehicle is only specifically modeled when it is being used to transport cargo. When its trip is finished, the vehicle designated as a capability asset goes back into the pool, and it can be used immediately in an entirely different location. No empty vehicle trips are modeled for a capability asset.

Second, the locations where vehicles can be used may be specified by setting up *asset pools*. Asset pools are collection of vehicles that serve specific locations within the theater network. An asset pool can also be set up to serve all locations. Line haul operations may be set up using asset pools with trailers that can serve only two nodes. Asset pools also have *home nodes* where all fully tracked vehicles congregate when they are idle.

Last, the analyst may specify time periods during which vehicles are available. By default, an asset is available throughout the scenario. However, specific intervals, initial times, or final times can be entered.

Infrastructure Data

A theater infrastructure is required for the area of operations and must include all the nodes (i.e., ports, staging areas, and destinations) referenced in the ETPFDD. Links — roads, railways, waterways, and pipelines — connect the nodes. All nodes have geographic coordinates for mapping and distance calculations. Infrastructure resources are modeled in four main ways within ELIST: as rate resources, gate resources, capacity resources, or discrete resources.

A rate resource is characterized by its ability to process a given amount of cargo in a given time; for example, the capability to load containers on railcars in containers/hour. The resource represents the men and equipment involved. The time consumed by an activity using a rate resource will be at least as long as the amount being processed divided by the rate. However, the activity may take longer than the time dictated by one resource, as in the case where multiple resources with different rate values are required.

A gate resource also represents a capability specified as a rate. However, this type of resource does not have any duration associated with its use. Road capacities, for example, are represented using gate resources; some number of vehicles may travel onto the road per hour.

A capacity resource is a nonconsumable resource that is used in some fraction of the whole for the duration of an activity. Its use, however, has no impact on the activity duration. An example is storage area at a port.

Some equipment is represented discretely. Cranes at a berth, for example, are acquired for a ship loading activity and released when the activity is complete.

The main node types modeled are seaports, airports, and intersections. The basic node, an intersection, can represent a staging area, a rail terminal, or any kind of intersection of links. At this type of node, trucks, railcars, and helicopters can be on- and off-loaded. Capabilities for loading cargo to and from vehicles are all modeled as rate resources. These capabilities are broken into three parts: infrastructure, MHE (Materials Handling Equipment), and personnel. This approach gives analysts flexibility in storing the static aspects of a terminal, such as ramp and dock capability, separately from more dynamic capabilities such as personnel and equipment. From these values, a rate resource is constructed for the simulation that has a capability that is the minimum of the three components. Attributes for POL, containers, breakbulk cargo, and RORO cargo loading for rail

Figure 2. Sample Unit History

30GB UTC:1E777 UIC:WAB7AA

Elem	Commodity	Cargo ID	Amount	Sq Ft	Time	Event	Location
3	Personnel	P2041	14.0	0.0	2 0:00	Available TOZEUR-NEFTA -TPAL-IAP	TOZEUR-NEFTA -TPAL-IAP
					2 0:00	Waiting for SAFAQIS DD Asset Buses	TOZEUR-NEFTA -TPAL-IAP
					2 0:00	Waiting for BIZERTE DD Asset Buses	TOZEUR-NEFTA -TPAL-IAP
					2 8:33	Road trip from TOZEUR-NEFTA -TPAL-IAP to UNKN TUNISIA -UNQU-RPA	TOZEUR-NEFTA -TPAL-IAP
					2 8:33	Road Onloading (Buses)	TOZEUR-NEFTA -TPAL-IAP
					2 9:03	Waiting for Serial for TOZEUR-NEFTA -TPAL-IAP to UNKN TUNISIA -UNQU-RPA	TOZEUR-NEFTA -TPAL-IAP
					2 9:03	Road Departure in Serial (Buses)	TOZEUR-NEFTA -TPAL-IAP
					2 18:36	Road Arrival (Buses)	UNKN TUNISIA -UNQU-RPA
					2 18:36	Road Enter Node (Buses)	UNKN TUNISIA -UNQU-RPA
					2 19:05	Road Offloading (Buses)	UNKN TUNISIA -UNQU-RPA
					2 19:20	Final Delivery	UNKN TUNISIA -UNQU-RPA
4	Oversized Ton...	D3306	207.3	2073.0	2 0:00	Available TOZEUR-NEFTA -TPAL-IAP	TOZEUR-NEFTA -TPAL-IAP
					2 0:00	Any mode trip from TOZEUR-NEFTA -TPAL-IAP to UNKN TUNISIA -UNQU-RPA	TOZEUR-NEFTA -TPAL-IAP
					2 0:00	Road Onloading (Commercial Trucks)	TOZEUR-NEFTA -TPAL-IAP
					2 1:59	Waiting for Serial for TOZEUR-NEFTA -TPAL-IAP to UNKN TUNISIA -UNQU-RPA	TOZEUR-NEFTA -TPAL-IAP
					2 1:59	Road Departure in Serial (Commercial Trucks)	TOZEUR-NEFTA -TPAL-IAP
					2 11:33	Road Arrival (Commercial Trucks)	UNKN TUNISIA -UNQU-RPA
					2 11:33	Road Enter Node (Commercial Trucks)	UNKN TUNISIA -UNQU-RPA
					2 12:02	Road Offloading (Commercial Trucks)	UNKN TUNISIA -UNQU-RPA
					2 12:02	Final Delivery	UNKN TUNISIA -UNQU-RPA

and road vehicles are all represented. Basic nodes also include resources for storage areas for different cargo types, as well as other resources.

Seaports have all the data associated with an intersection node, plus the data for ship berthing and loading. Berths are represented as separate entities with their own attributes and resources, which include physical dimensions, number and types of cranes at the berth, and RORO and POL load capabilities. Some resources, such as personnel, are considered to be port-wide, others are assigned to a single berth.

In order to collect or deliver cargo at a seaport, a ship must first be berthed at an appropriate length of dock. If needed, cranes are assigned to the ship. Offload takes place in fixed time intervals, with as much cargo off-loaded as possible in that time (e.g., 1 hour). In this way, aggregate cargo can be divided, off-loaded, and moved forward in a timely manner, rather than off-loaded in large quantities before moving forward. On-loading ships does not require this artificial parameter because the cargo waiting on the ship is not being held back — when the ship is fully loaded, it will embark.

Aircraft parking areas at Airports are explicitly modeled. Only a limited number of aircraft can be processed at a time because of tarmac area limitations. All aircraft loading resources can operate anywhere within the airport.

The primary attributes of infrastructure links that are used by the simulation are length, rate of march, and rate of entry. Limited link capacity is modeled by the rate at which vehicles can start onto the link (rate of entry.) Road and rail links can also be limited in the size and weight of vehicles that may traverse them.

Scenario Parameters

The analyst can specify a number of options and parameters to direct and tune the simulation; a few examples are given. The simulation can enforce the mode of travel specified in the ETPFDD, or it can select a mode on the basis of the situation. The maximum amount of time to wait for additional cargo and the percentage of capacity preferred prior to departure can be specified for various vehicle types. The analyst can decide whether the storage area at a node should constrain movement or the cargo should be allowed to simply overflow. The preferred number of railcars in a train can be input, and the analyst can decide whether trucks must travel in serials (groups of vehicles). Scenario parameters are stored in the database as are all other ELIST data.

SIMULATION

The simulation is driven by discrete events. Initially scheduled events are: unit availability, ship arrivals, and plane arrivals. These events all have participant lists that contain unit component entities. Whenever an activity is completed, the newly idle unit components look in their required activity lists and create and schedule new activities as appropriate.

Unit components keep detailed histories of each completed activity as well as time spent queuing, and this information is available to the analyst. Figure 2 shows sample histories of two components of ULN 30GB from the movements report. The first element, 14 personnel, became available to move on day 2 at 0:00 and waited in two queues (for two asset pools) for the asset Buses. At 8:33, a bus was acquired, a trip was scheduled, and on-loading began. At 9:03, the bus was ready to depart. It was required to travel in a serial, which was immediately available. The people arrived at their destination at 18:36 and off-loaded. They had no other movement requirements. The bottom section shows the activities of 207.3 short tons of oversized tonnage.

Activity Objects

Activities are implemented as objects in Java, each with an "execute" method. Some activities can be considered compound activities and are represented as a single object with multiple states. A trip with an asset, for example, actually consists of a fixed series of subactivities — cargo onload, travel, node entry or parking, and cargo offload — with the asset, route, and participant data remaining the same throughout. Different methods are executed on the basis of the state of the trip.

Planning a trip is also a scheduled activity. This activity consumes no time (except for queue time) but is required whenever travel occurs. Planning a trip occurs in a trip initialization event; this event's main function is acquiring transport vehicles. It also verifies that a route exists. If a movement does not have a required mode, and more than one mode is indeed possible for the movement, this activity selects the trip mode. If appropriate assets are immediately available, the highest preference asset/mode for the commodity type is selected. Otherwise, the activity waits until at least one vehicle is available, then commits to that mode. If no asset exists that can carry the cargo, or no route exists, the cargo will go into an error queue.

The subclass capability and interface construct of Java were found to be very effective in implementing the different activities of the simulation. This success is primarily because there are many similarities among the transport activities for different modes, different cargo types, trips with or without cargo, and trips with or without assets. Figure 3 shows the classification hierarchy of some activities to show the level of inheritance.

Figure 3. Partial Activity Hierarchy

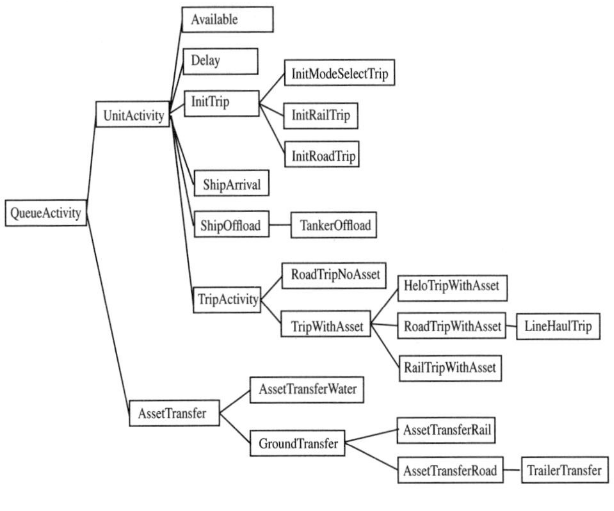

Event and Asset Managers

An event manager object handles the scheduling and execution of events. Events generate priorities on the basis of their participants' required delivery times. The simulation can be run to a specific time or run and stopped as desired. An asset manager object oversees the allocation of assets to activities. Vehicles are chosen on the basis of the commodity-asset preference rules, specific cargo dimensions, current location of the cargo and the vehicle (if it is fully tracked), and service area of the vehicle's asset pool. When an asset vehicle completes a trip, and there is a queue for the asset, it is either assigned immediately if it is needed at its current location, or the asset manager sends it to the location of the highest priority event in the queue. If there is no queue, the asset is sent to its home node.

RESULTS

Many reporting options are available to assist the analyst in evaluating the success of a plan, identifying bottlenecks, and analyzing asset usage. Plan success depends on the on-time arrival of all units at their final destinations. Summary arrival results can be viewed in total short tons for the entire scenario or by cargo type or destination. Figure 4 shows the total number of short tons required to be delivered to all destinations over time, the amount delivered in the simulation, and the short tons (of those delivered) that were also required at the time.

Figure 4. Total Delivery Graph

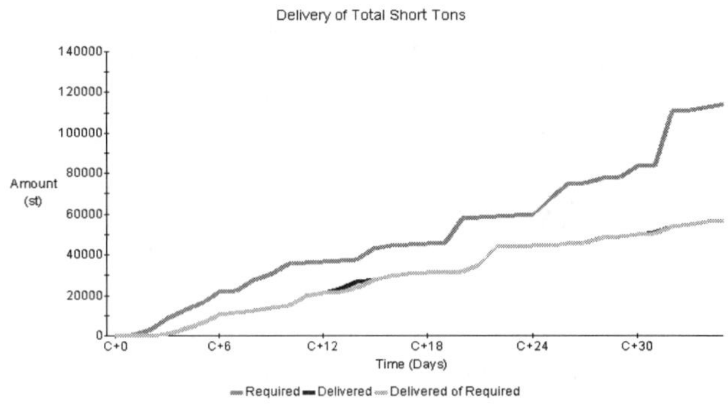

A query facility allows groups of units to be specified on the basis of name, location, delivery, and many other factors. These groups or individuals can then be reported and graphed. For example, all units traveling to a certain destination or all units not yet arrived could be reported.

Usage-over-time data are saved for all network and asset resources and all queues. The user interface allows easy selection (for reporting) from among all queues, destinations, seaports and airports, road links, routes, assets, asset pools, etc. Figure 5 shows a sample graph of the amount of cargo (in truck loads) waiting in the queue for Heavy Military Trucks. It is apparent that, although there was a backup of cargo waiting for this type of truck, the backup was not persistent throughout the scenario. Note that some of the cargo waiting for Heavy Military Trucks may actually have been moved by other assets. Other graphs are available to view the actual usage of each asset.

Figure 5. Queue Graph

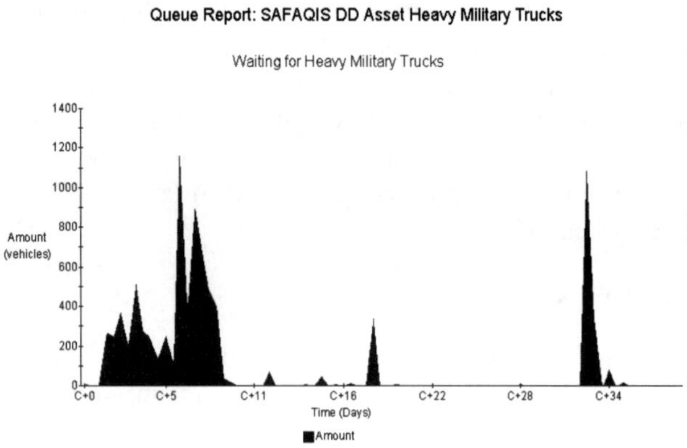

CONCLUSIONS

The ELIST8 simulation is a critical piece of an extensive system that includes import, export, visual editing, and error checking of vehicle data, asset and commodity data, network data, ETPFDD data, and scenario parameters. Mapping and query capabilities are included and continue to be enhanced. Simulation results can be saved to "projection" tables in the database. These tables are accessible to other tools to allow simulation and animation of an entire plan from U.S. bases to forward locations in a foreign theater. The capabilities provided by this expanding collection of tools will assist military logisticians with both their data management and analysis tasks. By providing greater ease and speed for modifying and analyzing the plans, these tools enable more "what if" scenarios to be examined and facilitate the logistical planning process.

The overall feeling of the team toward Java has been positive, but there have been problems. We have not found a development environment that satisfies everyone. The favorite seems to be VisualAge for Java (IBM). It has many useful features that facilitate development, a good visual debugger, and handles the scale of our system (over 680 classes not including third party). However, its method-based editors (as opposed to file-based) are not always desirable, especially when working with user interface classes. Also, VisualAge for Java is available on Windows NT but not Sun Solaris, our main development platform. The file-based Java environment Forte (Sun Microsystems) also works well on the PC. It is available for Solaris and Windows platforms, and it is free. We ran into numerous compile or path errors, and were unable to get our system running with JBuilder (free, Foundation version from Borland/Inprise.)

The immaturity of Java has led to time spent on "work-a-rounds," especially in relation to the Swing user interface classes. The Bug Parade at the Java Developer Connection site (http://developer.java.sun.com/index.html) has been beneficial in identifying Java problems and solutions, and the work-a-rounds have not consumed a significant portion of the development time.

Speed of execution continues to be a concern. It is easy to measure but difficult to quantify because of the large number of variables associated with the size of a scenario: the number of items being moved, the number of movements being made, how constrained the network and assets are, etc. However, as an illustration, a scenario with 717 units and approximately 140,000 short tons of men, supplies, and equipment, all moving to an average of one destination and using three modes (road, rail and water) was simulated in slightly more than 6 minutes on a Sun Ultra 10 workstation using JDK1.2. This is a relatively small scenario. Future work will involve thoroughly exploring the speed issue.

ACKNOWLEDGMENT

This work was supported under a military interdepartmental purchase request from the U.S. Department of Defense, Military Traffic Management Command Transportation Engineering Agency (MTMCTEA), through the U.S. Department of Energy contract W-31-109-ENG-109.

REFERENCE

Macal, C., C. Van Groningen, and M. Braun. 1995. "Simulation of Transportation Movements Over Constrained Infrastructure Networks." In *Proceedings of the 1995 Simulation Multi-Conference* (Phoenix, AZ, April). 27(4):97-102.

A Prototype Model for Traffic Networks

Tai-Chi Lee and Howard S. Travis
Department of Computer Science
Saginaw Valley State University
University Center, MI 48710
lee@svsu.edu

Keywords: Traffic Networks, Routing System, Track Segment, Transit Time, Segment Distance, Segment Speed.

Abstract

In the design of traffic network, a prototype model is often constructed first. Then, for the economical purpose an appropriate tool is chosen to simulate the model with various constraints. The purpose of this paper is to define a model for a traffic network in which the routing and the speed of a vehicle is under control of a computer program. Also, two proposed algorithms will be tested to compare safety and efficiency.

1. Introduction

The proposed traffic network will operate on monorail, without the use of cab drivers. The system will use remote sensors in each cab and in each monorail segment to control the speed and routing of each vehicle in the system that will direct each cab vehicle to it's destination in an efficient and timely manner. The following are Controlling Routines that will be required for the entire system:

Controlling Routines — Cab and Network Operations

1. Payment Routine (credit/debit card reader or token system).
2. Passenger Input, Destination (on-board display system).
3. Routing System (efficient delivery of cab to destination).
4. Departure Control (leaving the station).
5. Merging onto Network Segments.
6. Open Track Movement.
7. Intersection Control (approaching switching locations).
8. Switching Control (moving from one track segment to another).
9. Arrival Control (approaching Station).

2. Problem Assumptions

1. Each track segment allows cab traffic in one direction only. There are two track segments running between each station, allowing traffic to move in both directions.
2. Each track segment has an average cab speed, based on terrain and condition. The acceleration and deceleration time is included in the average cab speed when computing total travel time.
3. Station traffic (seen as potential segment traffic) will be ignored.
4. Each cab on a track segment that will be used in the calculation of travel time, will increase the travel time for that segment by 22%. The traffic on the network will be checked once, during the initial cab routing, to determine the best route of travel.
5. Additional traffic checks will not be performed during transit.
6. Two routes will be examined. The two routes will not use any of the same track segments (this is to minimize the odds that both routes will have out of service segments). The two routes were selected using the two shortest travel distances that meet the requirements as stated.
7. If the first and second routes both have out-of-service track segments, the passenger(s) will be required to select a new destination or choose alternate transportation methods.
8. The model will examine only twenty (20) stations, and two hundred (200) track segments that are part of the network. The same model could be extended to as many stations and segments as needed.

3. Constants, Variables, and Parameters

1. Station Numbers — S_n, will be a unique scalar number [parameter].
2. Segment Numbers (individual tracks) — n,

will be a unique identifier for a track between two stations [parameter].

3. Segment Distances (in miles) — D_n, where n is the Segment Number [constant].
4. Segment Speed (average) — V_n, in mph [parameter].
5. Number of Cabs on Segment — TR_n, variable reported by sensor system that monitors track usage. $TR_n = 10{,}000$ when segment "n" is out-of-service.
6. First Route Segment Flag — $f1_n$, set equal to 1 when segment is part of the first route. Set equal to 0 (default) when segment is not part of the route.
7. Second Route Segment Flag — $f2_n$, set equal to 1 when segment is part of the second route. Set equal to 0 (default) when segment is not part of the route.

4. Proposed Solution

A Microsoft Excel spreadsheet or a MODSIM program can be used to calculate the fastest route to any destination, based on examining the times required to transit the first and second programmed routes. The two routes provide the shortest distances between the two stations. The second route will not use any of the track segments used in the first route. When the passenger(s) enter the cab and select a destination, the system will examine the amount of traffic on the network at that time, and pick either the first or second route for travel. The equations for determining the time required to transit the first and second routes are as follows: (see [4])

$$TT_1 = 60 * \sum_{n=1}^{m} (f1_n * D_n * V_n^{-1} * (1 + .22 * TR_n)) \quad (1)$$

$$TT_2 = 60 * \sum_{n=1}^{m} (f2_n * D_n * V_n^{-1} * (1 + .22 * TR_n)) \quad (2)$$

where TT_1 is the first route transit time, in minutes;
and TT_2 is the second route transit time, in minutes;
and m is the total number of segments in the network.

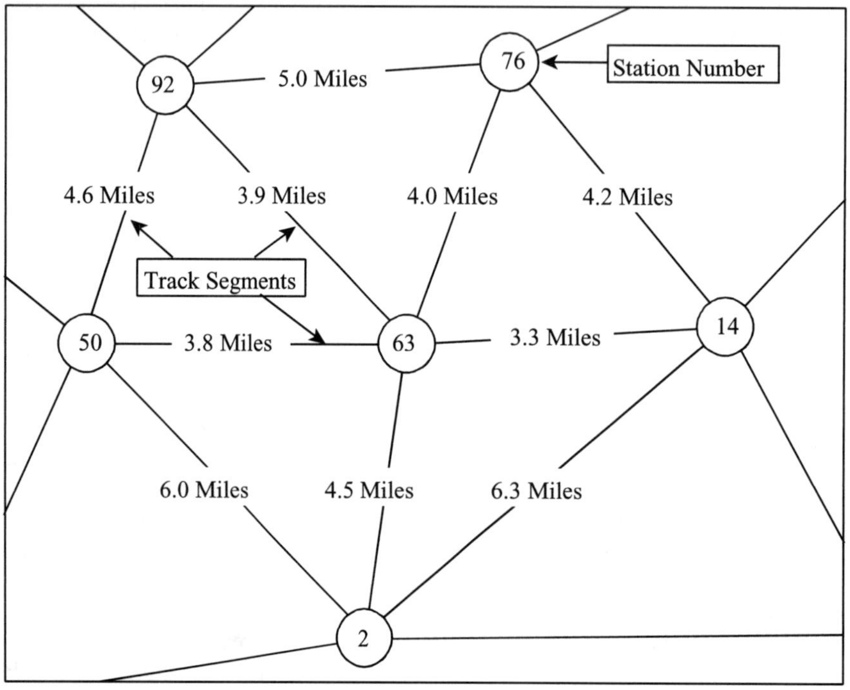

Figure 1 Network Layout shows Six Stations out of xx Stations

	51	52	53
51	Station	138+17+154+72+107	82+191+78+1+133
52	187+25+163+58+187	Station	36+118+127+146+157
53	71+80+72+196+94	24+80+163+133+18	Station

Table 1

The computer program will use several arrays, including the following that defines a route based on minimum distances. This would be a lookup table used to define flags $f1_n$ or $f2_n$:

The left-most column numbers are "from" a Station number, and the upper row are "to" numbers. To find a primary route, locate the appropriate box by using the "from" and "to" numbers. Each number in the box represents a segment number that will be traversed to move from one station to the other. By stringing the

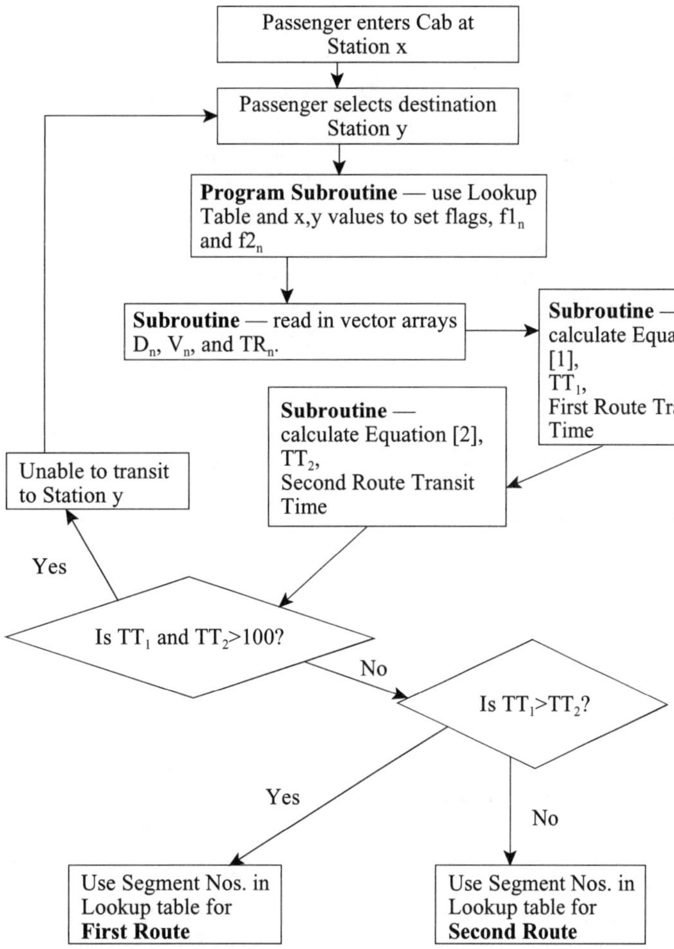

Figure 2 Program Flow Diagram — Proposed Solution

A	B	C	D	E	...
Seg. No.	**Seg. Dist. Miles**	**Seg. Speed MPH**	**Traffic Generator** Rand ( )	Rand ( )	**Traffic Volume Low**
0	0	1	0	0	1
1	4.261	44.70	0.72881	0.8697	0
2	6.834	61.42	0.88074	0.8316	1
3	9.247	77.10	0.84493	0.04981	1
...	...	...	...	...	...
198	4.281	31.70	0.77881	0.4877	0
199	3.834	71.42	0.58074	0.6313	0
200	9.747	78.10	0.94493	0.0898	1

Table 2

segments together, the cab can travel between any two points (stations). The flags, fl_n or $f2_n$, are set to unity when the number appears in the look-up table. Vector arrays are also stored for the constants D_n and V_n. The distance of average speed for each segment is assumed to be constant. The array for traffic on each segment, TR_n, is read in from the Traffic Reporting System, which is updated in real-time.

The requirement was for a system that can provide a route from one station to any other station at least 95% of the time. The system, as defined, meets this portion of the design requirement.

5. Validation of the Proposed Solution

Random number generators were used to establish the amount of traffic on each segment and the segments that were out-of-service. Random numbers were also used to select the track segment numbers between Stations (i.e., were used to fill-in the lookup tables). Care was taken to select equations that "indexed" the previous lookup table numbers so that random duplication of segment numbers did not occur. This was important since each segment on a route had to be "unique," not being duplicated. Also, the first and second routes could not share the same segment numbers.

A series of simulated runs were made between stations. The program computed transit times without mishap. No problems were noted. The design of the spreadsheet program turned out to be very stable, with little concern for bad code, since the "cutting and pasting" of cell equations left very little chance for error. Once an equation was tested and found to be mistake-free, the duplication of that cell meant that the use of this equation in other cells would also produce accurate results. This provides a definite advantage of eliminating the program development time.

6. Conclusion

A program in MODSIM [1,3] is being written to estimate the travel time that a cab would need to transit between two stations. Travel time was calculated for two routes, allowing the system to select the route with the shortest time. Two different spreadsheet layouts were used (Sheet 1 and Sheet 2). The first layout calculated only one transit at a time, showing the times for both routes and the total miles traveled on each route. The second layout calculated all possible transits (380) simultaneously and displayed information on the total number of closed segments, and how many transits were completely blocked by track construction or repair.

All of the Routing System Design Requirements were met, including displaying the fastest times for two routes, and providing a route between any two stations at least 95% of the time. The travel distance was also displayed, for the case when both routes would require an equal amount of time. In this case, the program was to pick the shortest route. A final step would be to provide an interface between the program output and the cab control system. While this wasn't specifically shown, programming the conditional arguments would be straight forward.

Improvements in this model could be made at several levels:

1) First, additional alternate routes could be added to the lookup table to help prevent out-of-service segments from blocking travel to the destination.
2) The array that contained segment speeds was assumed to be constant. Weather conditions, including rain, ice, and snow could affect certain portions of the network, changing the average speed, and affecting the route. Sensors in the track could be used to adjust the average speed, V_n, and slow all vehicles on the affected segment.
3) It may be more efficient to look at the closed segment as a "mini" transit within the total transit. In other words, the fastest time may be achieved by routing around a closed segment by running an imbedded version of this program that would select the fastest time around the closing and then embed that routing into the total transit routing.
4) Finally, the model could constantly check the route while the cab was underway, making mid-course corrections to keep the total transit time to a minimum.

7. References

1. T. Ramesh & T.C. Lee, "An Object-Oriented Simulation Model for a Split-Bus Multiprocessor Architecture," pp. 115–119, Proceedings of the 1996 Western Multi-Conference, Jan. 14–17, 1996, San Diego, CA.
2. Babatunde A. Ogunnaike & W. Harmon Ray, "Process Dynamic, Modeling, and Control," Oxford University Press, 1994.
3. MODSIM III — The Language for Object-Oriented Programming Tutorial, CACI Product Company.
4. Howard S. Travis, "A Routing System for An Automated Network of Small Vehicles, Term project for MSTP521

HLA SIMULATOR For LAND based TRANSPORTATION

Dietmar P. F. Möller[1,2, 3)] **and Hortensia Popescu**[1)]
[1)]University of Hamburg, Department Computer Science, Chair Computer Engineering
Vogt-Kölln-Str. 30, D. 22527 Hamburg, Germnay
[2)]McLeod Institute of Simulation Sciences, German Center
[3)]College of Engineering, Computer Science, and Technology, California State University, Chico
Department of Electrical and Computer Engineering, O´Connell Technology Center 313

Keywords:

Discrete Simulation, model design, queuing models, random number generation, transportation, HLA, federation, federate.

Abstract:

The paper describes modelling of queuing models for land-based transportation systems simulation using HLA. Modelling is done modular, based on road networks, driver-vehicle-elements, pedestrians, traffic lights and circadian influence on traffic-flows. Randomised probabilistic variables and normal distributed variables reflecting real word situations.

1. Introduction

1.1 HLA at the very first

The HLA is defined by three major elements, which is comparable to VHDL:

- HLA Rules or Federation Rules (FR), which ensure proper runtime interaction of simulations (or federates) in a federation, describing the simulation and federation responsibilities
- Interface Specification (IS), which defines the interfaces between federates and the Run-Time-Infrastructure (RTI) services and provides the means for federates to exchange data
- Object Model Template (OMT), which describes the data federates exchange providing a common method for recording information, establishing the format of key models
  ~ Federation Object Model (FOM)
  ~ Simulation Object Model (SOM)
  ~ Management Object Model (MOM)

1.2 Federation Rules

At the highest level, HLA consists of a set of HLA rules which must be obeyed if a federate or federation is to be regarded as HLA compliant.

HLA Rules for Federations

- Federations shall have a FOM, documented in accordance with the OMT
- All representation of object in the FOM shall be in the federates, not in the RTI
- During a federation execution, all exchange of FOM data among federates shall take place via the RTI
- During a federation execution, federates shall interact with the RTI in accordance with the HLA interface specification
- During a federation execution, an attribute of an instance of an object shall be owned by only one federate at any given time

HLA Rules for Federates

- Federates shall have a SOM, documented in accordance with the OMT
- Federates shall be able to update and/or reflect any attributes of objects in their SOM, and send and/or receive SOM interactions externally, as specified in their SOM
- Federates shall be able to transfer and/or accept ownership of attributes dynamically during a federation execution, as specified in their SOM
- Federates shall be able to vary the conditions under which they provide updates of attributes of objects, as specified in their SOM
- Federates shall be able to manage local time in a way which will allow them to co-ordinate data exchange with other members of a federation.

1.3 Interface Specification

Interface specification identifies how federates interact with federation and, ultimately, with one another.

Run Time Infrastructure (RTI)

- Software that provides common services to simulation systems
- Implementation of HLA Interface Specification
- Architectural foundation encouraging portability and interoperability

RTI Services

- Separate simulation and communication
- Improves on older standards
- Facilitates construction and destruction of federations
- Supports object declaration and management between federates
- Assists with federation time management
- Provides efficient communications to logical groups of federates

Interface Specification Management Areas

- Federation Management
- Declaration Management
- Object Management
- Ownership Management
- Data Distribution Management
- Time Management

1.4 Object Model Template (OMT)

Reusability and interoperability require that all objects and interactions managed by a federate, and visible outside the federate, should be specified in detail and with a common format. OMT provides a standard for documenting HLA object model information.

OMT

- Provides a common framework for HLA object model documentation
- Posters interoperability and reuse of simulations and their components

Required Information

- Object Class Structure Table
- Object Interaction Table
- Attribute/Parameter Table
- FOM/SOM Lexicon

Optional Information (OMT Extensions)

- Component Structure Table
- Associations Table
- Object Model Metadata

The OMT defines the FOM, the SOM and the MOM.

Federation Object Model (FOM)

- One per federation
- Introduces all shared information, e.g. objects, interactions
- Contemplates interfederate issues, e.g. data encoding schemes

Simulation Object Model (SOM)

- One per federate
- Describes salient characteristics of a federate
- Presents objects and interactions that can be used externally
- Focus on the federate´s internal operation

Management Object Model (MOM)

- Universal definition
- Identifies objects and interactions used to manage federations

1.5 Suggested steps for the very first

As reported in CSUC´s HLA electronic course material, federates shall have an HLA SOM, documented in accordance with the HLA OMT. The suggested steps are as follows:

1. Identify essential objects
2. Identify attributes used describing above objects
3. Build class hierarchy based on common attribute groupings
4. Classify each object and prepare object class structure table
5. Repeat steps 1-4 for interactions. Identify interactions and associated parameters, build hierarchy, classify interactions and prepare the interaction class table
6. Prepare initial attribute and parameter tables
7. While constructing data types, lexicons, and routing space tables, iterate with earlier tables, especially the attribute and parameter tables. Verify the potential attributes or parameters have not been overlooked and/or modify existing ones as necessary.

2. Land-based Transportation Simulator System

From a practical point of view, one has to restrict from the macroscopic aspects to a microscopic systems analysis strategy when modelling land-based transportation , based on positions and movements of transport vehicles, traffic lanes and crossings, traffic lights and traffic signs, municipal and individual traffic flows, people as discrete events etc. Microscopic land-based transportation structures could than be proper analysed by modelling and simulation.

Computer modelling of complex and heterogeneous land-based transportation is an iterative process, consisting of model building and computer simulation by changing the real structure of the model and its parameters in an effort to match the complex land-based transportation dynamic well. In fact, the derived model has served its purpose when an optimal match is obtained between the simulation results and the data obtained from the real land-based transportation system under test. In general the model building process of a land-based transportation system entails the utilisation of three types of information sources:

- goals and purposes of modelling, e.g. boundaries,
  components of relevance, level of details
- a priori knowledge of the traffic system modeled
- experimental data consisting of measurements on the system inputs and outputs.

With respect to the spectrum of modelling, a variety of levels of conceptual and mathematical representation of land-based transportation are evident, depending on the goals and purposes for which the model was intended, the extent of the a priori knowledge available, data gathers through experimentation, and measurements on real land-based transportation. For a HLA land-based transportation simulator we need:

- simulation of single transport vehicles
- simulation of transport vehicle bundles
- simulation of individual lanes
- simulation of any kind of road network
- realisation as distributed interactive simulator in order to fit big road network situations
- simple but flexible interface to adapt the control strategies e.g. traffic lights.

Building a realistic land-based transportation simulator, a library of simulation models is needed, contains

- different types of traffic situations
- different types of road conditions
- different types of car following behaviour
- different types of velocity profiles
- different interaction profiles traffic participants
- different types of lane changing
- different types of dangerous traffic situations
- different types of interactions with pedestrians,
- etc.

3. Land-based Transportation Simulation Model

Modelbuilding of land-based transportation situations could be based on assumptions like:

- traffic flow described as a sequence of situations
- within each situation the driver has a scope for action which could interact with different following situations
- each driver decides from his point of view for a scope of action.

With this situation-action-model assumptions, for each time segment the traffic specific situation can be analysed for decision support of the so called driver-vehicle-element. With this in mind, the following interactions of the discrete event land-based transportation simulator could be realised:

- driver-vehicle-element holds the actual lane, adapting to the actual traffic situation,
- driver-vehicle-element decides for lane changing in case of a slow vehicle in front or fall into line in case of branch off,
- driver-vehicle-element has to adapt to a right-of-way situation.

4. HLA Land-based Transportation Simulator

The distributed land-based transportation simulation system contains a federation and several federates which could run on a distributed computer network. Distribution of the computational load onto different computers yield in an effective simulation of big road networks because one single computer could not process the burden The components of the system are:

- RTIexec, a global process that manages the creation and destruction of federation execution,
- FedExec, one running process per executing federation that manages the federation, allows federates to join and resign from the federation and facilitates data exchange between federates,
- federates (simulation modules) which perform the computation of the different types of traffic flows,
- a graphic module which displays the actual intrinsic traffic dynamics of the involved driver-vehicle-elements within the road network.

as shown in Figure 1.

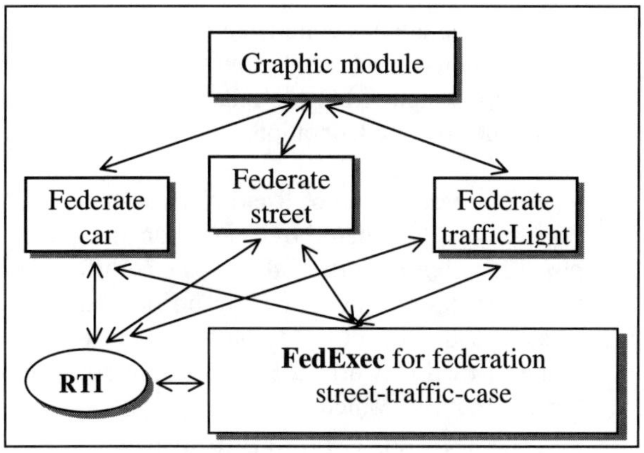

Figure 1: Schematic diagram of the HLA Traffic Simulation System

The realisation as distributed simulation system is to be state of the art, because decision making within the different simulation depends for each driver-vehicle-element only upon local boundaries. This means only driver-vehicle-elements in the near surroundings had to be taken into account. Therefore parts of the simulated road network can be simulated independently from each other. Only in the neighbourhood a transfer of data is necessary.

The initialisation of the RunTime Infrastructure contains the following steps:

- instantiation of the objects for the RTI ambassador and federate ambassador
- creating federation execution with specified name
- joining the federate to the federation
- setting the initial time management parameter

```
//---------------------------------
// Create RTI objects
//
// The federate communicates to the
// RTI through the RTIambassador
// object and the RTI communicates
// back to the federate through the

// FederateAmbassador object.
//---------------------------------
RTI::RTIambassador rtiAmb;
// libRTI provided
TrFederateAmbassador fedAmb;
// User-defined
// Named value placeholder for the
federates handle
RTI::FederateHandle federateId;
```

```
//-------------------------------
// Create federation execution.
// The RTI_CONFIG environment
// variable must be set in the
// shell's environment to the
// directory that contains the
// RTI.rid file and the Traffic.fed
//--------------------------------
try
  {
//-------------------------------
// A successful createFederation
// Execution will cause the fedex
//  process to be executed on this
// machine.
// A "Traffic.fed" file must exist
// in the current directory. This
// file specifies the FOM object,
// interaction class structures,
// default/initial transport and or
// dering informtion for object at
// tributes and interaction classes
//--------------------------------
  cout << "FED_TR: CREATING FEDERA-
       TION EXECUTION" << endl;
  rtiAmb.createFederationExecution(
     fedExecName, "Traffic.fed" );
  cout << "FED_TR: SUCCESSFUL CRE-
     ATE FEDERATION EXECUTION" <<
     endl;
  }
catch (RTI:: FederationExecutionAl-
readyExists& e )
  {
  cerr << "FED_TR: Note: Federation
     execution already exists." <<
     &e << endl;
  }
catch ( RTI::Exception& e )
  {
  cerr<<"FED_TR:ERROR:"<<&e<<endl;
  return -1;
  }
RTI::Boolean Joined=RTI::RTI_FALSE;
int numTries  = 0;

//--------------------------------
// Join federation execution
// Here we loop around the
// joinFederationExecution call
// until we try to many times or
// the Join is successful.
//--------------------------------
while(!Joined &&(numTries++ < 20))
  {
//-------------------------------
```

```
try
{
cout<<"FED_TR:   JOINING   FEDERATION
   EXECUTION: " << exeName << endl;
federateId =
rtiAmb.joinFederationExecution      (
myStreet->GetName(),     fedExecName,
&fedAmb);
      Joined = RTI::RTI_TRUE;
}
catch (RTI:: FederateAlreadyExecu-
tionMember& e)
{
cerr<<"FED_TR:ERROR:"<<
      myStreet->GetName()<<"already
      exists in the Federation Execu-
      tion"<<fedExecName<<"."<<endl;
cerr << &e << endl;
return -1;
}
catch
(RTI::FederationExecutionDoesNotExi
st&)
{
cerr<<"FED_TR:ERROR:"<<fedExecName
      <<"Federation Execution"<<"does
      not exists"<<endl;
rtiAmb.tick(2.0, 2.0);
}
catch ( RTI::Exception& e )
{
cerr<<"FED_TR:ERROR:"<<&e<<endl;
return -1;
}
} // end of while

cout<<"FED_TR:JOINED  SUCCESSFULLY:"
      <<exeName<<":Federate  Handle="
      << federateId << endl;
```

Each federate have to:

- define what data are to be published for each update or event and
- declare which updates and interaction (event) it is interested in receiving by subscribing to those attributes/messages
- specify if the federate is interested in controlling unnecessary message traffic

The simulation consist of:

- calculate state and update to RTI
- ask for time advance
- tick the RTI waiting the grant

When a federate has completed his simulation, it deletes the objects it created (streets, lane, intersection, cars etc.), resigns from the federation execution and tries to destroy the federation.

5. HLA Description of Road Networks

By using the land-based transportation simulator it is possible to optimise the traffic flows at different traffic nodes. Simulating a specific traffic node, the affiliated road network has to build up. For easy modelling of road networks a HLA specific notation had been introduced, which deal with:

- clear description of road networks
- separation of a global road network into local road networks as parts of the simulation modules.

The HLA-RTI land-based transportation Simulator is based on cars, streets and possible interrupt request for traffic lights or traffic signs. In accordance with the explanation in the previous chapter the streets assumed consisting of lanes for each direction, like west to east, east to west, north to south, and south to north, realised with blocks of equal length. For this case of study the streets are assumed to have one lane per direction. The cars are driving -as an simplification of the simulation system realised in case study 01- with the same speed. Hence traffic flow can be described as a sequence of blocks, as shown in Figure 2.

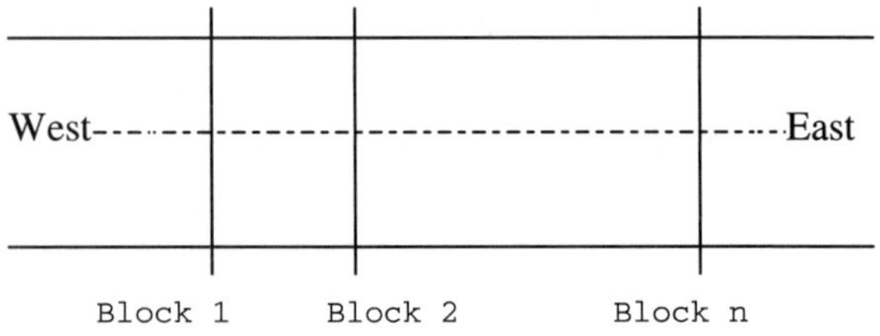

Figure 2: Schematic diagram of Federation Street Traffic West/East & vice versa

Within the HLA land-based transportation simulation system model the federation consists of more federates responsible for traffic flow. Due to that type of federates, the following object classes can be used: **Street**, **Lane**, **Block**, **Car**, **TrafficLight**, **Intersection**, **EntryInIntersection**.

Within the HLA land-based transportation simulation system model the object classes can be described as follows:

class Street contains:
name of the street
number of lane per direction
(1 lane in this case of study)
number of blocks per lane
direction *char[2];
(for example: direction (0) = "west"
direction (1) = "east")
lane for direction[0]
lane for direction[1]

class Lane contains:
direction
array of Block

class Block contains:
array of TrafficLight
array of TrafficSign
array of Car

class Car contains:
pointer to Street
pointer to Lane
pointer to Block
max velocity
current velocity

class TrafficLight characterised by:
ID
state(colour)
for entry in street
for entry in block

class Intersection contains:
array of EntryInIntersection

class EntryInIntersection characterised by:
street
lane
numberOfBlock

6. Outlook

The developed HLA land-based transportation simulator version can be expanded by more features like:
- streets with more then one lane for each direction,
- cars need not to have the same velocity profile; (in this case it has to be taken into account the fact that a driver-vehicle-element can decide to overtake another driver-vehicle-element driving with a slower velocity)
- more complex intersections, traffic sign etc.

In case of several streets, the **class Street** must contain supplemental an array with pointers to each street (a static variable), in order to access them and perform the communication.

```
static StreetPtr
  ms_StreetExtent[MAX_STREETS + 1];
```

In addition, instead of the two attributes of type **Lane**, (lane for direction[0] and lane for direction[1]), the class has two arrays of lanes, each of length "number of lane per direction".

7. References

Möller, D.P.F., S. Deigmüller: Distributed Interactive Simulation of Traffic Systems, In: Proceedings 1997 SCSC, pp. 619ff, Eds. M.S.Obaidat, J.Ilgen, SCS Pub. San Diego, 1997
McLeod Institute of Simulation Science, California State University Chico, http://www.ecst.csuchico.edu/~hla/
High Level Architecture (HLA), Module1: Basic Concepts of the High Level Architecture (HLA)

Medical and Pharmaceutical Applications

VALIDATION OF THE HUMAN MUSCLE MODEL

Aleš Belič, Nataša Knez, Rihard Karba, Vojko Valenčič
Faculty of Electrical Engineering
University of Ljubljana
Tržaška 25, 1000 Ljubljana, Slovenia
ales.belic@fe.uni-lj.si

Keywords: Dynamic models, Physiology, Pharmacokinetics, Optimization, Validation

ABSTRACT

Dynamic model of muscle belly displacement was composed to elucidate the involved processes. The corresponding non-evasive measurement technique was developed at the Faculty of Electrical Engineering, University of Ljubljana. The model was made for studying and improving the motion of persons with muscle disorders or athletes. The main problem of muscle belly displacement dynamics modelling poses Calcium (Ca^{2+}) dynamics. Measurements of Ca^{2+} in the muscle are difficult to perform, therefore, the data available in the literature are rare. However, understanding of Ca^{2+} dynamics is of key importance for the model. In spite of non-identifiability of the model, physiologically acceptable model structure and parameters could be obtained. It shows that there is a high correlation between muscle belly displacement and processes involved in muscle contraction. Genetic algorithms represent a powerful tool in the process of model parameters estimation.

INTRODUCTION

To study processes involved in muscle contraction and relaxation in humans a relatively simple model involving physiological properties of two major types of muscle fibers was developed. Since intra-cellular measurements are difficult to perform, a non-evasive measurement method was used to measure muscle responses to electrical stimulation. With the non-invasive measuring method radial displacement of muscle belly was measured. The model was based on known physiological properties of muscle fibers and measurements of muscle belly displacement on humans.

Chemical properties of the process were described with nonlinear compartment model. The structure of the model of chemical properties was derived from literature data. Mechanical properties of the muscle were modelled with combination of mechanical components which means springs and viscous dampers. Again, the structure of the mechanical submodel was derived from literature. Model parameters were determined by adaptive model scheme, where model response was fitted to measured muscle belly displacement by changing model parameters. Genetic algorithms were used as optimization routine. Model was composed in Matlab/Simulink, numerical analysis and simulation tool.

A great number of volunteers, mainly athletes, were involved in measurements. Twitch and tetanic responses of many skeletal muscles were measured. Model structure and parameters were determined from muscle belly displacement after one pulse of electrical stimulation. The lack of measurements of Ca^{2+}, ATP, ATP-aze in the muscle, make the model non-identifiable. Therefore, model parameters could not be uniquely identified. However, simplification of model structure was not possible if structural relations between model and real systems were to be preserved. Therefore, only general properties of muscle contraction or muscle belly displacement can be shown. Firstly, model was validated by comparing time courses of Ca^{2+} of the model with time courses found in the literature. Considerable accordance of model responses in Ca^{2+} time courses to literature data allowed for further testing of the model. Next the model responses were examined for multiple pulses of electrical stimulation. The model showed similar responses as were measured on muscles.

The work deals with modelling and validation of muscle dynamics model which was composed from a combination of physiological characteristics of muscles and measurements of muscle belly displacemnt.

GENETIC ALGORITHMS (GA)

Basic idea of GA (Goldberg 1989; Gen and Cheng 1997) is to search for optimal solution by applying natural laws of genetics and evolution. Different GAs (Belič et al. 2000) have been proposed and tested in the literature, each being optimal for a given problem. However, there was no universal solution for all optimisation problems and very likely never will be. It has been shown (Levine 1994) that larger populations exploration. It is suspected that best genetic material e.g. parameter set, prevails too slowly over less successful subjects than in smaller populations. Therefore, the convergence of algorithm is much slower and results are usually far away from optimum. On the other hand, parallel algorithm divides the whole population into smaller subpopulations. That enables faster convergence of the solution in subpopulations. Therefore, the parallel algorithm explores the problem space better than the simple algorithm, since each subpopulation usually distributes over different part of problem space. Migrations of subjects between subpopulations take place at regular intervals. This model is much closer to natural evolution of species and also works considerably better in problem space exploration.

Important stage in each modelling cycle (Matko et al. 1992; Cellier 1991) is model parameter estimation which is in biosciences often performed with identification with adaptive model. If the model structure is derived from physiological characteristics it is usually non-identifiable and unique solution of the problem does not exist. However, sometimes it is sufficient to find an acceptable solution in the set of solutions. That requires a method that is not very exact but can explore large parameter spaces in relatively short time. GAs represent a successful method for searching in large parameter spaces, when exact solution is not important.

MUSCLE DYNAMICS MODEL

The main problem of muscle belly displacement dynamics modelling poses Calcium (Ca^{2+}) dynamics. Measurements of Ca^{2+} in the muscle are difficult to perform, therefore, the data available in the literature are rare (Wetzel and Gros 1998). However, understanding of Ca^{2+} dynamics is of key importance for the model. A nonlinear compartment model, based on physiology of muscles including homeostatic control loop for ATP and ATP-aze levels was built to characterise the Ca^{2+} dynamics. The Ca^{2+} together with ATP contracts the muscle, whereas the ATP-aze enzyme enables muscle relaxation. Muscle motion is, therefore, mainly dependent on the ratio of those substances in the muscle. The compartment model, describing the dynamics of the three substances, was linked to the muscle mechanics model with the driving force. The driving force of the muscle was proportional to the bound Ca^{2+} levels. The muscle mechanics model was a composition of dampers and springs similar to those found in the literature (Huijing 1992). Since there are generally two types of muscles, fast and slow, differing mostly in Ca^{2+} dynamics, two structurally equal models of Ca^{2+} had to be used. Each model had, however, different set of parameters. The model of muscle mechanics described the muscle as whole, therefore, to couple the two models into one muscle dynamics model, bound Ca^{2+} levels of both muscle types were added the muscle before the driving force was calculated. Model parameters were determined by fitting the model responses to the measured data. Parallel genetic algorithm was used as optimization routine.

RESULTS

There were 16 parameters of the model to be set and only muscle belly displacement was measured. There were also some indications found in the literature about Ca^{2+} concentration in both muscle types that were also used in the fitting procedure (Wetzel and Gros 1998). The model was, therefore, not uniquely identifiable which lead to unreliable fitting procedure. Therefore, the procedure had to be repeated several times to obtain results of adequate significance. In all cases the results were optically and physiologically acceptable. Belly displacements on two muscles, brachioradialis and erector spinae could be successfully simulated by the model (Figures 1 and 2).

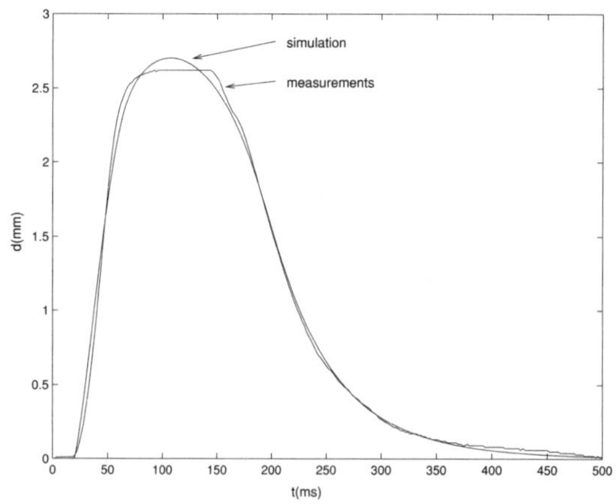

Figure 1: Model response vs. measured data for brachioradialis.

MODEL VALIDATION

Model was validated taking into account structural accordance of model to muscle physiology and simulation of model responses on muscle stimulation that was not used for model development.

In the model the following concepts of muscle contraction were taken into account:

- a certain amount of time is needed for electrical pulse to reach the stimulation site of the muscle,

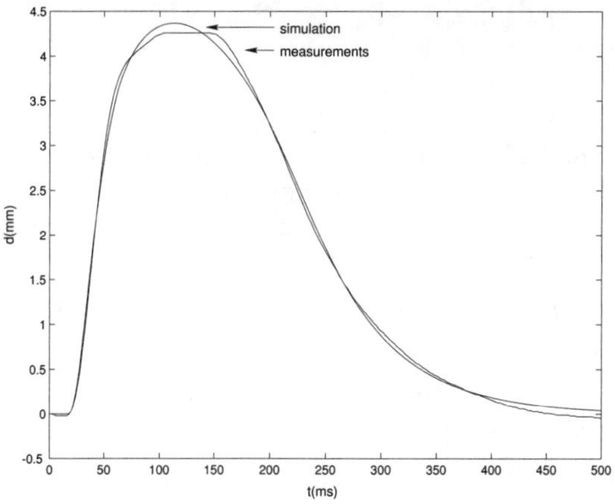

Figure 2: Model response vs. measured data for erector spinae.

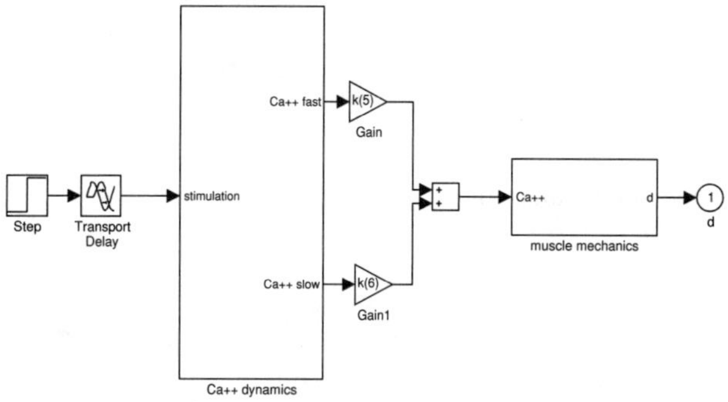

Figure 3: Model structure composed in SIMULINK

- muscle contraction is induced if the amplitude and the duration of the stimulative pulse is large enough,
- Ca^{2+} is released from the stores if pulse characteristics are above limits,
- the amount of released Ca^{2+} depends on pulse height,
- Ca^{2+} stores cannot be exhausted during the test,
- Ca^{2+} dynamics is different for each muscle type,
- ATP and ATP-aze stores are limited and the limits are specific for each muscle type,
- a control loop governs ATP and ATP-aze levels in the muscle and its characteristics depend on the muscle type,
- contraction force is proportional to Ca^{2+} levels,
- the force of both muscle types contracts the same tissue, therefore, a single model is used to characterise mechanical properties of the muscle.

The model structure can be seen in Figure 3, details can be seen in Appendix, in Figures 8 - 6. Muscle contraction after several pulses of stimulation was simulated next. As the model parameters were determined for single pulse of stimulation and as they are not uniquely identifiable, model response after several pulses of stimulation can be used for validation purposes. It is known, that if the pulse frequency is high enough (larger than 2 Hz), the muscles cannot relax completely between the pulses (Figure 4). At the frequencies of about 10 Hz and above tetanic contraction can be observed (Figure 5). The model responses are similar to those, measured on the real system.

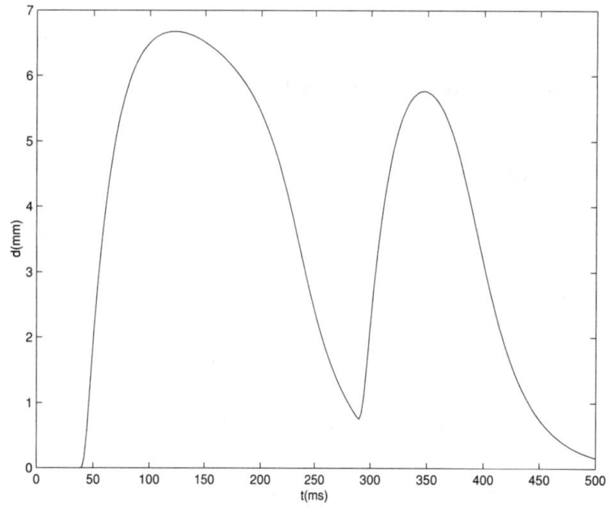

Figure 4: Non-tetanic muscle response to multiple-pulse stimulation

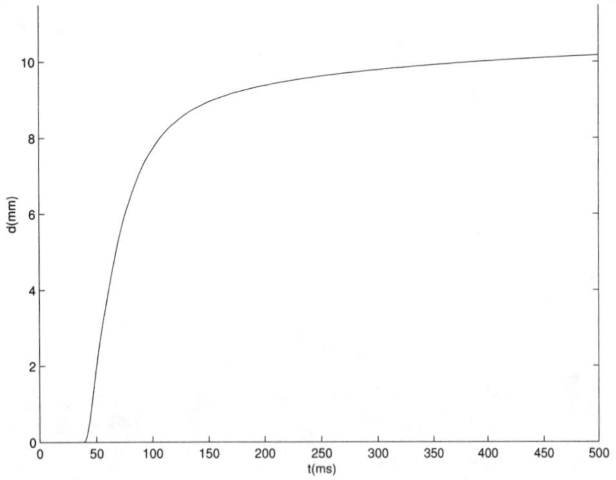

Figure 5: Tetanic muscle response to multiple-pulse stimulation

CONCLUSIONS

The following can be concluded:

- the model for dynamics of muscle belly displacement is composed according to muscle physiology and measured displacement,
- the model is non-identifiable, since there is not enough data to uniquely identify model parameters,
- genetic algorithm is efficient optimization routine in cases of non-identifiable models,
- in spite of non-identifiability, physiologically acceptable model structure and parameters could be obtained, therefore, there is a high correlation between muscle belly displacement and processes involved in muscle contraction and relaxation. This confirms the efficiency of the developed measurement technique when studying and improving the motion of persons with muscle disorders or athletes.

Significant difference between fast and slow muscle fibers is basic reason for such variety of measured muscle belly displacements. However, the reasons for the difference between the two fibers are still not completely understood. Model suggests that there is some control mechanism, controlling the levels of ATP-aze, that are crucial for muscle relaxation. In slow muscle fibers changes of ATP-aze are slower than in fast fibers, which could be the result of less agile controlling mechanism and larger amounts of stored enzymes in slow fibers.

Belič, A.; R. Karba; I. Grabnar; A. Mrhar; and D. Andrejič. 2000. "The role of Genetic Algorithms in Pharmacokinetic - Pharmacodynamic Modelling and Evaluation. " In *3rd Mathmod Proceedings*, Volume 2, (Vienna, Austria, February 2-4 2000), Vienna University of Technology, Argesim, 587–590.

Cellier, F. E. 1991. *Continuous System Modelling* Springer-Verlag, New York.

Gen, M. and R. Cheng. 1997. *Genetic Algorithms & Engineering Design* John Wiley & sons, inc, New York.

Goldberg, D. E. 1989. *Genetic Algorithms in Search, Optimization, and Machine Learning* Addison Wesley Publishing Company, New York.

Huijing, P. A. 1992. "Mechanical Muscle Models." In *Strength and Power in Sports*, Blackwell Science, Oxford, Great Britain, 130–150.

Levine, D. 1994. "A Parallel Genetic Algorithm for the set Partitioning Problem. " Technical Report ANL 94/23, Argonne National Laboratory, Argonne, IL, USA.

Matko, D.; R. Karba; and B. Zupančič. 1992. *Simulation and Modelling of Continuous Systems: A Case Study Approach* Prentice Hall, New York.

Wetzel, P. and G. Gros. 1998. "Decay of Ca^{2+} and Force Transients in Fast- and Slow-Twitch Skeletal Muscles from Rat, Mouse and Etruscan Shrew. " *The Journal of Experimental Biology,* NO. 201: 375–384.

APPENDIX

Submodels of muscle dynamics model:

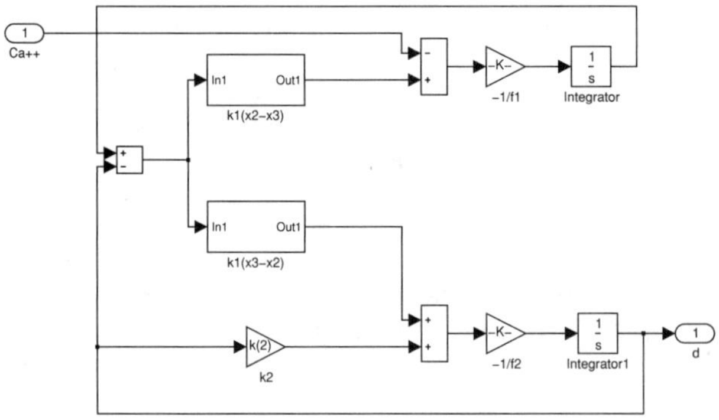

Figure 6: Muscle mechanics submodel

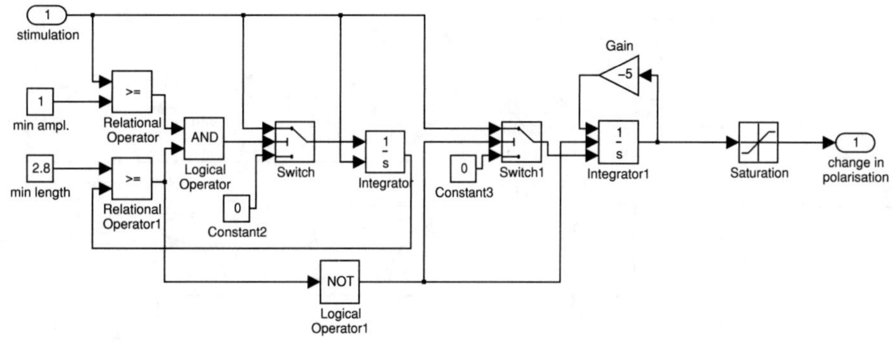

Figure 7: Submodel for triggering the Ca^{2+} release from strores

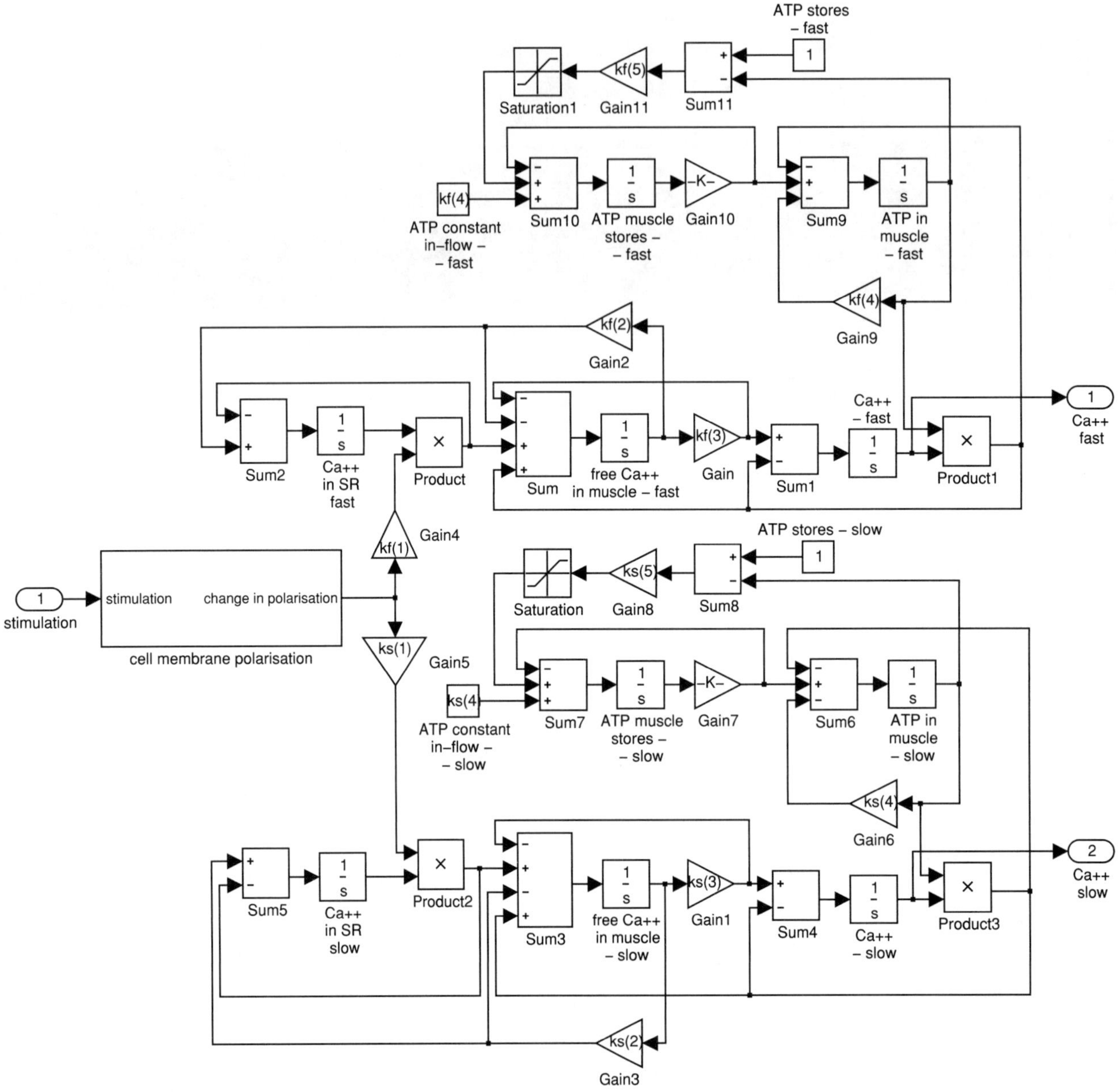

Figure 8: Submodel of Ca^{2+} dynamics

AN ENVIRONMENT FOR THE COMPARTMENTAL MODELING AND SIMULATION IN BIOLOGY AND MEDICINE

Yskandar Hamam, François Rocaries & René Natowicz
ESIEE
Cité Descartes, BP. 99
93162 Noisy le Grand CEDEX, France
hamam@esiee.fr

KEYWORDS

Biology, medicine, compartmental modeling, system dynamics.

ABSTRACT

In this paper, a MatLab environment for compartmental modeling is presented. In this environment, the user may select an interface between two compartments and write any available non linear Matlab expression to represent the behavior of the interface. He may also chose the differential equations of the compartments and use them within the simulation. All the functions are menu driven starting from the development of the model and ending with the display of results. The user may select the information to be displayed and the characteristics of the display window. Functions such as saving and retrieving a model are also menu driven such that the user needs a minimal knowledge of MatLab. An example of Ca^{++} dynamics is also presented.

1.0 INTRODUCTION

Compartmental modeling is a major tool in the study of the behavior of many biological systems. It may be used at all levels. At the micro level of modeling, such as the cell level, the different compartments are represented to obtain their kinetic and dynamic behavior. Such an example is that studied by the authors (Hamam *et al* 2000) in the field of the Ca^{++} exchange in the sarcolemmal and cytosolic compartments in cardiac myocytes. In this case, the cyclic behavior of the exchange which leads to the contraction and the relaxation of the cell through the fixation of Ca^{++} to the Myocin and Actin proteins is studied. The macro level is found at the other end. In this case the behavior of the various organs and media is studied (liver, kidneys, stomach, blood, ...). An example is that of the modeling of the gastric exchange within the stomach. Simulation is usually based on an artificial stomach in which duodenal compartments are used for the assessment of antiacid characteristics and the effect of drugs. The environment developed was used to replace the experimental tool by a numerical tool. Many other examples exist in biology as other fields.

In all these cases the interest is in the behavior of both the concentration in each compartment as well as the exchange between compartments. The compartment usually behaves as storage of different components and the variations of there level through time. This leads to non linear ordinary differential equations. The exchange process may be either in the direction of high to low concentration compartments which may be represented as a leakage or from low to high concentration compartments which may be represented as pumps. All the components may be either linear or non linear.

Using such models is of high interest to biologists and physicians that are interested in evaluation the effect of varying the various parameters in order to simulate the behavior under varying conditions. Some of the above practitioners are familiar with mathematical modeling in order to use their associated tools directly. In many cases, however, it is not the case. The authors have been working for several years with biologists, and as a result became aware of the need for tools that are accessible to them. Although a minimal knowledge of mathematics is necessary, it is important to have a tool that requires a minimal need from their part for modeling knowledge.

In this paper, the authors present this environment as well as an example of using this environment in biology. The example of the Ca^{++} dynamics in cardiac myocytes will be used throughout the paper to illustrate the environment. This presentation shows the capability of the environment from its various aspects: modeling compartments and interfaces, data and model input and output handling and graphics interfaces for displaying the simulation results.

The paper is organized as follows. In section two, the example of cardiac myocytes is presented. In section three, the environment is described and applied to the example. in section four, concluding remarks and future developments are considered.

2.0 CALCIUM DYNAMICS IN CARDIAC CELLS

In cardiac myocytes, the depolarization, evoked upon electrical stimulation, leads to Ca^{++} entry through the L-type voltage dependent channels into the sarcolemmal membrane. This influx results in the opening of RyR channels (ryanodine receptors) in the sarcoplasmic reticulum (SR). This in turn leads to the release into the cytosolic compartment of the Ca^{++} stored in the SR compartment which results in the contraction triggered by the Ca^{++} increase in the cytosolic compartment. Relaxation follows the re-uptake of Ca^{++} by the SERCA pump into the SR or its extrusion from the cell essentially by the Na/Ca exchanger. This mechanism is illustrated in figure 1.

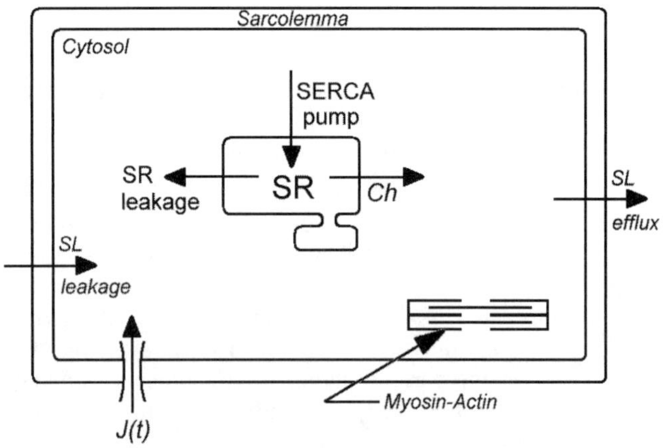

Figure 1: A schematic diagram of the compartments in cardiac myocytes

This representation may be extended to a more detailed one by increasing the number of compartments (Nordin 1993; Courtemanche *et al.*1998). The above model is however sufficient to illustrate our tool. (Tang and Othmer 1994) give the following differential equations for this model:

$$\begin{aligned}
\dot{x}_1 &= l_{-1}x_2 + l_{-2}(1 - x_1 - x_2 - x_3) - (l_1 + l_2)x_1x_4 \\
\dot{x}_2 &= -l_{-1}x_2 + l_{-2}x_3 + (l_1x_1 - l_2x_2)x_4 \\
\dot{x}_3 &= -(l_{-1} + l_{-2})x_3 + (l_2x_2 + l_1(1 - x_2 - x_3))x_4 \\
\dot{x}_4 &= -(V_r(g_1 + Chx_2) + g_2)x_4 + V_r(g_1 + Ch\,x_2)x_5 \\
&\quad - (Q(x_4) + V_rP(x_4)) + g_2C_0 + J(t) \\
\dot{x}_5 &= (g_1 + Ch\,x_2)x_4 - (g_1 + Ch\,x_2)x_5
\end{aligned}$$

such that

$$P(x_4) = \frac{p_1x_4^2}{x_4^2 + p_2^2} \text{ and } Q(x_4) = \frac{q_1x_4^2}{x_4^2 + q_2^2}$$

where the variables, constants and parameters are as follows.

Variables:

- x_1 is the proportion of activatable ryanodine channels;
- x_2 is theproportion of open ryanodine channels;
- x_3 is the proportion of closed ryanodine channels;
- x_4 is the calcium concentration in the cytosol (M);
- x_5 is the calcium concentration inside the SR (M);

Constants:

- g_1 is the leakage conductance between the SR and the cytosol (s^{-1});
- g_2 is the leakage conductance between the cytosol and extracellular medium (s^{-1});
- Ch is the conductance of the RyR channels (s^{-1});
- p_1 is the maximum rate of the sarcoplasmic pump ($M\times s^{-1}$);
- p_2 is the threshold concentration of the SERCA pump(M);
- q_1 is the maximum rate of the sarcolemma pump ($M\times s^{-1}$);
- q_1 is the threshold concentration of the sarcolemmal pump(M);

Other parameters:

- C_0 is the extracellular calcium concentration.

This example illustrates the various aspects of an environmental model.

- Media: in this example 3 media are concerned, the SR, the cytosol and the extracellular medium
- Interfaces: in this example two interfaces are considered, SR to cytosol and cytosol to the extracellar medium
- Objects: interfaces are composed of objects, e.g. three objects for the SR to cytosol interface
- Variables and constants as in the example.

In the following section, the representation of the above aspects of the model are considered.

3.0 THE MATLAB ENVIRONMENT

From the beginning two approaches were considered. The first is based on the Simulink Toolbox and the second uses directly the Matlab graphics tools. The latter approach was more convenient and was used for all the further development.

3.1 The Modeling Blocks

The interface based representation of the above described model is shown in figure 2. In this model two interfaces are implemented: the left interface is that between the cytosol and the extra-cellular media and the second between the sarcoplasmic reticulum and the cytosol media.

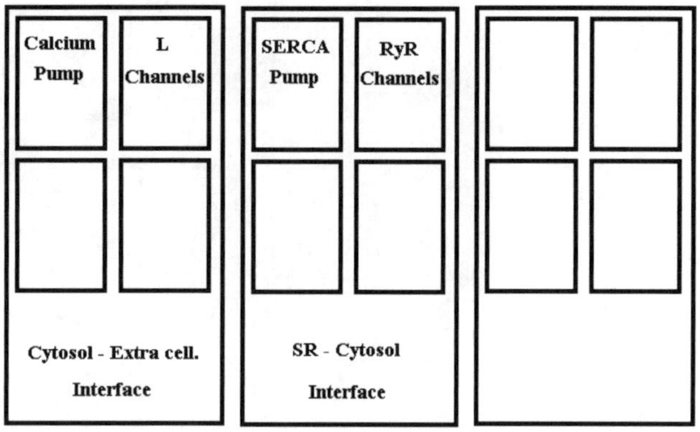

Figure 2: The interface model of the Tang and Othmer Model

3.2 The Steps for Creating a Model

Five steps are used for the development and the analysis of a model:

Step1: Creation of media and variables
Step 2: Creation of the interfaces
Step 3: Creation of objects
Step 4: Simulation
Step 5: Saving the model

In the following paragraphs, these steps are presented.

3.3 Creation of Media and Variables

When invoking the program the window in figure 3 appears. When the edit menu is then called and choosing the environment sub-menu, the window of figure 4 is obtained. Invoking the "Add new medium" submenu from the "Media and Variables" menu permits the addition of a new medium. Each medium is given an internal name and an external name. For each medium we may then add the corresponding variables by invoking the "Add new variables" menu. Having created the media and their variables, the interfaces may the be created.

3.4 Creation of Interfaces

Having created the media, all interfaces between these media become available. The user may then activate interfaces by choosing them from the available list. At the end of this step the user would have created all the user interfaces.

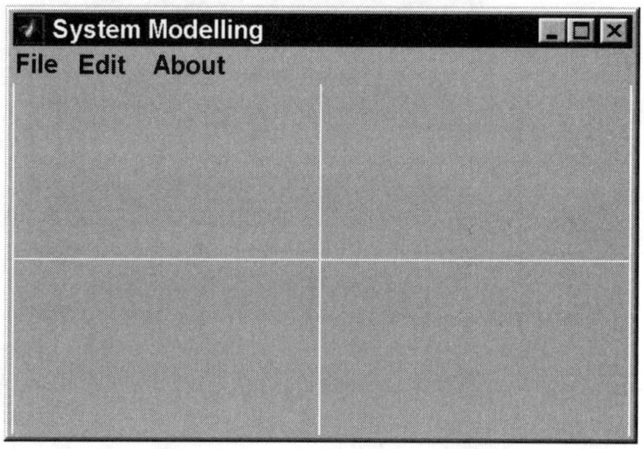

Figure 3: The main menu of the system modeling environment.

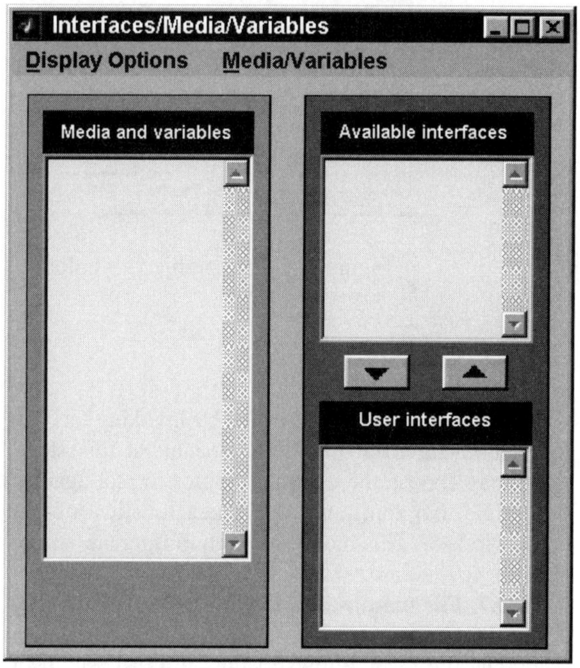

Figure 4: The environment window.

3.5 Creation of Objects

The user is now ready to create the objects associated to interfaces. This is done by the "Objects" submenu of the "Edit" menu. This opens the window associated to object parameters. The window is shown in figure 5.

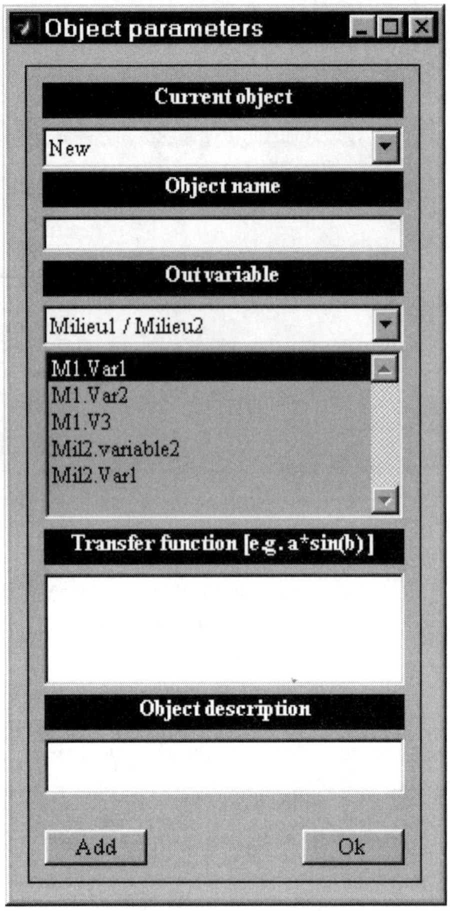

Figure 5: Creating objects window

3.6 Simulation

Simulating is then operated by invoking the "Simulation" submenu from the "Edit" menu. At this stage the user may choose the output variables to plot against time, the time horizon, and the characteristics of the display window. This menu is shown in figure 6.

3.7 File manipulation

The file menu allows loading ("Load" submenu), saving ("Save" submenu) and creating new models ("New" submenu). Models may also be added to the library .

3.8 Data Structure

The workspace is divided into two parts: the media and the interfaces parts. in turn these are divided each into two parts: general information and detailed data. As an example, the Tang and Othmer model is used for illustration. The corresponding data structure is given in figure 8.

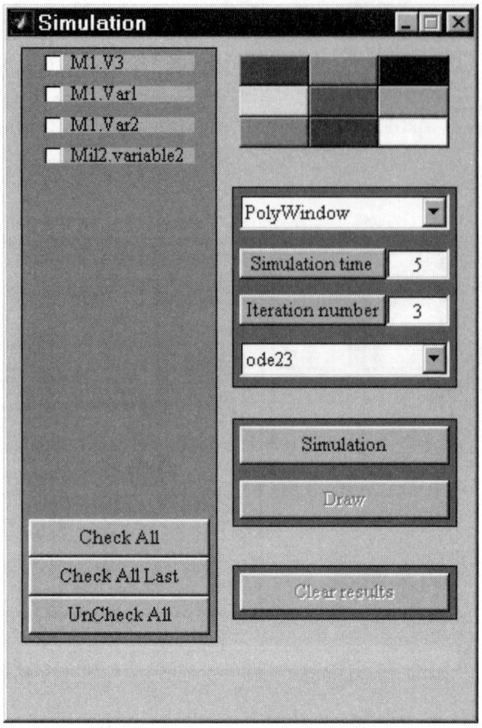

Figure 6: The simulation window

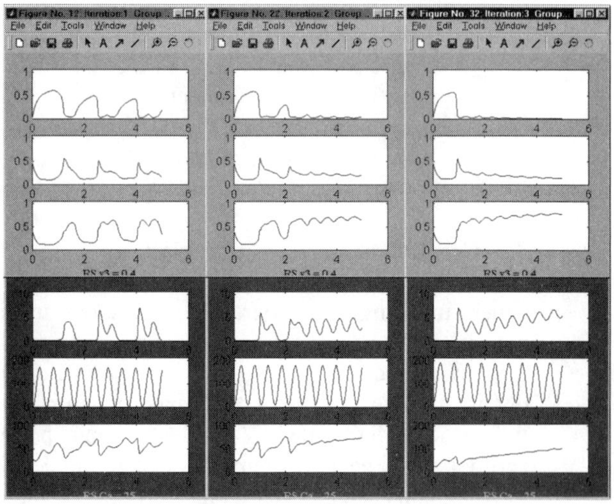

Figure 7: En example of a 3 windows - two groups output

4.0 CONCLUSIONS

In this paper, the authors presented a new environment for the analysis and simulation of models based on compartments. These models find their application, but are not limited to, biology and medicine. The real test of such environment is when given to users from the non modeling community. The authors are now testing this environment with biologists to validate the user friendliness of this software. Further work will be essentially oriented towards such aspects.

5.0 ACKNOWLEDGEMENT

The authors are grateful to Charles de la Ferriere, Laurent Labatte, Minh Tam Nguyen and Remy Wahnoun, students at ESIEE for their excellent work on this project.

6.0 REFERENCES

Courtemanche, M.; R.J. Ramirez; & S. Nattel. 1998. "Ionic mechanisms underlying human atrial action potential properties: insights from a mathematical model", *Journal of the American Physiological Society*, H, pp.301-321.

Hamam, Y.; F.Pecker; F.Rocaries; H.Lorino; C.Pavoine and R.Natowicz. 2000. "Identification and modeling of calcium dynamics in cardiac myocytes", *Simulation Practice and Theory*, June.

Nordin, C. 1993. "Computer model of membrane current and intracellular Ca^{++} flux in the isolated guinea pig ventricular myocyte", *Journal of the American Physiological Society*, H, pp.2117-2136.

Tang, Y. and H.G. Othmer. 1994. "A model of calcium dynamics in cardiac myocites based on the kinetics of ryanodine-sensitive calcium channels", *Biophysical Journal*, vol. 67 (December): pp.2223-2235.

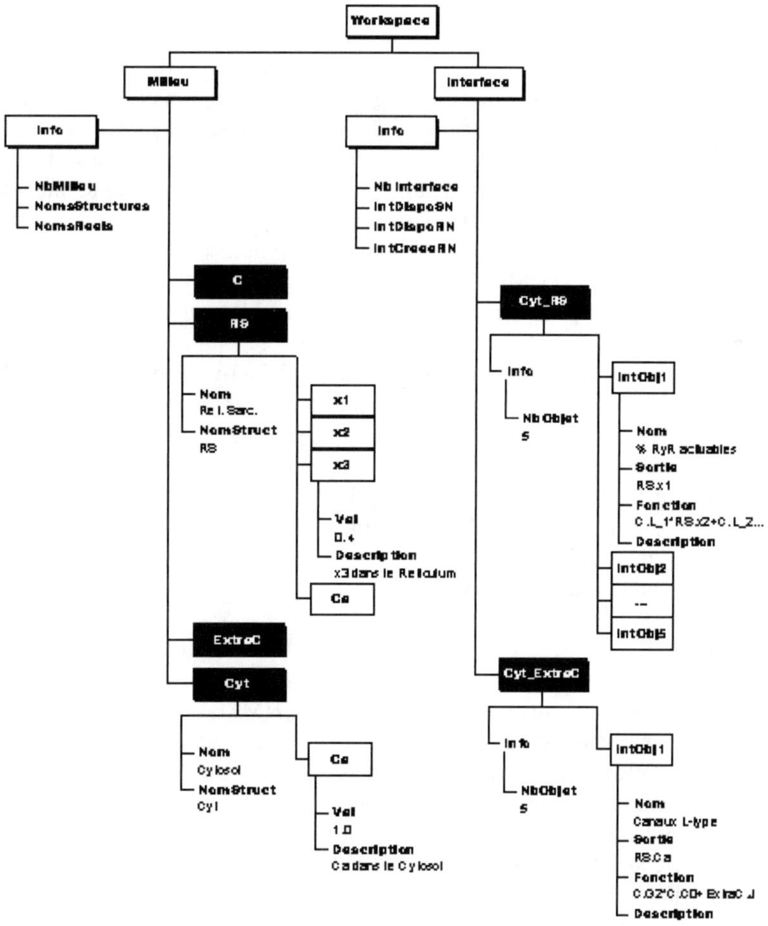

Figure 8: The data structure of the Tang and Othmer example

A LEARNING BASED STOCHASTIC MODELING APPROACH FOR CLINICAL DIAGNOSIS

Tarik AL ANI*, Yskandar HAMAM*, Redouane Fodil**, Frédéric Lofaso** and Daniel Isabey**

* ESIEE, Cité Descartes, BP 99,
3162 Noisy-le-Grand Cedex, France
emails: alanit@esiee.fr, hamamy@esiee.fr
** Inserm Unité 492, Faculté de Médecine, 8 rue du Général Sarrail, 94010, Créteil Cedex, France

KEYWORDS

Diagnosis, stochastic process, stochastic modeling, learning

ABSTRACT

A diagnosis toolbox is presented within the Scilab environment. This toolbox interprets sequences of data such as clinical measurements. It is based on a learning based stochastic methodology for constructing automated diagnosis architecture. The main idea behind our approach is the use of Hidden Markov Models (HMMs). The probabilistic concept of HMMs capture the uncertainty inherent in state interpretation. By applying off-line training procedures, different models may be constructed using only clinical measurements. Based on these models, off-line and on-line diagnosis and prediction may be achieved. In our toolbox popular methods and a new simulated annealing based method for the training of HMMs are incorporated. These methods cover both the training and recognition phases. Some practical aspects for using this toolbox are discussed and experimental results using clinical data are presented.

1.0 INTRODUCTION

The increasing sophistication of medical devices is generally advantageous in health-care environments. Increasing both safety and efficiency of the treatment is quite important. It is especially so in the case of difficult, unexpected, and time-critical situations (Morris 1993), (Wright et al. 1991), (Uckun 1993). Thus, automating monitoring and diagnosis of intensive-care unit patients becomes an important objective. Many approaches are based on expert or rule based systems (including fuzzy logic systems) (Steimann et al. 1993) and model based systems (Larsson 1995a), (Larssson 1995b). Expert systems have had a large impact on automated diagnosis. Expert systems, however, have several weaknesses, mainly due to the difficulty of building and maintaining large rule bases and also since the inference algorithms are not well-suited for real-time action or fast response. A current trend is to use models instead of rules. The advantage of this approach is that a true predictive inference may be obtained. In general, most of these approaches have traditionally been based on linear modeling techniques. This restricts the type of practical situations that can be modeled. However, obtaining linear or non linear analytical model of many patient monitoring domains is a difficult problem. A good approach is to construct empirical models using Adaptive and Interactive Modeling Systems.

Adaptive and Interactive Modeling Systems are machine learning based modeling systems for forming empirical models at different levels of abstraction according to the modeling objectives specified by users. The modeling process may be considered as a learning activity using inductive machine learning techniques from Artificial Intelligence (AI), stochastic schemes and optimization methods.

Learning based modeling approaches such as Artificial Neural Networks (ANNs) and Hidden Markov Models (HMMs) are promising for diagnosis and prediction. These approaches use a clinical data base to construct generalized or individual models for each patient.

This paper presents a diagnosis toolbox within the Scilab environment. Scilab is a scientific software package for numerical computations in a user-friendly environment (Scilab 2000). This toolbox interprets sequences of data such as clinical measurements. As a result our inference method may be referred to as **trend detection**. In recent years, new inference methods have been introduced to deal with sequences of data which traditionally cannot be dealt with efficiently because of problems such as missing, incomplete, and uncertain information. Such techniques complement established trend detection techniques such as Kalman filtering.

This toolbox concerns a learning based stochastic methodology for constructing automated diagnosis architecture. The main idea behind this approach is the use of Hidden Markov Models (HMMs). These models are based on an extension of the concept of Markov chains to include cases where the observation is a probabilistic function of the state.

A HMM is a finite model that describes a probability distribution over an infinite number of possible sequences. The HMM is composed of some number of states, which might correspond to pathophysiological states (e.g. respiratory events). Each state "emits" observations according to observation emission probabilities (e.g. clinical data using the technique of polysomnography), and the states are interconnected by state transition probabilities. Starting from some initial state, a sequence of states is generated by moving from state to state according to the state transition probabilities until an end state is reached. Each state then emits observations according to that state's emission probability distribution, creating an observable sequence of observations. A HMM is a double stochastic process with one underlying process that is not observable (state sequence) but may be estimated through a set of processes that produce a sequence of observations.

HMMs provide an effective approach for incorporating the temporal context. They may be employed directly using the measurement clinical signals of the process. These Models have been widely applied in automatic speech recognition and are now being extended to many fields such as pattern recognition, signal processing and control. In these field signals are encoded as temporal variation of short time power spectrum.

In our toolbox popular methods and a new simulated annealing based method for the training of HMMs are incorporated. These methods cover both the training and recognition phases.

By applying off-line training procedures, different models may be constructed using only clinical measurements. Based on these models, off-line and on-line diagnosis and prediction may be achieved.

The inference method of this toolbox synthesize interpretations of parameter values into interpretations of physiological and pathophysiological states. If the interpretation is extended to sequences of states in time, a state space trajectory may be obtained. The identification of state-space trajectories is a useful concept in diagnosis because some disorders may only be distinguished from each other by the sequences of pathophysiological states that they follow in time. The probabilistic concept of HMMs capture the uncertainty inherent in state interpretation.

A major interest of using HMMs is their capabilities for predictive inferences. These inferences make our toolbox useful in the

- evaluation of treatment plans,
- optimization of treatment plans,
- predictive alarming for example in anticipation of non desirable parameter values and pathophysiological states
- management of computational resources based on demand estimates.

In Section 2 we give a brief introduction to hidden Markov models. In section 3, the basic methodology and structure of the diagnostic toolbox are introduced. Section 4 gives some results of our approach using a real clinical data. The conclusions of this paper are presented in section 5.

2.0 BASIC HIDDEN MARKOV MODELS (HMMs)

Hidden Markov models (HMM) have been widely applied in automatic speech recognition. In this field, signals are encoded as temporal variation of short time power spectrum (Rabiner 1989), (Al Ani et al. 1996), (Al Ani et al. 1994). HMM applications are now being extended to many fields such as pattern recognition, signal processing, modeling and control of dynamic systems. In general, the HMMs approach seems to be promising in other fields such as in medical diagnosis and in other types of system monitoring (Bunks et al. 1998), (Smyth 1994). They are well suited for the classification of one or two dimensional signals. A HMM is a double stochastic process with one underlying process that is not observable but may be estimated through a set of processes that produce a sequence of observations. They may be used for the treatment of problems where information is uncertain and incomplete. Their use necessitates two stages: a training stage where the stochastic process is estimated through extensive observation and an application stage where the model may be used in real-time to obtain sequences of maximum probability. HMM models owe their success to the existence of many algorithms which are efficient and reliable. For the training stage, the Baum-Welsh algorithm (Baum 1967), (Baum 1970) has become very popular due to its reliability and efficiency. This algorithm has since been extended to include many different probability distribution functions and proofs of convergence are now available for these models. This method is based on the maximum likelihood criterion. Many works are now available on algorithms accounting for this as well as other criteria (Liporace 1982), (Bahl 1986, (Ephraim 87). Due to the non-convexity of the criterion, methods such as the simulated annealing are now used (Hamam et al. 1996), (Scilab 2000). The use of the trained HMM in real-time necessitates the use of an efficient algorithm which gives the state sequence of maximum probability. The Viterbi algorithm (Viterbi 1967) fulfills this need. This algorithm is a polynomial time dynamic programming algorithm. It is very efficient, very reliable and robust.

A Hidden Markov Model is defined by the triplet

$$\lambda = (\Pi, A, B)$$

where Π, A and B are the initial state distribution vector, matrix of state (q) transition probabilities and matrix of measurement probability distribution, respectively.

$$A = [\mathrm{a_{ij}}], \mathrm{a_{ij}} = P(q_{t+1} = j | q_t = i),$$
$$B = [b_j(O_t], \; b_j(O_t) = P(O_t | \mathrm{q_t} = \mathrm{j}),$$
$$\Pi = [\pi_1, \pi_2, \ldots, \pi_N], \pi_i = P(q_0 = i),$$
$$i, j \in \{1,2,\ldots,N\} t \in \{1,2,\ldots T\}$$

The observation may be discrete or continuous. In our case it is considered as continuous gaussian observation.

In general, at each instant of time t, the model is in one of the states q_i. It outputs $\mathbf{O}_t$ with probability $b_j(\mathbf{O}_t)$ and then jumps to state q_j with probability $\mathbf{a}_{ij}$. The model may be obtained off-line by training.

The state transition matrix represents the structure of the HMM. An example of three state HMM is shown in figure 1.

2.1 Structures of HMMs

It is possible to obtain two principal structures of models according to the restrictions of the elements in the state transition matrix **A**. These models are:

- **Ergodic Models**

  In these models there is no transition restriction on the elements of the matrix *A*. All the states can be reached from whatever other state with only one transition.

- **Left-Right Models**

  These models have the following properties:

  - The first observation is produced when the Markov chain is in the first state.
  - The last observation is generated when the Markov chain is in the final state.
  - There is not possibility to come back to a precedent state.

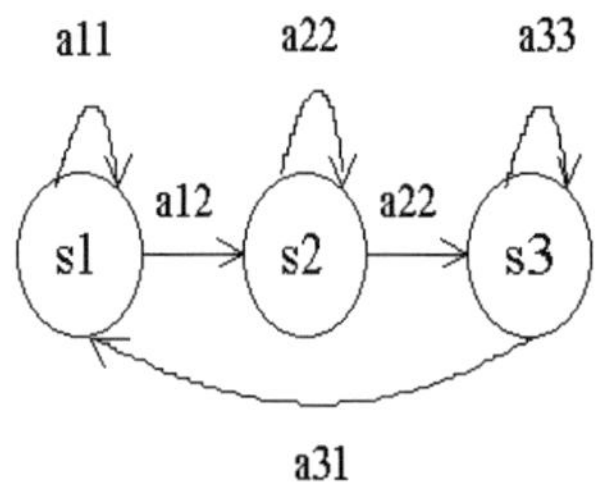

Figure 1: A three state HMM example

2.2 Training and recognition phases

In Patient monitoring, we may represent the evolution of by some hidden states corresponding to event 1, event 2,..., event n. For this process, the observations may be the continuous on-line or off-line clinical data.

To use HMM, two phases are needed: training phase and recognition phase.

Training phase: build one or many HMMs for the process (or processes w=1, ... , W) to be modeled. For example, in patient monitoring, we use a set of L different observation sequences to estimate the optimum parameters for each, i.e. creating a model for the w-th observation sequence.

Detection phase: For each hidden sequence in the test set characterized by an observation sequence O=$\mathbf{O}_1$, $\mathbf{O}_2$,..., $\mathbf{O}_T$, the occurrence probability

$$P_w = P(O|\lambda^w) \quad (1)$$

is calculated for each model. The unknown observation sequence O is then classified as the process

$$w^* = \arg\max_{w} P_w . \quad (2)$$

For the recognition phase, the forward probability function that evaluates probability of a partial observation sequence at node i may be used (Rabiner 1989)

$$\alpha_t(i) = P(o_1, o_2, \ldots, o_T, q_t = i|\lambda^w), \quad (3)$$

i.e. the probability of being in state i at time t given the model. This probability may be computed recursively.

The occurrence probability is obtained from

$$P(O|\lambda^w) = \sum_i \alpha_T(i). \quad (4)$$

In some applications of HMM, the most probable state sequence $Q^*_T = q^*_1\ q^*_2\ \ldots\ q^*_T$ that generates a given observation sequence $O = \mathbf{O}_1, \mathbf{O}_2, \ldots, \mathbf{O}_T$ is desired. To estimate the optimum state sequence, the Dynamic Programming Viterbi algorithm (Viterbi 1967) may be used.

For the training phase, there are many algorithms with different efficient approaches (Rabiner 1998). In this section we introduce briefly Viterbi and simulated annealing based training (Al Ani et al 1996), (Hamam et al. 1996).

- **Viterbi based training**

Starting from an initial model calculate iteratively

$$\tilde{\lambda}^w_{It+11} = \arg\max_{\tilde{\lambda}^w_{Itt}} \max_{Q} P(O, Q|\lambda^w_{It}), \quad (5)$$

until

$$\tilde{\lambda}^w_{It+11} = \tilde{\lambda}^w_{It} .$$

The subscripts here indicates the iteration number. The Viterbi algorithm and the new parameters are used here to trace the optimal state sequence Q^* for each training sequence. An observation vector is re-assigned a state if its original state assignment is different from the tracing result, i.e. assign Ot to i if q^*_t=i. If any observation vector is re-assigned a new state, use the new state assignment and repeat until $\tilde{\lambda}^w_{It+11} = \tilde{\lambda}^w_{It}$.

- **Simulated annealing based training**

Given the observation sequence O, a state sequence is generated at random. With the observations that are then assigned to each state, the mean and the variance of the sample are calculated. With these values the probability of generating O with the guessed state sequence is calculated. This is called the **initial cost**. Afterwards one state in the sequence is changed at random and the probability that this new state sequence has generated O is calculated, after changing the mean and the variance of the changed states. If the new probability is bigger than the old one, or the probability of acceptance

Paccept=exp((Pnew-Pold)/Temp),

where Temp is the temperature, is big enough, the change is saved. The probability of acceptance decreases with decreasing temperature so that for small values of Temp only better solutions are accepted. More details on this algorithm are found (Al Ani et al. 1998), (Hamam et al. 1996) and (Scilab 2000).

3.0 BASIC METHODOLOGIE

The toolbox is organized in such a manner to be interactive with the user. It is organized as three phases: **training phase**, **state interpretation phase** and **detection phase**.

1. **Training phase:** Using a given training data set, a corresponding set of modes is constructed using one of the following three approaches:

- **Baum-Welch_Liporace training approach:** In this case Maximum likelihood training based algoritm (Rabiner 1989), (Liporace 1982) .
- **Simulated annealing training approach:** Hamam's algorithm discussed in section 2 .
- **Viterbi training approach:** In this case Maximum a posteriori Viterbi training based algorithm discussed in section 2 is used .

In order to use Baum-Welch-Liporace or Viterbi algorithms, we need to cluster the data into a given number of states and initialize the parameters of the models. Thus, two clustering algorithms are implemented (Scilab 2000):

- K-mean algorithm and
- Simulated annealing vector quantization algorithm.

The simulated annealing training algorithm need no a priori clustering, however the number of states must be given.

2. State interpretation phase

Given training clinical observation sequences and their Hidden Markov Models, this phase allows to segment and interpret off-line the pathophysiological state sequence. The interpretation of each state will be useful for on-line detection and interpretation of the on-line state sequence. The identification of state-space trajectories is useful concept in diagnosis since some disorders can only be distinguished from each other by the sequences of pathophysiological states that they follow in time. The probabilistic concept of HMMs capture the uncertainty inherent in state interpretation.

3. Off-line or on-line Detection phase

Once the HMMs are available, the detection of hidden pathophysiological states in a given observation sequence is possible. This may be done by two consecutive steps:

- Step1: Selection of the model that gives the maximum likelihood (equation 1).

- Step 2: Pathophysiological state detection either by using Viterbi dynamic programming algorithm for off-line detection (equation 5) or by calculating the forward probability for on-line detection (equation 3). In the second case a sliding window is used on the observation sequence.

4.0 CASE STUDY

As an example, the respiratory activity diagnosis is considered to test the toolbox performances. Our experiment concern Sleep Apnea class detection (Chesson 1999). The main types of apneas are : obstructive, central and mixed We used real data from different patients. For apnea detection (pathophysiological state), only the measurements of the respiratory activities: Upper airway flow, esophagic pressure and gastric pressure are considered. These measurements are stochastic in nature and patient dependent. We considered that the number of these events are known a priori. The results of apnea and pathophysiological state detection are satisfactory and a good apnea detection was obtained. Figure 2 gives a simulation example for 2 states events: nominal and sleep apnea breathing case (this event lasts 10 seconds or longer).

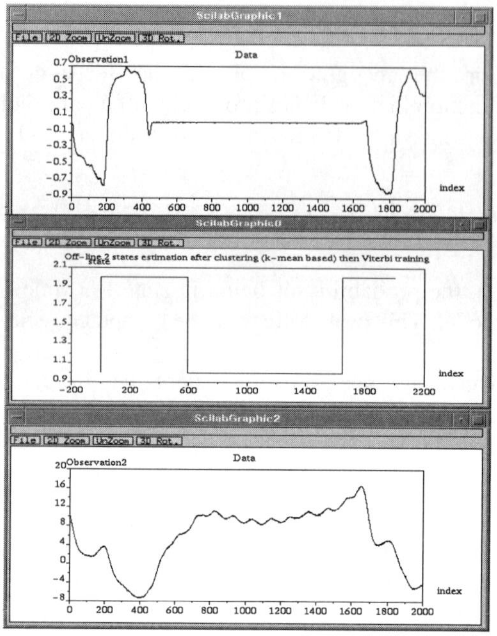

Figure 2. Sleep apnea simulation results. From top to down: airway flow, esophagic pressure and gastric pressure.

5. CONCLUSIONS

In this paper, a brief description of the elements of a HMM based diagnosis toolbox in Scilab environment is presented.

The HMMs may be used to provide a predictive estimate of pathophysiological states. However, to use them, some hypothesis must be satisfied. In this paper the following assumptions were made:

- The process is described by a first order Markov chain.

- A prior knowledge of the pathophysiological states and their measurement data are available for model training purpose.

- The pathophysiological states are assumed to be discrete.

Clearly, a learning based diagnosis system, such as our diagnosis system, is an interdisciplinary field which lies at the intersection of clinical medicine, computer science, AI and biomedical engineering. Thus the use of this system necessitates a balanced distribution of clinicians and computer scientists.

This toolbox is now being tested on many different breathing data for robustness and reliability.

5.0 REFERENCES

Chesson, A. Jr.; M. Littner; D. Davila; W. M. Anderson; M. Grigg-Damberger; K. Hartse; S. Johnson and M. Wise. 1999. "Sleep-Related Breathing Disorders in Adults: Recommendations for Syndrome Definition and Measurement Techniques in Clinical Research." SLEEP, Vol. 22, No. 5.

Al Ani, T. and Y. Hamam. 1996. "An Integrated Environment for Hidden Markov Models - A Scilab Toolbox". IEEE Int. Conf. on CACSD, Dearborn.

Al Ani, T. and H. Guellif. 1994. "Modèles de Markov cachées théorie et technique de base-Partie I." INRIA Report 2196.

Bunks, C.; T. Al Ani and D. McCarthy. 1998. "Using Hidden Markov Models on Acoustic Sensor Data for Machine Condition Monitoring and Prognostics". Workshop on Enhancement of Helicopter Fault Diagnostic Methodologies, Virginia Beach, VA. USA, 26-28 March 1998.

Baum, L. E.; T. Petrie; G. Soules and N. Weiss. 1970. "A maximization technique occurring in the statistical analysis of probabilistic functions of Markov chains," Ann. Math., 41(1), pp. 164-171.

Bahl, L. R.; P. F. Brown; P. V. De Souza and R. L. Mercer. 1986. "Maximum mutual information estimation of hidden Markov model parameters for speech recognition," Proc. ICASSP'86, Tokyo, pp. 49-52.

Baum, L.E. and J.A. Eagon. 1967. "An inequality with application to statistica estimation for probabilistic functions of Markov processe and to a modl for ecology." Bull. Armmer. Soc. 77, pp 360-363.

Ephraim, Y.; A. Dembo and L. R. Rabiner. 1987. "A minimum discrimination information approach for hidden Markov modeling." Proc. IEEE Int. Conf. Acoust. Speech and Signal Process, pp. 25-28, Dallas.

Hamam, Y. and T. Al Ani. 1996. "Simulated annealing approach for Hidden Markov Models." 4th WG-7.6 Working Conference onOptimization-Based Computer-Aided Modeling and Design, ESIEE,France, May 28-30.

Larsson, J. E.. 1995. "Model-Based Diagnosis of the Human Body." Yfantis, E. A., (Ed.), Intelligent Systems, Kluwer Academic Publishers, pp. 405-412.

Larsson, J. E.. 1995. "A toolbox for fast Model-Based Diagnosis." Knowledge Systems Laboratory, Technical report KSL-95-06, Stanford University.

Liporace, L. R.. 1982. "Maximum likelihood estimation for multivariate observations of Markov sources." IEEE Trans. Inform. Theory, IT-28, pp. 729-734.

Morris, A. H., 1993. "Paradigms in management, in Pathophysiologic Foundations of Critical Care." M. R. Pinsky and J.-F. A. Dhainaut, eds., Baltimore, MD, pp.193-206.

Rabiner, L. R.. 1989. "A Tutorial on Hidden Markov Models and Selected Application in Speech Recognition." Proc. IEEE, vol. 77, no. 2, pp. 267-296.

Scilab 2000, "A free CACSD Package by INRIA-France," http://wwwrocq.inria.fr/scilab/.

Smyth, P.. 1994. "Hidden Markov Models for fault detection in dynamic systems." Pattern Recognition," vol. 27, pp. 149-164.

Steimann, F. and K. P. Adlassnig. 1993. "Clinical monitoring with fuzzy automata." Technical Report MES-2, University of Vienna.

Uckun, S.. 1993. "Intelligent Systems in Patient Monitoring and Therapy Management: a survey of research projects." Knowledge Systems Laboratory, Technical report KSL-93-32, Stanford University.

Viterbi, A. J.. 1967. "Error bounds for convolutional codes and asymptotically optimum decoding algorithm." IEEE Trans. Inform. Theory, IT-13, pp. 260-269.

Wright, D. et al.. 1991. "Critical incidents in the intensive therapy unit." Lancet, 338: pp. 676-678.

AN OVERVIEW OF MODELING AND INTEGRATION OF NEUROLOGICAL DYNAMICS WITH SYMBOLIC STRUCTURES (MINDSS)

Troy D. Kelley
Army Research Laboratory

KEYWORDS - Cognitive Modeling, Hybrid Models, Machine Learning

ABSTRACT

The Human Research and Engineering Directorate (HRED) of the U.S. Army Research Laboratory (ARL) is developing a functional level, integrated computer simulation of human cognition. The computer simulation will run on ARL's high performance computing (HPC) center assets which include the ARL's "super computers." ARL is working closely with major U.S. universities (Harvard, Carnegie Mellon, and the University of California at Riverside) to host disparate models on high speed computers. Functional models of human cognition include but are not limited to language, problem solving, and perception. The Modeling and Integration of Neurological Dynamics with Symbolic Structures (MINDSS) program will have two goals: 1) functional level modeling and 2) functional level integration with subsymbolic models. Functional modeling at the symbolic level will allow for "reverse engineering" of the brain, which will reveal the lower neurological substrates. By understanding and computer modeling the higher level functional areas of the brain, we can begin to unravel the underlying neurological substrates that foster particular functionalities. The MINDSS program will eventually culminate in a functional representation of the brain at multiple levels, with various key areas of brain functionality being emphasized from the neural level through the subsymbolic level to the symbolic level.

INTRODUCTION

U.S. armed forces are rapidly moving toward an information-intensive, digital battlefield with potentially massive amounts of data being presented to the individual combatant. Typical combat scenarios now require each soldier to assume more of the decision making burden. Determining how decisions are affected in an information intensive, time critical, cognitively stressful environment and how different types of information presentation can affect overall human information processing are the essential goals of the Modeling and Integration of Neurological Dynamics with Symbolic Structures (MINDSS) program.

The modeling and simulation of human cognition has been called one of the most difficult tasks scientists have ever undertaken (Pew & Mavor, 1998). One difficulty in human cognitive simulation, especially within the neural network architectures, is the inability of the computer architecture to simulate the vast number of connections between neurons that comprise the human brain. Today's typical large computer encompasses about a hundred million transistors in its printed circuits, whereas the neurons in the human brain outnumber this figure by a factor of about a thousand (Cotterill, 1998). Not only are the vast numbers of neurons difficult to simulate, but the connections between neurons, which vary with different levels of connection strength, are difficult to simulate as well. Some conservative estimates have calculated that the average brain has approximately $10^{(100,000,000,000,000)}$ possible states in a synaptic connection space (Churchland, 1989).

A comprehensive computer model of the human brain, down to the neurological level, is technologically unachievable in the foreseeable future. Currently, computers that simulate human cognitive behavior do so in very specific domains (e.g., chess, medical diagnosis), and are designed to operate in a manner that employs a computer's strengths (i.e., multiple high-speed calculations), and are not designed in ways that exactly mimic human cognitive processes.

Currently, there are two primary approaches to the modeling human cognition: symbolic models and neural networks. High-level symbolic models, which are most often used by the human factors community, are primarily used for the simulation of high-level decision making and complex problem solving. These simulations do not require enormous amounts of processing power and can typically be accomplished on the average desktop personal computer. Neural network models, however, are typically used to simulate perceptual motor skills and can be limited by the computer's processing power.

Related work done within ARL's Human Research and Engineering Directorate (HRED) has typically concentrated on task-level human performance modeling; however, the importance of human cognitive performance is increasingly being emphasized and addressed (Wojciechowski & Knapp, 1999; Archer & Lockett, 1997). Human modeling at the task level has included work done in the Improved Performance Research Integration Tool, (IMPRINT) (Beideman, Munro, & Allender, in press.; Allender, McAnulty & Beiderman, 1992).

Related work in the scientific community in the area of cognitive architectures includes neural nets, ACT-R, SOAR, EPIC, OMAR, COGNET, SAMPLE. The SAMPLE architecture has been used in the analysis of flight landing procedures (Baron, Zacharias, Muralidharan and Lancraft, 1980), and the OMAR architecture has been used in modeling of command and control systems (Deutch and Adams, 1995). However, both SAMPLE and OMAR are not complete cognitive architectures in that they do not represent all aspects of cognition (e.g., learning). The only two high level symbolic cognitive modeling environments representative of a "unified theory of cognition" are ACT-R and SOAR. The cognitive modeling environment ACT-R is currently being used to model the tasks of the tactical action officer in submarines (Gray, Kirschenbaum, and Ehret, 1997) as well as modeling radar operators in Naval ships (Marshall, 1995); however, the work is still preliminary and it is difficult to assess its impact (Pew & Mavor, 1998). The SOAR architecture has been used to simulate fixed wing pilots in a theater of war, competing successfully with human adversaries (STOW-E in 1995, STOW-1997); however, numerous modifications had to be made to the SOAR architecture in order to allow it to behave in an appropriately competitive manner. SOAR and ACT-R both are high level symbolic architectures capable of representing human decision making. However, there is considerable debate as to whether lower level neurological architectures (i.e., neural nets) would be capable of simulating high-level reasoning skills (Sharkey & Sharkey, 1995; Touretzky, 1995).

APPROACH

Our approach to the MINDSS program has two major areas of concentration: 1) functional level modeling and 2) functional and neurological model integration.

The first goal of the MINDSS program is to model major functional areas of the brain using both high level symbolic representations as well as lower level neurological representations. It is our belief that the increased computing power afforded by the Department of Defense's high performance computing (HPC) (i.e., supercomputers) resources will allow for functional level modeling using neural nets. These key areas of functionality include but are not limited to language processing, decision making, problem solving, perceptual processing, emotion, skill acquisition, and knowledge organization. The importance of this step is that functional modeling of the brain provides more immediate applicability to practical areas of research interest (vision systems, decision support systems). Using both high level models and low level models will facilitate applicability to our research interests and will simultaneously, allow us to explore broader theoretical questions about the viability of neural nets to complex decision-making tasks.

The functional area development and modeling will lay the groundwork for the second major area of concentration for the MINDSS program. Functional modeling at the symbolic level will allow for "reverse engineering" of the brain which will reveal the lower neurological substrates. By understanding and computer modeling the higher level functional areas of the brain, we can begin to unravel the underlying neurological substrates that give rise to particular neurological functionalities.

The MINDSS program will then culminate in a functional representation of the brain at multiple levels, with various key areas of brain functionality being emphasized from the neural level, through the subsymbolic level, to the symbolic level. The integration of symbolic and neurological architectures into one model of the brain would allow for three major advances:

1) Prediction of brain states by using the cognitive symbolic level to predict neurological level dynamics and states. Such prediction would allow the effects of cognitive (symbolic) tasks to be understood at the neurological level and inform effects of neurological changes in brain states (from nutrition, fatigue, dehydration and stress).

2) Integration would also validate existing symbolic models for psychological plausibility. Symbolic level cognitive models would be tested against corresponding neurological data for fit and consistency.

3) Integration of the perceptual and motor components of perception (auditory and vision) to allow for understanding of the dynamics and interaction of cognition and perception.

UNIVERSITY PARTICIPATION

The MINDSS program has established interest from leading academic brain researchers from institutional, government, and academic settings from around the world. Cooperative research and development agreements (CRADAs) are currently being used to leverage the research activities of participating major universities who are interested in developing computational models of the human brain. The three universities who are currently participating in the CRADA sponsored research are Carnegie Mellon University, Harvard University, and the University of California at Riverside. These universities represent only the initial stages of larger university participation in the MINDSS program. Each university researcher will, in cooperation with HRED researchers, address a subset of the larger functional areas of brain operation (language, perception, motor skill, knowledge acquisition); thus, each functional subset of researchers will have its own technical goals and applicability to different research interests.

CURRENT RESEARCH

The three university participants from Harvard University, Carnegie Mellon University and the University of California at Riverside fall into the functional modeling category of language processing and language manipulation.

The University of California at Riverside is developing a large memory matrix from conversational text gathered from the news groups of the internet. This computer model develops a representation of the relationships between words, based on their co-occurrence rates within conversational text. This type of model has important implications for the MINDSS program. First, it begins to lay the groundwork for the automated creation of a knowledge base that represents lexical concepts and categories developed from textual input. Second, it has implications for a host of language specific models including language translation systems, bilingual research, text difficulty ratings and data mining.

Carnegie Mellon University is investigating the development of a computer model of human conceptual categorization, called ATRIUM (Erickson & Kruschke, 1998). The computer model uses both rules and exemplars to determine how to classify a particular stimulus. This line of research has implications for target recognition systems, as well as higher level human decision-making processes that rely on the categorization of information.

Harvard University is currently constructing and evaluating computational models of how one retrieves the pronunciations of words during speech. This model has implications for lower levels of language processing and speech generation systems.

MODELING INTEGRATION

Functional level models of human cognition will be developed by our university participants using CRADA agreements. These functional level models will correspond to major areas of human cognition including language, memory and decision-making. Further researcher participation will be conditional on developing functional areas not already covered by previous researchers. As the functional areas of research broaden, and as university participation increases, more and more aspects of the human cognitive system will be simulated and modeled. While much of the higher level functioning will be done with symbolic models, lower level processing will be done with neural nets.

The symbolic and neural networks that will comprise the hybrid MINDSS system will represent a diverse collection of models and modeling techniques. The cognitive models will most likely be developed in a variety of languages and architectures. The integration of these models could prove to be a most difficult challenge. As the MINDSS program progresses, it will come to be considered a "modular hybrid system" as described by McGarry, Wermter, and Macintrye (1999). Modular hybrid systems have rule and neural network-based architectures that cover the entire spectrum of integration: from two models that can send information in both directions, and can transform or change information in either model, to models that might simply share some bits of information, and only in one direction. This modular hybrid system, at least in its early stages, will represent all types of integration, at all levels of integration. Future development of the MINDSS program may build on the previous successes of the system and reduce or refine the amount of "overhead" among the different systems that are developed, but initial incarnations of the system will be very multi-modal and model specific.

To facilitate model integration the development of a concise and comprehensive data dictionary will be one of the foundations of the integration plan. The data dictionary will include all relevant data elements (variables) within each computational cognitive model developed for the MINDSS program. The development of a data dictionary will then in turn facilitate a data level integration. The goal is to enable models within MINDSS program to communicate with each other. This communication process, when possible and applicable, will be driven by the current research in brain functioning and cognitive mechanisms.

CONCLUSION

Computational simulation of the human cognitive processes can lead to wealth of knowledge and scientific discovery by revealing the dynamic intricacies of the human mind. Much of progress in modeling human cognition has been accomplished in the past 20 years, but advances in computer hardware technology will greatly enhance the capabilities of computationally intensive cognitive modeling environments. It is our intention to use a variety of established techniques (e.g., production systems, neural nets, hybrid architectures) to model the interactions and dynamics of the human cognitive system for the purpose of understanding a variety of human cognitive processes.

REFERENCES

Allender, L. McAnulty, D. M., & Bierbaum, C. (1992). Using Simulation to Support Testing: Implications of a HARDMAN III Application. In *Proceedings of the 34th Annual Military Testing Association* (San Diego, CA). Military Testing Association.

Archer, R. & Lockett, J. WinCrew- A Tool for analyzing Performance, Mental Workload and Function Allocation Among Operators. Published in *the Proceedings of the ALLFN'97: Revisiting the Allocation of Functions Issue.* Galway, Ireland. 1997. VOL II pp. 157-165.

Baron, S., Zacharias, G., Muralidharan R., & Lancraft, R., (1980). PROCUR: A model for analyzing flight crew procedures in approach to landing. *In Proceedings of the Eighth IFAC World Congress*, Tokyo, Japan.

Beideman, L. R., Munro, I. & Allender, L. (in press). *IMPRINT modeling for selected crusader research issues.* (Technical Report), Aberdeen Proving Ground, MD. U. S. Army Research Laboratory

Churchland, P.M. (1989). *On the nature of theories: A neurolocomputational perspective.* In "Mind Design II", Cambridge, MA: MIT Press.

Cotterill, R. (1998). *Enchanted Looms.* Cambridge, UK: Cambridge University Press,

Deutsch, S.E., & Adams, M. (1995). The operator-model architecture and its psychological framework. In *Proceedings of the Sixth IFAC Symposium on Man-Machine System.* Cambridge, MA: Massachusetts Institute of Technology.

Erickson, M. A., & Kruschke, J. K. (1998). Rules and exemplars in category learning. *Journal of Experimental Psychology: General, 127,* 107-140.

Gray, W. D., Kirschenbaum, S.S., and Ehret, B.D. (1997). The precis of Project Nemo, phase 1: Subgoaling and subschemas for submariners. In *Proceedings of the Nineteenth Annual Conference of the Cognitive Science Society.* Hillsdale, NJ: Lawrence Erlbaum.

Pew, W. R., & Mavor, A. S. (Eds.) (1998)., *Modeling human and organizational behavior.* Washington DC.:National Academy Press.

Marshall, S. P. (1995). *Learning in tactical decision-making situations: A hybrid model of schema development.* Presented at the ONR Hybrid Learning Kick-off Meeting, Washington, DC, August 3-4.

Sharkey, A.J.C., & Sharkey, N.E. (1995). Cognitive modeling: Psychology and connectionism. In the *Handbook of Brain Theory and Neural Networks,* M. A. Arbib, ed. Cambridge, MA: MIT Press.

McGarry, K., Wermter, S., & Macintrye, J. (1999). Hybrid Neural Systems: From Simple Coupling to Fully Integrated Networks. *Neural Computing Surveys, 2,* 62-93.

Touretzky, D. S. (1995). Connectionist and symbolic representations. In the *Handbook of Brain Theory and Neural Networks,* M. A. Arbib, ed. Cambridge, MA: MIT Press.

Wojciechowski, J. Q., & Knapp, B. G. (2000). *Command and control (C2) human performance modeling.* Preseneted to the Advanced Simulation Technologies Conference (ASTC 2000) Washington DC.

GOLEM – MEDICAL MULTIMEDIA TRAINING SIMULATOR OF BODY FLUIDS AND ACID-BASE DISORDERS

Jirí Kofránek, Tomáš Velan, Patrick Janicadis, Roman Kerekeš
Department of Pathological Physiology
1st Faculty of Medicine, Charles University
Prague, Czech Republic
e-mail:kofranek@cesnet.cz

KEYWORDS

Education, Interactive, Physiology, Simulators, Trainers

ABSTRACT

We have created the multimedia medical computerised training simulator "GOLEM" for learning diagnostics and therapy of the of the critical clinical disorders of body fluids homeostasis. Our aim was to enable students to try out solving of individual critical situations out of reality on simulator. The theoretical basis of the simulator is the mathematical formulation of the relationship of homeostasis of the internal environment (acid/base and electrolyte equilibrium, of transport of blood gases, of osmotic and volume homeostasis), respiration, circulation and kidneys inclusive of the regulatory influence of relevant hormones and the influence of some therapeutic procedures. Mathematical description consists of 38 non-linear differential equations and containing 89 input and 179 output variables. Despite this complexity, the simulation model represents real body function with sufficient fidelity. When building the multimedia components of the simulator we have used developer's tools from Macromedia and for the development of the simulation models we have used developer's tools from MathWorks (Matlab and Simulink). The integration of the multimedia components, hypertext and simulation models interface was realised using original software tool (Control Web, developed by Moravian Instruments), which was originally designed to realise long distance control and measurement using PC and Internet. The simulator was implemented as an teleeducation tool on University Intranet.

1. THE PHYSIOME PROJECT

Progress in the field of modelling in biology and medicine is closely associated with the topic of *mathematically formalised description of biological reality* – i.e. transformation of description of a network of relations from verbal description to formalised description in the mathematical language. Similarly to theoretical physics, where experimental research in physics and related sciences is being interpreted, a new physiological approach called *integrative physiology* attempts to formalize description of mutual regulations in physiology. Here, methodological tools are computer models. Activities in this field are summarized in the international project *PHYSIOME*, which is a descendant of the *GENOME* project, mapping the sequence of the nucleic acid of the human genome (*GENOME* is expected to be finished after the year 2002). The aim of the *PHYSIOME* project* is to integrate biophysical biochemical and physiological knowledge by application of models of physiological systems (Bassingthwaighte, 1999).

The results of this project can be immediately employed in medica[l] education. *Linking multimedia environment*, serving as a graphica[l] and sound interface, *with simulation models*, facilitate[s] demonstration of complex regulatory processes (and thei[r] disorders) by an interactive simulation game. Outputs of suc[h] models are visualized as curves in charts or as changing pictures, movement of objects etc. They represent, therefore, *idea[l] combination for explanation of causal relations and multipar[ametric] processes.* Computer models for biology and medicine are directly used in *sophisticated educational programmes and medica[l] simulators*, the importance of which will further increase with the expansion of computers and Internet.

With the possibility of commercial use, there is a *change in the view of formal description of physiologic reality that underlies simulation models*. Detailed formalised description (in the form of mathematical equations or better algorithms written in a text form of a programming language) as a *pure scientific subject* has now suddenly become a confidential *technological know-how*, because of potential competition. Since we have been involved in the work on simulation of biomedical systems for more than twenty years we accepted the current situation as a challenge. Our aim is to develop multimedia educational programmes that utilize various simulation games. One of those is a simulator of physiologica[l] functions called Golem**.

2 HOW TO DO IT?

Two kinds of problems were to be solved by construction of the medical simulator:

1. The development of the *simulation model of physiological functions* – the theoretical work itself based on formalization of physiological relations.

---

* http:// physiome.org

** This research was partially supported by the Charles University Grant No. 217/1998 and by the Research and Development Initiative MSM-111100008 (physiome.cz).

2. The *development of the simulator* of physiological functions (the working title Golem is used) and the use of the simulator in education – practical application of the theoretical results. In addition, we have always supported the Internet accessibility of the project results.

Each of the problems is specific and requires using different developer's tools (fig. 1).

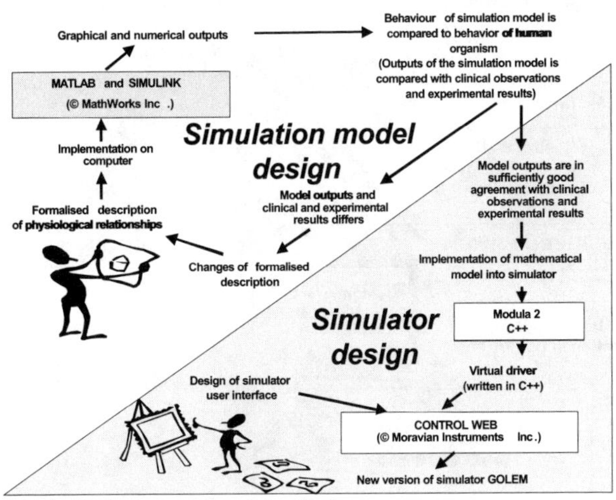

Fig. 1. Gradual generation of the simulator.

3. SIMULATION CHIPS

The *theoretical concept* of the simulator is a large simulation model based on mathematical formalization of the transfer of blood gasses, acid-base, electrolyte, volume and osmotic equilibrium, the function of the respiratory and urinary system, including the influence of hormones. The model design is based on classical models of Guyton *et al.* (1972), Cameron (1977), Ikeda *et al.* (1979), and Coleman *et al.* (1983), which we have sufficiently redesigned and extended. It consists of *38 non-linear differential equations* and contains *89 input* and *189 output* variables.

Whereas developing an educational simulator is a programmer's work, formalisation of global physiological relations is rather than creating software complicated scientific problem. The effective solution needs using adequate tools. Luckily for us, in the last years substantial progress has been made in the field of *software development tools for the design and testing of simulation models.* Therefore, we could utilize the advantage of professional tools by *Mathworks (Matlab, Simulink and related libraries).* These tools allow creating simulation models in an easy way and illustrating their structure graphically as linked simulation circuits associated into "simulation chips". In the same way as in electrical circuits electrical current is conveyed, in simulation chips information about the values of the variables is carried. The behaviour of the "software chips" can be easily tested with the help of adequate software tools for computer simulation: similarly to an electric scheme, where it is possible to carry current on individual "pins" of the chip, the same manner can be used to carry selected value (or some time course of values) of an appropriate variable to the software chip. At the same time, just by mouse, "measuring displays" can be "connected" to the outputs to register the values as long as the simulation is running (fig. 2-3).

The analogy with an electric schema resides also in the fact, that values of variables can be found not only on outputs of a subsystem (represented by the simulating "chip"), but also anywhere inside the system – display or virtual "oscilloscope" can be interactively with the mouse, connected to whatever contact (it means to whatever line) on the scheme. And eventually once the simulation programme has started selected values can be registered (or stored)

Furthermore, drawn structures are in the environment of Simulink "alive" – constant or variable values could be entered using mouse in the appropriate inputs of the software simulation "chips" (i.e subsystems of the simulation models) and output variables could be detected in digital or graphical representation on the outputs.

This way, the Simulink scheme can be a *very useful documentation* itself. Because of the international collaboration, it is very useful that Mathworks develops visualizator of Simulink schemes for Internet - e.g. in the PHYSIOME project it will be possible to describe the structure of the physiological regulatory circuits directly on WWW pages in Simulink schemes, which are becoming one of the industrial standards. Components (simulation chips) can be stored in *libraries*, and then withdrawn by a single mouse movement and reused in a new application. Using such a procedure we generated several libraries divided by physiological subsystems (acid-base equilibrium and transfer of blood gasses, respiration kidneys, water and ion equilibrium, circulation etc.)

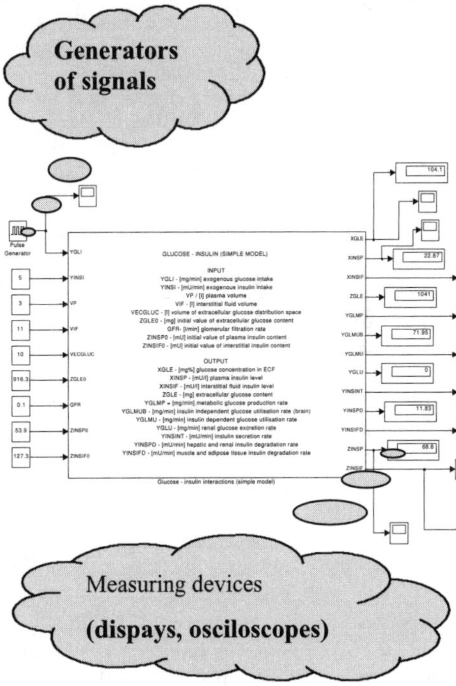

Fig. 2. Simulation chips and simulation circuits as the results of Simulink are analogical to electronic circuits. Here, however, information is conveyed instead of electrical current. In electrical circuits, controlled power supplies and generators of signals can be connected to the electrical joints and the course of the electrical voltage can be displayed with measuring devices or oscilloscopes. Similarly, in the graphical environment of the Simulink programme, simulation model input values can be connected to separated "pins" of the simulation chips and the time-course of the corresponding variables can be registered on the virtual displays or oscilloscopes.

Mathworks' simulation tools are designed for specialists and are not very suitable for an inexperienced user, who wants only to "play". Even though user-friendly interface could be developed, *for the application of the simulation model in medical education it is still too complicated*. Therefore, we had to use different developer's tools for the educational *simulator of physiological functions* itself.

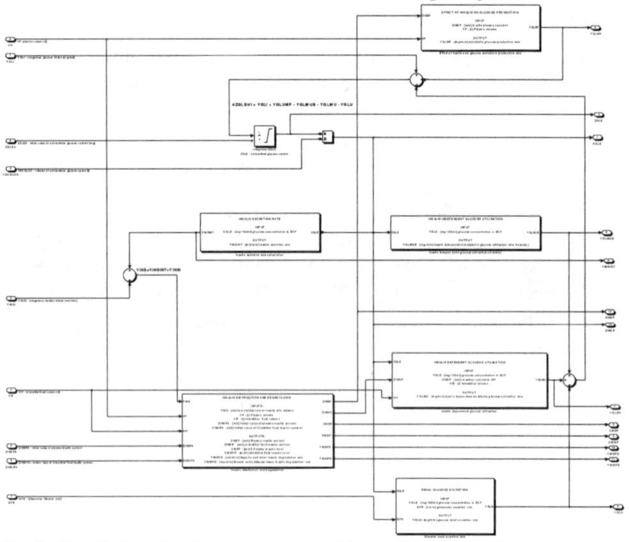

Fig. 3. Simulation circuits are constructed hierarchically, in the same way as in electronic circuits. In this figure, the inner structure of the simulation chip from the figure 2 is shown. Its structure resembles again an electrical network with interconnected integrated circuits. Small circles represent the inputs and outputs from the entire scheme to the corresponding input and output "pins" of the software chip. Rectangles represent another interconnected software simulation chips ("integrated circuits") of the lower hierarchical level.

4. COMPONENTS FOR GOLEM

"Svensk kvalitet (till Tjeckisa priser)" – "Swedish quality (for Czech prices)", is the motto on a handout of a Scandinavian distributor of a powerful software tool from the Czech Republic. Swedish people are very proud of the quality of their products, so if they claim in public that the development tool *Control Web* made by *Moravian Instruments Inc.* reached Swedish quality, it is a great honour for the group of authors who have been working very hard on the product from early 1990's. Nowadays, their effort peaked in the fact that their programme (its source code contains more than 2 million lines) is finding its way on the world market. Latest version of the programme could be used in Czech, English, German or even in Japanese characters. *Control Web* is mainly designed for development of *industrial visualization and control application for WIN32 platform** (collection, storing and processing of data, development of man-machine interfaces, etc.). The kernel of the Control Web system communicates trough a driver of a measuring/controlling adapter with an industrial appliance (fig. 4). User application created with the help of visualizing tools is then connected to the system kernel. Main structural components of the user application are *virtual devices* (communicating with each other by means of variables and messages).

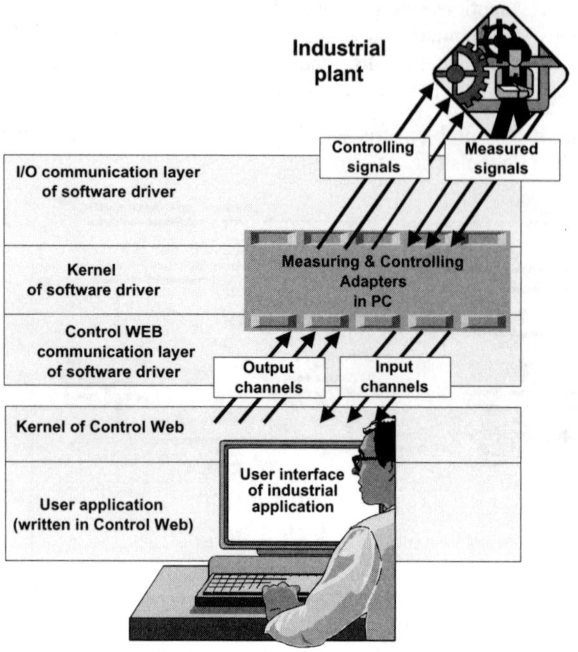

Fig. 4. Communication of the system Control Web with driver measuring controlling adapters during creation of industrial applications

Each of the virtual devices is a component, properties of which are easily modifiable using visualization and control elements. But not only this – each component is equipped with powerful programming tools as are local variables and user defined event-handling procedures. *Measured values* of the real world are delivered to the virtual devices through *input channels, control signals* from the environment are sent through *output channels*. Importantly, the system works in real time – every input/output channel is read in the moment when the virtual device (or a group of devices) asks for it. Real-time timing is monitored in detail and controlled. Virtual devices can be scheduled in exactly defined time and order.

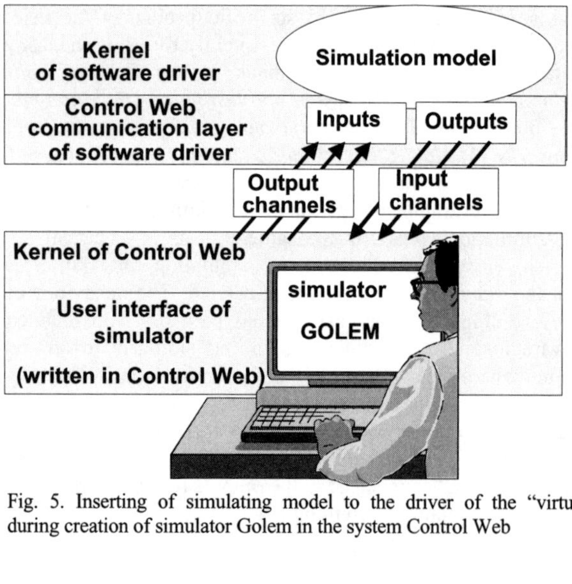

Fig. 5. Inserting of simulating model to the driver of the "virtual card" during creation of simulator Golem in the system Control Web

* http://www.mii.cz

The Control Web system supports very powerful means for development of the user interface of Golem simulator. For instance, it is easy to drag a device with the mouse from the group of virtual devices to the appropriate panel and then in an interactive dialog, set the values of its attributes, define its local variables or individual procedures (methods of the object) etc.

In order to take advantage of the developer's comfort of the Control Web system, *it was necessary to create a specific driver*, which would communicate (through software channels) with Control Web objects (see fig. 5). Contrasting to drivers for real measuring and control adapters, this *driver does not communicate with hardware of the adapters, but with the integrated simulation model.* If the driver is smart enough, the Control Web system is deceived. Input channels (leading to measuring devices) are treated as if they were measuring signals from a technological surrounding of the computer. In reality, they are the output variables of the simulation model. Through the driver, output channels of the Control Web control elements do not set active technological elements, but change inputs of the simulation model. The kernel of the simulator is a *virtual driver* containing the simulation model itself. The driver was implemented in C++. For its implementation, we used simulation model, of which the comfort of *Matlab* and *Simulink* convinced us. Furthermore, the virtual driver enables us to generate source code in C++ from the Simulink model using a special tool.

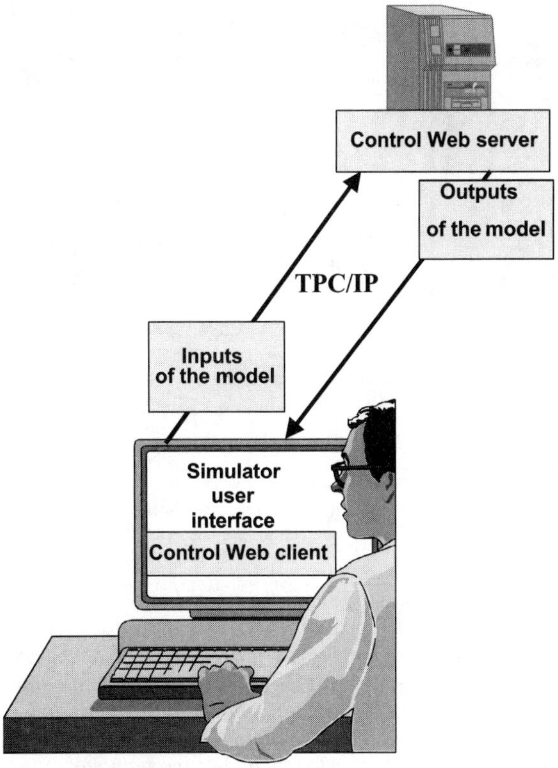

Fig. 6. Possibilities of the distributed educational simulating application.

Great advantage of the new version of Control Web is the *ActiveX container* included as one of the virtual devices, which represents a bridge connecting the Control Web system and the ActiveX properties and methods (OLE Automation). It is possible for example, to generate interactive educational animations in Macromedia Director system and store them as ActiveX components in the container.

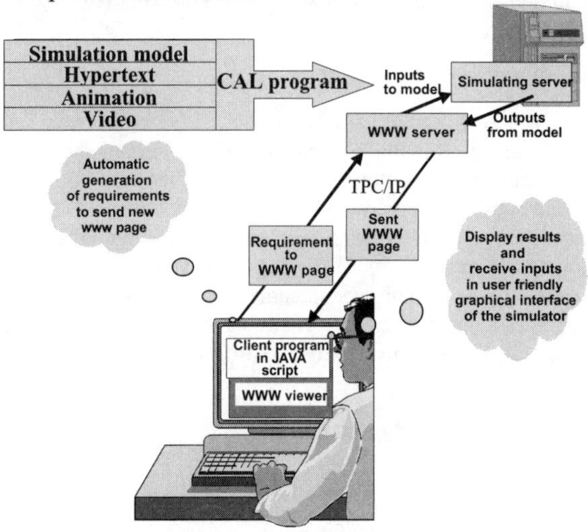

Fig. 7. Communication with distant educational simulating server, which was created in system Control Web by a common WWW browser.

Another indisputable advantage of the development of the simulator in the Control Web environment is that the system generates distributed solutions. This offers the possibility to develop a *distributed application*. Demanding numeric calculations of the simulator are processed on the server (Control Web) and visualization runs on the clients (fig. 6)

Apart from that, Control Web supports *visualization on any WWW clients*, because Control Web contains *full-value HTTP server*. This will help to *connect to the simulation educational server through a common WWW browser* (using Java applets for the display of basic virtual devices), which will be of great importance for distant educational programmes (fig.7).

5. GOLEM INSTEAD OF THE PATIENT

The practical result of our effort is Golem, a simulator of physiological functions. Simulator is drawn up so that its controlling would be as easy as possible. That is why the menus, buttons, switches (controlled by mouse), knobs (easy turnable by mouse and so appropriate values can be set), mouse controlled scroll bars, windows for inserting or displaying of numerical values etc.

Inputs of the simulator are:

- External conditions (as atmospheric pressure, concentration of gases in inspired air etc.) and initial values of some quantities.
- Amount of substances in the stores (before starting simulation).
- Rate of intake or loss of individual substances (ions, water, glucose) in/out of organism (through gastrointestinal tract or by infusion). Entering the rate of intake/loss enables arrangement of different scenarios of pathological disorders (for example diarrhoea, vomiting…) and their infusion therapy (by different types of infusion solution).

- Some of the internal parameters of physiological regulators in the model of simulation, their change can simulate different pathophysiological disorders of regulation (for example diabetes).

Outputs of the simulator appear:

- In windows with animated schemes of physiological subsystems: for quick orientation the colour of the window with numerical output is green in the case of normal parameters, the window is red if the physiological limit was exceeded, the window is light blue when the value is under the lower interval limit. Changing the values of individual quantities is often accompanied by changing animated schemes (for example by changing of "level", changing of dropping from a tap, changing direction of animated arrows etc.).
- In windows with graphical outputs: windows with physiological schemes and window with charts can be easily switched over using corresponding buttons.

From the pedagogic point of view it is very effective if we can *locally follow the response of individual physiological subsystems* to a change of values, which are regulated in other part of the organism. Therefore, we introduced to the simulator *the possibility of "detachment of regulation"* of some regulated physiological variables and their "switching over to setting input locally". A single push of the button under the window of appropriate variable (which is input to given subsystem) immediately disconnects the variable from the outer regulatory loop.

The values can be changed and the response of the subsystem to set values followed. It enables to confine during the simulation to specific physiological subsystem and study its behaviour independently of the complicated regulation relationships inside the whole organism and to observe behaviour of individual physiological relationships separately. This enables better understanding during the study.

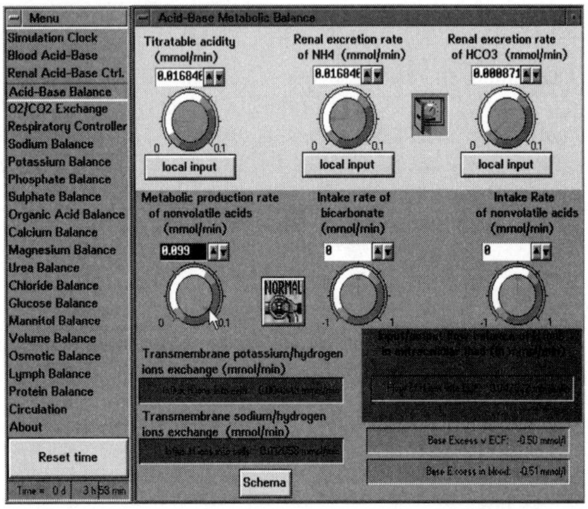

Fig. 8. Turning the knob we can increase the metabolic production rate of non volatile acids. By increasing the strong acid production, we cause metabolic acidosis.

After pushing the corresponding button the variable is connected to the regulatory loop again. By disconnecting of individual regulators we can observe separately the behaviour of independent regulatory loops and partial physiological subsystems. Thus, the simulator substitutes the whole scale of models of partial physiological subsystems and it can contribute to the understanding of a single physiological regulatory link.

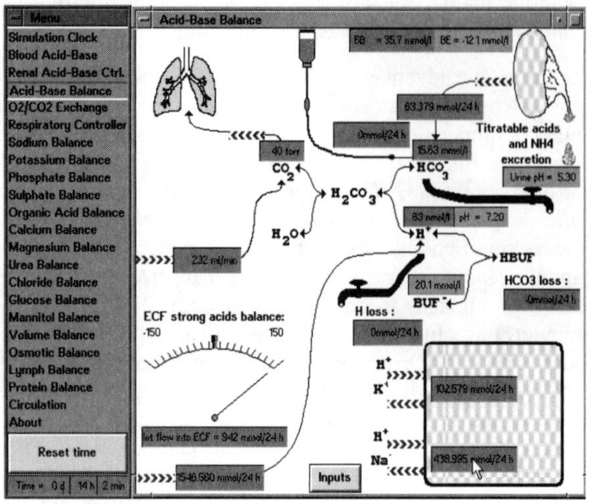

Fig. 9. Ratio of metabolic production and renal excretion of strong acids is highly increased. H^+/Na^+ and H^+/K^+ exchange on the cell membrane is activated. H^+ ions are buffered by intracellular and extracellular buffers.

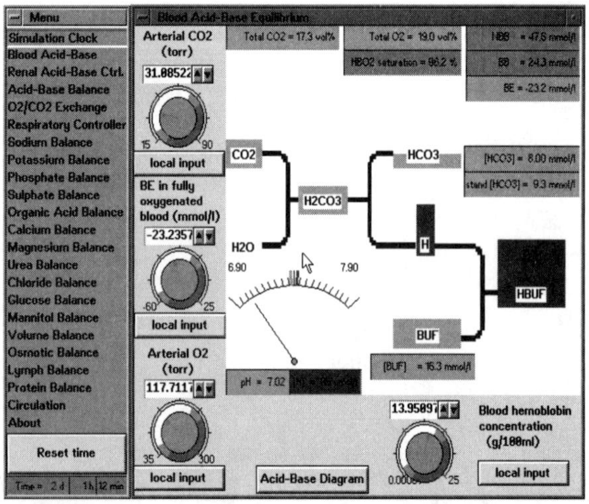

Fig. 10. Blood buffer system - the blood has been acidified, Base Excess and actual bicarbonate concentration are decreasing, and pCO_2 is also slowly decreasing.

Thanks to its complexity, the simulator enables practical demonstration of *continuity of physiological subsystems and how this continuity is manifested in different* pathophysiological situations. The simulator is able to simulate different *pathological situations and some therapeutic interventions by* changing rules its input values. The simple example of an acid-base disorder should demonstrate how easy it is to manipulate the simulator (fig. 8 – 14).

6. CONCLUSION

GOLEM is going to be a *very useful teaching device* to help understanding the basic rules of physiological regulations and the manifestations of their disorders in pathogenesis of different pathological conditions (Kofránek et al., 1997, 2000).

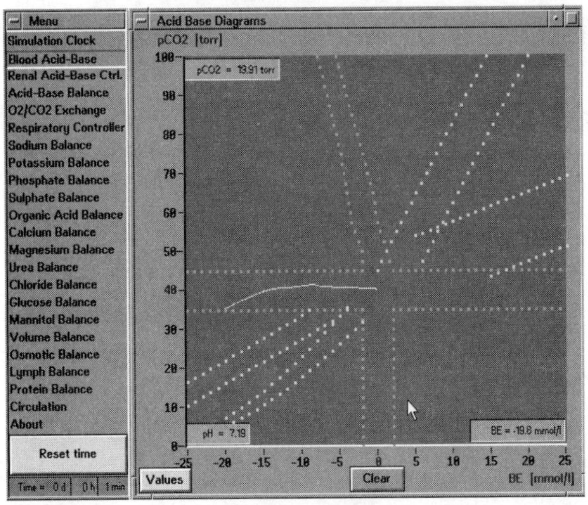

Fig. 11. Acid-base values on this compensatory diagram are in the acute metabolic acidosis range. This is the beginning of a progressive reaction by the ventilation centre to counteract metabolic acidosis.

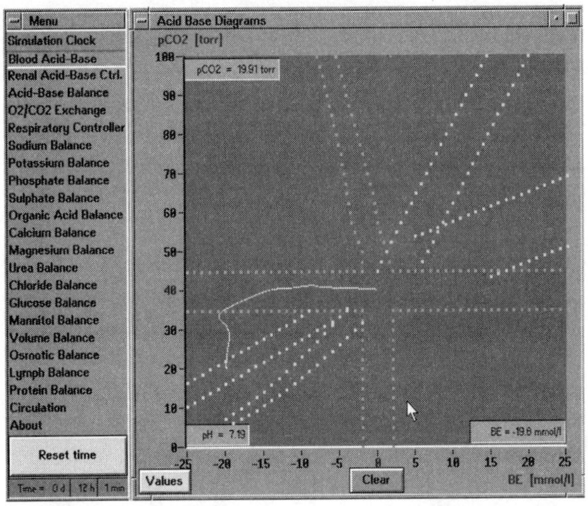

Fig. 12. Respiratory compensation is at a maximum in about 12 hours. Decreasing pCO2 is leading to a rise of arterial blood pH. Acid-base parameters are approaching a compensated metabolic acidosis range.

The simulator also allows carrying out *"virtual therapeutic interventions"*, so that we can start the therapy of a virtual patient in metabolic acidosis by an alkaline infusion. In virtual therapy we can also make a mistake. Nothing can happen, because the patient is virtual *(and his potential death is just only virtual) – but in the case of real patient this is not the true.* Our aim was to enable students to try out solving of individual critical situations out of reality on simulator.

REFERENCES

Bassingthwaighte, J.B. 1999. "Closing in on the Physiome Monster. Hierarchies, Independence and Interdependence in Strategies." In: *1999 Physiome Symposium in Seattle. Integrated biology of the heart.* (Yipintsoi, T., S. McCuloch, J. Caldwel, R.Reneman (Eds.)) University of Washington: 10-11.

Cameron, W.H. 1977. "A Model Framework for Computer Simulation of Overall Renal Function." *J. Theor. Biol.* vol. 66: 552-572.

Coleman, T. G. and J.E. Randall 1983. "HUMAN. A Comprehensive Physiological Model." *The Physiologist*, vol. 26, NO 1: 15-21.

Ikeda, N., F. Marumo and M. Shirsataka: "A Model of Overall Regulation of Body Fluids." *Ann. Biomed. Eng.* vol. 7: 135-166

J. Kofránek, T. Velan and R. Kerekeš. 1997. "Golem: A Computer Simulator of Physiological Functions as an Efficient Teaching Tool." In: *Legacy for 21st Cencury. Preceedings of the First Word Congress on Systems Simulation.*, (Teo, Z.M., W.C.Wong., T.I.Oren, R. Rimane (Eds.)), IEEE Singapore Section, Singapore., Singapore: 407-411.

J. Kofránek, T. Velan and P. Janicadis. 2000. "Computer Simulator of Body Fluids and Acid-Base Disorders as an Efficient Teleeducation Tool." In: *Modelling and Control Biomedical Systems 2000.* IFAC Symposium. (E. Carson, E. Salzeider (Eds.)). Pergamon, London 2000: 233-242

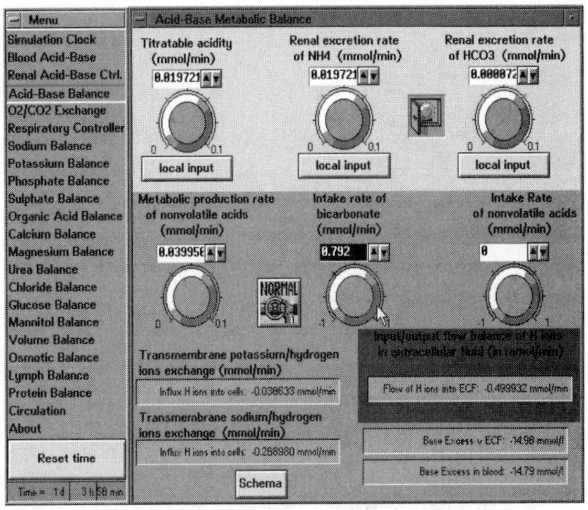

Fig. 13. The kidney's response progressively develops. Titratable acidity and NH_4^+ excretion increases, urine pH decreases. Renal response is in its maximum in 3-5 days. Only enough should be given to compensate pH. Turning the knob we are starting bicarbonate infusion therapy.

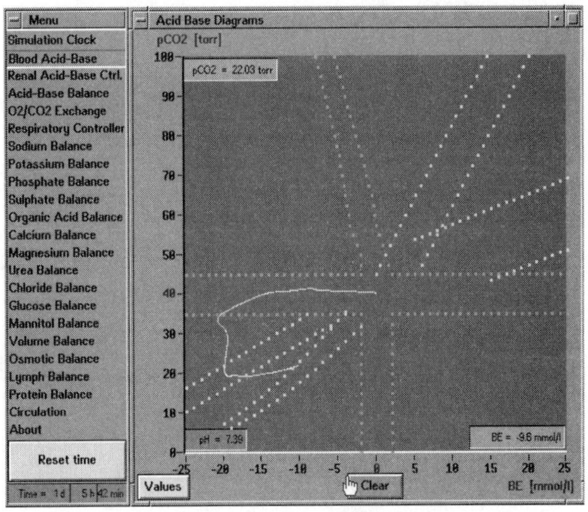

Fig. 14. BE and pH slowly increase after bicarbonate infusion. pCO_2 remains stable for a while (thanks to respiratory compensation), at its low level. We must take pCO_2 into account when choosing doses of alkaline infusion in order not to overdose, which can be dangerous.

RE-CONFIGURABLE DISTRIBUTED SIMULATION ENGINE FOR MULTIPLE USES

CAPT Joseph Celano, USN
Space and Naval Warfare Systems Command (SPAWAR)
PMW 131
celanoj@spawar.navy.mil

Jeffrey W. Wallace, Consultant
jeffrey.w.wallace@worldnet.att.net

Candace Conwell, SPAWAR PMW 131
clc@spawar.navy.mil

CDR Jeffrey McCampbell, USN, SPAWAR PMW 131
mccampbj@spawar.navy.mil

Yuh-Ling Su, SPAWAR PMW 131
yuhlings@spawar.navy.mil

KEYWORDS

Software engineering, distributed simulations, systems analysis, customer requirements, Kano

ABSTRACT

Most simulations are custom-built for a specific use case within a specific domain. As users become more sophisticated, the demand for non-domain simulation services increases. Users are demanding higher fidelity, faster runtimes, interfaces to real-world systems, common models, common components, and shared results. They want the option to use parallel processing for multiple replications or for increased resolution. Finally, users want use case-independent simulation services and to control use of the final product. User requirements evolve almost as fast as they can envision harnessing the technology they are watching evolve. Thus user requirements are never completely captured in a document and we refer to the growth in requirements as "unspoken requirements" for simulation. Many of these unspoken requirements will be fulfilled only with the application of distributed parallel processing. This paper offers an approach for addressing these types of "unspoken" user requirements By integrating key enabling technologies to build a re-configurable simulation engine that can be designed, coded and tested independent of the specific use-case applications software.

INTRODUCTION

A re-configurable distributed simulation engine (RDSE) provides application software a means to "snap-on" to a common engine consisting of a common set of simulation libraries or services. Possessing an open architecture, RDSE, while not fully designed and developed yet, is even in its beginning stages less brittle than those custom-built for specific use cases. Ideally, it could be used in a multiple situations including:

- Stand alone or distributed
- Single or multiple processors
- Single or multiple workstations
- Transparent to individual users
- Harnessing the power of sequential and/or parallel processing

In essence, the goal of a RDSE is to replicate in the simulation community what industry has done in computer gaming development. With RDSE focusing on the common elements of building a simulation, software developers are free to focus on constructing more robust applications for their customers.

Today's Situation

Approximately 80%of a simulation project's life cycle cost is spent on software maintenance, i.e.,. the testing, debugging and configuration management of the product. Despite insatiable user desires for more information technology, budgets continue to decline forcing the need for streamlining and savings while increasing quality of the product. The commercial gaming industry has adjusted by using common software engines to retain and expand its customer base. This is contrary to the simulation industry who continues to custom-build simulations for each user with a frustrated customer base who are craving more functionality.

Users are demanding high fidelity objects, interactions and environments. They want more speed with the higher fidelity and resolution. Realistic synthetic representation or stimulation of integrated systems is desired. At the same time, they want to run multiple simulations with and without real-world systems using common models with shared results. The big change is users now want to change how the simulation is used after delivery and want to use it differently than it was initially designed.

LOOKING BEYOND USER REQUIREMENTS

The Capability Maturity Model is widely recognized as a model for evaluating software process within an organization. However, it falls short in evaluating the user requirements. The Qualify Functional Diagram (QFD) offers a process improvement strategy, which can be used as a tool to aid a software design improvement process that provides insight in developing customer requirements (Richardson, 1997). In particular, QFD enables the software product development team to clearly specify and evaluate customer needs and wants and how those needs will be met.

Kano Requirements Model

To satisfy user requirements, one must understand how such requirements can be anticipated in order to meet user satisfaction. According the Kano Model, three types of user requirements must be considered to meet user needs (see Figure 1) (Kano, et al 1984).

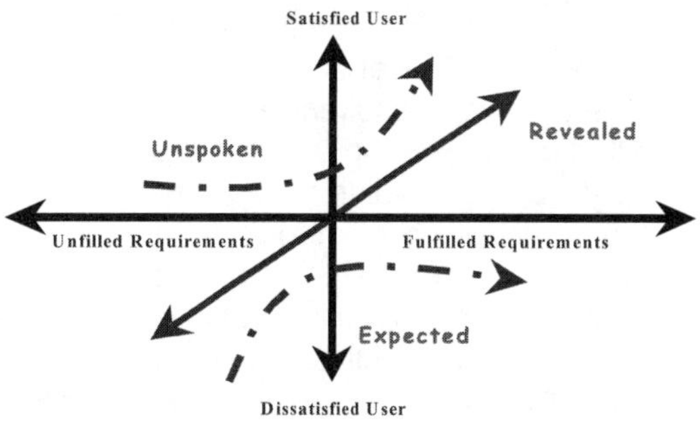

Figure 1. Kano Requirements Model

Revealed Requirements are typically what one is told by just asking the customer. Examples include an operational requirements document, market surveys, and requirements analysis. The level of satisfaction depends on proportion of the presence of the product. Custom-built simulation engines fall in this category.

Expected Requirements are those items the user fails to mention unless they are not delivered. These are basic expectations and sometimes called threshold requirements. Without fulfilling these requirements, the users become extremely dissatisfied. Meeting the expected requirements often goes unnoticed by the users. Products that do not meet these basic expectations will retain little or no value. Examples include a simulation having a graphical user interface and after action report generation.

Unspoken Requirements are difficult to discover since they are beyond customer expectations and often associated with outside software project's development objectives. Since the users do not envision them, their mere presence is excites them.

Again, these items are often unnoticed by the customer, but affords the greatest potential for increased market share if user requirements are satisfactorily met. For example, users would be delighted to get a 50:1 runtime speedup when they thought only a 10:1 was feasible with their particular simulation. This sets a new benchmark for customer satisfaction driving the user to thirst for more complex and different features.

User Increased Expectations

The Kano Model explains that the users desire to have unspoken requirements fulfilled as long as the features are perceived to add value. However, such new features are soon imitated by the competition resulting in the customers expecting them as routine (Mazur, 1996). As shown in Figure 2, fulfilled unspoken and revealed requirements eventually become expected. This generates new unspoken requirements. The goal for a simulation developer is to craft a technical strategy to anticipate these unspoken requirements prior to its competitors in order to gain and retain an unfair marketplace advantage.

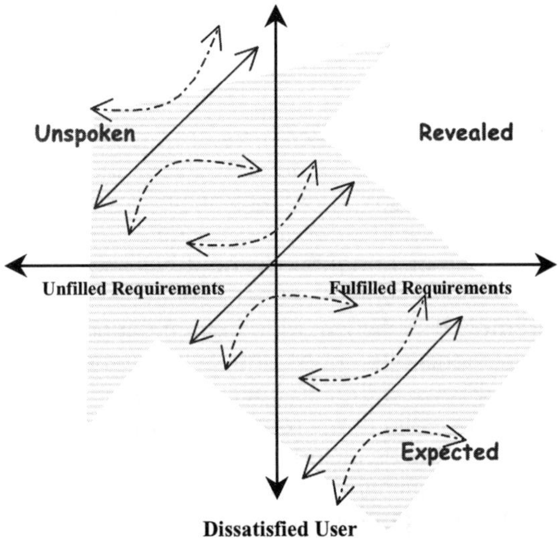

Figure 2. Fulfilled unspoken and reveal requirements eventually become expected. This generates new unspoken requirements.

- How does this relate the simulation industry? What are the users not saying, but want? Here are a few examples:

- Multiple repetitions of "what-if" analysis scenarios in MINUTES not HOURS;
- High-fidelity mission rehearsal with intelligent adversaries;
- High-fidelity wargaming that includes an ability to train on tactical decision aids;
- Process real time data;
- Visualize high-resolution environments and interactions; and,
- Do it all inside their competitor's business decision loop to assume an unfair advantage in their respective industry marketplace.

The Software Engineering Institute's "Product Line Program" suggests that future users requirements are best satisfied through a shared architecture built from common components (Carnegie Mellon University, 2000). This approach fosters strategic software reuse to achieve fast, efficient, predicable, low-cost, high quality production and maintenance.

One would then conclude that developing a re-configurable distributed simulation engine for multiple uses would provide an economically viable solution. This would be consistent with results of the Kano Model in asserting RDSE market opportunities as illustrated in Figure 3.

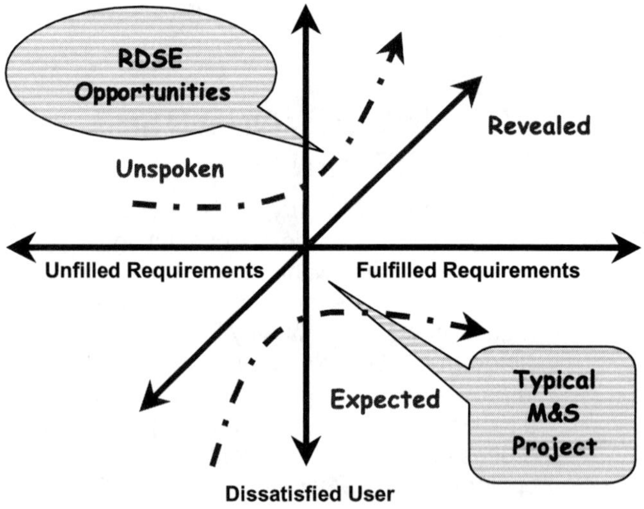

Figure 3. RDSE and the Kano Model

RDSE Requirements

What are the unspoken RDSE requirements? That is, what are the likely expectations of users once they become accustomed to the concept of having a simulation engine provided “off-the-shelf”? One must look beyond common objects and common components and build a simulation engine that utilizes "snap-together" product lines with interchangeable components. RDSE seeks to retain a development environment with inherent agility to flex to unanticipated customer needs. In essence, a simulation engine needs to be built under the same manufacturing philosophy current employed by the personal computer industry by quickly adapt to changing user requirements.

Simulation users are demanding M&S support that can only be accomplished by RDSE. These features include:

- Improved runtime with high volume entities
- Use of high fidelity models
- Improved connectivity, cognitive and adaptive behavior representations
- Fault tolerance
- Platform independence
- Processor independence
- Interface independence
- Multiple user
- Multiple views

Fitting into the SEI Product Line Program strategy and Kano Model, RDSE development applies business and acquisition guidelines that encourage development of common components. The objective is to entice future users to buy the simulation engine and write to the application program interface (API). This will result in freeing up customer funds to apply toward development of unique M&S application capabilities vice development and costly maintenance for a proprietary engine.

KEY TECHNOLOGY COMPONENTS

RDSE must include three essential simulation services modules that can be easily integrate in user-specified applications.

Modeling Services provide global time coordination between models as the overall simulation progresses in time. In addition, a uniform, inter-model interaction and synchronization mechanism, which hides the programming complexity of allowing the models to be distributed arbitrarily among some set of processors, is required. Additionally, the modeling service must scale to permit large numbers of models to be executed simultaneously.

Client Services provide a convenient mechanism to access data from the modeling service and permit interfaces and interactions to hardware-in-the-loop, human-in-the-loop, a variety of graphical displays, or data archiving applications.

Communications Services provide a variety of communications mechanisms to link either the clients to the modeling service, or the processors that host the modeling service. The Communications Services API should be sufficiently standardized to allow any useful communications service to be integrated into the architecture with little effort.

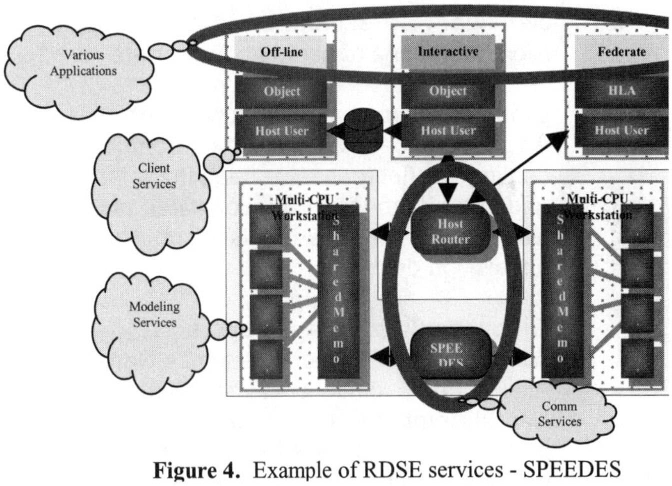

Figure 4. Example of RDSE services - SPEEDES

Figure 4 illustrates one such instantiation of these services using the SPEEDES framework (Steinman, 1998). The success of SPEEDES as a core technology component of RDSE is due primarily to adhering to the integration of these services within its architecture

Simulation Re-engineering

Unified Application Interface - Currently simulations within each domain are developing specific workarounds to make simulation High Level Architecture (HLA) compliant. However, such a HLA federation is often laborious to build which satisfies a specific use case. The problem occurs when these applications are desired in other federations. The process is again repeated to re-engineer the API's to make the simulations interoperable with other simulations adding risk to cost and schedule. In essence, a more general approach is needed which focuses on unified application interfaces and standards so applications can "snap-together" by design.

High Fidelity Modeling Environment

There are several areas that need more development before the goals of RDSE can be realized. While we understand how to model certain aspects of the real world quite well, such as those phenomena represented by Newtonian mechanics, increasing realism of representation is required in the following domains.

Behavior Representation - More realistic representations of human behavior are crucial to the success of future military simulation across all simulation domains. As our physical assets in the future military continue to decrease, we need to understand modern, joint, combined arms warfare in order to use M&S in our acquisition decisions.

Global Optimization - Adaptive computational techniques such as Genetic Algorithms, Evolutionary Programming, or Neural Computations are necessary to investigate alternatives for problems involving complex data spaces.

Fusion of Multi-spectral Data - This technology impacts not only the development of more realistic models of perception; i.e., multiple types of data being used in a decision process, but also the development of more comprehensive and accurate sensors.

Life Cycle Application Development Environment

Common and interoperable sets of simulation applications and tools are needed like those suggested in PANDA (Wallace *et al*, 2000) which maximizes the use of automated CASE tools in simulation engineering development.

Simulation Runtimes - Simulation runtime improvements will increase productivity and utility for the customer. The upfront investment in well-engineered component architecture will be returned many times over if the customer is able to increase the number of repetitions of an analysis or provide heretofore impossible resolution for mission rehearsal or environmental simulation in training. Furthermore, the customers across the spectrum of RDSE support will provide a wide financial base, and thus reduce the individual program investment.

Software Architecture - Good software architecture in all aspects - development environments, software components and frameworks, software development processes, are essential to the control of program cost, schedule, and performance. An architecture which provides common core components and APIs is one that is most likely to be well-managed and documented because the very purpose is re-use and availability. RDSE will be open source and will be fully-documented.

High Performance Computing - Users are demanding more realism in the computer simulations they use in all problem domains. Utilizing all possible hardware technology in concert with software architectures ensures proper development tasking and user satisfaction in the deployment phase. These demands require investment in solid applications like RDSE.

IMPLICATIONS OF RDSE

RDSE offers both common and multiple solutions that have implications in domain support and simulation support by encouraging WAN and wireless simulation interoperability, simulation integration within IT architectures and model validation. In all cases RDSE has the potential to provide replicated and scalable physics-based models in an operationally realistic distributed simulation. (See Figure 5.)

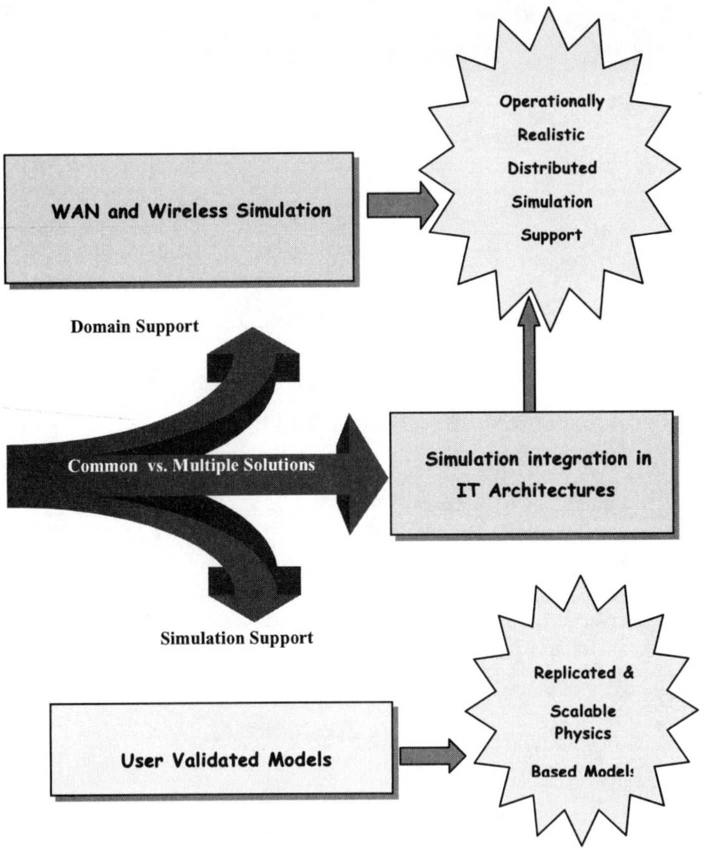

Figure 5. RDSE Technology Payback

RDSE applications

The idea of RDSE has arisen out of the shared experiences of several large DoD M&S programs: the Joint Simulation System (JSIMS); the Joint National Test Facility's Wargame 2000 (WG2K); the Joint Modeling and Simulation System (JMASS); the Extended Air Defense Testbed (EADTB); and the High Performance Computing Modernization Office's Common HPC Software Support Initiative (CHSSI). These programs have already organized themselves to coordinate the development of the SPEEDES framework mentioned above as a key element of RDSE. In addition, jointly authored and sponsored proposals among these collaborators are pending to advance several of the key technology areas listed above.

SUMMARY

RDSE is an architecture of simulation components and APIs that will support current and "unspoken" user requirements for increased resolution and speed in simulation. The "return on investment" will be realized when many simulation programs are able to use the open-source RDSE "off-the-shelf" distributed and parallel processing simulation engine. Like a good 5.0 Liter (302 ci.) Ford engine, or a 327 ci. Chevy engine, RDSE will provide a powerful, well-designed and capable engine for many applications. A software analogy is found on your desktop computer, where the (Windows, in our case) operating system is the baseline engine and the individual applications are written to the API, eliminating redundant development of utilities.

REFERENCES

Carnegie Mellon University, "Product Line Program," 2000. http://www.sei.cmu.edu/plp/plp_init.html

Kano, Noriaki, Nobuhiko Serako, Fumio Takahashi, and Shinichi Tsuji, "Attractive Quality and Must-Be Quality," *Hinshitsu* 14, no.2, 1984.

Mazur, Glenn H., "Elicit Service Customer Needs - Using Software Engineering Tools," In the *Proceedings of the Seventh Symposium on Quality Functional Deployment*, June 1995.

Mazur, Glenn H., "Voice of Customer Analysis - A Modern System of Front-end QFD Tools, with Case Studies," *AQC*, 1996

Richardson, Ita, "Quality Function Deployment - A Software Process Tool?" In the *Proceedings of the Third Annual International QFD Symposium*, 1997. http://www.csis.ul.ie./staff/ItaRichardson/intiqfd.htm

Steinman, Jeffrey, "Scalable Distributed Military Simulations using the SPEEDES Object-Oriented Simulation Framework," *Object-Oriented Simulation 1998*, Wallace, J. and J. Steinman eds., Society for Computer Simulation International, 1998.

Wallace, Jeffrey W., *et al*, "PANDA: Simulation Interoperability through Software Engineering," To appear in *The Proceedings of the 2000 Summer Computer Simulation Conference*, Society for Computer International, July 2000.

Science & Engineering

A NOVAL VOICE-OVER-ATM INTERFACE SIMULATION

H. S. Al-Raweshidy, M. M. Jahromi and L. Peil
Communication System Division
Electronic Engineering Laboratory
University of Kent at Canterbury
Canterbury, Kent, CT2 7NT, UK
e-mail: (H.Al-Raweshidy@ukc.ac.uk) or (mj8@ukc.ac.uk)

Telecommunications, Optimisation and Queuing.

ABSTRACT

This paper presents a novel simulation model for Voice-over-ATM interface that uses AAL2 protocol. Matlab programming and its Simulink package has been used in modelling this interface. The model is able to vary the signal coding modulation technique between PCM, ADPCM and E-ADPCM. The E-ADPCM technique illustrates more features of the AAL2 than the other two techniques. In addition to the voice compression and bit-dropping technique, this model optimises the voice packet delay via varying their sizes and packet filling delay to avoid traffic congestion. This novel optimiser reduces the average packet delay as the number of active voice sources increases while its effect over the mean bits per sample is negligible. According to the minimum requirement on mean bits per sample for good voice quality the optimiser provides 33% reduction on average packet delay.

INDRODUCTION

Voice communication, which is fundamental to all organisations, remains and will continue to remain a critical requirement to corporate the world. The most common telephony system is still analog that uses the modulation of electric signals along a wire to transport voice. For almost 40 years now, voice has been carried in ever-greater shares in digital format. In other hand, with competitiveness of today's market, organisations around the world have been continuously working to reduce rising communications costs and improving network efficiency. They recognised that significant economic saving can be achieved via integrating the data traffic and voice traffic onto a single network. The network operators and service providers are pursuing solutions, which will enable them to take advantage of excess capacity on broadband networks for voice and data transmission as well as utilise the Internet and company Intranets as alternatives to costlier mediums. A voice over packet application such as ATM meets the challenges of combining legacy voice networks and data networks by allowing both voice and data information to be transported over the packet network. (Chu 1997) and (Minoli 1998)

ATM is the technology of choice to achieve universal networking. It is designed to be the multimedia, multi-service technology with high-speed and efficient method of transferring information between users, irrespective to the nature of the traffic (voice, data or video). Early activity in the ATM Forum focused on data applications while voice transport was relegated to using ATM circuit emulation with AAL1 based upon CBR service class connections. Although this can provide high quality voice transport it does not deliver high bandwidth efficiency, flexibility or any PBX protocol intelligent features including voice compression, silence suppression and idle channel removal. (Minoli 1998

However, voice telephony over ATM is one of the key technologies for multimedia communications. In particular, low-cost real-time voice communication technology must be developed to effectively reduce the voice transmission cost per channel. Furthermore, as technology has evolved, the inherent burstiness of voice and many real-time applications can be exploited to decrease the cost of transmission significantly through the use of rt-VBR service class connections over ATM. In addition, many applications including wireless cellular communications and other trunking applications those have voice compression and silence suppression concerns mainly in packetisation delay and bandwidth efficiency. Therefore, ATM Forum has defined and standardised a new ATM adaptation layer (AAL2) that improves bandwidth efficiency and supports voice services demands. It is similar to AAL1 since both enhance the service provided by the ATM layer to support functions required by the next higher layer. Moreover, AAL2 goes beyond AAL1 by defining a structure, which includes functions supporting higher layer requirements neither considered nor possible within the structure of AAL1. (Minoli 1998) and (Subbiah and Dixit 1998)

AAL2 provides efficient transmission of low-rate, short and variable packets in delay sensitive applications. It supports both VBR and CBR service class connections within an ATM network. In addition, it enables multiple user channels on a single ATM virtual circuit with variable traffic conditions. This paper presents a novel voice-over-ATM interface that is modelled and simulated using Matlab programming and it s Simulink package. It illustrates the effects of AAL2 protocol in carrying voice telephony over ATM and introduced a novel voice packet delay optimiser that controls the traffic congestion problem via varying the packets sizes and their filling delay.

SIMULATED MODEL

Matlab programming and its Simulink package has been used in modelling a multi purpose voice telephony over ATM interface shown in figure 1 that implements AAL2. The voice signals as shown created and transmitted to the signal coding modulation block. According to the decided modulation technique the signals coded and passed to the AAL2 packetisation block. The filled packets placed in the queue after each packetisation interval that is controlled by the Timer-Composite Unit. The queuing load is reported to the controller, which obtains what to do with the next filled packets. The standard ATM cells created from the queued packets and transmitted through the VC connection. This process can be considered as voice assembly over ATM cell process, which forms %50 of the voice telephony transportation and the rest is the disassembly process. The ATM cells de-multiplexed into AAL2 packets that de-packetised into digital quantized codes and recover back to their original analog form via the invol ved signal decoder block. This model illustrates the advantages of using AAL2 protocol in carrying voice over ATM that provides:

I) Silence Detection and Suppression

In general, voice telephony consists of two periods: active and silent. An active period of a voice source corresponds to a talk spurt, whereas a silent period corresponds to durations during which the speaker pauses to breathe, gather thoughts or listen to the other speaker. The average active and silent periods are assumed to be respectively around 40% and 60% of voice call duration. During silent period there is no need to transmit bandwidth within a bundle. Therefore, an advanced silence detection algorithm is employed to detect and remove silence. The voice sources produce signals composed of silent periods and active periods in such a way that the overall activity factor for all sources over the full simulation time is 0.4 but each individual source has different activity factor. For instance, a group of ten sources is composed of two sources with an activity factor of 0.25, four sources with an activity factor of 0.375 and the last four sources with an activity factor of 0.5 that give the overall activity factor of 0.4. (Minoli 1998)

II) Idle Channel Removal

In addition to the silent periods that occur within voice calls, there is another common case in which the voice source is silent. The only difference between this case and the others is that the voice channel in this case is idle, in other words, there is no active voice call connection. Stopping cell transmission during such cases can reduce the bandwidth required for voice in the ATM network. However, in this simulation it is assumed when the channel becomes idle it is replaced with another active channel, therefore, the channels are always active. (Minoli 1998)

III) Voice Compression and VBR Service Class

The model uses these two features of AAL2 within three voice coding modulation techniques:

A) Pulse Code Modulation (PCM): It is the most commo technique used in coding voice signals, normally quantizes each analog sample into a 8 bits discrete value according to the μ-law characteristic (or A-law) that is defined by (1):

$$F_{\mu}(x) = \text{sgn}(x)\frac{\ln(1+\mu*|x|)}{\ln(1+\mu)} \quad (1$$

Then it will be recovered back to its original analog form using (2):

$$F_{\mu}^{-1}(y) = \text{sgn}(y)(\frac{1}{\mu})[(1+\mu)^{|y|}-1] \quad (2$$

The point of using this non-linear compression technique is to improve the coding procedure efficiency and minimise the quantization error. However, most signal processing functions involve linear operations that makes converting process of this non-linear compressed transmission format into a uniform format is necessary. To simplify the conversion process, μ is chosen to be 255 that have the property of being closely approximated by a set of eight straight-line segments. Furthermore, the slope of each successive segment is exactly one-half the slope of the previous segment. Thus an 8-bit μ255 code word is composed of 1 polarity bit, 3 bits to identify a major segment and 4 bits for identifying a quantizing interval within a segment. This technique supports CBR service class connections that applicable via both AAL1 and AAL2 protocols. (Minoli 1998)

B) Adaptive Differential Pulse Code Modulation: Which based on ITU-T G.726 algorithm, converts a uniform 64 kbit/s μ-law (or A-law) PCM channel to and from a 32 kbit/s channel. In practice, ADPCM applies a special algorithm to reduce the 8-bit sample to 4-bit words using

15 quantizing levels. These 4-bit words no longer represent sample amplitudes; instead they contain only enough information to reconstruct the amplitude at the destination. Therefore, this technique is compatible with the signal compression support in AAL2 protocol that leads to a reduction in the amount of required bandw idth. (Chu 1997), (ITU-I 1990a), (Minoli 1998) and (Sriram and Wang 1999)

C) Embedded ADPCM (E-ADPCM): This technique based on ITU-T G.727 algorithm, which is the extension of the ADPCM algorithm, illustrates one more advantage of using AAL2 in VATM interface. This technique has VBR coding algorithms with the capacity of bit dropping outside the encoder and decoder blocks. They consist of a series of algorithms such that the decision levels of the lower-rate quantizers are subsets of the quantizer at the highest rate. This allows bit reductions at any point in the network without the need of coordination between the transmitter and the receiver. This technique produces code words that contain enhancement bits and core bits. The feed-forward path utilises enhancement and core bits, while the feedback path uses core bits only. The inverse quantizer and the predictor of both the encoder and decoder use the core bits. Therefore, enhancement bits can be discarded or dropped during network congestion. (ITU-I 1990b), (Minoli 1998) and (Sriram and Wang 1999)

The controller block controls the process of these voice coding modulation techniques. It monitors the amount of instant queuing load Q(t) and compares it to the relative threshold value according to the in volved technique. Figure 2 indicates the controller block orders to the AAL2 packetisation block for all the possible cases. The thresholds value for all the cases depend on the link bandwidth.

VOICE PACKET DELAY OPTIMISER

When large number of voice sources in a common virtual circuit are active the amount of Q(t) increases sharply hence, existence of a mechanism that varies the packetisation interval (T) and decreases the input rate is useful. Moreover, when the amount of Q(t) is large enough ($Q(t) \geq Q_2$) the packets queuing delay will be quiet large that considers as a negative fact which affect the voice quality. However, this fact could be used positively in carrying more voice information over the AAL2 packets. Therefore, to support these two functions an additional statement has been added to the E-ADPCM (bit-dropping) technique statements that indicates:

$$If\ Q(t) \geq Q_T\ Then\ \ "T = T_1"\ Otherwise\ \ "T = T_0"$$

This means when the amount of Q(t) becomes greater or equal to Q_T, the value of T changes from its default value T_0 to the higher value T_1. The time difference between these two packetisation intervals uses in carrying more voice information over the AAL2 packets. Therefore, the controller block orders flowchart including the statement of the voice packet delay optimiser has been updated (see figure 3).

SIMULATION RESULTS AND DISCUTIONS

The model has been simulated over a link of 415 kbps for the following cases: PCM, ADPCM, E-ADPCM and the optimiser. The optimiser case has been simulated for three different threshold values $Q_T = Q_2$, $Q_T = (Q_2 + K_{ADPCM})/2$ and $Q_T = (K_{ADPCM} - 1)$. The following threshold values were obtained for this amount of bandwidth: $K_{PCM} = 16$, $K_{ADPCM} = 33$, $Q_1 = 11$ and $Q_2 = 22$. The default value for the packetisation interval T_0 is chosen to be 5ms and its higher value T_1 is 8ms.

Figure 4 shows a typical voice signal produced by a modelled voice source that composed of silent and active periods spread over the simulation time forming an overall activity factor of 0.375. The silent periods indicates as shown in the figure by setting the signal amplitude to zero.

A comparison between the input voice signal and the recovered output voice signal is plotted in figure 5. These signals are exactly the same, but the decoded signals is delayed for 5ms that corresponds to the packetisation delay.

Figure 6 shows the average voice packet delay as function of the number of instant active voice sources multiplexed over a single ATM VC. It is clear that as the model uses more features of AAL2 protocol better results obtained. Hence, as PCM techniques do not use any of the AAL2 protocol features, it has the worst results. The ADPCM technique due to involved voice compression mechanism supports almost twice the number of instant active voice sources in comparison to PCM technique with the same amount of average packet delay. In addition, E-ADPCM technique that enables bit-dropping mechanism, supports more instant active voice sources at lower average packet delay. Furthermore, optimiser technique reduces the average packet delay as the number of instant active voice sources increases.

To receive good voice quality, the average packet delay is considered to be acceptable up-to 5ms. From this view, figure 6 shows that the optimiser technique with threshold value equal to Q_2 gives the best results. Moreover, it is clear that the model by using PCM, ADPCM, E-ADPCM, optimiser-22, optimiser-27 and optimiser-32 for good voice quality supports 6, 15, 18, 31, 22 and 18 instant active voice sources respectively. (Sriram and Wang 1999)

However, when E-ADPCM and optimiser techniques are used, as bit-dropping mechanism involved, the voice quality in addition to the average voice packet delay depends also on the mean bits per sample. From this view, figure 7 plots the mean bits per sample as function of the number of instant active voice sources multiplexed over a single ATM VC. This figure shows that E-ADPCM technique gives better results than the optimiser, but the difference between these results is never greater than 0.09, which is not very significant. Furthermore, the minimum requirement on mean bits per sample is somewhere around 3.5 for good voice quality and both techniques have quite the same performance down-to 3.5 mean bits per sample. This fact reduces the number of instant active voice sources supported by the optimiser down-to 18 voice sources similar to E-ADPCM technique. (Sriram and Wang 1999)

Although, by using the optimiser the link capacity does not increase, it has the advantage of achieving the same voice quality at lower average voice packet delay. It reduces the average voice packet delay for 3.5 mean bits per sample from 5ms (E-ADPCM) to 3.35ms that means almost 33% reduction over the average packet delay.

CONCLUSIONS

From this paper it can be concluded that AAL2 adds significant advantages to the ATM technology for supporting low bit rate, delay sensitive applications. From the modelled voice telephony over ATM interface that is able to vary the voice coding modulation technique, it is clear that the embedded ADPCM technique illustrates more features of the AAL2 than the PCM and ADPCM techniques.

In addition to the voice compression and bit-dropping mechanism, this model optimises the voice packet delay via varying their sizes and packet filling delay to avoid traffic congestion. The effect of this optimiser starts when the embedded ADPCM starts dropping the second bit and its effect increases as the number of instant voice sources increases. This novel optimiser reduces the average packet delay as the number of active voice sources increases while its effect over the mean bits per sample is negligible.

From the simulation results it is clear that the best results for the optimiser technique were obtained in the case where the optimiser threshold value Q_T chosen to be equal to Q_2. For good voice quality according to the both average voice packet delay and mean bits per sample, the optimiser does not increases the link capacity. However, with 3.5 mean bits per sample it reduces the amount of average voice packet delay from 5ms (E-ADPCM) to 3.35ms i.e. 33% reduction over the average voice packet delay.

REFFERNCES

Chu, T. P., 1997, "Packetized Compressed Voice over ATM", SPIE Proceeding, Volume 3222: 120-127.

ITU-T. 1990a, Recommendation G.726: 40, 32, 24, 16 kbp Adaptive Differential Pulse Code Modulation (ADPCM), Geneva, Switzerland.

ITU-T. 1990b, Recommendation G.727: 5-, 4-, 3- and 2bit Sample Embedded Adaptive Differential Pulse Code Modulation (E-ADPCM), Geneva, Switzerland.

Minoli, Daniel and Minoli, Emma, 1998, Delivering Voice over Frame Relay and ATM, John Wiley & Sons Publisher

Sriram, K. and Wang, Y. T., 1999, "Voice over ATM Usir AAL2 and Bit-Dropping: Performance and Call Admission Control", IEEE Journal on Selected Areas in Communications, Volume 17, No. 1 (Jan.): 18-28.

Subbiah, Baranitharan and Dixit, Sudhir, 1998, "ATM Adaptation Layer 2 (AAL2) for Low Bit Rate Speech and Sata: Issues and Challenges", IEEE ATM Workshop: 225-233.

BIOGRAPHY

H. S. Al-Raweshidy (H.Al-Raweshidy@ukc.ac.uk) received his PhD degree from Strathclyde University for work in the area of spread spectrum multiplexing technique for optical communication networks. Currently, he is leadi a group of 15 researchers in the area of Radio-over-Fibre a Mobile IP at the Communication Systems Division, Electronic Engineering Laboratory, University of Kent. He a member of IEE and a senior member of IEEE. He acts as Guest editor for the International Journal of Wireless Personal Communications, he is a member of International Advisory Committees and Technical Program Committees of several conferences.

M. M. Jahromi (mj8@ukc.ac.uk) is a PhD student worki in ATM networking, Voice over ATM, Voice over IP and IP-ATM mobility at University of Kent at Canterbury. He received his MSc. in "Control and Information Technolog from the University of Manchester Institute of Since and Technology (UMIST) in 1996.

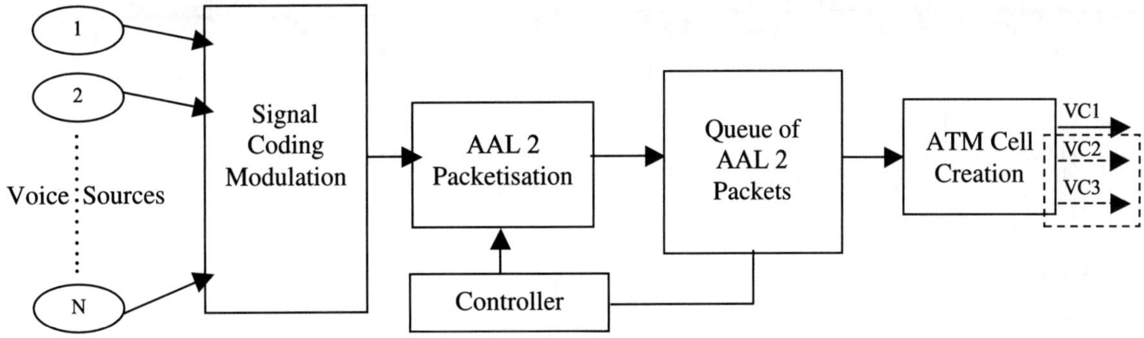

Figure 1: Voice Telephony over ATM Interface Model

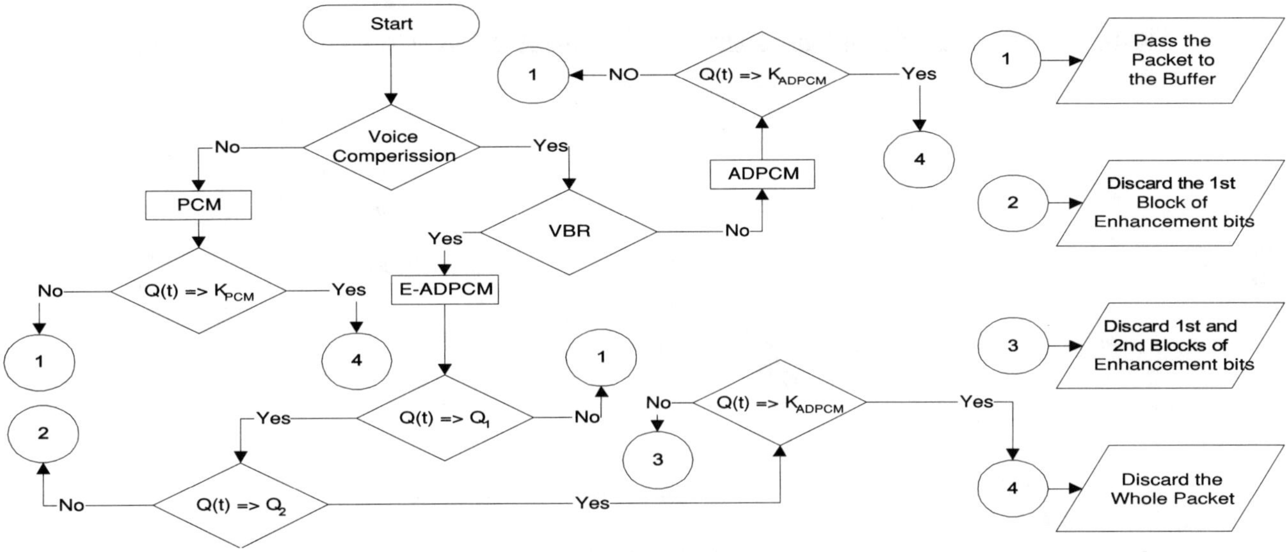

Figure 2: Controller Block Orders Flowchart for PCM, ADPCM and E-ADPCM

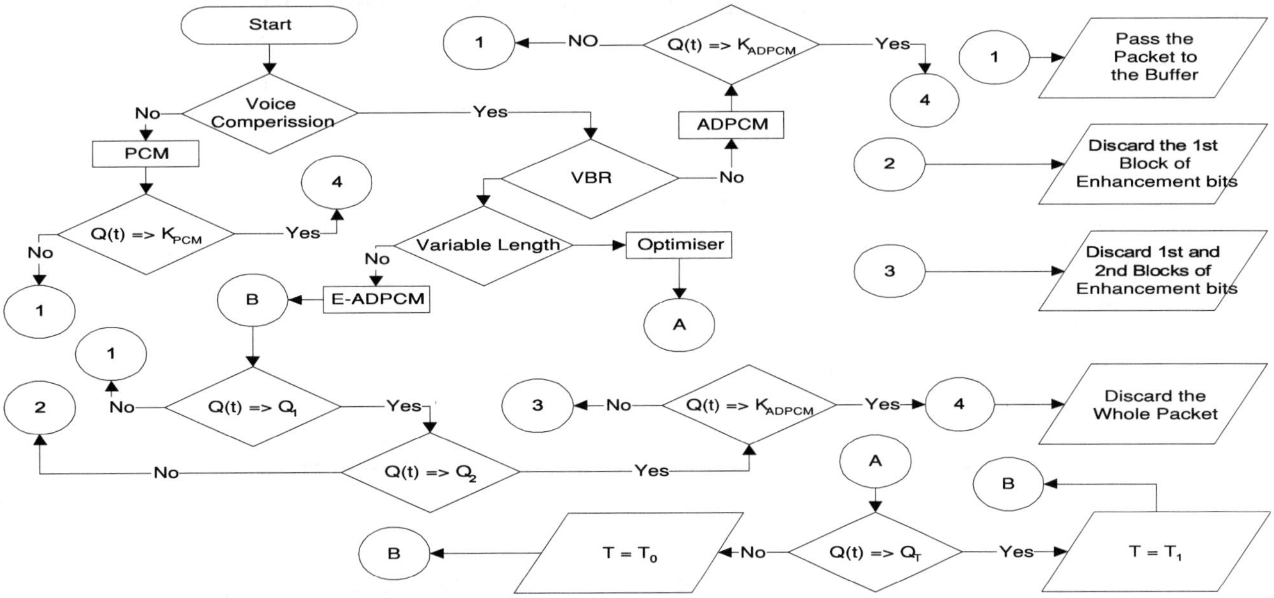

Figure 3: Controller Block Orders Flowchart for PCM, ADPCM, E-ADPCM and Optimiser

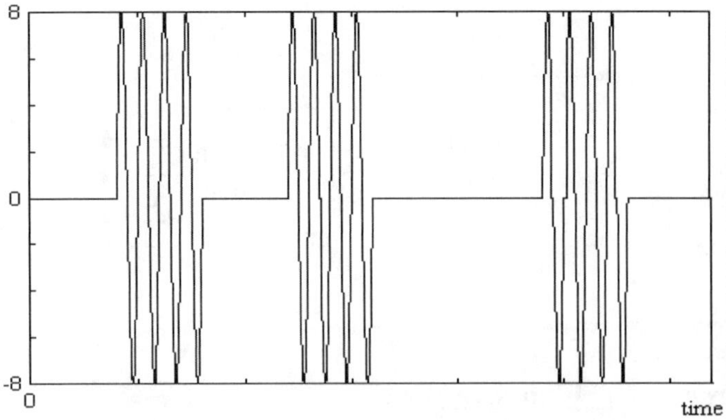

Figure 4: A Typical Produced Voice Signal

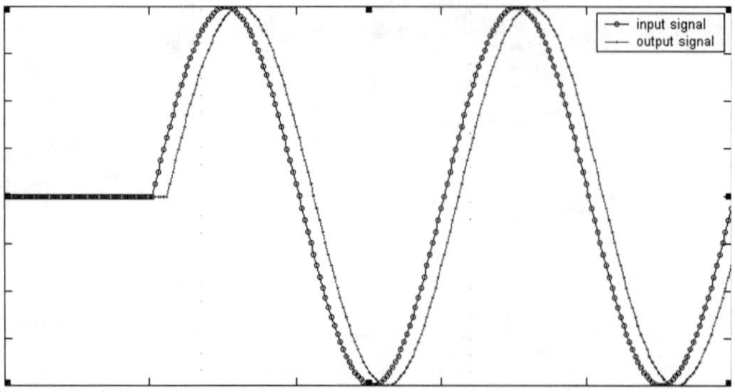

Figure 5: A Comparison Between Input and Output Signal

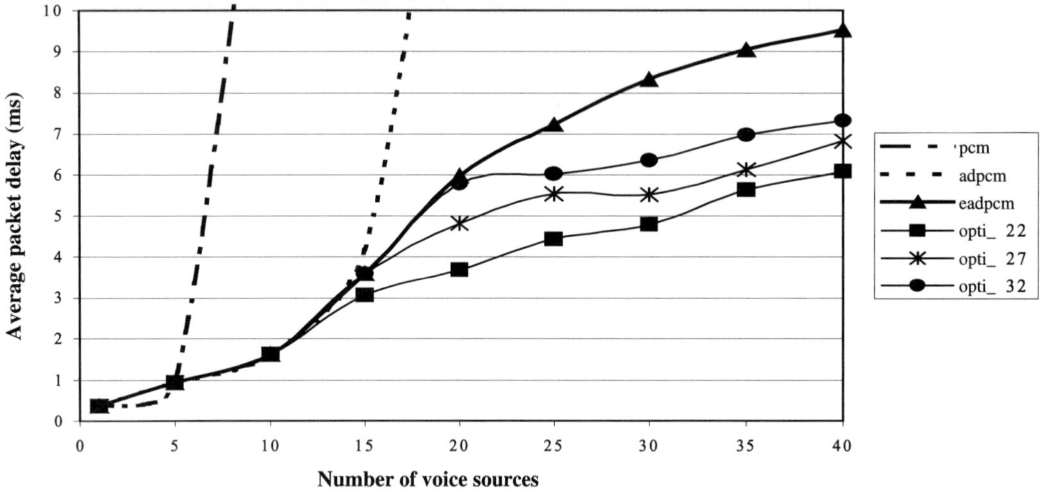

Figure 6: Average Voice Packet Delay & Number of Instant Active Voice Sources

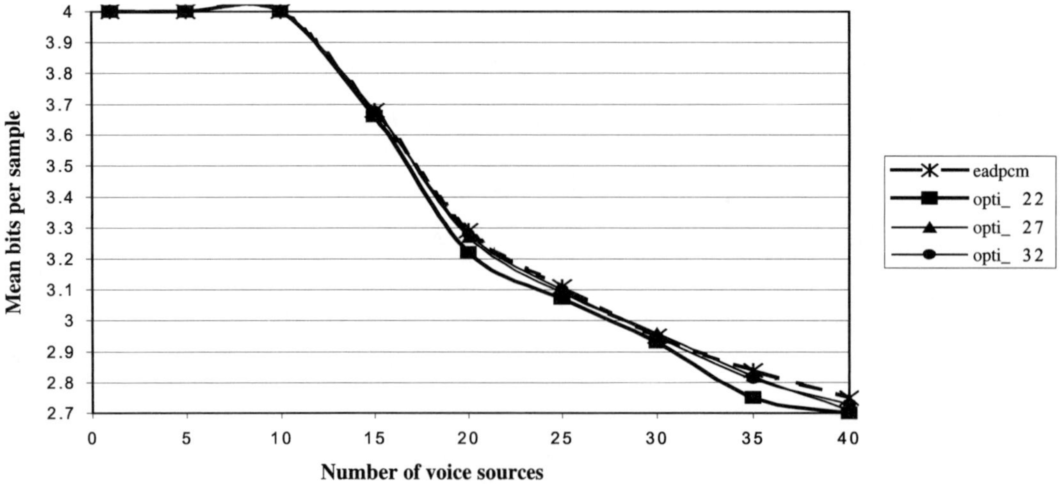

Figure 7: Mean Bits Per Sample & Number of Instant Active Voice Sources

THE COMPUTATIONAL REDUCTION AND PERFORMANCE EVALUATION FOR THE SIMULATION OF FADING COMMUNICATIONS CHANNELS

Yunxin Li and Xiaojing Huang
Motorola Australian Research Center
Locked Bag 5028, Botany, NSW 1455, Australia
e-mail: A12082@email.mot.com

KEYWORDS

Communications, Deterministic, Approximation techniques, Performance analysis

ABSTRACT

Two computational reduction methods for the simulation of multiple independent Rayleigh fading waveforms are analyzed and tested in this paper. The performance evaluation using different quality criteria shows that the table lookup method increases the second order moment of the simulated power spectral density considerably unless the size of lookup table is sufficiently large whereas the linear recursion method always provides both computational efficiency and performance acceptance.

I. INTRODUCTION

A number of different models have been proposed for the simulation of Rayleigh fading communications channels over the past decades. Generally, these models can be classified as statistic and deterministic ones. The statistic models are based on the shaping of the power spectral densities of white Gaussian noise processes by either time-domain or frequency-domain filtering(Verdin and Tozer 1993; Fechtel 1993; Young and Beaulieu 1998), whereas the deterministic models approximate the Rayleigh processes by finite superposition of properly selected sinusoids(Jakes 1974; Dent *et al.* 1993; Patzold et al. 1996; Crespo and Jimenez 1995). Conventional deterministic models are very popular because of their simplicity and good performance in generating single Rayleigh distributed waveform, but some undesirable properties have been found when they are used to generate multiple independent Rayleigh waveforms.

An improved deterministic method for the generation of multiple independent Rayleigh faders is proposed recently(Li and Huang 2000), which uses an asymmetrical arrival angle arrangement to guarantee the independence between different faders. The performances of this fading model are tested, which conform to the theoretical analyses. However, great computational effort is also showed because different sets of Doppler frequency shifts are used in different faders. Suppose that there are M independent Rayleigh waveforms need to be generated each using N equal-strength incident rays. The computation of these waveforms involves the evaluation of $\frac{MN}{2}$ sinusoids, which contributes to the most part of the computational load.

In this paper, two typical ways to reduce the computational effort for the simulation of multiple independent Rayleigh faders are analyzed and tested. The first straightforward way to reduce the execution time of the sinusoidal evaluation is using the table lookup method to generate approximate sinusoidal waves. The other way to efficiently generate accurate sinusoidal waves is to use the second order linear recursion with characteristic polynomial containing poles on the unit circle. Two different quality criteria are used to evaluate the performances of each computational reduction method. Theoretical analyses and simulation results show that the table lookup approximation degrades the fader's level crossing rate considerably because of the discontinuity of the simulated auto-correlation function of the fading waveform whereas the linear recursion method always demonstrates better performances.

In Section II, a short review of the improved independent fading model is presented. Then, the table lookup and linear recursion methods for efficiently generating sinusoidal waves are briefly described in Section III, with emphasis being placed on the theoretical development of the simulated auto-correlation function and power spectral density for the table lookup approximation. The performance evaluations for these two computational reduction schemes are conducted in Section IV using two different quality measures. Some numerical and simulation results are also given in order to draw the conclusions.

II. THE INDEPENDENT RAYLEIGH FADERS

As suggested in (Li and Huang 2000), by assuming uniform antenna pattern and uniform distributed incident power, and using an asymmetrical arrival angel arrangement given by

$$\alpha_{nk} = \frac{2\pi n}{N} + \frac{2\pi k}{MN} + \frac{\pi}{2MN}, \quad (1)$$

the k -th Rayleigh waveform can be formulated as

$$T_k(t) = \sqrt{\frac{1}{N_0}} \sum_{n=0}^{N_0-1} [\cos(\omega_M \cos\alpha_{nk} \cdot t + \phi_n)$$
$$+ j\sin(\omega_M \sin\alpha_{nk} \cdot t + \phi_n')], \ k = 0,1,2,\ldots, M-1, \quad (2)$$

where $N_0 = \frac{N}{4}$, $\omega_M = 2\pi f_M$ is the maximum Doppler frequency shift in rad/s, ϕ_n and ϕ_n' are random phases which can be considered as the seeds used to generate different realizations of $T_k(t)$. We see that both real and imaginary parts of $T_k(t)$ are the superposition of $\frac{N}{4}$ sinusoids with frequencies (called Doppler frequency shifts) $\omega_M \cos\alpha_{nk}$ and $\omega_M \sin\alpha_{nk}$ respectively. Thus, a total of $\frac{MN}{2}$ sinusoids need to be calculated in order to generate M complex-valued waveforms $T_k(t)$, $k = 0,1,2,\ldots, M-1$. With α_{nk} defined by (1), the $\frac{MN}{2}$ Doppler frequency shifts are different from each other, and therefore the independence between the real and imaginary parts of any $T_k(t)$ and the independence between any two waveforms $T_k(t)$ and $T_l(t)$, $k \neq l$, are guaranteed. The auto-correlation function of $T_k(t)$ is

$$R_k(\tau) = \langle T_k^*(t) T_k(t+\tau)\rangle = \frac{1}{2N_0} \sum_{n=0}^{N_0-1} [\cos(\omega_M \cos\alpha_{nk} \cdot \tau)$$
$$+ \cos(\omega_M \sin\alpha_{nk} \cdot \tau)], \quad (3)$$

and the corresponding power spectral density function is given by

$$S_k(f) = \frac{1}{4N_0} \sum_{n=0}^{N_0-1} [\delta(f - f_M \cos\alpha_{nk}) + \delta(f - f_M \sin$$
$$+ \delta(f + f_M \cos\alpha_{nk}) + \delta(f + f_M \sin\alpha_{nk})]. \quad (4)$$

(3) represents a very good approximation of the Bessel function $J_0(\omega_M \tau)$ and the n th moments, $n = 0,1,2,$ of $S_k(f)$ are found to be exactly the same as that of the ideal Jakes power spectral density function(Jakes 1974), i.e.,

$$b_0 = \int_{-\infty}^{+\infty} S_k(f) df = R_k(0) = 1, \quad (5)$$

$$b_1 = 2\pi \int_{-\infty}^{+\infty} f S_k(f) df = -j\dot{R}_k(0) = 0, \quad (6)$$

and

$$b_2 = (2\pi)^2 \int_{-\infty}^{+\infty} f^2 S_k(f) df = -\ddot{R}_k(0) = \frac{1}{2}\omega_M^2, \quad (7)$$

where $\dot{R}_k(\tau)$ and $\ddot{R}_k(\tau)$ denote the first and second derivatives of $R_k(\tau)$ respectively.

III. THE METHODS FOR COMPUTATIONAL REDUCTION

The evaluation of the $\frac{MN}{2}$ sinusoids contributes to the most part of the computational effort for the generation of M independent Rayleigh distributed waveforms each using N equal-strength incident rays. Therefore, if the operation for generating a sinusoidal wave is simplified, the total computational load of the M independent Rayleigh faders will be greatly reduced.

One straightforward way to simplify the generation of sinusoidal wave is using the table lookup method(Lin 1987). Suppose that the cosine values for L angles uniformly spaced around the unit circle are stored in a table which has the format as shown in Table 1. Then any cosine wave of frequency $\omega = 2\pi f$ with any initial phase φ is approximated by

$$\cos(\omega t+\varphi)\approx C_L\left[\left(Lft+\frac{L}{2\pi}\varphi\right)_L\right], \quad (8)$$

where $(\cdot)_L$ denotes the operation of taking integer part and modulo L. If the approximated sinusoidal wave is consecutively sampled at sampling period Δt and the sample at time Δtn is $C_L[(x_n)_L]$ with $x_n = Lf\Delta tn+\frac{L}{2\pi}\varphi$ denoting the phase variable, the next sample at $\Delta t(n+1)$ is then

$$C_L[(x_{n+1})_L]=C_L[(x_n+Lf\Delta t)_L]. \quad (9)$$

We see that the operation needed for generating one sample of sinusoidal wave by table lookup is only one addition and one modulo L.

Table 1. Sinusoidal Lookup Table

Index i	Cosine value $C_L[i]$
0	$\cos(0)$
1	$\cos\left(\frac{2\pi}{L}\right)$
⋮	⋮
$L-1$	$\cos\left(\frac{2\pi}{L}(L-1)\right)$

Mathematically, the table lookup approximation is equivalent to the replacement of the sinusoidal function $\cos(x)$ by its interpolated version $\cos_L(x)$ which can be expressed as

$$\cos_L(x)=\sum_{i=-\infty}^{+\infty}\cos\left(\frac{2\pi}{L}i\right)g\left(x-\frac{2\pi}{L}i\right), \quad (10)$$

where $g(x)$ is defined by

$$g(x)=\begin{cases}1 & 0\le x\le\frac{2\pi}{L}\\ 0 & elsewhere\end{cases}. \quad (11)$$

The approximated Rayleigh waveform now becomes

$$\tilde{T}_k(t)=\sqrt{\frac{1}{N_0}}\sum_{n=0}^{N_0-1}[\cos_L(\omega_M\cos\alpha_{nk}\cdot t+\phi_n)$$
$$+j\cos_L\left(\omega_M\sin\alpha_{nk}\cdot t+\phi_n^{'}-\frac{\pi}{2}\right)]$$
$$=\sqrt{\frac{1}{N_0}}\sum_{n=0}^{N_0-1}\sum_{i=-\infty}^{+\infty}\cos\left(\frac{2\pi}{L}i\right)\left[g\left(\omega_M\cos\alpha_{nk}\cdot t+\phi_n-\frac{2\pi}{L}i\right)\right.$$
$$\left.+jg\left(\omega_M\sin\alpha_{nk}\cdot t+\phi_n^{'}-\frac{\pi}{2}-\frac{2\pi}{L}i\right)\right]. \quad (12)$$

Therefore the auto-correlation function is derived to be

$$\tilde{R}_k(\tau)=\frac{1}{2N_0}\sum_{n=0}^{N_0-1}\sum_{i=-\infty}^{+\infty}\cos\left(\frac{2\pi}{L}i\right)\left[q\left(\omega_M\cos\alpha_{nk}\cdot\tau-\frac{2\pi}{L}i\right)\right.$$
$$\left.+q\left(\omega_M\sin\alpha_{nk}\cdot\tau-\frac{2\pi}{L}i\right)\right], \quad (13)$$

where $q(x)$ is defined by

$$q(x)=\frac{L}{2\pi}\int_{-\infty}^{+\infty}g(u)g(u+x)du, \quad (14)$$

and the corresponding power spectral density is

$$\tilde{S}_k(f)=\frac{1}{2N_0}\left(\frac{L}{2\pi}\right)^2\left(1-\cos\frac{2\pi}{L}\right)\sum_{n=0}^{N_0-1}$$
$$\{\left(\frac{f_M\cos\alpha_{nk}}{f}\right)^2\sum_{i=-\infty}^{+\infty}[\delta(f-f_M\cos\alpha_{nk}-Lf_M\cos\alpha_{nk}$$
$$+\delta(f+f_M\cos\alpha_{nk}-Lf_M\cos\alpha_{nk}i)]$$
$$+\left(\frac{f_M\sin\alpha_{nk}}{f}\right)^2\sum_{i=-\infty}^{+\infty}[\delta(f-f_M\sin\alpha_{nk}-Lf_M\sin\alpha_{nk}$$
$$+\delta(f+f_M\sin\alpha_{nk}-Lf_M\sin\alpha_{nk}i)]\}. \quad (15)$$

Note that $\tilde{S}_k(f)$ is no longer bandwidth-limited because of the discontinuity of the auto-correlation function $\tilde{R}_k(\tau)$ introduced by the table lookup approximation.

Another way to efficiently generate sinusoidal wave is based on the fact that a sinusoidal sequence can be considered as the zero-input response of a second-order discrete-time system with poles on the unit circle(Oppenheim and Schafer 1975). Suppose that the sequence $y(n)=\cos(\omega\Delta tn+\varphi)$ needs to be generated. The system function is therefore

$$H(z)=\frac{1}{1-2\cos(\omega\Delta t)z^{-1}+z^{-2}}, \tag{16}$$

and $y(n)$ can be calculated using the linear recursion

$$y(n)=2\cos(\omega\Delta t)y(n-1)-y(n-2), n=2,3,4,... \tag{17}$$

with the initial value

$$y(0)=\cos(\varphi), \tag{18}$$
$$y(1)=\cos(\omega\Delta t+\varphi). \tag{19}$$

We see that only one multiplication and one addition (subtraction) are needed for the evaluation of $y(n)$ by (17). The number of operations in generating one sample of sinusoidal wave using this linear recursion is similar to that of the table lookup method. However, two past samples must be stored for each sinusoid. Compared with the table lookup method, more memories are needed for the linear recursion when M and N_0 are large.

As long as the sampling period satisfies the Nyquist criterion, there will be no distortion introduced for the Rayleigh waveforms generated by this linear recursion method.

IV. THE EVALUATION OF PERFORMANCE

The performances of the independent Rayleigh faders after computational reduction can be evaluated using two different quality criteria. The first is to see how much the simulated auto-correlation function is close to the theoretical Bessel function $J_0(\omega_M\tau)$. The second is to compare the second-order moment of the simulated power spectral density with the ideal value given in (7).

The quality of the simulated auto-correlation function can be measured by the mean-square-error defined by

$$\varepsilon_k^2=\frac{1}{T_{mse}}\int_0^{T_{mse}}\left[\tilde{R}_k(\tau)-J_0(\omega_M\tau)\right]^2 d\tau, \tag{20}$$

where T_{mse} denotes the time interval over which the mean-square-error is evaluated. To adapt T_{mse} to the number of sinusoids used in the generation of the Rayleigh waveforms, we choose T_{mse} according to the relation

$$\omega_M T_{mse}=\pi N_0. \tag{21}$$

The relationship between ε_k^2 and N_0 is given in Figure 1 for both linear recursion method and table lookup approximation. It clearly shows that ε_k^2 becomes smaller when N_0 is larger. Also we see that, for a given N_0, the larger the lookup table size is, the smaller the mean-square-error will be. When the lookup table size $L=16$, ε_k^2 is nearly the same as that obtained using linear recursion. Figure 2 shows the auto-correlation functions of the Rayleigh waveforms generated after using the above two computational reduction methods, which confirm the analysis through Figure 1.

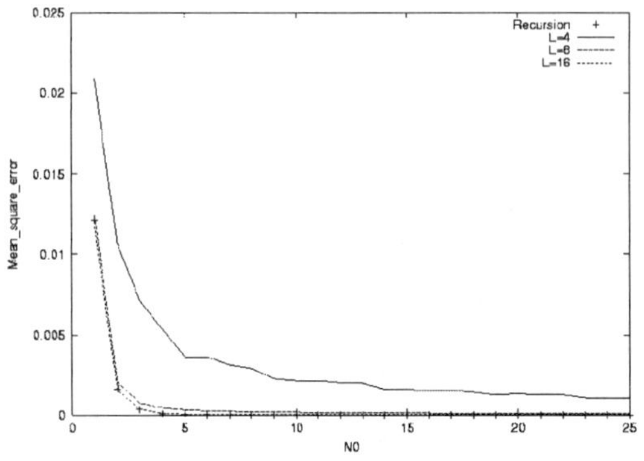

Figure 1. The mean-square-error ε_k^2 for linear recursion method and table lookup approximation ($M=8$, $k=0$).

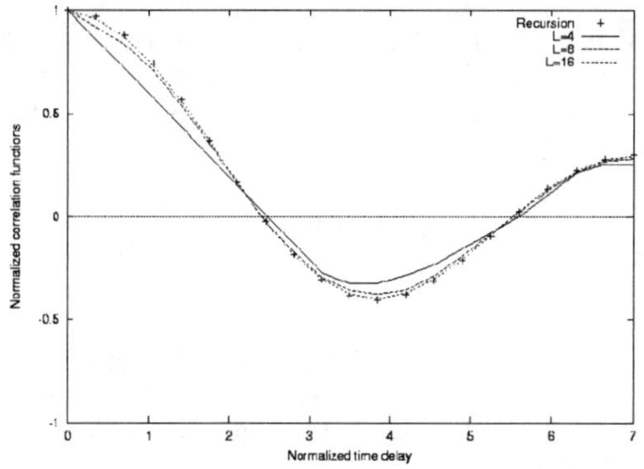

Figure 2. The auto-correlation functions of Rayleigh waveforms generated using linear recursion method and table lookup approximation ($N_0 = 8, M = 8, \quad k = 0$), where the normalized time delay is defined as $\omega_M \tau$.

The second-order moment of the simulated power spectral density of the Rayleigh waveform is another important quality measure because it is directly related to the level crossing rate and the average duration of fading time(Jakes 1974). For the linear recursion method, this moment will always be the same as the theoretical one (i.e., $\frac{1}{2}\omega_M^2$). When the table lookup approximation is used for the computational reduction purpose, the bandwidth of the simulated Rayleigh waveforms will exceed the maximum Doppler frequency shift. Suppose that an anti-aliasing filter is used, which limits the maximum frequency to the half of the sampling frequency f_s . Then, the second-order moment can be evaluated as

$$\tilde{b}_2 = (2\pi)^2 \int_{-\frac{f_s}{2}}^{\frac{f_s}{2}} f^2 \tilde{S}_k(f) df \approx \left(\frac{L}{2\pi}\right)^2 \left(1 - \cos\frac{2\pi}{L}\right) \cdot$$

$$\frac{1}{N_0} \sum_{n=0}^{N_0 - 1} \left\{ \left[\frac{f_s / f_M}{L \cos \alpha_{nk}} \right] (\cos \alpha_{nk})^2 + \left[\frac{f_s / f_M}{L \sin s \alpha_{nk}} \right] (\sin \alpha_{nk})^2 \right\} \omega_M^2 , \quad (22)$$

where $\lceil x \rceil$ denotes the nearest integer larger than x . Figure 3 shows that $\tilde{b}_2$ approaches the theoretical value only when very large lookup table size is used and that this moment increases as f_s becomes higher. Figure 4 shows how the simulated level crossing rate N_R (defined as the rate at which the envelope of the Rayleith waveform crosses a specified level in the positive direction) is affected by the large $\tilde{b}_2$ value. When $L = 16$, the normalized level crossing rates using table lookup approximation are always higher than that obtained by linear recursion method. To secure similar performance, L has to be as large as 512.

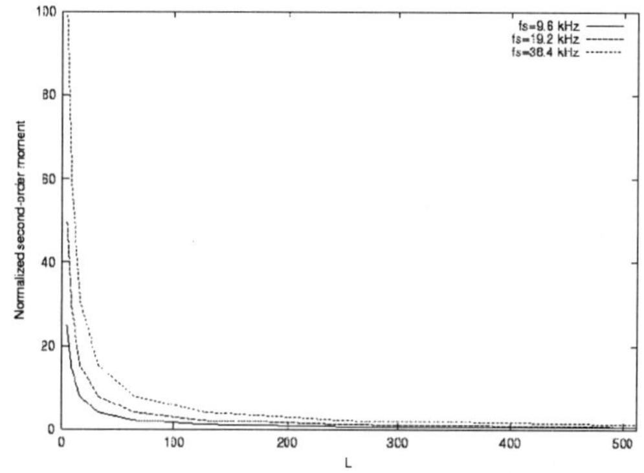

Figure 3. The normalized second order moments $\frac{\tilde{b}_2}{\omega_M^2}$ as a function of lookup table size L with different sampling frequencies f_s ($\omega_M = 2\pi \times 50$ rad/s, $N_0 = 8, M = 8$, $k = 0$).

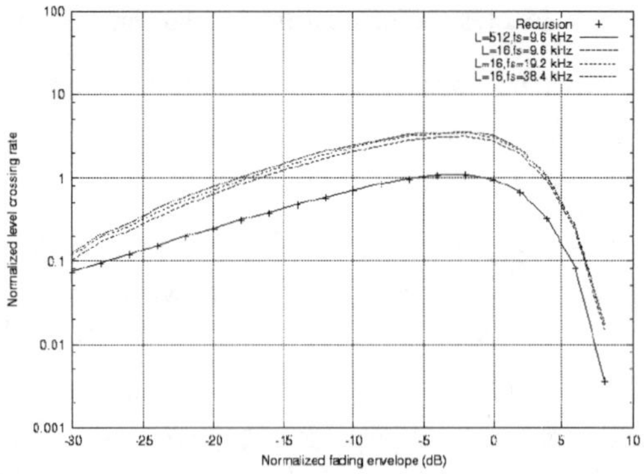

Figure 4. The normalized level crossing rates $\frac{N_R}{f_M}$ *for linear recursion method and table lookup approximation* ($\omega_M = 2\pi \times 50$ *rad/s,* $N_0 = 8$, $M = 8$, $k = 0$)*, where the normalized fading envelope is defined as the ratio of the fading envelope over its root-mean-square value.*

V. CONCLUSIONS

The improved multiple independent Rayleigh faders use different Doppler frequency shift sets to generate Rayleigh distributed waveforms which satisfy the independence requirement with each other. To reduce the computational effort involved in evaluating the sinusoids related to these Doppler frequency shifts, two computational reduction methods are analyzed and tested. The table lookup method provides good approximation to the ideal auto-correlation function according to the mean-square-error criterion even when the size of the lookup table is small. However, the second order moment of the simulated power spectral density is increased dramatically, which degrades the performance such as the level crossing rate of the simulated waveform. To secure better performance, sufficiently large lookup table size should be used. The linear recursion method can generate exact sinusoidal wave efficiently so that the performance will not be affected by the computational reduction. Consequently, the reduced-complexity independent Rayleigh faders with linear recursion provide both computational efficiency and performance acceptance for the simulation of multiple Rayleigh fading communication channels.

REFERENCES

Crespo, P. M. and J. Jimenez. 1995. "Computer Simulation of Radio Channels Using a Harmonic Decomposition Technique." IEEE Transactions on Vehcular Technology, Vol. 44, No. 3, August: 414-419.

Dent, P.; G. E. Bottomley; and T. Croft. 1993. "Jakes Fading Model Revisited." Electronics Letters, Vol. 29, No. 13, June: 1162-1163.

Fechtel, S. A. 1993. "A novel Approach to Modeling and Efficient Simulation of Frequency-Selective Fading Radio Channels." IEEE Journal on Selected Areas in Communications, Vol. 11, No. 3, April: 422-431.

Jakes, W. C. (Editor). 1974. *Microwave Mobile Communications.* AT&T IMP Corp., Reprinted by IEEE Press, 1994.

Li, Y. and X. Huang. 2000. "The Generation of Independent Rayleigh Faders." Presented at ICC'2000 on 19 June, 2000, New Orleans, USA.

Lin, K.-S. (Editor). 1987. *Digital Signal Processing Applications with the TMS320 Family, Volume 1.* Prentice-Hall, Inc., Englewood Cliffs, New Jersey.

Oppenheim, A. V. and R. W. Schafer, *Digital Signal Processing*, Prentice-Hall, Inc., Englewood Cliffs, New Jersey.

Patzold, M.; U. Killat; and F. Laue. 1996. "A Deterministic Digital Simulation Model for Suzuki Processes with Application to a Shadowed Rayleigh Land Mobil Radio Channel." IEEE Transactions on Vehicular Technology, Vol. 45, No. 2, May: 318-331.

Proakis, J. G. 1989. *Digital Communications.* McGraw-Hill Book Company.

Verdin, D. and T. C. Tozer. 1993. "Generating a Fading Process for the Simulation of Land-Mobile Radio Communications." Electronics Letters, Vol. 29, No. 23, 11 November: 2011-2012.

Young, D. J. and N. C. Beaulieu. 1998. "A Quantitative Evaluation of Generation Methods for Correlated Rayleigh Random Variates." In Proceedings of GLOBECOM'1998, 3332-3337.

A Novel Management Model for Distributing the Bandwidth Available over Active Connections

M. M. Jahromi and H. S. Al-Raweshidy
Communication System Division
Electronic Engineering Laboratory
University of Kent at Canterbury
Canterbury, Kent, CT2 7NT, UK
e-mail: (mj8@ukc.ac.uk) or (H.Al-Raweshidy@ukc.ac.uk)

Telecommunications, Dynamic and Traffic Management.

ABSTRACT

The purpose of this simulation was to setup and compare ABR service class connections to CBR service class connections. The modelled ABR system allocates to each active source a fair amount of bandwidth according to its production weight and traffic requirements by using closed-loop feedback controller. Active sources share the bandwidth with certain criteria to insure that at least all the active connections will be assigned with the amount of bandwidth negotiated for MCR guarantee and the rest will be distributed over them according to their traffic load and precedence. ABR improves the number of received cells and reduces the queuing delay, however, the amount of improvement in the number of received cells over all the sources can be added together while the amount of reduction in the queuing delay that depends on the traffic weight distribution cannot be added. Hence, the factor of total improvement in the number of received cells as a function of the percentage of un-used bandwidth has been modelled and fitted within an equation with six constant parameters and only one variable parameter (%un-used bandwidth). The mean value of the error between the model achievement and the fitted curve is 4.89E-5 and its standard deviation is 0.06587.

INDRODUCTION

The access to the Internet with multimedia applications will be one of the principal services of the next generation access networks. Multimedia consists of voice, video and data in the same application with high level of QoS requirement. Therefore, as dial-up IP connections run at fixed and low transmission bit rate without any QoS guarantees, it is not sufficient enough for such demands and services. The purpose of ATM is to provide a high trunk speed, low bit error rate, low delay multiplexing and switching network with high level of QoS guarantee irrespective to the nature of the traffic. This makes the ATM based access networks very suitable for future demands and services even for carrying IP-packets (datagrams). Furthermore, the task of multimedia traffic management and bandwidth allocation over ABR service class is the promising solution for highly cost-effective networks with very high bandwidth efficiency. The Block Oriented Network Discrete-event Simulator (BONeS) package has been used to setup and compare ABR service class connections with CBR service class connections. (Black 1998a), (Black 1998b), (Kerckeval 1998) and (Pryker 1995)

TRAFFIC MANAGEMENT

Unlike traditional forms of networking, ATM provides the capability to manage the traffic according to subscribers requirements and demands. This leads to fair bandwidth allocation, which means each connection will get its fair share whatever the fair is defined.

ATM Forum has defined and standardised five types of services: constant bit rate (CBR), real time variable bit rate (rt-VBR), non real time variable bit rate (nrt-VBR), unspecified bit rate (UBR) and available bit rate (ABR). The CBR service class, which has very high cost and its bandwidth utilisation is very low, negotiate the peak cell rate (PCR) parameter during connection setup and provides bandwidth and QoS guarantees. The PCR and sustainable cell rate (SCR) parameters are negotiated during VBR service class connection setup. This class guaranteed bandwidth and QoS with low bandwidth utilisation and high cost. The UBR service class is a simple service that gives no guarantees. The traditional Internet services would fall into this class while it is rarely used for transmitting multimedia applications, as they required high bet rate with QoS guaranteed.

To improve bandwidth utilisation, ATM Forum defined the ABR service class. In addition to the large number of parameters to be negotiated during connection setup, it allows bandwidth renegotiation during transmission using resource management cells and feedback controller. Although, ABR service class provides only minimum cell rate (MCR) as bandwidth guarantee, its QoS guarantee is acceptable at very low cost with high bandwidth efficiency. In such connection type, the sources are dynamically adjust their transmis sion rate based on the feedback controller decision, which monitor the network traffic constantly.

The traffic requirement classifications are related to three parameters: QoS guarantee, bandwidth efficiency and fairness. The key role in meeting these parameters is played by traffic management techniques. These techniques can be subdivided into three levels according to their area of operation and consideration. The first level, which is the lowest level of operation, called the node level controls. The controllers of this level that operate locally within each node control the parameters, which are assigned to this level via upper levels. This includes buffer scheduling, traffic shaping and packet discarding. The next level of traffic management techniques, which operates between first and third levels, is the network level controls. The operators at this level act as network nodes co-ordinators and control the network traffic. This level includes routing, call admission control and flow control. The third level, which is the main traffic management level, called network-engineering level. This level assigned the controllers values and commends to the other levels. This includes topology design, capacity assignment, routing design and server location.

However, all the three traffic management levels and techniques involved can be classified into six tasks as follows: bandwidth allocation, traffic shaping and rate control, flow control, scalable transmission, admission control, and congestion control. The main compatibility between these six tasks is that the feedback controller plays the main role in their management so it can be considered as the core of the various traffic management tasks. (Krunz 1999) and (Zheng and Atiquzzaman 1999)

SIMULATED SYSTEMS

As it was mentioned earlier, the purpose of this simulation was to setup and compare ABR service class connections to CBR service class connections with aims of reducing the cost and improving the bandwidth utilisation without loosing the QoS guarantees. Therefore, two identical systems were designed and modelled by using BONeS, block oriented network discrete event simulator, package; one setups CBR service class connections and the other setups ABR service class connections. The sources in both systems produces delay sensitive signals that requires the same PCR but with different production weights. The production weights are arranged in such a way that almost there will be an amount of the unused bandwidth overall the system all the time. This means the load over the sources buffers will vary, some will be lightly loaded, few will be heavily loaded and others will be loaded with sufficient amount of traffic. Therefore, in the CBR system that assigns to each source a fixed amount of bandwidth as a result of bandwidth negotiation during the connection setup, the bandwidth efficiency for the lightly loaded connections will be low while for the heavily loaded connections it will be over saturation with large amount of delay and cell loses.

Unlike the CBR system, the ABR system allocates to each active source a fair amount of bandwidth according to its production weight and traffic requirements. Active sources share the bandwidth with certain criteria to insure that at least all the active con nections will be assigned with the amount of bandwidth required for MCR guarantee and the rest will be distributed over them according to their traffic load and precedence. This distribution will be dynamically controlled and adjusted over instant active connections via feedback controller involved in ABR servic class connections.

From the feedback information the instant amount of un-used bandwidth (UB(t)) will be computed according to the following equation:

$$UB(t) = Total\ Bandwidth - \sum_{i=1}^{n(t)} MCR_i \qquad (1$$

Where n(t) is the instant number of the active connections. Then, the amount of UB(t) will be distributed over all the instant active connections fairly according to their traffic load as shown in (2):

$$B_i(t) = MCR_i + \left[UB(t) * \frac{TL_i(t)}{TL_T(t)} \right] \qquad (2$$

Where $B_i(t)$ is the instant allocated bandwidth to the connection i, $TL_i(t)$ is the instant traffic load over the connection i, and $TL_T(t)$ is the instant traffic load over all th connections. It consists of two parts, the first part is to insur the minimum cell rate guarantee and the other part is to manage fair distribution of the UB(t).

SIMULATION RESULTS AND DISCUTIONS

The systems were simulated for 11 cases via varying the average amount of unused bandwidth. Figures 1 and 2 are plots for a case with an average of 48% un-used bandwidth. It is clear that ABR system improves the number of receivec cells and reduces the queuing delay. Due to differences in the traffic weights over the shown sources A and B, the effect of the model over source B that has much higher traffic weight than source A, is more.

In CBR system, the number of received cells from both sources A and B is 5000 cells for each while in ABR system the number of received cells from sources A and B are 7877 and 16044 cells with 57.54% and 220.88% improvement respectively.

In other hand, the maximum cell queuing delay in CBR system for cells produced by sources A and B are 519.17 and 805.93 unit of transmission respectively. The corresponding values for the same amount of received cells from sources A and B in ABR system are 148.96 and 115.05 unit of transmission respectively. These values increase, as the number of received cells improves, up-to the maximum cell queuing delay 242.96 and 374.17 unit of transmission respectively.

However, the amount of improvement in the number of received cells over all the sources can be added together while the amount of reduction in the queuing delay that depends on the traffic weight distribution cannot be added. For the case of 48% un-used bandwidth the percentage of improvement in the number of received cells over all the sources is 92.75%. Hence, figure 3 is a plot of percentage improvement in the number of received cells over all the sources against the percentage of un-used bandwidth. The model given by (3) has been estimated from this curve by using curve-fitting technique.

$$Y(x) = a\log(bx) + cx^3 + dx^2 + f\sqrt{x} + g \qquad (3)$$

Where: $a = 3.58*10^{-9}$,
$b = 10.06$,
$c = 8.39$,
$d = -2.17$,
$f = 0.76$, and
$g = -0.045$.

The mean value of the error between the model achievement and the fitted curve is 4.89E-5 and its standard deviation is 0.06587.

CONCLUSIONS

This paper illustrates the benefits of ABR service class connections verses CBR service class connections. ABR service class connections provides maximum bandwidth utilisation at very low cost. It controls the traffic management issues and adjusts the sources transmission rates dynamically using a closed-loop feedback controller.

Active sources share the bandwidth with certain criteria to insure that at least all the active connections will be assigned with the amount of bandwidth negotiated for MCR guarantee and the rest will be distributed over them according to their traffic load and precedence. ABR improves the number of received cells and reduces the queuing delay, however, the amount of improvement in the number of received cells over all the sources can be added together while the amount of reduction in the queuing delay that depends on the traffic weight distribution cannot be added. Hence, the factor of total improvement in the number of received cells as a function of the percentage of un-used bandwidth has been modelled and fitted within an equation with six constant parameters and only one variable parameter (%un-used bandwidth). The mean value of the error between the model achievement and the fitted curve is 4.89E-5 and its standard deviation is 0.06587.

REFFERNCES

Black, Uyless, 1998a, ATM I: Foundation for broadband networks, 2nd edition, Prentice Hall PTR.

Black, Uyless, 1998b, ATM III: Internetworking, 1st edition Prentice Hall PTR.

Kerckeval, B., 1998, TCP/IP over ATM, 1st edition, Prentice Hall PTR.

Krunz, Marwan, 1999, "Bandwidth Allocation Strategies fo Transporting Variable-Bit-Rate Video Traffic", IEEE Communications Magazine, Vol. 37 No. 1 (Jan.): 40-46.

Pryker, Martin, 1995, Asynchronous Transfer Mode: Solution for Broadband ISDN, 3rd edition, Prentice Hall PTR.

Zheng, Bing and Atiquzzaman, Mohammed, 1999, "Traffic Management of Multimedia over ATM Networks", IEEE Communications Magazine, Vol. 37 No. 1 (Jan.): 33-38.

BIOGRAPHY

M. M. Jahromi (mj8@ukc.ac.uk) is a PhD student working in ATM networking, Voice over ATM, Voice over IP and IP-ATM mobility at University of Kent at Canterbury. He received his MSc. in "Control and Information Technology" from the University of Manchester Institute of Since and Technology (UMIST) in 1996

H. S. Al-Raweshidy (H.Al-Raweshidy@ukc.ac.uk) received his PhD degree from Strathclyde University for work in the area of spread spectrum multiplexing technique for optical communication networks. Currently, he is leading a group of 15 researchers in the area of Radio-over-Fibre and Mobile IP at the Communication Systems Division, Electronic Engineering Laboratory, University of Kent. He is a member of IEE and a senior member of IEEE. He acts as a Guest editor for the International Journal of Wireless Personal Communications, he is a member of International Advisory Committees and Technical Program Committees of several conferences.

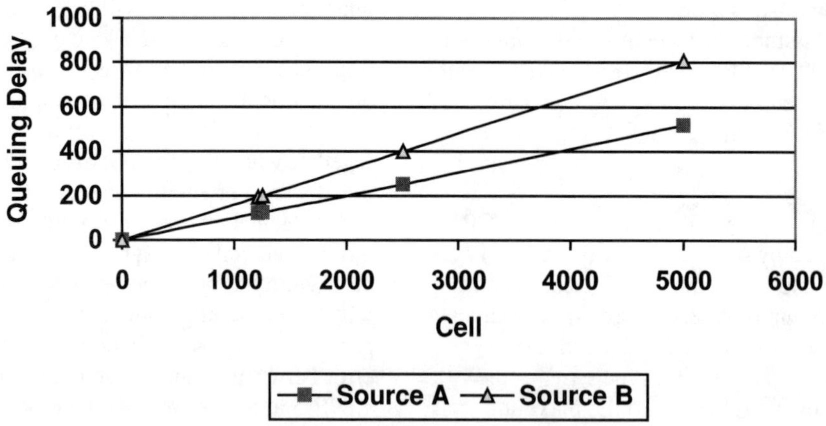

Figure 1: CBR system results for 48% UB

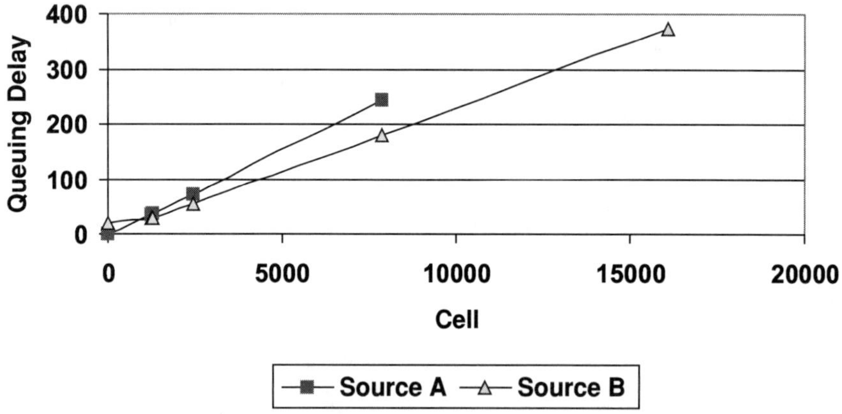

Figure 2: ABR system results for 48% UB

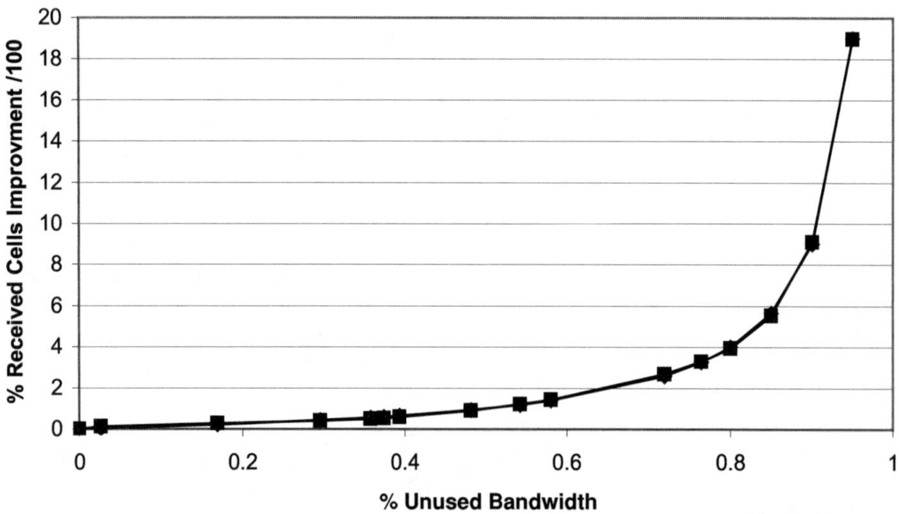

Figure 3: The effect of ABR over CBR model

ISSUES IN PARALLEL DISCRETE EVENT SIMULATION FOR AN INTERNET TELEPHONY CALL SIGNALING PROTOCOL

Phillip M. Dickens
Vijay K. Gurbani

Department of Computer Science and Applied Mathematics
Illinois Institute of Technology
Chicago, Illinois
Email: pmd@work.csam.iit.edu, vkg@rice.iit.edu

Paper code: S262

KEYWORDS: PDES, INTERNET, TELEPHONY, JAVA, FEATURES, SOFTSWITCH

ABSTRACT

In the world of Internet telephony, features are implemented somewhat differently than they are in the existing circuit-switched world. In Internet telephony, features can be implemented as Java applets that are controlled by an Internet call controller. As call signaling and feature deployment move towards the Internet as the network of choice, there is an increasing need to understand and predict the behavior of such systems in the Internet environment. One way to provide such insight is to develop discrete event simulation models of the entities involved in signaling and feature deployment. Given the size and complexity of such models, it is necessary to distribute the simulation across multiple computers to achieve reasonable performance.

In this paper, we discuss the issues involved in designing and implementing a parallel discrete event simulator for Internet telephony. In particular, we look at the issue of how to model network traffic contention within the Internet, how to best model the Java applets implementing the user features, how to synchronize the simulation, and how to maximize the performance of the simulation. While we discuss these issues within the context of Internet telephony, the solutions will be applicable to a wide range of simulation problems.

1 INTRODUCTION

In the world of Internet telephony, features[1] are implemented somewhat differently than they are in the existing circuit-switched telephony world. In the circuit-switched world, features are provided mostly by originating and terminating switches (it's actually a little bit more complicated than this since the features may not reside on the switch itself, but another host accessible to the switch; however, for our discussion, this abstraction will suffice). When a caller picks up a phone and dials a callee, the originating switch applies features to the caller's end point. When the call reaches the terminating switch, the callee's features are applied to the call.

In Internet telephony, with its emphasis on speed of creating and deploying features, the model of applying call features is somewhat different. In the circuit-switched world, a feature is written in special, often proprietary languages and, out of necessity, tied to a switch. In Internet telephony, a feature may well be a Java applet, spawned by an Internet call controller, and running on behalf of some user X. As an example, the feature being implemented may keep track of which of X's friends visit a certain web site, and upon her visit, invite her to a phone conference with X. The invited friend may herself have a feature applet to field such requests and deal with them appropriately. For instance, if it is between 9:00 AM and 12:00 PM, it is okay for X to call. Otherwise, X's call will be directed to her voicemail system.

User feature applets, once started, communicate between themselves using the Internet as the transmission medium and a call processing state machine to keep the call state

[1] A feature is a service provided by the telephone network; thus call waiting and caller ID are examples of telephony features.

synchronized between them. The call processing state machine is thus distributed by its very nature.

We are in the process of designing and implementing a distributed discrete event simulator to simulate the interactions of feature applets during the call setup phase, as they synchronize themselves based on the distributed call processing state machine. The simulator will answer the following basic question: given N users in a call, each with a feature applet, and the network throughput of the transmission medium being P (0 <= P <= 1) how long does it take to establish a call between the parties? It turns out however that developing such a simulator raises many interesting and difficult issues that have not yet been addressed by the simulation community. In this paper, we describe these issues and discuss possible solutions.

The rest of this paper is organized as follows: Section 2 gives a detailed look into the entities that comprise the call controller and feature applets, and the messages passed between them to successfully execute a user feature. Section 3 outlines the major issues to be addressed as this research moves forward, and Section 4 outlines related work.

2 ENTITIES INVOLVED IN THE SIMULATION

The Q.931 protocol [Itu98] is one of the primary UNI (User-to-Network Interface) protocols, and is the protocol used in our simulations. We begin by identifying the primary entities involved in the simulation, and the Q.931-like messages (signals) that are passed between these entities to establish a call.

The main entities in our simulation are:

1. The Internet softswitch running the call controller (coordinates the call). The softswitch is assumed to be executing on a general-purpose workstation or high-performance PC.
2. The device associated with the caller (phone, PC, etc.).
3. The user feature applet associated with the caller.
4. The device associated with the callee (phone, PC, etc.).
5. The user feature applet associated with the callee.

Note that there can be multiple callees participating in a call, each with its own device and user feature applet. However, there is only one caller (with its associated device and user feature applet).

Callers initiate the call; callees are recipients of the call. As the call signaling progresses, the devices communicate with the Internet call controller to inform it of certain events, which in turn causes the Internet call controller to send messages to the caller's and callee's user feature applets. The Internet call controller also sends messages to the devices to inform them of certain events. The set of messages a device sends to and receives from the Internet call controller consists of the following:

- **Call Request**: *Sent* by a caller's device when the user owning it wants to make a call. *Received* by the callee's device to indicate a call request has been initiated.
- **Call Proceeding**: *Sent* by the callee's device when call establishment procedures have been initiated. *Received* by the caller's device to indicate that call establishment procedures have been initiated.
- **Call Alerting**: *Sent* by the callee's device to indicate that the callee has been "alerted." *Received* by the caller's device
- **Call Connect**: *Sent* by the callee's device when the callee picks up her endpoint. *Received* by the caller's device to indicate that the callee has connected.
- **Call Disconnect**: sent by either callee or caller's device when the party hangs up.
- **Call Disconnect Ack** Sent by the party that receives the **Call Disconnect** message.

As noted, the user feature applet also receives messages from the Internet call controller. These messages are sent as the call state progresses and result in the execution of certain callback methods in the receiving applet. Note that it is also possible for user feature applets to send messages to each other through the Internet call controller. The callback methods executed by an applet in response to messages sent by the call controller include:

- **onInitCaller:** The caller's applet is being initialized.
- **onInitCallee:** The callee's applet is being initialized.
- **onCallProceeding:** Call is being sent to the callee.
- **onCallAlerting:** The callee is being alerted; callee hears audible ringing, for instance.
- **onCallConnect:** Callee has picked up her end device (i.e. telephone).
- **onCallDisconnect:** Callee or caller has hung up.
- **onCallDisconnectAck:** Call has been released.
- **onSendCallProceeding:** propagates a Call Proceeding message to all other participants in the call, except the participant who generated the Call Proceeding message.
- **onSendCallAlerting:** propagates a Call Alerting message to all other participants in the call, except the participant who generated the Call Alerting message.
- **onSendCallConnect:** propagates a Call Connect message to all other participants in the call, except the participant who generated the Call Connect message.
- **onSendCallDisconnect:** propagates a Call Disconnect message to all other participants in the call, except the participant who generated the Call Disconnect message.

Figure 1 depicts a time-line diagram representing the flow of messages for call establishment that occur between the caller's user feature applet, the Internet call controller, and the callee's user feature applet. The caller picks up her device and initiates a call, which results in a **Call Request** message to be transmitted to the call controller from the caller's device. The call controller then loads the caller's and the callee's user feature applets in memory and calls two callback methods: **onCallerInit()** for the caller and **onCalleeInit()** for the callee. The original **Call Request** message then makes its way to the callee's device, notifying it of the caller's desire to set up communication.

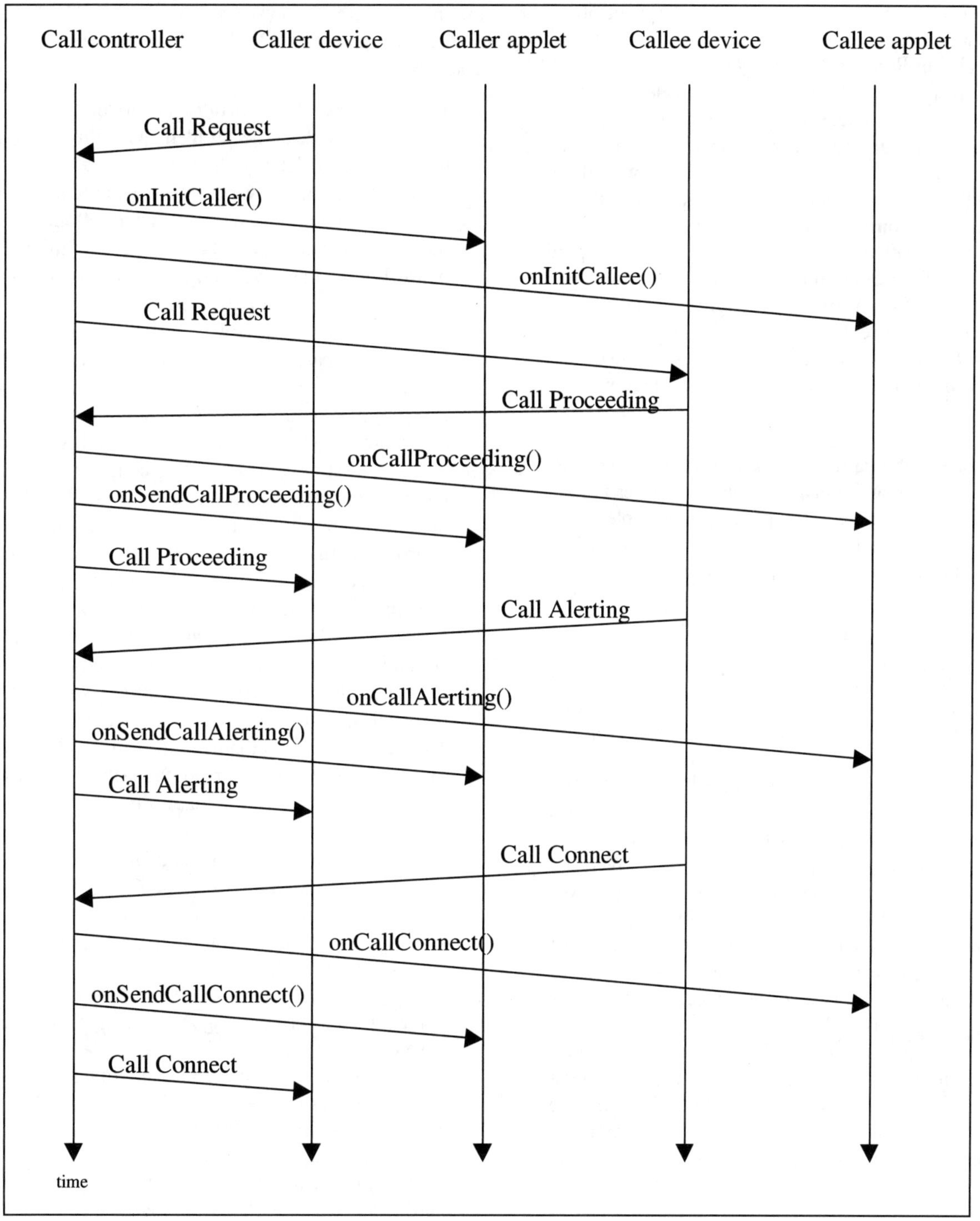

Figure 1: Call establishment messages and callbacks.

The callee's device, upon receiving the **Call Request** message, sends a **Call Proceeding** message to the call controller. This triggers the call controller to invoke two callback methods: **onCallProceeding()** and **onSendCallProceeding()** on the callee and caller respectively. The call controller then forwards the original **Call Proceeding** message from the callee's device to the caller's device.
Following the **Call Proceeding** message, the callee's device sends a **Call Alerting** message to the controller, which in turn invokes two callback methods: **onCallAlerting()** and **onSendCallAlerting()** on the callee and caller respectively. As before, the call controller then forwards the original **Call Alerting** message from the callee's device to the caller's device. When the callee's device gets the **Call Alerting** message, it emits an audible (or visible) indicator to the callee. As soon as the callee picks up its end point, a **Call Connect** message is sent from the callee's device to the call controller. The call controller, upon receiving the **Call Connect** message sends out an **onCallConnect()** and **onSendCallConnect()** to the caller and callee respectively. Once the **Call Connect** message makes its way to the caller's device, the call is established and voice data can begin to flow through the medium (the Internet in this case).

Eventually, one of the parties will hang up their end of the connection. When that happens, the call controller propagates disconnection events to the participating applets and devices, much as it did the connection-related events. We do not discuss further the call disconnect events.

3 ISSUES

There are a number of interesting issues that arise when designing a parallel discrete event simulation to model this system. Clearly, there is a significant amount of messaging activity that has to take place to perform this signaling, and this raises the question of how to best model Internet traffic contention within the simulation. Another issue has to do with the best way to model the activity of the user feature applets. One approach would be to model the applets by actually executing them and observing their behavior. Another approach would be to model the applet's execution with a random (or constant) completion time, and a set of predefined actions caused by its execution. The choice of implementation language is also an important consideration that will have a broad impact on the performance and scalability of the simulation. Finally, since the simulation model is executing across multiple platforms, there must be some mechanism to ensure simulation fidelity. The choice of this synchronization mechanism will have a significant impact on the performance and scalability of the simulation. In this section, we discuss each of these issues.

3.1 Modeling Network Contention

Consider the case of a caller's device sending a Call Request message to the call controller. It is clear that a certain amount of delay, say **t**, will be encountered by this message as it traverses the Internet from the caller's device to the call controller. This delay is clearly a function of the amount and type of Internet/Intranet traffic at that point in time plus the processing overhead at each of the hosts. So how do we quantify **t**? There are three possible approaches:

1. Write our own Internet/Intranet model as part of the simulation model. The problem with this approach is that such a model is extremely complex (and would thus make an already complicated simulation model even more complicated), and that developing such a model from scratch would duplicate a significant body of work aimed at developing scalable Internet simulation models (e.g. SSF[Cowi99]).
2. Another approach would be to build a model of the Intranet (or parts of the Internet) of interest using a pre-existing simulation package (such as SSF or ns [NS]) and execute the network simulation *offline* under various loads and configurations. This would provide some set of values for **t** that could be plugged into the simulation (for example, a value for **t** under light, medium and heavy loads). The disadvantage of this approach is that it is less flexible than simulating the network contention as the call signaling simulation is executing. In particular, it does not allow for the interaction of the call signaling simulation and the network simulation (e.g. in the real system the voice packets generated during a telephone call have an impact on the level of traffic on the common network medium).
3. The best approach, albeit the most difficult, would be to incorporate into our simulation a pre-existing simulation framework that simulates the Internet/Intranet traffic throughput. In this case, our simulator would input the call signaling message traffic into the external framework, and simply observe the time at which it reaches its destination. In effect, our simulator would be just another traffic source for the external framework.

   For example, consider Figure 2. In this example, the device associated with user 1 sends a Call Request message to the call controller at time $\mathbf{t_0}$. Thus this message enters into the network (being simulated by a an external simulation framework) at time $\mathbf{t_0}$. The message then competes for network bandwidth with the other traffic being modeled in the external framework (and any other call signaling messages already in the network). In this example, the Call Request message exits the external simulation framework (and arrives at the call controller) at time $\mathbf{t_1}$.

This approach of course requires an external simulation framework with well-defined inputs for our simulator to plug into. We are currently investigating existing simulation frameworks to determine if they can be used in this manner.

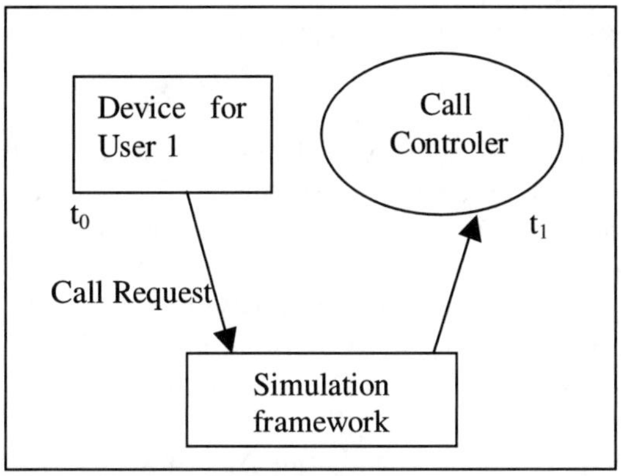

Figure 2: A simulation framework.

3.2 Direct execution simulation or "educated guess?"

A key component of the next generation Internet telephony will be the user feature applets that can be applied to the calls as they are being set up. Given the importance of this aspect of the system, it is critical to realistically model the feature applets in the simulation. So what is the best way to model such features? There are two basic options that we discuss in turn.

One way to model the user feature applets is to use the technique of direct *execution simulation.* In this approach, the behavior of a user feature applet is obtained by actually executing the applet and observing its behavior. Thus the call controller will actually spawn Java Virtual Machines (JVMs) when initializing the caller and callee applets. Subsequently, when a callback occurs the JVM previously spawned actually executes the callback method to determine its behavior. This of course provides the simulation with a very accurate model of the behavior of the applet being executed.

There are however difficult issues that must be addressed when using direct execution simulation. Perhaps the most important issue is how to determine the length of time it takes to execute a user feature applet. The problem presents itself when there are not enough computers available to dedicate a CPU to *each* of the user applets executing at a particular time in the simulation. To understand this issue, it is important to note that when an applet has a dedicated machine, hardware clocks can be used to provide an accurate accounting of the time the applet executes. When multiple applets are being multiplexed on the same CPU however, hardware clocks cannot provide this same service. The problem is that such clocks do not account for the time a process is swapped out due to the effects of multiprogramming. The issue then is how to factor out the length of time an applet is swapped out due to the effects of multiprogramming. (The interested reader is directed to [Dick96] for a detailed discussion of this problem.)

One solution to this problem would be to develop a model of the effects of multiprogramming, and to use this model to determine the amount of time an applet would have executed had it not been for the effects of multiprogramming. This certainly complicates the simulation model, but the more accurate picture of feature applet behavior may be worth the additional complexity.

The second approach to modeling the behavior of the user feature applets could be considered the "educated guess" scenario. In this approach, some reasonable estimate of applet execution time is developed and plugged into the simulation model. In a similar manner, some reasonable estimate of the behavior of the applets would have to be included in the model.

3.3 Implementation Language

We have chosen Java as the implementation language for a number of reasons. First, it has excellent support for distributed computing (including networking and serializing support). Also, Java supports multiple execution threads and handles the details of garbage collection. Perhaps the most important reason to use Java is that it is a highly portable language. In fact, previous research has demonstrated that Java's capabilities match very well with the requirements of distributed simulations [Kilg98, Pidd98].

The disadvantage of Java is that it is notoriously slow. However, as Java has grown in popularity its performance has been improving. An important aspect of this research will be the development of mechanisms to optimize Java's performance in this arena.

3.4 Synchronization protocol

The problem of maintaining temporal or causal fidelity between the various entities in a PDES is well studied [Fuji90]. The solution to this problem can be approached from two angles: using "conservative" techniques, or using "optimistic" techniques.

The "conservative" techniques work by ensuring that when a host processor processes an event with timestamp t, it will never receive an event with timestamp less then t from any other processor in the simulation [Lege96]. It has been well established that for conservative techniques to work well, good *lookahead* (defined as the simulator's ability to predict its future behavior) is required. Thus if a conservative approach is adopted, an important component of the research will be to identify and exploit the lookahead available in the simulation model.

"Optimistic" techniques, on the other hand, allow a processor to optimistically execute any event it receives (without waiting to ensure that it will never receive an event with a smaller timestamp). A state saving and rollback mechanism is employed to correct any out-of-order processing that does occur.

The decision to use either a conservative or an optimistic synchronization technique is still being investigated. Either of these techniques can be applied to the simulation being proposed, and we will perform some preliminary studies to determine which approach appears to be the most promising.

4 RELATED WORK

The work most closely related to this project is the call signaling simulation described in [Eyer00]. The primary difference is that their work pays close attention to the signaling aspect and does not consider the modeling of user feature applets, which is a significant component of this project.

[Lin95] studied PDES and its application to a specific field in telecommunication – Personal Communication Service (PCS). The goal of the PCS simulation is to optimally design cellular networks to minimize the blocking probability (a call is blocked if there are no channels available at a given cell). [Lin95] describes both conservative and optimistic simulations for PCS.

Other related work includes SSF[Cowi99] and ns[NS], both of which are network simulation packages. One of our goals is to incorporate the services of such packages in our simulation framework.

REFERENCES

[Cowi99] Jim Cowie, Hongbo Liu, et. al. Towards Realistic Million-Node Internet Simulations. *Proceedings of the 1999 International Conference on Parallel and Distributed Processing Techniques and Applications*, http://www.ssfnet.org/Papers/pdpta99.pdf.

[Dick96] P. Dickens, P. Heidelberger and D. Nicol. Parallelized Direct Execution Simulation of Message-Passing Parallel Programs. In *IEEE Transactions on Parallel and Distributed Systems.* Zvolume 7, Number 10, October 1996.

[Eyer00]Tony Eyers and Henning Schulzrinne. Predicting Internet Telephony Call Setup Delay. http://www.cs.columbia.edu/~hgs/papers/Eyer0004_Predicting.pdf

[Fuji90] Richard M. Fujimoto. Parallel discrete event simulation. *Communication of the ACM*, 33(10):30-53, October 1990.

[Itu98] ITU-T Recommendation Q.931 (1998) *ISDN user-network interface layer 3 specification for basic call control.*

[Kilg98] Richard A. Kilgore, Kevin J. Healy and George B. Kleindorfer. The future of Java-based simulation. In *Proceedings of the 1998 Winter Simulation Conference.*

[Lege96] Ulana Legedza and William E. Weihl. Reducing synchronization overhead in parallel simulation. *1996 Proceedings of the 10th Workshop on PADS*, pages 86-95.

[Lin95] Yi-Bing Lin and Paul A. Fishwick. Asynchronous Parallel Discrete Event Simulation. In *IEEE Transactions on Systems, Man, and Cybernetics, 1995.*

[NS] UCB/LBNL/VINT Network Simulator – ns (version 2), http://www-mash.cs.berkeley.edu/ns/

[Pidd98] M. Pidd and R.A. Cassel. Three phase simulation in Java. In *Proceedings of the 1998 Winter Simulation Conference.*

[Rapp96] Theodore S. Rappaport. Wirless Communications: Principles and Practices. *PrenticeHall Publishing Company, 1996.*

[Schu99] Henning Schulzrinne, Mark Handley, Eve Schooler, and Jonathan Rosenberg. SIP: Session Initiation Protocol. IETF RFC 2543.

HYDRODYNAMIC MODELLING AND SIMULATION OF OIL SANDS SLURRY FLOW IN FLEXIBLE PIPELINES

S. Frimpong, C. Meng, R.M.M. Changirwa and J.K. Szymanski
Centre for Advanced Mine Design Research
School of Mining and Petroleum Engineering
Room 220, Civil-Electrical Building
University of Alberta, Edmonton, Canada T6G 2G7
Email: sam.frimpong@ualberta.ca

Key Words: multi-phase flow, slurry flow, oil sand, flexible pipeline, hydraulic modeling

ABSTRACT

Excavation and haulage technology at Syncrude combines large-capacity dump trucks, shovels and the hydrotransport technology for mining operations. Currently, dump truck costs account for over 25 percent of the total production cost. Increasing haulage distances in the oil sands terrain at Syncrude will require many dump trucks to meet production targets and result in severe tire wear, frequent tire replacements and fleet maintenance and management problems. In addition, the need for reducing CO_2 and other exhaust pollutants emissions from diesel dump trucks warrants the use of a more efficient, less costly and an environmentally-friendly technology. A potential replacement technology is the 'at face slurrying' (AFS) technology. In this paper, the authors advance knowledge into the flexible pipeline hydraulics. Using the laws of mass and momentum conservation for both the fluid and the solid media and their interfaces, partial differential equations (PDEs) are formulated to study the fluid flow in the AFS system. The PDE models and their boundary conditions are solved using numerical modeling techniques. The mechanics of the flexible system are formulated and simulated over an extended period using data and information from Syncrude's North Mine. The results show that the flexible system is technically and economically viable for productivity between 6,300 and 6,500 tons per hour. The simulated head loss for the system is 15.66 m per 400 m, which compares with 20 m per 400 m for the existing stationary system at Syncrude. The pressure gradient-radius curves are assymptotic to the pipe boundaries, which indicates steep axial pressure gradient in the neighbourhood zone.

INTRODUCTION

Large-scale surface mining operations are increasingly demanding large-capacity shovels and dump trucks for excavation, loading and haulage operations [1]. Mine production cost, using haulage trucks, is expected to increase with increasing haulage distances. Slurry transportation is an economic haulage system in oil sands and coal mining operations characterized by long haulage distances and rugged terrain. A flexible arrangement of pipelines and slurry production system on mobile units capable of folding, extending and following the excavators, radially, horizontally and vertically is an appropriate technology for solving this problem. This technology will be used to create and transport oil sands slurry from a production face through a flexible system to join a fixed pipeline network. The objective of this study is to provide an understanding into the hydraulics of the oil sands slurry flow through flexible pipelines using mathematical modeling, experimentation and simulation modeling. The oil sands slurry is a three-phase medium with water, sand and bitumen as the main components. Theoretical models have been developed to study this problem by considering a multiphase mixture as a pseudo single-phase fluid with variable density [12,13]. However, due to the simplified boundary conditions in these models, they are limited in their applications to actual flow situations. Thomas (1963) used the same pseudo single-phase approach to model a two-phase flow system. The unique aspect of pseudo single-phase technique is that it enables conservation equations to be developed for single-phase fluid in the computation of various parameters. Depending on the application, the most important parameters may include pressure drop in the slurry transportation pipeline to the deposition and the critical velocity in solid-liquid. Multiphase systems are assumed to be homogeneous in most theoretical and experimental works.

Hinze (1963) studied the multiphase slurry transportation for dispersed multiphase flow systems by treating the phases as distinct and interacting. The stress tensor was treated as a composite velocity made up of the dispersed solids and the slurry vehicle phase velocities. In this way, he accounted for the velocity slippage between the two phases, leaving out the effect of particle concentration on the shear viscosity of the stress tensor. Later, Murray (1965) developed a model for the entire slurry system that contained a virtual term that varied from Newton's third law. In addition, multiple-phase flows have been studied by combining the second law of thermodynamic with three Langragian multipliers to account for the entropy inequality common in two-phase flows, and thus, established restrictions on the form of the constitutive equations – particularly those at the fluid-particle interface – for the fluid-particle mixtures [19]. The end result of this approach was the introduction of a distinct hydrostatic pressure for each phase, along with an interfacial pressure. Nunziato (1983) used a different approach to formulate the governing equations for disperse two-phase flow by analyzing the motion of a single bubble or particle of the disperse phase in the continuous fluid. Prosperetti and Jones (1984) have developed several mathematical models for solving various two-phase flow problems on the basis of one-dimensional stratified flow of two inviscid fields (or fluids), with distinct pressures ascribed for the two fields.

In this case of high particle concentrations, collisions among the particles also give rise to growth in the rapidly varying component of the pressure field. Unlike the models by several researchers [18, 7, 19, 20, 21], the rapidly varying pressure component appeared only in the equation of motion for the continuous fluid phase. An attempt was made to characterize the rheological behavior of dilute suspensions, due to non-uniform particle distributions, by extending Nunziato's model to plane Poiseuille flow [22]. Poiseuille flow of a suspension through a vertical, two-dimensional channel was modelled. Two different models were used: one having distinct pressures, one for the solid phase, and one for the fluid phase; and the other model in which there was only one pressure [23]. They showed that in the case of the first model settling particles moved ahead of the fluid, and buoyant particles lagged behind. In this study,

FLOW MECHANICS OF THE FLEXIBLE SYSTEM

The fundamental approach to the flexible piping system modelling employs the Bernoulli equation between two points, connected by a streamline, where the conditions are known. For adjacent flexible pipe units,

$$h_1+\frac{P_1}{\rho g}+\frac{\upsilon_1^2}{2g}+\Delta h_p=h_2+\frac{P_2}{\rho g}+\frac{\upsilon_2^2}{2g}+\Delta h_f+\Delta h_m \tag{1}$$

The total head at point 1 must match with the total head at point 2, adjusted for any increase in head due to pumps, losses due to pipe friction and other losses due to entries, exits and fittings. The pump head is generally a function of the flow through the system. Friction losses are a complex function of the system geometry, the fluid properties and the flow rate in the system. By observation, the head loss is roughly proportional to the square of the flow rate in most engineering flows (fully developed, turbulent pipe flow). This observation leads to the Darcy-Weisbach equation for head loss due to friction:

$$\Delta h_f = f\frac{L}{D}\frac{\upsilon^2}{2g} \tag{2}$$

It is insensitive to moderate changes in the flow and is constant for fully turbulent flow. Thus, it is often useful to estimate the relationship as the head being directly proportional to the square of the flow rate to simplify calculations.

$$f = f(\mathrm{Re},\frac{\varepsilon}{D},A) \tag{3}$$

The relative roughness relates the height of a typical roughness element to the scale of the flow, represented by the pipe diameter, ε/D. Pipe cross-section area, A, is important, as deviations from circular cross-section will cause secondary flows that increase the pressure drop. For laminar flow, the head loss is proportional to velocity rather than velocity squared, thus the friction factor is inversely proportional to velocity. The Reynolds number must be based on the hydraulic diameter. Here we are concerned with circular and therefore there is no need for k determination. For turbulent flow, Colebrook (1939) found an implicit correlation for the friction factor in round pipes. This correlation converges well in few iterations. Like pipe friction, these losses are roughly proportional to the square of the flow rate.

To calculate losses in flexible piping systems with both pipe friction and minor losses use in place of the Darcy-Weisbach equation. The procedures are the same except that the K values may also change as iteration progresses.

$$\Delta h_f=\left(f\frac{L}{D}+\sum K\right)\frac{\upsilon^2}{2g} \tag{4}$$

The velocity spectra in pipe flow are important in determining the overall flow performance. In cylindrical coordinates, the Navier-Stokes Equation, with the components in the radial, tangential and axial directions respectively, are:

$$\left(\frac{\partial\upsilon_r}{\partial t}+\upsilon_r\frac{\partial\upsilon_r}{\partial r}+\frac{\upsilon_\theta}{r}\frac{\partial\upsilon_r}{\partial\theta}+\upsilon_z\frac{\partial\upsilon_r}{\partial z}-\frac{\upsilon_\theta^2}{r}\right)$$
$$=-\frac{1}{\rho}\frac{\partial p^*}{\partial r}+\vartheta\left(\frac{\partial^2\upsilon_r}{\partial r^2}+\frac{1}{r}\frac{\partial\upsilon_r}{\partial r}+\frac{1}{r^2}\frac{\partial^2\upsilon_r}{\partial\theta^2}+\frac{\partial^2\upsilon_r}{\partial z^2}-\frac{\upsilon_r}{r^2}-\frac{2}{r^2}\frac{\partial\upsilon_\theta}{\partial\theta}\right) \tag{5}$$

$$\left(\frac{\partial \upsilon_\theta}{\partial t}+\upsilon_r\frac{\partial \upsilon_\theta}{\partial r}+\frac{\upsilon_\theta}{r}\frac{\partial \upsilon_\theta}{\partial \theta}+\upsilon_z\frac{\partial \upsilon_\theta}{\partial z}-\frac{\upsilon_\theta \upsilon_r}{r}\right)$$
$$=-\frac{1}{\rho r}\frac{\partial p^*}{\partial \theta}+\vartheta\left(\frac{\partial^2 \upsilon_\theta}{\partial r^2}+\frac{1}{r}\frac{\partial \upsilon_\theta}{\partial r}+\frac{1}{r^2}\frac{\partial^2 \upsilon_r}{\partial \theta^2}+\frac{\partial^2 \upsilon_\theta}{\partial z^2}-\frac{\upsilon_\theta}{r^2}+\frac{2}{r^2}\frac{\partial \upsilon_r}{\partial \theta}\right) \quad (6)$$

$$\left(\frac{\partial \upsilon_z}{\partial t}+\upsilon_r\frac{\partial \upsilon_z}{\partial r}+\frac{\upsilon_\theta}{r}\frac{\partial \upsilon_z}{\partial \theta}+\upsilon_z\frac{\partial \upsilon_z}{\partial z}\right)$$
$$=-\frac{1}{\rho}\frac{\partial p^*}{\partial r}+\vartheta\left(\frac{\partial^2 \upsilon_z}{\partial r^2}+\frac{1}{r}\frac{\partial \upsilon_z}{\partial r}+\frac{1}{r^2}\frac{\partial^2 \upsilon_z}{\partial \theta^2}+\frac{\partial^2 \upsilon_z}{\partial z^2}\right) \quad (7)$$

Consider the viscous oil sands slurry flows inside a very long flexible pipe of circular cross-section. The streamlines of the flow are all parallel to the pipe axis so that the fluid velocity components in the radial and tangential directions are zero (υ_r, υ_θ =0). As the flow has axial symmetry, the axial velocity component, υ_z, depends only upon the radial coordinate, r. Using this information, the Navier-Stokes equations can be simplified. That is, dropping all terms in equations 5-7 that contain, υ_r, υ_θ or the z or θ derivatives of υ_z, since these terms are all zero, and rearranging:

$$\frac{\partial p^*}{\partial r}=0; \quad \frac{\partial p^*}{\partial \theta}=0 \quad (8)$$

$$\frac{\partial^2 \upsilon_z}{\partial r^2}+\frac{1}{r}\frac{\partial \upsilon_z}{\partial r}-\frac{1}{\mu}\frac{\partial p^*}{\partial z}=0 \quad (9)$$

From Equations (5) to (7), p* does not depend on r. However, Equation (7) requires that dp*/dz be at most a function of r only. The only way to satisfy these requirements is for the differential to be a constant, which means that the bracketed term in equation (7) is also a constant. Flows through a circular pipe are of great practical interest because a circular cross-section is the most common form pipe as in FPS. Because of the circular symmetry, Poiseuille flow is an axially-symmetric flow best described by using cylindrical coordinates. The Navier-Stokes for this flow, in equation (9), simplifies to the form:

$$\frac{d^2\upsilon_z}{dr^2}+\frac{1}{r}\left(\frac{d\upsilon_z}{dr}\right)=\frac{1}{r}\frac{d}{dr}\left(r\frac{d\upsilon_z}{dr}\right)=\frac{1}{\mu}\frac{dp^*}{dz} \quad (10)$$

Total derivatives are used because velocity and pressure components are individual functions of radial and axial distances, respectively. Rearranging equation 10 and integrating results in equation (11).

$$r\frac{d\upsilon_z}{dr}=\frac{r^2}{2\mu}\frac{dp^*}{dz}+c_1 \quad (11)$$

Imposing boundary conditions, the shear stress at the pipe centreline, must be zero because of axial symmetry.

$$\left.\frac{d\upsilon_z}{dr}\right|_{r=0}=0 \quad (12)$$

With c_1=0, dividing equation (6) and integrating:

$$\upsilon_z=\frac{r^2}{4\mu}\frac{dp^*}{dz}+c_2 \quad (13)$$

By imposing boundary conditions that the velocity at the pipe wall is zero, assuming it is a stationary wall, the value of c_2 can be determined. Rearranging equation (13), the parabolic velocity distribution for the circular flow is:

$$\upsilon_z=\frac{a^2-r^2}{4\mu}\left(-\frac{dp^*}{dz}\right) \quad (14)$$

The volumetric flow rate Q may be found by integrating the axial velocity across the pipe's cross-section:

$$Q=\int_0^a \upsilon_z(2\pi r)dr=\frac{\pi}{2\mu}\left(-\frac{dp^*}{dz}\right)\int_0^a r(a^2-r^2)dr=\frac{\pi D^4}{128\mu}\left(-\frac{dp^*}{dz}\right) \quad (15)$$

The average flow velocity is obtained by dividing the volumetric flow rate Q by the pipe's cross-sectional area:

$$\upsilon_a=\frac{4Q}{\pi D^2}=\frac{D^2}{32\mu}\left(-\frac{dp^*}{dz}\right) \quad (16)$$

NUMERICAL AND STOCHASTIC MODELLING

The finite difference modelling technique is used to provide numerical approximations for the above equations. FORTRAN codes were also developed for the numerical models and simulated to obtain the relevant parameters for defining the flexible pipeline system.

DISCUSSIONS, ANALYSIS AND CONCLUSIONS

Modelling and simulation of the slurry flow through the dual lines (fresh water and slurry) was completed for the flexible system. The simulation models were validated with appropriate data from Syncrude. Figures 1 and 2 show the layout of a flexible pipeline system. Figure 1 shows the velocity profile. A head of 15.66m/400m of pipe length of slurry was obtained. It was assumed that the fittings account for a head loss of 10 m. The results were illustrated in Figure 2 and were found to concur with Syncrude's pipe head loss of 20 m/500m of slurry pipe [25]. Figures 3 and 4 show the secondary flow vortices in flexible pipelines. Figure illustrates the sequence of shovel excavation in a mining operation. Simulation was carried out by varying ψ, which enables the generation of various plots showing the effect of this value on axial velocity and pressure gradient in the flexible pipeline of fresh water and slurry as shown in Figures 6-9. The plot of axial velocity versus cross-sectional radius depicts a family of parabolic curves. The effect of ψ on pressure gradient is depicted in Figures 8-9 as plots of pressure gradient versus radius. This shows a family of curves that are asymptotic to the pipe boundary indicating steep axial pressure gradient in the region. Parametric variation in the dual lines can be attributed to the value ψ since it is a function of axial pressure gradient and dynamic viscosity.

Material conveyance in the system can be analyzed by considering the flow in each component as shown in Figure 10 that illustrates a conceptual daily-excavated envelope. The Computed and simulated material flow, rated as tonnes per hour, varied from 6300 tph to 6500 tph (see Figure 2). The material being excavated by the shovel and loaded to the mobile crusher is 6100 tph [2]. The mobile crusher has a capacity of 5000 tph and its short conveyor belt has a rated capacity of 3000 m^3/hr. The crusher-belt system produces an equivalent of 6300 tph. The slurry maker produces oil sands slurry of specific gravity of 1.6 and assuming a flowrate of 1.12 m^3/s, this is equivalent to a production of 6451 tph. The GAP flexible system conveys the material at the rate 6451 tph to join the hydro-transport system. The rate of excavation per day is 68000 cubic meters. This GAP system is likely to produce 0.9M BCM of oil sands in 15 days. The GAP system will work with a shovel, mobile crusher, and slurry maker system.

REFERENCES

1. Syncrude Mining Business Plan, 1997.
2. Syncrude Canada Ltd., Situation Appraisal – At Face Slurrying, 1998.
3. Noda, K., T. Kawashima and T. Masauyama, 1972, "Studies on Three-Phase Flow in an Inclined Pipe: Determination of Entrance Region of Pipe Measurements of Pressure Loss, Paper D5"; *Proc. of the 2nd Intl. Conference on Hydraulic Transport of Solids in Pipes*, Warwick, UK (September): 49-61.
4. Szymanski, J. and Mansour, N., Rheological Transient model of dense Coal/water suspensions, International Journal of Fuel Science Technology, Vol.4, No. 5, 1986.
5. Wasp, E.J., Kenny, J.P., and Gandhi, R.L., Solid-Liquid Flow Slurry Pipeline Transportation, Series on Bulk Materials Handling, Trans Tech Publications, Claustal, Germany, Vol. 1, No. 4, pp. 88-98, 1977.
6. Szymanski, J.K., and Gladysiewicz, L., Modelling of Long Conveyor Transients, Continuous Surface Mining, Vol. 1, No. 1-3, June 1987.
7. Stuhmiller, J.H., 1977, "The Influence of Interfacial Pressure Forces on the Character of Two-Phase Flow Model Equations"; *International Journal of Multiphase,* Vol. 3: 551-560.
8. Frimpong, S., and Whiting, J.M., A 3D numerical model of Mine value stochastic processes using dynamic arbitrage theory, Proceedings of the 26th APCOM Symposium, PennState University, State College, PA, September, 1996.
9. Warsi, Z.U.A., 1993, Fluid Dynamics: Theoretical and Computational Approaches; © Boca Raton, CRC Press, MA.
10. Szymanski, J. and N. Mansour, 1986, "An Experimental Investigation of Yield Stress of Western Canadian Coal Water Fuels"; *International Journal of Fuel Science Technology*, Vol. 5, No. 1:
11. Frimpong, S., J.M. Whiting and J. Szymanski, 1998, "Stochastic-Optimization Annealing of an Intelligent Open Pit Design;" *Journal of Mineral Resources Engineering*, © Imperial College Press, London, UK (in print).
12. Shook, C.A., and Daniel, S.M., A variable density model of the pipeline flow of suspensions, Can, J. of Chem. Eng., Vol. 47, pp. 196, 1969.
13. Shook, C.A., Slurry flow principles, Slurry Pipeline Manual, Saskatchewan Research Council Report No. 188, December 1986.
14. Thomas, D.G.: Non-Newtonian Suspensions, Part 1: Physical Properties and Laminar Transport Characteristics, Industrial and Engineering Chemistry, 55, 11. pp. 18-29, November 1963.
15. Durand, R.: Basic Relationships of the Transportation of Solids in Pipes – Experimental Research, Proc. of the 5th Congress, Intl. Association of Hydraulic Research, Minneapolis, Minnesota, 1953.
16. Kaskas, A.: Swarm Velocities in Sedimentation of Polydisperse Suspensions, Proc. of Particle Technology Seminar, edited by D. Venkateswarlu & A. Prabhakara Rao, Indian Institute of Technology, Madras, pp. 441-454, January, 1971.
17. Hinze, J.O.: Momentum and Mechanical-Energy Balance Equations for a Flowing Homogeneous Suspension with Slip Between the Two Phases, Applied Science Research, Section A, 11, pp. 33-46, 1963.
18. Murray, J.D.: On the Mathematics of Fluidization, Part 1. Fundamental Equations and Wave Propagation, Jour. of Fluid Mechanics, 21, 3., pp. 465-493, 1965.

19. Stewart, H.B. and Wendroff, B.: Two-phase Flow: Models and Methods, Jour. Of Computational Physics, 56, pp. 363-409, 1984.
20. Prosperetti, A. and Jones, A.V.: Pressure Forces in Disperse Two-phase Flow, Intl. Jour. Of Multiphase Flow, 10, 4,1984, pp. 425-440.
21. Nunziato, J.W.: A Multiphase Mixture Theory for Fluid-Particle Flows, Theory of Dispersed Multiphase Flow, Ed. R.E. Meyer, Academic Press, 1983, pp. 191-226.
22. McTigue, D.F., Givler, R.C. and Nunziato, J.W.: Rheological Effects of Non-uniform Particle Distributions in Dilute Suspensions, Jour. of Rheology, 30, 5, October 1986.
23. Hwang, G.J. and Shen, H.H.: Modelling the Phase Inter-action in the Momentum Equations of a Fluid-Solid Mixture, Intl. Jour. of Multiphase Flow, 17, 1, pp. 45, 1991.
24. McKee, W.N., An Overview Of The Syncrude Oilsands Mine, 90the Annual General Meeting of CIM, Edmonton, Alberta, May 8-12, 1988.
25. Coward, J, "Headloss Build-Up in North Mine Hydrotransport Pipelines due to Changing Feed Grades", Syncrude Canada Ltd., Research Department. Progress Report, 27 (4) 43-52, 1998.

NOMENCLATURE

D	GAP pipe diameter [m]
f	friction factor
P*	pressure component [N/m^2]
Q	flow rate [m^3/s]
r	GAP pipe radius [m]
Re	Reynolds number
ψ	constant, f(μ, dp*/dz) [N/cpm^3]
μ	dynamic viscosity [cp]
ϑ	kinematic viscosity [cp]
ε	pipe roughness
ρ	slurry density[kg/m^3]
υ_θ	tangential velocity component [m/s]
υ_a	average flow velocity [m/s]
Δh_f	pipe friction and minor losses
Δh_m	minor losses
υ_r	radial velocity component [m/s]
υ_z	axial velocity component [m/s]

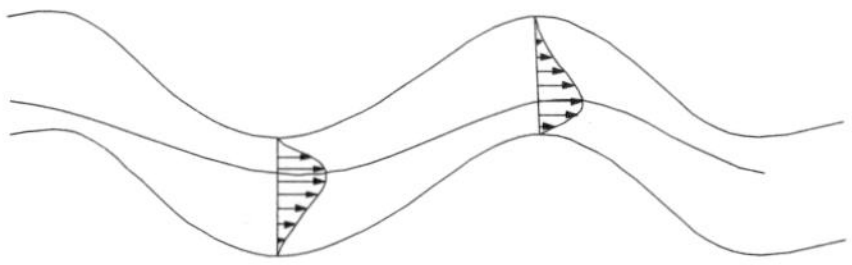

Figure 1 Velocity Profile in a Flexible Pipeline

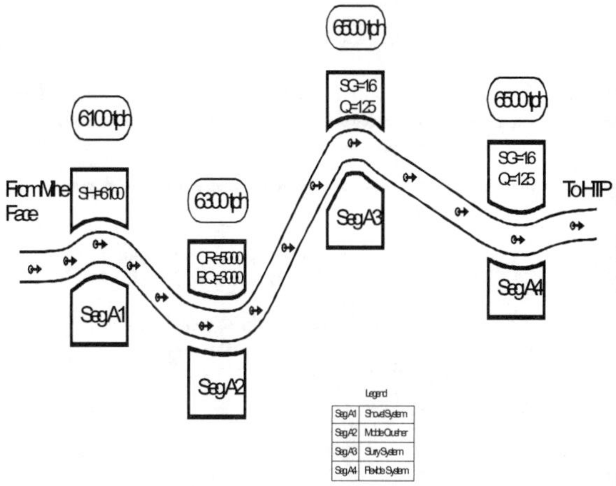

Figure 2: Material Analysis in Flexible Pipe

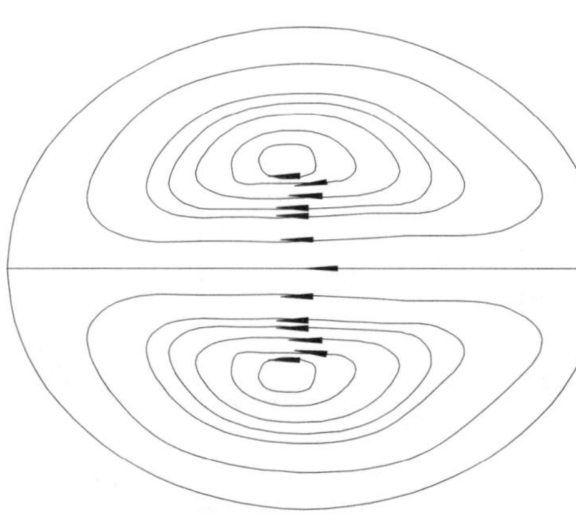

Figure 3 Schematic Secondary Flow Pattern

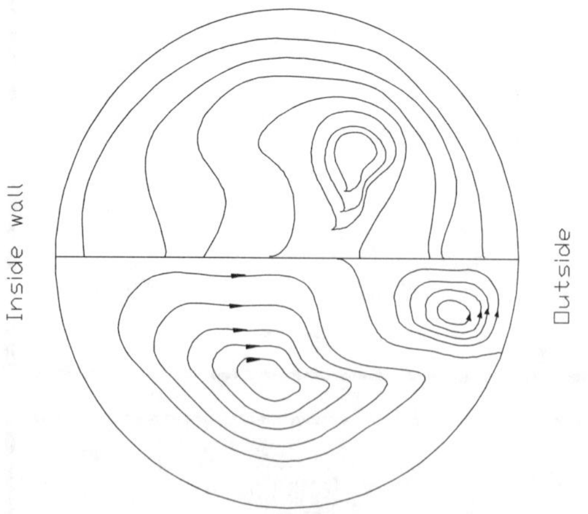

Figure 4 Four-vortex Laminar flow in a Curved Pipe

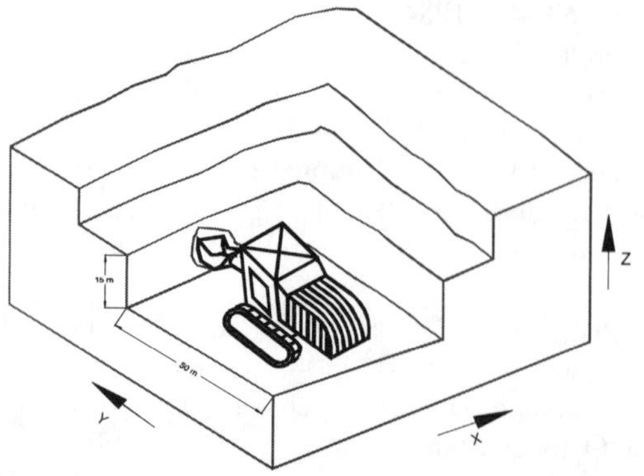

Figure 5 Conceptual Model of 3D Shovel Mining

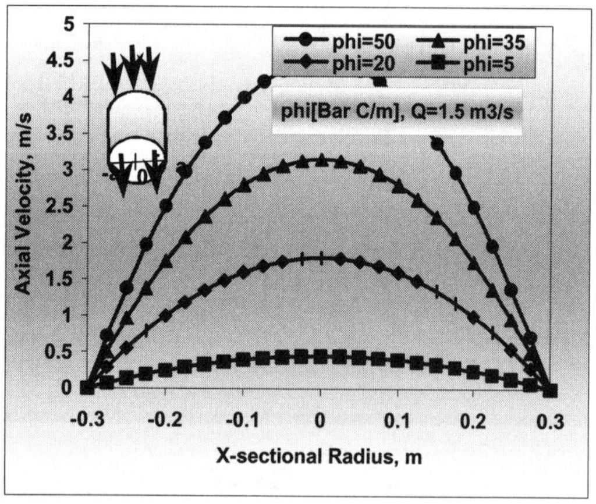

Figure 6: Axial Velocity Spectra for GAP's slurry line.

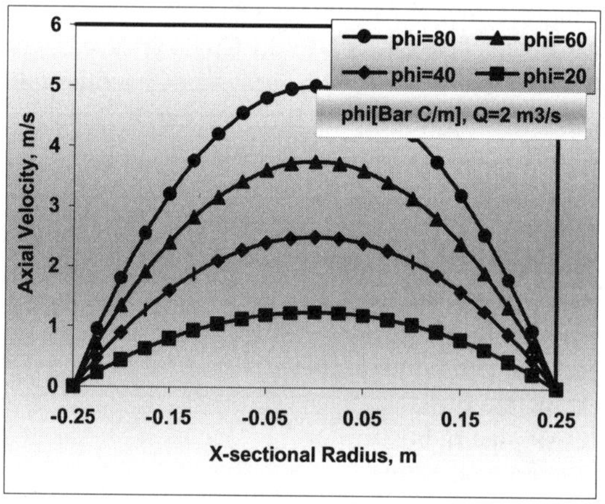

Figure 7: Axial Velocity Spectra for GAP's water line.

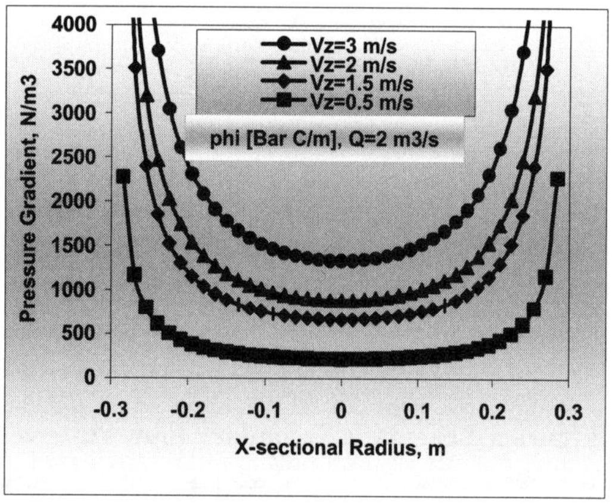

Figure 8: Pressure Profiles for GAP's Slurry Line.

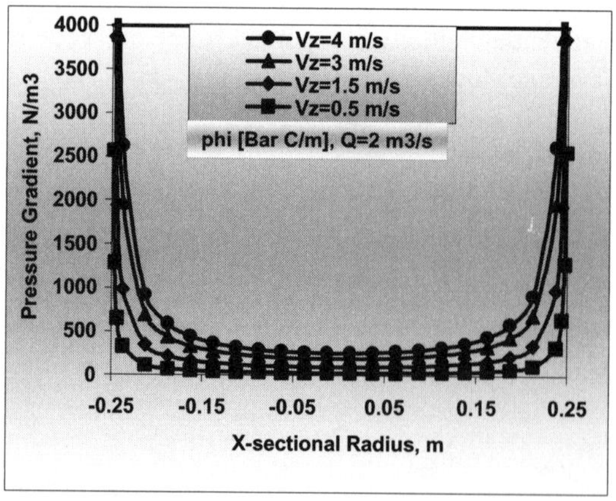

Figure 9: Pressure Profiles for GAP's Water Line.

GLOBAL MODEL FOR RETRACING U-EXCHANGE BETWEEN FOSSIL MOLLUSK SHELLS AND THEIR SURROUNDING ENVIRONMENT - GEOCHRONOLOGICAL APPLICATION.

S. SEMGHOULI*, T. El. KHOUKHI, R. CHERKAOUI EL MOURSILI *, E. JAHJOUH***, A.CHOUKRI***, M. DAHMANI* and A. CHOUAK***

*Laboratoire de Physique Nucléaire, Faculté des Sciences B.P 1014, Rabat Morocco.

**CNESTEN, 65 rue Tansift, Agdal Rabat – Morocco.

***Laboratoire des Faibles Radioactivité et d'Environnement, Faculté des Sciences, Kénitra, Morocco.

Abstract- In this study we present a new model for establishing the history of uranium exchange for mollusk shells after their burial. This model consists of numerical resolution of differential equations describing the decay phenomenon of uranium isotopes and their daughters. Our results imply that: (i) uranium was not uptake by mollusk shells during one relatively short diagenetic interval. (ii) A coefficient of U-exchange between these shells and their environment surrounding varies between -1×10^{-05} to $+1\times10^{-05}$ year^{-1}. (iii) It is more plausible to assume a different U-exchange modes by shells from a given site.

Key Words: Environmental science, Geophysics, Global Model, Numerical method, Differential equations.

Introduction

It is of fundamental importance to establish an absolute time scale and regional specificity of sea level and continental changes during the last 350.000 years. U-series dating methods allow the precise dating of corals and many speleothems which are essentially pure carbonates. Unfortunately, these materials are sparse around most of the world coastlines and continental terraces and attempt to date other fossils, such as mollusk shells, have to be made. Several results of mollusk shells from divers sites in the world have been reported. Some samples yielded reasonable age estimates whereas in other samples uranium migration was recognised (Brocker, 1963; Ivanonich et al 1983; Kaufman et al., 1971, 1996), since then mollusk shell ages have been suspected as it has become clear that buried faunal remains experience U-migration, mainly uptake, and this diminishes the reliability of the age results (Kaufman et al, 1971). Thus there are discrepancies between mollusk ages of the same stratigraphic sequence. These discrepancies provide strong evidence that the shells behaved as chemically open systems during the burial history, although the precise nature of such behaviour is obscure and probably variable. Since it is not yet possible to identify criteria that distinguish reliable dates from unreliable dates.

A several models based on geochimical assumption have been used to investigate uranium uptake history of fossils. In 1986, Rae and Ivanovich reported successful application of U-series dating to bones. A later study by Rae et al., (1989) cast doubt on the validity of this simple model. Other authors developed open system models. Chen and Yuan, (1988) measured $^{230}Th/^{234}U$ and $^{231}Pa/^{235}U$ ratios of bone samples from Chinese Palaeolithic sites. From 38 samples, the authors founds, 23 showing closed systems, 11 had signs of U-accumulation and 4 samples of U-leaching. The failure of this models is that the process of post-incorporation (or leakage) of uranium post-burial is possible only for one stage. The weakness of the model proposed by Bishoff et al, (1994), is that uranium migrates continuously into animals. The limitations of these models proposed by Grün et al, (1988) lies in uranium leaching for which the model does not have a solution.

This paper puts forward a several stages for open-system samples, which is strongly dependent on the hydrology of the site. This is modelized by the function of exchange with a surrounding environment. This function depends on the time and can take different forms. The model proposed here is based on a numerical resolution of differential radioactive decay equations. It is applicable to all samples. Nevertheless the model is based on as few assumptions as possible.

Mathematical model

Physical Equations

The uranium series dating methods are based on the measurement of the activity of uranium and its daughters in various geological materials. In this case a uranium radionuclides may be free of their daughters so that at subsequent time, the age of the deposit can be determined from the extent of the growth of the daughters to secular radioactive equilibrium, using the following differential equations system:

$$\begin{cases} \dfrac{dA_8(t)}{dt} = -\lambda_8 A_8(t) \\ \dfrac{dA_4(t)}{dt} = \lambda_8 A_8(t) - \lambda_4 A_4(t) \\ \dfrac{dA_0(t)}{dt} = \lambda_4 A_4(t) - \lambda_0 A_0(t) \end{cases} \quad [I]$$

Where $A_8(t)$, $A_4(t)$ and $A_0(t)$ represent the activities of the ^{238}U, ^{234}U and ^{230}Th respectively, λ_8 , λ_4 and λ_0 are the decay constants of these radionuclides and t is a time.

However, when a deposit is formed various geochimical processes occur that cause isotopic and elemental fractionation initiating a state of disequilibrium (Gascoyne, 1982). To take into account the mobility of isotopes the differential equations system become:

$$\begin{cases} \dfrac{dA_8(t)}{dt} = -\lambda_8 A_8(t) - K_8(t)A_8(t) \\ \dfrac{dA_4(t)}{dt} = \lambda_8 A_8(t) - \lambda_4 A_4(t) - K_4(t)A_4(t) \\ \dfrac{dA_0(t)}{dt} = \lambda_4 A_4(t) - \lambda_0 A_0(t) - K_0(t)A_0(t) \end{cases} \quad [II]$$

We introduce $K_8(t)$, $K_4(t)$ and $K_0(t)$ that represent the exchange factors in $year^{-1}$ respectively of ^{238}U, ^{234}U and ^{230}Th between mollusk shells and their burial environment.

Mollusk shells are generally assumed unreliable (Kaufman et al. 1971) comparably to corals because they constitute open system to uranium exchanges.

Model assumptions

The model treated in this work is based on the following assumptions:

(1) The initial $^{234}U/^{238}U$ ratio in the mollusk is supposed to be 1.14 with uranium concentration equal to 0.05ppm according to the results obtained by Kaufman et al (1971).

(2) The exchange process in the samples are confined to uranium isotopes only, and the coefficient characterizing this exchange is identical for either uranium isotopes: $K_4(t)=K_8(t)=K(t)$.

(3) The migration of thorium isotopes is not involved.

(4) The subsequent uptakes of uranium took place at the time T_j before present so that $T_j = D_j \times T$ where $0 \leq D_j \leq 1$ and T is the real age.

The differential equations system can be written in the case of our model as follows:

$$\begin{cases} \dfrac{dA_8(t)}{dt} = -\lambda_8 A_8(t) - K(t)A_8(t) \\ \dfrac{dA_4(t)}{dt} = \lambda_8 A_8(t) - \lambda_4 A_4(t) - K(t)A_4(t) \\ \dfrac{dA_0(t)}{dt} = \lambda_4 A_4(t) - \lambda_0 A_0(t) \end{cases} \quad [III]$$

The function that governs the discrepancies between the measured and the real $^{230}Th/^{234}U$ ratios is defined by the following equation:

$$\boldsymbol{R_i(K(t), T, D_j) = | R_t - R_m |}$$

Where:

- $R_t = (^{230}Th/U^{234})_{th}$ is the theoretical ratio determined from a numerical resolution of the system of equations (III),
- $R_m = (^{230}Th/U^{234})_m$ is the ratio calculated experimentally.

It is possible to find a value of K(t) and D_j for which $R_i(K(t), T, D_j)$ will pass through it's minimum. D_j and K(t) values that correspond to this minimum, allow us to know the time at which the exchange was made and the form of this exchange.

The numerical resolution of the system of equations [III] is done according to the Generalized Runge-Kutta method (Lambert 1973). We have established a Fortran 77 program allowing this numerical resolution.

RESULTS AND DISCUSSION

The application of the new model to four mollusk shells from the Atlantic Coast of Moroccan High Atlas will be discussed here. The measured isotopic ratios for these samples are listed in table 1 (Choukri, 1994). Three of four samples sampled from the same stratum show $^{230}Th/^{234}U$ ages younger than 120ky corresponding to the age of this unit (Hoang et al 1978). This implies a secondary uranium uptake by these mollusk shells during their burial.

In order to know the mode of uranium exchange for these samples, we study the variation of the minimum of Ri versus the coefficient of exchange K(t) considering three cases: constant exchange (C.E), linear exchange (L.E) and single episodic exchange (S.E.E).

Figures 1 and 5 show that the low value of Rimin is reached at $K = 10^{-7}$ (constant mode); this minima 0.0026 is less than the experimental statistical uncertainty 0.020 for $^{230}Th/^{234}U$ ratio (table 1). This value of K experience loses of uranium in the order of 10^{-7} per year but this value doesn't affect the evolution of the sample 92-20D in close mode.

For the same mode of exchange, the minimum of Rimin is found to be at -10^{-5} for the sample 92-20A and at -10^{-6} for the sample 92-20B (Fig. 2 and 3 respectively). This means that there was uranium uptake leading to their rejuvenation proportionally to K. Rather for the third sample 92-90C this mode of exchange can not explain the decrease of its age. Indeed, the minimum of Ri (fig. 4) corresponds to leakage of uranium.

The figures 6 to 9 present the evolution of Rimin in case of linear exchange. This mode can not explain the open system evolution of the samples dated because the only value of K where Rimin is smaller than the statistical uncertainty of $^{230}Th/^{234}U$ ratio is practically K = 0 i.e. no exchange occurred.

The last case based on simple episodic exchange seems to be more plausible to explain the evolution of the samples in the time. Indeed, on figures 10 to 13 where we have presented the curves for different D values giving the smallest Rimin, we can easily note that these values are small than the statistical uncertainty of $^{230}Th/^{234}U$ ratio and the K values indicate that the samples presenting ages less than 120ky had collected uranium in proportions explaining their respective rejuvenation. The instant of the assimilation was suspected to be for the sample 92-20C at 24ky before present with $K=-1\times10^{-05}$. For the forth sample supposed to evoluate in closed mode, the values of D showing the instant when the system could be considered open are 0.9 and 0.1 corresponding to 108ky and 12ky before now respectively with possibility of uranium uptake, characterized by relatively high K value (-10^{-3}), during the fossilisation period and recent weak ($K = 10^{-5}$) uranium runoff.

When we compare the minimum of Rimin for the constant and episodic exchange (table 2) we find that the samples 92-20A and 92-20B can be more probably affected by the constant mode rather than for the two other samples the more probable mode is the simple episodic one.

Conclusion

The results obtained for these samples permit us to conclude that:

- It is generally not possible to assume a single U-uptake model for a given site, which idea advanced by Grun et al (1994).
- The negative values of exchange coefficient K assigned to the three open samples provide an insight into the diagenetic processes responsible for U-uptake which is responsible of the rejuvenated of mollusks ages. Furthermore, the absolute value of K obtained is greater than the decay constants of ^{238}U and ^{234}U, which support the post-mortem uptake of uranium by mollusks after their burial.
- The coefficients of exchange obtained in this study for open shells are greater than these of the corals calculated by Ku et al. (1990). Such result can be explained by the fact that mollusk shells are more affected by the diagenetic processes than corals.
- The result for the sample 92-20D for which the uranium uptake has been carried out immediately after its burial, is supported by the suggestion that the uptake occurs within a few thousands of years (Brocker 1963) and (Ivanovich et al, 1983).
- The different values of exchange coefficient indicate that uranium uptake mode of these mollusk shells didn't involved the same continental source of uranium in this site or are dependent upon the mineralogy and specific shell structures.

The knowledge of the paleohydrology of the stratum is very important for retracing with success the history of uranium exchange and probably for thorium 230.

The new model presented in this paper can be completed by the multiple episodic exchange mode that will be treated in further study.

References

Bischoff, J., L., Robert J. Rosenbauer, Allen F. Moench and Ku T. -L.1995."U-series Age Equations for Uranium Assimilation by Fossil Bones". Radiochimica Acta 69, 127-135

Brocker, W.S.1963." A preliminary evaluation of uranium series in equilibrium as a tool for absolute age measurements on marine carbonates". Journal of Geophysical Research 72, 4745-4757.

Chen, T.M and Yuan. S.1988"Uranium-series dating of bones and teeth from Chinese Palaeolithic sites". Archaeometry, 30. 59-76

Choukri A,1994 " Application des methodes de datation par les series de l'uranium à l'identification des hauts niveaux marins sur la cote égyptienne de la Mer Rouge au moyen de coraux, radioles d'oursines et coquilles, et sur la cote atlantique du Haut Atlas au Maroc, au moyen de coquilles" Thèse d'état, Fac. Sci. Rabat.

Gascoyne, M and Schwarrcz, H.P.1982 " Carbonate and sulphate precipitates in uranium series disequilibrium: Applications to Environment Problems (eds. Ivanovich, M. and Harmon S.R) . pp. 487-512. Oxford Sciences Publications

Grun R. and McDermott F.1994." Open System Modelling for U-series and ESR dating of teeth". Quaternary Sciences Review, Vol 13 pp. 121-125

Hoang C.T, Ortlieb L. et Weisrock A.1978." Nouvelles datations $^{230}Th/^{234}U$ de terrases marines "ouljiennes" du sud-ouest du Maroc et leurs significations stratigrafiques et tectoniques." CRAcad.Sc.Paris, t, 286, Série D, pp. 1759-1762.

Ivanovich, M., Vita-Finzi, C. and Henning, G.J. .1983."Uranium-series dating of mollusks from uplifted Holocene beaches in the Persi an Gulf". Nature, 302, 408-410

Kaufman, A., Ghaleb, B., Wehmiller, J.F. and Hillaire-Marcel, C.1996. Uranium concentration and isotope ratio profiles within Mercenaria shells: geochronological implications. Geochimica et Cosmochimica Acta

Kaufman, A., Brocker, W.S., Ku, T.L. and Thurber, D.L.1971." The status of U-series methods of mollusk dating" Geochimica et Cosmochimica Acta, 35, 1115-1183.

Ku, T.L, Ivanovich. M, Luo. S.1990" U-series Dating of Last Interglacial High Sea Stands: Barbados Revisited" Quaternary Research 33, 129-147.

Lambert, J.D.1973 " Computational methods in Ordinary Differential Equations" Wiley

Rae A.M and Ivanovich. M.1986" Successful Application of uranium-series Dating to fossil Bones." Appl.Geochem. 1,pp. 419-

Rae A.M, Hedges, E.M. and Ivanovich. M.1989" Further studies of uranium series dating of fossil bone" Applied Geochemistry. 4, 331-337

Table1: U content, activity ratios and ^{230}Th ages of Mollusk shells from the Atlantic coast of Moroccan High Atlas (Choukri, 1994)

Sample	^{238}U(ppm)	$^{234}U/^{238}U$	$^{230}Th/^{234}U$	Age (ky)
92-20A	6.786±0.212	1.194±0.018	0.331±0.014	43±2
92-20B	5.411±0.144	1.240±0.020	0.465±0.021	67±4
92-20C	0.960±0.044	1.265±0.064	0.489±0.029	71±6
92-20D	0.214±0.006	1.149±0.053	0.684±0.020	122±10

Table 2: Rimin of constant and episodic modes for different samples

Sample	Rimin	
	Constant exchange	Simple episodic
92-20A	4. 10-4	1.3 10-3
92-20B	5. 10-5	1. 10-3
92-20C	6. 10-3	8. 10-4
92-20D	2. 10-3	1. 10-4

Figure 1: Variation of Ri vs a time in the case of constant exchange, 92-20D

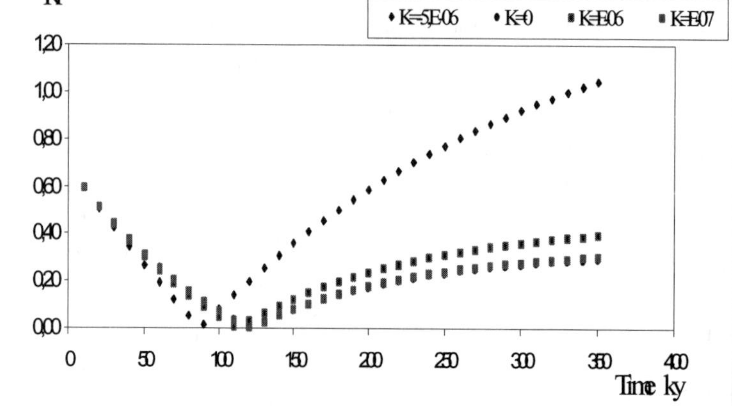

Figure 2: Variation of Rimin Vs K=Cste, 92-20A

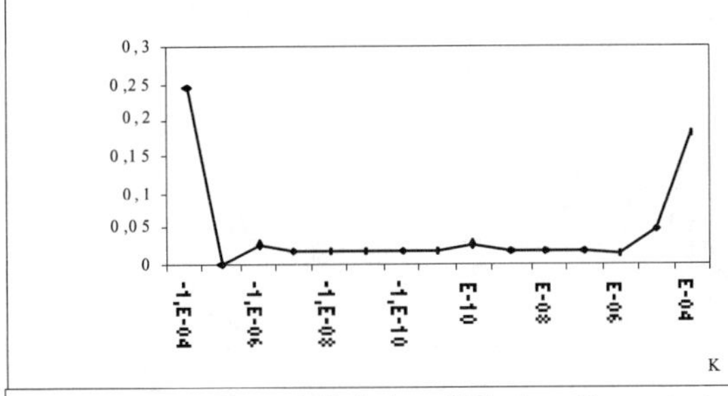

Figure3: Variat ion of Rimin Vs K=Cste, 92-20B

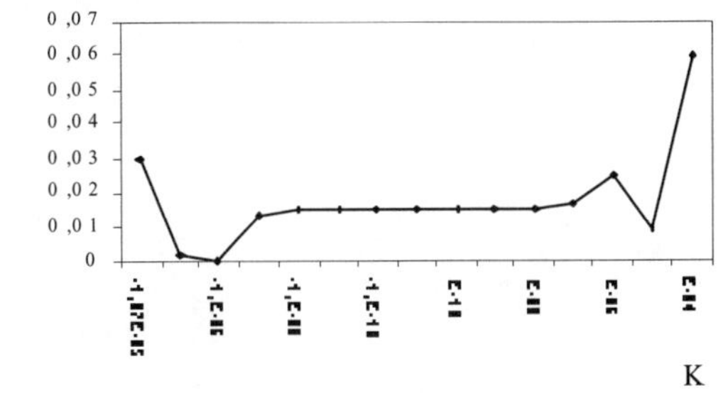

Figure 4: Variation of Ri min vs K=constant, 92-20C

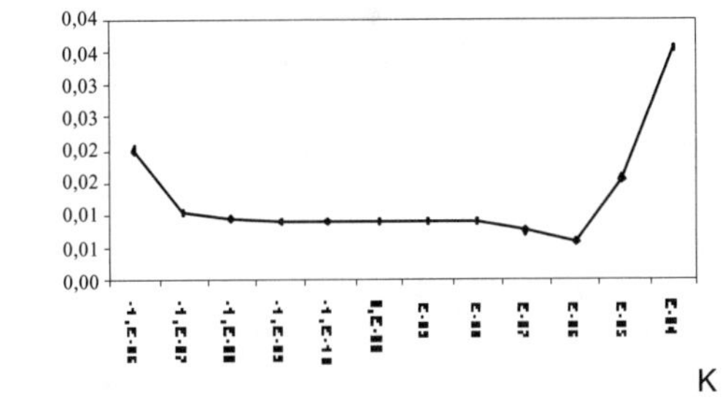

Figure5 : Variation of Ri min vs K(t)=cste 92-20 D

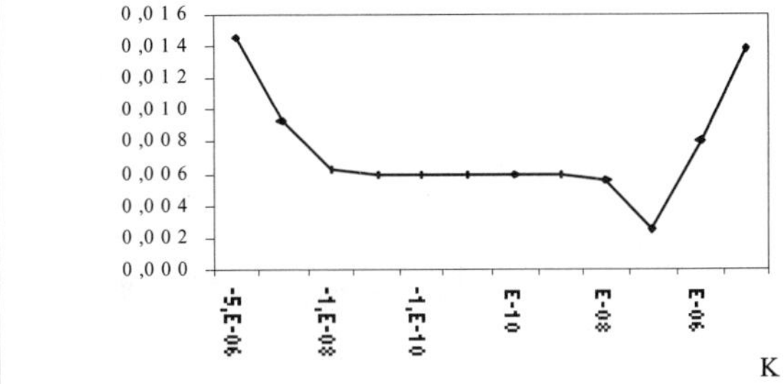

Figure 6:Variation of Rimin Vs K(t)=A*t, 92-20A

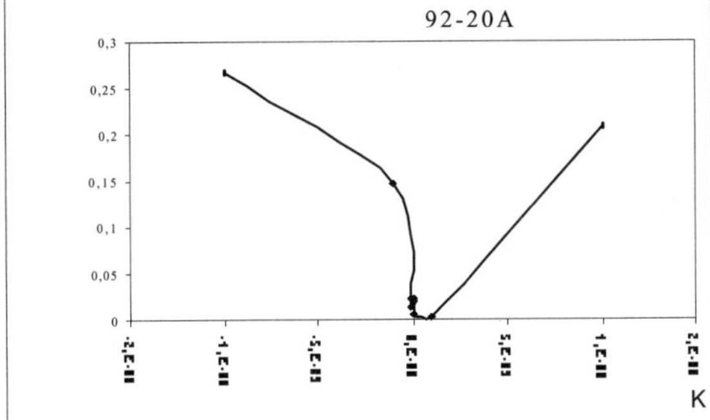

Figure 7: Variation of Rimin Vs K(t)=A*t, 92-20B

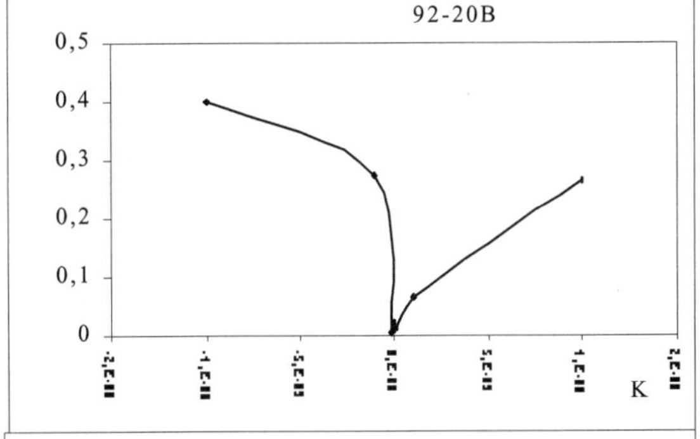

Figure 8:Variation of Rimin Vs K(t)=A*t. 92-20C

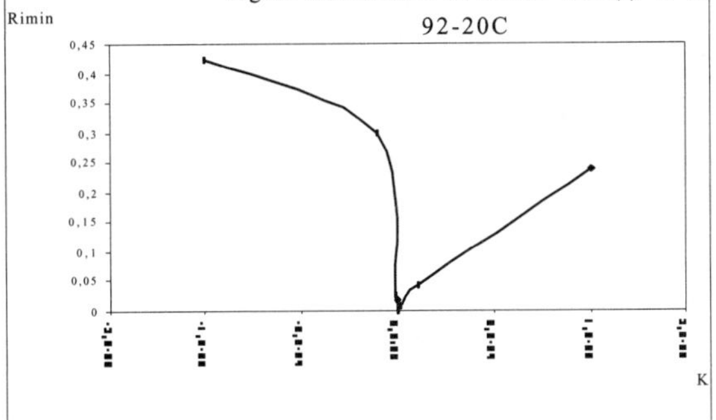

Figure 9: Variation of Rimin Vs K(t)=A*t. 92-20D

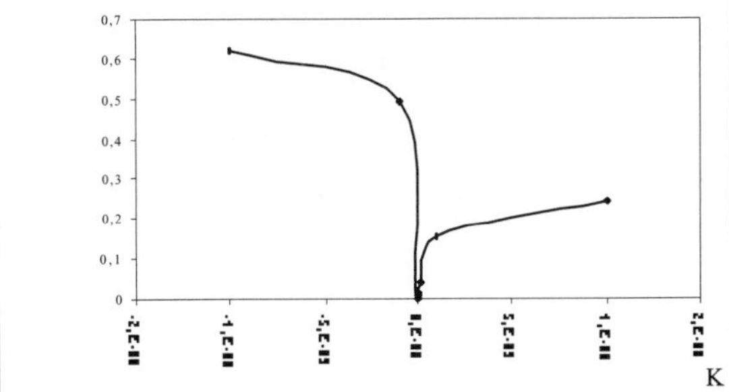

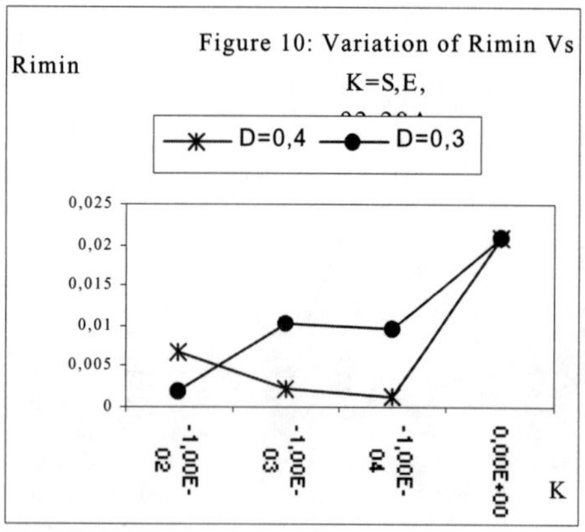

Figure 10: Variation of Rimin Vs K=S,E,

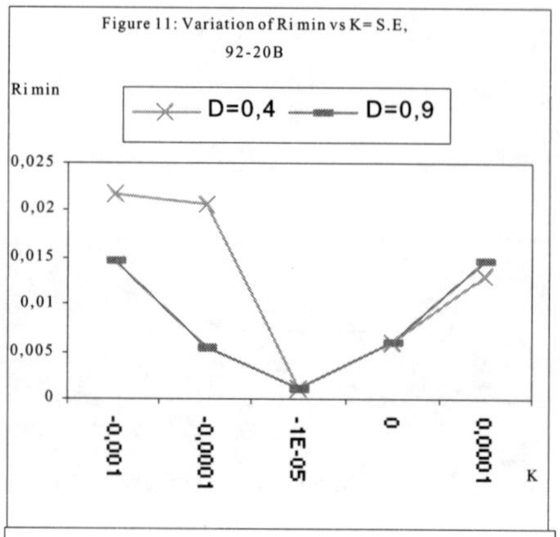

Figure 11: Variation of Ri min vs K= S.E, 92-20B

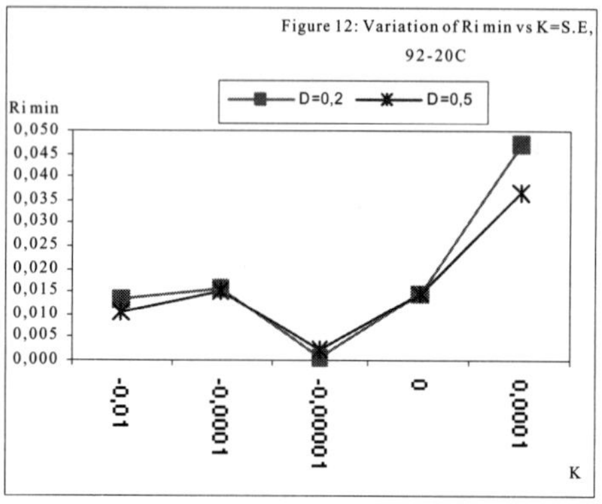

Figure 12: Variation of Ri min vs K=S.E, 92-20C

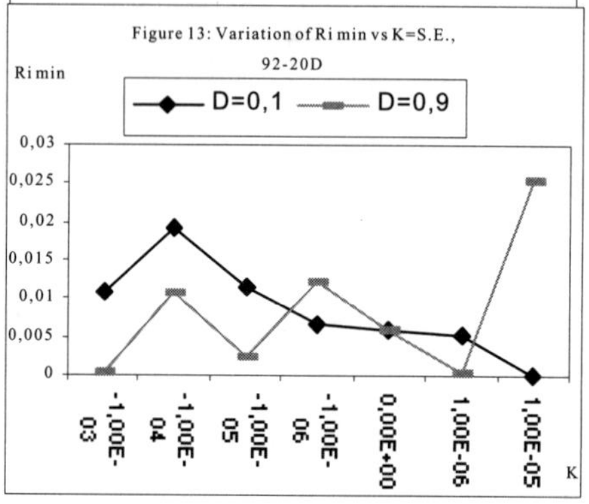

Figure 13: Variation of Ri min vs K=S.E., 92-20D

USING SIMULATION TO ASSIGN AGRICULTURAL MACHINERY IN MICHOACAN, MEXICO[1]

Enrique Arjona-Suarez and Graciela Bueno
Colegio de Postgraduados, Montecillo, Edo. de Mex. 56230, Mexico

J.Isabel Martinez-Cristobal
Universidad Tecnologica de Mexico, Mexico D.F. 11320, Mexico

KEYWORDS
Discrete-event simulation, Computer-aided analysis, Decision support systems, Agricultural systems.

ABSTRACT

This paper presents a decision support system (DSS) based in a simulation discrete event model. The DSS was developed for a group of farmers in the region of Tierra Caliente (hot land) in the state of Michoacán in Mexico, to serve as an aid in the assignment of agricultural machinery. Input of the DSS consists of data about a set of parcels and a set of crops of interest. Data about the parcels are their physical characteristics. Data about the crops are their labor and machine requirements and other requirements and restrictions. The output of the DSS consists of a list of minimum machinery and equipment required to realize all the crops simultaneously and a set of tables. Each table contains a feasible schedule of labors for the crops under the set of minimum machinery and all the restrictions given.

INTRODUCTION

This paper presents a decision support system (DSS) based in a simulation discrete event model. The DSS was developed for a group of farmers in the region of Tierra Caliente (hot land) in the state of Michoacán in Mexico, to serve as an aid in the assignment of agricultural machinery.

These farmers, as many other farmers in this region, each year have to choose a crop according to soil characteristics, machinery requirements, and market demands. Apparently an easy task at first sight, actually it is a complex one. This happens because the farmers are not the owners of the machinery and machinery for rental is scarce and in high demand. Usually, each farmer in an independent way plans well in advance his machinery rental timetable according to the crop selected. Crops require use of machinery at several stages and some crops can have up to 20 stages.

[1]This study was supported in part with a grant from the National Council of Science and Technology of Mexico (CONACYT) under project 31984-B.

Though implicit for the farmers, there is a high interdependence between their rental plans, and feasibility is frequently not obtained by many farmers because of simultaneity of machinery demands. Machinery is rented on a first come first served basis, and, once that a machine is rented or put in hold by a farmer, there is none or little opportunity of extra arrangements (subletting) between farmers.

Non feasibility of many of the farmers' machinery rental plans is a big problem for the farmers, resulting in economic losses. To attenuate losses, the farmers have been looking for an assignment plan satisfactory for all of them.

Obviously, to maximize the number of feasible machinery rental plans, it is necessary to consider the available machinery and all the farmers' plans together. Adjustment of plans has to be done when concurrence of requirements is impossible to satisfy. However, this is not an easy problem to solve intuitively by hand, and practically impossible to solve by the farmers without some technical assistance. Even for a few crops, the number of possible combinations that have to be tested is enormous. In this paper a solution method to the problem that uses both technical concepts and computer-aided analysis is described.

Being an assignment problem, mathematical programming (MP) techniques appear appropriate to solve the problem using commonly available software as LINDO (Schrage 1991), TORA (Taha 1992), etc. Diverse MP formulations of machinery assignment problems related to our problem can be found in the literature. (Danok et al. 1980) select machinery using mixed integer programming and considering several stochastic factors. (Ghassan et al. 1986) use mixed integer programming to select machinery for a single crop production. (Haffarr & Van Ee 1992) use dynamic programming to select machinery between three proposed alternatives. However, in our problem the use of MP techniques such as integer programming and networks result in formulations of the problem that are very large and cumbersome. The complexity of the formulations is due to the diversity of machinery and equipment, the restrictions on machinery maintenance and equipment useful life, and the restrictions on time that have to elapse between different stages of crops.

Due to the above facts, a DSS was developed as an alternative approach to solve the problem. The DSS comprises a discrete event simulation model and a heuristic algorithm to guide the use of the model. The model was built using the activity approach to allow a high degree of interaction between the final users and the model developers. This interaction occurred during the building, validation and experimentation stages.

Input of the DSS consists of data about a set of parcels and a set of crops of interest. Data about the parcels are their physical characteristics. Data about the crops are their labor and machine requirements and other requirements and restrictions. The output of the DSS consists of a list of minimum machinery and equipment required to realize all the crops simultaneously and a set of tables. Each table contains a feasible schedule of labors for the crops under the set of minimum machinery and all the restrictions given. The expertise of the farmers on stochastic events not considered in the system, is used to select the more suitable of the feasible schedules.

A FARMERS PROBLEM

Following one of the problems solved with the DSS is described. It involved four different crops in four different parcels. The crops considered were: Corn, Tomato, Watermelon, and Cantaloupe. The names of the parcels considered are: Tupiro, Playa (beach), Panteon (pantheon) and Cirian bajo.

Each one of these crops has particular requirements of soil, agricultural labors required and time to elapse between labors. Moreover, some labors may be done in different ways choosing between several alternatives of machinery, implements, and adjustments of the implements.

With respect to corn, soil should be clayey and labors required are: plowing, fallowing, dragging, sowing and fertilization, post fertilization, tilling, and harvesting. Plowing may be done with a tractor of 72 HP and a plow with one grid, or with a tractor of 105 HP and either a plow of one or two grids. Fallowing may be done either with a tractor of 72 HP or 105 HP, and a plow with three disks. The horizontal angle of the disks may be of 39, 42 or 45 degrees, the vertical angle may be of 15 or 25 degrees. Dragging may be done either with a tractor of 72 HP or 105 HP, and a harrow with two disk sets. The horizontal angle of the disks may be of 20, 22 or 25 degrees. Sowing and fertilization may be done either with a tractor of 72 HP or 105 HP and a unitary sower. Post fertilization may be done either with a tractor of 72 HP or 105 HP and a fertilizing machine. Tilling may be done either with a tractor of 72 HP or 105 HP and a tiller machine. Harvesting is done with a mechanical harvester. Time to elapse between plowing and fallowing is from 0 to 7 days. Time to elapse between fallowing and dragging is from 3 to 10 days. Time to elapse between dragging and sowing is from 0 to 2 days. Time to elapse between sowing and post fertilization is from 60 to 70 days. Time to elapse between post fertilization and tilling is from 0 to 1 days. Time to elapse between tilling and harvesting is from 60 to 80 days

With respect to tomato, soil should be slimy and labors required are: plowing, fallowing, dragging, sowing and fertilization, post fertilization, tilling, and harvesting. Plowing may be done either with a tractor of 72 HP or 105 HP and a plow with one grid. Fallowing may be done either with a tractor of 72 HP or 105 HP and a plow with three disks. The horizontal angle of the disks may be of 39, 42 or 45 degrees, the vertical angle may be of 15 or 25 degrees. Dragging may be done either with a tractor of 72 HP or 105 HP and a harrow with two disk sets. The horizontal angle of the disks may be of 20, 22 or 25 degrees. Sowing and fertilization may be done either with a tractor of 72 HP or 105 HP and a unitary sower. Post fertilization may be done either with a tractor of 72 HP or 105 HP and a fertilizing machine. Tilling may be done either with a tractor of 72 HP or 105 HP and a tiller machine. Harvesting is done manually with groups of five farm laborers or apprentices. Time to elapse between plowing and fallowing is from 0 to 4 days. Time to elapse between fallowing and dragging is from 0 to 5 ays. Time to elapse between dragging and sowing is from 0 to 6 days. Time to elapse between sowing and post fertilization is from 30 to 45 days. Time to elapse between post fertilization and tilling is from 0 to 1 days. Time to elapse between tilling and harvesting is from 60 to 70 days

With respect to watermelon, soil should be sandy and labors required are: plowing, fallowing, dragging, leveling, grooving and fertilization, sowing, post fertilization, tilling, and harvesting. Plowing may be done either with a tractor of 72 HP or 105 HP and a plow with one grid. Fallowing is done with a tractor of 105 HP, and a plow with four disks. Dragging is done with a tractor of 105 HP, and a drag harrow. Leveling may be done either with a tractor of 72 HP or 105 HP and a leveler. Growing and fertilization may be done either with a tractor of 72 HP or 105 HP and a fertilizing machine. Sowing is done manually with a group of five farm laborers or apprentices. Post fertilization may be done either with a tractor of 72 HP or 105 HP and a fertilizing machine. Tilling may be done either with a tractor of 72 HP or 105 HP and a tiller. Harvesting is done manually with groups of five farm laborers or apprentices. Time to elapse between plowing and fallowing is from 0 to 4 days Time to elapse between fallowing and dragging is from 0 to 5 days. Time to elapse between dragging and leveling is from 0 to 4 days. Time to elapse between leveling and grooving is from 0 to 4 days. Time to elapse between grooving and sowing is from 0 to 1 days. Time to elapse between sowing and post fertilization is from 32 to 48 days. Time to elapse between post fertilization and tilling is from 0 to 1 days. Time to elapse between tilling and harvesting is from 55 to 65 days.

With respect to cantaloupe, soil should be clayey and labors required are: fallowing, dragging, leveling, grooving and fertilization, sowing, post fertilization, tilling, and harvesting. Dragging should be done three times consecutively without intermediate resting times. Tilling should be done ten times consecutively with intermediate mandatory resting times. Harvesting should be done in five to six stages Fallowing is done with a tractor of 105 HP, and a plow with four disks. Dragging is done with a tractor of 105 HP, and a drag harrow. Leveling may be done either with a tractor of 72 HP or 105 HP and a leveler. Growing and fertilization may be done either with a tractor of 72 HP or 105 HP and a fertilizing machine. Sowing is done manually with a group of five farm laborers or apprentices. Post fertilization may be done either with a tractor of 72 HP or 105 HP and a fertilizing machine. Tilling may be done either with a tractor of 72 HP or 105 HP and a tiller. Harvesting is done manually with groups of five farm laborers or apprentices. Time to elapse between fallowing and dragging is from 0 to 5 days. Time to elapse between dragging and leveling is from 0 to 4 days. Time to elapse between leveling and grooving is from 0 to 5 days. Time to elapse between grooving and sowing is from 0 to 1 days. Time to elapse between sowing and post fertilization is from 30 to 45 days. Time to elapse between post fertilization and tilling is from 0 to 1 days. Time to elapse between consecutive tilling labors is from 8 to 10 days. Time to elapse between tilling and harvesting is from 65 to 75 days.

Duration of each labor depends on the size of the parcel and on the machinery, implements, and disk adjustments selected. The machinery and implements are rented in whole days so durations in hours have to be divided by 16, which is the length of the labor day, and rounded to the next higher integer.

Finally, all the machinery requires preventive and corrective maintenance and the implements have a useful span of life according to their conditions, so it is necessary to keep track of their use. For doing this, it is necessary to consider real times of labors instead of rounded ones.

THE SIMULATION MODEL

The simulation model that serves as a basis for the DSS, performs the simulation of the crops under a set of machinery and agricultural equipment given as input. Input data also includes human labor available, the parcel dimensions, the types of soils, and a set of priorities for the required labors. Besides the labors described in the above section, the model includes maintenance of equipment and bounds in the equipment useful life. For each piece of machinery or equipment, the model keeps an internal record of its use (both in hours of real use and in days of rentals) and of the maintenance given to it. The model allows six different soil textures, seven different crops, thirteen different labors, eleven different machines and implements and three types of human labor.

Soil textures allowed in the model are:

Clayey
Clayey-Sandy
Sandy
Slimy
Open
Open-Clayey.

Crops allowed in the model are:
Cantaloupe
Chili
Corn
Papaya
Tomato
Watermelon
Wheat.

Labors allowed in the model are:

Plowing
Fallowing
Dragging
Leveling
Grooving
Fertilization
Mechanical sowing
Manual sowing
Post fertilization
Maintenance
Tilling
Mechanical harvesting
Manual harvesting.

Machinery and implements allowed in the model are:

72 HP tractors
105 HP tractors
Sowers
Levelers
Fertilizing machines
Tillers
Reapers
Mechanical harvesters
One grid plows
Two grid plows
Three disk plows
Four disk plows
Two section harrows
Drag harrows.

Finally, human labors allowed in the model are:

drivers
farm laborers
apprentices

As it was said in the introduction, to allow the participation of the farmers in the development, validation and experimentation stages of the model it was built using the activity approach (Kreutzer, Martinez, Szymankiewicz). The model was implemented in a support software developed in C++ that uses a functional approach to describe the actions required by the model builder. Names of the functions resemble the actions required and many arguments of the functions may be omitted. Both names and arguments of the functions are given in natural like expressions built using declared and enumerate constants. In general, the computer model follows closely the hand model and implementation is straightforward.

In the model, labors are represented as activities, and time to elapse between consecutive labors by permanence of entities on waiting lines. To force a minimum time of permanence of an entity in a waiting line, two extra attributes are required in the entity. When an activity has to be realized consecutively several times on a same entity, the entity requires an extra attribute to keep track of how many times the activity has been performed on the entity. Some attributes of the entities are fixed (soil type, soil dimensions, tractor power, etc.) and others are variable (number of disks in a harrow, angle of a set of disks, hours accumulated since the last maintenance of a tractor, etc.). For the example given above, the model uses 12 entities, 14 waiting lines and 33 activities.

Entities used are: Soils, Tractors, Grid plows, Disk plows, Harrows, Levelers, Sowers, Fertilizing machines, Tillers, Mechanical harvesters, Farm laborers, Clock.

Waiting lines used are: Idle tractors, Idle implements, Idle harvesters, Idle laborers, Virgin soils, Plowed soils, Fallowed soils, Dragged soils, Leveled soils, Grooved soils, Fertilized soils, Tilled soils, Harvested soils, Idle clock.

Activities used are: Corn plowing, Tomato plowing, Watermelon plowing, Corn fallowing, Tomato fallowing, Watermelon fallowing, Cantaloupe fallowing, Corn dragging, Tomato dragging, Watermelon dragging, Cantaloupe dragging, Watermelon leveling, Cantaloupe leveling, Watermelon grooving, Cantaloupe grooving, Corn sowing, Tomato sowing, Watermelon sowing, Cantaloupe sowing, Corn post fertilization, Tomato post fertilization, Watermelon post fertilization, Cantaloupe post fertilization, Corn tilling, Tomato tilling, Watermelon tilling, Cantaloupe tilling, Corn harvesting, Tomato harvesting, Watermelon harvesting, Cantaloupe harvesting, Maintenance, Advance clock.

Most of the activities, as in the real problem, allow multiple choices of machinery and implements and some of them allow multiple choices of disk angles and human labor. In these activities, their durations have to be computed after the entities required for starting the activity are selected. For example, selection of alternative entities can be done as follows:

```
search_entity (TRACTOR, IN_ANY_POSITION_OF,
AVAILABLE_TRACTORS, WITH, POWER,
GREATER_OR_EQUAL_THAN, 72);
```

the duration of the activity, if it depends only of the power of a tractor, can be computed after choosing the tractor as follows:

```
if (attribute_value (POWER, OF, TRACTOR) ==72))
set_ activity_duration_to ( 2*PARCEL_SIZE);
else
set_activity_duration_to ( 1.8*PARCEL_SIZE);
```

Time to elapse between successive labors can be forced by using the values of two single attributes. In the following example, two such attributes were incorporated to the entity soil, and their values are tested with respect to the simulation time before starting an activity as follows:

```
search_entity (SOIL, IN_ANY_POSITION_OF,
PLOWED_SOIL, WITH, TEXTURE, EQUAL, CLAYEY,
MINIMUM_ELAPSED_TIME,
      LESS_OR_EQUAL_THAN, tsim,
MAXIMUM_ELAPSED_TIME,
      GREATER_OR_EQUAL_THAN, tsim);
```

where tsim is a global variable that contains the simulation time. When each activity is executed, the soil attributes values may be updated as in the following example:

```
assign_value (MINIMUM_ELAPSED_TIME, OF, SOIL, tsim);
assign_value (MAXIMUM_ELAPSED_TIME, OF, SOIL,
          tsim+4);
```

In general, as opposed to the MP formulation of the problem, the activity model is easy understandable by the lay man and only requires one artificial activity (ADVANCE_CLOCK) and one artificial entity (CLOCK). The purpose of this activity is to advance the simulation internal clock when some soil entities are in the waiting lines. This advancing was required because when soils are in a waiting line, they really are not in repose but under physical or chemical activities (plant germination, growing, ripening, etc.) and they may be not ready for the following labor. Times of permanence of soils in waiting lines correspond to elapsed times between labors. The artificial activity advances the simulation time a day at a time and so the discrete event model behaves also as a periodical one. The discrete event behavior of the model is used for timing labors (activities) and the periodical behavior of the model is used for timing soil reposes between labors. The activity ADVANCE_CLOCK has a duration of one labor day (16 hours) and only requires for starting the artificial attributeless entity CLOCK.

THE DECISION SUPPORT SYSTEM

The DSS controls the model. The purpose of the DSS is to find the minimum set of machinery and equipment required to realize all the crops simultaneously and to give feasible schedules for this set. Inputs to the DSS are only soil and crop input data. The DSS makes several runs of the model assigning different sets of machinery and assigning different priorities to the activities looking for a feasible schedule. Priorities and machinery are assigned by the DSS using an internal heuristic criterion to speed feasibility. Once a feasible schedule is obtained for a set of machinery, the DSS reduces the set of machinery looking for a feasible schedule for this new set. When the DSS has obtained the minimum machinery and equipment set required to realize all the crops simultaneously, it displays the set and a feasible schedule of labors under this set. Once this is done, the DSS can look for additional feasible schedules under the minimum set by changing only priorities to the activities.

The DSS needs to be run only once if all the parcels and crops are considered together as a unique set and the solutions obtained can be regarded as a global optimum This works very well when the number of parcels and crops is small as with the example given. However, for a considerable number of parcels or crops, the minimum set and the schedules obtained may be very sensible to small changes, so their utility may be very limited.

When the number of parcels or crops is big, an alternative solution, which can be regarded as a local optimum, can be obtained in a simple way grouping the parcels into several non overlapping sets and running separately the DSS once for each set. Solutions obtained in this way are usually more robust than the ones obtained when the DSS is run only once considering all the parcels as a unique set. Parcels can be organized into several non overlapping groups considering distances between parcels and types of crops. Parcels into each group should be situated at a reasonable distance to avoid lost moving times, and similar crops should be avoided as much as possible in a group to diminish simultaneity of identical requirements. Another factors that can be important to consider when building the groups are the size of the parcels. Groups usually work better with parcels with considerable variation of size. Robustness of solutions obtained with grouping is due to the fact that the agricultural equipment and machinery required by each group is implicitly assigned in an exclusive way to each group, and this may allow small changes in the scheduling of labors of farmers that are members of a same group.

Obviously, combining the two above uses of the DSS, with and without grouping, it is possible to evaluate how far is the sum of the requirements of the groups of parcels (local optimum) from the overall requirements of all the parcels as unique group (global optimum). So the grouping can be adjusted if desired. Small discrepancies are acceptable and often unavoidable. Great discrepancies can be acceptable when all the machinery required is available for rental, and differences in cost of rental of global and local optimum are negligible.

Finally, as it was mentioned above, when more than one feasible solution is obtained (overall or for grouping), the expertise of the farmers on stochastic events not considered in the system (delays in rain, freezes, etc.) can be very valuable to select the more suitable of the feasible schedules.

VALIDATION AND EXPERIMENTATION

The model was verified and validated using available historical data. Due that rental machinery and agricultural practices have remained practically unchanged for years in the region, historical data was very reliable.

Experimentation was done for several groups of parcels and crops stated by the farmers. All the results obtained by the DSS were very satisfactory. One of the experiments required by the farmers was the given in the above example.

With respect to this example, the minimum set of machinery and implements obtained by the DSS required the use of two tractors of 105 HP and a restricted set of implements. The restricted set of implements consisted of 19 items and 3 groups of farm laborers. Each group was constituted by 5 farm laborers. The DSS obtained five alternative schedules for the minimum set.

CONCLUSION

A DSS built to assign scarce agricultural machinery was described. The DSS is based in an activity discrete simulation model proposed as a very understandable solution alternative to mathematical programming techniques. The DSS proved very useful due to the high combinatory involved in the assignment of the machinery. Results and parts of the model of a real life application of the DSS were given in the paper.

The DSS, implemented in C++, was developed as part of a project aimed to convince Mexican farmers and industrial managers of the utility of simulation as a quantitative analysis and planning tool.

REFERENCES

Danok, A. B., B. A. McCar and T. K White. 1980. "Machinery Selection: Modeling Incorporation of Variability." *Amer. J. Econ.* 62:700-708.

Ghassan, A., A. K. Srivastava, T. H. Burkhardt and J. D.Kelly. 1986. "A Mixed Integer Programming (MILP) Machinery Selection Model for Navybean Production System". *Transactions of the ASAE* 29(1): 81-90.

Haffarr, Y. and G. Van Ee. 1992. "CUCHARV A Simulattion Model for Optimizing Mechanical Harvesting Returns of Pickling cucumbers." *Transactions of the ASAE* 35(1):45-51.

Kreutzer, W. 1986. *System Simulation: Programming Styles and Languages.* Addison Wesley, Great Britain

Martínez, J. C. 1996. *Stroboscope Manual.* University of Michigan.

Poole, T and J. Szymankiewicz. 1977. *Using Simulation to Solve Problems*. McGraw-Hill Co. (UK) Limited.

Schrage, L. 1991. *User's Manual for LINDO*. The Scientific Press. Palo Alto, CA.

Taha, H. A. 1992. *Operaations Research and Introduction*. 5th. Edition. MacMillan Publishing Co.

The Construction of Production Planning and Scheduling System for an IC Foundry in Ramp-up period

Shu-Hsing Chung[1], Yu-Chang Su[1] , Hsin-I Lee[2], Jing-Shi Liao[1], and An-Yi Chen[1]
[1]Dept. of Industrial Engineering and management, National Chiao-Tung University, Hsin-chu, Taiwan, ROC,
Tel: 886-3-5731638, Fax: 886-3-5722392, E-Mail: t7533@cc.nctu.edu.tw
[2]Department and Graduate Institute of Industrial Management, Chung-Hua University, Hsin-chu, Taiwan, R.O.C.

ABSTRACT

A good production planning in a ramp-up fab is difficult to be built due to the variation of production environment, such as the increase of capacity and throughput target, the changes of product mix and the development of new process technology. In this paper, we design a complete planning and scheduling system containing three models corresponding to three hierarchical level designs so as to solve scheduling problems for the ramp-up periods.

In the first planning level, the order-accepting model is used to determine the optimal product mix with the goal of profit maximization under the capacity limitation. The second planning level is responsible for the master production planning. Here, a heuristic model is designed to derive the utilization rate for each workstation so as to achieve the throughput target. With the workstation's utilization rate, the queueing model is applied for the bottleneck resource and the Conway's Laplace formula [3] is adopted for non-bottleneck resources to derive the expected flow time for each workstation, and then being transformed to the WIP level through the Little's formula [7]. Then, the fixed-WIP releasing policy is applied so as to set the wafer start time for each order. In the third level, the detail scheduling model is designed. The daily moves, the WIP level, and the cycle time for each layer of each product type is planned through the model.

The simulation tool "Mansim" is used to verify whether or not the developed hierarchical structure is reasonable and suitable for the IC foundry. Compare the simulation results with those of the heuristic models, we find that the planning system we proposed is effective and efficient. It thus is a rapid response mechanism to handle the scheduling problems for the wafer fab in ramp-up periods.

Keywords : foundry, ramp-up, production planning, wafer fab, simulation

I. INTRODUCTION

With the improvement of technology, semiconductor industry has been highly developed and become the focal industry in Taiwan. The enchanting profitability of IC foundry attracts more and more enterprises to invest a lot of money in building new foundries. However, there are many factors that make the production environment of a ramp-up foundry changing, including the increase of capacity and throughput target, the change of product mix and the development of new process. These phenomena cause the production planning difficult, and how to plan the production planning schedule more effectively and efficiently is the challenge most of the ramp-up IC foundries are facing nowadays.

In this study, a complete production planning and scheduling system is built for a ramp-up foundry to meet the goal of order due date completion and profit maximization. A simulation system is applied to support and verify the fitness of the model. This model as a result can be used to solve problems for ramp-up foundries even in an environment with no simulation system. This system can help a foundry to select the profitable orders, find its ideal WIP level, plan the feasible order releasing schedule, estimate production lead-time and assign the due-date in the ramp-up period.

The research is divided into three sections : (1) to determine the order mix for production, (2) to plan the master of the key machines. The photolithography layer is the basic object for building the hierarchical planning system. That is, the standard layer WIP and layer throughput for each product type will be planned and input to the shop floor control system.

This study is organized as follow: Section II reviews relevant research about production planning for wafer fabrication. Section III describes the procedure to construct production planning and scheduling system. Section IV demonstrates the implementation of this system using actual data from a ramp-up foundry and then compares the performance of the system with simulation results. Finally, section V analyzes the factors affecting the accuracy of this planning system and makes conclusion and direct the future research direction.

II. LITERATURE REVIEW

Atherton and Atherton [1] defined and classified the performance indexes in a wafer fab. They described and analyzed the relationships of these indexes in detail. The performance achieved by a wafer fab is often result of trade-offs among cost, capacity, production cycletime and throughput, ...etc.

Srivatsan and Kenpf [10] studied throughput time. The research indicated that both queueing model and simulation tools are not proper enough. Queueing model can not represent all aspects of a real fab and simulation often needs a lot of time and techniques for building a complex model. Therefore, they presented a simple method to estimate throughput time in IC fab. The model covered the dispatch of machines and personnel. It also provided "what-if" analysis function in order to manage and control WIP in a certain range.

Burman *et al.* [2] developed simulation planning model and queueing network model for IC fab manufacturing process. The performance of these two models on WIP and throughput time, exists 7% to 20% differences. But the execution time is 1/10 when using the simulation model.

In 1996, Hung and Leachman [5] combined looping and linear programming method to plan weekly input batches and applies uniform dispatch rule to develop the detail schedule. Using the developed detailed schedule as input, a real fab manufacturing process is simulated and flow time of each activity is collected. Then, the time parameter of constraints in the LP model is revised until the difference between the LP model and the simulation result is under an acceptable range.

The determination of WIP level is important in the overall planning system. Under the fixed-WIP releasing rule, Miller [8] in 1990 executed the simulation model to obtain the WIP level of a semiconductor line.

Conway *et al.* [3] derived the cycle time estimation formula for a single machine using the Laplace transformation formula:

$$E(X) = E(P) + \frac{\lambda E(P^2)}{2(1-\rho)} \tag{1}$$

where $E(X)$ is the expected product cycle time, $E(P)$ is the expected actual process time, $E(P^2)$ is the square of the expected process time, λ is the arrival rate of the product and ρ is the machine utilization.

(L) can be derived by the cycle time of the system (W) and input rate (λ), as shown in Little's law[7].

$$L = \lambda \times W \tag{2}$$

III. PRODUCTION PLANNING AND SCHEDULING SYSTEM

As a whole, this system is divided into three sections, shown as Figure 1. It contains : (1) decide the production order mix, (2) plan the master production schedule (MPS), and (3) plan the detailed schedule. The method of constructing three models is described as following.

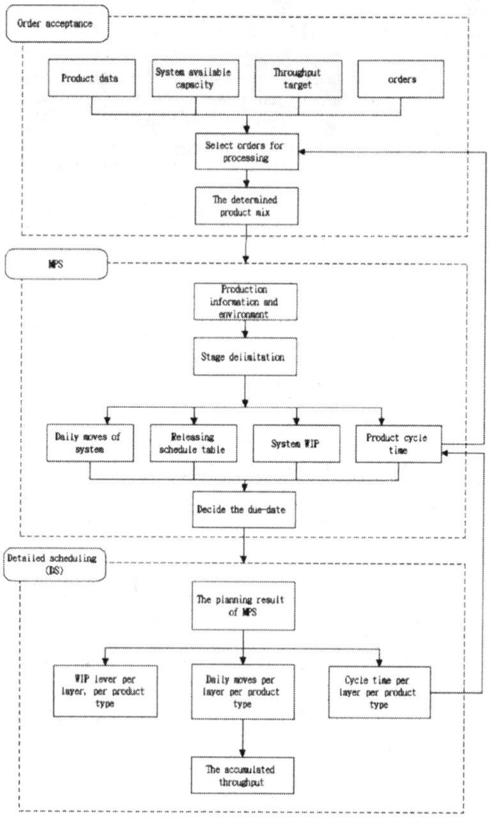

Figure 1. The whole planning control frame

1.Decide the production order mix

In the phase of order acceptance, some orders are selected so as to schedule their production in the planning period. The " revised TOC production mix rule", developed by Fredendall and Lea [4] , is adopted with considerations of the production characteristics of wafer fab. Before the decision of orders selection, the requested capacity of these orders must be estimated roughly to make sure where the capacity constraint resources are so as to arrange the schedule.

The machine with the highest utilization is recognized as the major capacity constraint resource (the bottleneck). The others with the utilization achieving 80% are named the capacity constraint resources (CCRs). The schedule of machines will be planned in order of decreasing utilization rate. In case, there is any resource which capacity supply could not satisfy the demand, then the one with the maximal difference between demand and supply will be the major constraint resource.

When selecting the orders for processing, there are several points must be considered, such as the margin profit per the capacity limit for each workstation. To prevent the bottleneck from wandering, the efficiency for every CCR is taken into account to plan the equilibrium between demand and supply. Moreover, in order to maximize the profit, we strive to achieve the throughput target by arranging product mix in the pre-defined acceptable range.

In other words, in the module of order acceptance, each order with higher profit will be chosen to set its product type and quantity and the product mix will be decided. Then, the due-date of every order will be determined through the feedback of the module of master production schedule (MPS).

2.Master production scheduling

To perform master production schedule in ramp-up fab, the first step is to check whether or not stage delimitation is needed when the production environment is changed within the planning horizon (H). A planning stage is ended whenever one of the following items changes: (1) target of throughput, (2) elevation of capacity, (3) product type mix, and (4) completion of the whole requests of an order.

Following is the procedure to perform the master production schedule.

(1) Calculating WIP level and cycle time

Atherton and Atherton described the impact of WIP [1]. It mentioned that high WIP level could ensure the stability of production, higher throughput, and higher utilization of resources. However, high WIP level also extends the production cycle time and reduces production yield. Even worse, the advantages mentioned above will disappear if the WIP level is much higher than the standard level. For this reason, controlling WIP level in an appropriate level is important for getting better planning results.

Consequently, when the duration and the product mix of a stage is determined, the system WIP level should be well controlled. This paper uses the "Fixed WIP" releasing rule because it is easy to control and can stabilize production. Under the goal of achieving throughput target, the reasonable lowest WIP level, an ideal WIP level, for each specific planned stage, needs to be found.

Lee and Lin [6] applied the M/M/S model of the queuing theory to estimate WIP level of the bottleneck workstation first and then derive the standard WIP level for each non-bottleneck workstation. Because the basic assumptions about the arrival rate and the service rate are not practical, the estimation of WIP level for each workstation is not close enough to the simulation result.

Contrarily, Shy [9] adopted Conway's Laplace transforms [3], named the Conway formula here, to estimate the expected flow time on each workstation. The expected flow time is then used to estimate the WIP level of the corresponding workstation through Little's low [3]. The application of Conway's formula does not need to make any specific assumptions for the processing times and for the arrival rates, and the performance of estimation has better performance than the M/M/S model.

However Conway's formula cannot derive good estimate of cycle time for the workstation with extremely high use rate. In this paper, we apply the queuing theory on the bottleneck and Conway's formula on non-bottleneck resources individually. The flow time of each workstation will be derived first and then the WIP level will be derived through Little's law [7]. Based on reaching system throughput target of the planning period, calculation of WIP level cycle time is stated as follows.

Subscript variable:

i : number of product type (i=1, 2, …, I)

j : product layer (j=1, 2, …, J_i)

k : number of resource type (k=1, 2, …, K)

$$\alpha_{ds} = T_s \div d_s \quad (3)$$

T_s: Throughput target in stage s

d_s: The length of the sth planning stage.

Step 2: The lot arrival rate(λ_{ks}) for workstation k, could be derived with T_s , the product mix ratio for product i in stage s (x_{is}), the requisite frequency of process i flows through workstation k (f_{ik}), and the rework rate for workstation k (γ_k). λ_{ks} can be written as

$$\lambda_{ks} = T_s \times \sum_i x_{is} f_{ik} (1+\gamma_k) \quad (4)$$

Step 3: The average service rate of workstation k, μ_{ks} , can be derived from d_s, the average operator efficiency on workstation k (e_k), and the average throughput rate of workstation k (O_k). The μ_{ks} can be written as

$$\mu_{ks} = d_s \times e_k \times O_k \quad (5)$$

Step 4: Estimate the utilization of each resource k in stage s

$$\rho_{ks} = \frac{\lambda_{ks}}{\mu_{ks}} \quad (6)$$

Step 5: Use the Conway's formula to estimate the cycle time, $E(T_k)$, for each part passing through workstation k with consideration of its batch size ABS_k .

$$E(T_k) = E(P_k) + \frac{\lambda_{ks} \times E(P_k)}{2(1-\rho_{ks}) \times ABS_k} \quad (7)$$

$E(P_k)$: expected effective service time of resource k

ABS_k : average batch size of batch type resource k

In that, $E(P_k{}^2) = E(P_k)^2 - V(P_k)$; For serial machine, ABS_k is 1.

Step 6: Apply the Little`s formula [3] to calculate WIP level of each workstation k, L_{ks} .

$$L_{ks} = \lambda_{ks} \times E(T_k) \quad (8)$$

Step 7: Derive standard WIP level L_s of stage s by summing up WIP level of each resource k, L_{ks}

$$L_s = \sum_k L_{ks} \quad (9)$$

(2)Moves on Bottleneck Resource

When the bottleneck resource finishes an operation, it means that one layer of a product is completed. Such a completion is named a move. Under fixed WIP environment, the daily throughput of each product type will be a multiple of its product mix ratio. To make the production smooth, every layer of a product shall have the same probability being processed by the bottleneck. Thus, the daily moves for product type i is derived as follows.

Step 1: Derive daily output of system (lot/day), α_{ds} in stage s as fomula (3).

Step 2: Calculate daily system throughput of each product type i according to the product mix ratio in stage s.

$$\alpha_{ids} = \alpha_{ds} \times x_{is} \quad (10)$$

Step 3: The daily moves for product type i is derived by multiplying its daily throughput by number of layers defined in its process plan (N_{iB}). Daily moves of the bottleneck in stage s (M_s) is calculated by summing up the daily moves of all product types.

$$M_s = \sum \alpha_{ids} \times N_{iB} \quad (11)$$

(3) Lot Releasing Schedule

By using the releasing rule "Fixed-WIP", the lot releasing time can be planned given the daily throughput target and the product mix. Each time, the releasing batch size for each product type is 6 lots. The selection of next product type for releasing is determined by the weight calculation equation. Before releasing wafers with the highest weight into the shop floor, the constraint must satisfied that such a release will not make the system WIP level over the planned level L_s .

$$\textit{Weighted of a product type} = \frac{\textit{Release batch size}}{\textit{Accumulated unreleased numbers of lots}} \quad (12)$$

(4) Planning production cycle time of products

The available system capacity, the throughput target, and/or the WIP level may be different between two planning stages. However, the time period for producing any product may across two or more stages. This paper adopts the way of "layer-splitting" to calculate the part-layer cycle time when the production of a layer is across two stages. The partial-layer cycle time in each stage will be estimated respectively. By summing up these fragmental cycle times, complete layer cycle time is derived.

The steps of estimating the production cycle time for each released batch are shown here.

Variables identification:

W_i : production cycle time of product i

W_{is} : part of cycle time of product i that occurred in stage s

W_{ils} : cycle time for operation l of product i occurred in stage s

W_{ijs} : partial cycle time for processing layer j in stage s for product i

s : the numbering of planning stage

$n_{i,s}$: the number of layers for product i which can be operated in stage s

$S_{(i,j)}$: the set which contains all operations belonging to layer j of product i

r_i : the release date of product i

Step1: For each stage, calculate the layer cycle time, W_{ijs} , for each layer of each product type by summing up the workstation cycle time of those operations belonging to the corresponding layer. Then, summing up all layer cycle times to get the product's cycle time in stage s, W_{is} .

$$W_{ijs} = \sum_{l \in S(i,j)} W_{ils} \quad (13)$$

$$W_{is} = \sum_{j=1}^{J_i} W_{ijs} \quad (14)$$

Step 2: For certain release batch of product i , if its processing is across more than one stage, the number of layers processed in each stage and the corresponding partial layer cycle time must be searched. For simplicity, we ignore the numbering expression of release batch. Following the procedure shown in Figure 2, the production cycle time, W_i , for product i can be derived.

(5) The throughput time table and the due-date setting

For each released batch, its throughput time is its releasing time plus its cycle time, as derived above. The safety slackness ratio is set as 10% here. Hence, the planned due date of one specific release batch is equal to the throughput date plus the safety slackness ratio times estimated production cycle time for this release batch. In case that an order requests more than 6 lots of wafers, the last release batch for the order

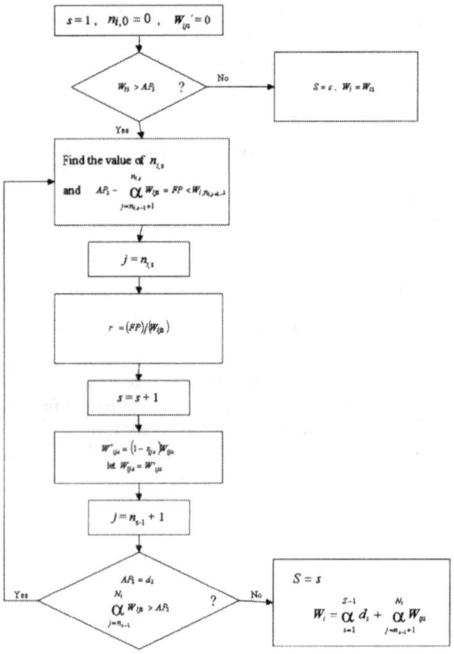

Figure 2. Procedure for deriving a product's cycle time if its processing is across more than one stage

3.Detail Scheduling (DS)

In this planning hierarchy, the model of DS receives the planning results from MPS and takes the influence caused by the constraint resources into considerations. This model takes each capacity constraint resource as the boundary to delimit the sub-layers of each layer. The sub-layers delimitation can help to make the input and output controls more precisely.

With the concept of smooth production, the higher the proportion of production mix is, the more throughput the product types are. Furthermore, according to the Little's law [7] , there is positive relation between WIP level and production cycle time. That is, the longer the layer cycle time is, the more WIP level is needed. The planning of WIP level and moves for sub-layers is based on the above idea.

The planning steps：

Step1: Calculate the planned WIP level for product i in stage s, L_{is}.

$$L_{is} = L_s \times \frac{x_{is} \times W_{is}}{\sum_i (x_{is} \times W_{is})} \tag{15}$$

Step2: Calculate the daily moves for product i in stage s, M_{is}

$$M_{is} = M_s \times \frac{x_{is} \times N_{iB}}{\sum_i (x_{is} \times N_{iB})} \tag{16}$$

Step3：Calculate the planned WIP level for the jth layer, L_{ijs}, or for the j'th sub-layer, $L_{ij's}$, of product i in stage s.

$$L_{ijs} = L_{is} \times \frac{W_{ijs}}{\sum_i W_{ijs}} \tag{17}$$

$$L_{ij's} = L_{is} \times \frac{W_{ij's}}{\sum_{j'} W_{ij's}} \tag{18}$$

i in stage s

Step4：Calculate the daily moves for layer j of product i in stage s, M_{ijs}.

$$M_{ijs} = \frac{M_{is}}{N_{iB}} \tag{19}$$

The above planning results will be offered to the production activity control (PAC) as the input data or the output control parameters so as to generate better production performance.

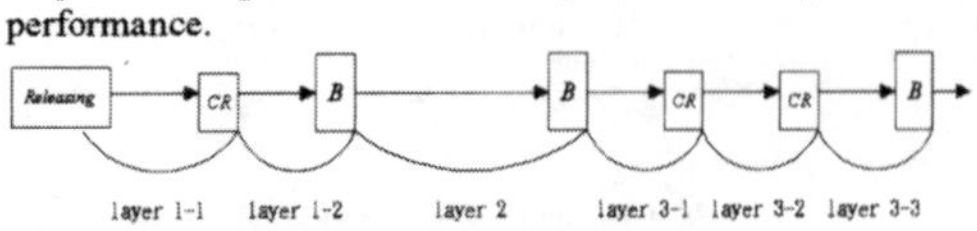

Figure 3. The graph of layer splitting

IV. EXPERIMENTAL DESIGN AND RESULTS

In order to evaluate a performance of the developed system, a wafer fab simulation model is constructed. The results of developed system are compared with the simulation results to validate the performance. The actual production data, obtained from a real wafer fab, are described below.

1. Environment setting

(1) Product related data

There are five products, Product-A, B, C, D and E, in the system. Product A and B are logic products and C, D, E are memory products. There is only one process for each product type.

(2) Equipment related data:

There are 236 machines in the model, separated into 83 kinds of workstations and of which 37 are batch workstations. There are 15, 3 and 9 workstations which process 6, 4 and 2 lots a time, respectively. Every workstation applies the FIFO dispatch rule, and every batch workstation applies the full-load batch rule.

(3) Workstation downtime distribution

Mean time between failure (MTBF) and mean time to repair (MTTR) of all the workstations are exponentially distributed, while mean time between prevention maintenance (MTBPM) and mean time to prevention maintenance (MTTPM) are known as constants.

(4) Capacity expansion plan

Assume that the IC fab capacity expansion plan is divided into three stages .The monthly throughput in the first stage (week 1 and 2) is 10 thousand pieces (10K). In the second stage (week 3 and 4), the monthly throughput increases from 10K to 16 thousand pieces (16K). In the third stage (from week 5 and up), the monthly throughput remains 16 thousand pieces (16K); however, its product-mix is changed.

Table 1. Related data for each stage

Stage	Time	Throughput target (pieces/month)	Product mix	Number of Bottleneck machines
1	Week 1，2	10K	5:7:3:4:1	8
2	Week 3，4	16K	5:7:3:4:1	13
3	Week 5 and up	16K	3:1:6:3:8	13

(5) Selecting simulation tool

Mansim is the simulation tool for constructing the model. The "Max WIP" function of Mansim is used to control the entry of materials into the system. Because the layer of order acceptance process is easy, the master production planning schedule and detail schedules are demonstrated directly in the next section.

2. Master production planning schedule and detail schedules

From the results of order acceptance, the product-mix for product A : B : C : D : E is 5 : 7 : 3 : 4 : 1, and the layer number for each product is 17, 19, 16, 20, 19 respectively. The accepted orders are scheduled, so as to set the due dates.

Table 2. Date for accepted orders

Order number	1	2	3	4	5	6	7	8	9	10
Product type	B	D	D	A	C	E	B	C	A	B
Quantity (*lot*)	18	6	18	12	12	6	12	6	18	12
Order number	11	12	13	14	15	16	17	18	19	20
Product type	B	A	C	D	A	B	C	E	B	D
Quantity(*lot*)	18	18	12	12	12	6	6	6	18	12

(1) Utilization

First of all, the results of the workstation's utilization rate from the designed model and from the simulation model utilization is quite the same. There is merely 0.72% different on average. Take the first stage for example. Figure 4 shows the workstation utilization under both the designed and simulation model and the difference between them. More than 95% of the workstations (79 workstations) have differences under 2%. The biggest differences are 14.26% on W32 and 10.52% on W40. In addition, the mean differences between designed model and simulation model on workstation utilization in stage 2 and stage3 are 1.02% and 0.59% respectively.

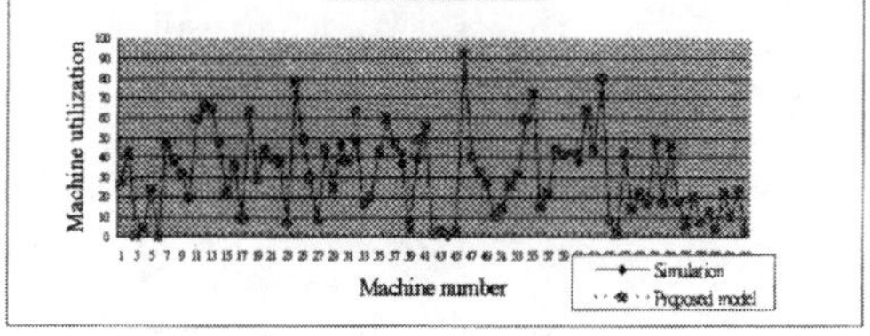

Figure 4. Comparison of the machine utilization

(2) WIP level

Figure 5. shows the comparison of WIP level for the designed and simulation model of each stage.

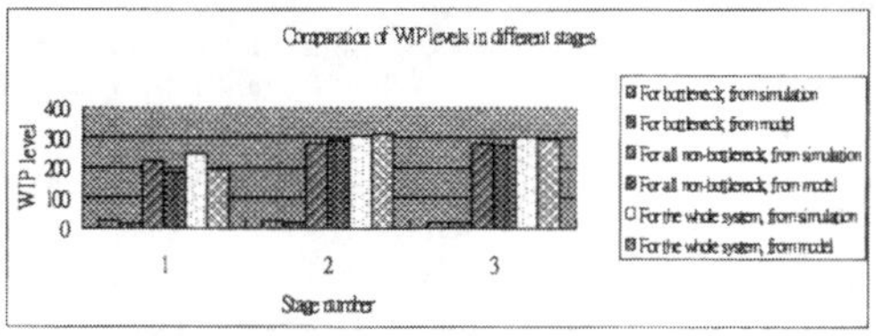

Figure 5. Comparison of WIP levels

(3) Order release schedule

Table 3 The order release schedule for the 20 accepted orders.

Product	Batch size	Releasing Date
A	6	2, 4, 6,7,9,1,12,14,15,16
B	6	2,3,4,5,6,8,9,10,11,12,14,15,15,16
C	6	3,6,9,12,14,16
D	6	3,5,7,9,11,13,15,16
E	6	9,16

(4) Layer cycle time for each product and due dates.

The layer cycle time of each product for the first stage is compared and shown in Figure 6. The planned due dates are also compared with that of simulation in Table 4. The difference of mean product cycle time is about 6.75% (29.07 hours) in the first stage, 16.33% in the second stage , and 11.57% in the third stage. The difference of the overall order due date is 5.58%.

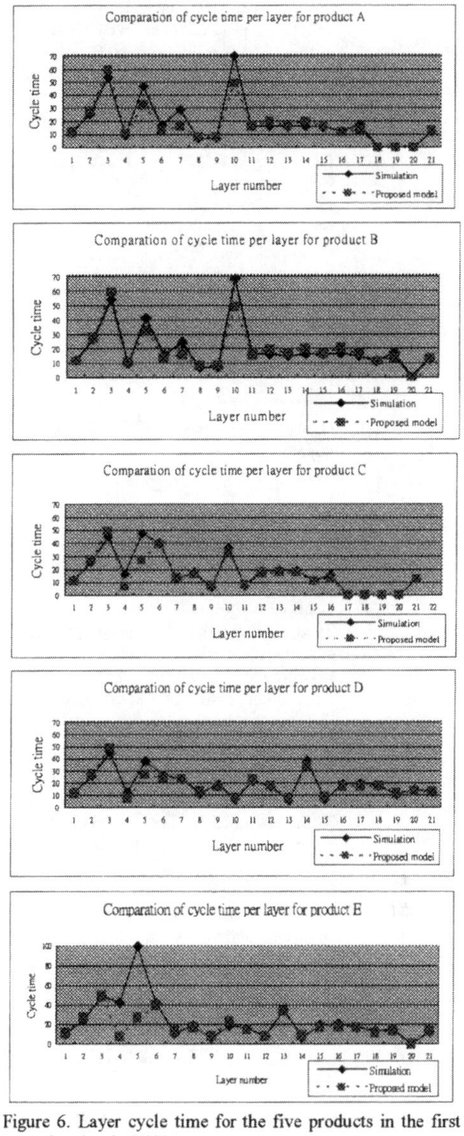

Figure 6. Layer cycle time for the five products in the first stage due date is 5.58%.

Table 4. Comparison of the scheduled due dates for orders

Order Number	1	2	3	4	5	6	7
Simulation	20.32	19.38	24.72	19.79	20.28	27.20	21.82
Model	21.15	19.69	25.44	19.55	20.10	25.08	23.08
Difference	0.83	0.31	0.72	0.24	0.18	2.12	1.26
Error (%)	4.08	1.60	2.91	1.21	0.89	7.79	5.77
Order Number	8	9	10	11	12	13	14
Simulation	23.06	23.59	24.02	26.15	27.15	26.83	27.82
Model	23.03	24.32	25.93	28.91	29.25	27.95	29.50
Difference	0.03	0.73	1.91	2.76	2.10	1.12	1.68
Error (%)	0.13	3.09	7.95	10.55	7.73	4.17	6.04
Order Number	15	16	17	18	19	20	
Simulation	28.92	27.67	28.59	32.08	29.41	30.28	
Model	31.06	30.82	29.99	31.76	32.25	32.30	
Difference	2.14	3.15	1.40	0.32	2.84	2.02	
Error (%)	7.40	11.38	4.90	1.00	9.66	6.67	

(5) Product layer WIP

WIP of each layer for the first stage is compared to that of simulation result in Figure 7. The designed model and simulation model has little difference in spreading system WIP to the product layer level. The largest difference appears in the 10th layer of product B with 3.78 *lots* of difference (about 27.19%). For the first stage, there are 88.54% of 96 layers having difference less than 1 lot, 6.25% in 1 to 2 *lots*, 3.13% in 2 to 3 *lots*, and 2.08% in 3 to 4 *lots*.

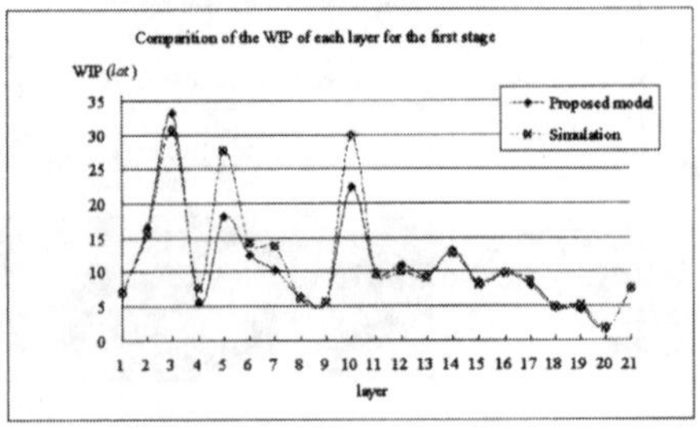

Figure 7. Comparison of the WIP of each layer for the first stage

V. CONCLUSIONS

For an IC foundry in ramp-up period, the production plan model has to consider both shop floor variation and rapid planning. In previous research, the environment is often set as fixed product mix or planned production. However, this paper develops a production planning system considering both environmental variation and response time. This paper focus on problem arising form the ramp-up period in an IC foundry, and plan the production plan model to assist the IC Foundry.

This paper, based on the queueing theory and the understanding of manufacturing characteristics, derives the utilization rate of each workstation and daily moves of the bottleneck quickly. Then by using Laplace formula [3] and Little's law [7], the cycle time and the WIP level are estimated for each workstation and for each layer of each product type. Moreover, dividing a layer into several sub-layers can exactly control the flow of a product so as to reduce the impact the environmental variation.

Under the designed system, the estimated workstation's utilization rate is more accurate than the estimation of WIP level for workstations. According to the simulation, the accuracy of estimation is related to four factors, including batch size of workstation, product priority, product mix, and throughput.

1. Batch size of the workstation

Batch size of a workstation may not affect the accuracy of estimation. However, notice that the releasing batch size being 6 lots is not a multiple of 4 lots. The accuracy of estimated utilization and WIP level for those workstations with batch size being 4 lots, such as W38, W39, and W42, thus is influenced.

2. Product priority

In the designed system, the releasing sequence of all product types is set as A, B, C, D, and E. Since the FIFO dispatching rule is adopted here, releasing sequence directly determinates the order of dispatching. Thus, the estimation result of product type with higher priority would be more accurate by comparison. However, the effect is not very significant, and the only exception is in the first and third stage.

3. Product mix

For the releasing batch size being 6 lots, the product of smaller product mix would wait a long interval for next releasing. This would elongate the time of rallying lots for for the product type of larger product mix, it rallies lots to meet the proper batch size more easily. Consequently, it could reduce the impact of fixed batch size.

4. Throughput

Increasing the planned throughput target would increase the daily releasing quantity. Under the releasing batch size being 6 lots, a larger quantity of releasing would reduce the impact of different batch sizes and make the estimation of product cycle time, and WIP level more accurate.

The future research could aim to develop mathematical model to decrease the estimation error between the proposed model and the simulation result by considering the preceding factors.

ACKNOWLEDGEMENT

This study was supported, in part, by the National Science Council, Republic of China, under Contract No. NS C87-2213-E-009-045.

REFERENCE

[1] Atherton, L. F. and P. W. Atherton. 1995. "Wafer Fabrication : Factory Performance and Analysis", *Kluwer Academic Pubishers, Norwell.*

[2] Burman, D. Y., F. J. Gurrola-Gal, A. Nozari, S. Sathaye, and J. P. Sitarik. 1986. " Performance analysis techniques for IC manufacturing lines." *AT&T Technical Journal*:46-56.

[3] Conway, R., Maxwell, W., and L. W. Miller. 1967. " Theory of Scheduling", *Addison-Wesley Publishing Company, Inc.*

[4] Fredendall, L. D. and B. R. Lea. 1997. "Improving the product mix heuristic in the theory of constraints." *International Journal of Production Research*, 35(6):1535-1544.

[5] Hung,Y. F. and R. C. Leachman. 1996. "A production planning methodology for semiconductor manufacturing based on interactive simulation and linear programming calculations." *IEEE Transactions on Semiconductor Manufacturing*, vol. 9, no. 2:257-269.

[6] Lee, C. E. and. Lin Y. H. 1998. "The Total Standard WIP Estimation Method for Wafer Fabrication." *European Journal of Operations Research*, (Accepted) (SCI).

[7] Little, J. D. C. 1961. "A proof for the queueing formula $L = \lambda \times w$." *Operations Research*, vol. 9: 383-387.

[8] Miller, D. J. 1990. "Simulation of a Semiconductor Manufacturing line." *Communication of the ACM*, vol. 33, no. 10:98-108.

[9] Shy Y. J. 1995. " The Planning and Control of WIP Level for Semiconductor Fabrication Factories." *The thesis of Industrial Engineering and Management Department in National Chiao Tung University.*

[10] Srivatsan, N. and K. Kenpf. 1995. "Effective Modeling of Factory Throughput Times." *IEEE/CPMT International Electronics Manufacturing Technology Symposium*. 377-383.

A Deadlock Avoidance and Scheduling Algorithm for Simulation of Product Flow in a Flexible Manufacturing System

Robert P. Judd
School of Electrical Engineering and Computer Science
Ohio University
Athens, Ohio 45701

Paul E. Deering
School of Electrical Engineering and Computer Science
Ohio University
Athens, Ohio 45701

Robert Lipset
Industrial and Manufacturing Systems Engineering Department
Ohio University
Athens, Ohio 45701

Keywords

Manufacturing, discrete simulation, system management

Abstract

Product flow deadlocks occur when parts become permanently blocked in a flexible manufacturing system (FMS). Most simulation and scheduling software packages do not address the problem of product flow deadlock. A system that is not in deadlock is said to be *live* and a system that is in deadlock is said to be *dead*. The method presented in this paper derives sufficient conditions for a manufacturing system to be live. This is accomplished by using the concept of *space* as a circuit parameter. It is proven that the space computation is sufficient for a manufacturing system to be live. An algorithmic strategy is employed to prove sufficient conditions. The strategy of the proof is, given a manufacturing system in its original state with *space* of all closed paths greater than zero, select any free resource. Then find an enabled part such that, when the part is virtually moved to that free resource, the space on all closed paths remains greater than zero. Then select another free resource in this new virtual state and repeat the process. If such part movements exist, then there exists a sequence of part movements that will empty the system. If the system can be emptied, then the original state of the system then can be declared *live*. A modification to the algorithm will include determining the set of all part movements that will satisfy the space conditions when moving into any free resource. From this set of possible moves an optimal part movement can be selected. An example showing the theory is presented.

1 Introduction

In recent years, researchers have shown considerable interest in methods for the design, scheduling, operation, and performance of flexible manufacturing systems (FMS). FMS are discrete event systems characterized by the availability of resources--e.g., robots, buffers, and machines--to produce a set of products. Raw parts, which belong to various product types, enter the system at discrete points in time and are processed concurrently, sharing a limited number of resources. In such a resource-sharing system, a situation may occur in which parts become permanently blocked. This is called *deadlock.*

Allowing a manufacturing system to enter only *live* states (deadlock-free states) and avoid any *dead* states (deadlocked states) can save both loss of production and labor costs as well as provide better resource utilization. Moving the wrong part in a live FMS can cause deadlock that can both cripple the entire manufacturing system and stall production. The only recourse is to manually resolve the deadlock and reset the FMS to a known state that is live. To prevent manual deadlock resolution in a FMS, a deadlock avoidance algorithm that can determine which parts to move must be incorporated into the controller of the FMS.

The problem is to develop a control policy to allocate shared resources such that deadlock is avoided. (Banaszak and Krogh 1990) proposed a *deadlock avoidance algorithm* (DAA) that developed a restriction policy based upon production route information to guarantee that no circular wait situations will occur. Their DAA is sufficient for avoiding deadlocks but is not an optimal solution. (Viswanadham, Narahari and Johnson 1990) developed a deadlock avoidance algorithm which employed a look-ahead policy. This algorithm did not detect all deadlocked states and suggested using a recovery mechanism in case of system deadlock. (Zhou and DiCesare 1992) and (Zhou 1996) generalized the *sequential mutual exclusions* (SME) and *parallel mutual exclusions* (PME) concepts and derived the sufficient conditions for a Petri net (PN) containing such structures to be bounded, live, and reversible. In general, PN solutions are suitable for manufacturing systems which contain few resources but become very complicated for larger systems.

Another formalism is to describe the manufacturing system using graphs (Cho, Kumaran, and Wysk 1995; Fanti, Maione, Turchiano 1996; Judd and Faiz 1995; Judd, Deering and Lipset 1997; Lipset, Deering, and Judd 1997; Lipset, Deering, and Judd 1998). In this approach, the vertices represent resources and the edges represent part flows between resources. (Cho, Kumaran, and Wysk 1995) used system status graphs to develop the concept of simple and non-simple bounded circuits with empty and non-empty shared resources to detect part flow deadlock and impending part flow deadlock. This method introduced the concept of a bounded circuit to detect deadlock. It detected deadlock based on characteristics of this bounded circuit. This method could only handle single capacity resources. (Fanti, Maione, Turchiano 1996) expanded the concept and developed a simple graph-theoretic method for deadlock detection and recovery in systems with multiple capacity resources. This algorithm did not prevent deadlock from occurring and suggested a suitable recovery strategy. (Judd and Faiz 1995) derived a set of static linear inequalities that could be satisfied to avoid deadlock. (Lipset, Deering and Judd 1997) expanded upon (Judd and Faiz 1995) to precisely quantify both necessary and sufficient conditions for deadlock. In this research they redefined the order of a knot, defined a special state called an evaluation state, and defined the concept of order reduction. The approach was to put the system into an evaluation state and then compute the order. The approach taken in this paper is similar to that of (Lipset, Deering and Judd 1997).

The focus of this research is to first develop an algorithmic approach to show sufficient condition for a manufacturing system to be live. Secondly, augment this algorithm approach to develop a method that can aid the user or controller in selecting optimal part movements for scheduling purposes.

This paper is organized as follows: Section 2 presents a short description of the model of a manufacturing system; Section 3 provides background on some results previously presented in (Lipset, Deering, and Judd 1997). Section 4 presents some preliminary results required in section 5. Section 5 develops sufficient conditions for a manufacturing system to be live by classifying four types of part movements to empty any manufacturing system. An algorithm is presented that determines safe part movements for simulating manufacturing systems. Section 6 presents an example illustrating the theory.

2 System Model

A manufacturing system consists of a set R of resources, e.g. robots, buffers, and machines, which produce a set P of products. Each resource $r \in R$ has a capacity of cap(r) units that can perform the required operations. The capacity function can be extended to a set of resources, that is

$$\text{cap}(R_1) = \sum_{\forall r \in R_1} \text{cap}(r), \quad \text{for any } R_1 \subseteq R.$$

For each product $p \in P$, the process plan $\text{plan}(p) = r_1 r_2 \ldots r_m$ defines the sequence of resources that are required to produce p. Resource r_m is the terminal resource for product p. It is assumed that all process plans are fixed, finite and sequential. A *part* is an instance of a product that flows through the system. At any given time, a manufacturing system is working on a set Q of parts. The function class(q) returns the product p to which part q belongs.

A manufacturing system can be represented by a *Wait Relation Graph* (WRG) $G = (V, A)$. Each vertex represents a resource; that is, V=R. A directed arc is drawn from vertex r_1 to vertex r_2, if r_2 immediately follows r_1 in at least one process plan. Each arc will be labeled with the part(s) that will flow through it. A *subgraph* $G_1 = (R_1, A_1) \subset G$ of a WRG consists of a subset of the resources and arcs of G so that all the arcs in A_1 connect resources in R_1. The union (intersection), denoted by $G_1 \cup G_2$ ($G_1 \cap G_2$), of two subgraphs is the union (intersection) of the component resource and arc sets. A *path* $P = (R_p, A_p)$ is a subgraph whose resources and arcs can be ordered in the list $r_1 a_1 r_2 a_2 \ldots a_{n-1} r_n$ where each arc in the list connects the resources on either side. When specifying a path, writing the arcs is redundant; therefore, only the resources will be enumerated when a path is defined. A *simple path* is a path with no repeated elements in the ordered list. A *closed path* is a path with the same first and last element. A *simple circuit* is a closed path with no repeated elements in the ordered list except the first and last element.

The function n(q) returns a positive integer that represents the position in plan(class(q)) of the operation that is currently processing q. When a new part q is added to the system, then $\text{n}(q) = 1$. As the part is moved from resource to resource according to its plan, n(q) is incremented until it reaches the end of its plan and exits the system. The *state n* of a manufacturing system is a vector containing the current n(q) for all $q \in Q$. A state n of a manufacturing system is *live* if a sequence of part movements exists that will empty the system. A state n of a manufacturing system is *dead,* or *deadlocked*, if it is not *live*.

Given a manufacturing system $G = (R, A)$, let $a \in A$ and $r \in R$. Then the function tail(a) returns the resource at the tail of the given arc; the function head(a) returns the resource at the head of the arc. A unit of the resource $r = \text{tail}(a)$ is said to be *committed* to arc a if it is processing a part q whose next resource in its process plan is head(a). It is important to note that the number of resource units committed to the outgoing arcs of r can be less than the number of busy units. This happens when some of the busy units are being used for terminal operations. A resource unit is *free* if it is not committed to an arc; by this definition a busy unit which is not committed is still termed free. A resource is *free* if any of its units are free. A resource is *empty* if it contains no parts. The commitment function com(a, n) returns the number of resource units that are committed to arc a when the system is in state n. The commitment function is extended to a set of arcs as follows:

$$\text{com}(A_1, n) = \sum_{\forall a \in A_1} \text{com}(a, n), \quad \text{for any } A_1 \subseteq A.$$

The function converge(r) returns true if more than one arc enters resource r. A resource r is said to be a *non-converging* resource if converge(r) is false. A part is *enabled* if either the next resource in its process plan contains at least one resource unit that is not busy or the part is in the last step of its process plan. Suppose that the system is in state n_0; there exists an arc a such that resource $r_2 = \text{head}(a)$ is free; and the part in the resource $r_1 = \text{tail}(a)$ is committed to a. Then, when r_1 finishes its operation, this part can be moved to resource r_2. This process is called *propagation*. The symbol n_k is used to denote the state of the system after the kth propagation. A part q in WRG G can be *shifted* to resource r if it can be propagated to r without propagating any other part in G. Let $\text{plan}(\text{class}(q)) = r_1 r_2 \ldots r_m$ be the process plan for part q in a WRG G. Then q can *freely exit* if part q can be shifted to r_m. If r is a free resource in a WRG G then the set $Q_s(r) = \{q : q \text{ can be shifted to } r\}$.

3 Previous Results

In (Judd and Faiz 1995) the *slack* of any subgraph

$G_1 = (R_1, A_1) \subseteq G$ is given by

$$\text{slack}(G_1, n) = \text{cap}(R_1) - \text{com}(A_1, n) . \quad (3.1)$$

A closed path c in a WRG G is in *primary deadlock* in state n if $\text{slack}(c,n) = 0$. An interesting property of slack is if G_1 and G_2 are two subgraphs of a WRG G in state n, then

$$\begin{aligned}\text{slack}(G_1 \cup G_2, n) = \text{slack}(G_1, n) + \text{slack}(G_2, n) \\ - \text{slack}(G_1 \cap G_2, n)\end{aligned} . \quad (3.2)$$

Let c_1 and c_2 be any two closed paths in a WRG of a manufacturing system. If $c_1 \cap c_2$ consists of exactly one resource with a capacity of one, then this resource is called a *knot* with respect to $c_1 \cup c_2$. Path c_1 is *connected* to c_2 if $c_1 \cap c_2 \neq 0$ and a part currently exists in the system that must propagate from c_1 to c_2 without leaving $c_1 \cup c_2$. Closed paths c_1 and c_2 are *cross connected* if c_1 is connected to c_2 and c_2 is connected to c_1. In state n, if $c = c_1 \cup c_2$ and $c_1 \cap c_2 = k$ where k is a knot, then the order of knot k with respect to the closed path c is defined as

$$\text{order}(k, c, n) = \begin{Bmatrix} 1, \text{if } c_1 \text{ and } c_2 \text{ are cross connected.} \\ 0, \text{otherwise.} \end{Bmatrix}$$

The order of any simple circuit is zero. If closed path c is in a WRG G in state n that contains m knots, the order of c is given by

$$\text{order}(c, n) = \sum_{i=1}^{m} \text{order}(k_i, c, n) .$$

The *free space* or *space* on a closed path c is the difference between the slack and the order; that is,

$$\text{space}(c, n) = \text{slack}(c, n) - \text{order}(c) \ \forall c \in C_G \quad (3.3)$$

where C_G is the set of all closed paths in G.

4 Preliminary Results

These results will be employed in the next section to show sufficient conditions for a manufacturing system to be live.

Lemma 4.1. Let G_1 be a subgraph of a WRG, and assume the graph is in state n_0. Assume that G_1 contains an enabled part. Let n_1 be the resulting state of the system after propagation. Then the order of any knot on G_1 cannot increase.

Proof: All connected closed paths are known in state n_0. This implies that the order of all knots is known in state n_0. After propagating a part, all the connected paths will either remain connected or become disconnected. That is, propagation cannot create a new set of connected closed paths. Clearly, if the set of connected closed paths cannot increase, the order cannot increase with respect to any of these connected closed paths. Therefore, the order of G_1 cannot increase. ■

The following corollary will show that the space of any subgraph cannot decrease due to part propagation along an arc within the subgraph.

Corollary 4.1. Let G_1 be a subgraph of a WRG in state n_0 and

$$\text{space}(G_1, n_0) > 0$$

Assume that the subgraph has an enabled part q committed to an arc a. Let n_1 be the resulting state of the system after part q is propagated along a. Then

$$\text{space}(G_1, n_1) \geq \text{space}(G_1, n_0) .$$

Proof: Substituting (3.3) into Corollary 4.1 from (Judd and Faiz 1995), we can write

$$\text{slack}(G_1, n_1) - \text{order}(G_1, n_1) \geq \text{slack}(G_1, n_0) - \text{order}(G_1, n_0) . \quad (4.1)$$

Then, combining (4.1) and Lemma 4.1, we can conclude

$$\text{space}(G_1, n_1) \geq \text{space}(G_1, n_0) .$$ ■

5 Sufficient Conditions for a System to be Live

This section will show sufficient conditions for a manufacturing system to be live. This will be accomplished by presenting four types of part movements, that when executed, do not cause a live system to become dead.

5.1 Part that can Freely Exit

Theorem 5.1. Given any part q in a WRG G that can freely exit, then removing part q from G will not decrease the space of any closed path in G.

Proof. Let n_0 be the state of G before part q is removed from G. Let n_1 be the state of G after part q is removed from G. Since part q no longer commits an arc in state n_1 then by Corollary 4.1, we can conclude

$$\text{space}(c, n_1) \geq \text{space}(c, n_0) \ \forall c \in C_G$$

where C_G is the set of all closed paths in G. ■

Corollary 5.1. Given any part q in a WRG G that can freely exit, then propagating part q to its next resource according to its process plan will not cause the space of any closed path in G to become zero.

5.2 Part Propagating into a Non-Converging Resource

Theorem 5.2. Let C_G be the set of closed paths in a non-empty WRG G in state n_0. Let a_0 be the arc part q commits in state n_0. Assume that $r = \text{head}(a_0)$ is a non-converging resource. If

$$\text{space}(c, n_0) > 0 \ \forall c \in C_G$$

then

$$\text{space}(c, n_1) > 0 \quad \forall c \in C_G .$$

Proof. Propagating part q to the non-converging resource r cannot commit q to any new circuits. Therefore, the space on any $c \in C_G$ in state n_1 can never change. ■

5.3 Part Propagating on a Circuit with Space Greater than One

Theorem 5.3. Let C_G be the set of closed paths in a non-empty WRG G in state n_0. Let a_0 be the arc part q commits in state n_0 and $r = \text{head}(a_0)$. Assume that propagating a part q in G to resource r commits arc a_1 in state n_1. If

$$\text{space}(c, n_0) > 1 \ \forall c \in C \text{ and } \text{space}(c, n_0) > 0 \ \forall c \in C_G - C$$

where $C = \{c \in C_G : a_0 \notin c \text{ and } a_1 \in c\}$ then

$$\text{space}(c, n_1) > 0 \quad \forall c \in C_G .$$

Proof. Two cases will be considered.

Case 1. $c \in C_G - C$. Since either $a_0 \in c$ or $a_1 \notin c$ we can conclude

$$\text{space}(c,n_1) \geq \text{space}(c,n_0) > 0 \quad \forall c \in C_G - C .$$

Case 2. $c \in C$. According to Lemma 4.1, propagating part q cannot increase the order of closed path c. By propagating part q to r and committing to arc a_1 in state n_1 the space on c will decrease by one. Therefore, we can write

$$\text{space}(c,n_1) = \text{space}(c,n_0) - 1 > 0 \quad \forall c \in C .$$

■

5.4 Shifting Parts on Circuits with Space Equal to One

Let C be a set of closed paths. If $c \in C$ has the property

$$c' \not\subset c \quad \forall c' \in C \text{ and } c' \neq c ,$$

then c is a *fundamental closed path* with respect to C. If all the elements of C are fundamental closed paths, then C is called a *fundamental set*. The function

$$\overline{C} = \text{reduce}(C)$$

returns the largest subset of C that is a fundamental set. Note that every element $c \in C$ can be expressed as the union of one or more elements of $\overline{C}$.

Algorithm 5.1 Let WRG G be in state n_0. Let C_G be all the closed paths in G. Suppose that

$$\text{space}(c,n_0) > 0 \quad \forall c \in C_G ,$$

and r is a free resource in G such that $\text{space}(c,n_0) = 1$ and c contains r. The algorithm in Figure 5.1 will find a part q^* on a circuit in C_G such that when q^* is shifted to r resulting in state n^*, then

$$\text{space}(c,n^*) > 0 \quad \forall c \in C_G .$$

1. $C_0 = \{c \in C_G : \text{space}(c,n_0) = 1, \text{and } r \in R_c \text{ where } c = (R_c, A_c)$
2. $\overline{C}_0 = \text{reduce}(C_0)$
3. $i = 1$
4. $\overline{c}_i \in \overline{C}_{i-1}$
5. Let $q_i \in Q_s(r)$ such that q_i is on $\overline{c}_i$
6. Let n_i be the state of the system after q_i is shifted to r
7. If $\text{space}(c,n_i) > 0 \; \forall c \in \overline{C}_{i-1}$ then go to step 11
8. $\overline{C}_i = \overline{C}_{i-1} - \{\overline{c}_i\}$
9. $i = i + 1$
10. Go to step 4
11. $q^* = q_i$
12. $n^* = n_i$
13. End

Figure 5.1 Listing of Algorithm 5.1

Lemma 5.1. If there is a closed path $c = (R, A)$ in a WRG G in state n such that $\text{space}(c,n) = 1$, then c must contain a part.

Proof. We prove this by contradiction. Assume c contains no parts. Since c contains no parts, we have $\text{com}(A,n) = 0$; therefore, we can write

$$\text{order}(c,n) = \text{cap}(R) - 1 .$$

Clearly, this cannot be the case since self-loops are not permitted and any closed path requires at least two resources that are not knots; thus, we can write

$$\text{order}(c,n) \leq \text{cap}(R) - 2 .$$

Hence this is a contradiction. ■

Lemma 5.2. Let C_G be a closed WRG in state n with at least one closed path c such that $\text{space}(c,n) = 1$. Let r be a free resource on c. Then there exists a part $q \in Q_s(r)$ on c.

Proof. By Lemma 5.1, circuit c contains a part. An input arc exists to r on c. By following this arc backwards, eventually an alternate part must be encountered before encountering r again. Therefore, a part q in c exists which can be shifted into r. ■

Corollary 5.1. A part $q \in Q_s(r)$ in step 5 of Algorithm 4.1 exists.

Lemma 5.3. Algorithm 5.1 terminates.

Proof. Clearly, $\overline{C}_0$ is not empty and is finite. In step 8 of Algorithm 5.1, an element is removed from set $\overline{C}_{i-1}$. Steps 4 through 10 can be repeated until $|\overline{C}_{i-1}| = 1$. In this case, the condition in Step 7 must be satisfied, since according to Corollary 4.1, propagating a part on a closed path cannot decrease its space. ■

Lemma 5.4. Shifting part q^* in C_G to resource r will not decrease the space of any element in the fundamental set $\overline{C}_0$.

Proof. We prove this by contradiction. Assume shifting q^* to r from state n_0 to n^* will decrease the space of some $\overline{c}_j \in \overline{C}_0$. Let $\overline{c}_i$ be the circuit in the step that terminates the algorithm. Since, by the check in Step 7, the space of all $c \in \overline{C}_i$ must be greater than zero, then c_j must have been removed from $\overline{C}_0$ in an earlier step. Define $C = \{c_j, c_{j+1}, \ldots c_i\}$. Now, Algorithm 5.1 terminates by identifying a part q^* that will be shifted from closed path $\overline{c}_i$ to r. As a result of the shift, it is assumed that $\text{space}(\overline{c}_j, n^*)$ went to zero. This implies that $\overline{c}_i$ is connected to $\overline{c}_j$. The operation of Algorithm 5.1 guarantees that path $\overline{c}_{k-1}$ is connected to $\overline{c}_k$ for $j \leq k \leq i$. Combining this observation with the previous one, we have $\overline{c}_i \to \overline{c}_j \to \overline{c}_{j+1} \to \ldots \overline{c}_i$ where $\to$ indicates "connected to". Therefore, resource r is an order-one knot.

Now

$$\text{space}(c,n_0) = 1 \; \forall c \in C \tag{5.1}$$

and since the circuits in c are cyclically connected then

$$\text{order}(r,c^*,n_0) = 1 , \tag{5.2}$$

where $c^* = \overline{c}_j \cup \overline{c}_{j+1} \cup \ldots \cup \overline{c}_i$. Combining (3.2), (5.1), (5.2) and and Corollary 4.1, we can write

$$\text{space}(c^*,n_0) = \sum_{i=1}^{m} \text{space}(c_i) - (m-1) - \text{order}(r,c^*,n_0)$$

$$= m - (m-1) - 1 = 0$$

This contradicts the hypothesis of Algorithm 5.1. ■

Lemma 5.5. Shifting q^* on a closed graph in C_G to resource r in Algorithm 5.1 will not decrease the space of any element in the set C_0 in state n^*.

Proof. By Lemma 5.4, $\text{space}(c,n^*) > 0 \; \forall c \in \overline{C}_0$. We need to show that the space of $c \in C_0 - \overline{C}_0$ will not decrease. Since c is the union of two or more elements in $\overline{C}_0$, then propagating q^* to resource r cannot commit any additional arcs on c. Therefore, the space of c can never decrease. ■

Theorem 5.4. Shifting q^* identified by Algorithm 5.1 on a closed graph in C_G to resource r will not decrease the space of any closed path to zero in G in state n^*.

Proof. By Lemma 5.4, $\text{space}(c,n^*) > 0 \ \forall c \in C_0$; therefore, we still need to show that the space of $c \in C_G - C_0$ will not decrease. Assume $c = (R_c, A_c)$. We have two cases to consider.

Case 1. $r \in R_c$. Since $c \notin C_0$ then $\text{space}(c,n_0) > 1$. Propagating q^* to resource r can only commit at most one arc on c and, by Lemma 4.1, the order of c cannot increase; therefore, we can conclude

$$\text{space}(c,n^*) \geq \text{space}(c,n_0) - 1 > 0 .$$

Case 2. $r \notin R_c$. Propagating q^* to r will not commit any arcs on c; therefore,

$$\text{space}(c,n^*) = \text{space}(c,n_0) > 1 .$$ ■

Corollary 5.2. Propagating q^* identified by Algorithm 4.1 on a closed graph in C_G to its next resource according to its process plan will not cause the space of any closed path in G to become zero.

5.5 Main Results

Algorithm 5.2. Let C_G be the set of all closed paths in a non-empty WRG G in state n. Suppose R^* is the set of free resources in G and

$$\text{space}(c,n) > 0 \quad \forall c \in C_G .$$

Then the algorithm listed in Figure 5.2 will find a set of parts Q^* such that, when propagated, G will remain live.

1. $E = \{q \in Q : q \text{ is enabled}\}$
2. $C = \{c \in C_G : a_0 \notin c \text{ and } a_1 \in c\}$ where a_0 is the arc part q commits before propagation and a_1 is the arc part q commits after propagating.
3. **for** each q in E **do**
4.   **if** q has a free exit **then**
5.   add q to Q^*
6.   **endif**
7.   **for** each r in R^* **do**
8.   **if** q is committed to r **then**
9.   **if** r is a non-converging resource **then**
10.   add q to Q^*
11.   **else** /* r is a converging resource */
12.   **if** r is on some $c \in C$ **and** $\text{space}(c,n_0) > 1 \ \forall c \in C$ **then**
13.   add q to Q^*
14.   **else**
15.   **if** $\text{space}(c,n_0) = 1$ for some $c \in C_G$ **then**
16.   Apply Algorithm 5.1 to find q^*
17.   add q^* to Q^*.
18.   **endif**
19.   **endif**
20.   **endif**
21.   **endif**
22.   **endfor**
23. **endfor**

Figure 5.2 Listing of Algorithm 5.2

Theorem 5.5. If any part in the set Q^* identified by Algorithm 5.2 is propagated, then G is live.

Proof. Since r is a free resource and G is not empty, then an enabled part q exists in G. We have four cases to consider in order show all possibilities.

Case 1. Part q has a free exit (Line 4). According to Theorem 5.1, removing part q from the system will not decrease the space of any closed path in G. Therefore, according to Corollary 5.1 propagating part q cannot reduce the space of any closed path in G to zero.

Next, assume that part q can be propagated to r, and n_1 is the state of the system after shifting the propagation. Let a_0 be the arc part q commits in state n_0 and a_1 be the arc part q commits in state n_1.

Case 2. Resource r is a non-converging resource (Line 9). According to Theorem 5.2 the space on any closed path in C_G can not decrease. Therefore, propagating part q to resource r, we can conclude

$$\text{space}(c,n_1) > 0 \quad \forall c \in C_G .$$

The next two cases assume that resource r is a converging resource and part q is being shifted onto a closed path in C_G.

Case 3. $\text{Space}(c,n_0) > 1 \ \forall c \in C$ (Line 12). According to Theorem 5.3, shifting part q on any circuit in C, we can conclude that

$$\text{space}(c,n_1) > 0 \quad \forall c \in C_G .$$

Case 4. $\text{Space}(c,n_0) = 1$ for some $c \in C_G$ (Line 15-16). By Theorem 5.4, Algorithm 5.1 will identify a part q^* that can be shifted to resource r such that

$$\text{space}(c,n_1) > 0 \quad \forall c \in C_G .$$

Therefore, according to Corollary 5.2, propagating part q will not cause the space on any closed path to become zero.

Applying case 1, case 2, case 3, and case 4 at each step, the space of all the closed paths in G will remain strictly positive; therefore, there will always be an empty resource into which a part can be propagated (that is, primary deadlock can never occur). Since all the process plans are finite, this process can continue until all parts exit G. A series of part movements exists to empty G. Hence, the system in its original state n is live. Therefore, propagating any part in Q^*, G will remain live. ■

6 Example

Example 6.1. Let the WRG G in Figure 6.1 be in state n_0. All resources are of unit capacity. Suppose the process plans for parts a, b and c are as presented in Table 6.1. Let $c_1 = r_1r_4r_2r_1$, $c_2 = r_2r_3r_4r_2$, and $c_3 = r_4r_5r_6r_4$. Assume that the state of the system is $n_0 = [n(a_1), n(a_2), n(b), n(c)] = [2,1,2,1]$.

Table 6.1 Process plans

Part	Process Plan
a_1, a_2	$r_2r_1r_4r_2$
b	$r_2r_3r_4r_5r_6$
c	$r_6r_4r_2$

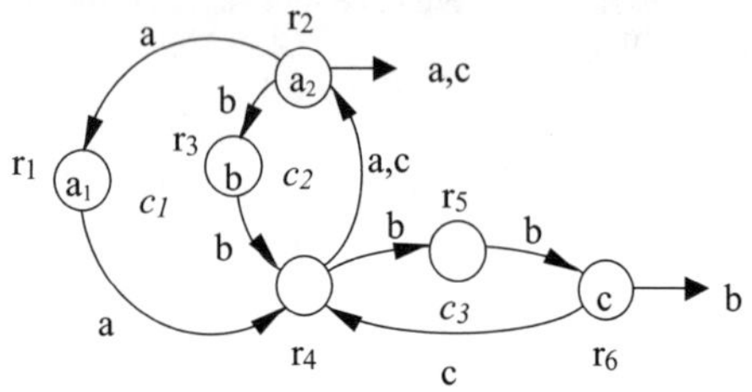

Figure 6.1 Manufacturing system

Table 6.2 Space of manufacturing system in state n_0

Subgraph	Space
c_1	1
c_2	2
c_3	2
$c_1 \cup c_2$	1
$c_1 \cup c_3$	2
$c_2 \cup c_3$	2
$c_1 \cup c_2 \cup c_3$	1

Clearly, the space of all closed paths is greater then zero. Table 6.3 shows the set Q^* from Algorithm 5.2 and one possible sequence of propagation to empty the system and conclude that the system is live.

7 References

Banaszak, Z. and B. Krogh. 1990. "Deadlock Avoidance in Flexible Manufacturing Systems with Concurrently Competing Process Flows." *IEEE Trans. on Robotics and Auto*. 6, no. 6: 724-733.

Cho, H., T.K. Kumaran, and R. Wysk. 1995. "Graph-Theoretic Deadlock Detection and Resolution for Flexible Manufacturing Systems." *IEEE Trans. on Robotics and Auto*. 11, no. 3: 550-527.

Fanti, M., G. Maione and B. Turchiano. 1996. "Deadlock detection and recovery in flexible production systems with multiple capacity resources." *Industrial Applications in Power Systems Computer Science and Telecommunications Procedings of the Mediterranean Electrotechnical Conference*, 237-241.

Judd, R. P. and T. Faiz. 1995. "Deadlock Detection and Avoidance for a Class of Manufacturing Systems." *Proceedings of the 1995 American Control Conference*, 3637-3641.

Judd, R. P., P. Deering, and R. Lipset. 1997. "Deadlock Detection in Simulation of Manufacturing Systems." *Proceedings of the 1997 Summer Computer Simulation Conference,* 317-322.

Lipset, R., P. Deering, and R. P. Judd. 1997. "Necessary and Sufficient Conditions for Deadlock in Manufacturing Systems." *Proceedings of the 1997 American Control Conference*, 1022-1026.

Lipset, R., P. Deering, and R. P. Judd. 1998. "A Stack-Based Algorithm for Deadlock Avoidance in Flexible Manufacturing Systems." *Proceedings of the 1998 American Control Conference*, 1252-1256.

Viswanadham, N., Y. Narahari, and T. Johnson. 1990. "Deadlock Prevention and Deadlock Avoidance in Flexible Manufacturing Systems Using Petri Net Models." *IEEE Trans. on Robotics and Auto*. 6, no. 6: 713-723.

Zhou, M. and F. DiCesare. 1992, "Parallel and Sequential Mutual Exclusion for Petri Net Modeling of Manufacturing Systems with Shared Resources." *IEEE Trans. on Robotics and Auto*. 7, no. 4: 550-527.

Zhou, M. 1996. "Generalizing parallel and sequential mutual exclusions for Petri net synthesis of manufacturing systems." *IEEE Symposium on Emerging Technologies & Factory Automation*, 49-55.

Table 6.3 Part movements to empty system

Set Q^*	Part	Apply Theorem	Resulting State
$\{a_1,b\}$	a_1 to r_4	5.4	3 1 2 1
$\{a_2\}$	a_2 to r_1	5.2	3 2 2 1
$\{a_1\}$	a_1 to r_2	5.1	4 2 2 1
$\{a_1,a_2,b\}$	b to r_4	5.3	4 2 3 1
$\{b\}$	b to r_5	5.2	4 2 4 1
$\{a_1,a_2,c\}$	a_1 exits	5.2	- 2 4 1
$\{a_2,c\}$	c to r_4	5.1	- 2 4 2
$\{b,c\}$	c to r_2	5.1	- 2 4 3
$\{a_2,b,c\}$	c exits	5.1	- 2 4 -
$\{a_2,b\}$	b to r_6	5.1	- 2 5 -
$\{a_2,b\}$	b exits	5.1	- 2 - -
$\{a_2\}$	a_2 to r_4	5.1	- 3 - -
$\{a_2\}$	a_2 to r_2	5.1	- 4 - -
$\{a_2\}$	a_2 exits	5.1	- - - -

Simulation Methodology for Testing Defects in Materials

M. S. Obaidat, M. A. Suhail and B. Sadoun

Monmouth University, KFUPM, and Applied Science University

***Corresponding Address: Professor M. S. Obaidat, Dept. of Computer Science,**

Monmouth University, W. Long Branch, NJ 07764, USA

***E-mail:* Obaidat@monmouth.edu**

Abstract

This paper presents a methodology to detect defects in materials using simulation. Wavelet transform and neural networks are used as feature extraction and classification tools, respectively. We first use the raw signal of the defect as an input to the neural networks. Then, the wavelet transform of the input defect signature is applied to the neural networks. The results of both methods are analyzed and their performance are compared and discussed. It is found that using Wavelet transform as a pre-clustering scheme before applying data to the neural networks can provide better classification results as compared to the case that does not use it. Our scheme is efficient and accurate.

Key Words: Nondestructive testing, defect classification, material characterization and testing, neural networks, wavelet transform.

1. Introduction

Nondestructive testing of materials and systems has become recently an important discipline due to the progress in the enabling technologies and the nature of many types of materials and systems that should be tested without any kind of damage or disruption [1]. Detecting defects in materials is an important process for many applications including quality control in manufacturing, maintenance of bridges, and machines, testing of nuclear reactors, and transducers embedded in many biomedical systems, to name a few. NDT enable us to check the performance of systems, devices, and materials in a cost-effective manner. Transducers, buildings, bridges, machines, aircarfts, space shuttles, power generation plants, nuclear plants, are some examples of complex systems used in a variety of diciplines that need to be tested without disturbing the system under testing. Nondestructive testing, NDT, is also called nondestructive evaluation, NDE, or nondestructive inspection, NDI. The American Society for NDT defines nondestructive evaluation as an examinataion of an object or material in a manner, which will not impair its future usefuleness [1-10]. It is important to measure the the operating characteristics of materials throughout their life cycles. Some devices such as transducers used in biomedical engineering systems, space shuttle systems, aircraft systems, bridges, to name a few examples, must be tested periodically to make sure that they operate properly so that we obtain correct measurements and indicators. Nondestructive evaluation/testing of materials can be performed using ultrasonic-based NDT, radiographic inspection, magnetic-particle inspection, and liquid-penetrate inspection.The work reported in this paper is concerned with ultrasonic-based NDT. Ultrasoic-based nondestructive testing is defined as a method used for detection of hidden flaws in the material being tested. It employs an ultrasonic signal that propagaes through the material, then the reflected echoes from defects and discontinuities in the material are received by an ultrasonic transducer and then recovered for further processing [1-10]. We will examine the use of neural networks for defect classification, where two approaches will be studied: (a) using the raw signal of the defect signature ($y(k)$) as an input to the neural network, and (b) the wavelet transform of $y(k)$ is applied to the neural network system. The result of both methods will be analyzed and their performance will be compared and discussed.

In this paper, we attempt to classify these defects according to three feature categories. These are the geometry, size and orientation in the case of angular flaws. To achieve such an objective, two approaches can be used to tackle this problem. These are the classical pattern recognition and artificial neural networks (ANNs) techniques [5-9]. The first approach is based on statistical pattern recognition simulation techniques such as Bayes or maximum likelihood decision rules, nearest neighbor decision rule, and tree classification method. The second approach is motivated by the universal approximation capabilities of ANN. Typically, a neural network consists of a set of sensory units (source nodes) that constitute the *input layer*, one or more *hidden layers*, and an *output layer* of computation nodes. The input signal propagates through the network in a forward direction, on a layer-by-layer basis. These types of neural networks are commonly referred to as *multilayer perceptrons* (MLPs), which represent a generalization of the single-layer perceptron [10]. Multilayer perceptrons have been applied successfully to solve some difficult and diverse problems by training them in a supervised manner with a highly popular algorithm known as the *error back-propagation algorithm*.

2. Previous Related Work

Sadoun [1] presented a new method for nondestructive testing of material. Obaidat *et al* [7] introduced a neural network simulation algorithm for defect classification of NDT. The results show a failure for the competitive learning when used for pre-clustering. The most successful paradigms for classification was backpropagation pardigm. They found out that the results of the backpropagation can be improved further if more hidden layers are added to the network, but the efficiency would decrease. Obaidat and Sadoun [8] devised a new neural network paradigm, the Hybrid Sum-Of-Product (HSOP), and applied it for the characterization of ultrasonic transducers and authentication of computer access. They found that the performance of HSOP is very good when applied to characterization of transducers. HSOP showed better performance that Sum of Product (SOP) paradigm when applied to the problem of characterization of ultrasonic transducers. Obaidat, Khalid and Sadoun [9] evaluated the performance several neural network paradigms to the charcetrization of ultrasonic transducers. The Moody-Darken Radial Basis Function Network (MD-RBFN), LVQ, and Fuzzy ARTMAP paradigms gave a rather excellent classification accuracy. Their results showed a failure for Probabilistic Neural Network (PNN) as applied to this problem.

Other related effortss include the work reported in [3, 11-13].

3. Problem Statement Proposed Solution

Artificial neural networks (ANNs) have been

used extensively for solving inverse problems in nondestructive testing. The inverse problem is recast as a problem in multidimensional interpolation, which consists of finding the unknown nonlinear relatiooship between inputs, *x* and outputs, *y*, in a space spanned by the activation functions associated with the neural network nodes. The input space, *x*, corresponds to the domain of the NDT signal generated by the inspection tool. In our case this is the ultrasonic transducer. The network output could be the signal class (defect / benign signal) or defect, characterization (length, width, depth and profile of the defect) or some other quantity related to the material properties of the test specimen. In this work, the signal class will be studied. Signal classification schemes typically employ multilayer perceptrons (MLP) networks while defect characterization techniques rely on radial basis function (RBF) type neural networks [10, 14]. Such conventional defect classification schemes methods suffer from the following drawbacks: (a) optimal selection of basis function centers is computationally intensive; often employing adaptive search methods, (b) network output accuracy cannot be reliably controlled in terms of the network parameters, and (c) defect related features occur at multiple resolutions in the NDT signal. Single resolution functional mapping schemes are not necessarily optimal. This work proposes an alternate new defect classification strategy by using a wavelet basis function neural network. We will examine the use of neural networks for defect classification, where two approaches will be studied. In the first approach, the raw signal *y(k)* is used as an input to the neural network. In the second approach, the wavelet transform [15-16] of *y(k)* is applied to the neural networks. We will investigate the two methods by means of computer simulation using synthetic data to verify the code of the simulation program. Then, we will check the validity of the simulation program by using real data. The performance of the two methods will be compared and discussed.

4. Neural Network Simulation Algorithm

In this paper, we use the MLP for classifying the signals obtained from NDT inspection into three classes. The network was trained using the well-known backpropagation algorithm. All subroutines used to develop this classification scheme were developed using a collection of functions built on MATLAB® Technical Computing Environment [17]. The neural network system has an input layer which has 20 neurons, and a hidden layer which has 10 neurons. The output layer has 3 neurons.

We used as an activation function the *tan-sigmoid* transfer function for all the hidden layers. However, the *log-sigmoid* linear transfer function is used at the output layer. The mean square error is considered to be .01. The size of the input layer depends on the input to the neural network. If the input is the raw-data *y(k)*, then the input size is 512. However, if the input is the discrete wavelet transform coefficients, the input size is 150. Next section elaborates more on this. The material used in our study is Aluminum. It is denoted by T15. T15 represents 15 MHz. transducer. We have three classes of defects. Therefore, there are three neurons in the output layer of the neural network. If the signal belongs to the ith type then the desired value for the ith neuron is 1 and the desired values for the others are 0. Table 1 shows the defect classes and their corresponding neural network outputs.

5. Discrete Wavelet Transform Simulation Algorithm

Discrete Wavelet Transform (DWT) is a very

effective signal compression and data reduction scheme. Because the energies of most signals are concentrated in a certain frequency band, all other frequencies are represented by very low amplitudes in the transform domain, and can be discarded without any loss of information. Figure 1 (a) and (b) show a typical ultrasonic 1 MHz crack signal sampled at 10 MHz and its DWT, respectively. The last 128 samples constituting level 1 DWT coefficients (samples 129 through 256) characterize the signal in the $[\pi/2,\pi]$ rad/s frequency band, which corresponds to frequency range of 2.5 to 5 MHz. These samples do not carry much information, because the signal does not have any spectral components in this frequency range. Level 2 DWT coefficients (samples 65 through 128) characterize the signal in the $[\pi/4,\pi/2]$ rad/s frequency band corresponding to the frequencies 1.25 to 2.5 MHz. The main energy of the signal appears in the Level 3 DWT coefficients (samples 33 through 64), which characterize the signal in the $[\pi/8,\pi/4]$ rad/s range, corresponding to frequency range of 625 kHz to 1.25 MHz. The relatively large negative peak appearing in the Level 4 DWT coefficients, samples 16 through 32, correspond to the lower frequencies in the signal, including the envelope of the signal. It can be easily seen that the 256 samples long signal can be represented by the first 128 samples of the DWT with little error, because the contribution of the last 128 coefficients is negligible. Therefore, the Level 1 DWT coefficients is negligible. This means that the Level 1 DWT coefficients can be discarded without any loss of information. In this respect, DWT not only provides a feature extraction scheme, but also provides significant data reduction, thereby reducing the computational burden considerably. The exculded samples are mainly due to noise, therefore, this data reduction also improves the classification accuracy which is a major goal.

6. Results and Discussion

Three types of defects are considered in our study, see table 1. After training the neural networks to classify the three signals, we examined the robustness of classification against noise. In other words, we calculated the percentage of miss-classification versus signal-to-noise ratio. The signal-to-noise ratio is varied from 0 to 14 dB and for each point in this range 1500 signals from each class are generated and applied to the neural network for classification. Then, the percentage of miss-classification as the number of miss-classified signals to the number of correctly classified signals is calculated. The results are shown in Figures 2, 3, and 4. From these figures we observe that for all

best performance is obtained when the discrete wavelet transform is used for pre-clustering.

10. Conclusions

In this paper, we devised a novel classification scheme for non-destructive testing of materials that uses neural networks and discrete wavelet transform (DWT) schemes. The study shows the superiority of the proposed scheme that uses DWT and neural networks over the classification of NDT signals using only neural networks. DWT not only provides an excellent feature extraction scheme, it also provides significant data reduction, thereby reducing the computational burden considerably. Furthermore, this data reduction improves the classification accuracy.

References

[1] B. Sadoun," Simulation Methodology for Nondestructive Testing of Materials,"

Proceedings of the Summer Computer Simulation Conference, SCSC'99, pp. 54-60, Chicago, IL, July 1999.

[2] R. B. Thompson and D. O. Thompson, "Ultrasonic in nondestructive evaluation," *IEEE Proceedings,* Vol. 73, No. 12, pp.1716 – 1755, Dec. 1985.

[3] S. K. Sin and C. H. Chen, "A comparison of deconvolution techniques for the ultrasonic nondestructive evaluation of materials", IEEE Trans. On Image Processing, Vol. 1, No. 1, pp. 3-10, January 1992.

[4] C.H. Chen and Tzu-Hung Cheng, "Signal processing in ultrasonic NDE using time-frequency representations". Proceedings of the *Intentional Conference on Experimental Mechanics: Advances and Applications,* PP 319-324, Dec. 1996.

[5] M. S. *Obaidat, and J. W. Ekis, " An Automated System for Characterizing Ultrasonic Transducers," IEEE Transactions on Instrumentation and Measurements, Vol. 40, N0-5, pp. 847-850, October 1999.*

[6] *M. S. Obaidat,* "On the characterization of ultrasonic transducers using pattern recognition.," IEEE Transactions on Systems, Man and Cybernetics, " Vol. 23, No. 5, pp. 1443-1450, Sept.-Oct. 1993.

[7] M. S. Obaidat and D. Abu-Saymeh," Methodologoies for Characterizing Ultrasonic Transducers Using Neural Network Paradigms," IEEE Transactions on Industrial Electronics, Vol. 39, No. 6, pp. 529-536, Dec. 1992.

[8] M. S. Obaidat and B. Sadoun, " HSOP: A Neural Network Paradigm and Its Applications," Neural Computing & Applications Journal, Springer, Vol. 2, No. 2, pp. 89-96, 1994.

[9] M. S. Obaidat, H. Khalid, and B. Sadoun," Ultrasonic Transducers Characterization by Neural Networks," Information Sciences Journal, Elsevier, Vol. 17, No. 1-4, pp. 195-215, June 1998.

[10] M. S. Obaidat, " Artificial Neural Networks to Systems, Man and Cybernetics: Characteristics, Structures, and Applications," IEEE Transactions on Systems, Man and Cybernetics, Part B, Vol. 28, No. 4, pp. 489-495, August 1998.

[11] L. Udpa and S. S. Udpa. Neural networks for the classification of nondestructive evaluation signals. *IEE Proceedings, Pt. F,* Vol. 138, No. 1, pp. 41 – 45, February 1991.

[12] M. S. Obaidat, A. Brodzik, and B. Sadoun, A Performance Evaluation Study of Four Wavelet Algorithms for Pitch Period Estimation of Speech Signals," Information Sciences Journal, Elsevier, Vol. 112, No. 1-4, pp. 213-221, Dec. 1998.

[13] M. S. Obaidat, C. Lee, B. Sadoun, and D. Nelson, " Estimation of Pitch Period of Speech Signal Using a New Dyadic Wavelet Algorithm," Information Sciences Journal, Vol. 119, pp. 21-39, Dec. 1999.

[14] Simon Haykin, "Neural Networks: A Comprehensive Foundation". Second Edition, Prentice Hall, 1998.

[15] C. Burrus, H. Guo, *"Introduction to Wavelets and Wavelet Transforms: A Primer,"* First Edition, Prentice Hall, 1998.

[16] C. K. Chui, *"Introduction to Wavelets,"* Academic Press, 1992.

[17] Michel Misiti et al., *"Matlab® Wavelet Tool Box Manul,"*, The Math Works Inc., March,1996.

Table 1. The defect classes and their corresponding neural network output.

Class Type	Output		
	y1	*y2*	*y3*
Class 0 (flawless specimen)	0	0	0
Class I (flat-top hole; d = 4 mm)	1	0	0
Class II (flat-top hole; d = 8 mm)	0	1	0
Class III (circular hole; d = 2 mm)	0	0	1

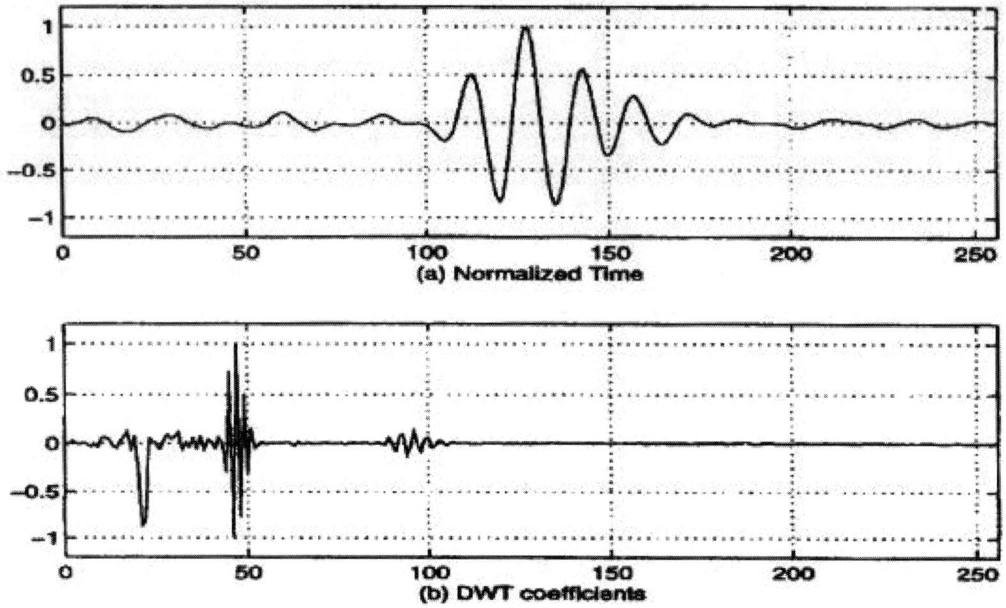

Figure 1. (a) A typical crack signal, and (b) its DWT.

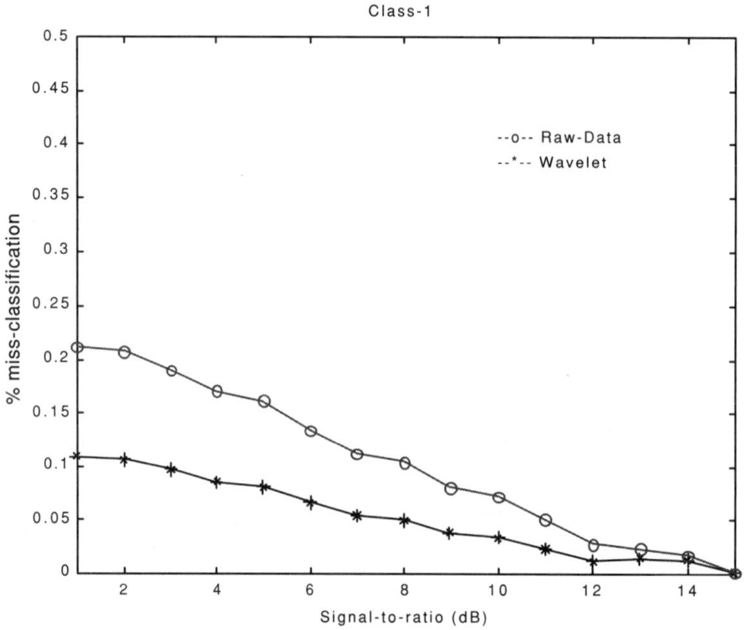

Figure 2. Percentage of miss-classification for class 1.

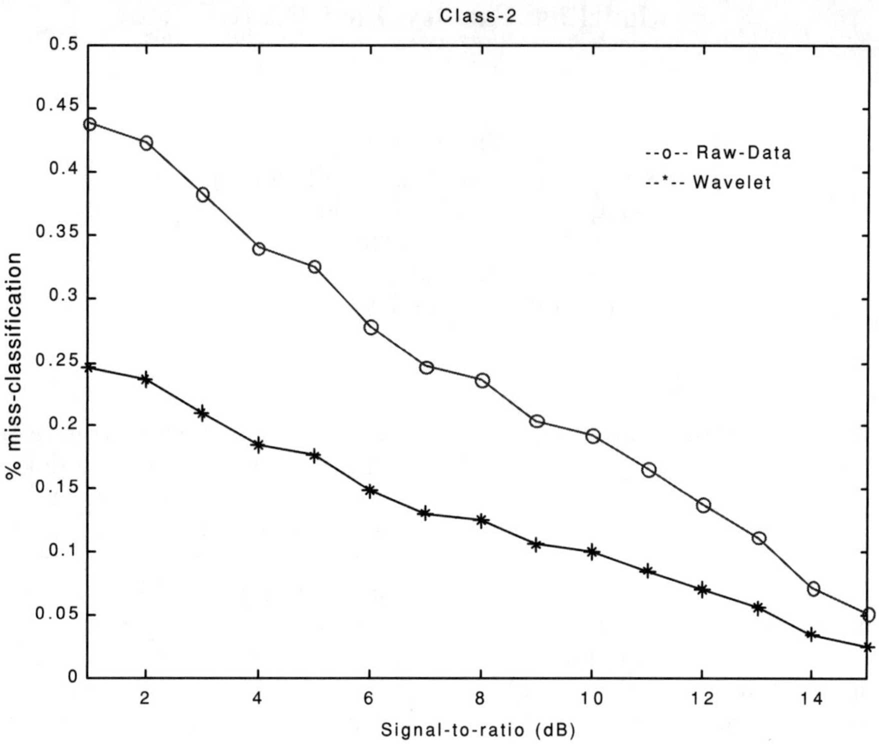

Figure 3. Percentage of missclassification for class II.

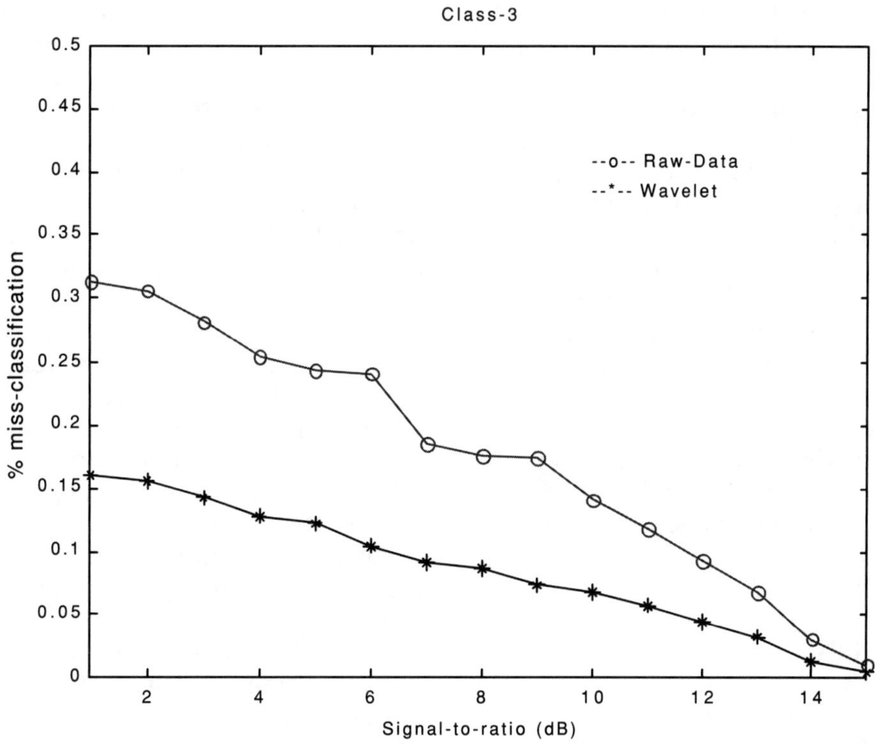

Figure 4. Percentage of miss-classification for class III.

Modeling Factory Logistics

By: Abe Nisanci
Professor of Industrial and Manufacturing Engineering and Technology
Bradley University
Peoria, IL 61625
e-mail: ibo@bradley.edu

KEY WORDS: Logistics, materials handling, storage and retrieval, simulation.

ABSTRACT

Simulation is an integral tool in designing factory logistics systems, which combines material management, material flow, and physical distribution systems into one overall flow system. Modern manufacturing approaches and the use of advanced manufacturing and material handling and storage systems are impacting the logistics systems in different and complex ways. These advanced manufacturing and material handling and storage systems are characterized by high degree of automation, complexity and cost. Simulation is a powerful tool that deals effectively with the complexities and challenges of designing and integrating the components of logistics systems. This presentation highlights the difficulties involved in modeling an integrated logistics system which consists of shuttle systems, multiple grip and gantry robot systems, automated guided vehicles, multi-layer conveyors, cranes, lift scissors, and automated storage and retrieval systems. The role of simulation in configuring these systems and modeling the scheduling and control systems, which integrate all these components, is also presented.

1. INTRODUCTION

A factory can be viewed as a network of transformation and temporary storage points or locations which are connected to each other through input and output relations. Well structured and operated network contributes significantly to the overall efficiency of a factory. Typical types of networks within a factory setting can be classified as coalescent or series. The coalescent network represents a large scale manufacturing in which a complex product is assembled from many parts and components. In other words, the final operation or the final assembly line assembles or coalesces these inputs into a final product. In a series network, products are shipped from one area to another for further processing. Shipping involves transfers from one machine to another, i.e. purely internal. It is also common to see a combination of these two types of networks in large scale manufacturing and assembly. However, these two types of networks are referred to as simple networks since each demand point is served by a single supply point, and each area is either a supply or a demand area, i.e. transshipment situation does not exist. Many complex logistics problems are encountered within this setting.

The design of an internal distribution and storage network, which is referred to as the materials handling system, is crucial to the success of any complex operation. Many issues are encountered and need to be addressed within this setting such as the appropriate means of transportation, methods of handling loads, receiving and in-process storage, in-process handling, workplace handling, warehousing of finished products etc. A material handling system transports the life blood of a manufacturing system. Advanced manufacturing systems which are characterized by increased complexity and cost are especially vulnerable to these issues. Depending on the configuration of an advanced manufacturing system, handling and storage subsystems may consist of various components such as automated storage and retrieval systems (ASRS), automated or self guided vehicles (AGVs, or SGVs), rail guided vehicles (RGVs), multi-directional lift tables, gantry robots, conveyors etc. These components also come in different types based on specific requirements They may be used at the process level serving a single or multiple machines or at the plant level to link various lines/areas. Furthermore, the machining, handling, and storage subsystems are all connected to each other through complicated scheduling and control algorithms which are executed by a central computer. Dynamic and probabilistic interactions of all these systems necessitate the use of a powerful tool like simulation.

The increased complexity and cost of modern service and manufacturing systems coupled with the advances in computer and simulation technologies have led to an extensive use of simulation. The use of simulation in designing these state of the art systems became a common practice enforced by corporate policies. The on-going developments in the computer and simulation technologies have made simulation a major tool for the efficient design, analysis and operation of these advanced manufacturing and handling systems. Currently, simulation plays a significant role in almost every major service and manufacturing industry throughout the world. The "Directory of Simulation Software" published by the Society for Computer Simulation (Rodrigues, 1994) lists 174 simulation products that are available in the marketplace. The annual "Buyer's Guide" of simulation software (Institute of Industrial Engineers, 1999) lists twenty-seven companies providing forty simulation software products. Twenty-eight simulation products are listed under the categories of general purpose simulation software, manufacturing oriented software, business process engineering, simulation-based scheduling, animators, simulation support software, and optimization (Banks 1998).

Simulation provides a realistic representation of the machining, handling, storage and scheduling systems. It is vital to have each of these systems to operate efficiently for the success of the entire system. Despite the advances in simulation, modeling these systems is always a challenging task with a myriad of complex problems which confront the simulation modeler throughout the study. The performance of one system affects the performance of another. More significantly, the scheduler of a system plays a central role in determining the performance of the material handling system. The scheduler links the dynamic and static system entities and ensures that the right actions are taken by the right components at the right times to optimize the performance of the entire system. The modeling of a scheduler and a controller requires the representation of complex decision rules for the dynamic allocation and monitoring of these subsystems for the production of parts over a time horizon. This study presents an overview of the modeling approaches and difficulties involved in modeling a factory logistics system. The emphasis is on material handling and storage systems, and scheduling and control policies. Modern simulation languages have modules or constructs which simplify the modeling of most frequently used materials handling systems. In fact, some are more materials handling oriented than the others. A module to simulate a specific materials handling system may also be flexible enough to model another system, e.g. modeling a simple crane system with an AGV module. The vendor of the package or the users of the package develop materials handling constructs upon a perceived need, e.g. specific material handling extensions or applications. Some of the simulation software feature a well developed array of pre-defined material handling systems including conveyors, automatic guided vehicle systems (AGVs), automated storage and retrieval systems (ASRS), bridge cranes, and power and free conveyors (Nisanci and Schwab 2000, and Nisanci 1998).

2. MODELING AGVs/SGVs

An Automated/Self guided vehicle (AGV/SGV) is a driverless industrial truck. SGVs are used as transport vehicles to move unit loads such as pallets, as tow vehicles such as carrying carts, as assembly transport vehicles, and as storage and retrieval vehicles etc. An AGV/SGV system consists of a fleet of AGVs which may consist of a combination of different types of vehicles all controlled by a central computer. Like any other material handling system, an AGV system plays a critical in determining throughput capability of a manufacturing subsystem or system. The AGVs are used to serve the machines or process centers in a given area and/or to link the various subsystems in a factory. They usually interface with a variety of handling equipment such as cranes, conveyors, shuttle systems etc. Computer simulation is widely used in determining the appropriate number of SGVs, load pick-up and delivery rules, transportation route selection etc. A realistic simulation study needs to take into consideration additional system design characteristics such as the capacities of the AGV pathways, path directions, vehicle interactions (e.g. collisions, blocking etc.), and vital vehicle characteristics such as velocity, acceleration, and deceleration. Unrealistic and oversimplifying assumptions regarding to the operation of an AGV system would render the results of a simulation study totally meaningless. Multi-million dollar projects would be delayed or even scrapped with considerable cost consequences.

To evaluate and test alternative system configurations and operating policies, it is important to model vehicle characteristics, pathways and travel restrictions, vehicle operating rules, and docking locations as configurable parameters. to evaluate alternative types of vehicles, traffic patterns, docking locations etc. A typical AGV/SGV system simulation model would consist of the following components:

1. Manufacturing and/or assembly centers:
* Variables and parameters related to machining, assembly operation times.
* Facilities layout.
* Locations of machines, assembly stations.
* Locations of raw material, in-process, and finished product storage areas.
* Entities such as parts, pallets etc., and entity flow logic.

2. Defining an AGV/SGV system:
* Battery charging and or maintenance locations
* Vehicle control points which are the locations and intersection points on the pathway at which a vehicle begins traveling on a path, or stops to load/unload, or waits for instructions from the host computer.
* Pathway segments, and their lengths, directions of travel, and capacities.
* AGV characteristics such as empty /loaded speeds, acceleration, deceleration, vehicle length, buffer distance, and check zone radius.
* Multiple fleet definition with each fleet consisting of vehicles with different characteristics, e.g. single versus double deck AGVs.

3. AGV/SGV Control policies:
* Deadlock prevention.
* Head-on contention: Rules to reverse the direction of vehicles based on vehicle status (loaded, empty), and priorities.
* Routing contention to allow a capture of a control point, e.g. FIFO, CLOSEST etc.
* Routing decisions for path selection, e.g. based on distance, congestion etc.
* Job/move assignments for allocating vehicles to move requests, e.g. FIFO, CLOSEST
* Positioning idle vehicles, i.e. staging at defined locations, or cruising etc.
* Vehicle selection rules, e.g. most idle, closest etc.
* User defined rules for any of the above to deal with system specific complex situations.

4. Performance statistics:
* Utilization of work/assembly, and machining stations.
* AGV performance (number of loads, unloads, percent blocked etc.), percent of time spent on loading, traveling, etc.
* Waiting for processes, and AGVs.
* Travel path congestion, utilization and trip statistics.
* Vehicle trip analysis
* User defined statistics

3. MODELING CONVEYORS

A conveyor system is another alternative handling system which may compete or complement an AGV system. They are used for frequent transfers over a fixed path. Various types of conveyors exist depending on the type of product transported, e.g. (bulk or unit loads), and where they are located (overhead, floor) etc. Furthermore, a conveyor system can also be multi-layer if there are space limitations and potential congestion, if a captive pallet system is used, and if there is a need for flow simplification. A multi-layer system may consist of upper and lower decks where the upper deck transfers the loaded pallets and the lower deck transfers the empty and partially full pallets. However, a multi-layer conveyors systems also need to be equipped with scissors or multi-directional lift tables to moves the pallets between the decks.

A conveyor system simulation model also requires the description of manufacturing and/or assembly centers as defined for the AGV system. A conveyor system may be modeled as a collection of series of resources of capacity one (segments), which are connected to each other. A conveyor system is modeled using the following components:

1 Defining a conveyor system:
* Conveyor dimensions, i.e. width, length.
* Type, i.e. accumulating or non-accumulating.
* Speed.
* Beginning and ending locations.
* Load routing rules if a conveyor branches out.
* Load exit rules for accumulating conveyors.
* Unit load dimensions, e.g. pallet width, length.
* Accessories, e.g. Scissors logic which may be needed to avoid blockage at intersections or if multi-layer conveyors are modeled;
  - Transfer two empty pallets at a time or
  - Transfer one empty and one partially full pallet at a time.
  -If a partially full pallet arrives first, transfer it right away, i.e. one at a time.
* Assignment rules for routing the exiting pallets
* Number of pallets on a conveyor if a captive pallet system is modeled.

2. Conveyor performance statistics:
* Percentage utilization.
* Maximum number of loads on the conveyor.
* Waiting statistics to get on and off the conveyor.
* Throughput of parts and pallets

4. MODELING AS/RS

Automated storage and retrieval systems are integral parts of modern manufacturing systems. Especially in fully automated advanced manufacturing environments such as Flexible Manufacturing Systems (FMSs), with expensive pallets/fixture requirements, AS/RS becomes a critical logistics support. In this setting, fixtures on which parts are mounted need to be moved tin and out of an FMS to transport the parts from one machining center to another till it is completed. The management of these fixtures becomes critical to provide a steady flow of parts to and from the machines. Each fixture in the system occupies a location in the AS/RS. Any time a fixture of a particular type is needed, its location in the AS/RS need to be determined. This requires keeping track of the contents of the AS/RS racks. A two dimensional array is used to define the racks. Each cell of an array represents a rack. The content of a rack is updated by assigning the identifier number of a fixture type which occupies the rack. An empty cell with "zero" assigned, indicates an empty rack.

The storage of fixtures used for manufacturing is done on multilevel racks organized in parallel rows with an automated retrieval and transportation vehicle operating between the rows. For finished or raw material storage and retrieval, the problems turns into a bigger warehousing organization and management problem. Storage, retrieval, and managing a fixed number of fixtures on storage racks represents a smaller problem considering the volume of moves, number of equipment involved etc. However, the complexities of bigger warehousing are also inherent in these smaller size automated fixture storage and retrieval systems. Modeling of such a system which is served by two rail guided vehicles could be achieved by using the AGV or crane constructs of a simulation software. If a single bi-directional pathway (runway) with multiple carriers is used, "crane constructs" may provide more realistic modeling. Usually, crane constructs provide complicated procedures to deal with complicated crane "interference" situations. The following modeling considerations are given using cranes to model rail guided vehicles.

* The location (x and y coordinate) of each rack needs to be defined.
* Content of each rack needs to be updated every time a change occurs. Each rack holds one fixture.
* Attributes such as assigned runway, maximum and minimum velocities, acceleration and deceleration, trolley velocity are defined.
* Priority rules for crane movements are defined, e.g. a crane moving to a drop-off location may have a higher priority over another crane moving to a pick-up point.
* Load selection/priority rules need to be defined

2. AS/RS performance statistics:
* Percentage utilization of locations and cranes
* Number of drops and picks for the gantry
* Waiting statistics to get location, and crane.
* Throughput of parts and pallets

5. LOGISTICS AND SCHEDULING

Scheduling significantly impacts the performance of a factory logistics system. A scheduling decision can easily deadlock an AGV, conveyor, crane etc. systems. Scheduling system needs to be tailored for a seamless integration of manufacturing and transportation operations. This may require user written codes using a general purpose language. Unlike the physical components, such as machining stations, carriers, storage equipment etc., the scheduling component is not visible and detailed information on scheduler and control logic does not exist or it is hard to get. Most often, the modeler has to conduct interviews with the software developers. Often the scheduling software is a product of a team effort and individuals can relay information only on the sections of the software which they have developed. This results in numerous loose ends which the modeler has to connect in order to build a realistic model. This is an iterative process which requires building the integrated scheduling and control flow chart from the piecemeal information obtained on the individual decision rules which make up the entire software system.

REFERENCES

Banks, J., 1998, "Software for Simulation," in Handbook of Simulation, J. Banks ed., John Wiley & Sons, New York., pp. 813-835.

Institute of Industrial Engineers, 1999, “Buyer’s Guide: Simulation Software,” Solutions, Vol. 31, No. 5, pp. 52-59.

Nisanci, A., and Schwab R.E., 2000, " Chapter 94: Simulation Packages", Handbook of Industrial Engineering, G. Salvendy ed., John Wiley & Sons, New York.

Nisanci, A. 1998, "Comparative Analysis of AGV and Multi-Layer Conveyor Systems Using Simulation," in Proceedings of Summer Computer Simulation Conference, M.S. Obaidat, F. Davoli, D. DeMarinis, Eds., The Society For Computer Simulation International, Reno, NV, pp. 15-20.

Rodrigues, J.M., 1994, Directory of Simulation Software, The Society for Computer Simulation, San Diego.

BIOGRAPHY

Dr. Abe Nisanci is a professor of Industrial and Manufacturing Engineering and Technology at Bradley University, Peoria, Illinois. He has Ph.D. and Ms. degrees in Manufacturing Engineering from Loughborough University, England, and Ms. and Bs. degrees in Industrial Engineering from Middle East Technical University, Ankara, Turkey. He has worked as a consultant with companies such as Caterpillar Inc., Cincinnati Milacron, Ingersoll Engineers, BDM, Allen Automated Systems, etc. His areas of interest and expertise include automated material handling and storage systems, flexible manufacturing systems, scheduling and control, simulation modeling, and pull systems. He has made numerous presentations at national and international conferences, and has published in various refereed journals. Dr. Nisanci is a member of ASEE, IIE, SCS, and SME.

BROADBAND HETEROGENEOUS NETWORK DESIGN BASED ON SIMULATED ANNEALING ALGORITHMS

Miguel Ríos, Vladimir Marianov, Cristián Abaroa

Department of Electrical Engineering
Universidad Católica de Chile
Casilla 306, Correo 22
Santiago-Chile
e-mail: mrios@ing.puc.cl

KEYWORDS: Broadband network design, optimization, modeling, system engineering.

ABSTRACT

The paper presents the global design of a heterogeneous broadband network. The problem to be solved involves a large number of variables (integer and real) and includes the topology definition, routing, capacity assignment, transfer mode, fault tolerance and traffic policy. Of these, only the fault tolerance is not considered in the paper. Three topics are discussed: a) the network model; b) the traffic model; and c) the resolution algorithms. Simulated annealing algorithms (SAA) are used to solve the problems. Computational experiments are presented showing that SAA gets to the optimum 10 times faster than a commercial AMPL-CPLEX solver.

INTRODUCTION

The global design of a heterogeneous broadband network is addressed. The ATM class networks are taken as examples, but the proposed methods can be used in any broadband network.

The problem to be solved involves a large number of variables (integer and real) and includes the topology definition, routing, capacity assignment, transfer mode, fault tolerance and traffic policy. Of these, only the fault tolerance is not considered in the paper.

These problems have been addressed in the literature from several points of view: capacity assignment through multiple origin-destination pairs (Bienstock 95), fault tolerant network dimensioning (Alevras 97), and uncapacitated network design (Balakrishnan 89). In (Bienstock 98) a virtual hierarchical network is designed that uses aggregated traffic distributed the same way considered in this paper.

This paper addresses three topics: a) the network model; b) the traffic model; and c) the resolution algorithms.

The network model is based on minimizing the cost of connecting a number of nodes, whose location is known, and also the traffic for each information type is also known. In addition an acceptable quality of service (QoS) is assured to each information type. QoS chosen parameters are delay and the cell loss probability.

The traffic model is a key element to ensure a reliable design. To facilitate the modeling and solving procedures, the equivalent bandwidth concept was used, and several traffic-modeling techniques were studied, including self-similarity and wide range dependency. Finally, the Fractional Brownian Motion (FBM) was selected.

In solving the design problem, two tools were used: a) AMPL-CPLEX (a commercial package), which finds the optimum solution of the linear model, in an exponential growing time, and b) a simulated annealing algorithm (SAA), which may also determine the optimum (it is not assured on all the problems though) or come close to the optimum solution.

Computational experiments are presented showing that SAA gets to the optimum 10 times faster than AMPL-CPLEX.

The experiments also show that for 50 node networks the AMPL-CPLEX is unable to deliver results due to the enormous processing time, while the SAA delivers good feasible solutions.

TRAFFIC MODEL

The paper uses the Fractional Brownian Model (due to Norros 95), which defines the equivalent bandwidth as

$$EBW = C = \lambda + \left(k(H)\cdot\sqrt{-2\cdot\ln(\alpha)}\right)^{\frac{1}{H}} \cdot a^{\frac{1}{2\cdot H}} \cdot B^{\frac{1-H}{H}} \cdot \lambda^{\frac{1}{2\cdot H}}$$

where λ is the mean arrival time (bps), $k(H)=H^H(1-H)^{1-H}$ with H being the Hurst parameter, B is the maximum queue length (buffer length), α is $P(x>B)$ or the cell loss probability, and a is the variance of cell arrival times.

NETWORK MODEL

The network model considers three types of traffic sources: video, sound and data, with the following parameters:

Parameter	Traffic source		
	Video	**Sound**	**Data**
Mean rate	50[Mbps]	2[Mbps]	100[kbps]
Variance	600[kbps]	400[kbps]	10[kbps]
Node Distribution	15%	100%	70%
Hurst	0.8	0.8	0.8
CLP	1e-8	1e-7	1e-5

The network model described below uses the following sets and variables:

Arc: Set of all possible undirected arcs among network nodes. Its size is given by $n(n-1)/2$ where n is the number of nodes.
Link: Set of all possible directed arcs among nodes. Its size is given by $n(n-1)$.
Cap: Set of arc capacities. Three of them were used (622, 155 and 45 Mbps).
Path: Set of all possible origin-destination (od) pairs. Its size is given by $n(n-1)$.
X_{ij}: Binary variable indicating if the arc between nodes i and j exists.
$Eflow_{ij}^{od,k}$: Binary variable indicating if flow between nodes i and j of pair od of type k exists.
n_i: Binary variable indicating if node i is linked.
$Flow_{ij}^{od,k}$: Real variable. Corresponds to the flow through link i,j of pair od and traffic type k.
$Traf^{od,k}$: amount of traffic of type k going from origin to destination node.
$DelN^k$: Switching delay
DelD: Transmission delay
dij: Distance between node i and j.
Ca: Cost per length unit.
Cs: Fixed costs of node
Cc: Cost of link capacity hardware.
$Vcap_r$: Capacity of link hardware (45-155 or 622 Mbps)
Y_{ij}^r: Integer variable. It is the quantity of links of type k in arc ij.

The network model then can be stated as:

$$\text{minimize} \sum_{(i,j)\in Arc} Ca \cdot d_{ij} \cdot X_{ij} + \sum_{i\in Node} Cs \cdot n_i + \sum_{(i,j)\in Link} \sum_{r\in Cap} Cc^r \cdot Y_{ij}^r$$

Subject to

1) Connection of nodes

$$n_i + n_j \geq 2 \cdot X_{ij} \qquad \forall (i,j) \in Arc$$

2) Traffic flow

$$flow_{ij}^{od,k} = traf_{od}^{k} \cdot Eflow_{ij}^{od,k}$$
$$\forall (i,j) \in Arc, (o,d) \in Path, k \in typeT$$

3) Arc presence

$$\sum_{k\in typeT} \left(flow_{ij}^{od,k} + flow_{ji}^{od,k}\right) \leq \sum_{k\in typeT} traf^{od,k} \cdot Carc_{ij}$$
$$\forall (i,j) \in Arc, (o,d) \in Path$$

4) Flow balance

$$\sum_{(x,j)\in Arc} flow_{ji}^{od,k} - \sum_{(x,j)\in Arc} flow_{ij}^{od,k} = \begin{cases} traf^{od,k} & \text{if } i = d \\ -traf^{od,k} & \text{if } i = o; \\ 0 & otherwise \end{cases}$$
$$\forall i \in Node, (o,d) \in Path, k \in typeT$$

5) Link capacity assignment

$$\sum_{(o,d)\in Path} \sum_{k\in typeT} flow_{ij}^{od,k} + flow_{ji}^{od,k} \leq \sum_{r\in cap} Vcap_r \cdot Y_{ij}^r$$
$$\forall (i,j) \in Arc$$

6) Delay restriction

$$DelN^k \cdot \left(\sum_{(i,j)\in Arc} Eflow_{ij}^{od,k} - 1 \right) + DelD \cdot \sum_{(i,j)\in Arc} (d_{ij} \cdot Eflow_{ij}^{od,k}) \leq Delay^k$$
$$\forall (o,d) \in Path, k \in typeT$$

7) Unidirectional flow restriction

$$Eflow_{ij}^{od,k} + Eflow_{ji}^{od,k} \leq 1$$
$$\forall (o,d) \in Path, (i,j) \in Arc \in typeT$$

SIMULATED ANNEALING METHODS

Simulated annealing is a Monte Carlo approach for minimizing multivariate functions. The term simulated annealing derives from the roughly analogous physical process of heating and then slowly cooling a substance to obtain a strong crystalline structure. In simulation, a minimum of the cost function corresponds to this ground state of the substance. The simulated annealing process lowers the temperature by slow stages until the system ``freezes" and no further changes occur. At each temperature the simulation must proceed long enough for the system to reach a steady state or equilibrium. This is known as thermalization.

The time required for thermalization is the decorrelation time; correlated microstates are eliminated. The sequence of temperatures and the number of iterations applied to thermalize the system at each temperature comprise an annealing schedule. To apply simulated annealing, the system is initialized with a particular configuration. A new configuration is constructed by imposing a random displacement. If the energy of this new state is lower than that of the previous one, the change is accepted unconditionally and the system is updated. If the energy is greater, the new configuration is accepted probabilistically. This is the Metropolis step, the fundamental procedure of simulated annealing. This procedure allows the system to move consistently towards lower energy states, yet still `jump' out of local minima due to the probabilistic acceptance of some upward moves. If the temperature is decreased logarithmically, simulated annealing guarantees an optimal solution.

Simulated annealing is a local search algorithm that is used frequently to solve problems where the solution space is very large and with many local minima. Among those problems are Travelling Salesman Problem (TSP), VLSI design, graph partitions, set covering design and other.

The algorithm was introduced by Kirkpatrik (Kirkpatrik 83). The energy initial state and temperature are defined first. Then a perturbation is generated and the energy of the resulting state is calculated. If this new state has less energy than the initial one, then it replaces it for the next iteration (storing the result). If not a higher level state, according to the formula $P_B=\exp(-\Delta E/T)$ is calculated and compared with a value P_{ran} obtained from a (0,1) uniform distribution. If $P_{ran} < P_B$ the initial state is replaced by the current one. Finally, the temperature is calculated (generally decreasing it) and the process is repeated. The energy state is the solution of the problem

COMPUTER EXPERIMENTS

The att48 problem was used as a test to observe the algorithm behavior. While there is no certainty the model will reach the optimum, the algorithm provided good and feasible solutions. Each running cycle took around 35 hours of CPU time in a Digital Alpha 433, running Digital Unix V4.0B.

Figure 1 shows the cost behavior in terms of the CPU time.

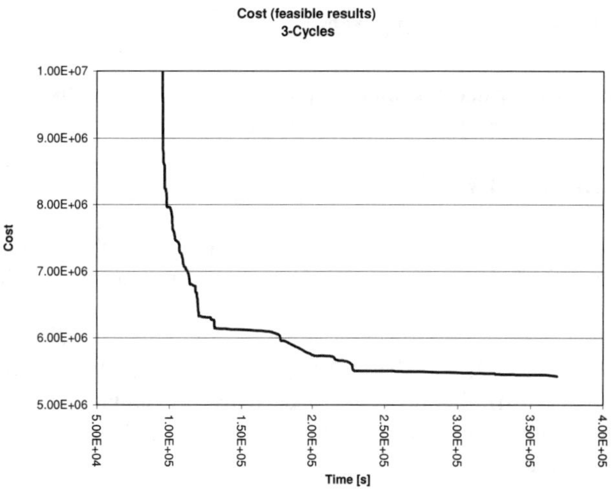

Figure 1. Cost in terms of CPU-time.

The following figure 2 shows the best solution found by the simulated annealing algorithm. It should be noted that it is unknown if that solution is close to the optimum solution. What is certain is that for such network, the AMPL-CPLEX package can't provide a solution.

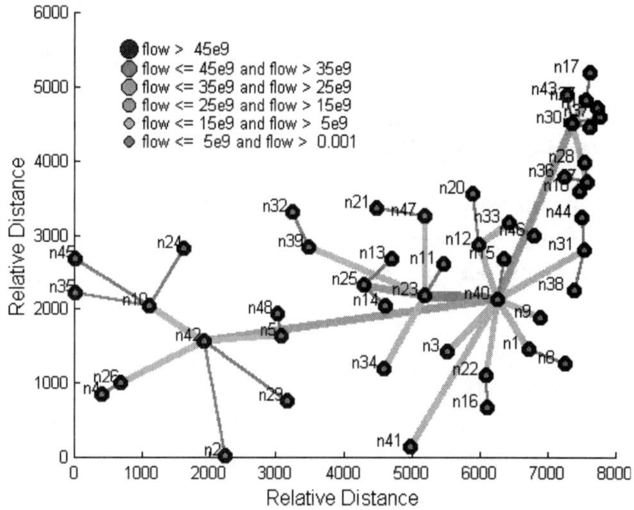

Figure 2. Best solution found by the simulated annealing algorithm.

CONCLUSIONS

The model presented considers all the basic elements used in a broadband network design: topology, routing and capacity assignment. It only requires knowledge about node locations and traffic distributions for each information type. The solution algorithm, which uses Simulated Annealing techniques, provides good solutions in reasonable computer time, even for a 48 node example carrying three information types.

ACKNOWLEDGEMENTS

This work was supported in part by grants from Fondecyt and Nortel Technology.

REFERENCES

-KIRKPATRIK, S., GELATT, C., VECCHI, M. (1983) Optimization by Simulated Annealing. Science, Vol. 220, N°4528, Mayo 1983.

-BIENSTOCK, D., CHOPRA, S., GÜNLÜK, O. Y TSAI, C. (1995) Minimum Cost Capacity Installations for multicommodity network flows. To Appear, Mathematical Programming.

-BIENSTOCK, D. Y SANIEE, I. (1998) ATM Network Design: Traffic Models and Optimization-Based Heuristics. Preprint. Bellcore. Morristown NJ 07960, iis@bellcore.com.

-ALEVRAS, D., GRÖTSCHEL, M. Y WESSÄLY, R. (1997) Capacity and Survivability Models for Telecommunication Networks. Preprint SC97-24. Konrad-Zuse-Zentrum für Informationstechnik. Berlin. Germany.

-BALAKRISHNAN, A., MAGNANTI, T. Y WONG, T. (1989) A Dual-Ascent Procedure for large-scale uncapacitated Network Design. INFORMS Operation Research, 37, pp. 716-740.

-ALLWRIGHT, R.J. Y CARPENTER, D.B. (1989) A Distributed Implementation of Simulated Annealing for the Traveling Salesman Problem. Parallel Computing, 10, p335-p338.

-LELAND, W. E., TAQQU, M. S., WILLINGER, W. Y WILSON, D.V. (1994) On The Self-Similar nature of Ethernet Traffic (Extended version). IEEE/ACM Trans. On Networking, vol2, N°1.

-NORROS, I. (1995) On the Use of Fractional Brownian Motion in the Theory of Connectionless Networks. JSAC, 13-6, August 1995.

BIOGRAPHIES

Miguel Ríos is an Electrical Engineer from the Universidad de Chile and Master of Applied Science and Doctor of Philosophy from the University of Ottawa. Since 1977 has been with the Department of Electrical Engineering at the Universidad Católica de Chile, where he is an Associate Professor of Electrical Engineering. His research interest include digital communications, network planning of telecommunications systems, computer networks and broadband networks.

Vladimir Marianov is an Electrical Engineer from the University of Chile, and Doctor of Philosophy from the Johns Hopkins University. Since 1981 he has been with the Department of Electrical Engineering at the Universidad Católica de Chile, where he is Professor of Electrical Engineering. His research interests include resource location, and network planning of telecommunications systems.

Cristián Abaroa is an Electrical Engineer, and Master of Engineering Sciences from the Universidad Católica de Chile. His research interests include communication network optimization and heuristics.

A SIMULATION OF A VALVE MANUFACTURING PLANT

Andrew Greasley
University of Derby
United Kingdom.
email: A.Greasley@derby.ac.uk

KEYWORDS

Simulation, Discrete, Manufacturing, Decision Making

ABSTRACT

This paper describes the construction of a simulation model of a valve manufacturing plant with the aim of assessing capacity requirements in response to a forecast increase in demand. The plant provides a weekly cycle of valves of varying types, based on a yearly production plan. Production control is provided by a just-in-time type system to minimise inventory. The simulation model investigates the effect on lead time of a range of valve sequences into the plant. The main benefit of the study was seen in its relatively close fit to the decision-making process, compared to alternative operational research 'optimisation' techniques. Thus the formation of a project team and the collection of information across departmental boundaries upon which informed decisions could be made was seen as an important part of the study process.

INTRODUCTION

It was proposed to build a simulation of a self-contained valve manufacturing plant for a subsidiary of one of Europe's major producers of pipeline products. The firm manufactures a range of valve products, all in SG iron sold through sales and service centres through accredited agents or from the company itself. A recent major product development is the 'Euro 16B' valve which eliminates the need for bolts or studs to secure the bonnet and seal housing thus reducing maintenance. It is also completely rubber covered by an epoxy process to avoid corrosion and increase operating life. The company had envisaged a sharp increase in demand for the product range, in particular for the new '16B' valve, and wished to use the simulation model to explore alternative strategies for increasing capacity to meet this demand.

THE PRODUCTION PROCESS

The production system is organised on a batch basis with a weekly batch size based on predicted yearly demand for a particular valve type. Each week a batch of castings for each valve type is released into the shop. There are 5 main types of valve, with varying sizes, producing a sequence of 15 separate batches. Each batch contains two or three components that are processed separately before assembly. The sequence of batches is termed a cycle with an identical weekly cycle being released into the shop over the planning period. The castings are machined, drilled, shot-blast and coated with epoxy resin were necessary to produce the valve parts which are then assembled and tested before delivery to the customer.

To reduce the amount of inventory no part is allowed to progress in the plant until the next machining centre becomes available. If more than one part is waiting for a particular station a priority system is activated. Parts are prioritised by their position in the valve cycle with parts earlier in the cycle (which consequently had spent more time in the plant) having priority for the available machine.

THE SIMULATION STUDY

Model Formulation

The main aim of the study was to investigate the steps needed to increase capacity. However much of the work centred upon a review of the current capacity in order to establish reliable data from which to build a model. Information on process routing, setup and process times was held in a variety of locations and forms within the company. This material was brought together and process flow diagrams were constructed to form a clear picture of the process.

Model Translation

The simulation was constructed using the SIMAN/CINEMA (Pegden, 1995) simulation system (see figure 1). A waiting cycle of parts is shown at the top of the screen. These are introduced into the system as the relevant machine in the plant becomes available. Each machine has an area adjacent to its position to show parts either waiting for process or waiting to leave for the next process. Thus a just-in-time type control system is in operation with only a single batch of parts allowed to wait at a machine at anytime.

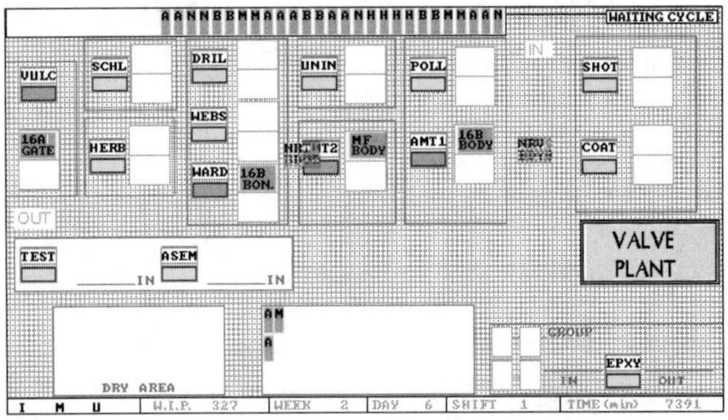

Figure 1. The Valve Plant Simulation Model

Model Experimentation

The company was keen to respond quickly to changing customer requirements, aiming to provide a response time of approximately one week. It was for this reason that they sought to get a batch for each job through the plant each week. The weekly production of each valve in each size in this way represented the weekly production cycle. However it was evident that with 5 types of valve in up to 4 sizes the cycle was complex. For this reason the simulation model was used to explore the impact of changes in the sequence of jobs processed (i.e. the processing order cycle) on overall throughput time. Initial experiments with the simulation model were with 8 sequences comprising 4 valve type sequences and 2 size sequences.

Results

The simulation experimentation revealed quite different results for valve cycle time and it was found that by simply altering the sequence in which the jobs were processed could reduce by 18 hours the length of time required to process the longest job and therefore the valve cycle. However this improvement was not able to provide sufficient capacity for the '16B' valve and the simulation was able to highlight the massive undercapacity of the epoxy plant in meeting this demand. In fact the implications for the manufacturing facility of the 16B valve caused the company to view the plant from a new perspective. Further investigations studied the effect of implementing a separate 16B line to maximise capacity utilisation. However the immediate recommendations from the study were as follows:-

- Change job sequence to minimise cycle time
- Purchase a new epoxy machine
- 3 shift working on bottleneck machines such as epoxy
- Use a batch splitting technique (Goldratt, 1993) to reduce waiting time for 16B valves

DISCUSSION

During the data collection phase of the simulation study i became clear that management had only a rough idea o present plant capacity on which to base decisions. Man Operational Research techniques provide an optimun answer to a problem based on given constraints whicl provides the basis on which options can be evaluated (e.g Linear Programming (Waters, 1998)). A simulation study however, more closely follows the decision making proces and this was shown in this case with the formation of project team working towards set objectives i.e. matchin capacity with demand for the facility. It was clear tha although the information was available across th departments within the company, this analysis had not bee undertaken and so an accurate assessment of capacity ha not been made. In order to carry out the simulation study thi information was vital, and with the project team in place, i was quickly provided and the analysis undertaken.

CONCLUSION

The simulation was important in not only evaluating option available to management, but highlighting the scale of th problems present. This required the collection of informatio from a variety of sources, and a model that reflected the tru capabilities of the production system. The effect of th increased demand for product could be clearly seen an convinced management that substantial changes were neede in order to meet demand.

This case highlights the use of simulation in enablin managers to quantify operational scenarios. This provides rational basis on which to take decisions on meetin performance criteria. For example the decision to study th creation of a new 16B line was taken on the basis of analysi provided by the simulation system quantifying the increas in demand.

REFERENCES

Goldratt, E.M.; Cox, J. (1993), *The Goal*, Second Edition Gower Publishing, Hampshire.

Law, A.M.; Kelton, W.D. (1991), *Simulation Modeling and Analysis*, Second Edition, McGraw-Hill, Singapore.

Pegden, C.D.; Shannon, R.E.; Sadowski, R.P. (1995), *Introduction to Simulation using SIMAN*, Second Edition, McGraw-Hill, Singapore.

Waters, D. (1998), *A practical introduction to management science*, Second Edition, Addison-Wesley, Singapore.

Organizational & Enterprise Simulation

LEAN ENTERPRISE SIMULATIONS

Mel Adams
Hank Czarnecki
Bernard J. Schroer

University of Alabama in Huntsville
Huntsville, AL 35899, U.S.A.

Bradley J. Schroer

Summa Technology, Inc.
Huntsville, AL 35805, U.S.A.

ABSTRACT

This paper presents the application of simulation to support the lean enterprise. Two areas for using simulation in lean manufacturing are as training tools and as design and analysis tools. The concept of lean manufacturing is the compression of time from an order, through manufacturing, to payment. To compress time requires continuous improvement. A discussion is given on combining simulation with continuous improvement along with several successful real world implementations.

INTRODUCTION

The Manufacturing Extension Partnership (MEP) is a nationwide network of over seventy centers whose sole purpose is to assist small and medium-size manufacturers. The centers are linked through the Department of Commerce's National Institute of Standards and Technology (NIST). The Alabama Technology Network (ATN) joined the MEP in 1996 and began operation as a nonprofit corporation through a partnership among the University of Alabama System, Auburn University and seven two-year colleges. The University of Alabama in Huntsville (UAH) is the Region 1 center serving six counties in North Alabama. The ATN/UAH Center has a staff of nine professionals visiting companies on a daily basis, identifying their needs and providing assistance on a fee for service basis. For FY98-99 the ATN/UAH Center completed 97 projects with 61 companies. A distribution of clients is 60% light manufacturing, 20% defense and aerospace, and 20% technology based start-ups. Also 57% of the projects were lean manufacturing, 23% business systems and management, and 20% product design and development.

LEAN MANUFACTURING

Lean manufacturing is a systematic approach to identifying and eliminating waste (all non-value-added activities) through continuous improvement by flowing the product at the pull of the customer in pursuit of perfection (NIST MEP 1998). Global competition is forcing companies to improve quality, reduce delivery time and at the same time lower cost. The essence of lean is to compress time from the receipt of an order all the way through to payment. The results of compressing time are greater productivity, shorter delivery times, lower costs, improved quality and increased customer satisfaction.

The key to lean manufacturing is to compress time by eliminating waste and thus continually improving the process. Kaizen is a Japanese word for continuous improvement. The essential elements of process improvement, or Kaizen, are good housekeeping, elimination of waste (seven wastes) and standardization of procedures. The NIST MEP has identified the following lean manufacturing tools: workplace organization (5 S's), standardized work, visuals, plant layout, quality at source, batch reduction, teams, pull/Kanban, point-of-use storage, quick changeover, one piece flow, cellular, and Takt time (NIST, 1998). A number of books have been written describing these tools (Greif, 1991; Imai, 1986; Nakajima, 1988; Ohno, 1988; Shingo, 1983; Shingo, 1986; Shingo, 1989, and Sekine, 1990).

A generally overlooked tool for lean manufacturing is simulation. This paper addresses the use of simulation as a lean manufacturing training tool, as a design and analysis tool and as support for the continuous improvement process, particularly in combination with Kaizen events.

LEAN MANUFACTURING TRAINING SIMULATIONS

Typical training simulation tools to support lean manufacturing that are used by the ATN/MEP are setup reduction simulation, tube factory simulation and electronics assembly simulation. In these simulations the goals are to train operators to work together as teams to learn problem-solving techniques and to continuously look for methods of eliminating waste and improving the process.

Setup Reduction Simulation

Single minute exchange of dies (SMED) is a lean manufacturing tool that allows the mixing of production without slowing output or creating higher costs associated with the waste of setup. Changeovers add no value and therefore should be as fast as possible. The goal of SMED is to eliminate downtime due to setups and changeovers.

The setup reduction simulation uses a set of wooden dies shown in Figure 1 (UAH, 2000). The exercise is to reduce the time to change the dies. The typical steps in the simulation are:

1. Select the continuous improvement team
2. Observe the operation and die changeover
3. Collect times for setup elements
4. Determine Takt time and establish improvement goal
5. Identify internal and external setup elements (Internal elements are steps that require machine to be turned off while doing changeover. External elements are steps that can be done without stopping production.)
6. Prepare bar chart of element times and compare with Takt time
7. Convert as many as possible internal elements to external elements using Kaizen teams
8. Reduce times of internal and external elements using Kaizen teams

For example, if the workday is eight hours and customer demand is 300 parts per day, then Takt time is 480 minutes/300 parts per day, or 96 seconds. This says that no operation can take more than 96 seconds to meet customer demand. If it does, then ways must be found to reduce cycle time, to improve the method or to add more machines or operators.

As part of the simulation, the team is free to make modifications to the dies and the process. Typical modifications are standardized bolts and nuts, quick disconnect clamps and redesigning both dies into one die. After each modification the above steps are repeated, thus demonstrating the concepts of continuous improvement. Using these lean techniques the initial 20-minute changeover in the simulation can be reduced to less than ten seconds.

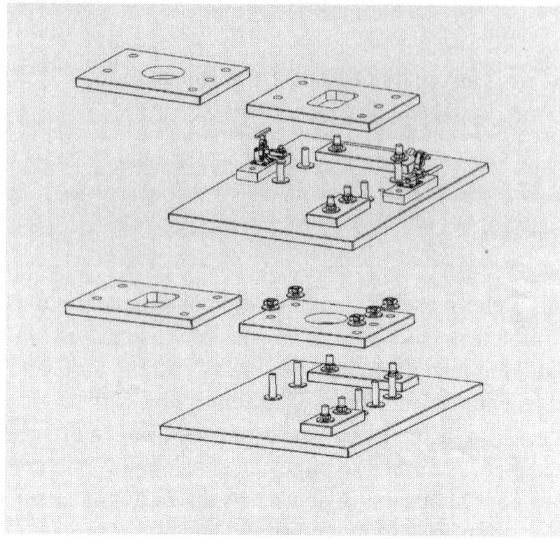

Figure 1: Setup Reduction Simulation

Tube Factory Simulation

In a push system parts are manufactured based on a sales forecast. As a result, parts are pushed through the plant to meet the forecast and work-in-process (WIP) is excessive. In a pull system parts are made, or replaced, based on customer orders. As a result, parts are pulled through the plant replenishing what was consumed and WIP is minimized.

The tube factory is a hands-on training simulation of a manufacturing line that assembles fifteen pieces of plastic tubes, elbows, and adapters into the final assembly shown in Figure 2 (UAH, 2000). The team members are assigned to four sub-assembly processes and to two material handling operations. Process sheets are given to each operator with instructions and a drawing of each sub-assembly. For the first round the team is given the task to make as many parts as possible in five minutes. This is equivalent to running the tube factory using the push system.

At the end of the first round a brief training session is given on the principles of lean manufacturing. The second round consists of having the team redesign the line based on the principles of lean. The team is given a

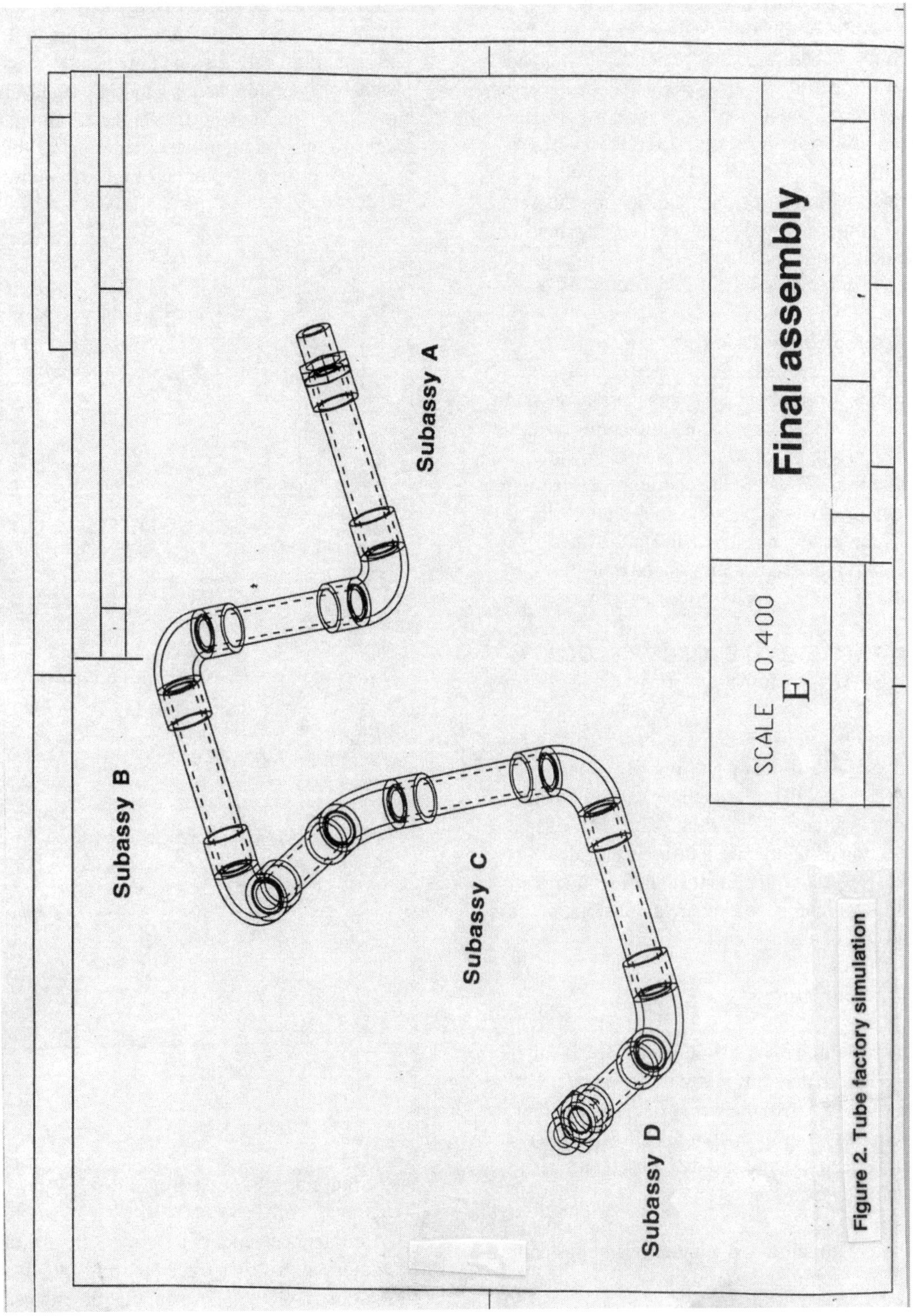

Figure 2. Tube factory simulation

production goal of 30 parts in five minutes. The simulation is run for another five minutes and the results compared with the first round. A third or fourth round may be necessary to meet the production goal. For example, Takt time is 10 seconds. Therefore, each sub-assembly cannot take more than 10 seconds. A time study may be necessary to improve the operation and to balance the work among the operators so each station does not exceed 10 seconds. Other modifications may include moving raw material closer to operators, eliminating chairs, arranging the line into a cell, using physical models rather than drawings at each sub-assembly, implementing one-piece-flow and incorporating a Kanban system.

Electronics Assembly Simulation

The electronics assembly simulation is also a hands-on training simulation of a factory that manufactures a simple electronics device (NIST, 1998). A typical eight-hour game consists of round 1 where the operators are instructed to make as many products as possible and rounds 2 through 4 after the team has made improvements to the line. Between each round the team is introduced to lean techniques and the continuous improvement process.

LEAN MANUFACTURING FACTORY FLOOR COMPUTER SIMULATIONS

Computer simulation has become an accepted tool in the design and analysis of manufacturing lines. Many companies will not install a new manufacturing line until the line has been evaluated using simulation. Management now sees simulation as inexpensive insurance against costly mistakes. Several typical factory floor simulation tools to support lean manufacturing are simulators, process simulators, and simulation systems.

Manufacturing Simulator

The Modular Manufacturing Simulator (MMS) can be used to rapidly (in less than thirty minutes) evaluate various alternatives to a manufacturing line, such as the addition of more machines or operators (MSFC, 1997). MMS is domain specific and can only be used on lines with the following characteristics:

- One line with unlimited number of stations and identical machines at each station
- Unlimited number of operators
- Unlimited space for WIP in front of each station
- Operators are fixed at specific stations or move between stations
- Work is done in lots of one part
- No machine breakdown

The following inputs are necessary to construct a MMS model: number of stations, number of machines at each station, number of operators, cycle time distribution at each station, and the assignment of operators to machines. Fixed operators are assigned to specific machines. Moveable operators are assigned to a set of machines and one of three movement rules selected: move when WIP reaches a maximum, move circular or "rabbit chase," or move in a push/pull manner. Figure 3 shows a sample line.

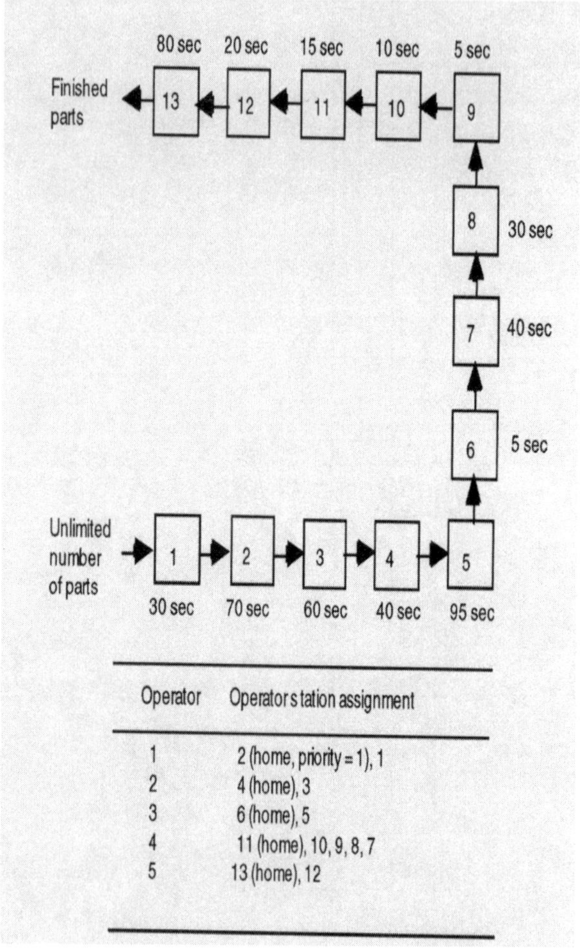

Figure 3: MMS Sample Problem

Manufacturing Process Simulator

A number of vendors have recently developed simulators to greatly reduce the time and effort to construct simulation models. These simulators are based on the concepts of having the user construct a flowchart of the process using a predefined set of icons, connecting the icons to define the flow of parts through the process, and then adding specific attributes to each icon. The simulator then automatically translates the layout into a simulation model and the model executed.

One of the process simulators is ProcessModel (1999). ProcessModel uses FlowCharter from Micrografix, Inc. to construct the flowchart of the manufacturing line and automatically translates the layout into a ProModel (1996) simulation model. Typically a user can construct a layout and have simulation results in several hours.

The basic building blocks of simulators such as ProcessModel are:

- Entities which are objects such as parts that are processed through the model
- Activities which perform operations on entities (generally machines)
- Resources which are generally people to process entities at activities
- Storages where entities wait (generally inventory areas)

Manufacturing Simulation Systems

A variety of simulation packages are commercially available to construct detailed simulation models. Almost all of these packages allow the overlaying of a model onto a scaled layout of the plant floor thus giving management a very realistic animation of the operation of the manufacturing process. Several common manufacturing simulation systems are Witness, SIMAN/Arena and ProModel.

With all this detailed accuracy and animation comes several drawbacks. One of the most serious is the time to develop, verify, and validate the simulation model. Quite often management cannot wait this length of time for the simulation results. A second drawback is that the firm needs someone trained in simulation. This person is not only difficult to locate, but generally cannot be justified on a full-time basis. As a result, many companies use simulators such as those described above as a quick and dirty method of obtaining results before investing in the more time consuming and expensive simulation systems.

COMBINING CONTINUOUS PROCESS IMPROVEMENT WITH SIMULATION

Productivity and quality can be greatly improved by the use of lean manufacturing tools. More sophisticated tools such as simulation can further enhance continuous improvement strategies by eliminating many trail-and-error attempts to find better methods to improve the process.

Figure 4 shows how computer simulation can be integrated with continuous improvement through the Plan, Do, Study and Act cycle (Deming, 1986). By using simulation the cycle can be restructured to Plan, Study, Do and Act. The key benefit is that simulation permits one to see and test an implementation of a plan before spending time and dollars in the Act phase. The process begins with constructing the simulation of the manufacturing process. Once verified and validated, the model is executed to expose problems. Management starts the continuous improvement process by requesting a Kaizen event with an aggressive goal, such as twenty-percent reduction in Takt time.

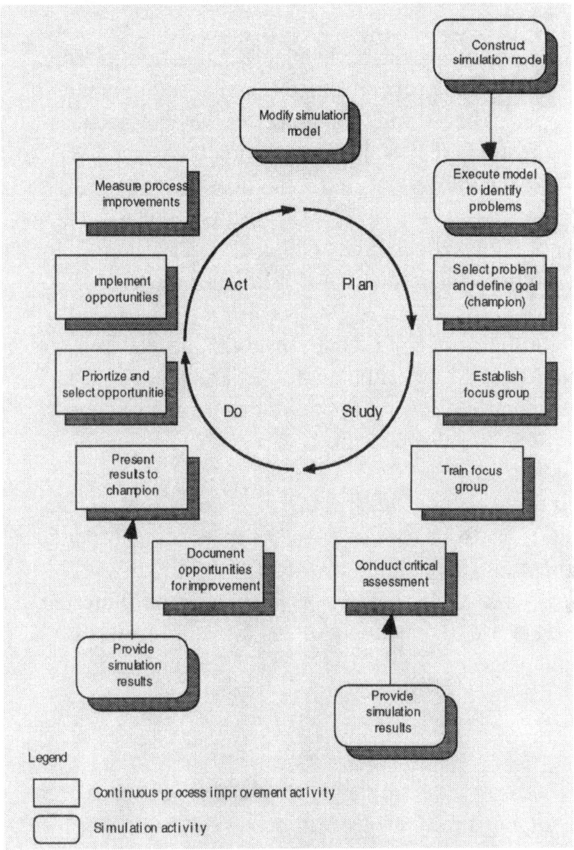

Figure 4: Simulation and Continuous Process Improvement

A team is established to conduct the Kaizen event. The team uses the simulation results to support the event. During the morning of the third day the Kaizen team documents the results of the assessment, brainstorm opportunities for improvement, and prepares the presentation. During the afternoon of the third day the team presents its findings to management. The results of the simulation are the key elements of the presentation. Management then prioritizes the opportunities for improvement and selects those opportunities for implementation with the quickest payback.

REAL WORLD IMPLEMENTATIONS

A recent project using simulation with lean manufacturing resulted in an estimated six months reduction in time in the design stage, shorter conveyors and fewer pallets with an estimated savings of $500,000 in up-front capital investment (Czarnecki, et. al., 1999). An unforeseen outcome was a new design of the proposed line. The simulation of this line indicated the same production as the initial design but with fewer operators and machines and a 50% reduction in conveyor length.

A second project started with the simulation training tools, followed by several Kaizen events, and then the development of a simulation model of the manufacturing line. The model focused on identifying the needed WIP to minimize the impact of interrupting the line with a rush order (Adams, et. al., 1999). The results indicated that an interruption of sixteen hours with a 48-hour changeover had no impact on production if WIP is ten parts.

A third project started with several Kaizen events and then a ProcessModel simulation (Miller, et. al., 1999). The results identified several opportunities for improvement and follow-on Kaizen events.

Since 1993 the NASA Marshall Space Flight Center (MSFC) has distributed over 1000 copies of the Modular Manufacturing Simulator at no cost to qualified manufacturers. MSFC follow-up surveys have indicated significant use of the simulator and large productivity improvements.

CONCLUSIONS

In summary, the following conclusions are made about simulation and the lean enterprise:

- Simulation provides a valuable training tool for implementing lean manufacturing. Kaizen teams consist of diverse groups of individuals; however, with training simulations the groups work better as teams and focus more quickly on identifying problem areas and suggestions for improvement.

- The setup reduction training simulation is an excellent hands-on exercise that helps managers and operators understand the potential for improvement in operations with changeovers. As competitive pressure forces manufacturers to be more responsive, setup reduction is the key to reducing batch size and thus shortening lead-time. The training exercise is particularly effective at helping people see the potential of relatively low cost changes in procedures.

- The training simulations are particularly effective in teaching the lean concepts and tools. The three training simulations provide vivid demonstration to participants of new behavioral approaches, involving and empowering individuals in teams, changing the role of management and helping create a new culture in the workplace.

- The electronics assembly simulation is an excellent presentation of the entire lean approach to systems management and continuous improvement. From a historical perspective it compares and contrasts lean manufacturing with craft/custom manufacturing, and traditional mass production. Participants understand the entire system and what is required for lasting improvements. After four rounds of the simulation, volume is usually increased by 1000% and inventory reduced by 90%.

- The tube factory also presents the basic lean approach and a few of the key tools during the transition from traditional chaotic push manufacturing to a lean pull system. This training simulation is particularly effective with new employee orientations and as the initial training for a new Kaizen team whose members have little exposure to lean. Again, dramatic improvements in output, quality, cost, delivery and lead-time are demonstrated. As one customer puts it "whatever that trainer's doing is working. Our new employees are pushing their supervisors with new ideas and some don't like it."

- Manufacturing simulation packages, such as simulators, can be used to support a number of the steps in the continuous improvement process. Computer simulation is most useful in supporting the Kaizen events, analyzing alternatives and opportunities for improvement before implementation and in presenting results to management.

- Computer simulation has the greatest impact if the models can be developed early in the Kaizen event. Used wisely, simulation makes everyone smarter about what and when to change.

- Animation and reporting features of computer simulation greatly improve the Kaizen team's ability to present its suggestions for improvement to management and for obtaining management commitment.

ACKNOWLEDGEMENTS

The Alabama Technology Network is funded in part by the U.S. Department of Commerce National Institute of Standards and Technology, the State of Alabama and Alabama Industrial Development Training.

REFERENCES

Adams, M., P. Componation, H. Czarnecki, and B. Schroer, 1999: "Simulation as a Tool for Continuous Process Improvement," *Proceedings Winter Simulation Conference*, Phoenix, AZ.

Czarnecki, H., B. Schroer, M. Adams, and M. Spann, 1999: *Continuous Process Improvement and Simulation*, Internal Research Report, University of Alabama in Huntsville, Huntsville, AL.

Deming, W.E., 1996: *Out of the Crisis*, Center for Advanced Engineering Studies, MIT Press, Cambridge, MA.

Greif, M., 1991: *The Visual Factory*, Productivity Press, Cambridge, MA.

Imai, M., 1986: *Kaizen: The Key to Japanese Competitive Success*, Random House, New York.

Miller, M., M. Adams, B. Schroer and C. Epps, 1999: "Simulation as a Lean Manufacturing Tool," Proceedings SouthEastern Simulation Conference, Huntsville, AL.

MSFC, 1997: *Modular Manufacturing Simulator Users Manual,* NASA Marshall Space Flight Center, Huntsville, AL.

Nakajima, S., 1988: *Introduction to Total Productive Maintenance*, Productivity Press, Portland, OR.

NIST, 1998: *Principles of Lean Manufacturing with Live Simulation Users Manual*, NIST Manufacturing Extension Partnership, Gaithersburg, MD.

Ohno, T., 1988: *Toyota Production System*, Productivity Press, Portland, OR.

ProcessModel, 1999: *ProcessModel Users Manual*, ProcessModel Corp., Provo, UT.

ProModel, 1996: *ProModel Users Manual*, ProModel Corp., Orem, UT.

Sekine, K., 1990: *One-Piece Flow*, Productivity Press, Portland, OR.

Shingo, S., 1983: Single Minute Exchange of Dies, Productivity Press, Cambridge, MA.

Shingo, S., 1986: *Zero Quality Control: Source Inspection and the Poka Yoke System*, Productivity Press, Portland, OR.

Shingo, S., 1989: *A Study of the Toyota Production System*, Productivity Press, Portland, OR.

UAH, 2000: *Lean Manufacturing Handbook,* University of Alabama in Huntsville, Huntsville, AL.

AUTHOR BIOGRAPHIES

MEL ADAMS is a senior research scientist in the Center for Automation and Robotics at the University of Alabama in Huntsville. He holds a Ph.D. in Strategic Management and MBA from the University of Tennessee. His research focuses on strategic change and entrepreneurship.

HANK CZARNECKI is a research scientist in the Center for Automation and Robotics at the University of Alabama in Huntsville. His areas of expertise are continuous process improvement, plant and manufacturing cell layout, and just-in-time systems. He has completed coursework for the Ph.D. in Industrial and Systems Engineering from the University of Alabama in Huntsville.

BERNARD J. SCHROER is director of the Center for Automation and Robotics, a professor in Industrial and Systems Engineering, and Associate Vice President for Research at the University of Alabama in Huntsville. He has a Ph.D. in Industrial Engineering from Oklahoma State University and is a registered professional engineer. His areas of research are manufacturing systems, systems simulation, and continuous process improvement.

BRADLEY J. SCHROER is a manufacturing engineer at SUMMA Technology, Inc. in Huntsville Alabama. His assignments include ISO, quality and continuous improvement. He is pursuing a MS in Engineering. He has a BS in Engineering from the University of Alabama in Huntsville.

USING ENTERPRISE SIMULATION TO SUPPORT SATS

Roland R. Mielke, Thomas W. Mastaglio and Mikel D. Petty
Virginia Modeling, Analysis and Simulation Center
Old Dominion University
Suffolk, Virginia 23435
e-mail: {rmielke, tmastaglio, mpetty}@vmasc.odu.edu

KEYWORDS
Simulation, enterprise models, decision support systems, general aviation, air transportation, high level architecture.

ABSTRACT

SATS or Small Aircraft Transportation System is a project concept designed to meet the public's private and short-haul commercial transportation needs using general aviation aircraft operating from local and regional public-use airports. Beginning in 2001, a prototype system called the Virginia SATSLab will be developed in Virginia for testing and evaluation. An enterprise simulation, the SATS Virtual Computer Environment, is proposed as a tool to help manage and coordinate the many industrial and academic research teams contributing to the SATS project. The SATS Virtual Computer Environment will provide a top-down perspective of the system that enables design collaboration, facilitates subsystem testing and evaluation, and creates a system visualization that supports efforts to explain and promote SATS. The enterprise simulation concept is explained and its application to the SATS project is developed. A system architecture based on the High Level Architecture (HLA) is described.

INTRODUCTION

The United States, under the leadership of NASA and the FAA, is developing a concept for and will prototype and evaluate a Small Aircraft Transportation System or SATS. SATS will be designed to meet the public's private and small commercial transportation needs using general aviation aircraft operating in a government-managed airspace from local and regional public-use airports. The development of SATS will occur over a period of years and will involve many research teams working on different components of the system. At some point, these components will be integrated to form the overall system. In system design, it is recognized that the integration of the components to form the whole is one of the most difficult steps. The reason for this is that in large complex systems the components are often developed in parallel and cannot be tested adequately during development because that process requires a complete system. Components which work fine in a stand-alone mode often can fail when interconnected. It is here that computer simulation can play an extremely important role.

The Virginia Modeling, Analysis and Simulation Center (VMASC) has proposed the design of a system-wide or enterprise simulation, called the SATS Virtual Computer Environment, to coordinate the development of SATS. Initially, this will be a very high-level simulation consisting of only the most basic system component objects: airports, airplanes, airspace control, local surface transportation, and weather. At first, these objects will be represented rather simply from a behavioral perspective and the simulation will capture the interaction of these objects. As the various research teams add definition to these objects, more detailed models can be developed and added hierarchically to the simulation. The availability of the SATS Virtual Computer Environment accomplishes several things. First, it provides individual research groups the ability to ask "what if" questions concerning design alternatives and to test their ideas in the context of the complete system. Second, it provides the collaborative environment in which the different research groups can communicate effectively their design decisions to other research groups. Third, it provides an effective visual environment in which to inform the public and to train potential SATS participants.

The successful development of the SATS Virtual Computer Environment requires a simulation architecture created using a top-down design approach very early in the project life. In this way, as system components are designed and prototyped, they easily can be integrated into the SATS Virtual Computer Environment making them available to other research groups and facilitating test and evaluation activities. The purpose of this paper is to explain our notion of enterprise simulation and to describe how the SATS Virtual Computer Environment is being developed as an instance of that concept. In the first section, SATS is briefly described and the SATS development strategy is presented. In the second section, the enterprise simulation concept is explained and its application to the SATS project is developed. Then, our preliminary design ideas for the SATS Virtual Computer Environment are presented in the third section. The fourth section is the conclusion.

SATS DESCRIPTION

Today in the United States there are approximately 5,400 public-use airports that are open for anyone to use. However, only 660 of these airports are served by commercial air service, and only 46 airports account for over

75% of all commercial airline traffic. In addition, the number of people traveling by airplane continues to increase. The resulting congestion of the nation's traditional hub-spoke commercial airline system has reduced the average doorstep-to-destination speed for the most common trips, trips of from 300 to 500 miles, to only 50-60 miles-per-hour. The idea behind SATS is to utilize the next generation of general aviation aircraft and the nation's public-use airports to create a safe travel alternative, freeing people and products from transportation delays by creating access to more communities in less time.

The planning and eventual success of SATS is based on four hypotheses (Hahne 2000): (1) the public can safely operate a SATS aircraft in nearly all weather conditions; (2) the public can afford to travel by SATS; (3) SATS infrastructure is an affordable option to national transportation system investments; and (4) SATS benefits all suburban, rural and remote communities in terms of accessibility, mobility, economic opportunity, environment and quality of life. The realization of these hypotheses will require an aggressive and coordinated research and development effort extending over the next five years. Significant technological challenges include development of the next generation of robust general aviation aircraft, deployment of a new digital airspace infrastructure, and the integration of SATS with the global intermodal transportation system. These challenges (Holmes 1999) are described briefly in the following.

The next generation general aviation aircraft will incorporate significant improvements in airframe construction, propulsion systems, and flight deck systems. Airframe structures will contain embedded sensors and communication devices to monitor maintenance and safety status, and embedded actuator devices that adjust aerodynamics as flight conditions change to attain more lift and to reduce drag. The structures will integrate new light weight composite materials and safety-enabling technologies, such as lightning and ice protection, with high-volume production techniques to achieve cost reductions of at least 50% over present materials and fabrication techniques. A new breed of small aircraft engines, both piston and turbine, are being developed which are environmentally friendly, have low maintenance requirements, and are capable of increasing aircraft cruising speeds by a factor of two. The single-crew SATS flight deck will utilize simplified decoupled controls and provide automated navigational assistance. The objective is to achieve commercial-aircraft-levels of safety and navigational capability while reducing the complexity of aircraft control to automobile-like simplicity.

The infrastructure that will support the new generation of general aviation airplanes will integrate modern digital communication, GPS navigation, and emerging surveillance technologies to produce, economically, new levels of utility for the thousands of small, public-use airports. A client-server architecture will provide information services over a satellite-based airborne internet to support collaborative air traffic management. Aircraft and airports will be interconnected nodes of a digital network capable of providing nearly instantaneous identification and information services on demand. Automated navigation assistance on virtual highways using highway-in-the-sky operating procedures will guide aircraft reliably to any airport via user-preferred trajectories. Intelligent landing facilities will provide automatic separation and sequencing control in non-towered, non-radar airspace. Digital landing facility information systems will deliver data on weather, traffic, and flight plans, while commercial information systems will deliver data on terminal support operations and intermodal transportation connections.

Some of the research required to meet the SATS technology challenges is already ongoing. A NASA-led government-industry partnership called Advanced General Aviation and Transportation Experiments (AGATE) is developing new technologies for avionics, airframe structures, and pilot training. A similar NASA-led partnership called the General Aviation Propulsion (GAP) Program is focused on developing new engine technologies for general aviation aircraft. Together, these programs already represent an investment of over $250 million in technologies to enhance civil aviation transportation. A next step in the development of SATS is to establish several federal-state partnerships to support the development of SATS testbeds. Initially, Virginia and Florida have been selected. In Virginia, NASA Langley Research Center and the Virginia Department of Aviation have teamed to form the Virginia SATSLab. This partnership will enlist university research and development expertise through the Virginia Space Grant Consortium (VGSC). A testbed consisting of three airports, located at Manassas, Newport News, and Blacksburg, will be developed beginning in 2001 for SATS field demonstrations scheduled to commence in 2003. The demonstrations will focus on the testing and evaluation of SATS enhanced airport technologies and the overall SATS operating strategies. In addition, market research will be conducted to determine the general market potential for SATS products and services. The results of these demonstrations will lead to a revised and enhanced planning template for the full-scale implementation of SATS. A major challenge for the Virginia SATSLab team will be the coordination of the many research groups developing components for the state wide testbed, and management of the integration of these components to produce a successful demonstration system. In addition, the team will need to convey to the public a very detailed and comprehensive vision of this complex system in order to conduct the necessary market research and to continue the process of developing support for the overall SATS program. It is for these Virginia SATSLab activities that we propose to develop and utilize initially the SATS Virtual Computer Environment.

ENTERPRISE SIMULATION

Enterprise simulation (Mastaglio 1999) refers to a dynamic model or simulation which is constructed with a top-down perspective and is intended to provide an overall conceptual view of the workings of a system. Systems which lend themselves to enterprise simulation frequently are comprised of a collection of entities interacting with one another in some context or environment according to a physical or behavioral set of accepted rules. In this case, the enterprise simulation is most easily viewed as the aggregation of the behaviors of the entities as they interact with each other and with their environment. Most often such systems are complex systems that have emergent behavioral properties (Casti 1996); therefore, it is imperative in enterprise simulations to accurately represent both the effects of the environment and the behavior of the individual entities.

A common characteristic of enterprise simulations is that they are developed to support human decision-making. They directly support the decision maker resulting in decisions which are either easier to make or are better informed (Mielke 1999). When confronted with the management of complex systems, humans conceptually build mental models of the system. A properly constructed enterprise simulation should present to the user an externalization of his mental model. Enterprise simulation allows the user to ask 'what if' questions about the enterprise. The simulation computes the probable system response to management decisions and policies so that managers can observe and better understand the cause and effect relationships between their decisions and system performance. Enterprise simulation provides the decision maker with a virtual environment in which to quickly, economically, and safely test and improve understanding and knowledge about the enterprise.

The use of an enterprise simulation is different from the way most simulation technology has been used in the past. Simulation has long been a tool the analyst used to evaluate potential solutions to a specific management problem they were assigned to help solve. The analyst's role was to derive a recommended point solution for management. This process might be called problem-centric simulation. Enterprise simulation, on the other hand, is used directly by decision makers to observe the dynamics of a system as it responds to stimuli introduced by the user. Notionally, the role of the analyst as a middleman in decision-making is eliminated; in actuality, the role of the analyst changes to one of simulation developer and validator only. Problem-centric modeling and simulation still has its place and continues to be a topic for research into improved methods. It is important to understand enterprise simulation as a different perspective on the use of simulation technology that may require some unique tools and capabilities (Veek 1999). It is a decision support tool, not a solution generator.

The Virginia SATSLab is an extremely large and complex system in which variability and uncertainty are essential components. The system will be expensive, and total costs will be highly sensitive to many of the early design decisions. In addition, the system will be developed and then utilized over a period of at least five years. These system characteristics suggest that enterprise simulation should play a key role in the design, implementation and operation of SATS. Advantages to using enterprise simulation in SATS include the following.

Collaborative Design Environment – Enterprise simulation will provide a common environment for the many contributing research and development groups to share their design decisions and to investigate the effects of design decisions of other groups.

Test and Evaluation – An enterprise simulation will allow preliminary designs and prototypes of system components to be fully tested and evaluated in the context of the entire system through simulation.

Improved Coordination and Management – Enterprise simulation will provide decision support essential to conduct of a successful project; it will help identify those areas requiring special emphasis or attention.

System Concept – Enterprise simulation can be used to create an animated, fully instrumented visualization of the entire system. This visualization will support efforts to explain and promote SATS to the public as well as potential funding sources. The visualization also will provide a realistic virtual environment in which to train and educate potential SATS participants.

In addition to the advantages gained through the use of enterprise simulation, it is very likely that the cost of developing the SATS Virtual Computer Environment would be recovered by the cost savings realized through its use. This presents a very compelling argument for the development and application of a SATS enterprise simulation.

SATS VIRTUAL COMPUTER ENVIRONMENT

Implementation Challenges

We have proposed the development of an enterprise simulation of SATS, the SATS Virtual Computer Environment. An actual SATS implementation will consist of interacting components; those components will include aircraft, airports, air traffic controllers, the environment, ground vehicles, and so on. A SATS Virtual Computer Environment would simulate those components, their behaviors, and their interactions. To derive full benefit from the simulation, the SATS components would be simulated before they are developed, indeed, even before they are completely designed. This would allow the simulation to determine if each component as specified and designed can operate within and meet the requirements of the overall system. Moreover, simulating the SATS components in advance of their final design and development will mitigate the previously mentioned integration difficulties by testing, within the simulation, the inter-component interactions and protocols earlier in the process. However, while the notion of simulating the SATS components before they are fully designed and built has benefits, it makes the task of constructing the SATS Virtual Computer Environment more difficult.

Two challenges follow from this idea.

Challenge 1 - The initial SATS component simulations are likely to be less detailed, in terms of both external attributes and interactions and internal models, than models developed later in the components' design processes, and so will need to be replaced in the SATS Virtual Computer Environment over time.

Challenge 2 - As the overall SATS design is developed, new and unanticipated SATS components may be identified, and simulations of those components within the SATS Virtual Computer Environment will be needed.

Two additional challenges also face the implementers of the SATS Virtual Computer Environment that will make integration of the simulations more difficult.

Challenge 3 - The consortium-based collaborative development of SATS implies that the SATS component simulations will be developed by a number of different organizations.

Challenge 4 - The SATS components vary widely, from aircraft to the environment, and it is reasonable to assume that differing simulation methodologies and implementation environments will be used for them.

The High Level Architecture

The High Level Architecture (HLA) is proposed as the supporting infrastructure and implementation paradigm for the SATS Virtual Computer Environment because it addresses all of these challenges. HLA is an architecture for constructing distributed simulations. It facilitates interoperability among different simulations and simulation types and promotes reuse of simulation software modules (Dahmann 1998). HLA can support virtual, constructive, and live simulations from a variety of application domains. HLA is defined by three documents:

1. The HLA Rules (DMSO 1998a), which define interoperability and what capabilities a simulation must have to achieve it within HLA.
2. The Object Model Template (DMSO 1998b), which is a methodology for specifying simulation data in terms of a hierarchy of object classes, and their attributes, and interactions between objects of those classes, and their parameters.
3. The Interface Specification (DMSO 1998c), which is a precise specification of the interoperability-related actions that a simulation may perform, or be asked to perform, during a simulation execution.

The HLA Run-Time Infrastructure (RTI) is an implementation of the Interface Specification, consisting of a set of services. The RTI provides services to start and stop a simulation execution, to pass data between simulations, to control the amount and routing of data that are passed, and to coordinate the passage of simulation time among the simulations.

Within the HLA, a set of collaborating simulations is called a federation; each of the collaborating simulations is a federate. Federates that adhere to the Rules can exchange data defined using the Object Model Template by invoking the services defined in the Interface Specification; those services are provided at run-time by the RTI.

HLA and the SATS Virtual Computer Environment

The SATS Virtual Computer Environment would be implemented as an HLA federation. Each of the simulations of the individual SATS components would be federates in the federation. An HLA object model defines the data (object classes and their attributes and interactions and their parameters), using the format prescribed in the Object Model Template, that would be sent and received between the federates. The SATS object classes (e.g., aircraft, airports, air traffic controllers, environment, ground vehicles) would be specified in a federation object model. The interactions between the objects (e.g., messages from an air traffic controller to an aircraft) would be specified as HLA interactions in the object model. A notional SATS federation is shown in Figure 1.

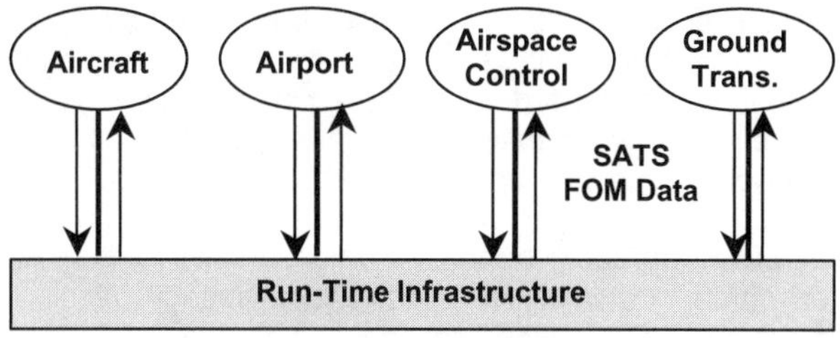

Figure 1. Notional SATS Federation

The features of HLA are just those needed to solve the challenges mentioned for the SATS Virtual Computer Environment. Each is considered in turn.

1. Replacing less detailed federates with more detailed federates over time. As long as the replacement federate sends and receives the same data as its predecessor, such replacements are quite simple in HLA. If the more detailed replacement federate adds new object classes, attributes, interactions, and parameters to the repertoire it generates, it may continue to interoperate with the other federates in the federation as long as it also continues to generate the less detailed data of its predecessor. This HLA version of "backward compatibility" is made possible by the Object Model Template, which, by organizing the federation's data in a hierarchical fashion, allows federates to request data at the level of detail desired. For example, suppose a federate that simulates a generic small aircraft exists in the federation and a corresponding object class is in the federation's object model. If that federate is later replaced by one which simulates Cessna 172 and Cessna Citation aircraft specifically in more detail, those object classes would be added to the object model as subclasses of the small aircraft class. Other federates in the federation could receive the attributes of objects of the more detailed subclasses if they could use that detail, or they could receive the data of the generic superclass if they could not.

2. Adding federates for unanticipated SATS components to the federation. Any HLA-compliant federate that sends and receives data specified in the federation's object model can be added to the federation and communicate with the other federates via the standard RTI services. If the new federate has additional capabilities that

includes generating new data, once those data are specified in the federation object model they can be accessed by other new or replacement federates.

3. Multiple developers of SATS component federates. The standard data definition methodology of the object model and the standard inter-federate communications mechanism of the RTI provide mechanisms that simplify the process of integrating federates produced by different developers by eliminating many potential types of incompatibility.

4. Varying simulation methodologies and environments. HLA constrains the external data communications of the federates but not their internal implementations. As long as the federates send and receive data defined in the federation object model using the RTI, they can communicate regardless of the simulation methodology used to implement them.

These interoperability benefits are not just claims; they have been demonstrated in HLA federations already developed. For example, all of these challenges were present during the development of the Combat Trauma Patient Simulation (CTPS), which is an HLA federation that simulates the military's casualty handling and treatment process (Petty 1999). CTPS federates were replaced during the development cycle with more detailed versions, unanticipated federates were later added to the CTPS federation more than once (Creech 1999) (Windyga 1999), CTPS federates were developed by multiple organizations, and those federates were built using different methodologies. The capabilities of HLA helped the CTPS implementers deal with these issues and it would support the needs of the SATS Virtual Computer Environment as well.

CONCLUSION

The purpose of this paper is to advocate the use of enterprise simulation in the development of the Small Aircraft Transportation System. Through the use of enterprise simulation, management and coordination of this very large and expensive project could be greatly enhanced. In addition, enterprise simulation could be an essential tool in explaining and promoting this complex system to program participants and the public.

A simulation architecture based on the High Level Architecture is proposed for development of the SATS Virtual Computer Environment. The use of HLA presents several very significant advantages. It facilitates the replacement of less detailed component models, developed early in the design process, with more detailed models as they become available. It supports the integration of many subsystem simulations developed by different research groups using dissimilar simulation methodologies and implementation environments. In addition, HLA eliminates many of the potential problems that might arise when it becomes necessary to enhance the SATS simulation by adding new subsystem simulations which were not anticipated during initial system design.

REFERENCES

Casti, J., 1996. *Would-Be Worlds: How Simulation is Changing the Frontiers of Science.* John Wiley & Sons, New York, NY.

Creech, G. S., 1999. "Increasing the Resolution of Simulated Combat Trauma Injuries in a High Level Architecture (HLA) Environment." M.S. Thesis, University of Central Florida, Department of Industrial Engineering and Management Systems.

Dahmann, J. S., F. Kuhl, and R. Weatherly, 1998. "Standards for Simulation: As Simple as Possible But Not Simpler: The High Level Architecture for Simulation." *Simulation*, Vol. 71, No. 6, pp. 378-387, December.

Defense Modeling and Simulation Office (DMSO), 1998. "Department of Defense High Level Architecture Rules, Version 1.3." Online document at http://hla.dmso.mil/hls/tech/rules/.

Defense Modeling and Simulation Office (DMSO), 1998. "Department of Defense High Level Architecture Object Model Template, Version 1.3." Online document at http://hla.dmso.mil/hls/tech/omtspec/.

Defense Modeling and Simulation Office (DMSO), 1998. "Department of Defense High Level Architecture Interface Specification, Version 1.3." Online document at http://hla.dmso.mil/hls/tech/ifspec/.

Hahne, D., 2000. "SATS High Density Operations." Presented at AGATE Review (Kissimmee, FL, Apr. 6). Online document at: http://sats.nasa.gov/satsarchive.html.

Holmes, B. J., 1999. "Small Aircraft Transportation System." Presented at SATS Space Grant Workshop (Hampton, VA, Nov. 16). Online document at: http://sats.nasa.gov/satsarchive.html.

Mastaglio, T. W., 1999. "Enterprise Simulation: Theoretical Foundations and a Practical Perspective." In Proceedings of the 1999 Winter Simulation Conference (Phoenix, AZ, Dec. 6-8).

Mielke, R. R., 1999. "Applications for Enterprise Simulation." In Proceedings of the 1999 Winter Simulation Conference (Phoenix. AZ, Dec. 6-8).

Petty, M. D. and P. S. Windyga, 1999. "A High Level Architecture-based Medical Simulation System." *Simulation*, Vol. 73, No. 5, pp. 281-287, November.

Veek, H., P. Ottjes, and A. Jaap, 1999. "Problem Oriented Modeling and Simulation." In Proceedings of the

Summer Computer Simulation Conference (Chicago, IL, July 11-15).

Windyga, P. S., J. P. Kincaid, B. C. Schricker, F. W. Feuerbacher, K. B. Anna, T. C. Johnson, and M. D. Petty, 2000. "Multiple Casualty Sources in the Combat Trauma Patient Simulation (CTPS)." In Proceedings of the Spring 2000 Simulation Interoperability Workshop (Orlando FL, March 26-31), pp. 424-433.

AUTHOR BIOGRAPHIES

ROLAND R. MIELKE is a Professor in the Department of Electrical and Computer Engineering at Old Dominion University. He is also Technical Director for the Virginia Modeling, Analysis and Simulation Center. He received the B.S., M.S. and Ph.D. in Electrical Engineering from the University of Wisconsin-Madison in 1968, 1970, and 1975, respectively. His research interests include system theory, graph theory, and enterprise simulation applications.

THOMAS W. MASTAGLIO is the Executive Director for the Virginia Modeling, Analysis and Simulation Center. He is also a Research Professor in the Department of Electrical and Computer Engineering at Old Dominion University. Previously he held positions with IBM, Loral and Lockheed Martin. He graduated from the U.S. Military Academy in 1969, earned the M.S. in Computer Science and Business Systems from the University of Colorado in 1978, and earned the Ph.D. in Computer and Cognitive Science from the University of Colorado in 1990. Dr. Mastaglio's research interests include the application of artificial intelligence to improving human-computer interaction and learning, usability engineering, cognitive modeling, and the development of large-scale enterprise models and simulations.

MIKEL D. PETTY is Chief Scientist of the Virginia Modeling, Analysis & Simulation Center at Old Dominion University. He was previously with the Institute for Simulation and Training at the University of Central Florida. Dr. Petty has worked in modeling and simulation since 1990 and has research interests in simulation interoperability, computer generated forces, and multi-resolution simulation. He received a Ph.D. from the University of Central Florida in 1997, a M.S. from UCF in 1988, and a B.S. from the California State University, Sacramento, in 1980, all in Computer Science. He is currently a member of a National Research Council committee on modeling and simulation.

ORGANIZATIONAL SIMULATION
CONCEPT & APPLICATION

Joseph Barjis

Department of Information Systems, Delft University of Technology, P.O. Box 356, 2600 AJ Delft, The Netherlands.
Tel: +31-15–2785827, Fax: +31-15–2786632 e-mail: J.Barjis@is.twi.tudelft.nl; http://is.twi.tudelft.nl/~barjis

Jan L.G. Dietz

Department of Information Systems, Delft University of Technology, P.O. Box 356, 2600 AJ Delft, The Netherlands.
Tel: +31-15-2787822, Fax: +31-15-2786632; e-mail: J.L.G.Dietz@is.twi.tudelft.nl

Luuk P.J. Groenewegen

Leiden Institute of Advanced Computer Science, Leiden University, P.O. Box 9512, 2300 RA Leiden, The Netherlands.
Tel: +31-71-5277139, Fax: +31-71-5276985; e-mail: luuk@liacs.nl

Keywords: *DEMO; Business Process Simulation; Organizational Simulation; Discrete Event Simulation*

ABSTRACT

The modeling formalisms and approaches, on which simulation is usually based, are quite technical. They are not very well suited for reflecting the activities of people in organizations. Nor are they suited for expressing the typically human negotiations between people involved in communication. DEMO takes a totally different approach towards organizational modeling, as it provides a communication perspective towards organizations based on speech act and social action theory.

The paper presents a first step towards systematic simulation of DEMO models for business processes. Based on the notions from DEMO we propose a first outline of a conceptual framework for organizational simulation. This outline reflects the so-called OER phases - Order, Execution and Result - occurring in any business transaction. Correspondences as well as dependencies between various transactions are expressed according to DEMO's transaction. It is shown how such a first outline of a simulation framework can be expressed in the simulation tool Arena.

1. INTRODUCTION

This paper introduces a language action based organizational simulation approach. Therefore, introduced definitions in this paper are given in the context of communication (business communication) between people (members, actors) within an organization. In order to better understand the concept behind this paper, a definition of an organization from the communication perspective is presented and discussed.

An *organization* consists of a large number of interdependent business processes that work together to generate products or services in a business environment (Alter, 1996). In the communication context, an organization can be understood as a network of commitments and the functioning of the organization can be explained in terms of the functioning of communication between people (Dietz, 1999). These commitments are created when the members of an organization are communicating for carrying out the mission of the organization.

Organizations are social systems that are composed of socially acting human beings and coordinated by performative (action-oriented) communication (Taylor, 1993; Winograd and Flores, 1986). In recent years, this communication oriented perspective on organizations has received considerable academic attention (Goldkuhl et al., 1998; Dignum and Dietz, 1997; Dignum et al., 1996).

When talking of organizational simulation for whatever purpose, e.g. optimizing organizational design, analyzing, training, business process simulation becomes an essential issue.

A *business process* is a related group of steps or activities that use people, information, and other resources to create value for internal or external customers. A business process consists of steps related in time and place, have a beginning and end, and have inputs and outputs (Alter, 1996). These features of the business process allow the business process to be investigated (treated) as a discrete system.

In (Davenport & Short, 1990) a business process is defined as "a set of logically related tasks performed to achieve a defined business outcome." A process is "a structured, measured set of activities designed to produce a specified output for a particular customer or market. It implies a strong emphasis on how work is done within an organization" (Davenport 1993). In their view processes have two important characteristics: (i) They have customers (internal or external), (ii) They cross organizational boundaries, i.e., they occur across or between organizational subunits.

There is a number of modeling techniques for investigating organizations and, consequently, identifying business processes in an organization, but in this paper we will emphasize the DEMO methodology as a sound and well tested methodology for this purpose.

The DEMO (Dynamic Essential Modeling of Organizations) methodology has been proposed to model the construction of an organization from the communication perspective. Founded in the Speech Act Theory and the Social Action Theory it provides a thorough understanding of the construction of an organization as well as of social co-ordination mechanisms. Next to a theory for explaining the construction of organizations, DEMO also provides a modeling technique. The modeling facility of DEMO provides an understanding and graphical representation of the transactional structure of organizations. A relevant set of publications on the DEMO methodology can be found in (Dietz, 1999; Dietz, 1999+; Dietz and Mulder, 1998; Reijswoud et al., 1999).

DEMO is proposed as a well formulated modeling technique for designing a model of the organization that to be further executed (run) using simulation tools. Although DEMO comprises five types of models, the action model of DEMO can serve on its own as an appropriate input model for simulation.

Optimization of the organization structure, in particular, strongly depends on the business process within the organization. Any change in the business process may cause positive or negative effects on the organizational design. Therefore business process redesign (BPR) is another related issue that has to be studied in the framework of organizational simulation. Business Process Redesign is the analysis and design of workflows and processes within and between organizations (Davenport and Short, 1990).

BPR gurus Michael Hammer and James Champy note in their book Reengineering the Corporation that only about 30 percent of reengineering projects they have reviewed are successful. One of the primary reasons for this low success rate is that the analysis behind performance estimates is often prepared with flowcharts and spreadsheets.

Business processes are way too complex and dynamic to be understood and analyzed by flowcharts and spreadsheets alone on the one hand. Organizations of competing/cooperating economic entities can exhibit surprising behavior on the other hand. Simulation can identify that behavior before it becomes expensive to fix.

Herein lies the opportunity for organizations to institutionalize simulation as the standard tool for BPR. Simulation is the only tool that can provide both accurate analysis and visualization of alternatives, comparison of various models of business process for optimization and best performance characteristics.

Although numerous papers (Davenport, 1993; Douglas et. al 1997; Hammer and Champy, 1993; Aguilar, 1999) dedicated to organizational and business process study or simulation, there is however still not enough conceptual framework concerning this issue. This paper will try to make a contribution towards this end, by proposing a conceptual framework for organizational simulation.

The paper concludes with some observations on current and future issues in the area of organizational simulation in general and business process simulation in particular. The provided bibliography is an essential support for the described concept.

2. THEORETICAL CONCEPT OF ORGANIZATIONAL SIMULATION

What is organizational simulation: Organizational simulation is the discipline of designing a model of an existing or planned organization, executing the model on a computer, and analyzing the execution output.

The most usual activities supported by organizational simulation are: analysis, design (redesign), optimization and training.

Simulation of organizations creates added value in understanding, analyzing, and designing organizations by introducing dynamic aspects. It provides decision support by anticipation of future changes in process design and improves understanding of processes (Aguilar et al. 1999).

Process simulation is the technique that allows representation of processes, people and technology in a dynamic computer model. A model, when simulated, mimics the operations of a business. This is accomplished by stepping through the events in compressed time while displaying an animated picture of the flow. Because simulation software keeps track of statistics about model elements, performance of a process can be evaluated by analyzing the model output data.

To understand an organization and all of its complexity, we must build artificial objects and dynamically act out roles with them. In (Fishwick, 1996) the overall task of simulation is generally divided into three primary sub-fields: model design, model execution and model analysis. If extend this confirmation to organizational simulation, then the overall task of organizational simulation generally comprises five subtasks that cover the entire simulation circle. These subtasks to be conducted in five steps are *process description*, *model design*, *model execution*, *model analysis* and alternative *scenarios evaluation* (see figure 1). Relations and order between these steps are also shown in this figure. Usually, results of the last two steps- model analysis and scenarios evaluation- cause redesign (changes) of the model and repetition of simulation. Actually this is the purpose of simulation: to repeat it until the optimal values are reached. Relations between the steps -model design, model analysis and scenarios evaluation- are called feedback, as shown in figure 1.

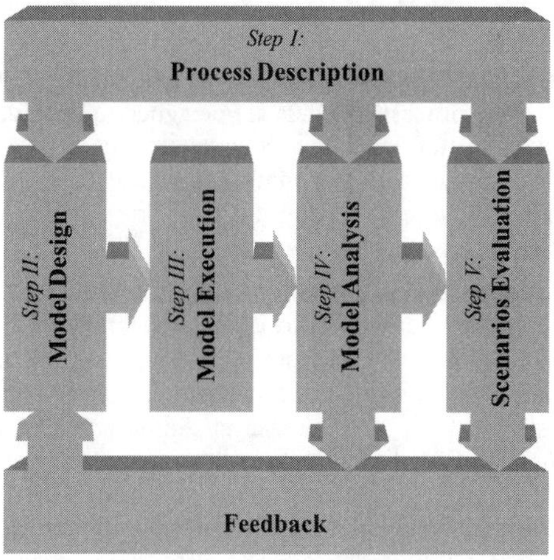

Figure 1. The basic steps in organizational simulation

Process description. In this step, firstly an organization under study is described. After a brief introduction of the organization, the order routing is presented. A description of the order routing is a good starting point for any analysis, especially when DEMO analysis is involved, because it presents an operational perspective of an organization and it normally and highlights clearly when and how the (communicative) actions in an organization are started. As we will see, this is also a good start for the identification of business transactions.

Model design. The most critical point in organizational simulation is to build a right model to represent properly the organization and address the problem to be solved. Simulation models can provide the most accurate and insightful means to analyze and predict the performance measures of business processes. for simulations to be successful, builders of organization models must invest significant effort into creating detailed models of organizational structure and work processes. Building accurate organization models requires the model builders to have a detailed understanding of the organization, the work that it does, and the interactions between the work process and the organization structure. If the model builders are successful, their model will reflect the structure and processes as they existed when the model is constructed. However, be aware of the dangers of using incorrect modeling and analysis procedures, which can lead to inaccurate results. This is another one reason why we have chosen the DEMO methodology as pre-simulation modeling technique for organizational simulation. This methodology is applied in numerous projects and case studies based on real life systems. Results of these works were reported in many international conferences, symposiums and scientific journals (Dietz, 1999; Dignum, et al., 1996; Dignum and Dietz, 1997; Reijswoud et al., 1999).

Model execution. In this step, when a model of an organization is built in such a manner that it is ready for being put into a computer using special simulation tools, simulation itself can be conducted. It is also possible to create a computer program which steps through time while updating the state and event variables in the developed model, but in the past few years, several new software tools have been developed specifically for simulating business processes. Most of these tools define business processes using graphical symbols or objects, with individual process activities depicted as a series of boxes and arrows. Special characteristics of each process or activity may then be attached as attributes of the process. Models are designed to provide answers at a given abstraction level, the more detailed the model, the more detailed the results and the more sophisticated the simulation process. The Arena tool, used in this paper for simulating a small model example, has the above features.

Model analysis. This final step concerns analysis of simulation results and consequently analysis of the model that was simulated. Most of simulation tools are designed in a way that the output data of simulation is formulated as numerical data or graphical dependencies. In both cases an analyst can observe characteristics of the simulated model with regard to the input data. For example, if a simulated model represents an insurance company then input data can be e.g. number of claims made by clients in a certain period of time. Characteristics in the claim process are e.g. reply time on the claim by the claim department, the period that financial department needs for paying off the claim etc. The simulation goal in this case can be the optimization of the business process in the related departments in order to reduce the backlog and operating cost, and speed up the claim processing time. Also simulation results can be used for redesigning business processes in the company. There are a lot of measures that can be taken in order to improve efficiency of the business within the insurance company. Based on the results of simulation a new model of the business can be designed and the analyst has to repeat simulation again and again comparing the results of each model. The simulation process continues until an optimal model (with respect to desired characteristics) is reached.

Scenarios evaluation. Simulation is a powerful problem solving technique to be used independently or in combination with well established modeling (or/and analytical) techniques. To solve a problem the analyst builds a conceptual model of the organization under study and explores the model trying to answer the posed questions.

As it was mentioned before, the features inherent to business systems demonstrate that business systems belong to the class of discrete systems and therefore they can be studied using discrete event simulation methods. Discrete event simulation is one way of building up models of an organization to observe its time based (or dynamic) behavior. There are formal methods for building simulation models and ensuring that they are valid. During the experimental phase the models are executed (run over time) in order to generate results. Then the results can be used to provide insight into an organization and its business process.

When using the DEMO modeling technique as a pre-simulation tool, organizational simulation takes as starting point a model of that organization (built by some analyst) as a network of interrelated business transactions. Then the execution of those transactions is being simulated in order to recommend possible changes in casual, conditional and optional links of these transactions. An analyst then implements these changes in the organization model and reruns the model. The result of this iterative model-simulate-analyze process is a model of an organization that is predicted to perform better on the originally modeled project.

The key insight behind the DEMO methodology in organizational modeling and design, is a structure that is capable of executing the amount of transactions required by its task (mission). Basically, in DEMO an organization is modeled as a network of transactions carried out by actors (people) communicating during carrying out mission of the organization. Actors communicate through a standard pattern of communication, called in DEMO the business transaction.

The transaction concept of DEMO is the universal building block of every business system. Conversely, a *business system* is a coherent structure of transactions, and a *business process* is the succession of statuses of these transactions.

3. A BRIEF INTRODUCTION TO DEMO

The DEMO methodology is built on a new and effective way of thinking about organizations. This new way of thinking has got the name 'OER-paradigm'. It fits in the so-called Language/Action Perspective (cf. Dignum and Dietz, 1997; Dignum et al.,1996; Goldkuhl et al., 1998). Contrary to the prevailing notion that communication is exchanging sentences, expressing some proposition with regard to some world, the Language/Action Perspective assumes that communication is a kind of action in that it creates commitments between the communicating parties. To communicate then is to perform language acts or communicative acts. The OER-paradigm, and accordingly DEMO, differs from other approaches in that it offers two useful additions. The first is the distinction between the essence of a business process and its realization. Otherwise said, while modeling business processes, we abstract fully from all information aspects (including calculations) and from all personnel aspects (including organizational/functional hierarchy). The second addition is that we conceive every business process to be some specific molecular structure of the 'atoms' having the same generic form. These atoms are called OER-transactions or business transactions. Some relevant papers/books are (Dietz, 1999; Dietz and Mulder, 1998).

An organization is conceived as a (discrete dynamic) system, of which the elements are social individuals or *subjects*, each of them having the *authority* to perform particular (*objective*) *actions* and a corresponding *responsibility* to do that in an appropriate and accountable way. For the coordination of their actions, the subjects enter into and comply with *commitments* towards each other. The changes that are brought about as the result of the actions of the subjects are discrete. This means that they are considered to take place instantaneously, and that there is a finite number of changes within a certain period. We thus classify organizations, in their essence, as social systems, where human beings play the role of social actor, distinct from their role as rational actor (i.e. knowing, communicating thoughts, and reasoning). Commitments are the effect of intersubjective actions, like requesting, promising, stating and accepting. The collective word for the *intersubjective* actions that actors perform in order to coordinate their (objective) actions is *'interaction'*. Objective actions and the related intersubjective actions appear to occur in a particular pattern, called the business transaction or *transaction* for short (cf. figure 1).

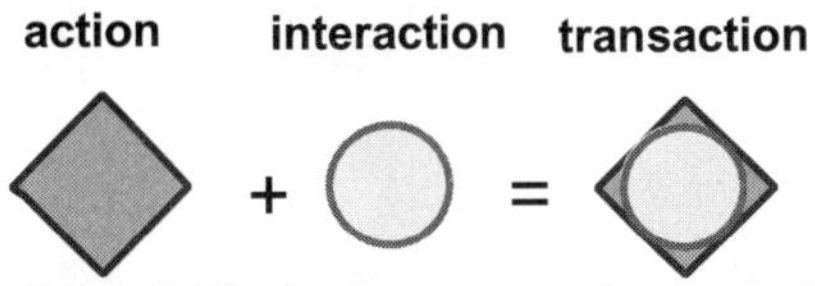

Figure 1. The business transaction concept

A transaction is carried through by two actors (human or machine), in a close cooperation. The generic pattern of a transaction is depicted in figure 2. The one who starts the transaction and eventually completes it, is called the customer or *initiator*, the other one, who actually performs the objective action, is called the supplier or *executor*. However, it should be noted that it is not necessarily that the transaction started by an actor must be completed by the same actor. Therefore we introduce notions of an original and a representation. A representation can be the original itself or really representation. That is why there are two actors-initiators in figure 2, the first one is the original initiator an the second one is representation of it. A transaction consists of three phases: the order phase or O-phase, the execution phase or E-phase, and the result phase or R-phase.

The order phase (O) is an interaction between the initiator and the executor that starts with the request of the initiator and ends with the promise by the executor. It is aimed at reaching agreement about some result in the object world to be achieved. For example, the assembler of a bicycle asks an assistant to mount a saddle and the assistant agrees to do that. The execution phase (E) starts with the promise and ends with the statement by the executor that the objective action, leading to the agreed upon result, is executed. This phase is performed by the executor solely. Example: the assistant mounts the saddle. The result phase (R) is again an interaction between the two actors, that starts with the statement and ends with the acceptance by the initiator of the result. It is aimed at reaching mutual agreement about the established result. The result is the establishment of a fact in the object world. Example: the assistant states towards the assembler that the saddle is mounted, and the assembler accepts this.

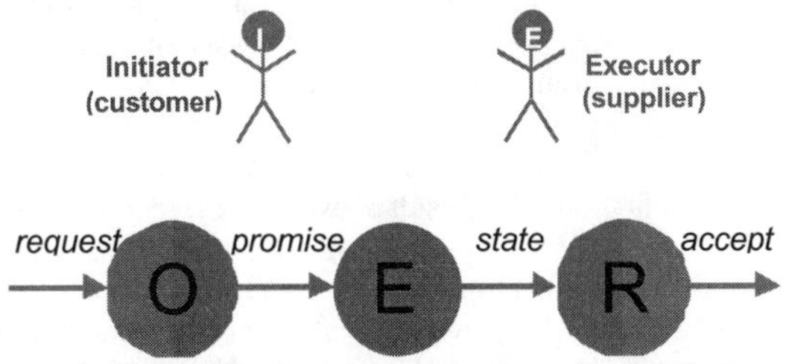

Figure 2. The transaction pattern: in actors' interrelation and graphical notion

At the moment of acceptance by the initiator, the result fact in the object world is said to come into existence, not at the moment of finishing the objective action. This principal position is important. On the one hand it stresses the supremacy of events in the intersubject world. On the other hand it allows material and immaterial objective acts (and resulting facts) to be dealt with in the same manner. For immaterial facts it is obvious that they cannot be said to exist unless they are stated and subsequently accepted, and thus that they come into existence at the moment of acceptance. Although at first sight, and intuitively, material facts seem to come into existence after having finished the objective action, this appears not to be the case on closer observation. In every organization with material objective actions (like manufacturing or transporting firms), there appears always to be someone who is held responsible for a particular material fact being the case. Only he or she has the authority to declare that something is the case, which then causes an event in the intersubject world.

During each of the phases of a transaction, new transactions may be initiated, the result of which is needed to proceed with the original one. In this way transactions are chained into arbitrarily large structures, called *business processes*.

The DEMO methodology comprises five types of models, together describing the complete essential model of an organization. One of them is the Inter Action Model. Another one is the Business Process Model (BPM). A BPM shows all identified (essential) transaction types, as well as the causal and conditional relationships between them. In this chapter these two of five DEMO models will be discussed and used in a concrete case study.

4. REPRESENTATION OF THE DEMO TRANSACTION USING ARENA SIMULATION TOOLS

We consider the Arena simulation tool to be one of the appropriate tools that can be used for simulating an organization, based on the transaction concept of DEMO. In this sense, one of the advantageous features of Arena is its animation facilities. This tool has rich and well formulated animation facilities that make simulation models interesting, attractive and easy for training people and demonstration purposes.

Arena is a general simulation tool, which can be used for business process simulation as well. There is an Arena business edition, which is made especially for this purpose. The way that Arena represents an activity, action or process is as follows. Each activity (action or process) in Arena can be represented as three interrelated elements like *Arrive*, *Server* and *Depart* or *Enter*, *Process* and *Leave*. When comparing this way of representation with the DEMO transaction concept, the similarity becomes obvious. The Order phase of a transaction can be treated as the Arrive (or enter) of a task, the Execution phase as the Server (or process) of the task and the Result phase as the Depart (or leave) of the task from the process (system). Or each of the phases separate Server, and initiation point by the Arrive, and the R-phase followed by the Depart. In order to demonstrate how it can be done in practice, some example fragments of DEMO process models are formulated in Arena according to this framework. By giving these examples we indeed cover all possible "relations between transactions". And it is through the translation of the various compositions of transactions that we actually get at the framework we are after.

These fragments are represented in figure 3. The upper part of each fragment represents a process according to the DEMO notations, and the lower part is its representation by the Arena elements. Fragments are gradually complicated. The first fragment (figure 3a) represents a process that has only one transaction (T1). For this transaction all the three phases are shown separately (T1/O, T1/E, T1/R), although it is possible to represent it in compact notation as one symbol- the disc with the bold line (cf. T2 in the second fragment).

The second fragment represents a process consisting of two transactions (T1, T2). Small disks represent the initiation points of transactions. They are connected by plain lines with arrowhead to the initiated transaction types. These arrows thus represent the *causal* links between transaction types. For example, T1 is initiated externally (represented by the single small disk). T2 is initiated during the execution phase of T1. To represent this, the disk of phase E of T1 is stretched out in order to contain the initiation disk for T2. The dotted lines with arrowheads represent *conditional* links. For example, the dotted arrow from T2 to T1/E indicates that T2 has to be completed before T1/E can be completed. In the Arena part of this fragment, the Duplicate serves for initiation of T1/E and T2 in parallel, and the Batch serves for synchronization of T2 and T1/E in order to reach T1/R.

Finally, the third fragment represents a process consisting of three transactions (T1, T2, T3). In addition to the second one, this fragment contains an optional transaction 'T3'. This transaction contains a new symbol, namely the bar across its causal link. This bar represents optionality. In the Arena part of this fragment, the Choose serves for checking the condition for initiation of the optional transaction T3. If the condition is true, the transaction will be executed, if not it will be skipped.

The Choose module provides entity branching based on the If conditional rule in conjunction with the deterministic Else and Always rules. Branch destinations are defined by connectors or by specifying a label destination.

Although self-activation (self-loop) example of DEMO process model is omitted in this figure, however it has to be noted that it can be also modeled as easily as the presented fragments.

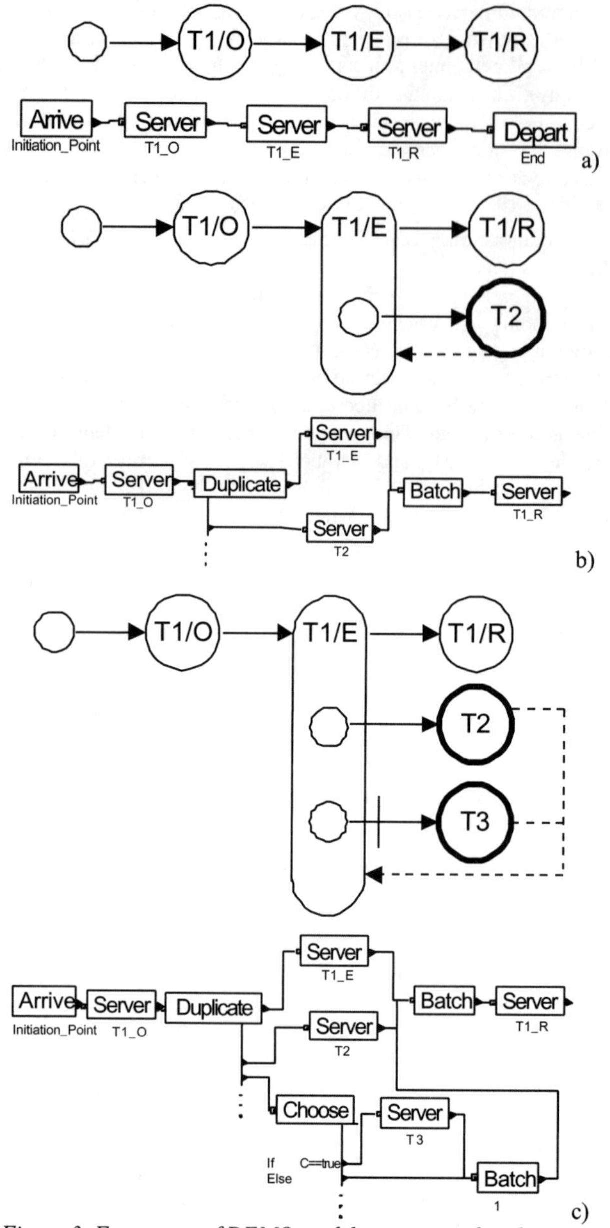

Figure 3. Fragments of DEMO models represented in the Arena notations

From the fragments, represented in figure 3, it becomes obvious that there exists a straightforward transformation scheme between DEMO process models and Arena simulation notations. It is also clear that to represent DEMO models of any complexity should not cause difficulty to be simulated using the Arena tools.

Actually the above fragments include almost all possible options of the process diagram such as causal, conditional and optional links, and also parallel initiation of several transactions and synchronization of several actions before succeeding further.

5. CONCLUSIONS

The results of the simulation of an organization lead the user in a directed search towards optimizing the organizational design, to recommend changes in the design of modeled organizations and to create better organizations. On the other hand, organizational simulation helps to improve the business (system) of an organization.

Up to now, systematic simulation of DEMO models has not been studied. In this paper the main research effort has been directed towards the integrated formalisms within DEMO and towards the DEMO methodology. Existing simulation tools have been developed mainly for simulating technical models. DEMO models of organizations are, however, rather different from the classical, technical models. So the problem is, how can we simulate DEMO models?

A solution to this problem is highly relevant, as the general benefits of simulation certainly apply to DEMO models, resulting in a better, more detailed analysis of the model, offering possibilities to vary many details of the model such as scenario's, priorities and selection criteria. Moreover, what makes simulation particularly promising for DEMO models, it might give rise to carefully and systematically investigating human negotiations and other forms of social activities occurring in organizations.

Future research will address the DEMO's submodels, probably leading to more refined analysis possibilities and results, embedded in a likewise more refined simulation framework.

REFERENCES

Aguilar, M.; Tankred Rautert and Lex Pater, 1999. Business Process Simulation: A Fundamental Step Supporting Process Centered Management. In the proceedings of *the 1999 Winter Simulation Conference (WSC '99)*, Phoenix, Arizona, December 5-8.

Alter, S., 1996. Information systems; a management perspective. Menlo Park : Benjamin/Cummings, USA.

Davenport, T.H. & Short, J.E., 1990. The New Industrial Engineering: Information Technology and Business Process Redesign. *Sloan Management Review*, pp. 11-27.

Davenport, T.H., 1993. Process Innovation, *Harvard Business School Press*, Boston.

Dietz J.L.G., 1999. Understanding Business Processes on the basis of Habermas' Theory of Communicative Action, in: Proceedings of *the AMCIS Conference*, Milwaukee USA, august.

Dietz, J.L.G., 1999+. Understanding and modeling business processes with DEMO, in: Proc. *ER'99, Annual International Conference on Conceptual Modeling*, Paris, November.

Dietz, J.L.G., J.B.F. Mulder, 1998. Organizational transformation requires constructional knowledge of business systems, *Proc. HICCS.*

Dignum, F., J.L.G. Dietz, 1997. Proceedings of the Second International Workshop on Communication Modeling. Computing Science Reports, Eindhoven University of Technology.

Dignum, F., J.L.G. Dietz, E. Verharen, H. Weigand, 1996. Communication Modeling - the Language/Action Perspective. *Electronic Workshops in Computing*, Springer, http://www.springcr.co.nk/cwic/workshops/CM96/.

Douglas B. Fridsma et al., 1997. Acquiring, Maintaining, and Customizing Organizational Work Process Descriptions. In *the proceedings of the AAAI Spring Symposium Artificial Intelligence in Knowledge Management*, Stanford University, March 24-26.

Fishwick, P.A., 1996. What is Simulation? *IEEE Potentials*, February.

Goldkuhl, G.; Lind, M.; Seigerroth, U., 1998. The Language Action Perspective on Communication Modeling, *Proceedings of the Third International Workshop*, Dept. Informatics, Jönköping International Business School, Sweden.

Hammer, M. and Champy, J., 1993. Reengineering the Corporation, Harper Collins Books, New York, NY.

Reijswoud, V. E. van, J.B.F. Mulder, J.L.G. Dietz, 1999. Speech Act Based Business Process and Information Modelling with DEMO, *Information Systems Journal.*

Taylor, J.R., 1993. Rethinking the Theory of Organizational Communication: How to Read an Organization. Ablex, Norwood.

Winograd, T, F. Flores, 1986. Understanding Computers and Cognition: A New Foundation for Design. Ablex, Norwood NJ.

About authors:

Joseph Barjis /Ph.D., Associate Academician of the International Informatization Academy, Chairman of the International Center of Information, headquartered in the Netherlands/ MSc. in Computer Science in 1991; Ph.D. in Computer Science in 1996; Ph.D. in Information Systems in 1999. He worked or works in: Russia, United Kingdom and the Netherlands.

Jan Dietz / Ph.D., Grand Ph.D., Professor, Academician of the International Informatization Academy/ started his scientific career in 1980 at Eindhoven University of Technology. In 1987 he obtained his Doctoral Degree. In January 1988 he was appointed Professor of Management Information Systems at the University of Maastricht. From September 1994 on he is Professor of Design of Information Systems at Delft University of Technology.

Luuk Groenewegen / Ph.D., Associate Professor / started his scientific career with a MSc. in Mathematics at Leiden University in 1972; PhD. in Operational Research at Eindhoven University in 1978; started in Computer Science at LeidenUniversity in 1979, first as Assistent Professor, since 1986 as Associate Professor.

SIMULATION OF ORGANIZATIONAL PROCESSES COMBINING SEMANTIC ANALYSIS AND PETRI NETS

Joseph Barjis

Department of Information Systems, Delft University of Technology, P.O. Box 356, 2600 AJ Delft, The Netherlands.
Tel: +31-15–2785827, Fax: +31-15–2786632; e-mail: J.Barjis@is.twi.tudelft.nl; http://is.twi.tudelft.nl/~barjis

Joaquim Filipe

Escola Superior de Tecnologia de Setúbal,Rua Vale de Chaves, Estefanilha, 2914 Setúbal, Portugal.
Tel.: +351 265 790 040; Fax : +351 265 721 869; e-mail: JFilipe@est.ips.pt; web: www.est.ips.pt/docentesweb/jfilipe

Keywords: *Semantic analysis, Petri net, Business process, Simulation*

ABSTRACT

This paper illustrates the application of semantic analysis in building a model of the organizational ontology and business processes. In this context, the ontology chart is a helpful diagram to build a final model of the organizational processes, using Petri nets. Our approach is aimed at combining two methods – a language action based semiotic method and a Petri net simulation technique – to provide a solid conceptual basis for the computer simulation models of an organization. Especially, it is demonstrated that semantic analysis is a helpful basis for developing a simulation model that can be analyzed using any available discrete simulation tools. In particular, ontology charts help analysts to observe all the business objects, relationships, activities, causal and conditional links within an organization.

1. INTRODUCTION

Human organizations are the subject of study for Organizational Theory, and many models of various types of organizations have been produced (Scott, 1992; Simon, 1996). On the other hand, computer simulation modeling is mainly a Computer Science subject, and computer science researchers often experience strong difficulties to model the human factors that must be reflected in any real-world model. In this paper we propose the Organizational Semiotics stance (Stamper, 1973; Liu, 1993) to overcome this difficulty and to provide a solid conceptual basis for the computer simulation models.

Organizations are seen in this paper as social information systems, where the overall activity is mainly the result of the coordinated behavior of several organizational agents. This focus on the semiotics social level (Stamper, 1973) is also shared, in the Computer Science community, by the Distributed Artificial Intelligence (DAI) research area, which we adopt as a second school of thought relevant to the research we present in this paper. In DAI, organizations are multi-agent systems, composed by autonomous agents acting in a coordinated way in order to achieve social goals, in a cooperative manner (Wooldridge and Jennings, 1995; Singh, 1996). Organizational agents, whether human or artificial, rely essentially on two mechanisms for behavior coordination: norms and communication. Organizations are social systems that are composed of socially acting human beings and coordinated by performative (action-oriented) communication (Taylor, 1993; Winograd, Flores, 1986). In recent years, this communication-oriented perspective on organizations has received considerable academic attention (Dietz, Mulder 1998; Dietz, 1999; Dignum, Dietz, 1997). But here, in this paper we will focus especially on normative models of agent behavior.

Organizations are complex, dynamic, non-linear adaptive, evolving systems. Since organizational behavior results from interactions among a variety of heterogeneous (human and artificial) agents, organizations are poor candidates for analytical models. Thus, computer simulation models become invaluable tools for theory building, where the models are not only hypotheses generators, but also provide the means to show the potential legitimacy of various theoretical claims. Since multi-agent logic is not sufficiently developed to achieve the logical consistency and completeness of organizational models, computational simulation provides a way to assess the adequacy of organizational models. Furthermore, computer simulation permits to gain insights into organizational phenomena and to explore processes and configurations that are difficult or impossible to investigate with other methods.

However, the immediate application of simulation methods to organizational processes faces some complexity unless a pre-simulation analysis is conducted. This difficulty especially arises when simulation is based on human factors and communication between these actors in order to carry out mission of the organization. The application domain must be very well understood before attempting to create a simulation model. This entails a requirements analysis phase, which is actually a preliminary phase of any software engineering project. Many methods have been proposed to tackle this important problem but, in spite of that, a high proportion of computer-based systems fail. Estimates vary between 40% and 50% of projects (Stamper, 2000). This indicates that the requirements specifications are often wrong.

Final step in the proposed in this paper approach after having a model in Petri net form is constructing an animated simulation model based on the Petri net model of the book acquisition process using Arena simulation tools. As business process simulation tools, Arena allows analysts to visualize, animate and simulate processes in a very easy and feasible way. As a result of simulation some histograms are drown that help analysts to improve and redesign processes.

2. SEMIOTICS

Semiotics was founded as a formal theory of signs by Peirce, which has established three distinct fields of semiotics: syntax, semantics and pragmatics. Stamper (1973) added three more levels to this theory, creating a framework which could be characterized as depicted in figure 1.

Andersen (1990) defined computer semiotics as a "*branch of semiotics that studies the special nature of computer-based signs and how they function in use.*" The semiotic approach to computing emphasizes the importance of the integration of computers in social reality. It is very important to make computer-based systems fit into a business organization and integrate information technology with the social aspects that enable the successful fulfillment of business goals.

The semiotic framework proposed by Stamper (1996) has been recommended by FRISCO (Falkenberg, 1998) as a philosophical foundation for information systems analysis. This approach is different from mainstream computer science because instead of adopting an objectivist stance – where it is assumed the existence of a single observable reality, external to the agent, which requirements modeling methods try to capture with the help of entity-relationship models and data-flow diagrams – it adopts a social subjectivist stance. This means that for all practical purposes nothing exists without a perceiving agent nor without an agent engaging in action (Stamper et. al., 2000). This philosophical stance ties every item of knowledge to an agent who is, in a sense, responsible for it. Thus, adopting this stance,

(...) the information model avoids the concept of truths that have been delivered from on high, independently of a knowing agent. Truth is something that the individual agents and group agents have to decide upon and for the consequence of which they have to take responsibility (Stamper, 1996 p.371).

The distinction between entity, attribute and relationship is therefore replaced by the concepts of agent, affordance (invariant that is perceived by an agent) and norm (a socially defined pattern). These concepts are related in a way that indicates ontological dependency.

Using this semiotics framework to cover the main stages of systems lifecycle, a collection of methods has been defined, which can be applied to all the systems development activities along the systems development lifecycle. These were developed under the MEASUR research program – Method for Eliciting, Analyzing and Specifying User Requirements (Stamper et al. 1988). This program actually developed a suite of methods, especially at the semantic level, providing the design of organizational ontology charts and the specification of the norms associated with the existing entities. These two outcomes of the semiotics approach to semantic analysis are explained below.

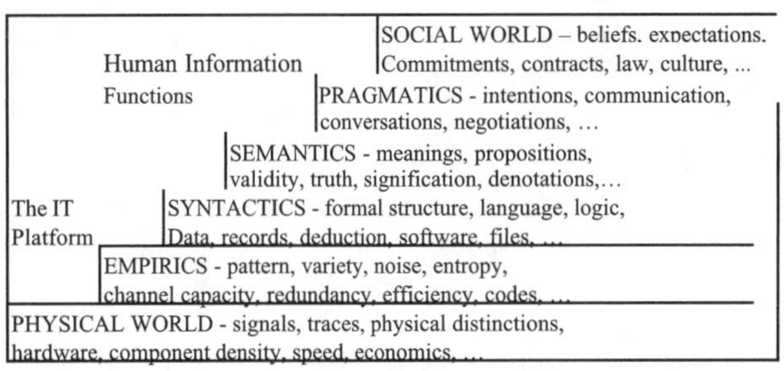

Figure 1. The semiotics framework (Stamper 1973)

2.1 Ontology Charts

The result of semantic analysis may be provide in a graphical format, using what is called a 'ontology chart', where nodes denote affordances, and arcs denote relationships of ontological dependency. Figure 3 shows an example of an ontology chart, obtained as result of the semantic analysis of the case study presented in section 3.

For example, the relationship between 'department' and 'school' is one of *ontological dependency* because it defines the existence of the first in terms of the existence of the second: 'school' is the ontological antecedent and 'department' is the ontological 'dependent'. The dot sign that marks this relationship means that the ontological dependency is that of part to whole.

The lines that link 'person' and 'works' (in both concepts of 'works' in the diagram) are labeled. These labels denote the roles that the antecedent plays, in each case, as agent of the action 'works'.

The '@' marking, for example, the link between 'approves', and 'request' means that the 'request' affordance is brought into existence conditionally to the validity of the 'approves' affordance: the head of the department may or may not 'approve' the 'request' – only after s/he exercises his discretion and approves the request will the 'request' actually start its existence.

For a complete description of the syntax of the *ontology chart*, the reader may consult (Stamper, 1996).

2.2 Norms

Meanings become clear when we know precisely when activities are performed. The ontology chart shows the ontological dependencies but not the starting and finishing times of each affordance. The dynamics of the organization, established by these start and finish events, may be determined either by norms or by an agent taking responsibility and exercising discretion.

Norms are a reflex of business rules, social goals, constraints and other structural aspects of the organization. Norms are an essential part of an agent's role, because they define all the regulated aspects that guide the agent in his activities, both by defining the agent's capabilities and obligations (to bring certain affordances into existence) and the agent's authorizations (to exercise its discretion, assuming responsibility for it).

Our approach views a business process as an activity network composed of autonomous agents. Agents represent individuals or collectives, including external stakeholders such as customers, regulators or suppliers, and internal entities such as staff, departments, or systems. In such a social environment, normative knowledge acquires a prominent role. Norms are needed to reduce the communicative overload that would occur if every action would require a process of negotiation before an agreement was reached. Norms are the result of social and often cultural, tacit, commitments for agents to achieve coordination without too much communication.

Although the responsibility for a discretionary action must rest ultimately with a human agent, it is possible to use artificial agents both to perform normative tasks, and to perform tasks with responsibilities clearly delegated from some human agent. For example, an ATM machine has been delegated the responsibility to deliver cash against the presentation of a proper plastic card and a correct personal identification code. However, if the machine delivers the wrong amount of money the responsibility ultimately lies with the bank, or a representative thereof, who must compensate the mistake, according to the proper norms.

3. CASE-STUDY

This case study reflects an organizational process of the Polytechnic Institute of Setúbal concerning the book acquisition process, initiated by a request from a lecturer, as depicted in figure 2.

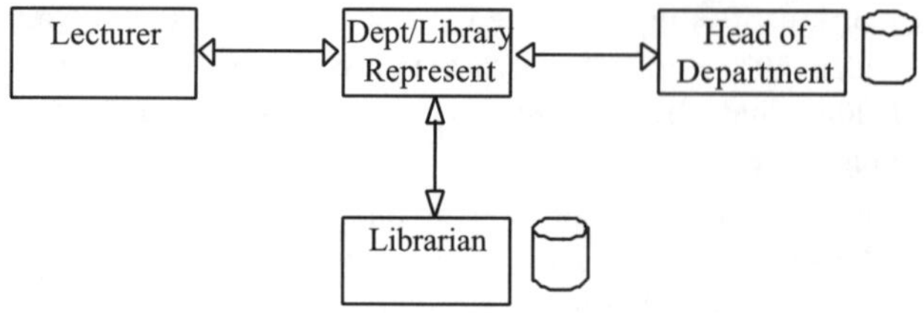

Figure 2. Book acquisition (informal description)

The book acquisition process is started by the lecturer, who expresses the desire to obtain a certain book. This is expressed as a book recommendation for acquisition, to the appreciation of the representative. The representative – who performs the role of mediator between the department and the library – will validate the recommendation. The mediator must ask the president of the department to approve the recommendation (if he considers the book worth being acquired and if the department has enough budget to buy it). If and only if all these conditions are fulfilled the book request will be brought into existence and the request processed by the library. The library will purchase the book and after the book entry into the library it will be classified (by the library). Only then the mediator will be informed that the book became available. The mediator will then inform the lecturer.

Figure 3 shows the ontology chart that corresponds to the semantic analysis of the case study described above.

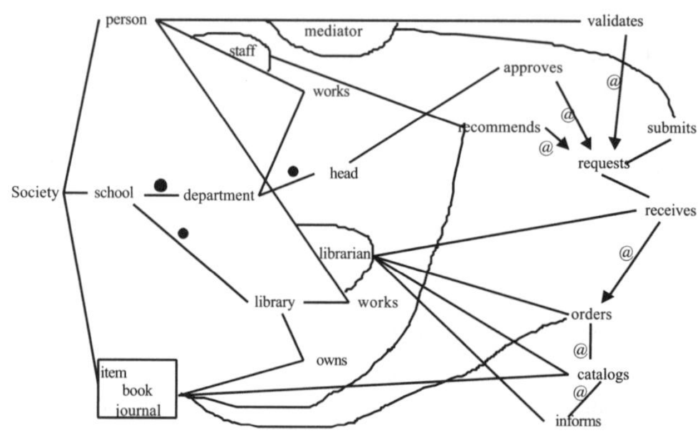

Figure 3. Ontology chart

4. PROCESS MODELING USING PETRI NETS

Results of the previous section provide a solid description of the processes for a book acquisition. After this primary analysis using the semantic method, it is easier to go on constructing a Petri net model of the book acquisition. Especially, information graphically represented by the ontology chart is helpful for this purpose. Semantic analysis, as a primary step in organizational simulation, helps to build a right model to represent properly processes and address the problem to be solved. As one can see from the previous section, semantic analysis in organizational simulation becomes especially important when organizations are considered as social systems.

Reading the case description and ontological chart, the following information can be easily derived:

There are at least 4 actions within the book acquisition process (1 recommendation, 2 validation, 3 ordering, 4 informing or acknowledging). One of these actions (validation) is conditional. It means that the head of the department may approve or not approve the request.

This information based on the semantic analysis can serve as input information for developing simulation model of the mentioned case. Simulation model cane be developed using Petri nets as well tested and supported technique.

As a modeling technique Petri Nets possess many advantages, including: their well-developed mathematical and practical foundation; compact representation of system behavior; available tools for both qualitative and quantitative analyses; and their graphical nature that aids in the understanding of processes.

Petri nets are a suitable tool for modeling static properties of processes as well as for dynamic properties that result from its execution.

Statically Petri nets represent processes as a network of two types of nodes - circles (places) and bars or rectangles (transitions).

Dynamically Petri nets represent processes through markers (tokens). Tokens are moved by the firing of transitions of the net.

A Petri net model of the book acquisition is represented in Figure 4. This model can be simulated (analyzed) using any discrete event simulation tools or Petri net tools.

In this figure, there are two rational transitions. These transitions, represented as double lined rectangles, model choice or decision between approved and not approved request. We call these transitions rational, because they don't represent any activity (process) and consequently have no duration.

Figure 5 represents an animated simulation model using the Arena simulation tool, based on the Petri net model of figure 4. There are two models in this figure. The first, on the upper part of the figure, is a logical model and the second, on the lower part, is animated model representing the lecturer, the mediator, the head of the department, the library and bookstore.

The flow of task (data) from actor to actor is animated using pictures of a document and information sign (see on the lift top of the logical model).

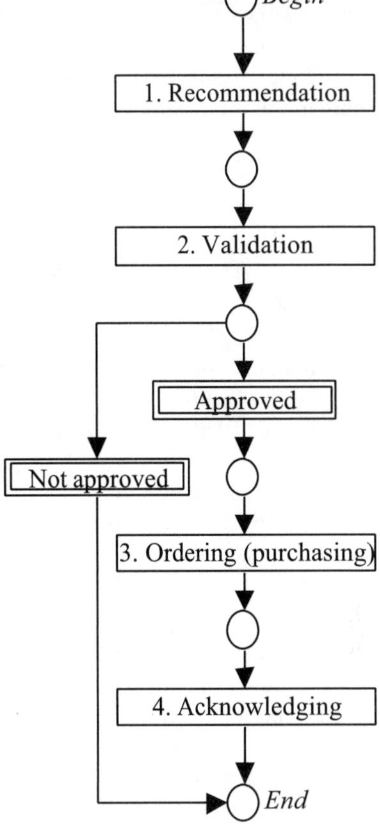

Figure 4. Petri net model of the book acquisition process

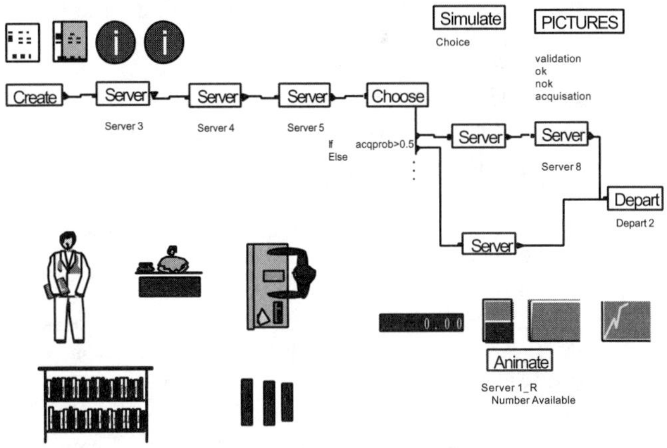

Figure 5. An animated simulation model of the book acquisition process using Arena tool

5. CONCLUSIONS

This paper illustrates the application of semantic analysis in building a simulation model of organizational processes. In this context, the ontological chart is a helpful diagram to build a final model of the organizational processes, using Petri nets.

It is demonstrated that immediate application of simulation methods to organizational processes faces some complexity unless there a pre-simulation analysis is conducted. This difficulty especially arises when simulation is based on human factors and communication between these actors in order to carry out mission of the organization.

Therefore, the proposed approach in this paper is aimed to combine two methods- language action based semiotic method and simulation technique Petri net- to provide a solid conceptual basis for the computer simulation models of an organization.

Especially it is demonstrated that semantic analysis and ontology chart are a helpful basis for developing a simulation model that can be analyzed using any available discrete simulation tools. In particular, ontology chart helps analysts to observe all activities and their strict logical sequences through all business processes within an organization. Complexity of the simulation model then depends on how many details of the ontology chart is captured by simulation model.

In the future authors are intended to apply this combined approach to more complex organizational process based on real life systems. And may be, towards this issue, the opportunity of hierarchical representation of ontology chart and then simulation model will be investigated. Because when considering complex organizational processes it becomes difficult to read and follow logical sequence of actions in the ontology chart. Perhaps it will be a good idea to compress a set of atomic actions into one core activity and represent them as one node or subnet of Petri net.

REFERENCES

Andersen, P. 1990. A Theory of Computer Semiotics: Semiotics approaches to Construction and Assessment of Computer Systems. Cambridge University Press, Cambridge, Mass.

Dietz, J.L.G., J.B.F. Mulder, Organizational transformation requires constructional knowledge of business systems, Proc. HICCS 1998, IEEE, 1998

Dietz, J.L.G., Understanding and Modeling Business Processes with DEMO, Proc. 18th International Conference on Conceptual Modeling (ER'99), Paris, 1999.

Dignum, F., J.L.G. Dietz, Proceedings of the Second International Workshop on Communication Modeling, Computing Science Reports, Eindhoven University of Technology, 1997.

Falkenberg, E., W. Hesse, P. Lindgreen, E. Nilsson, H. Oei, C. Rolland, R. Stamper, F. Assche, A. Verrijn-Stuart, K. Voss, 1998. FRISCO: A Framework of Information System Concepts, (web edition), IFIP, ftp://ftp.leidenuniv.nl/pub/rul/fri-full.zip.

Liu, K. 1993. Semiotics Applied to Information Systems Development. PhD Thesis, Twente University, The Netherlands.

Peirce, C. 1960. Collected papers of Ch. S. Peirce, C. Hartshorne and P. Weiss (Eds). Cambridge, Mass.

Scott, W., 1992. Organizations: Rational, Natural and Open Systems, third edition, Englewood Cliffs, N.J.: Prentice-Hall.

Simon, H. 1996. The Sciences of the Artificial (3rd Edition). MIT Press, USA.

Singh, M. 1996. Multiagent Systems as Spheres of Commitment. In Proceedings of the Int'l Conference on Multiagent Systems (ICMAS) - Workshop on Norms, Obligations and Conventions. Kyoto, Japan.

Stamper, R. 1973. Information in Business and Administrative Systems. John Wiley & Sons.

Stamper, R. 1992. Language and Computer in Organised Behavior. In Riet, R. and R. Meersman (Eds), Linguistic Instruments in Knowledge Engineering. Elsevier Science Publishers, North-Holland.

Stamper, R., 1996. Signs, Information, Norms and Systems. In: Signs of Work, Semiosis and Information Processing in Organizations, Holmqvist et al. (Eds.), Walter de Gruyter, Berlin, New York.

Stamper, R., K. Althaus and J. Backhouse, 1988. MEASUR: Method for Eliciting, Analyzing and Specifying User Requirements. In Computerised Assistance during the Information Systems Life Cycle, Olle, Verrijn-Stuart and Bhabuts (Eds). Elsevier-Science Publishers, Holland.

Stamper, R., K. Liu, M. Hafkamp and Y. Ades, 2000. Understanding the Roles of Signs and Norms in Organizations – a Semiotic Approach to Information Systems Design, Behavior and Information Technology (forthcoming).

Taylor, J.R., 1993. Rethinking the Theory of Organizational Communication: How to Read an Organization. Ablex, Norwood.

Winograd, T, F. Flores, 1986. Understanding Computers and Cognition: A New Foundation for Design. Ablex, Norwood NJ.

Winograd, T. and C. Flores 1986. Understanding Computers and Cognition. Addison Wesley Publishing Company.

Wooldridge, M. and N. Jennings 1995. Agent Theories, Architectures and Languages: a Survey. In M.Wooldridge and N. Jennings (Eds) Intelligent Agents, Springer-Verlag.

About authors:

Joseph Barjis /Ph.D., Associate Academician of the International Informatization Academy, Chairman of the International Center of Information, headquartered in the Netherlands/ MSc. in Computer Science in 1991; Ph.D. in Computer Science in 1996; Ph.D. in Information Systems in 1999. He worked or works in: Russia, United Kingdom and the Netherlands.

Joaquim Filipe /MSc., MBA, Adjunct Professor/ Started his scientific career at the Technical University of Lisbon, with an MSc. in 1989, in the area of Artificial Intelligence; is now finishing a PhD in Staffordshire University (UK) in the area of Multi-Agent Systems; started as research assistant in Computer Science at the Technical University of Lisbon in 1984 and is, since 1993, a Professor of Informatics at the Polytechnic Institute of Setubal (Portugal).

APPLYING BUSINESS OBJECTS FOR SIMULATION

Mohammad Abolhassani

Faculty of Information Technology and Systems, Delft University of Technology,
P.O. Box 356, 2600 AJ, Delft, The Netherlands, Tel: +31-15–2781530, Fax: +31-15–2786632, e-mail: m.abolhassani@its.tudelft.nl

Joseph Barjis

Faculty of Information Technology and Systems, Delft University of Technology,
P.O. Box 356, 2600 AJ, Delft, The Netherlands, Tel: +31-15–2785827, Fax: +31-15–2786632, e-mail: j.barjis@is.twi.tudelft.nl,
http://is.twi.tudelft.nl/~barjis

Keywords: *Business Objects, Object Oriented Method, Discrete Event Simulation, Petri-Nets*

ABSTRACT

Simulation can be used in many fields, including business management. For any simulation process, in order to achieve a satisfactory result, it is of great importance to be able to define the necessary and sufficient constituents of the process, in advance. Thus for any simulation process in the field of business management, the regarding business concepts should be defined and applied carefully and correctly. This paper suggests a new approach for this purpose.

The approach is founded on applying the notion of Business Objects. This notion imposes a strict distinction between the "pure" business concepts and any other issue, and divides these concepts into three categories. Analyzing the system in question and constructing the regarding models based on this notion can, in general, serve as input for the simulation process, and, in particular, result in the "right" Petri-Net models for simulation tools. The approach is explained using an example case.

1. INTRODUCTION

Simulation is helpful in many situations like analysis, design, training and study of dynamic behavior of a system. There are different areas where simulation is applicable, including business management, manufacturing, transportation and education.

The simulation process, in any field, encompasses different phases. The three main, interrelated, phases of the whole process are model design, model execution and model analysis [Fishwick, 1996]. However, to obtain a reasonable and satisfactory result, defining the concepts that should take part in the simulation process, and providing a correct representation thereof, using proper notations, is of crucial importance.

This paper emphasizes this "pre-simulation" phase and aims at proposing a new approach for this aspect of simulation regarding business management. The approach is founded on the notion of Business Objects. This notion is based on applying Object Oriented Method in business management and, at the same time, making a strict distinction between the business logic and any other issue out of its scope.

As simulation asks for a thorough insight in the concerning business, without any unnecessary details, we consider the notion of Business Objects as a suitable means for the recognition, categorization and preparation of those concepts that should participate in the simulation. In addition, Business Objects provide an organized, flexible and scalable basis for reacting to the changes in the business logic that may be needed due to different reasons. Furthermore, the standardization feature of Business Objects makes them suitable for serving as communication means among the involved parties, interoperation between different organizations and utilization for different applications within the same or different organizations.

To explain this approach and demonstrate its application and results, we have used an example case, namely an ordinary procedure within a travel agency. This example case underlines those processes that are related to the arrangement of a travel, including accommodation and transportation, within a specific time and price range. The goal of this simulation process is providing a better understanding of the mentioned processes in order to investigate the (possible) deficiencies.

Accordingly, the recognized Business Objects along with their properties are indicated and the example case is represented using various diagrams, including Petri-Net diagram, that highlight business processes within the travel agency from different viewpoints. These diagrams allow analysts to get a thorough picture of the business processes within organizations. Besides, they contain enough information to serve as input for building an animated simulation model using simulation tools, e.g., the Arena Simulation Tools. In particular, the resulting Petri-Net models can be used by different Petri-Net simulation tools that provide simulation, as well as analysis and edit of the Petri-Net models.

The benefits of simulation in business management

Business processes are too complex and dynamic to be understood and analyzed by flowcharting and diagrams alone. As such, simulation can be institutionalized as the standard tool for business processes analysis, design and redesign. In fact, simulation is the only means that can provide both accurate analysis and visualization of alternatives of the business processes. In brief, the key activities that can be supported by simulation in the field of business management are:

- Analysis
- Design & Redesign
- Optimization
- Training

- Visualization of work processes
- Capturing dynamic behavior of the system
- Testing the system before building it

Furthermore, simulation can be used for investigations about the issues like:

- Paralleling of processes
- Advancing initiation of processes
- Merging activities of different actors

Outline of the paper

The paper begins with a brief discussion about the Business Objects.

Then the example case, which will serve as the basis for the clarification of our approach is described, and the concerning Business Objects are specified. The example concerns a travel agency that wants to accomplish investigations about its existing methods regarding the treatment of its clients.

In the following chapters, first the graphical representations of the example case are presented, using different diagrams. Then, some points about the (intended) resulting animated simulation model are mentioned. Finally, A brief discussion about the advantages and shortcomings of this approach, and the ways to overcome these shortcomings in the future work concludes the paper.

2. BUSINESS OBJECTS

The notion of Business Objects (BOs) is concerned with applying Object Oriented Method in modeling business systems and realizing business software systems in distributed and heterogeneous environments. There are many different definitions for this notion. The most well known definition for BOs is the one presented by the Object Management Group (OMG) [OMG, 1995]:

A Business Object is a representation of a thing active in the business domain, including at least its business name and definition, attributes, behavior, relationships and constraints. A Business Object may represent, for example, a person, place or concept. The representation may be in a natural language, a modeling language or a programming language.

In an effort to provide a basis for a more globally accepted definition for BOs, they are defined as follows [Abolhassani, 1999]:

Business Objects are those Reflection Objects that comply with the standards devised for different concepts at different abstraction levels related to different business domains, and represent their functionality, characteristics, features, associations and peculiarities, in a clear and unambiguous manner.

Where Reflection Objects are defined as those *objects that reflect the semantics of the real-world concepts, and are the only objects that come into focus during the analysis process.*

This notion is in close relationship with the three-layer architecture [Edwards, 1997], which is based on the notion of excluding business logic, the set of rules and constraints that govern the procedures and manipulation of data related to business, from all other aspects.

In general, the BOs are divided into three main categories:

- Entity: Embraces the tangible and intangible business facets and represent enterprise data and their regarding manipulations according to the business rules and constraints.
- Process: Embraces the business activities and encapsulate units of enterprise work and their regarding data according to the business rules and constraints.
- Event: Embraces the persistent records of as well as notification means for business happenings and are concerned with state changes, action occurrences and time boundaries that are of importance within enterprise.

Realizing a successful simulation asks for an accurate, clear and thorough insight in the concerning business, without any unnecessary details. This is in conformance with the traits of Business Objects.

3. THE EXAMPLE CASE: TRAVEL AGENCY

3.1 Case Description*

When a client applies to the travel agency to book a trip, the desk clerk must check if he/she is already registered. Then the client can let the desk clerk know about his/her preferences regarding the intended trip. The preferences encompass destination, time, cost, accommodation and transportation. The desk clerk then surveys the options that match those preferences.

For the desired destination, and according to the specified time and cost (range), the desk clerk looks for the accommodation possibilities that match the client's desired properties. Then the desk clerk checks the outcomes with the client to see if the result is satisfactory. If not, the desk clerk asks the client to make some changes in his/her preferences regarding accommodation, and follows the same procedure with the new preferences. If after a certain number of trials the result is still not satisfactory, the desk clerk asks the client to change his/her preferences regarding other items, namely cost and time. In some cases it may even happen that the client is asked to change his/her destination, if possible. After each alteration the desk clerk begins the procedure with the new preferences.

When the right accommodation that matches all the (possibly changed) preferences is found, the (almost) similar procedure begins for the transportation. In this step, the desk clerk looks for the transportation means that matches all of the preferences (fixed at the previous step) and the client's desired properties. If no satisfactory result could be found, the other preferences regarding time and cost should be changed. In this case, if the changes in the preferences (may) affect the other items, the procedure must repeat again for those items. For instance, if the departure and/or arrival time change, the accommodation must be checked again. If this results in a satisfactory situation, the initiator step is succeeded, otherwise it must be repeated with new preference data.

*This example case is just meant for the demonstration of our approach and therefore may defer from the reality of the regarding business.

In case all the (possibly changed) preferences are fulfilled and the desired accommodation and transportation are found, the desk clerk informs the client and presents the achieved results to the counter clerk for the payment. After the payment is fulfilled by the client, the counter clerk informs the desk clerk and the desk clerk does the reservations.

On receiving the confirmation from the concerning reservation parties, the counter clerk informs the client about it. If there is no confirmation (received), the reservation is considered as failed. Accordingly, the client is invited to either change his preferences, what initiates the whole procedure from the very beginning, or get his money back.

Finally, in case the whole process succeeds, the accommodation and transportation documents will be sent to the client.

Note that this is a simplified procedure. For instance, arrangement for travel insurance is not included. Also, in an ideal situation, information about the destination attractions, accommodation, transportation, etc. should also be made available to the client.

3.2 The Business Objects

In conformance with the aforementioned common categorization of the Business Objects, the objects of the example case can be divided into three categories. In the following, the objects of each category, along with some of their main attributes and/or methods, are specified:

Entities:

Registration

Attributes: name, address, telephone-number, birth-date, birth-place, nationality, bank-number

Preferences

Attributes: destination, time, cost, accommodation, transportation

Client

Attributes: registration, preferences

Methods: do-application

Clerk

Attributes: name, work place, work-telephone-number, work-time

Desk

Methods: do-reservation, do-confirmation, do-cancellation

Counter

Methods: do-payment

Reservation-Form

Attributes: reservation-number, client, clerk, destination, time, accommodation, transportation, fee

Bill

Attributes: counter, reservation-form, to-or-from

Place

Attributes: name, city, country

Accommodation

Attributes: name, address, telephone-number, rooms

Room-Collection

Attributes: place-type, rank, facility, transportation-means, price, availability-number, availability-date

Room

Attributes: client-name, position-number, reserved

Transportation

Attributes: name, address, telephone-number, seats

Seat-Collection

Attributes: vehicle-type, rank, price, availability-number, availability-date

Seat

Attributes: client-name, position-number, reserved

Processes:

Application

Methods: set-registration, set-preferences

Reservation

Methods: check-registration, get-preferences, survey-accommodation, survey-transportation, set-reservation-form, set-bill

Payment

Methods: do-transaction, set-reception, reset-bill

Confirmation

Methods: inform-client, store-reservation-form, send-documents

Cancellation

Methods: inform-client, set-bill, initiate-application

Events:

Succeed

Attributes: reservation-form

Methods: initiate-confirmation

Fail

Attributes: reservation-form

Methods: initiate-cancellation

4. GRAPHICAL REPRESENTATION OF THE EXAMPLE CASE

4.1 Class Diagram

Figure 1 (see at the end of the paper) shows the Unified Modeling Language (UML) class diagram based on the BOs of the example case:

4.2 Sequence Diagram

The UML sequence diagrams of the Travel agency example case, represented in figure 2, are as follows. These diagrams depict three processes regarding the Reservation, Succeed and Fail.

Reservation

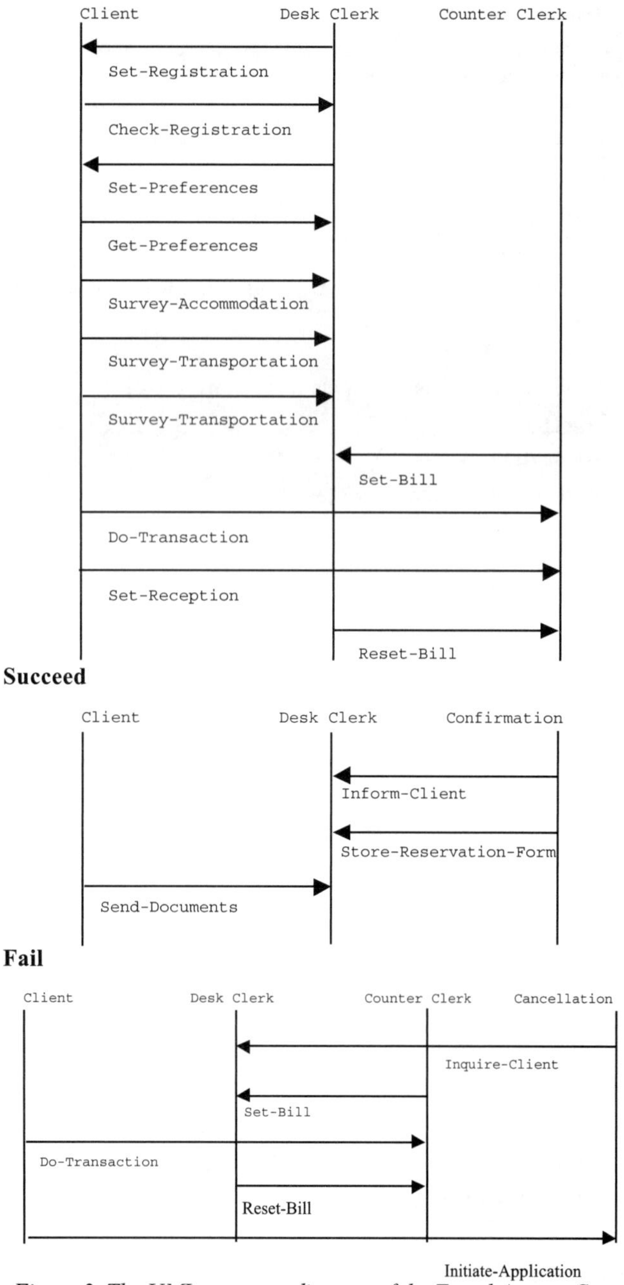

Figure 2. The UML sequence diagram of the Travel Agency Case

4.3 Petri-Net Diagram

Although there are numerous papers dedicated to the application of Petri-Nets in business process or workflow modeling and simulation [Aalst, 1998; Agostini and Michelis, 1998; Moelders et al., 1998], a sound and tested approach for identifying processes before constructing a Petri-Net model is still missing.

In order to build a correct Petri-Net model of the system under study, it is needed to identify all of the interrelated processes within the (business) system. The (process) BOs can be helpful for this task.

For the example case, the extracted (process) BOs help us to identify all of the business processes within the travel agency. In this way, five processes (or sub processes) that are contained in the entire business, namely: Application, Reservation, Payment, Confirmation and Cancellation, are recognized

Consequently, by identifying these processes, and establishing all causal and conditional links between them, constructing the regarding Petri-Net model is easier. We consider that the proposed model of the Petri-Net in this paper is process oriented.

The model shown in figure 3 represents all of the five processes as five transitions, graphically represented as five rectangles. Facts, created after each process, are included into ovals that follow the rectangles. For example, after the Application process two facts are created. These two facts are concerned with the setting of the Registration form and the Preference form.

All supplementary activities, contained in each process, are listed next to the corresponding rectangle. For example, Application process contains two activities: set registration and set preferences.

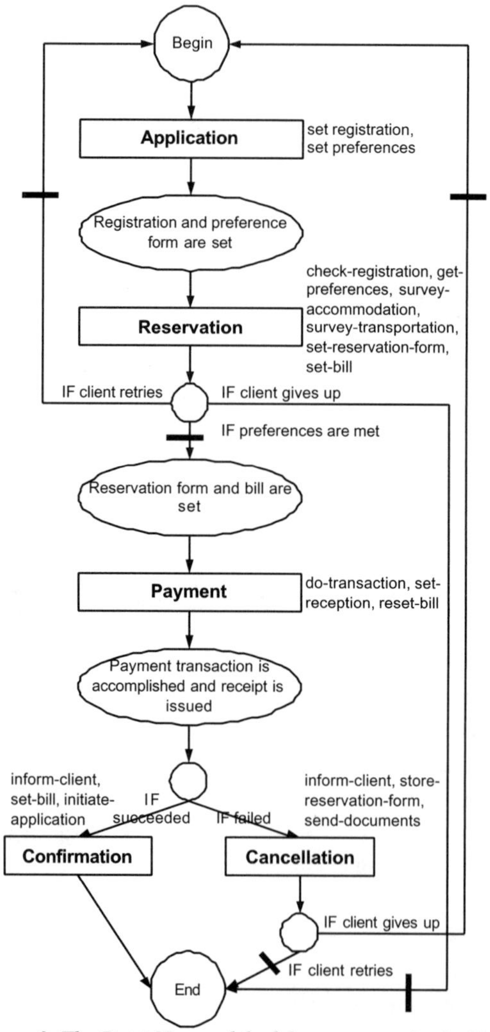

Figure 3. The Petri-Net model of the processes in the Travel Agency

5. THE RESULTING ANIMATED SIMULATION MODEL

Due to the limited scope of this paper we do not include the resulting animated simulation model into this paper. However, it can be asserted that the regarding simulation could help us in answering the following questions:

- Would it be better if the procedure began with the transportation and not the accommodation?
- Would it be better if the survey for the transportation ran parallel with the survey for the accommodation?
- Would it be better that the tasks of the desk clerk and the counter clerk was carried out by one person?
- Until which certain point is it reasonable to change the preferences?
- Which order is more efficient for changing the preferences?
- What other preferences can be taken into account?
- Would it be better to let (ask) the client (to) set different preferences for each item in advance?
- In case the client chooses for a new reservation after fail of his/her reservation, would it be better not to settle his/her payment until new reservation?

6. CONCLUSION

Constructing a business model based on the notion of BOs provides us with a (reasonable) straight way for the construction of Petri-Nets, which, in turn, form a good basis for the simulation process.

One of the advantages of the application of Petri-Nets for business systems is its compact representation of information in graphical and textual form. Also a Petri-Net model, like the one depicted in figure 3, can be easily simulated using Petri-Net simulation tools as well as discrete simulation tools. In the latter case, for example using Arena, Bewise, etc., the Petri-Net model can serve as an input data for developing an animated simulation model, as it contains all necessary information such as logical sequence of processes, causal and conditional links, synchronization and choice elements.

However, since the construction of Petri-Nets is directly related to the process BOs, this category of BOs plays an important role for this approach. Therefore, recognizing the right categories for BOs is of crucial importance, and mixing up the different categories of BOs can result in models that can not lead to the adequate Petri-Nets. As there are no strict lines for assigning a concept to a category, finding a way to alleviate this problem is a major subject of our future work.

As future research, authors will study how to make a proper interface between notions of BOs (consequently, its Petri net model) and the elements of Arena simulation tool. We consider that the Arena simulation tool can serve as one of appropriate tools for business process modeling, especially for building an animated simulation model.

REFERENCES

Aalst, W. van der, Finding Errors in the Design of a Workflow Process: A Petri-Net-based Approach, proceedings of the Workshop on Workflow Management: Net-based Concepts, Models, Techniques and Tools (WFM'98) within the 19th International Conference on Applications and Theory of Petri-Nets, Lisbon, Portugal, June 1998.

Abolhassani, M., Defining The Business Objects, proceedings of International Workshop on Information Integration and Web-based Application and Services (IIWAS'99), Yogyakarta, Indonesia, November 1999.

Agostini, A., Michelis, G. De, Simple Workflow Models, proceedings of the Workshop on Workflow Management: Net-based Concepts, Models, Techniques and Tools (WFM'98) within the 19th International Conference on Applications and Theory of Petri-Nets, Lisbon, Portugal, June 1998.

Edwards, J., 3-tier Client/Server At Work, John Wiley & Sons, Inc., 1997.

Fishwick, P., What is Simulation?, IEEE Potentials, February 1996.

Moelders, A., Wolf, M., Fengler, W., Object-Oriented and net-based modeling of business processes, proceedings of the Workshop on Workflow Management: Net-based Concepts, Models, Techniques and Tools (WFM'98) within the 19th International Conference on Applications and Theory of Petri-Nets, Lisbon, Portugal, June 1998.

Object Management Group (OMG), Glossary of Terms, Business Object Management Special Interest Group, OMG Document, 95-09-12.

About authors:

Mohammad Abolhassani, M.Sc.; Ph.D. candidate at the Delft University of Technology, Faculty of Information Technology and Systems; M.Sc. in Technical Informatics in 1997; B.Sc. in Computer Hardware in 1987; has worked/ works in Iran and the Netherlands.

Joseph Barjis, Ph.D.; Associate Academician of the International Informatization Academy; Chairman of the International Center of Information, headquartered in the Netherlands; Ph.D. in Information Systems in 1999; Ph.D. in Computer Science in 1996; M.Sc. in Computer Science in 1991; has worked/works in Russia, United Kingdom and the Netherlands.

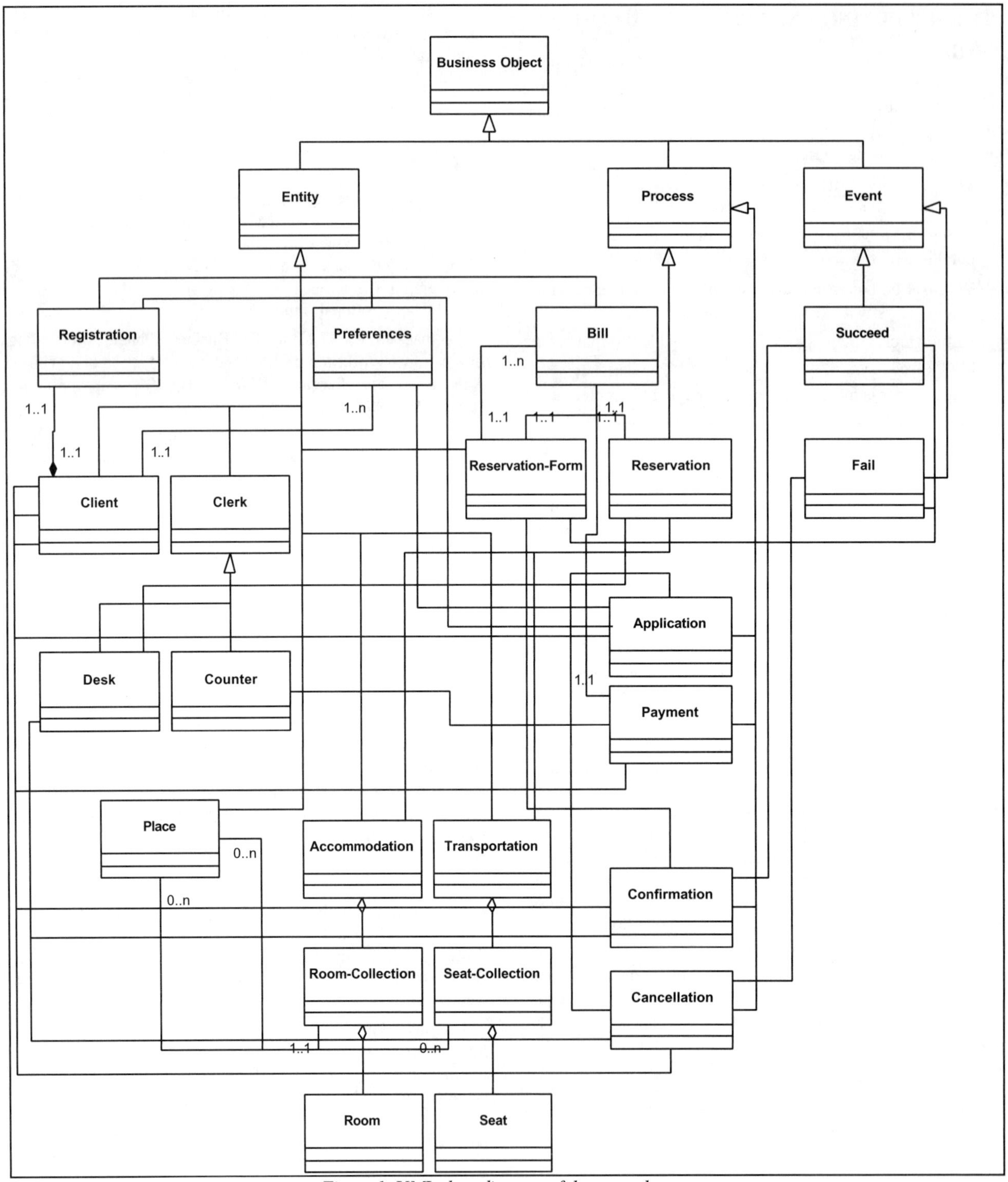

Figure 1. UML class diagram of the example case

AN APPROACH TO SIMULATING ICT MANAGEMENT PROCESSES

Ilian G. Ilkov
Department of Information Systems and Software Engineering, Delft University of Technology, P.O. Box 356, 2600 AJ Delft, The Netherlands. Tel.: +31 15 278 72 17, Fax: +31 15 278 66 32. E-mail: I.G.Ilkov@its.tudelft.nl

Prof. Dr. M. Looijen,
Department of Information Systems and Software Engineering, Delft University of Technology, P.O. Box 356, 2600 AJ Delft, The Netherlands. Tel.: +31 15 278 56 94, Fax: +31 15 278 66 32. E-mail: M.Looijen@its.tudelft.nl

ABSTRACT

In this paper an approach to simulating ICT management processes is described. The steps of the approach - the building of a conceptual model, a graphical representation and a simulation model of the processes under investigation - are presented. The way in which the conceptual model is obtained is discussed. The graphical representation based on this model and the three graphical models it consists of are described. The animated simulation model built on the basis of the models mentioned above and its functionality are presented. Finally, conclusions are made with regards to the use of the proposed approach, and directions for future research are outlined.

Keywords: Organisational simulation, conceptual framework, graphical process modelling, animated simulation modelling.

INTRODUCTION

The increasing dependency of contemporary organisations on Information Communication Technology (ICT) has lead to a rapid, and often uncontrollable, growth of technical infrastructure and applications in the last several decades. This in its turn has lead to an unstructured, and often even chaotic, approach to the management of ICT. The results of this are the growing ICT budgets, lack of qualified people and poor effectiveness and efficiency of the utilisation of ICT, which can be seen in many organisations nowadays. One of the ways to cope with this situation is to introduce more structured and process-oriented approaches to managing ICT. Therefore, a lot of efforts and resources are devoted to the reengineering of the current ICT management processes. Different techniques are used to support this reengineering. Animated simulation is one of these techniques. It has been used only recently in the field of business process reengineering, but has nevertheless shown promising results. However, simulation projects in this area have been plagued by the use of arbitrary approaches, poor structuring and low reusability of previously achieved results. The poor use of established techniques such as business process flowcharting and modelling together with simulation has also contributed to these problems. Therefore, a research project on using simulation for the reengineering of ICT management processes has been started at the department of Information Systems and Software Engineering of the Faculty Information Technology and Systems at the Delft University of Technology, The Netherlands. Among the goals of the project are to investigate the benefits which simulation offers for the modelling and reengineering of ICT management processes, to identify outstanding issues and problems in the field, and to propose a consistent framework for the investigation, modelling and simulation of such processes.

In this paper some intermediate results of this project are presented. These results are in the form of an approach to the simulation of ICT management processes. The aim of the approach is to propose a framework, within which the simulation projects can be carried out in an effective and efficient manner, and to provide a basis for better reusability of the results of previous simulation projects in the field.

The approach consists of three main steps: building a conceptual model of the processes under investigation, building a graphical representation of the processes, and building a simulation model of the processes. The conceptual model of the processes is built with the help of a conceptual framework for ICT management simulation, defined at an earlier stage of the research project. This model is used to build the graphical representation of the processes. This representation consists of three different models, namely the communication model, the process model and the workplace model. These models capture the communications and the information exchanged by the people participating in a certain process, the tasks of which the process consists and the sequence in which they have to be carried out, and the individual algorithms of work, which the people involved in the process follow. In this way, the graphical representation offers a good basis for initial modelling of the processes under investigation, as well as for depicting some process-related data and static characteristics, such as task executor, logical flow of information within the process and rules directing this flow. It is also a good means of communicating intermediate findings in a simulation project to the interested parties and for removing errors at an early stage. On the basis of the graphical representation, an animated simulation model of the processes under investigation is built. In this model, a time dimension is added to the static characteristics captured by the graphical model, and stochastic data are used to run the model. Animation is used to visualise and communicate the functioning of the model, and to monitor interactively some of the most important model parameters in the course of the simulation run. At the end of the run a thorough analysis of the simulation results is carried out. Potential bottlenecks and/or leverage points are identified. Different scenarios are tested with the model and an estimation of the obtained model parameters is made. Finally, suggestions for improvement are made on the basis of the simulation results to the involved parties.

Throughout this paper some results from a case study, done by one of the authors are used to illustrate the steps of the approach. The case study was carried out at the Production Monitoring (PM) department of the computer centre of a large Dutch organisation. The main function of this department is to monitor the technical infrastructure and applications used by the organisation, and to ensure the resolution of incidents and problems related to them within the predefined time and quality constraints. Several different activities are carried out in the department as part of this function. First, monitoring of the technical infrastructure and applications is carried out on a round-the-clock basis and actions are taken in case incidents and/or problems arise. These actions vary from applying standard solutions to making trouble tickets to initiating emergency procedures. Second, the quality of the resolution of problems initiated at the department is checked, and in case it is not satisfactory further resolution is demanded or escalation procedures are used. Third, some operation tasks related to PC operation and tape manipulation and backups are carried out. Finally, management activities are also carried out in the department in order to ensure that it is functioning according to the predefined cost and quality constraints.

As mentioned above, information about the organisational structure, process workflow and individual algorithms of work in the department is used in this paper. However, as the discussion is focused mainly on the steps of the approach, statistical data such as frequencies of occurrence, processing times and service times are omitted.

The structure of the paper is as follows. The discussion begins with a description of the first step of the approach, i.e., the building of the conceptual model. After that the way in which this model is used to obtain a graphical representation is explained and the three models used in that representation are discussed. A description of the way in which these models are used to build a simulation model follows. Finally, conclusions are made with regards to the use of the proposed approach and directions for future research are presented.

STEP 1: BUILDING THE CONCEPTUAL MODEL

The first step of the approach consists of building a conceptual model of the processes under investigation. This model is built with the help of a conceptual framework defined earlier in the project. The aim of the framework is to provide a consistent basis for initial modelling of the problem domain and the subsequent graphical representation and simulation of the processes under investigation. It can also improve the comparability and reusability of results from different simulation projects, thus increasing the effectiveness and efficiency of the modelling process.

The framework contains the following basic concepts:

- *Task* – a piece of work carried out by a person in the organisation. A distinction is made between simple tasks and complex tasks. Complex tasks consist of subtasks and rules for carrying them out. Simple tasks consist of a single action, which transforms the input into the desired output. Tasks are used as the building blocks for defining organisational structure, on the one hand, and processes and procedures, on the other.

- *Information object* – a piece of information exchanged among the people involved in the simulated processes. It can be in the form of a report, message, e-mail, phone call, etc.
- *Equipment* – the collection of hardware, software and communication facilities, which enable the employees of an (ICT) organisation to perform their tasks.
- *Procedure* – an ordered set of tasks carried out by one or more persons in the organisation.
- *Workplace* – a place in the organisation characterised by its position in the organisational structure, the tasks carried out there, and the equipment necessary for the successful fulfilment of these tasks.
- *ICT worker* – a person working at a specific workplace in the organisation. This is an auxiliary concept, which helps to model situations where several people carry out identical tasks, i.e., work at one and the same workplace.

For a more detailed description of the conceptual framework refer to (Ilkov, 1998).

In line with the example situation described in the previous section, we can describe the PM department as consisting of the following workplaces: Monitoring, Service Control, Operation and PM Manager. The people, working at these workplaces exchange the following information objects in the course of their work: Message (M), Trouble Ticket (TT), Problem Report (PR), Information Request (IR), etc. There are 1 or 2 ICT workers working at the Monitoring workplace, depending on the workload. The tasks carried out at this workplace are: Check Events, Make TTs, Apply Standard Solutions, Report Problems, Close Events. The equipment used at this workplace is a PC, connected to the Novell network of the organisation, an X-windows terminal, connected to the UNIX-based management server, and a telephone.

In this way, the process of building a conceptual model consists of describing all the workplaces in the department, the tasks, carried out at these workplaces, the equipment used, etc. This continues until a full description of the department in terms of the concepts described above and the relations among them is achieved. Some statistical data like duration of tasks, processing times and frequency of occurrence of some objects, can also be incorporated in the description. This description is the conceptual model, which is used in the next steps to obtain a graphical representation and a simulation model of the processes under investigation.

STEP 2: BUILDING THE GRAPHICAL REPRESENTATION

The second step of the simulation approach is the building of a graphical representation of the processes under investigation. This representation is a very good way of structuring the information obtained at the previous step, and contributes to improving the effectiveness and efficiency of the subsequent simulation model building process. As mentioned earlier, the graphical representation is a good means of communicating intermediate simulation results to the involved parties and can be very useful for discovering and removing errors at an early stage of the simulation project. It can be also used in the process of verification and validation of the simulation models.

The graphical representation consists of three different models, namely, the communication, the process and the workplace models. These models reflect different aspects of the processes under investigation and help for incorporating those aspects into the final animated simulation model. A more detailed description of the models follows.

The Communication Model

This model reflects the structure and the internal communications of the organisation (department) under investigation, as well as the information exchanged between this organisation and its environment. It consists of the workplaces, involved in the processes under investigation, the tasks, carried out at these workplaces and the information objects exchanged among them. The model also includes the information objects exchanged with other departments, which are not in the focus of the current simulation project, but are taking part in the investigated processes. In this way, the model gives a good overview of the workplaces included in the final simulation model, the input objects to these workplaces and the output objects sent by them to other workplaces in the model.

The communication model for the PM department is depicted on figure 1. As it can be seen from the figure, it includes the workplaces in the department, mentioned in the previous section. For each workplace a list of the tasks carried out there is provided.

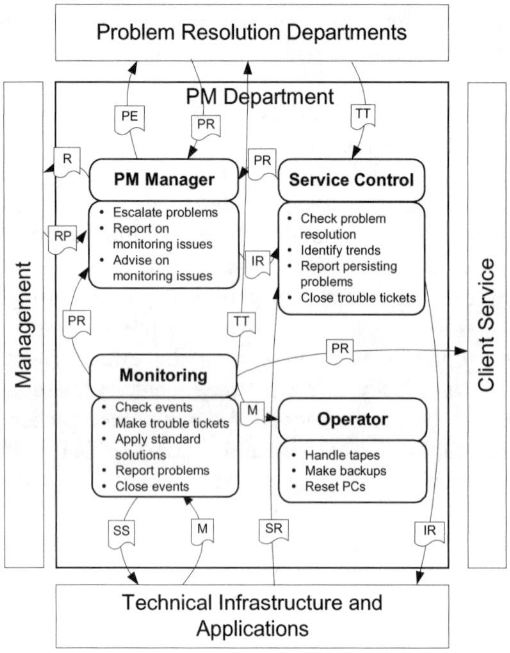

Figure 1: The Communication Model of the PM Department

The arrows connecting the workplaces with each other and with other parts of the organisation reflect the communications that take place, as well as the initiator and the recipient of each communication. Furthermore, information object icons are depicted on each of the arrows, indicating the exact information object exchanged during the communication. In this way, the communication model forms the basis for building the user view of the final simulation model, depicted on figure 4.

The Process Model

For each of the processes under investigation a process model is built. It provides information about the tasks, which the process consists of, the workplaces they are carried at, the order in which they are executed, and the conditions, which determine that order. Two symbols are used to represent the logic of the information flow in this model. The empty circle represents a choice (logical "OR"), in which one of the paths is taken depending on the value of the condition associated with the circle. A filled circle, on the other hand, represents a case when a certain output is sent to more than one task at the same time (logical "AND"). Icons, bounded by a dotted line represent workplaces or departments, which take place in the investigated process, but are not in the focus of the research. In case two tasks, belonging to different workplaces have to be carried out after each other, an information object icon is also added to indicate the kind of information exchanged. The letter "C" in the upper right corner of a task icon indicates that the task is complex, i.e., consists of subtasks. For each complex task a similar model can be build in order to capture the rules determining the order of execution of the subtasks. However, for simple processes these task models can be omitted, because the information they contain is also incorporated in the workplace models.

An illustration of the process model is provided on figure 2, where the model for the monitoring process carried out at the PM department is depicted. As it can be seen from the figure, the process begins with the arrival of a message indicating that a certain event has taken place.

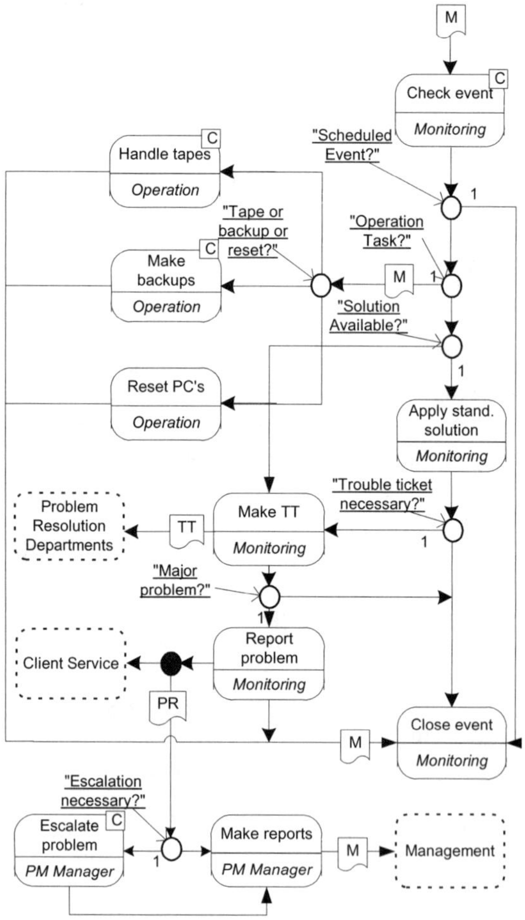

Figure 2: The Process Model of the PM Department

This event is checked at the Monitoring workplace. If it is a scheduled event, no further action is necessary and the message is simply sent to the archive, thus closing the event. If the event represents an operation task that has to be carried out, the message is sent to the Operator workplace, where the necessary action is taken. After that the event is closed by the Monitoring workplace. If neither of the first two cases is true, the event indicates an incident, and action has to be taken for its resolution. First of all, a check is made about whether a standard solution for exists for the incident. If such a solution does not exist, a TT is made and sent to the proper department. If a solution exists, it is applied. In case of a major problem, it is necessary to make a TT although a standard solution has already been applied. In such cases it is necessary sometimes to use also emergency procedures. A problem report is then sent from the Monitoring workplace to the PM manager and the Client Service, which take care of the further supervision of the problem resolution. After taking these actions the event is closed by sending the message to archive.

The process model is a good means of capturing the logic, which determines the flow of information (objects) in the organisation. Therefore it is used for defining the logical flow of entities among the workplaces represented in the simulation model.

The Workplace Model

For each of the workplaces in the organisation under investigation a workplace model is built. This model represents the activities carried out at the workplace and the conditions, which determine their execution. These activities can be tasks or subtasks. In case an activity is a subtask, the name of the task (in italic) to which it belongs is added to the icon representing the activity. This model also represents the interactions with the equipment necessary to carry out the activities.

The workplace model for the Monitoring workplace is depicted on fig. 3. As can be seen from the figure, the person working at this workplace waits until an event occurs. In case several events occur at the same time the one with the highest priority is chosen. The message, representing the event is then locked, using the X-windows terminal connected to the UNIX server. The next action that is taken is to check the Production Monitoring Agenda, a special distributed database available on the PC, which contains information about scheduled activities.

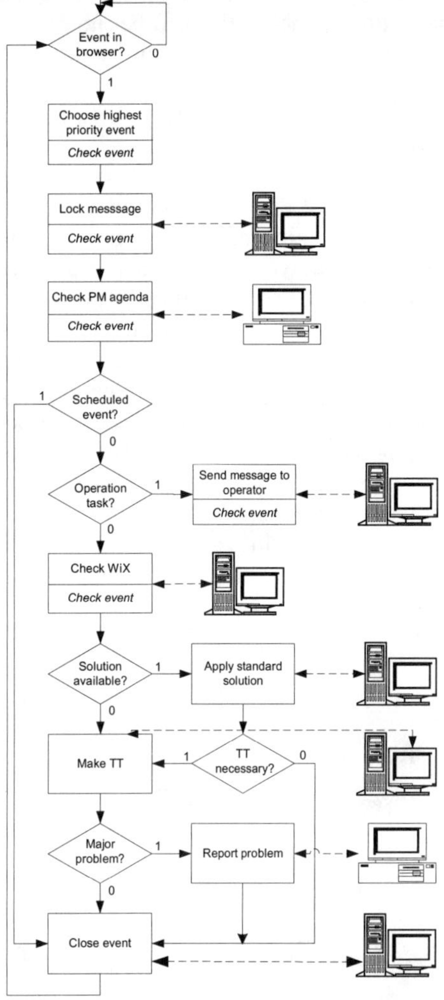

Figure 3: The Monitoring Workplace Model

If the activity is not scheduled a check is performed to see if it is an operation task. If that is not the case, a database called WiX, available on the UNIX server, is checked to see if a standard solution for the incident exists. If yes, the solution is applied using the X-windows terminal to access the management server. After that a check is made about whether a TT is necessary. If yes, the TT is created and sent to the proper department using a special trouble-ticket system available on the UNIX server. If the event indicates a major problem, a problem report is sent via the PC to the PM Manager and the Client Service, which take actions to limit the impact of the problem and ensure its further resolution.

The workplace model is very useful for building the logic in the simulation model, which controls the behaviour of the objects, representing the workplaces in the organisation. Due to the fact that it is very well structured and uses only basic flowcharting symbols, it can be implemented almost directly into the simulation model.

STEP 3: BUILDING THE SIMULATION MODEL

The final step of the simulation approach is the building of the animated simulation model of the processes under investigation. This model is built based on the models obtained at the previous two steps of the approach. These models provide almost all of the information necessary to build the structure and logic of the simulation model. However, stochastic data about occurrence of events, processing times, etc., also need to be incorporated in the model in order to obtain a quantitative estimation of the dynamic characteristics of the modelled organisation. Performance parameters, which help to model and determine these characteristics are also included.

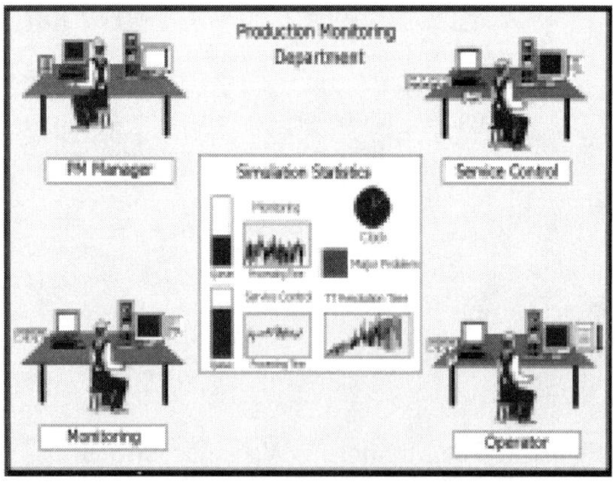

Figure 4: The Simulation Model of the PM Department

The (user view of the) simulation model built for the PM department is depicted on figure 4. The model visualises the workplaces in the department, the equipment used at these workplaces and the information objects processed and exchanged among them. Some important simulation statistics are also included in the user view, which allows for their interactive monitoring throughout the simulation run. These statistics include the number of information objects waiting for processing in the queues of the Monitoring and Service Control, the time it takes to process them, and the resolution time for the TTs created in the department. An alarm (warning light) is also included, which goes off if a major problem occurs, thus giving the users of the simulation model the possibility to follow more carefully the actions taken in such a case.

This simulation model can be used to assess the characteristics of the organisational structure and the implemented processes at the department, and to provide an estimation of the impact, which proposed changes might have on these characteristics.

FINAL REMARKS

In this paper an approach to simulating ICT management processes was presented. The steps of the approach were explained. The models that are built at each step, their interdependencies and the benefits they offer were described.

The approach offers a consistent framework for building ICT simulation models. Possible advantages of the use of the approach are better structuring of the research process, reducing the possibility of omitting an important aspect or characteristic in the final simulation model, and promoting the reusability of results obtained in different simulation projects. As a result of this, the effectiveness and efficiency of the process of model development can be improved.

Directions for future research on the topic will include the increasing and improving of the set of symbols used for the graphical representation in order to achieve greater flexibility and ease of use. Another step in this direction will be the development of a library of object classes, which will support and facilitate the implementation of the steps of the approach, and the building of the final simulation model.

REFERENCES

Harrell, Charles R. and Kevin C. Field, 1996. Integrating Process Mapping and Simulation, Proceedings of the Winter Simulation Conference, Coronado, California, 8-11 December, pp. 1292-1296.

Ilkov, I. G. and M. Looijen, A Library of Object Classes for ICT Management Simulation, in: Proceedings of the 13th International Conference on Systems for Automation of Engineering and Research, Varna, September 1999.

Kettinger, William J., James T. C. Teng and Subashish Guha, 1997. Business Process Change: A Study of Methodologies, Techniques and Tools, in MIS Quarterly, March, pp. 55-80.

Looijen, M., Information Systems Management, Control and Maintenance, 4th ed., Kluwer Bedrijfsinformatie, Deventer, 1999, (in Dutch).

INTEGRATING BUSINESS PROCESS MODELING AND SIMULATION

Joseph Barjis

Department of Information Systems, Delft University of Technology, P.O. Box 356, 2600 AJ Delft, The Netherlands. Tel: +31-15–2785827, Fax: +31-15–2786632; e-mail: J.Barjis@is.twi.tudelft.nl; http://is.twi.tudelft.nl/~barjis

Ilian G. Ilkov

Department of Information Systems Management, Delft University of Technology, P.O. Box 356, 2600 AJ Delft, The Netherlands. Tel: +31-15–2787217, Fax: +31-15–2786632. E-mail: ilkov@duticai.twi.tudelft.nl

KEY WORDS: *Business Process Reengineering, Business Process Simulation; Business Process Modeling, DEMO*

ABSTRACT

Business Process Modeling (BPM) and simulation are extensively used to facilitate Business Process Reengineering (BPR). Although these two techniques have very much in common and complement each other, they are often used separately, thus preventing business process modelers from fully utilizing their capabilities. In this paper the benefits, stemming from combining the DEMO (Dynamic Essential Modeling of Organization) business process modeling methodology with simulation are discussed. The discussion begins with a brief overview of the DEMO methodology and its capabilities. Then, the types of models, which DEMO uses to capture different aspects of business processes, are described by means of a library case example. These models are then used as a basis for building an animated simulation model of the library case in the ARENA™ simulation environment. The functionality of the simulation model and the benefits it offers are described. Finally, some problems in combining DEMO and simulation, and directions for future research are discussed.

1. INTRODUCTION

It is a well-known fact that the contemporary world of business is becoming increasingly dynamic and competitive. As a result of this, timely, effective and efficient change has become a critical success (and in many cases – survival) factor for many firms and organizations throughout the world. This has lead to a growth in business process reengineering consulting services, and consequently - to a proliferation of methods for conducting BPR (Kettinger, Teng and Guha, 1997). These methods include different approaches for business process modeling, and recently, animated simulation. However, BPM and simulation have been used rather independently from each other, which has prevented modelers from achieving all of the benefits, offered by these methods. In particular, BPM approaches often lack facilities for incorporating stochastic data into, and determining the dynamic characteristics of the modeled processes, e.g., waiting times, processing times, individual tasks and workloads. Simulation, on the other hand, often suffers from using unstructured process mapping approaches, and as a result simulation models are often built from scratch (Harrell and Field, 1996) and fail to capture important aspects and interdependencies of the processes.

In this paper an attempt is made to explore the benefits from combining the DEMO business process modeling methodology with animated simulation. The purpose of this is to enhance the functionality, offered by DEMO, and to increase the effectiveness and quality of the overall modeling process.

The paper is part of an ongoing research project on the simulation of ICT management processes, carried out at the Department of Information Systems and Software Engineering of the Faculty of Information Technology and Systems, Delft University of Technology, The Netherlands. The project is part of an overall research program carried out at the department, which encompasses the exploration, conceptualization and modeling of different aspects of ICT management (Looijen, 1998). Among the goals of the research project is to propose a consistent framework for the modeling and simulation of processes, carried out in the daily Management, Control and Maintenance (MCM) of Information Systems (Looijen, 1999). Some intermediate results of this project include a conceptual framework and a library of object classes for the simulation of ICT management processes (Ilkov and Looijen, 1999). However, there is still a need for a process modeling approach, which can help to translate the conceptual model of an ICT management simulation process into an animated simulation model. This problem is addressed in this paper.

The DEMO is a cross-disciplinary theory, rooted in the Language/Action Perspective (Dietz, 1999; Dignum and Dietz, 1997), for describing and explaining the operation of organizations, as well as a (re)engineering method based on this theory. The basis for the analysis of an organization with DEMO is the communication between the members of the organization (and between them and subjects in the environment). The elementary piece of communication is called the communicative action. The DEMO methodology contains several model types, each expressed in a specific diagram, that collectively provide the necessary knowledge for information systems development and business process redesign. The core concept is the notion of the essential (business) transaction. It is the 'atomic' building block of 'molecular' structures called business processes. By means of the DEMO models it is possible to achieve a solid understanding of the types of transactions that take place in an organization, the participants involved in these transactions, the information that is needed and created while carrying through the transactions, and the relationships between the different transaction types. The DEMO methodology comprises five types of models: the Interaction Model, the Business Process Model (BPM), the Action Model, the Interstriction Model and The Fact Model. In this paper the emphasis is laid on the first three models of the DEMO. Although the five models of the DEMO together describe the complete essential model of an organization, however one of the things that is still lacking in DEMO, is a facility to analyze and simulate the business processes, as modeled by the BPM of DEMO.

In order to overcome this, the models, obtained in DEMO, are used as a basis for building an animated simulation model of the business processes. The model is built in ARENA™ - a general – purpose, visual animated simulation environment, based on the SIMAN simulation language. ARENA™ has strong simulation and animation capabilities, as well as advanced facilities for data analysis and presentation. Recent versions include also tools for automatic generation of simulation models on the basis of process flowcharts. This makes ARENA™ suitable for modeling, visualizing and analyzing business processes.

The outline of the paper is as follows. In section 2 we provide a brief overview of organizational modeling using DEMO. In sections 3, 4 and 5 we describe the different models in DEMO – the interaction, the business process and the action models. In section 6 we describe the way in which these models can be enhanced and extended by building an animated simulation model of the processes under investigation. Finally, in section 7 some conclusions are drawn with regards to the benefits of using DEMO with simulation, and some problems and directions for future work are discussed.

2. ORGANIZATIONAL MODELING WITH DEMO

The DEMO methodology is built on a new and effective way of thinking about organizations. This new way of thinking has got the name 'OER-paradigm' ('OER' is a Dutch word meaning primal, original and essential). It fits in the so-called Language/Action Perspective (cf. Dignum and Dietz, 1997; Goldkuhl et al., 1998). Contrary to the prevailing notion that communication is exchanging sentences, expressing some proposition with regard to some world, the Language/Action Perspective assumes that communication is a kind of action in that it creates commitments between the communicating parties. To communicate then is to perform language acts or communicative acts. The OER-paradigm, and accordingly DEMO, differs from other approaches in that it offers two useful additions. The first is the distinction between the essence of a business process and its realization. Otherwise said, while modeling business processes, we abstract fully from all information aspects (including calculations) and from all personnel aspects (including organizational/functional hierarchy). The second addition is that we conceive every business process to be some specific molecular structure of the 'atoms' having the same generic form. These atoms are called OER-transactions or business transactions. Some relevant papers/books are (Dietz, 1999, Dignum and Dietz, 1997).

An organization is conceived as a (discrete dynamic) system, of which the elements are social individuals or *subjects*, each of them having the *authority* to perform particular (*objective*) *actions* and a corresponding *responsibility* to do that in an appropriate and accountable way. For the coordination of their actions, the subjects enter into and comply with *commitments* towards each other. The changes that are brought about as the result of the actions of the subjects are discrete. This means that they are considered to take place instantaneously, and that there is a finite number of changes within a certain period. We thus classify organizations, in their essence, as social systems, where human beings play the role of social actor, distinct from their role as rational actor (i.e. knowing, communicating thoughts, and reasoning). Commitments are the effect of intersubjective actions, like requesting, promising, stating and accepting. The collective word for the intersubjective actions that actors perform in order to coordinate their (objective) actions is *'interaction'*. Objective actions and the related intersubjective actions appear to occur in a particular pattern, called the business transaction or *transaction* for short (cf. figure 1).

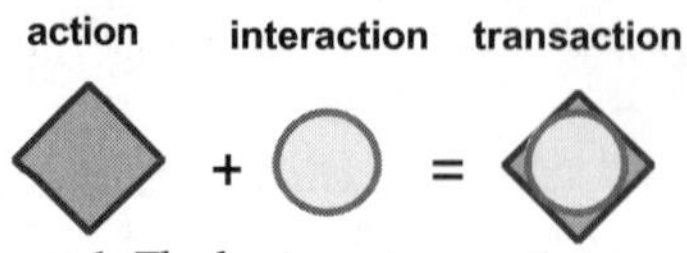

Figure 1. The business transaction concept

A transaction is carried through by two actors, in a close cooperation. The generic pattern of a transaction is depicted in figure 2. The one who starts the transaction and eventually completes it, is called the customer or *initiator*, the other one, who actually performs the objective action, is called the supplier or *executor*. A transaction consists of three phases: the order phase or O-phase, the execution phase or E-phase, and the result phase or R-phase.

The order phase (O) is an interaction between the initiator and the executor that starts with the request of the initiator and ends with the promise by the executor. It is aimed at reaching agreement about some result in the object world to be achieved. For example, the assembler of a bicycle asks an assistant to mount a saddle and the assistant agrees to do that. The execution phase (E) starts with the promise and ends with the statement by the executor that the objective action, leading to the agreed upon result, is executed. This phase is performed by the executor solely. Example: the assistant mounts the saddle. The result phase (R) is again an interaction between the two actors that starts with the statement and ends with the acceptance by the initiator of the result. It is aimed at reaching mutual agreement about the established result. The result is the establishment of a fact in the object world. Example: the assistant states towards the assembler that the saddle is mounted, and the assembler accepts this.

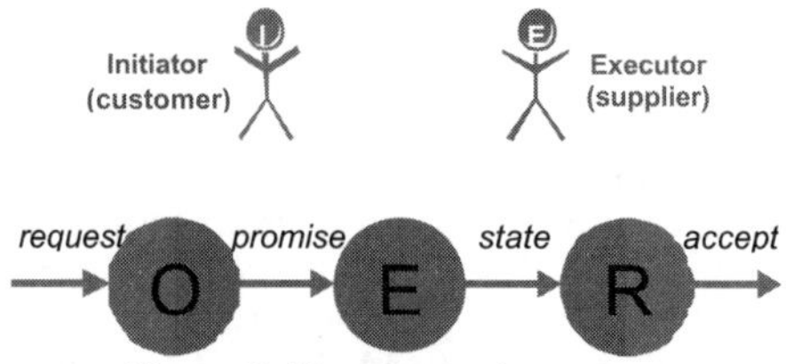

Figure 2. The transaction pattern

At the moment of acceptance by the initiator, the result fact in the object world is said to come into existence, not at the moment of finishing the objective action. This principal position is important. On the one hand it stresses the supremacy of events in the intersubject world. On the other hand it allows material and immaterial objective acts (and resulting facts) to be dealt with in the same manner. For immaterial facts it is obvious that they cannot be said to exist unless they are stated and subsequently accepted, and thus that they come into existence at the moment of acceptance. Although at first sight, and intuitively, material facts seem to come into existence after having finished the objective action, this appears not to be the case on closer observation. In every organization with material objective actions (like manufacturing or transporting firms), there appears always to be someone who is held responsible for a particular material fact being the case. Only he or she has the authority to declare that something is the case, which then causes an event in the intersubject world.

During each of the phases of a transaction, new transactions may be initiated, the result of which is needed to proceed with the original one. In this way transactions are chained into arbitrarily large structures, called *business processes*.

3. DEMO INTERACTION MODEL

The first model that is constructed in the DEMO analysis of an organization is the Interaction Model. The Interaction Model is a 'timeless' representation of the transactional structure of an organization. By term timeless we mean that the Interaction Model does not show the order in which the business transactions in an organization take place.

3.1 The Interaction Model

The focus of the Interaction Model is on the specification of (1) the types of business transactions that take place between the organization under investigation and its environment as well as in the organization, and (2) the initiating and executing actors of these identified transaction types. This specification of the transactional structure is, of course, performed parallel to the determination of the system boundary.

3.2 The interaction diagram

The interaction diagram is the graphical representation that is used for representing the DEMO Interaction Model. It provides symbols for all the aspects of the system that are identified in the Interaction Model. This means that transaction types, initiating and executing actors as well as the system boundary are included in the representation.

The most important element in the interaction diagram is the transaction type symbol. The transaction type symbol is a combined symbol of a disk and a diamond based on the basic structure of the business transaction.

In order to illustrate this and other models and methods discussed in this chapter, a small library example will be studied as illustration of application of these methods (the library case example originated by Dietz).

3.3 The library case description

In the public library of Delft town is a counter for returning books (the in-counter) and a counter for lending books (the out-counter). The in counter is occupied by Sanne and the out-counter by Tim. In addition, there is an information counter, occupied by Lisa. At this counter one can also be registered as member of the library. After having paid in cash, one receives a membership card with a bar code containing the membership number. If one wants to borrow a book, one has to take (a copy of) the book from the shelve. If one cannot find a book, one can go to Lisa for help. She has a computer on her desk that contains the complete library catalogue, sorted in several ways (on author, on subject and on title). If the book one wants to lend is found, one takes it to the out-counter. Tim will then scan the bar code on the membership card, as well as the code on the book. The book is now lent to the member. The lending period is three weeks. When one returns a book, one goes to the in-counter and hands the book to Sanne. She scans the book code and enters into her computer that the book is returned. On the screen she sees whether the lending period is exceeded, and in case it is, what is the fine to be paid. If so, the person who returns the book has to pay the fine. Then Sanne marks the book in her computer as returned.

3.4 The library interaction model

From the above concise description of the library services, the five transaction types that are listed in the table below, can be identified. For each of them a precise and unambiguous specification of the resulting fact type is provided. Thus, there are only five fact types in the object world that are relevant for modeling the operations of the library from the essential perspective.

transaction type	transaction result
T1 registration	F1 *membership/member M is registered*
T2 payment	F2 *membership M is paid*
T3 lending	F3 *loan L is started*
T4 returning	F4 *loan L is ended*
T5 fine_payment	F5 *the fine for loan L is paid*

Table 1. Transaction-result table

The next step is to identify the relevant actors and to determine their roles as initiator and executor of the transaction types. Once this is done, all interaction relationships are determined. These are drawn as exhibited in figure 3. Transaction types are represented by a symbol consisting of a disk with a diamond behind it. The disk represents the 'intersubject world part' of the transaction, the diamond represents the 'object world part'. Therefore, the disk can also be considered as a bank that contains the intersubject world states, and a diamond can be considered as a bank that contains the object world facts that are created as the result of successfully completed transactions. Boxes represent actors. A white box represents an elementary actor, i.e. an actor that is executor of precisely one transaction type, and a gray box represents a composite actor, also called system kernel. A transaction type is connected to its initiator by a plain line and to its executor by a line with a 'open' arrow point. The system boundary is represented by a gray round angle. The diagram exhibits e.g. that actor A1 is the executor of transaction type T1 and that (an elementary actor in) the system kernel S1 is its initiator. The converse holds for transaction type T2. There are only two elementary actors in the

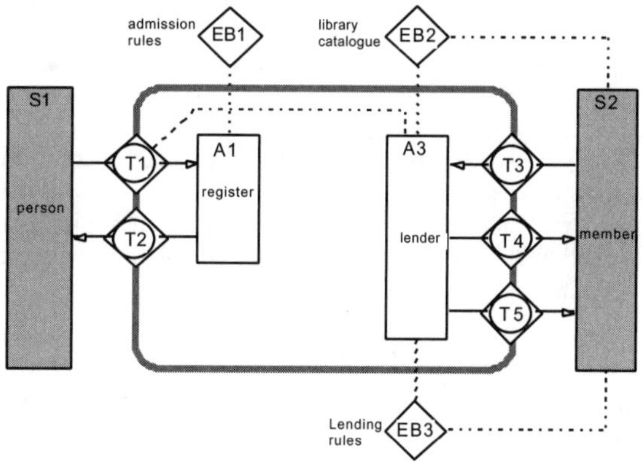

Figure 3: Interaction and interstriction model of the library

kernel of the system under consideration: A1 and A3. The role of Figure 3. Interaction and interstriction model of the library

A1 is actually played by Lisa. The role of A3 is partly played by Jim (complete executor role of T3 and initiator role in the O-phase of T4) and partly by Conny (initiator role in the R-phase of T4 and complete initiator role of T5).

Figure 3 also exhibits the interstriction relationships. For example, it shows that actor A3, the lender, has to have knowledge of transactions of type T1, the registrations. This is represented by the dotted line from the symbol of T1 to the symbol of A3. Furthermore, knowledge is needed from three external banks: EB1, containing the admission rules, EB2, containing the library catalogue, and EB3, containing the lending rules (like e.g. the lending period). It is also shown that the members (S2) are able to access EB2 and EB3.

4. DEMO BUSINESS PROCESS MODEL

The second model, after the Interaction Model, that is constructed in the DEMO analysis of an organization is the Business Process Model. The business process model shows all identified (essential) transaction types, as well as the causal and conditional relationships between them.

4.1 The Business Process Model

The business process model aims at providing a full specification of the causal and conditional relationships between business transactions. We speak of a *causal* relationship between two business transactions if one transaction causes the start of the other transaction. A causal relationship can be optional. This means that the start of a new business transaction is dependent on some condition. A *conditional* relationship between business transactions is defined as that the completion of one transaction forms the condition for the initiation or the completion of another transaction. Like the optional causal relationship a conditional relationship can also be optional.

4.2 The business process diagram

The business process diagram is the graphical representation that is used to represent the DEMO Business Process Model. It represents the Business Process Model either in a full or in a compact notation. In full notation all individual transaction phases are drawn while in the compact notation transaction phases are compressed into one symbol as much as possible. This business transaction symbol in the business process diagram is a disc with a bold line identified with the transaction number.

The three constituting transaction phases may be compressed into one business transaction symbol:

1. If there are no business transactions initiated during the transaction phases and;
2. If the completion of the Order-phase or Execution-phase are not conditions for initiation or the completion of other business transaction phases.

4.3 The library process model

The diagram of figure 3 does not show how the identified transaction types are put together to form the business process(es). To this end, another kind of diagram is developed, as shown in figure 4. It contains only the 'intersubject world part' of the transaction types, which are mostly split up into the three phases O, E and R, interconnected by plain lines. Small disks represent the initiation points of transactions. They are connected by plain lines with arrowhead to the initiated transaction types. These arrows thus represent the *causal* links between transaction types. For example, the upper part of figure 4 exhibits the structure of the first business process, which consists of transaction types T1 and T2. T1 is initiated externally (represented by the single small disk). T2 is initiated during the execution phase of T1. To represent this, the disk of phase E of T1 is stretched out in order to contain the initiation disk for T2. The dotted lines with arrowheads represent *conditional* links. For example, the dotted arrow from T2 to T1/E indicates that T2 has to be completed before T1/E can be completed. This reflects the fact that one becomes member after having paid the membership fee.

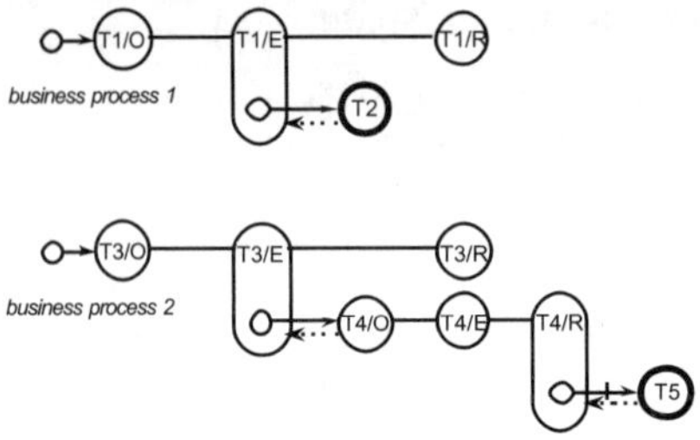

Figure 4. The (business) process structure of the library

The lower part of figure 4 exhibits the second process, consisting of transaction types T3, T4 and T5. This part contains a new symbol, namely the bar across the causal link of T5. This bar represents optionality. Otherwise said, during the result phase of T4 a T5 may be initiated, but not necessarily. In this way it is modeled that sometimes a fine has to be paid (T5) when returning a book (T4/R). If there is a T5, then the successful completion of it is a condition for completing T4.

5. ACTION MODEL

In this subsection we introduce the Action Model (AM) of DEMO and, its graphical representation, the Action Diagram (AD). The starting point for constructing the AM of a business system are its BPM and transaction process model of all transactions involved. As we can see from figure 2, a single business transaction consists of five actions, namely *request*, *promise*, *execute*, *state* and *accept*. These five actions in the AD are graphically represented as three separate boxes (see figure 5a). Since the *request* is logically followed by the *promise* and the accept follows after the *state*, they are represented as two action instead of four. Therefore, an entire business transaction is represented as three actions (request, execute, accept) and graphically as three boxes. Such a redundancy is made in order to make the AM and its AD more compact and easy for understanding.

Action according to the DEMO is either a communicative action or an objective action. The later is marked by painting the action box gray. As shown in figure 5a,b the AD represents the Action Model in a full or a compact notation. In full notation all three mentioned actions are drawn (figure 5a), while in the compact notation these actions are compressed into one symbol as much as possible (figure 5b). This business transaction symbol in the AD is a box with a bold line identified with the transaction number and duration of its execution (activity).

The three constituting actions within a transaction may be compressed into one box with a bold line according to the same rules as in the case of the business process diagram (see figure 5b).

Each box of the AD represents an activity and, consequently, has a definite duration. For example, imagine that we represent a business transaction the *request* action of which lasts just one day, execution of this request lasts seven days and results will be *accepted* lets say in two days (see figure 5a). In the small field on the right side of the activity box we insert duration of each action. If we use compact notation of the transaction (an activity) we insert the overall duration of actions in this small box (e.g., 10 days).

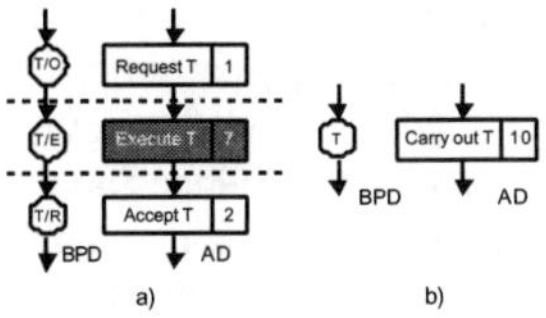

Figure 5: Representation of business transaction: a) in the notations of the BPD and AD; b) its compact representation

In addition to the described elements, the AD contains two more elements for representing rational (logical) actions with duration insufficient for modeling purposes. These two elements are *choice*, marked by C, and *exclusive-OR*. The element OR means that if any arc leading into it has been realized an arc emanating from it will be undertaken. Introduction of the last one (OR) is supposed to make the DEMO's action diagram as a standard flowchart, which can be analyzed with the common techniques for analyzing and simulating the behavior of discrete event systems (e.g., Petri nets). The choice element serves as probabilistic exit. It means that exactly one arc emanating from this element is undertaken if element is realized. The selection of the arc can be described, e.g., by means of a unique probability.

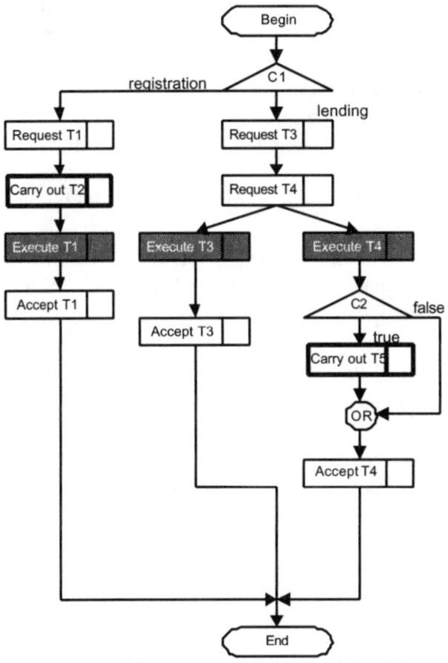

Figure 6: The action model of the library

For the best understanding syntax of the AD, it has to be noted that all boxes have AND-inputs and parallel outputs. It means that all arcs leading into a box must have been realized, in order to proceed and all arcs emanating from it will be undertaken in parallel once it is proceeded.

It should be noted that symbols in the BPD are timeless when symbols in the AD have certain duration. Also regarding choice conditions the BPD contain no information, when the AD contains complete information concerning choice conditions necessary for initiation (consequently execution) of optional transactions (see C1 and C2 in figure 6). Therefore, the AM is called most detailed and complete model of the DEMO models.

Figure 6 represents an action model of the library. For building this model, information represented in figures 4 and 5 is used.

6. THE SIMULATION MODEL

The three DEMO models described above help to capture the essence of the processes, carried out in an organization in terms of its transactional structure, the causal and conditional relationships of this structure, as well as the actions involved in the different transactions. These models, however, contain little information about how these transactions, and their accompanying actions can be distributed over the people, working in an organization, in order to form the structure of the reengineered organization, and what alternative solutions are available for this structure. Moreover, no information is available about the dynamic characteristics of a given organizational structure, thus leaving the modeler without an estimation of performance characteristics both on the individual level and of the reengineered organization as a whole.

In order to overcome this, an animated simulation model of the organization can be built. This model can be used for testing the dynamic behavior of the proposed organizational structure, for modeling business relationships among the people working in the organization, and for obtaining a detailed picture of individual workloads, processing times, organizational performance indicators, etc. Detailed data can be collected about the changes of these parameters over time. These data can then be analyzed and used to identify bottlenecks, adjust system parameters, and forecast system performance under a specific workload. This can serve as a basis for comparing alternative organizational structures and choosing the optimal one for a specific situation.

The simulation model can also be used for gaining deeper understanding of the processes carried out in the organization, for example by organizing brainstorming sessions with people involved in these processes, for resolving problems and generating ideas for improving the performance of the organization.

In order to illustrate the benefits of using animated simulation with DEMO, we will use a simulation model built for the example situation, described in the previous sections. The model is based on the DEMO models introduced above, and is built in the ARENA™ simulation environment. In particular, the business process model and the action model were very useful for building the simulation model, as the information they contained served as a basis for the simulation model logic. The interaction model, on the other hand, was useful for establishing the model functionality, relationships and boundaries on the conceptual level.

The (user view of the) simulation model for the library example is depicted in figure 7 (see at the end of the paper). As it can be seen from the figure, the three desks – In-, Out-, and Information – are modeled explicitly in the system. The same holds true for the system kernels S1 and S2, which are modeled by entities, representing people, coming to register, or members, coming to borrow or return books. The external databank, EB2, containing the library catalogue, is also included explicitly, as it plays an important role in the information-searching and borrowing processes. Some on-screen statistical indicators are also included, e.g., plots of the number of people waiting in each of the queues before the desks, and the time each of the workers is busy. The average service time in the library, as well as "control lights", indicating when a borrower is late and has to pay a fine, and when a book is found and a new member is registered, are also part of the indicators.

Although the model is based on an example situation and data used were arbitrarily chosen, it illustrates to a large extent the benefits of using simulation together with DEMO. Thus, next to the static analysis, we can obtain information about the dynamic characteristics of the system. These characteristics include the workload patterns for the different workers, the maximum and the average amount of time people have to wait before they can

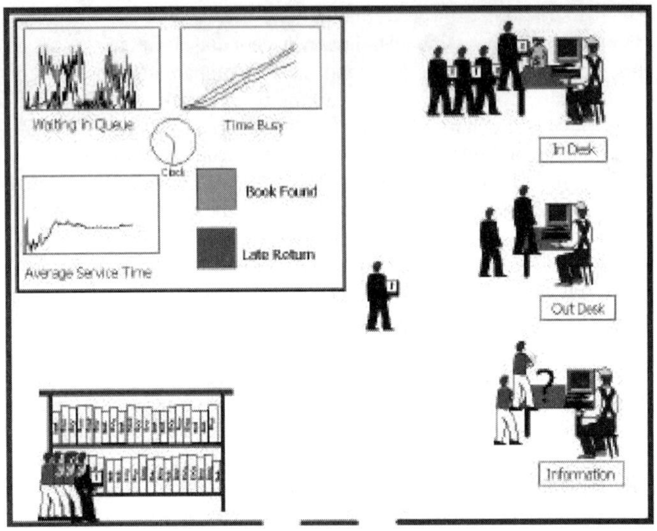

Figure 7: The simulation model of the library example

borrow or return a book, and the time it takes to obtain information and/or membership at the information desk. The animation also makes it possible to trace the movement of the people in the system as they proceed from one desk to the other.

On the basis of this information, conclusions can be drawn with regards to the utilization of organizational resources (people, hardware and software equipment, library inventory) and about the effectiveness and efficiency of the working procedures. Ideas about possible improvements can be generated and tested. Examples of such ideas could be redistribution of tasks, different working procedures, and implementation of new equipment. For our example case this could mean the joining of the functions of some of the desks into one desk with two workers, or the introduction of a faster library database. The feasibility of these ideas can then be tested with the simulation model, and forecasts about their effectiveness can be made.

7. FINAL REMARKS

In this paper an attempt to combine the DEMO business process modeling methodology with animated simulation was described. The DEMO methodology was introduced and it's underlying ideas and principles were explained. Three of the basic models used in DEMO were described by using a library case example, and their advantages and disadvantages were discussed. A simulation model based on the business process and action models was built for the library case example. The benefits this model adds to the DEMO methodology were discussed.

In the course of the work certain problems were also encountered. One of these problems was the collection of data about individual processing times and workloads, as well as data about the frequencies of arrival of members borrowing and returning books, and of new users asking for registration. These data are not part of the original DEMO methodology and need to be collected separately, which increases the development time and the organizational efforts, necessary to build the model. Another problem is that DEMO models contain very few guidelines about the way in which identified transactions (and the accompanying actions) can be distributed over the people, working in the organization. Therefore, additional efforts are necessary to define an initial organizational structure, on which a simulation model can be built. A third problem is that the form of the information, included in the business process and action models, is not suitable for direct use into a simulation model. Therefore, additional processing is necessary before it can be transformed in a ready-to-use form. These problems will be in the focus of the future research on the topic.

REFERENCES

ARENA User's Guide, Sewickley: Systems Modeling Co., 1996

Dietz, J.L.G., 1999. Understanding and modeling business processes with DEMO, in: Proc. ER'99, Annual International Conference on Conceptual Modeling, Paris, November.

Dietz, J.L.G., J.B.F. Mulder, 1998. Organizational transformation requires constructional knowledge of business systems, Proc. HICCS.

Dignum, F., J.L.G. Dietz, 1997. Proceedings of the Second International Workshop on Communication Modeling, Computing Science Reports, Eindhoven University of Technology.

Goldkuhl, G.; Lind, M.; Seigerroth, U., 1998. The Language Action Perspective on Communication Modeling, Proceedings of the Third International Workshop, Dept. Informatics, Jönköping International Business School, Sweden.

Harrell, Charles R. and Kevin C. Field, 1996. Integrating Process Mapping and Simulation, Proceedings of the Winter Simulation Conference, Coronado, California, 8-11 December, pp. 1292-1296.

Ilkov, I. G. and M. Looijen, A Library of Object Classes for ICT Management Simulation, in: Proceedings of the 13th International Conference on Systems for Automation of Engineering and Research, Varna, September 1999.

Kettinger, William J., James T. C. Teng and Subashish Guha, 1997. Business Process Change: A Study of Methodologies, Techniques and Tools, in MIS Quarterly, March, pp. 55-80.

Looijen, M., Conceptualization of IT Management as Integral Part of IT Research Projects, in: Proceedings of the 12th International Conference on Systems for Automation of Engineering and Research, Varna, September 1998.

Looijen, M., Information Systems Management, Control and Maintenance, 4th ed., Kluwer Bedrijfsinformatie, Deventer, 1999, (in Dutch).

A SIMULATION METHODOLOGY FOR INVESTIGATING BUSINESS PROCESSES IN SMALL COMPANIES

Joseph Barjis

Department of Information Systems, Delft University of Technology, P.O. Box 356, 2600 AJ Delft, The Netherlands. Tel: +31-15–2785827, Fax: +31-15–2786632; e-mail: J.Barjis@is.twi.tudelft.nl; http://is.twi.tudelft.nl/~barjis

Isan Barjis

International Center of Information, W. Barendsstraat 50c, 3814 AR Amersfoort, The Netherlands. Tel: +31-33–4758577, Fax: +31-33–4720089; e-mail: ib20@hotmail.com

Dokht, R.M.

Electro-Medics International B. V., Uranus 4, 2685 LZ Poeldijk, The Netherlands; Tel: +31-174–280324, Fax: +31-174–280715; e-mail: 101353.2602@compuserve.com

Chitchian, D.

Delft University of Technology, Faculty of Architecture, Technical Design and Information Group, Berlageweg 1, 2628 CR Delft, The Netherlands; e-mail: D.Chitchian@bk.tudelft.nl

Keywords: *Organizational simulation, Petri net, Business process, process refinements*

ABSTRACT

This paper introduces a methodology that allows to identify and capture business processes in a number of models. Granularity of these models is based on the growing insight into the business processes. If the initial, most abstracted, model represents a structural overview of business process, the final, most detailed, models are constructed in such a manner that they can serve as immediate input data for simulation purposes. The methodology is based on a type of Petri net, adapted for modeling business processes with respect to increasing granularity and capturing high risk activities (activities with time constraints).

To obtain a realistic simulation model of an organization one must correctly capture business processes and their characteristics. In the proposed methodology special attention is paid to this issue, how adequately identify business processes and construct their models. Another feature addressed in the proposed methodology is readability and comprehensibility of the constructed models. For this purpose we use a refinement procedure for processes. This procedure refines processes from a model to model until atomic actions (activities) are identified. To demonstrate application of the methodology in practice, business process in the EMI is discussed throughout the paper.

1. INTRODUCTION

Business process modeling and simulation are crucial but still poorly understood and controlled phase in the development cycle of information systems on one hand, for analyzing and understanding business itself on the other hand. A necessary precondition for a successful information systems development is undoubtedly an appropriate and precise understanding of processes to be supported. Moreover, it should be possible to share and validate such an understanding effectively and efficiently among the stakeholders in a development project. Thus, appropriate and precise models of the business system (or business process) have to be made. Most existing approaches to modeling business systems/processes however suffer from inappropriateness and/or imprecision. It is also often the case that developed models are hardly readable and comprehensible for non IT-people.

Although new, innovative ideas are upcoming (Aalst, 1998; Agostini and Michelis, 998; Moelders et al., 1998), the common approach to business process modeling and simulation are that the functional designers of the information system ask the future users to provide the requirements that must be met by the system.

The purpose of this paper is to demonstrate that it is possible to combine appropriateness and precision in a modeling approach. To this end, a methodology for refinement processes is combined with a type of Petri Net, adapted for modeling business processes.

This methodology is based on organizational theory and business process modeling. For more reading about organization, business processes and their related aspects, readers are referred to (Dietz and Barjis, 1999; Aguilar et al., 1999; Douglas et al., 1997).

The structure of this paper is as follows. As a theoretical aspect, the proposed methodology is discussed and introduced. In this part we also describe a refinement procedure for transferring business processes from the most abstracted level (structural overview of a business process) into the most detailed level (action-oriented representation). The refinement procedure is conducted at three levels of representation: business processes, core activities and atomic actions.

The granularity of the activities involved increases from model to model. This means that at one level, the most abstracted, the overall or structural aspects of the business processes is considered. At the other level, the most detailed, the same business process is viewed as an action-oriented diagram (flowchart). The step-by-step increase of complexity makes the models more readable and comprehensible, especially for non-IT people.

As an application aspect, the paper demonstrates a practical application of the proposed methodology based on a real life case study conducted in the Electro-Medics International (EMI) company. The EMI case is taken as a representative example for business process modeling and simulation.

2. A SMALL COMPANY

In this section we consider a small company from two points of view- business and modeling & simulation. As such a company, we consider the EMI as an example of small company, but first from the business point of view.

The EMI is considered to be a small service-oriented company established in 1990. In the year 1999, due to certain business environment it was identified that an entity with the location in Europe can function effectively and efficiently in order to serve the growing demand of developing countries.

The size of the company was subject to many conditions including:

High Risk Economies: In most cases the developing economies are considered high political/economic risk. The notion is that the conduct and future of any business is less predictable in comparison to the more advanced economies.

Efficiency: Creating a high cost center is not in the interest of any business activity especially with higher scarcity of funds in the developing economies. There is not enough fund to subsidize a business operation and it must be efficient. Subsequently, the operation must be small in every aspect (employees, location and equipment).

Limited Customers: The entity primarily was designed to provide special service to a group of specialists. Hence the customer base from the very beginning was designed to be limited. In case of expansion the new customers were going to be served via the well-established network locally.

Cost Center: The operation was designed to act as cost center versus profit center. From the very beginning there was a limited percentage of sales designed to cover the cost of the operation. Therefore the relation between higher turn-over and profitability was very limited.

So, in the concept of some business people and scholars, a small business can be defined in terms of its turn-over (may be less than US$ 1,000,000). This notion is based on certain objectives within a given economy and environment. However, in case of EMI, it has been designed to be a small operation in order to combine many elements (some have been identified) in order to respond to the interest of stakeholders. It could be argued that the difference in objectivity of the company has no bearings in the operation, but there is strong evidence that the objectives and environment has a great effect on the definition of the size of the company.

Now, from the modeling & simulation point of view, which is the goal of this paper.

We consider a company as a small, if it has a locally concentrated business system with one input and one output point. Although, the entire process can be consisted of many other processes (sub-processes), but in general it has one initiation point and one result point. Approach, proposed in this paper is based on modeling of such systems.

There are some definitions that we use in our paper, when investigating business processes in a company.

A **core activity** is an activity that is centered for a set of actions derived from it and oriented on execution of this core activity. These actions are built to complete (support) result of the core activity to which they belong. A core activity creates a specific fact in the objective world.

A **business process** is a related group of steps or activities that use people, information, and other resources to create value for internal or external customers. Business process consists of steps related in time and place, have a beginning and end, and have inputs and outputs. Examples of business process in a restaurant include taking orders, cooking food, and preparing a bill. Examples in a factory include manufacturing products, hiring employees, and maintaining equipment. Examples in doctor's office include making appointments, examining patients, and filling out insurance forms (Alter, 1996; Davenport, 1993).

A **firm** (or government organization) consists of a large number of interdependent business processes that work together to generate products or services in a business environment (Alter, 1996).

The **business environment** includes the firm itself and everything else that effects its success, such as competitors, suppliers, customers, regulatory agencies, and demographic, social, and economic conditions (Alter, 1996).

3. BUSINESS PROCESSES IN THE EMI

Electro-Medics International b.v. has been established in response to the growing need for a service company that could create an interface to two different business cultures- the developing countries and the developed countries. Hence, the medical profession in the developing countries is entirely dependent on the importation of such goods and services. However, the constraints on the availability of the hard currency on one hand and impatience of the business world in advanced societies make the conduct of the business a real challenge.

3.1 Basic Processes in the EMI

In order to conclude a business deal, there are several processes involved in the entire business process, namely they are *Product Awareness*, *Marketing*, *Contract Negotiation* and *Contract Execution*. Due to the limited scope of this paper only the Contract Execution process of the whole business process will be investigated in this paper.

3.2 Contract Execution

After finalization of the contract and negotiating the financing of the deal it is time to execute the order and deliver the goods. This stage involves as the placing of the order with the supplier by preparing the related documents of shipment of the goods. In this stage each activity requires different inputs.

(a) Placing the order: This requires a close attention about exact description of the goods and pricing. Afterwards, the agreement must be reached with the supplier for the payment, place of delivery and terms of the delivery.

(b) Documents preparation: In most cases the following documents are required:

- Invoice: to be certified by the chamber of commerce and the related embassy.
- Packing list: Identifies the packing with the exact description of the goods contained in the packing.
- Certificate of origin: This document is being issued by the local chamber of commerce and, in most cases, it must be legalized by the relevant embassy
- Inspection certificate: This is the third party verification designed to verify the contents of the shipment by independent authority.
- Airway bill (bill of lading): This document is related to the type of transportation meaning that the goods should be shipped to the customer. With the air transport it must be airway bill and with the land and sea transport it is bill of lading (B/L). This document is being prepared by the transport company and it indicates that the goods are already shipped/en route.

(c) Documents submission to the bank and finalization: The payment process is the last stage of the order execution. This stage is as important as any other stage. Any shortfall whether it is the document or discrepancy in the documents could lead to a fatal mistake. The consequence could be a very late payment or in some cases to the termination of the contract.

(d) Delivery to the customer: At this stage the goods are being cleared from the customs at the destination and are being physically delivered to the customer. This is the final stage where the goods are in the possession of the end-user and they become operational. At this stage the final check takes place and they are being installed, test-run and finally delivered in the operational form to the end-user. In most cases it is part of the contract that the end-user has already been trained or the training takes place at the site. In addition, there is a guarantee/warrantee period varying from one to five years and in some instances up to ten years. It is the responsibility of the supplier to keep the system functional during this period. Additionally, there is a maintenance contract plus the upgrading of the system(s) for its life-time. This includes periodical control of the equipment plus the trouble shooting.

As one can imagine the entire process is very dynamic and, in most cases, there are several projects that they are running in parallel. The monitoring of this process is very essential mainly due to the fact that each order has a limited validity time.

4. REFINEMENT OF PROCESSES

Process can be refined until the atomic actions are derived gradually adding information to models. In this section we demonstrate three levels of refinement. At the first level a structural overview of processes is represented. The second level shows a process oriented model. The third level represents an action oriented Petri net model of processes.

As it is obvious from the description of business in the EMI, reported in the previous section, there are three main processes and supporting actions (functions) identified. These processes include product awareness, marketing, contract negotiation and contract execution.

Figure 1 sketches a structural overview of these main processes. In this figure the gray roundangle represents the company (EMI) boundary with respect to the business environment. Each identified main process is represented by a circle labeled by the name of the process, e.g. *Contract execution*, and numbered as business process one, two, etc. (BP1, BP2, BP3…). Arcs between the main processes show the most possible interrelation of these processes.

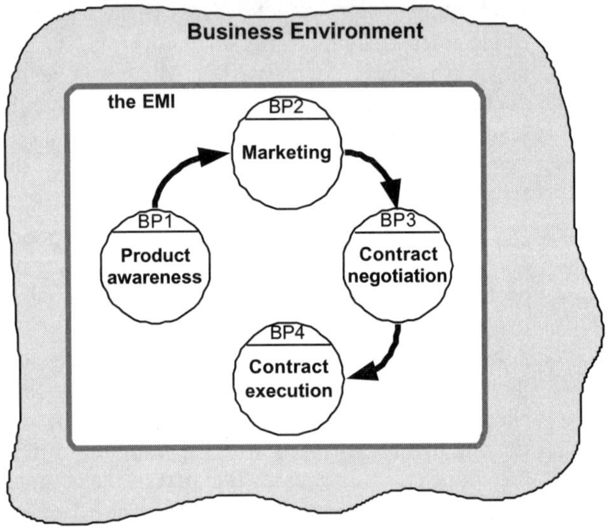

Figure 1. Structural diagram of business processes in the EMI

Figure 2 represents a process oriented diagram. In this figure the gray roundangle represents the cross processes boundary- boundary between the main processes, namely it represents the boundary for the contract execution process. In this step of refinement, the contract execution process is represented as a set of core activities e.g. CA1, CA2 etc. So, as shown, the contract execution process consists of three core activities such as *placing order*, *documents preparation* and *documents submission*. Each core activity, graphically represented by a rectangle, is identified by the name of the activity and also numbered accordingly. It should be noted that each core activity consists of a set of supplementary atomic actions. These actions are listed below each core activity correspondingly. In this figure the timing listed for CA3 means that there is a time constraint for this core activity. It will be explained later in figure 3c.

Another one feature inherent to the process oriented diagram of figure 2 is that each process e.g. BP4, has one beginning point (B) and one end point (E). in its turn, such a presentation makes it possible to represent more complex business structures in very compact notations. For example, each BP can be compacted as network represented by one symbol (see figure 1) having the beginning and end points.

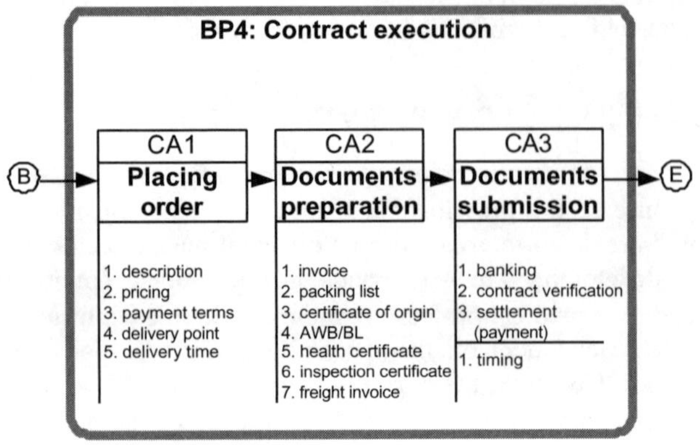

Figure 2. Process oriented diagram of the contract execution in the EMI

For the graphical representation of the detailed (action oriented) models, a type of Petri net has been used. In order to adapt the proposed type of Petri net for constructing the action oriented models including high risk activities (with time constraint), in particular we added to the standard Petri net elements a new element such as a timer (clock). The timer will trigger a timeout action, if the fixed time for the high risk activity is reached before completing its execution. To simulate the derived business process we deploy Arena simulation tools. Using these simulation tools, one is able to assign parameter values for the actions such as execution time or costs involved them. Then the result of the simulation gives some indications and verifications with which analysts can analyze the behavior of the business process for optimizing or redesign it.

A Petri net model captures the sequential and/or parallel processing order of the activities which are contained in the process. In figure 3b there are two choice elements within the flow of processing, represented by circles numbered as 2 and 4. The first choice concerns to find out if it is necessary to verify the contents of the shipment by independent authority. The second choice concerns if it is necessary to make freight invoice. Synchronization elements in this figure are used in order to synchronize the end of execution of several activities before proceeding further.

In figure 3b, one new element is represented. This new element (the bold bar) is a fictive (dummy) transition. Fictive because it doesn't have any duration or any action. It is only included for keeping syntactic correctness of the PN when dealing with optionality.

Figure 3c contains two new elements: the timer and subnet (represented by the double line rectangle and identified as CA2). Usually the duration for the document preparation process is seven days. If seven days are passed before finishing this process, then the timer will trigger a timeout token (signal). The subnet represents the document preparation process (figure 3b) in compact notation. It means, if after contract verification, it is found that some thing is wrong, then the document preparation process has to be repeated again.

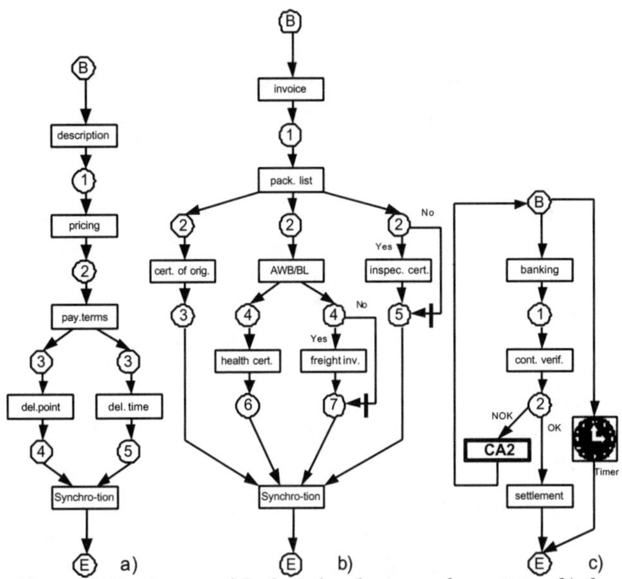

Figure 3. Petri net model of: a) the placing order activity; b) the documents preparation; c) documents submission.

Once, having models in the manner presented in figure 3, it is straightforward to conduct simulation of the business system under study. The only necessary value lacking in this model is duration of all the activities. However, in order to study dynamic behavior of the system it is not necessary to have an exact value for duration of all activities.

5. SIMULATION USING THE ARENA

Taking into account such advantagious features of the Arena simulation tool as animation facilities, hierarchical structure of models, object oriented feature, we consider this tool to be one of the appropriate tools for simulating models developed in this paper. Model hierarchy is possible due to the ability to formally separate Arena models into hierarchical views, called submodels, each with its own full workspace (resulting in unlimited workspace in any given model) for defining entity flow and displaying graphical animation. Submodels can contain any object supported in a model window (logic, static graphics, or animation.)

The use of submodels in simulated model not only increases the amount of workspace analysts have in which to build models, but it also allows the ability to better organize models. Each submodel is represented in its own view, allowing to partition visually a complex model flowchart into natural, easy-to-manipulate windows. Submodels themselves can contain deeper submodels; there is no limit to the amount of nesting that can occur.

Figure 4 depicts a simulation model of the contract execution process (BP4) in notations of the Arena tool. As it is seen from the figure, the beginning and end point are represented by standard elements 'Arrive' and 'Depart' used in the Arena. Each core activity is modeled as a submodel that in its turn contains another submodel (according to models represented in figure 3). The dot before the Arrive is a token that moves through all submodels and submodels within these them. This token imitates dynamic behavior of the model when it is simulated.

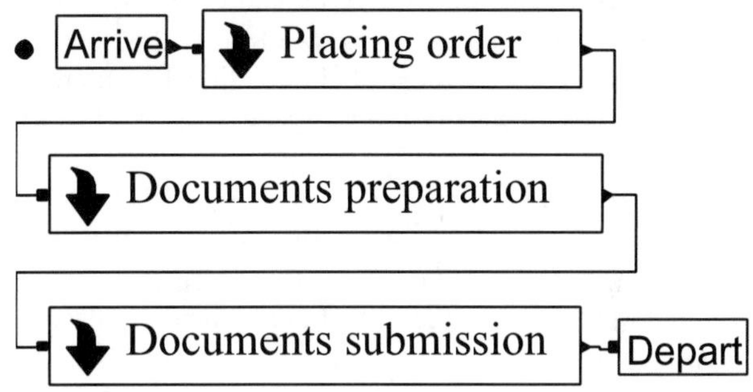

Figure 4. Simulation model of the contract execution

Submodels can be connected to other modules, other submodels, or can stand alone. Due to limited space in the paper, we will not disclose the inner structure of each submodel.

6. CONCLUSIONS

Petri net models, introduced in this paper are action oriented. It is possible to transform these models into high level Petri nets conform to the standard. This results in the ability to model more complex and large processes in a compact way.

As one can see, a simulation methodology introduced in this paper covers the entire investigation of business processes in a company. This entire investigation include business process description in natural language, constructing business process models, constructing simulation models, e.g. using Arena, and finally analysis of executed simulation models.

Concluding remarks about the proposed methodology are as follows. In the proposed methodology, each business processes is identified as a related group of activities with one initial and one final point. Such a representation of a business process allows the analyst to model each business process in isolation. Then these isolated models can be combined into one big complete model, or they can be represented as subnets within another model. This way of representation allows to portray the business processes in a more compact way. Compactness of models constructing becomes an important feature when dealing with complex business systems.

Finally, the derived models in Petri net notations can be simulated and analyzed using common discrete system tools like Petri net tools. These tools allow one to run simulation models of the business processes for observing the dynamic behavior of the business system and conducting performance analysis.

REFERENCES

Aalst, W.M.P. van der, 1998. Finding Errors in the Design of a Workflow Process: A Petri-net-based Approach. In the proceedings of the Workshop on Workflow Management: Net-based Concepts, Models, Techniques and Tools (WFM'98) within the 19th International Conference on Applications and Theory of Petri Nets, Lisbon, Portugal, June 22.

Agostini, A. ; Michelis, G. De. 1998. Simple Workflow Models. In the proceedings of the Workshop on Workflow Management: Net-based Concepts, Models, Techniques and Tools (WFM'98) within the 19th International Conference on Applications and Theory of Petri Nets, Lisbon, Portugal, June 22.

Aguilar, M. Tankred Rautert and Lex Pater. Business Process Simulation: A Fundamental Step Supporting Process Centered Management. In the proceedings of the 1999 Winter Simulation Conference (WSC '99) Phoenix, Arizona, December 5-8, 1999.

Alter, S., 1996. Information systems; a management perspective. Menlo Park : Benjamin/Cummings, USA.

Davenport, T.H., 1993. Process Innovation, Harvard Business School Press, Boston.

Dietz J.L.G.; Barjis J. Supporting the DEMO Methodology with a Business Oriented Petri Net. In the proceedings of the Fourth CAiSE/ IFIP8.1 International Workshop on Evaluation of Modeling Methods in Systems Analysis and Design (EMMSAD'99), Heidelberg, Germany, June 14-15, 1999.

Douglas B. Fridsma et al. Acquiring, Maintaining, and Customizing Organizational Work Process Descriptions. In the proceedings of the AAAI Spring Symposium Artificial Intelligence in Knowledge Management Stanford University, March 24-26, 1997.

Moelders, A.; Wolf, M.; Fengler, W., 1998. Object-oriented and net-based modelling of business processes. In the proceedings of the Workshop on Workflow Management: Net-based Concepts, Models, Techniques and Tools (WFM'98) within the 19th International Conference on Applications and Theory of Petri Nets, Lisbon, Portugal, June 22.

About authors:

Joseph Barjis /Ph.D., Associate Academician of the International Informatization Academy, Chairman of the International Center of Information, headquartered in the Netherlands/ MSc. in Computer Science in 1991; Ph.D. in Computer Science in 1996; Ph.D. in Information Systems in 1999. He worked or works in: Russia, United Kingdom and the Netherlands.

Isan Barjis /Ph.D. student/. He works in the Netherlands. From 1998 he started work with the International Center of Information, headquartered in the Netherlands, as a scientific researcher.

Dokht, R.M. 1990 on- Managing Director EMI and from 1995 on- Lecturer in MBA Program. 1996 to present- Haagse Hogeschool, the Hague, Adviser for Ph.D. students in various universities in the Netherlands. 1986 to present- Special adviser on Financial Structure for International Business (various organizations/banks). 1982-1985 Lecturing at the University of Tehran. 1980-1986 International Court of Justice Iran-United States Tribunal

Education

1997- Postgraduate in Business Program, University of Stanford. 1986-1997- Various seminars, workshops. 1975-1979- Graduate School, University of Taxas. Dallas. 1970-1974 - BA in Economics, National University of Iran.

Davood Chitchian /Ph.D./ MSc. in Computer Science from the University of Nevada Reno, USA, in 1989; Ph.D. in Computer Science from Delft University of Technology, the Netherlands, in 1997. Since 1997 on, Post Doctorate position at Delft University of Technology.

ANALYSIS IN SUPPORT OF A "HERD OF FELINES:"

SIMULATION, OUTCOME MEASUREMENT AND PLURALISTIC DECISION-MAKING

Desmond Saunders-Newton, Ph.D.
School of Policy, Planning and Development
University of Southern California
Los Angeles, California 90016
e-mail: DezSN@concentric.net

KEYWORDS: Policy-making, decision support system, management games

ABSTRACT

Elected officials who are members of local boards or legislative assemblies are challenged by a number of socio-political trends, such as accountability movements. In an attempt to respond to accountability pressures, elected decision-makers are formulating and implementing policies that will hopefully reform organizations so that they are more effective or efficient. It is not always easy for these decision makers to formulate effect policy given the complexity of some of the problems they are attempting to address. One aid to these officials is acquisition of information that enables improvement. Information of this type, that is also intuitive, is not often available. One means of getting such information, which can be incorporated into their choice making process, is through the use of a simulation modeling strategy that allows for interactive questioning. This paper presents this strategy in the context of issue of concern to an urban school board.

INTRODUCTION

A social and political trend that has become increasingly evident is a call for public sector organizations and agencies to decrease operational opaqueness, and improve organizational efficiency and efficacy. An overarching principle of this trend, which is often called accountability, is that efficiency and effectiveness improvements will result through the improved use of information. At least three assumptions underlie this realization of this principle. First, it is assumed that such "improvement-enabling" information is available. Second, the individuals with decision-making authority will make the most appropriate use of this information in order to improve an organization's outcomes. Third, and probably most important, is a first principle assertion made by many in the policy analysis and management science communities: *the choice-making process, and related organization outcomes, is improved by the systematic and consistent use of "information."*

Given the fulfillment of these assumptions, it is expected that public sector organizations and agencies will consequently demonstrate, as well as publicize, their achievements through the use of outcome measures. These measures, when most efficiently used, should be indicative of the organization's social impacts. As noted by Brooks, these measures reflect *estimates of how well organizations succeed at producing value for the public; for example, how well schools educate children and how well hospitals contain costs.* (Brooks-, 2000) No matter the substantive area of concern, e.g. education, healthcare, or defense, these measures should be both intuitive and useful to decision makers and citizens.

The challenge of using these measures, however, is their generation from data, and their incorporation into the decision-making and planning process. If an agency finds it in its best interest to invest in its decision support and planning capabilities, these same organizations must identify appropriate analytical tools for representing outcomes measures, identifying issues of interest and exploring potential outcomes in a comprehensible and credible fashion. Of particular interest is a tool that produces results that are easy to interpret and implement by elected officials, regardless of their analytical knowledge or political predispositions. Simulations of various types provide an appropriate decision support capability for public sector decision makers, particularly those elected to pluralistic bodies.

This paper describes the use of the simulation methodology to generate "improvement enabling" information that is easy to use by individuals with decision-making authority, and presents a framework for assessing the implications of using this generated information in support of organizational change consistent with accountability objectives. In support of this examination, this paper argues why simulation is an appropriate tool for representing and analyzing issues faced by an extremely demanding decisionmaking client, i.e. an elected body such as a school board or legislative assembly. In addition, the author presents a scheme for effectively using simulation model results to support planning choices in light of accountability concerns and organizational uncertainty. The paper also provides a case examination of using this simulation model strategy to address a major concern of a large urban school district, inequitable post-secondary outcomes. The modeling approach discussed illustrates an appropriate response to a major accountability concern as expressed by an elected board.

ACCOUNTABILITY, SIMULATION AND CREDIBILITY

One of the challenges faced by public sector decision makers is the ability to bring appropriate information or insights to bear on *issues of the day* in a timely and effective fashion. For many public sector organizations, judgments about organizational performance are made relative to the most effective or best private sector practice that can be identified. It is then assumed that the clientele and operational environment are "similar enough" such that one can assume that a public sector organization's performance can be equal to, at least in terms of outcome, the practice found in the private sector. This is often rarely the case, but such a fact does not change the perceptions often held by stakeholders. Moreover, it does not lessen the challenge faced by decision makers in an operating environment often characterized by a need for rapid reform and immediate improvements of a positive nature.

What follows in this section is a brief description of outcome measurement in support of the socio-political theme called accountability, and the role that can be played by simulation techniques in support of decision-making that must occur during the current *accountability zeitgeist*. This section will be concluded by a brief suggestion of how simulation can credibly influence choice making in a pluralistic setting.

Outcome Measurement & Pluralistic Decision Making

Accountability -- defined as the act of making agencies more responsible to a vested constituency -- is a *socio-political theme* that is currently framing organizational reform and decisionmaking in the United States. In an effort to increase the acceptability of public sector outcomes, elected officials as agents of society are expecting, as well as mandating, improvements in *outcome measures that are indicative of the organization's social impacts*.

It is important to note the italicized concept because it is not assured that the outcome measure is externally valid, i.e. reflects what actually happens in the "real" world. However, it is assumed that the selected measures have some close relationship with the events, outcomes or phenomenon the public cares about. If this type of validity exists, then the inherently logical nature of outcome measures should make easier policy formulation and assessment, or program improvements such as expansion, deletion or modification.

At present, most measurement systems focus on describing an agency's outcomes. Over time, it is likely that outcome measurement will become more integral to agency operations, and – more importantly – so will consequent sanctions and rewards. As the costs of unacceptable public sector performance – and conversely the benefits of acceptable performance – increase, agencies will become more concerned with effectively analyzing performance and planning for improved performance. This is particularly evident for individuals concerned with the administration of K-12 education.

Arguably, no sector is more scrutinized in terms of outcome measures than that of K-12 education. This is reflected by the general public disaffection with primary and secondary education. The high frequency of K-12 failures and follies are reported in local newspapers effectively illustrates the increased attempts to use measures to hold officials and public sector employees accountable to stakeholders. Moreover, these measures are being crafted and incorporated into legislation, administrative movements, and government programs in an effort to force the improvement of schools. Measures of school performance include standardized test scores, Advanced Placement examination performance, and enrollment and attainment in post-secondary institutions. While these measures are not perfect indicators of what occurs in a school or the experience created for a student while attending a particular school district, they would seem to suggest – at least as noted by stakeholders – the appropriate (or inappropriate) use of resources by K-12 institutions.

Based on these measures, decision makers attempt to promote success and alleviate failure through the formulation and implementation of policies and effective allocation or use of available resources in the form of programs. This endeavor is a challenge for a single executive, e.g. a superintendent, and a multiplicative challenge for a collective or pluralistic decision-making body, e.g. a school board or legislative assembly. The question of concern is how does a decision-making collective, rather than a single decision maker, best obtain and use information to support choices that require consensus and are often shaped by optimality-inhibiting factors such as political expediency and a lack of technical expertise.

In considering this question, it is necessary to consider the importance of information creation in using outcome measures, and recognizing the limitations associated the traditional use of these measures. A traditional view of the use of outcome or performance measures is provided by Harty as he notes two major problems that inhibit the successful use of performance measurement: (Harty 1996)

1. The collection of meaningful performance data requires resources (staff time and resources).
2. There is a considerable danger of overexpectation with respect to what performance measurement can accomplish.

If these aforementioned problems are overcome, performance measures can be effectively used to support program/policy formulation or change. Of course, *performance measurement information seldom explains why the measured results are the way they are and certainly doesn't intimate what can be done to improve results.* (Harty 1996) Improving results requires translating collected data into decision enabling information that is framed by the appropriate operational and policy context.

The actions that should occur following the acquisition of information, i.e. value-added data, that allows for action falls in the purview of the analyst -- or rather his or her model of the situation of interest -- and emerge from the subjective interaction that occurs between the decision maker and the generated knowledge. It is this interaction that is most appropriately supported by flexible methodologies that allow for representing complex relationships that are amenable to easy manipulation so as to consider "what if" scenarios.

Interactive-Intuitive Modeling Of Novel Policy Regimes

Simulation allows for the use of its modeling results, i.e. "improvement enabling" information, in a fashion that differs from the traditional way analyst communicates with pluralistic or legislative decision-making bodies. Typically, reports or modeling efforts for pluralistic decision-making bodies are less concerned with "knowledge for its own sake," and more concerned with the performance of particular programs or policies so as to support specific legislative action. As a result, analytical findings – as well as the method(s) that gave rise to these findings – offer *specific advice as whether to support a line item in the state budget or what to put in an amendment to a pending bill.* (Zajano and Lochtefeld 1999)

Beyond Traditional Modeling. In the current policy regime where choices are shaped by an effort to be "accountable," this aforementioned analytical style is not necessarily most appropriate. Many policy problems are difficult to resolve, such as K-12 education, because the factors that gave rise to the problem are either not well known or changing in magnitude and character over time and relative to other factors composing the social system of interest. Such complexity and dynamics makes it difficult to collect data for modeling and maintaining correct parameter values that illustrate the relative importance of factors. Thus, where the understanding of the decision makers is limited by the complex nature of the problem, then a traditional analytical approach is less desirable than a "exploratory" use of an analytical tool that will aid the choice or decision process.

The latter approach is called Exploratory Analysis, and is a methodology designed to improve comprehension and analysis of complex, highly uncertain, or poorly defined and understood systems. (Brooks *et al.* 1997) Whereas traditional model-based analysis is conducted to determine outcomes for the most likely conditions surrounding specific scenario(s), an approach that often requires the use of sensitivity analysis, exploratory analysis considers a "landscape of plausible outcomes." (Park and Lempert, 1998) This approach, given the exploration of the plausible outcomes associated with assumptions underlying decisions, coupled with an interactive computational environment can be of substantial use in developing the intuition of decision makers.

Flexible modeling frameworks, such as Exploratory Analysis, aid greatly in the policy and program planning process. One use of exploratory analysis is in Social Policy Gaming (SPG), which comprises exercises where individuals and groups make social policy decisions in a realistic but hypothetical environment, could be an effective decision aid and training device for community leaders who must struggle with seemingly intransigent domestic problems. (Kahan, et al. 1993) SPG is based on the assumption that decision makers benefit from exploring possible consequences of particular plans and decisions or for responding to crises, and that exploring a problem in the context of a particular scenario helps them understand the issues more completely--or at least differently--than contemplating actions in the abstract.

The SPG approach and rationale is consistent with the *systems modeling* strategy. This strategy, at least as used in support of legislative program evaluation, is based on the examination of scenarios by changing important parameters in a systematic manner during subsequent model estimations or simulations, i.e. computer experimentation. Most important, summarized results of multiple simulations allow policymakers to experience, conceptualize, and learn the effects of their decisions in a relatively safe manner, and afford analyst supporting the policymaker with the opportunity to test policy alternatives by comparative model assessment. (McIntire and Glaze 1999) Both the SPG and *systems modeling* approaches illustrate ways of generating deeper understanding that may allow for improved discourse and transitions to consensus.

This paper argues that considering choices based on outcome measures in an attempt to fulfill accountability commitments is a situation that benefits from this type of modeling. Given many accountability regimes are motivated by, and formulated in response to, anecdote - and in a few cases misguided abstraction - modeling of this type allows decision makers to expand or revise their understanding of social issues prior to policy or program implementation. Thus, by representing the vital policy assumptions and system interactions, it is possible to explore the complexities of social issues for decision makers who are not technically inclined. Moreover, an interactive approach that involves the decision maker, analyst and model, gives rise to the modeling trait called credibility. A credible model or simulation is less a near isomorphic representation of a real world event, but one whose is use is logically consistent with the modeling effort. (Dewar et al. 1996) More to the point, if the model is appropriately used, then it is more likely to be trusted by the decision maker. This results in decision makers who are more involved in the analytical process, and ultimately more informed users of outcome measures generated by the simulation model.

Methodology Du Jour. The tool or method of choice when making use of an Interactive-Intuitive Modeling approach should be characterized by flexible model formulation and an ability to represent complex systemic interactions. While not the perfect solution to modeling complex policy problems, simulation does afford an agency with greater flexibility in terms generating information on constrained data, and producing modeling results that account for varying expectations and assumptions. Thus, it provides a vehicle to address problems such as data scarcity. Unlike some analytical or statistical models that require extensive databases in order to estimate parameters of importance, simulation models provides an astute analyst with the ability to use appropriate synthetic data or to more simply explore plausible outcomes so as to deal with operating scenario uncertainty. In addition, expectations in the form of operating assumptions are easier to explicitly represent using simulation approaches. Subsequently, the method allows for "what if" considerations that will aid a collection of decision makers in gaining insights about social or policy issues even when assumptions or expectations are violated.

Without question, there exists numerous analytical techniques that can support the decision making process. These tools include those that make use of insights based on the aggregation of data, i.e. statistics and econometrics, as well as those that seek optimal allocative choices, i.e. mathematical programming. Each of these has a role in the illuminating the choices that are available to decision makers. However, the most appropriate methodological choice given the need to quickly model (and remodel) circumstances of concern as policies are changed is simulation. The general ability of the approach to represent complex social issues, make use of "soft" variables*, and capture the emergent phenomenon that occurs with the implementation of policy, is particularly important to decisions made in a world best characterized by complexity. In addition, certain simulation environments, e.g. *iThink* or *STELLA*, provide an incredibly visual means of representing the interplay between policy and social systems, and a relatively easy means of modifying the associated models. This ability allows for the development of a deeper understanding and intuition in the members who compose a pluralistic decision making body. And as noted earlier, this garnering of understanding and intuition is particularly important when considering the short and long-term implications of policy and program choices in response to socio-political themes such as accountability.

ACCOUNTABILITY EXEMPLAR: POST-SECONDARY OUTCOME MEASURES

An example of using the Interactive-Intuitive approach for modeling accountability is where we examine post-secondary outcomes for high school graduates. For this paper, we focus on a specific measure: college and university participation.

Modeling College Enrollment and Completion

While other measures exist, such as enlistment in the armed services and workforce entry, the proportion of high school seniors or graduates participating in the higher education process following their departure from high school is often of interest to stakeholders. A common measure of this participation is the number of students enrolling in

* Whereas hard variables reflect measured data, "soft" variables are those that not currently measurable.

college in the fall following high school graduation. This measure is often used for the following reasons: (Saunders-Newton and Rasmussen 2000)

- A high rate of college enrollment suggests a District's high schools are both enabling and motivating students to attend college.
- College-going rates can assist in determining the effectiveness of educational reform efforts being undertaken by the District.
- Post-secondary educational attainment, i.e. the completion of a higher education milestone in terms of a degree or certificate, makes more likely a contributing citizen who fulfills their civic responsibility to the community.
- Depending on the District, it indicates the degree to which a collection of schools are fulfilling the tenets of a court order that requires improving college attendance for minority students.

Based on these reasons, it is important to understand attendance rates so as to affirm effective high schools and to encourage improvement in schools with low college-going rates.

One question that often arises from review of such a measure is the rate of college completion for high school students. The concern is about the school or district's efficacy in preparing students to both enroll and complete college. In California, such a request from a Board member of an urban school district would be motivated by a number of concerns, including the adoption of policies by various higher education institutions that would result in disenrolling students not meeting remediation requirements and decreasing the acceptance rates of minority students into the most elite higher education institutions. In addition, an underlying issue reflects an opportunity cost issue, i.e. whether scarce instructional expenditures would be better allocated to instruction less oriented toward collegiate preparation.

Model "Evolution"

One possible analytical approach for generating a measure of college enrollment and completion is to represent the process as a pipeline through which students flow to college completion or out of the modeled system. It is important to note that this effort is an extreme simplification of what occurs post high school completion. By not explicitly accounting for other post-secondary choice making, "closing" the system off from inflows/reentrants, and not representing multiple interactions throughout the time horizon of the model, the analyst is unable to generate a "correct" answer, and creates more questions than answers. For example, what happened to the students who didn't re-enroll in college following their sophomore year, or how many students who originally enlisted in the military subsequently enrolled in college?

However, the aforementioned description suggests the formulation of the most correct model of the education participation dynamic. Such is not necessary or possible for at least several reasons. First, acquiring all the data necessary to develop such a model is at best difficult, if not impossible.

Figure 1: Educational Attainment & Post-Secondary Outcome Pipeline

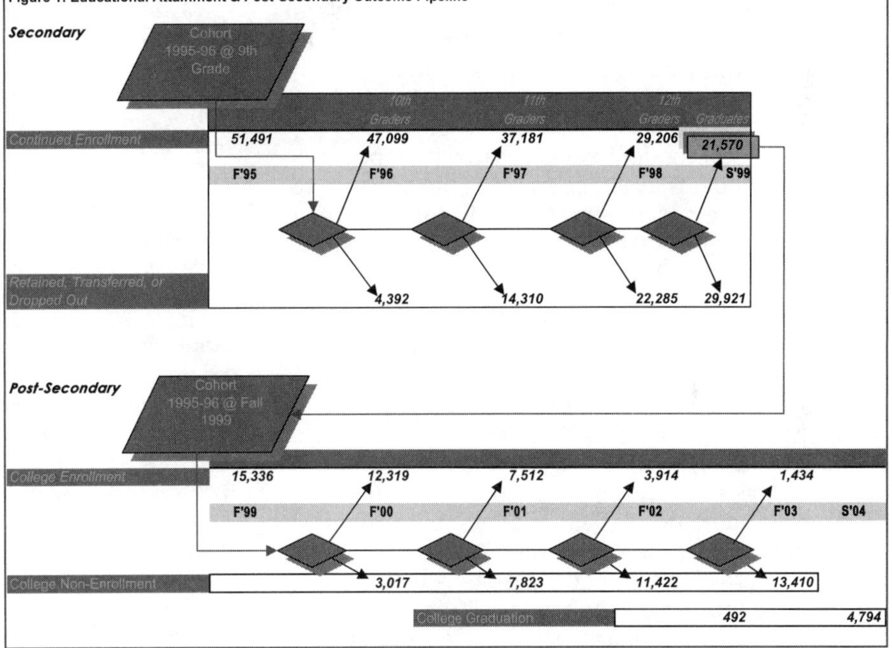

Second, the logical use of this model is not to find the "right" answer, but to suggest what may occur in the real world as a result of changing internal policy, implementing issue specific programs, and lobbying for external (exogenous) policy changes. Thus, estimation of specific values of statistical parameters is not the major focus.

Thus, the first attempt to generate accountability outcomes involved setting up a Monte Carlo experiment of the secondary-postsecondary pipeline. The model simulated 1000 experiments of various post-secondary outcomes that spanned a 10-year period. Beginning with the entry of the cohort into 9th grade, the model tracks school District level post-secondary outcomes 6 years post this cohort's anticipated high school graduation date. The measures of effectiveness considered included college enrollment into one of California's three state supported college systems, enrollment into one of California's private colleges, enrollment into any out-of-state college, work force entry, armed service enlistment, and incarceration. Figure 1 illustrates a snapshot of the base modeling results that focuses on college participation.

While the base model described above provided a means of answering questions about college completion, it did not necessarily address the plausible and likely questions that may arise from Board members after an initial viewing of the model results. In fact, it is likely that questions pertaining to how changes in economic conditions will impact post-secondary choices, and how has out-of-state enrollment changed due to recent Propositions passed in California will be asked. Thus, a more appropriate model construction proactively considers future questions in an attempt to build on past work and produce timely responses, and should incorporate the capabilities mentioned in the earlier discussion of the Interactive-Intuitive Approach. Such a simulation model begins to transition beyond just being a model that supports an initial analysis to a policy experimentation environment that considers issues – in a general fashion – that deal with post-secondary outcomes broadly defined.

This computational policy environment should afford the analyst/model-builder with an easy means of modifying the model, allowing for decision maker interaction, and an ability to provide multiple views or resolutions of the models output. With respect to the multiple views/resolutions, the District officials involved in this effort are interested in not only District-wide outcomes for all students, but school specific and ethnic group outcomes as well. The ability to generate these model results is a challenge but can be supported by the use of either the workbook paradigm of spreadsheets such as Excel or systems modeling environments such as iThink/STELLA.

CLOSING THOUGHTS

The appropriate formulation of any model is dependent on the logical use or uses of the model. In this case, it often known beforehand that certain decision makers will likely have a need to revisit questions due to the nature of the problem. Moreover, the likelihood and frequency of such *manager-model-analyst* interaction is increased when the problem/issue occurs in a realm best characterized by novelty and uncertainty. The current attempt to initiate large-scale reform in K-12 education in response to various accountability initiatives constitutes is an example of such a decision-making domain.

A means of addressing questions related of post-secondary choice, and of relating the results to organizational change in response to measures of accountability – or rather organizational effectiveness – is provided by the simulation strategy and model mentioned above. Ultimately, it provides a way of making pluralistic decision makers not only more accountable to their constituents, but to the available data and information as well.

REFERENCES

Brooks, A. 2000. "The Use and Misuse of Adjusted Performance Measures." *Journal of Policy Analysis and Management*, Vol. 19, No. 2 (Spring): 323-334.

Brooks, A.; B. Bennett; and S. Bankes. 1997. *An Application of Exploratory Analysis: The Weapons Mix Problem*. (65th MORS Symposium).

Dewar, J.A.; S. C. Bankes; J.S. Hodges; T. Lucas; D.K. Saunders-Newton; and P. Vye. 1996. *Credible Uses of Distributed Interactive Simulation (DIS) System*. RAND, Santa Monica, CA.

Hatry, H. P. 1996. "Foreward." *Organizational Performance and Measurement in the Public Sector* (Halachmi, A.; and G. Bouckaert, ed.) Quorum, Westport, Conneticut: ix-xii.

Kahan, J.P.; P.W. Greenwood; C.P. Rydell; W. Schwabe; and B.R. Williams. 1993. *Can Gaming of Social Policy Issues Help Translate Good Intentions into Change?* RAND, Santa Monica, CA.

McIntire, M.C.; and A.S. Glaze. 1999. "The Use of Systems Modeling in Legislative Program Evaluation." *New Directions for Evaluation*, No.8 (Spring): 45-60.

Park, G.S.; R.J. Lempert. 1998. *The Class of 2014: Preserving Access to California Higher Education*. RAND, Santa Monica, CA.

Saunders-Newton, D.; R. Rasmussen. 2000. "Enrollment of Los Angeles Unified School District Seniors in California Public Colleges and Universities: Years 1987-1998." Independent Analysis Unit, Los Angeles City Board of Education, CA (January).

Zajano, N.C.; and S.S. Lochtefeld. 1999. "The Nature of Knowledge and Language in the Legislative Arena." *New Directions for Evaluation*, No.8 (Spring): 85-94.

BIOGRAPHY

Desmond Saunders-Newton is currently an Adjunct Professor of Public Policy at the University of Southern California's School of Policy, Planning and Development, and the Program Analyst for Learning Outcomes & Performance Measurement for the L.A. City Board of Education's Independent Analysis Unit. He earned his Ph.D. from the RAND Graduate School, and focuses his research and professional practice on the use of computational and analytical models in support of decision-making in a variety of domains.

A SIMULATION OF AN ESTATE AGENCY WORKFLOW SYSTEM

Andrew Greasley and David Chaffey
University of Derby
United Kingdom
email: A.Greasley@derby.ac.uk

KEYWORDS

Simulation, Discrete, Workflow, Decision-making

ABSTRACT

A simulation model has been developed to simulate the behaviour of a workflow type Computer Supported Co-operative Work (CSCW) system. The value of being able to assess the frequency and volume of workflow transactions is indicated by a case study of CSCW software developed for estate agency co-workers. A simulation capability enables a range of alternative scenarios for workflow implementation to be assessed at the prototyping stage thus reducing time for testing. The model produced was based on a standard three-phase discrete-event simulation approach with implementation on a spreadsheet platform.

INTRODUCTION

Simulation of the workflow component of a Computer Supported Co-operative Work (CSCW) system has potential for reducing the costs of system implementation, while at the same time improving the quality of the delivered system. These benefits occur since simulating the behaviour of the system before implementation enables business analysts to assess the effectiveness of different approaches for enacting the workflow before costly prototypes are tested by end users. Despite this, the application of simulation to this problem is quite limited. Workflow Management Systems (WFMS) are a specialised type of computer system used increasingly in industry to assist in CSCW. This study focuses on implementation of this type of CSCW system. A WFMS can be defined as an automated method of co-ordinating business processes made up of tasks or activities undertaken by the human and computer resources of an organisation (Georgakopoulos et al, 1995). It is a significant technology since it can act as an enabler for the dramatic changes to businesses required for Business Process Re-engineering and the associated benefits this can bring (Hammer and Champy, 1993, Davenport, 1993). WFMS have been used in areas such as financial services applications for mortgage granting and document image processing and a wide range of standard business functions such as processin customer orders or purchase order requisitions.

WFMS include the following types of function, which can b simulated:

- a workflow queue of activities or tasks which need to b performed to achieve a business process often prioritised i a set order according to the business rules
- scheduling – assignment of tasks between a group o people, the workflow queue being queried to issu reminders to staff to perform tasks
- a routeing system for tasks and messages between tear members
- task performance metrics for managers - e.g. tas completion time

SIMULATION OF WFMS

The significance of simulation as a tool to aid WFM implementation has been noted as being of value by Giagli and Paul (1996) and Miller et. al.(1995). Giaglis and Pau (1996) outline a framework suggesting ways in whic simulation may be used to assist in Business Process Re engineering. This framework involves 5 steps of which two ar specific to workflow and CSCW software development. Thes are step 1; Identifying processes for innovation and step 5 designing and prototyping. Although the potential i recognised, this paper does not look at particular methods b which such simulations may be produced. More specificall Miller et al. (1995) consider how simulation may assist i workflow technology. They also propose general ways i which simulation may be used noting that "simulation may b used to design WFMS architectures and tune WFM implementations" and "simulation can be used to study an refine workflow specifications". More detailed descriptions o how simulation may assist in workflow implementation ar limited. Marazakis and Nikolau(1995) describe simulation o workflow transaction as a form of capacity planning, bu focusing on the volume of transactions that can be supporte by the IT infrastructure rather than how tasks are performed b the human operators of the system.

The importance of simulation to the effectiveness of a WFMS is recognised by the Workflow Management Coalition. They consider a simulation engine to be one of the main components in their reference model (WfMC, 1996) which recommends the key modules required for a WFMS (Figure 1). This diagram is indicative of the role of a simulation study in development of a WFMS. Before simulation can commence it is necessary to define the current workflow using process definition tools. At this point simulation can be used to determine the performance of the new workflow system in comparison with the existing system using measures such as the completion times for tasks in different scenarios. The results of the simulation can also be used to gauge the values that will be recorded by the administration and monitoring tools when the system is implemented. In the implementation described in this paper the simulation engine module in figure 1 can be considered to effectively replace the workflow scheduler.

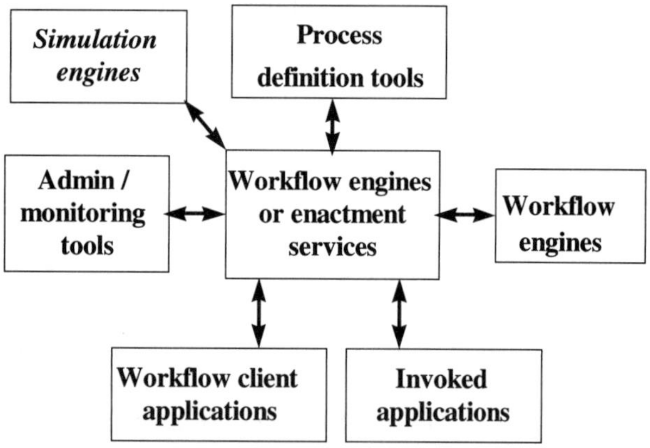

Figure 1. Components of a Workflow Management System - the Reference model of the Workflow Management Coalition

IMPLEMENTATION OF DISCRETE-EVENT SIMULATION ON A SPREADSHEET

Discrete-event simulation is a well known method of simulation modelling in which time is moved forward in discrete steps of differing lengths in duration from one event to the next. The time between events is not considered, unlike continuous simulation in which time is sampled continuously, usually at fixed intervals. In discrete event simulation the software model maintains a record of when future events will occur on a calendar and activates them in sequence. A number of alternative software control methods exist for performing discrete event simulation. These methods – Process Interactioi Event Based and Activity Based models are reviewed by Pid (1984). The simulation presented here is based on the thre‹ phase version of the activity-based approach. Paul (199] considers that three-phased activity based methods are a efficient method for simulation in terms of "mod‹ modifiability and model transparency". A spreadsheet-base simulation was developed using the Microsoft Visual Basic f‹ Applications™ (VBA) language and development environme‹ available for Microsoft Excel™. The spreadsheet simulatio implementation is described with a full code listing in Greasle (1998). This provides an accessible, low cost developme‹ environment with ready access to tools for numeric analysi tabulation and graphing.

CASE STUDY OF WFMS SIMULATION

An example of the application of the simulation model to service industry business where CSCW is beneficial described in this section. The business area is that of the sale ‹ properties (real estate or property sales through esta‹ agencies), the company involved is a national chain in the UK The users of the CSCW system that was developed includ sales negotiators who arrange the sale and purchase ‹ properties and are each assigned different properties an applicants they are responsible for; managers who monitor th negotiators and also handle some cases and branc administrators who prepare details of properties and dispatc routine correspondence to customers. In this busines teamwork is particularly important since the negotiators ma field enquiries from customers that are managed by other sta who are unavailable due to their showing a client round property. This arrangement requires each worker to perfor tasks on behalf of others and then inform them later of th outcome of the communication. A CSCW application appropriate to support the activities of the team members b issuing reminders to staff to perform tasks and recording th tasks and events that have occurred for reference by other tea members. A prototype system for this purpose was develope over a period of 6 months. Further details on busines requirements are given in Chaffey(1996a) and the technic solution in Chaffey(1996b). The system architecture comprise a Client-Server Wide Area Network (WAN) linking 1 branches and an area office where the server was locate‹ Shared data was stored on a Oracle™ database running o Windows NT.

In order to enact the tasks required by the business a tw‹ month period of process modelling to identify the task required was undertaken as described in Chaffey(1996a). This analysis identified approximately 40 tasks such as "Inspect Property", "Agree Offer" and "Process Sale to completion". These reminders to perform tasks were produced automatically by the system through a workflow scheduler based on Oracle™ database triggers that were fired following events involving customers. For example on registering a customer who wished to sell their property, a trigger would be fired when the new customer record was inserted into the customer table in the database to produce a task of inspecting the customers' property for valuation on a particular date.

The user interface of the part of the system used to manage collaboration between people was in two basic parts. The first for completing tasks (a task manager) and the second for reviewing the status of tasks, customers and properties (a task or event log), the latter being particularly useful for managers reviewing the status of all tasks in a branch or all branches. The task manager component consisted of a screen with a combined diary and a task list for each negotiator which contained a list of tasks to be performed and information necessary to complete the task, this included the type of task, the customer and/or property to which it referred, and a completion date. Tasks were completed through a conclusion button with which additional comments could be made. The task review component consisted of a table of significant events for each property and customer with corresponding dates and times on which they occurred.

A simulation model is useful for this type of application in order to identify, in advance the practicality of implementing a computer based system when the previous system was manual. Simulation is particularly important for identifying the volume of workflow that would be handled by each negotiator. This was not known previously since different tasks were undertaken by different negotiators although these were based on company guidelines. It was hoped that the workflow system would provide a better framework for undertaking operational activities to produce consistency between different operators and so enhance customer service.

In order to use a discrete event simulation approach for a WFMS it is necessary to relate the elements of a workflow system to the entities and events used in the discrete event simulation method. To achieve this, the workflow transactions are conceptualised as a series of tasks and events that occur through time. Tasks occur in response to events and are performed by actors (the human operators of the system) e.g. Georgakopoulos et.al.(1995). For this model development the relation between tasks and events can be best explained diagramatically. Figure 2 shows the sequential relationship between events and tasks through time that is represented b the x-axis. Note that a task consists of a start event (T_1) and a end event (T_2), with a set duration between the two, which i the average time it takes to complete a task. The y-axi provides a diagrammatic indication of how the state of a object changes through time as different events occur. Fc example a customer may change from unregistered t registered - this is a state change of the customer entity (objec and usually occurs at a single point in time.

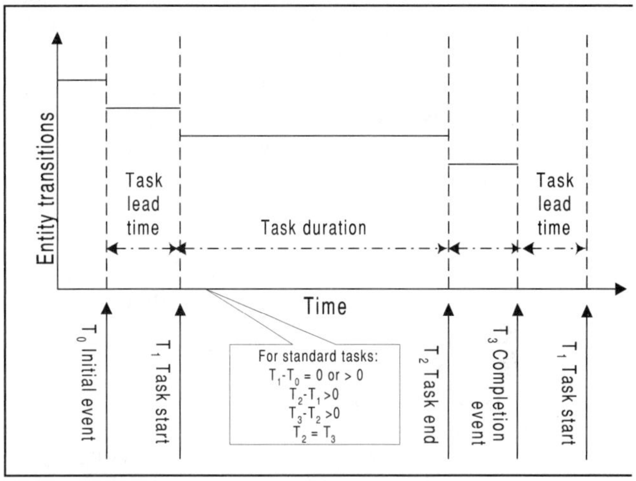

Figure 2. Diagram summarising relationships between task: events and entities

Two different types of events, which give rise to tasks, ca occur. T_0 is an initial or seed event that occurs when an evei occurs for the first time for a particular object. For exampl when a customer first enters a store before registration this i the first event that is recorded when they become part of th system. The simulation has to generate these seed events at particular frequency to represent the registration of ne customers and properties on the system. Seeds occur for thi system when a applicant customer is first registered, a vendc customer wishing to sell a house is first registered, when price change occurs to the property or when an offer is mad on the property. For this example only the first of these seed and the subsequent events that occur are described. Consequei or dependent events such as T_3 occur in response t completion of a previous task and are handled differentl These normally occur at the time of task completion. See events are generated according to a frequency distribution th is selected as being appropriate according to observations c system behaviour. The types of distributions that may b appropriate to a particular situation are given in Banks et. a

(1996). For this situation, observation suggested a negative exponential function with a mean new customer inter-arrival time of 1 day.

Task enactment occurs by specifying tasks in a generic process definition table that enables the simulation to be applicable to different business operations with minimal modification. To transform the physical workflow into the model workflow definition the following stages are involved:

1. Analyse existing and proposed systems in order to produce a logical workflow definition. In this case a flowchart (figure 3) is used to summarise the sequence of tasks that need to occur. In this example there is a single seed event (T_0) – Registration and multiple completion events (T_3) such as vendor registered which give rise to subsequent tasks (T_1).

2. Produce a physical workflow definition that forms an input to the simulation model in the form of a series of tasks. For each task it is necessary to define the following:-

- event name and identifier
- event type - is it a seed event (T_0) or a completion event (T_3)
- lead time before task needs to start (T_1- T_0 or T_1- T_3)
- task duration (T_2 - T_1)
- Next event relation and identifier

The task lead-time is specified as a minimum and a maximum probable according to observations of the real world system. If the minimum lead-time is 0 the next task may occur immediately on completion of the first. If it is greater than 0 there will be a practical reason for a delay before the next task can occur, for example it is normal to wait 1 day before attempting to follow up a viewing. The simulation time for the next task is calculated according to a negative exponential frequency distribution giving a range of times produced from the model between the minimum lead-time and the maximum lead-time. The time generated is used to insert a new event (task) into the calendar that will occur when the calendar is advanced to that time.

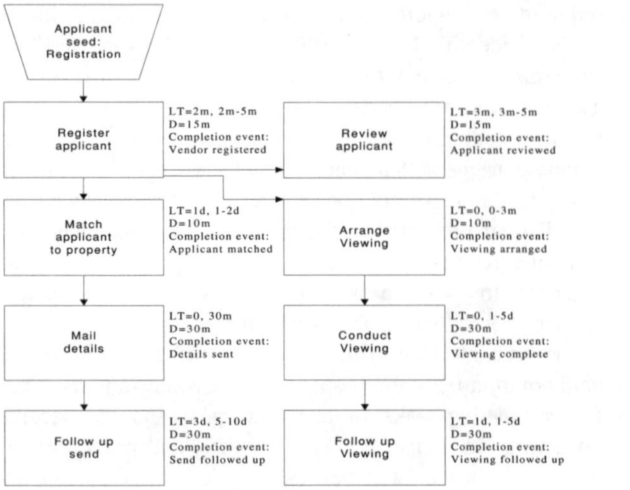

Figure 3. Workflow definition flowchart for estate agency applicant customer registration component

The only other model parameter that is varied for differer simulation runs is the duration. For this case it is necessary t run the simulation for an extended period of several week: since some tasks are only performed at the end of a proces that may take several months. The number of actors in th system are also specified in order to gauge the volume c workflow generated. These are the number of customers c applicant and vendor type and the number of service staf Typical results for this partial system are shown in Table I. It i seen that the main output from the system is equivalent to a activity or transaction log of a WFMS indicating the mai events and when they occurred.

Task	Task description	Date and time	Duration (mins)	Customer number
1	Enter store	01/12/97 18:35	0	1
2	Personal Contact	01/12/97 18:35	5	1
3	Register applicant	01/12/97 18:45	15	1
4	Enter store	02/12/97 09:05	0	2
5	Personal Contact	02/12/97 09:09	5	2
6	Register applicant	02/12/97 09:13	15	2
7	Match applicant to	02/12/97 18:46	10	1
8	Mail details	02/12/97 19:12	30	1
9	Match applicant to	03/12/97 09:17	10	2
10	Mail details	03/12/97 09:21	30	2
11	Arrange viewing	04/12/97 16:16	10	1
12	Enter store	04/12/97 16:50	0	3
13	Personal Contact	04/12/97 16:51	5	3
14	Register applicant	04/12/97 16:57	15	3
15	Match applicant to	05/12/97 10:02	10	3
16	Conduct viewing	05/12/97 16:16	30	1

Table I. Sample output from simulation transaction log

DISCUSSION

This paper has shown how a simple, yet functional discrete-event simulation system can be implemented on a spreadsheet to be used as a tool when developing CSCW systems that involve a workflow component.

Thus of the four functions of a WFMS described in the introduction, a workflow queue and corresponding metrics have been simulated, but with scheduling and routing to be added in future. Additionally, in future it is intended to develop more detailed metrics that can be used at different granularity's of time such as day, week and month. The model will also be applied to a full system and used in a range of situations where sequence types include AND and OR splits - this situation did not arise in this case study. With these modifications the range of applicable simulations will be extended further, giving additional opportunities for reducing implementation costs.

This paper has described the simulation implementation on a widely available and the well understood interface of a spreadsheet. However many specialised software packages for discrete-event simulation are available (e.g. ARENA™, MicroSaint™). Although these packages can be relatively expensive and often require knowledge of a proprietary simulation coding language they offer superior development and animation facilities that can be offered on the spreadsheet implementation presented here. Thus the spreadsheet implementation could be used to assess the usefulness of the simulation approach before investment in proprietary software for future sustained use of more complex models.

CONCLUSION

This paper has shown how a simulation capability enables a range of alternative scenarios for workflow implementation to be assessed at the prototyping stage thus reducing time for testing. The model produced was based on a standard three-phase discrete-event simulation approach with implementation using a spreadsheet platform. The spreadsheet simulation provides an accessible implementation platform that can be supplemented by a specialised simulation package for more complex analysis and more sustained use.

REFERENCES

Banks, J., Carson, J.S., Nelson, B.L. 1996 *Discrete-Event System Simulation* 2nd Edition, Prentice Hall.

Chaffey, D. 1996a. "Integration of IT Strategy, Process Analysis and System Implementation in an Office Automation based process improvement programme." In *Business process modelling*. 218-234. Scholz-Reiter, B. and Stickel, E. (eds), Springer Verlag, Berlin.

Chaffey, D. 1996b "Design and implementation factors in image retrieval across a Wide Area Network - a commercial example." *International Journa of Information Management*, Vol 15, No 6.

Davenport, T. 1993. *Process Innovation: Re-engineering work through Information Technology*. Harvard Business School Press, Boston.

Georgakopoulos, D., Hornick,M. AND Sheth, A. 1995. "An Overview of Workflow Management: From Process Modeling to Workflow Automation Infrastructure." *Distributed and Parallel databases*, Vol 3 119-153.

Giaglis, G.M. and Paul, R.J. 1996. "It's time to engineer re-engineering: Investigating the Potential of Simulation Modelling for Business Process Redesign." In *Business process modelling*. 313-332. Scholz-Reiter, B. and Stickel, E. (eds), Springer Verlag, Berlin.

Greasley, A. 1998. "An Example of a Discrete-Event Simulation on a Spreadsheet." *SIMULATION*, vol. 70, no. 3, pp. 148-166.

Hammer, M. & Champy, J. 1993. *Re-engineering the corporation: A manifesto for business revolution*. Harper Collins, New York.

Marazakis, M. and Nikolau, K. 1995. "Towards adaptive scheduling of tasks in transactional workflows." *Proceedings of the 1995 Winter Simulation Conference*. 604-611. ed. C.Alexopoulous, K.Kang, W.Lilegdon and D.Goldsman.

Miller, J., Sheth, A., Kochut, K., Wang, X. and Murugan, A. 1995. "Simulation modelling within workflow technology." *Proceedings of the 19 Winter Simulation Conference*. 612-619. ed. C.Alexopoulous, K.Kang, W.Lilegdon and D.Goldsman.

Paul, R.J. 1991. "Recent Developments in Simulation Modelling", *Journal c the Operational Research Society*, vol. 42, no. 3, 217-226.

Pidd, M. 1984. "Computer Simulation for Operational Research in 1984." I *Developments in Operational Research* (eds. R.W. Eglese & G.K. Rand), Pergamon Press.

Workflow Management Coalition (WfMC). 1996. *Reference model. Version 1. In The Workflow Management Coalition Specification. Terminology and glossary*. Document Number WFMC-TC-1011. Workflow Management Coalition, Avenue Marcel Thiry 204, 1200 Brussels, Belgium.

FACET: A SIMULATION SOFTWARE FRAMEWORK FOR MODELING COMPLEX SOCIETAL PROCESSES AND INTERACTIONS

John H. Christiansen
Decision and Information Sciences Division
Argonne National Laboratory
Argonne, Illinois 60439-4832
e-mail: jhc@anl.gov

KEYWORDS: object oriented, agent based, decision support systems, resource management, health care

ABSTRACT

FACET, the Framework for Addressing Cooperative Extended Transactions, was developed at Argonne National Laboratory to address the need for a simulation software architecture in the style of an "agent-based" approach, but with sufficient robustness, expressiveness, and flexibility to be able to deal with the levels of complexity seen in real-world social situations.

FACET is an object-oriented software framework for building models of complex, cooperative behaviors of agents. It can be used to implement simulation models of societal processes such as the complex interplay of participating individuals and organizations engaged in multiple concurrent transactions in pursuit of their various goals. These transactions can be patterned on, for example, clinical guidelines and procedures, business practices, government and corporate policies, etc. FACET can also address other complex behaviors such as biological life cycles or manufacturing processes.

To date, for example, FACET has been applied to such areas as land management, health care delivery, avian social behavior, and interactions between natural and social processes in ancient Mesopotamia.

INTRODUCTION

For most of the past decade, the Decision and Information Sciences Division (DIS) at Argonne National Laboratory (ANL) has had an on-going effort to develop robust object-based software architectures to address complex, multidisciplinary modeling and simulation problems. Most of our earlier object modeling work (ca. 1990-1995) focused on interactions among various natural processes (e.g., weather, hydrology, etc.). As the scope and complexity of our simulated domains grew to encompass human societal processes, we saw value in building a unifying software infrastructure to support construction and interoperation of societal process models, as well as interoperation of these societal process models with natural process models, within the same simulation frame of reference. The Framework for Addressing Cooperative Extended Transactions (FACET) is a product of this effort.

Certain general aspects of the behavior patterns embodied in societal processes tend to distinguish them from natural, or physics-based processes. Some of the hallmarks of societal processes are as follows.

- Processes involve some level of cooperation among the agents involved (though coercive behavior patterns are also possible).
- Agents may be concurrently involved in several behavior patterns and may need to prioritize their interactions and commitments to participate in these patterns.
- Behavior patterns can branch to follow several alternative paths and may segue into other patterns, based on social context.
- Processes can be interrupted and resumed at a later time.
- Processes can be preempted in progress, or be scheduled to occur but then be cancelled before they begin.

The FACET software infrastructure is designed to explicitly support modeling representation of these distinguishing characteristics. As a result of this design approach, FACET models can be more closely mapped to the often chaotic realities of social interchange, with less reliance on artificial abstractions and simplifications imposed by the modeling framework.

Fundamentally, FACET is a set of software objects that facilitate implementing and running models of complex, cooperative behaviors of agents. Here, the term, "agent," is used to denote simulation domain entities capable of autonomous, cooperative, and adaptive behavior. These agents are typically represented in a simulation by "Person" or "Organization" objects. FACET societal process models can be patterned on, for example, business practices, social mores and traditions, clinical practice guidelines and procedures, governmental and corporate policies, military doctrine, and so on. FACET can also be used to address complex behaviors not associated with human societal processes, such as zoological and botanical life cycles and manufacturing processes.

FACET SOFTWARE ARCHITECTURE

FACET models of complex, cooperative behaviors are run within a process-based discrete event simulation framework. At ANL, we have used the Dynamic Information Architecture System, or DIAS (Christiansen 2000), a distributed, object-based simulation framework, as the overarching discrete event simulation framework for FACET models.

Within the DIAS framework, new or legacy simulation models are provided with software object "wrappers" that formally define the model's capabilities and limitations, including specification of which abstractly defined behaviors of which classes of domain object they are qualified to implement. The set of models employed to implement domain object behaviors is then selected and linked to the objects whose behaviors they represent at run time, based on user-supplied information defining the context of the simulation. Although DIAS offers some strong advantages as an operating environment for FACET models, it is intended that FACET models be able to operate within other suitable discrete event modeling frameworks if desired.

FACET models can be run on workstations or personal computers under either UNIX or Windows NT. FACET was originally prototyped and built in the Smalltalk object-based language. A port of FACET from Smalltalk to Java is underway and should be completed by the end of summer 2000.

The FACET architecture relies on two main high-level software components, the "Course of Action" (COA) object class suite and the "Participant" object class. The suite of COA objects provides the infrastructure for building FACET behavior pattern models. Participant objects allow domain objects to take part as agents in FACET-based behavior patterns. Simulation domain objects of essentially any object class can participate as agents in FACET model behavior patterns, by associating them with FACET Participant objects.

Course of Action Object Class Suite

The COA object class suite defines a "collaborative extended transaction" model. A COA model is built as a network of individual steps, represented by "Step Template" objects, each of which is essentially a sub-model in its own right. Each step is roughly analogous to a scene in a play, with its own formally specified cast of characters (agents), props (agents' resources), and locale. Each step:

- Requires resources held by agents participating in the action;
- Consumes a specified (though variable) interval of time, during which the agents and resources are committed to the step and thus unavailable for other activities; and
- Results in changes to the state attributes of one or more of the participants, and/or changes to state attributes of other domain objects that had been declared to be of interest to the COA.

Although COAs are initially invoked by an agent as a response to a simulated situation, they are not necessarily "owned" by that agent. They are templates that provide a pattern for a number of different agents to collaborate to execute a complex dynamic behavior. For example, in a FACET health care simulation, a receptionist at an outpatient clinic, on receiving an event that indicates that a new patient has arrived in the waiting room with a cardiology appointment, may invoke a COA model that characterizes the detailed procedural flow for such an appointment. In this example, although the receptionist may launch the appointment COA model, the model actually represents a behavior of an *organization* - the clinic, or perhaps a particular medical department at the clinic - rather than a behavior of the receptionist. Several agents (doctors, nurses, technicians, receptionist, etc.) participate in the COA's behavior pattern on behalf of their organization. The COA is actually initiated by the organization when the receptionist sends a message that cues the organization to commence the appropriate behavior pattern. Once the behavior pattern is initiated, various agents representing doctors, nurses, etc. are cued to interact with each other and the patient on behalf of their organization.

The key object classes that make up the FACET COA object class suite, the COA Template, COA, and Step Template, are described below.

"Course of Action Template" Object Class (or "COA Template," see Figure 1) objects carry a directed graph of individual steps (Step Template objects). The Step Template objects specify the agents and other resources needed for each step and carry the instructions for what exactly is to be performed in the step. Generally, only one instance of each COA Template object class exists in the simulation frame of reference at any one time. Each unique behavior pattern, or FACET COA model, is a single instance of a subclass of the COA Template object class.

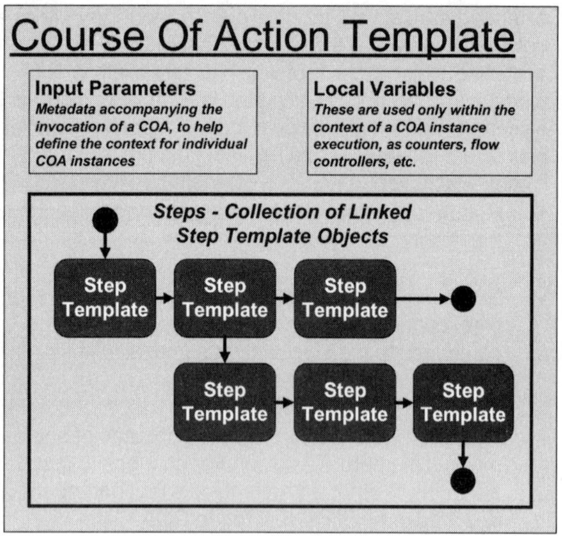

Figure 1. FACET Course of Action Template Object

The "Course of Action" Object Class (or "COA," see Figure 2) is associated with individual active instances of a behavior pattern, or COA Template.

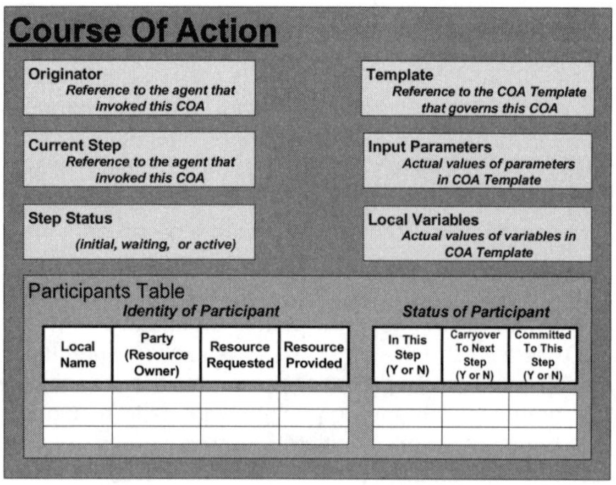

Figure 2. FACET Course Of Action Object

In contrast to the COA Template object class, there is only one *class* of COA object, but potentially a great number of *instances* of that class. Each COA object instance is, in essence, a "bookmark," indicating the current state of a *specific* extended transaction among simulation agents that is being modeled in accordance with a COA Template.

The centerpiece of the COA object class layout is the "Participants Table." This table correlates the generic names of actors and other resources declared in the Step Template objects' detailed step action layouts to specific resources requested from and provided by various agents in the simulation. Participants are added to and removed from the table as the COA proceeds through its steps. The Participants Table also indicates whether a resource is needed in the current step, whether it carries over from the previous step, and whether the resource has committed itself (or has been committed by its controlling agent) to participate in the step. Note that a domain object can be both an agent and a resource of another agent at the same time, as in the case of an organization (an agent) that employs individual persons. These persons are agents in their own right but can serve as resources within the employer organization's COAs.

Figure 3 provides a health care example of a COA object for a behavior pattern in progress. Here, the behavior pattern is a primary care routine return visit, and the pattern is performed on behalf of a family practice department at a hospital's medical clinic. As Figure 3 shows, the Participants Tables for steps in a COA are flexible. They can require either specific instances of an resource (e.g., a specific doctor at a clinic) or only a class of resource (e.g., "a nurse," or "an examination room").

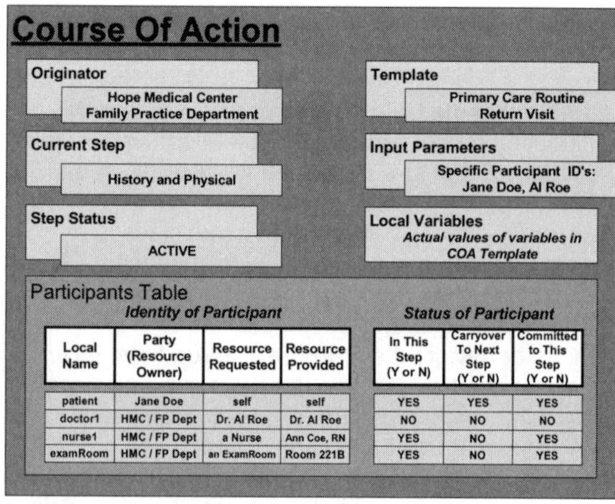

Figure 3. FACET Course of Action Object for a Health Care Behavior Pattern in Progress

The COA in Figure 3 shows a step in progress: a patient and a nurse are in an examining room cooperating in a "history and physical" step, in which the patient describes her symptoms, etc., and the nurse records this verbal information along with the patient's temperature, blood pressure, and possibly other measurements and observations. The doctor is not needed in this step, but is carried in the Participants Table because he is needed later in the office visit, for diagnosis, treatment, and/or referral steps.

A major simulation may have a very large number of agents or *ad hoc* groupings of agents embarked, in parallel, on the "same" COA. To continue with an example in the health care domain, thousands of individuals may be under the care of a health care organization for diabetes at any given time, and therefore nominally embarked on the same COA (although different individuals would be involved in different *steps* in the COA, both as patients and as health care providers). Figure 4 shows three active instances (COA's) of the same behavior pattern (COA Template) underway at a clinic. Note that the patterns happen to have progressed to different stages of completion (different steps). Also note that the participants in the different patterns have some overlap; the doctor, in particular, must have a means of resolving multiple concurrent demands for his/her time. This mechanism is provided by the "Participant " object class, discussed later in this paper.

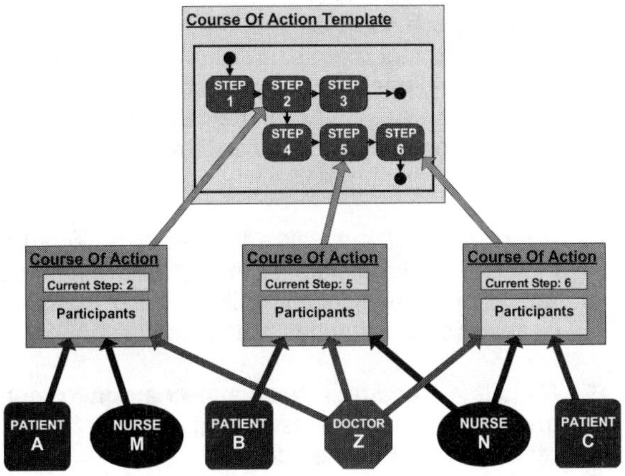

Figure 4. Simple Example of Relationship Between FACET COA Template Objects and COA Objects

The "Step Template" Object Class (Figure 5) carries the actual instructions to be carried out in a step of a COA. The Step Template also declares its own resource requirements. Each step can exist in one of three states:

- *Initial*: the previous step (if any) is over, and participants are being invited to participate in the current step.
- *Waiting*: all participants have been invited, but not all have committed to participate.
- *Active*: the step has begun, and has posted its own completion event for a future time, but has not yet run to completion.

The "Perform Step" code block does the actual work of a step, changing state variables of participating agents or other domain objects, and posting events and messages to other domain objects as needed. The "Decide Next Step" code block may have conditional logic for branching to alternate steps, based on values of participants' attributes, attributes of objects referenced in COA input parameters, and/or values of local variables relevant only to this instance of the COA. (The latter variables are held in a dictionary data structure in the COA object.)

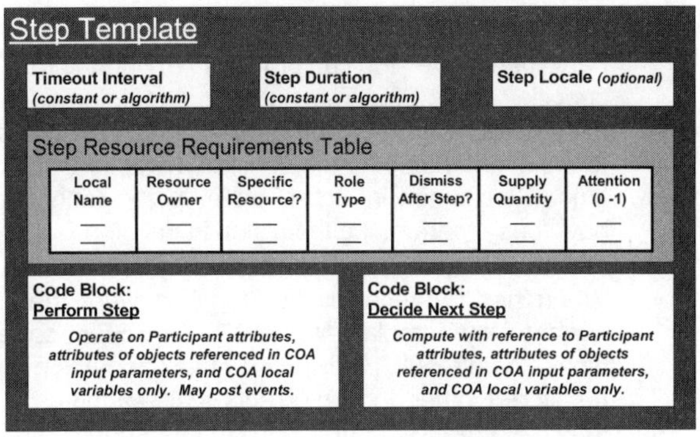

Figure 5. FACET Step Template Object

In Figure 5, the resource requirements table is used to drive the composition and generation of requests for participation in the step, and to update the COA's Participants Table. The "supply quantity" column addresses resource requests for consumables (fuel, food, etc.) as opposed to assets (staff, equipment, etc.). The "attention" column addresses the rather subtle problem of tasking agents in cases such as shift work, in which the task may not require the undivided attention of the agent for the full duration of the task. Via this FACET facility, it is possible to assign aggregate subtasks that are below the temporal resolution of the simulation. For example, a nurse in a hospital ward can be assigned a task such as making rounds to check patients' medications, for a full 8-hour shift but at, say, 0.15 attention. The practical constraint enforced by FACET is then that the nurse's tasks assigned for the shift may not exceed a total attention level of 1.0. In general, most agent participation requests tend to be assigned at an attention of 1.0. At the opposite extreme, however, patients may participate in some steps, such as wearing a portable cardiac monitor for a day, at an attention level of zero – the patient is definitely required for the step, but could in principle be doing something else concurrently as well.

The overall sequence of processing for a single step in a FACET COA can be characterized as follows. All processing described here is asynchronous and non-blocking.

- Enter step for the first time. Step is now in *initial* state.
- Step examines Step Template participants' requirements and posts invitations to all Step participants. Step is now in *waiting* state.
- Step waits for responses to invitations. If sufficient commitment of resources is not forthcoming before the step timeout interval has expired, exception

processing is performed (see "Exception" steps below).

- If sufficient response is received from the invited participants, the step can proceed. An algorithm specified in the Step Template is run to determine the step duration. A "Step End" event is then posted to the event queue for the computed step ending time. Step is now in "*active*" state - participants are now "busy" performing the action in the step.

- When the COA receives the Step End event, the current Step Template fires its "Perform Step" code block. As a result, participants' state attributes may be altered, other domain objects' state attributes may have been changed, participants' supply resources may be depleted or replenished, and events may be sent to other appropriate domain entities.

- The Step Template now fires its "Decide Next Step" code block, to determine which step will be invoked once the current step finishes.

- Participants are now released from the step; messages are sent to confirm this. The step then ends, and the next step begins.

The Step Template object class is subclassed to accommodate three somewhat different types of step: Actions, Expansions, and Exceptions. Most of the preceding discussion has focused on Actions, for simplicity, but the three types are handled quite similarly.

Actions are a type of step that has finite duration (in simulation time) and ties up assets and may consume supplies from among the agents participating in the Action.

Expansions are a type of step that implicitly calls for execution of another entire COA (thus "expands" a step into a COA). The sub-COA referenced in this Step then executes to completion and returns to the same Expansion step when done. Expansion steps facilitate the use of nested COAs, which is a very helpful capability and a key to ease of re-use of COA components

Exceptions are the key to the ability of FACET COA models to respond realistically to unusual circumstances. An Exception step is executed in place of the normal "current" step in a COA if a specified type of event is received by the COA object. Step timeout messages can also trigger an Exception step. An Exception step by definition has no participants, and takes no elapsed simulation time to perform, but carries the logic needed to route the COA onto a different sequence of steps, or to end the COA entirely. This allows COA's to preempt normal procedures, apply coping mechanisms or crisis management measures, etc., in response to changing conditions. FACET also supports the introduction of variability via randomly variable step durations and step timeout intervals, as well as random draws within a step's "Perform Step" and "Decide Next Step" logic blocks.

The "Participant" Object Class

The "Participant" object class provides the software infrastructure that allows a domain object to take part as an agent in FACET COA model behavior patterns. A Participant object is assigned as a delegate object to each simulation object for which COA model participation is desired. During the simulated duration of a COA step, the Participant object for each agent is cognizant of the existence, as well as the nature and extent, of the agent's participation, so that the resources (including the agent's personal attention, where appropriate) committed to the Action cannot be otherwise employed until the step terminates. Participant objects include the following key components:

- *Agenda Object*: maintains an up-to-date record of all unsatisfied requests for this agent's resources, and all of the agent's currently active and pending behavior patterns and resource commitments.

- *Resource Manager Object*: a mechanism to keep track of all commitments of, and requests for, resources held by the agent.

- *Role Objects*: a mechanism to allow agents to respond differently to requests depending on their current stance, or role, in the simulation. For example, a person who happens to be a doctor, a father, and a golfer might take on each of these roles at different times, but the resource allocation behaviors would likely be different for each role.

Agent Participation Negotiations

The FACET COA and Participant objects provide a highly flexible and expressive means for representing diverse transactions. The COA's essentially negotiate with the participating agents for their cooperation. The agendas of all potential participants are kept fully updated on the status of all *other* participants' commitment to a step, and each participant is free (subject to the constraints inherent in its own behavioral models) to join a step, refuse to join, defer joining pending other developments, join a different step on its agenda instead, designate specific resources from its resource pools to meet a general resource request, etc. For example, assume that a particular health care COA step requires a patient, examining room, nurse, and technician. A nurse might be assigned by his/her department to participate in the step, but if the technician fails to appear within a certain maximum wait time, the nurse can withdraw and await a different task or join a different step.

FACET APPLICATION EXAMPLES

At ANL, FACET has been applied to a diverse collection of application areas. Three such FACET applications are described here to illustrate the flexibility and range of applicability of the FACET architecture.

Sustainability of Ancient Mesopotamian Urban Centers under Environmental Stress

ANL is collaborating with the University of Chicago's Oriental Institute to build and exercise a dynamic object model of ancient Mesopotamian urban / agrarian life, using our DIAS and FACET object-based modeling frameworks. We are seeking a better understanding of the dynamics of ancient Mesopotamian urban centers – in particular their sustainability, growth, or decline in the face of environmental stress.

The initial simulation prototype represents a nucleated community of some 5,000 – 10,000 people, and its agricultural hinterlands, in northern Mesopotamia, circa 2,500 B.C. The actual historical prototype is the archaeological site now known as Tell Al-Hawa, near Mosul in northern Iraq (Ball et al. 1989). Simulations will address natural (weather, crop growth, hydrology, population dynamics, etc.) and societal (farming practices, kinship-driven behaviors, etc.) processes interweaving on a daily basis across 200-year simulations. This work is a substantial extension and expansion of earlier sustainability modeling work at the Oriental Institute (Wilkinson 1994). A key outcome of the FACET simulation is expected to be a new level of insight into the sensitivity of such a community to imposed environmental stresses such as droughts and soil erosion, in terms of ability to successfully handle such problems as labor shortages at harvest. Dynamic behaviors of software objects representing households, fields, crops, herds, etc. are simulated using (1) proven, existing natural systems models such as the U.S. Department of Agriculture's EPIC model for field crop dynamics and National Oceanographic and Atmospheric Administration paleoclimate models and (2) new FACET agent-based societal models based on archaeological and anthropological evidence.

Figure 6 depicts a simple subset of the COAs governing field crop management for individual family farming efforts in ancient northern Mesopotamia. In the step template flows shown, some steps have the option of repeating themselves. This reflects the notion that, once begun, those tasks tend to be addressed each day (or perhaps less often, for crop maintenance tasks) by appropriate teams of workers until they are completed. The processes illustrated here are undertaken each year by each of the several hundred to a few thousand extended families included in the Tell Al-Hawa urban area's simulation domain. Not included in the figure are the COA's that regulate the patronage relations between extended families and their lineage chiefs, nor between the lineage chiefs and the city's palace and temple households. Also not included here are the various economic behavior patterns, such as the undertaking of loans of grain, with repayment often in kind or in labor, as well as the pastoral component of the community and its continual interchange with the agricultural component.

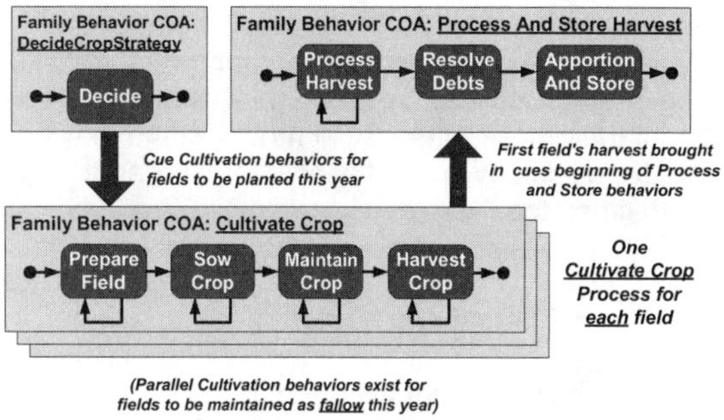

Figure 6. Course of Action Templates for Simplified Field Crop Management Behavior Patterns for a Single Ancient Mesopotamian Extended Family

Avian Social Dynamics in the Context of Integrated Land Management at U.S. Army Installations

ANL is currently completing a project for the U.S. Army Corps of Engineers Construction Engineering Research Laboratory aimed at exploring the social behaviors and population dynamics of an endangered bird species, the red-cockaded woodpecker (RCW), within the context of training activities and integrated land management initiatives at U.S. Army training facilities (Dolph et al. 2000). Using the FACET and DIAS frameworks, we have constructed an object-oriented individual-based, spatially explicit population dynamics model for the red-cockaded woodpecker, based on a model described by Letcher et al. (1998). This model can then be used to predict RCW populations dynamically in space and time, given that various land use and land management influences are acting within the ecosystem. FACET has been used to model the behavior patterns of the land management activities (planting, burning, etc.) that are included in the environmental stimuli impinging upon RCW populations.

For use in the RCW simulations, FACET models represent social behaviors of RCWs, such as the cooperative behaviors of a breeding pair. The FACET "agents" are in this case individual birds. The resource that each bird provides is simply its commitment to carry out the prescribed behaviors for the specified times and time intervals. RCW social dynamics, as prescribed in the Letcher et al. model, unfold on a seasonal basis. For each season, the following dynamics are addressed:

- Reproduction (1st season of each year only),
- Mortality,
- Movement (dispersal), and
- Competition (basically, males compete for territory, females for mates).

The FACET RCW model implementation uses regularly scheduled discrete events to move the simulated RCW population state forward in uniform seasonal time steps. Other dynamic processes (e.g., weather, hydrology, land management practices) can be running concurrently with the RCW model in the same simulation, allowing for inter-process feedbacks These other processes can be running with time steps different than those of the RCW model; some may be driven by irregularly spaced events rather than a uniform time step.

Health Care Clinical and Logistical Simulation

ANL has used both the FACET and DIAS software architectures to assemble HealthSim, a flexible software framework for addressing clinical and logistical aspects of health care delivery over a broad range of simulation level of detail and fidelity. HealthSim has been exercised in extensive applications for a large health care organization in California.

HealthSim uses scores of simulation models running in the same simulation, with many thousands of agents, to address the interplay of diverse dynamic behaviors, such as:

- Human physiological processes, including onset and progression of diseases, development of signs and symptoms, effects of interventions, etc. These are typically modeled using mathematical (e.g., differential equation integrator) biological models.

- Human cognitive behaviors, such as response to symptoms, making and keeping appointments, etc. FACET models are used here.

- Clinical / logistical processes, such as clinical practice guidelines, office procedures, personnel policies, etc. FACET has been used to represent all such processes.

- Medical monitoring equipment response. These are typically mathematical, engineering models.

In HealthSim, the FACET agent objects include organizations, such as medical departments, and individual persons in the occasionally overlapping roles of health care provider and patient. Individual "Person" objects include embedded "Physiology" objects with nested physiological subsystem objects. Models of normal physiological processes and pathophysiology are run as behaviors of these physiology objects. The Person objects experience symptoms by virtue of sign / symptom events they receive, posted by their own physiological objects in response to physiological changes.

Two brief examples illustrate the range of applicability of the HealthSim framework:

1. Access to Care. Multi-year simulations were performed for the entire 300,000 member population for a large medical center in Los Angeles, with over 400 doctors and other primary care providers. More than one million simulated health care service requests were processed through the system per simulated year. Over 30 medical departments were represented at fairly coarse resolution; the parent health care organization's Call Center was represented at fairly fine resolution. Issues addressed by these simulations included various aspects of the ability of the system to respond to shifting member service area demographics and overall increases in membership. Results from the simulation included wait times for appointments, bed and staff utilization, financial reports, etc.

2. Effectiveness of Cardiac Clinical Practice Guidelines. Multi-decade simulations were performed for the same medical center, for roughly 3,000 males at high risk for heart disease. Detailed normal physiology and heart disease pathophysiology and risk factor models were run for each patient. The dozen or so medical departments relevant to cardiac care, along with the Call Center, were modeled at fairly fine resolution. This required implementation of FACET COA models for the clinical, clerical and logistical detailed behavior patterns that come into play in providing care for heart disease patients. The range of procedures employed by the medical center in providing emergency and inpatient care for cardiac patients was represented by 33 separate COA models, covering behavior patterns, such as:
   - Emergency Room (ER) check-in and triage,
   - ER chest pain diagnosis,
   - Patient admission procedures,
   - Physician supervision in the Intensive Care Unit,
   - Inpatient EKG and echocardiogram tests,
   - Inpatient defibrillation, and
   - Transfer of a patient from one inpatient medical department to another.

The general question addressed by the fine-resolution heart disease simulations was what would be the effect of varying the rates of patient compliance with guidelines for administering cholesterol-lowering and blood-pressure-lowering drugs on outcomes for patients with high risk factors for heart disease?

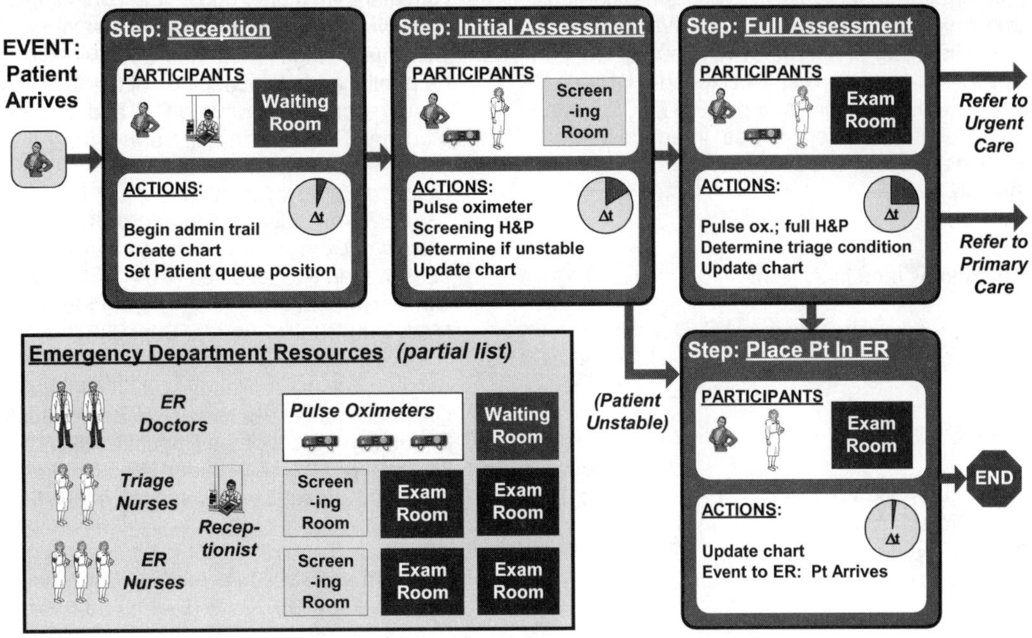

Figure 7. FACET Health Care COA Example:
Emergency Room Standard Check-In and Triage

Results included incidence of chest pains and heart attacks, rates of heart-disease-related hospital admissions, unplanned emergency room visits, etc.

Figure 7 is a simplified illustration of one of the 33 cardiac care COAs, "Emergency Room Standard Check-In and Triage," which is invoked by the medical center's Emergency Department in response to an event indicating that a new patient has presented in the ER. In our cardiac care simulations, the behavior pattern represented in Figure 7 is implemented by an active COA for each patient who has presented at the medical center's ER and has not yet been treated, admitted, referred to other health care services or otherwise provided for. All of these various follow-up activities are covered by other COAs that are cued to activate based on the possible outcomes of the ER Standard Check-In and Triage COA process. Each active instance of this COA has the patient as a participant in all steps. The COAs contend with each other for the other necessary participants - all of whom, or all of which, are resources of the Emergency Department, shown in the box in the lower left of the figure. The actual mechanisms for resolving precedence for patients' access to ER resources are carried within the "Perform Step" logic of the different steps.

PROSPECTS FOR FUTURE DEVELOPMENT AND APPLICATION OF FACET

Several diverse FACET application areas in addition to those described in this paper are planned or are in the early stages of development. They include:

- Military mission planning and resource management for "Operations Other Than War" applications (famine and flood relief, peacekeeping, etc.);
- Socioeconomic simulation of the South American cocaine industry, in the context of an effort to improve drug traffic interdiction effectiveness in the Caribbean, Central America, and Eastern Pacific regions;
- Operational risk assessment for financial institutions and others; and
- Cross-country logistics planning and management decision support.

It is ANL's intent to make the FACET package accessible to a wide range of users. One short-term measure undertaken to facilitate this goal is the porting of the framework from Smalltalk to Java. While Smalltalk was ideal for prototype development, we believe that a Java-based product will reach a larger audience. A longer-term goal is to provide FACET with a fully featured, intuitive graphical user interface to assist model developers in COA model implementation.

ACKNOWLEDGMENT

This work is sponsored by the U.S. Department of Energy under contract number W-31-109-ENG-38.

REFERENCES

Ball, W.; D. Tucker; and Wilkinson, T.J. 1989. "The Tell Al-Hawa Project: Archaeological Investigations in the North Jazira 1986-1987." *Iraq* 51: 1-66.

Christiansen, J.H. 2000. *"A Flexible Object-Based Software Framework for Modeling Complex Systems with Interacting Natural and Societal Processes."* To be published in Proceedings of the 4th International Conference on Integrating GIS and Environmental Modeling (Banff, Canada, Sept. 2-8).

Dolph, J.E.; J.H. Christiansen; and P.J. Sydelko. 2000. *"FACET: An Object-Oriented Software Framework for Modeling Complex Behavior Patterns."* To be published in Proceedings of the 4th International Conference on Integrating GIS and Environmental Modeling (Banff, Canada, Sept. 2-8).

Letcher, B.H.; J.A. Priddy; J.R. Walters; and L.B. Crowder. 1998. "An Individual-Based Spatially-Explicit Simulation Model of the Population Dynamics of the Endangered Red-Cockaded Woodpecker, *Picoides borealis*." *Biological Conservation* 86: 1-14.

Wilkinson, T.J. 1994. "The Structure and Dynamics of Dry-Farming States in Upper Mesopotamia." *Current Anthropology* 35, No. 5 (Dec.): 483-519.

SIMULATION INDUSTRY AND BUSINESS PRACTICES

SIMULATION ON THE NATIONAL AGENDA

CRITICAL ISSUES IN SIMULATION

Vince Amico
Consultant
831 Longhaven Drive
Maitland, FL 32751
407-644-7556
amico@cs.ucf.edu

Agostino G. Bruzzone
Professor
Instituto di Technologie
ed Impianti Meccanici
Universita degli Studi di Genova
via Opera Pia 15
16145 Genova, Italy
+39 010 353 2275
agostino@itim.unige.it

Ratan Guha
Professor
School of Electrical Engineering
and Computer Science
University of Central Florida
Orlando, FL 32816-2362
guha@cs.ucf.edu

Keywords Simulation, Modeling, Data, Computer Systems, Software, Validation

ABSTRACT

The four basic phases of a simulation project include; modeling, data and knowledge, implementation and validation. The critical issues associated with those phases determine the effectiveness of the simulation. This paper addresses the factors that contribute to those issues that may result in decreased effectiveness or invalidate the simulation. Suggestions are offered to assist in the early identification of potential for difficulties, thus leading to simulations that can achieve the objectives successfully.

1. INTRODUCTION

Simulation as a tool for analysis, design, experimentation, testing, training and logistics has became viable with the advent of practical computing technology. The era from 1940 through 1960 was dominated by analog computers especially for man in the loop real time simulations. Digital computers became prevalent in the late 1950's and early 1960's and ultimately replace analog computing as the platform of choice. Although the technology for the modeling process has significantly improved, the critical issues in the development of a simulation have remained the same.

Before discussing the Critical Issues in Simulation, the factors that make simulation a viable option in the development of emerging systems should be reviewed briefly. Modeling and simulation supports efforts in the development of new systems starting at the conceptual phase and continuing throughout the design, production, testing, training and logistics phases of a development.

The training phase continues as long as a system is in use. Simulators provide training for operators of complex man machine systems where safety and potential damage to equipment are involved. Simulation also enables the Armed Forces to conduct individual and team training as well as large-scale multi-unit exercises to develop and evaluate tactics and strategy. The resources required to conduct live exercises are generally impractical.

With the increased demand for modeling and simulation in all facets of government, industry and commerce it is important to define the process and the critical issues that are involved. It is this examination of the process that leads to the identification of the critical issues in simulation identified in this paper. Keeping these issues in mind will facilitate the creation of a simulation that satisfies the original requirement.

This paper is organized as follows: In section 2 we discuss the software development process and identify some other factors related to simulation that contribute to the effectiveness of a simulation. In section 3 we define a matrix of simulation framework to identify the purpose and level of simulation. In sections 4 – 7 we discuss the critical issues in all phases of the simulation development process and illustrate by examples from reported previous experiences. Finally, we summarize our discussion in section 8.

2. THE SIMULATION DEVELOPMENT PROCESS

The development of a simulation begins with the identification of a requirement. The verbal or conceptual statement of a requirement is then converted into a written document or a conceptual model.

Once a requirement for a simulation has been established, the development process consists of four basic phases. These phases are: development of the mathematical model(s); obtaining valid data including knowledge based data; implementation of the simulation models which consists of the selection of the computer hardware and development of the software programs and finally the validation of the simulation. These phases are directly related to the critical issues in simulation namely: 1. Modeling; 2. Data; 3. Implementation and 4. Validation. The first three critical issues; modeling, data and implementation are very closely related and thus one can impact the other areas.

In our experience, we find that there is several other factors, not directly a part of each phase mentioned above, contribute to the decreased effectiveness of a simulation. We briefly discuss those issues in the remainder of this section.

Budget Planning Limitations

The budget process may influence the direction of a project. If the development time and cost of the simulation system exceeds preliminary estimates, it may be necessary scale back the requirements to fit within the budget amount. These initial reductions in the scope of the simulation result in future problems if the scaling back is done, more from a cost cutting perspective, without making corresponding reductions in the requirements.

The Length of the Development Cycle

Another factor that contributes to the difficulties in developing useful simulation products is the development time involved. A major simulation systems or simulator can take as much as from 5 to 10 years to develop including the planning and budget cycle. During that time the system that you are planning to simulate probably has been changing. The intended application also may have changed. The people who originated the project may no longer be there to give their interpretation of the need. The length of the development process, which may take years, compounds the problems of developing a useful simulation.

Communications During the Development Cycle

The initial requirements document is the basis for subsequent validation testing through each phase of the development process. The conversion of this initial requirements document to a conceptual model is the most important step in the development of a simulation. (Pace 2000). The validation of the conceptual model is necessary to create a simulation, which reflects the original requirement. If the conceptual model does not reflect the objectives of the simulation and the project continues, major errors may not be detected until the final validation.

Subjective interpretation of each written document significantly contributes to the difficulties in developing a simulation the will meet the original requirement. As a requirement statement is translated into the next phase, it carries some element of bias or distortion resulting from the interpretations placed on the prior document. Experience indicates that a project usually continues despite the lack of a validity test at the completion of each phase. This propagation of errors, which continues through each of the phases of development, may result in a final product, which differs, from the requirement. At the completion of each phase, the simulation design must be evaluated in relation to the goals set forth in the requirements document.

3. SIMULATION FRAMEWORK

With the simulation development process defined, as well as its relationship to the critical issues, a framework with which to discuss these issues can now be establish.

Why is the selection of the correct models so important? Models that do not represent the behavior of the systems being simulated will give erroneous results. Rigorous models with details that are not significant or observable may result in unnecessary requirements for the computational system.

Consider a matrix that covers the levels of the simulation along one axis, and the simulation applications along the other axis. The levels of simulation would range from such items as components, sub-assemblies, systems and multi-systems. The simulation applications axis would range from: feasibility studies, analysis, design, development, testing, evaluation, training and logistics. A simulation framework is defined at each point of this space. This framework indicates the purpose of simulation and the level of simulation.

Three additional factors must be considered as we define the models. They are: the range of the variables in the models; the size of the gaming area; and environmental models that are associated with the simulation. Environmental models include terrain, atmosphere, and the ocean. If the requirements for the simulation include emergencies, then the models must be extended beyond their normal envelopes of operation.

4. CRITICAL ISSUE IN MODELING

Models define the behavior of such systems as; physical, biological, medical and environmental as well as human beings. These models then form the basis of a simulation.

Model Classification

The level of simulation models range from such items as components, sub-assemblies, systems and multi-systems. The objectives of each of these levels are not necessarily identical. At the component level there is a requirement for great detail and accuracy while at the multi-system level only state information on any one system is all that may be necessary.

Component Models. Component models form the basic building blocks for higher-level models such as sub-systems and systems models. Today's software tools, based on different approaches/philosophies, allow for easy and detailed modeling of components. In effect the integration of different paradigms allows one to reproduce components with complex behaviors dictated by different phenomena (electrical, mechanical, thermal etc.). Component modeling however, is very critical in complex systems, where the general behavior is driven by high-level interactions among many items (i.e. power plants). Thus in many cases general-purpose languages provide a common framework for defining components and their behavior/malfunctions.

Sub-Systems Models Sub-systems models are more concerned with the interaction of components, They may be treated as input-output functions rather than as detailed component behavior models.

System Models System models are in essence a collection of component and sub-systems models. The purpose of the simulation determines the level of detail and rigor. For the analysis or design stages one must use as complete and comprehensive a proven model as is available. When the application is training oriented, simplification can be made to the model and still achieve the required training objectives.

Multi-System Models Multi-System Models cover simulation that involve hundreds of units or platforms either manned or generated by the computer. Since the objective of these simulations is to develop, test and evaluate systems and their optimal tactical employment, and then to train task forces in their effective use, it is only necessary to provide state information of task force components to Command Centers. War Gaming models are generally completely computerized and are used to explore and evaluate various strategic policies and tactical doctrines. These models usually involve logistics, communications and other supporting systems that can influence the outcome of a given scenario.

Updating Models for Changes

Models must be updated to account for all the design changes that have been made to the system during its detail design, fabrication and test phases. Component and sub-system performance and dynamic data must be obtained to verify the elements of the model.

Model Applications

The applications of models range from the conceptual phase through the design, production and logistics phases of a project. At the conceptual phase of a project, the models must be theoretically correct and accurately represent the simulation objectives. In order to obtain valid results, no simplification should be made at this phase. The integrity of the model should be retained as the project moves from the component through the subsystem and finally the system phase for design, test and evaluation applications.

As the model application moves to the training and logistics phases, the objectives have more to do with the training of individuals to operate complex man machine safely and effectively. These simulations usually require large gaming area with sophisticated environmental models. These environmental models are required to support the vehicle motion computation, visual displays and a host of sensors systems. As the training objectives move up the matrix the model requirements can be adapted for the specific application.

Model Confidence

The detail level of the model as well as the model confidence must be directly related to the simulation project requirements and expectations. Exceeding the required level of detail usually results in increased costs and project delays. It is essential to verify that the confidence goals are reachable based on measurable data and available resources.

Model Reusability

The reuse of the simulation models is a major topic of discussion today. Software reusability will result in substantial savings of time and cost and could allow one to integrate modules, objects and models. However a deep knowledge of the original model is required to guarantee the success due to the intrinsic complexity of real industrial/military simulators. In addition, a complete validation must be performed on the new model to insure that validated objects will produce inconsistent results in new boundary conditions or in untested configurations.

Examples of Modeling Issues

Models can experience any one of a number of errors. These errors include: incorrect models, incomplete models, models are not revised when required, models are simplified because the accurate models are too complex for solution. Some examples are listed below.

Incorrect Model Initially the plan was to use a high frequency acoustic propagation model for a sonar simulation. However the sonar system was also capable of acquiring low frequency signals covering bottom bounce and convergence zone propagation paths. The revised acoustic models were much more complex.

Range of Variables A visual system developed for commercial airline application was installed on a fighter aircraft simulator. The aircraft roll rates for the fighter was much higher that those of commercial airline simulators and as a result the visual scene could not follow the fighter aircraft roll rates. The visual system had to be modified to accept the higher roll rates.

Rigorous Models Probably one of the most classical cases of debate over models is in the simulation of the main rotor of a helicopter. The model normally used, because of its relative simplicity, is the Vectored Thrust model. A much more detailed model is called the Blade Element model. That model requires an enormous amount of computing power.

Incomplete Models The surface ship dynamic models must include the forces that produce ship motion such as: wind, current, mooring lines, and tugs in addition to the internal ship controls. The modeling of these external forces is relatively complex. It took many years to develop effective models for docking. (Bruzzone et. al. 1997)

Correct Models When the correct model is used the results are very gratifying. Here is one example. In many facilities the material handling (from pallets in a production department to ammunitions inside a carrier) is a typical problem where simulation can improve efficiency and avoid operative problems. Obviously the model definition is critical for the successful application. In ATA, a corporation involved in environmental treatment, the use of proper simulation models improved the efficiency of transportation systems by 40%, just by re-engineering the management policy. (Bruzzone 1996)

Complex Models Environmental models are very complex and very dependent on conditions at a given time. It is not common to include unusual environmental conditions in the model. When severe down drafts are encountered that caused accidents in commercial airline operations, the simulators had to be modified to add this condition to the environmental model.

Model Simplification Simplifications are made to the model to accommodate available data or to facilitate programming? Do these models truly represent the behavior of the systems? Is some randomness introduced into the models in order to replicate the operational counterparts? These model issues also relate to degraded systems performance and the introduction of emergencies.

5. CRITICAL ISSUES IN DATA AND KNOWLEDGE

Given that the appropriate modeling for the system being simulated has been defined, the need for complete and accurate data is the next most important issue in developing a simulation. Data, in its broadest interpretation, must include the characteristics of physical systems, the environment, knowledge bases and the behavioral data that are an essential part of simulation models.

Obtaining Data and Knowledge for Models

The search for complete and accurate data is relentless. The results are frequently frustrating. In obtaining data for simulation models one or more of the following problems can be experienced; it can be incomplete, it may be inaccurate, some data may not be available. When data are obtained it must be evaluated and decisions made as to how to represent it mathematically. If data are not available, the creation of data based on best assumption is an area that must be viewed with suspicion. Assumed data should be tagged for replacement as soon as actual data becomes available.

Systems Data

The data used in models goes through an evolution starting with the data utilized in analytical and design models to that used in training and logistics models.

Data for models can be obtained from a variety of sources. The model for an emerging system has a greater probability for data errors. The initial design usually undergoes hundreds, if not thousands, of changes. The more mature the model and the actual system, the easier it is to obtain valid data. The developers should institute systems to track changes in the design of a system throughout its entire life cycle. Each change must be evaluated for its potential impact on the simulation. There should be a disciplined approach to the control of changes.

Environmental Data

The resolution of terrain data required for effective visual and sensor systems simulations are critical issues. Even with today's powerful computers, visual scenes are more like artistic representations than photographic images. Ocean modeling is another complex data area. Here again the variability of the ocean makes a universal model and a general data set impossible. Even when the variability of conditions is limited for a given scenario the data requirements are complex. (Heintzman 1984)

Knowledge Data

Obtaining real system behavior for a simulation project is very complex process (in effect this is the motivation for using Modeling & Simulation) The correlation and interactions among the components as well as their behavior is difficult to define either by, rules, equations or large scale databases. For these reasons it is very important to perform engineering analysis of the problem and to mix real system experts with simulationists in order to share the knowledge of internal processes.

Human Behavior Data

Many models for large military engagement systems or for interactive simulations such a driver training requires the modeling of human behavior to enable the computer to take on the roles of individuals or manned systems. (Klee, 2000). Research in the area of intelligent computer generated objects continues to improve the fidelity of modeling and thus broadens the applications and increases the validity of the simulations.

Examples Illustrating Issues with Data

The collection of valid data is a difficult process. A number of representative examples are cited below to give the range and depth of some of the difficulties.

Incorrect Aircraft Data Relating to Aircraft Model Changes A decision was made to use the simulation models and data from an earlier version of the aircraft on a new model of the same aircraft. When the simulator went into the test phase it came obvious that the results did not represent the new aircraft model. The entire simulation had to be redesigned. The program was delayed by about 2 years.

Data Availability and Changes When digital computers began to be incorporated into operational systems the first approach was to simulate the functions of the digital computer. An immediate problem arose because of the unavailability of the program data for that computer. Thus, when the onboard computer was simulated, the simulator was unable to keep up with the changes in the operational software. There are examples in aircraft simulators, submarine simulators and various sensor simulators. This situation has also occurred in the nuclear power plant simulators. (Amico 1984)

Incorrect Data A firm never achieved the car production target for few years. The analysts were complying with the low motivation, personnel skills, etc. for the area. The model was developed based on such productivity hypothesis. After a period of operation, an analysis based on field-collected data, demonstrated that the hypothesis for the initial design was based on a wrong market scenario. With the real market scenarios and with the optimal personnel efficiency at the production site included in the model, the painting tools and equipment parts were identified as the critical bottleneck in the process (Bruzzone & Giribone 1998)

Incomplete Data An automated filling line for mineral oil was developed by a leading company in that field. The site commissioning was successful and the target of 10,000 box/day was reached. However the real daily production never surpassed a 7,000-box/day threshold until a simulation study demonstrated that an elevator malfunctions was affecting the overall performance due to interactions with the automation control system. As a result of the simulation study, the firm was able to re-engineer the facility and achieve the design goal with reduced investments. (Giribone & Bruzzone 1997)

6. CRITICAL ISSUES IN IMPLEMENTATION

The implementation of a simulation consists of the computational system, hardware, and the software. The computational system must have sufficient speed and memory capacity to solve the simulation models for either real-time or non-real time simulations. The other component is the software programs that implement the models. These two closely related impact on the other.

Computational Systems

Non-Real Time Systems General-purpose digital computers are used to solve equations in non-real time. Outputs are either through printouts or a graphical interface or both. Non real time simulations in such area as nuclear weapons testing and environmental weather models require super computing facilities. If the run time for these simulations is too excessive, the computer may fail before a run is completed.

Real-Time Computational Systems The selection of a computer with adequate speed and memory for real-time man-in-the-loop simulations are very critical. The factors that contribute to this issue are related to the speed and memory capacity of the computer. Sizing is determined by the software representation of the models that must be solved with certain iteration rates. These rates are determined by the dynamics of the systems, its stiffness. The visual and sensor systems are another critical aspect of these simulations. In order for a visual system to be effective the display must be updated at least 30 frames per second..

Examples of Issues with Computational System Implementation

Computer Capacity The computer capacity was seriously underestimated for a system that included one of the first digital radar land mass simulators. There were also problems with estimating the complexity of the aircraft model itself. When system tests began it was determined that the computer capability had to be doubled. That resulted in major delays in delivery of the simulator.

Iteration Rates Aircraft cockpit control inputs to a computer were implemented through digital encoders on the controls. The computer was not able to accommodate the step inputs and the system failed. Prior control input technology was utilized to resolve the problem. In order to accommodate direct inputs an iteration rate of about 1500 Hz. is required instead of the 16 Hz. iteration rate of the flight equations. (Amico 1981)

Transport Delays One of the first Computer Generated Visual Systems ran into serious problems. The time delays in scene generation in response to pilot input were excessive. Human Factors studies were conducted to determine the cause of the problem and solution that would be necessary to make the system acceptable. This study concluded that the time delay should not greater than 80 to 90 milliseconds. These criteria placed a burden on the computational system because of the higher iteration rates that were required. This led to the 30 Hz. or 60 Hz. iteration rate requirement currently used when there are visual system attachments. These rates are also consistent with television frame rates. (NTEC Report TM-56 1977)

Software

Computer Software provides the tools for converting the models that have been developed into the form that the computer can execute. The computer programs must consider the characteristics of the system to insure that computations will be stable and provide the accuracy required for specific functions.

Software Errors The development of large-scale simulation model that involve thousand and perhaps million of instructions is a potential source of problems. Software is not perfect. What minimum error rate is acceptable? There must be sufficient independent software testing to determine if the software error rate is acceptable and will not cause computer systems shutdowns.

Vehicle Dynamics The major factors that influence the software requirements are the stiffness of the vehicles (iteration rate required for stable computation). The iteration rate establishes one of the key parameters in the software design as well as in the selection of the computational system. These parameters are also critical if any visual attachments are to be provided. (NTEC Report TM-56 1977), (Amico 1981)

Integrating Algorithms Another important issue is the selection of the most efficient integrating algorithms for the simulation application. There is a wide range of algorithms with varying degrees of accuracy. There has been much research directed toward improving the efficiency and accuracy of integrating algorithms. The accuracy of a platform track and location has been a major issue in implementing Distributed Interactive Simulations

Environmental Databases The size and resolution of any database used to generate sensor displays or visual imagery influence the size and complexity of the environmental database. Although substantial progress has been made in improving the resolution of sensor and visual systems, the processing of high-resolution environmental data is still a major computer speed and capacity problem.

Distributed Interactive Systems (DIS) And High Level Architecture (HLA) DIS and HLA are coping with the issues resulting from heterogeneous simulation systems interacting in a distributed multi-system environment. While there have been successes in applying HLA to distributed simulation scenarios, its application to more complex scenarios is still under development. The issues of uniform environmental models across all platforms and the data exchange efficiencies that will result in acceptable transport delays are areas that are still being addressed

Examples of Issues with Software Implementation

Software Design Errors A number of years ago there was a project that involved a major computer hardware and software development effort. The project started out with an estimate 10,000 instructions and ended up with over 80,000 instructions, small by today's standards but a major task in its time. The only way to test the software was to subject it to a major independent validation on a large mainframe computer. When test were started the error rate was about 10%. The software debugging process took about six months. After testing was completed the error rate was reduced to about .5%. The simulator could operate without experiencing any interruptions. But the entire hardware and software testing process took over 2 years on what was to have been an 18-month program. (Amico 1983)

7. CRITICAL ISSUE IN VALIDATION

Validation is the process of testing a simulation to determine if it accomplishes its stated objectives. Validation thus insures that the integrity of the initial requirement is maintained in the process of converting the original requirement into a useful product. Though it is usually associated with the final phase of a simulation project, validation should play an integral role in the project from the creation of the conceptual model. (Pace 2000). The user of the simulation models products and/or person defining the requirement should be involved in the validation of each phase of the simulation.

For simulation user and decision makers to trust the results of the simulation, conclusions and recommendations, experts in formal statistical analysis techniques with a trained staff for preparing and distributing the results of the simulations are essential. When simulation is utilized in the decision making process, the user greatly benefits from the timely delivery of a clear and concise presentation of the feasibility and drawbacks indicated by the results. If simulation is to be used as a final product, several critical tests must be demonstrated to convince the user of the applicability of the simulation.

Validation of the Models and Data

In the design phase, models are developed with the associated data. The computing system requirements are also determined as well as the software specifications. Each of the models and data elements should be reviewed against the stated requirement to validate the design.

Validation of the Implementation

Implementation the hardware and software design is the next phase. The development of a simulation is not any different than the development of any other kind of system. Thus one must expect that a number of changes will take place to correct errors in the design or to reflect changes in the Work Statement or for any number of other reasons. One might say that the process is one that is designed to meet an evolving Work Statement requirement by a process of continuous refinement. These changes will result in additional development time and associated costs.

Testing the Simulation

As the simulation advances into testing there are two distinct phases. One phase is primarily internal to the simulation developer. The objective of those tests is to determine if the simulation performs as designed. The next phase involves the agency for with the simulation was developed. Those test are conducted to determine if the requirements of the Work Statement are satisfied.

Testing to the Design As the simulation project advances into the component, sub-system and system testing phases, you experience another phenomena. That is, the level of test is directly related to, "who is testing the system to what criteria." At the lowest test level, the developers are usually interested in testing the element of the systems to determine if the simulation performs as designed. At this point there is usually no relationship to the ultimate user's needs.

Testing to the Work Statement This phase of testing determines if the simulation meets the requirements of the Work Statement. Representative of the system acquisition agency will conduct the test. Here again the focus is to determine if the simulation meets Work Statement requirements, not necessarily looking at the requirement's statement.

Validating the Simulation

The final phase of testing determines if the simulation meets the final version of the requirements statement. Tests are usually performed by agents of the user. The user will not only determine if simulation meets the requirement statement, but he will also determine if the simulation will accomplish the intended purpose. Sometimes they are not the same.

Examples of Issues with Validation

Correct Validation Criteria Simulators of military aircraft require much more comprehensive testing to determine if the simulator does in fact represent the performance and flying qualities of the actual aircraft. Obtaining aircraft test data required for validation testing is difficult. The application of FAA commercial aircraft standards will not cover the operating envelope of the military aircraft. (Galloway 1999)

Invalidated Simulations Sometime process re-engineering is performed based on qualitative analysis or untested simulations. The development of a new large automatic warehouse was assigned to a major automation company. The designer decided to use simulation to support their analysis. They developed a model that did not consider forklift interference based on the a-priori hypothesis that this phenomenon didn't have any influence. After the implementation no validation test was performed. The new warehouse design resulted in a 40% loss in productivity. The resulting claim was analyzed by third party experts using a new simulator that accounted for the mutual interference in the aisles. The results identified errors in the original automation policies the increased interference and generated deadlocks. The simulator supported the automation company's correction identification of the problem.

8. SUMMARY

The purpose of the paper is to present critical issues, which can impact a simulation. The applications span the entire spectrum of simulation projects from system analysis, design, development, production through training and logistics. These simulations have applications in government, business and industry. Examples have been presented to indicate what can occur if one or more of the critical issues avoid identification until the end of the project. The critical issues are interrelated and their interdependency should be recognized. The human element associated with communication and interpretation also plays an important roll. Thus, the vision of a simulation at the early stage of the process may not necessarily be the simulation that the user will ultimately require.

There is no question that simulations are very successful in performing a variety of functions if the proper design and validation procedures are followed. Their applications save lives and improve the efficiency and cost effectiveness of a wide variety of governmental, industrial and commercial systems.

9. ACKNOWLEDGMENTS

This work has been partially supported by ADSRC, a consortium funded by the Army Research Office (ARO), Grant No. DAAH04-95-1-250. The views and conclusions are those of the authors and do not represent the official policies of the funding agencies or the universities.

REFERENCES

Albers, F. Gerry, "Microcomputer Base for Control Loading". Proceedings for the 11th NTEC Industry Conference", NTEC Industry Conference. Nov. 14-16, 1978. Naval Training Equipment Center. Orlando, Florida. 109-112

Amico, G. V. and Lindahl, C. E., "The Evolution of Real Time Simulation of Aircraft for Training Applications", Summer Computer Simulation Conference, Seattle Washington, August 25-27 1980, 365-370

Amico, G. V. and Lindahl, C. E., "Real Time Simulation of Aircraft for Training Application; Past Present and Future", I/ITEC, 1981

Amico, G. Vince and Clymer, A Ben " Simulator Technology - Forty Years of Progress", Proceedings: All About Simulators 1984. Norfolk, VA. April 18-20, 1984 Vol. 14 No. 1. SCS San Diego, Ca., 175-188

Amico G. V. " High Performance, Low Cost Software; The key to Future Cost Effective Simulators and Training Systems", Proceeding: 1983 Summer Computer Simulation Conference. Seattle WA. SCS, 1106-1119

Bruzzone A.G. (1996) "Object-Oriented Simulation of Cleaning Operations in Urban Environments", Proc. of ESM'96, Budapest, June 2-6

Bruzzone A.G., Cotta G., Cerruto M.M.E. (1997) "Simulation & Virtual Reality To Support The Design Of Safety Procedures In Harbour Environments", Proceedings of ITEC 97, Lausanne (CH), April 22-25

Bruzzone A.G., Giribone P. (1998), "The Solution to the Problem: Why Applied to Industrial Production: the Key to Success for Total Quality Management", Proceedings of ToolMet 98, Oulu, April 16-18

Galloway, R. Thomas, Settle, Richard F., Maggio, Anthony F., "Flight Fidelity: Military Application and Commercial Practices", I/ITSEC 99 Conference, Orlando Florida, Nov. 29-Dec. 2, 1999

Giribone P., Bruzzone A.G. (1997) "Object-Oriented Simulation of Discrete Flows for Industrial Plants: An Application Example of an Automated Mineral Oil Filling Line", Proceedings of European Simulation Multiconference, ESM' 97, Istanbul, Turkey, June 1-4, 1997

Heintzman, Richard J. "Flight Simulator History, Evolution, and Future." Proceedings: All About Simulators, 1984 Norfolk, Va. Vol. 14 No. 1. SCS San Diego, Ca, April 18-20, 1984 177-175

Mosca R., Bruzzone A.G. (1997) "Re-Engineering of an Automated Warehouse System using Object-Oriented Simulation", Proceedings of Flexible Manufacturing & Intelligent Systems, Middlesbrough (UK), June 25-27

Pace, Dale K. "Simulation Conceptual Model Development". Proceedings of the Spring 2000 Simulation Interoperapability Workshop. March 26-31 2000, Orlando Florida. CD-ROM SISO

TM-56. NAVTRADEVCEN Report TM-56, "Delays of Visual Feedback in Aircraft Trainers," March 1977. Naval Training Device Center, Orlando, Florida.

BIOGRAPHIES

Vince Amico started his career in simulation when he joined the Special Devices Center in 1948 as a Project Engineer in the Flight Trainers Branch. He was promoted to Branch head, Division head, and then to Chief Engineer of the Special Projects Office. In 1969 he was selected for the Position of Director Of Engineering at the Senior Executive level. The was assigned to the position of Director of Research in 1979. He retired in 1981. Since then he did consulting, taught short course on simulation and presented papers at SCS and I/ITSEC Conferences. He was member of he Board of SCS and also served as VP Conferences. He is a member of AFCEA, AIAA, NDIA and SCS. He holds BofAE, MBA and MSE degrees. He is the Industrial Affiliates Coordinator for the School of Computer Science at UCF. He is a member of the Board of Directors of the National Center for Simulation.

Agostino G. Bruzzone began his engineering studies at the Italian Naval Academy and earned his Mechanical Engineering degree from the University of Genoa. He works with University of Genoa in the field of simulator-based applications for industrial plants, developing new methodologies and AI system integration techniques. Today he is teaching in Department of Production Engineering of the Genoa University" Management of Industrial Plants", "Project Management", "Industrial Plants". He is the Director of the McLeod Institute for Simulation Science, Genoa Centre and he is in charge as Industrial Relation Chair for the European Council of the SCS; he is founder member and president of the Liophant Simulation Club.

Ratan Guha is currently a Professor of Computer Science in the School of Electrical Engineering and Computer Science at the University of Central Florida. His research interests include parallel and distribute simulations, Petri Nets and performance evaluations, distribute computing, computing networks ands algorithms for computer graphics. He is a member of the ACM, IEEE AND SCS. He is a member of a consortium, "Advance Distribute Simulation Research Consortium" (ADSRC) supported by a grant for the Army Research Office.

DESIGN OF AN OBJECT ORIENTED SPACECRAFT COMPONENT LIBRARY FOR NASA INTERPLANETARY EXPLORATION

Daniel Charles McShan
Syzygyx Incorporated
Littleton, CO 80120
dcm@syzygyx.com

KEYWORDS

Aerospace, Software, Validation, Verification, Realtime Simulation, Library

ABSTRACT

NASA faces a challenging 21st century mission to explore space at an affordable cost and minimal risk, while maximizing science return. Fortunately, the basic needs of most agency spacecraft are very similar for most missions and it is not surprising that many of the same components are often reused. However, a significant redundant cost is spent by each mission in developing high fidelity models for all of these components. This will be particularly true as NASA tries to involve more industry partners to build the spacecraft. Ultimately, with time and budget constraints, these models are never as complete or robust as is desired. An open-source, object-based spacecraft component library is posited to address this issue. This common library will allow significantly more validation and verification of the spacecraft model than can be achieved in the ever decreasing design time allows for future missions. Finally, with a standard modeling ontology, the ability to leverage this commonality to define a infrastructure for all phases of mission simulation is presented. By making the library open source, increased product integrity is assured, to the mutual benefit of NASA and it's industry partners.

FASTER, BETTER, CHEAPER

Background

In 1992, NASA Administrator Dan Goldin set forth the Faster Better Cheaper challenge to NASA and it's academic and industry partners. This direction was due to a few expensive failures and overall NASA budget cuts. The days of multi-billion dollar mega-missions was (and still is) no longer politically feasible. In order to continue funding the shuttle and space station programs, the only option was to fly less expensive missions.

Successes

And so, over the next few years, NASA had several program successes on shoestring budgets.

Mars Pathfinder 96. Mars Pathfinder, in particular was dramatically, and publicly, an unquestionable success. The program took great risks, embodying new technologies, such as the airbag cushioned landing, and was rewarded with spectacular results. Without a doubt, NASA claimed, the "Faster, Better, Cheaper" approach was a resounding success.

Deep Space 1 Deep Space 1 was another undeniable success. The spacecraft has so far demonstrated several different technologies that will be utilized on future missions to reduce cost and risk for future science missions.

Failures

As if to counterpoint the overwhelming success of Mars Pathfinder, the Mars 98 missions, Mars Polar Lander and Mars Climate Orbiter, have served as glaring examples of the risks involved in the FBC approach.

Mars Climate Orbiter In October of 1999, the Mars Climate Orbiter failed to achieve orbit around Mars due to a miscommunication of units between the spacecraft designers and the mission analysts.

Mars Polar Lander In December of 1999, MCO's sister spacecraft, Mars Polar Lander, impacted the surface of Mars in what appears to be a result of a software failure.

Future Missions

As of the writing of this paper, the fate of future Mars missions is unclear. NASA is stepping back from the planned 01 Mars lander mission, and perhaps even the 03 launch window. Other Discovery missions are still in the works, and the current Stardust mission is well underway to rendezvous with a comet.

FASTER, BETTER, CHEAPER SIMULATION

For previous missions, the faster better cheaper mantra was applied to the entire spacecraft development process. Given the short development windows, the development of the flight software and the development of the testbeds will occur simultaneously and it is often difficult to tell who is testing who. It is impractical to assume that a small program will take on the burden of an independent verification and validation process. Inevitably, system information becomes available to flight software and simulations at the same time.

Subsystem Simulation

In general, each subsystem team will create some form of simulation of their domain for the purposes of validating whatever it will do. A general subsystem decomposition usually results in the following components:

Mechanical
Propulsion
Power
Thermal
Telecom
Dynamics
Guidance & Navigation Control
Attitude Control
Avionics
Harness

Each team will utilize tools appropriate to their domain to "test like they fly" the best that time and money allow. This often includes software simulations, hardware in the loop simulations, and subjecting flight articles to simulated use.

System Simulation

For spacecraft system simulation, the following incremental testbeds are generally deployed:

Software System Non-Realtime Simulation A "pure software" simulation. Most modern missions utilize the vxWorks operating system. Wind River offers a vxSim package which provides the operating system hooks that the flight software requires. A simulation can then be assembled modeling the entire spacecraft, including avionics.

Hardware-In-The-Loop Realtime Simulation The utilization of multi-tasking operating systems for flight software make an avionics-in-the-loop realtime simulation indispensable. At the very least, flight-like avionics is

Spacecraft-In-The-Loop Simulation There are several approaches for system testing on the spacecraft itself involving different fidelity simulations. Ultimately, testing on the vehicle is fundamentally limited by the fact that you are not, in fact, in space, and you have actual components rather than fully controllable simulations.

Social Realities

One of the major problems throughout the aerospace industry is the loss of talent to more commercial businesses. The field of design and testing of embedded real-time systems like spacecraft has been especially hit by the similar skill base requirements of the telecommunications industry. As a result, even the larger aerospace companies are having a difficult time maintaining the skills necessary to conduct adequate simulation based testing.

THE SPACECRAFT COMPONENT LIBRARY

The need for a common repository of spacecraft components was recently documented in the NASA FBC Task Final Report: "A common multi-agency, Internet Store for high-quality, modular, advanced components, supplied by multiple vending sources, must be a top national priority. This store would be fed by multi-agency advanced developments." And this statement, as much as any other, summarizes the requirement of and purpose for our Spacecraft Component Library.

Mission Component Commonality

Despite the vastly different mission objectives and industry differences, there are a large number of common parts to every spacecraft mission. Ultimately, there are a small set of manufacturers for most of the spacecraft components. "Electrons and photons cannot tell if they are participating in a reconnaissance mission or making noble scientific measurements at Mars. Spacecraft share most of the same equipment functionality." [Speer 2000]

Mission Database

As part of the initial study into the viability and usefulness of the Spacecraft Component Library, we are assembling a mission database to verify and quantify the claim that "spacecraft share most of the same equipment functionality." Some of the missions that we will be cataloging are:

Mars 96 Pathfinder
Mars 96 Global Surveyor
Mars 98 Polar Lander
Mars 98 Climate Orbiter
Mars 01 Orbiter
Genesis
Stardust
Deep Impact
Deep Space 1
SIRTF

Some of the components that we will be comparing include:

Inertial Measurement Units (IMU)
Reaction Wheels
Batteries
Solar Arrays
Antennae
Thrusters
Dynamics
Star Trackers
Cameras
Flight Processor

With this database in place, it should be fairly easy to determine where redundant efforts have been made, and where the greatest potential for outsourcing of component models lies.

Library Features

Ideally, the library will be a repository for all information relating to the component. This information will be gathered from the vendors, produced by Syzygyx, or donated from industry.

- Vendor Documentation
- Software & Hardware Simulator Documentation
- Specifications
- Software Simulation Objects
  - Functional
  - Power
  - Thermal

- Fault Modes
- Hardware Interface Simulator Specification
- Hardware Interface Stimulator Specification
- Hardware & Software Regression Tests
- CAD/CAM (iDEAS/CATIA)
- Finite Element Analysis (NASTRAN)
- Mass Equivalency Specification
- Interface Stimulator & Characterizer
- Electrical Interface
  - Simulator
  - Stimulator
  - Characterizer
  - Verifier
  - Configuration Control

Library Design Requirements

In general, the design of all facets of the library are dictated by a few requirements

Easily Accessible The models must be easily accessible to the various programs, preferably over the internet. Another facet of being easily available is that they must be cost effective and thus easily procurable.

Feedback Loop There must be a simple mechanism for bug reports and feature requests so that the user community can actively participate in the direction that the library proceeds.

Adaptable It is essential to allow the model components to be used with as many simulation infrastructures as possible.

Standardized It is important for the library to implement the industry standards for modeling in each domain.

Implementation Barriers

Not created here One of the biggest barriers to the acceptance of anything new is the inertial resistance against new ideas.

Legacy Systems Nearly every company in the industry already has models of the various components that make up the spacecraft they have built. The barrier here will be the cost and performance of the in-house reuse versus the cost of the out-sourced simulations. Also there will be existing personnel whose job it is to create the very simulations we are offering.

Proprietary designs Not all component designers may want every specification of their product so easily disseminated. This as true of programs as it is for vendors.

Cost to program This barrier is proportional to the perceived cost savings of in-house development rather than outsourcing.

Most of the barriers mentioned above are cost related. Some proposed solutions to these issues will be discussed in the Implementation section below.

SOFTWARE SIMULATION DESIGN

Most of the actual simulation work done by Syzygyx will be in the realm of subsystem simulations for use in validating flight software. Traditionally, this has been the largest share of simulation work done on a project, often eclipsing flight software development in time and complexity. This is where the Library will excel. We will focus on the requirements and preliminary design of the functional software simulator and the hardware simulator (below). The infrastructure to glue the software simulation to the hardware simulation is beyond the scope of the current paper, and will only be briefly reviewed.

Software Simulation Requirements

In designing the software simulations of the spacecraft components, the following requirements have been extracted.

Limit dependencies By limiting dependencies on other library components, we can maximize applicability of the simulation component for various infrastructures that may want to utilize it.

Multiple Fidelity Ideally, we will have a very high fidelity model that can be degraded to suit the purposes of a particular simulation.

Ontology It is desired to have a systematic approach to modeling. Fundamentally, this means designing a reification approach to the system and extracting the base classes which define the system.

System integration The library simulation components should be easily integrated into legacy or other architectures.

System Architecture independence The models should adhere to software standards and compile on most any platform.

State extraction The state of the model should be extractatable and reloadable for easy checkpointing.

Legacy Integration A general mechanism should be developed to develop simple hooks for legacy system integration.

Configuration Control As true for every library component, complete control over configuration is required. In addition, regression test suites are required to ensure quality.

Data driven All relevant data parameter must be settable at initialization time. This data may be loaded in via file IO or through accessors. The simulation should then check to know if it has been properly initialized.

Model Integrity The model should have a method to check all of it's input, state and reference parameters to ensure that they are within acceptable limits. This is for information use. The model should be able to deal with all physically acceptable values of a parameter.

Lookup Tables The model should have the ability to extract table information from a database.

Debuggable The simulation should have well defined debug hooks for runtime debugging. Ideally, these are runtime settable levels.

Fault Modes The simulation should model all known fault modes for the device. Faults should be able to be injected by the system. Approximate mean time between failures and probability of failures should be encoded if known.

Event Driven The models should have an event driven capability for all relevant interfaces, especially for discrete and serial events.

Time Driven The models will have a "clock" entry point which tell the model absolute and relative times. This clock is called be the infrastructures "realtime" clock and is used for time based events.

Frequency Independent Models should not require a particular integration time. It may be that in one system, it is necessary to run at 100Hz, another at 1Hz.

Encapsulation All model functionality and IO should be encapsulated within the model's scope. All IO to and from the system should occur through accessors or data objects.

Realtime Capable The models must have the capability to run in a hard realtime environment. Naturally this requirement is in conflict with the System Architecture Independence requirement above, as not all systems are realtime capable. In order to implement this capability, the model may be required to have a reduced fidelity mode in order to gain timeliness.

Software Simulation Design

As a result of these requirements, the following design decision have been make for the software simulation components of the library.

Object Based Design. The object oriented design approach has several advantages over conventional design approaches. The first task will be to establish a consistent ontology appropriate for our application.

C++ offers several advantages for engineering simulation. First, it offers the complete powers of the C language, effectively providing complete access to the underlying machine architecture. This is something that other object languages, like Java, cannot offer. It also means that the code can execute deterministically and can be easily debugged.

Another advantage is that C++ is also object oriented, which allows easy modularization if components. It allows for multiple inheritance, which is a very powerful tool for abstraction. The concept of abstract base classes is discussed below and provides a very useful mechanism for templating code. [McShan 2000]

Strong Typing There are several advantages in strong typing all simulation variables. First, it often improves code readability. Second, it allows the simulation system to have a lot more knowledge that can be exploited by "intelligent" applications. Finally, by using proper operator overloads, the strong types are easily replaced with the simple typesdefs to the types they represent.

Abstract Base Classes Abstract Base Classes (ABCs) contain only pure virtual methods. A pure virtual method consists of the function declaration only, without any implementation. A child class that inherits from the ABC is required to implement the method. One of the main advantages of ABCs over traditional base classes is that the dependency between child and parent class is easily severable by simply removing the relevant inheritance. Ultimately, the child has no real dependency on the parent other than implementing the required methods. The abstract base class can also provides a template for the development of new objects, requiring particular methods to be provided before the class will even compile.

MODEL class The Model Abstract Base Class will provide a template for model development. It provides basic functions that every model will have such as initialize, clock, and other generic methods.

STATE class For all operational modes, the model state will be stored in a STATE class. This class will have the capability of saving and loading itself from a stream for checkpoint and data display purposes.

FAULT class The fault base class encapsulates all the scheduling and injection for a given fault. There are two types of faults. One is the type of fault that can be linearly injected. I.e. as an entry point after processing inputs or after the model runs. Model execution will likely have a list of faults at each injection point. The other type of fault is a more complicated fault requiring model action. This will be implemented parametrically; either on/off or other appropriate mechanism, and is evaluated in the course of model execution.

Interface Description Language IDL will be provided for every model class. The IDL provides a language independent standardized description of the object for CORBA and Java accesses.

CORBA POA The C++ skeleton code necessary for distributing the model object will be provided. The Portable Object Adapter (POA) standard will facilitate the access of the simulation object by control and display programs, and even other objects.

Java Data Objects & Display Widgets The provided Java widgets will have the capability of accessing all of the parameters defined in the IDL (via a Java Data Object) for the component and display them in a meaningful format for that component. At a minimum, inputs, state and outputs widgets will be provided. The Display Widget is responsible for reading the Data Object at whatever rate it chooses. Mechanisms will be provided to populate the data object from a file, socket stream, and CORBA hooks. These mechanisms should be independent of the Display Widget (probably through an inheritance mechanism).

HARDWARE SIMULATION DESIGN

In order to test spacecraft components, non-realtime software simulation is seldom sufficient to validate flight products.

Particularly since many missions actively rely on the multitasking capabilities of the vxWorks operate

Hardware Simulation Requirements

Flight Like Connectors The hardware simulation will have flight like connectors for the component. These connectors should provide the only hardware interfaces required to simulate the interface.

Modular Design The design of the hardware simulator should be as modular as possible, ideally being able to be a standalone simulator apart from the rest of the system or to be a component of a larger, system simulator.

Stimulator Capable Each hardware simulator will have a corresponding "stimulator", preferable in the same packaging. The stimulator will have the interfaces required to test the simulator as well as an actual component. It should be equipped with a cable to connect to the flight like connectors.

Hardware Design

The hardware simulator is designed with the software simulator and device drivers in mind. Each chassis will contain one device, or subsystem, as appropriate. The design has the following components and features:

cPCI Compact-PCI is the chassis of choice for the interface simulators. Since it is expected that the simulators will be combined to create a system level test, the 3U cPCI form factor is ideal. If the device is sufficiently complicated, the 6U form factor will be used, without affecting any changes on the software.

Modular IO Modular IO will be used whenever feasible. This includes the families of Industry Pack (IP) IO and PCI Mezzanine Card (PMC) IO. This allows for maximum flexibility with regards to the underlying bus. Indeed, it would be very easy to implement this same architecture over the VME bus backplane.

Custom IO Custom IO will be implemented using the IP or the PMC form factor. PMC cards with FPGAs, a few chips of memory, and some IO circuitry can implement nearly every interface required. The IO will ideally connect through the backplane IO in the case of IP or through the front panel with PMC.

Flight Like Interface Card The Flight Like Interface Cards (FLICs) are intended to be 3U cPCI form factor with the flight like interface on the front panel, connected to a terminal block on the card. The cPCI backplane IO access is also connected to a terminal block, and signals are connected appropriately. Any signal conditioning necessary is implemented on the FLIC.

Stimulator The stimulator is an important component of the SCL. It will reside in the same chassis as the simulator, and is actually capable of performing a complete subsytem level test of the component. This is necessary in order to verify the simulator. The stimulator software will generate a test artifact which can then be compared between the simulator and a certified component. Components can also be validated against the ICD to ensure compliance. The stimulator will also be very useful in developing the realtime hardware in the loop simulator as it can provide the closed loop control necessary to check out the simulator independent of controlling avionics.

CONFIGURATION CONTROL

Configuration control is important for any library. We will provide software and hardware regression test suites to verify that the simulation matches the component to whatever fidelity is required.

CVS

Freely available, widely supported, and supports remote repositories, CVS is widely used for open source projects, and is the primary configuration control mechanism for the Library.

Process

A Configuration Control process will have to be developed which adequately allows users of the library to track revisions of the product as well as the simulations.

Feedback

A mechanism will be developed to allow for bug reporting and tracking. Since user feedback will be so important to the

OPEN SOURCE

The evolution of the gnu toolchain and linux as an open source operating system has brought light to the open source movement. Open source promotes software reliability and quality by supporting independent peer review and rapid evolution of source code.

In order to ensue quality and model integrity, a detailed regression test suite will be provided with each simulation component. Ideally, this regression test suite will actually be developed against the actual component and will have the actual empirical evidence used to generate the test suite included in the Library.

IMPLEMENTATION

As was mentioned above, the largest barrier to industry acceptance of the library is going to be cost. By leveraging the models across many users, the cost can be driven down. Programs will then have access to significantly higher quality simulations than they would be able to produce in-house at a fraction of the price.

NASA

It is hoped that NASA will realize the usefulness of such a library and will embrace the commercial attempt to make it a reality. Syzygyx is applying for a SBIR grant from NASA to help cover the significant starting research and development costs for this effort. In addition, we will be contacting the various NASA programs to ascertain their interest in funding this endeavor.

COTS Component Vendors

The commercial vendors of spacecraft components will also have a great incentive to participate in the library. The Library will offer links to the vendors websites for further information on their components. And the existence of a component entry in the Library will provide added value to their product.

Industry

Industry will have the most to benefit from the library as they will attain orders of magnitude improvement in simulation validity and time to implementation. These savings will allow faster simulation development time and consequently increased testing of the spacecraft. This will be especially true for smaller programs and companies that cannot afford to produce quality simulations for their spacecraft.

Open Source

Free software is not necessarily "free". The saying goes that it is "free as in freedom of speech, not free beer". Depending upon market conditions and initial interest, the simulation software will either be free for downloading, have a licensing fee attached, or perhaps funded through the Consortium memberships mentioned below. In any event, independent of cost, the code will be open source.

FUTURE DIRECTIONS

Consortium

As with all standards, industry acceptance is paramount if the spacecraft component library is to become successful. To this end, Syzygyx will be setting up a Consortium of governement, industry, and academia to discuss desired goals and directions for the library. Explicit in the design of the library is that it will be, at least for a time, a unilateral effort by syzygyx. This will allow for a faster time to market and quicker decision time. Consortium members will be charged dues which will help to allow Syzygyx to maintain existing models as well as simulate new components as they become available.

Component Database

Ultimately a component database of all the components in the SCL will be available. This will allow potential programs to compare and contrast similar components, download the simulations, and make important design based on mechanical, thermal, power and functional specifications earlier.

System Infrastructure

With a standard library of components in place, a powerful system infrastructure will be designed. This infrastructure will facilitate the development of system simulations significantly earlier in the design process.

Satellites

While the focus of the Spacecraft Component Library is on interplanetary missions, components used in deep space missions are also used in earth-orbiting satellites as well. The Library database will be expanded to include these satellites as well and satellite components will be added to the Library.

Other Space Agencies & Commecialization

As ESA, Japan, other nations and commercial companies venture into space, they will be confronted with the same challenges that NASA faces. It is likely that they will utilize the same fundamental components as NASA, and will be able to derive great benefit from the Library. Syzygyx will endeavor to include these spacecraft as well in the mission database as well as consider their requirements in developing the Library.

CONCLUSIONS

Increasing time and monetary constraints combined with the niche markets for space components has produced a great deal of component reuse for NASA interplanetary missions. Quality component simulations, while desperately required, can be time and budget consuming. To address these issues, Syzygyx is developing a Spacecraft Component Library to store open-sourced simulations of these components. This paper has developed some of the requirements and design decisions that will go into the Library. Over the next several months, Syzygyx will be continuing this design effort, developing a mission component database and designing the infrastructure necessary to make the Spacecraft Component Library a reality for NASA interplanetary missions.

REFERENCES

McShan, D., 2000, "Object Oriented Approaches to Faster, Better, Cheaper Testing", Aerospace Testing Seminar, October 2000.

Spear, T., "NASA FBC Task Final Report", 2000.

BIOGRAPHY

Dan McShan is the co-founder and Chief Science Officer of Syzygyx Incorporated. Syzygyx develops simulations for exploration of the extreme frontiers of knowledge. Before work at Syzygyx, Dan worked for four years at Lockheed Martin Space Systems designing and developing the realtime simulations for Mars 98 Lander & Orbiter, Stardust, Genesis, and Mars 01 Orbiter and proposals for Mars 03 and Mars 05 missions. Dan received his B.S.E.(Electrical) from the University of Michigan College of Engineering in 1994.

Verification and Validation of DEVS Models: Applying the Theory of Modeling and Simulation to the needs of Simulation Based Acquisition

Bernard P. Zeigler
Arizona Center for Integrative Modeling and Simulation
ECE Department
University of Arizona
Tucson, AZ 85721

Abstract

Formal representation of simulation models can contribute to a number of aspects in the modeling and simulation enterprise. Separation of models from simulation execution engines is a prerequisite for Simulation-Based Acquisition (SBA) which requires model transfer among phases of a project as well as from project to project. The Discrete Event System Specification (DEVS) formalism, drawing on its system theoretic basis, provides a number of important properties such as hierarchical, modular composition, universality and uniqueness that can better support development of simulation models and environments their development.

Simulation Based Acquisition (SBA) is a major initiative of the US Department of Defense to employ modeling and simulation (M&S) in all phases of system design , including for example, concept analysis, research, development, design, operation, and training. One of the main hoped-for benefits is the ability to reuse model code from phase to phase as well as from project to project. This requires that a number of supporting tools and other prerequisites be put in place that to put it mildly, stress the current state of the art. Among others, a framework is required that permits the models developed for a system to keep pace with the development of the actual system as its concept matures and transitions through the design stages. The Discrete Event System Specification (DEVS) formalism is an abstract basis for model specification that is independent of any particular simulation implementation. It thus has the potential to serve as the framework required for model transition through the phases of system development. Moreover, due to its system theoretic basis, DEVS enjoys a number of important properties such as closure under coupling, universality and uniqueness that are needed to support integration of the diverse kinds of models needed in the different phases of SBA. One example of a modeling and simulation environment build upon DEVS is Joint MEASURE^{TM} developed by Lockheed Martin. It is an industrial strength system-of-systems computational platform that has been used over several years in various system architecture assessment projects. It has been the focus of a deliberate effort to structure models in a manner that supports their subsequent reuse in later projects, making use of DEVS hierarchical, modular concepts to do so. While the issues needing consideration in the development of an infrastructure for SBA are too numerous to deal with in one paper, we will focus on a few of them to illustrate the approach suggested by the DEVS framework. Specifically, we will address the need to employ the separation of model specification from the form of its simulation execution to increase the likelihood of developing both better models and better simulation platforms for their execution. In what ways they are better is the focus of our subsequent discussion. We will begin by briefly reviewing the framework for M&S and the role of the DEVS formalism in it. An in-depth treatment can be found in reference (Zeigler, Kim et al. 2000). After this basis, we will suggest how today's M&S software development could greatly profit from the framework. Moreover, we'll show how the DEVS formalism provides some of the needed features for achieving SBA.

Formal Methods in Modeling and Simulation

Many developers of software adopt approaches to their craft that tend to be averse to formal methods despite the fact that such methods could improve the timeliness and reliability of their products (IEEE formal methods paper). In software development for modeling and simulation, aversion to theory is particularly deleterious, since successful systems require a good understanding of both the application domain as well as the principles underlying the M&S enterprise itself. In the past, one could argue that lack of theory in M&S to cover the difficulties faced in every-day development justified the anti-theory attitude that developed over the years. However, the culmination of theory development in the last quarter century is showing signs of significant progress toward meaningful support of today's simulation technology development

Elements of the Theory of Modeling and Simulation

The theory of modeling and simulation presented in (Zeigler, Kim et al. 2000) provides a conceptual framework and an associated computational approach to methodological problems in M&S. The framework (Figure 1) provides a set of entities (real system, model, simulator, experimental frame) and relations among the entities (model validity, simulator correctness, among others) that, in effect, present a model of the M&S domain.

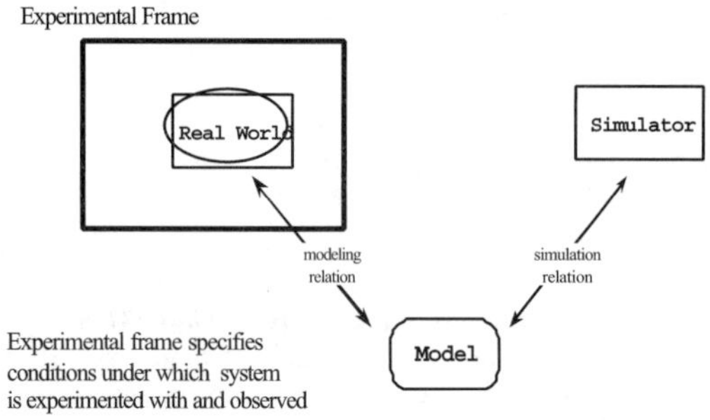

Figure 1 Entities and Relations of M&S in Framework

The computational approach is based on the mathematical theory of systems and works with object orientation and other computational paradigms. It is intended to provide a sound means to manipulate the framework elements and to derive logical relationships among them that are usefully applied to real world problems in simulation modeling. Interestingly, the framework and systems theory are intimately linked as suggested in Figure 2. The framework entities are formulated in terms of the system specifications provided by systems theory, and the framework relations are formulated in terms of the morphisms (preservation relations) among system specifications. Conversely, the abstractions provided by mathematical systems theory require interpretation, as provided by the framework, to be applicable to real world problems.

Verification: Theory-based versus Software-based Approaches to Simulation Environments

Our first example of application of the theory is to development and verification of simulation software. The theory distinguishes models from simulators and formalizes each and their relationships in mathematical system theory terms. But isn't this going too far in the formal direction? Proving theorems is not everyone's cup of tea. Can't we just remain at the informal level and write code based on our understanding?

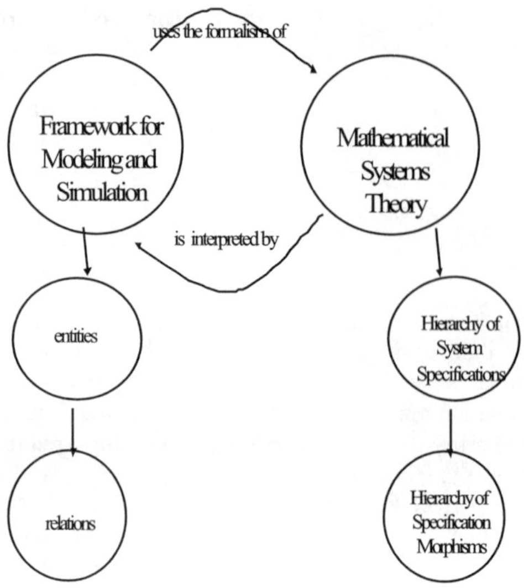

Figure 2

Let's look at a typical problem (Figure 3). We are asked to build a simulation environment that can handle both continuous and discrete event systems. One way to go about this task is an exclusively software-based approach. As illustrated below the grey separator, such an approach might separately examine existing continuous simulation and discrete packages, extracting the services offered by each, and combining them in some way to form the sought-after hybrid. Although this "software-only" solution is likely to work to some extent, it would be difficult to provide convincing assurance about its capabilities. Users would like to know whether this package can simulate any model of a combined nature they might come up with and that the software will correctly these models. In other words, one is unlikely to be able to prove – once and for all – that the environment is complete and correct. In contrast, the theory-based solution (upper half of Figure 3), concentrates first on the classes of systems formalized as DESS (differential equations) and DEVS (discrete event) and provides a synthesis of the two, DEV&DESS. Because of their mathematical formalization, properties of the combined formalisms can be, and have been, established (Zeigler, Kim et al. 2000). These include the properties of closure under coupling (guaranteeing well-defined coupled models and hierarchical composition) and universality of representation. Furthermore, abstract (implementation-independent) simulator algorithms have been developed and proven correct. Based on both the modeling and simulation foundation provided by the theory, a software developer is in a much better position to provide assurances to users concerning the capability and correctness of the simulation software.

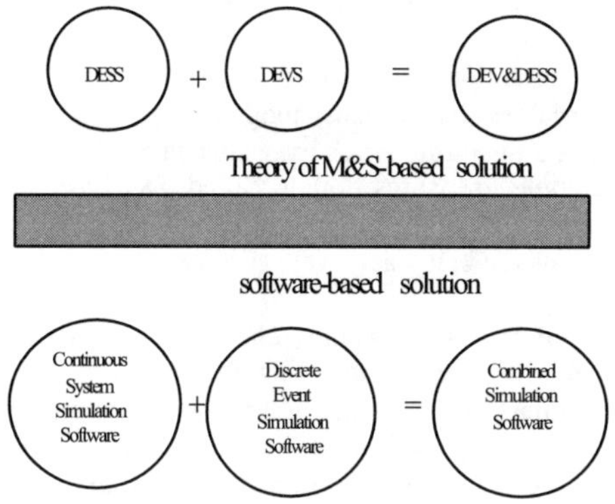

Figure 3 Theory-based vs Software-based Approaches

The DEVS Formalism and Issues in HLA Specification

The DEVS (Discrete Event System Specification) formalism, introduced in the first edition of "Theory of Modeling and Simulation" (Zeigler 1976), has undergone much development in the last quarter century, and is the focus of attention in the recently published second edition(Zeigler, Kim et al. 2000). Because of its computational properties, discrete event simulation is increasingly approaching parity with continuous simulation as the paradigm of preference for all types of application domains. One major indicator of this is the growing adoption of the High Level Architecture standard for distributed simulation promulgated by the U.S. Department of Defense (www.hla.mil). The time management services codified by HLA are essentially based on discrete event parallel and distributed concepts. Unfortunately, the specification of these services takes the software-based approach to combined continuous and discrete simulation just described. Indeed, there is no characterization available concerning the class of combined models that can be correctly simulated. Worse, there are discrete event models that are known not to be correctly executable with the services as currently specified (Zeigler, Ball et al. 1999)

The theoretical developments concerning DEVS portrayed in the second edition are timely in this regard. The book provides proof of the universality and uniqueness of the formalism for expressing the class of discrete event models. The situation is illustrated in Figure 4. The class of Parallel DEVS models is simulateable by a distributed simulation algorithm called the parallel DEVS simulation protocol. This means that any such model can be correctly simulated using this protocol. However, not all parallel DEVS models can be simulated using the time-management services of HLA. In fact it can be shown that the subclass of parallel DEVS with non-zero DEVS lookahead can be correctly simulated in HLA (Lake, Sarjoughian et al. 2000). Moreover, requiring non-zero lookahead severely restricts their behavior of DEVS since this requires that there is a lower bound on the time advance associated with all states, including those that result from external events. **The source of this difficulty is that HLA services were not designed within a framework which defines a class of discrete event models and which allows verification of simulation services by requiring that they handle all models in the defined class.**

Further, a concept called the DEVS Bus characterizes its capability to provide an efficient computational basis for simulation of systems in general, and continuous differential equation systems in particular. The DEVS Bus concepts are implemented in DEVS/HLA (Kim, Cho et al. 1999) an HLA-compliant modeling and simulation environment that supports high-level federation development and execution using the DEVS methodology.

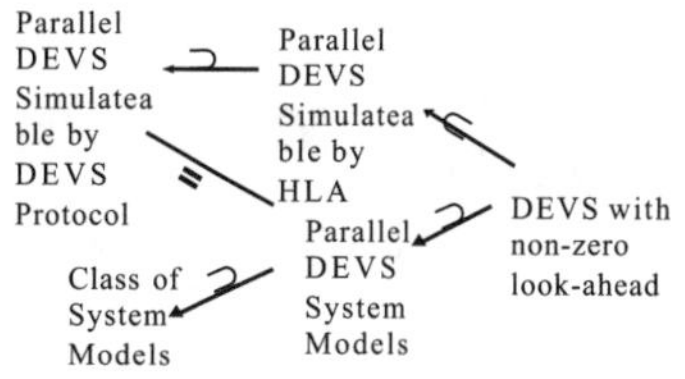

Figure 4. Simulation of Classes of DEVS Models

Validation: Experimental Frame Concepts

An *experimental frame* is a specification of the conditions under which the system is observed or experimented with. As such an experimental frame is the operational formulation of the objectives that motivate a modeling and simulation project. Many experimental frames can be formulated for the same system (both source system and model) and the same experimental frame may apply to many systems. Why would we want to define many frames for the same system? Or apply the same frame to many systems? For the same reason that we might have different objectives in modeling the same system, or have the same objective in modeling different systems. There are two equally valid views of an experimental frame. One, views a frame as a definition of the type of data elements that will go into the database. The second views a frame as a system that interacts with the system of interest to obtain the data of interest under specified conditions. In this view, the frame is characterized by its implementation as a measurement system or observer. In this implementation, a frame typically has three types of components (as shown in Figure 5): *generator,* that generates input segments to the system; *acceptor* that monitors an experiment to see the desired experimental conditions are met; and *transducer* that observes and analyzes the system output segments.

Objectives and Experimental Frames

Objectives for modeling relate to the role of the model in systems design, management or control. Experimental frames translate the objectives into more precise experimentation conditions for the source system or its models. A model is expected to be valid for the system in each such frame. Having stated our objectives, there is presumably a best level of resolution to answer the questions raised. The more demanding the questions, the greater the resolution likely to be needed to answer it. Thus, the choice of appropriate levels of abstraction also hinges on the objectives and their experimental frame counterparts.

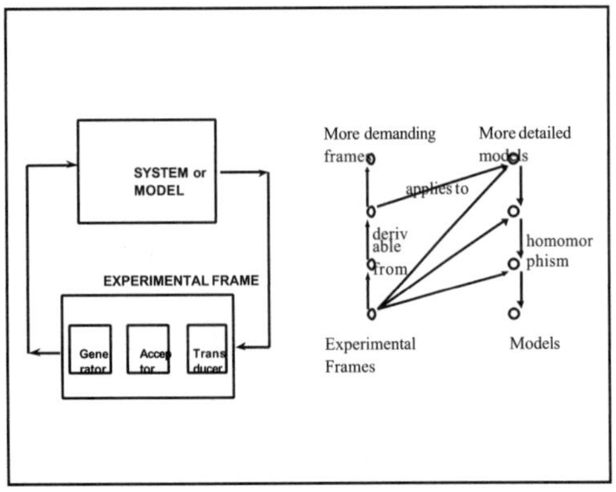

Figure 5 Experimental Frame and its Components.

There is a process for transforming objectives into experimental frames. Typically modeling objectives concern system design. Here measures of the effectiveness of a system in accomplishing its goal are required to evaluate the design alternatives. We call such measures, *outcome measures*. In order to compute such measures, the model must include variables, we'll call *output variables*, whose values are computed during execution runs of the model. The mapping of the output variables into outcome measures is performed by the transducer component of the experimental frame. Often there may be more than one layer of variables intervening between output variables and outcome measures. For example, in military simulations, *measures of performance* are output variables that typically judge how well parts of a system are operating. Such measures enter as factors into outcome measures, often called *measures of effectiveness*, that measure how well the overall system goals are being achieved.

Figure 5 also illustrates the relations that connect experimental frames to each other and to models. One of the pillars of SBA will be the support of repositories of models to enable reuse and collaborative development. Experimental frames can be used as the means to access models that are relevant to current objectives. The relation that determines if a frame can logically be applied to a model is called *applicability* and its converse, is called *accommodation.* Validity of a model in a particular experimental frame, requires, as a precondition, that the model accommodates the frame. The degree to which one experimental frame is more restrictive in its conditions than another is formulated in the *derivability* relation. A more restrictive frame leaves less room for experimentation or observation than one from which it is derivable. So, as illustrated in Figure 5, it is easier to find a model that is valid in a restrictive frame than one from which is derivable for a given system. It turns out that applicability may be reduced to derivability, i.e., a frame is applicable to a model, if it is derivable from the maximal frame applicable to the model. This means that a repository need only support the derivability relationship to answer queries concerning the existence of models that are relevant to current objectives.

Experimental Frames for Pollution Modeling and Simulation

A project involving collaboration among University of Arizona, University of Linz, Austria and GMD, Germany has been initiated to apply the theory of experimental frames to models developed for air pollution in urban regions. A family of models has been developed to predict ozone-concentration as dependent on wind (direction, velocity), diurnal variation of emissions (traffic and industry) and cloud cover. A family of experimental frames is being developed to provide a comprehensive view of the objectives and validity of the models in regard to the objectives.

One objective of using such models is to be able to issue credible alterts and warnings when ozone levels exceed acceptable limits. In Figure 6, the experimental frame corresponding to the issuance of a danger alert, called EF_{Alarm} specifies an output partition consisting of two equivalence classes, points below and above the alarm threshold, respectively. Another frame, $EF_{Envelope}$ requires agreement of the model predictions to within a specified envelope spanning the threshold level over some time period. This is a more stringent test of model validity. As defined, these frames are not in the derivability relation. However, by intersecting them we obtain a least upper bound , $EF_{Refined}$ from which each is derivable. The practical import of this is that it points out that a model may be valid in $EF_{Envelope}$ while still not being valid in the EF_{Alarm} frame. This is so since the model may do a good job of hovering around the alarm threshold while always staying below the threshold and thus not tripping the alarm when it should. However, we are sure that any model valid in $EF_{Refined}$ would indeed also be valid in both the other frames – so would correctly give alarm warnings over time. Thus, this would be the appropriate frame to use for model validation even though the simpler EF_{Alarm} frame is the ultimate application objective.

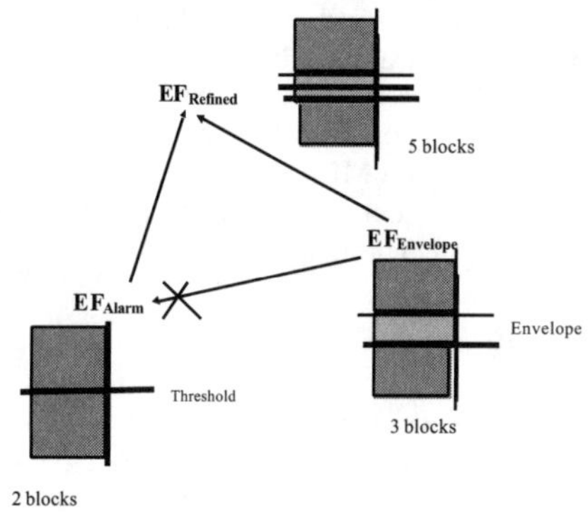

Figure 6 Experimental Frames for Ozone Alert

DEVS-Based Design Framework: Steps Toward SBA

The system design process transits among three phases, namely logical analysis, performance evaluation and implementation. each of which often employs a different model. Tag Gon Kim and colleagues (Kim, Cho et al. 2000) have been developing a unified modeling framework that provides a basis to specify models at different phases in common semantics. Based on DEVS, the framework provides a basis for modeling of discrete event systems in which logical analysis, performance evaluation, and implementation can be performed, all within a formal computer-operable notation for DEVS models, the DEVS Interface Specification Format. Although DEVS provides a general, theoretical basis for solving various problems, particular formalisms may address phase-specific design issues in more efficiently. In general, models developed for logical analysis typically reside at higher levels of abstraction than their performance-oriented counterparts.

Logical analysis within the proposed methodology occurs within the model verification phase. The phase not only verifies safeness and liveness of a designed model but checks operational correctness. The verification checks lower-level operational specification against higher-level assertional specification. Specifications for the two levels may employ either the same formalism or different formalisms. In the dual specification approach, the operational specification is expressed in the DEVS formalism and is checked against an assertional specification specified in temporal logic (Hong and Kim 1996) A single specification approach was recently developed in which both operational and assertional specifications are expressed in an extended DEVS formalism, called the Communicating DEVS(C-DEVS) formalism.

Performance evaluation within the framework employs object-oriented simulation of hierarchical DEVS models in HLA-compliant forms (Kim, Cho et al. 1999). In conventional methodologies, after logical and performance analysis, one typically must start from scratch to write a system implementation. In contrast, in the unified framework, a DEVS model used in the designed phase itself is an implementation which runs in real-time on a real-time simulation engine. An executable DEVS model is specified usimg an extension of DEVS, the real-time DEVS formalism and executes in a suitably developed real-time execution environment (Hong and Kim 1997).

DEVS Incursions into Simulation Technology

M&S environments based on the DEVS formalism have been incubating in academia for many years. Although none has yet reached the commercial market, these environments together with the underlying theory, are now gaining visibility and adoption in non-academic settings. A couple of examples will illustrate this point.

Joint MEASURE™ (Mission Effectiveness Analysis Simulator for Utility, Research and Evaluation.) was developed atop DEVS/HLA by Lockheed Martin, Sunnyvale, is intended to assist in evaluating a proposed defense system's mission effectiveness in the context of a specified set of possible design variations, operational utilization patterns and engagement scenarios (Zeigler, Hall et al. 1999). Joint Measure™ employs the DEVS modeling paraidigm to develop a library of sensor, weapon, and command/control communication platform models that can be composed to model military systems of systems operating in physically realistic environments. A full scale, industrial strength environment, it is intended to support Monte-Carlo and/or optimization simulation runs involving large numbers of runs with different random number seeds and parameter settings. It contains a visualization interface to display moving platforms the are spatially referenced within a Geographical Information System (GIS) and also contains a Data Modeling and Analysis Toolkit to support statistical analysis of simulation output.

As mentioned earlier, Joint MEASURE^{TM} can be considered a prototype environment for SBA. It exhibits many of the traits that would be required for fully-fledged SBA. Using the DEVS hierarchical, modular construction and system entity structuring concepts, models have been structured inin a manner that supports their subsequent reuse in later projects. Recently, a system-of-systems logical-time model was transformed to operate in real-time in a training mode demonstrating transition between phases of the same model.

DEVS has also been implemented to execute over CORBA (Common Object Request Broker Architecture) middleware in a distributed manner to address the requirements of scalable and efficient model execution. It also supports flexible extensibility based on the open industry standard, CORBA promulgated by the Object Management Group (OMG). DEVS/CORBA(Kim, Buckley et al. 1999) is a realization of a run-time infrastructure on top of CORBA middleware to support distributed simulation of DEVS components. Combining the advantages of CORBA and DEVS provides a heterogeneous, network-centric, distributed computing environment that includes modeling and simulation as well as other business objects.

In addition to incursions into current simulation software technology, many research directions are being pursued which are laying the basis for future commercial adoption. The following are some examples:

An extension of DEVS, called GDEVS, employs a polynomial representation of continuous behaviors to provide an alternative DEVS Bus realization of combined models. It has demonstrated a greater than ten fold increase in speed relative to the commercial Matlab package in representative benchmarks. One application of GDEVS is the redesign of hardware description languages whose capabilities have lagged behind the increasingly challenging demands that are being placed on them by hardware chip designers.

Combinations of DEVS with (non-simulation) software development formalisms such as Statecharts and Z are being developed to supplement the expressive power of DEVS with the verification capabilities of more abstract formal methods (Lake, Sarjoughian et al. 2000).

An approach to design of distributed object computing systems represents such systems as a two distinct layers (i.e., software/hardware) along with a mapping from one to the other. The software layer is denoted as *Distributed Cooperative Objects* and the hardware layer is denoted as *Loosely Coupled Network*. The *Object System Mapping* defines the allocation of software objects to hardware objects. DEVS-DOC, built on top of DEVSJAVA – a parallel DEVS-based modeling and simulation environment supports representation and of the layers and the association mapping (Sarjoughian, Hild et al. 2000). It thereby supports performance evaluation through simulation of alternatives for co-design of complex, heterogeneous distributed object systems that are emerging in network-centric applications.

Conclusions

The DEVS Interface Specification Format, introduced by Tag Gon Kim, is a potential standard for SBA in that is supports a framework for verification, performance evaluation, and real-time execution of DEVS models. Formal model specification stated in computer-operable notation can be analyzed for properties such as logical consistency that provide some degree of validation with respect to the objectives that motivate model development. Finally, such specification can be the basis of implementation to generate behavior both in simulation and in a real time execution.

As computing infrastructure (computers and networks) becomes ever more powerful and the types of models that are simulated become more and more sophisticated, the software-based approach to simulation technology becomes less and less viable and the theory-based approach becomes more and more critically necessary. This is especially true if the objectives of initiatives such as SBA are to be achieved. The DEVS formalism and its underlying system theory foundations provide a framework and a set of concepts to develop the infrastructure for SBA supporting reusable and well-validated models executed within well-verified and fully-capable simulation middleware. DEVS has already been demonstrated to support industrial strength precursors of SBA, such as Joint MEASURE^{TM}, and innovative modeling and simulation domain applications such as for distributed system design.

References

Hong, G. P. and T. G. Kim (1996). " A Framework for Verifying Discrete Event Models Using A Dual Specification Approach." SCS Transactions.

Hong, J. S. and T. G. Kim (1997). "Real-time Discrete Event System Specification Formalism for Seamless Real-time Software Development." Discrete Event Dynamic Systems: Theory and Applications, **7**: 355-375.

Kim, D., S. J. Buckley, et al. (1999). Distributed Supply Chain Simulation in a DEVS/CORBA Execution Environment. WSC, Phoenix.

Kim, T. G., S. M. Cho, et al. (2000). DEVS Framework for Systems Development: Unified Specification for Logical Analysis, Performance Evaluation and Implementation. Discrete Event Modeling and SImulation: Enabling Future Technologies. H. S. Sarjoughian. New York, NY, Springer-Verlag.

Kim, Y. J., J. H. Cho, et al. (1999). DEVS-HLA:Heterogeneous Simulation Framework Using DEVS Bus Implemented on RTI. Summer Computer Simulation Conference, Chicago, IL,.

Lake, T., H. Sarjoughian, et al. (2000). DEVS Simulation and HLA Lookahead. SIW, Orlando, FL.

Sarjoughian, H. S., D. Hild, et al. (2000). "Engineering Distributed Systems: Simulation-Based Co-Design." IEEE Computer **March**.

Zeigler, B. P. (1976). Theory of Modelling and Simulation. New York, John Wiley (Under Revision for 2nd Edition 1998).

Zeigler, B. P., G. Ball, et al. (1999). Implementation of the DEVS Formalism over the HLA/RTI: Problems and Solutions. SIW, Orlando, FL.

Zeigler, B. P., S. Hall, et al. (1999). "Exploiting HLA and DEVS to Promote Interoperability and Reuse in Lockheed's Corporate Environment." Simulation J. **74**(4): 288-295.

Zeigler, B. P., T. G. Kim, et al. (2000). Theory of Modeling and Simulation. New York, NY, Academic Press.

"PHYSICS, COMMUNICATION THEORY AND THE INTERACTIVE WORLD OF EXPERIENCE-BASED ENTERTAINMENT AND SIMULATION"

The Importance of Resonance

by
Priscilla Elfrey, Kennedy Space Center Liaison to the Simulation Community

The art and science of rehearsal and peak performance are of basic importance to the entertainment and simulation industries. Both build on similar technologies and the same physics. For each the test of success is that their products grab our attention, that they resonate with us.

Michael Pupin learned lessons, as a boy herding sheep in Serbia, contributing to his fame as the scientist for whom the physics building at Columbia University would be named. One lesson led to the loading coil that made long distance telephone calls possible before vacuum tubes. Another was the concept of tuning electrical coils. Both are examples of resonance rooted in Newton's law of action and reaction.

In those days, Serbian shepherd boys carried identical knives that they used to communicate with one another during the night. Each would drive a knife into the ground. By striking the handle, they sent messages to their friends across valleys and on other hills out of shouting range. They put their ears to the "receiving knives and, across great distances, heard the taps of 'transmitting' knives. Those identical knives were in resonance. Vibrations from one caused the other to move in sympathy. Natural vibration rates created energy waves that produced maximum results.

Also in those hills, Pupin heard bagpipers adjust their instruments until they were in sympathy with the notes produced by the others. When Pupin adjusted electrical circuits to respond to incoming waves, remembering those bagpipes, he used the word "tuning" to describe the process. To this day, we tune receivers to resonate with specific transmitters

If a disturbing force is tuned to it, we can stimulate anything in the physical world to an excessive response. If we know the natural vibration of an object; we can make it quiver without ever touching it. Examples include singers shattering a crystal goblet, bridges vibrating to the point of collapse from soldiers marching in cadence, and windows vibrating from a shuttle launch.

In the physical world, resonance, sympathetic vibration is the way to get maximum transfer of energy. In the world of the mind, including the world of simulation, resonance is the way to get a maximum transfer of idea content. (Boettinger)

If we send out messages that resonate with an audience --are in tune with their feelings and interests-- they will respond. As they respond, they can send messages back to the sender setting up a kind of feedback that amplifies the idea. This exchange can lead to enthusiasm, what actors, dancers, and musicians may describe as a "palpable energy."

Resonance creates the two-way communication typical of live performances where audiences sometimes make performers do better than they know how. It is a reason many people schooled in the theatre regard it as a more satisfying art form than cinema or television. Resonance can occur in television or film, of course, as when a nation shares poignant or telling moments, a feature film seems to touch a collective nerve, or a news event mesmerizes us all to the screen

We recently emerged from a century dominated by passive entertainment: film and television. Education, too, was often seen as something a teacher poured into an empty brain, like filling the fuel tank of an automobile (Postman).

With the Internet and related technology emphasizing experience-based entertainment and interactive learning, we face demands for different methods that will combine creativity, technical know-how, time-tested communication theory, research and discipline to achieve new goals

In August 1999, the Secretary of the Army signed a contract with the University of Southern California to establish an Institute for Creative Technology joining entertainment, the military and academia to improve the quality of training simulations in order to make them more true to life. The Army's Orlando-based Simulation Training and Instrumentation Command, STRICOM will administer the contract enabling Central Florida to be vitally involved in this cooperative effort to create new lifelike training. According to General William Bond, "We want to make our training more realistic." The Army wants soldiers to smell the cordite, feel that it is so real they perspire, their heartbeats go up, and they react as they would in the real environment.

The government-- --armed forces and the National Aeronautics and Space Agency (NASA)--is increasingly interested in applying advanced simulation technology to the full range of its work (mission planning, training, operations, testing and evaluation) to increase effectiveness. As Kennedy Space Center, Roy Bridges asserts, “When humans need to go where humans can not go; simulation is the only solution.

To create the virtual reality needed for the government’s Intelligent Synthetic Environments, experiential learning, and the interactive ”technosperience” the Florida entertainment industry envisions; we will require the highest fidelity in sensory applications. This includes visual, auditory, olfactory, and kinesthesia experience added to increasingly vivid visual and auditory technology and artistry. These technologies must be robust and low cost.

Central Florida has the necessary creative and technical capabilities to acquire and build this new expertise. Recent interchange with the experience-based, theme park, entertainment community and the simulation industry in Orlando, Florida under the auspices of the Mid-Florida Economic Development Council suggests that both the simulation and entertainment community might join in major research efforts in advanced sensory simulation.

To many people, today, "Florida" and "entertainment" mean its huge theme parks. Universal Studios, Sea World, Busch Garden, the Disney parks and the fantasies lining Downtown Disney and International Drive in Orlando are a key part of the state’s economy, attracting millions of visitors and earning billions of dollars.

Producers of these entertainment simulations understand how audio, video and graphic elements immerse the audience, be it for learning or recreation. Advances in government simulation, especially in creating ones that are increasingly true to life, will find their way back to special effects, theme park attractions, and filmmaking.

The entertainment industry already benefits hugely from government research in advanced computer systems, computer graphics, and the Internet. The Department of Defense, National Science Foundation, and NASA have supported the development of computer-aided design (CAD), 3D Graphics, algorithms, image generation as well as sophisticated simulator rendering and head-mounted displays. They also developed the Geometry Engine that produced custom integrated circuits for cost-effective high performance graphics systems and the virtual reality NASA uses for planning missions to Mars and beyond, and that the entertainment community offers now for our recreation. This is a technology of unlimited potential, offering solutions at every turn and promising to change our world. (

At the same time, we may remember that Socrates in Plato's Phaedrus warned us that the "discoverer of an art is not the best judge of the good or harm that will accrue to those who practice it." He was discussing writing, which, Neil Postman reminds us, is a technology. New technologies change what we mean by "knowing truth." They alter our symbols, habits, our conception of learning, and provide new concepts of what is real. Every technology has an ideological bias, constructs the world in one way rather than another, values one thing or group over another, and emphasizes some skills and thoughts over others. Technology can be friend or foe. As a program of social change, technology is never neutral [1].

Simulation starts with a reality rooted in technology and science, an ideological bias, a new idea, and old and new materials and puts this in a code based on numbers, words, action, images, sounds, and appreciation of limits of time. Learners, participants, the "others" receive the coded message and decode it based on their experience, education, imagination, mood, health, patience, and other factors.

.

A new idea is what might be, a solution. The attraction designer is asked to design a game beyond imagination. The general asks for a simulation that causes the participants to sweat. NASA wants an environment that allows people in California, Florida, and Maryland to work together as if time and distance were irrelevant.

These ideas begin, not in the mind, but in stored memories, some outside our consciousness (since much of what we are aware happens outside our awareness). A sound, an image, evens an odor or touch can start the process or awaken memory. Sometimes we see things we have always seen in a new way. We call this insight or understanding or creativity. It is the mark of the scientist and the artist.

Art lies in the arrangement of elements that create stories, lessons, and games that resonate with the "receivers." These must be presented in terms of reason, a single ultimate objective, common sense, that conservative knowledge that needs no explanation, plus emotion including as much sensory involvement and understanding as we can muster. It is not enough to lay out the facts. It is not enough to begin, as an engineer might, with the starting conditions, the situation, who is involved, and what resources are available. The real issue is to understand what the story is and how best to tell it.

The quest for a solution that will resonate involves knowledge of what's in the mind of the other, and how to attract what is desired while avoiding its opposite. There is also a lot of room for things to go wrong. The receiver may be distracted. The transmitter may have selected elements unwisely or packaged them poorly. Today, too much undifferentiated stimuli causes a numbness, a flatness of affect, that makes people indifferent to information that is not directly applicable and sensitive to their experience, learning, and knowledge.

It is easy, today, to look at simulation and interactive entertainment and see how far the technology has come. Nicholas Negroponte points out that improvement in television, and, we could add in simulation, has focused on improving the technology and not the artistry of its content. The point is to see how far we have to go to achieve simulation that truly resonates with virtual realism. We are beginning to see the variety and depth of talent we require. We are at a juncture, with the two industries where we can begin to examine the technology and its meaning. Negroponte and Neil Postman are critics of the new technology with vastly differing viewpoints who agree that when a people becomes an audience, a passive receiver, the nations and their cultures are at risk.

.

The Media Lab at MIT, in 1980, was marketed as the convergence of the sensory richness of television, the information depth of publishing, and the intricate interactivity of computers. Today as Negroponte admits, the Media Lab is the establishment but it was then seen as radical. Some saw it as "silly" and some colleagues at MIT branded them as "charlatans."

To map the new reality, today, both the simulation and entertainment industry require an integrated team of artists, storytellers, technicians, engineers and scientists working together as partners from the beginning of the project. The notion of Advanced Intelligent Multi-sensory Simulation Research – combining audio, visual, olfactory, kinesthesia, haptics with emotion and story making-- may strike some as unnecessary. Some may say it is, even, silly, but it will happen. It is necessary if simulation is to be truly true to life and as easy for people as talking to someone. "Smellovision" failed in commercial theatres, appears to have been rejected for Internet application, but, within the past two years, olfactory elements are increasingly recognized as contributing to virtual realism in simulation

The written word sparks images that get much of their meaning from the reader's imagination and background. Much of a poem or novel's color, motion, and sound comes from the reader's response and creates a kind of resonance.

"Dramatic skill," Henry Boettinger, the renowned, even, legendary, AT&T Director of Communication, advised " is essential" for easier and more correct comprehension, knowledge of what the story is and how to tell it. The desired outcome must be clear. And material must be ordered to give the impression of reality. He advised presenters and other communicators to use the simple direct code established by Vico of " statement, development, and resolution" in order to send an idea rolling down well-worn paths in the human brain.

This is foreign to the simulation engineer, as can be the entertainment industry's proposal to add their expertise and an integrated creative, technical and business team approach to simulation development while adding resonance, the emotional, as well as the physical and intellectual, content of either simulation or entertainment.

. The entertainment industry asserts that "detailed requirements" procedures, common to government, are limiting and, may inadvertently, focus test and evaluation on low level requirements. They point to entertainment's model for the rapid and aggressive rehearsal of the prototype Increasingly, they also talk with their counterparts in simulation about how, in particular, storytelling can enrich education and training.

They propose focusing on the "Big Story" with its conflict (the point to the story that it is trying to teach), its beginning, middle, and end. This is what Bran Ferran, President of Disney Imagineering and a member of the Army Science Board, calls "the Big Idea", such as the Army's initiative to "own the night." This dramatic idea suggests attention to the human reactions to simulation rather than accurate reality. By replicating nighttime battlefield emotions, for example, the attention would be on necessary standards and tasks that must be performed in those, often, harrowing circumstances.

The National Center for Simulation (NCS) as a Florida-based non-profit, education and research organization of industry, academia, the armed forces and NASA, recognized, in 1995 the need to bridge the entertainment and simulation industries. NCS into the organization independent producers and post production houses, along with the Florida Atlantic University's Center for Electronic Communication, offering a Master of Fine Arts degree in 3D computer graphics.

NCS Spacecraft Productions is a virtual incubator open to all NCS members. It recognizes that experience based entertainment simulation may well be at the core of the State's entertainment industry in five to ten years. Not only involved in production, this forum of engineers and artists can bring their best abilities to the table as a think tank for interchange of ideas. This could be a place to begin needed and serious dialogue on the impact of information technology so we can learn to understand what information is and how it gives direction to a culture (Goleman, Negroponte, Postman).

A DOD conference with entertainment and academic participants in 1996 concluded that regular interchange of information would be useful if only to identify research goals, which have already been achieved. It also surfaced research needs to keep both industries busy for many years. NCS outreach addresses workforce development, supporting simulation and entertainment that includes high definition television technologies, and the world's best amusement parks. NCS exists in large part to serve national armed forces and space interests and sees the agreement creating the USC program ram in entertainment and simulation as but a single step bringing these industries together.

Today, the simulation engineer is fascinated by the technical approach, rapid changes in the technology, and reports eagerly on the numbers in terms of speed, terabytes, pixels, voxel terrain, interpenetrating polygons, antialiasing and cost compared to a year ago. Outside the industry, in entertainment and elsewhere, people only want to know what they will experience, what they will see and do. The technology is amazing. No one else really wants to know why. People simply want to have it work and enjoy the results.

Interactivity is critical to achieving resonance since this phenomenon requires both transmitter and receiver who are in some way viscerally connected. The idea of the individual at the center of learning, at the center of the show, as the "receiver-transmitter" of resonance is one that is not only exciting but also demanding. There is a lot to be done, on our parts, if simulation and entertainment are to reach their potential—technically, artistically, and socially. Simulation is a technology that can literally touch the lives of everyone on Earth. That makes this a truly awesome responsibility.

Bibliography

Boettinger, Henry, *Moving Mountains*, Macmillan, 1969
Goleman, David; *Vital Lies, Simple Truth*; Simon and Schuster; 1985
Modeling and Simulation, Linking Entertainment an Defense, National Academy Press, 1997
Negroponte, Nicholas; *Being Digital*; Vintage 1996
Postman, Neil; *Technopoly*, Vintage Press; 1992

DOES SIMULATION NEED A REALITY CHECK?

William R. Swartout and Richard Lindheim
USC Institute for Creative Technologies
13274 Fiji Way, Fifth Floor
Marina del Rey, California 90292
Email: swartout@ict.usc.edu lindheim@ict.usc.edu

KEYWORDS: model credibility, real-time simulation

ABSTRACT

The military simulation community and entertainment community approach the simulation of reality in very different ways. Generally speaking, the military simulation community attempts to duplicate reality literally by reproducing real elements in a simulation. The entertainment community, on the other hand, creates the *appearance* of reality by bringing together a number of elements that *suggest* reality, but that may not be drawn from it. This paper examines these two approaches, gives examples of how the entertainment industry approaches the simulation of reality, and discusses some of the possible advantages that the entertainment industry's approach could have for military simulation.

INTRODUCTION

How can one best simulate reality? The military simulation community and the entertainment community take two very different approaches in answering this question. Generally, military simulation takes what might be called the literal approach to simulation. In this approach, one tries to create in the simulator an exact replica of the object being simulated. Thus, in the literal approach, a simulated helicopter cockpit would have all the switches, knobs, gauges and controls that one would find in a real helicopter. Often this is done by using in the simulator the same flight-qualified hardware that would be used in an actual helicopter. Similarly, the terrain databases that provide the out-the-window view for the simulator covers a large area represented at a uniform level of detail.

We see some important limitations to this approach. Using hardware from an actual vehicle in a simulator may significantly increase its cost while at the same time reduces its portability and ability to be reconfigured. If large areas of terrain are represented at a uniform level of detail, the graphical depiction of any particular part may not be very compelling due to processing limitations, even with today's powerful graphics engines.

In films, television and video games, the entertainment community also attempts to simulate reality--but using a very different methodology. Rather than trying to literally simulate everything, Hollywood begins by defining the ultimate objective. From their point of view these are criteria such as "What experiences should the audience have?" and "How should it feel." Once these goals are understood, they can guide how much effort is put into creating different aspects of the simulation. Some parts may be only roughly sketched, others represented very close to reality, while in some cases the simulation may be hyper-real, exaggerating reality for effect. For example, explosions in film and television are deliberately extended several times their normal clock time through a process called double-cutting. Another example: in the new movie, "Gladiator" only the lowest part of the Coliseum was actually built. The upper tiers and the thousands of screaming Roman participants were all done with CGI. If done skillfully, the audience is not be aware of the different levels of simulation used.

In this paper we will describe some of the techniques used by Hollywood to simulate reality selectively, and we will raise some questions: (1) When is it appropriate to use these techniques in military simulations and how could they contribute or detract from pedagogical goals and (2) Can training be equal or even more effective in a less real environment, where the participant can more easily suspend disbelief?

CASE STUDY: DIFFERENTIATING REAL AND ALMOST REAL

In personal communication with the authors, Alesya Paschal of STRICOM recounted an experience she had during the development of a simulator for the UH-1 helicopter. For the most part, the simulator cockpit was constructed using actual components from the UH-1. However, the contractor was unable to obtain the actual Air Speed Indicator used in the UH-1 (shown in Figure 1) due to availability. Instead, a commercially available indicator (shown in Figure 2) was used. The major differences are that the markings for the simulator indicator are equally spaced, while those on the indicator in the real helicopter have unequal spacing between 0 to 40 knots. On the real

Figure 1: Air Speed Indicator from actual UH-1

Figure 2: Air Speed Indicator from Simulator

aircraft, the marking for 10 knots is very close to zero, but much more widely spaced on the indicator used in the simulator.

When experienced pilots were debriefed after using the simulator, they stated that the indicator used in the simulator was *exactly* the same as the one they were accustomed to in the actual aircraft. They were quite surprised when they were shown photographs of the two obviously different gauges. One pilot told Alesya Paschal that the reason he did not notice the difference was that the major differences between the gauges are with their markings for slow speeds and he rarely went that slowly.

The lesson we take away from this case is that even very experienced users of a piece of equipment may have difficulty distinguishing between a real object and something that is close to the real thing, particularly if the major differences occur in areas that are usually not operationally relevant.

VERISIMILITUDE VS. REALITY

Whereas military simulations try to create realistic simulations by using actual components from real equipment, the entertainment industry attempts to create verisimilitude, or the appearance of reality, by weaving together a number of different elements, some of which may be real, while others may be completely synthetic. The key difference between the two approaches is that one attempts to *duplicate reality* to the highest fidelity possible, while the other attempts to *create an apparent reality.*

To create verisimilitude, the entertainment industry begins by asking some questions:

- What is the critical situation or story element that the user/viewer/participant should experience?
- How can we direct attention toward this element (and away from the irrelevant ones)?

The answers to these questions help direct effort and guide the process of creating verisimilitude. Depending on how the questions are answered, different degrees of reality may be required:

1. **Sketched reality.** If an element is not critical to the story or experience, it may be possible to just sketch it, leaving out much of the detail.
2. **Apparent reality.** If an element is central to the story it needs to appear as convincing as possible.
3. **Hyper-reality.** If an element is critical, but in real life it may escape notice or occur so quickly that it lacks impact, it may be necessary to exaggerate reality to create the appropriate impact.

In the next section we give examples of how these different approaches to reality are used in the entertainment industry and when each is useful.

DEGREES OF REALITY: EXAMPLES

Sketched Reality

A *cloze* is a "test of reading comprehension in which the test taker is asked to supply words that have been systematically deleted from the text" [American Heritage Dictionary]. People can successfully take such tests because they use the surrounding context to fill in the blank. The ability of people to supply missing details isn't limited to text. If one draws an almost complete circle on a blackboard, most people will call it a circle, even though it is in fact an arc.

Hollywood uses this trait and people's imaginations to fill in gaps similarly. For example, in the famous shoot-out in the office tower in the movie "Matrix" only the ground level was actually built. The remaining part of the impressive multi-story atrium was a painting. Another famous example can be found in Disneyland or Disney World, where the upper stories of the building on Main Street are built at a reduced scale.

By relying on the mind's ability to fill out missing details (as with painted upper stories) or correct erroneous information (as with upper stories at a reduced scale) it is possible to create perceptions that are effective and convincing, but at a much lower cost than would be required if all the details were constructed.

Apparent Reality

When greater fidelity is required to create a convincing environment, there still may be a number of possible ways to do it, each with its own set of tradeoffs. For example, consider the familiar movie scene of a couple driving down a road in a car.

The most straightforward, but also most difficult way to film such a scene is to use what is called a *tow shot.* The cameras are mounted on a truck or other vehicle that tows the actor's car down the street. This approach can provide very realistic results, but it can be difficult to execute. The street needs to be cleared of traffic.. If one of the actors blows a line, the whole parade needs to be moved back up the street before the shot can be started again. These complications make such shots expensive and cumbersome.

Another approach is the *process shot.* In this approach, the car is mounted on rockers and placed in front of a rear projection screen. While the scene is filmed a moving street scene is projected on the screen, so even though the car is stationary it appears to be moving. To make the motion of the car more convincing, grips may bounce the car while it is filmed to simulate going over a bumpy road. To be convincing, this shot must be done carefully. For example, at night the car must be illuminated with light that has the same color and direction as the light that illuminated the street scene when it was filmed. This approach also requires a considerable investment in equipment. The advantage of this approach is that the logistics are much easier. It is not necessary to close a city street, and re-taking a shot is simple. .

A third approach, sometimes called the *poor man's process shot,* provides many of the benefits of the process shot, but with almost no investment in equipment. The one restriction is that this shot must be set at night.

The car is set up on rockers as before, but because the scene is at night, there is no need for a rear projection system — it's supposed to be dark in the background, after all. As the scene is filmed, grips carry lights past the car to cast reflections on it and simulate driving at night down a lighted street. This shot can be extremely effective and very inexpensive.

These three different approaches to creating apparent reality represent different tradeoffs. The tow shot is similar to the approach used in military simulations: it incorporates real elements to create verisimilitude, but it is also the most expensive and cumbersome. The other two approaches move increasingly farther away from directly incorporating reality into simulations, with correspondingly reduced cost. But the latter approaches (particularly the poor man's process shot) are applicable in more limited circumstances. The lesson we take away from this is that by thinking carefully about the context in which a simulation will take place, it may be possible to significantly reduce its cost.

Hyper-reality

Sometimes it is necessary to exaggerate an event because a direct filming of the real event lacks the impact of actually experiencing the real event. One example of this is an explosion. In reality, it occurs very quickly and then is over. But it also has a major impact because it assaults all the senses (particularly if one is too close). In a direct filming of an explosion, one can see and hear the blast, but duplicating the chest-shaking thump is difficult. To compensate, filmmakers make the experience more intense by exaggerating the reality. One way to do this is to use slow motion so that the explosion lasts for a longer time than it does in reality. The audience has a longer time to see and hear the impact of the explosion and it intensifies the experience.

Another approach is to use a technique called *double-cutting,* which involves filming a critical scene (like an explosion or car wreck) from several different viewpoints simultaneously using multiple cameras. When the film is edited, the cuts from multiple cameras are used and spliced together in sequence, with some temporal overlap between the end of one cut and the beginning of the next. In this way, a viewer sees the same explosion from multiple points of view, and because the cuts are overlapped, the event lasts longer than it would in reality, increasing its intensity.

Movie soundtracks provide a number of examples of reality that has been altered or exaggerated for effect. In fact, in most major feature films, very little of the sound that was recorded when the film was shot ever makes it into the final cut. Instead, the soundtracks of most films are carefully constructed from sound effects, music and voices dubbed in after the fact. One example of this comes from the opening titles of the famous TV series *Hawaii Five O.* In one of the shots of the montage, a jet airliner lands on a runway. As it touches down, the tires squeal. This provides a nice punctuation for the landing. However, when a real jetliner lands, it is not possible to hear the tires squeak because the noise from the engines completely drowns it out. Nevertheless, the squealing-tires-on-landing effect, which started in *Hawaii Five O,* is now almost a sonic cliché. One rarely sees an airplane land in the movies today without hearing the tires squeak.

Another example of Hyper-reality is evidenced in the movie "Terminator II." Everyone who saw the movie remembers the famous scene where the kid on his motorbike is being chased by the bad Terminator in a 18 wheeler. The scene takes place in the concrete channel they call the L.A. River. Arnold, the good Terminator is on his motorcycle on the rim of the channel, and sees what is happening. He guns his hog, races along the rim and then leaps the fence and lands perfectly in the channel, placing himself between the boy and the bad Terminator. It is an exciting shot, and an impossible stunt. No one could do it, not even a Terminator.

How was it done? In one of the first uses of digital manipulation, director James Cameron had Arnold and the bike slowly lowered by wire into the channel. Then all the wires and apparatus to do this were digitally erased. When speeded up and enhanced with digital sparks and other effects, the impossible became possible. And no one in the audience complained that it was phony.

NON-REALITY: A CONJECTURE

The greatest words in literature are "Once Upon a Time" (or "a long time ago in a Galaxy far, far away.") Once the reader accepts this, he or she suspends disbelief.

Although military simulations generally try to be as realistic as possible, some of the most effective stories and films have been made about worlds that are completely made up. Film history is replete with works such as *Toy Story* and *Star Wars* (all of them) that take place in worlds that are imaginary. The fact that the story takes place in a fictional world is a great strength, because once the audience accepts that the world is fictional, they suspend disbelief and it is no longer necessary or expected that the world will duplicate our own. On the other hand, if a story is supposed to be set in the real world, then much more attention must be paid to getting all the details right.

What is most important, however, is that even though these stories may be set in imaginary places, it is still possible to learn from the stories and transfer these lessons back to the real world. Indeed, through out history, people have written allegorical stories set in unreal situations that are intended to teach lessons. An interesting question to explore is whether or not it would be possible to create military simulations that were set in unreal worlds, and use them to achieve pedagogical goals. Taking such an approach might make it possible to create effective simulations at a low cost.

SUMMARY

The point of this paper is to point out that for the entertainment industry, the most compelling experiences are not created by directly mimicking reality, but instead by using a wide variety of techniques that may be only loosely coupled to the underlying reality to be conveyed and potentially altering reality depending on the message that is to be delivered. The process of designing such an experience consists of answering a number of questions:

1) What are the objectives? What should the audience learn? How should they feel?
2) What techniques are available for achieving the desired objectives? Are they obtainable?
3) Are they affordable in terms of time and dollars? What is the acceptable trade-off that will do the job effectively?

In our view, military simulations could benefit from such an approach. Rather than using terrain data that renders thousands of square miles at the same level of resolution, consider first what the pedagogical goals are for a simulation system. Does all of the data need to be present? Is some more important than others? It may be possible to render the scene selectively, and draw attention to just the most relevant parts. While the specific techniques that we have outlined here may not be directly applicable to military simulations, we believe the general approach of altering reality to create a compelling experience will help us create simulations that are more effective and less costly.

William R. Swartout is the Director of Technology at USC's Institute for Creative Technology. Dr. Swartout is responsible for the overall technical direction of the ICT and oversight of technical projects and staff. He was formerly the Director of the Intelligent Systems Division at USC's Information Sciences Institute, and was elected in 1992 as a Fellow of the American Association of Artificial Intelligence (AAAI). Dr. Swartout has served as an Associate Research Professor at USC for the past ten years. He holds a PhD in Computer Science from MIT (1981), an M.S. in Electrical Engineering and Computer Science from MIT (1977), and a B.S. in Mathematical Sciences from Stanford (1974). Dr. Swartout's specific research interests in the area of artificial intelligence include: intelligent agents, knowledge-based systems, knowledge representation and acquisition, and natural language generation. He also served as the Conference Committee Chair for the AAAI (1992-1994), as Program Co-Chair at the Third International Conference on Principles and Knowledge Representation and Reasoning (1992), and as Program Co-Chair at the National Conference of Artificial Intelligence (1990).

Richard Lindheim is Executive Director of the ICT. He has over thirty-five years of experience in the entertainment industry. Initially working in the areas of audience testing and program research at NBC, Mr. Lindheim went on to hold various senior executive positions within MCA/Universal Television. Prior to joining the ICT, Mr. Lindheim was the Executive Vice President of the Paramount Television Group. In this capacity he was responsible for new business development and corporate strategy, and served as advisor to the Chairman and to the various divisions with in the television group. Among many other accomplishments, Mr. Lindheim formed Paramount Digital Entertainment, and later brought the military and the entertainment industry together as partners by developing the Story Drive Engine with DMSO. Mr. Lindheim received a B.S. degree in Electronic Engineering from the University of Redlands in California and completed interdisciplinary post-graduate studies at USC in Telecommunications and Engineering.

THE NAVAL POSTGRADUATE SCHOOL MOVES PROGRAM – ENTERTAINMENT RESEARCH DIRECTIONS

Michael Zyda
MOVES Academic Group
Naval Postgraduate School
Monterey, California 93943-5118 USA
http://www.npsnet.org/~zyda
zyda@acm.org

KEYWORDS

Defense and entertainment collaboration, modeling, virtual environments and simulation.

ABSTRACT

In 1997, the National Research Council issued a report that specified a joint research agenda for defense and entertainment modeling and simulation [NRC,97]. The NRC report provides a guide as to what research and development needs to be done to develop our future interactive entertainment and defense modeling and simulation systems. As a consequence of that report, a number of research laboratories have developed a joint entertainment/VR or entertainment/defense or entertainment/NASA focus. The Naval Postgraduate School MOVES Program, the largest modeling, virtual environments and simulation academic program, is one such organization following that report's research agenda with a number of active projects in defense and entertainment collaboration.

THE FUTURE OF NETWORKED ENTERTAINMENT

In the NRC report, we see that games and interactive entertainment (IE) have become the main technology drivers for networked virtual environments and not defense research expenditures. In order for the DoD to keep up with that evolving modeling, virtual environments and simulation technology, it then becomes important for DoD to examine the future of networked entertainment to see if there is the potential for a joint investment or collaboration. While we cannot say for certain what future networked entertainment looks like, we can hypothesize from what IE systems look like today. So we start out by looking at hypothetical versions of today's entertainment extrapolated into the future to identify perhaps what R&D we need to accomplish to get there. We need to look at what these IE systems will look like and how people will interact with such systems. We then examine how this can be aligned with DoD research desires for modeling, virtual environments and simulation.

To make our job a little bit easier, we make some assumptions on what we will have in the future:

- Infinite bandwidth to the home.
- Infinite 3D graphics capability and computing power in the home.
- Affordable for the home.

If these assumptions become true or nearly so, what will our games and IE systems be? Again, scenarios derived from today are the best we can do. We hypothesize a few such IE systems in order to motivate our research agenda.

Interactive TV

Probably the earliest vision of what Interactive TV will look like is captured in the 1966 motion picture "Fahrenheit 451," with Oskar Werner and Julie Christie. Interactive TV in that film shows Julie Christie participating in a television story with two on-screen characters. When it is time for Julie to respond, the characters look in her direction and a red light blinks on her wallscreen, appealing for a response. The message is that her response can possibly change story direction, that she can chat meaningfully with the on-screen characters and be "part of something". The technology necessary for such a system is networking to support two-way video/audio, entity streams (streams of state information for the involved characters) and sufficient resources that branching storylines based on user response can be "handled". Of course, the cynical tone of the film shows that no matter what her response, the story just goes on as planned. In our future, we really do want the story to change! So the requirement for autonomous characters and an interactive storyline engine is critical to being able to actually do this. The user experience with this system is reflected in the film piece. Julie has both individual and group concerns. She needs to know from people in the room how did she do. She also needs to know how her interactions were perceived by her friends watching elsewhere.

3D Avatar Chat & RPG

Chat rooms and role playing games (RPGs) are popular now and will be more so as we move to 3D avatar (3D character body) display and synchronized audio. With respect to interactivity, we want to have a 3D avatar, with animated face. We want to chat with others or with autonomous characters over the Internet. Autonomous characters are players not being run by a human but rather by a computer program that is compelling enough for the human player to believe that he/she is actually playing against some sort of intelligence. Our graphics are going to have to be very good for future 3D avatar chat. Our autonomy will have to be more compelling than today's. We want to see the lips move on the character to whom we are speaking. This has to be synched with the sound. Our character's movements cannot lag. The Internet is going to have to let us chat/play with people who are located just about anywhere. We will have audio and entity streams transiting the net. We are going to be a knight fighting the giant, our body motions tracked. We are going to find ourselves talking to Lara Croft of TombRaider and she's going to answer back. We are going to feel as if we are interacting with Lara.

Quake 2007/Shooters 2013!

We are going to go into a dark, 3D world and fight monsters off the 'Net. We're going to hear them breathe and we're going to hear them die. Our 3D virtual environment (VE) will have fully articulated monsters, monsters steered by body-suited, armed opponents or computed autonomously. We are going to team with distant friends to accomplish our missions. We will have an audio stream and an entity stream. We will feel as if we are in the Quake-2007 VE. Our roommates will be able to smell the fear and us the blood.

Our body motions will be tracked in our game cell unit, our fist will clench our weapon, our avatar may be altogether different from our corporeal norm. Our articulated avatars will be detailed and well-modeled and the behaviors so realistic that it will be difficult to tell if they are live or if they autonomous characters . Our demand will be for premium quality of service in our networking and we will insist on minimal lag. We will have entity streams for large numbers of players and audio streams from nearby players. And maybe video streams for offline chat. Our experience will be one of fear, comradery, excitement, sweaty palms, the entire gamut.

ExtremeSports 2015!

Imagine the view from the wrestler we will have and the thuds against our body as we perform ExtremeSports from the safety of our VR room. Our worlds will be rich in surface detail and there will not be a missed mogul in its depiction. The lag on our 'Net will be so low that we will be able to perform the most delicate motion. We will be Pele.

MartialArts Forever!

The tracking of our body movements in the VR cell with allow us to practice moves against fearsome opponents. The human avatars will be incredibly detailed, with each articulation smooth and the skin textures real. 'Net lag will be near zero as our quality of service is set to premium. We will feel that fist from Washington, DC. We will be in touch with our inner soldier and those out there too.

So if we want to be able to do all this, what do we need?

We need hardware, a fast network, software, input devices, a whole lot of things that we have now and a whole lot more not yet started on. Compute power – we need as many cycles as we can get for under $500. We have 1 Ghz clock rates now and will move to 300 Ghz by 2015! Graphics - we see game machines that are claiming 66M textured polygons per second this year [EETIMES,99]. We will have 300M+ to 5B textured polygons per second in two to five years [Smith,2000].

Network - we are seeing high-speed nets to the home. Broadband access will be available to over 100 million US homes by the year 2003 and deployed in some 28 million homes [Forrester,2000]. DSL speeds of 1.5Mbps downstream and 384K bps back allow us to interact with 500 players in a game and have a video stream at the same time. Cable modems promise greater speeds and allows us interactions with even greater numbers of simultaneous participants.

Latency reduction and predictive modeling research are key to us making usable IE systems. [Singhal/Zyda,99] indicates that latency must be less than 100ms for high interactivity, maybe 200ms for some gaming apps. Today we are seeing people live with 350ms or greater for some gaming now, with truly awful playability!

NPS MOVES & THE NRC REPORT

The Naval Postgraduate School's Modeling, Virtual Environments & Simulation (MOVES) Academic Program and Research Center has developed a research focus aligned with the NRC report. The following areas are our focus:

- Networked Virtual Environments
- Standards for Interoperability
- Technologies for Immersion
- Computer Generated Characters
- Human Factors & Human-Computer Interaction
- New Educational Paradigms

We look at these areas and particular relevant NPS MOVES projects below.

Networked Virtual Environments - A Vision

Eventually, there will exist a persistent virtual environment simultaneously shared by millions. There can never be a global reboot. All modifications must happen on the fly. The development of participant programs (live and autonomous characters) for that VE must be as simple as writing a web page is today. In order to accomplish that vision, we must develop a network software architecture (NSA) that is extensible, composable, and interoperable. We need cross-platform, component frameworks and dynamic behavior protocols. We need the ability to suspend/resume state so that we can have a persistent universe. We need to be able to develop area of interest management techniques in order to support the large number of expected players in our VE.

The motivation behind cross-platform component frameworks is that we want to build systems that are changeable overtime, systems whose updates are downloadable over the Internet, systems that can work on multiple platforms, systems whose pieces are small-enough that they are understandable and reusable. This is more than just extending memory. Dynamically loaded modules require a consistent plug-in framework. The system must establish a convention such that modules can integrate into already running applications.

Our desire for dynamic behavior protocols is that each entity in the VE be able to define its own protocol modules, modules that are dynamically loadable from the web. Our desire for the architecture for such protocols is that it is easy to maintain, always fully implemented, always optimized per individual, that it never consumes unused system resources and is updateable in real-time.

For the NSA, a three-tier approach seems the way to go. The first tier is Global, with an environment registry that helps find a particular virtual environment, i.e. VR-DNS. The second tier is Environment, with an object registry that tells what objects are in a particular environment. The third tier is Object, with a module registry that points to the location of the code for our objects and their input/output channels.

By using dynamic protocols, along with components of the existing Internet architecture, we can support the persistence of a large-scale distributed virtual environment. We hypothesize http Statelets, a platform independent file containing names of archived classes, URLs of the modules containing the classes, and the archived classes themselves.

Area of interest management through the use of multicasting for VEs has long been identified by NPS as being key to the scalability of networked virtual environments. The keys to success for such scalability are:

- Receive only what you need to process.
- Dynamic extensibility – the ability to dynamically add new protocols, environments.
- Must have the ability to handle "crowd" situations.
- Low overhead for interest management.

Issues in the mix of a successful solution to area of interest management include network latency, and available bandwidth, the long time to join a multicast group (0.5 seconds typical), multicast address space/allocation (think IPv6), the number of multicast groups supported by workstation/PC network interface cards, the number of multicast routes supported by network routers, and the current unreliable nature of large-scale multicast (need QoS support).

Standards for Interoperability - we must be designing standards for interoperability that are as simple to use as writing a web page. So once we have done all the net-VE research work above, we can then think about standardization.

Technologies for Immersion

The NPS focus on technologies for immersion is on the utilization of available, low-cost real-time graphics hardware such as the latest nVidia board sets and game machine development platforms like the Sony Playstation 2 and the Microsoft XBox. Trends from the game platform market are inspiring. The

Playstation 2 is listed as being capable of rasterizing 75M polygons/second and transforming 66M polygons/second and is being sold for $300. Plans for Playstation 3 six years from now are to be 1,000 times faster (66B polygons/second?) [EETIMES,99]! Silicon Graphics would do 20x increase in graphics in the same amount of time in previous generations. The Microsoft XBox is planned for 300M polygons per second. Where these numbers are taking us is closer to visual reality.

Ed Catmull defined visual reality as 80M polygons/picture [NRC,95, pg.252]. 80M polygons/picture at 60 pictures/second (fps) is 4.8B polygons/second. We are talking about machines that can visually display computer images indistinguishable from reality, speeds that game machines and PC boards are getting ever close to.

Tracking of human body motion in the networked VE is also a focus of NPS efforts. We are prototyping an inertial tracker that is capable of being deployed in a form factor the size of a wristwatch. We are going for sourceless, wireless, line-of-sight range tracking.

We are also looking at deployment of full sensory interfaces in order to include a wide range of sensory stimuli in our networked VEs including visual, auditory, olfactory, and haptic stimuli. We are looking at adopting location-based entertainment motion platforms like the LGM platform [LGM,2000].

Computer-Generated Characters

We want computer-characters in our net-VEs with whom we can interact in an intelligent fashion. We want autonomous behaviors for those characters. We want characters that can come in over the network and play with us, educate us, train us, characters that can learn and help guide the VE's story. We need software architectures that can provide:

- Adaptability - modify behavior automatically
- Learning - modify behavior over time, reinforcement learning.
- Agent-based - to allow for emergent behaviors.
- Behavior and Story Modeling
- High quality avatars

NPS MOVES Projects in Computer-Generated Autonomy

The NPS MOVES Research Center [MOVES,2000], in collaboration with the NPSNET Research Group [NPSNET,2000], has several projects in computer-generated autonomy. We are building a networked agent architecture in support of multiple game/defense development efforts. We are building videogames in support of various Army missions. We are building game-like simulations for training business managers in the operations of DoD clinics (SimClinic). We have constructed game-like simulations to explore the OPNAV management of the US Navy (SimNavy prototype).

The goal of the networked agent architecture project is to develop an NPS-owned agent-based simulation engine that operates in distributed fashion. We are developing tools for specifying the interiors and the interactions of the agents. Personnel in our research group have participated in the development of the engines underlying SimCity, SimAnt and SimFarm.

The motivation of our Army games project is to explore the development of web-based, instrumented, networked videogames. We are developing an integrated Career and Action game over a span of 48 months, fully instrumented, fully networked, developed for continual content refresh and update, using existing game development technology when possible, developing new technology when necessary. The Career game focuses on a simulated Army career, similar to an adventure game where experience through various schools and obtained objects moves the player forward in the action. The Action game is planned to be similar to Rainbow Six, with the focus on team play. The research focus in the development of these two games is to determine if games can be instrumented to be able to determine the aptitude, leadership abilities and psychological profile of the game player.

The goal of the SimNavy Prototype was to build an enterprise model of the US Navy in a fashion similar to Maxis' SimCity, with a dramatic computer-game interface, but with much higher resolution and Navy-relevant scenarios. The SimNavy concept was to simulate the OPNAV/N-code operation of the Navy, including resource allocation, the psychology of decision making, the zero sum economy, multilateral decisions and constraints, the conflict between political process and military requirements, and the dynamic nature of decision making. SimNavy's value was to provide an interactive experience through which Naval officers can learn how to make decisions at the various levels of the Navy's hierarchy. SimNavy was not a simulation for Navy war-fighting or tactics but rather a tool to examine the relationship between budget allocation and operational possibilities. A prototype of SimNavy was developed using commercial game artists for the Windows platform. The screens developed for that game are visible in the following online location [SimNavy,98].

NPS MOVES ACADEMIC PROGRAM

Besides providing a research agenda, the NRC report indicated that new educational paradigms were required to carry out that agenda, that Computer Science alone was not sufficient to build our future modeling and simulation systems. NPS has constructed a prototype educational program based on the NRC report - the MOVES (Modeling, Virtual Environments & Simulation) Academic Program [MOVES,2000]. The MOVES program is a blend of Computer Science and Operations Research, with the goal of producing graduates capable of understanding the mathematics behind modeling and simulation and the computer science required for the implementation of their models and simulations inside of a networked virtual environment. Both an M.S. and a Ph.D. in MOVES have been defined, with NPS having the only defined Ph.D. in M&S in the world (at the moment). The MOVES Program's Ph.D. specialization areas include physically-based modeling for virtual environments, networked virtual environments, human factors in virtual environments, adaptable software agents, modeling human and organizational behavior, discrete-event systems modeling, and data and model visualization.

CONCLUSION

Defense and entertainment collaboration are a natural considering the ability of the entertainment industry to outpace the DoD in many areas related to modeling, virtual environments and simulation. The Naval Postgraduate School MOVES Research Center, in conjunction with the NPSNET Research Group, is currently the largest funded effort aimed at developing DoD-relevant entertainment-derived, M&S systems. That research and development component, along with our strong MOVES Academic Program, are unmatched in focus and vision in this direction.

REFERENCES

[EETIMES,99] Yoshiko Hara, "Microprocessor Forum: Sony to use Playstation2 Technology for Workstation Line," EE Times, 8 October 1999, http://www.eetimes.com/story/OEG19991006S0040

[Forrester,2000] http://info.on2.com/broadband/bb_facts.html

[LGM,2000] LGM web site http://www.lgm.com

[MOVES,2000] MOVES Academic Program http://www.npsnet.org/~moves

[NPSNET,2000] NPSNET Research Group http://www.npsnet.org/~npsnet

[NRC,95] Virtual Reality: Scientific and Technological Challenges, Editors: Nathaniel I. Durlach and Anne S. Mavor, Committee on Virtual Reality Research and Development, National Research Council, National Academy of Sciences Press, Washington, DC 1995, ISBN 0-309-05135-5, http://www.amazon.com/exec/obidos/ASIN/0309051355/michaelzyda

[NRC,97] Zyda, Michael and Sheehan, Jerry (eds.), Modeling and Simulation: Linking Entertainment & Defense, National Academy Press, September 1997, ISBN 0-309-05842-2, 181 pages, http://books.nap.edu/catalog/5830.html

[SimNavy,98] Presentation slides for SimNavy on the web http://www.npsnet.org/~zyda/presentations/SimNavyTalk98.pdf

[Singhal/Zyda,1999] Sandeep Singhal and Michael Zyda, Networked Virtual Environments - Design and Implementation, ACM Press Books, SIGGRAPH Series, 23July 1999, ISBN 0-201-32557-8, 315 pages, http://www.amazon.com/exec/obidos/ASIN/0201325578/michaelzyda

[Smith, 2000] Mike Smith, "X-Box vs. PlayStation 2," MSN gaming Zone, 30 march 2000, http://www.zone.com/zzzz/gamesdomainxboxvsplay.asp

ACKNOWLEDGEMENTS

This work would not have been possible without the support of our sponsors: Advanced Network and Services, the Army Research Office, the Assistant Secretary of the Army for Manpower and Reserve Affairs, and the Navy Modeling and Simulation Management Office (N6M) through the MOVES Research Center.

BIOGRAPHY

Michael Zyda is a Professor in the Department of Computer Science at the Naval Postgraduate School, Monterey, California. Professor Zyda is also the Chair of the NPS Modeling, Virtual Environments and Simulation Academic Group. Since 1986, he has been the Director of the NPSNET Research Group. He has been at NPS since February of 1984. Professor Zyda's research interests include computer graphics, large-scale, networked 3D virtual environments, computer-generated characters, video production, entertainment/defense collaboration, and modeling and simulation. He is known for his work on software architectures for networked virtual environments.

Professor Zyda was a member of the National Research Council's Committee on "Virtual Reality Research and Development" and is one of the key authors of that report. Professor Zyda was the chair of the National Research Council's Computer Science and Telecommunications Board Committee on "Modeling and Simulation: Linking Entertainment & Defense". From that report, for the Deputy Assistant Secretary of the Army for Research and Technology, Professor Zyda drafted the operating plan and research agenda for the USC Institute for Creative Technologies (ICT).

Professor Zyda is a member of the National Research Council Committee on Advanced Engineering Environments. Professor Zyda is also a Senior Editor for Virtual Environments for the MIT Press quarterly PRESENCE, the journal of teleoperation and virtual environments. He is a member of the Editorial Advisory Board of the journal Computers & Graphics. Professor Zyda is also a member of the Technical Advisory Board of the Fraunhofer Center for Research in Computer Graphics, Providence, Rhode Island. He is a Member of the Board of Advisors for the Georgia Institute of Technology Modeling and Simulation Research and Education Center.

Professor Zyda has consulted for the White House Office of Science and Technology Policy, the Ministry of Industrial Development Sabah Province, Malaysia, Japan Tech Services Corporation, Tokyo, Hitachi Plant Construction & Engineering, Ohtsuka, SimGraphics Engineering, Pasadena, Silicon Graphics International, Geneva, Nihon Silicon Graphics KK, Advanced Telecommunications Inc., TecMagik, spiritChannel.com and Paramount Digital Entertainment, among others. He is a speaker with Celebrity Speakers, International .

Professor Zyda began his career in Computer Graphics in 1973 as part of an undergraduate research group, the Senses Bureau, at the University of California, San Diego. Professor Zyda received a BA in Bioengineering from the University of California, San Diego in La Jolla in 1976, an M.S. in Computer Science/Neurocybernetics from the University of Massachusetts, Amherst in 1978 and a D.Sc. in Computer Science from Washington University, St. Louis, Missouri in 1984.

COLABORATION OF THE ENTERTAINMENT INDUSTRY BY THE U. S. DEPARTMENT OF DEFENSE

Mr. Mark McAuliffe, Ms. Alesya Paschal, CPT Scott Sandback
U.S. Army Simulation, Training, and Instrumentation Command (STRICOM)
Orlando, FL 32826
Email: Mark_Mcauliffe@stricom.army.mil

Abstract: U. S. Department of Defense, with the Army as lead, has established a University Affiliated Research Center to leverage the Modeling and Simulation capabilities of the Nation's Entertainment Industry. In August 1999, the Army signed a five-year, $45M contract with the University of Southern California (USC), which established the Institute for Creative Technologies (ICT). The goal of ICT is to establish partnerships with the defense, Internet, and entertainment industries, strategically advance the Army's knowledge, expertise, and capabilities in modeling and simulation technologies. ICT research will support military acquisition, analysis, and training in the 21st century. The effort will leverage advances in modeling and simulation technologies to improve the realism and quality of Army training simulations, leader-development exercises, and even the capabilities the Army will look for in future weapons acquisition programs. This article discusses the economic reasons for this unique collaboration.

INTRODUCTION.

The stretch from the entertainment industry to the Department of Defense (DoD) isn't as big as one might initially think. In fact, DoD is already similar to Hollywood in many ways. The military currently uses mock towns to conduct mission rehearsals and training. Effects like smoke generators, sound effect systems, target systems, bullet strikes, mortar strikes, and roof top explosions similar to those used in Hollywood's back lots are used to immerse the participants into a more realistic environment. However, recent improvements taken from Hollywood's back lots could be applied to further enhance the training experience.

Another area is the Internet. The Internet created in 1969 for DoD and commercialized in 1991, has had a huge impact on the entertainment industry. This has effected games, music and movie distribution. And, there is a certain irony that the Internet, which was originally conceived as a communications structure to withstand a nuclear war, is now being examined for training a post Cold War military. Interactive games on the Internet have engaged people from around the world. Individuals meet globally in a common environment, and face each other or as "clans" face opponents. These opponents can either be computer generated or human opposing forces. The "first-person shooter" is a popular game genre that has matured to the point where the tactics for individual and team success are not too different from the tactics taught at the squad and team levels of military forces. Distributed training/gaming and mission execution in a virtual environment happen every day in the form of these online interactive games. This kind of training is a focus area for Army research.

The entertainment world also knows that complicated instructions quickly lose the interest of the user, resulting in loss of revenue. Therefore, the game developers made it a point to engineer and simplify its most complex products so that even a child can use them. For example, some game software packages require information for the user to operate their virtual equipment (i.e., a flight simulator). The game displays this information by means of virtual gauges placed so information is available to the player in an uncomplicated, yet effective way, so as not to distract from the game play. Some of these methods of displaying information are extremely elegant in their simplicity. Others mirror "real world" closely enough to allow high training transfer. DoD has complicated systems and even more complicated instructions. Often, DoD's systems require operator training and maintenance before the systems are available to the military. By applying the intuitive operation from the game industry to military systems, huge saving could result.

WHERE DoD IS GOING.

DoD is using game technology now; the Navy has a customized version of Microsoft Corp.'s Flight Simulator game for "all student pilots and undergraduates enrolled in Naval Reserve Officer Training Courses at 65 colleges."[1] The Navy has found that "students who use microsimulation products during early flight training tend to have higher scores than students who do not use the software."[1] In addition, the Army has adapted a commercial game Spearhead II to research the DoD High Level Architecture, and is evaluating its use in the Armor Training Curriculum.[2] "Game designers are experts in making their products fun and engrossing such that the player will become addicted to the experience. ... One of the biggest criticisms of using video games for training is that this 'fun factor' can result in depiction of unrealistic scenarios that lead to negative training. If DoD collaborates on the design of the game from the outset, these effects are largely eliminated, while still maintaining the 'fun factor'."[2] A senior army officer has stated that the fidelity in the Longbow game simulation exceeds the fidelity for the Longbow Combat Mission Simulator and the Longbow Crew Simulator. So, while the goal of simulation for the Army is such that participants "do not play, they experience", the same reality in games can be applied to the military.

HOW TO GET THERE.

It is apparent there is potential for cost savings through utilizing developments and applications of the entertainment industry, and collaboration for possible joint ventures of mutual benefit. Whether in a movie house, on a PC, or on a game console, technologies and their application by entertainment have developed to the point where military decision makers are taking a new look at the potential. To explore this new venue, the DoD, with the Army as lead, has established a University Affiliated Research Center to leverage the Modeling and Simulation capabilities of the Nation's Entertainment Industry. Last year, the Army signed a 45M dollar contract with the University of Southern California to link defense, Internet, and entertainment research in modeling and simulation. Initial applications include the use of modeling and simulation for the next generation fighting system and enhancing realistic training capability. This will strategically advance the Army's knowledge, expertise, and capabilities in modeling and simulation technologies. ICT research will support military acquisition, analysis, and training in the 21st century. The effort will leverage advances in modeling and simulation technologies to improve the realism and quality of Army training simulations, leader-development exercises, and even the capabilities the Army will look for in future weapons acquisition programs.

Common research between DoD and entertainment provides both industries the potential to reduce costs. The use of common technologies implementation can create a giant consumer market. In creating this giant consumer, the DoD would leverage the electronic game industry where "sales hit $6.9 billion just shy of movie box office receipt of $7.3 billion".[3] To create engaging experiences, the common core element is technology. The technology follows Moore's Law: " Each new chip contained roughly twice as much capacity as its predecessor, and each chip was released within 18-24 months of the previous chip",[4] and as the chip set improves, the simulations that supports games or DoD simulations improve. This computer revolution was the most critical element to provide the overall platform for games. One of the overarching constraints for both the game developer and the Government's materiel developer is the cost (recurring and non-recurring). Hardware seems to behave as Moore's Law predicts. However, another "break-point" is emerging. Manpower in the form of software developer's hourly rates has consistently increased. To offset this trend, new tools to aid in productivity and the use of creative talent (as opposed to technical talent) to develop content and story are finding their way into developers' shops. To expand the market, and capitalize on adjacent game technologies, there are now development tools-special software to help game developers process code for specific platforms. These tools aid in classical software development and support reusable code. In other words, the entertainment industry is working on a solution to simplify the complexity of using multiple technologies while minimizing the costs of doing so. As high capacity storage (CD-ROMs and DVDs) have dropped in price and microprocessors continue to increase in both speed and capability, game developers have been able to further enrich the game environment and add more and more realism to the end user experience.

One of the most economically productive areas for this collaboration is linking with the $7 billion game industry. But, the issue remains on "how" to affect collaboration with the game industry. Obviously the collaboration effort cannot be a one-way street. The Department of Defense must provide 'value added' to the game market if they want to capture their attention. Providing research funds, data and military expertise to the game industry is one way to contribute. The Army has provided these resources in a limited manner to game developers in the past. However, it is not feasible for the Army to support every game developer. With the creation of the Institute for Creative Technologies, a formal arrangement can be established for both the game industry and Department of Defense. This ICT arrangement is required because of the unique background and requirements of the two industries. Game developers need the commercial rights for product sales and overall software design control. DoD needs the right to use the software product for training, development, analysis and testing; but it has no direct interest in commercialization. Game development was based on a small aggressive software team that was in pursuit of the next " killer" game. Development was considered throwaway. After all, the game's graphics had to be redesigned and optimized, because better graphics hardware would be available. Software was generated without consideration of "reuse". The major threat for the game industry was a garage genius who would come online with a better game, or come to market with a similar idea ahead of your development. Although games are still schedule driven, words like art, story, and reuse have started to appear in the gamer's vernacular. There's also a new interest for "interactive games". Not too surprisingly, game developer and Department of Defense requirements may be converging.

By tapping into Hollywood, ICT will be able to exploit its story telling ability. With a Hollywood story, the "plot" in the form of situation and conditions is key and can add to the value of the training. The story can create an illusion that could also be applied to Army training. The training would then mirror a Hollywood project-writing, directing, and editing to produce a more compelling experience. All these steps will help ensure the illusion of a future mission. One effort that has applied these techniques is the Paramount Story Drive Engine project. The Story Drive Engine is a computer software system that merges the concepts of story, character, and simulation into a seamless user experience. This effort integrated news reports of live action with what was a paper drill. In its demonstration at Final Flurry, this resulted in the participants taking a personal interest in the outcome of events-truly engrossing the training audience. "In the Story Drive experience, the students are like a movie audience with the teacher as a director."[5] This demonstrated the power and training effectiveness of a well told story.

The production of a game now mirrors a Hollywood project-in its writing, directing, and editing to produce a more compelling experience. All these steps help ensure that "the [game] player has the illusion that they are in complete control of their character's destiny"[6]. In Don Carson's article on Environmental Storytelling: Creating Immersive 3D Worlds Using Lessons Learned from the Theme Park Industry [6], he discussed a desire for any computer game to "Take me to a place that: Lets me go somewhere I could never go. 'Lets me be someone I could never be.' Lets me do things I could never do!"[6] Games now use storytelling and sometimes actors to 'set the stage'. Who has control of what assets? What is your mission? What is success/ how are you evaluated? How much time do you have? Where are you? Furthermore, as more users jump onto the Internet to experience this virtual world, developers continue to refine and maximize the use of the always limited bandwidth.

RETURN ON INVESTMENT.

Many of the details which support this collaboration are contained in the National Research Council's 1997 report entitled "Modeling and Simulation: Linking Entertainment and Defense".[7] The concept identified in reference [7] supports cost reduction. This publication identifies common technologies and research vectors that would support collaboration.

THE PATH AHEAD.

The future for DoD may lie in the new Sony PlayStation2 or Microsoft Xbox as plug and play simulators with no maintenance costs, or as play and learn trainers. Perhaps, it is distributed shared virtual environments to conduct mission rehearsals, validate tactics, or simply to allow units to train together more often. It will likely include all of these, as well as the software development tools provided to the game developers (DoD simulation designers). It is apparent that the DoD has the opportunity to reduce costs while maintaining the forces necessary to insure national interests by applying some of the products offered by the entertainment industry.

REFERENCES

[1] Brewin, Bob "Navy takes PC game seriously Simulator- Software Helps Train Pilots", Federal Computer Week, February 07, 2000.

[2] Fullford, Deborah; Katz, Warren "Low-Cost Training Over the Internet", Proceedings of the International Conference on Web-Based Modeling and Simulation, January 23-27, 2000.

[3] Takahashi, Dean "How Four Renegades Persuaded Microsoft to Make a Game Machine", The Wall Street Journal.

[4] Intel Web Site, "What is Moore's Law?", http://www.intel.com/intel/museum/25anniv/hof/moore.htmil.

[5] http://208.201.97.5/pubs/fcw/1999/0830/fcw-newswargames-08-30-99.html.

[6] Carson, Don "Environmental Storytelling: Creating Immersive 3D Worlds Using Lessons Learned form the Theme Park Industry", March 01, 2000. http://www.gamasutra.com/features/20000301/carson_01.htm.

[7] Zyda, Michael "Modeling and Simulation Linking Entertainment and Defense", National Research Council 1997.

AUTHOR'S BIOGRAPHIES

MARK MCAULIFFE is a Principal Investigator for the Department of Defense Designated University Affiliated Research Center for Modeling and Simulation at the U.S. Army Simulation, Training, and Instrumentation Command (STRICOM) in Orlando, Florida. Mark has 25 years experience in the research and development of real time simulations. Mark holds a Master of Science degree in Systems Technology from the Navy Postgraduate School, a Master of Science in Management from Rollins College and a Bachelor of Science degree in Engineering from the University of Central Florida.

ALESYA PASCHAL is a Systems Engineer at U.S. Army Simulation, Training, and Instrumentation Command (STRICOM) in Orlando, Florida. Alesya has 10 years simulation experience to include efforts on Flight Simulators, Distributed Interactive Simulations, and Synthetic Environment Operational and Live Fire Testing. Most recently, her efforts include the Synthetic Theater of War-Architecture programs and STRICOM's SMART initiatives. Ms. Paschal holds a Master of Science degree in Engineering from Texas A&M University and a Bachelor of Science degree in Engineering from University of Tennessee.

CPT SCOTT SANDBACK is a research assistance attending the University of Central Florida in pursuit of his Master of Science degree in Interactive Simulation and Training Systems. His background in simulations include efforts in distributed interactive simulations, synthetic and live environment blending, and systems integration/interaction. He holds a Bachelor of Science degree in Computer Science from University of Southern Colorado.

Influences of Communications and Media

Secure Real Time Speech Transmission over the Internet: Performance Analysis and Simulation

Marco Roccetti

Dipartimento di Scienze dell'Informazione, Università di Bologna
Mura Anteo Zamboni 7, I-40127 Bologna, Italy
E.mail: roccetti@cs.unibo.it

Abstract

An adaptive packet audio control algorithm is presented that embodies a set of cryptography protocols designed to support secure, unicast, voice-based communications over the Internet. Performance results of a simulative/experimental analysis are reported that show that, with the proposed mechanism, secure audio communications may be conducted without sacrificing the quality of the transmitted speech.

Keywords

Internet, Multimedia, Privacy, Packet Audio, Jitter, Packet Loss, Simulation

1. INTRODUCTION

Sophisticated applications of Internet multimedia conferencing will become increasingly important only if the speech quality and the privacy provided by the communications will be perceived as sufficiently good by their users. The result of extensive experiments has shown that audio is frequently perceived as one of the most important component of multimedia conferencing. However, still Internet audio applications are often dismissed as impractical because of either the poor speech quality or the low security degree ensured by many existing Internet audio tools.

From a speech quality standpoint, two are the critical problems. One problem is represented by the fact that those audio applications are often constrained to work under very restrictive bandwidth. All the adopted solutions use codecs in order to reduce the quantity of data to be transmitted. Thus, an efficient coding of the signal is the first factor to consider in order (i) to work with the available transmission rates over networks, and (ii) to obtain the same speech quality as generated at the sender site. As an example, telephone quality of speech needs 64 Kbits, but in most cases such a bandwidth is not reachable over the Internet. Codecs are used in order to cope with this lack, but as the compression level increases (and the needed bandwidth decreases), the generated speech degrades itself, by turning misunderstandable. This issue has been passed down to the codec development efforts of the International Telecommunication Union (ITU), and several codecs have been designed that work well in the presence of the scarce network bandwidth constraint. As an example, the ITU codecs G.729 and G.723.1 have been designed for transmitting audio data at bit rates ranging from 8 Kbps to 5.3 Kbps.

The second problem affecting the speech quality amounts to the highly variable transmission delay that may be experienced over the Internet. The problem is that, since the current Internet routers operate on a FIFO basis and statistically multiplex traffic from different sources, only a flat, classless, best-effort service may be offered. The impact of this on real time audio traffic is to introduce delay variation (known as jitter) to the inter packet timing relationship and high packet loss rates. Unfortunately, user studies indicate that the most important factors that may disrupt the users' perception of audio are represented by the very large transmission delays experienced by packets while transversing the network and excessive packet loss rates. In particular, telephony users find round trip delays larger than 300 msec more like a half-duplex connection than a real time conversation. In addition, too large audio packet loss rates (over 10%) may have a tremendous impact on speech recognition. In the absence of network support to provide guarantees of quality to users of Internet voice software, an interesting alternative to cope with problems caused by jitter and high packet loss is to use adaptive control mechanisms. Typically, these mechanisms are based on the idea to use a voice reconstruction buffer at the receiver in order to add artificial delay to the audio stream to smooth out the impact of packet loss and jitter on the quality of the conversation. Clearly, the mechanisms have to be adaptive since jitter and packet loss on the Internet may vary significantly with time.

From a security viewpoint, only a few Internet audio conferencing tools exist that use speech compression and strong cryptography protocols to give users the ability to have a real time secure telephone conversation over the Internet [7]. Unfortunately, the typical problem with those tools is that the adopted strong cryptographic approach causes a computational overhead that is paid at the cost of further sacrificing the quality of the transmitted speech. In this paper, we focus our attention on two main factors: quality of speech and security degree. Indeed, it is worth observing that it is not possible to obtain the optimum conditions for both aspects; on the contrary, it is necessary to aim to an adequate trade-off between them. For instance, we can be interested in guaranteeing an absolutely secure service (e.g. by using long keys and strong cryptographic protocols) so that a "man in the middle" cannot decipher transmitted data neither during the conversation nor off-line. Unfortunately, such a service cannot be real time because of the extremely hard computing load of the privacy infrastructure. On the other hand, we can weaken the privacy conditions in order to obtain a soft or hard real time service. The key issue is to fix the minimal degree of security we must preserve. As far as a real time audio conversation is concerned, the minimal requirement is to avoid alteration from a third party during a conversation, so that a "man in the middle" cannot cut the communication channel and spoof by alterating the information exchanged between the two parties, in such a way they cannot become aware of this. In the following we refer to this level of secrecy and confidentiality as *real time security*. Based on the above considerations, it is worth noting that all the adopted encryption strategies in existing audio tools exploit symmetric cryptography (the same algorithm and key are used for both encryption and decryption) because symmetric algorithms are generally at least 1000 times faster than public-key algorithms, which are preferably used in less time dependent applications, such as authentication.

In this paper we show how a set of cryptography protocols (Sect. 3) may be embodied in a playot delay control mechanisms (designed by the author and detailed in Sect. 2) so as to conduct secure real time conversations over the Internet without sacrificing the quality of the transmitted speech. To confirm the efficacy of the approach, we report a set of performance results (Sect. 4) gathered from extensive simulative/experimentatal trials conducted over the Internet that show that, with our mechanism, a satisfiable privacy may be obtained in real time audio conversations while maintaining a good speech quality.

2. AUDIO CONTROL MECHANISM

During an audio communication, in order for the receiving site to reconstruct the audio conversation, the audio packets constituting a talkspurt must be played out in the order they were emitted at the sending site. Thus, to transport audio over a non-guaranteed packet switched network, such as the Internet, jitter has to be removed from audio packet streams since it causes the speech to be unintelligible. Typically, in order to compensate for variable network delays a smoothing playout buffer is used at the receiver. Received packets are queued into the buffer and the playout of each packet of a given talkspurt is delayed for some quantity of time beyond the reception of the first packet of that talkspurt. Playout control mechanisms adaptively adjust the talkspurt playout delay in order to keep this delay as small as possible, while minimizing the number of packets delayed past the point at which they are scheduled to be played out. Clearly, the longer the additional delay, the more likely it is that a packet will arrive before its scheduled playout deadline. However, too long playout delays may seriously compromise the quality of the conversation. We have devised a playout delay control scheme that (contrary to other audio tools, such as rat, FreePhone and NeVot [1, 2]) foregoes the traditional assumptions of externally synchronized systems clocks as well as the use of a specific jitter delay distribution of the audio packets, and is suitable for dynamically adjusting the talkspurt playout delay to the Internet traffic [3]. The scheme is based on obtaining, in periodic intervals (about 1 second), an estimation of the upper bound for the packet transmission delays experienced during an audio communication. Such an upper bound is periodically computed using round trip time (*RTT*) values obtained from packet exchanges of a three-way handshake protocol performed between the sender and the receiver of the audio communication. Prior to the beginning of the first talkspurt in an audio conversation, the sender initiates this packet protocol exchange activity by sending to the receiver a *probe* packet timestamped with the time value shown by its own clock (say *C*). At the reception of this probe packet, the receiver sets its own clock to *C* and sends immediately back to the sender a *response* packet with attached the same timestamp *C*. Upon the receiving of this response packet, the sender computes the value of the *RTT* by subtracting from the current value of its local clock the value of the timestamp *C*. At that moment, the difference between the two clocks is equal to an unknown quantity (say τ) which may range from a theoretical lower bound of 0 to a theoretical upper bound of *RTT*. Unfortunately, τ is unknown and a rough approximation of this value might result in both playout buffer overflow problems and packet loss due to late arrivals [3]. In order to master those problems, the sender, after having received the response packet from the receiver and calculated the *RTT* value, sends to the receiver a final *installation* packet, with attached the previously calculated *RTT* value. Upon receiving this installation packet, the receiver sets the time of its local clock, by subtracting from the value shown by its clock at the arrival of the installation packet the value of the transmitted *RTT*. Due to this setting of the receiver's clock, the time difference between the two clocks at the sender (C_S) and at the receiver (C_R), at the same time instant T^*, is equal to a value Δ, given by $\Delta = C_S(T^*) - C_R(T^*) = \tau + RTT$. It is easy to show that Δ is an unknown quantity that may range in the interval $[RTT, 2 \times RTT]$ depending on the unknown value of τ [3]. Based on the value of the time difference imposed by the protocol between the two clocks at the sender and at the receiver, the following playout/buffering strategy may be performed. Each audio packet emitted by the sender is timestamped by the sender with the time value shown by the sender's clock at the moment of its generation. When such an audio packet arrives at the receiver, its generation timestamp *t* is compared with the value *T* of the receiver's clock, and a decision is taken according to the following rules. If $t < T$, the packet is discarded having arrived too late to be played out. If $t > T + \Delta$, the packet is discarded having arrived too far in advance of its playout time. Instead, if $T < t \leq T + \Delta$, the packet is arrived in time for being played out and it is placed in the playout buffer at the receiver's site. Using the same rate *r* adopted for the sampling of the original audio signal at the sender, the playout process at the receiver's site fetches audio packets from the buffer and sends them to the audio device for playout, as discussed in the following. When the receiver's playout clock shows a value equal to *T*, the playout process searches in the buffer the audio packet with timestamp *T*. If such a packet is found, it is fetched from the buffer and sent to the audio device for immediate playout. If the packet timestamped with *T* is not in the buffer, then the playout process replaces the corresponding audio sample with a silence of length *r*. In essence, with the strategy summarized above, a maximum transmission delay equal to Δ is left to the audio packets to arrive at the receiver in time for playout. Consequently, a playout buffering space proportional to Δ is required at the receiver for packets with early arrivals. In order for the proposed scheme to adaptively adjust to the fluctuating network delays of the Internet, the clock *synchronization activity* (previously described) is first carried out prior to the beginning of the first talkspurt of the audio conversation, and then periodically repeated throughout the entire conversation. Each time a new synchronization activity is conducted, a new *RTT* value is computed on the basis of which the clocks' values, the buffering delay and the buffer dimension, at both the sender and the receiver, are updated.

2. 1. Codec

An Internet audio tool (termed BoAT) has been developed [5] that embodies the playout delay control algortihm described above and also uses compression (i) to allow speech to be reduced to a bandwidth fitting the network availability, and (ii) to reduce the quantity of data to be encrypted in order to speed up the encryption/decryption phase. BoAT exploits an adaptive control mechanism able to adjust the audio packet send rate to the current network conditions [4]. This send rate control mechanism exploits a wavelet based software audio codec designed to encode audio samples with a variable bit rate. The codec exploits a flexible compression scheme based on the discrete wavelet transform of audio data; the wavelet coefficients are quantized using a successive-approximation algorithm and encoded according to a run-length entropy coding strategy that uses variable length codes. The quantization scheme has the property that the bits in the audio stream are generated in order of importance, yielding a fully embedded code. In such a way, the encoder can terminate the encoding at any point thus allowing any precise (and variable) target bit rate. Based on this codec, a control mechanism has been devised that encodes and transmits audio samples with a data rate that is always proportional to the network traffic conditions. In essence, the control mechanism devised by the BoAT designers establishes a feedback channel between the sender and the receiver in order to assess periodically, in 5-second measurement intervals, the network congestion estimated under the form of average packet loss rate (and transmission delay variation). On the basis of this periodical feedback information, the following control process is carried out at the sender's site in order to match the send rate to the current network capacity. When the experienced average loss percentage surpasses a given upper threshold the control process gradually decreases the send rate according to a predefined decreasing scheme. Such one gradual decrease is obtained by exploiting the possibility of terminating at any point the encoding activity provided by the wavelet-based variable-bit-rate codec embedded in BoAT. Conversely, if the average loss rate falls below a certain lower threshold the send rate is gradually increased in order to match the improved connection capacity. As a final remark, it is worth mentioning that BoAT may guarantee a gradual adjustment of the send rate as ranging from 64 Kbps to 5.6 Kbps. The minimal and maximal values of this interval have been chosen on the basis of the fact that they correspond to the toll quality provided by PCM (64 Kbps) and to the synthetic quality provided by the LPC encoding strategy (5.6 Kbps).

3. SECURING THE MECHANISM

We define a *secure*, *real time* audio communication as an audio connection between two authenticated parties in which: i) only the authenticated parties may participate by exchanging (and playing out) audio streams with each other, ii) a not authenticated party cannot participate by exchanging (and playing out) audio streams with an authenticated party, and finally, iii) all the strategies adopted in order to meet the security requirements listed at the items i) and ii) above cannot jeopardize the real time behavior of the audio playout process. With item iii) in view, it is worth noticing that the encryption of entire audio samples (each of which may have length of several dozens of bytes) may result impractical in a time critical environment, since the time overhead caused by the encryption/decryption process could be unacceptable in most situations. Besides, since strong cryptographic schemes typically introduce additional delay and jitter to an audio stream, additional buffering would be required at the receiver to smooth out its impact. Based on these considerations, we have devised a modification of the playout mechanism previously illustrated that is able to satisfy the security requirements mentioned above without sacrificing the real time performances of the playout process. The idea behind our strategy is based on the fact that the correct temporal ordering of audio samples is fundamental in order to ensure that humans perceive the meaning of a transmitted speech. Nevertheless, it is well known that non-guaranteed networks (such as the Internet) typically deliver disordered packets at the destination site of a connection. Simply put, the timestamps piggybacked by our playout delay control mechanism on each emitted audio packet represent the only information that the receiving site of an audio communication may exploit in order to reconstruct the temporal order of the transmitted audio samples. Hence our decision to encrypt only the few bytes that constitute the timestamp attached to each audio packet. It is also important to mention that the encryption strategy we have designed to make our audio playout delay control policy secure exploits symmetric cryptography based on the already mentioned consideration that symmetric algorithms are generally at least 1000 times faster than public-key algorithms [6]. The adopted strategy is as follows. At the very beginning of an audio communication (i.e. prior to conducting the first *synchronization activity*), the two parties involved in the audio communication carry out a *preliminary authentication phase* where an authentication activity is combined with a symmetric key exchange. Such a preliminary phase is carried out only once at the beginning of an audio communication and may last even some few seconds since it has not any impact on the real time audio management process. Any well-known symmetric algorithm (such as those described in [6]) can be exploited to this aim. After having performed this preliminary phase, both the sender and the receiver of the audio communication are provided with a symmetric session key, and the first synchronization activity may take place. During such one first synchronization activity, prior to activating the third round of the synchronization activity (i.e. the installation phase), the sender exploits the symmetric session key (and a symmetric encryption algorithm) in order to encrypt the *RTT* value to be transmitted. Subsequently, the installation phase takes place and the encrypted *RTT* value is forwarded to the receiving site, where it is received, decrypted with the symmetric session key, and finally installed as described in the previous section. Then, after having emitted the installation packet, the sender may begin to execute the XORing of the timestamp of each audio packet to be transmitted with the current *RTT* value. Since XORing the same value twice restores the original, the decryption activity may be carried out, at the receiving site, using the installed *RTT* value. In order to make the proposed policy robust to trivial breaks [6], the mechanism we have described is repeated with each different synchronization activity performed during the audio communication and with each newly computed *RTT* value. In 1-second intervals the symmetric key (i.e. the *RTT* value) used to perform the XORing is changed, thereby making difficult for a not authenticated party to decode the encrypted timestamps and practically guarantees the real time security. In substance, each symmetric key is used to encrypt no more than a few dozens of timestamps and then updated. This policy is similar to some well-known protocols for radio communication which are spread spectrum frequency open, in the sense that during a conversation the transmission frequency is frequently changed in order to avoid interception and alteration.

It is easy to argue that the proposed approach has several advantages from both a cryptographic and a computational standpoint. To show those advantages we have developed the following experimentation.

4. RESULTS

In order to measure the performance of the mechanism we have proposed for making packetized audio secure, we wrote a simulator which takes the received packet trace file generated by running the BoAT audio tool, and simulates the behaviour of the securing mechanism. The audio traces were obtained (by exploiting BoAT and unicast UDP as transport protocol) on a 200 MHz MMX Pentium processor equipped with the Linux OS. 8-KHz sampled speech was used encoded with the BoAT's codec at a bit rate ranging from 64 Kbps to 5.6 Kbps. Each audio packet in the traces had length of 30 msec. BoAT was used on an IP-based internetworked infrastructure connecting the Laboratory of Computer Science of

Cesena (a remote site of the University of Bologna), with the C.E.R.N. Institute in Geneva. The route between Cesena and Geneva was typically quite lossy (20% in average); had about 20 hops and a bandwidth bottleneck (2 Mbps) in the link interconnecting Cesena with Bologna.

In Table 1, we report the computing time (expressed in msec) experienced during a second of audio conversation due to the coding, decoding, encryption/decription activities, as obtained by simulating the securing mechanism we have designed for packet audio over the Internet.

Comput. Time	BoAT 64 Kbps (Mean)	BoAT 64 Kbps (Var.)	BoAT 5.6 Kbps (Mean)	BoAT 5.6 Kbps (Var.)
Coding	105.5	46.5	31.03	12.11
Encrypt./ Decrypt.	0.14	13E-06	0.14	13E-06
Decod.	143.7	337.6	36.1	22.6

Table 1. Computing time (msec): coding, decoding, encryption/decryption.

It is worth noting that the results reported in Table 1 do not take into account transmission delays and are concentrated on the fixed delays due to the coding/decoding and encryption/decryption activities, only. Needless to say, in order to evaluate the total audio packet playout delay, the overhead per packet introduced with the described privacy scheme may be computed by adding the obtained values (divided by the number of packets transmitted during a second of audio conversation) to the end-to-end audio packet transmission latency measured by using BoAT.

With this in view, an overall example of the performance results is depicted in Table 2. In the second column of the Table, the playout delay and the packet loss are shown as obtained with our audio control mechanism and perceived by authenticated parties. In the third column, instead, the amount of packets is reported that are delivered out-of-order at the destination by the UDP layer. Given that an authenticated party should cope with such an amount of disordered packets, and based on the consideration that jitter and disorder make the speech unintelligible, we can deduce that it is impossible for an not authenticated party to reproduce in real time the temporal order of an audio stream.

Trial	Delay/ Loss	Disorder
1	201 msec / 7%	32%
2	205 msec / 6%	24%
3	217 msec / 5%	37%
4	185 msec / 7%	25%
5	183 msec / 8%	23%
6	199 msec / 6%	31%
7	193 msec / 6%	27%

Table 2. Performance results: average playout delay/ loss percentage, percentage of disordered packets.

Summarizing the obtained results reveal that equipping our audio control mechanism with security features do not affect the quality of the transmitted speech.

References

[1] V. Hardman, M.A. Sasse, I. Kouvelas, "Successful MultiParty Audio Communication over the Internet", Com. of ACM 41(5), 1998, 74-80

[2] S.B. Moon, J. Kurose, D. Towsley, "Packet Audio Playout Delay Adjustment: Performance Bounds and Algorithms", ACM Multim. Systems 6, 1998, 17-28

[3] M. Roccetti *et al.* "Design and Experimental Evaluation of an Adaptive Playout Delay Control Mechanism for Packetized Audio for Use over the Internet", Multimedia Tools and Applications, an International Journal, 2000, to appear

[4] M. Roccetti, "Adaptive Control Mechanisms for Packet Audio over the Internet", in Proc. of 2000 SCS Euromedia Conference (EUROMEDIA'2000), (F. Broeckx, L. Pauwels Eds.), pp. 151-155, SCS, Antwerp (Belgium), May 2000

[5] M. Roccetti *et al.*, "BoAT: the Bologna optimal Audio Tool": http://radiolab.csr.unibo.it/BoAT/src

[6] B. Schneier, "Applied Cryptography", J. Wiley & Sons, 1996

[7] P. Zimmermann, "PGPfone: Owner's Manual"", 1996: http://www.pgpi.com

Education and Training

RESULTS OF THE WORKSHOP "WHAT MAKES A MODELING AND SIMULATION PROFESSIONAL?"

Ralph V. Rogers

Department of Engineering Management
Old Dominion University
Norfolk, VA 23529

ABSTRACT

This paper addresses the results of an invited workshop conducted in Orlando, Florida in February, 1997. The workshop addressed the question: What makes a modeling and simulation professional? The workshop's results included a consensus ideal modeling and simulation professional characterized by eight categories and subsequent elements. Each of the eight categories and elements are presented as well as contextual narrative. The author provides an interpretation of the workshop results and implications for modeling and simulation professionals. Much of this paper appeared earlier as part of a panel session in the Proceedings of the 1997 Winter Simulation Conference [Rogers, 1997].

1 INTRODUCTION

On February 11, 12, and 13, 1997, the University of Central Florida (UCF) hosted an invited workshop on the modeling and simulation profession. The organizing themes and topics of the workshop were, "What makes a modeling and simulation professional?" The workshop's goal was the identification of the characteristics of an ideal modeling and simulation professional. The workshop included 25 national and international participants from academia, industry, government, and military. The North Star Institute and the National Training Systems Association provided financial support for the Workshop. UCF organized and ran the workshop..

A facilitator led workshop participants through a series of triggering questions, discussions, and activities focusing on the simulation professional, simulation education, simulation customers, and suppliers of simulation products and services. By the conclusion of the workshop, the participants reached a consensus on a set of characteristic elements of an ideal modeling and simulation professional and further partitioned those elements into eight categories. This paper identifies the categories and their elements and provides the author's interpretation and discussion of the consensus characteristics for modeling and simulation professionals.

2 BACKGROUND

In early 1996, a series of informal dialogs took place among organizations in government, military, academia and industry. The series topic focused on current demands for modeling and simulation personnel. From these dialogs, a belief emerged among many in the organizations that a shortage of modeling and simulation professionals existed to meet current world needs.

What was not clear, however, was exactly what was meant by a modeling and simulation professional. Confounding this issue was the extreme diversity of the simulation community and the general lack of a common taxonomy of simulation. Many organizations indicated a shortage of modeling and simulation personnel, but few had job classifications for modeling and simulation professionals. (As a result, for purposes of this paper, a modeling and simulation professional will be referred to a simulationist).

Thus, even if the belief in a shortage of personnel were correct, establishing valid evidence would be difficult because there are few common titles or terms (i.e. frames of reference) to define or discuss the information sought. Characterization or description of a representative or ideal simulationist was needed. To this end, the North Star Institute and the National Training Systems Association provided funds to the UCF to conduct the workshop.

3 CONSENSUS IDEAL SIMULATIONIST

For classification, the elements of the ideal simulationists were placed into the following categories:

- Attributes
- People Skills
- Basic Skills
- Modeling
- Systems Approach
- Human Factors
- Domain Knowledge
- Simulation methods

Each of these categories and the elements assigned to them are presented in the following sections. Narrative accompanies these presentations. The narratives are singularly those of the paper's author and do not signify a consensus opinion of the workshop participants or imply the endorsement of any workshop participant.

3.1 Attributes

- *Creative Problem Solving*
- *Practical Experience*
- *Have leadership skills: the ability to facilitate a collaborative interdisciplinary group effort.*
- *Ability to recognize/adapt to technology changes*
- *Interdisciplinary Skills*

The attribute elements of the simulationist reflect two distinct characterizations. One characterization emphasizes experience and demonstrable achievements. The other emphasizes personality/character. The latter set includes creative problem solving, leadership, and, to some degree, interdisciplinary skills. The element *Ability to recognize and adapt to changes in technology* also fall under this characterization, although it might be more appropriately represented by the terms visionary (or insightful) and adaptable. The *interdisciplinary skills* elements implies two levels of consideration. On one level it is about personality or, perhaps even, intellectual capability associated with open-mindedness and tolerance for ambiguity necessary for an individual to hold simultaneous competing paradigms and explanatory worldviews while observing phenomena.

The experience aspects of the *interdisciplinary skills elements* emphasizes direct experience in a interdisciplinary environment or situations. One interpretation would indicate the ideal simulationist has experienced the realities of confronting the challenges and ambiguity attaining some goal in a risk filled dynamic environment.

The real factor of the experience area of the Attribute Category is simply life experience. The requirement is for a certain maturing or development in the individual to temper his discipline canon knowledge (i.e knowledge not from direct experience) with direct experiential knowledge. The expectation is for the simulationist to have experience with situations where the ideal form or generalized problem of science or technology is matched against the uniqueness of the details of a specific problem/system. The underlying belief (if not the fact) for the requirement of practical experience is that real life is often a rather untidy affair that overwhelms the general forms of science and engineering with specifics which continually confound the desires and plans of managers, designers, scientists, engineers, analyst, educators, and even parents. The implicit assumption in the desire for experience is that encounters of direct experience are the most reliable markers to indicate an individual possesses skills in how to recognize and cope with life's rude challenges to human expectations and plans.

Thus, the ideal simulationist should have two kinds of experience:

- Practical pragmatic experience of trying to achieve a project goal, though not necessarily simulation experience.
- Interdisciplinary experience drawing on more than one discipline's canons.

Further, the ideal simulationist should have the following personality/character attributes:

- Creative
- Problem Solver
- Leader
- Adaptable
- Visionary
- Open-minded
- Tolerant

3.2 People Skills

- *Excellent written and verbal communications skills.*
- *Group interaction skills. An ability to accept and tolerate the ideas and perspectives of others.*
- *A commitment to life-long learning.*

The People Skills Category emphasizes interpersonal skills. The participants emphasized the simulationist's need to be an effective writer and speaker. Beyond this however, the simulationist should possess effective group and team interaction skills. Group or team interpersonal skills were considered more than the ability to present ones position or ideas. They emphasize working and dealing with other people in team efforts. Again, the desired skill places an emphasis on the simulationist attributes of tolerance and open-mindedness.

Whether *a commitment to life-long learning* is a People Skill is a reasonable question. An argument can be made that life-long learning element should be an Attribute. However, regardless of the partitioning, it is fair to say that the desire for life-long learning is a quality sought in the ideal simulationists. Perhaps, the placing of this element in the People Skill category merely emphasizes the participant's belief in the importance of interpersonal skills to the learning.

3.3 Basic Skills

- *Good analytic skills in probability and statistics, experimental design, and stochastic methods.*
- *Computing competence/skill.*
- *Mathematics and Operations Research.*
- *Project management skills.*
- *Cost Modeling*

- *A foundation in the physical sciences.*
- *An understanding and appreciation for the scie*ntific method.

The element *an understanding and appreciation of the scientific method* underscores all elements of the Basic Skills category. The scientific method is the unifying principle and foundation of modern science and scientific philosophy. Consequently, the scientific method is the starting point for exploration and thought as man tries to understand the universe he occupies, as well as, the starting point for discussing Basic Skills for the simulationist.

First and foremost, science is a system to find things out about the universe we inhabit and the scientific method represents the elements of that system [Checkland, 1981]. Science is generally characterized by the application of rational thinking (i.e. the application of the principle of causality) to experience. Specifically, the *practice* of science is the establishment of chains of causality to explain observations from deliberately designed experiments. Science's goal is the concise expression of the laws that govern the regularities of the universe. Ideally, these laws are expressed mathematically. Such laws or models derive their validity from the rigor imposed by the scientific method. The scientific method has three main characteristics:

- Reductionism: the reduction of complexity under experimental conditions,
- Repeatability: the validation of experimental results by repetition;
- Refutation: knowledge building by the refutation of hypotheses through hypothesis testing.

The development process for the scientific method clearly depends on experimentation and the application of the theory of reductionism. From this perspective, science is both empirical and reductionist.

There are three senses in which science is 'reductionist' and important to the simulationist. In first sense, reductionism is ingrained in the way science has been practiced since Decartes's published his *Discourses* [Eaton, 1927.] Science deeply absorbed Decartes's advice to break down problems into smaller and smaller components and analyze them piecemeal, components by component. This breaking into separate parts is the central principle of scientific practice. All of this, however, rests on the assumption that dividing up the problems being examined into separate parts will not distort the phenomenon being studied. So, science is reductionist in method.

The second sense in which science is reductionist lies with the principle known as Ockham's Razor and its importance in framing scientific explanations. Ockham's Razor states: "when faced with competing explanations, accept the most simple." [Checkland, 1981]. Science, under Ockham's Razor, provides the minimum explanation necessary to explain the observations under consideration. Its importance stems from the fact that only one explanation or description can be minimum. Thus, application of Ockham's Razor results in the simplest model necessary to explain the observed phenomenon. In this sense, science is reductionist in explanation.

The third sense in which science is reductionists concerns observations and experimental data. Collecting data in the real world is challenging. The real world is messy, noisy, chaotic, and complex. To make coherent investigations, scientists simplify their tasks by selecting some items to observe and investigate out of all those items that could be observed. The designed experiment is a special type of observation inexorably linked to the scientific method. In designed experiments, the investigator seeks through reduction in the extent of his experiment, the complete control over the investigation. He does this so that the changes that occur are the results of his actions, rather than the results of complex interactions of which he is unaware. Simply, to define an experiment is to reduce the universe of observations. Therefore, science is reductionist in observation.

The other category elements are disciplinary partitions of modern science and engineering. They are the paradigms and the tool sets necessary to describe, explain, and explore observable phenomena. They are also more; they embody the worldviews, explanatory paradigms, validated models, and accepted doctrine of the different disciplines. Consequently, the Basic Skills Category provides the disciplinary reference, analytical methods, and explanatory power that are the basic building blocks for the simulationist to work with in the prevailing disciplinary paradigms.

The Basic Skills Category identified the following specific disciplinary threads of a simulationist:

- Probability & Statistics
- Experiment Design
- Stochastic Methods
- Mathematics
- Physical Science
- Operations Research
- Project Management
- Cost Modeling
- Cost Engineering

The participants generally believed that these skills should be encountered through formal classes or disciplinary integrated programs (i.e. subjects encountered in more than one class). This category reflects a belief that an ideal simulationist requires a strong education in a science or engineering curriculum. The uniqueness in this set is the emphasis on the mix of traditional (i.e. hard) science areas (e.g. math and physics) and operations/human activities (e.g.

organization, planning, scheduling, managing and costing).

Traditional science provides the skills to observe phenomena, describe it, represent it, model it, categorize it, gather it, analyze its data, and developed associated inductive and deductive knowledge. More importantly, traditional sciences represent disciplines that arose from and were firmly anchored in the application of the scientific method to provide explanation of the physical phenomena.

The operations/human activities area reflects the workshop's participant belief that the ideal simulationist requires skills to address problems of managing time and resources within constraints. Moreover, the workshop's participants believe that managing time and resources within limits while successfully accomplishing the specified goal is the major (some argue the only) effective measure of performance for a successful simulationist. Thus, the emphasis placed by the workshop's participants on the Basic Skill threads of project management, economics, and cost engineering.

High levels of computer competency and all it implies is mandatory for the simulationist because of modern simulation's dependency on computer technology. For current simulationists, computer software is the principal target media for representing a model and computer systems are the cosmic engines of the model's universe. To these reasons, the workshop participants believed a simulationist must know, to a "sufficient" level of competency, how to use computer operating systems, high level programming languages, simulation languages, spreadsheets, word processing, presentation packages and data bases. Additionally, the simulationist must be more than a cursory users of software packages. An ideal simulationist has studied and understands basic principles of data structures, algorithms, and software engineering. Specific current areas of topical importance to simulationist include object-oriented programming and distributed/parallel processing.

3.4 Modeling

- *Model builder.*
  - *Conceptualization---high level tools provide a framework and vocabulary*
- *Empiricist.*
- *Simulation is an experimental technique; appreciate the capabilities and limitations of experimental methods.*
- *Ability to use abstraction, look at system from different perspectives*
  - *Using different perspectives to map to simulation "world views"*
  - *Adjusting level of abstraction to achieve proper degree of fidelity*
  - *Tradeoff in cost/level of detail/effectiveness*
  - *Retain clarity of causality where warranted (NOTE: The ability to use abstraction is the most essential capability for successful modeling and simulation studies.)*
- *Ability to use various paradigms in building models*
  - *representational form can be critical in the expression and communication of concepts.*
- *Model human, physical and hypothetical systems*
- *Feasibility assessments*
  - *Cost-benefit considerations and risk analysis.*
- *Knowledge engineering*
  - *Understand data gathering and validation techniques and structural relationships..*
  - *Linking analysis techniques to presentation methods and media.*

The Modeling Category may be the most important and pivotal category for the establishing the ideal simulationist. At the same time, the Modeling Category is the most "problematic" category with regards to the workshop participant's responses. The elements of this category refer to concepts, ideas, and methodologies that are contextually sensitive. Their meaning, importance, and application can vary with how and why the model was created, as well as, with the degree of objectivity and subjectivity associated with a particular model. As such, the category's elements refer to factors and issues that are pertinent within a continuum of model types and modeling issues. Recognizing and understanding the elements within this reference of multiple model types is primary in establishing the importance of modeling to the simulationist, as well as, identifying the model knowledge and modeling skills required of the ideal simulationist.

Part of the problem associated with discussing the Modeling Category is the semantics of models and modeling. While no attempt was made during the workshop to build a consensus definition for model, a starting point that most of the workshop participants would probably agree is "a model is something used in place of something else". Beyond this, agreement may breakdown. However, for the needs of this discussion it is necessary to narrow the definition further. Based on the previous review of the scientific method, for these discussions, a model is: "a representation of a system or phenomenon that is associated with any hypotheses required to describe the system or explain the phenomenon." (While generally neutral, this definition is still certainly potentially contentious.)

Models of the scientific method are minimal explanations of the observations of a designed experiment composed of the simplest possible components of nature under the complete control of an investigator trying to disprove a specific hypothesis. Models, consequently, are the essence of reductionism and are endemic to science and the scientific method. In this context, models should be characterized and considered in some minimalist criteria with respect to its referent phenomenon. Therefore, models should be made up of: the minimal elements which make up the whole (constituents), the minimal structure of the constitutes in the whole (composition), and the minimal processes introducing the dimension time (interactions). The only additional point to be made here is that minimal has meaning only with respect to some objective or purpose (e.g. the hypothesis under consideration). The two criteria of 1) minimum in constituents, composition, and interaction and 2) created for some purpose or objective, establish the fundamental standard for all models and model types.

After the fundamental criteria, the most important question of modeling and models is: When is a constituent, composition or an interaction so significantly involved in the phenomenon of interest that it warrants inclusion in the model? The Principle of Ockham's Razor coupled with designed experimentation provides, at least in theory, the principle and mechanism to answer this question. (If model does not explain the phenomenon, a constituent, composition, or interaction is added until the model explanation is consistent with the designed experiment's observations). It is important to remember that the tradition and roots of the scientific method are grounded in the discovery of fundamental laws of the physical universe. Specifically, the scientific method's designed experiments, are to be carried out in the real world on real elements. The success of this approach is predicated on the investigator, through reduction, maintaining complete control over the variables and environment of his experiment.

Of course, the real phenomenon of interest may not be available, or may be too expensive, or may be too complex, or may be too dangerous to use in a designed experiment with the extent of control required to rigorously and iteratively apply the Principle of Ockham's Razor. Such situations require relaxing the rigor of the scientific method's designed experiment. Rigor relaxation affects the degree of control of the designed experiment and the concept of minimal observation. In this sense, the designed experiments move from the highly controlled idealized environment of the laboratory to less controlled environments of somewhere else. These other-than-laboratory experiments vary in degree of controllable and uncontrollable variables. In these situations, science stills tries to discover the laws associated with the observed phenomenon and the scientific method is still the basis for discovery of the underlying laws. What is different from the designed experiments of the strict scientific method is the uncertainty introduced in the observations. The challenge is how to use these observations to create a model that meets the two criteria of the fundamental standard for models. In such situations, data parsimony (i.e. reduction to level of usefulness but not beyond) to meet the fundamental standard may be realized through technique or human interpretation [Flood and Carson, 1988]. Such techniques and interpretations are often referred to as data filtering.

Data filtering is the root concern of many of the elements identified by the workshop participants in the Modeling Category. It is important to note, however, the workshop participants were much less concerned with the *techniques* of data filtering (e.g. mathematical tools, statistical, pattern recognition, clustering analysis). (This could be because many of the data filtering techniques were identified in the elemental threads of the Basic Skills Category). Most data filtering concerned human interpretation. This can be attributable to the belief that while many techniques are available and used in data filtering to support data parsimony, the investigator, both consciously and unconsciously, intuitively performs data filtering---sometimes a little, sometimes a lot.

Intuitive judgments are inevitable even in the strictest sense of the scientific method. Consider the formulation of a conceptual model (i.e. conceptualization). The conceptual model provides an account (often in narrative) of what the components must do in order to explain the observations. During conceptualization, both constituents (i.e. complexity) and composition (i.e. structure) are largely determined [Flood and Carson, 1989]. A number of assumptions (i.e. judgments) must be addressed during conceptualization including aggregation (the extent to which different components are lumped into a single entity), abstraction (the degree to which certain aspects are considered in a model), and idealization (the approximation of structure and behavior when observed structure and behavior is difficult to describe). The investigator must make personal judgments about the constituents, composition, and interactions of a model.

An important point must be remembered: The choice of significance, while often made by human judgment, is not arbitrary. The choice still must satisfy the standard criteria for models and explain, in a chain of causality, the observations. Repeatability still must be satisfied. Objectively proving satisfaction of the standard criteria, however, becomes more difficult as the uncertainty in the observations increases and the data filtering depends more on human judgment.

So far, discussions have centered on models to explain natural laws of the physical universe as derived from the scientific method. Other elements and elements aspects identified at the workshop pertain to models associated technology's purposeful create of things. Specifically, models associated with engineering, operations research, training, and entertainment. While the standard reference for such models are based in the scientific method, these contexts reflect different aims and purposes of models.

The strategy of engineering is to obtain (or develop) a model of the process, system, or object concerned. The model in which the overall performance is expressed in some explicit measures of performance. The engineer improves or optimizes the model in terms of the chosen performance criterion. This evaluation of improvement is done through experimentation on the model. The engineer applies the same standards for designed experiments of the scientific method to experiments conducted on his engineering models Finally, the engineer attempts to transfer the solution derived from the model to the real-world situation. This is an heroic attempt to be scientific in the real-world (as opposed to the laboratory) and the difficulties are great. The strategy obviously requires the model to be shown to be valid.

Not surprisingly, the defining characteristic of engineering and other applied science disciplines are the validated models each claims as their own. Most of these models arose from physical laws validate through the scientific method. But not all models of the applied science disciplines meet this requirement. Many are heuristics and simply standard practices that are accepted as part of a discipline's model set and do not meet the rigorous standards of the scientific method. In the applied sciences, data filtering most often consists of matching observations or conceptual situations to the models of the discipline of the specific engineer or applied scientist.

Human interpretation in applied science modeling building efforts is different from the modeling building of the scientific method. In the scientific method of modeling building, human judgment is used to provide hypotheses for the components and structure necessary to explain the observed phenomenon. Science is concerned with why. In applied science modeling building, human judgment is used to provide hypotheses of which validated or accepted models match the observed phenomenon and then use the knowledge from science to achieve some desired manipulation of the physical universe (e.g. cure polio). Applied science is concerned with how.

As an applied science, engineering extends the concern with *how* to hypothetical phenomenon or systems. That is, models for referents which do not yet exist anywhere except the in modeler's or engineer's mind. Here human judgment is almost exclusively used to select component models and model structure. Such model's validation is often described by terms like face validity, standard engineering practice and reasonable performance. The engineer's design, while guided by the laws of science, are initially mostly matters of human judgment. The analysis and experimentation of the engineering approach brings the rigors of science into the process and contributes to eliminating design errors and uncertainty.

As the elements of the Modeling Category reflect, the ideal simulationist requires a range of modeling perspectives and skills most of which can only be described as qualitative or judgmental. While grounded in the scientific method as the fundamental arbiter on matters of validity, the simulationist's modeling demands also must draw on experience, creativity, intuition, and understanding the limits of his resources and the certainty of his knowledge. Moreover, the ideal simulationist is expected to grasp the entire continuum of model issues discussed not because it is desirable to have such breath, but because any simulationist will, out of necessity, have to address the range of modeling issues associated with the continuum of models in almost any modeling situation that he/she may face.

3.5 Systems Approach

- *Define the problem.*
- *Systems perspective to identify critical items of the systems (what to include in model).*
- *Determine correct level of abstraction.*
- *Develop a functional specification of the model.*
- *Apply a systematic approach to analysis (i.e. systems approach should be applied to planning this analysis just as it is to building the model.)*
- *Possesses assessment heuristics (sanity checks, cause and effect) to insure reasonableness.*

The systems approach refers to a set of closely related methodologies that attempt to select an efficient means of achieving a known and defined goal. A large number of system methodologies have been proposed under the general headings of systems analysis, systems engineering and operations research. Typical is the method proposed by Jenkins [Flood and Carson, 1988]. Jenkins' method consisted of four phases: a) Systems Analysis, b) Systems Design, c) Implementation, and d) Operation. System Analysis consisted eight stages: 1) recognition and formulation of the problem, 2) organization of the project, 3) Definition of the system, 4) definition of the wider system, 5) definition of the wider system objectives, 6) definition of the objectives of the system, 7) definition of the overall economic criterion, and 8) information and data collection. Systems Design consists of: 1) forecasting, 2) model building and simulation, 3) optimization, and 4) control. Implementation consists of: 1)documentation and sanction approval and 2)construction. Operation consists of: 1) initial operation and 2) retrospective appraisal of the project.

Although founded on the tradition and principles of the scientific method, the systems approach is, in one sense, its complement. While the scientific method's focus is on understanding of universe around us, the systems approach's focus is on creating something in the universe for a purpose or goal. The systems approach starts from an organizational definition of systems as a complex grouping of objects and/or phenomenon for which there is an overall objective. The system approach then selects the system that will achieve the goal. Science establishes a rational explanation for observed phenomenon. Reductionism and empiricism underpin the scientific method. Emergence and hierarchy underpin the systems approach.

Emergence assumes the existence at certain levels of complexity in nature and systems "emergent" properties that cannot be reduced in explanation to lower levels. That is, some properties (or phenomenon) only appears (emerges) when a certain level of complexity is reached. More commonly stated, the whole is greater than the sum of its parts. As implied, the concern is with wholes and their properties. Hierarchy looks at phenomenon in terms of the fundamental differences between one level of complexity and another.

The ideal simulationist is expected to be able to effectively apply the systems methodologies to the range of problems that he encounters. What is heavily implied for the simulationist is the importance of understanding the life cycle of a model or simulation and that a simulation is a goal oriented system that typically part of some other system with higher order but different objectives. All systems methodologies reflect some variation of this theme. Another issue in the Systems Approach Category is the consideration of complexity as a confounding factor in understanding the real-world phenomenon. Specifically, the simulationist recognizes the implications of the concept of emergence and hierarchy when trying to model phenomenon.

3.6 Human Factors

- *Understanding Human/Computer Interaction Including: Sensory perception and limitations for key senses such as haptic, visual and aural; appreciation for the psycho-physiological factors involved in derivation of perception and creation of meaning.*
- *Understanding of Cognitive Representation: That is, Artificial Intelligence (e.g. knowledge representation, expert systems, logic methods, planning, symbolic reasoning and cognitive science.*
- *Understanding of Behavioral Representation for individuals and groups*
- *Interpret and present results deriving meaning through techniques including data reduction, visualization and other sensory methods.*
- *Understanding of Ergonomics*

The concern with the Human Factors category falls under two considerations. First, the simulationists should understand the issues and difficulties in modeling both individual and group human behavior. This may be thought of understanding the problems more than knowing how to solve it. The second consideration involves the Human /computer interface with the simulation. This includes issues of data representation and man-in-the-loop issues. Generally, this issue recognizes that humans may be a user of simulation, a part of the simulation itself, or both and that human factors and ergonomics are important considerations for these humans. The ideal simulationist is expected to be aware of both considerations, as well as, conscientious about addressing human factor related issues.

3.7 Domain Knowledge

- *Experiential education (e.g. on-the-job, internship, cooperative education, exchanges, etc.)*
- *Sample Domains: (e.g. Medical systems, Legal systems, Social systems, entertainment systems, military systems. business and industrial systems). NOTE: exposure of simulationists to various domain uses and interests as well as exposure of domain experts to nature and use of simulation.*
- *Domain and technique interaction*
- *Bring simulation support to the domain expert.*
- *Important concept: only the domain expert can judge domain-specific assumptions.*

The simulationist should have knowledge of the domain with which he working. However, if the simulationist is part of team, the domain expert must provide the judgment of domain assumptions.

3.8 Simulation methods

- *Definition: simulation methods are techniques to design, develop, produce, implement, operate and assess simulations)*
- *Aware of the broad perspective of simulation methods and can do one or two areas well.*
- *Integrate new technologies with simulation where appropriate.*

- *Translate current knowledge to new and unique applications.*
- *Knowledge of current simulation and modeling tools and their appropriate use.*

The workshop participants recognized the extensive range of simulation technologies and methodologies associated with the equally broad range of domains and applications with which modeling and simulation is used. The participants saw no need to declare one method superior to another. What was deemed important for a simulationist was that he knows of the breath of methods and, as a practical case, they use well one or two methods within the limits of the methodologies.

4 DISUSSION

The elements of the ideal simulationist in the categories of Attributes, People Skills, Basic Skills, and Domain Knowledge are typical of those identified for any ideal engineer or applied scientist. Indeed, one can conclude from these results that an ideal simulationist begins as an engineer or applied scientist. Moreover, if a cursory interpretation of the other four categories where used, then most engineers and scientists could claim to be simulationist for most could claim the necessary breath from their undergraduate education. Most are heavily exposed to models, have a nodding to extensive exposure in systems approaches, have been admonished to recognize the human component of technology and science, and have experienced the use of some form of simulation. However, clearly from the narratives, a simulationist requires more depth of knowledge and experience than suggested in this interpretation and, actually, much greater breath.

Indeed, workshop participants emphasized specialized knowledge and direct experience as essential characteristics of a simulationist. Additionally, most purposeful attempts at creating simulationist have relied on highly specialized training and on-the-job (i.e. direct) experience. Several workshop participants from industry which hire people to perform simulation studies and develop simulation products, indicated what they looked for were individuals with strong fundamental skill associated with categories of Attributes, People Skills, Basic Skills, and Domain Knowledge. They assert that they can train such individuals to do their job with specialized training from vendors on specific simulation products and on-the-job training. I do not doubt this approach is successful for companies involved. But, I question the efficiency and cost effectiveness of this apprenticeship approach. I also believe this approach falls short of developing the ideal simulationist the workshop identified with the interdisciplinary skill and breath of knowledge desired.

The keys to the ideal simulationist, I believe, are in the categories of Modeling and Systems Approach. Simulationist are asked to concurrently model with a reductionist and emergence viewpoint They are also asked to consider designed experiments and hierarchical issues while creating their models. The simulationist must be able to transition from the paradigms of asking the why question to the paradigms of asking the how question within the same simulation project; he goes from recognizing structure to creating structure with a limited set of constructs. I believe the emphasis on interdisciplinary and differing worldviews reflects the need to provide the simulationist with greater powers to interpret his model and more fundamental constructs to represent those interpretations.

Unfortunately, I see little in the conscious efforts to develop the ideal simulationist identified by the workshop participants with the polar but necessarily broading perspectives and skills.

REFERENCES

Checkland, P. 1981. *Systems Thinking, Systems Practice.* New York: John Wiley & Sons.

Decartes, R. Discourse on the Method of Rightly Conducting the Reason and Seeking for Truth in the Sciences. In *Descartes Selections,* (1927), R.M. Eaton (ed). New York: Charles Scribner's Sons.

Flood, F.L. and E.R. Carson. 1988. *Dealing with Complexity: An Introduction to the Theory and Application of Systems Science.* New York: Plenum Press.

Rogers, R. What makes a modeling and Simulation Professional?: The consensus view from one workshop. *Proceedings of the 1997 Winter Simulation Conference.* S. Andradottir, K. Healy, D. Withers, B. Nelson (eds). Atlanta, Georgia, December 7-10, 1997.

AUTHOR BIOGRAPHY

RALPH V. ROGERS organized the simulation workshop of February 1997 at UCF. He is currently Chair of the Department of Engineering Management and Graduate Program Director for Modeling and Simulation Programs at Old Dominion University. His Ph.D. is in Systems Engineering from the University of Virginia, Charlottesville, Virginia.

THE 1998 NSF WORKSHOP ON TEACHING SIMULATION TO UNDERGRADUATE COMPUTER SCIENCE MAJORS

William Yurcik
Department of Applied Computer Science
Illinois State University
Normal, IL 61790
wjyurci@ilstu.edu

Ruth Silverman
Center for Automation Research (CFAR)
University of Maryland
College Park, MD 20742
ruth@cfar.umd.edu

KEYWORDS: simulation resources, instruction, curricula, education methodologies

ABSTRACT:

Both novice and experienced educators across different disciplines have expressed the need for resources to help orient them to teach computer simulation. This paper presents a NSF-sponsored workshop held in August 1998 in Washington D.C. to directly address this problem. With input from leading simulation educators, simulation education was discussed during this workshop with the result being several tangible products: a simulation laboratory manual, a simulation education Internet world wide web homepage, sharing and development of simulation curricula/software, and active participation at several leading computer science conferences. Lastly we propose future directions for further enhancing simulation education by building upon the results of this workshop.

INTRODUCTION

With the support of National Science Foundation (NSF) DUE (Department of Undergraduate Education) Course and Curriculum Development (CCD) Grant #DUE-9554863, "Simulation for Computer Science Majors", Ruth Silverman revised and restructured an existing simulation course designed for senior computer science majors. She presented papers about the project at the 1996 and 1997 Winter Simulation Conferences (WSC) (Silverman 1996, 1997a).

Continuing this effort, Dr. Silverman worked with several consultants[1] to produce the following: (1) a set of simulation laboratory exercises using commercially available software (GPSS/H); (2) a computer simulation laboratory manual integrating the exercises with related computer science reference materials and instructions in the use of the GPSS/H software (Silverman 1997b); (3) a pilot computer simulation course (Fall 1996 and following semesters) using this manual together with a single theory of simulation textbook; (4) student questionnaires to be used to evaluate the new computer simulation courses; and (5) computer simulation curricula materials and published academic papers which were distributed to interested faculty who responded to notices posted on the Internet.

With additional NSF support under the Undergraduate Faculty Enhancement (UFE) program, Dr. Silverman organized and held a workshop on teaching simulation to computer science majors. This workshop for 20 faculty participants from around the world was designed to enhance skills for teaching simulation to undergraduate computer science majors, to produce resources and modules for teaching computer simulation, and to promote interaction among simulation educators. Dr. Silverman held the workshop August 2-8 1998 at the University of the District of Columbia. International experts in teaching simulation were guest lecturers, including Maurice Aburdene (Bucknell University), Jerry Banks (Georgia Institute of Technology), and Thomas Schriber (University

[1] Th consultants were (in alphabetical order): Maurice Aburdene (Chair and Professor, Department of Electrical Engineering, Bucknell University); Dick Elnicki (Professor, Department of Decision and Information Sciences, University of Florida); Richard Fujimoto (Professor, College of Computing, Georgia Institute of Technology); and Thomas Schriber (Professor, Department of Computer and Information Systems, University of Michigan).

of Michigan). Several software manufacturers supported the workshop by demonstrating their products and providing software, instruction and documentation, including OPNET, Visual Thinking International, and Wolverine Software.

The faculty were brought together to enhance skills for teaching simulation, produce resources for teaching simulation, and promote interaction among simulation educators. Feedback from participants indicated that the main reasons for coming to workshop were: training in teaching simulation (rather than training in simulation), selecting and experimenting with simulation software, and meeting with others who teach simulation. Goals included individual growth, sharing resources, and continuing faculty interaction.

Results of the workshop included recommendations of software packages and textbooks for courses, formulation of goals and content for courses, and suggestions for use of general systems theory as a unifying theme for courses. These materials are contained within the Simulation Education Homepage (Yurcik 1999). A Birds-of-a-Feather (BOF) Session in Simulation Education served as an informal follow-up to the Workshop continuing the sharing of resources with additional faculty. This BOF took place at the ACM Special Interest Group on Computer Science Education (SIGCSE) Conference meeting in New Orleans March 25 1999. The Simulation Education Homepage was first publicly announced at this event.

The remainder of this paper is organized into the following sections: "Computer Science Curriculum" defines the motivation behind the Workshop; "Workshop Details" documents what occurred during the workshop; an introduction to the "Computer Simulation Laboratory Manual"; a description of the "Simulation Education Homepage" which serves as a repository for Workshop; and a summary of the workshop and future directions in the last section.

COMPUTER SCIENCE CURRICULUM

In Computer Curricula 91, Tucker notes that existing computer science curricular often lack an established infrastructure for upper-level undergraduates (Tucker 1991). He identifies a number of curriculum needs including the need for more hands-on laboratory experience, the need to integrate abstraction, the need for collaborative learning, and the need for active learning. To address these needs, Tucker recommends establishment of an advanced undergraduate course in Modeling and Simulation but does not establish a syllabus or content for the course.

Most computer science majors have very limited exposure to simulation (Silverman 1996). Simulation courses have largely been mathematical and when hands-on experience in the use of simulation software is provided, it is often limited to applications in business and manufacturing (Silverman 1996). Computer science students are thus not adequately prepared for employment opportunities involving the use of simulation as a tool in solving problems.

Computer simulation is a dynamic field and difficult to teach due to the wide range of skills required in addition to domain specific knowledge of an application area, skills such as computer programming, mathematics, probability, statistics, and experimental design. From the educator's perspective, optimized instructional materials are needed for teaching simulation on an international basis to avoid duplication of effort and to promote best practices. Both novice and experienced educators across different disciplines have expressed the need for resources to help orient them to teach computer simulation. The usefulness of available simulation textbooks would be improved if they were supplemented with a substantial laboratory component based on the use of new object-oriented, visual, and animated simulation packages that are now available.

WORKSHOP DETAILS

The goals of the workshop are individual growth, sharing resources, and continuing interaction throughout the workshop and beyond. The workshop was designed for three groups: (1) faculty who already teach simulation; (2) faculty with limited background related to simulation or new Ph.D.'s with limited teaching experience; (3) faculty from small institutions with limited resources (these faculty may also fit into 1 and 2). All participants were encouraged to make short presentations and/or lead a discussion group on a specific topic. Faculty in (1) formed small groups planning syllabi, prepared a preliminary annotated list of resources that faculty in (2) found useful, made short presentations and lead discussions, used the laboratory to try new software, planned course exercises, and examined reference materials. Faculty in (2) were especially interested in having an overview of selected topics, viewing software demonstrations, and using software to run sample lab exercises with the assistance of workshop staff. Faculty in (3) were especially interested in group discussion about teaching simulation with limited resources.

Each participant received the following:

- A loose leaf binder containing the Simulation Laboratory Manual (Silverman 1997b)
- Presentation materials by lecturers and participants
- A copy of Thomas Schriber's textbook on GPSS/H (Schriber 1991)
- Classic simulation reference papers.

Formal workshop presentations included the following (in approximate chronological order):

- "Workshop Agenda and Organization Details" (Ruth Silverman, CFAR)
- "Simulation Teaching Needs and Goals: A Guided Tour to the Simulation Manual" (Ruth Silverman, CFAR)
- "Modeling and Simulation and Their Effective Teaching" (Martha Centeno, Florida International University)
- "Statistics and Queues and Their Effective Use In a Course in Simulation" (Ralph Rogers, Old Dominion University)
- "Simulation of Computer Networks" (Maurice Aburdene, Bucknell University)
- "Perspectives on Simulation Using GPSS" (Thomas Schriber, University of Michigan)
- "Inside Simulation Software: How It Works and Why It Matters" (Thomas Schriber, University of Michigan)
- "Simulation Software and Its Selection" (Jerry Banks, Georgia Institute of Technology)
- "Activate This Classroom at Time Now" (Manual Rossetti, University of Arkansas)
- "DEVS: Discrete-Event Modeling and Simulation" (Hessam Sarjoughian, University of Arizona)
- "High Level Architecture (HLA) for Simulation: An Update" (Katherine Morse, SAIC)
- "HLA University Outreach Program" (Katherine Morse, SAIC)
- "SLX – Stretching the Boundaries of Simulation Software" (Jim Henriksen, Wolverine Software)
- "AutoMod Animation" (Matt Rohrer, AutoSimulations)
- "SIMUL8" (Jaret Hauge, Visual Thinking)

Small group discussion self-selected on the following topics:

- Software selection and small college resources
- Textbook selection
- Goals, approaches, content and student skills for a course in simulation. Promoting hands-on active learning in laboratory sessions and team projects.
- Preparing new and improved resources including syllabi and bibliography, modules, graded exercises, instructor aids, lecture outlines, notes for specific simulation topics, and annotated assignment units for inclusion in a course or module.
- Preparing preliminary annotated list of current resources.
- Simulation manual – improvements and additions.
- Simulation module development for use in a course other than simulation (such as Civil Engineering).
- Enhancing faculty skills
- Planning world wide web (www) or other repository and interaction after workshop ends.

At the end of the workshop there was a roundup session which summarized accomplishments, formalized the Simulation Education Homepage as a repository if educational resources, planned a follow-up meeting for 1999, discussed future interactions, and lastly evaluated the workshop.

SIMULATION LABORATORY MANUAL

From upper-level undergraduate courses in computer simulation for computer science majors, there is an expressed need for simulation exercises in applied disciplines (e.g., communication networks, computing systems) for students to solve problems and as well as appropriate reference material in probability, queues, networks, and computing systems. The benefits of a manual incorporating exercises and reference material include: integration of student knowledge of theory and practice at an upper division level; increasing student problem-solving ability especially in applied areas such as networks, operating systems, performance analysis, and scheduling; more hands-on laboratory experience to learn by doing (active learning), and low-cost exposure to simulation software.

A manual was developed under a team headed by Ruth Silverman (Silverman 1997b). After a primer on queues, communications networks and computer systems, the manual offers a discussion of: networks, operating systems, resource management, performance analysis, and scheduling, and some possible performance metrics. The manual contains a collection of graded exercises in these areas, for students to solve using simulation. Also included are instructor's aids such as syllabi and team projects. The aim is to increase student problem-solving ability by hands-on laboratory experience and learning by doing, and to integrate theory and practice at an upper division level. The manual can be used for a required capstone course for majors. The Manual's Table of Contents is listed below:

0. Introduction
1. Getting Started with GPSS/H
2. Primer on Queues, Communication Networks, and Computer Systems
3. Graded Exercises Using Simulation
4. Instructor's Aids Including Syllabi and Team Projects
5. Bibliography and References

In Section 1 GPSS/H was selected a low-cost and widely used commercial software especially suited for underfunded colleges. Section 2 introduces how to develop simulation models as a middle ground between analytic modeling and prototypes – providing appropriately accurate results for moderate investment in time and money. Queues occur in many computer systems, for example in waiting lines of computer processes awaiting service from a processor. Specific systems to study include CPUs, databases, and networks with performance evaluations of packet response times, time to service a request, and system throughput (transactions per second). The manual points to textbooks for instruction in the basics by providing an annotated bibliography (Fishwick 1995, Stallings 1996, Jain 1991). Section 3 includes 35 graded problems starting with introductory exercises to more advanced exercises. Several problems are solved using different simulation languages to contrast languages (for example a single queue/single server system). Section 4 suggests 21 different team projects such as operating systems, data flow architectures, transaction processing systems, database systems, and network programs. Section 4 also includes advanced supplementary problems and a student questionnaire for pre/post simulation course testing.

SIMULATION EDUCATION HOMEPAGE

http://www.acs.ilstu.edu/faculty/wjyurci/nsfteachsim/indexnew.html

Workshop participants decided the most effective repository for workshop materials would be a website which was eventually created by William Yurcik in 1999 and is currently supported by him as a service to the simulation community (Yurcik 1999). Given the title of "The Simulation Education Homepage" (SimEdHome) this website contains all the presentations from the workshop, the Simulation Manual, and links to all participants as well as the following unique listings: different definitions of simulation, simulation education resource articles, a LISTSERV Email discussion list, simulation course syllabi worldwide, simulation textbooks and references, simulation software for the classroom, simulation organizations, simulation education conferences, people in the simulation community, simulation applications, and simulation career opportunities.

The website serves conflicting goals successfully: (1) to illuminate best practices in the teaching of simulation and (2) a view the breadth of simulation education resources to allow educators academic autonomy to pick and choose what is best for their unique environment. SimEdHome accomplishes the first goal by cross-referencing resources so that patterns of usage clearly emerge such as which textbook/ software is used by the most courses or the consensus definitions of simulation and modeling. SimEdHome accomplishes the second goal by incorporating unsolicited and solicited input from the simulation community worldwide on the breadth of SimEdHome topics such that unique/minority/innovative simulation education ideas are represented and available to anyone over the Internet.

The NSF workshop highlighted the fractured state of simulation education knowledge - a situation ripe for a community effort to solve. As a result of this homepage, web-based simulation resources have been organized in one location which has served as a virtual meeting place for discussion about teaching computer simulation. Cross-referencing simulation resources in one virtual location has not only integrated knowledge from the entire field in a logical and useful tool but also revealed unexpected insights into the current state of computer simulation education. Response from the entire computer simulation community, both educators and researchers, has been immediate, continuous, and growing (20,000+ hits since March 2000).

CONCLUSIONS

This paper summarizes the 1998 NSF Simulation Education Workshop. With input from leading simulation educators, the workshop resulted in several tangible products including a simulation laboratory manual, a simulation education Internet world wide web homepage, sharing and development of simulation curricula/software, and active participation at several leading computer science conferences. Future directions for further enhancing simulation education by building upon the results of this workshop include continuing to inform the simulation community about the SimEdHome website and enhancing the SimEdHome website with interactivity using XML integrated with database processing such that the website may be queried for desired information.

In conclusion, the impact of the 1998 NSF Simulation Education Workshop has been dramatic, continuing to produce instructional material for defined methods of teaching computer simulation for the foreseeable future. We feel that this work may serve as a model for improving education in other topic areas, especially interdisciplinary topic areas, where knowledge is spread across a breadth of different disciplines.

ACKNOWLEDGMENTS

This research was funded in part by the following NSF grants: NSF #DUE-9554863 (2/1/96 – 7/31/98) and NSF #DUE-9752706 (2/1/98 – 7/31/00). A special thanks to Dr. Lillian "Boots" Cassel and NSF staff for guidance and support. Lastly, we would like to acknowledge the significant intellectual contributions of the workshop participants (in alphabetical order): Maurice Aburdene, Scott Anderson, Vijay Arora, Hossein Arsham, Jerry Banks, Ahmed Barbour, John Bonomo, Ben Burrell, Martha Centeno, David Gross, Laveen Kanal, William Katcher, Andrew Kornecki, Uwe Langer, Johannes Luethi, Kevin McCarthy, Nieves McNulty, John Najarian, Mufit Ozden, Jeffrey Popyack, Amelia Regan, Ralph Rogers, Manual Rosetti, Hessem Sarjoughian, Thomas Schriber, Duane Shie, Chen-Chi Shing, Robert Strader, John Trimble, and Susan Wallace. We could not have asked for a more outstanding group of simulation professionals to help initiate this work and they have continued to contribute "virtually".

REFERENCES

Fishwick, P. 1995. *Simulation Modeling, Design, and Execution*, Prentice Hall.

Jain, R. 1991. *Art of Computer Systems and Performance Analysis*, Wiley Publishers.

Schriber, T. J. 1991 *An Introduction to Simulation Using GPSS/H.* John Wiley and Sons.

Silverman, R. 1996. "Simulation for Computer Science Majors: A Preliminary Report," *Winter Simulation Conference*, pp. 1395-1400.

Silverman, R. 1997a. "Simulation for Computer Science Majors: A Progress Report," *Winter Simulation Conference*.

Silverman, R. revised edition October 1997b. *A Laboratory Manual for Simulation with GPSS/H for Computer Science Majors: an Integrated Approach,* consultants: Maurice F. Aburdene, Richard Elnicki, Richard Fujimoto, Thomas J.

Schriber, (see link on The Simulation Education Homepage).

Stallings, W. 1996. *Data and Computer Communications* 5th edition, Macmillan Publishers.

Tucker, A. editor. Curricula 91. June 1991. "A Summary of the ACM/IEEE-CS Joint Curriculum Task Force Report Computing Curricula," *Communications of the ACM*, Vol. 34 No. 6, pp. 69-84.

Yurcik, W. 1999. *The Simulation Education Homepage*
http://www.acs.ilstu.edu/faculty/wjyurci/nsfteachsim/indexnew.html

SIMULATIONISTS: WHAT DOES INDUSTRY WANT?

William V. Tucker, Bruce T. Fairchild and David C. Gross
The Boeing Company
Huntsville, Alabama 35824
william.v.tucker@boeing.com, bruce.fairchild@boeing.com, david.c.gross@boeing.com

KEYWORDS
Education, Training, Professional Development

ABSTRACT

Boeing applies simulation to a very broad array of applications, ranging from financial, to product concept development, to actual product requirement compliance verification. Consequently, the company has a great and ongoing need for Simulationists. Industry and academic agencies such as the Accreditation Board for Engineering and Technology (ABET) do not recognize a simulation undergraduate degree program, nor does any university grant such a degree. Therefore, we recruit and apply systems, software, electrical, and mechanical engineers with applicable course work and experience and expose them to simulation techniques via on-the-job training. The company has developed a three-level, informal program for engineers to use in their own professional development. We have summarized this program at other simulation professional development fora, and review it here. We summarize our current development strategy and describe our views about needed improvements in academic preparation for this field.

DISCLAIMER

The opinions expressed herein do not represent an official position of The Boeing Company, but of the authors, and sometimes just one of them. The experience categories described correlate to the company's professional development levels, but the names and descriptions have been changed to broaden their context and increase their clarity for a broad audience.

WHAT DOES A SIMULATIONIST DO?

A simulation project is like any other development project in that it requires good management and design skills if it is to succeed. However, a simulation is a *meta*-problem. First, simulation developers must resolve all of the usual issues associated with developing any software intensive system, such as user interface, timing and sizing, reliability, etc. But in addition and more important, simulation developers must design a representation of the system of interest – and not only that system, but the environment within which it operates and the other systems with which it interacts. One should not underestimate the difficulty of designing this system within a system! There may, or may not, be a real world simuland, from which the simulationist picks the aspects to be represented and those to be left out, but these decisions are crucial, subtle, and complex. All of the value in a simulation comes out of the design decisions made about the fidelity of the representation of the system of interest, and the guesses made about its behavior in unknown circumstances (e.g., in a crash). It is more complex to design and build than the thing simulated. It is less complex because at least one aspect of the simuland must be left out of the simulation, or else the simulation would be the thing.

A complete simulationist, like the systems engineer, brings to bear a broad range of knowledge and skills, which may be grouped into four general classes. Figure 1 illustrates some of the broadly assorted knowledge the simulationist must acquire to claim mastery.

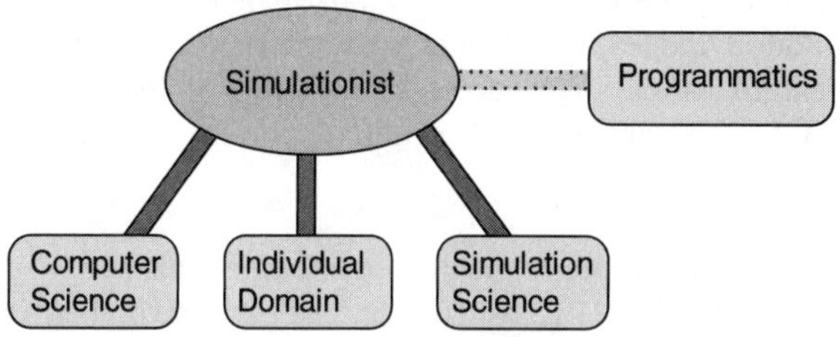

Figure 1: The Simulationist's Depends on Differing Kinds of Knowledge

First: Understanding the simuland is crucial. One must know what to simulate. Many, if not most, current simulationists have at least undergraduate training in an engineering discipline, or other fundamental grounding in the process being simulated. A simulationist need not know as much about the simuland as a domain expert, but must possess sufficient understanding to elicit and translate a domain expert's knowledge into a valid representation.

Second: The ability to make computers behave is central. The simulationist applies much of mathematics and most of software engineering.

Third: A simulationist is one who has a command of the tools and skills unique to simulation; that is, the knowledge and capabilities necessary to use computer hardware and software to represent a simuland.

Fourth: A simulationist eventually needs knowledge of programmatics, i.e., the business of developing and fielding a product. Once again, simulation creates special demands for its developers, since the simulation itself is rarely the point of the program. More often, the simulation is being developed in support of some larger program: a training simulator for new power plant operators, or a analytical tool for selecting a mix of weapon systems.

WHAT DOES INDUSTRY NEED?

In today's engineering world of unprecedented product complexity and reliability demands, industry wants and needs to apply simulations to very complex problems. As the Boeing 777 demonstrates (the first "paperless" airliner design), simulation is no longer a supplement to the engineering process, simulation is at the core. Therefore, Industry must be able to develop and utilize complex simulations at an affordable price.

Despite Industry's need for developing highly capable simulations at a reasonable cost, Industry does not widely recognize simulation as a career field. In fact, if one introduces oneself as a simulationist or even as a simulation professional (away from the gentle shelter of an SCS conference), questioning eyebrows rise. Industry does simulation, indeed a tremendous amount of it, but there is no mature simulationist career field, in the way that there are systems engineering or software engineering career fields.

Simulation projects, like other software intensive projects, are often late, insufficient, and expensive. Part of the reason is that simulations (like software) are frequently developed by well meaning amateurs. Most engineers, if not all, occasionally develop special purpose analytical models. The engineers' success in these small projects creates confidence in their analytic skills. Unfortunately, these special purpose models are either thrown away, or maintained and grown into large, inefficient, incomprehensible, but indispensable, simulations. Improving the professionalism of simulationists would clearly address this problem.

IS SIMULATION A PROFESSION?

In a conference opening paper, *The Simulation Profession* (McLeod 1985) analyzes the question specifically for the "Professional Simulationist." Because simulationists seldom interface one-on-one with an individual client who directly pays them, it will always be difficult to establish a profession on a par with medicine or law. Certainly, we could move toward a standard of professionalism using the template of the professional engineer. There is no question that if simulation is to fulfill its potential for improving engineering, and if the needs of industry are to be met, then simulationists will have to be more professional

IS THERE A SHORTAGE OF SIMULATIONISTS?

Before considering the quality of simulationists, we should consider the quantity. We have anecdotal evidence of both over supply and under supply. Just a few years ago we could name qualified, experienced, simulationists who failed to find positions in the field, after trying for extended periods. Some gave up and changed direction. Then, as now, some companies cited shortages and inability to attract qualified help. Now we observe the scene slowly changing. Demand has been increasing and employers are learning how to calibrate the job seekers.

The differences may have been regional, domain specific, or seen from different points of view. Academic, industrial, government, and professional society leaders all have a vested interest in a growing base of technically trained professionals, while, contrariwise, promoting an oversupply is bad for individuals. Without clear definition of the field and hard employment data we cannot be sure. One significant benefit of simulation as a legitimate career field would be the availability of employment data. Employment data is useful to both companies and individuals planning relocation or retraining.

HOW DO SIMULATIONISTS DEVELOP?

Here is a representative job description for an industrial simulationist: "Responsible for the definition, development and use of computer-based simulations, simulators, stimulators and supporting technologies including mathematical techniques and algorithms, software and software engineering and computing hardware. Beyond these technical skills, the simulationist accepts other assignments such as proposals, planning, reviews, marketing, etc., and supports mentoring and training of fellow simulationists."

Certainly, this knowledge base can only be developed through experience. So, simulationists like many other professions might be classified according to their expertise and experience. The greenest simulationist is a apprentice, a beginner or learner, just entering into an apprenticeship, given relatively close supervision and small bounded tasks. The ink is still drying on the apprentice's Bachelor's Degree. A good heuristic is that an apprenticeship lasts three projects, or five years.

The second level is journeyman, considered competent to work on large, complex tasks with infrequent supervision. The journeyman simulationist has the tools of the software design engineer, including the capability to perform software architecture development, object-oriented design, extensive software reuse, and algorithm and data structure development. The journeyman is equipped with simulation tools and techniques for both discrete and continuous simulation, understands user interfaces and controls, and can build models using common simulation computer languages. The journeyman's apprenticeship provides insulation from inexperience and overconfidence.

The master simulationist adds the skills of program management (cost, schedule, risk management, proposal development, etc.) and interfacing with the customer to those of the journeyman. An important obligation of the master simulationist is to mentor and develop apprentices.

Table 1 illustrates a matrix of capabilities used to describe the career growth of a Boeing real-time simulation engineer.

	Knowledge	**Skills**	**Experience**
Apprentice (entry level)	• Modeling • Simulation • Programming • Statistics • Data structures • Standards • Knowledge of a Domain	• Basic computer and software tools • Basic Simulation tools • Verification	• Multiple Computers • Multiple Software Tools • One or a Few Simulation Projects • Model Development
Journeyman (engineer)	• Systems Engineering • Object-oriented Design • Multiple Domains • System Architectures	• Proposal Preparation • Validation • Simulation Requirements Elucidation • Fidelity Requirements Specification • Sensitivity Analysis • Object-oriented Programming • Customer Coordination	• Multiple Projects within a Domain • Multiple Lifecycle Phases • Application of Simulation • One or more publications
Master (senior engineer)	• Simulation in Support of Operational Systems • Advanced Simulation Techniques • Alternative Simulation Concepts	• Accreditation • Domain Evolution Planning • Simulation Program Management • Simulation Lifecycle Cost Analysis • Simulation Risk Management	• Projects in Multiple Domains • Multiple customer Interfaces • National/ International Conference Committees • Simulation Innovation • Multiple Publications

Table 1: A Simulationist Should Grow in Skills, Knowledge, and Experience.

WHAT DOES INDUSTRY WANT FROM ACADEMIA?

The authors see the primary need for academia is to develop educational programs to speed the creation of journeymen. Industry is inefficient in providing the technical skill base required for the rite of passage through journeyman. Academic programs can also efficiently provide the basics of program management while industry must provide the specifics for our own processes. While academia can increase the slope of the learning curve by imparting technical skills, industry experience is needed to gain mastery of the processes through practical experience that is needed for a journeyman to become a master simulationist.

A dilemma for all technology training is that curricula are constrained by time and must provide solid grounding in fundamentals. This means that problems posed are small, well defined, with information sources well known, usually in a few preceding pages in a text and are solved by an individual as entirely new work. Industrial tasks normally have mushy and often rapidly changing definitions, are extremely large or are part of something large and little information is readily available to apply to the solution. The work is performed by teams, strongly encouraged to reuse previous designs.

Thus, students can gain much by being required to work in teams, on problems largely developed and defined by the team, and expected to search out information sources that may not exist. For example, a term project given to a class might be to determine, via simulation, how much and how often a creek through campus could cause property damage. One legitimate answer might be that the creek has not, over several previous decades, risen anywhere near its banks, and that there is no property within reach of the creek with value close to the cost of doing the simulation. Another might realize that even though the creek won't rise, it could infiltrate underground into a nearby library basement where valuable books are stored; therefore the need is to simulate the water table, not the creek. Yet another team might look into changes in weather patterns, or drainage in the area that might invalidate historical data.

Certainly, industry looks to academia to teach fundamentals. For the example, the student needs to be aware of the stochastic nature of some data (rainfall), continuous equations to model level in the creek, partial differential equations describing the movement of fluid in a porous media, and applicable tools and techniques to translate these fundamentals into useful results. But the student also needs to be astute enough to find rainfall records, to find or generate geologic data, to estimate the cost of obtaining results and the value of results when obtained. Most important, the student must critically examine the problem statement, to determine whether the right problem is being attacked and that the answer will be useful.

ARE UNIVERSITIES TRAINING SIMULATIONISTS?

Professions look to academia to set standards and provide general education. However, as we have pointed out, no university today offers an accredited degree in simulation, at least at the undergraduate level. It is easy to conclude that the clear and present need for professional simulationists is largely unmet by academia, at least at the undergraduate level. This situation, of course, can change, but such changes come slowly. However, it is not clear that this need is best met at the undergraduate degree level.

Though written primarily for training simulator engineers after employment, a paper *All About Simulators* (Bradley, et. al. 1984) provides some useful guidance toward a body of knowledge for simulationists.

IS SIMULATION A SCIENCE OR A TECHNOLOGY?

Before deciding how universities should respond to the need for professional simulationists, we should think just what kind of professional we mean. Within the university, schools of science are organized differently than schools of engineering and technology. Consider Table 2. Different kinds of professions have different kinds and correspondingly differing education paradigms.

Profession	Primary Interest	Education Paradigm
Entrepreneur	Exploitation	School of "Hard Knocks" Experience Oriented (Case Studies)
Engineer	Use of Knowledge	Undergraduate, Masters Technology Orientation
Scientist	Expansion of Knowledge	Graduate School, PhD and post-doc. Theoretic Orientation
Simulationist	?	

Table 2: What Kind of Professional Simulationist?

We see a need for simulation scientists to move the science of simulation forward, as well as simulation technologists who apply simulation in new ways to new problems. But let us ask, what is simulation science? It is easy to think of physics as an underlying science applied by engineering specialties such as electrical, civil, and mechanical. But what is the body of simulation science? The cupboard, while not quite bare, is very nearly so. Astoundingly for a technique so broadly applied, there are fewer fundamental theorems of simulation, and less consensus on what they would be if they existed! Simulation seems to be defined more by practice than defined and unified by theory.

IS SIMULATION BEST AS A GRADUATE PROGRAM?

Figure 2 shows other professions, defined more by practice than theory. Law and medicine begin specific training at the graduate level. Masters in Business Administration programs draw from both business and technical undergraduate degrees. Engineering and most science graduate programs require a similar undergraduate degree, by contrast. Which model best fits simulation?

The present university approach to simulation is essentially modeled along the lines of law and medicine. In contrast to the undergraduate situation, there are very advanced graduate simulation courses offered at many universities, these courses tend to be distributed around different academic departments and aimed at specific problems in the engineering specialties rather than providing general simulation education. Of course, this begs the question as to whether or not this is the best organization.

For one intending to become a simulation scientist, an undergraduate degree in simulation may be appropriate. But for industry's needs, application knowledge obtained via an undergraduate degree in engineering or physics is vital, and the advanced degree model seems best. We suggest an undergraduate degree in a specific discipline of interest followed by graduate work as the best preparation.

ABOUT THE AUTHORS

William V. Tucker is Manager - Modeling and Simulation Technology in the Boeing Company Phantom Works, with responsibilities for tracking, improving and transitioning modeling and simulation technology capabilities in support of internal and Department of Defense customer objectives. He has served in several leadership roles in the Workshops on Standards for the Interoperability of Distributed Simulations and more recently in the successor to DIS, the Simulation Interoperability Standards Organization. He holds a BS in Electrical Engineering from Wichita State University.

Bruce T. Fairchild is a Principal Engineer - Modeling and Simulation Technology in the Boeing Phantom Works Modeling and Simulation organization. He has served in several capacities within the Society for Computer International, currently as Senior Vice President. He holds a Ph.D. with major in Chemical Engineering from the University of Florida.

David C. Gross is an associate technical fellow in the Boeing Phantom Works Modeling and Simulation organization. He is a doctoral candidate in the Industrial Engineering Department at the University of Central Florida, with emphasis in simulation and visualization. He holds a MSE in Operations Research from The University of Alabama in Huntsville.

REFERENCES

Bradley, James H., A. Ben Clymer and Bruce T. Fairchild. 1984. "Training for Simulator Engineers," All About Simulators, 1984, Proceedings of the SCS Simulators Conference, (Norfolk, Virginia, April 18-20), Society for Computer Simulation International, San Diego, CA., pp. 148-154.

McLeod, John. 1985. "Fantasies of Professionalism versus Real-World Facts," Proceedings of the Conference on The Simulation Profession, (Norfolk, Virginia, March 3-8), Society for Computer Simulation International, San Diego, CA., pp. 3-5.

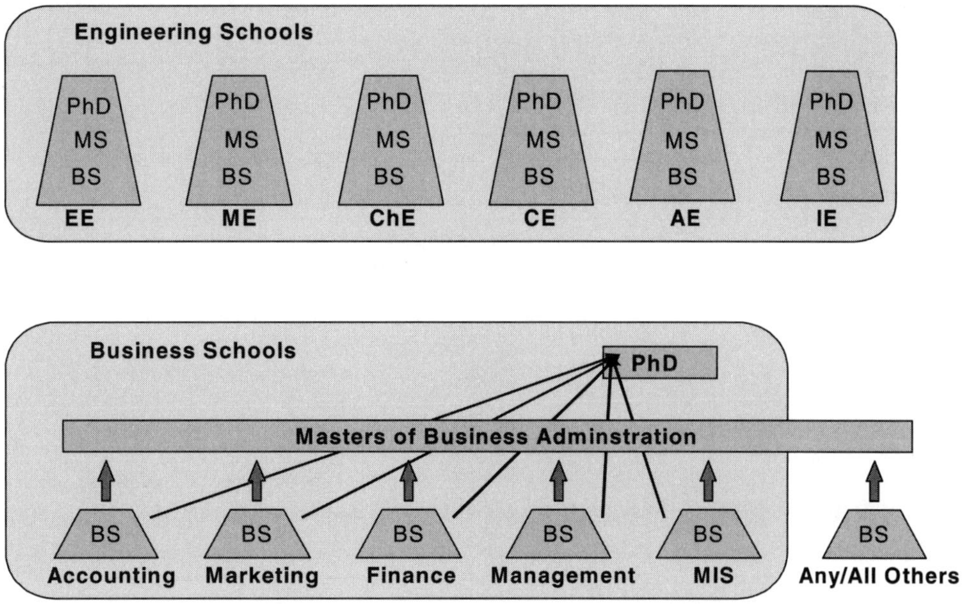

Figure 2: Which Model Best Fits Simulation?

Economics of Modeling and Simulation

DETERMINING THE VALUE OF SIMULATION

Dr. Steven C. Gordon
Technical Director, Air Force Agency for Modeling and Simulation (M&S)
12350 Research Parkway, Orlando, Fl 32826-3276
email: steve.gordon@afams.af.mil
(407) 208-5776

KEYWORDS: Military, aerospace, combined simulation, decision-making, policy-making.

ABSTRACT

It is both logical and appropriate for decision-makers to ask for ways to judge the value of simulation. Often, the request is even more pointed than just wanting a report of the value of simulation, and specifics on the economics of simulation are requested. Clearly, undertaking to answer questions about the economics of simulation will be critical to building an understanding of how to spend future marginal National Defense dollars. One can evaluate the economics of simulation where it supports our ability to develop, build, and test new weapon systems. Here, historically derived returns on investment, cost avoidance, cycle time reductions, and lifecycle cost savings have been documented and warrant further investigation. However, there is a larger area of use for simulation where judging its value must go beyond economics. The underlying thesis of this paper will be that simulation, in some areas, has a value beyond economics. The broader question of the value of simulation, too, must be tackled because simulation must prove its worth in order to protect and increase its funding share.

INTRODUCTION

As the only accepted tool used to perform many specific defense tasks, simulation is key to the way we build combat readiness today, and it will expand in usefulness to be integral in how we employ forces in the future. This paper will look at ways to judge the value of simulation by looking at its use in wargaming, experimentation, assessment, acquisition, evaluation, training, and decision support for combat operations. Ways to judge economic return, cost avoidance, and readiness impacts will be discussed. Simulation has become a fundamental enabler of combat readiness, and it has an integral impact across Air Force responsibilities to organize, equip, train, and sustain forces for employment. As we increase our ability to exploit the power of simulation to prepare for and conduct combat operations, we must document the value of simulation and use this documentation and the efficacy of simulation to persuade decision makers to invest in the right simulation tools with the right funding levels. Unfortunately, we are not yet at the point where we can answer the boss' question, "How much do I save if I fund this M&S program?" This question is often asked, yet cost may not be the most important metric for M&S.

PARTITIONING OF THE M&S "PIE"

M&S is used within DoD and industry to support many activities, and it has been found to be valuable for several reasons. M&S provides risk reduction by providing training where mistakes are not fatal, minimizing environmental impact, allowing covert rehearsal, and ensuring information security. M&S is efficient because it reduces the cost to assemble the training team, reduces stress on high value assets, provides a standard instructional environment, and reduces the use of expendables. M&S is effective because it accelerates creation of scenarios, allows rapid changes in combat arenas, provides a testbed for concepts and strategies, increases availability and portability, and reduces personnel and operational tempos. A standard approach to partitioning the M&S "pie" may be useful in further discussions of the value or economics of simulation. The approach used in this work is to divide the uses of M&S into wargaming, experimentation, acquisition, evaluation, assessment, training, and decision support for combat operations. Other approaches are, of course, possible (Oswalt 1999). The division or partitioning of M&S used in this paper does not assume that such "stovepipes" are beneficial or permanent. In fact, M&S programs are increasingly crossing these boundaries and finding use within areas not originally envisioned for the individual M&S programs. The crossover (the blurring of M&S use across distinct tasks) is yet one more indication of the value of M&S.

Wargaming

Wargames generally look well beyond the current Program Objective Memorandum (POM); sometimes they focus 15 to 20 years or more in the future. Wargames are used to evaluate future doctrine, strategy, or concepts, using a mixture of current and hypothesized weapons systems, against anticipated enemy forces in presumed future scenarios. Wargames, or future studies, have historically used role players and control staffs to generate the future scenarios and responses; however, M&S use in wargames is growing as increased fidelity, immersive scenarios, and reduction in the number of support personnel are desired. For most wargames, M&S has become the only acceptable means to generate the immersive future battlespaces. The M&S used in wargames usually does not require human-in-the-loop or links to real-world systems. The M&S often is closed-loop with multiple complete runs of the scenario used to determine an average outcome. In order to further the understanding of the economics of M&S, cost trade-off analyses should be conducted for wargames such as Army After Next, Navy Global, or Global Engagement to compare the cost savings and benefits of using M&S vice using alternatives to M&S, such as additional role players and support staff.

Experimentation

Experiments generally look within the timeframe of the current or next POM and are focused on evaluating innovations in operational concepts, procedures, or weapon systems. Experiments such as Joint Expeditionary Force Experiment (JEFX) look at new ways to use current equipment (perhaps with minor modifications) in scenarios using anticipated nearterm adversary forces. M&S is used extensively in experiments; yet, the M&S systems have not been developed exclusively for experimentation, which ideally calls for the ability to use multiple Air Tasking Order paths with both fast-forward and rewind of the simulation (HQ USAF/XOC 1998). In JEFX 99, nearly 100 simulations were used to drive the experiment. For JEFX 99, M&S generated an immersive environment of 2500 intelligence messages and 2106 mission updates per day through the Theater Battle Management Control System and over 12,000 intelligence updates every 10 minutes through other real-world systems (HQ USAF/XOC 1998). Role players and support staff could not have generated such a torrent of real-world message traffic; realism and experiment effectiveness would have declined and costs in terms of staff tempo and TDY funding would have increased markedly without M&S. The key function of M&S in experimentation has been cited by Lieutenant General Santarelli, PACAF/CV, "*Computer simulation has become a must. In fact, it may be the only way to represent the complexities of future warfare*" (Santarelli 1998). It is recommended that analyses should be conducted to evaluate the resource savings and increased realism generated through M&S use in experimentation.

Assessment

One of the first uses of M&S was for force structure analyses to evaluate the future force structure needs of the individual Services. For instance, force structure studies that evaluate the required mix of air superiority, ground attack, and mixed-use platforms now rely on simulation. Studies like the Deep Attack Weapon Mix Study or the Quadrennial Defense Review use several M&S systems to estimate the required size of each Service to meet the challenge of presumed future conflict scenarios and taskings. For many types of analyses, there is simply no alternative to M&S tools; therefore, there has been little need to justify investment in them. The cost-benefit analysis for M&S use here should include not only the use of role players in lengthy analyses, but also the quality of the analyses that would result if M&S were not used. An undersized future force might be very costly to the United States and our allies.

Other assessments are focused on improvement in procedures or processes. For instance, an analysis of the weapons storage area at Nellis AFB using legacy M&S resulted in recommended system upgrades and improved security effectiveness. The approach devised via M&S saved $7M at Nellis AFB alone and resulted in double the security effectiveness of the previously planned approach (Force Protection Battlelab 1999). Similar cost savings are anticipated at other weapons storage sites.

Acquisition

M&S use in acquisition of new or improved weapons systems is one area of M&S use where economic benefit is a most natural computation. This is also the area of greatest pay-off for M&S use. Of the total budget controlled by acquisition program managers, 3% to 15% is being spent on M&S; with over 200 defense programs between $1M and $50B in size, the investment in M&S and the potential pay-off is high (O'Bryon 1999). Estimates derived from industry and government acquisitions indicate that intelligent use of M&S can reduce design cycle time by 50% on average (SBA Task Force 1998). The use of appropriate M&S from program initiation potentially saves 2% in system life cycle costs—easily $Bs in savings. Furthermore, for small acquisition programs with no more than $20M invested in simulation, M&S use has an estimated return on investment[*] of approximately 25:1 (National Academy of Sciences 1997).

The most convincing testimonials to the power of M&S are in comparisons of concurrent or nearly concurrent programs that can be used to illustrate acquisition with or without the use of M&S (SBA Task Force 1998). For instance, The Boeing Corporation invested heavily in M&S for design and development of the 777 aircraft. Results from the 777 model acquisition compare very favorably to the design and development of the earlier 747 aircraft for which M&S use was limited. The 747 model required 10,000 shims for ill-fitting parts, while the 777 aircraft required just 50 shims per aircraft. Scrap was reduced by 30% on the 777 aircraft.

[*] Return on investment (ROI) can be calculated as (Benefit - Cost of M&S) / (Cost of M&S)

Rework of parts was reduced from 30% for the 747 aircraft to 3% for the 777 aircraft.

Other comparisons for military procurements help explain the value of simulation (SBA Task Force 1998). In one example using the F-15E aircraft, virtual manufacturing assistance using M&S (in 1997) was contrasted to traditional methods (from the early 1990s). The use of M&S to support the manufacturing process led to a 33% reduction in design release time, 27% reduction in design cost, 19% reduction in manufacturing cycle time, 20% reduction in factory floor space, 24% reduction in parts count, and a 78% reduction in fasteners required for assembly. For a Defense Advanced Research Projects Agency initiative for concurrent engineering, a radar warning system was redesigned using traditional versus concurrent M&S-supported design techniques. The traditional approach required 96 man-months, while the M&S-supported concurrent design approach required 46 man-months for completion. The F-22 is being developed using extensive M&S support, and it has been subject to some Congressional interest due to the amount of simulation used in place of initial flight testing. Secretary of the Air Force Peters testified to the Senate Armed Services Committee in 1999 that M&S was cheaper than flying the F-22 for early developmental testing.

Further work to capture the true economics of M&S use in a variety of acquisition programs will be of great value for decision-makers. Definition of terms, business cases, and market models for the use of M&S will assist in the accurate analysis of the economics of M&S from program inception to logistical support.

Evaluation

The aggressive use of M&S in test and evaluation saves (or at least cost avoids) huge amounts of funding each year—over $100M per year across the Services (SBA Task Force 1998). Intelligent use of M&S to support evaluation reduces live testing, destruction of valuable assets, use of overtasked test ranges and equipment, and decisions based on sparse data. For instance, the testing of the Advanced Medium Range Air-to-Air Missile would cost $3M for each supported test launch; yet M&S allowed up to 300 runs for the same price as one live test. Such cost trade-offs allow more complete evaluation of the launch envelope and less uncertainty in the operation of the weapon. As another example detailed at the 2000 Air Armament Summit, 8500 M&S runs for the AGM-65 Maverick missile pinpointed areas in the launch envelope where live testing was beneficial and preceded 12 perfect flight tests. The use of M&S for test and evaluation can also be used to pinpoint where live testing can be focused, or it can be used to terminate unworthy programs early before too many resources have been expended in live evaluation and fielding.

Training

The cost avoidance attributed to M&S for training is considerable. Across DoD, success in M&S training has outpaced M&S success in other areas. For battlestaff training exercises, Joint Task Forces and/or Component staffs are trained to plan and execute a Joint or Coalition campaign. Simulation has grown in importance for these exercises due to resource savings and improved training quality. In the early 1980's, the scenario control staff typically scripted the entire exercise with weeks of pre-exercise meetings to script all inputs. A ratio of 1:1 for support staff to trainees was needed because every engagement was decided by dice roll and manual input. Real-world systems were seldom used to input exercise events, and "training like we intend to fight" was not fully possible. POSITIVE LEAP 1980 was the first Rapid Deployment Task Force Exercise and 2800 controllers were needed to drive the exercise for a 2800-person training audience.

Since the early 1980s, M&S has increasingly been relied on to support battlestaff training exercises. With minimal M&S support, REFORGER 1988 trained 35 maneuver headquarters and used 97,000 soldiers, 7,000 tracked vehicles, and 1,080 tanks throughout Europe as training aids at a cost of $53.9M plus $20M maneuver damage. Using more robust M&S, REFORGER 1992 trained 35 maneuver headquarters using 20,000 soldiers and 135 tracked vehicles as training aids in Europe and the United States at a cost of $19.5M with no maneuver damage. Currently, the ratio of training audience to control force is 3:1 in a typical battlestaff training exercise, saving 500 or more personnel per exercise. This cost savings attributed to M&S amounts to at least $9.0M per year for Air Force key exercises versus a cost of approximately $4.0M for M&S maintenance. This return on investment is much less than the cited 25:1 for acquisition programs because training simulations are changed to link to new or revised command and control systems, and the value of M&S in terms of improved training and reduced personnel burdens is not factored in. M&S for battlestaff training is improving the quality of training by linking the training audience to the scenario, using real-world systems, providing repeatable standards for training, while saving personnel tempo and expenses. The value of M&S to combat readiness has been stated by the Headquarters PACAF staff: "*M&S...has improved air component readiness...*" (HQ PACAF/DOQ Message 031915z Nov. 98).

For battlestaff training exercises, the economics of simulation can be further documented by estimating the cost of using live forces as training aids for battlestaffs. If about one-half of the sorties in a typical Blue Flag battlestaff training exercise were live sorties, the cost would be over $7.3M per day. For a typical annual Air Force battlestaff training exercise schedule, the cost of live flying about one-half of the exercise sorties would be over $500M per year. Of course, personnel tempo, operational tempo, safety, and resource limitations would make this an impossible choice today and in the future.

For mission-level training, M&S is growing in use. For instance, each Service now has a mission training system for weapons system-level training in immersive, multi-player synthetic environments either being fielded now or in the near future. These systems will provide improved individual and team training in environments and scenarios that would be impossible to create in live training outside of combat. In 1998, General Richard E. Hawley, Commander of Air Combat Command, stated[**] the need for a distributed mission training system: *"Do you have any idea how hard it is for us to pull all these disparate elements of our warfighting team together to train in the same place at the same time in peacetime? What better way to prepare that force than with a high fidelity, synthetic joint training environment..."* to build combat readiness. These systems are an improved adjunct to live training and they also save resources. Simulator operating costs are one-tenth to one-third the cost of operating the actual weapons system. The cost of purchasing an entire mission training system, such as the Close Combat Tactical Trainer, based at several United States Army posts is approximately equivalent to the cost of three new tanks and some operations tempo trade-offs.

M&S is proving to be a valuable training tool in many other fields, including medicine. New systems with interactive "dummies" train soldiers and physicians to treat wounds on the battlefield and conduct patient care in hospitals. New virtual reality systems allow trainee surgeons to feel and see their knifework. They can see high-resolution three-dimentional images of the human body and feel the pressure of the instrument as it "cuts" through tissue (OPTICS.ORG NewsAlert 2000). The growing field of Advanced Distributed Learning will also, to some extent, provide training to deployed forces and may include M&S tools. One measure of the value of simulation is in its spread through many disciplines, from medicine to security force training, to improve readiness in widely disparate specialties. This popularity proves the value of M&S and further justifies the need for investigation of the economics of simulation.

[**] Keynote speech to the Interservice/Industry Training, Simulation and Education Conference sponsored by the National Training Systems Association in Orlando, Florida on December 1, 1998.

Decision Support for Combat Operations

Probably the first use of M&S for support to operations was for mission rehearsal in the special operations and tactical aircraft mission areas. The importance of M&S has grown through technology improvements and better understanding of its capabilities to facilitate use of M&S for battlestaff rehearsal and decision support to operations. In 1998, the Warrior Preparation Center in Germany conducted NIMBLE LION using air power simulations normally used for training to improve the Air Tasking Order (ATO) build process (WPC 1998). NIMBLE LION was successful and was improved upon to assist planning and execution of the Air War Over Serbia (AWOS) in Operation ALLIED FORCE. Analysis support, often using M&S assistance, to ALLIED FORCE Senior Commanders was a key innovation. From both NIMBLE LION and AWOS, lessons learned point to the need for improved decision support tools, including predictive M&S tools that can screen courses of action and ATOs and predict enemy actions. M&S will be used to accelerate contingency planning and response and improve execution of campaigns; yet the value of this asset to operations will be difficult to quantify.

WHAT'S NEXT

The use of anecdotal information is currently the primary means used to judge the economics or value of simulation. The anecdotes, even if accompanied by numerical estimates, are viewed, for the most part, with some skepticism and do not provide sufficient insight into M&S value to tailor investments or answer critics. Concerning the economics of M&S, further definition of the questions to be answered and whom the answers are intended for is necessary. Both M&S support to acquisition and evaluation are logical areas for further evaluation of the economics of simulation. In order to explore these areas further, one could design a study plan to look at alternatives to M&S (decision approaches, man-in-the-loop, range testing, do nothing, etc.) using a cost-effectiveness methodology. An analysis of alternatives approach could shed light on the value of M&S (personal communication with Ms Audree D. Newman). Useful ways to describe the uses of M&S in common terminology, business cases, and market models can improve understanding of the economics of M&S. Ongoing impressive work to describe ways to explore the value of simulation is continuing (Oswalt 1999).

CONCLUSION

This paper illustrates one way to organize M&S systems in terms of wargaming, experimentation, assessment, acquisition, evaluation, training, and decision support to combat operations. New ways of describing the value of simulation beyond economics have been explored. In the nearterm, however, economic considerations will still be a primary driver of decisions on M&S programs, and standard ways to evaluate the economics and value of simulation must be stipulated for progress to be made. Simulation has become a fundamental enabler of combat readiness, and it has an integral impact across Air Force responsibilities to organize, equip, train, and sustain forces for employment. As we increase our ability to exploit the power of simulation to prepare for and conduct combat operations, we must document the value of simulation. This documentation and the efficacy of simulation can be used to convince decision-makers and policy makers to invest in the right simulation tools with the right funding levels. Perhaps the typical question "How much do I save if I fund this M&S" can be changed to "How much combat readiness do I gain if I fund this M&S?"

REFERENCES

ABIS. 1996. "Advanced Battlespace Information System (ABIS) Task Force Report." Director of Defense Research and Engineering (OSD), Director of Command, Control, Communications, and Computer Systems (Joint Staff). www.ca.dtic.mil/dstp/96_docs/abis/.

Force Protection Battlelab. 1999. "Force Protection Battlelab Initiatives MAJCOM Security Forces Directors' Update." 1631 Stewart Street, Suite 102, Lackland AFB, Tx. 78236-5255, (210) 671-0051.

Gerth, J. 1997. "Simulator Training Effectiveness for F-15 Aircrews." Report to ACC/DRSM from Georgia Tech (GTRI/SEV/HFB), Atlanta, Ga. (July 11).

Gordon, S. C. 1998. "Modeling and Simulation Support to Warfighters." Technical Report. Project A-5815. Georgia Tech, Atlanta, Ga. (Dec. 15).

HQ USAF/XOC. 1998. "M&S After Action Report EFX98." VectorCheck. AF/XOC Newsletter, Volume 2, Issue 5, Winter. USAF/XOC, Pentagon, Washington DC, 22015. (703) 695-1833.

National Academy of Sciences. 1997. "Technology for the United States Navy and Marine Corps, 2000-2035." Naval Studies Board. Commission on Physical Sciences, Mathematics, and Applications. Vol. 9, Chapt. 2. www.nas.edu/cpsma/nsb/tfnf.htm.

O'Bryon, J. F. 1999. "Meet 'MASTER'—Modeling & Simulation Test & Evaluation Reform." Program Manager. March-April 1999. pp. 8-14.

OPTIC.ORG NewsAlert. 2000. "Week 19: OPTICS.ORG News" electronic mail. Web site: optics.org. (May 5).

Oswalt, I. 1999. "Defining M&S Value." Briefing from Kapos Associates Inc, Suite 1900, 1101 Wilson Blvd, Arlington, Virginia 22209, (703) 528-4575 (Aug. 7).

Patenaude, A. 1996. "Study on the Effectiveness of Modeling and Simulation in Weapons Systems Acquisition Process." (study conducted for the Deputy Director, Test, Systems Engineering and Evaluation, Office of the Secretary of Defense), Science Applications International Corporation, McLean, Va. (Oct.).

Santerelli, E. D. 1998. "Air Component Support to Joint Exercises." Joint Force Quarterly. (Autumn/Winter 1997-1998): pp 71-75.

SBA Task Force. 1998. "A Roadmap for Simulation Based Acquisition, Report of the Joint Simulation Based Acquisition Task Force (Coordinating Draft)." (Dec. 8). www.msiac.dmso.mil/sba/documents.asp.

"Strawman Implementation Plan for Simulation Based Acquisition." 1999. (Jun. 14). www.msiac.dmso.mil/sba_documents/master022599.doc.

WPC. 1998. "Warrior Preparation Center (WPC) NIMBLE LION Initial After-Action Report." HQ USAFE, Ramstein AFB, Germany.

Worley, D. R.; H. Simpson; F. Moses; M. Aylward; M. Bailey; and D. Fish. 1996. "Utility of Modeling and Simulation in the Department of Defense: Initial Data Collection." Institute for Defense Analyses, Alexandria, Va. (Aug.).

BIOGRAPHY

Dr Steve "Flash" Gordon has served as the Technical Director of the Air Force Agency for Modeling and Simulation since October of 1998. Dr Gordon retired from the United States Air Force in 1998 after 26 years of service, including assignments as an F-111E Instructor Weapon Systems Officer, F-111E Wing Electronic Warfare Officer, F-111E Flight Commander, Professor and Head of the Department of Mathematical Sciences at the United States Air Force Academy, Air Operations Center Director and Joint Force Air Component Commander at 13th Air Force, and as Division Chiefs on the Air Staff. Dr Gordon's academic degrees are in Aeronautical and Astronautical Engineering from Purdue University, Industrial Engineering and Operations Research from Purdue University, Human Development Counseling from Peabody College of Vanderbilt University, and Mathematics from Marymount College.

MANAGING MODELING AND SIMULATION AS A SINGLE PROGRAM

Dr. W. A. Watkins, Computer Sciences Corp. and C. F. Booth, Dynamics Research Corp.
Consolidated Support Facility, Suite 750
1901 N. Moore Street, Arlington, VA
Wwatkin3@csc.com and cbooth@drc.com

KEYWORDS: Model Acceptance, Model Credibility, Validation, Return on the Investment, Ballistic Missile Defense

ABSTRACT

The rationale behind its recent decision to manage Modeling and Simulation (M&S) as a single program and the anticipated return on the investment for the Ballistic Missile Defense Program (BMDO) is compared to past practices and contrasted to the needs of the warfighter. The paper provides a short history of M&S within BMDO pointing out the parallelism in the M&S management approach with the evolution of Ballistic Missile Defense (BMD) Systems. BMDO undertaking of a two-year internal audit and several management changes that culminated in the preparation of a business case for restructuring M&S management within BMDO into a single program is discussed, along with the rationale for the business case in terms of the anticipated payoff of Core M&S capability to predict BMD performance with confidence and fully support the user needs across all the domains.

INTRODUCTION

The Ballistic Missile Defense Organization (BMDO), previously the Strategic Defense Initiative Organization, has undergone many changes since its inception in 1983. Most notable are the changes in the system architecture driven by changes in the threat environment. The initial Phase I Strategic Defense System (SDS) architecture focused on space-based systems to defend worldwide against large numbers of Intercontinental Ballistic Missiles (ICBMs). With the end of the cold war, the focus shifted to a Global Protection Against Limited Strikes (GPALS) architecture designed to defend the United States against a small number of missiles launched by a rogue state. This architecture, while still incorporating space-based Command, Control and Communication, Intelligence Surveillance, and Reconnaissance components, was primarily a ground-based missile-to-missile intercept system. Lessons learned in the Gulf War, improved sensor and precision hit to kill (HTK) technologies and the continuing evolution of the threat environment motivated defense planners to move beyond fixed, ground based systems. Figure 1 illustrates the evolution of the Ballistic Missile Defense (BMD) program.

Figure 1 BMD Roadmap

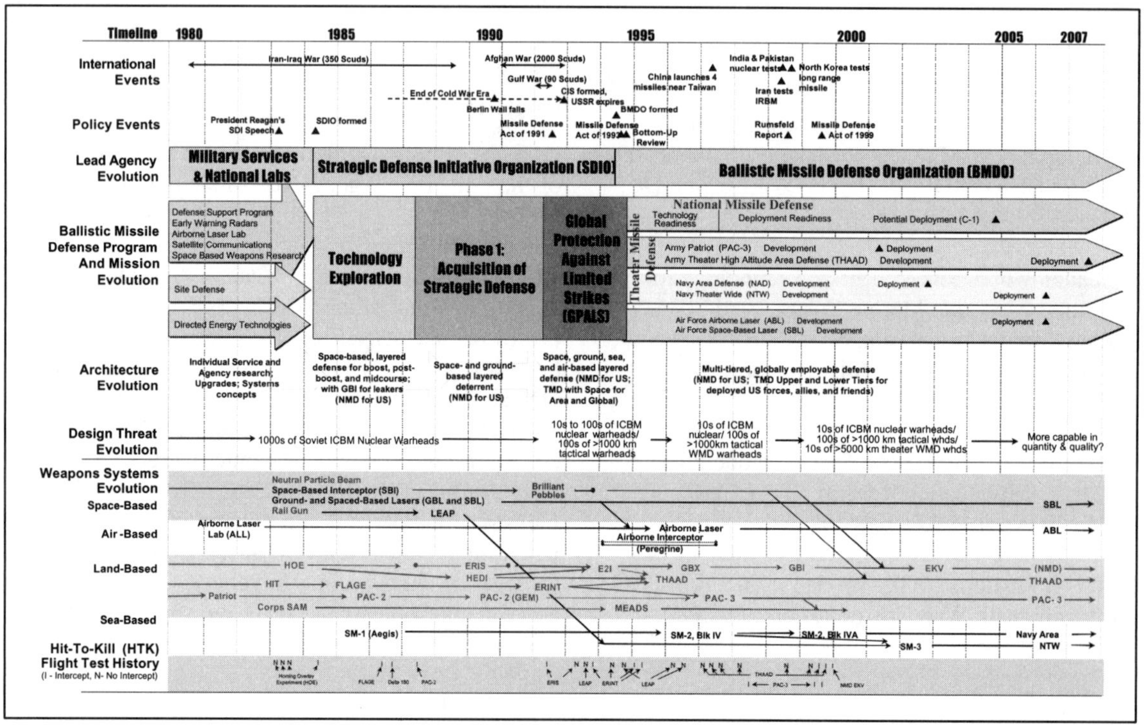

During the past decade, the evolving threat challenged the existing BMD mission performance requirements stressing the capability of autonomous BMD systems, even when deployed in large numbers. New mission requirements demanded a form of collective engagement of the threat by interoperable, multi-layered, air, sea and land defense systems. Figure 2 depicts the current multi-layered, Theater Missile Defense (TMD) system of systems

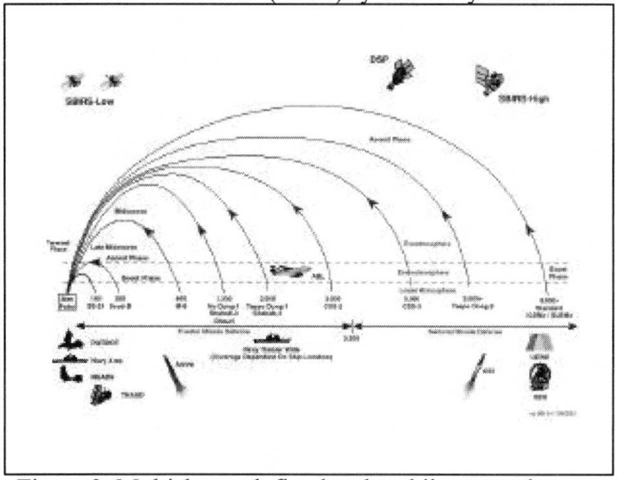

Figure 2 Multi-layered, fixed and mobile, ground, sea and air-based Theater Missile Defense (TMD) architecture

Similarly, National Missile Defense (NMD) requires developing, testing, and integrating five major components or elements[1].

To implement the BMD architectures, Congress directed the Department of Defense (DoD) to establish Major Defense Acquisition Programs (MDAP) to develop air, land and sea based systems with attributes incorporating emerging sensor and precision HTK technologies. BMDO's role was to:

- Foster these technologies - Conduct experiments and engineering studies, sponsor the build and testin g of prototypes, collect threat, signature and environmental data.
- Substantiate the evolving architectures - Conduct concept evaluation, architecture analysis, design trade studies and system engineering evaluation for mission effectiveness (cost, schedule and performance).
- Guide, with budgetary oversight, the development of these systems.

[1] These five elements include: the Ground Based Interceptor (GBI); Upgraded Early Warning Radars (UEWR); U.S.-based X-Band Radars (XBR); Battle Management/ Command, Control, and Communications (BM/C3); and the Space Based Infrared System (SBIRS) in high and low earth orbits.

BMDO MODELING AND SIMULATION

To carry out their role, BMDO developed models and simulations (M&S). BMDO emphasized use of low fidelity M&S to study architecture variants, medium fidelity for engagement effectiveness and higher fidelity engineering models to conduct evaluation for technology payoff. BMDO chose to manage M&S within each of the user communities (i.e., analysis, system engineering, test and evaluation, and technology). This approach optimized support to individual users and provided quick turnaround of changes to the M&S.

In parallel, the individual MDAP managers[2] developed and evolved M&S in step with program maturation to evaluate performance as part of their acquisition process. MDAPs typically moved their M&S from lower to higher fidelity system representations consistent with evolution of system design and development understanding. If the MDAP followed this process with discipline throughout the acquisition the M&S would embody an authoritative representation of system hardware performance understanding. The payoff would be credibility and ability to predict performance in tactically representative synthetic and test, environments and scenario s, for operational acceptance testing. To represent the synthetic threat, environment and scenarios, both BMDO and the MDAPs developed threat models, stimulators, emulators and synthetic scene generation M&S for signatures of sensing systems, and characterizations of the environment. BMDO, the MDAPs and their supporting contractors built a large number of M&S of varied type (i.e., Constructive, Virtual (Operator in the Loop (OITL) and Hardware in the Loop (HWIL)) and Live) with mixed fidelity for use in all the use domains (Campaign, Mission, Engagement, Engineering (includes physics based models)). For the most part, these M&S activities were independent, managed within the MDAP and the BMDO user communities leading to redundancy and disconnects (e.g., failure to provide an integrated M&S providing an "end-to-end"[3] capability) across the use domains.

In 1998, Gen (ret) Larry Welch, USAF conducting an independent review of a series of BMD flight failures,[4]

[2] Generally, the US Air Force, US Navy and US Army manage air-, sea- and ground-based systems, respectively.
[3] End to end is the analytic chain of BMD performance that starts with defensive planning and laydowns through early warning/detection/ engagement process and ends with kill assessment that now includes ground effects.
[4] Report of the Panel on Reducing Risk in Ballistic Missile Defense Flight Test Programs, 27 February 1998. Available at http://www.acq.osd.mil/bmdo/bmdolink/html/docs.html

criticized BMDO for failing to predict or anticipate BMD ground and flight test problems. His review also cited disconnects in the existing M&S Program. This criticism together with today's more challenging system requirements, prompted the BMDO and MDAP user communities to look for a more robust M&S tool set that:

- Represented BMD end-to-end performance with combinations of MDAP systems performing on a level playing field under operational scenarios that stressed their autonomous performance.
- Represented levels of integration and interoperability to identify the mission and performance effectiveness of joint data exchange, command and control and fire control.
- Facilitated the comparisons and evaluation of data, data elements and syntax for establishing joint communication protocols and standards
- Represented the integration and near -real-time assessment of critical system performance elements into a common tactical picture for command and control decision making
- Represent the ability of humans to execute effective command and control in a time critic al, information dominant environment[5].

In response, BMDO undertook a two-year internal audit of the existing M&S Program. This included a review of all M&S used within BMDO and the MDAP community. After eliminating the many M&S tools that were used within the contractor community but not directly funded nor sponsored by either the BMDO or the MDAPs, the initial list contained 282 M&S.

An extensive and comprehensive evaluation of each of the 282 M&S was conducted. This included site visits to the M&S developer and user locations. 194 M&S were judged to not substantially support current BMDO and MDAP test and evaluation needs or acquisition milestones. BMDO M&S that were redundant, did not to support current key technology, or contribute to understanding of integration and interoperability performance were eliminated. The remaining 88 M&S were designated BMD Primary M&S. 68 of the primary M&S were funded, managed and used solely by the individual MDAPs. The remaining 20 M&S were used by multiple MDAPs or used for TMD system of systems integration and interoperability evaluations. They were designated "Core M&S." The Core M&S covered the use domains but the existing capability did not meet all the user community requirements. BMDO needed to identify how to manage and fund the evolution[6] of the Core M&S into a comprehensive, integrated, accredited set of tools. M&S of the joint data network, cooperative threat engagement dynamics, kill assessment, ground effects were needed to resolve the representation disconnects of BMD end-to-end performance. Several engineering M&S needed threat, environment and signature enhancements to reduce MDAP performance risk. The Core M&S also needed to be connected together, federated where simultaneous processing was required and anchored for cross validation. Once integrated, the M&S could pace system of systems design and development evaluation and testing necessary to block upgrade and field integrated, interoperable missile defense systems.

A Corporate M&S approach was established to guide the integration and use of the Core M&S. An M&S Strategic Plan was written to describe the M&S end state vision and identify the way ahead. It provided the initial thinking for an approach to bring the Core M&S into an integrated, accredited and supportable capability to predict BMD end to end performance. Figure 3 pictorially represents that end state as a coherent hierarchy of Core M&S supporting analysis, system engineering and test and evaluation user activities, tied together by the data and traceable to requirements.

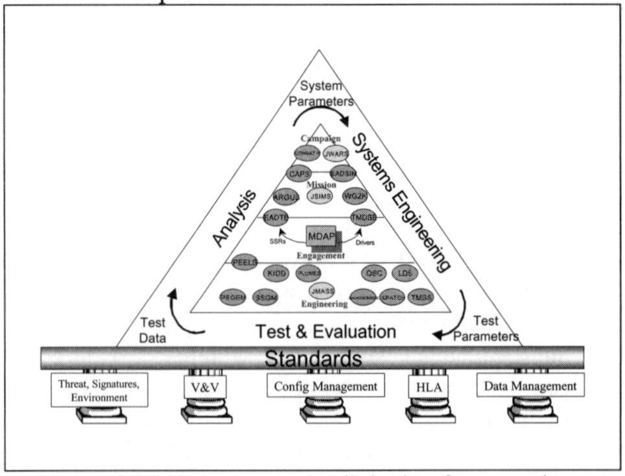

Figure 3 BMDO Core M&S linked to form a coherent hierarchy

The Core M&S, when fully developed, will represent the end-to-end BMD performance. Through consistent, repeated use and several accreditations the M&S will

[5] High data content and rate is required to engage fast moving threat. Connectivity of multiple systems leads to engagements based on autonomic and command and control data with decision intervals down to as low as tens of seconds. This drives the need for, at least, medium fidelity M&S to parameterize the essential elements of messages and message content.

[6] Evolution not revolution was predicated on a limited budget and aggressive schedule driven by M&S user need and funding competition from the hardware side of acquisition and test.

achieve confidence levels that support the traceable linkage of analysis, system engineering and test and evaluation data results. The Core M&S hierarchy is intended to evolve consistently with spiral acquisition development. This approach ultimately provides an M&S capability that can predict ground and test performance within a disciplined process that is traceable to requirements. The disciplined process starts with M&S in analysis that identifies the critical system parameters, passes them traceably to M&S into system engineering that evaluates and establishes test parameters, evolves M&S to predict those test parameters, conducts ground or flight test and feeds the data back to M&S for comparison and iteration. Underpinning the coherent hierarchy is the M&S standards processes essential to maintain consistency in use and critical for establishing the basis for validation.

The evolution of the Core M&S into this coherent hierarchy requires the phased integration of M&S sustainment, enhancement, VV&A and federation to meet user requirements. The user community has time-urgent requirements that have to be met in a prioritized manner consistent with available funding. Limited funding means these requirements have to be phased within the long-range goal of building the coherent hierarchy. Funding limitations and time-urgent requirements necessitate consideration of every cost saving opportunity. M&S overhead reduction was a prime candidate. The M&S infrastructure also needed to be streamlined. Managing the M&S capability as a single program with a single point of responsibility and accountability made good business sense. A business case expressing this rationale was presented to the new BMDO, Director and he approved.

ESTABLISHING A SINGLE PROGRAM

Implementation of M&S as a single program required two components:

1) A collaborative environment to collect all the Core M&S users requirements, provide a cadre of M&S technical expertise to assess the need for change, identify their priorities and build an overall investment plan to deliver accredited M&S to the users in time to support key T&E events and acquisition milestone decisions.
2) An M&S organization within BMDO to manage all the Core M&S.

These two components were implemented as the BMDO M&S Working Group (MSWG) and the BMDO/TEM organization. The MSWG is a collaborative environment that brings together all BMDO and MDAP (including NMD) stakeholder requirements for the Core M&S. This collaborative process will ensure that the Core M&S is able to provide confident ability to predict system performance. BMDO/TEM implements the Core M&S single program. TEM provides product leaders for all Core M&S to ensure disciplined model development responsive to user requirements. A TEM M&S Support Team provides centralized management of the Core M&S compliance to standards and assessment of M&S capability facilitating earlier user acceptance.

User acceptance begins with user requirements specifying the type of M&S and the intended use. That information is brought to the MSWG via three working groups. Each working group is charged with presenting the M&S capability necessary to meet the MDAP and TMD FoS requirements for their portion of the Core M&S. The MSWG integrates working group recommendations to establish the overall Core M&S support plan (cost, development schedule, and M&S capability). The MSWG reports to the BMDO Test and Simulation Director for funding approval. Together, BMDO/TEM and the MSWG organizations working as a single program provide a stable program that leads to an integrated and accredited set of Core M&S tools supporting MDAP and TMD FoS Analysis, System Engineering, and T&E.

RETURN ON INVESTMENT

A single M&S program providing an integrated capability provides several payoffs or M&S Returns On the Investment (ROI). Consolidating management functions streamlines infrastructure and eliminates redundant efforts providing cost savings. The more important pay-off, however, comes from a higher acceptance rate during operational test and warfighter confidence that the fielded system will meet the tactical mission requirements. The BMDO M&S Program is designed to achieve these payoffs by establishing this integrated hierarchy of credible M&S using the user-M&S developer collaborative process. The collaborative process is key since user acceptance of M&S is critical to realizing payoff in operational testing and establishing confidence that the system will perform in the tactical environment.

If M&S data is of sufficient credibility, it can be used for test planning and pre-test prediction during the development and operational test phase of acquisition. A few hardware tests and several runs of M&S test performance prediction can be merged to reach a statistically significant performance data sample size earlier and at a lower cost to certify hardware performance. The M&S ROI is a higher acceptance rate during operational tests.

From the perspective of the warfighter, a ROI exists if M&S provides confidence that the fielded system will meet the tactical mission requirements. Why M&S? Because the operational testing environment falls far short of representing the tactical environment. These limitations include:

- Funding constraints limit the number of tests, test articles and assets, length of test, configuration of the hardware and the extent of the operational threat scenario.
- Political considerations and security control the execution of sensitive tactics, the characteristics of the threat scenario and possibly the configuration of hardware.
- Range safety controls the environment, the test location, engagement scenario, tactics, techniques and procedures and who conducts the test.
- Operational constraints limit the use of a real threat, the hardware is usually pre-production and the mission dynamics are scripted thus red, blue and white force reactions are not measured.

As a result, extrapolation of operational test results without M&S to confidently predict performance in a tactical environment becomes mostly subjective, based on the performance of similar systems in a combat environment.

M&S, especially constructive simulations with the synthetic threat, sensor signatures, environment and scenarios, dynamically interacting together, are the only tools that can come close to representing the tactical environment. But, can the M&S prediction of tactical performance be believed? To achieve the warfighter ROI, the M&S must be credible, and users must accept the validity of the representation of tactical performance.

Two M&S users play a major role certifying the suitability of systems for tactical use, the operational tester and the warfighter. The Director of Operational Test and Evaluation (DOT&E) conducts operational test to establish the suitability of systems for production. The operational test data is valuable because of the controlled and measurable conditions of the test, but not sufficient to certify tactical performance. The warfighter, in the joint exercise environment, evaluates combat readiness. This test mixes combat troops operating live hardware systems or component of systems together with M&S, emulators and stimulators. The joint exercise environment offers some gains in tactical representation relative to operational testing but the threat is still not real, the scenario is scripted and range safety limits tactical reality. The bottom line is no one testing environment provides all the necessary data for certifying tactical representation, each contributes a part to the whole. The important point that follows is that M&S is essential to completing the whole. M&S can represent a credible repository of system knowledge, able to manifest all the implications of system test data with a methodology that is traceable to requirements and describes the expected performance of the critical system or system of systems parameters. For M&S to be a credible repository requires the consistent, continuous and, repeatable use of M&S integrated with testing and validated with a basis built over time. The end state is a quantified M&S user confidence to predict tactical performance. The investment required to support a disciplined process using M&S consistently in test and evaluation returns credible prediction of performance in the tactical environment. The process is called STEP[7]. Figure 4 illustrates application of the STEP process.

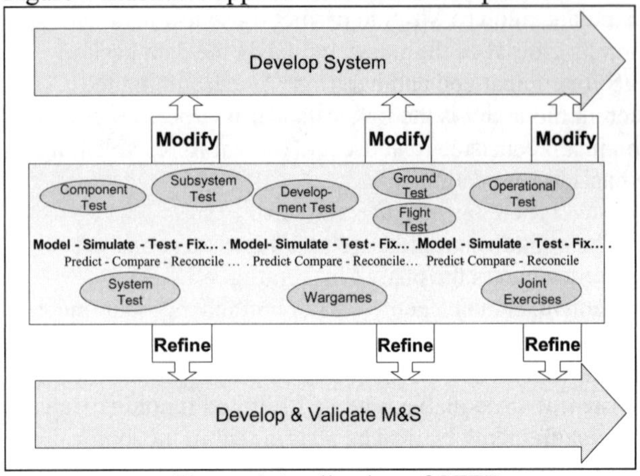

Figure 4 Application of STEP

The key to the STEP process is the consistent discipline to use M&S as a predictor of the event (test or evaluation) followed by the comparison with test or evaluation data. The most important part of the process is the reconciliation of the M&S differences, with rigor[8]. If this process is used consistently the ultimate user, the warfighter, is able to run M&S at a measured level of confidence in a synthetic combat environment, threat and scenario thus predict combat performance. If that confidence level is acceptable, the M&S ROI payoff to the warfighter is mission confidence. Mission performance confidence mitigates the low confidence tendency to over-invest in other mission areas during overall war plan evaluation.

PROCESS TO ENABLE ALL M&S ROI

The ability to generate acceptable confidence levels in M&S output is critical. The methodology is not new. The strategic programs of the 70s and the 80s used this process very successfully with M&S much less

[7] The Simulation, Test and Evaluation Process (STEP) process, "model-simulate-fix-test-iterate." Is described in the STEP Guideline 4 December 1997, available at http://www.acq.osd.mil/te/programs/tfr/step.htm

[8] The M&S output and test data are compared and statistically determined, to some level of confidence, whether or not they represent the same entity (sample). If not, system engineering must resolve (this is where it may be costly and where the discipline usually weakens)

sophisticated and with less computing power than is on a desktop today. The process does not start in operational test. M&S predictions that match a single test result are not statistically significant. How many matches is enough? How do you handle the differences, fix the model or believe the model and fix the hardware? A daunting task if M&S validation rigor and discipline starts in development and operational test. That task is not as daunting if M&S validation occurs consistently, throughout acquisition. Users must validate each M&S use and look for anchoring[9] opportunities to cross validate the M&S in different use domains. This facilitates comparisons with all the M&S tools that predict and compare component, subsystem and system design and development data and builds the validation basis over time. This follows the tenets of Simulation Based Acquisition[10], and if accomplished with rigor, interpolations and extrapolations are possible to fill in the gaps with statistical techniques that measure the confidence level of the integrated set of M&S output over a large domain of use.

The system engineer is key player to establish the path to M&S confidence. They turn the hardware and operational requirements into system parameters that guide M&S development. They also manage the performance risk giving the M&S developers and other M&S users the ground rules for how accurate or valid the M&S must be. They are also the traffic cops of acquisition. They review and monitor the results of system development and M&S analysis, establish the scope of the M&S constructive and virtual simulations that evaluate performance parameters and recommend the test parameters for M&S to plan and predict test performance. The system engineer also monitors the statistical data that establishes model confidence. By using M&S to also predict system performance risk and comparing those results with M&S reconciliation's with, component, subsystem, and system test data the system engineer recommends M&S enhancements to explore hardware performance changes commensurate with performance risk. Each of these activities build the validation basis for feeding back to the end-to-end constructive simulation to provide a prediction capability based on statistical confidence intervals. As the hardware is designed and developed the component, subsystem and system data should be fed back (using the STEP process) into the associated M&S. As the hardware is pro-typed and hardware-in-the-loop or operator-in-the-loop type tools are built their data should also be fed back to the constructive simulation to reconcile any difference and maintain the confidence levels consistent with the system engineer's performance risk assessment. If this is done with rigor and discipline, then the M&S constructive simulation has a more complete validation basis to predict the development test results. The development test data adds to this validation basis because the test is reflective of a mature design and when used in combination with a confident M&S prediction, the reconciliation between the model and the test data is conducted on a traceable record of rigor. In addition, a confident M&S predictive ability can be used to structure the overall development and operational test plan. M&S predictions for parameters with high confidence, representing the known will guide the testing to verify that knowledge and build confidence in those lesser known parameters. The return to the T&E user should be a more efficient testing program with tests focused to rapidly build and verify understanding in a structured orderly fashion leading to a focused risk reduction, a significant ROI for M&S.

SUMMARY

A coherent hierarchy of accredited M&S tools that builds confidence in a constructive simulation that predicts end state performance delivers ROI to many users. BMDO task is difficult. The set of Core M&S comes from a legacy of M&S development of many defense programs in varying phases of acquisition. A credible constructive M&S requires a level playing field to be credible to the user and the stakeholders whose system performance is represented. M&S representing BMD system of systems requires a middle ground of medium fidelity representation that strikes a balance among the range of individual system knowledge's Bringing together M&S into a coherent hierarchy of accreditation that satisfy the scrutiny of all the users and stakeholders is the objective of the Core M&S managed, as a single program. The ROI end state for BMDO is to deliver a credible M&S that can predict of tactical performance to the most important user, the warfighter.

---

[9] The process of comparing the outputs of two or more M&S that match (similar parameters) when run with the same input conditions.

[10] Johnson, LTC Michael V. R. Sr., McKeon, Lt.Col Mark F., and Szanto, LtCol Terence R., Simulation Based Acquisition: A New Approach – Report of the Military Research Fellows CSMC 1997-1998, Defense Systems Management College Press, Fort Belvoir, VA, December 1998. Define Simulation Based Acquisition as." . . an iterative, integrated product and process approach to acquisition, using modeling and simulation, that enables the warfighting, resource allocation, and acquisition communities to fulfill the warfighter's materiel needs, while maintaining Cost As an Independent Variable (CAIV) over the system's entire life cycle and within the DoD's system of systems."

THE MODELING AND SIMULATION INFORMATION ANALYSIS CENTER (MSIAC)

Dr. Jerry M. Feinberg
MSIAC Chief Scientist / IIT Research Institute
1901 N. Beauregard St., Suite 400
Alexandria, VA 22311-1705
e-mail: jfeinberg@msiac.dmso.mil

KEYWORDS

Model analysis, Model transfer, Forecasting, Decision-making, Policy-making

ABSTRACT

This paper presents the roles and missions of the MSIAC, a DoD Information Analysis Center sponsored by the Defense Technical Information Center and the Defense Modeling and Simulation Office. The MSIAC's goal is to be a single, integrated support activity for the use, employment, and sustainment of M&S. The MSIAC's objective is to facilitate warfighters' and developers' missions by applying knowledge created from scientific, technical, and operational support information.

The MSIAC provides scientific, technical, and operational assistance in conducting joint training, building doctrine and tactics, developing operational plans, assessing warfighting situations, assessing technologies, and structuring forces. Current knowledge products include help desk responses, state-of-the-art reports, education and training courses, and simulation/software/database distribution. The MSIAC also leads special projects in operational support; scientific and technical analysis; M&S resource repositories; verification, validation, and accreditation technical assistance; High Level Architecture compliance testing; and simulation impact assessments.

The MSIAC's success relies on experienced people with extensive knowledge of community needs. The MSIAC is uniquely able to serve both developers and military users, and to act as a link between them, because of expertise in M&S-related technology, experience applying advanced technology, strong military operations experience, and extensive warfighter experience and perspective.

INTRODUCTION

The Modeling and Simulation Information Analysis Center, or MSIAC, is a Department of Defense Information Analysis Center sponsored by the Defense Technical Information Center and the Defense Modeling and Simulation Office. The MSIAC is dedicated to creating and applying knowledge for the M&S community through collecting, processing, analyzing, and disseminating scientific, technical, and operational support information.

The specific objectives of the MSIAC are to:

- facilitate use of scientific, technical, and operational support information relating to M&S in research and development, design, analysis, testing, evaluation, training, operations, and maintenance of DoD systems, military systems operated by allied and friendly nations, and the industry/research base which produces and supports these systems,
- maintain and develop methods for the collection, analysis, and dissemination of M&S-related information,
- transfer M&S information within the U.S. Government and between the U.S. Government and authorized users,

- facilitate the reuse and interoperability of M&S through use of the M&S Common Technical Framework, and
- support the M&S community as a single integrated support activity for the use, employment and sustainment of M&S.

The MSIAC's mission is to increase the productivity of DoD scientific and engineering functions through timely dissemination of authoritative, accurate, and high-quality knowledge in the M&S field and through promotion of standardization across M&S. We are accomplishing these missions by providing in-depth analysis services and by creating specialized technical knowledge products. For example, the MSIAC responds to technical inquiries; prepares state-of-the-art reports, handbooks and data books; performs technology assessments; and supports exchanges of information among scientists, engineers, and M&S practitioners.

Technical areas of interest to the MSIAC include:

- models and simulations used within the DoD, evaluated for potential use by DoD components, or developed outside the DoD but which have application to DoD M&S requirements;
- DoD component M&S plans, policies, directives, instructions, procedures, and publications such as users' guides, training materials, and configuration management techniques;
- verification, validation, and accreditation policies, procedures, and guidelines for M&S applications;
- M&S assessment and evaluation techniques, including measurement techniques to assess M&S accuracy, fidelity, efficiency, effectiveness, reliability, interoperability, and reuse potential; and
- standards, specifications, and best practices with respect to the design, development, and implementation of M&S.

For example, the MSIAC is engaged in researching and analyzing all classes of M&S; the interfaces between M&S and command and control systems, intelligence systems, weapon systems on instrumented ranges, weapon system components, and sensors; standards, specifications, and evaluation techniques for models and simulations; system descriptions, interfaces, data communication methods, and data elements and data interchange standards used in M&S; and applications of M&S to the evaluation of operational effectiveness of forces, systems, subsystems, doctrines, tactics, and plans in support of training, analysis, and acquisition.

The MSIAC's scope includes M&S information necessary to support:

- basic and applied Research, Development, Test, and Evaluation (RDT&E) activities,
- military operations,
- acquisition, logistics support and maintenance,
- basic and applied research, and acquisition activities, and
- operational employment and support of M&S.

MSIAC KNOWLEDGE FUNCTIONS AND OPERATIONS

The MSIAC functions with a set of basic (or core) operations and a set of extended operations that are funded separately. The basic operations are information collection, information processing and management, information analysis, and information dissemination. The extended operations are called Technical Area Tasks and are separately funded by government and private customers.

Basic Operations - Information Collection

To increase the productivity of the DoD scientific and engineering functions, the MSIAC is chartered to monitor, access, collect, and extract M&S-related knowledge from worldwide engineering, technical, scientific, and operational support information. To support this collection, the MSIAC stays abreast of the cutting edge of M&S technology through information channels such as publications; conferences and workshops; professional societies; technical interchange meetings and briefings; and face-to-face, telephone, and e-mail communications with knowledgeable organizations and individuals.

Currently, we have assigned specific MSIAC personnel to monitor and collect information in various areas of M&S. Our current "cut" at these focus areas includes acquisition, test and evaluation, training, operational analysis, advanced concepts and requirements, experimentation, C^4ISR, complex contingency operations, weapons of mass destruction, logistics, engineering level models, and technologies. Each area has many subareas. For example, under technologies, the MSIAC is collecting knowledge in verification, validation and accreditation; natural environment; human and organizational behavioral modeling; data standards; interoperability; and commercial trends.

Basic Operations - Information Processing and Management

The MSIAC is chartered to record and store M&S information. To execute this function, the MSIAC maintains libraries of reports, studies and analyses, and symposia proceedings that we use as M&S resource material. We also provide the registrar, help desk, systems administration, and management to sustain the DoD Modeling and Simulation Resource Repository (MSRR), a system designed to facilitate developer and end-user access to and reuse of M&S resources. Also, in our role as a software distribution activity, the MSIAC stores and maintains computer-based models, simulations, databases, and supporting software tools.

Since the extensive scope of M&S precludes having in-house expertise in all possible areas of the field, the MSIAC has developed and is expanding an extensive database of subject matter experts. These subject matter experts are qualified expert persons or organizations who have agreed to provide assistance in instances when the MSIAC does not have requested information, or when the expert has additional information or skills needed to provide better answers to users' inquiries.

Basic Operations - Information Analysis

In anticipating and responding to our users' needs, the MSIAC synthesizes and analyzes information to create and distribute knowledge products and to offer advisory services. In preparing for our users' future information needs, we are constantly monitoring the social, political, and technical environment that influences the course of M&S activities in Government, industry, and academia.

As a national resource of information relevant to M&S, the MSIAC provides timely analyses and responses to user inquiries for M&S information. We assist users in the formulation, scoping and modification of their perceived questions or problems, and we attempt to span the entire M&S spectrum in providing the required information.

As an example of MSIAC technical research, we are monitoring and analyzing M&S topics which offer potential for being significant contributors to M&S advancements over the next five years. These topics include:

- Human and Organizational Behavior Modeling (HOBM) and its potential applications to improve simulation fidelity, reduce the need for humans-in-the-loop, and significantly improve the faithful representation of events in simulations,
- Distributed Mission Training (DMT) and its ability to allow geographically dispersed units to train, plan, and eventually execute military operations using their go-to-war C^2 systems,
- Simulation Based Acquisition (SBA) and its cradle-to-grave approach of using standard data models and simulations to achieve significant savings in acquisition functions, phases, and programs, and
- Joint experimentation with a promise to revolutionize the adoption of warfighting concepts and leading edge technologies.

As part of our analysis function, the MSIAC is also promoting value-added exchanges of information between researchers and technology developers, and between technology developers and warfighters. The MSIAC is helping technology developers investigate and understand functional requirements and technological capabilities, and is helping the warfighters understand how to use, train for, and maintain the M&S technologies pushed (and about to be pushed) upon them.

Basic Operations - Information Dissemination

To accomplish its objectives and missions, the MSIAC disseminates products and services to information users in Government, industry, and academia, as well as to decision and policy makers in the acquisition and broader M&S community. The MSIAC is responsible for disseminating answers to technical inquiries, products to promote customer awareness, bibliographies, training materials, analysis reports, databases, handbooks/databooks, and state-of-the-art reports.

The MSIAC maintains an extensive website containing information on a wealth of M&S activities. The homepage contains links to the MSIAC help desk, a list of frequently asked questions, M&S calendar, M&S news reports, electronic journal, and the MSRR. The URL for the MSIAC website is http://www.msiac.dmso.mil.

The MSIAC prepares and issues an electronic journal to the user community every three months; the journal is available through the MSIAC home page. The journal contains articles on cutting edge technology within M&S; synopses and critiques of newly acquired reports and journal articles; summaries of the initiation or completion of M&S programs; listings of future conferences and symposia; and summaries of significant technology breakthroughs and new technological applications.

The MSIAC develops, maintains, and presents education and training courses for disseminating M&S technology and information to the entire community. Current courses are the M&S Staff Officer Course (a 5 day overview), MS 101 (a 1/2 day tutorial), M&S Orientation (a 1 hour high level overview), and the PMO M&S Workshop (a 1 day workshop). Attendees include DoD operators, PMOs/PEOs, RDT&E staff and acquisition specialists, plus industry and university representatives.

The MSIAC prepares and issues state-of-the-art reports in response to the community's needs in M&S related subjects. To support these reports and other analysis and dissemination activities, the MSIAC is establishing electronic collaboration areas. Members of the M&S community can utilize these areas to access all of the available MSIAC resources including special interest areas, online knowledge bases, and resource repositories; to receive direct support from online subject matter experts; and to hold online meetings.

Finally, the MSIAC serves as a software distribution activity. We disseminate computer-based models, simulations, databases, and supporting software tools. For each of these, we have a working knowledge of the key attributes (e.g., strengths, weaknesses, level of detail) and are fully capable of advising potential users on any resource's appropriateness for a particular application. The MSIAC is currently providing and supporting the distribution of products such as the Master Environmental Library, Conceptual Model of the Mission Space, Unit Order of Battle, and Authoritative Data Sources. These products, and others like them, are becoming a mainstay of services offered by the MSIAC to users in every domain from concept development to training.

Extended Operations - Technical Area Tasks (TATS)

TATs are analytical and technical tasks that are separately-funded efforts over and above the MSIAC basic center operations. These tasks have their basis in emerging Government requirements that necessitate a rapid and authoritative response. A corollary basis for TATs is to derive and create knowledge products which, in turn, feed the MSIAC M&S knowledge base.

In the overall MSIAC concept, these technical area tasks:

- provide for the preparation of specialized projects or services that are useful to the M&S community,
- contribute to the growth of the M&S information base, benefiting a wide range of users,

- provide a means to develop specialized information collections or databases for specific organizations,
- transfer the results of M&S engineering efforts to other DoD and U.S. Government activities, and
- promote awareness, education and use of available M&S resources by applying the results of previous M&S investment to current problems, thereby increasing the economy, efficiency, and effectiveness of current DoD scientific, technical, acquisition, logistics, training, and operational activities.

TATs can be conducted in the areas of operational support services, scientific and technical analysis, M&S education and training, M&S employment assistance, technical and management support to the MSRR, software and documentation distribution, M&S conference support; verification, validation, and accreditation technical assistance; High Level Architecture compliance testing; simulation impact assessments; and communications requirements definition and service allocation.

SUMMARY

The MSIAC is becoming the single, integrated support activity for the use, employment, and sustainment of M&S. We are creating knowledge products through collecting, processing, analyzing, and disseminating scientific, technical, and operational support information. We are already providing assistance in conducting joint training, building doctrine and tactics, developing operational plans, assessing warfighting situations, assessing technologies, and structuring forces. Ongoing MSIAC products include help desk responses; state-of-the-art reports; model, simulation, supporting software and database distribution; education and training; and knowledge products. Additional MSIAC projects include scientific and technical analysis; M&S resource repositories; verification, validation and accreditation technical assistance; High Level Architecture compliance testing; and simulation impact assessments.

We are encouraging and facilitating M&S reuse and interoperability throughout all of our activities and efforts. The MSIAC's information collection, analysis, and dissemination promote the use of existing information, while reducing unnecessary duplication of research, information collection, analysis, and dissemination.

Finally, the MSIAC's successful customer support relies on experienced people with extensive knowledge of customer needs. We have the unique ability to serve as a link between developers and military users because of our staff's strong expertise in M&S-related technology, experience applying advanced technology, military operations experience, and extensive warfighter experience and perspective.

AUTHOR BIOGRAPHY

Jerry M. Feinberg is a Senior Technical Advisor for IIT Research Institute and the Chief Scientist for the MSIAC in Alexandria, Virginia. Associated with the MSIAC from its inception, he is currently concentrating on outreach to the commercial, academic, and Government (non-DoD) sectors of the modeling and simulation community. Dr. Feinberg holds a Ph.D. and M.S. in Mathematics, and an M.S. in Physics, from Stanford University, and a B.S. in Mathematics from the California Institute of Technology. He is a member of Tau Beta Pi and is a Hertz Foundation Fellow.

SCSC '99 Papers

External and Internal Interoperability of the Enhanced ModSAF Architecture

Mark D. Roberts, Jill McCutcheon, John W. Willcox III
COLSA Corporation
6726 Odyssey Drive
Huntsville, AL 35806
(205) 922-1512
mroberts@colsa.com, jmccutch@colsa.com, jwillcox@colsa.com

Jacqueline G. Steele
United States Army Space and Missile Defense Command (USASMDC)
P.O. Box 1500
Huntsville, AL 35807
(205) 955-3572
SteeleJ@smdc.army.mil

Keywords: ModSAF; Enhanced ModSAF, Shared Memory, Interoperability, Scalability, Load Balancing, Fault Tolerance, HLA, Simulation, Modeling, Object Ownership Negotiation

ABSTRACT: The Enhanced Modular Semi-Automated Forces (E-ModSAF) project involves modification of the ModSAF ground forces modeling simulation to utilize shared memory on multiple-processor high-performance computers. Redundant network traffic processing and database management overheads are eliminated, providing significant and scalable performance increases per processor. The E-ModSAF architecture leverages the existing ModSAF design and provides three additional components: Protocol Data Unit (PDU) Reader, PDU Writer and an Executive. The PDU Reader processes incoming network messages into a shared memory state database utilized by all SAFsims (modeling processes) and SAFstations (graphical user interface processes). The optional PDU Writer allows outgoing network message processing to be centralized into a single process. The Executive controls, monitors and provides fault tolerance for processes under its control. It dynamically balances entity-modeling load among SAFsims, allowing maximum usage of computational resources.

The paper focuses on external and internal interoperability of the E-ModSAF architecture. Interoperability with external simulations is discussed with emphasis on object ownership negotiation. Interoperability of E-ModSAF components is described, emphasizing the use of shared memory for common data storage and inter-process communications, and the relationship between fault tolerance and dynamic load balancing capabilities is explained. A discussion of E-ModSAF interoperability in relation to the High Level Architecture (HLA) is also provided.

1. Introduction

Distributed simulation applications are used to support the full range of military activities including: Research, Development and Acquisition (RDA), Training, Exercises and Military Operations (TEMO), and Advanced Concepts and Requirements (ACR). As distributed simulation applications have matured and their usage has proliferated, the need for higher fidelity models involving large numbers of entities has also grown, applying an increasing pressure on computing resources. Current hardware and software limitations must be overcome in order to support the orders of magnitude increases in entity counts which are required to support future military activities involving distributed simulation applications.

The Office of the Secretary of Defense has initiated the Department of Defense (DOD) High-performance Computing Modernization Program (HPCMP) to provide the United States military the technological resources needed to support warfighting requirements. The HPCMP is investing over a billion dollars over five years to provide advanced hardware, software, tools and training to DOD researchers in support of the warfighter. The HPCMP has resulted in the creation of several high-performance computing centers known as Major Shared Resource Centers (MSRCs) and Distributed Centers

(DCs) where large numbers of high-performance computers are now available. Additionally, the Defense Research and Engineering Network (DREN) is undergoing a major upgrade to increase its performance. Under the HPCMP, the Common High-performance Computing Software Support Initiative (CHSSI) was formed to provide DOD researchers applications that exploit scalable computing resources.

The Enhanced ModSAF (E-ModSAF) effort is the United States Army Space and Missile Defense Command (USASMDC) portion of what is a collaborative Army-Navy project being conducted under the CHSSI program in the Forces Modeling and Simulation (FMS)/C4I Computational Technology Area (CTA). The effort involves the enhancement of the Modular Semi-Automated Forces (ModSAF) ground forces modeling simulation to leverage the capabilities of HPC large scale shared memory multiprocessor computer architectures in order to increase ModSAF performance. For the Navy portion of the project, the Naval Research Laboratory (NRL) is sponsoring Metron, Inc. in an effort to port the Navy Simulation System (NSS) to the Synchronous Parallel Environment for Emulation and Discrete-Event Simulation (SPEEDES) to support quick reaction analysis and rapid mission planning.

This paper focuses on interoperability of the E-ModSAF architecture. Interoperability with external distributed applications is discussed with emphasis given to the roles and responsibilities of specific E-ModSAF components in relation to network communications, and the perceived singularity of E-ModSAF by distributed applications. The interoperability of internal E-ModSAF components is described, including collaborative use of shared memory, inter-process communications, and process management. A discussion of E-ModSAF interoperability in relation to HLA is also given.

2. Scalability Limitations of ModSAF

ModSAF was designed to support Distributed Interactive Simulation (DIS) and consists of SAFsims and SAFstations that communicate with each other and with other DIS applications by utilizing network communications and the DIS protocol. DIS applications send PDUs across the network describing the current state of the entities they are modeling (hosting). Each SAFsim and SAFstation reads and processes all messages from the network and places processed message data into its own state database that describes all entities being simulated. In this manner, ModSAF processes ghost entities modeled by other SAFsims or other DIS applications.

When the current ModSAF architecture was designed, SAFsims and SAFstations participating in an exercise were expected normally to be executing on different computers. Since large scale shared memory architectures were very expensive and not readily available, no effort was made to leverage their capabilities. However, the current ModSAF architecture does support multiprocessor computers in that multiple SAFsims and SAFstations can be executed on multiple-processors and will function the same as if executing on different computers. Figure 2.1 illustrates multiple ModSAF processes executing on a multiprocessor computer with the current ModSAF architecture. SAFsims and SAFstations communicate with each other via network message traffic in the same manner as they do with distributed applications executing on other computers. Each SAFsim and SAFstation maintains virtually an identical copy of the state data describing all entities being modeled by all SAFsims.

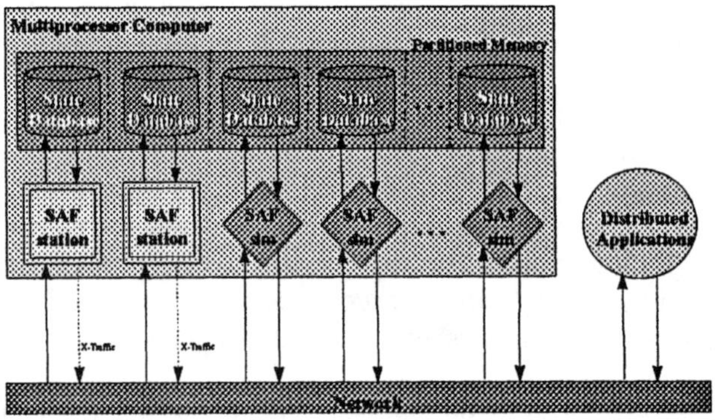

Figure 2.1 Conventional ModSAF Architecture on Multiprocessor Computer

Although multiple instances of ModSAF SAFsims and SAFstations will execute and collaborate on a large scale multiprocessor computer, the current ModSAF architecture has limited scalablility. Consequently, the number of entities that can be modeled by executing additional SAFsims on separate processors eventually approaches a limit. Table 2.1 presents the results of recent testing using the standard ModSAF 3.0 benchmark on a Silicon Graphics Origin 2000 computer where multiple instances of SAFsims were added on separate processors. A SAFstation process was executed on a separate processor during the tests in order to monitor the benchmarks and to emulate actual usage.

Table 2.1 ModSAF 3.0 Benchmark Results on the Silicon Graphics Origin 2000

Number of SAFsims (Processors)	Total Entities Modeled by all SAFsims	Average Entities Per Processor
1	160	160
2	264	132
4	384	96
8	640	80
15	720	48

The limited scalability of conventional ModSAF is a direct result of the increasing PDU processing load imposed on each SAFsim as additional SAFsims are executed. Because each message must be read from the network and processed by each SAFsim into its own state database, SAFsims must spend more and more time processing message traffic, and as a consequence, have less and less time available for modeling. Since ModSAF distributes the modeling load among available SAFsims, the average number of entities modeled per SAFsim decreases as additional SAFsims are added. Figure 2.2 compares the measured performance of ModSAF to 100% scalable performance. The difference between the two curves represents the potential performance increase targeted by the E-ModSAF project.

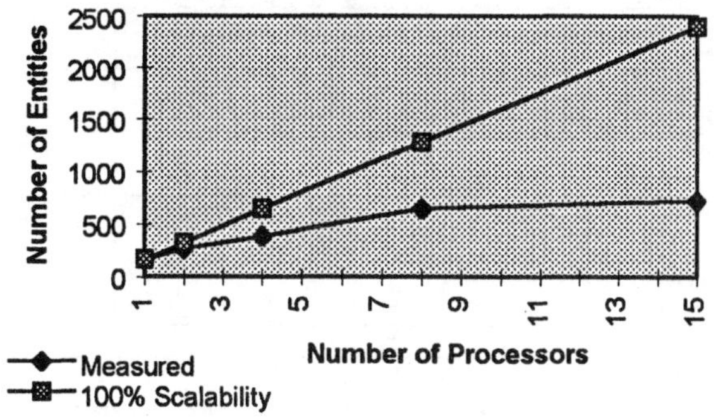

Figure 2.2 Measured vs. 100% Scalable Performance of ModSAF 3.0 on the Silicon Graphics Origin 2000

3. E-ModSAF Project Overview

The E-ModSAF project is a three-year effort that began in March of 1997. As a HPCMO CHSSI task, E-ModSAF is being developed using a formal software development process that includes a Software Development Plan [1], Requirements Document [2], Design Document [3], a comprehensive testing phase, and user and maintenance documentation. The Test and Evaluation Master Plan [4] incorporates Alpha and Beta testing and several formal reviews to determine compliance against extensive critical technical parameters.

3.1 Technical Objectives

The goal of the E-ModSAF project is to modify the ModSAF architecture to enable it to fully utilize high-performance computing resources. Technical objectives established to achieve this goal are as follows:

- Utilize shared memory to eliminate data storage redundancies.
- Utilize inter-process communications for internal message passing.
- Monitor and optimize processor utilization.
- Provide centralized control of SAFsims and SAFstations.
- Provide a fault tolerance recovery mechanism for ModSAF processes.
- Dynamically balance modeling load among SAFsims.
- Implement enhancements in such a manner that existing ModSAF modeling functionality is not compromised.
- Minimize intrusion into existing ModSAF code to allow E-ModSAF code to be easily recognized and placed into future versions of ModSAF.
- Demonstrate E-ModSAF with a HLA-compliant version of ModSAF.
- Implement enhancements using POSIX-compliant code whenever possible.
- Demonstrate E-ModSAF on two or more computer architectures.

3.2 Programmatic Objectives

In addition to technical objectives, several programmatic objectives were established for the project including:

- Coordinate with the Simulation, Training and Instrumentation Command (STRICOM) to incorporate the E-ModSAF architecture into the ModSAF baseline.
- Involve the ModSAF User Community in E-ModSAF Beta testing
- Collaborate with the Navy-sponsored SPEEDES project in order to transition technologies between the Army and Navy.

4. E-ModSAF Architecture Overview

The E-ModSAF architecture proposes to eliminate redundancies pertaining to network traffic and data storage by utilizing a Shared Memory State Database (SMSDB) and by introducing three new components: the

PDU Reader, the PDU Writer, and the Executive. As depicted in Figure 4.1, the PDU Reader provides for network messages to be read once and placed into the SMSDB. It also is responsible for dead reckoning. SAFsims and SAFstations read from and write to the SMSDB, and the PDU Writer reads data from the SMSDB and sends PDUs out across the network. The Executive provides a centralized control interface for configuring, starting and stopping E-ModSAF component processes and monitoring processor utilization in order to optimize run-time system performance. It also provides a fault tolerance recovery mechanism for processes it controls, dynamically balances modeling load among E-ModSAF SAFsim processes, and negotiates object ownership with external distributed applications. An inter-process communications (IPC) system is used for internal message traffic among E-ModSAF component processes.

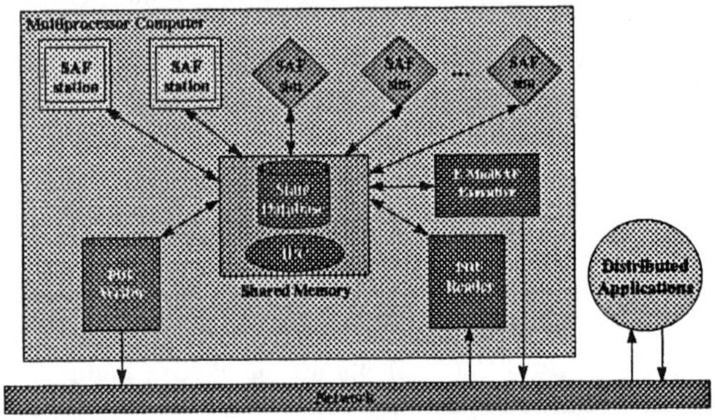

Figure 4.1 Enhanced ModSAF Architecture on Multiprocessor Computer

5. E-ModSAF Interoperability with External Simulations

E-ModSAF network communications with distributed applications are functionally equivalent to that of a single instance of conventional ModSAF, with DIS and Persistent Object (PO) PDUs being sent and received in a normal manner. Although E-ModSAF consists of separately executing SAFsim and SAFstation processes, it interacts with external applications as if it were a single distributed application. It outputs simulatorPresent PDUs as required to represent E-ModSAF as a single application and negotiates object ownership with distributed applications as a single application. E-ModSAF maintains a single vehicle table in shared memory used by all local SAFsims and SAFstations. Within the E-ModSAF vehicle table, entities continue to be designated as local or remote, with the local entity designation representing an entity that is the responsibility of E-ModSAF. The simulator address field for each local entity in the vehicle table is used to assign modeling responsibility to local SAFsims under the control of the Executive. Distributed applications are provided a single simulator address for E-ModSAF, causing the combined modeling load of all SAFsims under the control of the Executive to be viewed by distributed applications as a single E-ModSAF modeling load. The distribution of the E-ModSAF modeling load to the SAFsims under the control of the Executive is entirely transparent to distributed applications.

Although the PDUs emanating from and being received by E-ModSAF are the same as with conventional ModSAF, multiple E-ModSAF processes collaboratively communicate with distributed applications. All incoming PDUs (DIS and PO) are read by the PDU Reader and processed into the SMSDB. All outgoing DIS PDUs are output by SAFsims and SAFstations or by the optional PDU Writer. However, outgoing PO PDUs emanate from several E-ModSAF processes. Table 5.1 lists six PO PDUs and the processes from which they are output.

Table 5.1 Persistent Object PDUs Emanate from Multiple E-ModSAF Processes

PO PDU	Executive	PDU Writer	SAF-station	SAFsim
simulator-Present	W			
describe-Object	W*	W	w	w
object-Present		W	w	w
object-Request	W			
delete-Object		W	w	w**
nomination	W			

* Sent only in response to objectRequest PDU.
** SAFsim may output deleteObject PDU in response to Parser Window command.
Legend: W= PDUs written to network
w= PDUs written to network when PDU Writer not used

The Executive is responsible for coordinating and synchronizing actions with distributed applications. The Executive outputs simulatorPresent PDUs representing E-ModSAF as a single application, objectRequest PDUs requesting information concerning unknown objects, and describeObject PDUs providing object information in response to like requests from distributed applications. It also outputs nomination PDUs as part of object ownership negotiation. The PDU Writer, SAFstations, and SAFsims are responsible for providing entity state information to distributed applications. Either the optional PDU Writer or SAFstations and SAFsims output describeObject PDUs as the object states change and objectPresent PDUs when objects remain unchanged.

6. Interoperability Among E-ModSAF Processes

Interoperability among E-ModSAF processes is accomplished by collaborative use of the SMSDB, internal message passing via the inter-process communications system, and by process management provided by the Executive.

6.1 Collaborative Use of the SMSDB

The Executive process is responsible for initializing shared memory for the SMSDB and for the IPC system. Much of the interoperability among E-ModSAF processes is a direct result of the collaborative use of the data placed into the SMSDB and does not require internal message passing via the IPC. The Executive distributes the local entity modeling load by setting the simulator address fields in the vehicle table to the addresses of the SAFsims it controls. Each SAFsim accesses the vehicle table as part of its normal processing and models the entities designated as local entities that have been assigned its simulator address. The PDU Reader places remote entity data into the SMSDB as PDUs are received or as it performs dead reckoning calculations. SAFsims place data pertaining to the entities they are responsible for hosting directly into the SMSDB and can access the SMSDB to retrieve data pertaining to any entity. The PDU Writer continually monitors the SMSDB and outputs describeObject or objectPresent PDUs as necessary. Because each process maintains memory pointers into the same data, all processes respond to changes in the SMSDB, regardless of the specific process making the change.

The E-ModSAF architecture combines the conventional DIS method of subdividing entity modeling responsibility into local and remote entities with its own method for distributing local entity modeling load among SAFsims it controls. This method minimizes opportunities for data contention involving the SMSDB. Only the PDU Reader writes to locations containing remote entity data. Each local entity is the responsibility of only one SAFsim and only that SAFsim writes to locations pertaining to that entity. Because two processes never write to the same memory location at the same time, processes must only wait to read a location while it is being written to by another process. In addition, multiple processes can read the same location simultaneously.

6.2 Inter-Process Communications

Although collaborative use of the SMSDB provides for much of the interoperability among E-ModSAF components, inter-process communications are required between the Executive and PDU Reader. As part of its coordinating and synchronizing role, the Executive is responsible for negotiating ownership of objects with distributed applications and managing the shared vehicle table. These functions require two-way communications with external distributed applications. Because, the PDU Reader processes all incoming network traffic, certain rarely encountered messages are forwarded to the Executive using the IPC system. Table 6.1 lists the three PO PDUs that are forwarded by the PDU Reader to the Executive.

Table 6.1 Persistent Object PDUs Forwarded to the Executive by the PDU Reader

PO PDU	PDU Reader Action	Executive Action
objectPresent	Forwards objectPresent PDUs for unknown entities	Modifies vehicle table and outputs objectRequest PDU
objectRequest	Forwards all received objectRequest PDUs	Outputs describeObject PDU
nomination	Forwards all received nomination PDUs	Modifies vehicle table

As the PDU Reader processes incoming PDUs, they are parsed, and the message data is normally placed directly into the SMSDB. However, when the PDU Reader encounters an objectPresent PDU for an unknown entity, it places the PDU into the IPC system. The Executive receives and processes the PDU, modifies the vehicle table as required, and outputs to the network a objectRequest PDU requesting additional entity information. All objectRequest and nomination PDUs are also placed into the IPC system when recognized by the PDU Reader. The Executive outputs describeObject PDUs in response to objectRequest PDUs and modifies the vehicle table in response to nomination PDUs. This inter-process message forwarding method minimizes incoming message processing, allows E-ModSAF to be perceived as a single application by distributed applications, and provides behavior consistent to that of conventional ModSAF.

6.3 Executive Process Management

The Executive combines centralized control, dynamic load balancing, and fault tolerance in order to manage E-

ModSAF component processes. Its graphical user interface provides a centralized control point for starting, stopping and monitoring SAFsims and SAFstations. It dynamically balances local entity modeling load among SAFsims it controls by changing simulator addresses in the shared vehicle table based on periodic processor utilization measurements, and provides a fault tolerance recovery mechanism. Given a SAFsim failure, the Executive detects the failure, redistributes its modeling load to other SAFsims, and automatically restarts the process. When the SAFsim has been fully initialized and is able to resume modeling responsibilities, the Executive redistributes modeling load back to the restarted SAFsim.

7. E-ModSAF Interoperability in Relation to HLA

One of the stated technical objectives of the project is to demonstrate E-ModSAF with an HLA-compliant version of ModSAF. Beginning with ModSAF 5.0, future ModSAF releases will have varying degrees of HLA compliance. In relation to HLA, E-ModSAF interoperability is expected to be minimally impacted. E-ModSAF will be treated as a single application, having its own Simulation Object Model (SOM) and will be incorporated in Federation Object Models (FOMs) as if it were a single application. Since the E-ModSAF architecture affects the storage and handling of data and not the contents or logical processing of data, changes to the data being passed should be transparent to E-ModSAF. As the E-ModSAF project continues and efforts to incorporate its architecture into an HLA-compliant ModSAF version progress, additional knowledge will be gained and technical issues will be addressed as required.

Data Distribution Management (DDM) services should be of special interest once an HLA-compliant E-ModSAF is fully functional. DDM's interest management techniques should enable multiple E-ModSAFs to be executed on multiple HPC resources, with each achieving high entity counts while communicating with optimized message traffic that does not overload network resources. Until the HLA DDM service is available to E-ModSAF, the conventional DIS broadcast approach to network message passing could strain network resources precluding such experiments.

8. Current Project Status

Build 1 of E-ModSAF is currently undergoing Beta testing.

9. Conclusions

The E-ModSAF project has demonstrated that a large scale, limited scalability simulation can be enhanced to leverage large-scale HPC resources. Efforts applied in the architecture design effort have shown the importance of defining roles and responsibilities among multiple collaborating processes and the value of shared memory and inter-process communications for eliminating data processing and storage redundancies. Test results to date have demonstrated that the architecture is scalable and achieves significant performance increases over conventional ModSAF.

10. References

[1] "Software Development Plan for the FMS-3 Project: Efficient PDES for Analysis", Naval Research Laboratory, May 1997

[2] Roberts, M., McCutcheon, J., Willcox III, J.: "Requirements for the HPC-Enhanced ModSAF", COLSA Corporation, June 1997

[3] Roberts, M., McCutcheon, J., Willcox III, J.: "E-ModSAF Design Document", COLSA Corporation, January 1998

[4] "FMS-3 TEMP ADDENDUM, Efficient PDES for Analysis", Naval Research Laboratory, November 1997

Author Biographies

MARK D. ROBERTS is a Senior Software Analyst at COLSA Corporation. He received a BS in Electrical Engineering from the University of Alabama in Huntsville in 1985. He is the principal investigator for the Enhanced ModSAF project.

JILL MCCUTCHEON is a Senior Systems Analyst at COLSA Corporation. She received a Math/Computer Science degree from the University of Alabama in Huntsville in 1981. She is an investigator for the Enhanced ModSAF project focusing on shared memory and inter-process communications.

JOHN W. WILLCOX III is a Systems Analyst at COLSA Corporation. He received a BS in Bioengineering from Texas A&M University in 1985. He is an investigator for the Enhanced ModSAF project focusing on process control and monitoring, load balancing, and fault tolerance.

JACQUELINE G. STEELE is a Senior Engineer in the Simulations Directorate of the United States Army Space and Missile Defense Battle Lab. She received Bachelors degrees in Mechanical Engineering and Textile Engineering from Auburn University and a MS in Administrative Science from the University of Alabama in Huntsville. She is the sponsor of the Enhanced ModSAF project.

DEVELOPMENT OF PAREMETER-BASED SIMULATOR FOR THE ANALYSIS OF AUTOMATED MANUFACTURING SYSTEM

Jung-wook Kim, Kwan-hee Han, Gi-tae Kim and Chung-wha Lee

Virtual Manufacturing and Research Center Department
Daewoo Information System Co.
526 Namdaemoonno 5ga,
Chung-Gu, Seoul, Korea

Keywords : parameter, simulator, generator, resource information, database

ABSTRACT

When we analyze automated manufacturing systems having large material-handling facilities, one of the most powerful method is a discrete-event simulation. During the simulation phase, many alternatives are experimented before real system is constructed, so we can find out some problems at earlier stage which would deteriorate the real system. Especially in building a new manufacturing system, there are many changes in design phase, and therefore many simulation experiments have to be performed to reflect the design changes such as layout, operation logic and so on.

To evaluate the performance of each design alternative, we have to build simulation models for each alternative and it leads to time-consuming and inefficient tasks. Therefore, it is necessary to build a parameter-based simulator(PBS) for analyzing many design alternatives rather than make new simulation models for each alternative. It is a 'single-model, multiple-use' approach.

In this paper, we identify the generic structure of PBS for material-handling system and apply it to tire manufacturing production line. The PBS described in this paper consists of three parts; part generator, define of resource information and part database. The first part is the 'Part Generator' which is used for preparing the simulation execution such as type of product, the number of each product, working day, working condition and so on. After preparing such part information and the condition of execution, we have to setup for the attribute information of the facility, human and transfer. It is a second part of PBS, "Define Resource Information". It is a important condition because it means that the users can experiment for the various alternatives in design step. And by using a "Part Database", the last part of PBS, each part can automatically create the attributes. The part database consists of the necessary fields abstracting from the original database. By using the PBS, the designers and operators of automated manufacturing system can make a decision in a more efficient way and they can shorten the time to design the new system or improve the existing system.

In later section of this paper, the usefulness of the proposed PBS framework is demonstrated by applying it to the inspection line and AS/RS(automated storage/retrieval system) of H company which is a Korea tire manufacturer.

1. INTRODUCTION

Simulation is the outstanding tool analyzing the performance of systems in advance by describing various phases of systems. Therefore, the simulation method is being introduced in many fields recently. Especially, various layout alternatives exist at the construction phase of new plants, and sometimes we face a decision-making of operation logic or transfer facilities or resources. Most manufacturing companies have the advanced plant layout teams for this reason, and these teams are using more simulation tools than other cases are. This simulation method should be able to forecast the possible situation at operation stage of plants; for example, facilities trouble, 100% performance by urgent request, changes of labors, and so on need to be analyzed. Besides, this team is responsible for finding out bottleneck process by experimenting or forecasting the possibility of attaining production target. However, it's not easy for simulation method to react fast enough in various alternatives. In fact, many engineers in actual plants do experiments with lots of conditions during the project period. Also, most engineers don't have much knowledge about not only simulation modeling skill but experiment plan or analyzing skill. In this case, most experiments are limited to certain alternatives and the experimental model won't be useful any more after the project is over.

The PBS (Parameter Based Simulator) is a kind of simulator for us to develop to assist Window users by introducing the simulation skill in more efficient ways. It covers customers' complaint occurred past a few years in projects. The PBS is being performed automatically, and users are able to observe the results when users in GUI environment provide required conditions for the experiment analysis at the stage of new plant layout. In other word, the PBS allows simulation S/W beginners to perform the experiment and supports key function for analyzing the results. So this method is being well used by new plant teams due to convenience of experiment analysis for various alternatives.

This paper introduces brief outline for the PBS composition at chapter 2, and how it applied an example based on a certain tire company in Korea.

2. THE STRUCTURE OF SIMULATOR

The PBS we propose has been implemented easily because that recently, most common S/Ws or specific S/Ws are performed in Windows environment. As a matter of fact, a general simulation S/W has almost the same function as the PBS; however, the PBS we propose is composed of various modules utilizing the characteristics of simulation S/W. In other word, users decide the alternatives and use simulation S/W engine modules doing experiments the defined alternatives and database modules inducing process information for experiment based on GUI environment modules able to observe the results. The PBS is performed in MS Windows 95, 98, or NT, and the develop S/Ws such as FoxPro, Excel, Oracle, MS-Access create GUI easily. It is also easy to interface with simulation S/Ws, and any kinds of S/Ws with database function are able to do. The next Figure 1 shows the entire outline of the PBS and the composition, and the required function for each modules is following.

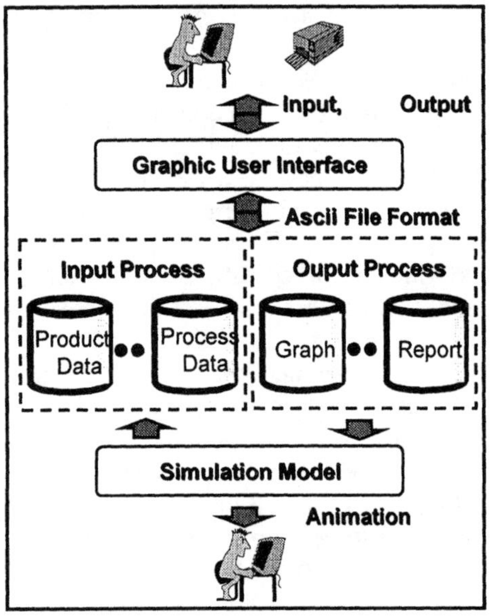

Figure 1 : PBS Architecture

2.1 Part Generator

Generally during the simulation project period there have a number of limitation of alternatives creation or experimental analysis due to part type, rapid information, condition, etc. Besides, there are many difficulties to implement the model reflecting the information. The PBS allows users to implement the condition model and use it in convenient way.

The next Figure 2 shows the typical part generator.

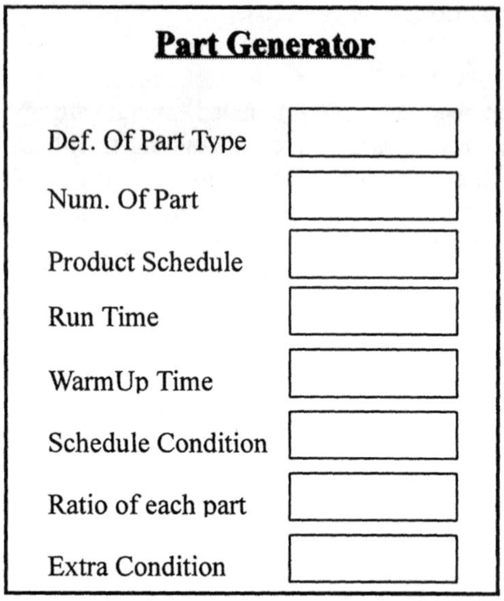

Figure 2 : Typical form of Part Generator

First of all, users define the part type. Generally, users need to define the part type suitable for required site because only one kind of part case has not been frequently occurred. And users decide the number of part and define the products' schedule which contains the period users' request. The next, users can define the Run Time and WarmUp Time. These become the conditions of the simulation experiment. The last, users define the Schedule Condition and Extra Condition such as the productivity in labor unit or production target. The production rate for each part types needs to be controlled as well. "Part Generator" is the part defined as general experimental conditions. The data defined in "Part Generator" is stored as ASCII file type, and assigned to define the pre-required condition of simulation S/W.

2.2 Define Resource Information

As referred, various requested conditions such as change in facility specification, reorganization of control logic, and labor plan changes are occurred during the project period. The "Define Resource Information" module is the one to react against users' request in convenient way. The next Figure 3 shows the typical "Define Resource Information".

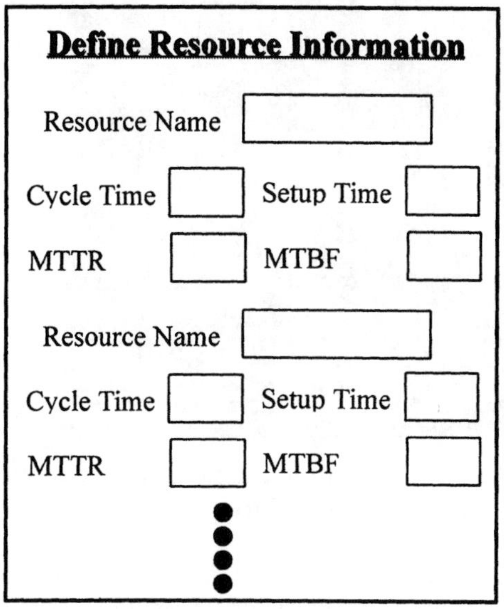

Figure 3 : Define Resource Information

The users are able to define process time, setup time, MTTR(Mean Time To Repair), MTBF(Mean Time Between Failure), various kinds of control logic, the number of labors, and job schedule. These mean that users can experiment for various alternatives. Perhaps, referred new plant teams would take advantage of easy defining or doing some useful experiments. The data defined in "Define Resource Information" is stored as ASCII file type and assigned to the part that defines each resource and logic.

2.3 Part Database

In many cases, each part has many attributes which are imported from existing database. However, some irrelevant jobs occur because the information is imported from only filed users are interested in. Also, it's difficult to manage the part of chosen field and not easy for the original database managers to support the actual managers in real project. Therefore, most actual managers prefer to handle the simulator only related filed that they need in original database. The Part Database is the module that reflects actual users' requirement. In order for users to manage the particular filed, the interface module, which includes output display that users want to look, was constructed. This function impressed the actual users, and this kind of request is frequently occurred.

The next Figure 4 shows the typical "Typical form of Part Generator".

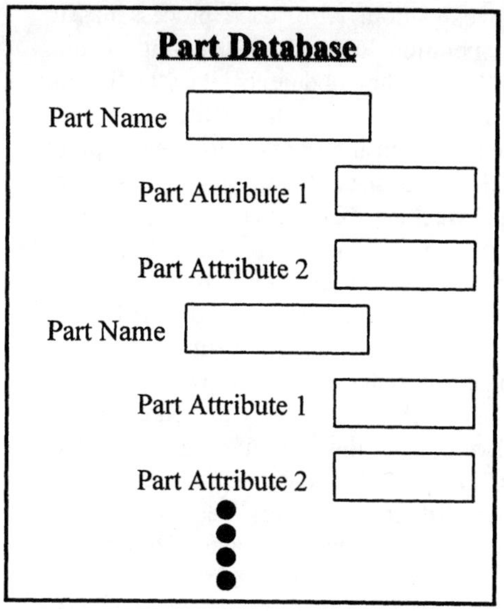

Figure 4 : Typical form of Part Database

3. APPLICATION EXAMPLES

3.1 Definition of site

Among the project sites having the similar composition type as the PBS we applied it to H tire manufacturing company in Korea. The H tire is the well-developed company that was about to build a large scale of new plant due to increase in sales and uprising economic situation. So the new plant team inquired us the simulation analysis based on layout plan. Especially, the H tire tried to focus on inspection process, distribute process and storing at the AS/RS(Automated storage and retrieval system) after the tires were produced in the facility for tire generating. Also, H tire wanted to do experiments with many kinds of facility conditions, production plan, and operating logic till the final AS/RS. For this, we decided to implement the process simulator of tires based on the PBS. This project was in progress for total 8 months, and the Visual FoxPro software and AutoMod were used. As a matter of fact, the H tire selected the Visual FoxPro because they already used it, and we decided a simulation software, AutoMod because it is appropriate for logistics system analysis.

3.2 Project performance

The PBS we developed was used for simulator at the H tire. In other word, the "Part Generator" was implemented as the first module, which defines production schedule, production rate, productivity, etc for each types of tire. These values can say the typical factors for "Part Generator". Second, the many machines, exist from the facility for tire generating to AS/RS warehouse, need the various information for simulation execution. Also, each process has to have the operation logic for distributing of tire. We could apply the module of the "Define of resource information" in the PBS which can define the operation information for each type of tire. The H tire consists of many facilities such as Trimming Machine, Conveyer, Elevator, Folk Liter, AGV, AS/RS, labor, etc. The tire process has specific characteristics that many kinds of tires are produced, and tires are loaded as lot unit base for each cell after a type sorting. For this, users decide different operating logic for each tire. It means that each tire has many attributes. So we could also apply the module of the "Part Database" in the PBS. The Part Database includes the attributes of tire, and users' required display. This module is for managing and defining the various attributes for each type of tire. The next three Figure 5, Figure 6, Figure 7 show the module capturing each display.

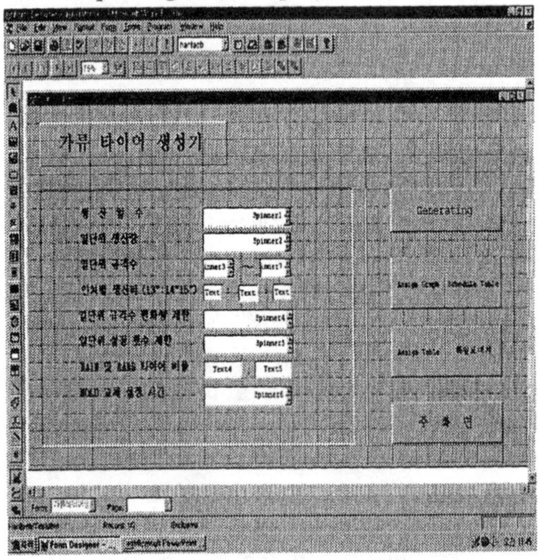

Figure 5 : The Application example of Part Generator for H Tire

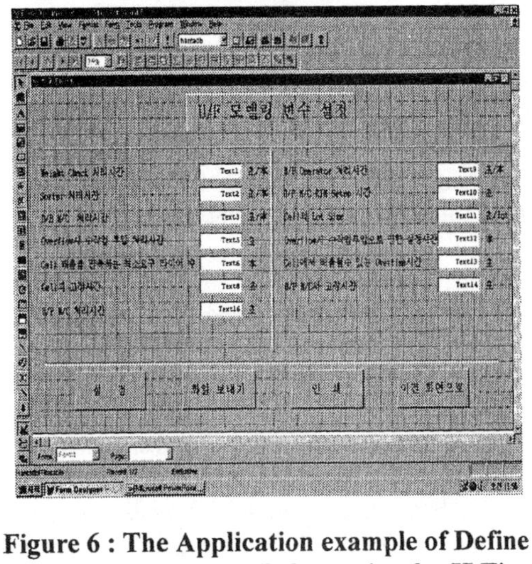

Figure 6 : The Application example of Define of Resouce Information for H Tire

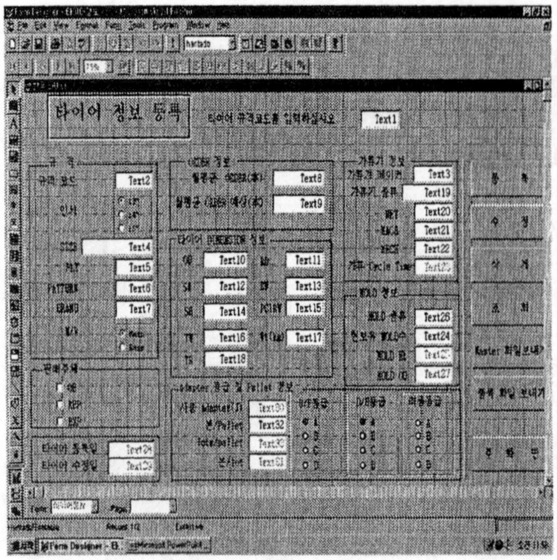

Figure 7 : The Application example of Part Database for H Tire

When using the PBS, users first define the various attributes of tire in each type accurately in module 3, then decide the performance conditions by pressing the send file button after setting the experimental plan in module 1, after deciding each facility information and control logic in module 2. Once pressing the send button, those conditions are automatically reflected to the AutoMod software. So the users are able to look at the result by just clicking the run button at AutoMod. The next Figure 8 shows the one of result after the simulation performed by capturing a graph, which was provided by the AutoMod.

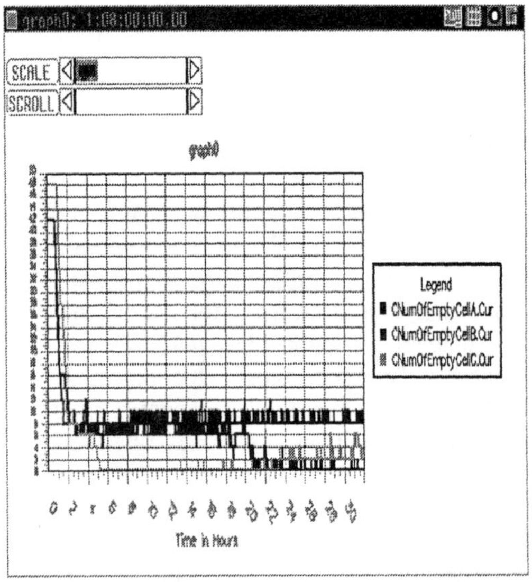

Figure 8 : The Application example of the Simulation result for H Tire

3.3 Application result

There were a number of errors at the beginning

of the PBS we applied. The users' requirements were so broad that the simulator implement was too difficult to reflect them. However, the result from H tire was quite satisfactory. At the beginning we spent a lot of time implementing interface after developing the PBS and simulation modeling. But, there were no more users' request due to our various experiments of the PBS. Because we made an agreement of limitation and definition of the PBS module at the beginning it was possible. Most people who experienced such projects feel that the simulation project is something that endless requests exist. The PBS is the tool to solve this problem. The H tire kept experiments by the PBS after our team was discharged, and obtained outstanding results. In fact, the new plant has lately been finished building, and entered the production stage. The H tire made compliment to our analysis result, and announced that that's because of the PBS.

4. CONCLUSION

The PBS is the simulator developed for actual users to operate very conveniently. As a matter of fact, it's almost impossible for actual users to understand and operate very complex simulation software. Moreover, in many cases the simulation models aren't be used after the project is over, and the simulation experts are discharged. We desperately felt the need to implement the PBS after we kept facing this problem. In other word, users operate by themselves after the project ends, was developed. In fact, the sites implementing the PBS would get very successful results. In addition, the PBS brings many strong points to not just actual users but also system developers in a way that it creates models and performs analysis.

It's easy to apply and analyze the data due to pre-database implementing, and also save a lot of time remodeling due to setting variables function of resources. Also, it brings convenience when designing and implementing the algorithm for operating logic. In other word, it brings strong points to both the post-usage of users' side and the modeling of developer side.

Now, we are implementing the result analysis module that the PBS is insufficient. It's not that easy for actual users to analyze the simulation result. Existing simulation S/Ws or specific analysis tool such SIMSTAT aren't suitable for actual users to understand easily. Therefore, our analysis module must be easy using tool for users. For this reason, we need to develop the module that capable to display the results as graphs or tables after importing critical information using the PBS. We are implementing along with real plants' situation, and will bring out our module, PBS II next time soon.

REFERENCE

Kieran L. Coughlan; Paul J. Nolan. 1995. "Developing Special Purpose Simulators Under Microsoft Windows". *In proceedings of the 1995 Winter Simulation Conference*. pp.969~976.

Dankbar, G. C.; J. L. Shellum;K. E. Bennet. 1992. "The Use of Simulation to Evaluate Automated Equipment for Clinical Process Laboratory", *In proceedings of the 1992 Winter Simulation Conference*. pp.1065~1070.

Drews, P. and M. Weyrich; 1997. "Virtual Manufacturing -An Overview", *VR News*, Vol.6, No.3, pp.18~22.

Buzacott, John A. and J. George Shanthikumar. 1993. *"Stochastic Models of Manufacturing Systems"*, Prentice-Hall International.

Hoskins, Jerry W. 1997. "Improve Profits and Reduce Cycle Time with Manufacturing Cells and Simulation", *In proceedings of the International Lean Manufacturing Conference*,

Seppanen, Marvin S. 1993. "Kanban Simulator Using SIMAN and LOTUS 1-2-3", In *proceedings of the 1993 Winter Simulation Conference*, pp.838 ~ 844.

Autosimulations Inc, 1998. " *AutoMod Reference Manual*".

Microsoft Inc, 1998. *"Visual Foxpro Reference Manual."*

Byoung K. Choi, Kwan H. Han, Tea Y. Park, "Object-Oriented Graphical Modeling of FMSs", The International Journal of Flexible Manufacturing Systems, Vol.8, No.2, p159-182, 1996.

Kwan H. Han and Byoung K. Choi, "An Object-Oriented Modeling Framework for Automated Manufacturing Systems", International Journal of Computer Integrated Manufacturing, Vol.10, No.5, p324-334, 1997.

BIOGRAPH

Jung-wook Kim is the team member of Virtual Manufacturing Department in Daewoo Information Systems Co. Ltd. in Korea. He received his B.S. and M.S. degrees in Industrial Engineering from the Dongguk University in Seoul, Korea. He accomplished over 20 projects and his research interests are in simulation modeling, virtual manufacturing, and supply chain management. His e-mail address is jungwook@mail.disc.co.kr

Kwan-hee Han is the general manager of Institute of Information Technology in Daewoo Information Systems Co. Ltd. in Korea. He received his B.S. in Industrial Engineering from Ajou University, M.S and Ph.D degree in Industrial Engineering from Korea Advanced Institute of Science and Technology, Korea. He has 15 years experiences in implementing CIM systems and conducted over 10 major projects in manufacturing industry and his research interests are in simulation modeling of automated manufacturing systems, virtual manufacturing, VR applications at design & manufacturing areas and knowledge management systems. His e-mail address is hankh@mail.disc.co.kr

Gi-tae Kim is the deputy general manager of Virtual Manufacturing Department in Daewoo Information Systems Co. Ltd. in Korea. He received his B.S. in Mechanical Engineering from Inha University. He has 14 years experiences in implementing system integration for manufacturing site and conducted over 10 major projects in manufacturing industry and his research interests are in simulation, virtual reality, product data management and CAD. His e-mail address is gtkim@mail.disc.co.kr

Chung-wha Lee the director of Institute of Information Technology in Daewoo Information Systems Co. Ltd. in Korea. He received his B.S. in Industrial Engineering from Seoul University, M.S in Industrial Engineering from Korea Advanced Institute of Science and Technology, Korea. And Ph.D degree in Industrial Engineering from Penn. State University in U.S.A.

AUTHOR INDEX

AUTHOR INDEX

Author Index

AUTHOR INDEX

Author Index

Author Index

Author Index

AUTHOR INDEX